A companion to medical studies

Editorial board

A companion to
medical studies

IN THREE VOLUMES

Volume 1

Anatomy, biochemistry, physiology and
related subjects

EDITORS-IN-CHIEF

R. PASSMORE

J. S. ROBSON

BLACKWELL SCIENTIFIC PUBLICATIONS

OXFORD AND EDINBURGH

632 03250 2   Cloth
632 05810 2   Limp

For the three-volume set

632 05840 4   Cloth
632 05850 1   Limp

Printed and bound in Great Britain by
WILLIAM CLOWES AND SONS LTD, LONDON AND BECCLES

Contents

THE STRUCTURE AND FUNCTION OF TISSUES

THE STRUCTURE AND FUNCTION OF THE SYSTEMS

MAN IN HIS ENVIRONMENT

Volume II

General pathology and pharmacology

Volume III
Medicine, surgery, obstetrics, therapeutics and social medicine

Contributors to volume 1

E. Asmussen *Universitetets Gymnastikteoretiske Laboratorium, Copenhagen, Denmark*

Joyce D. Baird *Department of Medicine, University of Edinburgh*

G.S. Boyd *Department of Biochemistry, University of Edinburgh*

J. Chalmers *Department of Orthopaedic Surgery, University of Edinburgh*

D.R. Cullen *Royal Infirmary, Edinburgh*

S.H. Davies *Department of Medicine, University of Edinburgh*

P.R. Davis *Department of Biological Studies, University of Surrey*

A.N. Davison *Department of Biochemistry, Charing Cross Hospital Medical School, London*

M.H. Draper *Department of Physiology, University of Edinburgh*

O.G. Edholm *Medical Research Council, Division of Human Physiology, London*

Hamad Elneil *Department of Physiology, University of Khartoum, Sudan*

R.B.L. Ewart *Department of Medicine, University of Edinburgh*

R.B. Fisher *Department of Biochemistry, University of Edinburgh*

D.C. Flenley *Department of Medicine, University of Edinburgh*

S. Fletcher *Department of Pathology, University of Edinburgh*

J.M. Forrester *Department of Physiology, University of Edinburgh*

T.W. Glenister *Department of Anatomy, Charing Cross Hospital Medical School, London*

A.D. Hally *Department of Anatomy, University of Newcastle upon Tyne*

D.G. Harnden *Medical Research Council, Clinical and Population Cytogenetics Research Unit, Edinburgh*

E.A. Harris *Clinical Physiology Department, Green Lane Hospital, Auckland, New Zealand*

E.R. Hitchcock *Department of Neurological Surgery, University of Edinburgh*

F.E. Hytten *Medical Research Council, Reproduction and Growth Research Unit, University of Newcastle upon Tyne*

W.J. Irvine *Department of Therapeutics, University of Edinburgh*

R.J. Johnson *Department of Physiology, University of Edinburgh*

D.G. Julian *Department of Medicine, University of Edinburgh*

A.W.S. Kerr *Department of Anatomy, University of Edinburgh*

M.G. KERR *Department of Obstetrics and Gynaecology, University of Edinburgh*

A.H. KITCHIN *Department of Physiology, University of Edinburgh*

K. KUCZYNSKI *Department of Anatomy, University of Edinburgh*

ANNE T. LAMBIE *Department of Therapeutics, University of Edinburgh*

T.R. LEE *Department of Psychology, University of Dundee*

SYBIL M. LLOYD *Department of Physiology, University of Edinburgh*

A. MCGHIE *Department of Psychology, University of Dundee*

I.B. MACLEOD *Department of Clinical Surgery, University of Edinburgh*

J.N. MILLS *Department of Physiology, University of Manchester*

J.A. MILNE *Department of Dermatology, University of Glasgow*

A.R. MUIR *Department of Veterinary Anatomy, University of Edinburgh*

P.R. MYERSCOUGH *Department of Obstetrics and Gynaecology, University of Edinburgh*

J.E. NEWSAM *Western General Hospital, Edinburgh*

J.H. OTTAWAY *Department of Biochemistry, University of Edinburgh*

R.PASSMORE *Department of Physiology, University of Edinburgh*

W.L.M. PERRY *Department of Pharmacology, University of Edinburgh*

A. PETERS *Department of Anatomy, Boston University, U.S.A.*

L. MARY PICKFORD *Department of Physiology, University of Edinburgh*

W.N.M. RAMSAY *Department of Biochemistry, University of Edinburgh*

J. RICHMOND *Department of Medicine, University of Edinburgh*

M.H. RICHMOND *Department of Molecular Biology, University of Edinburgh*

A.P. RYLE *Department of Biochemistry, University of Edinburgh*

R.J. SCOTHORNE *Department of Anatomy, University of Newcastle upon Tyne*

D.C. SINCLAIR *Department of Anatomy, University of Aberdeen*

J.W. SMITH *Department of Anatomy, University of St Andrews*

WINIFRED L. STAFFORD *Department of Biochemistry, University of Edinburgh*

A.G. STEWART *Department of Therapeutics, University of Dundee*

L.G. WHITBY *Department of Clinical Chemistry, University of Edinburgh*

I. MAUREEN YOUNG *Department of Gynaecology, St Thomas's Hospital Medical School, London*

Preface

This book is the preclinical part of a comprehensive work in three volumes written for undergraduate medical students. The whole work aims to give them an interesting, intelligent and exciting account of modern medicine and the medical sciences. The student will find in it more than sufficient information to enable him to pass his examinations and thereafter to begin to discharge clinical responsibility under supervision. Its aim is to set out concisely the scientific achievements on which modern practice is based; it also indicates important growing points and prepares its readers for medical practice in the twenty-first century when they will be at the height of their professional careers.

Today there is much criticism of medical education by both teachers and students. A common complaint is that teaching is carried out in various departments whose staff may have little idea of what is being taught in other departments. Throughout this book unnecessary departmental barriers are broken down. The editors, who represent the major medical disciplines, come from the same medical school; it has been possible for them to meet frequently so that together they have been responsible for planning each part and for the detailed editing of the contributions. One important consequence of these arrangements has been a great reduction in the repetition of material which appears inescapable in a series of departmentally-orientated books.

As we were finishing the correction of the proofs, the Report of the Royal Commission on Medical Education 1965–8 was published. The Commission recommends attention to four subjects, not often taught in the preclinical period, but which are dealt with in this volume. These are statistics (chap. 3), human genetics (chap. 38), behavioural sciences (chaps. 36 and 45) and sex education (chap. 47). In addition we give in chaps. 4 and 5 a fuller account of nutrition than is customary; this is a practical subject which profoundly influences the welfare of mankind and which also escapes attention in many courses. The account of anatomy is much shorter than in textbooks of former days. However, we believe that a thorough grounding in the structure of the human body is an essential basis for medical practice. The anatomical sections have been read carefully by editors who are not professional anatomists and unnecessary detail has been pruned. The anatomy of all the internal organs and systems and the structure of the tissues is presented together with the physiology and biochemistry and is thus, in the words of the Commission, an 'approach to the teaching of human structure and function on a genuine co-operative basis'.

We are indebted to Mr T.C. Dodds for help in producing the colour plates and to the artists, Miss Ann McNeil, Miss Dorothy Mustart, Miss Yvonne Prince, Mr Colin Judge and Mr Martin Miller, who have drawn or redrawn all the illustrations; to the secretaries, especially Mrs Margaret Simpson and Miss Barbara Chisholm, who have typed vast quantities of manuscript; and to Miss Elizabeth MacKenzie, Mrs Esme Passmore, Dr Winifred Stafford and Dr James Smith, who have undertaken the onerous task of producing the index.

We are grateful to the authors who have made this volume possible. Some of them have spent many hours with the editors going over their manuscripts and have patiently acquiesced when sections of their work have disappeared either into the waste paper basket or into another chapter. Many of them have allowed large alterations in their scripts and the editors must take responsibility for such errors as remain.

This book owes much to the publishers. Without Mr Per Saugman's vision and encouragement we should never have begun. Without Mr Nigel Palmer's industry and perseverance we should never have finished.

Edinburgh   R. Passmore
May 1968   J.S. Robson

Acknowledgements

We wish to thank all publishers, editors and authors who have allowed us to reproduce illustrations but especially Professor Romanes and the Oxford University Press for the use of *Cunningham's Textbook of Anatomy* on which many of our anatomical illustrations are based. Others include Academic Press Inc.; American Chemical Society; American Society of Biological Chemists Inc.; American Physiological Society; Appleton–Century–Crofts; Edward Arnold (Publishers) Ltd; Baillière, Tindall & Cassell Ltd; Blackwell Scientific Publications Ltd; Butterworths; Cambridge University Press; Chatto & Windus; University of Chicago Press; J. & A. Churchill Ltd; CIBA; G. Doin; Elsevier Publishing Co.; Society for Endocrinology; J.R. Geigy S.A.; Grune & Stratton Inc.; Heffers; William Heinemann Medical Books Ltd; Johns Hopkins Press; Henry Kimpton; Lange Medical Publications; H.K. Lewis & Co. Ltd; J.B. Lippincott Co.; Little, Brown, & Co.; E. & S. Livingstone Ltd; Longmans, Green & Co. Ltd; Macmillan & Co.; McGraw–Hill Publishing Co. Ltd; C.V. Mosby Co.; Munksgaard; National Coal Board; New York Academy of Sciences; Oxford University Press; Prentice–Hall Inc.; W.B. Saunders Co.; Scientific American Inc.; H.M. Stationery Office; Charles C. Thomas; John Wiley & Sons Ltd; Williams & Wilkins Co.; Yale University Press; *Acta Physiologica Scandinavica*; *American Journal of Medicine*; *American Journal of Obstetrics and Gynecology*; *American Journal of Physiology*; *Annals of the New York Academy of Sciences*; *Biochemistry*; *Biochimica et biophysica acta*; *Brain*; *British Medical Bulletin*; *British Medical Journal*; *Bulletin of the Johns Hopkins Hospital*; *Clinical Science*; *Cold Spring Harbor Symposia on Quantitative Biology*; *Contributions to Embryology*; *Developmental Medicine and Child Neurology*; *Endocrinology*; *Progress in Hormone Research*; *Journal of the American Medical Association*; *Journal of the American Oil Chemists Society*; *Journal of Applied Physiology*; *Journal of Biological Chemistry*; *Journal of Clinical Investigation*; *Journal of Endocrinology*; *Journal of Histochemistry and Cytochemistry*; *Journal of Neurophysiology*; *Journal of Obstetrics and Gynaecology of the British Commonwealth*; *Journal of Pediatrics*; *Journal of Physiology*; *Lancet*; *Nature*; *Physiological Reviews*; *Progress in Cardiovascular Diseases*; *Quarterly Journal of Experimental Physiology*; *Science*; *Scientific American*; *Veterinary Record*.

Finally, we would like to acknowledge our indebtedness to other publications if through inadvertence this list is incomplete.

Chapter 1
Man and his environment

A struggle in which all,
The elderly, the amorous, the young, the handy and the
  thoughtful,
Those to whom feeling is a science, those to whom study
Of all that can be added and compared is a consuming love,
In cities, deserts, ships, in lodgings near the port,
Discovering the past of strangers in a library,
Creating their own future on a bed, each with his treasure,
Self-confident among the laughter and the *petits verres*,
Or motionless and lonely like a moping cormorant,
In all their living are profoundly implicated.

THE EXTERNAL ENVIRONMENT, WHICH IS ALWAYS CHANGING

Thus W.H. Auden reports the struggle which the human biologist must analyse in detail. Man is a tough and ubiquitous animal. He can be found in little colonies in the polar regions or living as a nomad in arid deserts. He may inhabit small villages in the rarefied air of the higher ranges of the Andes or huge towns in the humid heat on the sea coast of southern Asia. He is capable of exploring outer space. He must come to terms with a great variety of other animals of all sizes. He may be both hunter and hunted. He is engaged in a constant struggle with viruses, bacteria, protozoa and worms, many species of which may become his parasites. With the majority of these a *modus vivendi* is established, but not a few can seriously incapacitate or even kill him. Man is also a social animal, normally utterly dependent on other men and women for his simplest necessities, and harmonious relations with our fellows are always difficult to achieve.

The essence of human biology is the study of adaptive processes made necessary by struggles with an ever-changing environment. The doctor is particularly concerned with the responses to parasites, social maladjustments and violence, often the result of motor, industrial and home accidents. He must know the effects of unsuitable or defective diets. Nowadays he is more and more concerned with the responses to new chemicals to which man is being exposed for the first time. Many of these chemicals are essential features of the environment in a modern industrial civilization. Others have been introduced as drugs for their healing properties. The doctor is concerned also with the adaptive changes that occur in the mother during pregnancy and with the effects of a great variety of degenerative diseases, the consequence of the wearing out of parts of the mechanisms of the body with increasing age.

On account of its continuous exposure to a changing environment, the human body must be considered as an **open system**. This distinguishes it from most of the chemical reactions and the physical behaviour of matter, which can be studied as a **closed system** in a fixed and constant environment. The behaviour of a closed system is more susceptible to scientific study and can often be described in terms of the limits imposed by precise natural laws. The student will already be familiar with many such laws, for instance, those associated with the names of Avogadro, Boyle, Dalton, Gay-Lussac, Henry, Hooke, Joule, Newton and Ohm. Fewer biologists have had their names perpetuated in a similar manner.

THE INTERNAL ENVIRONMENT, WHICH IS RELATIVELY CONSTANT

Perhaps the best known physiological principle is that first set out in 1857 by Claude Bernard in a lecture at the Sorbonne in Paris: 'All the vital mechanisms, however varied they may be, have always but one end, that of preserving the constancy of the conditions of life in the internal environment'.

The blood and the lymph which bathe the cells are conceived of as an internal environment, which protects the cells of the organs of the body from variations in the external environment. The American physiologist Cannon, in 1929, introduced the term **homeostasis** to describe this principle. *Homoios* is a Greek word meaning the like or the same. Homeostatic processes are those physiological reactions which tend to restore the internal environment to a steady or resting state; here are four examples. Heavy physical exercise raises the temperature of the blood and also its acidity. A meal raises the level of blood sugar, and drinking water lowers the osmolality of the blood. Exercise, food and drink each initiate responses which cause the blood to return to the normal state.

EXERCISE AND BLOOD TEMPERATURE

The normal temperature of the blood is around 37–38°C. A man running for 20 min produces some 200 kilocalories (kcal) of heat. The specific heat of the body is 0·83. So this heat is sufficient to raise the temperature of a 65 kg man by

$$\frac{200 \times 0.83}{65} = 2.6°C$$

Whilst running, the man starts to perspire and may lose 200 g of sweat; as the latent heat of evaporation of water is 0·580 kcal/g this is equivalent to 116 kcal of heat. The sweating reduces the rise in body temperature and helps to return it to the normal level soon after the end of the run. Sweating is a physiological cooling mechanism that is brought into action rapidly as soon as the body temperature rises.

EXERCISE AND THE ACIDITY OF THE BLOOD

The blood is normally slightly alkaline. The hydrogen ion concentration is about 40 ng/l (1 nanogram = 10^{-9} g), corresponding to a pH value of 7·4. During exercise the muscles produce carbon dioxide, which is an acid in solution. During a 20 min run, 40 litres of CO_2 may be produced. This is equivalent to 1·8 moles of carbonic acid. However, the acidity of the blood rises only slightly during exercise and the pH seldom falls by more than 0·05. This is partly due to the buffering power of the blood (p. 6.4), but also to the fact that as soon as exercise starts, the rate and depth of breathing are increased so that the carbon dioxide is blown off almost as rapidly as it is formed. Panting at the end of the run returns the pH of the blood to normal in a few minutes.

FASTING AND THE GLUCOSE CONTENT OF THE BLOOD

The blood of a fasting man contains about 70 mg/100 ml of glucose. This sugar is utilized continuously by the tissues and the level is normally maintained by the absorption of dietary carbohydrate from the intestines. After a meal the blood sugar may rise to 140–160 mg/100 ml. This excess is stored temporarily as glycogen in the liver and muscles, a process which requires insulin, a hormone secreted by the pancreas. Yet a man may fast for two or three weeks or even longer and his blood sugar is well maintained and will probably not fall below 50 mg/100 ml. During this time glucose is still being used; the brain alone requires 80 g/day. The level in the blood is kept constant by the formation of glucose (gluconeogenesis) from protein and glycerol derived from fat. The liver has a predominant role in this adaptive reaction.

DRINKING AND THE OSMOTIC CONCENTRATION OF THE BLOOD

If you drink 3 pints of beer (1·7 litres of water), it is rapidly absorbed into the blood from the alimentary canal. This might be expected to dilute the blood greatly; the osmotic pressure of the crystalloid substances in the blood is about 300 milliosmoles/litre. In fact it falls by only about 3 per cent. A precipitous fall in the osmolality of the blood is prevented, because a small fall is rapidly sensed by osmoreceptors in the brain. From a controlling centre in the hypothalamus, the secretion of a pituitary hormone, vasopressin, is regulated. The level of this hormone in the blood determines the rate at which the kidneys excrete water. In this instance, the excretion of water in the urine is almost as rapid as the water absorption from the intestines.

These four examples of homeostasis illustrate how the internal environment of the body is kept constant, despite the imposition of considerable external stresses. The effector organs in these examples are the sweat glands, lungs, liver and kidneys. The mechanisms by which these organs are brought into play involve elaborate control systems both chemical and nervous in nature.

In various disease states homeostasis may break down. The temperature may rise to 41°C as a result of infection by parasitic organisms; the acidity of the blood may rise (to pH 7·1–7·2) in disease of the lungs preventing the normal excretion of CO_2; the blood sugar may fall to levels below 40 mg/100 ml in patients with insulin-producing tumours of the pancreas. Under each of these conditions the patient is seriously ill and, unless they are remedied rapidly, may die.

THE COMPOSITION OF THE BODY AND THE SIZE OF THE INTERNAL ENVIRONMENT

The body can be considered as composed of three compartments. Firstly there is the **cell mass**, comprising all the cells of the body where most of the chemical work of the body is done; this compartment is sometimes referred to as the active mass. Secondly there is the **supporting tissue**. This includes the **extracellular fluid** in the blood and the fluid surrounding the cells in the various organs. This fluid makes up the **internal environment** of the cells. The supporting tissue also includes the minerals in the skeleton and the protein in connective tissue fibres. The third compartment is the **energy reserve**, composed largely of fat held mainly in the cells of adipose tissue beneath the skin and surrounding the principal internal organs.

It is, of course, impossible to separate out these compartments by physical dissection. There are, however, indirect ways of measuring the size of each. In a healthy young man, the body weight is divided approximately: 55 per cent cell mass, 30 per cent supporting tissue and 15 per cent energy reserve. In a young woman the energy reserve is usually almost twice as large.

The **dilution principle** is one of the means that are used to measure the size of the compartments of the body. Suppose you want to measure the volume of water in a small ornamental fishpond in a garden. It would be tedious and difficult to empty it into measuring cylinders. A simpler procedure is to add to the pond a small quantity (Q) of a water-soluble dye. After a short interval, to allow the dye to diffuse throughout the pond, a sample of the water is taken and the concentration (C) of the dye determined. The volume (V) of water in the pond is then given by

$$V = \frac{Q}{C}$$

A variety of substances, deuterium oxide or heavy water, tritiated water, the drugs antipyrine and amino-antipyrine, and also ethyl alcohol, appear to diffuse evenly throughout the water in all the tissues of the body. They can be used to measure **total body water** by the dilution technique. A known amount of the substance is given either by mouth or intravenous injection; after an interval to allow for absorption and diffusion, a sample of venous blood is taken and the concentration of the substance in the plasma determined. Then the volume of the 'space' occupied by the substance in the body can be calculated. This 'space' then equals the total body water, provided the assumption that the diffusion of the substance throughout the total body water is uniform is correct.

Another group of substances, including the polysaccharide inulin, sucrose and mannitol, sodium thiocyanate and the ions $^{35}SO_4$, ^{82}Br and ^{24}Na, if injected into the body, occupy approximately the same 'space', which is much smaller than the deuterium space. These substances either do not cross the membranes of the cell walls or are extruded as a result of active processes within the cells. In consequence they can be used to measure the space occupied by extracellular fluids. The measurement of the extracellular water is not as precise as the measurement of total body water, because none of the substances used completely meet the requirements of the test. They are either found in the cells in small amounts (Na thiocyanate) or do not diffuse evenly throughout all the extracellular water (inulin).

In a healthy man weighing 65 kg, a normal value for the total body water is 40 litres and for the extracellular water is 15 litres. These figures are convenient to remember. They correspond to about two-thirds and one-fifth of the body weight. These proportions are higher in thin people and much less in the obese.

The extracellular water can be further subdivided into the **plasma water**, in the circulating blood, and the **interstitial water**, in the tissue spaces surrounding the cells. The plasma volume can be determined by the dilution technique, using the dye Evans blue or serum albumin labelled with radioactive iodine as an indicator. A normal value is 3 litres. This leaves 12 litres of fluid actually surrounding the tissue cells and forming the internal environment which determines their behaviour (table 1.1). The **cell water** can be determined only by difference, and in our example of a healthy man it amounts to 25 litres.

TABLE 1.1. The distribution of water in the body of a healthy man weighing 65 kg (in litres).

Interstitial water	12		
Plasma water	3	Extracellular water	15
		Intracellular water	25

Total body water 40

The water content of the various types of cells differs and is not always easily determined. Muscle cells are 75 per cent water, but the water content of red blood cells is less than 70 per cent, as also is probably the water content of connective tissue cells. If the cells are assumed to be on average 70 per cent water, then

$$\text{cell mass} = \text{cell water} \times \frac{100}{70}$$

The size of the energy reserve, the fat in the body, can be determined by density measurements (p. 4.8). A normal figure for a man is 9 kg. Women of course are usually fatter.

We can now divide our normal man quantitatively into his three compartments (table 1.2). There is no method

TABLE 1.2. The compartments of a normal man.

	kg
Active tissue	
Cell mass	36
Supporting tissue	
Internal environment or extracellular fluid	15
Bone minerals and extracellular proteins	5
Energy reserve	
Fat	9
Body weight	65

as yet for determining the mass of the bone minerals and the extracellular proteins in life. The value of 5 kg in the table is obtained by difference.

The measurement of the body weight is frequently made in physiological studies and in clinical practice. Changes in body weight are rightly considered of great importance in assessing the progress of many diseases. The weighing-machine may not reflect accurately what is happening in the body. Thus our man might be suffering from a wasting disease and his cell mass diminish by 2 kg and his energy reserve by 4 kg during a month. At the same time fluid may accumulate in the body (oedema) and his extracellular water increase by 6 kg. He would then still weigh 65 kg, although seriously wasted.

It is frequently necessary to make corrections for the great variations in size of human beings. Thus in therapeutics the dose of drugs may be given as so many mg/kg body weight. This is sound provided the distribution of the body weight amongst the three compartments is approximately normal. Such a system of dosage is unreliable for very thin or very fat people.

The measurement of the size of the various compartments of the body demands laboratory skills and equipment. It is an important part of clinical science and is leading to a new understanding of how the body works in health and in disease. It is not an essential in routine hospital practice. Yet every doctor makes frequent use of a weighing-machine. It must be remembered that what goes on the scales is not a uniform mass. Body weight is a measure of the sum of the size of three compartments of the body, each with very different functions.

The size of the internal environment is reduced when there is insufficient water to drink or if there are excessive water losses due to sweating. Diarrhoea and vomiting lead to losses of water and electrolytes and a reduced internal environment. This is important, especially in babies and young children. A significant increase probably never occurs in health in response to any stress from the external environment, but increased extracellular water giving rise to oedema is a common feature of many diseases. It is found in starvation and other nutritional disorders and is characteristic of many cardiac, renal and liver diseases.

The size of the internal environment is regulated but not with great precision. If you weigh yourself every morning immediately after waking and emptying the bladder, you will often find a variation of up to 1 kg from day to day and occasionally greater. This is largely due to variations in extracellular fluid. How the control of the size of this volume is effected is only partially understood and is further discussed on p. 33.17.

THE COMPOSITION OF THE INTERNAL ENVIRONMENT

This is relatively easy to determine. The capillaries of the circulation allow, for the most part, a free exchange between the electrolytes and crystalloid substances in the blood and interstitial fluid. Thus an analysis of a sample of blood plasma gives a good indication of the composition of the internal environment. Proteins do not pass readily across the capillary barrier and whereas the plasma contains 5–8 g/100 ml of protein, the concentration in the interstitial fluids is very small. Table 1.3 sets out the normal values for the electrolyte content of the extracellular fluid, based on analyses of plasma. For

comparison, figures for the intracellular fluid are also given. It is, of course, very difficult to obtain cell water for analysis; the figures given are estimates based on analyses of whole tissues from which values for the extracellular electrolytes are subtracted.

TABLE 1.3. A normal distribution of ions in intracellular and extracellular fluids.

	Intracellular (mEq/l)	Extracellular (mEq/l)
Cations		
Na^+	10	145
K^+	150	5
Ca^{++}	2	2
Mg^{++}	15	2
	177	154
Anions		
Cl^-	10	100
HCO_3^-	10	25
SO_4^{--}	15	1
Organic acids		5
PO_4^{---}	142	2
Proteins		21
	177	154

Sodium is the principal cation in the extracellular water and potassium in the intracellular water. The ability of cells to survive and to respond to nervous and chemical stimulation depends on ionic gradients across the cell wall. In the plasma the principal anions are Cl^- and HCO_3^-. In the cells phosphate and protein provide the chief anions for maintaining the electrochemical balance with the K^+ ions. The amount of HCO_3^- in the plasma is altered by changing the rate and depth of breathing. These determine the gaseous CO_2 output. Respiration in this way influences the HCO_3^- content of the extracellular fluid and is a fine adjustment in the control of the pH of the internal environment. Measurements of plasma bicarbonate are of great value in investigating disturbances of the acid-base balance. These occur in health during exercise, as already mentioned, and in acclimatization to high altitude; they are a common feature of many diseases, especially those associated with failure of the lungs and kidney.

The fact that the internal environment is primarily a solution of sodium chloride may be a reflection of the marine origin of mammals in the remote evolutionary past. In most parts of the oceans, the sea water contains about 3 per cent NaCl, corresponding to 500 mEq/litre of Na, more than three times the amount in the internal environment. Such a load of sodium is beyond the capacity of the kidneys, which are the guardians of the internal environment and accurately maintain its chemical composition. For this reason castaways on the ocean should not drink sea water, which will only exaggerate their thirst and accelerate their death (p. 41.3).

THE STABILITY OF THE INTERNAL ENVIRONMENT

Few men have submitted their bodies to severe environmental stress in the interests of physiology as frequently as Sir Joseph Barcroft. In his laboratory at Cambridge there was a small room in which the chemical composition and pressure of the atmosphere could be varied experimentally. Barcroft once spent 14 days in this room in an atmosphere equivalent to that on the higher slopes of Everest. He has pointed out that many, perhaps most, essential functions of the body can proceed over a fairly wide range of conditions, but the mental processes are much more restricted. He describes how a small change of hydrogen ion concentration in the blood over a short period can affect the higher nervous system causing inability to concentrate, which may last for two or three days. Most of us are aware of how a trivial degree of fever can seriously impair mental effort. Perhaps the development of an accurate control over the internal environment has been a necessary prerequisite for the development of the higher nervous functions, which are characteristic of man. To quote Barcroft:

'The chemical and physical processes associated with the working of the mind are of so delicate a character that beside them the changes measured by the thermometer or the hydrogen electrode must be catastrophic— overwhelming. Processes (probably rhythmic) of such delicacy must surely require a medium of great constancy in which to attain ordered development. How often have I watched the ripples on the surface of a still lake made by a passing boat, noted their regularity and admired the patterns formed when two ripple-systems meet, but the lake must be perfectly calm, just as the atmosphere must be free from atmospherics if you are to find beauty in the subtle passages of a symphony. To look for high intellectual development in a *milieu* whose properties have not become stabilized is to seek music amongst the crashings of a rudimentary wireless or the ripple patterns on the surface of the stormy Atlantic.'

LEVELS OF ORGANIZATION

A complex organization is necessary to make the adaptive changes in a system open to a constantly changing environment. Enzymes are the catalysts that determine the rate and course of all the organic chemical reactions in the body; in composition they are proteins. When studied in aqueous solution in test tubes, the behaviour of enzymic reactions is described by a well-defined set of laws. Enzymic kinetics is a precise and elegant branch of science. However, the behaviour of an enzyme is not always readily explained by these rules, because their activity within the cell is influenced by many other concurrent chemical reactions. Reactions of the cells appear more complex than those of the enzyme systems of which they are composed. Similarly the function of each of the organs of the body cannot be fully described in terms of the functions of the cells, of which they are composed. The behaviour of a whole man is more adaptable than that of the individual organs; the whole body possesses the ability to co-ordinate the individual organs. Finally, a human society becomes a powerful and effective unit when it is able to co-ordinate the behaviour of its individuals. The great physiologist J.S. Haldane stressed the importance of the different levels of organization in living systems. He taught that:

'The life of an organism must be regarded as an objective active unity which embraces its environment, and manifests itself not merely in the mutual relations between parts of the organism itself, but also between the organism and its environment. The use of this conception in biology separates it from the physical sciences.'

J. Barcroft and J.S. Haldane in England and L.J. Henderson and W.B. Cannon in the United States were four great physiologists, who in the first quarter of the twentieth century developed Bernard's conception of the stability of the internal environment. It is the most important theoretical generalization within the medical sciences. No student will regret spending a few evenings browsing through one or more of the books by these masters, which are listed at the end of this chapter.

Physiology and biochemistry are difficult subjects. Unfortunately pathology and the clinical sciences are no easier. The difficulty arises because you cannot understand how the whole body works, either in health or disease, unless you first have some knowledge of the function of its component systems. Yet a detailed study of the parts easily obscures the whole. It is difficult to know where to begin. In pre-medical courses, it is possible to set out concisely and dogmatically, the essentials of physics and chemistry. The student starting physiology will soon realize that the human body is a complex mechanism about which we know much, but understand little. In these respects the human mind is no better. In whatever branch of medicine the student chooses for his final career, he will have to make important decisions, which may affect the health and even the lives of people, lacking a full understanding of what he is doing. The difficulties of the medical sciences will present a challenge that lasts a life time. The recurring glimpses of understanding are the intellectual rewards.

FURTHER READING

BARCROFT J. (1934) *Features in the Architecture of Physiological Function.* London: Cambridge University Press.

CANNON W.B. (1932) *The Wisdom of the Body.* New York: Norton.

HALDANE J.S. & PRIESTLEY J.G. (1935) *Respiration.* New Haven: Yale University Press.

HENDERSON L.J. (1928) *Blood—a Study in General Physiology.* New Haven: Yale University Press.

MOORE F.D. (1963) *The Body Cell Mass and its Supporting Environment.* Philadelphia: Saunders.

OLMSTEAD J.M.D. (1939) *Claude Bernard.* (An excellent short account of Bernard's life and work.) London: Cassell.

PASSMORE R. & DRAPER M.H. (1968) The chemical anatomy of the human body in *Biochemical Disorders in Human Disease*, 3rd Edition, ed. Thompson R.H.S. & King E.J. London: Churchill.

Chapter 2
Control theory and systems

The dependence of life on the control of Man's internal environment is outlined in chap. 1. The constancy of the blood hydrogen ion concentration is given as an example. In health this varies within the range 35–45 ng/litre, and no chemical method is known which detects such a small change in H^+ in solution. In fact, in the laboratory, only elaborate electronic methods can be used to measure concentration changes of this order. Specialized cells, situated in the respiratory area of the brain stem are sufficiently sensitive to detect these small changes and bring about appropriate adjustments in breathing and so the excretion of CO_2. Little is known about the details of their operation at a quantitative level, and they constitute only a part of the entire mechanism controlling blood hydrogen ion concentration. This control system is only one of a large number of others which detect and stabilize changes in many physiological variables, e.g. the blood pressure, the osmolality of the blood, the supply of oxygen to the tissues, body temperature, the amount of light falling on the retinae, and many others. Detectors also monitor the position of the limbs and so allow control of posture and movement with fine precision.

The relative constancy of the concentration of the blood glucose, despite a varying rate of utilization by the tissues and an irregular dietary supply, has already been mentioned. In diabetes mellitus, the control of blood glucose by the insulin secreted from the pancreas is disturbed. Since the 1920's it has been possible, using injected insulin or other means, to keep the blood glucose level nearly within normal limits in these patients. This control, unlike the natural one, is not self-regulating, and the blood glucose level after an injection of insulin in the absence of food may fall dramatically, giving the condition of hypoglycemia. The treatment of diabetes with insulin in doses graded to the dietary intake is one example of normal physiological control being approximated by modern therapeutics. Correction of a failure of thyroid gland function by giving preparations of thyroid secretion is a similar example. The maintenance of the heart's normal rhythm using electronic pacemakers, and the replacement of kidney function by machines using dialysis, are other examples of Man's ability to remedy failures in physiological control systems.

Man also modifies his external environment, so as to bring it within the compass of the physiological control system which maintains the deep body temperature at about 37°C. In some millions of years he has learned to make clothes and provide himself with shelter and in this way to extend his habitat almost to the North Pole and to exist in other hostile environments. The Eskimo is an example of man adjusting his external body temperature to a level where his own control systems can maintain life. This he does by decreasing his heat loss by clothing himself in animal skins and by building insulated houses of snow (p. 40.46).

Few people today appreciate how great was the exchange of knowledge between biologist and physical scientist in the eighteenth and nineteenth centuries. Fick, regarded nowadays as a physicist because of his outstanding mathematical work about the diffusion of non-ionic substances, was in fact an anatomist. Helmholtz, whom all scientists regard as one of the great physicists, was a physiologist of note. Black, who helped to lay the foundations of the chemistry of oxygen and of respiration, was a Professor of Chemistry at Edinburgh, where he presented his famous M.D. thesis, and later became Professor of Medicine at Glasgow. Andrews held simultaneously the Chairs of Chemistry and of Medicine in Belfast and, although known internationally for his work on the liquefaction of gases, he was responsible for the control of two outbreaks of cholera in that city. Cross fertilization between the physical and the biological sciences reached its nadir before the beginning of the twentieth century. The introduction of quantum theory virtually revolutionized the study of mathematical physics, physics and chemistry, but did not assist the understanding of the biology of that time. The discoveries of anaesthetics and antisepsis which allowed the development of surgery and the rapid advance of laboratory diagnostic methods, led to greater specialization in Medicine so that by 1930, as today, one could no longer imagine an Andrews being Professor of both Chemistry and Medicine.

The steam-engine governor, invented in 1775 by James Watt, was one of the first automatic control devices. It was analysed in 1868 in a classic paper by Clerk Maxwell *On*

Governors. The problem was to adjust the amount of steam delivered to the engine to the variable load to be overcome. By linking the throttle to the engine speed, the delivery of power was adjusted to overcome any departure from the desired speed. While early mechanical control systems existed it was not until 1934 with Hazen's paper, *Theory of Servomechanisms*, that the general study of control systems began. Much of the modern control equipment has been designed to replace or complement a human operator, and once again engineer and biologist are on common ground.

The engineer's task is to design a device with a single definable object, e.g. to keep the temperature constant inside a large building. This is a comparatively simple problem; it needs a temperature detector or receptor which, if the temperature falls below the desired value, switches on a heating system and, if the temperature goes above this value, switches it off. The temperature in any room or part of the building in which receptors are sited may be set to any desired level and it oscillates around the set level. This phenomenon is called **hunting**.

The biologist's task is to understand or analyse existing systems of great complexity in the light of current knowledge. The engineer's problem is to build a system to serve a specific end. In spite of this, however, the theory of operation of an automatic pilot which lands a jet aircraft and of the stretch reflex system which controls the position of an arm as it turns the page of this book have a great deal in common.

Control systems analysis

When designing a control system an engineer tries to simplify it and the equations which describe it as much as possible, whilst preserving the standards of performance that are set. Almost all control systems can be simplified to the form shown in fig. 2.1.

In the first place, it is necessary to measure the variable being controlled by a device shown as B. In order that the system may handle only one type of signal, the desired input quantity is measured with a device A, producing a signal in similar form. These signals are nearly always in the form of varying electrical quantities, and many devices exist to change output quantities such as temperature, pressure, humidity, position, angular velocity and others into electrical signals. Electrical quantities are not invariably used, however, and outputs may be transformed into mechanical signals such as hydraulic pressures, lengths of rods or cables, rotation of shafts and many others. The two signals, representing present output and desired input, are compared in a comparator and the difference is used to give a **misalignment** or **error signal**. This signal is then amplified in the error amplifier and used to drive an effector or output controller to change the output in such a way as to reduce the error. The concept of comparing the desired input with the actual out-

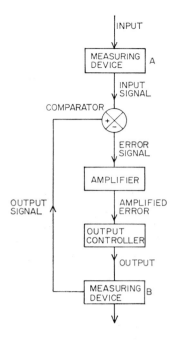

Fig. 2.1. Model of a control system.

put, i.e. of measuring the error, and then using this error to show what action is needed to eliminate the error, is the basis of control systems. A second essential feature is the amplification of the error signal to enable it to drive large outputs. This often is the main purpose of a control system, e.g. the steering mechanism of a large ship enables a man to move a rudder weighing many tons with fingertip control. The third essential feature is the closing of the loop from the output to the input by a feedback element which allows the output to be added or subtracted from the input in the comparator. This permits the system to provide complete automatic closed loop working of which homeostasis is an example.

In summary, a servo system is actuated by an error signal, possesses power amplification, and operates automatically in a closed loop.

A modern example of the design of a servo system for use in medicine is a powered artificial hand. The gripping force is controlled by electrical activity in the muscles of the stump; this electromyographic signal is picked up by electrodes in the socket and is approximately proportional to the tension in the muscle. This is compared at the input to amplified signals fed back from pressure sensors at the finger tips. Any difference is amplified and used to drive a motor which controls the grip of the fingers. If the electromyographic signal is increased and exceeds the feedback signal, the motor is arranged to increase the grip, increasing the feedback signal from the pressure sensors and reducing the error until the motor stops. Should the object gripped react so as to increase the pressure and thus the feedback signal, then this signal exceeds the input and the amplified signal to the motor causes it to reduce the pressure until the two signals balance. The system is thus arranged both to follow variation in input and to compensate for alterations in output conditions or loading.

MATHEMATICAL MODELS

The study of control engineering was facilitated when the systems began to be described mathematically using differential equations. Mathematical models could then be made and the likely performance of any system analysed and predicted.

Consider a simple system such as a motor driving a pointer to follow the movements of a remote shaft rotated by hand. Potentiometers can be fitted to both shafts to change the output and input angles into electrical signals.

Let the input and output angles be θ_1 and θ_0 and the corresponding signals e_1 and e_0. Then

$$e_0 = K\theta_0 \quad \text{and} \quad e_1 = K\theta_1$$

where K is a constant of the potentiometer. The two signals are compared and the difference is an angular positional error,

$$e = e_1 - e_0$$
$$= K(\theta_1 - \theta_0)$$

This is then amplified by a factor, e.g. A to give from the amplifier an amplified error E.

$$E = Ae$$
$$= AK(\theta_1 - \theta_0)$$

If the torque output, T, of the motor is related to the signal from the amplifier thus:

$$T = M \times E$$

where M is a constant of the motor; then

$$T = MAK(\theta_1 - \theta_0) \tag{1}$$

If there is friction present in the system which presents a load to the motor proportional to speed, this friction load can be represented as $F(d\theta_0/dt)$, where $d\theta_0/dt$ is the rate of change of output angle with time and F is a constant for the particular friction in the system.

Suppose the total inertia of the load is I, then the motor torque less the frictional load is used to accelerate this inertia, i.e.

$$T - F\frac{d\theta_0}{dt} = I\frac{d^2\theta_0}{dt^2} \tag{2}$$

where $d^2\theta_0/dt^2$ is $d(d\theta_0/dt)/dt$ which is the rate of change of angular velocity, that is, angular acceleration. Equation 1 is only a particular form of the Newtonian equation of motion,

$$\text{Force} = \text{mass} \times \text{acceleration}$$

Combining 1 and 2 gives

$$MAK(\theta_1 - \theta_0) = I\frac{d^2\theta_0}{dt^2} + F\frac{d\theta_0}{dt}$$

or

$$\theta_1 - \theta_0 = \frac{I}{C} \cdot \frac{d^2\theta_0}{dt^2} + \frac{F}{C}\frac{d\theta_0}{dt} \tag{3}$$

where $C = MAK$

This is a differential equation describing the performance of the simple system in terms of its output acceleration, speed, position and the input signal. Many biological systems can be usefully studied considering them as control systems and modelling them in a similar way to this example using differential equations of greater or lesser complexity. This fact has led to the increasing collaboration between engineers and biologists in an effort to extend their understanding of both systems, but the present rate of development would have been impossible without the use of analogue computers as an aid to the solution of these differential equations, which may be far too complex to allow of manual solution.

Analogue computation

Analogue computers work by simulating accurately physical quantities in terms of varying electrical signals which can be more easily and quickly manipulated and measured. In essence, the elements of an analogue computer may be used to produce electrical models of the differential equations which describe the mathematical models of control systems.

The computer contains devices (simulators) to do all the mathematical operations, such as integration, differentiation, multiplication (amplification) or division, addition and subtraction, sign changing and many others. In each of these devices constants, representing the constants of the various elements of the system, such as the I, M, A, K, etc. of equation 3, can be inserted or altered at will. A flow diagram, such as shown in fig. 2.1 or 2, is compiled from the differential equations of the system to be analysed and each block in the diagram then represents a

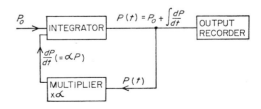

FIG. 2.2. A flow diagram.

simulation element of the computer. These elements are connected together in the same way as in the flow diagram, with the appropriate constants inserted as desired, and then represent an electrical model of the system being studied. If an electrical input similar in form to an actual input to the system is applied, then the output of the computer is related, in an exactly similar way, to the actual output of the system.

For example, if the computer is set up to represent the motion of a bouncing ball and the output on an oscilloscope and the ball studied together, then the output will bounce and decay with the ball and its magnitude is proportional to the bounce of the ball at any time.

The input for the system model in the computer is usually derived from a **function generator**, a device which can provide inputs such as sine, square or triangular waves, continuously increasing or decreasing quantities (ramp functions) or sudden increases and decreases (step functions), trains of pulses and many others.

The output may be displayed on an oscilloscope as mentioned, and observed or photographed, or it may be recorded directly on tape or paper chart recorders. A major advantage of analogue computers is that the solution need not only be presented at the rate at which it naturally occurs in real time, as in the ball example, but may be condensed in the time scale for rapidity and economy, or expanded for detailed study of a transient phenomena. A further advantage is that following any alteration of the constants of the system the changed response appears almost at once and therefore the effect of a wide range of variation of constants can be quickly seen.

By comparison the digital computer deals directly with numbers and is essentially an arithmetic machine for the solution of problems which can be resolved into sequences of numerical operations. It can only solve differential equations by approximate step by step methods. By making these steps as small as one wishes and using many places of decimals these solutions may, in fact, be more accurate than those of an analogue machine but lack the instantaneous nature of the other's solution.

As an example of the study of a biological system on an analogue computer, consider the growth of a natural breeding population in the absence of restraining influences. It is not a control system because it is difficult to discern a desired input figure and hence an error. Nor does there seem to be any 'gain' or an obvious 'closed loop'. However, the growth can be described by a simple exponential equation.

$$P(t) = P(o) \, e^{\alpha t} \qquad (4)$$

where $P(t)$ is the population at any time, t, $P(o)$ is the initial population when t is zero, e is the exponential constant (2·7183) and α is a constant. The form of this growth curve is shown in fig. 2.3 for various values of α.

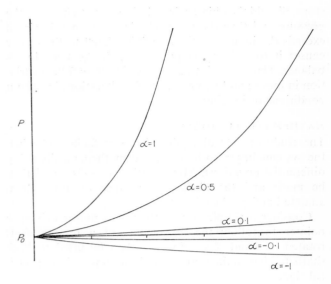

FIG. 2.3. Exponential curves (see text).

The expression in equation 4 can be expressed more simply as a differential equation:

$$\frac{dP}{dt} = \alpha P \qquad (5)$$

where d/dt as before expresses **rate of change** of population P. The actual rate of change is now seen to depend on the constant α. If α is negative the population declines, if positive it increases; the larger the value of α the faster the population increases.

Equation 5 is the simplest form of differential equation. It is termed a **first order equation** because the highest order of differential which occurs is dP/dt. Equation 3 is a **second order equation** because $d^2\theta_o/dt^2$ occurs, and if the highest order term is of the form d^n/dt^n the equation is an **nth order equation**. Both equations 2 and 3 are **linear** since they do not contain functions and their differentials multiplied together such as $(dP/dt)^2$ or $P \times (d^2P/dt^2)$. Such equations are non-linear and far more complex and difficult to solve, if indeed this is possible. A first order differential equation is simple to solve, thus

$$\frac{dP}{dt} = \alpha P$$

$$\frac{1}{P} \, dP = \alpha dt$$

Integrating once

$$\int \frac{1}{P} dP = \int \alpha dt$$

$$\log_e P = \alpha t + \text{a constant}$$

Various values of $P(o)$ and of α can be used to produce families of curves for different initial populations and rates of growth but this is extremely tedious, even in such a simple case. To solve the problem on an analogue computer, a flow diagram is drawn, and integrator and multiplier elements of the machine connected as shown in fig. 2.2. Various values of $P(o)$ can be fed in at the input together with various values of α (by altering the constant of the multiplier which can be done readily) and the effects rapidly and easily studied or recorded. More complex mathematical expressions for population growth may be adopted and as easily simulated on the computer.

As an example of a physiological problem to which the method of analysis might be applied, let us take only one simple stage of the complex control system which regulates the temperature of the human body. Man's deep body or core temperature (θ) varies with time and this relationship may be described by a simple differential equation:

$$mc\frac{d\theta}{dt} = H_g - H_i$$

where m is the deep core mass, c its specific heat and $d\theta/dt$ represents the rate of change of temperature with time. H_g is the heat gain and H_i the heat loss of the system.

We must, however, consider in detail how heat is either gained or lost, and decide whether it is possible to state a mathematical law for each circumstance. Heat is produced by metabolic processes, or gained by ingesting food or fluid at temperatures above that of the body. In addition, industrial workers may be exposed for intervals of time to high external temperatures, miners and steelworkers being obvious examples. Under such circumstances they may gain heat from their surroundings. On the other hand, heat loss results from sweating, from conduction, convection and radiation of heat from the body to cooler surroundings, from respiration as the inspired air is warmed by the body before it is expired, and in urine and faeces. A few of these processes are immediately susceptible to mathematical analysis; for example the heat loss in the urine is (mass of urine) × (specific heat of urine) × (body temperature). But the complex gain or loss of heat by someone working under conditions where there is no external control of temperature or humidity cannot be written in any simple mathematical form. The process is outlined in fig. 2.4; heat gain and loss are represented as being fed into a comparator; the difference $(H_g - H_i)$ (the error signal) determines the final body core temperature, through an output controller. At a physiological level this entire process is extremely complicated, and is discussed on p. 40.4.

In fig. 2.5 we 'translate' the control diagram of fig. 2.4 into the 'language' of the analogue computer. Fig. 2.5 introduces two new computer symbols and of necessity their representation has been oversimplified. The **summer** simultaneously adds and subtracts incoming voltages

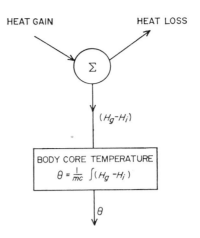

FIG. 2.4. Model of the control of body temperature.

which are proportional to physical factors. But as we have said, H_g and H_i are each the sum of many variables. In more detail the summer would have many input voltages, each one representing the factors for heat gain where the sign is positive or the heat loss where the signal is negative. In some cases it is possible to define one of the H_g or H_i factors by a known physical law. But in many cases this is not possible, and the input requires a function generator, by the use of which it may eventually be possible to understand the temperature control at a quantitative level.

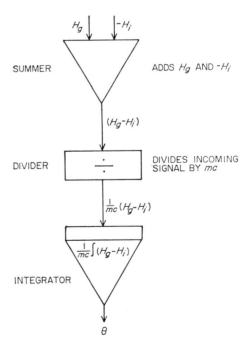

FIG. 2.5. Model of a control system containing a summer and a divider.

Although for at least 30 years the fundamental anatomical pathways and physiological control regions have been known, it has always been difficult to define such central processes in a quantitative way. It is now appreciated that few biological problems can be stated even approximately by linear differential equations. Obviously this introduces immense difficulties in tackling physiological problems mathematically. Because of this the introduction of the analogue computer to the world of medicine is of vital importance. As an example, a research worker in Edinburgh University who was studying heart function used to spend 28 hours calculating the results of one of his experiments with a standard calculating machine. When an analogue computer became available about 30 min was needed to programme the machine to this particular problem, a process professionally known as **patching**; thereafter 28 hours of tedious work was reduced to 5 min! Once programmed the machine can carry out any number of identical calculations in 5 min. The opportunity for advance in physiological research through the introduction of such apparatus should be obvious. Apart from the arithmetical fact that the time needed for a single calculation was reduced by a computer by 99·64 per cent, much more important is that the rapid feedback of information to a research worker may within weeks rather than years, help to lead an entire research programme quickly into the most productive channel.

FURTHER READING

BAYLISS L.E. (1966) *Living Control Systems*. London: English Universities Press.

FAGG S.V. (1956) *Differential Equations*. London : English Universities Press.

MILHORN H.T. (1966) *The Application of Control Theory to Physiological Systems*. Philadelphia : Saunders.

Chapter 3
Biological variation and its measurement

Statistical techniques are used in every branch of medicine. As all may use the same techniques, illustrative examples of their application may be drawn from any branch of preclinical or clinical study. Perhaps the most frequent use of statistical methods is made by pharmacologists and by workers in social science and public health. For this reason some of the examples given in this chapter are taken, not from anatomy, physiology or biochemistry, but refer to subjects which the student will encounter in later studies.

It is not possible to provide, in the space of a single chapter, more than a very short account of actual methods. The aim is to provide enough to lead to some understanding of the potential and the limitations of statistical techniques. Those who find it necessary to apply the techniques should consult a statistician before starting their experiments, since he may give invaluable advice not only on the ultimate calculation but, prospectively, on the design of the experiments themselves.

Errors of measurement

Scientific work depends upon measurement, and all measurements are subject to error. Some of the sources of error are common to all sciences. There is the error associated with measuring instruments. Thus if we measure length with a good ruler graduated in millimetres we would expect to get a figure correct at least to the nearest millimetre, i.e. our measurement has an error of ± 0.5 mm. If, on the other hand, we measure length with a micrometer gauge the error may be reduced to ± 0.005 mm; however accurate our instruments, there is still a finite error. This is often overlooked since people who use complicated measuring instruments may be unaware of the error associated with the apparently precise readings on the dials of the machine. There is also the error associated with the operator. This may result from boredom or fatigue; for example it arises in those who have to watch a panel of instruments for long periods such as radar operators and also in people who use calculating machines, who make a predictable number of mistakes in entering figures. Errors may also arise from conscious or unconscious bias in that one individual may consistently overestimate and another consistently under-

estimate the end point of a titration. All of these sources of error arise in chemistry and physics as well as in biology.

Biological variation

In biology there is a further source of error which is so large that it overshadows all other errors; usually in the physical sciences, it is so small that it can be ignored. This is called **biological variation** and stems from the fact that individuals in a biological population are not identical. Thus, whereas all individual molecules in a population of hydrogen molecules may usually be considered as identical and indistinguishable, no two men or muscle cells or amoebae or bacteria or virus particles can be regarded as identical. The more complex the biological individual, the more variable the population is likely to be. This variability between individuals means that measurements made on any **sample** of individuals do not necessarily reflect the measurements of any other sample drawn from the same **population**. This is perfectly obvious but is readily forgotten. If we draw a sample of one nail from a bag of nails bought from the ironmonger, measure it with a ruler and find that it is 2.5 cm long, it is a fair inference that all the other nails have the same length. Of course, if a micrometer gauge is used the nails will be found to vary in size a little; on the other hand, if we measure one medical student and find that his height is 178 cm it is not a fair inference, even if only a ruler is used, that all other medical students are of the same height.

Purposes of measurement

Measurements are made for two main reasons. The first is to make inferences about the population of things in which we are interested. For example, what is the blood pressure of a healthy man of 40 years? We could measure the blood pressure of one such man and infer that this value represents the value for the population. In this case there would be an infinite population of healthy 40-year-old men and a sample of one such man. Common sense warns us that our inference might well be wrong. In other words our **estimate** of the true value in the population is subject to error. Common sense also tells us that if we want to decrease the error and have a better chance of drawing the right inference, the size of the sample should be increased. The second reason for making measurements is to discover whether the individual on whom we made the measurement is normal or abnormal. This presupposes that the normal measurements are already known. In this case the individual is compared with previously acquired knowledge and the appropriate inferences drawn. Such inferences may be right or wrong; all that can be done is to assess the **probability** of the inference being right. Much of statistics is concerned with such assessments.

We must also define our terms, sample and population, very precisely. If we measure the blood pressures of a sample of healthy 40-year-old men when they are recumbent, any inference drawn can apply only to a population of healthy recumbent 40-year-old men. To make any inference about the same men when they are running in a marathon is obviously fallacious. Thus inferences must be limited to conditions identical to those under which sample measurements are made.

Measurements of central tendency

The most usual question asked about measurements is of the form: 'What is the blood pressure of a healthy 40-year-old man?' Since we know that individuals vary the only answer available is some sort of **average value** or, in other words, a measurement of the **central tendency** of all the values in the population. The most usual of these measurements is the **arithmetic mean**, usually called the **mean**. Other measurements such as the most commonly occurring value, the **mode**, or the value intermediate between the highest and the lowest individual value in the sample, the **median**, may be used. One other measure of central tendency is of especial importance in medical biology; for reasons, some of which are discussed later, it is often convenient to use the average of the logarithms of the measurements. This is the **logarithmic mean**.

In a sample of n values of a measurement y, we can express the mean, usually written as $\bar{y}$, algebraically as follows:

$$\bar{y} = \frac{\sum y}{n} \tag{1}$$

where $\sum$ signifies the sum of all the values of y.

Measurements of scatter

Just as individual values in a sample show a central tendency, they also show a tendency to dispersal or scatter, depending on the degree of variability. Once again this tendency can be expressed in various ways. The simplest is to state the lowest and highest individual values, i.e. the **range** of the measurements. Another way is to measure the difference between each individual value

and the mean value; this difference is usually called the **deviation** from the mean. If we sum all the deviations the result is, of course, zero. A common way of calculating the mean is to guess the mean, to sum the deviations, and then adjust the guessed value of the mean by the average deviation. Algebraically this can be expressed as follows:

$$\sum (y - \bar{y}) = \sum y - \sum \bar{y}$$
$$= \sum y - n.\bar{y}$$
$$= \sum y - n.\frac{\sum y}{n}$$
$$= \sum y - \sum y$$
$$= 0$$

Since the sum of the deviations is always zero, then the mean deviation must also be zero.

This difficulty can be avoided in two ways. Firstly we can calculate the sum of the deviations ignoring the sign, and dividing this sum by n gives a **mean deviation**.

$$\text{Mean deviation} = \frac{\sum |(y - \bar{y})|}{n}$$

Alternatively the sign can be eliminated by squaring each individual deviation, thus making all the values positive. The sum of these values is called the **sum of squares**. The **mean square deviation** can then be reduced to the original scale by extracting its square root. This value, which, for reasons discussed below, has other major advantages, is the most commonly used measure of scatter and is called the **standard deviation (s)**. It is calculated algebraically:

$$s = \sqrt{\frac{\sum (y - \bar{y})^2}{n}} \tag{2}$$

This is the correct equation for the standard deviation when n is large. When the sample size is small, as it usually is in biology, the equation tends systematically to underestimate the real value of the standard deviation. This is corrected by adjusting the equation to

$$s = \sqrt{\frac{\sum (y - \bar{y})^2}{n - 1}} \tag{3}$$

With large samples the difference in the estimate of s using equations 2 and 3 is negligible, but with small samples it may be considerable. Thus nothing is lost by using equation 3 on all occasions.

CALCULATION OF SUM OF SQUARES

When using a machine one can calculate $\sum (y - y)^2$ without doing any tedious subtraction from the following equation:

$$\sum (y - \bar{y})^2 = \sum y^2 - \frac{(\sum y)^2}{n} \tag{4}$$

This equation is derived as follows:

$$\sum (y - \bar{y})^2 = \sum y^2 - 2 \sum y \cdot \bar{y} + \sum \bar{y}^2$$
$$= \sum y^2 - 2 \sum y \cdot \frac{\sum y}{n} + n \cdot \bar{y}^2$$
$$= \sum y^2 - 2 \frac{(\sum y)^2}{n} + n \cdot \frac{(\sum y)^2}{n^2}$$
$$= \sum y^2 - 2 \frac{(\sum y)^2}{n} + \frac{(\sum y)^2}{n}$$
$$= \sum y^2 - \frac{(\sum y)^2}{n}$$

The mean square deviation, s^2, is usually referred to as the **variance** (V).

DISTRIBUTIONS

If we measure the systolic blood pressure of 100 healthy 40-year-old men a series of values is obtained from which the measurements of central tendency and of scatter may be calculated (table 3.1a). The instrumental and operator

TABLE 3.1a. Systolic blood pressures (mm Hg) measured on 100 healthy 40-year-old men

112	134	164	104	142	121	150	133	134	157
140	119	126	151	135	110	108	112	147	127
95	124	128	117	128	117	128	125	127	124
127	130	131	125	117	129	127	136	132	128
136	125	118	130	114	114	140	130	91	126
123	98	130	136	129	127	133	123	126	120
132	127	138	130	123	126	111	154	128	130
134	126	127	116	122	101	132	136	129	145
137	152	134	132	124	156	116	113	160	131
123	119	133	121	132	126	124	115	111	132

Mean = 127·48 ($\sum y/n$)
Median = 127·5 (Midpoint of range)
Mode = 127 (Commonest value, occurring seven times)
Range = 91–164
Mean
  deviation = 9
Standard
  deviation = 13

Calculations
$\sum y$ = 12748
$\sum y^2$ = 1641874
$(\sum y)^2/n$ = 1625115
$\sum (y - \bar{y})^2$ = 16759
V = 169
s = 13
$\bar{y}$ = 127·48

errors are so small in relation to the biological variation that they are not considered separately. The first thing to note is that the mean, median and mode, which are defined in the table, all lie close together. Table 3.1b gives the marks obtained in an examination by 100 medical students. These have been adjusted so that the mean and standard deviations are the same as those for the blood pressure values. In this case, however, the mean and the

2

TABLE 3.1b. Marks obtained in class examination by 100 medical students (maximum mark = 242)

124	126	117	126	121	117	185	120	126	124
139	118	125	124	121	123	123	123	121	126
122	122	123	119	122	120	127	128	120	124
134	130	117	123	123	122	119	123	125	122
122	121	124	127	160	123	126	142	128	123
119	122	158	122	127	122	124	127	154	136
130	146	127	116	125	166	124	118	124	125
121	169	120	119	175	128	121	125	122	125
121	118	130	124	126	124	128	125	126	120
127	124	117	172	127	119	125	126	123	120

Mean = 127·48
Median = 150·5
Mode = 124
Range = 116–185
Mean
  deviation = 7·8
Standard
  deviation = 13

Calculations
$\sum y$ = 12748
$\sum y^2$ = 1641922
$(\sum y)^2/n$ = 1625115
$\sum (y - \bar{y})^2$ = 16807
V = 169
s = 13
$\bar{y}$ = 127·48

mode are not the same but are similar, and the median is very different. How can the differences between the two series of values be shown? One obvious way is to draw a diagram or graph to illustrate the **distribution** of the values. The simplest form of diagram is a **histogram**. The figures are arranged in groups and the **frequency** of the occurrence of values in each group is plotted against the range of that group, as shown in fig. 3.1. It is clear that,

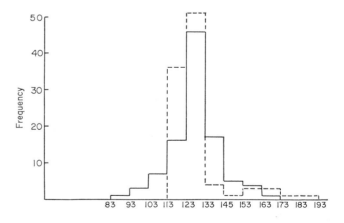

FIG. 3.1. Histograms of distributions in tables 3.1a & b. Systolic blood pressure (mm Hg), solid line; examination mark, broken line.

despite the fact that both distributions have the same mean and standard deviation, they are very different in shape. In the case of the values for blood pressure the distribution is roughly symmetrical about the mean. If the samples are made bigger and the range of each group made narrower, a smoother set of smaller blocks is obtained; ultimately, with an infinite sample and an infinitely small

FIG. 3.2. Frequency distribution of population of systolic blood pressure (BP) of healthy 40-year-old men. Abscissa, (a) BP in mm Hg; (b) BP in units of standard deviation (*s*) from mean.

range for each group, a curve called the **frequency distribution curve** may be drawn (fig. 3.2). In many biological measurements, the shape of this curve approximates closely to the so-called **normal distribution** or **Gaussian distribution** after the man who first described it mathematically. On the other hand the distribution of examination marks (fig. 3.1) is not normal; it is asymmetric and is said to be **skew**.

These are essentially empiric findings although various theoretical arguments have been advanced to account for them. The equation for the normal distribution is, of course, known and contains only two variables, the mean and the standard deviation. The mathematical relationship between these variables is the primary reason for using them as common descriptions of central tendency and of scatter. It is tacitly assumed, whenever statistical methods based on the normal distribution are used, that the measurements being examined have been drawn from a normal distribution of such measurements. Certain tests of the validity of this assumption are available, but normally they are not carried out. In fact, many statistical tests based on the normal distribution actually work quite well when applied even to very skew distributions.

THE RELATIONSHIP OF THE MEAN AND THE STANDARD DEVIATION TO THE NORMAL DISTRIBUTION

Fig. 3.2a shows the normal frequency distribution curve; this is the distribution which is being assumed for the whole population of individuals from which a sample is drawn. The maximum frequency, the mode, and the median both coincide with the mean of the distribution, i.e. the distribution is symmetrical about the mean. This is characteristic of the normal distribution and is clearly not true for skew distributions. The abscissa in fig. 3.2a is the actual value of the blood pressure. Now that the mean and the standard deviation are known we can redraw the distribution using for the abscissa a scale of standard deviations on either side of the mean (fig. 3.2b.) If the area under the curve is now taken as unity, we can

calculate, on the basis of the equation for the normal distribution curve, the proportion of the area under the curve that lies within the range ± 1 standard deviation or ± 2 standard deviations from the mean and so on for any number of standard deviations we wish to choose. Tables of these integrals are published and can be found in standard works.

In fig. 3.2b the areas of the normal curve enclosed are roughly:

mean ± 1 standard deviation
 = 66 per cent (horizontal shading)
mean ± 2 standard deviations
 = 95 per cent (horizontal plus diagonal shading)
mean ± 3 standard deviations
 = 99 per cent (horizontal, diagonal and vertical shading).

The value of this exercise should now be obvious. If the mean and the standard deviation of the population are known, then, for a sample of one individual, there is only one chance in a hundred that, if he is really a member of the population, his value will deviate from the mean by more than three times the standard deviation. Thus if a 40-year-old man has a blood pressure of 170 mm Hg, which lies more than three times the standard deviation away from the mean, we would be tempted to assume that he is not a member of the population of healthy 40-year-old men; i.e. his blood pressure is abnormal. Even so this assumption would be wrong once in every hundred times that it was made and the possibility of an error of this type is unavoidable although we can set any **chance** we like. The levels of probability of being wrong that are usually chosen are 1 in 20 or 1 in 100.

While all this seems plain sailing, we must remember two points.

(1) The mean and standard deviation of a population are seldom known. We usually are obliged to estimate them from previous samples and these estimates may be wrong.

(2) If too high a standard is set for excluding a value from the population, then values which really are not part of the population will appear to belong to it. Thus if we say that a blood pressure is only abnormal or unhealthy if it is more than 166 mm Hg, we may accept many blood pressure values of less than 166 mm Hg as healthy when they are not. Failure to spot an abnormality may be as dangerous as to regard a normal individual as abnormal. For these reasons it is difficult to lay down the normal ranges for any measurement with any real accuracy.

Design of experiments

One of the simplest forms of experimental design consists of choosing two comparable samples of individuals from the same population and then applying to one of the two samples some form of treatment. Treatment is used here to mean any change imposed upon the sample and does not necessarily mean a form of medical treatment. This sounds easy but is actually, in many circumstances, very difficult. The main problems are to ensure, firstly that the two samples are comparable and, secondly, that all the individuals in both samples are members of the same population throughout the experiment with the single exception of the treatment applied to the one sample.

It may suffice to give two examples. The result of a laboratory experiment on two samples of ten mice, could be invalidated if from a box of twenty mice, ten are picked out by hand and put in another box. By this technique one would tend to catch the least active mice in making the transfer, so that the two groups would not be comparable in this respect. One could improve on this by catching and putting the mice successively into two boxes, but it is better to allocate them in a truly **random fashion**. This can be accomplished by identifying each animal, e.g. with a colour code, numbering each and allocating each to one or other sample by using a table of random numbers. This is a time-consuming exercise but is worth the trouble since any individual mouse has the same chance of ending up in the first sample as in the second. This technique of **random sampling** is adequate if all the mice in the original box are to be regarded as members of the same population. If they are all males then an imbalance of the sexes in the two samples cannot arise; if they are of mixed sex then random sampling may give incomparable samples in that one sample may have a preponderance of one sex.

The second example is the selection of human subjects to form two comparable samples. Let us consider the problem of finding out if a particular drug is effective in preventing seasickness. If the subjects are allocated to the two samples completely at random, then imbalances may easily arise in such factors as sex, age, previous experience of sea voyages and so on. In these circumstances they can be regarded as members of the same population only in that they are all exposed to the same stress but not in respect of these other features. The usual answer to this problem is to impose some restraints upon the random sampling process. Thus men and women might be dealt with as separate groups allocating the members of each group at random to the two samples. The problem is that the more restraints that are imposed, the less certain is it that two unbiased samples have been obtained, even if the two samples are balanced in respect of the restraints imposed. We are often obliged to compromise between these two competing features in designing experiments.

The two samples are then kept under identical conditions throughout the experiment, save that the treatment is given to one of the samples. This, too, raises problems.

If a drug is given to one sample, and not to the other, we not only apply the action of the drug, we also apply a psychological stimulus so that the individuals may feel they are being looked after and cared for and may respond to this stimulus even if the drug is inactive. This is an extremely potent and well-recognized stimulus. Giving inert tablets of lactose (an inert medicine is usually called a placebo) causes improvement in the subjective feelings or symptoms in a large proportion of patients. Such people are called **placebo reactors**. Subjective effects may also appear to improve physical performance. The history of athletic training is full of accounts of special diets, vitamins, tonics and nowadays more dangerous drugs recommended by trainers and coaches. These are nearly always based on the subjective reports of athletes and not on their records.

It is therefore necessary to give the untreated sample the same apparent treatment as the treated sample, thus limiting the treatment to the actual action of the drug or other treatment.

Furthermore, the experimenter or the doctor, who is assessing the results of the experiment, is often swayed or biased in his judgement if he knows which subjects or patients have been treated. This unconscious bias becomes an operator error which may invalidate the experiments when the final assessment is made. Nowadays experiments are often designed to ensure that the operator does not know which individuals are in the treated group. This situation, where neither the individuals (the patients) nor the operator (the doctor) knows which individual is in which sample, is called a **double-blind trial.** Where patients are severely ill there may be ethical objections to such a design; but if it is not used, great care must be exercised in interpreting the results.

Analysis of results

When a properly designed experiment is completed, the measurement, whatever it may be, is made on all the individuals in both samples. How can the results be assessed? The fundamental basis of examining the data is called the **null hypothesis**; this is an hypothesis that the treatment applied to the one sample has had no effect. In this case both samples may be regarded as random samples of individuals from the same normally distributed population. The true values of the mean and the standard deviation of this population are unknown but estimates of these can be made from data on one or both samples. On the basis of these estimates the probability that both samples are drawn from the same population may be calculated. This calculation was developed by Grossett who wrote under the pseudonym of *Student.* He worked for the brewing firm of Guinness and was one of the pioneers of statistical theory. The test depends upon the distribution of the statistic *t*. When the sample size is infinitely large, then, for any given value of the integral of

[handwritten margin note: should be Gossett ≠ Gosset]

the normal distribution, t is the corresponding value of the abscissa expressed in terms of the standard deviation. Thus on p. 3.4 we made the approximate statement that 95 per cent of all values lay 'within the range of the mean ± 2 standard deviations'. The accurate statement would be: 'within the range of the mean ± 1.96 standard deviations', 1.96 being the value of t corresponding to a probability or frequency of 0.95 when the sample size is infinite or equals the population. Values for t have been calculated and tabulated for various sample sizes and for various probabilities.

Standard error of the mean

As already described the standard deviation is a measure of the variability of individuals about the mean of the population. Individuals may be regarded as samples of one. What would be the variability, about the mean of the population, of the averages of samples of two, or of three, or of more individuals? These sample averages, or sample means, would be expected to deviate from the population mean by a smaller amount as the sample size increased; and the two would coincide when one sample equalled the total population. It is easier to understand this if an actual example is considered. Let us say that we measure the height of 1000 male medical students and assume that this population is normally distributed, with a mean, $\bar{y}$, and a standard deviation, s. We then draw, at random, sixteen samples (m samples) each of nine (n) students. This will give sixteen estimates of $\bar{y}$. How will these estimates be distributed about the true value of $\bar{y}$? The mean of the sixteen values of $\bar{y}$, written $\bar{\bar{y}}$ is calculated thus,

$$\bar{\bar{y}} = \frac{\sum \bar{y}}{m}$$

We can also calculate the standard deviation of the sixteen values of $\bar{y}$, written $s_{\bar{y}}$. Thus,

$$s_{\bar{y}} = \sqrt{\frac{\sum (\bar{y} - \bar{\bar{y}})^2}{m - 1}}$$

This statistic, $s_{\bar{y}}$, which is the standard deviation of the means of samples, is called the **standard error**. It can be calculated directly when we draw several samples; when only one sample is drawn it can be estimated from the equation;

$$s_{\bar{y}} = \frac{s}{\sqrt{n}} \qquad (5)$$

where n is the number of individuals in the sample. Thus, in our example, when $n=9$ each estimate of $s_{\bar{y}}$ is one-third ($1/\sqrt{9}$) of the corresponding estimate of s. When $s_{\bar{y}}$ is calculated directly, by drawing several samples it also is approximately one-third of the value of s. Thus $s/\sqrt{n}$ is approximately equal to $\sum (\bar{y} - \bar{\bar{y}})^2/(m-1)$.

As the sample gets bigger the standard error of the mean gets smaller. In the case where a population is of infinite size, then as the sample size approaches infinity, the standard error of the mean approaches zero; in other words the mean is known without error. We are now in a position to calculate three statistics from the information obtained by drawing a single sample. Thus:

$$\text{Mean} \quad \bar{y} = \frac{\sum y}{n} \qquad (1)$$

$$\text{Standard deviation} \quad s = \sqrt{\frac{\sum (y - \bar{y})^2}{n - 1}} \qquad (3)$$

$$\text{Standard error of the mean} \quad s_{\bar{y}} = \frac{s}{\sqrt{n}} \qquad (5)$$

or

$$s_{\bar{y}} = \sqrt{\frac{\sum (y - \bar{y})^2}{n(n - 1)}} \qquad (5a)$$

Difference between two means

We can now return to the problem that faced *Student* in designing his t test to compare the means of two different samples. It is possible to measure the probability that any one sample mean deviates from the true mean by any given number of standard errors of that mean, but the true mean and the true standard error of the mean are unknown. We can only compare the estimates of the mean derived from two samples and use as the standard error an estimate based on the standard errors calculated for each sample. *Student* thus gave the following equation for calculating t from such data:

$$t = \frac{\bar{y}_1 - \bar{y}_2}{s_{(\bar{y}_1 - \bar{y}_2)}} \qquad (6)$$

where $s_{(\bar{y}_1 - \bar{y}_2)}$ is the standard error of the difference between the two means (see below). Having calculated the value of t, the probability that, if the two samples had been drawn from the same population, this value would be reached or exceeded, can be obtained from a table of t, entering the table for the value of $n=n_1+n_2-2$. If the value found for the probability is less than 0.05 then there is less than one chance in twenty that the samples are drawn from the same population, or less than one chance in twenty that the treatment applied to one sample has had no effect.

The reason why the table of t is entered for the value corresponding to $n=n_1+n_2-2$ is that this is the number of **degrees of freedom** associated with the comparison being made. The concept of degrees of freedom is used widely in statistics and is at first difficult to follow. If, however, we were told that the mean height of a sample of sixteen medical students was 170 cm we could create our own hypothetical series of sixteen individual heights with complete freedom to choose any values at all for the first fifteen students, but the sixteenth value would be fixed for us since the mean was given. We can be said to have only fifteen degrees of freedom in this exercise. Thus if we assigned a hypothetical height of 180 cm to fifteen students our last student must be only 20 cm tall. This follows from the fact that:

$$\bar{y} = \frac{\sum y}{n}$$

$$\therefore 170 = \frac{\sum y}{16}$$

$$\therefore \sum y = 16 \times 170$$

$$= 2720 \text{ cm}$$

and

$$\sum y \text{ for 15 students} = 15 \times 180$$

$$= 2700 \text{ cm}$$

Thus, once we have calculated the mean of a sample of n values, only $(n-1)$ degrees of freedom are left; and in comparing two means the sum of the degrees of freedom associated with each, i.e. (n_1-1) and (n_2-1) is n_1+n_2-2.

The **standard error of the difference between two means** may be calculated in one of two different ways. The first depends upon the theorem that the variance of a difference is equal to the sum of the variances of each of the terms. Thus:

$$V(\bar{y}_1 - \bar{y}_2) = V(\bar{y}_1) + V(\bar{y}_2)$$

$$= s_{\bar{y}_1}{}^2 + s_{\bar{y}_2}{}^2$$

$$= \frac{\sum(y_1-\bar{y}_1)^2}{n_1(n_1-1)} + \frac{\sum(y_2-\bar{y}_2)^2}{n_2(n_2-1)}$$

$$\text{(from equation 5a)}$$

Where $n_1 = n_2$ this expression becomes

$$V(\bar{y}_1 - \bar{y}_2) = \frac{\sum(y_1-\bar{y}_1)^2 + \sum(y_2-\bar{y}_2)^2}{n(n-1)}$$

The alternative method of calculating the standard error to be used in equation 6 is to assume that, since the null hypothesis requires that both samples are drawn from the same population, the best estimate of the variance is that calculated from both samples combined together. For this purpose we calculate the overall mean, $\bar{\bar{y}}$, and estimate the variance from the equation:

$$V(y) = \frac{\sum(y-\bar{\bar{y}})^2}{(n_1+n_2-1)}$$

Hence

$$V(\bar{y}_1) = \frac{V(y)}{n_1}$$

$$V(\bar{y}_2) = \frac{V(y)}{n_2}$$

so that, summing the variances of the two means

$$V(\bar{y}_1 - \bar{y}_2) = \frac{V(y)}{n_1} + \frac{V(y)}{n_2}$$

$$= \frac{n_1+n_2}{n_1 n_2} \cdot V(y)$$

Where $n_1 = n_2$, this becomes

$$\frac{2n}{n^2} V(y) = \frac{2V(y)}{n}$$

Analysis of variance

The t test is a method of comparing two samples. It cannot be used for more than two samples without making separate analyses for each pair of samples. R.A. Fisher developed a wholly different technique for coping with the problem of examining the differences between a number of samples, and it is instructive to examine this technique in relation to the simple case of two samples at this stage.

Fisher's technique consists of examining not the differences between means but the ratio between variances. His ideas are beautifully simple in concept but often extremely difficult in practice. He showed mathematically, that the sum of squares of deviations from the mean could be partitioned into additive components. Let us consider the heights of two samples of sixteen medical students. On the basis that all the individuals in both samples are members of the same population we can calculate an overall mean for the thirty-two values and an overall variance. Thus:

$$\bar{\bar{y}} = \frac{\sum y_1 + \sum y_2}{n_1 + n_2} = \frac{\sum y}{32}$$

$$V = \frac{\sum(y-\bar{\bar{y}})^2}{n_1+n_2-1} = \frac{\sum(y-\bar{\bar{y}})^2}{31}$$

There are thus thirty-one degrees of freedom associated with the overall variance. When we consider each sample separately we get:

$$\bar{y}_1 = \frac{\sum y_1}{n_1} = \frac{\sum y_1}{16}$$

and

$$V_1 = \frac{\sum(y_1-\bar{y}_1)^2}{n_1-1} = \frac{\sum(y_1-\bar{y}_1)^2}{15}$$

Similarly,

$$V_2 = \frac{\sum(y_2-\bar{y}_2)^2}{n_2-1} = \frac{\sum(y_2-\bar{y}_2)^2}{15}$$

There are thus (n_1-1) and (n_2-1) degrees of freedom associated with the sample variances, i.e. in this case thirty. We thus have a component of the variance associated with the individual samples with thirty degrees of freedom, and a total variance associated with thirty-one degrees of freedom. The remaining degree of freedom is associated with the variance of the two sample means about the overall mean. Thus we can write:

$$V_{\bar{y}} = \frac{\sum (\bar{y} - \bar{\bar{y}})^2}{2 - 1}$$

Fisher's mathematics showed that the sums of squares, not the variances, were additive. Thus:

$$\sum (y - \bar{\bar{y}})^2 = \sum (y_1 - \bar{y}_1)^2 \\ + \sum (y_2 - \bar{y}_2)^2 + \sum n.(\bar{y} - \bar{\bar{y}})^2 \quad (7)$$

We can look at this semi-diagrammatically in table 3.2. It is clear that the last term in equation 7 would be very much bigger in the second example than it would be in the first and also that the other terms on the right hand side in equation 7 would be smaller in the second example than in the first. We can regard the last term as a source of variation 'between samples'. Since the mean of each sample represents n values its squared deviation is multiplied by n to bring it into line with the other sources of variation which are to be regarded as 'within samples'.

Fisher went on to compare the variances derived from the separate components of the overall sum of squares. This gave rise to the descriptive term **analysis of variance**. If the variance 'between samples' is large compared to the variance 'within samples', as in the second example, then it is improbable that the samples have been drawn from the same population, even though the values for the combined data on all thirty two students looks like a homogeneous population. He therefore calculated a statistic called the **variance ratio**, usually written F, and derived the probabilities of getting various values of F with different sample sizes. Tables of F are available just as are tables of t. The usual form of expressing an analysis of variance of the data we have been describing is in table 3.2b, and the general form in table 3.3. Since within any one sample the individuals have been treated in exactly the same way, the within samples variance depends only on the essential biological variation between individuals. We can regard this inescapable minimum variation as basic to any experimental situation. Thus the within samples variance is often called the **error variance** and is used to calculate the significance of the other estimates of variance, in this case the variance between samples. This is the simplest case of the

TABLE 3.2a. Heights of thirty-two medical students. The heights are arranged as two samples of sixteen medical students on the basis of two hypothetical examples. Each individual height in the table is represented by a dot.

Height in cms	All 32 students	Example 1		Example 2	
		Sample 1	Sample 2	Sample 1	Sample 2
182	.	.		.	
179	...	.	..	...	
176	....	..	..	....	
173	.....	..	...	....	.
170	......	...	...	...	...
167	.....	...	..	.	....
164	....	..	..		....
161	...	..	.		...
158	.		.		.

TABLE 3.2b. Analysis of variance.

Source of variation	Example 1				Example 2			
	Sum of squares	Degrees of freedom (d.f.)	V	F	Sum of squares	Degrees of freedom (d.f.)	V	F
Between samples	0	1	0	0	648	1	648	39
Within samples	1152	30	38·4	—	504	30	16·8	—
Total	1152	31	37·16		1152	31	37·16	

TABLE 3.3.

Source of variation	Sum of squares	d.f.	V	F
Between samples	$\sum n(\bar{y}-\bar{\bar{y}})^2$	I	(B) $\dfrac{\sum n(\bar{y}-\bar{\bar{y}})^2}{I}$	B/E
Within samples	$\sum (y_1-\bar{y}_1)^2 + \sum (y_2-\bar{y}_2)^2$	30	(E) $\dfrac{\sum (y_1-\bar{y}_1)^2 + \sum (y_2-\bar{y}_2)^2}{30}$	
Total	$\sum (y-\bar{y})^2$	31	$\dfrac{\sum (y-\bar{y})^2}{31}$	

analysis of variance. The result obtained is very nearly identical to that obtained using a *t* test. The technique is, however, very much more versatile as we shall see.

PAIRED DATA

Sometimes it is very difficult to design an experiment of this kind because the variability of the individuals within the samples is so great that it may require very large samples indeed to show up the effect of a treatment which is applied to one sample. In such cases it may be possible to improve the design if the same samples of individuals can be used on two occasions, testing the control and the treatment on each individual. Thus we might be interested to discover whether a drug made patients sleep longer at night. For example, if the drug is given to ten patients and a placebo to another ten we might get results as shown in table 3.4a. The mean

TABLE 3.4a. Results of experiments to determine the activity of a drug believed to induce sleep. First experiment.

Hours of sleep	
Untreated patients y_1	Treated patients y_2
7·2	5·3
4·8	4·6
6·7	7·7
8·9	9·4
4·1	7·2
6·8	7·9
7·4	8·9
5·7	7·3
8·4	7·5
7·0	6·2

Calculations

$\sum y$	= 67		= 72
$\sum y^2$	= 468·84		= 538·34
$(\sum y)^2/n$	= 448·9		= 518·4
$\sum (y-\bar{y})^2$	= 19·94		= 19·94
V	= 2·216		= 2·216
$V\bar{y}$	= 0·2216		= 0·2216

$$V(y-\bar{y}) = 0\cdot4432$$
$$s_{(y-\bar{y})} = 0\cdot666$$
$$\bar{y}_1 - \bar{y}_2 = 0\cdot5$$
$$t = 0\cdot75$$

TABLE 3.4b. Second experiment.

Patient number	Sleeping time		Difference in sleeping time $y = y_2 - y_1$
	Control night y_1	Treatment night y_2	
I	7·2	7·7	+0·5
2	4·8	6·2	+1·4
3	6·7	7·3	+0·6
4	8·9	8·9	0
5	4·1	4·6	+0·5
6	6·8	7·5	+0·7
7	7·4	7·9	+0·5
8	5·7	5·3	−0·4
9	8·4	9·4	+1·0
10	7·0	7·2	+0·2

Calculations

$\sum y$	= 5·0	V	= 0·2511
$\sum y^2$	= 4·76	$V\bar{y}$	= 0·0251
$(\sum y)^2/n$	= 2·5	$s\bar{y}$	= 0·159
$\sum (y-\bar{y})^2$	= 2·26	t	= 3·15

sleeping time for the treated individuals is 7·2 hr as compared with 6·7 hr for the controls. A *t* test between the means gives a value of only 0·75 which would be expected to occur by chance in almost half of all the cases where the two samples had been drawn from the same population. In other words there is no evidence that the drug has had any effect. In fact, however, the same ten individuals had been given the drug on one occasion and the placebo on another occasion, giving the data shown in table 3.4b. The actual sleeping times are the same as in table 3.4a, but they are in pairs, each pair applying to a single person. If we disregard the pairing, a *t* test would yield the identical result to that obtained from the data of table 3.4a. We can, however, now consider the difference in sleeping time for each individual. On the basis of the null hypothesis, i.e. that the treatment has no effect, we would expect the mean difference to be zero. Thus we know the population mean in this case and we can test the difference of the observed mean from the population mean directly. Thus, in this case;

$$t = \frac{\bar{y}-0}{s_{\bar{y}}}$$

and from this calculation we obtain a value of $t = 3 \cdot 15$ which would occur by chance less than once in a hundred times if the drug had no effect. This example shows clearly the importance of using paired data whenever possible.

A word of warning is, however, necessary at this point. If all ten subjects were given the placebo on one night and the drug on the following night we would have to pause before jumping to the conclusion that the drug was effective. It might well be that some factor other than the drug had caused the change; thus the hospital ward might have been noisy on the first night and quiet on the second. We can protect ourselves against such extraneous factors by giving half the subjects the drug on the first occasion, the other half receiving the placebo; and then, on the second occasion reversing the situation. This type of design is often called a **cross-over experiment**.

Relationship between two variables

So far we have discussed the analysis of data where only one measurement is made on each individual studied. Frequently in biological observations or experiments, we are interested in the relationship that may exist between two measurements. Thus we may want to know the relationship, if any, between the blood pressure and the weight of a series of men or animals. This involves us in the further statistical technique of **correlation**.

TABLE 3.5. Weights and systolic blood pressures of a group of ten men.

Man number	x Weight kg	y Systolic blood pressure mm Hg
1	110·0	160
2	93·0	123
3	75·0	98
4	105·5	138
5	71·5	110
6	125·0	147
7	97·0	139
8	88·5	121
9	84·0	151
10	76·5	130

Calculations

$\sum x$	$= 926$	$\sum y$	$= 658 \cdot 5$
$\bar{x}$	$= 92 \cdot 6$	$\bar{y}$	$= 65 \cdot 85$
$\sum x^2$	$= 176782$	$\sum y^2$	$= 88374 \cdot 5$
$(\sum x)^2/n$	$= 171495 \cdot 2$	$(\sum y)^2/n$	$= 86724 \cdot 45$
$\sum (x - \bar{x})^2$	$= 5286 \cdot 8$	$\sum (y - \bar{y})^2$	$= 1650 \cdot 05$
$V(x)$	$= 587 \cdot 42$	$V(y)$	$= 183 \cdot 335$
s_x	$= 24 \cdot 24$	s_y	$= 13 \cdot 55$

$$\sum xy = 124008 \cdot 5$$
$$\sum xy/n = 12400 \cdot 85$$
$$\bar{x} \cdot \bar{y} = 12195 \cdot 42$$
$$r = 0 \cdot 626$$

If we made the two measurements on a sample of ten men we might get the data shown in table 3.5. The simplest way of illustrating any possible relationship between the two sets of measurements is to plot a **scatter diagram** as shown in fig. 3.3. Although the points are

FIG. 3.3. Scatter diagram relating weight and systolic blood pressure of a group of men.

widely scattered a line can be drawn through the points indicating that as the weight increases so also does the blood pressure. When the scatter diagram shows this relationship the two measurements are said to be correlated. The **correlation coefficient** is a measure of this linear trend, and should not be used for relationships that follow patterns more complicated than a straight line. If the apparent relationship is obviously a curve there may, of course, be a linear relationship between some function of the data; e.g. the logarithm or square root of one measurement might be linearly related to the other measurement.

If there is a linear relation then it follows that, to some extent, the value of one measurement can be predicted if the other is known. If all the points lie on the line the prediction is without error; if there is no relationship we cannot predict at all. In the first instance the correlation coefficient is unity; in the second it is zero. Partial correlations lie between these values. Correlation may be positive or negative. In the example in fig. 3.3 the blood pressure (BP) rises as the weight rises and the correlation is positive. If the BP fell as the weight rose the correlation would be negative.

If there is no correlation then the value of the BP is independent of the weight. Therefore the error of prediction of the BP for any individual whose weight is known would be the deviation of his BP from the mean BP of all individuals whatever their weight. The estimate of this error can be taken as the variance of the BP values, calculated in the usual way (V). On the other hand, if there is a linear relationship, the error of the prediction is the deviation of the BP from the value predicted by the line. The line is drawn to minimize the total of these errors, i.e. in such a way as to minimize the sum of squares of these deviations. This is called fitting a line by the **method of least squares**. A variance based upon these deviations (V_L) can be calculated. The correlation coefficient, usually written as r, is obtained from the equation:

$$r = \sqrt{1 - \frac{V}{V_L}} \qquad (8)$$

Equation 8 cannot be easily used to calculate the correlation coefficient, since we must first fit the line. The two procedures are combined by using the following equation:

$$r = \frac{\dfrac{\sum (x - \bar{x}) \times \sum (y - \bar{y})}{n}}{s_x \times s_y} \qquad (9)$$

or, if we avoid calculating deviations altogether, by:

$$r = \frac{\dfrac{\sum xy}{n} - \bar{x}.\bar{y}}{s_x \times s_y} \qquad (9a)$$

If equation 9a is applied to the figures in table 3.4 we get $r = +0.626$ which is a value that would occur by chance, in the absence of any real correlation less, than once in twenty times. We can therefore conclude that there is probably a real correlation. The value of r corresponding to various probabilities is provided in published tables for different values of n.

INTERPRETATION OF A CORRELATION

Even if a significant correlation between two variables is demonstrated, careful interpretation is necessary. It does not mean that a change in one variable causes a change in the other. Thus the fact that a correlation was established between the populations of storks in various provinces of Germany and the birth rates in these provinces did not mean that if more storks had been introduced the birth rate would inevitably have risen.

Secondly we must not extrapolate beyond the limits of the data. Thus if weight and blood pressure are shown to be correlated in men between the weights of 70 and 125 kg it does not follow that they are still correlated in lighter or heavier men.

REGRESSION

The correlation coefficient measures the degree to which two independent variables are associated. Often, experi-

ments are done in which one variable is fixed independently and changes that occur in the other variable which is dependent are observed. The amount of contraction of smooth muscle after various doses of a drug may be measured. Here we plot not a scatter diagram but a graph relating the contraction (the **response**) to the dose or the log. dose of the drug given (fig. 3.4). There is

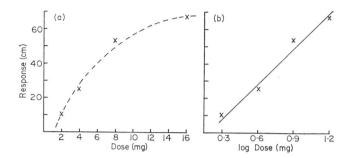

FIG. 3.4. Graphs relating (a) dose and (b) log dose of a drug to response, e.g. cm of contraction of smooth muscles.

usually a linear relationship with the log. dose over a certain dose range; and this is a useful fact as will be seen on p. 3.12.

Since we want to calculate the change in the response for a given change in the dose the normal equation for a straight line can be used:

$$y = a + bx \quad \text{(where } a \text{ and } b \text{ are constants)}$$

In this case y is the response, x the dose, and b is the slope of the line (the **dose response line**) relating them. The constant, b, is called the **regression coefficient**.

USE OF DOSE RESPONSE LINES

The main use of dose response lines is in bioassay, where the strength of one sample of an active biological preparation, hormone or drug is measured in terms of the strength of another. Extracts of biological material are not pure chemicals and no two preparations can be relied on to be of equal strength. Hence bioassay is the normal method of controlling the strength of, for example, insulin preparations and most vaccines and antitoxins. Thus, to control the dose in experimental work or to protect the patient from fluctuations in strength when used clinically, each preparation must be tested against a standard preparation prepared and held for this purpose, and containing a definite number of units of activity per unit weight. This subject constitutes an important part of pharmacology and is not discussed in detail here but certain features are worthy of comment.

Relative potency

If two preparations are compared by bioassay two dose-response lines can be plotted from the results. This usually gives the sort of data illustrated in fig. 3.5. Here the log. of the dose has been plotted against the mean response obtained with each preparation. It follows, if the lines are parallel, that for any level of response the horizontal distance between the lines (AB) is constant. This distance

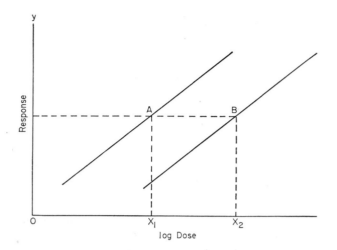

FIG. 3.5. Dose response lines in bioassay.

is the difference between the logarithms of the two doses that produce the same response ($OX_2 - OX_1$). Since the antilogarithm of the difference between two logarithms is the ratio of the two arithmetic values, we can therefore say that the ratio of equipotent doses is constant. This ratio is called the **potency ratio**. If the potency ratio of a preparation is 2·0 as compared with the standard, then all doses given must be halved to produce the same biological effect.

Limits of error

Since all measurements of response represent the means of varying responses in a number of animals, the dose response lines are not known without error. The potency ratio is thus only an estimate of the true value. It is thus customary to attach limits to the estimate beyond which it is improbable that the true value lies. The calculation of such limits is very complex.

It is important to remember that the best that can be done is to make a statement of probability. We can say: 'Unless a 1 in 20 chance has come off, the real potency lies within these limits and the best estimate of the real potency is thus and thus'; but it follows that, if the 1 in 20 chance has come off, the real potency may lie well outside our limits.

This is one of the reasons why it is hard to control the potency of biological extracts of this kind. Thus a manufacturer may sell insulin labelled with a potency of 100 units/ml. This label is based on assays against the standard preparation of insulin tested by its potency to

lower blood glucose and will, by law, have limits of error such that, unless a 1 in 20 chance has come off, the real potency will lie between 90 and 111 units/ml. But, occasionally, and despite the fact that most manufacturers work to even closer limits, the chance does come off, and the preparation is either stronger or weaker than is claimed. It is of the essence of statistics that this chance cannot be eliminated; it can only be quantified, thus allowing for reduction in the chance by proper experimental design.

ANALYSIS OF VARIANCE IN BIOASSAY

The power of the analysis of variance as a statistical tool is well illustrated by its application to bioassay. Suppose that a preparation of a biological preparation is given at two different dose levels and that the standard preparation is given at the same two dose levels, the responses of ten animals being measured for each dose. Thus forty animals in all are used in the test and four responses measured. An analysis of variance can be done in the following form:

Source of variation	d.f.	
Between doses	3	
Within doses	36	(9 within each
	—	of 4 doses)
Total	39	

But we can further partition the three degrees of freedom between doses as follows:

(1) between standard and test preparations　　1
(2) between high and low doses　　1
(3) interactions between preparations and doses　　1
　　　　　　　　　　　　　　　　　　　　　　　　　—
　　　　　　　　　　　　　　　　　　　　　　　　　3

Here we are calculating the variance, about the overall mean, of the forty responses, attributable to:

(1) the means of the twenty responses to each preparation **independent of dose,**

(2) the means of the twenty responses to each dose **independent of preparation,**

(3) the mean of the ten responses to the high dose of the standard combined with the ten responses to the low dose of the test preparation, and of the ten responses to the low dose of the standard combined with the ten responses to the high dose of the test preparation.

These variances are compared with the error variance (the within doses variance) which is the irreducible measure of the biological variation of response in animals treated in exactly the same way.

If variance (1) is significantly larger than the error variance it means that the preparations vary significantly in strength. If variance (2) is significantly larger than the error variance it means that the slope of the dose response line is significantly greater than zero. If this is not true then there is no evidence that a larger dose will produce a larger response and the whole assay is worthless. If variance (3) is significantly larger than the error variance it means that the two dose-response lines differ significantly from parallelism. This, in turn, means that the ratio of equipotent doses will vary depending on the level of the response; hence no valid potency ratio can be calculated and the assay is invalid. This may be the result of impurities in the test preparation modifying the responses.

Thus the analysis of variance can be used to test the validity of the assay in a number of ways. The more degrees of freedom that are available between doses, the more refined can the examination of the data become. Thus, when three doses of test and standard preparation are used, a further test is possible to see whether the dose response line is really linear or whether there is significant curvature. The concept is simple but the mathematics becomes increasingly complex.

Proportions

We have dealt so far with measurements made of various variables. In medicine there are many situations where the response that is observed is not continuously graded but is of the all-or-nothing variety. Thus a patient may live or die; a physiological event either does or does not take place. These responses are often called **quantal responses** to differentiate them from **graded responses**.

The logic of dealing with the statistics of quantal responses is the same as that used for graded responses, but the mathematics is different. One example must suffice for our argument.

Let us assume that we know that, of the population of patients who develop a given disease, the proportion who die is 30 per cent. We draw a sample of 100 patients, and treat them by some new method. If the null hypothesis is correct then the expectation is that thirty patients will die. If only ten die, what is the probability that this would happen by chance and that the null hypothesis should be rejected? We need a method of calculating the standard error of a proportion.

In a simple case, e.g. where there are only three patients in our sample, we can calculate the probabilities directly

Chance that any one patient will live $= 7/10$
Chance that all three patients live
$\qquad = (7/10)^3 = 343/1000 = 34\cdot3$ per cent
Chance that two patients live and one dies
$\qquad = 3 \times (7/10)^2 \times 3/10 = 441/1000 = 44\cdot1$ per cent
Chance that one patient lives and two die
$\qquad = 3 \times (7/10) \times (3/10)^2 = 189/1000 = 18\cdot9$ per cent
Chance that all three patients die
$\qquad = (3/10)^3 = 27/1000 = 2\cdot7$ per cent
Total $\qquad\qquad = 1000/1000 = 100$ per cent

Direct calculation is not practical with large numbers. In such cases the standard error of a percentage is calculated from the following expression

$$s = \sqrt{\frac{p \times q}{n}} \qquad (10)$$

where $p =$ percentage dying, $q =$ percentage recovering and $n =$ number in sample.

Thus in our simple example

$$s = \sqrt{\frac{30 \times 70}{3}} = \sqrt{\frac{2100}{3}} = \sqrt{700} = 26\cdot5$$

If the expected death rate of 30 per cent were to vary by more than twice its standard error, i.e. if it were in excess of 83 per cent, we would regard it as improbable that this should occur by chance. As we saw by direct calculation the chance of all three patients dying is only 2·7 per cent. The standard error method thus agrees with the direct method.

If a sample of 100 patients with the same disease are given a new drug and it is observed that only fifteen died, can we say that it is probable that the treatment is effective? Here we obtain

$$s = \sqrt{\frac{30 \times 70}{100}}$$
$$= \sqrt{21}$$
$$= 4\cdot5$$

Our observed death rate is 15 per cent, differing from expectation by 15 per cent or, in other words, by more than three times the standard error. Thus, unless a 1 in 100 chance has come off, the treatment has had some effect.

Usually we do not know the value of the proportion in the population. This is the same problem as we discussed for graded responses. Here we rely on a comparison between a treated sample and a control sample.

DIFFERENCE BETWEEN PROPORTIONS

The same theorem applies, namely that the variance of a difference is the sum of the variances of the two separate values. Since

$$s = \sqrt{\frac{p \times q}{n}} \qquad V = \frac{pq}{n}$$

the sum of the variances is thus

$$\frac{p_1 q_1}{n_1} + \frac{p_2 q_2}{n_2}$$

and the standard error of the difference is therefore

$$s_{\text{difference}} = \sqrt{\frac{pq}{n_1} + \frac{pq}{n_2}} \qquad (11)$$

Thus if we had two samples of 100 patients and one sample was treated and fifteen died, whereas in the other sample, used as controls, thirty died, there would be, as in the graded response (p. 3.7) two possible ways of proceeding. We can take the observed proportions for each sample separately, thus

$$V_1 = \frac{p_1 q_1}{n_1} \qquad V_2 = \frac{p_2 q_2}{n_2}$$

$$= \frac{30 \times 70}{100} \qquad = \frac{15 \times 85}{100}$$

$$= 21 \qquad = 12\cdot75$$

$$\therefore s_{\text{difference}} = \sqrt{V_1 + V_2}$$

$$= \sqrt{33\cdot75}$$

$$= 5\cdot75$$

and, hence,

$$t = \frac{p_1 - p_2}{s_{\text{diff}}} = \frac{15}{5\cdot75} = 2\cdot6$$

Alternatively we can regard, on the null hypothesis, the combined proportion for both samples as the best estimate of p. Thus, of 200 patients, forty-five died, giving a value for p of 22·5. We thus have

$$s = \sqrt{\frac{22\cdot5 \times 77\cdot5}{100} + \frac{22\cdot5 \times 77\cdot5}{100}}$$

$$= \sqrt{34\cdot87}$$

$$= 5\cdot9$$

The χ^2 test

When we wish to compare more than two proportions we must use another technique than that just described. This is comparable to the progression from the t test to the analysis of variance for graded responses. The χ^2 test, developed by Pearson, serves this purpose. χ^2 is a value computed from the difference between observed numbers and expected numbers. In a general form it can be calculated from

$$\chi^2 = \frac{(\text{Observed number} - \text{Expected number})^2}{\text{Expected number}} \quad (12)$$

It is thus the sum of the squared deviations from expectation expressed as a ratio in relation to expectation. Tabulated values of χ^2 in relation to probability are available for any given number of summed differences.

Let us assume that the death rates from a disease of childhood are arranged in relation to the age. We might get figures such as those shown in table 3.6a. We might suspect from the data that the chance of a child dying was greater the younger the age. How can this theory be tested? Once again the null hypothesis is used.

TABLE 3.6a. Death rates for a disease of childhood arranged according to the age of the child.

Age in years	Number of cases of disease	Number of dying	Per cent dying
< 1	12	4	33·3
1	19	5	26·3
2	37	8	21·6
3	46	8	17·4
4	30	6	20·0
5	18	2	11·1
Total	162	33	20·4

TABLE 3.6b. Comparison of observed with expected deaths from diseases of childhood at different ages.

Age in years	Number of cases of disease	Number dying Observed (O)	Number dying Expected (E)	$\frac{(O-E)^2}{E}$ χ^2	Number recovering Observed (O)	Number recovering Expected (E)	$\frac{(O-E)^2}{E}$ χ^2
1	12	4	2·4	1·07	8	9·6	0·27
1	19	5	3·9	0·31	14	15·1	0·08
2	37	8	7·5	0·03	29	29·5	0·01
3	46	8	9·4	0·21	38	36·6	0·05
4	30	6	6·1	0	24	23·9	0
5	18	2	3·7	0·78	16	14·3	0·20
Total	162	33	33	2·4	129	129	0·61

Total $\chi^2 = 2\cdot4 + 0\cdot61$
$= 3\cdot01$
$n = 6$

If it is assumed that there is no difference in the mortality at different ages, then we would expect that the overall mortality rate of 20·4 per cent would apply to all age groups. We can thus construct a new table giving the expected number of deaths at each age (table 3.6b). The total χ^2 as calculated is 3·01. It must always be remembered that there is a value of χ^2 obtained both from the number dying and from the number recovering, although, since these are not independent figures, there are only six separate comparisons, so $n = 6$. This value of χ^2, on consulting a table, would be expected to occur by chance in no less than 80 per cent of samples. There is thus no reason to reject the null hypothesis and no reason to think the disease more lethal in younger children.

THE FOURFOLD TABLE

When there is only one real comparison being made, there is a special quick way of calculating χ^2. This is a frequent situation in medicine. Thus, for example, we have thirty patients with coronary thrombosis treated with a new drug to prevent clotting of the blood and nineteen survive for 3 months; while of forty-one comparable cases not so treated only fifteen survive for 3 months. Is the treatment of any benefit as judged on this criterion of 3 months' survival? We can arrange the data as a fourfold table with marginal totals (table 3.7a). The general

Table 3.7. The fourfold table. Relationship between the number of patients, treated and untreated, who live or die.
(a) Figures for quoted example.

	Number living	Number dying	Total
Number treated	19	11	30
Number untreated	15	26	41
Total	34	37	71

(b) The general form of the fourfold table.

	Number living	Number dying	Total
Number treated	a	c	$a+c$
Number untreated	b	d	$b+d$
Total	$a+b$	$c+d$	$a+b+c+d$

case is given in table 3.7b and the general equation for χ^2 is

$$\chi^2 = \frac{(ad-bc)^2(a+b+c+d)}{(a+b)(c+d)(a+c)(b+d)} \qquad (13)$$

$$\text{where } n = 1$$

In our example

$$\chi^2 = \frac{(26 \times 19 - 11 \times 15)^2 \times 71}{34 \times 37 \times 30 \times 41}$$

$$= 4 \cdot 97$$

This value will occur by chance in just over 1 in 100 samples. There is thus some reason for rejecting the null hypothesis and accepting that the treatment is of value.

It has been found that, when the numbers are small, the equation tends to overestimate χ^2. A correction is therefore used. Thus

$$\chi^2 = \frac{[ad-bc-\frac{1}{2}(a+b+c+d)]^2(a+b+c+d)}{(a+b)(c+d)(a+c)(b+d)} \qquad (14)$$

Recalculating we get $\chi^2 = 3 \cdot 95$. This is a value which will occur by chance almost exactly once in twenty samples. Our conclusion is therefore still justified but not so firmly justified.

Quantal response assays

We may want to measure the regression line relating the proportion of individuals who recover when treated with varying doses of a drug. In this case we have to relate the percentage recovering to the dose, or preferably to the logarithm of the dose (p. 3.11). When such a log. dose response line is plotted (fig. 3.6a) a **sigmoid** (S-shaped)

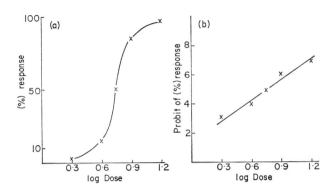

FIG. 3.6. Dose response relationships in a quantal response assay.

curve is usually obtained. This created much statistical difficulty which was solved by Gaddum. His method, later modified by Bliss, depends on the transformation of the percentage response to a function called the **probit**. Probits are symmetrical about a central value 5·0 corresponding to a percentage response of 50 per cent; and the differences between probits get bigger the further away the response gets, in either direction, from 50 per cent. This has the effect of turning the sigmoid curve into a straight line (fig. 3.6b). When two preparations are being compared this linear relationship permits the calculation of a potency ratio and limits of error. The arithmetic is very complex, although the concept is simple. Values for probits are obtained in standard tables.

Errors of blood counting or radioactive counting

The distribution of the counts of cells or of disintegrating atoms follows a peculiar pattern called the **Poisson distribution**. This is a limiting case of the binomial distribution when the probability of an event is vanishingly small. Thus the probability that any one blood cell in a sample will actually be counted on the haemocytometer slide is very small; and the probability that in the time of a radioactive count any particular atom will disintegrate is also very small.

The peculiar feature of a Poisson distribution is that its variance is equal to its mean. Thus if we count 100 cells, the total count is the mean, the variance of the count is 100, and the standard deviation of the count is $\sqrt{100} = 10$ or 10 per cent. If we count 400 cells the standard deviation is 20 or 5 per cent; and if we count 10,000 cells it is 100 or 1 per cent. The same applies to radioactivity counts. The standard deviation is a measure of the error of the count. If the total number of cells actually counted is 100 or more, we can compare two separate counts by calculating the variance of the difference between them, using as before the theorem that the variance of a difference is the sum of the variances of the components.

Thus, if we have two counts of 180 and 220 respectively, we have a variance for the difference between them of $180 + 220 = 400$ and a standard error of this difference of 20. Since the difference (40) is twice its own standard error we might suspect that the two counts are not from the same population. This is a crude test since we are not dealing with a normal distribution and more refined methods of test applicable to the Poisson distribution are available but beyond the scope of this book.

FURTHER READING

BERNSTEIN L. & WEATHERALL M. (1952) *Statistics for Medical and Other Biological Students*. Edinburgh: Livingstone.

BRADFORD HILL A. (1966) *Principles of Medical Statistics*. London: The Lancet.

MORONEY M.J. (1951) *Facts from Figures*. Harmondsworth: Penguin.

Chapter 4
The supply and use of energy

Light, absorbed by plants for photosynthesis, is the initiator of all biological processes. Heat, given off by both animals and plants, is the final waste. Between light and heat, useful mechanical work is possible. Energy is a Greek word meaning work. In the nineteenth century, physicists made it a technical term, the capacity to do mechanical work. The interconversion of the various forms of energy such as light, heat, and the motions of wind, water or electricity and that stored in various fuels or reservoirs is possible but it is limited. The limits are set down and described by the science of energetics or thermodynamics. In 1923, Lewis and Randall eulogized this science in the following passage:

'Aside from the logical and mathematical sciences there are three great branches of natural science which stand apart by reason of the variety of far-reaching deductions drawn from a small number of primary postulates. These are mechanics, electromagnetics and thermodynamics. These sciences are monuments to the power of the human mind and their intensive study is amply repaid by the aesthetic and intellectual satisfaction derived from a recognition of the order and simplicity which has been discovered among the most complex of natural phenomena.'

The study of the biological aspects of thermodynamics, using either whole living animals and human bodies or isolated fragments of the tissues, provides the biologist with a satisfaction similar to that described above.

Basic definitions

The definition of energy as the capacity to do work is derived from mechanics, the first of the branches of natural science referred to by Lewis and Randall. **Work** is defined as the overcoming of a force; for example, the lifting of a weight by a man is work done on the weight by some biological machinery against the force of gravity. The work done by the biological machinery must be at least equal to the obvious mechanical work done on the weight, i.e. work done = force × distant = m × g × h (where m = mass, g = acceleration due to gravity and h = height). In the absolute metric system, the unit of force is called a **dyne** and is the force necessary to give a mass of 1 g an acceleration of 1 cm/sec/sec. If this force moves the unit mass 1 cm, then 1 work unit (or **erg**) has been expended on the mass. The erg is inconveniently small, and for most practical purposes the basic unit of work, or the capacity to do work, is the joule which equals 10^7 ergs. If we lift 1 kg 1 metre above the ground, then we have done (m × g × h) units of work or 1000 × 981 × 100 = 9·81 × 10^7 ergs or 9·81 joules of work. This elementary but fundamental definition is derived from the basic ideas of Newtonian mechanics.

The muscles which carry out the aforementioned work are not only mechanical engines, but chemical engines. We are concerned with a quantitative description of the various energy transformations that can occur in such a system. When a muscle contracts, some of the **chemical energy** bound in its components is released and converted, partly into mechanical work and partly into heat. The First Law of Thermodynamics states that energy can only be transformed from one form to another and is indestructible. This carries the practical corollary that we can express quantities of any kind of energy in terms of a single unit of any other kind. In 1843, Joule first measured the mechanical equivalent of heat, and this is accepted to be 4·1855 × 10^7 ergs for one heat unit, which is defined as the amount of heat necessary to raise the temperature of 1 g of water from 14·5° to 15·5 °C. This is the **gramme calorie** (15 °C), and it is usually known simply as a calorie. The principal unit of energy employed by physiologists is the **kilocalorie** (= 1000 cal). The natural unit of choice could have been the erg or joule as previously defined. However, all forms of energy tend ultimately to appear in the form of heat, and thus it can be argued that units of heat should be the universal coinage of energetics.

It is important to discuss the significance of the term heat, because it is often confused with temperature in everyday speech. If a quantity of heat is supplied to a gramme of water at room temperature, there will be an increase in motion of the molecules of water, and the volume of water will expand. We describe this by saying that the temperature of the water has increased. What we mean is that heat will tend to escape from the mass of water until its temperature is once again the same as that of the room. The temperature indicates the gradient of heat energy between the gramme of water and the room, in exactly the same sense that is understood by the pressure head of water in a reservoir. This gives information about the force with which water escapes from the reservoir via a pipeline, but it gives no information about the quantity of water in the reservoir. However, it would be possible to learn something about the capacity of the reservoir, by adding or subtracting a known quantity of water and observing the resultant pressure change. It is not possible to manipulate heat in the same way as water, just as it is not possible to pick up a handful of sunshine. This means that when measurements have to be made about quantities of radiant or vibrational energy such as heat, this must be done indirectly by seeing what happens to a standard of reference, such as a known volume of water, when some heat is added to it. This is how the heat given off in a chemical reaction, such as combustion, is measured in a bomb calorimeter. Here careful arrangements are made so that all the heat given off is transferred to water, and the increase in temperature is observed, classically by a volume change in another liquid, mercury.

The manifestations of electrical energy are commonplace in daily life, but it is not often appreciated that temperature is strictly analogous to voltage, which is in turn equivalent to pressure. These are the intensity factors, whereas calories, coulombs, and litres are units of the capacity aspects of heat, electrical, and volume energy. A battery is a system of two compartments, in one of which is an accumulation of free electrons. The voltage of the battery gives information about the 'pressure' head of the electrons in the negative side of the battery, but tells nothing about how many electrons are in the compartment. However, it is the number of free electrons in the compartment which determines how much energy can be obtained from that particular battery. This remains **potential energy** until the battery is placed in a situation where the electrons can be made to do work. This is achieved by the movement of electrons along a conducting circuit, and the greater the force driving the electrons around the circuit (electromotive force, commonly expressed as a voltage) and the more electrons that are available, the more work can be done, and thus the greater the available energy. This approach to electrical energy introduces the concept of a flow of energy along a wire, and thus introduces a rate factor. The rate of transfer of energy from one system to another is expressed as the transfer of power. **Power** is a measure of the rate of doing work. Thus 1 joule/sec is equivalent to 1 coulomb of charge transferred against a gradient of 1 volt in 1 sec or 1 ampere of current flowing for 1 sec. This unit is known as the **watt**. In our domestic life, the common unit of electricity is the kilowatt-hour, and electrical appliances are commonly labelled in terms of their wattage or power consumption. Thus an electrical heater for a small room would need an element dissipating electrical power at the rate of 1000 watts or transferring heat into the room at a rate of 239 cal/sec. This is 14.3 kcal/min, or about the same amount of heat that would be transferred to the room by ten people sitting quietly, as many hostesses know. The usual physiological unit of power is the kcal/min. The connections between the various units of energy and power are important, and they are set out in tables 4.18–20 in an appendix on p. 4.15.

These tables and the above account of energy have been taken from Passmore and Draper (1965) Energy Metabolism in *New Methods of Nutritional Biochemistry*, Volume II, ed. Albanese A.A.; New York and London: Academic Press and reproduced by kind permission of the publishers.

FUELS OF THE BODY

The fuels of the body are carbohydrate, fat, protein and ethyl alcohol, taken in the diet. Most of the energy bound in the carbon and hydrogen linkages of the molecules of these substances can be made available to the body, in the course of their breakdown by processes which are mostly oxidative. This energy is ultimately derived from the sun. The energy of solar radiation is fixed by the photosynthetic processes, when water and carbon dioxide are converted by green plants into carbohydrate. The energy so fixed can be utilized by plants for synthesis of other carbohydrates, fats, proteins and alcohols. Photosynthesis takes place only in the green leaves of plants, which are of limited use as human foods. Firstly, the cell walls of plants contain large amounts of cellulose, which cannot be digested in the human alimentary canal. Secondly, the concentration of energy in green leaves is low. Animals, such as ruminants, whose diet is composed largely of green fodder, have to spend the greater part of their lives eating in order to obtain sufficient energy. Farmers aim to concentrate the energy originally present in green leaves either into the seeds of cereal grains and oil seeds or into the muscles, adipose tissue and milk and eggs of farm animals. Cereal grains, vegetable oils, meat and dairy products are the principal sources of energy in human diets. Farming can legitimately be considered a branch of chemical industry. Crops and farm animals are the 'plant' which the farmer uses to convert solar radiation into human food.

THE ENERGY CONTENT OF FOODS

Since the gramme-molecular weight of glucose is 180 and by Avogadro's Law 1 gramme-molecule of a gas occupies

22·4 litres, the combustion of 1 mole of glucose can be described thus:

$$C_6H_{12}O_6 + 6O_2 = 6CO_2 + 6H_2O + \text{heat}$$
$$180 \text{ g} \quad 6\times22\cdot4 \text{ l} \quad 6\times22\cdot4 \text{ l} \quad 6\times18 \text{ g} \quad 686 \text{ kcal}$$

The quantitative aspects of this equation are of great importance to physiologists. Glucose, of course, will not normally ignite until it has been raised to a high temperature and then the energy will be liberated instantaneously. For glucose to serve as a fuel in the body, combustion must take place at a temperature around 38°C and it must be controlled so that the energy is liberated in small quantities, accurately graded to meet the local requirements of the tissues. Enzyme systems in the body effect the oxidation of glucose in a series of stages, of which at least six are associated with the liberation of energy. These reactions allow sufficient energy to become available to meet the needs of the tissues with a dissipation of heat so small that local temperature does not rise by more than 3 or 4°C at the most. How this is brought about will be described in chaps. 7, 8 & 9. The additive result of all these stages is the same as if the glucose had been ignited spontaneously and is given in the above equation. It also follows that the combustion of 1 g of glucose yields 3·81 kcal (**heat of combustion**) and 0·6 g of H_2O (**metabolic water**). Further the volume of CO_2 produced is equal to the volume of O_2 utilized, so that the ratio,

$$\frac{CO_2 \text{ produced}}{O_2 \text{ used}} \text{ (respiratory quotient, RQ)} = 1$$

This ratio is nowadays often known as the **respiratory exchange**. Furthermore 1 litre of O_2, when used to oxidize glucose liberates 4·93 kcal (**calorie equivalent of oxygen**). Each of these values is of physiological importance, as will appear later.

These terms have been defined and explained with reference to glucose, because it is a foodstuff with a comparatively simple molecular structure. A similar procedure could have been employed, using a fat such as a triglyceride or a protein. As these molecules are larger and more complicated, equations are more cumbersome. Similar, but not identical, values for heat of combustion, metabolic water, respiratory quotient and calorie equivalent of oxygen can be derived for these substances.

HEATS OF COMBUSTION

These are measured experimentally using a **bomb calorimeter** (Fig. 4.1). This depends on the fact that foodstuffs can be readily ignited by a small electric current, when under high oxygen pressure. The bomb is a small steel cylinder, into which the food is placed in a platinum crucible. A small wire through which a current can be

FIG. 4.1. The bomb calorimeter.

passed is placed on the food. The bomb has a screw top, containing a valve through which oxygen can be passed to raise the pressure in the bomb. When the bomb is charged with food and the pressure raised, it is placed in a water calorimeter. The food is then ignited and the heat of combustion calculated from the rise in temperature in the calorimeter. Table 4.1 gives in the first column the heats of combustion of proteins, fats and carbohydrates derived from common foods and also of alcohol. These are precise physical measurements which represent the total energy available on oxidation. They do not represent the physiological values for the energy available to the tissues. Since the food is not completely digested and absorbed from the alimentary canal, and oxidation in the tissues is not always complete, and some losses of energy are inevitable.

Losses in the faeces

The human alimentary tract is remarkably efficient. Many studies have shown that with a normal diet about 99 per cent of the carbohydrate, 95 per cent of the fat and 92 per cent of the protein is absorbed (table 4.1). The calorie loss in the faeces is seldom more than 5 per cent of the intake. The figures above are not fixed values, but vary slightly from individual to individual and also according to the nature of the diet. With a diet based on undermilled cereals and coarse vegetables, the bulk of the faeces is large owing to the big intake of indigestible cellulose

TABLE 4.1. Heats of combustion and availability of energy in the principal types of food.

	Heat of combustion kcal/g	Loss in urine kcal/g	Availability per cent	Atwater factors kcal/g
Protein				
Meat	5·35 ⎫	1·25	92	4
Egg	5·58 ⎭			
Fat				
Butter	9·12 ⎫			
Animal fat	9·37 ⎬	—	95	9
Olive oil	9·38 ⎭			
Carbohydrate				
Starch	4·12 ⎫			
Sucrose	3·96 ⎬	—	99	4
Glucose	3·81 ⎭			
Ethyl alcohol	7·10	trace*	—	7

* Traces also lost in expired air.

and this is usually associated with a slight diminution in the absorption of the digestible components.

Losses in the urine

Proteins are not completely broken down in the tissues. The nitrogen is excreted in the urine largely in the form of urea, but also as uric acid, creatinine and other substances. Energy is lost in the urine, in amounts corresponding to about 1·25 kcal/g of dietary protein. About one-quarter of the energy present in the dietary protein is thus not available to the tissues. In health, the breakdown of carbohydrates and fats is for practical purposes complete. A large number of organic acids and other substances derived from fat and carbohydrate appear in

the urine but the daily output of each is measured in milligrams and the total output does not normally amount to 1 g. In disease, however, large amounts of energy may be lost in the urine. For example, in diabetes up to 25 per cent of the dietary intake of energy may be excreted in the urine in the form of glucose and acetoacetate.

CALCULATION OF THE ENERGY VALUE OF HUMAN DIETS

Table 4.2 gives values for the protein, fat, carbohydrate and energy content of some common foods. The figures are taken from a report prepared by McCance and Widdowson, which gives analyses of 663 foods commonly eaten in Great Britain. Tables giving analyses of American, Indian, Australian, South African and Singapore foods are also available. Any particular food gives approximately the same analysis in whatever part of the world the sample is taken, but it is best to use tables prepared from analyses of local foods. With the aid of such tables it is possible to prescribe a diet in which the calorie content is known with an accuracy of ± 10 per cent. This degree of accuracy usually suffices in laying down ration scales (e.g. for boarding schools and other institutions and also for the armed services) and for clinical purposes (e.g. the treatment of obesity and diabetes). If in any investigation it is necessary to know more accurately the energy intake of a given person, it is essential to weigh out and homogenize a duplicate portion of everything that is eaten and then to analyse an aliquot.

In practical dietetics, physiological values for the energy content of the nutrients in a human diet, which take into account the losses of energy in the urine and faeces,

TABLE 4.2. The energy value and nutrient content of some common foods (values per 100 g). From McCance and Widdowson (1960).

	Energy kcal	Water g	Protein g	Fat g	Carbo- hydrate g	Alcohol g
Whole wheat flour	339	15·0	13·6	2·5	69·1	—
White bread	243	38·3	7·8	1·4	52·7	—
Rice, raw	361	11·7	6·2	1·0	86·8	—
Milk, fresh, whole	66	87·0	3·4	3·7	4·8	—
Butter	793	13·9	0·4	85·1	tr	—
Cheese, Cheddar	425	37·0	25·4	34·5	tr	—
Beef steak, fried	273	56·9	20·4	20·4	0	—
Haddock, fried	175	65·1	20·4	8·3	3·6	—
Potatoes, raw	70	80·0	2·5	tr	15·9	—
Peas, canned	86	72·7	5·9	tr	16·5	—
Cabbage, boiled	9	95·7	1·3	tr	1·1	—
Orange, with peel	27	64·8	0·6	tr	6·4	—
Apple	47	84·1	0·3	tr	12·2	—
White sugar	394	tr	tr	0	105·0	—
Beer,* bitter	31	96·7	0·2	tr	2·2	3·1
Spirits* (gin, whisky 70% proof)	222	63·5	tr	0	tr	31·5

* Values per 100 ml.

must be used. Many years ago, the American physiologist Atwater rounded off the figures in the first three columns in table 4.1 to give the values 4, 9, 4 kcal/g for the energy available to the tissues from protein, fat and carbohydrate respectively. The **Atwater factors** are useful approximations widely used in making up dietary prescriptions. Physiological losses of alcohol in the urine and expired air are small, and a value of 7 kcal/g may be taken as correct.

The detailed prescription of the items of food in a diet is properly the task of a dietitian, who is trained in the use of food tables.

THE SOURCES OF ENERGY IN DIETS

Within fairly wide limits proteins, fats and carbohydrate are exchangeable as a source of energy. All diets must contain some protein to provide nitrogen and essential amino acids (p. 11.13). Throughout the world most national diets provide between 10 per cent and 15 per cent of the energy as protein. Eskimos, South American gauchos and pastoral tribes such as the Masai in East Africa, who may live almost entirely on foods of animal origin, may take more protein, and there is no evidence that this does them any good or any harm. It is possible to live on diets containing very little of either fat or carbohydrate. Poor people whose diet is based largely on cereal grains have a predominantly carbohydrate diet. In many peasant communities energy may be provided by 12 per cent protein, 10 per cent fat and 78 per cent carbohydrate, although such a diet must be unappetizing and may well be lacking in vitamins. With increasing wealth a family always increases its fat intake. In prosperous western countries about 40 per cent of the energy is derived from fat. In the national diets of the

United Kingdom, U.S.A. and other countries whose population is well fed, the energy distribution is approximately 12 per cent protein, 40 per cent fat and 48 per cent carbohydrate. Increasing material prosperity, increasing dietary fat and increasing heart disease have been common features of many countries in the twentieth century and it has been held widely that these associations are causal.

Table 4.3 sets out how the calories might be distributed in the diet of a healthy adult man and of a middle aged woman who wishes to reduce weight.

ENERGY EXPENDITURE AND HUMAN CALORIMETRY

The great French chemist Lavoisier, who first established the role of oxygen in the combustion of inorganic substances, defined clearly the problems associated with the use of energy in animals. He put a guinea-pig in a box surrounded by ice and measured the rate at which the ice melted and at which CO_2 was produced and showed that the two rates were related. He also measured the rate of oxygen consumption by a man at rest and showed that it was increased three or four times by light exercise. Lavoisier died on the guillotine during the Reign of Terror in 1794. After his death many chemists and physiologists in the nineteenth century developed methods to study the relationship between heat output, work done and the respiratory exchanges in man and animals.

By 1900, the American physiologist Atwater, assisted by an engineer Rosa, had developed a human calorimeter. This consisted of a chamber in which a man could live and work for several days, and at the same time the total output of heat could be measured (fig. 4.2). This could be related to the net energy intake, which is the energy in the food minus the energy lost in the urine and faeces. In experiments lasting 4 days he measured both the energy intake and the energy output of his subjects and was able to get agreement within ± 1 per cent. This demonstration, that the law of conservation of energy applies to man, was a great technical achievement. It was also important in killing the idea, common in the nineteenth century, that living creatures possessed 'a vital force' which in some way allowed them to operate outside of the laws of physics and chemistry. This idea is not yet quite dead and many obese people think that their fat accumulates in some mysterious way unrelated to the caloric content of their diet. Unfortunately they are sometimes supported in this view by their physicians. 'Calories don't count' is a slogan of some advertised slimming regimes. Atwater counted them very accurately.

The measurement of the total heat output of a man (**direct calorimetry**) remains a very difficult procedure

TABLE 4.3. The provision of energy in two diets. (a) Diet suitable for an adult man. (b) Diet low in calories and in carbohydrate, suitable for a middle-aged woman who wishes to reduce her weight.

Nutrient	Daily intake g	Energy value kcal/g	Energy intake kcal
(a) Protein	100	4	400
Fat	100	9	900
Carbohydrate	400	4	1600
			2900
(b) Protein	60	4	240
Fat	40	9	360
Carbohydrate	100	4	400
			1000

FIG. 4.2. The Atwater–Rosa human calorimeter.

and is seldom attempted nowadays. The heat output is, however, quantitatively related to the oxygen utilization. The measurement of oxygen consumption (**indirect calorimetry**) is a relatively easy technical procedure, which can be used to measure rates of energy expenditure in daily activities at work and during recreations, and any changes in the rates that may be brought about by disease.

The theoretical background of indirect calorimetry

If the reader turns back to p. 4.3, he will find the calorie equivalent of oxygen, when glucose is being utilized. Values for each of the other nutrients can be similarly calculated and accepted values are set out in table 4.4, together with the respiratory quotients. It will be seen that the values of the calorie equivalent do not differ greatly. In practice, the human body is nearly always running on a mixture of fuels. The usual assumption that the utilization of 1 litre of O_2 corresponds to the production of 4·8 kcal of energy will involve an error of at most ±4 per cent.

As fats have a much lower proportion of oxygen in

TABLE 4.4. The calorie equivalent of oxygen and the respiratory quotient associated with the combustion of the principal nutrients.

Nutrient	kcal/l O_2	RQ
Protein	4·60	0·81
Fat	4·69	0·71
Carbohydrate (starch)	5·01	1·00
Ethyl alcohol	4·86	0·66

their molecules than carbohydrates, the RQ associated with their oxidation is lower than the value of 1·0 for carbohydrate. An observed value of the RQ of below 0·80 or over 0·90 indicates that the energy is being produced predominantly from fat or carbohydrate respectively.

The amount of protein broken down in the tissues can be determined from the amount of nitrogen excreted in the urine (p. 5.3) provided kidney function is normal. If over a given period of time the intake of O_2 and the output of CO_2 by the lungs and the excretion of N_2 by the kidneys is determined, then it is possible to calculate the amount of protein, fat and carbohydrate utilized by the tissues (**metabolic mixture**) and the relative proportion of the energy derived from each fuel. The arithmetic necessary for this calculation is essentially simple but is cumbersome. It can be found in the books recommended for further reading.

THE MEASUREMENT OF OXYGEN CONSUMPTION

There are three established methods in common use. The Benedict–Roth spirometer is the simplest when the subject is at rest and is employed for measuring metabolic rates in hospital patients. The Douglas bag method is the most accurate and reliable and is the method of choice in the physiology laboratory. The Max Planck Respirometer is a convenient instrument to use in industry and in field conditions.

The Benedict–Roth spirometer (fig. 4.3) is a closed-circuit breathing apparatus, which is filled with oxygen. It has a capacity of about 6 litres. The O_2 is contained in

FIG. 4.3. The Benedict–Roth spirometer.

a metal drum which floats on a water seal. The subject breathes in from this drum through an inspiratory valve. His expired air passes back into the drum through an expiratory valve and a soda lime canister, in which the CO_2 produced is absorbed. As the O_2 is used up, the drum sinks and its movement is recorded on a paper chart; from this the rate of O_2 consumption can be read. The apparatus is simple to use and accurate. It has the disadvantage that it can be used only when the subject is at rest or doing very light exercise and that, as the CO_2 output is not measured, the RQ cannot be calculated.

The Douglas bag (fig. 4.4) is a canvas or plastic bag, normally of 100 litre capacity. The subject breathes

FIG. 4.4. The Douglas bag

through a metal or plastic mouthpiece which houses inspiratory and expiratory valves. Room air is breathed in and all the expired air is collected in the bag. The bag is then emptied through a gas meter and a sample of the expired air taken for analysis of the O_2 and CO_2 content. Rates of O_2 utilization and CO_2 production can then be calculated. The method is ideal for subjects either at rest or exercising on a treadmill or bicycle ergometer.

The Max Planck Respirometer (fig. 4.5) was introduced in Germany for use in industry. The principle is the same as that in the Douglas bag method, but the volume of the expired air is measured directly in a dry gas meter. This is worn on the subject's back, like a haversack, and weighs 3–4 kg. The spirometer contains a sampling de-

FIG. 4.5. The Max Planck respirometer.

vice, which diverts an adjustable portion of the expired air, less than 1 per cent, into a small rubber football bladder. This will not fill up for 5–10 min, even if the work is heavy. The sample of expired air in the bag is then analysed. This instrument is ideal for measuring O_2 consumption rates during light and moderate work. With very heavy work involving an expiratory output of more than 50 l/min, the meter tends to under-record and it also imposes a significant resistance on the subjects breathing at high rates.

Other apparatus is available for measuring very high rates of O_2 consumption, as in competitive athletics, and also for the continuous recording for several hours of both O_2 intake and CO_2 output by hospital patients or subjects at rest. In both these circumstances, there are considerable technical difficulties and the methods are suitable only for use by experienced workers.

RATES OF ENERGY EXPENDITURE

The amount of energy which each of us requires to take in our food is determined by the amount of energy that we put out in the activities of everyday life. In many of the poor and underdeveloped countries the food supply is insufficient to meet the energy of a working population and of their growing children. In rich countries, where food is abundant, intake of energy frequently exceeds output. Inevitably then the excess is stored as fat, and obesity with its attendant disadvantages results. There is now much interest in determining rates of energy expenditure, and the findings are used for assessing dietary requirements, both at national and at individual level.

Energy expenditure lying at rest

An adult male lying at rest may use O_2 at the rate of some 250 ml/min corresponding to an energy output of about

1·25 kcal/min. This figure may be modified according to his size, and for sex and age, by climate and diet and also by disease. As there are 1440 min in the day, 1800 kcal is approximately the amount of energy which should be provided by the diet for a man confined to bed.

For over 60 years it has been customary to refer to the resting energy output as the **basal metabolic rate** (BMR). The BMR is described and discussed in all textbooks and has an immense literature. This is largely theoretical. The term implies that for each individual there is a fixed minimum level of metabolism on which life depends. However, the minimum level of metabolism of any individual is not always the same. It depends on the previous nutritional history, on the body temperature and may be affected by drugs and hormones. It is impossible to define a 'vital minimum' or basal metabolism. A more accurate and descriptive term is **resting metabolism**, which has no theoretical overtones.

THE EFFECT OF BODY SIZE

Table 4.5 illustrates a general biological law. The metabolic rate of a mouse is more than ten times that of an ox, expressed per unit of weight, but is of the same order for all mammals when expressed per unit of surface area. The small animal has a big surface, relative to weight, from which heat is lost. To maintain body temperature relatively more heat must be produced. Accordingly it became conventional to express values of resting metabolism in units of surface area. Standard values for a man and a woman aged 20 are 38·6 and 35·3 kcal/m²/hr. The surface area of human subjects is by tradition derived from a measurement of height and weight using a nomogram (fig. 4.6). This nomogram was constructed over 50 years ago and is based on measurements of the area of paper required to cover completely the nude bodies of less than twenty United States citizens.

It is generally agreed that women have a lower resting metabolic rate than men when the rates are expressed per unit of surface area. However, this does not mean, Mary, that the 'fire of life' burns less intensely in you than in Tom. It is only a reflection of the fact that you are fatter than he is. Table 4.6 presents data obtained

FIG. 4.6. Nomogram for calculating surface area.

by Edinburgh students in one of their physiological practical classes. The resting O_2 consumption was measured using the Benedict–Roth spirometer. The percentage of body fat was calculated from body density, determined by weighing each subject first in air and then under water. As the density of fat is about 0·9 and of the fat free tissues or lean body mass is about 1·1, the proportion of fat in the body can be calculated from a measurement of the density. The average O_2 consumption is higher for the men than for the women and this difference remains after correction for surface area (141 and 115 ml/m²/min respectively). If the fat free body or lean body mass is used as the index of comparison, the sex difference disappears. The average O_2 consumptions are 4·2 and 4·3 ml/kg lean body mass/min for the men and women.

Several workers have now shown that the lean body mass predicts resting metabolic rates more accurately than does surface area and that there is no sex difference

TABLE 4.5. Resting metabolism in various species related to size.

Species	Weight kg	Surface area m²	Resting metabolism		
			kcal/day	kcal/kg	kcal/m²
Mouse	0·0285	0·007	5·2	180	739
Rat	0·3	0·0384	26·3	90	686
Monkey	3·22	0·257	156·0	50	608
Dog	14·9	0·652	542·0	36	831
Sheep	29·5	0·805	692·0	23	860
Man	65·0	1·83	1667·0	27	910
Pig	186·0	2·67	2647·0	14	993
Cattle	366·0	4·56	5678·0	15	1245

TABLE 4.6. Body fat, lean body mass and resting oxygen consumption of young men and women.

	Height cm	Weight kg	Surface area m²	Lean body mass kg	Body fat kg	Body fat %	Resting oxygen ml/min
24 young men							
Mean	176	68·5	1·83	61·1	7·5	10·7	258
Range	168–190	53·1–88·3	1·60–2·16	44·8–74·6	3·1–20·7	4·5–26·9	188–326
Standard deviation	5·9	8·2	0·13	6·93	4·3	5·6	30
25 young women							
Mean	165	58·2	1·62	43·1	15·1	25·6	186
Range	156–179	42·4–70·5	1·35–1·87	37·8–55·3	9·0–23·7	18·4–34·8	148–225
Standard deviation	4·2	7·1	0·10	4·1	4·0	4·57	22

TABLE 4.7. Normal values for the resting rate of energy expenditure of adults (kcal/min).

Men	Women	Fat %	Weight kg							
			45	50	55	60	65	70	75	80
Thin	—	5		0·99	1·06	1·12	1·19	1·26	1·32	1·39
Average	—	10		0·94	1·01	1·08	1·14	1·21	1·28	1·34
Plump	Thin	15	0·82	0·89	0·96	1·03	1·09	1·16	1·23	1·30
Fat	Average	20	0·78	0·84	0·91	0·98	1·05	1·11	1·18	1·25
—	Plump	25		0·80	0·86	0·93	1·00	1·07	1·13	1·20
—	Fat	30			0·81	0·88	0·95	1·02	1·08	1·15

with the use of this parameter. This is important theoretically. The surface area law implies that energy production is graded accurately to meet heat losses. This is not so, at least in civilized human communities. We adjust our body temperature so that we are comfortable by altering our clothing, going closer to or farther away from a fire, opening a window or putting on a fan. The rate of energy production is more probably determined by inherent properties within the cells. In 1902, the great German pioneer of human energy studies, Carl Voit, wrote: 'The unknown causes of metabolism are found in the cells of the organism. The mass of these cells and their power to decompose materials determines the metabolism. All kinds of influences may act upon the cells to modify their ability to metabolize, some increasing it or others decreasing it.'

Table 4.7 sets out standards for the normal resting metabolism related to body size. Figures are given for a range of body weight and fat content. The student is warned that this table differs from the conventional table found in textbooks for over 50 years and based on surface area. The table is simple to use. Unfortunately, there is as yet no method of measuring the fat content of the body, suitable for routine clinical examinations, but the use of the visual assessments given in the table may well be less inaccurate than calculation of surface area from the conventional nomogram.

Most people spend about 8 out of the 24 hours resting in bed. During this period the mean metabolic rate does not differ significantly from the value predicted in table 4.7. Measurements made throughout the night have shown that values are usually a little higher on first going to bed, probably due to the effect of the last meal (p. 4.10), but they generally fall a little below the standard between 2 and 4 in the morning when the body's temperature is at a minimum. A night's rest normally costs 400–500 kcal.

THE PARTITIONING OF RESTING O₂ UTILIZATION AMONGST THE SEVERAL ORGANS

Table 4.8 shows how the resting metabolism may be divided among the principal organs of the body. To obtain

TABLE 4.8. The partition of the resting oxygen utilization among the principal organs of a healthy man weighing 65 kg.

Organ	Oxygen used ml/min	Resting metabolism %
Liver (including the splanchnic area)	67	27
Brain	47	19
Heart	17	7
Kidney	26	10
Skeletal muscle	45	18
Remainder (by difference)	48	19
Total	250	100

this data it is necessary to measure the rate of blood flow in the organs (p. 28.28) and also the O_2 content of their arterial and venous blood and then apply the Fick principle (p. 28.28). The development in the last 20 years of small plastic catheters which enable samples of blood from deep veins to be taken in man has made this possible. The brain, which makes up less than 2·5 per cent of the body weight, is responsible for about 20 per cent of the energy consumption at rest. Students and office workers may be disappointed to learn that their hard work at the books involves no appreciable extra energy. In many experiments it has been impossible to show any increase in O_2 uptake when a subject previously resting and dozing is suddenly set complicated problems in mental arithmetic. By contrast, the rate of O_2 consumption of a resting muscle may be increased a hundredfold on exercise. The reader may also be surprised to find that his kidneys do more work than his heart—at least when he is resting. After chap. 33, he will appreciate what a complex task is the manufacture of urine.

THE EFFECT OF AGE
A newborn baby has an O_2 consumption of about 7·0 ml/kg/min of body weight, twice the rate of an adult on a basis of weight. The high rate of metabolism is caused by the energy requirements for growth. As the growth rate declines, the metabolism approaches the adult level. Table 4.9 gives values for the resting meta-

TABLE 4.9. Resting metabolism of infants and young children.

Weight kg	Resting metabolism kcal/24 hr	Weight kg	Resting metabolism kcal/24 hr
3	145	11	585
5	270	13	660
7	390	15	720
9	495	17	780

bolism of infants and very young children. As is customary, the figures are given in kcal/24 hr, which are convenient for calculating dietary energy needs. Table 4.10 gives values for older children and adolescents, which

TABLE 4.10. Resting metabolism of older children and adolescents.

Weight kg	Boys kcal/min	Girls kcal/min	Weight kg	Boys kcal/min	Girls kcal/min
15	0·50	0·50	40	0·93	0·86
20	0·60	0·59	45	0·98	0·92
25	0·71	0·67	50	1·03	0·97
30	0·79	0·74	55	1·09	1·02
35	0·87	0·80	60	1·13	1·07

may be compared with the adult values in table 4.7. It can be seen that adolescents have a slightly higher metabolic rate than adults of the same weight. The sex difference in table 4.10 arises because little girls are fatter than little boys; a distinction that occurs long before puberty.

The resting metabolic rate continues to decline throughout adult life, but slowly at a rate of about 2 per cent per decade. Standard values for octogenarians are about 85 per cent of those for young adults (table 4.7).

THE EFFECT OF FOOD
The metabolic rate is raised soon after a meal has been eaten and may continue above the fasting level for 4–6 hr. This is known as the **specific dynamic action** (SDA) of food. This is a very variable phenomenon. After most meals, it usually amounts to an increase of about 10–15 per cent, but if the meal is rich in protein the SDA may be as much as 30 per cent. After a test meal consisting of fat or carbohydrate only, it is usually absent or less than 5 per cent. The SDA immediately after a meal rich in protein is probably due to work done by the stomach in secreting digestive juices; later the effect certainly arises from the liver, associated with the handling of amino acids. Even after a large meal the metabolic rate will be back to the normal resting level in the small hours of the next morning. Man has no means of 'burning off' the effects of gluttony. A dietary energy excess must either be worked off by exercise or stored as fat.

Starvation, either partial or complete and due either to disease or famine, invariably causes a fall in the resting metabolic rate. This is certainly due to a shrinkage of the cell mass and probably also to a reduction in the metabolism in the tissues. This is an adaptive mechanism which helps to protect the body in times of scarcity.

THE EFFECT OF CLIMATE
Standards for resting metabolic rates were first drawn up in North America and in Western Europe. It was later shown that these were about 10 per cent too high for Calcutta, Singapore and elsewhere in the tropics. A racial difference was first suggested, but this is almost certainly not a fact. Careful studies on European visitors to Asia have shown that a fall in resting metabolic rate usually occurs in them, but this is not invariable. The change takes place slowly over 3–6 months. Conversely many students from tropical countries who have measured their resting metabolism in our laboratory have usually found values similar to those obtained by natives of Edinburgh. How climatic changes bring about these alterations is not understood.

THE EFFECT OF THYROID ACTIVITY
The thyroid hormones stimulate oxidations and heat production within the cells. In experimental animals, removal of the gland causes a marked fall in resting O_2

consumption, which is increased by injections of extracts of the gland. The disease, myxoedema due to atrophy of the thyroid gland, is associated with very low levels of resting metabolic rates, which can be raised by treatment with thyroid hormones. Overactivity of the gland (hyperthyroidism) raises the metabolic rates sometimes to as much as double the normal rate. How the thyroid hormones work is discussed in chap. 25.

With a careful technique, measurements for resting metabolism should usually fall within ± 15 per cent of the standard values, but a few individuals with normal thyroid gland activity may have higher or lower rates. Hyperthyroidism and hypothyroidism cannot be diagnosed confidently until the metabolism is raised or lowered by 30 per cent. For many years the measurement of the resting metabolic rate was the most reliable method of assessing thyroid function and of checking progress in thyroid disease. It is now out of fashion, having been replaced by various tests for iodine metabolism which are found more convenient both for patient and doctor. It remains, however, a good guide which may be used when results with modern methods are equivocal or where facilities for their use are not available.

THE EFFECTS OF PREGNANCY AND LACTATION
These are discussed in chap. 37.

Energy expenditure in everyday life
MAXIMUM RATES OF WORK
A student who is physically fit should be able to undertake exercise which involves an O_2 consumption of 4 l/min. This means multiplying his resting rate by sixteen times. In a few exceptional athletes, a **maximum oxygen uptake** of 5 l/min or even higher has been recorded. Many students can do no better than 3 l/min. An ability to work at these rates is essential for those who undertake heavy manual labour or compete in strenuous sports and recreations. However, a middle-aged or elderly man or someone with a disability of the heart or lungs is able to move around comfortably, do light

work and enjoy light exercise, provided he can increase his resting O_2 consumption rate four times, i.e. up to 1 l/min with an energy expenditure of 5 kcal/min. The details of the respiratory and cardiovascular adjustments needed to increase the supply of O_2 to the tissues are a main theme of chaps. 28 and 29.

CLASSIFICATION OF PHYSICAL ACTIVITIES
Table 4.11 gives a classification based on rates of energy expenditure. This was first drawn up from the measurements of rates of O_2 consumption by men in the Swedish iron-industry. However, it is also applicable to other industries and to sports and games. With a suitable modification for body weight, it can be applied to women. The figures in table 4.11 are given in units of

TABLE 4.11. The grading of industrial work and physical activity.

	Energy expenditure	
Grade	Men kcal/min/65 kg	Women kcal/min/55 kg
Light	2·0–4·9	1·5–3·4
Moderate	5·0–7·4	3·5–5·4
Heavy	7·5–9·9	5·5–7·4
Very heavy	10·0–12·4	7·5–9·4
Unduly heavy	12·5–	9·5–

kcal/min. This is convenient, as will soon become clear, when assessing food requirements for persons with varying ways of life. By dividing by five, the figures can be transposed into rates of O_2 consumption in l/min. This is the more convenient unit for the physiologist or physician concerned with studies on the heart and lungs. The table provides a numerical definition of **light, moderate** and **heavy work.**

Table 4.12 gives examples of the energy expenditure of various physical activities. It is based on many thousands of measurements by indirect calorimetry. Obviously the grading can be only approximate. Thus most jobs

TABLE 4.12. Examples of the energy expenditure of various physical activities.

Light work at 2·5–4·9 kcal/min		Moderate work at 5·0–7·4 kcal/min	Heavy work at 7·5–9·9 kcal/min	Very heavy work at over 10 kcal/min
Assemby work	Building industry	General labouring (pick and shovel)	Coal mining (hewing and loading)	Lumber work
Light industry	Bricklaying	Agricultural work (non-mechanized)	Football	Furnace men (steel industry)
Electrical industry	Plastering	Route march with rifle and pack	Country dancing	Swimming (crawl)
Carpentry	Painting	Ballroom dancing		Cross country running
Military drill	Agricultural work (mechanized)	Gardening		Hill climbing
Most domestic work with modern appliances	Driving a truck	Tennis		
Gymnastic exercises	Golf	Cycling (up to 10 miles/hr)		
	Bowling			

on a farm involve **moderate** work, but some are **heavy** and a few **light**. Similarly for most of us tennis is a sport demanding **moderate** physical activity, but a Wimbledon champion must do **heavy** work and some performers on our public courts appear to be taking very **light** exercise.

Sitting and standing

Each of us spends a large part of the day sitting and standing, when energy is needed by the muscles responsible for maintaining the posture of the body. Work may also be done using the muscles of the arms. These factors do not greatly increase the metabolic rate. When we are mobile and active, the major part of the work done is usually expended in moving the weight of the body. The energy expenditure of some 160 Glasgow men and women has been measured when sitting and standing in their homes and engaged in reading, listening to radio and watching television, etc. The mean values were above the mean resting value by 20 per cent when sitting and 50 per cent when standing. The maximum increases were 70 per cent when sitting and 100 per cent when standing. Fidgeting and apparent 'tension' does not raise the energy expenditure greatly. It is impossible to increase your rate of energy expenditure significantly without getting up and moving about.

Walking

Walking at moderate speed (3·5 miles/hr) involves increasing the energy expenditure fourfold, up to 5 kcal/min for an average man. Most of the work involved in walking is utilized in raising the centre of gravity at each step. The energy cost of walking is directly proportional to body weight and also to the speed, except at very low and very fast speeds, when the movements become relatively less efficient. The cost of walking is the same in both sexes. Table 4.13 gives predicted values for the cost of walking by persons of varying weight at different speeds. These predictions are based on many hundreds of measurements and are unlikely to be out by more

TABLE 4.13. Normal values for the energy expenditure when walking (kcal/min).

Speed		Weight (kg)					
km/hr	miles/hr	45	55	65	75	85	95
3	1·9	2·1	2·5	2·8	3·2	3·5	3·8
4	2·5	2·7	3·2	3·6	4·0	4·3	4·6
5	3·1	3·2	3·7	4·2	4·7	5·1	5·5
6	3·8	3·8	4·4	4·9	5·4	5·9	6·4
7	4·4	4·4	5·0	5·5	6·1	6·6	7·1

than ± 15 per cent. Walking is the most common physical activity. It may be prescribed by a physician who wishes to alter the energy balance of an obese patient, with as much precision as an alteration in the diet.

DAILY RATES OF ENERGY EXPENDITURE

If the time spent by an individual in each of his various activities throughout the 24 hours is recorded and also the metabolic cost of each activity determined, then the daily energy expenditure rate can be calculated.

Energy expenditure (kcal/day) = time spent in activity (min) × metabolic cost of activity (kcal/min).

Tables 4.14 and 4.15 show examples of how a normal man and woman might each spend a day. Energy expenditure amounts to 3200 and 2300 kcal/day respectively. These two examples are taken from a report by the Food and Agricultural Organization (FAO) of the United Nations on Calorie Requirements; this report is used as a basis for calculating the food requirements of the various counties of the world. Its central feature is a reference man and a reference woman, each aged 25 years and weighing 65 kg and 55 kg respectively, whose energy requirements are set out in tables 4.14 and 4.15.

How far the requirement indicated in these two tables represents a true value for any population is uncertain. Table 4.16 sets out the results of surveys of the energy expenditure of various occupational groups amongst the

TABLE 4.14. The energy expenditure of a Reference Man.*

Time spent	Activity	kcal/day	kcal/day
8 hr	Working activities: mostly standing (over-all rate, 2·5 kcal/min)		1200
8 hr	Nonoccupational activities:		
	1 hr washing, dressing, etc. at 3 kcal/min	180	
	1·5 hr walking at about 6 km/hr at 5·3 kcal/min	480	
	4 hr sitting activities at 1·54 kcal/min	370	
	1·5 hr active recreations and/or domestic work at 5·2 kcal/min	470	
			1500
8 hr	Rest in bed at basal metabolic rate		500
	Total		3200

* Weight, 65 kg; age, 25 years; mean annual environmental temperature, 10°C.

TABLE 4.15. The energy expenditure of a Reference Woman.*

Time spent	Activity	kcal/day	kcal/day
8 hr	Working activities in the house or in industry: mostly standing (over-all rate, 1·83 kcal/min)		880
8 hr	Nonoccupational activities:		
	1 hr washing, dressing, etc. at 2·5 kcal/min	150	
	1 hr walking at about 5 km/hr at 3·6 kcal/min	220	
	5 hr sitting activities at 1·41 kcal/min	420	
	1 hr active recreation and/or heavier domestic work at 3·5 kcal/min	210	
			1000
8 hr	Rest in bed at basal metabolic rate		420
		Total	2300

* Weight, 55 kg; age, 25 years; mean annual environmental temperature, 10°C.

TABLE 4.16. Daily rates of energy expenditure by individuals with varying occupations.

	Energy expenditure kcal/day		
Occupation	Mean	Minimum	Maximum
Men			
Elderly retired	2330	1750	2810
Office workers	2520	1820	3270
Colliery clerks	2800	2320	3290
Laboratory technicians	2840	2240	3820
Elderly industrial workers	2840	2180	3710
University students	2930	2270	4410
Building workers	3000	2440	3750
Steel workers	3280	2600	3960
Farmers	3420	2900	4000
Coal miners	3660	2970	4560
Forestry workers	3670	2860	4600
Women			
Elderly housewives	1900	1490	2410
Middle-aged housewives	2090	1760	2320
Laboratory technicians	2130	1340	2540
Assistants in department stores	2258	1820	2850
University students	2290	1380	2600
Factory workers	2320	1970	2980
Bakery workers	2510	1980	3390

people of Scotland, carried out by Dr John Durnin of Glasgow University. Each survey covered a whole week. The reader will notice the enormous variations in each group; thus the most active university student, both male and female, expended almost twice as much energy as the most sedentary. This is due to the different uses of leisure time. In a modern industrial society very few people do much heavy work in the course of earning their living and this is usually achieved by a man with about 1200 kcal/day or less. He may expend far more energy, over 2000 kcal/day, if he pursues active recreations enthusiastically. On the other hand there is nowadays an increasing number of people who prefer to spend their leisure time sitting, perhaps watching television, or driving around in their car admiring what is left of the countryside. The new modern man, *homo sedentarius*, expends much less energy than the 3200 kcal/day, as set out in the FAO standard (table 4.14). So does the modern woman. Housework may appear tiring, but this is usually because so many women find it boring. Except in a large house, where there are several small children, it seldom involves heavy work.

The existence of *homo sedentarius* is well recognized in the United States. The Food and Nutrition Board of the United States Academy of Science in 1964 reduced the food allowances from the FAO standards to 2880 kcal/day for men and 2100 kcal/day for women. This certainly is in keeping with the modern American way of life, in which no one appears to walk a yard if this can possibly be avoided. Yet this recommendation that Americans need less food may be unsound and perhaps the real need is for more exercise. *Homo sedentarius* may not be a healthy specimen. He is certainly prone to obesity, and obesity, as the figures of the American life insurance companies show, predisposes to heart disease and diabetes.

PEASANT AGRICULTURALISTS

The majority of the people of the world do not live in prosperous industrial urban societies. They are peasants, who get their living from their land. How hard do peasants work? Certainly the answer is very heavy at harvest and seed time, when 12 hours a day may be spent in the fields. Much agricultural work involves energy expenditure rates of 5 kcal/day or over. However, all agricultural work is seasonal. Surveys in Africa and India have indicated that peasants spend from 855 to 1700 hr a year at work in their fields. These figures correspond to 17–34 hr/week. Thus the overall rate may be no more than that of an industrial population.

THE FUTURE

Until 200 years ago, when the industrial revolution began, human muscles, supplemented by those of horses and oxen, provided the power that made civilization possible. Muscles did the work of the field, built the great temples and cathedrals, transported men and their armies about the world, spun and wove the fibres for clothing and tapestries, thrashed and ground the corn. Only in the last respect was a little power available from wind and water mills. In industrial societies all this has changed. Man and woman have become creatures who flick switches that control large sources of power. In such societies, there is little necessity for them to use their muscles for anything but the lightest activity. At the same time working hours have been greatly reduced and the 40-hour week is now commonplace. With the better organization of industries, there is little doubt that a 20-hour week would suffice for doing the necessary work in a modern technical society. There is already much more time for leisure than formerly and this is likely to increase greatly.

NATIONAL FOOD NEEDS

It is well known that the countries of the world can be divided roughly into two groups. In the rich countries in North America, Europe and in Oceania, agriculture and trade produce a plentiful supply of food. Indeed surplus crops have become an economic embarrassment. In these countries obesity is common, with all its consequent ill health. In the poor countries mostly in Asia, Africa and in Latin America, where the majority of the world's population live as peasant farmers, the food supply rarely measures up to the energy needs of the population. Hunger is commonplace, especially at the season before the harvest is due. The threat of famine and starvation is often not far away. Table 4.17 shows estimates of the average daily food supply and requirement of some selected countries; each is expressed in calories. The estimates of requirements are based on the physiological considerations, already outlined in brief. It will be seen that in many countries the supply is far ahead of need, whereas in others the need is not being met.

The transfer of the surplus crops and food products of the rich countries to the poor countries has been effectively carried out on occasions to meet special needs. Many millions of children have benefited from the dried milk supplied through the United Nations and national agencies. Surplus grains from the U.S.A. and other countries have averted serious famine in Asia and in Africa. However, the economic processes of normal trade have proved unable to distribute the world's food according to the physiological needs of the people and there is no sign that this will ever become possible. The poor countries have, for the most part, little to export which can balance their imports of foods. In most poor countries, agricultural production is increasing, but at a

TABLE 4.17. Calorie supplies compared with requirements. From FAO (1965). Calorie requirements are calculated on the basis of the current age and sex structure of the population.

Country	Average supplies 1953–4	1962–3	Estimated requirements
	Calories/head/day		
Western Europe			
Austria	2700	2970	2610
Denmark	3330	3370	2750
Finland	3070	3110	2760
France	2840	—	2530
Germany, Federal Republic of	2880	2960	2590
Greece	2590	2940	2410
Ireland	3460	3450	2620
Italy	2480	2740	2460
Netherlands	2900	3030	2610
Norway	3100	2930	2780
Sweden	3020	2990	2800
Switzerland	3110	3220	2660
United Kingdom	3110	3270	2630
Yugoslavia	2690	2990	2620
North America			
Canada	3050	3060	2640
United States	3130	3100	2590
Oceania			
Australia	3170	3140	2600
New Zealand	3350	3490	2640
Latin America			
Argentina	2980	2810	2580
Brazil	3280	2800	2310
Chile	2450	2410	2610
Guatemala	—	2080	2370
Mexico	2360	2600	2450
Peru	2260	2310	2500
Venezuela	2050	2370	2390
Far East			
Ceylon	1990	2080	2290
India	1740	2000	2240
Japan	1930	2230	2360
Pakistan	2000	2010	2250
Philippines	1690	1810	2200
Near East and Africa			
Israel	2780	2820	2530
Jordan	—	2160	2410
Lebanon	—	2460	2410
Turkey	2730	3110	2410
United Arab Republic	2340	2670	2380
Mauritius	—	2370	2250
South Africa	2680	2820	2570

rate which is barely keeping up with the increase in population and in some countries it is falling behind. The only solution to the problem other than a catastrophic increase in the death rate due to war, famine or epidemic disease appears to be a rational and planned limitation of the birth rate. Fortunately, this is at last becoming generally realized and many poor countries have now commenced active family planning programmes. Whether these can be developed sufficiently rapidly to prevent the catastrophes which must arise when a people outgrow their food supplies, only the future can tell.

It is probable that many, perhaps most, of the present generation of medical students will practise their profession in a country where there is either a superabundance of food or an inadequate supply. In either instance their clinical practice will include many difficult nutritional problems resulting from caloric imbalance. They will also have the opportunity to use their influence to bring about administrative measures to alleviate or reduce such imbalances. In planning and carrying out a sound food policy for their country, all governments depend upon the advice of their medical profession.

Appendix

TABLE 14.18. Conversion factors for units of force*

Name of unit (unit system)	Significance	Dynes
Dyne (cgs)	Accelerates 1 g by 1 cm sec^{-2}	1×1
Newton (mks)	Accelerates 1 kg by 1 m sec^{-2}	1×10^5
Pond (cgs)	Accelerates 1 g by 981 cm sec^{-2}	$9 \cdot 81 \times 10^2$
Kilopond (mks) (kilogram force)	Accelerates 1 kg by 981 cm sec^{-2}	$9 \cdot 81 \times 10^5$
Poundal (fps)	Accelerates 1 lb by 1 ft sec^{-2}	$1 \cdot 382 \times 10^4$
Pound weight (fps)	Accelerates 1 lb by 32·174 ft sec^{-2}	$4 \cdot 448 \times 10^5$

* Mass × length × time^{-2} as expressed in centimetre-gramme-second (cgs), metre-kilogram-second (mks), and foot-pound-second (fps) unit systems.

TABLE 4.19. Conversion factors for units of energy.*

Name of unit (unit system)	Significance	Ergs	Joules	Calories	BTU
Ergs (cgs) (dyne cm)	1 g moved 1 cm by 1 dyne	1×1	1×10^{-7}	$2 \cdot 389 \times 10^{-8}$	$9 \cdot 472 \times 10^{-11}$
Joule (mks)	1 kg moved 1 m by 1 newton	1×10^7	1×1	$2 \cdot 389 \times 10^{-1}$	$9 \cdot 472 \times 10^{-4}$
Calorie (cgs)	1 g H$_2$O heated 1°C	$4 \cdot 186 \times 10^7$	$4 \cdot 186 \times 1$	1×1	$3 \cdot 964 \times 10^{-3}$
Kilocalorie (cgs)	1 kg H$_2$O heated 1°C	$4 \cdot 186 \times 10^{10}$	$4 \cdot 186 \times 10^3$	1×10^3	$3 \cdot 964 \times 1$
Meter-kilogram force (mks)	1 kg moved 1 m against gravity	$9 \cdot 806 \times 10^7$	$9 \cdot 806 \times 1$	$2 \cdot 343 \times 1$	$9 \cdot 288 \times 10^{-3}$
British thermal unit (fps)	1 lb H$_2$O heated 1°F	$1 \cdot 056 \times 10^{10}$	$1 \cdot 056 \times 10^3$	$2 \cdot 522 \times 10^2$	1×1
Foot-poundal (fps)	1 lb moved 1 ft by 1 poundal	$4 \cdot 214 \times 10^5$	$4 \cdot 214 \times 10^{-2}$	$1 \cdot 007 \times 10^{-2}$	$3 \cdot 992 \times 10^{-5}$
Foot-pound force (fps)	1 lb moved 1 ft against gravity	$1 \cdot 356 \times 10^7$	$1 \cdot 356 \times 1$	$3 \cdot 239 \times 10^{-1}$	$1 \cdot 284 \times 10^{-3}$

* Mass × length^2 × time^{-2} = energy = capacity to do work (force × distance) as expressed in centimetre-gramme-second (cgs), metre-kilogram-second (mks), and foot-pound-second (fps) unit systems.

TABLE 4.20. Useful physiological power conversion factors (the time unit is the minute).

Name of unit	kcal/min	Kwatts	Mkg force/min	BTU/min	H.P./min	Ft-lb/min
Kilocalories/min	1×1	$6 \cdot 978 \times 10^{-2}$	$4 \cdot 268 \times 10^2$	$3 \cdot 964 \times 1$	$9 \cdot 354 \times 10^{-2}$	$3 \cdot 087 \times 10^3$
Kwatts	$1 \cdot 433 \times 10$	1×1	$6 \cdot 116 \times 10^3$	$5 \cdot 681 \times 10$	$1 \cdot 340 \times 1$	$4 \cdot 424 \times 10^2$
Metre-kilogram force/min	$2 \cdot 343 \times 10^{-3}$	$1 \cdot 635 \times 10^{-4}$	1×1	$9 \cdot 288 \times 10^{-3}$	$2 \cdot 192 \times 10^{-4}$	$7 \cdot 233 \times 1$
British thermal units/min	$2 \cdot 523 \times 10^{-1}$	$1 \cdot 761 \times 10^{-2}$	$1 \cdot 077 \times 10^2$	1×1	$2 \cdot 360 \times 10^{-2}$	$7 \cdot 789 \times 10^{-2}$
Horsepower/min (U.S. and British)	$1 \cdot 069 \times 10$	$7 \cdot 459 \times 10^{-1}$	$4 \cdot 562 \times 10^3$	$4 \cdot 237 \times 10$	1×1	$3 \cdot 300 \times 10^4$
Foot-pounds/min	$3 \cdot 239 \times 10^{-4}$	$2 \cdot 260 \times 10^{-5}$	$1 \cdot 382 \times 10^{-1}$	$1 \cdot 285 \times 10^{-3}$	$3 \cdot 030 \times 10^{-5}$	1×1

FURTHER READING

DURNIN J.V.G.A. & PASSMORE R. (1967) *Energy, Work and Leisure*. London: Heinemann.

Food and Agriculture Organization of the United Nations. (1957) *Calorie Requirements*, Nutrition Studies, No. 15. Rome: FAO.

Food and Agriculture Organization of the United Nations (1966) *The State of Food and Agriculture* published annually. Rome: FAO.

McCANCE R.A. & WIDDOWSON E.M. (1960) *The Composition of Foods*. Med. Res. Coun. (London) Spec. Rep. Ser. No. 298.

Chapter 5
Essential materials and waste

A policeman in the course of his duty may have to observe carefully everything and everybody who enters and leaves a house. His observations are likely to provide police headquarters with valuable clues, but not with sufficient evidence to charge anyone for criminal behaviour within the house. Before this can be done, it is usually necessary to get a warrant to enter and search.

It is comparatively easy for a physiologist to study both qualitatively and quantitatively the food and water consumed by a human body, and also the expired air, urine and faeces that leave it. Material is also lost in the sweat, in the menstrual fluid and milk, and in the form of a new-born baby. This chapter is concerned with the daily credits and debits of material, which are required to maintain the structures within the body and provide its energy. The cells and tissues of the body are not static structures. They are continually being turned over, and substances replaced at varying rates. Many of the chemical components set free by the breakdown of substances within the cells are utilized again to synthesize new tissues. Some, however, cannot be so used and are lost in the excreta, and these have to be made good from the diet. In a healthy adult, who is neither gaining nor losing weight, the dietary intake of each of the elements must exactly balance the excretory losses. It is a common practice both in clinical medicine and in research to draw up a balance for N, Ca, Na and K. It is also possible, but much more difficult, to determine the balance for C, H, Fe, S and indeed for any element which forms part of the structure of the body.

NUTRIENTS

The chemical components of a diet are referred to as nutrients. These may be classified as carbohydrates, fats, proteins and alcohol (the sources of energy), water and electrolytes, minerals and vitamins.

CARBOHYDRATES

These provide the chief source of energy in most diets. About 50 per cent of the total calories in the diet of a prosperous industrial community come from carbohydrate. In a poor agricultural community, living largely on cereals, the proportion is higher and may be up to 85 per cent.

Masai warriors, Eskimos, South American gauchos and others who may live on foods entirely of animal origin have practically no carbohydrate in their diet. As these people are vigorous and healthy, carbohydrate is not a dietary essential. The explanation is that the body can form glucose from certain amino acids (p. 11.21) and probably from glycerol which is a component of fat (p. 10.3).

Starch

The chief dietary carbohydrate is starch, which is present in all cereal grains, roots and tubers. The starch molecule is a polysaccharide composed of several hundred glucose units linked together and forming two chains (p. 9.4). The small amount of glycogen (animal starch, p. 9.9) present in meat and other tissues makes only a trivial contribution to the diet.

Cellulose

Plant cells have walls which are mainly composed of cellulose. This, like starch, is composed of chains of smaller molecules, mainly glucose. These chains cannot be broken down by the digestive juices of man and other mammals. However, protozoa and bacteria present in the alimentary canal of ruminants (cattle and sheep) and herbivores (rabbits and horses) can digest the celluloses and make the resultant material available as a source of energy for the animal host. Human diets may contain up to 15 g of cellulose daily, depending on their content of fruit, vegetables and coarse cereals. This passes through the intestine unchanged and has a mild laxative action by adding bulk to the faeces.

Sugar

The familiar table sugar is **sucrose**, a disaccharide (p. 9.3) in which the constituent hexose units are glucose and fructose. Sucrose is manufactured from sugar-cane in the tropics and from sugar-beet in temperate regions. **Lactose** is the disaccharide (p. 9.3) present in the milk of all mammals and is made up of glucose and galactose units. **Maltose** is a disaccharide (p. 9.3) composed of two glucose units. It is formed from starch in the malting of barley and other cereals for brewing. The two mono-saccharides **glucose** and **fructose** are made commercially by the hydrolysis of sucrose. They are present, in small quantities, in most fruits. Significant amounts of glucose may be present in grapes and of fructose in honey.

A normal diet may contain from 300 to 500 g of carbohydrate daily, providing 1200–2000 kcal. In traditional diets most of this is provided as starch in cereal grains, but in recent years in all prosperous countries an increasing proportion has come from sugar.

Nearly all the dietary carbohydrate is oxidized in the body to carbon dioxide and water, and the carbon is excreted as CO_2 in the expired air. The faeces contain all the cellulose present in the diet, but negligible amounts of other carbohydrates. The urine contains citric acid, lactic acid and other intermediary products of carbohydrate metabolism and it may also contain traces of sugars. In health, the daily excretion of these substances is measured in milligrams. Less than 0·2 per cent of the carbon in the dietary intake of carbohydrate appears in the urine.

FATS

This is the second largest source of energy in most diets. In the United Kingdom fat supplies about 40 per cent of our calories. A normal diet for an active man may contain 140 g of fat, providing 1260 kcal/day. In a modern diet about half the fat is eaten as table fat and about half is 'hidden fat', present in cakes, puddings, sauces, etc. Foods rich in fat are expensive and there is a close association between average national income and fat intake. Many people living in poverty get only 10–20 g of fat/day and such diets are almost always deficient in the fat-soluble vitamin A (p. 5.11). There are also certain fatty acids, the essential fatty acids (EFA), which animal tissues cannot synthesize and which must be supplied in the diet. These are polyunsaturated fatty acids (p. 10.1). Animals fed on artificial diets devoid of these acids fail to thrive and develop a scaly dermatitis, but EFA deficiency has never been satisfactorily demonstrated in human beings on natural diets. Human requirements for EFA are certainly low, probably only 2–3 g/day, an amount which is provided by even the poorest natural diets. Diets rich in EFA lower the concentration of cholesterol and other lipids in the plasma and this may have a protective action against the development of arterial disease (atherosclerosis).

Fat has a calorie value more than twice that of carbohydrate and hence it provides a more concentrated form of energy. Polar explorers and others who may need 6000 kcal/day may eat up to 300 g of fat daily, otherwise their diet would be impossibly bulky. Such large amounts of fat can be digested, absorbed and metabolized by very active men.

The diet contains many lipids, but the most important as a source of energy are the triglycerides, whose chemical structure is discussed in detail on p. 10.2. Here it is sufficient to state that a high proportion of saturated fatty acids in the triglyceride molecule gives fat, which is solid at room temperature. This includes all animal and dairy fats, except marine fats. The triglycerides present in plants and in marine oils contain relatively more unsaturated fatty acids and are liquid at room temperature. The artificial hardening of these oils by hydrogenation of the double bonds in the unsaturated fatty acids is the basis of the margarine industry.

Fats play an important part in making foods palatable and a good cook needs a plentiful and varied supply. During World War II, the supply of oils and fats in the United Kingdom fell from the pre-war figures of 45·3 to 37·0 lb/head/year. This caused much grumbling and discontent, although the supply remained far greater than was essential for physiological purposes.

The greater part of the dietary fat is oxidized in the body and the carbon is excreted as CO_2. The faeces always contain some fat, usually less than 5 per cent of the intake. The urine also contains traces of an intermediary product of fat metabolism, aceto-acetic acid, and of its derivative β-hydroxybutyric acid. Normally the amounts are so small that they can be neglected, but if the metabolism of carbohydrate is greatly reduced, as may happen in partial starvation or in diabetes mellitus, these acids are produced in large amounts and are then excreted in the urine. This condition is known as ketosis and is discussed on p. 10.25.

PROTEINS

Protein in the diet is essential to replace the continuous breakdown of the body proteins. Each day in a normal man 200–400 g of protein, about 3·5 per cent of the total protein present in the body, may be destroyed and resynthesized. The amino acids formed by the breakdown may in part be used again, but an additional dietary source is also necessary. The national diet in the United Kingdom provides on average 93 g/day of protein, but this is certainly more than is necessary to maintain the tissues. This could be done by most adults with a daily dietary intake of 20–40 g. Many years ago it was recommended that the diet should contain 1 g protein/kg body weight and this is still sound advice. It provides a wide margin of safety and allows for the great variation in the minimal needs of individuals which are known to exist.

The protein needs of children are relatively far greater than those of adults. A newborn baby requires about five times as much protein as an adult per unit of body weight. This requirement falls as the rate of growth declines, but toddlers need about two and a half times as much as adults and adolescents about one and a half times more. Unless these amounts are provided in the diet the child will not grow to its full potential. Poor children in all countries are liable to get an inadequate supply of protein. As a result they grow up small and stunted. In the poorer countries of the world, many children are weaned from the breast on to a diet containing little or no milk and in which the main constituent is carbohydrate of cereal origin. Amongst such children a severe and often fatal wasting disease with the East African name of kwashiorkor is common. The production and distribution of protein foods suitable for very young children and the education of mothers in their use is perhaps the most important medical problem in many undeveloped countries of the world.

Amino acids

Proteins are made up of about twenty different amino acids, which are joined together by peptide bonds. The varying arrangements of the sequence of the amino acids in protein molecules give them different chemical properties and also their individuality. Each of us contains some proteins which are different from those of our neighbour (unless he is our identical twin). The number of amino acids commonly found in the proteins of the human body is approximately the same as the numbers of letters in the alphabet. The various combinations in which they can be arranged (p. 12.4) allow an infinite variety of proteins to be synthesized, in the same way as the letters of the alphabet allow an infinite number of sentences to be constructed. Some of the amino acids cannot be synthesized in the body and a dietary supply is necessary. These are known as essential amino acids and are discussed on p. 11.13.

The quality of proteins

Certain proteins, e.g. those in eggs and human milk, supply the amino acids in proportions well suited for the synthesis of human proteins. Other proteins are relatively deficient in one or more amino acids. These proteins are thus of relatively less value in the diet. Maize proteins are relatively lacking in tryptophan, wheat proteins in lysine, potato, cassava and many other vegetable proteins in the sulphur-containing amino acids. These amino acids are called the **limiting amino acid** of the particular protein, because the relative amount of this acid determines the **biological value** (p. 11.13) of the protein in the diet. Most dietary proteins have a biological value of 40–80 per cent of that of an ideal mixture of proteins such as is present in egg. Fortunately different vegetable proteins have different limiting amino acids and they are able to **supplement** each other. Thus it is possible, by blending

suitable vegetable proteins, to produce a mixture which has almost the same biological value as casein in milk. In underdeveloped countries, where the milk supply is defective, artificial vegetable 'milks' can be manufactured and this is an important public health measure. For adults also, especially in underdeveloped countries, it is important that too large a proportion of the dietary protein should not come from one source. Traditional mixtures such as 'bread and cheese' and 'rice and dhal' are practical examples of the value of a mixture of proteins in a poor man's diet.

The nitrogen balance

As already mentioned the N present in the proteins is excreted in the urine mostly in the form of urea. By comparing the N in the diet with the total N excreted it is possible to tell whether a subject is gaining or losing protein from the tissues. A negative N balance (N excretion greater than the dietary N intake) occurs in starvation and in wasting diseases such as prolonged infections or fevers. A positive N balance occurs in a growing child or in a patient who is recovering from a wasting disease. Table 5.1 is an example of the effect of varying the dietary protein intake on the N balance. The subject was a young woman whose diet was restricted because of obesity and contained only 24 g of protein. The intake of N was 3·9 g/day and the total excretion estimated at 6·5 g/day. The N balance was therefore $3·9 - 6·5 = -2·6$ g/day. This is equivalent to a loss of tissue protein of $2·6 \times 6·25 = 16·25$ g/day. Her dietary protein was therefore insufficient and, as the object of the diet was to remove excess fat and not to cause wasting of muscle and other tissues, the diet was changed; part of the carbohydrate and fat was replaced by protein to make the total protein intake 80 g/day. Table 5.1 shows that on this diet she was in positive N

TABLE 5.1. Nitrogen balances of a young woman on two reducing diets A containing 24, and B containing 80 g protein/day. All values expressed as g N/day.

	A	B
Intake		
Food	3·9	12·7
Output		
Urine	5·3	9·3
Faeces	0·7	0·6
Skin	(0·5)	(0·5)
	6·5	10·4
Balance	−2·6	+2·3

balance, indicating that the dietary protein was now more than adequate for her needs.

It will be seen that most of the N output is in the urine

and the amount in the faeces is small and in this instance not increased by the extra dietary protein. The faecal N comes in part from undigested food, but also from the protein present in the digestive juices and in the epithelial lining of the gut, which is being continuously shed and renewed. There is also a continuous loss of N in the dead, superficial cells, which are rubbed off the skin, in sweat and in the growth of nails and hair. These losses are small compared with those in the urine and are also extremely difficult to measure. In table 5.1 an arbitrary figure has been inserted, based on figures in the literature. It is much easier to collect and analyse urine than the faeces. As the faecal losses are relatively small, in the absence of diarrhoea, faecal collection is often omitted. The subject can usually be assumed to be in positive balance if less than 90 per cent of the dietary intake of N appears in the urine.

Sulphur

The sulphur-containing amino acids, cysteine and methionine, provide from 0·6 to 1·6 g of sulphur in the diet. The exact amount depends on both the quantity and quality of the dietary protein. Most of this sulphur is converted to sulphate and excreted as sulphate ions in the urine. A high protein diet in this way contributes to the acidity of the urine (p. 5.27). The diet also contains a little sulphate and the total urinary sulphur may be up to 2 g day. Most of this is excreted as sulphate, but there is always a little organic sulphur present.

Carbon and hydrogen

In the nineteenth century physiologists and organic chemists worked together to measure the carbon and hydrogen balances of human subjects on various diets. Even today this would be a tedious and difficult procedure and it is seldom, if ever, carried out.

WATER

The body has three sources of water: (1) the water present in the food, (2) the water drunk and (3) the water formed by the oxidation in the tissues of the hydrogen present in the foodstuffs (metabolic water).

Water is lost in three ways: (1) in the urine, (2) in the alimentary canal and (3) by evaporation. There is an obligatory water loss by evaporation from the lungs and skin. The expired air is always saturated with water vapour at body temperature and water is evaporated from the skin, even when there is no sweating. Much of this is absorbed by underclothes, which are heavier and damper in the evening than when they were put on fresh in the morning.

Table 5.2 shows the measured intake and output of water by a young man leading a sedentary life in a tem-

perate climate. These are normal values. The amount of water in the food depends on the nature of the diet and is normally about 1000 g but may be much less on a dry diet. The water drunk is also variable and usually amounts to between 1000 and 1500 g/day. However, several litres may be drunk in a hot climate or by someone who works in a hot environment. The metabolic water depends on how much carbohydrate, fat and protein is oxidized and amounts to between 200 and 400 g/day.

TABLE 5.2. The water balance in a young man leading a sedentary life (data are g/day and the mean of measurements over a 4 day period).

Intake		Output	
Water in food	801	Urinary water	1516
Water drunk	1300	Faecal water	26
Metabolic water	254	Evaporative water	809
	2355		2351

The urinary water is usually between 1000 and 1500 g/day. Normally very little water is lost from the alimentary canal and in formed faeces the output is up to 150 g/day. The evaporative water plays an important part in cooling the body. It is related to energy expenditure and usually accounts for about 25 per cent of total heat losses.

A negative water balance can arise in the following ways:

(1) if the water supply is curtailed or if, for any reason, a patient is unable to drink,

(2) if there are excessive losses from the alimentary canal, as occurs in diarrhoea and vomiting. Many litres of fluid may be lost in this way,

(3) if there is excessive sweating. Men working in hot climates may readily lose 6 kg/day of water in the sweat and losses as high as 12 kg/day have been reported,

(4) if there is excessive loss in the expired air. On high mountains the air is very cold and dry and so more water is required to humidify the expired air. Further, the volume of expired air is increased owing to the stimulus to respiration from the lowered oxygen pressure in the atmosphere (p. 43.2). It has been estimated that Everest climbers may lose water at the rate of 2–3 kg/day by this route and it is probable that members of several expeditions became dehydrated in this way,

(5) if the kidneys fail to retain water, as may occur in diabetes insipidus and in other rare diseases.

There is no true reserve of water in the human body. A normal adult male contains about 40 litres in his body. If he is 2 litres short, he is likely to be very thirsty; if he is 4 litres short he may well be very ill; and he will probably be dead before he has lost 8 litres. Even in a cold climate with no excessive sweating, a man will not survive more than about 4–6 days without water on account of the continuous obligatory water losses.

It is probably impossible to create a positive water balance, and so overhydrate a healthy man. As any beer drinker can verify, the more water that is taken in, the more is passed out in the urine.

The full water balance that is set out in table 5.2 cannot easily be determined and a well equipped laboratory or metabolic ward is needed to do so. Fortunately it is seldom necessary for this to be done. It will be observed that in the table the water drunk approximately equals the urinary water. A fluid chart, on which all that a patient drinks and all the fluid that may be injected intravenously and also the urinary output, are recorded, is frequently kept in hospitals.

ELECTROLYTES AND MINERALS

Sodium

The dietary intake is very variable and in different individuals usually ranges from 70 to 350 mEq/day, corresponding to about 5–20 g of NaCl. The sodium content of the earth is not high and most natural foods contain little sodium. There are still a few primitive people in the world who are ignorant of the use of common salt and their daily intake may be only 30 mEq/day or less. Early in all civilizations common salt came into use as a food preservative and man rapidly developed a taste for it. Besides the table salt we each may add to our food, bakers and dairymen add salt to our bread and to our butter. All preserved and canned meats contain large amounts, as do most sauces, and cooks salt all vegetables. A diet low in salt is valuable in several types of diseases of the kidneys, the heart and the liver. All patients find even a minor restriction of their salt intake unpleasant and a severe restriction is almost intolerable and can seldom be borne for more than two or three weeks. Civilized man is certainly habituated to salt and perhaps can even be described as addicted to it.

The output of salt by the kidneys closely parallels the dietary intake. However large the dietary intake, salt will not be retained by a healthy individual and is promptly excreted in the urine. All land animals have evolved in an environment which is poor in sodium. The ability to conserve this element has been essential for survival. The human kidney is capable of protecting the salt content of the body and, if the need arises, can secrete a urine which is almost free of sodium and chloride.

The faeces normally only contain about 5 mEq/day, but considerable loss may occur if there is diarrhoea.

Visible sweat contains from 20–80 mEq/l. No salt is lost in the normal evaporative water losses from the skin. Table 5.3 shows the balance in a young man leading a sedentary life in a temperate climate.

A negative sodium balance leading to sodium deficiency

TABLE 5.3. The daily sodium and potassium balance of a young man leading a sedentary life on a normal diet. Mean of five daily measurements.

	Sodium mEq/day	Potassium mEq/day
Intake		
Food	135	60
Condiments	0	0
	135	60
Output		
Urine	130	55
Faeces	5	10
Skin	negligible	negligible
	135	65
Balance	0	−5

is common in hospital patients in the tropics. Their normal diet is often low in sodium and there is a continual loss in the sweat, which may easily amount to 200 mEq/day. A fever with the consequent increase in sweating or a minor gastrointestinal disturbance with diarrhoea, each increases sodium losses and hence may precipitate sodium deficiency. Sodium deficiency occurs less commonly in temperate climates, and arises from severe or prolonged vomiting or diarrhoea, and in some forms of kidney and endocrine disease.

Salt deficiency leads to a reduction in the volume of the extracellular fluid and of the blood. When it develops slowly and is of moderate severity, the symptoms are dizziness, fainting, weakness and mental confusion; there may be hypotension on standing. Acute severe deficiency leads to shock with a marked fall in blood pressure. It is also the cause of miner's cramp, well known to those who work underground in hot mines in any part of the world. A traditional remedy is for the miner to add salt to his beer.

Potassium

All cells in both animals and plants are rich in potassium and in consequence most natural whole foods contain the element. Fruit juices are a particularly rich source. Probably potassium deficiency never occurs as a result of a natural dietary deficiency. Intakes usually range between 40 and 90 mEq/day. The faeces contain a little more potassium than sodium, usually about 10 mEq/day. The sweat contains very little potassium. The urinary potassium normally approximates to the dietary intake. Table 5.3 shows the potassium balance in a young man.

Potassium deficiency commonly arises from the increased losses associated with vomiting and diarrhoea.

It may also follow from the continued use of purgatives. Excessive loss in the urine may occur in renal disease.

In all wasting diseases and trauma where there is a breakdown in the cell structure, the intracellular potassium escapes into the extracellular fluid and blood and is in part excreted in the urine. All patients who are wasted, from whatever the cause, are liable to be deficient in potassium, which must be made good as part of their rehabilitation.

Deficiency of potassium causes muscle weakness, dizziness, thirst and mental confusion. It also interferes with the excitability of tissues, demonstrable in the heart by changes in the electrocardiogram (p. 28.10).

Anions

The chief anions in the diet are chloride and phosphate. The chloride intake is similar to the sodium intake because of their association in dietary salt. The excretory losses of chloride run parallel to those of sodium. Intake and output of phosphate are best discussed in relation to calcium, because of their close association in bone formation.

Calcium

Calcium is necessary for the formation and maintenance of bone, as is iron for the manufacture of the pigment haemoglobin, present in the red blood corpuscles. An adequate dietary supply of these two minerals is of the utmost importance.

It has been mentioned already that very little sodium and potassium is present in the faeces. This is because the salts of these two elements are soluble in water and so are readily absorbed from the gut. In contrast, calcium and iron form many salts which are either insoluble or only sparingly soluble in water. All diets contain calcium and iron in quantities which could easily meet the body's need, if they could be absorbed. However, the greater part of the dietary calcium and iron simply passes through the alimentary canal and is lost in the faeces. The problems of the supply of both calcium and iron are essentially the provision of a diet from which they can be absorbed in adequate amounts.

An adult human skeleton contains about 1·2 kg of calcium. This takes about 20 years to manufacture, so the growing child and adolescent must retain on average about 160 mg/day of calcium. The skeleton is not a permanent structure, but is being continually renewed. Studies with isotopes indicate that in an adult about 700 mg of calcium are resorbed from bone and replaced daily. Some of this calcium can be utilized again, but there is always a loss in the urine which must be made good from the diet. Fig. 5.1 shows the calcium exchanges in a young European.

Typical European diets provide about 1000 mg/day of calcium and about 800 mg pass into the faeces. The only

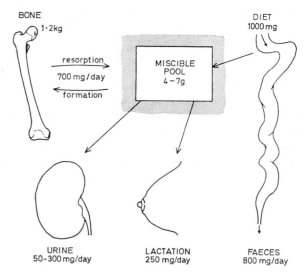

FIG. 5.1. The calcium exchanges in the human body.

rich dietary source is milk. Cow's milk contains about 120 mg/100 ml, so 0·5 litre (just under 1 pint) goes a long way to meet the requirements of either a child or adult. The calcium in milk is concentrated in cheese and most cheeses are very rich sources, providing up to 1200 mg/100 g. Human milk contains much less calcium than cow's milk, usually between 20–40 mg/100 ml. A mother who is nursing her baby will put out up to 250 mg/day of calcium in her milk, and this must be replaced in her diet. Milk is a good source of protein as well as calcium and the protein probably facilitates the absorption of calcium, as the calcium salts of amino acids are relatively soluble.

Cereals, fruits and vegetables all contain calcium, but in very varying amounts. The calcium in cereals is made in part unavailable by the presence in the whole cereal grain of an organic acid, phytic acid, which forms an insoluble calcium salt. Phytic acid is not absorbed from the gut and calcium phytate is lost in the faeces. Most of the phytic acid is in the germ and outer pericarp of the grain, which is removed by milling. Thus calcium is much more readily absorbed from bread made from highly-milled white flour than from bread made from wholemeal flour. In the United Kingdom calcium lactate is artificially added to flour. The reason for this is as follows.

In making white bread about 70 per cent of the whole wheat grain is used. The remaining 30 per cent, which includes the indigestible cellulose (p. 5.1) in the outer coats, is sold by the millers as cattle food. In 1940–1, many ships carrying grain from Canada and the U.S.A. to the U.K. were sunk by German submarines in the Battle of the Atlantic. In these circumstances, it seemed wasteful to use only 70 per cent of the cargo for human food, so it was decided to make all bread from a flour in which 85 per cent of the whole grain was extracted. This 'national flour' contained more phytic acid than white flour: experiments on man showed that its use increased the losses of calcium in the faeces. To make good these losses, the flour was 'enriched' by the addition of calcium lactate. This was sensible. However, when in peace time we reverted to bread made from white flour, the order to enrich the flour was not repealed. We continue to add calcium to our bread. Whether anyone now derives any benefit from this measure is uncertain.

Other substances that may make calcium unavailable include oxalic acid and free fatty acids. Rhubarb and certain other vegetables and fruits contain oxalates, but the amounts normally eaten are not sufficient to have any practical effect on calcium absorption. If fats are improperly absorbed as may happen in disease of the small intestine, there is an excess of unesterified fatty acids in the gut and these form insoluble calcium soaps, which are excreted in the faeces. Thinning and weakening of the bones, arising in this way, is a common consequence of long standing intestinal disease.

It was formerly thought that the intake of phosphates had an important effect on calcium absorption. However, it has been shown in adults that large intakes of phosphorus do not inhibit calcium absorption. Nevertheless, the phosphate intake may be more important for infants, and in artificial milk preparations for infant feeding it is probably wise to keep the phosphate and calcium proportions within the limits normally found in natural milk (table 5.6, p. 5.21.).

So far this account of calcium has been an essentially European one. Table 5.4 sets out the national intake of

TABLE 5.4. The principal sources of calcium in national diets (mg/head/day).

	Total calcium	Calcium from milk	Calcium from cereals	Calcium from vegetables
United Kingdom	1024	591	290*	46
U.S.A.	1116	856	29	135
India	347	147	165†	23

* of this 243 mg was artificially added calcium.
† of this 67 mg was provided by pulses.

calcium in the United Kingdom, the U.S.A., where European diets are eaten, and in India. The figures for India are typical of many countries in Asia and Africa where the milk supply is small. Despite the low calcium intake there is no evidence that Asian and African bones are in any way inferior to European and American bones. They have the same calcium content and are no more liable to fractures. It is certain that on these low calcium diets, Asians and Africans absorb a higher proportion of the calcium than Europeans do on their diets. Those who live on diets rich in calcium are probably 'disadapted' to calcium absorption in some way. This may

be due to the loss of an enzyme phytase in the alimentary canal, which can split the calcium phytate. When Europeans have been given low calcium diets experimentally, most of them have acquired the ability to absorb a greater proportion of the calcium than when on their usual diets. This change, however, takes place gradually over many weeks or months.

Although the bones of people who are brought up in countries where there is little milk are of good quality, they are usually small. Milk provides protein and calcium necessary for bone formation, but the lack of dietary protein is probably the factor that most commonly limits growth. It has been shown that giving calcium lactate to children on diets which contain little milk does not accelerate growth. Giving extra protein does. It would be relatively much easier and cheaper for a country such as India to enrich rice with calcium than to provide extra protein for the growing children. Unfortunately this measure would probably do no good.

The urinary output of calcium varies widely in individuals and 50–300 mg/day is the normal range in health. This may be related to variations in intestinal absorption and in turnover rates in bone.

Calcium besides being necessary for bone development is also essential for the normal excitability of tissues. In severe calcium deficiency the motor nerves become readily excitable and twitching and spasm of the muscles, especially of the face, hands and feet occurs. This is known as tetany.

Magnesium

The body contains about 25 g of magnesium most of which is present in bone. It is the second most important intracellular cation after potassium; the concentration in cells is about 15 mEq/l. and the ion plays an essential role in many enzymic reactions.

A typical diet contains 200–400 mg most of which is not absorbed and appears in the faeces. Like potassium, magnesium is widely distributed in foods and a primary dietary deficiency probably never arises. Magnesium deficiency, however, is often present in patients with prolonged diarrhoea whatever the cause. The chief features are weakness and depression. The magnesium content of all muscle cells is lowered and the electrocardiogram shows changes similar to those in potassium deficiency.

Strontium

Interest in this metal arose when it was discovered that the radioactive isotope ^{90}Sr was present in the fall-out of atomic explosions. This contaminates crops and the isotope becomes incorporated into plants and animals, which are used as human food.

Strontium is a divalent metal in the same group in the periodic table as magnesium and calcium. It is treated biologically in a similar manner, being stored in bone.

As ^{90}Sr has a half-life of 28 years, it is a potential danger to bone marrow and other tissues. The testing of nuclear weapons led to significant amounts of ^{90}Sr being found in milk and vegetables in many parts of the world. The amount of ^{90}Sr detectable in the bones of young children also rose, but not sufficiently to cause a level of radio-activity, which is considered dangerous. Accidents at local atomic power stations are another potential danger. The Agricultural Research Council Radiobiological Laboratory in the U.K. and the Atomic Energy Commission in the U.S.A. each publish at regular intervals analyses of the radioactivity of samples of food.

Strontium derives its name from Strontian a village in Argyllshire in the West of Scotland. It was first isolated at the end of the eighteenth century from mineral ore obtained from local lead mines.

Phosphorus

The human body contains from 600 to 900 g of phosphorus, of which over 80 per cent is present in bone and most of the remainder is within the cells. Phosphates are widely distributed in the earth's crust and are present in all plants and animals tissues. Phosphorus deficiency is known to veterinarians as occurring occasionally in cattle who graze on very poor land. A primary dietary deficiency of phosphorus probably never occurs in man. A diet that is adequate in calcium certainly contains sufficient phosphorus.

The roles of phosphates in the body are numerous and are discussed frequently in future chapters.

Iron

The body contains about 4 g of iron, approximately the weight of a 2 inch nail. About 2·5 g are present in the pigment haemoglobin and about 1 g as ferritin and haemosiderin, the form in which iron is stored in the cells. The remainder is present in myoglobin, the cytochromes and other cell constituents.

The life of a human red cell is about 120 days and just under 1 per cent of the total haemoglobin in the body must be resynthesized daily. For this purpose about 20 mg of iron are needed. Most of this is obtained from the haemoglobin in the broken down red cells, but about 1 mg is needed to make good body losses and this must be provided by the diet.

The body does not excrete iron. All the iron present in the plasma is bound to protein and this does not appear in the urine. A small iron loss occurs in the desquamation of cells from the skin and from the epithelium of urinary and respiratory tracts. More important is the iron loss in the menstrual blood. This normally amounts to about 28 mg/menstrual period or the equivalent of 1 mg/day but it may be much more. Furthermore if a woman becomes pregnant she needs additional iron to supply the needs of the foetus and later for her milk. During reproductive life a woman requires about 2 mg/day of iron, about twice as much as a man.

All human diets contain more iron than the body needs; yet anaemia due to iron deficiency is extremely common in women, though it rarely occurs in men unless there is a chronic source of blood loss (e.g. bleeding piles or infection with the blood-sucking hookworm). This is due to the fact that most of the dietary iron is present in a form which cannot be absorbed. Good human diets provide 12–15 mg iron daily and with this intake the 1 mg of iron needed by adult men is readily absorbed, but it is only marginally adequate for women and mild degrees of anaemia are likely to be found. When diets provide only 8–9 mg/day, anaemia is widespread and often severe in women.

Some iron is present in all natural foods. Liver and other offal are rich sources; meat, fruit and vegetables are usually good sources. Whole cereal grains also contain much iron, but it is mostly made unavailable by the presence of phytic acid (p. 5.6), which forms insoluble iron phytate, similar to calcium phytate. Ferric iron is not absorbed and dietary iron must first be reduced to ferrous iron before it can pass across the gut wall and this reduction is probably assisted by ascorbic acid and the —SH groups in the sulphur-containing amino acids. A good mixed diet by providing plenty of ascorbic acid and protein facilitates iron absorption.

The role of the stomach and hydrochloric acid in iron absorption has been much disputed. Atrophic gastric mucous membrane, producing little or no hydrochloric acid, and anaemia due to iron deficiency are frequently found together. Which of these is cause and which is effect has been disputed for 50 years and the problem is not yet solved.

Iron absorption is greatly increased if the body stores are reduced or the rate of formation of red cells is increased. For instance after a severe haemorrhage a man, instead of absorbing only 10 per cent of his dietary intake, may absorb 20–30 per cent. Clearly there is some control of the alimentary absorption of iron and this is related to iron needs. The nature of this control, which is situated in the walls of the small intestines, is discussed on p. 30.39.

In many parts of Africa iron cooking-vessels are used and extraneous iron gets into the diet so that intakes of iron may reach 100 mg/day. Cheap wines and cider may be very rich in iron, possibly due to contamination from vessels in which they have been stored or prepared. In France and in the poorer section of the U.S.A. many heavy wine-drinkers have a large dietary intake of iron. In these circumstances the control of absorption may break down and part of the dietary excess enters the body. As there is no means of excreting excess iron, it accumulates in the tissues and a condition known as siderosis arises (Greek *sideros* = iron). Siderosis may be found by chemical analysis in the organs at post mortem in a person who has died as a result of an accident, who was otherwise well. However, severe siderosis may contribute to the liver cirrhosis which is common in many parts of Africa and also in heavy wine-drinkers.

Acute iron poisoning may also occur and fatalities have been reported in children who have consumed a bottle of their mother's iron tablets, thinking them to be sweets.

Trace elements

These elements are defined as those that occur in not more than one part in 20,000 in the tissues of the body. Some of these elements are essential dietary constituents; others are probably not required, but are incorporated from the soil into crops used for human and animal food.

IODINE

Iodine is an essential component of thyroxine and other secretions of the thyroid gland. In the absence of an adequate supply the gland enlarges and a visible swelling appears in the neck, known as a goitre. Goitres may become very large and unsightly; they are associated with a varying degree of failure of thyroid function.

The body contains from 20 to 50 mg of iodine and a daily intake of about 150 μg is required. The iodine content of foods is very variable and depends on the iodine content of the soil on which they are grown. The sea contains much more iodine than the land. Iodine was first discovered in seaweed by Courtois in 1811, who was using it as a source of nitre for gunpowder for Napoleon's army. All sea foods are rich sources of iodine.

There are at least a million people in the world suffering from goitre. They are mostly found in isolated villages high up in the Himalayas and in the Andes and in many parts of Africa. Goitre can be prevented by adding potassium iodide to table salt. This is done in many countries, but not in Great Britain. Sporadic cases of goitre are still found in most countries and this is due to the fact that individual needs for iodine vary greatly. Goitres are most common in adolescent girls. Sea fish eaten at one or two meals a week provides more than 150 μg/day of iodine and goitre is prevented.

FLUORIDE

Water may contain up to 10 parts per million of fluoride. Epidemiological studies have shown that where the water contains less than one part per million dental caries is more common than elsewhere. In many districts of the world with water supplies low in fluoride it has been shown that the addition of fluoride to bring the concentration to one part per million reduces the incidence of dental decay in children.

If the fluoride content of the water is high (3–5 parts per million) a brown mottling of the teeth occurs. This is unsightly, but the teeth are sound. Mottling of the teeth

and fluoride intakes of this level are common in many countries and are not associated with any disease or signs of ill health. However, there are a few isolated villages where wells provide water containing 10 parts per million or even more of fluoride. This high intake causes an increased density of the bones and calcification of the ligaments. The spine is especially affected and the resulting poker back is a serious disability.

Medical and dental authorities are agreed that where the fluoride content of the drinking water is low, the addition of fluoride to bring the concentration up to 1 part per million is safe and will reduce the incidence of dental decay in children. Water engineers are also agreed that this procedure is cheap and practical. However, the provision of adequate water supplies to a community is a responsibility of local governments. Although local authorities in Europe and America have fluorinated their water with a consequent improvement in the teeth of their children, many others, including we regret to say Edinburgh, have not done so. Fluoridation has been bitterly opposed in local councils by those who state that it is an unnatural tampering with the water and that individuals have no choice to opt out of a scheme and drink, if they wish, unfluorinated water. Fluoridation is claimed to be a governmental interference with the rights of the individual. Most anti-fluoridators have an irrational fear of 'chemicals' without which a modern society could not exist. Undoubtedly they are responsible for many of our children continuing to have bad teeth.

COPPER

Deficiency of copper is well known to the veterinary profession, as occurring in sheep grazing on poor soils and causing anaemia. Copper is almost certainly an essential dietary element for all animals. A normal human diet contains about 2 mg Cu/day and copper deficiency has not been reported in man. There is no evidence that human beings ever require extra copper.

COBALT

This element is a component of the molecule of vitamin B_{12} (p. 5.15) and so is an essential dietary component. Traces of cobalt are present in many foods and there is no evidence that man ever suffers from a primary lack of cobalt.

ZINC

Human diets provide from 10 to 15 mg of zinc and the human body contains about 1–2 g. Zinc is an essential component of several enzyme systems. Zinc deficiency has been reported to be the cause of some children in Irani villages failing to mature normally.

MANGANESE

This is certainly an essential element. Manganese is a component of many enzyme systems and manganese deficiency occurs in cattle grazing on pastures containing peat, which contains very small amounts of the element. Manganese deficiency has not been reported in man and the diet usually provides 5–10 mg/day.

SELENIUM

There is a disease of lambs and calves in New Zealand and the U.S.A. known as 'white muscle disease', which usually responds well to selenium therapy, but no human counterpart is known. In laboratory animals, extra selenium can reduce the effects of vitamin E deficiency. Selenium is widespread in most soils.

In conclusion it may be said that copper, cobalt, zinc, manganese, selenium and in addition molybdenum, nickel and arsenic and perhaps other elements are of interest to biochemists and of practical importance to the veterinary profession, but not to doctors. However, poisoning by some of these elements has been reported in industrial workers, miners and others who are exposed to high concentrations of dusts and vapours in which they are present.

VITAMINS

Vitamins are organic compounds which the body is unable to synthesize and which must be supplied in the diet. Many of them have been shown to be components of enzyme systems (p. 7.13).

Five major diseases: scurvy, beriberi, pellagra, keratomalacia and rickets, arise as a result of a dietary lack of one of the vitamins. In the past these diseases have been responsible for much ill health and many deaths. As each can be prevented by appropriate dietary means, they should no longer be seen. However, even in prosperous communities they are not extinct though nowadays rare and in many parts of the world they remain important medical problems. Only by the education of the public and the constant vigilance of individual doctors and the public health authorities is their prevention assured.

The discovery of vitamins is comparatively recent. The concept of dietary deficiencies was unknown to ancient and medieval physicians. In 1497 on Vasco de Gama's voyage from Portugal round the Cape of Good Hope to the Malabar coast in South India, one hundred out of his one hundred and sixty men died of scurvy. Thereafter scurvy was a common scourge of all those who went on long sea voyages. Some people, notably the great explorer Captain Cook and the Scottish Naval surgeon James Lind, were well aware that the disease could be prevented by an adequate supply of fresh fruit or vegetables. In the late eighteenth century, Americans began to use the term 'limeys' for the British because lime juice was then a regular issue on ships of the British Navy. Yet the general concept of deficiency diseases was still not appreciated.

In the nineteenth century, nutritional research was directed primarily to elucidating the roles of protein, fat and carbohydrate of the diet in supplying the energy needs of the body. In the last third of the century, the discovery of bacteria and the realization of the enormous role which they and other parasites play in causing infectious diseases emphasized the importance of positive environmental factors in pathological processes. This led to a great search for infective agents and toxic factors to account for all diseases, which distracted the attention of most physicians and research workers from considering the possible role of dietary deficiences as a cause of disease. Although a few far-sighted men realized that an inadequate diet might be a primary cause of disease, this was not generally appreciated, until the publication in 1912 of a famous experiment by Hopkins, the first Professor of Biochemistry in Cambridge. One group of rats were fed on a diet of pure protein, fat and carbohydrate together with minerals. Another group received the same diet but in addition each rat was given 3 ml of milk. Those rats on the pure diet failed to grow, but those receiving the milk developed normally. After 18 days the milk was taken away from the second group, which then ceased to grow, and given to the first group, which then grew normally. Clearly there was an 'accessory factor' in the milk.

It was soon shown that there were several accessory factors and as these were discovered they were called vitamin A, B, C, D etc. The word vitamine was introduced by the Polish biochemist Funk because he thought that all the factors were vital amines. It is now known that only a few of the vitamins are amines, but the name has stuck although the final 'e' was soon removed. In the last 40 years most of the vitamins have been isolated, synthesized and given new names, according to accepted chemical terminology. In general these new names will be used in this book. The old letters are, however, still in use and some of them are likely to remain. They are simpler, though less informative than the chemical names, and are preferable in popular expositions for the education of the general public.

The vitamins can be divided into two great classes: the fat-soluble and water-soluble vitamins. The body cannot maintain a large store of the water-soluble vitamins, and so deficiency disease is likely to arise after only a few weeks on a diet deficient in these vitamins. By contrast there is a large store of most of the fat-soluble vitamins in the liver fats and in a previously well-fed adult these stores are sufficient to prevent the appearance of evidence of deficiency even after many months or perhaps years on an inadequate diet. Diseases due to deficiency of the fat-soluble vitamins usually occur in children who have been on a defective diet since weaning.

The water-soluble vitamins circulate freely in the blood and are readily excreted by the kidneys. If for therapeutic purposes a large excess is given, the excess is rapidly lost in the urine and so they are not toxic. By contrast the fat-soluble vitamins are not excreted. If an excess is given, it is stored in the liver and after a time toxic symptoms may arise. A popular and mistaken belief is that, if a little of something does one good, more of it will do you more good. It is very important to see that children are not overdosed with fat-soluble vitamins. An over-conscientious mother can be as great a danger to her child as a feckless one. This has practical aspects in the prevention of rickets.

Fat-soluble vitamins

VITAMIN A OR RETINOL

This vitamin is a highly unsaturated aromatic hydrocarbon which is soluble in fats, but not in water. It is present only in some foods of animal origin. Dairy products, butter, cheese and milk are rich sources as is margarine, to which the vitamin is now added artificially. Liver is also a rich source since it is the site where the vitamin is stored in the body. Fish-liver oils are exceptionally rich. Meats contain only traces of the vitamin as it is not stored or concentrated in any body fat outside the liver.

The body is not entirely dependent on a dietary source of vitamin A, as it can be formed in the body from carotene precursors, especially beta carotene. The carotenes are pigments which are widespread in fruits and vegetables. Dietary beta carotene can be converted into vitamin A in the wall of the small intestine. How much of the dietary carotene is converted is always uncertain; it is probably about one-third and may be less. In this country most of us get about half of our vitamin A direct from dairy products and about half from the precursors in fruits and vegetables. Vitamin A deficiency is now a rare condition in prosperous communities. It is still very common in many parts of the tropics, where there are few productive dairy cattle and where fruits and vegetables may be scarce and expensive.

The first sign of vitamin A deficiency is difficulty in vision when the light is dim (night blindness). The rods of the retina are stimulated when a retinal pigment, rhodospin or visual purple, is bleached by light p. 10.9. An aldehyde formed from retinol, the chemical name for the vitamin, is an essential part of the visual purple. Vitamin A is also necessary for growth, normal bone formation and the normal process of shedding and repair of epithelial tissues. In the absence of an adequate supply, epithelial surfaces fail to shed their dead cells and become dry and thickened (keratinized). In particular this may affect the cornea of the eye, which becomes opaque and soft (keratomalacia). If not promptly treated, the cornea may collapse, disorganization and infection follow and lead to the loss of the eye. Every year, tens of thousands of young children in the poorer countries of the world go permanently blind for lack of a milligram or so of vitamin A. Did that last sentence make you feel uncomfortable? There is no cause in medicine that is more worth fighting than a campaign against keratomalacia.

An international unit of vitamin A was set up with beta carotene as a reference, before the vitamin was available in pure form. By definition 1 i.u. is equal to 0·6 μg of beta carotene, but only half the carotene molecule can be converted into the vitamin, so 1 i.u. also equals 0·3 μg of vitamin A. As under physiological conditions only about one-third of the beta carotene is converted into the vitamin, the dietary requirements, expressed in i.u./day, depend on how much is provided as preformed vitamin and how much as the precursor. A recommended allowance is 2000 i.u./day for a young child and 5000 for an adult (p. 5.25) provided one-fifth of these totals is as preformed vitamin, mostly in dairy produce, and the remainder from vegetable sources. The chemical structure of vitamin A is given on p. 10.8.

VITAMIN D OR CALCIFEROL

The word rickets comes from the Anglo-Saxon *wrikken* meaning to twist. It describes the twisting of the long bones, especially of the legs, and of the spine. The pelvis may also be twisted and contracted and this was formerly responsible for many difficult labours. The disease was first described by English physicians in the seventeenth century. At this time London began to take on the appearance of an industrial city and was often covered by a cloud of smoke. Rickets became a common disease amongst poor children in industrial cities throughout the world and was particularly severe amongst the families of Muslims living in purdah. The children of wealthy parents and country children, though not immune, were less often and less severely affected.

Soon after Hopkins had discovered vitamins, Mellanby and others were able to show that rickets was due to deficiency of a fat-soluble vitamin, vitamin D. The disease was produced experimentally by dietary means in dogs. Young puppies are very susceptible to rickets, and today medical students are perhaps more likely to see a case of rickets in a young puppy than in a child. It is easy to gain prestige by advising the owner to give her pup some cod liver oil. The bow legs will then soon straighten. Cod liver oil, like many other fish-liver oils, is a rich source of the vitamin. Vitamin D is found in dairy products, butter, milk and cheese, and also in eggs and liver. It is not naturally present in other foods, but is artificially added to margarines and to some infant foods.

The body is not entirely dependent on a dietary source of this vitamin, for it can be synthesized from precursors in the skin by the action of ultraviolet light. Industrial smoke and the purdah system each reduce the exposure of children to sunlight and so contribute to rickets. It is still not accurately known how much vitamin D can be synthesized in the skin, and the relative importance of lack of sunlight and lack of dairy produce in the causation of the disease is uncertain.

Vitamin D was soon shown not to be a single compound. There are at least two substances, both sterols, which have vitamin D activity. Their chemical structure and properties are described on p. 10.9.

Vitamin D acts in two ways. It promotes the absorption of calcium from the small intestine and it facilitates the deposition of bone by the formation of insoluble calcium salts. Overdosage with vitamin D leads to a high level of calcium in the blood, followed by pathological calcification of various organs of the body and is sometimes fatal.

Several closely related substances have vitamin D activity. They can all be obtained by the irradiation of sterols (p. 10.9). The international standard of vitamin D is calciferol, obtained from the irradiation of ergosterol which is present in yeast and 1 mg of calciferol contains 40,000 i.u. of vitamin D. The dietary requirements of vitamin D are difficult to estimate precisely, partly because how much is synthesized in the skin cannot be determined. A dietary intake of 400 i.u./day is probably sufficient. Higher intakes, as already stated, may be toxic and some children appear especially susceptible to this hazard.

VITAMIN E

When rats are fed on certain artificial diets, they fail to reproduce. The females abort and the males become sterile. In addition degenerative processes occur in the muscle which become partially converted into fibrous tissue. All these changes can be prevented by adding vegetable oils to the diet. A concentrate obtained from wheat germ oil proved very effective and was named vitamin E. Vitamin E is now known to be a mixture of tocopherols (p. 10.9). These are oily liquids, which have the property of protecting other substances against oxidation. There are a number of other antioxidants present in biological material.

There is no good evidence that vitamin E deficiency ever occurs in man, and probably all human diets contain a sufficiency of the necessary tocopherols. Vitamin E therapy has been tried for a wide variety of human ailments, including repeated abortions and various muscular dystrophies. Extravagant claims have been made which have not stood up to critical analysis. Vitamin E has no place in modern therapy.

VITAMIN K

The Danish biochemist, Dam, described how a bleeding disease of chicks could be prevented by feeding them with a number of foodstuffs, including lucerne and putrid fish-meal. From these he extracted a vitamin, which was called vitamin K (Koagulation Vitamin). There are several substances with vitamin K activity. All are fat-soluble and derivatives of naphthoquinone (p. 10.9).

Vitamin K is essential for the formation of prothrombin in the liver. Prothrombin is a necessary component of the complex mechanism for the clotting of blood (p. 26.14).

Vitamin K preparations are used in medicine in a variety of bleeding conditions. These may arise as a result of a failure to absorb vitamin K in disorders of the alimentary tract.

A primary dietary deficiency of vitamin K has not been produced in laboratory animals and probably never arises in man. It is readily synthesized by *Escherichia coli* and other bacteria that inhibit the intestines.

Water-soluble vitamins

ASCORBIC ACID OR VITAMIN C

The widespread incidence of scurvy at one time in ships' crews and the fact that the disease could be prevented by fresh fruit and vegetables have already been described (p. 5.10). The essential feature of scurvy is haemorrhage, which may occur in the skin, giving the appearance of large bruises, or in the internal organs, where the consequence may be fatal. The disease is often most conspicuous in the gums, which appear swollen and bleeding.

The elucidation of the nature of the responsible vitamin had to await the discovery of a suitable experimental animal. In 1907, guinea-pigs were shown to be very susceptible to scurvy. Only guinea-pigs and primates develop the disease on experimental diets. Although all animals need a supply of this protective vitamin, other species were able to synthesize it in their own tissues. Man and other susceptible animals appear to have lost the mechanism for doing this.

Using the guinea-pig as an experimental animal, various extracts of citrus fruit juices were concentrated and tested. In 1928, the vitamin was obtained in a crystalline form and soon after synthesized. Previously referred to as vitamin C, it was renamed ascorbic acid and shown to be a simple sugar. The formula of ascorbic acid and its chief chemical properties are described on p. 9.4. Here it is sufficient to state that it is water soluble and easily destroyed by oxidation at moderate temperatures. In consequence there may be large losses of the vitamin in washing, preparing, cooking and serving vegetables and fruit. These losses may be minimized by good techniques in the kitchen, but a serving of cooked vegetables or fruit is unlikely to contain more than half of the vitamin originally present. Often much less remains. The pleasant American custom of starting the day with a glass of fresh fruit juice at breakfast ensures an adequate intake of the vitamin.

Apart from fruit and vegetables there are no other

important dietary sources. Milk, meat and eggs contain only traces. Of vegetable sources, green, leafy vegetables such as cabbage are the richest. The concentration of the vitamin in potatoes is not high, but as large amounts are eaten they are a useful source. In Scotland, much less fruit and vegetables are eaten than in the south of England, and potatoes provide the major portion of the supply of the vitamin. The amount present in potatoes falls off on storage and in the spring and early summer, before new potatoes become available, they contain very little. At this season of the year it is not unusual to find a case of scurvy in Edinburgh. The patient is usually an old man living alone, who either dislikes or cannot afford to buy fruit and fresh vegetables.

As already stated, milk contains very little ascorbic acid and what there is will be destroyed if the milk is boiled. In consequence young children are especially liable to scurvy and at one time infantile scurvy was very common. Nowadays, due to the better education of mothers in child feeding and in part to the availability of orange juice as a Welfare Food for children, it has become rare. However, some 50 cases are diagnosed in young children in the United Kingdom each year.

Adult scurvy is specially likely to occur in dry and semi-desert countries, where vegetable gardens and orchards are difficult to maintain. In such countries scurvy is not uncommonly found when famine conditions arise. Less than 10 mg/day of ascorbic acid is needed to prevent the onset of scurvy and many people appear to be perfectly healthy on such an intake. However, as an insurance 20 mg/day is recommended by British authorities. In America the recommended intake is 70 mg/day—a very liberal 'safety margin' which is generally considered in Britain to be unnecessary.

An ordinary helping of cabbage or other green vegetables (30–60 g or 1–2 oz) provides 20–25 mg of ascorbic acid. A good helping of boiled potatoes (100 g or 3 oz) gives 5–15 mg. An orange or other citrus fruit provides about 10–20 mg in 30 g or 1 oz either of the fresh fruit or the juice.

THIAMINE OR VITAMIN B$_1$

Beriberi is an ancient oriental disease, which affects chiefly rice eaters. There are two forms. In **dry beriberi** the patient is wasted and may be partially paralysed; he may be able to walk only with the aid of sticks; there may be a severe loss of function of the peripheral nerves. In **wet beriberi,** the heart is affected and the peripheral tissues become waterlogged, partly due to a loss of function of the capillary walls and partly due to heart failure. Large numbers of persons may be incapacitated by the disease and deaths are not infrequent.

Our understanding of the nature of beriberi began in 1890. A Dutch military physician, Eijkman, working in Indonesia, found that fowls fed on the food provided for

his hospital patients developed weakness and paralysis similar in some ways to that present in his beriberi patients. It was found possible to produce a disease resembling in many ways human beriberi in a convenient laboratory animal, the pigeon, by feeding the birds on highly-milled, polished rice. This could be prevented if the birds were given a small portion of the outer pericarp or germ of the rice grain; this is normally removed in the milling process. Active extracts of rice germ were concentrated and finally a pure crystalline product was obtained. As little as 5 mg of the crystals, if given to a patient with beriberi dying of heart failure can transform him in less than one hour. The laboured breathing is eased, the rapid pulse slows and the congestion relieved. There is perhaps no more dramatic spectacle in medicine than the relief of acute beriberi with a few crystals of the vitamin.

The responsible vitamin was first called vitamin B and subsequently vitamin B$_1$ to distinguish it from other soluble vitamins present in the crude extract. The structure of the vitamin was soon elucidated and found to be an amine containing a sulphur atom. Thereupon it was renamed thiamine. The structure of thiamine is given on p. 7.13, together with its principal chemical functions.

The brain of a pigeon suffering from beriberi, if minced or sliced and suspended in physiological saline, takes up oxygen in the presence of carbohydrate more slowly than the brain of a normal pigeon. In 1931, the writer, then a medical student, was one of a group of assistants in the Biochemistry Department at Oxford who helped Professor Peters to show that if the vitamin was added to the brain suspension *in vitro* in catalytic amounts the defect in oxidation of carbohydrates was reversed. In beriberi the biochemical lesion, a term introduced by Peters, has been shown to be a specific defect in the complex mechanism for the breakdown of carbohydrate in the cells. The exact role of the vitamin is described on p. 9.12. This was the first demonstration that a vitamin was part of a specific enzyme system, essential for the metabolism of living cells. Subsequently many other vitamins have been shown to play an essential role in cell metabolism.

Thiamine is present in small amounts in all living cells. Consequently it is found in all whole natural foods. Not being soluble in fats, it is absent from butter, animal fats and vegetable oils. It is also absent or present in very small quantities in refined foods such as sugar and some cereal flours. Thiamine can be stored in relatively large amounts in the seed grains of cereals and pulses. Consequently rich sources are whole cereal grains and pulses (peas and beans). Yeast is also rich and a well-known remedy for beriberi. Wholemeal wheat flour and hand-pounded rice provide ample thiamine. In the machine milling of both wheat and rice most of the thiamine is removed. Orientals are largely protected against beriberi by the thiamine in the pulses traditionally eaten with rice.

In the past, outbreaks of beriberi have on occasions been reported in the West associated with excessive consumption of white bread. Nowadays synthetic thiamine is cheap and in many countries it must be added to white flour used for bread making. Synthetic thiamine tablets are widely available in most big Eastern towns, where beriberi is now a rare disease. It is still an important problem in many rice-eating villages. The traditional methods of hand pounding the rice are often replaced by small mills, which can mill the rice very finely. They are sometimes the property of the village headman. The finer he can mill the rice, the more bran he has to sell as cattle food. In such circumstances beriberi may break out.

Thiamine circulates in the blood and is present in all the body fluids. If a mother is on a diet deficient in the vitamin, her milk will also be defective and her infant may suffer from beriberi.

Thiamine is not needed for the metabolism of fats and thiamine requirements are related to the carbohydrate content of the diet. A margin of safety is provided by an intake of 0·6 mg/100 non-fat kcal. It is more usual, but less accurate, to equate thiamine intake with total calories and 0·4 mg/1000 total kcal has been recommended. For an adult active man the total daily intake should be about 1·3 mg/day. Nursing mothers should have a little more and 1·4 mg/day is recommended.

NICOTINIC ACID

Maize or Indian corn is one of the gifts of the New World to the Old. Wherever it has been widely cultivated—in the southern states of the U.S.A., in Central America, in Spain, Italy, the Balkans, Egypt, North Africa and many other countries—there have been widespread outbreaks of pellagra. It first occurred in Southern Europe in the eighteenth century. The word is of Italian origin and derived from *pelle* skin and *agra* sour. A characteristic feature is an eczematous condition of the skin, occurring over those parts of the body exposed to sunlight. There are also mental changes and diarrhoea which may lead to severe wasting. It may be remembered as the disease of the three D's—dermatitis, dementia and diarrhoea. It is a chronic disease recurring every spring with the increasing sunlight. Many thousands of people in any maize-eating area may be affected with a mild form, but there are also severe cases with some deaths.

At one time it was thought that maize contained some toxin or carried some infective agent, but the fact that it is a deficiency disease was proved by a series of classical epidemiological studies and human dietary studies carried out by an American doctor, Goldberger, in the Southern States between 1913 and 1928. He was able to show that pellagra could be prevented by the addition of milk and a variety of other foods to the diet and that it could be cured rapidly by yeast and yeast extractives. The accessory factor was shown to be heat stable and water soluble.

It was first called vitamin B_2 or vitamin P-P (pellagra-preventing). At first the elucidation of its nature was held back by the lack of a suitable laboratory animal and all testing of extracts had to be carried out on human patients. When a condition known as black tongue in dogs was found to be in many ways analogous to pellagra, progress was rapid and in 1937 it was found that nicotinic acid or its derivative nicotinamide was the active substance. A dose of 100 mg of either substance, or even less, will relieve the symptoms of a severe case of pellagra within a few hours.

The chemical structure and roles is given on p. 7.13.

Maize is a poor source of nicotinic acid, but highly milled rice usually contains even less. Although cases of pellagra may be found not infrequently amongst rice-eaters they do not suffer from large epidemics of the disease. The explanation is that the body is not entirely dependent on a dietary source of nicotinic acid. It has a limited power of synthesis from the amino acid tryptophan. Maize protein contains little of this amino acid, but it is present in good amounts in rice and other cereals. About 60 mg of tryptophan are equivalent to 1 mg of nicotinic acid. Occasional cases of pellagra are still found in all countries, due usually to chronic intestinal disease interfering with absorption or to an inadequate diet associated with alcoholism. At one time it was not uncommon in the old lunatic asylums in Europe. Occasionally the characteristic and obvious skin condition is absent and the mental features predominate. Such a patient may receive psychotherapy for many months before it is realized that all he needs is a little nicotinic acid.

Like thiamine, nicotinic acid is present in the whole-wheat grain in good quantities, but most is removed by the millers in preparing fine flours or polished rice. In Great Britain, the U.S.A. and many other countries, nicotinamide must by law be added to white flour used for bread making. Butcher's meat, especially offal, and fish are good sources. Yeast and yeast extracts are very rich, but the vitamin does not pass in significant amounts into fermented liquors. Fruit and vegetables are poor sources, as are milk and dairy products. The pellagra-preventing action of milk, well known to Goldberger, is due largely to the rich content of tryptophan. The nicotine which smokers absorb cannot be converted into the vitamin.

A daily intake of 12 mg of nicotinic acid provides an ample safety margin against pellagra.

RIBOFLAVINE

In the early days of accessory food factors, rats were found to need for normal growth, a heat-stable water-soluble substance. This could be extracted from milk. In 1932, the German Nobel laureate, Warburg, described a yellow pigment, which acted as a respiratory catalyst in many tissue preparations. These were soon shown to be the same substance. The chemical structure and role are given on p. 7.13.

Riboflavine is certainly an essential dietary factor for man. In people subsisting on poor diets, a variety of degenerative conditions of the skin and mucous membranes is found. The junction of the skin with a mucous membrane is likely to be involved and particularly at the angle of the mouth, where the appearance of raw and often infected fissures radiating outwards is known as angular stomatitis. This condition, very common in many parts of the tropics, often responds promptly to treatment with riboflavine. Other causes, such as ill-fitting dentures and iron deficiency, are more likely to be responsible for angular stomatitis in Britain. The conditions, which have been attributed to riboflavine deficiency are common in some parts of the world, where they serve as a useful index of an unsatisfactory diet. Lack of riboflavine, unlike ascorbic acid, thiamine and nicotinic acid, is not associated with the appearance of a major disease.

The reason for this is not quite clear. Perhaps it is because the vitamin is widely distributed and almost all foods contain a little. Milk is a good source and whole cereals, pulses and offal are rich. It is the only vitamin present in significant amounts in British beer. A dietary intake of 1–2 mg/day appears to be sufficient for human needs.

The anti-anaemic vitamins

The red blood cells have a life span of about 120 days. The continuous production of new blood cells is a major synthetic task for the body. If any one of three substances, iron and the two vitamins, cyanocobalamin and folic acid, are present in inadequate amounts, production is liable to be limited and anaemia may arise. As already stated, iron is an essential component of haemoglobin. Iron deficiency leads to a type of anaemia in which the haemoglobin level of the blood is reduced disproportionately to the number of red cells. By contrast when the supply of vitamins is defective, pigment production is not primarily affected, but the mature red cells do not develop normally from their large primitive precursors in the bone marrow (p. 26.9). There is a marked reduction in the number of cells, but these each contain a normal amount of haemoglobin.

CYANOCOBALAMIN OR VITAMIN B_{12}

The story of the discovery of this vitamin is one of the most exciting in medicine. A severe and invariably fatal form of anaemia was described first by Addison and known as pernicious anaemia. Thomas Addison (1793–1860) was a distinguished physician who, after graduating at Edinburgh, made his reputation at Guy's Hospital in London, where he was a contemporary of Bright and Hodgkin. His name is also associated with the disease that arises from destructive lesions of the adrenal glands. There was no hope for patients with pernicious or Addisonian anaemia. They invariably went down hill slowly and after many months or a few years died with the numbers of red cells in the blood reduced to only about one-fifth the normal level. This outlook was changed when Minot, Professor of Medicine in Harvard, showed in 1921 that the anaemia could be relieved if the patient consumed a pound of raw or lightly cooked liver each day. The writer well remembers when he was a schoolboy watching an uncle, who visited his home, struggling with this therapy. This desperate remedy at least provided hope.

Minot's pupil, Castle, made the next important discovery. He showed that if beef was digested by gastric juice obtained from a healthy person and then fed to a patient with Addisonian anaemia, a rapid improvement in the blood occurred. Beef previously digested by gastric juice from a patient with Addisonian anaemia had no such effect. He postulated that to cure the anaemia a dietary substance (the extrinsic factor) was necessary, but that this could only be effective in the presence of substance produced by normal gastric juice (the intrinsic factor). In patients with Addisonian anaemia, the defect was a failure to produce intrinsic factor, which was necessary either for the absorption or utilization of extrinsic factor. This has now been shown to be correct, but the discovery produced no immediate benefit to patients.

Throughout the 1930's, chemists prepared various extracts from liver containing the active blood forming principle. These extracts could be given by injection, a great advantage for the patients. Progress was slow, because each stage of the extractions could be tested only on a patient suffering from Addisonian anaemia, which fortunately was not a common disease. When it was discovered that the active factor was also a growth factor for the micro-organism *Lactobacillus lactis dorner* the pace quickened. Finally 20 mg of crystalline substance was extracted from 1 ton of fresh liver. A dose as small as 1 µg of this substance given to an anaemic patient stimulated red cell formation and produced remission in a few days. The substance was first known as vitamin B_{12}. When it was synthesized and shown to be a complex porphyrin derivative containing the element cobalt, it was renamed cyanocobalamin. The structure and role of the vitamin is given on p. 7.14.

The patient with pernicious anaemia formerly died, because he was unable to transport one-millionth of a gram of the vitamin daily across one or two millimetres of the gut wall. Nowadays he receives an injection of the vitamin at fortnightly or monthly intervals. With this, he is in every respect a normal healthy person.

The nature of the intrinsic factor and of the defect in the gastric mucosa responsible for the failure of production are still not fully understood.

How the vitamin may act in the tissues is discussed on p. 26.9. It probably is essential for all growing tissue. Deficiency manifests itself first as a failure in blood formation because of the rapid turnover of blood in the body.

Cyanocobalamin is absent from all plant products. The dietary source is from foods of animal origin and usually amounts to around 15 μg/day, but poor diets may contain as little as 3 μg or even less. The vitamin is formed by many moulds and fungi. Commercially it is made cheaply as a by-product in the manufacture of streptomycin.

Many animals grow more rapidly if they have a small addition of foods of animal origin to their diet. This is probably due to the action of vitamin B_{12}, which has been used for this purpose in animal husbandry. Antibiotics, such as penicillin and aureomycin, have been widely used by farmers to accelerate growth of chicks, pigs and young cattle. They probably act by so altering the intestinal flora as to favour the production or stabilization of vitamin B_{12}.

At one time it was thought that vitamin B_{12} deficiency arose only as a result of a failure of the absorption mechanism and never as a primary dietary deficiency disease. There is now no doubt that a dietary lack of the vitamin is responsible for the anaemia that arises in some young Indian children, who have been suckled by mothers who are strict vegetarians or whose diet is otherwise unsatisfactory.

FOLIC ACID

At the time when only crude liver extracts were available for the treatment of pernicious anaemia, Dr Lucy Wills was studying in Bombay the severe anaemias that frequently occur in pregnant women in India. She found that some women had anaemia, in which the blood picture was identical with that in pernicious anaemia. Yet these patients did not respond to liver extracts known to be able to cure pernicious anaemia, but they did respond to dried yeast and yeast extracts. Here was another 'accessory factor'.

Later a substance obtained from spinach and called folic acid was shown to be an essential growth factor for certain micro-organisms. It was subsequently isolated and synthesized. The pure folic acid was found to be identical with the 'Wills factor'. Anaemia due directly to dietary deficiency of folic acid is common in many tropical countries, especially in pregnancy. Pregnancy appears to increase the requirements of this vitamin and folic acid deficiency is responsible for a proportion of the anaemias that occur in pregnancy in all countries. Anaemia due to a failure of absorption of the vitamin occurs in some patients with chronic disease of the alimentary canal.

The structure of folic acid and its role in tissue metabolism, is given on p. 7.13.

Green vegetables and liver are rich sources of the vitamin. Cereals contain small quantities, but much may be lost in the milling process. Meat and fish contain the vitamin in variable amounts, but are not rich sources. Most fruits contain very little. Human diets in this country provide between 50 and 200 μg/day of folic acid which seems to be an adequate amount.

OTHER WATER-SOLUBLE VITAMINS

Many other substances have been shown to be essential dietary factors for experimental animals or for micro-organisms. Some of them, such as pyridoxine and pantothenic acid, are almost certainly essential in the diet of man. However, they appear to be so widely distributed in human foods that it is doubtful if dietary deficiences ever arise. Very rarely an infant becomes increasingly irritable and develops convulsions, which can be immediately relieved by an injection of 10 mg of pyridoxine, far more than an ordinary infant receives in the diet. This is important as an example of a dietary idiosyncrasy. Human beings undoubtedly vary considerably in their requirements for vitamins. Occasionally a patient is found suffering from a deficiency disease, although his diet appears to be adequate in every respect. Such patients may respond well to large doses of a vitamin. The student must appreciate the variability of man. Inevitably his teachers and textbooks must concentrate on describing the properties of the average or normal individual.

Although pyridoxine and pantothenic acid are vitamins which appear to have very little clinical importance, each is a component of an essential enzyme system. Their chemical structures and biochemical roles are given on p. 7.13.

FOODS

So far we have been considering the proteins, fats, carbohydrates, minerals and vitamins needed by the body. These are the essential nutrients. It is now time to desscribe the principal foods of man and how they can be mixed together to form suitable diets. Foods can be conveniently classified as follows: cereals and cereal products; starchy roots; pulses and legumes; vegetables and fruits; sugars, preserves and syrups; meat, fish and eggs; milk and milk products; fats and oils; beverages.

A good diet often contains foods from all nine classes, although no single one is essential.

CEREALS

Primitive man was a hunter who also collected wild fruits and berries. Civilization was not possible until the art of domesticating grasses was acquired. Grass seeds (cereals) could be harvested and stored for many months and so provided a source of food which was not dependent on the day-to-day activities of hunters. Cereals now form the principal food of the overwhelming majority of mankind. For many poor peasants in Asia and Africa they provide 80 per cent or more of the total calories in the diet. With increasing wealth, diets become more mixed but even in the richest countries cereals provide 25 per cent of total calories and are the largest single item of food.

The principal cereals of the world are rice, wheat, maize, the millets, barley, oats and rye. Corn is an old Saxon word which can properly be used to describe any cereal grain. In the U.S.A. its use has been restricted to maize, which is usually referred to as corn, but in other parts of the world corn may be used to describe the main cereal crop.

Botanically the cereals are closely allied. The seeds have the same general structure and chemical composition and so all whole cereals have similar nutritive properties; their value may be profoundly altered by the millers. Fig. 5.2 shows a diagram of a typical grain. The main bulk is the starchy inner endosperm to which at one end is attached the germ or embryo by a structure

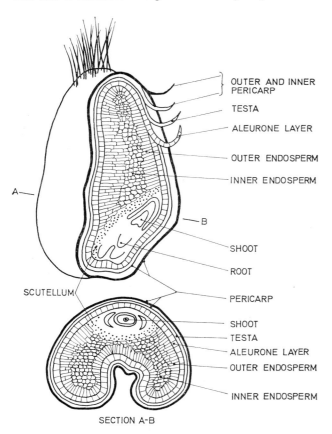

FIG. 5.2. The structure of the wheat grain. From McCance, *Lancet*, **i**, (1946) 77.

known as the scutellum. The outer endosperm and aleurone layer and pericarp surround the grain; the whole is encased in a woody husk.

The whole grain contains very little water and over 80 per cent is made up of starch. Contrary to a popular view, cereals contain a considerable amount of protein, which usually provides from 8 to 12 per cent of the calories present in the grain. However, as already described (p. 5.3), the quality of the protein in a single cereal is not ideally suited to human needs and a mixture of suitable sources of plant proteins is required. The whole grain contains about 3 per cent of fat.

Cereals provide significant amounts of the minerals calcium and iron, but owing to the presence of phytic acid, which forms insoluble phytates with these elements, they are poorly absorbed. Diets based largely on cereals are thus often barely adequate in these nutrients.

Whole cereal grains are rich sources of most of the B group of vitamins, especially thiamine. They contain no vitamin C. Of the fat-soluble vitamins, A and D are completely absent. Most cereals contain no significant amount of the vitamin A precursor, beta carotene, but several varieties of maize are comparatively rich. Vitamin E is present in the oil which can be extracted from cereals.

Wheat and rice

Wheat and rice are always eaten after part of the grain has been removed by milling. Milling removes the indigestible cellulose, which is present in the outer coats of the grain and adds bulk to the faeces. A sudden change to a diet based on whole or lightly-milled cereals may cause slight diarrhoea but this is only temporary. Milling also makes the resulting wheat flour or rice grain white. Whiteness has always been prized as a quality in flour and rice, perhaps because of its association with purity. White flour and white rice were available to the ancient Greeks and Romans and to their contemporary Indians, but it was expensive. To grind and sieve a white flour by traditional methods with stone mills and to prepare a white rice by hand pounding were arduous tasks and such foods were only for the rich. With the advent of the industrial revolution, steel mills have become available, which can readily produce fine white flour and rice. These then became the staple food of the poor. By tradition millers have always kept the millings, which they sell as cattle food. To make white flour or rice about 30 per cent of the whole grain must be removed. Mills have always spread rapidly with industrialization. They spare the peasant cultivators an arduous task and provide them with a white food, which gives social prestige. The millers appreciate the extra millings, which they can sell. The removal of the small amount of oil improves the keeping qualities of flour or rice and so makes a more suitable product for trade.

However, a high extraction wheat or rice containing only 70 per cent of the whole cereal has lost most of the B vitamins present and particularly nearly all the thiamine. This matters little in contemporary Western diets, where there are many other sources of the vitamins, but it is of paramount importance to poor rice-eaters. Beriberi, due to thiamine deficiency became common in rice-eating countries after the introduction of mills producing polished white rice. India and Pakistan are exceptions, and beriberi in epidemic proportions has been confined to a region on the east coast of India. This is because in these countries most paddy (rice in the husk) is parboiled or steamed before milling. Parboiling partially protects the grain against losses in milling, probably by making the germ more adherent.

Nowadays it is possible to replace some of the losses in milling by the addition of synthetic vitamins. White flour in Britain is enriched with thiamine, nicotinic acid and iron, but it is not possible to replace all the losses. It is much more difficult technically to enrich rice in this way.

Wheat or rice is the cereal of choice for most people. Improved varieties enable both crops to be cultivated on poor soils and under climatic conditions which were previously impossible.

Millets

The millets are the poor man's cereal. They grow well under conditions where the cultivation of rice or wheat is difficult or impossible. There are large numbers of millets, with an even greater number of names. The commonest are:

(1) *Sorghum vulgare* or the large millet, also known as dura in Africa and juar or cholam in India,

(2) *Eleusine coracanna* or finger millet, known as ragi in South India,

(3) *Pennisetum typhoideum*, known as barja or cambu in India.

Millets are nutritious foods; like all cereals they have to be husked, but they are not highly milled. They are usually eaten after making into a porridge.

Maize

Maize is a cereal of American origin, but now grown widely in the Mediterranean region and in many parts of Africa and Asia. Although associated with pellagra (p. 5.14), it is an excellent food, provided it does not form too high a proportion of the diet. It is eaten by many of us as a breakfast cereal.

Barley, oats and rye

Barley and oats are good cereals formerly widely eaten in Europe. Barley is nowadays grown mostly for brewing, and oats as a cattle food. Even the Scots are eating less and less porridge. Rye is a hardy cereal formerly widely grown in north and east Europe. It is now being replaced by wheat, but rye is still grown in many parts of eastern Europe and rye bread is widely appreciated especially in Scandinavia and the United States.

Bread

Wheat is the only cereal which can be made into bread. This is because it contains two proteins, gliadin and glutelin, which give wheat flour its characteristic stickiness. Wheat may be eaten unleavened as is traditional in the Middle East and in Pakistan and North India, and for this purpose wholemeal flour is used. Wheat flour may also be leavened by yeast; the dough so formed is then made into bread by baking. Wholemeal flour yields a dough which does not rise well and to get a good large loaf white flour is best. U.S.A. and Canadian wheats give a 'strong' flour which makes bread with a firm texture, so that the loaf stands up well. British wheats are 'weak' and are not good for breadmaking, but are ideal for biscuits. British biscuits are the best in the world.

Most bread contains about one-third of its weight as water. Bread is often made into toast; dry heat applied has little or no effect on the nutritive value, but a variable part of the moisture is driven off. An ounce of toast thus will have a higher calorie content than an ounce of bread, an important fact for those on a reducing diet. Italian wheats have a high content of gliadin and glutelin and are very hard. They are ideal for making 'pasta' which can then be moulded into macaroni and spaghetti.

In conclusion it may be said that the nutritive value of cereals is often underestimated in prosperous countries. Good bread and good rice are excellent foods. They are tasty and nutritious, providing calories, proteins and the B group of vitamins, and some calcium and iron. Only when an excessive proportion of the calories are derived from cereals does a diet become unbalanced.

STARCHY ROOTS

Potatoes

This American plant was introduced into Europe early in the sixteenth century and by the middle of the seventeenth century its cultivation was widespead. Potatoes were more easily cultivated than cereals and they give a higher yield of calories per acre. This provision of an alternative crop providing a second source of energy-rich food ended the history of famines in Western Europe, which had previously arisen from failure of the cereal harvests. However, in Ireland, potatoes completely replaced cereals in agriculture. When in 1845 and again in 1846 and 1847, the potato crops were almost entirely destroyed by blight, famine, perhaps the most disastrous in human history, occurred. Over a million people died and probably as many emigrated. Their descendants form an important part of the modern populations of such cities as Boston, Glasgow and Liverpool.

The potato is an excellent food. In 1910, a Danish 'keep fit' man lived for a year on a diet consisting solely of potatoes. He was investigated carefully by physiologists and shown to remain in good health. On no other single food could an adult man survive indefinitely. This is because, unlike cereals, potatoes contain a significant amount of vitamin C and small quantities of carotene. Potatoes contain a little less protein than cereals and are not so rich in the B group of vitamins, but the amounts present are at least adequate for an adult. Potatoes contain about 70 per cent of water. A given weight of potatoes thus provides about one-third of the starch and one-third of the calories present in the same weight of a cereal.

Potatoes have a reputation for being fattening. If you eat so many potatoes that the calorie intake exceeds the expenditure, then inevitably excess fat is laid down. Potatoes have, however, no specific fattening properties and, eaten in moderation, are an excellent food.

The sweet potato is a traditional dish in the Southern States of the U.S.A. It is grown extensively in many hot climates. The roots have the same general properties as other potatoes. Many varieties are coloured and the carotene present may be an important source of vitamin A activity.

Cassava and other tropical roots

Cassava shrubs, of which there are many varieties, come from South America, but are now widely grown in tropical Africa and in some parts of Asia. As they are easily cultivated and give a high yield, they are valuable as a source of energy. However, the roots contain little protein, which contributes only 3 per cent to the total calories. In any tropical area where cassava is a principal food, evidence of protein deficiency is usually widespread especially in the children. Many of the varieties are poisonous when freshly harvested owing to the presence of cyanides. These can be removed by washing and drying in the sun. Tapioca is prepared from cassava. The products available in Western shops are usually highly refined and nutritionally may be considered as pure starch.

Yams are climbing plants and **taro** a herbaceous perennial of the *colocasia* family, which are grown in many tropical areas. They are easily cultivated and the yield of tubers, which in the case of some yams may be as big as a football, is large. Hence, they are invaluable to many communties as a source of energy. Their protein content is not high; it may be sufficient to meet the needs of adults, but is inadequate for growing children.

Sago is another starchy food, but it is not a root, being derived from the pith of the sago palm.

Many invalid foods available in western countries are based on tapioca, sago or ground rice. For practical purposes they are little more than pure starch, but as an easily digestible form of energy they have a place in the diets of convalescents. It is of course necessary to supplement them with a good source of protein and other nutrients, such as milk and eggs.

PULSES AND LEGUMES

Pulses, lentils or dhals are the dried seeds of various species of *leguminosae*. They have a traditional place in cereal diets in tropical and subtropical countries, where rice and dhal may be the equivalent of the poor man's bread and cheese in the west. Pulses are invaluable in supplementing the protein content of cereal diets. Their protein content is usually about double that of cereals. They also supplement the amino acid mixture, being especially rich in lysine, in which many cereals are poor. Pulses are not milled and all species are rich in the B group of vitamins in which cereal diets are often deficient. Greater cultivation and so more consumption of pulses would improve greatly many types of poor diet and reduce the incidence of protein deficiency in young children.

The soya bean is a pulse which forms the basis of much of the culinary art of the Chinese. It differs from other pulses in containing about 18 per cent of fat, but this gives it no nutritional advantages over the pulses more commonly used in other countries.

In Western diets there may be a great variety of peas and beans. They are eaten in many different ways, but are far less important from the nutritional viewpoint than are the pulses in tropical diets. They are generally classified as 'vegetables' and their nutritive properties are discussed below under this general heading.

VEGETABLES AND FRUITS

A number of plant structures serve as vegetables in human diets. These are green leaves (cabbage and lettuce), flowers (cauliflower and artichoke), seeds (peas and broad beans), gourds (egg plant, ladies finger and cucumber), stems (leeks and celery) and roots (beetroot and onion). Broadly speaking, all have similar nutritive values and they can be discussed together as a class of food. First we eat vegetables because they are pleasant and their flavours add to the variety of our foods. Secondly, all vegetables contain 70 per cent or more of water. They contribute few calories and little protein. Vegetables are recommended to those on reducing diets, because they may fill the stomach and give a sense of repletion without providing many calories. The cellulose present in the plant structures adds bulk to the faeces and so prevents constipation. Most vegetables contain calcium and iron in amounts that could be useful, but they are often in a form that is poorly absorbed from the gut. The water-soluble B group of vitamins is present in all vegetables, but none is a particularly rich source. Vegetables also contain vitamin C, but the amounts are very variable and the vitamin is often lost during storage, preparation and cooking. Vegetables are chiefly valuable as a source of carotene, the precursor of vitamin A. The amount present is again extremely variable, but there is a rough relation between the colour of the vegetable and the carotene content. Carrots are exceptionally rich and are the chief source of vitamin A activity in the diet of many British people.

The minerals and vitamins present in vegetables can make a valuable contribution to the nutritive value of poor cereal diets. There is no doubt that in many village communities in the tropics, vitamin deficiencies could be abolished and general health improved if the people were persuaded to cultivate vegetable gardens. The importance of the nutritive value of vegetables in mixed western diets has probably been exaggerated in popular teaching. The Scots don't like vegetables; at least they eat only about half as much as Londoners. There is no evidence that their health is any worse on this account.

Fruits in general contain more water and even less energy and protein than vegetables. Most contain small quantities of minerals and also vitamins of the B group and carotene. The main nutritional value of fruits lies in their vitamin C content: almost all fruits are good sources and some are very rich. A single helping of fresh fruit, canned fruit or fruit juice each day ensures that the vitamin C intake is adequate. Fruits and fruit juices are a pleasant and valuable source of potassium for many patients. Fruits contain a great number of organic acids. Citric acid derives its name from lemons, malic acid from apples and pyruvic acid from burnt grapes. These acids are all readily broken down and metabolized by enzyme systems within the body and do not contribute significantly to the acid–base balance.

Bananas require a special mention. They are a fruit which provides carbohydrate in quantities as much as 20 g/100 g. A great many varieties are grown and in some parts of the tropics they form a major food of the population. However, they contain little protein and children fed on diets in which bananas are the chief constituent are likely to suffer severely from protein deficiency. Of course in small quantities bananas are a pleasant food, easily digestible and especially appreciated by invalids and convalescents.

SUGAR, PRESERVES AND SYRUPS

In the United Kingdom we eat just over 120 lb/head/year of sugar. Table 5.5 shows the great increase in sugar consumption in the last 80 years and a corresponding decline in cereal consumption. Similar figures are available from the U.S.A. This is the largest change in our dietary habits that has taken place this century. The cane sugar or sucrose that the grocer sells is a pure chemical

TABLE 5.5. Changes in the amounts of sugar and cereal grains in the food supplies of the United Kingdom (lb/head/year).

	1880	1924–8	1953	1962
Sugar	64	87	98	111
Wheat flour	280	198	193	161
Other cereals	?	16	16	16

almost up to the standard of an analytical reagent. It provides calories, but no other nutrients. The same is almost true of many fats and most alcoholic drinks, and these foods are said to provide 'empty calories'. This large sugar intake has to be complemented by foods rich in proteins, minerals and vitamins. It certainly contributes to the high incidence of dental caries, obesity, diabetes and possibly atherosclerosis in numerous countries. Many people said to have 'a sweet tooth' can be more accurately described as sugar addicts.

Sugar is a food preservative and it is used to make jams and preserves, which usually contain about 70 per cent of sucrose. Most jams retain only a small portion of the vitamin C originally present in the fruit.

Syrups such as molasses, treacles and Golden Syrup ® are concentrated sugar solutions. They contain 20–30 per cent of water, but negligible amounts of nutrients except sucrose. There are some natural syrups such as the famous maple syrup in North America, but these have no nutritive property other than their sugar content. Honey also contains about 75 per cent of sugars, mostly fructose; regrettably the bees neglect to add vitamins. It is a pleasant food, but the reputation for medicinal properties which it has acquired with some people is unmerited.

Sugar is the main ingredient in boiled sweets, which may contain 90 per cent. Toffees and candy are a mixture of sugar, syrup and fats. Most chocolates are a mixture of cane sugar and cocoa powder. These sweets contribute energy but little else to the diet.

MEAT, FISH AND EGGS

Muscle contains about 18 per cent of protein. Meat, as ordinarily eaten, always contains a large amount of fat and a composition of 20 per cent protein, 20 per cent fat and 60 per cent water is usual. There is, however, a wide range for all these values. The protein present in meat is of a high biological value. Meats contain little calcium, but are good sources of iron. They contain useful amounts of the B group of vitamins, especially nicotinic acid and riboflavine; pork muscle is rich in thiamine. There is a little vitamin C in fresh meat, but most of this is destroyed in cooking. Animal fats contain only very little vitamin A, except those from the liver.

All meats have approximately the same nutritive value, although they may differ markedly in their flavour and tenderness, which give them 'their quality'. At one time physicians taught that white meat (poultry and game) was more easily digested than red meat (beef and mutton) and so more suitable for invalids. This is a myth. All muscle is readily digested; however, the fibrous connective tissue, fascia and tendon, which may be present in a helping of any meat is less digestible. As animals age, their muscle develops more fibrous tissue and their meat becomes less tender.

Most people are very conservative in their taste for meats and normally eat the flesh of only a few species. Many Englishmen are revolted by the thought of eating frogs and snails, which a Frenchman considers a delicacy. A laboratory worker would be appalled if told to eat a guinea-pig, which may be much appreciated in many South American homes. Necessity may change established habits. Soldiers in beleaguered garrisons, after eating their horses, have turned to cats and dogs and even rats have been eaten. In many parts of Africa and in some areas in Asia a great variety of animal foods may be eaten, including locusts, lizards, snakes and monkeys. All these may be useful foods, especially as sources of protein, and so can contribute to health.

Liver, kidneys and other offal are of good nutritional value. In general they resemble butchers' meat, but liver is much richer in vitamins and in iron.

Beef teas, Oxo ®, Bovril ® and other meat extractives have a reputation as nourishing food. In fact they contain very little solid matter and so provide few nutrients. They do, however, contain the flavouring agents present in meat. These may well promote the appetite and so make a valuable contribution to the feeding of invalids.

Fish and other sea foods are a valuable source of protein. Many species have a high oil content, which may be rich in vitamins A and D. Small fish, if eaten whole, including the bones, provides calcium. This may be important in many tropical areas, especially in the deltas of great rivers, where the calcium intake is often low.

A hen's egg weighing 2 oz or 60 g contains about 6 g of first class protein, 6 g of fat and provides 80 kcal and also some calcium and iron. The yolk is rich in vitamin A and also contains the water soluble vitamins. Eggs have a deservedly high reputation as a human food.

MILK AND MILK PRODUCTS

Table 5.6 shows the composition of typical samples of human and cow's milk. Milk serves as a complete food for an infant during the early months, and although human milk is perhaps ideally suited to this purpose, cow's milk after some modification is also effective. There are many different reasons which may make a mother decide to breast feed or bottle feed her baby. She need have no fear that her baby will not receive adequate nourishment from a suitable preparation based on cow's milk made by reputable firms. The table shows that cow's milk is richer in protein and poorer in carbohydrate than human milk. An approximation to human milk can be made by diluting cow's milk with water and adding sugar.

TABLE 5.6. The composition of human and cows' milk

	Human	Cows'
	all values per 100 g	
Calories	70	66
Carbohydrate (g)	7	5
Protein (g)	2	3·5
Fat (g)	4·0	3·5
Calcium (mg)	25	120
Phosphorus (mg)	16	95
Iron (mg)	0·1	0·1
Vitamin A (i.u.)	170	150
Vitamin D (i.u.)	1·0	1·5
Thiamine (μg)	17	40
Riboflavine (μg)	30	150
Nicotinic acid (μg)	170	80
Ascorbic acid (mg)	3·5	2·0

All milks are rich in calcium, but poor in iron. An infant usually starts life with some reserves of iron laid down mostly in the liver in the later stages of uterine life. If mixed feeding with foods rich in iron is delayed for more than 6 months, anaemia due to iron deficiency is likely to occur. Indeed in all countries this type of anaemia is common in infants and young children. Milk contains all the vitamins that an infant requires. If, however, a mother receives a diet lacking in thiamine, her milk will be low in this vitamin and beriberi may develop in the infant. If a baby is being fed on a cow's milk preparation and this milk is boiled, all the vitamin C may be destroyed. In these circumstances infantile scurvy may arise. Many studies have shown that mothers on inadequate diets generally produce milk of good quality. The quantity of milk, however, may be insufficient to allow the baby to grow at the normal rate. Milk production appears to receive high priority in the metabolism of starving or undernourished women who are lactating.

It would be difficult, though not impossible, to feed young children or adolescents so that they could attain their normal growth potential without some milk in the diet. If milk is not available or available in only small amounts, then special care must be taken to see that both the quantity and quality of the protein intake is satisfactory and that there are good alternative sources of vitamin A and calcium.

Milk is a suitable food for those adults who like it, but it is not an essential constituent in adult diets. Milk fat is composed mainly of triglycerides containing saturated fatty acids. It is widely believed that a high intake of such acids predisposes to arterial disease, though the evidence is far from conclusive. Milk preparations are now available in the U.S.A. in which the butter fat has been removed and replaced by fats of vegetable origin containing a high proportion of unsaturated fatty acids. This is a good example of the sophisticated foods which may be produced in a society which possesses great technical ability.

Sour milks

In many countries it is the custom deliberately to sour milk by fermenting it with bacteria. *Lactobacillus acidophilus* is used for this purpose. It breaks down the lactose in the milk, but the protein, calcium and vitamins remain. There are many local recipes for making sour milk or yoghurt and all yield a product of high nutritive value. As the fermenting bacteria overgrow and destroy any pathogenic bacteria that may be present in the original milk, it is hygienic; it is also delicious.

Butter

It has long been the custom to separate the fats from surplus milk and make butter. The nutritive value of butter is discussed in the next section.

Skimmed milk

This is milk from which the butter fat has been removed. Traditionally in European farms it was given to young pigs, who thrived on it. Large quantities are now available from the big butter industries in the U.S.A., New Zealand and elsewhere. It is easily dried and then forms a stable powder. As it contains all the protein and calcium present in the original milk, it forms, after reconstitution with water, a valuable food for growing children. With the aid of the United Nations, many thousands of tons of dried skim milk have been distributed in countries where the local milk supply is inadequate. There is much evidence that this has benefited the health of the children.

Cheese

Cheese making is an ancient art, used by farmers' wives to dispose of surplus milk. The basic process is to allow the milk to clot, usually under the action of the enzyme rennet. The clot is then separated and this contains most of the protein and a variable proportion of the fat present in the original milk. The clot is then dried and pressed. Cheeses are thus highly nutritious foods, rich in protein.

There are many recipes, which provide cheeses of different flavour and consistency. These are named after villages and small towns in the countries of Europe where they originated. Nowadays few farmers' wives find the time to make cheese, which is almost all produced commercially. You can no longer buy a Stilton cheese in Stilton.

FATS AND OILS

The chief fats of animal origin used in human diets are dairy fats, butter and ghee, suet from beef and lard from pork. Important vegetable oils include olive oil, groundnut oil, cotton seed oil, sesame or gingelli oil, mustard oil, coconut oil, red palm oil and corn oil from maize. Margarine is an artificial fat made largely from mixtures of vegetable oil and whale oil. It will be noticed that animal fats, except those of marine origin, are solid, whereas vegetable fats are liquid. The melting point of a fat is determined by the relative proportion of unsaturated to saturated fatty acids present. Margarine is made by reducing the proportion of unsaturated fats in natural oils by hydrogenation.

Fats are a concentrated source of calories. The diets of active men who do much work, such as lumber men and arctic explorers, would be very bulky, if they did not contain a large amount of fat. Some fats are important because they carry the fat soluble vitamins. However, fats are used in diets chiefly because we like them and they are essential for good cooking. In most prosperous countries, fats provide 35–40 per cent of the total calories, far more than is necessary to meet the physiological needs for essential fatty acids.

Butter fat contains vitamin A and D. The amounts of vitamin A depend on the quality of the pasture on which the cattle graze. Summer butter is usually very rich in this vitamin and there is appreciably less in winter butter. Vitamins A and D are artificially added to margarines to the levels present in summer butter. It is impossible to distinguish by feeding experiments between the nutritive values of margarine and butter and nowadays many people cannot distinguish their tastes. Margarine is perhaps the best example of the skill of food technologists in producing an artificial food.

Vegetable oils contain no vitamins, but are valuable as a source of calories and for their culinary properties. An exception to this is the red palm oil, which is rich in carotene. This palm, *Elaeis guineensis*, is a native of West Africa, but plantations are now present in other parts of Africa and also in Asia. In Nigeria it has been shown that children are healthier in areas where red palm oil is used than in areas where the diets are similar, except that they contain other vegetable oils. A great extension in the plantation of these palm trees would be of immense benefit to the health of many tropical communities.

BEVERAGES

Although a man drinks from 1 to 2 litres of water each day, he does not appear to like it very much, at least in its pure form. He prefers to drink one of a number of beverages. These are appreciated for their flavours and perhaps for the drugs which may be present; they may also contain nutrients. Flavours are provided by the essential oils of herbs, berries, fruits and grains. Their chemistry is little understood. Many traditional skills are employed to produce the aroma of a fine tea or the bouquet of a good whisky. Their manufacture is still a craft rather than a science.

Alcoholic beverages

A wit has said that *homo sapiens* can be distinguished from the other primates by the fact that wherever two or three of them are gathered together, there you will find theological argument and fermented liquor. Ethanol is produced by the fermentation of carbohydrates present in grain or fruit by wild or cultivated yeasts. Ethanol is a remarkable substance. It is a nutrient, which is easily absorbed, and so may be a valuable source of energy. On the other hand if taken regularly, it may contribute to the excess calories which cause obesity. As a drug, its sedative action gives it a place in medical practice. By inhibiting those centres in the brain on which the most developed mental faculties depend, it produces a sense of well-being and so promotes social intercourse. In many men and women the critical faculties are overdeveloped, so that it is difficult for them to appreciate the views of others. Alcohol may help to bring about the compromises which are essential in a good society. On the other hand excessive use of alcohol causes loss of judgement and, if continued, leads to addiction, which disrupts the person and may ruin his family. Alcohol is also a disinfectant and a preservative; these properties give it a useful, if small, place in medicine and in the food industry. Many people are so impressed by the evils which arise from the improper use of alcohol that they are total abstainers. Some of these try to enforce their views on others and sometimes succeed in bringing about a legal prohibition of alcohol in their country or community. Experience has shown that the law cannot prevent the abuses of alcohol. This is a matter of education.

Beers are made from cereal grains, chiefly barley. The starch is first converted to the disaccharide maltose, by the enzyme maltase; this is allowed to act by keeping the grain in the warm, damp atmosphere of a malting house. The malt is then fermented by yeast. Beers contain from 2 to 6 per cent of alcohol according to their strength and similar amounts of carbohydrate. The caloric value of beer ranges from 25 to 70 kcal/100 ml. Although yeasts are very rich in the B group of vitamins, these do not come out of the cells. Beers are almost totally devoid of vitamins, except for riboflavine, significant amounts of which are found in most beers. These remarks do not always apply to home made and country beers, especially those in which wild yeasts are used. There have been reports of missionary teachers, ardent for total abstinence, causing the appearance in primitive rural people of multiple vitamin deficiencies by prohibiting the brewing of their country beer.

Wines are made by the fermentation of grapes and occasionally other fruits. Table wines contain from 8 to 10 per cent of alcohol and provide from 60 to 80 kcal/100 ml. Port and sherry are strengthened by the addition of extra alcohol to bring the concentration up to 15 per cent. Wines are devoid of vitamins, but they sometimes contain large amounts of iron, parts of which may be absorbed and contribute to liver disease.

Spirits are made by the distillation of various fermented liquors. Brandy, whisky and rum contain just over 30 per cent of ethanol and provide 220 kcal/100 ml. For practical purposes they are devoid of other nutrients. The distiller's art in forming the bouquet is most subtle and a fine brandy or a good whisky provides one of the elegant luxuries of European civilization. Illicit distillation by crooks or amateurs is a dangerous process; spirits so produced may contain methanol and other alcohols which are very toxic. The drinking of such crude liquor may cause permanent blindness and death.

Coffee and tea

It is difficult to appreciate what European society was like less than 400 years ago when there was no tea or coffee. The coffee beans and tea leaves came from shrubs grown in tropical or subtropical gardens which are very beautiful. Much art is required in the preparation of the final products so as to preserve the aromas for which they are appreciated. The first infusions contain xanthine derivatives which have pharmacological properties. Caffeine, theophylline and theobromine are present, of which caffeine is the most important. It stimulates the nervous system and so often prevents fatigue; it also acts on the kidneys to increase the flow of urine. Tannins which are weak protein precipitants are present in both tea and coffee. There are no harmful effects from one or two cups of coffee or tea and probably no medical contra-indications to their use. The caffeine in excessive amounts of coffee may cause sleeplessness. Gastritis, which is sometimes found in those who drink many cups of strong tea, has been attributed, on no good grounds, to the tannin present. Tea and coffee by themselves are of no nutritive value. They are often drunk with added sugar and milk. In this way the tea and coffee drinking habit may contribute to the excess calories which cause obesity.

Soft drinks

Fruit juices, lemonades and squashes are pleasant drinks. If freshly prepared they are rich sources of vitamin C, as are many commercial preparations. The calorie content is variable and depends on the amount of sugar added. This may be up to 15 per cent, or occasionally even more, giving a value of about 60 kcal/100 ml. Fruit juices are all rich in potassium and so helpful in the diets of convalescents, who have to rebuild lost tissue.

'Colas' and many other synthetic soft drinks on the market are widely advertised. The exact composition of most of these is a trade secret. Many people find them pleasant drinks, but the advertisements, in so far as they claim any special nutritive or health promoting properties, may be misleading.

Mineral waters

Many natural waters contain inorganic salts to which medicinal properties have been attributed. The well at Epsom near London from which Epsom salts, magnesium sulphate, was first isolated, proved in the seventeenth century very profitable to its owner. Mineral waters contain carbonates, bicarbonates and sulphates and sometimes iron and hydrogen sulphite. For the most part these are present in such low concentrations that they have no medicinal or toxic properties. Mineral waters are pleasant drinks, but quite discredited as therapeutic agents. Nevertheless spa treatment remains popular. It is nowadays fashionable in Western Germany and the famous old Bohemian spas are well patronized by modern Czechoslovakians. For many successful and prosperous men and women, whose way of life may have led them to dietary excesses of calories and alcohol, a period on a disciplined regime will be beneficial. Water, applied either internally or externally will do no harm; its use may serve as a ritual which can help to a more balanced way of life.

CHEMICALS ON THE FARM AND IN THE FOOD INDUSTRY

Farmers use artificial chemicals as fertilizers, to control weeds and to destroy insects and other pests. Food technologists use chemicals as preservatives, colouring agents, flavouring agents, anti-oxidants, flour improvers, fat extenders and emulsifiers. Some of these chemicals inevitably find their way in small quantities into the diet. It would be idle to pretend that they do not involve a hazard to health. However, in all advanced countries their use is controlled by legislation. For this purpose governments are advised by expert committees, who can draw on the findings of analytical and pharmacological laboratories. A doctor cannot be expected to appreciate the details of these problems, though some knowledge of their pharmacological testing is necessary. Suffice it to say that there is no evidence that any of the many permissible chemicals used in the concentrations and in the manner prescribed by law, represents a significant hazard to health.

There are people who think that the artificial use of chemicals in the preparation of food is wrong. These are the 'natural farmers' and 'health food' advocates. They are enthusiastic for the traditional way of life, which our ancestors found good. One may sympathize with their views, but in the modern world they are quite impractical. Farmers could not possibly produce the crops needed to feed the present population of the world without the use of chemicals. Nor could the shops provide the modern city dweller with the food to which he has become accustomed without the aid of chemicals used by the food industry. You may have had for breakfast fruit juice (from California), a cereal (from Iowa), some fish (caught off Iceland), bread (from Canadian flour), butter (from New Zealand), marmalade (from Seville oranges), coffee (from Brazil) with sugar (from Jamaica) and milk (from a dairy herd 200 miles from your home). It would be quite impossible to enjoy such a breakfast, unless there was an elaborate food industry able to use intelligently a variety of chemicals.

We cannot go back to the traditional way of life in which 80 per cent of the population lived in the country and grew food for themselves and also sufficient to sell in the markets of the nearby towns to meet the needs of the small numbers in the urban population. All the evidence, and there is much of it, indicates that the nutritive value of the diets of those who live in great cities like London and New York is as good as that of the diets eaten by their grandfathers and great grandfathers, who were mostly countrymen. The modern townsman is also immune from the effects of local failures of crops. He can enjoy any of the luxuries of the table all the year round, many of them at a low cost. All this is owed to an efficient food industry, which uses chemicals widely, but carefully. Whether modern foods taste better or worse than country fare can only be a matter of opinion.

Frozen and canned foods

No manufacturer can sell foods preserved by freezing or canning or indeed by any method, unless they taste good. In general, the chemical substances responsible for flavour are more unstable than vitamins and other nutrients. Any frozen or canned foods in which the original flavours are well preserved are therefore likely to contain most of their original nutrients. It would be foolish to claim that such foods are always as good as those fresh from one's garden or a nearby orchard or farm, but they may well be more nutritious than 'fresh' foods which have spent days in city markets and shops.

RECOMMENDED ALLOWANCES

Ration scales have to be drawn up for the armed services and for those who live in institutions such as boarding schools, hospitals, prisons, etc. It is important that such scales provide nutrients in sufficient amounts to meet the physiological needs of the people for whom they are intended. Physiological standards of requirements are also needed to assess the significance of the findings in dietary surveys in which the food consumption of sections of a community may be measured. National governments nowadays direct agricultural and trade policies to try to ensure an adequate food supply for the people. Such policies are ultimately based on estimates of physiological needs.

Many countries and also the Food and Agricultural Organization of the United Nations have drawn up recommended dietary allowances. Table 5.7 is from the Food and Nutrition Board of the United States. The recommendations are for groups of people and not for individuals and provide a margin of safety to cover individual variations and common stresses. An individual whose dietary intake does not come up to these standards in all respects will not necessarily be malnourished. The United States standards would be generally accepted in other countries with two exceptions. First, most nutritionists in other countries do not agree with American nutritionists that any extra benefit to health is derived from an intake of ascorbic acid as high as 70 mg/day. The British standard is 20 mg/day, which is about what most of us consume and is far more than is needed to prevent scurvy. There is no evidence that the people of Great Britain are in any respect less healthy than the Americans on account of the fact that they drink less fruit juice. Secondly, the calorie allowances for adults in U.S. standards have been set a little lower than those in most other countries. The reason for this is that the majority of Americans appear to live relatively sedentary and physically inactive lives.

The standards in table 5.7 are liberal and provide a

TABLE 5.7. Food and Nutrition Board, National Academy of Sciences—National Research Council recommended daily dietary allowances,* revised 1963. Designed for the maintenance of good nutrition of practically all healthy persons in the U.S.A. Allowances are intended for persons normally active in a temperate climate.

	Age Years	Weight kg (lb)	Height cm (in)	Calories	Protein g	Calcium g	Iron mg	Vitamin A value† i.u.	Thiamine mg	Riboflavine mg	Niacin equiv.‡ mg	Ascorbic acid mg	Vitamin D i.u.
Men	18–35	70 (154)	175 (69)	2900	70	0·8	10	5000	1·2	1·7	19	70	—
	35–55	70 (154)	175 (69)	2600	70	0·8	10	5000	1·0	1·6	17	70	—
	55–75	70 (154)	175 (69)	2200	70	0·8	10	5000	0·9	1·3	15	70	—
Women	18–35	58 (128)	163 (64)	2100	58	0·8	15	5000	0·8	1·3	14	70	—
	35–55	58 (128)	163 (64)	1900	58	0·8	15	5000	0·8	1·2	13	70	—
	55–75	58 (128)	163 (64)	1600	58	0·8	10	5000	0·8	1·2	13	70	—
	Pregnant (second and third trimester)			+200	+20	+0·5	+5	+1000	+0·2	+0·3	+3	+30	400
	Lactating			+1000	+40	+0·5	+5	+3000	+0·4	+0·6	+7	+30	400
Infants§	0–1	8 (18)	—	kg×115 ±15	kg×2·5 ±0·5	0·7	kg×1·0	1500	0·4	0·6	6	30	400
Children	1–3	13 (29)	87 (34)	1300	32	0·8	8	2000	0·5	0·8	9	40	400
	3–6	18 (40)	107 (42)	1600	40	0·8	10	2500	0·6	1·0	11	50	400
	6–9	24 (53)	124 (49)	2100	52	0·8	12	3500	0·8	1·3	14	60	400
Boys	9–12	33 (72)	140 (55)	2400	60	1·1	15	4500	1·0	1·4	16	70	400
	12–15	45 (98)	156 (61)	3000	75	1·4	15	5000	1·2	1·8	20	80	400
	15–18	61 (134)	172 (68)	3400	85	1·4	15	5000	1·4	2·0	22	80	400
Girls	9–12	33 (72)	140 (55)	2200	55	1·1	15	4500	0·9	1·3	15	80	400
	12–15	47 (103)	158 (62)	2500	62	1·3	15	5000	1·0	1·5	17	80	400
	15–18	53 (117)	163 (64)	2300	58	1·3	15	5000	0·9	1·3	15	70	400

* The allowance levels are intended to cover individual variations among most normal persons as they live in the United States under usual environmental stresses. The recommended allowances can be attained with a variety of common foods, providing other nutrients for which human requirements have been less well defined.

† 100 i.u. from preformed Vitamin A and 4000 i.u. from beta-carotene.

‡ Niacin equivalents include dietary sources of the preformed vitamin and the precursor, tryptophan. 60 mg tryptophan represents 1 mg niacin.

§ The calorie and protein allowances per kg for infants are considered to decrease progressively from birth. Allowances for calcium, thiamine, riboflavin and niacin increase proportionately with calories to the maximum values shown.

TABLE 5.8. Daily allowances recommended by the Nutrition Advisory Committee, Indian Medical Research Council, revised by Patwardhan (1960). All values per day.

	Calories	Protein g	Calcium g	Iron mg	Vitamin A i.u.	Vitamin D i.u.	Thiamine mg	Ascorbic acid, mg
Man (55 kg, 120 lb)								
Light or sedentary work	2400							
Moderate work	2800	55						
Very hard work	3900							
Woman (45 kg, 100 lb)			1·0					
Light or sedentary work	2000							
Moderate work	2300	45		20–30	3000–4000		1·0–2·0	50
Very hard work	3000		—					
Pregnancy (later half)	2300	100	1·5			400–800		
Lactation	2700	110	2·0					
Children								
0–6 months	120/kg							
7–12 months	100/kg							
1–3 years	1200	3·5/kg						
4–6 years	1500							
7–9 years	1800	3·0/kg						
10–12 years	2100							
13–15 *years*		2·5/kg	1·0–1·5	10–30	3000–4000	400 800	0·5–1·0	30–50 and over
Girls	2100							
Boys	2500							
Adolescents								
16–19 *years*								
Girls	2100	2·0/kg						
Boys	3150							

N.B. The estimates of the protein requirements are subject to the proviso that dietary protein is derived from more than one foodstuff.

wide margin of safety. However, they are quite impractical for many relatively poor countries in Asia, Africa and Latin America. Table 5.8 sets out standards drawn up for India. In many parts of the world there will be an immense task to improve agricultural production so that the food supply could meet these lower standards. To reach them, however, would improve the health of the people immeasurably.

WASTE

Waste products leave the body by four routes, in the expired air, in the urine, in the faeces and in the sweat.

EXPIRED AIR

This usually contains from 3 to 5 per cent CO_2. The total amount of CO_2 expired daily normally ranges from 350–600 litres and contains about 200–300 g of carbon. The lungs excrete a far greater bulk of waste matter than do the kidneys, the amount of CO_2 excreted daily being sufficient to neutralize 16–26 litres of normal sodium hydroxide. The minute-volume of expired air is controlled by the necessity to excrete CO_2 in amounts which maintain the level of pH of the blood within the normal range (p. 29.24).

The expired air is always saturated with water vapour at approximately body temperature and from 250 to 500 g of water are lost from the body daily in this way. This is an obligatory water loss and not subject to physiological control.

The volatile substances ethanol and acetone can be detected in the expired air, if they are present in the blood in sufficient concentrations. These substances diffuse across the lung membranes and into the expired air in amounts directly proportional to concentration in the blood. Hence an analysis of the alcohol content of the expired air can indicate to a police surgeon the level in the blood. The total quantity of both alcohol and acetone that can be lost from the body in this way is small and the lungs play an insignificant role in the clearing of these substances from the blood.

Nitrogenous waste products are not excreted via the lungs.

URINE

Table 5.9 shows the composition of a 24-hour specimen of urine from a healthy young man.

TABLE 5.9. The usual range of the amounts of the main constituents in a 24-hr specimen of urine from a healthy young man.

WATER (ml)	1000–2500
ELECTROLYTES (mEq)	
Cations	
Sodium	100–250
Potassium	40–80
Magnesium	8–16
Calcium	3–8
Ammonia	up to 80
Hydrogen	up to pH 4·0
Titratable acidity	50–100
Anions	
Chloride	100–250
Inorganic sulphate	50–120
Bicarbonate	up to 50
Phosphate (mM)	20–50
NITROGEN CONTAINING SUBSTANCES (g)*	
Urea	20–40
Creatinine	1–2
Uric acid	0·5–0·8
Ammonia	0·5–1·3
Total amino acids	up to 1·5

* The urine also contains protein in amounts up to 50 mg/day. This is not detectable by the methods of analysis in common clinical use.

Water

The urinary output of water is regulated so that the concentration of the plasma is kept within very narrow limits just under 300 mOsm/l. It is also the means by which the total water content of the body is controlled. This varies slightly from day to day and anyone who weighs himself regularly before breakfast frequently finds daily variations of 0·5 kg, and a gain or loss of 1 kg is not unusual. Most of this variation in body weight is due to changes in body water.

The water also acts as vehicle for the other urinary constituents, which for a healthy man on a normal diet amount to about 50 g/day, most of which is urea and sodium chloride. Consider a subject eating 100 g of protein daily. There will be 16 g of N to excrete. By far the greater part of this is excreted as urea and there will be about 30 g of urea in the urine (60 g of urea contain 28 g of N). If the diet contains 10 g NaCl, about the same amount will appear in the urine. The other urinary constituents may number over one hundred, but together they do not add up to more than 10 g.

The amount of water necessary for the excretion of these substances is determined by the ability of the kidney to concentrate urine. In health the kidney cannot produce a urine with a concentration greater than about 1200 mOsm/l. This is about four times the concentration of plasma. About 30 g of urea (mol. wt. 60) is equivalent to 500 mOsm, and 10 g of NaCl (Na 23 Cl 35·5) is equivalent to 2×170 mOsm. The protein and salt in the diet of our subjects thus produce between them an osmolal load of 840 mOsm and the other urinary substances may increase the load to about 1000 mOsm/day. To excrete this the kidneys must be provided with a minimum of $1000/1200 = 830$ ml of water. This is the **obligatory water** in the urine. Its volume is dependent on the value of the diet. If this amount of water is not available from the normal intake, water is drawn from the tissues and the body becomes dehydrated, as may happen to the castaway in a lifeboat. Most of us drink more water than is necessary to excrete the urinary solids and it is unusual for urine to be excreted at its maximum concentration. With a urinary output of 1500, the 1000 mOsm solute load will give a concentration of 660 mOsm/l.

The osmolal concentration of urine can be derived from a determination of its freezing point, which can be easily carried out in the laboratory on a small sample. A doctor can, however, get a good approximation in his consulting room or office by simply measuring its specific gravity using a simple hydrometer. The relation between sp. gr. and osmolality varies with the composition of the urine and the molecular weights of its constituents. Urine from a healthy subject on a normal diet shows the following general relationships:

sp. gr.	1·010	1·015	1·020	1·025	1·030	1·035
mOsm/l.	400	600	800	1000	1200	1400

The 24-hour sample of urine from the subject on the diet described above thus has a specific gravity of approximately 1·017.

It is very difficult to dry urine and so determine directly the urinary solids. However, it was pointed out in a German thesis over one hundred years ago that the last two figures in the specific gravity multiplied by two give the grammes of solids present in a litre of urine. For our subject 1 litre of urine will be calculated to contain $17 \times 2 = 34$ g of solids, and so his daily output of 1500 ml would contain 51 g of solids. This is approximately the figure suggested for the urinary solids based on a consideration of his diet.

Acid

Human urine is usually acid and the pH may range from 4·0 to 8·0. In health, the degree of acidity is determined by the amount of metabolic acid produced in the body and eliminated in the urine. By far the most important of these is sulphuric acid produced by the oxidation of sulphur containing proteins and 100 g protein produce about 60 mEq of sulphuric acid to be excreted. This acid is of course buffered in the urine mainly by phosphate and NH_3 secreted into the urine by the kidney. In fruits and some vegetables, potassium and to a lesser extent sodium may be present as salts of organic acids, which are metabolized in the body and not excreted in significant amounts in the urine. Those who eat large quantities of fruits and vegetables may have alkaline urines. Alkaline urine is, of course, commonly found in patients who have been taking sodium bicarbonate. The kidney is able to manufacture ammonia and to excrete ammonium ions in the urine. In this way it can contribute to the acid–base balance of the body (p. 6.4). The role of the kidney in regulating the acid–base balance is very important in many pathological states. However the amount of acid that the kidney normally secretes is relatively small and amounts to between 50–100 mEq/day.

Nitrogenous substances

In the healthy adult the total amount of nitrogen in the urine is determined by the dietary intake and with typical European diets about 85 per cent is excreted as urea. By contrast in Asian diets the proportion of the urinary nitrogen excreted as urea is often less and may be as low as 60 per cent, but the reason for this is unknown.

The creatinine excretion in the urine is remarkably constant in any one individual and is independent of the diet. It is probably related to the muscle mass and, indeed, creatinine excretion is sometimes taken as a measure of the muscle mass in studies of body composition.

Uric acid is derived from purine metabolism. The urinary output comes mostly from the endogenous breakdown of the purines of the body and it is little affected, if at all, by the purine content of the diet.

The urinary ammonia is discussed on p. 33.24. The kidney normally conserves amino acids and only small amounts of these substances are found in the urine in health. There are a number of diseases, each fortunately rare, when, owing to an hereditary defect of kidney function, one or more of the amino acids may appear in the urine. A very small amount of protein is present in the urine, derived from the serum and perhaps by exudation from the urinary tract.

Other urinary constituents

The urine contains small amounts of almost all other soluble body constituents. Its yellow colour is due to the presence of urochrome which is derived from one of the bile pigments. All the water-soluble vitamins and hormones and their metabolites can be detected in the urine. The amounts present are small and the losses are normally of no significance. However, the urinary output of a particular vitamin or hormone is often of interest both in physiological and pathological studies.

The kidney is readily conceived of as an organ for removing waste products from the body. It is much more than this, for it is the principal means of regulating the chemical composition of the internal environment of the body. This aspect is the main theme of chap. 33.

In the last decade with the development of the artificial kidney and the possibility of renal transplantation, the kidney has become 'news'. These and other advances in our ability to assist renal function by elaborate procedures may overshadow the important fact that the composition of the urine and its volume is largely determined by the nature of the diet. Modification of the composition of the urine by the control of the diet is an important aid in the treatment of many renal diseases. Recently we saw a patient receiving an elaborate and expensive treatment for assisting the removal of an excess of sodium from the body. This patient had been given a kipper for breakfast.

FAECES

Table 5.10 gives the composition of the normal faecal output over 24 hours of a young man on a European diet. Both the formation and output of faeces is irregular. So an analysis of a single sample cannot give an accurate picture of the daily output. Such an assessment is best made by collecting the faeces passed over at least 3 and preferably 5 days.

TABLE 5.10. The usual range of the amounts of main constituents in the faeces over a 24-hr period in a healthy young man on a European diet.

Total weight (g)	75–200
Water (g)	50–175
Dry weight (g)	15–30
Protein* (g)	4–7
Fat (g)	3–5
Soluble carbohydrate	trace
Insoluble carbohydrate (cellulose or roughage) (g)	up to 15
Sodium (mEq)	5–10
Potassium (mEq)	8–15
Calcium (mg)	500–900
Iron (mg)	10–15
Total ash (g)	3–6

* the figures for protein are analyses of $N \times 6.25$. About half the N in the faeces is actually present as protein.

Faeces consist of dietary matter which the alimentary canal has been unable to absorb, together with the remnants of the mucous membranes of the alimentary tract, which are constantly being shed and renewed. Other substances are excreted into the gut lumen with the digestive juices. It is not easy to determine how much of any constituent of the faeces is dietary waste (exogenous) and how much is a true excretion (endogenous).

The bulk of the faeces depends largely on the cellulose content of the diet. Most diets provide 5–10 g of cellulose daily, but 15 g would not be unusual in a vegetarian. All of this appears in the faeces as 'roughage'.

The intestinal contents are greatly modified by bacterial action in the large intestine. Bacteria form from 5 to 10 per cent of the dry weight of the faeces. They produce gas and most people pass up to 200 ml of flatus daily, part of which is probably derived from swallowed air. Flatus contains up to 30 per cent of methane, but the loss of energy in this way by man is very small. Cattle lose about 10 per cent of the gross energy content of the diets as methane.

SWEAT

The sweat is a means of getting rid of waste heat. The body is cooled by the evaporation of the sweat on the skin and sweat which simply drips off is ineffective in this regard. The evaporation of 1 litre of sweat removes 580 kcal of heat from the body. The usual range for rates of sweating is from 100 to 1000 ml/hr and this corresponds to heat losses of from 0·6 to 6·0 kcal/min (figures which may be compared with rates of energy expenditure given in chap. 4). When the temperature of the environment is greater than the temperature of the surface of the skin, cooling by radiation and convection is impossible (p. 40.4). All heat loss can then take place only by evaporation of sweat. In very hot climates as much as 3000–5000 kcal/day may be lost in the sweat.

Sweat varies greatly in chemical composition, but is essentially a weak solution of sodium chloride. The osmolality lies between 100 and 200 mOsm/l. (plasma 300 mOsm/l.). Table 5.11 gives some normal values for sweat. Losses of sodium can easily be as much as 250 mEq/day, which might require a doubling of the normal intake. In exceptional cases the losses can be greater.

TABLE 5.11. The composition of normal sweat

Cations	
Sodium	20–70 mEq/l.
Potassium	5–15 mEq/l.
Anions	
Chloride	20–76 mEq/l.
Lactate	10–30 mEq/l.
Urea	4–20 m Mole/l.
pH	4–6·5
Freezing point	−0·08−−0·37°C
Osmolality	100–200 mOsm/l.

Excretion of urea in the sweat is small and sweating is not of practical assistance to patients with kidney disease.

FURTHER READING

DAVIDSON SIR STANLEY & PASSMORE R. (1966) *Human Nutrition and Dietetics*, 3rd Edition. Edinburgh: Livingstone.

TAYLOR C.M. & PYE O.F. (1966) *Foundation of Nutrition*, 6th Edition. New York: MacMillan.

TABLES OF FOOD ANALYSES

AYKROYD W.R., GOPALAN C. & BALASUBRAMANIAN S.C. (1963) *The Nutritive Value of Indian Foods*, 6th Edition. Indian Coun. Med. Res. Spec. Rep. Ser. No. 42.

McCANCE R.A. & WIDDOWSON E.M. (1960) *The Composition of Foods*. Med. Res. Coun. (London) Spec. Rep. Ser. No. 298.

PLATT B.S. (1962) *Tables of Representative Values of Food Commonly used in Tropical Countries*. Med. Res. Coun. (London) Spec. Rep. Ser. No. 302.

WATT B.K. & MERRILL A.L. (1963) *Composition of Foods* U.S. Dept. Agric. Handbook No. 8 Washington D.C.

Structure and function of cells

Chapter 6
Acids, bases and buffer mechanisms

This chapter is concerned with the physicochemical properties of biological fluids which are involved in the control of their reaction, i.e. their degree of acidity or alkalinity. Mammalian cells derive energy from oxidative processes which produce acidic waste products. These substances pass into the fluids of the body and are subsequently excreted (p. 33.22). A series of mechanisms stabilize the concentration of hydrogen ions in the body fluids within relatively narrow limits. This degree of control of hydrogen ion concentration is characteristic of mammals and greater variation in the reaction of body fluids occurs in fishes or insects. It is not known why the hydrogen concentration is so finely regulated because, although enzymes are sensitive to changes in acidity, they usually exhibit optimum activity (p. 7.6) over a much wider range of hydrogen ion concentration than is maintained in the plasma. However, cell membranes and subcellular particle membranes consist of specific proteins which are amphoteric (p. 11.3) and are sensitive to small changes in the hydrogen ion concentration of their environment. It seems likely that the high degree of specificity shown by cell membranes may be attributed to highly organized lipoproteins arranged in a specific orientation (p. 13.6). It is possible that the tertiary and quaternary structure of the lipoprotein membranes, and hence the membrane characteristics, may be altered by the hydrogen ion concentration of the bathing fluid. Thus the normal metabolic activity of the cell and of the whole animal will be adversely affected by wide changes in hydrogen ion concentration.

Acids

In 1923, Bronsted in Denmark and Lowry in England suggested that an acid be defined as a proton donor while, conversely, a base be defined as a proton acceptor. Thus the relationship between acids and bases can be described as follows:

$$AH \rightleftharpoons A^- + H^+ \qquad (1)$$
$$\text{Acid} \quad \text{Base} \quad \text{Hydrogen ion or proton}$$

In aqueous solution hydrogen ions exist in hydrated form $[H_3O^+]$ and are termed **hydroxonium ions**. So when an acid ionizes in water this equation is more correctly written:

$$AH + H_2O \rightleftharpoons A^- + H_3O^+ \qquad (2)$$
$$\text{Acid} \quad \text{Water} \quad \text{Base} \quad \text{Hydroxonium ion}$$

By custom, however, the symbol for the concentration of hydrogen ions is usually represented as $[H^+]$ rather than in its hydrated form $[H_3O^+]$, the square brackets denoting concentration. An acid and its equivalent base are described as **conjugate** or a **conjugate pair**. Table 6.1

TABLE 6.1. The ionization of acids, the formation of the hydroxonium ions and the resultant conjugate bases.

	Acids	Conjugate bases
Water	$H_2O + H_2O$	$\rightleftharpoons H_3O^+ + OH^-$
Hydrochloric acid	$HCl + H_2O$	$\rightleftharpoons H_3O^+ + Cl^-$
Carbonic acid	$H_2CO_3 + H_2O$	$\rightleftharpoons H_3O^+ + HCO_3^-$
	$HCO_3^- + H_2O$	$\rightleftharpoons H_3O^+ + CO_3^{--}$
Phosphoric acid	$H_3PO_4 + H_2O$	$\rightleftharpoons H_3O^+ + H_2PO_4^-$
	$H_2PO_4^- + H_2O$	$\rightleftharpoons H_3O^+ + HPO_4^{--}$
	$HPO_4^{--} + H_2O$	$\rightleftharpoons H_3O^+ + PO_4^{---}$
Ammonia	$NH_4^+ + H_2O$	$\rightleftharpoons H_3O^+ + NH_3$
Protein	H. Protein $+ H_2O \rightleftharpoons H_3O^+ +$ Proteinate$^-$	

illustrates the ionization of acids, the formation of the hydroxonium ions and the resultant conjugate bases. The list also shows that acids may be neutral molecules, anions or cations. It will be noted that some acids ionize to give a single hydrogen ion or proton and the appropriate conjugate base, for example, water or HCl. These acids are monobasic acids because each molecule of the acid produces one hydrogen ion. On the other hand, carbonic acid dissociates into two hydrogen ions and is a dibasic acid. The two ionizations of the acid are quite distinct and there is experimental evidence to support the concept of the reaction occurring in two separate steps.

(1) $\quad H_2CO_3 + H_2O \rightleftharpoons HCO_3^- + H_3O^+$
$\quad\quad$ Carbonic acid $\quad\quad$ Bicarbonate

(2) $\quad HCO_3^- + H_2O \rightleftharpoons CO_3^{--} + H_3O^+$
$\quad\quad$ Bicarbonate $\quad\quad$ Carbonate

According to the law of mass action the velocity of any

chemical reaction is directly proportional to the product of the molal concentrations of the reactants and at equilibrium the dissociations are represented by two distinct dissociation constants, K_1 and K_2. Thus for carbonic acid,

$$K_1 = \frac{[HCO_3^-][H^+]}{[H_2CO_3][H_2O]} \quad or \quad \frac{[HCO_3^-][H^+]}{[H_2CO_3]} \quad (3)$$

because the concentration of water can be considered to be constant as it is present in such great excess;

and

$$K_2 = \frac{[CO_3^{--}][H^+]}{[HCO_3^-][H_2O]} \quad or \quad \frac{[CO_3^{--}][H^+]}{[HCO_3^-]} \quad (4)$$

Similarly there are acids, such as phosphoric acid, which are capable of ionizing to yield three hydrogen ions. In these cases the conjugate base produced in the first ionization is the acid of the second ionization, and similarly the conjugate base produced in the second ionization is the acid involved in the third ionization.

Thus monobasic acids have only a single K value, while diabasic acids have K_1 and K_2 values, while for tribasic acids there are K_1, K_2 and K_3 values. The strength of an acid depends upon the degree to which the acid is dissociated in solution and a strong acid is almost completely ionized. In other words a strong acid is one in which the tendency to release H^+ is much greater than for the conjugate base to accept them. A strong acid is therefore always associated with a weak base. An example, HCl is almost entirely ionized and yields the chloride ion, a very weak base. By contrast carbonic acid is a weak acid and is only slightly dissociated in aqueous solution to yield the strong base, HCO_3^-. The value of the dissociation constant of the acid K_a indicates the strength of the acid. It is normally given as the negative logarithm to the base 10 of the dissociation constant of the appropriate reaction. A list of common acids of biological importance with values for K_a and pK_a is given in table 6.2.

TABLE 6.2. K_a and pK_a values for acids of biological importance.

Acids		K_a	pK_a
Acetoacetic acid		$1 \cdot 6 \times 10^{-4}$	3·8
Benzoic acid		$6 \cdot 6 \times 10^{-5}$	4·2
Acetic acid		$1 \cdot 8 \times 10^{-5}$	4·7
β-Hydroxybutyric acid		$1 \cdot 6 \times 10^{-5}$	4·8
Carbonic acid	K_1	$7 \cdot 95 \times 10^{-9}$	6·1
	K_2		9·8
Phosphoric acid	K_1		2·0
	K_2	$1 \cdot 59 \times 10^{-9}$	6·8
	K_3		12·4
Ammonium ion		$0 \cdot 43 \times 10^{-9}$	9·4
Lactic acid		$1 \cdot 38 \times 10^{-4}$	3·9

$$pK = -\log_{10} K.$$

Water can behave as an acid and a base because it dissociates into a $H^+ + OH^-$ and it can also accept an H^+ to give H_3O^+. A substance that behaves as an acid and a base is said to be amphoteric. Many biological substances, notably proteins and amino acids, are amphoteric (p. 11.3).

The ionization product of water and the pH scale

The ionization of water may be written:

$$H_2O \rightleftharpoons H^+ + OH^- \quad (5)$$

or

$$H_2O + H^+ \rightleftharpoons H_3O^+ \quad (6)$$

The equilibrium constant of the first reaction is given by:

$$K = \frac{[H^+][OH^-]}{[H_2O]} \quad (7)$$

The equilibrium point of this reaction falls very far to the left hand side of the ionization equation so that for all practical purposes the concentration of undissociated water remains constant and hence K is very small. This means that for a given temperature:

$$[H^+][OH^-] = K_w \quad (8)$$

At 24°C the ionic product of water is 10^{-14}; since $[H^+]$ must equal $[OH^-]$ at neutrality, $[H^+]$ of water under these conditions is 10^{-7} g ion/l. The constancy of the ionization constant for water at any given temperature means that if $[H^+]$ is increased, $[OH^-]$ must be correspondingly decreased. It follows that the reaction of an aqueous solution may be expressed either in terms of $[H^+]$ or $[OH^+]$. Conventionally $[H^+]$ is used for this purpose. Furthermore if $[H^+]$ of an aqueous solution is greater than it is in pure water, i.e. 10^{-7} g ion/l, the solution is said to be acid while if less than this it is said to be alkaline.

Following the studies of Sorensen in 1909 and others, the method of expressing hydrogen ion concentrations as g ion/l was changed to employ the common logarithmic expression of those values. In this nomenclature the hydrogen ion concentration is related to its $\log_{10}$ value (pH).

$$pH = \log_{10} \frac{1}{[H^+]} \quad (9)$$

Thus, water with $[H^+]$ of 10^{-7} g ion/l has a pH of 7·0. Acid solutions then have a pH less than 7·0 and alkaline solutions a pH greater than 7·0 and the pH scale representing $[H^+]$ ranges as a series of simple numbers from 0 to 14. Although the above equation relating pH and the logarithm of the reciprocal of $[H^+]$ is widely used in biology and medicine, it is more correctly expressed as the $\log_{10}$ of the reciprocal of the activity of the H^+, i.e.

$$pH = \log \frac{1}{a_{H^+}} \quad (10)$$

The concept of the activity of an ion in solution has been evolved to explain deviations from ideal thermodynamic behaviour of ions at certain concentrations.

Ideally when an electrolyte is dissolved in a liquid of high dielectric constant such as water, the resultant ions should, apart from hydration, be free from the influence of other substances in the solution. This ideal state is rarely achieved except at infinite dilution, because the electrostatic and other influences of other ions in the solution affect the behaviour of the ions under study. Thus an activity function has been evolved to designate the apparent concentration of an electrolyte in solution. In general the activity coefficient may be calculated from the following ratio:

$$\text{Activity Coefficient} = \frac{\text{Observed activity of ionic species}}{\text{Molal concentration of ionic species}} \quad (11)$$

The activity of an ionic species is dependent upon the concentration of charged particles of all species present in the solution. Thus, as the concentration of an electrolyte decreases so the activity coefficient tends towards unity. This coefficient is influenced by temperature, valence of the ions and by the concentration of ions or ionic strength.

On the Debye–Huckel treatment of activities, if Z is the valence of the ion and μ the ionic strength of the solution, then at a given temperature the activity coefficient in a dilute solution is given by:

$$-\log_{10} \text{ activity coefficient} = 0.5\, Z^2 \sqrt{\mu} \quad (12)$$

The activity coefficient for H^+ is not accurately known so that the pH measured electrometrically by a glass electrode and a pH meter is not in fact a precise measure of actual hydrogen ion concentration and bears a complex and indeterminate relation to it. For these reasons the pH of a solution is always determined by reference to pH of one or more standards whose assigned pH is given by the National Bureau of Standards in Washington.

These considerations do not reduce the meaning or importance of pH determinations in biological work. Absolute values for pH and changes which occur in pH of biological fluids closely reflect changes in the activity of hydrogen ions. Furthermore, the expression of the reaction of a complex biological solution in terms of $[H^+]$ is also often valuable and does not lead to misconceptions provided the above reservations are kept in mind.

The concept of buffers

Many intracellular metabolic processes such as those which result in the decarboxylation of keto acids producing CO_2, the anhydride of H_2CO_3, or the oxidation of S or P derived from dietary proteins and fats, and many others which yield hydrogen ions, could result in a marked change in the tissue fluid hydrogen ion concentration. As discussed previously, body fluids contain special physicochemical mechanisms which resist changes in hydrogen ion concentration. These are called buffers.

A weak acid dissociates in aqueous solution to a limited extent so that at equilibration most of the acid is undissociated. The equilibrium constant of this reaction is:

$$K = \frac{[A^-][H^+]}{[HA]} \quad (13)$$

in which the value of K is small. By transposition:

$$[H^+] = K\frac{[HA]}{[A^-]} \quad (14)$$

This indicates that the $[H^+]$ in a solution of a weak acid is a function of the ratio of the concentration of the undissociated acid and its conjugate base. If a solution of the salt of the acid is now added to the weak acid, the concentration of the conjugate base will be greatly increased since almost all the A^- ions will be derived from the salt.

Acid $HA \rightleftharpoons H^+ + A^-$ (weakly dissociated)

Salt $BA \rightleftharpoons B^+ + A^-$ (completely dissociated)

From the mass action equation the increase in $[A^-]$ must reduce the degree of dissociation of HA and so the $[H^+]$ falls. Furthermore equation 14 becomes approximately equal to

$$[H^+] = K\frac{[\text{acid}]}{[\text{salt}]} \quad (15)$$

This means that $[H^+]$ of a solution of a weak acid and its salt is proportional to the ratio of the concentration of the acid to the salt. Now if H^+ are added to such a solution the great bulk of them combine with the strong conjugate base (A^-) to form the weak largely undissociated acid (HA) and free H^+ are removed from the solution. The $[H^+]$ is therefore very much less than would have occurred if the same number had been added to water. Conversely if H^+ are removed from such a solution further ionization of the weak acid occurs so that the $[H^+]$ is maintained. In so far as such a solution tends to remove H^+ when these are added, and contribute H^+ when they are removed, this type of solution tends to stabilize the $[H^+]$ due to the presence of the conjugate pairs. For this reason the solution is said to be buffered and the conjugate pairs constitute a buffer solution or a buffer system.

The classic mass action equation 15 may be used to determine the hydrogen ion concentration if the dissociation constant K_a of the acid and the molar ratio of the acid to salt in the buffer solution are known. The equation is customarily expressed in logarithms and was converted to this form by a German physiologist, Hasselbalch, from the original devised in 1909 by Henderson in America. Consequently it is known as the Henderson–Hasselbalch equation:

$$\begin{aligned} pH &= -\log[H^+] \\ &= -\log K_a - \log\frac{[HA]}{[BA]} \end{aligned} \quad (16)$$

4

since $-\log K_a$ is pK_a by definition

and $-\log \dfrac{[HA]}{[BA]} = \log \dfrac{[BA]}{[HA]}$ we may write equation 16

$$pH = pK_a + \log \frac{[salt]}{[acid]} \qquad (17)$$

or

$$pH = pK_a + \log \frac{[proton\ acceptor]}{[proton\ donor]} \qquad (18)$$

$$= pK_a + \log \frac{[base]}{[acid]} \qquad (19)$$

The effectiveness of a buffer system can be illustrated by the so-called pH–titration curve. Such a curve for NaOH and H_3PO_4 is shown in fig. 6.1. In this diagram the

FIG. 6.1. Titration of H_3PO_4 with NaOH.

change in pH with respect to the volume of standard NaOH added $\left(\dfrac{d\mathrm{pH}}{dA^-}\right)$ is minimal in the regions of pK_1, pK_2 and pK_3. It is clear from equation 18 that at the values of pH which correspond to the values of pK, the ratios $\dfrac{[conjugate\ base]}{[conjugate\ acid]} = 1$.

Physiological buffer solutions

The weak acids and their conjugate bases, whose ionization is given in table 6.1, constitute the principal buffers in tissue and body fluids and help to maintain hydrogen ion concentration within limits compatible with life.

(1) The carbonic acid-bicarbonate buffer system,
(2) The phosphoric acid buffer system,
(3) The protein buffer system,
(4) The ammonia buffer system.

THE BICARBONATE SYSTEM

The gas CO_2 is the anhydride of carbonic acid and the concentration of carbonic acid in an aqueous solution is related to the partial pressure of CO_2 in equilibrium with this solution (Henry's law)

$$[CO_2] = k_0 \cdot P_{CO_2} \qquad (20)$$

where $[CO_2]$ is the concentration of CO_2 in liquid
k_0 is the solubility coefficient
P_{CO_2} is the partial pressure of CO_2 in the gas phase in equilibrium with the liquid.

When CO_2 is dissolved in an aqueous solution such as plasma the dissolved gas slowly undergoes hydration with water to produce carbonic acid. This reaction is quite slow in plasma but in red blood cells there is an enzyme, carbonic anhydrase, which catalyzes this hydration reaction (p. 29.19). As carbonic acid is a weak acid, it only weakly dissociates to H^+ and its conjugate bases. The equilibrium falls very far to the left hand side of this equation. The bicarbonate buffer system consists of an aqueous solution containing a highly dissociated bicarbonate salt in equilibrium with a gas phase containing CO_2 at a fixed partial pressure.

$$CO_2 + H_2O \rightleftharpoons H_2CO_3 \rightleftharpoons H^+ + HCO_3^- \qquad (21)$$

$$BHCO_3 \rightleftharpoons B^+ + HCO_3^- \qquad (22)$$

Thus the P_{CO_2} dictates the concentration of H_2CO_3, and the concentration of the bicarbonate ions (base) depends upon the particular solution under study. Since the pK_1 of carbonic acid is a constant, at a given temperature, the pH of the buffer solution depends upon the P_{CO_2} and $[HCO_3^-]$, and is given by the Henderson–Hasselbalch equation:

$$pH = pK_1 + \log_{10} \frac{[HCO_3^-]}{[H_2CO_3]} \qquad (23)$$

The apparent pK_1 of carbonic acid is 6·1. Thus the pH of a solution buffered by this system will be:

$$pH = 6\cdot1 + \log_{10} \frac{[HCO_3^-]}{[H_2CO_3]} \qquad (24)$$

$$= 6\cdot1 + \log_{10} \frac{[salt]}{[acid]} \qquad (25)$$

The partial pressure of CO_2 in human blood is 40 mm Hg (p. 29.22). The solubility of CO_2 in water at 37°C is 0·0334 mM/kg water. Hence when equilibrium is attained the $[CO_2]$ in solution is 0·0334 × 40 which is approximately 1·35 mM/l. Although only a small part of dissolved CO_2 is combined with water to form H_2CO_3 it is customary to regard the whole of the CO_2, dissolved and combined, as carbonic acid, i.e. as 1·35 mM/l. Each litre of human plasma also contains approximately 25 mEq HCO_3^-. The ratio of HCO_3^-/H_2CO_3 is therefore approximately 20, the log of which is 1·3. When this is added to the pK of carbonic acid, 6·1, the calculated value for pH is 7·4 which is the pH of the blood. The bicarbonate ion is the principal buffer base in extracellular fluids and the control of its concentration within narrow limits is one of the most important functions of the kidney (chap. 33). The concentration of the conjugate acid carbonic acid is also subject to accurate physiological control by the lungs (chap. 29). The system is of great importance in clinical medicine because P_{CO_2} and $[HCO_3^-]$ in blood may be relatively easily measured or calculated and estimates of the two are widely used to detect and assess abnormalities in acid-base balance which arise in the course of disease.

THE PHOSPHORIC ACID BUFFER SYSTEM

On purely chemical grounds the phosphate buffer system should provide a better buffering system than the carbonic acid–bicarbonate system over the physiological range of pH. This arises from the fact that its pK_2 is 6·8 and is near the pH of extracellular fluids. The total concentration of phosphate in the extracellular fluid is however too low for the phosphate system to make a major contribution to buffering in this compartment. Phosphate, however, is present in urine in large amounts and it constitutes an important urinary buffer, the role of which is described on p. 33.23.

THE PROTEIN BUFFER SYSTEM

Plasma and tissue proteins are buffers because they possess a number of groups listed in table 6.3 which are

TABLE 6.3. Titratable groups present in proteins.

Ⓟ, protein molecule.

capable of acting as proton acceptors or donors. These include the amino and carboxyl groups which occur at the ends of protein chains (p. 11.3). In addition, the dicarboxylic amino acids, aspartic and glutamic acids provide free carboxyl groups. Tyrosine possesses a phenolic group, lysine contains free amino groups, while arginine and histidine provide guanidine and imidazole groups respectively. Since protein molecules composed of many amino acids contain large numbers of acidic and basic groups each with its own dissociation constant, they can act as buffers over a wide range of $[H^+]$.

Haemoglobin plays a specially important role in buffering carbonic acid which is mainly due to the imidazole groups of histidines. This is described on p. 29.20.

THE AMMONIUM BUFFER SYSTEM

The contribution of ammonia to the control of hydrogen ion concentration is confined to the urine and is described on p. 33.24.

The whole body as a buffer system

The body contains a complex system of buffers which are contained within the proteins of tissues and the cellular and extracellular fluids. In a solution containing a mixture of buffers the conjugate acid base ratio is determined at any pH by its pK. Any change in pH is reflected in a change in the acid base ratios of all the buffers accessible to the hydrogen ions. In experiments in which acids have been given to dogs it has been shown that the majority of acids are buffered within cells but the bicarbonate system is the most important in the extracellular fluids.

Concentration of hydrogen ions in body fluids

Normal human plasma is usually described as being blandly alkaline with a pH of between 7·45–7·35 (mean 7·40). This corresponds to a mean $[H^+]$ of 40 nEq/l. It seems likely that pH of interstitial fluid is similar to that of the plasma after allowance has been made for the Donnan effect. Much less is known of the intracellular $[H^+]$ but both direct and indirect observations suggest that the majority of cells are appreciably more acid and possess an aggregate pH of about 6·8. The hydrogen ion concentration of some body fluids is given in table 6.4,

TABLE 6.4. Hydrogen ion concentration of some body fluids

	pH units	$[H^+]$ nEq/l
Plasma	7·4 (7·35–7·45)	40
Urine	4·0–8·0	100,000–10
Gastric juice	1·0	100,000,000
Pancreatic juice	8	10
CSF	7·33	47
Bile	5·7–8·6	2000–2·5
Intracellular fluid*		
muscle	6·8	160
RBC	7·2	63

*Determined indirectly.

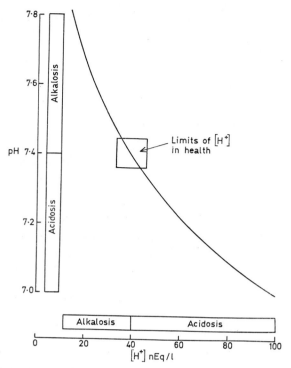

FIG. 6.2. Range of [H$^+$] in blood compatible with life.

proportional to their activity. The relationship pH bears to [H$^+$] is, however, complex as it is both curvilinear and inverse. Fig. 6.2 gives the range of [H$^+$] in blood compatible with human life and the corresponding values for pH on the vertical axis, with the limits for [H$^+$] and pH in health. Clearly the conversion from one nomenclature to the other cannot be done in the head.

The main danger of the use of the pH notation in medicine is that it obscures the fact that the difference in [H$^+$] between two pH units low in the scale is greater than the difference between two pH units in the higher reaches of the scale. Thus a rise in the pH of from 7·2 to 7·4 represents a fall in [H$^+$] of 23 nEq/l while a rise in pH from 7·4 to 7·6 represents a fall in [H$^+$] of only 15 nEq/l.

The range from pH 7·0 to 7·8 compatible with life corresponds to [H$^+$] of from 16 to 100 nEq/l. The extreme values are only found in serious disease. Since the mean normal [H$^+$] in blood is about 40 nEq/l it will be seen that the body is better able to survive an increase in [H$^+$] (**acidosis**) than to withstand a fall in its concentration (**alkalosis**). This may have an evolutionary origin and be due to the fact that mammalian tissues are obliged to dispose of acid produced by their metabolism.

where their values are expressed as nEq/l and in the pH notation.

A word of warning is needed concerning the use of the pH notation. The hydrogen ion concentrations in most body fluids are very small fractions of a m-mole. The pH notation was introduced to avoid the use of cumbersome small numbers and because electrodes used in the measurements of [H$^+$] give readings logarithmically

FURTHER READING

BAYLISS L.E. (1960) *General Physiology*, 2nd Edition, Vol. 1, pp. 151–165. London: Longman.

GLASSTONE S. (1960) *Textbook of Physical Chemistry*, 2nd Edition, pp. 974–1009. London: Macmillan.

NAHAS G.G. ed. (1966) Current concepts of acid-base measurement. *Ann. New York Acad. Med.* **133**.

ROBINSON J.R. (1967) *Fundamentals of Acid-Base Balance*, 3rd Edition. Oxford: Blackwell Scientific Publications.

Chapter 7
Enzymes

The vast majority of the metabolic reactions which occur in organisms, both inside and outside cells, proceed at measurable rates only in the presence of a suitable catalyst. Enzymes are proteins, each of which catalyses one or a small group of these reactions. Many enzymes have been isolated in a pure state, and in the case of many more, in which this has not been done, their metabolic importance is well understood.

The rate of reaction catalysed by an enzyme is proportional to its concentration. The rate of reaction also depends on the concentration of the compound whose reaction is catalysed (the substrate), on pH and temperature as well as on the concentration of various types of activators, coenzymes and inhibitors. The study of the effects of these variables has led to important conclusions about the way in which enzymes act and to reliable methods for their estimation or assay.

In living tissues, complex metabolic reactions must be co-ordinated, and this is achieved largely through regulation of the activity of particular enzymes by alteration of the concentrations of the enzyme, its substrates, inhibitors, activators or coenzymes. Many coenzymes are chemically related to and formed from vitamins so that it is not surprising that vitamin deficiencies lead to serious and widespread disturbances of metabolism.

Protein biosynthesis is catalysed by a complex of enzymes and some structural proteins, e.g. the contractile protein of muscle, also have enzymic properties. Thus enzymes are not only important functional units but also act as units of structure. These generalizations are as true for disease-causing bacteria as they are for their human or animal hosts, and the successful use of antibiotics must ultimately be based on a sound understanding of the enzymology of both host and pathogen. It is possible now to describe a few comparatively uncommon diseases in terms of a failure of enzyme function, and this number is likely to increase. It is reasonable to think that in the not too distant future, practising doctors will need a much fuller understanding of the properties of enzymes than they do now.

SYMBOLS AND ABBREVIATIONS

Throughout this chapter the following symbols and abbreviations are used:

E	enzyme
S	substrate
ES	enzyme-substrate complex
P	products
I	inhibitor
[ ]	concentration of the substance in the brackets
T	temperature ($^\circ$K)
t	time
K	a constant having the dimensions of an equilibrium constant
K_a	an acid dissociation constant
pK_a	$-\log K_a$
K_m	Michaelis constant
k	a velocity constant
v	initial velocity of a reaction
V	maximum initial velocity of a reaction

In chemical equations:

Ⓔ or ⒺH	an enzyme
P_i	inorganic orthophosphate
PP_i	inorganic pyrophosphate
	an organic phosphate radical

$$-P{=}O\diagup^{OH}_{\diagdown OH}$$, without reference to its state of ionization

ATP, ADP, AMP	adenosine triphosphate, adenosine diphosphate, adenosine monophosphate
NAD, NADH$_2$	oxidized and reduced forms of nicotinamide adenine dinucleotide
CoA, CoASH	coenzyme A
FAD	flavin-adenine-dinucleotide

BIOLOGICAL CATALYSIS

Within living organisms a host of organic compounds takes part in degradative and synthetic reactions and undergo interconversion. A few of these metabolic reactions, like the reversible combination of water and carbon dioxide to form carbonic acid, occur at a measurable rate at physiological pH and temperature outside living systems but the majority proceed immeasurably slowly in the absence of a suitable catalyst.

Enzymes, like other catalysts, are active in small amounts and do not alter the equilibrium constant; therefore the free energy change of the reaction catalysed remains the same (p. 8.2); they simply increase the rate of approach of the reaction to equilibrium. Like inorganic catalysts enzymes can be poisoned or inhibited and this is, as will be seen later, of great biological importance.

As they are proteins, enzymes are denatured by extremes of pH, by heat, and by high concentrations of organic solvents, the ions of heavy metals or bulky anions like trichloroacetate. All enzymes lose their enzymic activity on denaturation and, for an enzyme, the terms denaturation and inactivation merely reflect different ways of looking at the same phenomenon.

ENZYME SPECIFICITY

Inorganic catalysts like platinum black can catalyse a wide variety of reactions; enzymes differ markedly from such catalysts in that they show a high degree of specificity. With few exceptions each individual enzyme catalyses only one reaction or a group of closely related reactions. Since so many different metabolic reactions are known, it follows that there are very many enzymes and the list of the International Enzyme Commission includes about 1000 well-defined enzymic activities from different animals, plants and micro-organisms. It seems likely that no two of these catalytic activities are due to the same protein.

Degrees of specificity

A great many enzymes show a specificity which is absolute, i.e. they are found to catalyse, in forward and reverse directions, only one reaction. Many others, especially hydrolysing enzymes, show a lower degree of specificity and are capable of catalysing the reactions of a group of related compounds. Thus a β-galactosidase catalyses the hydrolysis of a variety of β-D-galactosides at rates which vary somewhat with the nature of the aglycone R, but it does not catalyse the hydrolysis of α-galactosides or of glucosides.

Proteolytic enzymes also generally show a low degree of specificity and catalyse the hydrolysis of peptide bonds linking many different types of amino acid residues, though they may show preferences for particular residues on one side or the other of the bond. The pancreatic enzyme trypsin is more specific than most and it hydrolyses only those bonds in which the acyl group is part of the basic amino acids, lysine or arginine.

Sites of attack by trypsin

Chymotrypsin, also produced by the pancreas, hydrolyses rapidly bonds involving the carbonyl groups of amino acids with aromatic or bulky aliphatic side chains. Neither enzyme is entirely specific for peptides and they also catalyse the hydrolysis of unsubstituted amides and even of esters while showing the same specificity for the amino acid residue providing the carbonyl group. In fact, esters of arginine and of tyrosine are often used in the laboratory as substrates for trypsin and chymotrypsin respectively.

The high specificity of most enzymes, together with much other evidence, some of which is discussed later, suggests that on the surface of the enzyme molecule there is one or perhaps a few sites specifically adapted for binding the correct substrate and bringing about the reaction. This region of the enzyme surface is called the **active centre** or **active site**.

Stereospecificity

The β-galactosidase quoted above attacks only derivatives of D-galactose, and trypsin and chymotrypsin catalyse only the hydrolysis of peptide or ester bonds of amino acids of the L-configuration. This enzymic requirement, for only one optical isomer of a substrate is another general feature of enzymic catalysis. Also if an asymmetric product is formed from symmetric substrates, the reaction is found to proceed stereospecifically, and only one optical isomer is formed. Thus, the enzyme in the liver which converts glycerol to α-glycerophosphate forms only the L-isomer. Using Fischer projection formulae:

$$
\begin{array}{ccc}
\mathrm{CH_2OH} & & \mathrm{CH_2OH} \\
| & & | \\
\mathrm{HO-C-H+ATP} & \longrightarrow & \mathrm{HO-C-H+ADP} \\
| & & | \\
\mathrm{CH_2OH} & & \mathrm{CH_2O\textcircled{P}} \\
\text{Glycerol} & & \text{L-α-Glycerophosphate}
\end{array}
$$

Similarly citrate synthase which catalyses the formation of citrate in the citric acid cycle (p. 9.14) does so stereospecifically. The citrate is then dehydrated and rehydrated by aconitate hydratase. This occurs stereospecifically on the side of the molecule which originated from oxaloacetate to form D-(+)-isocitrate, possibly via the intermediate cis-aconitate. This was demonstrated by the use of isotopically labelled oxaloacetate:

(a, b and c in fig. 7.1). In the aconitate hydratase—citrate system, the groups on the substrate with which a, b and c respectively interact may be the 3-OH and 3-COOH and

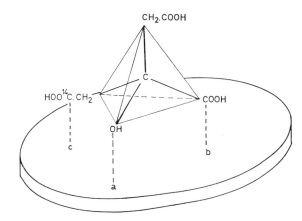

FIG. 7.1. Hypothetical interaction of citrate (formed enzymatically from ^{14}C-labelled oxaloacetate) with the surface of aconitate hydratase.

one of the terminal —CH$_2$COOH groups of the citrate. There is only one side of the tetrahedral arrangement of the groups around the symmetric C-3 atom that presents the three groups in the correct spatial arrangement for interaction with the three specific groups on the enzyme

$$
\underset{\text{Oxalaocetate}}{
\begin{array}{c}
\mathrm{COOH} \\
| \\
\mathrm{CO} \\
| \\
\mathrm{CH_2} \\
| \\
\mathrm{^{14}COOH}
\end{array}
}
\;
\begin{array}{c}
+\mathrm{CH_3CO.SCoA} \\
+\mathrm{H_2O}
\end{array}
\;
\underset{\text{synthase}}{\overset{\text{citrate}}{\rightleftharpoons}}
\;
\underset{\text{Citrate}}{
\begin{array}{c}
\mathrm{COOH} \\
| \\
\mathrm{CH_2} \\
| \\
\mathrm{HO-C-COOH} \\
| \\
\mathrm{CH_2} \\
| \\
\mathrm{^{14}COOH}
\end{array}
}
\;
\underset{\text{hydratase}}{\overset{\text{aconitate}}{\rightleftharpoons}}
\;
\underset{\textit{Cis}\text{-aconitate}}{
\left[
\begin{array}{c}
\mathrm{COOH} \\
| \\
\mathrm{CH_2} \\
| \\
\mathrm{C-COOH} \\
\| \\
\mathrm{CH} \\
| \\
\mathrm{^{14}COOH}
\end{array}
\right]
}
\;
\begin{array}{c}
+\mathrm{H_2O}
\end{array}
\;
\underset{\text{hydratase}}{\overset{\text{aconitate}}{\rightleftharpoons}}
\;
\underset{\text{D-}\textit{Iso}\text{-citrate}}{
\begin{array}{c}
\mathrm{COOH} \\
| \\
\mathrm{CH_2} \\
| \\
\mathrm{H-C-COOH} \\
| \\
\mathrm{HO-C-H} \\
| \\
\mathrm{^{14}COOH}
\end{array}
}
$$

The ability of an enzyme to distinguish between the two chemically identical —CH$_2$COOH groups of the symmetric citrate molecule is at first sight surprising, but it stems from the fact that the enzyme, being made from asymmetric L-amino acid units, is itself asymmetric. Just as our own inherent asymmetry (right- or left-handedness) enables us to recognize the right side of another outwardly symmetric human being, without having to consider such minutiae as the side on which the hair is parted or the hand which wields a tennis racquet, so the enzyme is able to distinguish two like sides of a symmetric molecule, which a symmetric agent cannot do. More particularly it is only necessary that the enzyme showing such stereospecificity should interact with the substrate at three specific groups on its surface

surface. Thus, binding always takes place at the same face of the tetrahedron and the dehydration occurs stereospecifically. For a further explanation of stereoisomerism and other examples of stereospecificity see p. 9.4.

Enzyme specificity and metabolic regulation

The high degree of specificity shown by enzymes is of great biological importance, since it allows the rate of individual enzymic reactions to be independently regulated by variation of either the concentration of the particular enzyme or its degree of activity. The whole pattern of enzymes in a cell thus becomes a very sensitive and flexible instrument for the regulation of the cellular metabolism.

CLASSIFICATION AND NOMENCLATURE OF ENZYMES

The specificity of the enzymes leads naturally to a system of classification based on the nature of the reaction catalysed. In the systematic nomenclature, the name of each enzyme denotes the substrate or substrates and the type of reaction catalysed, and all the systematic names have the suffix -ase. Trivial names of abbreviated form are more generally used but those based on the name of the substrate only are no longer recommended. Thus aconitate hydratase has the systematic name citrate (iso-citrate) hydrolyase but the old trivial name aconitase is no longer used. Some of the best known enzymes (e.g., pepsin, trypsin) have names which do not end in -ase.

The enzymes fall into six main divisions; examples of each with trivial and systematic names appear below.

(1) **Oxidoreductases**: *lactate dehydrogenase* (L-lactate: NAD oxidoreductase)

$$CH_3CHOHCOOH + NAD \rightleftharpoons$$
$$CH_3COCOOH + NADH_2$$

cytochrome oxidase (ferrocytochrome *c*: oxygen oxidoreductase)

$$4 \text{ ferrocytochrome } c + O_2 \rightleftharpoons$$
$$4 \text{ ferricytochrome } c + 2O^{--}$$

(2) **Transferases**: *aspartate aminotransferase* (formerly glutamic- oxaloacetic transaminase) (L-aspartate: 2-oxo-glutarate aminotransferase).

2-Oxo-glutarate	L-Aspartate		L-Glutamate	Oxalo-acetate

Hexokinase (ATP:D-hexose-6-phosphatephosphotransferase)

D-Glucose

D-Glucose-6-phosphate

Glycogen phosphorylase (α-1,4-glucan: orthophosphate glucosyl transferase)

(3) **Hydrolases**: *alkaline phosphatase* (orthophosphoric monoester phosphohydrolase)

$$RO\text{P} + H_2O \longrightarrow ROH + \text{P}OH$$

Phosphoester   Alcohol   Orthophosphate

Lipase (glycerol ester hydrolase)

Triglyceride   Diglyceride   Fatty acid

(4) **Lyases (splitting enzymes)**: *fumarate hydratase* (L-malate hydro-lyase)

L-Malate   Fumarate

Oxaloacetate decarboxylase (oxaloacetate carboxylyase)

$$COOHCOCH_2COOH \longrightarrow COOHCOCH_3 + CO_2$$

Oxaloacetate   Pyruvate

Carbonic anhydrase (carbonate hydrolase)

$$H_2CO_3 \rightleftharpoons H_2O + CO_2$$

(5) **Isomerases**: *triose phosphate isomerase* (D-glyceraldehyde-3-phosphate ketolisomerase)

D-Glyceraldehyde-3-phosphate   Dihydroxyacetone phosphate

(6) Ligases (joining enzymes): *acetyl CoA synthetase*
(acetate: CoA ligase (AMP))

$$ATP + CH_3COOH + CoASH \longrightarrow$$
$$CH_3CO.SCoA + AMP + PP$$

A close examination of these divisions show that some of them are rather arbitrary; hydrolases are just a special group of transferases as indeed are most enzymes.

PURIFICATION OF ENZYMES

Although some enzymic investigations can be successfully pursued with crude or only partially purified preparations, it is essential for many purposes, like the detailed investigation of the mode of action of an enzyme, to use a pure preparation. One of the first requirements when attempting to purify an enzyme is a suitable method of assay, or measurement of the amount of the enzyme, and a discussion of assay methods is given on p. 7.19.

Since enzymes are proteins, they are purified by the methods of protein fractionation (chap. 10), including isoelectric precipitation, salting-out, precipitation with organic solvents, ion exchange chromatography, exclusion chromatography and zone electrophoresis. By a combination of these techniques many enzymes have been obtained in a pure, sometimes crystalline, state. In the development of a new purification scheme, each projected step is tested on a small sample of the material, and the total amount of protein and total amount of enzyme is determined before and after the treatment. If the step provides a good increase in the specific activity (units of enzyme/mg protein) and a good percentage recovery of the activity, the whole batch is treated in the same way and the next step is then investigated. There is no set recipe for the purification of an enzyme.

THE RATE OF ENZYME-CATALYSED REACTIONS

Measurement of the rate

In order to measure the rate or velocity of a reaction, it is necessary to measure, either continuously or at suitably chosen intervals of time, the concentration of products formed or the concentration of substrate remaining. It is usually better to measure the concentration of a product since estimation of quite small decreases in the initially high substrate concentration is likely to be less accurate. Colorimetric and spectrophotometric methods are most commonly used, because they are both sensitive and convenient for routine purposes, and may readily be used in continuous fashion with automatic recording of the

absorbance of the reaction mixture so that a permanent record of the course of the reaction is obtained. When the reaction involves removal of hydrogen ions from the solution or their addition to the solution the technique of continuous titration at constant pH can be employed. Here an unbuffered solution is used and acid or alkali is added so as to keep the pH constant; the method can also be used with automatic recording. Reactions involving uptake or liberation of a gas can be followed by manometric methods.

Fig. 7.2 shows a typical progress curve for an enzymic

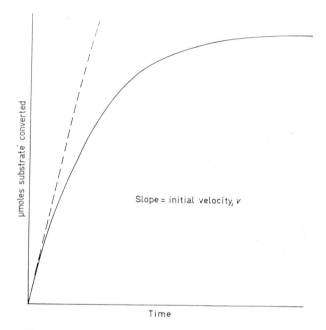

FIG. 7.2. Typical progress curve of an enzyme catalysed reaction. The initial velocity v is given by the slope of the dotted line. From Hendley & Beers (1961) *J. biol. Chem.* **236** 2051.

reaction. In this, as in all reactions whether catalysed or not, the slope of the curve, i.e. the rate of the reaction, eventually falls to zero but in an enzyme-catalysed reaction the rate in the initial stages may be very nearly constant. The eventual decline in rate in both an enzymic and a non-enzymic reaction may be caused by the approach of the reaction to equilibrium, but in an enzymic reaction there are other possible causes. These include inhibition of the enzyme by one of the products of the reaction, fall of the concentration of substrate below levels which effectively saturate the enzyme (p. 7.8) and instability of the enzyme at the temperature and pH of the assay. The initial rate of the reaction, given by the slope of the progress curve at zero time, cannot be affected by any of these causes and it is therefore with this measure of the rate of the reaction that we shall be concerned. Valuable information can sometimes be obtained by analysis of the rest of the curve but such methods are beyond the scope of this book.

Effect of enzyme concentration on the rate

It is found empirically that at a fixed temperature, pH and initial concentration of substrate, the initial velocity of an enzymic reaction is directly proportional to the concentration of the enzyme, provided that the molar concentration of the enzyme is very much less than that of the substrate.

Effect of hydrogen ion concentration on the rate

Although enzymes *in vivo* act at a nearly constant pH, this effect is important in choosing a suitable pH for an enzymic assay and also because its study has helped the understanding of the way in which enzymes catalyse reactions.

If the initial rate of an enzymic reaction is determined at a number of different pH values (all other conditions being unchanged) it is usually found that there is one value (fig. 7.3a) or a range of values (fig. 7.3b) at which the rate is greatest. This optimal pH is usually not far from neutrality, in the range pH 5 to pH 9, but a few enzymes have optima outside this range; pepsin attacks some substrates optimally at pH 2 and arginase hydrolyses arginine optimally at about pH 10.

It is noticeable that the ascending and descending limbs of a plot of activity against pH, at least where the two limbs are separated by a marked plateau as in fig. 7.3b, are sigmoid. That is to say, they have the same shape as the titration curve of an acid or base. This observation leads to an explanation of the pH optimum. Enzymes, being proteins, possess numerous ionizable groups on the surface of their molecules, largely those of the side chains of aspartic acid, glutamic acid, arginine, lysine and histidine and the phenolic hydroxyl of tyrosine and the thiol group of cysteine. There may also be free α-amino and α-carboxyl groups from the ends of the polypeptide chain or chains. Table 7.1 shows

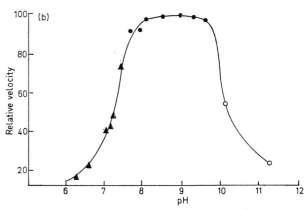

FIG. 7.3. pH-optima of enzymes (a) acetylcholinesterase (b) proline iminopeptidase. The different symbols show experiments conducted in different buffer systems. From Wilson & Bergmann (1950) *J. biol. Chem.* **186**, 683, and Sarid *et al.* (1959) *J. biol. Chem.* **234**, 1742.

TABLE 7.1. pK_a values of ionizable groups in proteins

Group	pK_a
α-Carboxyl	3·0–3·2
β-Carboxyl (aspartic acid)	3·0–4·7
γ-Carboxyl (glutamic acid)	3·0–4·7
Imidazolium (histidine)	5·6–7·0
α-Amino	7·6–8·4
Sulphydryl (cysteine)	8·3–8·6
ε-Amino (lysine)	9·4–10·6
Phenolic hydroxyl (tyrosine)	9·8–10·4
Guanidinium (arginine)	11·6–12·6

the pK_a values of these groups as they occur in proteins, but they may in particular cases be considerably altered by neighbouring charged groups. At the optimal pH of an enzyme, some of these groups are protonated and some unprotonated. Consider in an enzyme two such ionizable groups, —AH and —BH, which have well separated pK_a values, that of —AH being the lower. The absence of a written positive charge does not mean that either may not be an imidazolium, guanidinium or substituted ammonium group. A plot, against pH, of the fraction of the enzyme molecules in which —AH is dissociated and —BH undissociated, without regard to the state of ionization of any other groups, would be like that of fig. 7.4. The points of inflection of the ascending and descending limbs are at the pK_a values of —AH and —BH respectively. This curve is clearly very similar to that of fig. 7.3.b, and it suggests that, for any enzyme showing a curve of this sort, there are two ionizable groups which must be in a particular state of ionization for the enzyme to be active, and that a pH-activity curve is simply a plot of the fraction of the enzyme present in this state against pH. There may be other ionizable groups essential for the activity, either for binding the substrate to the enzyme or

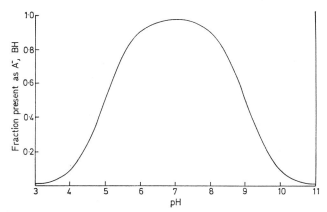

FIG. 7.4. Dissociation of molecule with two dissociable groups AH and BH whose pK_a values are 5·0 and 9·0 respectively.

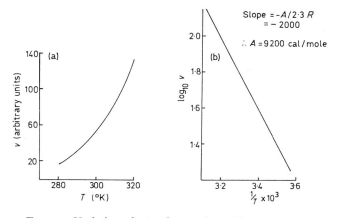

FIG. 7.5. Variation of rate of a reaction with temperature.

bringing about its conversion, but if their pK_a values are further removed from the pH optimum of the enzyme they will have little effect on the shape of the curve. When the substrate is capable of ionization the curve may reflect the pK_a value of a substrate rather than an enzyme group.

It is possible from a detailed analysis of the effects of pH on activity to determine the pK_a values of essential groups and so to start to identify their nature.

Effect of temperature on the rate

The relationship between temperature and the rate of any chemical reaction is given by the Arrhenius equation:

$$\ln k = C - A/RT; \qquad 2.3 \log_{10} k = C - A/RT$$

or

$$\frac{d \ln k}{dT} = \frac{A}{RT^2}; \qquad \frac{d \log_{10} k}{dT} = \frac{A}{2\cdot3 RT^2}$$

where k is the velocity constant of the reaction, R the gas constant (approx. 2 cal.degree^{-1}mole^{-1}), T the absolute temperature, A the energy of activation and C a constant. Enzyme-catalysed reactions show the same relationship so that a plot of initial velocity against temperature would look like that shown in fig. 7.5a, and a plot of log v against $1/T$ is a straight line whose slope is $-A/2\cdot3R$ as in fig. 7.5b. From such a plot, the value of A, the energy of activation of the reaction, can be obtained. In the few cases where the spontaneous reaction is sufficiently fast to measure, it is found that the energy of activation for the catalysed reaction is lower than that for the spontaneous one; this is, of course, the expected result since catalysts lower the energy of activation of the reactions they catalyse (p. 8.2).

It is often difficult to measure the initial velocity of an enzymic reaction over a wide range of temperatures and one sometimes sees curves relating 'enzymic activity' to

temperature with an optimum somewhere about 50°C. Such a curve appears in fig. 7.6. Here 'enzymic activity' is not the initial rate of the reaction, but is the amount of products formed in some fixed time and an 'optimum temperature' is found because two processes are involved i.e. the simple increase in the rate of the catalysed reaction and the increase in the rate of denaturation (inactivation) of the enzyme. Proteins generally have high energies of activation of denaturation which means a marked temperature dependence of the rate of denaturation. This rate may increase several hundredfold over a 10°C rise in temperature in contrast to the approximate doubling of the rate for most reactions including those catalysed by enzymes. At temperatures over about 60°C, the enzyme is rapidly inactivated and has little opportunity to act at all. The rising part of the temperature activity curve re-

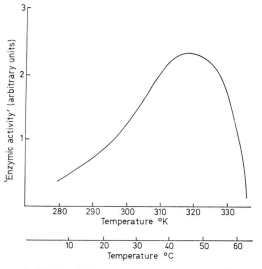

FIG. 7.6. Effect of temperature on amount of catalysed reaction occurring in a fixed time. 'Enzyme activity' is the amount of substrate converted in a fixed time.

flects the increase in the rate of the catalysed reaction and the falling part reflects the inactivation of the enzyme.

This lability of enzymes to heat allows preparations which have been inactivated at 100°C for 5 min to serve as 'controls' in enzyme studies. However, not all enzymes are irreversibly and totally inactivated by such treatment.

Effect of concentration of substrate on the rate

Fig. 7.7 shows measurements of initial velocity plotted against initial substrate concentration for an enzyme in a series of experiments in which the pH, temperature and enzyme concentration are unchanged. At low substrate

FIG. 7.7. Variation of velocity of a catalysed reaction with substrate concentration. $V = 0.01\,\mu\text{mole ml}^{-1}\,\text{min}^{-1}$, $K_m = 0.4\,\text{mM}$

concentrations the velocity increases with substrate concentration but eventually a plateau of maximum velocity is reached. This behaviour was explained by Michaelis and Menten in 1913 on the assumption that enzyme and substrate combined together to form an enzyme-substrate complex with which they were in equilibrium:

$$E + S \rightleftharpoons ES$$

This explanation was modified by Briggs and Haldane who made the less demanding assumption that the complex is not in equilibrium with the enzyme and substrate but that a steady state is rapidly reached in which the concentration of the complex is constant. The reactions to be considered are:

$$E + S \underset{k_{-1}}{\overset{k_{+1}}{\rightleftharpoons}} ES \overset{k_{+2}}{\longrightarrow} E + P$$

to which we assign the velocity constants shown on the appropriate arrows. The reverse reaction:

$$ES \underset{k_{-2}}{\longleftarrow} E + P$$

is ignored because only the initial velocity of the reaction is being considered so that there are no products and hence no back reaction.

Usually the total concentration of enzyme $[E]$ is very much smaller than the concentration of substrate $[S]$; the substrate concentrations investigated may be in the range 10^{-5} to 10^{-3} M, while the enzyme may well be as dilute as 1 μg/ml which, assuming a molecular weight of 50,000, corresponds to 2×10^{-8} M. When the steady state concentration of the enzyme-substrate complex has been attained, its rate of formation must be equal to its rate of breakdown in the forward and backward directions. Each of these rates is given by the product of the appropriate velocity constant and the concentrations of the interacting compounds. If $[E]$ is the total concentration of enzyme the concentration of free enzyme is $([E]-[ES])$. The concentration of free substrate will be very nearly equal to $[S]$ since $[ES] < [E] \ll [S]$.

Describing the steady state algebraically:

$$[S]([E]-[ES])k_{+1} = [ES]k_{-1} + [ES]k_{+2}$$

The velocity $v = k_{+2}[ES]$. We therefore extract $[ES]$, a variable often difficult to measure experimentally:

$$k_{+1}[E][S] - k_{+1}[ES][S] = (k_{-1}+k_{+2})[ES]$$

$$\therefore (k_{-1}+k_{+2})ES + k_{+1}[ES][S] = k_{+1}[E][S]$$

$$\therefore ES(k_{-1}+k_{+2}+k_{+1}[S]) = k_{+1}[E][S]$$

$$\therefore [ES] = \frac{k_{+1}[E][S]}{k_{-1}+k_{+2}+k_{+1}[S]}$$

$$\therefore [ES] = \frac{[E][S]}{\dfrac{k_{-1}+k_{+2}}{k_{+1}}+[S]}$$

and multiply both sides by k_{+2}:

$$k_{+2}[ES] = \frac{k_{+2}[E][S]}{\dfrac{k_{-1}+k_{+2}}{k_{+1}}+[S]} \tag{1}$$

The velocity $v = k_{+2}[ES]$ and at high substrate concentrations the maximum initial velocity, V, is reached when the enzyme is saturated with substrate, and is all present as enzyme-substrate complex whose maximal concentration is $[E]$, i.e.,

$$V = k_{+2}[E]$$

The expression $(k_{-1}+k_{+2})/k_{+1}$ is itself a constant, known as the **Michaelis constant**, K_m, and making the appropriate substitutions equation (1) becomes

$$v = \frac{V[S]}{K_m + [S]} \tag{2}$$

This equation has the form of a rectangular hyperbola, as does a plot of initial velocity against substrate concentration (fig. 7.7).

In equation (2) v and V have the dimensions mole litre^{-1}sec^{-1}; K_m, being the ratio of the first order velocity constants k_{-1} and k_{+2} (sec^{-1}), and the second order constant k_{+1}(litre.mole^{-1}sec^{-1}) has the dimensions of mole.litre^{-1}, i.e., of concentration.

If the situation where the substrate concentration is such that the initial velocity is half the maximal initial velocity is considered:

$$\frac{V}{2} = \frac{V[S]}{K_m+[S]}$$

$$\therefore\ K_m+[S] = 2[S]$$

$$\therefore\ K_m = [S]$$

The value of K_m is therefore given by the substrate concentration which gives half the maximal initial velocity and this may, in some cases, be found from a curve like that in fig. 7.7. The Michaelis constant is a characteristic of the enzyme (for a given substrate and given reaction conditions) and can be determined even if the enzyme concentration is unknown, as is clear from equation (2) in which $[E]$ does not appear. V is dependent on the enzyme concentration, but if this is known in molar terms, k_{+2} may be found since $V = k_{+2}[E]$.

K_m is sometimes regarded as though it were the dissociation constant of the enzyme-substrate complex, k_{-1}/k_{+1}, but this is valid only when $k_{-1} \gg k_{+2}$ which is not always the case. When K_m does approximate to this dissociation constant it becomes analogous to the inverse of the binding constant used in pharmacological studies.

Determination of K_m and V

The determination of K_m and V from curves such as that of fig. 7.7 is not always possible or convenient; it may not be possible to reach the theoretical maximal velocity because the substrate is insufficiently soluble, or because high concentrations of substrate inhibit the enzyme (p. 7.11) or merely because the substrate can be obtained only in small amounts. It is in any case more convenient to use a linear expression and one is obtained in the following way.

Inverting equation (2) we get

$$\frac{1}{v} = \frac{K_m+[S]}{V[S]} \qquad (3)$$

$$\frac{[S]}{v} = \frac{[S]}{V}+\frac{K_m}{V} \qquad (4)$$

If S/v is plotted against S, a straight line is obtained (fig. 7.8 plotted for the same data as fig. 7.7) having slope $1/V$ and intercepts on the ordinate and abscissa of K_m/V and $-K_m$. This method of plotting results has advantages over the plot of $1/v$ against $1/[S]$, based on equation (3), in that the points at higher substrate concentrations, which tend to be more accurate, are better

FIG. 7.8. Graphical determination of K_m and V
$K_m = 0.4$ mM (0.4 μmole.ml)
$V = 0.01$ mM min^{-1} (0.01 μmole.ml^{-1}min^{-1})
The figure shows a linear plot of the data of fig. 7.7

spaced out, and thus have more weight in the fitting of the best straight line.

Determinations of K_m and k_{+2}, particularly under varying conditions of pH or solvent, or with different substrates, are valuable in investigations into the specific mode of action of individual enzymes; on such evidence it has been concluded that cholinesterase has a cationic site important in binding the substrate acetyl choline. Values of K_m are important in assessing the physiological significance of enzymes especially when the regulation of alternate paths of reactions by changes in the concentrations of metabolites is involved. Values of k_{+2} have less importance in metabolic studies. If one is interested in deciding whether a tissue contains enough of a particular enzyme to account for the observed rate of a metabolic conversion, it is sufficient to be able to measure the amount of the enzyme in terms of the rate of the catalysed reaction, and it is not necessary to know the molar concentrations of the enzyme or the value of k_{+2}.

INHIBITORS

Enzyme-catalysed reactions are affected also by agents which reduce their rates and investigation of how this effect is produced has been of great importance in inquiries into the mode of action of enzymes and more recently in understanding the ways in which the complex of metabolic reactions is regulated *in vivo*.

Many agents destroy the activity of enzymes unspecifically by denaturing the protein irreversibly. Such agents as strong acids or alkalis, trichloroacetic acid, detergents and high concentrations of heavy metal ions or organic solvents all act in this way and though they are useful experimentally when one wishes to stop an enzymic reaction, they are not of great theoretical interest and are not usually classed as inhibitors.

Competitive and non-competitive inhibition

The more interesting and informative inhibitors are those which show some degree of specificity, that is to say they lower the activity of only a few enzymes and do so at low concentrations. Such inhibition may be either reversible or irreversible; if the inhibitor can be removed and activity restored by dialysis or chromatography or precipitation of the enzyme, it is classed as reversible. Detailed analysis of specific, reversible inhibitors shows that they may be divided into two broad classes of competitive and non-competitive inhibitors, although examples with intermediate properties are known.

The difference between the two classes is illustrated in fig. 7.9 which shows data for the hypothetical enzyme of figs. 7.7 and 7.8. At a constant concentration of inhibitor, the initial velocity of reaction given by a constant concentration of enzyme at constant pH and temperature increases with substrate concentration, in a manner similar to that found in the absence of any inhibitor. If, at high substrate concentrations, the inhibition is eventually abolished so that V is the same as that found in the absence of inhibitor, the inhibitor is said to be competitive. It appears that the substrate and inhibitor, which

often have similar chemical structures, compete with one another in binding at the active centre. Either one or the other can be bound but not both. Examples of such competition include the inhibition of succinate dehydrogenase by other dicarboxylic acids such as malate and oxaloacetate, which like succinate are intermediates in the citric acid cycle (chap. 8), and malonate which is not a metabolite. The fraction of enzyme molecules which bind substrate at any instant depends on the concentration of the substrate and of the inhibitor and on the dissociation constant of the enzyme-inhibitor complex K_i, and on the value of K_m. Only the enzyme-substrate complex can break down to give products. The reactions involved are:

$$E+S \rightleftharpoons ES \longrightarrow E+P$$
$$E+I \overset{K_i}{\rightleftharpoons} EI$$

At a sufficiently high substrate concentration the enzyme is almost entirely bound to substrate and the normal maximum velocity is found.

A non-competitive inhibitor at constant concentration produces the same fractional inhibition of the enzyme no matter what the concentration of the substrate, and such inhibitors show no chemical similarity to the substrate. Fumarate hydratase, for example, is non-competitively inhibited by thiocyanate ions. In a case of truly non-competitive inhibition, binding of inhibitor to the enzyme does not affect the binding of the substrate, nor does binding of the substrate affect the binding of the inhibitor, but binding of the inhibitor does prevent the breakdown of the enzyme-substrate complex in the forward direction to enzyme and products.

We must now introduce K_s, the true dissociation constant of the enzyme substrate complex, which must also be the constant for dissociation of the substrate from the enzyme-inhibitor-substrate complex; the reactions involved are:

$$E+S \rightleftharpoons ES \longrightarrow E+P$$
$$E+I \overset{K_i}{\rightleftharpoons} EI$$
$$EI+S \overset{K_s}{\rightleftharpoons} EIS$$
$$ES+I \overset{K_i}{\rightleftharpoons} EIS$$

Analysis of the competitive and non-competitive situations by arguments similar to those used on p. 7.8 leads to the modified Michaelis equations shown below:

No inhibitor

$$v = \frac{V[S]}{K_m+[S]} \qquad \text{or} \quad \frac{[S]}{v} = \frac{[S]}{V} + \frac{K_m}{V}$$

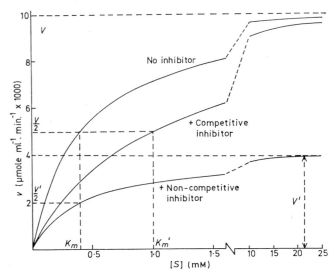

FIG. 7.9. Variation of velocity of a catalysed reaction with substrate concentration in the presence of a constant concentration of a competitive and of a non-competitive inhibitor.
$K_m = 0.4$ mM, $V = 0.01$ μmole.ml^{-1}min^{-1};
$[I] = 3.0$ mM, $K_i = 2.0$ mM.

Competitive inhibition

$$v = \frac{V[S]}{K_m(1+[I]/K_i)+[S]} \quad \text{or} \quad \frac{[S]}{v} = \frac{[S]}{V} + \frac{K_m(1+[I]/K_i)}{V}$$

Non-competitive inhibition

$$v = \frac{V[S]}{(K_m+[S])(1+[I]/K_i)} \quad \text{or} \quad \frac{[S]}{v} = \left(\frac{[S]}{V} + \frac{K_m}{V}\right)(1+[I]/K_i)$$

These equations mean that in the case of competitive inhibition, an apparent value for K_m is found, higher than that found in the absence of inhibitor, being

$$K_m' = K_m(1+[I]/K_i)$$

but the value of V is unchanged. With a non-competitive inhibitor K_m is unchanged, but a lower value is found for the maximal initial velocity, being

$$V' = V/(1+[I]/K_i)$$

The nature of an inhibition and the value of K_i may thus be found by plotting S/v against S for the reaction in the absence of inhibitor and in the presence of a constant known concentration of inhibitor. As shown in fig. 7.10 (the data of fig. 7.9. replotted) non-competitive inhibition gives a line of increased slope and unchanged intercept on the abscissa, while competitive inhibition gives a line with unchanged slope but increased intercepts on both axes.

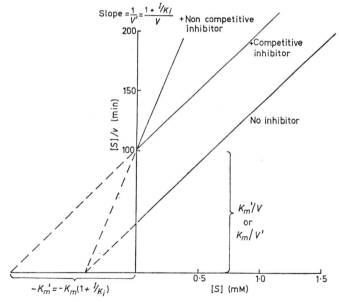

FIG. 7.10. Linear plots of competitive and non-competitive inhibition.
$K_m = 0.4$ mM; $V = 0.01$ mM.min^{-1}. For both inhibitors $[I] = 3.0$ mM, $K_i = 2.0$ mM.

Specific irreversible inhibitors

Some of the most potent enzyme inhibitors are those which react with the enzyme stoicheiometrically and irreversibly with the formation of a new covalent bond.

The inhibition of a number of esterases by organophosphorus compounds or of many thiol-enzymes by alkylating agents like iodoacetic acid are reactions of this type

$$\text{\textcircled{E}}H + F\text{—}P(OR)_2 \longrightarrow \text{\textcircled{E}}\text{—}P(OR)_2 + HF$$

with the P double-bonded to O in both.

$$\text{\textcircled{E}}\text{—}SH + ICH_2COOH \longrightarrow \text{\textcircled{E}}\text{—}S.CH_2COOH + HI$$

In many such cases, as for example the inhibition of cholinesterase with di*iso*propylphosphorofluoridate (DFP) it has been shown that prior addition of substrate or a reversible competitive inhibitor at least partly protects the enzyme from the irreversible inhibition. This suggests that there is competition between the agents for the active site of the enzyme, so that it seems likely that the irreversible inhibitor reacts with a group in the active centre.

Metallic inhibitors

Many enzymes, especially those containing thiol groups essential for their activity are inhibited by low concentrations of the ions of heavy metals or by metallo-organic compounds like p-chloromercuribenzoate,

$$\text{Cl}^- \dots \text{Hg}^+ \langle\text{ring}\rangle \text{COO}^-$$

This effect should be distinguished from the denaturation of proteins produced by high concentrations (of the order of 0.1 M or more) of the salts of heavy metals. It is usually reversible, especially by the addition of metal-binding agents like cyanide, cysteine or ethylenediamine-tetra-acetate (EDTA, Versene). Sensitive enzymes are inhibited even by the concentrations of metal ions found in ordinary distilled water so that glass distilled or de-ionized water is often necessary in work with enzymes, and addition of EDTA is often useful during their isolation.

Inhibition by excess of substrate

It was mentioned earlier (p. 7.9) that with some enzymes it is not possible in practice to attain the theoretical maximum velocity (determined from a plot of S/v against S), because at high substrate concentrations the substrate itself acts as an inhibitor (fig. 7.11). In some of these cases it has been shown that the substrate finally inhibits by removing from the enzyme an essential activating metal ion or by competing with a second substrate, often water, for its binding site. In others it appears that two substrate molecules are bound at one site on the enzyme surface, but neither is correctly bound and so no reaction takes place. Cholinesterase is inhibited by excess of acetyl choline in this way.

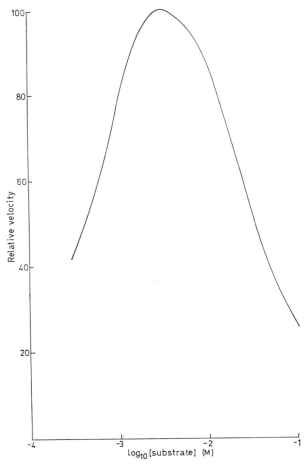

FIG. 7.11. Inhibition by excess of substrate. Erythrocyte acetylcholinesterase acting on acetylcholine. From Augustinsson K-B (1949) *Arch. Biochem. Biophys.* **23**, 111.

ACTIVATORS

The rates of some enzyme catalysed reactions are found to be increased by the presence of compounds or ions which do not themselves appear in the overall reaction and which are termed activators. Carbonic anhydrase requires Zn^{++} ions for its activity and phosphokinases are activated by Mg^{++}. Many other examples of activation by metal ions are known and for some there is evidence that the metal ion is involved in binding the substrate to the enzyme.

With other enzymes the activator may be an organic molecule, perhaps a metabolite in some chain of metabolic reactions, a hormone, or even the substrate itself. If the substrate acts as an activator, the relationship between the velocity and substrate concentration is not the normal one (p. 7.8); the rate of reaction increases faster than the substrate concentration at low substrate concentrations, so that the curve becomes S-shaped (fig. 7.12).

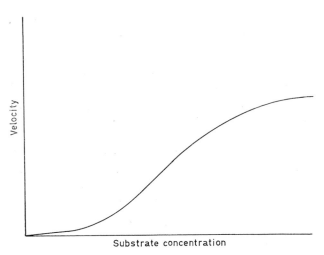

FIG. 7.12. Activation by substrate. From Okagski & Kornberg (1964) *J. Biol. Chem.* **239**, 269.

The activation and inhibition of enzymes by metabolites may play an important part in the regulation of the metabolism of both micro-organisms and mammals and these effects are discussed on p. 7.17.

PROSTHETIC GROUPS, COENZYMES AND VITAMINS

Although the majority of enzymes are proteins composed only of amino acids joined to one another by peptide bonds, some are conjugated proteins and contain in addition a relatively firmly, even covalently, bound organic compound which plays an important part in the catalytic activity. Such non-amino acid components are called prosthetic groups and the protein without its prosthetic group is called an apo-enzyme. Each prosthetic group acts as a temporary acceptor of some metabolic fragment in its transfer from one compound to another. Since the prosthetic group remains attached to one apo-enzyme molecule and since the enzymes are highly specific the fate of the fragment is determined when it is transferred to the prosthetic group.

The coenzymes are also organic compounds essential for the activity of some enzymes and they too act as intermediate acceptors of metabolic fragments. Unlike prosthetic groups they are not firmly bound to their enzymes but are freely dissociable.

Many of the substances which act as vitamins of the B group in the diet of man or animals, or which are essential growth factors for certain micro-organisms, are found to be chemically closely related to compounds which act as coenzymes or prosthetic groups of enzymes. Nicotinamide, riboflavin, thiamine, biotin, pantothenic acid,

TABLE 7.2. Prosthetic groups, coenzymes and vitamins.

Growth factor or vitamin	Structure	Related prosthetic group or coenzyme	Function
Thiamine (B_1)	Pyrimidine ring Thiazole ring	Thiamine pyrophosphate	Transfer of some aldehyde groups e.g. pyruvate dehydrogenase system, transketolase.
Lipoic acid		Enzyme-bound lipoic acid	Acceptance of some aldehyde groups and their oxidation to acyl complexes, e.g. pyruvate dehydrogenase complex.
Pantothenic acid	$HOCH_2-\overset{\overset{\displaystyle CH_3}{|}}{\underset{\underset{\displaystyle CH_3}{|}}{C}}-CH(OH)CONHCH_2CH_2COOH$	Coenzyme A	Acyl transfer and alteration, e.g. pyruvate dehydrogenase system, fatty acid oxidation.
Nicotinic acid (niacin)	Nicotinic acid (niacin) Nicotinamide	NAD, NADP	Transfer of $H \equiv e^- + H^+$
Riboflavine		FMN, FAD	Transfer of $H \equiv e^- + H^+$
Pyridoxal and derivatives (B_6)	Pyridoxine Pyridoxamine	Pyridoxal phosphate	Transfer of amino groups, generally by the formation of Schiff's bases, e.g. aminotransferases, serine hydroxymethyltransferase.
Folic acid	Pterin residue *p*-Amino-benzoic acid residue Glutamic acid residue	Tetrahydrofolic acid	Transfer and interconversion of C_1 units at level of oxidation of formate, formaldehyde and methanol, e.g. in purine synthesis, serine transhydroxymethylase, methionine synthesis.

TABLE 7.2—*continued*.

Growth factor or vitamin	Structure	Related prosthetic group or coenzyme	Function
Cyanocobalamin (B₁₂)		Cobamide coenzymes	Molecular rearrangements and formation of methyl groups.
Biotin		Enzyme-bound biotin	Carboxylations, e.g. acetyl-CoA carboxylase.
—	—	Nucleoside diphosphates	Phosphate transfer (ATP, GTP), glycosyl transfer (UDP-glucose).
—	—	Haem	Electron transfer (cytochromes), oxygen transport (haemoglobin).

folic acid, vitamin B_{12} and pyridoxal and its related compounds, all show this relationship. These substances cannot be synthesized either at all or at an adequate rate by the organisms requiring them, but if provided in the diet or growth medium they can be utilized for the synthesis of the essential coenzymes and prosthetic groups. Typical examples of prosthetic groups and coenzymes along with the growth factors or vitamins which are an essential part if their structure are shown in Table 7.2.

THE ACTION OF COENZYMES

The first coenzyme (nicotinamide adenine dinucleotide, NAD) was discovered as a factor necessary for the fermentation of sugar by cell-free yeast extracts. It was diffusible and stable to heat and was clearly not itself an enzyme. The name coenzyme was given to indicate its role in co-operating with the enzymes to produce the fermentation reactions. Many other coenzymes have been discovered since.

The function of this co-enzyme in yeast fermentation is to accept hydrogen from glyceraldehyde-3-phosphate in a reaction catalysed by a specific dehydrogenase (and involving phosphorylation of the substrate) and then to donate it in a reaction catalysed by alcohol dehydrogenase in which acetaldehyde is reduced to ethanol. In glycolysis in muscle the role is similar; the NAD is reduced in the same reaction but is reoxidized by transferring the hydrogen to pyruvate to form lactate in a reaction catalysed by lactate dehydrogenase.

D-Glyceraldehyde-3-phosphate → 1,3-Diphosphoglycerate (glyceraldehyde phosphate dehydrogenase, Muscle and yeast)

Acetaldehyde + NADH₂ → NAD + Ethanol (Alcohol dehydrogenase, yeast)

Pyruvate + NADH₂ → NAD + L-Lactate (Lactate dehydrogenase, muscle)

Under aerobic conditions in both yeast and muscle the $NADH_2$ may be oxidized by yet another series of reactions ultimately involving the oxidation of the hydrogen to water. Most of the $NADH_2$ is oxidized in one of these ways, but there are many other reactions in which it may be oxidized. There are also many ways in which NAD may be reduced to $NADH_2$. Thus neither the origin nor the fate of the hydrogen attached to NAD is in any way determined. The coenzyme can carry the hydrogen from any reaction in which it may become available to any reaction in which it can be utilized. Coenzyme A acts as a carrier of acyl groups and nucleoside diphosphates act as carriers of phosphate in an analogous way.

The manner in which the above reactions are written indicates that it would be legitimate to regard the coenzyme as a substrate in the reactions, and indeed the rate of the catalysed reaction depends on the coenzyme concentration in the same way as it depends on substrate concentration. The distinction between a coenzyme and a substrate lies more in the metabolic role of the compound than on the way in which it behaves in any enzymic reaction. A molecule of a coenzyme may be used over and over again in the same group of reactions, while in general a substrate molecule passes only once down one particular pathway.

Even the distinction based on metabolic role is not always clear. Phosphoglucomutase catalyses as overall reaction the interconversion of glucose-1-phosphate and glucose-6-phosphate but does so only in the presence of small amounts of glucose-1,6-diphosphate. This has been shown by isotopic labelling studies to donate its phosphate to one reactant, converting it to the diphosphate, while it itself becomes the monophosphate product.

Glucose-1,6-diphosphate ⇌ Glucose-6-phosphate
+ +
Glucose-1-phosphate Glucose-1,6-diphosphate

Thus, although the concentration of the diphosphate remains constant the individual molecules are continually being changed. In fact, the reaction is more complex than that shown above; the enzyme itself acts as an intermediate acceptor of the phosphate between the glucose mono- and diphosphate.

ENZYME SUBSTRATE COMPLEXES AND THE ACTIVE CENTRES OF ENZYMES

The kinetic analysis, given on p. 7.8, of the effect of varying substrate concentration on the rate of enzymic reactions, was based on the assumption that the enzyme and substrate bind together to form a complex. In some cases the formation of such a complex has been shown more directly. Several metal containing or metal activated enzymes undergo a change of absorption spectrum on addition of substrate. Thus peroxidase which is a haem-enzyme catalysing reactions of the type

$$AH_2 + H_2O_2 \longrightarrow A + 2H_2O$$

shows a change in the absorption spectrum of the haem group when hydrogen peroxide is added to the solution, and this has been used for following the rate of formation of the peroxidase-hydrogen peroxide complex in detailed studies of the kinetics of the system. The enzyme D-amino acid oxidase contains an FAD prosthetic group and is, like all flavin compounds, yellow, but a crystalline complex of the enzyme with D-alanine has been obtained which contains FAD and D-alanine in equimolar proportions and is deep purple. This is apparently a crystalline form of the enzyme-substrate complex.

Since enzymes usually attack substrates much smaller than themselves, and since, in those studied, only one or a few substrate molecules are bound to the enzyme at one time, it seems likely that the substrate is bound at one or a few special parts of the enzyme surface, i.e. the active site or centre. The nature of the groups involved in binding the substrate and of the groups with which it is thus brought into close proximity must be such that they induce changes in the electronic configuration of the substrate or substrates, so that their conversion into products occurs more easily (i.e. with a lower energy of activation) than is the case for substrate not bound to the active centre.

It is obviously of interest to obtain more detailed information on the nature of active centres and their mechanism of action and studies of this sort have been undertaken in many laboratories on a variety of different enzymes. The techniques used include studies of the changes in the kinetic parameters brought about by alterations in the substrate molecule or by changes of pH, dielectric constant or temperature, and chemical studies using specific irreversible inhibitors.

This last approach can best be illustrated by the experiments performed with a group of esterases and peptidases which includes trypsin, the cholinesterase of the plasma and the acetylcholinesterase of the erythrocytes. These enzymes are all rapidly and irreversibly inhibited by a number of organophosphorus compounds including DFP and the inhibition is due to the attachment of one di-isopropylphosphoryl group to the active centre of each enzyme molecule:

$$CH_3-CH(CH_3)-O \quad O \\ \underset{CH_3-CH(CH_3)-O}{\overset{}{P}}-F+H\textcircled{E} \longrightarrow$$

$$CH_3-CH(CH_3)-O \quad O \\ \underset{CH_3-CH(CH_3)-O}{\overset{}{P}}-\textcircled{E}+HF$$

The amino acid residue at the active site to which the di-isopropylphosphoryl group is attached has been investigated in several of these enzymes by chemical or enzymic degradation. In every instance the reaction is found to have occurred by formation of a serine phosphoester derivative. The serine is always found in one of two sequences, either -Asp.Ser.Gly- or -Glu.Ser.Ala- and with trypsin and chymotrypsin the similarity of the sequence extends even further. It thus seems likely that this serine sequence lies at or near the active centre of each enzyme.

There is also kinetic evidence for the involvement of histidine at the active site of these enzymes, but in chymotrypsin, for which the complete amino acid sequence is known, this residue has been identified at position 57 (numbering from the N-terminus) far from the serine residue at position 195. The two residues are presumably brought close together by the secondary and tertiary folding of the polypeptide chain. It seems that it will not be long before we can explain with certainty the catalytic activities of at least one or two enzymes.

ISOENZYMES

In the preceding discussion it has been tacitly assumed that in any one tissue only one protein is responsible for any one catalytic activity. The development of refined techniques of protein fractionation has shown that this is by no means always true. The important method of electrophoresis in starch or polyacrylamide gel allows one to separate proteins by small differences in their molecular charge and size and by this means many enzymes have been shown to exist in tissues in multiple molecular forms, which are known as isoenzymes or isozymes.

The best known example is lactate dehydrogenase. It exists in five forms which can be separated by electrophoresis in starch gel or starch grains at a mildly alkaline

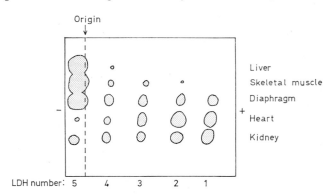

FIG. 7.13. Separation of the lactate dehydrogenases of tissues of the adult rat by electrophoresis in a bed of starch grains. Modified from Fine, Kaplan & Kuftinec (1963) *Biochemistry* **2**, 116.

pH; they are detected in the gel by their specific enzymic activity, the reduction of NAD by lactate being coupled to the reduction of a colourless compound to an insoluble dye (fig. 7.13).

Analysis of tissue extracts by this method shows that tissues differ from one another in the proportions of the five isoenzymes they contain. Each isoenzyme of mammalian lactate dehydrogenase consists of four sub-units (polypeptide chains), each with an active centre for binding NAD and lactate, but there are only two types of subunit (H and M). The isoenzyme which migrates fastest towards the anode (LDH 1) is found in greatest abundance in heart muscle and consists of four H sub-units; the slowest migrating, (LDH 5) is most abundant in skeletal muscle, and consists of four M sub-units; three intermediate forms have the compositions H_3M, H_2M_2, and HM_3. The physiological significance of this and other systems of isoenzymes is not certain.

Lactate dehydrogenases are also found in the serum and the identification of the particular isoenzymes present is becoming of clinical importance as a diagnostic aid since damaged tissues release their enzymes into the blood; thus the pattern of isoenzymes in the serum may identify the tissue which has been damaged.

REGULATION OF METABOLISM AT THE ENZYME LEVEL

In a complex organism like a mammal the metabolic activity of the organs and tissues is regulated in a number of ways, usually involving the nervous and endocrine systems. At a lower level within the cell the properties of the enzymes suggest ways in which the flow of substrates along a metabolic pathway might be regulated. The rate of an enzyme-catalysed reaction is dependent on pH, temperature, and concentrations of the enzyme, substrates, coenzymes, activators and inhibitors. The activity of some enzymes is also sensitive to changes in the ionic strength of the medium, although these have not been discussed. Three of these variables, pH, temperature and ionic strength, seem unlikely to play a role as part of a sensitive regulatory mechanism. Changes in any one of them would result in changes in the rates of a great number of metabolic reactions, and of course organisms regulate their internal pH and ionic strength, and warm blooded animals their temperature too, within narrow limits.

Mass action effects

Variations of the concentrations of substrates or coenzymes affect the rate of catalysed reactions in which they play a part in a way which depends on the relationship between the K_m of the enzyme and the concentration of the substrate concerned. If the initial concentration of a substrate is of the same order as or lower than the K_m of the enzyme, so that the enzyme is not saturated and this concentration is then increased, for example by dietary intake, the rate of conversion of the substrate to products will automatically increase so that the concentration of the substrate tends to return to its original lower level. The reverse effect would operate if the initial substrate concentration should fall by a reduction

in its rate of supply or by increase in the rate of some competing pathway. If, however, the concentration of the substrate is already much higher than the K_m of the enzyme, so that the enzyme is effectively saturated, changes in the concentration of the substrate do not produce changes in its rate of conversion to products. An interesting situation arises when a metabolite is a substrate for two different enzymes, each catalysing the initial reaction of a different chain as in the scheme below:

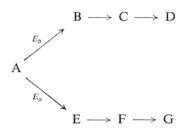

If we assume that in this scheme the enzyme E_b has a low K_m so that it is always saturated with the substrate A, the rate of conversion of A to B will not depend on the concentration of A. If the enzyme E_e has a higher K_m so that it is only one third saturated at the initial concentration of A, the rate of conversion of A to E will be only one third of the maximum. If now the concentration of A is raised tenfold, the enzyme E_e will become five-sixths saturated (you should check this figure for yourself), and the rate of conversion of A to E will be 2·5 times what it was before. The important result is that a change occurs in the ratio in which A is divided between the two pathways. Such a situation is found in yeast where pyruvate is oxidized by an enzyme with a K_m of about 10^{-4} M and decarboxylated to aldehyde by an enzyme with a K_m of about 10^{-3} M. When the supply of pyruvate increases a greater fraction of it is used for acetaldehyde formation (fermentation) while the rate of oxidation remains relatively unchanged. Changes in the concentration of coenzymes produce similar effects, and since the same coenzymes are used by many different enzyme systems these effects provide a means of coordinating the rates of different metabolic pathways, e.g. the Pasteur effect, p. 9.13.

Changes of enzymic activity

Another possible means of metabolic regulation depends on alteration of the activity of an enzyme by changes in the concentrations of activators or inhibitors which may be hormones or metabolites or coenzymes involved in other metabolic pathways or may even be the substrate or the product of the reaction, as in the inhibition of hexokinase by glucose-6-phosphate. There are many examples of such activation and inhibition, but it is as well to bear in mind that it is much easier to demonstrate the effect on the enzyme than to show that the effect is in fact important in the regulation of the metabolism of the organism.

Some interesting examples of activation and inhibition have recently been found, mainly in micro-organisms, in which the effect is thought to be produced by a change in the conformation of the enzyme induced by binding of the activator or inhibitor; binding of an activator stabilizes the conformation which has the greater activity, binding of an inhibitor has the reverse effect. Such effects are called allosteric. One such example is the allosteric inhibition of the threonine dehydratase of the bacterium *Escherichia coli* by isoleucine which is a distant end product of the reaction in which threonine undergoes dehydration deamination:

$$
\begin{array}{cccc}
CH_3 & NH_3 & CH_3 & CH_3 \\
| & \nwarrow & | & | \\
CHOH & & CH_2 & CH_2 \\
| & \xrightarrow[\text{dehydratase}]{\text{Threonine}} & | & CHCH_3 \\
CHNH_2 & & CO & | \\
| & & | & CHNH_2 \\
COOH & & COOH & | \\
& & & COOH \\
\text{Threonine} & & \alpha\text{-Oxobutyrate} & \text{Isoleucine}
\end{array}
$$

No other amino acid inhibits the dehydratase as effectively and since there is little structural resemblance between isoleucine and threonine it seems unlikely, despite the competitive nature of the inhibition, that they can be bound at the same site on the enzyme. It is more likely that there is a specific isoleucine-binding site as well as a threonine-binding site and that binding of either amino acid at its own specific site alters the conformation of the enzyme in such a way that binding of the other amino acid is impossible, so that competitive kinetics are observed. This notion is supported by the finding that both the ability to bind isoleucine and the inhibition can be destroyed by mild heating and are absent in the enzyme produced by some mutant organisms.

The inhibition of threonine dehydratase by isoleucine is an example of the general phenomenon of end product inhibition. The end product of a pathway inhibits the enzyme catalysing the first step which leads exclusively to its formation. Since the pathway involved may be long, the end product often has little structural similarity to the substrate of the enzyme catalysing the first step and in such cases the inhibition is likely to be allosteric, at least if it shows competitive kinetics. Other allosteric inhibitors however need not be direct or indirect products of the enzymes they inhibit.

It seems likely that the importance of isoenzymes may lie in the possibility they provide for the catalytic activity of different tissues to show different degrees of sensitivity to metabolites which act as activators or inhibitors.

Changes in the concentration of enzyme; induction and repression

The control of the rate of an enzymic reaction by inhibition or activation produces a rapid, fine control but the rate may also be altered more coarsely, and more slowly, by changes in the concentration of the enzyme itself.

Induction is a process in which the substrate of a reaction or a closely related compound specifically provokes an increase in the rate of synthesis of the enzyme. Repression is the converse process in which an intermediate or final product of an enzyme reaction reduces the rate of synthesis of the enzyme. The effect is to increase the rate of removal of the inducing substrate or to reduce the rate of formation of a product which is already present. In *E. coli* the formation of the threonine dehydratase discussed above is repressed by isoleucine in the growth medium. In a growing culture of cells the pre-existing enzyme is continuously diluted by division of the cells so that isoleucine not only inhibits the enzyme already present but also allows its concentration in the cells to fall. The bacterium thus not only stops synthesizing an amino acid it can obtain from the growth medium but also stops synthesizing an enzyme for which it has no current need.

Induction and repression have been studied most in bacterial systems but there are some examples in mammalian metabolism in which changes in the concentration of an enzyme seem to be important.

Zymogens

Some of the proteolytic enzymes of the digestive tract are secreted into the tract not as the active enzyme but in the form of an inactive precursor or zymogen. Thus pepsinogen is secreted into the stomach by the gastric mucosa and is activated by the acid of the stomach as well as by pepsin itself. The pancreas also secretes its major proteases or peptidases as the zymogens trypsinogen, chymotrypsinogen and procarboxypeptidase. Trypsinogen is activated by the enterokinase of the small intestine and by trypsin which also acts as the activator for chymotrypsinogen and procarboxypeptidase. All these activation reactions start when the pancreatic juice is mixed with enterokinase in the small intestine and involve selective hydrolysis of a few of the peptide bonds of the zymogens. It seems likely that the proteolytic enzymes of the pancreas are produced in an inactive form because the active enzymes would hydrolyse the proteins of the cells which form them. This would be biologically disadvantageous and does occur in acute pancreatitis. Pepsin is rapidly inactivated at pH values above 6 so that it would be rapidly destroyed at the intracellular pH and here the zymogen mechanism may be a protection for the enzyme rather than the cell.

ASSAY OF ENZYMES

The assay or measurement of the amount of an enzyme is important in experimental biochemistry. A suitable assay system is essential in any attempt at purification of an enzyme and is also important in metabolic studies where it is necessary to show that the amounts of all the enzymes involved in a proposed metabolic pathway in a tissue are sufficient to account for the observed rate of metabolic conversion. The proper assay of enzymes is also of great and growing importance in clinical practice where measurement of the amounts of particular enzymes in tissues or fluids is used as an aid in diagnosis, prognosis and control of treatment.

The isolation of an enzyme in pure state is usually a tedious process involving many different treatments in succession and the final recovery may often be less than 10 per cent of the enzyme in the starting material. Isolation and weighing of the purified enzyme would be a hopelessly impractical way of determining the amount of the enzyme in a tissue. The obvious practical way is to make use of the fact that the initial rate of the catalysed reaction is proportional to the concentration of the enzyme, other conditions being constant, and to measure initial velocities under suitably chosen conditions.

Assay conditions

The conditions to be considered are those whose effects have been discussed in the previous sections. The pH must be kept constant either by using a buffer or by continuous titration. The pH chosen is usually the optimum pH of the enzyme not only because the assay is most sensitive at this pH but also because the rate of reaction varies only slightly with small variations in pH in this region and errors are minimized.

The temperature must be kept constant with a thermostatically controlled water bath. The assay is more sensitive at higher temperatures because the reaction is faster, but a limit is set by the instability of the enzyme. Temperatures of 25°, 30° or 37°C are often employed. If the enzyme is found to be unstable at the pH and temperature first chosen it may be necessary to work at a lower temperature or even at a pH other than the optimum.

The substrate concentration should be high enough to keep the enzyme saturated during the reaction so that the rate does not decline because of removal of the substrate, but it may not be possible to achieve this condition if the substrate has a very low solubility or is merely very expensive. In such cases a declining rate of reaction is to be expected.

If the enzyme requires activators or coenzymes these should also be present in saturating concentrations, and ideally the incubation mixture should contain no inhibitors of the enzyme. This last condition may not be easily achieved in assays of enzymes in tissue extracts, and one may not even know whether inhibitors are present or not; it must be borne in mind that the activity found may be less than the maximum activity of the uninhibited enzyme.

In every enzyme assay it is necessary to carry out a suitable blank reaction using boiled or otherwise inactivated enzyme in order to be able to correct the rate found for any spontaneous or non-enzymic reaction or for any apparent reaction due only to the reagents used for analysis. The intensity of the reagent blank reaction will vary from one method of following the reaction to another; methods of following the course of the reactions have already been discussed in general terms.

Units of enzymic activity

The International Commission on Enzymes has recommended that one unit of enzyme be defined as that amount of enzyme which causes the conversion of one micromole of substrate per minute under standard conditions, usually optimum pH, 30°C and saturating concentrations of substrate, etc. With these units one can express the specific activity of an enzyme preparation as units of activity per milligram of protein or per milligram of protein nitrogen. The latter measure of the amount of protein is often used since dry protein preparations may contain high and variable proportions of water or of the salts used in their precipitation or crystallization and the nitrogen content of a dialysed protein preparation is easily determined.

If the enzyme preparation is pure and the molecular weight is determined, one can calculate the molecular activity. This is the number of moles of substrate converted per mole of enzyme per minute at optimal substrate concentration, and is related to the older, less well-defined term, turnover number, which is no longer in use. The catalytic activity of an enzyme is defined as the number of moles of substrate converted per active centre per minute at optimal substrate concentration and is thus identical with the molecular activity for enzymes having only one active centre per molecule.

For some enzymes it is not possible to express the activity in micromoles of a substrate converted because the substrate or the reaction is ill defined. This is especially so with enzymes like proteases and nucleases which attack substrates of high molecular weight and catalyse the hydrolysis of several bonds in each substrate molecule. In such cases the units of activity have to be arbitrarily defined as for example the amount of enzyme giving a specified increase in the optical absorption of the products of the reaction soluble in a suitable precipitating reagent.

FURTHER READING

DIXON M. & WEBB E.C. (1964) *Enzymes*, 2nd Edition. London: Longmans, Green.

Chapter 8
Energetics of living cells

Energy is the capacity to perform work. It may be stored or appear in different forms such as potential, kinetic, chemical, electrical, thermal and radiant energy, the basic units of which are discussed on p. 4.1.

The continued viability of living matter depends on controlled energy transformations. As described on p. 4.2, solar energy is harnessed by the photosynthetic apparatus of the green plants in which it is converted into chemical energy, first in the form of a simple carbohydrate. Plants then convert this into other molecules such as complex sugars, proteins and lipids which may then be consumed by an animal. Subsequently the energy may be utilized for mechanical, osmotic, electrical or other work in the animal organism. These animal tissues may in turn be consumed as a source of potential energy and essential nutrients by another animal or by man. The energy cycle is then completed by the oxidative sequences of reactions occurring in animal tissues in which dietary and tissue metabolites merge and the molecules are converted by various chemical transformations to substances of lower potential energy. These are carbon dioxide, water, urea, etc. and are excreted as waste products to serve in turn other living systems such as plants and bacteria. Much of the science of biochemistry is concerned with studies of the specific processes whereby animal tissues transfer energy between different molecules and store and utilize it to perform work.

The combustion of glucose in a bomb calorimeter where it is converted almost instantaneously into carbon dioxide and water with the liberation of energy as heat is described on p. 4.3. In the body at 37°C glucose is broken down slowly to the same products and some of the energy liberated can be used to do work, the remainder being dissipated as heat. On the other hand, glucose remains unchanged almost indefinitely if kept in a bottle on the laboratory bench or in the larder. Further, in green plants carbon dioxide and water can be converted into glucose by solar radiation and at the same time oxygen is given off.

Dynamic equilibrium

Consider a general reaction in which an equilibrium is reached:

$$A + B \rightleftharpoons C + D$$

According to the Law of Mass Action the rate (v) of the forward reaction is proportional to the concentrations of A and B

$$v_1 \text{ (forward)} = k_{+1}[A] \times [B]$$

similarly for the backward reaction

$$v_2 \text{ (backward)} = k_{-1}(C) \times (D)$$

At equilibrium the two rates must be the same and so,

$$K = \frac{[C] \times [D]}{[A] \times [B]}$$

K is defined as the **equilibrium constant**.

The correct expression for true or thermodynamic equilibrium involves activities rather than molar concentrations, as the velocity of a chemical reaction depends upon activities rather than the concentration of the reacting substances. In biological work it is usual to assume that solutes and solutions behave in an ideal thermodynamic fashion in which case the activities and concentrations may be taken as identical.

For reactions which proceed forwards and far to the right K is large and for reactions which do not proceed far to the right K is small. The equilibrium constant is dependent upon temperature and many reactions can be forced in the desired direction by raising or lowering the temperature. Unfortunately this device is not available to mammals who are obliged to operate at a constant temperature. The equilibrium constant K is therefore a useful measure of the degree of spontaneity of a given chemical reaction. However, a favourable equilibrium constant implies only that the reaction may proceed and is theoretically possible. There may be impediments to its progress.

Thermodynamic considerations

All energy transformations that take place in living systems obey the fundamental laws of thermodynamics which is a branch of science devoted to the study of energy exchanges. Thermodynamics is concerned with the conditions under which a reaction will proceed and with the overall energy transformations, not with the route through which this transformation occurs or the rate at which the reaction occurs.

The **first law of thermodynamics** states that the total energy within a closed system, such as the universe, remains constant. Thus, energy cannot be created or destroyed. As indicated on p. 4.1 this law implies an exact equivalence between different forms of energy such as chemical energy, kinetic energy, electrical energy and heat.

The **second law of thermodynamics** sets the limits which restrict the transformation of one type of energy into another which then may become available for useful work. This energy (G) is called free energy. The relation it bears to the total energy of a system (enthalpy H) and the energy not available for work (entropy TS) is concisely stated in the form of the equation.

$$H = G + TS$$

These terms must now be defined.

Enthalpy (H) is the sum of the total energy initially present in a system. In a biological system this is usually equivalent to the heats of combustion of the reactants. Thus it can be readily measured.

Free energy (G) of a system is that fraction of the total energy which is available for useful work. When a chemical reaction occurs the reaction proceeds with a decrease in free energy until an equilibrium point is reached. The symbol G is taken from the name of the American physical chemist Willard Gibbs.

Entropy is a measure of that part of the total energy of the system that is not available for work. Entropy is a function of the temperature (T) of the molecules involved in a particular system. The symbol S is a capacity factor expressed as calories/degree. The total entropy is obtained by multiplying it by the intensity factor T.

Entropy is related to the degree of disorder or randomness in a system. At the molecular level it reflects the probability that a particular reaction will occur. Thus in a freely reversible reaction the change in entropy is zero while in an irreversible process the entropy steadily increases. In a closed system entropy can only increase and is reduced only if a source of energy is introduced from outside.

THE CALCULATION OF FREE ENERGY CHANGES

Biochemists are concerned with the problem of whether reactions can proceed by themselves in the presence of suitable catalysts, or whether an extraneous source of energy is needed to drive them. This involves consideration of the changes in free energy involved in reactions. The changes that can occur in a system are more important than the absolute amounts of energy present. In consequence the second law is more useful if written in the following form:

$$\Delta G = \Delta H - T\,\Delta S$$

ΔG cannot be determined directly by experiment, but can be derived in the following manner. It can be shown on theoretical grounds that:

$$\Delta G^0 = -RT \log_e K$$

G^0 is the **standard free energy** when the concentrations of all the components of a reaction are molal. R is the gas constant and equals $1\cdot987$ cal/mole/deg. T is the absolute temperature and K the equilibrium constant of a reversible reaction. Hence, for reactions taking place at 37°C

$$\Delta G^0 = -1\cdot987 \times 310 \times 2\cdot3 \log_{10} K.$$

Thus for a reaction with an equilibrium constant of 1000

$$\Delta G^0 = -1\cdot987 \times 310 \times 2\cdot3 \times 3$$
$$= -43 \text{ kcal}$$

Provided the value of ΔG^0 is negative (at a fixed temperature and pressure), then the reaction theoretically can proceed of its own accord and will be energy yielding or **exergonic**. On the other hand if a reaction has a positive ΔG^0, it cannot proceed unless it is coupled to another process which provides energy. Such reactions are said to be **endergonic**. There are many examples of exergonic reactions being coupled to endergonic processes. If ΔG^0 is zero the reaction is in chemical equilibrium.

Because a reaction is capable of proceeding, it does not follow that it will necessarily take place. Petrol can be combusted and the energy used to drive a car. Yet it can remain stable indefinitely in the tank. Before combustion can begin, it has to be ignited by a spark. This provides **activation energy** which raises the total energy level sufficiently to allow combustion to take place. In the case of a

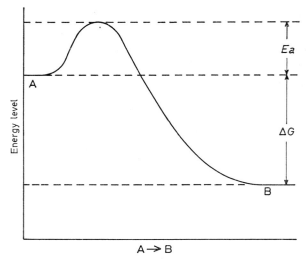

FIG. 8.1. For the conversion of A to B, energy of activation *Ea* is required. This energy is recovered and made available together with the change of free energy ΔG of the reaction.

petrol engine the activation energy is provided by the heat from the spark. In general, cells do not influence the rate of metabolic reactions by changes in temperature. Enzymes and other catalysts are able in some ways to decrease the activation energy of biological reactions sufficiently to allow them to proceed. No enzyme or catalyst, however, can cause a reaction to proceed that is not capable of taking place on energetic grounds. Fig. 8.1 illustrates diagrammatically the changes in energy level in the course of a reaction.

The immediate source of energy in cells

One of the problems is to unravel the precise mechanisms by which living tissues control the release of energy with only very small changes in temperature. In all cells there is a continuous process of repair and maintenance in which the chemical components are disassembled and resynthesized. This cellular activity requires energy and is expensive from the short term energetic standpoint. However, on a long term view it is efficient because these processes allow the entire cellular architecture to be replaced without disturbing the normal activity of the cell. The value of this system will become apparent when problems arising from cell injury are encountered.

Many cells vary their rates of metabolic activity greatly. They must be geared to the demands made upon them by other cells and tissues and this necessitates the use of energy which must be immediately available. In the case of a resting muscle called upon to contract and so do work, the energy must be available in a matter of milliseconds. The cells of the kidneys and cardiac muscle, for instance, have to adjust their metabolic rates to provide the energy necessary for the concentration of ions or for the work of the heart.

Nutrients derived from the diet provide the energy necessary for all these processes. Supplied at irregular intervals, they must be stored in suitable compounds which act as energy reserves. The main store, of course, is in the form of fat in the adipose tissue, but it takes time for this to be mobilized and transported to cells which require it. Certain organic phosphorylated compounds play a key role in this capacity and their contribution to the energetics of living tissues is now described.

'HIGH ENERGY PHOSPHATE' COMPOUNDS

Phosphoric acid is a weak inorganic tribasic acid whose function in bodily buffer systems is discussed on p. 6.5. This acid has the structure

$$HO-\overset{\overset{\displaystyle O}{\|}}{\underset{\underset{\displaystyle OH}{|}}{P}}-OH \quad \text{or} \quad H_3PO_4$$

Phosphoric acid can react with alcohols to form esters, e.g.

$$H_3PO_4 + ROH \rightleftharpoons RO\overset{\overset{\displaystyle O}{\|}}{P}(OH)_2 + H_2O$$

The acid can also react with amines,

$$H_3PO_4 + RNH_2 \rightleftharpoons RNH\overset{\overset{\displaystyle O}{\|}}{P}(OH)_2 + H_2O$$

or combine with organic acids to form mixed anhydrides, e.g.

$$H_3PO_4 + RCOOH \rightleftharpoons RCOO\overset{\overset{\displaystyle O}{\|}}{P}(OH)_2 + H_2O$$

In living tissues there is a wide range of phosphorylated compounds, including phosphorylated derivatives of carbohydrates, proteins and lipids (phospholipids), many of which have complex structures. Some of the phosphorylated derivatives are phosphate esters or phosphate anhydrides, and fig. 8.2 shows the specific groupings between the phosphate moiety and the rest of the molecule. The **free energy of hydrolysis** of most phosphate esters is low and for these ΔG^0 lies between -1 and -4 kcal/mole; α-glycerophosphate and glucose 6-phosphate are examples of this group. In a much smaller group, of which the other substances in fig. 8.2 are examples, the free energy of hydrolysis is high and ΔG^0 lies between -5 and -11 kcal/mole. This distinction, first made by Lipmann, has been modified from its original form and they are now called 'low energy phosphate' compounds or 'high energy phosphate' compounds. This is a loose, albeit convenient, terminology and refers to the actual free energy of hydrolysis of the bonds and not to a specific energy state of the compound as a whole. One example helps to illustrate this point.

$$\text{Adenosine triphosphate} \xrightarrow{\text{H}_2\text{O}}$$
$$\text{(ATP)}$$
$$\text{adenosine diphosphate} + H_3PO_4 + \text{energy}$$
$$\text{(ADP)}$$

Here ATP is hydrolysed in the presence of water and perhaps by an enzyme such as an ATPase to give rise to ADP with the release of the free energy of hydrolysis of the terminal phosphate bond. For this reaction ΔG^0 is about 8 kcal. Consider a second reaction in which ADP is hydrolysed in the presence of water to yield adenosine monophosphate (AMP) + inorganic phosphate + energy.

$$\text{ADP} \xrightarrow{\text{H}_2\text{O}} \text{AMP} + H_3PO_4 + \text{energy}$$

Again ΔG^0 for the hydrolysis of the terminal phosphate bond of ADP is comparable to that of the terminal phosphate bond of ATP and about 8 kcals. Consider now the third hydrolysis of AMP to yield adenosine + inorganic phosphate. This reaction results in a lower release of free energy of hydrolysis and consequently the bond which

CH$_2$OH

CHOH

CH$_2$—O—P=O

α-Glycerophosphate

Glucose-6-phosphate

Adenine

Adenosine triphosphate (ATP)

1,3-Diphosphoglyceric acid

Phosphoenolpyruvic acid

CH$_3$

HN=C—N—CH$_2$—COOH

Creatine phosphate

Acetyl phosphate

CH$_3$—C—O~P=O

FIG. 8.2. Phosphorylated derivatives which are phosphate esters or phosphate anhydrides.

links the sugar moiety of adenosine to the phosphoric acid moiety is a 'low energy phosphate bond' whereas, more correctly, the observation is that the bond had a low free energy of hydrolysis. The overall energy changes in the controlled hydrolysis of the phosphate moieties of ATP are as follows:

ATP $\longrightarrow$ ADP + inorganic phosphate + 8 kcal

ADP $\longrightarrow$ AMP + inorganic phosphate + 8 kcal

AMP $\longrightarrow$ adenosine + inorganic phosphate + about 3 kcal

It is customary to represent the high energy phosphate groups as $\sim$Ⓟ. Thus the structure of ATP may be expressed as A—P$\sim$Ⓟ$\sim$Ⓟ. The reasons for high levels of energy of the phosphate bonds are complex and no simple explanation is satisfactory. The high free energy of hydrolysis of the terminal phosphate group of ATP is in part due to the stabilization by resonance of one of the products of the reaction, ADP. Similar considerations apply to the conversion of ADP to AMP. In the breakdown of carbohydrates, phosphorylated derivatives are first formed at the expense of ATP. A typical example is the phosphorylation of glucose by the enzyme hexokinase to form glucose-6-phosphate (G-6-P).

It is possible to predict the direction in which such a reaction is likely to proceed by breaking it down to its component parts. As stated previously ATP is hydrolysed as follows:

$$ATP + H_2O \longrightarrow ADP + H_3PO_4 + 8 \text{ kcal}$$

G-6-P has a low free energy of hydrolysis and the reaction is:

$$G\text{-}6\text{-}P + H_2O \longrightarrow glucose + H_3PO_4 + 3 \text{ kcal}$$

Hence when glucose is phosphorylated at the expense of ATP there is a decrease in free energy so that this is a spontaneous reaction:

$$Glucose + ATP \longrightarrow G\text{-}6\text{-}P + ADP + 5 \text{ kcal}$$

Here we have an example of a low energy phosphate compound being synthesized at the expense of a high energy compound.

The above values are for the standard free energy changes (ΔG^0) and so are obtainable only under standard conditions where the concentrations of the reactants are Molal. As a rule reactants are not at this concentration and hence changes are usually expressed as ΔG values and related to ΔG^0 by the equation:

$$\Delta G = \Delta G^0 + RT \log_e \frac{(\text{products})}{(\text{reactants})}$$

It is important to note this effect of concentration on ΔG because where the ΔG in a reaction is small, the direction of the reaction can be affected by the change in the concentration of one or other of the reactants. This is demonstrated by the reactions which lead to the storage of high energy phosphate bonds in compounds like creatine phosphate as follows:

$$\text{ATP} + \text{creatine} \rightleftharpoons \text{ADP} + \text{creatine phosphate}$$

This reaction has a ΔG^0 which is positive, although small and about 2 kcal. However, it is possible for the reaction to proceed in the direction of creatine phosphate in spite of this by increasing the concentration of ATP. This is the situation in the living cell where for reasons not understood the intracellular concentrations of ATP and ADP are kept low, usually about 10^{-3} M. As ATP is essential to the economy of the cell, a ready source must be available. When reactions in the cell generate ATP and other high energy phosphate compounds, any excess of high energy phosphates is thus stored as creatine phosphate. If a demand for ATP arises, the creatine phosphate reacts with the ADP to give ATP and creatine. Thus, although ΔG^0 of the above reaction is small and positive, the manipulation of the concentrations of the ADP and ATP in the cell makes it possible to drive the reaction in the forward or backward direction depending upon whether there is a need to restore the ATP levels or to increase the energy reserve of creatine phosphate.

In certain instances phosphorylated intermediate products of metabolism may be modified by further enzymic action which changes the structure of the bond linking the organic moiety to the phosphate moiety. For example, in the oxidation of an alcoholic phospho-ester to a carboxylic acid phosphate anhydride, a phosphate ester bond with a low free energy of hydrolysis is transformed into a phospho-anhydride bond with a high free energy of hydrolysis. This is a reaction in which electrons are withdrawn from the molecule.

$$\text{RCH}_2\text{CH}_2\text{O}\textcircled{P} \longrightarrow \text{RCH}_2\text{COO} \sim \textcircled{P} + 4\,e$$

In the chemical laboratory, an alcohol is converted into a carboxylic acid by heating with acidified dichromate:

$$\text{CH}_3\text{CH}_2\text{OH} \longrightarrow \text{CH}_3\text{CHO} \longrightarrow \text{CH}_3\text{COOH}$$

This is a spontaneous reaction and the free energy associated with the conversion is dissipated as heat. However, in the animal organism the oxidation of such an alcohol into a carboxylic acid results in much of the energy of the reaction being trapped in high energy phosphate compounds. Subsequently this energy may either be utilized or transferred to a store by a suitable controlled exchange reaction.

Many of the key mechanisms which link oxidative reactions with the regeneration of ATP from ADP + inorganic phosphate occur in subcellular particles called mitochondria (p. 13.7). These are extremely active in cell respiration. The resultant oxidation reactions are the principal energy yielding reactions in the cell, and much effort has been exerted towards elucidating the links between oxidation and high energy phosphate bond formation.

Oxidation

Oxidation is defined as a reaction involving loss of electrons and conversely reduction is a reaction in which electrons are gained. The oxidation of a substance may therefore be written:

$$A \longrightarrow A^+ + 1\,e^-$$

Clearly there must be provision for some suitable electron acceptor. In general, oxidation reactions are coupled to reduction reactions and electrons flow from the substance which is undergoing oxidation to the substance which is undergoing reduction.

$$A + B \rightleftharpoons A^+ + B^-$$

It is also characteristic of biological oxidations that they are often linked together to form a chain along which the electrons flow. Further stages in the above reaction might be:

$$B^- + C \rightleftharpoons B + C^-$$

$$C^- + D \rightleftharpoons C + D^-$$

The net result of such a chain of reactions would be:

$$A + D \longrightarrow A^+ + D^-$$

In biological systems a common oxidizing agent is molecular oxygen which accepts either two or four electrons as follows:

$$O_2 \xrightarrow{+2e^-} O_2^= \xrightarrow{+2e^-} 2O^=$$

These reactions ultimately lead to the conversion of molecular oxygen into metabolic water since

$$2O^= + 4H^+ \longrightarrow 2H_2O$$

It is a simple matter to calculate the volume of water produced per day (metabolic water) by an individual at rest, given that the oxygen consumption is about 250 ml/min and about one-half of the oxygen is used as an electron acceptor.

RESPIRATORY COENZYMES

An important group of substances, respiratory coenzymes, act as intermediary links in such a chain of oxidations and these are now described. They serve as intermediates in the chain of events between the initial stage of the oxidation of a substrate in a cell and the final stage of oxidation which is the formation of water by molecular oxidation. A brief account of their role as coenzymes or prosthetic groups is given on p. 7.12. Before describing in more detail their modes of action in the cell, their chemical structures are discussed.

Pyridine nucleotides
Two electron acceptors widely distributed in the cells are **nicotinamide-adenine dinucleotide (NAD)** and **nicotinamide-adenine dinucleotide phosphate (NADP)**. The structure of NAD is:

Nicotinamide-adenine dinucleotide (NAD)

NADP has the same structure as NAD with the addition of a phosphate on position 2′ of the ribose portion of the molecule.

The business part of the molecules is the pyridine ring of nicotinamide. A substrate provides the oxidized form with two electrons, in this instance accompanied by $2H^+$, i.e. $2H^+ + 2e = 2(H)$. The pyridine ring takes up two electrons and one proton and the other proton is set free in the medium.

In the reverse direction $NADH_2$ gives up two electrons and one H^+.

The reaction can be followed easily because there are big differences between the ultra-violet absorption spectra of NAD and $NADH_2$. Changes in the concentrations of the two forms are measured by determining the optical density of a solution at 340 nm.

Flavoproteins
Flavine-adenine dinucleotide (FAD) is a derivative of adenosine and the vitamin riboflavine with the following structure:

Flavine-adenine dinucleotide (FAD)

FAD can take up to two electrons and two H^+ (two hydrogen atoms) on two nitrogen atoms in the *iso*alloxazine ring of riboflavine to form $FADH_2$ as follows:

Flavine mononucleotide (FMN), which is a phosphate of riboflavine, also takes up to two electrons and two H^+ in a similar manner, to form $FMNH_2$.

Both these substances act as prosthetic groups to a variety of proteins to form flavoproteins (Fp). Fp are enzymes for a variety of reactions involving oxidation and reduction. As they are for the most part yellow and highly coloured, the course of such reactions is readily followed.

The electron transporting quinones

These are present in most cells and an example is the **ubiquinones** which have the general formula below with n varying from 6 to 10 in different species.

$$CH_3O-\underset{O}{\overset{O}{\diamond}}-CH_3 \qquad \overset{CH_3}{\underset{|}{}}$$
$$CH_3O-\diamond-(CH_2-CH=C-CH_2)_nH$$

Ubiquinones accept one or two electrons to form stable semiquinones on reduction.

Vitamin K (p. 10.9) may also act as an electron carrier but the quantitative significance of this in the tissues is uncertain.

Cytochromes

These are respiratory pigments found in all cells. Each molecule contains one atom of iron in a porphyrin structure, bound to protein as a prosthetic group. One of the most common, cytochrome c, has a molecular weight of about 12,500 and its structure is represented as follows:

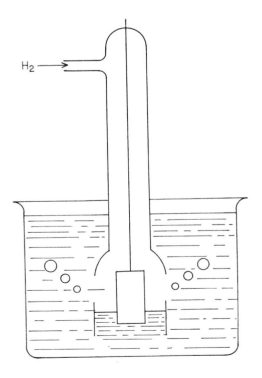

Porphyrin

$$M = CH_3 \qquad P = CH_2CH_2COOH$$

Cytochrome c

The vinyl groups ($-CH=CH_2$) in the porphyrin component are reduced and linked to cysteine residues of the protein by thioester bonds. The iron atom is associated with the resonating porphyrin structure and linked to amino acids in the protein. Such a structure is called a metallic ligand.

The cytochromes, of which there are many, are readily reduced and oxidized by the transfer of electrons from the iron ligand

$$\underset{reduced}{Fe^2} \rightleftharpoons \underset{oxidized}{Fe^3} + e^-$$

In this way they act in the chain of electron transfers in the cells. Cytochrome a_3 transfers its electrons to oxygen with the formation of metabolic water (p. 8.5). In this manner it forms the final stage in a chain of oxidative processes.

The cytochromes were observed as long ago as 1885 by means of their characteristic absorption spectra. Keilin in Cambridge was the pioneer in using these to identify and name the different cytochromes. Nowadays, absorption spectroscopy provides a ready means of determining changes in the amounts of the reduced and oxidized forms of the various cytochromes in the tissues.

OXIDATION REDUCTION POTENTIALS

The questions now arise of the order in which the links are arranged in an oxidative chain, how the substrate is related to the chain and the circumstances which allow electrons to flow down it.

In oxidation reduction studies the hydrogen electrode (fig. 8.3) is used as the reference system. It consists of a cell in which hydrogen gas at 1 atmosphere pressure is bubbled over a platinum black electrode which is partly

Fig. 8.3 Diagram of the hydrogen electrode.

immersed in a solution of hydrogen ions whose activity is unity. In actual practice this corresponds to an aqueous solution of hydrochloric acid about $1 \cdot 18$ N. The overall reaction is therefore that two hydrogen ions plus two electrons give rise to hydrogen gas.

$$2H^+ + 2e^- \underset{Pt}{\overset{Pt}{\rightleftharpoons}} H_2 \text{ gas}$$

Oxidation reduction (redox) systems can be directly or indirectly compared with this reference electrode. Since the ease with which an electron leaves one molecular species differs from the ease with which an electron leaves another, it is possible to compare the redox potential of pairs of molecules or ions, provided they can undergo an electron transfer reaction. Thus the oxidized over the reduced forms of a number of inorganic or organic molecules can be compared, e.g. Fe^{+++}/Fe^{++}, $NAD/NADH_2$, pyruvate/lactate and $2H^+/H_2$. In each case the oxidized form can be transformed into the reduced form by the addition of one or two electrons. While in some cases H^+ are also involved, their role is passive and they interfere little with the overall energetics. The oxidation–reduction equations involving the transference of electrons can be treated as normal chemical reactions:

$$\begin{array}{cccc} X & + \quad Y & \rightleftharpoons & X^+ & + \quad Y^- \\ \text{(reductant)} & \text{(oxidant)} & & \text{(oxidant)} & \text{(reductant)} \end{array}$$

The equilibrium constant (K) will be

$$K = \frac{[X^+][Y^-]}{[X]\ [Y]}$$

It is possible to treat this reaction as two dependent functions, namely the loss of an electron by X to yield X^+ and the gain of this electron by Y to yield Y^-. The actual value of K is then dependent on the relative affinities of X and Y for the electron. By means of the hydrogen electrode and suitable equipment it is possible to set up 'half cells' to establish the relative affinities of different systems for electrons.

In this way the $2H^+/H_2$ system can be connected to the Fe^{+++}/Fe^{++} system or to the $NAD/NADH_2$ system or to any other redox couple. Such observations make it possible to arrange redox systems in an electrochemical order and those with a more positive electrode potential value are capable of oxidizing a less positive system. Thus the flavoproteins (Fp) can oxidize $NADH_2$ since they have a more positive electrode potential value than the $NAD/NADH_2$ system. Naturally in order to standardize the electrode potentials it is necessary to specify the concentration of the reactants in the general equation:

$$\text{Oxidant} \rightleftharpoons \text{reductant} + \text{electron(s)}$$

The usual conditions are that the oxidant and reductant are both Molal. Hence the electrode potentials are compared under standardized physical conditions and in an aqueous solution where the concentrations of the reductants and oxidants are equal. As most biological redox systems are measured at pH $7 \cdot 0$, standard potentials (E'_0) are quoted in comparison with the hydrogen reference electrode at this pH. This has a value E'_0 of $-0 \cdot 42$ of a volt with reference to the hydrogen electrode at pH 0. Consequently by means of tables of standard redox potentials it is possible to predict the tendency for electrons to pass from one system to another. Table 8.1 sets out a selection of redox potentials of biological

TABLE 8.1. Redox potentials E'_0 in aqueous solution at pH $7 \cdot 0$

Respiratory coenzymes	E'_0
O_2/H_2O	$+0 \cdot 82$
Cytochrome a	$+0 \cdot 29$
Cytochrome c	$+0 \cdot 23$
Ubiquinone (CoQ)	$+0 \cdot 10$
Cytochrome b	$-0 \cdot 04$
Flavoproteins (Fp)	$-0 \cdot 06$
FAD	$-0 \cdot 20$
NAD (or NADP)	$-0 \cdot 32$
H^+/H	$-0 \cdot 42$
Other redox systems	
Ascorbic/Dehydroascorbic acid	$+0 \cdot 08$
Fumarate/Succinate	$0 \cdot 00$
Pyruvate/Lactate	$-0 \cdot 18$
Pyruvate/Malate	$-0 \cdot 33$
GSSG/GSH (Glutathione)	$-0 \cdot 34$
α Oxoglutarate/Succinate	$-0 \cdot 67$

interest. The upper part shows the values for the important respiratory coenzymes and these lie between $+0 \cdot 82$ volts for molecular oxygen and $-0 \cdot 42$ volts for the hydrogen electrode. The lower part contains E_0 values for six important biochemical reactions and also for ascorbic acid and glutathione. These two substances which are readily oxidized are both widespread in the tissues, but their functional role is still largely unknown. From table 8.1 it would therefore be predicted that a redox coupled system such as $NAD/NADH_2$ ($E'_0 - 0 \cdot 32$ volts) would be capable of reducing a flavoprotein to the corresponding reduced flavoprotein. Similarly one might predict that flavoproteins could in turn reduce the succinate-fumarate system. However, because a system has a redox potential which is more negative than some other system, this does not imply that the reduction reaction necessarily occurs. It only indicates that, other considerations being favourable, the system moves in the direction of the more positive E'_0.

The energetics of redox reactions

Redox potentials are valuable physical constants because they are precisely related to free energy changes. It will be apparent that the energy available as a consequence of the electron moving from a more negative system to a more positive system and ultimately to oxygen can be made available for useful work.

Redox potentials allow us to calculate the free energy change, since when one or more electrons move from a donor redox system to an acceptor redox system ΔG is directly related to (E) the difference in redox potential.

If E_1 is the standard redox potential of system A the donor and E_2 is the standard redox potential of system B the acceptor then

$$E_1 - E_2 = \Delta E$$

It can be shown that $\Delta G^0 = -nF \Delta E_0$ where n is the number of electrons transferred and F is the charge/mole $= 96,500$ coulombs $= 23 \cdot 07$ kcal.

In redox systems it is desirable to separate the donor and acceptor systems and consider the overall reaction as being composed of two 'half cells'.
Thus if

$$K = \frac{\text{oxidized}}{\text{reduced}}$$

then

$$\Delta G^\circ = -RT \log_e K = -RT \log_e \frac{\text{oxidized}}{\text{reduced}}$$

$$\Delta G^\circ = -nF \Delta E = -RT \log_e \frac{\text{oxidized}}{\text{reduced}}$$

$$\Delta E = \frac{RT}{nF} \log_e \frac{\text{oxidized}}{\text{reduced}}$$

For example in the oxidation of lactic acid to pyruvic acid we have the following reaction:

$$\text{lactic acid} + \text{NAD} \rightleftharpoons \text{pyruvic acid} + \text{NADH}_2$$

The free energy of a redox system in terms of the electrical energy available for useful work can be measured in terms of the number of electrons involved in the movement and the relative electrode potentials of the two systems involved, that is the electrode potential of the donor system and the electrode potential of the acceptor system. Thus in the former reaction the equilibrium constant K for the reaction is given as follows:

$$K = \frac{[\text{pyruvate}][\text{NADH}_2]}{[\text{lactate}] \quad [\text{NAD}]}$$

The actual value of the change in free energy in this reaction is given by the equation which was derived previously:

$$n\Delta G^\circ = -RT \log_e K$$

It is therefore easy to deduce that the change in free energy in a redox system is related to the change in the standard potential of the oxidized system compared to the standard potential of the reduced system. Thus the

5

general equation for the change in free energy in a redox system is given by

$$\Delta G^0 = -nF\Delta E$$

Mitochondria and cellular energetics

Fractionation procedures permit the separation of cellular components into nuclei, mitochondria, lysosomes, endoplasmic reticulum and cell sap (p. 13.7). Of these subcellular particles the mitochondria have the highest rate of oxygen uptake *in vitro*. Mitochondria are bounded by sensitive membranes which are easily distorted by a wide range of physiological agents including magnesium ions, thyroxine and glutathione. This leads to swelling or shrinkage of the particles and the rate of respiration of mitochondria is influenced by these changes and also by other factors such as the availability of oxygen, inorganic phosphate (P_i) and ADP. Mitochondria have a large range of enzymes and coenzymes of the redox system. These include dehydrogenases which have NAD as a coenzyme, flavoproteins and the various cytochromes.

When mitochondria are incubated with certain oxidizable substrates in the presence of ADP and P_i there is a decrease in the concentration of ADP and P_i associated with the uptake of oxygen and the appearance of ATP. Thus the overall equation for a reaction can be represented as follows:

$$O_2 + 2XH_2 + P_i + ADP \longrightarrow ATP + 2H_2O + 2X$$

This process is called **oxidative phosphorylation**.

By a combination of sophisticated absorption spectroscopic methods, coupled to selective respiratory inhibitors, it is possible to elucidate the individual steps in the oxidation of a substrate. Thus when a compound is oxidized using NAD as the electron acceptor $NADH_2$ is formed. This redox system has an extremely negative electrode potential (E_0 $-0 \cdot 32$). As there is only a limited amount of NAD in the mitochondria it is important that the $NADH_2$ should be re-oxidized to NAD. This can be achieved by coupling the $NAD/NADH_2$ system to a suitable redox couple with a less negative electrode potential. Such a system is provided by the mitochondrial flavoproteins (E $-0 \cdot 06$). Thus when two electrons move from $NADH_2$ to a flavoprotein the change in electrode potential will be

$$E_1 - E_2 = -0 \cdot 32 - (-0 \cdot 06) = -0 \cdot 26 \text{ v}$$
$$\Delta G^0 = nF \Delta E$$
$$= 2 \times 23 \cdot 07 \times 0 \cdot 26$$
$$= \text{about 12 kcal}$$

This change in potential is associated with the generation of one high energy phosphate bond.

Similarly there is only a limited amount of flavoprotein in the mitochondria and hence, when the flavoprotein is in the reduced state, a suitable electron acceptor is needed

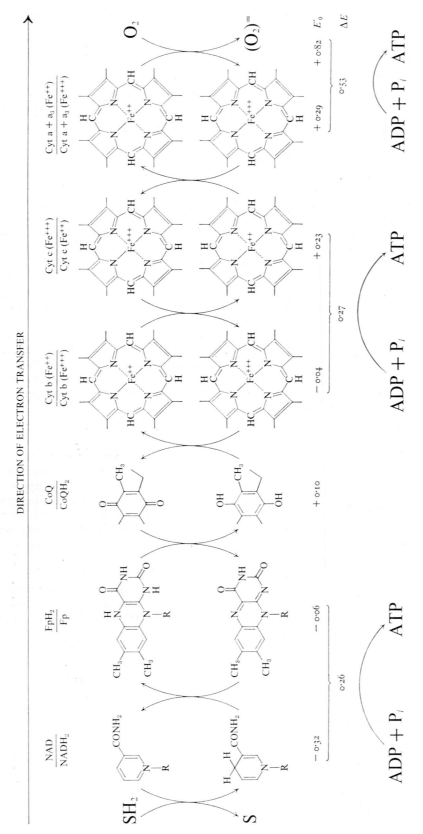

FIG. 8.4. A typical reconstruction of the events in the respiratory chain. SH_2 is the substrate undergoing oxidation. The redox potentials and the possible energy trapping sites are shown. The apparently anomalous position of CoQ in relation to its redox potential is explicable on its higher concentration. There is also doubt regarding the position of CoQ in the main electron transfer line. The cytochromes have similar prosthetic groups but different protein moieties. The enzymes involved in electron transport are arranged in sequences in macromolecular complexes in the cristae of the mitochondria. Each respiratory enzyme sequence as shown above may be about 18nm in length.

to bring about the re-oxidation of the flavoprotein. For this purpose cytochrome c ($E+0\cdot26$) is available. In this case ΔE will be $-0\cdot06 - 0\cdot26 = -0\cdot32$. From this ΔG can be calculated and is about 15 kcal. Again, this ΔE is the force behind the generation of another high energy phosphate bond.

There are also present in mitochondria other cytochromes which can bridge the gap between cytochrome c ($E+0\cdot23$) volt and the electrode potential of the $O_2/2O^=$ ($E+0\cdot82$) volt. If finally the electrons were moved from cytochrome c directly to molecular oxygen, which serves as the electron sink, ΔE would be $0\cdot59$ and ΔG equivalent to about 27 kcal (fig. 8.4).

By a combination of precise methods for the determination of electrode potentials of different redox couples and for the measurement of metabolic changes in intact mitochondria, it has been shown that mitochondria respiring in the presence of substrates known to employ NAD as an electron acceptor generate about three ATP molecules from three ADP molecules for each atom of oxygen consumed. This is frequently referred to as a P/O ratio of 3. Applying the concept of energetics, as the electrode potential of the $NADH_2/NAD$ system is $-0\cdot32$ and that of oxygen is $+0\cdot82$, ΔE is $1\cdot14$ and ΔG about 52 kcal. This is the maximum energy available from the system and as the mitochondrial particles appear capable of producing three phosphate bonds of high free energy of hydrolysis, each with a ΔG of about 8 kcal, per two electrons transported through the chain, the efficiency of the process is probably of the order of $(3 \times 8)/52$ or about 50 per cent.

The mechanism by which these phosphorylations are coupled to the oxidation of coenzymes and prosthetic groups is not known. It is, however, certain that a phosphorylated form of the hydrogen or electron carriers is not involved in ATP synthesis. A simple model system which is consistent with most of the known facts is shown below:

$$AH_2 + B + I \rightleftharpoons A \sim I + BH_2$$

$$A \sim I + X \rightleftharpoons A + X \sim I$$

$$X \sim I + P_1 \rightleftharpoons X \sim P + I$$

$$X \sim P + ADP \rightleftharpoons X + ATP$$

AH_2 and B represent components of the electron transport chain. I and X have not yet been identified, but may be active centres on the appropriate enzyme molecules, rather than independent compounds of small molecular weight. Indirect evidence for the existence of $X \sim I$ and

$X \sim P$ has been obtained, in the sense that mitochondria which have been 'loaded' with oxidizable substrate can carry out a strictly limited amount of chemical work in the absence of ADP and ATP. It has proved unexpectedly difficult to elucidate the mechanism of oxidative phosphorylation, possibly because the system is effective only when the proteins catalysing the reactions are built into the native mitochondrial membrane structure, and this cannot easily be investigated chemically.

The four reactions above have all been shown as reversible (with double arrows $\rightleftharpoons$) because in certain circumstances it is possible to reverse the direction of electron flow, e.g. to reduce NAD with a donor of more positive redox potential, using ATP to overcome the energy barrier. It is doubtful whether this has any physiological significance in animals, but the reduction of NADP by H atoms from water, using energy from sunlight, is an important part of the process of CO_2 fixation in photosynthesis by plants.

Some physiological and pharmacological agents interfere *in vitro* with the efficiency of oxidative phosphorylation. Thyroxine, free fatty acids, dicoumarol, dinitrophenol and some antibiotics can all decrease the P/O ratio in mitochondrial preparations. This separation of oxidation from phosphorylation is termed **uncoupling.**

The entire concept of the respiratory chain and oxidative phosphorylation has slowly evolved over a number of years. Much of the information has had to be derived by indirect methods and the application of physicochemical logic to biological experimentation. The account of electron transporting enzymes and coenzymes given here is not intended to be exhaustive because apart from the substances discussed in this chapter there are many other redox couples present in mitochondria, such as ubiquinone and proteins in which there is a non-haem iron prosthetic group. As yet we do not understand the mechanism by which the energy associated with the transference of an electron or electrons from a donor system to an acceptor system can be coupled to the generation of certain specific phosphate bonds. Nevertheless such events do occur and it is for the future to elucidate the chemical and biochemical mechanism of oxidative phosphorylation.

FURTHER READING

LEHNINGER A.L. (1965) *Bioenergetics*. New York: Benjamin.

Chapter 9
Carbohydrate metabolism

D-Glucose is probably the most abundant organic chemical on earth, surpassing in quantity even the vast masses of paraffin hydrocarbons which are known to be hidden beneath the earth's crust. Glucose can be made from the simplest chemicals, water and carbon dioxide, using only the energy of sunlight, and it can act as the sole source of carbon for a vast number of living organisms. Even in man glucose need be supplemented by only a very few chemicals, including, of course, amino acids as a source of nitrogen, for it to be able to support life indefinitely. It is clear, therefore, that knowledge of the pathways of metabolism open to glucose and its derivatives is important in the study of human biology.

When the word 'glucose' is used it must be remembered that free glucose occurs only rarely and it is polymers of glucose, mostly of high molecular weight, which are so abundant. For better or worse, the most abundant of all these polymers, cellulose, cannot be utilized directly by vertebrates, which can metabolize only the partial breakdown products provided by symbiotic bacteria. This symbiosis is most highly developed in ruminants, e.g. cattle or sheep, and hardly exists at all in man. Empirical recognition of these facts by our forefathers led first to organized herding of ruminants and later to the intensive production of the glucose polymer which can be digested by man, i.e. starch, in cereal agriculture.

CHEMISTRY OF CARBOHYDRATES

Narrowly defined, carbohydrates are chemicals of the composition $(CH_2O)_n$, where n is usually greater than 3. The presence of so many oxygen atoms in the molecule, together with the strict tetravalency of carbon, imposes stringent limitations on the structural possibilities. The word carbohydrate is now taken to mean not only this type of organic compound but also carbohydrate derivatives, and di- and polysaccharides, whose empirical formulae depart somewhat from the basic pattern.

The formula $(CH_2O)_n$ implies a linear array of carbon atoms, one of which must carry a carbonyl group (aldehyde or ketone), and all the rest must carry an alcohol (−OH) group. The simplest such compound is glyoxal, but **glyceraldehyde**

$$
\begin{array}{ll}
1 & CHO \\
& | \\
2 & CHOH \\
& | \\
3 & CH_2OH
\end{array}
$$

is usually taken to be the parent compound, because it is the simplest carbohydrate to show stereoisomerism which is explained on p. 9.4; all optically active carbohydrates are named with reference to L- or D-glyceraldehyde. The most common carbohydrates, the **monosaccharides**, have five or six carbon atoms and are called pentoses and hexoses, and their carbon atoms are numbered from the aldehyde or ketone end.

The presence of so many hydroxyl groups makes the molecule **polar**, which means in effect that carbohydrates are chemically reactive, notably soluble in water and insoluble in non-polar or fat solvents. This is not true, however, of cellulose. Carbohydrates and related sugar alcohols are also, as a class, sweet to the taste; this is even true of glycerol.

The main chemical reactions of carbohydrates which occur in the body depend on the carbonyl and the alcohol groups. These reactions are acetal formation, oxidation-reduction and esterification.

ACETALS AND HEMI-ACETAL FORMATION

Many of the properties of aldehydes and ketones are better understood if the carbonyl form is written in the hydrated form as it largely exists in aqueous solution:

$$
\begin{array}{c}
R \\
\diagdown \\
\quad CO + H_2O \rightleftharpoons \\
\diagup \\
R_1 \\
\mathrm{I}
\end{array}
\qquad
\begin{array}{c}
R \qquad OH \\
\diagdown \diagup \\
C \\
\diagup \diagdown \\
R_1 \qquad OH \\
\mathrm{II}
\end{array}
$$

Acetal formation can then be regarded as a reaction of

molecule II with one or more alcohols with the elimination of water:

Hemi-acetal

Acetal

Hemi-acetals are sufficiently unstable to form and break up spontaneously, especially in aqueous solution; acetals are more stable, although easily hydrolysed by acid.

The importance of this in sugar chemistry is that the alcohols R_2—OH and R_3—OH can be hydroxyl groups in the same molecule, or in similar molecules. Thus the aldehyde group of D-glucose can form a hemi-acetal with the —OH on either C-4 or C-5 of its own chain:

D-Glucose

The dotted lines joining C-1 with the new —OH indicate the existence of two stereoisomers, denoted as α- and β-D-glucose. The three compounds in the diagram form and reform spontaneously in a solution of glucose, a phenomenon known as **mutarotation.**

The hemi-acetal ring forms of the sugars can clearly react with a second alcohol. While this can be of almost any type, the most interesting acetals are those in which the second hydroxyl belongs to another monosaccharide giving, for example, the **disaccharide** maltose:

Since the second sugar molecule in this example still has a free carbonyl group, it can also form an acetal, and so long chains or **polysaccharides** can be built up. The —OH-donating monosaccharide used need not be identical with the hemi-acetal, so that non-symmetrical disaccharides, such as lactose, or polysaccharides with repeating patterns, such as in the **mucopolysaccharides,** may be built up.

The acetals, whether polysaccharide or not, are called **glycosides**, and energy is necessary for their formation; an interesting point in carbohydrate metabolism is the method by which the reactants are activated in nature. They are stable once formed, unless attacked by acids or enzymes. In particular, both the pyranose or furanose configuration of the hemi-acetal ring, and the α- or β-configuration of the hydroxyl, are frozen until the glycoside bond is destroyed.

OXIDATION AND REDUCTION

In sugars containing an aldehyde group (aldoses), the aldehyde can easily be oxidized to the corresponding carboxylic acid and somewhat less readily reduced to the alcohol. In ketoses, the ketone cannot be oxidized without breaking the carbon chain, but it can be reduced just like an aldose. The **sugar alcohols** do not occur widely in nature, and are not readily metabolized in man. For this reason they can be used as sweetening agents for diabetic patients, who should not eat sugar in excess. Fructose and glucose both give the same alcohol, **sorbitol.**

Aldoses can also be oxidized at the primary alcohol group to the corresponding **-uronic acids** by gentle oxidizing agents, e.g. hypoiodite. This test distinguishes

D-Glucose   D-Glucose   Maltose

between aldoses and ketoses. The formation of uronic acids is important and **glucuronic acid** $COOH(CHOH)_4$-CHO is widely distributed in the body (p. 16.7). The

D-Sorbitol

usual oxidizing agents used in the laboratory, e.g. hot alkaline copper solutions, oxidize both aldoses and ketoses with break-up of the molecule.

ESTER FORMATION

Any of the primary or secondary alcohol groups of a monosaccharide or polysaccharide can be esterified by reaction with an acid. The most common biological esters are those of phosphoric and sulphuric acids.

Both sulphuric and phosphoric acids are polybasic. It follows that the mono-esters are acids, and also that the possibility of di-ester formation exists. The phosphoric acid di-esters are widely distributed in nature, and are important, e.g. cyclic adenosine monophosphate, the dinucleotides, and the polynucleotides or nucleic acids.

Sulphate di-esters are not known, but the acidity of the sulphate-containing mucopolysaccharides gives them considerable solubility in water, while on the other hand their calcium salts may have a rigid structure which is important in explaining the physical properties of bone.

Some important mono- and polysaccharides
As already explained, there are two trioses; D- and L-glyceraldehyde. The occurrence of stereoisomerism means that there are four tetroses, eight pentoses and sixteen hexoses in the aldose series and eight ketohexoses. Most of these occur in traces in nature; three hexoses, two pentoses and three disaccharides of importance are:

D-Glucose

D-Galactose

D-Fructose

D-Ribose

D-Deoxyribose

α-Maltose
(α-D-glucosyl-1,4-D-glucose)

α-Lactose
(β-D-galactosyl-1,4-D-glucose)

Sucrose
(α-D-glucosyl-β-D-fructoside)

Starch has two components, amylopectin, whose structure is like that of glycogen but is less highly branched, and amylose, which is a straight-chain polymer of α-1,4-glucosyl residues. **Cellulose** is a straight-chain polymer of β-1,4-glucosyl residues. **Acid polysaccharides** containing either sulphate esters or uronic acids are discussed on p. 16.7 and **glycogen** on p. 9.8.

Ascorbic acid, the antiscorbutic vitamin is a hexose derivative:

$$
\begin{array}{l}
\text{CO} \longrightarrow \\
\text{HO} \!-\! \text{C} \quad\;\; \\
\quad\;\; \| \qquad \text{O} \\
\text{HO} \!-\! \text{C} \quad\;\; \\
\quad\;\; | \\
\text{HC} \longrightarrow \\
\quad | \\
\text{HO} \!-\! \text{CH} \\
\quad\;\; | \\
\text{CH}_2\text{OH}
\end{array}
$$

It is the lactone of a uronic acid, and is strongly acidic, because the proton of the —OH on C-2 dissociates readily. The **enediol** grouping can be oxidized by very mild oxidizing agents:

$$
\begin{array}{ccc}
\text{HO} \!-\! \text{C} & & \text{O} \!=\! \text{C} \\
\quad\; \| & \rightleftharpoons & \quad\; \| \\
\text{HO} \!-\! \text{C} & & \text{O} \!=\! \text{C}
\end{array}
$$

and the product, **dehydroascorbic acid**, retains antiscorbutic activity. With more vigorous oxidation, however, the molecule splits up into oxalic acid and other products. Even dissolved O_2 in aqueous solution does this, and the process is greatly accelerated by traces of copper ions, alkaline pH, sunlight and heat. Solutions of ascorbic acid can to some extent be stabilized by strong acids, but the crystalline solid is stable indefinitely in the dark. It is very soluble in water. Although ascorbic acid is made biologically from D-glucose, the active form is the L-isomer.

Stereoisomerism

The electron orbitals (valency bonds) of individual atoms are orientated in three-dimensional space. The four single bonds of carbon are directed towards the apices of a regular tetrahedron, if the nucleus is imagined to be at the centre of the polygon. It follows that if the four bonds of a single carbon atom are united with four different atoms or groups, two arrangements are possible which are not identical, and therefore two different isomers of the compound exist.

The situation is sometimes described by saying that the mirror image of one isomer is not identical with the isomer itself. What this means can be seen in fig. 9.1.

If the forms in the diagram are regarded as tetrahedra

(a) Two isomers

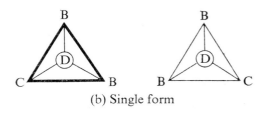

(b) Single form

FIG. 9.1. Stereoisomers.

with their bases resting on the paper, and their apices projecting upwards, so that the radical 'D' is in each case pointing towards the reader's face, it will be appreciated that the right hand tetrahedron in both instances is the mirror image of the left. In the upper part of the figure the right hand tetrahedron cannot be superimposed on the left, e.g. by twisting it round; the only way in which A can be superimposed on A, B on B, and C on C, is by inverting one tetrahedron, and then, of course, it is impossible to superimpose D on D. In the lower part of the figure, the right-hand tetrahedron can be imposed on the left by rotating it 120° clockwise. This is to say that there are two isomers of the compound (ABCD) but only one of the compound (BBCD).

In a molecule containing more than one carbon atom, each may be asymmetric, and the number of possible isomers is then 2^n. There are 2^4, or 16, isomers of a hexose and 2^5 or 32 if it is in the hemi-acetal form. The physical differences between the isomers are very small, if there is only one asymmetric atom, but with several, real differences begin to appear. For example, there are noticeable differences between the hexoses in chemical reactivity, solubility and sweetness.

The most remarkable differences between stereoisomers are, however, in their biological activity and in optical properties. All stereoisomers, unless they are internally compensated, rotate the plane of polarized light. There is no satisfactory explanation of this phenomenon. However a ray of light may be thought of as a bundle of wave forms, each vibrating in a different fixed plane stretching between the light source and the receptor. If the ray passes through certain crystals which have non-symmetrical lattices, only wave forms vibrating in certain preferred planes may be let through, the rest of the beam being absorbed. The emergent light beam is said to be **plane polarized**. If it passes through a second similar crystal, all the remaining light is absorbed unless the orientation of the lattice of the second crystal in space is identical with that of the first. This is the principle of the polarimeter.

Optically active substances, i.e. those containing an asymmetric carbon atom, rotate the plane of polarized light to an extent dependent on the substance, its concentration in solution, and the length of the light path. The rotation may be to the right (dextrorotatory) or to the left (laevorotatory) when viewed along the light path. The extent of the rotation may be measured by observing how much the second of a pair of polarizing crystals must be rotated to let the beam of light through again, after the stereoisomer has been introduced into the light path.

Stereoisomerism would be of academic interest were it not that the great majority of biological processes make use of only one of a pair of stereoisomers. All but one of the amino acids are optically active and naturally occurring proteins are constructed only from L-amino acids. It is in fact impossible to construct a helical protein from random mixtures of L- and D-amino acids. Moreover the great majority of enzymes accept only one of the possible stereoisomers of a compound as a substrate (p. 7.3).

Furthermore even certain coenzymes exhibit stereoisomerism. C-4 of NAD or NADP accepts 1 e and 1 H^+ and then contains 2 H atoms which project on opposite sides of the pyridine ring. Thus these 2 H atoms at C-4 are not equivalent. Certain enzymes selectively remove an $H^+ + e$ from one face of the reduced coenzyme. When the reduced coenzyme structure is written with the —$CONH_2$ to the right hand side of the formula the plane facing the reader is termed A and the hydrogen atom sticking out of this plane towards the reader at C-4 is termed H_A. The other hydrogen atom is then H_B. Certain dehydrogenases are A or B specific with respect to the donor $NADH_2$ or $NADPH_2$ systems.

Thus cells and tissues not only contain, in general, a large number of optically active compounds, but the 'unnatural' isomers are either biologically inactive or have biological properties differing from the natural ones. For example, D-ascorbic acid is not an antiscorbutic substance. D-thyroxine has no more than one third of the effect of L-thyroxine on the basal metabolism. The unnatural isomer of acyl-carnitine is a competitive inhibitor of the natural isomer, and so may block transfer of fatty acid metabolites in and out of mitochondria. These examples show that at least an awareness of the need to specify a stereoisomer in considering biological phenomena is essential in medical science.

RACEMIZATION

A mixture containing equal proportions of both isomers of an optically active compound shows no optical activity because the effects of the two isomers cancel each other out. The biological activity is usually only 50 per cent of that of the pure natural isomer. Such a mixture is called a **racemic mixture**, and is the usual product when a compound is made chemically.

Racemization also occurs when a compound with an asymmetric carbon atom acquires a double bond and loses it in a subsequent reaction, unless the process is under stereospecific control. For example, L-lactic acid can be oxidized to pyruvic acid, where C-2 is no longer a centre of asymmetry. If pyruvic acid is reduced, the product is DL-lactic acid, unless a specific D-lactate dehydrogenase is used.

NOMENCLATURE

Originally optically active compounds were called **dextrorotatory** or **laevorotatory** on the basis of their rotation of polarized light, hence dextrose (glucose) and laevulose (fructose). The prefixes D- or L- were also used. The system fell into confusion when it was found that closely-related compounds could have opposite rotations. For example, we know that lactic acid is made in nature from dextrorotatory glyceraldehyde (phosphate) but in animals the lactic acid is laevorotatory, although its salts are dextrorotatory. The difficulty has been avoided by establishing chemically the relationship of each natural isomer to a reference compound. All carbohydrates are classified by reference to D-glyceraldehyde (with a capital letter); amino acids with reference to L serine. The actual rotation is then indicated by a sign (+) or (−); thus lactic acid produced in animals is D(−) lactic acid; bacteria may produce the L(+) compound.

CARBOHYDRATE METABOLISM

The catabolism of glucose

Only one reaction directly involving glucose is of importance in animals. This consists of a transfer of a phosphate radical from adenosine triphosphate (ATP) to the OH group on carbon atom 6 of glucose. The other product is adenosine diphosphate (ADP). This reaction is catalysed by the enzyme **hexokinase** and is in practice irreversible for thermodynamic reasons.

Glucose-6-phosphate (G-6-P) is a substrate for several enzymes; one catalyses isomerization to glucose-1-phosphate (G-1-P), one to fructose-6-phosphate (F-6-P), and one the oxidation to 6-phosphogluconic acid (6-P-G). A fourth enzyme, found only in certain tissues, is a specific **glucose-6-phosphatase** which converts the ester back to free glucose and inorganic phosphate (P_i). Thus the multiplicity of pathways of the carbon atoms of glucose really begins with G-6-P and not with glucose (fig. 9.2).

Each of these pathways is considered in turn, beginning with that initiated by the conversion to F-6-P. The final product of this pathway is the C-3 compound pyruvate, each molecule of glucose being split into two. In most cells pyruvate can be readily oxidized to CO_2 and water, and in animal tissues this route to the complete oxidation of glucose is the most important. The sequence of reactions leading to pyruvate is usually known as the **Embden–Meyerhof pathway** (fig. 9.4).

While the interconversion of G-6-P and F-6-P is freely reversible, the next step, involving the transfer of another phosphate radical from ATP to form F-1,6-di-P (FDP),

is almost irreversible. The enzyme responsible, **phosphofructokinase,** has several interesting properties. It quickly loses activity in tissue extracts exposed to air, although there is no evidence that it is directly affected by oxygen in intact cells. It is inhibited by ATP, its own substrate, at concentrations of about 4 mM which is towards the upper end of the concentrations found in tissues, and

FIG. 9.2. Interrelationships of glucose-6-phosphate.

FIG. 9.3. The conversion of glyceraldehyde-3-phosphate (GAP) to 3-phosphoglycerate (3-PGA).

FIG. 9.4. The Embden–Meyerhof pathway.

the inhibition is relieved by adenosine monophosphate (AMP), which is neither a substrate nor a product of the enzyme. The enzyme is inhibited also by citrate. For these reasons it is believed that phosphofructokinase is very important in the regulation of carbohydrate metabolism.

In the next reaction FDP splits between C-3 and C-4 to yield the trioses, glyceraldehyde-3-phosphate (GAP) and dehydroxyacetone phosphate (DHAP). In spite of its apparent complexity the reaction is freely reversible at the concentrations of reactants found in tissues. DHAP is metabolized only by a side reaction and so might be expected to accumulate. It does not do so, because an **isomerase** catalyses the interconversion of DHAP and GAP, and the latter compound is continuously removed.

The reaction which follows is an oxidation, accompanied by a considerable decrease in the free energy of the system. In this case, however, a new phosphate compound is synthesized, a mixed anhydride, and the phosphate radical is then transferred to ADP, forming ATP. This was the first example of 'energy-trapping' to be discovered. The details of the overall reaction are given in fig. 9.3. The active site of the responsible enzyme (E) contains an SH group, probably firmly bound as glutathione.

A reactive thio-ester is formed as an intermediate, and this is phosphorylated to yield 1:3 diphosphoglycerate and the free enzyme once again. Thus the net result is:

$$GAP + P_i + NAD + ADP \longrightarrow 3\text{-}PGA + ATP + NADH_2$$

3-phosphoglycerate is isomerized to 2-phosphoglycerate and the latter readily loses a molecule of water, with the formation of phospho-enolpyruvate. This enol ester grouping is again very reactive and the transfer of the phosphate radical to ADP occurs readily, catalysed by

pyruvate kinase. The pathway can be summarized as follows:

$$Glucose + 2ATP \longrightarrow FDP + 2ADP$$
$$FDP + 4ADP + 2P_i + 2NAD \longrightarrow$$
$$Pyruvate + 4ATP + 2NADH_2$$

Thus there is a net gain of 2ATP for each molecule of glucose catabolized.

Pyruvate is an important intermediate compound, but before describing its metabolism, the other three possible reactions of glucose-6-phosphate are considered.

HEXOSE MONOPHOSPHATE (PENTOSE) PATHWAY (fig. 9.5)

In many tissues, but not in muscle, there exists a pattern of enzymes in addition to those already described, which are capable of directly oxidizing G-6-P to pentose phosphates, and which together with the enzymes of the Embden–Meyerhof pathway, can oxidize G-6-P completely to CO_2 and H_2O (or $NADPH_2$). The enzymes are first **glucose-6-phosphate dehydrogenase**, which oxidizes the ring form of G-6-P to the acid lactone; a **lactonase** catalyses the production of the straight-chain form of the acid. The dehydrogenase requires NADP specifically as hydrogen acceptor, as does the associated enzyme, **phosphogluconic acid dehydrogenase**. Although the product of this latter reaction should be a β-keto acid, it must spontaneously decarboxylate at the enzyme site, as it has never been isolated, and the observed products are ribulose-5-phosphate and CO_2.

Ribulose-5-phosphate can be isomerized to ribose-5-phosphate, the starting material for purine nucleotide synthesis (p. 12.21.) It may be that in some tissues this is the main function of this enzyme sequence; in other tissues, however, e.g. liver, the rate at which G-6-P is metabolized by this alternative pathway can be shown to be much faster than the rate of nucleic acid synthesis and the pentose phosphates must therefore be metabolized in some other way. With the help of two enzymes, **transketolase** and **transaldolase**, which have been found to occur together with G-6-P dehydrogenase, it is possible to rearrange the thirty carbon atoms present in six molecules of the pentose ribulose-5-phosphate into five molecules of the hexose glucose-6-phosphate, as shown in fig. 9.5. In summary, the sequence gives

$$6G\text{-}6\text{-}P + 12NADP \longrightarrow 5G\text{-}6\text{-}P + 12NADPH_2 + 6CO_2.$$

In effect, one molecule of glucose has been completely oxidized. Since no energy has been directly trapped as in the Embden–Meyerhof scheme, the value of this oxidation may be questioned. Its importance may well be the production of twelve molecules of $NADPH_2$ per molecule of glucose oxidized; this is required for fatty acid synthesis, since this and most synthetic reac-

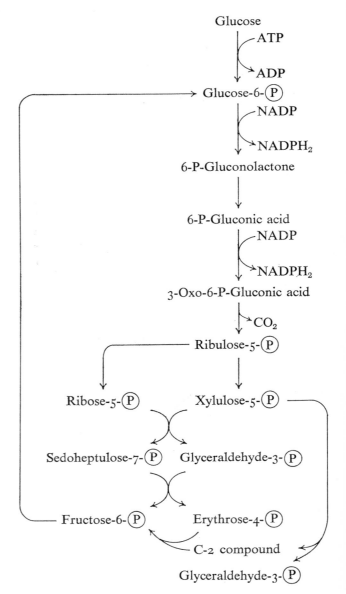

FIG. 9.5. The hexose monophosphate pathway.

tions in cells which involve reduction are catalysed by enzymes specific for $NADPH_2$, whereas most cell dehydrogenases are specific for NAD. The point of the alternative pathway may therefore be in providing the appropriate reduced coenzyme, rather than in producing ATP directly.

Glycogen metabolism

Glycogen is found in most animal cells, but more particularly in muscle and liver. The concentration in muscle is about 1 per cent of the wet weight, and may vary from 0 to 5 per cent; in the liver the concentration is usually about 5 per cent, but may be as high as 10 per cent; it falls in starvation and other circumstances practically to zero, for reasons which will become apparent later.

Glycogen is a large polymer of glucose, mol. wt. 1–5 million; it contains only α-glucose residues. These are connected to each other mostly by 1:4 linkages thus:

but there also occur 1:6 linkages at so-called branch points. In the inner part of the molecule there is a branch point every three to four residues and the outer branches are six to eight residues long.

The whole structure has a tree-like appearance, as shown in fig. 9.6. This highly branched structure of the molecule is very significant for the metabolism of glycogen.

BREAKDOWN OF GLYCOGEN

Residues which are attached at the outermost end of the terminal branches by a 1:4 link can be transferred to inorganic phosphate and so form α-glucose-1-phosphate (G-1-P). This reaction is catalysed by an enzyme called **phosphorylase**, which has complicated properties. It exists in tissues in two forms, one active (phosphorylase *a*) and one inactive (phosphorylase *b*). Muscle phosphorylase *b* has half the molecular weight of the muscle *a* enzyme.

FIG. 9.6. Structure of glycogen. ○, glucose residues linked at carbon 1 and 4; ●, branch points with linkage at carbon 1, 4 and 6.

The conversion of *a* to *b* is accompanied by the release of inorganic phosphate, and conversely the reactivation process requires phosphorylation by ATP. Thus we have:

$$\left.\begin{array}{l} \text{Phosphorylase } a \longrightarrow \\ \qquad \text{phosphorylase } b + 2\text{P}_1 \\ \text{Phosphorylase } b + 2\text{ATP} \longrightarrow \\ \qquad \text{phosphorylase } a + 2\text{ADP} \end{array}\right\} \text{Liver}$$

$$\left.\begin{array}{l} \text{Phosphorylase } a \longrightarrow \\ \qquad 2 \text{ phosphorylase } b + 4\text{P}_1 \\ 2 \text{ phosphorylase } b + 4\text{ATP} \longrightarrow \\ \qquad \text{phosphorylase } a + 4\text{ADP} \end{array}\right\} \text{Muscle}$$

The dephosphorylating and rephosphorylating processes are each catalysed by a specific enzyme.

In normal aerobic tissues it is found that most of the phosphorylase and most of the rephosphorylating enzyme are inactive. The latter can be reactivated by yet a third enzyme which requires **3′5′ cyclic AMP**. This nucleotide which appears to have a key role in metabolism is a cyclic compound with the phosphoric acid moiety doubly esterified between the alcoholic hydroxyls on carbon atoms 3 and 5 of the ribose portion of the nucleotide as follows:

It is formed from ATP by the action of an enzyme, **adenyl cyclase**

$$\text{ATP} \longrightarrow 3'5'\text{AMP} + \text{PP}_i \text{ (pyrophosphate)}$$

The 3′5′ cyclic AMP is also attacked by an enzyme or enzymes present in most tissues termed **phosphodiesterases** which hydrolytically split the cyclic phosphate structure between the C-3 of the ribose and the phosphate as follows

$$3'5'\text{AMP} \longrightarrow 5'\text{AMP}$$

The concentration of 3′5′ cyclic AMP in a given tissue is accordingly dependent upon the supply of ATP and the relative activities of the adenyl cyclase enzyme and the phosphodiesterase enzymes. It is never present in a concentration more than a few per cent of the concentration of either ATP or 5′AMP.

3′5′ cyclic AMP appears to be a chemical mediator in the mechanism of action of various hormones. Thus glucagon and adrenaline activate the adenyl cyclase system and quickly increase the tissue concentration of $3'5'$ AMP. In liver an increased $3'5'$AMP level facilitates the conversion of inactive phosphorylase (phosphorylase *b*) into active phosphorylase (phosphorylase *a*). This is quite distinct from the activation of phosphorylase *b* itself by $5'$AMP.

Thus the explanation of the glycogenolytic effect of adrenaline is that it facilitates the conversion of ATP $\rightarrow$ $3'5'$AMP. This latter substance in turn enhances the formation of phosphorylase *a* which then attacks the glycogen molecule to give G-1-P and so triggers off glycogenolysis. Insulin also increases the concentration $3'5'$ cyclic AMP in liver and muscle.

In adipose tissue adrenaline raises the concentration of $3'5'$ cyclic AMP which activates a lipolytic enzyme system so that 'free fatty acids' are released from the storage triglycerides (p. 32.6).

G-1-P and G-6-P are in equilibrium catalysed by **phosphohexose isomerase**. This reaction is shown in fig. 9.2. Thus the glucose residues liberated from glycogen by phosphorylase can enter either the Embden–Meyerhof or hexose monophosphate pathways of glucose metabolism.

It is only the α-1:4 linked glucose residues of glycogen which can be broken off by phosphorylase and the enzyme is unable to attack 1:4 bonds interior to a 1:6 branch point. For the complete breakdown of glycogen, another system is required, which can attack the 1:6 bonds. This enzyme, the debranching enzyme or **amylo-6-glucosidase**, simply hydrolyses the glucose residue attached by a 1:6 bond to produce free glucose.

To produce the branched structure of glycogen a **branching enzyme** (transglycosylase) is necessary. This is in fact a transferase, acting as shown in the diagram below:

($\bigcirc$ represents a glucose residue)

The reaction catalysed by phosphorylase is essentially reversible and *in vitro* glycogen can be synthesized in a system consisting of a primer (a fragment of polysaccharide), a suitably high concentration of G-1-P, a low concentration of inorganic phosphate and branching enzyme. The concentrations of G-1-P and P_i found *in vivo* do not favour the synthetic reaction; furthermore patients have been found whose liver or muscle cells contain no phosphorylase, but yet are loaded with glycogen. An independent mechanism of glycogen synthesis has been discovered, which explains these awkward facts.

GLYCOGEN SYNTHESIS

This mechanism of glycogen synthesis depends on glycosyl transfer from a coenzyme called uridine diphosphate glucose (UDPG). The following sequence of reactions occurs:

$$UTP + G\text{-}1\text{-}P \longrightarrow UDPG + PP_i$$
$$UDPG + (glucose)_n \rightleftharpoons UDP + (glucose)_{n+1}$$
$$UDP + ATP \longrightarrow UTP + ADP$$

This reaction sequence is energetically less economical for the cell, since one molecule of ATP is required for each glucose residue added. On the other hand, the large drop in free energy on the scission of the UDP–G bond means that the transfer reaction is essentially irreversible and synthesis is therefore always favoured. All the evidence suggests that glycogen synthesis and breakdown proceeds by the action of the two enzymes systems **UDP glucosyl transferase** and **phosphorylase** respectively.

INBORN ERRORS OF GLYCOGEN METABOLISM

A number of uncommon disorders are associated with increased storage of glycogen in the various tissues. These do not arise from increased formation of glycogen but are due to a lack of one of several enzymes involved in its breakdown. The defect usually becomes obvious in infancy and often leads to death before adult life.

Table 9.1 gives a summary of the various types of glycogen storage disease with the enzymes whose absence leads to glycogenosis. In some patients more than one enzyme may be absent or have a very low activity.

TABLE 9.1. Enzyme defects in glycogen storage diseases.

Type	Enzyme defect	Tissues Affected
I	Glucose-6-phosphatase	Liver, kidney, gut
II	Lysosomal acid glucosidase	Generalized, particularly heart, tongue, brain
III	Amylo-6-glucosidase (Debranching enzyme)	Liver, heart, muscle, RBC, WBC
IV	Branching enzyme (amylo 1,4–1,6 transglycosylase)	Liver, spleen, heart, muscle, RBC, CNS
V	Muscle phosphorylase	Skeletal muscle
VI	Liver phosphorylase	Liver, WBC

Other carbohydrate pathways

UDPG is a component of a number of other important pathways in carbohydrate metabolism:

LACTOSE SYNTHESIS

Lactose is the disaccharide found in milk and formed from glucose and galactose (Gal). It is synthesized only in mammary tissue.

$$UDPG \longrightarrow UDP\ Gal$$
$$UDPGal + G\text{-}1\text{-}P \longrightarrow UDP + Lactose\text{-}1\text{-}P$$
$$Lactose\text{-}1\text{-}P \longrightarrow Lactose + P_i$$

GALACTOSE METABOLISM

Lactose in the diet is hydrolysed in the gut wall to glucose and galactose. The latter sugar is transformed to glucose.

$$Gal + ATP \longrightarrow Gal\text{-}I\text{-}P + ADP$$

$$Gal\text{-}I\text{-}P + UDPG \longrightarrow UDPGal + G\text{-}I\text{-}P$$

$$UDPGal \longrightarrow UDPG$$

The enzyme which catalyses the first reaction is an epimerase. It inverts the configuration of —H and —OH at C-4, thus converting the galactose residue into a glucose residue.

disaccharide sucrose is consumed in large quantities. It is hydrolysed in the gut wall to equimolar amounts of fructose and glucose. Fructose can be phosphorylated to F-6-P by hexokinase, but this reaction is inhibited in the presence of glucose and it seems likely that fructose is metabolized by means of a special fructokinase.

$$Fructose + ATP \longrightarrow F\text{-}I\text{-}P + ADP$$

F-1-P can be split by an aldolase to form dihydroxyacetone phosphate and glyceraldehyde. The latter is phosphorylated either directly or after oxidation to glyceric acid. In either case the two trioses join the Embden–Meyerhof pathway.

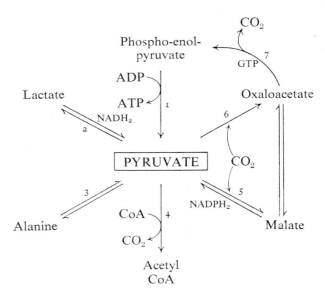

Fig. 9.7. The formation of glucuronides.

The epimerase is found in liver and curiously also in erythrocytes. Clearly the immediate formation of UDPG favours direct synthesis of glycogen from galactose in liver.

Due to a lack of one or other of the enzymes in the above sequence a child may be unable to convert galactose to glucose. Galactose accumulates in the blood and tissues. These children do not thrive and develop cataracts and mental defects, unless on an artificial diet without galactose.

GLUCURONIC ACID METABOLISM

The oxidation of glucose residues is shown in fig. 9.7. Glucuronic acid occurs combined in two types of compound. Firstly it is present in many of the mucopolysaccharides which act as lubricants and are also important constituents of connective tissue (p. 16.7). Secondly, in the liver it can combine with many toxic or potentially toxic substances to form water soluble glucuronides, which may then be excreted in the bile. The bile pigment, bilirubin diglucuronide, a product of haemoglobin catabolism, is an important example. The mechanism by which this is formed is described on p. 31.8. Free glucuronic acid is seldom found in the body.

FRUCTOSE METABOLISM

Fructose is not normally a constituent of the diet but the

Pyruvic acid metabolism

Pyruvate has a central position in carbohydrate metabolism (fig. 9.8).

Fig. 9.8. Interrelationships of pyruvate.

There are thus at least seven reactions involving pyruvate or the close relative, phospho-enolpyruvate. These are numbered in the figure and discussed in turn.

(1) The reaction catalysed by **pyruvate kinase** has already been mentioned as converting phospho-enol pyruvate to pyruvate at the end of the Embden–Meyerhof pathway. For all practical purposes it is irreversible, so that phospho-enolpyruvate and thus other triose phosphates cannot be made directly from pyruvate.

(2) Most animal cells contain in their cytoplasm large quantities of **lactic dehydrogenase**, which requires NAD and catalyses the reversible oxidation of lactate. Lactate undergoes no other known reaction in animals. Its formation is important under anaerobic circumstances since it allows the reoxidation of $NADH_2$ formed in the oxidation

Lipoic acid I   Lipoic acid II

The acetaldehyde is transferred to form I, which becomes reduced, while the acetaldehyde group is oxidized to an acetyl residue (fig. 9.9).

FIG. 9.9. The formation of acetyl CoA.

of glyceraldehyde phosphate. The $NADH_2$ is normally oxidized by the aerobic pathway described later in the chapter. If for any reason the cells have an inadequate supply of oxygen, this reoxidation does not occur fast enough for their energy needs; glucose can still be catabolized and ATP consequently produced by the coupling of the two reactions and the whole of the Embden–Meyerhof pathway then becomes self-contained. Anaerobiosis is thus usually accompanied by increased lactate formation (see opposite).

The activity of the lactic dehydrogenase is so great that the redox couples pyruvate/lactate and $NAD/NADH_2$ are nearly always in equilibrium (p. 8.8). The pyruvate/lactate ratio in blood is quite frequently used as an indicator of the $NAD/NADH_2$ ratio or redox state of cells. It is, however, unwise to draw conclusions from changes in the ratio without a knowledge of other factors which might affect it (e.g. pH). It is also certain that the $NAD/NADH_2$ ratio is different in the mitochondria and in the cytoplasm.

(3) Two transaminases, widely distributed in cells, can convert alanine (ala) to pyruvate (pyr):

ala + keto acid $\rightleftharpoons$ pyr + amino acid

ala + α-oxoglutaric acid $\rightleftharpoons$ pyr + glutamic acid

(4) The oxidative decarboxylation of pyruvate is the main pathway of metabolism for this compound and thus for carbohydrate. Essentially, pyruvate is split into CO_2 and acetaldehyde. In animal tissues the latter is not set free but combines first with the prosthetic group thiamine pyrophosphate, from which it is transferred to a second prosthetic group, lipoic acid. This can exist in two forms:

This acetyl residue is then transferred to Coenzyme A, and the reduced lipoic acid is re-oxidized to form I by NAD. The overall reaction is:

$CH_3COCOOH + CoASH + NAD \longrightarrow$

$CH_3CO.SCoA + NADH_2 + CO_2$

The acetyl group can be oxidized to CO_2 and H_2O as described on p. 9.14, or it can be used to synthesize fatty acids or other lipids. The decarboxylation reaction is almost irreversible, so that the acetyl cannot be used to synthesize pyruvate.

Reactions 5, 6 and 7 in fig. 9.8 represent various ways in which a connection can be made between pyruvate and the 4-carbon acids of the citric acid cycle (p. 9.14). There may be, in addition, another enzyme catalysing the straight decarboxylation of oxaloacetate to pyruvate, but this is a reaction which can in any case occur spontaneously.

(5) The **malic enzyme** catalyses the reversible reaction to malic acid.

$CH_3COCOOH + CO_2 + NADPH_2 \longrightarrow$

$COOHCH_2CHOHCOOH + NADP$

(6) **Pyruvate carboxylase** is an enzyme found in mitochondria which catalyses the reaction to oxaloacetic acid.

$CH_3COCOOH + CO_2 \longrightarrow HOOCCH_2COCOOH$

It contains biotin as prosthetic group and, as with acetyl-CoA carboxylase, ATP has to be used to activate the CO_2 before it can be used. The reaction, therefore, goes only from left to right, as written, and not in the reverse direction, as might be expected.

Pyruvate carboxylase is active only in the presence of acetyl-CoA although this compound is not used in the reaction. It appears that this requirement for activity could be a very important control mechanism regulating the oxaloacetate concentration in the mitochondria, and hence their ability to oxidize acetyl groups.

(7) **Phospho-enol pyruvic acid carboxylase**, the last enzyme of this group, does not involve pyruvate directly but converts oxaloacetate to phospho-enol pyruvate. Guanosine triphosphate (GTP), an energy rich compound, is involved.

$$HOOCCH_2COCOOH + GTP \longrightarrow$$
$$CH_2CO\textcircled{P}COOH + GDP + CO_2$$

The enzyme is found in the cytoplasm and is thought to be very important in enabling hexoses to be formed from non-carbohydrate precursors. It permits the pyruvate kinase reaction to be by-passed and hence carbohydrate to be formed from amino acids and lactate.

Although we are concerned here with the metabolism of carbohydrates, it is worth pointing out that the citric acid cycle alone will not catalyse the complete oxidation of the carbon skeleton of amino acids, because it contains no mechanism for converting the 4-carbon acids to acetyl groups. It is the latter which are actually completely oxidized in the cycle. The rather complicated arrangement of enzymes in fig. 9.10 provides an explanation for the complete oxidation of amino acids as well as for their partial conversion to carbohydrate, since the carbon skeletons of the glucogenic amino acids can be converted either to pyruvate, or to a member of the citric acid cycle, and hence to oxaloacetate or malate.

If the pyruvate kinase barrier is passed, fructose diphosphate can relatively easily be formed from phospho-enol pyruvate, provided the ATP and $NADH_2$ levels in the cytoplasm are sufficiently high to force the reversal of the triose phosphate dehydrogenase step. The phosphorylations which produce FDP (and G-6-P) are on energetic grounds not reversible, however, and fructose-6-phosphate (and free glucose) can be formed only by 'by-pass' reactions. In some tissues there exists a concentration of a **fructose-diphosphatase** which can catalyse the reaction:

$$FDP \longrightarrow F\text{-}6\text{-}P + P_i$$

In liver, and also to a small extent in kidney, there exists a specific **glucose-6-phosphatase**.

The liver is thus, in effect, the only organ which can form free glucose, either from glycogen or from small molecule precursors. This is a very important function of this organ, since in man the blood sugar is not permitted to fall below certain limits, even when carbohydrate is not being consumed in the diet, yet there is a continual uptake of glucose from the blood by many organs, notably the brain, which probably cannot utilize other sources of energy.

The Pasteur effect

A phenomenon which is very widely observed in both animal tissues and micro-organisms was first pointed out by Pasteur. If the conditions are made wholly or partially anaerobic, as by restricting the O_2 supply, there is not only an increase in the rate of production of lactic acid (or of ethanol, by yeasts) but also an increase in the rate of utilization of glucose or of glycogen. The rates fall to their normal level again on the re-admission of air.

The value of this phenomenon is quite clear. The major part of the ATP synthesis in most cells is a product of the oxidative reactions going on in mitochondria. If these stop because of lack of oxygen, the corresponding ATP output ceases too. Nevertheless, the cell's demand for ATP may be unchanged or even increased. Glycolysis does produce some ATP, as already described, and it is the only kind of metabolism which can continue in the absence of an adequate supply of oxygen, because of the self-contained reduction of pyruvate to lactate (or acetaldehyde to ethanol in yeast). One might therefore expect, in theory, the aerobic rate of utilization of glucose to be increased nineteenfold when the oxygen source is removed, since this is the ratio of ATP produced aerobically to anaerobically per mole of glucose. In practice, the ratio does not increase beyond five, so some cell functions must be starved of energy.

The anaerobic breakdown of glucose is not in itself inefficient, since most of the free energy of the glucose is still present in the lactic acid. The latter must, however, be disposed of; in animals it is usually reoxidized to pyruvate in the liver when aerobic conditions return.

It is of considerable interest to find out the mechanism of the Pasteur effect, in terms of enzymology, since this would provide insight into the control of cell metabolism in general. In a linear sequence of enzyme reactions which are more or less reversible, the rate of each is controlled by the rate of substrate supply from its predecessors and the rate of product removal by its successor. There needs to be only one rate-limiting or pace-making reaction, not necessarily the first. Application of this idea to the Embden–Meyerhof pathway is complicated by the fact that there are three reactions generally thought of as irreversible, those catalysed by hexokinase, phosphohexokinase and pyruvate kinase, and one which is reversible only with difficulty, the oxidation of glyceraldehyde phosphate. It is difficult to see how the rate of earlier reactions can be controlled by later ones in the sequence.

The breakdown of glycogen in anaerobic conditions can readily be explained in terms of the known properties of enzymes. Phosphorylase *b* is rapidly reactivated to phosphorylase *a*, and muscle phosphorylase *b* is in any case active in the presence of AMP (see below). This leads to a greater rate of formation of hexose phosphates. Phosphohexokinase will be activated by a slight fall in the concentration of ATP, a rise in the concentration of AMP, and an increase in concentration of F-6-P. It is at this point appropriate to explain why a rise in concentration of AMP is to be expected. An enzyme known originally as Lohmann's enzyme, or myokinase, and now known as **adenylate kinase**, is present in most tissues and is very active. It catalyses the reaction:

$$ATP + AMP \rightleftharpoons 2\ ADP$$

In anaerobic circumstances, when the concentration of ADP might originally start to rise and of ATP to fall, because of the cessation of oxidative phosphorylation, adenylate kinase, working from right to left of the equation given above, rapidly reforms ATP, and the net result is an increase in AMP concentration in the tissue, and, for a short time at least, little change in ATP or ADP levels. Changes of this kind have been observed to occur within a few seconds of stopping the blood flow to the liver.

The rate of the triose phosphate dehydrogenase reaction increases largely because of increased concentrations of the substrate, rather than of the co-factors ADP and P_i. The over-riding requirement is that NAD should continuously be supplied, and this can happen because the $NADH_2$ produced in the oxidation of glyceraldehyde phosphate is re-oxidised by the reduction of pyruvate to lactate. All the other enzymes in the pathway respond to increased rates of production of their substrates, and the overall effect is an increase in the rate of production of lactate at the expense of glycogen.

It is more difficult to explain an increase in the rate of consumption of glucose by cells and tissues in anaerobic conditions, because there is no way in which hexokinase can be activated. We are forced to conclude that the rate of utilization of glucose is controlled by the rate at which it permeates the cell membrane, without being able at present to specify how the latter might be affected by changes in Po_2 or demands for ATP.

Glycerol phosphate

A dehydrogenase is known which catalyses the reaction:

$$
\begin{array}{ccc}
CH_2OH & & CH_2OH \\
| & & | \\
CHOH & + NAD \longrightarrow & CO \quad + NADH_2 \\
| & & | \\
CH_2O\textcircled{P} & & CH_2O\textcircled{P}
\end{array}
$$

Glycerol phosphate is necessary for the formation of triglycerides and phospholipids, and it can in this way be made from carbohydrate. The system GAP/DHAP is also a possible candidate for the transfer of reducing equivalents to or from mitochondria and cytoplasm, as explained in the next section, but in general the levels of the two enzymes are too low in animal tissues for this to be very effective.

The citric acid cycle

The complete oxidation of carbohydrate and indeed also of fats and amino acids is accomplished by means of a cyclic sequence of enzymic reactions, whose substrates and products are present only in catalytic quantities within the cell. This sequence is commonly known as the citric acid cycle, but sometimes as the tricarboxylic acid or Krebs cycle.

We have already seen that pyruvate, the sole end product of the catabolism of glucose, can be oxidized to acetyl-CoA ($CH_3CO.SCoA$), and CO_2. In chap. 10, it is also shown that the long-chain fatty acids, the most important constituents of fats, are oxidized to acetyl-CoA by means of the β-oxidation cycle. Since these two nutrients, glucose and fatty acids, provide between them over 85 per cent of the energy intake in almost all diets, the further fate of acetyl-CoA is clearly of considerable interest. Although the acetyl residue can be used for a number of syntheses, it is mostly oxidized by way of the citric acid cycle to provide energy for tissue functions.

Acetyl-CoA reacts with oxaloacetic acid to produce citric acid; free CoA is also released.

$$
\begin{array}{ccc}
CH_3CO.SCoA & & CH_2COOH + HSCoA \\
+ & & | \\
COCOOH & \longrightarrow & HOCCOOH \\
| & & | \\
CH_2COOH & & CH_2COOH \\
\text{Oxaloacetic acid} & & \text{Citric acid}
\end{array}
$$

The enzyme which catalyses this reaction is the **condensing enzyme**. It is inhibited by ATP.

Citric acid is converted into *iso*citric acid by the action of the enzyme **aconitase**:

$$
\begin{array}{ccc}
CH_2COOH & & CH_2COOH \\
| & & | \\
HOCCOOH & \longrightarrow & CCOOH \\
| & & \| \\
CH_2COOH & & CHCOOH \\
\text{Citric acid} & & \textit{Cis}\text{aconitic acid}
\end{array}
$$

$$
\begin{array}{c}
CH_2COOH \\
| \\
HCCOOH \\
| \\
HOCHCOOH \\
\textit{Iso}\text{citric acid}
\end{array}
$$

It is doubtful whether the intermediate *cis*aconitic acid has a separate existence.

*Iso*citric acid is oxidized by two enzymes, one specific for NAD and occurring in mitochondria, and the other specific for NADP and found in cytoplasm. The product, oxalosuccinic acid, is extremely unstable and decomposes spontaneously, especially in the presence of *iso*citric dehydrogenase, to give α-oxoglutaric acid and CO_2.

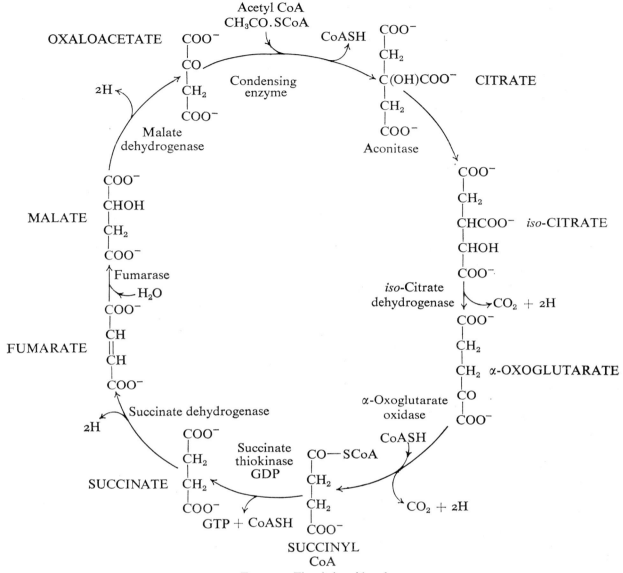

FIG. 9.10. The citric acid cycle.

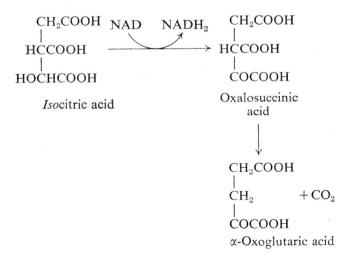

Isocitric acid

Oxalosuccinic acid

α-Oxoglutaric acid

The oxidation of α-oxoglutaric acid which follows proceeds by a mechanism similar to that by which pyruvic acid is oxidized (p. 9.12). The enzyme contains thiamine pyrophosphate as a prosthetic group and a CoA derivative, succinyl SCoA, is the product. The latter is immediately converted to free succinic acid by the following reaction:

$$\begin{matrix} \text{CO.SCoA} \\ | \\ \text{CH}_2 \\ | \\ \text{CH}_2 \\ | \\ \text{COOH} \\ \text{Succinyl CoA} \end{matrix} + \text{GDP} + \text{P}_i \rightleftharpoons \begin{matrix} \text{COOH} \\ | \\ \text{CH}_2 \\ | \\ \text{CH} \\ | \\ \text{COOH} \\ \text{Succinic acid} \end{matrix} + \text{GTP} + \text{CoASH}$$

Notice that the free energy of the succinyl CoA thio-ester

link is preserved by the formation of a high-energy bond in guanosine triphosphate (GTP).

Succinic acid is oxidized to fumaric acid by **succinic dehydrogenase**, which contains an atypical flavin as a prosthetic group.

$$COOHCH_2CH_2COOH \longrightarrow$$
$$COOHCH=CHCOOH+2H$$

Fumaric acid is converted to malic acid by the addition of a molecule of water, catalysed by **fumarase.**

$$COOHCH=CHCOOH+H_2O \longrightarrow$$
$$COOHCH_2CHOHCOOH$$

Finally, malic acid is oxidized to oxaloacetic acid to complete the cycle:

$$COOHCH_2CHOHCOOH+NAD\ (NADP) \longrightarrow$$
$$COOHCH_2COCOOH+NADH_2(NADPH_2)$$

The net result of this cyclic process, set out in schematic form in fig. 9.10, is the oxidation of the acetyl group CH_3CO-, to two molecules of CO_2 and four sets each of two electrons and two H^+ (2H). In the cycle three $NADH_2$ and one FpH_2 are formed. More hydrogen appears here than in the original CH_3CO- radical because two molecules of H_2O are consumed, one in the formation of citrate and one in the formation of malate.

ELECTRON TRANSPORT REACTIONS

The oxidation of these reduced co-factors is carried out by a complex sequence of enzymes. The enzymes of the citric acid cycle, with the exception of special forms of *iso*citric and malic dehydrogenases, are in mitochondria to which the electron transport chain is confined. The substrate oxidizing and co-factor oxidizing enzymes are co-ordinated in a way that allows the efficient trapping of the energy yielded by the oxidations.

The probable sequence of reactions in the oxidation of mitochondrial $NADH_2$ is shown in fig. 9.11. The precise nature of the flavoprotein coupling $NADH_2$ to the cytochromes has not been elucidated, and there is some dis-

agreement about the relative positions of cytochrome b and ubiquinone (p. 8.10). Cytochromes a and a_3 have been distinguished spectrographically, but as cytochrome oxidase is a complex enzyme it is quite possible that the two different haem groups are attached to the same lipoprotein.

The linkage between Fp redox steps and the cytochromes, each prosthetic group of which can accept only one electron, is by means of the —SH and Fe groups shown in fig. 9.11. These are probably not separate prosthetic groups; the —SH groups at least are part of the appropriate flavoproteins, and it has long been known that these enzymes are accompanied by non-haem iron.

Succinate is oxidized directly by a flavoprotein, and the electrons from this arrive in the main chain at the level of cytochrome b–ubiquinone. This can be shown by the use of poisons, e.g. certain barbiturates, which block the oxidation of $NADH_2$, but not of succinate. Antimycin A, on the other hand, blocks the oxidation of cytochrome b, and inhibits the oxidation of both $NADH_2$ and succinate.

The oxidation of fatty acids also takes place in mitochondria, and the flavoprotein acyl-CoA dehydrogenases are said to be re-oxidized by an electron-transferring factor which links to the main chain at the level of cytochrome c.

Mitochondria freshly prepared from tissues do not oxidize added $NADH_2$, and it is not known how cytoplasmic $NADH_2$ is re-oxidized. A 'shuttle', i.e. the reduction in the cytoplasm by $NADH_2$ of a compound, the reduced form of which can enter the mitochondria and there be re-oxidized, is one possible solution of this difficulty. A number of possible shuttle redox pairs of this type have been proposed.

The energetics of intermediary metabolism

As discussed in chap. 8 the oxidation of one mole of $NADH_2$ by molecular oxygen leads to a decrease in free energy of about 50 kcal. This energy does not all appear as heat, but the oxidation is accompanied by the synthesis of 3 moles of ATP per mole of $NADH_2$, the efficiency of

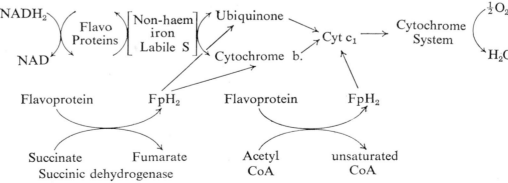

FIG. 9.11. Sequence of reaction in the oxidation of mitochondrial $NADH_2$.

energy trapping being about 50 per cent (p. 8.11). When the concentrations of reactants and products actually present are taken into account, the efficiency is probably greater. If succinate is used as a substrate, rather than a compound which produces $NADH_2$, the ratio of ATP formed to the electrons transferred (the P/O ratio) approaches 2 rather than 3. From this it is clear that one ATP is synthesized during the transfer of two electrons from $NADH_2$ to cytochrome b, and two ATP are synthesized during the transfer of electrons from cytochrome b to oxygen.

The complete oxidation of 1 mole of glucose to CO_2 and H_2O yields 686 kcal. The oxidation of glycogen yields a little more energy from the splitting of the glycosidic bond. Table 9.2 shows the free energy still available at various stages of the process, and makes it clear how much of the total energy is released during the oxidation of acetyl-CoA (about 60 per cent of the total). For lactate G^0 is 650 and for the conversion of glucose to lactate

TABLE 9.2. Free energy available during intermediary metabolism.

	Free energy of oxidation to CO_2 and H_2O (kcal/mole)		NAD reduced (moles)
	$-\triangle G^0$ to CO_2	Partial $-\triangle G^0$	
Glycogen (per mole glucose)	700		
		14	
Glucose	686		
		122	2
2 Pyruvate	564		
		132	2
2 Acetyl-CoA	432		
		432	6 (and 2 flavoprotein directly)
$4CO_2 + 4H_2O$	0		

$\Delta G^0 = -36$ which is about 5 per cent of the total energy available. There is a close correlation between the amount

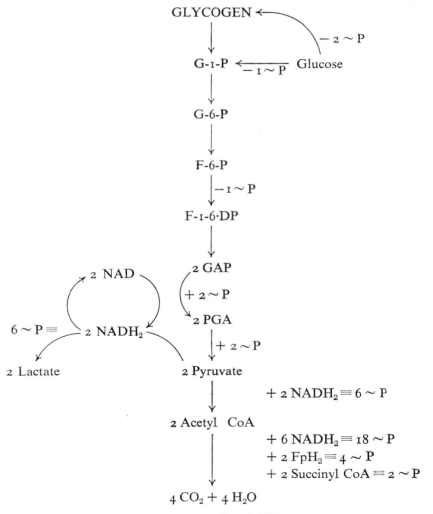

FIG. 9.12. Formation of ATP.

of $NADH_2$ formed and the free energy released. In the oxidation of carbohydrate almost all the energy is transferred to NAD, producing $NADH_2$. Subsequently this energy is released in the re-oxidation to NAD.

Since the amount of ATP formed during intramitochondrial oxidation of $NADH_2$ is known from direct measurement, and the stages at which substrate level phosphorylation occur are also known, we can now estimate both the moles of ATP formed per mole of carbohydrate oxidized, and the efficiency with which energy is 'trapped' as chemical energy useful to the cell during the oxidation (fig. 9.12).

If it is allowed that the standard free energy of hydrolysis of ATP is about 7 kcal/mole, using the values for free energy change in the various stages given in table 9.2, the net ATP yield is therefore:

from glucose to 2 pyruvate	+ 8 ATP
from glucose to 2 lactate	+ 2 ATP
from glycogen to 2 lactate	+ 3 ATP
from 2 pyruvate to CO_2 and H_2O	+30 ATP
from glucose to CO_2 and H_2O	+38 ATP

The following estimates of efficiency are appropriate:

Glucose to 2 pyruvate	$8 \times 7/122 = 46\%$
Glucose to 2 lactate	$2 \times 7/36 = 39\%$
Glycogen to 2 lactate	$3 \times 7/50 = 42\%$
2 Pyruvate to CO_2 and H_2O	$30 \times 7/564 = 37\%$
Glucose to CO_2 and H_2O	$38 \times 7/686 = 39\%$

These figures can be refined in various ways, and in particular if $NADH_2$ is used directly in reductive synthesis, the efficiencies may be very different from those quoted. Nevertheless, the figures indicate the order of magnitude of energy trapping through ATP and stress once again the dominant role of mitochondrial oxidations in the provision of energy for cellular functions.

FURTHER READING

DICKENS F., RANDLE P.J. & WHELAN W.J., eds. (1967) *Carbohydrate Metabolism and its Disorders.* 2 vol. New York: Academic Press.

LEHNINGER M.J. (1964) *The Mitochondrion.* New York: Benjamin.

RACKER E. (1965) *Mechanisms in Bioenergetics.* New York: Academic Press.

Scientific American Offprints No. 36, 41, 69 & 91. San Francisco: W.H. Freeman.

Chapter 10
Lipid metabolism

Some account of the importance of fat in the diet has already been given (p. 5.2). This chapter is concerned with the metabolism of fats in the body, where they are of the utmost importance in providing a compact store of fuel, which can be rapidly mobilized when needed. The housewife knows well what she means when she uses the word fat, but she includes a number of different types of chemical substances which collectively biochemists call **lipids**. They are all characterized by being soluble in fat solvents such as chloroform or ether, but almost insoluble in water. Although all lipids share this property, they possess a wide variety of chemical structures, physicochemical properties and metabolic characteristics. Lipids may be divided into five classes:

(1) fatty acids,
(2) triglycerides and waxes,
(3) phospholipids and glycolipids,
(4) cholesterol and its derivatives,
(5) vitamins A, D, E and K.

CHEMISTRY OF LIPIDS

Fatty acids

These are monocarboxylic acids, homologues of acetic acid with longer, almost invariably unbranched chains. Only about eighteen are found in significant amounts in mammalian tissues and these are shown in table 10.1. All the important acids have an even number of carbon atoms which are referred to by numbers or by Greek letters, as follows:

$$\underset{\omega}{\overset{16}{CH_3}}(CH_2)_{11}\underset{\gamma}{\overset{4}{CH_2}}\underset{\beta}{\overset{3}{CH_2}}\underset{\alpha}{\overset{2}{CH_2}}\overset{1}{COOH}$$

In addition an acid is described as mono-, di-, tri- or polyenoic depending on whether it has one, two, three or more double bonds. The shorthand designation for linolenic acid with eighteen carbon atoms and three double bonds is $C_{18:3}$, or in more detail $C_{18\Delta9,12,15}$ which indicates the position of the double bonds in the chain. There are two geometrically isomeric configurations at each double bond. The naturally occurring unsaturated fatty acids are all cis form with the molecules bent back at

TABLE 10.1. Structure of fatty acids of biological importance.

Molecular formula	Common name	Systematic name
Saturated acids		
$C_4H_8O_2$	Butyric	n-Butanoic
$C_6H_{12}O_2$	Caproic	n-Hexanoic
$C_{10}H_{20}O_2$	Capric	Decanoic
$C_{12}H_{24}O_2$	Lauric	Dodecanoic
$C_{14}H_{28}O_2$	Myristic	Tetradecanoic
$C_{16}H_{32}O_2$	Palmitic	Hexadecanoic
$C_{18}H_{36}O_2$	Stearic	Octadecanoic
$C_{20}H_{40}O_2$	Arachidic	Eicosadecanoic
$C_{24}H_{48}O_2$	Lignoceric	Tetracosanoic
Unsaturated acids		
$C_{16}H_{30}O_2$	Palmitoleic	Hexadec-9-enoic
$C_{18}H_{34}O_2$	Oleic	Octadec-9-enoic
$C_{22}H_{42}O_2$	Erucic	Docos-13-enoic
$C_{24}H_{46}O_2$	Nervonic	Tetracos-15-enoic
$C_{18}H_{32}O_2$	Linoleic	Octadeca-9,12-dienoic
$C_{18}H_{30}O_2$	Linolenic	Octadeca-9,12,15-trienoic
$C_{20}H_{32}O_2$	Arachidonic	Eicosa-5,8,11,14-tetraenoic
Hydroxy acids		
$C_{24}H_{48}O_3$	Cerebronic	α-HO-Tetracosanoic
$C_{24}H_{46}O_3$	α-HO-Nervonic	α-HO-Tetracos-15-enoic

the double bond. Thus they cannot pack as closely together as saturated chains or those in the trans form:

Cis: natural form

Trans: not found in nature

When multiple double bonds are present in natural fatty acids, the double and single bonds do not alternate and are therefore not conjugated. A model of the linolenic acid molecule is illustrated in plate 10.1a, facing p. 10.10.

Because butyric acid has a short chain, it is slightly soluble in water (pK 4·76). The acids with longer chains are almost insoluble and have much higher pK values. These acids form esters with alcohols.

$$RCOOH + R'OH \rightleftharpoons RCOOR' + H_2O$$

They also form salts with alkalis which are the familiar soaps of commerce. The detergent properties of soaps are due to the ability to form a stable emulsion in water which dissolves oily material in its fatty chains.

The melting point of a fatty acid of a given chain length decreases with the increase in the number of double bonds. Thus oleic, linoleic and linolenic acids are oils, liquid at room temperature, unlike stearic and palmitic acids. The degree of unsaturation of a sample of fatty acids may be defined by the iodine number. This is the amount of iodine taken up by unit weight of the material.

$$\underset{\begin{array}{c}|\\ \mathrm{H}\end{array}\ \begin{array}{c}|\\ \mathrm{H}\end{array}}{\mathrm{R-C=C-R}} \xrightarrow{I_2} \underset{\begin{array}{c}|\\ \mathrm{I}\end{array}\ \begin{array}{c}|\\ \mathrm{I}\end{array}}{\overset{\begin{array}{c}\mathrm{H}\\ |\end{array}\ \begin{array}{c}\mathrm{H}\\ |\end{array}}{\mathrm{R-C-C-R}}}$$

Saturated acids are formed commercially in some margarines by hydrogenating unsaturated fatty acids using metallic catalysts. In this way the more unsaturated vegetable oils are altered to resemble animal fats. Unsaturated fatty acid chains tend to become oxidized in air, yielding unstable products, probably peroxides, which decompose to keto and hydroxy acids; these have a characteristic rancid smell.

The nature and proportion of each fatty acid in a mixture is determined by gas liquid chromatography. In this method the acids are converted to their more volatile methyl esters and a sample (a few μg only) of the mixture is swept by a stream of inert gas at elevated temperature over a liquid such as a silicone oil spread on an inert solid. The components of the vapour partition between the gas and liquid phases as they pass along the tube, the more volatile and shorter chain esters emerging before the longer chain esters. By recording the presence of a vapour in the effluent gas and the retention time, the relative amounts of each component may be compared with those of standard fatty acid esters (fig. 10.1). Since for each series of saturated, mono-, di- and tri-enoic acids, the log of the retention time is proportional to the chain length, it is possible to determine the identity of an unknown fatty acid.

Triglycerides and waxes

Most of the dietary fat is composed of a mixture of tri-

FIG. 10.1. Separation of a mixture of fatty methyl esters on a column of synthetic polymer-containing ester groups.

glycerides (TG). Each TG molecule has three fatty acid chains esterified by the trihydric alcohol glycerol to give a single neutral molecule. The waxes are esters of fatty acids with long chain alcohols.

$$\begin{array}{c}
\qquad\qquad\qquad\qquad\overset{O}{\underset{\|}{}}\\
\qquad\qquad H_2COC(CH_2)_{14}CH_3\\
\qquad\overset{O}{\underset{\|}{}}\qquad\qquad |\\
CH_3(CH_2)_7CH{=}CH(CH_2)_7COCH\\
\qquad\qquad\qquad\qquad |\qquad\overset{O}{\underset{\|}{}}\\
\qquad\qquad H_2COC\,(CH_2)_{16}CH_3
\end{array}$$

A triglyceride

α-Stearyl-β-oleyl-palmitin

$$\overset{O}{\underset{\|}{}}$$
$$CH_3(CH_2)_8CH_2OC\,(CH_2)_{14}CH_3$$

Bees wax

Myricyl palmitate

Fats used in the food industry may be of animal origin, e.g. lard, butter and fish liver oil, or of vegetable origin, e.g. groundnut, maize (corn), cotton seed, sesame, coconut and olive oils. Since they are all triglycerides, the difference between them lies in the nature and proportions of the particular fatty acids esterified to the glycerol moieties (table 10.2). Milk fats are exceptional in that 10 per cent of the fatty acids have short chains of four to twelve carbon atoms. Mammalian tissues, including human fat, contain predominantly C_{16} and C_{18} acids, some saturated and others unsaturated. Olive oil has $C_{18:1}$ as a major component and corn oil $C_{18:2}$. The high proportion of polyunsaturated fatty acids in fish oils keeps them liquid at the temperature of sea water, whereas the solid fat, lard, has about 50 per cent of fatty acids $C_{16:0}$ and $C_{18:0}$. It must be emphasized that a fat such as butter is not a chemically pure substance consisting of millions of identical molecules, as is the case with a spoonful of cane sugar.

TABLE 10.2. Fatty acids present in common foods (approximate percentage of total fatty acids).

	C_{4-6}	C_{8-12}	C_{14}	C_{16}	C_{18}	$C_{16:1}$	$C_{18:1}$	$C_{18:2}$	Poly-unsaturated
Milk	5	6	8	26	11	3	33	4	2
Egg	–	–	trace	25	8	3	52	9	3
Ox fat	–	–	3	29	21	3	41	2	trace
Pig fat	–	–	1	28	15	2	47	4	3
Herring	–	–	8	12	trace	6	←21→		51
Cod liver	–	–	6	9	trace	20	←29→		36
Olive oil	–	–	1	16	2	1	65	15	trace
Corn oil	–	–	–	8	2	1	30	56	2
Cotton seed	–	–	1	17	2	1	41	37	trace
Sesame seed	–	–	–	8	4	trace	45	41	trace
Sunflower seed	–	–	–	4	4	trace	14	73	1
Ground nut oil	–	–	trace	9	3	trace	65	17	trace
Soya bean oil	–	–	trace	10	2	trace	29	51	6
Red palm oil	–	–	2	35	5	trace	52	5	trace

It is a mixture of different triglyceride molecules. Thus a sample of human fat, in which the fatty acids are oleic acid (R_1) 50 per cent, palmitic acid (R_2) 23 per cent, linolenic acid (R_3) 10 per cent, stearic acid (R_4) 6 per cent and palmitoleic acid (R_5) 5 per cent, consists of many different molecules such as:

The glycerol portion may be esterified with any three of these five acids in any one of the three positions on the molecule.

The triglycerides can be separated by gas liquid chromatography without prior hydrolysis. Obviously saponification and subsequent analysis of the liberated fatty acids by gas liquid chromatography, which is easier to perform, gives an overall picture rather than information about the individual triglyceride molecules which are present. A molecule in which all three fatty acids are the same is very seldom encountered in nature and each usually contains at least one saturated and one unsaturated fatty acid.

Phospholipids and sphingolipids

The phospholipids, unlike the triglycerides, contain phosphorus and frequently nitrogen as well as carbon, hydrogen and oxygen. They are important constituents of biological membranes, blood plasma and egg yolk.

GROUP I PHOSPHATIDES

The first group are derived from L-**phosphatidic acid** and have the general formula:

One of the α-positions on the glycerol molecule is esterified by phosphoric acid and the other two by fatty acids. The hydroxyl group on the phosphate is also esterified by one of the following alcohols:

Choline	$HO-CH_2CH_2\overset{+}{N}(CH_3)_3$	basic
Ethanolamine	$HO-CH_2CH_2NH_2$	basic
Serine	$HO-CH_2CHNH_2COOH$	ampho-teric
Inositol		neutral

Glycerol $HOCH_2CHOHCH_2OH$ neutral
Phosphorylated
   inositol $C_6H_6(OH)_4[OPO(OH)_2]_2$ acidic

The structures of some important phospholipids as they exist at physiological pH are shown below, where R_1, and R_2 are long hydrocarbon chains and R_2 is generally unsaturated.

Phosphatidyl choline (lecithin) (nearly neutral)

Phosphatidyl ethanolamine (weakly acidic)

Phosphatidyl serine (acidic)

Phosphatidyl inositol diphosphate (acidic)

The mitochondrial lipid in heart muscle contains cardiolipin. Unlike the other phospholipids it is not found in brain. The structure is given below; the esterified fatty acids are mainly polyenoic.

Cardiolipin
(acidic)

It can be seen that phospholipids, unlike triglycerides, are charged polar compounds. Since some are neutral and others show varying acidity, it is possible to separate the classes by partition chromatography on silicic acid columns. In general the fatty acids on the β position are unsaturated, while those on the α position are saturated. One or other of these may be absent, for example in the 1-acyl and 2-acylglyceryl phosphoryl cholines. These substances are called lysolecithins as they have the ability to lyse or break cell membranes.

β-Lysolecithin

α-Lysolecithin

The **plasmalogens** have an unsaturated ether group, rather than an ester group, on the α position. Those of ethanolamine and choline form a big proportion of the phospholipids of brain and heart.

$$H_2C-O-CH=CH(CH_2)_{13}CH_3$$
$$R_2C\overset{O}{=}O-CH$$
$$H_2C-O-\overset{O^-}{\underset{O}{P}}-O-CHCHNH_2$$

An ethanolamine plasmalogen

The suffix 'alogen' in their name is used since, on mild hydrolysis, they yield an aldehyde. In the compound shown, this would be $CH_3(CH_2)_{13}CHO$.

GROUP 2 SPHINGOLIPIDS

These contain **sphingosine**, a complex base which is in some ways structurally similar to a monoglyceride.

$$CH_3(CH_2)_{12}CH=CH\underset{OH}{\overset{H}{C}}-\underset{NH_2}{\overset{H}{C}}-\underset{OH}{CH_2}$$

Sphingomyelins found in nervous tissue, particularly myelin sheath, and in blood contain sphingosine, phosphoryl choline and a molecule of fatty acid. The phosphoryl choline is esterified to the primary alcohol group and an amide link joins the fatty acid to the amino group.

$$CH_3(CH_2)_{12}CH=CH\underset{OH}{\overset{H}{C}}-\underset{NH}{\overset{H}{C}}-CH_2-O-\overset{O^-}{\underset{CH_2CH_2\overset{+}{N}(CH_3)_3}{P=O}}$$
$$\underset{R_1}{\overset{C=O}{|}}$$

N-acylsphingosine   phosphoryl choline

Cerebrosides are similar compounds with a hexose joined by an ether link to sphingosine in place of the phosphoryl choline, i.e. they contain no phosphorus. The sugar residue is usually galactose. The fatty acid mixture obtained after hydrolysing brain cerebrosides contains $C_{24:0}$ and C_{24}-α-hydroxyacids as major components.

$$CH_3(CH_2)_{12}CH=CH\underset{OH}{\overset{H}{C}}-\underset{NH}{\overset{H}{C}}CH_2-O-$$
$$\underset{R_1}{\overset{C=O}{|}}$$

A cerebroside (glycolipid)

Gangliosides are found in erythrocytes, spleen and nervous tissue, and resemble cerebrosides but are more complex. They have the following structure:

N-acylsphingosine-
 glucose-galactose-N-acetylglucosamine
  |
  N-acetylneuraminic acid

Brain ganglioside

The carbohydrate side chain is longer and contains one molecule of N-acetyl glucosamine and at least one of N-acetyl neuraminic acid.

$$HOOC\overset{O}{=}C-CH_2-\underset{H}{\overset{OH}{C}}-\underset{HN}{\overset{H}{C}}-\underset{OH}{\overset{H}{C}}-\underset{H}{\overset{OH}{C}}-\underset{H}{\overset{OH}{C}}-CH_2OH$$
$$\underset{CH_3}{\overset{C=O}{|}}$$

N-acetylneuraminic acid

Phospholipids have been known for nearly 100 years but their function is still uncertain and is discussed on p. 10.17. The distribution of lipids in the nervous system is shown in table 24.5.

Cholesterol

The steroids form a large class of lipids, which includes the hormones of the adrenal and sex glands, vitamin D and the bile acids. These substances are produced in the body from cholesterol which is widespread in nature and present in all normal diets in amounts up to 1 g daily, but larger quantities are synthesized throughout the tissues, mainly in the liver. Cholesterol has the structural formula:

Many biological compounds have the same ring structure but with different substituents especially at positions 3, 11 and 17.

The essential functions of cholesterol and related compounds at the molecular level are not precisely known. These are undoubtedly related to the shape and general configuration of the basic steroid structure.

Steroids may be regarded as derivatives of a parent substance, perhydro*cyclo*pentenophenanthrene.

As its rings, unlike those of aromatic compounds such as benzene, are fully saturated, the bond angle of the six membered rings is 120°. Now the tetrahedral angles of the bonds about an isolated carbon atom are about 109°. Consequently in these rings the carbon–carbon bonds would be strained from this optimum angle, if the rings did not buckle.

Consider first the single ring compound, *cyclo*hexane, C_6H_{12}, which can exist in two non-planar forms, the chair and the boat (fig. 10.2). The chair form has carbon

FIG. 10.2. The *cyclo*hexane ring in two non-planar forms.

atoms 1, 3 and 5 in one plane and the rest in a parallel plane a little above. It is the form in which most of the molecules exist. In it there are two kinds of bonds, those parallel to the threefold axis of symmetry of the molecule (axial) and those which make an angle of 109° with the axis of the ring (equatorial). By rotating the ring valence bonds two chair forms can be visualized (fig. 10.3).

FIG. 10.3. Two chair forms of *cyclo*hexane.

They are equivalent, unless the groups represented in the open and closed circles are different, as in the mono-

substituted compound, *cyclo*hexanol. Then the two forms exist in equilibrium with one another. The one with the hydroxyl group in the equatorial position is more stable and present in greater amount.

When two groups are substituted on adjoining carbon atoms in a *cyclo*hexane ring, if one substituent is axial and the other equatorial, the arrangement is cis. If both are axial, the arrangement is trans (fig. 10.4).

FIG. 10.4. Trans and cis forms of 1:2-disubstituted *cyclo*hexanes.

Turning now to the situation in which two rings are fused together, as in the steroids, we can visualize two ways in which this could be done. One is the trans form in which the bonds to hydrogen at the ends of the ring junction are both axial (fig. 10.5). In the cis form they lie in the

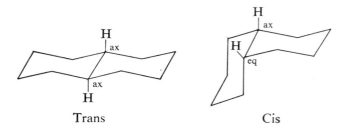

FIG. 10.5. Two ways in which *cyclo*hexane rings may be fused together.

equatorial and axial positions. If a group is substituted for hydrogen, to regain stability, i.e. with minimum interference from other groups, this larger group should be in the equatorial position (fig. 10.6.). By convention a group which sticks down below the junction of the rings is described as α to the junction, while the other possibility is described as β to the junction. Consequently, for stability the 3-hydroxyl should be α in a cis form and β in the trans form. This is the situation in the common sterols. Cholestanol, derived from cholesterol, a compound with the trans configuration, is a 3-β-ol while the bile acids are cis 3-α-ols. Using the easier flat diagrams it is customary to indicate that a group is α or below the

Trans -β   Cis -α

Trans -α   Cis -β

(HO lies below plane   (HO lies above plane
of ring A)   of ring A)

FIG. 10.6. Four forms of 3-HO-*cyclo*decalin.

plane of the ring junction by using a dotted bond. In this way the formulae below show part of the molecules of the bile acids and of cholestanol.

Cis-3-α-ol   Trans-3-β-ol
Bile acid   Cholestanol

Cholesterol is generally written as on p. 10.5. Notice that the double bond is adjacent to the junction between rings A and B. Cholestanol is shown in fig. 10.7, in which the spatial relationships between the atoms is indicated.

FIG. 10.7. Cholestanol.

The rings are locked together along 5/10 and 8/9, resulting in the occurrence of asymmetric centres at carbon atoms 3, 5, 8, 9, 10, 13, 14, 17 and 20. The groups pointing to the back of the molecule (downwards on the paper) are α orientated. They are written joined to the nucleus by broken lines, while those to the front (β groups) are joined by continuous lines. The 3-hydroxy and angular methyl groups at 18 and 19 and the side chain are all β orientated. Plate 10.1c-d, facing p. 10.10, shows models of the cholesterol and cholic acid molecules.

Since cholesterol with its hydroxyl group is an alcohol, it is capable of forming esters with acids. Those of biological importance are with long chain fatty acids or with sulphate. On reduction of the double bond at position 5, two arrangements at C_5 are possible. The products of microbial reduction in the gut are in the trans form while the cis one is found in the bile acids.

BILE ACIDS
These are oxidation products of cholesterol in which the side chain has been partially removed with formation of a carboxyl group. There are also one, two or three α-hydroxy groups and the double bond at C_{5-6} has been reduced. The cis configuration is found at the junction of rings A and B.

Cholic acid and chenodeoxycholic acid are the primary bile acids. Fig. 10.8 indicates their structure and the mechanism of their formation. Two other bile acids, deoxycholic acid and lithocholic acid, are formed by intestinal bacterial action (p. 31.8).

Compounds with a free 3-β-hydroxy group, e.g. cholesterol, are precipitated by a digitonin which is itself a steroid glycoside. This provides a method of separating cholesterol from other steroids and 3-α-hydroxy acids. A quantitative method of assaying cholesterol is the Liebermann–Burchardt reaction. It is based on the blue–green colour formed when cholest-5-en-3-β-ol is mixed with concentrated sulphuric acid and acetic anhydride. The bile acids with three α hydroxy groups at 3, 7 and 12, or two hydroxy groups at 3 and 7 or 3 and 12, give a pink colour with furfural under acid conditions. This is the Pettenkofer reaction.

The fat-soluble vitamins
An account of the nutritional aspects of these substances is given on p. 5.11.

VITAMIN A
Vitamin A or retinol is a pale yellow substance quite insoluble in water. As already described part is supplied preformed in the diet and part is derived by oxidation in the body of carotenes, which are water soluble, coloured pigments present in plants. β carotene, which is orange in colour, is the main source of retinol and the conversion is shown in fig. 10.9.

Retinol and carotene are stable to heat and temperatures normally used in cooking but are readily oxidized. With the high temperatures used in frying, losses are small if exposure to air is limited as in deep frying, but with shallow frying pans all vitamin activity may be lost.

FIG. 10.8. The conversion of cholesterol to bile acids in the liver.

Chenodeoxycholic acid

Cholic acid

β-Carotene

Retinol

FIG. 10.9. The conversion of β-Carotene to retinol.

Retinol reacts with antimony trichloride to form a bright blue compound with an absorption maximum at 620 μm and this property is used for assay purposes both in foods and in tissues.

VITAMIN D

Vitamin D exists in several forms. The natural form, vitamin D_3, has the following structure:

C_8H_{17}

HO

7-Dehydrocholesterol

C_8H_{17}

H_2C

HO

Vitamin D_3

It is formed by the action of sunlight on 7-dehydrocholesterol, a sterol widely distributed in the skin and all animal fats. Vitamin D_2 (calciferol), used in therapeutics, is formed from the irradiation of ergosterol, a sterol found in fungi and yeast. This compound differs from 7-dehydrocholesterol in having as a side chain —C_9H_{17}. There is as yet no satisfactory chemical method of estimating vitamin D in foodstuffs. The vitamin can be estimated only by bioassay, usually the ability to prevent rickets occurring in rats or chicks on a vitamin-free diet. The lack of a good chemical test greatly handicaps the control of the vitamin D content of infant foods and the study of its metabolism.

VITAMIN E

Vitamin E is a mixture of tocopherols, which are yellow oily liquids remarkably stable to heat. α-Tocopherol has the following structure:

$$H_3C \quad \overset{CH_3}{\underset{8}{|}} \quad O \quad \overset{CH_3}{|} \quad \overset{CH_3}{|} \quad \overset{CH_3}{|} \quad \overset{CH_3}{|}$$
$$\overset{7}{} \quad \overset{}{} \quad -(CH_2)_3 CH(CH_2)_3 CH(CH_2)_3 CH$$
$$HO \quad \overset{6}{} \quad \overset{5}{} \qquad \qquad \qquad \overset{|}{CH_3}$$
$$\overset{|}{CH_3}$$

Vitamin E; α-(or trimethyl)-tocopherol

Five other tocopherols have vitamin E activity; they differ structurally in having only one or two methyl groups in the 5, 7, 8 positions.

VITAMIN K

Vitamin K exists in nature in two forms and several synthetic analogues are used clinically. Vitamins K_1 and K_2 are both derivatives of the cyclic structure naphthoquinone and each has a long side chain designated R in the formula:

O

CH_3

R

O

In K_1, 2-methyl-3-phytyl-1,4-naphthoquinone, R is

$$-CH_2-CH=\overset{CH_3}{\underset{|}{C}}-(CH_2-CH_2-CH_2-\overset{CH_3}{\underset{|}{CH}}-)_3CH_3$$

In K_2, 2-methyl-3-difarnesyl-1, 4-naphthoquinone, R is

$$-CH_2-(CH=\overset{CH_3}{\underset{|}{C}}-CH_2-CH_2-)_5CH=\overset{CH_3}{\underset{|}{C}}-CH_3$$

METABOLIC ROLES OF THE FAT-SOLUBLE VITAMINS

While the cellular function of most of the B group of vitamins may be described in precise biochemical terms, the detailed functions of the fat-soluble vitamins are virtually unknown. For instance, how vitamin A affects growth and the development of bone and connective tissue is not established though there is evidence that it is essential for the normal lipoprotein structure of cell membranes.

The precise role of vitamin A is established only in respect of its action in night vision. The cis form of the aldehyde retinene, which is derived from the vitamin, combines with a protein (opsin) to form the visual pigment, rhodopsin. When this is bleached by light, it breaks down into opsin and retinene, this time in the trans form. This is converted back into the vitamin which then undergoes conversion to the cis form, which is ready for reoxidation to retinene (cis). The conversions may be summarized diagrammatically:

Rhodopsin

Light

Opsin + retinene (cis)
(Vitamin A aldehyde) → Retinene (trans) + opsin

Dark ‖ NAD   ‖ NADH₂

11-cis retinol ⇌ All-trans retinol

Other aspects of night vision are found on pp. 5.11 and 24.60. As the regeneration process is slow, a sufficient quantity of vitamin A aldehyde must be present if vision in poor light is to be maintained.

Although vitamin D is essential for the normal absorption of calcium from the small intestine and for its deposition in growing bone, how these effects are brought about is not known.

The polyunsaturated fatty acids such as linoleic acid are sensitive to autoxidation in the presence of oxygen. This is a free radical attack.

$$R_1CH_2CH{=}CHCH_2R_2 \xrightarrow{O_2} RCH_2CH{-}CH_2CH_2R_2$$
$$\underset{\displaystyle OOH}{|} \quad \text{(peroxide)}$$

It can be suppressed by anti-oxidants such as the tocopherols. This autoxidation is most readily demonstrated in chicks fed a diet rich in polyunsaturated fatty acids and low in vitamin E. Whether vitamin E has a significant action in this respect in healthy tissues is uncertain.

Vitamin K is necessary for the formation of prothrombin by the liver, but how it affects the synthesis of this protein is not known. Uncoupling of oxidative phosphorylation in mitochondria obtained from vitamin K deficient chicks has been observed.

METABOLISM OF LIPIDS

Alimentary absorption

Adults on a normal western diet absorb 100–120 g of lipid per day; most of this is triglyceride but there is also cholesterol and phospholipid. The ingested material enters the duodenum as a coarse emulsion. Here some of the fatty acids are split off the TG molecules by pancreatic lipase and 2-monoglycerides and a little glycerol are liberated (30.37).

Since the fatty acids and monoglycerides are not water soluble, one might foresee difficulties in transporting them into the intestinal mucosal cells. This is overcome by the action of bile salts which combine with them to form aggregates or micelles. These particles are less than 0·5 μm in diameter, about one-hundredth the size of those in the original TG emulsion. They form a clear liquid which is able to enter the villi of the mucosal cells, along with the glycerol and other water-soluble compounds. Within the cells the monoglycerides are then re-esterified by activated fatty acids. The resulting TG droplets are not identical with those ingested, since the dietary fatty acids change position on the glycerol molecule, and are mixed with those entering the mucosal cells from the blood. Some short chain acids with fewer than fourteen carbon atoms pass directly into the portal blood along with any free glycerol, due probably to their greater water solubility and rejection by the esterifying enzymes. The bile salts do not appear to enter the intestinal cells but pass into the ileum where they diffuse into the blood and recirculate to the liver. The cholesterol and phosphatidyl choline added in bile are also largely reabsorbed.

Dietary cholesterol esters are hydrolysed in the gut along with TG. The products pass into the intestinal epithelial cells where they mix with cholesterol formed endogenously and are almost all esterified. The acids used are mainly unsaturated, presumably selected from the fatty acid pool by the enzymes involved. Phospholipids are also formed within the intestinal cells.

The lipids accumulating in the cells pass out into the lymph in the form of **chylomicrons**. These are particles consisting mostly of TG with some cholesterol, phospholipid and protein in proportions which vary slightly and are indicated in table 10.4. Being 0·1–1 μm in diameter, they scatter light and so a suspension of chylomicrons appears milky. This is readily observed in lymph or plasma sampled 3 or 4 hr after a meal rich in fat.

Transport of lipids in the blood

The chylomicrons pass into the lymph, through the thoracic duct and into the blood in the great veins of the neck. There they join the other lipoproteins formed by the liver from endogenous TG. The normal range of the lipid content of serum is shown in table 10.3. The lipids are

TABLE 10.3. The normal range of values of serum lipids in healthy young adults (mg/100 ml).

	Range
Cholesterol	140–260
Phospholipids	165–275
Triglyceride (fasting)	50–300

transported in the plasma as lipoproteins. These macromolecules consist of a central core of TG surrounded by cholesterol and its esters, phospholipid and a little protein, the apoprotein. The phosphate groups of phosphatidyl choline and sphingomyelin are in contact with the aqueous phase and their charge may stabilize the colloid. Phospholipid and protein in lipoproteins turn over more slowly than the triglyceride portion. Lipoproteins may be looked upon as transporters which carry TG. In the tissues the TG is unloaded for use and the transporter is returned for reloading, usually in the liver.

The three types of lipoprotein formed in the liver are designated α, pre-β and β from their mobility relative to the globulins during the electrophoresis of serum (p. 11.4). Each has its own structure and chemical composition, although in fact each consists of many lipid components. The apoprotein of α-lipoproteins appears to differ from that of the β-lipoproteins, judging from their amino acid content and their antigenicity. The pre-β-lipoproteins probably contain both the α-and β-apoproteins and

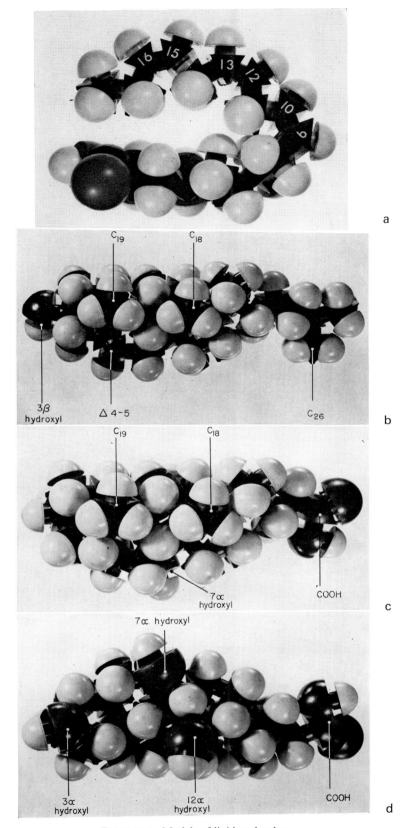

PLATE 10.1. Models of lipid molecules.
(a) Linolenic acid, (b) cholesterol, (c) cholic acid from β-face, (d) cholic acid from α-face.

PLATE 11.1. Model of a haemoglobin molecule.
From Perutz M.F. (1960) *Nature (Lond.)*.

another peptide. The proteins are formed in the liver and have a half-life (3–4 days) shorter than that of other plasma proteins.

When the lipoproteins are considered in order of increasing density (table 10.4), it will be seen that the TG

extent. The cholesterol esters of the high density lipoproteins contain a larger proportion of arachidonic acid and other polyunsaturated essential fatty acids than do those in the low density fraction which resemble the liver cholesterol esters. High levels of total plasma cholesterol

TABLE 10.4. The lipoproteins in serum.

Lipoprotein	Electrophoretic Mobility	Density	Average concentration mg/100 ml	Percentage composition			
				Protein	T.G.	Total cholesterol	Phospholipid
Chylomicrons	None	<0·96	0–50	2	82	9	7
Very low density	pre β (or α_2)	0·96–1·006	150	7	52	23	18
Low density	β	1·006–1·063	400	21	9	47	23
High density	α_1	>1·063	350	46	8	19	27

content falls, while that of the phospholipid and protein rises. The analyses also show that β or low density lipoproteins contain a higher proportion of cholesterol than the others. When the β-lipoprotein level rises in the plasma the cholesterol level rises inevitably. In the same way the chylomicrons and very low density lipoproteins parallel changes in the TG level. It is possible to achieve a large scale separation of the different plasma lipoproteins by making stepwise additions of sodium bromide in order to raise the specific gravity to fixed values. The lipoproteins lighter than the density of the solution can then be centrifuged at high speeds to the top of the tube. In this way successive lipoprotein fractions of defined density can be obtained. Normally about 70 per cent of the cholesterol is esterified. When in a fasting man, the TG level in the serum falls to about 50 mg/100 ml, only about 30 per cent of the fatty acid present is in TG molecules. After a meal containing at least 30 g of fat, however, the quantity of TG rises and chylomicrons appear. The cholesterol and phospholipid concentrations remain virtually unchanged.

The lipoprotein content of the blood depends on the quantities of the different types of lipids to be transported, the availability of amino acids and phospholipids and on a normally functioning liver.

In certain rare hereditary conditions, in which high density lipoprotein is deficient, cholesterol accumulates in the cells of the reticuloendothelial system. From this it can be deduced that this lipoprotein is involved in cholesterol transport. It has also been observed that in the normal individual the rate of turnover of ^{14}C-cholesterol carried on high density lipoprotein is greater than for cholesterol carried on low density lipoprotein. Possibly the high density lipoproteins are required to carry cholesterol from the peripheral sites to the liver for conversion to bile salts and excretion. Those of lower density are necessary for the transport of triglycerides from the liver and intestinal mucosal cells. Tissues other than the liver remove ^{14}C-cholesterol from the plasma, though to a much smaller

fall if unsaturated vegetable oils are substituted in the diet for saturated fats. It seems probable that this effect is produced by changing the distribution of cholesterol between the plasma and cellular compartments of the body rather than by decreasing its rate of synthesis or increasing that of its degradation.

Atherosclerosis, a condition in which lipid is deposited in the intima of the arteries, leads to coronary artery disease and other vascular disorders. The probability of an individual developing one of these diseases has been correlated with the quantity of cholesterol (or more precisely of β-lipoprotein) circulating in the blood. As a consequence much effort has gone into studying the causes of abnormal elevation of blood cholesterol which

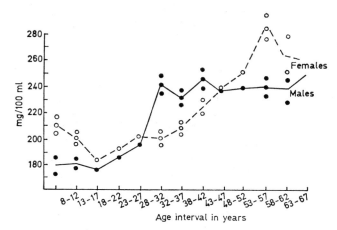

FIG. 10.10. The relation of total serum cholesterol to age in male and female. From Adlersbeg *et al.* (1956) *J. Amer. Med. Ass.* **162**, 619.

may be defined as a value above 240 mg/100 ml. Fig. 10.10 shows the mean serum cholesterol levels of apparently healthy New Yorkers of both sexes at different ages. The rise which begins in males in the third decade is delayed in females until the mid forties, apparently through the

6

protective action of female sex hormones. Other factors predisposing to a high plasma cholesterol are lack of exercise and the diet, which in prosperous countries is high in saturated fatty acid and sucrose. These may exaggerate the genetic tendency of some individuals to maintain a high serum cholesterol level. It should be emphasized however that a direct cause and effect relationship between hypercholesterolaemia and atherosclerosis has not been proved.

Breakdown of lipoprotein

The lipoprotein TG is removed from the blood by the adipose tissue and muscle through the action of an enzyme, **lipoprotein lipase** (LPL). In this way the plasma is 'cleared' of its milky appearance. The fatty acids which are split off the TG core by the enzyme enter the tissues. In adipose cells they are reformed into TG with α-glycerophosphate derived from blood glucose. In muscle they are used directly for oxidation. The liberated glycerol and other components remain in the blood and return to the liver. The activity of plasma LPL is increased after a meal. It is decreased in fasting, but on the other hand the **TG lipase** present in adipose tissue has its activity increased by fasting and decreased by feeding. The function of the two enzymes is different. LPL is used to put triglycerides into the stores and is required only when there is already sufficient metabolic fuel (carbohydrate). The other lipase breaks down stored TG when it is needed as an energy source. LPL seems to be located near the walls of the blood capillaries. After an injection of heparin the activity of the enzyme in the plasma is increased. This is probably due to activation of the enzyme but perhaps also to stimulation of its release from a storage site. It may be that heparin or a closely related substance forms an integral part of the enzyme, either stabilizing it or allowing it to combine with the lipoprotein substrate.

The liver differs from other tissues in that lipoproteins are taken up directly without prior breakdown by lipase. Within the parenchymal cells they are dismantled, yielding oily drops of TG which may be subsequently hydrolysed. As labelled plasma FFA (defined in the next paragraph) are not incorporated into plasma lipoproteins in hepatectomized animals, the probable site of lipoprotein formation is the liver. The fatty acid pattern of the lipoprotein-TG resembles less closely that of the recently ingested triglycerides than does that of the chylomicrons. This is because the liver fatty acids from which they are built up include those brought in as FFA from the adipose stores (laid down over a considerable period) and those formed endogenously by the liver. In the liver, FFA molecules are replaced into TG molecules and also tailored by the lengthening and desaturation of their chains.

Breakdown of fatty acids

Fatty acids on oxidation yield a large quantity of energy and function principally as an energy store in the form of TG. When they are required by the body, TG is broken down by lipases to yield glycerol and free fatty acids (FFA). Both products pass out of the fat storage cells into the blood stream, where the fatty acids are transported bound to plasma albumin, being otherwise insoluble in water.

Injection of isotopically labelled fatty acids into the blood has shown that the molecules are taken up by the liver, heart, kidney, muscle and other organs. There they may be reformed into TG and other lipids or oxidized within the mitochondria of the cells. To cross from the cytoplasm into the mitochondrial membranes the fatty acids must probably first be esterified with coenzyme A and then with carnitine.

$$RCO.SCoA + (CH_3)_3 \overset{+}{N}-CH_2-CH-CH_2-CO\overset{-}{O}$$
$$\underset{OH}{|}$$

$$Carnitine$$
$$\downarrow$$

$$(CH_3)_3\overset{+}{N}-CH_2-CH-CH_2\ CO\overset{-}{O} + CoASH$$
$$\underset{OCOR}{|}$$

The necessary transferase enzyme is more active when cytoplasmic FFA concentration is rising, as in starvation. At the same time glycolysis is inhibited and so entry of pyruvate into the mitochondria is reduced.

Oxidation of fatty acids.

Four classes of enzymes, found in the mitochondria of liver and other tissues, break down fatty acid chains by stepwise removal of two carbon fragments. The removal of a fragment involves:

(1) activation by esterification with coenzyme A,
(2) oxidation at the β position,
(3) hydration,
(4) reoxidation, followed by
(5) liberation of acetyl CoA.

The chain is then shorter by two carbon atoms (fig. 10.11). Thus in a series of steps a C_{18} chain is broken down to nine acetyl units. This is termed the β-oxidation pathway. When all the necessary enzymes are present, no fatty acids with C_4 to C_{14} chains or other intermediates can be isolated. Each step is apparently co-ordinated with the following one in such a way that the products do not accumulate but pass straight down through the reaction sequence to acetyl CoA. The polyunsaturated fatty acids, linoleic and arachidonic, are as rapidly oxidized as the saturated ones apparently by the same route.

(1) $RCH_2CH_2COOH + ATP + CoASH \xrightarrow[\text{thiokinase}]{Mg^{++}}$

$\qquad RCH_2CH_2CO.SCoA + AMP + PP$

(2) $RCH_2CH_2CO.SCoA + FAD \xrightarrow[\text{dehydrogenase}]{\text{acyl}}$

$\qquad \overset{\beta}{R}CH = \overset{\alpha}{CH}CO.SCoA + FADH_2$

(3) $RCH = CHCO.SCoA + H_2O \xrightarrow[\text{hydrase}]{\text{enoyl}}$

$\qquad \overset{\beta}{R}CHOH\,\overset{\alpha}{CH_2}CO.SCoA$

(4) $RCHOH\,CH_2CO.SCoA + NAD \xrightarrow[\text{dehydrogenase}]{\beta\text{-HO—acyl}}$

$\qquad RCOCH_2CO.SCoA + NADH_2$

(5) $RCOCH_2CO.SCoA + CoASH \xrightarrow{\text{thiolase}}$

$\qquad RCO.SCoA + CH_3COSCoA$

FIG. 10.11. β-oxidation of fatty acids.

For every two carbon atoms split off, one molecule of FAD and one of NAD is reduced (steps 2 and 4). These enter the respiratory chain for oxidation by the cytochromes and generate five ATP molecules. The liberated acetyl CoA molecules join the common pool, mixing with those formed by oxidation of pyruvate derived from glucose or amino acids. They may also be used to form fatty acids or cholesterol (p. 10.20). However, in the tissues of a fasted individual who has little carbohydrate available most of the acetyl CoA present has been derived from fat and is used for energy production rather than for synthetic purposes.

The energy which may be obtained by the oxidation of one molecule of stearic acid ($C_{18:0}$) may be calculated as follows; for each of the eight stages where an acetyl CoA molecule is formed five molecules of ATP are produced as described above. Each of the nine acetyl CoA units may enter the citric acid cycle and generate twelve ATP molecules on one revolution. Thus the C_{18} acid forms $(8 \times 5) + (9 \times 12) = 148$ ATP molecules. This may be compared with three molecules of glucose (also eighteen carbon atoms) which can form $3 \times 39 = 117$ ATP molecules. Alternatively, since one mole of stearic acid weighs 258 g and three moles of glucose 540 g, one gram stearic acid can provide $\dfrac{148}{117} \times \dfrac{540}{258} = 2\cdot6$ times more energy than one gram of glucose. The ratio of the heats of combustion of stearic acid and of glucose is $\dfrac{9\cdot3}{3\cdot69} = 2\cdot5$. Fat (TG) is thus a more concentrated store of chemical energy than carbohydrate.

It has been observed that in brain tissue palmitic acid is oxidized *in vitro* more rapidly than palmityl CoA. This is contrary to the findings for other tissue and suggests that a different oxidative pathway is followed. A hint is given by the presence of odd numbered and α-hydroxy fatty acids in the cerebrosides of the white matter. It is estimated that the fatty acids used in the brain and also by plant chloroplasts are oxidized predominantly to α-hydroxy acids, and then via the aldehydes to acids with one less carbon atom.

$CH_3(CH_2)_{22}COOH \xrightarrow{O_2} CH_3(CH_2)_{21}\overset{\alpha}{CH}OH\,COOH$

$CH_3(CH_2)_{21}COOH \xrightarrow[\underset{NADH_2\ \ NAD}{}]{} CH_3(CH_2)_{21}CHO + CO_2$

$CH_3(CH_2)_{20}CHOH\,COOH \dashrightarrow CH_3(CH_2)_{20}COOH$, etc.

Enzymes capable of activating fatty acids with CoA do exist in the brain. They are probably involved in the synthetic pathways.

Liver microsomes and also certain bacteria can oxidize fatty acids of intermediate chain length at the final or ω position by a process involving molecular oxygen, ferrous ions and $NADH_2$. The resulting ω-hydroxy compounds are further oxidized to the dicarboxylic acids which may be excreted or split by the β-oxidative pathway. The physiological importance of the ω-oxidation of fatty acids is not yet clear.

$\overset{\omega}{CH_3}(CH_2)_8COOH \longrightarrow HOCH_2(CH_2)_8COOH \longrightarrow$

$\qquad HOOC(CH_2)_8COOH \longrightarrow 5CH_3CO.SCoA$

These oxidations are brought about by mixed function oxidases (p. 7.4). Some of the enzymes involved in the chain of reactions have been separated from the microorganism *Pseudomonas* and partly purified. They consist of a non-haem iron electron carrier rubredoxin, an $NADH_2$ rubredoxin reductase and the ω-hydroxylase. The reactive sequence may be postulated as follows:

Fatty acid synthesis

It is a common observation that the body appears to lay down fat when the diet is rich in carbohydrate. The conversion of carbohydrate into fat was demonstrated in 1853 by Lawes and Gilbert, the pioneers of agricultural chemistry. They showed that the carcasses of young pigs contained more than four times as much fat as had been present in their previous diet. In recent experiments performed *in vivo* and *in vitro* the labelled carbon atoms of ^{14}C-glucose have been traced to both the fatty acid and glycerol parts of the tissue TG molecules. Not unexpectedly, ^{14}C-acetate is also converted to fatty acids, suggesting that glucose may first be broken down to this two-carbon fragment before the long chains are built up. The action of the mitochondrial enzymes which oxidize fatty acids is not reversible and so these enzymes are incapable of forming fatty acid from acetate. As this synthesis occurs in cell homogenates from which all the subcellular particles have been removed, a different system containing only soluble enzymes must be involved. A cytoplasmic enzyme preparation can synthesize fatty acids from acetyl CoA, if NADPH$_2$ and manganese are added. When acetate is used as substrate, then ATP and CoA must also be supplied.

When the unfractioned enzyme system is used palmitic acid is the only product which can be isolated. However, by using ^{14}CO$_2$ and only one fraction of the enzyme mixture, the formation of malonyl CoA by the carboxylation of acetyl CoA can be demonstrated.

$$CH_3 CO.SCoA + {}^*CO_2 + ATP \xrightarrow{Mn^{++}}$$

$$H_2C \overset{\displaystyle {}^*COOH}{\underset{\displaystyle CO.SCoA}{\Big\langle}} + ADP + P_i$$

The asterisk indicates an isotopically labelled carbon atom which can be followed through a series of reactions. The single enzyme involved is acetyl CoA carboxylase. The step which it catalyses appears to be the slowest or limiting one in the whole pathway from acetyl CoA to long chain fatty acid. As a consequence, it is a probable site for the operation of physiological controls. The compound biotin acts as a carrier of carbon dioxide and is bound to the enzyme. Its role has been described by the following series of reactions.

$$H\overset{*}{C}O_3{}' + biotin\ enzyme + ATP \longrightarrow$$

$$\overset{*}{C}O_2\text{-biotin enzyme} + ADP + P_i$$

$$\overset{*}{C}O_2\text{-biotin enzyme} + acetyl\ CoA \longrightarrow$$

$$\overset{*}{malonyl}\ CoA + biotin\ enzyme$$

The biotin enzyme complex

When 1-^{14}C-malonyl CoA is provided as substrate along with acetyl CoA, the resulting palmitic acid contains no ^{14}C. On the other hand, if 2-^{14}C-malonyl CoA is used, the even carbon atoms 2–14 in the palmitic acid are labelled. This allows the system to be visualized overall as:

$$acetyl\ SCoA + 7\ 1\text{-}^{14}C\text{-malonyl}\ SCoA + 14NADPH_2$$
$$\longrightarrow CH_3(CH_2)_{14}COOH + 7{}^{14}CO_2 + 14NADP +$$
$$6H_2O + 8CoASH$$

Experimentally the quantity of NADPH$_2$ oxidized per mole of palmitic acid formed was found to be almost fourteen moles or two for each 2C residue added to the original acetyl group.

The multi-enzyme called fatty acid synthetase, which links on the malonyl groups and performs the remainder of the synthesis, has a molecular weight of many hundreds of thousands when isolated from mammalian tissue. It has still to be resolved into its constituent enzymes. However, when the bacterium, *E. coli*, was used rather than mammalian cells as source of the synthetase, the various enzymes could be separated out, along with an 'acyl-carrier' protein (ACP) of molecular weight about 10,000. The latter contained one —SH group as a 4-phospho-pantotheine residue (fig. 7.13). Its role may be as a carrier of the substrate molecules to the condensing enzyme. The activated malonyl group may then condense with the acetyl group on the carrier, yielding acetoacetyl-S-ACP, with release of a carbon atom as carbon dioxide.

$$\left. \begin{array}{l} Acetyl\ SCoA + ACP\text{-}SH \longrightarrow acetyl\ S\text{-}ACP \\ malonyl\ SCoA + ACP\text{-}SH \longrightarrow malonyl\ S\text{-}ACP \end{array} \right\} \longrightarrow$$
$$CH_3COCH_2CO.S\text{-}ACP + CO_2 + ACP\text{-}SH$$

Subsequently the acetoacetyl S-ACP is reduced to β-hydroxybutyryl S-ACP using NADPH$_2$ as hydrogen donor. The product is then dehydrated and again reduced, to butyryl S-ACP, by a process involving FMNH$_2$ and NADPH$_2$.

$$CH_3COCH_2CO.S\text{-}ACP + NADPH_2$$
$$\longrightarrow CH_3CHOHCH_2CO.S\text{-}ACP + NADP$$
$$\xrightarrow{-H_2O} CH_3CH{=}CHCO.S\text{-}ACP$$
$$CH_3CH{=}CHCO.S\text{-}ACP + FMNH_2 + NADPH_2$$
$$\longrightarrow CH_3CH_2CH_2CO.S\text{-}ACP + NADP + FMN$$

The product is a saturated chain bound to the 'acyl carrier' protein and able to pick up another molecule of malonyl S-ACP. This leads to the formation of hexanoyl S-ACP with a 6C chain. The process can be continued until the 16C acyl S-ACP is reached. At this point, the palmitic acid is freed from the carrier protein.

A carrier protein of mammalian origin has not yet been isolated but the fatty acid synthetase in mammals appears to resemble that in yeast, which has been extensively investigated. In this organism the various enzyme components required to perform the different steps of the synthesis have not yet been separated in an active state as they have been in the bacterium, but evidence has been obtained for the presence in the multi-enzyme complex of two functional thiol groups. One binds the acyl group and the other the malonyl group and subsequently the elongated chain during the reductive steps in the formation of the saturated chain.

$$HOOC\ CH_2CO—S$$
$$\searrow E$$
$$R(CH_2CH_2)_nCO—S$$
$$\downarrow$$
$$R(CH_2CH_2)_nCOCH_2\ CO—S$$
$$\searrow E+CO_2$$
reductive steps   HS
$$R(CH_2CH_2)_{n+1}\ CO—S$$
$$\searrow E$$
$$HS$$

The major difference between the bacterial enzyme system and that of the higher organisms appears to lie in the strength of the forces binding these catalytic proteins to the structural components of the cell. However, a mixture of acetyl S-ACP and malonyl S-ACP derived from *E. coli* can be converted to a long chain fatty acid by the fatty acid synthetase system of rat adipose tissue. This and the fact that both adipose tissue and lactating mammary gland require carbon dioxide and biotin for fatty acid synthesis lead to the conclusion that the cytoplasmic system is operative in these tissues as well as in the cells of micro-organisms.

Formation of unsaturated fatty acids

These arise from the corresponding saturated acids. The process requires $NADPH_2$ and molecular oxygen. For this reason yeasts grown anaerobically need a supply of oleic acid, but not when in air. In yeasts and rat liver microsomes, there are particulate enzyme systems which can convert stearic acid to oleic acid and also $C_{20\Delta8,11,14}$ to arachidonic acid $C_{20\Delta5,8,11,14}$.

In *Euglena*, a primitive green organism, the desaturase enzymes which are soluble, include ferredoxin (a nonhaem iron electron carrier protein which is also

involved in photosynthesis), a flavin nucleotide, an $NADPH_2$ dependent oxidase and a desaturase. The mechanism is probably similar to that envisaged for the ω-oxidation of fatty acids. The substrate is the fatty acid linked to the acyl carrier protein. Note that in the cytoplasmic synthesis of fatty acids the chains appear to leave the carrier when they reach C_{16}, whereas here in the particulate systems longer chain -ACPs act as intermediates in the desaturation process and possibly also in chain lengthening.

In experimental diabetic animals there is poor conversion of saturated to unsaturated fatty acids. Injection of insulin allows recovery of this process to take place, but only after a delay of about 24 hr. Actinomycin, an inhibitor of protein synthesis, also inhibits this response to insulin. Perhaps insulin promotes the synthesis of the desaturation enzymes by lifting the repression of the appropriate genes. The thyroid hormones appear to have a similar action.

Path A
$$CH_3(CH_2)_6CHOHCH_2\ CO.S\text{-}ACP$$
$$\beta\downarrow\ \alpha$$
$$CH_3(CH_2)_6CH{=}CH\ CO.S\text{-}ACP$$
$$\downarrow$$
$$CH_3(CH_2)_8CO.S\text{-}ACP$$
↓ 3 Malonyl S CoA
$$CH_3(CH_2)_{14}\ COOH+3CO_2$$
palmitic acid $C_{16\cdot0}$

Path B
$$CH_3(CH_2)_6CHOHCH_2\ CO.S\text{-}ACP$$
$$\gamma\quad\beta\downarrow\ \alpha$$
$$CH_3(CH_2)_5CH{=}CH\ CH_2CO.S\text{-}ACP$$
↓ Malonyl S CoA
$$CH_3(CH_2)_5CH{=}CH\ CH_2CO\ CH_2CO.S\text{-}ACP$$
$$\downarrow$$
$$CH_3(CH_2)_5CH{=}CH\ (CH_2)_3\ CO.S\text{-}ACP$$
↓ 3 Malonyl S-ACP
$$CH_3(CH_2)_5CH{=}CH\ (CH_2)_9\ COOH\ +3CO_2$$
cis Vaccenic acid $C_{18}\ \Delta11$

Fɪɢ. 10.12. Pathways of fatty acid formation.

An alternative route for the synthesis of unsaturated acids must exist in anaerobic organisms. Here the cytoplasmic synthesis proceeds as already described. When β-hydroxydecanoyl-ACP is formed, it can be dehydrated in the α-β position and then reduced to the saturated acyl-ACP (path A, fig. 10.12); alternatively dehydration can occur in the β-γ position. The resulting double bond is not reduced, but persists throughout the subsequent chain lengthening steps, path B.

Ingested or synthesized fatty acids may be transformed, mainly in the liver, into fatty acids particular to the specific lipids of the body (table 10.5). The unsaturated fatty acids and intermediate length saturated acids are elongated in the microsomes by addition of 2C units reacting as malonyl CoA. In contrast, chain lengthening in the mitochondrial fraction of liver occurs also by a second route, which is independent of biotin, apparently a reversal of β-oxidation. Evidence for this was provided by incubating mitochondria with 2-^{14}C-acetyl CoA and a number of cofactors. Most of the incorporated ^{14}C became located in the second carbon atom of the chain rather than on alternate atoms right along the chain. Existing or added fatty acids were being lengthened in the mitochondria rather than *de novo* synthesis taking place.

Essential fatty acids

The chain lengthening and desaturation processes are important for the provision of adequate supplies of the essential fatty acids. Dietary linoleic acid is converted by the microsomes to arachidonic acid (fig. 10.13).

TABLE 10.5. Some analytical data for major fatty acids of tissues (percentage of total fatty acids).

	C_{14}	C_{16}	C_{18}	C_{20}	$C_{16\Delta9}$	$C_{18\Delta9}$	polyunsaturated	
							$C_{18\Delta9,12}$	C_{18}, C_{20}, C_{22}
Plasma (*human*)								
Triglyceride	1	27	3	trace	3	44	15	6
Cholesterol ester	trace	12	1	1	2	23	51	8
Phospholipid	trace	35	15	1	trace	12	18	18
Sphingomyelin		42	10	20		trace		14
Erythrocytes (*human*)	1	25	19		trace	16	11	22
Depot fat (*human*)	3	24	8		5	47	10	3
Milk (*human*)	*16	22	9		4	33	8	3
Liver (*ox*)								
Neutral fat	1	30	7	trace	10	40		10
Phosphatidylcholine	1	28	14	trace	4	12	20	20
Adrenal (*ox*)	1	24	11			40		22
Brain (*human*)								
Grey: phosphatidylcholine		45	9			31		
phosphatidyl ethanolamine			27			12		39
phosphatidyl serine			25			22		37
White: phosphatidyl choline		34	13			45		
phosphatidyl ethanolamine			36			38		23
phosphatidyl serine			9			42		9

* C_4–C_{14}.

Thus
$$\overset{18}{C}H_3CH_2CH_2CH_2CH_2CH=\overset{12}{C}H\,CH_2CH=\overset{9}{C}H\,CH_2CH_2CH_2CH_2CH_2CH_2CH_2\,COOH$$
Linoleic

Desaturase | O_2 NADPH$_2$

$$\overset{18}{C}H_3CH_2CH_2CH_2CH_2CH=\overset{12}{C}H\,CH_2CH=\overset{9}{C}H\,CH_2CH=\overset{6}{C}H\,CH_2CH_2CH_2CH_2\,COOH$$
γ-Linolenic

Malonyl CoA and desaturase | O_2 NADPH$_2$

$$\overset{20}{C}H_3CH_2CH_2CH_2CH_2CH=\overset{14}{C}H\,CH_2CH=\overset{11}{C}H\,CH_2CH=\overset{8}{C}H\,CH_2CH=\overset{5}{C}H\,CH_2CH_2CH_2\,COOH$$
Arachidonic

FIG. 10.13. The conversion of lineolic to arachidonic acid

Note that these essential acids have their last double bond six places away from the methyl end. An isomeric form of linolenic acid $C_{18\Delta 9,12 \text{ and } 15}$ is transformed into $C_{20\Delta,11,14, \text{ and } 17}$. These substances are present in the tissues but are not essential fatty acids. Oleic acid is also useless in preventing the symptoms of essential fatty acid deficiency, for desaturation can occur only at a site on the carboxyl side of the existing double bond, i.e. $C_{18\Delta 9}$ cannot be converted to $C_{18\Delta 9,12}$ with the necessary double bond six places away from the methyl group.

The distribution of the fatty acids in the tissues is described in table 10.5. Arachidonic acid is found in highest concentration in the lipids of the endocrine organs, adrenal cortex, ovary, testis and pituitary, and in the brain.

To be effective, the polyunsaturated acids must be in the all-cis form. Thus arachidonic acid all cis $C_{20\Delta 5,8,11,14}$ is curved, (fig. 10.14). The all trans form would be linear, similar to a saturated chain (fig. 10.14). A phospholipid or cholesterol ester containing an all-cis polyunsaturated acid is therefore of a very different shape from one with a saturated or trans unsaturated acid.

Apart from the special role of arachidonic acid as a precursor of the prostaglandins (p. 25.48), provision of phospholipids containing the essential fatty acids appears to be necessary for the integrity of membranes and for the electron transport system of mitochondria (p. 8.9). Why the linolenic series of acids should be less effective in this regard is not known since they differ only in having their double bonds lying nearer the methyl end of the chain.

Triglyceride synthesis

The microsomes of liver and adipose tissue cells appear to be the principal sites of TG synthesis. The glyceride portion of the molecule is provided by L-α-glycerophosphate formed by phosphorylation of glycerol, except in the adipose tissue which has little of the necessary enzyme, glycerokinase. In the fat cell of adipose tissue the compound is derived by reduction of the triose phosphate, dihydroxyacetone phosphate, formed in glycolysis. Fat synthesis in adipose tissue is therefore dependent on carbohydrate metabolism and does not take place or

is greatly reduced in starvation when carbohydrate is not readily available.

The condensing fatty acids are first activated by CoA and then possibly transferred to an acyl carrier protein. Two of them esterify the free hydroxyl groups of α glycerophosphate to give a phosphatidic acid. Usually an unsaturated fatty acid condenses at the β position, while either a saturated or an unsaturated acid may go on the other hydroxyl. The phosphate group is finally split off by a phosphatase, and a third fatty acid substituted to give a molecule of TG (fig. 10.17) In intestinal mucosal cells 2-acylglycerols may be acylated directly to diglycerides and triglycerides.

Breakdown of triglycerides

The TG are stacks of energy-yielding fatty acid chains; since the tissues in which they are synthesized also contain lipases which break them down again to free glycerol and FFA, the laying down and removal occurs freely, providing a flexible system. The control by means of hormones as well as by the availability of substrates is considered on p. 32.7. Pancreatic lipase differs from the other lipases so far studied in that it splits off only the α and α' fatty acids from TG. The bulk of the dietary TG is therefore broken down in the duodenum and first part of the jejunum only as far as the 2-monoglyceride.

Synthesis of phospholipids

The use of isotopically labelled precursors, such as ^{32}P-phosphate, ^{14}C-choline and ^{14}C-fatty acids, shows that phospholipids are formed in all tissues. The pathways involved have been deduced by adding possible co-enzymes and intermediates and observing the effect on the incorporation of the isotope into the product.

Thus when phosphatidic acid is mixed with ^{14}C^{32}P-phosphoryl choline and a preparation from rat brain, the ^{32}P is found to be incorporated into the newly formed phosphatidyl choline and is not split out during condensation, i.e. no labelled inorganic P is produced. As the incorporation is stimulated by the addition of cytidine triphosphate (CTP) p. 12.2, it is deduced that the steps are as shown in fig. 10.15.

FIG. 10.14. Cis and trans forms of arachidonic acid.

$$HOCH_2{}^{14}CH_2\overset{+}{N}(CH_3)_3 + AT^{32}P \longrightarrow HO-{}^{32}\overset{\overset{O}{\|}}{\underset{\underset{O}{\|}}{P}}-O-CH_2{}^{14}CH_2\overset{+}{N}(CH_3)_3$$

Choline   Phosphoryl choline

Fig. 10.15. Synthesis of phosphatidyl choline. DG = diglyceride.

The same argument applies to the formation of phosphatidyl ethanolamine from ethanolamine and probably also for the plasmalogens. However, the formation of phosphatidyl serine is shown in fig. 10.16. In this case phosphoryl serine is not on the route. Phosphatidic acid reacts with CTP to form CDP-diglyceride which then condenses with serine or inositol to yield phosphatidyl serine or phosphatidyl inositol. No enzyme for the phosphorylation of serine has been found so far.

Fig. 10.16. Synthesis of phosphatidyl ethanolamine, phosphatidyl serine and phosphatidyl inositol.

Fig. 10.17. Pathways of lipid synthesis.

More evidence has been obtained by adding CTP or CDP-diglyceride to the brain preparations along with ^{14}C-inositol. The activated diglyceride is more stimulatory and therefore enters the pathway closer to the formation of the final product, phosphatidyl inositol.

Although phosphatidic acid is on the pathway to triglycerides as well as to phospholipids, they may not be formed within the cell from the same precursor pools. There is some evidence that high concentrations of palmityl CoA inhibit phosphatidic acid phosphatase. This might be expected to divert phosphatidic acids to phospholipids by the route shown on the left of fig. 10.17 rather than to di- and triglyceride formation.

Synthesis of sphingolipids

Experiments with labelled serine and acyl CoA or palmityl CoA show these to be precursors of sphingosine. Palmityl aldehyde is first formed and then condenses with serine, the product being subsequently oxidized by a flavoprotein yielding sphingosine (fig. 10.18).

$$CH_3(CH_2)_{14}CHO + HOOCCHNH_2CH_2OH$$

Serine

$$\downarrow CO_2$$

$$CH_3(CH_2)_{14}\underset{|}{\overset{HO}{C}}H\underset{|}{\overset{NH_2}{C}}HCH_2OH$$

$$\downarrow \begin{array}{l} Fp\ ox \\ Fp\ red \end{array}$$

$$CH_3(CH_2)_{12}CH = CH\underset{|}{\overset{HO}{C}}H\underset{|}{\overset{NH_2}{C}}HCH_2OH$$

FIG. 10.18. Sphingosine.

This is acylated by an activated fatty acid and may further react with cytidine diphosphate choline to give sphingomyelin. The synthetic routes to the cerebrosides and gangliosides are shown in fig. 10.19.

PAPS = 3'-phosphoadenosine-5'-phosphosulphate
NANA = N-acetylneuraminic acid

FIG. 10.19. Formation of complex phospholipids.

Degradation of phospholipids

The phospholipids are broken down by enzymes called phospholipases. Those which attack glyceryl phosphoryl compounds are divided into four categories according to the bond severed (fig. 10.20).

The product of the attack by phospholipase A on phosphatidyl choline (lecithin) is lysolecithin (1-acyl glycerylphosphoryl). Two molecules of this can dissimulate (fig. 10.21) yielding phosphatidyl choline and glycerylphosphoryl choline. Phospholipase A is a constituent of the pancreatic secretion, while phospholipase B is active in intestinal mucosal cells. An additional substrate for phospholipase C is sphingomyelin, but enzymes exist which are specific for the degradation of sphingomyelin, as well as for the cerebrosides and gangliosides. Rarely in individuals these enzymes are absent. Then undegraded phospholipids accumulate, especially in nervous tissues. Mental retardation and other defects develop.

The liberated acyl groups are probably used to acylate other compounds such as cholesterol. The specificity of these lipases and the enzymes involved in reacylating to phosphatidyl choline, etc., is such that compounds are formed of the required structure, i.e. those with a particular saturated fatty acid at the 1-position and an unsaturated one at position 2.

Synthesis of cholesterol

The basic building block of cholesterol, like that of fatty acids, is acetate of which three molecules after activation unite to form hydroxymethylglutaryl CoA (fig. 10.22).

It is not yet clear how much goes by each of the routes in fig. 10.23. It may be that the intermediates link to an acyl carrier protein, route (b), prior to condensation.

Next the product is reduced to mevalonate, a process requiring $NADPH_2$ (fig. 10.24). Successive phosphorylations with ATP yield a triphospho compound which then splits off P_i and CO_2. In this way mevalonate is converted to isopentenyl pyrophosphate which is a derivative of the isoprene unit, a building block of long chain naturally occurring compounds, common also to rubber and the carotenoid pigments (p. 10.8).

Three of these C_5 units join to form the C_{15} farnesyl pyrophosphate (fig. 10.25), two molecules of which condense to the C_{30} squalene by a reductive step utilizing $NADPH_2$. The whole process from acetate to squalene goes on in an anaerobic environment.

The subsequent steps are oxidative. The C_{30} chain is folded and tailored to the 3-β-hydroxy steroid molecule, cholesterol (fig. 10.26). The sequence of steps involves oxidation by oxygen and migration of CH_3 groups from the positions held in squalene. Three other CH_3 groups are lost as CO_2. This biosynthesis is stereospecific with regard to each of the sixteen asymmetric centres of the sterol molecule. It is presumably achieved by rigid fixing of the molecule to the enzymes performing the cyclization steps.

Cholesterol is synthesized in all the tissues of the body. The slowest step which therefore determines the rate is the reduction to mevalonate. At this point a negative feedback mechanism operates in the liver, when as is usual the diet contains significant amounts of cholesterol. The responsible agent may be the bile acids derived in part from the dietary cholesterol. Starvation also depresses the formation of cholesterol by the liver, hydroxymethylglutaryl CoA being degraded instead to ketone bodies (p. 10.25). In contrast, the synthesis in the extrahepatic tissues, thought to be the source of 70 per cent of the plasma cholesterol, is not controlled in the same way.

FIG. 10.20. Sites of attack by phospholipases.

FIG. 10.21. Dissimulation of lysolecithin.

$$CH_3CO.SCoA + H_2C \overset{COOH}{\underset{CO.SCoA}{<}} \longrightarrow CH_3COCH_2CO.SCoA + CO_2$$

Acetoacetyl CoA

CH₃CO.SCoA

$$\underset{\overset{|}{CH_2COOH}}{CH_3\overset{OH}{\overset{|}{C}}{-}CH_2CO.SCoA} + HSCoA$$

Hydroxymethylglutaryl CoA

FIG. 10.22. Formation of hydroxymethylglutaryl.

Malonyl-S-ACP + Acetyl-S-ACP (b) → Acetoacetyl-S-ACP

CO₂

Acetyl CoA

Hydroxymethylglutaryl-S-ACP

CoA

ACP-SH

Acetoacetyl CoA (a) Hydroxymethylglutaryl CoA

FIG. 10.23. Alternative pathways to hydroxymethylglutaryl CoA.

FIG. 10.24. Formation of an isoprene unit from hydroxymethylglutaryl CoA.

FIG. 10.25. Formation of squalene from isoprene units.

FIG. 10.26. Formation of cholesterol from squalene.

Cholesterol esters

Cholesterol can be esterified at its free hydroxyl group by fatty acids, which are activated to fatty acyl CoA, except in the intestinal mucosal cell. Here esterification of the entering cholesterol is obligatory for its release into the lymph. A variety of fatty acids is found in the cholesterol esters in man, the composition depending on the tissue examined. Little of the cholesterol in the liver is esterified compared with 70 per cent of that in plasma or the adrenal gland.

Plasma cholesterol esters may be formed in the liver where they enter the lipoprotein fraction and subsequently appear in the blood. Alternatively, free cholesterol in the plasma lipoproteins may be transesterified from the 2-fatty acyl groups of the serum phosphatidyl choline. The importance of the two sources of plasma cholesterol esters is not clear but after injecting ^{14}C-mevalonate into an animal there is a delay between the label appearing in the free cholesterol and in the cholesterol esters of the plasma. This suggests that the free cholesterol of liver and plasma is a precursor of plasma cholesterol esters.

Since in man all the cholesterol esters of a given plasma lipoprotein fraction turn over at the same rate, they are probably formed by the same mechanism, regardless of the fatty acid residue present. These may be saturated, mono-, di- or polyunsaturated C_{16} to C_{20} acids. The biggest proportion of plasma cholesterol esters are found in the high density lipoproteins (p. 10.11) which turn over more rapidly than the low density ones. Cholesterol esters may stabilize the lipoproteins in some way through their hydrophobic long fatty acid chains. They do not appear to be involved in transport of cholesterol from one tissue to another.

The cholesterol esters of the tissues are probably formed by esterification of cholesterol synthesized within the tissues themselves. They predominate over free cholesterol in those tissues in which cholesterol is a metabolic intermediate, as in the adrenal gland where steroid hormones are formed. Thus the cholesterol esters may be a reservoir of cholesterol 'nuclei' and of fatty acids available on hydrolysis for synthetic purposes. Cholesterol is present in the free rather than the esterified form in subcellular or plasma membranes.

The functions of phospholipids

The phospholipids are found in the cellular and subcellular membranes of all organisms to the extent of 20–30 per cent of the dry weight. An obvious molecular property is their dual nature, for like bile salts they consist of hydrophilic and hydrophobic portions.

AS COMPONENTS OF MEMBRANES

Membranes consist of proteins and a small quantity of cholesterol, both solubilized by phospholipid. The three types of molecule are held together by hydrophobic association which leaves the ionic or hydrophilic portions free to bind other charged molecules, e.g. cytochrome c as shown in fig. 10.27. As the basic framework of the

Protein

Hydrophobic bonding of phospholipid to protein

Ionic bonding of cytochrome c to phosphate groups in cardiolipin

Cytochrome c

FIG. 10.27. Representation of the proposed complex between a cytochrome and a phospholipid–protein component of the mitochondrial inner membrane. From Green D. E. & Fleischer S. (1964). *Metabolism and Physiological Significance of Lipids.* New York: Wiley.

membrane remains after removal of the lipid, the structural skeleton is the protein moiety. It is now generally accepted that the double layer of lipid observed in EM pictures of stained preparations may not represent the situation *in vivo*, except for the myelin membrane. Membranes are now considered to be aggregates of subunits which are coiled proteins with which the lipids associate. These are represented in fig. 10.28.

FIG. 10.28. Equilibria involved in hydrophobic association of phospholipid and membrane protein. From Benson A. A. (1966) *J. Amer. Oil Chem. Soc.* **43**, 265.

In the plasma membrane the subunits appear to aggregate to flat vesicular closed structures whereas in the inner mitochondrial membrane, containing the enzymes involved in electron transport, the sheets may be rolled into tubes capable of being flattened out, e.g. by the presence of calcium or sodium ions.

In this inner membrane the globular repeating units have a molecular weight of about a million and are of at least ten types, differing chemically and enzymically. It has been calculated that each contains about forty protein and four hundred phospholipid monomers.

The plasma membrane separates the extracellular fluid from the cytoplasm of the cell. In addition it allows the controlled entry and exit of small molecules, nutrients and waste products and the free passage of water. Studies on the rate of entry of glucose and cations into cells have led to the hypothesis that this is limited by the availability of carriers existing in the cell membrane. We can visualize the acidic phosphatides, phosphatidyl serine and phosphatidyl inositol on the outside of the lipoprotein subunit binding calcium ions and also perhaps being a component of the lipoprotein ATPase, the basis of movement of sodium and potassium ions in and out of cells (p. 14.7). The barrier may be crossed by changes in the conformation of the protein coil resulting in the bound ions reaching the other side of the reconstituted membrane polymer. Thus the ability of calcium to increase the permeability of the cell membrane to other small molecules may lie in its ability to alter the spatial structure of the constituent subunits. Such a transformation can be used to describe the process whereby the plasma membrane of an isolated fat cell becomes more permeable to glucose after controlled treatment with phospholipase C. Presumably the phospholipids are digested away, changing the characteristics of the membrane, while the unknown carrier mechanism, common also to the insulin facilitated transport of glucose, is unaffected.

The phospholipids of membranes are not chemically inert building blocks but are dynamic components continually broken down by phospholipases and replaced. The mean half-life of the lipids in mitochondrial membranes is about 10 days in liver and 30 days in brain. However, in each tissue there is a structural fraction turning over more slowly than the rest. The enzymes involved in the breakdown have greater affinity for fatty acid chains of a particular length or degree of unsaturation, thus allowing the structural pattern to be retained.

IN SUBCELLULAR PARTICLES

It is probable that the phospholipids present in the endoplasmic reticulum are involved in protein synthesis through their capacity to orientate the messenger-RNA molecules (p. 12.5). Within the cell nucleus the small amount of phospholipid rapidly incorporates ^{34}P in periods of great mitotic activity. More conclusive information is available from studies of mitochondria.

In mitochondria the oxidation of $NADH_2$ and its coupling to the synthesis of ATP depends on the lipid components of the inner membrane. In subcellular particles respiration stops after they have been subjected to the action of phospholipases or lipid solvents. Moreover the activity of the oxidizing enzymes, e.g. cytochrome oxidase, is restored by adding phospholipid extracts. Thus removal of the lipid results in destruction of the organized systems, as shown by loss of activity, which is restored by returning the phospholipid. The mitochondrial enzymes appear to be located together in groups according to their function, e.g. those for electron transport (p. 8.5) and those for fatty acid oxidation. The functional constituents, flavin, haem and nonhaem iron, are all hydrophobic, and the lipoprotein may provide a medium necessary for the electron flow and for the correct conformation of the enzymic proteins.

An additional role has been allocated to mitochondrial phospholipids. They are known to promote the activities of certain of the enzymes. Thus cytochrome c oxidase requires an acidic lipid, its substrate apparently being a phospholipid complex of cytochrome c. Perhaps this is to bind NAD and provide a hydrophobic environment for the enzymic reaction. In a similar way, β-hydroxybutyrate dehydrogenase requires phosphatidyl choline. As the mechanism of the active transport processes becomes known, so the role of the phospholipids in the plasma membrane may be shown to be more than structural.

Phospholipids in blood plasma

These are known to have two important functions in the blood, one as constituents of the plasma lipoproteins (p. 10.11) and the other in blood coagulation (p. 26.14). A phospholipoprotein is contributed by the platelets to the mechanism involved in prothrombin activation; it perhaps provides a catalytic surface on the platelet.

The role of free fatty acid (FFA) in metabolism

FFA is the form in which lipid is transported in the blood from adipose tissue depots to the tissues where it is used as a source of energy. The concentration of FFA in plasma is low but very variable. Whereas after an overnight fast the level of blood glucose usually lies between 4 and 5 m-moles/l, the level of plasma FFA is usually between 400 and 600 μEq/l. The level is sensitive to the nutritional state of the subject. If he continues to fast but takes exercise, the level rises rapidly and in one to two hours may reach as high as 2000 μEq/l. On the other hand if a normal breakfast or 50 g of glucose is taken, it falls in about 30 min to 200 μEq/l or sometimes less.

The level in the plasma differs in different blood vessels. In one fasting subject after a short period of light exercise blood was drawn from an artery and two veins in the leg, a superficial vein draining mostly adipose tissue and a deep vein draining muscle. The levels of plasma FFA were 820 (artery), 1390 (superficial vein) and 540 (deep vein) μEq/l. These figures indicate an entry of FFA into the circulation from adipose tissue and an uptake by muscle. After giving glucose and an injection of insulin, the plasma FFA level fell to 190 μEq/l in the superficial vein. Hence the utilization of glucose shuts off the outflow of FFA from adipose tissue and prevents its uptake by muscle. Using the same technique in animals it has been shown that the brain does not remove FFA from the blood even in the fasting state.

By injecting palmitic acid labelled with ^{14}C into the circulation, it is possible to calculate the turnover rate of FFA in the blood. Surprisingly it has been found that each molecule of FFA exists on average in the plasma for only a few minutes. In one experiment the value was 2·7 minutes. Now if 750 μEq, the amount normally present in the plasma, is replaced every 2·7 min, then about 100 g of lipid is carried into and out of the blood as FFA in 24 hours. This is equivalent to just under 1000 kcal/day which is sufficient to meet about two-thirds of the energy needs at rest. Obviously this FFA component of the blood is of the utmost importance in the metabolic economy of the body.

Dynamic aspects of lipid metabolism

The classical methods of analysis of plasma and tissue lipids give limited information as to where the constituents have come from, how they are transformed and to what extent this occurs. By injecting ^{14}C-fatty acids into animals it has been found that 30 per cent is taken up by the liver. Within 5 min this is practically all esterified, being found mainly in the neutral lipid rather than in the phospholipids which have a slower turnover rate. The ^{14}C leaves the liver first in the very low density lipoproteins and later appears in those of higher density.

The slower turnover of ^{14}C-labelled chylomicrons in fasted dogs after hepatectomy, indicates that the liver is the major site of removal of lipoprotein from the blood–liver pool. TG is hydrolysed there and the fatty acids oxidized or converted to ketone bodies. In contrast, in the fed animal, removal from the plasma by other tissues becomes more important and about one-third is removed by the liver, and one-fifth by the adipose tissues. The triglyceride fatty acid of lipoprotein enters adipose and muscle cells in the fed animal through activation or formation of lipoprotein lipase. It is not necessary for the triglyceride fatty acids present in the chylomicrons to pass first through the liver for transformation to low density lipoproteins before being taken up by the peripheral tissues.

Isotope studies also show that the exchange of cholesterol phospholipid or fatty acid molecules from one component (plasma lipoprotein, cell membrane or storage depot) to another takes place without necessarily involving a net change of that component. Lipid molecules, except those in the nervous system, are being continuously transformed and transported about the body. Thus, the apparent constancy of the body fat has been shown to be illusory.

Ketosis

In fasting or during prolonged exercise energy is obtained by mobilization of the fat stores and there is a tendency towards overproduction of acetyl CoA in the liver. More is formed than can enter the citric acid cycle. Instead it is converted to acetoacetyl CoA and thence to acetoacetate, which enters the blood stream (fig. 10.29).

The metabolism of acetoacetate is described on p. 31.6. In the tissues other than liver, such as muscle and kidney, which can reactivate the ketone bodies acetoacetate and hydroxybutyrate, the resulting compounds are utilized as metabolic fuel along with the lipid stored in these tissues. However, the rate of utilization of these ketone bodies is limited. When the rate of production by the liver exceeds that of removal by the peripheral tissues, then the blood level rises. As the pKs of hydroxybutyric acid and acetoacetic acid are 4·8 and 3·8 respectively, the ketone bodies circulate in the blood plasma in ionized form. Consequently the dissociation of the carbonic acid (pK 6·1) is repressed, and the ratio $[HCO_3^-][H_2CO_3]$ falls (ketoacidosis).

The only means of controlling acetoacetate formation in the body appears to be by the secretion of insulin. This tapers off as the level of blood sugar falls. A low insulin level seems rapidly to activate the enzymes involved in acetoacetate synthesis. It also allows FA mobilization to occur by suppressing re-esterification. In this way substrate for ketone body production is provided.

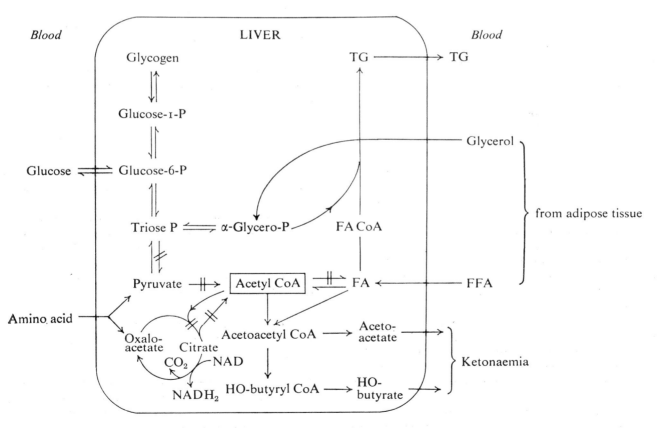

FIG. 10.29. Reactions occurring in the liver during ketosis. When the pathways marked ⫽ are used relatively less than the pathways for FA metabolism, ketonaemia is likely to develop.

However, even in prolonged fasting, gluconeogenesis seems to be sufficient to keep up some insulin secretion. There is evidence that this hormone acts directly on the lipase present in the adipose tissue which is particularly active in this situation (p. 32.6). As a consequence, the flow of FFA into the blood, and thence to the liver is controlled. Without insulin, the acetoacetate derived from the flood of FFA entering the liver would be poured out unchecked. This may lead to a grave condition and occurs in some patients with diabetes mellitus in which the supply of endogenous insulin is inadequate.

Interrelations between lipid and carbohydrate metabolism

Since fatty acids and carbohydrate are broken down to acetyl CoA, both can supply energy to the body through the citric acid cycle and the respiratory chain. Table 10.6 is an estimate of the sources of energy used by the tissues of a man at rest in the postabsorptive state. Great accuracy

TABLE 10.6. An estimate of the fuels used by a normal man at rest in the postabsorptive state, modified from Fritz (1961) *Physiol. Rev.* **41**, 52.

Fuel	Site of oxidation	m.moles/min oxidized	O_2 used ml/min	Per cent
Glucose	Chiefly brain	0·33	45	18
FFA—Ketones	Liver	0·04 ⎫		
FFA—CO_2	Liver	0·10 ⎬ 0·32	149	60
FFA—CO_2	Extrahepatic tissues	0·18 ⎭		
Ketones	All tissues, except liver	0·16	15	6
Glycerol	All tissues	0·09	7	3
Amino acids	Chiefly liver	35 mg	34	13
			250	100

cannot be claimed for any individual figure. However, there is little doubt that FFA provides the major part of the energy under these conditions, glucose provides about one-fifth, nearly all used by the brain, amino acids about one-tenth and ketones and glycerol significant but smaller amounts. The proportions utilized may be altered greatly by a meal and by exercise. After giving glucose or taking a meal containing carbohydrate, the RQ rises to close to unity, suggesting that during carbohydrate absorption, glucose rather than fat is used to provide energy. More direct evidence for this may be obtained by injecting ^{14}C labelled palmitic acid. After taking glucose, the specific activity of the exhaled carbon dioxide is lower than it is when fasting, indicating that a larger proportion has come from unlabelled carbohydrate. The mechanism for the switch over of fuels is probably as follows; glucose

entering the blood from the intestines causes a rise in the amount of circulating insulin (p. 25.44), which facilitates the passage of glucose into the cells and so allows it to be metabolized. Part of this glucose is converted in the liver and adipose tissue to glycogen, and the remainder is broken down to triose phosphate by the glycolytic pathway and the hexose monophosphate pathway. In this way, α-glycerophosphate becomes available, particularly in the adipose cells to lock up most of the liberated FFA by re-esterifying them to TG. As a consequence the FFA leave the adipose cells at a reduced rate and the lowered plasma level no longer allows the tissues to use FFA as a fuel. Instead, glucose is readily available for oxidation, by breaking down to pyruvate and on to acetyl CoA, finally yielding carbon dioxide and $NADH_2$. Acetyl CoA produced in excess of energy requirements is transformed within the liver and adipose cells to fatty acid. The hexose monophosphate pathway can provide much of the $NADPH_2$ necessary for this synthesis. Thus excess of dietary carbohydrate may be stored as glycogen or converted to fat. The amount converted into fat may depend upon how full is the limited capacity of the glycogen store.

During short sharp bursts of exercise, carbohydrate (glycogen) is the immediate source of the extra fuel and is provided by glycolysis within the muscle cells. Within a few minutes of the start of exercise muscles begin to withdraw large amounts of FFA from the blood. The factors responsible for the mobilization of fat during muscular exercise are discussed on p. 32.7.

In fasting when glucose is no longer being absorbed, depletion of the liver glycogen occurs and the blood glucose falls to a level between 50 and 70 mg/100 ml. Glucose utilization is reduced in the tissues, other than nervous, and this keeps the blood level from falling further, a situation which would soon cause damage to the brain. The body has a number of mechanisms to make its metabolism shift over to fat, its main reserve fuel tank.

The major change is that less glucose enters the adipose cell to act as a brake on the output of FFA. As a result, the concentration of plasma FFA may be doubled or more by an 18 hour fast in spite of the FFA being removed by the tissues in increasing amounts. The FFA are oxidized and the resulting $NADH_2$ passes to the respiratory chain and the acetyl CoA enters the citric acid cycle for conversion to carbon dioxide and more reduced co-enzymes (fig. 10.30). The acetyl groups seem to be prevented from condensing back to long chain fatty acids (site a) by the elevated fatty acid concentration which inhibits acetyl CoA carboxylase. It is thought that a similar end product inhibition, this time by acetyl CoA, reduces the oxidation of pyruvate to acetyl CoA (site b). Thus less pyruvate derived from carbohydrate enters the cycle for oxidation.

FIG. 10.30. *The formation of reduced forms of pyridine nucleotide co-enzymes.* $NADH_2$ in cytoplasm: 1, oxidation of malate to oxaloacetic acid; 2, glycolysis. In mitochondria: 3, oxidation of fatty acids; 4, oxidation of pyruvate; 5, oxidation of acetyl units in citric acid cycle. $NADPH_2$ in cytoplasm: 6, oxidation of malate to pyruvate; 7, in the pentose pathway. *Utilization of reduced forms of pyridine nucleotide co-enzymes.* $NADH_2$ in cytoplasm: I, reduction of oxaloacetate to malate; II, gluconeogenesis; III, reduction of dihydroxyacetone phosphate to α-glycerophosphate. In mitochondria: IV, generation of ATP by the cytochrome system. $NADPH_2$ in cytoplasm: V, reductive carboxylation of pyruvate to malate; VI, synthesis of fatty acids, cholesterol, hydroxylations, etc.

Sites of control a, b, c, d, e, and f (see text).

FIG. 10.31. Stimulation of gluconeogenesis by acetyl CoA.

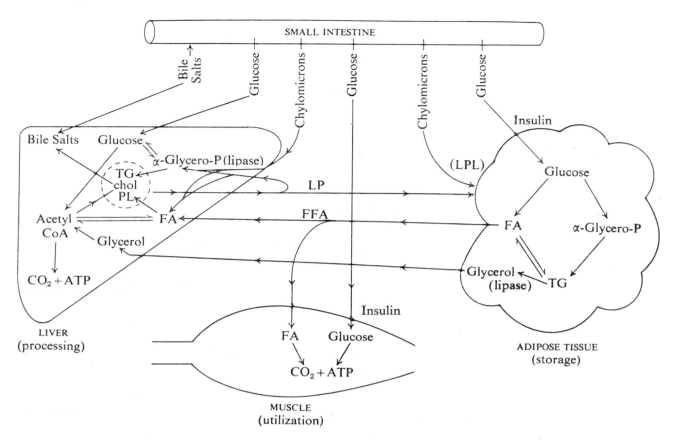

FIG. 10.32. Transport, storage and utilization of fat in the tissues related to carbohydrate metabolism. FA, fatty acid; FFA, free fatty acid; LP, lipoprotein; LPL, lipoprotein lipase; PL, phospholipid; TG, triglyceride.

Simultaneously the high acetyl CoA concentration accompanying fatty acid oxidation has been shown *in vitro* to inhibit phosphofructokinase (site c) and to have an activating effect on pyruvate carboxylase (site d) (fig. 10.31). The former might be expected to reduce glycolysis while the latter promoted gluconeogenesis through the formation of oxaloacetate and therefore of phosphoenolpyruvate. Fatty acid oxidation, which reduces NAD in mitochondria, probably also stimulates the reductive steps in the cytoplasmic transformation of phosphoenolpyruvate to triose phosphate (site e). The necessary transference of this reductive capacity to the cytoplasm is probably achieved by the reduction of oxaloacetate to malate which moves outwards across the mitochondrial membrane. In the cytoplasm the $NADH_2$ can be regenerated by the reformation of oxaloacetate.

Fatty acids have been shown in isolated tissue to prevent the uptake of glucose by muscle cells; since the metabolic effects of fasting have been mimicked by adding palmitic acid to tissues from fed animals, they appear to be mediated largely by the availability of this substrate and not by other direct actions, e.g. hormones.

It has been observed that the activity of the citrate cleavage enzyme (site f) is enhanced in tissue from carbohydrate fed animals and reduced by fasting. This has led to the belief that citrate, formed in the mitochondria and passing out into the cytoplasm, where it is split by this enzyme, is the source of the acetyl CoA used in fatty acid synthesis.

Fig. 10.32 attempts to summarize the sites of the main reactions in the transport, storage and utilization of fat in the tissues and its relation to carbohydrate metabolism.

Comment

It will be clear to the reader that the metabolism of triglycerides is fairly well established. The physiological role of the phospholipids and cholesterol is less well understood but knowledge of these subjects is important for the understanding of various nervous and arterial diseases.

FURTHER READING

Advances in Lipid Research. New York: Academic Press.
HANAHAN D.J. (ed) (1960) *Lipid Chemistry*. New York: Wiley.

Chapter 11
Protein metabolism

The proteins form a group of macromolecular nitrogenous substances with such a wide range of physical and chemical properties that they serve diverse physiological functions. Some highly insoluble proteins, such as the keratins of skin, hair and nails appear to be comparatively inert, albeit indispensable structural components; others, including the proteins of muscle and connective tissue, are concerned with mechanical function as well as structure. Some more soluble proteins are used for transporting oxygen, iron, copper, lipids and a variety of hormones about the body. Perhaps the most striking fact is that all enzymes are proteins.

Living organisms must therefore obtain compounds containing nitrogen as well as carbon, hydrogen and oxygen for the synthesis of proteins. Higher animals, including man, are unable to utilize inorganic nitrogenous compounds to a significant extent, and are therefore dependent on other forms of life for a suitable dietary supply of nitrogen. For them protein is an important and indispensable constituent of the diet. More than 90 per cent of the nitrogen of all living cells is present in the form of protein, which is the ultimate product of a complex system of intracellular synthetic machinery.

In spite of the great diversity of their properties, all proteins can be hydrolysed, either by treatment with a series of enzymes or by boiling for some hours with moderately concentrated acid (5–6N HCl) to give a mixture of amino acids. **Simple proteins** give only amino acids on hydrolysis. **Conjugated proteins** give, in addition, small quantities of other substances. A molecule, other than an amino acid, obtained by the hydrolysis of a conjugated protein is called a **prosthetic group** (p. 7.12). These vary greatly in the nature and strength of the bonds which link them to the main part of the protein molecule, and many of them are liberated by treatment which is too mild to hydrolyse the protein into its constituent amino acids.

AMINO ACIDS

As their name indicates, amino acids are substances which contain both amino and acidic groups. Very large numbers of such compounds are known to organic chemistry, but only about twenty are found as products of the hydrolysis of proteins. All but two of these are α-amino acids, i.e. the amino group is linked to the carbon atom adjacent to the carboxyl group:

$$R-CH \big\langle \begin{matrix} COOH \\ NH_2 \end{matrix}$$

In the simplest amino acid, aminoacetic acid or glycine, $R = H$. In other amino acids, R may be a straight chain or branched aliphatic radical; it may contain a hydroxyl group, a thiol or a thioether group; it may possess additional basic or acidic groups or a cyclic radical. The important amino acids are given, with their formulae and commonly used abbreviations, in table 11.1. The table also lists the two exceptions to the α-amino acid rule and a few amino acids which are not found in proteins although they are of biological importance.

The formulae show that all the amino acids except glycine ought to be optically active and this has been found to be so. However, only the L-form of each acid, i.e. the isomer which is theoretically derived from L(—)serine, is found as a product of protein hydrolysis, although there are rare instances of the biological occurrence of D-amino acids, particularly D-glutamic acid.

General chemical properties

The individual amino acids possess specific properties which depend on the nature of R and general properties which are determined largely by the α-amino-carboxyl group. The latter vary slightly on account of the influence of R. The amino group itself is responsible for a purple colour produced when amino acids are warmed with ninhydrin, a complex triketone. This reaction is useful for the detection of amino acids on paper chromatograms or electrophoresis strips. Proteins give a similar but much weaker reaction.

TABLE 11.1. Some biologically important amino acids

Name	Standard abbreviation	R	Present in proteins
Glycine	Gly	$H-$	+
Alanine	Ala	CH_3-	+
Valine	Val	$(CH_3)_2CH-$	+
Leucine	Leu	$(CH_3)_2CH-CH_2-$	+
Isoleucine	Ile	$C_2H_5-CH(CH_3)-$	+
Serine	Ser	CH_2OH-	+
Threonine	Thr	$CH_3-CHOH-$	+
Aspartic acid	Asp	$HOOC-CH_2-$	+
Asparagine	Asp(NH$_2$)	$H_2NOC-CH_2-$	+
Glutamic acid	Glu	$HOOC-CH_2-CH_2-$	+
Glutamine	Glu(NH$_2$)	$H_2NOC-CH_2-CH_2-$	+
Lysine	Lys	$H_2N(CH_2)_4-$	+
Ornithine	Orn	$H_2N(CH_2)_3-$	−
Arginine	Arg		+
Histidine	His		+
Phenylalanine	Phe		+
Tyrosine	Tyr		+
Tryptophan	Trp		+
Cysteine	Cys	$HSCH_2-$	+
Cystine half	CyS	Double molecule formed by oxidation of pairs of cysteines to give $-S-S-$ structure	+
Methionine	Met	$CH_3-S-(CH_2)_2-$	+
		FORMULA	
Proline	Pro		+
Hydroxyproline	Hyp		+
β-Alanine		$H_2N-CH_2-CH_2-COOH$	−
γ-Aminobutyric acid		$H_2N-CH_2-CH_2-CH_2-COOH$	−
Cysteic acid		$HO_3S-CH_2-CH(NH_2)COOH$	−*

* Sometimes formed by oxidation in protein hydrolysates.

The amino group reacts readily with 1-fluoro-2-4-dinitrobenzene to give a dinitrophenyl derivative of the amino acid:

$$R-\overset{\displaystyle COOH}{\underset{\displaystyle NH_2}{CH}} + \underset{\displaystyle NO_2}{\overset{\displaystyle F}{\underset{}{\bigcirc}} NO_2} \longrightarrow \underset{\displaystyle NO_2}{\overset{\displaystyle R-\overset{\displaystyle COOH}{\underset{\displaystyle NH}{CH}}}{\underset{}{\bigcirc}} NO_2} + HF$$

The compounds produced are bright yellow and easily identified on chromatograms. The reaction is useful for identifying free amino groups in protein molecules. Where R contains a free amino group, as in the case of lysine, this reacts as well as the α-amino group, so that the product contains two dinitrophenyl radicals.

When an amino acid is dissolved in water, the carboxyl group tends to lose a proton while the amino group becomes protonated:

$$R-\overset{\displaystyle COOH}{\underset{\displaystyle NH_2}{CH}} \rightleftharpoons R-\overset{\displaystyle COO^-}{\underset{\displaystyle NH_3^+}{CH}}$$

The resulting structure has both a positive and a negative charge, but the net charge is zero unless there are other ionizable groups in the molecule. Such a structure is called a **zwitterion**. In an electric field it migrates neither to the cathode nor the anode (fig. 11.2).

The addition of acid to a solution containing the zwitterion form of an amino acid causes the carboxyl group to become protonated:

$$R-\overset{\displaystyle COO^-}{\underset{\displaystyle NH_3^+}{CH}} + H^+ \rightleftharpoons R-\overset{\displaystyle COOH}{\underset{\displaystyle NH_3^+}{CH}}$$

This equilibrium depends to some extent on the influence of R, but for most amino acids pK_{a_1} is around 2·6.

Conversely, the addition of base to a zwitterion solution detaches the proton from the amino group, leaving the carboxyl fully dissociated:

$$R-\overset{\displaystyle COO^-}{\underset{\displaystyle NH_3^+}{CH}} + OH^- \rightleftharpoons H_2O + R-\overset{\displaystyle COO^-}{\underset{\displaystyle NH_2}{CH}}$$

This dissociation again depends slightly on R, but for most amino acids pK_{a_2} is about 9·6.

The pH range over which an amino acid assumes the zwitterion structure is called the isoelectric region and the arithmetic midpoint of this is the **isoelectric point**.

Both above and below the isoelectric region the solution acts as a buffer. These important physiochemical points are summarized in fig. 11.1, which shows graphically the

FIG. 11.1. Titration curve of alanine, showing p*K* values, isoelectric point, and the structural formulae corresponding to the stages of the titration.

pH changes which follow the addition of base to the acid form of the amino acid alanine.

Separation of amino acid mixtures

Electrophoresis is the migration of a charged solute, e.g. an amino acid in an electric field. Unless the pH is near the isoelectric point, the amino acid migrates towards one of the electrodes. In a buffer of suitably chosen pH the properties of a wide range of amino acids are sufficiently different for effective separations to be made by electrophoresis on supporting media like paper, cellulose acetate or polyacrylamide gel. Fig. 11.2 shows a paper electropherogram of the amino acids found in the urine of a healthy subject and one suffering from cystinuria, a hereditary condition in which the patient's urine contains excessive quantities of cystine and the basic amino acids (p. 33.10).

Ion exchange is a more effective technique of separation for larger quantities of amino acids when quantitative analysis is required. This process also depends on the presence of ionized groups in the molecule; a buffered amino acid solution is allowed to percolate slowly through a long narrow glass column packed with an ion exchanger, a highly polymerized insoluble substance containing free acidic or basic groups. If the hydrogen ion concentration is suitable, the amino acid ions are electrostatically bonded to the ion exchanger and may be liberated serially, according to their properties, by altering the composition of the buffer which drips through the column. The process, which is illustrated in fig. 11.3, is

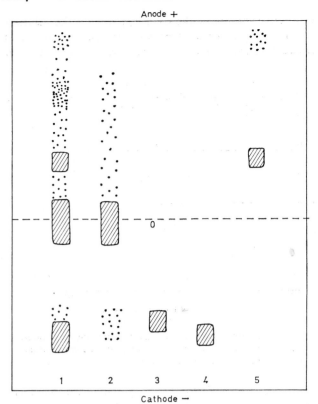

FIG. 11.2. Amino acid patterns of urines after paper electrophoresis at pH 8·6. 0, line on which the spots of urine or amino acid solution were applied. 1, Cystinuric urine; 2, Normal urine; 3, 4, 5, standards of lysine, arginine and cystine, respectively. The monobasic, monoacidic amino acids migrate very little at pH 8·6 and are clustered round the point of application of the urine. From Goulden B.E. & Leaver J.L. (1967) *Vet. Rec.*, **80**, 244.

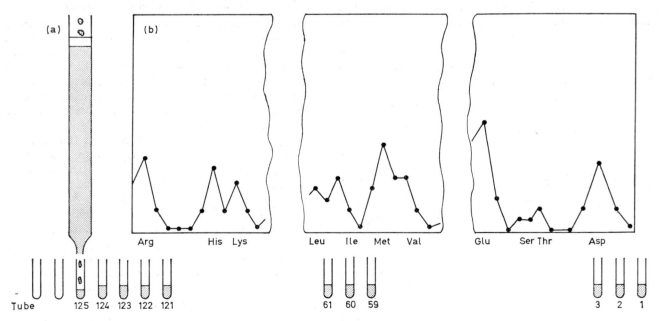

FIG. 11.3. Separation of amino acids by ion exchange chromatography. (a) Column packed with ion exchange resin and loaded with amino acid mixture through which is dripped a series of buffer solutions. The eluate is collected in constant volume fractions which are analysed quantitatively by the ninhydrin reaction. The points on the chart (b) represent intensities of colour given with ninhydrin in individual tubes.

widely used in studying the composition of the amino acid mixtures obtained by the hydrolysis of purified proteins.

Paper chromatography is an ingenious and popular separation technique which makes use of the differences both in distribution coefficients of amino acids between various pairs of solvent mixtures and in the extent to which different amino acids are adsorbed to paper. The wide diversity in the structure of R (table 11.1) causes distinct differences in the solubilities of the amino acids in different solvents. In an atmosphere containing solvent vapours, the fibres of a piece of filter paper become saturated with the solvent. Even in the absence of other solvents, paper contains a good deal of water. If a small spot of a solution of amino acids is placed near one end of a piece of filter paper and a suitable mixture of solvents, e.g. *n*-butanol, water and acetic acid, is allowed to flow across the paper, the amino acids migrate across the paper at different rates, determined partly by differential adsorption but chiefly by differences between their relative solubilities in the mobile solvent mixture and the solvent (water) in the paper fibres. When the paper has been almost completely covered by the moving solvent it is dried, sprayed with ninhydrin and warmed to colour the amino acid spots. Individual compounds can be identified by comparing the rate of flow (R_f = distance travelled by substance/distance travelled by solvent front) with that of known amino acids applied to the paper as separate spots. Separations by paper chromatography can often be improved by turning the dried paper (without staining it) through 90° and making a second run with a different

solvent mixture. Fig. 11.4 illustrates such a two-dimensional paper chromatogram given by a protein hydrolysate.

Properties of individual amino acids

The radical R confers on the individual amino acids many specific chemical properties. Thus glutamic and asparatic acids have each an additional carboxyl group, the properties of which are superimposed on those of the amino-carboxyl group. Sometimes the additional carboxyl groups are found as amides, e.g. in glutamine and asparagine, which are no longer markedly acidic. Other amino acids have additional amino groups (lysine, ornithine) or other basic groups (histidine, arginine).

Several of the more complex radicals found in the amino acids, e.g. the phenolic ring in tyrosine, the indole ring in tryptophan and the guanidinyl group in arginine, give characteristic colour reactions which are useful for either identifying the compounds or their quantitative determination. Usually the reaction is given not only by the free amino acid but also, perhaps in a modified form, by proteins which contain it.

Although all the amino acids are colourless, some, notably tyrosine and tryptophan, have striking absorption bands in the ultraviolet, with maxima close to 275 and 280 nm respectively. The intensity of absorption in this region of the spectrum is often used for the quantitative estimation of these amino acids or of proteins which contain them, in the same way as absorption at 260 nm is used as a measure of nucleic acid concentration.

The sulphydryl group of cysteine is readily split off by warming with dilute alkali and, in the presence of lead acetate, a black precipitate or dark brown colouration of lead sulphide is produced. The sulphydryl group is also very susceptible to oxidation, when two of the groups react together to give a disulphide:

$$\underset{\text{CH}_2\text{.SH}+\text{HS.CH}_2}{\overset{\text{COOH}}{\underset{|}{\text{CHNH}_2}}} \overset{-2e-2H^+}{\underset{+2e+2H^+}{\rightleftharpoons}} \underset{\text{CH}_2\text{—S—S—CH}_2}{\overset{\text{COOH}}{\underset{|}{\text{CHNH}_2}}} \overset{\text{COOH}}{\underset{|}{\text{CHNH}_2}}$$

The double molecule of the free amino acid is called cystine. This redox reaction is freely reversible.

PEPTIDES

When a protein free extract of yeast is treated with cuprous oxide, the insoluble cuprous salt of an amino acid derivative called **glutathione** is precipitated. Although first isolated in this way from yeast, glutathione is present in most, perhaps in all living cells. It has a molecular weight of 307 and belongs to the class of substances known as peptides. When boiled with acid it gives equimolar proportions of glutamic acid, glycine and cysteine.

FIG. 11.4. Two-dimensional paper chromatography of amino acids. ○, point of application of mixture. From McElroy W.D. (1964) *Cell Physiology and Biochemistry*, 2nd Edition. New Jersey : Prentice-Hall.

The last named is usually obtained in the oxidized form, cystine. On treatment with dilute NaOH and a trace of copper sulphate, glutathione gives a purple colour. This test is positive with biuret (NH_2—CO—NH—CO—NH_2) and with all substances containing more than one peptide link or bond (—CO—NH—). In glutathione the three amino acids are linked together by two peptide bonds:

$$
\begin{array}{ccc}
\text{COOH} & & \\
| & & \\
\text{CHNH}_2 & \text{Peptide bonds} & \\
| & & \\
\text{CH}_2 & \quad\quad \text{CH}_2\text{SH} & \\
| & \quad\quad | & \\
\text{CH}_2\text{---CO---NH---CH---CO---NH---CH}_2\text{---COOH} \\
\gamma\text{-Glutamyl} \quad\quad \text{Cysteyl} \quad\quad \text{Glycine}
\end{array}
$$

One unusual feature of the structure is the linking of the glutamic acid to the rest of the molecule by a peptide bond involving the γ-carboxyl group. Even in the case of the dicarboxylic acids, almost all peptide bonds involve the α-carboxyl group, next to the —NH_2.

A characteristic property of glutathione is its reversible oxidation to the disulphide form:

$$2GSH \underset{+2e+2H^+}{\overset{-2e-2H^+}{\rightleftharpoons}} G\text{---S---S---G}$$

The reaction takes place with all peptide structures, including proteins, which contain cysteine.

Glutathione, which contains three amino acid residues, is a tripeptide. The molecules of oxytocin and vasopressin, the neurohypophysial hormones (p. 25.15) each contain nine amino acid residues while those of the hormones glucagon and ACTH contain twenty-nine and thirty-nine respectively. Such compounds are called polypeptides. Peptides of varying molecular weights are widespread in low concentrations and fulfil an assortment of functions. They are also formed in the gut by the action of digestives enzymes on proteins in food.

PROTEINS

Proteins, like peptides, give a positive biuret test and can be hydrolysed to give a mixture of amino acids. Protein solutions give many of the amino acid tests which do not depend on the α-aminocarboxyl radical. Analysis shows that —COOH and —NH_2 are produced in equivalent amounts during the hydrolysis of a protein. It therefore appears that protein molecules consist of amino acids linked together by peptide bonds:

$$
\begin{array}{ccc}
\text{R}_1 & \text{R}_2 & \text{R}_3 \\
| & | & | \\
\text{---NH---CH---CO---NH---CH---CO---NH---CH---CO---}
\end{array}
$$

Such a statement, however, only begins to describe the structure of a protein molecule. How large is the molecule? How many molecules of each amino acid are present in a protein molecule? In what order are the amino acids arranged? Does the molecule consist of one large polypeptide chain, or of two or more linked together? Is the molecule freely flexible or does it assume some definite shape? What forces or bonds maintain the shape of a protein? In the case of a conjugated protein, it is also necessary to consider the location of the prosthetic group and the way in which it is bound to the polypeptide chain.

The answers to these questions are of two kinds: those which deal with such purely chemical matters as amino acid numbers and sequence, and those which deal with physical matters like the actual shape of the molecules. The first group is said to deal with the primary structure of proteins, the second with secondary and tertiary structure.

Purification of proteins

No solution can be found to these problems until a protein has been isolated in a pure state, free from other proteins. Protein molecules with rare exceptions are insoluble in organic solvents. These often also damage their delicate structure and consequently interfere with their properties. Even moderate heat is often harmful. Hence the common techniques for the purification of organic compounds are usually not applicable to proteins. Special techniques have been developed, many of which have found applications in clinical biochemistry and other fields of medical interest.

Early in the history of proteins it was observed that they are not dialyzable; if a protein solution containing also substances of low molecular weight (salts, sugars, urea or amino acids) is placed in a cellophane sac, permeable only to substances of low molecular weight, and the sac is suspended in a vessel of water, then the protein remains in the sac while the other substances diffuse out. If the external liquid contains salts or a buffer or some other dialyzable substance, then this passes into the sac, so that by using repeated changes of the external liquid, or a continuous flow, the other constituents of a protein solution can be changed in any desired way. Dialysis is widely used in the isolation and purification of proteins and is also a step in the automated clinical chemical analysis of blood plasma or serum, and in procedures where the separation of proteins from small molecules is required. The discovery that proteins are not dialyzable gave an early indication that they are substances of high molecular weight.

Gel filtration is a modern development of dialysis in which a small volume of protein solution, followed by a continuous flow of water or a salt solution or a buffer, is passed down a vertical glass column packed with fine particles of gel (dextran or polyacrylamide). The gel particles function as tiny dialysis sacs into which substances of low molecular weight diffuse freely, while the protein molecules, are excluded by their large size, being restricted to the space between the gel particles. Hence, as the constituents of the original protein solution flow down the column, solutes of low molecular weight pass more or less freely in and out of the gel particles, while the proteins, not being delayed in this way, flow more rapidly and therefore emerge from the foot of the column first. The procedure is illustrated in fig. 11.5. Gel filtration can

FIG. 11.5. Gel filtration: (a) prepared column; ○, gel particles, magnified several thousand times. (b) Application of sample; ●, large protein molecules, ⋮⋮⋮ solutes of low-molecular weight. (c, d); Separation commences; low molecular weight solutes travel more slowly because the molecules permeate the gel particles. (e, f) Collection of the separated materials in different flasks.

be adapted to the separation of proteins of different molecular weight by the use of gel particles specially made to have exclusion limits well into the range of molecular weights of proteins.

Other methods of protein separation and purification depend on the presence of ionizable groups, mainly in the amino acid side-chains, although the terminal groups of the polypeptide chain are also ionizable.

In the molecule of a protein there are very many ionizable groups and, as the properties of these are modified by neighbouring groups, the pattern of change in ionization with change in pH is very much more complex than in the case of any of the amino acids. As the pH moves from the acid side, where the positive charges of protonated amino groups predominate, to the alkaline side, where the negative charges of ionized carboxyls are more numerous, a definite point is passed where the sums of the charges of opposite sign are equal. This is the isoelectric point, and at this pH the protein does not migrate in an electric field. Strictly speaking, the above definition refers to the theoretical **isoionic point,** and the experimentally observed isoelectric point is slightly different

because of the effects of adsorbed ions from the chosen buffer. However, in general there will be an excess of positively and negatively charged groups, and it is possible to separate proteins in a mixture into groups which have similar ratios of net charge to mass. Electrophoresis is commonly carried out on a strip of filter paper or cellulose acetate, either to check the homogeneity of some preparation or to ascertain the relative proportions of different groups of proteins in serum in disease. The proteins themselves are colourless, but the strips can be dried, soaked in a solution of a suitable dye, washed and dried. The various bands of protein are stained blue with an intensity which corresponds approximately to the amount of protein present. A paper electropherogram of the proteins of normal serum is shown in fig. 11.6 (see also p. 31.3).

FIG. 11.6. Paper electrophoresis of normal serum proteins. The origin is the line of application of serum. All protein fractions except γ-globulin migrate towards the anode, albumin being the fastest. The density of hatching indicates the approximate depth of staining. From Datta, J.S. & Ottaway, J.H. (1965) *Biochemistry*. London: Baillière, Tindall & Cassell.

Proteins can also be separated by ion exchange (p. 11.3). With such complex mixtures of proteins as are found in plasma, this is too tedious for routine analysis, but the technique is invaluable for the purification of many individual proteins.

An older but still useful technique makes use of the fact that many proteins are precipitated from solution by high concentrations of inorganic salts, e.g. ammonium sulphate. A once popular classification of the proteins was based on differences in solubility in water and salt solutions of different concentration. By definition, albumins are proteins which are soluble in water and dilute salt solutions and are only precipitated by complete saturation of the solution with ammonium sulphate. Globulins are insoluble in water, soluble in dilute salt and precipitated by lower concentrations of ammonium sulphate; the original standard was half the concentration required to saturate the solution, but many globulins are more easily precipitated. An interesting clinical application of the salting out technique is the distinction of haemoglobin from the closely related pigment myoglobin; this distinction may be important, because both pigments may be present in the urine after crush injuries. Haemoglobin is precipitated in 2·8 M-ammonium sulphate, but myoglobin remains soluble until the concentration reaches 3·4 M.

Although protein molecules are too large to pass through a dialysis membrane, those of the common soluble proteins are much too small to settle out of solution under the simple force of gravity. Modern centrifugal methods, however, can easily give gravitational fields of the order of 10^5–10^6 g, and under these conditions the molecules of proteins can be sedimented and to some extent separated according to their size and weight.

Molecular weights of proteins

Most of the recorded molecular weights of proteins have been determined by centrifugal methods. The rate at which the molecules of a protein sediment in the gravitational field of a high-speed centrifuge depends on several factors:

(1) the molecular weight of the protein,

(2) the partial specific volume, which is a measure of the contribution of the protein to the total volume of the solution,

(3) the gravitational force, which is related to the angular velocity (a function of the speed of revolution) and the effective radius of the centrifuge rotor,

(4) the diffusion coefficient, which is a measure of the effect of the solvent (usually water) and the salts, buffer components or other solutes of low mol. wt. on the movement of the protein molecules.

Since there are independent methods for the evaluation of both diffusion coefficients and partial specific volumes, and the gravitational force is easily calculated for the particular centrifuge used, it is possible to estimate the mol. wt. of any protein by measuring, usually by an optical method, its rate of sedimentation.

Sometimes the molecule, usually of a conjugated protein, contains such a small proportion of some element or chemical grouping that this gives a minimum value for the mol. wt. For example, both haemoglobin and myoglobin contain about 0·34 per cent Fe. If it is assumed that each protein molecule contains one atom of iron, the mol. wt. in both cases works out at about 16,400. Osmotic and centrifugal methods show that in fact the mol. wt. of myoglobin is close to this figure, but that of haemoglobin is about four times as high, 65,000. The original assumption is therefore correct for myoglobin, but not for haemoglobin. The exercise thus discloses that the molecule of haemoglobin must contain four atoms of iron.

Table 11.2 gives examples of the mol. wt. of proteins ranging from about 10,000 to several millions. Since the mol. wt. of the individual amino acids range from 75 (glycine) to 204 (tryptophan), any protein molecule must contain over 100 amino acid residues and some contain many thousands.

TABLE 11.2. The molecular weights of some proteins (see also Table 11.3).

Protein	Molecular weight
Cytochrome c	12,500
Haemoglobin (human)	65,000
Pepsin	35,000
Catalase	250,000
Fibrinogen	450,000
Haemocyanin (octopus)	2,800,000

Primary structure of proteins

The proportions of the different amino acids which make up a protein molecule can be ascertained by quantitative hydrolysis, ion-exchange separation and estimation of the amounts of the individual amino acids. Representative figures are given in table 11.3. For the complete elucidation of structure the next task is the immense one of determining the order in which the various amino acid residues are linked together. A useful starting point is the amino acid bearing a free amino group at one end of the polypeptide chain. This can be identified by application of the fluorodinitrobenzene reaction (p. 11.3). The pure protein is allowed to react with the reagent, when only free amino groups, present at the end of the chain and in any lysine residues form the yellow dinitrophenyl derivatives. Subsequent hydrolysis, paper chromatography and identification of the yellow spot or spots should disclose the number and nature of the end groups. Each polypeptide chain present in the original material should yield one α-2,4-dinitrophenyl derivative, so that the finding of two or more indicates a complex molecule with more than one polypeptide chain. The presence of a single N-terminal amino acid does not, of course, exclude the possibility of the existence of multiple chains in the molecule. For example, the molecule of normal adult human haemoglobin contains a pair of α- and a pair of β-chains. Although these differ in amino acid make-up, the N-terminal amino acid in both cases is valine. Where a molecule proves to have more than one chain, the links between the chains may be stable covalent disulphide bonds between cysteine residues or weaker bonds of the type of hydrogen bonds.

Identification of the carboxyl terminal amino acid is more difficult, because no reagent has yet come into use which reacts specifically with the terminal —COOH quite as effectively and simply as fluorodinitrobenzene reacts with the —NH$_2$. Useful information can sometimes be obtained by brief treatment of the protein in solution with carboxypeptidase, an enzyme which specifically catalyses the hydrolysis of the peptide bond nearest to the free —COOH. The results of such experiments need critical study, because the removal of the terminal amino

TABLE 11.3. The amino acid composition (molecules amino acid/molecule of protein) of some typical proteins.

	Haemoglobin (Human) mol. wt. 65,000	Albumin (Human serum) mol. wt. 68,000	Cytochrome c (Human heart) mol. wt. 12,500	Apoferritin (Horse spleen) mol. wt. 480,000	Insulin (Beef) mol. wt. 5700	Myosin (Rabbit) mol. wt. 470,000	Collagen (Rat skin) —*
Gly	40	15	13	251	4	188	138*
Ala	72	—	6	348	3	367	44
Ser	32	24	2	196	3	183	18
Thr	32	29	7	140	1	207	8
Pro	28	30	7	106	1	103	51
Hyp	0	0	0	0	0	0	39
Val	64	45	3	173	5	202	10
Ileu	0	9	8	85	1	197	5
Leu	70	62	6	599	6	381	10
Phe	32	32	3	175	3	136	5
Tyr	12	18	5	134	4	94	1*
Trp	6	1	1	21	0	0	0
Cys†	6	37	2	48	6	41	0
Met	6	6	3	77	0	108	3
Asp	50	53	8	435	3	399	19
Glu	32	81	10	577	7	738	30
Amide N	32	43	7	549	6	432	17
Arg	12	24	2	213	1	202	21
His	38	15	3	124	2	75	2
Lys	44	58	18	194	1	432	12
Total	576	539	107	3896	51	4,053	416*

* The mol. wt. of native collagen is not known; the values in this column are given as molecules of each amino acid/molecule of tyrosine, which is the least plentiful of the amino acids present.

† Cysteine + cystine.

Haemoglobin figures compiled from complete amino acid sequence given by Perutz M.F. (1962). *Proteins and Nucleic Acids*, Amsterdam: Elsevier. Other figures recalculated from data of Tristram G. R. & Smith R.H. (1963): *Adv. Prot. Chem.*, **18**, 227.

acid automatically exposes a new one, also capable of removal by the enzyme. It is rare to be able to identify conclusively the carboxyl end of a chain in this way.

The complete sequence of the amino acid residues in a polypeptide chain involves an extremely rigorous and painstaking analysis. In a series of experiments the protein (or, if the molecule contains multiple chains, a preparation containing only one kind of chain) is subjected to partial hydrolysis by a range of different techniques, e.g. varying concentrations of acid, allowed to act for different times at different temperatures or a variety of specific enzymes, used singly or in sequence. The peptides obtained in each case must be separated, hydrolysed and identified. Application of the fluorodinitrobenzene reaction either to the original material or to the mixture of peptides may assist in the identification. The use of hydrolytic reagents of different specificities and different rates of reaction gives a series of peptides which overlap when placed in correct sequence along the chain, and in favourable cases it may be possible to build up gradually a picture of the complete structure. So far the task has only been completed for a few proteins, including the enzyme ribonuclease and a number of haemoglobins, and for a larger and rapidly growing number of polypeptides e.g. insulin, glucagon,

gastrin, parathormone, ACTH. It is natural that attention should have been directed first to substances of surpassing physiological interest.

A simple variant of this technique has proved of great value in the study of differences between the structures of closely related polypeptides and proteins. The hydrolysis of a pure protein with a pure peptidase of high specificity should always give the same mixture of peptides. If these are separated by a standard procedure involving electrophoresis followed by chromatography the same final pattern (**finger print**) should always be observed. If the same procedure is applied to a protein which differs only slightly from the first, perhaps in the identity of only a single amino acid, the peptide pattern or finger print should also show a slight, but clearly defined difference. This technique was first used for the study of species differences in the structure of insulin, but is best known for its application to the study of abnormal genetic variants of human haemoglobin. Over fifty of these variants have now been recognized. In many of these, the abnormality consists only of a difference in a single amino acid in the β-chain. For example, in sickle-cell haemoglobin, commonly called haemoglobin S, a single glutamic acid in the normal β-chain is replaced by valine. Such a difference would be almost impossible to detect by any conventional method of analysis, but, as may be seen from fig. 11.7, it is easily disclosed by finger printing.

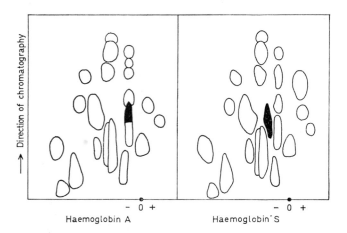

FIG. 11.7. Fingerprints of tryptic hydrolysates of haemoglobins A and S. ○, point of application of hydrolysate; + −, direction of electric field. The peptides which differ in behaviour and composition are marked black, the one containing valine (in HbS) has moved slightly further towards the cathode. Modified from Ingram V. (1958) *Biochem. Biophys. Acta*, 28, 539.

Secondary and tertiary structure of proteins

The backbone of the polypeptide chain contains the repeating unit —N—C—C— of which the atoms are linked by single covalent bonds. If there were free rotation about these bonds, the chain would twist and coil at random, without assuming any definite and reproducible structure or shape. Measurements of the rates of diffusion and sedimentation of protein molecules in solution show that the facts are not consistent with such an hypothesis. Haemoglobin, serum albumin, many enzymes and a host of other proteins behave as if the molecules were uniform, relatively compact particles (**globular proteins**). The molecules of other proteins, e.g. collagen, fibrin, silk fibroin, appear to exist in a more or less rigid, greatly elongated form (**fibrous proteins**). Many fibrous proteins are insoluble and information about their shape has been obtained by the use of the EM and other techniques, such as X-ray crystallography, which are also applicable to crystals prepared from soluble proteins.

When a beam of X-rays traverses a molecule, the rays are diffracted by the component atoms to an extent which depends on the number of electrons in each atom. In a crystal, where the molecules are orientated in a regular manner, and to some extent in other organized molecular structures, the diffraction effects accumulate to give a well-defined pattern. The patterns given by complete crystals can be photographed, and the analysis of many photographs taken from different angles enables a picture to be built up of the location and spacing of the

atoms in the repeating unit of the crystal, i.e. the molecule. The interpretation of the diffraction patterns given by the crystals of substances composed of atoms of elements of low atomic number is much easier if crystals can be made which incorporate occasional atoms of heavy metals such as mercury, and where possible this device is utilized in the X-ray crystallography of proteins.

The X-ray diffraction patterns given by many proteins give prominence to a frequently repeated interatomic spacing of such a magnitude that it could not occur in extended polypeptide chains. This indicates some permanent folding or twisting in a way which must be conditioned and maintained by the groups of atoms (—NH— —CH—CO—) of which the backbone of the polypeptide is constructed. The kind of twist which best fits the experimental results is illustrated in fig. 11.8. Each turn of the helix contains 3·6 amino acid residues. The figure shows how each —NH— or —CO— is in close proximity to a —CO— or —NH— in the neighbouring turn, so that the structure is maintained by —CO····HN— hydrogen bonds. The term **secondary structure** is used to refer to this helical folding of the polypeptide chain, without reference to the final shape of the molecule as a whole, which is described as **tertiary structure**. In cases where the complete molecule is comprised of a number of subunits, each of which is itself a polypeptide, tertiary structure is sometimes used to describe only the shape of the individual polypeptides, while the name **quaternary structure** is reserved for the entire molecule.

Since many proteins are found in solution in the living body, it is important to know whether the α-helical secondary structure is characteristic only of the crystalline state, or whether it persists when the molecule is dissolved. The optical rotatory properties of protein solutions suggest that in most proteins there is a marked tendency for the α-helix to persist in solution. The extent to which this occurs depends partly on pH, so that electrostatic bonds between side chain groups must play a part in the maintenance of the helix. Among the few proteins which show little or no evidence of α-helical structure in solution are the milk phosphoprotein casein and the immunologically important γ-globulins of plasma.

Wherever the amino acids proline or hydroxyproline occur in a polypeptide chain, the common α-helical secondary structure cannot be formed. This situation, which is found in collagen and other connective tissue proteins, as well as sporadically elsewhere, develops partly because the nitrogen atom forms part of a rigid heterocyclic ring which does not fit perfectly into the shape of the α-helix, and partly because the nitrogen carries no hydrogen to form a hydrogen bond. The difficulty is surmounted in different ways. In most proteins, where there is only an occasional proline molecule, the α-helix is temporarily interrupted and the chain as a whole takes an angle determined by the other forces

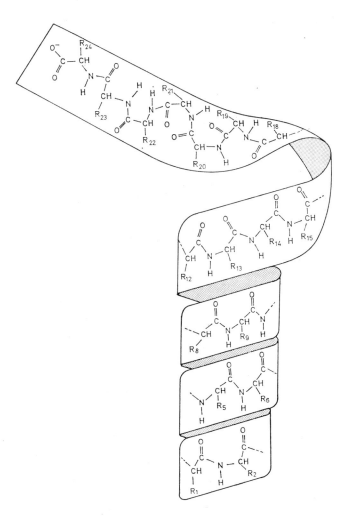

FIG. 11.8. The right-handed α-helix. The lower part of the ribbon, with the polypeptide structure drawn upon it, shows the helical structure. Note that the relative positions of —NH— and —CO— in successive coils are favourable for hydrogen bond formation. Further up the ribbon there is random folding, with full extension of the chain at the upper end. From Haggis G. *et al.* (1964) *Introduction to Molecular Biology*. London : Longmans.

involved. In collagen there is about 22 per cent of proline and hydroxyproline, spread evenly along the chain, so that the common α-helix cannot be stabilized at all. A different type of helix develops, in which three similar polypeptide chains are twisted together. The formation of the structure is facilitated by the fact that every third position in the collagen polypeptide chains is occupied by glycine, which has only a hydrogen atom for side chain and therefore occupies little space.

The formation of the α-helix cannot itself account for the observed fact that the molecules of many proteins adopt a globular shape, both in solution and in the crystalline state. The stability of the α-helix depends to

some extent on bonds between side-chain groups in neighbouring parts of the chain. There seems no *a priori* reason why the formation of hydrogen bonds or electrostatic interaction should not take place between side chain groups in different parts of the molecule thrown sufficiently close together. Such bonds would then hold together different parts of the polypeptide chain in much the same way as —S—S— bonds between remotely separated cysteine residues, and a sufficient number of these points of interaction might well produce an approximately globular structure. The tertiary structure of a few proteins has been worked out in great detail. Among these myoglobin and haemoglobin are now classical examples. The full quaternary structure of haemoglobin, in which the two α- and two β-chains are knit together in a roughly spherical shape, involves the interaction of side-chain groups in different polypeptide chains. A model of the haemoglobin molecule is illustrated in plate 11.1, facing p. 10.11. Careful inspection indicates that the α-helix, indicated by flat discs piled on top of one another, breaks down at various points and at many of these there is a definite inflexion of the axis of the chain. This happens because here and there the forces tending to draw the amino acids away from their neighbours are stronger than those which tend to knit the α-helix together. Some, but by no means all, of the corners occur, as would be expected, at points where the chain contains proline.

The secondary, tertiary and quaternary structures of proteins are a matter of highly complex physical chemistry with, however, an increasing number of repercussions in physiology and medicine. Changes in the quaternary structure of haemoglobin are associated with the equilibrium between haemoglobin and oxygen and also with important differences between the acid-base properties of haemoglobin and oxyhaemoglobin (p. 29.20). The difference in the primary structures of haemoglobin A and haemoglobin S, to which reference has already been made, is associated with differences in shape and solubility. The changes in the structure of γ-globulins which confer on them a wide range of specific immunochemical properties are of immense importance, although the changes themselves are not yet understood.

Denaturation

The bonds which maintain the spatial configuration of protein molecules are weak and easily broken, with consequent loss of structural integrity, by heat or sometimes even by alteration of the physicochemical conditions, such as by the addition of acid or alkali. The loss of structure caused by any such method is called denaturation, provided that the treatment is not vigorous enough to alter the primary structure; the reductive fission of disulphide bonds is, however, sometimes regarded as denaturation. Denaturation is associated with the loss of such biochemical properties as enzymic activity and with marked alterations in physicochemical properties. For example, solubility more especially near the isoelectric point, is often greatly diminished by denaturation.

AMINO ACIDS AND PROTEINS IN NUTRITION

Broadly speaking, nutrition serves two purposes which are inextricably woven together. These are the building and maintenance of body structure and its essential constituents, and the provision of energy for all the activities of life (chap. 4). While fats, carbohydrates and proteins can all serve as sources of energy, only proteins supply the nitrogen and also the sulphur required for the synthesis of proteins and other compounds essential for maintenance, growth and related purposes such as pregnancy and lactation.

The quantitative study of protein requirements is of practical importance from several points of view, not least because in many parts of the world it is necessary to find the best way of sharing out what at present are manifestly inadequate supplies. When attempts are made to ascertain protein requirements, for example, by feeding young animals on experimental diets, it is found that even when the diet is adequate in all other respects the rate of growth depends on the kind of protein as well as the amount which is fed. Some remarkable differences between individual proteins are illustrated by the results of classical experiments carried out in New York between 1912 and 1916 (fig. 11.9). Osborne and Mendel found that ovovitellin, from egg yolk, and lactalbumin from milk promoted growth extremely well, but casein, also from milk,

less satisfactorily. The wheat protein, gliadin, barely maintained the weight of young rats, while with zein from maize, the animals lost weight continuously. Increasing the proportions in the diet improved the growth promoting properties of casein, gave a slight benefit with gliadin, but had no effect with zein. That these differences were attributable to differences in amino acid composition was shown by giving supplements of amino acids. Gliadin contains all the amino acids but only a very small proportion of lysine. The addition of lysine to the gliadin diet conferred on it good growth promoting properties. Zein contains little lysine and no tryptophan and supplements of both these amino acids are required.

Essential amino acids

The fact that even a large increase in the zein content of the diet does not increase its growth promoting properties, whereas a small supplement of lysine and tryptophan does, suggests that these two amino acids cannot be synthesized in the animal body, even with the aid of an ample supply of nitrogen. They were, in fact, the first members of the group of essential or indispensable amino acids to be discovered. An essential amino acid is one which cannot be synthesized in the body from readily available precursors at a rate sufficient to meet metabolic needs, so that it must be supplied in the diet. The list of essential amino acids varies somewhat from one species to another, and young animals may require a dietary supply of an amino acid which can be synthesized sufficiently rapidly by the mature animal. Chicks, for example, require a dietary supply of glycine, but mature fowls do not; young rats cannot synthesize arginine rapidly enough to permit full growth on an arginine deficient diet. In the same way, histidine is an essential amino acid for man during infancy. In qualitative terms, human requirements for essential amino acids have been worked out carefully by feeding young men and women on protein free diets containing mixtures of purified amino acids. Table 11.4 lists the amino acids which have been shown to be essential for man. Some progress has been made in ascertaining the quantities of the various individual amino acids required.

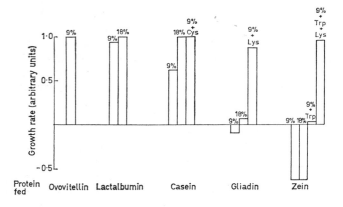

FIG. 11.9. Comparison of the growth promoting properties of different proteins. The proteins were fed to young rats at a level of 9 per cent and 18 per cent of the weight of an otherwise adequate diet with and without supplements of amino acids as indicated. Data from Osborne & Mendel (1912–16).

TABLE 11.4. Amino acids essential in human diets.

Isoleucine	Methionine
Leucine	(Cystine)
Lysine	Threonine
Phenylalanine	Tryptophan
(Tyrosine)	Valine
Histidine*	

* Only essential for infants.

Two of the amino acids, although not strictly essential, occupy a rather special position. Tyrosine can be synthesized in the animal body but only from phenylalanine. A deficiency of the essential amino acid, phenylalanine, therefore leads to a deficiency of tyrosine unless that substance is present in the diet. Conversely, if the dietary supply of tyrosine is ample, the phenylalanine requirement is lower because tyrosine synthesis is not required. In practice, therefore, the two aromatic amino acids are bracketed together when considering the essential amino acid content of dietary proteins. There is a somewhat similar relation between the two sulphur containing amino acids, for methionine is essential but cystine is not. If synthesis of cystine is required because the intake from the diet is insufficient, the necessary sulphur can be supplied only by methionine. Hence, in nutritional work it is important to consider the two sulphur-containing amino acids together. Casein contains much the same proportion of methionine as many other proteins, but less cystine. The supply of cystine can be augmented in three ways, by increasing the casein content of the diet, by supplementing the diet with cystine or by supplementing the diet with methionine. The first two are illustrated in fig. 11.9. The third could not be tested at the time when those experiments were first done because methionine was not discovered until seven years later.

From a practical point of view, a dietary protein which is absolutely or relatively deficient in one or more of the essential amino acids can be supplemented not only by feeding the missing amino acid but also, and much more easily, by feeding other proteins rich in the amino acid in question. This is one of the most important reasons for the oft-repeated advice that the diet should consist of a wide range of foods. Among the people who are in constant danger of protein deficiency are those who, from custom or necessity, rely largely on food from a single source such as rice, maize or cassava.

The division of the amino acids into essential and nonessential groups is concerned only with the question of their provision in the diet and not at all with metabolism. Amino acids which are not dietetically essential are synthesized in the body, when required for protein production, and some of them have other very important metabolic functions to fulfil.

Quantitative comparison of nutritional value of proteins

Proteins like zein which are totally deficient in some essential amino acid are rare, but large numbers of proteins including the mixed proteins in a natural food range in properties between gliadin, which just maintains the weight of animals when fed at a comparatively high level, and casein which supports growth well. At the other end of the scale, no proteins or naturally occurring mixtures of proteins promote growth in the young rat

better than vitellin or the mixed proteins of whole eggs. Studies on infants suggest that for them the proteins of human milk are most effective. These mixtures appear to fulfil the theoretical criteria for an ideal **reference protein**, which are complete digestibility and utilization for anabolic purposes when fed at a suitable level. Whole egg protein is the most conveniently available and is widely used as a reference standard. Its essential amino acid composition is given in table 11.5. Although an artificial

TABLE 11.5. The essential amino acids of reference protein (whole egg protein).

Amino acid	mg/g N
Isoleucine	415
Leucine	553
Lysine	403
Phenylalanine	365
(Tyrosine)	(262)
(Total aromatic amino acids)	(627)
Methionine	197
(Cystine)	(149)
(Total sulphur-containing acids)	(346)
Threonine	317
Tryptophan	100
Valine	454

mixture of pure amino acids might, in theory, be more satisfactory as a reference standard, and tentative reference patterns of amino acids have been suggested, there are still difficulties in their use and it seems better in the meantime to use the egg protein standard.

The value of a particular source of protein is estimated by feeding a standard diet containing a constant proportion of the protein source under investigation. The dietary intake of nitrogen (I) is measured, as are also the output in the faeces (F) and the urine (U). Tests are best carried out during the period of growth when amino acid requirements are more stringent. Tests on humans are laborious and require a high degree of co-operation from the subjects. Young rats are convenient experimental animals for this purpose, because they require amino acids in proportions broadly similar to those required by man.

The **biological value** is an index of nutritional quality calculated as the fraction of absorbed nitrogen which is retained in the body for maintenance and growth:

$$BV = \frac{I - F - U}{I - F}$$

In fact, the faecal nitrogen does not represent entirely the unabsorbed residue of dietary protein (p. 5.28), and in any case from a practical point of view absorbed nitrogen is less important than ingested nitrogen. Allowance can be made for such considerations by using **net protein utilization**, which is the ratio of nitrogen retained to nitrogen taken in:

$$NPU = \frac{I-F-U}{I}$$

BV and NPU can only be measured on suboptimal intakes of protein, because once the optimum intake is passed there is no increase in retention with further increase in intake. Falsely low values of the numerical expression are thus obtained. Careful attention to this point and making measurements under conditions in which the prevailing living conditions are imitated give **net protein utilization operative** (NPU_{op}).

By definition, NPU or BV of reference protein must be unity, or 100 per cent. Proteins which are less well utilized give lower values. If the requirement of a given subject for ideal reference protein can be found, then the necessary intake of protein of known NPU can be calculated very simply. Thus, if a given subject requires 45 g reference protein per day, and NPU for the available diet is 70 per cent, the intake of protein in that diet should be $45 \times 100/70 = 64$ g.

Modern analytical methods make it possible to determine the amino acid composition of natural diets as well as of individual purified proteins. Since the limiting factor in the nutritional quality of protein is often the proportion of one of the essential amino acids present, the nutritional value can be described in terms of a **chemical score** or **protein score**, which is the ratio of the quantity of the limiting amino acid, expressed as a fraction of the total quantity of essential amino acids, to that of the same amino acid in reference protein, expressed in the same way. In practice, the ratio must be evaluated for each of the essential amino acids in turn (taking cystine with methionine and tyrosine with phenylalanine). The lowest ratio found indicates the limiting amino acid and, when expressed as a percentage, gives the protein score. An example of the calculation is given in table 11.6.

Table 11.7 gives some examples of limiting amino acids and protein scores. Fig. 11.10 gives a graphical comparison of NPU with protein score for a number of foods of animal and vegetable origin. There is fair but far from perfect agreement between the chemical and biological methods of assay. This shows that present techniques are only partially adequate and emphasizes the wisdom of allowing a substantial safety margin in calculating protein requirements. When the indices disagree it is wiser to rely at present on the biologically determined NPU, although in the long run it will probably be easier and more satisfactory to use a reliable index depending on chemical analysis of the foodstuffs. It is worth noting that some amino acids may be partially destroyed by cooking (some of the lysine in wheat proteins is destroyed

during the baking and toasting of bread), so that it is better to evaluate the quality of a protein prepared in the way in which it is actually eaten.

TABLE 11.6. Calculation of the chemical or protein score of soya flour protein.

	Reference protein	Soya flour protein
Total essential amino acids (g/100 g protein)	51·3	41·4
Methionine + cystine (g/100 g protein)	5·5	3·1
Methionine + cystine (% of total essential amino acids)	10·8	7·5
Apparent chemical score (based on sulphur-containing amino acids)	$\frac{7·5}{10·8} \times 100 = 70\%$	
Lysine (g/100 g protein)	6·4	6·3
Lysine (% of total essential amino acids)	12·4	15·3
Apparent chemical score (based on lysine)	$\frac{15·3}{12·4} \times 100 = 123\%$	
Tryptophan (g/100 g protein)	1·6	1·4
Tryptophan (% of essential amino acids)	3·1	3·3
Apparent chemical score (based on tryptophan)	$\frac{3·3}{3·1} \times 100 = 106\%$	

Similar calculations are made for all the essential amino acids. The lowest apparent chemical score (given here by the sulphur-containing amino acids) indicates the limiting amino acid and gives the numerical value of the chemical score.

TABLE 11.7. Chemical scores of the protein in some natural foods, based on whole egg reference protein as standard.

Food	Limiting amino acid	Chemical score
Egg	—	100
Milk	S*	60
Egg albumin	Trp	90
Beef muscle	S	80
Beef liver	S	70
Fish	Trp	75
Oats	Lys	70
Rye	Thr	90
Rice	Lys	75
White flour (wheat)	Lys	50
Potato	S	70
Peas	S	60

* Methionine + cystine.

a

6–12 +X

b

PLATE 12.1. Human chromosomes.

Chromosomes of a normal human male cell from a culture of peripheral blood; (a) orcein (×2700); (b) chromosomes of the same cell arranged in pairs according to the Denver convention.

PLATE 15.1. A cardiac muscle cell.

An electron micrograph of a rat cardiac muscle cell showing the sarcolemma (S), myofilaments (F), mitochondria (M), Z-discs (Z) and glycogen granules (G); osmium fixation, araldite embedding (× 63,000).

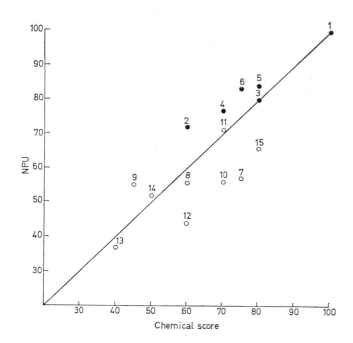

FIG. 11.10. Comparison of NPU and protein score for some animal ●, and vegetable ○, proteins. If agreement were perfect all the points would lie on the straight line. (1) Egg protein (reference); (2) Casein; (3) Beef muscle; (4) Beef kidney; (5) Pork tenderloin; (6) Fish; (7) Rice; (8) Millet; (9) Corn (maize); (10) Soya flour; (11) Potato; (12) Peas; (13) Wheat gluten; (14) Wheat flour (white); (15) Cottonseed meal.

Nitrogen losses and requirements for growth

The techniques which are used for assessing BV and NPU are not suitable for assessing the minimal daily intake of protein necessary to ensure good health, particularly in adult subjects who are no longer growing. In all age groups, except perhaps young infants, protein requirements can be satisfactorily calculated from nitrogen requirements, which are comprised of the nitrogen needed to replace obligatory losses together with any supplement which it may be necessary to allow in respect of growth, pregnancy, lactation, convalescence, etc.

Measurement of the loss of nitrogen from the body while the subject is on a protein-free diet should give a value for the obligatory loss. Nitrogen is lost from the body surface (in sweat, hair and nails and by loss of the superficial layers of the skin), in the faeces and in the urine. Surface losses under normal conditions amount to not more than 20 mg N/kg body weight/day and are usually much less. The figure is not affected by the amount of protein in the diet. Prolonged heavy work in hot climates has been reported to increase losses of nitrogen in sweat, but the point has not been established and such losses are probably of little practical significance. The faecal nitrogen is largely derived from digestive

secretions and exfoliated cells and only depends to a small extent on dietary nitrogen (some vegetable proteins are slightly less completely digested than animal proteins). Faecal nitrogen does, however, increase somewhat with the bulk of the diet, and this factor also is greater with foodstuffs of vegetable origin. Faecal nitrogen normally ranges from 10 to 20 mg/kg body weight/day.

Although the nitrogen content of the diet makes little difference to faecal and integumental losses, the same is by no means true of the urinary nitrogen, which varies very greatly with the dietary nitrogen. When a well-fed subject is given a protein-free diet adequate in calories, the nitrogen content of the urine falls steeply for 4 or 5 days, until a daily output of about 3 g from a normal adult (about 45 mg/kg/day) is reached (fig. 11.11). Thereafter the fall is much slower, although the

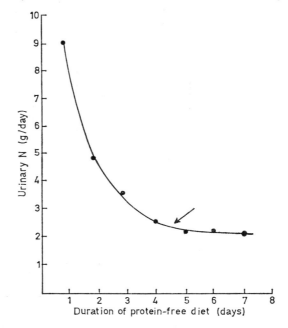

FIG. 11.11. Nitrogen excretion in a man on a protein-free diet.

constant tissue wastage which is suffered on a protein free diet causes continuing nitrogen excretion. The obligatory loss is taken as the value already quoted, found at the fairly definite point of inflection seen after 4 or 5 days in the graph of nitrogen loss against time.

The urinary nitrogen is found in compounds which are produced in the course of normal metabolic processes. The obligatory loss of nitrogen in the urine should therefore bear some relation to the basal metabolic rate, and experiment has shown that this is true; for each kcal produced in basal metabolism there is an excretion of 2 mg N in the urine. This calculation is in good agreement with the adult value already given, and is probably more reliable in children.

7

The total obligatory loss of nitrogen ranges from about 115 mg/kg/day in children at one year old to about 80 mg/kg/day in adults. Actual values are illustrated in fig. 11.12, for which maximum rather than average figures for faecal N and body surface N have been used. The supplement required for growth is calculated from the known rates of growth of well-nourished children and the

80 per cent is needed during the second half and only 4 per cent during the first 10 weeks. The daily loss of nitrogen in the milk of a lactating woman is variable, but may be as much as 2·5 g/day. Fever, wounds, accidents and surgical operations all stimulate protein catabolism markedly, but it is difficult to make an exact evaluation of the amount of additional protein required during con-

FIG. 11.12. Approximate nitrogen requirements of normal human subjects (mg/kg/day).

assumption, based on experimental observation, that nitrogen (mainly in protein) accounts for 2·9 per cent of the weight gained during growth. Fig. 11.12 includes illustrative values for children from 1 year of age upwards. Notice that the values are quoted in mg/kg/day so that although a child of 2 years and one of 8 both require 13 mg N/kg/day for growth, this represents nearly 0·4 g N in the older child and only 0·18 g N in the younger.

Infections, physical injury, excitement and indeed all stresses stimulate protein catabolism. Calculations of normal protein requirements should therefore include a component to allow for the stress of normal living. The value may be set, somewhat arbitrarily, at 10 per cent of the figure calculated by taking all the other components together. This allowance is included in the histograms given in fig. 11.12. Other allowances and supplements may be calculated separately. A single pregnancy imposes a total additional requirement of about 150 g N, of which

valescence. The need for supplements in other conditions is not well established. Thus, there is no good evidence to support the popular belief that the heavy expenditure of energy in severe manual labour carries with it an increased requirement for protein. Again, trained athletes have been said to perform better on a diet rich in protein, but there is no scientific basis for this. However, in the early stages of training, muscle tissue is being built up and for this extra protein is required.

When the minimal nitrogen requirements have been computed in the ways described, it is easy to calculate the quantity of ideal reference protein which could supply them, since the average nitrogen content of protein is 16 per cent. The nitrogen requirement is multiplied by 6·25 to give the chemically equivalent weight of protein. For an ideal subject, this should give a satisfactory intake of reference protein. Not all subjects, however, behave ideally, and the protein of ordinary mixed diets does not behave like reference protein. The calculated figure must therefore be corrected, in the way already shown, for the NPU of the actual diet, and it is advisable to allow for individual variation by adding 20 per cent to the final figure. Table 11.8 gives some figures showing that adults

TABLE 11.8. Nitrogen requirements and daily dietary allowances of protein.

| Age, years | N required mg/kg | Allowance of protein* | |
		Reference g/kg	NPU = 75% g/kg
Up to 3/12	—	2·3†	(3·1)‡
4/12 to 12/12	—	1·3†	1·7
1	148	1·11	1·48
5	130	0·97	1·30
10	114	0·86	1·14
15	110	0·83	1·10
18	101	0·76	1·01
Adult	95	0·71	0·95

* Includes 20% to allow for individual variation.
† From known intakes of healthy infants.
‡ For comparison only.

ought, on the basis of these calculations, to receive about 1 g protein/kg/day if the protein has an NPU of 75 per cent. This is about the value usually found for a good mixed diet in which half or nearly half the protein comes from animal sources. For each kg body weight, children require more protein than adults, and the younger the child, the more protein it requires because the rate of growth (expressed as a fraction of the body weight) declines progressively from birth onwards. The figures for infants have not been calculated in the same way, but are taken from the normal protein intakes of healthy breast-fed infants.

Quantitatively speaking, investigations in different parts of the world have reached similar conclusions, although it is recognized that many individuals whose intake of protein is below the recommended levels may show no obvious signs of protein deficiency. In most developed countries the average intake of protein is somewhat higher than the recommended level and in some individual cases NPU may be above 75 per cent.

Protein nutrition and energy supply

The calculations which have been made so far are all based on the assumption that the total calorie intake is adequate, but in some cases it may be important to take into account the twofold relation between protein nutrition and the provision of calories. At one end of the scale, the utilization of protein is more effective when energy needs are met largely by other foodstuffs, especially carbohydrate. When the diet lacks carbohydrate as well as protein, protein is diverted to supply energy and

protein deficiency develops more easily. On the other hand, the gross intake of food is limited by its calorie content, so that if the proportion of protein in the diet is below a certain level, it is impossible for the subject to consume sufficient food to supply his needs for protein. It is therefore important to consider the proportion of total calories provided by protein and ideally it is necessary to take variations in NPU into account. This is significant in the case of a diet containing protein of low NPU, where the intake might be satisfactory if NPU were higher. The index which has been developed to aid the study of this aspect of protein requirements is rather clumsily termed **net dietary protein calories per cent** (NDpCal%). This is evaluated by multiplying the fraction of the total calories of the diet which is derived from protein by the NPU_{op}, so that it is equivalent to the fraction of the total calories which would be derived from protein if the protein were of reference quality. Thus, if a diet yields 2700 kcal/day of which 270 come from protein with an NPU_{op} of 70, then

$$NDpCal\% = \frac{270}{2700} \times 70 = 7.$$

In practice, it is found that if NDPCal% is less than 5 the diet is incapable of meeting the protein requirements of adults, while if the value is less than 8 the diet is unsuitable for infants. It can be calculated that the calorie requirements of children older than one year are so high that although their need for protein is also great, NDpCal% is of little significance. A child of four, given free access to a palatable diet of NDpCal% as low as 4, should be able to satisfy his protein requirements. On the other hand, if the quantity and quality of the protein in the diet are low, protein deficiency is certain to complicate any calorie deficiency that may develop. Where NDpCal% is low, it can be raised by supplementing the diet with dried skimmed cows' milk, which has a high NDpCal% of about 25. Other supplements rich in protein may prove suitable where milk is scarce. Many milk substitutes, prepared from suitable mixtures of vegetable proteins, are now available in countries with an inadequate milk supply and have been shown to promote satisfactory growth in children.

INTERMEDIATE METABOLISM OF AMINO ACIDS AND PROTEINS

The intermediate metabolism of amino acids embraces a wider range of biochemical reactions than that of either carbohydrates or fats. There are several reasons for this; firstly, proteins always contain nitrogen and almost always sulphur as well as carbon, hydrogen and oxygen, so that the metabolism of amino acids includes the elaboration of nitrogenous and sulphur-containing end products (mainly urea and sulphate); secondly, many different types of structure are found among the carbon skeletons of amino acids, and each is metabolized in its own more or less specific way. While the ultimate end products are carbon dioxide and water, produced in the citric acid cycle and by the re-oxidation of dehydrogenase coenzymes, the various amino acids enter the cycle only after conversion to intermediate products, most of which also arise in carbohydrate and fat metabolism. Again, since proteins are, apart from traces of some of the vitamins and other highly specialized compounds, the only source of nitrogen available to the animal body, amino acid metabolism includes the biosynthesis not only of proteins (chap. 12) but also of almost all other nitrogenous compounds, including non-essential amino acids. The carbon skeletons of these are

synthesized mainly but not exclusively from precursors which are not amino acids, although the nitrogen is provided by other amino acids. Many other nitrogenous compounds, including purine and pyrimidine bases, porphyrins and creatine are synthesized in specific reactions from particular amino acids. Fig. 11.13 summarizes the main pathways.

Such a wide variety of biochemical processes necessarily involves a large number of enzymes. Many of these require the presence of coenzymes. As there are so many possibilities for the development of a nutritional or metabolic defect leading to error in, or failure of, the synthesis of a coenzyme or enzyme, it is not surprising to find a large variety of pathological conditions, fortunately many of them exceedingly rare, associated with specific failures of reactions in the metabolism of one or more of the amino

FIG. 11.13. Amino acid metabolism.

acids. When the basic defect is an inherited failure to synthesize a specific enzyme, the condition is known as a hereditary or **inborn error of metabolism**. Where a reaction fails because of some other cause, such as deficiency of a vitamin, leading to lack of a particular coenzyme, the condition is an **acquired error of metabolism**. The study of metabolic errors, is important in specific cases for clinical reasons and has also been of great value in the elucidation of metabolic processes. Failure of one link in a chain of reactions may lead either to accumulation of an intermediate, as in alkaptonuria (an inborn error of tyrosine metabolism) or to diversion into an abnormal metabolic pathway, as in phenylketonuria (an inborn error of the metabolism of phenylalanine). Inborn errors were first recognized in the field of amino acid metabolism.

Amino acids in body fluids

In comparison with the amounts present in chemical combination as protein, concentrations of free amino acids in body fluids are low. Plasma contains a total concentration of 2–4 mM, to which the individual amino acids make very different contributions. Glutamine, alanine and lysine are among the most plentiful, methionine and aspartic acid the least so.

The amino acids in all the body fluids are of mixed origin, and, while there is free diffusion between plasma and interstitial fluid, there is no simple relation between extracellular and intracellular amino acids. The plasma amino acids are derived from the products of protein digestion, which are actively absorbed across the wall of the small intestine (p. 30.38) and from the products of hydrolysis of extracellular proteins, those of dead or decaying cells (e.g. aged erythrocytes) or, in the case of the non-essential acids, new synthesis. It has been known for half a century that all cells take up amino acids avidly from the interstitial fluid and may accumulate them against the concentration gradient. Inside the cell the molecules mingle with those of newly synthesized amino acids and those, perhaps, liberated from proteins hydrolysed in the course of the life of the cell. The intracellular concentration of amino acids varies greatly, but is about five to ten times greater than that outside the cells.

The composition of the mixture of amino acids available to the enzyme systems of any cell depends not only on the mixture in the extracellular fluid bathing that cell (and this may vary from one part of the body to another) but also on the extent to which metabolism in in that cell contributes to the mixture.

Urinary losses normally amount to no more than about 5 mM per day of free amino acids, with about as much again in the form of some easily hydrolysed substances of unknown nature. Losses are small because amino acids are actively reabsorbed in the renal tubules by mechanisms which resemble those involved in intestinal absorption. In cystinuria, an inborn error, there is a failure of the active absorption of cystine as well as of the diamino acids, lysine and arginine, in both the kidney and the intestine. As might be expected, the pattern of renal excretion of amino acids is altered both qualitatively and quantitatively in a number of pathological conditions, including nutritional disorders and diseases of the liver.

The fate of the nitrogen of amino acids

Many of the biochemical processes which effect the removal of the α-amino group and its subsequent metabolism are common to all the amino acids and are conveniently treated before discussion of the metabolism of the individual amino acids.

One method by which the amino group can be removed from an amino acid molecule is **oxidative deamination**, in which the amino acid is converted to an α-keto acid and the amino group to ammonia. An imino acid is formed as a transient intermediate.

$$RCHNH_2COOH \rightleftharpoons 2e + 2H^+ + \underset{\underset{NH_3 + RCOCOOH}{\overset{\downarrow}{NH}}}{\overset{\|}{RCCOOH}}$$

The first enzyme found to catalyse oxidative deamination in animal tissues, mainly kidney, was a flavoprotein named D-amino acid oxidase because of its surprising specificity for the D-amino acids. Its natural function remains obscure. Even the more recently discovered L-amino acid oxidase, another flavoprotein, is only weakly active with most amino acids. It appears to be identical with glycine oxidase or glycine dehydrogenase, which catalyses the same type of reaction with glycine as substrate.

Another specific oxidative deamination is that catalysed by L-glutamate dehydrogenase which utilizes NAD or NADP as coenzyme.

$$COOHCH_2CH_2CHNH_2COOH + NAD$$
Glutamic acid
$$\downarrow$$
$$COOHCH_2CH_2C{=}NHCOOH + NADH_2$$
α-Iminoglutaric acid
$$\downarrow$$
$$COOHCH_2CH_2COCOOH + NH_3$$
α-Oxoglutaric acid

This reaction is important partly because in conjunction with a series of transaminations it serves as a general method of deamination and also because it is readily reversible and is believed to play an important part in the transfer of energy across the membranes of mitochondria. The thermodynamic equilibrium point lies far in favour of glutamate synthesis, and the reaction is also of importance in connection with amino acid synthesis. It is one of the fundamental reactions of nitrogen fixation in plants.

In 1937 the Russian biochemist Braunstein discovered a process of very wide significance, **transamination**. This is the reaction in which an amino acid reacts with an α-keto acid. The α-keto acid is converted to the amino acid with the same carbon skeleton, while the original amino acid is deaminated with the production of the corresponding keto acid. These reactions are reversible and are catalysed by a series of enzymes called transaminases or aminotransferases.

$$R_1CHNH_2COOH + R_2COCOOH \rightleftharpoons$$
$$R_1COCOOH + R_2CHNH_2COOH$$

Transaminases are widespread throughout the body, and two of them, glutamic oxaloacetic transaminase (GOT) and glutamic pyruvic transaminase (GPT) have a special clinical interest because they escape into the plasma when there is damage to various tissues, notably the myocardium and the liver (p. 31.17). Aminotransferases require a phosphorylated derivative of pyridoxine, vitamin B_6, as coenzyme. The active compound is an aldehyde, pyridoxal 5-phosphate, which is reversibly converted in the course of its action to the corresponding amine, pyridoxamine 5-phosphate:

Pyridoxine   Pyridoxal 5-phosphate

Pyridoxamine 5-phosphate

The course of the reaction can be represented in fig. 11.14:

For simplicity, one-way arrows have been used, but all the reactions are reversible.

All the amino acids, except threonine and lysine, can undergo transamination and glutamate, aspartate and alanine or one of the corresponding oxo compounds appear to participate in every reaction. Furthermore, the wide distribution of aminotransferases link glutamate with aspartate or alanine means that the nitrogen of any other amino acid can very easily appear in one of these three acids. If it should appear in glutamate, this may then be oxidatively deaminated by the action of glutamic dehydrogenase to give ammonia and α-oxoglutarate. The latter substance can then serve as the acceptor for another amino group, so that we have here the machinery for the continuous deamination of a wide range of amino acids:

Carbamyl phosphate is an intermediate in the synthesis of urea and some other nitrogenous compounds. It is an amide of the mixed anhydride of carbonic and phosphoric acids $NH_2COO\textcircled{P}$, which is synthesized with the aid of ATP. It is not stable, only present in tissues in low concentration (pp. 12.22 and 31.2).

Glutamine, on the other hand, is much more stable. It is found, in greater quantities, all over the body and is also synthesized with the aid of ATP:

$$HOOCCH_2CH_2CHNH_2COOH + ATP + NH_3$$
$$\downarrow$$
$$H_2NOCCH_2CH_2CHNH_2COOH + ADP + P_i$$
Glutamine

Ammonia is highly toxic and, either free or in the protonated form, is present only in minute concentration in the body fluids, with the exception of urine. Ammonia produced in the bodies of mammals is converted in the end to urea by a cyclic process which takes place in the liver (p. 31.2).

FIG. 11.14 Action af aminotransferase

The formation of glutamine may be regarded as either a temporary storage or a detoxication mechanism. The ammonia can be liberated through the action of a specific hydrolase, glutaminase, which is of importance in the kidney (p. 33.24).

$$H_2NOCCH_2CH_2CHNH_2COOH + H_2O$$
Glutamine
↓
$$NH_3 + HOOCCH_2CH_2CHNH_2COOH$$
Glutamic acid

The fate of the carbon of amino acids

Most of the carbon in amino acids is finally oxidized to carbon dioxide. The use of alanine as the donor of an amino group in a transamination leaves pyruvate which may then undergo oxidative decarboxylation to acetyl coenzyme A. The keto acids formed from glutamic and aspartic acids are themselves intermediates in the citric acid cycle, so that their oxidation presents no new problem. The question also arises, however, whether these intermediates may be converted to glucose or other carbohydrate derivatives, rather than to carbon dioxide. Evidence of this has been available for a long time from experiments in which lean meat, proteins or amino acids were fed to phlorizinized dogs. Phlorizin poisons the renal tubules, inhibits the reabsorption of glucose and leads to large losses of sugar in the urine. Lean meat and purified proteins caused the excretion of glucose corresponding, on the average, to 58 per cent of the protein fed and also to the excretion of a little aceto-acetate and β-hydroxybutyrate. After amino acids were given the products varied; most of the amino acids were converted largely to glucose, but leucine, isoleucine, phenylalanine and tyrosine gave rise to acetoacetate. Thus, in this experiment many amino acids were gluco-genic and a few ketogenic. Modern evidence confirms that gluconeogenesis from amino acids is a process of meta-bolic significance. As the older evidence suggests, it involves many more amino acids than the few which have been mentioned. The glucogenic pathways for individual amino acids are described below.

Metabolism of individual amino acids

ASPARTIC ACID

The fate of the carbon and the general importance of this amino acid in transamination have already been noted, as well as the part it plays in donating the nitrogen for the final stages of the synthesis of arginine and adenylic acid (p. 31.2 and 12.21). A carbamyl derivative of aspartic acid is the starting point for the synthesis of pyrimidine bases (p. 12.19).

GLUTAMIC ACID AND GLUTAMINE

The general importance of glutamic acid should be al-ready obvious. It has a few highly specialized functions, e.g. in brain where it is decarboxylated to give γ-amino-butyric acid (p. 24.88). Glutamine serves as the donor of an amino group in the synthesis of many important com-pounds, including aminosugars and purine bases (p. 12.18).

CYSTEINE AND CYSTINE

The first step in the metabolism of the disulphide cystine is reduction to cysteine which is then oxidized at the sul-phur atom to give cysteine sulphinic acid. This compound undergoes transamination with the formation of β-sulphinylpyruvic acid. Loss of sulphur dioxide, which is hydrated to sulphite and oxidized to sulphate, leaves pyruvate and this may then be oxidized, converted to car-bohydrate or transaminated to alanine. In the liver cysteine sulphinic acid may also be oxidized to cysteic acid and decarboxylated to taurine, which is conjugated with bile acids to give bile salts (p. 31.8).

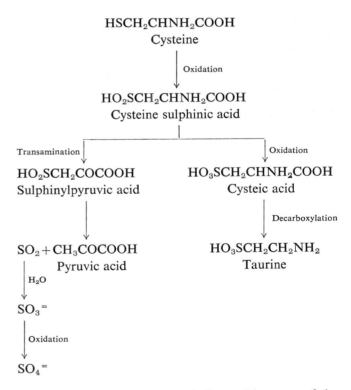

Although cysteine is not, strictly speaking, one of the essential amino acids, it can only be synthesized if methionine is present to provide the sulphur. The other compound required is serine, which is easily syn-thesized from 3-phosphoglyceric acid. Methionine is de-methylated to give homocysteine, which condenses with serine to form a thioether, cystathionine. Hydrolysis of cystathionine gives cysteine and homoserine:

$$CH_3SCH_2CH_2CHNH_2COOH$$
Methionine

$$\downarrow$$

$$HSCH_2CH_2CHNH_2COOH$$
Homocysteine

$$HOCH_2CHNH_2COOH—H_2O \curvearrowleft$$
Serine

$$HOOCCHNH_2CH_2SCH_2CH_2CHNH_2COOH$$
Cystathionine

$$\downarrow$$

$$HOOCCHNH_2CH_2SH + HOCH_2CH_2CHNH_2COOH$$
Cysteine $\qquad$ Homoserine

As cystine is sparingly soluble, patients with cystinuria are liable to form urinary calculi consisting almost entirely of cystine.

METHIONINE

This is an essential amino acid and also serves as the source of sulphur for the synthesis of cysteine and cystine. The complete catabolism of methionine follows the same pathway as far as the formation of homoserine (see above). It then undergoes simultaneous deamination and reduction at the terminal hydroxyl group to give α-oxobutyric acid. Oxidative decarboxylation in the same way as occurs with pyruvate or α-oxoglutarate yields propionyl coenzyme A, which is converted to succinyl coenzyme A after carboxylation to methylmalonyl coenzyme A.

$$HOCH_2CH_2CHNH_2COOH$$
Homoserine

$$\downarrow$$

$$CH_3CH_2COCOOH$$
α-Oxobutyric acid

$$\downarrow -CO_2$$

$$CH_3CH_2CO.SCoA$$
Propionyl coenzyme A

$$\downarrow +CO_2$$

$$CH_3CHCO.SCoA$$
$$|$$
$$COOH$$
Methylmalonyl coenzyme A

$$\downarrow B_{12}\ \text{coenzyme}$$

$$HOOCCH_2CH_2CO.SCoA$$
Succinyl coenzyme A

Succinyl coenzyme A is an intermediate in the citric acid cycle and may be either oxidized or converted to carbohydrate, hence the glucogenic properties of methionine.

The details of the utilization of the methyl group of methionine are dealt with under 'one-carbon' metabolism (p. 11.28).

SULPHUR METABOLISM

The excretion of sulphur in the urine varies mainly with the intake of the amino acids containing sulphur and hence with the intake of protein, although there is a little preformed sulphate in most foods. With most satisfactory diets the total daily output is of the order of 1g sulphur. About three-quarters of this is inorganic sulphate formed from cysteine and methionine in the way outlined above. Most of the remainder consists of sulphate esters of organic hydroxy compounds but there are traces of numerous inorganic as well as organic compounds including the sulphur containing amino acids themselves. Some rather unusual compounds, e.g. bromobenzene, are detoxicated on excretion by conjugation with cysteine to form mercapturic acids.

Important sulphate derivatives in the body are the sugar sulphates found in the molecules of many mucopolysaccharides and related compounds e.g. heparin and chondroitin sulphate. These, like the sulphate esters found in urine, are synthesized with the aid of the coenzyme 3'-phosphoadenosine 5'-phosphosulphate.

VALINE

This glucogenic essential amino acid is catabolized in a long series of reactions involving transamination, oxidative deamination and oxidation of one of the methyl groups to methylmalonyl coenzyme A and hence to succinyl coenzyme A.

$$\begin{array}{c} H_3C \\ \diagdown \\ \quad CHCHNH_2COOH \\ \diagup \\ H_3C \end{array}$$
Valine

$$\downarrow$$

$$\begin{array}{c} H_3C \\ \diagdown \\ \quad CHCOCOOH \\ \diagup \\ H_3C \end{array}$$
α-Oxoisovaleric acid

$$\downarrow$$

$$\begin{array}{c} H_3C \\ \diagdown \\ \quad CHCO.SCoA \\ \diagup \\ H_3C \end{array}$$
Isobutyryl coenzyme A

$$\downarrow$$

$$\begin{array}{c} HOOC \\ \diagdown \\ \quad CHCO.SCoA \\ \diagup \\ H_3C \end{array}$$
Methylmalonyl coenzyme A

LEUCINE

Transamination to an α-keto acid is again followed by oxidative decarboxylation. After further oxidation and other metabolic manipulations the products are equimolar amounts of acetoacetate (which accounts for the ketogenic properties of leucine) and acetyl coenzyme A.

$$H_3C$$
$$\diagdown$$
$$CHCH_2CHNH_2COOH$$
$$\diagup \qquad \text{Leucine}$$
$$H_3C$$
$$\downarrow$$
$$CH_3COCH_2COOH + CH_3CO.SCoA$$
Acetoacetic acid   Acetyl coenzyme A

ISOLEUCINE

The third branched-chain essential amino acid is also transaminated to an α-keto acid, oxidatively decarboxylated and subjected to several further reactions, with the formation in the end of equimolar proportions of acetyl coenzyme A and propionyl coenzyme A.

The branched-chain α-keto acids which are produced from valine, leucine and isoleucine are normally all oxidatively decarboxylated by the same enzyme. Maple syrup disease, so rare as to be a clinical curiosity, is an inborn error of metabolism in which there is a deficiency of this enzyme. The α-keto acids are excreted in the urine to which they impart a characteristic odour. The condition is associated with severe mental insufficiency and patients rarely survive longer than a few months.

The metabolism of valine leads directly, and that of methionine and isoleucine indirectly, after carboxylation of propionyl coenzyme A, to the formation of methylmalonyl coenzyme A. The intramolecular rearrangement by which this is transformed to succinyl coenzyme A requires a coenzyme derived from vitamin B_{12}. In pernicious anaemia deficiency of the vitamin leads to a deficiency of the coenzyme and the methylmalonyl coenzyme A is hydrolyzed to the free acid, which is excreted in the urine. This acquired metabolic error forms the basis of a test for vitamin B_{12} deficiency.

THREONINE

This is metabolized in two different ways. The more important is by way of a reaction catalyzed by an enzyme requiring pyridoxal phosphate, threonine deaminase. Its action gives ammonia and α-oxobutyric acid, which is also an intermediate in methionine metabolism. Threonine can also be metabolized after being split by threonine aldolase to acetaldehyde and glycine.

$$CH_3CHOHCHNH_2COOH$$
Threonine

$$\swarrow \qquad \qquad \downarrow$$

$$NH_3 + CH_3CH_2COCOOH$$
α-Oxobutyric acid

$$CH_3CHO + CH_2NH_2COOH$$
Acetaldehyde   Glycine

PROLINE AND HYDROXYPROLINE

These non-essential amino acids are synthesized from glutamic acid. The γ-carboxyl group is reduced to —CHO and the five-membered ring is then formed by condensation. Reduction then gives proline. Hydroxyproline is formed only by hydroxylation of proline in the course of the synthesis of collagen. The catabolism of proline apparently follows the reverse pathway to glutamic acid. The urinary excretion of hydroxyproline is used as an index of collagen metabolism in malnutrition and in diseases of supporting tissues.

LYSINE

Lysine is an essential amino acid. Although no evidence has been found that it can be transaminated, it is undoubtedly metabolized, presumably after oxidative deamination by L-amino acid oxidase. The subsequent reactions are complex and lead to one molecule of acetoacetyl coenzyme A for each molecule of lysine catabolized.

HISTIDINE

This can be transaminated, but is chiefly catabolized through a long series of reactions which starts with a specific deamination of an unusual kind and leads to the formation of formiminoglutamic acid (FIGLU). In the presence of a coenzyme derived from the vitamin folic acid, FIGLU is converted to glutamic acid. In folic acid deficiency, which is sometimes difficult to distinguish from vitamin B_{12} deficiency, FIGLU is excreted in the urine, where it can be estimated readily (p. 26.9).

Histidine   FIGLU   Glutamic acid

The biosynthesis of histidine is not sufficiently rapid in young children to meet all their needs. For them histidine is an essential amino acid.

Histidine is the parent of the pharmacologically important substance **histamine,** which is formed by decarboxylation and subsequently metabolized after oxidation to ammonia and imidazolylacetaldehyde by the enzyme diamine oxidase.

Other metabolic products formed from histamine include an acetyl derivative and a methyl derivative. These, as well as methylated derivatives of the parent amino acid, histidine, are excreted in the urine.

ARGININE

This is of immense importance in urea synthesis (p. 31.2), and since the raw material of arginine, ornithine, is

readily synthesized from glutamic acid, arginine itself is non-essential. The catabolism of arginine again takes place through ornithine to glutamic acid. Arginine serves as a source of the guanidinyl group for the synthesis of other compounds containing this group, notably creatine.

Creatine is synthesized from arginine, glycine and methionine. The first two are condensed together in the kidney in the presence of the enzyme glycine transamidinase with the formation of glycocyamine or guanidinoacetic acid, which is subsequently methylated in the liver to give creatine.

Creatine is transported to the muscles where it is converted to phosphoryl creatine (p. 15.10). Creatine is excreted in varying amounts by women and children, but only traces are present in the urine of men. A cyclic anhydride, **creatinine,** is excreted by both sexes. The creatinine output is used as an index of the muscle mass. The daily excretion by any given individual is so constant that in metabolic studies its measurement provides a check that the urinary collection for each day has been complete.

PHENYLALANINE AND TYROSINE (fig. 11.15)

Phenylalanine is an essential amino acid, but tyrosine is not, since it can be synthesized from phenylalanine. Indeed, the normal catabolism of phenylalanine proceeds by hydroxylation to tyrosine. Hereditary lack of the necessary enzyme, phenylalanine hydroxylase, leads to an inborn error of metabolism, phenylketonuria, in which phenylalanine, instead, is transaminated extensively to phenylpyruvic acid. This is excreted to the extent of 1–2 g/day and is also metabolized further to phenyllactic acid and related compounds. When the hydroxylase system is present, these other pathways are not followed to any extent. Presence of phenylpyruvic acid in the blood and central nervous system leads to mental retardation. Arrangements to test the urine of every child soon after birth for phenylpyruvic acid have been made in many places. Restriction of the intake of phenylalanine at a sufficiently early age has a beneficial effect. Such a treatment is expensive for the community, but the cost is less than that of keeping a mental defective for life.

After transamination to p-hydroxyphenylpyruvic acid the catabolism of the aromatic amino acids proceeds by the formation of homogentisic acid, 2,6-dihydroxyphenylacetic acid. Compounds like this are readily oxidized, the ring is split open and the resulting dicarboxylic acid, 4-maleylacetoacetic acid, is converted to a mixture of equimolar amounts of fumaric acid and acetoacetic acid. Alkaptonuria is an inborn error of metabolism in which there is a lack of homogentisic acid oxidase. The free acid is excreted in the urine, which darkens greatly as a result of atmospheric oxidation. The connective tissue of people with this inborn error may become pigmented and they are prone to arthritis.

FIG. 11.15. Phenylalanine and tyrosine metabolism. (1) Site of metabolic 'block' in phenylketonuria. (2) Abnormal pathway followed when there is a block at (1). (3) Site of cleavage of the aromatic ring. (4) Site of metabolic 'block' in alkaptonuria.

A small amount of tyrosine is metabolized by further hydroxylation to 3,4-dihydroxyphenylalanine (DOPA) a reaction which is catalyzed by the liver enzyme tyrosinase. DOPA serves as a precursor of the skin pigment melanin (p. 35.7). In the adrenal medulla DOPA is decarboxylated to give an amine which is used for the synthesis of noradrenaline and adrenaline.

The hormones of the thyroid gland are also derivatives of tyrosine.

TRYPTOPHAN

The bulk of the tryptophan which is metabolized passes under the influence of the enzyme tryptophan pyrrolase. This opens the five membered ring to give N-formyl kynurenine. Removal of the formyl group leaves kynurenine which may enter several metabolic pathways. The products include anthranilic acid and xanthurenic acid, which are excreted in excessive amounts in pyridoxine deficiency, and nicotinic acid. The formation of nicotinic acid involves the synthesis of a pyridine ring from the residue of the original indole (fig. 11.16).

Tryptophan is thus to be regarded as a provitamin for nicotinamide. In Hartnup disease, a rare inborn error, there is mental retardation associated with a markedly subnormal conversion of tryptophan to N-formylkynurenine. (See also p. 31.15 and fig. 31.13.)

Tryptophan can also be hydroxylated. (fig 11.17) to 5-hydroxytryptophan, which undergoes decarboxylation to 5-hydroxytryptamine (5-HT). 5-HT has powerful pharmacological actions on the circulation and the central nervous system and may have important physiological roles (p. 24.88). Its formation, however, does not account for much of the daily utilization of tryptophan. 5-HT is deaminated to 5-hydroxyindoleacetic acid before excretion. Another minor pathway of tryptophan metabolism involves transamination to indole pyruvic acid and oxidative decarboxylation to give indoleacetic acid, also known as a plant hormone.

Melatonin is a derivative of 5-HT which has been isolated from the pineal gland, hypothalamic tissue and peripheral nerve. It promotes the aggregation of melanin granules in melanocytes (p. 24.36).

* These arrows do not indicate single chemical reactions.

FIG. 11.16. Formation of nicotinic acid and xanthurenic acid from tryptophan.

FIG. 11.17. Tryptophan and 5-hydroxytryptophan metabolism

CH_3O — Melatonin structure with $CH_2CH_2NHCOCH_3$

Melatonin (N-acetyl-5-methoxytryptamine)

Intestinal micro-organisms convert tryptophan to free indole itself and derivatives such as skatole and indoxyl. These may be absorbed and re-excreted. Indoxyl is conjugated in the liver with sulphate to give an ester of which the K salt, named indican, is excreted in the urine.

Indole   Skatole CH_3 Indoxyl OH

Indican $O—SO_3K$

SERINE

This is important partly because of the high proportion of it in the phosphoproteins of milk and eggs, where the terminal hydroxyl groups of the serine residues are esterified with phosphoric acid, and partly because of its close

$$\begin{array}{ccc} CH_2O\,\textcircled{P} & & CH_2O\,\textcircled{P} \\ | & \rightleftharpoons & | \\ CHOH & & CO \\ | & & | \\ COOH & & COOH \end{array}$$

3-Phosphoglyceric acid   3-Phosphohydroxypyruvic acid

$$\big\Updownarrow$$

$$\begin{array}{ccc} CH_2OH & & CH_2O\,\textcircled{P} \\ | & & | \\ CHNH_2 & \leftarrow & CHNH_2 \\ | & & | \\ COOH & & COOH \end{array}$$

Serine   3-Phosphoserine

metabolic relations with glycine and 'one-carbon' metabolism. Serine is non-essential. It is synthesized from 3-phosphoglyceric acid as shown in the opposite column. Serine can also be formed from glycine in a reversible reaction with N^{10}-hydroxymethyltetrahydrofolic acid (see below).

Although serine can be transaminated, its oxidation proceeds mainly by a reaction which yields pyruvic acid directly, under the catalytic influence of serine dehydrase, a pyridoxal–phosphate dependent enzyme. The formation of pyruvate in this way accounts for the glucogenic properties of the amino acid.

$$\begin{array}{ccc} CH_2OH & & CH_3 \\ | & & | \\ CHNH_2 & \longrightarrow & CO \quad + NH_3 \\ | & & | \\ COOH & & COOH \end{array}$$

Serine   Pyruvic acid

GLYCINE

Although glycine is the simplest amino acid and is readily formed from carbohydrate, e.g. via 3-phosphoglyceric acid and serine, it is important because it takes part in several biosynthetic processes. These include, the synthesis of creatine (p. 11.24) and the synthesis of purine nucleotides (p. 12.18). It reacts with succinyl coenzyme A to give δ-aminolaevulic acid, an intermediate in the synthesis of porphyrins and haem (p. 26.7).

$$\begin{array}{ccccc} COOH & & & COOH & \\ | & & COOH & | & \\ CH_2 & & | & CH_2 & \\ | & + & CH_2 & \longrightarrow & CH_2 & +CO_2+HSCoA \\ CH_2 & & | & | & \\ | & & NH_2 & CO & \\ CO.SCoA & & Glycine & | & \\ Succinyl & & & CH_2 & \\ coenzyme\ A & & & NH_2 & \text{δ-Aminolaevulic} \\ & & & & acid \end{array}$$

Since the reaction which gives glycine from serine is reversible, it is possible for the catabolism of glycine to take place in the same way as that of serine. There are, however, other pathways, notably that in which the amino acid is deaminated by glycine oxidase with the formation of glyoxylic acid and ammonia. The glyoxylic acid may either be oxidized to oxalic acid and excreted in the urine or oxidatively split to formic acid and carbon dioxide. The formic acid may then enter the pathways of 'one-carbon' metabolism.

$$\underset{\text{Glycine}}{\overset{\text{CH}_2\text{NH}_2}{\underset{|}{\text{COOH}}}} \xrightarrow{-\text{NH}_3} \underset{\text{Glyoxylic acid}}{\overset{\text{CHO}}{\underset{|}{\text{COOH}}}} \begin{array}{l} \longrightarrow \underset{\text{Oxalic acid}}{\overset{\text{COOH}}{\underset{|}{\text{COOH}}}} \\ \longrightarrow \underset{\text{Formic acid}}{\text{CO}_2 + \text{HCOOH}} \end{array}$$

One-carbon metabolism

In the course of this outline of amino acid metabolism, at least three radicals containing only one carbon atom have been encountered: $-CH_3$, $-CH_2OH$ and $-CHO$. The last of these is familiar as an aldehyde group, but it is also a formyl radical and is usually known by this name in relation to one-carbon metabolism. These radicals appear in the course of the metabolism of methionine, glycine, serine, histidine and tryptophan and may be used in the synthesis of methylated compounds like creatine or choline, or in processes where single carbon atoms have to be inserted into complex structures, as in the synthesis of purine nucleotides (p. 12.18). Isotopic studies show that these radicals, no matter what their origin, pass through a common metabolic pathway. Their metabolism involves the participation of a coenzyme, tetrahydrofolic acid (THF), derived from the water-soluble vitamin folic acid. THF (p. 7.13) has two active binding sites for one-carbon radicals, both of them nitrogen atoms, which are named N^5 and N^{10}. When serine is converted to glycine, the hydroxymethyl group is transferred to the coenzyme to give N^{10}-hydroxymethyl THF. Dehydration gives N^5, N^{10}-methylene THF which can also be formed reversibly from methionine via the intermediate N^5-methyl THF. The N^5, N^{10}-methylene compound can be reversibly oxidized to N^5, N^{10}-anhydroformyl THF which is also produced by the deamination of N^5-formimino THF. The anhydroformyl compound is derived from N^{10}-formyl THF which is itself formed from formate and THF with the help of ATP. Apart from their role in amino acid metabolism, these substances are important because both N^5,N^{10}-anhydroformyl THF and the N^{10}-formyl THF are used in the synthesis of purine nucleotides (p. 12.18). Moreover, the other one-carbon

derivatives can all be transformed to N^5-methyl THF, an intermediate source of methyl groups for transmethylation. The interrelations of these various substances are illustrated as follows:

$$\text{THF}_{N^{10}}^{N^5} + \text{serine}$$
$$\big\Updownarrow$$
$$\text{THF}_{N^{10}}^{N^5} + \text{methionine} \qquad \text{THF}_{N^{10}-CH_2OH}^{N^5} + \text{glycine}$$
$$\underset{B_{12}}{\overset{\text{Homocysteine}}{\Big\Updownarrow}} \Big\Updownarrow \qquad\qquad\qquad -H_2O \Big\Updownarrow$$
$$\text{THF}_{N^{10}-CH_3}^{N^5} \underset{\text{NAD}}{\overset{\text{NADH}_2}{\rightleftharpoons}} \text{THF}_{N^{10}}^{N^5}\!\!>\!CH_2$$
$$\text{NADP} \Big\Updownarrow \text{NADPH}_2$$
$$\text{THF}_{N^{10}}^{N^5}-CH=NH \xrightarrow{-NH_3} \text{THF}_{N^{10}}^{N^5}\!\!>\!CH$$
$$\uparrow \qquad\qquad\qquad \uparrow$$
$$\text{THF}_{N^{10}}^{N^5} + \text{formiminoglutamic} \qquad \text{THF}_{N^{10}-CHO}^{N^5}$$
$$\text{acid} \qquad\qquad\qquad \uparrow \text{ATP}$$
$$\uparrow \qquad\qquad\qquad$$
$$\text{Histidine} \qquad\qquad \text{THF}_{N^{10}}^{N^5} + \text{formate}$$

Transmethylation

Transmethylation is the name given to the process in which methyl groups are transferred to the precursors of methylated compounds, e.g. creatine, choline, adrenaline. At one time it was believed that methyl groups could not be synthesized in the body and that some source of them, usually choline or methionine, was a dietetic necessity. It is now clear that methyl groups can be synthesized by the pathways outlined above, but usually most of the methyl groups used are derived from dietary methionine.

Methionine is an obligatory intermediate in transmethylation. Apart from the dietary supply, it may be derived by the methylation of homocysteine with methyl groups from N^5-methyltetrahydrofolic acid or from betaine, an oxidation product of choline. Before transmethylation can take place, methionine is converted to a

$$\underset{\text{Methionine}}{\begin{array}{c} \text{COOH} \\ | \\ \text{CHNH}_2 \\ | \\ \text{CH}_2 \\ | \\ \text{CH}_2 + \text{RCH}_2\text{O}\,\circledP \sim P \sim P \\ | \\ \text{S} \\ | \\ \text{CH}_3 \end{array}} \longrightarrow \underset{\text{S-Adenosylmethionine}}{\begin{array}{c} \text{COOH} \\ | \\ \text{CHNH}_2 \\ | \\ \text{CH}_2 \\ | \\ \text{CH}_2 \\ | \\ {}^+\text{S}-\text{CH}_2-\text{R} \\ | \\ \text{CH}_3 \end{array}} + \underset{\begin{array}{c}\text{Guanido-}\\\text{acetic acid}\end{array}}{\begin{array}{c} \text{COOH} \\ | \\ \text{CH}_2 \\ | \\ \text{NH} \\ | \\ \text{C}=\text{NH} \\ | \\ \text{NH}_2 \end{array}} \longrightarrow \underset{\begin{array}{c}\text{Homo-}\\\text{cysteine}\end{array}}{\begin{array}{c} \text{COOH} \\ | \\ \text{CHNH}_2 \\ | \\ \text{CH}_2 \\ | \\ \text{CH}_2 \\ | \\ \text{SH} \end{array}} + \underset{\text{Creatine}}{\begin{array}{c} \text{COOH} \\ | \\ \text{CH}_2 \\ | \\ \text{NCH}_3 \\ | \\ \text{C}=\text{NH} \\ | \\ \text{NH}_2 \end{array}}$$

FIG. 11.18. Transmethylation, $RCH_2 = $ adenosyl, where the carbon represents C^5 of the ribose residue.

high energy derivative, S-adenosylmethionine. This sulphonium compound is formed by reaction of methionine with ATP. All the phosphate appears as pyrophosphate and inorganic orthophosphate.

S-adenosylmethionine then reacts with a methyl acceptor (e.g. guanidoacetic acid). The loss of the methyl group leaves S-adenosylhomocysteine, which is immediately cleaved, probably hydrolytically, to give homocysteine and adenosine. The homocysteine is used as a sulphur donor for cysteine synthesis. Other examples of transmethylation are shown in fig. 31.12.

THE TURNOVER OF PROTEINS

The picture of amino acid and protein metabolism is incomplete without some knowledge of the ways in which body proteins are destroyed and the rate at which they are replaced. Apart from the specialized case of the proteins of skin, hair and nails, which are lost altogether, the body proteins are believed to be destroyed by hydrolysis. Isotopic labelling experiments show that there is some re-utilization of the amino acids during the replacement of intracellular proteins, which indicates that the destructive process must be one in which amino acids are liberated. Proteolytic enzymes, the cathepsins, are widely distributed in tissues. They are found especially in lysosomes (p. 13.8), but the extent to which they are active during life is unknown.

How long the molecules of any given protein persist before replacement is a complex problem. Experiment shows that many extracellular proteins are destroyed at random, but at very different rates. At one extreme, measurement of the rate of disappearance of the label after an initial brief period of synthesis from isotopically labelled amino acids has shown that, in the rat, bone collagen synthesized in infancy persists with little destruction for at least 300 days (half the life span). Collagen from other sources is less persistent. On the other hand, the use of purified proteins labelled with ^{131}I has shown that human serum albumin is replaced at a rate of about 10 per cent/day (180 mg/kg/day) and fibrinogen at 35 per cent/day (35 mg/kg/day).

The position with intracellular proteins is more complicated, because the pattern of cell life, with the synthesis of protein during cell division balanced by protein destruction on the death of the cell, is superimposed on possible metabolic patterns during the life of the cell. The study of individual proteins, e.g. liver aldolase and muscle myosin, indicates that some turnover takes place during the life of the cell. This varies greatly from tissue to tissue and from protein to protein, e.g. liver proteins are more labile than those of muscle, but is small compared with the initial rate of synthesis or the final rate of degradation when the cell is destroyed. In the case of erythrocytes, no metabolism of haemoglobin takes place while the mature cell is circulating and the daily renewal of 0·8 per cent of the

cells accounts for a turnover of about 90 mg protein/kg/day. At the other extreme the cells of the jejunal mucosa undergo renewal every 1–2 days and even although the rate of protein replacement might in other circumstances appear quite substantial, it is negligible in comparison with the high turnover of protein associated with the rapid replacement of the cells themselves. It should be observed that the proteins of the intestinal mucosal cells, like those of the secretions in the alimentary tract, join the dietary proteins in digestion.

It is difficult to arrive at a sound overall value for the rate of replacement of protein in the entire body, largely because the extent to which the re-utilization of amino acids takes place cannot yet be fully evaluated. Published figures range from about 120 to over 400 g/day for a normal man. The upper figure represents some 3·5 per cent of the total body protein.

When a subject consumes a protein free diet the output of nitrogen in the urine takes several days to fall to the value which reflects inevitable wastage of tissue proteins (fig. 11.12). Negative nitrogen balance is thus most marked in the early stages of such an experiment. The weight and protein content of certain organs, notably the liver, spleen and other visceral structures, follow a similar downward curve. Some of the plasma proteins, in particular albumin and transferrin, behave similarly. There is a fall in haemoglobin which is secondary to a diminution in the numbers of erythrocytes. If the diet is low in protein, the changes are qualitatively similar but quantitatively less, although different organs and proteins are affected to different extents. The protein content and weight of the liver, for example, fall even when the change in protein intake is not sufficient to cause overt signs of protein deficiency. When normal protein intake is resumed, all these changes are reversed. The subject goes into positive nitrogen balance which only reverts to equilibrium after several days. The nitrogen retained appears as an increase in the total protein of the body, distributed appropriately over those organs which lose protein on a protein deficient diet. That part of the body protein which fluctuates according to the dietary intake is called **labile body protein**. Even under the most favourable conditions, the labile body protein is not more than 5 per cent of the total body protein or 600 g in an adult male. It is usually much less. It is generally assumed that modest diminution in the various components of labile body protein does no harm, so that at times this fraction has been regarded as a short term store. Even if this view is correct the effect does not seem to be important. There is also no evidence that those of us in prosperous countries, who are accustomed to eat much more protein than the amounts necessary to ensure that physiological needs are met, derive any benefit thereby.

The control of protein turnover by dietary intake probably operates in two different ways. On the one hand, a diminished supply of amino acids is likely to lead to a diminished rate of protein synthesis and, in so far as protein destruction is kinetically dependent on the supply, this leads to a correspondingly diminished rate of destruction. The period at the beginning of a low protein dietary regime when the output of nitrogen is falling corresponds to the gradual adjustment of protein and amino acid catabolism to the reduced rate of protein synthesis.

There is also an effect at the level of cell multiplication. One example of this is seen in the subnormal level of red cells which is found characteristically in protein deficiency. Again, the fall in weight of the viscera is paralleled by a fall in the rate of replacement of the small intestinal mucosal cells. This has been demonstrated by autoradiography after the administration of tritiated thymidine to experimental animals. The DNA of the cells in course of formation at the time of the dose becomes labelled, so that their passage towards the tips of the villi can be followed.

FURTHER READING

MUNRO H.N. & ALLISON J.B. ed. (1964) *Mammalian Protein Metabolism*. New York: Academic Press.

ROSE W. C. (1957) The amino acid requirements of adult man. *Nutr. Abs. Rev.* **27**, 631.

Food and Agricultural Organization/World Health Organization (1965). *Protein Requirements. Tech. Rep. Wld. Hlth. Org.* No. 301.

The figures used in discussing protein requirements have been taken from the above.

Ministry of Health (1964) *Requirements of Man for Protein. Rep. publ. Hlth. med. Subj.* (*Lond.*), No. 111.

GARROD, A.E. (1963) *Inborn Errors of Metabolism* (reprinted with a supplement by H. Harris) London: Oxford University Press.

Chapter 12
Cell growth and division

The growth and division of a unicellular organism, such as a **bacterial** or a **protozoal** cell, leads ultimately to the formation of two copies of a structure of which there was originally only one. If, as is usually the case, the two daughter cells are identical, every molecule and atom of the parent cell is duplicated in the daughter. With **metazoan** cells the duplication is frequently less clear cut since differentiation of the daughter cells is more likely to occur in the course of growth. However, in general, the growth and division of a metazoan cell requires the duplication of the great majority of the molecules and structures in the parent.

The distribution of newly-synthesized cell material between the daughter cells broadly follows one of two patterns; it is either shared between the daughters, or it all finds its way to one of them. Most mammalian cells share their cell compounds more or less equally between their daughters, but the second type of division, usually called **budding**, is encountered in some plants and primitive animals. Among the yeasts, for example, both types of division are found and this leads to the description of a yeast as a 'budding' or a 'fission' yeast.

The duplication of cell material involves the synthesis of many types of macromolecules, apart from the provision of sufficient compounds of low molecular weight to allow macromolecular synthesis to occur. The biosynthesis of most types of macromolecules is described in chaps. 9 & 10. This chapter is primarily concerned with two processes:

(1) the method by which inherited information is interpreted and used to make the protein part of the new cell material, i.e. the mechanism of protein synthesis and the role of the gene,

(2) the method by which the information necessary to synthesize a cell or indeed a whole new organism is transferred from cell to cell and from organism to organism.

The key molecule in both these processes is deoxyribonucleic acid (DNA), since the information needed to allow the synthesis of all the proteins and enzymes of the cell, bacterial or mammalian, lies in the nucleotide base sequence of the DNA (p. 12.2). It is the same base sequence that provides the information which allows a duplicate copy of the DNA to be made for the daughter cell. In this section therefore, the structure of DNA is discussed first in some detail since the informational role of this molecule is implicit in its structure. Then the way in which the information in the DNA is used to make proteins is considered; finally the method whereby the information is passed to daughter cells and organisms is described.

THE STRUCTURE OF DNA

The DNA molecule is an extremely long chemical thread made up of two strands. Unlike most threads, however, the strands are not wound round one another but are held as a pair which are wound round an imaginary central core to form a spiral or 'double helix' (fig. 12.1). This arrangement means that the gross structure of the helix looks like a long screw from the side; but if it is examined from one end, a hole can be seen passing from one end to the other up the centre of the helix.

Each strand of the double helix consists of a long chain of the sugar deoxyribose and phosphate residues arranged as shown in fig. 12.2. These chains are formed by the loss of two water molecules to condense a phosphoric acid residue with two deoxyribose molecules, one being attached through its 5'-hydroxyl and the other through its 3'-hydroxyl. Each of these deoxyribose molecules is, in turn, connected to further phosphate residues, and so the chain is built up. Every sugar molecule in the chain is substituted through its 3- and 5-hydroxyl groups and all the phosphates are doubly substituted except the residues at the ends of the chain. One end is a singly-substituted phosphate on a 3'-hydroxyl of a deoxyribose, and the other is a similar phosphate on a deoxyribose 5'-hydroxyl. This difference allows the chemical identification of the two ends of a DNA strand; and any process, such as a stepwise enzyme action (p. 12.11), which moves along the strand, can be considered to move in a definite direction, either $5' \rightarrow 3'$ or $3' \rightarrow 5'$. This concept of 'direction' along a DNA deoxyribose-phosphate backbone is important since the two strands that go to make up the double helical thread are arranged to lie in

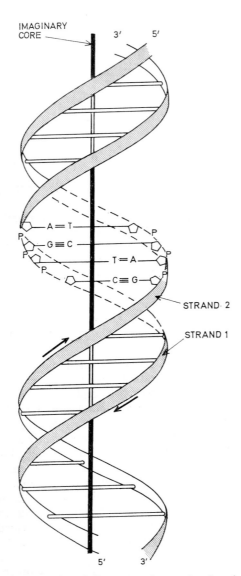

FIG. 12.1. DNA thread of two strands round an imaginary core in an anti-parallel manner. A, T, G and C represent complementary base pairs (p. 12.3)

FIG. 12.2. Three residues from the middle of the poly-deoxyribose-phosphate backbone of DNA.

FIG. 12.3. Structure of the purine and pyrimidine bases found in DNA. The asterisk marks the atom involved in bonding to the C-1 of deoxyribose.

opposite directions: reading along the strands from one end of the double helix to the other, one strand runs in the direction 3′→5′ and the other 5′→3′. For this reason, the DNA thread is said to consist of an anti-parallel double helix.

In addition to the phosphate residues at the 3′ and 5′ positions, each of the deoxyribose residues in the strands is further substituted at the C-1 position with a purine or pyrimidine base (fig. 12.2). Two purines, adenine and guanine, and two pyrimidines, thymine and cytosine, are commonly found in DNA (fig. 12.3). Although no intrinsic pattern seems to emerge when the order of the bases along the strand is examined, the bases on one strand are clearly related to the bases on the strand opposite. In the DNA double-helical thread the purine and pyrimidine bases of the two strands lie opposite one another in the structure (fig. 12.4) and the pattern is always one in which

FIG. 12.4. Complementary base pairs drawn to show intermolecular hydrogen bonds (dotted lines).

a thymine on one strand is faced by an adenine and a guanine by a cytosine. Thus thymine and adenine are said to be a complementary base pair and so are guanine and cytosine. This arrangement is largely responsible for holding the two strands in their correct juxtaposition in the double-helical thread; adenine–thymine and guanine–cytosine base pairs are particularly effective in doing this because they form closely-fitting intermolecular links through hydrogen bonds, two in the case of the adenine–thymine pair and three with guanine–cytosine (fig. 12.4). The presence of an adenine opposite a thymine and a guanine opposite a cytosine means that there is always one molecule of adenine to every molecule of thymine and one guanine for every cytosine in DNA; chemical analysis shows this to be so (fig. 12.1).

Although the ratio of each base in a pair is 1:1, the ratio of the two types of base pairs, (adenine+thymine) to (guanine+cytosine), varies widely in DNA from different species. Examination of the (adenine+thymine) to (guanine+cytosine) ratios for various organisms shows that the more extreme ratios are carried by bac-

teria, whereas the mammalia form a closer group around an (adenine+thymine)/(guanine+cytosine) ratio of 60:40 (table 12.1). The similar base ratio of all mammalia is usually taken to indicate a relatively close evolutionary relationship when compared with different species of bacteria.

TABLE 12.1. Guanine+cytosine per cent of base pairs in DNA of some bacteria, invertebrates and vertebrates.

Bacteria and rickettsiae		Invertebrates		Vertebrates	
30	*Clostridium welchii*				
32	*Rickettsia prowazeki*				
34	*Staphylococcus aureus,*	34	Sea urchin sp.		
36	*Proteus vulgaris*	36	Sea urchin sp.		
38	*Pneumococcus*	38	Clam		
40				40	MAN
42	*Bacillus subtilis*	42	Earthworm, locust	42	Ox, sheep, pig, mouse, rat, salmon, trout, herring, frog.
44	*Rickettsia burneti*			44	Horse, hen, turtle
46					
48	*Corynebacterium acne*				
50	*Neisseria gonorrhoeae*				
52	*Escherichia coli*				
54	*Salmonella typhi*				
56	*Aerobacter aerogenes*				
58	*Brucella abortus*				
60					
64	*Pseudomonas fluorescens*				
66	*Pseudomonas aeruginosa*				
68	*Mycobacterium tuberculosis*				
70					
72	*Micrococcus lysodeikticus*				
74	*Actinomyces bovis*				

The very precise alignment of base pairs in the double-stranded molecule of DNA leads to a structure of great regularity, whatever the ratio of (A+T)/(G+C). The overall diameter of the helical thread is about 1·8 nm and there are about ten base pairs per turn. The base pairs, being virtually planar structures, are stacked on top of one another like a pile of pennies and their interaction with the other atoms of the helix ensures that they are spaced regularly about 0·34 nm apart. The intramolecular hydrogen bonding also holds the —C-3′—O—P—O—C-5′—polydeoxyribophosphate strands in a fixed position at an angle of about 70° to the longitudinal axis of the DNA.

When the double helix is looked at from the side, the polydeoxyribophosphate chains, which contribute most to the screw-like appearance of the structure, are seen to be unequally spaced to give a major and a minor groove. This arrangement is also a direct consequence of the interatomic hydrogen bonds and the precise geometry of the grooves is very important in the action of certain antibiotics used in clinical medicine.

It must be stressed that all the dimensions given so far refer to double-stranded DNA when examined in the crystalline state by X-ray crystallography. In this state the structure is very compressed and the extent of inter-atomic bonding within the molecule at its greatest. In solution, or in the cell, there is little doubt that base pairing exists, but it is clear that the rigidly crystalline structure cannot occur. The molecular weight of DNA isolated from cells is usually between 5×10^6 and 1.5×10^7 (average about 8×10^6) and such DNA is usually somewhat degraded. A molecular weight of 8×10^6 corresponds to a helical length of about 0.5 μm or more and clearly therefore some super-coiling of the helix is essential if it is to be accommodated in the chromosome. A well-documented case of the impossibility of accommodating helical DNA in a cell concerns the DNA from bacteriophage (bacterial viruses). In this case the DNA from the phage is about 3 μm long, if stretched out in the helical state, yet the phage head is only about 0.08 μm in diameter.

Single-stranded DNA

Although virtually all the DNA in cell nuclei is double stranded, some bacterial viruses have single-stranded DNA. The molecular weight of the DNA in these viruses is about 1.7×10^6, and they are organisms with probably the smallest quantity of genetic information. These viruses are probably single stranded only when outside the host cell; once within the cell they immediately set about synthesizing the strand complementary to the one carried by the free virus.

Determination of DNA structure

The structure of DNA outlined above has been deduced from extensive study of the products of chemical and enzyme hydrolysis together with the X-ray crystallographic examination of crystalline DNA. The polydeoxyribonucleotide nature of the molecule was deduced by chemical means and careful analysis gave the following molecular characteristics:

(1) The sum of the purine nucleotides in hydrolysates equals the sum of pyrimidine nucleotides, i.e. $(A+G) = (T+C)$.

(2) Adenine and thymine are present in equal amounts, and so are guanine and cytosine, i.e. $(A=T)$ and $(G=C)$.

(3) The number of 6-amino groups on the purine and pyrimidine bases equals the number of 6-keto or hydroxyl groups. In this respect, $(A+C) = (G+T)$. The underlying structural reason for these constants, however, was not apparent until the actual position of the atoms in a crystal of DNA was visualized by X-ray crystallographic analysis. When this was done, Watson and Crick were able to suggest the complementary anti-parallel base pairing model to rationalize all the analytical and crystallographic evidence on DNA structure.

Although the overall structural features of the DNA molecule are now clear, little is yet known about the order of bases along the polydeoxyribose strands in any piece of DNA of biological importance. Methods exist for determining whether the distribution of bases along the DNA strand is random but no evidence for a non-random distribution has been forthcoming so far. The determination of the base sequence of a gene is one of the most important outstanding problems of molecular biology.

The genetic code

As mentioned previously, the order of the base pairs in the DNA double helix appears to be completely random apart from the specific pairing across from strand to strand, but actually it contains very precise information. In the process of protein synthesis (p. 12.8) the order of the amino acids in the strand-like polypeptide chains of a protein is determined by the order of purine and pyrimidine bases on one of the strands of the DNA double helix. Thus the essentially linear molecule of DNA determines the structure of the essentially linear polypeptide chain, and the apparently random order of bases on the DNA reflects the apparently random order of amino acids in a polypeptide chain. In practice it is found that only one strand of the DNA is used in protein synthesis and that sets of three adjacent bases on this strand provide the information that leads ultimately to the insertion of one amino acid into the growing polypeptide chain. For this reason the DNA is said to carry a code constructed out of 'base triplets'.

Since four different purine and pyrimidine bases are found in DNA, sixty-four different base triplets are possible, if it is assumed that the base order can only be read in one direction along the DNA strand and that the triplets do not overlap (see p. 12.1 for a discussion of 'direction' in DNA). Since only twenty different amino acids are found in proteins under natural conditions (p. 11.1) more than one 'triplet' is available for each type of amino acid. Identification of the triplets that correspond to each amino acid, the problem of 'cracking the genetic code', has shown that certain amino acids can be coded by up to six different base triplets whereas others only have one (see p. 12.11). The reason for this variation is not yet understood.

PROTEIN SYNTHESIS: THE COMPONENTS OF THE SYSTEM

Introduction

It has already been stated that one of the central roles of DNA in the cell is to provide information to enable

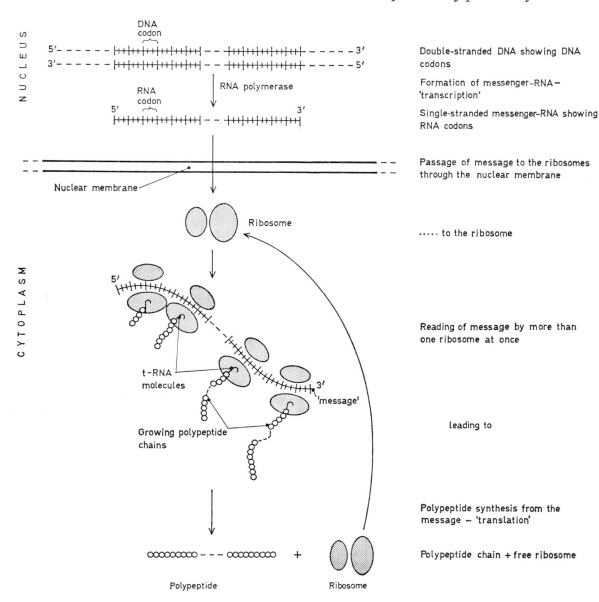

FIG. 12.5. Schematic representation of the mechanism of protein synthesis (not to scale).

amino acids to be inserted into their correct places in a growing polypeptide chain during protein synthesis. Proteins are synthesized on ribosomes by the stepwise addition of amino acids to a growing polypeptide chain (p. 12.9); one problem in protein synthesis can therefore be stated precisely. How can the information contained in the DNA as a succession of base triplets be translated to ensure the correct order of insertion of amino acids in a growing protein? This problem is exacerbated in most cells by the fact that the DNA lies in a nucleus whereas most of the ribosomal sites of protein synthesis are outside the nuclear membrane.

The problem is solved in the cell by the use of a second type of informational macromolecule, once again a strand-like nucleic acid with repeating structure (fig. 12.5). The information is transcribed from the purine–pyrimidine 'language' of the DNA to the similar language of ribonucleic acid (RNA) and then translated to the amino acid language of protein at the ribosome. The intermediary nucleic acid molecule is a special type of RNA, often called **messenger RNA** in recognition of its role. Once at the ribosome the information in the messenger RNA is translated into a polypeptide chain by the use of a number of further RNA molecules which are adapted to recognize both specific purine–pyrimidine triplets of the message and also amino acids. These **translating**

RNAs are often called the **transfer or t-RNAs**. They do not seem to be bound permanently to the message on the ribosome, but are free in solution in the neighbourhood of the protein–synthesizing sites and appear to be drawn into the system when required to insert a given amino acid. After carrying out this process they are then liberated until required again.

In the succeeding sections, therefore, the chemical structure of the messenger RNA, transfer RNAs and ribosomes are examined to see how their structure is adapted to their role in protein synthesis before proceeding to discuss the mechanism of protein synthesis itself in detail.

The structure of messenger RNA (m-RNA)

Superficially, messenger RNA has considerable structural similarities to DNA. Once again there is the long chain of alternating sugar–phosphate residues; although in RNA the sugar is ribose not deoxyribose. As in DNA, the phosphates are doubly substituted, one bond being to the 3′-hydroxyl of the sugar and the other to the 5′. Once again the ends of the strand can be distinguished, one by having a free 5′-phosphate and the other by a 3′-phosphate. Unlike DNA, however, there is no evidence that messenger RNA contains base pairs and therefore the molecule is probably single stranded. Furthermore, since there are no base pairs there is no mechanism for forming a stable helical structure and a length of messenger RNA is probably a great deal more flexible than an equivalent length of DNA.

DNA chains are extremely long, and they are not transcribed into messenger RNA in one piece. Rather, the DNA is transcribed section by section, as a series of messages, so the RNA transcripts are much shorter than the DNA. At the lower limit, messenger RNAs may be as little as 150 bases long, and it seems unlikely that they can ever contain more than 7000–10,000 bases. The means whereby the DNA is transcribed section by section, rather than as a continuous messenger-RNA molecule, are unknown.

As with DNA, the information necessary to ensure the insertion of an amino acid in the correct position in a growing polypeptide chain is carried in the sequence of purines and pyrimidines substituted at the C-1 position of the ribose residues of messenger RNA. However, the bases found in RNA are not all the same as in DNA. The purines, adenine and guanine and the pyrimidine cytosine are present in both DNA and RNA, but thymine does not occur in RNA whereas another related pyrimidine (uracil, fig. 12.6) does. So the sixty-four base triplets of DNA, which are constructed from the four bases adenine, guanine, cytosine and thymine, are transcribed into sixty-four RNA triplets compiled from adenine, guanine, cytosine and uracil. These RNA base triplets are frequently called **RNA codons**, since they are the

Uracil

FIG. 12.6. Structure of the pyrimidine uracil.

code units carrying the essential information to ensure the unamibiguous insertion of a single amino acid when the message comes to be translated into protein. Because of the method of synthesis, however, the base sequence of a given piece of DNA is not transcribed into a piece of messenger-RNA having an identical base sequence, even excepting the replacement of thymine by uracil. Rather the messenger-RNA base sequence is complementary to the DNA sequence, as if a base-paired double strand had formed between the informational strand of the DNA and a strand of messenger RNA during synthesis (see p. 12.3). Thus the messenger carries a complementary cytosine when DNA carries guanine (or vice versa) and uracil where DNA has adenine (or vice versa).

The structure of transfer RNAs (t-RNAs)

Since the messenger RNAs are transcripts of portions of the DNA and are capable of leaving the nucleus to reach the ribosomal sites of protein synthesis (p. 12.5), their use solves the first problem of the transfer of information from the DNA to the ribosome, the problem of translocation. However, the messenger-RNA molecules, as in DNA, carry their information in terms of their purine and pyrimidine base sequence and there remains the problem of 'translating' the language of purine–pyrimidine triplets into amino acid sequence. This step is achieved by the transfer RNAs with the help of the ribosomes.

The structure of the transfer RNAs, of which there are certainly large numbers of different types in a cell, is based in each case on the polyribophosphate backbone characteristic of the nucleic acid molecules examined so far. Once more the molecule has 'ends' consisting of free 3′- and 5′-phosphates, and the ribose molecules are substituted at C-1 with purine and pyrimidine bases. As with the messenger RNAs, the bases adenine, guanine, cytosine and uracil are common, but the transfer RNAs often contain an additional sprinkling of other purines and pyrimidines, often called the 'unnatural' or 'abnormal' bases (fig. 12.7). Transfer RNAs are considerably smaller than most messenger RNAs, and the complete structure of one of the alanine transfer–RNAs from yeast has been worked out (fig. 12.8).

So far, two parts of the structure have been identified as being directly involved in the activity of alanine

FIG. 12.7. The 'unnatural' purines and pyrimidines found in alanine transfer-RNA from yeast. In addition to these compounds, thymine (normally considered to be a pyrimidine characteristic of DNA) is found in alanine transfer-RNA.

FIG. 12.8. Structure of alanine transfer-RNA from yeast.

A = adenine, G = guanine, C = cytosine, U = uracil

'Abnormal' bases
I: hypoxanthine (base pairs as guanine)
T: thymine (normally a DNA component)
DiH.U: 5, 6 dihydrouracil
DiMe.G: N, N demethylguanine
Me.G: 1-methylguanine
Me.I: methylhypoxanthine
ψ: pseudouracil

transfer–RNA, and similar regions probably occur in all transfer RNAs:

(1) the series of residues at the 3′ end of the molecule, residues 75–77 in fig. 12.8,

(2) a group of bases about the middle of the molecule which lie near a region rich in 'abnormal' purine and pyrimidine bases (36–38).

The first of these two regions is responsible for binding the amino acid alanine. In all the transfer RNAs that have been examined so far, this terminal sequence is 3′-P-adenosyl-5′-P-3′-cytidyl-5′-P-3′-cytidyl-5′-P···, and therefore, apart from actually reacting with the amino acid, this region does not itself confer any specificity on the t-RNA.

The second region has been identified less certainly than the first, but it is almost without doubt the region responsible for recognizing the relevant base triplet on the messenger RNA. As we have seen, the sequence of base triplets, each of which specifies an amino acid, is transcribed from DNA into the complementary base sequence of messenger RNA and it is these RNA triplets, or RNA codons, that have each to be identified by part of the transfer-RNA structure. The part of the t-RNA which recognizes the codon is called the **anticodon** and is

probably residues 36–38 in the structure shown in fig. 12.8. Recognition probably consists of 'base pairing' between purine–pyrimidine residues in the codon and anticodon.

As far as is known, the remainder of the t-RNA structure is concerned with recognition of the enzyme responsible for loading relevant amino acid (via the amino acid adenylate, p. 12.8) on to the carrier adenine residue at the 3′ end of the molecule.

The ribosomes

The ribosomes are the site of protein synthesis and their microscopic structure and location in the cell are described on p. 13.8. Chemically they are fairly uniform in composition regardless of their source, and usually contain about 60 per cent protein and 40 per cent RNA. The protein component is not a single protein but a relatively large number of different proteins, the majority of which appear to be basic, and the RNA has the polyribophosphate structure, substituted with purine and pyrimidine bases, which has become familiar from the discussion of messenger and transfer RNA. In the laboratory, ribosomes can be made to fall into two unequal pieces, one about 65 per cent of the total and the other about 35 per cent, although whether this occurs in the cell is very doubtful. The relative proportion of protein to nucleic acid in these fragments seems to be about the same as in the parent structure, but it is likely that the larger fragment carries two RNA chains whereas the smaller has only one. Each RNA chain contains about 1500–2000 bases but the extent of inter-base pairing and helical structure is much disputed. Certain experiments, however, tentatively suggest that the helical content of ribosomal RNA is high.

PROTEIN SYNTHESIS: THE MECHANISM

The process of protein synthesis involves two separate series of biochemical reactions:

(1) the reactions that each amino acid has to undergo to achieve an activated chemical state from which it can form a peptide bond and thus extend the growing peptide chain by one unit,

(2) the reactions by which the information in the DNA is transferred via the messenger RNA to the site of protein synthesis on the ribosome.

These two biochemical processes impinge at the site of protein synthesis on the ribosome and are co-ordinated there by the transfer RNAs. The process is shown diagrammatically in fig. 12.5.

AMINO ACID ACTIVATION

This process occurs in two stages and is carried out by enzymes called **aminoacyl-RNA synthetases.** The first reaction consists of the coupling of an amino acid with adenosine triphosphate (ATP) to form an aminoacyl-adenylate, with the liberation of pyrophosphate, as shown in reaction 1.

$$NH_2CHRCOOH + \begin{array}{c} Synthetase \\ enzyme \end{array} + ATP \longrightarrow$$
$$NH_2CHRCO.AMP.ENZYME + PP \quad (1)$$

The amino acid adenylate is not liberated from the enzyme surface during this reaction but the pyrophosphate is, and the course of amino acid activation may be followed experimentally by measuring the liberation of this compound.

The second stage of the reaction involves transfer of the amino acid residue from adenosine monophosphate (AMP), still on the surface of the enzyme, to the terminal adenine residue of the *adenyl.cytidyl.cytidyl*··· portion of the relevant transfer RNA (p. 12.7) as shown in reaction 2.

Synthetase enzyme. AMP.COCHRNH$_2$
+ t-RNA—C-3′—P—5′-C-3′—P—5′-A-3′—P

$$\downarrow$$

Synthetase enzyme + AMP + t-RNA—C-3′—P—
—5′-C-3′—P—5′-A—COCHRNH$_2$ + P   (2)

Once formed, the cleavage of the bond joining the amino acid to the t-RNA can provide the free energy for the formation of a peptide bond.

There is probably a synthetase enzyme for each type of transfer RNA found in the cell and the specificity of interaction between these molecules lies in the structure of the enzyme and the RNA sequence of those parts of the t-RNA not involved in accepting the amino acid or binding to the RNA codon in the message.

PEPTIDE BOND SYNTHESIS

Once activated in this way and carried on a specific transfer RNA, the amino acid is capable of reacting with the carboxyl end of a growing polypeptide chain according to reaction 3a. During the synthesis of the protein chain, the end of the growing peptide chain is occupied by an amino acid (R$_1$, reaction 3a) still attached through its carboxyl group to the terminal adenine of its own transfer RNA (t-RNA$_1$); thus its terminal amino acid is still in the activated state. The incoming activated amino acid (R$_2$, coupled to t-RNA$_2$) reacts through its free amino group to form a peptide bond with the activated terminal carboxyl of the peptide chain (reaction 3a). The energy necessary for this chemical reaction comes from the splitting of the bond between the terminal carboxyl group and the adenine of t-RNA$_1$. At the end of this reaction, therefore, the amino acid chain has been lengthened by an amino acid which is still activated with t-RNA$_2$ on its carboxyl group, and t-RNA$_1$ is liberated. The next amino acid (R$_3$, carried by t-RNA$_3$) is then added to the growing chain by an identical series of reactions (reaction 3b), and in this way the polypeptide chain grows to the full length determined by the number of triplets in the message. Which of the twenty amino acids is inserted at each position in the peptide chain seems to be determined solely by the coding triplet in the message attracting an anticodon grouping on a t-RNA which is already loaded with an amino acid.

POLYRIBOSOMES

Since the ribosome is intimately involved in the processes described above, the point of contact between the message and the ribosome must move along the messenger RNA as the polypeptide chain grows. Electron microscope (EM) studies of ribosomes photographed in the act of synthesizing proteins suggest that more than one ribosome can pass along a messenger–RNA molecule at one time; that is, synthesis of a second polypeptide chain may start before the previous one is complete. The structures in which the ribosomes are found at intervals along the length of a messenger–RNA molecule are often called polyribosomes.

$$\begin{array}{c} \text{t-RNA}_1 \qquad\qquad \text{t-RNA}_2 \\ | \qquad\qquad\qquad | \\ \underset{|}{R} \quad \underset{|}{R} \quad \underset{|}{R} \quad \underset{|}{R_1}\,3' \qquad \underset{|}{R_2}\,3' \\ \mathrm{NH_2CHCONHCHCONHCHCONHCHCO} \quad + \quad \mathrm{NH_2CHCO} \end{array}$$

$$\downarrow \qquad\qquad (3a)$$

$$\begin{array}{c} \text{t-RNA}_2 \qquad\qquad \text{t-RNA}_1 \\ | \qquad\qquad\qquad | \\ \underset{|}{R} \quad \underset{|}{R} \quad \underset{|}{R} \quad \underset{|}{R_1} \quad \underset{|}{R_2}\,3' \qquad 3' \\ \mathrm{NH_2CHCONHCHCONHCHCONHCHCONHCHCO} \quad + \quad \mathrm{OH} \\ \text{(released)} \end{array}$$

$$\begin{array}{c} \text{t-RNA}_2 \qquad\qquad \text{t-RNA}_3 \\ | \qquad\qquad\qquad | \\ \underset{|}{R} \quad \underset{|}{R} \quad \underset{|}{R} \quad \underset{|}{R_1} \quad \underset{|}{R_2}\,3' \qquad \underset{|}{R_3}\,3' \\ \mathrm{NH_2CHCONHCHCONHCHCONHCHCONHCHCO} \quad + \quad \mathrm{NH_2CHCO} \end{array}$$

$$\downarrow \qquad\qquad (3b)$$

$$\begin{array}{c} \text{t-RNA}_3 \qquad\qquad \text{t-RNA}_2 \\ | \qquad\qquad\qquad | \\ \underset{|}{R} \quad \underset{|}{R} \quad \underset{|}{R} \quad \underset{|}{R_1} \quad \underset{|}{R_2} \quad \underset{|}{R_3}\,3' \qquad 3' \\ \mathrm{NH_2CHCONHCHCONHCHCONHCHCONHCHCONHCHCO} \quad + \quad \mathrm{OH} \\ \text{(released)} \end{array}$$

FORMATION OF MESSENGER RNA

We have seen how the amino acids are activated and are inserted one at a time into the growing polypeptide chain at the behest of the triplet codons on the messenger RNA. The only biochemical process that remains to be described is the formation of messenger RNA. The exact biochemical reactions involved in messenger-RNA synthesis are unknown although *in vitro* studies have given an indication of what must be involved. The synthesis of RNA in normal cells appears to be brought about by an enzyme known as **DNA-dependent RNA polymerase.** This enzyme is capable of synthesizing RNA by the stepwise addition of nucleotides according to the following general reaction, where XTP represents the nucleotide triphosphates of adenine, guanine, cytosine and uracil.

$$\begin{array}{c} \underset{|}{\text{RNA}} \qquad\qquad \underset{|}{\text{RNA}} \\ \underset{|}{5'} \;+\; \text{XTP} \;\rightarrow\; \underset{|}{5'} \;+\; \text{PP} \\ \text{P} \qquad\qquad \text{P} \\ \qquad\qquad\;\; | \\ \qquad\qquad\;\; 3' \\ \qquad\qquad\;\; | \\ \qquad\qquad\;\; X \\ \qquad\qquad\;\; | \\ \qquad\qquad\;\; 5' \\ \qquad\qquad\;\; | \\ \qquad\qquad\;\; P \end{array}$$

The enzyme requires a 'primer' of double-stranded DNA and the order which the nucleotides are inserted into the growing nucleotide chains is determined by the nucleotide order of the primer DNA. When studied in the test tube, using double-stranded DNA, two types of RNA chain are synthesized, each complementary in structure to one of the DNA strands of the double helix. Thus the action of the enzyme on a piece of DNA having the following composition,

$$3'\text{—A—G—C—T—T—C—G—A}\cdots 5' \quad (1)$$
$$5'\text{—T—C—G—A—A—G—C—T}\cdots 3' \quad (2)$$

would be to yield two single-stranded RNA chains, one having the sequence 5′—U—C—G—A—A—G—C—U—3′ (i.e. complementary to strand 1) and the other having the sequence 3′—A—G—C—U—U—C—G—A—5′ (complementary to strand 2). In the living cell, however, it is fairly certain that only one of the DNA strands is transcribed into an RNA chain, but the mechanism whereby only one of the DNA strands is chosen is unknown.

The antibiotic actinomycin D inhibits DNA–primed RNA polymerase *in vitro* at very low concentrations and probably acts *in vivo* by inhibiting this enzyme.

'CRACKING THE GENETIC CODE'

Before leaving the topic of protein synthesis and the involvement of DNA in the process, it is valuable to examine briefly the experimental approaches that have been used to elucidate the genetic code, that is, to decide which of the sixty-four possible DNA and RNA base triplets can lead to the insertion of given amino acids in the growing peptide chain.

The main experimental routes which have been used are:

(1) determination of the amino acid sequence of pure proteins,

(2) examination of the effect of mutagens on amino acid sequence,

(3) synthesis of model polynucleotide 'messengers' and their use for protein synthesis *in vitro*.

The first step was the discovery that minor differences in amino acid sequence existed in the structure of proteins and enzymes obtained from various species. Even within a species, genetically-determined variations in protein structure can be found. In man the haemoglobins provide an example (p. 26.6). The amino acid sequence of haemoglobin from most individuals conforms to a structure now accepted as 'normal' haemoglobin, but rarely, molecular variants of the 'normal' structure are found. One of these is the haemoglobin associated with sickle-cell anaemia, a very common disorder in the negro race. This haemoglobin differs from 'normal' in the substitution of a single amino acid in the structure (valine) for another (glutamic acid). Since the sickle-cell trait is heritable it was assumed that the change of amino acids in the haemoglobin was genetically determined and due to a one-step mutation. Other 'variant' haemoglobins have been detected in the human population and these can be shown to be due to a single, or at the most two, amino acid transpositions. Examination of all the alternative amino acids which are found at a single point in these variants of the haemoglobin molecule has shown that certain amino acid transpositions are common while others have never yet appeared. These results suggest, therefore, that amino acids that can be exchanged are separated by a single mutational step, whereas those which cannot are separated more widely. Since one mutation will change the nature of one of the bases in a coding triplet in the DNA, it follows that amino acids which can be exchanged at a single point in the structure in haemoglobin, or any other protein for that matter, will have DNA codons which differ in the nature of only one of the three bases. Although this approach gives some idea of the relationships between the amino acids and their codons it gives no idea of the nature of the bases involved.

In view of these results the next stage was clearly to try to induce mutations with mutagens known to have specific chemical effects, in an attempt to link certain types of chemical change in the DNA to certain types of amino acid transposition in the proteins. By and large this approach has been bedevilled by the broad specificity of most mutagens and it is never possible to be absolutely sure that a given chemical change has actually occurred in the DNA.

Despite these difficulties, however, two mutagens yielded useful results. The first was nitrous acid, which was known from previous chemical work to change an —NH$_2$ group to an —OH group; for example, adenine to hypoxanthine and cytosine to uracil. Although neither of these products are normal components of DNA, it became clear that they could act, at least in the coding role, and by the careful study of HNO$_2$ mutations certain amino acid transpositions could be identified as associated with changes in either guanine or cytosine.

The other mutagens that yielded valuable results were members of the acridine series of dyes. Their action was either to add or subtract a base from DNA by insertion or excision during synthesis. Although the line of argument is involved it become clear that insertion or excision of one base leads to disappearance of the product protein in recognizable form and that the insertion or excision of two additional bases was necessary for the reappearance of recognizable protein. These arguments were the first to hint at the presence of a **triplet code**, a solution that had been anticipated on theoretical grounds.

The final proof of the triplet nature of the code came from experiments in which the composition of the protein synthesized was examined after certain model messenger–RNA molecules had been added to an *in vitro* protein–synthesizing system. In the first experiments of this kind a 'message' or polyuridylic acid led to the synthesis of polyphenylalanine, suggesting that the RNA triplet UUU coded for phenylalanine. More complex messages, such as poly UC, caused the synthesis of polypeptides consisting of two alternating amino acids, thus:

UCU, CUC, UCU, CUC, UCU, · · ·

↓

Ser, Leu, Ser, Leu, Ser,   · · ·

These results suggested that the 'code' was probably triplet but could theoretically involve any odd number of bases. The clinching experiment was one in which the primers were poly AAG, poly AGA, and poly GAA. These three polymers led to the synthesis of three different polypeptides each containing one amino acid, thus:

AAG, AAG, AAG, AAG, AAG, · · ·

↓

Lys, Lys, Lys, Lys, Lys,   · · ·

and

$$AGA, AGA, AGA, AGA, AGA, \cdots$$

$$\downarrow$$

$$Arg, \quad Arg, \quad Arg, \quad Arg, \quad Arg, \quad \cdots$$

and

$$GAA, GAA, GAA, GAA, GAA, \cdots$$

$$\downarrow$$

$$Glu, \quad Glu, \quad Glu, \quad Glu, \quad Glu, \quad \cdots$$

Thus the code must be 'triplet' and AAG, AGA and GAA are RNA codons for Lys, Arg and Glu respectively. The complete list of RNA codons is shown in table 12.2.

TABLE 12.2. The RNA version of the genetic code.

First base	Second base				Third base
	U	C	A	G	
U	Phe	Ser	Tyr	Cys	U
	Phe	Ser	Tyr	Cys	C
	Leu	Ser	C.T.	?	A
	Leu	Ser	C.T.	Trp	G
C	Leu	Pro	His	Arg	U
	Leu	Pro	His	Arg	C
	Leu	Pro	GluNH$_2$	Arg	A
	Leu	Pro	GluNH$_2$	Arg	G
A	Ile	Thr	AspNH$_2$	Ser	U
	Ile	Thr	AspNH$_2$	Ser	C
	Ile	Thr	Lys	Arg	A
	Met	Thr	Lys	Arg	G
G	Val	Ala	Asp	Gly	U
	Val	Ala	Asp	Gly	C
	Val	Ala	Glu	Gly	A
	Val	Ala	Glu	Gly	G

C.T., chain termination triplets.

The DNA version consists of the complementary sequences of deoxyribonucleotides. It is interesting that this list now contains two codons which can lead to chain termination in the polypeptide. Whether they are active normally *in vivo* is not yet clear.

NUCLEAR DIVISION

Up to this point we have been concerned with the biochemical reactions by which the information carried in the genetic material of the cell is used in the synthesis of the protein components of new cell material. The primary concern from now on will be with the replication of genetic material and its distribution into the daughter cells. This process may be considered in two separate parts:

(1) the biochemical reactions whereby a second copy of the parental DNA is prepared for distribution to the daughter cell,

(2) the processes whereby the two copies of the genetic material are separated and one copy passed to each daughter cell.

The second of these processes probably always involves the use of specialized cell structures which are strictly nothing to do with the replication of the DNA molecule itself; and in diploid cells, where there are many chromosomes to distribute equally to the daughter cells, these structures can be seen with a microscope in appropriately stained preparations.

The overall process of duplication of chromosomes and their distribution to the daughter cells in diploid organisms is called **mitosis,** and nuclei undergoing this process have a very characteristic appearance when stained by methods which distinguish the chromosomes. In diploid organisms, the formation of gametes is accompanied by a halving of the total number of chromosomes in the nucleus and this process of reduction division or **meiosis,** involves further variations in the pattern of DNA replication and chromosomal transfer. The succeeding section deals with the chemical process of DNA replication and the movements of chromosomes during mitosis and meiosis.

Replication of DNA

For the genetic information in a cell to be transferred to its progeny on division, replication of parental DNA must precede cell separation. At the present time enzymes from bacterial and mammalian sources which fulfil most of the biochemical requirements for replication of DNA have been studied *in vitro*; but it is not yet known whether these are the enzymes which carry out the duplication in the living cell. The DNA synthesizing enzymes which are active in the test tube are known as the DNA polymerases and they catalyse the formation of DNA from the 5′-triphosphates of deoxyadenine, deoxyguanosine, deoxycytidine and deoxythymidine.

The actual chemical reactions involved are shown in fig. 12.9. As with the DNA-primed RNA polymerase (p. 12.9) the overall reaction involves the transfer of a nucleotide to the 5′ end of a DNA chain with the concomitant liberation of pyrophosphate. As with the DNA-primed RNA polymerase (p. 12.9), the enzymes will not act without the presence of some 'primer' DNA, and as with the RNA enzyme, the product of polymerase action has the same overall base composition as the primer.

The way in which the primer may be involved in this process is shown in fig. 12.9. Moreover, with the DNA polymerases, the product has the base-paired double helical form of native DNA and it seems extremely likely that two DNA strands which are synthesized by the enzyme, and which form the base-paired double helix of the product, are complementary in structure to the two strands of the 'primer' DNA.

One difficulty that is not yet resolved concerns the direction of synthesis of the DNA polymerase. Since DNA consists of an anti-parallel double helix (p. 12.2), the 3'-phosphate on one strand of the helix will lie opposite a 5'-phosphate on the complementary strand. Yet autoradiograph studies in bacteria show that DNA replication passes in one direction only along a DNA helix; that is, one strand would seem to be synthesized in the 3'→5' direction and the other in the direction 5'→3'. The isolated DNA polymerases are all most active *in vitro* in the 3'→5' direction, and the means by which the synthesis of both complementary strands is achieved *in vivo* is not understood. Furthermore, there is some doubt as to whether the DNA polymerases that have been isolated so far are sufficiently active to achieve the amount of DNA synthesis needed to duplicate all the DNA of a cell within one cycle. Despite all these difficulties, however, there is little doubt that the replication of DNA in the living cell involves an enzyme (or enzymes) which form a replica molecule by synthesizing two DNA strands complementary in structure to the two strands of the parental helix. Fig. 12.10 shows that such a product is indistinguishable from the parent structure.

In organisms, such as bacteria, which have a single chromosome, DNA replication is continuous throughout the division cycle, but in nucleated cells, the replication of DNA is completed before the distribution of the chromosomes to the daughter cells commences. Thus autoradiograph studies show that the maximum rate of DNA synthesis occurs in nucleated cells during interphase and little during mitosis or meiosis.

Arrangement of DNA into chromosomes

In bacteriophages, which are viruses which live within the bodies of bacteria, the genetic material consists of a single molecule of DNA which in a number of instances has been

FIG. 12.9. The possible chemical reactions involved in DNA replication. (a) The existing double-stranded DNA molecule has opened to give a free thymidine residue. To retain the base-paired structure of the original DNA, this thymidine must be faced by deoxyadenosine triphosphate (dATP). (b) The incoming dATP residue is aligned opposite the thymidine residue. (c) A chemical reaction occurs between the dATP molecule and the 3'-OH group of the preceding residue of the same strand, with the concomitant liberation of the pyrophosphate (PP) residue.

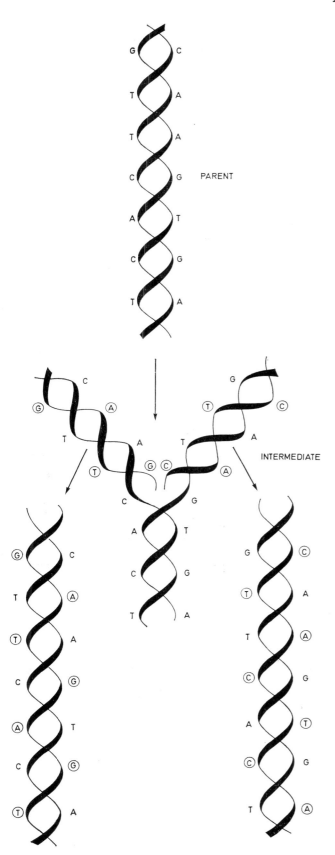

shown to be circular. The replication of the DNA molecule is therefore the same thing as the replication of the genetic material of the organism. In bacteria also, genetic and cytological evidence indicates that the genetic material is composed of one large DNA molecule. In higher organisms, however, the situation is much more complicated. Firstly, there is a great increase in the total amount of DNA. The length of DNA molecules is usually measured in terms of the number of 'base pairs' and the length found in various species increases in step with the complexity of the organism and its position in the evolutionary tree. Virus particles have between 10^4 and 10^5 base pairs, bacterial have between 10^6 and 10^7 and higher organisms have anything up to 10^9. Secondly, in mammalian cells the DNA is closely associated with a protein. This nucleoprotein complex is termed **chromatin** and confers on nuclear material special staining properties. Feulgen stain is highly specific for chromatin but is difficult to apply in practice. Orcein though less specific is more widely used because of its ease of use and its permanence. Recently acridine dyes have been used to stain DNA. In a cell stained with acridine-orange, DNA containing structures show a yellow fluorescence when examined in ultra-violet light while RNA structures show a red fluorescence. Thus in the nucleus the red fluorescence of the nucleoli can be clearly seen against the yellow chromatin.

The proteins which are found complexed with DNA in nucleated cells are basic proteins, often containing large amounts of the amino acids lysine and arginine. In general these basic proteins are called histones but in certain specific locations they may have special names; for example, the protamines that are found with the DNA of spermatozoa. There has been much speculation over the years about the role of the histones in the mammalian cell and this has been sharpened by the realization that they are absent in bacteria and viruses. One hypothesis is that they 'blank off' portions of the DNA of the chromosomes to limit expression of some of the genetic material in differentiated cells.

The DNA of the mammalian cell along with its associated protein is divided into a number of separate blocks, the **chromosomes**, so called because of the staining properties already described. The single DNA thread of bacteria and viruses is often loosely called a 'chromosome' but it differs considerably in structure from those of mammals and other nucleated cells. The number of chromosomes in a cell is characteristic of the species (table 12.3). All the cells of the body with the exception of the gametes and a few cells in the liver and bone marrow have the same number of chromosomes. The precise arrangement of the DNA and histone in the chromosome is not known. There are several hypotheses. There

FIG. 12.10. Biosynthesis of DNA. Ringed bases are components of the newly-synthesized strand.

TABLE 12.3. Diploid chromosome numbers.

Moulds				
Neurospora sp.	14		*Mollusc*	
Plants			Snail	54
Cucumber	14		*Vertebrates*	
Pea	14		Cat	38
Onion	16		Mouse, pig	40
Cabbage	18		Monkey	42
Bean	22		Rabbit	44
Water melon	22		MAN	46
Tomato	24		Sheep	54
Pine tree	24		Cattle	60
Insects			Guinea-pig	64
Drosophila	8		Horse	66
House fly	12		Dog	78
Bee	32		Hen	78
			Pigeon	80

the chromosome is a coiled structure, with, sometimes, a suggestion of secondary coiling. This coiling should not, however, be confused with the helical structure of the DNA molecule because there is a difference of several orders of magnitude in the scale. In short, the detailed structure of the chromosomes of higher organisms is not known in spite of intense study.

Mitosis

In order to conserve the specific number of chromosomes (the diploid or 2n number) the division of the genetic material of the cell occurs by the precisely controlled process of mitosis (fig. 12.11). Mitotic division is the type of cell division which occurs in somatic cells during periods of growth when the total number of cells is increasing, or during repair processes when lost or damaged cells are being replaced. In the resting cell (interphase) the chromosomes cannot be detected inside the nucleus as discrete structures. There are sometimes a few condensations of DNA (chromocenters) which can be recognized in the interphase nucleus. One of these, the sex chromatin body or Barr body, occurs only in female cells and is discussed in more detail on p. 12.16. The interphase part of the cell cycle is normally split into three periods. During the G1 phase RNA synthesis, protein

may be a number of DNA molecules lying parallel to each other along the length of the chromosome or lying end to end and joined by protein bridges. Another suggestion is that the entire chromosome is a single DNA molecule of enormous size. Autoradiographic evidence suggests that the chromosome is not multistranded. If the DNA is in the form of a single long thread its packing into a chromosome is bound to be complex. EM has so far shed little light on this problem. The light microscope shows that

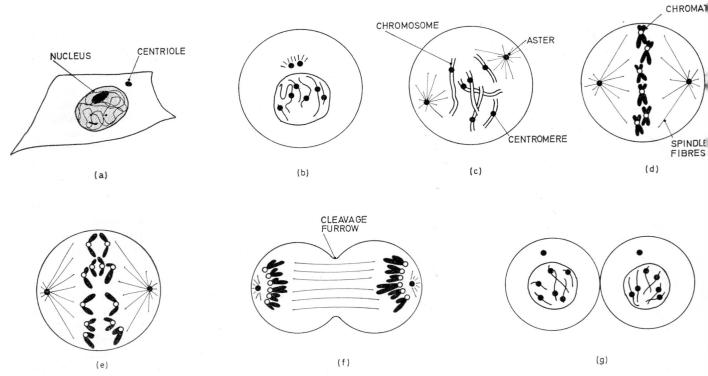

FIG. 12.11. Mitosis. (a) Interphase (46 chromosomes). (b) Early prophase. Centriole divides, chromosomes appear as threads. (c) Late prophase. Centrioles separate. Aster and spindles form, chromosomes seen to be double, nuclear membrane disappears. (d) Metaphase. Chromosomes line up in equatorial plane. (e) Early anaphase. Centromeres divide, chromatids begin to separate. (f) Late anaphase. Separation of chromatids continues, cleavage furrow forms. (g) Telophase. Two daughter cells each with 46 chromosomes.

synthesis and cell growth proceed, but there is no DNA synthesis. In the second stage (the S phase) the DNA of the chromosomes is replicated. The replication is not exactly synchronous, some chromosomes completing their synthesis before others. Between the end of DNA synthesis and the next cell division there is a second growth period (G2).

As a cell approaches mitosis, the chromosomes become visible as threads within the nucleus (prophase). At the same time cytoplasmic bodies, the centrioles, divide and the two new centrioles move to opposite poles of the cell. It is from these bodies that the protein fibres (the spindle) which control the mechanical separation of the chromosomes radiate. At the end of prophase the nuclear membrane disappears and the chromosomes which are now obviously double structures continue to contract. Each half of these double structures is known as a chromatid (fig. 12.12). They are held together at one

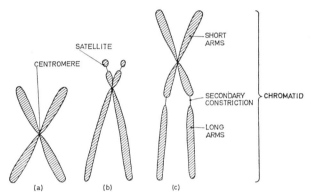

Fig. 12.12. Metaphase chromosomes. (a) metacentric (b) acrocentric (c) submetacentric.

point, the centromere, which is the point of attachment of the chromosome to the spindle. The chromosomes line up in the equatorial plane of the cell (metaphase) and it is at this stage that the chromosomes are normally examined. The two chromatids separate following a longitudinal division of the centromere. The spindle fibres now appear to contract, pulling the chromatids which become the chromosomes of the two daughter nuclei towards opposite poles of the cell (anaphase). A cleavage furrow begins to divide the cytoplasm of the cell, the chromosomes elongate and a nuclear membrane reforms around them. This stage is termed telophase and it results in the reconstitution of two daughter nuclei which are genetically identical with the parent nucleus.

Normal human chromosomes

The chromosomes of man can be examined directly using the light microscope. Some tissues, for example bone marrow, are dividing sufficiently rapidly for preparations to be made directly from the body, while other tissues such as peripheral blood cells or skin fibroblasts can be made to divide out of the body by growing in tissue culture for a short period. A large number of dividing cells is accumulated in the culture with the use of the drug Colchicine which inhibits the formation of the spindle so that cells enter mitosis but are arrested at the metaphase stage. The cells are now treated with a hypotonic solution which helps to improve the spreading of the chromosomes at a later stage. They are fixed to preserve their morphology and then flattened by drying the cells out onto a glass microscope slide. The chromosomes are stained usually with orcein or Feulgen stains both of which are specific for DNA (plate 12.1a, facing p. 11.14). These chromosomes which are forty-six in number can be arranged as twenty-three pairs (plate 12.1b, facing p. 11.14). One member of each pair is derived from the mother and one member from the father (homologous chromosomes). There is one pair of chromosomes, the sex chromosomes, which is involved in the determination of sex. The other twenty-two pairs, which are not involved in sex determination, are termed **autosomes.** For the description of chromosomes, the length and the position of the centromere are taken into account. A chromosome with the centromere near the middle is said to be metacentric, while a chromosome with the centromere near one end is said to be acrocentric. If the centromere occupies an intermediate position it is said to be submetacentric (fig. 12.11). The presence of satellites or secondary constrictions can also help in identification. The chromosomes are normally numbered according to an international convention (Denver system) the largest chromosome being number 1 and the smallest number 22. Some of the chromosomes can be recognized individually, e.g. Nos. 1, 2, 3 and 16, but most of the chromosomes can be recognized only as one member of a group of similar chromosomes. It is usual to assign letters to these groups as follows: chromosomes 1–3 group A, chromosomes 4 and 5 group B, chromosomes 6–12 group C, chromosomes 13–15 group D, chromosomes 16–18 group E, chromosomes 19–20 group F, chromosomes 21–22 group G. This grouping simplifies the description of certain types of chromosome abnormality.

The sex chromosomes are not assigned numbers. In the female the two sex chromosomes are alike and are called X chromosomes which belong to the C group. In the male, however, there is one X chromosome like those of the female and one Y chromosome which is quite different in appearance. It resembles chromosomes 21–22 and is therefore a G group chromosome, but it can normally be distinguished from 21–22 in good preparations.

The Y chromosome in man is strongly male determining and in certain abnormal situations can ensure masculinization in the presence of as many as four X chromosomes. Two X chromosomes are necessary for normal female sexual development. However, there is evidence to suggest that all or part of one X chromosome is inactive after a certain stage in development. Autoradiographic evidence shows that this X chromosome synthesizes DNA much later in the S period than do the other chromosomes. This late labelling X can be seen in a proportion of female interphase nuclei as the sex chromatin body (=Barr body). This body stains deeply with DNA specific stains but it can also be recognized with less specific stains such as cresyl violet. It is normally seen applied to the inside of the nuclear membrane (fig. 12.13).

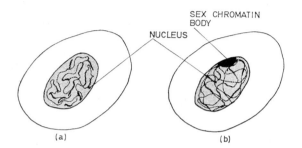

FIG. 12.13. Sex chromatin. (a) Male cell, chromatin negative. (b) Female cell, chromatin positive.

Normal females have 40–70 per cent of cells with a single sex chromatin body (chromatin positive) while male cells have no sex chromatin body (chromatin negative). This is of great practical importance since the number of X chromosomes carried by an individual can be determined very simply by examining cells from the oral mucosa in a buccal smear. Certain abnormalities of sexual development can be detected in this way. The number of sex chromatin bodies is always one less than the number of X chromosomes in the cell. Morphological

abnormalities of the X chromosome may be reflected in the altered size of the sex chromatin body, while chromosome mosaic individuals may have an unusually low percentage of cells with a sex chromatin body.

Meiosis

As we have seen mitosis is the mechanism for maintaining the constancy of the genetic material from cell to cell, but as the chromosome number is characteristic of the species there must also be a mechanism for maintaining the constancy of the chromosome number from generation to generation. The cells in all tissues of the body have forty-six chromosomes with the exception of some cells in the bone marrow and in the liver which have 2, 4 or 8 times the normal number of chromosomes (polyploid cells). If, however, the gametes also contained forty-six chromosomes the fusion of an egg and a sperm would result in the production of an individual with ninety-two chromosomes. During the formation of the gametes, therefore, a special type cell division, meiosis, reduces the number of chromosomes in the gametes to half the number found in the somatic cells, in this case twenty-three chromosomes, the haploid or n number of chromosomes. It is important to note, however, that meiosis is not merely a reduction division, since during this process a mixing of genetic material takes place between homologous chromosomes. In simple organisms reproduction can occur by simple fission of the genetic material and the cell into two identical daughter cells. However, in many instances even in lower organisms reproduction cannot be continued indefinitely in this way, e.g. if a stock of Paramecium is kept under conditions which permit only asexual reproduction it quite rapidly becomes degenerate. The stock can be rejuvenated by permitting sexual reproduction which involves the mixing of genetic material

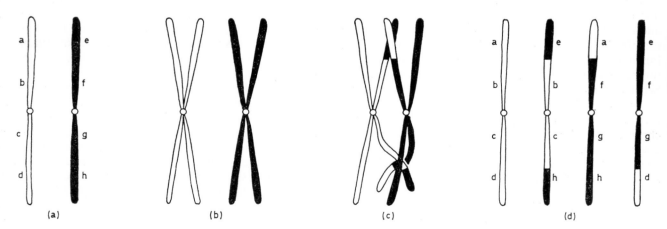

FIG. 12.14. Crossing over. (a) Pairing of homologous chromosomes; a–e, b–f, c–g, d–h are pairs of allelic genes. (b) Each chromosome replicates and is now composed of two chromatids. (c) Crossing over occurs. (d) Four new chromosomes in which crossing over has resulted in the recombination of the genetic material.

from two separate individuals to occur. Similarly mammalian cells in tissue culture, which of course divide by mitosis, have a finite lifetime after which they cease to divide and they eventually degenerate. During meiosis

breaks occur when the two homologous chromosomes are lying close together, and in the rejoining process 'crossing over' occurs so that each individual chromosome in the mature gamete will have a portion of its genetic

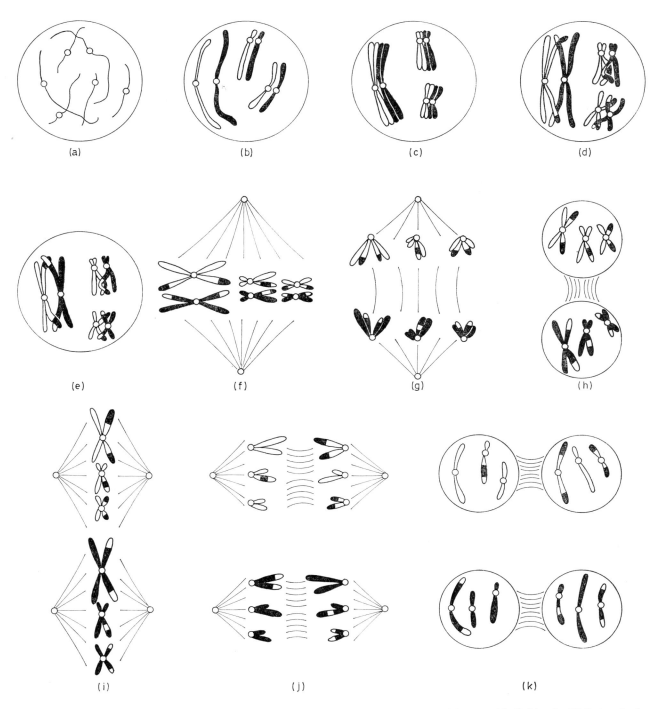

FIG. 12.15. Meiosis. (a) Leptotene, 46 chromosomes; (b) zygotene; (c) pachytene; (d) diplotene; (e) diakinesis; (f) first metaphase; (g) first anaphase; (h) first telophase, 23 pairs of chromatids; (i) second metaphase; (j) second anaphase; (k) second telophase, 23 chromosomes in each of four cells.

material derived from the maternal chromosome and part derived from a paternal chromosome. This breakage and rejoining is an essential feature of the normal process of meiosis (fig. 12.14), and is responsible for maintaining the genetic variability which ensures the uniqueness of each individual, and probably the continued existence of this species.

The process of meiosis consists essentially of two separate divisions which follow one closely upon the other (fig. 12.15). The first division is the reduction division, and it has an elongated prophase which can be subdivided into several different stages. In the first stage (**leptotene**) the chromosomes appear within the nucleus as unpaired thread-like structures, but very soon homologous chromosomes come to lie closely together (**zygotene**). Each of these paired structures is termed a bivalent. In the next stage (**pachytene**), each chromosome reduplicates itself so that each bivalent is composed of four threads lying closely parallel to each other. As the shortening of the chromosome progresses it becomes apparent that the homologous chromosomes are not held together along their entire length, but only at particular points (**diplotene**). These points, termed **chiasmata,** are the points where crossing over occurs. Meiosis in the female is normally arrested at this point for a prolonged period (the dictyate phase) which lasts from the late intra-uterine period of development until just prior to the shedding of the ovum from the ovary several decades later. During spermatogenesis there is no such delay. In either case meiosis proceeds by further contraction of the chromosomes (**diakinesis**) and the chiasmata begin to move towards the ends of the chromosome (terminalization). Shortly after this process is complete the nuclear membrane disappears marking the end of prophase. The chromosomes, still in homologous pairs, line up in the equatorial plane of the cell (first meiotic metaphase). One member of each homologous pair then moves to opposite poles of the cell without any division of the centromeres (first meiotic anaphase). The mechanical processes involved appear to be the same as those underlying mitosis, but the result is quite different in that the two daughter nuclei which reconstitute at the first telophase each have only twenty-three chromosomes, each of which is composed of two chromatids. The second meiotic division usually follows closely after the first, and resembles an ordinary mitotic division. The overall result of meiosis, therefore, is the production of four cells each with twenty-three chromosomes from a single primary germ cell with forty-six chromosomes. In the male each of these four cells undergoes differentiation to form a spermatozoon but in the female unequal division of cytoplasm between the divisions results in the reduction of one very large cell which matures to form the ovum and three small cells termed polar bodies which degenerate. At fertilization the diploid number is re-

constituted by the union of two nuclei each containing twenty-three chromosomes. A female has two X chromosomes and therefore all the ova will have a single X chromosome (**homogametic**) but in the male half of the spermatozoa will contain an X chromosome and half will contain a Y chromosome (**heterogametic**). Fertilization of an ovum by a Y–bearing sperm results in a male fertilized egg or zygote and fertilization by an X–bearing sperm results in a female zygote. Thus sex determination occurs at the instant of conception. Abnormalities of cell division are discussed on pp. 38.11 and 12.

THE SYNTHESIS OF NUCLEIC ACID PRECURSORS AND THE BREAKDOWN OF MACROMOLECULAR RNA AND DNA

For nucleic acid synthesis to occur the cell must have a ready supply of the precursor nucleotides, which in turn, require the availability of adenine, guanine, cytosine, uracil, thymine, ribose and deoxyribose in suitable molecular combination. It is the biosynthesis of these compounds which is first described here.

Nucleic acid components are liberated from macromolecular RNA and DNA by the concerted action of nucleases and phosphatases, and the purines and pyrimidines liberated are further degraded by pathways completely unrelated to their synthesis. The specificity of nucleolytic enzymes and the subsequent degradation of purines and pyrimidines is dealt with in the second part of this section. The names, structures and abbreviations of the various (chiefly) nucleotide derivatives of the purine and pyrimidine bases are set out in table 12.4.

Purine and pyrimidine biosynthesis
SYNTHESIS OF PURINE RIBONUCLEOTIDE MONOPHOSPHATES

The basic molecular structure of all purines is shown in fig. 12.16; while adenine has no amino group at position 6, guanine has an —OH at that position and —NH$_2$ at position 2. Both adenine and guanine are synthesized via inosinic acid, IMP, by the same biosynthetic pathway. In the course of this process the purine nucleus is built up stepwise from glycine, NH$_3$ and a source of C-1 units. Fig. 12.16 shows also how the various nitrogen and carbon atoms of the purine ring are derived from their precursors; thus C-4, C-5 and N-7 come from glycine; C-6 comes from CO$_2$; N-1 from NH$_3$ via the α-amino of aspartic acid; N-3 and N-9 come from NH$_3$ via the amino group of glutamine; and C-2 and C-8 come from the C-1 pool with the intervention of formyltetrahydrofolic acid. The exact sequence of biosynthetic reactions is shown in fig. 12.17. Since the immediate precursors of the nucleic acids are the purine and pyrimidine nucleotide triphosphates, it is these compounds rather than the free bases, which are the end

TABLE 12.4 Names and abbreviations of purine and pyrimidine nucleotides and related compounds

Base	Nucleoside	Nucleotide (nucleotide monophosphate)	Nucleotide diphosphate	Nucleotide triphosphate
Adenine	Adenosine Adenine riboside	Adenine ribotide Adenosine monophosphate (adenylic acid) AMP A-5′-P	Adenosine diphosphate ADP	Adenosine triphosphate ATP
Guanine	Guanosine Guanine riboside	Guanine ribotide Guanosine monophosphate (guanylic acid) GMP G-5′-P	Guanosine diphosphate GDP	Guanosine triphosphate GTP
Cytosine	Cytidine Cytosine riboside	Cytosine ribotide Cytidine monophosphate (cytidylic acid) CMP C-5′-P	Cytidine diphosphate CDP	Cytidine triphosphate CTP
Uracil	Uridine Uracil riboside	Uracil ribotide Uridine monophosphate (uridylic acid) UMP U-5′-P	Uridine diphosphate UDP	Uridine triphosphat UTP
Thymine	Thymidine Thymine deoxyriboside	Thymine deoxyribotide Thymidine monophosphate (thymidylic acid) d-TMP* d-T-5′-P*	Thymidine diphosphate d-TDP*	Thymidine triphosphate d-TTP*
Orotic acid	Orotidine Orotic acid riboside	Orotic acid ribotide Orotidine monophosphate (orotidylic acid) OMP O-5′-P	—	—
Hypoxanthine	Inosine Hypoxanthine riboside	Hypoxanthine ribotide Inosine monophosphate (inosinic acid) IMP I-5′-P	—	—

Where *deoxy*ribosides and *deoxy*ribotides are involved, the abbreviations are prefixed with d-, e.g. *deoxy*guanosine diphosphate is d-GDP.

* Thymine derivatives, although containing *deoxy*ribose, are frequently abbreviated without the d-: thymine deoxyriboside diphosphate = thymidine diphosphate = TDP.

FIG. 12.16. Basic purine structure showing the metabolic origin of the C, O and N atoms that go to make up the ring structure.

FIG. 12.17. Purine nucleotide biosynthetic pathway. Formyltetrahydrofolic acid (Formyl THFA).

products of the biosynthetic pathways. Free bases, if found at all, occur transiently as intermediates in the breakdown of nucleic acids and possibly in the formation of deoxyribonucleotides. The biosynthetic pathways proper end at the nucleotide monophosphates, and since the pathway starts with ribose 5-phosphate every molecule up to the final adenine and guanine ribonucleotide is already in the nucleotide monophosphate state.

Two antibiotic compounds, azaserine and diazo-oxo-norleucine exert their action by inhibiting those steps of the purine biosynthetic pathway which involve the use of glutamine. The antibiotics are drawn to the active sites of these enzymes by their structural resemblance to gluta-mine. Once at the active centre, they inactivate the en-zyme by blocking an essential —SH group.

PURINE NUCLEOTIDES, NUCLEOSIDES AND FREE BASES

Once in the form of the ribonucleotide monophosphates, the nucleotides can be converted freely, if a sufficient

supply of energy is available, to the related nucleotide di- and triphosphates, and it is as the triphosphates that they are used in the biosynthesis of RNA (fig. 12.18). Alterna-

FIG. 12.18. Interconversion of nucleotide mono-, di- and triphosphates. X, any purine or pyrimidine base; XMP, nucleotide monophosphate; XDP, nucleotide diphosphate; XTP, nucleotide triphosphate.

tively the terminal phosphate may be removed by phos-phomonoesterase to form purine ribosides and thence, by removal of the ribose, to form the free bases. It is this last reaction that liberates free adenine and guanine from RNA and DNA during hydrolysis by a combination of nucleases and phosphatases (p. 12.25).

CONVERSION OF PURINE RIBONUCLEOTIDES TO DEOXYRIBONUCLEOTIDES

Just as adenine and guanine *ribo*nucleotide triphosphates are the precursors of RNA, so the *deoxyribo*nucleotide triphosphates are the precursors of DNA (p. 12.12). The conversion from the ribonucleotide to the deoxyribonucleotide is thought to occur at the nucleotide diphosphate level; guanosine diphosphate (GDP) is reduced to deoxyguanosine diphosphate (d-GDP), and adenosine diphosphate (ADP) to deoxyadenosine diphosphate

mine being shown in fig. 12.3. All pyrimidines are synthesized by the same pathway, the ring structure being built up from CO_2, NH_3 and aspartic acid. Fig. 12.19 also shows how the various atoms of the pyrimidine ring are derived from its precursors: N-1 from NH_3 and C-2 from CO_2 via carbamyl phosphate; N-3, C-4, C-5 and C-6 from the α-amino group and C-2, C-3 and C-4 of aspartic acid, respectively. The α-carboxyl group of aspartic acid is lost as CO_2 during this synthesis. The exact sequence of reactions is shown in fig. 12.20.

FIG. 12.19. Basic pyrimidine structure showing the metabolic origin of the C, O and N atoms that go to make up the ring structure.

(d-ADP). These deoxyribonucleotide diphosphates are then converted, exactly as with the ribonucleotide diphosphates, to the triphosphates before being used for DNA synthesis.

PYRIMIDINE RIBONUCLEOTIDES AND DEOXYRIBONUCLEOTIDES

The basic structure of all pyrimidines is shown in fig. 12.19, the actual structures of uracil, cytosine and thy-

As in the case of purines, the end product of the pathway is in the ribonucleotide. Uridine ribonucleotide (UMP) is derived from orotidine 5-phosphate by decarboxylation, and cytidine ribonucleotide (CMP) from UMP by replacement of an —OH group by —NH_2. The amino group for this conversion is supplied by the amide residue glutamine (fig. 12.21).

As with the purine ribonucleotides, conversion of the pyrimidine ribonucleotides to the di- and triphosphates

FIG. 12.20. Pyrimidine biosynthetic pathway. PRPP, phosphoribosylpyrophosphate.

FIG. 12.21 Conversion of uridine monophosphate to cytidine monophosphate.

occurs readily in the presence of a suitable energy source, and the triphosphates are used for RNA synthesis (p. 12.9). Hydrolysis by the appropriate monosterases yield uridine and cytidine from which uracil and cytosine are formed, in turn, by nucleosidase action (p. 12.25). As in the case of purines, these routes are normally only degradative.

The origin of the pyrimidine deoxyribonucleotides is unclear. Probably, as with the purines, the conversion occurs at the diphosphate level, i.e. uridine ribonucleotide

'ABNORMAL' PURINES AND PYRIMIDINES

Certain RNA fractions, notably transfer RNA (p. 12.6), contain about 10 per cent of their purine and pyrimidine residues in the form of bases other than those commonly associated with DNA and RNA. Little is known about their synthesis except that 2,6-diaminopurine, 6-methyl purine and N,N-dimethylaminopurine are almost certainly synthesized as the ribonucleotide monophosphates from AMP. Among the pyrimidines, dihydrouracil is on

FIG. 12.22. Conversion of deoxyuridine monophosphate to thymidine monophosphate.

diphosphate (UDP) is reduced to uridine deoxyribonucleotide diphosphate (d-UDP) and cytidine ribonucleotide diphosphate (CDP) is reduced to cytidine deoxyribonucleotide diphosphate (d-CDP).

The thymine derivatives necessary for DNA synthesis probably arise from d-UMP by methylation at the C-5 position using formyltetrahydrofolic acid as the C-1 source (fig. 12.22). The involvement of folic acid at this stage is shown by the extreme sensitivity of this reaction to inhibition by antifolic drugs such as aminopterin and amethopterin. Once thymine deoxyribonucleotide (d-TMP) is formed, interconversion to d-TDP and d-TTP occurs in the same way as is found with d-CMP (p. 12.21).

the degradative pathway from uracil, and thymine *ribo*nucleotide is probably synthesized via the nucleoside from free thymine. Pseudouridine (p. 12.7) is derived from uracil, possibly with the intervention of phosphoribosyl pyrophosphate.

Biosynthesis of ribose and deoxyribose

D-ribose is used for the biosynthesis of purine and pyrimidine ribonucleosides and ribonucleotides as 5-phosphoribosyl-1-pyrophosphate (fig. 12.17), and this compound is synthesized in the cell from ribose 5-phosphate and ATP, according to the reaction:

ribose 5-P + ATP $\longrightarrow$ 5-phosphoribosyl-1-pyrophosphate + AMP

In some organisms, the ribose 5-phosphate used for RNA synthesis is a by-product of the hexose monophosphate pathway of glucose metabolism (p. 9.8). In this series of reactions, glucose is converted to ribulose 5-phosphate via 6-phosphogluconic acid and 6-phospho-3-ketogluconic acid. The ribulose 5-phosphate is then isomerised to ribose 5-phosphate by the widely distributed ribulose 5-phosphate isomerase enzyme. Although this reaction sequence occurs widely, it may not be used to make the majority of ribose in the cell. An alternative pathway to ribose 5-phosphate has been postulated in which there is a transketolase-catalysed transfer of a $CH_2(OH)C=O$... residue from fructose to glyceraldehyde-3-phosphate.

Deoxyribose, as stated above, can certainly be formed by reduction of a ribose residue which is already part of a nucleotide (p. 12.22). However, there is a possibility that a condensation of glyceraldehyde 3-phosphate with acetaldehyde to form deoxyribose 5-phosphate can be catalysed by an enzyme present in many types of cell. How

this compound is used for deoxyribonucleotide synthesis is not yet clear.

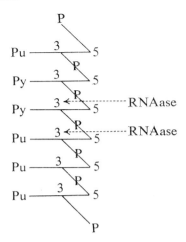

FIG. 12.23. Ribonuclease specificity; see text for details.

FIG. 12.24. Intermediate structures formed during ribonuclease action. (a) Intact RNA structure. (b) Intermediate cyclic 2′-, 3′-diphosphate. (c) Final product.

Enzymic breakdown of RNA and DNA

A large number of different enzymes which hydrolyse macromolecular RNA and DNA have been classified among the broad group of nucleases, but only in relatively few cases has the exact specificity of the enzyme been worked out. The enzymes, which act on nucleic acids and their breakdown products, may be classified as follows:

(1) depolymerases: ribonucleases and deoxyribonucleases. In general, enzymes in this group which are active on RNA, are inactive on DNA and vice versa.

(2) phosphodiesterases and phosphomonoesterases. These enzymes act on the oligonucleotide breakdown products of both RNA and DNA.

(3) nucleosidases.

DEPOLYMERASES

In man, the large molecular weight nucleic acids which enter the alimentary tract as part of the food, are degraded in the duodenum by ribonuclease and deoxyribonuclease which are part of the pancreatic secretion. Both enzymes have been purified and a considerable amount is known about their properties.

Ribonuclease

Pancreatic ribonuclease is specifically adapted to split the bond linking the phosphoryl group of pyrimidine nucleoside 3′-phosphate to the 5-hydroxyl of the adjacent purine or pyrimidine nucleoside (fig. 12.23, see p. 12.6 for the details of RNA structures). With model compounds as substrates, the enzyme can be shown to produce a 2′,3′-cyclic phosphate as an intermediate in the hydrolytic process (fig. 12.24). When the enzyme acts on intact RNA the macromolecule is degraded to free cytidine 3′-phosphate and uridine 3′-phosphate together with some larger oligonucleotides which, as a consequence of the enzyme specificity, are rich in purines.

Deoxyribonuclease

Pancreatic deoxyribonuclease hydrolyses DNA with the formation of 5′-nucleotides, dinucleotides and relatively large amounts of material that are partly degraded but

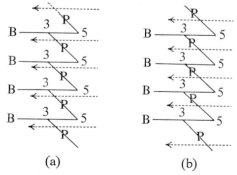

(a)   (b)

FIG. 12.25. Specificity of different types of deoxyribonuclease. (a) Pancreatic DNAase. (b) Spleen DNAase.

which can be hydrolysed no further (fig. 12.25a). The exact specificity of the enzyme is not known. Spleen tissue contains a second type of deoxyribonuclease which degrades DNA to oligonucleotides having a free 3′-phosphate and group (fig. 12.25b). Streptococci produce an enzyme similar in action to pancreatic deoxyribonuclease except that little free mononucleotides are produced.

PHOSPHODIESTERASES

These enzymes hydrolyse the phosphodiester bonds which link ribose and deoxyribose moieties to phosphate in the polynucleotide chain. Two types of diesterase are known, one hydrolyses the polynucleotide chain to 3′-monophosphates (spleen diesterase is commonly used for this purpose) and the other yields 5′-monophosphates (fig. 12.26). The latter type of enzyme is found in the

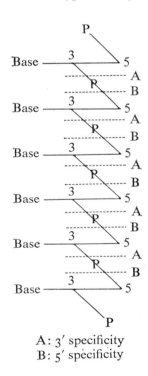

A: 3′ specificity
B: 5′ specificity

FIG. 12.26. Specificity of 3′- and 5′-phosphodiesterase.

venom of several species of snakes. Both these enzymes have been used extensively for the preparation of specific nucleotides from nucleic acids and also in structure determination on oligonucleotides from RNA and DNA.

PHOSPHOMONOESTERASE

These enzymes remove orthophosphate from the terminal esterified phosphate group in mono- or oligonucleotides (fig. 12.27). A 5′-nucleotidase is present with the diest-

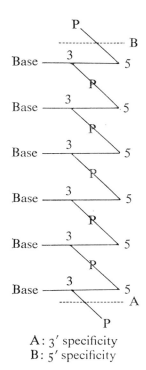

A: 3' specificity
B: 5' specificity

FIG. 12.27. Specificity of 3'- and 5'-phosphomonoesterase.

erase in snake venom and rye-grass is a source of 3'-monoesterase.

NUCLEOSIDASES

The combined action of the depolymerases, phosphodi-esterases and phosphomonoesterases is to degrade RNA and DNA to the state of nucleosides. The nucleosidases then split the sugar-base bond in these compounds to liberate the free purine or pyrimidine and ribose or deoxyribose (fig. 12.28).

Breakdown of free purines and pyrimidines

BREAKDOWN OF PURINES

Once adenine and guanine have been liberated from the

nucleic acids by the appropriate degradative enzymes, they may be degraded further by a series of reactions which in certain organisms ultimately yield urea (fig. 12.29). The first step in this pathway is the conversion of both adenine and guanine to xanthine (via hypoxanthine in the case of adenine) and this compound is then converted to uric acid by the action of xanthine oxidase. In some cases, uric acid can then be further degraded to urea via allantoin and allantoic acid

Although not all the enzymes necessary to achieve these reactions are found in all species, they seem to form the main route of degradation of the purines, at least in metazoa. Man and the apes are unusual since they have no uricase and therefore uric acid is excreted as the end product of the purine breakdown. In most mammals, however, uric acid is degraded to allantoin, which is excreted, whereas many fish excrete allantoic acid. Further pathways exist in micro-organisms; thus some *Pseudomonas* species degrade purines to urea + glyoxylic acid, while the anaerobic *Clostridia* yield glycine via 5-aminoimidazole.

Purine catabolism is directly implicated in at least one disease since over-production of uric acid is responsible for the symptoms of gout. This condition occurs in primates and some birds and is characterized by the deposition of crystals of uric acid salts in the joints.

BREAKDOWN OF PYRIMIDINES

The free pyrimidines liberated from RNA and DNA by the concerted action of nucleases and phosphatases may be further degraded to one of three β-substituted amino acids, depending whether uracil, cytosine or thymine is involved (fig. 12.30). These β-amino acids are the main nitrogenous excretory products derived from pyrimidines in mammals.

An alternative degradative pathway to urea + malonic acid exists in some bacteria. In this case the first step of the pathway is the conversion of pyrimidines to the corresponding substituted barbituric acids.

Purine riboside

Free purine   Ribose

FIG. 12.28 Nucleosidase action.

FIG. 12.29. Purine degradative pathway

FIG. 12.30. Pyrimidine degradative pathway.

FURTHER READING

ALLFREY V.G. & MIRKSEY A.E. (1961) How cells make molecules, *Scientific American*, **205**, 3.

DAVIDSON J.N. (1960) *The Biochemistry of the Nucleic Acids*, 4th Edition. New York: Wiley.

HOLLEY R.W. (1965) The nucleotide sequence of a nucleic acid. *Scientific American* **214**, 2.

NIRENBERG M. (1962) The genetic code. *Scientific American* **208**, 3.

OCHOA S. (1963) Synthetic polynucleotides and the genetic code. In *Informational Macromolecules*, ed. by H. Vogel, V. Bryson & J.O. Lampen. New York: Academic.

STEIN W.H. & MOORE S. (1960) The chemical structure of proteins. *Scientific American*, **204**, 3.

THOMPSON J.S. & THOMPSON M.W. (1966) *Genetics in Medicine*. Philadelphia: Saunders.

Chapter 13
Cell structure

The fertilized ovum is one of the largest human cells; against a dark background, it can just be seen by the naked eye. By repeated mitotic division, this cell produces the co-ordinated population of cells and their products which we recognize as an adult human. The number of generations of cells between the adult and its ovum is surprisingly small; a series of 50 mitoses produce over 10^{15} cells. The processes of intermediary metabolism occur within each of these cells, but during this period of cellular multiplication differentiation is taking place so that groups of cells become specialized for their particular role in the body.

Differentiation
The earliest changes in differentiation affect the nucleic acids and thus the types of proteins produced in any particular cell; these changes cannot be seen in microscopic preparations as alterations in cell structure. Chemical differentiation is followed by cellular differentiation when the shape or contents of the cell can be seen to be different from those of its unspecialized neighbours. Tissue differentiation, **histogenesis**, occurs when differentiated cells aggregate to form tissues, and organ differentiation, **organogenesis**, follows as groups of tissues combine to form functioning organs. The division of the ovum and its subsequent differentiation produce all the cells of the body, but as this differentiation proceeds so cells become restricted in the range of cell types which they can produce. As they specialize, they also lose the capacity for cell division. A complex organism contains highly specialized cells, which cannot divide, and it also produces dividing cells for repair and replacement. So the cells of the body can be graded according to their mitotic capabilities; it is a continuous gradation which can be roughly separated into three groups.

Cells which cannot divide in the adult: a full complement is obtained during development and the life of these cells may be as long as that of the individual. Any damage or loss is irrevocable as they cannot be replaced from less specialized cells. The nerve cells, which establish complex connexions during their differentiation, and the muscle cells which combine to form a skeletal muscle fibre are examples of this group of mitotically inactive cells.

Cells which divide slowly and irregularly in health: these can be stimulated to rapid division. The connective tissue cells belong to this group, as after injury a burst of mitotic activity will produce the cells necessary for repair. Similarly, the cells of adipose tissue and glands proliferate in response to a demand for increased function.

Cells which reproduce rapidly and regularly in the healthy adult: in these populations, the offspring of the rapidly dividing cells differentiate into specialized cells which have a short life span. The epithelia of the skin and alimentary tract and the precursors of erythrocytes are good examples of this type, for an adult produces and destroys about a million erythrocytes every second and replaces the lining of the intestine every few days.

Size and shape of differentiated cells
The large independent protozoon cell performs all the functions of living matter and is directly exposed to the external environment. The small size and varied shapes of higher animal cells are incompatible with an exposed independent existence. Human specialized cells can live only in an environment whose limits of temperature, osmolality and ionic balance are controlled by the activities of other specialized cells. Most of the cells of the body are between 10 and 40 μm in diameter, the erythrocyte (7–8 μm) being the smallest and the ovum (about 100 μm) the largest. Many cells have adopted extraordinary shapes. Consider first a nerve cell which supplies the skin of the big toe. The cell body and nucleus are in the 5th lumbar intervertebral space, just above the sacrum; a process from the cell body branches, one part going down to the toe, and the other up the spinal cord to reach the medulla oblongata in the skull. The cell body has a diameter of about 50 μm and the cylindrical processes are only about 5 μm in diameter, but they extend almost 2 m (2,000,000 μm). At the magnification of fig. 13.1 these processes would run for almost half a mile. Similarly, skeletal muscle is formed of multinucleated cylindrical fibres which run the whole length of most of our muscles, while to facilitate diffusion through the walls of blood

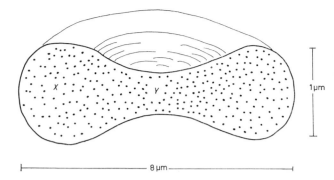

FIG. 13.2. An erythrocyte.

FIG. 13.1. Variations in the size and shape of cells.

vessels the lining endothelial cells are flattened so that they are less than 1 μm thick. The erythrocyte provides another example of modification of external shape (fig. 13.2). This non-nucleated disc is packed with haemoglobin and as oxygen combines with and is released from the haemoglobin it must diffuse into and out of the cell. Near the periphery of a disc (X), the contents are exposed to a greater surface area of membrane than at the centre (Y). Hence it is possible to contain at the periphery more haemoglobin which is effective, thus the biconcave disc is the most efficient shape.

Internal structure is modified, so that each type of cell becomes adapted for its particular role. Thus it is difficult to describe a 'typical cell'. It is best to consider first those features which are common to all cells and necessary for the maintenance of the cell's life; later the components which are found only in specialized cells are discussed.

No single technique can show all the features of cell structure; the concept of a cell to be described is a synthesis of the information provided by several methods. It is unnecessary for students to know the details of these techniques, but it is worthwhile understanding the particular contributions and limitations of each method.

HISTOLOGICAL TECHNIQUES

LIGHT MICROSCOPY

With an ordinary **light microscope** little can be seen in a living cell. Almost all its constituents are colourless so that it appears as a drop of clear jelly. Although the absorption of light by cell constituents is similar, some of these possess different refractive indices. This fact is used in the **phase contrast microscope**, where the combination of two beams of light, one of which has been retarded by a quarter of its wavelength, succeeds in converting slight differences in refractive index into different intensities. If the cell contains closely packed orientated material, this can be demonstrated by its effect on polarized light, so that when viewed through a **polarizing microscope** with a polarizer and analyser at right angles, oriented fibrils and membranes appear bright against a black background. These structures are then said to be birefringent or anisotropic. The detection and even measurement of certain constituents of living cells, of which nucleic acids and haemoglobins are examples, can be accomplished by illuminating them with monochromatic light of appropriate wavelength and measuring its absorption in a **microspectroscope**.

All these microscopes can be used on single free cells, like blood cells and spermatozoa, and can also be applied to intact cells dispersed from complex organs. They are useful for examining cells growing outside the body in organ, tissue and cell culture. Cell movements, growth and multiplication can be directly observed in cultured cells and the changes in structure produced by irradiation, toxic agents and deprivation of essential nutrients can be seen. As a tissue cell growing in culture has lost the environment and intercellular contacts of the intact tissue, changes in the cell shape are inevitable and obvious, but other changes may be undetected. The value of cell culture as employed in the study of human chromosomes is described on p. 12.15.

FIXATION AND EMBEDDING

Attainment of satisfactory resolution with the light microscope depends on the specimen being thin; to separate objects which are less than 1 μm apart the whole thickness should not be more than 10 μm. Small free cells satisfy this criterion, but many cells are larger than 10 μm and in the tissues they are so tightly packed that adequate resolution can be achieved only by cutting the tissue into very thin slices. A microtome will obviously transect many cells. As it is difficult to cut fresh tissues, it is usual first to kill the cells hoping to retain their contents as at the moment of death. This process of **fixation** can be achieved by chemicals such as alcohol, formaldehyde and osmium tetroxide which denature the cell proteins and so prevent the autolysis which would otherwise follow cell death. After the tissue is fixed it must be supported in a medium such as paraffin wax which allows it to be cut into thin slices. The fixed tissue must first be dehydrated with alcohol and then infiltrated with molten paraffin wax before it is cast into a block and cooled. The paraffin block can then be cut on a microtome and a continuous series of thin sections produced. These consecutive sections can be used to construct a three dimensional picture of the tissue.

STAINING

If the sections are examined immediately, after the wax has been removed with a solvent such as benzene or xylol, no more can be seen than in the direct examination of a living cell. It is therefore necessary to stain selectively certain cell components. A multitude of staining methods are used; many of the best, like the old dyer's art, are empirical. Nowadays new methods are often based on known chemical reactions and these are termed **histochemical** methods. **Haematoxylin and eosin** is the best known empirical method; it stains the nuclei blue-black, and the cytoplasm and extracellular fibrils pink. Certain basic dyes, like toluidine blue, stain the nucleic acids in both the nucleus and cytoplasm. Metallic impregnation methods demonstrate fine nerve processes, delicate reticulin fibres and even intracellular organelles. Collagen can be specifically stained with aniline dyes and if this is combined with a cytoplasmic and nuclear stain, the triple staining method will distinguish extracellular connective tissues from the cells themselves. Elastin protein can be stained by an empirical method in elastic connective tissues.

Typical examples of histochemical methods are provided by the prussian blue staining of iron and the periodic-acid-Schiff (PAS) method for polysaccharides. In this method, the periodic acid first oxidizes the glycol groups which will then react with the Schiff's reagent and produce a red colour. If the section is first treated with salivary amylase this will hydrolyse the glycogen present; this procedure makes it possible to distinguish this polysaccharide from the mucopolysaccharides of connective tissues and mucin.

All information obtained from fixed, embedded and sectioned cells is static, and any dynamic changes can be inferred only by examining cells at different periods in their life span or secretory cycle. Dynamic interpretations from static material can be assisted by studying the sites of incorporation of radioactive materials. The cells or animals are first exposed to a radioactive substance for a certain time; the tissue is then fixed and sections cut; these are then covered with a photographic emulsion. The emissions from the radioactive elements incorporated into the tissue components affect the overlying emulsion and silver grains are produced at these sites. After subsequent staining of this section, the position of the radioactivity can be related to the structure of the tissues. This method of **autoradiography** can demonstrate cell production and migration by identifying those cells which have incorporated radioactive thymidine into their DNA. It is thus largely responsible for the present knowledge of the dynamics of cell populations (p. 13.1).

It should be appreciated that in sections of chemically fixed tissues which have been cut in paraffin wax, all the water and those components which are soluble in water, alcohol, benzene or molten wax have been removed. The residue of insoluble material is merely a scaffolding composed of precipitated, denatured fibrous proteins, effete enzymes and highly polymerized insoluble molecules such as nucleic acids and polysaccharides. Some lipoprotein complexes remain but all other lipoids have been dissolved. Conceding that only a travesty of the original cell remains, it must be recognized that the technique of chemical fixation and wax embedding has provided most of our present knowledge of the arrangement and shape of tissue cells and the pathological changes in diseased tissues. It is probable that almost all the slides in a student's collection will be such specimens and it is essential that the drastic treatment given to the material should be remembered during their examination.

FROZEN SECTIONS

Many methods attempt to preserve more of the cell's structure. The removal of lipid can be avoided by freezing chemically fixed tissue; the ice block provides sufficient support to produce **frozen sections**, in which the lipid can be stained with a dye like Sudan III. These frozen sections are useful also as a rapid method of diagnosis on tissues removed at a surgical operation, and can be prepared in the operating theatre. Some enzymes retain part of their activity after certain chemical fixatives, but apart from the phosphatases, practically no enzymes survive paraffin embedding. So for **enzyme histochemistry, fresh frozen** sections are widely used; autolysis is prevented by rapid freezing and the resulting ice block is cut on a cold microtome. Rapidly frozen tissue can also be dehydrated for embedding in paraffin wax by sublimation of the ice in a vacuum. This **freeze-dried** tissue preserves some enzyme activity and retains small soluble molecules which are washed away in any form of aqueous chemical fixation. The enzymes are located in the cells by incubating the section with an appropriate substrate in a medium which precipitates one of the end products at the site of enzyme activity.

IMMUNOFLUORESCENCE

The highly selective nature of immunological reactions can be used to identify and localize particular proteins in cells and tissues. This complicated technique is easily explained by taking a specific example. To locate the protein heavy meromyosin (HMM), a pure preparation of HMM is injected into a rabbit and, after a suitable period, the animal produces an antibody to this protein (Anti-HMM). This antibody is a protein present in the plasma of the rabbit. Blood can then be removed and the antibody is chemically combined with a fluorescent dye to form Anti-HMM-F. If frozen sections or fragments of muscle are now treated with Anti-HMM-F, the strong bonds between HMM and Anti-HMM-F hold the fluorescent dye at the sites where HMM is distributed in the muscle. The uncombined Anti-HMM-F is then washed away and the fluorescence revealed by illumination in ultraviolet light. This ingenious technique of **immuno-fluorescence** has proved valuable in many investigations of normal structure and of human immunological diseases.

ELECTRON MICROSCOPY

All the methods mentioned so far are ultimately limited by the resolving power of the light microscope (0·3 μm) which is about three orders of magnitude greater than the size of the smaller molecular components of the cells. It follows that much of the organization of the cell would forever remain unknown if investigations were limited by this resolution. Employment of the **electron microscope** (EM) for greater resolution (1·0 nm) increases the technical difficulties, since the tissue must be in a vacuum and the specimen must be less than 50 nm thick. These conditions virtually exclude the examination of living cells, which cannot therefore be used as a criterion for the faithfulness of the preservation of the fine structure revealed by the EM. The most successful method of examining tissues in the EM has been a copy of the chemical fixation paraffin embedding method of light microscopy. The fixative is osmium tetroxide but comparable results

can be obtained after fixation with potassium permanganate and glutaraldehyde and on frozen dried specimens. Cutting sections thin enough for the EM presented a technical problem, which was conquered by replacing paraffin wax by plastic embedding media. Finely engineered **ultramicrotomes** using broken glass or diamond knives cut the tissues in these plastics into sections, less than 10 nm thick. These sections are supported on copper mesh grids for examination and photography in the EM. The autoradiographic, histochemical and immunological methods of light microscopy are all being adapted so that they can be employed in the electron microscope.

Much useful information about intracellular structures has come from a combination of electron microscopy and **differential centrifugation**. Small portions of a tissue are fixed, embedded and sectioned for electron microscopy to determine the form of its intracellular structures. If a large portion of the same tissue is homogenized, various constituents can be separated from the soup obtained by centrifuging at different speeds. These pellets of segregated constituents can then be prepared for electron microscope examination. Similar pellets can be analysed for their chemical constitution and enzymic activity. In this way, chemical structure and function can be assigned to the particular components of the original intact cell. As an example, mitochondria can be isolated by centrifugation and shown to possess oxidative phosphorylating enzymes.

The resolving power of the EM and, especially, the inadequacies of methods of fixation and sectioning prevent these techniques revealing actual atomic structure. The general form of macromolecules can be seen, but the atomic structure of a collagen fibre or myosin filament cannot be revealed by EM. **X-ray diffraction** patterns from pure crystalline biological materials will indicate their atomic architecture. The necessary purity can be achieved only by chemical isolation of the material, but if the location of a macromolecule can be determined by EM then it is justifiable to interpolate the known atomic structure to this site.

Hence by combining the information produced by all the techniques of structural examination it is possible to create a mental image of the atomic architecture of the whole body. This goal has been achieved only in a few instances like that demonstrated (fig. 13.3) where it is possible to draw the plan for the whole range. The techniques are available and only time is needed to complete the picture.

FUNDAMENTAL CELL STRUCTURE

There are certain features of cell structure which are present in all cells capable of continued life. These features are listed opposite and are described before consider-

Cell Boundary
Cytoplasm
    Cytoplasmic matrix
    Endoplasmic reticulum
    Golgi apparatus
    Mitochondria
    Ribosomes
    Lysosomes
    Centrioles (in cells capable
      of division)

Nucleus
    Nuclear envelope
    Nucleoplasm
    Sex chromatin
    Nucleolus

ing more specialized cellular structures which are found only in cells which are adapted for particular functions.

The mature erythrocyte, blood platelets and squamous cells in a keratinized epithelium are non-nucleated; they have a brief life and cannot reproduce, so they must be regarded as exceptions to the scheme.

The cell boundary

When a living cell moves in its supporting medium, its edge can be detected in the phase contrast microscope as a sudden change in refractive index. Even after staining the cytoplasm, little can be seen at the boundary of most cells by light microscopy. With the EM however, a clearly defined membrane separates the contained cytoplasm

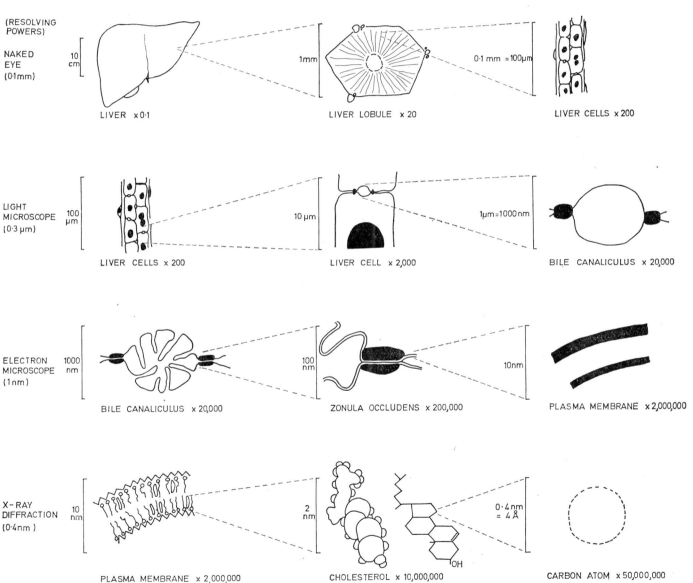

FIG. 13.3. Naked eye examination, light microscopy, electron microscopy and X-ray diffraction each give different views of the body. These sketches of the liver show the contribution of each method. If they are combined, an understanding of the molecular architecture of the organ is obtained.

from the surrounding medium. In a thin section of osmium fixed material, the membrane appears as shown in fig. 13.4; this structure is a feature of all animal and plant cells. It had been predicted from studies of cell permeability that the cell surface would include a membrane composed of a bimolecular leaflet of phospholi-

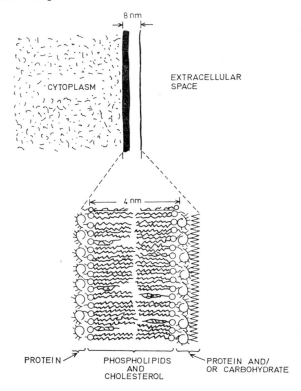

FIG. 13.4. The plasma membrane as it appears in an electron micrograph and showing its molecular architecture.

pids. The dimensions of the membrane now observed with the EM fit such a structure; for this and other reasons, it is now interpreted that the tripartite membrane illustrated in the upper part of fig. 13.4 has the general chemical architecture shown in the lower part. This limiting membrane is known as the **plasma membrane** and is, by definition, the layer which provides the main control of the exit and entry of ions and small molecules. Changes in the plasma membrane's permeability to ions affect the normal negative electrical potential of the cytoplasm, and the consequent electrical events can be recorded as the action potential.

The plasma membrane is not static or rigid; it is in active motion, extending pseudopodia and contributing to the movement of the whole cell. These activities are probably caused by forces developed in the underlying cytoplasmic proteins.

The structure with two rows of packed lipids seen in the EM (fig. 13.4) is analogous to the micellar arrangement assumed by phospholipids in the absence of protein.

Nevertheless one cannot be certain that this is the arrangement of phospholipid and protein in membranes in the living cell. The complex permeability properties of membranes indicate that the structure is less simple; it is possible that protein-lined pores penetrate the phospholipid portion or even that the protein extends throughout the central portion (p. 10.23).

The surface of the cell also carries identification marks which are characteristic of the cell, the species and even the individual. Our capacity to reject tissues grafted from other people is effected by the reactions which follow the recognition of a foreign cell surface. So the proteins and possibly carbohydrates in the outer lamella of the plasma membrane must incorporate specific antigenic patterns which are determined by the genetic machinery of the cell.

The cytoplasm

The term cytoplasm refers to all the material within the cell, except that contained in the nucleus. As more and more cytoplasmic structures have been discovered and named, the definition of cytoplasm has become confused. If it refers to all the extranuclear material, the term **cytoplasmic matrix** can be used for the portion which is not contained in any recognizable organelle. The cytoplasmic matrix of a living cell appears homogeneous in the phase contrast microscope. This amorphous mass of colloidal proteins, carbohydrates and simple solutions of all the small molecules and ions involved in metabolism is maintained in an internal cellular environment. The internal medium is partially insulated from changes in the extracellular fluid by the plasma membrane. This is necessary as precise physicochemical conditions must prevail within the cell to maintain the colloidal dispersion and intrinsic shape of the protein molecules. The cytoplasm has a uniform affinity for stains like eosin, although chemical fixation can cause artefactual clumping. Rapid freezing avoids this coalescence and by preserving enzyme activity allows subsequent histochemical incubation to show the presence of cytoplasmic enzymes.

The EM shows that, beyond the resolution of the light microscope, internal cell membranes produce an elaborate division of the cytoplasm into compartments with different chemical constitutions. These internal membranes have structures similar to those of the plasma membrane and are made of phospholipid. The EM allows their description and classification. A satisfactory nomenclature is not available and with the variations which accompany any cell specialization it is difficult to describe a general arrangement. However, in all cells membranous sacs, tubes and vesicles are present; their lumina usually appear empty in contrast to the surrounding cytoplasmic matrix with its denatured proteins, polymerized carbohydrates and nucleic acids. Originally this internal organization was thought to be a network confined to the centre of the cell, and it was thus named **endoplasmic reticulum**. Although this form and distribution is not constant, the name has been preserved.

The **Golgi apparatus** is one portion of the endoplasmic reticulum which forms an organelle present near the nucleus of all cells. It consists of a stack of flattened sacs surrounded by a cloud of small vesicles and often a few small lipid droplets (fig. 13.5). This complex can be

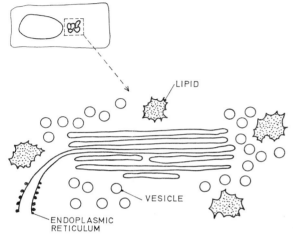

FIG. 13.5. A Golgi apparatus, in section.

impregnated with silver and gold salts for light microscopic examination, where it appears as a network around the nucleus. The more detailed knowledge of its structure which is now available has not elucidated its function; it is possibly a site of internal membrane synthesis. It is a prominent feature of secreting cells where it lies on the side of the nucleus nearest to the secreting surface.

Mitochondria are also membranous organelles; since they have a unique structure and are not known to be continuous with or formed from the endoplasmic reticulum, they are considered as separate bodies. Mitochondria can be seen by phase contrast microscopy, often as long thread-like bodies about 1 μm wide, and this is the origin of their name (Gr. *mitos* = thread, *chondros* = granule). They number thousands in a single cell, and are in continuous motion, segmenting and rejoining and they can be seen to grow in length. If cells are exposed to the dye Janus green during life (intravital staining) the mitochondria are specifically stained. The ultrastructure of mitochondria is very characteristic (fig. 13.6); the internal membrane is invaginated to form cristae and between the cristae the dense matrix contains some dark granules. Differential centrifugation, EM and direct histochemical methods show that the mitochondria contain the enzymes for aerobic glycolysis and the cytochromes of the electron transfer system. Thus the mitochondria should be regarded as the furnaces where the cell's fuel is burnt and the released energy is harnessed.

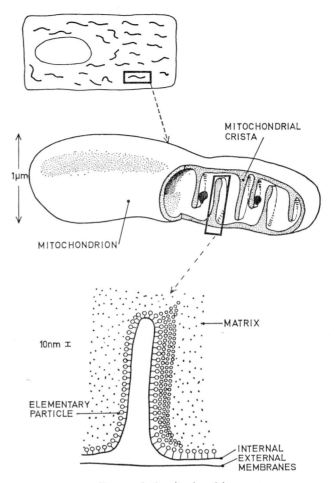

FIG. 13.6. A mitochondrion.

The enzymes and cytochromes are an integral part of the phospholipid mitochondrial membranes and the matrix contains the pyridine nucleotides. At very high resolution, electron micrographs show bead-like projections on the cristae which are probably the individual molecules of the enzymes. The cristae appear to act as a scaffolding which holds the enzymes in relation to each other, very probably in the order in which they operate. Mitochondria seem to contain a very small proportion of the DNA in the cell and they may be selfmultiplying organelles containing the genetic information necessary for the synthesis of their own proteins.

Most of the RNA of the cell is found in the cytoplasm; it can be demonstrated by its absorption of ultraviolet light, even in a living cell. Although fixation and embedding removes the lower molecular weight transfer RNA, cytoplasmic nucleic acids can be shown in these specimens as cytoplasmic basophilia after staining with basic dyes like toluidine blue. Since the DNA is virtually restricted to the nucleus, this staining demonstrates the presence of RNA in the cytoplasm and the previous treatment indicates that this RNA is in an insoluble form. Dense particles, 15 nm in diameter, are seen by EM in the cytoplasmic matrix of all cells; after isolation by centrifugation, these particles are shown to be a RNA-protein complex and they are known as **ribosomes**. A string of ribosomes is attached to a strand of messenger RNA to produce a polyribosome in the synthesis of a protein (fig. 13.16). Hence a ribosome particle in an EM indicates the point where a protein molecule can be produced. If a cell is not growing or secreting protein there are few ribosomes, but some are always present to replace the proteins lost in normal turnover.

Most cells contain organelles which are smaller and denser than mitochondria, and these are the **lysosomes**. They have a single limiting membrane and contain hydrolytic and proteolytic enzymes, some lipid droplets and often ferritin molecules (fig. 13.7). The lysosomes also possess acid phosphatase activity and so they differ from mitochondria in structure and enzyme content. Their function is not entirely clear; they may be involved in digesting phagocytosed material whether this arises from outside the cell or by a process of autodigestion in organelles known as autophagic vacuoles (fig. 13.17). Autophagic vacuoles contain cytoplasmic material surrounded by two layers of membrane and they probably represent zones of internal scavenging.

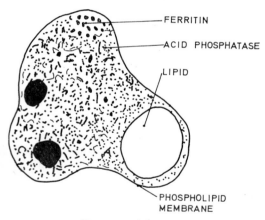

FIG. 13.7. A lysosome.

Apart from the group of cells (p. 13.1) which have relinquished the power to divide, all other cells contain bodies which lie close to the nucleus, near the Golgi apparatus; these are the **centrioles**. Each is an open ended barrel shaped body, less than 0·5 μm long and 0·2 μm in diameter; the wall is made of nine sets of three longitudinal tubules arranged in an overlapping fashion (fig. 13.8). Throughout the interphase period, the cell contains a pair of centrioles which are orientated at right angles to each other. Immediately before prophase, both centrioles divide to produce two pairs, which move to the opposite sides of the nucleus. Only one member of each

FIG. 13.8. The centrioles in an interphase cell.

pair seems to be involved in mitosis, and from this one, a leash of microtubules extends into the nucleus to form the spindle (p. 12.15). Microtubules are a normal constituent of the cytoplasm of interphase cells, but only in mitosis are they seen to connect with the centriole to form the spindle.

The nucleus

The margins of the nucleus are sharply defined in living and stained cells. Intact nuclei can be isolated from cells. Water and small molecules penetrate the nucleus rapidly but there is a barrier to the passage of macromolecules. Thus there is a **nuclear membrane or envelope** which can constrain the DNA and histones of the nucleus without interfering with the passage of metabolites. The fine structure of the nuclear envelope shows that it is an extension of the endoplasmic reticulum, which forms a flattened sac, the perinuclear cisterna, surrounding the **nucleoplasm**. The inner phospholipid membrane is applied to the nucleoplasm and the outer layer to the cytoplasm. The perinuclear cisterna is a part of the lumen of the endoplasmic reticulum, since in places the outer layer is continuous with the membranes of the endoplasmic reticulum in the cytoplasm (fig. 13.9). Circular pores between the nucleoplasm and cytoplasm are formed by the fusion of the outer and inner layers of the nuclear envelope; these pores are about 50 nm in diameter and they are probably partially occluded. When the prophase stage of cell division is completed the nuclear envelope breaks up into a series of vesicles which reaggregate around the nuclei of the two daughter cells at telophase.

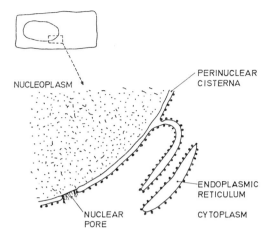

FIG. 13.9. A nuclear envelope.

The changes in the nucleus which are associated with the appearance of chromosomes and their movements during cell division are described on p. 12.14, so we are now concerned with the 'resting nucleus'. This structure is badly named because it is during this interphase period that the DNA controls the production of RNA and at the appropriate time the DNA replicates, ready for the next division. As these efforts are invisible and follow the dramatic microscopic events of mitosis, a false impression of leisure is given.

In the living cell under phase contrast, the nucleus appears homogeneous, with a slightly higher refractive index than the cytoplasm, in which it moves and gently rotates during life. In the interphase nucleus, the DNA is uncoiled and extended to its full length making the actual length of the DNA molecules in each nucleus about a metre. Even remembering that each double helix is only 1·8 nm wide, it is hard to visualize so much being

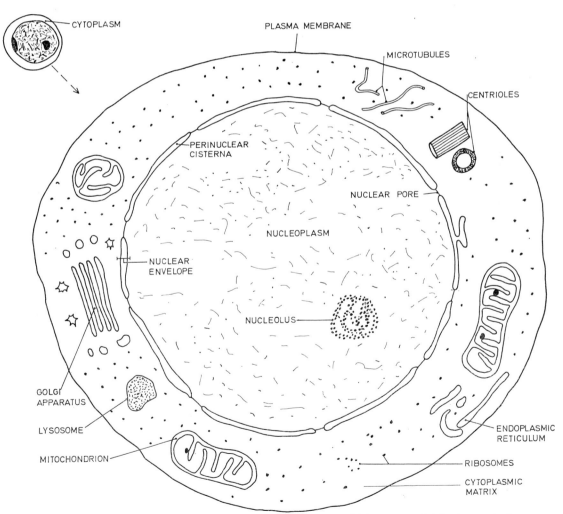

FIG. 13.10. A section of a cell containing the structures which are essential for its survival.

packed into a sphere perhaps 5 μm in diameter; the nucleus also contains the special nuclear proteins, the histones. The packing is random, so the nucleus can be likened to a ball of very fine thread; thin sections for the EM confirm this arrangement as the nucleoplasm appears as a uniform mass of dots and short lengths of fine fibres.

The nucleic acid attracts stains such as haematoxylin, and the DNA can be specifically stained with Schiff's reagent after partial hydrolysis, the **Feulgen reaction**. Most fixatives for light microscopy cause some clumping of the nuclear contents, so that the nucleus appears to contain darkly staining masses which may be condensed near the nuclear membrane or form a network throughout the nucleus. This artefact is called **chromatin** and since there is some constancy in its arrangement in particular cells treated in standard fashion, its distribution can be useful in identification.

The sex chromatin or Barr body, which is present in the nuclei of normal interphase female cells, represents a mass of unextended DNA. It is not an artefact and as the number and distribution of these bodies indicate the fate of the sex chromosome during division and fertilization they are clinically important.

Apart from the chromatin produced from the DNA content, the nuclei usually contain normal aggregations of RNA which are called **nucleoli**. Nucleoli are dark spheres about 1 μm in diameter; they are known to contain RNA because they disappear after ribonuclease digestion, they do not stain with the Feulgen reaction and yet they attract the nucleic acid stains. The nucleoli are especially prominent in protein-secreting cells and they always disappear before mitosis.

Nuclei vary in size and shape, their size increasing with that of the cell. Very large cells such as osteoclasts and skeletal muscle fibres are multinucleated. The shape of the nucleus conforms to the shape of the cell, thin flat discs in compressed endothelial cells, long ovoids in smooth muscle cells and spheres in cubical epithelial cells. Some nuclei acquire bizarre shapes, being multilobulated in the polymorphonuclear leucocyte and kidney shaped in monocytes.

If all the cellular constituents so far described were assembled in their simplest form, the cell produced would appear as in fig. 13.10. This cell would be capable of movement, maintenance and cell division. It could absorb from the surrounding medium the nutrients and oxygen necessary to produce energy. It could discharge its waste products and could synthesize its own constituents. It would, however, be an ineffective, unproductive member of the population, contributing nothing to the common weal. This theoretical cell is strikingly similar to an actual cell, the lymphocyte. The immunological functions which are currently assigned to this important white blood cell do not make any functional demands which could not be accomplished by this fundamental cell structure.

SPECIALIZED CELL STRUCTURES

In differentiated cells, certain features of the fundamental structure just described become exaggerated and other cellular structures appear. It is these specialized features which by increasing the mobility, absorptive capacity, synthetic ability etc., determine the role of any particular cell, and it is the recognition of these features which makes it possible to identify a cell in the tissues. No cell possesses more than a few of these special features and they are conveniently described as modifications of the fundamental structure under these headings:

The cell boundary
    Extracellular constituents
    Intercellular adhesion
    Pinocytosis, phagocytosis and secretion
    Increase in surface area
    Cilia and flagellae
Cytoplasmic membranous organelles
    Rough-surfaced endoplasmic reticulum
    Smooth-surfaced endoplasmic reticulum
    Mitochondria
Cytoplasmic proteins, lipids and carbohydrates
Pigments

The cell boundary

EXTRACELLULAR CONSTITUENTS

When two tissue cells are in apposition, their plasma membranes do not usually come into direct contact, there being an extracellular gap about 15 nm wide. This gap is permeable to water and ions and probably serves to expose a large area of the plasma membranes of closely packed cells to the interstitial fluid. This space between cells exists because each membrane has an outer coating of mucopolysaccharide, the carbohydrate protein complexes in the extracellular spaces of the body which form the basis of the connective tissue ground substance. The bonds between these opposed cells are not strong as the gap can be enlarged by osmotic changes and other cells, e.g. lymphocytes, can migrate into the gap (fig. 13.11).

The strength of the surface can be increased by incorporating a fine meshwork of the fibrous protein, reticulin, in the surrounding mucopolysaccharide coat. This stronger investment is called a **basement membrane**, and it can be shown by light microscopy either by impregnating the reticulin fibres with silver salts or by staining the polysaccharide with the PAS reaction. Different surfaces of a single cell can have varying amounts of extracellular covering. Thus an epithelial cell (fig. 13.11) has a naked plasma membrane facing the surface, a polysaccharide-containing extracellular space along its sides and a well-developed basement membrane at the base of the cell.

FIG. 13.11. Intercellular adhesions.

More than half of the human body is extracellular and the physical characteristics of this part can vary from a watery interstitial fluid to the calcified collagenous matrix of bone. The form of the extracellular materials determines the properties of the connective tissues (chap. 16). Here it is only necessary to recognize that these tissues are extensions of the extracellular coats around cells. Cellular activity is responsible for the synthesis of the connective tissue proteins (collagen, reticulin, elastin, plasma proteins, etc.) and carbohydrates, e.g. sulphated mucopolysaccharide in cartilage; it also maintains them during life and controls the deposition of minerals in these tissues.

INTERCELLULAR ADHESION

If body cells did not stick together, we would collapse into a slimy mass of assorted cells around our skeletal remains. The attachments of cells to each other create organs and provide barriers to enclose such fluids as bile, blood and urine (chap. 17). The specific adherence of cells is an important factor in controlling differentiation and the loss of this property, which is one of the features of malignant change, releases the cancer cell to roam the body.

Where cells adhere strongly to their neighbours, special structures are seen at the surface. These structures are found only between cells of a similar type, muscle to muscle and epithelial cell to epithelial cells and although their distribution varies in different tissues they are constant in structure. A useful nomenclature for these specialized regions of adhesion is as follows.

Macula adhaerens or desmosome (fig. 13.11) is a 'spot-weld' between adjacent cells, where the cytoplasmic sides of the plasma membranes are thickened to receive the attachment of intracellular fibrils. In the gap between these thickenings, an organization of the intercellular materials reveals itself as a bisecting line. Structures like half desmosomes attach cells to the surrounding connective tissue. This is well seen at the end of a muscle cell where the contractile force of a myofibril is transmitted through the plasma membrane to the collagen fibres of the tendon.

Zonula adhaerens (fig. 13.11) is similar to a desmosome but more extensive; in epithelia it forms a continuous girdle around the cell, formerly known as the terminal bar. A zonula adhaerens does not have such a prominent bisecting line and may not have intracellular filaments radiating out into the cytoplasm.

Zonula occludens (fig. 13.11) is the junction where intercellular space is obliterated by the cohesion of the outer layers of the apposed plasma membranes. An obvious function of this tight junction is to eliminate intercellular diffusion and thus it is an essential feature of epithelial organization.

Some cells fuse even closer to each other, so that the intervening plasma membranes disappear. This is seen in the syncytial structure of the skeletal muscle fibre, the syncytiotrophoblast and the large osteoclasts.

PINOCYTOSIS, PHAGOCYTOSIS AND SECRETION

While the passage of water, gases, ions and small molecules through the plasma membrane occurs by passive diffusion or by active (molecular) transport mechanisms built into the plasma membrane itself, a special method is apparently employed for the entry and exit of larger molecules and particles. Fig. 13.12a shows how the formation of a small vesicle can carry such a macromolecule into the cell without disrupting the ionic permeability characteristics of the surface. These minute vesicles, 20–40 nm in diameter, are present at the surface of most cells and the name of the process is pinocytosis or 'cell drinking'. The production of the vesicle and its movement depends on energy and ATPase can be demonstrated in the walls of pinocytotic vesicles. As the first step in the process is adhesion of the particle to the surface, pinocytosis can select molecules from the surrounding medium.

Phagocytosis or 'cell-eating' is a similar process, where the ingested objects are large enough to be seen by the light microscope. Bacteria, effete erythrocytes and dead cells

(a)

(c)

(b)

(d)

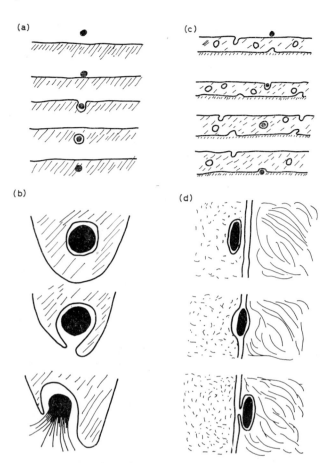

FIG. 13.12. Various forms of membrane transport. (a) pinocytosis: a macromolecular particle is indicated as a black dot; its entrance into the cytoplasm through a small vesicle is shown. (b) The discharge of a secretory droplet. (c) The passage of a particle through a cell as seen in capillary endothelia; note that the particle remains enclosed in a membranous vesicle. (d) The transfer of material from one cell to its neighbour: this could indicate the passage of a melanin granule from a melanocyte on the left to an epithelial cell on the right.

are ingested by phagocytosis. Compared with the almost universal ability to pinocytose, phagocytosis is an accomplishment reserved for a few cell types known as macrophages and histiocytes (chap. 27).

Just as these contortions of the cell surface take substances into the cell, so the reverse process is used for the discharge of macromolecular material into the surrounding medium. At the apex of an enzyme-secreting cell, the stored protein enzymes approach the surface as secretory granules: their membranous envelopes join the plasma membrane and the contents are liberated (fig. 13.12b). Many thousands of small vesicles are held at nerve terminals, to release their contained transmitter material on stimulation of the nerve (p. 14.28).

A combination of these input and output mechanisms

allows material to be transferred directly from one cell to another. For instance the melanocytes in the skin which manufacture the pigment melanin pass it directly to the ordinary epithelial cells where it is stored (fig. 13.12d). Pinocytosis is also a means of transfer straight through a cell without the material coming into direct contact with the other cell contents; the permeability of capillary walls probably depends partly on this process (fig. 13.12c).

INCREASE IN SURFACE AREA

The area of exposed plasma membrane can be increased by various geometric patterns. Finger-like projections are common and if packed close together they form a refractile surface to the cell known as a brush border (fig. 13.13). Similarly, intussusceptions of the membrane

FIG. 13.13. Microvilli forming a brush border.

which accommodate the processes of adjacent cells increase the surface area (fig. 13.14). These adaptations are probably more complex than a simple increase in the surface area, for the membranes of the brush border and

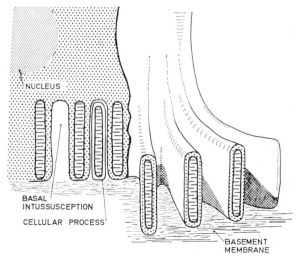

FIG. 13.14. Increase in the surface area by basal intussusceptions, as found in the renal tubules.

basal intussusceptions carry specific enzymes; these contortions should therefore be regarded as supports for the enzymes concerned with ion pumping and active transport. They thus have a supporting role similar to that of the cristae in mitochondria. A further example of membranes playing a supportive role is provided by the retinal rods and cones, where invaginations of the plasma membranes carry the photosensitive pigments.

The surface area can be increased also by tubular invaginations. Intracellular canaliculi provide a passage for acid secretion by the oxyntic cells of the stomach (p. 30.14) and the very fine T-tubules of striated muscle carry the surface action potential deep into the fibre (p. 14.25).

The myelin sheath of a nerve fibre is also an extension and modification of the surface plasma membrane (p. 14.4).

CILIA AND FLAGELLAE

A cilium is a cell projection which is actively motile; they are like oars which can move a protozoan cell. In tissues composed of stationary cells the cilia move the fluid bathing the surface. Ciliary movement has a sense of direction, all the cilia on one cell or on an epithelial sheet of cells beating the same way. During the forceful stroke the cilium is a rigid rod, about 4 μm long, which recoils in a bent flaccid state ready for the next cycle (fig. 13.15). The ultrastructure of a cilium is intriguing and complicated: it is attached to a root body which resembles a centriole (p. 13.8). Fine tubules extend from the root

body up the axis of the cilium, nine pairs of tubules being arranged peripherally around a central thicker pair.

Flagellae are much longer than cilia, the human sperm tail reaching 50 μm, but their basic structure is the same as a cilium with some extrafibrillar material symmetrically arranged around the ring of $(9 \times 2) + 2$ tubules (fig. 13.15).

On some secreting cells, very long tapered processes provide sites for the discharge of secretion; these are called stereocilia. They are easily seen by light microscopy, being 10–20 μm long, and their resemblance to cilia is only superficial as they are non-motile and do not have an organized internal structure.

Cytoplasmic membranous organelles

As described on p. 13.8, some **ribosomes** are always present in cells for the natural turnover of the cell's own proteins. A high concentration of ribosomes in the cytoplasm indicates more active protein synthesis. If the proteins produced are for the growth of the cell, as in embryonic development, or if they are retained in the cell then the polyribosomes are found floating freely in the cytoplasm. This concentration of RNA causes an intense cytoplasmic basophilia; the deep-blue-staining cytoplasm of the immature red cell which is synthesizing haemoglobin provides a good example.

ENDOPLASMIC RETICULUM

When a large number of ribosomes is attached to the

FIG. 13.15. Cilia, movements and ultrastructure.

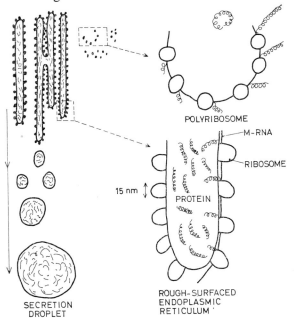

FIG. 13.16. Protein synthesis at polyribosomes. At the top right this is shown as it would occur free in the cytoplasm. On the left the ribosomes are attached to membranes of the endoplasmic reticulum and the synthesized proteins pass into the lumen of the reticulum.

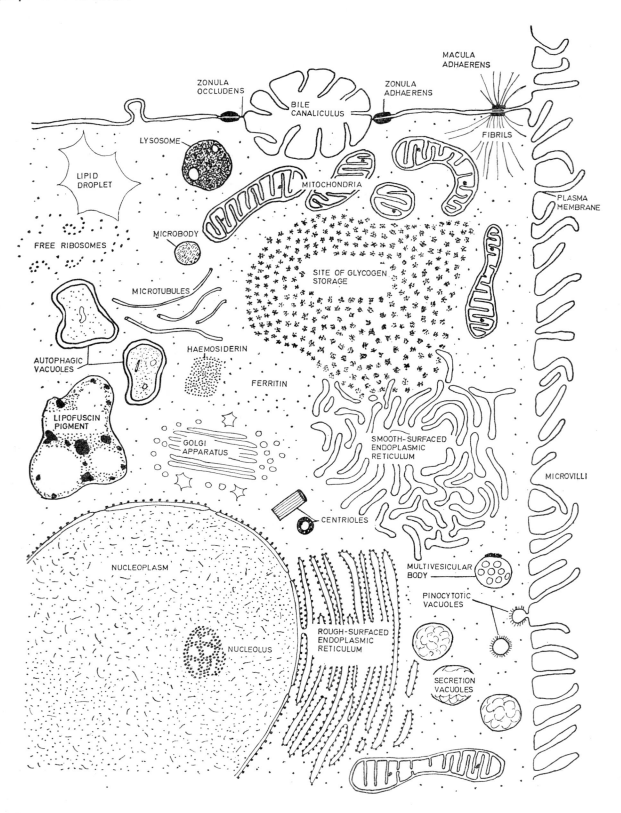

Fɪɢ. 13.17. A composite diagram showing the structures which can be seen in a parenchymal cell (hepatocyte) in the liver.

membranes of the endoplasmic reticulum, this is described as **rough-surfaced ER** (fig. 13.16). This combination also indicates protein synthesis, but here the newly formed protein molecules pass into the lumen of the endoplasmic reticulum where they aggregate to form secretory granules. The secretory granules move towards the Golgi region of the cell before passing to the surface for discharge. Thus the endoplasmic reticulum can be regarded as a packaging and delivery apparatus. Note that these cells will also be basophilic in the light microscope; the EM, by showing the relationship between the ribosomes and the internal membranes, can show whether the products are mainly exported or stored. Hence the protein-secreting cells of the pancreas and the plasma cells secreting antibodies contain large amounts of rough-surfaced ER. Elaborate proliferations of membranous tubules and sacs, without attached ribosomes, are known as **smooth-surfaced ER** (fig. 13.17). This is found in cells which are synthesizing carbohydrates, like glycogen, and steroids. In striated muscle, smooth-surfaced endoplasmic reticulum is called the sarcoplasmic reticulum. It is concerned with calcium ion binding and constituting a support for the enzymes of anaerobic glycolysis.

Microsomes are an artefact of homogenization. When the endoplasmic reticulum is disrupted, it forms vesicles which can be separated by ultracentrifugation (fig. 24.121). These may be derived from rough- or smooth-surfaced reticulum; microsomes from the former contain ribosomes.

MITOCHONDRIA

As the main site for energy conversion in cells, a complement of these organelles is almost always present. An obvious specialization is the provision of large numbers of large mitochondria with an increased area of closely packed cristae in those cells which need a great deal of energy. The continually beating heart muscle, the cells of the kidney tubules pumping ions back into the plasma and the oxyntic cells of the stomach secreting hydrochloric acid are all packed with large complex mitochondria.

Cytoplasmic proteins, lipids and carbohydrates

PROTEINS

Many of the enzymatic and structural proteins form an integral part of the organelles already described, but some are in colloidal solution in the cytoplasmic matrix. Cellular differentiation can be shown by locating an enzyme system associated with a particular function; for instance, the epithelial cells of the prostate have a high acid phosphatase activity. In the EM, a diffuse density in the cytoplasmic matrix is all that remains of this colloidal solution. However, one particular globular protein (ferritin) is made obvious by its extraordinary capacity to store iron. Ferritin has an iron-containing core which by

scattering electrons appears as a dense particle 5 nm in diameter.

Fibrous proteins fulfil diverse roles in the cytoplasm of many cells. They are responsible for the movement of cilia and flagellae and for the contraction of muscle (p. 15.3). They confer strength and turgidity on the cytoplasm as tonofibrils in the epithelial layers of the skin. Similarly, in a cell with a brush border an underlying feltwork of fibrils sends a core of fibrils into each microvillus, and this is known as the terminal web (fig. 13.13). The outermost layers of the epidermis contain the fibrous protein keratin, the substance which forms nails and hair.

LIPIDS

Phospholipid protein complexes are the basis of the plasma and internal membranes; as such they are present in the organelles and bodies like the myelin sheath and myelin figures. The simpler lipids, the triglycerides, are present in varying quantities, and as they are immiscible with water, even a small amount will aggregate to form a lipid droplet. Large amounts form a single spherical droplet around which the cell is reduced to a thin cytoplasmic film, as in an adipose tissue cell (p. 32.1). Numerous smaller lipid droplets are seen in the cells of brown adipose tissue and in cells which secrete and store steroid hormones or the fat-soluble vitamins A and D.

Embedding in paraffin wax removes all the simple lipids, so a lipid-containing cytoplasm can appear either frothy or show a single large empty vacuole. Frozen sections retain the lipid which can then be stained. In EM, osmium fixation by combining with the lipids makes them less soluble, so they can be recognized as homogeneous inclusions in the cytoplasm; they may or may not have an enclosing phospholipid membrane.

CARBOHYDRATES

Monosaccharides and disaccharides, being soluble, are removed by all preparative procedures except freeze drying. Histochemical staining with the PAS type of reaction can show only the highly polymerized and relatively insoluble polysaccharides, like starch and glycogen. Digestion with salivary amylase provides a useful control, since this treatment hydrolyses glycogen. Glycogen is present in most cells but is stored mainly in muscle and liver. In EM, glycogen particles can be recognized as clumps of dense granules each larger than a ribosome.

Mucous secretions contain large amounts of mucoprotein and glycoprotein which are polysaccharide protein combinations. These substances are also PAS positive but they resist digestion with amylase. If they are stained with certain dyes, they take on a colour different from that of the original dye, that is, they exhibit metachromasia. Metachromasia is shown also by the sulphated mucopolysaccharides of cartilage and by another similar substance, heparin.

Pigments

Compared with the vivid colours of plants, insects and birds, mammals are drab creatures and man is one of the least colourful. Much of our colour we receive fortuitously from the iron-containing haemoglobin and its iron-free but coloured derivatives, bilirubin, urobilinogen and stercobilin. Likewise our muscles are reddish because the iron-containing myoglobin is present in them. Even the subtle and seductive natural colours of the eyes and hair are merely interference patterns formed by a black pigment, melanin, synthesized from tyrosine. Tyrosine is first converted to dihydroxyphenylalanine (DOPA) and subsequently to melanin. Melanocytes which are capable of forming melanin can be identified by incubation with DOPA. In the cytoplasm, melanin appears as black spherical granules in which the actual melanin is combined with protein.

In pathological conditions, many pigments may be present but in normal unstained cells, apart from melanin, only visual purple, lipofuscin, haemosiderin and ingested foreign matter can be seen. Visual purple is a photosensitive pigment, present in the rods and cones of the retina where it is presented to the light, in monomolecular layers, by being attached to flat sheets of lipoprotein membrane. Carotene and other carotenoid substances can also colour cells if they are present in sufficient amounts.

Lipofuscin, one of the commonest cellular pigments, is known by a variety of names (wear and tear pigment, haemofuscin, lipochrome, brown atrophy and age pigment), a selection which demonstrates its complexity as well as ignorance of its function, and indicates that it contains some lipid and some iron. The lipofuscin content increases with the age of a cell. In nerve cells of old people large masses of this yellow pigment may surround the nucleus. There are structural resemblances and so possibly a functional relationship between lysosomes (p. 13.8) and lipofuscin granules, although the latter do not have the acid phosphatase activity of the former. Haemosiderin, which contains a large aggregation of ferritin molecules, also appears as yellowish-brown granules, but its intense prussian blue staining distinguishes it from lipofuscin.

Exogenous substances, such as dust, carbon particles or tattooed dyes remain obvious in the cells which have phagocytosed these particles.

COMMENT

This survey of the types of organelles and structures found in cells is not comprehensive. Additional features are still being discovered and biochemical and functional information is being allotted to known structures. Continued research, even with existing techniques, should clarify many points in the immediate future. It is bound to be difficult to determine precisely the relation between structure and function in the cell; the size of the structures, their interdependence and the disturbance which any method of examination produces, all make the task formidable. This is not surprising since a complete understanding of the machinery of the cell would mean an explanation of life itself. It is encouraging to compare a modern description of the cell with an account written before the application of electron microscopy, X-ray diffraction and refined biochemical techniques.

As illustrative of the present position, the parenchymal cell of the liver may be used as an example. It fulfils many functions, as an endocrine and exocrine gland, as the main site for a multitude of reactions in intermediary metabolism and as a store of materials (p. 30.32); it is therefore not surprising that this cell contains a larger collection of organelles than most of our more limited cells. In fig. 13.17, all the structures mentioned in the preceding pages are illustrated as they appear in the liver cell.

Finally, although the general pattern of cell structure has been summarized, descriptions of the infinite variety of different cells have not been attempted. Many of these differences, in secreting cells, are due to the nature of the secretion product. Even when this product cannot be chemically defined, empirical staining methods can distinguish these cells from their neighbours. Consideration of all these cells is best deferred until the structure and function of the systems is considered (chaps. 24–37).

FURTHER READING

An illustrated account of preparative methods showing the hazards in interpretation:

HAM A.W. (1965) *Histology*, 5th Edition. London: Pitman Medical Publishing.

Practical details of various techniques:

BAKER J.R. (1950) *Cytological Technique*, 3rd Edition. London: Methuen's Monographs on Biological Subjects.

KAY D. (1965) *Techniques for Electron Microscopy*, 2nd Edition. Oxford: Blackwell Scientific Publications.

PEARSE A.G.E. (1960) *Histochemistry, Theoretical and Applied*, 2nd Edition. London: Churchill.

A well-illustrated histology textbook:

BLOOM W. & FAWCETT D.W. (1968) *A Textbook of Histology*, 9th Edition. Philadelphia: Saunders.

A fuller account of cell structure which emphasizes dynamic aspects:

DE ROBERTIS E.D.P., NOWINSKI W.W. & SAEZ F.A. (1960) *General Cytology*, 3rd Edition. Philadelphia: Saunders.

Comprehensive review of the available literature:

BRACHET J. & MIRSKY A.E. (1958–64) *The Cell*, 6 Vols. New York: Academic Press.

The structure and function of tissues

Chapter 14
The conducting tissues

Excitability is a characteristic of all living tissues and is present in both unicellular and multicellular organisms. A stimulus such as that applied by an electric current at one site may be transmitted to another part where it excites movement or other activity. A stimulus may also be inhibitory when it diminishes activity or movement. Although a general property of all cells, excitability and its spread or transmission is especially developed in nerve and muscle cells. Conduction occurs not only from one part of a cell to another but also from one nerve cell to another and from nerve to muscle cells. In nerve cells conduction is relatively fast and is observed as a single voltage pulse of fixed wave form. By this means excitatory or inhibitory impulses are carried quickly to all parts of the body.

STRUCTURE OF NERVOUS TISSUE

In higher animals the nervous system is divided into two main parts, the central nervous system (brain and spinal cord) and the peripheral nervous system. The peripheral system consists of long nerve cables or fibres attached centrally to a nerve cell. It transmits information from peripheral sensory receptors by **afferent impulses** to the brain or spinal cord, where they are appreciated and co-ordinated. Cells within the central nervous system then transmit outgoing or **efferent impulses** to the appropriate organ such as muscles or glands. In addition, concentrations of nerve cells are found throughout the body, autonomic ganglia, whose activity is less dependent on central nervous control and mainly concerned with the control of the internal organs such as the heart, intestine and glands. The nervous system is composed of the following structural units.

The nerve cells or neurones are the conducting units and although a great number of morphological variations exists, they are all able to receive impulses and transmit them to other cells.

The supporting cells of the central nervous system are called the **neuroglial cells. Schwann cells** play a similar role in the peripheral nervous system. The neuroglial cells are intimately related to the neurones and play an important part in the metabolism of the nervous system. In addition, they form the myelin sheaths which surround the larger nerve fibres and act as insulating covers for rapidly conducting nerves.

Connective tissue consists of the fibrous tissue sheaths which surround the nerve fibres and ganglia of the peripheral nervous system. It is not normally present within the central nervous system, but connective tissue forms the protective meningeal membranes that cover the outsides of the brain and spinal cord. In addition many sensory nerve endings have elaborate connective tissue capsules (p. 24.67).

The neurone

A neurone is a complete cell and consists of a nerve cell body or perikaryon (*peri*, around, *karyon*, kernel or nucleus) and its associated processes. There are many varieties of neurones depending upon their shape and size and the number, length and form of their processes. There are two types of process, **axon** and **dendrite**, and although it is usually possible to distinguish them morphologically, it is simpler to define the processes on the basis of the direction in which they conduct nerve impulses. Dendrites, of which each neurone may have one or more, conduct impulses towards the perikaryon. There is only one axon to each neurone and this usually conducts impulses away from the perikaryon (fig. 14.1).

On the basis of the number of processes arising from the perikaryon, neurones may be classified in the following way.

Multipolar neurones are by far the most common type within the central nervous system; they have a single axon with numerous dendrites arising from the perikaryon. The form of the cell body varies greatly; sometimes the dendrites arise in an apparently random fashion as in the ventral horn cells of the spinal cord (fig. 14.1). In other neurones the dendrites arise from more localized portions of the perikaryon as in the large Purkinje cells of the cerebellum (p. 24.39) where they arise from only one pole of the pear-shaped neurone, and although there are only a few main stem dendrites these branch profusely to produce an extensive dendritic tree (fig. 14.2b). The pyramidal neurones of the cerebral cortex on the other hand have a single large dendrite arising from the apex of a cone-shaped perikaryon and in addition a number of small dendrites arise from the base of this type of cell (fig. 14.2a).

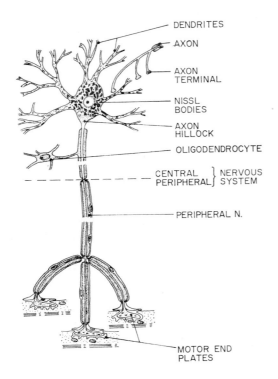

FIG. 14.1. Diagram of a ventral horn cell from the spinal cord.

FIG. 14.2. Various types of neurones. Golgi preparations, redrawn from Cajal. (a) Pyramidal neurone from cerebral cortex, (b) Purkinje cell from cerebellum, (c) bipolar cells from olfactory mucosa, (d) dorsal root ganglion cells, (e) unipolar neurones from the mesencephalic nucleus of the trigeminal nerve.

Bipolar neurones have only two processes arising from the perikaryon, one axon and one dendrite. Such neurones are present in the vestibular and spiral ganglia of the eighth cranial nerve and somewhat modified bipolar neurones form the receptor cells of the retina and olfactory epithelium (fig. 14.2c).

Unipolar neurones occur within the mesencephalic nucleus of the trigeminal nerve (p. 24.26) and the majority of neurones in the spinal and cranial nerve ganglia have this form. They possess a single process which arises from the perikaryon before dividing into two processes (fig. 14.2d and e). In the case of the ganglion cells one of these two processes is peripherally directed and carries impulses towards the cell body, while the other process is directed centrally to enter the brain or spinal cord (fig. 14.2d). When first formed, neurones of the spinal ganglia are bipolar in form, having a process arising from each end of the perikaryon. During development, these processes come together on one side of the cell body and their bases fuse into a single, short stem. Thus the neurone becomes unipolar or, as it is sometimes termed because of its mode of development, pseudo-unipolar. In this particular instance, there is no structural difference between the peripherally and centrally directed processes of the neurone. They have the same characteristics and both are invested with myelin sheaths. Also, since the nerve impulse may bypass the perikaryon in this type of neurone, it is not usual to differentiate between the centrally directed axon and the peripheral dendrite but both are called by the noncommittal term of 'nerve fibre'.

CYTOLOGY OF THE NEURONE

The structure of the neurone so far presented is the one obtained when histologists apply the Golgi technique to stain their material. This technique was used to great effect by the Spanish neuroanatomist, Ramon y Cajal, and it is almost the only method of staining which shows the full extent of the neurone and all its processes in three dimensions. After staining by the Golgi method, a neurone appears brown or black and none of its internal cytological structure can be seen. Other stains show these features and amongst the most useful are the basic aniline dyes. These dyes stain the **Nissl granules** of the cytoplasm. Nissl granules are present in the perikaryons of all neurones and they may vary from the rather large coarse granules of the motor cells (fig. 14.1) to the small dust-like particles in the sensory neurones. The granules extend also into the dendrites, but in contrast they are absent from axons and also from the point where the axon arises from the perikaryon. This region is known as the **axon hillock**. EM studies show that Nissl granules are made up of endoplasmic reticulum and the basic staining with aniline dyes is due to their high content of ribosomes.

Dissolution of the Nissl granules, **chromatolysis,** is usually associated with injury to the neurone or its processes. Sectioning the axon of a neurone causes chromatolysis and this procedure is often used by neuroanatomists to determine the neurones from which the axons in a nerve are derived.

Basic dyes stain also the nucleus of a neurone. This is usually spherical in shape and situated in the centre of the perikaryon. One or two prominent nucleoli are normally present within the nucleus whose membrane is quite distinct. Since dendrites contain only a few Nissl granules and no granules are present in the axons, basic dyes cannot be used to stain these processes. Instead, a variety of silver staining methods is employed since, if the correct conditions are used, silver is deposited within the neurone in the form of filaments that have been called neurofibrils. These neurofibrils run nearly parallel to each other throughout both the perikaryon and the processes, and are particularly prominent within the axon. In EM studies, structures with the sizes and characteristics of neurofibrils have not been observed, but neurones and their processes contain many fine filaments, neurofilaments, each about 10 nm in diameter, as well as microtubules (p. 13.17) which are about twice as thick. It is probably upon these tubules and filaments that the silver is deposited during staining.

In addition to the neurofilaments and tubules and the ribosomes which form the Nissl granules, the cytoplasm of neurones contain mitochondria; those within the dendrites and axons are long, thin, threads. In neurones the Golgi apparatus is well developed and it was here that Golgi first saw this structure. Vacuoles, vesicles, glycogen and pigment may occur as cytoplasmic inclusions within neurones. The pigment may be brown or black, as in the cells of the substantia nigra. (p. 24.20).

DENDRITES

In general, the dendrites do not extend far from the perikaryon and are characterized by their repeated branching and irregular outlines; their surfaces often give rise to spines and thorns (fig. 14.1). Cytologically, the dendrites are like the perikaryon of which, for most purposes, they may be regarded as extensions, adapted for the reception of nerve impulses from other neurones. In other words, the dendrites, along with the perikaryon, form the receptor area of a neurone.

AXONS

Usually, an axon arises from the perikaryon at an axon hillock (fig. 14.1). Structurally, axons differ from dendrites in that they contain more neurofilaments than tubules; they do not contain ribosomes and they may be myelinated. Axons branch at varying distances from the perikaryon but they do not ramify like a dendrite; instead their branches come off the main stem at right angles and within the central nervous system the terminal branches always form bulbous expansions that are applied to the surfaces of dendrites, the perikaryon or axons of other neurones (fig. 14.1). These axon terminals are called **boutons**; these may occur also along the length of an axon when they are known as **boutons en passage.**

Axons that leave the central nervous system to form peripheral efferent nerves also end in expansions that may be applied either to the surface of another neurone, as in the case of those axons of the sympathetic nervous system which form the synapses upon the neurones of the ganglia, or to the surface of a striated muscle fibre to form a motor end plate, or they may end within the interstices of glandular tissue or smooth muscle fibres.

Before these axon terminals are considered, the various means by which an axon may be ensheathed are described, as these affect the mode of conduction.

SHEATHS OF PERIPHERAL NERVE FIBRES

The sheath-forming cells of the peripheral nervous system are the Schwann cells. These are elongated cells with spindle shaped nuclei which lie parallel to the length of the nerve fibres. The Schwann cells usually ensheath each nerve fibre both completely and separately. It is on the basis of the form of the sheath that peripheral nerve fibres are said to be either myelinated or unmyelinated.

In the following account, the term 'nerve fibre' covers all neuronal processes which may be carrying impulses towards the central nervous system (afferent fibres) or away from it (efferent fibres). Such nerve fibres may be **myelinated** or **unmyelinated** and, as pointed out above, both the centrally and peripherally directed processes of the sensory ganglion cells have the same structure.

Most peripheral nerves contain a mixture of myelinated and unmyelinated nerve fibres, but it is common for one type to predominate. In the living body, nerves that contain many unmyelinated nerve fibres appear dull and grey, while those that contain mostly myelinated nerve fibres are white and glistening. This white appearance is due to the presence of myelin, a complex lipoprotein which blackens with osmic acid (fig. 14.3).

Unmyelinated nerve fibres are associated with somatic and visceral functions and are between 0·1 and 1·0 μm in diameter. EM studies show that each of these nerve fibres is separately ensheathed by a Schwann cell, but in such a way that many of them occupy the same Schwann cell (fig. 14.4). The separation between nerve fibres is achieved by each one being invaginated at a different site on the Schwann cell surface, so that in effect each one lies in its own groove. Sometimes a nerve fibre is only partially enclosed by the Schwann cell but in other instances the fibres are completely enfolded in such a way that the edges of the groove come together to form a mesaxon (fig. 14.4). A mesaxon is formed by apposition of the surfaces of two different areas of the plasma membrane of the same Schwann cell and the apposition is such that the outer layers of the triple layered plasma membrane fuse to form

9

FIG. 14.3. Internodal segments of two nerves from a young animal. Stained with osmic acid.

a five layered structure (fig. 14.4) that is equivalent to a zonula occludens (p. 13.11).

Since each Schwann cell extends for only a short distance along a group of nerve fibres, the total ensheathing of a peripheral unmyelinated nerve fibre is achieved by a series of Schwann cells lying end to end.

Myelinated nerve fibres include practically all those with a diameter of more than 2 μm. When myelin is blackened with osmic acid it is found that the myelin sheath is interrupted at regular intervals along its length by indentations. These indentations are the **nodes of Ranvier** (fig. 14.3) and the length of myelin between two adjacent nodes is referred to as an **internode**. Generally, the greater the diameter of the fibre the less frequent are the nodes of Ranvier, so that the internodal length of a nerve fibre 5 μm in diameter is about 0·5 mm while that of a 10 μm fibre is about 2 mm (fig. 14.5). Another observation made with the light microscope is that only one Schwann cell nucleus is associated with one internodal length of myelin (fig. 14.3), since this length represents the extent of that Schwann cell.

Polarized light and X-ray diffraction techniques show

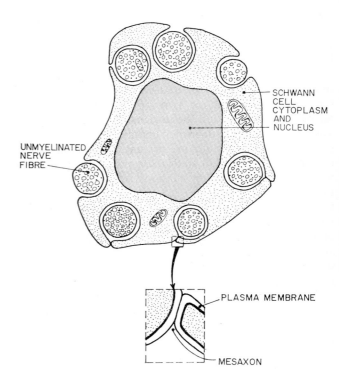

FIG. 14.4. Diagram to show the arrangement of unmyelinated nerve fibres within a Schwann cell, details of how plasma membrane surfaces come together to form a mesaxon are also given.

FIG. 14.5. Short segments of different diameter peripheral nerve fibres to show the internodal lengths of myelin. Drawn to scale.

that myelin is composed of lipid and protein laid down in a series of concentric layers or lamellae, each of which has a radial thickness of 17–18 nm. EM observations confirm this finding and show that the lamellae are formed from the plasma membrane of the Schwann cell and it is for this reason, of course, that myelin has a high lipoprotein content. To understand the structure of the myelin sheath, it is necessary to refer to its development. In the first stage of myelin formation, a single nerve fibre is enclosed by a Schwann cell (fig. 14.6a), in such a way that it indents the surface of that cell to lie within a groove. Next, the free edges of the Schwann cell come together to form a mesaxon (fig. 14.4), so that the two opposed plasma membranes fuse on their outer surfaces (fig. 14.6b). The mesaxon then elongates in a spiral manner around the enclosed axon (fig. 14.6c). Initially the spiral is loose, but

FIG. 14.6. The myelin sheath of peripheral nerve fibres. a–c; the development of the sheath; d, the structure of the adult sheath.

FIG. 14.7. Diagram of a longitudinal section through a node of Ranvier of a peripheral myelinated nerve fibre.

later the cytoplasm is lost from between the successive turns. At the site of fusion of the cytoplasmic surfaces of the plasma membrane forming the myelin sheath, a dense line is formed. This major dense line within the sheath alternates with the thinner, intraperiod lines (fig. 14.6d), formed by the fusion of the outer surfaces of the same membrane. Thus compact myelin is formed, and each turn of the spiral is termed a lamella. Cytoplasm remains on the inside of the sheath, between the myelin and the axon as well as on the outside where the nucleus of the Schwann cell is seen.

At a node of Ranvier (fig. 14.3 and 14.7) the successive layers of the spirally arranged lamellae of myelin end. Each layer overlaps the one lying internal to it and at the site of overlap the lamellae of the sheath open up along the major dense line to enclose Schwann cell cytoplasm. Consequently, in longitudinal sections through a node there appears to be a series of cytoplasmic pockets (fig. 14.7). In reality, of course, these loops represent sections through a continuous spiral of cytoplasm whose ends are in direct continuity with the cytoplasm on the inside and outside of the myelin sheath.

In the region of these loops the gap between the plasma membrane of the Schwann cell and that of the axon is very small, being only about 3 nm. It is thought that this is to limit the passage of ions into the extracellular space between the sheath and the axon. At a node, the myelin is interrupted, the interdigitating processes of the adjacent Schwann cells do not fuse together and the continuous basement membrane and endoneurium are permeable to ions (fig. 14.7). So here the plasma membrane of the axon is bathed with extracellular ions. Ionic insulation of the internodal segment and exposure at the nodes are necessary for saltatory conduction (p. 14.20).

Nerve bundles, which make up a peripheral nerve, contain both myelinated and unmyelinated fibres. On the outside of each Schwann cell there is a basement membrane (fig. 14.7) and into this are inserted the delicate reticular and collagen fibres that constitute the **endoneurium** (fig. 14.7). This is hardly visible in the light microscope. Around each bundle of nerve fibres there is a sheath of connective tissue, the **perineurium**, which consists of layers of connective tissue fibres between which are fibroblasts (fig. 14.8). Binding these bundles together and forming the outer connective tissue sheath of the whole nerve is the **epineurium** (fig. 14.8).

FIG. 14.8. Diagram of the structure of a peripheral nerve containing myelinated and unmyelinated nerve fibres, to show the neural sheaths.

SHEATHS OF FIBRES IN THE CENTRAL NERVOUS SYSTEM

The majority of nerve fibres within the central nervous system do not have sheaths and so intermingle with each other, being separated by spaces only 20 nm wide. The sheaths of the myelinated axons, which are of course few in grey matter and predominate in white matter, are similar to those of peripheral nerves in that the myelin is formed by the spiral wrapping of the plasma membrane of the myelin-forming cell, in this case the oligodendrocyte (fig. 14.1 and 14.9). The main differences between the

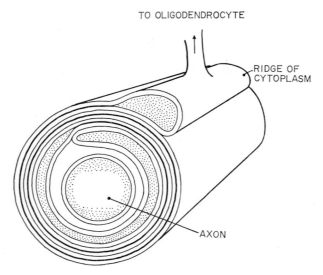

FIG. 14.9. The structure of the myelin sheath of the central nervous system. While the nucleus of the Schwann cell of the peripheral nervous system is contained within the cytoplasm on the outside of the sheath, the nucleus of the oligodendrocyte is within the cell body situated some distance away from the site of myelin formation. Also see fig. 14.6.

myelin sheaths in the peripheral and central nervous systems are as follows.

(1) An oligodendrocyte is responsible for the formation of a number of internodal lengths of myelin, not upon the same axon, but upon different axons. For this reason the oligodendrocyte nucleus is not found in intimate association with the outside of the sheath, as is the Schwann cell nucleus. Instead it is some distance away, the myelin sheath being formed at the end of an oligodendrocyte process. It is not yet known how many sheaths are formed by each oligodendrocyte.

(2) There is an incomplete layer of cytoplasm on the outside of a myelin sheath in the central nervous system, so that the outsides of adjacent myelin sheaths can come into direct contact with each other.

(3) At a node of Ranvier in the central nervous system the axon is bare and not covered by cytoplasmic processes of the myelin-forming cell as in peripheral nerves.

Thus a nerve fibre within the central nervous system has a myelin sheath formed by oligodendrocytes, but once that nerve fibre leaves the central nervous system its myelin is formed by Schwann cells (fig. 14.1).

Neuroglia

The neuroglia are the supporting cells of the central nervous system. They are of three different types, the astrocytes, the oligodendrocytes and microglia. The structural features of these cells are not apparent in preparations normally used for the histological study of the nervous system, since only their nuclei are visible. Consequently, special stains and EM methods have to be used for their study.

Astrocytes have numerous processes arising from the perikaryon and this star shape accounts for their name. They are of two types, fibrous astrocytes, which predominate in white matter, and protoplasmic astrocytes, which are found mainly in grey matter. The difference between the two types lies in the number of intracellular fibrils which they contain. Astrocytes occur throughout the central nervous system and their processes course between those of neurones. Single processes in grey matter may isolate certain neuronal components such as synapses from the surrounding structures, while, in white matter groups of processes of fibrous astrocytes surround bundles of nerve fibres.

Some processes of astrocytes extend to the outside of the nervous tissue and expand into end feet which separate neurones and their processes from both the fluid and meninges on the outside of the central nervous system, as well as from the blood vessels that penetrate into it. Thus, end feet of astrocytes separate the nerve cells from all other tissues. It is now thought that any substance entering or leaving the central nervous system has to pass through these end feet and that one of the functions of astrocytes is the transport of metabolites. In this same role, they might also retard the passage of certain substances and so contribute to the formation of the blood–brain barrier (p. 24.86). Astrocytes react to pathological conditions by producing extensive scars that are thought to prevent the breakdown of remaining nervous tissue.

Oligodendrocytes are smaller and have fewer processes than astrocytes. They are found throughout the central nervous system and in white matter lie in rows between the myelinated nerve fibres, where one of their functions is the formation and maintenance of central myelin sheaths. In grey matter, oligodendrocytes are often found close to neurones, where they are referred to as perineuronal satellite cells. The role of these satellite cells is not certain, but their metabolism seems to be closely linked with that of the neurones, which they may help to support.

Microglial cells are characterized by nuclei which stain deeply and have either an elongated or a rounded shape. Long branching processes arise from the cell bodies. Unlike the other two glial types, microglial cells are not derived from ectoderm, but have a mesodermal origin similar to reticuloendothelial cells (p. 27.1). Under normal conditions microglia appear to play no part in the maintenance of the central nervous system, but in pathological conditions they migrate towards the site of inflammation or degeneration and carry out phagocytosis until their cytoplasm becomes filled with lipid substances and cell debris.

NERVE CONDUCTION

Much of our knowledge about the physiology of nerve and muscle cells comes from the study of the giant axon of the squid and of sartorius muscle of the frog. Both preparations are large enough for chemical analysis and remain excitable for several hours after excision. Excitability depends on the differences between the ionic composition, especially of the $[Na^+]$ and $[K^+]$, of their extracellular and intracellular fluid (fig. 14.10). These differ quantitatively but not qualitatively from those in man (p. 1.4).

Squid axon membrane		Frog muscle membrane	
Outside (o)	Inside (i)	Outside (o)	Inside (i)
Na^+ 460	Na^+ 50	Na^+ 120	Na^+ 9
K^+ 10	K^+ 400	K^+ 3	K^+ 140
Cl^- 540	Cl^- 40–100	Cl^- 120	Cl^- 4
with additional cations, e.g. Ca^{++}	P^- and other anions	with additional cations, e.g. Ca^{++}	P^- and other anions
+	−	+	−
← 60 mV →		← 90 mV →	

FIG. 14.10. Concentrations of ions in mEq/l and electrical potential differences in millivolts across the cell membranes of the squid axon and frog muscle. P^- represents a negatively charged protein group, for which the membrane is impermeable.

Membrane equilibrium and resting potential

Physical systems in which two phases are separated by a membrane with one phase having a large impermeable ion were originally described by Nernst and by Donnan. Their work was based on that of a modest but outstanding member of Yale University, Professor Josiah Willard Gibbs, who by 1875 had described the general theoretical conditions for ionic equilibrium in such systems. By 1902 an equilibrium system had been described for phases separated by a membrane with ionic distributions comparable to those in biological cells. In its simplest form this considers two solutions separated by a membrane freely permeable to the small ions present in the solution, e.g. Na^+, K^+ and Cl^-, but impermeable to others, e.g. protein ions (P^-) (fig. 14.11). Then if (i) represents the inner compartment containing P^-, (o) the outer compartment and the square brackets concentration, there are two conditions for equilibrium:

(1) the hydrostatic pressure in the compartment (i) must be greater than that for the compartment (o). This difference in pressure is called the osmotic pressure,

(2) there must be an electrical potential difference ($E_i - E_o$) between the two phases related to the concentrations of the permeable ions. For Na^+ and K^+ this relationship is given by the Nernst equation:

$$E_i - E_o = \frac{RT}{F} \ln \frac{[K^+]_o}{[K^+]_i} = \frac{RT}{F} \ln \frac{[Na^+]_o}{[Na^+]_i}$$

For the negative ion Cl^- it becomes:

$$E_i - E_o = \frac{RT}{F} \ln \frac{[Cl^-]_i}{[Cl^-]_o}$$

Where R is the gas constant, T the absolute temperature and F is the faraday.

About this time, such a PD was demonstrated across biological cell membranes and is now called the **resting potential** or the **transmembrane potential**. Using the string galvanometer, it was shown that during nervous and muscular activity a zone of altered transmembrane potential, the **action potential**, moved along the axis of the cell and could be detected as it passed recording electrodes on the surface of the cell. The speed with which this zone of depolarization (fig. 14.12) moves along the axon or muscle cell is called the **conduction velocity** (p. 14.22). This had been measured in 1850 by Helmholtz who found values up to 30 m/sec in frog sciatic nerve muscle preparations.

Membrane

Inside (i)	Outside (o)
K^+	K^+
Na^+	Na^+
Cl^-	Cl^-
P^-	
−mV(E_i)	+mV(E_o)

PD

FIG. 14.11. The effect of a semipermeable membrane on ionic potential distribution. The membrane is permeable to Na^+ and Cl^- but not to P^-.

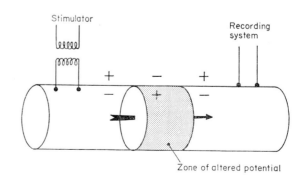

FIG. 14.12. Depolarization in a conducting nerve.

THE BERNSTEIN THEORY

In 1902 Bernstein applied these new electrochemical theories to biological cells and suggested the following.

(1) In the resting state, only K^+ could pass through the membrane, which was impermeable to all other ions.

(2) As a result there was an equilibrium system similar to that demonstrated by Donnan with an electrical PD across the membrane (fig. 14.11). The value of this potential would be decided by K^+, the only permeable ion, and would have the value:

$$E_i - E_o = \frac{RT}{F} \ln \frac{[K^+]_o}{[K^+]_i}$$

(3) On excitation Bernstein postulated that the permeability of the cell membrane changed especially to anions, so that the cell was no longer in equilibrium with the extracellular fluid, but became a diffusion system of the kind described by Gibbs. Under these circumstances there would be diffusion of ions between the compartments. Gibbs had also demonstrated that such a system would give a potential difference between phases, and that this diffusion potential would be different in value and sign from the resting potential;

(4) Transmission of the action potential resulted because this region of altered permeability moved along the axon.

(5) Following the passage of the zone of altered permeability, the membrane reverted to its original state. The axon was then capable of further excitation.

Bernstein's view prevailed for over forty years and apparently explained the ionic composition of cell and extracellular fluid and the magnitude and direction of the resting potential. However, a critical test of the theory needed: ·

(1) accurate measurements of the resting potentials of individual cells in solutions identical with their normal extracellular fluid,

(2) better knowledge of the ions permeable to the cell membrane,

(3) accurate chemical analysis of intracellular and extracellular ionic content,

(4) detailed analysis of the transmembrane voltage change and its time course when an action potential passes along the cell.

These measurements were not technically possible during the years when Bernstein's theory held and the factors which led to its modification illustrate the close interplay between new experimental techniques and theoretical ideas.

MODERN DEVELOPMENTS

In early apparatus for measuring resting potentials (fig. 14.13) one silver electrode was in contact with the cell

FIG. 14.13. Early apparatus for measuring resting potential.

contents through a damaged area of the membrane and the other with the bathing solution, which represented the extracellular fluid. Short circuiting was prevented as far as possible by a barrier dividing the bath into two parts, in which the uninjured and damaged portion of the nerve or muscle lay. Precision depended largely on the effectiveness of this barrier. Values of up to -30 mV were obtained from frog muscle, whereas the value accepted today is -90 mV. In stating the values for transmembrane potentials, it is conventional to represent the potential inside the cell as E_i and that outside the cell as E_o; the transmembrane potential is then $E_i - E_o$. Thus a transmembrane potential of -90 mV means that the inside of the cell is 90 mV negative relative to the outside, and not that the inside is -90 mV and the outside zero. Before 1940, chemical estimation of Na^+, K^+ and Ca^{++} was always difficult and often impossible in small samples; a single sodium estimation could take up to two days of tedious work and it was difficult to be certain whether these ions were permeable or impermeable. Chloride analysis was easier and Conway in Dublin had deduced that Cl^- was permeable.

In the late 1930s accurate extracellular recording of action potentials was advanced by the improved design of amplifiers and oscilloscopes, but the biologist of that day usually designed and built all his equipment and had a restricted budget. The second World War which began in 1939 indirectly contributed much to our present biological knowledge. In that year, Hodgkin and Huxley in Cambridge developed the experimental approach which led to the revision of ideas about ionic distributions and their relation to excitability in the cell. The contribution of these two workers was recognized by the award of a Nobel prize. The new techniques developed about this time included:

(1) intracellular microelectrodes which gave accurate measurements of transmembrane potentials,

(2) recording equipment which became commercially

available as a result of rapid war time development of the electronics industry,

(3) the flame photometer which allowed accurate and rapid analysis of very small samples of fluids containing Na^+, K^+ and other ions and

(4) artificial radioactive isotopes which made possible the study of the membrane permeability of all important ions.

Although the original physical and electrochemical theories are still accepted, the Bernstein hypothesis has been considerably modified by these experimental techniques and their use has established the following experimental findings:

(1) K^+, Na^+, and Cl^- are all permeable to the cell membrane,

(2) neither Na^+ nor K^+ is in equilibrium when the cell is in its resting state. The position for Cl^- is still controversial, but it is unlikely to be in equilibrium,

(3) even in the resting state Na^+ diffuse into the cell continually, and K^+ diffuse out.

The new findings show that the resting transmembrane potential is a diffusion potential, i.e. an electrical potential between the two phases caused by the interdiffusion of ions. The value of this potential is given by the Goldman equation and is:

$$E_i - E_o = \frac{RT}{F} \ln \frac{P_{K^+}[K^+]_o + P_{Na^+}[Na^+]_o + P_{Cl^-}[Cl^-]_i}{P_{K^+}[K^+]_i + P_{Na^+}[Na^+]_i + P_{Cl^-}[Cl^-]_o} \quad (1)$$

where the subscript i refers to the intracellular phase and o to the extracellular phase. E is electrical potential, $[K^+]$, $[Na^+]$, and $[Cl^-]$ the concentrations of K^+, Na^+ and Cl^+ respectively, R the gas constant, T the absolute temperature and F the faraday. The expression ln signifies natural logarithms i.e. logarithms to the base e. P is the membrane permeability coefficient of any ion e.g. P_{K^+} is a measure of the ease with which the K^+ passes through the membrane.

At 20°C (293°A) the term $RT/F \ln$ is 58 mV $\log_{10}$ and the equation becomes,

$$E_i - E_o$$
$$= 58 \log_{10} \frac{P_{K^+}[K^+]_o + P_{Na^+}[Na^+]_o + P_{Cl^-}[Cl^-]_i}{P_{K^+}[K^+]_i + P_{Na^+}[Na^+]_i + P_{Cl^-}[Cl^-]_o} mV$$

The derivation of the Goldman equation is discussed on p. 14.11 together with the significance of P^-. The equation shows that the transmembrane potential at any instant depends not only on the intra- and extra-cellular composition, but also on the instantaneous permeability of the membrane to any ion. In the resting state for squid axon and frog sartorius muscle, the permeability to K^+ is much greater than that to Na^+ or Cl^-. Under these circumstances the Goldman equation approximates closely to the Nernst equation.

$$E_i - E_o = \frac{RT}{F} \ln \frac{[K^+]_o}{[K^+]_i} \quad (2)$$

This was the equation used by Bernstein, and with the experimental results available to him in 1902 his original error in interpreting the origin of the resting potential may be readily understood.

The findings that Na^+ diffuse into and K^+ diffuse out of the cell and yet the chemical composition of the cell remain constant can be explained only if Na^+ is actively removed and K^+ actively brought back. To maintain this steady state energy is required and a significant proportion of the metabolism of the body at rest is utilized in this way. A Na^+/K^+ pump must exist, but the mechanism of the pump has yet to be explained at a molecular level. Such an explanation would contribute much to a detailed understanding of cellular physiology.

Bernstein's interpretation of the transmission of the action potential is still fundamentally correct, but it is now known that the movement of the zone of positive potential results from changes in permeability not only of K^+ but also of Na^+ and other ions. The details of this transmission are discussed on p. 14.16. The next section deals in more detail with the study of equilibrium and diffusion systems. It is summarized for the non-mathematical reader on p. 14.12.

THEORETICAL CONSIDERATIONS

Basic to the study of both equilibrium and diffusion systems is the concept of **chemical potential** introduced by Gibbs and for which the symbol μ is used; its units are Joules/mole. Gibbs demonstrated that any species in equilibrium between phases had the same value for its chemical potential in those phases. In the case of a two-phase system with phases (i) and (o), at equilibrium for each permeable substance $\mu_i = \mu_o$.

For substances not in equilibrium Gibbs suggested the flux at any point x in the diffusion system would be proportional to both the concentration of the substance and the gradient of its chemical potential at that point. Flux is defined as that number of g moles or g ions passing in one second through an area 1 cm² at right angles to the direction of diffusion of that substance. For diffusion systems we write:

$$J = -UC \frac{d\mu}{dx} \quad (3)$$

where J is the flux, U the thermodynamic mobility and C the concentration, in g moles or g ions/c.c. The use of the c.c. rather than the ml is deliberate, since J is defined in terms of cm² and hence the c.c. is the only unit of volume which gives an intelligible equation. The negative sign is necessary because the flux is always down the chemical potential gradient.

Theoretical studies suggest that the relationship between μ and C of a non-ionic substance is

$$\mu = {}^*\mu + RT \ln C \qquad (4)$$

${}^*\mu$ is the standard reference chemical potential; as with all potential functions, values of μ must be related to some arbitrary reference state. The value of ${}^*\mu$ depends upon the solvent and it is important to stress that this relation applies to solute species only.

The flux of any non-ionic species diffusing in a single solvent is obtained by combining equations (3) and (4)

$$J = -UC\frac{d}{dx}({}^*\mu + RT \ln C) \qquad (5)$$

and since ${}^*\mu$ is constant

$$J = -UC\frac{d}{dx}(RT \ln C) \qquad (6)$$

this reduces to

$$J = -URT\frac{dC}{dx} \qquad (7)$$

This is a theoretical derivation of Fick's experimental law for non-ionic solutes under similar conditions

$$J = -D\frac{dC}{dx} \qquad (8)$$

where D is the diffusion coefficient. Hence for non-ionic solutes flux depends only on their concentration gradient.

For ionic solute species in a phase at a voltage E there is an additional energy of ZFE Joules/mole because of ionic charge, where Z is the valency number and F the faraday (coulomb/mole of charge). The chemical potential for ions is written formally:

$$\bar{\mu} = {}^*\mu + RT \ln C + ZFE \qquad (9)$$

It is divided into a chemical and an electrical component and is commonly referred to as the **electrochemical potential** and given the symbol $\bar{\mu}$. In equation (9) the standard state ${}^*\mu$ depends on the solvent of the phase but not on the electrical state.

Gibb's original relationship for non-ionic solutes is for ideal solutions only and although such solutions exist, the relationship does not hold for most real solutions. The situation is comparable with that for the gas laws which treat an idealized perfect gas, but are modified for real gases. For real non-ionic solutions it is common to write

$$\mu = {}^*\mu + RT \ln Cf \qquad (10)$$

where f is an activity coefficient, and is a function of the concentration of the solutes present. The comparable expression for single ionic components is

$$\bar{\mu} = {}^*\mu + RT \ln Cf + ZFE \qquad (11)$$

There are experimental methods for measuring f for non-ionic, but not for ionic components. Though f values can be calculated for extremely dilute solutions of ions, this is not possible at physiological concentrations.

As with non-ionic substances, the condition for equilibrium with permeable ions is that the electrochemical potential of any ion is the same in all phases. In the case of two phases i and o separated by a membrane, for any permeable ions $\bar{\mu}_i = \bar{\mu}_o$. Hence

$${}^*\mu_i + RT \ln C_i + ZFE_i = {}^*\mu_o + RT \ln C_o + ZFE_o \quad (12)$$

If the solvent is the same for each phase, then ${}^*\mu_i = {}^*\mu_o$ and rearrangement gives

$$E_i - E_o = \frac{RT}{ZF} \ln \frac{C_o}{C_i} \qquad (13)$$

This is, of course, the Nernst equation for equilibrium given on p. 14.7. As set out there Z is omitted, because its value is 1 for Na^+ and K^+ but -1 for Cl^-.

For ionic diffusion systems the flux of any ion is

$$J = -UC\frac{d\bar{\mu}}{dx} \qquad (14)$$

It is the simplicity of this expression which makes the concept of electrochemical potential so important. An ion always diffuses down its electrochemical potential gradient. However combining equations (9) and (14), gives the following expression for flux:

$$J = -UC\frac{d}{dx}({}^*\mu + RT \ln C + ZFE)$$

$$= -URT\frac{dC}{dx} - UCZF\frac{dE}{dx} \qquad (15)$$

Hence the flux of any ion is not only a function of its concentration gradient but also of the electrical potential gradient; these two gradients may act in opposition.

In these equations the ionic thermodynamic mobility U is not identical with the conventional ionic mobility U', as measured in solutions without concentration gradients. The relationship between U and U' is however linear and is $U = U'/F$. If the mobility factor is not clearly defined, apparent contradictions may arise in the details of equations used in electrophysiology.

Origin of the Electrical Potential in diffusion systems

Consider the ionic system in fig. 14.14 with 1 M KCl and 1 M NaCl in compartment (i) but 0·1 M KCl and 0·1 M NaCl in compartment (o). The barrier prevents mixing due to density differences and allows the formation of a diffusion zone without turbulence. For the moment any suggestion that it behaves as a selective membrane is not considered. When the cell is filled, Na^+ (mobility of 5·2 μsec/volts/cm) diffuses less rapidly from (i) to (o) than K^+ (mobility 7·6) or Cl^- (mobility 7·9); for an instant, too

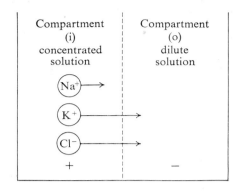

FIG. 14.14. Movements of ions in a diffusion zone.

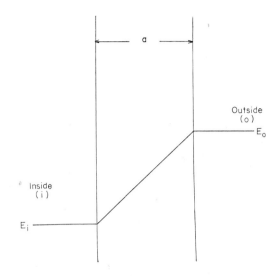

FIG. 14.15. The electrical gradient through a cell membrane.

short for practical measurement, there is an excess of Na^+ in compartment (i) and an excess of Cl^- in compartment (o) giving rise to an electrical potential difference with a finite value across the interface between phases. The potential thus created opposes the movement of negative ions from (i) to (o) and aids the movement of positive ions. The excess of unmatched charge is very small, perhaps of the order of 10^{-12} g ions in each compartment, and so cannot be detected by chemical means; only the electrical effect is observable. At any given concentration of ions in each compartment and allowing free ionic diffusion in water from one compartment to the other a unique diffusion potential $E_i - E_o$ is set up and at any region in the barrier the flux of any diffusing ion is given by equation 15. There is a diffusion rate for each ion from (i) to (o), which is for any ion at any instant a compromise between dC/dx and dE/dx. Such a system runs down in time. Ions diffuse from one compartment to the other until the composition of each is identical and $E_i - E_o$ is zero.

Once the idea of electrochemical potential and its relationship to chemical composition and electrical potential had been realized, it was an elementary step to devise the conditions for ionic equilibrium between phases and so to arrive at the Nernst equation. But is it equally possible using the flux equations to formulate a relationship between the diffusion potential $(E_i - E_o)$ and the concentration of ions in compartments (i) and (o)? This intriguing problem roused the interest of many of the great men of science at the beginning of the twentieth century. Gibbs, Nernst, Planck and Einstein are all associated with attempted solutions, but the fact remains that without some simplifying assumption either about concentration gradients or electrical potential gradient, no answer can be reached.

For electrophysiologists the most useful attempt is the Goldman equation (p. 14.9) published in 1943. This treatment assumes a layer between phases (o) and (i) where diffusion takes place, of width a (fig. 14.15). The

simplifying assumption is that the gradient of electrical potential in this zone is linear, and that

$$\frac{dE}{dx} = \frac{E_i - E_o}{a} \qquad (16)$$

With this assumption it becomes possible to integrate the individual ionic flux equations. For example, for Na^+ the equation

$$J_{Na^+} = -U_{Na^+} RT \frac{d[Na^+]}{dx} - U_{Na^+} CF \frac{E_i - E_o}{a} \qquad (17)$$

can now be integrated. If, as is usual, only the ions K^+, Na^+ and Cl^- are considered, the Goldman equation is obtained. It is now possible to define P, the permeability coefficient precisely. For any ion P has the value URT/a, but as each ion species has a different U value, so it also has a different P value. P is not a permeability constant since in a biological membrane its value may change depending on the value of $E_i - E_o$. The Goldman equation was originally developed for a free diffusion zone. If a system is now considered where the barrier, like the biological membrane, has ionic selective properties, the value of U for any ion may be different depending upon whether the ion is in free solution outside the membrane or in a less well defined solution inside the membrane. But the Goldman integration still applies, although only from one inner surface of the membrane to the other inner surface, and values of $[K^+]$, $[Na^+]$ and $[Cl^-]$ must be those existing just on the insides of the membrane surface (fig. 14.16). These concentrations are not readily available and the Goldman treatment has been modified by Hodgkin and Huxley using the membrane/solvent partition coefficient β for any ion. This is incorporated

Inside (i)	Membrane		Outside (o)
$[K^+]_i \rightleftharpoons [K^+_{membrane}]_i$		$[K^+_{membrane}]_o \rightleftharpoons [K^+]_o$	
$[Na^+]_i \rightleftharpoons [Na^+_{membrane}]_i$		$[Na^+_{membrane}]_o \rightleftharpoons [Na^+]_o$	
$[Cl^-]_i \rightleftharpoons [Cl^-_{membrane}]_i$		$[Cl^-_{membrane}]_o \rightleftharpoons [Cl^-]_o$	

FIG. 14.16. Ionic concentrations within and without the cell membrane. $[K^+_{membrane}]_o = \beta[K^+]_o$, etc, see text.

into the permeability coefficient term. For example, if $[K^+_{membrane}]_o$ is the concentration of K^+ in the membrane at the interface membrane/outside solution, then $[K^+_{membrane}]_o = \beta[K^+]_o$. The permeability coefficient is then modified to $RTU_K{}^+ \beta/a$. With this new value for P the Goldman equation retains its original form for membrane systems, and ionic concentrations are still those inside and outside the cell. This newly defined P may be measured experimentally for some ions, using the measured values for the resting potential and the flux of the radioactive ion across the membrane.

Recently Hogg in Edinburgh has shown that the Goldman equation may be deduced by the kinetic methods introduced by Eyring to the study of reaction rates and later extended to diffusion systems. The significance of Hogg's work is that it shows the equation applies to electrical *PD* gradients across the membrane which are antisymmetrical (fig. 14.17) about a plane at the midpoint

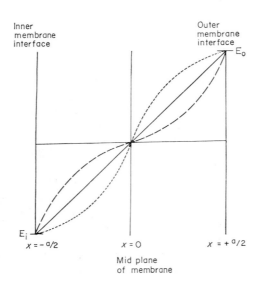

FIG. 14.17. Antisymmetric potential changes about membrane mid plane.

of the membrane. This is theoretically a more satisfying condition than the narrow restriction of a linear potential change across the membrane.

The idea of permeability coefficients is of importance.

Any change in the values of P for a membrane, for any ion, gives a different value of $E_i - E_o$ even without gross changes in the concentrations of ions in either phase.

THEORETICAL SUMMARY

In the previous section it was shown that:

(1) any ion in equilibrium across a membrane obeys the Nernst equation (p. 14.7);

(2) if the system is not in equilibrium but is a diffusion system, the value of the electrical potential across the membrane ($E_i - E_o$) for any set of conditions is given by the Goldman equation (p. 14.9). It was stressed that the permeability coefficient of the membrane (P) to any ion is not constant, but may vary with the value of $E_i - E_o$, e.g. changes in the ionic concentration outside the cell may produce changes in the value of P for any ion. This makes interpretation of experimental data difficult;

(3) changes in the permeability coefficient of any one ion produce changes in the value of $E_i - E_o$ without changes which are detectable by chemical methods in either the internal or external concentrations of that ion. Fig. 14.18 may help in understanding how increases in

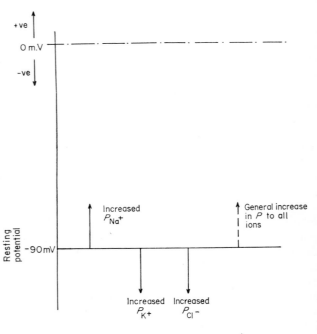

FIG. 14.18. The effect on changes in permeability coefficient on resting potential.

the value of P for the ions Na^+, K^+ and Cl^- affects the value of the transmembrane potential.

The resting potential in the diagram is that for frog sartorious muscle, although the changes are true for other systems. With the normal concentrations of ions outside and inside the cell, an increase in P_{Na^+} makes the resting potential more positive i.e., it moves its value towards zero and may even put it into the positive region. Increases in P_{K^+} and P_{Cl^-} make the resting potential more negative. The changes may be calculated from the Goldman equation. In the case of a general increase in P_{Na^+}, P_{K^+} and P_{Cl^-}, the trend is to make the transmembrane potential less negative (more positive). This is not immediately obvious from the Goldman equation but is an experimental fact. One must assume that the effect of an increase in P_{Na^+} is greater than the combined effects of increasing P_{K^+} and P_{Cl^-}. The summary of information about changes in permeability coefficients in fig. 14.18 is needed to understand the electrophysiology of the action potential, pre- and post-synaptic potentials and the neuromuscular junction.

EVIDENCE FOR ACTIVE TRANSPORT

If either Na^+ or K^+ is in equilibrium, then since $Z = 1$ (p. 14.10) the relationship

$$E_i - E_o = \frac{RT}{F} \ln \frac{[Na^+]_o}{[Na^+]_i} \qquad (18)$$

or

$$E_i - E_o = \frac{RT}{F} \ln \frac{[K^+]_o}{[K^+]_i} \qquad (19)$$

holds. Values for E_i and E_o for squid axon and frog sartorius muscle cells may now be measured directly using Hodgkin–Huxley glass microelectrodes. These consist of thin fine bore glass tubing drawn to sharp, very fine points, about 0·5 μm diameter; this is just below the limit of resolution of the light microscope. These are filled with 3N KCl. Since the mobilities of K^+ and Cl^- are almost the same, there should be no diffusion potential as the microelectrode is at the same potential as the fluid in the region at the electrode tip. The resistance of microelectrodes is very high, at least 10^7 Ω and for accurate measurement the resistance, more widely called the impedance, of the potential measuring instrument must be at least a thousand times greater. Such a device commonly uses a special electrometer valve, which may only be the first stage in an electronic voltmeter, but it is a valve with a specially designed grid which responds to voltage changes but draws only a minute current of the order 10^{-13} amp from the voltage source. It is in fact a high impedance system because from Ohm's law,

$$\frac{V \text{ measured}}{I \text{ taken}} = R \text{ impedance of instrument}$$

Connections from the 3N KCl to the electrometer valve are by Ag wire which has been chlorided and, for this reason, the electrodes are usually called micro silver/silver chloride electrodes. The system is represented schematically in fig. 14.19. In practice the electrometer valve is used as a cathode follower, as this technique allows a more versatile use of the valve and helps decrease

FIG. 14.19 Arrangement for recording from an internal electrode.

its output impedance. Excellent accounts of the basic circuitry of high impedance devices exist, and such instruments are now commercially available. Analysis of the cell contents for larger cells, such as the squid axon or muscle cells, is not difficult so that values for ionic concentrations may be found experimentally. It is therefore feasible to calculate the transmembrane potential which would exist if either the Na^+ or K^+ are in equilibrium. That the system cannot be a simple Donnan one is however immediately obvious without measuring $E_i - E_o$.

If the Nernst equation applies to both Na^+ and K^+, since $E_i - E_o$ is identical for each ion

$$\frac{RT}{F} \ln \frac{[K^+]_o}{[K^+]_i} = \frac{RT}{F} \ln \frac{[Na^+]_o}{[Na^+]_i}$$

or

$$\frac{[K^+]_o}{[K^+]_i} = \frac{[Na^+]_o}{[Na^+]_i}$$

This is the Donnan Equilibrium condition for two positively charged permeable ions in a physical system with two phases (o) and (i), separated by a membrane. This relationship clearly does not hold for those nerve or muscle cells so far studied, and so at least one of the ions Na^+ or K^+ cannot be in equilibrium. To resolve the problem, the Nernst calculated equilibrium value of $E_i - E_o$ must be compared with the measured value. Table 14.1 gives the calculated equilibrium values of $E_i - E_o$ for Na^+ and K^+. As will be seen neither agrees with the measured value of -60 mV (fig. 14.10). In the case of Na^+ the sign of the transmembrane potential for equilibrium is in fact the reverse of that experimentally observed. Neither Na^+ nor K^+ are in equilibrium.

TABLE 14.1. Calculated values for $E_i - E_o$, if K^+ and Na^+ are to be in equilibrium across the squid axon membrane.

	Concentration (mEq/l)		$E_i - E_o$ (mV) required for equilibrium
	Inside cell	Outside cell	
Na^+	50	460	$+58$
K^+	400	10	-89

In ionic diffusion the electrical potential gradient may assist or oppose that of the concentration gradient (p. 14.10). This is well illustrated for Na^+ in the squid axon. For equilibrium the concentration gradient would need to be opposed by a potential gradient of 58 mV with the inside positive relative to the outside. However the electrical potential gradient acts in the same direction as the concentration gradient; (i) is in fact at -60 mV relative to (o) and both gradients assist the diffusion of Na^+ into the axon. There can be no doubt whatever from these measurements that Na^+ diffuses down its electrochemical potential gradient into the squid axon. The case for K^+ requires a little more thought. For equilibrium the concentration gradient would need to be opposed by an electrical gradient such that the inside would be -89 mV relative to the outside. In fact the inside is -60 mV relative to the outside. So although the electrical potential gradient does oppose the chemical potential gradient, it is not sufficiently large to prevent net diffusion of K^+ out of the cell. Again there is no doubt from the experimental data that K^+ continually diffuses down its electrochemical potential gradient from the inside of the cell to the outside. $E_i - E_o$ must therefore be a diffusion potential and its value at any instant is given by the Goldman equation as modified by Hodgkin.

THE ENERGY REQUIREMENT FOR THE RESTING POTENTIAL

It has been suggested that the electrical potential across the cell membrane is a diffusion potential. But diffusion processes run down, unlike the living cell which keeps a constant composition. If there is continuous diffusion of Na^+ into the cell and of K^+ out, and the cell's ionic composition does not change, then there must be an active transporting system in the framework of the membrane which pumps out Na^+ and pumps in K^+. Fig. 14.20 represents such a system, in which a pump compensates for the influx of Na^+ and the efflux of K^+. Such a mechanism working against chemical and electrochemical potential gradients requires energy. Experimentally it has been established that this energy is supplied by the metabolic processes of the cell.

If a cell is poisoned with dinitrophenol (DNP), the formation of ATP is blocked and this decreases the rate at

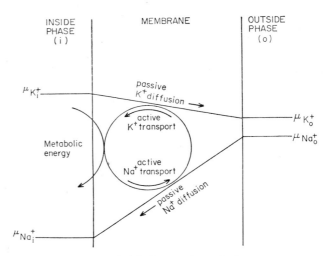

FIG. 14.20. Model of a membrane ionic pump.

which Na^+ is extruded from the interior of the squid axon. An axon can be loaded with ^{24}Na by stimulating it in the radioactive solution; if it is then placed in an extracellular fluid containing no ^{24}Na, the rate at which the labelled Na^+ leaves the axon is easily measured by counting the radioactivity in the extracellular fluid. The addition of DNP markedly decreases the rate at which ^{24}Na is extruded from the axon (fig. 14.21). When the DNP is removed from the medium, sodium is extruded at the original rate, when allowance has been made for the decreasing concentration of ^{24}Na inside the axon. That the reaction $ATP \longrightarrow ADP + \Delta G$ is an essential step in the active extrusion of Na^+ is shown by poisoning an axon with cyanide. Cyanide blocks the oxidative processes

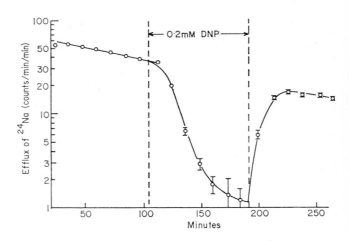

FIG. 14.21. Sodium efflux from a Sepia axon during treatment with dinitrophenol. At the beginning and end of the experiment the axon was in artificial water. Abscissa: time after end of stimulation in ^{24}Na sea water. Ordinate: rate at which ^{24}Na leaves axon. Vertical lines are $\pm 2 \times$ S.E. Temperature 18°C. From Hodgkin (1964).

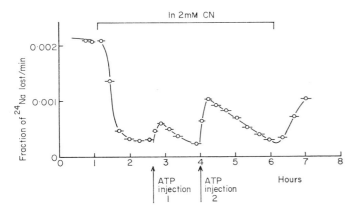

FIG. 14.22. The effect of injecting two different amounts of ATP into an axon poisoned with cyanide; injection 1 raised the ATP concentration in the axon by 1·2 mM and injection 2 by 6·2 mM. From Hodgkin (1964).

necessary for the formation of ATP and the rate of extrusion of Na^+ from the cell drops, but rises again when ATP is injected into the axon (fig. 14.22).

Experiments with ^{42}K have shown that when the cell is poisoned, the influx of K^+ also decreased and this led to the concept of a Na^+/K^+ linked pump. More exact measurements, however, show that in some cells the 1 : 1 ratio between these ions does not hold. The attractive theory that for each Na^+ actively transported out of the cell a K^+ is transported in is an oversimplification. A detailed study of the contribution to the system by Cl^- is needed, but the half life of ^{35}Cl is so short (37 min) that experimental studies are difficult to carry out.

An enzyme which hydrolyses ATP to ADP was first identified in the membranes of red blood corpuscles and is known as **adenosine triphosphatase** or **ATPase**. It is probably present in all cell membranes and is activated by a rise in either $[Na^+]_i$ or $[K^+]_o$, and by Mg^{++} in the presence of Na^+. It is inhibited by digoxin and other cardiac glycosides which inhibit the transport of Na^+ against a gradient. An $(Na^+ + K^+)$ activated ATPase has now been isolated from all tissues in which an active transport of Na^+ and K^+ is known to occur and it is probably responsible for the directional pumping of Na^+ and K^+ in all cells.

While this concept of the ionic state of the cell may be modified in the future, the idea of a diffusion system generating a transmembrane potential and an active transport maintaining a constant ionic cell composition, is likely to persist. As yet, the mechanism cannot be described at a molecular level and presents a fascinating problem in cellular biology; mathematical physics cannot at the moment relate chemical energy changes and the movement of ions across membranes.

The energy required must be provided by metabolic processes that go to make up the resting metabolism. What proportion of the energy utilization by resting man goes to maintain ionic concentrations cannot be calculated.

The nerve impulse

Information is transmitted along nerves by means of a voltage change, which is of uniform shape in unmyelinated nerves. Because the frequency and the velocity at which nervous impulses are transmitted are both limited, the biological method differs in several respects from the methods used in telecommunication. Nevertheless, electrical engineering techniques and theory illustrate some points in the relation between structure and function in the nerve axons. Since the axon consists of an inner conducting medium separated from an outer extracellular conducting medium, it may be compared with the co-axial cable (fig. 14.23) used to join a television aerial to the set. Much time and thought has gone into the designing of cables, which transmit complex voltage wave forms with a minimum voltage loss or distortion.

FIG. 14.23. Comparison of the structure of an axon (a) and a cable (b).

CABLE THEORY

A theoretical model of a co-axial cable is shown in fig. 14.24. Each unit of length (i) of the inner conductor has a resistance r_i. The inner conductor is separated from the outer one by an insulator. No insulator has infinite resistance and the leakage resistance across a unit length is r_m. The two conductors separated by an insulator form a condensor with capacity (C_m). If a square voltage pulse

FIG. 14.24. The electrical properties of a cable.

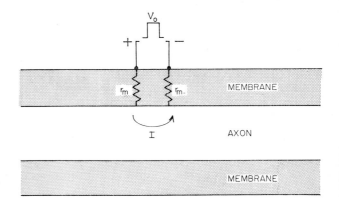

FIG. 14.25. The changes in form in a pulse wave during transmission in a cable.

FIG. 14.26. Diagram showing the current (I) from an external stimulus flowing through the membrane and inside the axon.

(V_0) is injected into the cable at o, the pulse decreases the further along the cable it goes and at points $a, b, \ldots, n$ $V_a, V_b, \ldots, V_n$ become progressively less. The pulse wave also changes its shape and is no longer square, but the rising edge is curved in an exponential manner, as is the falling edge (fig. 14.25). Using the ratio V_0/V_n and the distance required for V_0 to reach V_n, it is possible to calculate values for r_1, r_m and C_m. V_0 decreases exponentially and the distance required for it to fall to $1/e$ ($e = 2.73$) is known as the characteristic length λ and equals $\sqrt{r_m/r_1}$. In the squid axon λ is about 3 mm and so all voltage and current would have disappeared long before the end of the axon, if it behaved as a co-axial cable. Obviously transmission in nerves cannot be explained solely in terms of electrical engineering. For a motor neurone in the spinal cord of an adult man which gives off an axon which reaches the big toe, about one metre away, a different conducting process is necessary.

THE ACTION POTENTIAL

On increasing an electrical stimulus (V_0) to a nerve, it behaves locally as a co-axial cable until the transmembrane potential is increased, i.e. made more positive, by about one-third of its resting value. Then a new mechanism, unknown to electrical engineers, is observed. If a voltage pulse (fig. 14.26) is applied to an axon, current flows from the positive to the negative electrode. Some of this current (I) flowing through the membrane resistance decreases the transmembrane potential, i.e. it depolarizes the membrane. When this current is sufficiently great to change the potential from about -60 mV to -40 mV, a change takes place in the physical properties of the mem-

brane. In the region of stimulation the permeability to sodium (P_{Na^+}) suddenly increases, and Na^+, with their positive charge, cross the membrane into the cell. The number of ions involved is minute and may be as small as 10^{-24} g ions/cm length. This has very little effect on the $[Na^+]$ of the interior of the axon and cannot be detected chemically, but the electrical effect is easily observed. The movement of Na^+ further changes the transmembrane potential until it is reversed, the inside becoming positive relative to the outside (fig. 14.27a). A feed back now operates at the level of the single cell membrane which serves to limit this potential change. Hodgkin and Huxley showed that the voltage change across the membrane caused by the increase in P_{Na^+} induces an increase in P_{K^+} and that an outflow of K^+ restores the transmembrane potential to its pre-excitation value (fig. 14.27b). The movements of ions resulting from these changes in P_{K^+} and P_{Na^+} account for the changes in transmembrane potential across an axon when it is stimulated locally. The local electrical potential rises from -60 mV to about $+20$ mV and back again to -60 mV. This change is called an **action potential** or **spike potential** (fig. 14.28). This transmembrane voltage change is transmitted along the axon in an undistorted form and at a velocity much less than that at which any physical voltage impulse would be passed in a co-axial cable.

Although the experimental technique for depolarizing the membrane may seem artificial, in fact the physiological initiation of a nerve impulse is brought about by such a depolarization. In afferent nerve fibres this arises from

FIG. 14.27. (a) Na^+ entering the axon during the initial rising phase of the action potential, (b) K^+ leaving the axon during the final falling phase.

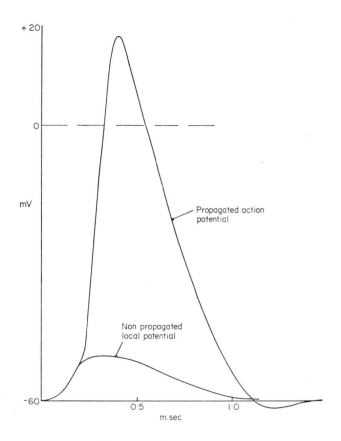

FIG. 14.28. Transmembrane voltage changes measured near the point of stimulation. A subthreshold stimulus produces local changes which are not propagated. A threshold stimulus produces a propagated action potential.

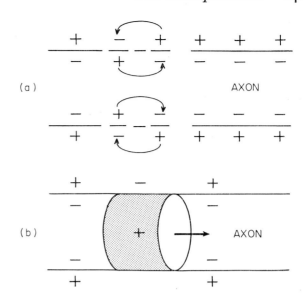

FIG. 14.29. (a) Local currents inside and outside the axon, (b) passage of reversed polarity down the axon.

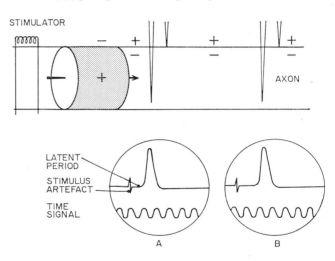

FIG. 14.30. The action potential recorded at two different sites, A and B, on a nerve.

sensory receptor cells, as a result of specific responses to changes in the body's internal or external environments; in efferent fibres the voltage is generated within the motor neurone by the action of the afferent nerves at the synapse (p. 14.26). How this biological voltage change is transmitted must now be considered.

Once a local depolarization of the membrane has taken place, the situation arises where in effect two batteries are joined in series. Local currents flow in the directions shown by the arrows (fig. 14.29a). These local currents passing through the membrane depolarize it in the same manner as does an artificial stimulus. So a region of reversed polarity passes down the axon (fig. 14.29b). The velocity is slow, in terms of physical conduction, being about 15 m/sec; in the squid giant axon in general in un-myelinated axons the velocity of transmission is roughly proportional to the axon diameter. When two pairs of glass microelectrodes are used to measure the transmembrane potential, the action potential can be detected on an oscilloscope as it passes each point (fig. 14.30). The stimulus artefact is a voltage change induced physically in the recording system at the instant of stimulation. On the oscilloscope screen the distance between this artefact and the action potential is a measure of the time it takes for the action potential to reach the recording electrodes. This time, **the latent period** is illustrated for the two sets of electrodes A and B in fig. 14.30. The latent period increases with the distance from the point of stimulation; such observations are used to calculate the velocity of conduction in nerves.

After the passage of the action potential there is a brief period of time, of the order 0·5 msec. during which it is impossible to stimulate the axon. This period is known as the **refractory period**.

THEORY OF THE ACTION POTENTIAL

Confirmation for the theory that the origin of the action potential is a function solely of the interplay between sodium and potassium permeability has been given by Hodgkin and Huxley. Direct measurement of P_{Na^+} and P_{K^+} is not possible in the msec. duration of the nerve impulse. Instead, a new quantity, the **membrane conductance** (g) to these ions, which is more readily measured has been defined on the basis of an empirical model of the membrane. However, Gibbs had already laid the theoretical foundations for such a model.

Equation 15 (p. 14.10) gives the flux for any ion and multiplying by ZF gives the current I carried by that ion

$$I = ZFJ = -URTZF\frac{dC}{dx} - UCZ^2F^2\frac{dE}{dx}$$

and rearranging

$$I \cdot \frac{1}{UCZ^2F^2} = -\frac{RT}{ZF}\frac{1}{C}\frac{dC}{dx} - \frac{dE}{dx} \qquad (18)$$

Integrating from the outside to the inside of the membrane and multiplying by dx, the equation becomes

$$I\int_0^1 \frac{dx}{UCZ^2F^2} = -\frac{RT}{ZF}\int_0^1 \frac{1}{C}\cdot dC - \int_0^1 dE$$

On the right hand side both integrals are readily solved and this gives

$$I\int_0^1 \frac{dx}{UCZ^2F^2} = -\frac{RT}{ZF}\log_e\frac{C_i}{C_o} - (E_i - E_o)$$

or

$$I\int_0^1 \frac{dx}{UCZ^2F^2} = E_{Nernst} - E_{membrane} \qquad (19)$$

where E_{Nernst} is the equilibrium potential for the ion (p. 14.7), and $E_{membrane}$ the cell transmembrane potential. On the right side the expressions are in terms of electrical voltage only, while on the left current is multiplied by an integral, which cannot be immediately evaluated, but by Ohm's Law it must have the dimensions of resistance and $\int_0^1 \frac{dx}{UCZ^2F^2}$ becomes the transmembrane resistance for any ion being considered. Taking Na^+ as an example we may write

$$I_{Na^+}(R_{Na^+}) = E_{Na^+}_{Nernst} - E_{membrane} \qquad (20)$$

Fig. 14.31 gives the electrical analogue to this equation.

The Hodgkin model is based on a number of ionic units of this type (fig. 14.32). For Na^+ the positive pole of the Nernst potential is directed towards the inside of the cell and for K^+ to the outside of the cell. Hodgkin also added another system (L, fig. 14.32) for the flux of ions other than Na^+ and K^+. At the moment little is known about the contribution of these other ions; the most important are Ca^{++}

FIG. 14.31. Electrical analogue for the current flow by Na^+ through the membrane. $E_m = E_{membrane}$.

FIG. 14.32. The Hodgkin model for membrane ionic currents.

and Cl^-, but neither of these alter the conclusions about the interplay between the permeability of Na^+ and K^+. For squid axon in the resting state there can be no net flow of current across the cell membrane, i.e. any current carried into the cell by an ion must be equal and opposite to that carried out of the cell by other ions. It is now necessary to look more closely at the concept of membrane conductance. Equation 20 may be rewritten as

$$I_{Na^+} = \frac{1}{R_{Na^+}}\left(E_{Na^+}_{Nernst} - E_{membrane}\right) \qquad (21)$$

and the quantity $1/R_{Na^+}$ is called the **conductance,** which is the inverse of resistance, and given the symbol g_{Na^+}. Any permeable ion has its own membrane conductance. We have already seen (p. 14.11) that the greater the value of the thermodynamic mobility for any ion the greater the permeability to that ion. Equations 19 and 20 relate g to the thermodynamic mobility as

$$g = \frac{UZ^2F^2}{\int_0^1 dx/C} \qquad (22)$$

During the passage of an action potential the ionic concentration in the membrane does not change appreciably since only 10^{-24} g ions/cm^2 are involved. Therefore any change in ionic mobility (U) is directly proportional to conductance; but permeability is also directly proportional to U (p. 14.11). Therefore during the action potential the behaviour of g reflects changes in P, and hence $P \propto g$.

Experimental studies of the quantity g use the technique known as the **voltage clamp**.

The voltage clamp experiment changes the transmembrane potential along the entire axon to some predetermined value. In theory this can be done as shown in fig. 14.33. A battery of negligible internal resistance and of electrical potential 56 mV is connected suddenly to two lengths of silver wire, extending the full length of the axon internally and externally. The electrical analogue is shown in fig. 14.34 which considers the effect only on Na^+ and K^+. This limitation is justified for squid axon, because only these ions are responsible for the passage of current. Effectively the transmembrane potential has now been set to -56 mV, the EMF of the battery connected to the outside and to the inside of the cell by two electrodes with zero resistance. Fig. 14.34 shows that the problem at a physical level should be a simple demonstration of Kirchoff's Laws. The addition of the extra 56 mV battery gives a new current distribution in the circuit. Apart from current from the recharging of the membrane capacitance (an event which takes place within µsec.) a new current distribution is set up, and if the value of R_{Na^+} and R_{K^+} remain constant, current flows in only one direction and there is no possibility in such a physical analogue of a reversal, at any time, of current flow. However, when an experiment of this kind is applied to a length of squid axon immersed in artificial extracellular fluid the results, as shown in fig. 14.35, suggest that once more physics or physical chemistry cannot be applied in their most elementary form to the biological membrane. Clamping the transmembrane potential at -56 mV certainly shows a µsec fluctuation potential due to the recharging of the membrane capacitance. In fact in most experimental records the time

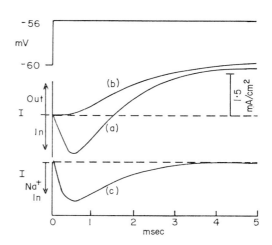

FIG. 14.35. Changes in current following a voltage clamp.

interval is so short relative to the phenomena of interest that the effect is seldom reproduced. Of greater interest (fig. 14.35a) is that for the first 1·5 msec current (I) flows into the cell, reaching a maximal influx at about 0·5 msec, returning to zero, and after 1·5 msec current flows out of the cell the value increasing to a steady 1·5 m.amps/cm² for as long as this particular clamping voltage is applied. Hence the membrane system cannot be a simple physical arrangement as in fig. 14.34. The only possible interpretation is that the values of R_{Na^+} and R_{K^+} are changing during the time course of the experiment. That this is so has been demonstrated by Hodgkin and Huxley. They repeated the experiment using an extracellular fluid with the sodium replaced by choline, an ion impermeable to the membrane, to maintain the osmolality. Fig. 14.35b shows that on applying the clamping voltage there is no inward flow of current, but a slow increase of outflowing current to a similar maximal value after about 3 msec. It was suggested from this experiment that the inward flow of current was caused by Na^+ and the outward flow by K^+, and that subtracting curve (b) from (a) would give the sodium current (c). Experiments of this type allow calculations from I_{Na^+} and I_{K^+} of how the conductance (g) of each ion varies with time. These show that g_{Na^+} increases to reach a maximum at about 0·5 msec and then returns to its original value within 3 msec and that g_{K^+} increases more slowly, reaching a maximum and keeping that value at about 5 msec (fig. 14.36). But if the transmembrane potential is returned to its normal value after 0·6 msec, g_{Na^+} returns almost immediately to its resting value. In such a short time any change in g_{K^+} is not easily measured, but it returns to its original value if the transmembrane potential is restored to normal at 6·3 msec. Thus g_{Na^+} and g_{K^+} are not only functions of transmembrane potential, but also of the time during which such a potential is applied. Hodgkin and Huxley have

FIG. 14.33. Arrangement for a voltage clamp experiment.

FIG. 14.34. Electrical circuit with a voltage clamp.

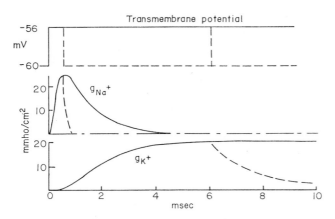

FIG. 14.36. Changes in conductance following a voltage clamp.

FIG. 14.37. Theoretical solution for propagated action potential and conductances at 18·5°C. Total entry of sodium = 4·33 pmole/cm²; total exit of potassium = 4·26 pmole/cm². From Hodgkin and Huxley (1952).

studied the relationships of g_{Na^+} and g_{K^+} with time for a number of clamped transmembrane potentials in the squid axon, and derived a complex equation which describes changes in g_{Na^+} and g_{K^+} once the squid axon is depolarized. An equation has also been derived relating the theoretical change in V against time for the transmembrane potential, if the squid axon is depolarized sufficiently to initiate an action potential. From this the shape and size of the action potential can be calculated, and the velocity of propagation worked out. There is little doubt that the transmission of an action potential is a feed back system involving changes in g_{Na^+} followed by changes in g_{K^+}. The calculated changes of these, and the calculated shape and duration of the transmitted action potential are given in fig. 14.37. The correlation between the calculated properties of the action potential and the observed experimental values is perhaps one of the most outstanding examples of the application of chemical physics to biology. The Na^+/K^+ permeability theory can account for both the origin and transmission of the voltage change, known as the action potential, but this phenomenon cannot yet be explained in molecular terms.

The all or none rule
Provided that the duration of the stimulating pulse is sufficiently long, the propagation of an action potential begins at a critical value of stimulating voltage, below which there is no propagation. Further increase of voltage does not change the shape of the propagated action potential, not does it alter the conduction velocity or the refractory period. The action potential follows an all or none rule, i.e. if the voltage is just sufficient to generate it, the response is maximal and in no way changed by a further increase of the stimulus.

Duration of the action potential
It is of interest to calculate the length of the squid axon occupied by the passage of a single action potential. If the velocity is 15 m/sec and the duration of the impulse is 1 msec, the length of the axon occupied, like that of a train running past the platform of a station will be,

$$\text{velocity} \times \text{duration}$$

which in this case is 1·5 cm. This may seem a surprising length of nerve to be occupied by the action potential, but in human motor nerve axons up to 10 cm may be taken up by the passage of a single action potential.

CONDUCTION IN MYELINATED FIBRES
In these myelin is present in regions round the axon, but the nodes of Ranvier are left unmyelinated (p. 14.4). The result is an interesting compromise between the biological mechanism of transmission and that of the co-axial cable. The thick myelin sheath increases the transmembrane resistance and decreases the transmembrane capacitance so that the myelinated regions of an axon behave as a co-axial cable (fig. 14.38). At a node transmission takes place as already described in the unmyelinated squid axon. When an action potential is generated at one node, then local currents tend to flow at the next node and depolarize it. The action potentials thus jump from one node to the next, i.e. **saltatory conduction**. However, between nodes the nerve behaves as a co-axial conductor and the velocity of conduction approximates to that of engineered cable.

The shape and size of the action potential between the nodes follows physical laws and is attenuated, i.e. the height decreases and the shape is distorted, but the voltage change at each node remains sufficient to bring about the same change in membrane ionic permeability to regenerate the action potential. Conduction in myelinated nerves is not unlike transmission in a transatlantic cable, containing amplifiers sunk at intervals so that they can restore the shape and form of the impulses before there is serious attenuation.

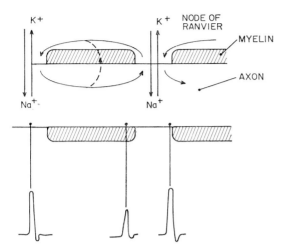

FIG. 14.38. Saltatory conduction. An action potential at a node causes a local current to flow down the interior of the axon. A small part of this current leaks through the myelin and the potential is alternated. Sufficient current reaches the next node to depolarize it and so regenerate the full action potential.

EXTERNAL RECORDING OF THE ACTION POTENTIAL

It is possible to use intracellular microelectrodes to study transmission only in large nerve axons. In most nerves the action potential can be recorded only by placing silver electrodes on the surface of the axon. Fig. 14.39 shows the electrical events, recorded at external electrodes, as the action potential passes down an axon. Such a record is a diphasic action potential. In practice it is difficult to obtain the symmetry suggested in the figure because the zone of altered polarity may overlap both recording electrodes. A better record is obtained if the axon membrane is crushed between the electrodes, thereby destroying the membrane, but keeping the electrical continuity of the axoplasm (fig. 14.39 f). Then only the first phase of the action potential is recorded, because the zone of altered polarity cannot reach the second electrode. Conventionally the direction in which the oscilloscope beam is displaced is reversed when recording the external monophasic action potential. This record must not be confused with that recorded from internal electrodes. In these, as we have seen, the potential changes from about -60 mV to about $+20$ mV and returns to the original value, i.e. it is positive going. With external recording the potential changes from o mV to a negative value, the size of which depends on the geometry of the axon, and back to o mV, i.e. it is negative going.

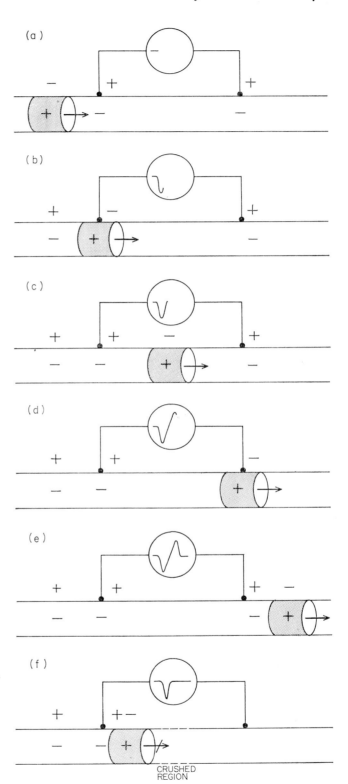

FIG. 14.39 (a–e). The electrical events recorded by surface electrodes as an impulse passes down an axon; (f) the effect of crushing the axon.

The technique of recording externally from single axons has been widely used with fibres carefully dissected from mixed nerves.

EXTERNALLY RECORDED ACTION POTENTIALS FROM MIXED NERVES

Fig. 14.40 shows a record obtained by stimulating a frog sciatic nerve with a gradually increasing stimulus. The record is a summation of a number of responses from different axons. With a small stimulus only a few of the large axons respond. With increasing stimulus more and more of the large fibres respond until a maximum is reached (e) and further small increases (f and g) produce no change in the size or shape of the response. This is because more and more of the large fibres conduct until all become active. Only a much larger increase in stimulus excites the smaller fibres.

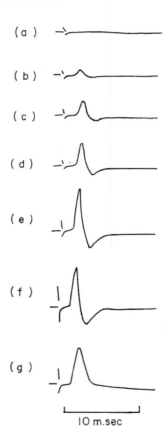

FIG. 14.40. Response of frog sciatic nerve to gradually increasing strength of stimulus. From Bures, Petran & Zachar (1967). *Electrophysiological Methods in Biological Research.* New York: Academic Press.

The speed of conduction of the impulse depends on the diameter of the fibre, being slowest in the small ones (fig. 14.41). Hence the electrical changes produced in the small fibres reach the recording electrodes after those produced in the large fibres. The result is a **compound action potential** (fig. 14.42) in which three distinct peaks may be seen.

FIG. 14.41. The separation of the action potential of fibres of different size.

FIG. 14.42. A Compound action potential recorded from frog sciatic nerve, showing the α, β and γ components of the A wave. Time scale 5 msec. From Bures, Petran & Zachar.

Fibre size and speed of conduction

A large nerve bundle contains fibres which vary in diameter from < 1 to 22 μm. For mammalian medullated fibres at 37°C the speed of conduction in m/sec is approximately 6 times the diameter measured in μm. Both fibre size and speed of conduction are used to classify nerve fibres.

The compound action potential shows three waves A, B, C. The major A wave is the contribution of the large rapidly-conducting fibres and these include the ordinary motor neurone fibres running to muscle. Conduction rates range from 15 to 120 m/sec in this group, which is further subdivided into α, β and γ fibres. The γ fibres are the smallest and slowest conducting fibres running to striated muscle.

The B wave arises from fibres with a speed of 3–15 m/sec and are efferent preganglionic sympathetic fibres. C fibres are unmyelinated and conduct slowly at 0·5–1 m/sec.

Experimentally it is difficult to demonstrate the existence of the B and C waves in student practical classes. Large stimulating voltages are required because of their small size and a logarithmic time base display is needed because of their slow conduction.

A different classification, which depends on fibre diameter, and not on conduction velocity is generally used for sensory fibres. Fibres of different size usually carry information from different sources (table 14.2).

TABLE 14.2. The classification of sensory fibres.

Group	Diameter (μm)	From
I	12–20	Muscle spindles and Golgi tendon organs
II	8–9	Skin; some fibres from muscle spindles
III	3–4	Various sources
IV	1·5	Various sources

RELATIVE AND ABSOLUTE REFRACTORY PERIOD

If a frog sciatic nerve preparation is stimulated twice then provided the time interval between stimuli is sufficiently great, two identical action potentials are recorded (fig. 14.43a). If the time interval is then decreased in stages, the stimulus strength being kept constant, the height of the second action potential starts to fall (b). The

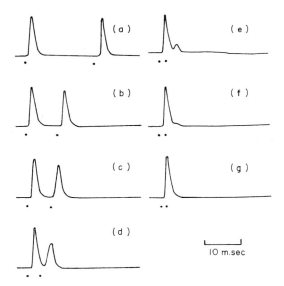

FIG. 14.43. The responses of a frog sciatic nerve to two identical stimuli separated by a decreasing interval of time (a–g). The spike amplitude from the second stimulus declines as the interval between the two stimuli is reduced. A measure of the absolute refractory period is provided by (g). From Bures, Petran & Zachar.

time between the stimuli at this point is the **relative refractory period**, and as the time interval is further decreased, the height continues to fall (c–f) and eventually disappears (g). At this point the second stimulus is said to fall within the **absolute refractory period.** During the absolute refractory period no increase in stimulus can produce a second action potential, but during the relative refractory period the size of the second action potential may be restored by increasing the strength of the second stimulus.

TRANSMISSION OF EXCITATION FROM CELL TO CELL

The electron microscope has shown that in vertebrates there appears to be no direct continuity between the end of an axon and another nerve cell or cell of an effector organ such as muscle. The cytoplasm of the axon and of the excitable tissue to which the impulse is transmitted are each enclosed within its own membrane and these are separated by a space. The nerve impulse has to cross this gap, and if, as seems likely, the electrical resistance and capacities of the junctional membrane and intercellular space possess the same properties as the nerve fibres, the axon potential cannot cross it directly and depolarize the post junctional tissue. The discontinuity of the junction is overcome by the liberation of a chemical substance which crosses the gap between the cells and stimulates or inhibits the next cell. This it does by altering the membrane permeability of the cell so as to set up or inhibit another potential, which in turn is transmitted onwards. The first example of chemical transmission was provided by the experiments of Otto Loewi in 1920. The heart is slowed by stimulating the vagus nerve and Loewi showed that if this is done with the heart of a frog, perfusion of the blood from this heart through the heart of a second frog causes it also to be slowed. He concluded that vagal stimulation liberated a substance, 'vagusstoffe', which affected the excitability of cardiac muscle. It is now known that this substance is **acetylcholine.** The drug atropine causes the heart to beat faster. It does this by interfering with the action of acetylcholine at the nerve-muscle junction.

The heart is innervated by a second group of nerves which accelerate it, the sympathetic nerves p. 24.89. Loewi showed that a similar 'accelerator substance' was liberated by sympathetic nerve stimulation. The similarity between the effect of sympathetic nerve stimulation and the actions of adrenaline, called by Cannon sympathin, had already been pointed out by Langley and Eliot at the turn of the twentieth century, and it is now clear that the accelerator substance is **noradrenaline**, a close derivative of adrenaline.

Neuromuscular transmission

THE STRUCTURE OF THE NEUROMUSCULAR JUNCTION

Somatic efferent nerve fibres end upon the surfaces of skeletal muscle cells to form **end plates.** The neurones giving rise to these nerve fibres are the motor cells of the ventral horn of the spinal cord and of the cranial nerve nuclei (p. 24.24). A nerve fibre reaching a muscle enters the perimysium of the muscle before it terminates by bifurcating several times, each bifurcation occurring at a node of Ranvier. By this means, each motor neurone may innervate a number of muscle fibres which collectively form a motor unit (p. 15.8).

When the terminal branch of a motor nerve fibre reaches the muscle cell, it loses its myelin sheath and the axon expands on to the surface of the muscle in the form of a number of terminal arborizations to form the **motor end plate** (figs. 14.44–14.46). At the end plate these short

FIG. 14.44. Drawing of a silver stained motor end plate from the rat. Note the terminal arborization of the axon and the accumulation of nuclei in this region.

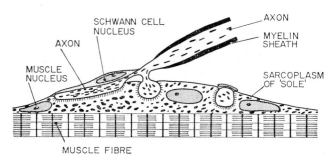

FIG. 14.45. Representation of a motor end plate as seen in longitudinal section. The terminal nerve branches lie in synaptic gutters in which the plasma membrane of the sarcolemma is thrown into folds. In the muscle fibre there is an accumulation of sarcoplasm, the sole, that contains many mitochondria and muscle cell nuclei. Modified after Couteaux (1960).

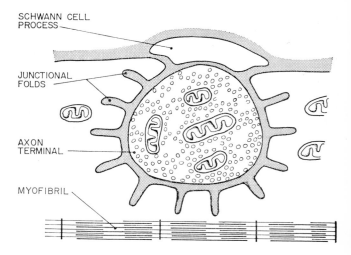

FIG. 14.46. Diagram of portion of a motor end plate to show the axon terminal lying within the synaptic gutter. The sarcolemma, which forms the junctional folds, is separated from the axon terminal by a distance of 50 nm.

terminal branches lie in finger-like **synaptic gutters,** and there they are covered by thin extensions of the last Schwann cell. At the bottoms of these synaptic gutters, the sarcolemma or plasma membrane of the muscle cell is thrown into a series of folds, the junctional folds, which run at right angles to the terminal branch of the nerve; these branch in such a way that when viewed from above they appear as a finger print. The sarcolemma at the tops of these folds is separated from the plasma membrane of the axon terminal by a distance of about 50 nm, and in the interval between the two plasma membranes there is an ill defined layer, about 20 nm thick, that probably represents the fused basement membranes of the muscle cell and axon (figs. 14.45 and 46).

The region of a muscle cell which receives the end of a nerve is called the sole. This is an elevation of muscle fibre characterized by an accumulation of sacroplasm containing numerous mitochondria and nuclei.

TRANSMISSION AT THE NEUROMUSCULAR JUNCTION

In those regions of the axon which lie in close proximity to the muscle cell there are many vesicles (fig. 14.45). These vesicles have been shown to contain acetylcholine. Current theory is that the action potential which is transmitted down each of the branches of the axon liberates the acetyl choline from the vesicles. When the nerve ending is depolarized, this **transmitter substance** diffuses or is transported across the gap between it and the muscle cell. The acetylcholine appears to act at specific receptor sites in the muscle membrane at the end plate, causing an increase in permeability to Na^+ and K^+ simultaneously and to other cations. The ionic movements resulting from the permeability increase cause the membrane potential in the end plate to become more positive (depolarized). An end plate potential (EPP) is set up and local currents flow, which are sufficient to depolarize the nearby muscle cell membrane to a point where the membrane permeability to Na^+ increases markedly; and at this region an action potential originates in the muscle cell and is generated by the processes previously described for the nerve axon. The duration of the action potential is longer and in skeletal muscle may be as much as 5 msec.

Experimental evidence

The classical preparation is the frog sartorius muscle with its attached nerve, but mammalian tissues have also been used. The transmission of the impulse across the neuromuscular junction can be shown by placing a microelectrode between the nerve and the muscle at the point of junction. The potential generated in the nerve as the impulse arrives at the junction is distinct from the action potential in the post junctional tissue which occurs 0.8 msec later. This delay indicates electrical discontinuity and strongly favours the idea of non electrical transmission.

That the acetylcholine comes from the nerve and not as a result of the muscle contraction can be shown by adding eserine and curare to a nerve muscle preparation. Eserine, the active principle of the Calabar bean and used as an ordeal poison in West Africa, competitively inhibits the enzyme responsible for the destruction of acetylcholine (p. 14.28). When the nerve is stimulated increasing amounts of acetylcholine can be detected in the perfusate. Curare is used as an arrow poison by Peruvian Indians and has the effect of paralysing the man or animal injured by the arrow. If the nerve of a curarized muscle-nerve preparation is stimulated, the muscle does not contract, but acetylcholine appears in the perfusate in amounts similar to those when contraction occurs.

That acetylcholine acts only on the end plate can be shown by applying it by a micropipette to the postsynaptic junction of a neuromuscular junction. Very small amounts (10^{-15} mole) of acetylcholine are able to excite a muscle fibre if applied directly on an end plate. Movement of the pipette a fraction of a millimetre or so to the surface of the muscle results in failure to induce a response.

THE SPREAD OF THE IMPULSE IN MUSCLE

When an end plate potential reaches a sufficient level, it generates an action potential which spreads through the muscle fibre in a manner similar to the spread in a nerve fibre. There is a resting potential with the inside of the cell negative compared to the surface and the potential is due to the passage of Na^+ into the cell from the extracellular fluid. The shape of the action potential depends on the nature and position of the recording electrodes. In muscle it travels at a rate of several m/sec and is able to activate the contractile apparatus within the cell. In animals it is possible to record from intracellular electrodes as with the squid axon. It is also possible to record the electrical activity of human muscles.

The electromyogram can be obtained using an electrode about the size of a hypodermic needle which is inserted through the skin into the belly of the muscle; the electrode is insulated except at the tip. Recordings can also be made using surface electrodes on the skin. The activity so recorded comes in each case from many fibres, often composing several motor units (p. 15.8) whose nerve fibres may not be firing synchronously; hence it is not a precise record of the activity in any one fibre. There is little electrical activity from a resting muscle, although spontaneous random discharges may occur, but a burst of discharges arises whenever a muscle contracts voluntarily. Electromyography has a limited clinical application in the investigation of certain diseases of muscle and motor neurones. If simultaneous records can be made from several groups of muscles, these can be used to analyse the muscles employed and their timing in a complex movement. Golfers have had their swings studied in this way.

SMOOTH MUSCLE AND OTHER TISSUES

There is little information available about the terminations of visceral motor fibres that innervate cardiac muscle, smooth muscle and glandular tissue. Their nerve fibres form plexuses within the viscera and there are dilations of the nerve fibres that contain vesicles but do not form synaptic junctions with the surrounding cells; the chemical transmitter is discharged into the surrounding extracellular space.

The electrical activity of smooth muscle varies greatly from time to time and from tissue to tissue. Spikes of potential can be recorded from the gut, but here and in other sites the potential changes are small and represent only partial depolarization. Stretching a smooth muscle depolarizes the membrane and may cause firing and subsequent contraction.

Smooth muscle may continue to function after it has been separated from its nerve supply. After the nerves to a skeletal muscle have been cut, the muscle is completely paralysed and is flaccid. Smooth muscle after section of the nerves may still contract and show electrical activity. The nerves regulate rather than initiate activity. Many smooth muscles have a double nerve supply, receiving one set of fibres which release acetylcholine and another set which release noradrenaline. These oppose each other, one being excitatory and the other inhibitory, but their roles in this respect differ in different parts of the body. Both the spontaneous activity of smooth muscle and the responses to nervous stimulation may be modified greatly by hormones and this is most marked in the case of uterine muscle.

Transmission in the nervous system

THE STRUCTURE OF THE SYNAPSE

Synapses are places of contact between two neurones at which an impulse is transmitted from one neurone to another. Knowledge of these structures has been increased by EM studies, for almost all that can be seen with the light microscope is the expansion of an axon into a terminal bouton (fig. 14.47). Any axon, by branching, may give rise to a large number of terminals and the transmission of an impulse at a synapse can occur only in one direction. In all cases, a bouton is the presynaptic component, but the postsynaptic side of a synapse may be formed by any part of the surface of a second neurone. Usually the postsynaptic component is a dendrite (axodendritic synapse) but it may be a perikaryon (axosomatic synapse), or even the surface of another axon (axoaxonic synapse). The number of synapses on the surface of a neurone is roughly proportional to the area of the receptor surface, i.e. the area of the dendrites and perikaryon. While each of the synapses may be formed by the axons of quite different neurones, there is evidence that an individual axon may form a number of synapses upon the surface of the same cell. A ventral horn cell within the spinal cord may have as many as 30,000 synapses upon its surface and these cover almost all the surface of the cell.

In synapses in mammalian central nervous tissue the EM shows that the plasma membrane of the presynaptic axon terminal is separated from the postsynaptic component by a cleft of about 20 nm (fig. 14.47). At these sites of apposition, the two plasma membranes possess an accumulation of electron dense material on their cytoplasmic surfaces and this material may either be symmetrically disposed, or more prominent on the postsynaptic side. Within the presynaptic bouton, there are vesicles, 20–50 nm in diameter. These are the synaptic vesicles and in addition there is often a collection of mitochondria. The synaptic vesicles tend to accumulate against the electron dense material of the presynaptic membrane and it is now generally believed that they contain the chemical mediator for synaptic transmission. The vesicles are thought to discharge their contents into the cleft between the pre- and postsynaptic membranes (fig. 14.47b).

SYNAPTIC FUNCTION

The work of Sherrington on the properties of reflexes in the nervous system (p. 24.8) showed that impulses from peripheral receptors on reaching the synaptic junctions with motor neurones responsible for movement produced both excitatory and inhibitory effects. These effects could be added or subtracted quantitatively at the synapses and they could persist or be stored for a definite, though brief, period of time. Sherrington postulated the existence of a central excitatory state and a central in-

PRESYNAPTIC AXON TERMINAL

SYNAPSE

POST SYNAPTIC MEMBRANE

(a)

SYNAPTIC VESICLES

(b)

20nm CLEFT

Fig. 14.47. Generalized diagram of a synapse within the central nervous system. (a) shows the pre-synaptic axon terminal with its content of synaptic vesicles and accumulation of electron-dense material at the synaptic junction, (b) is a higher power of the synaptic region to show the 20 nm cleft and two synaptic vesicles bursting into the cleft.

hibitory state which could be produced at the synapses and it was the relationship between these two states, graded by the incoming stimuli, that determined motor activity. At that time it was impossible to study directly events at the synapse. However, the techniques used for studying the electrical properties of the squid axon have now been developed for use in the central nervous system; thus a microelectrode can be inserted into the interior of a single motor neurone in the spinal cord of a cat and the electrical effects in the neurone correlated with the reflex effects.

Excitatory postsynaptic potential (EPSP)

A microelectrode impaled in a motor neurone in the spinal cord can record the changes of potential within the cell when the neurone is stimulated through an excitatory afferent nerve. After a short latent period (0·5 to 1·0 msec), the potential rises from a resting level of -70 mV to as much as $+30$ mV, the size of the rise being dependent on the strength of the afferent stimulus (fig. 14.48). This EPSP is a depolarization analogous to the end plate potential (EPP) in the neuromuscular junction and it is probably associated with the same ionic movements. There is a critical rise, about 10 to 18 mV, above which a sharp secondary rise, the axon spike, occurs (fig. 14.48c); this is due to the initiation of an impulse in the axon hillock, the most excitable part of the neurone, from which the impulse leaves to travel down the motor nerve.

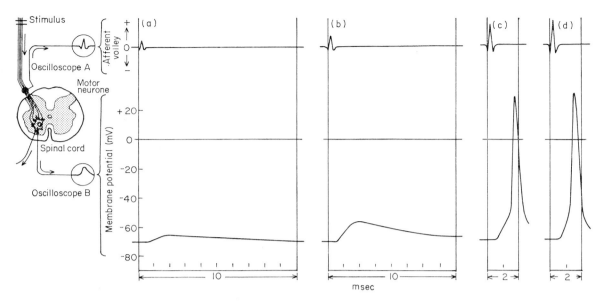

FIG. 14.48. Excitation of a motor neurone is studied by stimulating the sensory fibres that send impulses to it. The size of the afferent volleys reaching the motor neurone is displayed on oscilloscope A. A microelectrode implanted in the motor neurone measures the EPSP which appears on oscilloscope B. The size of the afferent volley is proportional to the number of fibres stimulated to fire. It is assumed that one to four fibres can be activated. When only one fibre is activated (a) the potential inside the motor neurone shifts only slightly. When two fibres are activated (b) the shift is somewhat greater. When three fibres are activated (c) the potential reaches the threshold at which depolarization proceeds swiftly and a spike appears on oscilloscope B. The spike signifies that the motor neurone has generated a nerve impulse of its own. When four or more fibres are activated (d) the motor neurone reaches the threshold more quickly. From Eccles, J.C. (1965). *Scientific American* reprint No. 1001.

There are probably over one thousand axon terminals synapsing on the dendrites of a single motor neurone. Many of these may be a long distance, as far as 1 mm away from the main axon hillock. How a small EPSP generated at a distant dendrite is able to reach the axon hillock without being attenuated to such an extent that it is no longer capable of excitation is an unresolved problem.

Inhibitory postsynaptic potential (IPSP)
The stimulation of afferent nerve fibres which inhibit reflexly muscle movement produces a hyperpolarization of the membrane of the motor neurone. This increase in potential is called the inhibitory postsynaptic potential. IPSP subtracts from EPSP and makes it harder for the latter to reach a level sufficient to make the neurone fire. If anions, especially Cl⁻, are injected by ionophoresis into the neurone from which the record is being obtained, they have a marked effect on the IPSP, reducing it or even reversing it. It is probable that the IPSP acts by making the cell membrane more permeable to Cl⁻; these then enter the cell from the extracellular space and make the interior more negative. Fig. 14.49a shows a normal IPSP converted into a false EPSP by the injection of Cl⁻ into the neurone. Fig. 14.49b shows the injection of Cl⁻ has no effect on the depolarization of a normal EPSP.

It is not possible to account for all the effects of an inhibitory stimulus in terms of IPSP. There is an additional **presynaptic inhibitory action,** in which nerves carrying inhibitory impulses can synapse on the axon terminal of nerves carrying excitatory impulses. Stimulation of

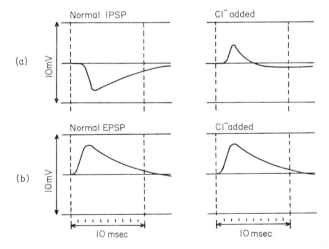

FIG. 14.49. Recording of (a) inhibitory postsynaptic potential (IPSP) and (b) excitatory postsynaptic potential (EPSP) from a motor neurone. The effect of altering the internal Cl⁻ is shown. From Eccles, J.C. (1965) *Scientific American*, reprint No. 1001.

inhibitory nerves reduces the presynaptic potential in the axon and may lower this sufficiently to prevent the axon firing the motor neurone.

Motor neurones may also inhibit themselves by a feed back mechanism involving cells with very short axons which lie adjacent to them in the grey matter of the spinal cord, **Renshaw cells**, (fig. 14.50). Shortly after leaving the

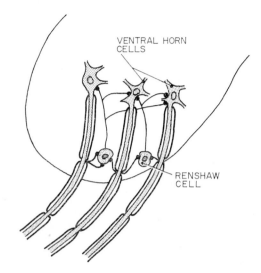

FIG. 14.50. Feedback inhibition through Renshaw cells in the ventral horn of the spinal cord.

axon hillock, the axon of the motor nerve sends off short branches which synapse with the Renshaw cell. When this cell fires, it inhibits the original motor neurone and also adjacent ones. Similar local inhibitory circuits exist in the cerebellum and in the motor cortex.

EPSP, IPSP and the other inhibitory processes can explain how a motor neurone either fires or does not fire in response to the arrival of a large variety of afferent impulses. How the electrical change is able to cross the synaptic gap remains to be discussed.

CHEMICAL MEDIATORS IN THE NERVOUS SYSTEM
There is a close similarity between the structure of axon terminals at a synapse and at a neuromuscular junction in skeletal muscles where chemical transmission by acetyl-choline is known to occur.

Direct evidence of chemical transmission between two nerve cells has been obtained by stimulating a nerve going to a sympathetic ganglion, i.e. the **preganglionic fibre**. Acetylcholine has been detected in the perfusate from the ganglion and this substance has been shown to be capable of stimulating the nerve cell in the ganglion and so the axon leaving it, i.e. the **postganglionic fibre**, either when injected or applied to it. Nerves which secrete acetyl-choline at the axon terminals are called **cholinergic nerves**. Postganglionic nerves which arise from autonomic ganglia secrete either acetylcholine or noradrenaline; in the latter case they are called **adrenergic nerves**. With a few important exceptions adrenergic nerves constitute the efferent nerves of the **sympathetic system** while cholin-ergic nerves constitute the efferent nerves of another part of the autonomic nervous system the **parasympathetic system**. Anatomical and physiological features of these two parts of the autonomic nervous system are described on pp. 19.12, 20.39 and 24.88.

Acetylcholine is synthesized by choline acetyl transferase (acetylase) from choline and acetyl CoA.

$$\text{Acetate} \longrightarrow \underset{\text{Acetyl CoA}}{\overset{\text{CoA}}{\diagdown}} \underset{\text{Choline}}{\overset{\text{Acetylcholine}}{\diagup}}$$

The enzyme is present in neurones whose axons liberate acetylcholine. It is manufactured in the cell bodies and is carried down the axon. When a cholinergic nerve fibre is cut the enzyme is detectable at the cut end while the cell body becomes depleted. Acetylcholine is manufactured throughout the neurone but especially at nerve endings and is rapidly replaced as it is secreted. The choline is continuously absorbed from the extracellular fluid by nerve endings and when sympathetic ganglia are suspended in a medium free of choline they soon become depleted of acetylcholine. The vesicles in the prejunctional nerve endings visible under the EM contain physiologically inactive acetylcholine.

Small amounts of acetylcholine are released from nerve endings even at rest. This is shown by the existence in resting muscle of spontaneous minute EPPs which occur about one/sec. and do not fully depolarise the post-junctional membrane. When a nerve impulse reaches the prejunctional nerve terminal a large increase in the secretory rate occurs. By comparing the responses of acetylcholine applied to an end plate by ionophoresis it can be calculated that acetylcholine is released in quanta or packets containing thousands of molecules at a time.

Acetylcholine release is associated with the migration of Ca^{++} into the cytoplasm of the nerve terminal and the amount released is proportional to the concentration of Ca^{++} in the ECF. Magnesium ions have an effect oppo-site to Ca^{++}; increasing the Mg^{++} in the ECF depresses acetylcholine secretion.

Acetylcholine must be rapidly removed from the myo-neural or synaptic junction if repolarization is to take place and an enzymatic mechanism to carry this out was postulated by Dale in 1914. Acetylcholine is hydrolysed extremely quickly by one of a series of enzymes called cholinesterases. Cholinesterases are found in red cells, nervous tissue and striated muscle and are responsible for the destruction of acetylcholine.

Noradrenaline is synthesized in adrenergic nerves from phenylalanine and tyrosine as described on p.11.25 the final stage involving the methylation of adrenaline by phenyl ethanolamine N methyltransferase. The phenylalanine and tyrosine are taken up by the nerve cell from the ECF. Noradrenaline-containing granules are visible microscopically in nerve fibres and their terminals. Section of nerve cell from its axon causes the noradrenaline to disappear from the severed axon. Stimulation of the post-ganglionic adrenergic nerve by e.g. acetylcholine causes a rapid release of noradrenaline which must be rapidly replaced since the nerve content of noradrenaline is not reduced. The process of release causes increased synthesis and some of the released noradrenaline is taken back into the terminal nerve fibres.

Noradrenaline is disposed of by two enzymes which are found widely distributed in many tissues of the body. These are catechol O methyltransferase (COMT) and monoamineoxidase (MAO). COMT catalyses the transfer of methyl groups to the meta OH group of noradrenaline to form normetadrenaline (p. 25.30), and MAO oxidizes the amine to 3·4 dehydroxyvandelic acid. It is also conjugated in the liver (p. 31.14).

Chemical mediators in the central nervous system
Chemical mediators for synaptic transmission in the brain are much less well defined than in the peripheral autonomic ganglia and are discussed on p. 24.87.

FURTHER READING

COUTEAUX R. (1960) The motor end plate, in *Structure and Function of Muscle* (Ed. Bourne), vol. 1, pp. 337–80. New York: Academic Press.

CAJAL S.R. (1911) *Histologie du Systeme Nerveux de l'Homme et des Vertebres*. Paris: A Maloine.

ECCLES J.C. (1965) *Scientific American* Reprint No. 1001.

HODGKIN A.L. (1964) *The Conduction of the Nerve Impulse*. Liverpool: Liverpool University Press.

HYDEN H. (1960) *The neuron in the Cell* (Ed. Brachet J. and Mirscky A.E.), pp. 215–323. New York: Academic Press.

KATZ B. (1966) *Nerve, Muscle, and Synapse*. New York: McGraw-Hill.

WHITTAKER V.P. & GRAY E.G. (1962) The synapse: biology and morphology, *Brit. med. Bull.* **18**, 223–8.

Chapter 15
The contracting tissues

Apart from trivial movements due to cilia and flagellae, all motion in and of the body is the result of contraction in muscle cells. The finger movements of a violinist, the punch of a boxer, the beat of the heart, the expulsion of a foetus and the constriction and dilatation of the pupil of the eye illustrate the variety of these movements. Muscular tissues must be capable of contractions which are variable in speed, power and extent. Some of these tissues are under somatic nervous control and others are controlled by the autonomic nervous system or circulating hormones. Some normally contract only when stimulated by their nerve, while others have an inherent rhythmic contraction but this can be modified by external influences. These different contractile functions and methods of control are associated with differences in the structure of muscular tissues. The main differences lie in the shape, size and content of the muscle cells themselves. For reasons explained later, some muscle cells appear **striated** in the light microscope and others are **non-striated or smooth.**

In most mammals, including man, skeletal muscle makes up about half the body weight, contains more than half the body water and has an extracellular fluid content which is about one and a half times the volume of the blood plasma. When mild exercise is taken, such as walking at 4 miles/hr, the oxygen consumption can increase to between five and six times the basal level. Thus the pattern of energy metabolism in the body is determined almost entirely by skeletal muscle.

STRUCTURE OF MUSCLE

It is useful to classify muscle, histologically, into three types:

SKELETAL (SOMATIC) VOLUNTARY STRIATED MUSCLE (fig. 15.1a)
The cross-striated cells are very long, up to 10 cm. Some run from the origin of a muscle to its insertion. The diameter of these cylindrical cells is from 30–60 μm, and each contains thousands of nuclei, which usually lie near the surface of the cell. Each cell receives, near its centre,

the termination of a spinal or cranial nerve fibre. At the site of the nerve ending, the muscle cell and the nerve combine to produce a complex structure, the myoneural junction or motor end plate (p. 14.24).

CARDIAC INVOLUNTARY STRIATED MUSCLE (fig. 15.1b)
These cells are much shorter than in skeletal muscle. They do not exceed 100 μm in length. They have an irregular shape and are often branched. Individual cells stick to their neighbours and so the whole muscle consists of a network. The points of adhesion between adjacent cells can be recognized as transverse dark lines called intercalated discs. The cross striations are similar to those in skeletal muscle, but there are only two to eight nuclei in each cell and these are near the centre.

Each of these cells has its own inherent rhythm but, since they are all joined together, the cell with the most rapid rhythm drives all the others. After an impulse has been produced, it spreads over the intercalated discs to affect the whole muscle. The fastest cells are usually located in the sinu-atrial node (p. 28.9), but all the other cells are capable of driving the heart at slower rates, if the nodal cells are ineffective.

SMOOTH (VISCERAL) INVOLUNTARY NON-STRIATED MUSCLE (fig. 15.1c)
These non-striated spindle-shaped cells are narrower than either of the other types. Usually they are about 200 μm long and less than 10 μm in diameter; in the pregnant uterus (p. 37.48) they increase to at least twice this normal size. One long ovoid nucleus occupies the middle of each cell.

All the smooth muscles are under the control of the autonomic nervous system, but the degree of control varies greatly. Some smooth muscle, like that in the pupil or the wall of the ductus deferens, is richly supplied with sympathetic and parasympathetic nerves, while other smooth muscle, e.g. in the intestinal wall, resembles cardiac muscle in having an inherent rhythm which is only modulated by its motor nerve supply. Smooth muscle is stimulated to contract by being stretched and this property accounts for much of its activity.

FIG. 15.1. Three types of muscle (a) skeletal; (b) cardiac; (c) smooth.

Muscular tissue also includes the connective tissues, lymphatic and blood vessels, motor nerves to the muscle and to the vessels, and sensory nerves from receptors in the muscle (pp. 14.24 and 24.13). The macroscopic arrangement of muscular tissues is described on p. 19.11 As the cells are always elongated, they are often called muscle fibres, but this term is confusing as it may be applied not to a single cell or line of cells, but also to the bundles of cells which can be seen with the naked eye. Also, in muscle the word fibre refers to a living cell while, in the connective tissues, it means the extracellular components which give the connective tissues their properties.

The muscle cell

It is convenient to consider the design of a general muscle cell, which includes the features found in all histological types of muscle. It has many of the features of the typical cell (chap. 13) but it has been adapted for the conversion of chemical energy into a contractile force. The cell is always elongated in the line of contraction and it is surrounded by an excitable membrane known as the **sarcolemma** (plate 15.1, facing p. 11.15). The cytoplasm has the special name of **sarcoplasm**; it possesses all the normal elements of cytoplasm (p. 13.6) and also the contractile protein filaments, **myofilaments**, which run along the long axis of the cell. When these filaments group together and become visible in the light microscope, they are called **myofibrils**. The mitochondria are usually large and numerous. The smooth endoplasmic reticulum is disposed around the myofibrils and is known as the **sarcoplasmic reticulum**; this seems to be involved in carrying the impulse from the sarcolemma to the contractile myofibrils.

The special cytology of muscle cells is described under the following headings:

(1) myofilaments,
(2) sarcolemma and sarcoplasmic reticulum,
(3) development, growth and regeneration.

MYOFILAMENTS

All myofilaments contain at least three proteins, actin, myosin and tropomyosin and are of two types, thick and thin.

Tropomyosins

Tropomyosins are very long molecules which are apparently enzymically inactive and their polypeptide chains are all in the α-helical form (p. 11.10). They do not contain proline or hydroxyproline. They act as scaffolding and supports for the actin and myosin molecules.

Actin

Actin can exist in a globular form **G–actin** (mol. wt. 60,000) with a diameter of 5·5 nm. G–actin readily aggregates in moderately concentrated salt solutions to form long filaments, each filament containing two strands of spherical actin molecules, twisted on each other (fig. 15.2). This fibrillar form is called **F–actin**. The thin filaments in muscle consist of F–actin, probably combined with tropomyosin. Each G–actin unit in F–actin contains a group capable of combining with myosin.

Myosin

Myosin is a much larger protein (mol. wt. 500,000) and it has a more complex shape. One portion contains extended α-helices and resembles tropomyosin. This portion is 160 nm long and joins a globular head about 4 nm in diameter (fig. 15.2). When the molecules aggregate to form

FIG. 15.2 The molecular structure of myofilaments.

filaments, their tails fit in parallel to form the core of the thick filaments which, like the thin actin-containing filaments, include also some tropomyosin. The heads of the myosin molecules project, in a radial fashion, from the sides of the thick filaments. As the heads all point in the same direction, the intrinsic structure of the myosin-containing filament is polarized in one direction (fig. 15.2).

Although the actin filaments are apparently unpolarized (fig. 15.2), it can be shown that, on each globular molecule, the myosin-combining site points to the same end of the filament (fig. 15.3).

In the sarcoplasm these myosin- and actin-containing filaments lie side by side and the contractile force is produced at the points of apposition between the projecting heads of the myosin molecules and the globular actin molecules. Since both filaments are polarized, the force

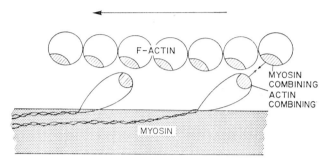

FIG. 15.3. The interaction of myosin and actin.

can be exerted in only one direction. A muscle can contract actively but it cannot lengthen actively. If shortening occurs, successive G–actin molecules come into contact with a myosin molecule. When shortening is not allowed, as in isometric contraction (p. 15.7), the same pairs of G–actin molecules and myosin molecule heads are interacting throughout the attempted contraction (fig. 15.3).

In smooth muscle, the filaments run along the long axis of the cell, but do not group together to form myofibrils. There is no regular pattern of particular lengths of each type of filament, so cross striations are not evident by light microscopy. This arrangement of filaments imposes no limit to the range of shortening as one filament can continue sliding past its counterpart. The power of the movement is directly related to the number of filaments and hence to the number of contact points between actin and myosin molecules; power is not necessarily affected by this simple arrangement. The expulsive force exerted by the uterus at parturition demonstrates the power of smooth muscle. Smooth muscles contract relatively slowly but are capable of maintaining the same tension for long periods. This **tonic activity** of smooth muscles in the visceral and vascular walls, which is controlled by the autonomic nervous system and by circulating hormones, plays an important part in regulating the function of the cardiovascular, gastrointestinal, urogenital and respiratory systems.

Rapid contraction in mammalian skeletal muscles is associated with a regular arrangement of the two types of filaments. This results in a cross-striated pattern being seen in the light microscope. It is associated with clear grouping of the filaments to form definite myofibrils.

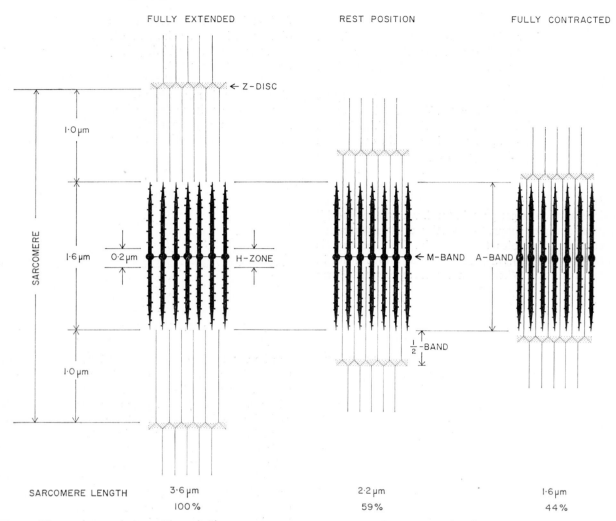

FIG. 15.4. The arrangement of myofilaments in a myofibril. For ½-band read ½ I-band. From Muir A. R. *Vet. Rec.* **80**, 456 (1967).

The dimensions and disposition of the filaments in a myofibril from striated muscle are shown in fig. 15.4. The thick myosin-containing filaments are 1·6 μm long and they are held in a regular hexagonal packing by cross connections situated halfway along their length. At this point the polarity of the myosin molecules changes so that all the heads point away from the centre. Thus the contractile force is directed towards the centre. Where the polarity changes, the tails of the myosin molecules overlap so there are no projecting heads for a distance of 200 nm in the centre. The thin actin-containing filaments are 1 μm long and they are anchored at one end to a meshwork of tropomyosin known as the **Z-disc** (plate 15.1, facing p. 11.15). These two arrays of filaments fit into each other, so that each thin filament is surrounded by three thick ones and each thick filament is directly related to six thin filaments (fig. 15.5).

In this manner a composite contractile unit, the **sarcomere**, is formed. Its various parts are known by the letters

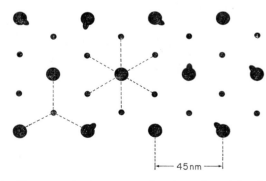

FIG. 15.5. A transverse section through an A-band.

shown in figs. 15.4 & 6. A myofibril from the biceps muscle runs perhaps 6 cm from origin to insertion and contains about 30,000 sarcomeres. The thick filaments produce birefringence in polarized light (Anisotropy) and so are called the A-band. The width of the A-band

a

b

PLATE 16.1. Bone cells.
(a) Osteoblasts, which during bone growth form a continuous layer of cuboidal cells on the bone surface. A few become entrapped in the matrix and then assume the role of osteocytes ($\times 600$).
(b) An osteoclast; at the zone of contact between osteoclast and bone a 'brush border' can be seen. Sites of resorption may be recognized after the departure of the osteoclast by the scalloped appearance of the bone surface ($\times 960$).

a

b

PLATE 16.2. Bone structure.

(a) Woven bone in an immature form seen only at sites of rapid growth. The osteocytes are large and numerous, and the bone matrix forms a random woven pattern without the lamellae characteristic of matrix bone (×120).

(b) Cortical bone in which several osteones are shown in cross-section. Each contains a central neurovascular canal. The lamellar structure of the bone is clearly visible. A 'cement line' delineates each osteone. The irregular cavity in the centre is a resorption cavity showing the scalloped border left by the action of osteoclasts. Such cavities become occupied by a new osteone and so bone is slowly but constantly repaired and replaced throughout life (×136).

does not change, but a paler, isotropic I-band contains only thin filaments and this band narrows during contraction. The architecture of the sarcomere imposes precise limits on the amount of shortening which can occur. It is obvious from fig. 15.4 that the total range of movement of one sarcomere is 2 μm, that is from 3·6 μm to 1·6 μm. Thus a muscle fibre can shorten by more than 50 per cent. In fact, our skeletal muscles need to shorten to 43 per cent of their fully extended length to produce the full movement at the single joint where they act. This shortening is almost exactly the same, proportionately, as the shortening which can occur at each of its sarcomeres.

A myofibril is about 1 μm thick and the regular series of A- and I-bands is due to its constituent sarcomeres. All the myofibrils in a cell are placed and kept in register with each other; this remarkable fact is still unexplained. Thus the whole cell shows the cross-striated pattern which is truly the property of single myofibrils. Fig. 15.6 shows how myofilaments are assembled and organized in a whole skeletal muscle fibre.

Connective tissue, largely composed of collagen, surrounds all the cells and limits extension of the cells beyond the physiological range which is dictated by the sarcomere design. The connective tissue is organized in three ways:

(1) the sheath around the whole muscle is called **epimysium**.

(2) the sheath around the bundles of cells producing the 'muscle fibres' visible to the naked eye is **perimysium**.

(3) each cell has a connective tissue tube called the **endomysium**.

All these sheaths are continuous with and form a large part of the tendon or bony attachment. The contractile force produced in the myofibrils is transmitted to the tendon at the end of the cell. Here the myofibrils are attached to the inside of the plasma membrane, from the outside of which reticulin and collagen fibres run to the ultimate attachment.

SARCOLEMMA AND SARCOPLASMIC RETICULUM

The sarcolemma forms the boundary of individual muscle cells (plate 15.1, facing p. 11.15). It has a structure similar to the boundary of all other cells (p. 13.5) consisting of a plasma membrane with an outer condensation of connective tissue forming a basement membrane. Changes in the permeability of this membrane allow the ionic movements which create an action potential (p. 14.25).

The basement membrane is well developed around a multinucleated skeletal muscle cell and it blends with the collagenous endomysial tube. So the plasma membrane of a skeletal muscle fibre is always separated from the plasma membrane of neighbouring cells. Each skeletal muscle cell receives a nerve ending, and depolarization of its plasma membrane is normally due to nerve impulses causing discharge of transmitter substance at this motor

end plate. Smooth-muscle cells which receive a rich autonomic nerve supply are similarly isolated from each other, although the basement membrane sheath is thinner. This fact explains the older view that smooth muscle did not possess a sarcolemma.

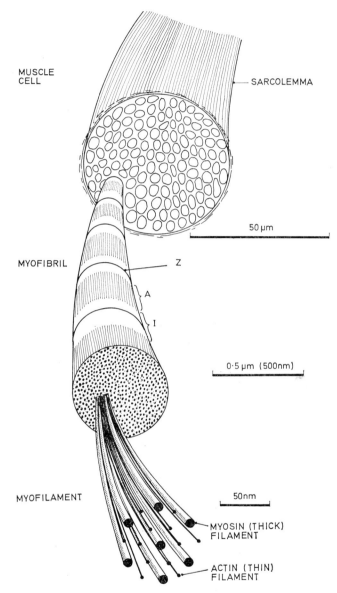

Fig. 15.6. The arrangement of myofilaments and myofibrils in a skeletal muscle fibre.

In cardiac muscle, the ends of the short muscle cells are stuck together at the intercalated discs to form the fibres. The basement membrane covers only the sides of the fibres, so at the discs the plasma membranes of the two cells come into contact and fuse to become a structure similar to a zonula occludens (p. 13.11). Because of the fusion, depolarization of one cell spreads to its neighbours and so through the whole heart. Hence cardiac muscle is often said to be a syncytium. Smooth muscle which has a meagre nerve supply also has groups of cells joined together by plasma cell fusions with the same spread of depolarization.

The ionic changes in the sarcoplasm due to depolarization lead to contraction of the myofibrils. This process is called excitation–contraction coupling and recently two aspects of the process have been clarified.

Firstly, it has been shown that the sarcolemma is not confined to the surface of striated muscle cells. Tubules of plasma membrane leave the sarcolemma to penetrate the cell, passing close to all the contained myofibrils. These

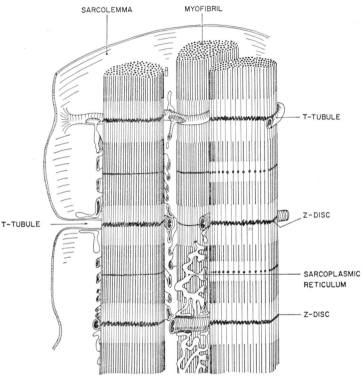

FIG. 15.7. The internal cellular membranes of cardiac muscle.

are the T-tubules and they are spatially related to the cross striations, being at the level of the Z-disc in cardiac muscle (fig. 15.7) and at the junction of the A and I bands in skeletal muscle. Thus the impulse to contract spreads along these tubules to permeate the whole cell as well as spreading along the surface.

Secondly, the myofibrils are embraced by a system of fine intracellular tubules called the sarcoplasmic reticulum. The membranes of this reticulum have peculiar Ca^{++} binding properties and it is thought that they initiate contraction by liberating Ca^{++} into the sarcoplasm. It will be seen (p. 15.12) that Ca^{++} are necessary for the ATPase activity of the myosin. The sarcoplasmic reticu-

lum comes into contact with the sarcolemma and the T-tubule and it may be here that the signal passes from the surface membrane to the sarcoplasmic reticulum.

DEVELOPMENT, GROWTH AND REGENERATION OF MUSCLE

All striated muscle and practically all smooth muscle develops from mesoderm. The smooth muscles of the iris, the arrector pili muscles (p. 35.5) and the contractile cells in secreting epithelia, myoepithelial cells (p. 17.7), are exceptions in that they may arise from ectoderm. The cells which are to become striated muscle are seen first in the segmentally arranged somites. Clusters of spindle-shaped cells, **myoblasts**, form discrete lateral masses in the somites known as **myotomes**. Some of the muscles remain segmentally arranged, e.g. the intercostal muscles, but most of the myoblasts migrate and rearrange to form the non-segmented muscles. In the limbs there is probably also some differentiation of myoblasts, but the early migration of myoblasts does seem to be followed by the outgrowth from the central nervous system of the motor nerve supply. In this manner the pattern of muscle innervation is determined even if there is differentiation of myoblasts at the site of the final muscle. The migration of the myoblasts from the myotomes in the occipital region into the tongue is established in evolution even though it cannot be observed in human embryos; it explains the course and distribution of the hypoglossal nerve.

Prior to the differentiation of a muscle, the myoblasts proliferate and then stick together to form long columns of cells. Suddenly, the intercellular barriers disappear and a multinucleated tube is formed. Myofibrils with cross striations first appear just inside the sarcolemma of this multinucleated cell and the content of myofibrils gradually increases. At a later stage, the nuclei move from the centre of the cell to take up their mature position under the sarcolemma. When the sarcomeres are seen first in the early embryo, they have the same dimensions as in the adult, so growth in length of the muscle is associated with the addition of new sarcomeres. Not quite all the myoblasts fuse together; a small proportion, perhaps 5–10 per cent of the nuclei in a skeletal muscle, remain as undifferentiated cells sandwiched between the basement membrane and the sarcolemma of the adult muscle cell. These are the **satellite cells** and they play an important part in muscle regeneration. For regeneration of skeletal muscle to occur the damage must not be severe enough to impair the blood or nerve supply or to destroy completely the endomysial tubes. Under these conditions proliferation of myoblasts, probably derived from satellite cells, is followed by a recapitulation of the process of embryonic development.

The myoblasts which are to form cardiac muscle appear in the cephalic part of the lateral plate mesoderm (fig. 18.6). As in skeletal muscle they adhere to each other, but in this tissue the intervening cell membranes do not disintegrate since the adhesions form the intercalated discs. Myofibrils appear in the same position as in skeletal muscle but the nuclei do not move out to the periphery of the cell. Division of the nuclei in each cell produces the two to eight nuclei of an adult cardiac muscle cell. There are no satellite cells in cardiac muscle and there is no regeneration of myocardium.

The differentiation of smooth muscle is much simpler as the mesodermal cells need only to elongate and to synthesize the contractile proteins. In contrast to the striated varieties, the body remains capable of developing smooth muscle throughout adult life. In the uterine wall during pregnancy, for instance, there is an actual increase in the number of smooth muscle cells (hyperplasia) as well as an increase in the size of individual cells (hypertrophy).

Hyperplasia does not occur in skeletal or cardiac muscle after birth, so all the growth is due to increase in size of the cells. This hypertrophy is augmented by exercise and by sex hormones, particularly testosterone, at puberty. Disuse leads rapidly to atrophy of skeletal muscle, for it can be detected within a few hours of the immobilization of a limb in plaster. Loss of the motor nerve supply produces severe wasting of muscles, but central nervous system lesions do not have the same effect.

Whole skeletal muscle

There are numerous patterns for the arrangement of the muscle cells (p. 19.11), which are determined by the available sites for skeletal attachment and the need to ensure that the cells are just long enough to produce the movements at the joints affected by the muscle. A fusiform muscle belly with a tendinous insertion is the simplest arrangement. The muscle cells are bound together, fasciculated and supported by the epi-, peri- and endomysium mentioned above. The collagen of the tendon is derived partly from these sheaths and partly from fibres arising from the ends of the muscle cells themselves. The muscle cells may either run the whole length of the belly or end at intermediate points by being attached to other muscle cells. In the former case all the motor end plates are in a band at the centre of the belly; in the latter they are scattered through the whole substance of the muscle.

Each cell has only one motor end plate, which includes the end of a spinal or cranial nerve fibre. Each ventral horn nerve cell, or its cranial equivalent, sends one axon which branches in the muscle to supply a number of muscle cells. Since the nerve cell exhibits an 'all or none' property and as the arrival of an impulse at its motor end plates causes a similar 'all or none' depolarization of the muscle cells it supplies, this combination of muscle cells and their innervating neurone forms a structural and functional unit. It is known as the **motor unit** and the number of muscle cells in such a unit varies with the delicacy of the movement which that muscle produces. In the small muscles moving the eyes and fingers one nerve cell supplies only 10–12 muscle cells; in the coarse muscles of the limbs and back a motor unit may have as many as 300 muscle cells. The individual muscle cells in a motor unit are scattered throughout the substance of the muscle; they do not correspond to the bundles of cells enclosed by perimysium. As well as these motor axons, every skeletal muscle contains sensory axons attached to receptors such as muscle spindles and tendon organs (p. 24.13).

An electrode placed over a muscle, or inserted into the extracellular tissue in the muscle, can detect the electrical activities of adjacent motor units. When these are amplified and recorded they produce an electromyograph which demonstrates the activity of that muscle in a particular action (p. 14.25).

FUNCTION OF SKELETAL MUSCLE

Excitability

Skeletal muscle can be stimulated to contract in precisely the same way as nerve. It exhibits a threshold to electrical stimulation, a latent period between stimulation and response and absolute and relative refractory periods, i.e. a period of unresponsiveness to any stimulus, which is followed by a period in which there is an increase in the magnitude of the threshold stimulus.

All skeletal muscles have motor nerve supplies, which are the normal channels of excitation, and all can be excited by stimulation of their motor nerves. But the region of the muscle fibre which does not have a motor end plate is also electrically excitable and manifests all the properties cited above. Thus it can be taken that the muscle cell itself belongs to the same class of irritable tissue as the nerve fibre.

Characteristics of muscular contraction

If a muscle is excited by applying a single shock to its motor nerve it responds by exhibiting:

(1) an action potential which appears after a short latency,

(2) a contraction which occurs after a further latent period.

If the nerve is stimulated repetitively at a sufficiently low frequency there is a series of discrete action potentials but the contractile activity is of a continuous nature.

The form taken by the contractile activity depends on circumstances. If the attachments of the muscle are fixed, the activity takes the form of development of tension in the muscle, and the contraction is called **isometric**. If one or both of the attachments can move, then the muscle may be able to shorten without the development of any increase in tension, and this sort of contraction is called **isotonic**. If one sets out to draw a cork from a bottle, the arm muscles used initially contract isometrically until the tension developed is sufficient to put the cork into motion. They contract isotonically during withdrawal until the cork is practically free and thereafter contraction is neither purely isotonic nor purely isometric. Thus when we speak of muscular contraction we use 'contraction' in a technical sense. In common speech, contraction means shortening. In muscle physiology it means that physiological activity which can lead to shortening if the circumstances allow. One should always be on guard in medical science to keep general and technical meanings separate.

TWITCH AND TETANUS

A single shock to a motor nerve produces a contraction which is called a **twitch**. Depending on the species and on the anatomical site and the temperature of the muscle, the time before return to resting tension in an isometric twitch may be 100–600 msec.

If a second stimulus is applied after an interval exceeding the refractory period, which is usually of the order of a millisecond, the tension rises further than in a twitch, even if the peak of twitch tension has been passed before the second stimulus is applied. If a series of stimuli at regular intervals is applied, the tension continues to rise more and more slowly until it becomes constant or oscillates at the frequency of stimulation around a constant mean which can be several times as great as maximum twitch tension. Tension declines to zero 100–600 msec after the last stimulus, as in a twitch. This kind of contraction is called a **tetanus**. This word must be distinguished from tetany, a state of increased excitability of motor nerves. Tetanus is also the name of a disease in which tetanic contractions of muscle arise as a result of poisoning by a bacterial toxin.

During a tetanus (or tetanic contraction) action potentials can be observed in the muscle. There is one action potential of a normal kind for every stimulus applied. Thus action potentials remain discrete, whilst contractions fuse, but fusion takes place only if the interval between stimuli is much shorter than twitch time. A frequency of 10/sec may give fused contraction, but a smooth tetanic contraction needs a frequency of 100/sec or more.

ACTIVE STATE

It is difficult to devise apparatus for recording muscular contractions in which there is no lag in response and no distortion. The isometric contraction should be the easier to record faithfully, but the maximum isometric twitch tension of the medial head of the cat gastrocnemius can exceed 6 kg and even the gastrocnemius of the small English frog (*Rana temporaria*) gives a tension of 2 kg, so fairly substantial devices are needed.

Further difficulties arise within the muscle itself. What one is trying to record is the tension that the muscle fibres themselves would develop if they were directly attached to undistortable and immediately responsive detectors. But the muscle cells are attached to each other and to the attachments of the muscle by the connective tissue elements already described which are being stretched in some measure all the time that the tension in the muscle cells is rising. These elements will therefore not have achieved full stretch at the moment at which tension in the muscle cells begins to fall, and the tension transmitted by them to their attachments will not be, at its maximum, the maximum tension which the muscle cells can develop.

This same argument can be applied to the relation between the muscle as a whole and the recording apparatus, in which a tension must be developed if a tension is to be recorded. So we expect the recorded twitch tension to be lower than the tension that the muscle is capable of developing in a twitch. The tension that we ought to be able to record if there were none of these obstacles has been called the **active state**.

The technique of determining the time course of the active state is too complex to be described here, but the outcome is important; active state tension rises almost instantaneously to its maximal value which is equal to maximal tetanic tension (fig. 15.8). The active state tension is maintained for a little shorter time than that taken for a twitch to reach peak tension and then declines. Since this has been established, several other pieces of evidence have been shown to fit in. For instance, the effects of a number of drugs which change the form of the normally recorded isometric twitch have been shown to be explicable by their effect on the length of the plateau of active state tension.

Thus the picture of a contracting muscle is very different from what we should expect from personal experience of the fineness with which it can be adapted to our needs. The individual elements have to be thought of as contracting maximally or not at all, with no gradations possible except those inherent in the transition between fully isometric and fully isotonic. The picture that emerges from the work on active state reinforces the notion of the individual muscle cell as something that acts in an all or none fashion, and this is of importance in theories of muscular contraction.

Gradation of muscular activity

So far we have considered the properties of muscle maximally stimulated either directly or through its motor nerve so that all the muscle cells act together. The muscles, however, consist of numerous motor units, normally acting independently, each consisting of the muscle cells which are innervated by the terminal branches of the axon of the single motor neurone. Since motor neurones in the ventral horn of the spinal cord are stimulated individually, it is very unlikely that the twitches of different motor units will be synchronous. In any sustained muscular activity a set of motor units contracts asynchronously in such a way that some are fully active, some are relaxing and some are quiescent at any given instant.

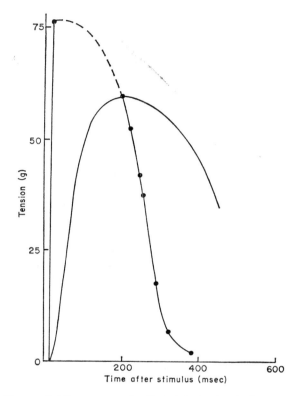

FIG. 15.8. Time-course of active state tension in frog sartorius at 0°C. The interrupted part of the line was drawn by extrapolation. An ordinary muscle twitch is also shown. From Ritchie (1954) *J. Physiol.* **126**, 155.

If there is a rotation of states of activity among a constant number of such units, the muscle will be in a more or less steady state of activity, although no single unit will be in a steady state of tetanic contraction. The all-or-none responses of the individual contractile units are masked by the asynchronous nature of the activity and by the non-rigid nature of the connective structure of the muscle through which the contractile activity has to be transmitted to origins and insertions.

Fatigue

When an isolated frog gastrocnemius muscle is made to twitch repetitively by electrical stimulation of its nerve, the contraction steadily becomes smaller, even if the muscle is kept in oxygen. A sufficiently long period of rest restores the ability to contract.

This effect is usually due to the circumstances of the experiment. Every contraction causes an efflux of potassium from the excited cells, as with nerve. The potassium added to the extracellular water cannot be removed by the circulation, as would happen *in vivo*, and accumulates. Increase in extracellular potassium renders the muscle cells inexcitable. If such muscles are soaked in fresh physiological saline they regain excitability. If a small volume of saline is used for a series of such muscles it ultimately loses its ability to restore excitability and is then found to contain three to four times the normal potassium concentration.

Isolated muscles can become exhausted as well as inexcitable. They require energy for contraction, even if they are not doing external work. Muscle cells store carbohydrate in the form of glycogen and lipid in the form of triglyceride, but these stores are limited and in isolated muscle failure to respond may be due to exhaustion of reserves of nutrients.

Rigor

When muscles become exhausted they fail to relax, i.e., they go into rigor, rather than fail to contract. Although there are complicating factors, the onset of rigor is determined chiefly by failure of energy supply. As soon as oxygen is no longer supplied by the circulation the sole available energy source is glycogen, which can be converted anaerobically to lactic acid. When this is exhausted rigor follows. The onset of rigor is accelerated in an animal which has been violently exercised immediately before death, and rigor is instantaneous in an animal which has been poisoned with iodoacetic acid, which prevents the formation of lactic acid. It is important to keep in mind that lack of energy seems to destroy the capacity to relax, not the capacity to contract.

Rigor mortis passes off with time. This probably has no significance for an understanding of muscle function. Autolytic processes occur in cells after death and their internal structure gradually disintegrates; this disintegration involves the contractile elements.

Relation between muscle length and contraction

If the ability of a muscle to contract is due to interaction between the myosin and actin filaments in its sarcomeres, it is to be expected that passive stretching to the point where there is no overlap of these filaments would make it incapable of contraction. When muscles are stretched in this way and then stimulated it can be seen under the light microscope that sarcomeres do not in fact contract.

The amount of work which a muscle can perform when it is maximally stimulated depends on its initial length. If it is initially not under tension, the contractile elements must shorten and the connective tissue must be stretched before tension can be developed at the attachments of the muscle, and the development of such tension is a prerequisite of the performance of external work. During these preliminaries work is done in overcoming internal friction and in deforming the connective tissue elements. Only a fraction of the energy liberated in each twitch can be used for external work in such circumstances. With increase in initial extension of the muscle less energy is needed for these unproductive activities so that more external work can be done; when the degree of initial extension is reached at which some of the sarcomeres have attained such lengths that they can no longer contract, the ability to perform work begins to fall. Thus there is an optimal extension, at which the muscle can perform maximal work in a single twitch.

This relation is not directly applicable to normal muscular activity *in vivo*. In these circumstances some of the muscle fibres undergo passive stretching every time a twitch takes place in adjacent motor units, so that the passive viscous and elastic properties of muscle fibres enter more into this situation than into the experimental one. But as the pattern of excitation of motor units in any voluntary contraction *in vivo* is at present impossible to determine, it is not possible to analyse profitably the performance of muscle *in situ*.

Heat production in muscle

Metabolic energy which cannot be used to perform mechanical, electrical or chemical work must be dissipated as heat. Frog sartorius muscle at rest, metabolizing nutrients at the rest rate, dissipates about 2 cal/kg/min at 20°C. The only way of measuring such small heat production is by means of a sensitive thermopile. Accurate measurements on active muscle can be made only with muscles that can be brought into close contact with a suitable thermopile and kept in contact. In the frog sartorius the heat production during a single maximal isometric twitch is about 3 cal/kg, the exact value depending on the amount of work done. Energy is liberated in a twitch in three forms:

(1) initial heat, which starts before a mechanical response is seen; this is sometimes called the heat of activation,

(2) heat of shortening which is directly proportional to the extent of shortening,

(3) mechanical work.

It has been pointed out that the magnitudes of these components are quite independent of one another; there is never any question of reducing the amount of activation or shortening heat by making the muscle do more work. No heat is liberated during relaxation. These changes occur equally well in the presence or absence of oxygen. If oxygen is available, there is a subsequent slow production of additional heat which is about equal in magnitude to the sum total of activation heat, shortening heat and external work. Comparable data are not available for the muscles of warm-blooded animals. The general similarity in structure of amphibian and mammalian muscle, however, makes it unlikely that there are fundamental differences between their basic modes of action, so we may take it that a similar pattern of energy liberation would occur in mammalian muscle, and that any effective theory of muscular contraction should take into account this pattern of heat production.

The sarcoplasm contains all the enzymes of the Embden–Meyerhof pathway, which was indeed first studied in muscle, and all the enzymes of β-oxidation of fatty acids, together with all the enzymes of the citric acid cycle and of the terminal respiratory pathway. It can therefore generate ATP at the expense of energy derived from carbohydrate or fat.

The energy source for contraction

ATP is generally held to be the specific means by which the energy produced in the oxidation of nutrients can be utilized for the performance of work by muscles. If this is true, the theory of muscular contraction must find a central place for ATP, although it is generated outside the contractile myofibrils.

There is nothing specialized in the processes of ATP generation in muscle cells. It arises in the ways described on p. 8.9. But there is something specialized about the pattern of needs for it. As we have seen, individual muscle cells go into activity in all-or-none fashion and they do this repetitively in any overt muscular activity. In addition, the increased energy requirement of the muscles in mild activity is large, judging from the increase in oxygen requirement of the whole animal, so individual muscle cells need a great deal of ATP frequently at very short notice.

On the other hand, we shall see that muscular contraction would be difficult or impossible if the ATP concentration was very high, so that it is not feasible to store a large reserve of ATP in the cell.

The difficulty is overcome by storing the reserve of high energy phosphate in another form, phosphocreatine:

$$\text{Phosphocreatine} + \text{ADP} \underset{\text{phosphokinase}}{\overset{\text{creatine}}{\rightleftharpoons}} \text{Creatine} + \text{ATP}$$

This tends to go to the left, so that the equilibrium concentration of ATP is low. In resting mammalian muscle the ATP concentration is about 5 μmoles/g and the phosphocreatine concentration about 20–30 μmoles/g. The creatine phosphokinase activity in muscle is sufficiently high to make re-equilibration almost instantaneous; if oxidative phosphorylation cannot generate ATP from ADP as rapidly as necessary, the creatine phosphokinase automatically makes up the deficit to a limited extent. The total store of energy as ATP and phosphocreatine in human muscle is sufficient to keep a man running for less than 5 sec.

Muscle logistics

Muscle is ultimately dependent for its supply of ATP on the nutrients and oxygen brought to it in the bloodstream. But the circulation cannot supply these things just at the time when they are most needed. It has been shown that in vigorous contraction the pressure set up within the muscle is enough to arrest blood flow. It may be expected that in parts of a muscle where units are contracting the capillaries will be squeezed and supplies will often be temporarily cut off. Thus, there is a tendency for the muscle to be deprived at its time of greatest need.

There is another supply difficulty; at rest, muscle blood flow is about 2–5 ml/100 g/min. If all the oxygen were abstracted from this it would supply 120–300 ml O_2/min to all the muscles of the body. This compares with a resting oxygen requirement of the whole body of 250 ml/min. The oxygen requirement for walking at 4 miles/hr is more than four times the resting requirement, and almost all this extra oxygen is used by the muscles. Thus, even in mild exercise there has to be a considerable adaptation of the circulation, involving increased cardiac output and redistribution of the output between destinations to give a larger share to the muscles. This adaptation is rapid, but not instantaneous. During it the muscles have to get energy from somewhere, and it cannot be obtained on credit. Muscle glycogen can be broken down by the normal pathways to pyruvate. In the absence of adequate oxygen, the pyruvate can act as hydrogen acceptor from NADH generated in the oxidation of triose phosphate to phosphoglyceric acid. The pyruvate is reduced to lactate. The overall effect of this transformation is to liberate about one-fifth of the energy of the glycogen for use by the muscle. If oxygen is available, the pyruvate can be completely oxidized by way of the citric acid cycle. It is in this stage that the remaining four-fifths of the energy of the glycogen is liberated.

Muscle normally contains 5–10 g of glycogen/kg but the lipid content is appreciably higher and can be oxidized to provide energy. However when muscles most urgently need a store of utilizable energy they are also most deficient in oxygen, and therefore tend to be restricted to the partial use of their glycogen by converting it to lactate.

This ability of muscle to obtain energy anaerobically was responsible for the early belief that carbohydrate was the fuel of muscle. In fact, it appears that carbohydrate is important because of its availability as a short term anaerobic source of energy at the beginning of exercise, but in sustained activity the major source of energy supply is the free fatty acids of the blood. However, quite a lot can be done without external supplies. The athlete who runs 100 yards is unlikely to obtain more than a tiny fraction of the energy he dissipates from anything other than glycolysis of muscle glycogen. A fuller discussion of the effects of muscular exercise is given in chap. 42.

Oxygen supply to muscle

For the same reasons that make it difficult to supply nutrients to muscle there is a problem in maintaining oxygen supply. Muscles used rhythymically as in rowing or running may have a highly intermittent blood supply and may be forced to depend on glycolysis of a diminishing glycogen supply if they lack adequate continuous oxygen supply. However, they can make their glycogen last five times as long if they can oxidize it.

Some muscles of birds and mammals are equipped with a means of ameliorating the effects of oxygen deprivation. These are the red muscles. They owe their darker colour to their content of myoglobin, which is a haem protein of the same general character as haemoglobin, and has the property of combining with oxygen in the same way. The haemoglobin molecule is made up of four sub-units whose molecular weight is about 17,000 (p. 11.8). The myoglobin molecule consists of one such unit, but this unit is not identical in amino acid composition with any of the subunits in the haemoglobin of the same species.

Myoglobin differs from haemoglobin also in its oxygen dissociation curve. As described on p. 29.17, myoglobin can pick up and store in the cells the oxygen brought by the blood even when the circulation is too inadequate to maintain a high oxygen tension in the tissue fluid interposed between capillaries and muscle cells.

Red muscles and white muscles

In the blood-free state, all organs have some colour due to the natural intracellular pigments such as the yellow flavins, the orange carotenoids and the red cytochromes. But these are pale shades usually, compared with the colour of myoglobin, so that muscles containing much of this pigment are strikingly red, The difference in colour between pectoral muscle of the domestic fowl and that of the pigeon, partridge or grouse shows that corresponding muscles in different species can contain a lot of myoglobin or a little. Muscles which have to maintain activity for long periods, such as the pectoral muscles of flying birds and the extensors of the limbs used in walking, are more likely to contain red muscle.

In some species it has been found that the time course of the maximal twitch of a red muscle is much more prolonged than that of a white muscle. This is true in the cat. If the motor nerves of a pair of muscles in the hind limb of a kitten are cut, one muscle being red and one white, and if the distal end of each cut nerve is sutured to the proximal end of the other nerve, so that, after regeneration, each nerve comes to innervate the wrong muscle, then the twitch of the red muscle becomes brisker and that of the white muscle less brisk. However, it is doubtful if this association between whiteness and speed of contraction is a general one. More work on more muscles, and analyses of contraction in terms of active state is desirable before too much is built on this evidence.

Limiting oxygen tension in muscle

As the oxygen tension in arterial blood is of the order of 100 mm Hg, we tend to think that muscles need to be supplied with oxygen at quite high oxygen tension, measurable in tens of millimetres of mercury. Since the advent of oxygen electrodes it has become clear that the oxygen tension needed at the surface of a cell in order to provide a high enough concentration to meet the needs of the cell can be very low indeed. A diagram which gives oxygen tensions at various sites in the human body is on p. 43.2. No figures are available for human muscle, but in general the critical concentration is a fraction of a millimetre of mercury. Since intracellular concentrations must be lower than extracellular ones in order that there shall be diffusion of oxygen into and across the cells, the ability of myoglobin to hold on to oxygen until the oxygen tension is a few mm Hg is of no disadvantage.

The need for relatively high oxygen tensions in blood arises because the oxygen has to diffuse across the capillary wall and through the extracellular fluid to reach the cell. There must therefore be a concentration gradient from capillary lumen to cell surface and this must be capable of being made large enough to meet the needs for rapid transport in conditions of vigorous activity. Since one cannot raise the arterial tension appreciably, the cells need to be able to operate energetically when the oxygen tension at their surfaces is low.

The gradient of concentration of oxygen, and incidentally of any other metabolite, between capillary and muscle cell is affected not only by the concentration difference between these structures but also by their mean distance apart. This distance is dependent on the mean number of patent capillaries per unit cross-sectional area of the muscle. This number rises markedly during muscular activity (p. 28.23).

Contraction process in muscle

The work of A.F. Huxley has shown that when single frog sartorius muscle cells are stretched they exhibit the length-tension relation illustrated in fig. 15.9. The scheme below the graph illustrates the relation between sarcomere length and the overlap between actin and myosin filaments.

It is clear from what has been said earlier that contraction involves an interaction between the actin and myosin filaments in the sarcomere. Precisely what happens is not clear but a theory can be built on the following evidence:

(1) It has been shown that if actin and myosin are put together in solution, the viscosity of the solution is much greater than would be expected if the two kinds of molecules had remained apart from one another in solution.

(2) If ATP is added to the mixture the viscosity falls to the value expected for a mixture of independent molecules and the ATP is gradually hydrolysed to ADP and inorganic phosphate; the viscosity rises in parallel with this disappearance of ATP

(3) The disappearance of ATP is due to enzymic activity of the myosin and the active centre is in the heads of the myosin molecules which protrude from the sides of the myosin-containing filaments.

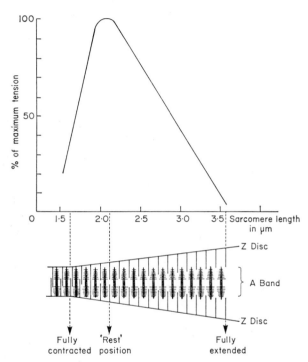

FIG. 15.9. The relationship between the length of a sarcomere and the isometric tension which its muscle cell can produce. From data of Gordon, Huxley & Julian (1966) *J. Physiol.* **184**, 143.

(4) This ATPase activity is markedly increased by the presence of calcium.

If we suppose that the interaction between the actin and myosin which occurs in solution is the same as that which occurs in contraction, the ATP, produced by metabolic activity in the sarcoplasm, which diffuses into the myofibrils would be expected to maintain the actin and myosin filaments in a state of dissociation from one another. Stimulation of the muscle, which is known to involve calcium, would bring about:

(1) release of calcium into the myofibrils,

(2) activation of the ATPase activity of myosin,

(3) removal of the inhibitory action of ATP on association between actin and myosin.

Consequently contraction would occur.

Each molecule of G–actin in the F–actin chain contains a firmly bound adenosine diphosphate residue which seems to be concerned with the linking together of the F–actin molecules. It is not clear whether it is concerned also with the link between myosin and actin. If it were, it would be easy to see how ATP could break the link by competition for the active centres of the myosin ATPase.

This explanation of muscular contraction would account for the occurrence of rigor when energy supply ran out, since there would then be no ATP to bring about dissociation of actin-myosin links. But there are still uncertainties. Most of the work on the ultrastructure of muscle has been carried out on muscle broken up in concentrated glycerol water mixtures. This material resembles muscle in rigor much more than it resembles normal muscle, which is to be expected, because it is dead. But what is unexpected is that it contracts when ATP is added. It has been necessary to make most of the studies of the ultrastructure of contracted muscle on this material, and it has still to be established that the appearances correspond with those of normal contraction. The connections between the heads of the myosin molecules in the thick filaments and the actin in the thin filaments, seen in this sort of material (fig. 15.3), are not easily explained in terms of direct association between actin and myosin. However, this is not incompatible with the explanation offered here of the mechanism of muscular contraction.

FURTHER READING

All aspects of the subject are covered and reviewed in:
BOURNE G.H. ed. (1960) *The Structure and Function of Muscle*, vols. I–III. New York : Academic Press.

A review of the function of muscle appears in:
DAVSON H. (1964) *General Physiology* 3rd Edition. London: Churchill.

Chapter 16
Supporting tissue

Since the middle of the last century, when the cell theory became widely accepted, medicine has been primarily concerned with cellular functions in organs. This is understandable because breakdown in a cellular system such as the heart, the liver or the kidney often produces dramatic effects within a few hours. However, as knowledge of organ functions has increased and therapeutic procedures have become more effective, more attention has been directed to a group of diseases whose progress is usually measured in years or decades. Examples of these are the hardening of the walls of the arteries, the various rheumatic diseases and the slow decalcification of bones in old people. These diseases arise because of a metabolic failure in tissues which are rich in extracellular fibrous proteins but poor in cells. In consequence the metabolism of such tissue is slow compared with that of the cellular tissues of such organs as the liver, kidney or heart, but the tissue is far from inert as was once believed.

CONNECTIVE TISSUE

Connective tissues are derived from mesenchyme and they make up a large part of the body, including all tissues which are not epithelial, nervous or muscle. This covers such widely varying tissues as bone, cartilage, fibrous tissue, elastic tissue, blood and lymph. In spite of their variety, these tissues share the common property that their function is dependent on the quality of their extracellular component.

Supporting tissue consists of extracellular fluid, proteins and minerals which support the cells in their various organs and by means of the bony skeleton support the whole body. Connective tissue contains cells which are responsible for manufacturing and maintaining the extracellular material but they themselves play only a small part in its actual function.

The properties of most connective tissues are due to their content and arrangement of **fibrous proteins.** They also contain an interfibrillar substance commonly known as connective tissue **ground substance**, the properties of which are dependent upon complex mucopolysaccharide macromolecules. These compounds constitute an impor-

tant and ubiquitous system of polysaccharide molecules present in all extracellular fluid phases of the body. These complicated molecules tend to make the aqueous phase more like a jelly; the more polysaccharide present the firmer the consistency, and this can vary from the rigidity of hyaline cartilage through the jelly-like content of the umbilical cord to the watery extracellular fluid found in skeletal muscle, which is the extracellular fluid of the physiologists.

Fat cells are widely distributed throughout connective tissue and in places such as the skin they have the important physical functions of insulation and padding. In view of the metabolic importance of adipose tissue in health and disease, it is considered later as a separate tissue (chap. 32).

Quantitative aspects of connective tissues

The significance of connective tissue is better appreciated if the components of the body are considered in terms of their functional contribution. Thus there are tissues which are predominantly cellular, though they include a little fibrous tissue in their stroma; typical examples are the liver, skeletal muscle and brain, and in these organs the major part of the metabolism takes place. Then there are those tissues which are predominantly fibrous, but which include a few cells. The function of these tissues is mostly mechanical; the rigidity and strength of bone is produced by a highly organized mineralization of the fibrous protein collagen which is found in bone, as well as in tendons and fasciae. Bone can be regarded as a tendon systematically calcified where much of the water has been displaced by crystals of a complex inorganic salt of calcium phosphate (p. 16.10). A third group of tissues, not often regarded as connective tissue, is the blood and extracellular fluids whose function is essentially nutritive.

Table 16.1 sets out the composition of a 65 kg man in terms of tissues and organs. If the predominantly cellular organs, such as the muscles, liver, brain and endocrine organs, are added together they come to about 38 kg. This cell or organ mass includes some connective tissue in the form of stromal collagen, the collagen of the arteries and some extracellular fluid. Making allowance for these, the

TABLE 16.1. The tissues of a 65 kg man (kg fresh tissue).

Cells ('organ mass')	38·3
Bone	8·0
Skin subcutaneous tissue	7·8
Adipose tissue	4·0
Blood	5·5
Structural connective tissue (tendons, fasciae, etc.)	1·0
Loculated fluids (joints, eye balls, etc.) and miscellaneous connective tissue fluids	0·4
Total	65·0

true cell mass is about 34 kg or just over half the total weight of the standard man (65 kg). Thus the cells of the body which are most concerned with the processes of metabolism and movement are supported structurally and nutritionally by about their own weight of connective tissue. Tissues such as skin and bone contain relatively few cells, and so cytoplasm makes up a smaller proportion of their total volume. It can be seen that skin and bone together make up a large part of the body (15·8 kg) and that the contribution of all the other structural components such as tendons is relatively small (1 kg). The remaining mass of the body is largely accounted for by two tissues of great nutritional importance, these are blood and fat (9·5 kg).

TABLE 16.2. A normal chemical composition of a man weighing 65 kg and the distribution of substances in supporting tissue.

Component	Mass in kg	Amount in supporting tissue in kg
Protein	11·0	3·0 Connective tissue including bone
Fat	9·0	6·2 Adipose tissue and skin
Water	40·0	12·0 Interstitial fluid
		3·0 Loosely bound in bones, joint capsules, eyes, etc.
		3·0 Plasma
Minerals	4·0	3·8 Bone
Carbohydrate	1·0	0.5 Connective tissue mucopolysaccharides
Totals	65·0	31·5 (48·5 per cent of body weight)

Table 16.2 sets out the chemical composition of the normal body in terms of protein, fat, carbohydrate, minerals and water, and gives an estimated partition of these constituents between the cells and supporting tissue. Inspection shows, not unexpectedly, that the bulk of the protein and water of the body is found in association with cells, whereas 95 per cent of all the minerals in the body is in the connective tissue, principally in the skeleton. Cells and connective tissue have a small quantity of carbohydrate attached to them. The polysaccharide of the cell (glycogen) can be easily broken down to glucose and so made available as a source of energy. However, the complex polysaccharides of the connective tissue are relatively inert as befits their structural and polyanionic function which is discussed on p. 16.7.

Chemical composition of individual tissues

Table 16.3 gives the chemical constituents of some typical tissues. Here skin is considered as a connective tissue organ because the ectodermal contribution of cells and keratin is relatively small. About 95 per cent of all protein in the skin is collagen and is thus mesenchymal tissue. It can be seen that protein is an important component of all structural tissues and tendon has the highest concentration of protein of any tissue, although as mentioned previously, the total mass of all tendons is small. In contrast, the protein content of plasma and adipose tissue is low. It is perhaps surprising that the protein content of tissues as widely different as bone and muscle is virtually the same although it is, of course, extracellular in bone and intracellular in muscle.

Each of the tissues listed in table 16.3 has an extracellular fluid (ECF) compartment, the composition of which corresponds closely to that of plasma as far as the minerals listed are concerned. Since ECF occupies only a small part of the volume of the tissue, the content of each mineral should be less than that found in a kg of plasma provided it is largely extracellular in distribution. If this is not so then the mineral must be present attached to a special compartment in the tissue. As table 16.3 shows, connective tissues have a mineral composition very

TABLE 16.3. Composition of 1 kg of various fresh tissues.

Constituent	Tendons	Cartilage	Bone	Skin	Adipose tissue	Skeletal muscle	Plasma
Protein (g)	360	170	200	270	20	210	66
Fat (g)	—	—	50	100	850	75	7
Water (g)	600	740	250	620	130	700	913
K (mEq)	12	12	40	22	5	105	5
Na (mEq)	90	170	230	70	22	25	144
Ca (mEq)	7	48	9000	8	—	2	5
Mg (mEq)	14	10	390	3	—	20	1·8
Cl (mEq)	90	40	30	80	—	16	104
Polysaccharide (g)	30	80	30	10	—	10	1

different from a typical cellular tissue such as muscle. A further discrepancy is that each connective tissue shows a characteristic difference from the expected content of sodium and to a lesser extent of calcium and magnesium judged by comparison with plasma. In bone this is at first sight not surprising, particularly for calcium, but the actual site of the large amount of magnesium and sodium present is unknown. Similarly in tendon there is slight excess of sodium and chloride, and surprisingly a large excess of magnesium which is essentially an intracellular mineral. In bone, sodium is held mainly in a water free state in association with the mineral crystals of the matrix. Studies with ^{24}Na have shown that part of bone sodium is readily exchangeable with plasma sodium. The calcium and phosphate of bone play an important role in maintaining the concentrations of these substances in the blood, and in some diseases demineralization of the skeleton can proceed to such an extent that the bones become very weak and may break after trivial injuries.

Structure of connective tissues

The basic ingredients of connective tissues remain similar in different parts of the body but the relative proportions of the constituents vary widely. There are two main systems of fibres, each composed of a characteristic protein, **collagen** and **elastin**, associated with which there are numbers of mucopolysaccharide macromolecules. These mucopolysaccharides are characteristic of the ground substance phase of connective tissue, i.e. the watery phase bathing the fibres and cells. Three types of cell are found:

(1) **fibroblasts** which manufacture the fibre systems,
(2) **mast cells** which are concerned with mucopolysaccharide metabolism,
(3) **macrophages**, also called histiocytes or phagocytes, which may be fixed or free to move about and scavenge for cellular and other debris.

The fibrous proteins and mucopolysaccharides of connective tissue are different from any intracellular substances and can be stained characteristically by simple histological procedures. Elastin, the chief protein of elastic tissue, is stained by the dyes orcein and resorcin-fuchsin, brown and dark blue respectively, but is not stained selectively by acidic dyes like eosin. Whether or not collagen stains with aniline dyes seems to depend on the size of the strands, which are made up of small subunit fibrils of collagen associated with mucopolysaccharides. Thus, in loose connective tissue the EM reveals many small strands of collagen less than 0·5 μm in diameter which do not stain with dyes such as aniline blue, which stain the larger strands (1–5 μm). In addition, some delicate fibres commonly found in the connective tissue of glandular organs do not stain easily, although the EM shows that

fine collagen fibrils are their principal components; they are known as **reticulin fibres.** Impregnation with silver under special conditions is the best way to demonstrate this particular system of supporting tissue. Finally, mention should be made of a structure called the **basement membrane** or more accurately the basal lamina (p. 17.1). Very fine elements of collagen are important constituents of basement membranes, but they are overshadowed by mucopolysaccharide components which can be stained with the PAS method (plate 17.1b facing p. 17.2).

In growing tissues, where cells and fibrous proteins are being manufactured, the nucleic acids of the nucleus and cytoplasm stain with a basic dye such as haematoxylin, and the cell population stands out clearly against the background of extracellular components which take up acidic counterstains such as eosin or aniline blue. In mature non-proliferating tissues the cell nuclei still stain prominently a deep purple with haematoxylin but the cytoplasm now stains, if at all, with the counterstain, and thus a superficial examination can give the impression that some cells are virtually all nucleus.

One further staining phenomenon is of importance, i.e. metachromasia or metachromatic staining. This means that certain stains of a single colour stain some elements of tissues a different colour. An example of this is the staining red of the cytoplasmic granules of mast cells by toluidine blue. This is because of the granule's content of the sulphated mucopolysaccharide heparin. The explanation of the important phenomenon of metachromatic staining is thought to be that groups of molecules of the dye are coupled to macromolecules, such as sulphated mucopolysaccharides, in such a way that the absorptive behaviour of the molecular complex is altered and thus the colour of the transmitted light observed down the microscope is changed.

LOOSE CONNECTIVE TISSUE

This is also known as areolar connective tissue because in stained preparations there are many small areas in which no structural organization is apparent. This tissue can serve as a model for the structure of all connective tissue. It is found typically beneath the skin, around viscera, in serous membranes, around organs and muscles and in the nooks and crannies of the body such as occur between the tendons and around joints. Fig. 16.1 is a drawing of a section of typical areolar tissue stained with haematoxylin and eosin. Large numbers of strands, 2–10 μm in diameter, are each made up of fibres smaller than 1 μm, which in turn are formed of bundles of microfibrils. The fibres branch by splitting and can be fanned out like the cords making up a rope. These are collagen fibres. Another and different kind of fibrous material can also be seen. These are the elastic fibres, which occur less frequently than the collagen fibres in most connective

FIG. 16.1. Diagram of the structure of loose connective tissue, × 500.

tissues. The EM shows that elastic fibres have a homogeneous structure unlike collagen fibres; furthermore the branching of elastic fibres is different from that of collagen strands in that branches may link up with each other to form a loose irregular net.

The fibrous structure of loose connective tissue resembles a loosely woven woollen cloth which gives easily when it is pulled and has sufficient elasticity to return to its original shape when released. The loose mesh is ideal for holding the weak gel-like ground substance and water. Because of the content of mucopolysaccharides and the mesh of fibres, the water is not free to move about easily in loose connective tissue, and yet like water in a filter-paper there is no barrier to diffusion.

The cells of loose connective tissue are few in number but characteristic. Fibroblasts, macrophages, mast cells and fat cells are found scattered through the meshwork of fibrils. Loose connective tissue is a living tissue and it contains a blood supply. Furthermore, because the slow movement of water is an important part of its function some lymphatic capillaries are also present in association with the blood capillaries.

FIBROBLASTS

The fibroblast is the cell type most commonly seen in connective tissue (fig. 16.1). It has a prominent round or slightly elongated vesiculate nucleus with a prominent nucleolus and the cell body tends to be drawn out into a number of projections. In the EM abundant rough surfaced endoplasmic reticulum, pinocytotic vesicles, lysosomes, modest numbers of mitochondria and granules of varying size are seen. In tissues that are actively growing, e.g. in young animals or around a healing wound, the cytoplasm of the fibroblast is basophilic and easily seen in light microscopy. In old tissues such as a contracted scar the fibroblasts become less active and protein synthesis diminishes. The nucleus elongates and there is only a thin layer of cytoplasm, hard to demonstrate in conventional histological preparations. These changes are reflected in fine structure; rough surfaced endoplasmic reticulum decreases and the Golgi zone is less prominent. The term fibroblast should be reserved for those cells that are actively dividing or synthesizing new fibrous material and cells found in old stable tissues are called fibrocytes.

MACROPHAGES

Macrophages are known also by other names such as fixed and wandering histiocytes, phagocytic cells, monocytes or clasmatocytes. They are present in most connective tissue and are approximately as numerous as the fibroblasts from which they are distinguished by having a darker, more indented bean-shaped nucleus. If a supravital dye such as colloidal trypan blue is injected into connective tissue a day or two before the tissue is taken for histological examination, the difference between a macrophage and a fibroblast is apparent, for only the cytoplasm of the macrophage contains appreciable numbers of granules of dye. This experiment demonstrates that one of the important functions of the macrophage is to scavenge for foreign particles, fragments of cells or extracellular material. The adjectives fixed or wandering are largely superfluous as, given an appropriate stimulus, fixed cells become amoeboid and move about the tissue. After injection of colloidal material, macrophages move into the site from adjacent regions and monocytes may move through capillary walls and become indistinguishable from tissue macrophages. In such situations some neutrophil polymorphs from the blood also move into the site. These cells are actively phagocytic but are smaller than the macrophages; indeed they are sometimes called microphages. They are easily distinguished by their characteristic lobed nuclei. The oxygen consumption of macrophages rises during phagocytosis.

Another distinction between macrophages and fibroblasts is found in their general disposition. Fibroblasts tend to occur in relation to collagen fibres, whereas macrophages congregate, sometimes in clusters, in the region of blood vessels. Some tissues such as tendons or ligaments may be practically free of macrophages, while other tissues such as the omentum have many.

MAST CELLS

Mast cells are relatively common in connective tissue, particularly in association with the blood vessels in adipose tissue. The name comes from the German word, *masten* to feed, and they were so named because these prominent cells are full of granules and were thought to be phagocytic. We now know that they manufacture macromolecules of carbohydrate and are producers of granules and not overfed cells. The granules are not seen well in sections stained with haematoxylin and eosin, but in squashed preparations of connective tissue, methylene blue stains the mast cells and their masses of granules clearly. Mast cells are about the same size as fibroblasts and are more spherical with round nuclei, when this is visible through the granules (fig. 16.1).

Mast cells are known to produce a number of substances, including the mucopolysaccharide heparin, which is used to prevent clotting of blood and has other possibly important roles. These granules of complex macromolecules are responsible for the characteristic metachromasia of mast cells. Thus the dye, toluidine blue, stains them red instead of the expected blue. Histamine and 5-hydroxytryptamine are also made by mast cells although the latter is produced in very low concentrations, if at all, in human mast cells.

FAT CELLS

The fat cell is highly specialized and plays a big role in metabolism; they occur in most loose connective tissues in small clumps or even singly and in some situations they form large aggregates organized into lobules by strands of connective tissue (chap. 32).

The four types of cell described are not the only cells that can be found in connective tissue, but they are the most common. White cells from the blood, polymorphs, lymphocytes and monocytes are occasionally found in loose connective tissue particularly, and these cells appear in large numbers when there is inflammation. A specialized cell known as a **plasma cell** is frequently found. This cell has a basophilic cytoplasm and an eccentrically placed nucleus with a prominent Golgi region which usually shows up as a pale area, centrally placed, near the nucleus. Plasma cells have an important function in the manufacture of antibodies (chap. 27). As might be expected, plasma cells are found where foreign proteins are likely to gain entrance to the body, e.g. beneath the epithelial membranes lining the respiratory and alimentary tracts.

DENSE CONNECTIVE TISSUE

This tissue is found in tendons and fasciae where strength and flexibility are needed and in such structures as the ligamentum nuchae or the aortic wall where distensibility as well as strength is required. The strength is achieved by a great increase in fibrous material which in tendons is produced almost entirely by collagen fibrils arranged in parallel bundles. Although collagen has little elasticity in comparison with elastin, it is nevertheless very strong by absolute standards. The tension imposed on the Achilles tendon during games such as tennis is a measure of its strength. In terms of loading, the ability of the fibrocartilaginous intervertebral discs, largely collagen, to withstand pressures of up to 250 kg/cm² is an index of the resistance of collagen to distortion. In big tendons groups of collagen bundles are organized into fascicles by loose connective tissue in which the blood vessels run, but both the blood supply and cell population are relatively small. The only cells seen in sections of tendons are strings of flattened fibrocytes running between groups of fibres (fig. 16.2). In structures where distensibility as well as

FIG. 16.2. Dense connective tissue. A section cut from a large mature tendon. This shows the flattened fibrocytes sparsely distributed among the collagen fibres, × 200.

strength is important, such as the aortic wall, elastic tissue is prominent. Fresh elastic tissue is yellow and tissues with a predominance of elastic tissue have a distinct yellow tint. In sections the elastic tissue is characteristically coiled and branched in configurations which are quite distinct from the regular arrangement found in collagen fibre bundles.

Fascial sheets of tissue as in the fascia lata need strength and flexibility in many directions and so the collagen fibres are randomly arranged in thick bundles somewhat similar to the cellulose fibres in a sheet of paper.

Mesothelial or serosal membranes

These tissues form the lining of pleural, pericardial and peritoneal cavities and include mesentery and omental tissues. The only difference between these membranous sheets and fasciae is the presence of a single layer of squamous cells on the inner surface or, in the case of a mesentery supporting an organ such as the gut, on both sides of a lining membrane (p. 17.2). The connective tissue elements in these membranes are essentially similar to those in loose connective tissue In the mesenteries and omental tissues large amounts of adipose tissue may develop in well-nourished subjects. The lining membranes have important properties concerning water movements. This is illustrated by the fact that in disease there may be large quantities of fluid in the peritoneal, pericardial, or pleural cavities. The normal thin films of fluid make these membranes slippery. This is a most important property of the membranes which allows, for example, the coils of the gut to glide over each other without difficulty. The lubricant is a mucopolysaccharide, chiefly hyaluronic acid which is discussed more fully on p. 16.8.

The proteins and mucopolysaccharides of connective tissue

COLLAGEN

Collagen is remarkable both because of its amino acid composition and because of the amazingly regular way in which the molecules of protein are put together to make the basic fibre unit. The microfibril is in register with neighbouring microfibrils so that it produces a charac-

FIG. 16.3. Diagrammatic view of the way tropocollagen molecules are arranged in the formation of collagen microfibrils.

teristic banded appearance under the EM. This is diagnostic of collagen as no other fibrous protein possesses this particular periodicity. Fig. 16.3 shows a diagrammatic EM view of a collagen microfibril. The major periodicity of about 70 nm is illustrated. In tissues the microfibrils line up when running parallel, so that the corresponding part of each band matches. Thus characteristic dark and light bands run across bundles of microfibrils.

At higher magnifications and with different preparative techniques, the basic 2 band 70 nm periodicity can be seen to be itself made up of some 10 or 11 sub-bands (fig. 16.3). In the actual formation of a microfibril the basic molecular units must aggregate in an overlapping ordered fashion. The ordering of the tens of thousands of molecules so precisely in a microfibril is a most remarkable phenomenon.

The basic molecule is **tropocollagen.** These molecules are synthesized inside the fibroblast cell, but the microfibrils are put together outside the cell. It has been possible to disintegrate collagen into tropocollagen and to demonstrate the ability of these molecules to aggregate side by side in suitable environments, and so build the microfibril complete with periodicity in a test tube. Thus the fibroblasts secrete tropocollagen into the regions about the cells where the molecules line up end to end and side by side to form long microfibrils which can be seen to grow thicker as they are pushed away from the cell of origin by more secretion. The fibrils near a cell are thin and gradually become thicker at a distance from the cell. The long fibrils found in connective tissue imply a remarkable degree of co-ordination between neighbouring fibroblasts.

The secreted tropocollagen molecules have a length of about 280 nm and a diameter of some 1·5 nm with a molecular weight of about 350,000. Each molecule consists of three separate polypeptide chains, each made of about a thousand amino acids. In the chain of amino acids, nearly every fourth one is glycine, followed by either a hydroxyproline or a proline molecule. Collagen is unique in containing about 13 per cent of hydroxyproline. This can be estimated chemically and thus the amount of collagen in a tissue can be calculated from the amount of hydroxyproline present. Hydroxyproline excretion in urine is also used to study collagen metabolism.

FIG. 16.4. Collagen formation. After Gross (1961)

Normally it is about 60 mg/24 hr in growing children, falling to half this value in healthy adults. In some diseases, such as hyperthyroidism or Paget's disease of bone, hydroxyproline excretion is increased. An interesting feature concerning the hydroxyproline and hydroxylysine of collagen is that they are formed by hydroxylation of proline and lysine in the formation of tropocollagen molecules. This is unusual because most other amino acids in proteins are supplied from the pool of amino acids. The content of sulphur containing amino acids and aromatic amino acids is small in collagen.

ELASTIN

Elastin is, like collagen, a fibrous protein, but its rod-like molecules are packed in a random fashion and so the EM reveals no ordered ultrastructure. Elastin occurs in tissues either as interconnected threads, as in the skin, or as more massive fibres, as in the ligamentum nuchae, or as fenestrated plates, as in the wall of the aorta, where as many as fifty plates may make up the thickness of the elastic tissue in the wall. Elastin is resistant to drying and survives in good condition in Egyptian mummies.

The amino acid composition of elastin differs from that of collagen most notably in that its content of hydroxyproline is low, as is its content of dicarboxylic amino acids. Apart from these differences the proteins have a similar composition. Each has important associated carbohydrate complexes and are therefore glycoproteins. The dicarboxylic acid groups may help to bind mucopolysaccharides to the collagen protofibrils; these giant molecules may lace the protein molecules together to give the highly ordered collagen structure. Elastin is associated with lipid material and sphingolipid and galactosides have been extracted from it.

MUCOPOLYSACCHARIDES

The mucopolysaccharides of connective tissue account for only 1–5 g/kg of fresh tissue, but their relationship to water and hormone metabolism is important. Thus in the myxoedema of hypothyroid disease, the thickening of the skin may be due to excessive hydration of mucopolysaccharide. The dramatic water holding capacity of mucopolysaccharides is apparent in the tissues of the cock's comb. In the mature bird this is a massive headpiece of firm consistency yet it is over 90 per cent water. It contains some 2 per cent of collagen and about 7 per cent of the mucopolysaccharide, hyaluronic acid. The mass of the comb is dependent upon the levels of androgens in the blood, so much so that the weight of the castrated cock's comb can be used to assay quantities of androgens. The size of the tissue and its turgidity is due to the quantity of hyaluronic acid present and this in turn is dependent on the quantity of androgens present. Wharton's jelly of the umbilical cord and the vitreous humour of the eye are other examples of mucopolysaccharide gels.

There are many complex carbohydrates present in biological systems and the elucidation of their structures and functions is difficult. The term mucopolysaccharide was originally introduced to describe the hexosamine-containing polysaccharides found in animal tissues, particularly in viscous secretions, hence the prefix muco. Now the term refers to those substances which contain residues of both a uronic acid and a hexosamine and are thus acidic mucopolysaccharides. The acidic nature of these molecules is probably responsible for their ion binding properties which are often enhanced by the presence of one or more sulphate groups. There are at least seven well characterized mucopolysaccharides associated with connective tissue and some of their properties are set out in table 16.4.

TABLE 16.4. Properties of some common mucopolysaccharides.

Mucopolysaccharide	Component monosaccharides	Approximate mol. wt.	Occurrence
Hyaluronic acid	D-Glucuronic acid, 2-acetamido-2-deoxy-D-glucose	1,500,000	Vitreous humour, ground substance of connective tissues, umbilical cord, plasma, synovial fluids, cardiac valves
Chondroitin	D-Glucuronic acid, 2-acetamido-2-deoxy-D-galactose	50,000	Bovine cornea, septal cartilage
Chondroitin sulphate A (chondroitin 4-sulphate)	D-Glucuronic acid, 2-acetamido-2-deoxy-4-o-sulpho-D-galactose	50,000	Aortic tissue, cartilage, adult bone, ligamentum nuchae, cornea
Chondroitin sulphate B (dermatan sulphate)	L-Iduronic acid, 2-acetamido-2-deoxy-4-o-sulpho-D-galactose	50,000	Cardiac valves, pig skin, bovine lung tissue, bovine sclera
Chondroitin sulphate C (chondroitin 6-sulphate)	D-Glucuronic acid, 2-acetamido-2-deoxy-6-o-sulpho-D-galactose	5000	Aortic tissue, cartilage, adult bone, cardiac valves, umbilical cord
Keratosulphate (keratan sulphate)	D-Galactose, 2-acetamido-2-deoxy-6-o-sulpho-D-glucose	?10,000	Nucleus pulposus, costal cartilage, corneal tissue, aortic tissue
Heparin	D-Glucuronic acid, 2-deoxy-2-sulphoamino-D-glucose with additional o-sulphate groups	20,000	Liver, mast cells, spleen, muscle, lung, thymus, blood, heart

There are three hexose bricks in the mucopolysaccharides, namely, D-glucose, L-idose and D-galactose. Fig. 16.5 shows that the essential difference is the position of the OH or CHOH groups above or below the plane of the pyranose ring of the molecule. In the common hexuronic acids the CHOH group at position C-5 is replaced by COOH to give D-glucuronic acid or L-iduronic acid. The hexosamines have NH_2 at C-2 instead of OH;

which are derived from them. For example, the basic unit of chondroitin sulphate A and chondroitin sulphate B (table 16.4) differ only in the orientation of the aldehyde groups on C-5 of the hexuronic acid (glucose and idose, 2 and 3 of fig. 16.5). Such small changes in orientation are not easy to identify, and this is one reason why knowledge of these important molecules has lagged behind that of proteins and lipids. Another factor is that the polysac-

FIG. 16.5. Basic structural elements of acidic mucopolysaccharides.

glucosamine and galactosamine are the usual hexosamines found in mucopolysaccharides. The repetitive unit is usually a disaccharide hexuronic acid-acetylated hexosamine combination. This is shown in fig. 16.5 where the basic structure of hyaluronic acid is depicted. The sulphate groups are found on the C-4 or C-6 positions of the hexosamine. Heparin is more complex in that it is based on a tetrasaccharide unit with five or six sulphate groups, one of which is found attached to the nitrogen group at C-2 of the hexosamine and another at the C-2 carbon position of the hexuronic acid.

In the same way as proteins are composed of twenty or so amino acids, polysaccharides are built up from a few basic molecules. The shape of the monomer appears to be of importance in carbohydrate polymers because small changes in the configuration of the side groups makes a difference in the properties of the mucopolysaccharides

charides are intimately associated with proteins and lipids to form macromolecular complexes which are difficult to break down into consistent and stable degradation products.

HYALURONIC ACID

Hyaluronic acid is the best known of the mucopolysaccharides and it has the widest distribution in connective tissue. In tissues it is closely associated with a protein, forming a highly hydrated complex with a molecular weight of about 10^7. The different properties of hyaluronic acid extracted from tissue ground substance and from synovial fluid may be due to the nature of the associated proteins.

Apart from its water holding capacity hyaluronic acid has the property of increasing the slipperiness of fluids and the lubricating and shock absorbing system of joints is dependent on the state of the hyaluronic acid complexes in the synovial fluid. In rheumatic diseases of joints, upsets in hyaluronic acid metabolism occur.

CHONDROITIN

Chondroitin and the chondroitin sulphates A and C have a wide distribution in tissues but as their name suggests they are particularly important in the structure of cartilage. The intercellular elements of hyaline cartilage consist of a network of fine collagen fibrils, visible only with the EM, supported by a chondroitin–sulphate–protein complex which varies in different parts, as is shown by staining with toluidine blue which reacts metachromatically with chondroitin sulphates. Radioactive sulphur has been used to study the sulphate metabolism of cartilage.

Table 16.4 shows that mucopolysaccharides such as chondroitin sulphate B and keratosulphate have a wide distribution, the only systematic difference between them being an association of chondroitin sulphate B with tissues in which coarse collagen strands are prominent. The list of tissues in table 16.4 reflects merely those tissues which have been studied.

SKELETAL TISSUES

Bone and cartilage are also specialized connective tissues of mesodermal origin. Like the other connective tissues, their main function is mechanical. Together with their attached ligaments, they provide a framework for the support and protection of soft tissues and a system of levers which enable muscles to act effectively. The range of mechanical functions performed by the skeleton varies from such delicate tasks as the transmission of sound waves in the middle ear to withstanding loads of many times the body weight. For example, the femoral neck during normal walking is subjected to a load of three times the body weight, while during athletic activity, such as running or jumping, the load may be increased to five or six times the body weight, i.e. about half a ton.

In addition to these mechanical functions, bone plays a role in the metabolism of calcium and magnesium and is the major reservoir of these elements. The mechanical and biochemical functions of bone are dependent on one another. Excessive metabolic demand for calcium, as in hyperparathyroidism, may result in mechanical failure. Immobilization of a limb similarly leads to decalcification of the bones.

BONE

Physical characteristics of bone

The structure of bone is well suited to its mechanical purpose. The upper end of the femur in a young adult, for example, can withstand a vertical load of nearly 1 ton, i.e. twice the load that would be imposed in the course of maximal athletic activity. When this safety margin is exceeded, a fracture results. In old age and in a great variety of diseases the strength of bones is impaired, and they break more readily (pathological fractures).

The forces to which bones are subjected include compression, tension and a combination of these in twisting or bending strains. Table 16.5 shows that bone compares

TABLE 16.5. Forces to which materials can be subjected.

	Ultimate tensile stress (kg/mm^2)	Ultimate compressive strength (kg/mm^2)	Modulus of elasticity
Human cortical bone	7–10	14–21	1·6
Cast iron	7–21	42–100	20·0
Mild steel	42–63	45	30·0
Mahogany	8	4	1·3
Granite	10–20	9–26	—

well with other structural materials. Another useful mechanical property of bone is elasticity, i.e. its ability to return to its original shape after the deforming force has been applied. The lower the modulus of elasticity of a material the greater its flexibility and therefore the less its liability to fracture with a given stress. Further protection against sudden impact is provided by the soft tissues which cover bone; it had been shown for example, that the cranium without the protection of the scalp may be fractured by a force of 0·5 kiloponds whereas with the intact covering of the scalp a force of 5 kiloponds is necessary.

The strength of bone depends upon two properties, the nature of bone tissue, and the design or architecture of the whole bone.

The nature of bone tissue

Bone tissue has two main components, an organic matrix consisting largely of collagen and a mineral matrix consisting of calcium, phosphate and other elements in a crystalline form.

Each matrix contributes to the strength of bone, the collagen being responsible for its tensile strength, as it is in tendons and fascia, and the mineral for its compressive strength and rigidity.

THE ORGANIC MATRIX

The organic matrix which is called **osteoid** accounts for 25 per cent of the weight and 38 per cent of the volume of adult bone; 95 per cent of the organic matrix consists of collagen and the remaining 5 per cent of interfibrillar ground substance containing small amounts of mucopolysaccharides which include hyaluronic acid and chondroitin sulphate and some proteins. The collagen of bone appears indistinguishable from that of other connective tissues and yet it differs from these in that it can accumulate minerals in an ordered fashion during bone formation.

THE MINERAL MATRIX

Bone mineral has a rigid crystalline structure with an X-ray diffraction pattern characteristic of the 'apatites' and is called **hydroxyapatite**. Its probable composition is $Ca_{10}(PO_4)_6(OH)_2$ with the addition of small and variable amounts of other ions, notably Mg^{++}, Na^+, $CO_3^=$, Citrate$^=$ and F^-.

The mechanism of calcification is not yet fully understood. It is a property shared by the osteoid tissue of bone, the matrix of growth cartilage, teeth and by a number of other tissues when damaged or diseased, such as atheromatous blood vessels or tuberculous lymph nodes. Two factors appear to be necessary for the process of calcification:

(1) a suitable matrix such as collagen which can act as a site for the initiation of crystallization of the bone minerals from a solution of calcium and phosphate which exists in the tissue fluids,

(2) phosphatase activity which produces a local concentration of phosphate ions and so favours crystal growth in the presence of calcium ions.

The hydroxyapatite crystals are first formed at regular intervals along the collagen fibrils and thereafter enlarge to form needle shaped or flat plaques along and perhaps within the collagen fibre. The small amounts of mucopolysaccharides present in association with the bone collagen may be the factor which allows mineralization to proceed.

In health, mineralization proceeds so rapidly that osteoid or unmineralized bone matrix is found only in minute quantity at sites of bone formation. Where mineralization is impaired as in rickets or osteomalacia, excess of osteoid occurs leading to softening and mechanical failure of the skeleton.

The surface ions of the lattice of the apatite crystal are hydrated and this binds a layer of ions and water around the crystal, the **hydration shell**. Water thus forms an integral part of the apatite crystal as well as of the interstitial fluid of bone. With increasing age the water content diminishes and the amount of mineral increases. The water content of bone is important for the maintenance of its elastic property and provides a means by which bone salts take part in a dynamic metabolic exchange with ions in the body fluids.

The surface area of the bone crystals in the adult amounts to many acres and exchange of ions with body fluids occurs over this area through the hydration shell. Normally these include Na^+, Mg^+ and Ca^{++}, citrate and carbonate but other ions taken by mouth or inhaled which have a affinity for bone may also become incorporated, e.g. strontium, radium or lead and fluoride, and persist there for many years.

The ionic exchange provides a physical basis for the continuous process of remoulding and replacement of bone which continues throughout life. About 700 mg of Ca is exchanged between blood and bone each day and the calcium in blood is in dynamic equilibrium with that in bone. This process is assisted by the activity of bone cells and influenced by parathyroid hormone, thyrocalcitonin, vitamin D and the pH of the environment. An analysis of the human skeleton shows that it contains 99 per cent of the total calcium, 88 per cent of the phosphate, 70 per cent of the citrate, 80 per cent of the carbonate, 50 per cent of the magnesium, 30 per cent of the sodium and 9 per cent of the water in the body.

While all these substances either form an integral part of the bone crystal or are associated with it as part of ionic exchange, the high concentration of citrate has for long been a puzzle. There is evidence to suggest it plays a more active metabolic role and is formed in bone. Parathyroid hormone increases citrate production by bone and vitamin D, which is essential for the normal calcification of osteoid tissue, restores the blood level of citrate which is reduced in rickets or vitamin D deficiency.

The cells of bone

Bone tissue is formed by **osteoblasts**, maintained by **osteocytes** and resorbed by the action of **osteoclasts**. These cells can each assume the role of the others depending upon their situation and environment.

Bone cells originate from mesenchymal cells capable of differentiating into fibroblasts, bone or cartilaginous cells. So closely related are the different types of connective tissues that more than one type may develop in response to certain diseased and injured states. Thus in the healing of fractures, cartilage is frequently found in the callus of new bone, and in damaged muscle bone may form (myositis ossificans) as well as fibrous tissue.

OSTEOBLASTS

Osteoblasts are most readily recognized at the site of new bone formation where they form a continuous layer of cuboidal cells with basophilic cytoplasm and large nuclei covering the growing bone surfaces (plate 16.1a, facing p. 15.4). When bone formation ceases, they become inconspicuous spindle cells which continue to line all bone surfaces and are capable of emerging from this resting phase to resume osteogenic function in response to a variety of stimuli including mechanical stress or trauma. The osteoblasts form the organic matrix of bone. During their active phase they contain alkaline phosphatase which assists in a way not fully understood in the process of mineralization.

OSTEOCYTES

As the bone matrix is elaborated by the osteoblasts a number of these cells become trapped in the new bone tissue and are then referred to as osteocytes (fig. 16.6 and

FIG. 16.6. Osteocytes are spindle-shaped cells lying in lacunae within bone. Processes from these cells permeate the bone in fine canaliculi through which the cells make contact with the tissue fluids at the bone surfaces.

plate 16.1a, facing p. 15.4). The osteocytes occupy lacunae in the bone matrix and are connected to each other and to the bone surfaces by a large number of cytoplasmic processes which lie in canaliculi permeating the bone and so providing a route for metabolic exchange between the bone and the tissue fluids. The osteocytes exert an influence on the hydration shell of bone matrix in their immediate vicinity from which they can withdraw or deposit bone mineral as the biochemical needs of the body dictate.

OSTEOCLASTS

Osteoclasts occur in mononucleated or multinucleated forms; the nuclei resemble those of the osteoblasts and osteocytes. These cells have a common origin. They lie on the bone surfaces at sites of bone resorption and their activity is revealed by the presence of eroded areas in the adjacent bone (plate 16.1b, facing p. 15.4). Osteoclasts are the only cells known to be capable of bone resorption. They are found therefore at sites of bone remodelling and their number increases in response to parathyroid hormone.

They have a dual function; together with osteoblasts they shape and organize the architecture of bone structure in response to mechanical stress, and they share with the osteocytes the function of making calcium and other ions available for the physiological requirements of the body.

Bone architecture

Bone tissue occurs in two main forms: woven (fibre bone) and lamellar bone.

WOVEN BONE (plate 16.2a, facing p. 15.5)

This is a transient form which is seen during phases of rapid bone formation, as in embryonic life or at zones of endochondral ossification. It is found also in the early callus which first appears in the healing of a fracture. Woven bone consists of a loose framework of delicate bone trabeculae which, as its name implies, appears like a loosely woven material in a histological section. It is mechanically inefficient as a structural material and is normally succeeded rapidly by the formation of lamellar bone, but in the rare disease of fragilitas ossium this transition is incomplete and affected infants have fragile skeletons.

LAMELLAR BONE

This is made up of a series of layers in each of which the collagen fibres have a distinct orientation which differs from the adjoining layers, rather like the structure of plywood; this is one of the many features contributing to bone strength. Lamellar bone occurs in two distinct structural forms, described as cortical (compact) and cancellous (spongy) bone.

FIG. 16.7. Diagram of cortical bone showing the structure of an osteone. These rod-shaped units of bone structure are made up of series of lamellae. In each layer the collagen fibres are orientated in a direction different from those in the adjacent layers. From Bassett C.A.L. Electrical effects on bone. *Sci. Amer.* 213, **18**.

FIG. 16.8. Three-dimensional diagram of cancellous bone structure at a bone end. Note the cross linkage between the trabeculae supporting the predominantly vertical orientation. From *Documenta Geigy* (1963) Osteoarthritis of the knee joint II, *Acta clinica*.

Cortical bone (fig. 16.7 and plate 16.2b, facing p. 15.5)
This forms the cylindrical shafts of the long bones. It is made up of a large number of rod like units known as Haversian systems or osteones which consist of a central canal containing vessels and nerve fibres surrounded by up to fourteen concentric lamellae. The osteones branch and interweave one with another, their long axes coinciding with the major lines of stress, again revealing the structural design of bone.

Cancellous bone (fig. 16.8)
This is found at the expanded ends of the long bones and occupies most of the irregular bones of the skeleton. It is composed of lamellar bone, arranged in the form of trabeculae which are laid down in an orderly pattern

FIG. 16.9. The arrangement of trabeculae shown in this X-ray of a femoral head is as characteristic of the femur as its external form. Like cancellous bone elsewhere in the body its structure is so organized as to provide great strength with economy of material.

constant in any individual bone. Wherever the architectural arrangement of these trabeculae has been studied it has been found to be the most efficient structure for withstanding the stresses experienced by that particular bone (fig. 16.9).

The fact that the internal structure of bone develops in response to mechanical stress has been recognized for many years. If the stresses applied to a bone are altered the trabeculae become rearranged to meet the new stresses. For example, if a joint is surgically fused, new trabecular patterns develop in the participating bones. Again, when a fracture heals, an excess of bone first forms at the fracture site but with the passage of time the callus is gradually remodelled in an attempt to restore the original form of the bone. In childhood this responsiveness of bone is so marked that malaligned fractures may straighten out completely in a few years. This capacity diminishes and the accuracy of fracture reduction is more critical in adult life than in childhood.

The mechanism by which bone adapts to stress has until recently remained obscure. John Hunter, in 1770, was the first to recognize that bone, hitherto regarded as an inert tissue, was in fact 'constantly changing in its matter'. It is now known that osteoblasts and osteoclasts effect this process and that mechanical stress is one of the stimuli to which they respond. Recently it has been shown that when bone is stressed, small electrical potentials are generated within it which may be the ultimate stimulus to which the cells of bone respond.

As discussed in chap. 18 the basic shape of an individual bone is conferred upon it by a preceding model of cartilage or membrane. Growth cartilage is endowed from early embryonic life with a potential for reproducing a specific bone form and subject to certain hormonal and nutritional influences it dictates the ultimate size of each bone. This development is independent of mechanical stresses or normal anatomical relationships, since undifferentiated mesenchymal tissue from an embryonic limb bud can grow even in tissue culture into recognizable bone forms. Thus the external shape and size of the individual bones of the skeleton are controlled by intrinsic factors inherent within the early growth cartilage. Once bone has replaced cartilage, however, extrinsic factors such as mechanical stress are necessary for the maintenance of its form and for the development of its internal architecture.

Skeletal turnover

The amount of bone in the skeleton depends upon the balance between bone formation and bone resorption, i.e. between osteoblastic and osteoclastic activity. During the growing period both processes are highly active although bone formation clearly exceeds destruction. In adult life until middle age the amount of bone remains constant, but during this time there is a continuous process of repair and replacement of the skeleton so that there is a complete turnover of bone approximately every 20 years.

In old age resorption exceeds formation leading to an atrophy of the skeleton which is called osteoporosis. If this atrophic process is severe the safety margin of skeletal strength is reduced and fractures may result from slight trauma.

Periosteum

The periosteum is the ensheathing membrane which covers bone, except where it is covered by articular cartilage. It consists of an inner layer composed of osteoblasts which is conspicuous during the growing period and contributes largely to the increase in diameter of the bone, and an outer fibrous layer which carries part of the blood supply to the bone and provides attachment for muscles and ligaments. During the growing period the periosteum is firmly attached only at the circumference of the epiphyseal cartilage plate. Elsewhere it can be peeled off the bone as easily as a banana skin. Because of this loose attachment the muscles and ligaments which are attached to the periosteum may move their attachments over the underlying bone, during the growth of the bone. If this were not so, the fact that bone growth in length takes place only at the epiphyseal cartilage plates would result in a bizarre situation where many muscle origins and insertions were

restricted to a narrow zone somewhere near the centre of each long bone.

It is only after growth ceases and the periosteum no longer slides like an elastic sheet over the underlying bone that firmer attachments develop and muscles acquire an anchorage through collagen fibres which pass directly into the bone tissue itself.

For powerful muscles such as the biceps, quadriceps and gastrocnemius, the periosteal attachment described above would not be strong enough and in these instances the muscles acquire a direct attachment to bone during the growth period through the medium of secondary centres of ossification.

Blood supply of bone

As with many other features of the anatomy of bone the blood supply has a different arrangement before and after growth has ceased. A typical long bone has four principal groups of vessels (fig. 16.10).

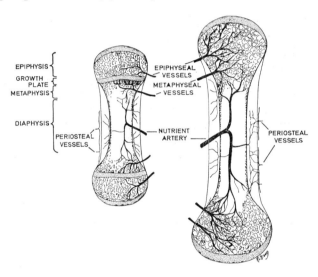

Fig. 16.10. Diagram showing the arrangement of blood vessels in bone before and after the growth period. Note that the growth plate isolates the epiphyseal from the metaphyseal circulation during the growing period, but that they anastomose freely after growth has ceased. The periosteal vessels supply the osteogenic layer on the bone surface during the growth period, but penetrate the cortex and supplement the nutrient artery in adult life.

The **epiphyseal** vessels supply the epiphyseal centres of ossification and are concerned also with the nutrition of growth cartilage. These vessels do not anastomose with the **metaphyseal** vessels since the cartilage acts as an avascular septum. The metaphyseal vessels sustain the vigorous new bone formation and remodelling which takes place on the metaphyseal side of the growth cartilage. The diaphysis is supplied mainly by one or more large **nutrient arteries** which penetrate the cortex to branch within the medullary cavity supplying the marrow and the greater part of the bone shaft.

The **periosteal** contribution to the blood supply of bone is slight during the growing period but increases when growth ceases and the periosteum acquires a firm and stable relationship to the underlying bone. As the growth plate disappears a free anastomosis develops between the epiphyseal and metaphyseal circulations.

The separate sources of blood supply in the growth period leads to a risk of avascular necrosis of bone. Thus infection of bone which may thrombose the nutrient artery can lead to death and sequestration of an entire diaphysis in childhood, whereas this complication is less common in adult life when loss of the nutrient artery can be replaced by the periosteal blood supply.

Relationship of bone and marrow

At first sight the association of bone and haemopoietic marrow appears to be a marriage of convenience; bone in order to combine strength with lightness is arranged in a tubular form which affords ideal protection for the delicate marrow tissue. However, the relationship is more profound than this for frequently haemopoietic marrow tends to develop in association with bone which forms outside the skeleton, e.g. in damaged muscle or tendon. When this happens, the bone simultaneously becomes organized into a capsular form with a thin cortex containing the marrow. From evidence such as this it has been suggested that the marrow may be one of the several factors which help to determine the structure of bone.

CARTILAGE

Structure and function of cartilage

Cartilage is the other major component of the skeleton and like bone has several roles to perform. The greater part of the skeleton is first represented by cartilage, which in due course is replaced by bone through the process of endochondral ossification considered in chap. 18. The cartilage model is responsible for both the shape and ultimate size of the individual bones. During foetal life or soon after birth the cartilage in each bone becomes restricted to two regions, the epiphyseal cartilage plate or plates which are responsible for the continued growth in length of the long bones and which disappear in adolescence, and the articular surface of bone. The articular cartilage contributes to the size of the epiphyses, or the whole bone in the case of the carpal and tarsal bones which lack separate cartilage plates.

The superficial layers form a highly efficient joint surface which possesses enduring low friction properties which are the envy of engineers. The coefficient of friction of articular cartilage is approximately 0·013 which is almost three times more slippery than ice articulating

with ice. Finally articular cartilage serves as a cushion which helps to protect the underlying bone from the effects of sudden loading. Cartilage also persists into adult life as an integral part of the skeleton notably in the rib cartilages.

Other types of cartilage tissues exist outside the skeleton in the framework of the ear and respiratory system.

Structure of cartilage

Cartilage is a firm gel bound together by the fibrous proteins collagen and elastin in varying proportions. The descriptive terms hyaline, fibrous or elastic are applied to it according to the relative amount of collagen or elastin. Hyaline cartilage is clear homogeneous tissue (Greek *hyalos*: glass) from which articular and rib cartilage is formed. Fibrocartilage is a firmer opaque material found in the menisci of the knee joint and elastic cartilage, which is yellow in colour, is found in the structure of the ear and epiglottis.

Hyaline cartilage contains 80 per cent water, 6 per cent mineral salt and 14 per cent organic substance which includes the fibrous proteins and chondromucoprotein, a complex protein molecule to which are bound sulphated polysaccharides, chiefly chondroitin sulphate. The chondromucoprotein holds the large amount of water present in cartilage, and is largely responsible for its resilience.

As in bone the fibrous protein of cartilage shows a high degree of organization which varies with the particular function and type of cartilage and with age. For example, in articular cartilage the fibres tend to arise more or less perpendicularly from the underlying bone to form arches with the fibres at the summit running roughly parallel with the joint surface (fig. 16.11). This arrangement becomes more obvious with increasing age.

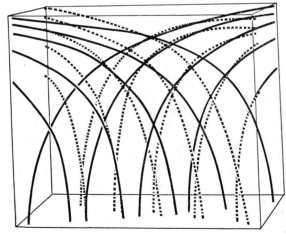

FIG. 16.11. Diagram illustrating the arched arrangement of collagen fibres in articular cartilage. As the fibres approach the surface they become parallel with it. From *Documenta Geigy* (1963) Osteoarthritis of the knee joint, II. *Acta clinica.*

The chondroblast and chondrocyte

The chondroblast is the cell responsible for the formation of cartilage. The appearance and distribution of these cells alters with the degree of activity and the type of cartilage. In a resting phase (chondrocyte) the cell is plump and circular, with a large rounded nucleus, filling a lacuna within the cartilage matrix, and usually uniformly distributed throughout (plate 16.3a, facing p. 17.6). During the growing phase they are smaller and more flattened in appearance. The different forms are well shown in the epiphyseal cartilage plate (plate 16.3b, facing p. 17.6). Here the cells are organized into columns in the axis of growth, the smaller proliferating cells lying in the epiphyseal side. As they move down the column they become hypertrophied while the surrounding matrix becomes calcified. Eventually the cells degenerate and become invaded by capillary loops in the metaphysis and bone becomes deposited upon the scaffold of calcified matrix in the process of endochondral ossification described more fully in chap. 18. Cartilage growth is mainly interstitial, i.e. the proliferating cells divide within their matrix, whereas bone growth is appositional, taking place at the surfaces; this is the only type of growth which can occur in a rigid structure.

Calcification

Cartilage shares with bone the property of calcification. This is most evident in the epiphyseal cartilage plate where it occurs in the matrix of the hypertrophic zone and is an essential precursor to the subsequent endochondral ossification. If mineralization is prevented as in the disease of rickets the invasion by vascular tissue and bone is inhibited and the hypertrophic zone becomes greatly widened. Calcification may occur in other areas of cartilage such as the rib cartilages, a process which becomes more marked in old age. The mineral is a calcium apatite crystal similar to that of bone.

Nutrition

Cartilage is largely avascular and acquires its nutrition by diffusion of nutrients from the surrounding tissue fluids. In the epiphyseal cartilage plate the major source of nutrition is the vascular plexus on the epiphyseal side of the plate next to the proliferating zone, the rich metaphyseal blood supply being concerned mainly with endochondral ossification. This observation has clinical importance, for fractures commonly take place in childhood through the hypertrophied zone of cartilage, a site of considerable structural weakness. These fractures never disturb the nutrition and growth of the cartilage plate, whereas the more unusual epiphyseal fracture which may damage the epiphyseal vessels frequently disturbs cartilage growth, with subsequent shortening or deformity of the affected bone. Articular cartilage derives its nutrition largely by diffusion from the joint synovial fluid, except during the growth period when the deeper layers receive a supply from the epiphyseal vessels. Mechanical activity acts as a pump which aids diffusion of nutrients through cartilage. If for any reason a joint or limb is disused, nutrition is impaired and both articular and growth cartilage may degenerate and may even become wholly destroyed; a limb severely paralyzed by poliomyelitis in childhood is frequently shorter than the unaffected limb for this reason.

Synovial tissue

The lining membrane of joints and tendon sheaths is referred to as the synovial membrane; it consists of two or more layers of polygonal cells which form a discontinuous covering. Synovial membrane presents a smooth glistening surface with occasional villi. On its deep surface it is supported by a highly vascular fibrous tissue. The synovial tissue plays an important part in maintaining the efficiency of a joint, by secreting synovial fluid which serves to lubricate and nourish the cartilage and by acting as scavenger to remove metabolites and detritus such as separated fragments of cartilage from the joint. In a synovial membrane, one type of cell has a phagocytic function and another type secretes synovial fluid. Synovial fluid is a clear viscous fluid which in health is present only in small amount. Chemically it is a dialysate of blood plasma with the addition of the mucopolysaccharide hyaluronic acid which is responsible for its high viscosity and lubricating properties. (See also pp. 19.8 & 19.9).

FURTHER READING

BLOOM W. & FAWCETT D.W. (1968) *A Textbook of Histology*, 9th Edition, chaps. Philadelphia: Saunders.

BRIMACOMBE J.S. & WEBBER J.M. (1964) *Mucopolysaccharides. Chemical structure, distribution and isolation.* BBA Library, 6 Amsterdam: Elsevier.

GROSS J. (1961) Collagen in *Readings from Scientific American: The Living Cell.* San Francisco: Freeman.

HAM A.W. (1965) *Histology*, 5th Edition, chaps. 10, 17, 18. Philadelphia: Lippincott.

HARKNESS R.D. (1961) Biological functions of collagen. *Biol. Rev.* **36**, 399.

LACROIX P. (1951) *Organization of Bones.* London: Churchill.

McLEAN F.C. & URIST M.R. (1961) *Bone. An Introduction to the Physiology of the Skeletal Tissue.* Chicago: Chicago University Press.

MANNERY J.F. (1954) Water and electrolyte metabolism. *Physiol. Rev.* **34**, 334.

SMILEY J.D. & ZIFF M. (1964) Urinary hydroxyproline excretion and growth. *Physiol. Rev.* **44**, 30.

THOMSON D'ARCY W. (1961) *On Growth and Form*, abridged edition. Cambridge University Press.

WIDDOWSON E.M. & DICKERSON J.W.T. (1964) Chemical Composition of the Body in *Mineral Metabolism*, vol. II, part A, Ed. Comar & Bronner. New York: Academic Press.

Chapter 17
Lining and secreting tissues

LINING TISSUE

Blood, bile, urine and intestinal contents are four examples of fluids which are found in the body, and life demands that they should be kept separate from each other and from the rest of the tissues. Sheets of cells which are capable of maintaining this separation are called **epithelia**. Since materials must pass from one side to the other of these sheets of cells, the epithelial tissues can absorb and secrete particular substances and they often establish and maintain a chemical or electrical gradient across their surface.

The epithelia form both the internal and external surfaces of the body and they possess two characteristic features. Firstly, they are separated from the underlying tissue by a layer called the **basement membrane**, which is composed mainly of mucopolysaccharide (p. 16.7). The basement membrane of epithelia can be demonstrated by staining its mucopolysaccharide component by the PAS reaction (plate 17.1b, facing p. 17.2). Secondly, they consist almost entirely of cells with little intervening extracellular space and no blood vessels. The uninterrupted layer of cells is needed to control the passage of material across their surface. The details of the close adhesions between adjacent epithelial cells have already been described (p. 13.11).

After fulfilling these two general requirements, there is variation in the arrangement, shape and number of cells which make up the various types of epithelia. This variety arises from different functional requirements and the wide range of physical, chemical and osmotic forces to which the surfaces are exposed.

Classification of epithelia

The first character used to classify an epithelium is that of the number of cells in the layer which separates the basement membrane from the external surface or lumen. If the layer is only one cell thick and all the cells have a luminal and basement membrane surface, then it is called a **simple epithelium**. If it is more than one cell thick and no single cell extends through the whole depth of the layer, it is a **stratified epithelium**. A less common form of **pseudostratified epithelium** contains some cells which

extend from the basement membrane to the lumen and some which are in contact only with the basement membrane.

The next characteristic which is used is the shape of the cell which abuts on the lumen; these can be **squamous, cubical** or **columnar**. Various other features such as the possession of cilia or a brush border characterize some epithelial cells.

Types of epithelia

SIMPLE SQUAMOUS EPITHELIUM (fig. 17.1 and plate 17.1a, facing p. 17.2)

The single layer of cells is very thin, often less than 2 μm and the cells are like scales: hence the term squamous.

FIG. 17.1. Simple squamous epithelium.

Each cell extends over a large surface area, perhaps 1000 μm², and its edges are stuck to those of its neighbours. From the surface this epithelium resembles crazy paving. The EM shows that there are two types of simple squamous epithelium, **non-fenestrated** and **fenestrated**. In the latter the thin cells are perforated by numerous circular pores each about 40 nm in diameter. In the cytoplasm of the non-fenestrated type many small pinocytotic vesicles are present and, since some of these fuse with the inner and outer plasma membranes, they are probably involved in transporting macromolecular materials.

SIMPLE CUBICAL EPITHELIUM (fig. 17.2)
This consists of a regular palisade of cubical cells, each one having a centrally placed nucleus.

FIG. 17.2. Simple cubical and columnar epithelium.

SIMPLE COLUMNAR EPITHELIUM (fig. 17.2 and plate 17.1c)
Columnar cells are taller than they are broad, and their nucleus is nearer to the basal side of the cell. Simple columnar epithelium can possess a brush border or cilia on its luminal side, and when present these features should be added to its description.

STRATIFIED SQUAMOUS EPITHELIUM (fig. 17.3)
Many layers of polygonal cells underlie the flattened cells of the surface. The squamous cells on the surface may retain their nuclei or they may become non-nucleated squames, full of the protein keratin. Thus there are two varieties of stratified squamous epithelium, **cornified (keratinized)** and **non-cornified (non-keratinized)**.

STRATIFIED COLUMNAR EPITHELIUM (fig. 17.3 and plate 17.1d)
The adherent columnar cells on the surface are separated from the basement membrane by at least one layer of smaller cells. Like simple columnar epithelium the stratified type can also support cilia.

TRANSITIONAL EPITHELIUM (fig. 17.3)
Epithelium of this type presents a line of swollen cells to the lumen and has a number of layers of smaller cells below the surface. This name is confusing and inappropriate but there does not appear to be an acceptable alternative.

Functions and distribution of epithelia
The thinness of a simple squamous epithelial layer facilitates passive diffusion, but as it has such a small cytoplasmic volume in relation to surface area it cannot perform active transport of material or secretion. Its flat moist surface provides a frictionless boundary. Phago-

FIG. 17.3. The stratified epithelia.

cytosis is performed by these cells and some of them are specially adapted for this function. Since the cells allow diffusion, they provide a suitable lining for the blood and lymph vessels; the fenestrated type is distributed where the material transfer is greater than usual, for example in the capillaries of the endocrine glands, renal glomerulus and mucosa of the small intestine. The alveolar epithelium in the lung is simple squamous, which allows the passage of gases. The serous cavities, such as the pleura and peritoneum, have a simple squamous lining which allows the contained organs to slide over each other. Another name applied to the simple squamous lining of the blood and lymph vessels and of the sinusoids of the liver, spleen and bone marrow, where it has marked phagocytic powers, is **endothelium**, and the cells are known as endothelial cells. In these sites it forms the basis of the **reticulo-endothelial system** (chap. 27); the reticulin of the basement membrane provides the prefix of the term.

PLATE 17.1. Histology of the lining and secreting tissues.

(a) Simple squamous epithelium, lining the capsule of the glomerulus, appears as a line of flattened nuclei. Simple cubical epithelium forms the two distal convoluted tubules in the lower right part of the field. Human kidney cortex, haem & eosin (×500).

(c) Simple columnar epithelium with mucus secreting goblet cells from a small intestinal villus. The brush border and the mucus is stained red by the PAS stain. Human jejunum, PAS (×400).

(e) Myoepithelial cells in the walls of a sweat gland. The elongated, reddish myoepithelial cells are seen in a tangential section of this coiled tubular gland. Pulp of human finger, Masson (×250).

(b) The basement membranes of the proximal and distal convoluted tubules appear as fine red lines; the brush border of the proximal tubule is also stained. Dog kidney cortex, PAS (×500).

(d) Stratified, ciliated, columnar epithelium. Human trachea, haem & eosin (×500).

(f) Serous and mucous acini with striated muscle fibres from the tongue. The pale cells with small basal nuclei in the mucous acini, on the right, are easily distinguished from the darker serous cells. Rabbit tongue, Van Gieson (×250).

Mesothelium is another synonym for the simple squamous epithelium applied to the linings of the serous cavities. It is wiser to think of the similarity of these linings rather than to multiply their nomenclature but there is justification for considering endothelia and mesothelia as types of lining different from other epithelia. They always develop from mesoderm and retain, in the adult, the capacity of regeneration from primitive mesenchymal cells. Pathological conditions, such as tumours, arising in the endothelia and mesothelia differ in many respects from those arising in epithelia, so pathologists usually consider them as separate categories and apply the term 'epithelia' only to the other lining tissues. In pathology therefore, the term 'simple squamous epithelium' is not used to any extent.

Active absorption requires the use of energy and the volume of cytoplasm necessary to contain the mitochondria is provided by a cubical or columnar epithelium. The luminal surface of the cells is often increased by the formation of a brush border (p. 13.12). Absorption would be hindered by a stratified type of epithelium and absorptive surfaces are of the simple cubical or columnar type. Good examples are provided by the lining of the small intestine and the proximal convoluted tubules in the kidney, which have brush borders. Less active absorption occurs in the large intestine, gall bladder, stomach and the larger ducts of glands, where the epithelium is simple cubical or columnar and does not have a true brush border, although there are a few microvilli on each cell. The simple cubical epithelium forming the distal convoluted renal tubules absorbs actively but here it is the basal surface area of the cell which is increased (pp. 13.12 and 33.3).

Ciliary activity also consumes energy and so cilia are always associated with a columnar type of cell. Ciliated columnar epithelium may be simple, stratified or pseudo-stratified. It is present in the respiratory passages, and the uterine tube.

Secretion is another important epithelial function and the height of the epithelial cells can indicate their secretory activity. This is shown in the thyroid gland where the lining of a thyroid follicle is simple squamous in a quiescent follicle but may become cubical or columnar with increasing activity. The secretory products are usually stored in the cytoplasm of the epithelial cell; mucus for instance can be stained in the inner half of the cells which line the surface of the gastric mucosa. Goblet cells in a columnar epithelium are specialized mucus-secreting cells which have this shape because of their large store of mucus (fig. 17.4 and plate 17.1c, facing p. 17.2). Some secreting epithelial cells have long non-motile processes which project into the lumen; these stereocilia are best seen on the simple columnar cells of the ductus epididymis (fig. 17.4).

Resistance to surface friction is the characteristic

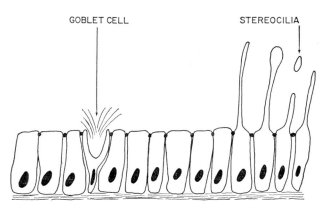

GOBLET CELL   STEREOCILIA

Fig. 17.4. Secretory modifications of simple columnar epithelium.

feature of stratified squamous epithelium. It also provides a relatively impervious layer, and so it forms the epidermis of the skin, and the linings of the mouth, pharynx, oesophagus and vagina. If it is non-keratinized with nuclei in the surface layer of cells, then it is lining a moist surface such as the mouth or conjunctival sac. On the dry surfaces there is always a layer of cells without nuclei but loaded with keratin which form a stratum corneum, and the thickness of this layer is directly related to the amount of surface friction. A series of elaborate modifications allows this type of epithelium to withstand friction; the basement membrane is indented by the underlying connective tissue so that it forms an irregular plane which helps to prevent the whole epithelium from shearing away from its support; the epithelial cells are toughened by a fibrous protein forming tonofibrils within the cells; and at the adhesion points between adjacent cells, desmosomes, the tonofibrils are attached to the adhesion plaques. Thus a stratified squamous epithelium provides a thin, tough, almost watertight surface layer which is firmly tacked down to the tissue beneath.

Transitional epithelium seems to be the only variety which can withstand the hypertonicity and special composition of urine. It is therefore always and only found on surfaces like those of the ureter and bladder which are constantly in contact with urine. These organs vary their contained volume and transitional epithelium allows for stretching.

Origins of epithelia

Epithelia develop from all three germ layers. Since epithelial structure has to conform to the function of a surface, it is not influenced by its embryological origin. Non-keratinized stratified squamous epithelium, for instance, is derived from all three germ layers; from ectoderm in the conjunctiva, from entoderm in the oesophagus and from mesoderm in the upper part of the vagina. Endothelia and mesothelia arise only from mesoderm.

Regeneration of epithelia

The relatively undifferentiated simple squamous type of epithelium lining blood vessels (endothelium) and serous cavities (mesothelium), seems to be able to recruit cells from the surrounding mesenchyme. In the healing of a wound, some of the new capillaries differentiate *in situ* and they are not all produced by outgrowths from neighbouring vessels. This is exceptional; most epithelia, after the earliest embryonic stages, can grow only from themselves. The basement membrane does not always prevent the migration of cells into an epithelium, and lymphocytes are regular visitors, but none of these migratory cells seem capable of differentiating into epithelial cells. Conversely epithelial cell proliferation is confined by the basement membrane which epithelial cells do not normally penetrate. A carcinoma is a malignant tumour in which epithelial cells lose their mutual adhesion and penetrate into the underlying tissue.

The loss of a cell in the single layer of a simple epithelium is replaced by cell division and lateral movement to fill the gap. If there are large numbers of undifferentiated epithelial cells interposed in a simple epithelium, the pseudostratified variety is produced. When the number of regenerating cells is sufficient to separate all the surface cells from the basement membrane a true stratified epithelium is present. Hence the exposed epithelia which suffer damage tend to be of the stratified variety. A journey down the air passages of the respiratory system shows the epithelium changing from stratified to simple as more protected cavities are reached. In the stratified squamous epithelia there is a constant replacement of the surface cells as they die; the basal cells of this epithelium tend to divide at night when the body is at rest.

It is initially surprising that the intestinal epithelium, which is so exposed to dietary indiscretions, should be of a simple type. Its absorptive function is assisted by its being only one cell thick and its replacement is now known to be effected by a rapid migration from regenerating cells which enjoy the seclusion of the tubular crypts. So each intestinal epithelial cell has a short active life.

If an area of an epithelium is destroyed, an ulcer is produced. The ulcerated region can be repaired only by epithelial proliferation from the intact epithelium around the edges of the ulcer. Another example of the independent property of epithelia is given by skin grafting, for a surface slice of skin, including epidermis, can be cut off and transplanted to carry epithelial cells to a completely denuded area. The epidermis at the site of removal is renewed by epithelial cells growing out of the truncated sweat glands and hair follicles to populate the surface.

EPITHELIAL DERIVATIVES

The epithelia are modified to produce a variety of structures. The origin of hairs and nails from the stratum corneum of the stratified squamous epithelium of the epidermis is described with the skin (p. 35.5). The manner in which the enamel of the teeth develops on the basal surface of the epithelium forming an enamel organ is mentioned elsewhere (p. 21.46). Glands are also derived from epithelia and, as described below, some lose their connection with the surface.

SECRETORY TISSUE

All cells, of course, must be able to transport substances across their membranes; they must be able to take up nutrients and extrude waste matter. Some cells, however, extrude substances which are useful to the body, and these are called **secretory cells**. These cells may be part of the structure of an organ, as in the kidney tubules, or they may be grouped together and organized as glands which are developed as epithelial outgrowths.

In order to increase the volume of secretory epithelial cytoplasm which discharges on to a surface, the glandular outgrowths assume different shapes (fig. 17.5). Tubular outgrowths can be simple, branched and coiled, while saccular outgrowths are, in man, only branched. A compound gland is one in which the original outgrowth forms a complex branching duct system before becoming the secretory portion. The secretory portion of a compound gland can be tubular or saccular or, as in the liver, exhibit a laminar arrangement of its secretory cells. The saccules of a compound gland are called **acini**, because each one resembles a berry (*L. acinus*) on the end of the branching stalk or duct.

The type of secretory product affects the structure of a gland. If it is synthesizing enzymes, it has **serous acini** whose cells have basophilic cytoplasm due to their high RNA content. A large oval nucleus with prominent nucleoli lies near the centre of the serous cell and its apical cytoplasm contains stores of its protein secretion as zymogen granules. Mucopolysaccharides forming the basis of mucous secretion appear clear after routine staining methods, so the **mucous acini** have an empty appearance with compressed nuclei near the base of each cell (fig. 17.6 & plate 17.1f, facing p. 17.2). The mucus can be selectively stained by the PAS reaction (p. 13.3). The goblet cells mentioned above are isolated mucus secreting cells.

Most glands are either mucus secreting, e.g. sublingual, or serous in type, e.g. parotid and pancreas. In a mixed gland, such as the submandibular, the acini are usually of one or other type with the mixing occurring in the duct. There are, however, sometimes serous cells associated with a mucous acinus, and since these have a crescentic shape they are known as serous demilunes. The secretory cells themselves in the submucosal glands of the duodenum have mixed mucous and serous features.

Apart from proteins and polysaccharides, some gland

FIG. 17.5. Types of glands.

cells secrete electrolytes and water. The secretory cells of the sweat glands expel a hypotonic salt solution but the outstanding example of this type of secretion is the oxyntic cell of the stomach which produces a hydrochloric acid solution. Lipoid materials are also secreted by certain glands, notably the cutaneous sebaceous and apocrine sweat glands.

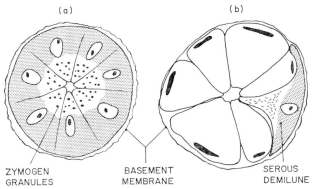

FIG. 17.6. Serous (a) and mucous (b) acini.

Where the glands retain a connection with the surface from which they are developed and discharge their secretion on to it, such as the sweat glands and those which produce digestive juices, they are called **exocrine** glands. Those which lose their connection with the surface, and secrete directly into the blood stream, are called **endocrine** glands. These glands produce hormones, which travel in the blood stream to act on target organs at a distant site. In all cases, however, the secretory processes are similar, i.e. water and electrolytes must be transferred across the cells from the blood of the surrounding capillaries to the lumen of the gland, and enzymes or hormones elaborated in the secretory cells themselves must be passed into the ducts or blood stream.

The range of secretory products mentioned above demands different methods of discharge. Electrolytes and water can be pumped through the cell membrane without any structural change being observed in that membrane; this is **eccrine** secretion. In **apocrine** secretion the materials accumulate in the luminal part of the cell, which then breaks off into the lumen. Stereocilia represent a form of apocrine secretion as these long cytoplasmic processes project into the lumen and accumulate blebs of secretion before pinching them off. A third method of secretion is **holocrine**, where the whole cell accumulates the product; the sebaceous glands of the hair follicles are a characteristic example of this type of discharge. The testes secreting spermatozoa and the stratified squamous epithelia secreting keratin-loaded cells are other examples of holocrine secretion.

Appearance of cells during secretion

In many of the enzyme-producing exocrine glands, such as those of the pancreas, microscopic examination shows the presence of granules, which are the precursors or storage forms of the active enzymes secreted by the cells. By time–lapse cinephotography of living tissues, it can be shown that these **zymogen granules** are in constant motion in the cells, and that their numbers are depleted when the gland is active. They build up again in the resting cells. They appear to be semi-fluid in nature, and dissolve when they are liberated into the ducts of the glands. EM studies show that the granules are first formed in the rough-surfaced endoplasmic reticulum, which is studded with ribosomes. Later they aggregate in the Golgi region where they are surrounded by smooth-surfaced membranes, which become continuous with the membrane of the free surface of the cell during secretion. The granule can then break through this membrane, while the cell membrane remains intact (fig. 13.12b).

Secretory granules may be seen also in the cells of endocrine glands, though these have been less intensively studied. The secretory granules demonstrated in the anterior pituitary gland appear to be similar to those seen in the exocrine pancreas. The EM also emphasizes their essential similarity, since here too the granules appear to be surrounded by a smooth membrane, and are formed near the Golgi apparatus. The mechanism of release of the hormone from these granules may be similar to the release of enzyme from exocrine glands. Hormones may be stored in glands by the formation of follicles, where the precursors of the secretion accumulate.

Secretory processes

Many transport mechanisms across cells can be explained entirely by the laws of physical chemistry, i.e. by osmosis, diffusion or filtration. In these cases the structure of the cell membrane is the determining factor in the interchanges which occur, and metabolic activity of the cells is not involved. Such processes are said to be **passive**. In secretion, however, there is a gain in free energy, which must be supplied by metabolic processes in the cell, and the system is said to be **active**. For example, substances may be elaborated which are not present in the blood at all, such as the HCl produced by the oxyntic cells of the stomach, and the pressure in the ducts of glands may exceed the blood pressure.

The work of secretion

If the standard free energy changes in the chemical reactions involved in secretion are known, together with the activities of the secreted substances, the minimum work done in secretion can be calculated. However, these values are extremely difficult, if not impossible, to determine for complex molecules such as enzymes and hormones. Estimates, based on many unsupported assumptions, suggest that 0·4 kcal energy are required to produce the protein present in the gastric juice secreted by a dog after a meal of 200 g meat.

For the energy requirements for the secretion of ions, the calculation is simpler. If we consider the transport of H^+ from the blood (pH 7·4) to gastric juice (pH 1·0), we use the formula:

$$W = RT \ln \frac{C_1}{C_2}$$

where W is the work done per mole HCl transported, R is the gas constant, T the absolute temperature, and C_1 and C_2 the pH values (negative logarithms of the H^+ concentration). Rewriting, and using $\log_{10}$, we have, at 37°C

$$W = RT \times 2 \cdot 303 \, (\log_{10} C_1 - \log_{10} C_2) \text{ calories}$$
$$= RT \times 2 \cdot 303 \times 6 \cdot 4 \text{ calories}$$
$$= 9 \cdot 1 \text{ kcal}$$

Blood flow during secretion

During secretory activity the blood supply of a gland is increased by four to eight times, thereby ensuring a plentiful supply of nutrients and oxygen to produce the energy required and the water and electrolytes necessary for elaboration into the secretion. This transport of water from the capillaries and across the cells helps to flush out the protein secreted by the cells themselves.

In three situations a specific mechanism to achieve this vasodilatation has been described. These are in salivary secretion, sweat production, and the exocrine secretion of the pancreas. Here it is believed that when activity of the glands begins, a proteolytic enzyme is released, which reacts with tissue fluid protein to form the polypeptide **bradykinin**. This is a potent vasodilator substance, and probably has a local effect in increasing blood flow. This increase in blood flow has, of course, no necessary influence on the rate of secretion from the gland, but may aid it by supplying increased amounts of oxygen and nutrients. Bradykinin is likely to be active in other secretory tissues.

Control of secretion

Some glands secrete continuously, while others are activated only by specific stimuli. This applies to both exo-

a
b

PLATE 16.3. Cartilage structure.

(a) Articular cartilage, in which the chondrocytes are large circular cells, fairly uniformly distributed throughout the matrix. Near the surface they are flattened (× 375).

(b) Epiphysial cartilage plate, in which the cartilage cells are organized into columns in the axis of growth. Towards the epiphysial side (top) the cells are actively proliferating and appear small and flattened. Further down the column the cells enlarge and eventually degenerate. They are then invaded by the metaphysial blood vessels and new bone is laid down on the persisting scaffold of cartilage matrix. Note that the nutrition of the cartilage plate is derived from the vessels on the epiphysial side (× 90).

PLATE 24.1. EM of grey matter from the parietal cortex of an adult rat.
In this section, tangential to the surface, the apical dendrites (DD) of pyramidal cells are transected and between them large numbers of smaller dendrites (D), axons (A) and boutons (B) are seen. Astrocyte cytoplasm (G) is also present. The marker is 1 μm long and the section is approximately 0·05 μm thick. EM from Dr A. Peters.

crine and endocrine glands. The type of control is intimately related to the resting rate of secretion, the duration of secretion in response to the stimulus, and the feedback systems inhibiting the process. The following factors influence the rate of secretion.

NERVOUS FACTORS

Nervous control mechanisms occur when a rapid onset of secretion is required from an otherwise inactive gland or a rapid increase above a low resting rate of secretion. The adrenal medulla and salivary glands are examples of secretory tissues under nervous control.

CHEMICAL FACTORS

Chemical control of secretion occurs in glands such as the parathyroids, where the level of plasma calcium determines the rate of secretion of parathormone, which in turn regulates the plasma calcium concentration.

HORMONAL FACTORS

Hormonal control mechanisms exist where a less rapid, less finely graded but prolonged secretion is required, such as the production of the hormones by the adrenal cortex and bile by the liver.

Some glands require both a rapid onset of secretion and a prolonged response, and in these cases a combination of nervous and hormonal control is found. For example, the secretion of gastric juice is rapidly raised above the resting level by nerve impulses and its secretion is maintained by a hormone (p. 30.17).

PHYSICAL FACTORS

Physical factors are involved in sweat secretion, which depends ultimately on deep body temperature, though this information is transmitted by nerve impulses.

MECHANICAL FACTORS

Mechanical stimuli are probably involved in the secretion of mucus. Its secretion in the gastrointestinal tract is thought to be caused by mechanical stimulation of the mucosa.

These and other examples of simple and mixed control of secretory processes are described more fully in other chapters, where the mechanisms are dealt with in greater detail.

Myoepithelium

Around the cells of some glands (sweat, salivary, mammary and lacrimal), there are specialized cells of ectodermal origin, which resemble smooth muscle in appearance (plate 17.1e, facing p. 17.2). The cytoplasmic processes of these **myoepithelial** cells surround the secretory units, and have been shown by EM studies to contain myofilaments. The contraction of these is thought to assist in expelling the secretion of the glands. This may be brought about by either nervous or hormonal mechanisms.

Other secretory processes

By our original definition that secretory cells are those which extrude substances useful to the body, we should include also nerve synapses, nerve endings, and the neurosecretory cells of the hypothalamus. The synapses and nerve endings produce the chemical mediators necessary for the transmission of the nerve impulse. The hypothalamus produces the hormones which are stored in the posterior pituitary gland, usually referred to as posterior pituitary hormones. These forms of neurosecretion are, however, outside the usual concept of secretory tissue, and are dealt with in chaps 14 and 24.

FURTHER READING

BLOOM W. and FAWCETT D.W. (1968) Epithelium in *A Textbook of Histology*, 9th Edition. Philadelphia: Saunders.
DAVSON H. (1964) *A Textbook of General Physiology* 3rd Edition. London: Churchill.

Chapter 18
Early development

For the new individual, life begins in the ampulla of the uterine tube with the act of fertilization, when the nucleus of the ovum fuses with that of the sperm. At fertilization the diploid number of chromosomes is restored, the chromosomal sex of the new individual is determined and the ovum is activated to proceed to the first **cleavage division** (fig. 18.1).

EMBRYOGENESIS

After fertilization a series of divisions known as **cleavage** converts the single fertilized ovum, **zygote**, into a large

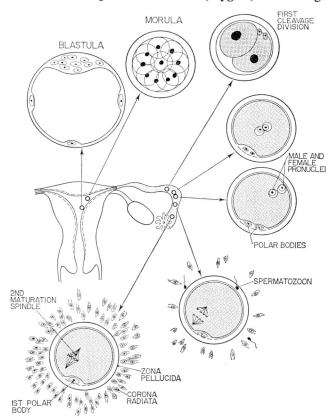

FIG. 18.1. The development of the conceptus during the first 6 days after fertilization.

number of cells or **blastomeres**. The first few cleavage divisions take place in fixed symmetrical planes, but subsequent divisions appear to be irregular. Since the human zygote, as that of other mammals, contains little yolk in the cytoplasm, cleavage involves the whole zygote and all the blastomeres are of about equal size. Cleavage divisions occur within an intact zona pellucida, which limits the size of the **conceptus**. The blastomeres are arranged as a solid ball of cells called the **morula.** With continuing cell division, the cells form a hollow ball, the **blastula** or **blastocyst**, whose wall is closely applied to the inner surface of the zona pellucida. The cavity of the blastocyst is the **blastocoele**; its outer wall is a single layer of cells called the **trophoblast**. Attached to the inner surface of the trophoblast is a small cluster of cells, the **inner cell mass**. The trophoblast makes no direct contribution to the embryo but is concerned with its nutrition. It is the part of the conceptus which will make intimate contact with the maternal tissues. The inner cell mass, on the other hand, is the source of cells of the embryo itself and of two of its membranes, the **amnion** and the **yolk sac**. At this stage the blastocyst is distended with fluid.

The conceptus is now nearing the end of its first week of life. Three or four days are spent in passage down the uterine tube and two or three days lying free within the narrow uterine lumen (fig. 18.1). The investing cells of the corona radiata have been shed and the zona pellucida becomes thin and shortly disappears. The conceptus is still only a little larger than the fertilized ovum. Cleavage produces a large number of small cells, with a normal ratio of nuclear to cytoplasmic mass, from a single large ovum which had a disproportionately large amount of cytoplasm.

The conceptus is now ready to implant in the endometrium and this phenomenon is described on p. 37.34.

THE CONCEPTUS AT 7 DAYS

Fig. 18.2a shows a section through the youngest known implanted human embryo. It is not yet completely buried in the endometrium, but its point of penetration has still to be repaired by regeneration of uterine epithelium. The primitive blastocyst cavity has temporarily collapsed. Where the trophoblastic wall of the blastocyst is not in direct contact with maternal tissue it remains a simple squamous epithelium. Elsewhere it has grown rapidly by ingesting and digesting cells of the endometrium.

The embryo itself is forming from the inner cell mass (fig. 18.2b). A slit-like **amniotic cavity** has just appeared. Its roof is a thin layer of **amniotic ectoderm**, probably formed by splitting off from the trophoblast; its floor is

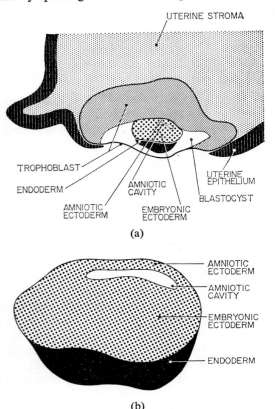

(a)

(b)

FIG. 18.2. Human conceptus, aged about 7½ days after fertilization; (a) in section (b) detail of the inner cell mass. After Hertig & Rock (1945) *Contr. Embryol.* **31**.

a thicker layer, the **primitive embryonic ectoderm**. The **endoderm** is a thin layer of cells, which has split off from and remains closely applied to the lower surface of the primitive ectoderm.

THE CONCEPTUS IN THE SECOND WEEK (fig. 18.3)

At fourteen days, the conceptus is completely implanted within the endometrium. It consists of a roughly spherical sac, whose thick wall is the trophoblast, and whose cavity may now be called the **extraembryonic coelom**, since it surrounds the embryo. Two epithelial sacs, the amniotic cavity and the yolk sac, are suspended within this coelom. They are roughly spherical and are flattened where they lie in contact with one another, like two hollow rubber balls pressed together. The embryo itself consists of two flat sheets of epithelial cells at this area of contact. One layer, which is continuous at its

margins with the epithelium of the amnion, is the **embryonic ectoderm**, the other, continuous at its margins with the epithelium of the yolk sac, is the **embryonic endoderm**.

The inner surface of the trophoblast and the outer surface of the amniotic and yolk sacs, in fact all surfaces facing into the extraembryonic coelom, are covered by a layer of a loose, primitive mesenchymal tissue, the **extraembryonic mesoderm**. This is thought to have developed initially from the trophoblast and forms, with it, the outermost layer of the conceptus, the **chorion**. Strands

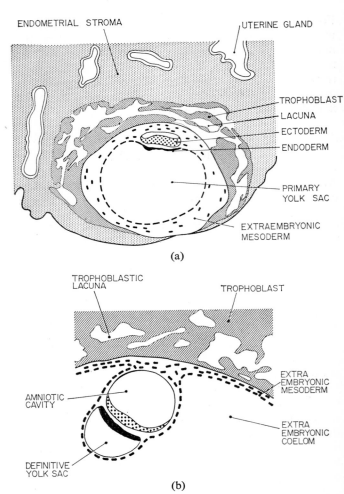

(a)

(b)

FIG. 18.3. Human embryos and adjacent membranes (a) aged about 12 days after fertilization, (b) at about 16 days. After Hertig & Rock (1941), *Contr. Embryol.* **29**, & Brewer (1945), *Contr. Embryol.* **31**.

of extraembryonic mesoderm suspend the amniotic and yolk sacs from the inner surface of the chorion, and form the **connecting stalk** which provides the main mesodermal basis of the umbilical cord.

It is important to appreciate that the whole conceptus is still minute at this stage, the external diameter being about 1–2 mm. It is superficially embedded in an endometrium which is about 8 mm thick. Small though it is, however, the conceptus has grown rapidly during the week since implantation began; its diameter has increased about five times. Some of this increase is due to distension of the extraembryonic coelom by fluid derived from the endometrium, but comparison of figs. 18.2a & 3a shows that the trophoblast in particular has grown rapidly. The outer shell shows no cellular boundaries and is therefore called **syncytiotrophoblast**; the inner layer remains cellular and is called **cytotrophoblast**.

Nutrients required for this rapid trophoblastic growth are obtained from maternal tissues. The syncytiotrophoblast is spongy and is penetrated by irregular, intercommunicating spaces, or lacunae. The invading trophoblast necessarily erodes maternal vessels, mostly enlarged capillaries and venules, and these discharge blood into the lacunae. The trophoblast is nourished by the fluid element of this extravasated blood, by interstitial fluid of the succulent endometrial stroma and by maternal blood and connective tissue cells which it ingests by phagocytosis. Nutritive material for the growing embryo itself can be derived only from the same sources. This primitive nutritive material is called **histotrophe**. It provides for the survival and growth of the conceptus during these early stages before circulation of maternal blood through the trophoblastic lacunae is fully active and before any embryonic vessels have developed in the chorion.

THE CONCEPTUS IN THE THIRD WEEK

The third week is a period of rapid development. The **chorionic sac** increases in diameter from about 2 mm to between 5 and 15 mm. It is covered externally by well-developed **chorionic villi**. These are bathed in maternal blood which now circulates through **intervillous spaces**, and, within their mesodermal cores, chorionic blood vessels develop (p. 37.39).

The most important change in the embryo itself is the establishment of the third of the germ layers, the **intra-embryonic mesoderm**. It is best appreciated by imagining the chorionic sac to be opened and the amnion cut away close to the margin of the bilaminar germ disc where it becomes continuous with the embryonic ectoderm. The dorsal surface of the embryonic disc may now be inspected (fig. 18.4a). A linear thickening of the ectoderm appears in the midline of the disc and establishes both the polarity of the disc, since it lies at what will be the caudal end, and its bilateral symmetry. If one could study fresh human embryos at this stage, this **primitive streak** would appear opaque as compared with the rest of the ectoderm which would be almost translucent. A transverse section through the primitive streak (fig. 18.4b) shows that it lies at the bottom of a shallow **primitive groove**. Streams of mesodermal cells arise from it and spread laterally and forwards towards the head end of the disc. These form

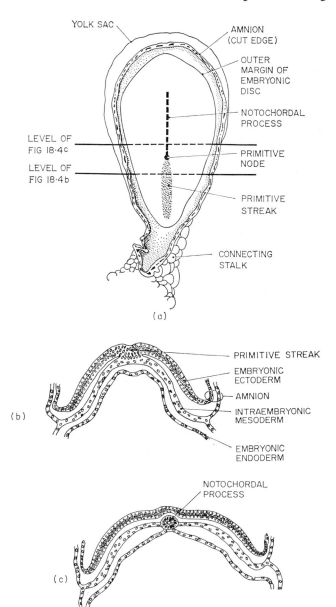

Fig. 18.4. Embryonic disc of estimated age 20 days after fertilization. (a) Dorsal view exposed by removal of the amnion to show the primitive streak. Transverse sections through the embryonic disc at the level of the primitive streak (b) and notochordal process (c). After Heuser (1932), *Contr. Embryol.* **23**.

the intraembryonic mesoderm which occupies the interval between ectoderm dorsally and endoderm ventrally.

At the cranial end of the streak there is a slight thickening, the **primitive node**, from which a rod of cells, the **notochordal** or **head process**, extends forwards in a plane between ectoderm and endoderm (fig. 18.4c). In its forward growth, the cranial end of the notochordal process soon meets the **buccopharyngeal membrane**, which is a small circular mid-line area where ectoderm and endoderm remain in contact, not having been separated from one another by the spreading intraembryonic mesoderm. The notochordal process extends to the hinder edge of the buccopharyngeal membrane and no further (fig. 18.11).

A similar area of immediate contact between ectoderm and endoderm is found at the caudal end of the primitive streak. This is the **cloacal membrane**.

With the development of the intraembryonic mesoderm, the germ disc is now three-layered. The notochordal process, and with it the disc as a whole, elongates rapidly, and the primitive streak comes to lie more and more caudally. The primitive streak plays the dominant role in these changes (fig. 18.5)

Quite apart from forming a primitive, temporary, mid-line skeletal axis, the notochordal process plays an important part in the next major event in embryonic development, the formation of the **neural plate**, the forerunner of the **neural tube**. The **neural plate** arises as a

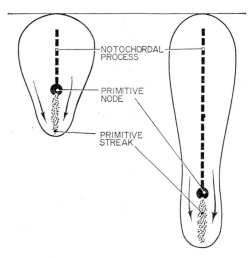

FIG. 18.5. Dorsal views of the germ disc to show how the disc grows in length by the proliferation of new cells from the primitive node and primitive streak. Based on Streeter.

thickened area of embryonic ectoderm overlying the notochordal process and its associated (paraxial) mesoderm. This relationship is not simply topographical; the ectoderm is induced to form the neural plate by the underlying tissue which acts as a primary inductor.

THE CONCEPTUS IN THE FOURTH WEEK
The following changes occur during this week.
Changes in the intraembryonic mesoderm
These are most easily understood in a transverse section through the middle of the germ disc (fig. 18.6).

(1) The **paraxial mesoderm** which lies on either side of the axially placed notochord divides into a series of seg-

mental blocks, the **mesodermal somites**. These develop in craniocaudal sequence; the caudally retreating primitive node and streak add new somites to the caudal end of the series, until the total of about forty-two pairs is completed. The number of somites present in a particular embryo is a better guide to its general developmental state than is its length.

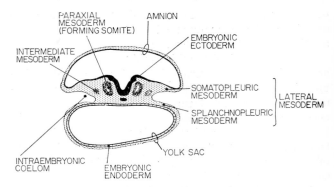

FIG. 18.6. Transverse section through the three-layered germ disc, showing subdivisions of the intraembryonic mesoderm.

(2) The **lateral mesoderm** lies towards the lateral edge of the flat, trilaminar embryonic disc. It is not segmented. A cavity, **the intraembryonic coelom** appears within it, dividing the mesoderm into two layers. The upper of these two layers, together with the embryonic ectoderm, forms the **somatopleure**, so called because it is the forerunner of the body wall. The lower layer, together with the embryonic endoderm, forms the **splanchnopleure** as the forerunner of the wall of the gut.

The intra- and extraembryonic coeloms soon communicate with one another. This provides a route of entry into the embryo of fluid from the maternal tissues, via the chorion and extraembryonic coelom. It should be noted that the embryonic somatopleure may be traced without interruption into the amniotic somatopleure, and the embryonic splanchnopleure into the yolk sac splanchnopleure.

(3) The **intermediate mesoderm** lies between paraxial and lateral mesoderm. It is neither segmented into somites nor divided into two layers. Most of the genito-urinary system develops in this mesoderm.

The pericardial coelom and pericardioperitoneal canals
The intraembryonic coelom forms a continuous, horse-shoe-shaped cavity (fig. 18.7). The **pericardial coelom** lies towards the cranial end of the germ disc. The mesoderm in front of it remains intact, separating the pericardial and extraembryonic coeloms. It is called the **septum transversum**. The **pericardioperitoneal canals** are paired tubes which link the pericardial and peritoneal coeloms. It is important to realize that so long as the embryo remains a

flat, trilaminar disc, the various parts of the coelom all lie in the same flat plane, and that only the peritoneal part of the coelom communicates with the extraembryonic coelom.

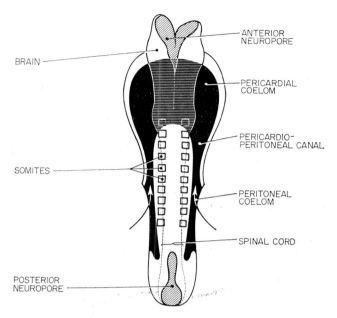

FIG. 18.7. Dorsal view of the embryo at the beginning of the fourth week showing the outline of intraembryonic coelom, a continuous series of spaces within the intraembryonic mesoderm. The amnion has been removed and the coelom is shown as if seen through a translucent ectoderm. The peritoneal part of the coelom communicates with the extraembryonic coelom (arrows).

Formation of the neural tube (fig. 18.8)

The thickened ectoderm of the neural plate forms a pair of longitudinal neural folds, one on each side of the midline neural groove. The **neural folds** fuse with one another dorsally to form a closed **neural tube**, forerunner of the brain and spinal cord. Fusion begins in the centre of the tube in embryos with seven paired somites and extends cranially and caudally. As the embryo grows in length, the neural tube is progressively added to at its caudal end. New neural plate ectoderm arises by cellular proliferation from the primitive streak, and this in turn thickens, folds, and closes. The importance of the primitive streak as a growth centre is again apparent.

For a time, the neural tube remains open both cranially and caudally. The cranial opening or **anterior neuropore** closes at the end of the 4th week. Because the neural tube grows by additions to its caudal end, closure of the caudal or **posterior neuropore** is delayed until the 6th week, when new somite formation from the primitive streak ceases.

When the neural folds fuse, some neural ectoderm at the lateral edges of the neural plate is not included within

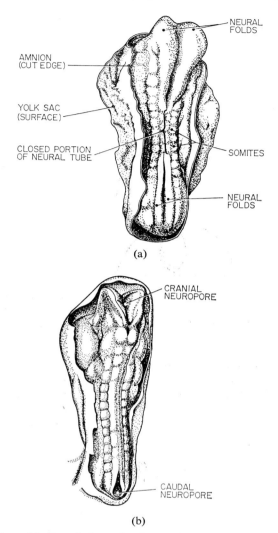

FIG. 18.8. Dorsal views of embryos of 7 somites (a) and 10 somites (b) showing the formation of the neural tube by fusion of the neural folds. After Payne (a) and Corner (b).

the neural tube. This is the **neural crest** (fig. 18.9). In the spinal region of the neural tube, this forms a series of segmental masses, corresponding to the mesodermal somites. In the cranial region, the neural crest forms irregular non-segmental masses. From both the cranial and the spinal neural crest a wide variety of cells arise:

(1) **primitive neuroblasts**, from which develop the first order sensory neurones, whose cell bodies are found in the cranial and spinal sensory ganglia (fig. 24.107),

(2) **lemnoblasts**, the forerunners of Schwann cells of peripheral nerve fibres,

(3) **sympathoblasts**, which give rise to the postganglionic effector neurones of the autonomic nervous system,

(4) **phaeochromoblasts**, which migrate to form the adrenal medulla and other chromaffin tissue,

(5) **melanoblasts,** which migrate to the epidermis where they form the pigmented melanocytes.

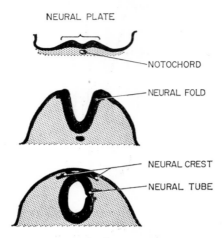

FIG. 18.9. Cross-sections to show successive stages in the formation of the neural folds, their fusion to form the neural tube, and the origin of the neural crest.

Folding of the body

The trilaminar germ disc lies upon the yolk sac. This flat plate is converted into a cylindrical embryo by bending or folding in both transverse and longitudinal planes.

FIG. 18.10. Transverse sections showing development of the lateral body folds which convert the flat germ disc into a cylindrical embryo.

Transverse folding produces the **lateral body folds** (fig. 18.10). A number of important changes should be noted.

(1) After folding is complete, the embryo lies almost entirely within the amniotic cavity.

(2) The lateral and ventral abdominal wall has been formed from the somatopleure.

(3) The continuity between intra- and extraembryonic coeloms has been restricted.

(4) The gut tube has been pinched off from the yolk sac, but the two still communicate by a **vitello-intestinal duct.**

(5) As the gut tube separates from the yolk sac, it draws away from the dorsal abdominal wall, and the initially broad mesodermal attachment becomes thinned to form a **dorsal mesentery.**

(6) The intermediate mesoderm comes to lie ventral to the somites and as it thickens, it bulges into the coelom as the **urogenital ridge.**

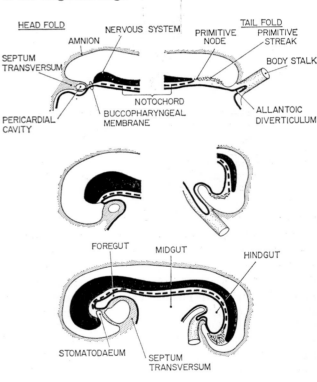

FIG. 18.11. Sagittal sections showing the formation of head and tail folds.

Similarly longitudinal folding forms the head and tail folds (fig. 18.11). This folding occurs because dorsal structures, particularly the neural tube, grow more rapidly than ventral structures. Several changes should be noted.

(1) As the septum transversum and the pericardial cavity have swung into a ventral position, a diverticulum of the gut has been pinched off from the yolk sac. This diverticulum is the **foregut**; it lies between the pericardial

coelom and the neural tube and ends blindly in front at the **buccopharyngeal membrane**.

(2) The brain is now the most cranial part of the embryo. The ectoderm-lined diverticulum which lies between neural tube dorsally and pericardium ventrally is the **stomatodaeum**; it is separated from the foregut by the buccopharyngeal membrane.

(3) The septum transversum, originally the most cranial structure in the embryo, now forms the caudal wall of the pericardial coelom. It lies beneath the endoderm of the ventral wall of the caudal part of the foregut. When the liver develops as a ventral outgrowth from this part of the gut wall it grows immediately into the septum transversum.

The effect of the formation of the head fold on the pericardioperitoneal canals obviously cannot be seen in a midsagittal section. Fig. 18.12 shows the canal leading

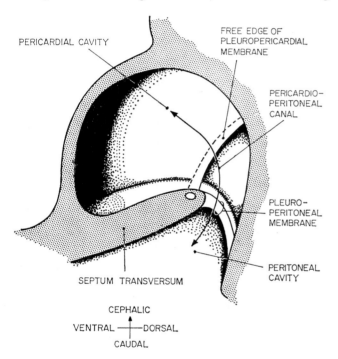

FIG. 18.12. The pericardioperitoneal canal. The embryo has been sectioned in a parasagittal plane, to the right of the midline, and the heart removed. The diagram shows the inner cut surface of the right hand portion of the sectioned embryo.

dorsally from the pericardial coelom to lie at the side of the caudal end of the foregut, and passing dorsal to the septum transversum before opening into the peritoneal coelom.

The **tail fold** appears somewhat later than the head fold, and again a blind-ending diverticulum, the **hindgut**, is pinched off from the yolk sac. It is separated from the amniotic cavity by the cloacal membrane. Note, too, the

changed relations of the primitive node, primitive streak, cloacal membrane, **body (connecting) stalk** and its contained endodermal **allantoic diverticulum**. In the formation of the tail fold the craniocaudal sequence of these structures is reversed, and the formation of the head fold has a similar effect on the craniocaudal sequence of septum transversum, pericardial cavity and buccopharyngeal membrane. For this reason, this sequence of changes is sometimes called **reversal** of the embryo.

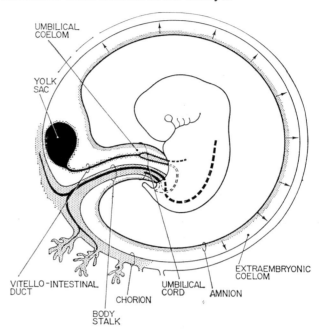

FIG. 18.13. The mode of formation of the umbilical cord. As the amnion expands, it obliterates the extraembryonic coelom by fusing with the chorion, and provides an investment for the umbilical cord. Part of the extraembryonic coelom persists for a time within the umbilical cord as the umbilical coelom. The body (connecting) stalk contains the allantoic diverticulum and umbilical vessels, only one of the two umbilical arteries is shown.

The formation of the lateral body, head and tail folds is not a sequence of separate events, but part of a general process of constriction at the junction between embryo and yolk sac. As the amnion expands to obliterate the extraembryonic coelom, it forms an external investment for the **umbilical cord**. The body stalk provides the mesoderm for the umbilical cord and it also contains the umbilical vessels, the endodermal allantoic diverticulum, the vitello-intestinal duct, and the remains of the extraembryonic coelom (fig. 18.13).

MAIN FEATURES OF THE EMBRYO

The following account presents a composite picture of embryos of about one month of age. The somites are almost completely formed. The embryonic length ranges from 4–7 mm, and the diameter of the chorionic sac from 20–38 mm. Most of the organ systems are now present in rudimentary form, and the student should find this a useful general baseline from which he can proceed to their more detailed study.

The outer surface of the **chorionic sac** is thickly clothed by villi which have an outer covering of trophoblast and a central core of extraembryonic mesoderm, containing blood vessels through which circulates embryonic blood. The chorionic villi are bathed in circulating extravasated maternal blood and exchange of nutritive and waste material and of respiratory gases takes place between the two blood streams. This type of nutrition is called haemotrophic, in contradistinction to the histotrophic nutrition of the early conceptus.

The embryo is suspended from the inner surface of the chorion by the body stalk, through which run two umbilical arteries carrying blood to the chorionic circulation and two umbilical veins returning blood to the embryo. The amnion invests the embryo and contains the amniotic fluid. The watery environment of the amniotic fluid is particularly important in providing physical support in these early stages, when the embryo has the consistency of a soft jelly. A narrow tubular stalk (the yolk stalk or vitello-intestinal duct) connects the embryonic gut with the yolk sac, which lies within the extraembryonic coelom. The yolk sac is bathed in coelomic fluid, and its

wall is richly supplied with embryonic blood by the vitelline artery.

THE MAIN EXTERNAL FEATURES (fig. 18.14)

The C-shaped curvature is characteristic; this is a further effect of the growth of the nervous system which has already helped to form the head and tail folds.

FIG. 18.14. Embryo aged about 4 weeks.

FIG. 18.15. The nervous system in an embryo of about 4 weeks, (a) subdivisions (b) cranial and spinal ganglia. After Streeter.

WALL OF FOREBRAIN

Ⅲ VENTRICLE

CAVITY OF OPTIC VESICLE

LENS PLACODE

(a)

FOREBRAIN

OLFACTORY PLACODE

FRONTONASAL PROCESS

OLFACTORY PIT

(b)

HINDBRAIN

OTIC VESICLE

OTIC PLACODE

OTIC PIT

PRIMITIVE PHARYNX

(c)

FIG. 18.16. The forerunners of the special sense organs in embryos of about 4 weeks. (a) The optic vesicle, a hollow outgrowth from the forebrain will form, among other things, the future retina. The lens develops from the surface ectoderm, under the inductive influence of the optic vesicle; (b) olfactory epithelium develops from areas of surface ectoderm, the olfactory placodes; (c) the lining epithelium of the inner ear develops from the otic vesicle, a derivative of the otic placode.

The head is disproportionately large, mainly because of the precocious development and growth of the brain. The **pharyngeal** or **branchial arches**, from whose mesoderm develop, among other things, the skeleton and musculature of the jaws, are conspicuous. In the absence of a neck the developing face and jaws rest directly on the primitive pericardium through whose translucent wall the heart can be seen.

On each side of the dorsal part of the trunk, flanking the spinal cord, is a series of segmental mesodermal blocks, the somites. Ventral to these are the **limb buds**, simple stubby outgrowths from the trunk. The upper limb is more advanced in development than the lower, in keeping with the general precocity of the front end of the embryo. The surface bulge between the heart and the upper limb bud is produced by the liver. The ventral abdominal wall, between the pericardium and the root of the tail, is occupied entirely by the umbilical ring, the line of continuity between amniotic ectoderm and the embryonic epidermis.

THE NERVOUS SYSTEM (fig. 18.15)

The **neural tube** extends throughout the length of the embryo and possesses a large **neural canal** and a wall which is still essentially epithelial. Brain and spinal cord are not sharply demarcated but the divisions into fore-, mid- and hindbrain are recognizable.

The ganglia of cranial and spinal nerves develop from the **neural crest** which, in the spinal region, forms a series of cell clumps lying beside the neural tube, in segmental arrangement corresponding to the mesodermal somites. The cranial neural crest, on the other hand, is not arranged segmentally, but in clusters from which develop the ganglia of V, VII, VIII, IX and X cranial nerves. The young nerve cells, **neuroblasts**, of the craniospinal neural crest develop in a basically similar fashion. Each sends an axonic outgrowth into the neural tube, the **central process**, and an axonic outgrowth to a peripheral sensory terminal, the **peripheral process**. It is worth noting that these precursors of first order afferent neurones are initially isolated structures and establish secondarily their connections both with the central nervous system (the neural tube) and with peripheral sensory receptors (fig. 24.107).

The precocious appearance of the eye is matched by that of the **olfactory placodes**, thickened areas of surface ectoderm which sink beneath the surface as the olfactory pits. From the placodal epithelium will develop the smell receptors. The epithelial lining of the internal ear is already present as the **otic vesicle**, which lies beside the hind brain, close to the VII and VIII ganglia, an early association which persists into the adult. The otic vesicle develops as a localized ectodermal thickening, the **otic placode**, which sinks beneath the surface to form a pit and then becomes pinched off from the surface as a closed ectodermal vesicle (fig. 18.16).

The subsequent development of the nervous system is described on p. 24.77.

THE NOTOCHORD AND MESODERMAL SOMITES

The pairs of segmentally arranged somites, derived from the paraxial mesoderm, are described in regional groupings; four occipital, eight cervical, twelve thoracic, five lumbar, five sacral and eight or nine coccygeal. A small, short lived cavity appears within each somite, dividing it into an outer sheet of cells, which constitutes the **myotome** and the so called **dermatome**, and an inner, more loosely-arranged collection of cells, the **sclerotome** (fig. 18.17).

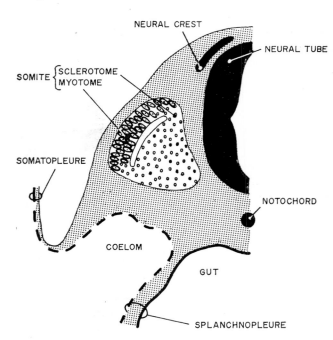

FIG. 18.17. The mesodermal somites are wedge-shaped blocks of paraxial mesoderm. Each shows an outer myotome and an inner sclerotome.

The myotome gives rise to much of the skeletal muscle whose histological development is described on p. 15.6. The more general features of rearrangement of the myotomal contributions may be summarized as follows.

(1) The early muscle fibres are arranged in a craniocaudal orientation, which is commonly lost later.

(2) Muscle primordia commonly undergo extensive migration, e.g. the latissimus dorsi which develops from cervical myotomes has attachments in the adult as far caudally as the iliac crest. Similarly the muscle of the diaphragm arises from cervical myotomes and undergoes an extensive shift caudally. These migrating muscle primordia draw after them their nerves of supply and the course followed by these nerves gives an indication of the direction and extent of migration.

(3) Few muscles arise from single myotomes; most are formed by fusion of parts of adjacent somites.

(4) Two muscles may arise by longitudinal splitting of a single primordium.

(5) Layers of muscles, such as those of the abdominal wall, may be formed by tangential splitting of primordia.

(6) Part, or all, of a myotomal primordium may degenerate, leaving, as a connective tissue remnant, an aponeurotic sheet or a ligament.

These various morphogenetic mechanisms lead to the laying down of the musculature of the trunk. Although the details are complex, the general pattern is simple and of some importance (fig. 18.18).

A **dorsal column** develops on a plane dorsal to the vertebral transverse processes and forms the postvertebral extensor muscles of the spine, which are innervated by the dorsal primary rami of the spinal nerves.

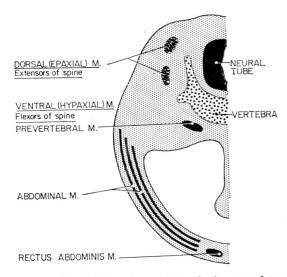

FIG. 18.18. The basic pattern of the body musculature derived by migration from the myotomes.

A **ventral column** forms the prevertebral musculature and, by migrating into the somatopleuric mesoderm, the lateral and ventral muscles of the thoracic and abdominal walls. These are innervated by the ventral primary rami of spinal nerves.

Branchial muscles which arise from the branchial arch mesoderm (p. 18.32) are not of somite origin.

The dermatome was so named because its cells were believed to migrate to a position beneath the ectoderm, there to form the dermis, the connective tissue layer of the skin. At best, such a contribution is small, and the only justification for retaining the name is the segmental distribution of nerve fibres to the skin (p. 24.3).

The sclerotome contributes, by proliferation and migration, to the general body mesenchyme. It also provides

cellular streams, originally segmental like the somite, which flow medially to surround the notochord and the neural tube (fig. 18.19). These segmental masses become rearranged to form intersegmental blocks from which develop the **centra of the vertebrae**. From sclerotomic material surrounding the neural tube arise the **neural arches** of the vertebrae, and ventrolateral extensions into the body wall form the **costal processes**. The three constituent elements of each vertebra, centrum, neural arch and costal process,

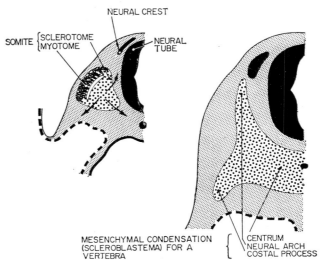

FIG. 18.19. Migrating streams of cells from the sclerotome form, among other things, the vertebrae and ribs.

are thus established in an intersegmental position and alternate therefore with the segmental spinal nerves and with the myotomic muscles. Each vertebra is laid down as a densely cellular mesenchymal precursor, the **scleroblastema**; this transforms into a cartilage model which is subsequently replaced by bone by the process of endochondral ossification (p. 18.37).

The notochord disappears where it is surrounded by the developing centra; between them it expands to form the gelatinous centre of the intervertebral disc, the **nucleus pulposus**.

THE GUT TUBE AND ITS DERIVATIVES (fig. 18.20).
The gut tube, lined throughout by endodermal epithelium, extends from the buccopharyngeal membrane, now ruptured, to the cloacal membrane, by which it is closed off from the amniotic cavity. It is relatively simple at this stage, following the general C-curvature of the neural tube and the notochord. From it will develop a great variety of structures. The cranial end of the tube is the **primitive pharynx**. It is the broadest part of the gut, flattened between the pericardium which lies below its floor and the nervous system and notochord which lie above its roof. From each lateral wall there project four

pouch-like extensions or bays, the **pharyngeal pouches.**

Behind the primitive pharynx the gut tube narrows into the **oesophagus**; from its ventral wall arises a blind-ending tube which provides the epithelial lining of the **trachea, bronchial tree** and **respiratory portion of the lungs.** The respiratory function of the branchial region has been lost, to be replaced in air-breathing animals by the lungs which still arise, however, from the gut endoderm.

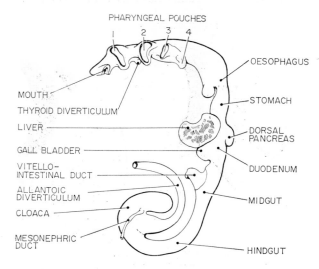

FIG. 18.20. Outline drawing, from the left side, of the gut tube and its derivatives, in an embryo of about 4 weeks. After Streeter (1945) *Contr. Embryol.* **31.**

The **stomach** is already recognizable as a spindle-shaped dilatation, which leads in turn into the **duodenum.** Two outgrowths of endodermal epithelium arise from the duodenum; a dorsal one that forms the major part of the **pancreas,** and a ventral one, from which develop the epithelial components of the **liver, gall bladder, bile ducts** and a minor part of the **pancreas.** The site of outgrowth of the liver bud is a valuable landmark as it defines the junction between the **foregut** and the **midgut.**

From the embryonic midgut there will develop part of the duodenum, distal to the entry of the common bile duct, the rest of the small intestine, the **caecum, appendix** and **ascending colon,** and the greater part of the **transverse colon.** It is that part of the gut which in younger embryos was widely continuous with the yolk sac, and which is still connected with it by the vitello-intestinal duct. The midgut is that part of the gut which is supplied, in the adult, by the superior mesenteric artery, bordering cranially on the vascular territory of the coeliac artery, and caudally on that of the inferior mesenteric artery.

The midgut continues without demarcation into the **hindgut**; this in turn opens into the **cloaca** (latin, a sewer) which receives the **mesonephric ducts** and the **allantoic diverticulum.**

When the general form of the endodermal gut tube has been appreciated we can look at its surroundings. It is immediately invested throughout its length by a loose cellular mesenchyme from which will develop the connective tissue and muscle layers of the gut. The gut is also related to a rather complex series of spaces which together form the **coelomic cavity** of the embryo.

THE COELOMIC TRACT

The three portions of the intraembryonic coelom: the pericardial cavity, pericardioperitoneal canals and peritoneal cavity, are continuous with one another. The peritoneal part of the coelom communicates with the extraembryonic coelom. This communication may be important for the survival of the embryo, since it provides a route for circulation of fluid and dissolved nutrients from the extraembryonic coelom into the intraembryonic coelomic tract. This may serve as an accessory route of supply for the early embryo.

The gut is closely related to the coelom. The primitive pharynx lies dorsally to the pericardial cavity (fig. 18.21a). The oesophagus and the tracheal outgrowth are flanked on either side by the pericardioperitoneal canals, forerunners of the pleural cavities (fig. 18.21b). The remainder of the foregut and the midgut lie within the peritoneal cavity, suspended from the dorsal abdominal wall by the dorsal mesentery (fig. 18.21c and d).

The **diaphragm,** which later separates the pleural and pericardial cavities from the peritoneal cavity, is represented at this stage by the **septum transversum.** As its name implies this is a mesodermal sheet lying transversely across the body. Ventrally it is continuous with the ventral abdominal wall; dorsally it is incomplete where it is traversed on either side of the midline by the pericardioperitoneal canals. Its cranial surface faces into the pericardium, its caudal surface is being invaded by cords of liver cells derived from the hepatic bud (fig. 18.22). The **pleural cavity** develops as an extension of the pericardioperitoneal canal. The forerunner of the lung is called the **lung bud,** consisting of one of the primary divisions of the epithelial tracheal tube, with a covering layer of splanchnopleuric mesoderm.

To understand later changes in the coelomic cavities it is important to appreciate that, at this stage, the lung buds are very small relative to the heart and pericardial cavity. The primitive pleural cavities into which the lung buds grow are also relatively small, and they lie entirely dorsal to the pericardial cavity and open freely into its dorsal wall. The lung bud grows into a pleural cavity which expands before it. The cavity grows ventrally around the heart. It expands into the thick layer of loose mesenchyme which forms the wall of the pericardial cavity (fig. 18.23). Extension of the pleural cavity into this mesenchyme splits it into an outer layer which will form the **chest wall** and an inner layer, the **pleuropericardial**

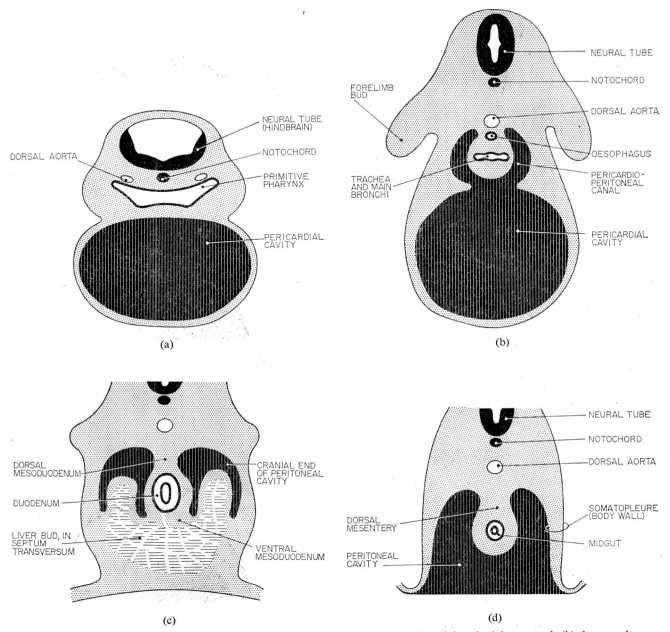

Fig. 18.21. Transverse sections through (a) the primitive pharynx with the pericardial cavity lying ventral; (b) the oesophagus and trachea, flanked by the pericardioperitoneal canals, which open from the dorsal wall of the pericardial cavity; (c) the septum transversum; (d) the midgut level.

membrane, which will form the definitive **fibrous pericardium**. Hence this is clothed internally with serous pericardium and externally by parietal pleura. Each pleuropericardial membrane has a free edge dorsally; fusion of the two free edges in the midline with one another and with the mesoderm ventral to the oesophagus will later close off the pericardial from the two pleural cavities.

Expansion of the pleural cavities into the thick mesodermal bed of the primitive pericardial wall brings into existence a second membrane lying between the pleural cavity and the peritoneal cavity and called, therefore, the **pleuroperitoneal membrane** (fig. 18.24). Like the pleuropericardial membrane this too has a free edge dorsally and medially. Fusion between the mesoderm which surrounds the oesophagus in the midline and the free edge of the pleuroperitoneal membrane on each side will at about the 6th week separate each pleural cavity above from the peritoneal cavity below.

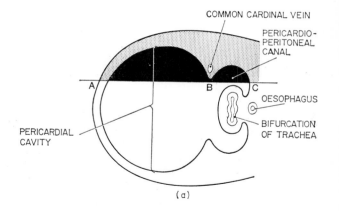

FIG. 18.22. Sagittal section to show the relationships of the septum transversum to the coelomic cavities, the gut and the liver. The dotted line marks the limit of the head fold (fig. 18.11).

THE HEART AND CIRCULATION

The heart in an embryo of about 4 weeks is already an active pump, with rhythmical co-ordinated contractions passing from the venous (input) end of the heart to its arterial (output) end, which projects through the roof of the pericardium and, therefore, comes to lie below the floor of the primitive pharynx. The arterial and venous ends are relatively fixed points of anchorage; between them the heart is a free tubular loop lying within the pericardial coelom. It is essentially uniform in structure throughout its length (fig. 18.25).

(1) An inner lining of simple squamous epithelium, similar to the endothelial lining of the entire vascular tree, is called **endocardium**.

(2) An outer layer of developing muscle forms the **myocardium**. The outermost cells of this layer develop into connective tissue and form the **epicardium**.

(3) The **cardiac jelly** is a layer of connective tissue between the endocardium and the myocardium. It is sparsely cellular and rich in gelatinous intercellular matrix.

Regional variations in shape and thickness of myocardium and cardiac jelly distinguish the various chambers. Starting at the venous end these are: **sinus venosus, primitive atrium, primitive ventricle, bulbus cordis** and **truncus arteriosus**.

The arteries are little more than endothelial tubes, relatively larger than they are in the adult and lacking the connective tissue and muscle elements which develop later from the surrounding mesenchyme. Their basic pattern is shown in fig. 18.26. The truncus arteriosus pierces the dorsal wall of the pericardium and opens into a dilated **aortic sac** which lies below (ventral to) the pharyngeal floor. From it arise on each side a series of

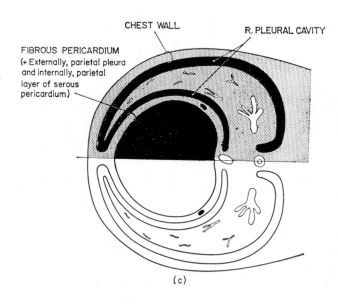

FIG. 18.23. Transverse sections to show (a) how the pleural cavity develops as an extension of the pericardioperitoneal canal, by splitting of the mesoderm of the primitive pericardial wall, (b) how the lung grows into the enlarging cavity prepared for it, (c) the adult relationships.

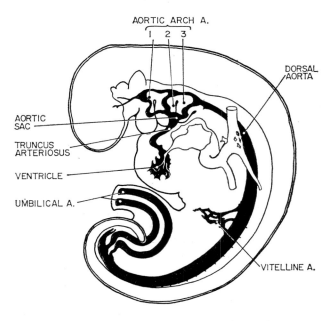

FIG. 18.24. Drawing to show the development of the pleural cavity from the pericardio peritoneal canal. As in fig. 18.12, the embryo has been sectioned in a parasagittal plane, to the right of the midline, and the diagram shows the medial cut surface of the right hand part of the sectioned embryo. Cf. fig. 18.23a which shows the upper surface of a section cut in plane ABC. Based on Frazer, *Manual of Human Embryology.*

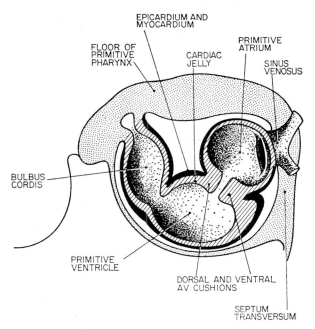

FIG. 18.25. Diagrammatic longitudinal section of primitive heart tube showing the basic structure of its wall and its fundamental subdivisions.

aortic arch arteries. These run round the primitive pharynx to open into the paired dorsal aortae which lie dorsal to the pharynx. Each aortic arch artery lies within the mesoderm of a pharyngeal arch between two adjacent pharyngeal pouches.

The **paired dorsal aortae** extend caudally to the tail of the embryo, lying dorsally to the gut, ventrally to the neural tube, and following the C-curve of each. Their branches are distributed to a surface network of capillaries investing the neural tube, to arterial plexuses in the visceral mesoderm surrounding the gut tube, trachea and lung buds and to the intermediate mesoderm from which will develop, among other things, the kidneys and gonads.

FIG. 18.26. The main arteries in an embryo of about 4 weeks. After Streeter (1942) *Contr. Embryol.* **30.**

The largest branches of the dorsal aortae are their terminal ones, the **umbilical arteries**, which arise from plexuses lying beside the cloaca, and run in the body stalk on either side of the allantoic diverticulum, to the chorionic circulation. It is, of course, not surprising that the chorionic circulation should take the major share of the blood; by allowing exchange between embryonic and maternal circulations the chorion provides for the nutritive, respiratory and excretory needs of the embryo, quite apart from the endocrine function of its trophoblastic component.

The veins are distributed on a simple basic plan (fig. 18.27).

(1) From the head, and particularly the brain, blood is drained by the paired **anterior cardinal veins**; from the body caudal to the heart run the paired **posterior cardinal**

veins. These join the anterior veins to form the **common cardinal veins.**

(2) Blood returns from the chorionic circulation by the paired **umbilical veins.**

(3) From the vascular yolk sac blood returns by paired **vitelline veins.**

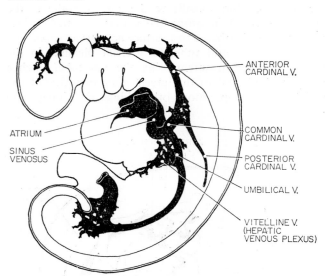

FIG. 18.27. The main veins in an embryo of about 4 weeks. After Streeter (1942) *Contr. Embryol.* 30.

These three pairs of veins converge on the **sinus venosus**, a common venous reservoir embedded within the mesoderm of the septum transversum. The routes by which they reach the septum transversum are worthy of attention.

(1) The common cardinal veins which run caudally to enter the septum transversum lie in the pleuropericardial membrane close to its free border. The lung bud grows laterally into the expanding pleural cavity behind (dorsal to) this vein (fig. 18.28).

(2) The umbilical veins enter the embryo by way of the body stalk and run in the body wall mesoderm (somatopleure) to enter the septum transversum at its lateral edges. The umbilical veins do not, therefore, at this stage become involved with the cords of liver cells which are beginning to invade the septum transversum.

(3) The vitelline veins enter the embryo in the visceral mesoderm which surrounds the yolk sac stalk and turn cranially to enter the septum transversum where they are broken up into a complicated plexus of thin-walled vessels. This **hepatic venous plexus** becomes intimately intermingled with growing liver cords. Having circulated through the liver, this vitelline vein blood is collected into a symmetrical pair of **right** and **left hepatocardiac veins.**

These important relationships may be best illustrated by a semi-schematic ventral view (fig. 18.29). This shows that (1) the sinus venosus occupies the full width of the

septum transversum, extending laterally as **right** and **left horns,** (2) the common cardinal and umbilical veins enter the sinus laterally at the extremity of each horn, (3) the hepatocardiac veins enter the sinus nearer to the midline and (4) the opening of the sinus venosus into the primitive atrium, the sinuatrial orifice, is no longer in the midline but has moved to the right. This is one of the earliest indications of a developing asymmetry in the pattern of the major veins as they enter the heart.

The right hepatocardiac vein enlarges and forms the terminal segment of the inferior vena cava (fig. 18.30); the left closes off. The right umbilical vein becomes closed. The left umbilical vein establishes an anastomosis with the left vitelline vein as they enter the septum transversum.

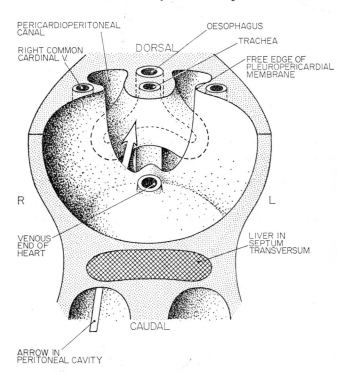

FIG. 18.28. The front wall of the pericardial cavity has been cut away, and the heart removed. The openings into the pericardioperitoneal canals lie on each side of the splanchnopleuric mesoderm which surrounds the oesophagus and trachea. The common cardinal veins run in the free edges of the pleuropericardial membranes. As the lung bud grows laterally into the primitive pleural cavity it passes dorsal to the vein. Modified from Frazer, *Manual of Human Embryology.*

This anastomosis diverts umbilical vein blood into the hepatic venous plexus. We have already seen that the chorionic circulation is the largest recipient of blood; a major part of the venous return is, therefore, through the left umbilical vein into the hepatic venous plexus. Because the left hepatocardiac vein is closing, umbilical vein blood runs obliquely through the hepatic plexus towards

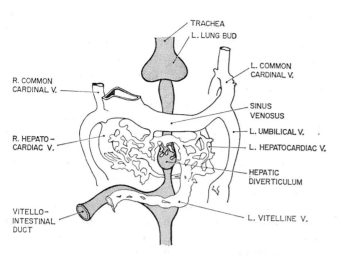

FIG. 18.29. Ventral view of the arrangement of veins entering the sinus venosus in an embryo of about 4 weeks. After Streeter (1945) *Contr. Embryol.* **31**.

the right hepatocardiac vein near its entrance to the sinus venosus. The increased venous flow, obliquely from left to right, through the hepatic plexus, brings about the formation of a large venous channel, the **ductus venosus**, which provides a direct route of flow for oxygenated blood from the left umbilical vein to the inferior vena cava.

FIG. 18.30. Ventral view of the arrangement of veins entering the sinus venosus, at a later stage than fig. 18.29. The portal vein is derived from the vitelline veins.

THE URINARY SYSTEM

The intermediate mesoderm which lies between the paraxial and lateral mesoderms forms an extended cellular mass, the **nephrogenic** (kidney forming) **cord**, which is found between lower cervical and sacral levels. Kidney tubules develop directly from the cellular meso-

derm of the nephrogenic cord; this development begins at the upper end of the cord and extends progressively towards its caudal end. As new tubules are added caudally, those at the head end of the cord regress. In essence, therefore, a wave of kidney tubule formation spreads caudally through the nephrogenic cord.

The tubules which thus arise in succession are not identical and may be grouped into three sets (fig. 18.31).

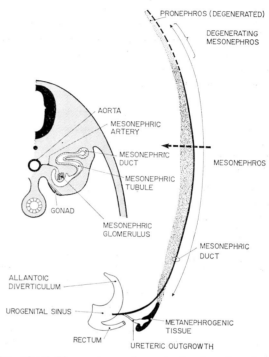

FIG. 18.31. The nephrogenic cord, showing the relative positions of pro-, meso- and metanephros. A transverse section of the mesonephros is shown on the left.

(1) The **pronephros** (the head kidney) is confined to the extreme upper end of the cord, and is vestigial and functionless in the human embryo.

(2) The **mesonephros** (the middle kidney) extends from upper thoracic to lower lumbar segments, although it is not fully developed throughout its length at any one time. Its tubules are probably functional in the human embryo and open into a duct, the **mesonephric duct**, which began its development in connection with the pronephros, and which grows caudally to open into the **cloaca**.

(3) The **metanephros** forms the permanent, definitive kidney of man and other mammals, birds and reptiles. Its development is described with the urinary tract (p. 34.1).

THE GENITAL SYSTEM

The development of the genital system is described in detail on p. 37.53. Here we need say only that the **gonads** develop as paired swellings on the inner side of the mesonephros. They bulge into the peritoneal coelom and form the **urogenital ridge**.

SUMMARY

This account has sketched the outline of early embryogenesis and the further development of most of the systems is considered in the appropriate chapters. However, the cardiovascular system and the branchial arches form such integral parts of the embryo that their whole development is described here.

Embryologists usually define the stage of development of an embryo by reference to its length or number of paired somites, but in this chapter the timing of events is related to postconceptional age. Interest in the timing of embryogenesis has increased greatly in recent years because of the recognition that various environmental influences may distort development. Severe damage occurs

TABLE 18.1.   Timetable of human development

Age after fertilization (weeks)	Crown-rump length (mm)	
0–1		Fertilization and cleavage
1–2		Implantation
2–3		Embryo two layered
3–4		Embryo three layered, first somites formed, neural folds appear, intraembryonic coelom develops
4–5	4–7	35–38 pairs of somites, leg buds appear, lens placode develops, division of atrium in progress, one way circulation through heart
5–6	11–14	Limb bones, skull base and vertebrae are precartilaginous, closure of IV foramen, division of truncus arteriosus complete, palate development begins (completed at 12 weeks)
6–7	22	First bone formed, sex recognizable externally

when dramatic changes are taking place in the development of an organ, and so the timing of exposure to the hazards determines the nature of the lesion. It must not be assumed that all developmental anomalies are the result of external influences. There is evidence that many defects are genetic in origin. Table 18.1 relates age and length with some important developmental events.

THE DEVELOPMENT OF THE HEART

The circulation of blood is well established in embryos at the end of the 4th week of development. The heart at this stage is a simple tubular structure which forms a U loop within the pericardial cavity. Blood returns to the heart at its venous end, the sinus venosus, which is embedded in the septum transversum. The sinus venosus opens into the single primitive atrium by way of the sinu-atrial orifice which lies in the midline, is elongated dorso-ventrally and is guarded by two flaps of endocardium, the right and left venous valves which prevent reflux of blood from atrium to sinus. The primitive atrium, in its turn, leads into the primitive ventricle. The atrioventricular (AV) orifice is soon encroached upon by two local thickenings of the cardiac jelly (fig. 18.32a). Imagine yourself within the cavity of the primitive ventricle, looking towards the AV orifice and the primitive atrium (fig. 18.32b). As the dorsal and ventral cushions thicken and grow towards one another, the orifice becomes H shaped; later, when the cushions meet and fuse, the AV orifice is divided into right and left channels, separated by the **septum intermedium**, so called because of its position intermediate between atrium and ventricle.

FIG. 18.32. Atrioventricular (AV) junction and the AV cushions. (a) Schematic longitudinal section; (b) diagrammatic view of the AV orifice and the AV cushions which encroach upon it, as seen from within the cavity of the ventricle.

From the primitive ventricle the blood flows into the bulbus cordis which gradually narrows and passes without a sharp line of demarcation into the truncus arteriosus. This is the arterial end of the heart; it pierces the pericardial roof to open into a thin-walled midline structure, the **aortic sac**, from which arise the aortic arteries.

In understanding the complex changes which follow, it is important to keep in mind several features of the primitive heart tube.

(1) It is attached to the pericardial wall only at its venous and arterial ends. Between these two fixed points it loops freely into the pericardial cavity. The dorsal mesocardium, a mesentery which at an earlier stage suspended it within the pericardium, has disappeared.

(2) It lies in the midsagittal plane.

(3) It shows little regional specialization and the layers which constitute its wall are continuous without interruption from one chamber to the next. In particular, there is no interruption of the musculature at the junction between atrium and ventricle and the impulse for contraction spreads directly from the venous end, where it is initiated, to the arterial end. The venous end of the heart is already established as the **pacemaker**; a unidirectional

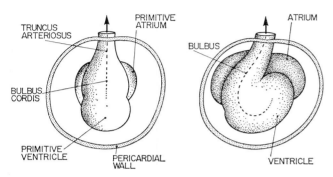

FIG. 18.33. Ventral views of the heart tube, showing the displacement of the bulbus cordis to the right and the ventricle to the left; changes brought about by the rapid elongation of the heart. Based on Frazer, *Manual of Human Embryology.*

flow of blood from venous to arterial end is maintained by the peristaltic wave of contraction. This is aided by the peculiar inelastic property of the cardiac jelly which is thickened to form the endocardial cushions at the AV

orifice. As the wave of contraction passes over the AV junction, the AV cushions are pressed together, effectively preventing reflux of blood and anticipating the effect, but not the mechanism, of the AV valves which develop later.

The heart tube now enters a period of rapid growth and becomes bent in the transverse as well as in the sagittal plane. The result of this can be seen by looking at the heart from the front (fig. 18.33); the bulbus cordis is now displaced towards the right and the ventricle towards the left. The primitive atrium lies dorsal and caudal to the ventricle and may be seen bulging forward on either side of the bulbus cordis.

The various chambers of the simple heart tube now become divided by septal partitions. To simplify understanding, these changes are dealt with chamber by chamber, although they occur more or less simultaneously.

PARTITIONING OF THE ATRIUM

The sinu-atrial opening moves from its original midline position on the dorso-caudal wall of the atrium to a position to the right of the midline. Division of the atrium into right and left sides by a flimsy **septum primum** now begins (fig. 18.34). This develops from the dorso-caudal wall of the atrium and extends in the midsagittal plane as a crescentric sheet of tissue which approaches and fuses with the septum intermedium. The hole which is bounded by its free edge is the **foramen primum**. This becomes progressively smaller as the septum primum grows to meet the septum intermedium and, before communication between the right and left sides of the

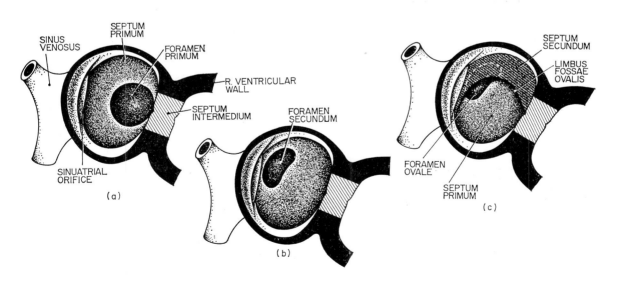

FIG. 18.34. The development of the interatrial septa. The right wall of the primitive atrium and of the ventricle have been removed and the developing septa are viewed from the right. (a) Septum primum and foramen primum, (b) septum primum and foramen secundum, (c) septum secundum.

atrium is cut off, a new opening, the **foramen secundum,** appears, high up in the septum primum. This communication allows blood to flow into the left side of the atrium because the only venous return to the heart at this stage is via the sinus venosus which now opens into the right side of the atrium.

A second septum, **septum secundum,** later develops on the right side of septum primum. It differs from septum primum in certain important respects. Although it grows towards septum intermedium, it does not reach it; its growing margin remains as a free edge to form a conspicuous landmark on the right side of the atrial septum, the **limbus fossae ovalis** of the adult heart (fig. 28.5). It is also a thicker and more substantial structure than septum primum. Its growth normally continues until it overlaps foramen secundum completely. It does not, however, prevent the flow of blood from right to left atrium because the diaphanous septum primum is easily displaced to the left by the stream of blood which flows through the oblique passage between the two septa (fig. 18.35). So long as pressure in the right atrium is higher than that in the left, this flow of blood through the septum will continue. This is the state of affairs until pulmonary respiration begins at birth; then the venous return from the greatly increased pulmonary circulation brings the pres-

sure in the left atrium to a level equal to or slightly greater than that in the right, and septum primum is pressed up against septum secundum. Thus it acts as a valve which closes off the passage through the septum. The oblique passage is the **foramen ovale**; the entrance to it is in the right atrium, bounded by the limbus fossae ovalis, the free margin of septum secundum; the exit from it is foramen secundum, opening into the left atrium.

PARTITIONING OF THE VENTRICLE

This is brought about by a very different mechanism. The greater parts of both the right and left ventricles develop from the single ventricle by expansion of its wall externally and hollowing out of its wall internally (fig. 18.36c). The interventricular septum is, as it were, left behind as a crescentic sheet of cardiac muscle, lying more or less in the sagittal plane, between the expanding right and left ventricles. We can only guess at the factors which bring about this expansion of right and left ventricles; perhaps the two streams of blood which enter the ventricle through the right and left AV orifices have a sculpturing action on the thick trabeculated ventricular muscle. Be this as it may, the muscular part of the interventricular septum does not grow upwards into the ventricle; the ventricles expand on either side of it. The free edge of the **muscular septum** which is produced in this fashion obviously does not meet the septum intermedium; between the two is an **interventricular foramen** allowing communication between right and left ventricles. This is closed later by cardiac jelly from a variety of sources; the closing tissue is fibrous rather than muscular and forms the **membranous portion** of the interventricular septum (fig. 18.42). The mechanism of its formation is inseparable from the method of division of the bulbus cordis and truncus arteriosus.

PARTITIONING OF THE BULBUS CORDIS AND TRUNCUS ARTERIOSUS

The bulbus cordis and the truncus arteriosus together constitute the outflow tract of the developing heart which eventually delivers blood into a **systemic** circuit (derived from the fourth aortic arch) and a **pulmonary** circuit (derived from the sixth aortic arch). The bulbus cordis and truncus arteriosus must be divided in such a way that the right ventricle discharges into the pulmonary circuit, and the left into the systemic circuit.

Fig. 18.37 illustrates the interior of the ventricles and of the bulbus at the beginning of development of the continuous spiralling septum which will divide the bulbus and truncus throughout their length. It is important to appreciate the relationships of the ventricles to one another and to the bulbus at this stage. The ventricles lie side by side, the right lying slightly ventral to the left; each receives its own stream of blood through its own AV orifice. The bulbus lies in such a position that it can re-

FIG. 18.35. Section of the heart to show the mechanism of the foramen ovale (a) prenatal, (b) postnatal.

jelly project into the bulbus from its right and left sides; these are the **right** and **left bulbar ridges**. Soon they meet and fuse, to form the **bulbar septum** which divides the bulbus into **anterior** and **posterior** channels. This septum is not confined to the bulbus but continues upwards into the truncus, spiralling as it goes. In the truncus it is called the **aorticopulmonary septum** because it divides the truncus into aortic and pulmonary channels. At the upper end of the truncus the **aortic channel** lies in front and ejects its

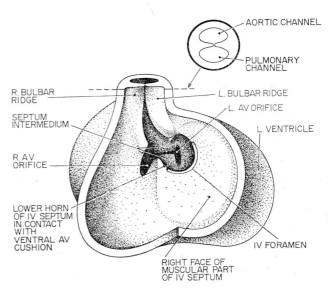

FIG. 18.36. The origin of the right and left ventricles from the primitive ventricle. (a) Ventral view of the unopened heart, (b) ventral view of the heart after removal of its ventral wall, (c) diagrammatic section of the heart cut in the plane shown. (a) and (b) based on Frazer, *Manual of Human Embryology*.

FIG. 18.37. The front wall of the bulbus cordis and of the right ventricle has been removed and the heart is viewed obliquely from the front and the right. This view allows the right face of the interventricular (IV) septum to be seen. Note (1) the relation of the two 'horns' of the interventricular septum to the septum intermedium, (2) the right and left bulbar ridges, thickenings of the cardiac jelly of the bulbus cordis shown also in a transverse section. After Frazer, *Manual of Human Embryology*.

ceive two streams of blood, one from the right ventricle and one from the left.

Because the right ventricle lies slightly ventral to the left, the right ventricular stream is ejected into the front or ventral half of the bulbus, the left ventricular stream into the back or dorsal half. It is known from the study of hydrodynamic models that two fluid streams, ejected in parallel into a single tube, spiral around one another, the spiral turning clockwise as the two streams travel through the tube. There are good grounds for believing that the same sort of thing happens in the outflow tract of the heart at this stage and that the two spiralling streams exert a moulding effect on the thick layer of cardiac jelly which lies beneath the endocardium of the bulbus and truncus.

The effect of this moulding can be illustrated most simply by a transverse section through the bulbus cordis at the level indicated in fig. 18.37. Ridges of thickened cardiac

blood into the 4th aortic arches (systemic circuit), while the **pulmonary channel** lies behind and ejects its blood into the 6th aortic arches (pulmonary circuit) (fig. 18.38).

The bulbar ridges also extend downwards towards the ventricles; as they do so they spiral in such a way that the **right bulbar ridge** comes to lie on the caudal wall of the ventricle, where it grows across the dorsal end of the right AV orifice, before meeting and fusing with the free edge of the muscular part of the interventricular septum. The **left bulbar ridge** similarly spirals on to the cranial wall of the ventricle to meet and fuse with the free edge of the muscular part of the interventricular septum. The right and left bulbar ridges form a coronally disposed septum at level A (fig. 18.39), dividing the bulbus at this level into an anterior (pulmonary) channel and a posterior (aortic)

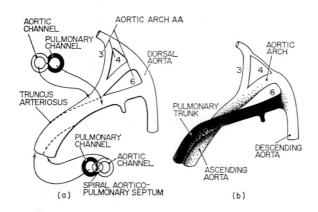

Fig. 18.38. (a) View of truncus arteriosus, aortic arch arteries 3, 4 and 6, and dorsal aorta from left side. The dotted lines trace the course of the attachment of the spiral aortico-pulmonary septum to the wall of the truncus. (b) Similar to (a), after splitting of the truncus into two separate channels, one of which, the aortic, leads into the 4th aortic arch, the other, the pulmonary, into the 6th arch.

channel. This septum spirals as it descends through the bulbus so that when it meets and fuses with the free edge of the muscular portion of the interventricular septum, it lies in the sagittal plane. The septum has divided the bulbus into two channels, one communicating with the right ventricle and forming the **infundibulum** of the adult right ventricle, the other communicating with the left ventricle and forming the **aortic vestibule** of the adult left ventricle.

Fig. 18.39. A view of the opened heart, similar to that shown in fig. 18.37, at a later stage of development. The right and left bulbar ridges, which lie in the coronal plane at level A, spiral as they descend so that, when they reach the ventricles, they lie in the sagittal plane and can therefore fuse with the free edge of the muscular interventricular (IV) septum and seal off the interventricular foramen. After Frazer, *Manual of Human Embryology.*

The bulbar septum has not only divided the bulbus, however; it has also sealed off the interventricular foramen, being the main contributor to the **membranous portion** of the interventricular septum (fig. 18.39).

ABSORPTION OF SINUS VENOSUS INTO RIGHT ATRIUM

Originally the sinus venosus is embedded within the septum transversum and is an independent chamber, opening in the midline into the caudal wall of the primitive atrium. It is symmetrical, receiving on each side the common cardinal, umbilical and vitelline veins (fig. 18.29). This pattern is soon replaced by a less complicated but asymmetrical one as the result of the following changes.

(1) The right anterior cardinal vein, the right common cardinal vein and the right horn of the sinus venosus form the **superior vena cava**. The right posterior cardinal vein remains as the arch of the vena azygos.

(2) The left common cardinal vein and the left horn of the sinus venosus cease to receive blood from the body wall. Their territory becomes restricted, at a later stage, to the wall of the heart itself, when they form the **coronary sinus**.

(3) The vitelline and umbilical veins undergo great modification, largely because of the invasion of the septum transversum by the developing liver.

In summary, the sinus venosus now receives three veins, the superior vena cava, inferior vena cava and coronary sinus, and opens into the back wall of the right atrium through an elongated sinu-atrial orifice, guarded by right and left venous valves.

The sinus venosus now becomes freed from the septum transversum and is absorbed or 'taken up' into the back wall of the right atrium. Thus, each of the three tributaries of the sinus venosus develops an independent opening (fig. 18.40). The part of the definitive atrial wall derived from sinus venosus is smooth internally, as befits its venous origin, while the remainder of the definitive atrium has a rough trabeculated interior, being derived from the primitive atrium. The venous valves lose their original significance with the disappearance of the single sinu-atrial orifice. The left venous valve fuses with the atrial septum; the right forms, dorsally, the **crista terminalis** and, ventrally, the valve of the inferior vena cava and the valve of the coronary sinus. Of these three structures, only the valve of the inferior vena cava has any functional importance. During foetal life it may help to direct the inferior caval blood stream across the right atrium towards the foramen ovale (fig. 39.2).

DEVELOPMENT OF PULMONARY VEINS

From the back wall of the left atrium a single pulmonary vein develops and divides; each branch in turn divides, so that two pulmonary veins from each lung return blood by

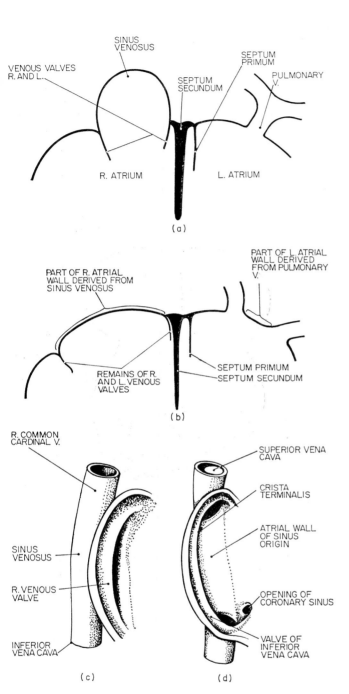

FIG. 18.40. The absorption of the sinus venosus in the back wall of the right atrium. Transverse sections (a) before and (b) after absorption of sinus venosus into back of right atrium and of pulmonary veins into body of left atrium. Right lateral views (c) before and (d) after absorption.

a single common trunk to the left atrium. In much the same way that the sinus venosus was absorbed into the back of the right atrium, so the **common pulmonary vein** and its two primary divisions are absorbed into the back of the left atrium. Each of the four pulmonary veins now opens independently into the left atrium and the rectangular area bounded by their four orifices is smooth, being of venous origin, while the remainder of the interior of the definitive atrium is trabeculated, being derived from the primitive atrium (fig. 18.40).

DEVELOPMENT OF THE ATRIOVENTRICULAR VALVES

The right and left AV openings derive from the originally single AV opening which is divided by the septum intermedium. Each opening is surrounded by cardiac jelly from which the AV valves develop by growth, excavation and thinning.

The **left AV orifice** is the simpler. One valve cusp develops on each side of the slit, giving rise to the (bicuspid) **mitral valve**.

The **right AV orifice** is originally like the left, but the right bulbar ridge, as it grows down the back wall of the ventricle towards the free edge of the interventricular septum, cuts across the dorsal end of the opening, converting it from a slit into a triangular opening. Each boundary of the triangle is composed of cardiac jelly from which the three cusps of the **tricuspid valve** are sculptured.

DEVELOPMENT OF THE AORTIC AND PULMONARY VALVES

These develop from cardiac jelly. At the upper end of the bulbus cordis, the right and left bulbar ridges form a coronally disposed bulbar septum (fig. 18.37). Additional dorsal and ventral intercalated cushions of cardiac jelly develop at this level. When the upper bulbus divides to form aortic and pulmonary channels it does so in the plane of the bulbar septum. The anterior (pulmonary) channel and the posterior (aortic) channel each has three masses of cardiac jelly from which the three cusps of its valve will be fashioned (fig. 18.41). In later development the entire heart rotates about its long axis, so that the right atrium and ventricle come to lie anteriorly and the left chambers posteriorly. This rotation alters the relative positions of the great vessels as they leave the heart; in the adult the pulmonary trunk, at the level of the valve, lies mainly to the left of the aorta.

DEVELOPMENT OF THE CONDUCTING SYSTEM

Peristaltic contraction of the primitive heart tube occurs in the absence both of a conducting system and of autonomic innervation, the sinus venosus acting as pacemaker. Initial continuity of atrial and ventricular muscle allows the spread of the impulse for contraction. This continuity is progressively interrupted in embryos of

30 days and older and the development of specialized conducting tissue becomes necessary. The **SA** and **AV nodes** appear as specializations of the myocardium and the **AV bundle**, continuous with the AV node, differentiates in the interventricular septum where it divides into **right** and **left bundle branches** (p. 28.9).

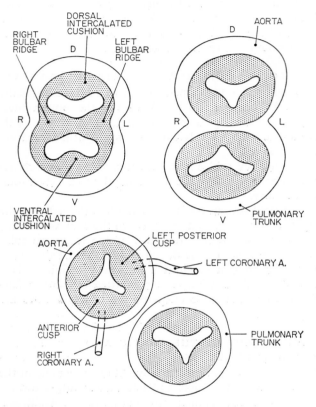

FIG. 18.41. Transverse sections of the bulbus cordis, seen from above, to show the mode of origin of the pulmonary and aortic valves.

So far the development of the heart has been described in a piecemeal fashion, chamber by chamber. Fig. 18.42 brings together, in a simple diagram, most of the important and clinically useful information about the septa of the heart. It shows schematically the appearance of a sectional plane passing through the atria and ventricles.

Interest in cardiac development has increased greatly in recent years, partly because of the development of surgical correction of several different kinds of cardiac malformation and partly because of the demonstration that some virus infections, notably rubella, of the mother at certain stages of pregnancy may cause cardiac defects.

Development of the aortic arch arteries

The aortic arch arteries are simple endothelial tubes which arise from the aortic sac; this lies in the midline, below the floor of the primitive pharynx and above the roof of the pericardium. These arteries run dorsally around the primitive pharynx within mesoderm of the pharyngeal (branchial) arches, and open dorsally into the dorsal aorta.

Initially, the aortic arch arteries form a bilaterally symmetrical pattern, but symmetry is lost as development proceeds. There are six pairs of them, numbered from 1–6, in order of their sequence of development. As more caudal members of the series appear, arteries 1 and 2 dwindle and largely disappear. Artery 5, while of some interest to the comparative embryologist, is ephemeral and can be disregarded.

Because later development is asymmetrical, it is convenient to study the changes which occur on each side in turn, as seen in lateral views of the embryo.

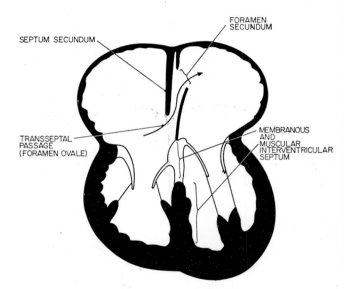

FIG. 18.42. Section through atria and ventricles, to show the developmental origin of the septa of the heart.

THE LEFT SIDE

Fig. 18.43a shows the aortic arch arteries in an embryo of about 4 weeks. The 1st and 2nd arteries have disappeared, the 3rd and 4th are large and arise in common from the aortic sac ventrally. It is worth noting that there is no ventral aorta in the human embryo. The 6th or **pulmonary arch** is still small; it lies close to the site of origin of the lung buds, and the future left pulmonary artery arises from the middle of its caudal wall by sprouting of endothelial cells. The relation of the arteries to the pharyngeal pouches is also of importance. The 3rd pouch lies between the 3rd and 4th arteries; the caudal pharyngeal complex (p. 18.29) lies between the 4th and 6th arteries.

At 5 weeks (fig. 18.43b) division of the truncus arteriosus by the spiral aorticopulmonary septum is nearly complete. The upper end of the truncus and the aortic sac are divided into an anterior portion, from which arise the

3rd and 4th arteries, and a posterior portion, from which arises the 6th artery. The basic pattern of transformation on the left side is completed with the disappearance of the short segment of dorsal aorta between the points of entrance into it of 3rd and 4th arteries.

The left external carotid artery arises as a new outgrowth from the proximal end of the left 3rd aortic arch. The left subclavian artery is formed from the left 7th cervical intersegmental artery, which at this stage arises from the dorsal aorta below the opening into it of the 6th aortic arch. The left subclavian artery subsequently migrates headwards up the aorta to its definitive position.

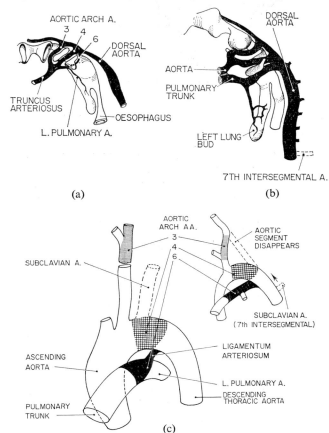

FIG. 18.43. (a) Aortic arch arteries of the left side in an embryo of about 4 weeks (5 mm). After Congdon. (b) Aortic arch arteries of the left side in an embryo of about 5 weeks (11 mm). (c) Scheme of the great vessels of the adult, seen from the left side, for comparison.

Fig. 18.43c shows schematically the appearance of the great vessels as seen from the left side in the adult, and should make clear the developmental origin of the various vessels.

THE RIGHT SIDE

Fig. 18.44a shows the situation on the right, when the pattern is essentially the same as that on the left; fig.

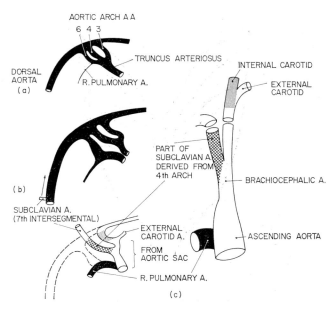

FIG. 18.44. (a) Aortic arch arteries of the right side in an embryo of about 4 weeks (5 mm). (b) Aortic arch arteries of the right side in an embryo of about 5 weeks (11 mm). (c) Scheme of the great vessels of the adult seen from the right side, for comparison.

18.44b shows the later changes and fig. 18.44c presents schematically the situation in the adult.

Once the pattern of development of the aortic arches as seen separately on right and left sides is understood, fig. 18.45, which is a diagram summarizing the entire story, may be appreciated. In studying and using this diagram the distortions which are necessary to depict the aortic sac and the dorsal aortae in the same plane should be remembered.

CAUSATIVE FACTORS IN AORTIC ARCH DEVELOPMENT

It would be unfortunate if preoccupation with the complex changes in the aortic arch system prevented brief comment on some of the factors thought to be responsible for the changing pattern.

(1) Embryonic vessels first appear as capillary-like tubes lined by a simple squamous epithelium, the endothelium, which arises from the flattening of aggregates of **angioblasts** of mesenchymal origin.

(2) Reduction of blood flow through one of these primitive endothelial tubes usually leads to a reduction in its size and eventual disappearance. This fate overtakes the 1st and 2nd aortic arches, for example, when the 3rd and 4th vessels take over most of the output from the aortic sac.

(3) Contrariwise, increased blood flow through a primitive endothelial channel leads to its enlargement and subsequently to the differentiation of the various supporting layers which make up the definitive artery or vein.

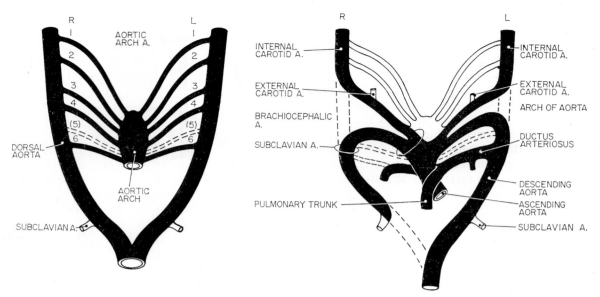

Fig. 18.45. Schematic drawing showing, in ventral view, the fate of the aortic arches. The brachiocephalic artery is circled, but unlabelled.

(4) Genetic factors play an important part in shaping the pattern of development of the aortic arches and of other parts of the vascular system. For example, in mammals it is the left 4th aortic arch which persists as the main systemic vessel, in birds the right. It is not clear to what extent the genes operate indirectly through haemodynamic mechanisms. It is known, however, that experimental ligation of the right 4th arch in the chick embryo results in the left 4th arch taking over the blood flow from the aorta and persisting as the systemic trunk. Altered haemodynamic factors can, then, override genetic control.

(5) New vessels may arise from existing endothelial tubes as sprouts of solid endothelial cords which subsequently acquire a lumen. The distal portions of the pulmonary arteries arise in this way from the 6th aortic arches. In normal development actively growing parts seem to attract invasion by capillaries. In the adult, defects resulting from loss of tissue may be made good by granulation tissue, a mass of young connective tissue, richly vascularized by new capillary sprouts.

FUNCTIONAL IMPORTANCE OF THE DUCTUS ARTERIOSUS

The ductus arteriosus is a wide channel linking the left pulmonary artery with the aorta, and, in foetal life, carries a large part of the output of the right ventricle into the systemic circulation. Its fate at and after birth is discussed on p. 39.4. The lung, functionless throughout foetal life, must be prepared for function at birth. This involves the development of a pulmonary circulation, of no functional value to the foetus but vital to the establishment of pulmonary respiration. The capillaries in the un-

expanded lung of the foetus offer high resistance to pulmonary circulation and there are two mechanisms by which blood may be short-circuited away from the pulmonary circulation. First, the foramen ovale provides a

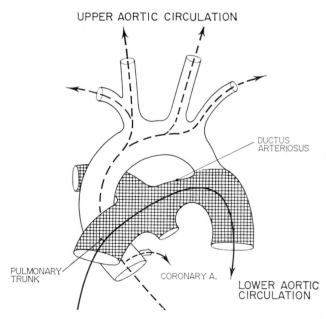

Fig. 18.46. To show the two aortic circulations, an upper, to the head and neck, brain, upper limbs and the heart itself and a lower, distributed to the remainder of the body.

route by which some of the blood returning to the right atrium is shunted to the left atrium and thence to the systemic circulation, by-passing the lungs. Secondly, much of the blood leaving the right ventricle via the pulmonary trunk follows the low pressure route into the aorta via the ductus arteriosus, rather than the high pressure route through the pulmonary circulation.

These two bypasses of the pulmonary circulation may be thought of as providing two aortic circulations (fig. 18.46). (1) An **upper aortic circulation**, derives its blood from the placenta, via inferior vena cava, foramen ovale, left atrium, left ventricle and upper aorta, i.e. that part proximal to a conical narrowing on the proximal side of the opening of the ductus arteriosus. Blood to the upper aortic circulation is distributed to the head and neck, brain, upper limbs and to the heart itself. (2) A **lower aortic circulation** derives its blood from the superior vena cava, via the right atrium, right ventricle, pulmonary trunk, left pulmonary artery and ductus arteriosus and distributed to the rest of the body.

This concept is based essentially on two facts. First, the oxygen saturation in the upper circulation, e.g. in carotid blood, is consistently higher than that in the lower e.g. in femoral artery blood. Secondly, ligation of the aorta proximal to the ductus in the sheep foetus scarcely reduces blood flow in the lower aortic circulation. The two aortic circulations are of importance to the foetus in that blood of higher oxygen saturation is directed to the brain and the heart itself, while blood of lower oxygen saturation goes to the placenta.

At birth the ductus closes, and the events leading to its closure are discussed on p. 39.4. Here it need only be emphasized that the late foetal ductus has a structure different from the vessels which it connects; its wall contains substantial amounts of smooth muscle, arranged in interlacing spirals. Contraction of this muscle at birth brings about closure of the ductus by a combination of kinking, shortening and narrowing of the channel.

DEVELOPMENT OF PRIMITIVE PHARYNX AND OF THE PHARYNGEAL DERIVATIVES

GENERAL FEATURES

The **primitive pharynx** is the front end of the foregut. It is the widest part of the endodermal gut tube, is rather flattened between the pericardium ventrally and the neural tube dorsally and is at first closed anteriorly, and separated from the stomatodaeum, by the buccopharyngeal membrane.

The **pharyngeal (branchial) pouches** grow outwards as hollow balloon-like extensions of the pharynx. They develop in sequence, pouch 1 the first to appear, being most cranial. In the human embryo there are four true pouches on each side; they meet the surface ectoderm to form a two layered epithelial **closing membrane**. As the pouches develop and extend outwards, they divide the mesoderm which lies between the pharynx and the surface ectoderm into a series of bars, the **pharyngeal** or **branchial arches**. Each pouch lies between two arches, the first pouch, for example, lying between the 1st and 2nd arches. In the earlier stages of pharyngeal development, the mesoderm of the arches is readily distinguished from neighbouring paraxial mesoderm by being much more densely cellular.

From the mesoderm of each arch there develop
(1) an aortic arch **artery** running round the pharynx from aortic sac to dorsal aorta,
(2) a cartilaginous **skeletal** element and
(3) a branchial **muscle** element.

Within the mesoderm of each arch there also runs a **nervous** element, consisting of branchial (special visceral) motor fibres, which supplies the branchial muscle arising from that arch.

The whole complex of pouches and arches makes sense only in an evolutionary context. In aquatic vertebrates, the pouches and arches of the embryo form the gill pouches and bars of the adult; the aortic arch arteries carry blood to and from the gills (afferent and efferent branchial vessels); the branchial cartilages provide the supporting skeleton of the gill arch and are moved by the muscle element. All these structures have persisted in the earlier stages of avian and mammalian embryos. The development of pulmonary respiration makes them redundant as respiratory organs, but they have been retained and made use of in other ways.

The general form of the pouches and their immediate surroundings are illustrated in fig. 18.47 which shows the pharyngeal region from the exterior, and in two different sectional planes. Each pouch is, at first, widely continuous with the pharynx. It is flattened between two adjacent arches and has a cranial and a caudal wall, a dorsal and a ventral end and laterally it makes contact with the surface ectoderm at an elongated closing membrane. As seen from the outside of the embryo, the closing membrane lies in the depths of a furrow between two arches, an **external pharyngeal groove**.

The relations of a typical pouch to the aortic arch arteries and to the pericardium are particularly important. The 3rd pouch, for example, lies between the 3rd and 4th arteries and its ventral end lies close to the roof of the pericardium. At this early stage, the embryo has no neck; the floor of the primitive pharynx, from which the tongue and the floor of the mouth develop, is immediately above the pericardium.

MORPHOGENETIC FACTORS

A major morphogenetic factor in subsequent development of the region is the so-called descent of the heart. While it is not a strictly accurate description of what happens, it is a useful phrase. The extent of descent of the heart is made clear in fig. 18.48 which shows the level of the septum transversum relative to the somites in two embryos. In the younger, about 24 days, the dorsal

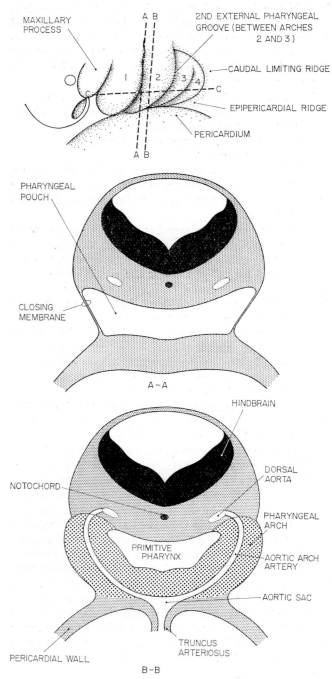

FIG. 18.47. External view of the pharyngeal region of an embryo aged about 4 weeks (5 mm). Schematic coronal sections in planes A–A and B–B are shown below. The floor of the pharynx after cutting in plane C–C is shown as fig. 18.55.

edge of the septum transversum lies opposite the upper cervical somites; by the 7th week it has 'descended' to the level of the first lumbar somite. The change in position is, of course, a relative one and is due to the dorsal part of

the body, including the somites, growing faster than the ventral, which, in lagging behind, suffers a relative 'descent.' An important result of these changes is that the head, and with it the floor of the mouth, is lifted off the pericardium, as a neck comes into existence. Which of the various structures of the neck is the pace setter is unknown but the developing vertebral column is probably responsible. Several structures in the neck keep pace with this growth; the 3rd aortic arch (common and internal carotid arteries) is a simple example. It is, in a sense, drawn out between its lower end in the thorax and its

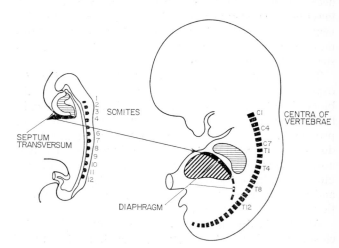

FIG. 18.48. The 'descent of the heart' indicated by the relation of the septum transversum (future diaphragm) to the somites. Based on Patten, *Human Embryology*.

upper end in the head. The process is not, of course, simply one of passive elongation; if it were, the vessel would narrow and break; growth of the vessel wall must also occur. In similar fashion the oesophagus, the larynx and trachea and the vagus nerves grow with the growing neck.

This concept is useful in following the development of the pouches. Consider the 3rd pouch; at an early stage it lies between the 3rd and 4th aortic arches, with its dorsal end close to the dorsal aorta and its ventral end close to the pericardium. Its subsequent growth does not fully keep pace with that of the neck as a whole. Its ventral end maintains its primitive relationship to the pericardium; its dorsal end, however, does not maintain its position in the head but is left behind in the lower neck (fig. 18.50).

The fundamental developmental changes in the form and position of the 3rd and 4th pouches are largely determined by traction in the growing neck; they are made possible by the severance of the connection between the pouches and the primitive pharynx and between the pouches and the surface ectoderm. In other words, the 3rd and 4th pouches become free epithelial structures, subject to relative displacements among the tissues of the neck.

FATE OF THE POUCHES (fig. 18.50)

Pouch 1 lies between the 1st (mandibular) and 2nd (hyoid) arches. It incorporates part of the 2nd pouch and retains both its original continuity with the pharynx and its original contact with the ectoderm at the 1st closing membrane. Because it gives rise to the epithelial lining of the auditory tube and the tympanic cavity it is called the **tubotympanic recess**. The 1st closing membrane contributes to the formation of the **tympanic membrane**.

Pouch 2 in the main loses its identity in the tubotympanic recess. Part of it remains independent, however, and is said to be represented in the adult by the **intratonsillar fossa**. The development of the palatine tonsil in relation to this part of the 2nd pouch is one of a number

derm. Its ventral end remains in contact with the pericardium and the thymic cord of cells becomes drawn out away from it, retaining for a time its connection with parathyroid III. The final positioning of parathyroid III and thymus III, and the histogenesis of the thymus are discussed on p. 18.30.

Pouch 4 appears later than pouch 3, is smaller and makes less contact with the surface ectoderm. In general, its behaviour follows that of pouch 3. However, from its caudal wall there arises a hollow outgrowth, the so-called **ultimobranchial body**. This grows rapidly and soon the boundaries between the pouch itself and the ultimobranchial body become obscure; the whole structure is now called the **caudal pharyngeal complex**. The

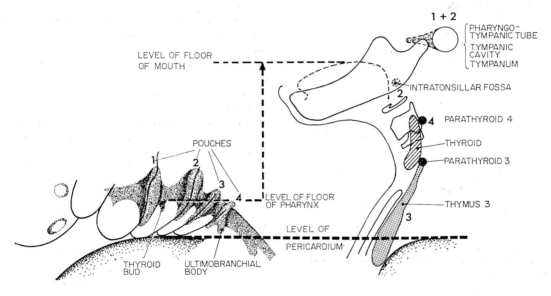

FIG. 18.49. The pharyngeal pouches, as seen from the left side. The overlying pharyngeal arches are imagined as transparent. Note particularly the position of the ventral ends of the pouches, immediately above the pericardium.

FIG. 18.50. The derivatives of the pharyngeal pouches. With the development and growth of the neck, the head has been lifted off the pericardium. The floor of the mouth has moved upwards, leaving the thyroid and the derivatives of pouches 3 and 4 behind, at various levels, in the neck. Note particularly that the ventral (lower) end of pouch 3 retains its primitive relation to the pericardium.

of interesting lymphoepithelial associations, discussed more fully later in connection with the thymus.

Pouch 3 is the most typical of the series. In embryos of about 5 weeks, while the pouch is still a hollow structure attached to the pharyngeal wall, a **parathyroid gland (parathyroid III)** begins to differentiate from the endodermal epithelium of the wall of the dorsal end of the pouch. It lies close to the 3rd aortic arch artery from which it is precociously vascularized. There is experimental evidence of the very early onset of function in the mammalian parathyroid. The remainder of the pouch forms a solid cord of compactly arranged epithelial cells, the forerunner of the **thymus (thymus III)**. The pouch loses its connection with the pharynx and with the surface ecto-

other **parathyroid gland (parathyroid IV)** arises from the dorsal end of pouch 4; it is clearly serially homologous with parathyroid III. The connection between the caudal complex and the pharynx becomes attenuated and ruptures and the entire complex follows the 'descending' heart as the neck elongates. Just as pouch 3 lay between the 3rd and 4th aortic arches so the caudal pharyngeal complex lies between the 4th and 6th arteries. The final positioning of the complex and the fate of that part of it which does not give rise to parathyroid are considered later.

DEVELOPMENT OF THE THYROID GLAND

This is derived not from a pouch, but from the endodermal epithelium in the midline of the pharyngeal floor, between the 1st and 2nd arches. The aggregation of epithelial cells forms a **thyroid bud** which grows ventrally, away from the pharyngeal floor and towards the aortic sac, with which it soon comes into intimate contact (fig. 18.51). It follows the 'descending' heart and the growth of the slender solid cord of cells which links it to the parent pharyngeal endoderm fails to keep pace with that of the

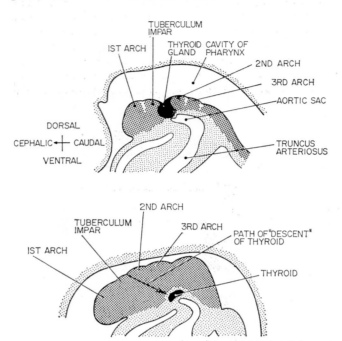

FIG. 18.51. Sagittal sections, to show the development of the thyroid gland from the endodermal epithelium of the floor of the pharynx.

surrounding tissues and normally it soon ruptures. As the neck elongates the thyroid leaves the 'descending' heart, losing its earlier contact with the aortic sac, and becoming stranded in the lower part of the neck. Its cells proliferate actively, producing bilaminar cords of cells which spread out on either side of the midline, giving the gland a U-shaped appearance. The caudal pharyngeal complex becomes attached to the posterior aspect of the lateral lobe of the thyroid near its upper pole. Parathyroid III similarly is related to the back of the lateral lobe near the lower pole. Here it remains as the inferior parathyroid of the adult, severing its connection with the anlage of thymus III. Parathyroid IV forms the superior parathyroid, after severing its connection with the rest of the caudal pharyngeal complex. The fate of that part of the complex which does not form parathyroid IV is still in some doubt. It becomes completely embedded in the substance of the lateral lobe and its very intimate association with the thyroid has been taken by some to indicate that it makes a contribution to the follicular epithelium of the gland. Recent work strongly suggests that

the ultimobranchial body forms epithelial cells scattered between the thyroid follicles, the so-called **parafollicular cells**. These cells are thought to be the source of calcitonin, a hormone involved, with parathyroid hormone, in calcium homeostasis (p. 25.17).

Between the bilaminar cords of thyroid epithelium is vascular connective tissue derived from surrounding mesenchyme. Precursors of secretion may be detected within thyroid cells of experimental animals by the use of ^{131}I, shortly before colloid-containing follicles are found. In man, follicles containing stainable colloid are first seen in embryos of 10 to 11 weeks.

Developmental anomalies

The thyroid may fail to follow the descending heart and then develops at the site of its formation in the developing tongue. Such a **lingual thyroid** is usually the patient's only thyroid tissue. The thyroid bud, in whole or in part, may follow the heart all the way in its descent, giving rise to thoracic ectopic thyroid tissue.

The slender cellular cord which links the thyroid bud and the pharyngeal floor until $5\frac{1}{2}$ weeks may persist as a tubular **thyroglossal duct**, lined by epithelium and reinforced externally by connective tissue. Its persistence, in whole or in part, may lead to the formation of cysts, sinuses or fistulae anywhere in the midline of the neck from the base of the tongue to the thyroid gland. Because of their origin, these remnants may be lined by a variety of epithelia and they may form ectopic thyroid tissue (fig. 18.57).

THE DEVELOPMENT OF THE THYMUS

The human thymus is a thymus III, derived from the ventral part of the 3rd pouch. Initially it is obviously epithelial, forming an elongated densely cellular cord on either side of the lower neck and extending into the thorax. At about 10 weeks the epithelium forms a looser cytoreticulum and lymphocytes begin to appear. Blood vessels and connective tissue invade the thymus from the surrounding mesenchyme, dividing it into the characteristic lobules. The epithelial cytoreticulum becomes obscured in the **cortex** because of the dense accumulation of lymphocytes, but it remains more obvious in the **medulla**, where lymphocytes are less abundant. **Hassall's corpuscles** are specialized differentiations of the epithelial cytoreticulum (p. 27.16).

The origin of the thymic lymphocytes is an embryological problem of long standing, whose solution has acquired a new urgency in recent years with the recognition of the great importance of the thymus in immune reactions. There have been two conflicting views, one that the thymic lymphocytes arise directly from the epithelial cytoreticulum, the other that they are derived from invading mesenchymal cells. Experiments of Auerbach who cultured thymic epithelium uncontaminated by mesenchyme, in chambers of millipore membrane which prevents the entrance of cells but not of soluble nutrients suggest, that lymphocytes develop from epithelial cells.

Several other important features of the developmental history of the thymus are summarized below.

(1) Its growth pattern is almost unique; it reaches its greatest relative size at birth, its greatest absolute size before puberty and thereafter undergoes a progressive involution, which leaves it in the adult as an atrophic remnant. A somewhat similar pattern is seen in lymph nodes and intestinal lymphoid tissue.

(2) It is precocious, among all the lymphoid organs, in the development of its lymphocytic element, which appears in thymus at about 10 weeks; in spleen, lymph nodes and alimentary tract it does not appear until 20 weeks or later.

(3) Its experimental removal from newborn animals interferes with the subsequent capacity of the mature animal to mount immune reactions of various kinds (p. 27.19).

(4) Although the initial embryonic population of thymic lymphocytes is probably of epithelial origin, regeneration of thymic lymphocytes following experimental depletion in the adult depends upon mesenchymal precursors being available.

THE DEVELOPMENT OF THE PHARYNGEAL ARCHES

Only four of the six arches can be seen externally; the 5th is small and short lived, while the 6th is deeply placed and lies in the parasagittal plane flanking the entrance to the respiratory tract in the floor of the caudal end of the pharynx.

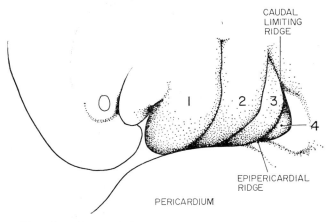

FIG. 18.52. External view of pharyngeal arches, showing the 3rd and 4th arches in the depths of the cervical sinus.

Arches 1 and 2 are the most prominent externally; 3 and 4 soon sink beneath the surface in the so-called **cervical sinus**, a depression in the side of the developing neck, bounded by the 2nd arch and by two low mesoder-
12

mal ridges, the **caudal limiting** and **epipericardial ridges** (fig. 18.52).

Skeletal elements

Within each arch a skeletal element develops by condensation and chondrification of mesoderm. In the 1st and 2nd arches these **cartilage bars** extend throughout the length of the arch, but in the 3rd, 4th and 6th caudal arches they are present only at the ventral end of the arch. The fates of arch cartilages are varied; they may disappear, they may be replaced by bone, or they may be represented in the adult by 'ligaments' which are the remains of the perichondrium. Fig. 18.53 summarizes the fate of the cartilage bars.

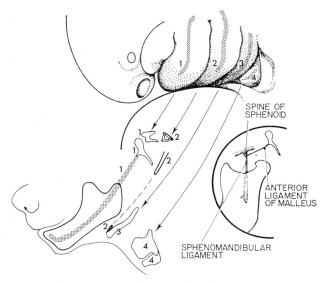

FIG. 18.53. Scheme of the fate of the pharyngeal arch cartilages.

The **first arch cartilage (Meckel's cartilage)** is closely related, at its dorsal end, to the tubotympanic recess, forerunner of the tympanic cavity, and from it develop two of the auditory ossicles, the **malleus** and the **incus**. The intermediate portion regresses, leaving its perichondrial sheath to form the **anterior 'ligament' of the malleus** and the **sphenomandibular 'ligament'**. The major ventral portion of Meckel's cartilage extends ventrally to the midline where it meets its fellow. The **mandible** develops in relation to Meckel's cartilage, but almost exclusively as a membrane bone, to which the cartilage makes essentially no contribution.

The **second arch cartilage**, like Meckel's cartilage, is related at its dorsal end to the developing middle ear, to which it contributes the **stapes**. From the rest of the cartilage, or its perichondrium, there develop the **styloid process** of the temporal bone, the **stylohyoid ligament** and the lesser cornu and upper part of the body of the **hyoid bone**.

The **third arch cartilage** is deficient dorsally; its ventral end forms the lower part of the body of the hyoid bone and its greater cornu.

The cartilages of the 4th and 6th arches are restricted to the ventral region; their fate is less precisely known than that of the 1st and 2nd arches but in general they form the **laryngeal cartilages**.

Muscular and branchial motor nervous elements. These may be considered together. The muscles derived from pharyngeal arch mesoderm consist of skeletal striated muscle but, because of their origin, they are called branchial. The nerves which supply them are classified as branchial efferent. The fate of the muscle elements and the innervation of the muscle groups derived from them are summarized in table 18.2.

Sensory nervous elements

Some of the mesoderm of each arch contributes to the development of a particular area of skin, or mucous membrane, or both; this area, in a general way, receives its sensory innervation from the sensory component of the nerve appropriate to that arch.

Fig. 18.54 shows the pattern of sensory nerves in the arches. The sensory fibres have their cell bodies in ganglia of nerves V, VII, IX and X, which are derived mainly from the cranial neural crest. The ganglia of VII, IX and

FIG. 18.54. Sensory components of the nerves of the pharyngeal arches. Early stage showing arches and cranial nerves (a) and superficial (b) and deep (c) distribution in the adult.

X receive additional contributions from the **epibranchial placodes**, which are localized thickenings of the ectoderm overlying the dorsal ends of the 2nd, 3rd and 4th arches. *The Vth cranial (trigeminal) nerve* is the nerve of the 1st arch. Its extensive distribution to skin and mucous membranes in the head reflects the widespread contributions of mesoderm of the 1st arch to skin and mucous membrane. The **ophthalmic division** of V is a nerve of the paraxial mesoderm, which forms the frontonasal process, and is not considered further here. The **maxillary division** of V is the nerve of the **maxillary process**, whose mesoderm contributes to the skin of the face, and to the mucous membrane of the nasal cavity and of the palate. These areas accordingly are innervated by the maxillary nerve.

TABLE 18.2

Arch	Muscles derived	Motor innervation
1 (Mandibular)	Muscles of mastication Anterior belly of digastric Mylohyoid Tensor veli palatini Tensor tympani	Mandibular division of trigeminal nerve (V)
2 (Hyoid)	Muscles of facial expression (including platysma) Stylohyoid Posterior belly of digastric Stapedius	Facial nerve (VII)
3	Stylopharyngeus	Glossopharyngeal nerve (IX)
4	Cricothyroid muscle	External laryngeal branch of superior laryngeal nerve (branch of vagus, X)
6	Constrictors of pharynx Intrinsic muscles of larynx Striated muscle of upper oesophagus	Vagus nerve (X) (principally fibres of the cranial accessory nerve, XI)

The **mandibular division** of V is the nerve of the mandibular arch itself, which contributes mesoderm to the skin of the face and the mucous membrane of the mouth and tongue, again determining the general pattern of sensory innervation.

The VII, IX and X nerves have little cutaneous sensory distribution, but they supply sensory fibres to the mucous membrane of the tongue, pharynx and larynx, whose distribution is related to developmental migrations of the appropriate arch mesoderm.

Relations of arteries and nerves of the arches
Relations in the neck can be understood only in terms of its development; the course of the recurrent laryngeal nerves serves as an example. These nerves are branches of the vagi and enter the 6th arch caudal to the 6th arch

artery. Descent of the heart carries the 6th arch artery caudally and, on the left side, the recurrent laryngeal nerve must follow a looped course below the ductus arteriosus. On the right side, disappearance of the distal end of the 6th artery, and of the 5th artery, allows the recurrent nerve to loop below the 4th aortic arch, which forms the subclavian artery.

There is also an important functional relation between the nerves and arteries of the arches. Baroreceptor areas develop on the 3rd aortic arch (carotid sinus) innervated by the IX nerve, and on the 4th aortic arch (aorta and right subclavian) innervated by the Xth nerve.

DEVELOPMENT OF THE TONGUE
The tongue develops from the pharyngeal arches in the floor of the primitive pharynx (fig. 18.55). The first pair

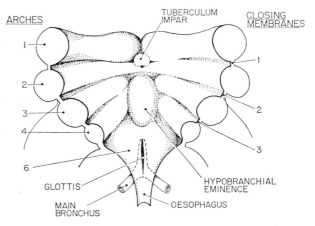

FIG. 18.55. The floor of the pharynx viewed from above. See plane C–C on fig. 18.47a.

of arches meet in the midline and contribute to the formation of a small unpaired midline elevation, the **tuberculum impar**. The second pair of arches also meet in the midline, but the third and fourth pairs fall short of the midline, their inner ends running into a low ridge on the pharyngeal floor, the **hypobranchial eminence**. Behind this and also in the midline is the **glottis**, flanked by the 6th pair of arches. This view of the pharynx makes clear why the sixth arches do not appear on the external surface.

The surface is covered by a mucous membrane, an epithelium and its supporting connective tissue. The epithelium covering the pharyngeal surface of the first arch is ectodermal; that of the remainder is endodermal.

Principal contributions to the tongue are made by paired **lingual swellings**, derived from the inner ends of the 1st pair of arches, and by mesoderm of the 3rd pair of arches which is said to migrate forwards beneath the epithelium and, in so doing, excludes the second pair of arches from the tongue (fig. 18.56). The sulcus terminalis,

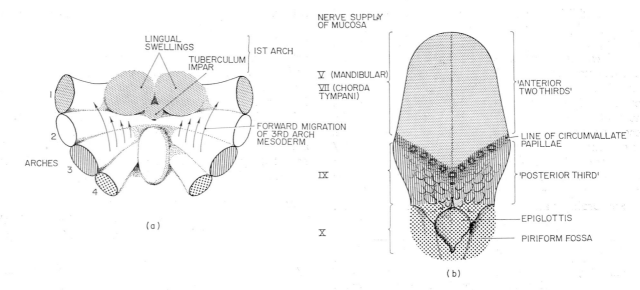

FIG. 18.56. The contributions of pharyngeal arch mesoderm to the development of the tongue.

or rather the line of circumvallate papillae immediately in front of it, marks the junction of the body (anterior two-thirds) and the root (posterior third) of the tongue. These are derived respectively from first and third arches, and are innervated by the nerves of those arches, V and IX. The **foramen caecum** marks the site of origin of the thyroid diverticulum, which grew downwards from the pharyngeal floor between the tuberculum impar in front and the 2nd arches behind. This relationship is shown in fig. 18.57.

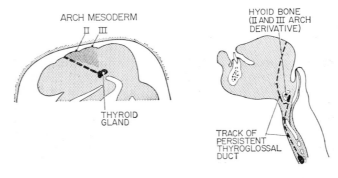

FIG. 18.57. Sagittal section showing the relationship of a thyroglossal duct to the 2nd and 3rd pharyngeal arches.

which shows why a persistent thyroglossal duct lies in front of the body of the hyoid which develops, as we have seen, from the cartilage bars of the 2nd and 3rd arches.

The innervation of the taste buds of the body of the tongue by the **chorda tympani** (VII) is, at first sight, embryologically unsatisfactory, until it is recalled that chorda tympani may represent the **pretrematic branch** (pre—in front; trema—a hole) of VII, i.e. the branch which, in ancestral forms, came from the facial (VII), the nerve of the second arch, and ran in the first arch, in front of the **gill cleft** (fig. 18.54a).

The origin of the musculature of the tongue presents some interesting problems. The motor nerve is the hypoglossal (XII) which arises by a series of rootlets from the medulla, in line with the ventral roots of spinal nerves, and which is associated, in phylogeny, with the occipital somites. In forms below the mammals, there seems no doubt that the tongue musculature arises by migration of occipital somite material which invades the developing tongue, accompanied by the XII nerve. In mammals, on the other hand, although premuscle tissue can be traced into the tongue from the caudal limiting ridge by way of the epipericardial ridge, the evidence for the origin of this material from occipital somites is very slender.

Formation and closure of the cervical sinus

The cervical sinus, as we have already seen, is a depression on the exterior of the pharyngeal region, bounded by the 2nd arch and the caudal limiting and epipericardial ridges. In its floor lie the 3rd and 4th arches and the 2nd, 3rd and 4th external grooves. These relationships are best seen in a section cutting horizontally through the sinus (fig. 18.58). The placode which contributes to the IX ganglion is an area of thickened ectoderm overlying the dorsal end of the 2nd external groove, while the placode of X covers the dorsal end of the 4th arch (fig. 18.54).

Growth of the boundaries of the sinus results in their gradual approximation to one another and in the closure of the sinus. The placodal ectoderm is buried beneath the surface as two vesicles (vesicle II = placode of IX, vesicle IV = placode of X) which normally disappear. The two **cervical vesicles** are of importance clinically because occasionally they may persist to form **branchial cysts**

FIG. 18.58. Horizontal section through the cervical sinus before and after closure of the sinus. Two ectodermal vesicles are buried beneath the surface; they normally disappear.

in the neck. **Branchial fistula** may also result from developmental aberrations during closure of the sinus. This is an epithelial tract running from an internal opening, in the pharyngeal region, to an external opening on the skin of the neck. The formation of such a fistula

FIG. 18.59. Scheme to show the developmental origin of a fistulous connection between the pharynx and the skin of the neck.

implies a combination of abnormal events (fig. 18.59) which includes (1) the persistence of a pharyngobranchial duct, the tubular connection between a pouch and the pharynx, (2) the establishment and persistence of a connection between one or other of the cervical vesicles and

its associated pouch and (3) the persistence of a cord or tube of ectodermal epithelium between the vesicle and the surface ectoderm.

GROWTH OF THE BODY

Growth is a complex process and it is not made easier to understand by the numerous definitions proposed for it. These range from the forthright and oversimplified, 'growth is increase in size' (T.H.Huxley) to the over-elaborate and almost meaningless 'growth is the co-ordinated expression of incremental and developmental factors and functions.'

We begin by looking at growth in length, or stature, before and after birth. Fig. 18.60 shows two kinds of growth curve: (a) a 'distance travelled' curve, giving **height achieved** at a particular age and (b) a 'velocity curve,' which gives the **rate of growth** during the journey. These curves show several features of interest.

(1) The rate of foetal growth is considerable. After a slow start during the first two months, which is the main period of embryogenesis and organogenesis, growth accelerates to a maximum at about four and a half months when it slows again. The newborn baby measures about 50 cm, representing an average increment in length of about 1·5 mm/day. If this rate of growth continued after birth, a 10-year-old child would stand 7 metres tall.

(2) Growth slows in late pregnancy and accelerates temporarily after birth.

(3) The rate of growth declines fairly rapidly in the first four years after birth and more slowly until puberty, when a rapid acceleration occurs, the **adolescent growth spurt**.

(4) Growth in stature virtually ceases at about 18 years in boys, and 16 years in girls. This marks the end of the period of growth of long bones; the vertebral column continues to grow by a small amount, 3–5 mm in all, up to the age of about 30 years.

Height remains stationary until about 50 years when it begins to decline: 'In extreme old age the old man's

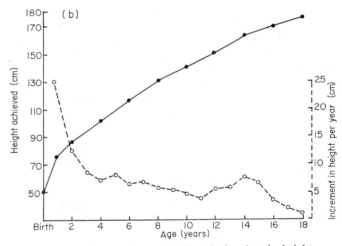

FIG. 18.60. Graphs of growth in length showing the height achieved (solid line) and the rate of growth (broken line), (a) prenatal, (b) postnatal at various ages. Based on Tanner (1964).

frame is shrunken and it is but a memory that "he once was tall".' (D'Arcy Thompson).

In analysing growth in stature, we have examined what is really the simplest measure of growth, essentially the growth in one dimension, length, of a single tissue, bone. On closer examination, even this apparently simple measurement is found to be more complex. A man's height is the sum of the lengths of head, trunk and lower limbs and these make widely differing proportionate con-

tributions to total height at different ages. This point is clearly seen in fig. 18.61; at the 4th month of foetal life, the head is a major contributor to body height, reflecting the precocious development of the brain, while the lower limbs make the smallest contribution. At maturity, on the contrary, the lower limbs make a larger contribution than the trunk, and the head is a poor third.

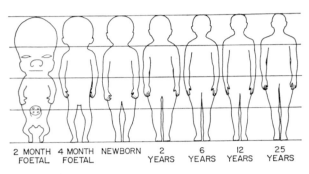

FIG. 18.61. To show the changing proportions of the body during growth and development.

The child is father to the man, but the transformation of one to the other is not simply a matter of proportionate increase in stature. Before puberty, the legs grow faster than the trunk; boys are on average taller than girls after adolescence and this seems to be due to the longer period of prepubertal lower limb growth in boys. Most of the adolescent growth spurt in stature occurs in the trunk rather than in the limbs.

Before the factors which control growth in stature are analysed, the way in which long bones develop and grow must be examined and this is most easily done in a developing limb.

Development of limbs and growth of long bones

The **limb buds** first appear as simple paddle-like outgrowths from the trunk. The forelimb buds appear first and are always in advance of the hindlimb buds in their development. The limb bud is essentially a mass of primitive mesenchyme, a loose gelatinous embryonic connective tissue, surrounded by a layer of ectodermal epithelium, the forerunner of the epidermis (fig. 18.62a). From the mesenchymal core of the limb bud there develops: (1) the skeletal axis of the limb, bones and periosteum, cartilage, joints and their capsules and ligaments, (2) the muscles, tendons and fasciae, (3) the dermis, the connective tissue layer of the skin, and the subcutaneous connective tissue and (4) the blood vessels and lymphatics.

The nerves of the limb do not develop in situ, but by the invasion of the limb bud at an early stage by axonic sprouts from cell bodies in the ventral grey horn, dorsal root ganglia or sympathetic ganglia.

DEVELOPMENT OF LONG BONE

The **scleroblastema** (fig. 18.62b) is formed by the aggregation and proliferation of mesenchymal cells to form a compact cellular mass which roughly anticipates the form of the future bone. Its cells differentiate into chondroblasts, which actively elaborate the matrix of cartilage.

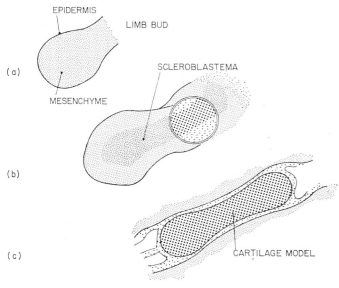

FIG. 18.62. Successive stages in the development of a long bone; (a) the limb bud, (b) the scleroblastema, (c) the cartilage model.

In short, the mesenchymal scleroblastema is transformed into embryonic hyaline cartilage which forms a rough but recognizable model of the future bone and is therefore called the **cartilage model**.

The cartilage model (fig. 18.62c) is everywhere surrounded by the primitive mesenchyme from which it developed. Where the cartilage models of adjacent bones meet, a joint space develops, lined by a connective tissue membrane, the synovial membrane, reinforced externally by the joint capsule. Over all the remaining surface of the cartilage model the surrounding mesenchyme forms an investing membrane, the perichondrium, within which two rather poorly demarcated layers may be recognized, an inner, which is looser and more cellular, and an outer, which is more fibrous.

Growth of the cartilage model occurs by two mechanisms (figs. 18.63): (1) **interstitial growth** in which chondroblasts within the model divide and the daughter cells elaborate more matrix about themselves, and (2) **appositional growth** in which new chondroblasts are formed by differentiation of primitive mesenchymal cells of the inner, cellular, layer of the perichondrium. These newly formed chondroblasts produce matrix and the cartilage model increases in girth by the successive addition of cartilage to the external surface.

It is important to distinguish between these two methods of growth of cartilage because, as we shall see, the capacity of cartilage to grow interstitially is fundamental to the continued growth in length of long bones.

Division of cartilage cells is more active in two disc-shaped areas, each lying in a plane at right angles to the long axis of the cartilage model and at some distance from each end. The plane of division of each dividing cartilage cell is also in a plane at right angles to the long axis of the model. As the result of repeated cell divisions and the accompanying production of cartilage matrix, the cells of the model assume a characteristic pattern (fig. 18.64). While those at either end of the model, in the future epiphyses, divide in more random fashion and therefore retain a uniform pattern, cartilage cells of the future shaft or diaphysis are arranged in lines or rows along the long axis of the model. These lines or rows of cartilage cells are usually called cartilage columns.

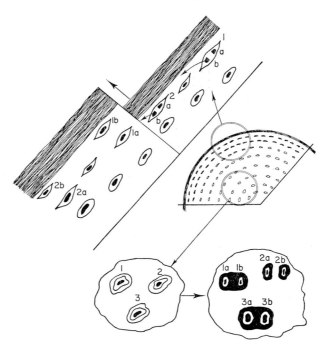

FIG. 18.63. Two mechanisms of growth of cartilage; above, appositional or growth by surface accretion; below, interstitial or growth from within.

The primary ossification centre

Two important events now occur at about the same time, but for convenience are described separately. The first consists of **degeneration of cartilage** in the centre of the cartilage model (fig. 18.65a). Cartilage cells at the centre of the future shaft enlarge greatly. This hypertrophy is associated with a corresponding enlargement of the spaces in the matrix, the **lacunae**, within which the cells lie, and with the deposition of calcium salts in the matrix which lies between the enlarged lacunae. Calcified cartilage matrix is apparently poorly permeable to tissue fluid and the hypertrophied cartilage cells die and shrivel. The centre of the shaft of the cartilage model now presents the appearance of a honeycomb; the spaces are empty lacunae, and the walls are calcified cartilage matrix. The

FIG. 18.64. To show the orientation of cartilage cells within the cartilage model; the pattern is determined by the plane of cell division in two disc shaped areas, the future epiphyseal plates.

second event is the **formation of the periosteal collar of bone** (fig. 18.65b). While these degenerative changes are going on, cells in the inner cellular layer of the perichondrium differentiate into bone forming cells or **osteoblasts**. These lay down a thin layer of **membrane bone**, so-called because it is developing within a connective tissue membrane. The essential stages in the formation of this periosteal collar are those involved in bone formation whenever or wherever it occurs in the body (p. 16.10).

The perichondrium within which the periosteal collar of bone has developed is now called **periosteum**. The change is one of name only, and neither of appearance nor developmental potentiality.

From the inner layer of the periosteum one or more **periosteal buds** now pass through spaces in the periosteal collar and invade the honeycomb of calcified cartilage matrix at the centre of the shaft (fig. 18.65c). The periosteal bud is essentially a loose vascular cellular connective tissue. It extends into the empty cartilage lacunae by breaking down the thin partitions of calcified cartilage matrix which lie between them. Its cells have a wide range of developmental potentiality and give rise to the following:

(1) **Osteoblasts** which align themselves on the surface of the bars, or trabeculae, of calcified cartilage matrix, and produce bone. This is called **endochondral bone** because it has developed within the cartilage model; it is distinguished from membrane bone by the fact that each trabecula contains a central core of calcified cartilage matrix. It must be stressed that, in endochondral ossification, cartilage is not transformed into bone; it is replaced by bone, the calcified cartilage matrix merely serving as an inert scaffolding upon which bone is deposited.

(2) **Osteoclasts** which play an important part in the removal or resorption of bone (p. 16.11).

(3) Bone marrow precursors (p. 26.5).

(4) Blood vessels which are initially large thin walled sinusoids. These extend into the medullary cavity by sprouting of solid endothelial buds, which subsequently acquire a lumen.

The region of bone formation at the centre of the shaft which has now been established is called the **primary centre of ossification**. It appears in most long bones in the 7th–8th week of intra-uterine life and consists of the membrane bone of the periosteal collar and the endochondral bone within the cartilage model.

Having begun at the centre of the shaft, the process of ossification extends towards each end. It is preceded by the same sequence of events that has already been described at the primary centre; hypertrophy of cartilage cells, enlargement of lacunae, calcification of cartilage matrix, degeneration of cartilage cells, invasion of empty lacunae by vascular loose connective tissue of the osteogenetic bud and the deposition of bone on the surface of calcified cartilage trabeculae.

The pattern in which this bone is produced is determined by the orientation of the columns of cartilage cells already referred to. In each column, the youngest cartilage cell, that most recently produced by cell division, lies furthest from the centre of the shaft; the oldest cell lies nearest to the centre of the shaft. Each column of cartilage cells is steadily encroached upon by degenerative change.

The osteogenetic tissue extends in succession into each new, empty, enlarged lacuna (fig. 18.66). Between the columns of empty lacunae the calcified cartilage matrix forms scalloped bars or trabeculae on the surface of which new bone is deposited. Although cartilage cells at the inner (central) end of each column are continually degenerating and disappearing, the length of the column is not thereby reduced, because there occurs continued cartilage cell division at the outer end of the column. The

FIG. 18.65. Four stages in the establishment of the primary ossification centre in the middle of the shaft. (a) Enlargement and degeneration of cartilage cells and calcification of the cartilage matrix, (b) the formation of the periosteal collar of bone, (c) and (d) the invasion of the empty lacunae by the periosteal (osteogenetic) bud, consisting of bone-forming and bone-destroying cells, and developing blood vessels and bone marrow elements.

processes of new cartilage cell production at one end of the column, and cartilage cell degeneration at the other are nicely balanced; new endochondral bone is continually laid down on trabeculae of calcified cartilage matrix and the bone as a whole steadily increases in length. It cannot be emphasized too strongly that the continued growth of the bone in length is dependent on the continued multiplication of cartilage cells at the outer end of each cartilage cell column. Hence, the growth in length of a long bone depends upon the interstitial growth of cartilage.

That part of the bone which is ossified from the primary

FIG. 18.66. Scheme to show the extension of the ossification process towards the end of the shaft.

ossification centre is the **diaphysis**; the plate or disc of proliferating, hypertrophying and degenerating cartilage cells is the **epiphysial plate**; the area of most recently formed endochondral bone, on the diaphysial side of the epiphysial plate, is the **metaphysis**.

Ossification of the epiphyses

At birth, the ends of most long bones still consist of cartilage; **secondary centres of ossification** appear within them in the first few years after birth. The sequence of changes is similar to that at the primary centre, with the important exception that no periosteal collar is formed at the surface. Cartilage cells at the centre of the epiphysis enlarge and die, leaving enlarged lacunae with walls of calcified cartilage matrix. In human epiphyses a periosteal bud is not the usual source of osteogenic and haemopoietic cells. These arise instead from the **cartilage canals**, irregular branching channels which carry vascular mesenchyme from the surface deep into the centre of the epiphysis. Endochondral bone is now formed by the usual mechanism (fig. 18.67).

It is worth emphasizing that the epiphyses of a long bone are ossified later than and independently of the diaphysis. In fact, the epiphyses and diaphysis are three separate bones, united by the cartilaginous epiphysial plates. These plates are the representatives, in postnatal life, of the original cartilage model, not yet replaced by bone. The continuing interstitial growth of the epiphysial plate provides for continuing growth in length of a long bone; bone itself cannot grow interstitially.

Epiphysial union

At the end of the growing period, division of cartilage cells in the epiphysial plate ceases and the continuing invasion of the plate, from the diaphysial side, by bone-forming tissue results in the complete replacement of the cartilaginous plate by bone. Epiphysis and diaphysis are now one, united by a thin disc of bone, somewhat denser than the remainder and, therefore, recognizable in a radiograph as the epiphysial 'scar.' The process of bony union of epiphyses and diaphysis is called **synostosis**. In a typical long bone, with an epiphyseal plate at either end, one plate may make a larger contribution than the other to the total growth in length of the bone, either because its cartilage cells proliferate more rapidly, or because they proliferate for a longer period, or by a combination of the two reasons. This end of the bone is often referred to as 'the growing end'; clinically important examples are the lower end of the femur and the upper end of the tibia, the upper end of the humerus and the lower ends of radius and ulna. Premature arrest of growth may result from accidental damage to the epiphysial plate. Occasionally the surgeon may use this as a therapeutic device.

Final shaping of the bone

The articular cartilage, which clothes the articulating surface of the epiphysis, persists throughout life. It represents part of the original cartilage model which has not been replaced by bone of the secondary ossification centre.

Growth in girth of the bone occurs by the continuing production of new bone within the cellular layer of the

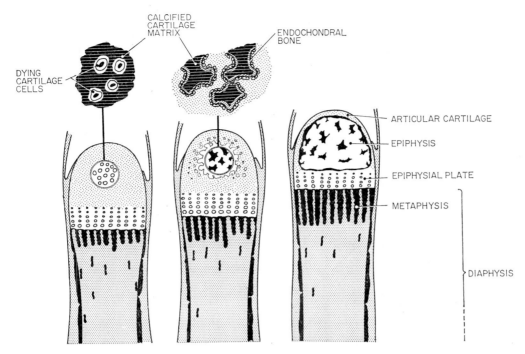

FIG. 18.67. Ossification of the epiphysis, at a secondary centre of ossification (plate 16.3b, facing p. 17.6).

periosteum. This is appositional growth of bone and is intramembranous. As bone is added externally, it is removed internally (fig. 18.68); the shaft, therefore, retains a tubular form, which not only gives strength without excessive weight, but also provides space for the bone marrow. This combination of external deposition and

FIG. 18.68. Transverse sections of a growing bone to show increase in girth by external deposition and internal resorption.

internal resorption is the simplest example of a process of shaping of growing bone called **remodelling.**

Remodelling occurs also in the metaphyses, the two regions most recently formed by endochondral ossification on the diaphysial side of the epiphysial plate. Because the plate is a circular disc, the new bone formed at the metaphysis is a cylinder whose diameter is the same as

that of the disc. The shaft retains its graceful form, widening slightly from its centre to its extremities, because, in the region of the metaphyses, bone is removed externally and added internally. Note that this is the reverse of what happens at the centre of the shaft (see fig. 18.69).

Control of growth in stature

Growth in stature of the whole body is largely determined by the growth in length of the long bones which, in turn, is finally dependent upon interstitial growth of the epiphysial plates of cartilage. The rate of linear growth and the final stature attained are, therefore, essentially determined by the rate of proliferation of cartilage cells in the epiphysial plate and the duration of the proliferative period.

Many factors affect the rate and duration of this proliferation.

Genetic

Studies on identical twins make it clear that genetic factors are of paramount importance in determining the final adult height. Even when reared apart, adult identical twins differ in height much less than do fraternal twins brought up together.

There is a popularly held view that there has been a secular increase in average adult height, but the evidence suggests that men of the Old Stone Age were no shorter than the average 167–170 cm today. However, when undernutrition is widespread and prolonged, the average height of adults falls.

The final expression of genetic constitution as adult height has become stable. It also appears that the genetic constitution manifests itself in early childhood; a child taller than average tends to remain taller and achieves a greater than average adult height. A reasonably accurate prediction of final height can be made by doubling the height of the child on its second birthday. It must be stressed, however, that there are greater differences in height between identical twins during the growing period

FIG. 18.69. Longitudinal sections of a growing bone to show remodelling of bone at the metaphysis. (a) Shows the change in shape and (b) shows the sites of new bone deposition.

than at the end of it. Further, there is no doubt that adult stature is achieved earlier, i.e. growth in childhood is accelerated, in children today.

Hormonal

(1) **Anterior pituitary somatotrophic hormone** or **growth hormone** is of major importance in controlling growth from birth to adolescence, exerting its main effect on cartilage cell proliferation and, therefore, on the growth in length of long bones. This is made clear by the dwarfism which results from deficient secretion of the hormone and gigantism when secretion is excessive (p. 25.13).

(2) **Thyroid hormones** affect both the rate and the duration of cartilage cell proliferation in the epiphysial plate; if secretion is deficient in the postnatal growing period, growth in stature, and particularly in length of long bones, is stunted.

(3) **Adrenal androgens**, which are first secreted in quantity at adolescence, are responsible for the adolescent growth spurt.

(4) **Testicular androgens** in boys are also involved. These hormones act upon the vertebral column rather than upon the long bones. Castration during the growth period leads to a failure of synostosis between epiphysis and diaphysis and, as a result, the period of growth in length of the limbs is prolonged.

Nutritional

Growth in stature is slowed by malnutrition but may accelerate, to return the individual almost to his genetically appropriate stature when normal nutrition is restored.

Growth may also be retarded by non-specific factors such as severe illness. While cartilage proliferation and therefore growth in length are retarded, ossification in the metaphysis may proceed with little disturbance; a rather denser, thin plate of bone may be laid down during this period of growth retardation and may persist as a **line of arrested growth**, easily visible in a radiograph.

THE ADOLESCENT GROWTH SPURT

Although the rate of growth is greater in early embryonic life and in infancy than it is at puberty, the period of the adolescent growth spurt is more dramatic, not only be-

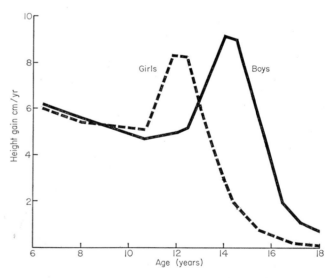

FIG. 18.70 Graphs to show the 'adolescent growth spurt'. Based on Tanner (1964).

cause it is a period of accelerated growth rate and follows a period of slowly declining rate but because of its associated changes and the onset of sexual maturity.

Fig. 18.70 gives velocity curves for growth in boys and girls and shows several important features.

(1) The growth spurt is of sudden onset. It is, in fact, the only substantial, sudden change of rate in the whole growth curve; apart from the adolescent spurt, children

do not usually grow, as is sometimes popularly believed, by 'fits and starts.'

(2) The rate of growth accelerates from about 6 cm to about 10 cm/year (the foetus grows to a birth length of 50 cm in 10 months).

(3) Girls enter the growth spurt on average at age 11–13½ years, earlier than boys by some two years. The intensity of the spurt is, however, greater in boys than in girls. These two facts help to explain the greater average height of men; boys continue their prepubertal growth in stature, mainly growth of the limbs, for a longer period than girls; growth in stature in the adolescent period involves the trunk rather than the limbs, and the boys now benefit from the greater velocity of the spurt.

One important fact about the adolescent growth spurt does not emerge from fig. 18.70; it is the variability of its time of onset. The range is from 10½–16 in boys and from 9½–14½ in girls.

ASSOCIATED EVENTS AT PUBERTY

The changes which occur at puberty are probably triggered by the hypothalamus, bringing about release of

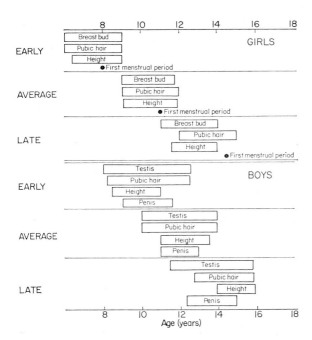

FIG. 18.71. The chronology of events at puberty. The chart shows the period of accelerated growth of organs, e.g. 'testis' and of the body as a whole, 'height'. Based on data of Tanner (1962) *Growth at Adolescence*. Oxford: Blackwell Scientific Publications.

pituitary gonadotrophins, which stimulate growth of the gonads and later the secretion of sex hormones, which evoke the secondary sex characters.

Fig. 18.71 summarizes the chronology of the major events in boys and girls. Again, the variability of their time of onset must be stressed. This means, of course, that chronological age, i.e. age by the calendar, is a poor index of physiological maturity; as Tanner points out, 'the statement that a boy is 14 is . . . hopelessly vague'; he may still be a boy, or almost a man. It is obviously important, therefore, for the doctor to be aware of the normal range of variation of onset of, for example, menstruation. Neither onset at age 10 nor delay until age 17 need necessarily, in the absence of other findings, be a matter for concern.

The doctor obviously needs a better yardstick than chronological age to measure the progress of the child and adolescent along the route to physiological maturity. Of various measures of **developmental age**, the developmental status of the skeleton is one of the most conveniently and objectively assessed. The times of appearance of ossification centres in short bones, e.g. of the carpus, and in the epiphyses of long bones, and their union with the diaphysis correlate well with the time of appearance of secondary sex characters. Thus skeletal maturity is a better index of physiological maturity than chronological age. Skeletal maturity is most conveniently assessed from radiographs of the wrist; appearances are compared with standards derived from similar radiographs of large numbers of 'normal' children. Menstruation begins in girls of 'bone age' of 12–14½, although their chronological ages range from 10–16½.

Using skeletal age as an index, it appears that the girl who begins to menstruate early was already more mature physiologically at age 7, and probably earlier, than her more tardy classmates. The tempo of development of physiological maturity, i.e. the skeletal age, and the age of onset of puberty and of the growth spurt, is, in part at least, under genetic control; there is, for example, less difference between the time of onset of menstruation in identical than in non-identical twins.

CHRONOLOGICAL AND DEVELOPMENTAL AGE IN FOETAL LIFE

In the first two-thirds of intrauterine life, chronological age correlates well with the developmental state of various organs and with the size, both weight and length, of the body as a whole. Towards the end of pregnancy, however, the weight of a particular foetus is no longer entirely reliable as a guide to its chronological, i.e. gestational, age or to its developmental status. An inadequate uterine environment may inhibit foetal growth. So it is important to distinguish between babies who are of low birth weight because of foetal growth retardation and those who are light because of shortened gestation. The former show a characteristic lack of subcutaneous fat and the skin is loose and wrinkled, suggesting that fat has actually been lost. Brown fat which plays an important part in temperature regulation in the newborn is also reduced or absent (p. 39.6). Skeletal and brain size, and the maturity of the brain, as indicated by the complexity of the cerebral gyral pattern, are, however, little affected. Similarly, the developmental maturity of the lung is normal, as judged by histological appearances. In short, the baby who has suffered foetal growth retardation, shows signs of malnutrition rather than of a curtailed period of gestation.

While genetic factors are paramount in determining final adult stature this is not true of birth weight. Here maternal environment is more important; a small mother tends to produce a small baby because uterus and placenta are small and cannot provide for a large baby.

Tissue growth

SKELETAL MUSCLE

The development of the skeletal muscle fibres is described on p. 15.6. The formation of new fibres ceases about the fourth month of foetal life. Further growth of the muscle as a whole, therefore, depends upon (1) increase in length and diameter of existing fibres and (2) increase in the amount of noncontractile interstitial connective tissue. The growth in length of individual fibres commonly does not keep pace with the elongation of the whole muscle; the constituent fibres slide over one another, so that few of them eventually run the whole length of the muscle from tendon to tendon. Increase in diameter results from synthesis of new cytoplasm, both sarcoplasm and myofibrils; in the rat gastrocnemius muscle the weight of cytoplasm per nucleus increases more than five times between 17 and 95 days of age.

Several factors affect the final diameter of the muscle fibre; it varies from muscle to muscle in the same individual and in the same muscle in different species. Thus, fibres of the diaphragm of the shrew are several times smaller than those of the cow, but the difference is much less than that in the total bulk of the two animals. It seems that there are upper size limits for muscle fibres, beyond which they cannot grow without sacrificing efficiency. Androgenic hormones play an important part in development of the greater muscular bulk and strength in boys than in girls after puberty, the differences before puberty being small. The enlargement of muscle in response to increased work is a matter of common knowledge; it results from the enlargement (hypertrophy) of individual fibres, in which additional myofibrils appear. Since a muscle contains a substantial population of connective tissue cells, the total bulk of the muscle may not alter much in the earlier stages of work hypertrophy because the muscle fibres enlarge at the expense of the interstitial connective tissue.

The atrophy of muscle which occurs with disuse is no less familiar than work hypertrophy but is equally complex; its mechanisms involve such factors as increased interstitial connective tissue, reduced blood supply and, possibly, the purely 'trophic' effects of neuromuscular contact.

SKIN

As the body grows, the skin grows with it, maintaining itself as a well fitting tight covering. How is its growth so nicely adjusted to that of the underlying tissues? Experimental evidence suggests that skin grows interstitially in response to tension generated by growth of deeper structures. In the epidermis, interstitial growth involves proliferation of cells in the basal, germinative layer. In the dermis, proliferation of connective tissue cells is predominant in the earlier stages of growth; later, the production of fibrous intercellular material is of major importance. There are occasions when tensions arise so rapidly in the skin that it cannot grow pari passu with the deeper tissues; it becomes thinned and shiny, and tearing of the dermal connective tissue may occur.

FAT

The cells of adipose tissue arise from a cell resembling a fibroblast. Many small discrete droplets of fat appear within the cytoplasm, and eventually coalesce in a single large droplet, which displaces the flattened nucleus into the thin peripheral rim of cytoplasm. Adipose tissue grows by recruitment of new fat cells and by marked cell enlargement from the continued accumulation of fat. Deposition of subcutaneous fat in the human foetus does not begin until about 34 weeks. It increases in thickness until about 9 months postnatally, then decreases until 7 or 8 years, when it increases again.

The familiar sex differences become marked at adolescence. In boys, subcutaneous fat in the limbs is reduced, but changes little in the trunk; in girls, limb fat continues to increase and trunk fat even more so. These differences provide an obvious illustration of the importance of differential rates of growth in shaping body form.

NERVOUS TISSUE

Growth in the nervous system is complex, but involves, at least, the following:

(1) formation and proliferation of young nerve cells, neuroblasts, in the neural tube and in peripheral ganglia, somatic and autonomic;

(2) formation and proliferation of precursors of the special supporting tissue of the nervous system, the glia and sheath cells;

(3) growth of cell processes, axons and dendrites from the neuroblasts, i.e. the differentiation of the neurones;

(4) formation of investing sheaths, particularly myelin, round the nerve cell processes.

It is a commonplace of adult human anatomy that the spinal cord is larger where the nerves of the limb plexuses arise from it. Experiments on lower animals have shown that the size of central nuclear aggregates of nerve cells is largely determined by the size of the peripheral field innervated. Thus unilateral limb amputation in the chick embryo results in reduced growth of the appropriate part of the spinal cord. This is caused by the degeneration of large numbers of nerve cells. On the other hand increasing the peripheral field, as by transplanting supernumerary limbs in larval amphibians, leads to enlargement of those parts of the nervous system which supply the additional tissue. This response seems to be due to an increased differentiation of cells to form neurones, rather than to increased proliferation.

Axons and dendrites arise as protoplasmic sprouts from the cell body or perikaryon; the new cytoplasm is synthesized in the cell body and flows along the processes, whose tips make their way to peripheral connections by pseudopodial extensions, spinning out the fibre behind them as they advance. The factors which determine the direction followed by growing processes remain obscure, but the ultrastructural orientation of the region through which they are advancing seems to be of greatest significance. The diameter of the developing processes is determined by the size of neuroblast from which they arise.

Once an axon has established a peripheral connection it is, in a sense, anchored at each end; further growth occurs interstitially, the stimulus for growth probably being provided by the traction of, for example, the growing limb in which it lies.

It is generally believed that the child is born with his full complement of nerve cells and that he will outlive substantial numbers of them; a reduction of cell counts with age has been found in both cerebral and cerebellar cortices.

Reference has been made to the precocious development and growth of the neural tube in the embryo, and this precocity continues to be evident after birth.

Myelin is formed round processes of nerve cells by the supporting cells (p. 14.4). Myelin formation begins in the spinal cord at about mid-foetal life and the process is not completed for several years. At birth, fibres of the brain are still largely unmyelinated, and continuing myelination accounts largely for the continuing increase of weight of the brain until adolescence.

Maintenance, regeneration and repair

So far, growth processes have been considered largely in relation to those changes which constitute the development of the individual; the same processes are no less important in maintenance, repair and regeneration of body tissues.

MAINTENANCE

The life span of the individual may differ greatly from that of his constituent cells. Thus dead cornified cells are constantly rubbed away from the surface of the epidermal layer of the skin and, since the epidermis maintains a relatively constant thickness, this loss must as constantly be made good by new cell production. This occurs by cell division in the deepest layer of the epidermis, the basal or germinative layer. Daughter cells move towards the surface, driven by the pressure of new cell production behind them, and undergo the series of structural changes, **cytomorphosis**, which in turn leads to their death and shedding in the cornified layer. Thus, the epidermis is maintained, although its constituent cells are constantly changing. This continual replacement of cells is called **cell turnover**, and its rate may be measured either by determining the proportion of cells which divide in unit time, or by autoradiography after labelling of dividing cells by tritiated thymidine. Cell populations have been classified, according to their rates of turnover, as renewing, expanding and static (p. 11.29).

REGENERATION AND REPAIR

In many tissues, growth by cell division virtually ceases in the adult, but may be resumed to make good losses due to disease or accident. The liver provides a model example; its cells constitute an expanding population during the growth period, but cell division declines to a normal rate of about 0·01 per cent in the adult. After partial excision of the liver, the remaining portion shows a great increase in mitotic activity, with rates estimated at more than 3·5 per cent. In a few days it declines to about 1 per cent and then more gradually to normal levels.

Damage to nerve cells, on the other hand, does not elicit a return of mitotic activity; if the axon is cut, regeneration may occur by outflow of cytoplasm from the cut end of the proximal stump, essentially an increase in the rate of the normal proximodistal flow.

In mammals, unlike some lower vertebrates, regeneration of parts such as a limb, or organs such as the eye, does not occur: regeneration is restricted to the cellular and tissue level. Regeneration in mammals is not, however, an unorganized process. In the repair of fractures of bones, essentially a process of regeneration of lost tissue, osteogenic cells inside and outside the shaft at the fracture site produce new bone, both directly by intramembranous ossification and by replacement of cartilaginous callus, endochondral ossification. Initially, an excess of bone is formed at the fracture site, but a remodelling process similar to that described in long bone development restores the normal contours of the bone, often so effectively that the original fracture site is scarcely evident. Not only has bone tissue been regenerated, but a bone organ has been repaired.

In liver regeneration, too, an essentially normal microscopic structural pattern may be restored.

GENERAL ASPECTS OF DEVELOPMENT

Morphogenesis

Although each system of the body presents its own complexities of developmental pattern, the processes of morphogenesis are few and relatively simple. They may involve increase in size of the constituent cells or, more commonly, in their number, through local proliferation or by migration of cells from surrounding areas. The production of intercellular material may make an important contribution. These processes are not, of course, in themselves responsible for the appearance of characteristic patterns of shape in the developing embryo. These patterns arise rather from **differential growth rates** of various parts of the embryo.

The formation of sheets or layers of cells is one of the basic developmental manoeuvres, and particularly the establishment of the three germ layers. The formation of the endoderm by delamination from the inner cell mass, and of the mesoderm by migrations of cells from the primitive streak is described on pp. 18.3.

The formation of tubular structures may occur in a variety of ways, by the fusion of folds, e.g. neural tube, by the appearance of a lumen in a solid rod of cells, e.g. the duct of many glands, or even by the adhesion and subsequent disappearance of the epithelial walls at the centre of a hollow disc, e.g. semicircular canals. Undoubtedly, however, the most important event in development is cell differentiation.

Cell differentiation

The fertilized ovum, the embryo, the foetus and the adult are simply stages in the life of the individual. The developmental changes through which the individual passes involve great increases in size and in complexity. The single, large and apparently simple fertilized ovum gives way to the much larger and more complex embryo and adult, in whom there have appeared different regions (head, trunk, limbs) different organ systems and organs, different tissues, different cells, and different cell constituents. The term differentiation is used to describe the complex processes involved in the establishment of all these differences. On closer analysis the problem of differentiation is basically one of cell differentiation, whose nature and control are the fundamental problems of modern biology.

The differences between fully differentiated cells, e.g. an erythrocyte, a neurone and a skeletal muscle fibre, are obvious; each shows structural specializations which reflect specialized functions. Each is a discrete cell type; as Weiss pointed out long ago, there are no cells intermediate between any of them, and the transformation of one into either of the others is impossible. They are the stable end stages of differentiation; the erythrocyte is a dying cell, whereas the neurone and the skeletal muscle fibre are long lived but, under most conditions, are incapable of division.

The differences are less obvious between cells which are more closely related, e.g. cells of the epithelial layer of the cornea and cells of the epidermis. Both develop from the ectoderm and each forms part of a surface layer. One cell type, however, is transparent and non-cornified, while the other becomes fully cornified and is soon shed as a dead squame. These structural differences reflect functional differences and are appropriate to the different environments in which the cells occur naturally. Would a corneal epithelial cell retain its 'corneal' characters if it were transplanted to a skin site? In fact, it does; slivers of cornea transplanted to a defect in the skin of the chest in rabbits continue to behave like cornea, retaining their transparency.

Now let us look at two cell types even more closely related to one another; epidermal cells from body skin and from skin of the sole of the foot in the guinea-pig. Sole of foot epidermis is thick, with a prominent cornified layer, while body epidermis is thin and its cornified layer is poorly developed. Stimuli of various kinds, mechanical, chemical or thermal, may produce thickening of body skin epidermis, so that it comes to resemble epidermis on the sole of the foot, but the change is not permanent and is reversed when the stimulus is removed. Moreover, if skin from the sole of the foot is transplanted to an area of body skin, it continues to behave indefinitely as if it were still on the sole of the foot, exposed to mechanical trauma. There are, then, inherent differences between the cells of the two types of epidermis. These differences spring from a higher innate rate of cell proliferation in epidermis of the sole of the foot; they are evident in the foetus, before mechanical stimuli can act and they are altered only temporarily or not at all by environmental change.

Each of these three examples of the permanent character of cellular differentiation has been drawn from the adult organism. That presumptive epidermal cells can be permanently diverted into a different developmental pattern may be shown by growing skin from a 5-day chick embryo in a tissue culture medium containing an excess of vitamin A. Cells which normally would become epidermal cells synthesizing keratin, become mucus secreting and sometimes produce cilia. This experiment indicates that in the earlier stages of development, cells are more plastic and their developmental course is more easily altered by changes in their environment.

At still earlier stages of development, even more striking redirection of development may be shown to occur experimentally. If a patch of cells which would have formed the neural plate of an early amphibian embryo is transplanted to an area of potential epidermis, the potential nerve cells develop into epidermal cells. Contrariwise, potential epidermis transplanted to the future neural plate area develops into neural tissue. It appears from this that, in the earlier stages of development, prospective potency is much wider than presumptive fate, i.e. the direction in which a cell normally develops if left undisturbed is only one of several possibilities; it is, in fact, pluripotent and the full range of its developmental potentiality can be revealed only by experimental alterations in its environment.

EMBRYONIC INDUCTION

What factors determine the direction in which a particular cell or group of cells develop? In all vertebrates, the so-called **chorda mesoderm** plays a prime role in determining the basic structural plan of the embryo. Its mode of formation varies in different species; in mammals it is represented by the notochordal process and the paraxial mesoderm which flanks it. Experimental evidence indicates that the chorda mesoderm induces the ectodermal tissue, which overlies it, to form the neural plate. The evidence for this is threefold.

(1) If contact between the ectoderm and the chorda mesoderm is prevented, the neural tube fails to develop.

(2) Ectoderm normally destined to form epidermis, i.e. presumptive epidermis, forms neural plate if transplanted to a position overlying the chorda mesoderm.

(3) Chorda mesoderm transplanted to a new site beneath presumptive epidermis induces ectopic neural plate formation.

In amphibians the chorda mesoderm arises by the rolling in of cells into the blastocoele cavity, the invagination taking place at the blastopore. If tissue of the dorsal lip of the blastopore is transplanted beneath ectoderm of another amphibian embryo at the same stage, not only is a neural tube induced, but also most of the essential organs of a second embryo. It was for this reason that Spemann called the dorsal lip of the blastopore the **organizer** or **primary organizer**. There is no reason to doubt that the primitive streak and the cells which migrate from it, notochordal process and intraembryonic mesoderm, serve a similar function in mammals.

Once the direction of development of the main axial organs has been induced by the primary organizer, a series of **secondary inductions** is set in train. This can best be illustrated by the example of the eye. The formation of the optic vesicle is the result of an inductive action on the neural plate. The optic vesicle in turn induces the formation of a lens placode, and subsequently of a lens, from the surface ectoderm with which it lies in contact. The evidence for the inductive action of the optic outgrowth is the same as that already given for the primary inductive action of the chorda mesoderm.

The chain reaction of induction does not end here. In amphibians the characteristic transparency of the cornea is due to the disappearance of pigment from its epithelial layer, and to the failure of pigment cells to appear in its stromal layer. These important events are induced by the lens and the optic cup.

Although the initial development of the optic vesicle is an induction, dependent upon another tissue, once the eye rudiment is established its development continues more or less normally when it is transplanted to a site removed from its inducer. This capacity for autonomous development is called **self differentiation**.

SELF REGULATION

That the development of an organ rudiment is already determined in a particular direction does not imply that each cell within it is irrevocably committed to a particular fate. The broad plan of future development may be laid down within the rudiment, but the individual cells can still follow a number of different developmental paths. This is illustrated very clearly in the development of a limb. The limb bud is already determined; if explanted to another site it continues its development normally. However, if it is split, it forms two limbs, each smaller than normal; if a second limb bud is transplanted alongside it, a single limb is formed, larger than normal; if it is excised, a new limb bud arises from the general area of the limb field. This ability of an experimentally altered rudiment to redirect its constituent cells so that they form a harmonious whole is called **self regulation**.

COMPETENCE

Induction involves two parties; the inducing tissue or inductor and the tissue which is induced. Competence is the ability of a particular tissue, at a particular time, to respond to a particular inductor.

Let us use the presumptive ectoderm of a young amphibian blastula as an example. As already described, when left undisturbed it will normally develop into epidermis; but if transplanted to the presumptive neural plate area it forms neural plate. Under a variety of normal or experimental circumstances it may develop into structures as diverse as pigment cells in the skin, cartilage cells in a branchial arch, craniospinal or autonomic ganglion cells, Schwann cells, the lens, the otic vesicle, or the anterior lobe of the pituitary. Under certain conditions it may form mesodermal or even endodermal structures.

As development proceeds, the wide range of competence of the presumptive ectoderm becomes restricted. Restriction of developmental potential, i.e. differentiation, is not, at first, expressed as structural change within the cell. That development is now determined in a particular direction is made clear by transferring the cells to the neutral environment of tissue culture when they self differentiate. The state of determination which precedes the histological signs of differentiation is sometimes called **chemodifferentiation**, a useful term in which to cloak our ignorance.

ROLE OF THE NUCLEUS IN DIFFERENTIATION

Differentiation is seen, then, as the result of the inter-action of inducing agents, which are external and environmental, and the inherited potentialities of the tissue, transmitted by the genes. Does nuclear differentiation occur, or is the genetic complement of all the cells of an individual embryo the same? When the nucleus from one of the presumptive ectodermal cells of a frog blastula is transplanted to an enucleated activated frog ovum, normal development sometimes follows, indicating that, at this stage, the nuclei of the presumptive ectoderm, at least, are genetically equivalent. A similar conclusion may be drawn from the fact that small fragments of early chick blastoderm, which contains up to 60,000 cells or more, may, on rich culture medium, produce a small but complete embryo. In some of these fragments, none of the cells would normally have contributed to the embryo itself but would have formed extraembryonic membranes.

It must be said, however, that the nucleus from an endodermal cell of a frog blastula, when transplanted to an enucleated frog ovum, is less capable of directing normal development; it seems already to have undergone some differentiation. Moreover, in later stages of development there is clear evidence that nuclear differentiation has occurred. Indeed, some cells, such as lens epithelium or erythrocytes, lose their nuclei altogether, and the nuclei from postgastrulation stages of frog are not capable of directing normal development when transplanted to an enucleated frog egg.

These evidences of nuclear differentiation do not, however, establish that cell differentiation results from nuclear differentiation as a primary event. Rather are the nuclear changes to be regarded as the result of suppression or activation of gene loci by the local micro-environment, cytoplasmic or extracellular.

CHROMOSOMAL DIFFERENTIATION

There is direct evidence that environmental factors can affect the structure of chromosomes and, presumably, the activity of their genes. In certain flies, the giant chromosomes show, at various sites, cloud-like thickenings called puffs. At the site of puffing, there is evidence of RNA synthesis, and there are sound reasons for believing that puffing is the morphological expression of gene activation (p. 38.2). The time and site of appearance of puffs correlates with particular stages of differentiation. Most significantly it has been shown that the time of appearance of certain puffs is altered when premature moulting of the larva is induced by injections of the moulting hormone.

REVERSAL OF DIFFERENTIATION

The possibility of reversal depends largely on what is meant by differentiation.

Cells in tissue culture appear to lose some of their specific structural attributes, and tend to form sheet-like epithelial aggregates or more loosely associated cells like fibroblasts or isolated cells of macrophage type. This 'dedifferentiation' is often only apparent, however, and the cells may resume their former differential characters when restored to a more normal environment.

In a similar way, some cells look strikingly different under different conditions of hormonal stimulation. The epithelial cells of the prostate and seminal vesicle, for example, are shrunken and non-secreting in castrated animals, and resume their normal structure and functional activity under the influence of testosterone. The uterine epithelium responds similarly to oestrogens. There is good reason to believe that these hormones exert their effects by gene activation. It is doubtful, however, if these changes should be regarded as differentiation; the term **modulation**, with its implication that the changes are reversible and do not involve any fundamental change in the cell, is to be preferred.

Evidence is accumulating, however, that true dedifferentiation may occur. Cartilage cells, freed from their matrix and grown in tissue culture, may lose the capacity to synthesize matrix and may, apparently, differentiate again into other cells of the connective tissue lineage.

It is clear that purely cytological criteria are not sufficiently refined to allow the earlier stages of cell differentiation to be recognized. If differentiation is fundamentally the development of a specific pattern of protein synthesis, then studies of isoenzyme content and of tissue specific antigens will enable us to describe more precisely the sequence of differentiation.

SELECTIVE CELL ASSOCIATIONS

There are other, even more subtle, differences between cells, which are revealed by their interactions with one another. If the cells of a developing organ, such as the kidney, are dissociated by trypsin, and the resulting cell suspension is sown on the chorioallantoic membrane of the chick, they reorganize themselves into a mass which is recognizable as kidney. Moreover, kidney and liver cells, mixed together, sort themselves out into histologically organized fragments of liver and of kidney; no mixtures of the two cell types are found.

This preferential attachment of cells of like origin is believed to depend upon their surface properties. Its basis is probably the same as that of **contact inhibition**. Isolated cells, grown in culture on a glass surface, move about on the surface, and divide. When they make contact with other cells, movement and frequently division are inhibited. If the same phenomenon occurs in vivo, it is clearly important in the regulation of cell movement and cell division, both in normal tissues and at sites of repair of lost tissue. The spread of epithelial cells over a denuded surface, and the cessation of movement when the defect is covered may be described, although not explained, in terms of the removal and then the return of contact inhibition.

FURTHER READING

BELL E. Ed. (1965) *Molecular and Cellular Aspects of Development* (a collection of important original papers on modern developmental biology). New York: Harper and Row.

DAVIES J. (1963) *Human Developmental Anatomy.* New York: The Ronald Press Co.

SPRATT N.T. (1964) *An Introduction to Cell Differentiation.* London: Chapman and Hall.

STREETER G.L. Developmental horizons in human embryos. *Contrib. Embry.*, Carnegie Institution of Washington, **30**, 1942; **31**, 1945; **32**, 1945; **34**, 1951.

TANNER J.M. (1964) Human growth and constitution, in *Human Biology*, Ed. Harrison G.A., Weiner J.S., Tanner J.M. and Barnicot N.A. Oxford University Press.

Chapter 19
Introduction to topographical anatomy

Topographical anatomy deals with the form, relationships and mechanical functioning of the component parts of the body. It is commonly studied regionally, by examining the arrangement of the organs and tissues in a given region and determining their function by appropriate methods.

The traditional method of obtaining topographical information is to dissect a dead body, and much present knowledge was originally obtained in this way. The advantages are that a leisurely investigation can be made, and that deep structures may be examined as easily as superficial ones. But most of the bodies used for this purpose are those of elderly people; their muscles are feeble and small, and many of their organs may be diseased or wasted. The embalming process shrinks and hardens the soft tissues, and may distort their relationships. It is therefore necessary to check much of the information provided by the dead body against the living subject before it can be accepted. New methods of study of the living body have led to a considerable revision of anatomical ideas, and this revision is by no means complete, especially as regards function.

Inspection of the intact living body reveals the swelling of muscles and their behaviour when a movement is made, the pulsation of arteries, and the position of superficial bones, tendons and veins. Examination by touch (**palpation**) detects more detail, and gives additional data, the resistance of bone, the contraction of buried muscles, the position of nerve trunks, dense connective tissue and solid viscera. Manipulation of joints demonstrates their construction and the types and ranges of movement of which they are capable. **Percussion**, in which the finger of one hand is laid flat on the body and struck firmly with a finger of the other hand, can map the boundaries of air-containing organs such as the lungs and stomach by the 'feel' of the vibrations set up and the dullness or resonance of the note produced.

With instruments, more is possible. The stethoscope can give an idea of the position and size of the heart and lungs, for their normal functioning creates noises which can be heard through it (**auscultation**). Recording electrodes can illustrate the part played by muscles in various movements. Instruments can be introduced through the orifices of the body to inspect such viscera as the urinary bladder, the stomach, the nose and the larynx, the rectum and the uterus. The eardrum and the retina can also be examined, using special equipment.

Surgical exploration of the living body is a fruitful source of information, and so is radiology. A plain radiograph can show not only the bones but also the shape, position and size of the heart and lungs in different phases of activity and in different postures. The hollow organs can be made visible if radio-opaque substances are swallowed or injected into them; air may be introduced to outline body cavities. Cineradiography demonstrates the mechanical functioning of the joints, the heart, lungs, and alimentary canal.

Surface anatomy
This is the name given to the rules describing the projection of deep structures on to the surface of the body; the importance of being able to locate and identify a given structure through the intact skin needs no emphasis.

Wherever possible bony prominences are used as reference points from which to take bearings, and measurements are often expressed in units derived from the patient's own body rather than in inches or centimetres. If we say that in the average adult a given artery lies three centimetres away from a bony projection, we are faced with a complicated calculation when we try to work out how far away it would be in a 3-year-old child. But if it is described as lying three fingers' breadths away from the bone, we are expressing a universal rule which does not vary with age or body size, since the patient's fingers grow with him, and large people have larger fingers than small ones. Other units used in this way are thumb's breadths and hand's breadths.

In many instances it is possible to avoid even this kind of measurement if two bony points are available. It may be said, for example, that a nerve can be found two-thirds of the way along a line joining one bony point to the other, and this also is a universal rule. In the abdomen, where easily identified bony landmarks are scanty, a grid of artificial lines can be superimposed as a substitute, and this grid will be used in the description of the abdominal viscera (fig. 20.30).

The mobility of the internal organs was not appreciated until quite recently, and the 'surface markings' of viscera were given in terms of the dead and embalmed body. Simple acts such as breathing, sitting, bending down, etc., may alter the relationships of the internal organs to each other and to the surface of the body.

Language of anatomy

The language of anatomy is the basis of the language of medicine. It must therefore be clear, precise and unequivocal. In the early days of anatomy the same structure received different names in different countries. In 1895, an international conference at Basle adopted an agreed terminology based upon Latin; a language admirably suited for the purpose, since it was understood the world over, was sufficiently adaptable to accommodate new ideas and discoveries, and was not tainted with ideas of national prestige. The Basle Nomina Anatomica (BNA) represented a considerable advance from chaos, but several countries subsequently found some of the terms in it unsuitable and proceeded to make unilateral revisions: the Birmingham Revised terminology (BR) of 1933 and the Jena Nomina Anatomica (JNA) of 1936 are examples.

In 1955, another international Latin terminology was accepted; this Paris Nomina Anatomica (PNA) allows each country to make translations but not alterations of the basic terms.

Complete adoption of a new terminology cannot be achieved by a stroke of the pen. Clinicians and anatomists still tend to refer to structures by the names which they learned as students. Some of these eponymous terms perpetuate (often with little justification) the name of the supposed discoverer of the structure and this practice has some historical interest. But the Latin terms are more useful because they usually give some idea of the position, function, shape or construction of the structures to which they are applied. Those who have no Latin should use a medical dictionary to find out their meaning; it is much easier to do this than to try to remember the 5,500 terms in the PNA parrot-wise.

Descriptive terms

Anatomical descriptions are based on the **anatomical position**, in which the body stands erect with the feet together and parallel; the arms are by the side, and the palms of the hands, the head, and the eyes all face directly forwards. Relationships described in this position retain their validity no matter what position the body subsequently takes up. For example, structures further away from the ground in the anatomical position are said to be **superior** to structures which are closer to the ground; the converse of superior is **inferior**. Thus the head is superior to the heart, and the heart is inferior to the head. This relationship is still expressed in the same way even if the patient stands on his head. A similar convention is used in map reading, where one place remains north of another on the map, even though the map may be twisted round or picked up and held in a different plane. In descriptive embryology the word **cranial** is often used instead of superior, and the word **caudal** may be substituted for inferior.

Structures near the front of the body are **anterior** to those near the back; conversely, structures near the back are **posterior** to those near the front. The spine is always posterior to the heart, even though the patient may be lying down or on his face. Here again there are alternatives; **ventral** is a synonym for anterior and **dorsal** for posterior. The words **lateral** and **medial** refer to structures respectively further away from and nearer to the mid-line of the body; something exactly in the mid-line is said to be **median**.

In the limbs, other words may be used. In the forearm **ulnar** is equivalent to medial, and **radial** means lateral (the ulna is the medial bone of the forearm, and the radius the lateral bone). Similarly in the leg, **tibial** is the same as medial, and **fibular** the same as lateral. The words **palmar** and **plantar** describe respectively the anterior surface of the hand and the inferior surface of the foot (the palm and the sole), while the posterior surface of the hand and the superior surface of the foot are both usually called the **dorsum**. The pair of words **proximal** and **distal** substitute for superior and inferior respectively.

Other pairs of more ordinary words are often employed. **Superficial** and **deep** refer to relative distance from the surface of the body, and the use of **external** and **internal** is usually restricted to the description of hollow viscera or the walls of cavities such as that of the chest. The words **central** and **peripheral** refer to relative distance from the centre of the body. Several ordinary words take on a more precise meaning. Thus **arm**, which in everyday speech may mean the whole upper limb, in anatomical description refers only to the territory between the shoulder and the elbow, and **leg** means only the part of the lower limb between knee and ankle.

Description of movements is often difficult, and the movements permitted at individual joints are explained when these joints are considered. The word **abduction** refers to movement away from the mid-line of the body, and its converse is **adduction**. In the hand, however, abduction and adduction are considered to occur away from and towards an arbitrary line through the middle digit, since this simplifies the description of the small muscles of the hand. In the foot a similar convention holds, but the arbitrary line is through the second, not the third, digit. **Flexion** is defined as a movement of a joint in which the two movable parts are brought towards apposition, and its converse is **extension**. **Medial rotation** of a limb is a movement in which the anterior surface of the limb turns to face medially; **lateral rotation** turns the anterior surface to face laterally.

Lastly, it is necessary to know the terms used to describe sections made through the body in various planes. An anteroposterior section exactly in the mid-line, dividing the body into two equal halves, is said to be in the **median sagittal plane**, and any other section parallel to this is known as a **sagittal section**. The reason for this is that one of the joints of the skull, known as the sagittal suture because of its resemblance to an arrow, lies in the median plane. A section at right angles to the median plane, dividing the body into anterior and posterior portions, is known as a **coronal section**, from the name of another skull suture. The terms **horizontal**, **transverse** and **oblique** as applied to sections of the body are self-explanatory, but it must be remembered that all such terms refer to the anatomical position.

Variation

In topographical anatomy quantitative variation is of considerable importance. The figures given in this book for the weights of different organs and the dimensions of cavities represent arithmetic means, and theoretically standard deviations or ranges should also be given. These are usually omitted for reasons of space and clarity but it should be remembered that the mean figure gives limited information about the values likely to be obtained in individual patients.

Topographical anatomy also deals with qualitative variation. Such matters as the shape of a tooth, the position of an organ, the path of a blood vessel, or the pattern of cutaneous innervation, are important even though it is difficult to define them in mathematical terms. This book contains descriptions of the commonest anatomical arrangements which may occur in only a minority of the population (chap. 3).

ORGANIZATION OF TISSUES

FASCIA

Superficial fascia

The connective tissue which surrounds and permeates the more highly differentiated tissues is itself organized, in certain situations, into specialized structures. The superficial fascia (panniculus adiposus) is a layer of loose areolar tissue deep to, and merging with, the dermis of the skin. Where it is plentiful, as in the forearm, it allows the skin to move freely over the underlying structures, but where it is virtually absent, as in the nose and the ear, the skin is firmly tacked down. In the loose meshes of the superficial fascia the vessels and nerves running to the skin are protected and escape injuries they might suffer if they were rigidly fixed in position.

In certain places the superficial fascia contains muscle fibres. These may be voluntary muscle, as in the muscles of facial expression and the platysma (p. 21.16), or involuntary, as in the nipple or the scrotum. In the region of the lower abdomen and groin the superficial fascia contains elastic and collagen fibres in sufficient numbers to make a recognizable membranous layer which helps the muscles of the abdominal wall to resist the intra-abdominal pressure (p. 20.29).

The main constituent of the superficial fascia is fat, which forms an insulating layer protecting the body against loss of heat; people with a heavy deposit of subcutaneous fat survive prolonged immersion in cold water longer than those not so well favoured. It is worth noting that whales and walruses have an immensely thick layer of blubber under their skins; hairy animals have little fat in the superficial fascia, the hair providing a sufficient insulation.

The fat in the superficial fascia also acts as a storage depot to be called upon in starvation, and it protects the underlying structures from rough usage by the environment. The rounded contours of the female body are due to the fact that females have relatively more subcutaneous fat than males. The distribution of this fat is a secondary sexual characteristic. For example, the female breast develops in the superficial fascia, and at puberty the glandular tissue of the breast is embedded in fat. Fat is also laid down at this time in the buttocks and thighs, and on the posterior aspect of the arms. Later in life fat is often deposited between the scapulae and at the back of the neck, forming the dowager's hump, and also in the subcutaneous tissue of the lower part of the abdomen. In the male abdominal wall fat tends to accumulate in the upper rather than the lower part of the region; no explanation is known to account for the sexual difference.

In certain places there is overgrowth and specialization of the superficial fascia. For example, in the pads of the fingers it consists of dense fibrous strands which form a kind of honeycomb structure enclosing small collections of fat. A similar arrangement is found in the toes, and in the pad of the heel; the fatty tissue of the lower part of the buttock is honeycombed in much the same way. It is thought that this is a protective device developed in areas which are subjected to considerable pressure, by standing, sitting, handling tools, etc., to minimize damage to the underlying structures.

Deep fascia

Immediately deep to the superficial fascia lies a layer of connective tissue, consisting largely of collagen fibres, which is known as the deep fascia. Its thickness and strength vary considerably from one part of the body to another. It is thin and filmy over the small muscles of the thumb, and in the face it is so tenuous as to be considered absent. In contrast, it is immensely thick and strong in the lower part of the back and on the outer side of the thigh.

In the limbs, the deep fascia forms a sleeve which surrounds the muscles and dips between them to become attached to the periosteum of the bones. This arrangement divides the limb into compartments, and many muscles attach themselves to the fascial walls of the compartment in which they lie. The fixation of the fascia to the bone is important in stabilizing and supporting these muscles.

The division of the limb into osteofascial compartments has also an important influence on the circulation. When a muscle contracts within its tight tube of bone and fascia, the swelling of its belly compresses the veins and lymphatics which lie with it inside the tube. Since both veins and lymphatics are provided with non-return valves (p. 28.20), the compression always forces the venous blood and lymph towards the thorax. If this action is prevented through paralysis of the muscles or because the limb is enclosed in plaster of Paris, tissue fluid tends to accumulate in the periphery, particularly if the limb is dependent.

In the front of the leg there is no separate layer of deep fascia over the subcutaneous surface of the tibia, and similar fusions of fascia and periosteum occur over the mandible and the crest of the ilium. Sometimes the fascia is thickened to form specialized fibrous structures. In the front of the fingers it is represented by the fibrous sheath of the flexor tendons, and it is replaced on the back by the fibrous extensor hood (p. 22.26).

At the wrist and ankle the investing deep fascia is thickened and strengthened to strap the tendons down and prevent them from bow-stringing away from the bones when they are pulled on by their muscle bellies. Elsewhere special pulleys or slings may be formed to alter the direction of pull of tendons or to check their action. A good example is found in the orbit, where the tendon of the superior oblique muscle passes through such a pulley and turns back on itself to be attached to the eyeball (p. 21.13).

The deep fascia is not easily penetrated by fluid, and collections of fluid such as blood or pus tend to take the line of least resistance and spread along the 'fascial planes' Thus the various layers of deep fascia in the neck determine the direction in which infection may spread from the throat or mouth, and are therefore of clinical importance. Some glands have a dense layer of fascia immediately surrounding them, restricting them from expansion. If the gland becomes inflamed and swollen, the fibrous capsule is stretched, and since it is usually well supplied with sensory nerves, the process is very painful. This is part of the explanation of the pain in mumps.

LIGAMENTS

A ligament is a well-defined band or cord of white fibrous tissue, usually connecting two bones. Most ligaments are developed to resist movement of a joint in a particular direction; some of them are local thickenings of the fibrous joint capsule, and are called **intrinsic ligaments**, but others are completely isolated from the joint capsule, and are known as **extrinsic ligaments**. An example is the sacrotuberous ligament (p. 20.15), which helps to prevent the sacrum tilting on the ilium, but is some distance away from the sacroiliac joint. It is possible that such ligaments may be laid down by fibroblasts in response to unidirectional stresses tending to pull the bones apart, but the existence of other ligaments is more difficult to explain; thus, the coraco-acromial ligament and the ligament which bridges across the suprascapular notch of the scapula merely connect two different parts of the same bone, though the coraco-acromial ligament may play a protective role in the mechanism of the shoulder joint (p. 22.4).

Some structures which receive the name of ligaments are not strictly ligaments at all; the inguinal ligament and its extensions (p. 20.23) are simply the tendinous attachments of the external oblique muscle of the abdomen. Others, such as the round ligaments of the liver and the uterus, are remnants of embryological structures which have no function in the adult. The name is also given to certain double folds of peritoneum, containing blood vessels and connective tissue, which connect one viscus to another or to the body wall; in this category are included the broad ligament of the uterus and the ligament of the ovary (pp. 37.1 and 2).

CARTILAGE

Cartilage is a light, strong, resilient material, which can survive prolonged pressure or friction without damage. It is classified according to the number and type of the fibres which occur in the matrix surrounding the cells (p. 16.14). If only a few fine fibres of collagen are present, it is called **hyaline cartilage**; if the collagen fibres are numerous the name is **fibrocartilage**, and if elastic fibres predominate, the tissue is called **elastic cartilage**.

Hyaline cartilage is found in the adult in the respiratory tract (p. 29.9) where it stiffens and holds open the trachea and bronchi, in the costal cartilages which join the ribs to the sternum and to each other (p. 20.7), and as the articular cartilage of synovial joints (p. 16.14). In the infant and child its distribution is more widespread, since it forms the precursor of the whole bony skeleton except the clavicle and the bones of the vault of the skull. The cartilaginous template is gradually invaded by bone-forming cells in the process of ossification (p. 18.37) and ultimately replaced by bone except at the joints. This replacement is complete in most bones by the age of 21, but a certain amount of conversion of hyaline cartilage to fibrocartilage and ultimately to bone or bone-like tissue may continue in restricted situations until old age. This calcification or ossification of the costal cartilages is of importance as it may impede the free movements of the chest in respiration.

The thin cap of hyaline cartilage left at the ends of the bones to take part in the synovial joints is exceedingly smooth and almost frictionless. Thin layers of hyaline cartilage receive an adequate nutrition by diffusion and thus require no blood vessels. This is true for many of the smaller joints, where the cartilage is no more than 1 or 2 mm thick. In the larger joints, where the cartilage may reach a thickness of about 0·5 cm in a young person, it is tunnelled through by cartilage canals, which contain blood vessels, derived from the adjacent bone, and a certain amount of connective tissue. The bearing surface, however, is always free from blood vessels. Articular cartilage is devoid of nerve fibres.

Fibrocartilage is found in symphyseal joints, such as those between the bodies of adjacent vertebrae (p. 20.3) and it also forms the intra-articular discs (menisci) which are found in many joints (p. 19.8), and which differ from most cartilage in having a considerable nerve supply. It is found in tendons where they are exposed to pressure, and sometimes where they are attached to bone. It is often difficult to distinguish between fibrocartilage and fibrous tissue, since the collagen fibres may be so numerous as to obscure the scanty cartilage cells.

Elastic cartilage is very much less common; it is found only in mobile parts of the external ear, the nose and the epiglottis, and its elastic qualities are shown by the springy return of these structures to their original shape if they are pulled or distorted. It has little tendency to ossify in old age.

If cartilage is injured or partly destroyed, a certain amount of regeneration can take place, through the activity of the cells of the thin covering membrane which is called the **perichondrium**, though cartilage may also be formed in ordinary connective tissue in response to friction, possibly through the conversion of fibroblasts to chondroblasts (p. 16.15). The surface of articular cartilage is continually being worn away because of the movements of the joint, and continuous growth is necessary to maintain its normal thickness. In this case the perichondrium can play no part, since the free surface has no covering of perichondrium.

BONE

The human skeleton has two embryological sources. The **visceral bones** are derived from the branchial arches, and comprise the mandible, the hyoid bone, the auditory ossicles, and such bone as may replace the cartilaginous elements of the larynx in old age. The **somatic bones** of the rest of the body are formed in the body wall, and belong to the axial skeleton, formed by the skull and vertebral column, or to the appendicular skeleton of the limbs. Some somatic bones occur in tendons of muscles, and are known as **sesamoids**. Most are small, and many are inconstant, but the patella (p. 23.9) is both large and important.

The bones form a supporting scaffolding and protection for the soft tissues, and enable the body to resist the action of gravity and other external forces. They act as a system of levers allowing one part of the body to move relative to another; this permits the body to move about in space, propelled along by the thrust of the lower limbs, or pulled about by the grasping hands. Some sesamoids apparently act as roller-bearings, such as those in the ball of the great toe (p. 23.20). Other bones have a protective function. The skull consists of several bones fixed together to form a box for the vulnerable brain; the ribs protect the thoracic and upper abdominal viscera. The skeleton is a store of calcium phosphate which can be called on when required; about 99 per cent of the calcium of the body is found in the bones. Lastly, the bones serve as a receptacle for the marrow which produces the formed elements of the blood; in the embryo most of the skeleton is used in this way, but after birth haemopoiesis becomes restricted to such places as the proximal ends of the limb bones, the bodies of the vertebrae, the sternum and the skull.

Bones vary greatly in shape and to a lesser extent in structure. The **long bones** of the limbs consist essentially of a shaft and two ends, which are expanded to provide stable surfaces for the adjacent joints. The shaft is a tube of dense compact bony tissue (p. 16.11), and the medullary cavity in the centre is filled with marrow (p. 26.4). In the adult this is fatty and yellow, though in response to a need for extra blood formation it can revert to haemopoietic function and become red marrow again. The ends of long bones consist of spongy cancellous bone (p. 16.12) covered over by a thin rind of compact bone; the meshes of the spongy bone are filled by red marrow.

The same basic construction is found in the metacarpals, metatarsals and phalanges, which are also classed as long bones, though their dimensions are tiny when compared with the humerus or the femur; the term miniature long bone describes them adequately.

The short bones of the carpus and tarsus have no recognizable shaft, and tend towards a roughly cubical shape; they are made of spongy bone surrounded by a thin layer of compact bone, like the ends of the long bones.

Flat bones consist of a sandwich of spongy bone between two layers of compact bone. Their surfaces are usually curved, as in the 'flat' bones of the vault of the skull. In this situation the layers of compact bone are known as **inner and outer tables,** and the spongy bone in the middle is called the **diploe.**

Any bones which cannot conveniently be included in the foregoing categories are classed as irregular bones; the vertebrae and the bones of the face are irregular. The central portion of some of the skull bones is absorbed and replaced, not by marrow, but by air sinuses extending from the nasal cavity. Such bones are sometimes included in a separate class of **pneumatic bones.**

The surface of a bone is roughened where ligaments, tendons or fibrous insertions of muscle are attached. Fleshy muscle attachments leave the surface relatively smooth. Vessels, nerves or tendons may make grooves or actually pierce the bone. These features on the surface of a bone are readily identified and given special names. Some are exclusive to a particular bone, such as the groove for the tendon of flexor hallucis longus on the talus (p. 23.17), other terms are more generally used.

For example, any localized elevation or projection is called a **process**; sharp pointed processes may be called **spines,** and large round ones are **tuberosities** or **tubercles.** A hooked process may be called a **hamulus,** and a horn-shaped one a **cornu.** A sharply defined ridge is known as a **crest,** and a low one is called a **line.** Grooves are known as **sulci,** and tunnels as **canals**; a hole in the bone is a **foramen,** and a depression is called a **fossa.** An **articular surface** is a smooth area participating in a joint; it is covered in the living state by cartilage (p. 19.4). A **facet** is a small articular surface, a **condyle** a rounded one, and a **trochlea** is one shaped like a pulley. An **epicondyle** is a small process closely related to a condyle.

The internal construction of bones also varies according to local stresses and strains. If the bones were solid masses of compact bone, they would be very heavy, and enormous muscles would be needed to move them. On the other hand, cancellous bone is not so strong as compact bone, and a compromise is necessary. Every bone has an outer crust of compact bone, which varies in thickness according to the strains it must resist. In the short and irregular bones it is thin, but in the middle of the shafts of the long bones it is relatively thick and strong. Secondly, the spongy bone becomes modified according to its situation. Spongy bone is formed by a honeycomb arrangement of thin irregular plates of bone called trabeculae, and these trabeculae are so disposed as to resist the stresses normally applied to the bone. In this way a characteristic pattern is formed for each bone of the skeleton (fig. 16.9).

Very little strength is lost by the shafts of the long bones being tubular instead of solid, since bending stresses are taken by the surfaces of the cylindrical shaft, and there is little need for a solid core. In the same way, bones such as the maxilla can be hollowed out with impunity; its surface must be large in order to make room for the teeth and the facial muscles, but a solid maxilla would impose a strain on the muscles at the back of the neck which hold the head upright.

Bone must also be strong where other tissues are attached to it. At such points the outer, fibrous layer of the periosteum (p. 16.13) becomes modified. The collagenous perforating fibres which fix it to the surface layers of the compact bone become more numerous and crowded together, forming a strong attachment continuous with the collagen of the tendon, muscle, or ligament and binding together the compact bone which it perforates. In the adult, a tendon may gradually become transformed into bone; as it approaches the bony surface, it develops a zone of fibrocartilage (p. 16.14), which is succeeded by a zone of calcified cartilage, and this in turn merges into the true compact bone.

The process of ossification and growth is described in chap. 18. Most of the primary centres of ossification appear before birth, as do some of the secondary centres. Since closure of the epiphyseal plates does not begin to occur until late adolescence, the skeleton in childhood consists of a growing framework of cartilage and membrane, in which growing islands of bone are separated from each other by progressively diminishing intervals. The epiphyseal lines, which mark the site of the epiphyseal cartilages, are visible not only on the bone itself, but on its radiographic shadows, where they must be distinguished from the appearances caused by fractures. It is for this reason that the position of all epiphyseal lines has to be learned, though it is not necessary to commit to memory the exact times of appearance and closure of the individual centres of ossification. Such times vary within wide limits, and the average figure may be misleading in an individual patient. Detailed information is of course needed when attempting to assess the age of an unidentified body, or the stage of growth reached by a patient whose development does not appear to be proceeding satisfactorily. It is usual for more growth to occur at one end of a long bone than the other, and the end at which most activity takes place is often called the **growing end.** This is a misleading term, for both ends grow, but it is of value in calling attention to the fact that an injury to this end will produce a much more serious impairment of growth than damage to the other.

Secondary centres of ossification also play a part in the growth of some of the prominences and processes of individual bones, not only those which are found at the ends of the bone. For example, there are secondary centres for the medial border of the scapula and for its coracoid process (p. 22.41), but not, as a rule, for its lateral or superior border, which manage to grow satisfactorily without such an apparatus. This underlines the fact that very little is known about the reasons for the appearance of epiphyses. It was formerly customary to account for them as due to pressure, traction, or evolutionary fusion of bones which are separate in other animals. Such explanations leave as many problems unaccounted for as they solve. Pressure-bearing points on bone frequently fail to develop epiphyses, and so do localized muscular or ligamentous attachments.

The region of the shaft of a long bone which immediately adjoins the epiphyseal plate is known as the **metaphysis,** and is important because it is here that infection tends to lodge. There is a very rich supply of blood to this area from vessels which encircle the bone and enter it through numerous small foramina. If the epiphyseal plate, or part of it, with the corresponding portion of metaphysis, is included within the line of attachment of the adjacent joint capsule, an abscess at the end of the bone may burst into the joint cavity; if the epiphyseal line is outside the joint capsule, this cannot occur. The relationship of the epiphyseal lines to the corresponding joint capsules is thus important clinically.

The metaphysis is the most vascular portion of the bone, but the most obvious of the arteries supplying a long bone is the **nutrient artery**, which enters the shaft through the **nutrient foramen** at a position which is characteristic for the particular bone. The name is misleading, since most of the blood brought by this artery is destined for the bone marrow. The terminal branches of the blood vessels supplying compact bone lie in the Haversian canals (p. 16.11). These canals also convey fine sensory nerve fibres derived from the deeper layer of the periosteum covering the bone.

The blood and nerve supply of short and irregular bones is less stereotyped, but is often sufficiently constant to be of clinical importance; in the scaphoid bone, the pattern of the blood vessels and scanty blood supply slows the healing of a fracture in this bone.

Normal healthy bone resists bending and twisting nearly as well as cast iron, and there is a considerable safety factor protecting it against overloading. Nevertheless it is not proof against leverage, and violence applied to a part of the body some distance away may succeed in breaking a bone at its weakest point. It is even possible to snap a bone by a violent contraction of the patient's own muscles, if this happens to catch the protective mechanisms unawares.

In young people bones may crack in a spiral fashion, part of the bone remaining intact. This is called a **greenstick** fracture, from the resemblance to the way in which a green twig breaks incompletely. It is relatively easy to repair, since the ends of the bone remain closely applied. In old people the bones are more brittle, and the break is often complete, with the result that the direction of the force applied and the contraction of the muscles attached to the fragments may produce a considerable deformity by twisting or pulling them apart.

The process of repair of a fracture is essentially similar to the process of ossification, and the bone-forming cells are derived from the periosteum. A large unwieldy lump of bony tissue called provisional callus is formed round the site of the fracture, and this has then to be remodelled to form a more streamlined structure known as the definitive callus. Sometimes bone formed by displaced periosteum may constitute a danger to the adjacent blood vessels; this is particularly liable to occur in the region of the elbow.

JOINTS

Joints occur where one component of the skeleton meets another; like a carpenter's or engineer's joints, they are not necessarily associated with movement. Nor are they necessarily permanent. For example, the epiphysis and metaphysis of a long bone are united by hyaline cartilage in what is called a **primary cartilaginous joint,** which allows no movement, and disappears when growth of the bone ceases.

There are three main classes of permanent joints. In **fibrous joints** the bones are united by fibrous tissue. In the variety known as a **suture**, the attachment is tight enough to prevent all movement, and such joints are found only in the skull, where they allow the bones to grow. Many of them are not strictly permanent, since after growth is finished they too tend to be invaded by bone and may eventually disappear in old age. A **syndesmosis** is a fibrous joint in which some stretching or twisting movement is possible, such as the distal tibiofibular joint (p. 23.15).

In the second kind of permanent joint the ends of the bones are covered by hyaline cartilage, and the two cartilaginous surfaces are then united by a plate of fibrocartilage to form a secondary cartilaginous joint, or **symphysis.** The middle of the plate of fibrocartilage may become softened, as in the intervertebral discs (p. 20.3), or it may develop a small cavity, as in the pubic symphysis (p. 20.14). Movement at such joints is naturally limited, but the sum total of the individual movements between adjacent vertebrae can be considerable.

The third type of permanent joint is the **synovial joint,** which usually permits free movement (fig. 19.1). The moving surfaces are as a rule covered by a layer of hyaline cartilage, but in a few joints, such as the temporomandibular joint (p. 21.19) this may be replaced by fibrocartilage or even fibrous tissue. Stretching from one bone to another, and continuous with the fibrous periosteum on each, is the joint capsule, forming a sleeve of collagen fibres encircling the joint. Many of these fibres run randomly, but here and there are definite bands of parallel fibres known as intrinsic ligaments to distinguish them from the extrinsic ligaments which do not form part of the joint capsule. The intrinsic ligaments may be connected to such structures as the cartilaginous discs or menisci which are found in certain joints, and most of them afford attachments for muscles and tendons. Some ligaments extend a considerable distance beyond the joint which they protect, as, for example, the tibial collateral ligament of the knee joint (p. 23 10), and others may pass over two or more joints, being functionally concerned with several movements.

The joint capsule is lined by a thin, smooth, vascular mesothelium called the **synovial membrane**, which covers all the surfaces enclosed by the capsule but not covered

FIG. 19.1. Synovial joints (highly schematic). The synovial cavity is greatly exaggerated; in reality the cartilaginous surfaces are in contact, separated only by a thin film of synovial fluid. (a) Essential features. (b) Joint containing an incomplete disc of fibrocartilage. (c) Joint containing a complete disc. The joint cavity is divided into two, and the synovial membrane is attached to the margins of the disc. (d) Formation of a bursa. Its walls consist of synovial membrane plus a thin layer derived from the capsule; these are fused together in the living joint.

by articular cartilage. It also excludes from the joint cavity any tendons or ligaments which may lie within the capsule, and is attached to the margins of the articular cartilage and the discs or menisci which may be present.

In certain parts of the joint, where the bones do not fit each other well and the capsule might tend to slacken in certain phases of movement, there may be pads of fat between the fibrous capsule and the synovial membrane; these pads, which bulge into the dead space during movement, may help in the lubrication of the joint.

The synovial membrane usually develops folds and fringes in places well clear of the articular surfaces; occasionally some of them may be nipped by an unexpected movement, thereby causing one variety of internal injury of the joint. The fringes are highly vascular, and are the main source of synovial fluid. This clear or slightly yellow viscid fluid is secreted from the blood by the synovial membrane; it lubricates the joint, nourishes the articular cartilage, and provides macrophages to scavenge the debris from the working surfaces. Synovial fluid is present in very small quantities, even the largest joints containing only a few drops. But if the joint is injured, as by a sprain, fluid may accumulate in the joint cavity, separating the working surfaces and stretching the already damaged capsule. If this fluid becomes infected, the synovial membrane allows locally produced toxins to pass into the blood stream. The synovial cavity can be regarded as a specialized connective tissue space.

Occasionally pieces of fibrocartilage are interposed between the two bearing surfaces (fig. 19.1b & c). In the ball and socket joints at the shoulder and hip a thin ring or labrum of fibrocartilage, triangular in cross-section, is attached round the margin of the socket, so deepening it to enclose more of the ball. In the knee joint (p. 23.7) the flat surfaces of the condyles of the tibia are deepened in a very similar manner by two crescentic pieces of fibrocartilage which are known as semilunar cartilages, or menisci. Other joints, such as the sternoclavicular joint (p. 22.3) have a complete disc of fibrocartilage dividing the joint into two separate compartments. Such discs may be complete or perforated, and need not be as round as their name suggests; for example, the 'disc' in the radiocarpal joint (p. 22.15) is triangular in shape.

Several functions have been suggested for these cartilaginous structures. They may increase the stability of the joint because they can adapt themselves to the different profiles of the articular surfaces during movement; they may act as shock absorbers protecting the margins of the articular surfaces. It is probable that they help to distribute the synovial fluid more evenly through the joint cavity and so act as 'oilers' reducing friction. Finally, discs and menisci may allow different movements to take place in the two compartments into which the joint is divided; in the temporomandibular joint, for example (p. 21.19), a gliding movement occurs in the upper compartment and a hinge movement in the lower.

In many joints the fibrous capsule has weaknesses or gaps through which the synovial membrane may protrude to form pockets lying on the surface of the joint (fig. 19.1d). Such **bursae**, as they are called, help to reduce friction, for instead of muscles rubbing against the capsule, one smooth surface of the bursa slips over the other, lubricated by synovial fluid. Bursae are not necessarily connected with the synovial cavity of a joint, and can develop in the connective tissue round muscles or tendons as smooth-walled cavities containing a tiny quantity of viscid lubricant fluid closely resembling synovial fluid. Sometimes a bursa may be wrapped round a tendon as to enclose it almost completely (fig. 19.2) for a considerable part of its length; such elongated bursae are known as **synovial sheaths.**

Voluntary movements at synovial joints are naturally determined by the shape of the articular surfaces. **Hinge joints** permit flexion and extension (p. 19.2), but movements in other planes are limited. **Pivot joints** resemble the hinges of a gate, and, like them, allow a movement of rotation; the superior radio-ulnar joint allows the radius to rotate around its axis in the movements of pronation and supination of the forearm (p. 22.14).

FIG. 19.2. Construction of synovial tendon sheath. (a) Surface view. (b) Longitudinal section. (c) Cross section. Note how the blood supply enters the tendon.

Plane joints, such as those which occur between the bones of the carpus and tarsus (pp. 22.16 and 23.19) have surfaces which are more or less flat, and consequently permit gliding movements in several directions in the plane of the surface.

In a **condylar joint** one bone articulates with the other by two distinct and often completely separate articular condyles. Such joints in general behave like hinge joints, but if one condyle is made to rotate on its own axis the other describes an arc centred on the point round which rotation takes place. In the knee joint (p. 23.12) the two condyles share a common synovial cavity, but in the atlanto-occipital joint (p. 21.23) there is a separate cavity for each condyle. Other joints, not normally described as condylar joints, have similar capacities for movement; the two temporomandibular joints (p. 21.19) together form a condylar joint in which the two condyles are separated by the width of the skull.

Saddle-shaped joints have surfaces shaped like two saddles, one placed cross-wise and upside-down on top of the other. Such joints allow rocking movements in two main planes at right angles to each other, and slight movements in other intermediate planes; a little rotation can also occur. The type specimen of such joints is the carpometacarpal joint of the thumb (p. 22.16), but this kind of surface can be detected in many other joints, though the curvatures of the saddles are not so marked.

Ball and socket joints allow very free movement round any axis drawn through the middle of the ball; thus flexion and extension, abduction and adduction, rotation, and any combination of these movements are all possible. If they occur sequentially, as when the toe is used to trace out a circle on the ground, the combination of movements is known as circumduction.

Ellipsoid joints, such as the radiocarpal joint, are ball and socket joints in which both ball and socket are ellipsoidal rather than spheroidal. They permit flexion and extension, abduction and adduction, and circumduction. Rotation is impossible.

This classification of synovial joints by the movements they permit is an oversimplification. The articular surfaces of any joint are not such as would be obtained by sectioning any regular geometric solid, and all voluntary movements are necessarily compound rather than simple. For example, the profiles of the trochlear surfaces of the humerus and talus have a screw-like spiral twist, so that flexion and extension at the elbow and ankle, which are both classed as hinge joints, are always accompanied by some axial rotation. In a similar manner most other movements, of whatever basic kind, are transformed into circumductions. Nor are voluntary movements the only movements which can occur at a joint. When a ball is gripped by the hand there is an easily observable rotation of the proximal phalanges of the fingers on the heads of the metacarpals. This movement results largely from the fingers meeting the resistance of the curved surface of the ball. It is of great functional importance. Movements of this kind are sometimes known as accessory movements.

Very few movements in the intact body involve only one joint. Certain joints are coupled together, such as those between the radius and ulna; rotation of the radius round the ulna must take place at both joints or it cannot take place at all. Again, many muscles and ligaments take part in the working of two or more joints, and a movement in one automatically produces a movement in the other; a good example is afforded by the movements of the shoulder girdle (p. 22.8), which necessarily involve several joints. Finally, the postures of the body, such as standing, are dependent on many joints, and an injury to one of them can lead to far-reaching alterations in the behaviour of the others.

Many factors limit the movements permitted at a joint,

and some may be more important than others. For example, flexion of the elbow is limited by the development of the muscles on the front of the arm, for the soft parts are brought into apposition with each other. The bigger the biceps, the more it restricts the range of flexion. In most joints the first line of defence is the tension of the antagonist muscles. In cases where the muscles are paralysed, a greatly increased range of passive movement becomes possible, leading to stretching of the joint capsule and the formation of what is called a flail joint. On the other hand, if the tone of the muscles is increased, as in spastic paralysis, movements will be reduced in range. Should the muscles be inadequate, the duty of restricting movement falls to the ligaments, either intrinsic or extrinsic. Ligaments are inextensible, and are therefore ill-adapted to withstand a suddenly imposed maximal strain, which might rupture their fibres. Sudden movements are therefore probably always restricted by muscles. On the other hand it appears that the continued stresses imposed on the hip joint and the arches of the foot by the maintenance of the upright posture (p. 23.23) may be taken largely by the ligaments.

The stability of a joint is determined largely by the muscles which surround it and hold the articular surfaces together. Muscles have the advantage that they remain tense throughout the movement they resist, and pay out gradually as their opponents contract, in a manner which is impossible for the inelastic ligaments. Muscles such as those comprising the rotator cuff of the shoulder joint (p. 22.10) are sometimes referred to as **extensile ligaments.**

The action of muscles in maintaining stability may be assisted, in certain instances, by the tension of ligaments. For example, in hinge joints it is theoretically possible for the ligaments at either side of the joint to remain tense throughout the whole range of flexion and extension. The ligaments in the plane of movement can become tense only in extreme flexion or extreme extension, and are therefore of no use in holding the bones together during the movement.

A third factor in joint stability is the degree of congruence of the articular surfaces. In the sacroiliac joint (p. 20.14) many protuberances on one bone fit into depressions on the other, giving a mechanically strong joint. Such an arrangement naturally interferes with movement, and indeed one must think of strength and mobility as being to a certain extent incompatible. The factors which make for strength are good fit of bones, strong tight capsule and closely applied strong muscles; these necessarily interfere with freedom of movement. In contrast, joints with weak, lax capsules, marked incongruity of the articular surfaces, and controlling muscles situated some distance away from the capsule, have lost strength but gained mobility.

The congruence of the articular surfaces is usually minimal during the movement, and maximal at both extremes, when the joint is described as reaching a close-packed position. Not only do the bones achieve the best fit in this position, but the ligaments are wound up and tensed by the rotation which is inherent in all simple movements. In contrast to the 'close-packed' position, in which the joint is well adapted to resist stresses, is the **position of rest.** This is the position taken up by the joint when it is not in use and when all the muscles acting on it are relaxed. The position of rest is naturally about the mid-point of the various movements undertaken by the joint.

The blood supply of joints is derived from a plexus of vessels lying outside the joint capsule, and its nerve supply comes from the adjacent nerve trunks. The fibrous capsule is freely supplied by sensory fibres, and so are any inclusions of fibrocartilage in the joint. The synovial membrane has a few sensory fibres, and the articular cartilage has none. The rich supply of the joint capsule is associated with pressure and tension receptors which play a part in the feedback from the joint to the central nervous system. Since the capsule is supplied by nerves which also supply the muscles acting on the joint there is a possibility of establishing local reflex arcs which may play a part in maintaining stability.

MUSCLE

Visceral muscle
(Involuntary or smooth)

Visceral muscle tends to be arranged in sheets rather than in discrete bundles. It occurs in the walls of blood-vessels, where it regulates the blood supply to the tissues and helps to control the blood pressure. In the walls of the alimentary canal it mixes food and digestive secretions, propels them onwards, and expels their residues. Visceral muscle is concerned with the propulsion and ejection of urine, the passage of the ovum along the uterine tube to the uterus, and the movement of spermatozoa during ejaculation. It provides the motive force which empties the uterus at childbirth, and it may assist in supporting certain parts of the gut. Visceral and somatic muscle fibres may be mixed together, as in the middle third of the oesophagus (p. 30.6) or the levator palpebrae superioris muscle (p. 21.14).

When simple constriction of a tube is required, as in the anal canal (p. 30.25) and urethra (p. 34.5) the visceral muscle fibres are arranged circularly to form a **sphincter.** When propulsion is called for, they tend to form two layers, which are usually termed **longitudinal and circular,** but which are in reality both spirals, one being loose and the other tight. The mechanics of this arrangement cause waves of contraction and relaxation to pass along the tube as the muscle is excited by its nerve supply.

Cardiac muscle
(Involuntary striated)
Cardiac muscle is restricted to the heart and the roots of the great vessels which enter and leave it. Like visceral muscle, it is arranged in sheets, which have a characteristic spiral twist, and this is important in the emptying of the heart).

Somatic muscle
(Voluntary, striated or skeletal)
Somatic muscle fibres occur in bundles called fasciculi. Each fibre ends in a collagenous tip, which may be very short, or may form part of a recognizable tendon or aponeurosis.

Many muscles have attachments to several different structures, and are described as having two or more **heads**: this is often reflected in their name: biceps, triceps, quadriceps. Some of the attachments move relatively little when the muscle contracts: these are known as the **origin** of the muscle, while the more movable ones are called its **insertion**. These are only relative terms, and if the insertion of the muscle can be fixed the origin will then move towards it. For example, the pectoralis major muscle (p. 22.6) is described as taking origin from the chest wall and being inserted into the arm. But in climbing the upper limb is fixed by the grip of the hand, and the pectoralis major then acts from its fixed insertion to pull the chest towards the arm. Similarly, many muscles in the lower limb act from their insertions on their origins during walking, when the foot is fixed to the ground by friction.

The arrangement of the bundles within a muscle determines its external form and its range of movement. The fibres may run parallel to each other throughout the whole length of the muscle (fig. 19.3a). Since a muscle fibre can only shorten by a known proportion of its extended length, the arrangement of the fibres in a **strap muscle** allows the maximum range of contraction. In the rectus abdominis muscles (p. 20.22) the strap arrangement is broken up into several segments by tendinous intersections which cross the muscle at intervals (fig. 19.3b). In places such as the hand, where bulky muscles would get in the way of movement, the fleshy parts of the muscles are located up in the forearm, and attached to their insertions by long thin **tendons**. Muscles of this kind are called **fusiform**, from the shape of their fleshy bellies (fig. 19.3c), and the gain in the mobility of the part involves a sacrifice of range of movement, since the tendon is inextensible, and the contracting fibres are shorter than in a strap muscle of similar length. Occasionally a muscle has a belly at either end, with a connecting tendon in the middle (fig. 19.3d); it is then said to be **digastric**. Finally, the muscle fibres may not form a straight line with the tendon, as in the fusiform muscle, but may

run into it at an angle. In this way are formed the unipennate and bipennate muscles (fig. 19.3e, f), named because of the resemblance of the arrangement to a feather.

A fixed volume of muscle tissue can accommodate either a few long fibres or many short fibres. The range of movement depends on the average length of the fibres, but the strength of the muscle is a function of the number of fibres contracting. A pennate muscle therefore gains in strength what it loses in range, though some of the advantage is lost because of the angulated pull, which has a component at right angles to the tendon as well as one in line with it.

Fig. 19.3. Arrangement of fibres in somatic muscle (schematic). (a) Strap muscle. (b) Intersected muscle. (c) Fusiform muscle. (d) Digastric muscle. (e) Unipennate muscle. (f) Bipennate muscle.

The actions of a muscle depend on its attachments, and there are very few muscles in the body with only one action. Again, no muscle acts alone; it is always set into play together with several others as an integrated group. It is therefore misleading to think of one muscle in isolation, and better to consider the group as a whole. A muscle which crosses a joint in such a way that its contraction produces abduction and lateral rotation (p. 19.2) cannot be made to produce either of these movements separately. But when it acts as a member of a group, some of the other members can be employed to cancel out the unwanted action. Thus, if abduction is required, the lateral rotation can be nullified by combining its action with one or more medial rotators. Similarly if lateral rotation is desired, the muscle can be combined with a group of adductors which cancels the unwanted abduction.

A muscle is said to act as a **prime mover** in a given movement when it contracts primarily for the purpose of producing the movement. When it acts in a subsidiary capacity it is called a **synergist**. Synergists prevent the unwanted movements inherent in the contraction of the prime movers, and may also help them by fixing other joints to provide a stable base from which the prime movers can act. Muscles which oppose the prime movers are called their **antagonists**, and play a very important part in the movement because they pay out gradually as the prime movers contract, so providing a steady control.

Not all somatic muscles act on joints, and some produce movement of soft tissues only; as examples may be cited the muscles which move the eyeball and the soft palate. It is also necessary to distinguish between the actions of which a muscle is capable, and the functions which it normally performs in the intact body. Thus a number of the muscles which closely invest the shoulder joint and form the rotator cuff (p. 22.10) are capable of rotating the humerus in its socket, but their chief task is to act as extensile ligaments which prevent the bones from being separated during movement.

Fine movements, such as writing, are performed with the prime movers and antagonists contracting throughout, the necessary motions resulting from variations in the opposing forces. On the other hand, in movements such as kicking a football or serving at tennis, the prime movers and antagonists tend to relax once the stroke has been made, the continuation of the movement being due to momentum. Such movements are terminated by contraction of the antagonists in order to prevent damage to inextensible structures.

NERVE

The basic unit of the nervous system is the neurone (p. 14.1), and the central nervous system, comprising the brain and spinal cord, consists of large numbers of neurones supported in a framework of connective tissue cells known as neuroglia (p. 14.6). Sections through the central nervous system exhibit grey and white areas; the white matter is white because light is reflected from the myelin sheaths of the nerve fibres which preponderate in it; the grey matter is largely made up of cell bodies.

Masses of grey matter are called **nuclei**, some of which, e.g. the basal nuclei, are large and embedded in the depths of the brain. Other collections of neurones, forming grey matter, are outside the central nervous system; they are then known as **ganglia**. In the spinal cord the grey matter lies in a column surrounded by white matter, like the pattern in a stick of rock. In the cerebral hemispheres of the brain (p. 24.44) a thin cortex of grey matter on the surface is separated from the basal nuclei by white matter.

The peripheral nervous system is the name given to the nerves which bring information to the central nervous system and carry instructions from it to the periphery. Those which spring from the spinal cord are called the **spinal nerves**, while those attached to the brain are known as **cranial nerves**. The cell bodies of the motor neurones in the peripheral nerves lie in the grey matter of the central nervous system, while those of the sensory neurones lie in ganglia just outside it. The **autonomic**

system is the collective name for the neurones concerned in the supply of visceral muscle, cardiac muscle, and the cells of certain glands; the cerebrospinal system supplies the whole of the rest of the body. The autonomic system is purely motor, while the cerebrospinal system contains both motor and sensory neurones.

The spinal nerves are segmental structures, and are attached to the spinal cord in an orderly series. There are eight cervical nerves, twelve thoracic, five lumbar, five sacral and one coccygeal nerve. The first cervical nerve emerges from the spinal canal between the occipital bone and the first cervical vertebra (fig. 21.25) and the first seven cervical nerves therefore lie superior to the correspondingly numbered cervical vertebra. Because there are only seven cervical vertebrae and there are eight cervical nerves, the eighth cervical nerve emerges inferior to the seventh cervical vertebra, and from this point downwards the nerves emerge inferior to the correspondingly numbered vertebrae.

Each spinal nerve is attached to the spinal cord by two roots, ventral and dorsal. The dorsal root is almost entirely composed of sensory fibres, and their cell bodies lie in the dorsal root ganglion, which is situated in the

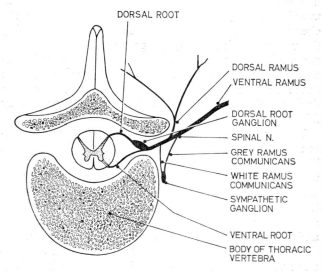

FIG. 19.4. Formation and branching of a thoracic spinal nerve. The coverings of the spinal cord and nerve roots have been omitted for the sake of clarity.

intervertebral foramen (fig. 19.4). Their central processes enter the spinal cord along a vertical posterolateral furrow. The ventral roots leave the cord from its anterolateral aspect in a series of more compact bunches; they are exclusively composed of motor fibres whose cell bodies lie in the spinal grey matter.

The roots of the cervical nerves run more or less horizontally from the cord to emerge through the appropriate intervertebral foramen. But because the cord is shorter than the vertebral column, successive pairs of roots have to run more and more obliquely in order to escape. In consequence the length of the nerve roots increases from above downwards, and the lower part of the spinal canal, below the termination of the spinal cord, is occupied by a leash of nerve roots called the cauda equina (p. 24.2).

Just peripheral to the spinal ganglion, the dorsal and ventral nerve roots unite to form the spinal nerve, which therefore contains both motor and sensory fibres. After a very short course, the spinal nerve divides into two main branches, a dorsal primary ramus destined for structures on the posterior aspect of the trunk, and a larger ventral primary ramus, which is distributed to the ventral part of the body and to the limbs. Each ramus, like the parent trunk, contains both motor and sensory fibres.

Immediately after they are formed, the ventral rami of the thoracic and first two lumbar nerves give branches to a chain of ganglia lying alongside the bodies of the vertebrae and extending from the skull down to the coccyx. These white rami communicantes constitute the sympathetic outflow of the autonomic system (p. 24.88), and the ganglia and the vertical communications between them are known as the sympathetic trunk. The fibres of the white ramus communicans may end locally in the corresponding ganglion, or they may turn upwards or downwards in the sympathetic trunk to reach another ganglion. In either case they synapse with a secondary sympathetic neurone, which then sends its axon, either directly back into the corresponding spinal nerve, or

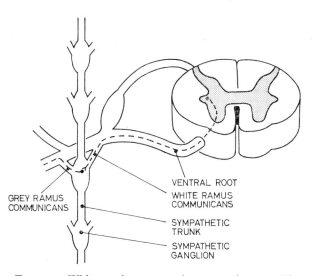

GREY RAMUS
COMMUNICANS

VENTRAL ROOT
WHITE RAMUS
COMMUNICANS

SYMPATHETIC
TRUNK

SYMPATHETIC
GANGLION

FIG. 19.5. White and grey rami communicantes. The dotted line shows the path of a sympathetic fibre originating in the thoracic part of the spinal cord. It runs through the ventral root of the spinal nerve and the white ramus communicans into the sympathetic ganglion, where it relays. The second order neurone runs in the grey ramus communicans to the ventral ramus of the nerve and will be distributed in one or more of its branches.

through the sympathetic truck to enter another spinal nerve. The bundles of such secondary sympathetic neurones look grey because they have a negligible coating of myelin, and are therefore known as grey rami communicantes. In contrast to the white rami communicantes, which are restricted to the thoracic and first two lumbar nerves, the grey rami communicantes can and do reach every spinal nerve (fig. 19.5). On reaching the ventral ramus some of the fibres of the grey ramus communicans are distributed with it, while others find their way into the dorsal ramus of the nerve.

Each dorsal ramus is connected to the one above and the one below by bundles of nerve fibres passing from one to the other and so forming what is called a simple loop plexus. The arrangement allows a nerve fibre emerging in one spinal nerve either to continue to the periphery in a branch of that nerve, or, by passing along the connecting loops, to enter another nerve at a different level.

The plexuses connecting the ventral rami are more complicated because of the difficulties introduced by the limbs, but the principle is similar. The rami which feed the plexus communicate or combine, and from the peripheral side of the resulting plexus there spring branches, which may or may not receive special names. All these branches, like the rami from which they are derived, contain both motor and sensory fibres, and many of them supply both muscle and skin; these are known as mixed nerves. Others may be solely destined for skin, and are commonly called sensory nerves; others again supply muscle only, and are referred to as motor nerves. Nevertheless, the sensory branches contain sympathetic motor fibres for the visceral muscles of the blood vessels and hairs of the skin, and the motor branches contain sensory fibres coming from the sense organs in the muscle.

The general redistribution of fibres in a plexus (fig. 19.6) means that a given branch of the plexus may contain fibres originating in several different nerve roots. Thus, the musculocutaneous nerve (p. 22.31), a mixed branch of the brachial plexus, contains fibres derived from the fifth, sixth and seventh cervical nerve roots. Conversely, the fibres leaving or entering the spinal cord in any one nerve root may be distributed along several different pathways to the periphery. For example, the fifth cervical nerve contributes fibres to seven other named branches of the brachial plexus, as well as giving off several branches before taking part in the plexus at all. The group of muscles to which fibres from a given ventral root are ultimately conveyed, possibly by many different peripheral pathways, is called a **myotome**. The motor nerve which eventually enters the muscle usually contains fibres derived from two or more central roots, so there is a degree of overlap between adjacent myotomes.

The skin supplied by a given dorsal nerve root is called its **dermatome**. Adjacent dermatomes overlap each other

FIG. 19.6. Diagram of simple nerve plexus. The spinal rami running into the plexus are labelled A to E, and those running away from it are labelled a to e. The fibres in B are mainly distributed through its direct continuation b, but some find their way into a, c, d and e. Conversely, the fibres in d can be traced back, not only to D, but also to B, C and E.

very extensively, and because of this it is difficult to map accurately the territory supplied by one spinal nerve root.

The cranial nerves differ from the spinal nerves in several ways. They do not form plexuses, though they may communicate with their neighbours on leaving the skull. Not all of them are mixed nerves, and there is no regular arrangement of motor and sensory roots. Some have a specialized role in connection with the organs of special sense, and one, the optic nerve, is really part of the brain and not a peripheral nerve at all. Several contain autonomic fibres derived from the cranial parasympathetic component of the autonomic system, but others contain no autonomic fibres at all.

In summary, a peripheral nerve may contain both motor and sensory fibres of the cerebrospinal system; if it is a branch of a spinal nerve or plexus it will also contain

sympathetic motor fibres. If it is a branch of a cranial nerve it may or may not contain parasympathetic fibres. The largest fibres in a peripheral nerve are those derived from the sensory endings in a somatic muscle, which reach a diameter of about twenty micrometres, and the smallest are the axons of the secondary sympathetic neurones, which may be less than one micrometre in thickness.

Each nerve fibre is surrounded by a delicate connective tissue called **endoneurium**, and is wrapped into a bundle or funiculus with other fibres by a denser material known as **perineurium**. Finally, the funiculi which make up the nerve are enclosed by an outer covering of tough fibrous

FIG. 19.7. (a) Cross section through a peripheral nerve trunk containing six funiculi. (b) Enlarged portion of (a) showing the coverings of the nerve fibres.

tissue called the **epineurium** (fig. 19.7). The connective tissue gives the nerve its tensile strength, and some nerves such as the sciatic, may contain much more connective tissue than nervous material.

FURTHER READING

BARNETT C.H., DAVIES D.V., & MacCONAILL M.A. (1961) *Synovial Joints.* London : Longmans.
CLARK W.E. LE GROS (1965) *The Tissues of the Body* 5th Edition. Oxford: Clarendon.
SINCLAIR D. (1966) *An Introduction to Functional Anatomy* 3rd Edition, Oxford: Blackwell Scientific Publications.
TABER C.W. (1965) *Cyclopedic Medical Dictionary,* 10th Edition. Oxford: Blackwell Scientific Publications.

Chapter 20
The trunk

My book is wrote . . . in order, by a more frequent and a more convulsive elevation and depression of the diaphragm, and the succussations of the intercostal and abdominal muscles in laughter, to drive the *gall* and *bitter juices* from the gall-bladder, liver, and sweet-bread of his majesty's subjects with all the inimicitious passions which belong to them, down into their duodenums.

T<small>RISTAM</small> S<small>HANDY</small>

The trunk is the central part of the body and is continuous, above with the neck, on either side with the upper limbs and below with the lower limbs. The outer tissues of the trunk constitute the **body wall**. This encloses two regions (fig. 20.1) which are described as cavities, al-

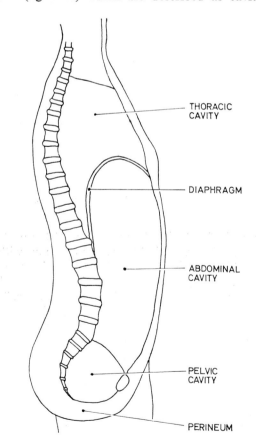

THORACIC CAVITY

DIAPHRAGM

ABDOMINAL CAVITY

PELVIC CAVITY

PERINEUM

F<small>IG</small>. 20.1. Median section of trunk showing compartments.

though in the natural state they are completely occupied by organs and their associated vessels, nerves and connective tissues. In other words they are cavities only in the sense that the inside of a box is a cavity when it is filled with china and sawdust. The two cavities are separated by the **diaphragm,** a dome-shaped sheet of muscle in which muscle fibres arise from the body wall and are inserted into a central tendon. The **thoracic cavity** lies above the diaphragm and the corresponding part of the trunk is described as the thorax. The **abdominal cavity** lies below the diaphragm and consists of two parts in wide communication. The larger upper part is the **abdominal cavity** proper. The smaller lower part is called the **pelvic cavity**; it is surrounded by the bony pelvis, and is limited below by an inverted dome-shaped muscle sheet, the **pelvic diaphragm.** Below the pelvic cavity and between the thighs there is a region of the body wall which is traversed by the terminal parts of the gastro-intestinal and genito-urinary tracts; this is the **perineum.**

THE RELATIONSHIP OF STRUCTURE TO FUNCTION IN THE BODY WALL

The body wall, as well as providing protection to the internal organs, has other functions which vary in different parts and the structure is correspondingly modified. The common **posterior wall** of the thoracic, abdominal and pelvic cavities is formed by the relevant parts of the vertebral column and the related muscles. The vertebral column has three functions, namely, to surround and protect the spinal cord, to transmit body weight and to allow movement between one part of the trunk and another. Consequently it consists of a large number of bony rings of rather elaborate form, which articulate in series by intervertebral joints. The **wall of the pelvic cavity** is continuous laterally with the tissues of the lower limb and must consequently transmit much of the weight of the body from the vertebral column to the lower limb skeleton. For this reason it consists largely of bones, the joints between which allow little movement. The **lateral** and **anterior walls of the abdominal cavity** are largely formed by three layers of flat muscles, which run concentrically around it. On contraction, these muscles not only move the thorax in relation to the pelvis, but raise the intra-abdominal pressure, an essential step in defaecation and parturition.

In the **thoracic cavity**, on the other hand, a negative, or more accurately subatmospheric, pressure is necessary for respiration (chap. 29). Consequently the lateral and anterior walls of the thoracic cavity consist, not of muscle alone as in the abdominal wall, but of muscles and bones together. The bones are the sternum, anteriorly, and the ribs which extend round the chest wall between the sternum and the vertebral column. Three layers of intercostal muscles occupy each intercostal space and attach adjacent ribs to one another, while other larger muscles pass to the ribs from surrounding parts such as the neck, upper limbs and pelvis. Contraction of these muscles move the ribs in relation to the vertebral column and sternum so that the volume of the thoracic cavity is increased, and the pressure within the cavity is diminished.

The **diaphragm** is concave towards the abdominal cavity and convex towards the thoracic cavity. Thus when this muscle contracts it reduces intrathoracic pressure and increases intra-abdominal pressure. Intrathoracic pressure can be raised only indirectly, by contracting the abdominal muscles and relaxing the diaphragm. The raised intra-abdominal pressure then displaces the diaphragm upwards and, by reducing the volume of the thoracic cavity, increases the pressure within it.

GENERAL ORGANIZATION OF THE BODY WALL

Developmentally the organization of the body wall is essentially segmental, and although in the adult this early pattern is partially obscured, much of the region still consists of a series of segments or zones, each of which contains similar structures. Thus each successive segment contains a vertebra, a costal or rib element in one form or another, a spinal nerve and a sympathetic ganglion, a somatic or body wall artery and a somatic vein.

The vertebral column

The vertebral column, which consists of the vertebrae and the joints and ligaments uniting these bones to one another, contains the spinal cord and its meninges within the vertebral canal. Each vertebra is thus a ring of bone surrounding a vertebral foramen which may be regarded as one segment of the vertebral canal (figs. 20.2 and 20.3).

The anterior part of the ring, the **body**, is roughly cylindrical, with more or less flat upper and lower surfaces. The posterior part of the ring, the **vertebral arch**, consists of paired **pedicles** and **laminae**. The pedicles are

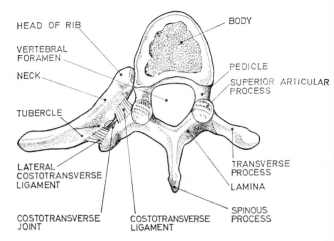

FIG. 20.2. Thoracic vertebra and rib seen from above.

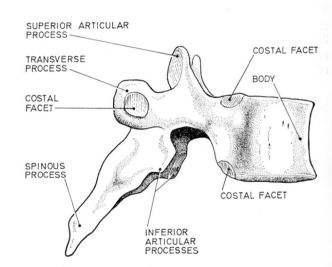

FIG. 20.3. Side view of thoracic vertebra.

continuous in front with the upper part of the posterior surface of the body. Behind they are continuous with the laminae which extends backwards and medially to fuse posteriorly. The **spinous process** projects backwards in the median plane from the junction of the laminae. Three additional processes project from the junction between each pedicle and lamina. The **transverse process** extends laterally; the **superior articular process** extends upwards and carries an articular facet on its posterior surface, and the **inferior articular process** extends downwards and has an articular facet on its anterior surface.

The vertebral column may conveniently be divided into five zones in which the individual vertebrae exhibit characteristic features. The seven cervical, the twelve thoracic and the five lumbar vertebrae are associated with the neck, the thorax and the abdomen proper, respectively. In the pelvic cavity and perineum, five sacral vertebrae are fused to form the single **sacrum** and three or four small and incomplete vertebrae are described collectively as the **coccyx**.

THE INTERVERTEBRAL JOINTS

The **intervertebral disc** (figs. 20.4 and 20.5) is a unique type of secondary cartilaginous joint which lies between adjacent vertebral bodies. The adjacent bony surfaces each present a central plate of avascular hyaline cartilage surrounded by a raised rim of bone. The peripheral parts of these surfaces are united by a ring of dense collagenous tissue, the **anulus fibrosus**, in which the fibres follow oblique circular courses from one bone to another. The region within the anulus fibrosus and between the cartilage plates is occupied by the **nucleus pulposus**. In the newborn this is a gelatinous material containing a high concentration of mucopolysaccharides; it is traversed by fine collagen fibres and contains groups of large vesiculated multinucleated cells derived from the notochord. In infancy and childhood the cells disappear, and throughout life the rigidity of the tissue progressively increases owing to an increase in its collagen.

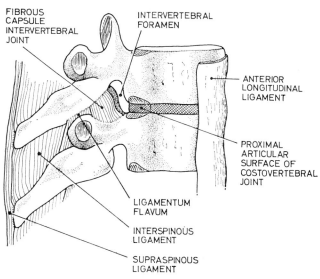

FIG. 20.4. Side view of articulation between two thoracic vertebrae.

This joint permits small degrees of angulation and rotation between adjacent vertebral bodies. At the same time the anulus fibrosus elastically resists these movements, so that, when the moving force ceases, the bones tend to recoil to a neutral position. The elasticity of the anulus and nucleus pulposus also absorbs a large part of the strain energy created by sudden stresses acting along the vertebral column. If these stresses are greater than the elastic limit of either the anulus or the cartilage plates, these tissues may rupture and allow herniation of the

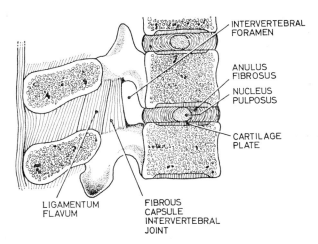

FIG. 20.5. Median section of articulating thoracic vertebrae.

nucleus pulposus either to the exterior or into the spongy bone of the vertebral body.

The common accessory ligaments of all the intervertebral discs are the **anterior** and **posterior longitudinal ligaments**. The anterior ligament (fig. 20.4) is a broad band which covers, and is attached to, the anterior aspects of the vertebrae and intervertebral discs. The posterior ligament (fig. 20.6) lies on the anterior wall of the vertebral canal. It is broad over the posterior aspects of the intervertebral discs to which it is very firmly attached;

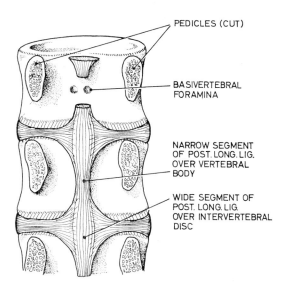

FIG. 20.6. The anterior wall of the vertebral canal.

between the discs it is a narrow band which is quite separate from the posterior surfaces of the vertebral bodies. Both ligaments end at the upper border of the sacrum because below this level the sacral vertebrae are fused.

The **intervertebral joints** (figs. 20.4 and 20.5) are small paired synovial joints between the apposed articular facets on the superior and inferior articular processes of adjacent vertebrae; each is surrounded by a synovial capsule and a simple fibrous capsule. The shape and orientation of these joints dictate the kind and range of movement which can occur between vertebrae. The accessory ligaments of the intervertebral joints are the **ligamenta flava**, and the **interspinous** and **supraspinous ligaments** (figs. 20.4 and 20.5). The ligamenta flava are paired ligaments containing a high proportion of elastic fibres. Each pair joins the adjacent laminae of the articulating vertebrae. Behind they fuse and become continuous with the interspinous ligament, while in front each fuses with the fibrous capsule of the corresponding intervertebral joint. Adjacent spinous processes are joined by a mass of collagenous tissue; between these processes this is described as the interspinous ligaments, whereas the tissue surmounting the tips of the processes is designated the supraspinous ligament.

The **intervertebral foramina** (figs. 20.4 and 20.5) are paired gaps in the wall of the vertebral canal between each adjacent pair of vertebrae. They allow spinal nerves and veins to leave the canal and spinal arteries to enter it. In the sacral region their form is modified by the fusion of the vertebra to one another, but in the thoracic and lumbar regions all have the same general form. Here each foramen is bounded above and below by a pedicle, behind by an intervertebral joint, and in front by the upper vertebral body and an intervertebral disc. The foramina are only slightly larger than the structures which traverse them, so any narrowing of the foramina causes compression of these structures.

The ribs

A costal element is associated developmentally with each vertebra but the extent to which this element develops and its eventual fate varies greatly in different regions.

In the thoracic region, because of the need to produce negative intrathoracic pressures, the costal elements develop as twelve separate ribs each of which is continued anteriorly as a costal cartilage (fig. 20.7). Posteriorly each articulates with one or two adjacent vertebral bodies at the **costovertebral joints**, and the upper ten articulate with the corresponding transverse processes at the **costotransverse joints** (figs. 20.2 and 20.8). The upper seven ribs extend round the body wall and their costal cartilages

FIG 20.7. The thoracic skeleton. The costal cartilages are stippled.

FIG. 20.8. The articulation of typical ribs with the thoracic vertebral column. Refer to figs. 20.3 and 20.4.

articulate anteriorly with the sternum at the **sternocostal joints**. The lower five, sometimes known as false ribs, become progressively shorter and their costal cartilages end either as free extremities or by articulation with the costal cartilages immediately above at the **interchondral joints** (fig. 20.7). Because of the presence of the ribs, the segmental nature of the body wall is very evident in the thorax, and each **intercostal space** contains three intercostal muscles, an intercostal nerve, intercostal arteries and intercostal veins.

In the lumbar region the costal elements remain small and do not survive as separate bones. They become fused with the developing transverse processes so that an adult lumbar transverse process consists of a true transverse element and a costal element. As a result the segmentation of the body wall is less obvious in the lumbar than in the thoracic region.

Similarly in the sacral region the transverse and costal elements fuse to form the lateral part of the sacrum.

The spinal nerves

The spinal nerves emerge from the vertebral canal into the tissues of the body wall through intervertebral foramina. The relationships they bear to their corresponding vertebrae is described on p. 19.13.

Immediately beyond the intervertebral foramen each spinal nerve divides into **ventral** and **dorsal primary rami**, of which the dorsal is usually the smaller (fig. 20.9). The dorsal primary rami turn backwards around the corresponding intervertebral joints, and, dividing into medial

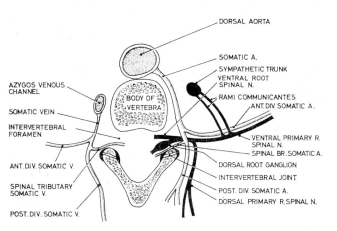

FIG. 20.9. Schematic diagram of the relationship of the main vessels and nerves of the trunk to the vertebral column.

and lateral branches, supply the postvertebral group of muscles and segmental strips of skin on the posterior aspect of the trunk. Each ventral primary ramus (VPR) passes laterally and its subsequent distribution depends on the extent of its association with the limbs. The VPR

of T3–T12, which have no association with the limbs, extend round the body wall lying in the corresponding intercostal spaces (fig. 20.29). The other thoracic, lumbar and sacral VPR contribute in varying measure to the innervation of the body wall. Additionally, and in some cases predominantly, they contribute to the nerve plexuses which lie lateral to the cervical, lumbar, sacral and coccygeal parts of the vertebral column; from these plexuses nerves carrying fibres from more than one spinal segment are distributed to the tissues of the upper and lower limbs.

The sympathetic trunk

Although its position varies in different regions of the body, in general the sympathetic trunk lies anterolateral to the vertebral bodies along the whole length of the vertebral column, and consequently anterior to the spinal nerves as they emerge from the intervertebral foramina (figs. 20.9, 20.27 and p. 19.12).

The VPR of T1–L2 or 3 are connected to the corresponding sympathetic ganglia by white rami communicantes (figs. 19.4 and 20.50). These are composed predominantly of the axons of the preganglionic cells in the lateral horn of the spinal grey matter and represent the entire outflow of sympathetic fibres from the central nervous system. Many of these fibres synapse with cells in the sympathetic ganglion which they reach first; others pass upwards or downwards along the trunk to synapse in the cervical, lower lumbar or sacral ganglia which have no white rami and therefore no direct supply of preganglionic fibres; some pass directly into the visceral branches of the sympathetic trunk to synapse in one of the central autonomic plexuses.

In contrast to the narrow inflow of fibres to the sympathetic trunk through the T1–L3 segments, postganglionic fibres leave all the ganglia of the trunk and pass through grey rami communicantes to the VPR of all the spinal nerves (figs. 19.4 and 20.50). Thereafter they are distributed through both the ventral and dorsal primary rami of these nerves to blood vessels, sweat glands and hair follicles.

Thus the VPR of T1–L3 are associated with both the inflow and outflow of fibres from the sympathetic trunk, through the white and grey rami communicantes respectively. All other spinal nerves are associated only with the outflow through grey rami.

The somatic arteries

The **dorsal aorta** extends along the posterior wall of the trunk from T4–L4 where it divides into two **common iliac arteries** (fig. 20.10). Each common iliac artery subsequently divides into an **external iliac artery** to the lower limb and an **internal iliac artery** to the pelvic cavity and

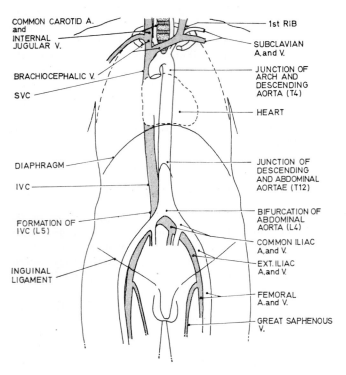

FIG. 20.10. The large arteries and veins of the trunk.

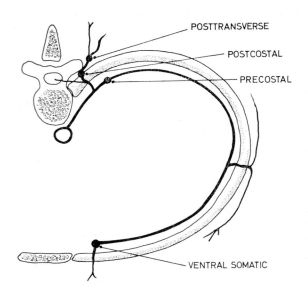

FIG. 20.11. The sites of longitudinal anastomoses between the somatic arteries.

perineum. The aorta lies more or less on the anterior aspect of the vertebral column and anterior to the sympathetic trunk and the spinal nerves. From the posterolateral aspects of the aorta, somatic branches arise at regular intervals (fig. 20.9), and passing laterally and backwards behind the sympathetic trunk, become associated with the spinal nerves from T3–L4 just lateral to the intervertebral foramina. Here they divide into anterior and posterior branches which thereafter run in close association with the ventral and dorsal primary rami of the corresponding nerve. Each posterior branch gives off, in addition, a spinal branch which traverses the corresponding intervertebral foramen and takes part in the formation of the arterial plexuses which lie in the extradural space and on the surface of the spinal cord.

In early development the branches of these somatic arteries are linked by a series of longitudinal anastomotic channels (fig. 20.11). The anterior branches are joined by the precostal anastomosis in front of the posterior ends of the ribs or costal elements, and by the ventral somatic anastomosis in the anterior part of the body wall. The dorsal branches are joined by the postcostal and posttransverse anastomoses which lie in front of and behind the transverse processes respectively.

Beyond the region T3–L4 the somatic arteries are not derived directly from the dorsal aorta. Above, the somatic arteries are derived from subclavian arteries (fig. 20.10) which are arterial trunks to the upper limbs. Below they arise from the external and internal iliac arteries.

The somatic veins

In the region T3–L4 the somatic veins follow courses similar to those of the corresponding arteries. Like the arteries they are linked together in the anterior part of the body wall by a ventral somatic anastomotic channel, and each receives a spinal tributary, through the intervertebral foramen from the venous plexuses in in the spinal extradural space.

The veins end in a series of longitudinal venous channels which lie lateral to the vertebral bodies (figs. 20.9 and 20.27) and drain upwards to end in the **superior vena cava** (SVC) (fig. 20.10) in the upper part of the thoracic cavity. Collectively these longitudinal channels constitute the **azygos system of veins**.

Above T3 the somatic veins drain into the **brachiocephalic veins** (fig. 20.10) which receive the venous blood from the upper limbs and are tributaries of the **superior vena cava**. Below L4 they drain predominantly into the external and internal iliac veins which are tributaries of the **inferior vena cava** (IVC) (fig. 20.10).

The body wall as a whole

Between T3 and the middle lumbar region the arrangement of the nerves, arteries and veins of the body wall is strictly segmental. However, above and below this region the simple segmental arrangement is less evident, due to the demands of the upper and lower limbs.

THE SKELETON OF THE TRUNK

THE THORACIC SKELETON

The thoracic skeleton or cage surrounds and partially encloses the thoracic cavity. In the coronal plane its shape is parabolic (fig. 20.7), while in the transverse plane it is reniform, the anterior wall being convex and the posterior concave (fig. 20.33).

The anterior wall is comparatively short and is formed by the sternum (fig. 20.7). The longer posterior wall extends above and below the limits of the sternum and is composed of all the thoracic vertebrae (fig. 20.1). The incomplete lateral walls consist of the ribs and costal cartilages separated from one another by the intercostal spaces (fig. 20.7).

Below, the thoracic cavity is separated from the abdomen by the dome of the diaphragm. Above it is directly continuous with the tissues of the neck. The oblique plane of this continuity is surrounded by the first ribs and costal cartilages, the first thoracic vertebra and the upper border of the sternum, and is conveniently described as the **thoracic inlet** at the root of the neck (fig. 21.35).

The thoracic vertebrae

In this region of the vertebral column the intervertebral discs have the same depth anteriorly and posteriorly; but the vertebral bodies are slightly deeper behind than in front, and consequently, the column is concave forwards. The twelve thoracic vertebrae increase gradually in size from above down. The upper nine are all similar whereas the lower three are atypical in certain respects.

In a typical vertebra (figs. 20.2 and 20.3), the body is roughly cylindrical, the vertebral foramen is small and circular, and the spine is long and directed downwards and backwards. The facets on the superior articular processes are flat and face backwards, upwards and a little laterally, while the similar inferior articular facets face in the opposite directions. The transverse process is directed laterally and somewhat backwards. Each vertebra carries three small costal articular facets. Two of these lie on the posterolateral aspect of the body and abut against the upper and lower surfaces, while the third lies near the lateral end of the transverse process.

In the atypical thoracic vertebrae, the lower costal facets are absent on the bodies of T10, T11 and T12, and the upper costal facets are displaced backwards on to the pedicles; the costal facets are absent from the transverse processes of T11 and T12, and the inferior articular processes of T12 resemble the lumbar processes with which they articulate.

The sternum

This is a flat bone, in the anterior thoracic wall (fig. 20.7). In the adult it consists of three parts named, from above down, the **manubrium, body** and **xiphoid process**. The manubrium and body articulate at the secondary cartilaginous **manubriosternal joint**, and the body and xiphoid process at the similar **xiphisternal joint**.

The manubrium extends downwards and forwards, and its transverse diameter is greater above than below. Its upper border is marked by the wide **jugular (suprasternal) notch**, and on either side of this by a cartilaginous facet for articulation with the medial end of the clavicle. Its shorter lower border articulates with the body. The forward inclination of the body is less than that of the manubrium, and the two parts thus make a very obtuse angle open backwards. The slight ridge formed by this **sternal angle** can be readily felt through the skin and is an important landmark. The body increases in width from above down throughout its upper three-quarters and subsequently becomes narrower as far as its lower end. The shape of the xiphoid process varies considerably, but usually it is roughly triangular. The lateral borders of the manubrium, body and xiphoid process articulate in various ways with the costal cartilages of the upper seven ribs (p. 20.8).

The ribs

The twelve ribs are long curved bones. Each articulates posteriorly with the vertebral column and thereafter extends forwards and downwards round the chest wall before becoming continuous with a costal cartilage. The ribs become progressively longer from 1–7 and then shorter from 7–12.

The posterior end of each rib (fig. 20.8), is called the **head**, the adjacent 2 cm the **neck**, and the rest is described as the **shaft**. Neck and shaft are separated by the **tubercle** on the posterior aspect. Ribs 1, 11 and 12 exhibit features which are atypical of the series, whereas the others are very similar.

The head of a **typical rib** carries upper and lower articular facets separated by a horizontal non-articular zone. The lower facet on the rib head articulates with the upper costal facet on the numerically corresponding vertebral body, and the upper facet on the rib head with the lower costal facet on the vertebral body immediately above (fig. 20.8). This **costovertebral joint** is enclosed by an articular capsule and its synovial cavity is divided into two compartments by an intra-articular ligament which extends from the non-articular zone on the rib head to the adjacent intervertebral disc. The neck of a typical rib (figs. 20.2 and 20.8) extends laterally and backwards, anterior to the numerically corresponding transverse process. At its lateral end, a small cartilage facet on the lower medial part of the tubercle articulates with the costal facet on the transverse process at the **costotransverse joint**. In the upper part of the series the costal facet lies on the anterior aspect of the transverse process and the plane of the costotransverse joint is concave forwards. On the other hand the costal facets associated with ribs 8, 9 and 10 lie on the upper surfaces of the transverse process and the plane of the joint is flat and nearly horizontal. Each costotransverse joint is enclosed by an articular capsule and is associated with a number of accessory ligaments. Two costotransverse ligaments join the neck and the tubercle of the rib to the corresponding transverse process on either side of the joint (fig. 20.2), and the **superior costotransverse ligament** is a broad sheet which extends from each rib neck to the transverse process immediately above it (fig. 20.8). The shaft of a typical rib has inner and outer surfaces, and upper and lower borders, and the lowest part of the inner surface is marked in its posterior two-thirds by the **costal groove** (fig. 20.8). From the tubercle the shaft first extends laterally, more or less in line with the neck, but it then turns, quite abruptly, into the curvature of the chest wall. This sharp bend is called the **angle** of the rib shaft, and its distance from the tubercle is proportional to the length of the whole rib.

The head of the **first rib**, carries one facet and the costovertebral joint which it forms with the upper costal facet on the first thoracic vertebral body has a single synovial cavity. The neck is not associated with a superior costotransverse ligament. The angle coincides with the tubercle and the shaft subsequently follows an acute and even curvature, downwards and forwards round the thoracic inlet (fig. 20.7). Its surfaces face upwards and downwards so that its borders are described as inner and outer. There is no costal groove on the lower surface, but the upper surface carries a number of features associated with structures in the neck and upper limb.

The heads of the **eleventh** and **twelfth ribs**, carry one facet, which articulates with the single costal facet on the body and pedicle of the corresponding vertebra. There are no tubercles and no costotransverse joints. Both ribs are short and the twelfth is usually confined to the posterior wall of the trunk.

The costal cartilages

The distal end of each rib shaft is fused to the corresponding costal cartilage which thereafter continues round the chest wall (fig. 20.7). These bars of hyaline cartilage vary in length in the same way as the ribs, increasing in length from the first to the seventh and decreasing from the seventh to the twelfth rib. The first costal cartilage is fused to the lateral angle of the manubrium of the sternum and thus forms a primary cartilaginous joint between that bone and the first rib. This is the only joint of this type which persists into adult life; all others lie between centres of ossification which fuse when growth ceases and they have consequently disappeared by early adult life. The second cartilage extends horizontally and

articulates by a synovial **sternocostal joint** with twin facets on the adjacent parts of the lateral margins of the manubrium and body of the sternum. The cavity of the joint is split into two compartments by an intra-articular ligament which is continuous with the manubriosternal joint. The cartilages from the third to the seventh extend upwards and medially, the upward obliquity increasing progressively from above down. The third to the sixth articulate with the lateral margin of the body of the sternum at synovial sternocostal joints. The seventh costal cartilage articulates with the body and xiphoid process. All the sternocostal joints tend to degenerate in old age, the costal cartilage becoming continuous with the sternum, either directly or through a zone of fibrous tissue. The eighth, ninth and tenth costal cartilages also turn upwards and medially, but, becoming progressively shorter from above down, they end, short of the sternum, by articulating with the costal cartilage immediately above at the synovial **interchondral joints**. The eleventh and twelfth cartilages are very short and pointed, and they end freely, without articulation, in the lateral part of the body wall.

MOVEMENTS AT THE JOINTS OF THE THORACIC SKELETON

Vertebral movement

Changes in the form of the vertebral column are the result of small displacements of adjacent vertebrae upon one another, and although individual displacements are small, in summation their effect may be considerable. Intervertebral movement is essentially an elastic distortion of the intervertebral disc, controlled and limited by the intervertebral joints and intervertebral ligaments. Consequently the extent of movement is proportional to the moving force and when this force ceases the displaced bones recoil to their neutral relationship.

Although intervertebral movement can occur in any direction as at a synovial ball and socket joint, it is convenient to regard any particular movement as being a combination of certain cardinal movements. Thus flexion and extension describe angulations forwards and backwards by the vertebrae in the sagittal plane. Lateral flexion is angulation in either direction in the coronal plane, and rotation is a twisting of one vertebra on its neighbour about a vertical axis through the intervertebral disc.

In the thoracic region flexion, extension and lateral flexion are all somewhat limited in range by the presence of the rib cage. On the other hand rotation is comparatively free because the curvatures of the facets of the intervertebral joints form arcs of a circle which is concentric with the intervertebral disc.

The movements of the ribs and costal cartilages

In the upper seven or true ribs, the rib head lies higher than the anterior end of the corresponding costal cartilage, and the most lateral part of the rib shaft lies below the transverse plane which traverses these two points. Movements of these ribs on the vertebral column may be regarded as occurring simultaneously about two axes of rotation. The transverse axis extends from the costovertebral joint to the centre of curvature of the facets of the costotransverse joint; because of the obliquity of the rib, movement upwards round this axis displaces the costal cartilage and the related part of the sternum upwards and forwards (fig. 20.12a). The anteroposterior axis traverses the costotransverse and sternocostal joints; elevation of the rib round this axis causes the lateral part of the shaft to move upwards and laterally (the so-called bucket handle movement) while the rib head is displaced very slightly downwards (fig. 20.12b).

(b)

(a)

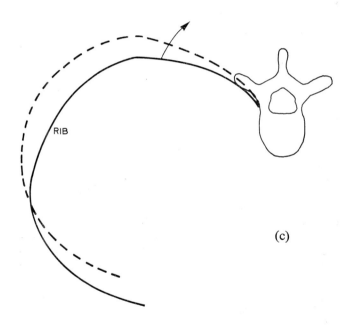

(c)

FIG. 20.12. Movements of the ribs (a) lateral view showing increase of anteroposterior thoracic diameter by true ribs (1–7) during inspiration; (b) anterior view showing increase of transverse thoracic diameter by true ribs during inspiration; (c) increase of transverse thoracic diameter by lower ribs during inspiration.

Rotation of the eighth, ninth and tenth ribs at the costotransverse joint around either a transverse or an anteroposterior axis is largely prevented by the plane form and almost horizontal disposition of the articular surfaces. On the other hand, the costal cartilage is free to move laterally because of its lack of attachment to the sternum. Consequently, movement is restricted to rotation of the rib about a vertical axis traversing the costovertebral joint, such that the rib tubercle slides backwards or forwards on the upper surface of the transverse process and the costal cartilage is carried laterally or medially (fig. 20.12c). In simultaneous lateral movement of the three ribs, the relationship of their anterior ends at the interchondral joints remains unchanged, but the eighth costal cartilage tends to move on to a more lateral and therefore a lower part of the seventh (fig. 20.7). The downward

displacement of the eighth rib, which would thus be expected, does not occur, for in practice, lateral displacement of the eighth, ninth and tenth ribs is always associated with upward displacement of the upper seven.

The eleventh and twelfth ribs articulate with the rest of the thoracic skeleton at costovertebral joints only, and are consequently capable of small movements in any direction. This mobility is of little value.

Sternal movements

Movements between the segments of the sternum at the manubriosternal and xiphisternal joints are restricted to small angulations of one segment or another in the sagittal plane, and are always secondary to movements of the upper seven ribs.

Respiratory movements of the thoracic skeleton

Inspiration depends on an increase in the volume of the thoracic cavity by increase of one or more of its three diameters, vertical, anteroposterior and transverse. As a result air is sucked into the lungs and, incidentally, venous blood and lymph are drawn into the thoracic vessels from surrounding parts.

The vertical diameter is increased in small part by extension of the normally concave thoracic vertebral column, but predominantly by contraction of the diaphragm which is displaced towards the abdominal cavity. The efficiency of diaphragmatic contraction is dependent both on the stability of the ribs from which it arises and on the accommodation of the abdominal viscera which are displaced by its downward movement. Stability of the diaphragmatic origin is achieved by fixation of the eleventh and twelfth ribs by the posterior abdominal muscles and by the natural restriction of movement, in the eighth, ninth and tenth ribs to a transverse plane (see above). Accommodation for the displaced abdominal viscera is found in part by relaxation of the anterior abdominal muscles, and in part by an increase in the transverse diameter of the upper part of the abdominal cavity resulting from a passive lateral displacement of the eighth, ninth and tenth ribs by the pressure of the displaced abdominal viscera. This passive lateral displacement of the lower ribs increases the transverse diameter of the lower thorax as well as that of the upper abdomen.

It has just been noted that diaphragmatic contraction results indirectly in an increase in the transverse diameter of the lower part of the thorax. The transverse and anteroposterior diameter of the rest of the thorax are increased by elevation of the upper seven ribs by muscles in the thoracic wall and neck. Each rib is moved simultaneously about its transverse and anteroposterior axes and the resulting forward displacement of the costal cartilages and sternum and the lateral displacement of the rib shafts increase the anteroposterior and transverse diameter respectively. It is evident that the magnitude of these increases is always proportional to the length of the rib concerned. It follows that the forward displacement of the body of the sternum is greater than that of the manubrium and that this disparity must be accommodated by a slight reduction of the sternal angle.

At birth the ribs are almost horizontal and do not achieve their adult obliquity until about the seventh year. Thus during infancy, and to a lesser degree in childhood, inspiration depends almost entirely on diaphragmatic movement.

Expiration, in quiet respiration, is produced largely by the recoil of the elastic lung tissue. The additional force required in forced expiration, as in blowing a trumpet, is derived from contraction of the anterior abdominal muscles.

THE ABDOMINAL AND PERINEAL SKELETON

The lumbar vertebrae

In the adult, the lumbar part of the vertebral column, composed of the five lumbar vertebrae and the corresponding intervertebral articulations, is convex forwards. This convexity increases from above down and is more pronounced in the female than the male. It is due largely to a disparity between the anterior and posterior dimensions of the intervertebral discs.

In this region the costal element is small and is incorporated into the definitive transverse process early in development; there are therefore no ribs and no costal facets on the vertebral bodies.

The lumbar vertebrae continue the progressive increase in size noted in the thoracic region. The bodies are wider in the coronal than in the sagittal plane, the vertebral foramina are triangular and larger than in the thoracic region, and the spines are rectangular and project horizontally backwards (figs. 20.13 and 20.14). The most characteristic feature is the orientation of the facets

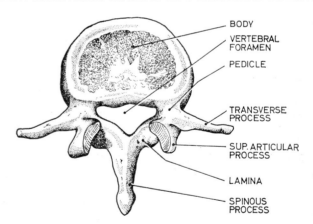

FIG. 20.13. Lumbar vertebra seen from above.

on the articular processes. The superior facets are concave and face medially and backwards, whereas the inferior are convex and face laterally and forwards. The upper four transverse processes are long, thin and spatulate, and their anterior surfaces are divided into medial and lateral halves by a vertical ridge. The fifth transverse process is conical and its base is continuous with the pedicle rather than with the junction between the pedicle and lamina.

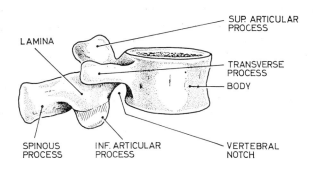

FIG. 20.14. Side view of lumbar vertebra.

The movements in the lumbar vertebral column are the same as those in the thoracic region but their individual extents are different. The range of flexion and extension is greater than in the thorax, partly because of the absence of the restricting influence of the ribs and sternum, and partly because the intervertebral discs are deeper and more easily deformed. Extension is greater than flexion; flexion reduces the resting curvature and usually ends when the column is straight. Lateral flexion is also greater in the lumbar than in the thoracic region for the same reasons. On the other hand rotation is very limited in the lumbar column, because the facets on the articular processes are radial rather than circumferential to the axis of rotation which passes vertically through the intervertebral discs.

The sacrum

The adult sacrum is formed by the fusion of five sacral vertebrae which diminish in size from above down. These vertebrae possess two important peculiarities; short but comparatively massive costal elements are fused to the transverse processes, pedicles and bodies (fig. 20.15a); and the vertebral foramina of the fourth and fifth vertebrae are incomplete posteriorly because of the absence of laminae and spines (figs. 20.15c and 20.17).

Fusion between the sacral vertebrae involves the whole of their adjacent surfaces except for that T-shaped zone on either side which is related to the corresponding spinal nerve and its ventral and dorsal primary rami (fig. 20.15b).

During fusion, the five vertebral foramina become continuous as the **sacral canal**, but the lower part of the posterior wall of this canal remains deficient at the **sacral hiatus**. From the sacral canal, four paired, T-shaped canals lead laterally through the regions originally occupied by the intervertebral foramina and subsequently open on to the pelvic and dorsal surfaces at the **pelvic** and **dorsal sacral foramina**. Lateral to these foramina the transverse and costal elements fuse completely to form the **lateral mass** (figs. 20.15b, 20.16 and 20.17).

The adult sacrum is triangular in form and presents a broad base above, a narrow blunt apex below, and pelvic, dorsal and lateral surfaces.

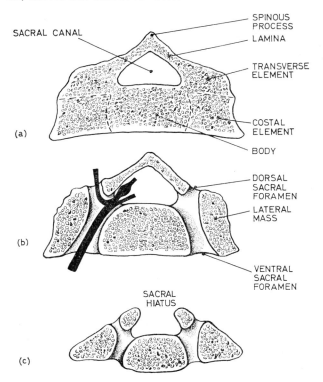

FIG. 20.15. Cross sections of sacrum: (a) through upper sacral segment, (b) between upper sacral segments, (c) between lower sacral segments.

On the **base** (figs. 20.16 and 20.17), the upper end of the sacral canal is surrounded by the upper aspects of the body and vertebral arch of the first sacral vertebra which resemble in form and attachments the corresponding surface of a lumbar vertebra. The body is surmounted by the lumbosacral intervertebral disc, the pedicles form the lower margins of the fifth lumbar intervertebral foramina and the superior articular processes, the laminae and the spine are joined to the corresponding features on the fifth lumbar vertebrae by intervertebral joints, ligamenta flava and an interspinous ligament. The smooth upper surface of the lateral mass extends laterally from the body, pedicle and articular process and is named the **ala**.

The **apex of the sacrum** is formed by the inferior surface of the fifth sacral vertebral body and is attached to the coccyx below by the sacrococcygeal intervertebral disc (fig. 20.16).

The **pelvic surface of the sacrum** (fig. 20.16) is smooth, concave in the sagittal plane and faces downwards and forwards towards the pelvic cavity (fig. 20.39). It exhibits two rows of four pelvic foramina, and each pair of foramina is joined across the midline by a ridge which

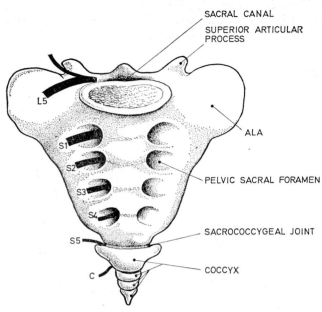

FIG. 20.16. Upper and pelvic surfaces of sacrum and coccyx. Ventral rami of the related nerves are shown in black.

demarcates two fused vertebral bodies. The upper border of the first sacral vertebral body forms a prominent ridge which lies just below the lumbosacral intervertebral disc and is named the **sacral promontory.**

The **dorsal surface** (fig. 20.17) is rough, convex and faces upwards and backwards. It presents two rows of four dorsal foramina. The upper foramina are separated by

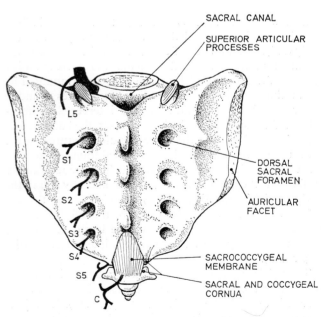

FIG. 20.17. Dorsal surface of sacrum and coccyx. The dorsal rami of the related nerves are shown in black.

a median row of tubercles which represent the spines of the fused vertebrae, while the lower foramina are separated by the sacral hiatus. The lowest parts of the lateral margins of the hiatus project downwards as two processes named the **sacral cornua.**

The **lateral surface** (fig. 20.18), is broad above where it is associated with the first three sacral vertebrae, but narrows to a mere border in its lower part. On the broad

FIG. 20.18. Side view of sacrum and coccyx.

upper part, the dorsal third is rough whereas the pelvic two-thirds carries a large cartilage facet for articulation with the ilium at the sacroiliac joint. The facet is ear-shaped, the concave border being directed dorsally, and it is consequently named the **auricular facet.**

The coccyx

The three or four vertebrae caudal to the sacrum are small and incomplete, and are more or less fused to form the coccyx (figs. 20.16 and 20.17). The lower two or three are mere nodules of bone, but the first consists of a body with small transverse processes and rudimentary superior articular processes, the coccygeal cornua.

The triangular coccyx is attached to the apex of the sacrum on which it is angulated forwards. The sacro-coccygeal joint is formed, anteriorly, by a rudimentary intervertebral disc and posteriorly by the sacrococcygeal membrane which extends from the dorsal surface of the coccyx and its cornua, to the margins of the sacral hiatus and the sacral cornua. The intervals between these two elements represent intervertebral foramina and are traversed by the fifth sacral nerves. The tiny coccygeal nerves pierce the lowest part of the sacrococcygeal membrane and turn laterally below the coccygeal cornua.

The osteoligamentous pelvis

This is formed by the two hip bones, the sacrum and coccyx, and the ligaments which join these bones to one another (fig. 20.22). Anteriorly the hip bones articulate in the median plane at the symphysis pubis, and posteriorly each hip bone articulates with the upper part of the lateral surface of the sacrum at a sacroiliac joint.

It is important to note that, despite its name, the osteoligamentous pelvis is not co-extensive with the pelvic cavity. It forms the side walls of both the pelvic cavity and the perineum and projects upwards into the posterolateral walls of the abdominal cavity proper.

THE HIP BONE

Each hip bone is ossified in cartilage from three primary centres of ossification (fig. 20.26) and the three regions of bone so formed are named the **ilium**, the **pubis** and the **ischium.** These remain separated by thin zones of cartilage until after puberty, and although thereafter they fuse to form the single hip bone, the corresponding regions of the adult bone retain their original names.

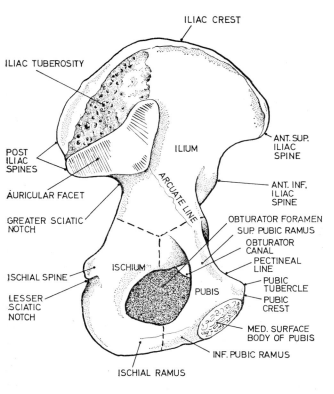

FIG. 20.19. Inner aspect of left hip bone.

The general features of the inner and outer aspects of the hip bone, and the extents of its three component parts are shown in figs. 20.19 and 20.20.

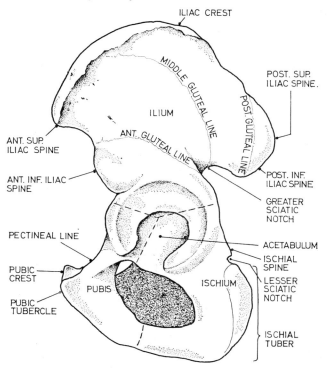

FIG. 20.20. Outer aspect of left hip bone.

The large oval aperture in the lower part of the bone is the **obturator foramen**. It is occupied by the fibrous **obturator membrane** except at its anterosuperior corner, where the pelvic cavity and the thigh communicate through the **obturator canal**.

The obturator foramen separates the pubis in front from the ischium behind. The body of the pubis lies in front of the foramen and articulates with its counterpart at the symphysis pubis. The **superior** and **inferior pubic rami** extend backwards from the body, above and below the foramen. Similarly, the comparatively thick body of the ischium lies behind the foramen and the single **ramus of the ischium** extends forwards below it. The lower boundary of the obturator foramen is thus formed by both the inferior pubic ramus and the ischial ramus, and so is called the **ischiopubic** or **conjoined ramus**.

The large cup shaped hollow on the outer surface of the hip bone is the **acetabulum** which articulates with the head of the femur at the hip joint. It is contributed to by all three components of the hip bone, the superior pubic ramus forming its anterior part, the body of the ischium its postero-inferior part, and the ilium its postero-superior part. The ilium forms the whole of the hip bone above the level of the acetabulum and its free upper margin is named the **iliac crest**.

Because the main function of the pelvis is the transmission of body weight, its orientations in sitting and in standing are important. In sitting, a coronal plane which passes through the anterior ends of the iliac crests traverses the acetabula. In standing, the upper part of the pelvis is farther forwards in relation to its lower part so that the anterior ends of the iliac crests and the upper border of the pubic symphysis all lie in the same coronal plane. It is in this position that the pelvis is described.

THE PUBIS

The **body of the pubis** has a rough medial surface which is involved in the formation of the pubic symphysis, an outer surface which faces downwards, forwards and laterally towards the thigh, and an inner surface which faces upwards and backwards. Its upper border, the **pubic crest,** ends laterally in the distinct prominence of the **pubic tubercle.** The **superior pubic ramus** extends from the body, backwards, upwards and laterally to the anterior part of the acetabulum. A sharp ridge, the **pectineal line,** runs laterally along its upper aspect from the pubic tubercle. The **inferior pubic ramus** passes backwards, downwards and laterally, and the interval between the diverging inferior pubic rami in the articulated pelvis is described as the **subpubic angle.** The inner surface of this ramus, in the male, is usually divided by a faint ridge into upper vertical and lower everted zones.

THE ISCHIUM

The notable features of the **body of the ischium** lie along its posterior aspect. Below, and just behind the acetabulum, the **spine of the ischium** projects backwards and medially as a spatulate process with inner and outer surfaces. At the lower end of the body the massive, oval prominence of the **ischial tuber** faces backwards. Its surface is divided by two ridges into upper lateral, upper medial, lower medial and lower lateral quadrants. The ischial spine and tuber are separated by the smoothly rounded **lesser sciatic notch.** The inner surface of the ramus of the ischium is divided, as on the inferior pubic ramus, into upper and lower parts.

THE ILIUM

The S-shaped **iliac crest** (fig. 20.21), which is the free upper border of the ilium, ends anteriorly at the **anterior superior iliac spine** and posteriorly at the **posterior superior iliac spine.** The anterior two-thirds is convex laterally while the posterior one-third is concave laterally and lies above and behind the dorsal surface of the sacrum.

The anterior border extends from the anterior superior iliac spine to the acetabulum and exhibits the blunt eminence of the **anterior inferior iliac spine** on its lower part. The posterior border runs from the posterior

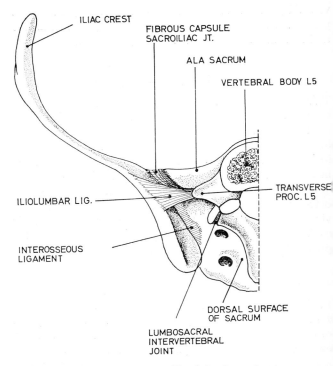

FIG. 20.21. Left sacroiliac joint from above.

superior iliac spine to the acetabulum. Its lower part exhibits the deep and extensive **greater sciatic notch** with the **posterior inferior iliac spine** at its posterior and upper limit.

The outer surface of the ilium is demarcated from the posterior part of the iliac crest by the rough **posterior gluteal line** which diverges upwards and forwards from the greater sciatic notch. On the inner surface of the crest the rough area of the **iliac tuberosity** is above and behind the ear-shaped auricular surface, which is the distal articular surface of the sacroiliac joints. In front of this facet the bone is smooth; it is crossed obliquely by the blunt ridge of the **arcuate line,** which runs from the auricular facet, downwards and forwards, to the pectineal line of the pubis.

THE PELVIC JOINTS

The **pubic symphysis** is a secondary cartilaginous joint which lies in the median plane between the medial surfaces of the bodies of the pubic bones. Thin plates of hyaline cartilage cover the rough bone surfaces and are joined by a dense zone of fibrocartilage. The peripheral fibres of this zone extend directly on to the neighbouring aspects of the pubis while the central part of the zone frequently degenerates in middle life to form a cavity.

The **sacroiliac joint** is a synovial joint between the auricular surfaces on the ilium and the upper two or three segments of the sacrum. Anterior to the joint is the upper part of the pelvic cavity while below it is the greater sciatic notch. Behind and above the joint the iliac crest and tuberosity overlap the dorsal surface of the sacrum, and the two bones are separated by a narrow deep crevice.

The plane of the joint is more or less vertical and extends backwards and medially at a small angle to the sagittal plane. In general, the articular surfaces are plane, but in detail they are covered by small reciprocal depressions and elevations. After middle age fibrous bands frequently join the articular surfaces to one another.

The joint cavity is surrounded and enclosed by a fibrous capsule which is attached to the adjoining surfaces of the ilium and the sacrum. In front and below, the capsule is thin, but behind it consists of an extremely thick mass of short fibres. These extend between the iliac tuberosity and the closely adjacent dorsal surface of the sacrum and are often described as the **interosseous ligament** (fig. 20.21).

The joint is additionally strengthened by four accessory ligaments. The **iliolumbar** and **lumbosacral ligaments** (fig. 20.21) have a common medial attachment to the conical transverse process of the fifth lumbar vertebra. The former extends laterally to the most anterior part of the iliac tuberosity whereas the latter turns downwards to blend with the fibrous capsule. The **sacrotuberous**

ligament (fig. 20.22) arises from the greater part of the dorsal surfaces of the sacrum and coccyx and from the posterior border of the ilium above the greater sciatic notch. The fibres extend downwards and laterally, converging rapidly as they go, and are attached to the medial edge of the ischial tuber. The **sacrospinous ligament** (fig. 20.22) is triangular. It has a broad attachment to the lateral aspects of the lower part of the sacrum and the coccyx, and extends laterally and forwards across the inner aspect of the sacrotuberous ligament to the spine of the ischium.

THE FORM AND FUNCTIONS OF THE VERTEBRAL COLUMN AS A WHOLE

Up to the time of birth and for some time afterwards, the shape of the vertebral column conforms to the wall of the uterine cavity and is uniformly concave forwards (fig. 20.23a). This **primary curvature** persists into adult life in the thoracic and sacrococcygeal regions. On the other hand the cervical curvature is obliterated and then replaced by an anterior convexity when the child begins to hold up its head, and a similar reversal occurs in the lumbar region when walking begins during the second year (fig. 20.23b). The formation of these **secondary curvatures** is largely the result of the development of a disparity between the anterior and posterior dimensions of the intervertebral discs. The cervical and lumbar convexities merge smoothly with the thoracic concavity, but the lumbar and sacral regions join at the abrupt

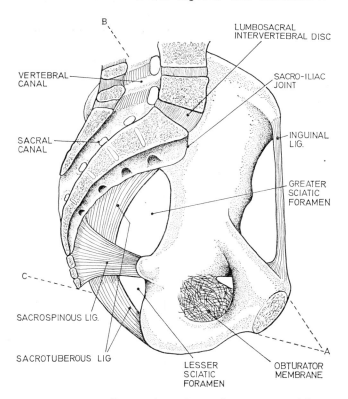

FIG. 20.22. Median section of osteoligamentous pelvis. Refer to fig. 20.19. AB and AC indicate planes of pelvic inlet and outlet in the erect posture. Details of the vertebral canal are given in fig. 20.5.

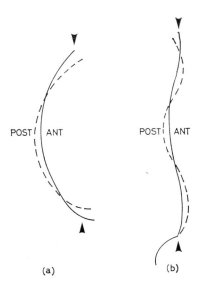

FIG. 20.23. The sagittal curvatures of the vertebral column: (a) in the infant, (b) in the adult. The interrupted lines indicate the changes in the curvatures produced by longitudinal forces.

lumbosacral angle. This is of the order of 140–150° and hence the lumbosacral intervertebral disc is wedge shaped.

The vertebral column affords protection to the spinal cord, permits movement between adjacent parts of the trunk and gives attachment to numerous muscles. Its main function, however, is to support the weight of the greater part of the body and to transmit the weight across the sacroiliac joints to the hip bones. In conformity with this function the vertebral bodies increase progressively in size from the skull to the level of the sacroiliac joints and thereafter they decrease rapidly. Similarly, the trabeculae of the spongy bone within the vertebral bodies are predominantly vertical and are larger and more numerous on the concave side, i.e. the compression side, of the relevant curvature. The readily deformable nature of the intervertebral discs under compressive stress combined with their elasticity allows the efficient absorption of the strain energy involved in sudden loading of the column. This strain energy is absorbed also by another mechanism. Any long column tends to bend under axial compression. General experience, from a superficial understanding of springs to the knowledge that it is advisable to land, after a jump, with bent rather than straight knees, tells us that strain energy is more efficiently absorbed in bending than in compression. It has already been noted that all intervertebral movement depends on distortion of intervertebral discs and is resisted elastically. Thus the strain energy of sudden loading can be absorbed by bending the vertebral column as well as by compression of the intervertebral discs. However, if the vertebral column were straight or uniformly curved, bending would distort the erect posture and the orientation of the head. The alternation of convex and concave regions through the length of the column allows bending under axial compression without disturbance of the erect posture (fig. 20.23b).

THE OSTEOLIGAMENTOUS PELVIS AS A WHOLE

It has been noted already that the osteoligamentous pelvis is not co-extensive with the pelvic cavity, but forms part of the boundaries of the abdominal cavity proper and the perineum. The plane of continuity between the abdominal and pelvic cavities, which is called the **pelvic inlet**, extends upwards and backwards at an angle of about 50° to the horizontal (fig. 20.22). It is surrounded by a circular bony margin which is known as the **pelvic brim**, and consists of the sacral promontory, the alae of the sacrum, the arcuate lines, the pectineal lines, the pubic tubercles and crests, and the upper border of the pubic symphysis, in broad continuity with one another. The part of the osteoligamentous pelvis which lies above the pelvic

brim is associated with the abdominal cavity proper and is consequently described as the **false pelvis**, while the part which lies below the brim is associated with the pelvic cavity and the perineum and is described as the **true pelvis**. Thus the pelvic inlet is the entrance to the pelvic cavity from the abdominal cavity proper and is also the entrance into the true pelvis from the false pelvis.

The lower margin of the true pelvis (figs. 20.22 and 20.41) is diamond shaped and is formed by the inferior aspect of the pubic symphysis, the ischiopubic rami, the ischial tubers, the sacrotuberous ligaments and the coccyx. The **pelvic outlet** which is enclosed by this margin extends backwards and upwards at an angle of about 15° to the horizontal. Because the margin lies entirely in the perineum and indeed forms the boundaries of that region, the term pelvic outlet means the outlet from the true part of the osteoligamentous pelvis and not the outlet from the pelvic cavity. The two terms, pelvic inlet and pelvic outlet are important in obstetrical practice.

The cavity of the osteoligamentous true pelvis has three communications with neighbouring regions (fig. 20.22):

(1) the **obturator canal** leads into the medial part of the thigh.

(2) the aperture bounded by the greater sciatic notch, the spine of the ischium and the sacrotuberous and sacrospinous ligaments is named the **greater sciatic foramen**, and leads into the buttock.

(3) the aperture bounded by the ischial spine and tuber and the sacrospinous and sacrotuberous ligaments is named the **lesser sciatic foramen**; it too leads into the buttock.

THE OSTEOLIGAMENTOUS PELVIS IN THE FEMALE

The shape of the true osteoligamentous pelvis tends to differ in the female and male subject, but it is important to note that the differences may be small. In the female the distances between the paired arcuate lines, ischial spines and ischial tubers are all greater, the sacrum is wider and shorter, and the sub-pubic angle is larger, approximating to a right angle. Furthermore the anterior concavity of the sacrum is mainly at its lower part, and the lumbosacral angle is more acute.

These differences mean that the female true pelvis is wider both anteroposteriorly and transversely, and is more cylindrical in form than funnel shaped. The size and form of the female true pelvis can be assessed both radiographically and by vaginal examination, the more important diameters being:

(1) the distance from the back of the pubic symphysis to the sacral promontory, which is known as the obstetrical conjugate diameter and has an average value of about 11 cm,

(2) the transverse diameter of the inlet which has an average value of about 13·5 cm,

(3) the transverse distances between the ischial spines and the ischial tubers which have average values of 12·5 cm and 11·5 cm respectively.

The function of the osteoligamentous pelvis

Like other bones, those of the pelvis protect underlying structures and give attachment to muscles. The main purpose of these bones is to transmit body weight from the vertebral column, either to the acetabula and so to the lower limbs in standing, or to the ischial tubers in sitting. Accordingly the zones within the hip bone through which these stresses are transmitted, namely the arcuate line of the ilium and the body of the ischium, are thicker and stronger than the rest of the bone. The sacroiliac joint lies across both these lines of stress and also is a joint at which little purposeful movement is required. Consequently, like the fibrous joints of the skull and the small synovial joints in the middle part of the foot the sacroiliac joint is a shock absorber. By virtue of the elastic deformability of its cartilaginous and collagenous tissues it absorbs a large part of the strain energy involved in stress transmission. During late pregnancy, its ligaments become more easily deformed and allow some joint movement which increases the capacity of the true pelvis; in all other circumstances its movements are of little importance. The efficiency of the joint depends on its stability and its ability to resist displace-ments which body weight tends to produce. This is achieved by the interlocking form of its articular surfaces and by the size and disposition of its ligaments. In standing the tendency of body weight to drive the sacrum downwards in relation to the hip bones is restricted by the strong interosseous sacroiliac ligaments, while the tendency to rotate the sacrum so that its posterior part moves backwards and upwards is controlled by the sacrotuberous and sacrospinous ligaments (fig. 20.24a). At the same time the upward pressure of the femoral head on the acetabulum is resolved into one component acting along the arcuate line towards the vertebral column, and another which tends to separate the hip bones from one another (fig. 20.24b). Actual separation is prevented by tensile stress in the pubic bones and the pubic symphysis which thus constitute a tie bar between the two acetabula.

The posture of the trunk affects the tilt of the pelvis. The angle of the brim of the pelvis is usually 50°–60° to the horizontal, and is determined by the postural pull of the abdominal, spinal and thigh muscles on the pelvis. Abnormal forward tilting of the pelvis is compensated for by an increased lumbar curvature (**lordosis**). Similarly abnormal backward tilting is compensated by increasing the thoracic spinal curvature (**kyphosis**).

These abnormal postures are usually acquired during childhood and adolescence and frequently bring trouble in later life because of the excessive strain they throw on muscles and ligaments.

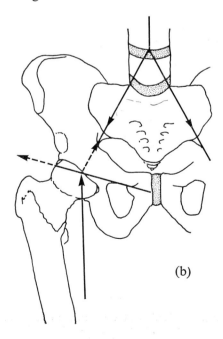

Fig. 20.24. (a) The effect of body weight at the sacroiliac joint. (b) Diagrammatic representation of the directions of the stresses operative during standing.

THE DEVELOPMENT OF THE SKELETON OF THE TRUNK

Each bone in the trunk is formed by ossification of a cartilage model.

THE VERTEBRAE

In all the **thoracic** and **lumbar vertebrae** the process of ossification is similar (fig. 20.25). Each half of the vertebral arch with the posterolateral corner of the vertebral body is ossified from a primary centre, while the rest of the body is ossified from a

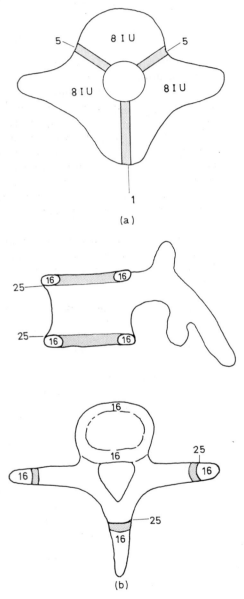

FIG. 20.25. Ossification of vertebrae, (a) at birth, (b) at about eighteen years. Numerals on the figures indicate age, in years, of appearance of ossification centre. Stippled areas are cartilaginous at birth. Leaders show time of fusion in years. I.U., age in weeks of intra-uterine life.

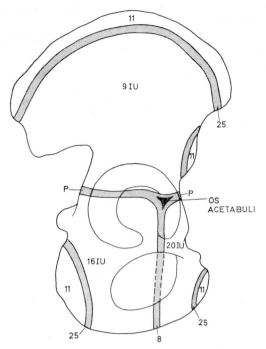

FIG. 20.26. Ossification of hip bone. Leaders show time of fusion in years. I.U., age in weeks of intra-uterine life, P, puberty.

separate primary centre, the **centrum**. These primary centres appear about the eighth week of intra-uterine life and at birth the ossified halves of the vertebral arch are still separated from one another and from the bone of the centrum by persistent zones of cartilage. The median zone is ossified during the first year and the two lateral zones during the fourth or fifth year. At this age cartilaginous epiphyses persist at the extremities of the transverse and spinous processes and on the upper and lower surfaces of the vertebral bodies. Secondary centres appear in these epiphyses about the sixteenth year. Those related to the upper and lower surfaces of the body are confined to anular peripheral zones. The secondary centres fuse with the primary at the twenty-fifth year. Thereafter the upper and lower surfaces of the vertebral body present a raised peripheral bony strip surrounding a thin central plate of persistent cartilage.

Each **sacral vertebra** is ossified from the same three primary centres as in the thoracolumbar region. In the upper three vertebrae, however, additional primary centres form in the anterior, or costal, region of the lateral mass. The primary centres appear rather later in the sacral than in the thoracic and lumbar vertebrae, between the twelfth and twenty-fourth intrauterine week.

By the ninth year the primary centres within each sacral vertebra have fused, but cartilaginous epiphyses persist on the upper and lower aspects of each body and on the lateral aspects of the lateral masses.

At puberty the hitherto separate sacral vertebrae fuse with one another except in the regions of the bodies. And at about the same time secondary centres of ossification appear in the upper and lower parts of the lateral mass epiphyses, while anular secondary centres form in the upper and lower epiphyses of the bodies. These secondary centres fuse with the primary part of the sacrum at between twenty and twenty-five years of age, and it is only then, with the final fusion of the vertebral bodies, that the consolidation of the sacrum becomes complete.

Each piece of the **coccyx** is ossified from a single primary centre. The centres appear, from above down, between the ages of one and fifteen years.

THE HIP BONES

Three primary centres of ossification appear, respectively, in the ilium at the eighth week, in the ischium at the third month and in the pubis at the fourth month of intra-uterine life.

At birth, the ilium, ischium and pubis are separated, across the region of the acetabulum, by a Y-shaped, or triradiate, strip of cartilage, while the ischium and pubis are separated across the ischiopubic ramus by a second cartilaginous zone (fig. 20.26). Moreover the whole length of the iliac crest, the anterior inferior iliac spine and the ischial tuber consist of cartilaginous epiphyses.

At eight years the ischiopubic ramus is consolidated by fusion of the ischial ramus with the inferior pubic ramus, and at puberty secondary centres form in the three epiphyses and as the os acetabuli, in the iliopubic part of the triradiate cartilage.

Obliteration of the triradiate cartilage occurs soon after puberty, but fusion of the other secondary centres with the primary part of the bone does not occur until between the twentieth and twenty-fifth years.

THE STERNUM

Early in development the sternum is represented by two separate and symmetrical cartilaginous **sternal plates** which fuse to form the cartilaginous sternum. One primary centre of ossification appears in the future manubrium in the 24th week and four centres, one above the other, appear in the body between then and birth. The centre for the xiphoid process may appear at any time after the third year of life. The four centres in the body fuse between puberty and the twenty-fifth year. The manubriosternal and xiphisternal joints persist between the body and the manubrial and xiphoid centres.

THE RIBS

The primary centre of ossification in each rib appears near the angle about the eighth intra-uterine week. The head, and the tubercles where they are present, are ossified from secondary centres which appear, much later than most centres of this kind, at or after the age of puberty. The primary and secondary centres fuse at about the twenty-fifth year.

Congenital abnormalities of the trunk skeleton

An appreciable proportion of the population exhibit variations in the number of vertebrae which have the characteristic features of the several regions of the vertebral column. Thus:

(1) a **cervical rib** may be associated with the seventh cervical vertebra or the first thoracic rib may be absent.

(2) a **lumbar rib** may be associated with the first lumbar vertebra or the twelfth thoracic rib may be absent.

(3) the fifth lumbar vertebra may be partially or completely fused to the sacrum (**sacralization of the fifth lumbar**) or the first piece of the sacrum may persist as a separate vertebra (**lumbarization of the first sacral**).

(4) the first piece of the coccyx may be incorporated into the sacrum.

In a smaller number of people, individual vertebrae are malformed. (1) One-half of a vertebra may fail to develop and the corresponding rib is usually absent. (2) In spina bifida, the two halves of the vertebral arch fail to fuse. Abnormalities of the sternum can usually be traced to incomplete fusion of the paired cartilaginous sternal plates. Therefore they tend to occur in the lower part of the sternum and take the form either of a central foramen in the body or of a complete division of the lower part of the body or the xiphoid into bilateral halves.

THE MUSCLES AND FASCIA OF THE TRUNK

These muscles fall naturally into three groups, first, those which are attached solely to the trunk skeleton, secondly those which arise from the trunk skeleton but are inserted into the bones of the lower limb and thirdly, several large superficial muscles which arise from the trunk skeleton and are inserted into the shoulder girdle and the humerus. In this chapter the first group and one member of the second (iliopsoas) are considered. These are conveniently divided, both functionally and topographically, into the pre- and postvertebral muscles, the diaphragm, and the anterolateral muscles of the thorax and abdomen. The muscles of the pelvis and perineum form a rather separate functional group and are considered on p. 20.29.

The postvertebral muscles of the trunk (sacrospinalis)

This group forms a massive band of muscle, which, because it extends from the bony pelvis to the cervical region of the vertebral column, is conveniently described collectively as **sacrospinalis**. The group lies in a groove bounded medially by the vertebral spines and laminae and their associated ligaments, and in front by the transverse processes and by the ribs between the tubercles and angles (fig. 20.28). All the components of sacrospinalis share a common nerve supply from the dorsal primary rami of the spinal nerves.

The **superficial fibres of sacrospinalis** are predominantly vertical and comparatively long so that they extend over several vertebrae. They arise from the greater part of the dorsal surface of the sacrum from the adjacent inner slope of the dorsal part of the iliac crest (p. 20.14), and from the lumbar and lower thoracic spines. Passing upwards they are attached, successively, to the spines of the thoracic vertebrae, the transverse processes of the lumbar and thoracic vertebrae, and the outer aspects of the ribs between the tubercles and angles.

The **deep fibres of sacrospinalis** are short and oblique, extending, from below, upwards and medially over one or two vertebrae. They arise from the posterior aspects of the lumbar and thoracic transverse processes and are inserted into the spines and laminae of higher vertebrae.

The prevertebral muscles of the trunk

Unlike the postvertebral group, these muscles are restricted to certain regions of the vertebral column. **Longus colli (cervicis)** lies in the cervical and upper thoracic regions, **iliopsoas** and **quadratus lumborum** are associated with the lumbar region.

Longus colli may be divided conveniently into three sets of fibres. The vertical set extend along the anterior aspects of the cervical and upper thoracic vertebral bodies; the superior oblique set extend, from the upper cervical transverse processes, upwards and medially to blend with the vertical fibres; and the inferior oblique set arise from the transverse processes of the lower cervical vertebrae except the seventh, and extend downwards

and medially to join the vertical fibres. In the trunk itself, the vertical and inferior oblique fibres of longus colli extend downwards over the anterior aspects of the vertebral bodies as far as the fourth thoracic level (fig. 20.45).

Iliopsoas arises in the lumbar region as separate psoas and iliacus heads. The large, fusiform **psoas head** has multiple origins (1) from the medial halves of the anterior aspects of the upper four lumbar transverse processes (fig. 20.28), (2) from the lateral aspects of the upper four lumbar intervertebral discs and from the adjacent regions of the vertebral bodies (i.e. the highest and lowest fibres come from the twelfth thoracic and fifth lumbar bodies respectively) and (3) from four fibrous arches

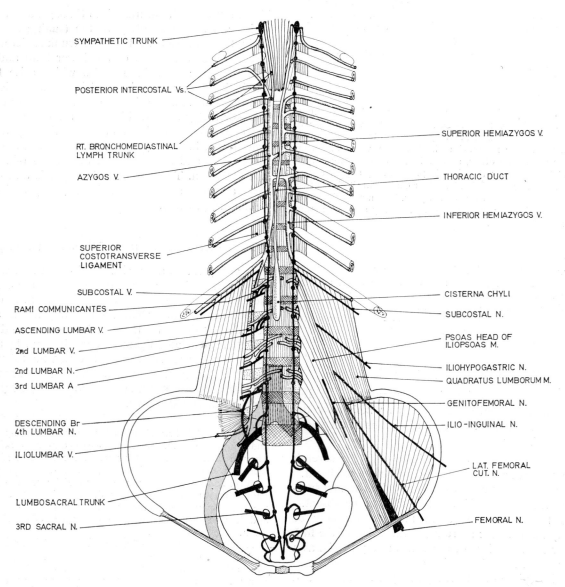

FIG. 20.27. The posterior walls of the thoracic, abdominal and pelvic cavities.

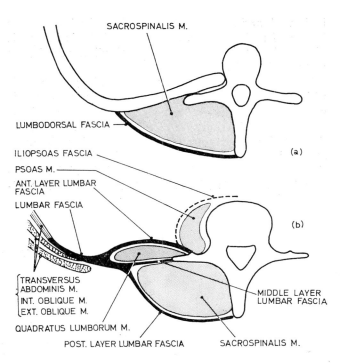

SACROSPINALIS M.

LUMBODORSAL FASCIA

ILIOPSOAS FASCIA

PSOAS M.

ANT. LAYER LUMBAR FASCIA

LUMBAR FASCIA

(a)

(b)

TRANSVERSUS ABDOMINIS M.
INT. OBLIQUE M.
EXT. OBLIQUE M.

QUADRATUS LUMBORUM M.

POST. LAYER LUMBAR FASCIA

MIDDLE LAYER LUMBAR FASCIA

SACROSPINALIS M.

FIG. 20.28. The lumbodorsal fascia (a) in thoracic region, (b) in lumbar region.

which extend across the concave anterolateral aspects of the upper four lumbar vertebral bodies (fig. 20.27).

The muscle passes downwards and laterally along the lateral aspects of the lumbar vertebral bodies, along the arcuate line of the ilium, and then across the superior pubic ramus, lateral to the pectineal line. Thereafter it passes beneath the inguinal ligament (p. 20.23) and enters the thigh (figs. 20.27 and 20.39).

Because of the discontinuous origin of the muscle, four separate spaces exist between the fibrous arches and the psoas muscle fibres on the one hand, and the upper four lumbar vertebral bodies on the other. These spaces form important neurovascular pathways from the prevertebral region, in front, to the intervertebral foramina behind (figs. 20.27 and 20.28).

The fan-shaped **iliacus head** arises from the inner surface of the ilium above the arcuate line. The fibres extend downwards and, converging towards the lateral aspect of the psoas head, pass with psoas beneath the inguinal ligament and into the thigh (figs. 20.27 and 20.39).

In the upper part of the thigh the two heads fuse to form the common tendon of iliopsoas which is inserted into the lesser trochanter of the femur (p. 23.2).

Quadratus lumborum (figs. 20.27 and 20.28) is attached below to the iliolumbar ligament and the adjacent part of the iliac crest. Extending upwards, lateral to psoas and in the plane of the lumbar transverse processes, it becomes attached to the lateral halves of the anterior

aspects of the upper four lumbar transverse processes and to the medial half of the lower border of the twelfth rib.

The deep fascia of the vertebral region

The **lumbodorsal fascia** is a collective term describing a series of interconnected fascial layers which are intimately associated with the vertebral muscles (fig. 20.28).

In the thoracic region, a single layer covers the posterior aspect of the sacrospinalis and extends from the thoracic spines medially to the angles of the ribs laterally.

In the lumbar region three layers of fascia are attached to the vertebral column and fuse into a single layer as they are traced laterally. The **posterior layer** extends from the lumbar spines across the posterior surface of sacrospinalis. Above it is continuous with the thoracic part of the lumbodorsal fascia while below it is attached to the sacrum and iliac crest. The **middle layer** arises from the tips of lumbar transverse processes and extends laterally between sacrospinalis and quadratus lumborum. Above it reaches the twelfth rib, and below, the iliac crest and iliolumbar ligament. The **anterior layer** is attached to the ridges on the anterior aspects of the lumbar transverse processes between the regions associated with psoas and quadratus lumborum, and passes laterally across the anterior surface of quadratus lumborum. Above it reaches the twelfth rib, and below, the iliac crest and iliolumbar ligament. Traced laterally the three layers fuse at the lateral border of quadratus lumborum. The single **lumbar fascia** so formed, is a thick collagenous sheet which extends laterally for two inches or so in the interval between the lateral half of the twelfth rib and the iliac crest.

The **iliopsoas fascia** is a comparatively thin layer which covers the free surface of both the iliacus and psoas heads of iliopsoas.

The **arcuate ligaments** are thickened and strengthened zones in the deep fascia of the vertebral region, which give origin to some of the muscle fibres of the diaphragm (fig. 20.34). The **medial arcuate ligament** is such a thick zone in the fascia covering the upper part of the psoas head of iliopsoas; it extends across that muscle between the body and the middle of the transverse process of either the first or the second lumbar vertebra. The **lateral arcuate ligament** is a thickening of the anterior layer of the lumbodorsal fascia over the upper part of quadratus lumborum; it extends from the middle of the first or second lumbar transverse process to the middle of the lower border of the twelfth rib.

The anterolateral muscles of the thorax

In the thoracic region the characteristic three concentric layers of the body wall are divided into intercostal segments by the ribs and costal cartilages. Each layer consist in part of muscle and in part of collagenous tissue, and the inner and middle layers are separated by a neurovascular plane.

In each intercostal space (fig. 20.29), the **outer layer** is formed by the fibrous **external intercostal membrane** which extends from the sternum to the costochondral junctions, by the **external intercostal muscle** from the costochondral junctions to the rib tubercles, and thereafter by the **superior costotransverse ligament**. Each external intercostal muscle is attached to the adjacent borders of two ribs and its fibres run downwards, and at the same time forwards round the chest wall.

body wall, and the neurovascular plane lies between the inner and middle layers. Anteriorly this basic pattern is disturbed by the presence of a longitudinal muscle, the rectus abdominis.

The **rectus abdominis** (fig. 20.30) is a long flat muscle which is attached below by tendinous fibres to the pubic crest and the outer surface of the pubic symphysis. It extends through the length of the abdominal wall on to the anterior aspect of the thorax, and there becomes attached, from the lateral to the medial side, to the fifth, sixth and seventh costal cartilages and the xiphoid process. The muscle is wider above than below so that, al-

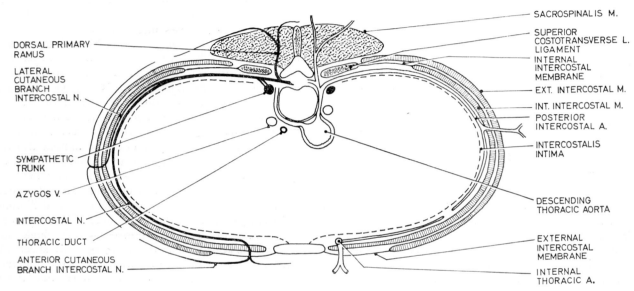

FIG. 20.29. Main relations of somatic arteries and nerves in an upper intercostal space.

In the **middle layer**, the **internal intercostal muscle** extends from the sternum to the rib angles, and the **internal intercostal membrane** from the rib angles to the rib tubercles. Thereafter this layer is also completed by the superior costotransverse ligament. The fibres of each internal intercostal muscle are attached to the costal groove of one rib, and extend downwards and at the same time backwards round the chest wall, to reach the upper margin of the rib immediately below (fig. 20.45). The constitution of the **inner layer** is very variable. It is to be regarded as a fibrous sheet which may or may not contain thin laminae of muscle fibres in its anterior, central and posterior parts. These muscle fibres are described collectively as the **intercostalis intima**.

The anterolateral muscles of the abdomen

The greater parts of the anterior and lateral regions of the abdominal wall consist of the three partly muscular and partly fibrous layers which are characteristic of the whole

though its medial border is vertical, its lateral border is gently curved and extends upwards and a little laterally to cross the costal margin over the ninth costal cartilage. In thin people the slight prominence of the lateral border creates a parallel groove on the skin surface, which is named the **linea semilunaris**. The muscle is usually incompletely divided into segments by three transverse **tendinous intersections**, which lie at the levels of the umbilicus and xiphoid process and midway between. Each intersection extends to the anterior surface of the muscle, but does not reach the posterior surface which is purely muscular.

The **external oblique muscle** (fig. 20.31), is the most superficial of the three concentric, flat muscles of the abdominal wall, and it corresponds both in plane and in fibre direction to the external intercostal muscle in the thorax. It arises by eight digitations from the outer surfaces of the lower eight ribs along a straight oblique line extending from the anterior extremity of the fifth rib to

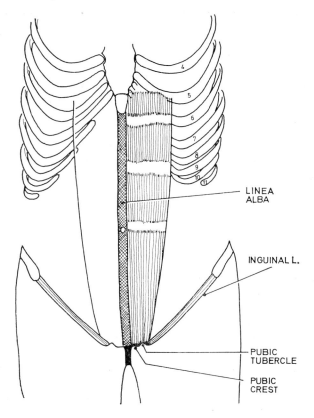

FIG. 20.30. The rectus abdominis muscle.

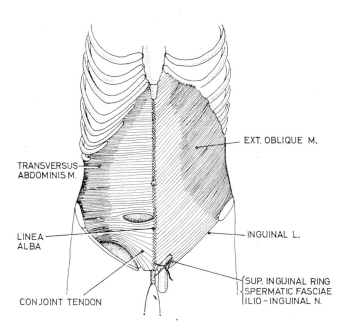

FIG. 20.31. The external oblique and transversus abdominis muscles.

the twelfth costal cartilage. The posterior part of the muscle passes downwards and forwards to the anterior third of the iliac crest, so that the posterior border is free and overlies the lumbodorsal fascia (fig. 20.28). The remaining fibres extend in a parallel direction into the anterior abdominal wall. Here they give way to an extensive aponeurosis along a line which runs from the anterior superior iliac spine towards the umbilicus, and thereafter passes vertically upwards to the ninth costal cartilage.

The **aponeurosis of external oblique** continues medially in front of the abdominal and thoracic parts of rectus abdominis. Reaching the midline its greater part achieves an insertion by becoming continuous with the aponeurosis of the opposite side. The linear zone in which the fibres of the two aponeuroses interdigitate runs from the xiphoid process to the symphysis pubis and is named the **linea alba**.

The part of the aponeurosis immediately below that which reaches the linea alba splits, about 2 cm above the pubis, into two diverging parts which are attached to the pubic symphysis and the pubic tubercle respectively. The triangular aperture, so formed, is larger in the male than the female, and is named the **superficial inguinal ring**. Its base is formed by the pubic crest and the diverging aponeurotic fibres which form its medial and lateral boundaries are the **crura of the ring**. The apex is directed upwards and laterally and the centre of the ring lies 1 cm above the pubic tubercle.

The lowest part of the aponeurosis is described as the **inguinal ligament** (figs. 20.31, 20.36 and 20.38). It is curled backwards so that it presents a grooved upper surface, a free posterior border, and an anterior border which is directly continuous with the rest of the aponeurosis. The ligament is attached at its lateral end to the anterior superior iliac spine, from which it extends medially and downwards. At its medial end all its anterior fibres are attached to the pubic tubercle, but its posterior fibres curve, first backwards and then backwards and laterally, to become attached to the pectineal line on the superior pubic ramus. The latter part is distinguished as the **lacunar ligament**.

The fascia lata of the thigh is fused to the under surface of the inguinal ligament (fig. 20.38), and consequently although the ligament is straight when the hip joint is flexed it is convex downwards when the joint is extended. The large space between the inguinal ligament and the hip bone is one of the major pathways through which structures may pass from the abdominal cavity to the thigh, the greater part of the space is occupied by the iliopsoas muscle (fig. 20.39).

The **internal oblique muscle** (fig. 20.32) lies deep to the external oblique. It is homologous with the internal intercostal muscle in the thorax and its fibres in general follow a similar direction, from behind, upwards and forwards, round the body wall. It arises continuously from (1) the lateral two-thirds of the grooved upper surface of the inguinal ligament (fig. 20.37), (2) the anterior part of the iliac crest, and (3) the outer surface of the lumbar fascia between the iliac crest and the twelfth rib (fig. 20.28). The uppermost muscle fibres are short and are inserted into the lower three costal cartilages, becoming contiguous with the anterior parts of the internal intercostal muscles of the tenth and eleventh intercostal spaces (fig. 20.32). The remaining fibres join a broad aponeurosis along a line which runs downwards from the tenth

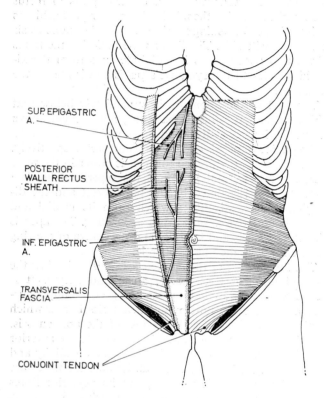

SUP EPIGASTRIC A.

POSTERIOR WALL RECTUS SHEATH

INF. EPIGASTRIC A.

TRANSVERSALIS FASCIA

CONJOINT TENDON

FIG. 20.32. The internal oblique muscles.

costal cartilage and gradually approaches the lateral border of rectus abdominis. This aponeurosis is described below.

The **transversus abdominis muscle** (fig. 20.31) lies deep to the internal oblique, but although it thus corresponds in position to the intercostalis intima in the thorax, its fibres are horizontal. The muscle fibres arise mainly continuously from (1) the lateral one-third of the grooved upper surface of the inguinal ligament (fig. 20.36), (2) the anterior part of the iliac crest, (3) the lateral edge of the lumbar fascia (fig. 20.28), and (4) the costal cartilages of the lower six ribs. Those coming from the eighth, seventh and sixth arise deep to rectus abdominis (fig. 20.31). All these fibres join an aponeurosis along a line which ex-

tends from the xiphoid process towards the midpoint of the inguinal ligament. The line is slightly convex laterally and crosses the lateral border of rectus abdominis midway between the xiphoid process and the umbilicus.

The **aponeuroses of internal oblique and transversus abdominis** both extend towards the midline deep to that of external oblique, but their form and relationship to rectus abdominis vary at different levels.

(1) The aponeuroses derived from the lowest fibres of both muscles fuse to form the **conjoint tendon** (figs. 20.36 and 20.37). This curves medially and downwards, and, after passing behind the superficial inguinal ring and in front of rectus abdominis, is attached to the pubic crest and tubercle and the medial part of the pectineal line on the superior pubic ramus.

(2) From the conjoint tendon to a level midway between the umbilicus and the pubic symphyses, the two aponeuroses fuse and, after passing in front of rectus abdominis, blend with the linea alba (figs. 20.31, 20.32 and 20.35).

(3) Above this level the aponeurosis of transversus abdominis passes entirely behind rectus abdominis to reach the linea alba (figs. 20.31 and 20.35). On the other hand that of internal oblique splits at the lateral border of rectus abdominis into anterior and posterior layers which cross the corresponding aspects of rectus abdominis before fusing again in the linea alba (figs. 20.32 and 20.35). The anterior layer is closely associated with the aponeurosis of external oblique, and both extend on to the thoracic part of rectus abdominis to become attached to the ribs and costal cartilages around its margins. The posterior layer is similarly associated with the aponeurosis of transversus abdominis; the two layers are attached above to the sixth, seventh and eighth costal cartilages, while their free lower margin is named the **arcuate line.**

The diaphragm

This dome shaped muscle separates the thoracic from the abdominal cavity (fig. 20.1). When the muscle is seen from above (fig. 20.33), it is evident that, because of the considerable forward projection of the vertebral column, it consists of extensive right and left parts, which are separated by and lie slightly above the smaller central part. The lateral parts are named the **cupulae.**

The reniform origin of the muscle from the bones and fasciae of the body wall is obliquely placed, the anterior part lying at a considerably higher level than the posterior (fig. 20.1). The fibres are inserted into an aponeurotic **central tendon** which is crescentic and convex forwards (fig. 20.33). The highest part of the diaphragm is tendinous and consequently the anterior muscle fibres are much shorter than those lying posteriorly or laterally.

It is convenient to divide the origin into three parts. The **sternal origin** arises from the posterior aspect of the xiphoid process, and the **costal origin** from the

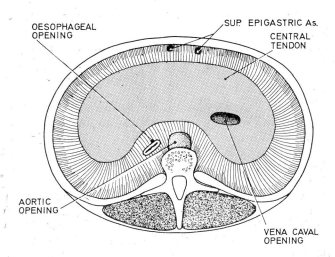

FIG. 20.33. The diaphragm from above.

deep aspects of the lower six ribs and costal cartilages. The **vertebral origin** (fig. 20.34), arises from the medial and lateral arcuate ligaments (p. 20.21) of both sides and by two separate, fusiform, tendinous bundles or **crura** from the anterior aspect of the lumbar vertebral column. The right crus arises from the upper three lumbar bodies and the intervening intervertebral discs, whereas the left arises from only the upper two. The initially separate crura pass upwards and forwards and eventually fuse in

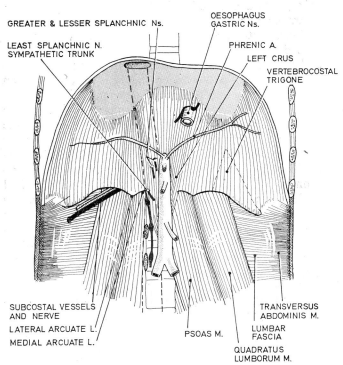

FIG. 20.34. The abdominal surface of the diaphragm and the posterior abdominal wall.

front of the lower border of the twelfth thoracic vertebral body. The junction is coated by tendinous fibres which are described as the **median arcuate ligament**.

In the mid-phase of quiet respiration, in the erect posture, the right cupula is a little higher than the left at the level of the eighth thoracic vertebra (fig. 20.34). In the supine position the resting level rises because of the absence of the gravitational pull of the abdominal viscera, and the thoracic volume is reduced. When the body is on one side the lower cupula rises to a higher level than the upper, but its excursion during respiration is increased.

The diaphragm presents a number of openings in its substance (figs. 20.33 and 20.34).

(1) The small **sternocostal gap** between the sternal and costal fibres transmits the superior epigastric vessels from the thorax to the abdomen.

(2) The large median **aortic opening** lies between the right and left crura. It is obliquely placed and bordered, above, at the twelfth thoracic level, by the median arcuate ligament, and below by the second lumbar vertebral body. It contains the aorta and thoracic duct.

(3) The **vertebrocostal trigone**, present in some people, is an interval between the vertebral and costal fibres of the diaphragm which varies considerably in size.

(4) The round **vena caval opening** lies within the central tendon in the right cupula of the diaphragm, about 3 cm to the right of the midline and at about the eighth thoracic level in quiet respiration.

(5) The **oesophageal opening** lies in the vertebral part of the muscular substance of the diaphragm, above and about 2 cm to the left of the aortic opening and at the level of the tenth thoracic vertebra. The vagus nerves accompany the oesophagus through this opening.

The fascial envelope of the abdominal cavity

The inside of the wall of the abdominal cavity is formed by the deep surface of several muscles and their aponeuroses, by bones and by the lumbar fascia. All these elements are lined by a continuous fascial envelope. Over the muscles it is a distinct layer, over the bones it joins the periosteum, while elsewhere it blends with the lumbar fascia and the muscle aponeuroses. Different parts of the envelope are given distinct names, often corresponding to the muscle to which the part is related. Thus over the diaphragm and the iliopsoas muscles it is named the **diaphragmatic fascia** and the **iliopsoas fascia** respectively; in relation to the transversus abdominis and rectus abdominis it is described as the **transversalis fascia**, and over the quadratus lumborum it is known as the anterior layer of the lumbodorsal fascia (p. 20.21.)

Nevertheless these layers of fascia are continuous with one another and form a single envelope lining the abdominal cavity. The envelope is separated internally from the viscera and peritoneum by a layer of fatty areolar tissue. This varies in thickness and adiposity in different people and is described collectively as the **extraperitoneal tissue**. Within the abdominal cavity it is a useful, though not an invariable rule, that the somatic nerves lie outside the fascial envelope whereas the large arteries and veins and the splanchnic nerves lie inside the fascial envelope within the extraperitoneal tissue.

Special regions of the abdominal wall

RECTUS SHEATH (fig. 20.35)

This is formed by the several tissues which encapsulate the rectus abdominis muscle and its character varies at different levels. The thoracic part of the rectus abdominis is covered anteriorly by the aponeurosis of external oblique and by the anterior layer of the aponeurosis of internal oblique. Posteriorly the muscle lies directly

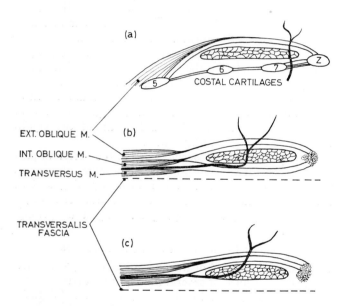

FIG. 20.35. The rectus sheath (a) above the costal margin, (b) between the costal margin and the arcuate line, (c) below the arcuate line.

against the sixth, seventh and eighth costal cartilages and the corresponding external intercostal membranes. From the costal margin to the arcuate line the anterior relations of the muscle remain the same, but it is now related posteriorly to the posterior layer of the internal oblique aponeurosis, to the aponeurosis and the uppermost muscle fibres of transversus abdominis (fig. 20.31), and to the tranversalis fascia. Below the arcuate line the aponeuroses of all three flat muscles pass in front of rectus abdominis, which consequently is related posteriorly to the transversalis fascia alone.

It is important to note that the tendinous intersections in the upper part of rectus abdominis (p. 20.22) are fused to the anterior wall of the rectus sheath whereas they have no attachment to the posterior wall.

INGUINAL CANAL

This is a pathway which traverses that part of the abdominal wall immediately above the inguinal ligament. It is convenient to recall certain features of this region. The inguinal ligament presents a grooved upper surface, the medial end of which is formed by the lacunar ligament. The aponeurosis of external oblique is continuous with the anterior margin of the inguinal ligament and exhibits the triangular superficial inguinal ring above the pubic crest. The lower muscle fibres of internal oblique and transversus abdominis arise from the lateral two-thirds and the lateral one-third respectively of the upper surface of the inguinal ligament, and, arching medially and then downwards, end in the conjoint tendon. This tendon passes behind the superficial inguinal ring and is inserted into the pubic crest and tubercle and into the medial part of the pectineal line.

In the male the transversalis fascia descends as a distinct sheet from the lower border of transversus abdominis and the conjoint tendon and becomes attached to the free posterior margin of the inguinal ligament and its lacunar part (figs. 20.36 and 20.38). At the mid-point between the pubic symphysis and anterior superior iliac spine, 1 cm above the inguinal ligament, below the fibres of transversus abdominis but deep to those of internal oblique, the transversalis fascia gives off a tubular process named the **internal spermatic fascia** (figs. 20.36, 20.37 and 20.38). The opening into this process from the abdominal cavity is the **deep inguinal ring**, which can be seen as a ring only from within. From the deep inguinal ring, the internal spermatic fascia runs an oblique course through the abdominal wall; it emerges through the superficial inguinal ring (fig. 20.31), and turns downwards into the scrotum. As it follows this course it acquires two additional, concentric fascial coverings. The first corresponds to the internal oblique layer of the abdominal wall and is named the **cremasteric fascia**. It is partly fibrous, but also contains the **cremaster muscle** whose fibres, after arising from the middle of the inguinal ligament, descend in the cremasteric fascia into the scrotum and thereafter ascend again to reach the pubic tubercle (fig. 20.37). The outermost layer, the **external spermatic fascia**, is entirely fibrous, and is continuous at its upper end with the margins of the superficial inguinal ring (fig. 20.31). These three fascial sheaths continue into the scrotum where they surround the testis and its serous covering, the tunica vaginalis (p. 37.21).

Several structures pass from the extraperitoneal tissues of the abdominal cavity through the deep inguinal ring, and pass within the three concentric fascial layers into the scrotum. These structures plus the surrounding layers of fascia constitute the **spermatic cord**. The oblique track through the abdominal wall which the spermatic cord follows between the deep and superficial inguinal rings is the **inguinal canal**. In the adult male it is about 10 cm long.

The anterior wall of the canal has three distinct parts. Laterally it is formed by both the muscular fibres of internal oblique and the aponeurosis of external oblique, its central part consists of the external oblique aponeurosis alone, and medially it is deficient at the superficial

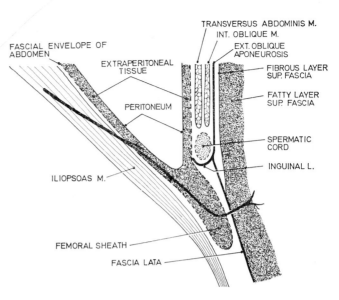

FIG. 20.38. Sagittal section showing course of genito-femoral nerve and its femoral branch in black.

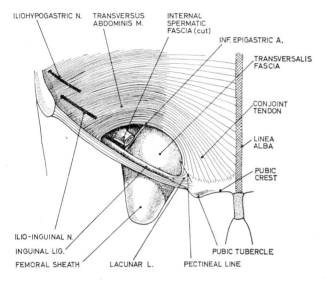

FIG. 20.36. The inguinal region after removal of the external and internal oblique muscles.

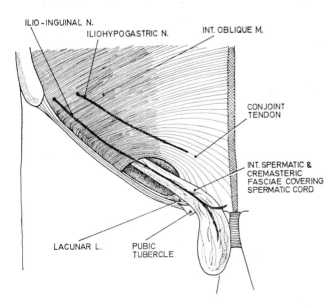

FIG. 20.37 The inguinal region after removal of the external oblique muscles. Refer to fig. 20.31.

inguinal ring. In contrast, in the posterior wall, the lateral part is deficient at the deep inguinal ring, the central part is formed by transversalis fascia and the medial part consists of this fascia and the conjoint tendon. Above the canal, the fibres of internal oblique and transversus abdominis arch from the anterior to the posterior wall. Below, the floor of the canal is formed by the grooved upper surface of the inguinal ligament including the lacunar ligament.

In the female the inguinal canal is narrower and both the deep and superficial inguinal rings are smaller. The canal is traversed by the **round ligament of the uterus**, which is invested by fascial layers corresponding to, but more tenuous than, those in the male.

The inguinal canal offers less resistance to intra-abdominal pressure than other parts of the anterior abdominal wall. However, the two inguinal rings which contribute to this weakness are each related to the strongest part of the opposite wall of the canal.

The inguinal canal is of considerable surgical importance because protrusions of the abdominal contents known as **inguinal herniae** occur through it.

FEMORAL SHEATH (figs. 20.38 and 23.40)

This is a conical protrusion of the fascial envelope of the abdominal cavity into the thigh. It traverses the interval bounded, in front, by the medial half of the inguinal ligament, medially, by the lacunar ligament, and behind, by the pectineal line on the superior pubic ramus. The cavity of the sheath is divided by two sagittal septa into lateral, intermediate and medial compartments, each of which is continuous at its upper end

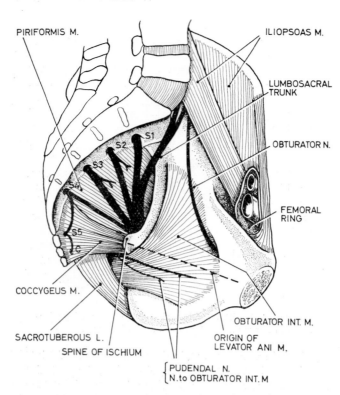

PIRIFORMIS M.

ILIOPSOAS M.

LUMBOSACRAL TRUNK

OBTURATOR N.

FEMORAL RING

OBTURATOR INT. M.

ORIGIN OF LEVATOR ANI M.

COCCYGEUS M.

SACROTUBEROUS L.

SPINE OF ISCHIUM

PUDENDAL N.
N. to OBTURATOR INT. M

S1 S2 S3 S4 S5 C

FIG. 20.39. Median section of osteoligamentous pelvis. Nerves in black. Refer to figs. 20.16, 20.19 and 20.22.

with the abdominal extraperitoneal tissue (fig. 20.39). The lateral and intermediate compartments are largely occupied by the femoral artery and vein respectively. On the other hand the medial compartment, which is named the **femoral canal,** contains only one or two deep inguinal lymph nodes and loose connective tissue. The upper end of the canal is limited laterally by the femoral vein and is described as the **femoral ring** (fig. 20.39). Protrusion of abdominal contents through this ring constitutes a **femoral hernia.**

The functions of the trunk muscles

Excluding the muscles of the pelvis and perineum, the muscles of the trunk have two functions. Firstly, they create pressure changes in the thoracic and abdominal cavities, including those involved in respiration. Secondly, they are concerned with displacements of one part of the trunk in relation to another, through movements of the vertebral column.

The mechanism by which the volume of the thoracic cavity is increased in inspiration is considered on p. 20.10. It can now be appreciated that this mechanism involves several factors.

(1) Contraction of the diaphragm displaces its central tendon downwards and increases the vertical diameter of the thorax. This displacement depends on the fixation of the lowest ribs by the quadratus lumborum, and on the displaced abdominal viscera being accommodated partly by the relaxation of the abdominal muscles, and also by the passive lateral displacement of the eighth, ninth and tenth ribs.

(2) The anteroposterior and transverse diameters of the thorax are increased by elevation of the upper seven ribs. In quiet respiration this is achieved by the intercostal muscles, particularly the external intercostals. In more vigorous inspiration these muscles are augmented by the scalene and sternomastoid muscles in the neck and even in exceptional circumstances, by muscles acting on the ribs from the fixed upper limbs.

(3) Increase in the vertical diameter of the thorax is effected through extension of the thoracic vertebral column by the sacrospinalis muscles.

Quiet expiration is a passive process which is achieved by the elastic recoil of the expanded lungs, the extended vertebral column and the distended abdominal wall. In forced expiration contraction of the oblique and transversus muscles increases intra-abdominal pressure and thereby passively raises the diaphragm. Contraction of the intercostal muscles prevents bulging of the intercostal spaces by the raised intrathoracic pressure.

Raising intra-abdominal pressure for defaecation and parturition involves the same mechanism as that of forced expiration, except that actual expiration of air is prevented by closure of the laryngeal lumen. Inspiration displaces the diaphragm downwards, closure of the larynx then fixes the diaphragm, and thereafter the intra-abdominal pressure is raised by contraction of the oblique and transversus muscles of the abdominal wall.

Ignoring the effects of gravity, it is evident that in movements of the spine:

(1) thoracolumbar extension is produced by the superficial fibres of sacrospinalis;

(2) rotation is by the deep fibres of sacrospinalis;

(3) flexion is caused by the muscles of the anterior abdominal wall, particularly rectus abdominis, and to a lesser extent by iliopsoas;

(4) lateral flexion is produced by all the muscles of one side of the trunk, particularly sacrospinalis, quadratus lumborum and the oblique and transversus muscles of the abdominal wall.

However, these actions are of little significance unless they are considered in relation to gravity.

In standing, because of the different curvatures of the lumbar and thoracic regions, the force of gravity tends to cause flexion of the thoracic column and extension of the lumbar (fig. 20.23). The maintenance of posture depends on the prevention of these displacements. It has been noted (p. 20.8) that flexion and extension both involve elastic deformation of the tissues of the intervertebral articulations. It will be appreciated, therefore, that gravitational displacement of the vertebral column in standing is prevented largely by the stresses in the deformed joint tissues, and to only a small degree by activity in the relevant muscle groups.

Deviations from the normal metastable standing position, e.g. flexion or lateral flexion, are, of course, initiated by the relevant muscle groups. Thereafter they are assisted by gravity, and are controlled and limited by a combination of elastic joint resistance and the antagonistic muscle group. Thus flexion from standing is initiated by the flexor muscles, but thereafter, gravitational flexion is controlled by both the activity of sacrospinalis and elastic joint resistance. As flexion proceeds, joint resistance increases and consequently muscular activity decreases, until, in full flexion, sacrospinalis is totally inactive. On the other hand, flexion of the vertebral column when lying supine is achieved by the flexor muscles acting against both the force of gravity and elastic joint resistance.

In walking, the trailing leg exerts an upward and forward force which maintains the body's forward momentum. But, because this force is unilateral, it also tilts the trunk towards the opposite i.e., the supported side, so that gravity tends to carry the vertebral column into lateral flexion. Some lateral flexion is necessary to carry the centre of gravity of the body, from its original central position, to a position over the single supporting foot. Once this relationship has been established, further lateral flexion must be prevented by the lateral flexor muscles of the opposite side. Thus throughout walking, each time the left foot leaves the ground, the trunk inclines towards the right and the sacrospinalis, the quadratus lumborum and the lateral abdominal muscles of the left side become active (p. 23.25).

The superficial fascia of the trunk

The trunk is completely invested by fatty superficial fascia which is directly continuous with that of the limbs and neck. Its thickness varies enormously, from a few millimetres to several centimetres, in different individuals. Over the lower part of the anterior abdominal wall, the deep part of the superficial fascia is a membranous layer. It contains a relatively high proportion of elastic fibres and acts as a natural corset over that part of the abdominal wall against which gravity exerts the greatest force. Below, the central part of this membranous layer extends down to envelop the scrotum and penis and eventually turns backwards into the perineum (p. 20.31, fig. 20.40). Each lateral part of the same layer crosses the inguinal ligament and becomes fused to the deep fascia of that part of the thigh, the fascia lata (fig. 20.38).

On the anterior aspect of the thoracic wall the mammary gland is contained within the superficial fascia.

THE PELVIC CAVITY AND THE PERINEUM

The muscles which lie within the true osteoligamentous pelvis are associated with the pelvic cavity and the perineum.

Obturator internus (fig. 20.39) arises from the deep aspect of the obturator membrane, the immediately surrounding bone, and that part of the ilium which lies below the arcuate line. Its fibres converge like a fan on the deep aspect of the lesser sciatic foramen and, becoming tendinous, turn at right angles through the foramen into the buttock. After being joined by two small additional heads, the **gemelli**, the tendon is inserted into the greater trochanter of the femur (p. 23.4). Functionally the muscle is concerned entirely with the lower limb.

Piriformis (fig. 20.40) arises from the pelvic surface of the second, third and fourth pieces of the sacrum, between and lateral to the corresponding sacral foramina. Its fibres pass laterally through the greater sciatic foramen into the buttock and, becoming tendinous, they are inserted into the greater trochanter of the femur. Like the obturator internus, the muscle acts on the lower limb.

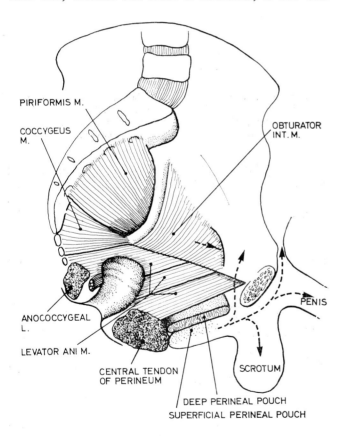

PIRIFORMIS M.

COCCYGEUS M.

OBTURATOR INT. M.

PENIS

ANOCOCCYGEAL L.

LEVATOR ANI M.

CENTRAL TENDON OF PERINEUM

SCROTUM

DEEP PERINEAL POUCH

SUPERFICIAL PERINEAL POUCH

FIG. 20.40. Median section of osteoligamentous pelvis showing division into pelvic cavity and perineum. Arrows show the obturator canal, and routes from superficial perineal pouch to pelvic cavity, scotum, penis and anterior abdominal wall. Refer to figs. 20.39 and 20.41.

The **pelvic diaphragm** is an incomplete muscular partition, convex downwards, which extends across the true osteoligamentous pelvis and divides it into the **pelvic cavity** above and the **perineum** below. It is deficient anteriorly and is traversed posteriorly by the anorectal junction.

The partition consists of two symmetrical pairs of muscles; the coccygeus muscles form its posterior part and the levator ani muscles form the remainder. Each **coccygeus muscle** (fig. 20.39) overlies the pelvic aspect of the corresponding sacrospinous ligament (p. 20.15). Laterally its apex is attached to the ischial spine while medially it is inserted into the lateral margins of the lower part of the sacrum and the upper part of the coccyx. Each **levator ani** muscle has a linear origin on the side wall of the true pelvis and its fibres extend downwards, medially and backwards to reach the median plane. The line of origin (fig. 20.39) reaches from the pelvic aspect of the body of the pubis to the pelvic aspect of the ischial spine, and between these bony origins the muscle arises from a dense layer of fascia which covers the inner surface of the obturator internus muscle. The posterior fibres run parallel to and in close proximity to the lower margin of coccygeus and are inserted into the lowest part of the coccyx (fig. 20.40). The fibres immediately in front of these, end in a median fibromuscular region named the **anococcygeal ligament** (figs. 20.40 and 20.41). It occupies the interval between the tip of the coccyx and the anorectal junction and extends downwards into continuity with peri-anal skin. The succeeding fibres of the levator ani become directly continuous with the corresponding fibres of the opposite side around the lateral and posterior aspects of the anorectal junction; although they are part of levator ani, they may be distinguished under the name of the **puborectalis muscle** (figs. 20.40 and 20.41). The most anterior fibres of levator ani are inserted into a second median fibromuscular region, the **central tendon of the perineum** (perineal body) which lies in front of the anorectal junction and is continuous with the perineal skin (figs. 20.40 and 20.41). Between the pubic symphysis and the central tendon of the perineum, and limited on either side by the most anterior fibres of the levator ani muscles, is a large gap in the pelvic diaphragm through which the pelvic cavity and perineum communicate (fig. 20.41).

The pelvic cavity

The pelvic cavity is shaped like a bowl, obliquely placed so that its axis is directed upwards and forwards. It is in broad continuity above with the abdominal cavity proper at the level of the brim of the pelvis. Its lateral wall is formed by bone and that part of obturator internus which lies between the pelvic brim and the origin of levator ani (fig. 20.40). Its dorsal wall faces predominantly downwards and consists of the sacrum, the coccyx, the

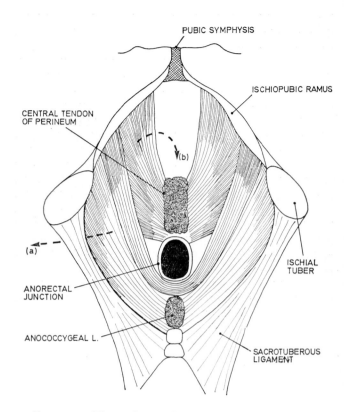

FIG. 20.41. The perineum from below showing the inferior surfaces of the levatores ani muscles. Arrows indicate exits from perineum (a) through lesser sciatic foramen into the buttock and (b) into the pelvic cavity.

sacroiliac joints and piriformis muscles. The short ventral wall faces upwards and backwards and is formed by the bodies of the pubic bones and the pubic symphysis. Below, the walls merge smoothly into the concave floor formed by the coccygeus and levator ani muscles.

Apart from its continuity with the abdominal cavity proper, the pelvic cavity communicates with several other adjacent regions. The obturator canal leads into the medial part of the thigh, the greater sciatic foramen into the buttock, and the median gap in the pelvic diaphragm into the perineum.

The bony and muscular walls of the pelvic cavity are lined by a layer of fascia which is continuous, through periosteum, with the fascial envelope of the abdominal cavity proper (p. 20.25). This fascia is separated from the pelvic peritoneum by extraperitoneal tissue. In the upper part of the pelvic cavity this layer is comparatively thin but below it forms an extensive zone in which the extraperitoneal parts of many of the pelvic viscera are embedded. Although different zones of this tissue vary in density and may be given distinct names, it is to be appreciated that they are only subdivisions of the continuous pelvic fascia.

The perineum

The perineum is the lowest part of the cavity of the true osteoligamentous pelvis, and lies between the pelvic diaphragm and the area of skin between the thighs. It differs from the other three divisions of the trunk in that it contains no serous cavity. It is occupied by connective tissue of various densities and is traversed by the terminal parts of the intestinal and genitourinary tracts.

In the horizontal plane it is diamond shaped (fig. 20.41) while in coronal section its depth is greater in its lateral than in its median part (figs. 20.43 and 20.44).

The roof of the perineum (fig. 20.41) is the convex under-surface of the pelvic diaphragm and is therefore deficient anteriorly between the pubic symphysis and the central tendon of the perineum. The side walls (figs. 20.39, 20.43 and 20.46) consist of those parts of the osteoligamentous pelvis and its associated muscles which lie below the level of levator ani and coccygeus. From before back these are the lower parts of the pubic symphysis and the pubic bodies, the ischiopubic rami and the lower parts of the obturator internus muscles, the ischial tubers, the lesser sciatic foramina and the sacrotuberous ligaments. Posteriorly, the coccyx, to which the pelvic diaphragm is attached, comes into contact with the skin. In other words the roof and floor join and there is no side wall.

The floor of the perineum is skin. Posteriorly this skin lies in the lower part of the natal cleft and contains the anus; anteriorly it differs in the two sexes and so is described with the reproductive system (chap. 37, figs. 20.42 and 20.43).

The perineum communicates with the pelvic cavity through the anterior gap in the pelvic diaphragm (fig. 20.41), and with the buttock through the lesser sciatic foramen (figs. 20.41 and 20.44).

The compartments of the perineum

The diamond-shaped perineum may be divided into anterior and posterior triangular parts by a coronal plane through the central tendon of the perineum and the anterior parts of the ischial tubers. The anterior region contains the genital and urinary tracts and is named the **urogenital triangle**. The posterior region contains the anal canal and is named the **anal triangle**.

The **urogenital triangle** is divided into several compartments by three horizontal, triangular layers of fascia lying one above the other (figs. 20.40, 20.42 and 20.43). The middle and thickest layer is the **inferior fascia of the urogenital diaphragm (perineal membrane)**; above this lies the **superior fascia of the urogenital diaphragm** and, below, the **membranous layer of the superficial fascia**. The three layers are attached by their lateral margins to the upper, middle and inferior parts of the ischiopubic rami. Posteriorly they fuse with one another and also, near the median plane, with the central tendon of the perineum.

14

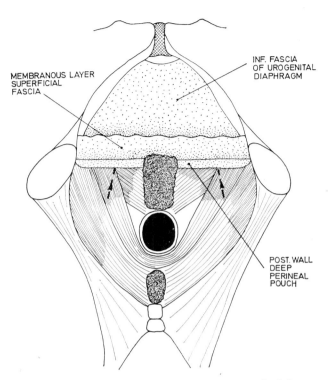

FIG. 20.42. The perineum from below. Arrows lead from ischiorectal fossae into anterior recesses. Refer to figs 20.40, 20.41, 20.43 and 20.44.

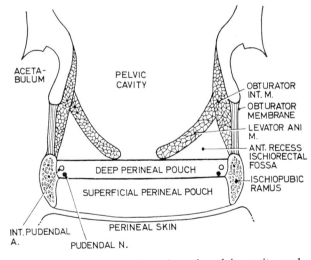

FIG. 20.43. Coronal section through pelvic cavity and urogenital triangle of perineum.

Anteriorly the superior and inferior fasciae of the urogenital diaphragm end by fusing with one another a short distance behind the lower part of the pubic symphysis. A gap is thus left between the symphysis and the fasciae. The anterior part of the membranous layer of the superficial fascia extends forwards beneath the pubic symphysis and envelops the scrotum and penis before becoming continuous with the membranous superficial fascia on the abdominal wall (p. 20.29). In the scrotum, the fascia contains involuntary muscle fibres which are inserted into the overlying skin and are named the **dartos muscle**; they contract in response to cold and fear, and wrinkle and thicken the scrotal skin. A thick septum of this fascia traverses the scrotum to reach the under surface of the penis and thereby divides the scrotum into two compartments.

The **deep perineal pouch** is that part of the urogenital triangle which lies between the superior and inferior fasciae of the urogenital diaphragm. It is completely separated from the surrounding regions by these two fascial layers and by the ischiopubic rami. It contains the transverse perineal muscles, the sphincter urethrae and the terminations of the pudendal vessels and nerve. In the male the bulbourethral glands are lodged in the deep perineal pouch.

The **superficial perineal pouch** lies between the inferior fascia of the urogenital diaphragm and the membranous layer of the superficial fascia. It is completely enclosed behind and on either side but anteriorly it is in direct communication with other neighbouring regions (fig. 20.40). Through the gap between the pubic symphysis and the deep perineal pouch, and subsequently through the gap in the anterior part of the pelvic diaphragm, it communicates with the pelvic cavity. Anteriorly it is in continuity with the tissues of the scrotum, the penis and the anterior abdominal wall.

On either side of the midline, and between the pelvic diaphragm, the superior fascia of the urogenital diaphragm and the obturator internus, lies a tissue space which is triangular in coronal section (fig. 20.43). Anteriorly it is limited by the body of the pubis, but posteriorly it is in continuity with an ischiorectal fossa. It is consequently named the **anterior recess of the ischiorectal fossa.**

The **anal triangle** (figs. 20.42 and 20.44) of the perineum is almost completely divided into two symmetrical parts by the central tendon of the perineum, anal canal, and anococcygeal ligament which all extend from the roof of the region to its floor, that is from the pelvic diaphragm to the skin. These lateral parts, the **ischiorectal fossae**, are wedge-shaped regions largely occupied by fatty tissue. In each fossa the medial wall consists of the pelvic diaphragm, the central tendon, anal canal, and anococcygeal ligament, whereas the lateral wall is formed by the obturator internus, the ischial tuber and the sacrotuberous ligament. The lateral wall is traversed by the lesser sciatic foramen. These walls meet above along the attachment of the pelvic diaphragm and, behind, at the attachments of the pelvic diaphragm and the sacrotuberous ligament to the coccyx and sacrum. Anteriorly, the fossa is separated from the superficial and deep perineal pouches by the posterior walls of those compartments, but continues forwards at a higher level as the

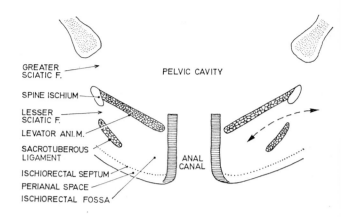

FIG. 20.44 Coronal section through pelvic cavity and anal triangle of perineum. Arrows indicate communication of ischiorectal fossa and buttock through lesser sciatic foramen.

anterior recess. The base of the fossa is formed by the perineal skin. The fatty tissue immediately deep to this skin has a finer texture than that in the rest of the fossa and is separated from it by a thin fascial septum. This part of the ischiorectal fossa is known as the **perianal space.**

THE ARTERIES OF THE BODY WALL

The main arterial trunks

The main systemic artery of the body is the aorta which arises directly from the left ventricle of the heart. In its course it undergoes several changes in direction and on the basis of these changes it is divided into three parts (fig. 20.10). The short first part, the **ascending aorta**, passes upwards, forwards and to the right, close to the anterior thoracic wall. Reaching the deep aspect of the second costal cartilage it becomes continuous with the second part, named the **arch of the aorta**. The arch is convex upwards and passes backwards and to the left to end in contact with the left side of the fourth thoracic vertebra. It gives off three large branches from its upper surface. The **brachiocephalic artery**, after a short upward course, divides into the **right subclavian** and the **right common carotid arteries**. The **left common carotid** and the **left subclavian arteries** arise directly from the arch beyond the origin of the brachiocephalic. Each subclavian artery turns laterally at the thoracic inlet and arches laterally over the upper surface of the first rib. Here it becomes the axillary artery which supplies the upper limb (p. 22.34). Each common carotid artery ascends into the corresponding side of the neck (p. 21.27).

The third part of the aorta, the **dorsal aorta**, begins as a continuation of the arch at the left side of the lower border of the fourth thoracic vertebra, and ends by bifurcating slightly to the left of the midline on the anterior aspect of the fourth lumbar vertebra. In the thorax it follows the curvature of the vertebral column and gradually shifts from its lateral to its anterior aspect. It then traverses the aortic opening in the diaphragm (fig. 20.34) and continues vertically downwards to its termination. The vessel is divisible at the level of the median arcuate ligament into the **descending thoracic aorta** and the **abdominal aorta.**

The **common iliac arteries** (figs. 20.27 and 20.46) arise at the terminal bifurcation of the abdominal aorta and run downwards and laterally. Each ends in front of the corresponding sacroiliac joint and at the level of the lumbosacral intervertebral disc by dividing into internal and external iliac arteries. The common iliac arteries are about 5 cm long in the adult, but because their origins are to the left of the midline, the right artery is a little longer than the left.

The **internal iliac artery** (fig. 20.46) is about 2·5 cm long. From its origin it turns downwards and backwards along the side wall of the pelvic cavity and ends at the upper border of the greater sciatic foramen by dividing into a spray of branches.

The **external iliac artery** (fig. 20.46) runs downwards and forwards along the medial border of iliopsoas. It passes beneath the midpoint of the inguinal ligament, and, changing its name to that of the femoral artery, enters the lateral compartment of the femoral sheath (p. 23.37).

Most of the tissues of the body wall are supplied by somatic branches arising from the major vessels named above. Many of these vessels also give off branches to the tissues of the neck, to the upper or lower limbs, or to the thoracic, abdominal, pelvic or perineal viscera, but these are considered in the appropriate sections. Moreover the muscles which, though overlying the thorax, are functionally associated with the shoulder girdle and upper limbs are supplied to a large extent from the upper limb arteries.

The blood supply of the deep tissues of the thoracic and abdominal walls

THE SEGMENTAL VESSELS

The **costocervical trunk** (fig. 20.47) arises from the subclavian artery in the region of the thoracic inlet, and runs backwards to the neck of the first rib. There it divides into a **deep cervical branch** which continues backwards into the cervical part of sacrospinalis, and a **superior intercostal branch** which descends into the thoracic cavity, where it represents a persistence of the embryonic precostal anastomosis (fig. 20.11). The superior intercostal artery gives off **posterior intercostal arteries** to the first and second intercostal spaces where their subsequent course corresponds to the posterior intercostal arteries arising from the descending thoracic aorta (see below).

The **posterior intercostal arteries** to the remaining intercostal spaces arise from the descending thoracic aorta (fig. 20.45). Because the descending thoracic aorta begins at the lower border of the fourth vertebra and lies to the left of the midline the upper intercostal arteries ascend to reach their intercostal spaces, and those of the right side cross the anterior aspects of the vertebral bodies from the left to the right. Reaching their proper intercostal spaces each posterior intercostal artery runs laterally midway between two ribs, lying between the superior costotransverse ligament and the internal intercostal membrane externally, and the intercostalis intima (when present) and the pleura internally. At the rib angles it ascends into the costal groove, where it is lodged between the internal intercostal muscle and the intercostalis intima (fig. 20.45), and thereafter continues in the same plane to the anterior end of the intercostal space. The lower two arteries continue forwards from the tenth and eleventh intercostal spaces into the abdominal wall where they lie between the internal oblique and transversus abdominis muscles. The posterior intercostal arteries supply branches to the tissues associated with the intercostal spaces, spinal branches which pass through the intervertebral foramina into the vertebral canal, and posterior branches which pass between the superior costotransverse ligaments and the vertebrae to reach the postvertebral tissues (fig. 20.29).

FIG. 20.45. (a) The descending thoracic aorta and its somatic branches. (b) Section of intercostal space.

The **subcostal artery** is in series with the posterior intercostal vessels, and, early in its course, gives off typical **spinal** and **posterior branches**. Running below the twelfth rib on quadratus lumborum it passes behind the lateral arcuate ligament into the abdominal cavity (fig. 20.34). It reaches and pierces the lumbar fascia and then continues round the body wall in the neurovascular plane between the internal oblique and transversus abdominis muscles. The vessel ends lateral to the rectus sheath.

The **lumbar arteries** arise from the posterolateral aspects of the abdominal aorta, in front of the upper four lumbar vertebrae, and pass laterally to reach the spaces beneath the fibrous arches of the psoas head of iliopsoas (fig. 20.27). Turning backwards deep to the fibrous arches, the arteries pass between psoas and the vertebrae to the intervertebral foramina, and there give off **posterior and spinal branches** similar to those of the posterior intercostal arteries. Thereafter the vessels turn laterally, behind psoas and quadratus lumborum, into the substance of the lumbar fascia, and from here they pass round the body wall in the neurovascular plane to the lateral border of the rectus sheath. The arteries give off branches to the surrounding muscles and overlying skin.

The **iliolumbar artery** arises from the internal iliac but is in series with the posterior intercostal, subcostal and lumbar arteries. It passes upwards, deep to the external iliac vessels, to the medial border of psoas where it divides into two branches. The **lumbar branch** corresponds closely to the posterior branch of a lumbar artery. It gives off a spinal twig which passes through the fifth lumbar intervertebral foramen and thereafter passes backwards into sacrospinalis. The **iliac branch** turns laterally and supplies both heads of iliopsoas.

THE DEEP VENTRAL VESSELS OF THE BODY WALL

The **internal thoracic artery** (fig. 20.29) arises from the subclavian artery in the thoracic inlet. It passes downwards in the anterior thoracic wall lying just lateral to the sternum and immediately external to the pleura and to the intercostalis intima when that layer is present. At the sixth intercostal space it divides into **superior epigastric** and **musculophrenic branches**.

The vessel gives off several small branches to the thoracic viscera some of which reach the upper surface of the diaphragm. But its major branches are the **anterior intercostal arteries** which run laterally in the upper six intercostal spaces, and the **perforating branches** which pierce the anterior ends of the same intercostal spaces to reach the overlying muscles, fascia, skin and mammary glands.

The **musculophrenic artery** passes downwards and laterally towards the twelfth rib along the line of origin of the diaphragm. It distributes twigs to neighbouring parts of the thoracic and abdominal walls and the diaphragm.

The **superior epigastric artery** descends through the sternocostal gap in the diaphragm and passes into the rectus sheath behind the rectus abdominis (figs. 20.32 and 20.33). It is considerably smaller than the inferior epigastric artery and anastomoses with it between the xiphoid process and the umbilicus. It gives branches to the structures in its vicinity including the overlying skin.

The **inferior epigastric artery** arises from the external iliac immediately above the midpoint of the inguinal ligament (fig. 20.46) and passes upwards and medially in the anterior abdominal wall, in the general direction of the umbilicus. The initial part of its course is in the extraperitoneal tissues and lies just to the medial side of the deep inguinal ring (fig. 20.36). It pierces the transversalis fascia below the arcuate line and continues upwards within the rectus sheath lying deep to the rectus abdominis (fig. 20.32). It gives branches to the neighbouring tissues of the body wall,

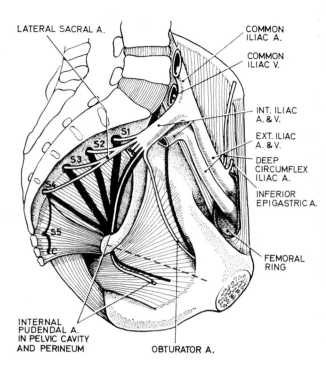

FIG. 20.46. Parietal vessels of pelvic cavity and perineum. Refer to figs. 20.39 and 20.40.

but only two of these are important. A small **pubic branch** passes close beside the femoral ring, either on its lateral or its medial side, and turns downwards on to the side wall of the pelvic cavity. In about 25 per cent of individuals this branch replaces the obturator artery (see below). It is then of considerable size and its proximity to the femoral ring makes it of surgical interest. In the male a small **cremasteric branch** enters the spermatic cord through the deep inguinal ring and supplies its fascial coverings.

The **deep circumflex iliac artery** arises from the external iliac close to the inferior epigastric (fig. 20.46). Running behind the inguinal ligament to the anterior superior iliac spine it ramifies amongst the muscles of the lateral abdominal wall.

THE BLOOD SUPPLY OF THE SUPERFICIAL TISSUES OF THE THORACIC AND ABDOMINAL WALLS

The deep vessels described in the previous sections contribute superficial branches to the overlying superficial fascia and skin, and these tend to be located in rows on the anterior, lateral and posterior aspects of the trunk. In addition, these superficial tissues are supplied by arteries which arise from the proximal parts of the arterial stems of the upper and lower limbs (fig. 20.48). Thus the **lateral thoracic artery** (p. 22.36) arises from the axillary artery and runs downwards and forwards to reach the superficial fascia on the anterolateral aspect of the chest wall. Similarly, the **superficial epigastric artery** arises from the proximal part of the femoral artery and, passing over the inguinal ligament, extends upwards through the superficial fascia of the anterior abdominal wall.

The only structure of individual importance in the superficial fascia of the trunk is the **mammary gland** (p. 37.51). It is supplied by the lateral thoracic artery, the perforating branches of the

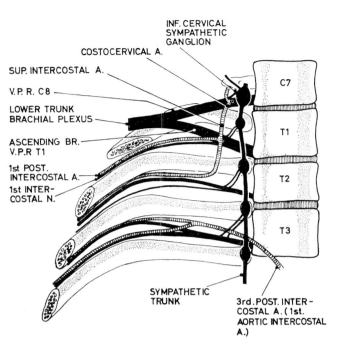

FIG. 20.47. Nerves and arteries of upper intercostal spaces. V.P.R., ventral primary ramus.

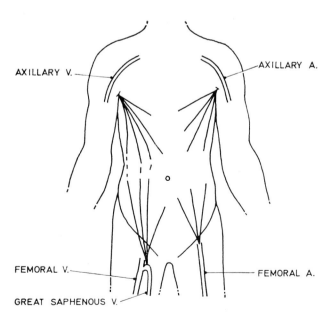

FIG. 20.48. Schematic diagram of arteries (right) and veins (left) of the superficial fascia of the trunk.

internal thoracic artery and some smaller twigs from the corresponding intercostal arteries.

THE ARTERIAL SUPPLY TO THE DIAPHRAGM

The diaphragm receives its blood supply in part from neighbouring arteries of the body wall, the internal thoracic, the musculophrenic and the lower posterior intercostals. In addition two **phrenic arteries** arise from the anterior aspect of the uppermost part of the abdominal aorta, pass laterally across the corresponding crura and ramify on the undersurface of the diaphragm behind the oesophageal and vena caval openings (fig. 20.34).

THE ARTERIES OF THE PELVIC WALL AND THE PERINEUM

The great majority of the vessels in these regions arise from the internal iliac artery opposite the upper border of the greater sciatic foramen (fig. 20.46). This vessel also gives off visceral branches and branches to the lower limb which are considered in the appropriate sections (pp. 23.36, 30.44, 37.7).

The **lateral sacral artery** represents the posterior branches of the lower segmental arteries of the body wall. It passes medially and downwards across the piriformis and the ventral primary rami of the sacral nerves towards the coccyx, and gives off four branches which pass through the pelvic sacral foramina to reach the sacral canal and the tissues on the dorsal part of the sacrum.

The **obturator artery** runs downwards and forwards over the obturator internus and its fascia. Traversing the obturator canal it passes into the thigh and its subsequent course is described later (p. 23.37). It gives branches to the surrounding tissues including a pubic branch which ascends and anastomoses with the pubic branch of the inferior epigastric artery.

The **internal pudendal artery** runs downwards across piriformis and the ventral primary rami of the sacral nerves to the lower border of the greater sciatic foramen, through which it passes into the buttock. Here it turns downwards across the outer aspect of the ischial spine to the lesser sciatic foramen. Turning medially and forwards it passes through this opening into the perineum where it lies high on the lateral wall of the ischiorectal fossa, about 4 cm above the ischial tuber (fig. 20.46). In this position it is embedded in the fascia covering the perineal part of obturator internus, the fascial tunnel containing it being known as the **pudendal canal**. The artery continues forwards and downwards and pierces the posterior fascial wall of the deep perineal pouch (fig. 20.42). In the pouch it lies against the deep aspect of the inferior pubic ramus (fig. 20.43). The vessel gives off a few muscular twigs in the pelvic cavity and the buttock, but its main branches arise in the perineum. The **inferior rectal artery** arises in the pudendal canal and spreads medially as several branches to the anal canal and the skin of the anal triangle. In the anterior part of the ischiorectal fossa the **scrotal or labial branches** radiate forwards through the superficial perineal pouch to the corresponding areas of skin. The several branches arising in the deep perineal pouch supply structures in that region and in the superficial perineal pouch (p. 20.32).

In addition to these three branches of the internal iliac certain other small arteries are involved in the blood supply of the pelvic cavity and perineum.

The **median sacral artery** arises from the bifurcation of the abdominal aorta. It descends along the dorsal wall of the pelvic cavity to the coccyx and anastomoses freely with the lateral sacral arteries on either side.

One or two **external pudendal arteries** arise from the femoral in the proximal part of the thigh, and, crossing the ischiopubic ramus, anastomose with the scrotal or labial branches of the internal pudendal.

THE VEINS OF THE BODY WALL

The main venous channels

The **axillary vein**, which receives the greater part of the blood from the upper limb, leaves the axilla to become the **subclavian vein** and this is joined in the thoracic inlet by the **internal jugular vein** descending from the tissues of head and neck (fig. 20.10). The confluence of these two large vessels at symmetrical points on either side of the midline forms the **brachiocephalic veins**, which join one another behind the first right costal cartilage to form the **superior vena cava**. Because of the eccentricity of their termination, the two brachiocephalic veins are dissimilar in course and length, that on the right being about 2·5 cm long and descending almost vertically, and that on the left being some 6 cm long and running to the right with only a slight downward inclination. The superior vena cava descends vertically to open into the right atrium of the heart.

The **femoral vein**, which carries a large part of the venous blood of the lower limb, traverses the intermediate compartment of the femoral sheath where it is joined by the great saphenous vein which drains much of the superficial fascia of the thigh and leg. Passing behind the inguinal ligaments each femoral vein becomes the corresponding **external iliac vein**, and these ascend along the brim of the pelvic cavity, medial to iliopsoas (figs. 20.10 and 20.46). Their relationships to the corresponding external iliac arteries are dissimilar. That on the right begins on the medial side of the artery and later lies behind it, whereas that on the left remains medial to the artery throughout its course. The **internal iliac vein** of each side begins by the confluence of numerous tributaries at the upper border of the greater sciatic foramen and ascends to the pelvic brim behind the corresponding artery and in front of the sacroiliac joint (fig. 20.46).

The **common iliac veins** are formed on either side by the confluence of the external and internal iliac veins (figs. 20.10, 20.27 and 20.46). On the right, the origin lies behind the bifurcation of the common iliac artery whereas on the left it lies to the medial side of that vessel. Both veins extend upwards and medially and join one another, slightly to the right of the midline, on the anterior aspect of the fifth lumbar vertebral body, to form the **inferior vena cava**. The right common iliac begins behind the corresponding artery and ends on its right side, whereas that on the left extends along the medial side of the corresponding artery and then passes behind the right common iliac artery.

The **inferior vena cava** (figs. 20.10 and 20.34) passes upwards, lying slightly to the right of the median plane, in contact with the right side of the abdominal aorta and anterior to the fifth, fourth and third lumbar vertebral bodies and the fourth and third right lumbar arteries.

Coming into association with the right crus of the diaphragm it begins to move forwards and to the right, becoming separated from the abdominal aorta and the vertebral column. It then continues upwards and to the right in front of the vertebral fibres of the diaphragm, and passes through the vena caval opening in the central tendon of the diaphragm. In the thorax the vein immediately opens into the right atrium of the heart.

The main venous channels described above are associated with an additional system of veins, named the azygos system, which has no direct counterpart on the arterial side.

In the **azygos system** (fig. 20.27) the **ascending lumbar vein** begins below as a branch of the corresponding common iliac vein and passes deep to the psoas head of iliopsoas. It extends upwards lying deep to these muscle fibres, in front of the transverse processes of the lumbar vertebrae and immediately lateral to the lumbar intervertebral foramina. Above it leaves the upper part of psoas in the thorax and turns medially on to the anterolateral aspect of the twelfth thoracic vertebra. Here each ascending lumbar vein is joined by the **subcostal vein** (see below) and the vessel so formed is known on the right side as the **azygos vein** and on the left as the **inferior hemiazygos vein**.

The **azygos vein** (figs. 20.27, 20.29 and 20.45) passes upwards along the anterolateral aspect of the thoracic vertebral bodies, but separated from them by the right posterior intercostal arteries. Reaching the fourth thoracic level it arches forwards away from the vertebral column, above the root of the right lung, and opens into the posterior wall of the superior vena cava.

The **inferior hemiazygos vein** (figs. 20.27 and 20.29) follows a similar course on the left side, where it lies behind the descending thoracic aorta and lateral to the left posterior intercostal arteries. At the eighth thoracic level, or thereabouts, it turns abruptly to the right and passing behind the aorta joins the azygos vein.

The **superior hemiazygos vein** (fig. 20.27) runs along the left anterolateral aspect of the thoracic vertebrae from the fourth to the ninth, lying behind the aorta and lateral to the left posterior intercostal arteries. At its lower end it also turns to the right, passes behind the aorta, and joins the azygos vein.

Thus all the venous blood from the azygos system of vessels on both sides of the body eventually enters the terminal arch of the azygos vein and drains into the superior vena cava.

VENOUS DRAINAGE OF THE DEEP TISSUES OF THE THORACIC AND ABDOMINAL WALLS

The great majority of the veins involved in the venous drainage of the body wall follow courses which are similar to those of the corresponding arteries, and descriptions are required only for their terminal parts.

THE SEGMENTAL VESSELS

The segmental veins of the body wall correspond in name and course to the posterior intercostal, subcostal, lumbar and iliolumbar arteries, and each receives close to its termination a **posterior tributary** from sacrospinalis and the overlying skin, and a **spinal tributary** which issues from the vertebral canal through the appropriate intervertebral foramen.

The **posterior intercostal veins** lie above the corresponding arteries (fig. 20.45b). Reaching the posterior end of the intercostal space (fig. 20.27) the first posterior intercostal vein of each side turns upwards in front of the neck of the first rib and in close association with the superior intercostal artery. It then turns forwards in the thoracic inlet and joins the corresponding brachiocephalic vein. The second and third veins on the left join to form the **left superior intercostal vein** which turns forwards across the left side of the arch of the aorta to join the left brachiocephalic vein.

All the remaining posterior intercostal veins drain into the azygos system. On the left the fourth to the ninth join the superior hemiazygos, and the ninth, tenth and eleventh join the inferior hemiazygos. On the right the second, third and fourth join and open into the beginning of the arch of the azygos vein by a common trunk named the **right superior intercostal vein**, while all the others join the azygos vein directly.

The **subcostal veins** (figs. 20.27 and 20.34) join the upper ends of the ascending lumbar veins at the commencement of the azygos and inferior hemiazygos veins.

The **four lumbar veins** follow the corresponding arteries on to the deep aspect of the psoas head of iliopsoas (fig. 20.27). In this situation they are connected to the ascending lumbar veins. The first and second usually terminate by this connection, but the third and fourth usually continue beyond it and, passing between psoas and the lumbar vertebrae, they appear from beneath the fibrous arches of psoas and join the inferior vena cava. Those of the left side pass behind the abdominal aorta.

The **iliolumbar vein** is similarly connected to the initial part of the ascending lumbar deep to psoas, but usually continues beyond this to join the common iliac vein.

THE VENTRAL VESSELS

The **superior epigastric, musculophrenic, internal thoracic, inferior epigastric** and **deep circumflex iliac veins** follow the corresponding arteries usually as venae commitantes. The **internal thoracic** drains into the brachiocephalic vein, and the **inferior epigastric** and **deep circumflex iliac** into the external iliac vein.

THE VENOUS DRAINAGE OF THE SUPERFICIAL TISSUES OF THE THORACIC AND ABDOMINAL WALLS

The skin and superficial fascia of the trunk are drained in large measure by the terminal tributaries of the deep veins. In addition, however, the anterolateral aspect of the thorax and the anterior aspect of the abdomen are drained by the lateral thoracic and superficial epigastric veins (fig. 20.48). The **lateral thoracic vein** is formed by the confluence of tributaries from the superficial fascia as far down as the umbilicus, and passes upwards to the axilla to join the axillary vein. The **superficial epigastric vein** is formed by tributaries from below the umbilicus. It passes downwards into the proximal part of the thigh where it joins the terminal part of the great saphenous vein (p. 23.39).

Thus the venous drainage of the superficial fascia presents a kind of watershed at the level of the umbilicus. But this watershed is not complete; many connections exist between the lateral thoracic and superficial epigastric vessels and frequently the two are continuous and form the **thoraco-epigastric venous channel**. When the venous drainage of the whole lower limb is obstructed, the blood from the isolated region may return by way of the femoral, great saphenous, superficial epigastric, lateral thoracic, axillary, subclavian, and brachiocephalic veins to the superior vena cava.

THE VENOUS DRAINAGE OF THE DIAPHRAGM

This corresponds closely to the arterial supply. The **phrenic veins** open into the upper part of the inferior vena cava.

THE VENOUS DRAINAGE OF THE PELVIC WALL AND THE PERINEUM

The **lateral sacral, obturator** and **internal pudendal veins** follow the courses of the corresponding arteries, usually as venae commitantes, and drain into the internal iliac vein.

The **median sacral venae commitantes** join either the beginning of the inferior vena cava or the left common iliac vein. The two **external pudendal veins** pass laterally into the thigh and join the terminal part of the great saphenous vein.

THE SOMATIC LYMPHATICS OF THE TRUNK

The main lymphatic trunks

The terminal lymphatic trunks which drain into the great veins at the root of the neck are shown in figs. 20.49 & 21.35. The thoracic parts of the thoracic duct and the right bronchomediastinal trunk are described below.

The sacculated lower end of the **thoracic duct** is named the **cisterna chyli**. About 5 to 8 cm in length, it lies within the aortic opening in the diaphragm, on the right side of the aorta. It has the first and second lumbar vertebrae and the corresponding right lumbar arteries behind it, and the right crus of the diaphragm on its right side (figs. 20.27 and 20.34). Its lower end re-

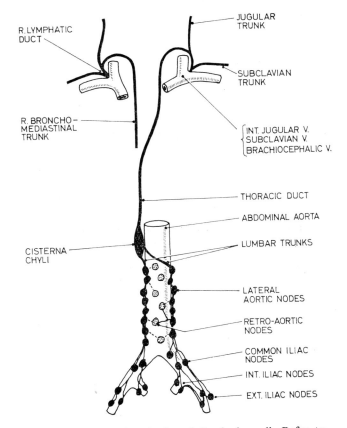

FIG. 20.49. The lymphatics of the body wall. Refer to fig. 20.27.

ceives the right and left **lumbar trunks** (fig. 20.49) and the **intestinal trunk**, and its upper end is continuous with the thoracic duct.

The duct runs upwards, in front of the thoracic vertebral column, to the thoracic inlet where it opens into the junction between the left internal jugular and subclavian veins. In the lower part of its course it is slightly to the right of the median plane, between the azygos vein and the aorta, and anterior to the right posterior intercostal arteries (fig. 20.27). Approximately at the middle of the thorax it moves to the left of the midline, and lies close to the superior hemiazygos vein and the aorta and anterior to the right posterior intercostal arteries. Above, it rests on the left border of the longus cervicis muscle and is in close association with the left recurrent laryngeal nerve (p. 21.30 and fig. 21.35).

The **right bronchomediastinal trunk** begins about the middle of the thorax and runs upwards in close association with the azygos vein (fig. 20.27). Thereafter it continues along the right border of the longus cervicis muscle to the root of the neck.

Lymph vessels and nodes of the deep tissues of the thoracic wall

In the anterior thoracic wall, the lymph vessels run with the anterior intercostal arteries and veins and reach the **internal thoracic chain** of lymph nodes. These are placed along the course of the internal thoracic vessels, and their efferents ascend to join the right lymphatic duct or the thoracic duct in the root of the neck.

The lymph vessels of the lateral and posterior parts of the thoracic wall follow the posterior intercostal arteries and veins to reach the **intercostal** lymph nodes in the posterior parts of the intercostal spaces. The efferents from the upper intercostal nodes on the right side join the right bronchomediastinal trunk, whereas those of all the other intercostal nodes join the thoracic duct.

Lymph vessels and nodes of the deep tissues of the abdominal and pelvic cavities and the perineum

The lymph vessels from these tissues follow the corresponding blood vessels and the majority reach two long chains of lymph nodes placed along the abdominal aorta and the common, external and internal iliac vessels. The efferents of these chains are the lumbar trunks which join the cisterna chyli (fig. 20.49).

From the deep tissues of the anterior abdominal wall above the umbilicus the lymph vessels follow the superior epigastric artery and vein to reach the internal thoracic lymph nodes. From the deep tissues of the lower part of the anterior abdominal wall, the lymph vessels follow the inferior epigastric and deep circumflex iliac arteries to reach the external iliac lymph nodes.

The lymph vessels from the deep tissue of the lateral and posterior parts of the abdominal wall pass alongside the lumbar arteries and veins to the lateral aortic and retro-aortic lymph nodes. Lymph vessels from the walls of the pelvic cavity and from the deep tissues of the perineum run with the corresponding arteries and veins to the internal iliac lymph nodes.

Lymph vessels of the superficial tissues of the trunk

These lymph vessels are in communication with the deep vessels described above and throughout their course they follow closely the arteries and veins of the superficial fascia (fig. 20.49). Those from areas below the umbilicus, including the superficial tissues of the perineum, converge on the inguinal nodes at the root of the lower limb (p. 23.40). Those from areas above the umbilicus, including the mammary gland, converge on the axillary nodes at the root of the upper limb (p. 22.39).

THE NERVES OF THE TRUNK

The nerves of the trunk contain four functional types of fibres. **General somatic efferent fibres** are concerned solely with the innervation of voluntary muscle fibres. **General visceral efferent fibres** constitute the **autonomic system** and may be either of **sympathetic** or **parasympathetic** type. Parasympathetic fibres in the trunk are concerned only with the innervation of the viscera. On the other hand sympathetic fibres are involved in the innervation both of the viscera and certain somatic structures, namely, the involuntary muscle fibres associated with arterial walls, hair follicles, superficial fascia, the dartos muscle, and the sweat glands of the skin. **General somatic afferent fibres** carry sensory impulses from many tissues in the body wall. **General visceral afferent fibres** transmit sensory impulses from viscera and from the walls of both visceral and somatic blood vessels.

THE GROSS FORM OF THE NERVOUS SYSTEM OF THE TRUNK

The **thoracic nerves** emerge through the intervertebral foramina of that region. Their ventral primary rami pass into the intercostal spaces while their dorsal primary rami turn backwards between the superior costotransverse ligaments and the vertebral bodies into the sacrospinalis muscle (fig. 20.29). The **lumbar nerves** appear through the corresponding intervertebral foramina deep to the psoas head of iliopsoas. The ventral primary rami run laterally into the body wall whereas the dorsal primary rami turn backwards between adjacent transverse processes into the sacrospinalis muscle (fig. 20.27). The **upper four sacral nerves** leave the sacral canal through bony canals from which the primary rami emerge through the pelvic and dorsal sacral foramina (figs. 20.15, 20.17 and 20.46). The **fifth sacral** nerve emerges from the vertebral canal through an aperture which is bordered, in front, by the sacrococcygeal intervertebral disc and, behind, by the sacral and coccygeal cornua and the posterior sacrococcygeal membrane (fig. 20.17). At this point it lies outside the pelvic cavity on the outer surface of the coccygeus muscle, and divides into its primary rami. The dorsal ramus turns backwards into sacrospinalis, whereas the ventral turns forwards, and passes through coccygeus and the sacrospinous ligament into the pelvic cavity (fig. 20.46). The tiny **coccygeal nerve** emerges from the lowest part of the vertebral canal by piercing the posterior sacrococcygeal membrane, and the courses of its primary rami are similar to those noted in the fifth sacral nerve (figs. 20.17 and 20.46).

The **sympathetic trunks** (figs. 20.27, 20.45 and 20.50) extend, on either side of the vertebral column, from the base of the skull to the coccyx. Developmentally the number of ganglia corresponds to the number of spinal nerves, but fusion of adjacent ganglia reduces the number in each region. The definitive number in the cervical region is three, in the thoracic region it is usually eleven or twelve, in the lumbar region four and in the sacral, four or five. The lower ends of the sympathetic trunks join in front of the coccyx in the single **ganglion impar**. The thoracic part of each trunk (figs. 20.27, 20.45 and 20.47) lies anterior to the heads of the ribs and anterior to the posterior intercostal vessels as they lie in the posterior ends of the intercostal spaces. It is thus lateral to the vertebral column and behind and lateral to the azygos or hemiazygos veins (fig. 20.29). In the lower part of the thorax the trunk inclines medially on to the uppermost part of the psoas head of iliopsoas (fig. 20.27), and enters the abdominal cavity by passing beneath the medial arcuate ligament (fig. 20.34). It then passes downwards, anterior to the lumbar vertebral column and the lumbar vessels, and just medial to the fibrous arches of psoas (fig. 20.27). The right trunk is partially covered by the inferior vena cava and the left trunk by the abdominal aorta. Below, the trunk passes behind the corresponding common iliac vessels and turns over the sacral promontory into the pelvic cavity. Here it extends downwards and medially on the pelvic surface of the sacrum, lying just to the medial side of the pelvic sacral foramina.

The **central autonomic plexuses** (fig. 20.50) are dense and extensive collections of autonomic nerve fibres, of both the sympathetic and the parasympathetic type, which are interspersed with autonomic nerve cells. Where the concentration of nerve cells is high, that part of the plexus is called a ganglion. In the thorax, the **thoracic aortic plexus** lies along the wall of the aorta, and additional plexuses, such as the **cardiac, pulmonary** and **oesophageal**, are closely associated with individual viscera.

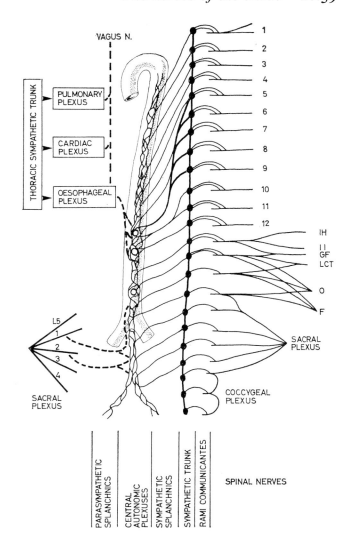

FIG. 20.50. Schematic diagram of distribution of autonomic nerves to autonomic plexuses and spinal nerves.

In the abdominal cavity the **pre-aortic plexus** extends along the anterior aspect of the abdominal aorta and its branch plexuses pass along the several branches of that vessel to the viscera with which they are associated. At the bifurcation of the abdominal aorta the pre-aortic plexus is continued downwards, in and around the median plane, as the **hypogastric plexus**. This passes anterior to the left common iliac vein and, crossing the sacral promontory, descends on the pelvic aspect of the sacrum between the sympathetic trunks. In the lower part of the pelvic cavity the hypogastric plexus divides into two symmetrical **pelvic plexuses**, which extend forwards across the pelvic diaphragm on either side of the midline pelvic viscera.

Connections of the sympathetic trunk

(1) Every ganglion on the sympathetic trunk is connected to the ventral primary ramus or rami with which it is developmentally associated by one or more **grey rami communicantes** (figs. 20.27 and 20.50). In addition each of the ganglia between T1 and L2 (L3 in some individuals) is connected to its corresponding ventral primary ramus (p. 19.13 and 24.3) by **white rami communicantes** (p. 19.13 and 24.3). In the thoracic region (figs. 20.27 and 20.47) the rami lie in the posterior ends of the intercostal spaces and run laterally from the sympathetic trunk for a distance of about 1 cm. In the lumbar region (fig. 20.27), because of the more anterior position of the sympathetic trunk, the rami are about three times as long, and extend backwards with the lumbar vessels deep to the fibrous arches of the psoas head of iliopsoas. In the pelvic cavity the rami are very short and run laterally from the sympathetic trunk on the pelvic aspects of the sacrum and coccyx.

(2) Each ganglion gives off medial (splanchnic) branches which run forwards and usually downwards to reach the central autonomic plexuses (fig. 20.50). The thoracic plexuses receive branches from both the cervical and thoracic ganglia. The pre-aortic plexus receives splanchnic branches from the lower thoracic and lumbar ganglia. The contributions from the lower thoracic ganglia are three large branches, which are named the **greater**, the **lesser** and the **least splanchnic nerves** and arise respectively from T5–9, T10 and 11, and T12. They run downwards on the lateral aspect of the vertebral bodies between the azygos or hemiazygos vein and the sympathetic trunk. The greater and lesser splanchnic nerves pierce the corresponding crus of the diaphragm (fig. 20.34), while the least splanchnic passes behind the medial arcuate ligament just medial to the sympathetic trunk. The hypogastric and pelvic plexuses receive fine medial branches from the lumbar and sacral parts of the sympathetic trunk.

(3) Direct vascular branches pass from the sympathetic trunk to the walls of many large arteries.

Parasympathetic connections with the central autonomic plexuses

(1) Several large branches arise from the ventral primary rami of S2 and 3 within the pelvic cavity and are named the **pelvic splanchnic nerves** (figs. 20.39 and 20.50). These are quite distinct from the grey rami communicantes which join the ventral primary rami to the sympathetic chain, and they must also be differentiated from the medial or splanchnic branches of the sympathetic chain which pass to the hypogastric and pelvic plexuses. The pelvic splanchnic nerves are parasympathetic in character and run directly from the spinal nerves into the hypogastric and pelvic plexuses.

(2) The **vagus** or **tenth cranial nerve** descends from the brain stem, through the neck and into the thorax and abdomen (figs. 20.50 and 21.31). It gives all the parasympathetic fibres to the thoracic autonomic plexuses and further fibres of the same type to the pre-aortic plexus.

COURSE AND DISTRIBUTION OF THE SPINAL NERVES

Each spinal nerve carries several different functional types of nerve fibres, namely, general somatic efferent and afferent fibres, a few general visceral afferent fibres and general visceral efferent fibres of sympathetic type, innervating sweat glands, and involuntary muscle fibres in blood vessels, skin and superficial fascia.

Dorsal primary rami

All the dorsal primary rami supply the sacrospinalis muscle. In addition, with the exception of those arising from the fourth and fifth lumbar and certain cervical nerves (p. 21.25) which are devoid of cutaneous fibres, they innervate a continuous strip of skin on the posterior aspect of the trunk (fig. 20.51). This extends from the posterior part of the neck to the tip of the coccyx; it

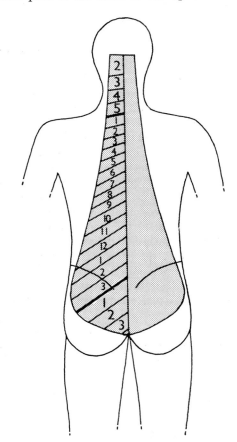

FIG. 20.51. Cutaneous distribution of the dorsal primary rami of spinal nerves.

widens progressively from above down as far as the middle of the sacrum, where it reaches the lateral aspect of the buttock, and thereafter narrows rapidly. The cutaneous branches of the dorsal primary rami exhibit a general downward inclination which becomes increasingly acute as far as L3. Those derived from L1, 2 and 3 cross the posterior part of the iliac crest and run downwards and laterally across the upper part of the buttock. Those derived from S1, 2 and 3 supply the medial part of the buttock, and those from lowest three spinal nerves supply the skin of the natal cleft over the coccyx (fig. 20.53).

Ventral primary rami

The basically segmental distribution of the ventral rami in the trunk is modified in the first and second thoracic nerves, and in the nerves between the first lumbar and the fourth sacral, by the partial or complete incorporation of these rami into the plexuses of the upper and lower limbs. From the third to the sixth thoracic each ventral ramus runs its entire course in the thoracic wall within an intercostal space (fig. 20.29). On the other hand, from the seventh to the twelfth thoracic, the ventral rami begin their course in the thoracic wall, but later emerge from the intercostal spaces into the abdominal wall.

The **ventral rami T3–T4 are intercostal nerves**. Each extends along the length of the corresponding intercostal space (fig. 20.29) lying in the upper part of its neurovascular plane (fig. 20.45b) and immediately below the corresponding intercostal arteries and veins. Eventually it passes anterior to the internal thoracic artery and pierces the overlying tissues as a spray of anterior cutaneous twigs. The branches are as follows:

(1) A collateral branch arises from the proximal part of the nerve and follows it in the lower part of the same intercostal space to end as additional anterior cutaneous twigs.

(2) A lateral cutaneous branch arises near the angles of the ribs and follows the parent nerve to the midaxillary plane. There it pierces the overlying muscles, in vertical alignment with the corresponding branches of the other intercostal nerves, and divides into anterior and posterior parts.

(3) Motor branches to the corresponding intercostal muscles and sensory branches to the related part of the parietal pleura arise throughout the course of the nerve.

The anterior and lateral cutaneous branches given off by one of these intercostal nerves, together supply a strip of skin, which is continuous posteriorly with the skin area supplied by the corresponding dorsal primary ramus. They also 'overlap' on to the skin areas associated with the nerves immediately above and below. Consequently interruption of one of these nerves does not result in an area of complete anaesthesia.

The **ventral ramus of T1** (fig. 20.47) passes behind the superior intercostal artery (p. 20.33) in the interval between the necks of the first and second ribs and there divides into a large **ascending branch** and a small **first intercostal nerve**. The latter extends round the neurovascular plane of the first intercostal space and is concerned purely with the innervation of the muscles of the first intercostal space and the related parietal pleura. Because it carries no cutaneous fibres it has neither lateral nor anterior cutaneous branches. The lateral part of the first intercostal space is related to the axilla, and is thus not directly covered by skin, whereas the skin which covers the anterior part of the space is supplied by the supraclavicular nerves which descend from the ventral rami of C3 and 4. The ascending branch passes upwards and laterally across the neck of the first rib, lateral to the sympathetic trunk and the superior intercostal vessels. Turning laterally on to the upper surface of the first rib it joins the ventral ramus of C8 to form the lower trunk of the brachial plexus, and is thereafter distributed to the tissues of the upper limb.

The **ventral ramus of T2** is atypical only in respect of its lateral cutaneous branch. This emerges through the chest wall in line with those of the succeeding intercostal nerves. However, it does not divide into anterior and posterior branches, but crosses the axilla to be distributed to the skin on the upper half of the medial aspect of the arm. Because of this distribution it is named the **intercostobrachial nerve**.

The **ventral rami T7–T11** extend laterally as intercostal nerves along their respective intercostal spaces. Reaching the anterior ends of these spaces, however, they pass between the adjacent digitations of the diaphragm and those of transversus abdominis and enter the abdominal wall in the neurovascular plane between transversus abdominis and internal oblique. Here the nerves diverge from one another, the seventh and eighth passing upwards and medially, the ninth horizontally and the tenth and eleventh downwards and medially. At the lateral border of the rectus sheath each nerve pierces the posterior lamella of the aponeurosis of internal oblique (fig. 20.35). It then traverses the substance of rectus abdominis and the anterior wall of the sheath to reach the overlying skin as the terminal **anterior cutaneous branch**. The anterior cutaneous branch of T10 lies about the level of the umbilicus. Like the higher intercostal nerves each member of this group gives off both **collateral** and **lateral cutaneous branches**. The former run parallel to and below the parent nerves and terminate like them as additional anterior cutaneous branches. The lateral cutaneous branches emerge through the overlying muscles in the midaxillary plane, and consequently in vertical alignment with the higher lateral cutaneous branches. Thereafter they divide into anterior and posterior divisions and, in association with the corresponding anterior cutaneous branches and the corresponding dorsal primary rami, they supply continuous strips of skin extending in succession round one half of the body wall. As was noted in the thoracic wall, each strip is additionally innervated by the nerves immediately above and below it.

The lower intercostal nerves also supply their respective intercostal muscles, the peripheral fibres of the diaphragm, the three flat muscles of the abdominal wall and rectus abdominis. Throughout their course they supply sensory twigs to the adjacent regions of the parietal pleura and the parietal peritoneum.

The **subcostal nerve** is the ventral ramus of T12. It is in series with the intercostal nerves and has a similar distribution. It runs across the quadratus lumborum immediately below the subcostal vessels and the twelfth rib and, passing deep to the lateral arcuate ligament, reaches the abdominal aspect of the lumbar fascia (fig. 20.34). Piercing this fascia, it enters the neurovascular plane between transversus abdominis and internal oblique, and passes round the abdominal wall. It then passes through the overlying aponeuroses and ends as an anterior cutaneous branch. Throughout its course the nerve gives motor branches to the flat abdominal muscles and sensory filaments to the parietal peritoneum. The collateral branch of the subcostal nerve follows a course similar to those at higher levels. However, the lateral cutaneous branch is rather atypical. It pierces the internal and external oblique muscles in line with the rest of its kind, and divides into anterior and posterior parts, but many of its filaments descend over the iliac crest. Consequently the strip of skin supplied by the dorsal and ventral rami of T12 is not entirely confined to the body wall but overlaps on to the anterolateral aspect of the thigh immediately below the anterior superior iliac spine (fig. 20.52).

The **ventral rami of L1–L4** run laterally into the substance of the psoas head of iliopsoas (fig. 20.27). Within this muscle L4 gives off a descending branch which becomes incorporated into the sacral plexus (p. 20.43). On the other hand, the rest of L4 and the ventral rami of L1, 2 and 3 form the **lumbar plexus**. This plexus is comparatively simple and involves the separation of the roots into a number of divisions and the formation of branches from one or more of these divisions (fig. 20.50). The branches so formed emerge from the lateral, anterior and medial aspects of psoas.

(1) Direct motor branches arise from the roots of the plexus to the quadratus lumborum and the psoas head of iliopsoas

(2) The **iliohypogastric nerve** derives its fibres entirely from L1. Emerging from the upper part of the lateral border of psoas, it runs, outside the fascial envelope of the abdominal cavity (p. 20.25), across quadratus lumborum and the lumbar fascia (fig. 20.27). It pierces the transversus abdominis immediately above the iliac crest (fig. 20.36) and runs forwards in the neurovascular plane

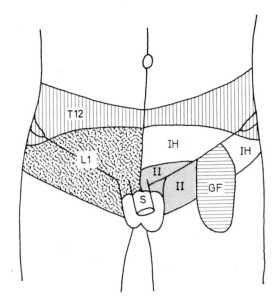

FIG. 20.52. Cutaneous distribution of the ventral primary rami of T12 and L1. IH, Iliohypogastric; II, ilio-inguinal; GF, genitofemoral; S, sacral nerves.

of the abdominal wall. It pierces internal oblique about 2 cm medial to the anterior superior iliac spine (fig. 20.37) and finally appears through the aponeurosis of external oblique a little above the superficial inguinal ring (p. 20.23) as a terminal anterior cutaneous branch. In its course the nerve supplies the adjacent part of the parietal peritoneum and gives motor branches to the flat abdominal muscles but not to rectus abdominis. Its lateral cutaneous branch pierces the internal and external oblique muscles, in line with those of the thoracic nerves, and descends over the iliac crest, behind the lateral cutaneous branch of the subcostal nerve, to supply skin in the thigh below the anterior superior iliac spine (fig. 20.52).

(3) The **ilio-inguinal nerve** also arises solely from L1. It emerges from the lateral border of psoas immediately below the iliohypogastric nerve and passes downwards and laterally, outside the fascial envelope of the abdomen, and across the quadratus lumborum, the iliac crest and the upper fibres of the iliacus head of iliopsoas (fig. 20.27). Recrossing the iliac crest, it pierces transversus abdominis and internal oblique in rapid succession just above the anterior superior iliac spine (figs. 20.36 and 20.37) and continues downwards and medially into close association with the spermatic cord, or the round ligament. The nerve then follows the spermatic cord through the superficial inguinal ring and divides into cutaneous branches (fig. 20.31). These are distributed to the skin of the thigh below the medial end of the inguinal ligament and to the proximal part of the penis and scrotum, or the mons pubis and the anterior part of the labium majus

(fig. 20.53). The ilioinguinal nerve gives off neither a collateral nor a lateral cutaneous branch, but throughout its course distributes twigs to the flat abdominal muscles and the parietal peritoneum.

(4) The **genitofemoral nerve** is formed by contributions from both L1 and L2. It emerges from the anterior surface of psoas, and, turning downwards, divides almost immediately into femoral and genital branches (fig. 20.27). Unlike the other branches of the lumbar plexus, these traverse the fascial envelope of the abdomen and come to lie in the extraperitoneal tissue (fig. 20.38). This peculiarity is associated with the fact that each branch eventually leaves the abdominal cavity within a protrusion of the fascial envelope. The femoral branch, which carries only cutaneous fibres, descends just lateral to the external iliac artery, and follows that vessel into the lateral compartment of the femoral sheath. Passing through the anterior wall of the sheath and the overlying fascia lata, (fig. 20.38) it supplies a considerable area of skin below the central part of the inguinal ligament (fig. 20.52). The genital branch, which carries only motor fibres, descends lateral to the femoral branch. It turns forwards across the deep aspect of the inguinal ligament, and passes through the deep inguinal ring into the spermatic cord, where it supplies the cremaster muscle.

The cutaneous distribution of the first lumbar nerve (figs. 20.52 and 20.53) comprises the skin areas supplied by the dorsal primary ramus and the iliohypogastric and ilioinguinal nerves, together with the upper part of the area supplied by the genitofemoral nerve.

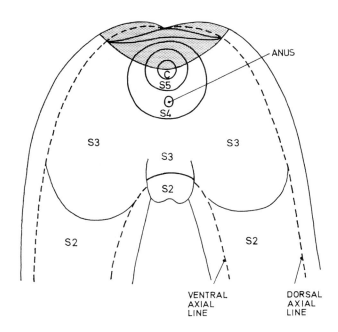

FIG. 20.53. Segmental cutaneous innervation of the perineum. Dark areas dorsal rami, white areas ventral rami.

(5) The **lateral cutaneous nerve** of the thigh (fig. 20.27) arises from L2 and L3 and leaves the lateral border of psoas below the level of the iliac crest. It runs between iliacus and the fascial envelope of the abdomen to the anterior superior iliac spine, and, thereafter, passes beneath the lateral end of the inguinal ligament into the thigh.

(6) The **femoral nerve** (fig. 20.27) is the largest branch of the lumbar plexus and draws its fibres from L2, 3 and 4. It emerges from the lateral border of psoas and descends, outside the fascial envelope of the abdomen, in the deep groove between the psoas and iliacus heads of iliopsoas. The nerve then passes deep to the inguinal ligament and enters the thigh outside and lateral to the femoral sheath. In the abdomen it supplies the iliacus. Its later course and distribution are described with the lower limb (chap. 23).

(7) The **obturator nerve** is formed by branches from L2, 3 and 4 and emerges from the medial border of psoas (figs. 20.39 and 20.46). It turns over the brim of the pelvic cavity, passing behind the common iliac vessels and lateral to the internal iliac vessels. Thereafter it extends downwards and forwards between the obturator internus muscle and its fascia, and gradually approaches the obturator vessels which lie below it. It then passes through the obturator canal into the medial part of the thigh where all its branches arise. In about 30 per cent of the population some of the fibres of the obturator nerve follow a separate course as the **accessory obturator nerve**. When present this follows the medial border of psoas and passes into the thigh between the inguinal ligament and the superior pubic ramus.

The **ventral rami of L5, S1, 2, 3 and 4** take part, together with the descending branch of the ventral ramus of L4, in the formation of the sacral plexus (figs. 20.39 and 20.50).

The descending branch of L4 emerges from the medial border of psoas in close association with the obturator nerve and the iliolumbar artery, and turns downwards over the brim of the pelvis behind the common iliac vessels. The ventral ramus of L5 runs laterally from its intervertebral foramen, into the interval between the fifth lumbar transverse process and the ala of the sacrum. It then turns downwards into the pelvic cavity and joins the descending branch of L4 to form the **lumbosacral trunk**. This trunk continues downwards between the sacroiliac joint and the bifurcation of the common iliac vessels, and then across the surface of piriformis to the lower part of the greater sciatic foramen. The ventral rami of S1, 2 and 3 emerge through the upper three pelvic sacral foramina. That of S1 is large and comparable in size to the lumbosacral trunk, that of S2 is considerably smaller and that of S3 smaller still. The three nerves pass laterally across piriformis and converge with the lumbosacral trunk on the lower part of the greater sciatic foramen. The ventral ramus of S4 is very small. It emerges through the lowest pelvic sacral foramen and gives off (like the ventral ramus of L4) a descending branch. The nerve then extends laterally to join the other roots of the sacral plexus. Close to the lower part of the greater sciatic foramen the roots of the plexus unite to form a broad band from which the branches of the plexus arise. The great majority of these branches are concerned with the innervation of the lower limb tissues (chap. 23). The branches considered below are those which innervate abdominal, pelvic and perineal tissues.

The **pelvic splanchnic nerves** are parasympathetic branches arising from the ventral rami of S2 and 3. (p. 20.40).

Muscular branches arise from the roots of the plexus, and supply piriformis (S1 and 2) coccygeus (S4) and levator ani (S4).

The **perineal branch of S4** arises from the corresponding root of the plexus and passes through the pelvic diaphragm between coccygeus and levator ani into the ischiorectal fossa. It supplies cutaneous filaments to the perineal skin around the anus and contributes to the innervation of the anal musculature.

The **nerve to obturator internus** arises from L5, S1 and 2 in the greater sciatic foramen. It first passes into the buttock where it lies on the outer aspect of the ischial spine, lateral to the internal pudendal vessels. At the lower border of the ischial spine it turns forwards through the lesser sciatic foramen into the perineum and runs into the substance of the obturator internus (fig. 20.39).

The **pudendal nerve** is formed at the lower part of the greater sciatic foramen by contributions from S2, 3 and 4 and follows the same course as the previous nerve into the ischiorectal fossa, except that it lies on the medial side of the internal pudendal vessels. Thereafter it follows the internal pudendal vessels through the pudendal canal and the deep perineal pouch (p. 20.35, figs. 20.39 and 20.43). In the pudendal canal the nerve gives off a spray of **inferior rectal branches** which follow the corresponding arteries across the ischiorectal fossa towards the anal canal. They are distributed to the musculature and lining membrane of the anal canal, and to the skin around the anus. In the same region a spray of **scrotal** or **labial branches** extend forwards into the superficial perineal pouch and supply the skin of the urogenital triangle and the distal part of the scrotum. In the cutaneous distribution of the pudendal nerve, S2 fibres are distributed anteriorly and S4 fibres posteriorly. The other branches of the pudendal nerve are concerned with the innervation of the penis or clitoris, the urethra and the muscles associated with these structures.

The **ventral rami of S5** and the **coccygeal nerves** are very small. Initially they lie on the outer surface of coccygeus, but passing through that muscle they enter the pelvic cavity just lateral to the coccyx. There the ventral ramus of S5 divides into ascending and descending branches which form loops with the descending branch of S4 and the coccygeal nerve respectively. These two loops constitute the **coccygeal plexus** (fig. 20.39). From the plexus, minute branches arise which pierce coccygeus and supply the perineal skin between the tip of the coccyx and the anus (fig. 20.53).

Cutaneous innervation of the perineum and scrotum
(fig. 20.53)

The skin immediately behind the tip of the coccyx is innervated by the dorsal primary rami of the lower sacral and the coccygeal nerves. That in front of the coccyx and over the anococcygeal ligament is supplied by branches of the coccygeal plexus. The skin around the anus, over the central tendon of the perineum and over the urogenital triangle and the distal part of the scrotum is innervated by the pudendal nerve, the perineal branch of S4, and by the perineal branch of the posterior femoral cutaneous nerve (p. 23.31). These nerves are not associated with individual areas. Their distributions overlap so that successive areas from the scrotum to the anococcygeal ligament are supplied by the ventral rami of S2, 3 and 4, in that order (fig. 20.53). The proximal part of the scrotal skin is innervated by fibres from the ventral ramus of L1 through the ilio-inguinal nerve.

THE SURFACE ANATOMY OF THE TRUNK

In clinical practice it is necessary to relate particular structures in the walls and cavities of the trunk to its skin surface. With one or two exceptions soft tissue features on the trunk, such as the nipples and the umbilicus, are too variable in position to be used for this purpose, and in practice the deep structures are usually related to bony features which can be palpated through the skin.

Three soft tissue features are of value. Unless there is a great deal of fat in the superficial fascia, the lateral border of the rectus abdominis muscle can usually be seen as a slightly curved ridge on the anterior abdominal wall. This ridge is named the **linea semilunaris** and it crosses the costal margin over the ninth costal cartilage. The position of the **inguinal ligament** can usually be seen and felt as a round ridge between the abdomen and the thigh. When the hip joint is flexed the ridge is straight, whereas when the hip joint is extended the ridge is somewhat convex towards the thigh. On the posterior aspect of the trunk, and immediately above the natal cleft which separates the buttocks, paired dimples on the skin usually mark the positions of the **posterior superior iliac spines** of the hip bones. These overlie the upper parts of the corresponding sacro-iliac joints.

Many bony features can be palpated through the skin. The **sternal notch**, the **sternal angle**, the **xiphisternal joint** and the **lateral border of the body of the sternum** are all readily palpable.

Most of the **ribs** and **costal cartilages** can be palpated on the anterior aspect of the thoracic wall. However, it is very important to note that the ease with which the first rib can be felt varies greatly in different individuals. Consequently, it is usual, in numbering the ribs, to begin from the second costal cartilage, which can always be identified by its relationship to the sternal angle (see p. 20.7).

When the **costal margin** is palpated the extremities of the eighth, ninth and tenth costal cartilages can usually be identified and the free end of the eleventh costal cartialge can be clearly felt, but the identification of the twelfth costal cartilage depends very much on the length of the corresponding rib.

In the lower part of the trunk, the upper border of the **pubic symphysis**, the **pubic crest and tubercle**, the **anterior superior iliac spine**, the **iliac crest** and its **tuberosity**, and the **posterior superior iliac spine** can all be felt through the skin. In the male the pubic crest and tubercle are most readily palpated by invaginating the thin skin of the scrotum behind the testis and the spermatic cord.

In the perineum, the inferior border of the **pubic symphysis**, the inferior margins of the **ischiopubic rami**, the **ischial tubers** and the **coccyx** can be palpated.

On the posterior aspect of the trunk the **spines of the thoracic and lumbar vertebrae** and the **posterior surface of the sacrum** can be identified. In numbering these features it must be noted that although most of the cervical spines are impalpable, the highest spine which is readily palpable, in most individuals, is that of the seventh cervical vertebra.

The surface anatomy of the anterior abdominal wall

(1) The **lateral border of the rectus abdominis** is identified by the **linea semilunaris**.

(2) The muscle fibres of the **external oblique** may be demarcated from the aponeurosis by a line running from the anterior superior iliac spine towards the umbilicus and, thereafter, vertically upwards to the ninth costal cartialge.

(3) The musculo-aponeurotic junction of the **internal oblique** muscle is gently convex forwards. It begins at the tenth costal cartilage and becomes confluent with the linea semilunaris in the lower part of the abdominal wall.

(4) The aponeurosis of the **transversus abdominis** muscle begins along a line which is concave forwards, and extends from the xiphoid process to the mid part of the inguinal ligament.

(5) The **inguinal canal** is about 5 cm long and lies parallel to, and a little above, the inguinal ligament. It begins at the **deep inguinal ring** which is 1 cm above the mid-inguinal point, and ends at the **superficial inguinal ring**, whose centre is 1 cm above and lateral to the pubic tubercle.

(6) The **inferior epigastric artery** arises immediately above the midinguinal point and runs in the direction of the umbilicus.

The surface lines and regions of the trunk

The palpable bony points of the trunk may be used to construct two horizontal and two vertical planes which divide the body wall into regions (fig. 20.54).

The horizontal planes are the **transpyloric plane**, which lies midway between the sternal notch and the upper border of the pubic symphysis and the **transtubercular** plane which traverses the tubercles of the iliac crests. The right and left **lateral** or **midclavicular planes** extend vertically through the mid-inguinal points and the mid-points of the clavicles. The three abdominal regions which lie between the lateral planes are named **epigastric, umbilical** and **hypogastric** from above down, while the three corresponding regions which lie lateral to each lateral plane are described as **hypochondriac, lumbar** and **iliac**.

The projection of the vertebrae on the anterior body wall

(1) The sternal notch corresponds to the lower border of T2 in the adult male and the upper border of T3 in the adult female. At birth the sternum lies at a relatively higher level.

(2) The transpyloric plane traverses the lower border of L1.

(3) The transtubercular plane cuts the upper part of L5.

(4) In standing the upper border of the pubic symphysis is level with the sacrococcygeal joint.

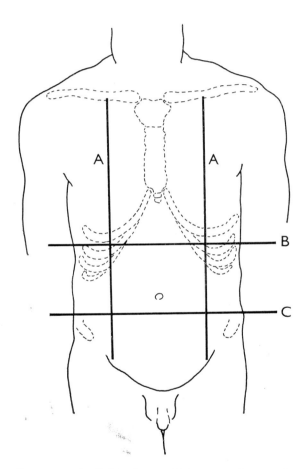

FIG. 20.54. Artificial planes which are used as surface markings from the abdomen. A, lateral or midclavicular plane; B, transpyloric plane; C, transtubercular plane.

Chapter 21
The head and neck

The head can be considered as being made up of two parts:

(1) the upper end of the central nervous system with its protective coverings. In this the neurocranium is the bony support and extends to form the bony orbit;

(2) the structures which surround and support the upper ends of the alimentary and respiratory systems. These are both derived from the gut tube of the embryo. The rigid supporting structures are the bones of the upper and lower jaws. The muscles for chewing and swallowing and for facial expression, along with their nervous and vascular supply, are built on to this scaffolding.

All these components are intimately related to each other and in a descriptive anatomical account it is not possible to separate them. Hence the region is described under the following regional headings:

(1) the cranial cavity,
(2) the orbit,
(3) the face and scalp,
(4) the neck,
(5) the median hollow viscera,
(6) the middle ear and related cavities.

THE CRANIAL CAVITY

The central nervous system is the largest single organ in the human embryo, and although its later growth lags behind that of other parts of the body, it is the most important of all the organs of the body. The head is constructed around the greatly enlarged upper end.

The subdivision of the central nervous system into brain and spinal cord at the level of the foramen magnum is arbitrary as far as its organization is concerned. This is not true, however, of the covering and protective structures which surround it. The cranium is, for all practical purposes, a rigid container. By contrast, the vertebral canal is surrounded by a series of jointed bony segments and its walls are mobile. The mobility is most marked in the cervical region immediately inferior to the base of the skull, where vulnerability to indirect violence is increased. Moreover, the interposition of soft

tissues between adjacent segments of the vertebral column allows a needle to be inserted into the subarachnoid space for the collection of cerebrospinal fluid.

The skull is formed by the interlocking of a number of bones. Those at the base are mainly ossified in cartilage, while those in the vault are entirely developed in membrane. When ossification is complete, these bones fuse to form a single structural unit. Although capable of deformation during the period of growth, the skull becomes less malleable as age advances and by the age of forty becomes virtually rigid with the fusion of the sutures.

The interior of the bony skull is identical with the cranial cavity that is identified radiographically. It is not equivalent to the cavity which encloses the brain as this is separated from the radio-opaque shell of bone by soft tissues.

A midline section of the skull reveals that its interior is not of uniform height. The base is divided into three

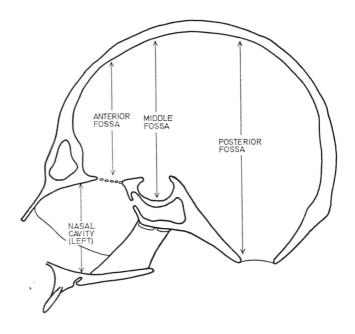

FIG. 21.1 Midline sagittal section of skull.

21.1

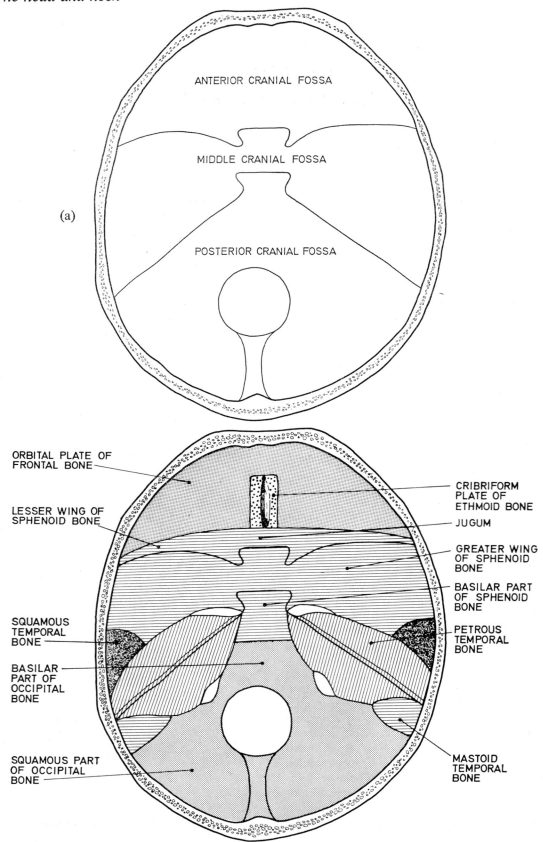

Fig. 21.2. Interior of skull base (a) fossae, (b) bones.

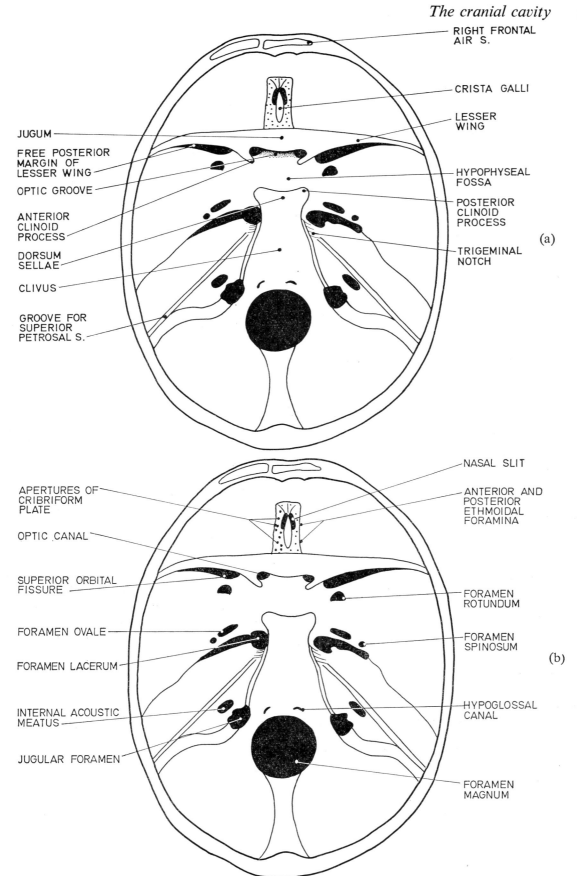

FIG. 21.3. The base of the skull (a) bony land marks, (b) foramina.

regions or fossae by two transverse boundaries. The anterior fossa, the shallowest of the three, lies above the nasal cavity in the midline and above the orbits, which are extensions of the neurocranium. Below the middle fossa lie the sphenoidal air sinuses and the nasopharynx, with masticatory structures on either side of them. The posterior fossa is directly continuous with the vertebral canal at the foramen magnum. It is the deepest of the three fossae, and the vertical height of the cranial cavity is greatest between the vault of the skull and the foramen magnum (fig. 21.1).

The division of the interior of the basal part of the cavity into three fossae is precisely defined when the interior of the base of the skull is viewed from above. The boundaries are shown in fig. 21.2a.

Anterior cranial fossa

The floor of the fossa is not level but is depressed where it overlies the nasal cavity and bulges upwards over the orbits. It is made up of the following bones:

The **ethmoid bone** occupies the central part of the fossa and from its upper surface projects the **crista galli**, a sharp-edged midline keel of bone. On either side, the floor of the fossa is depressed and consists of the thin, heavily-perforated bone of the **cribriform plate**. Near the anterior end of the plate, close to the side of the crista galli, is a narrow elongated aperture, the **nasal slit** which is larger than the other perforations of the plate. All these apertures connect directly with the nasal cavity. At the lateral edge of the cribriform plate, two fine apertures, the **anterior** and **posterior ethmoidal foramina**, run laterally between the upper surface of the ethmoid labyrinth and the medial edge of the frontal bone to the orbit.

The **frontal bone** articulates with both the lateral and the anterior edges of the ethmoid bone, enclosing it on three sides. The two **orbital plates** form the anterolateral parts of the fossa and bulge upwards. The frontal air sinuses frequently extend into them, separating the bone of the roof of the orbit from the bone of the floor of the fossa. The part of the frontal bone which connects the two orbital plates across the midline in front of the cribriform plate and the crista galli has a sagittally placed groove on its cranial aspect. This groove is occupied by the superior sagittal sinus.

The lesser wings of the **sphenoid bone** spread laterally along the posterior margin of the fossa and are connected to each other across the midline by the **jugum of the sphenoid**.

FORAMINA AND THEIR CONTENTS IN THE ANTERIOR CRANIAL FOSSA (fig. 21.3b).

The **nasal slit** contains the anterior ethmoidal nerve and vessels. The **foramina of the cribriform plate** hold the nerve fibres from the olfactory mucous membrane to the olfactory bulbs. The **anterior** and **posterior ethmoidal foramina** contain the anterior and posterior ethmoidal nerves and vessels.

Middle cranial fossa

The raised central part of the fossa, the **sella turcica**, is comparatively short from front to back. It lies between the anterior and posterior clinoid processes and contains a concave fossa to accommodate the hypophysis and its enclosing dura mater. Lateral to the sella, the floor of the fossa slopes downwards and outwards. The two lateral regions form the greater part of the fossa and extend forwards for a short distance below the free posterior margins of the lesser wings of the sphenoid bones. Their floors are composed of parts of both temporal and sphenoidal bones and are pierced by a number of foramina. The parts of the individual bones involved are as follows:

The **body of the sphenoid bone** forms the median part of the middle fossa, including its anterior and posterior boundaries. Immediately behind the jugum of the sphenoid is the shallow **optic groove**; at each end of the groove, where the lesser wing unites with the body of the sphenoid, there is a rounded aperture, the optic canal. Posterior to the groove on the upper surface of the sphenoidal body is the concavity for the accommodation of the pituitary gland, with grooves for the two internal carotid arteries on either side. The **lesser** and **greater wings of the sphenoid bone** project laterally from the body of the bone and form the anterior wall and floor of the anterior half of the extensive lateral part of the fossa.

The **upper surface of the petrous temporal bone** completes the fossa posteriorly. It is separated from the body of the sphenoid bone by a jagged aperture called the **foramen lacerum**. A wide suture, between the petrous temporal bone and the greater wing of the sphenoid, contains a smooth canal for the intrapetrous part of the internal carotid artery. The apex of the petrous temporal bone is marked by a notch which runs forwards, interrupting the groove for the superior petrosal sinus. This is occupied by the motor and sensory roots of the trigeminal nerve, whose ganglion overlies the suture mentioned above.

Laterally, the **squamous temporal bone** fits into the angle between the petrous temporal and the greater wing of the sphenoid bone. The suture between it and the lateral part of the petrous bone is normally obliterated by the age of five but forms a potential route for the spread of infection. In early life an otitis media may extend through it and involve the temporal lobe of the brain.

FORAMINA AND THEIR CONTENTS IN THE MIDDLE CRANIAL FOSSA (fig. 21.3b)

The **optic canal** lies between the roots of the lesser wing and the body of the sphenoid bone. It is a tube rather than a foramen which during its course may protrude into the upper lateral corner of the sphenoidal air sinus. It connects the fossa to the orbit and contains the optic nerve, its meningeal coverings and the ophthalmic artery.

The **superior orbital fissure** passes between the greater and the lesser wings of the sphenoid bone and contains the oculomotor, trochlear and abducent nerves, the ophthalmic division of the trigeminal nerve, a sympathetic root from the internal carotid plexus and the ophthalmic veins (fig. 21.11).

The **foramen rotundum** lies immediately below the superior orbital fissure. It connects the middle fossa with the pterygopalatine fossa and contains the maxillary nerve.

The **foramen spinosum** contains the middle meningeal vessels. These run in grooves to the pterion and lambda.

The **foramen ovale** is larger than the previous foramen and is situated in an anteromedial position. It contains the mandibular division and motor root of the trigeminal nerve, the accessory meningeal artery, the lesser petrosal nerve and emissary veins.

The **sphenoidal emissary foramen** contains only emissary veins.

The **foramen lacerum** is blocked in its lower half by fibrous tissue and cartilage. The carotid canal enters its posterolateral aspect and so connects the middle fossa with the part of the neck alongside the pharyngeal wall. The upper part of the foramen is occupied by the internal carotid artery, its sympathetic plexus of nerves and some emissary veins.

The **foramina for the greater and lesser petrosal nerves** are minute holes on the superior surface of the petrous temporal bone. They allow these nerves to run from the geniculate ganglion and the tympanic plexus through the middle fossa to the nerve of the pterygoid canal and the otic ganglion respectively.

Posterior cranial fossa

The floor is made up of parts of the occipital and temporal bones, with small contributions from both the body of the sphenoid and the parietal bones. The parts of the individual bones involved are as follows:

The **body of the sphenoid bone** projects downwards and backwards from the **dorsum sellae** to the middle of the sloping **clivus**, which forms the midline part of the anterior wall of the fossa.

The **occipital bone** forms the major part of the floor of the fossa and completely surrounds the centrally placed foramen magnum. Posterior to the foramen, the occipital bone expands into the flattened concave **squamous part**. A midline ridge called the **internal occipital crest** joins the posterior margin of the foramen magnum to the prominence of the **internal occipital protuberance**. From this point on each side of the midline, a groove runs laterally in a horizontal plane to the parietal bone and is occupied by the transverse venous sinus. Between this groove and the posterior margin of the foramen magnum, the bone is concave for the accommodation of the cerebellum, the **cerebellar fossa**. The groove for the transverse sinus turns downwards at its lateral end to follow an S-shaped course to the jugular foramen.

The **petrous** and **mastoid temporal bones** are commonly described as a single unit, the **petromastoid**. Together they form the anterolateral wall of the fossa.

The posterior inferior angle of the **parietal bone** fits into the angle between the petromastoid and squamous occipital bone.

FORAMINA AND THEIR CONTENTS IN THE POSTERIOR CRANIAL FOSSA. (fig. 21.3b)

The **internal acoustic meatus** penetrates and ends in the petrous temporal bone. It is connected by canaliculi with the vestibular and cochlear apparatuses, and with the stylomastoid foramen. It contains nerve VIII, the facial nerve, and its sensory parasympathetic root and the labyrinthine vessels.

The **jugular foramen** lies inferior to the internal acoustic meatus and its shape varies even on the two sides of the one skull. Immediately below the internal acoustic meatus, the upper margin of the foramen shows a well-marked notch for the glossopharyngeal nerve. The termination of the sigmoid sinus in the superior bulb of the internal jugular vein occupies the posterior and lateral part of the aperture; the inferior petrosal sinus lies in the anteromedial angle of the opening; between these two venous sinuses lie the glossopharyngeal, vagus and accessory nerves. The vagus and both parts of the accessory nerve share the same opening in the dura mater.

The **hypoglossal canal** is below and medial to the jugular foramen and wholly within the occipital bone. A bony prominence, the jugular tubercle, overhangs and partly conceals it and separates it from the jugular foramen. It contains the hypoglossal nerve.

The **foramen magnum** is occupied by the junction of the medulla oblongata and the spinal cord, the intradural part of the vertebral artery and its branches, vertebral veins, the spinal part of the accessory nerve and the meninges.

The **mastoid emissary foramen** connects the groove for the sigmoid sinus to the retroauricular surface of the mastoid bone.

The **posterior condylar canal** connects the same groove to the lower surface of the occipital bone, behind the condyle.

Both of these two foramina transmit emissary veins only.

The regions with which the cranial cavity is directly connected by foramina are as follows:

Connection	*Foramina*
Nasal cavity	Nasal slit
	Cribriform plate
Orbit	Optic canal
	Superior orbital fissure
	Ethmoidal foramina
Pterygopalatine fossa	Foramen rotundum
Infratemporal fossa	Foramen spinosum
	Foramen ovale
Neck	Carotid canal
	Jugular foramen
	Hypoglossal canal
Petrous temporal bone	Internal acoustic meatus
	Petrosal foramina
Vertebral canal	Foramen magnum

Cranial vault

The roof of the cranium is formed by the fusion of the frontal, parietal and occipital bones at the coronal, sagittal and lambdoidal sutures. In young adults when the individual bones are still separate, the connection between the adjacent edges of these flat bones is by a serrate arrangement of peg and socket joints, the individual components of which are about 1 mm long and sealed by fibrous tissue.

The interior of the vault is grooved in the midline for the superior sagittal sinus. The venous blood within the sinus flows backwards towards the external occipital protuberance and the grooves become wider when traced in this direction. The bone, within and alongside the groove, is often deeply pitted, particularly in aged skulls. Such pitting marks the site of the arachnoid granulations (p. 21.8). The parietal bone is often perforated, usually near its posterior end by emissary veins.

From either side of the vault, grooves run upwards and medially on the internal surface of the bone, breaking up into progressively finer channels. These grooves are occupied by the middle meningeal vessels. These supply only the bone and dura mater; the veins are closer to the bone.

Structures separating the intracranial part of the central nervous system from the surface of the head

The skull develops in the foetus from a number of isolated centres of ossification which gradually grow together, cutting off the brain from the superficial structures of the head. Nevertheless, some communications remain between intracranial and extracranial structures. Such communications, usually in the form of small venous channels, permit infection in superficial sites to extend across the cranial barrier and invade the cavity. The protective structures around the intracranial central nervous system is made up of the following:

(1) skin and superficial fascia,

(2) deep fascia and epicranial aponeurosis in the scalp,

(3) skeletal muscle, e.g. in the temporal fossa and the occipital region,

(4) the periosteum of the exterior of the skull,

(5) bone of the cranium consisting of two layers of compact bone, the inner and outer tables of the skull, separated by marrow-containing cancellous bone, the **diplöe**,

(6) periosteum of the interior of the skull,

(7) the dura mater which is fused to the periosteum, except where venous spaces, the intracranial venous sinuses, occur between these two layers,

(8) the pia-arachnoid investing the central nervous system.

Interior of the brain case (fig. 21.4)

The dura mater encloses the entire central nervous system and is separated from the pia-arachnoid by a capillary interval, the subdural space. The dura mater is not interrupted at the foramen magnum. The spinal part of the membrane, however, is free of the surrounding bony structures, except for a loose connection to the

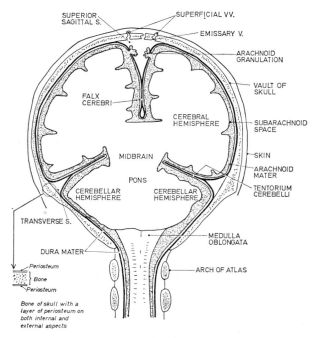

FIG. 21.4. Tentorium and falx.

posterior longitudinal ligament. Movement of a vertebra has accordingly little effect on the spinal cord and its meninges. In contrast, the intracranial part of the dura mater is firmly bound to the surrounding bone and changes in the latter closely affect both the dura mater and the vascular and nervous structures connected to it.

The dura mater exhibits three major folds, the **tentorium cerebelli**, the **falx cerebri** and the **falx cerebelli**. These form incomplete partitions within the cranium. In separating adjacent parts of the brain, this dural arrangement acts as a set of baffles. In movements of the head they prevent massive shift of the brain within the cranial cavity.

The partitions intersect along a line which runs downwards and backwards in the cranial cavity to end on the internal occipital protuberance. This is the position of the straight sinus. Above and to each side of the sinus are situated the two occipital lobes of the cerebrum, and below lies the superior vermis of the cerebellum. From the dura mater of the upper wall of the sinus, the falx cerebri extends upwards and forwards between the two cerebral hemispheres. From the lower surface of the posterior part of the sinus, the smaller falx cerebelli runs downwards and backwards on the wall of the posterior cranial fossa. On either side of the sinus, the two halves of the tentorium cerebelli extend laterally and forwards, enclosing the U-shaped tentorial notch.

The **supratentorial space** contains the two cerebral hemispheres, which are united across the midline by the corpus callosum. On the under surface of the hemispheres lie the olfactory bulbs and tracts, and the optic nerves, chiasma and tracts. Behind, above and in front of the corpus callosum, the hemispheres are separated by the falx cerebri.

The **infratentorial space** accommodates the remainder of the cranial contents. These include the brain stem, the cerebellum and all the cranial nerves from the trigeminal to the hypoglossal nerves. Although the trigeminal nerve crosses the posterior margin of the middle cranial fossa in order to connect with its ganglion, it remains concealed from the other structures by the roof of the cavum trigeminale in which it lies. The cavum connects only with the infratentorial space.

The oculomotor and trochlear nerves emerge from the superficial surface of the brainstem at the level of the tentorial notch, where the supratentorial and infratentorial spaces intercommunicate. Both the nerves pierce the dura mater at that level and their position is at the natural boundary between the two spaces.

The **tentorium cerebelli** slopes upwards and inwards from its fixed peripheral margin towards its centrally placed free edge. The fixed margin extends laterally on each side of the internal occipital protuberance along the lips of the groove for the transverse sinus. Here the two layers of dura mater diverge to form the upper and lower walls of the sinus. At the lateral end of the transverse groove, the fixed margin of the tentorium continues medially and forwards along the lips of the groove for the superior petrosal sinus to the posterior clinoid process. The **cavum trigeminale** connects with the infratentorial space by its opening below the superior petrosal sinus at the trigeminal notch. The superior petrosal sinus, which lies above the opening of the cavum, and the inferior petrosal sinus which lies in the posterior cranial fossa below and medial to the opening, are continuous here with the cavernous sinus. The opening of the cavum is therefore at the apex of the angle between the converging superior and inferior petrosal sinuses.

The free anterior margin of the tentorium cerebelli forms the boundary of the tentorial notch, within which lies the midbrain and the oculomotor and trochlear nerves. This border is U-shaped and the two free ends are attached to the anterior clinoid processes. Where the free edges of the falx cerebri and of the tentorium cerebelli are continuous, the great cerebral vein pierces the dura mater to enter the straight sinus.

The **falx cerebri** at its anterior end blends with the dura mater of the anterior cranial fossa around the crista galli. Superiorly, its two layers separate to enclose the superior sagittal sinus and become continuous with the dura mater of the cranial vault. Posteriorly, its layers are continuous with the dura mater of the upper surface of the tentorium cerebelli around the straight sinus. The depth of the falx cerebri is greatest posteriorly. The inconstant inferior sagittal sinus is enclosed in its free inferior edge.

The central nervous system is connected to the dura mater by nerves and blood vessels which cross the subarachnoid space to their destinations. Changes in the relative positions of parts of the brain, due to local or general alterations in intracranial pressure, exert traction on these connecting structures. This produces clinical effects which are not directly related to the site of the primary lesion. For example, a rise in supratentorial pressure, with a downward shift of the brain stem towards the foramen magnum, often stretches the abducent nerves and so paralyses the lateral rectus muscles.

Intracranial venous sinuses (fig. 21.5)

The system of venous sinuses is extradural. Venous blood from the brain traverses the subarachnoid space and the dura mater to enter a sinus. Usually, the shortest

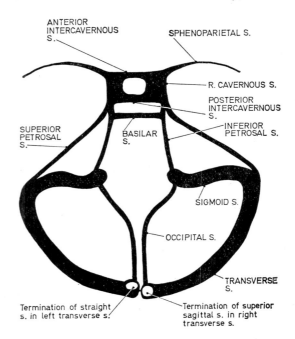

FIG. 21.5. Venous drainage of the cranial cavity.

possible route is taken and drainage is into the nearest sinus.

Some sinuses are connected to extracranial veins by emissary venous channels which occur at a number of points in the neurocranial wall. The diploic veins which are situated between the tables of the skull drain into superficial or intracranial venous channels, or into the emissary vessels which connect them. The venous sinuses possess no valves.

Their walls are of dense connective tissue and cannot distend or collapse. The main drainage to the exterior of the skull is through the sigmoid sinus and internal jugular vein.

The **superior sagittal sinus** begins at the crista galli. It may drain blood from the upper part of the nose and frontal air sinuses. Its course is in the midline, in contact with the deep aspect of the frontal bone, the sagittal suture and the occipital bone, following the upward curve of the vault of the skull in the attached margin of the falx cerebri. It terminates usually by turning sharply to the right to become continuous with the right transverse sinus at the internal occipital protuberance. Here also it communicates with the straight and left transverse sinuses and, if an occipital emissary vein is present, with the superficial veins at the back of the neck.

The sinus is connected with wide, laterally placed extensions called **lacunae laterales.** There may be as many as three of these on each side of the midline. The most constant overlies the upper part of the precentral gyrus of the cerebrum.

The **arachnoid villi** are concentrated along the walls of the superior sagittal sinus and around the walls of the lacunae laterales. These villi are buds of cellular connective tissue, derived from the arachnoid mater. They pierce the dural wall of the sinus and project into its lumen, where they are covered by the endothelial lining of the sinus. Each villus possesses a central channel, through which cerebrospinal fluid percolates into the sinus when pressure within the latter is low. When the intracranial venous pressure rises the villus functions as a valve, to prevent blood flowing into the subarachnoid space (fig. 24.106). Large groups of villi are described as granulations. When they are large enough, they lie in shallow depressions on the internal surface of the skull.

The superior sagittal sinus drains the upper parts of the superolateral and medial surfaces of the cerebral hemispheres. It receives the parietal emissary vein and connections from the lacunae laterales.

The **inferior sagittal sinus** lies in the posterior part of the free inferior edge of the falx cerebri. It terminates at the anterior end of the straight sinus, where it joins the great cerebral vein.

The **straight sinus** runs posteriorly from the junction of the inferior sagittal sinus and great cerebral vein to the region of the internal occipital protuberance, where it turns sharply to the left to form the left transverse sinus. The confluence of sinuses at the internal protuberance leads to the risk of extensive intracranial bleeding following direct injury to this part. In addition to the inferior sagittal sinus and the great cerebral vein, tributaries from the adjacent surfaces of the occipital lobes and cerebellum enter the sinus.

The **transverse sinuses** follow symmetrical courses in the attached margin of the tentorium cerebelli. Each sinus terminates at the posterior end of the petrous temporal bone by turning downwards to become the corresponding sigmoid sinus. The course of each sinus can be traced on the exterior of the skull from the external occipital protuberance, along the superior nuchal line, to the root of the auricle.

The **sigmoid sinuses** are directly continuous with the transverse sinuses. Turning downwards, each sinus leaves the tentorial margin and follows the general line of the junction of the petromastoid and occipital bones. In the floor of the posterior fossa, the sinus turns forwards to the jugular foramen and passes through its posterolateral part to become the superior bulb of the internal jugular vein.

The transverse and sigmoid sinuses receive superficial veins from the adjacent parts of the brain. The sigmoid sinus is connected with the posterior auricular and occipital regions by the **mastoid and posterior condylar emissary veins.** The mastoid vein drains the parietal diploë. In addition, the beginning and the end of the sigmoid sinus are connected to the cavernous sinus of the same side by the narrow superior petrosal and inferior petrosal sinuses, and the terminal part of each sigmoid sinus communicates with the confluence of sinuses by means of the corresponding occipital sinus.

The **superior petrosal sinuses** are channels, lying in the anterior part of the attached border of the tentorium cerebelli. At the opening of the cavum trigeminale, each lies in the double layer of dura mater in the roof of the opening and drains adjacent parts of the brain.

The **inferior petrosal sinuses** separate the clivus from the petromastoids and leave the cranial cavity through the anteromedial part of the jugular foramina. Along with the sigmoid and superior petrosal sinus, each forms the third side of a triangle of sinuses around the internal acoustic meatus. In addition to veins from the adjacent part of the cerebellum, the sinus receives the labyrinthine vein from the internal acoustic meatus.

The **occipital sinuses** unite the confluence of sinuses to the terminal parts of the sigmoid sinuses, running as parallel channels in the attached margin of the falx cerebelli, and diverging to their separate terminations on either side of the foramen magnum.

The **cavernous sinuses** are situated on either side of the fossa for the hypophysis (fig. 21.6). This endocrine gland lies on the upper surface of the sella turcica, connected to the base of the brain by a thin stalk of neural tissue. The dura mater which condenses around it in foetal life encloses the gland to leave only a small median aperture for this connection. At the edges of the aperture for the connecting stalk, the dura mater which encloses the hypophysis is continuous with that which lines the remainder of the middle cranial fossa. But, around the aperture, between the anterior and posterior clinoid processes, there is a raised area of dura mater, the **diaphragma sellae.** Separating the diaphragma and the adjacent dura mater of the middle fossa from the underlying periosteum and bone is an arrangement of venous spaces, the cavernous and intercavernous sinuses.

FIG. 21.6. Coronal section of cavernous sinus

Across the lumen of each cavernous sinus pass fibrous tissue partitions, lined with vascular endothelium, which break up the sinus cavity into a number of venous channels. Each sinus contains part of the internal carotid artery, surrounded by its sympathetic plexus. This artery enters the sinus through the upper part of the foramen lacerum and runs anteriorly in a groove on the body of the sphenoid. On its lateral side, and also within the sinus, is the abducent nerve. Both artery and nerve are enclosed in fibrous tissue, continuous with the partitions of the sinus, and also separated from the lumen of the sinus by vascular endothelium. The artery leaves the sinus by turning upwards on the medial side of the anterior clinoid process to pierce the dura and arachnoid to enter the subarachnoid space. At this point, the thin-walled artery, well supported within the sinus by its connective tissue covering, enters a fluid-filled space where support is minimal and movement is free. Within the lateral wall of the sinus, and separated from the artery and the abducent nerve by venous channels, are the oculomotor, trochlear, ophthalmic and maxillary nerves in that order from above downwards.

The two cavernous sinuses intercommunicate across the midline by means of the anterior and posterior inter-cavernous sinuses, which lie on the sella turcica in front of and behind the dural sac of the hypophysis, and through the basilar sinus, which runs posterior to the base of the dorsum sellae.

Posteriorly, the cavernous sinus receives the superior and inferior petrosal sinuses and the basilar sinus. Anteriorly, it receives the ophthalmic veins, and the small sphenoparietal sinus, which runs along the posterior margin of the lesser wing of the sphenoid bone. Superiorly, the superficial middle cerebral and other cerebral veins enter the roof of the sinus. Inferiorly, it is

freely connected with the veins outside the skull by means of emissary veins which pass through the foramen ovale and the foramen lacerum.

The cavernous sinus is deeply placed within the cranial cavity and yet is connected with extracranial veins by means of emissary channels. These potential routes for the extension of infection into the sinus are as follows:

(1) from the face, via the connections between the facial and ophthalmic veins at the orbital margin,

(2) from the pterygoid region, via veins in the foramen ovale and the sphenoidal emissary foramen,

(3) from the pharynx via veins which surround the intrapetrous part of the internal carotid artery.

Cranial nerves (fig. 24.29)

The point at which a cranial nerve emerges from or enters the substance of the brain is its superficial point of origin or attachment. Cranial nerves may be classified in accordance with the position of their superficial attachments as follows:

Cerebral hemispheres—I or olfactory nerve.
Junction of the midbrain and the cerebral hemispheres—II or optic nerve through the optic chiasma and tract.
Midbrain—III or oculomotor nerve and IV or trochlear nerve.
Pons—V or trigeminal nerve.
Ponto-medullary junction—VI or abducent nerve, VII or facial nerve, and VIII or vestibulocochlear nerve.
Medulla—IX or glossopharyngeal nerve, X or vagus nerve, the cranial part of XI or accessory nerve and XII or hypoglossal nerve.
Spinal cord—the spinal part of XI or accessory nerve.

As with spinal nerves, a dural sheath becomes applied to the nerve as it leaves the skull, and blends with its fibrous tissue coverings. The deep origins of the cranial nerves within the brain and the points where they leave that organ are described on pp. 24.16–24.26. Here we are concerned only with their course inside the skull and their passage through the foramina.

The cranial nerves can also be classified according to their exit points from the cranial cavity.

CRIBRIFORM PLATE GROUP OF NERVES

The dura mater of the anterior fossa is tightly bound down to the margins of the foramina which exist in the ethmoid bone on either side of the crista galli. The axons of the receptor cells of the olfactory zone of the nose occupy these foramina and pierce the dural and arachnoid membranes at their upper ends. Thereafter, they cross the subarachnoid space to enter the olfactory bulbs.

The anterior ethmoidal nerves and vessels, which pass from the orbit to the nasal cavity, lie within the dura mater of the cribriform plate. More posteriorly, terminal branches of the posterior ethmoidal group of neuro-vascular structures supply the dura mater.

CAVERNOUS SINUS GROUP (fig. 21.6)

The **optic nerves** lie immediately superior to the sinus. Each is enclosed in a sheath of the dura, arachnoid and pia. Cerebrospinal fluid separates the pia-arachnoid here as elsewhere, and extends as far as the back of the eyeball where the dura mater tube blends directly with the sclera. At the point where the optic nerve emerges from the optic canal and enters the main cranial cavity, the internal carotid artery also emerges from the dura mater of the upper surface of the cavernous sinus and comes to lie on the lateral side of the nerve, between it and the anterior clinoid process. At this point, the ophthalmic artery branches off from the internal carotid, passes below the optic nerve into the canal, and enters the orbit on its lateral side, piercing the dura mater sheath of the nerve as it does so. Either just before or just after it becomes extradural, the ophthalmic artery gives off the central artery of the retina, which crosses the pia-arachnoid sheath of the optic nerve to enter its substance. The vena comitans of this central artery drains into one of the veins of the orbit. Increase in the cerebrospinal fluid pressure is transmitted along the optic sheath to the back of the eyeball. Thus the central retinal vein, and to a lesser extent the retinal artery, may be partially or completely occluded as they pass through the subarachnoid space of the optic nerve.

The **abducent nerve** pierces the pia mater at the ponto-medullary junction, and runs upwards and forwards on the clivus, within the subarachnoid space. Two-thirds of the way up the clivus, it pierces the arachnoid and dura and continues in the same direction as before outside the dura mater. It enters the middle cranial fossa immediately medial to the opening of the cavum trigeminale. Thereafter, it runs forward within the cavernous sinus, on the lateral side of the internal carotid artery, to the superior orbital fissure, where it passes into the orbit through the fibrous ring at the apex of the rectus cone. The major part of its intracranial course is therefore extra-dural.

The **oculomotor nerve** is superficially attached at the medial side of the crus cerebri of the midbrain. It runs anteriorly between the posterior cerebral and the superior cerebellar arteries, and pierces the arachnoidal and dural membranes. It continues on its course in the lateral wall of the cavernous sinus, and leaves the cranial cavity by passing through the superior orbital fissure, within the fibrous ring at the apex of the rectus cone. It divides into an upper and a lower branch just before leaving the cranial cavity.

The **trochlear nerve** arises superficially from the dorsal surface of the lowest part of the midbrain, just below the inferior colliculus, passes around the brain stem and runs anteriorly in the lateral wall of the cavernous sinus, at first below and later lateral to the oculomotor nerve. It enters the orbit by passing through the upper lateral part of the superior orbital fissure, outside the fibrous ring of the rectus cone.

The **trigeminal nerve** is the only nerve that is superficially attached to the pons. Its sensory and motor roots enter and leave the brain stem at the junction of the pons and the middle cerebellar peduncle. These two roots cross the posterior boundary of the middle cranial fossa at the trigeminal notch at the apex of the petrous temporal bone. The motor root passes below the trigeminal ganglion to pierce the arachnoid and dural meninges at the foramen ovale. It may have a dural exit separate from the sensory part of the mandibular nerve, which also passes through this foramen, a fact which may permit the preservation of the motor root in surgical destruction of the sensory fibres of the mandibular nerve. The three terminal sensory branches of the trigeminal ganglion, ophthalmic, maxillary and mandibular, run forwards from the ganglion, each piercing the dura mater separately. The mandibular division has virtually no intracranial course. It leaves the cavity by the foramen ovale almost at the anterior margin of the ganglion, while the maxillary and ophthalmic nerves run forward in the lateral wall of the cavernous sinus. The maxillary nerve leaves the cavity at the foramen rotundum. The ophthalmic nerve, by contrast, breaks up into its lacrimal, frontal and nasociliary branches while still within the wall of the cavernous sinus. The lacrimal and frontal branches pass into the orbit through the upper lateral part of the superior orbital fissure, outside the fibrous ring of the rectus cone. The nasociliary nerve, however, enters the fissure through its lower medial part, within the ring and within the rectus cone (fig. 21.11).

INTERNAL ACOUSTIC MEATUS GROUP

The **facial nerve**, along with its autonomic sensory root, the nervus intermedius, and the **vestibulocochlear nerve** all join the brain stem at the pontomedullary junction. The cochlear element of the vestibulocochlear nerve is the most lateral, and the motor root of the facial nerve the most medial of the entire group. All these nerves are enclosed in a tunnel of dura and arachnoid mater, and a thin layer of cerebrospinal fluid, within the internal acoustic meatus. They are accompanied by the labyrinthine artery, a branch of the basilar vessel, and its vena comitans. The nerves and the blood vessels pierce the meninges at the lateral end of the meatus and are distributed to the interior of the petrous temporal bone through a number of foramina in the lateral wall of the meatus.

JUGULAR FORAMEN GROUP

In spite of its size, the jugular foramen is almost completely obscured by its covering of dura mater. Two apertures exist in the dura mater between the inferior petrosal and sigmoid sinuses, a small one directly below the internal acoustic meatus, and a larger one a little lower down. The **glossopharyngeal nerve** occupies the superior opening, while the **vagus** and cranial and spinal parts of the **accessory nerve** share the lower one.

All these nerves, excluding the spinal part of the accessory nerve, arise from the medulla oblongata by a series of rootlets which run in the longitudinal axis of the brain stem well posterior to the olive. The spinal accessory nerve pierces the lateral aspect of the upper six segments of the spinal medulla in the same longitudinal plane as the cranial roots. Gathering into a single trunk, the spinal accessory fibres enter the cranial cavity through the foramen magnum, and hook over the intracranial part of the vertebral artery, which is running upwards and medially at that point on its way to the lower border of the pons. The spinal and cranial parts of the accessory nerve then converge upon the jugular foramen, crossing the jugular tubercle of the occipital bone to do so. Upon this tubercle, the glossopharyngeal, vagus and cranial and spinal parts of the accessory nerve are in contact with the dura mater covering the bone, in that order from before backwards. Thereafter, the glossopharyngeal nerve follows its separate route. Two sensory ganglia are found on the course of the nerve just after it pierces the dura mater, the upper one within and the lower one just below the jugular foramen. From the inferior ganglion arises the tympanic branch, which enters the middle ear through a small foramen on the undersurface of the base of the skull. It carries secretomotor fibres to the parotid gland, and sensory fibres to the middle ear and its related cavities.

After the vagus and the cranial and spinal parts of the accessory nerves pierce the dura mater, the two components of the accessory nerve separate and the cranial part joins the vagus nerve. Two sensory ganglia also occur on the vagus. The spinal accessory nerve takes a separate course to the sternomastoid and trapezius muscles.

HYPOGLOSSAL CANAL

The **hypoglossal nerve** is superficially attached to the medulla oblongata by a vertical series of rootlets, which coalesce into two trunks which often pierce the dura mater separately. Both trunks hook over the intracranial part of the vertebral artery, and leave the cranial cavity through the hypoglossal canal, forming a single trunk after piercing the dura mater.

Surface relationships of the brain (fig. 21.7)

The frontal poles of the **cerebral hemispheres** lie immediately above and lateral at the root of the nose and are separated from the surface of the head by the frontal bone and its contained air sinuses. The occipital poles are placed above and lateral to the external occipital protuberance and between them lies the terminal part of the superior sagittal sinus.

The stem of the lateral sulcus fits against the free posterior margin of the lesser wing of the sphenoid bone, and both lie opposite the **pterion**. This is a point which lies about 3 cm posterior to the frontozygomatic suture, and 1 cm above that level. It is situated at the upper end of the greater wing of the sphenoid bone on the outside of the skull. Within the cavity and opposite this point, lie the anterior division of the middle meningeal vessels external to the dura mater.

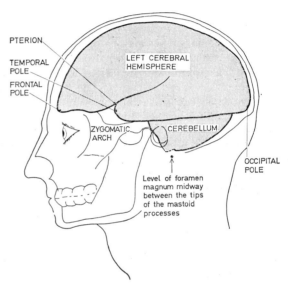

FIG. 21.7. Surface relations of the brain.

The lower lateral margin of the frontal lobe runs from the frontal pole along the supraorbital margin to its lateral end, and then upwards to the pterion. The temporal pole can be indicated by a line which runs, convex forwards, to connect the pterion to the upper margin of the zygomatic arch. Its most anterior point fails to reach the lateral margin of the orbit. The floor of the middle fossa lies opposite the upper margin of the zygomatic arch, and the inferolateral margin of the temporal lobe coincides with this level. A continuation of the line of this through the upper margin of the external acoustic meatus, and along the superior nuchal line to the external occipital protuberance indicates the position of the inferolateral border of the occipital lobe. In the last part of its course, it coincides in position with the transverse sinus. The upper medial margins of the cerebral hemispheres with the superior sagittal sinus run in parallel lines across the top of the head.

The **brain stem** is placed too deeply within the cranium

to permit accurate surface marking. The anterior surface of the pons does not extend any further forward than the the anterior edge of the external acoustic meatus. The junction of the brain stem and the spinal cord at the foramen magnum lies midway between the tips of the mastoid processes.

The parts of the **cerebellum** which lie in relationship to the walls of the posterior cranial fossa are the posterior and inferior aspects of the two hemispheres, and the inferior vermis which unites them in the midline. This part of the cerebellum which is in contact with the interior of the skull is therefore situated inferior to the superior nuchal line, and is separated from the skin of the upper part of the posterior surface of the neck by the insertions of the postvertebral muscles. The upper, deeper surface of the cerebellum is situated immediately below the tentorium cerebelli.

The **middle meningeal vessels** lie opposite the midpoint of the upper border of the zygomatic arch and end by dividing into a frontal and a parietal branch about a thumb's breadth above that point. The frontal division runs upwards and forwards from the point of bifurcation to the pterion, and from there upwards and backwards to the middle of the vertex. Both artery and vein frequently run in a tunnel of bone at the pterion and are easily damaged. The less important parietal division runs upwards and backwards towards the lambda, at the apex of the occipital bone.

THE ORBIT

The orbit is an extension of the neurocranium around the eye and the optic nerve and consists of soft tissues and a bony shell. The bony shell is like a hollow pyramid with the base anteriorly and the apex posteriorly. The medial walls of the two pyramids are parallel, while the lateral walls, if projected backwards, would meet at a right angle. The anterior cranial fossa lies above the orbits, while the bones of the upper jaw, including the maxillary air sinuses, lie below. Medial to each orbit are the ethmoidal air sinuses and the upper part of the nasal cavity, and laterally is the temporal fossa. The apex of the orbit is directed into the middle cranial fossa.

The following features of the bony orbit are of importance.

(1) The optic canal is situated just medial to the apex of the orbit. It is a rounded aperture which transmits the optic nerve, with its meningeal coverings, and the ophthalmic artery.

(2) Immediately lateral to the optic canal is a right-angled slit. The angle points medially, and lies at the apex of the orbit. The upper limb of the slit is the superior orbital fissure, the lower the inferior orbital fissure. From the middle of the latter, a groove runs

forwards in the floor of the orbit, becoming progessively deeper and more enclosed. This is the infraorbital groove and canal. It opens on to the face as the infraorbital foramen.

(3) On the upper part of the medial wall of the orbit, two small apertures, the anterior and posterior ethmoidal foramina, lead into the anterior cranial fossa.

(4) Also on the medial wall, just behind the medial margin of the orbit, is a hemicylindrical groove which is occupied by the nasolacrimal sac, the nasolacrimal fossa. Its well marked posterior margin is the posterior lacrimal crest.

SOFT TISSUE STRUCTURES OF THE ORBIT (fig. 21.8) The orbits are completely shut off from the face, when the eyes are shut, by the dense fibrous tissue plates or **tarsi**

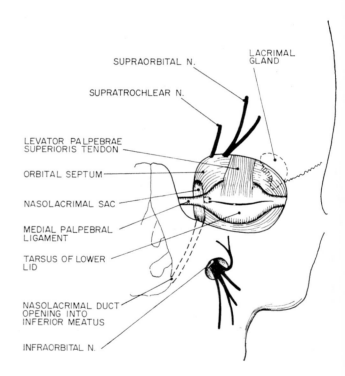

FIG. 21.8. Frontal view of the left orbit with eye closed.

which support the eyelids, and by the thin orbital septum which connects the periphery of the tarsi to the orbital margin.

Both the tarsi and the two parts, upper and lower, of the orbital septum are covered superficially by the orbicularis oculi muscle. From the medial ends of the tarsi, the **medial palpebral ligament** stretches in front of the nasolacrimal sac to be attached to the anterior margin of its fossa. A less well-defined lateral palpebral ligament stretches to the lateral margin of the orbit.

The internal surfaces of the tarsi are lined by the conjunctiva, which is reflected on to the eyeball superiorly and inferiorly at the fornices. The stratified columnar conjunctival epithelium blends with the stratified squamous epithelium of the cornea at the corneoscleral junction. When the eyelids are closed, the conjunctiva is virtually a closed sac. Opening on to the free edges of the eyelids are modified sebaceous and sweat glands, whose secretion prevents adhesion of the margins of the lids.

The movements of the eyeball

These are the result of a combination of the individual actions of the extraocular muscles (fig. 21.9).

changes direction entirely and runs backwards, laterally and downwards. It becomes flattened, and passes below the superior rectus muscle, between it and the eyeball, to be inserted into the posterior half of the upper lateral quadrant of the eyeball.

The **inferior oblique muscle** comes from the maxillary bone in the floor of the orbit, just lateral to the nasolacrimal fossa and runs laterally. It passes below the inferior rectus muscle, but medial to the lateral rectus. It is inserted into the upper lateral quadrant of the eyeball, mainly in its posterior half. Thus, although their routes to their respective linear attachments are different, both oblique muscles are inserted very close together on the eyeball.

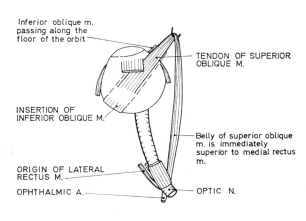

FIG. 21.9. Extraocular muscles of left eye seen from above.

The **rectus muscles, superior, inferior, medial** and **lateral** are arranged around the eyeball to form the **rectus cone**. The apex of this cone is formed by a tough fibrous ring, which surrounds the optic canal and the medial part of the superior orbital fissure. Each rectus muscle arises from the corresponding part of the ring and runs anteriorly to be inserted into the sclerotic coat of the eyeball about 0·5 cm from the corneoscleral junction. The cone is completed by a double sheet of fine fibrous tissue which covers and lines the recti, and connects them to each other, separating the fat within the cone around the optic nerve from the remainder of the orbital fat, and this can limit the spread of infection. Structures entering the orbit within the fibrous ring commence their course within the rectus cone. Those structures, however, which utilize routes outside the ring remain outside the cone.

The **superior oblique muscle** arises from the roof of the orbit, above and medial to the optic canal and runs forwards in the upper medial corner of the orbit to a point just posterior to its medial margin. There the muscle becomes tendinous and is suspended from the frontal bone by a fibrous ring-like pulley, the **trochlea**. At the trochlea, the superior oblique tendon

ACTIONS OF THE EXTRAOCULAR MUSCLES

The optical axis of the eye may be directed upwards, downwards, medially and laterally. In medial deviation the medial rectus, and in lateral deviation the lateral rectus are the all-important muscles. In looking upwards and downwards, the situation is less simple. Owing to the oblique orientation of the orbits, the superior and inferior recti pass medial to a vertical axis running through the centre of the eyeball, and therefore exert their effect most powerfully when the eye is directed laterally. The superior and inferior oblique muscles also pass slightly medial to the same axis, but their direction is at right angles to that of the recti. The eye is therefore directed upwards by the superior rectus when it is deviated laterally, and by the inferior oblique when it is deviated medially. It is directed downwards by the inferior rectus when deviated laterally, and by the superior oblique when deviated medially. When one muscle is paralysed, its failure to contract is most noticeable when an attempt is made to look in the direction in which its effect is maximal. For instance, superior oblique paralysis gives double vision when the patient attempts to look downwards and medially with the affected eye. Thus, a patient whose right superior oblique muscle is paralysed can fire a shotgun accurately at partridges passing overhead, but fails to park his car correctly, because he sees two kerbs on his left hand side.

The nerve supply of the extraocular muscles is as follows:

Superior rectus muscle—oculomotor nerve.
Inferior rectus muscle—oculomotor nerve.
Inferior oblique muscle—oculomotor nerve.
Medial rectus muscle—oculomotor nerve.
Superior oblique muscle—trochlear nerve.
Lateral rectus muscle—abducent nerve.

The **levator palpebrae superioris muscle** arises from the roof of the orbit just above the attachment of the fibrous ring of the recti (fig. 21.11). It is a narrow ribbon of muscle at its origin, but widens as it passes anteriorly. From its medial and lateral edges,

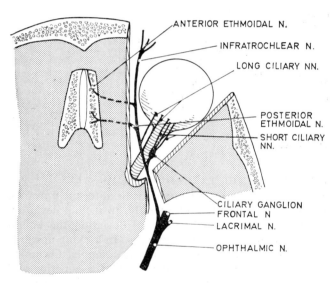

ANTERIOR ETHMOIDAL N.
INFRATROCHLEAR N.
LONG CILIARY NN.
POSTERIOR ETHMOIDAL N.
SHORT CILIARY NN.
CILIARY GANGLION
FRONTAL N
LACRIMAL N.
OPHTHALMIC N.

FIG. 21.10. The nasociliary nerve.

expansions spread out to the medial and lateral margins of the orbit. The central part of the muscle passes anterior to the superior tarsus, partially inserting itself into its superficial surface, and spreading through the overlying fibres of the orbicularis oculi muscle to be attached more diffusely to the skin of the upper eyelid. From the deep surface of the intraorbital part of the muscle, a sheet of smooth muscle fibres passes to the upper edge of the tarsus. The fibrous tissue sheath of the levator palpebrae superioris muscle blends with that of the underlying superior rectus muscle, and the resulting fibrous tissue lamella is attached to the superior fornix of the conjunctiva. As a result, elevation of both the upper lid and the fornix occur when looking upwards.

The skeletal muscle fibres are supplied by the oculomotor nerve; the smooth muscle by the sympathetic fibres derived from the internal carotid plexus.

FASCIAL SHEATH OF THE EYEBALL

The whole of the eye, except the cornea and the optic nerve and its sheath, is enclosed in a thin sheath of fascia. Anteriorly, this sheath blends with the sclera and conjunctiva at the corneoscleral junction. Posteriorly, it is loosely connected to the dura mater of the optic nerve sheath, a few millimetres behind the lamina cribrosa. A layer of fine connective tissue strands, most obvious posteriorly, intervenes between the sheath and the sclera. Ciliary arteries and nerves, venae vorticosae and the tendons of the extraocular muscles must traverse the fascial sheath and its underlying connective tissue space. Extensions of the sheath surround the flattened tendons of the extraocular muscles.

The eyeball is maintained in position by thickenings of the sheath. These constitute a soft tissue socket within which it can rotate. Stretching from the lateral to the medial margins of the orbit is the **suspensory ligament**. This condensation involves the fascial sheaths around the inferior rectus and inferior oblique tendons and resembles a hammock supporting the eyeball. Provided that it is intact, even destruction of the maxilla fails to affect the position of the eye. From the medial and lateral rectus muscles triangular fascial connections blend with the bony attachments of the suspensory ligament. These are the **medial** and **lateral check ligaments** which limit the amount of movement of the eye. The union of the sheaths of the superior rectus and levator palpebrae superioris muscles with the upper part of the fascial sheath, and the union of the sheaths of the inferior rectus and oblique tendons with the suspensory ligament on the lower aspect of the eyeball, similarly limit upwards and downward movement.

Blood supply of the orbit

The **ophthalmic artery** shares the optic canal with the optic nerve and its meningeal sheaths and so enters the orbit within the rectus cone. At the start of its intraorbital course it lies on the lateral side of the optic nerve. The **lacrimal branch** is given off, which keeps to the lateral side of nerve and eyeball. The main trunk of the ophthalmic artery, however, crosses above the optic nerve, and runs forward on the medial side of the eyeball. The artery and its lacrimal branch together form a V-shape above the optic nerve and eyeball; the medial limb is the thicker and has more branches. The distribution of both arteries is to the extraocular muscles and skin, to the dura mater, parts of the lacrimal apparatus and to the choroidal circulation of the eyeball. In addition, the ophthalmic artery supplies the retina, parts of the nasal cavity and some of the paranasal sinuses. The important branches to the eyeball are as follows.

(1) The **central artery of the retina** is an end artery (p. 28.15) and is the sole source of supply to the retina. Its terminal branches and their accompanying veins can be seen with an ophthalmoscope.

(2) The **ciliary arteries** supply the choroidal circulation, and enter the eyeball posteriorly around the optic nerve and anteriorly just behind the corneoscleral junction. The lateral group of anterior choroidal arteries come from the lacrimal branch of the ophthalmic artery.

The **ophthalmic veins** drain posteriorly through the superior orbital fissure to the cavernous sinus. They receive the central retinal vein and the venae vorticosae of the eyeball, and all the venae comitantes from the ophthalmic arterial area, except the cutaneous ones, most of which flow into the facial vein. These latter, however, communicate with the ophthalmic veins, and link the cavernous sinus to the superficial veins in the danger area of the face, above the ear-mouth line.

Nerve supply of the orbit (fig. 21.10 and 11)

Three nerves, one motor and two sensory, enter the orbit through the lateral part of the superior orbital fissure, above and lateral to the fibrous ring of the rectus muscles. They are distributed outside the rectus cone.

FIG. 21.11. The rectus cone and the superior orbital fissure.

The **trochlear nerve** passes medially above the levator palpebrae superioris to supply the superior oblique muscle. It contains motor and proprioceptive fibres for this muscle alone.

The **frontal** and **lacrimal nerves** are lateral to the trochlear nerve in the fissure. They are two of the three terminal branches of the ophthalmic division of the trigeminal nerve. The larger frontal branch runs forward in the roof of the orbit to break up into a small supra-trochlear and a large supraorbital branch, which together supply the upper eyelid and the anterior half of the scalp. The lacrimal nerve, which is lateral to the frontal, runs in the upper lateral part of the orbit to supply the lacrimal gland and the lateral part of the upper eyelid. It communicates in the orbit with the zygomatic branch of the maxillary nerve, so receiving from the ganglion secretory fibres to the lacrimal gland.

A large group of nerves enters the orbit through the fibrous ring of the recti, and therefore lies within the rectus cone.

The **nasociliary nerve** is the third terminal branch of the ophthalmic division of the trigeminal nerve, and, like the remainder of that nerve, is purely sensory. It connects with the ciliary ganglion, but the fibres transmitted pass through the ganglion without interruption. Following the ophthalmic artery, it passes medially above the optic nerve and ends as the anterior ethmoidal branch by supplying the skin of the tip of the nose, after passing through the anterior cranial fossa and the nasal cavity. It sends, in addition to its sensory root to the ciliary ganglion, two long cilary branches to the back of the eyeball. In the medial half of the orbit, it gives off a posterior ethmoidal branch to the sphenoidal and posterior ethmoidal air sinuses, and an infratrochlear branch to the skin at the root of the nose. The main trunk continues through the anterior ethmoidal foramen to be distributed with the corresponding vessels to the ophthalmic area of supply in the interior of the nasal cavity. It communicates with the oculomotor nerve in the orbit.

The **oculomotor nerve** enters the orbit as two branches, an upper and a lower, both within the rectus cone. The upper branch supplies the superior rectus and levator palpebrae superioris muscles. The lower division is distributed to the medial and inferior recti and the inferior oblique muscle. In addition, preganglionic parasympathetic efferent fibres, originating in the accessory oculomotor (Edinger–Westphal, p. 24.24) nucleus, pass through the lower division of the nerve to the ciliary ganglion, where they synapse with cells whose processes are distributed via the short ciliary nerves to the sphincter pupillae and ciliary muscles of the eyeball.

The **ciliary ganglion** is simply a parasympathetic relay station for the pathway just described. It is situated on the lateral side of the optic nerve, and its sole functional connection is with the oculomotor nerve. Other roots, sensory and sympathetic, merely use the ganglion and its short ciliary branches as a route to the eyeball.

The **abducent nerve** is distributed only to the lateral rectus muscle, which it supplies as it enters the orbit.

The extraocular muscles contain large numbers of muscle spindles. Their afferent fibres run within the abducent and oculo-motor nerves before being transferred to the nasociliary nerve in the orbit. Within this trigeminal nerve branch they run to its mesencephalic nucleus. The afferent fibres in the trochlear nerve pass directly to the mesencephalic nucleus (p. 24.26).

The **sympathetic supply** of the orbit is derived ultimately from the headward end of the thoracolumbar outflow, and enters the cranial cavity as the internal carotid plexus. It reaches the orbit as a separate sympathetic root which passes through the apex of the rectus cone, and as a plexus around the ophthalmic artery. It supplies the dilator pupillae muscle of the eye, the smooth muscle in levator palpebrae superioris, the vessels of the eyeball and orbit, and the strands of smooth muscle known as the orbitalis, which surrounds and constricts the veins passing through the superior and inferior orbital fissures. Paralysis of the orbital sympathetic fibres produces Horner's triple syndrome of constricted pupil, drooping upper eyelid (ptosis) and a sunken eye (enophthalmos).

Lacrimal apparatus

The structures responsible for the production and re-sorption of tears include the lacrimal gland, the con-junctival sac, the lacrimal punctae on the medial ends of the upper and lower eyelids, the canaliculi leading from them, the nasolacrimal sac into which they drain and the duct which carries the lacrimal fluid to the nasal cavity (fig. 21.8).

The gland is situated in a shallow fossa in the upper lateral part of the orbit, and has a palpebral process which extends around the lateral edge of the levator palpebrae superioris muscle. Some twelve ducts open into the lateral part of the superior fornix of the conjunctiva. Secretions flow from the upper lateral to the medial side of the con-junctival sac, where they are taken up by the lacrimal punctae. In order to operate effectively, these minute apertures must be applied to the surface of the con-junctiva. This is effected by the tone of the lacrimal part of the orbicularis oculi muscle. The main sheet of this muscle contracts reflexly to massage the lacrimal secre-tions across the conjunctiva and cornea. After passing into the canaliculi, the secretions reach the nasolacrimal sac, which lies in its fossa at the medial side of the orbit, and from here they are passed down the nasolacrimal duct to be discharged into the inferior meatus of the nose.

THE FACE AND SCALP

Muscles of the face and scalp

Over the face and scalp, the skin and the superficial fascia are bound to an underlying stratum of skeletal muscle which becomes an aponeurosis over the vertex of the head. This layer is of uneven depth and where it is fleshy, its fibres are frequently inserted into the dermis. The activity of this musculo-aponeurotic layer is re-sponsible for the production of the variations in the ex-pression of the face and brow. This layer is derived from the mesoderm of the second or hyoid arch, and the muscle fibres in it accordingly obtain their motor nerve supply from the second arch nerve, the facial nerve. A continu-ous sheet of the same muscle extends into the neck as the platysma muscle.

The muscle in the face is arranged as three sphincters, one over each orbit and one around the mouth, linked by poorly defined bands. These latter features radiate on each side of the face from a point a little lateral to the angle of the mouth. All these muscles, linear and sphinc-ter, have limited connections with the underlying bones.

The **orbicularis oculi muscle** is the sphincter muscle of the orbit and surrounds the palpebral fissure. The main sheet of the muscle, the orbital part, is attached to the medial margin of the orbit from the supraorbital notch to the region of the infraorbital foramen, and includes the medial palpebral ligament in its attachments. These fibres loop around the tarsi, but do not become attached to the lateral part of the orbital margin. Finer fibres, the palpebral part, form a layer on the superficial aspect of the tarsi, and are traversed by some of the fibres of the levator palpebrae superioris, as they pass from the orbit to the skin of the upper eyelid. The lacrimal part is deep to the rest of the muscle; it arises posterior to the naso-lacrimal sac and is inserted into the medial ends of the tarsi.

The **buccinator-orbicularis oris muscle** forms the con-tractile element in the lips and the cheeks. The buc-cinator is a sheet of muscle which continues posteriorly as the superior constrictor muscle of the pharynx. The line of junction between the two is a vertically placed fibrous intersection, the pterygomandibular raphe. Superiorly and inferiorly, the buccinator is attached to the maxilla and the mandible on the lateral aspects of their alveolar processes, at the line of reflec-tion of the gingival mucous membrane. It blends medially with the fibres of the orbicularis oris, which form an elliptical sphincter around the lips. The oral aspect of the buccinator is lined by a thick layer of connective tissue, the inner cheek pad, which supports the stratified squamous non-keratinizing epithelium of the vestibule of the mouth. The duct of the parotid salivary gland pierces both the buccinator and the inner cheek pad to open into the vestibule of the mouth at the level of the second upper molar tooth.

The **occipitofrontalis muscle** extends from the superior margins of the orbits to the superior nuchal lines. Anteriorly, it is mainly connected to the other muscles of the face, posteriorly to bone. Laterally, it blends with a layer of deep fascia, which extends in the tem-poral region down to the zygomatic arch. Over the top of the skull, it is aponeurotic. Its importance lies in its intimate attachment to the overlying skin, particu-larly over the vertex of the skull, where there is one com-posite layer of skin, dense connective tissue and apo-neurosis. Within this triple layer the nerves and vessels of the scalp are distributed, entering from the periphery. This permits free movement of the skin-aponeurosis as one layer, when either frontal or occipital fibres of the muscle contract. Except where the parietal emissary veins enter their foramina alongside the sagittal suture, the anatomical separation of the scalp from the underlying periosteum of the cranial vault is complete. In industrial scalping injuries and when this skin-aponeurosis layer is raised in surgical operations, the survival of the scalp flap depends on an adequate peripheral attachment.

The **platysma muscle** is a subcutaneous sheet of skeletal muscle. It extends from the upper part of the pectoral region to the lower jaw, where it blends with the muscles around the mouth. It has an interrupted attachment on its deep aspect to the lower margin of the body of the mandible.

NERVE SUPPLY TO THE MUSCLES OF FACIAL EXPRESSION

The **facial nerve** emerges from the stylomastoid foramen, turns on to the lateral aspect of the styloid process, and enters the parenchyma of the parotid gland. Fibres pass to the posterior part of the occipitofrontalis, the posterior belly of the digastric muscle and to the stylohyoid muscles prior to its entry into the gland. Within the substance of the parotid, the remainder of the nerve breaks up into five bundles of fibres, which penetrate the secretory tissue and emerge along the whole extent of the anterior border of the gland from its upper to its lower poles. In the face, they are distributed to the muscles by numerous small branches. The presence of these motor fibres in the superficial layers of the face must be remembered during facial surgery.

In its course through the parotid gland, the main trunk of the facial nerve passes superficial to the retromandibular vein and the external carotid artery, both of which are within the gland.

When the facial nerve is paralysed, the affected half of the face is immobile and expressionless. More serious complications arise from the loss of function of the orbicularis oculi and the orbicularis oris-buccinator muscles. Paralysis of the orbicularis oculi abolishes the blinking response, so that the affected eye is totally unprotected from direct injury. Since the punctae are not kept in contact with the ocular conjunctive, the resorption of lacrimal fluid ceases and tears flow down over the surface of the cheek. As the eyelids cannot be closed, the eye has to be turned upwards during sleep. The loss of function in the orbicularis oris-buccinator sheet prevents effective closure of the lips and occlusion of the vestibule of the mouth during chewing, which itself is unimpaired. The vestibule becomes distended with partially masticated food, which cannot be retained between the teeth, and which eventually dribbles from the affected corner of the mouth.

CUTANEOUS NERVE SUPPLY OF THE HEAD AND NECK

The nerves involved are partly cranial and partly spinal in origin. The detailed distribution of these nerves is shown in figs. 21.12 and 13.

BLOOD SUPPLY OF THE FACE AND SCALP

The arterial supply is unequally divided between the external and internal carotid arteries, the contribution of external predominating. The internal carotid artery, through its ophthalmic branch, supplies the regions which receive branches from the ophthalmic nerve. The external carotid artery supplies the skin through the following branches:

The **facial artery** runs from the anterior margin of the masseter muscle to the medial angle of the eye, supplying the lower and

upper lips, the face and the side of the external nose. It anastomoses freely in its terminal part with branches of the ophthalmic artery. Blood can reach the bed of a ligated ophthalmic artery through the facial arterial route.

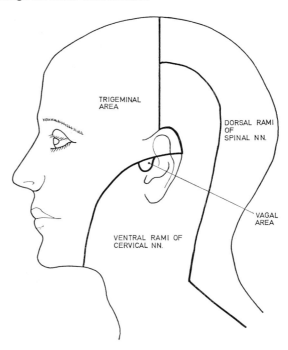

FIG. 21.12. Cutaneous distribution of trigeminal and spinal nerves.

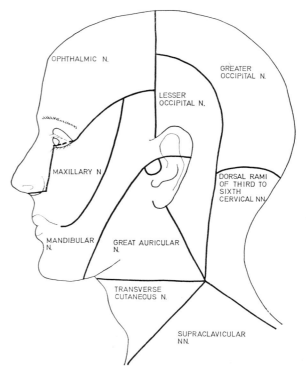

FIG. 21.13. Cutaneous nerve supply of the head and neck.

15

The **superficial temporal artery** accompanies the auriculotemporal nerve, and crosses the zygomatic arch with it, immediately in front of the ear. It is distributed to the temporal region and the scalp.

The **posterior auricular artery** is small, and supplies the region immediately behind the ear.

The **occipital artery** enters the posterior part of the scalp region at the superior nuchal line, about an inch from the midline, and accompanies the greater occipital nerve to the skin and superficial tissues of the posterior half of the scalp.

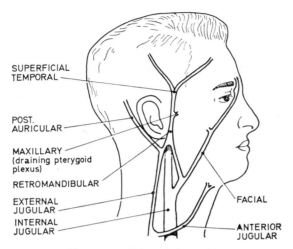

SUPERFICIAL TEMPORAL

POST. AURICULAR

MAXILLARY (draining pterygoid plexus)

RETROMANDIBULAR

EXTERNAL JUGULAR

INTERNAL JUGULAR

FACIAL

ANTERIOR JUGULAR

FIG. 21.14. Veins of the neck.

In the face and scalp regions, the main veins run as follows:

The **facial vein** is formed by veins from the front of the scalp which converge at the medial angle of the eye. Here the skin is very thin so the vein is usually clearly visible and is commonly termed the **angular vein**. This is one of the sites of facial-ophthalmic venous anastomosis. The main trunk of the vein runs posterior to the artery to the anterior margin of masseter communicating with the pterygoid venous plexus by means of the deep facial vein. It finally drains into the internal jugular system, often in common with the lingual vein. It receives the anterior division of the retromandibular vein prior to doing so.

The **superficial temporal vein** drains the area of supply of the corresponding artery and accompanies it on its course. At the zygomatic arch, it enters the substance of the parotid gland, and joins the retromandibular venous channel. This vessel leaves the parotid gland at its lower pole, and divides into a small anterior division which enters the facial vein, and a larger posterior division which constitutes the main part of the external jugular vein.

The **posterior auricular vein** joins the posterior division of the retromandibular vein to form the external jugular vein.

The **occipital vein** accompanies the occipital artery only as far as the upper part of the back of the neck, where it ends in the suboccipital venous plexus. The deep cervical vein connects the plexus to the brachiocephalic vein at the root of the neck.

Emissary veins, of which the facial-ophthalmic connection is only one example, connect the superficial veins of the scalp, face and the back of the neck to the intracranial venous sinuses.

Parotid salivary gland

The parotid gland fits into the space between the posterior border of the mandible and the anterior borders of the mastoid process and the sternomastoid muscle.

Its lateral surface is smooth, and conforms to the contours of the face. It has a diamond shape with sharp upper and lower angles. These fit between the temporomandibular joint and the external acoustic meatus at the upper end, and between the angle of the mandible and the anterior margin of the sternomastoid muscle at the lower. From the blunt anterior angle of the gland, the parotid duct runs across the masseter, at the anterior border of which it turns sharply medially, pierces the buccinator and the inner cheek pad and opens into the vestibule of the mouth.

Because the deep surface of the gland is moulded into the cleft between the mandible and the sternomastoid, it is irregular. It has an anteromedial surface, related to the masseter, the mandible and the medial pterygoid muscle, and a posteromedial surface related to the sternomastoid, the posterior belly of the digastric muscle and the styloid process. Between these two surfaces, the medial edge of the parotid gland may extend as far as the internal carotid artery and the internal jugular vein (fig. 21.18).

During prenatal growth the parotid gland comes to surround the external carotid artery, the retromandibular vein, the facial nerve, and the deep and superficial parotid lymph nodes. The external carotid artery enters the parotid from the lateral aspect of the styloid process, and soon divides in the gland into the superficial temporal and maxillary arteries. The maxillary artery runs forward deep to the neck of the mandible, and enters the pterygomaxillary fissure. The retromandibular vein, which is formed within the gland, runs superficial to the artery, while the facial nerve passes through the gland superficial to them both. The deep parotid lymph nodes form part of the deep cervical group, while the superficial ones are part of the collar chain and drain the skin of the temporal region, the forehead and the front of the auricle. The whole parotid gland is enclosed in a strong envelope of deep fascia. A superficial layer spreads upwards over the lateral surface of the gland to blend with the periosteum of the zygomatic arch and with the perichondrium of the external acoustic meatus. Another layer passes deep to the gland, blending with the periosteum of the tympanic plate and the styloid process. A thickened layer, the stylomandibular ligament, extends from the styloid process to the angle of the mandible, separating the parotid from the posterior pole of the submandibular gland and from the medial pterygoid muscle.

The external acoustic meatus and the external ear

The external ear is a plate of elastic cartilage, covered with skin. This cartilage support is continued into the external meatus, whose lateral third is an incomplete cylinder of the same material. Where the cylinder is incomplete, the deficiency is supplied by fibrous tissue

The remainder of the adult external meatus is formed in bone, the tympanic plate forming the walls and floor, and the squamous temporal bone the roof. The entire canal of the external acoustic meatus is curved along its course with its convexity facing upwards and slightly backwards; the tympanic membrane, which closes its medial end, faces somewhat downwards and forwards as well as laterally. The skin which lines both meatus and membrane is tightly bound down to the underlying connective tissue. In the meatus, it is supplied with large coiled glands which secrete wax, and with sebaceous glands and hair follicles. The nerve supply comes mainly from small branches of the auriculotemporal nerve and from the auricular branch of the vagus with a few filaments from the facial and the glosso-pharyngeal nerves. In herpes of the sensory ganglion of the facial nerve, the few filaments derived from it may produce bullae in the external meatus (fig. 21.12).

The skin of the lower part of both surfaces of the auricle is supplied by fibres of the great auricular nerve. The lateral side of the upper part is supplied by the auriculotemporal nerve, and the medial surface by the lesser occipital nerve.

Masticatory apparatus

During mastication, the maxilla, which is firmly fixed to the rest of the skull, is immobile; while the mandible

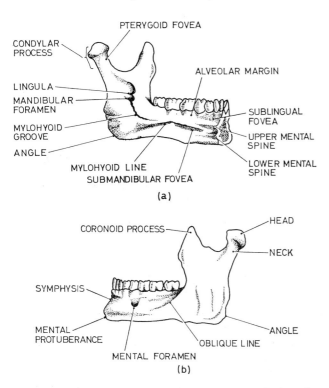

FIG. 21.15. The mandible (a) medial aspect (b) lateral aspect.

is moved in relation to it by the four pairs of muscles of mastication.

THE TEMPOROMANDIBULAR JOINT

Because the mandible is a single bone from the age of two onwards, the two temporomandibular joints function as a single unit; thus they may be regarded as a bicondylar joint with two separate cavities divided by the total width of the base of the skull.

Each temporomandibular joint is formed by the head of the condylar process of the mandible and the mandibular fossa and articular tubercle of the squamous temporal bone. These two bony surfaces are not congruent.

The superior surface forms a wide shallow groove, facing downwards, whose anterior edge is enlarged into a ridge, the articular tubercle. The long axes of both groove and ridges run transversely. The articular upper surface of the head of the mandible is ellipsoidal and has a long axis which runs medially and slightly backwards. The neck of the mandible below it is flattened anteroposteriorly and exhibits a fossa, the pterygoid fovea, on its anteromedial aspect. The lateral pterygoid muscle, which is intimately associated with the joint both structurally and functionally, is mainly inserted into the fovea but also passes through the capsule of the joint to become continuous with the intra-articular disc. This structure compensates for the differences in shape between the opposing surfaces of the two bones. It completely divides the cavity of the temporomandibular joint into an upper and a lower compartment, since the edge of the disc fuses with the capsule.

The capsule of the joint is attached superiorly to the margins of the mandibular fossa, except anteriorly, where it extends on to the anterior aspect of the articular tubercle. Inferiorly it surrounds the neck of the mandible. It is thickened laterally to form the **lateral ligament**, whose fibres run downwards and backwards from the lateral margin of the fossa and the tubercle to the lateral side and posterior aspect of the neck of the mandible. It has no counterpart of comparable strength on the medial aspect of the joint, since the two temporomandibular joints are separate parts of the same functional articulation. The two lateral ligaments are the widely separated **collateral ligaments** of the mandibulocranial articulation.

The fibres of the capsule which connect the superior articular surface of the joint to the intra-articular disc are lax. Those connecting the disc to the lower articular surface are, by contrast, shorter and tighter. Movement between the disc and the squamous temporal bone is accordingly easier to achieve than movement between the disc and the mandible.

The **sphenomandibular** and **stylomandibular ligaments** are situated close to the temporomandibular joint, but have little functional connection with it. The former is the remnant of the perichondrium of the first arch cartilage of the embyro (Meckel's cartilage), and the latter is a thickening in the fascia between the parotid and submandibular glands.

MUSCLES OF MASTICATION

This group of four muscles is supplied by motor fibres of the trigeminal nerve, which reach them through its mandibular division. The muscles are derivatives of the first or mandibular arch mesoderm. The masseter lies on the lateral aspect of the plane of the mandible, the temporalis is situated in that plane, and the lateral and medial pterygoid muscles lie deep to it. These are shown in figs. 21.16 and 17 where O and I represent the origin and insertion respectively.

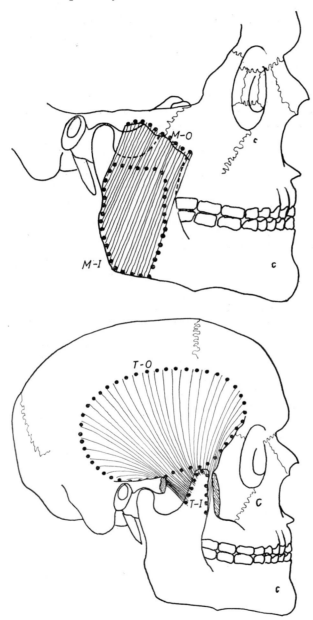

FIG. 21.16. Muscles of mastication.

Masseter (M)

M-O Lower border of zygomatic arch.
M-I Lateral aspect of the ramus of the mandible.

Temporalis (T)

T-O Floor of temporal fossa and overlying fascia.
T-I Tip and margins of the coronoid process of the mandible.

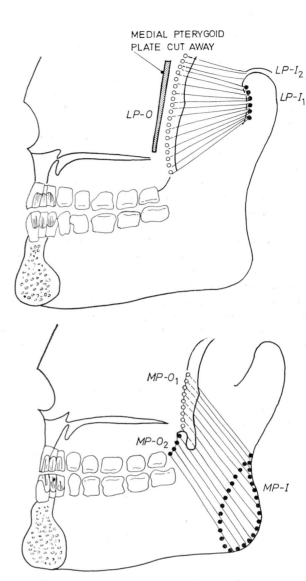

FIG. 21.17. Muscles of mastication; medial view.

Lateral Pterygoid (LP)

LP-O Lateral surface of lateral pterygoid plate and the infratemporal surface of the greater wing of the sphenoid.
LP-I_1 Pterygoid fovea on the neck of the mandible.
LP-I_2 Intra-articular disc of the joint.

Medial Pterygoid (MP)

MP-O_1 Pterygoid fossa.
MP-O_2 Tuberosity of the maxilla.
MP-I Medial aspect of the angle of the mandible.

MOVEMENTS OF THE TEMPOROMANDIBULAR JOINT

Movements at this joint are mainly, but not exclusively, produced by the masticatory muscles. The mouth is opened by the lateral pterygoid muscle, the combined suprahyoid and infrahyoid muscles, the platysma and gravity. In this action, two movements occur within the double joint cavity. First, the head of the mandible and the disc move together under the traction of the lateral pterygoid muscle, sliding downwards and forwards until they lie directly under the tubercle. Because of the direction of the fibres of the lateral ligament of the temporomandibular joint, no resistance is encountered from it. Secondly, and occurring at the end of the first movement, the head of the mandible rotates in a hinge movement on the undersurface of the intra-articular disc. In both movements, the region of the mandibular foramen remains nearly static, thus avoiding traction on the inferior alveolar nerve and vessels.

line posteriorly down to the thoracic inlet. The structures which lie in front of the cervical vertebrae are, however, continued upwards, deep to the mandible, as the midline hollow visceral spaces of the head, and as the laterally placed neurovascular bundles as far as the under surfaces of the middle and anterior cranial fossae. The infratemporal and submandibular regions are simply upward extensions of the neck.

The structures which form the neck can be divided into: the **central supporting structures** (the cervical vertebral column with its prevertebral, paravertebral and post-

FIG. 21.18. Horizontal section of head.

Apposition of the teeth, or occlusion, is achieved by the combined actions of the masseters, medial pterygoids and the temporals. Protrusion of the chin is produced by the contraction of the medial and lateral pterygoids, assisted by the masseters, while retraction is effected by the posterior fibres of the temporales. A slewing of the jaw to one side is achieved by combining protrusion by the muscles of one side of the head with retraction by the muscles of the other.

THE NECK

The neck extends from the level of the lower margin of the mandible anteriorly and from the superior nuchal

vertebral muscles), the **neurovascular bundle of the head** and the superficially placed **muscle sheet** with its enclosing layers of deep fascia (figs. 21.18 and 19).

Anterior to the prevertebral muscles with between the neurovascular bundles, the hollow viscera run through the neck into the thorax.

Central supporting structures

CERVICAL VERTEBRAL COLUMN

The individual vertebrae differ from each other more sharply than do those of the thoracic, lumbar or sacral regions. They fall into the following groups:

(1) atlas-axis complex, which is modified from the basic vertebral pattern,

INFRAGLOTTIC PART OF LARYNX

LARYNGOPHARYNX

SCALENUS ANTERIOR M.

INFRAHYOID MM.

STERNOMASTOID M.

NEUROVASCULAR BUNDLE

SCALENUS MEDIUS M.

C6

LEVATOR SCAPULAE M.

TRAPEZIUS M.

SPLENIUS AND SUBSPLENIAL MM.

FIG. 21.19. Horizontal section of neck.

(2) typical cervical vertebrae, the third to the sixth,

(3) seventh cervical vertebra, which is transitional in form between the typical cervical and the upper thoracic vertebrae.

Atlas-axis complex

The part of the skull which surrounds the foramen magnum is a series of modified vertebrae, which have fused into a single mass. The synovial joints between this mass and the upper surface of the atlas, and between the atlas and the axis, are of the same nature.

The **atlas** (fig. 21.20) is unique in possessing no apparent supporting structure in the form of a vertebral body. Instead, two lateral masses are connected by two bony arches, the posterior arch being longer and more slender. Elongated kidney shaped facets on the superior aspect of each lateral mass articulate with the occipital condyles. On the corresponding parts of the inferior

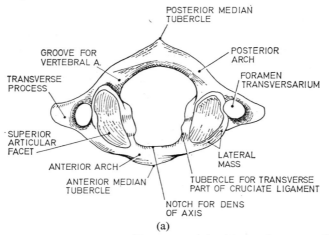

POSTERIOR MEDIAN TUBERCLE

GROOVE FOR VERTEBRAL A.

POSTERIOR ARCH

TRANSVERSE PROCESS

FORAMEN TRANSVERSARIUM

SUPERIOR ARTICULAR FACET

ANTERIOR ARCH

ANTERIOR MEDIAN TUBERCLE

LATERAL MASS

TUBERCLE FOR TRANSVERSE PART OF CRUCIATE LIGAMENT

NOTCH FOR DENS OF AXIS

(a)

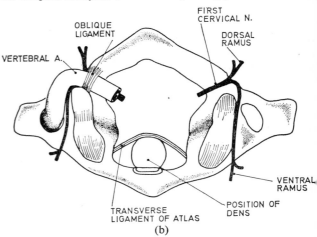

OBLIQUE LIGAMENT

FIRST CERVICAL N.

DORSAL RAMUS

VERTEBRAL A.

VENTRAL RAMUS

POSITION OF DENS

TRANSVERSE LIGAMENT OF ATLAS

(b)

FIG. 21.20. Atlas (a) superior aspect, (b) vertebral artery and first cervical nerve.

aspects of the lateral masses are circular, flattened facets, set at a light angle to the horizontal plane, for articulation with facets on either side of the dens of the axis.

The **anterior arch** of the atlas is slightly anterior to the plane of the anterior aspects of the succeeding vertebral bodies. It unites the two lateral masses of the atlas, whose centrum has become separated and fused to the axis forming a pivot for the dens. There is a tubercle on the anterior aspect of the arch to which are attached the upper ends of the anterior longitudinal ligament of the vertebral column and the longus colli muscles. On the posterior aspect of this arch there is a synovial area for articulation with the dens of the axis.

The **posterior arch** is grooved on its upper surface, at the point at which it blends with the lateral mass, immediately posterior to the condyle. The first cervical nerve lies in the floor of this groove, and divides while within it. The ventral ramus turns anteriorly round the lateral margin of the condyle, while the dorsal ramus runs straight backwards in the groove. Above the nerve, the vertebral artery fills the whole width of the groove as it turns backwards and medially around the posterior margin of the condyle, before turning forwards on its medial side to pierce the posterior atlanto-occipital membrane (fig. 21.20b).

From the lateral aspect of the lateral mass projects the **transverse process**, within which is the **foramen transversarium** for the vertebral artery and its venae comitantes. The tubercle on its lateral margin is the posterior one. Neither the atlas nor the axis has a readily demonstrable anterior tubercle on its transverse process.

The transverse processes of the atlas are prominent on the lateral aspect of the neck, just below the external acoustic meatus.

The **axis** (fig. 21.21) is a compound of the centrum of the atlas

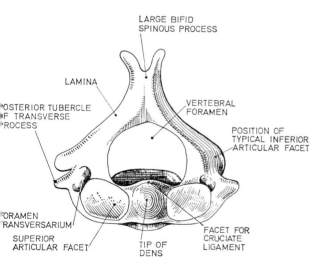

FIG. 21.21. Axis.

and the whole of the second cervical vertebra. It is further modified on its superior surface by the absence of typical articular facets, which would hinder rotation of the atlas and skull around the dens of the axis. The inferior aspect of the axis, however, exhibits none of these specialized features, and conforms to that of any typical cervical vertebra. The superior articular facets are therefore anterior to its inferior facets and consequently also to the articular facets of the other vertebrae. These superior facets correspond to those involved in the atlanto-occipital articulation. They consist of flat circular areas on either side of the dens and are inclined slightly downwards and outwards.

In contrast to the atlas, which has no true spine, the axis possesses a very strong, prominent bifid spinous process. The ligamentum nuchae is attached to the groove between the two parts of the split spinous process. When an attempt is made to tap the cisterna magna, the palpable prominence of the spinous process of the axis is used to direct the point of the needle towards the posterior atlanto-occipital membrane.

The **occipito-atlanto-axial** joints differ from those uniting other vertebrae (p. 20.3). The movement of nodding involves the articulating surfaces of the atlas and the occipital bone. The rotary movement, however, only takes place between the dens of the axis and the anterior arch of the atlas, and involves the movement of the combined skull and atlas as a single mobile unit upon the axis and the remainder of the cervical column. Fusion of the atlas and axis virtually prevents rotation of the head.

The specialized articulations (fig. 21.22) involving the base of the skull, the atlas and the axis are therefore:

(1) atlanto-occipital.
(2) atlanto-axial.
(3) occipito-axial.

(a)

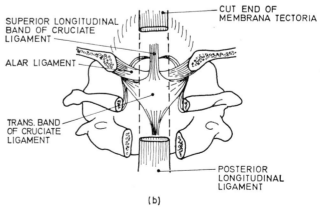

(b)

FIG. 21.22. The occipito-atlanto-axial connection. (a) posterior view, (b) internal ligaments.

The atlas and the occipital bone are united by the two articular capsules of the joints between the condyles of the two bones, and by membranes uniting the arches of the atlas to the margins of the foramen magnum. These membranes are continuous at their edges with the capsules of the synovial joints. The anterior **atlanto-occipital membrane** is uninterrupted, but the larger posterior membrane is pierced laterally by the vertebral artery and its venae comitantes and by the emerging first cervical nerve.

The union of the atlas and the axis is also achieved by synovial joints which connect the opposed articular surfaces of the two bones. The posterior arch of the atlas is united to the arch of the axis by the **atlanto-axial membrane.** The undivided trunk of the second cervical nerve pierces this membrane, and its large dorsal ramus lies in contact with the upper surface of the arch of the axis. The posterior aspect of the body of the axis is connected to the lateral masses of the atlas by two diverging accessory atlanto-axial ligaments.

The apex of the dens of the axis is connected to the base of the skull at the anterior margin of the foramen magnum by the vestigial apical ligament. From either side of this slender structure, two much stronger **alar ligaments** radiate from the dens to the foramen magnum. Posterior to the dens the **cruciate ligament** covers the atlas and axis to reach the occipital bone. It consists of a thin longitudinal band, running from the posterior surface of the body of the axis to the anterior margin of the foramen magnum, blended with a much stronger transverse band which connects the two tubercles on the lateral masses of the atlas. This transverse band holds the dens against the arch of the atlas. Behind the cruciate ligament, the posterior longitudinal ligament extends upwards as the membrana tectoria to the anterior margin of the foramen magnum.

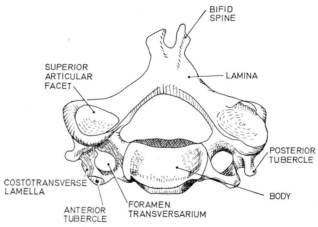

FIG. 21.23. Typical cervical vertebra.

Typical cervical vertebra.

The third, fourth, fifth and sixth cervical vertebrae are alike in all but minor details. Their bodies, when viewed from above or below, are kidney shaped (fig. 21.23). The posterolateral margins of the upper surfaces of the bodies are drawn upwards like the seat of a chair. Correspondingly, on the inferior surfaces, the posterolateral margins are bevelled off.

The neural arch is connected to the back of the body by a pair of pedicles which project backwards and laterally. The enclosed vertebral foramen is triangular in outline. The articular facets are supported by a short pillar of bone, which runs from the superior to the inferior articular surfaces. The upper facet faces upwards and backwards, the lower downwards and forwards.

The transverse process projects from the lateral aspect of the body and the anterior part of the neural arch of the vertebra. It contains the foramen transversarium for the vertebral artery. The lateral edge of the transverse process is drawn up into two tubercles, an anterior and a posterior, united by a thin bar of bone, the **costotransverse lamella.** This bar is bent downwards in the middle and so accommodates the ventral ramus of the cervical nerve corresponding in number to the vertebra. The anterior tubercle is only present on the typical vertebra and is most marked on the sixth where it is termed the **carotid tubercle,** since it is possible to compress the common carotid artery against it. To these tubercles are attached the longus colli, the longus capitis and the scalenus anterior muscles, whose origins are therefore restricted to the typical vertebrae. This is in contrast to scalenus medius and all the muscles posterior to it, which are attached to posterior tubercles and so arise at any level of the cervical column. The anterior tubercle and the costotransverse lamella are homologues of the ribs.

The seventh vertebra

This differs from the typical members of the series in having a long, nonbifid spine. Because this spinous process can usually be seen in the back of the neck, it is referred to as the **vertebra prominens.** The anterior tubercle of the transverse process of this vertebra, as in the atlas and axis, is suppressed. The foramen transversarium of the process is often as large as that of any other cervical vertebra, but usually only contains a vein. The general appearance is therefore intermediate between that of a typical cervical and a typical thoracic vertebra.

CERVICAL VERTEBRAL MUSCLES

The prevertebral muscles. The **longus colli** is a strip of skeletal muscle fibres and tendon, which lies on the fronts of the cervical and upper three thoracic vertebrae, immediately lateral to the anterior longitudinal ligament.

The **longus capitis** arises in common with the longus colli. Its fibres run upwards and medially on the anterior surface of the latter muscle to be inserted into the basilar part of the occipital bone, lateral to the pharyngeal tubercle. The two longus muscles form the immediate posterior relations of the midline hollow viscera and the neurovascular bundle, separated from them by the prevertebral layer of fascia.

The paravertebral muscles are grouped around the brachial and cervical plexuses, and the subclavian artery. The **scalenus anterior muscle**, arising from the anterior tubercles of the typical cervical vertebrae, forms the anterior wall of the cleft for the plexuses and the artery. The posterior wall is composed of the scalenus medius and posterior muscle and the levator scapulae (p. 22.6).

The course of the scalenus anterior muscle is downwards, forwards and laterally from its origin on the cervical column to the scalene tubercle on the superior surface of the first rib. Here it is inserted behind the groove for the subclavian vein and in front of the groove for the subclavian artery.

The **scalenus medius muscle** extends downwards and laterally from its extensive origin from all or most of the posterior tubercles of the transverse processes of the cervical column to the posterior part of upper surface of the first rib (fig. 21.24). The posterior fibres of the muscle extend downwards as far as the second rib, and are called the **scalenus posterior muscle.**

The prevertebral and paravertebral groups of muscles are supplied directly by the ventral rami of the cervical nerves. The longi flex the vertebral column, in opposition to the postvertebral group of muscles, the scaleni bend the cervical column, and indirectly the head, to their own side of the body. They play a very small part in elevation of the first and second ribs in forced inspiration.

The postvertebral muscles. The posterior aspects of the laminae of the cervical vertebrae below the level of the first give attachment to an irregular series of obliquely placed muscle bundles, **the multifidus.** Superficial to these bundles, a more clearly defined layer of muscle runs obliquely from transverse processes to spines, ending at the spine of the axis. This is the **semispinalis cervicis muscle.** From the spine of the axis two muscles extend in the same plane as the semispinalis cervicis; the **inferior oblique**

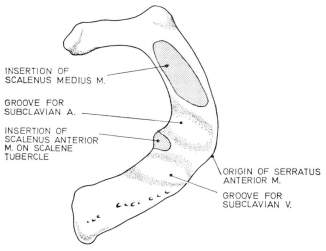

INSERTION OF
SCALENUS MEDIUS M.

GROOVE FOR
SUBCLAVIAN A.

INSERTION OF
SCALENUS ANTERIOR
M. ON SCALENE
TUBERCLE

ORIGIN OF SERRATUS
ANTERIOR M.

GROOVE FOR
SUBCLAVIAN V.

FIG. 21.24. The first rib from above.

muscle which goes to the transverse process of the atlas and the **rectus capitis posterior major,** which is attached superiorly between the inferior nuchal line and the foramen magnum.

The angle between the inferior oblique and the rectus major muscles is closed above and laterally by the **superior oblique muscle,** which extends from the transverse process of the atlas to the lateral part of the occipital bone. The three cornered recess enclosed by the two obliqui and the rectus major is the **suboccipital triangle** (fig. 21.25).

The muscles of the triangle are supplied by the dorsal ramus of the first cervical nerve. The nerve breaks immediately into bundles to the individual muscles within the suboccipital triangle.

Immediately superficial to the semispinalis cervicis and the

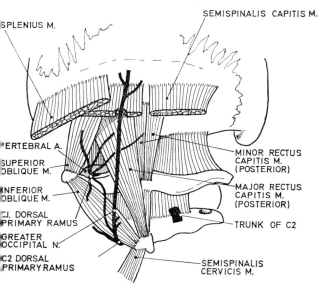

SPLENIUS M.

SEMISPINALIS CAPITIS M.

VERTEBRAL A.

SUPERIOR
OBLIQUE M.

INFERIOR
OBLIQUE M.

CI. DORSAL
PRIMARY RAMUS

GREATER
OCCIPITAL N.

C2 DORSAL
PRIMARY RAMUS

MINOR RECTUS
CAPITIS M.
(POSTERIOR)

MAJOR RECTUS
CAPITIS M.
(POSTERIOR)

TRUNK OF C2

SEMISPINALIS
CERVICIS M.

FIG. 21.25. The suboccipital triangle.

The cervical spinal nerves 21.25

suboccipital muscles lies the **semispinalis capitis.** This is a thick, powerful structure and gives rise to the longitudinal prominence on either side of the midline of the back of the neck. It arises from the transverse processes of the upper half of the thoracic column and from the articular processes of the lower half of the cervical column, and is inserted into the medial posterior part of the infranuchal area of the occipital bone. It lies in contact with the ligamentum nuchae, but usually has no attachment to it. Other ill defined slender muscles complement semispinalis.

The **splenius capitis** and **cervicis muscles** form a single continuous sheet which arises from the lower half of the ligamentum nuchae and the upper thoracic spinous processes and radiates upwards, laterally and forwards to be inserted into the lateral part of the superior nuchal line, the mastoid process, and the posterior tubercles of the upper cervical vertebrae. The splenius muscular sheet separates the deep postvertebral muscles from the levator scapulae, scaleni, the trapezius and the sternomastoid muscles.

All the postvertebral muscles are supplied by the dorsal rami of the cervical and upper thoracic spinal nerves. They extend the head and neck.

THE CERVICAL SPINAL NERVES (fig. 21.26)

The cervicothoracic enlargement lies at the region of attachment of the nerves forming the brachial plexus. This enlargement commences gradually a little below the foramen magnum, reaches its greatest size at the level of the fifth cervical vertebra and tapers off at the second thoracic vertebral level.

The cervical spinal nerves are attached to the spinal cord, like all spinal nerves, by a ventral efferent and a dorsal afferent root. In the first cervical segment, however, the dorsal afferent attachment is very small, and may be absent since there is no cutaneous distribution of this nerve. Between the dorsal and ventral roots of the upper five or six cervical nerves, and situated dorsal to the ligamentum denticulatum, the rootlets of the spinal part of the accessory nerve ascend to the foramen magnum.

The cervical nerves divide into dorsal and ventral rami. In the first two of the series, the dorsal ramus is by far the larger; the remainder conform to the pattern of the other spinal nerves, with a large ventral and a small dorsal ramus. The ventral rami of the second to the fourth nerves send cutaneous branches to the side of the head, the angle of the jaw, part of the external ear and the anterior part of the neck. The fifth and succeeding cervical ventral rami supply the upper limb. The dorsal rami supply the back of the head and the posterior part of the neck as far down as the vertebra prominens with cutaneous branches derived from the second to the sixth segments only, the remaining segments having no cutaneous representation through the dorsal rami.

The prevertebral and paravertebral muscles are supplied by ventral rami, while the dorsal rami supply all of the postvertebral muscles. Since any one muscle, for example, semispinalis capitis, may be supplied from a series of cervical and upper thoracic segmental nerves, defects of motor innervation become clinically obvious only when an extensive lesion exists.

The **first cervical nerve** has a very small dorsal afferent root since this nerve has no cutaneous distribution. The nerve emerges from the vertebral canal dorsal to the synovial joint of the atlanto-occipital articulation. Its ventral ramus turns forward on the lateral side of the lateral mass of the atlas to appear as a descending nerve bundle which joins the larger ventral ramus of the second cervical nerve. A large part of the ventral ramus of the

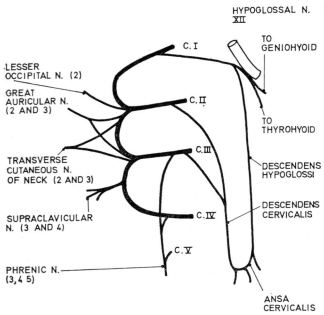

FIG. 21.26. Cervical plexus plan.

first cervical nerve is distributed with the hypoglossal nerve which it joins just below the base of the skull. This is distributed to muscles of the infrahyoid group by the ansa cervicalis. The dorsal ramus of the first cervical nerve is distributed to the muscles of the suboccipital triangle.

The **second cervical nerve** pierces the atlanto-axial membrane and then divides into a large dorsal and a smaller ventral ramus. The latter is distributed partly to skin with the cutaneous branches of the cervical plexus, and partly to the adjacent muscles, including the sterno-mastoid. From the point of division, it passes forwards around the lateral aspect of the vertebral artery as it lies between the transverse processes of the axis and atlas, and joins the first and third cervical rami on the front of the vertebral column. The dorsal ramus supplies fibres to some of the postvertebral muscles, but the major part of the nerve is distributed to the skin of the back of the head as the **greater occipital nerve**. It passes below the inferior oblique muscle, crosses the suboccipital triangle, pierces semispinalis capitis and trapezius to enter the superficial fascia at the superior nuchal line.

The **ansa cervicalis** is a loop of nerve fibres which runs

with the neurovascular bundle in the neck. It has two roots, a superior one derived from the trunk of the hypoglossal nerve, but containing cervical fibres only, and an inferior root of fibres from the second and third cervical ventral rami. The branches of the ansa pass to the infrahyoid group of muscles (p. 21.51).

Cutaneous branches (fig. 21.27) are derived from the interconnected ventral rami of the second, third and fourth cervical nerves. The combination of the second and third rami produces the **lesser occipital, great auricular** and **transverse cutaneous nerves**. From the third and fourth nerves are derived the **medial, intermediate** and **lateral supraclavicular nerves**.

FIG. 21.27. Cutaneous branches of the cervical plexus.

The **phrenic nerve** (fig. 21.28) supplies the diaphragm which develops in the neck and so its efferent nerve supply comes from the fourth cervical segment, with additional fibres from the third and fifth segments. These roots pass on to the anterior aspect of the scalenus anterior muscle deep to its fascial covering. There they combine to form a single trunk, which passes off the medial margin of the muscle at the root of the neck to enter the superior mediastinum. An accessory phrenic nerve, composed of fibres of the fifth cervical nerve, often arises from the nerve to the subclavius muscle.

The ventral rami of the lower four cervical nerves,

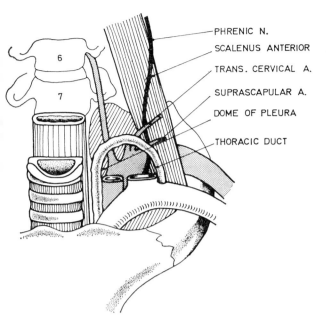

FIG. 21.28. Phrenic nerve in the neck.

with some fibres from the fourth nerve as well, are distributed to the upper limb and shoulder girdle. Along with the ventral ramus of the first thoracic nerve, they

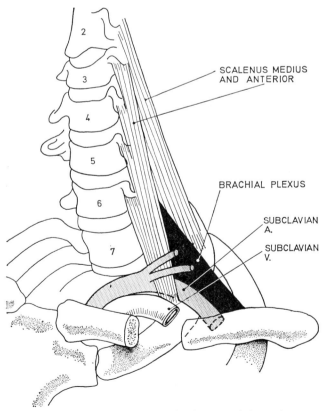

FIG. 21.29. Brachial plexus in the root of the neck.

form the **brachial plexus** (p. 22.30). This occupies the posterior part of the interval between the scalenus anterior and scalenus medius muscles, and the upper surface of the first rib. The subclavian artery lies anterior to the plexus in the lowest part of the interval. The combined bundle of nerves and artery passes through the cervicoaxillary canal to the axilla. The subclavian vein, which completes the neurovascular bundle of the upper limb, lies slightly more anterior than the artery and nerves and is separated from them at the root of the neck by the scalenus anterior muscle (fig. 21.29).

Neurovascular bundle (figs. 21.18 and 19)

The blood vessels and nerves passing through the neck either to or from the head occupy the triangular interval between the prevertebral muscles, the midline hollow viscera and the superficial muscle, sternomastoid. They form a bundle which extends from behind the medial third of the clavicle to the base of the skull at the carotid canal and jugular foramen, medial to the lower part of the external acoustic meatus. The common carotid artery and its internal and external branches, the vagus nerve and the internal jugular vein are the major components of the bundle. The relationships of these components to each other vary at different levels of the bundle. They are together enclosed in a tubular sheath of deep fascia, the **carotid sheath**. Posteriorly, it fuses with the prevertebral layer of fascia which covers the longi and the scaleni, and anteriorly it blends with the fascia which encloses the thyroid gland.

THE CAROTID ARTERY (fig. 21.30)

The **internal carotid artery** supplies the major part of the cerebral hemisphere of its own side, and communicates by means of the circulus arteriosus (circle of Willis) at the base of the brain, with the opposite internal carotid artery, and, usually, with both vertebral arteries. By contrast, the **external carotid artery** supplies muscles, fasciae, skin and bone, and plays no part in the arterial supply to the central nervous system.

Although the cervical part of the courses of the two common carotid arteries is practically identical, their origins differ on the two sides of the body. The right common carotid and subclavian arteries originate as the two branches of the brachiocephalic artery at the level of the upper part of the right sternoclavicular joint. The left common carotid artery arises, as does the left subclavian, from the arch of the aorta, and has a short intrathoracic course between the trachea and the left lung. It enters the neck opposite the left sternoclavicular joint. The left subclavian artery is likewise sandwiched between the superior mediastinal structures and the left lung. It enters the root of the neck medial and slightly anterior to the apex of the left lung and runs laterally in a groove on its upper surface.

The **common carotid artery** ascends in the neck, just under cover of the anterior border of the sternomastoid muscle and divides at the level of the upper margin of the thyroid cartilage, opposite the lower border of the third cervical vertebra. The internal carotid artery

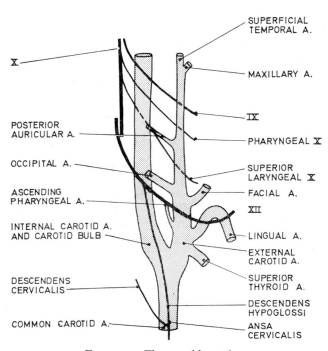

FIG. 21.30. The carotid arteries.

continues in exactly the same direction as the common carotid, while the external carotid artery commences anteromedial to its internal counterpart, but progressively moves to an anterolateral position as it ascends in the neck. It becomes smaller as it is followed headwards, since it gives off a series of branches. It ends posteromedial to the neck of the mandible by dividing into the superficial temporal and maxillary arteries. By contrast, the internal carotid artery, which gives off no branches in the neck, remains the same size until it enters the petrous temporal bone through the carotid canal. At its origin there is a slight dilatation of its wall, the **carotid sinus**. Between the two branches of the common carotid artery is found a small group of chemoreceptor cells embedded in fibrous tissue, the **carotid body** (p. 29.24). Both the body and the sinus are supplied by the glossopharyngeal nerve through its sinus branch, to which some vagus fibres are added.

Branches of the external carotid artery

The **superior thyroid artery** supplies the thyroid gland

where it anastomoses with the inferior thyroid artery (p. 21.33). A large branch, the superior laryngeal, pierces the thyrohyoid membrane to supply the larynx.

The **ascending pharyngeal artery** is a long vessel which runs up to the base of the skull and supplies the wall of the oropharynx, the nasopharynx and the palatine tonsil.

The **lingual artery** passes deep to the hyoglossus muscle to supply the tongue, the sublingual gland and the floor of the mouth.

The **facial artery** passes upwards on the lateral aspects of the middle and superior constrictors of the pharynx, before turning sharply downwards, directly opposite the bed of the palatine tonsil, from which it is separated only by the thin superior constrictor muscle. At this point, it gives off the ascending palatine and tonsillar branches. It then descends well lateral to its ascending course, lying in a groove in the posterior pole of the submandibular salivary gland, to which it gives an arterial supply. Thereafter it lies between the gland and the medial surface of the medial pterygoid muscle before it appears at the lower margin of the mandible, and turns upwards on the anterior edge of the masseter to enter the face. Its branches are distributed to the palatine tonsil, the pharynx, the soft palate, the submandibular gland and the skin and superficial muscles of the face.

The **occipital artery** arises from the posterior aspect of the external carotid at the point at which the hypoglossal nerve turns from its posterior to its lateral aspect. Its course is first below and then medial to the posterior belly of the digastric muscle. It grooves the base of the skull just medial to the mastoid notch, from which the digastric muscle arises, and then runs across the occipital bone to appear at the superior nuchal line with the greater occipital nerve and supplies the posterior part of the scalp. It gives branches to the muscles of the neck, including the sternomastoid.

The **posterior auricular artery** is a small branch whose only importance is that it gives rise to the stylomastoid branch which supplies the distal part of the facial nerve.

The **superficial temporal artery,** one of the two terminal branches, supplies the parotid gland and the temporomandibular joint behind which it passes. Thereafter it crosses the zygomatic arch and breaks up into branches to the temporal part of the scalp.

The **maxillary artery,** the other terminal branch, runs forward and medially, deep to the mandible to reach the pterygo-maxillary fissure, where it breaks up into branches to the nose, nasopharynx and palate. It gives off numerous branches in the infratemporal region. Of these, only two are of importance. The **middle meningeal artery** enters the middle cranial fossa via the foramen spinosum to supply only dura mater and bone. The **inferior alveolar artery** accompanies the inferior alveolar nerve through the mandibular foramen to the teeth of the lower jaw and to the skin of the chin and mucous membrane of the lower lip.

INTERNAL JUGULAR VEIN

The internal jugular system drains the cranial cavity and only a few of the superficial veins of the head and the neck end in it. Its course is downwards, forwards and medially from its start at its superior bulb in the jugular foramen to its end at its inferior bulb at the root of the neck, where it joins the subclavian vein to form the brachiocephalic venous trunk.

The relationship of the internal jugular vein to the axis of the internal carotid and common carotid arteries and the vagus nerve alters as it descends. As it emerges from the jugular foramen, it is posterior and very slightly lateral to the internal carotid artery, as this latter vessel is entering the carotid canal. Between the artery and the vein, the last four cranial nerves pass from the cranial cavity to the neck. The glossopharyngeal, vagus and spinal accessory nerves leave the jugular foramen anterior to the vein, while the hypoglossal nerve gains its exit medial to the others through the hypoglossal canal, and runs laterally between the vagus nerve and the internal jugular vein to the lateral aspect of the external carotid artery. The glossopharyngeal nerve turns anteriorly around the internal carotid artery, and comes to lie on its lateral aspect, where it becomes one of a group of structures separating the internal and external carotid arteries. The spinal accessory nerve turns posteriorly on one or other side of the internal jugular vein, before supplying and piercing the sternomastoid muscle. The vagus nerve descends vertically, initially between the artery and the vein, but later posterior to both of them, lying in the interval between them.

In the neck, the internal jugular vein swings on to the lateral aspect of the arterial axis, often overlapping it anteriorly, and permitting the vagus nerve to lie against the prevertebral muscles. As the vein descends it passes to a plane anterior to that of the common carotid artery, which it is accompanying at this point. The brachiocephalic vein, in which the internal jugular vein terminates, lies on a plane anterior to that of the three large branches of the aortic arch, the brachiocephalic, left common carotid and left subclavian arteries. As the venous drainage is to the right atrium, both veins deviate to the right and the right vein is often larger than the left.

The internal jugular vein receives the inferior petrosal sinus just below the base of the skull. The venous efferents from the pharyngeal plexus of veins, the facial, lingual and superior and middle thyroid veins join it in the neck.

THE VAGUS NERVE (fig. 21.31)

The two vagi follow similar courses from the base of the skull to the lower part of the neck. Thereafter, differences in the great blood vessels on the two sides affect the course of the two nerves.

Within the jugular foramen and for a short distance below, the vagus nerve has two longitudinal swellings, the superior and inferior sensory ganglia. These contain pseudo-unipolar cells concerned in the transmission of somatic sensation, taste and sensation from viscera. From the superior ganglion, a small twig is given off to the dura mater of the posterior cranial fossa, and a

slightly larger one, the auricular branch, proceeds through the lateral part of the temporal bone to emerge on the lateral aspect of the skull at the tympanomastoid fissure, and supplies the skin of the external acoustic meatus and the lateral aspect of the tympanic membrane with sensory fibres, in association with fibres of the auriculotemporal nerve (fig. 21.12).

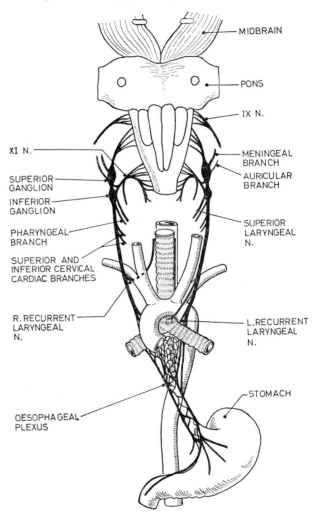

FIG. 21.31. Vagus nerve.

Two branches of greater importance leave the inferior sensory ganglion just below the base of the skull. These are as follows.

The **pharyngeal branch,** which passes between the internal and external carotid arteries to reach the pharyngeal plexus of nerves on the lateral aspect of the middle constrictor of the pharynx. The nerve contains mainly efferent fibres, derived from the cranial part of the accessory nerve.

The **superior laryngeal nerve,** which passes medial to both the internal and external carotid arteries to run downwards and forwards on the side of the pharynx, where it breaks up into an internal and an external branch. The former pierces the thyrohyoid membrane to supply the upper part of the larynx and the epiglottis with sensory fibres, including taste fibres to the latter structure. The external laryngeal nerve sends motor fibres to the cricothyroid muscle and to the inferior constrictor of the pharynx.

Although these two branches arise from the parent trunk of the vagus at the site of the inferior sensory ganglion, many of their fibres come from nerve cell nuclei within the medulla oblongata. True sensory fibres, the peripheral processes of the cell bodies of the ganglia, form only a small proportion of the whole of these nerves.

The vagus nerve descends in the neck within the carotid sheath, coming to lie directly on the prevertebral structures a short distance below the jugular foramen, as the internal jugular vein swings laterally on its descending course. It gives off two further branches to the cardiac plexuses.

At the root of the neck, the courses of the two vagi differ. On the right, the nerve passes anterior to the beginning of the subclavian artery and then runs downwards and backwards, inclining medially to become applied to the right lateral aspect of the trachea. As it crosses the subclavian artery, it gives off the **right recurrent laryngeal nerve,** which passes around the artery to reach the interval between the trachea and the oesophagus. There it ascends to the lower border of the cricopharyngeus muscle, on to whose deep surface it passes as it enters the larynx. On the left side, however, the vagus nerve passes from the posterior wall of the carotid sheath into the interval between the carotid and subclavian arteries, and runs downwards on to the left lateral aspect of the arch of the aorta. The **left recurrent laryngeal nerve** arises from the vagus in the thorax, passes below the aortic arch and ascends into the neck on its medial aspect, in the tracheo-oesophageal groove, to end in the same way as the right nerve.

THE GLOSSOPHARYNGEAL NERVE (fig. 22.32)

Like the vagus, the glossopharyngeal nerve has two ill-defined swellings on its course in the jugular foramen. These are likewise composed of sensory cells, whose peripheral processes are distributed with the branches of the nerve. From the better defined inferior ganglion, arises the **tympanic nerve** which enters the petrous temporal bone by means of a canaliculus on the crest which separates the lower openings of the carotid canal and the jugular foramen. This is a mixed nerve, containing sensory fibres from the middle ear and the auditory tube and secretomotor fibres for the parotid gland.

In the upper part of the neurovascular bundle the nerve runs laterally, anterior to the vagus and posterior to the internal carotid artery, to gain the lateral aspect of the

artery. It then passes downwards and forwards between the internal and external carotid arteries, gradually sliding round the stylopharyngeus muscle which it supplies. From the anterior margin of the stylopharyngeus muscle, the nerve runs forward on the side of the pharynx, deep to the stylohyoid ligament, to break up into its terminal branches. These supply the posterior third of the tongue and the circumvallate papillae, the palatine tonsil and its bed, and the lateral part of the soft palate. The various fibres concerned are sensory from mucous membrane, taste fibres from the tongue and the

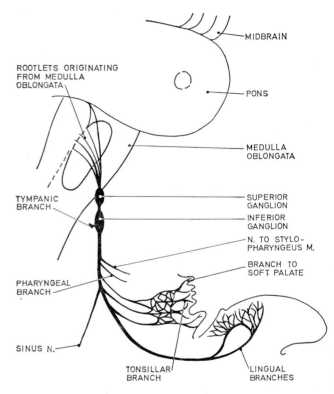

FIG. 21.32. Glossopharyngeal nerve.

circumvallate papillae, and secretomotor fibres to the mucous and serous glands of the tongue and oropharynx. These parasympathetic fibres are postganglionic efferents, whose cell bodies lie in a number of scattered unnamed ganglia on the course of the main nerve trunk.

In addition to these branches, the glossopharyngeal nerve gives off a sinus branch to the carotid sinus and body, and a pharyngeal branch, which distributes sensory and secretomotor fibres to the wall of the pharynx.

THE SPINAL PART OF THE ACCESSORY NERVE

This nerve leaves the neurovascular bundle just below the jugular foramen to reach and supply the sternomastoid and trapezius muscles (pp. 21.33 and 22.5).

THE HYPOGLOSSAL NERVE (figs. 21.33 and 37)

After passing between the vagus nerve and the internal jugular vein, the hypoglossal nerve slips around the external carotid artery on to its lateral aspect where the occipital artery arises. Thereafter, it runs anteriorly on the lateral aspect of both carotid arteries, passing deep to

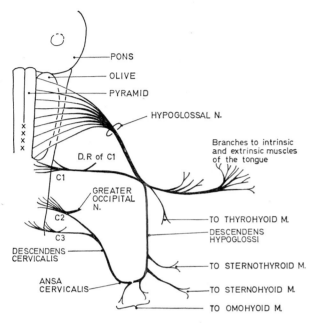

FIG. 21.33. Hypoglossal nerve.

the posterior belly of the digastric and stylohyoid muscles, the submandibular gland and the mylohyoid muscle, to break up into branches to the intrinsic and extrinsic muscles of the tongue. It communicates with the first and second cervical nerves at the lower surface of the base of the skull and gives a root to the ansa cervicalis.

THE CERVICAL SYMPATHETIC TRUNK (fig. 21.34)

All the fibres from the central nervous system, to the sympathetic trunk enter below the neck (pp. 20.40, 24.88). The cervical part of the trunk is connected to the spinal nerves only by grey rami communicantes (p. 19.13). Usually, the cervical part consists of three ganglia, the superior, middle and inferior. The inferior cervical ganglion is, however, usually fused with the first, and even the second thoracic sympathetic ganglia, to form a mass called the cervicothoracic ganglion.

The general position of the cervical part of the sympathetic trunk is within the prevertebral layer of fascia, on the front of the longus capitis and longus colli muscles, posteromedial to the carotid sheath. It is not, however, uniformly orientated in the vertical plane. The superior cervical ganglion, spindle shaped and 2–3 cm long, lies on the front of the longus capitis muscle at the level

of the second and third cervical vertebrae. The variable middle ganglion is often found near the inferior thyroid artery at the level of the sixth cervical vertebra. Below this, the trunk deviates laterally as it descends to the neck of the first rib, over the front of which it is continuous with the remainder of the sympathetic trunk.

All three ganglia give off grey rami communicantes to the adjacent spinal nerves. Thus, the superior ganglion gives off four, the middle ganglion two, and the cervicothoracic ganglion three or more grey rami. In addition, all three give branches to the cardiac plexuses.

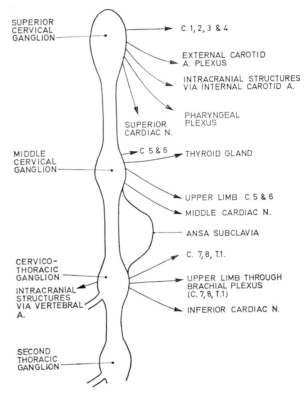

FIG. 21.34. Cervical sympathetic trunk.

Additional branches are given off by the individual ganglia as follows.

The **superior ganglion** gives branches to form plexuses around the internal and external carotid arteries and to the pharyngeal plexus of nerves.

The **middle cervical ganglion** forms a plexus around the inferior thyroid artery and provides an upper root to the ansa subclavia.

The **cervicothoracic ganglion** gives branches which form a plexus around the vertebral artery and provide a lower root to the ansa subclavia.

The **ansa subclavia** is an additional connecting bundle between the cervicothoracic and middle cervical ganglia, which passes in front of the proximal part of the sub-clavian artery, giving a plexus to that part of the vessel only. Fibres passing to the middle and superior ganglia from the second thoracic segment may utilize this route.

THE THORACIC DUCT IN THE NECK (fig. 21.35)

Although not a part of the neurovascular bundle, the thoracic duct is closely related to the lower part of the bundle on the left side of the root of the neck. It ascends

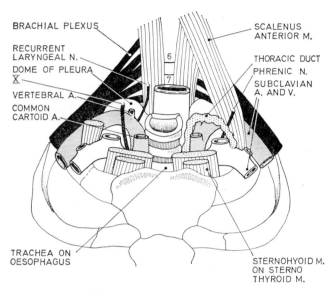

FIG. 21.35. Root of the neck.

on the left side of the oesophagus, and is therefore very deeply placed at the cervicothoracic junction. Passing upwards to the level of the seventh cervical vertebra, it turns sharply laterally between the carotid sheath and the structures immediately anterior to the vertebral column. It then passes forwards, lateral to the neurovascular bundle of the neck, to end at the junction of the internal jugular and subclavian veins. It may receive the jugular, subclavian and broncho-mediastinal lymph trunks of the left side of the body before it ends in the vein, or these may find separate entrances into the venous circulation. The corresponding three lymph trunks on the right side of the neck may also obtain separate openings into the junction of the right internal jugular and subclavian veins, or they may unite prior to doing so to form a right lymphatic duct (p. 20.37).

ADDITIONAL RELATIONSHIPS OF THE NEUROVASCULAR BUNDLE

(1) Between the internal and external carotid arteries at the upper part of their course are the styloid process, the stylopharyngeus muscle, the glossopharyngeal nerve

and the pharyngeal branch of the vagus. The uppermost part of the external carotid artery runs through the deep part of the parotid salivary gland, which also separates it from the internal carotid artery.

(2) On the medial aspect of the bundle lie the median hollow viscera. At the root of the neck these are represented by the trachea and oesophagus. At a higher level, the larynx and laryngopharynx and finally, extending to the base of the skull, the nasopharynx. Intervening between the bundle and the hollow viscera are the superior laryngeal nerve and its internal and external laryngeal branches, the pharyngeal branch of the superior cervical sympathetic ganglion, the pharyngeal venous plexus and the ascending pharyngeal artery.

(3) In the neck, the neurovascular bundle is covered by parts of the infrahyoid muscles and the thyroid gland and its capsule, the sternomastoid muscle and its enclosing fascia, and the structures in the superficial fascia of the neck overlying it. Superiorly, the posterior belly of the digastric and the stylohyoid cross superficial to the bundle just below the angle of the mandible. Above that level, the bundle lies deep to the parotid gland and its enclosed structures, and to the mandible and the attached muscles of mastication.

(4) The internal jugular vein is surrounded by the deep cervical chain of lymph nodes which begins superiorly as the retropharyngeal nodes, and which receives afferents from the collar chain and other superficial groups of nodes in the head and neck region (p. 21.54). The efferents from this series of nodes drain into the jugular lymph trunk.

THE SUBCLAVIAN VESSELS IN THE ROOT OF THE NECK

These are components of the neurovascular bundle of the upper limb (p. 22.34). In the neck each **subclavian artery** runs in a groove immediately anterior to the apex of the lung, forming a smooth curve, convex upwards. Passing through the narrow vertical slit between the scalenus anterior and the scalenus medius muscles and anterior to the brachial plexus, each artery crosses the upper surface of the first rib to enter the cervico-axillary canal. In the neck they give off the following branches.

The **vertebral artery** arises from the parent trunk well medial to the scalenus anterior muscle and runs upwards and medially behind the neurovascular bundle and enters the foramen transversarium of the sixth cervical vertebra. Thereafter, it runs upwards in the foramina transversaria of the remaining cervical vertebrae, with the ventral rami of the cervical nerves emerging posterior to it. Above the transverse process of the atlas, it turns backwards and medially, pierces the posterior atlanto-occipital membrane and enters the foramen magnum. After piercing the dural and arachnoid membranes, it runs upwards and forwards on the front of the medulla to unite with the artery of the opposite side to form the **midline basilar artery**. In its course in the neck it is accompanied by venae comitantes, which drain often as a single vertebral vein into the brachiocephalic vein. The vertebral artery is surrounded by its sympathetic plexus of nerves, derived from the cervicothoracic ganglion. Its only important branch below the foramen magnum is the **radicular branch** to the spinal cord. Within the cranial cavity, it gives off anterior and posterior **spinal branches**, which descend through the foramen magnum to supply the spinal cord (p. 24.4).

The **internal thoracic artery** leaves the subclavian trunk just lateral to the origin of the vertebral artery and runs inferiorly to enter the thorax behind the first costal cartilage (p. 20.8).

The **thyrocervical trunk** arises from the upper surface of the subclavian artery just at the medial edge of the scalenus anterior muscle. It breaks up into three branches, two of which run laterally, anterior to the scalenus anterior muscle and the phrenic nerve, to supply structures in the posterior triangle of the neck and the scapular region. The upper of these two branches, the **transverse cervical artery**, sends a deep branch to accompany the dorsal scapular nerve, and a superficial branch which joins the spinal accessory nerve on the deep surface of the trapezius muscle. The lower branch, the **suprascapular artery**, runs laterally behind the clavicle to pass above the suprascapular ligament into the supraspinous fossa.

The third branch of the thyrocervical trunk is the **inferior thyroid artery**, which ascends on the medial edge of the scalenus anterior muscle to the level of the sixth cervical vertebra, and then turns sharply medially to enter the posterior aspect of the lateral lobe of the thyroid gland, supplying both it and the parathyroid glands. The transverse part of the inferior thyroid artery lies posterior to the neurovascular bundle of the head, but anterior to the vertebral artery and the prevertebral structures.

The **costocervical trunk** takes origin from the subclavian artery deep to the scalenus anterior muscle. It runs backwards across the apex of the lung to end at the neck of the first rib by dividing into the **superior intercostal artery,** to the first two intercostal spaces, and the **deep cervical artery** to the postvertebral muscles.

The **subclavian vein,** running anterior to the scalenus anterior muscle, is at a slightly lower level than the artery because of the inclination of the first rib. It is the terminal section of the main upper limb vein, and extends from the outer margin of the first rib to its junction with the internal jugular vein behind the medial third of the clavicle. It receives the external jugular vein, which pierces the deep fascia in the roof of the posterior triangle of the neck to join it.

Superficial structures of the neck

These structures include the sternomastoid and trapezius muscles, the deep fascial layer that splits to enclose them and which forms the roofs of the anterior and posterior triangles of the neck, the platysma muscle and the superficial vessels and nerves.

The **trapezius** and the **sternomastoid** muscles are parts of the same muscular sheet, but are usually separated by an interval, the **posterior triangle of the neck**. Occasionally, this interval may be almost obliterated, with nerves and blood vessels issuing from a narrow slit in an almost complete sheet of muscle fibres. The **trapezius** is a muscle of the shoulder girdle (p. 22.5). The fibres of insertion of the **sternomastoid** are attached along the lateral part of the superior nuchal line and the lateral aspect of the base of the mastoid process in exactly the same plane as the fibres of origin of the trapezius. The inferior attachment of the sternomastoid muscle is its origin. This consists of a tendinous attachment to the front of the manubrium sterni, and a thin musculoaponeurotic origin from the superior surface of the medial third of the clavicle. The interval between the anterior margin of the sternomastoid and the midline of the front of the neck is the **anterior triangle of the neck**. The lower margin of the mandible forms its remaining side.

The nerve supply of the sternomastoid and trapezius muscles is mainly derived from the spinal part of the accessory nerve. This nerve runs in the deep fascia which forms the roof of the posterior triangle of the neck where it is superficial and easily damaged. Its course across the posterior triangle can be marked by joining the midpoint of the posterior margin of the sternomastoid to a point two fingers' breadths above the clavicle on the anterior border of trapezius. There is an additional supply to the sternomastoid from the second cervical nerve, and to the trapezius from the third and fourth cervical nerves.

One sternomastoid muscle acting alone turns the face to the opposite side of the body. The two acting together, can flex the neck and the head on to the trunk. But if the head is first extended by the postvertebral muscles, the sternomastoids will operate together to maintain it in forcible hyperextension. When respiration is impeded, the sternomastoids act as accessory muscles of respiration.

The deep fascia of the neck encloses sternomastoid, the spinal accessory nerve and the trapezius and forms the roof of the posterior triangle between the two muscles and the roof of the anterior triangle anterior to the sternomastoid. Between the two manubrial heads of the sternomastoids, it splits into two layers just above the jugular notch, in order to enclose the jugal venous arch, which connects the two anterior jugular veins across the midline of the neck. More superiorly, the deep fascia blends with the perichondrium of the thyroid cartilage and with the periosteum of the hyoid bone, mandible and zygomatic arch. It splits to enclose the submandibular gland anteriorly and the parotid gland posteriorly. At the attachments of the sternomastoid and trapezius muscles to the mastoid process and the superior nuchal line, it blends with the periosteum of the skull.

The superficial veins of the neck are the **external** and **anterior jugular veins**. The former begins just below the external acoustic meatus where the posterior division of the retromandibular vein joins the small posterior auricular vein (fig. 21.14). It runs vertically downwards across the lateral surface of the sternomastoid muscle, and pierces the deep fascia of the posterior triangle of the neck to enter the subclavian vein. It receives the anterior jugular, transverse cervical and suprascapular veins just before doing so.

The **anterior jugular vein** commences in the submental region and runs downwards in the anterior triangle of the neck, superficial to the infrahyoid muscles. It is connected with the vein of the opposite side by the jugal venous arch, and ends by passing behind the sternomastoid muscle to join the external jugular vein.

Infratemporal fossa and submandibular region

The mandible is separated from the wall of the pharynx and mouth by muscle, glands, blood vessels and nerves. Posteriorly, the region intervening between the ramus of the mandible and the pharyngeal wall is termed the infratemporal fossa. More anteriorly, the structures lying between the body of the mandible and the tongue are described as lying in the submandibular region. The infratemporal fossa and submandibular regions are continuous and are described together.

The lateral and medial pterygoid muscles (p. 21.20) separate the ramus of the mandible from the tensor veli palatini and superior and middle constrictor muscles of the pharynx. The two pterygoid muscles are separated by the inferior alveolar and lingual branches of the mandibular nerve which occupy the **interpterygoid plane**. This plane slopes downwards and laterally from the foramen ovale to the ramus of the mandible. The maxillary artery runs, in the majority of cases, between the lateral pterygoid muscle and the ramus of the mandible. Less frequently it lies superficial to the inferior alveolar and lingual nerve in the interpterygoid plane. The veins which drain the area supplied by this artery form a plexus around the lateral pterygoid muscle, the **pterygoid venous plexus**. From this plexus, blood is drained via the short maxillary vein into the retromandibular vein.

THE MANDIBULAR NERVE (fig. 21.36)

The mandibular nerve and the motor root of the trigeminal nerve frequently leave the cranial cavity by separate openings in the dura mater covering the foramen ovale. The two become united within or just below the foramen, and the motor root is distributed as a component of the mandibular nerve through some of its branches. Immediately medial to the emerging nerve, and separating it from the tensor veli palatini muscle, lies a small parasympathetic ganglion, the **otic ganglion**. Preganglionic fibres reach this ganglion from the glossopharyngeal nerve by way of its tympanic branch, the tympanic plexus in the middle ear, and the lesser petrosal nerve. Postganglionic fibres pass to the auriculotemporal nerve, which conveys them to the parotid gland. Fibres from the mandibular nerve, such as those supplying the medial pterygoid, tensor veli palatini and tensor tympani muscles directly from the undivided trunk of the nerve, may pass through the ganglion on their way to their respective muscles.

The mandibular nerve breaks up into a small anterior and a larger posterior division. The former passes through the fibres of the lateral pterygoid muscle to end as the sensory **buccal branch** to the skin and mucous membrane of the cheek, but gives off efferent twigs to the masseter, temporalis and lateral pterygoid muscles prior to doing so. The posterior division gives rise to the **auriculotemporal nerve** which passes posterolaterally to supply the temporomandibular joint and the parotid gland. It passes behind the mandibular fossa and climbs over the zygomatic arch to enter the temporal region where it supplies the overlying skin and the upper lateral aspect of the auricle. The posterior division of the mandibular nerve then breaks up into an anterior branch, the lingual nerve, and a posterior branch, the inferior alveolar nerve.

The **lingual nerve** passes from the deep surface of the lateral pterygoid muscle on to the medial aspect of the mandibular ramus, posterior to the tendon of insertion of the temporalis. It passes below the lowest fibres of the superior constrictor of the pharynx, and comes to lie above the posterior part of the mylohyoid muscle. Here it is immediately deep to the mucous membrane of the linguogingival sulcus in the floor of the mouth. It then runs on the lateral surface of the hyoglossus muscle just above the hypoglossal nerve (fig. 21.37). The main part of the submandibular gland lies on its lateral side. The nerve turns below the submandibular duct and passes from its lateral to its medial side. It then turns upwards and forwards into the anterior two-thirds of the tongue, whose mucous membrane it supplies with sensory fibres. The lingual nerve is joined by a branch of the nervus intermedius of the facial nerve, the **chorda tympani**, a short distance below the base of the skull. This nerve leaves the middle ear and passes medial to the spine of the sphenoid, the middle meningeal artery and vein and the inferior alveolar nerve before joining the lingual nerve. The chorda tympani contains taste fibres whose cell bodies lie in the geniculate ganglion, and parasympathetic fibres to the glands of the floor of the mouth. This latter group of nerves fibres relays in the **submandibular ganglion**, which is suspended from or fused with the lingual nerve on the lateral surface of the hyoglossus muscle. The taste fibres are distributed to the oral surface of the tongue, which is its anterior

the mandibular foramen. It runs within the bone of the mandible in the mandibular canal, together with the inferior alveolar branch of the maxillary artery and its accompanying vein. It sends twigs to the pulp cavities of the mandibular teeth, and gives off a large mental branch near its termination. This mental branch leaves

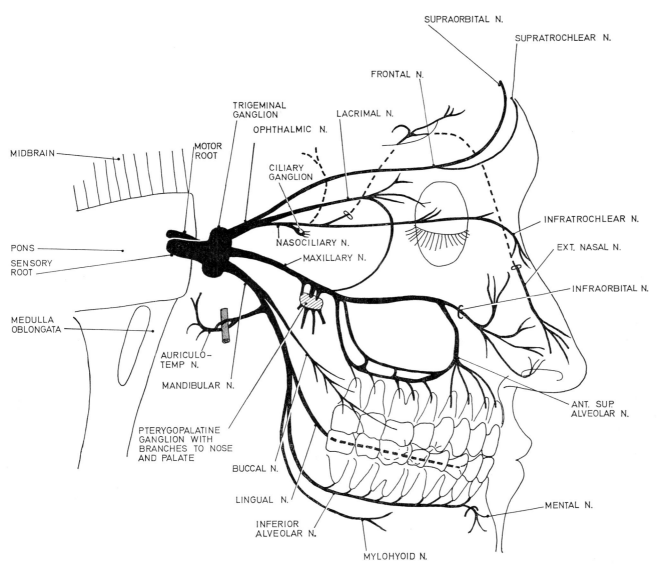

FIG. 21.36. Trigeminal nerve.

two-thirds, but not to the taste buds of the circumvallate papillae, which are supplied by the lingual branch of the glossopharyngeal nerve. The parasympathetic fibres are distributed to the glands of the tongue and to the submandibular and sublingual salivary glands.

The **inferior alveolar nerve** passes across the deep surface of the lower fibres of the lateral pterygoid muscle, lateral to the sphenomandibular ligament, and enters

the mandibular canal by the mental foramen, and breaks up into branches which supply the skin of the region of the chin and the mucous membrane and skin of the lower lip. Before entering the mandibular foramen, the inferior alveolar nerve gives off a small motor branch, the mylohyoid nerve, which runs forwards and downwards in the mylohyoid groove on the medial aspect of the mandible, lateral to the medial pterygoid muscle. As it runs forwards, it slips between the sub-mandibular gland and the mylohyoid muscle, supplying that muscle along with the anterior belly of the digastric.

THE MAXILLARY AND INFRAORBITAL NERVES

These nerves form a single trunk, the name changing at the posterior end of the infraorbital groove.

The trunk of the maxillary nerve leaves the cranial cavity through the foramen rotundum, and immediately enters the pterygopalatine fossa. Leaving the fossa by turning sharply laterally through the upper part of the pterygomaxillary fissure, it lies for a very short part of its course in the deepest part of the infratemporal fossa. From there, it turns forward into the inferior orbital fissure, and runs anteriorly in the infraorbital groove and canal to enter the superficial fascia through the infra-orbital foramen. Its terminal branches are distributed to the skin of the lower eyelid, cheek, side of the nose and the skin and mucous membrane of the upper lip. The infraorbital part of the nerve is accompanied by the infraorbital branch of the maxillary artery.

Within the pterygopalatine fossa, the trunk of the maxillary nerve is connected by two pterygopalatine branches to a small mass of parasympathetic nerve cells, the **pterygopalatine ganglion**. From the inferior aspect of this ganglion a number of nerves are directed to the nasal cavity, the palate and the nasopharynx. These are mainly sensory branches of the maxillary nerve, but contain other fibres, some of which are derived from the parasympathetic cells of the ganglion. The largest of these branches is the **greater palatine nerve** which occupies the greater palatine canal and fora-men, and supplies the major part of the hard palate. The **lesser palatine nerves** leave the greater palatine canal to open on to the soft palate which they supply with taste fibres, as well as the general sensory, parasympathetic secreto-motor and sympathetic fibres which are present in all the other branches. The **nasopalatine** and **lateral** and **medial nasal branches** leave the pterygopalatine fossa by the sphenopalatine foramen to be distributed to the septum and lateral wall of the nasal cavity. The pharyngeal branch reaches the upper part of the wall of the nasopharynx. All these nerves are accompanied by similarly named branches of the maxillary artery and their venae comi-tantes (p. 21.42.)

In the infratemporal fossa, a zygomatic and two or more posterior superior alveolar branches are given off. The **zygomatic nerve** enters the orbit through the lateral part of the inferior orbital fissure. It gives off the zygo-maticofacial and zygomaticotemporal branches to the skin of the face, and its communication with the lacrimal nerve transmits secretomotor fibres from the pterygo-palatine ganglion. The **posterior superior alveolar nerves** enter fine canaliculi in the bone of the posterolateral wall of the maxillary air sinus, and are distributed with the neurovascular bundles to the molar and premolar teeth and adjoining gum.

The **infraorbital nerve** gives off an anterior superior alveolar branch while in the infraorbital groove. This nerve runs in a bony canal, along with the corresponding vessels, across the anterolateral surface of the maxillary air sinus, passing lateral to the infraorbital foramen, to the region of the anterior nasal spine. At this point, a small twig is given off to the anterior part of the floor of the nose. The greater part of the nerve passes in the neurovascular bundles, present in the walls of the maxillary air sinus, from which branches go the pulp cavities of the incisor and canine teeth, and to the mucous membrane lining the maxillary sinus.

The function of the pterygopalatine ganglion is to act as the relay station for preganglionic fibres derived from the nervus intermedius of the facial nerve, which are destined for the area of maxillary nerve distribution. Fibres subserving the special sense of taste, whose cell bodies are in the geniculate ganglion, are also con-tained among the nerve bundle passing to the pterygopalatine ganglion from the nervus intermedius, but they just pass through the ganglion. The route followed by these two sets of fibres from the facial nerve is by the greater petrosal nerve to the foramen lacerum, where they are joined by sympathetic fibres from the internal carotid plexus, and thence by the nerve trunk which occupies the pterygoid canal to the ganglion in the pterygopalatine fossa. The sympathetic fibres which join the greater petrosal nerve in the foramen lacerum are derived from the upper end of the thoracolumbar outflow and reach the cranial cavity in the form of a plexus around the internal carotid artery. These are postganglionic fibres, whose cell bodies are situated in the superior cervical ganglion in the neck.

The tongue

The tongue (fig. 21.37) is formed from the blended fibres of the extrinsic muscles, described below, and the longi-tudinal, transverse and vertical intrinsic fibres. Numerous serous and mucous glands are enclosed between the inter-lacing strands of these muscles. Their ducts open on to the dorsum and side of the tongue, which are covered with a layer of non-keratinizing stratified squamous epithelium, which is modified on the dorsum of the tongue into the various kinds of papillae. At the junction of the anterior two-thirds and the posterior third of the dorsum of the tongue, there is a V-shaped row of prominent sessile projections, the circumvallate papillae, so arranged that the apex of the V points backwards. Immediately behind the row of papillae is an ill-defined groove, the sulcus terminalis. At its posteriorly pointing apex, there is a slight pit, the foramen caecum, indi-cating the position of the thyroglossal downgrowth of the embryo. The mucous membrane of the tongue

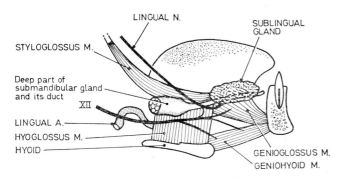

FIG. 21.37. Lateral view of the tongue.

posterior to the sulcus and foramen is raised and made irregular by subepithelial lymphoid tissue, the lingual tonsil.

NERVE SUPPLY

The sensory supply to the anterior two-thirds of the tongue is derived from the lingual nerve, which also carries taste and secretomotor fibres from the chorda tympani, ultimately derived from the nervus intermedius. The circumvallate papillae and the posterior third of the tongue, the pharyngeal surface, is supplied by the glosso-pharyngeal nerve with fibres subserving general and special taste sensation, and with secretomotor fibres. A few fibres of the internal laryngeal branch of the superior laryngeal nerve, derived from the vagus, reach the most posterior part of the tongue. The motor supply to the intrinsic and extrinsic muscles of the tongue reaches them through the hypoglossal nerve. The palato-glossus, whose fibres blend with the posterior part of the side of the tongue, is a muscle of the soft palate, and is supplied by the pharyngeal branch of the vagus.

VASCULAR SUPPLY

This is mainly derived from the lingual artery, which passes forwards from its origin from the external carotid deep to the hyoglossus muscle. It terminates as the deep artery of the tongue, and supplies the organ to its tip. The veins which drain the area are both deep and superficial to the hyoglossus muscle and drain into the internal jugular system, either directly or through the facial vein.

THE SUPRAHYOID MUSCLES AND THE MUSCLES OF THE TONGUE (fig. 21.38)

The **geniolossi** radiate backwards into the substance of the tongue from origins on the upper mental spines (fig. 21.15). Their fibres blend with the intrinsic muscles of the tongue on a plane which is medial to that of the styloglossus and hyoglossus muscles. Their upper edges are covered by the mucous membrane of the linguogingival sulcus, while their lower edges are in contact with the geniohyoids.

The **geniohyoid muscles** arise from the lower mental spines, and are inserted into the upper surface of the body of the hyoid bone on either side of the midline.

The **styloglossus muscle** obtains an origin from the styloid process, at the point at which it becomes continuous with the stylohyoid ligament. Its fibres gather together to form a bundle which runs forwards and downwards through the lowest part of the superior constrictor of the pharynx, to blend with the upper fibres of the hyoglossus at the side of the tongue.

The **hyoglossus** is a sheet of muscle which arises from the upper margin of the greater horn and body of the hyoid bone, and runs upwards and forwards to blend with the styloglossus and the intrinsic muscles of the tongue. It is situated lateral to the plane of the middle constrictor of the pharynx and the genioglossus, and is medial to the submandibular gland and the mylohyoid. The lingual artery and its venae comitantes lie on the medial side of the lowest fibres of the hyoglossus, while the lingual and hypo-glossal nerves run across its lateral surface.

The **mylohyoid muscle** arises from the mylohyoid line of the mandible, and its anterior fibres run downwards and medially to meet in a median fibrous raphe. The posterior fibres gain an attachment into the upper surface of the body of the hyoid bone. Associated with it, and often partly blended with it, is the **anterior belly of the digastric muscle**. Arising from a shallow depression on the lower margin of the mandible just lateral to the symphysis, the fibres of this muscle run downwards and backwards to become continuous with a tendon which unites them to the fibres of the posterior belly. This tendon is slung from the junction of the body and greater horn of the hyoid bone by a pulley formed from a loop of deep fascia. The **posterior belly of the digastric muscle** arises from the floor of the digastric notch, and is joined in its course in the uppermost part of the neck by a slender band of

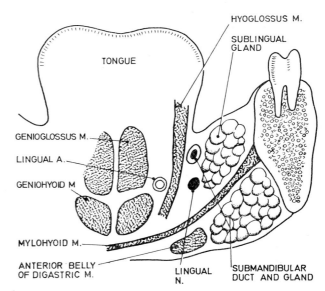

FIG. 21.38. Coronal section of the floor of the mouth.

fibres which arises from the styloid process, and passes antero-inferiorly to reach the digastric tendon, around the sides of which it passes to its insertion on the hyoid bone. This is the **stylohyoid muscle**.

Actions of the muscles of the tongue and the suprahyoid muscles

The extrinsic and intrinsic muscles of the tongue act as a group in modifying the whole organ in phonation and in the action of guiding the food between the teeth during mastication. Protrusion of the tongue is effected by the genioglossi, assisted by the intrinsic muscles. In the voluntary part of the act of swallowing, the tongue is drawn upwards and backwards by the combined actions of the styloglossi and mylohyoids. The digastric, stylohyoid and mylohyoid muscles raise the hyoid bone, and with it the larynx, during the second or involuntary phase of swallowing (p. 21.47).

Nerve supply of the suprahyoid muscles

The anterior belly of the digastric and the mylohyoid muscles are derived from the mesoderm of the first pharyngeal arch of the embryo, and are accordingly supplied from the first arch, or mandibular, nerve through its mylohyoid branch. The posterior belly of the digastric and stylohyoid muscles are derived from second arch mesoderm and are therefore supplied by the second arch, or facial, nerve (p. 18.32).

The salivary glands of the floor of the mouth (figs. 21.37 and 38)

The main or superficial part of the **submandibular salivary gland** is situated in the angle between the mylohyoid muscle and the inner side of the mandible. A layer of deep fascia extends upwards from the body of the hyoid bone and splits to enclose the gland and to bind it to the mandible. The two bellies of the digastric muscle, which are also enclosed within this fascial capsule, form a hammock-like arrangement for the lower edge of the gland. The inferolateral surface extends from this hammock arrangement to the lower margin of the mandible and is related to the superficial structures of the upper part of the neck. The posterior pole of the gland extends backwards beyond the mylohyoid and lies between the hyoglossus and the insertion of the medial pterygoid muscle. The ascending part of the facial artery turns laterally above the stylohyoid muscle into a groove on the posterior pole of the submandibular gland. Emerging from this groove, the descending part of the vessel runs to the lower margin of the mandible between the gland and the lowest part of the medial pterygoid muscle. Between the bone of the mandible and the lateral aspect of the gland lie several small lymph nodes, the submandibular lymphatic nodules. These are members of the collar chain of lymph nodes, and drain the adjacent parts of the face and the side of the tongue.

The deep part of the gland extends forwards from the medial surface of the main mass of the structure and is accompanied by the submandibular duct. Both structures occupy the gutter between the mylohyoid and hyoglossus muscles. The duct runs anteriorly, passes medial to the sublingual gland, and discharges into the floor of the mouth by the opening in the summit of the sublingual papilla, which lies immediately lateral to the frenulum of the tongue (p. 21.45).

The **sublingual salivary gland** lies in the anterior part of the floor of the mouth, and raises a ridge in the linguogingival sulcus. On the summit of this ridge, a row of small apertures allows the secretions of the gland to reach the cavity of the mouth. Laterally, it is in contact with the

medial surface of the mandible at the sublingual fovea, and below that with the anterior fibres of origin of the mylohyoid muscle. Its medial surface is in contact with the hyoglossus and genioglossus muscles.

MEDIAN HOLLOW VISCERA

Sections of the head and neck (fig. 21.39 and fig. 21.40) show the vertical extent of the hollow viscera which lie within it. From the spheno-ethmoidal recess, which lies immediately below the cribriform plate of the ethmoid bone, a series of cavities stretches downwards to the upper part of the thorax.

FIG. 21.39. Vertical section of skull.

The bony plate of the **hard palate** (fig. 21.41) supplemented posteriorly by the soft palate forms a horizontal dividing wall between the paired nasal cavities and the median nasopharynx above, and the mouth and oropharynx below. The septum of the nose is fused with the upper surface of this dividing wall in the midline, and the free posterior edge of the septum meets the hard and soft palates at their point of junction. The **soft palate** in addition to its central aponeurotic support, includes fibres of skeletal muscle, and a small bundle of this is continued backwards to form the **uvula.** Both the upper and lower surfaces of the hard and soft palates are clothed with connective tissue, glands and epithelium. On the superior or nasal surface, this epithelium is of the respiratory columnar ciliated type, while on the inferior or oral aspect, it is of the stratified squamous non-keratinizing type. When the narrow, transversely placed slit which connects the nasal and oral parts of the pharynx is closed by the combined action of the palatine and pharyngeal muscles, as in swallowing, the upper respiratory cavity and the lower alimentary cavity are separated completely.

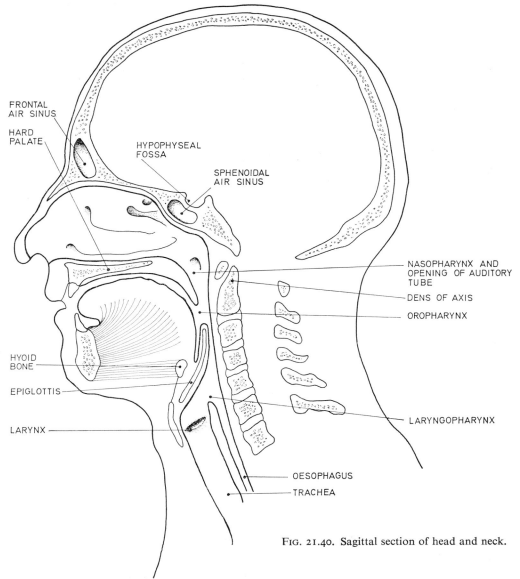

FRONTAL AIR SINUS

HARD PALATE

HYPOPHYSEAL FOSSA

SPHENOIDAL AIR SINUS

NASOPHARYNX AND OPENING OF AUDITORY TUBE

DENS OF AXIS

OROPHARYNX

HYOID BONE

EPIGLOTTIS

LARYNX

LARYNGOPHARYNX

OESOPHAGUS

TRACHEA

FIG. 21.40. Sagittal section of head and neck.

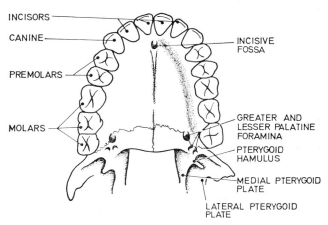

INCISORS

CANINE

PREMOLARS

MOLARS

INCISIVE FOSSA

GREATER AND LESSER PALATINE FORAMINA

PTERYGOID HAMULUS

MEDIAL PTERYGOID PLATE

LATERAL PTERYGOID PLATE

FIG. 21.41. The hard palate.

The cervical part of the visceral space is divided by a vertical septum; in front lie the larynx and trachea and behind laryngopharynx and oesophagus. This septum is formed by the muscles and cartilages of the posterior wall of the larynx and by the adjacent walls of the trachea and oesophagus. The cricoid cartilage forms the major part of the dividing wall between the larynx and laryngopharynx. Its rigid nature and almost circular outline determines the form of the interior of the larynx, while the laryngopharynx, which is applied to the convex posterior aspect of the cartilage is a curved slit with an anterior concavity (fig. 21.19).

Nose and nasopharynx

The nasal cavities are situated on either side of a midline septum. In coronal section each forms an inverted wedge, with its base on the upper surface of the hard palate and its apex in the narrowest part of the cavity, immediately below the cribriform plate of the ethmoid bone. Each nasal cavity opens on to the surface of the face anteriorly and into the nasopharynx posteriorly. Both openings are immediately adjacent to the floor of the nose, so that during normal respiration air is directed through the lower part of the cavity. Only a small proportion of the inspired air is drawn up into the cul-de-sac lined by olfactory epithelium.

The nasopharynx is a single slit-like cavity, slightly convex anteriorly. The lateral angles of the slit lie in the pharyngeal recesses, posterior to the expanded medial ends of the auditory tubes. The posterior wall of the cavity bulges downwards and forwards because of an aggregation of lymphoid tissue, the nasopharyngeal tonsil.

THE ROOF OF THE NASAL CAVITIES

The nasal cavities and the nasopharynx are placed behind the median part of the face, above the hard palate and below the median parts of the cranial fossae. The roof extends from the cartilaginous external nose, along the under surface of the nasal and frontal bones to the inferior aspect of the cribriform plate of the ethmoid bone, where it reaches its highest point and is separated from the anterior cranial fossa only by that thin, perforated lamina of bone. Injury to the bone at this point may establish a connection between the subarachnoid and nasal cavities, through which cerebrospinal fluid flows down the nose. Posterior to the cribriform plate lies the body of the sphenoid with its two enclosed air sinuses which open on each side of the midline, where the bony septum and the sphenoid articulate. The lower part of the sphenoid body and the basiocciput with which it articulates posteriorly, continue downwards and backwards as the roof of the nasopharynx. The pharyngeal tubercle on the under surface of the basilar part of the occipital bone indicates the most posterior extent of the nasopharyngeal mucous membrane on the base of the skull and the point of its reflexion on to the muscular part of the posterior pharyngeal wall.

THE LATERAL WALL OF THE NASAL CAVITY (fig. 21.42)

The major part of the lateral wall of the nose is composed of the ethmoid bone above and the maxilla below. From these two bones project the delicate conchae or turbinate bones; when covered with mucous membrane, they give a characteristic appearance to the interior of the nose. There are three of these conchae in each nasal cavity, two from the ethmoid bone, and the largest, the **inferior nasal concha** being a bone in its own right. The small superior concha projects from the medial surface of the ethmoid bone immediately below the cribriform plate. It is grooved vertically on its medial surface for the axones of the receptor nerve cells of the olfactory mucous membrane, as they converge on the cribriform plate. The space above the superior concha is the **sphenoethmoidal recess,** while that lateral to it is the superior meatus of the nose. From the lower part of the ethmoid bone, the middle concha, a much larger horizontal lamina of bone with a downward turned medial edge, projects into the cavity. The space below and lateral to it is the middle meatus. The lateral wall of this meatus is distended medially by a group of air sacs, whose thin bony walls are translucent. The prominence so produced is the **bulla ethmoidalis.** The middle ethmoidal air sinuses open on to the surface of the bulla; below and in front of it, a gap in the bone of the lateral wall of the nose,

the **hiatus semilunaris,** leads directly into the maxillary air sinus. Because of the size of the inferior concha, the inferior meatus which lies below and lateral to it is the largest of the three. The only aperture in its lateral wall is the **nasolacrimal duct.**

The maxillary bone completes the antero-inferior part of the lateral wall of the nose. Posterior to the ethmoid and inferior conchal bones, the perpendicular plate of the palatine bone and the medial pterygoid lamina form the lateral wall. The nasal and frontal bones provide the anterior part of the roof and a small part of the lateral wall of the cavity, while the lacrimal bone, in the medial wall of the nasolacrimal duct, also forms a small part of the lateral wall of the middle meatus.

At the upper end of the perpendicular plate of the palatine bone, the **sphenopalatine foramen,** intervenes between the central part of the edge of the plate and the body of the sphenoid bone with which it is articulating. In life, the foramen is covered with mucous membrane, deep to which the nerves and vessels from the pterygopalatine fossa pass into the lateral wall and septum of the nose.

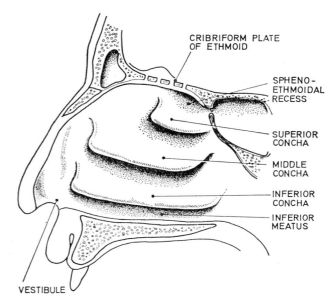

FIG. 21.42. The lateral wall of the nasal cavity.

NASAL SEPTUM (fig. 21.43)

This is composed of the perpendicular plate of the ethmoid, the septal cartilage and of the vomer. The free posterior edge of the vomer, smooth and slightly concave, forms the medial boundary of the posterior nasal aperture (posterior naris, posterior choana). A groove runs downwards and forwards on each side of the vomer, from the body of the sphenoid to the incisive fossa in the anterior part of the hard palate. This lodges the nasopalatine nerve and associated blood vessels.

That part of the perpendicular plate of the ethmoid bone which is situated below the cribriform plate is grooved like the medial surface of the superior concha; these grooves also carry olfactory nerve bundles.

THE FIBROCARTILAGINOUS PART OF THE AUDITORY (PHARYNGOTYMPANIC, EUSTACHIAN) TUBE

The medial part of the tube connecting the nasopharynx and the middle ear is an incomplete roll of hyaline cartilage, with the deficiency in its anterolateral aspect filled in with fibrous tissue. It occupies the suture on the under surface of the base of the skull between the posterior margin of the greater wing of the sphenoid and the quadrate area of the petrous temporal bone. Its expanded pharyngeal end is directed medially and anteriorly into the aperture enclosed by the upper part of the posterior margin of the medial pterygoid plate and the body

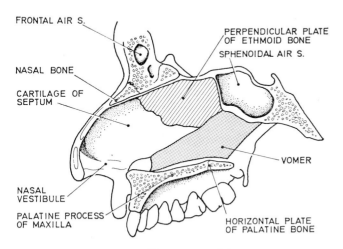

FIG. 21.43. The septum of the nose.

of the sphenoid bone, and is often supported inferiorly by a spine projecting backwards from the middle of the posterior edge of the plate. When covered with mucous membrane, the edges of the tubal opening form a prominence in the lateral wall of the nasopharynx, the **tubal elevation**. Posterior to its opening, the recess of the pharynx wall extends laterally to the under surface of the foramen lacerum, which is, of course, blocked off inferiorly by fibrous tissue.

THE SOFT TISSUE LINING OF THE NOSE AND NASO-PHARYNX

The mucous membrane of the nose and of most of the nasopharynx consists of columnar ciliated epithelium intermixed with goblet cells and supported by connective tissue. This latter layer contains both serous and mucous acini, and numerous vascular spaces of a venous nature, over and above the normal blood supply, and sensory and secretomotor nerve fibres. In the olfactory area the epithelium contains both receptor and supporting cells.

As well as the **nasopharyngeal tonsil** on the posterior wall of the nasopharynx, other deposits of lymphoid tissue occur around the openings of the auditory tubes, the **tubal tonsils.** These collections of lymphoid tissue form part of a ring around the upper parts of the respiratory and alimentary passages. The palatine and lingual tonsils complete the encirclement.

The epithelial lining of the nasal cavities is continuous anteriorly with the skin which lines the nostrils. Laterally, it blends with the columnar ciliated epithelium of the paranasal sinuses, and with the lining of the nasolacrimal duct. Posteriorly, it continues onwards from the bony walls of the nose to the internal surface of the superior constrictor muscle of the pharynx, where it is supported by the thickened connective tissue of the pharyngeal wall, the pharyngobasilar fascia. At a line running around the interior of the nasopharynx from the dorsum of the soft palate to the opening of the auditory tube and onwards to the posterior pharyngeal wall there is an irregular transition from respiratory epithelium to one of a stratified squamous non-keratinizing kind.

SPACES CONNECTED WITH THE NASAL CAVITY AND THE NASOPHARYNX (fig. 21.44)

These spaces, the paranasal air sinuses, the nasolacrimal duct and the auditory tube, have connections with the nasal cavity which have existed from the very earliest phase in their development. Thus, the paranasal sinuses develop initially as grooves in the roof or lateral wall of

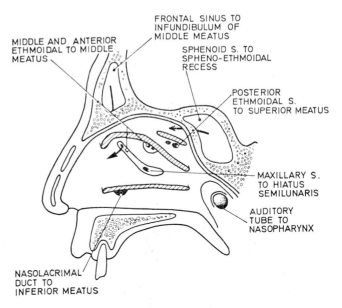

FIG. 21.44. The meatuses and the lateral wall of the nose, showing the connections and drainage of air sinuses.

the nose. The auditory tube is part of the tubotympanic recess which develops from the first internal pouch of the primitive pharynx (p. 18.29). The nasolacrimal duct is completed by the fusion of the lips of the groove separating the maxillary and frontonasal processes of the embryonic face to enclose a canal which is drawn into the substance of the face, with its lower end opening into the lower part of the nasal cavity (p. 21.56).

The arrangement of the openings of these cavities and

tubes in the lateral wall of the nose and nasopharynx is as follows:

(1) the sphenoidal air sinus opens into the spheno-ethmoidal recess,

(2) the posterior ethmoidal air sinuses open by several pinhole apertures into the superior meatus of the nose,

(3) the nasolacrimal duct opens into the anterior part of the inferior meatus,

(4) the auditory tube opens into the nasopharynx,

(5) all the remaining cavities, the frontal, maxillary, anterior and middle ethmoidal air sinuses open into the middle meatus. The middle ethmoidal sinuses open on to the summit of the ethmoidal bulla, while the anterior ethmoidal group of sinuses has an aperture into the upper anterior part of the hiatus semilunaris. The maxillary sinus opening occupies the central part of the hiatus. The frontal sinus, which is an extension of an anterior ethmoidal air sac between the tables of the frontal bone, opens by its infundibulum, which has to pass through the ethmoidal labyrinth to do so, into the uppermost anterior part of the middle meatus of the nose.

THE NERVE SUPPLY OF THE NOSE AND NASOPHARYNX (figs. 21.45 and 21.46)

The special sense of smell. See olfactory nerves (p. 24.47).

The general sensory supply of the nose. Both the septum and the lateral walls of the nasal cavity are innervated by the ophthalmic

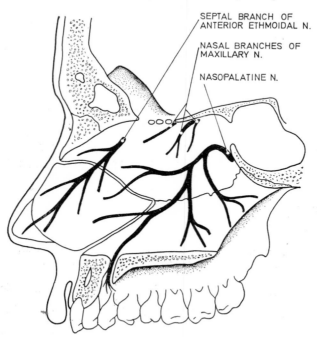

FIG. 21.45. Nerve supply of the nasal septum.

and maxillary divisions of the trigeminal nerve. The ophthalmic region of supply is confined to the upper anterior part of the mucous membrane of lateral wall and septum, while the maxillary nerve supplies the larger lower and posterior parts of

both. The ophthalmic supply is derived from the **anterior ethmoidal nerve,** which goes to the lateral wall and septum, before becoming the external nasal nerve to the skin of the tip of the nose.

Most of the maxillary supply enters the nasal cavity from the pterygopalatine fossa through the sphenopalatine fora-

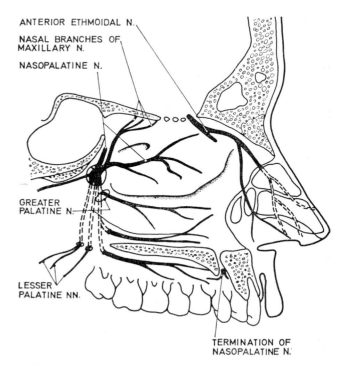

FIG. 21.46. Nerve supply of the lateral wall of the nose.

men. The **nasopalatine nerve** crosses the most posterior part of the roof of the nose to the septum, and runs downwards and forwards on the vomer, innervating the adjacent mucous membrane. Anteriorly, it penetrates the hard palate at the incisive fossa, and supplies the gum in the premaxillary region. Other shorter **nasal branches** leave the sphenopalatine foramen to supply the more posterior part of the septum, and the lateral wall in the region of the posterior ends of the superior and middle conchae. Branches of the greater palatine, anterior superior alveolar, infraorbital nerves and pharyngeal branches of the maxillary nerve complete the innervation of the nasal cavity.

THE VASCULAR SUPPLY OF THE NOSE AND NASOPHARYNX

The ophthalmic area of nerve supply receives branches of the anterior ethmoidal branch of the ophthalmic artery, derived from the intracranial part of the internal carotid artery. These follow the arrangements of the nerves. The area supplied by branches of the maxillary nerve also receives branches of the maxillary artery. On the septum, the artery accompanying the nasopalatine nerve forms an anastomosis with the terminal part of the greater palatine artery, which enters the nasal cavity through the incisive fossa. They are joined by branches of the anterior ethmoidal and facial arteries, the latter entering deep to the skin of the upper lip and the vestibule of the nose. This septal anastomosis is where epistaxis is likely to occur.

The venae comitantes of these arteries drain to the sphenopalatine foramen, the nasal slit, the incisive fossa and the vestibule of the nose, following the general direction of venous flow from these areas.

Paranasal sinuses

These air-filled cavities communicate with the nose and are lined by ciliated columnar epithelium. Nasal infections often spread into these sinuses.

The **maxillary air sinus** occupies the interior of the maxillary bone from the floor of the orbit to the hard palate, and may extend into the alveolar process, often as much as half an inch below the general level of the floor of the rest of the cavity. Its shape is roughly pyramidal, with its base in the lateral wall of the nose. The drainage exit of the sinus is, in fact, in the substance of the ethmoid bone, high up in the medial wall. The apex of the sinus is in the zygomatic process, and often extends into the zygomatic bone itself. The cavity may be subdivided by a number of thin bony septa.

It is by far the largest of the paranasal sinuses; the orbit lies immediately above it, the nose on its medial side, the oral cavity below it, and the pterygopalatine fossa immediately posteriorly. Posterolaterally, it faces into the infratemporal region, and anterolaterally into the face. Its most important immediately related structures are the trunk and branches of the maxillary nerve, and the terminal part of the maxillary artery and its accompanying veins. Thus, the infraorbital neurovascular group lies in its roof, the posterior superior alveolar group in its posterolateral wall, and the anterior superior alveolar group in its anterolateral wall. The greater palatine group lies inferiorly, below the hard palate, and the nerves and vessels supplying the lateral wall of the nose are related to its medial surface. It is from these nerves and blood vessels that the walls and mucous membrane of the sinus are supplied.

The **ethmoidal air sinuses** are situated between the upper part of the nasal cavity and the medial wall of the orbit. Superiorly, they are separated from the anterior cranial fossa by part of the orbital plate of the frontal bone. They are supplied by the ethmoidal arteries and nerves.

The **sphenoidal air sinuses** are paired and occupy most of the substance of the body of the sphenoid bone (fig. 21.40). They are situated behind the upper part of the cavity of the nose, and above the nasopharynx. They are related superiorly to the pituitary and its coverings, and laterally to the cavernous sinus and its contents, particularly to the internal carotid artery (fig. 21.6). Its neurovascular supply is posterior ethmoidal in origin.

The **frontal air sinuses** penetrate the frontal bone immediately above and lateral to the root of the nose and frequently extend backwards into the roof of the orbit. They are usually asymmetrical, the dividing septum not being in the midline. The anterior ethmoidal arteries and nerves supply them.

Mouth, oropharynx, laryngopharynx and oesophagus

MUSCLES OF THE PHARYNX AND THE SOFT PALATE (fig. 21.47)

The pharynx, unlike the remainder of the alimentary tract, possesses a double layer of skeletal muscle in its wall, comprising an inner longitudinal and an outer

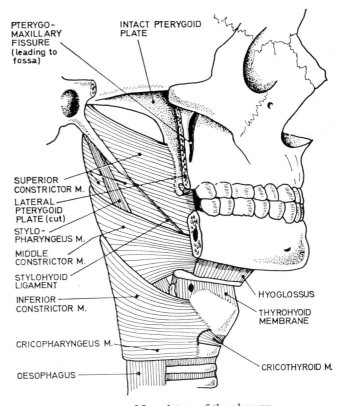

FIG. 21.47. Musculature of the pharynx.

circular lamella. The outer circular layer is better developed and consists of three constrictor muscles, superior, middle and inferior.

The attachments of the pharyngeal constrictors. A poorly defined median fibrous raphe stretches from the pharyngeal tubercle on the inferior aspect of the basilar part of the occipital bone down almost to the oesophagus. The three constrictor muscles are inserted into it.

The **superior constrictor** arises from the lower half of the posterior border of the medial pterygoid plate, the pterygomandibular raphe, the posterior end of the mylohyoid line of the mandible and the side of the tongue. Through the pterygomandibular raphe it is continuous with the buccinator muscle.

The **middle constrictor** arises from the lower part of the stylohyoid ligament, and the lesser and greater horns of the hyoid bone.

The **inferior constrictor** arises from the oblique line on the lateral aspect of the thyroid cartilage, from a fibrous band which connects the lower end of the line to the cricoid cartilage, and from the lateral aspect of that cartilage. Its lowest fibres are horizontal, and form the **cricopharyngeal sphincter** at the pharyngo-oesophageal junction. Its fibres are continuous with those of the other side, with no intervening raphe.

The internal longitudinal layer of pharyngeal muscle is poorly defined. It is provided by the stylopharyngeus, the palatopharyngeus and the salpingopharyngeus, in that order from anterior to posterior. The first of these three muscles commences its course outside the plane of the pharyngeal wall, while the other two are situated within it throughout their length. Their fibres blend into a single longitudinal sheet in the lower part of the wall of the pharynx.

The **stylopharyngeus** arises from the medial aspect of the base of the styloid process, and passes between the superior and middle constrictor sheets to enter the longitudinal layer of muscle. It is inserted into the posterior margin of the thyroid cartilage, and into the lamina propria of the mucous membrane of the pharynx. The **palatopharyngeus** arises from the soft palate, and blends with the posterior margin of the stylopharyngeus. It is inserted into the subepithelial connective tissue of the pharyngeal wall. The **salpingopharyngeus** arises from the posterior margin of the tubal elevation. It forms the muscular interior of the salpingopharyngeal fold. Inferiorly, it blends with the posterior margin of the palatopharyngeus, with whose fibres it is inserted.

SOFT PALATE

The central supporting structure of the soft palate is the palatine aponeurosis, formed by the union in the midline of the posterior part of the roof of the mouth of the expanded tendons of the tensores veli palatini muscles. The remaining muscles of the soft palate are attached to either the upper or lower surface of this aponeurosis. The anterior margin of this latter structure is attached to the palatine crests of the hard palate, and to the posterior nasal spine at its posterior margin. The aponeurosis blends posteriorly with the lamina propria of the mucous membrane of the free edge of the soft palate.

The **tensor veli palatini** arises from the cartilage and fibrous tissue on the anterolateral aspect of the auditory tube, and from the adjoining bone by an attachment extending from the spine of the sphenoid to the scaphoid fossa. Its fibres pass downwards and converge on the lateral side of the inferior end of the medial pterygoid plate of the sphenoid bone. Here the muscle blends with its tendon, which turns sharply around the lower margin of the plate to pass medially to the palatine aponeurosis, with which it becomes continuous. In doing so, it passes through the buccinator muscle immediately anterior to the hamulus (fig. 21.41).

The **levator veli palatini muscle** arises from the medial aspect of the auditory tube, and from the adjoining part of the petrous temporal bone. Its fibres descend and turn medially to be inserted into the upper surface of the palatine aponeurosis. Together with the tensor and the pharyngeal end of the auditory tube, it obliterates the triangular aperture between the superior margin of the superior constrictor muscle and the inferior surface of the base of the skull.

The **palatoglossus** is a muscular band which arises from the lower surface of the palatine aponeurosis and descends on the lateral boundary of the oropharyngeal isthmus to the lateral side of the tongue, where it blends with the musculature of that organ. It is covered with mucous membrane, and, as the **palatoglossal fold**, forms the anterior boundary of the tonsillar fossa. Posterior to that fossa, the **palatopharyngeus muscle** descends in a similar fashion, and is likewise clothed in mucous membrane forming the **palatopharyngeal fold**. This muscle arises from the soft palate, mainly by a layer of fibres which separates the levator veli pala-

tini from the upper surface of the palatine aponeurosis, and sweeps downwards and backwards in the wall of the oropharynx.

The uvula contains a few muscle fibres, the musculus uvulae. The exterior of the pharyngeal muscles is clothed by a thin, poorly defined layer of connective tissue, the buccopharyngeal fascia. Their internal aspect is in direct contact with the lamina propria of the pharyngeal mucous membrane, the **pharyngobasilar fascia**, which is thickest, in the triangular area above the upper edge of the superior constrictor muscle where it blends with the other structures filling in the deficiency.

PALATINE TONSIL (fig. 21.48)

The two palatine tonsils are the largest of the collections of lymphoid tissue which surrounds the lumina of the upper ends of the alimentary and respiratory tracts (p. 21.41). Each tonsil is situated in the lateral wall of the

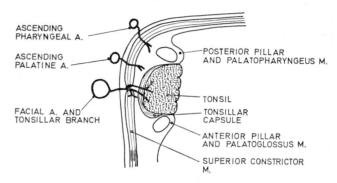

FIG. 21.48. A horizontal section of the tonsil showing its relations.

oropharynx between the palatoglossal and palatopharyngeal folds, above the side of the posterior third of the tongue. Laterally, it is separated by a layer of strong connective tissue, the tonsillar capsule, from the superior constrictor of the pharynx, and from the loop of the facial artery which lies lateral to the muscle. It receives an arterial supply from the tonsillar and ascending palatine branches of that loop, and from the ascending pharyngeal artery.

ORAL CAVITY

The teeth and gums divide the cavity into the mouth proper and the vestibule, which lies between the gums and the cheeks. Within the cheeks is found the buccinator muscle (p. 21.16), which is covered with superficial fascia and skin externally, and lined by the dense connective tissue of the inner cheek pad and the oral mucous membrane internally. The parotid duct opens through the buccinator sheet into the vestibule of the mouth opposite the second upper molar tooth.

The mouth proper lies within the line of the teeth and gums, and is anterior to the palatoglossal fold. Its roof is formed by the hard and soft palates, and its floor by the tongue and the sulcus which separates it from the gums, the linguogingival sulcus. In this sulcus, the epithelium is raised up over the ridge of the sublingual salivary gland, and a row of about a dozen small ducts from this gland open through it. At its anteromedial end, the aperture of the submandibular salivary duct opens into the floor of the mouth alongside the midline, separated from its opposite number by a thin fold of epithelium on the under surface of the tongue, the **frennlum linguae.** The deep vein of the tongue may be seen shining through the epithelium on the inferior aspect of the organ. It is the vena comitans of the terminal part of the lingual artery.

THE TEETH

There are twenty deciduous teeth in man. Each half of each dental arcade holds two incisors, one canine and two milk molars. These erupt between the sixth and the twenty-fourth months of postnatal life, and are progressively shed as the permanent dentition appears. This consists of a total of thirty-two teeth. Each half of each dental arcade contains two incisors, one canine, two premolars and three molars. They erupt between the seventh and twenty-fifth years of postnatal life.

Individual eruption times

Deciduous dentition. Medial incisor, 6th month.
Lateral incisor, 8th month.
First molar, 12th month.
Canine, 18th month.
Second molar, 24th month.

Permanent dentition. First molar, 6–7 years.
Medial incisor, 7–8 years.
Lateral incisor, 8–9 years.
First premolar, 10–11 years.
Canine, 10–12 years.
Second premolar, 11–12 years.
Second molar, 12 years.
Third molar, 13–25 years.

STRUCTURE OF TEETH (fig. 21.49)

The deep part of a tooth, known as the root, is embedded in a bony socket. The shape of the projecting crown varies in different teeth, being sharp like a chisel on an incisor, pointed on a canine and capped by rounded tubercles on premolars and molars. The centre of the crown and root contain the pulp with its vessels and nerves which enter the tooth through a small canal at the tip of the root. A tooth is composed mainly of a thick mass of **dentine,** which surrounds the pulp. Over the crown the dentine is protected by **enamel,** which ends at the neck where the mucous membrane of gum is attached. Around the root the dentine is covered by a thin layer of modified bone called cement. Between the cement and the bone of the

jaw there is a layer of collagenous tissue called the **periodontal membrane;** from it fibres penetrate the cement and the bone and so secure the tooth. The periodontal membrane is equivalent to periosteum and so is highly vascular and supplied with nerves.

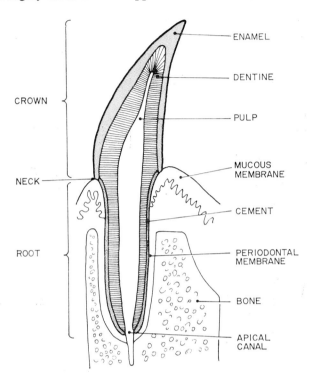

FIG. 21.49. A longitudinal section of an incisor tooth.

Enamel is a non-cellular calcified matrix which is the hardest tissue in the body. Over 98 per cent of the solid matter is a mineral containing calcium and phosphate with a trivial remainder of protein. The enamel is disposed in the form of rods, which have been formed by single **ameloblasts,** and which run from the surface of the crown to the junction with the dentine. These rods are bound together by the small amount of protein present. This is similar to keratin, which is of interest since the enamel is an ectodermal derivative.

Dentine has the same constituent minerals and collagenous scaffolding as bone, but it is harder and does not contain cells in lacunae. Instead its cells, the **odontoblasts,** lie along the inner wall and extend long fine processes through tubules in the dentine. These dentinal tubules run radially from the pulp to the junction with the enamel and anastomose with each other. Dentine is a living tissue, like bone, and it can repair itself although there are no blood vessels or cells within the actual dentinal matrix. As with bone formation, a non-calcified collagenous scaffolding, predentine, is formed before the deposition of calcium salts.

The pulp is a central core of loose mesenchyme containing blood vessels, nerves, phagocytic cells and, of course, odontoblasts. The extent to which the pulp nerves penetrate the dentinal tubules is debated, but we can all vouch for the extreme sensitivity of the dentine.

DEVELOPMENT OF TEETH (fig. 21.50).

The enamel of the crowns of the teeth is produced by ectodermal invaginations from the gingival epithelium while the pulp, dentine, cement and periodontal membrane are mesodermal like the surrounding bone. Along

FIG. 21.50. Stages in the development of a tooth; (a) the dental lamina, (b) formation of an enamel organ, (c) first appearance of enamel and dentine inside a bell-shaped enamel organ, (d) later development, (e) higher magnification of enamel and dentine formation.

the crest of the developing gum in each jaw, the epithelium grows as a sheet into the deeper tissue so forming the **dental lamina.** Although originally continuous, this sheet soon breaks up into the ten deciduous tooth germs for each jaw. From the lingual side of the lamina further germs appear which later form the permanent teeth.

The epithelial portion of the tooth germ is at first a little bag filled with loose cells, the stellate reticulum; then the deeper side of the bag invaginates so that it becomes a bell shaped **enamel organ.** It is the cells on the concave aspect of the bag, the **ameloblasts,** which synthesize the enamel. The mesodermal contents of the bell become the pulp, cement and odontoblasts which form the dentine. Each ameloblast secretes an enamel rod on its basal aspect and the opposed odontoblast forms predentine which soon calcifies to become dentine. So the two sheets of cells, ameloblasts and odontoblasts, march away from each other leaving the enamel and dentine behind them. The odontoblasts leave fine cytoplasmic processes in the dentinal tubules as they move towards the centre and reduce the size of the pulp cavity. The plane of the amelodentinal junction is the permanent indication of where a tooth began to form, since once the first enamel is laid down, the shape of the tooth is determined. While the tooth is in the jaw, the enamel organ continues to deposit enamel but on eruption the organ is reduced to a thin sheet of cells, the enamel cuticle, which soon wears off. Hence no change in the size of a tooth can occur after eruption. The small deciduous teeth, which are adapted to the size of a child's jaw are replaced during adolescence by the larger permanent teeth, which have been formed within the jaw.

OROPHARYNX AND LARYNGOPHARYNX (fig. 21.56).

The oropharynx extends from the palatoglossal folds to the posterior wall of the pharynx. Its roof is formed by the soft palate. The tonsillar bed and palatopharyngeal fold lies in its lateral wall. Its floor extends from the circumvallate papillae to the tip of the epiglottis, and includes the pharyngeal surface of the tongue with its lingual tonsil, and the median glosso-epiglottic fold which connects it to the front of the epiglottis. On either side of this fold, there is a hollow, the **vallecula.** Its posterior boundary is a poorly defined fold of mucous membrane, the lateral glosso-epiglottic fold, which sweeps around the posterior and lateral aspects of the hollow to fade away in the lateral part of the tongue.

The laryngopharynx lies between the upper edge of the epiglottis and the pharyngo-oesophageal junction. In the median part of its anterior wall lies the inlet of the larynx, bounded by the epiglottis, and the two aryepiglottic folds which spread laterally and posteriorly from its margins to converge posteriorly at the posterior margin of the laryngeal orifice. Here in each fold there are two tubercles composed of cartilage nodules covered with mucous membrane, the medial being the corniculate and the lateral the cuneiform tubercles. On either side of the laryngeal opening lie the deep pyriform fossae. Below the tubercles, the anterior wall of the laryngopharynx bulges backwards, so that its lumen is reduced to a curved slit with an anterior concavity, which gradually merges inferiorly with the oesophageal lumen.

THE CERVICAL PART OF THE OESOPHAGUS

This is continuous with the laryngopharynx at the level of the lower border of the sixth cervical vertebra. It is suspended from the posterior aspect of the cricoid cartilage by an upward extension of its outer longitudinal layer of muscle, which is skeletal at this level. It is placed immediately anterior to the anterior longitudinal ligament and the prevertebral muscles, and directly posterior to the trachea. The recurrent laryngeal nerves lie on either side in the tracheo-oesophageal grooves, and the thoracic duct is situated posteriorly on the left side, tucked into the interval between the left margin of the oesophagus and the front of the prevertebral structures.

THE ACTION OF SWALLOWING

This takes place in two stages. In the first or voluntary phase, a bolus of food is lifted upwards and backwards into the space between the palatoglossal folds by the combined action of the mylohyoid and styloglossus muscles. Respiration is restrained, and the palatopharyngeal isthmus is reflexly occluded by the coordinated action of the tensores and levatores veli palatini, which draw the soft palate upwards and backwards. The superior constrictor muscles contract to bring the posterior pharyngeal wall into contact with the upper surface of the soft palate, thus completing the occlusion of the isthmus.

In the course of the second or involuntary phase, the bolus passes through the oropharynx and laryngopharynx

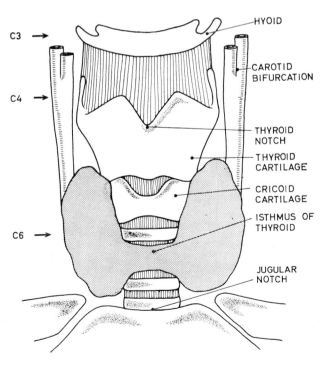

C3 →

C4 →

C6 →

HYOID

CAROTID BIFURCATION

THYROID NOTCH

THYROID CARTILAGE

CRICOID CARTILAGE

ISTHMUS OF THYROID

JUGULAR NOTCH

FIG. 21.51. Anterior view of the larynx.

to the upper end of the oesophagus, where it is temporarily retarded by the cricopharyngeal sphincter. During this phase, the opening of the larynx is shut off. The epiglottis is drawn downwards and backwards towards the tubercles of the posterior margin of the inlet by the action of the aryepiglottici, while the thyroepiglottici widen the inlet, reducing it to a transverse slit. The food mass passes to either side of the epiglottis, pouring as two streams through the lateral pyriform fossae. At the same time, the whole larynx is drawn upwards by the suprahyoid muscles, removing the obstruction produced by the backward pressure of the rigid posterior surface of the cricoid cartilage against the anterior aspect of the body of the sixth cervical vertebra. The food mass now collects at the lower end of the laryngopharynx, and the cricopharyngeal sphincter relaxes to permit it to pass into the oesophagus. The larynx returns to its normal position under the traction of the infrahyoid muscles and gravity.

It is usual for the lips to be closed during the act of swallowing, and it is difficult to carry out the act without this assisting factor. Non-occlusion of the jaw margins renders swallowing practically impossible.

The larynx

The larynx extends from the level of the third cervical vertebra to the lower border of the sixth, where it is continuous with the trachea. It is a semirigid structure with a framework of bone and cartilage, connected together by ligamentous sheets and bands and by synovial joints. Its lowest or infraglottic division is shaped like a nozzle pointing upwards; its rigid wall is due to the cricoid cartilage (fig. 21.51). This part of the larynx is not capable of deformation by the food bolus and is an obstacle to be overcome in the act of swallowing. The outlet of this rigid nozzle, the **rima glottidis**, can be altered in length, breadth and outline, so enabling air to be puffed or bubbled in varying quantities and at varying rates over the resonators of the oral cavity.

THE LARYNGEAL CARTILAGES

The support of the larynx is provided by three rigid elements, two of which are cartilaginous, while the third is bony from childhood onwards. These are the thyroid and cricoid cartilages, and the hyoid bone (fig. 21.52). The last structure represents the fused anterior ends of the second and third arch cartilages of the embryo.

The **hyoid bone** is U-shaped with the convexity of the letter forming the body and the greater horns are the two free extremities. The lesser horns project upwards from the junctions of the body with the greater horns. The bone is ossified from a hyaline cartilage model from centres which appear during the first year of postnatal life and fuse in middle age. It is subcutaneous, the deep fascia of the anterior triangles of the neck blending with the periosteum of the outer surfaces of the body and greater horns.

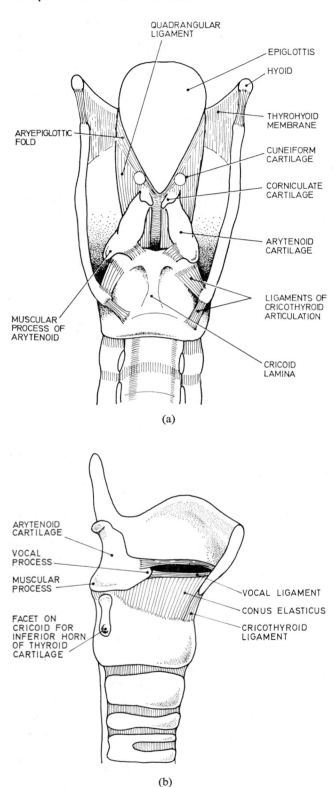

QUADRANGULAR
LIGAMENT

EPIGLOTTIS

HYOID

THYROHYOID
MEMBRANE

ARYEPIGLOTTIC
FOLD

CUNEIFORM
CARTILAGE

CORNICULATE
CARTILAGE

ARYTENOID
CARTILAGE

MUSCULAR
PROCESS OF
ARYTENOID

LIGAMENTS OF
CRICOTHYROID
ARTICULATION

CRICOID
LAMINA

(a)

ARYTENOID
CARTILAGE

VOCAL
PROCESS

MUSCULAR
PROCESS

FACET ON
CRICOID FOR
INFERIOR HORN
OF THYROID
CARTILAGE

VOCAL LIGAMENT

CONUS ELASTICUS

CRICOTHYROID
LIGAMENT

(b)

FIG. 21.52. Cartilages and ligaments of the larynx; (a) posterior view, (b) lateral view with the right half of the thyroid cartilage removed.

Its deep surface is in contact with the submucosa of the pharynx, except in the midline, where it is separated from the front of the epiglottis by the loose tissue below the glossoepiglottic fold, and by the hyoepiglottic ligament.

The **thyroid cartilage** is composed of two hyaline cartilaginous laminae united anteriorly. The angle between these two plates is about a right angle in the male, and up to 120° in the female. The free posterior border of each lamina is prolonged upwards and downwards into superior and inferior horns. A raised oblique line runs downwards and forwards across the lateral surface of each lamina, converging on the inferior part of the fused anterior margins.

The **cricoid cartilage** is roughly circular in outline when viewed from above, and is in the form of a short cylinder, whose posterior wall projects above its upper margin. Facets on the lateral aspects of the cartilage articulate with the inferior horns of the thyroid cartilage, and others on the upper surface of the posterior part of the body articulate with the arytenoids. The posterior aspect of the cartilage has a midline ridge for the attachment of the upper end of the external longitudinal layer of muscle of the oesophagus, and two lateral hollows for the origins of the posterior cricoarytenoid muscles.

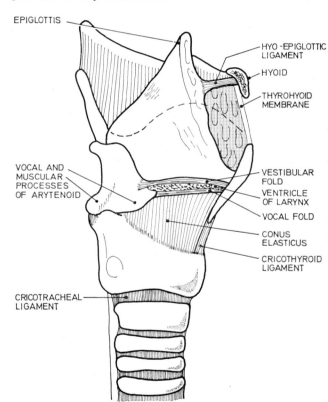

EPIGLOTTIS

HYO-EPIGLOTTIC
LIGAMENT

HYOID

THYROHYOID
MEMBRANE

VOCAL AND
MUSCULAR
PROCESSES
OF ARYTENOID

VESTIBULAR
FOLD

VENTRICLE
OF LARYNX

VOCAL FOLD

CONUS
ELASTICUS

CRICOTHYROID
LIGAMENT

CRICOTRACHEAL
LIGAMENT

FIG. 21.53. Cartilages and ligaments of the interior of larynx, shown by removing right half of the thyroid cartilage.

On the upper edge of the posterior part of the cricoid cartilage lie the two **arytenoid cartilages**, each of which resembles a quarter of a pyramid, with an apex, a medial angle placed alongside the middle of the larynx, a muscular process which is the lateral angle, and a vocal process which points directly forwards (figs. 21.52 and 21.53). The vocal process is composed of non-calcifiable elastic cartilage, while the remainder is hyaline.

The medial surface of the arytenoid cartilage is covered with the mucous membrane of the larynx, and the lower margins of the two cartilages form the boundaries of the intracartilaginous part of the rima glottidis. In the fresh larynx, the remaining aspects of the arytenoids are obscured by muscular and ligamentous attachments.

The **epiglottic cartilage** is composed entirely of the elastic variety and is not subject to ossification. It is attached to the posterior aspects of the median parts of the hyoid bone and thyroid cartilage by the hyoepiglottic and thyroepiglottic ligaments. Its posterior surface and upper margins, with some of the upper part of its anterior surface, are covered with mucous membrane. It is linked by a fold of mucous membrane to the apex of the arytenoid cartilage on each side of the laryngeal orifice, the **aryepiglottic folds** (fig. 21.56).

THE JOINTS OF THE LARYNX

The upper margin of the thyroid cartilage is attached to the posterior edge of the hyoid bone by a tough sheet of fibrous tissue, the **thyrohyoid membrane**, which passes deep to the hyoid bone to reach its upper attachment. The free posterior edges of this membrane are thickened to form the lateral thyrohyoid ligaments which contain small cartilaginous aggregations. The lateral aspect of the membrane is pierced by the internal laryngeal branch of the superior laryngeal nerve, accompanied by the superior laryngeal branch of the superior thyroid artery, and its

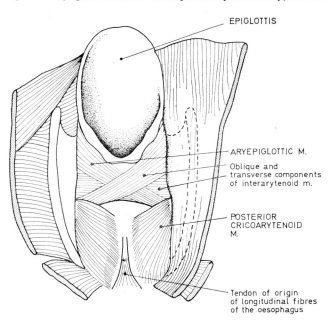

EPIGLOTTIS

ARYEPIGLOTTIC M.

Oblique and transverse components of interarytenoid m.

POSTERIOR CRICOARYTENOID M.

Tendon of origin of longitudinal fibres of the oesophagus

FIG. 21.54. Posterior view of the muscles of the larynx.

venae comitantes. These ramify in the floor of the pyriform fossa, which lies on the immediate medial aspect of the membrane. A bursa separates the upper median part of the membrane from the posterior aspect of the body of the hyoid bone. Remnants of the thyroglossal duct may be found tucked up deep to the anterior edge of the body of the hyoid bone (p. 18.30).

A band of fibrous tissue, the median cricothyroid ligament, unites the anterior parts of the thyroid and cricoid cartilages. More posteriorly and separate from it, a strong sheet of connective tissue extends from the upper margin of the cricoid cartilage and the vocal process of the arytenoid cartilage to the posterior aspect of the fused median part of the thyroid cartilage,

16

about halfway up its length. This is the **conus elasticus**. The upper free margin, extending from the vocal process to the back of the thyroid cartilage is the **vocal ligament**. The space between the edges of the vocal ligaments is the anterior or interligamentous part of the rima glottidis. A few millimetres above this level a thin ligamentous band, the **vestibular ligament**, connects the lateral aspect of the arytenoid cartilage with the back of the median fused part of the thyroid cartilage a little above the attachment of the vocal ligament. It is the supporting structure of the vestibular fold, which is the upper boundary of the ventricle of the larynx.

A thin sheet of connective tissue runs from the lateral margin of the epiglottis to the anterior margin of the arytenoid cartilage blending with the vestibular ligament below and having a free superior margin in the aryepiglottic fold. This is the **quadrangular ligament** which forms part of the lateral wall of the vestibule or uppermost part of the interior of the larynx. It also forms the medial wall of the pyriform fossa.

Two pairs of synovial joints occur in the larynx. The **cricothyroid articulations**, which involve the inferior horns of the thyroid cartilage, and the lateral aspects of the cricoid, are involved in flexion-extension of these two cartilages on each other. The **cricoarytenoid articulations**, involving the bases of the arytenoid and the upper surface of the cricoid cartilages, have incongruent surfaces in most positions of the arytenoids. They are capable of permitting rotation of the arytenoids around a vertical axis, and lateral traction of these cartilages.

THE LARYNGEAL MUSCLES

Unlike the remainder of the intrinsic muscles of the larynx, the **cricothyroid muscle** is placed largely on the external aspect of the supporting cartilages. It arises from the anterior surface of the cricoid cartilage close to the median plane, and runs upwards and backwards to be inserted into the deep surface and inferior margin of the thyroid cartilage. Its lateral surface is partly obscured by the fibrous band which gives origin to some of the muscle fibres of the inferior constrictor of the pharynx. The muscle flexes the thyroid cartilage upon the cricoid, approximating the anterior margins of these two structures, and increasing the tension in the vocal ligament. The **thyroarytenoid muscle** (fig. 21.55) extends from the lateral aspect of the arytenoid cartilage to the posterior aspect of the median part of the thyroid cartilage. The medial fibres are placed parallel to the vocal ligament, and are connected to its lateral edge, constituting the **vocalis muscle**. The main part of the muscle draws the arytenoid cartilage towards the posterior aspect of the thyroid cartilage, opposing the action of the cricothyroid and relaxing the tension in the vocal ligaments. The vocalis portion can alter the tension within individual parts of the vocal ligament.

Continuous with the thyroarytenoid posteriorly, and connecting the posterior surfaces of the two arytenoid cartilages is the thin **interarytenoid muscle**. The central part of its anterior aspect, between the two arytenoid attachments, is clothed with the mucous membrane of the larynx, and so forms the posterior boundary of the rima glottidis. Its posterior aspect is traversed by two slender obliquely placed muscle bundles, the oblique arytenoid muscles, which connect the muscular process of one arytenoid cartilage with the apex of the other and which are continuous with the aryepiglottici. The transverse and oblique muscles separate the backs of the arytenoid cartilages from the mucous membrane of the laryngopharynx. The transverse fibres draw the two arytenoid cartilages together, and thereby reduce the width of the aperture of the rima glottidis. The two obliqui act as part of the aryepiglottici.

The **aryepiglotticus muscle** (fig. 21.55) runs from the tip of the arytenoid cartilage, where it is continuous with the oblique muscle, to the lateral margin of the upper edge of the epiglottis. It blends with the upper margin of the quadrangular ligament. At its upper end, it is associated with muscle fibres which arise from the deep aspect of the thyroid cartilage, close to the insertion of the thyroarytenoids, the **thyroepiglotticus muscle**. It also is blended with the quadrangular ligament. The aryepiglotticus closes the laryngeal inlet by drawing the epiglottis and the arytenoid cartilages together, and the thyroepiglotticus assists by changing the inlet to a transverse slit.

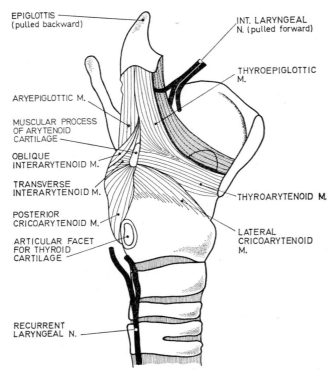

FIG. 21.55. Lateral view of the muscles of the larynx.

Two muscles gain an insertion into the muscular processes of the arytenoid cartilages. The **posterior cricoarytenoid muscle** arises from the concavity lateral to the median ridge on the posterior surface of the cricoid cartilage, while the much smaller **lateral cricoarytenoid muscle** gains an origin from the upper margin of the lateral part of the same cartilage. The tendons of insertion of the two muscles therefore pull upon the muscular process of the arytenoid cartilage from opposite directions. Consequently, when acting alone, the posterior cricoarytenoid muscle abducts the vocal ligament from the midline position, while the lateral muscle reverses this action. When both the posterior and lateral muscles contract together, they oppose the action of the transverse arytenoid muscle and draw the two arytenoid cartilages apart, widening the rima glottidis, particularly its posterior inter-cartilaginous part.

THE INTERIOR OF THE LARYNX

The inlet of the larynx is covered by the same stratified squamous non-keratinizing epithelium that occurs in the oral and laryngeal parts of the pharynx. Inside the orifice, this changes to a pseudostratified columnar ciliated epithelium, as found in the nose and trachea. This epi-

thelium is supported by connective tissue which contains serous and mucous acini, and lines the whole of the interior of the larynx except over the vocal folds, where it is replaced by a stratified squamous non-keratinizing variety.

When viewed with a laryngoscope, the interior wall exhibits a transversely placed elliptical recess, the **ventricle of the larynx** (fig. 21.56). At its posterior end, the arytenoid cartilage can be seen shining through the lining epithelium. The upper lip of the ventricle is the vestibular fold, and the lower lip the vocal fold. The interior of the larynx is subdivided into a superior portion, **the vestibule**, above the vestibular folds, an **intermediate region** between the vestibular and vocal folds, including the ventricles, and an **infraglottic region** below the vocal folds.

FIG. 21.56. Rima glottidis and vestibule of larynx.

THE NERVE AND BLOOD SUPPLY OF THE LARYNX

The *sensory innervation* of the mucous membrane comes from the internal and recurrent laryngeal nerves, both of which are ultimately derived from the vagus. The former supplies the region between the epiglottis and the vocal folds, while the latter innervates the region below that level and also sends fibres to the trachea. The rima glottidis is thus the dividing level between superior and recurrent laryngeal zones of innervation.

The *motor supply* to the cricothyroid muscle is obtained from the external laryngeal branch of the superior laryngeal nerve. The remainder of the intrinsic muscles of the larynx are supplied by branches of the recurrent laryngeal nerve.

The *blood supply* follows much the same course as these nerves. The superior laryngeal branch of the superior thyroid artery accompanies the internal laryngeal nerve through the thyrohyoid membrane to the upper part of the larynx. The lower part is supplied by the inferior laryngeal branch of the inferior thyroid artery, which enters the larynx, along with the terminal part of the recurrent laryngeal nerve.

Structures related to the trachea in the neck

The trachea is directly continuous with the infraglottic part of the laryngopharynx, the lower margin of the cricoid cartilage being connected by the cricotracheal membrane to the first ring of the trachea. Like the oesophagus, the trachea is inclined backwards as well as downwards, following the curve of the vertebral column. This is demonstrable in a lateral radiograph. The cervical part of the trachea is clothed anteriorly and laterally by the isthmus and lateral lobes of the thyroid gland. The recurrent laryngeal nerves run in the tracheo-oesophageal grooves, and so lie posterolateral to the viscus. The common carotid arteries lie posterior to the lateral lobes of the thyroid gland, and therefore posterolateral to the trachea in the neck. The subsequent course of the trachea is described on p. 29.3.

THE THYROID AND PARATHYROID GLANDS (fig. 21.57)

The thyroid gland has a median isthmus and two lateral lobes. The former lies across the third, fourth and fifth

- EXTERNAL CAROTID A.
- SUPERIOR THYROID A. AND V.
- INTERNAL JUGULAR V.
- MIDDLE THYROID V.
- INFERIOR THYROID A.
- THYROCERVICAL TRUNK
- SUBCLAVIAN A.
- INFERIOR THYROID V.
- L. BRACHIOCEPHALIC V.

FIG. 21.57. Blood supply of the thyroid gland.

tracheal rings, and blends with the two lateral lobes which extend superiorly on each side of the larynx as far as the oblique lines. The whole gland is enclosed in a capsule formed from the pretracheal fascia which binds it to the trachea. It lies in a plane which is superficial to the inferior pharyngeal constrictor and the external laryngeal nerve, and deep to the sternothyroid muscle, which is attached along with the fascial capsule of the gland to the oblique line of the thyroid cartilage. Two parathyroid glands are embedded in each lateral lobe (p. 25.23).

The *arterial supply* is derived from the superior and inferior thyroid arteries, which anastomose freely. The recurrent laryngeal nerve may run among or even superficial to the branches of the latter vessel and so is at risk in thyroidectomy. An additional arterial supply may be obtained from the brachiocephalic artery by its thyroidea ima branch, which supplies the region of the isthmus.

The *thyroid veins* drain by three main routes, a superior and middle to the internal jugular vein, and an inferior to the brachiocephalic veins within the thorax.

The developments of these glands and other structural features are found on p. 18.29 and 25.17.

THE PRETRACHEAL (INFRAHYOID, STRAP) MUSCLES

This group includes both bellies of omohyoid, sternohyoid, sternothyroid and thyrohyoid. Their importance lies in their close relationship to the thyroid gland.

All these muscles are supplied by the first three cervical nerves from the ansa cervicalis, except the thyrohyoid, which receives a twig from the hypoglossal nerve, which contains fibres derived from the first cervical nerve. Their action is to draw the larynx downwards at the end of the second or involuntary phase of swallowing, acting as an antagonist to the suprahyoid muscles.

The **sternohyoid** connects the posterior aspect of the sternoclavicular joint to the medial part of the front of the body of the hyoid bone. On the lateral side of its superior attachment arises the superior belly of the **omohyoid.** This slender band of muscle runs downwards and laterally across the neurovascular bundle of the neck, where it narrows to blend with a tendon which connects it to the inferior belly, which arises from the scapula medial to the suprascapular notch. Deep to these two muscles run the **sternothyroid** and **thyrohyoid,** both of which are rather wider than the sternohyoid. The sternothyroid connects the back of the sternoclavicular joint to the oblique line of the thyroid cartilage, and the thyrohyoid continues from this attachment to the front of the hyoid bone.

MIDDLE EAR AND RELATED CAVITIES

The auditory tube, the middle ear cavity, the mastoid antrum and the mastoid air cells are modifications of the simple tubotympanic recess of the embryo. This recess is formed from the first internal pouch of the primitive pharynx with some small addition from the second pouch. The series of cavities which develops from this outgrowth becomes enclosed posteriorly within the parts of the temporal bone.

The middle ear cavity lies in the petrous temporal bone at the medial end of the external acoustic meatus, and some millimetres lateral to the blind end of the internal meatus. A line connecting these two openings passes straight through the centre of the middle ear cavity. Superiorly, the cavity is related to the floor of the middle cranial fossa. The floor of the cavity of the middle ear is placed immediately above that part of the jugular foramen

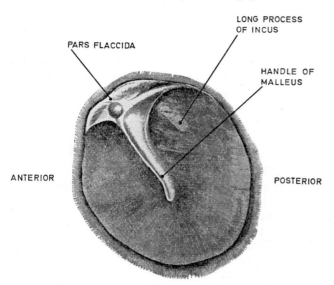

FIG. 21.58. Lateral aspect of left tympanic membrane.

which contains the superior bulb of the internal jugular vein. The internal carotid artery ascends within the bone which forms the anterior wall below the opening of the bony canal of the auditory tube. The terminal part of the sigmoid sinus lies posterior to the lower part of the posterior wall of the cavity.

The cavity of the middle ear is a narrow vertical slit within the temporal bone. It has practically no anterior wall above the level of the slight convexity created by the carotid canal, since the bony auditory tube and the canal for tensor tympani muscle are continuous with it on this aspect. Its posterior wall has the aditus to the mastoid antrum in its upper part and a small pyramidal projection for the stapedius muscle below.

The lateral wall of the cavity is largely occupied by the tympanic membrane, with the attached handle of the malleus. Most of this membrane is kept tense by the tensor tympani muscle, which is inserted into the malleus near the upper margin of the membrane. A very small segment of it however, stretching from the malleolar attachment to the upper margin, is flaccid. The larger, tense part of the membrane consists of a sheet of connective tissue, containing both radial and circular fibres, with skin on the external and flattened epithelium on the internal aspects; the flaccid part consists of the epithelial layers only. The periphery of the tense area of the membrane shows a fibrocartilaginous thickening at its attachment to bone. The entire tympanic membrane

slopes downwards and medially, with an anterior inclination, so that it makes an angle of roughly 55° with the anterior and inferior walls of the external acoustic meatus (fig. 21.59). The centre of the membrane is drawn medially, and the point of maximum concavity when viewed from the lateral aspect is called the **umbo**. The part of the tympanic cavity which arises above the level of the upper margin of the tympanic membrane is the epitympanic recess which contains the greater part of the malleus and incus.

The medial wall separates the middle ear cavity from the cochlear and vestibular apparatuses. A convexity, occupying most of the lower part of that wall, the **promontory**, is produced by the bulging of the first coil of the cochlea. Its surface is marked by a network of fine grooves for the fibres of the tympanic branch of the glossopharyngeal nerve and sympathetic fibres derived from the plexus around the internal carotid artery. In the upper part of the medial wall a transverse bony ridge inclines downwards at its posterior end. This marks the position of the bony canal for the facial nerve, as it passes from the geniculate ganglion to the stylomastoid foramen.

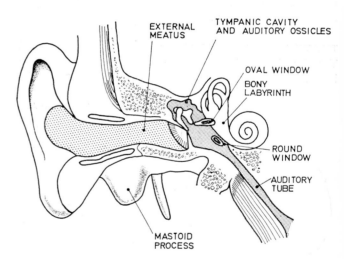

FIG. 21.59. Coronal section of the right ear.

On the upper margin of the promontory and below the facial canal, is an oval opening in the bone, the **fenestra vestibuli**, which is closed by the footplate of the stapes and its anular ligament. At the lower margin of the promontory is another aperture, the **fenestra cochleae**, which is closed by the secondary tympanic membrane. These two apertures lead into the scala vestibuli and scala tympani respectively. The perilymph within these scalae is sealed off from the middle ear cavity by the structures which close the fenestrae. At the posterior margin of the promontory is a small indentation, the sinus tympani, which fortuitously marks the position of the ampulla of the posterior semi-circular canal of the vestibular apparatus (p. 24.26)

THE MUCOUS MEMBRANE OF THE TYMPANIC CAVITY

The lining of the cavity of the middle ear consists of a single layer of epithelium, which varies from a columnar ciliated at the opening of the auditory tube to a flattened type on the inner surface of the tympanic membrane. This epithelium is connected to the periosteum of the bony walls of the cavity by a thin layer of connective tissue which contains nerves and blood vessels. Both epithelium and connective tissue are continuous over the ossicles. The mucous membrane receives a sensory supply from the glossopharyngeal nerve, via its tympanic branch.

THE AUDITORY OSSICLES

The medial surface of the tympanic membrane is connected to the fenestra vestibuli by a system of small bones united by synovial joints. The upper part of this system is in the epitympanic recess, above the level of the upper margin of the tympanic membrane. This system of bony segments forms the connecting link which transmits impulses from the tympanic membrane to the fluid-filled system of the cochlea at the fenestra vestibuli. The **malleus**, a club-shaped bone with an expanded upper end, is connected to the roof of the cavity by a superior ligament. Its lower thinner part or handle is bound to the medial surface of the tympanic membrane. At the upper margin of the tympanic membrane, the anterior ligament connects the neck of the malleus to the anterior wall of the tympanic cavity. The posterior aspect of the head of the malleus articulates with the body of the **incus**, a true synovial joint intervening. This ossicle consists of a body and two posteriorly projecting processes, a short upper one and a longer lower one. The former is connected to the posterior wall of the cavity by a ligament, while the longer process articulates by a minute synovial joint with the head of the third ossicle, the **stapes**. This structure is shaped like a stirrup, with a footplate bound by its anular ligament into the fenestra vestibuli. A fluid wave from the footplate of the stapes, travels along the scala vestibuli through the duct of the cochlea to the scala tympani, where its force is absorbed by the secondary tympanic membrane (p. 24.26).

The ossicles may be regarded as being connected to the bone of the tympanic cavity and to each other by a series of five joints, three tethered and two mobile, all of which are involved in ossicular movement. The ligament attachments of the ossicles to the bony wall of the cavity form the tethered joints, and involve the superior and anterior ligaments of the malleus, the posterior ligament of the incus, and the anular ligament of the stapes. The mobile joints are free to move in more than one plane, and consist of the malleo-incudal and the incudo-stapedial articulations.

THE MUSCLES OF THE MIDDLE EAR

The **tensor tympani** arises from the roof and walls of the canal in which it lies. As it passes to its insertion into the neck of the malleus, it turns sharply laterally around a bony spur at the posterior end of its bony canal, the processus cochlearformis. Its tone maintains the medial convexity of the membrane and presses the footplate of the stapes into the fenestra vestibuli. The **stapedius** arises from the interior of the small bony pyramid on the posterior wall of the middle ear cavity and is inserted into the head of the stapes at the point of convergence of the two limbs of the ossicle. It contracts to draw the footplate of the stapes backwards and out of the fenestra vestibuli.

The ossicles are derived from the dorsal ends of the first and second arch cartilages of the embryo, and the two muscles are developed from the mesoderm of these arches. Thus, the malleus is derived from the first arch cartilage, the tensor tympani which is inserted into it from first arch mesoderm, and the nerve supplying the muscle is a branch of the first arch nerve, the mandibular division of the trigeminal nerve. The stapes is developed from the dorsal end of the second arch cartilage, the stapedius which is inserted into it is derived from second arch mesoderm and the nerve which supplies the muscle is a branch of the second arch nerve, the facial nerve. A paralysis of the stapedius muscle of whatever cause gives rise to discomfort, almost amounting to pain, upon the hearing of a loud noise (p. 24.29).

The incus, which is not directly attached to either muscle, is probably of first arch cartilage derivation.

THE FACIAL NERVE IN THE PETROUS TEMPORAL BONE (fig. 21.60).

The main trunk of the facial nerve and the nervus intermedius enter the petrous temporal bone through a canal in the lateral end of the internal acoustic meatus. The two nerves blend to form a single trunk within the bone. Just above the vestibule of the internal ear, this trunk takes a sharp turn backwards, the genu of the facial nerve. At the genu, the nerve is swollen as a result of the presence within it at this point of ganglion cells forming the **geniculate ganglion**, which is mainly concerned with the sense of taste. From the ganglion, the facial nerve runs backwards in the medial wall of the middle ear, and then downwards in its posterior wall, emerging from the base of the skull at the stylomastoid foramen (p. 21.17). When within the petrous temporal bone, it gives off branches, most of which are fibres from the nervus intermedius; no part of that nerve reaches the stylomastoid foramen. At the ganglion, the **greater petrosal nerve** runs forwards to pierce the floor of the middle cranial fossa

(p. 21.5). Also within the petrous bone, a small branch is given off to join the fibres of the tympanic plexus which are secretomotor in type and which are derived from the glossopharyngeal nerve, to form the **lesser petrosal nerve**, which passes through the floor of the fossa anterolateral to the greater nerve. As the facial nerve descends in the posterior wall of the middle ear, it supplies the stapedius

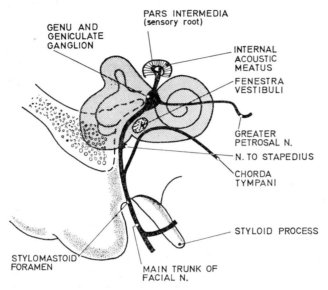

FIG. 21.60. The intrapetrous part of the facia nerve.

muscle, and then loses the remainder of its nervus inter-media fibres in the **chorda tympani**; this branch arises just above the stylomastoid foramen, pierces the posterior wall of the middle ear and runs across the cavity. It passes lateral to the long process of the incus and medial to the handle of the malleus, and leaves by a small canaliculus in the lower part of the anterior wall of that cavity. Emerging from the base of the skull, it is distributed with the lingual nerve.

THE MASTOID ANTRUM AND THE MASTOID AIR CELLS

The antrum lies directly posterior to the middle ear cavity, connected to it by the **aditus** in the upper part of their common wall. It can be surface marked as lying 1 to 2 cm medial to the suprameatal triangle which is above and behind the external acoustic meatus.

The extensive system of air sacs which usually fills the mastoid process opens into the periphery of the antrum. The mucous membrane of these sacs is continuous with that of the antrum, and through it with the middle ear cavity. Sometimes the mastoid air cells are greatly reduced or even absent.

THE BONY PART OF THE AUDITORY TUBE

The bony auditory tube is situated immediately inferior to the canal for the tensor tympani muscle. It runs parallel and anterolateral to the bony carotid canal for the internal carotid artery, and opens into the posterior end of the suture between the posterior margin of the greater wing of the sphenoid bone and the quadrate area of the petrous temporal bone. Here it is continuous with its fibrocartilaginous continuation, which it meets at a slight angle (p. 21.40). Both the bony and fibrocartilaginous parts of the auditory tube are lined by a pseudo-stratified columnar ciliated epithelium.

LYMPH DRAINAGE OF THE HEAD AND NECK (fig. 21.61)

The **deep cervical chain of lymph nodes** surrounds the structures of the neurovascular bundle in the neck, and is particularly associated with the internal jugular vein. Superiorly, this chain can be traced to a small node occupying the angle between the posterior wall of the nasopharynx and the prevertebral muscles, the **retro-pharyngeal node**. Posteriorly, individual members of the deep cervical chain appear in the posterior triangle of the neck, spreading from the border of the sternomastoid muscle. One of these, the **jugulo-omohyoid node**, lies at the point at which the inferior belly of the omohyoid muscle crosses the neurovascular bundle. Among its afferent vessels are a few which come directly from the tip of the tongue. At the anterior border of the sternomastoid, where it crosses the posterior belly of the digastric muscle, is another member of the deep cervical chain, the **jugulodigastric** or **tonsillar node**, which receives afferents from the posterior third of the tongue, the tonsillar bed

FIG. 21.61. Main groups of lymph nodes in the head and neck.

and the adjacent wall of the oropharynx. The efferent lymphatic vessels from the deep cervical nodes converge on the **jugular lymph trunk**, which drains into the junction of the internal jugular and subclavian veins through the thoracic duct or right lymphatic duct (p. 20.37).

The superficial region of the head is drained by a series of small groups of lymph nodes, which also receive some deeply placed afferents. This arrangement of nodes is described as the **collar chain**. It consists of the following groups:

The **submental nodes** lie between the diverging anterior bellies of the digastric muscles, on the under surface of the mylohyoids, and drain the median parts of the tongue, gum and lower lip.

The **submandibular nodes** are wedged between the submandibular gland and the medial surface of the mandible, and drain the remainder of the lower jaw and the side of the tongue.

The **superficial parotid group** drains the upper part of the face and the temporal region. It continues downwards over the superficial aspect of the sternomastoid muscle as the superficial group of cervical nodes, which drain into the lower posterior group of deep nodes. They follow the course of the external jugular vein. The **deep parotid nodes** do not belong to the collar chain series but are members of the deep cervical group.

The **mastoid group** lies on the lateral aspect of the mastoid process, and drains the side of the head.

The **occipital group** lies on the superficial aspect of the upper fibres of the trapezius, and drains the posterior part of the scalp.

All these nodes drain into the deep cervical series of nodes. The submental group tends to send its efferent vessels to the more inferiorly placed nodes, particularly the jugulo-omohyoid.

In addition to these, there are scattered groups of lymph nodes in the anterior part of the neck, the **anterior cervical nodes**. These include the infrahyoid group on the thyrohyoid membrane, the prelaryngeal group on the cricothyroid ligament, the pretracheal nodes at the lower end of the thyroid gland, and some upper members of the paratracheal series in the tracheo-oesophageal groove. All these nodes drain into the lower deep cervical nodes.

FIG. 21.62. Lymph drainage of the tongue.

The tongue is drained by lymph vessels which pass from its tip to the submental and jugulo-omohyoid nodes, from its lateral edge into the submandibular group, from the median part of its dorsum into submandibular and deep cervical nodes of both sides of the neck, and from its posterior third into the upper deep cervical group (fig. 21.62). The nasopharynx sends vessels into the retropharyngeal nodes. The oropharynx, including the palatine tonsil, drains mainly to the jugulodigastric node. The larynx sends vessels from its upper part, above the vocal ligament, to the infrahyoid group, and thence to the upper deep cervical nodes. From its infraglottic part, vessels pass to the prelaryngeal, pretracheal and paratracheal nodes.

The lymphatic vessels from the thyroid gland run to the upper deep cervical, pretracheal, paratracheal, lower deep cervical and anterior mediastinal nodes. Some of its vessels may bypass all nodes and end in the thoracic duct or subclavian vein. The vessels of the cervical part of the trachea end in the prelaryngeal and pretracheal nodes, and in some members of the deep cervical group. The cervical part of the oesophagus drains to the paratracheal nodes.

THE DEVELOPMENT OF THE FACE

The face develops from that part of the embryo which immediately surrounds the buccopharyngeal membrane. A thickening develops in the epithelium on either side of the midline of the surface of the embryo, immediately superficial to the forebrain. These are the two olfactory placodes, and they are destined to form the olfactory mucous membrane of the definitive nose. The mesoderm in the regions surrounding the placodes grows faster than that deep to them. As a result, the placodes become buried in the surface of the embryo. The depressions thus produced are the **olfactory pits** (fig. 21.63). Between them, the mesoderm and overlying ectoderm are raised up into a **median nasal process**, whose lateral margins are the **globular processes**. Lateral to the placodes, the elevated mesoderm in similar fashion forms the **lateral nasal processes**. The placodes sink progressively dorsally and caudally into the substance of the embryonic head, until they meet the cephalic boundary of the primitive pharynx, into which they achieve a temporary opening. This is later occluded by epithelial proliferation. The region between the primitive nostrils provided by this pair of nasal pits, and the cephalic edge of the stomatodaeum, is the rudimentary palate. This latter structure, along with the median and lateral nasal processes, together constitute the **frontonasal process**. Branches of the ophthalmic nerve grow into this process. Mesoderm proceeds to proliferate also between the ectoderm and endoderm at the sides of the stomatodaeum, forming the **maxillary process** at either lateral end of the primitive mouth. The primitive mouth is completed inferiorly by the two mandibular arches which grow forwards to fuse in the midline.

Associated with the maxillary process is the maxillary division of the trigeminal nerve, which grows into the mesoderm of the process. Similarly, the mandibular division of the same nerve, along with the motor root, grows into the mandibular arch, supplying its derivatives, including the skeletal muscle which develops from its mesoderm.

As growth continues the optic outgrowths extend laterally from the diencephalon, until they come into contact with the epithelium of the surface of the embryo at the dorsal end of the groove which separates the frontonasal and maxillary processes. The overlying ectoderm becomes invaginated to form the lens vesicle, and the eye develops at the extreme dorsal end of the maxillo-frontonasal groove.

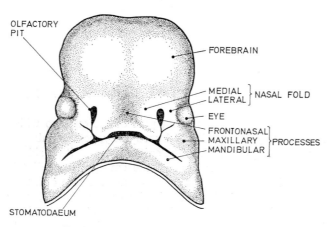

FIG. 21.63. Ventral aspect of foetal head.

By this time, the buccopharyngeal membrane has broken down, and the primitive oral cavity and the pharynx are in direct continuity. The maxillary processes grow ventrally, separating the primitive frontonasal palate from the oral cavity, and the medial edges of the two maxillary processes fuse with the very narrow downward projecting portion of the frontonasal process which forms the philtrum of the upper lip. A more limited fusion takes place between the adjacent edges of the maxillary process and mandibular arch, and upon the extent of this depends the size of the definitive mouth.

The lateral part of the groove between the maxillary and frontonasal processes is progressively lengthened by the ventral growth of the former, and deepened by the proliferation of mesoderm within the adjacent parts of both processes. It is designated the **nasolacrimal groove**, since the apposition of its growing lips eventually converts it into a canal, the nasolacrimal duct of the full-term foetus. Where the apposed edges fail to fuse, an oblique fissure extends from the medial angle of the eye to the lateral margin of the oral fissure of that side of the face, a condition of **cleft face**.

From the floor of the oral cavity, the tongue is developed initially from the internal aspects of the fused ventral ends of the first and second pharyngeal arches. Later, the third arch grows cranially to contribute to the posterior third of the tongue, and obliterates all

traces of the second arch in doing so. In the early stages of foetal development, the tongue projects headwards, sufficiently to virtually fill the primitive oral cavity. While this situation exists, epithelially covered ridges grow medially from the oral aspects of the maxillary processes. These are the **palatine processes**. At first,

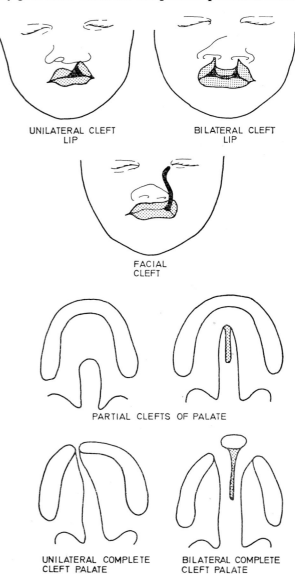

FIG. 21.64. Congenital abnormalities of the face and palate.

their free medial edges are turned caudally. Later, as the cavity of the mouth increases in size relative to the tongue, the medial edges of these two processes meet, and their ventral ends fuse with the margins of the primitive frontonasal palate, and, dorsal to that, with each other. A septum is thus formed between the nasal and oral cavities. When a failure of fusion between the ventral ends of the frontonasal and maxillary processes occurs, a false or paramedian hare lip exists (fig. 21.64). If this failure is more extensive and involves the palatine contributions of both processes, partial or complete cleft palate may result. This may be further complicated by a failure to join up with the nasal septum. In its extreme form, no roof exists in the mouth, and a median tag of tissue is suspended from the septum of the nose, just above the oral cavity.

FURTHER READING

SARNAT B.G. (1951) *The Temporomandibular Joint.* Springfield, Ill. : Thomas.

TRUEX R.C. & KELLNER C.E. (1948) *Detailed Atlas of the Head and Neck.* London : Oxford University Press.

WOLFF E. (1948) *The Anatomy of the Eye and Orbit,* 3rd Edition. London : Lewis.

Chapter 22
The upper limb

The upper limb (fig. 22.1) is composed of the shoulder girdle, the upper arm, the forearm and the hand. In ordinary speech the distal part of the forearm is called the wrist. The hand is divided into three parts, the carpus (anatomical wrist), the hand proper (the dorsum and the palm) supported by the bones of the metacarpus, and five

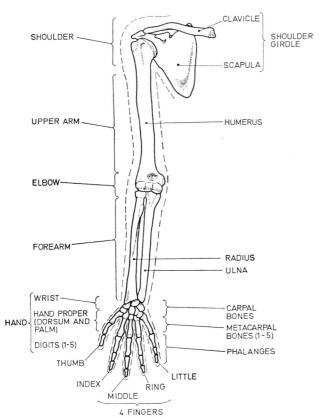

FIG. 22.1. General plan of the upper limb.

digits, the thumb and four fingers (index, middle, ring, little).

Both the upper and lower limbs are built on a similar plan. Both have the girdles (shoulder and pelvic) which connect them to the trunk, a single bone in the upper arm and in the thigh, two bones each in the forearm and leg, the carpus and metacarpus in the hand and the tarsus

and metatarsus in the foot and both have phalangeal bones.

There are, however, considerable functional differences between the two limbs. The pelvic girdle has no free movement, while the shoulder girdle possesses great mobility. The lower limb, specialized for simpler tasks of weight-bearing, locomotion and balance, differs from the upper limb which is a mobile system of joints and levers for positioning the hand, a delicate organ capable of the complicated tasks of exploration, gripping and manipulation. Like sight and hearing, the hand is an extension of the scope of the brain into the environment, providing important information about our body and the surrounding world. The palm and the pulp of the digits, possess many sensory endings. It has been said that man owes his progress to the development of the cerebral hemisphere and to being equipped with an opposable thumb, since the contact between the thumb and the pulps of the other digits is necessary for fine and delicate processes of exploration and manipulation. Even computers and automation systems cannot be built without a skilful hand being applied during their production.

Hence any diminution in the efficiency of the hand affects our livelihood; unfortunately injuries to the upper limb and particularly to the hand are common in a mechanical age. In their treatment special care needs to be given to preserving function.

BONES, JOINTS AND MUSCLES OF THE SHOULDER GIRDLE AND SHOULDER

The shoulder girdle is made up of two bones, the clavicle and the scapula (fig. 22.2), united by the strong coraco-clavicular ligament and a synovial acromioclavicular joint, an arrangement which allows slight movement between the two bones. The girdle is attached to the axial skeleton in front by the synovial sternoclavicular joint and its ligaments, and by muscles (pectoralis minor, fig. 22.16; subclavius, fig. 22.16 and serratus anterior, fig. 22.17), whilst at the back the link is purely muscular (trapezius, fig. 22.13; levator scapulae, fig. 22.14 and rhomboids, fig. 22.14).

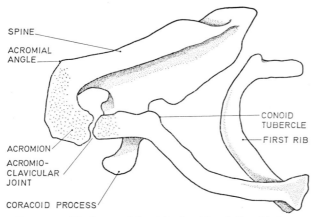

FIG. 22.2. The bones of the right shoulder girdle with the first rib, seen from above.

Functionally the shoulder girdle should be considered together with the upper part of the arm, with the shoulder joint and its muscles (deltoid, fig. 22.19; supraspinatus, infraspinatus, teres major and minor, fig. 22.20; subscapularis, fig. 22.21) and with the muscle links between the humerus and trunk (pectoralis major in front, fig. 22.15, and latissimus dorsi at the back fig. 22.18).

In contrast to the pelvis, the shoulder girdles are separate from each other; this together with the method of their attachment to the axial skeleton gives considerable mobility to these regions, their stability depending largely on the action of the muscles.

BONES OF THE SHOULDER REGION

The clavicle (fig. 22.3)

This is a curved strut extending from the sternum to the acromion process of the scapula and holding the point of the shoulder at its proper distance from the trunk. If the strut is broken, which usually happens at the junction of the middle and lateral thirds, the shoulder falls forwards and medially.

The medial end is expanded and overrides the sternum

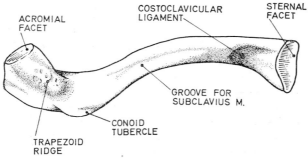

FIG. 22.3. The inferior surface of the right clavicle.

where it forms the sternoclavicular joint. The suprasternal notch intervenes between the medial ends of the two clavicles. The lateral end is flattened and articulates with the acromion of the scapula. The medial two-thirds of the shaft is convex forwards since it is applied to the anterior curvature of the chest wall; near the medial end of the bone the inferior surface is rough for the attachment of the costoclavicular ligament and more laterally grooved for the attachment of the subclavius muscle. The lateral third of the shaft overlies the shoulder and is flattened from above downwards with its inferior surface marked by a **conoid tubercle** near the posterior border and by a **trapezoid ridge** running forwards and laterally from the tubercle.

The scapula

The scapula is a triangular plate of bone whose anterior surface is applied to the posterior curvature of the chest so that its plane makes an angle of 30° with the coronal plane when the arm is by the side (fig. 22.4). The posterior

FIG. 22.4. The position of the scapula in relation to the coronal plane and the head of the humerus.

surface is divided into **supraspinous** and **infraspinous fossae** (fig. 22.5) by the **spine** which projects backwards and continues laterally and forwards as the **acromion process**. The **acromial angle,** which can be readily palpated at the back of the shoulder, is the point where the acromion bends forwards to meet the lateral end of the clavicle. The scapula has superior, lateral and medial borders, and superior, inferior and lateral angles, the last being thickened to form the neck and head of the bone. The lateral surface of the head faces forwards and laterally (fig. 22.6) and is slightly hollowed out to form the shallow **glenoid fossa** which articulates with the almost hemispherical head of the humerus. Supraglenoid and infraglenoid tubercles are to be found just above and below the rim of the glenoid fossa. The **coracoid process** projects anteriorly from the upper part of the neck of the scapula. From its vertical portion or root it bends forwards at its angle into a horizontal part which ends in its tip. The blade-like body of the scapula is covered by muscles and only the inferior angle, the lower part of the medial border, spine, acromion and the coracoid tip can be felt through the skin. With the arm by the side,

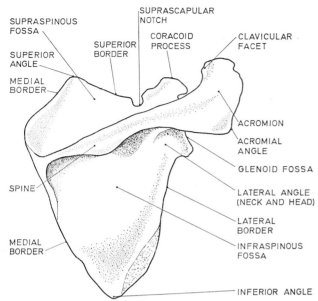

FIG. 22.5. Posterior view of the scapula.

the root of the spine lies at the level of the third thoracic vertebral spine and the inferior angle at the seventh spine.

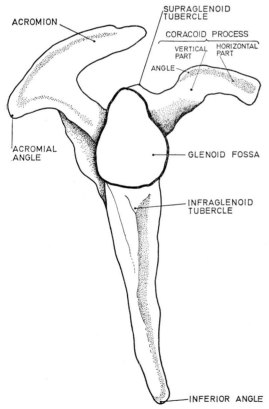

FIG. 22.6. Lateral view of the scapula.

The humerus (fig. 22.7)

The almost hemispherical **head**, covered by articular cartilage, faces upwards, medially and slightly backwards in the plane of the scapula to meet the shallow and much smaller glenoid fossa. The head is separated from the rest of the bone by the shallow constriction called the **anatomical neck**. The **greater tubercle** is the large prominence, lateral to the head, which forms the point of the shoulder. The **lesser tubercle** on the anterior

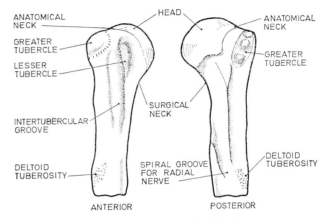

FIG. 22.7. The upper part of the right humerus.

aspect of the proximal end of the bone is separated by the intertubercular groove from the greater tubercle. The **surgical neck** is the region immediately below the head and the tubercles. The **deltoid tuberosity**, the rough V-shaped impression at the attachment of the deltoid muscle, is found around the midpoint of the lateral aspect of the shaft. On the posterior surface of the shaft a shallow groove for the radial nerve runs obliquely downwards and laterally.

JOINTS OF THE SHOULDER REGION

The sternoclavicular joint (fig. 22.8)

The shoulder girdle is united to the trunk by the muscles and by the synovial sternoclavicular joint. The large medial end of the clavicle fits into a socket formed by a notch on the manubrium sterni and by the first costal cartilage. A strong fibrous capsule surrounds the joint. Two accessory ligaments are the **interclavicular ligament** extending from clavicle to clavicle, and the **costoclavicular ligament** from the under surface of the clavicle to the upper surface of the first costal cartilage. An articular disc attached to the clavicle above and to the first costal cartilage below blends with the capsule and divides the joint into two compartments, medial and lateral. These ligaments and the articular disc prevent medial

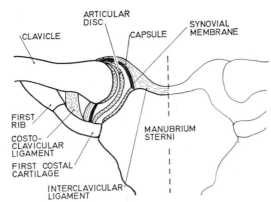

FIG. 22.8. Sternoclavicular joint. Synovial membrane is black and cartilage is dotted.

dislocation of the clavicle even when an impact on the shoulder is sufficient to break the bone.

The acromioclavicular joint (fig. 22.9)

This joint unites the two bones of the girdle. It has a weak capsule and usually contains an incomplete articular disc. The plane of the joint is oblique so that the lateral end of the clavicle tends to override the acromion,

FIG. 22.9. Acromioclavicular joint.

and the security of the joint depends on the strong **coracoclavicular ligament** which anchors the clavicle to the coracoid process. Attachments of this important ligament are the conoid tubercle and trapezoid ridge on the clavicle, and the coracoid process in the region of its angle.

The shoulder (glenohumeral) joint (fig. 22.10)

The shoulder joint which is of the synovial ball and socket variety has a very free range of movement. Neither the fit of the bones, nor the capsule and ligaments contribute much to its stability, as this depends almost entirely on the surrounding muscles.

The **capsular ligament** is very loose and it presents

FIG. 22.10. The shoulder joint. The cavity is distended as normally only potential spaces exist. The section is in the plane of the tendon of the long head of biceps.

inferiorly a dependent pouch when the arm is by the side; if the arm is immobilized in this position, the walls of the pouch may become permanently fused together, causing a stiff joint. The capsule is attached around the anatomical neck of the humerus except medially where it descends on to the surgical neck; on the scapula it is attached to a fibrocartilaginous rim called **labrum glenoidale**, bound to the periphery of the glenoid fossa. The capsule extends above to include the supraglenoid tubercle and the attachment of the tendon of the long head of the biceps muscle. The **transverse ligament** bridges across the upper part of the intertubercular groove to hold the tendon in position. The **coracohumeral ligament** runs from the lateral part of the root of the coracoid process to the anatomical neck and greater tubercle, blending with the capsule. The tendons of the rotator cuff muscles (p. 22.10) fuse with and strengthen the capsular ligament.

The synovial membrane lines the deep aspect of the capsule, covers the labrum glenoidale, surrounds the tendon of the long head of biceps and lines the intracapsular bone which is not covered by articular cartilage. There are two bursae communicating with the synovial cavity, one surrounds the bicipital tendon, the other lies anteriorly under the subscapularis muscle.

The weakest part of the capsule is at the inferior aspect and this is the area which is usually torn when the head of the humerus comes out in dislocation of the shoulder joint. The axillary nerve which lies inferior to the joint may then be injured.

The coraco-acromial arch and subacromial bursa (fig. 22.11)

These should be regarded as a functional extension of the shoulder joint. One of the commonest causes of pain

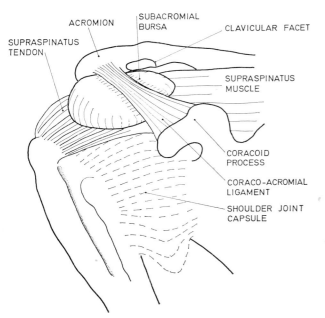

FIG. 22.11. Coraco-acromial arch and subacromial bursa. The bursa is distended.

and disability in the shoulder region is due to the disturbance of this bursal joint.

The **coraco-acromial arch** forms a shelf above the shoulder joint. It is composed of the horizontal part of the coracoid process, the coraco-acromial ligament and the acromion. The ligament is attached to the lateral border of the horizontal part of the coracoid and to the acromion in front of the acromioclavicular joint. The arch is separated from the shoulder joint by the supraspinatus tendon blending with the superior aspect of the capsule. To ensure a smooth movement the subacromial

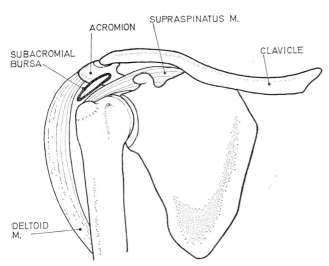

FIG. 22.12. A diagram illustrating the relations of the subacromial bursa.

bursa lies between the upper surface of the supraspinatus tendon and the capsule of the shoulder joint below, and the arch and overlying deltoid muscle above. This bursa does not normally communicate with the cavity of the shoulder joint, but it may do so in disease or following changes due to age.

MUSCLES OF THE SHOULDER REGION

The muscles connecting the upper limb to the axial skeleton are shown in figs. 22.13–18 and consist of trapezius, rhomboids, levator scapulae, pectoralis major, pectoralis minor, subclavius, serratus anterior and latissimus dorsi. In all these figures O and I represent the origin and insertion of the muscles respectively.

The muscles of the shoulder are shown in figs. 22.19–21

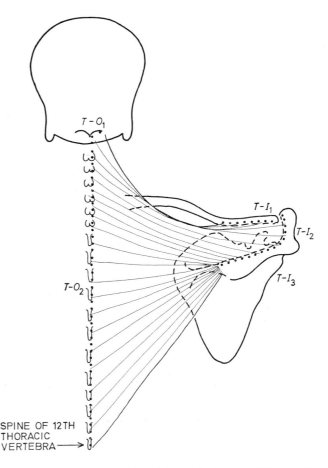

FIG. 22.13. **Trapezius muscle** (T). which lies superficial to the levator scapulae and rhomboid.

$T\text{-}O_1$ Medial third of superior nuchal line of occipital bone and external occipital protuberance.

$T\text{-}O_2$ Ligamentum nuchae, the spines of the seventh cervical and all thoracic vertebrae.

$T\text{-}I_1$ Lateral third of clavicle.

$T\text{-}I_2$ Medial border of acromion.

$T\text{-}I_3$ Crest of the spine of scapula.

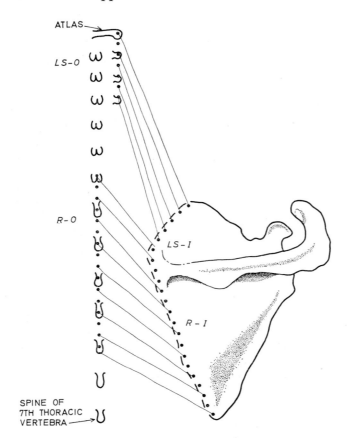

FIG. 22.14. The levator scapulae and the rhomboid muscles, which lie deep to trapezius.

Levator scapulae muscle (*LS*).

LS-O Posterior tubercles of the transverse processes of the first three or four cervical vertebrae.

LS-I Medial margin of scapula from the upper angle to the spine.

Rhomboid muscles (R).

R-O Lower part of ligamentum nuchae, spines of seventh cervical and first five thoracic vertebrae.

R-I Medial border of scapula from the spine to the inferior angle.

FIG. 22.16. The pectoralis minor, subclavius and coracobrachialis muscles.

Pectoralis minor muscle (*PM*).

PM-O Third, fourth and fifth ribs.
PM-I Medial border of coracoid process.

Subclavius muscle (*S*)

S-O First rib and its cartilage.
S-I Floor of groove on the inferior surface of the clavicle.

Coracobrachialis muscle (*CB*)

CB-O Tip of coracoid process.
CB-I Middle of medial border of the shaft of the humerus.

FIG. 22.15. Pectoralis major which lies superficial to the pectoralis minor, subclavius and coracobrachialis muscles.

Pectoralis major muscle (*P*).

P-O₁ Medial half of the clavicle.

P-O₂ Manubrium and body of sternum, first six costal cartilages.

P-O₃ Aponeurosis of external oblique muscle of the abdomen.

P-I Lateral lip of the intertubercular groove.

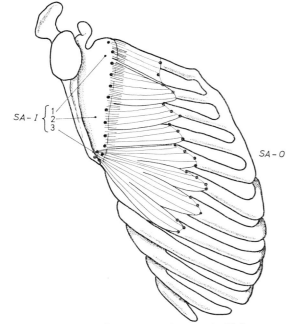

FIG. 22.17. **Serratus anterior muscle** (*SA*)

SA-O Outer surfaces of the upper eight ribs.
SA-I(1) Costal surface of the superior angle, (2) medial border, (3) inferior angle of the scapula.

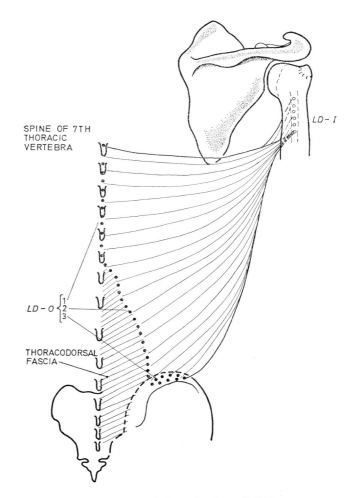

FIG. 22.18. **Latissimus dorsi muscle** (*LD*).

LD-O₁ Spines of lower six thoracic vertebrae.
LD-O₂ Through thoracolumbar fascia from the spines of the lumbar and sacral vertebrae.
LD-O₃ Posterior part of the iliac crest.
LD-I Floor of the intertubercular groove of the humerus.

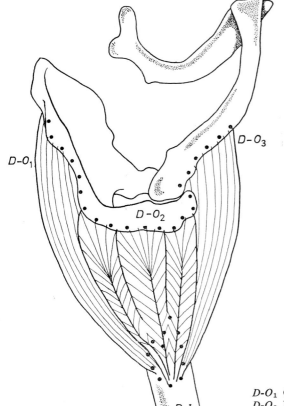

FIG. 22.19. **Deltoid muscle** (*D*).

D-O₁ Crest of the spine of the scapula.
D-O₂ Lateral border of acromion.
D-O₃ Lateral third of the clavicle.
D-I Deltoid tuberosity of the humerus.

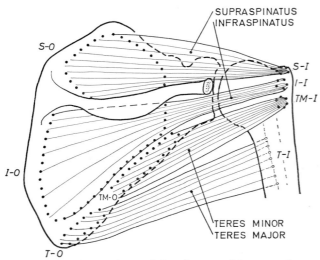

FIG. 22.20. Supraspinatus, infraspinatus and teres muscles.

Supraspinatus muscle (S).

S-O Walls of the supraspinous fossa, except near the neck of the scapula.

S-I Facet on the top of the greater tubercle of the humerus.

Infraspinatus muscle (I)

I-O Walls of the infraspinous fossa except at the neck of the scapula.

I-I Middle facet on the greater tubercle of the humerus.

Teres major muscle (T)

T-O Dorsal aspect of the lower third of the lateral border of the scapula.

T-I Inner lip of the intertubercular groove.

Teres minor muscle (TM)

TM-O Dorsal aspect of the upper two-thirds of the lateral border of the scapula.

TM-I Lowest facet on the greater tubercle of the humerus.

and consist of deltoid, supraspinatus, infraspinatus, teres major and minor, subscapularis and coracobrachialis.

MOVEMENTS OF THE SHOULDER REGION

The mobility of the structures associated with the shoulder girdle and the shoulder itself has been emphasized. Before the individual movements are described it is necessary to discuss the important concept of the **scapulothoracic mechanism.** The scapula is joined directly to the trunk only by muscles and is freely movable on the chest wall. As these muscles have much greater leverage than those acting on the shoulder joint itself, the scapulothoracic mechanism makes an important contribution to the range and power of the movements of the shoulder girdle and arm.

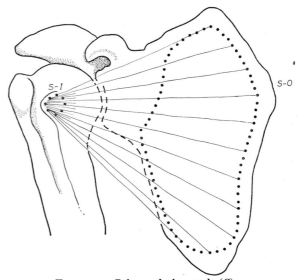

FIG. 22.21. **Subscapularis muscle** (*S*).

S-O Anterior surface of the scapula.

S-I Lesser tubercle of the humerus.

The position of the socket for the head of the humerus can be altered either by translation or rotation of the scapula on the trunk. Even if surgical fixation of the shoulder joint is carried out, increase in the movements of the scapula on the trunk preserves considerable mobility. Some movement of the scapula on the clavicle is possible in spite of the strong coracoclavicular ligament and it occurs at the acromioclavicular joint when the scapula moves on the trunk. The contribution of this joint to the mobility of the shoulder region does not seem to be of importance, since its surgical fixation does not cause any appreciable disability. The contribution of the sternoclavicular joint is also important since with the elevation of the shoulder, the clavicle rotates in this joint until its anterior surface inclines upwards. When the lateral end of the clavicle moves forwards or backwards, downwards or upwards, the medial end moves in the opposite direction because of the strong fulcrum formed by the costoclavicular ligament.

Movements at the joints of the shoulder girdle

The shoulder with the attached limb can be elevated, depressed, moved forwards and backwards. Elevation is achieved by the upper fibres of the trapezius, levator scapulae and rhomboids. It is checked by the costoclavicular ligament. Depression is achieved by subclavius, pectoralis minor and the lower fibres of the trapezius. It is checked by the articular disc of the sternoclavicular joint and by the interclavicular ligament. Serratus anterior and pectoralis minor are responsible for forward movement and trapezius and rhomboids for backward movement.

Pectoralis major and latissimus dorsi muscles, although

acting primarily at the shoulder joint, assist in the movements of the girdle, the former in the forward and the latter in the backward direction.

Movements of the arm in relation to the trunk

These occur at the shoulder girdle and at the shoulder joint itself in a well co-ordinated and synchronized manner. Abduction and adduction, by definition, occur in the plane of the scapula and flexion and extension at right angles to this plane (fig. 22.4). Circumduction is a combination of the above four movements. Rotation can occur at any given position of the arm and consists of movement of the limb around the long axis of the humerus (fig. 22.22).

CIRCUMDUCTION   ROTATION

FIG. 22.22. Lateral and medial rotation and circumduction.

Flexion is achieved by pectoralis major, the anterior fibres of deltoid, coracobrachialis and the short head of biceps. Extension is brought about by latissimus dorsi, teres major and minor, posterior fibres of the deltoid, infraspinatus and long head of triceps. Pectoralis major, latissimus dorsi, teres major and minor are responsible for adduction. Lateral rotation is carried out by infraspinatus, teres minor, posterior fibres of deltoid and medial rotation by pectoralis major, anterior fibres of deltoid, subscapularis, latissimus dorsi and teres major. Medial rotation is stronger than lateral rotation.

The three muscles of the arm: biceps, coracobrachialis and triceps, are shown on figs. 22.16 and 22.29.

The movement of abduction deserves separate description because of its importance and complexity and because it is a good example of the functional co-ordination of many structures. As already indicated, abduction occurs in the plane of the scapula and only in this plane is the capsule of the shoulder joint not twisted. This is an important consideration when it is necessary to rest the joint for some time. The range of abduction is from the dependent position to above the head, approximately two-thirds of the movement occurring at the shoulder joint and one-third by rotation of the scapula. Some degree of lateral rotation accompanies abduction.

The joints and links concerned with the abduction of the upper limb are sternoclavicular, acromioclavicular

FIG. 22.23. Diagram showing the effect of the deltoid pull in early and middle range of abduction.

and shoulder (glenohumeral) joints, the coracoacromial arch with the bursal joint and the scapulothoracic link.

The muscles effecting abduction are the deltoid, supraspinatus, trapezius and serratus anterior. A powerful middle multipennate portion of the deltoid abducts while the anterior and posterior fibres prevent anteroposterior sway of the humeral head in the shallow glenoid fossa.

FIG. 22.24. Diagram showing the rotation of the scapula on the trunk. From D. C. Sinclair (1966) *An Introduction to Functional Anatomy*. Oxford: Blackwell Scientific Publications.

Supraspinatus, owing to its position above the shoulder joint, assists in the early stages of abduction, but together with the rest of the **rotator-cuff muscles** (infraspinatus, teres minor and subscapularis) it has a much more important synergistic action in preventing the powerfully contracting deltoid from pulling the head of the humerus upwards out of the joint in the early stages of abduction (fig. 22.23). When further stages are reached the deltoid is at a mechanical advantage and tends to press the head into the joint. The scapula and thus the glenoid fossa are rotated by the **trapezius** and **serratus anterior** (fig. 22.24) in such a way that the socket for the humeral head looks more and more upwards, increasing the extent of the abduction of the arm.

It is important to realize that all these muscles are involved together throughout abduction, and act in unison and balance; they differ in the degree and timing of their contribution. The so-called rhythm of abduction refers to the co-ordinated movement of the humerus on the scapula with the movement of the scapula on the chest wall. This rhythm is subject to individual variations, but usually some movement of the scapula can be felt in the very early stages by grasping and following the inferior angle of the scapula through the soft tissues. This movement of the scapula begins at the same time on both sides of the body when both arms are being abducted.

BONES, JOINTS AND MUSCLES OF THE ELBOW REGION

BONES OF THE ELBOW REGION

The distal end of the humerus is compressed antero-posteriorly and bent forwards (fig. 22.25). The **capitulum**

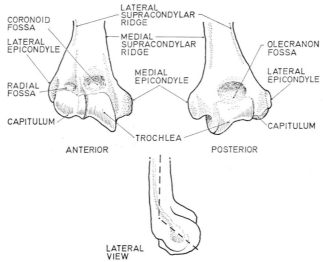

FIG. 22.25. Lower part of the right humerus. Lateral view shows the angle between the shaft and lower end.

is on the lateral part of the distal end, convex for articulation with the head of the radius. The **trochlea**, pulley-shaped, is on the medial part of the distal end and articulates with the ulna; its medial lip projects lower than the lateral. The **medial** and **lateral epicondyles** are two prominences above the articular surface of the distal end; their anterior and distal aspects serve for attachment of many muscles and ligaments. Medial and lateral supra-condylar ridges extend from the epicondyles proximally on to the shaft. There are three fossae above the capitulum and the trochlea between the epicondyles, two in front (**radial** and **coronoid**) and one at the back called the **olecranon fossa**; these three accommodate the proximal ends of the forearm bones in movements at the elbow joint.

The posterior and most proximal part of the ulna is called the **olecranon** and where it embraces the humerus it is lined with articular cartilage of the elbow joint (fig. 22.26). Projecting forwards and continuous with the olecranon is the **coronoid process**, its upper surface being articular and together with the olecranon forming the **trochlear notch** of ulna. On the lateral aspect of the coronoid process, facing the head of the radius, is the **radial notch**. The **tuberosity of ulna** is below the coronoid and, below the radial notch a large depression the supinator fossa is limited posteriorly by a supinator crest.

The radius does not overlap the humerus. The proximal end (fig. 22.26) consists of head, neck and tuberosity. The head is a thick disc with the superior surface concave; the distal part of the circumference of the head is narrower than the proximal; this confers stability to the joint. The **neck** is the constricted portion supporting the head; below the neck on the medial side there is a projection called the **tuberosity of the radius**.

THE ELBOW JOINT

The elbow joint (fig. 22.27) is a synovial joint of the hinge variety but has some characteristics of a saddle-shaped joint in that it allows some movement of the ulna on the humerus besides flexion and extension (see supination and pronation). Essentially the elbow joint is an articulation of ulna with the humerus, the radius being attached to the ulna and moving with it. Stability of the elbow joint depends on the ulna, since it does not seem to be affected by surgical removal of the head of the radius. The concave superior surface of the radius matches the round capitulum and the trochlear notch of the ulna fits the pulley shaped trochlea of the humerus. The capsule is attached:

(1) around the articular surface of the humerus including the fossae situated above it (only the lower half of the olecranon fossa),

(2) to the **anular ligament** of the superior radio-ulnar joint,

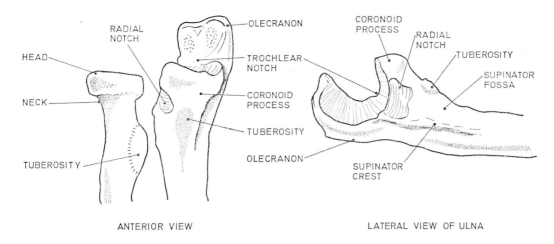

FIG. 22.26. Upper part of the ulna and radius.

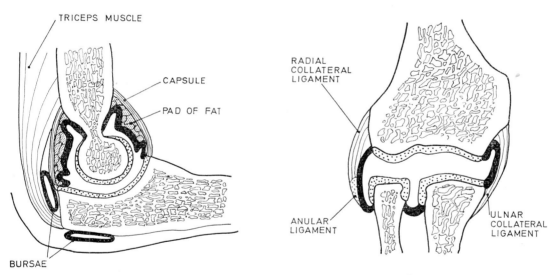

FIG. 22.27. Longitudinal and coronal sections of the elbow joint.

(3) to the olecranon,

(4) to the coronoid process.

Being mainly a hinge joint, the anterior and posterior parts of the capsule are weak while the lateral and medial parts are strongly reinforced by **collateral ligaments.** The radial ligament extends from the lower part of the lateral epicondyle to the anular ligament and the ulnar extends from the lower edge of the medial epicondyle to the coronoid process and olecranon (fig. 22.28). The synovial cavity is continuous with that of the superior radio-ulnar joint. The synovial membrane lines the deep aspect of the capsule and the bone not covered by the articular cartilage. Pads of fat are interposed between the synovial membrane

FIG. 22.28. Ligaments of the elbow joint.

and the capsule in the region of the three fossae, improving the lubrication of the joint.

MUSCLES OF THE ELBOW REGION

Fig. 22.29 shows the attachments of the biceps, brachialis, triceps and anconeus muscles which act primarily at the elbow joint.

Acting primarily on the more distal parts of the limb, but assisting in movements at the elbow joint, are brachioradialis, pronator teres, and flexor and extensor groups of the forearm muscles (figs. 21.41–43).

FIG. 22.29. Muscles which act primarily on the elbow joint.

Biceps brachii muscle (*BB*).

BB-O₁ Long head from the supraglenoid tubercle of the scapula.

BB-O₂ Short head from the tip of the coracoid process.

BB-I Posterior part of the tuberosity of the radius and through the bicipital aponeurosis to the deep fascia of the forearm.

Brachialis muscle (*B*) which lies deep to *BB*

B-O Distal two-thirds of the front of the shaft of the humerus.

B-I Tuberosity of the ulna.

Triceps muscle (*T*)

T-O₁ Long head from the infraglenoid tubercle of the scapula.

T-O₂ Lateral head from the back of the humerus, above the radial nerve groove.

T-O₃ Medial head from the back of the humerus, below the radial nerve groove.

T-I Posterior part of the proximal surface of the olecranon.

Anconeus muscle (*A*)

A-O Distal part of the back of the lateral epicondyle of the humerus and from the capsule of the elbow joint.

A-I Triangular area on the lateral aspect of the olecranon and the posterior surface of the ulna.

MOVEMENTS AT THE ELBOW JOINT

The main movements are flexion and extension but some contribution is made to supination and pronation, by adduction and abduction respectively of the ulna at the saddle-shaped humero-ulnar compartment of the elbow joint. Flexion is achieved by biceps, brachialis (the strongest), pronator teres and brachioradialis, assisted by the flexor and extensor groups of the forearm muscles attached to the front of the epicondyles. Extension is brought about by triceps and anconeus.

BONES, JOINTS AND MUSCLES OF THE FOREARM

BONES OF THE FOREARM

The shafts of the ulna and radius (fig. 22.30) face each other by their interosseous borders to which the tough interosseous membrane is attached. The shaft of the radius is convex medially in the proximal quarter and

FIG. 22.30. Bones of the right forearm.

laterally in the distal three-quarters. The shaft of the ulna is subcutaneous posteriorly. The ulnar **styloid process** juts down from the posteromedial aspect of the rounded head of the ulna.

The distal end of the radius is expanded and bent anteriorly (fig. 22.31). Its **styloid process** juts down from the lateral side and the **dorsal tubercle** is the most prominent of the ridges on the back. The ulnar notch, situated on the medial side, articulates with the head of ulna.

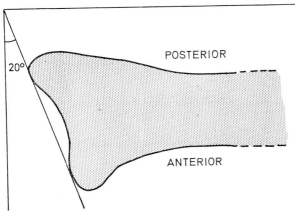

FIG. 22.31. Distal end of radius traced from a lateral radiographic view in pronation.

JOINTS OF THE FOREARM

The proximal radio-ulnar joint

The head of the radius is encircled by the anular ligament and the radial notch of ulna (fig. 22.32). The **anular**

ligament is a strong band attached to the anterior and posterior borders of the radial notch of ulna forming a ring which is narrower below than above. The upper margin of the ligament is attached to the lateral epicondyle and to the lateral part of the elbow capsule. The lower margin of the ligament allows for rotation by being very loosely attached to the neck of the radius. The synovial membrane of the elbow joint lines the inner surface of the ligament and is reflected on to the neck of the radius.

The interosseous membrane (fig. 22.30)

The interosseous membrane is thin and strong and attached to the interosseous margins of ulna and radius. Its fibres are directed downwards and medially.

The distal radio-ulnar joint (fig. 22.33)

The head of the ulna articulates with the ulnar notch of the radius laterally and with a triangular articular

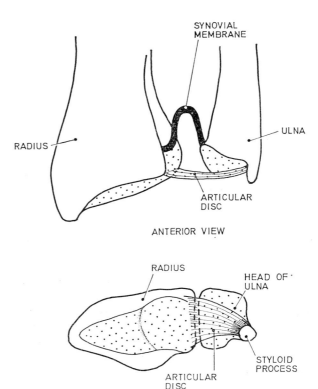

FIG. 22.33. Distal radio-ulnar joint.

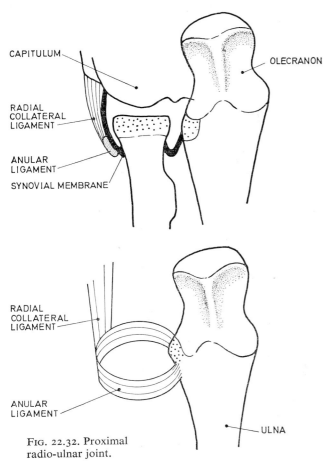

FIG. 22.32. Proximal radio-ulnar joint.

disc inferiorly. This disc is attached by its apex to the pit at the root of the ulnar styloid and by its base to the edge between the carpal and medial surfaces of the distal end of radius. Its upper surface articulates at the inferior radio-ulnar joint with the head of the ulna, and its lower surface forms part of the articular surface of the wrist joint; thus this disc separates these two joint cavities and excludes the ulna from the wrist joint.

MUSCLES EFFECTING MOVEMENTS AT RADIO-ULNAR JOINTS

The prime movers are biceps (powerful supinator figs. 22.29 and 22.34) supinator (figs. 22.34 and 22.43) pronator teres (fig. 22.41) and pronator quadratus (fig. 22.43). Other muscles which pass obliquely across the forearm

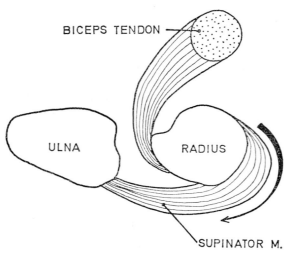

FIG. 22.34. The supinating action of supinator and biceps muscles.

contribute to these movements. These are flexor carpi radialis and palmaris longus in pronation (fig. 22.41), and extensor pollicis longus in supination (fig. 22.43).

MOVEMENTS AT THE RADIO-ULNAR JOINTS

The supine position of the forearm is when its bones are parallel, while in the prone position the radius crosses the ulna (fig. 22.35). The movement of pronation starts from the supine position, carries the radius and the hand forwards around the lower end of the ulna which at the same time moves slightly back and laterally (p. 22.12). The axis of these movements passes through the centre of the radial head to the pit at the root of the ulnar styloid.

To these radio-ulnar movements, the rotation of the humerus in the glenohumeral joints should be added, medial rotation increasing the range of pronation and lateral rotation the range of supination. The glenohumeral contribution is most marked when the elbow is extended, so that the range of radio-ulnar rotation alone is best tested by fixing the flexed elbow at the side of the body. The range of radio-ulnar supination or pronation is

approximately 130–140°, the rotation at the shoulder adds another 140–160° and the full combined range may reach almost 360°.

Owing to the slant of the trochlear surface of the distal end of the humerus (fig. 22.25) the arm and the forearm are not in a straight line when the limb is straightened and supinated; the angle between them, about 170°, is

(a)   (b)

FIG. 22.35. Diagram showing (a) supine and (b) prone positions. The broken line represents the axis of the humerus and the continuous line the axis of supination and pronation. From Sinclair D.C. (1966) *Introduction to Functional Anatomy.* Blackwell Scientific Publications.

called the carrying angle. This angle is masked by pronation. It makes it easier for the hand to be brought to the mouth when the elbow is flexed and the forearm in mid-pronation and it also allows the forearm to fall in line with the arm when the elbow is straightened with the forearm in mid-pronation. This arrangement gives minimal strain and maximal stability when weights are carried (fig. 22.35). When stability of the hand is required for fine manipulation, the elbow is flexed to a right angle and the forearm held midway between pronation and supination.

BONES, JOINTS AND MUSCLES OF THE HAND

BONES OF THE HAND

The bones of the hand can be considered in three parts: the skeleton of the wrist or carpus; the skeleton of the hand proper (palm and dorsum), the metacarpal bones; and the skeleton of the digits (thumb and fingers), the phalanges.

The carpus (fig. 22.36)

This is composed of eight bones in two rows which together form a transverse arch spanned by a strong tiebeam called the flexor retinaculum (fig. 22.48). The proximal surface of the carpus is convex both anteroposteriorly

FIG. 22.36. Bones of the carpus. (a) Antero-superior view; the bones are distracted. (b) Inferior view showing carpal arch and sulcus; S. scaphoid, L. lunate, Tr. triquetrum, H. hamate, C. capitate, Td. trapezoid, Tm. trapezium.

and from side to side. Blood supply is carried to the carpal bones with the ligaments attached to them, so it may be interrupted by injuries to the ligaments. The blood supply to the scaphoid is peculiar as the blood vessels often run from the distal to the proximal end of the bone and in some fractures the supply to the proximal part may be interrupted.

The metacarpus (fig. 22.37)

All metacarpal bones have a base, shaft and a large rounded head. The second, third, fourth and fifth metacarpal bones can be considered together. Their heads have articular cartilage on their distal and anterior surfaces. Near the posterior and proximal part of the side of the

head there is a tubercle and a pit just in front of it. The shafts are curved, being concave towards the palm. The bases conform to the carpus and its arch, the metacarpal bones being arranged like a fan diverging from the distal row of the carpal bones.

The first metacarpal has a shorter and flatter shaft than the rest; it does not lie in the plane of the palm as its broad anterior surface faces medially. Its base has a saddle-shaped articular surface which fits a similar surface on the trapezium. The setting of this metacarpal and the nature of its joint at the base are important in gripping and opposing with the thumb.

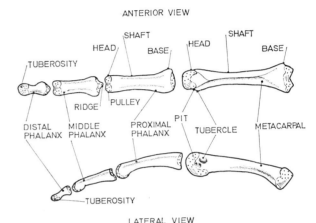

FIG. 22.37. The metacarpal and phalangeal bones of a finger.

The phalanges (fig. 22.37)

Each finger has a proximal, middle and distal phalanx. The thumb has only two; proximal and distal, they are shorter and broader than those of the fingers. Each phalanx has a base, shaft and head. All phalanges are concave towards the palmar aspect of the hand. The proximal phalanx has a concave oval facet on the base for the head of the metacarpal. The head of this phalanx has a pulley-shaped articular surface for articulation with the base of the middle phalanx, which has a median ridge fitting the groove on the head pulley. A similar arrangement exists at the distal joint. The distal phalanx has a tuberosity instead of the head.

JOINTS OF THE HAND

The wrist (radiocarpal) joint (fig. 22.38)

This is of the synovial type and ellipsoid variety. The distal end of the radius and the triangular articular disc form a socket for the convex surface of the scaphoid, lunate and triquetral bones. The triquetrum is related to the medial ligament of the joint in the anatomical

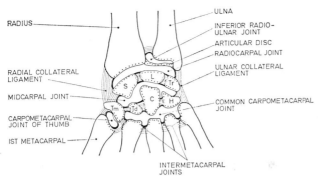

FIG. 22.38. Joints in the wrist region. Bones shown distracted.

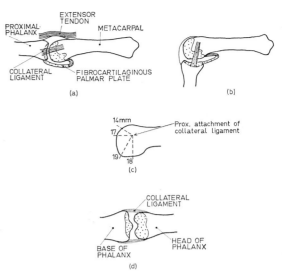

FIG. 22.39. Metacarpophalangeal and interphalangeal joints. Extended (a) and flexed (b) metacarpophalangeal joints. (c) Profile of metacarpal head. (d) Interphalangeal joint.

position and makes contact with the socket only in adduction. The capsule is attached to the margins of the articular surfaces and is strengthened by anterior, posterior, medial and lateral ligaments. The medial ligament extends from the ulnar styloid to triquetrum and pisiform and the lateral one from the radial styloid to scaphoid and trapezium.

The midcarpal joint (intercarpal joints) (fig. 22.38)

Bones of the proximal row are united to the distal row by dorsal, palmar, medial and lateral ligaments. This synovial joint is of the ellipsoid variety, the same as the wrist joint; and both are concerned with the movements at the wrist.

The carpometacarpal joints (fig. 22.38)

Except for the first and fifth digits, these irregular, synovial, joints are of little importance. The carpometacarpal joint of the thumb on the other hand is important because of the mobility of this digit; the saddle shaped base of the first metacarpal fits into the corresponding saddle of the trapezium. The carpometacarpal joint of the little finger is also often almost a saddle joint since this finger has more mobility at this joint than the rest.

The intermetacarpal joints (fig. 22.38)

These are between the bases of the second, third, fourth and fifth metacarpal bones. The joint between the last two is concavo-convex to allow for the mobility of the little finger.

Except for the carpometacarpal joint of the thumb and the joint between triquetrum and pisiform, the midcarpal, carpometacarpal and intercarpal joints share a common synovial cavity.

The metacarpophalangeal (MP) joints (fig. 22.39a and b)

These synovial joints allow flexion and extension, adduction and abduction, and some rotation. The latter movement can be observed during opposition; thus they have some features of ball and socket joints. The rounded

head of the metacarpal articulates distally with the concave surface of the base of the proximal phalanx and anteriorly with the palmar ligament of the joint. The capsule is strengthened at the sides by eccentrically attached

FIG. 22.40. Individual fingers in flexion point to the scaphoid.

collateral ligaments which, as can be seen in fig. 22.39c, become slack in extension and taut in flexion. On the dorsum the capsule is very thin as it is replaced by the expanded extensor tendon. The palmar ligament of the joint is a plate of fibrocartilage firmly attached to the proximal phalanx but connected only loosely to the metacarpal bone. At the sides this plate fuses with the collateral capsule and is connected to the deep transverse

ligaments of the palm which unite the four medial metacarpophalangeal joints.

These joints are important in the prehensile (gripping, seizing) movements of the hand. Owing to the manner of attachment of the collateral ligaments and the profile of the metacarpal head (fig. 22.39c) it is clear that if the ligaments become contracted in the extended position, flexion of the joint is impossible and the power grip

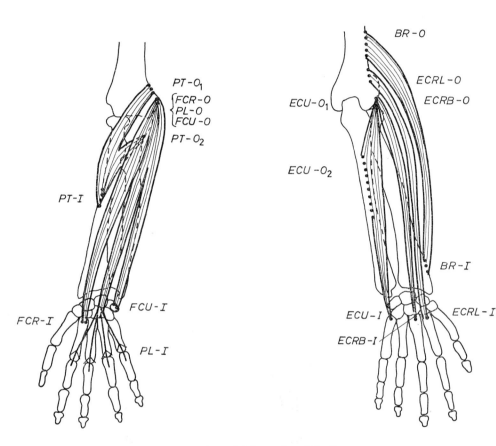

FIG. 22.41. Superficial muscles of the forearm.

Pronator teres (*PT*).

PT-O₁ Humeral attachment: lowest part of medial supracondylar ridge, medial epicondyle.

PT-O₂ Ulnar attachment: coronoid process.

PT-I Middle of lateral surface of radius.

Flexor carpi radialis (*FCR*)

FCR-O Common flexor origin on the medial epicondyle.

FCR-I Base of second metacarpal.

Palmaris longus (absent in 10%) (*PL*)

PL-O Medial epicondyle.

PL-I Flexor retinaculum and palmar aponeurosis (see later).

Flexor carpi ulnaris (*FCU*)

FCU-O Medial epicondyle, medial border of olecranon and upper part of posterior border of ulna.

FCU-I Pisiform bone.

Brachioradialis (*BR*)

BR-O Upper two-thirds of lateral supracondylar ridge.

BR-I Lateral side of lower end of radius.

Extensor carpi radialis longus (*ECRL*)

ECRL-O Distal third of lateral supracondylar ridge.

ECRL-I Base of second metacarpal.

Extensor carpi radialis brevis (*ECRB*)

ECRB-O Lateral epicondyle of humerus (common extensor origin).

ECRB-I Base of third metacarpal.

Extensor carpi ulnaris (*ECU*)

ECU-O₁ Lateral epicondyle.

ECU-O₂ Middle part of posterior border of ulna.

ECU-I Base of fifth metacarpal.

against palm is lost and against the thumb very much less efficient.

The interphalangeal (IP) joints (fig. 22.39d)

These are synovial of the hinge variety. At the proximal joints (PIP) the flexion extension arc is about 110°. Extension is limited by the palmar structures. The distal joints (DIP) have 60–90° range of movement. The collateral ligaments in both joints are represented by the thickening of the medial and lateral aspects of the capsule. No active rotation occurs in these joints, but if the fingers are flexed individually, they all point to the tubercle of the scaphoid bone (fig. 22.40). This is due to the setting of the metacarpal bones in their joints, their different lengths and the arrangements within the individual joints.

The interphalangeal joints are more vulnerable than the MP joints owing to their superficial position between rigid bones, fibrous flexor sheaths and the skin. The PIP joints are the most important since if they are damaged, the function of the hand is seriously impaired.

MUSCLES CONCERNED WITH MOVEMENTS OF THE HAND

The flexor carpi radialis, palmaris longus, flexor carpi ulnaris, extensor carpi ulnaris, and extensor carpi radialis longus and brevis act only at the wrist (fig. 22.41).

Muscles acting on the digits and at the wrist secondarily are:

(1) on the fingers, flexor digitorum superficialis (fig. 22.42), flexor digitorum profundus (fig. 22.43), extensor

FIG. 22.42. Muscles of the forearm.

Flexor digitorum superficialis (sublimis) (FDS)

FDS-O₁ Humero-ulnar attachments: medial epicondyle of humerus, ulnar collateral ligament, medial border of coroncid process.

FDS-O₂ Upper two-thirds of anterior border of radius.

FDS-I Margins of palmar surface of middle phalanx (see insert).

Extensor digitorum (ED)

ED-O Lateral epicondyle of humerus.

ED-I Bones of the fingers and to the extensor expansion (fig. 22.54).

Extensor digiti minimi (EDM)

EDM-O Lateral epicondyle of humerus.

EDM-I Joins the tendon of ED to the little finger.

FIG. 22.43. Deep muscles of the forearm.

Flexor pollicis longus (FPL).

FPL-O Middle 2/4 of anterior surface of radius and adjoining interosseous membrane.

FPL-I Base of distal phalanx of thumb.

Flexor digitorum profundus (FDP)

FDP-O Upper two-thirds of anterior and medial surface of ulna and adjoining interosseous membrane.

FDP-I Base of distal phalanges after passing through the split in the tendon of *FDS* (fig. 22.42).

Pronator quadratus (PQ)

PQ-O Distal part of anterior surface of ulna.

PQ-I Distal part of anterior and medial surfaces of radius.

Supinator (S)

S-O₁ Superficial humeral attachments: lateral epicondyle of humerus, radial collateral ligament, anular ligament.

S-O₂ Deep ulnar attachment: supinator fossa and crest of ulna.

S-I Round the upper third of shaft of radius.

Extensor indicis (EI)

EI-O Back of lower part of ulna and adjoining interosseous membrane.

EI-I Extensor insertion of index finger (see *ED*).

Abductor pollicis longus (APL)

APL-O Posterior surface of radius, posterior and lateral surface of ulna, intervening interosseous membrane.

APL-I Base of first metacarpal.

Extensor pollicis longus (EPL)

EPL-O Middle third of posterior surface of ulna and adjoining interosseous membrane.

EPL-I Base of distal phalanx of thumb.

Extensor pollicis brevis (EPB)

EPB-O Posterior surface of radius and adjoining interosseous membrane.

EPB-I Base of proximal phalanx of thumb.

digitorum (fig. 22.42), extensor indicis (fig. 22.43) and extensor digiti minimi (fig. 22.42);

(2) on the thumb, are flexor pollicis longus, extensor pollicis longus, extensor pollicis brevis and abductor pollicis longus (fig. 22.43).

The intrinsic muscles of the fingers are palmar and dorsal interossei, lumbricals (fig. 22.44), and hypothenar

FIG. 22.44. Intrinsic muscles of the fingers.

Lumbrical muscles (*L*) of the right hand.

L-O Tendons of flexor digitorum profundus (*FDP*, fig. 22.43).

L-I Distal wings of extensor expansion.

Palmar interossei muscles (*PI*)

PI-O Palmar aspect of second, fourth and fifth metacarpal shafts.

PI-I Almost all fibres inserted into the distal wings of the extensor expansion (like lumbricals].

Dorsal interossei muscles (*DI*)

DI-O Adjacent sides of two metacarpal bones. Abductor digiti minimi (ADM) completes the series.

DI-I Considerable variation as distal attachment is divided in variable amounts between: base of proximal phalanx, proximal and distal wings of extensor expansion.

muscles, i.e. flexor digiti minimi brevis, abductor digiti minimi and opponens digiti minimi (fig. 22.45). Intrinsic muscles of the thumb are the thenar muscles, i.e. flexor pollicis brevis, abductor pollicis brevis, opponens pollicis and adductor pollicis (fig. 22.45). The first dorsal interosseus muscle is included since it also stabilizes and adducts the thumb.

MOVEMENTS AT THE WRIST
The radiocarpal and midcarpal joints are one functional unit and flexion, extension, abduction, adduction and

FIG. 22.45. Muscles of thumb and little finger.

Abductor digiti minimi (*ADM*).
ADM-O Pisiform bone.
ADM-I Base of proximal phalanx.

Flexor digiti minimi brevis (*FDM*)
FDM-O Flexor retinaculum and hook of hamate.
FDM-I Base of proximal phalanx of little finger.

Opponens digiti minimi (*ODM*)
ODM-O Flexor retinaculum, hook of hamate.
ODM-I Medial aspect of fifth metacarpal.

Abductor pollicis brevis (*APB*)
APB-O Flexor retinaculum, scaphoid, trapezium.
APB-I Radial side of proximal phalanx of thumb.

Flexor pollicis brevis (*FPB*)
FPB-O Flexor retinaculum and trapezium.
FPB-I Radial side of base of proximal phalanx.

Opponens pollicis (*OP*)
OP-O Flexor retinaculum and trapezium.
OP-I Whole length of radial aspect of first metacarpal.

Adductor pollicis (*AD*)
AD-O_1 Front of third metacarpal.
AD-O_2 Front of carpus and bases of metacarpal bones.
AD-I Ulnar side of base of proximal phalanx.

circumduction can take place there. The muscles which are mainly concerned are the radial and ulnar flexor and extensors of the carpus, abduction being performed by a combination of radial flexors and extensors and adduction by the ulnar groups of the corresponding muscles. Abduction which occurs mostly in the midcarpal joint is assisted by abductor pollicis longus and extensors pollicis longus and brevis. Flexion, occurring mostly in the midcarpal joint, is assisted by palmaris longus, long flexors of the digits and abductor pollicis longus. Extension which occurs mostly in the radiocarpal joint is assisted by the digital extensors. The extensors of the carpus act as synergists during flexion of the digits as they fix the wrist in an extended position. Lack of this synergistic action is obvious when gripping with the fingers when the wrist is markedly flexed.

MOVEMENTS OF THE HAND

All movements in the upper limb as far as the wrist obviously serve to position the business end of the limb, the hand. The movements of the hand can be arbitrarily divided into **non-prehensile**, e.g. pushing, hitting with the flat hand, karate, swimming, and **prehensile**, movements concerned with seizing and gripping. The hand is not a specialized tool and its versatility is shown by its uses as a chuck, pliers, hook and ring (fig. 22.46).

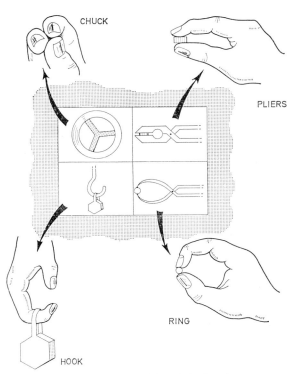

FIG. 22.46. Versatility of the hand.

These functions of the hand are effected by:
Opposition, when the pulp of the thumb is brought into

(a) (b) (c)

FIG. 22.47. (a) Opposition, (b) power grip, (c) precision grip.

contact with the pulp of any of the other digits (fig. 22.47a).

Power grip, when the object is clamped against the palm (fig. 22.47b).

Precision grip, when the object is held by the opposing surfaces of the digits (fig. 22.47c).

Fine movements of the individual digits are controlled mostly by the intrinsic muscles of the hand, and are used in activities such as piano playing and typing.

For these various functions it is necessary that the bones and joints should be assembled and functioning normally and that their movements are accurately co-ordinated by contraction, relaxation and fixation of the appropriate muscles. The hand is represented in the central nervous system by large motor and sensory areas.

Each type of tissue in the hand makes a special contribution to all these functions.

Skin

Without the normal mobile skin cover the hand would be absolutely useless. The blanching of the knuckles when making a fist shows that the hand is covered with just a sufficient area of skin. Palmar skin protected by thick epidermis is fixed by strong anteroposterior fibres to the

FIG. 22.48. Retaining structures in the hand. (a) Flexor retinaculum, (b) extensor retinaculum, (c) fibrous flexor sheath, (d) transverse section of the finger showing digital ligaments. *APL*, Abductor pollicis longus; *ECRB*, Extensor carpi radialis brevis; *ECRL*, Extensor carpi radialis longus; *ECU*, Extensor carpi ulnaris; *ED*, Extensor digitorum; *EDM*, Extensor digiti minimi; *EI*, Extensor indicis; *EPL*, Extensor pollicis longus; *FCR*, Flexor carpi radialis; *FDP*, Flexor digitorum profundus; *FDS*, Flexor digitorum superficialis (sublimis); *FPL*, Flexor pollicis longus.

deep palmar fascia (fig. 22.49) and this stabilizes it on the underlying tissues for gripping. Surface ridges and grooves on the palm increase its surface friction. In contrast the mobile skin of the dorsum allows for flexion and prehension. Any loss or contracture of the skin of the hand is disabling, particularly so over the pulp of the digits where there is a special concentration of the sensory end organs. Grafting skin cover for the pulp is of limited value, unless it is transferred from the pulp of another digit with its blood and nerve supply.

Superficial and deep layers of the connective tissue of the hand

SUPERFICIAL FASCIA

The superficial fascia of the palmar aspect of the hand is a layer of fatty and areolar tissue arranged like sponge rubber in the spaces of a network of collagen fibres which connect the skin to the deep fascia (fig. 22.49). This serves as an elastic protective cushion taking the brunt of the pressure in the palm associated with the power grip. The superficial fascia on the dorsal aspect is much thinner and stretches easily.

DEEP FASCIA

The deep fascia of the hand is arranged in a specific manner for retention and gliding.

Retention

If tendons were not retained in position during grasping, they would prolapse and instead of the hollow palm there would be ridges of the skin stretched over the long flexor tendons. This bowstringing is prevented in five ways.

The **flexor retinaculum** is attached to the bones of the carpus and stretches over the transverse arch of the carpus, so forming a carpal tunnel, which contains nine long flexor tendons and one nerve (fig. 22.48a).

The **palmar aponeurosis** is found in front of the tendons in the palm (fig. 22.49). It consists of two layers fused together, the superficial one being a continuation of the tendon of the palmaris longus and the deep layer continuous with the distal edge of the flexor retinaculum. On both sides the palmar aponeurosis is continuous with the much thinner deep fascia covering the thenar and hypothenar groups of muscles. The palmar aponeurosis is anchored to the skin by superficial anteroposterior fibres, and to the deep metacarpal and interosseous fasciae by the deep anteroposterior fibres which form septa in the distal part of the central palm. These septa lie on each side of the long tendons and on each side of the neurovascular bundles and lumbrical muscles. One of these deep septa extends from the shaft of the third metacarpal to the radial border of the triangular palmar aponeurosis at its junction with the thenar part of the deep fascia. This is known as the **oblique septum,**

17

PALMAR APONEUROSIS

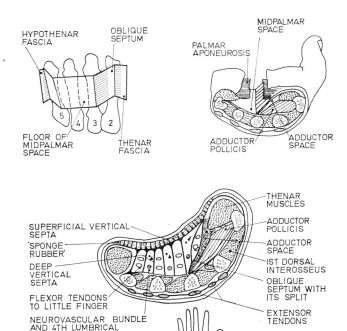

FIG. 22.49. Arrangement of the superficial and deep fascia of the hand.

and it is separated from the anterior surface of the adductor pollicis by a space filled with loose areolar tissue. This is the **adductor** or **thenar space.** The space on the medial side of the oblique septum extending deep to the palmar aponeurosis as far as the hypothenar muscles is the **midpalmar space.** It is filled with loose areolar and fatty padding arranged around the structures and between the deep septa which separate them. The distal edge of the palmar aponeurosis is divided over the level of the metacarpal heads into four slips each of which in turn splits into three bands; a central one is continuous along the palmar aspect of the finger with the fibrous flexor sheath and one on each side is attached to the deep transverse ligament of palm.

The **fibrous flexor sheath** is attached to the sides of the proximal and middle phalanges and to the base of the distal phalanx (fig. 22.48c). It is thin over the joints and rigid opposite the shafts of the phalanges. This arrangement provides an osteofascial tunnel for the flexor tendons and prevents bowstringing in the fingers. The thumb has its own fibrous sheath attached to the sides of the proximal phalanx and to the base of the distal phalanx.

The **extensor retinaculum** is simpler as the fingers cannot be extended much beyond the straight line. An extensor retinaculum is attached laterally to the distal part of the anterior border of radius and medially to the medial carpal bones, sending an extension round the distal end of the ulna to blend with the deep fascia on the palmar aspect of the lower part of the forearm (fig. 22.48b). The septa, which extend from the retinaculum to the bony points lying deep to it, form separate compartments for the tendons.

The **digital ligaments** are sheets of connective tissue extending from the sides of the phalanges to the skin, and which contain the neurovascular bundles of the digits (fig. 22.48d).

FIG. 22.50. Gliding mechanisms in the hand. (a) Paratenon and synovial sheath; (b) Palmar and dorsal synovial sheaths; (c) Arrangement of connective tissue around a flexor tendon.

Gliding

The sliding movements of the tendons are facilitated by the loose surrounding connective tissue, which forms a paratenon, when more or less straight line movement occurs (fig. 22.50a). Where a tendon slides round a corner or a bend the paratenon is replaced by a synovial sheath formed by substitution of the middle areolar layer of the paratenon by a space filled with a film of synovial fluid (fig. 22.50a). The position of the synovial sheaths of flexor and extensor tendons is shown in fig. 22.50b. Obviously some areas have tough and unyielding walls surrounding the tendons, e.g. fibrous flexor sheaths of the digits, carpal tunnel (fig. 22.50c) where the fit of the tendon is very tight and there is hardly any surrounding loose areolar tissue. In other areas, like the palm, the tendons move in much softer, looser spaces.

Assembly of the skeletal elements of the hand

Although the forces created in the hand during its movements are transmitted along multiple lines and surfaces, a general account of the arches of the hand is useful for a clear picture of its functions and their disturbances. The following arches (fig. 22.51a) can be recognized:

(1) transverse carpal arch, fixed and rigid,
(2) transverse metacarpal arch, second and third fixed; first, fourth and fifth mobile,
(3) longitudinal metacarpal arch, fixed concavity of the metacarpal shaft,
(4) longitudinal metacarpophalangeal and digital arch,

mobile and continuous with the longitudinal metacarpal arch.

These arches are maintained by fibrous and muscular elements and differ considerably in the degree of their mobility. The principal **fixed axis of the hand** is continuous with the radius through the fixed carpal arch and consists of the second and third metacarpal bones, which are fixed and positioned for function by synergistic action of the radial extensor and flexor muscles of the carpus. Around the principal axis the mobile elements can be moved into many positions. These mobile elements (fig. 22.51b) are:

(1) first metacarpal with the bones and joints of the thumb which possesses the greatest mobility,
(2) the index finger which possesses considerable independence from the other fingers,
(3) fourth and fifth metacarpal bones with the middle, ring and little fingers.

Action of the muscles in the movements of the hand

Appropriate positioning of the mobile elements of the hand around its fixed axis is carried out by the integrated action of many muscles through their complicated attachments; stressing the action of a single muscle is an oversimplification if the functional balance of all the other elements is not considered.

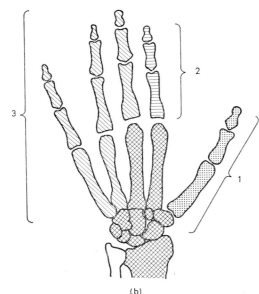

Fig. 22.51. Assembly of the skeletal elements of the hand. (a) Arches, (b) mobile elements (see text).

Before the actions of the muscles are described it is useful to consider the posture of the hand at rest. This can be seen in one's own hand. There is a moderate degree of dorsiflexion of the wrist with slight ulnar deviation. From index to little finger, there is a gradual increase in the flexion of the MP and IP joints of the fingers, and the pulp of the thumb is near the radial aspect of the DIP joint of the index.

MOVEMENTS OF THE THUMB

The functional value of the thumb is about half that of the whole hand. The notable feature is a wide range of movement at the carpometacarpal joint. The movements (fig. 22.52a) are as follows.

Abduction: abductor pollicis brevis assisted by abductor pollicis longus.

Adduction: adductor pollicis.

Flexion: flexor pollicis brevis, flexor pollicis longus, opponens and abductor pollicis brevis.

Extension: extensor pollicis longus and brevis, assisted by abductor pollicis longus.

Medial rotation: opponens pollicis.

Lateral rotation: extensor muscles of the thumb.

Circumduction: a combination of the above.

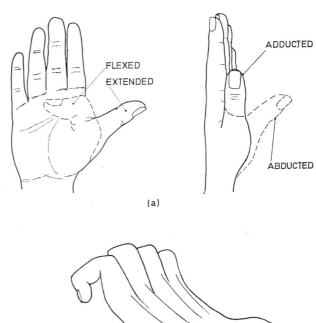

Fig. 22.52. (a) Movements of the thumb, (b) position of claw hand, the MP joints are hyperextended and the IP joints are flexed.

The muscles of the thenar compartment act, like stay ropes on a mast, in positioning and stabilizing the thumb; they bring the thumb away from the rest of the hand in readiness for gripping and pinching. In all these movements, the ability to oppose is most important. The thumb is brought into the starting position, i.e. abduction, and from there on, the composite **movement of opposition** consists of some flexion, adduction and medial rotation of the thumb. This brings the most important sensory areas of the hand, i.e. the pulp of the digits, into functional contact (fig. 22.47a). The mobile transverse metacarpal arch is produced by the thenar and hypothenar muscles. The arch is deepened and the integrated action of the long flexors, extensors and intrinsic muscles of the digits completes the opposition.

MOVEMENTS OF THE FINGERS

The normal longitudinal arch of the digit, which is so important in the final stages of opposition, is necessary for small object prehension and for the power grip. For the same reason the arch is balanced in favour of flexion (fig. 22.51a). The arch is maintained by four factors:

(1) shape of bones, i.e. concavity of palmar aspects of metacarpals and phalanges,

(2) arrangements of joints, i.e. articular surfaces present on the palmar aspects of the heads of bones,

(3) palmar structures at the IP joints and the fibrous sheaths prevent hyperextension,

(4) muscles.

A finger controlled only by long flexors and extensors cannot be kept in equilibrium. Such a finger assumes the position of clawing, with hypertension at the MP and flexion at the IP joints (fig. 22.52b). Normally this deformity is prevented by the action of the intrinsic muscles which flex at the MP and extend at the IP joints. When these intrinsic muscles are put out of action, for instance in ulnar nerve paralysis, the 'clawed hand' is produced. The normal longitudinal arch of the finger ray therefore depends on three muscular elements, long flexors, long extensors and intrinsic muscles. The distal insertions of the long flexors has already been given. The other two require more consideration.

The extensor and intrinsic components are applied through the complicated mechanism of the **extensor expansion.** This lies in the shallow connective tissue bed, gliding immediately beneath the skin and closely related to the bones and joints of the fingers, and is therefore vulnerable. It can be visualized as a plexiform arrangement of bands and flat thin membranes sandwiched between two thin layers of connective tissue (fig. 22.53a) in which it can slide not only longitudinally but also transversely, changing the position of one band in relation to the others and also to the axes of the joints over which they act.

Extensor extrinsic component (fig. 22.53b)

The long extensor tendon at the MP level divides into three bands. Its direct continuation proceeds along the dorsum of the proximal phalanx, while two side bands, embedded in the proximal edge of the hood of the extensor expansion, encircle the metacarpal head to fuse with the deep transverse ligament of the palm. This last attachment of the long extensor limits its proximal retraction.

(a)

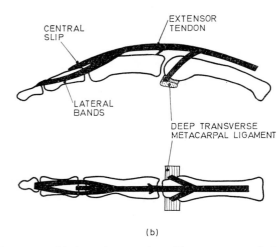

(b)

FIG. 22.53. (a) Dorsal expansion, (b) extensor extrinsic component.

The main portion of the tendon gives a slip attached to the dorsum of the base of the proximal phalanx and then continues towards the PIP joint. Before reaching it, the tendon again divides into three terminal bands. A central one is attached to the base of the middle phalanx. Two lateral bands, which at first lie in the grooves over the lateral part of the dorsum of the PIP joint, converge to be attached to the base of the distal phalanx. All these elements of the extrinsic component are bound together by oblique and transverse fibres embedded in the flat triangular extensor expansion with its hood, and proximal and distal wings (fig. 22.54c).

Intrinsic component (fig. 22.54a)

Although the **interossei muscles** are posterior to the deep transverse ligament of the palm, they lie anterior to the axis of flexion at the MP joint and so flex this joint. Four dorsal interossei together with abductor pollicis brevis and abductor digiti minimi are strong digital abductors from the axial line of the third digit, while palmar interossei are concerned with adduction towards this line (fig. 22.44). Both dorsal and palmar interossei, however, send most of their insertions into the extensor expansion contributing with the lumbricals to its proximal and distal wings so they extend at the IP joints (fig. 22.54b).

The **lumbrical muscles** lying palmar to the MP joint axis and dorsal to the IP joints axes also assist in flexion of the former and extension of the latter. They serve as an adjustable, contractile link between the flexor and extensor systems of the fingers where their muscle spindles can function as an important nervous feed back mechanism.

Fig. 22.54b shows the combined extrinsic and intrinsic components of the extensor expansion.

Before the function of the dorsal apparatus is discussed, the **link** or **retinacular ligament** should be considered. This is a strong fibrous band extending from the palmar aspect of the fibrous flexor sheath and the adjoining bone; it passes obliquely on the palmar side of the axis of the PIP joint towards the dorsum of the finger, joining the lateral band of the dorsal expansion, dorsal to the DIP joint axis. The mechanical effect of this ligament can be seen when passively flexing the DIP joint; this causes the ligament to become taut and forces the PIP joint into flexion simultaneously and automatically (fig. 22.55a and observe on your own finger). If now the PIP joint is passively extended, the DIP joint is forced into extension as well. With this link it might be thought unnecessary to have muscles for active extension of the DIP joint, since this would be automatically accomplished by the extensor muscles of the PIP joint. However, the passive extension of the DIP joint by the retinacular ligament is not complete and some active force is necessary to complete the extension of DIP joint.

When measured along the dorsum, the finger is about 2·5 cm longer in flexion than in extension. This is because of the palmar projection of the heads of the metacarpals and phalanges. Obviously this feature augments the effect of the retinacular ligament during flexion, but diminishes it when the flexed finger is extended. Complete extension at the DIP joints is due to the tension in the terminal parts of the lateral bands and follows the contraction of

(a)

(b)

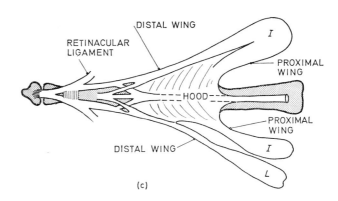

(c)

FIG. 22.54. (a) Intrinsic component, (b) combined extrinsic and intrinsic components, (c) the extensor expansion. *L*, Lumbrical; *I*, Interosseous muscle.

During flexion   (a)   During extension

(b)

(c)

Fig. 22.55. Mechanism of extension of the interphalangeal joints (see text).

the muscles attached to the distal wings of the extensor expansion. This contraction relaxes the central band so that the force (A–B, fig. 22.55b) of the long extensor is transferred to the lateral bands to act on the DIP joint and complete its full extension. This resembles a servo mechanism, since the force from the long extensor has its point of application changed from the PIP to the DIP joint by the contraction of the muscles attached to the distal wings of the extensor expansion.

When extending the fully flexed finger, contraction of the long extensor tendon extends the MP joint; it is also involved in the extension of the IP joints by a more complex mechanism. In the fully flexed position of the PIP joint the distal wings and lateral bands of the extensor expansion lie on the sides of the head of the proximal phalanx (fig. 22.55c). In these circumstances the pull of the extensor muscles is applied to the central slip and extends the middle phalanx at the PIP joint, and not to the lateral bands which in the flexed PIP joint are relaxed as they lie along the short cut, i.e. in the line of the shortest distance to the base of the distal phalanx. Any further pull on the lateral bands in this position shifts them more towards the palm and makes them less able to extend the DIP joint. Thus the pull on the central fibres extends only the PIP joint, but as a result of this extension the retinacular ligament partially extends the DIP joint. After extension of the PIP joint, the lateral bands have moved dorsally and the distal wing muscles now pull on them to cause the active final extension of the DIP joint.

In summary, the normal phalangeal movements are co-ordinated by the retinacular ligament, while the MP joint moves independently being extended by extensor digitorum, extensor digiti minimi and extensor indicis, and flexed by the long flexors and intrinsic muscles.

Electromyographic studies and clinical observation show that the flexor digitorum profundus is very important in flexion of both IP joints, and it assists the intrinsic muscles in flexion of the MP joint. Flexor digitorum superficialis is less important, coming into action when additional power is required.

FASCIAE OF THE UPPER LIMB

Superficial **fascia of the pectoral region** contains fat in which the breast is embedded. Deep fascia is attached above to the clavicle and medially to the sternum. It invests the pectoralis major muscle and is continuous below with the fascia of the abdominal wall. Beyond the inferolateral border of this muscle it is thickened to form the floor of the armpit. This axillary fascia is continued posteriorly on to the posterior fold of the armpit and laterally joins the deep fascial sleeve of the upper arm. Deep to the pectoralis major muscle another layer of connective tissue invests the pectoralis minor muscle. From the superomedial border of the muscle this deep connective tissue, called here the **clavipectoral fascia** (fig. 22.56), extends upwards and is attached to the inferior surface of the clavicle, where it splits to enclose the subclavius muscle. Medially the clavipectoral fascia is attached to the first costal cartilage, laterally to the coracoid process and coracoclavicular ligament. Below the pectoralis minor muscle, a continuation of this fascia passes down to join the axillary fascia and is called the **suspensory ligament of the axilla.**

The deep **fascia of the upper arm** is arranged as a strong tubular investment for the muscles. It is continuous above with the deep fascia of the shoulder and with the axillary

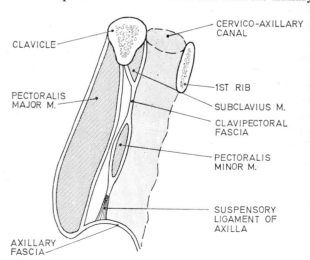

Fig. 22.56. Almost sagittal section through the axilla showing the arrangement of the deep fascia.

fascia; below it is attached to the olecranon and the epicondyles of the humerus and becomes continuous with the deep fascia of the forearm. Two intermuscular septa extend from this sleeve to the supracondylar ridges of the humerus. The medial one, which is stronger, provides origin for the medial head of the triceps posteriorly, and for the brachialis anteriorly. The lateral septum provides origin for the medial and lateral heads of the triceps posteriorly, and for the brachialis and brachioradialis anteriorly.

The superficial **fascia in the forearm** does not present any special features, but in the hand it is modified already described. A small muscle, palmaris brevis, is found in the deep layer of the superficial fascia. It extends from the medial border of the flexor retinaculum and palmar aponeurosis to the skin of the medial border of the hand. It deepens the hollow of the hand.

The deep aspect of the deep fascia provides an extensive area for the attachment of the muscles and plays an important part in the return of fluid from the upper limb by providing tough walls for the muscular compartments in which active muscle contraction can exert pressure on the venous and lymphatic channels. Being relatively impervious to fluid, the deep fascia determines the location and spread of extravasated fluids and inflammatory processes.

The muscles and the deep fascia of the upper limb form the boundaries of three important regions.

The **axilla** is the space between the upper arm and the chest wall. The narrow cervicoaxillary canal, at the apex of the axilla, accommodates the main nerves and vessels of the upper limb. It is bounded in front by the middle portion of the clavicle, medially by the outer border of the first rib and posteriorly by the superior border of the scapula. The anterior wall of the axilla is composed of two layers, the pectoralis major muscle and posterior to this, from above downwards, the subclavius muscle, clavipectoral fascia, pectoralis minor muscle, and the suspensory ligament of the axilla (fig. 22.56). Medially, the chest wall lies covered by the serratus anterior muscle. The posterior wall of the axilla is formed by subscapularis, latissimus dorsi and teres major muscles, while laterally the biceps and coracobrachialis muscles separate the axilla from the intertubercular groove. The floor of the space is formed by the axillary fascia which is held up by the suspensory ligament of axilla. The **axillary sheath** is the continuation of the deep cervical fascia which is drawn into the axilla through its apex around the main neurovascular bundle. Distally it fuses with the connective tissue coats of the bundle. The axilla contains the axillary vessels, lower part of the brachial plexus, its branches and numerous lymph nodes and vessels, all set in areolar tissue and fat.

The **cubital fossa** is a triangular hollow in front of the elbow. Superficially it is covered by skin, superficial and deep fascia which includes the **bicipital aponeurosis,** a flat fibrous band extending down and medially from the bicipital tendon to blend with the deep fascia of the forearm. The floor of the fossa consists of two muscles, brachialis and supinator. It contains the brachial, radial and ulnar vessels, tendon of biceps and median nerve (fig. 22.57).

The **anatomical snuff box** on the lateral aspect of the wrist; it is bounded in front by the tendons of the long

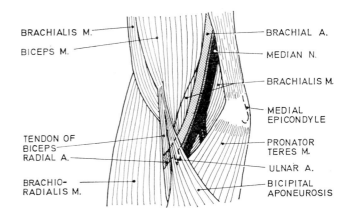

FIG. 22.57. Right cubital fossa.

abductor and short extensor of the thumb, posteriorly by the tendon of the long extensor of the thumb. In its floor the tip of the radial styloid, scaphoid and trapezium, are spanned by the lateral ligament of the wrist. The radial artery crosses this ligament in the floor of the snuff box.

NERVES OF THE UPPER LIMB

Almost all of the upper limb is supplied by the ventral rami of the fifth, sixth, seventh, eighth cervical and the first thoracic nerves which form the brachial plexus. The fifth cervical usually receives a contribution to the plexus from the fourth cervical, and the second thoracic may send fibres to join the first thoracic. There is some variation in the position of the plexus; it may be **prefixed**, i.e. when the fourth cervical contribution is large and the thoracic segment contributions small or absent. In a **postfixed plexus** the second thoracic contribution is large while the fourth cervical does not contribute and only a few fibres come from the fifth cervical.

The second thoracic always contributes to the cutaneous supply of the upper limb, not through the brachial plexus, but by an independent intercostobrachial nerve which crosses the axilla to reach the arm. The lateral supraclavicular nerves from the third and fourth cervical ventral rami supply part of the skin of the shoulder region. The skin over the upper part of the scapula is supplied from the ventral rami of the third and fourth cervical nerves

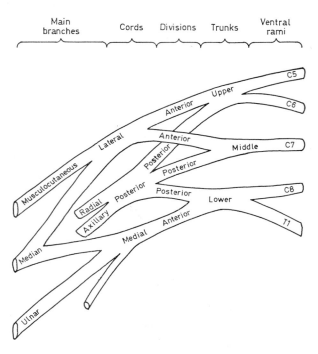

FIG. 22.58. General plan of the brachial plexus. From *Cunningham's Textbook of Anatomy*. 10th Edition (1964), London: Oxford University Press.

while that of the lower part is supplied from the cutaneous branches of the dorsal rami of the upper thoracic nerves.

Two muscles acting on the upper limb do not receive their nerve supply through the brachial plexus; trapezius is supplied from the spinal part of the accessory nerve and from the ventral rami of the third and fourth cervical nerves, and levator scapulae, which is supplied by the same cervical nerves, often also receives a branch from the plexus through the dorsal scapular nerve. The pathways of the **brachial plexus** are contained in its roots (ventral rami), trunks, divisions and cords (fig. 22.58) and they follow a complicated course through the plexus. The cords finally divide into the main nerves of the upper limb. Before that, however, branches are given off to the upper limb from the plexus itself. These are the long thoracic nerve which supplies serratus anterior, nerve to subclavius, suprascapular nerve, and dorsal scapular nerve which supplies the rhomboid muscles (fig. 22.59).

The roots and trunks are found in the neck above the clavicle, while the divisions and cords are in the axilla. The divisions lie posterior to the clavicle and the cords, with the commencement of the main nerves of the upper limb, lie below the clavicle.

The three cords of the brachial plexus give off the following nerves:

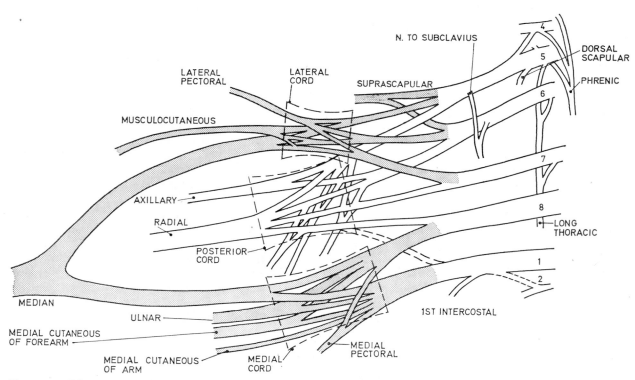

FIG. 22.59. Diagram of brachial plexus, showing the origin of its branches. Dorsal divisions are clear and ventral divisions stippled (Cf. fig. 23.44). From *Cunningham's Textbook of Anatomy*. 10th Edition (1964), London: Oxford University Press.

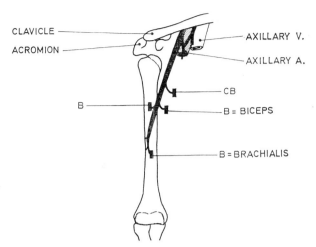

CLAVICLE
ACROMION
AXILLARY V.
AXILLARY A.
CB
B
B = BICEPS
B = BRACHIALIS

Fig. 22.60. Diagram of the musculocutaneous nerve and the muscles which it supplies. Modified from Pitres and Testut.

Lateral cord gives off the lateral pectoral, musculocutaneous and lateral root of the median.

Medial cord gives off the medial pectoral, medial root of the median, ulnar, medial cutaneous nerve of the arm and medial cutaneous nerve of the forearm.

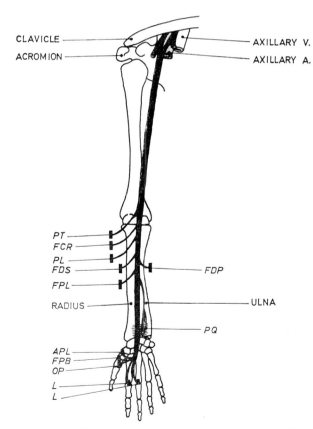

CLAVICLE
ACROMION
AXILLARY V.
AXILLARY A.
PT
FCR
PL
FDS
FPL
RADIUS
FDP
ULNA
PQ
APL
FPB
OP
L
L

Fig. 22.61. Diagram of the median nerve and the muscles which it supplies. Modified from Pitres and Testut.

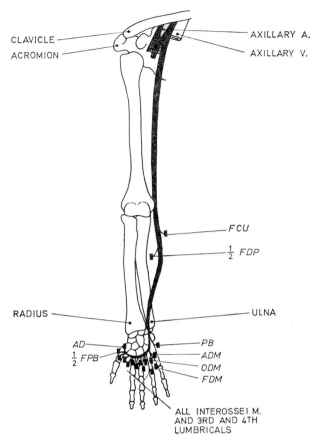

CLAVICLE
ACROMION
AXILLARY A.
AXILLARY V.
FCU
½ FDP
RADIUS
ULNA
AD
½ FPB
PB
ADM
ODM
FDM
ALL INTEROSSEI M. AND 3RD AND 4TH LUMBRICALS

Fig. 22.62. Diagram of the ulnar nerve and the muscles which it supplies. Modified from Pitres and Testut. All interosseous muscles are supplied by the deep branch of the ulnar nerve.

Posterior cord gives off the radial, axillary, upper and lower subscapular and thoracodorsal which supplies latissimus dorsi.

The **lateral pectoral nerve** supplies the pectoralis major muscle, while the **medial pectoral nerve** supplies both pectoralis major and minor muscles.

The **musculocutaneous nerve** (C5, 6, 7) pierces the coracobrachialis muscle to supply the muscles shown in fig. 22.60. Its sensory terminal part pierces the deep fascial sleeve, just above the elbow, to become the lateral cutaneous nerve of the forearm (fig. 22.64).

The **median nerve** (C5, 6, 7, 8, T1) is formed from its lateral and medial roots; these usually join in the axilla, but may join lower. The median nerve runs with the brachial artery, passes in the forearm between the superficial and deep muscles and ends in the hand. Its muscular branches are shown in fig. 22.61. The anterior interosseous nerve arises from the median nerve at the upper part of the forearm and runs downwards in front of the interosseous membrane, contributing to the supply of the flexor pollicis longus and the lateral half of the flexor digitorum

CLAVICLE
ACROMION
D
AXILLARY N.
T_1
T_2

AXILLARY A.
AXILLARY V.
RADIAL N.
TM
T_3

BR
ECRL
ECRB
S
A
ED
EDM
ECU
APL
EPL
EPB
EI

ULNA
RADIUS

FIG. 22.63. Diagram of the axillary and radial nerves and the muscles which they supply. Modified from Pitres and Testut.

profundus, and supplying pronator quadratus muscle. The cutaneous distribution of the median nerve is represented on fig. 22.64.

The **ulnar nerve** (C8, T1) often receives a contribution from C7 either through the lateral cord or through the lateral root of the median nerve. It follows the course of the axillary and brachial arteries as far down as the middle of the upper arm, where it deviates from the artery by piercing the medial intermuscular septum. Then it lies posterior to the medial epicondyle, before passing medial to the elbow joint, to descend on the medial side of the forearm to supply the hand. It crosses in front of the flexor retinaculum and divides into its two terminal branches, superficial and deep. Its muscular branches are shown in fig. 22.62 and the cutaneous distribution in fig. 22.64.

The **medial cutaneous nerves** of the arm (T1) and forearm (CB, T1), are distributed as shown in fig. 22.64.

The **axillary nerve** (C5, 6) leaves the axilla together with the posterior circumflex humeral artery inferior to the shoulder joint and divides into anterior and posterior branches, both of which pass across the back of the upper end of the humerus. Its muscular branches are shown in fig. 22.63 and the cutaneous distribution in fig. 22.64.

The **radial nerve** [(C5) C6, 7, 8 (T1)] extends from the axilla round the posterior aspect of the shaft of the humerus to the front of the lateral epicondyle just above the elbow joint, where it ends by dividing into its superficial and deep terminal branches. The muscular branches of the trunk of the radial nerve and of its deep branch are shown in fig. 22.63. The cutaneous distribution of both the trunk and its superficial terminal branch is shown in fig. 22.64.

The **thoracodorsal nerve** (C6, 7, 8) supplies the latissimus dorsi. The **subscapular nerves** (C5, 6). The upper supplies the subscapular muscle, the lower supplies the lateral part of the same muscle and the teres major.

Cutaneous innervation of the upper limb is shown in fig. 22.64 and the areas of dermatomes in fig. 22.66. Innervation of the joints of the upper limb is derived from the adjoining nerves:

(1) sternoclavicular joint by the medial supraclavicular,
(2) acromioclavicular and shoulder joints by the lateral pectoral, suprascapular and axillary,
(3) elbow joints by musculocutaneous, median, ulnar and radial.
(4) superior radio-ulnar joint by anterior interosseus and deep branch of radial,
(5) radiocarpal, midcarpal and carpometacarpal joints by the anterior interosseus, deep branch of radial and ulnar,
(6) metacarpophalangeal and interphalangeal joints by the digital branches of the median and ulna.

The nervous control of movements at the particular joints as effected by the roots of the brachial plexus is shown in table 22.1.

TABLE 22.1. Root innervation of movements.

Shoulder		Elbow		Forearm		Wrist		Fingers (long muscles)		Hand
Abduction Lateral rotation	C5	Flexion	C5, 6	Pronation	C6	Flexion	C6, 7	Flexion	C7, 8	Movements effected by intrinsic muscles T1
Adduction Medial rotation	C6, 7(8)	Extension	C7, 8	Supination	C6	Extension	C6, 7	Extension	C7, 8	

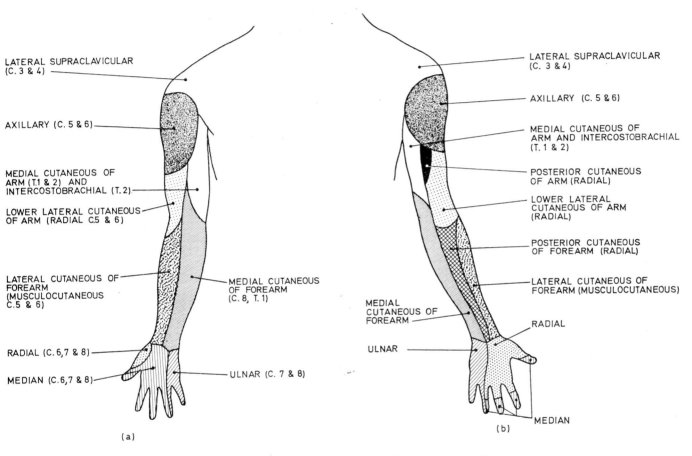

LATERAL SUPRACLAVICULAR
(C. 3 & 4)

AXILLARY (C. 5 & 6)

MEDIAL CUTANEOUS OF
ARM (T.1 & 2) AND
INTERCOSTOBRACHIAL (T. 2)

LOWER LATERAL CUTANEOUS
OF ARM (RADIAL C.5 & 6)

LATERAL CUTANEOUS OF
FOREARM
(MUSCULOCUTANEOUS
C.5 & 6)

RADIAL (C.6,7 & 8)

MEDIAN (C.6,7 & 8)

MEDIAL CUTANEOUS
OF FOREARM
(C. 8, T. 1)

ULNAR (C. 7 & 8)

(a)

LATERAL SUPRACLAVICULAR
(C. 3 & 4)

AXILLARY (C. 5 & 6)

MEDIAL CUTANEOUS OF
ARM AND INTERCOSTOBRACHIAL
(T. 1 & 2)

POSTERIOR CUTANEOUS
OF ARM (RADIAL)

LOWER LATERAL
CUTANEOUS OF ARM
(RADIAL)

POSTERIOR CUTANEOUS
OF FOREARM (RADIAL)

LATERAL CUTANEOUS OF
FOREARM (MUSCULOCUTANEOUS)

RADIAL

MEDIAL
CUTANEOUS OF
FOREARM

ULNAR

MEDIAN

(b)

FIG. 22.64. Distribution of cutaneous nerves. (a) on the front; (b) on the back of the upper limb. From *Cunningham's Textbook of Anatomy*. 10th Edition (1964), London : Oxford University Press.

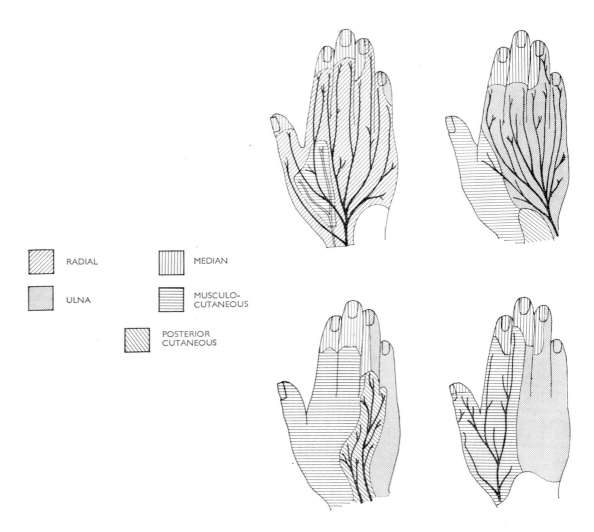

RADIAL

MEDIAN

ULNA

MUSCULO-
CUTANEOUS

POSTERIOR
CUTANEOUS

FIG. 22.65. Variations in the pattern of the cutaneous nerves to dorsum of the hand. From J. C. B. Grant (1962) *An Atlas of Anatomy*. London : Baillière.

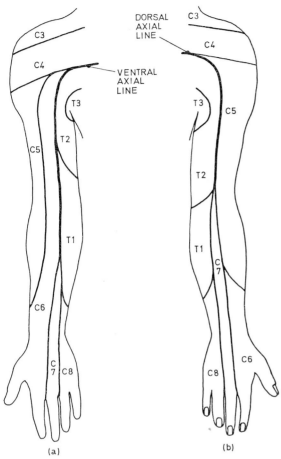

FIG. 22.66. Dermatomes of upper limb, showing segmental cutaneous distribution of spinal nerves on (a) the front, and (b) the back of the limb. From *Cunningham's Textbook of Anatomy.* 10th Edition (1964), London: Oxford University Press.

Nerve supply of the hand

The **cutaneous** distribution and important variations are shown in fig. 22.65. The afferent impulses are of great importance for the sensory feedback, from the skin, joints and muscles, and for protection against injury. The sensory function of the hand can be classified as:

(1) informative of position, size, shape, weight, etc. of objects,

(2) 'grip sight' for fine sensory appreciation and tactile discrimination both in precision and power grip,

(3) protective.

The **muscular** branches to the intrinsic muscles of the hand, derived from the ventral ramus of the first thoracic nerve, are distributed through the ulnar and median nerves, the latter supplying the thenar muscles, except adductor pollicis, and two lateral lumbricals, while the former supplies the rest. An important variation is the nerve supply to the flexor pollicis brevis which is usually double, from median and ulnar, but may be only from the ulnar.

The functional deficit caused by interruption of the activity of the nerves of the upper limb depends on the level of interruption. To understand this deficit knowledge of the levels at which the particular muscular branches are given off from the parent trunks is necessary. Examples of the common motor tests for the main nerves of the upper limb are given below:

(1) Radial nerve damage in the middle of the arm is tested by trying to dorsiflex the wrist or extend the metacarpophalangeal joints.

(2) Ulnar nerve damage at the wrist is tested by trying to abduct and adduct the fingers (interossei muscles).

(3) Median nerve damaged at the wrist is shown when trying to abduct the thumb, as the only muscle which can carry out this movement, abductor pollicis brevis, is supplied by the median nerve.

Autonomic nerve supply of the upper limb

There is no evidence for the presence of the parasympathetic fibres in the upper limb. The efferent fibres of the sympathetic system are distributed to the blood vessels, sweat glands and to the arrector pili muscles. The preganglionic fibres are derived from the lateral horn of the upper thoracic spinal cord, and they synapse in the first thoracic and inferior cervical sympathetic ganglia, and probably in the middle cervical ganglion. From these ganglia the postganglionic fibres, transmitted mostly in the lower trunk of the brachial plexus, accompany the peripheral nerves and are distributed in their field of supply. The vessels of the upper limb have, however, a double source of vasomotor fibres. Some of the postganglionic fibres are distributed directly, often by the ansa subclavia, to the subclavian artery to form a periarterial sympathetic plexus on the wall of the artery. These probably do not extend beyond the axilla and the continuation of this plexus on the arteries of the upper limb is provided by contributions from the adjacent peripheral nerves.

BLOOD VESSELS OF THE UPPER LIMB

ARTERIES (fig. 22.67)

The blood for the right upper limb leaves the aortic arch through the short, wide brachiocephalic trunk which divides into the right common carotid and right subclavian arteries, the latter delivering the blood to the limb. On the left side, the subclavian artery is a direct branch of the arch of the aorta. At the outer border of the first rib, on entering the axilla, the main stem of the subclavian artery changes its name to **axillary artery**. At the lower border of the teres major muscle, it is called the **brachial artery**. This vessel ends in the cubital fossa,

FIG. 22.67. Diagram of the named arteries of the upper limb. From Grant's *Atlas of Anatomy*.

by dividing into **radial** and **ulnar arteries.** The radial artery runs down the forearm to the lateral aspect of the wrist, where it curves round to the back of the hand before passing anteriorly through the interosseous space between the first and second metacarpal bones. Entering the palm in this way it ends by anastomosing with the deep palmar branch of the ulnar artery. The ulnar artery runs from the cubital fossa to the flexor retinaculum on the ulnar side of the forearm. It ends on the retinaculum, lateral to the pisiform bone, by dividing into a superficial palmar arch and the deep palmar branch which joins the radial to form the **deep palmar arch.** The **superficial palmar arch** lies just beneath the palmar aponeurosis. Four arteries arise from it; the palmar digital artery goes to the ulnar border of the little finger and three common palmar digital arteries divide distally into branches supplying the contiguous sides of the fingers.

The **deep palmar arch** lies deeply in the proximal part of the palm and gives off three palmar metacarpal arteries which join distally the common palmar digital arteries.

THE SUBCLAVIAN ARTERY

Besides being a stem vessel it supplies some upper limb structures through two branches in the neck. The **transverse cervical** with its superficial branch is associated with the deep surface of the trapezius muscle and its deep branch is associated with the levator scapulae, supraspinous, infraspinous and subscapular regions. The **suprascapular,** which crosses anteriorly to the brachial plexus, reaches the suprascapular notch and is distributed in the supraspinous and infraspinous fossae of the scapula and gives branches to the adjacent muscles and joints.

THE AXILLARY ARTERY

This is divided into three parts: the first, above the pectoralis minor muscle, the second, posterior to it and the third, inferior to it. The branches of the axillary artery are:

(1) one from the first part; **superior thoracic artery** is distributed to the first intercostal space.

(2) two from the second part; **thoraco-acromial** pierces the clavipectoral fascia and divides into acromial, clavicular, deltoid and pectoral branches and **lateral thoracic** descends along the inferolateral border of the pectoralis minor muscle.

(3) three from the third part; the largest, **subscapular** is distributed to the subscapular region, to the infraspinous region (through its circumflex branch), to the chest wall and the latissimus dorsi muscle, the **posterior circumflex humeral artery** passes backwards together with the axillary nerve round the back of the surgical neck of the humerus and ends under cover of the deltoid muscle, and the smallest of the three, the **anterior circumflex humeral artery** passes around the front of the surgical neck.

THE BRACHIAL ARTERY

This has the following named branches:
Profunda brachii artery runs with the radial nerve at the back of the humerus to divide into a radial collateral artery which accompanies the radial nerve to the front of the lateral epicondyle and a posterior descending branch which passes behind the lateral epicondyle. An ascending branch of this last artery anastomoses with the posterior circumflex humeral artery. **Superior ulnar collateral artery** runs towards the back of the medial epicondyle. **Inferior ulnar collateral artery** 'Supratrochlear', gives branches both in front and behind the medial epicondyle.

A small nutrient artery to the humerus is given off from the middle of the brachial artery.

THE RADIAL ARTERY

The branches are: **Radial recurrent artery** arises in the cubital fossa. **Superficial palmar branch** arises just above the wrist and passes into the palm, often taking part in the formation of the superficial palmar arch. **Palmar carpal branch** runs to the palmar carpal arch. **Dorsal carpal branch** is given off at the side of the wrist to the dorsal carpal arch; from the dorsal carpal arch three dorsal metacarpal arteries pass distally and near the knuckles each divides into two **dorsal digital arteries.** Each dorsal metacarpal artery communicates with the deep palmar branch and with digital palmar arteries through the intermetacarpal spaces. The dorsal digital arteries of the thumb and the radial side of the index arise independently from the radial artery. **Princeps pollicis artery** is given off in the palm and divides into two digital palmar arteries to the thumb. **Radialis indicis artery** supplies the palmar aspect of the radial side of the index.

THE ULNAR ARTERY

It gives the following branches: The anterior and posterior **ulnar recurrents** pass in front of and behind the medial epicondyle.

FIG. 22.68. Anastomoses. X denotes the anastomotic branches and the heavy lines the segments of the vessels which are linked.

Common interosseous artery passes to the upper border of the interosseous membrane and divides into: (1) **anterior interosseous artery** which runs in front of the membrane to the upper border of the pronatus quadratus muscle where it sends one branch to the palmar carpal arch and another perforating to the back of the forearm to join the dorsal carpal arch, (2) **posterior interosseous artery** which passes to the back of the forearm above the upper border of the interosseous membrane, supplies the muscles on the back of the forearm and ends in the dorsal carpal arch. At its origin it gives off the interosseous recurrent artery which passes to the back of the lateral epicondyle.

The **palmar carpal branch** of the ulnar artery completes the palmar carpal arch. The **dorsal carpal branch** ends in the dorsal carpal arch. The **deep palmar branch** joins the radial artery in the depths of the palm to complete the deep palmar arch.

The upper limb is provided with many anastomotic arterial communications which may open up to provide an adequate collateral circulation in case of blockage of the main arteries. These are illustrated in fig. 22.68 and may be listed as follows: scapular anastomosis; communication between the intercostal arteries in the chest wall and lateral thoracic, subscapular arteries and branches of the thoracoacromial artery; between the descending branch from the posterior humeral circumflex and the ascending branch from the profunda brachii; anastomosis around the elbow; between the muscular branches of the radial, ulnar and anterior interosseous arteries in the forearm; free anastomoses in the hand between the carpal and palmar arches, intermetacarpal communications and between the dorsal and palmar arteries in the digits.

VENOUS DRAINAGE

The main venous return from the upper limb is through the axillary vein which continues as the subclavian and brachiocephalic veins before opening into the superior vena cava. The veins of the upper limb can be divided into **superficial veins** which lie for most of their course outside the sleeve of the deep fascia, and **deep veins** which accompany the arteries inside the fascial sleeve.

Superficial veins (fig. 22.69)

The digits are drained of venous blood through anastomosing palmar and dorsal digital veins. From the palm most of the venous return goes to the dorsum, particularly through the intercapitular veins between the heads of the metacarpal bones and around the margins of the hand. The blood from the digits and the palm thus drains to the dorsal venous network (fig. 22.69) on the back of the hand. The cephalic vein issues from the radial end of this network and the basilic vein arises from the ulnar end. The further course of these veins is shown in fig. 22.69. The cephalic vein pierces the clavipectoral fascia to end in the axillary vein. The basilic vein runs to the axilla where it continues as the axillary vein.

The superficial veins of the forearm are extremely variable, but, at the elbow, the superficial veins are usually arranged as shown in fig. 22.69.

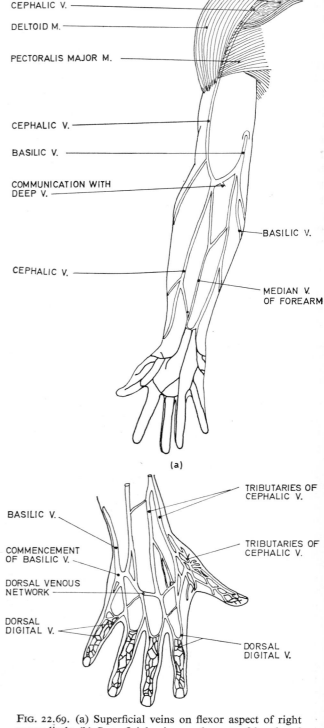

FIG. 22.69. (a) Superficial veins on flexor aspect of right upper limb. (b) Superficial veins on dorsum of hand and digits. From *Cunningham's Textbook of Anatomy.* 10th Edition (1964), London: Oxford University Press.

Deep veins

The deep veins, except for the axillary vein, are arranged in pairs, one on each side of the various arteries. The axillary vein, a direct continuation of the basilic vein, traverses the axilla and becomes the subclavian vein at the outer border of the first rib. Its tributaries correspond to the branches of the axillary arteries except for the thoraco-acromial which joins the cephalic vein. The axillary vein receives the brachial veins in the lower part of the axilla and the cephalic vein in its upper part.

LYMPH DRAINAGE
(fig. 22.70)

The collecting system is arranged in superficial or sub-cutaneous and deep layers, which remain practically separate until the main trunks of the superficial set pierce the deep fascia in the upper arm.

The palmar surfaces of the digits and the palm itself have a rich plexus of **superficial lymphatics**. Most of these drain into the vessels of the dorsum around the sides of the digits, margins of the palm and through the inter-digital clefts. In their further course they accompany the main superficial veins. Some are interrupted at the superficial lymph nodes, but nearly all run to the axilla before they pierce the deep fascia.

Deep lymphatics accompany the deeper blood vessels. Most of the superficial and deep lymphatics end in the axillary lymph nodes from whence the lymph passes to the **subclavian lymph trunk**. There is also a communication between the axillary and lower deep cervical nodes and some lymph from the axilla may drain to the jugular lymph trunk. The left subclavian trunk drains into the thoracic duct and the right one joins the right lymphatic duct (p. 20.37).

Lymph nodes

Superficial nodes include cubital nodes lying a little above the medial epicondyle. Infraclavicular nodes lie anterior to the clavipectoral fascia and drain some of the shoulder area. Deltopectoral nodes lie in the groove between the two muscles and drain part of the arm and shoulder.

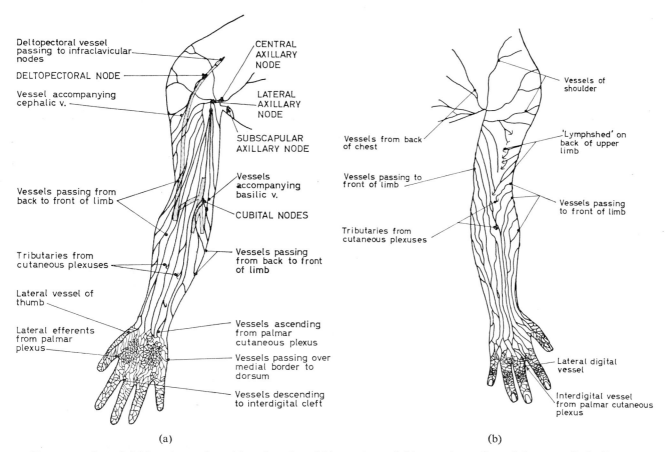

(a)   (b)

FIG. 22.70. Superficial lymph vessels and lymph nodes of (a) anterior and (b) posterior surface of the upper limb. From *Cunningham's Textbook of Anatomy*. 10th Edition (1964), London: Oxford University Press.

Small **deep nodes** may occur along the course of the deep blood vessels. **Axillary lymph nodes** (fig. 22.71) are divided into the following groups which intercommunicate freely:

Lateral, along the axillary vein.
Pectoral, in the anterior part of the axilla.
Subscapular, in the posterior part of the axilla.
Central, in the middle.
Apical, in the apex of the axilla; they convey the collected lymph to the subclavian trunk.

The axillary lymph nodes drain a large part of the trunk (p. 20.38). Most of the lymph from the upper limb passes into the lateral group of nodes.

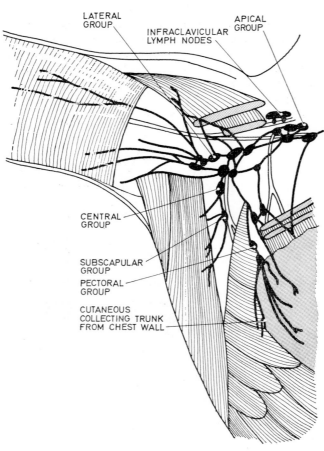

FIG. 22.71. Axillary lymph nodes. From *Gray's Anatomy* (1962). London: Longmans.

MECHANISM OF FLUID RETURN

The main bulk of the centripetal flow of the fluid passes from the dorsal aspect of the hand through the venous and lymphatic channels. Compression of these channels by the active contractions of the muscles within the fascial compartments creates a pumping action which maintains this backflow, its direction being determined by the valves in the vessels. In the upper limb this mechanism is particularly active in the axilla and hand. In the axilla, the veins and the lymphatics are surrounded by muscles and fasciae; thus the movements of the shoulder region facilitate the fluid return. In the hand, the veins can be emptied by repeated clenching of the fist; the venous blood and lymph are squeezed into the dorsal region of the hand where they can accumulate since the connective tissue is loose and mobile on the back of the hand. Interference with normal movement of the shoulder and hand therefore causes swelling. If a normal upper limb, even in a young person, is immobilized in a dependent position, the pumping mechanism is ineffective and swelling develops in less than 12 hours. As there is just enough skin on the hand (p. 22.22) any accumulation of fluid on the dorsum makes the skin tighter and impairs the range of flexion, so creating a vicious circle.

It is important to realize that immobilization of the shoulder and the hand has its inherent risks and if possible in injury or disease one or both of these regions should be kept mobile.

SHORT NOTES ON THE COURSE OF NEUROVASCULAR BUNDLES

The axilla

In the axilla the **axillary artery**, surrounded by the cords and branches of the brachial plexus, with the **axillary vein** lying on its medial aspect, enters the axilla at the apex, but then deviates towards its lateral wall so the main neurovascular bundle in the lower part of the axilla follows the movements of the arm. However, the **axillary nerve** and **posterior circumflex humeral vessels** leave the axilla at the level of the surgical neck of the humerus, inferior to the capsule of the shoulder joint. The **radial nerve** lying behind the axillary artery enters the upper arm directed towards the back of the humerus where it is found in its groove accompanied by the **profunda brachii artery**. The **musculocutaneous nerve** having pierced the coracobrachialis muscle traverses the upper arm between brachialis and biceps muscles.

The upper arm

In the upper arm the **brachial artery** together with the **median nerve, medial cutaneous nerve of the forearm and the ulnar nerve** runs down from the lower border of the axilla along the medial aspect of the arm in the groove between the brachialis and biceps muscles. The **ulnar nerve** passes backwards, at the mid-point of the arm, pierces the medial intermuscular septum, reaches the back of the medial epicondyle and then crosses the medial ligament of the elbow joint (fig. 22.28). The **brachial artery** with the **median nerve**, which has crossed it from the lateral to medial side, reaches its end in the cubital fossa (fig. 22.57). The **radial nerve** together with the **profunda brachii artery** traverses the spiral groove on the back of the humerus, the anterior descending branch of the artery accompanying the nerve as it pierces the lateral intermuscular septum and descends to the front of the elbow.

The forearm

In the forearm the **ulnar nerve** continues down the medial part of the forearm towards the radial side of the pisiform bone under cover of the flexor digitorum superficialis and flexor carpi ulnaris muscles, accompanied on the lateral side in its lower two-thirds by the **ulnar artery** which reaches it from its point of origin in the cubital fossa.

The **superficial branch of the radial nerve** continues from the front of the lateral epicondyle down the lateral part of the forearm under cover of the brachioradialis muscle, lying a little lateral to the middle third of the radial artery. In the distal third of the forearm it inclines backwards across the distal end of the radius to end on the dorsum of the hand. The **radial artery** begins in the cubital fossa and runs downwards and slightly lateral to the distal end of the radius where it turns posteriorly to leave the forearm by entering the anatomical snuff box, where it lies on the lateral ligament of the wrist joint. It is under cover of the brachioradialis muscle as far as the distal third of the forearm where it is covered only by the skin and fasciae and so its pulsation can be felt just above the wrist.

The **median nerve** leaves the cubital fossa by passing between the heads of the pronator teres muscle; here it crosses superficially to the ulnar artery and then runs downwards through the middle of the forearm in front of the flexor digitorum profundus and behind the flexor digitorum superficialis to which it is closely adherent. Just below the pronator teres it gives off the **anterior interosseous nerve** which reaches the wrist region lying on the anterior surface of the interosseous membrane. The **deep branch** of the radial nerve runs in front of the elbow joint, enters the supinator muscle in whose substance it winds round the lateral side of the upper part of the radius, and reaches the dorsum of the forearm between the superficial and deep muscles where it divides almost immediately into its multiple terminal branches.

The wrist

Just above the wrist, at the common site of cut wounds, the disposition of the main nerves and vessels on the palmar aspect is shown in fig. 22.72. The most lateral structure is the radial artery, as the superficial branch of

FIG. 22.72. The anterior aspect of the wrist.

the radial nerve is already on the lateral aspect of the region. The median nerve appears on the lateral aspect of the tendons of the flexor digitorum superficialis and is found between the tendons of the flexor carpi radialis and palmaris longus, superficial to the tendon of the flexor pollicis longus. The ulnar artery with the ulnar nerve on its medial side lies in the medial part of this region partly under cover of the flexor carpi ulnaris. The median nerve enters the carpal tunnel alongside the tendons of the flexor digitorum superficialis, while the ulnar artery and nerve lie anterior to the flexor retinaculum, but under cover of the palmaris brevis muscle.

The hand

In the palm, the common digital nerves lie posteriorly to the superficial palmar arch and its branches, which are immediately behind the palmar aponeurosis. Near the fingers they cross each other, the arteries lying now posterior to the nerves. The neurovascular bundles in the digits are enclosed in the digital ligaments and lie against the sides of the fibrous flexor sheaths (fig. 22.48d).

OSSIFICATION OF THE BONES OF THE UPPER LIMB

The general features and principles of ossification are discussed on p. 18.36. The diagrams below show the parts of the bones of the upper limb ossified from the primary and secondary centres and their approximate times of appearance and fusion (fig. 22.73). The variations in these times caused by racial, nutritional and sexual factors are omitted for simplicity.

LINE OF IMPACT
(fig. 22.74)

A fall on the outstretched hand or striking a blow causes an impact which is taken mainly by the third metacarpal bone, from which it is transmitted to the capitate and scaphoid bones of the carpus. The force then passes along

Fig. 22.73. Numbers on the bones indicate age, in years, of appearance of ossification centres. Stippled areas are cartilaginous at birth. Leaders show the time of fusion in years. IU, age in weeks of intra-uterine life; B, birth; P, puberty.

FIG. 22.74. Line of impact in the upper limb.

the radius, but in normal conditions does not reach the humerus directly as it is taken up by the obliquely disposed fibres of the strong interosseous membrane which transfer it to the ulna and so to the humerus and scapula. The impact is then partially absorbed by the muscular attachment of the scapula to the trunk, but if severe or unexpected, the bony strut of the clavicle is strained or broken.

REVERSE ACTION OF THE MUSCLES

Usually, the muscles of the upper limb act from the trunk on limb, in other words from their origin on their insertion and from their more proximal to their more distal attachments. However, there are many instances when the opposite occurs, as for example in swimming or climbing. It is important to realize this as there are circumstances in which the reverse action of the muscles can be used to assist or replace the action of one which is weakened or lost. For example, after loss of the musculocutaneous nerve and hence the action of the biceps and brachialis muscles, flexion at the elbow can be produced by the muscles in the forearm. Their reverse action at the elbow can be helped by moving their origins up the humerus surgically.

SURFACE ANATOMY

Bony landmarks

The **clavicle** is subcutaneous throughout and can be palpated from its rounded sternal end to the lateral edge of the acromial end, which is 3 cm medial to the lateral border of the acromion. If this border is followed posteriorly for about 5 cm a sharp **acromial angle** can be felt, from which the **crest of the spine of the scapula** can be traced medially towards the third thoracic spine. The **tip of the coracoid process** can be felt indistinctly on pressing backwards 2 cm below the junction of the lateral and intermediate thirds of the clavicle. The **greater tubercle of the humerus** forms the most lateral point in this region and is known as 'the point of the shoulder'. The **lesser tubercle** lies 2·5 cm lateral to the tip of the coracoid process.

Both **epicondyles of the humerus** are subcutaneous and easily palpated. The line joining them passes through the tip of the **olecranon** when the elbow is extended, but in full flexion the tip is 2 cm distal to this line. The **head of the radius** lies 2·5 cm distal to the lateral epicondyle and its position can be verified by feeling it to rotate when the forearm is pronated or supinated. The **posterior border of the ulna** is subcutaneous throughout and can be traced from the olecranon down to the **head of the ulna** which stands out prominently in pronation. On its posteromedial aspect the **styloid process** can be felt. The **anterior border of the lower end of the radius** is felt as a distinct transverse ridge on the front of the forearm about 2–3 cm proximal to the base of the thenar eminence. The **styloid process of the radius** may be felt projecting down from the lateral aspect of the distal end of the radius and its tip is 1 cm distal to the tip of the ulnar styloid. The **dorsal tubercle of the radius** can be felt on the back of the distal end of the radius in line with the second intermetacarpal space. The four points of the attachments of the flexor retinaculum can be identified on the palmar aspect of the carpus. The **tubercle of the scaphoid** can be felt at the proximal border of the thenar eminence and the **crest of the trapezium** immediately distal to it; the **pisiform** is a prominence felt at the base of the hypothenar eminence and the **hook of the hamate** lies 2–3 cm distal and lateral to the pisiform. When the fist is made the prominences of the heads of the metacarpals and phalanges are easily felt and identified as the knuckles.

Soft-tissue landmarks

Most of the superficial muscles and tendons of the upper limb can be easily identified by palpation and in lean individuals can be observed particularly when in action. Some of the soft tissue landmarks are described below.

AXILLARY FOLDS

The anterior fold, formed by the lower part of the pectoralis major muscle can be gripped by the hand and palpated throughout; the posterior fold is formed by the latissimus dorsi and teres major muscles. It extends to a lower level than the anterior one. The **biceps muscle** forms a longitudinal prominence on the front of the arm. In the cubital fossa, with the elbow flexed, the **tendon of the biceps** can be felt in the middle with the sharp upper edge of the **bicipital aponeurosis** passing medially and distally. On the back of the pronated forearm with the hand clenched, a groove can be seen and palpated which extends from the lateral epicondyle towards the dorsal tubercle of the radius (see fig. 22.75). This groove overlies the **intermuscular septum** separating the radial extensors of the wrist from the digital extensors. **Tendons** near the palmar aspect of the **wrist** can be easily palpated; from the radial to the ulnar side they are: tendon of the flexor carpi radialis, then of the palmaris longus (absent in 10 per cent), of the flexor digitorum superficialis and lastly of the flexor carpi ulnaris. There are

FIG. 22.75. Surface anatomy of the dorsum of the forearm.

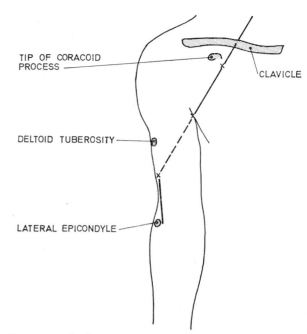

FIG. 22.77. Surface anatomy of the brachial plexus and radial nerve.

usually two distinct **creases at the wrist**; the proximal one overlying the line of the wrist joint and the distal one over the upper border of the flexor retinaculum.

Using the above mentioned bony and soft tissue landmarks the following structures can be mapped out on the surface of the upper limb.

Axillary and brachial arteries. With the arm abducted to a right angle and the forearm supinated (fig. 22.76) a line is drawn from the midpoint of the clavicle to the midpoint of the cubital fossa.

FIG. 22.76. Surface anatomy of the main neurovascular bundle.

Proximal to the junction of the posterior axillary fold with the arm, this line represents the axillary artery; the rest denotes the brachial artery.

Brachial plexus. Its main elements in the upper limb are indicated by a line joining the midpoint of the clavicle to a point one finger's breadth distal and medial to the tip of the coracoid process (fig. 22.77).

Axillary nerve. Most of its course can be indicated on the skin by a transverse line at the back of the shoulder a hand's breadth below the acromial angle.

Radial nerve (fig. 22.77). The radial nerve is represented by a line joining the following points: point of termination of the brachial plexus (see above), point of junction of the posterior axillary fold with the arm, point at the junction of the upper and intermediate thirds of the distance between the insertion of the deltoid and the lateral epicondyle and finally the anterior aspect of the lateral epicondyle. The *deep branch of the radial nerve* appears on the back of the forearm at a point on a line joining the lateral epicondyle to the dorsal tubercle of the radius shown in fig. 22.75, which also shows other structures found along this line.

Median nerve (fig. 22.78). In the arm it follows the line of the

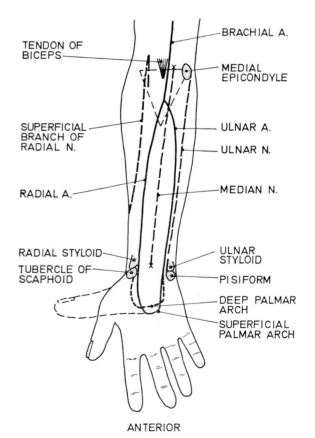

FIG. 22.78. Surface anatomy of the anterior aspect of the forearm and hand.

brachial artery and is found in the cubital fossa halfway between the biceps tendon and the medial epicondyle. From this point the line continues in the forearm to the point halfway between the radial and ulnar styloids.

Ulnar nerve (fig. 22.78). In the arm it follows the line of the brachial artery as far as the midpoint of the arm: at this point it deviates to the back of the medial epicondyle; from there a line drawn to the distal and radial aspect of the pisiform represents the nerve in the forearm.

Ulnar artery (fig. 22.78). From the point of termination of the brachial artery it joins the line of the ulnar nerve at the junction of its upper and intermediate thirds.

Radial artery (fig. 22.78). Represented by a line convex laterally from the points of termination of the brachial artery to the scaphoid tubercle.

Superficial palmar arch reaches as far distally as the lower border of the extended thumb (fig. 22.78), with the deep arch being about 1.5 cm more proximal, accompanied here by the deep branch of the ulnar nerve.

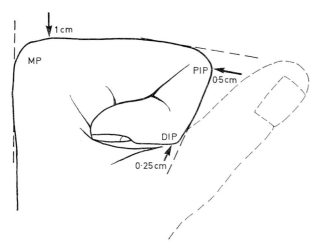

FIG. 22.79. Surface anatomy of the joints of the fingers.

Metacarpophalangeal joints on the palmar aspect are 2 cm proximal to the digital webs, posterior to the lower transverse skin crease of the palm. The *proximal interphalangeal joints* are 0.5 cm and the *distal joints* 0.25 cm from their knuckles (fig. 22.79).

FURTHER READING

Many concepts and diagrams in this chapter are based on the following works.

HOLLINSHEAD W.H. (1958) *Anatomy for Surgeons*, Vol. 3. The limbs, London: Cassell.

JAMIESON J.G. (1950) *Brit. J. Surg.* 38, 193.

JONES F.W. (1948) *The Principles of Anatomy as seen in the Hand*, 2nd Edition. London: Baillière.

KAPLAN E.B. (1965) *Functional and Surgical Anatomy of the Hand*, 2nd Edition. Philadelphia: Lippincott.

LITTLER J.W.W. (1964) Textbook of Reconstructive and Plastic Surgery, ed. by J.M. Converse. Vol. 4. Philadelphia: Saunders.

LANDSMEER J.M.F. (1949) The anatomy of the dorsal aponeurosis of the human finger and its functional significance. *Anat. Rec.* **104**, 1.

LANDSMEER J.M.F. (1955) Anatomical and functional investigations of the human fingers. *Acta anat. (Basel)* **25** (Suppl. 24).

LANDSMEER J.M.F. (1963) The co-ordination of finger-joint motions. *J. Bone Jt Surg.* **45**-A, 1654.

PITRES J.A. & TESTUT L. (1925) *Les Nerfs en Schemas; Anatomie et Physiopathologie.* Paris: G. Doin.

STACK G.H. (1962) Muscle function in the fingers. *J. Bone Jt Surg.* **44**-B, 899.

STACK G.H. (1963) A study of muscle function in the fingers. *Ann. roy. coll. Surg. Engl.* **33**, 307.

Chapter 23
The lower limb

As in other vertebrates, the human upper and lower limbs have a similar basic design; attached to the trunk by a specialized bony girdle, the free limb consists of a single proximal bone, paired intermediate bones and a distal hand or foot (fig. 23.1). The primary function of the upper

FIG. 23.1. General plan of the lower limb.

limb is to orient the hand in space so that its delicate and specialized movements may be performed. The principal functions of the lower limb in man are locomotion and to provide support for the upright trunk.

The differentiation of upper and lower limbs with the

adoption of the erect posture accounts for many of the differences between them. The hand is freely movable with highly mobile digits, while the foot is a grosser structure, adapted to the distribution and transfer of body weight to the ground; the digits are much less mobile. In tragic cases of congenital absence of the hands, however, the foot may be trained to a high degree of manipulative dexterity indicating a functional similarity.

Other differences in form between the two limbs have arisen with adoption of the erect posture. In the foetal position, both upper and lower limbs are flexed upon the trunk. After birth, the lower limbs become extended and the femur undergoes medial rotation at the hip, while the leg below the knee adopts a position comparable to pronation of the forearm. Thus the anterior aspect of the knee corresponds to the posterior aspect of the elbow, and the great toe can be compared to the thumb with the hand held in full pronation.

The bones of the leg, the tibia and fibula, do not rotate around one another as do the radius and ulna. However, movements of the foot known as inversion and eversion occur at the subtalar and midtarsal joints. These movements may be compared loosely with supination and pronation respectively.

BONES, JOINTS AND MUSCLES OF THE HIP

THE BONES OF THE HIP

The pelvic girdle is described on p. 20.13.

The femora are the longest bones in the body. Each articulates above, with the hip bone at the acetabulum, and below, with the tibia and patella. Their upper ends are separated by the width of the pelvis, while their lower ends come together at the knee, so that the femora slope obliquely downwards and medially with the subject standing at attention. This obliquity is greater in the female due to the relatively broader pelvis.

The femur (figs. 23.2 and 3)

The upper end of the femur is characterized by an almost

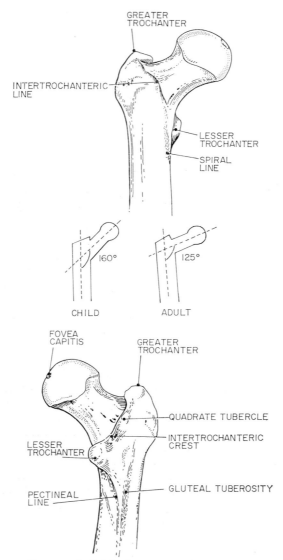

FIG. 23.2. Upper end of right femur; top, anterior and bottom, posterior view.

spherical head which is connected to the shaft by a long neck set obliquely into the shaft.

The head is covered by articular cartilage to form two-thirds of a sphere for articulation with the acetabulum. A depression on the head, the **fovea capitis femoris,** is for the attachment of the ligamentum teres. Through this pit a number of small blood vessels enter and supply the head.

The neck is relatively narrow above and expands downwards and slightly posteriorly towards its insertion into the shaft at an angle of 125° in the adult and 160° in the child (fig. 23.2).

It is ridged longitudinally, and many small vessels enter it to run upwards forming the major blood supply of the femoral head. In fractures of the neck of the femur, these vessels may be damaged, resulting in death (ischaemic necrosis) of the head.

The **greater trochanter** projects above the neck laterally to receive the attachments of the gluteal muscles. On the medial surface of the greater trochanter is the **trochanteric fossa** for the attachment of the obturator externus muscle (fig. 23.3). The greater trochanter is a useful landmark easily palpable on the lateral aspect of the hip.

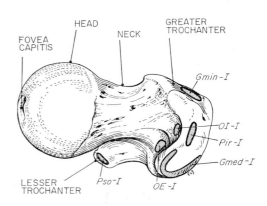

FIG. 23.3. Upper end of right femur seen from above, showing the insertions (*I*) of gluteus minimus (*G min*) and medius (*G med*), obturator internus (*OI*) and piriformis (*Pir*) to the greater trochanter. Iliopsoas (*Pso*) is inserted into the lesser trochanter. The insertion of obturator externus (*OE*) is into the deep trochanteric fossa.

The **lesser trochanter** lies below the femoral neck on the posteromedial aspect of the bone, and receives the attachment of the iliopsoas tendon. Posteriorly, the two trochanters are joined by a prominent **intertrochanteric crest.** This crest is partially interrupted by another tubercle, the **quadrate tubercle,** to which the quadratus femoris muscle is attached. Anteriorly, the two tubercles are joined by a less prominent ridge, the **intertrochanteric line.**

The shaft of the femur is slightly bowed anteriorly and is triangular in cross-section, with anterior, medial and lateral surfaces. The medial and lateral borders are rounded, while the sharp, rough posterior border is known as the **linea aspera.** This line receives the attachment of the adductor and other muscles and it extends from the level of the lesser trochanter down to the junction of the middle and lower thirds of the femur, where it separates into the medial and lateral **supracondylar lines** (p. 23.7).

The **pectineal line,** for attachment of pectineus muscle, passes from the lesser trochanter to the linea aspera (fig. 23.2). The spiral line, to which a portion of vastus medialis muscle is attached, runs below the pectineal line from the linea aspera across the medial surface of the shaft, towards the lower part of the intertrochanteric line. The **gluteal tuberosity,** a roughened longitudinal ridge on the posterior aspect of the upper femoral shaft, lies lateral to the linea aspera (fig. 23.2) and receives the attachment of the lower part of gluteus maximus.

THE HIP JOINT

The femoral head articulates with the hip bone at the acetabulum forming the hip joint. This is a good example of a ball and socket joint, the acetabulum partially enclosing the femoral head. Although it is less mobile than the shoulder joint, it has greater stability which is necessary for weight transfer.

The **acetabulum** forms a cup-shaped cavity which is defective below at the **acetabular notch.** This notch is bridged by the strong transverse acetabular ligament. The articular surface of the acetabulum is horse-shoe shaped (fig. 20.13) enclosing the **acetabular fossa** which contains a small fat-pad. The ligamentum teres is attached partially to the transverse ligament and to the floor of the acetabular fossa. The concavity of the acetabulum is deepened by a ridge of fibrocartilage which extends around its rim, the **labrum acetabulare.** The labrum narrows the mouth of the acetabulum and as its diameter is slightly less than the maximum diameter of the femoral head, it helps to prevent dislocation.

The joint capsule is very strong and surrounds the joint on all sides. Proximally it is attached around the acetabulum, and distally it grasps the neck of the femur, reaching anteriorly to the intertrochanteric line, but posteriorly falling short of the intertrochanteric crest by about 2 cm.

In the erect posture, the axis of the weight of the trunk passes slightly behind the hip joint, so that there is a tendency for the posterior part of the pelvis to tip downwards (fig. 23.4). To prevent this rotation, the anterior part of the joint capsule is stronger than the posterior aspect.

FIG. 23.4. The iliofemoral ligament resists the tendency of the pelvis to rotate.

Certain parts of the capsule show further thickening, and are named as ligaments. The strongest part of the joint capsule is the **iliofemoral ligament,** which is anterior to the joint, extending from the ilium just below the anterior inferior spine to the femur where it is attached to the intertrochanteric line. Its fibres are thinnest centrally giving it the appearance of an inverted Y (fig. 23.5).

FIG. 23.5. Ligaments of the hip joint, (a) anterior, (b) posterior view.

The **pubofemoral ligament** arises from the pubis in the region of the iliopubic eminence and from the obturator membrane; it is attached to the intertrochanteric line along with the lower limb of the iliofemoral ligament. The **ischiofemoral ligament** is a weak band of fibres extending from the ischium below the acetabulum to blend with the posterior fibres of the capsule. Certain fibres can also be demonstrated encircling the neck of the femur, being most distinct posteriorly. These form the **zona orbicularis** and lie deep to the three named ligaments.

The synovial membrane lines all parts of the interior of the joint, except over cartilage or fibrocartilage. It stretches across the acetabular fossa; anteriorly it lines the neck of the femur completely but, posteriorly, it extends only as far as the attachment of the capsule 2 cm from the intertrochanteric crest. Here, it usually protrudes

between the capsule and the neck to form a bursa for the obturator externus tendon (fig. 23.6.). Anteriorly, the synovial cavity frequently communicates with the iliopsoas bursa through the 'weak area' indicated in fig. 23.5a. The **ligamentum teres,** or ligament of head of femur, really represents a flattened portion of synovial membrane, carrying a few vessels to the femoral head.

THE MUSCLES OF THE HIP REGION
(figs. 23.6–9)

The muscles around the hip joint can be compared to those around the shoulder joint. The deltoid muscle of the upper limb corresponds to the mass of gluteus maximus posteriorly and tensor fasciae latae anteriorly. In both upper and lower limbs these muscles cover short muscles which

FIG. 23.6. Short lateral rotating muscles of the hip joint. *O* and *I* represent the origin and insertion of the muscles.

Piriformis (*Pir*)
Pir–O Pelvic surface of middle three pieces of sacrum.
Pir–I Tip of greater trochanter.

Obturator internus (*OI*)
OI–O Internal surface of the true pelvis (see fig. 20.39).
OI–I Medial surface of greater trochanter. The tendon curves around the lesser sciatic notch and the gemelli muscles then accompany the tendon to its insertion.

Quadratus femoris (*QF*)
QF–O Lateral margin of ischial tuber.
QF–I Quadrate tubercle and intertrochanteric crest.

Obturator externus (*OE*)
OE–O External surface of obturator membrane.
OE–I Trochanteric fossa (see fig. 23.3).

FIG. 23.7. Gluteal and tensor fasciae latae muscles.

Gluteus minimus (G min)
G min–O Gluteal surface of ilium between middle and anterior gluteal lines (fig. 20.20).
G min–I Anterior surface of greater trochanter (fig. 23.3).

Gluteus maximus (G max)
G max–O$_1$ Gluteal surface of ilium behind posterior gluteal line.
G max–O$_2$ Posterior surface of sacrum.
G max–O$_3$ Sacrotuberous ligament.
G max–I$_1$ Gluteal tuberosity of femur.
G max–I$_2$ Iliotibial tract.

Gluteus medius (G med)
G med–O Gluteal surface of ilium between posterior and middle gluteal lines (fig. 20.20).
G med–I Lateral surface of greater trochanter (fig. 23.3).

Tensor fasciae latae (*TFL*)
TFL–O Anterior superior iliac spine and part of ilium.
TFL–I Iliotibial tract and fascia lata.

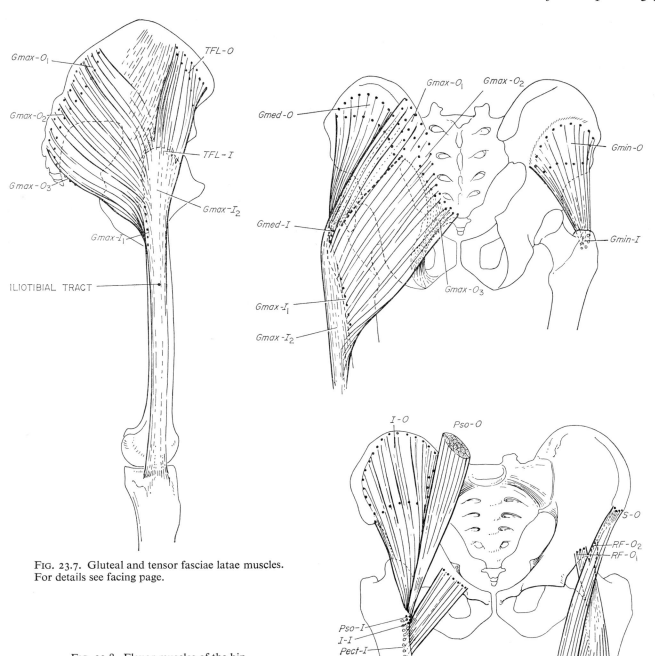

FIG. 23.7. Gluteal and tensor fasciae latae muscles.
For details see facing page.

FIG. 23.8. Flexor muscles of the hip.

Psoas major (*Pso*)

Pso–I Transverse processes, bodies and intervertebral discs of lumbar vertebrae (fig. 20.10).
Pso–I Lesser trochanter.

Iliacus (*I*)

I–O Iliac fossa.
I–I With psoas as iliopsoas into lesser trochanter and area below between spiral and pectineal lines.

Pectineus (*Pect*)

Pect–O Pectineal surface of pubis.
Pect–I Pectineal line below lesser trochanter.

Sartorius (*S*)

S–O Anterior superior iliac spine.
S–I Medial surface of tibia (fig. 23.21).

Rectus femoris (*RF*)

$RF–O_1$ Straight head: anterior inferior iliac spine.
$RF–O_2$ Reflected head: groove above the acetabulum.
RF–I With quadriceps tendon (fig. 23.17 and 19).

are inserted closely around the upper end of the bone; in the upper limb these are the rotator cuff muscles, and in the lower limb, gluteus medius and minimus, piriformis, the obturator muscles and quadratus femoris. The short muscles act primarily as rotators and stabilizers of the shoulder and hip joints. The hamstring muscles which extend the hip joint and flex the knee are shown in fig. 23.18.

Flexion of the hip is achieved mainly by iliopsoas and sartorius, with some assistance from rectus femoris and

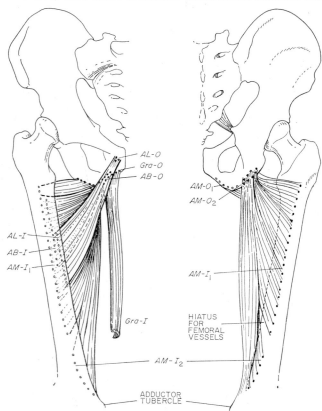

FIG. 23.9. Adductor muscles of the hip.

Gracilis (*Gra*)
Gra–O Medial margin of inferior ramus of pubis.
Gra–I Medial surface of upper end of shaft of tibia.

Adductor longus (*AL*)
AL–O Round tendon from body of pubis.
AL–I Lower part of linea aspera.

Adductor brevis (*AB*)
AB–O Femoral surface of body and inferior ramus of pubis.
AB–I Upper part of linea aspera.

Adductor magnus (*AM*)
(Adductor portion supplied by obturator nerve)
AM–O$_1$ Inferior pubic ramus.
AM–I$_1$ Linea aspera.
   (Hamstring portion supplied by sciatic nerve)
AM–O$_2$ Lower lateral part of ischial tuber.
AM–I$_2$ Medial supracondylar line and adductor tubercle.

pectineus (fig. 23.8). As flexion of the hip is often associated with flexion of the knee, the rectus femoris muscle usually functions as an extensible ligament which couples these two movements. Extension is produced by the hamstring muscles (fig. 23.18) and again, since it is usually accompanied by extension of the knee, these muscles change their length little during this combination of movements at the hip and knee joints. The contractile nature of the hamstring and rectus femoris muscles enables them to act independently at one of the two joints, as for example when contraction of the hamstrings raises the body after touching the toes with straight knees. If the hamstrings and rectus femoris were replaced by fibrous cords, relatively normal walking movements could be produced by flexing both the knee and hip joints through the action of iliopsoas at the hip; similarly both joints would extend through the action at the knee of the vasti muscles (fig. 23.19). The adductor muscles are shown in fig. 23.9, which shows that the vertical fibres of the adductor magnus (AM-O_2I_2) are mainly extensors of the hip. The abducting muscles, gluteus medius and minimus are important in walking since they tilt the pelvis up from the supported side to allow the other leg to swing through (p. 23.26).

MOVEMENTS AT THE HIP REGION
These are similar to movements in any ball and socket joint. Extension and flexion occurs around a transverse axis. Flexion is free and is limited by apposition of the thigh

FIG. 23.10. Axis of rotation of the femur.

against the trunk when the knee is bent. With the knee straight, flexion is limited by tension in the hamstring muscles. Extension is relatively limited, primarily by tension in the joint capsule, particularly of the iliofemoral and pubofemoral ligaments. However, all parts of the joint capsule become tight in extension. Conversely, in flexion, all parts of the capsule are relaxed, and dislocation is most likely to occur with the joint in this position. Abduction is limited by tension of the adductor muscles and the pubofemoral ligament. Adduction is limited by the abductor muscles and by the lateral part of the iliofemoral ligament. Circumduction consists of a combination of the above four movements.

Rotation at the hip joint is a confusing concept since the axis of rotation is not the shaft of the femur but is a line joining the head and the lower end of the femur (fig. 23.10). Thus during rotation, the femur swings around this axis like a gate on its hinges. Medial rotation therefore occurs when the femur is pulled anteriorly around its axis. Lateral rotation obviously occurs in the reverse direction. Hence rotator muscles which arise from the pelvis anterior to the axis of rotation pull the femur anteriorly around the axis and produce medial rotation. It makes no difference whether these muscles are inserted anteriorly or posteriorly, like iliopsoas, on the femur. A similar concept exists for lateral rotation. If the neck of the femur is fractured, true lateral rotation of the femur occurs. This is because the axis of rotation then becomes the shaft of the femur, and as the majority of rotators are inserted into the posterior aspect of the femur, lateral rotation around this axis is produced.

BONES, JOINTS AND MUSCLES OF THE KNEE REGION

THE BONES OF THE KNEE REGION

The lower end of the femur articulates with the upper end of the tibia and the patella to form the knee joint. The head of the fibula articulates with the lateral side of the lateral tibial condyle forming the superior tibiofibular joint (fig. 23.11).

The femur (fig. 23.12)

The shaft of the femur expands below to form the lower end of the femur. From the lower end of the linea aspera, the well-marked medial and lateral **supracondylar lines** run towards the epicondyles. The flat posterior surface of the lower end of the femur forms part of the floor of the popliteal fossa, and is known as the **popliteal surface.**

The large mass of the lower end of the femur is made up of the **medial and lateral condyles,** which are separated posteriorly by the deep **intercondylar notch.** Anteriorly, the condyles are joined by an articular surface known as the patellar surface, the patella coming into contact with this

area of the femur during full flexion of the knee. The anterior surfaces of the condyles lie in the line of the femoral shaft, but posteriorly they project beyond it. The **epicondyles** are small projections on the surface of each condyle. A more marked projection at the upper end of the medial condyle is the **adductor tubercle,** to which is attached the tendinous portion of adductor magnus muscle. On the lateral surface of the lateral condyle, posterior to the epicondyle, there is a well marked groove for the tendon of popliteus muscle.

The tibia (fig. 23.13)

The upper end of the tibia is large and expanded to form a plateau for articulation with the lower end of the femur, and is composed principally of two condyles and the tibial tuberosity. The two **condyles** are separated by a roughened intercondylar area, to which the intra-articular structures, i.e. cartilages and ligaments (p. 23.10) are attached. The **intercondylar eminence** is a sharp projection in this region. The upper surface of each condyle is smooth and oval for articulation with the corresponding femoral condyle, the medial articular surface being slightly the larger. On the back of the medial condyle is a rough horizontal groove to which part of the semimembranosus tendon is attached. The lateral condyle stands out from the shaft more than the medial condyle. This gives it a distal surface, on the posterior aspect of which is a circular facet for articulation with the head of the fibula. On the anterior part of the lateral surface of the lateral condyle, the attachment of the iliotibial tract creates an impression.

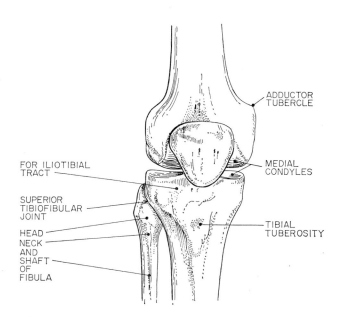

FIG. 23.11. Articulation of bones of right knee and superior tibiofibular joints.

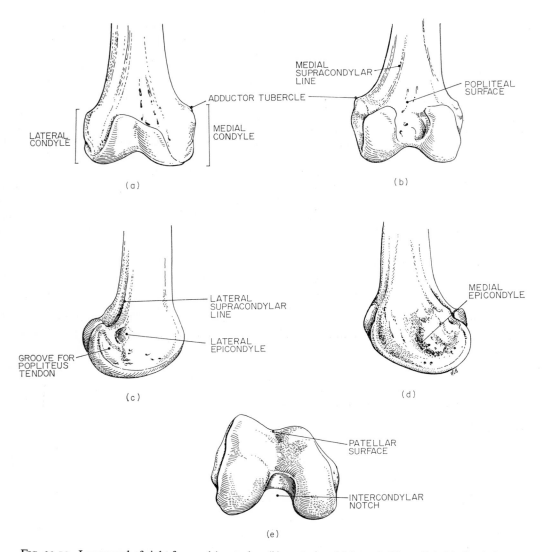

FIG. 23.12. Lower end of right femur, (a) anterior, (b) posterior, (c) lateral, (d) medial, (e) distal views.

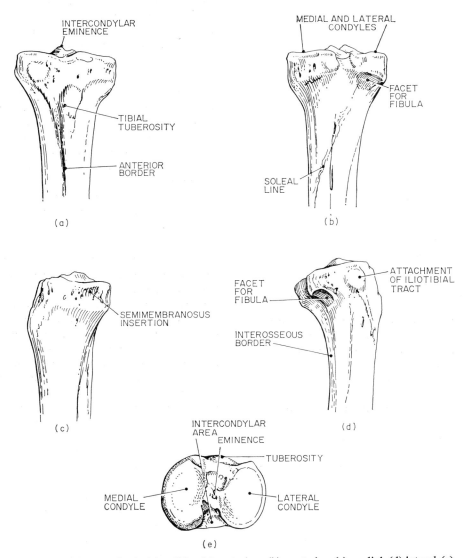

FIG. 23.13. Upper end of right tibia, (a) anterior, (b) posterior, (c) medial, (d) lateral, (e) proximal views.

The **tuberosity of the tibia** is situated anteriorly where the upper end joins the shaft. The upper part of this tubercle is smooth, and receives the ligamentum patellae.

The shaft of the tibia is triangular in cross section, with anterior, lateral (interosseous) and medial borders. The anterior border can be felt subcutaneously in all its length running down the front of the shin. The posterior surface has an oblique ridge near its upper end which runs downwards and medially from the region of the fibular facet. This is the **soleal line** caused by the origin of a portion of the soleus muscle.

The patella (fig. 23.14)

The patella is a roughly triangular sesamoid bone situated in the common tendon of the quadriceps muscles. Its

anterior surface is subcutaneous, and roughly marked with vertical grooves. The posterior surface articulates with the femur, and is roughly divided into medial and lateral halves by a gentle ridge which fits into the intercondylar ridge in full flexion of the knee. The **ligamentum patellae,** the continuation of the quadriceps tendon, is attached proximally to the lower pole of the patella, and distally to the tibial tuberosity.

The fibula (fig. 23.11)

The fibula is the smaller, lateral bone of the leg, and articulates with the tibia at the superior and inferior tibiofibular joints. The upper end is composed of the head and neck, and can be palpated on the lateral side just below the knee.

18

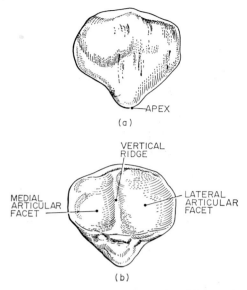

FIG. 23.14. Right patella, (a) anterior, (b) posterior.

A large oval articular facet for articulation with the lateral tibial condyle is present on the proximal surface of the head. The **apex** of the fibula projects upwards posterolateral to the articular surface, and receives the attachment of the fibular collateral ligament of the knee joint.

A narrow neck connects the head with the shaft of the bone. The common peroneal nerve (p. 23.32) winds round the lateral side of the fibular neck, and can be felt against the bone in this region.

The shaft of the fibula is slender, with a slight spiral twist. It has anterior, posterior, and medial (interosseous) borders which separate the anterior, posterior and lateral surfaces. The posterior surface has a pronounced longitudinal ridge, the medial crest, which further divides it. The markings on the fibular shaft are very variable.

THE KNEE JOINT

The knee joint is basically a synovial joint of the simple hinge type. It is the largest joint in the body, and the presence of many intra-articular structures makes its structure complex.

As in all hinge joints the strongest parts of the joint capsule (fig. 23.15) lie on the sides of the joint forming inextensible ligaments, which prevent medial or lateral displacement. The anterior and posterior parts of the capsule are weaker to allow flexion and extension.

The capsule is thin and membranous posteriorly; anteriorly, it is largely replaced by the quadriceps tendon, patella and ligamentum patellae. It is attached to the femur around the articular margins of the femoral condyles and the intercondylar line posteriorly. Its lower attachment is to the posterior surfaces and sides of the tibial condyles and to the anterior surfaces of the condyles along oblique lines extending to the tibial tuberosity. The capsule is considerably strengthened in certain regions by expansions from surrounding muscles.

DEFICIENCIES IN THE CAPSULE

The capsule is absent between the quadriceps tendon and anterior aspect of the femur, allowing the synovial membrane to bulge upwards, forming the **suprapatellar bursa** (fig. 23.17a). Posteriorly the popliteus muscle emerges from the knee joint through a gap in the capsule (fig. 23.15e). In addition, posterior to the medial femoral condyle, there is frequently a deficiency through which the synovial membrane may communicate with bursae under semimembranosus and the medial head of gastrocnemius.

THICKENINGS AND EXPANSIONS OF THE CAPSULE

The continuation of the quadriceps tendon, extending between the lower pole of the patella and the tibial tuberosity is called the **ligamentum patellae** (fig. 23.19).

The **quadriceps expansion** extends from the quadriceps tendon and patella to the oblique lines on the anterior surfaces of the tibial condyles (fig. 23.19). The **oblique posterior ligament** is an extension from the semimembranosus tendon which runs upwards and laterally on the posterior aspect of the capsule (fig. 23.15e). The **arcuate ligament** is a thickening in the capsule above the deficiency through which the popliteus tendon emerges (fig. 23.15e).

EXTRACAPSULAR STRUCTURES

The **tibial collateral ligament** (fig. 23.15d) is a broad strap-like ligament extending from the medial epicondyle of the femur to the upper quarter of the anteromedial surface of the tibia. Its deep surface is closely attached to the capsule and thus to the intermediate part of the medial meniscus. The **fibular collateral ligament** (fig. 23.15c) is a strong cord-like band about 5 cm long, which extends from the lateral femoral epicondyle to the apex of the fibula. For most of its length it is quite separate from the joint capsule, with vessels and nerves to the joint passing through the gap.

INTRACAPSULAR STRUCTURES

The **menisci** or **semilunar cartilages** (fig. 23.17b), are two intracapsular structures attached to the tibial condyles which reduce the disparity between the lower femoral and upper tibial surfaces and thus permit smoother movements of the tibia on the femur during flexion and extension. They also act to a lesser degree as shock absorbers during walking.

The medial and lateral menisci are attached to the tibial condyles and, being thicker at their outer margins, increase the concavities on these condyles to receive the

FIG. 23.15. The knee joint. The attachments of the joint capsule are shown from the front (a), and back (b). The collateral ligaments are shown in lateral (c), and medial (d) views. The ligaments on the back of the joint are shown in (e).

femoral condyles. Each meniscus is curved, the medial meniscus forming a letter 'C', while the lateral meniscus forms almost a complete circle. The menisci are attached to the intercondylar eminence at their anterior and posterior horns and at their periphery to the tibial condyles by short ligamentous fibres, the **coronary ligaments.** The medial meniscus is also closely attached to the joint capsule, and particularly to the tibial collateral ligament of the knee, and is therefore less mobile than the lateral meniscus. This reduced mobility renders the medial meniscus more liable to injury during sudden rotatory strains of the knee joint such as may occur during a game of football. The lateral meniscus moves during such strains, while the more fixed medial cartilage is subject to shearing forces and may tear, particularly towards its posterior part. The **transverse ligament** is a small ligament joining the anterior parts of the medial and lateral menisci (fig. 23.17b).

The bony dissimilarities between tibia and femur do not confer anteroposterior stability. The **cruciate ligaments** (figs. 23.16 and 17b) play an important part in preventing

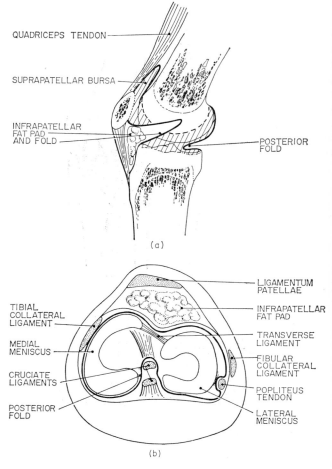

FIG. 23.17. Synovial membrane of the knee joint in vertical (a) and horizontal (b) section.

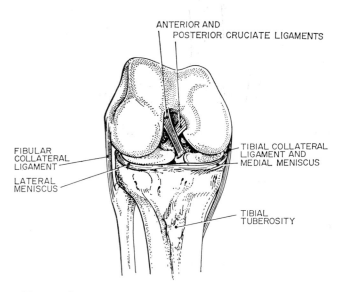

FIG. 23.16. The cruciate ligaments. The joint is viewed from the front after removing the patella and ligamentum patellae.

dislocation in these directions. They are attached to the intercondylar eminence of the tibia below and pass upwards to the internal surfaces of the two femoral condyles. As they ascend they cross each other and so earn the name cruciate.

The anterior cruciate ligament passes upwards, laterally and backwards from the anterior part of the intercondylar eminence to attach to the medial surface of the lateral femoral condyle. The posterior cruciate ligament passes upwards, forwards and medially from the most posterior part of the intercondylar eminence to be attached to the lateral surface of the medial femoral condyle. While these two ligaments are relatively taut in all stages of joint movement, they are most taut when the knee is fully extended. The anterior ligament prevents backward displacement of the femur on the tibia, while the posterior ligament blocks anterior displacement of the femur on the tibia.

The **synovial membrane of the knee joint** lines the capsule of the joint and the intra-articular structures, some of which throw it into rather complicated folds. Superiorly it bulges above the patella, deep to the quadriceps tendon, forming the **suprapatellar bursa.** When there is an excess of fluid in the joint, e.g. in an infection or following trauma, this bursa becomes prominent and may be easily demonstrated clinically. An infrapatellar fat pad lies posterior to the ligamentum patellae and is surrounded by synovial membrane. The relationships of the synovial membrane are shown in fig. 23.17 where it is seen that the intra-articular structures, with the exception of the menisci, are in fact extrasynovial.

MUSCLES OF THE KNEE REGION

Extension is achieved by vastus medialis, lateralis, intermedius and rectus femoris, which combine to form quadriceps (figs. 23.8, 19 and 20). Flexion is due mainly to the hamstrings (fig.23.18), with some assistance from gracilis and sartorius (figs. 23.8, 9 and 21). The calf muscles, gastrocnemius and plantaris, also assist in flexion of the knee (fig. 23.30). The popliteus is partially intra-articular and plays an important part in initiating flexion at the knee joint by laterally rotating the femur on the tibia (fig. 23.22).

FIG. 23.18. Hamstring muscles.

Biceps femoris (*BF*)

BF–O₁ Long head: medial part of ischial tuber with *ST–O*.
BF–O₂ Short head: linea aspera.
BF–I Apex of head of fibula.

Semitendinosus (*ST*)

ST–O Medial part of ischial tuber.
ST–I Upper part of medial surface of tibia (fig. 23.21).

Semimembranosus (*SM*)

SM–O Lateral part of ischial tuber.
SM–I₁ Groove on back of medial condyle of tibia.
SM–I₂ Through fascia over popliteus to the soleal line.
SM–I₃ Oblique posterior ligament of knee joint (fig. 23.15e).

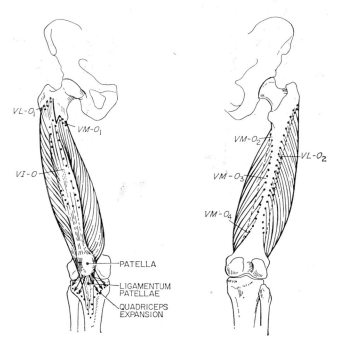

FIG. 23.19. Extensor muscles of the knee.

Vastus medialis (*VM*)

VM–O₁ Intertrochanteric line.
VM–O₂ Spiral line.
VM–O₃ Medial edge of linea aspera.
VM–O₄ Medial supracondylar line and adductor magnus tendon.

Vastus lateralis (*VL*)

VL–O₁ Anterior surface of greater trochanter.
VL–O₂ Lateral edge of linea aspera.

Vastus intermedius (*VI*)

VI–O Anterior and lateral surfaces of the shaft of femur.
With rectus femoris (fig. 23.8) they are inserted into the patella (fig. 23.17a) and thence to the tibial tuberosity as ligamentum patellae with expansions to adjoining parts of upper end of tibia.

FIG. 23.20. Muscles of the thigh. In the right diagram the rectus femoris muscle has been turned forwards to reveal vastus intermedius.

FIG. 23.21. Insertions of sartorius (*S–I*), gracilis (*Gra–I*) and semitendinosus (*ST–I*) to the anteromedial surface of tibia.

FIG. 23.22. **Popliteus (*Pop*)**
Pop–O₁ Pit at anterior end of groove on lateral condyle.
Pop–O₂ Lateral meniscus.
Pop–I Posterior surface of tibia above soleal line.

MOVEMENTS AT THE KNEE JOINT

At the limit of extension there is an additional movement of medial rotation of the femur on the tibia, the tibia being considered as fixed, as it is during weight-bearing. This rotatory movement occurs during the final 5° of extension and tightens up all the ligaments of the joint; thus it increases stability. Before flexion of the knee from the fully extended position can begin, this medial rotation of the femur must be reversed to unlock the joint. The necessary lateral rotation of femur on the tibia is achieved by popliteus, whose tendinous attachment to the lateral femoral condyle pulls back the lateral condyle, while the muscular attachment to the posterior part of the lateral meniscus prevents this portion of the meniscus being damaged. Once this rotation has occurred, simple flexion may begin and can continue until the calf muscles come into contact with the posterior thigh muscles.

Medial rotation of the tibia on the femur, especially in the flexed knee, is due to the sartorius, gracilis and semitendinosus muscles with biceps femoris opposing this movement.

The patella increases the leverage of the quadriceps muscle in extending the knee from the fully flexed position. When this extension is proceeding, the patella is jammed hard against the femoral condyles and is immobile from side to side. When the quadriceps muscle is relaxed, the patella is freely mobile from side to side. The patella occasionally has to be removed surgically and, although the quadriceps muscle functions remarkably well in its absence, the power of knee extension never quite matches that of the normal side.

The femur makes a laterally oriented oblique angle with the tibia and so contraction of the quadriceps muscle tends to dislocate the patella towards the lateral side (fig. 23.19). This is normally prevented by the more prominent lateral margin to the patellar groove on the femur and by the medial pull of the lowest fibres of vastus medialis ($VM–O_4$). Nevertheless lateral dislocation of the patella is more common in women as their femora are more oblique.

BONES, JOINTS AND MUSCLES OF THE LEG

BONES OF THE LEG

The lower end of the tibia (fig. 23.23) is a continuation of the triangular shaft, which is thinnest about the junction of the middle and lower thirds of the bone and thickens

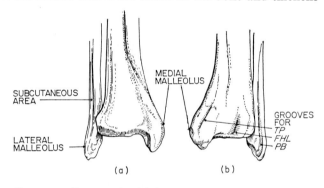

SUBCUTANEOUS AREA

MEDIAL MALLEOLUS

GROOVES FOR
TP
FHL
PB

LATERAL MALLEOLUS

(a) (b)

FIG. 23.23. Lower ends of right tibia and fibula, (a) anterior, (b) posterior views. *TP*, tibialis posterior; *FHL*, flexor hallucis longus; *PB*, peroneus brevis.

towards the lower end where it becomes four-sided. The subcutaneous medial surface becomes the **medial malleolus,** which is easily felt at the medial side of the ankle. The lateral surface of the malleolus is smooth and has an articular surface, continuous with that on the distal surface of the bone, for articulation with the talus. The lateral surface is characterized by the triangular **fibular notch** into which the lower end of fibula is firmly attached by a fibrous interosseous ligament.

The shaft of the fibula continues downwards to the distal end of the bone (fig. 23.23) which is named the **lateral malleolus.** This is easily palpable and visible on the lateral aspect of the ankle joint and is pyramidal in shape. The subcutaneous lateral surface is smooth and convex, and it extends to a slightly lower level than the medial malleolus. The medial surface has a large articular area for articulation with the lateral surface of the talus, while above this there is a rough area for attachment of the interosseous tibiofibular ligament. Posterior to the articular area, a deep

malleolar fossa indents the medial surface of the malleolus. The posterior surface of the malleolus is grooved for the peroneus brevis and peroneus longus tendons.

JOINTS OF THE LEG

The proximal tibiofibular joint

The head of the fibula articulates with the lateral condyle of the tibia by a small plane synovial joint. It is surrounded by a circular capsular ligament and allows only slight gliding movements of the head of the fibula when stress is applied to the ankle joint.

The interosseous membrane

The interosseous membrane, which stretches between the interosseous borders of the tibia and fibula, is similar to that in the forearm.

The distal tibiofibular joint (figs. 23.27 and 28)

This is a very strong fibrous joint. The lower ends of the tibia and fibula are held together by the thick **interosseous ligament** passing between the floor of the fibular notch of the tibia and the rough area on the medial surface of the fibula above the lateral malleolus. Three further ligaments are associated with this joint; the strong **anterior** and **posterior tibiofibular ligaments** stretch downwards and laterally from the anterior and posterior margins of the lower end of tibia to the anterior and posterior surfaces of the lateral malleolus, and the **transverse tibiofibular ligament** passes from the posterior margin of the lower end of the tibia to the malleolar fossa on the lateral malleolus.

These ligaments maintain the integrity of the ankle joint, as they prevent the tendency for the talus to be forced upwards between the malleoli during weight bearing. If the upward force becomes too great, as in landing on the feet from a great height, the ligaments may rupture and the tibia and fibula are split apart.

BONES, JOINTS AND MUSCLES OF THE FOOT

THE BONES OF THE FOOT

These consist of the tarsal and metatarsal bones and the phalanges (fig. 23.24).

The tarsus

There are seven tarsal bones (cf. eight carpal bones).

The **talus** (fig. 23.25) provides the link between the leg bones, tibia and fibula, and the remaining bones of the foot. It has no direct muscular attachments. The talus consists of a body and a head joined by a narrow neck. The body lies posteriorly and fits between both malleoli,

FIG. 23.24. Skeleton of right foot, (a) superior, (b) inferior, (c) lateral, (d) medial views.

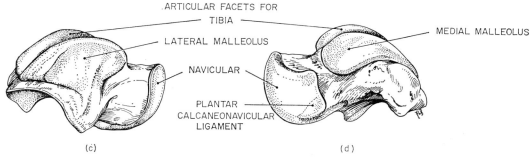

FIG. 23.25. Right talus, (a) superior, (b) inferior, (c) lateral, (d) medial views.

articulating with them and with the distal end of the tibia superiorly. The superior articular surface tapers posteriorly and is convex anteroposteriorly and slightly concave from side to side.

A large articular area on the lateral surface articulates with the lateral malleolus and is continuous with the superior articular surface. A smaller comma-shaped facet for articulation with the medial malleolus is on the medial side and is also continuous with the superior articular surface.

These three contiguous articular surfaces are known as the **trochlear surface** of the talus and are surrounded by the attachments of the capsule of the ankle joint. Like the articular surface on the distal end of the tibia, the trochlear surface is wider anteriorly. The inferior surface is concave and articulates with the posterior articular facet on the calcaneus. The posterior margin of the inferior surface bears two projections, the posterior and medial tubercles, with a groove between them for the tendon of flexor hallucis longus.

The head of the talus is directed anteromedially. It is hemispherical and covered by articular cartilage. It articulates with the navicular bone anteriorly, the anterior

and middle calcaneal facets inferiorly and the plantar calcaneonavicular (spring) ligament which lies between the navicular bone and the sustentaculum tali (fig. 23.29). The neck of the talus is constricted with a deep groove inferiorly, the **sulcus tali.**

The **calcaneus** (fig. 23.26), or heel bone, has six irregular surfaces and is roughly rectangular in shape. The posterior part of this bone forms the prominence of the heel. The **sustentaculum tali** projects from the upper part of the medial surface. The lateral surface bears a short ridge, the **peroneal tubercle,** which separates the tendons of peroneus longus and brevis. Anteriorly, the calcaneus articulates with the cuboid bone. The tendo calcaneus is attached to the posterior surface in its middle third and there is a smooth area above this where a bursa lies between the tendon and the bone.

The upper surface bears three articular facets; the posterior articulates with the body of talus, and the middle and anterior articulate with the head of talus.

The middle facet lies on the upper aspect of the sustentaculum tali, and is separated from the posterior facet by a deep sulcus, the **sulcus calcanei.** This corresponds to the sulcus tali, so that when the bones are articulating, a narrow

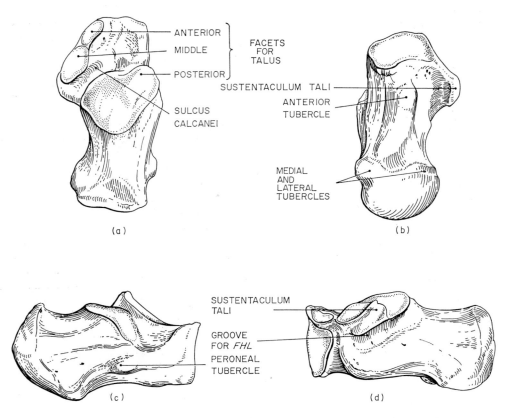

FIG. 23.26. Right calcaneus, (a) superior, (b) inferior, (c) lateral, (d) medial views.

tunnel directed anterolaterally is formed. This is the **sinus tarsi,** which contains the interosseous talocalcanean ligament.

The inferior surface is concave and ridged and bears three tubercles, the anterior tubercle, and the medial and lateral posterior tubercles.

The **navicular** bone lies between the head of the talus posteriorly, and the three cuneiform bones. Its posterior surface is concave and smooth, while its anterior surface has three facets for the cuneiforms. A prominent tuberosity arises from its medial surface, and this may be palpated about 2 cm below and anterior to the medial malleolus.

The **cuboid** bone is a large bone, described by its name, which lies on the lateral side of the foot between the calcaneus posteriorly, and the fourth and fifth metatarsals anteriorly. There is a prominent groove on the anterior part of the inferior surface through which the peroneus longus tendon passes.

Three **cuneiform** bones are wedge shaped and they articulate with the navicular posteriorly, and with the bases of the first three metatarsals anteriorly. The medial cuneiform is the largest, and it is narrowest superiorly, while the intermediate and lateral bones are narrower inferiorly. The intermediate bone is shorter than the other

two, so that the base of the second metatarsal lies more proximally than the other metatarsals and thus it also articulates with the sides of the medial and lateral cuneiforms. This feature complicates the operation of disarticulation through the second tarsometatarsal joint.

The metatarsals and phalanges

These are similar to the metacarpal bones and phalanges of the hands (p. 22.14), but some differences are worth noting.

With the exception of the first, the metatarsals are longer and more slender than the metacarpals. The articular base of the first metatarsal is not saddle shaped. The fifth metatarsal has a styloid process projecting from the lateral side of its base which is easily palpable. The phalanges of the toes are shorter than in the fingers, and the fifth toe frequently has only two phalanges.

JOINTS OF THE FOOT

The ankle (tibiotarsal) joint (figs. 23.27 and 28)
The ankle joint is a synovial joint of the hinge variety. The trochlear surface of the talus fits between the malleoli and

articulates with them and the distal surface of the tibia. The posterior tibiofibular ligament completes the socket posteriorly.

FIG. 23.27. Posterior view of the ankle joint.

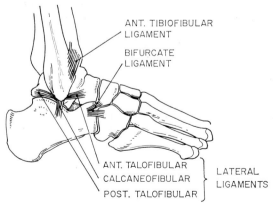

FIG. 23.28. Ligaments around the ankle.

As this is a hinge joint, the medial and lateral ligaments are strong. The medial ligament is named the **deltoid ligament** on account of its shape. Proximally it is attached to the distal end of the medial malleolus and it fans out distally to be attached to the upper surface of the navicular bone, the neck of the talus, the plantar calcaneonavicular (spring) ligament, the sustentaculum tali and the medial surface of body of talus. The **lateral ligament** extends from the distal end of the lateral malleolus and is divided into three parts, the posterior talofibular, calcaneofibular and anterior talofibular ligaments (fig. 23.28).

The anterior and posterior parts of the joint capsule are relatively weak to allow the movements of flexion and extension. The synovial membrane lines the anterior of the joint capsule.

Because the trochlear surface of the talus is wider anteriorly than posteriorly, this surface is gripped more tightly between the malleoli when the foot is dorsiflexed than when it is plantarflexed. With the foot in plantar flexion the slight side-to-side rocking movements of the talus permit abduction and adduction of the foot.

The tarsal joints

The individual tarsal joints are plane joints of varying degrees of complexity, at any one of which movement is relatively slight. Their summation however, results in the movements of inversion and eversion. Functionally, the most important joints in this respect are the joints between the talus above and the calcaneus and navicular below.

THE TALOCALCANEAN JOINT

This is a synovial joint between the concave facet on the inferior surface of the body of the talus and the posterior convex facet on the calcaneus. The capsule of this joint is thickened anteriorly to form the **interosseous talocalcanean ligament.**

THE TALOCALCANEONAVICULAR JOINT

This synovial joint is of the ball and socket variety. The head of the talus lies in the socket which is made by the navicular bone anteriorly, the middle and anterior articular facets of the calcaneus posteriorly, and inferomedially between these two by the **plantar calcaneonavicular (spring) ligament.** This strong ligament passes between the sustentaculum tali posteriorly and the tuberosity and inferior margin of navicular anteriorly.

A fibrous capsule surrounds the joint, and this is supported medially by the navicular extension of the deltoid ligament and laterally by the navicular extension of the bifurcate ligament (fig. 23.28).

Though anatomically the talocalcanean and talocalcaneonavicular joints are separate, they act functionally as the **subtalar** joint, allowing movements of the calcaneus, and so the rest of the foot, around an axis which passes from the point of the heel up through the neck of the talus (fig. 23.36).

THE MIDTARSAL JOINT

The articulation between the head of the talus and the navicular lies roughly in the same transverse line in the foot as the articulation between the calcaneus and cuboid. Though these articulations have separate joint cavities and capsules, they function as one unit, the midtarsal joint; movements at ¡this joint are additive to the movements of the calcaneus (p. 23.23), at the talocalcaneonavicular and talocalcanean joints. This is because the muscles which produce these movements of the calcaneus are all attached to the foot in front of the midtarsal joint. The midtarsal joint has three important accessory ligaments (figs. 23.28 and 29).

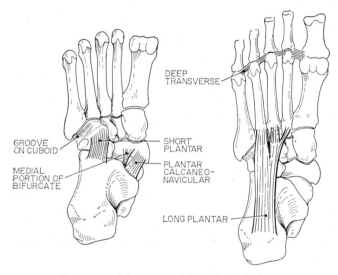

GROOVE
ON CUBOID

MEDIAL
PORTION OF
BIFURCATE

DEEP
TRANSVERSE

SHORT
PLANTAR

PLANTAR
CALCANEO-
NAVICULAR

LONG PLANTAR

FIG. 23.29. Ligaments of the sole of the foot.

The **short plantar ligament** is a thick ligament which passes between the anterior tubercle of the calcaneus and the posterior ridge of the groove on the cuboid. The **bifurcate ligament** is attached posteriorly to the upper surface of the calcaneus behind its anterior margin, the ligament bifurcates anteriorly; the medial limb is attached to the inferomedial aspect of the navicular, and forms part of the socket for the head of the talus; the lateral limb is attached to the upper surface of cuboid. The **long plantar ligament,** lying superficial to the short plantar ligament, is attached posteriorly to the plantar surface of the calcaneus and passes forwards to be attached to the bases of the middle three metatarsals. Some deeper fibres are attached to both anterior and posterior margins of the groove in

the cuboid, converting this into a tunnel for peroneus longus tendon.

The remaining intertarsal joints do not warrant special description, other than to state that the plantar aspects of their joint capsules are always stronger than the dorsal aspects.

THE TARSOMETATARSAL JOINTS

These joints are relatively immobile, plane, synovial joints. The first is the most mobile, while the second, being wedged between medial and lateral cuneiforms, is the least mobile. This fact may account for the frequency with which the second metatarsal is fractured (March fracture) during relatively light exercise.

The metatarsophalangeal and interphalangeal joints

Though less mobile than the corresponding joints of the fingers (p. 22.16) these joints resemble them closely in structure and function. The heads of the metatarsals are bound together by a deep transverse ligament which unites the plantar thickenings of all the joint capsules.

The movements at these joints are very similar to those in the hand, though the range of movement is smaller.

The big toe or hallux is considerably less mobile than the thumb, though it has similar muscle attachments. Its main functions are concerned with weight distribution and with propulsion during walking or running; hence there are sesamoid bones in the tendons of flexor hallucis brevis. Thus since stability rather than mobility is required, the deep transverse ligament of the foot connects the metatarsophalangeal joint of the hallux to that of the second toe, whereas the thumb is free of such restraint.

MUSCLES AND MOVEMENTS OF THE ANKLE

The ankle joint is essentially a hinge joint and provides mainly for the movements of dorsiflexion and plantar-flexion. Dorsiflexion at the joint is produced by muscles passing to the foot anterior to the ankle joint, i.e. tibialis anterior, extensor hallucis longus, extensor digitorum longus and peroneus tertius (fig. 23.34). This movement results in elevation of the forefoot in relation to the heel.

The opposite movement of plantarflexion is produced by calf muscles gastrocnemius, plantaris and soleus (figs. 23.30 and 31), assisted by tibialis posterior (fig. 23.32), flexor digitorum and hallucis longus (fig. 23.31), and the peroneal muscles (fig. 23.35).

It has been noted already that the trochlear surface of the talus is rather broader anteriorly than posteriorly, so that in dorsiflexion, the talus fits more compactly between the malleoli; in fact dorsiflexion is limited by this locking mechanism. The joint is most stable in this position.

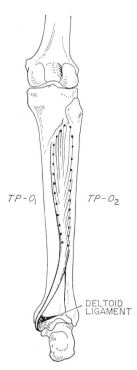

FIG. 23.30. Muscles of the calf.

Gastrocnemius (G)

G–O₁ Lateral head: upper part of lateral surface of lateral femoral condyle, and lower part of lateral supracondylar line.

G–O₂ Medial head: popliteal surface of femur above medial condyle.

G–I Tendo calcaneus in company with plantaris and soleus (*Sol* fig. 23.31).

Plantaris (Pla)

Pla–O Popliteal surface of femur above lateral condyle.
Pla–I Medial side of tendo calcaneus.

FIG. 23.32. **Tibialis posterior (TP)**
TP–O₁ Lateral part of upper two-thirds of posterior surface of tibia below soleal line.

TP–O₂ Posterior surface of fibula and interosseous membrane.

TP–I See figs. 23.33 and 37.

FIG. 23.31. Muscles of the calf.

Soleus (Sol)

Sol–O₁ Posterior surface of upper one-quarter of fibula.
Sol–O₂ Soleal line of tibia.
Sol–O₃ Tendinous arch between *O₁* and *O₂*.
Sol–I Middle one-third of posterior surface of calcaneus after joining gastrocnemius to form tendo calcaneus.

Flexor digitorum longus (FDL)

FDL–O Upper two-thirds of posterior surface of tibia below soleal line and medial to *TP–O₁* (fig. 23.32).
FDL–I See fig. 23.33 and 37.

Flexor hallucis longus (FHL)

FHL–O Lower two-thirds of posterior surface of fibula.
FHL–I See figs. 23.33 and 37.

FIG. 23.33. Arrangement of tendons of deep calf muscles.

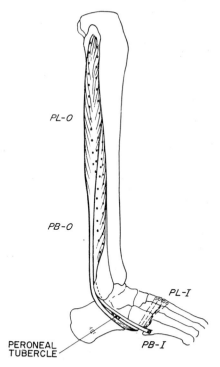

FIG. 23.35. The peroneal muscles.
Peroneus longus (*PL*)

PL–O Upper two-thirds of lateral surface of fibula.

PL–I Base of first metatarsal and medial cuneiform bone. Its tendon runs in a deep groove on the plantar aspect of the cuboid.

Peroneus brevis (*PB*)

PB–O Lower two-thirds of lateral surface of fibula.

PB–I Tuberosity on base of fifth metatarsal. Its tendon lies in a groove on the posterior aspect of the lateral malleolus.

FIG. 23.34. Muscles of the anterior compartment of the leg.
Extensor hallucis longus (*EHL*)

EHL–O Anterior surface of fibula and adjacent interosseous membrane.

EHL–I Base of distal phalanx of big toe. This muscle lies between extensor digitorum longus and tibialis anterior and is partially concealed by them.

Tibialis anterior (*TA*)

TA–O Upper two-thirds of lateral surface of shaft of tibia.

TA–I Medial surface of medial cuneiform and base of first metatarsal.

Extensor digitorum longus (*EDL*)

EDL–O Upper two-thirds of anterior surface of fibula.

EDL–I Bones of the toes and extensor expansions.

Peroneus tertius (*PT*)

PT–O Lower one-third of anterior surface of fibula.

PT–I Base of fifth metatarsal.

MOVEMENTS OF THE FOREFOOT

Four movements may be described; adduction occurs when the forefoot is moved horizontally towards a line running forwards between the feet, abduction when it is moved horizontally away from this line; inversion takes place as the medial border of the foot is raised so that the sole of the foot tends to face medially, and eversion when the lateral border of the foot is raised so that the sole tends to face laterally.

Though these movements may be quite separate, adduction and inversion are frequently combined, as are abduction and eversion. Inversion is produced mainly by tibialis posterior and tibialis anterior assisted by flexor hallucis longus. The principal evertors of the foot are the peroneal muscles. These muscles are all attached to the foot in front of the midtarsal joint, and the major part of these two movements occurs at the subtalar joint around an oblique axis (fig. 23.36). This can be checked by the

FIG. 23.36. The muscles which produce inversion and the axis of inversion and eversion.

student if he attempts inversion or eversion while holding his own calcaneus still with the hand. Minor gliding movements at the other tarsal joints add only slightly to the range of movement achieved.

Adduction and abduction of the forefoot are relatively limited movements, more particularly in the dorsiflexed position. Tibialis anterior and posterior are the principal adductors, assisted by the long muscles to the big toe, while peroneus longus and brevis are the important abductors. Movements of the toes are similar to but much less important than those at the fingers. The intrinsic muscles of the foot and the long flexors and extensors of the toes are shown in figs. 23.37 and 38.

In considering the movements of abduction and adduction of the toes, the line of reference passes along the second toe and not, as in the case of the hand, along the third digit. Thus the arrangement of the interossei muscles is slightly different (fig. 23.37). The plantar interossei adduct, and the dorsal interossei abduct as in the hand; however, the second toe cannot be adducted into itself

and so has no plantar interossei. Since the hallux has its own adductor, there are only three plantar interossei, which pass to the lateral three toes. The hallux and the fifth toe have their own abductors. The second toe has attached to it the medial two dorsal interossei, while the lateral two muscles pass to the lateral sides of the third and fourth toe respectively.

The flexor digitorum accessorius muscle (fig. 23.37) has no counterpart in the hand. Its function is to alter the pull of the flexor digitorum tendons from a slightly oblique angle so that they act along the longitudinal line of the toes thus increasing efficiency. It can also maintain flexion of the toes when the long flexor muscles are in different states of contraction, as during marked plantar flexion of the foot.

THE ARCHES OF THE FOOT

The normal foot displays a well-marked longitudinal arching which is present from birth. The medial side of the foot is normally arched more prominently than the lateral side so that there is also a transverse arch of the foot, this arch being completed by the transverse arch of the other foot when standing with the feet together.

The **longitudinal arch** is in two parts (fig. 23.39); the medial longitudinal arch consists of the talus, calcaneus, navicular, cuneiforms, metatarsals and phalanges of the medial three toes. The lateral longitudinal arch consists of the calcaneus, cuboid, metatarsals and phalanges of the lateral two toes.

The **transverse arch** is most marked at the height of the longitudinal arches, namely across the distal row of tarsal bones.

Four interdependent factors maintain the integrity of the arches:

(1) The first is the shape of the bones and their interlocking nature. The head of the talus fitting into the socket of the talocalcaneonavicular joint may be regarded as the keystone in the medial longitudinal arch.

(2) The ligaments of the foot joints are all stronger on the plantar side of the joints. Two of these ligaments deserve further mention; the plantar calcaneonavicular (spring) ligament is important since it completes the socket of the talocalcaneonavicular joint into which the head of the talus fits; the long plantar ligament acts like a bow string between the posterior tubercles of the calcaneus and the heads of the metatarsals.

(3) The muscles may be divided into two groups. Firstly, those which maintain an upward pull on the arches consist of tibialis posterior and anterior acting on the medial arch and peroneus brevis and tertius maintaining the elevation of the lateral arch. Secondly, tendons which function as bowstring supports consist of the long flexor tendons which assist in the maintenance of the longitudinal arches and peroneus longus which helps to maintain the

First (superficial) layer

Abductor digiti minimi (*ADM*)

ADM–O Medial and lateral tubercles of calcaneus.

ADM–I Lateral side of base of proximal phalanx of the little toe.

Flexor digitorum brevis (*FDB*)

FDB–O Medial tubercle of calcaneus.

FDB–I Palmar surface of base of middle phalanx of second, third, fourth and fifth toes. The tendons split to allow the *FDL* tendons to reach the distal phalanx.

Abductor hallucis (*AbH*)

AbH–O Medial tubercle of calcaneus.

AbH–I Medial side of base of proximal phalanx of the big toe.

Second layer

Flexor digitorum longus (*FDL*)

FDL–O Posterior surface of tibia.

FDL–I Base of distal phalanges after passing through the split in the tendon of flexor digitorum brevis.

Flexor hallucis longus (*FHL*)

FHL–O Posterior surface of fibula.

FHL–I Base of distal phalanx of big toe.

Flexor digitorum accessorius (*FDA*)

FDA–O$_1$ Lateral edge of plantar surface of calcaneus.

FDA–O$_2$ Long plantar ligament and medial surface of calcaneus.

FDA–I Tendon of *FDL*.

Lumbricals (*L*)

L–O Tendons of flexor digitorum longus.

L–I Extensor expansions.

Third layer

Flexor digiti minimi brevis (*FDM*)

FDM–O Base of fifth metatarsal and long plantar ligament.

FDM–I Lateral side of base of proximal phalanx of the little toe with *ADM*.

Adductor hallucis (*AdH*)

AdH–O$_1$ Transverse head; palmar aspect of joint casules of second, third, fourth and fifth metatarsophalangeal joints.

AdH–O$_2$ Oblique head: long plantar ligament and bases of metatarsals 2-4.

AdH–I Lateral side of base of proximal phalanx of the big toe, together with *FHB*.

Flexor hallucis brevis (*FHB*)

FHB–O Cuboid and lateral two cuneiforms.

FHB–I Medial and lateral sides of base of the proximal phalanx of the big toe in association with adductor hallucis (*AdH*) and abductor hallucis (*AbH*).

Fourth layer

Peroneus longus (*PL*)

PL–O Upper two-thirds of fibula.

FIRST LAYER

SECOND LAYER

THIRD LAYER

FOURTH LAYER

Fig. 23.37. The muscles in the sole of the foot.

PL–I Base of first metatarsal and medial cuneiform bone.

Tibialis posterior (*TP*)

TP–O Posterior surface of interosseous membrane (fig. 23.32).

TP–I$_1$ Tuberosity of the navicular.

TP–I$_2$ All the bones of the tarsus, except the talus, and the bases of the second, third and fourth metatarsals.

Plantar interossei (*PI*)

PI–O Medial side of the plantar aspect of third, fourth and fifth metatarsals.

PI–I Medial side of the extensor expansions.

Dorsal interossei (*DI*)

DI–O Contiguous sides of metatarsals.

DI–I As shown with their centre of action at the second toe (cf. fig. 22.44).

FIG. 23.38. Muscles of the dorsum of the foot.

Extensor digitorum brevis (*EDB*)

EDB–O Anterior part of upper surface of calcaneus.
EDB–I₁ Dorsal surface of base of proximal phalanx of the big toe.
EDB–I₂ Extensor expansions of second, third and fourth toes.

Extensor hallucis longus (*EHL*)

EHL–O Anterior surface of fibula (fig. 23.34).
EHL–I Dorsal surface of base of distal phalanx of the big toe.

Extensor digitorum longus (*EDL*)

EDL–O Anterior surface of fibula (fig. 23.34).
EDL–I Extensor expansions of second, third, fourth and fifth toes.

Peroneus tertius (*PT*)

PT–O Anterior surface of fibula (fig. 23.34).
PT–I Base of fifth metatarsal.

transverse arch. The short muscles of the hallux and little toe also contribute to the integrity of the medial and lateral arches respectively.

(4) The plantar aponeurosis is described on p. 23.28 and assists in maintaining the longitudinal arches.

The arches of the foot distribute the weight of the body from the tibia and hence talus to the ground over as wide an area as possible. This reduces the pressure on individual areas of the foot. The mechanism is illustrated by fig. 23.39. The jointed nature of the arches confers spring to the foot, which increases the propulsive efficiency of the foot during walking; this resilience absorbs the shock during weight transference. The arches also protect the nerves and vessels running in the sole of the foot.

FIG. 23.39. The longitudinal arches of the foot and the directions of weight transmission.

THE MECHANISMS OF STANDING, WALKING AND RUNNING

Posture and standing

When standing normally, the centre of gravity of the body is just in front of the second piece of the sacrum. The effective body weight thus acts along a perpendicular line from this point to the ground (fig. 23.4). This line passes just behind the hip joints and just in front of the knee joint and the ankle joint. Thus the trunk tends to fall backwards at the hip joint and forwards in front of the knee joint and ankle joint, producing extension at the hip joint and the knee joint, and dorsiflexion at the ankle joint.

These tendencies bring each of these major joints into their most stable position:

(1) The strong iliofemoral ligament of the hip joint is tightest in extension.

(2) The final phase of extension at the knee joint is accompanied by a medial rotation of the femur on the tibia, which tightens all the ligaments of the knee joint.

(3) Dorsiflexion at the ankle brings the broadest portion of the trochlear surface of the talus between the malleoli.

When standing in such a position, electromyography of the leg muscles reveals remarkably little muscular activity. However, minor alterations in the posture cause a stabilizing activity of muscles around these joints.

Walking and running

During walking, one leg supports the body weight while the other leg is swung forwards. Thus each leg alternates between a swinging and a supporting phase.

The movement of walking is initiated by tilting forward the body which advances the centre of gravity and line of body weight. This forward movement is now increased by pushing off with one leg by plantar flexion at the ankle, while the other leg swings forward. This movement also pushes the body weight to the opposite side, so that it arrives over the other leg as this reaches the ground ready to enter the supporting phase.

THE SWINGING PHASE

The leg moves from a position behind the centre of gravity to pass in front of it so that it is ready to take up the body weight during the supporting phase. In order to prevent the foot trailing along the ground during this phase, the hip is flexed and laterally rotated, the knee is flexed, and the foot is dorsiflexed. Clearance is also assisted by tilting the pelvis to elevate the whole swinging limb; this is achieved by contracting the hip abductors, principally gluteus medius and minimus, on the side of the supporting limb. Once momentum has been achieved by the swinging limb, little muscular effort is required, and as the leg passes its supporting companion the knee extends and the foot becomes slightly plantar flexed and inverted as the heel reaches the ground for the supporting phase.

THE SUPPORTING PHASE

The body weight is initially taken on the heel and then passes along the outer border of the foot to be distributed across the metatarsal heads. The knee is kept extended while weight is being borne, but at the end of the supporting phase, the knee is unlocked by lateral rotation of the femur on the tibia. At the ankle joint plantarflexion gives way to active dorsiflexion, pulling the body weight over the ankle. The foot now becomes slightly everted, and push off occurs by strong plantarflexion at the ankle, the final thrust being given by flexor hallucis longus as the leg moves once more into the swinging phase.

It will be noted that during walking many muscles act in the opposite manner to that usually described, in that the distal attachment, insertion, remains fairly static while the contracting muscle moves the proximal bone from which it arises. This reverse action of muscles is of greater importance in the lower than the upper limbs (p. 22.42).

MAINTENANCE OF BALANCE DURING WALKING

The tilting action of the pelvis during walking tends to move the centre of gravity and line of the body weight from side to side. This tilt is steadied and compensated for by contraction of the erector spinae and abdominal muscles on the side opposite to the contracting hip abductors, i.e. on the side of the swinging limb, to prevent the thorax falling over too far laterally. This tilting action is also counterbalanced by the swinging of the arms, the right arm swinging forward as the left leg is swinging. Arm swinging also contributes to the forward momentum achieved during walking.

The invertors and evertors of the foot keep the body stable on each foot during walking, another example of reverse action, and they are particularly active when walking over uneven ground. The short flexors of the toes, the flexor accessorius, interossei and lumbricals are important in improving the grip of the foot on the ground.

RUNNING

The mechanics of running are similar to those of walking. The main differences are that the trunk is inclined further forward, the movements are more powerful and exaggerated and there is an interval of time between push off of the supporting leg and the landing of the swinging leg, so that body is momentarily unsupported. In running the touch down is not made with the heel, but on the metatarsal heads.

FASCIA OF THE LOWER LIMB

The whole lower limb, like the upper limb, is enclosed in a sleeve of deep fascia which blends proximally with the deep fascia of the trunk. It is attached to bone along the outer lip of the iliac crest and along the pubic crest and ischiopubic ramus of the pelvis. In the leg it is attached to the anterior and medial margins of the tibia, so that the anteromedial surface of the tibia, the shin, is devoid of deep fascia.

The deep fascia maintains the smooth shape of the limb and assists the muscles in returning venous blood. From the covering sleeve of deep fascia various septa pass deeply to be attached to the long bones of the limb. These septa divide the muscles into groups, each muscle in a group having a similar action; they are known as **intermuscular septa** and produce functional muscle compartments.

Various portions of the deep fascia of the lower limb show special peculiarities which deserve more detailed description. The deep fascia of the thigh is thick, and is given the name **fascia lata.** This fascia is attached proximally to the inguinal ligament and, to the whole of the outer lip of the iliac crest; it blends with the fascia on the posterior aspect of the sacrum and is attached medially to the ischial tuber and ischiopubic ramus, to the body of the pubis and to the pubic crest.

In its upper part it splits to enclose two muscles, the tensor fasciae latae anterolaterally and the gluteus maximus muscle posteriorly. These two muscles converge on and are attached to a considerably thickened portion of the fascia lata, the **iliotibial tract** (fig. 23.7). This tract commences about the level of the greater trochanter and, passing vertically down the posterolateral aspect of the thigh, it passes lateral to the knee joint to be attached to the anterior surface of the lateral tibial condyle. Gluteus maximus and tensor fasciae latae thus exert an action on the knee joint. Their pull through the tract maintains the knee in the extended position and acts most powerfully in stabilizing the knee when weight is being taken on the semiflexed knee. During this movement, which is important in walking, the tract can be felt most easily.

The fascia lata is attached distally to the patella, to the inferior margins of the tibial condyles and to the head of the fibula. Posteriorly it blends with the popliteal fascia. A defect is present over the upper part of the femoral triangle. This defect, known as the **saphenous opening,** is about 1 cm in diameter and in the adult is situated about 4 cm below and lateral to the pubic tubercle. Through this opening the great saphenous vein reaches the femoral vein. Lymphatics from the superficial inguinal nodes and superficial branches of the femoral artery also pass through the opening. A thin layer of loose fascia which covers the saphenous opening is perforated by all these structures and hence receives the name of **cribriform fascia** (fig. 23.61).

The femoral vessels, as they pass out of the abdomen into the thigh, draw with them an extension of the extra-peritoneal transversalis fascia (fig. 23.40). This funnel-shaped prolongation of fascia fuses with the adventitia of the femoral vessels about 2 cm below the inguinal ligament and is known as the **femoral sheath** (p. 20.27). The femoral nerve, which is not included in the femoral sheath, lies lateral to the artery.

Three **intermuscular septa** pass in from the deep fascia of the thigh to be attached to the linea aspera of the femur (fig. 23.41). The lateral intermuscular septum arises from the deep surface of the iliotibial tract. The three functional muscular compartments produced by these

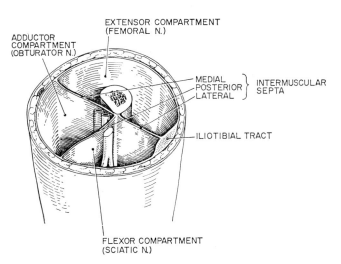

FIG. 23.41. Fascial compartments of the thigh.

septa contain respectively adductors of the hip, extensors of the knee and flexors of the knee. Note that the femoral vessels leave the adductor compartment to pass into the flexor compartment through the opening in adductor magnus.

The fascial arrangements in the leg are shown in fig. 23.42; the posterior compartment is divided into anterior and posterior subdivisions by a deep septum. This separates the superficial plantar flexors, soleus and gastrocnemius, from the long flexors passing to the foot. The tibial nerve and vessels lie deep to this layer of fascia.

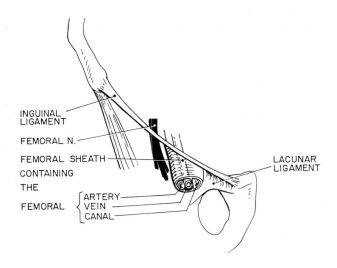

FIG. 23.40. Femoral sheath and canal.

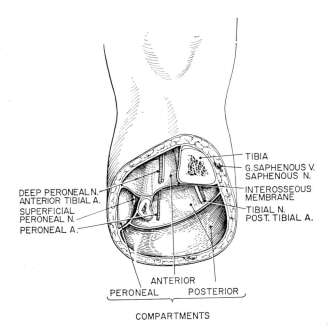

FIG. 23.42. Osteofascial compartments of the leg.

Fig. 23.43. Retinacula at the ankle.

The thickenings of the deep fascia which form **retinacula** at the ankle, and the associated synovial sheaths, are shown in fig. 23.43. The fibrous flexor sheaths in the toes are lined with synovial sheaths and are similar to those described in the fingers (p. 22.24).

The deep fascia of the sole of the foot is similar to that in the hand. The central part is thickened and is known as the **plantar aponeurosis.** Attached posteriorly to the posterior tubercles of the calcaneum, this aponeurosis covers the flexor digitorum brevis and widens as it runs forward to divide into five slips, one for each toe. As in the hand, these slips are attached to the proximal borders of the fibrous flexor sheaths and to the sides of the metatarsophalangeal joints. In contrast to the big toe, however, the thumb does not receive a slip from the palmar aponeurosis, as this would limit its mobility. The plantar aponeurosis assists in the maintenance of the longitudinal arches of the foot (p. 23.25).

Bursae

The important bursa at the hip joint lies between the iliopsoas tendon and the capsule of the hip joint. This often communicates with the joint through the weak area in the capsule (fig. 23.5a).

Many bursae are present around the knee and five are worth special mention:

(1) A prepatellar bursa lies between the skin and patella.

(2) An infrapatellar bursa lies between the skin and ligamentum patellae.

(3) Two bursae lie between the heads of gastrocnemius and the posterior aspect of the knee joint. The bursa beneath the medial head always communicates with the knee joint.

(4) One bursa lies between semimembranosus and the knee joint and usually opens into the joint.

(5) The suprapatellar bursa, deep to the quadriceps tendon, is a direct extension of the synovial membrane of the knee joint (p. 23.10).

When kneeling, friction between the skin and these underlying hard structures can cause inflammation; housemaid's knee is inflammation of the prepatellar bursa and clergyman's knee affects the infrapatellar bursa.

At the ankle the important bursa lies between tendo calcaneus and the upper third of posterior surface of calcaneus.

NERVES OF THE LOWER LIMB

The nerves supplying the lower limb arise over a wide area of the spinal cord, from the twelfth thoracic segment above to the fifth sacral segment below (fig. 23.44). The

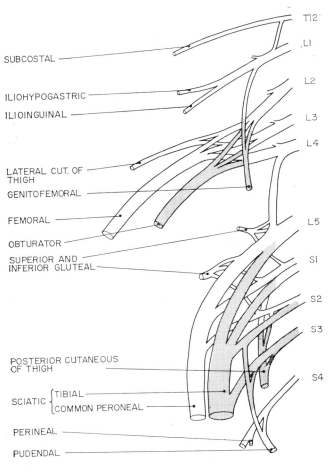

FIG. 23.44. Simplified diagram of the lumbosacral plexus, which omits small muscular branches. Dorsal divisions are clear and ventral divisions stippled (cf. fig. 22.59).

muscles are supplied entirely by the ventral primary rami of the nerves. The dorsal primary rami of the first three lumbar nerves and the sacral nerves assist in the cutaneous innervation of the limb by supplying the skin over the buttock (fig. 23.52 and 20.53).

The ventral primary rami of the lumbar and sacral regions form two complex plexuses, the **lumbar plexus** and the **sacral plexus,** which share a common nerve at L4. These are described on p. 20.42, and only the nerves which supply the limb are discussed here.

Branches of the lumbar plexus

The **genitofemoral nerve** (L1, 2) emerges on the anterior surface of psoas major near the pelvic brim and runs down to leave the abdomen on the anterior aspect of the external iliac artery. Its genital branch traverses the inguinal canal, supplying cremaster muscle, while the femoral branch supplies the skin over the upper part of the thigh (fig. 23.53).

The **lateral cutaneous nerve of thigh** (L2, 3) traverses the iliac fossa lying on iliacus to leave the abdomen by piercing the inguinal ligament near the anterior superior iliac spine. It is distributed to the skin on the lateral side of the thigh (figs. 23.53).

The **obturator nerve** (L2, 3, 4) emerges in the pelvis from behind the medial border of psoas and runs on the side wall of the pelvis towards the obturator foramen. It is accompanied in the pelvic part of its course by the obturator vessels and escapes from the pelvis through the obturator groove at the upper part of the foramen. The obturator nerve supplies the obturator externus muscle, the adductor muscles of the hip (fig. 23.51) and the hip joint itself. A cutaneous branch often accompanies the saphenous nerve to supply the medial aspect of the lower third of the thigh, and a genicular branch descends on adductor magnus to reach the knee joint posteriorly.

The **femoral nerve** (L2, 3 and 4) is the largest branch of the lumbar plexus. It emerges from the lateral border of psoas major below the iliac crest and runs between psoas major and iliacus to enter the thigh by passing behind the inguinal ligament. As it enters the thigh it is an immediate lateral relation of the femoral artery, which separates it from the femoral vein (fig. 23.40). The nerve runs only a very short course in the thigh before breaking up into numerous branches (fig. 23.45).

The muscular branches separate to the four components of quadriceps, to sartorius and pectineus. The nerve thus supplies the flexors of the hip joint and the extensor muscle of the knee. The cutaneous branches run into the medial and intermediate cutaneous nerves of the thigh and the saphenous nerve which is distributed to the medial side of knee, calf and heel (fig. 23.53).

The region of the thigh where the femoral nerve breaks up is known as the **femoral triangle,** the boundaries of which are the inguinal ligament above, the sartorius muscle laterally and the medial border of adductor longus medially (fig. 23.45). The floor of this triangle is gutter shaped and is made up of iliacus, psoas major, pectineus and adductor longus. The roof of the triangle is the strong fascia lata of the leg, and it is pierced by the great saphenous vein which joins the femoral vein in the triangle. The profunda femoris artery arises from the femoral artery in the triangle and passes posteriorly behind adductor longus. The femoral vein lies posterior to its artery in the lower part of the triangle and is separated from the profunda

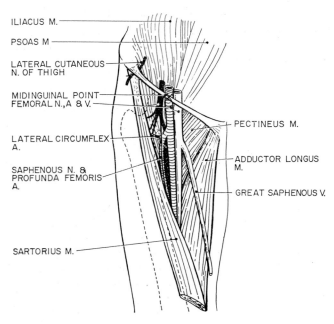

FIG. 23.45. The femoral triangle. Superficial branches of the femoral artery are omitted.

FIG. 23.46. The adductor canal. The roof, formed by the sartorius muscle, has been removed and the femoral vein is omitted for clarity. In the section through X–X shown below, the vessels and nerve occupy part of the adductor canal.

femoris vein lying anterior to its artery by the adductor longus muscle.

The **saphenous nerve** leaves the femoral triangle at its apex on the lateral side of the femoral artery, and enters the **adductor canal** (fig. 23.46). This canal lies between the vastus medialis laterally and the adductor muscles posteriorly. It has a roof of fascia, which is covered by the sartorius muscle. The femoral artery and vein leave the canal at the opening in adductor magnus to reach the popliteal fossa. The saphenous nerve spirals round the artery, passing first on to the anterior aspect of the artery and then lying slightly medial to it. Below the adductor hiatus, the nerve is accompanied by the descending genicular branch of the femoral artery. It emerges from the canal posterior to sartorius and in front of gracilis, just below the knee, and runs down in the company of the great saphenous vein to supply the skin of the medial side of the leg and heel. Just before it leaves the adductor canal it gives off an infrapatellar branch to the skin around the knee and to the knee joint (fig. 23.46).

Branches of the sacral plexus

The **sciatic nerve** is the largest nerve in the body and the main nerve of the lower limb (figs. 23.44 and 47). It is formed by contributions from all the ventral rami concerned in the sacral plexus; the ventral divisions of the rami eventually form the tibial nerve, and the dorsal divisions form the common peroneal nerve. The sciatic

nerve leaves the pelvis below the lower border of the piriformis muscle and enters the gluteal region. There it inclines laterally across obturator internus tendon to reach the space between the ischial tuber and the greater trochanter of the femur. It then runs downwards in the thigh on the posterior surface of the adductor magnus muscle. Intramuscular injections into the buttock should always be given into the upper outer quadrant to avoid damage to the sciatic nerve.

The sciatic nerve gives off no branches in the gluteal region, and its course in the thigh and its distribution is considered in more detail on the next page.

The **superior gluteal nerve** (L4, 5, S1) leaves the pelvis above the piriformis muscle in the company of the gluteal artery. In the buttock it passes laterally between the gluteus medius and minimus muscles, along with the deep division

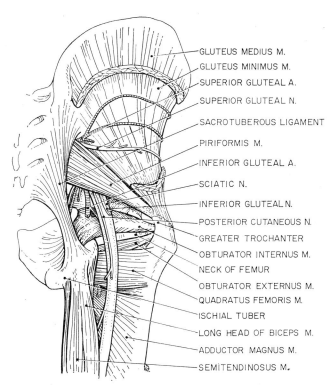

FIG. 23.47. The gluteal region after removal of gluteus maximus muscle. A portion of the gluteus medius muscle has been resected and the gemelli muscles, above and below the tendon of obturator internus, have been omitted to reveal the back of the hip joint capsule.

of the superior gluteal artery. After supplying both these muscles it reaches the deep surface of tensor fasciae latae in which it ends (fig. 23.47).

The **inferior gluteal nerve** (L5, S1, 2) leaves the pelvis below the piriformis, lying posterior to the sciatic nerve, and at once enters the overlying gluteus maximus muscle which is all it supplies.

The **nerve to quadratus femoris** (L4, 5, S1) passes out of the lower part of the greater sciatic foramen, and closely applied to the ischium it runs deep to obturator internus and gemelli to reach quadratus femoris. It also supplies the inferior gemellus.

The **nerve to obturator internus** (L5, S1, 2) is described on p. 20.44.

The **posterior cutaneous nerve of thigh** (S1, 2, 3) is the largest purely cutaneous branch of the sacral plexus. It enters the gluteal region along with the inferior gluteal artery and nerve and then runs downwards on the posterior surface of the sciatic nerve. Several small gluteal branches curve upwards over the lower border of gluteus maximus to supply the skin of the lower part of the buttock while a perineal branch runs forward to supply the skin of the perineum and posterior part of the scrotum. The main trunk of the nerve gives off branches to the posterior

aspect of the thigh, finally becoming expended behind the knee.

The **perforating cutaneous nerve** (S2, 3) pierces the sacrotuberous ligament and lower part of gluteus maximus to supply a small area of skin in the inferomedial region of the buttock.

The course and distribution of the sciatic nerve

In the thigh, the sciatic nerve runs downwards on the posterior surface of adductor magnus. It passes deep to the long head of biceps femoris (fig. 23.48) and at a variable position in the thigh divides into its two major components, the tibial and common peroneal nerves. Unlike the other major nerves of the limb, femoral and obturator, it does not have an accompanying large artery, but a small branch of the inferior gluteal artery accompanies and supplies it.

The sciatic nerve supplies muscular branches to the hamstring muscles. With the exception of the branch to the short head of the biceps, which arises from the common peroneal part, these branches all arise from the tibial component of the nerve. The adductor magnus muscle is innervated by two nerves, the sciatic and the obturator (fig. 23.9). The sciatic nerve supplies the vertical fibres of this muscle, those attached to the ischial tuber, which act as a hamstring muscle to extend the hip, while the obturator nerve supplies the more oblique fibres to the shaft of the femur which act as an adductor muscle.

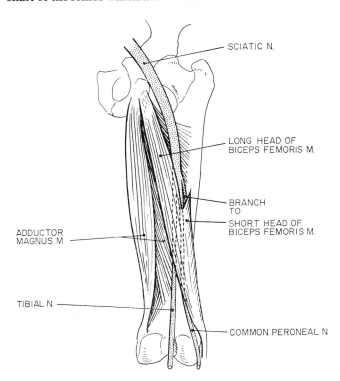

FIG. 23.48. The course of the sciatic nerve.

The two terminal branches of the sciatic nerve enter the **popliteal fossa** near its apex (fig. 23.49). This diamond-shaped fossa is situated behind the knee and lower femur,

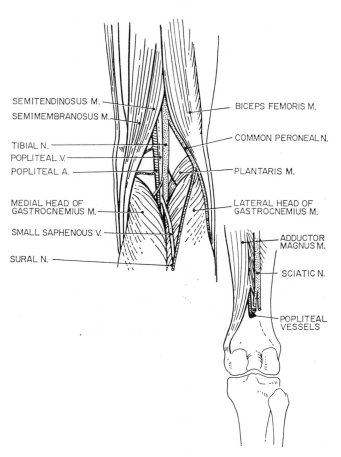

FIG. 23.49. Right popliteal fossa.

and is bounded above and laterally by the biceps femoris and above and medially by the semimembranosus and semitendinosus muscles. Its lower boundaries are formed by the two heads of the gastrocnemius muscle. The floor of the fossa is the popliteal surface of the femur and the upper part of the posterior capsule of the knee joint. The fossa is covered superficially by deep fascia of the leg, which is slightly thickened in this region, and called the **popliteal fascia**.

The **common peroneal (lateral popliteal) nerve** (L4, 5, S1, 2 and 3) inclines laterally across the upper part of the fossa to pass superficial to the lateral head of gastrocnemius. It continues on this superficial course behind the head of the fibula and winds around the neck of this bone, where it can easily be felt, to enter the substance of peroneus longus. It gives off branches in the fossa. The lateral cutaneous nerve of the calf pierces the popliteal fascia to reach its cutaneous distribution over the lateral aspect of

the upper calf. A branch descends deep to the deep fascia to join the sural nerve in the back of the calf.

The **tibial (medial popliteal) nerve** (L4, 5, S1 and 2) crosses the popliteal fossa with the popliteal vessels to leave the fossa by passing deep to the gastrocnemius. In its course through the fossa, the nerve is superficial to the vein and the popliteal artery runs deep to them both. In the lower part of the fossa, the small saphenous vein pierces the popliteal fascia to enter the popliteal vein. After leaving the popliteal fossa, the tibial nerve descends on the posterior surface of the popliteus muscle and enters the calf by passing deep to the tendinous arch between the tibial and fibular attachments of soleus (fig. 23.50). In the popliteal fossa, the tibial nerve gives off numerous branches. One cutaneous branch, the **sural nerve**, runs downwards beneath the deep fascia, which it pierces near the middle of the back of the calf, and continues to the lateral side of the foot. Branches from the upper part of this nerve pierce the deep fascia to reach the skin of the posterior part of the upper calf. Muscular branches pass to plantaris, both heads of gastrocnemius, popliteus and soleus. Articular branches accompany the genicular arteries to the knee joint.

The nerves in the leg and foot

In the substance of peroneus longus on the neck of the fibula, the common peroneal nerve divides into superficial and deep peroneal nerves.

The **deep peroneal (anterior tibial) nerve** continues to spiral round the neck of the fibula, deep to extensor digitorum longus, until it reaches the interosseous membrane

FIG. 23.50. Vessels and nerves of the leg. The tibialis anterior muscle has been removed from the anterior view, seen on the left.

lateral to the anterior tibial vessels (fig. 23.50). It runs down the leg with these vessels lying between tibialis anterior medially and extensor digitorum longus and then extensor hallucis longus laterally. In the lower part of the leg the extensor hallucis longus muscle crosses superficially to reach the medial side of the nerve, so that at the ankle joint it lies between tibialis anterior and extensor hallucis longus tendons medially, and extensor digitorum longus and peroneus tertius tendons laterally.

The nerve continues forward on the dorsum of the foot lying deep to the extensor digitorum tendons to reach the first interdigital cleft, the skin of which it supplies; this is the only cutaneous branch of the deep peroneal nerve. Muscular branches pass to the long extensors, tibialis anterior and peroneus tertius in the leg and extensor digitorum brevis in the foot (fig. 23.51). These muscles dorsiflex the ankle, extend the toes, and contribute to inversion and eversion of the foot. It also sends articular branches to the ankle joint.

The **superficial peroneal (musculocutaneous) nerve** runs downwards in the substance of peroneus longus and then comes to lie between peroneus brevis and longus, which it supplies before becoming subcutaneous by piercing the deep fascia two thirds of the way down the leg. It then passes on to the dorsum of the foot and breaks up into digital branches into the toes, supplying the dorsum of all the toes apart from the lateral side of the fifth toe (sural nerve) and the adjacent sides of hallux and second toe (deep peroneal nerve).

The **tibial nerve** runs vertically down the leg closely applied to the fascia covering the deep surface of soleus. It emerges from the cover of soleus in the lower third of the leg, and passes behind the medial malleolus lying between the tendons of tibialis posterior and flexor digitorum longus medially, and flexor hallucis longus laterally. In its course in the calf it is accompanied by the posterior tibial vessels. At a point midway between the medial malleolus and the medial prominence of the heel, the tibial nerve divides into its terminal branches, the medial and lateral plantar nerves. It supplies the muscular branches to the deep surface of soleus muscle, to tibialis posterior and to the flexors digitorum and hallucis longus. These muscles contribute to plantar flexion at the ankle, to inversion of the foot, and flexion of the toes. Through the cutaneous branches it supplies a small area of skin on the medial side of the heel. Finally it supplies the ankle joint via the articular branches.

The two **plantar nerves** supply all the small muscles in the sole of the foot and the skin of the sole. They follow the course of the plantar arteries (fig. 23.60).

The **medial plantar nerve** runs forward under cover of abductor hallucis and crosses superficial to the flexor hallucis longus and flexor digitorum longus tendon to lie on flexor hallucis brevis. It gives off cutaneous branches to the sole which pass through the interval between ab-ductor hallucis and flexor digitorum brevis and then pierce the deep fascia of the foot. It then divides into digital cutaneous branches for the medial three and a half toes. Its muscular supply is limited to muscles close to its course i.e. abductor hallucis, flexor digitorum brevis, flexor hallucis brevis and, usually, the first lumbrical (fig. 23.51).

The remaining muscles of the foot are supplied by the **lateral plantar nerve**, which crosses the sole of the foot on the medial side of the lateral plantar artery, passing between flexor digitorum brevis and flexor accessorius to the deep surface of abductor digiti minimi. It supplies both flexor accessorius and abductor digiti minimi and sends cutaneous branches to the lateral part of the sole before dividing into superficial and deep branches under the base of the fifth metatarsal. The superficial branch sends a cutaneous branch which divides to supply the skin of the plantar surface of the little toe and the lateral part of the fourth toe. It supplies muscular branches to the flexor digiti minimi brevis, and the interosseous muscles of the fourth interosseous space (third plantar and fourth dorsal). The deep branch passes deeply into the sole and lies in the concavity of the plantar arch across the bases of the metatarsals deep to the long flexor tendons. It supplies branches to the remaining muscles of the foot and ends in the substance of the oblique head of adductor hallucis.

The lateral plantar nerve is similar to the ulnar nerve in the hand, while the medial plantar nerve resembles the median nerve.

Nerve distribution in the lower limb

Movements at joints are regulated by centres in the spinal cord, and fig. 23.55 illustrates the spinal segments involved in leg movements. Familiarity with this diagram and a knowledge of the action of any muscle, determines the segmental supply of that muscle. Such knowledge is of importance in localizing injury or disease in the spinal cord. The segmental nerve supply of the joints of the limb is the same as that of the muscles producing movement at the joints.

The muscular distribution of the main nerves is given in fig. 23.51 and the cutaneous nerve distribution and the segmental dermatomes are shown in fig. 23.52 and 53.

Autonomic nerve supply to the lower limb

The sympathetic nerve supply to the blood vessels, arrector pili muscles and sweat glands of the lower limb arise in the spinal cord from segments T12 to L2.

White rami pass to the sympathetic ganglia from these nerves. Branches from the ganglia pass into the aortic plexus and also back to the peripheral nerves. From the aortic plexus, sympathetic fibres accompany the iliac arteries and pass to the limb. These fibres tend to supply only the more proximal part of the limb, the more distal parts being supplied by fibres carried in the peripheral nerves.

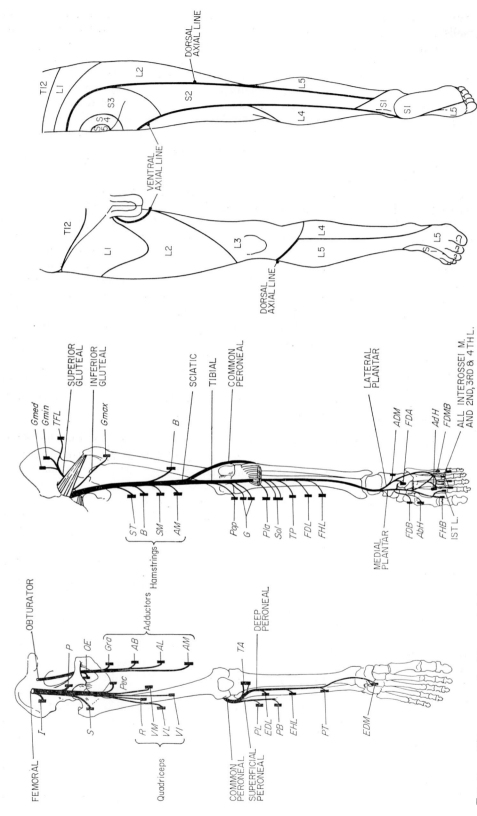

FIG. 23.52. Dermatomes of lower limb, showing segmental cutaneous distribution of spinal nerves on (a) the front, and (b) the back of the limb. From Cunningham (1961) *Textbook of Anatomy*, London: Oxford University Press.

FIG. 23.51. The nerve supply of the muscles of the lower limb. Abbreviations are as given on the diagrams of the muscles.

FIG. 23.54. Main arteries of the lower limb, seen from in front.

FIG. 23.53. Distribution of cutaneous nerves on (a) the front, and (b) the back of the lower limb. There is considerable variation in these territories and the extent to which they overlap each other.

FIG. 23.55. Segmental nerves and movements in the lower limb. From Last R.J. (1963) *Anatomy: Regional and Applied*, 3rd edition. London : Churchill.

BLOOD VESSELS OF THE LOWER LIMB
ARTERIES

Each limb has a single main artery which carries the blood necessary for the function of the limb (fig. 23.54). Branches of this artery supply the various muscles, bones and joints. Such a simple arrangement suffers from the disadvantage that an injury or disease of the main arterial trunk causing blockage would result in the death of the limb distal to the obstruction unless alternative pathways to the distal parts were available. Hence, many of the branches of the main arterial vessel anastomose with branches given off lower down the vessel, providing a collateral circulation.

The collateral circulation of the lower limbs is not so efficient as in the upper limb but is important since in old age arterial disease and obstruction is common. It is discussed in greater detail following a brief description of the arteries of the limb.

The major blood supply to the lower limb is carried by the **femoral artery,** though the gluteal region is supplied from within the pelvis by the **gluteal arteries,** branches of the internal iliac; the upper part of the adductor muscles of the thigh receive their blood supply from the **obturator artery.**

Branches from the internal iliac artery

The superior and inferior gluteal arteries both arise inside the pelvis. The **superior gluteal artery** enters the gluteal region by passing through the greater sciatic notch above piriformis, and divides into a superficial and deep branch (fig. 23.47). The superficial branch supplies mainly gluteus maximus, while the deep branch runs forward between gluteus medius and minimus. Both these divisions anastomose freely with one another, with branches of the inferior gluteal artery, and particularly with ascending branches of the medial and lateral circumflex vessels. The **inferior gluteal artery** passes out of the pelvis through the greater sciatic notch below piriformis and runs downwards posteromedial to the sciatic nerve to reach the proximal part of the thigh. It supplies numerous muscular branches to the buttock muscles and hip joint before anastomosing freely with neighbouring vessels.

The **obturator artery** is a small branch of the internal iliac artery, which leaves the pelvis through the obturator foramen. It sends a branch to the hip joint, and muscular branches to the proximal parts of the adductor muscles. By anastomosing with the profunda femoris, it contributes to the anastomosis around the hip (fig. 23.56).

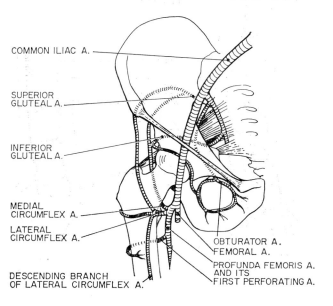

FIG. 23.56. Anastomoses around the hip joint.

The femoral artery

The aorta bifurcates in the abdomen at the level of the fourth lumbar vertebra into the common iliac arteries. At the pelvic brim the common iliac artery divides into the internal iliac artery, which supplies blood to the pelvis and gluteal region, and the external iliac artery which continues along the pelvic brim, carrying the major part of the blood supply to the limb. The external iliac artery gives off the inferior epigastric artery immediately before it passes from the abdomen behind the inguinal ligament at the midinguinal point. As it enters the thigh, it is called the **femoral artery,** and its pulsations can easily be felt below the midinguinal point. The femoral artery gives off four small branches below the inguinal ligament, which supply the skin of the upper thigh, the scrotum and adjoining abdominal wall.

The femoral artery continues down the leg, carrying blood to the knee, leg and foot. It passes downwards in the adductor canal deep to sartorius muscle and reaches the back of the thigh by passing through the opening in adductor magnus (figs. 23.46 and 49). This part of the femoral artery is often called, by clinicians, the superficial femoral artery to distinguish it from the **profunda femoris artery,**

a large branch of the femoral which arises 4 cm below the inguinal ligament. The profunda femoris artery passes deep to the femoral artery to reach the posteromedial aspect of the femur. It supplies many branches to the muscles of the thigh, **perforating branches** passing through the adductor magnus to curve round the posterior surface of the femur; medial and lateral circumflex arteries are the other named branches of the profunda femoris artery (figs. 23.56 and 57). The **lateral circumflex artery** is more superficial, and supplies branches to the muscles in front

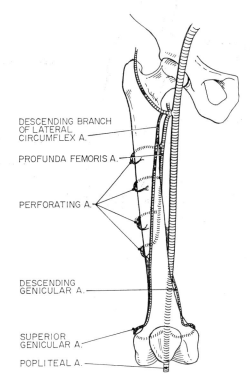

FIG. 23.57. Anastomoses in the thigh.

of the hip joint and to vastus lateralis, and sends an ascending branch anterior to the hip joint to reach the tensor fasciae latae. The **medial circumflex artery** passes deeply into the thigh to pass medial to the femur below the hip joint, supplying muscles as it goes. It supplies branches to the hip joint and its surrounding short muscles. The branches of the profunda femoris artery play an important part in providing a collateral circulation when the flow through the femoral artery is obstructed.

THE POPLITEAL ARTERY

When the femoral artery passes through the opening in adductor magnus to reach the back of the thigh, it becomes the popliteal artery. The popliteal artery passes downwards lying close to the popliteal surface of the femur, where it is liable to injury in fractures of the femur. The artery then passes posterior to the capsule of the knee joint and to popliteus, at the lower margin of which muscle it ends by dividing into the anterior and posterior tibial arteries (fig. 23.50). This is about the level of the neck of the fibula. The popliteal artery gives off muscular and genicular branches (fig. 23.58) which supply the knee joint and its capsule.

FIG. 23.58. Anastomoses around the knee, showing the genicular arteries.

THE POSTERIOR TIBIAL ARTERY

The posterior tibial artery is the larger of the two divisions of the popliteal artery and passes deep to soleus muscle and the fascia clothing the deep surface of this muscle (fig. 23.50). As it passes down the leg, it remains close to the tibial nerve (p. 23.32). It can be palpated easily at the ankle, halfway between the medial malleolus and the medial prominence of the heel. The artery ends at this point, dividing into the main arteries of the sole of the foot, the medial and lateral plantar arteries.

The main branch of the posterior tibial artery is the **peroneal artery,** which is given off about 5 cm below popliteus. As it passes down the limb it inclines laterally across the posterior aspect of the tibialis posterior to lie between that muscle and flexor hallucis longus in close relationship to the fibula. It gives off a **perforating branch** which passes through the interosseous membrane just

above the inferior tibiofibular joint (fig. 23.59). The peroneal artery then passes behind the lateral malleolus to end as branches on the lateral side of the heel.

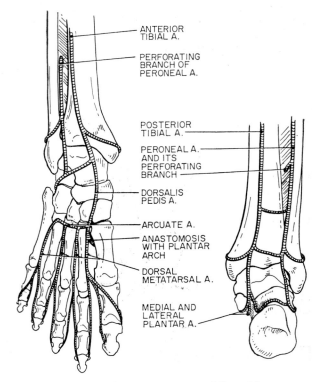

FIG. 23.59. Anastomoses around the ankle.

The posterior tibial and peroneal arteries supply branches to the muscles of the calf, to the ankle and inferior tibiofibular joints and to the tibia and fibula respectively.

THE PLANTAR ARTERIES

The medial and lateral plantar arteries arise from the termination of the posterior tibial artery below the medial malleolus (fig. 23.60).

The **medial plantar artery,** which corresponds to the radial artery in the hand, is the smaller of the two and runs forward along the medial side of the foot between abductor hallucis brevis and flexor digitorum brevis to end as the medial digital artery of the big toe. Near the first metatarsophalangeal joint it anastomoses with the medial branch of the first plantar metatarsal artery. It supplies muscular branches to the two adjacent muscles, and cutaneous branches to the skin on the medial side of the foot.

The **lateral plantar artery** is much larger and corresponds to the ulnar artery in the hand. It crosses to the lateral side of the foot, accompanying the lateral plantar nerve, and passes between flexor digitorum brevis and flexor digitorum accessorius; it then runs forward between abductor

FIG. 23.60. Arteries in the sole of the foot.

digiti minimi and flexor digitorum brevis to reach the medial side of the base of the fifth metatarsal. It then passes deep, and arches across the sole of the foot, under the bases of the metatarsals, to anastomose with the dorsalis pedis artery; this portion of the artery is known as the **plantar arch.**

The lateral plantar artery gives off cutaneous branches to the sole and lateral side of the foot, and muscular branches to the small vessels of the foot. From the plantar arch arise the **four plantar metatarsal arteries,** each of which runs forward on the interosseous muscles to divide near the heads of the metatarsals into two **digital arteries** which supply the medial and lateral sides of adjacent digits (fig. 23.60). Three **perforating arteries** also rise from the plantar arch, passing through the lateral three inter-metatarsal spaces to anastomose with the corresponding **dorsal metatarsal arteries.**

THE ANTERIOR TIBIAL ARTERY

From its origin this artery passes forwards below the popliteus muscle to reach the anterior compartment of the leg by passing over the upper border of the interosseous membrane (fig. 23.50). It runs down the leg with the deep peroneal nerve (p. 23.32). Passing in front of the ankle joint it lies between the tendons of extensor hallucis longus and extensor digitorum longus to reach the dorsum of the foot, where it becomes known as the dorsalis pedis artery. The anterior tibial artery may be palpated at the level of the ankle joint, and the dorsalis pedis may be palpated in its course over the dorsum of the foot.

The artery gives off muscular branches and two recurrent arteries supply the knee joint.

DORSALIS PEDIS ARTERY (fig. 23.59)

The direct continuation of the anterior tibial artery, this vessel begins in front of the ankle joint and runs forward over the dorsum of the tarsus. It ends by passing downwards between the heads of the first dorsal interosseous muscle to anastomose in the sole with the lateral plantar artery (plantar arch). A branch called the **arcuate artery** runs laterally deep to the extensor tendons and gives off three dorsal metatarsal arteries.

Collateral circulation of the limb

The anastomoses which provide for the collateral circulation tend to be best developed around the major joints like the hip, knee and ankle. Additionally there is an important anastomotic chain in the thigh. These are all illustrated in figs. 23.56–59. The anastomosis around the hip is important since it allows communication between branches of the internal iliac artery, which supplies the pelvis and gluteal region, and branches of the femoral artery from the limb itself. Thus an arterial obstruction even as high as the external iliac artery does not prevent blood reaching the leg provided this anastomotic pathway is patent.

VENOUS DRAINAGE

The veins of the leg may be divided into two groups, superficial and deep, which are united at intervals by communicating veins.

Superficial veins (fig. 23.61)

These veins drain the skin and subcutaneous tissues. The veins from the toes form metatarsal veins which run into a small plantar and a larger dorsal venous arch on the foot. The medial ends of these arches join the great saphenous vein, while the lateral ends join the small saphenous vein.

The **great (long) saphenous vein** ascends in the subcutaneous tissues across the medial malleolus, and as it passes up the leg with the saphenous nerve it receives further tributaries. It crosses the knee posteromedially to the medial condyles of the femur and then inclines slightly medially across the thigh. It pierces the deep fascia of the leg, at a point 4 cm below and lateral to the pubic tubercle, to enter the femoral vein. Just before it pierces the deep fascia, it receives quite large tributaries from the medial aspect of the thigh, from the lower abdominal wall and from the scrotum.

The **small (short) saphenous vein** ascends posterior to the lateral malleolus and runs upwards in the subcutaneous tissues of the calf alongside the sural nerve. It pierces the deep fascia behind the knee and enters the popliteal vein.

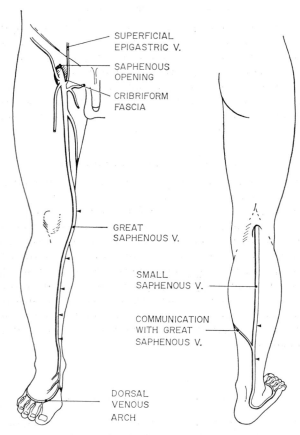

FIG. 23.61 Superficial veins of the lower limb. Many tributaries are omitted and the common sites of communication with deep veins are shown by arrows.

Deep veins

The deep veins are formed by tributaries arising in the muscles, bones and joints of the leg. The small muscular veins join to form venae comitantes which accompany the arteries, and there are no named deep veins until the venae comitantes of the anterior and posterior tibial arteries unite at the lower border of popliteus to form the **popliteal vein,** which initially lies posteromedial to the artery. As the vein ascends, it crosses posterior to the artery separating it from the tibial nerve (fig. 23.49) to lie posterolateral to it as it passes through the adductor magnus opening into the thigh and becomes the femoral vein.

The femoral vein ascends alongside the femoral artery and inclines slightly medially to become a posterior relation of the artery. The **profunda femoris vein** joins the femoral vein 5 cm below the inguinal ligament and at this point these two large veins separate the femoral and profunda femoris arteries. The femoral vein now inclines more medially, and as it leaves the thigh by passing behind the inguinal ligament to become the external iliac vein, it lies medial to the artery (fig. 23.40).

LYMPH DRAINAGE

The lymphatic drainage tends to follow the venous drainage, with the lymphatics from tissues deep to the deep fascia following the deep veins, and the lymphatics from skin and superficial tissues following the saphenous veins. The superficial lymphatic drainage is shown in fig. 23.62.

FIG. 23.62. Superficial lymphatic drainage of the lower limb.

Lymph nodes

The lymphatic vessels drain into lymph nodes, which are situated in two places, behind the knee and in the groin.

The **popliteal nodes** are situated deep to the popliteal fascia. Lymphatic vessels accompanying the short saphenous vein enter these nodes and the lymph then passes onwards in the deep lymphatics which accompany the popliteal and femoral vein to the deep group of inguinal nodes.

The deep fascia divides the **inguinal nodes** into superficial and deep groups. The superficial nodes lie along the line of the inguinal ligament and along the upper part of the great saphenous vein. The former group receive lymph from the upper thigh, buttock and lower abdominal wall. The saphenous vein group drains the lymph from the superficial tissues of the leg. From both these groups of nodes the lymph passes through the cribriform fascia to the deep group of nodes.

The deep inguinal lymph nodes lie around the upper part of the femoral vein, and in addition to receiving lymph from the superficial nodes, they collect the lymph rom all the deep lymphatics in the leg. From the deep nguinal nodes, lymphatics accompany the external iliac vein to reach the abdominal lymph nodes. Like the veins, he lymphatic vessels are supplied with numerous valves and so again muscular activity aids the upward movement of the fluid.

MECHANISM OF FLUID RETURN

In order to assist the return of blood, the limb veins are supplied with valves, which prevent reflux of venous blood towards the periphery.

In the lower limb, these valves are particularly important, since the erect posture adds a considerable hydrostatic pressure opposing return of blood to the heart. The sucking action of the thorax during inspiration and the transmitted pressure from the arteries assist the venous return, but the most important mechanism promoting venous return from the limb is the contraction and relaxation of the limb muscles.

The whole limb and its muscular compartments are surrounded by tough, relatively inelastic, deep fascia (p. 23.26). When a muscle contracts, it squeezes on the blood contained in the deep veins within the deep fascial envelope. The blood is then pushed out of the muscular compartment, and because of the arrangement of the valves in the leg veins, it must pass upwards towards the heart. When the muscle relaxes, more blood enters the muscle from the arterial side, and from veins below it. Blood also enters the deep veins during this phase from the superficial veins, via the communicating veins, which also have valves to prevent reflux into the superficial veins. Repeated muscular contractions and relaxations thus keep the venous blood flowing.

These skeletal muscles can thus be compared to a peripheral muscle pump; the soleus muscle is particularly important. Guardsmen on parade faint because they do not move their leg muscles for long periods so that blood pools in their legs, resulting in impaired venous return and hence cardiac output, and the diminished cerebral arterial flow causes the faint.

Failure of function of the venous valves in the leg results in increased pressure on valves below them which may themselves fail, creating a further increase in pressure on lower valves. Failure of the valves in the communicating veins is particularly serious as the flow of blood in these veins during muscular contraction is reversed, so that blood flows from the deep to the superficial veins, resulting in localized dilatations of the superficial veins called **varicose veins.** Blockage of the deep veins by thrombosis also produces dilatation of superficial veins.

OSSIFICATION

As for the upper limbs (p. 22.41) the diagrams in fig. 23.63

19

show the parts of the bones ossified from primary and secondary centres. The approximate dates given for their appearance and fusion show the usual sequence.

SURFACE ANATOMY

The length and direction of the long bones determine the basic form of the limb, which may be long, short, straight, knock-kneed or bowed. The femora slant inwards from the acetabula to the knees, and in the adult female this angulation is more marked than in the male because of the shorter length of the femur and the greater width of the pelvis. As discussed on p. 23.23 the shape of the bones in the foot is an important factor in maintaining the arches and hence the shape of the foot.

The general shape of the limb is given by the muscles within their fascial envelopes surrounding the bones. The rather stark outline which this produces is smoothed out by the layer of subcutaneous fat. In females, this layer is thicker than in males, particularly in the thighs and buttocks, giving a more rounded appearance to the female limb. In obese females excess fat deposits first appear in the buttocks and upper thighs.

The fullness of the buttock is due to the gluteus maximus muscle, and the size of the gluteal fat pad determines its final shape. The gluteal fold or buttock crease does not represent the lower border of gluteus maximus, which extends well below the gluteal fold on its way to its insertions into the gluteal tuberosity of the femur and the iliotibial tract.

The fusiform shape of the thigh is produced mainly by vastus intermedius and lateralis. The rounded muscular prominence above the anteromedial aspect of the knee is due to the lower fibres of vastus medialis. If the subject stands on one leg, with the knee slightly flexed, the iliotibial tract is easily felt, and is sometimes seen, passing to its insertion into the lateral condyle of the tibia. When the thigh is flexed, abducted and slightly laterally rotated, the sartorius muscle becomes prominent, coursing across the thigh. Posteriorly, the tendons of the hamstring muscles bordering the popliteal fossa may be seen and felt, particularly when the knee is flexed.

The shape of the calf is produced by the two heads of gastrocnemius and the underlying soleus. These muscles become tendinous forming the tendo calcaneus, which is easily seen and felt behind the ankle passing to its insertion into the calcaneus. The medial belly of gastrocnemius extends lower down than the lateral belly.

On the dorsum of the foot, the fleshy belly of the extensor digitorum brevis is felt proximally, and the tendons of tibialis anterior and the long extensor muscles can be seen and felt passing to their insertions.

Bony landmarks

The **anterior superior iliac spine** can be palpated at the anterior end of the iliac crest, and the **posterior superior iliac spine** is palpable at the posterior end.

The **pubic crest,** and the **pubic tubercle** at its lateral end can be palpated easily. The **inguinal ligament** passes between the pubic tubercle and the anterior superior iliac spine. The **midinguinal point** is that point on the inguinal ligament which lies midway between the anterior superior iliac spine and the pubic symphysis.

The **ischial tuber** is readily palpated as a thick bony mass in the lower part of the buttock, being separated from the tuber of the opposite side by a distance of one hand's breadth. The **greater trochanter** of the femur is subcutaneous and hence easily palpable in the lateral aspect of the upper thigh. If a line be drawn around the side of the buttock from the anterior superior iliac spine to the ischial tuber, it crosses the tip of the greater trochanter. This is known as **Nelaton's line,** and use is made of it in diagnosing dislocation of the hip or fracture of the femoral neck.

FIG. 23.63. Numbers on the bones indicate age, in years, of appearance of ossification centres. Stippled areas are cartilaginous at birth. Leaders show the time of fusion in years. IU, age in weeks of intrauterine life; B birth; P, puberty.

The shaft of the femur is clothed by muscles and hence is not readily palpable.

The **condyles** of the femur and tibia are subcutaneous and easily palpated at the knee. Between the femoral and tibial condyles anteriorly, the joint line can be palpated, particularly when the knee is flexed and the **patella** lies just above the level of the plane of the knee joint.

The **adductor tubercle** of the femur is felt as a sharp prominence immediately above the medial femoral condyle. The **tibial tuberosity** is palpated at the upper border of the shin, and the **ligamentum patellae** may be felt stretching between this tubercle and the lower pole of the patella.

The **head of the fibula** is seen and felt as a posterolateral prominence below the lateral tibial condyle. The tendon of biceps femoris is inserted into the apex of the head of the fibula and is easily felt here. The **neck of the fibula,** with the common peroneal nerve crossing it, is palpable immediately below the head.

The anteromedial surface of the **tibia,** and its sharp anterior border, forming the shin, are subcutaneous throughout their length, and hence easily palpable.

The **medial** (tibia) and **lateral** (fibula) **malleoli** form the subcutaneous prominences at each side of the ankle. The lateral malleolus extends 1 cm lower than the medial one. The prominence of the heel is produced by the calcaneum.

The **sustentaculum tali** can be palpated 2.5 cm distal to the tip of the medial malleolus, while 2·5 cm. anterior to the sustentaculum the **tuberosity of the navicular** is easily felt.

The **styloid process** of the fifth metatarsal forms the prominent projection half-way along the lateral border of the foot.

Soft tissue landmarks

The **femoral artery** may be felt pulsating in the upper part of the femoral triangle, below the midinguinal point. With the thigh laterally rotated and slightly flexed, draw a line between the midinguinal point and the adductor tubercle. The femoral artery follows a course corresponding to the upper two-thirds of this line.

The **great saphenous vein** passes through the saphenous opening in the deep fascia to join the femoral vein. This is surface marked by a point 4 cm below and lateral to the pubic tubercle.

The **sciatic nerve** enters the gluteal region at a point opposite the junction of the upper and middle thirds of a line joining the posterior superior iliac spine and the ischial tuber. It curves downwards and slightly laterally to pass into the thigh midway between the greater trochanter and the ischial tuber. The nerve therefore occupies the lower medial quadrant of the buttock.

In the thigh, the nerve runs slightly medial to the midline of the thigh, and it normally divides into its two main branches in the upper part of the popliteal fossa.

The **popliteal artery** may be represented by a line extending from a point just medial to the apex of the popliteal fossa above, to a point in the midline of the leg just below the level of the tibial condyle. The arterial pulsation may be palpated in the popliteal fossa, though this is sometimes difficult as the artery lies deep in the fossa. Palpation is facilitated by flexing the knee and compressing the artery against the popliteal surface of the femur.

The **common peroneal nerve** is easily felt at the lateral side of the neck of the fibula as it passes from the popliteal fossa into the peroneal compartment of the leg.

The pulses in the ankle and in the foot

The **anterior tibial artery** is palpable anteriorly mid-way between the medial and lateral malleoli. It lies lateral to the tendons of tibialis anterior and extensor hallucis longus, and medial to the tendons of extensor digitorum longus and peroneus tertius.

The **dorsalis pedis artery** is the continuation of the anterior tibial artery, and may be palpated on the dorsum of the foot lateral to the tendon of extensor hallucis longus until it passes into the sole of the foot between the first and second metatarsal bones.

The **posterior tibial artery** is palpable at the medial side of the ankle midway between the tip of the malleolus and the medial tubercle of the calcaneus.

The **perforating branch of the peroneal artery** can be palpated at the anterior border of the lateral malleolus.

FURTHER READING

BARNETT C.H. (1961) *Recent Advances in Anatomy*, 2nd Edition. Joints and Movement, p. 404. London: Churchill.

BARNETT C.H., DAVIES D.V. & MACCONNAILL M.A. (1961) *Synovial Joints; Their Structure and Mechanics.* London: Longmans.

BREATHNACH A.S. (1965) *Frazer's Anatomy of the Human Skeleton*, 6th Edition. London: Churchill.

BRUCE J., WALMSLEY R. & ROSS J.A. (1964) *Manual of Surgical Anatomy*. Edinburgh: Livingstone.

CROUCH J.E. (1965) *Functional Human Anatomy*. London: Kimpton.

HOLLINSHEAD W.H. (1954) *Anatomy for Surgeons*, Vol. 3. The Limbs. London: Cassell.

HOLLINSHEAD W.H. (1960) *Functional Anatomy of the Limbs and Back*, 2nd Edition. Philadelphia: Saunders.

LAST R.J. (1967) *Anatomy: Regional and Applied*, 4rd Edition. London: Churchill.

The structure and function of the systems

Chapter 24
The nervous system

And afterwards I showed what must be the fabric of the nerves and muscles of the human body to give the animal spirits contained in it the power to move the members; what changes must take place in the brain to produce waking, sleep and dreams; how light, sound, odours, tastes, heat and all the other qualities of external objects impress it with different ideas by means of the senses; how hunger, thirst and the other internal affections can likewise impress upon it divers ideas; what must be understood by the common sense (sensus communis) in which these ideas are received, by the memory which retains them, by the fantasy which can change them in various ways, and out of them compose new ideas, and which can cause the members of such a body to move in as many different ways as can take place in our own case apart from the guidance of the will.

Descartes, R. (1637)   *Discourse on Method.*

The cells of the nervous system are described in chap. 14, where it is shown that the neurones have very long, slender, branching and tortuous processes which are supported and ensheathed by neuroglial cells. The human brain and spinal cord weighs over 1·5 kg and consists almost entirely of neurones and neuroglia and their processes. Since understanding of the activity of the brain must be based on a knowledge of its structure, a study of its detailed anatomy is a challenge which has been readily accepted.

The macroscopic structure can be described and named as in any other organ, and by cutting it in slices the distribution of grey and white matter can be defined. Various simple methods stain the cells so that even small collections forming nuclei, ganglia and columns can be located. The real technical difficulties arise when attempts are made to trace the course and distribution of the nerve fibres which issue from these aggregations of cells. This is because the fibres have microscopic dimensions and yet travel long distances. The difficulties are increased by the extensive branching of processes and by the close packing of fibres which have very different courses. So on normal brains after staining the myelin sheaths, by revealing their lipoprotein, or the neurites, by impregnating with silver salts, only relatively simple and circumscribed pathways can be traced through serial sections. One of the silver impregnation methods, that of Golgi, is

very informative just because for some unknown reason it stains only a small proportion of the total number of cells. However, the cells are picked at random, and when selected the whole of the cell and its processes are blackened. This means that the geometry of the cell can be revealed in a thick section without being hidden by all its neighbours. Examination with the EM is disheartening because it shows that there are many fibres which are too small to be resolved by light microscopy, and the thinness of the specimen makes any large scale reconstruction virtually impossible. Anyone intending to pursue the study of the nervous system should examine an electronmicrograph of central nervous tissue (plate 24.1, facing p. 17.7), and then reflect on its magnification and depth. If he then continues with the pursuit, he will at least be aware of the difficulties.

Some assistance in unravelling the tracts comes from the fact that, during development, certain pathways myelinate at different ages. Also, after damage or disease, tracts may disappear completely so that the resultant gap shows the previous course of large bundles of fibres, and the patient's symptoms can then be a clue to the function of that pathway.

Fortunately, other methods are available but they are experimental, and therefore can usually only be applied to experimental animals. If a nerve fibre is cut, changes take place in its cell body, myelin sheath, and at the boutons of its synapses; for instance, cutting a peripheral nerve causes chromatolysis in those cell bodies which give rise to the cut fibres, and the position of the chromatolytic cells then determines their origin (p. 14.2). Similarly, degenerating myelin and denervated boutons can be shown by staining with the Marchi and Glees methods respectively. All these methods depend on catching a fibre or cell at the right stage of its degeneration. After a suitably timed accident, it is rarely possible to apply them to human postmortem material. Although these degenerative methods are tedious and often capricious, they are the most precise tools of the neurohistologist.

A very different group of methods for tracing pathways is based on the electrophysiological study of the course of impulses. After either a natural or direct electrical stimulus, a recording electrode can map and time the traffic in the tracts, and the time delay can indicate the presence of intercalated synapses. This form of neuro-anatomy using physiological tools is very effective and particularly useful for tracing the course of afferent impulses from peripheral receptors in the skin, muscles and retina. Cutting or freezing at points along the journey of the impulse while recording elaborates and confirms the value of this method. Similarly, stimulation in certain regions can produce measurable motor effects, and likewise be used to map the course of the traffic. These techniques are of less value in unravelling the connections within the central nervous system, as distinct from those closely connected to the input and output fibres. Apart from relatively simple stimulation experiments, like the classic work of Penfield on human brains exposed at operation, these types of investigation are also restricted to laboratory animals.

Finally, mention should be made of the contribution of modern neurosurgery to the investigation of the role of certain parts of the brain in human behaviour. By stereotactic methods, lesions can be made in definite parts of the brain and their effects observed after and during the operation. Initially, the sites were chosen empirically, but with experience lesions of precise size and location can produce predictable effects. Apart from helping the patient, these lesions provide direct evidence of the role of parts of the cerebrum in determining behaviour. Although this evidence cannot be as precise as that of the neuro-anatomist, it is included in this chapter because it is clinically important and adds to our understanding.

THE SPINAL CORD

The spinal cord lies within the vertebral canal and extends from the foramen magnum to the region of the first or second lumbar vertebra; below this level a fibrous cord, the **filum terminale**, passes down the vertebral canal to fuse with the second sacral vertebra. In embryonic life, the spinal cord extends throughout the entire length of the vertebral canal, but due to the faster growth of mesoderm the neural elements reach finally only as far as the upper lumbar vertebrae. Because of this, the lumbar and sacral nerve roots have a long course from the cord to the intervertebral foramina and within the vertebral canal form the **cauda equina** (fig. 24.1). This **vertebrosegmental discrepancy** is of clinical importance. At upper cervical levels it is slight and can be ignored but the lumbosacral segments are so compressed that they only extend over two or three vertebrae.

Spinal nerves

In the embryo, neural processes emerge from the ventral part of the cord to innervate effector organs and are thus motor (fig. 24.107). At the same time other neural elements outside the cord form the primitive dorsal root ganglia. One process of each cell in the ganglion grows into the posterior part of the cord whilst another process grows out to receptor organs and is thus sensory. These two elements form the ventral (anterior) or motor roots

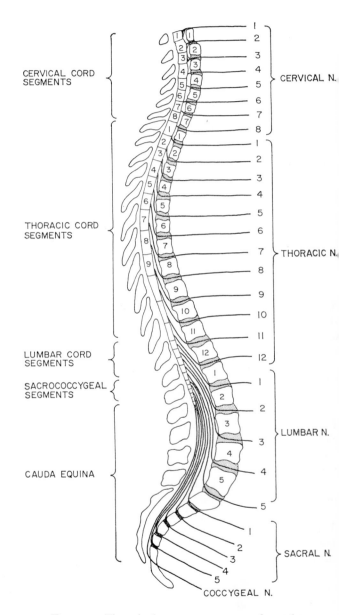

FIG. 24.1. The spinal segments, nerves and vertebrae.

and dorsal (posterior) or sensory roots of the cord. The two roots join to form a spinal nerve (fig. 24.2). Each nerve passes through an intervertebral foramen, the ganglion lying in the foramen itself.

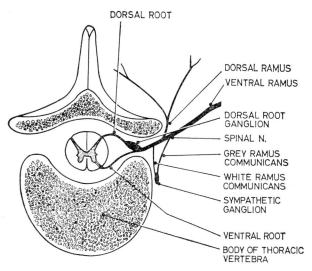

FIG. 24.2. The thoracic spinal nerve with the coverings of the spinal cord and of the nerve roots omitted.

FIG. 24.3. The dermatomes.

SEGMENTAL DISTRIBUTION OF SPINAL NERVES

In segmented invertebrates, such as the earthworm, each segment of the nerve cord innervates its own somite, receiving and giving impulses only to that segment. In man, this arrangement is only partly preserved and is best demonstrated in the thoracic region where the intercostal nerves act as typical segmental nerves. With the outgrowth of limbs this segmental pattern becomes blurred. The legs are innervated by a plexus composed of motor and sensory nerves from the lumbosacral segments of the cord. Nerves related to the lower cervical and first thoracic segments form a plexus innervating the upper limb. These two plexuses spring from segments somewhat larger than adjoining segments and are called the **cervical** (C4–T2) and **lumbosacral enlargements** (L2–S3). Despite the complex branching and unions of these plexuses the sensory innervation of the skin still demonstrates its segmental origin as **dermatomes** (fig. 24.3). More detailed dermatome maps are given in the regional chapters (figs. 20.51, 21.12, 22.66, 23.53).

Spinal meninges

Within the vertebral canal the cord is surrounded by a number of membranes termed the meninges (fig. 24.4).

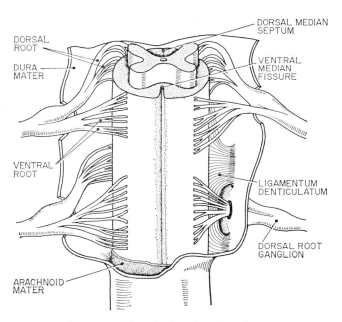

FIG. 24.4. The spinal cord and meninges.

Closely investing the cord is a thin membrane, the **pia mater**. The **subarachnoid space**, which is continuous with that round the brain and filled with cerebrospinal fluid (CSF), separates the pia from the thin enveloping **arachnoid membrane**. The spinal nerve roots also lie within the CSF which may be readily tapped by puncturing the intervertebral space posteriorly in the lumbar region (lumbar puncture). The arachnoid membrane is separated by only a narrow **subdural space** from a thicker fibrous membrane, the **dura mater**, which is continuous with that covering the brain. At each thoracic and cervical segment the pia, arachnoid and dura mater fuse to form the **ligamentum denticulatum** which fixes the cord on both sides to the dura. Finally, the **epidural veins** and fat fill the **epidural space** which lies between the dura and the vertebral canal.

A deep midline groove, the **ventral median fissure**, divides the cord into right and left halves and encloses the anterior spinal arteries. A fibrous **dorsal median septum** lies posteriorly and is continued inwards almost as far as the central canal. On either side of the midline lie the **dorsolateral** and **ventrolateral sulci**.

Blood supply

Most of the blood to the cervical spinal cord comes via the vertebral arteries (fig. 24.5). The **anterior spinal artery**

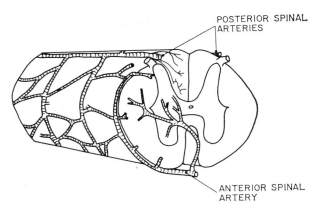

FIG. 24.5. Sectional view of spinal cord showing blood supply.

is formed from branches arising from both vertebral arteries and passes down the front of the cord in the midline receiving contributions from ventral radicular arteries especially on the roots of C7, 8 and T1 which ultimately come from branches of the subclavian arteries. The **posterior spinal arteries** are also branches of the vertebral or sometimes the posterior inferior cerebellar artery and these receive contributions from the dorsal radicular arteries.

Anastomoses between the anterior and posterior systems lie in the superficial part of the cord and in the pia mater. Thus both systems supply the periphery of the cord both anteriorly and posteriorly. The central part of the cord is largely supplied by the anterior spinal artery which gives off perforating branches in the ventral median fissure. The distribution of the radicular arteries to the cord varies greatly but a point of practical impor-

tance is that both ventral and dorsal radicular arteries lie on the anterior aspects of the spinal nerve roots and are hidden from view and may possibly be injured during surgical procedures. The anterior spinal artery is, in fact, an anastomotic system rather than one long artery with the major contributions coming from the radicular arteries. Some of the more important connections arise in the cervical region, and the largest is in the lumbosacral portion of the cord, being a large artery usually arising from the tenth intercostal artery. The venous drainage follows a pattern similar to that of the arteries.

The spinal grey matter

The spinal cord has a roughly H shaped central mass of grey matter and peripheral white matter which can be distinguished on cross section with the naked eye (fig. 24.6). In the thoracic cord the cross bar of the H is prolonged beyond the uprights to form the **lateral horns**. In the centre of the cross bar lies the

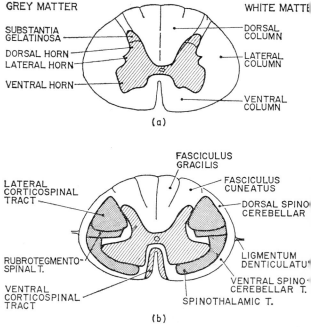

FIG. 24.6. (a) White and grey columns in the spinal cord. (b) The position of the major tracts in the cervical region.

poorly defined central canal separating **ventral and dorsal commissures**. The grey matter also contains the **dorsal or posterior horns** and the **ventral or anterior horns**. The white matter is divided into the **dorsal, lateral and ventral columns**. The ratio between grey and white matter varies at different levels of the cord (fig. 24.7). At the cervical cord accommodates fibres connecting higher parts of the central nervous system with all the rest of the

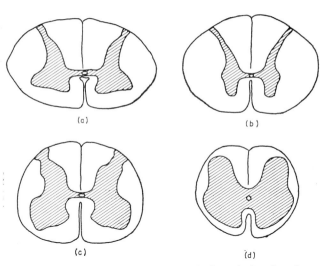

FIG. 24.7. Sections through the spinal cord showing the different proportions of grey and white matter at various levels. (a) cervical, (b) thoracic, (c) lumbar and (d) sacral.

spinal cord, more white matter is present than elsewhere in the cord. The lumbar enlargement has little white matter because there are relatively few connecting fibres.

The term horn is misleading, since the grey matter extends the whole length of the cord. Within it, columns of cells extend for its whole length or for shorter distances.

THE DORSAL CELL COLUMN (fig. 24.11)

The grey matter closest to the dorsal root is termed the apical portion and lies immediately posterior to **substantia gelatinosa** which, extending throughout the grey column, is continuous with the spinal nucleus of the trigeminal nerve (p. 24.25). Substantia gelatinosa receives impulses of pain and temperature conveyed by small fibres in the sensory root. The **dorsal funicular grey** receives impulses providing information on muscle tone and joint position and movement. Touch impulses also arrive in this area, as do pain and temperature impulses which arrive both directly and after relay in substantia gelatinosa. Anterior to the dorsal funicular grey matter lies the **thoracic nucleus** extending from C8–L2 (fig. 24.14). It receives proprioceptive impulses and then conveys them to the spinocerebellar tract. Immediately lateral to the thoracic nucleus lies the **secondary visceral grey**, the small column of cells which receive sensory impulses from viscera. The dorsal column therefore is entirely sensory in function receiving impulses from the primary neurone in the dorsal root ganglion and relaying them into the ascending systems of the cord. Some impulses, however, synapse in the dorsal column with internuncial or connector neurones which pass directly to motor neurones on the same or opposite sides of the cord. A fibre carrying a pain impulse, for example, may synapse with a cell or cells in substantia gelatinosa which conveys the impulse to a motor

neurone on the same side, resulting in a reflex withdrawal of the injured area.

THE INTERMEDIATE OR LATERAL CELL COLUMN

This extends laterally between T1 and L3 in the same coronal plane as the central canal. Cells in this region give off axons passing to sympathetic ganglia and are therefore preganglionic sympathetic efferent neurones. In the sacral level a similar column of cells gives rise to parasympathetic preganglionic efferents (pelvic splanchnic nerves).

THE VENTRAL CELL COLUMN

Clinical and experimental evidence suggests that particular groups of ventral column cells supply particular muscles. There is also a functional representation in that muscle groups concerned with extension and adduction are represented more superficially than those concerned with flexion and abduction (fig. 24.8). Special groups of

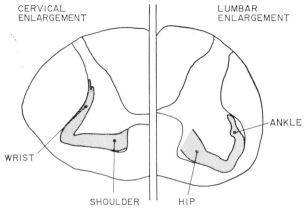

FIG. 24.8. Functional localization of motor cells in the ventral horns of the cervical and lumbar segments.

cells appear in the cervical region and are termed accessory and phrenic nuclei. The spinal accessory nucleus extends through the upper cervical cord, its rootlets emerging between the ventral and dorsal roots to ascend and join the cranial accessory nerve leaving the skull through the jugular foramen. The phrenic nucleus contains the motor neurones of the diaphragm.

The spinal white matter

DESCENDING (MOTOR) PATHWAYS

In man, the principal motor pathway is the **corticospinal tract**. Fibres originating in motor neurones in the cerebral cortex descend through the midbrain to the medulla and before entering the cord they cross the midline to a more posterior position as the **lateral corticospinal tract** (fig. 24.9). A small number of fibres fail to cross over until lower levels; these continue as the **ventral corticospinal tract**. As the tracts descend the cord they give off

FIG. 24.9. The corticospinal tracts from the midbrain to the spinal cord.

axons to motor neurones of the ventral column, becoming smaller as they descend. The lateral corticospinal tract lies immediately lateral to the dorsal horn and deep to some ascending pathways.

The **rubrospinal tract** arises from the red nucleus and after decussation passes through the pons and medulla to lie immediately in front of the lateral corticospinal tract. In man it probably does not descend below cervical levels and much of it is composed of fibres arising from the tegmentum of the midbrain (p. 24.18) It probably co-ordinates head and trunk movements. The **tectotegmentospinal tract** is an important descending pathway concerned with pupillary dilation. Fibres arising from the superior colliculus, tectum and tegmentum pass through the pons and medulla to lie directly anterior

to the rubrospinal tract. Although many of these fibres are probably concerned with motor co-ordination of head and trunk, some pass into the thoracic cord to end in the intermediate grey matter around the preganglionic sympathetic motor neurones. Impulses are then relayed in the superior cervical ganglion, and postganglionic fibres go to the iris (fig. 24.10). Lesions of this pathway may therefore produce a pinpoint pupil, a sign not uncommonly found in diseases of the brain stem. The vestibular apparatus has a marked influence on motor function, some of its effects being through the **vestibulospinal tract** which lies in the ventral part of the cord on the same side as the nucleus of origin. The **reticulospinal tracts** pass into the lateral white column as the lateral reticulospinal and into the ventral column as the medial reticulospinal tracts. They probably influence respiration

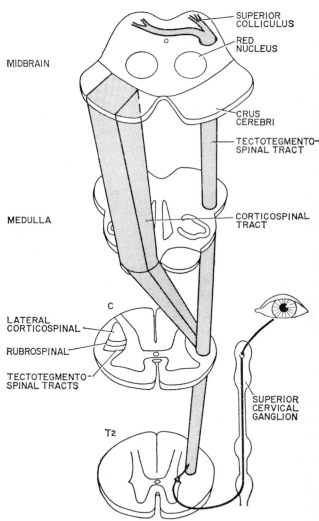

FIG. 24.10. The connections with the pupil from the descending pathways. Modified from Crosby E.C., Humphrey T. & Lawer E.W. (1962) *Correlative Anatomy of the Nervous System*. New York: Macmillan.

and temperature regulation. The **olivospinal tract** arises in the olive, crosses the midline, and probably co-ordinates head and arm movements.

ASCENDING (SENSORY) PATHWAYS

Before entry into the cord the fibres in a dorsal sensory root are grouped into two major divisions.

The lateral division (fig. 24.11)

After entering the cord, the axons divide into ascending and descending fibres in the **dorsolateral fasciculus** before ending in the substantia gelatinosa and the dorsal funicular grey. Pain and temperature impulses from the skin probably relay in substantia gelatinosa; such impulses from

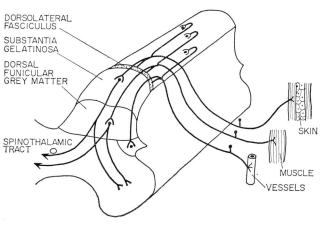

Fig. 24.11. The lateral division of the dorsal root (pain and temperature sensation.)

deep structures, i.e. bone, joints and muscle probably enter the dorsal funicular grey. It is probable that visceral impulses are distributed to the secondary visceral grey matter, relaying at successively higher intervals on the same and opposite sides of the cord. Visceral collaterals may synapse in substantia gelatinosa with cells common to both somatic and visceral synapses and this provides one explanation for referred pain (p. 24.70). After giving off collaterals to ventral horn cells, fibres pass from both substantia gelatinosa and the dorsal funicular grey across the midline in the ventral commissure to enter the anterior part of the lateral column and ascend as the **spinothalamic tract**. As the tract ascends the cord, successive fibres are added to it and this produces a lamination. In the lower levels of the cord each successive addition of fibres from each segment displaces the previous fibres posterolaterally, each segment overlapping the next (fig. 24.12). Thus lower levels tend to lie posterior and lateral to higher levels. This knowledge enables the neurosurgeon to perform fractional section of the tract to relieve pain in particular areas. The ligamentum denticulatum delineates the posterior boundary of the spinothala-

mic tract. However not all pain impulses are relayed along the spinothalamic tract and some pass along multisynaptic pathways in the dorsal horns.

Fig. 24.12. The spinothalamic tract. C, T, and L represent cervical, thoracic and lumbar.

The medial division (fig. 24.13)

This consists of thick myelinated fibres which ascend several segments in the dorsal white column. Those from the upper part of the body displace fibres from the lower part into a more medial position so that by the midthoracic part of the cord two distinct fasciculi are recognized. The more medial, conveying impulses from the lower part of the body, is **fasciculus gracilis**, and the lateral, conveying impulses from the upper part of the body, is **fasciculus cuneatus**. They end in **nucleus gracilis** and **nucleus cuneatus** respectively.

Sensory organization

A principle of sensory organization important for the cerebral cortex is already apparent. The first neurone with its cell body in the dorsal ganglion synapses with cells on the same side of the cord, i.e. in the substantia gelatinosa, the dorsal funicular grey or the nuclei gracilis and cuneatus. The second neurone crosses the midline. Impulses relayed from substantia gelatinosa and dorsal funicular grey cells cross over in the anterior commissure to ascend in the opposite spinothalamic tract. Those from the nuclei at the top of the dorsal columns cross over as the **internal arcuate fibres**. Both groups finally enter the opposite thalamus and from thence are relayed to the sensory cortex (p. 24.22).

These pathways carry all impulses conveying sensory information from the body to the brain. How the different sensations are divided amongst the different pathways is not known with precision. Pain and temperature are almost entirely carried in pathways which cross over early and ascend in the spinothalamic tract. Impulses carrying sensations of pressure and positional sense in

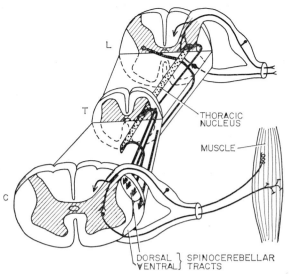

FIG. 24.14. The formation of the dorsal and ventral spinocerebellar tracts.

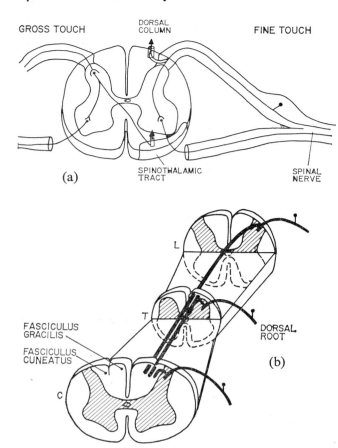

FIG. 24.13. The medial division of the dorsal root: (a) course of fibres in a spinal segment, (b) the formation of fasciculus gracilis from the lower part of the body and fasciculus cuneatus from the upper part.

tracts which ascend the cord and brain stem to end in the cerebellum of the same side through the inferior cerebellar peduncle (fig. 24.31). From the cervical region, where there is no thoracic nucleus, this proprioceptive information ascends in the fasciculus to the nucleus cuneatus where collateral branches synapse on the accessory cuneate nucleus. Cells in this accessory nucleus send their axons to join the rest of the dorsal spinocerebellar tract in the inferior cerebellar peduncle. Some impulses cross the midline of the anterior commissure and ascend to end in the olive. From here, however, axons cross the midline as the olivocerebellar fibres to the contralateral cerebellum, preserving the homolateral relationship for the passage of these impulses. The **spinovestibular tract** ends in the vestibular nuclei after its origin from cells in the dorsal funicular grey.

REFLEX ACTIVITY

Reflexes are the functional units by which muscular action is graded according to the peripheral stimuli. The muscular action which follows the stimulus is in general carried out by striated muscle, but can involve smooth or cardiac muscle. When studied as part of a reflex, movement seems automatic, reliable and free from transient and unpredictable activity. The link between the stimulus and the response is a nervous path which usually traverses the spinal cord, but many reflexes are conducted through higher parts of the central nervous system; the contraction of the pupil of the eye in response to light is mediated by a reflex path through the midbrain.

Reflexes are not necessarily all present at birth. Some develop later, like the normal plantar response (p. 24.14);

muscles and joints (proprioceptive impulses) follow ascending pathways on the same side of the cord and cross over in the internal arcuate fibres in the medulla. Many workers recognize two varieties of touch; fine touch is the ability to localize a stimulus and discriminate between it and a similar nearby stimulus; gross touch is the recognition of a stimulus without accurate localization. Impulses conveying both these sensations enter by the medial division; those conveying fine touch mostly go up the cord in the dorsal columns on the same side, whilst those responsible for gross touch probably relay in the dorsal funicular grey and then cross over to ascend in the opposite spinothalamic tract.

A number of ascending pathways carry information which does not reach the cerebral cortex but is used to organize movement (fig. 24.14). Proprioceptive impulses enter the cord through the medial division and synapse in the dorsal funicular grey and thoracic nucleus. The second neurone, however, instead of crossing the cord, passes laterally to the posterior periphery of the lateral column to form the **dorsal** and **ventral spinocerebellar** others are present at birth and subsequently vanish, like the Moro startle reflex (p. 24.20). Voluntary movements play no part in reflexes; and a habit, arising as it does out of earlier deliberate actions, is not a reflex. 'Conditioned reflexes' are a special type of reflex discussed on p. 24.92.

We understand the spinal reflex better because we can stand upon the shoulders of Sir Charles Sherrington (1857–1952), who shared a Nobel prize and was appointed to the Order of Merit for his 'discoveries regarding the function of the neurones'. He analysed the behaviour of the **reflex arc** which is the conducting path between a stimulus and the ensuing response. He drew comparisons between the behaviour of a nerve trunk and the behaviour of a reflex arc. These include:

Speed of conduction

The reflex arc conducts more slowly; the weaker the stimulus, the more slowly it conducts. Fig. 24.15 shows the scratching movements of a dog in response to electrical stimulation of its skin. Stimulation starts at 'on'

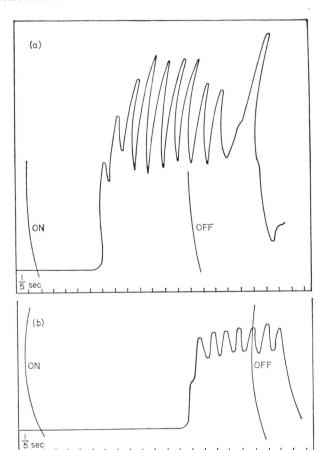

FIG. 24.15. Scratching movements of a dog in response to stimulation of skin from 'on' to 'off'. (a) stronger stimulation, (b) weaker stimulation. After Sherrington C. (1906) *Intergrative Action of the Nervous System*. London: Cambridge University Press.

and is continued till 'off'. Note the length of time elapsing from the start of the stimulus until scratching begins. This is much longer than the time that would elapse during conduction along any large nerve fibre from the skin via the spinal cord to the scratching muscles. Is it possible that this reflex is conducted along slowly conducting nerve fibres only? This explanation is ruled out by the second part of the figure. Here the stimulus is reduced in intensity, but not in duration (note the slightly altered time scale); the delay before scratching starts is clearly greater. So the reflex arc is conducting more slowly than any but the tiniest nerve fibre and, unlike any nerve fibre, at a variable speed depending on the intensity of stimulation. The speed can be shown to vary during conduction through the spinal cord and not during conduction to or from the cord.

After discharge

The response, or the muscular movement, does not end exactly when the stimulus ceases, even allowing for conduction time along the reflex arc. There may be marked after discharge prolonging the response. Fig. 24.16 records

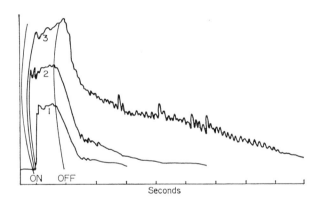

FIG. 24.16. Flexion of cat's leg in response to stimulation to skin lasting 1 sec from 'on' to 'off'. Traces 1 to 3 evoked by increasing strength of stimulus. After Sherrington.

the withdrawal of a cat's leg in response to electrical stimulation of the skin, more intense than the delicate stimulation which evokes scratching. Three different intensities of stimulation were employed and three degrees of response recorded. The record was made by using levers pivoted at the right of the figure and so the time of starting stimulation is shown by an arc of a circle, marked 'on'. The interval between this arc and the start of the upswing produced by the retreating leg is the **latent period**, the gap during which conduction is occurring along the reflex arc but before the response begins. This latent period is evidently brief and clearly well below one-tenth second, especially with the higher strengths of stimulus.

The stimulus was stopped at time 'off', shown by another similar arc of a circle. But the response does not end until rather less than one-tenth second later. The leg has not resumed its initial position for a number of seconds, and with the highest intensity of stimulation, rhythmic jerking (**clonus**, p. 24.66) persists practically to the end of the record.

After discharge is not a feature of a nerve trunk but is shown here to occur in a reflex arc. A brief stimulus gives rise to a much more prolonged response; the spinal cord processes operate over a much longer time scale than the impulses in peripheral nerve fibres. This is true even though in the long, jerky clonus the spinal cord is not itself setting up a rhythm but is being restimulated by the incoming sensory traffic from the jerking limb.

A peripheral nerve trunk responds to a single stimulus, if this is sufficiently strong, with a single impulse. Repeated impulses are the product of repeated stimulation. But the scratch reflex is a rhythmic, repeated response in a reflex arc which can occur after a single stimulus (fig. 24.17). A single shock in the skin at the time marked

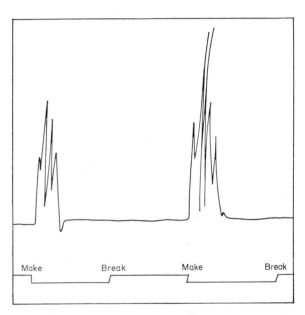

FIG. 24.17. Scratch reflexes of a dog in response to faradic stimulation of the skin. The second stimulus is stronger than the first. After Sherrington.

'make' gives rise to four scratches, and the weaker shock at 'break' to none; a stronger shock then produces five scratches. The rhythm of a reflex response does not conform strictly to the rhythm of stimulation.

Graded responses

A single nerve fibre exhibits the **all-or-none phenomenon**. When sufficiently strongly stimulated, it conveys an impulse, but it cannot convey half an impulse or a double sized impulse. Conduction in a reflex arc shows

much more gradation. Fig. 24.18 is a record of a dog's flexion reflex, in which the leg is withdrawn in response to electrical stimulation of a digit. As the strength of stimulation is increased, the response increases, but not in a linear fashion.

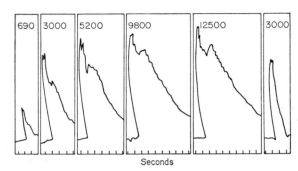

FIG. 24.18. Flexion reflex: withdrawal of a dog's leg in response to stimulation of varying intensity. Strength of stimulus is given in arbitrary units for each response. After Sherrington.

Temporal summation

The dog's scratch reflex is difficult to elicit by any single stimulus of whatever strength. But the reflex arc concerned is capable of adding together successive stimuli; two weak stimuli, one after the other, can be successful when either alone fails. Admittedly a single nerve fibre can respond in a similar way, but only when the stimuli are a mere fraction of a millisecond apart. Enormously greater intervals can be dealt with by a reflex arc, which possesses a property termed **temporal summation** permitting the summing of incoming traffic spaced apart in time. In the case of the scratch reflex, the interval may be as long as 1·4 sec. In other words, if a dog's skin is stimulated at a strength insufficient to make it scratch, and the same small stimulus is repeated as long as 1·4 sec later, the second stimulus may prove effective; the spinal cord has a holding capacity of that length. The beginnings of this holding capacity can be seen when one notes how much longer an excitatory postsynaptic potential lasts than the nerve impulse responsible for it (p. 14.17). But in the case of a simple monosynaptic reflex, such as a tendon jerk (p. 24.12), the holding capacity may not extend further than about 10 msec.

One way conduction

Another distinction between a nerve trunk and a reflex arc is the 'one way only' property of the arc. When a nerve trunk is artificially stimulated in the middle of its length, impulses are generated in its fibres which proceed both ways, i.e. towards the end of the fibre and back towards the neurone body (**antidromic conduction**). But the antidromic impulse is unable to proceed backwards round a reflex arc and reach the receptors which normally originate the reflex activity. Nor is it possible to stimulate a ventral spinal root and produce impulses in dorsal spinal roots.

Fatigue

A healthy nerve fibre, adequately supplied with blood, is extremely difficult to fatigue and will continue to respond to stimulation much longer than a reflex arc. Fig. 24.19 shows a record of a scratch reflex being elicited

Seconds

Fig. 24.19. Scratch reflex of a dog in response to stimulation at two different places on skin. After Sherrington.

by a tickle, first at one point on the skin (stimulus A) and then at another (stimulus B). After some 21 secs of continuous stimulation, the rhythm and amplitude are much reduced; but it is hard to believe that the stimulated skin is the site of the fatigue since some recovery appears during the persistence of the stimulus. It is impossible to believe that the outward path from the spinal cord or the responding muscles are fatigued, because changing the position of the stimulus restores completely the vigour of the response. The fatigue occurs in the central element of the reflex arc, i.e. in the spinal cord.

Similarly conduction through the spinal cord is much more susceptible to anoxia and anaesthetics than conduction through nerve fibres. The higher parts of the central nervous system are even more susceptible. But it should not be assumed that fatigue is a word which has a constant physiological accompaniment. It describes human experience and needs careful interpretation. The weak link in the chain which gives way in fatigue may be one of many. For instance, if one uses a thumb muscle to press continuously, fatigue makes one stop in the end. Here the weak link is in the muscle fibres themselves. During severe physical exercise, the weak link may lie outside the neuromuscular system altogether and the transport of oxygen or the availability of glucose may be deficient. Other forms of human fatigue may defeat analysis, except by those who sell popular remedies.

Inhibition

A further property of a reflex arc is that conduction in it can be impaired by inhibition. Fig. 24.20 shows withdrawal of a cat's leg in response to electrical stimulation

FIG. 24.20. Flexion reflex of leg. From time A to time C, the foot of the same leg was being stimulated. From time B to time C the opposite foot was being stimulated also. After Sherrington.

of the foot of the same leg, a flexion reflex. The stimulation lasts from A to C. From B to C, the other foot is stimulated as well and the reflex response is reduced. No interference occurs within the spinal cord; the afferent impulses from the second foot, on reaching the spinal cord, excite neurones on their own side of the cord, which is the opposite side from the one traversed by the reflex arc. The axons of these neurones cross the midline (fig. 24.21) and reach the nervous elements of the reflex arc.

There they can interfere with conduction in two ways:
(a) by producing **inhibitory postsynaptic potentials** (IPSPs, p. 14.27) at the neurones where they synapse, thus

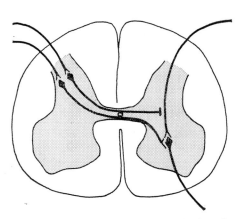

FIG. 24.21. Inhibitory pathways in a spinal cord segment.

making them less excitable. Strychnine poisoning is capable of blocking this type of inhibition and even results in 'release' excitation.

(b) by **presynaptic inhibition**. Nerve impulses which have entered the spinal cord along sensory axons can be reduced in amplitude below the normal level by activity in special nerve endings alongside the axon. This occurs at afferent terminals, just before the impulse reaches the synapse, and is therefore called presynaptic inhibition. Afferent impulses are thus subject to suppression within the central nervous system even before they reach their destination at the end of the axon along which they are travelling. The suppression occurs over a much longer time course than inhibition operating by IPSPs.

What this presynaptic mechanism means in the normal working of the central nervous system is not yet plain. It can be brought into action by impulse traffic either in other afferent fibres entering the cord, via a sequence of two interneurones, or in fibres descending from higher centres.

Inhibition always involves one or more interneurones within the spinal cord, which intervene between the afferent fibres (for instance from the opposite foot in fig. 24.20) and the reflex arc in which conduction is impaired. So inhibition, like repentance, is always late; if both feet were stimulated simultaneously, the flexor reflex would appear at full amplitude before the inhibition took effect. It seems that interneurones are essential for inhibition, because the same neurone cannot produce both excitatory and inhibitory effects at its axon's synaptic terminations. The afferent axons from a foot can bring a flexion reflex into action, an excitatory function; these same axons cannot inhibit a reflex directly, but can do so only by exciting an inhibitory interneurone or a chain of such interneurones.

Spatial summation

A flexion reflex can be produced when two stimuli are applied at different places on a limb, even when neither alone would be effective. Here the cord is showing an ability termed spatial summation; two stimuli at different places are being summed. So one can think provisionally of the spinal cord as a system capable of addition (spatial summation), subtraction (inhibition), and of holding information over a period of time (temporal summation). But this is still to underestimate its capacity. It is certainly capable of evolving one response rather than another, when simple arithmetic would produce a different solution. Fig. 24.22 shows what happens when a scratch reflex is first induced alone and then what happens when it is superimposed upon a flexion reflex. The two do not add, or the trace would rise off the record; instead, the new reflex displaces the old temporarily after a second or so of confusion.

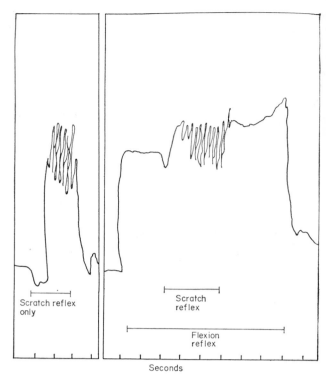

FIG. 24.22. Interaction of flexion reflex and scratch reflex in a dog. After Sherrington.

Tendon jerks

These are simple reflexes of great clinical importance. The **knee jerk** can be elicited by crossing one leg over the other while sitting down, and allowing it to hang freely. When the patellar tendon is tapped sharply, quadriceps contracts briefly and partially extends the knee. This jerk is one of a whole family of tendon jerks, most readily found in the antigravity muscles. They include the **Achilles tendon** or **ankle jerk**, since soleus and gastrocnemius support the body when one is on tiptoe, the **biceps** and **triceps jerks,** which do the same when one hangs from one's hands or does a press-up, and the **masseter-temporalis** or **jaw jerk**. The reflex arc concerned, like all reflex arcs, comprises a receptor, a conducting nervous path, and an effector organ. The receptor here is a muscle spindle.

A **muscle spindle** is a complicated structure, which has a fusiform capsule of connective tissue lying parallel with the muscle fibres. It contains a few short and very slender striated muscle cells; these are the intrafusal fibres which contrast with the main mass of extrafusal fibres. The intrafusal fibres receive motor nerve terminals, but their axons come from small cells in the ventral horn of the spinal cord and although myelinated they are much smaller ($8-2\ \mu$m) than the $20-12\mu$m motor nerve fibres to the rest of the muscle. These motor fibres to the intrafusal muscle are known as γ efferents because of their fibre

classification (Aγ, p. 14.22). Two sets of sensory endings
are present on the intrafusal muscle fibres (fig. 24.23). One,
the annulospiral ending, is wrapped around the muscle
cell and the other is described by its name, the flower-spray
ending. The afferent fibres from the annulospiral endings
are large and myelinated (20–12 μm) but those from the
flower-spray endings are rather smaller. Large numbers
of spindles lie within striated muscles, in parallel with the
muscle fibres; in a human lumbrical muscle, they are
about 2 mm long. When such a spindle is stretched,
it generates impulses in a large, group IA (p. 14.23) nerve

FIG. 24.24. Response of muscle spindles in anterior tibial
muscle to (a) stretch and (b) release. A, muscle length; B,
muscle tension; C, response of primary ending; D, response
of secondary ending. From Alnaes *et al.* (1965). *Acta
physiol. Scand.* **63**, 200.

A tendon jerk is a monosynaptic reflex, since the conducting nervous path traverses one synapse only in the
spinal cord. By stimulating electrically IA fibres from a
muscle and recording the impulse traffic at two stages on
the reflex arc, one can time its progress. Fig. 24.25 shows
the record of such an experiment. Here, the time taken to
reach the spinal cord along the afferent nerve from the
point of stimulus at A was 1·4 msec, and a further
1·1 msec saw the traffic a short distance down the
efferent nerve, having passed through the cord. If the
time allowed for the short distance of travel down the
efferent nerve is 0·3 msec, it follows that a mere 0·8 msec
elapsed during conduction through the cord and synaptic
transmission. This is not long enough to cross more than
one synapse. So one branch of a IA afferent fibre ends at
the motor neurone; it is worth bearing in mind that other
branches of the same fibre terminate in the thoracic nucleus
of the spinal cord, and the traffic is relayed from there to
the cerebellum. Conduction from afferent fibre to motor
neurone occurs through the generation of an EPSP (p.
14.26), which happens when even a single impulse

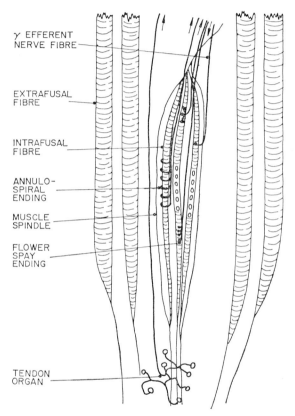

γ EFFERENT
NERVE FIBRE

EXTRAFUSAL
FIBRE

INTRAFUSAL
FIBRE

ANNULO-
SPIRAL
ENDING

MUSCLE
SPINDLE

FLOWER
SPAY
ENDING

TENDON
ORGAN

FIG. 24.23. Sensory innervation of muscle, showing a
flower spray ending, an annulospiral ending, a Golgi tendon organ and a γ efferent fibre.

fibre. The impulse traffic from these is relatively easy
to record in animals, since the large fibres are simpler
to isolate than small ones (fig. 24.24). Fig. 24.24 shows
the traffic provoked, not by a brief stretch as in the knee
jerk, but by sudden and maintained stretch of a muscle.
The group IA fibre fires vigorously at the onset of the
stretch, but soon slows, though continuing to fire at a
higher rate than before the stretch. A steadier increase in
rate of firing is recorded from the other fibre which is a
group II afferent from a muscle spindle, conducting
more slowly.

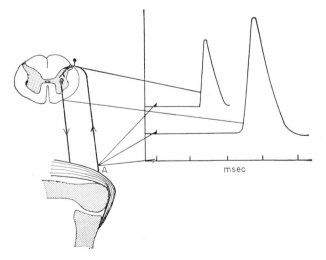

FIG. 24.25. The nervous pathway involved in a knee jerk,
and the electrical recordings obtained in a cat from two
sides of the path after electrical stimulation at point A.
After Lloyd.

arrives and has a much longer duration than the impulse itself. If the EPSP rises sufficiently, the motor neurone fires, and the impulse then proceeds along its axon to reach the motor endplate in quadriceps.

The reflex arc of a tendon jerk crosses only one segment of the cord. The presence of a normal jerk shows that the receptors are sensitive, the relevant afferent and efferent nerves are intact, the spinal cord segment, including the motor neurones, is working normally, and the responding muscle is in order.

Stretch reflexes

A tendon jerk is elicited artificially and it is difficult to assign a clear cut function to it. When a joint is moved passively and the new position is maintained, a rather different response, the stretch reflex, comes into play. The stretched muscles respond by increased tension, but the response is **multisynaptic** and depends on factors to which a tendon jerk is practically immune. For instance, the subject can affect the response, and if he intends to retaliate by pulling back when the muscle is stretched it makes the response much larger. Again, cerebellar damage may reduce a stretch reflex but not the tendon jerk at the same joint. When the tone of muscles is tested by moving a joint passively to and fro, an impression is gained of whether the stretch reflexes are normally active, i.e. whether a limb appears limp or stiff. If they are overactive, the joint is moved only with difficulty. It may suddenly give (the claspknife response). The receptors in this reflex of giving way to strong bending are the **Golgi tendon organs,** which are sprays of unmyelinated nerve terminals, penetrating the tendon close to the myotendinous junction (fig. 24.23). These receptors are less sensitive (higher threshold) than muscle spindles, but feed large afferent nerve fibres (group IB).

Flexion reflexes

These act so as to withdraw out of harm's way a limb that is being hurt, and responses of this kind of reflex are shown in figs. 24.16 and 18. A human being will naturally behave in this way if he is pricked, burnt or pinched; pulling body hairs may be used in clinical testing as a stimulus. A flexion reflex is a more complex reflex than a tendon jerk. It is multisynaptic, the reflex arc traversing more than one synapse in the spinal cord, and shows greater variability.

For instance, a tendon jerk is normally confined to the muscle that is stretched; there is no response from other muscles. But a varying number of muscles may be involved in a flexion reflex. A very slight prick on one toe makes only that toe move upwards out of the way. If the prick is sharper, the movement is more extensive. The whole limb may be drawn up, and in addition, the other limb may be extended (**crossed extension reflex**). The value of such a response in helping to get the injured toe

clear of trouble is obvious. So here a stimulus at one site can produce a muscular response of very variable extent, depending on how strong it is.

Again, a tendon jerk has a sharply defined latency. In a monosynaptic arc this is composed mostly of delays in the excitation of the muscle spindle by the sudden stretch of the muscle. In contrast, the latency of a flexion reflex can vary greatly; it is greatest when the stimulus is smallest and becomes less with more effective stimulation. The synaptic chain in the spinal cord conducts with variable speed.

Plantar response

When the skin of the sole of the foot is firmly stroked, so as not to tickle, yet not to hurt, especially in the area shown in fig. 24.26, the normal response is a downgoing

FIG. 24.26. The area on the sole of the foot over which the plantar response is best obtained. From Walshe F. (1965) *Further Critical Studies in Neurology.* Edinburgh: Livingstone.

or 'clenching' of the big toe, which in some sense attempts to grasp the source of the stroking. The abnormal or Babinski response consists in an upgoing of the toe, a dorsiflexion (sometimes ambiguously called 'extension'), together with fanning out of the other toes. In early infancy the response is normally upgoing, but before the child walks it takes on the adult downgoing pattern. The abnormal sign is a clinical index of faulty function of the corticospinal (pyramidal) tracts and is found also during anaesthesia and sleep. However, conversely a normal plantar response is not proof positive that the corticospinal tracts are operating normally.

Other reflexes affected by corticospinal pathways are

the abdominal and cremasteric reflexes. The former takes place when the skin of the abdomen is lightly scratched; the underlying part of the abdominal wall musculature contracts, pulling over the umbilicus. The response may fail when the corticospinal paths are interrupted; it may also fail in normal health. The cremasteric reflex consists in retraction of the testis when the skin of the medial upper thigh is stroked and this too may fail in disorders of the corticospinal paths. In both cases a difference between the two sides is much more conclusive evidence than bilateral absence of the reflexes.

Control and modification of reflexes

Even a tendon jerk is a variable phenomenon. The sensitivity of the receptor, the muscle spindle, can be altered. The intrafusal fibres, when their γ motor neurone activity causes them to contract, pull upon the receptor portion of the spindle, making it more sensitive to stretch. When the intrafusal fibre is taut, even a slight or brief pull on the whole muscle increases the activity of the spindle receptor. When it is slack, a longer or faster pull is necessary. Fig. 24.27 shows diagrammatically a muscle being

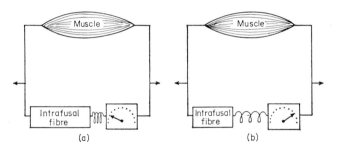

FIG. 24.27. Muscle and muscle spindle being stretched by constant force. (a) The intrafusal fibre is relaxed, and little tension is recorded by the spindle. (b) The intrafusal fibre is contracting, and more tension is recorded by the spindle.

stretched by the same force all the time; but clearly on the right where the intrafusal fibre is short, the meter is recording a larger apparent pull than on the left where the intrafusal fibre is long. The stretching force operates virtually entirely on the muscle; negligible force is required to stretch the intrafusal fibre (operating on the little spring in the diagram). The intrafusal fibres, when they contract, contribute nothing to the tension produced by the whole muscle in which they lie.

This arrangement should not be seen simply as a means by which activity in the spinal cord can make tendon jerks more or less sensitive. Consider what happens if the initial event is γ motor neurone activity. The spindle receptor becomes more active and a stretch reflex may result even though no actual stretch has occurred; the muscle shortens to a length determined by the γ motor

neurone activity. Thus movement can be initiated by γ motor neurones, although they do not themselves produce it. The place of such activity in normal movements is not yet entirely clear.

Tendon jerks can be modified by a procedure called **reinforcement** or Jendrassik's manoeuvre; in Jendrassik's words: 'If when the patellar tendon is struck, the patient clenches the hand, or makes other violent movement, the coincident jerk is increased.' It is simple to make the subject link the fingers of his two hands together and then instruct him to pull them apart, without letting go, just before one strikes the patellar tendon. The increase in the jerk could occur because Jendrassik's manoeuvre increases γ motor neurone activity. But there is another site on the reflex arc where its conduction can be altered. This is at the synapse; on the motor neurone's surface there may be no less than 30,000 synaptic knobs. Only a small number of these are the endings of afferent fibres from muscle spindles. There are also terminations from many other sources, including those responsible for voluntary movement (p. 24.66), and some of these are inhibitory. Their activity can affect the excitability of the motor neurone and hence the conduction in the tendon jerk reflex arc.

So any motor neurone serving as the efferent path of a tendon jerk can also serve as the **final common path** for a large number of reflexes, including complex reflexes organized from higher levels of the central nervous system than the spinal cord itself. These include tonic neck reflexes (p. 24.26) and, more complex still, conditioned reflexes (p. 24.92).

Is it possible to say how much of the behaviour of a motor neurone consists of reflex responses, and how much of directed activity or acts of free will, which are not tethered to the compulsion of reflex arcs, like travellers on Procrustes' bed? It is important to realize how difficult it is to make the behaviour of a reflex arc really dependable and rigorous. This ought to be most easily achieved in the simplest arc: the monosynaptic arc of the tendon jerk. But, as Sherrington pointed out, the knee jerk as tested clinically in normal man is 'delicately variable'; to make it reasonably dependable, a standard position must be adopted and the subject's attention must not vary. Changes in many higher parts of the nervous system alter the response. Really consistent records of spinal reflexes are generally obtained in animals in which the spinal cord has been isolated from the rest of the nervous system, and so in a very real sense a reflex is a 'convenient fiction' (Sherrington). If it were possible to assemble all the reflexes there are and to assess all their interactions, one might then begin to look for a residue of behaviour which is non-reflex, the place where Mind intervenes. But no picture can be even outlined of the sum of all reflexes, and to obtain dependable reflexes at all demands careful and deliberate simplification. One cannot guess all the contents of a black box by supposing that they must all be like the one fraction that can be made understandable.

'Knowledge is proud that he has learned so much;
Wisdom is humble that he knows no more.'

(Cowper).

Reflexes operating on smooth muscle and on glands

Efferent paths from the spinal cord run not only to voluntary muscle but also to other organs, such as the smooth muscle of blood vessels and the cells of the adrenal medulla. Reflex paths through the spinal cord end in them too. Fig. 24.28 shows a huge rise in blood pressure following electrical stimulation of a toe nerve; this occurred

FIG. 24.28. Rise in arterial blood pressure in a dog in response to electrical stimulation of the hind leg. The dog's spinal cord has been transected in the cervical region. After Sherrington C. (1906). *Integrative Action of the Nervous System*. London: Cambridge University Press.

in a dog which had previously undergone transection of the spinal cord at the eighth cervical level and the path is a spinal reflex arc. Similarly, reflexes affecting the urinary system can be organized by the spinal cord alone p. 34.8.

Spinal transection

When the spinal cord is severed, no sensory impulses can pass to the brain from the region below the cut, and so nothing can be felt in the lower part of the body. This part is also incapable of voluntary movement, since the necessary paths are interrupted. But the mechanism of spinal reflexes still remains in the separated part of the cord. Immediately after the injury there is a period of **spinal shock**, with absence of any activity in the separated spinal cord below the cut. The higher nervous system transmits to the spinal cord impulse traffic which is predominantly excitatory. Remove this source of excitation and all activity ceases for a time. No reconnection of the severed parts of the cord ever occurs, but reflex activity is recovered in the isolated portion.

The time is long in man and recovery may not be maximal for many weeks. It is much shorter in other animals. A cat recovers activity in its cord below a transection in a few hours and a frog in a few minutes. The greater the importance of higher parts of the nervous system to an animal, the more prolonged the effect of their disconnection.

In man, during spinal shock, the part of the body innervated by the spinal cord below the lesion is at first entirely flaccid. Pulling hairs and tapping tendons call forth no movement whatever, and are of course not felt by the victim. The bladder is inert and fills up; when it is sufficiently overstretched, the excess dribbles out but only a small part of its contents is evacuated.

After some days, recovery begins and cord function appears gradually, as shown by recovery of reflexes. Flexion reflexes in response to quite trivial stimuli may be troublesome; before injury, the extensor muscle system seems to depend much on excitatory influences from higher levels of the nervous system and it never recovers proper activity; hence the victim may become bent up in a flexed position. The bladder recovers reflex activity enough to empty itself fairly completely when full; vascular and sweating reflexes can now be demonstrated which are being handled by the isolated part of the cord. Until these vascular responses return, whenever the victim is tilted up, pooling of blood occurs in the venous vessels in the part of the body below the injury so that a marked fall in arterial blood pressure occurs.

THE BRAIN STEM AND CRANIAL NERVES

External appearance (fig. 24.29)

The brain stem lies almost entirely in the posterior cranial fossa, and may be divided into **medulla oblongata, pons** and **midbrain**.

In the lower medulla the ventral median fissure is obscured by the decussation of the pyramids. The **olive** lies lateral to the pyramid and is formed by the underlying **olivary nucleus**. Rootlets of the **hypoglossal nerve** emerge between the olive and pyramid. Immediately lateral to the olive the **inferior cerebellar peduncle** fans back into the cerebellum. In the shallow groove between olive and peduncle emerge the rootlets of the **cranial accessory the vagus** and the **glossopharyngeal nerves**. Immediately above the pyramid and olive the transverse fibres of the pons form the **middle cerebellar peduncle**, and in the groove between these fibres and the olive the **abducent nerve** emerges and more laterally the **facial nerve** and **auditory nerve**. The large sensory and small motor root of the **trigeminal nerve** penetrate the middle of the transverse pontine fibres laterally. The **crura cerebri** converge to enter the pons from above, separated from

FIG. 24.29. (a) Dorsal and (b) ventral views of the brain stem. From Noback C.P. (1967) *The Human Nervous System*. New York: McGraw-Hill.

one another by the deep interpeduncular fossa from which the **oculomotor nerve** leaves the midbrain just above the transverse pontine fibres. The **trochlear nerve** is the only one to leave the back of the brain stem and runs anteriorly around the cerebral peduncles between peduncle and pontine fibres. The **optic tracts** pass around the peduncle from the optic chiasma to the lateral geniculate bodies, enclosing the hypothalamus. Anteriorly behind the chiasma lies the **pituitary stalk** and structures of the anterior hypothalamus and behind these the posterior hypothalamus and mamillary bodies deep within the interpeduncular fossa.

The midbrain encloses a small central channel, the

aqueduct, which opens out in the pons and upper medulla as the fourth ventricle and narrows again in the lower medulla before becoming the central canal of the spinal cord.

The dorsal columns of the spinal cord end in the prominences overlying the dorsal column nuclei. Medially and forming the lower boundary of the floor of the fourth ventricle is the **gracile tubercle** and above it and laterally the **cuneate tubercle**. The flat **superior cerebellar peduncle** leaves the cerebellum to enter the midbrain and above it lie four rounded elevations, the **superior** and **inferior colliculi**. The trochlear nerve emerges from the centre of the midbrain just below the inferior colliculus. A faint elevation, the **brachium of the inferior colliculus**, passes from the inferior colliculus to the medial geniculate body which lies immediately lateral to the superior colliculus. Both inferior colliculus and medial geniculate body are relay stations in the auditory pathway. Lateral to the medial geniculate lies the lateral geniculate body, the main termination of the optic tracts. A brachium of the superior colliculus runs to the lateral geniculate body. Above the superior colliculus lies the **pineal gland** which is often calcified and in radiographs of the skull this is a useful indicator of displacement of the brain. The posterior wall of the third ventricle becomes continuous with the aqueduct.

The **floor of the fourth ventricle** (fig. 24.30) has a median groove and is divided into superior and inferior

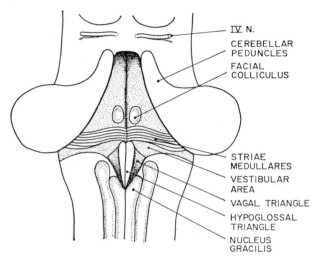

FIG. 24.30. Floor of the fourth ventricle.

parts by a raised transverse band of fibres, the **striae medullares**. Just below this band lies a small triangular area on either side of the median groove, the **hypoglossal triangle**. Immediately lateral to it, the **vagal triangle** overlies the **vagus and solitarius system**. In the superior half of the fourth ventricle a small prominence, the **facial colliculus**, lies on either side of the midline. It is produced by fibres of the facial nerve crossing over the abducent nucleus. Below the striae medullares there is another triangular area which overlies the vestibular nuclei, termed the **vestibular area**.

Transition from cord to brain stem (fig. 24.40)

Many of the structures found in the spinal cord continue into the brain stem, maintaining the same general relationship one to another although modified by the widening out of the central canal into the fourth ventricle. In the cord, the grey matter ventral to the central canal is motor and that dorsal to the canal is sensory in function. This functional arrangement is continued throughout the brain stem, the widening of the central canal into the

fourth ventricle pushing the sensory grey column into a more lateral position. The ventral horns of the spinal grey become continuous with a column of cells forming the motor nuclei of the cranial nerves. Similarly the visceral efferent cell column of the spinal cord continues into the brain stem as the cranial visceral motor column supplying smooth muscle, glands and blood vessels; the visceral afferent column becomes the brain stem's visceral sensory nuclei. The sensory grey matter of the spinal cord continues as the sensory nuclei of the cranial nerves. Substantia gelatinosa, for example, becomes continuous with the spinal nucleus of the trigeminal nerve (fig. 24.43).

Ascending tracts are normally interrupted by relays in nuclei from which fibres ascend in new tracts such as the medial lemniscus, but the spinothalamic tract continues throughout the brain stem with the addition of pain and temperature fibres from the head. The corticospinal tract occupies the ventral portion of the brain stem until the decussation when it passes into the lateral part of the cord.

Outline of the internal anatomy of the brain stem

THE MEDULLA OBLONGATA (fig. 24.31)
The ventral portion of the medulla is formed by the pyramids. In the lower medulla the dorsal column nuclei appear dorsal to the central canal but higher up these nuclei disappear after giving off fibres which cross the midline as the internal arcuate fibres to form the **medial lemniscus** lying on either side of the midline behind the pyramids. In the upper medulla the spinocerebellar tract forms most of the inferior cerebellar peduncle and the olivary nucleus appears on either side of the medial lemniscus. Posterior to the olive lies the spinothalamic tract, and posterior to this the spinal tract and nucleus of the trigeminal nerve.

THE PONS (fig. 24.32)
The anterior portion contains down going fibres from the cortex, interspersed by the transverse fibres of the pons forming the middle cerebellar peduncles. Within this network of fibres lie scattered cell groups, the **pontine nuclei**. The posterior portion of pons or **tegmentum** is continuous with and similar to the posterior part of the medulla, although the medial lemniscus has rotated into a transverse position posterior to the pontine fibres. In the upper pons the medial lemniscus becomes more lateral and the fourth ventricle begins to narrow into the cerebral aqueduct of the midbrain.

THE MIDBRAIN (fig. 24.33)
The midbrain or mesencephalon consists of a large anterior and a small posterior portion. The posterior portion which roofs the aqueduct is the **tectum** and the anterior portion the **cerebral peduncles**. Each of these is

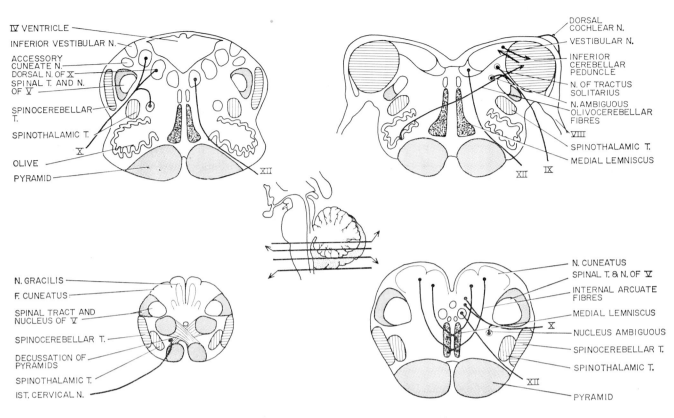

IV VENTRICLE
INFERIOR VESTIBULAR N.
ACCESSORY CUNEATE N.
DORSAL N. OF X
SPINAL T. AND N. OF V
SPINOCEREBELLAR T.
SPINOTHALAMIC T.
X
OLIVE
PYRAMID
XII

DORSAL COCHLEAR N.
VESTIBULAR N.
INFERIOR CEREBELLAR PEDUNCLE
N. OF TRACTUS SOLITARIUS
N. AMBIGUOUS
OLIVOCEREBELLAR FIBRES
VIII
SPINOTHALAMIC T.
MEDIAL LEMNISCUS
XII
IX

N. GRACILIS
F. CUNEATUS
SPINAL TRACT AND NUCLEUS OF V
SPINOCEREBELLAR T.
DECUSSATION OF PYRAMIDS
SPINOTHALAMIC T.
IST. CERVICAL N.

N. CUNEATUS
SPINAL T. & N. OF V
INTERNAL ARCUATE FIBRES
MEDIAL LEMNISCUS
X
NUCLEUS AMBIGUOUS
SPINOCEREBELLAR T.
SPINOTHALAMIC T.
XII
PYRAMID

FIG. 24.31. Transverse sections of the medulla oblongata.

SUPERIOR CEREBELLAR PEDUNCLE
LATERAL LEMNISCUS
MESENCEPHALIC T. AND N. OF V
MEDIAL LONGITUDINAL FASCICULUS
MEDIAL LEMNISCUS
CORTICOPONTINE AND CORTICOSPINAL FIBRES
NUCLEI PONTIS

MESENCEPHALIC T. AND N. OF V
IV
LATERAL LEMNISCUS
IV NERVE N.
MEDIAL LONGITUDINAL FASCICULUS
MEDIAL LEMNISCUS
DESCENDING AND TRANSVERSE FIBRES OF PONS

SUPERIOR CEREBELLAR PEDUNCLE
DENTATE N.
INFERIOR CEREBELLAR PEDUNCLE
SUPERIOR VESTIBULAR N.
SPINAL T. AND N. OF V
VII NERVE N.
SPINOTHALAMIC TRACT
MEDIAL LEMNISCUS
CORTICOSPINAL TRACT (PYRAMIDS)
VII
VI

IV VENTRICLE
MAIN SENSORY N. OF V
MOTOR N. OF V
PONTOCEREBELLAR FIBRES IN MIDDLE CEREBELLAR PEDUNCLE
MEDIAL LEMNISCUS AND SPINOTHALAMIC T.
PONS
V

FIG. 24.32. Transverse sections of the pons.

FIG. 24.33. Transverse section of midbrain.

subdivided into the **tegmentum substantia nigra** and **crus cerebri**. The crura carry fibres from the cerebral cortex to the pons, medulla and spinal cord. The tegmentum and the descending systems in the crura are separated by the substantia nigra, a column of pigmented cells occupying the whole length of the midbrain. It has a crescent shape extending in transverse section from the medial to the lateral sulcus. The **red nuclei** which are somewhat red when freshly cut, appear to either side of the midline and occupy the tegmentum immediately medial to the medial lemniscus. Fibres of the oculomotor nerve pass through its substance to emerge in the medial sulcus.

THE RETICULAR FORMATION

Groups of cells and fibres are arranged in a diffuse network throughout the brain stem filling the spaces between and having numerous connections with ascending and descending systems. These neurones can be excited from a variety of sources, skin stimulation, painful or otherwise, by sound, in some cases by light reaching the eye or by changes within the alimentary canal and other viscera. They also respond to stimulation of the descending pathways, such as the pyramidal tract. In fact, they might seem on first consideration only a means of jumbling the information that travels in the central nervous system. Yet the reticular formation has numerous definite functions. Through its upper connections with the thalamus and cerebral hemispheres, it controls alertness, waking or sleeping. When the thalamus and cerebral hemispheres are cut off from it by injury, they fall asleep, at least as judged by their pattern of electrical activity; this is not simply because all their afferent channels are silenced, since the optic nerves are still connected normally. Electrical stimulation within the reticular formation rouses the sleeping animal and alerts the waking animal. It seems that consciousness is determined by the activity of the reticular formation and many anaesthetics act particularly upon it.

Rousing, the response to any alerting stimulus, can take complex forms. If a normal baby up to about 5 months old is startled, especially by the possibility of falling or being dropped as when his cot is shaken, he exhibits the **Moro reflex.** He blinks and throws his arms out and then flexes and adducts them, as if to take a firm grasp of his mother. Normally this reflex becomes unrecognizable as development proceeds. The adult, when similarly startled, may jump and show **orienting reflexes**; he is able to localize the stimulus, and so turns his head and eyes to the source of a noise or a flash, in advance of any voluntary decision.

The reticular formation also possesses downward connections with the spinal cord. The operation of these connections is complex because different parts of the formation exert opposed effects. The more lateral part when stimulated facilitates extensor muscle stretch reflexes which become larger and more brisk. The more medial part produces the reverse effect; stretch reflexes become brisk in the flexor muscles. If the brain stem is transected immediately above the pons, a balance is struck in what remains of the reticular formation still connected with the spinal cord, to the advantage of the lateral part, and **decerebrate rigidity** occurs; stretch reflexes in extensor muscles become very active and the limbs are stiff and may be outstretched. The increased activity is chiefly due to increased firing of the γ motor neurones.

Also in the reticular formation are the neurones of the principal **cardiovascular controlling system**, often called the **vasomotor centre.** The isolated spinal cord can maintain some tone in the arterioles of the body and from the spinal cord at levels T1–L2 the sympathetic preganglionic fibres emerge to form the first link in the efferent path to the arterioles. Indeed, painful stimulation of the skin, or distension of a hollow viscus such as the bladder, can lead to vasoconstriction and often a reflex rise in blood pressure which can be mediated by the cord in isolation (fig. 24.28 and 34). Normally, however, an over-riding control is exerted by the medullary system, which receives information from the baro- and chemoreceptors of the carotid region (p. 28.31) and commands as efferent paths not only the sympathetic outflow already mentioned, but also the vagus nerve which includes fibres supplying the atria. Fig. 24.35 shows that cardiovascular control is conducted by two regions with opposing effects, an upper and more lateral pressor region, where stimulation increases vascular tone, and a lower, more medial part, from which reverse effects arise. **Control of respiration** is conducted by a system of neurones in a similar position (fig. 24.36). Those respon-

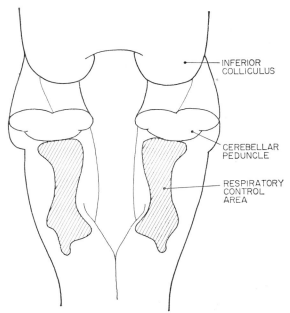

FIG. 24.36. Dorsal view of cat medulla, to show location of respiratory neurones. After Salmoiraghi G.C. & Burns B. (1960). *J. Neurophysiol.* **23**, 2.

sible for expiration are on the whole more posterior, but are not so clearly segregated as in the cardiovascular control system, since they overlap those responsible for inspiration. The respiratory rhythm is the product of their interaction. Sneezing and swallowing interrupt the normal respiratory rhythm, as does speech. This link clearly involves traffic from higher up in the nervous system. When the medulla is cut off from the pons and the higher parts of the CNS, it generates a jerky gasping type of rhythm, lacking the smoothness of normal breathing.

Detailed anatomy of brain stem

It is convenient to describe this in two parts, first the ascending and descending pathways and second the nuclear masses. As a general rule the ascending systems lie in the dorsal part of the brain stem and the descending systems in the ventral part.

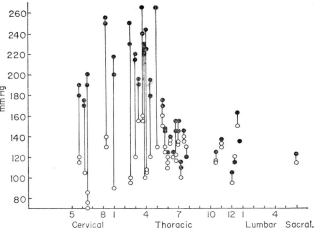

FIG. 24.34. Systolic blood pressure. (○) before and (●) after distension of the bladder in patients with traumatic section of the spinal cord at the levels shown. When the transection is low in the cord, most or even all of the sympathetic outflow to the blood vessels is still linked to the medulla and therefore to the baroceptor system; hence when bladder distension evokes vasoconstriction in the body below the transection, there is compensatory vasodilation above the transection and little or no rise in systemic blood pressure occurs. However, when the transection is high the path for compensatory vasodilation is blocked and a gross rise in blood pressure is seen. From Guttmann L. & Whitteridge D. (1947). *Brain* **70**, 387.

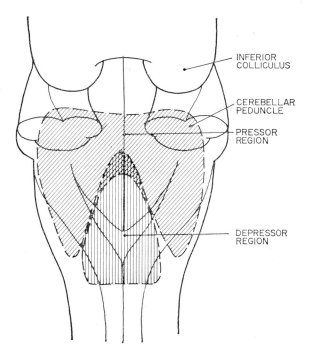

FIG. 24.35. Dorsal view of medulla and pons of the cat, after removal of cerebellum, to show the location of the cardiovascular control system. After Alexander (1946) *J. Neurophysiol.* **9**, 205.

THE MEDIAL LEMNISCUS (fig. 24.37)

The fibres from the dorsal column nuclei cross the mid-line as the **internal arcuate fibres** in the lower part of the medulla. The first fibres to cross arise in the gracile nucleus and ascend the brain stem immediately behind the pyramid to be joined by fibres from the cuneate nucleus, the whole ascending together as the medial lemniscus. As the lemniscus ascends the medulla, the leg fibres move laterally and the lemniscus assumes a right-

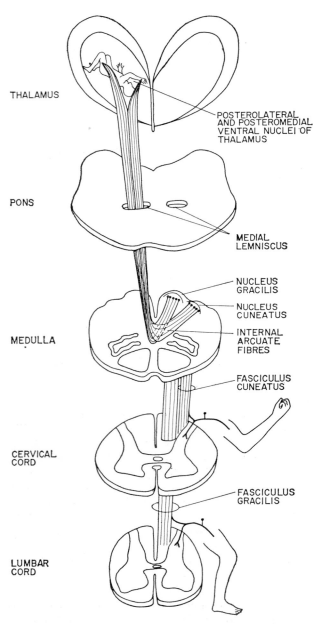

THALAMUS

POSTEROLATERAL
AND POSTEROMEDIAL
VENTRAL NUCLEI OF
THALAMUS

PONS

MEDIAL
LEMNISCUS

NUCLEUS
GRACILIS

NUCLEUS
CUNEATUS

INTERNAL
ARCUATE
FIBRES

MEDULLA

FASCICULUS
CUNEATUS

CERVICAL
CORD

FASCICULUS
GRACILIS

LUMBAR
CORD

FIG. 24.37. The dorsal columns and the formation of the medial lemniscus. Modified from Crosby E.C., Humphrey T. & Lawer E.W. (1962). *Correlative Anatomy of the Nervous System.* New York: Macmillan.

angled shape. The relationship of the fibres is such that it is convenient to imagine each half as a headless body slumping into a sitting position on the pyramid, back to back with each other and with their feet against the olive. As the lemniscus reaches the midbrain it is joined medially by fibres probably conveying touch and pressure sensation from the head. This relationship is maintained until the lemniscus ends in the thalamus, so that the medial part of the thalamus (ventralis posteromedialis) receives fibres from the face, and the lateral part of the thalamus (ventralis posterolateralis) receives fibres from the body. Fibres conveying gross touch travelling in the spinothalamic tract also join the lemniscus.

THE SPINOTHALAMIC TRACT (figs. 24.12, 31 and 32)

The spinothalamic tract ascends the medulla, passing posterior and lateral to the olive and separated only by the rootlets of the glossopharyngeal, vagus and accessory nerves from the spinal tract of the trigeminal nerve. As the tract ascends the brain stem, fibres from the lower part of the body become more lateral than those from the upper part, which become related to the trigeminal lemniscus, also carrying pain and temperature sensation. The medial lemniscus and the spinothalamic tract ascend the midbrain in close association, most of the spinothalamic tract ending in the medial thalamic nuclei particularly the centromedian (p. 24.32); many fibres take a multisynaptic pathway through the reticular system.

THE SPINOCEREBELLAR TRACTS (figs. 24.14 and 31)

These tracts pass up the posterolateral aspect of the medulla in two portions. The dorsal spinocerebellar tract forms most of the inferior cerebellar peduncle which enters the cerebellum to synapse in the cerebellar cortex. The ventral spinocerebellar tract continues up the brain stem lateral to the medial lemniscus until it reaches the upper pons where it curves back into the superior cerebellar peduncle to end in the cerebellar cortex.

THE CRUS CEREBRI (figs. 24.33 and 38)

This contains fibres from the cerebral cortex which emerge from the internal capsule. They are arranged in a pattern similar to that of the motor fibres in the internal capsule (p. 24.36). Thus the most anterior part consists of frontopontine fibres arising from the frontal lobe and ending in pontine nuclei. The most posterior part carries temporo-parieto-occipito-pontine fibres arising in those parts of the cortex and conveyed to the pontine nuclei, which give fibres to the opposite cerebellar hemisphere. This is an important and predictable connection since movement of one side of the body is controlled by the same side of the cerebellum and by the opposite cerebral hemisphere. The middle of the crus is composed of corticobulbar and corticospinal fibres. Corticobulbar fibres lie anteriorly and end in the motor nuclei of the cranial nerves. Some of these fibres are crossed, others uncrossed. Nuclei such as the oculomotor, trigeminal and nucleus ambiguus (motor nucleus of glossopharyngeal and vagus) receive both crossed and uncrossed fibres, as does the part of the facial nucleus supplying the upper part of the face. Thus unilateral lesions of the peduncle have little effect upon these nerves. However, the lower part of the face is

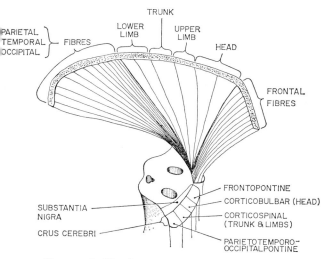

FIG. 24.38. The formation of the crus cerebri.

innervated from a portion of the facial nucleus which receives only crossed fibres, as do the nuclei of the abducent and hypoglossal nerves. Hence, a unilateral lesion of the crus produces a gross weakness of the lower face and tongue and an abducent palsy on the opposite side. The corticospinal fibres continue into the pyramid.

THE MEDIAL LONGITUDINAL FASCICULUS (figs. 24.32, 33 and 39)

This is a pathway between many cranial nerve nuclei, especially those supplying the external ocular muscles. It extends from the floor of the third ventricle into the spinal cord, passing close to the abducent, trochlear and oculomotor nuclei. Many different fibres pass within the fasciculus but its major connections are with vestibular and extrapyramidal systems. In the spinal cord the medial longitudinal fasciculus runs in the ventral column but with the formation of the medial lemniscus, it is displaced dorsally and in the brain stem it remains in the midline close to the ventricular system.

The cranial nerve nuclei (figs. 24.40 and 41)

The division of the grey matter of the spinal cord and brain stem into distinct functional groups has already been indicated. In the brain stem the motor column lies medial to the sensory column and many cranial nerves have nuclei in both.

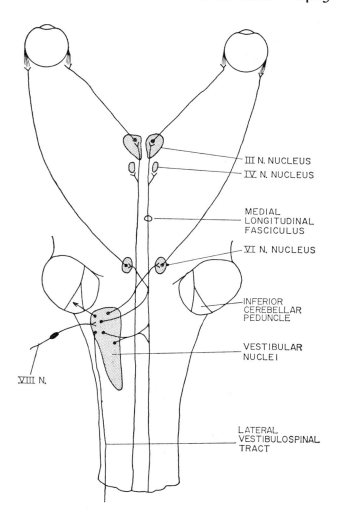

FIG. 24.39. The medial longitudinal fasciculus.

THE MOTOR COLUMNS (figs. 24.40 and 41)

The motor columns may be subdivided into a **visceral group** which innervate smooth muscle, glands and vessels and a **somatic group** which innervate skeletal muscle. The somatic group has a **branchial** sub-group innervating striated muscles derived from the branchial arches. The branchial cell column migrates from its embryonic position. Nucleus ambiguus and the facial nucleus are good examples. In embryonic life the nerves emerge directly from the nuclei through the lateral aspect of the brain stem like all branchial nerves. Because of migration into a more anterior and lateral position the internal course of the fibres is curved.

The **somatic cell column** occupies a position close to the midline. From it come the fibres which make up the oculomotor, trochlear and abducent and hypoglossal nerves which supply the extraocular and tongue muscles. With the exception of the trochlear which arises at the

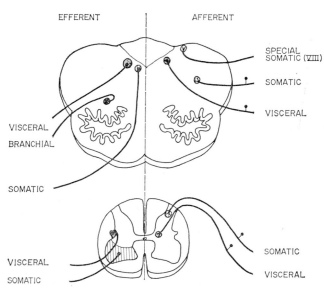

EFFERENT AFFERENT

SPECIAL SOMATIC (VIII)

SOMATIC

VISCERAL

VISCERAL BRANCHIAL

SOMATIC

VISCERAL

SOMATIC

VISCERAL

SOMATIC

SOMATIC

VISCERAL

FIG. 24.40. Functional components of cranial nerve nuclei in the medulla and the spinal nerve nuclei in the spinal cord.

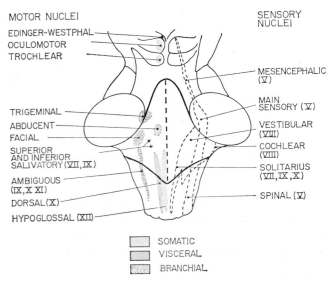

MOTOR NUCLEI

SENSORY NUCLEI

EDINGER-WESTPHAL
OCULOMOTOR
TROCHLEAR

MESENCEPHALIC (V)

MAIN SENSORY (V)

TRIGEMINAL
ABDUCENT
FACIAL
SUPERIOR AND INFERIOR SALIVATORY (VII, IX)
AMBIGUOUS (IX, X XI)
DORSAL (X)
HYPOGLOSSAL (XII)

VESTIBULAR (VIII)

COCHLEAR (VIII)

SOLITARIUS (VII, IX, X)

SPINAL (V)

SOMATIC
VISCERAL
BRANCHIAL

FIG. 24.41. Cranial nerve nuclei, showing relationships to the floor of the fourth ventricle. Modified from Crosby E.C., Humphrey T. & Lawer E.W. (1962). *Correlative Anatomy of the Nervous System*. New York: Macmillan.

back of the brain stem, these nerves emerge from the ventral aspect near the midline.

Nerves with cell bodies in the **branchial cell column** supply the muscles of mastication, expression and swallowing which are derived from branchial arches. Muscles of mastication are innervated by the trigeminal nerve, those of expression by the facial nerve and those of swallowing and vocalization by the glossopharyngeal,

vagus and cranial accessory nerves. The branchial motor fibres in these three nerves arise from the **nucleus ambiguus**. The spinal accessory nerve supplies the trapezius and sternomastoid muscles which are branchial muscles.

The **visceral cell column** continues from the spinal cord up into the midbrain where it is the most lateral of the cranial motor cell groups. In the thoracic cord the cell column is sympathetic and in the sacral and cranial parts parasympathetic. Nerves arising in this column supply the visceral structures including those of the head and neck. The vagus or wandering nerve innervates the thoracic and abdominal viscera. The smooth muscles of the eye, the iris and ciliary muscles are innervated by fibres arising in this column, which emerge with other fibres of the oculomotor nerve. Finally most of the fibres of the glossopharyngeal and vagus nerves originate from this column. The part of the column supplying fibres to the oculomotor nerve is termed the **Edinger-Westphal nucleus**, to the facial nerve the **superior salivatory nucleus**, to the glossopharyngeal the **inferior salivatory nucleus** and to the vagus the **dorsal motor nucleus of the vagus**.

Many of these nuclei are concerned with feeding. Mastication and salivation, swallowing and digestion are co-ordinated by a fibre pathway the **dorsal longitudinal fasciculus** lying between the somatic and visceral motor columns, e.g. between the hypoglossal and dorsal motor nucleus of the vagus.

Summary of motor nuclei of cranial nerves

Somatic	3	4	—	6	—	—	—	—	12
Branchial	—	—	5	—	7	9	10	11	—
Visceral	3	—	—	—	7	9	10	—	—

The larynx, pharynx and oesophagus are the site of complex reflexes which are mediated through the brain stem nuclei. Mucus from the nose and saliva arrive continuously in the upper pharynx, and mucus from the lungs arrives similarly via the larynx in the lower pharynx. Both are automatically swallowed down the oesophagus and from time to time food and drink are swallowed in addition. During swallowing the bolus of liquid or solid is transferred in an orderly fashion, and the larynx is temporarily closed so that none goes the wrong way, into the lungs by the trachea. Any that does so excites the **cough reflex** and is returned. So if this group of reflexes is impaired by disease of the brain stem or relevant cranial nerves, the patient is in danger of drowning in his own secretions which are not being properly swallowed, and so form a pool in the pharynx and leak through the ill-closed larynx into the trachea. Giving fluid by mouth then makes matters worse still. The proper temporary remedy is to lower the patient's head and let the pool empty out of his mouth.

Besides such complex activities, quite simple reflexes are organized by the brain stem, for instance, the **corneal**

reflex. If the cornea is lightly touched or even blown upon, the eyelids are immediately closed. The afferent path of this reflex is in the ophthalmic division of the trigeminal nerve, and the efferent path in the motor fibres of the facial nerve, terminating in the muscle orbicularis oculi. The link between the two paths lies in the brain stem, and there too the response becomes bilateral, since touching one cornea brings about blinking of both eyes.

THE SENSORY CELL COLUMN

This is divided into visceral and somatic parts but there is no branchial column. Somatic sensation enters the **trigeminal system** and visceral sensation, including taste, enters the **solitarius system**.

The special senses, hearing, equilibration and vision, form a new cell column of **special somatic** sensation which lies most laterally.

The **trigeminal sensory system** (fig. 24.42) accepts

FIG. 24.42. The central sensory connections of the trigeminal nerve. Modified from Noback C.P. (1967). *The Human Nervous System.* New York: McGraw-Hill.

somatic impulses from the head and thus includes fibres not only from the trigeminal nerve but also from the facial, glossopharyngeal and vagus nerves which carry cutaneous sensation from small areas of the ear and the posterior third of the tongue and pharynx. It may be helpful to point out the similarities between a spinal nerve and the trigeminal nerve. In the trigeminal nerve the ganglion contains cell bodies of axons coming

from the three different segments of the face. Instead of having a separate ganglion to each division they are fused into one large trigeminal ganglion. The ventral or motor root of the nerve passes separately, close to the dorsal or sensory root. Spinal nerve fibres containing pain and temperature enter the dorsolateral fasciculus and ascend and descend for short distances. The spinal tract of the trigeminal nerve is the equivalent of the dorsolateral fasciculus, and it descends the cord as low as C4. The spinal tract synapses with its nucleus, just as the dorsolateral fasciculus synapses in the substantia gelatinosa.

Pain and temperature impulses from the trigeminal, facial, glossopharyngeal and vagal nerves are conveyed to their ganglionic cells. In the case of the trigeminal nerve the three sensory divisions have their cell bodies in the trigeminal ganglion and in the case of the facial in the geniculate ganglion. The glossopharyngeal and the vagus nerves have sensory ganglia near the base of the skull (p. 21.11). After the entry of the nerves into the pons or medulla, pain and temperature impulses descend the brain stem and synapse with cells in the spinal part of the nucleus of the trigeminal nerve. These descending fibres form the spinal tract which merges with the dorsolateral fasciculus lateral to the nucleus. Both the spinal tract and the spinal nucleus of the trigeminal nerve are arranged so that fibres from the ophthalmic division of the trigeminal nerve are represented most anteriorly,

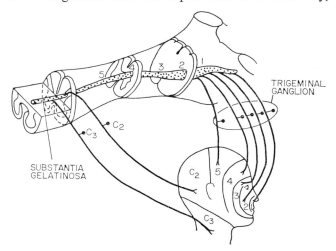

FIG. 24.43. Somatotopic arrangement in the spinal nucleus of the trigeminal nerve V.

those from the maxillary division next and those from the mandibular division most posteriorly (fig. 24.43). Immediately anterior to the ophthalmic fibres there is the spinothalamic tract carrying impulses from the opposite side of the body and immediately posterior to the mandibular fibres are the descending fibres from the facial, glossopharyngeal and vagal nerves conveying somatic sensation. The most anterior, i.e. the ophthalmic fibres, extend further down the cord. Fibres from the periphery of the face end in the lower part of the spinal nucleus and fibres from the central part of the face higher up. This overlapping 'onion skin' pattern is imposed upon the ophthalmic, maxillary and mandibular territories The neurosurgeon uses this knowledge to denervate part of the head by medullary tractotomy in the treatment of intractable facial pain.

Fibres are relayed from the spinal nucleus across the midline to ascend in the trigeminal lemniscus medial to the spinothalamic tract and posterior to the medial lemniscus. During its course the tract gives off numerous collaterals to other cranial nerves and to the reticular formation, where it may act as part of the arousal mechanism. Touch and pressure sensation end partly in the **main sensory nucleus of the trigeminal** which lies in the pons and partly in the spinal nucleus. After crossing the midline, the secondary sensory neurones ascend to join the medial lemniscus putting the 'head' on the 'headless man' of the lemniscus (p. 24.22). Proprioceptive impulses from muscles of the jaws, face, tongue and eyes pass to the **mesencephalic nucleus** of the nerve and are probably relayed to end in the cerebellum.

The solitarius system accepts visceral afferents from the facial, glossopharyngeal and vagus nerves, the somatic afferents of these nerves entering the trigeminal system. In both systems the cell bodies of the nerves lie in peripheral ganglia.

Fibres leaving the ganglion cells enter the medulla descending to form a tract known as **tractus solitarius**. This descends through the centre of a cylinder of cells which is **nucleus solitarius** with which the fibres synapse. The nuclei on either side of the brain stem converge and fuse in the lower part of the medulla. The upper part of the nucleus is concerned with taste and here taste fibres from the tongue end after passage in the facial nerve. The lower part of the nucleus is concerned with general visceral sensation and receives the termination of the vagus nerve. The intermediate portion serves both taste and general visceral sensation; here the glossopharyngeal nerve enters, conveying general visceral sensation from the pharynx and larynx. The secondary fibres are relayed from the nucleus solitarius across the midline to ascend in the medial lemniscus to the thalamus.

The inner ear

The **inner ear** consists of two components, the **bony labyrinth,** a complex cavity within the petrous temporal bone, and the **membranous labyrinth,** an assembly of interconnected sacs and channels lying inside the bony labyrinth. The whole inner ear is filled with fluid, unlike the middle ear.

The bony labyrinth (fig. 24.44) has three parts. The central part is the **vestibule,** which lies immediately medial to the inner wall of the tympanic cavity; thus the foot-

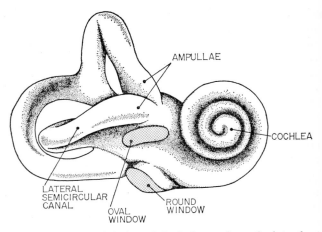

FIG. 24.44. The right bony labyrinth seen from the lateral side.

plate of the stapes (p. 21.53), held by its anular ligament in the oval window in this inner wall, can transmit sound waves through the wall into the vestibule, where they enter the fluid filling the vestibule.

The **cochlea** (p. 24.28) lies in front of, and the **semicircular canals** behind the vestibule. These are three in number and open into the vestibule at each end. Each lies in a plane approximately at right angles to the others and each has a dilated section at one end adjoining the vestibule, termed the **ampulla.**

EQUILIBRATION

The membranous labyrinth lies inside the bony labyrinth, and is filled with fluid, **endolymph**; the fluid surrounding it and filling the bony labyrinth is **perilymph**. In the vestibule lie the **utricle** and **saccule,** two membranous chambers which show on the lining of their cavities a patch of epithelium containing hair cells. The hairs project into the cavity and support gelatinous masses containing deposits of calcium carbonate, the **otoliths**. In the saccule the hair cells lie on the side wall and may serve as detectors of low frequency vibrations. The hair cells of the utricle serve as receptors sensing gravitational forces acting upon the otoliths. They generate impulses in the utricular branch of the vestibular nerve which correspond to the position of the head; if the head is tilted to a new angle, the pattern of impulses alters, because gravity acts upon the otoliths along a different axis. It is possible in crayfish larvae to substitute iron filings for the otoliths. When a magnet is then placed above the creature, its iron otoliths move in such a way that it responds by turning upside down.

In man, responses to the information from the utricle are hard to distinguish separately and form one component in **tonic neck reflexes**. When the posture of the head is altered, alterations of the whole posture of the body follow. This type of postural change may sometimes be seen

n a premature baby, not yet endowed with a full repertoire of behaviour. Its limbs take up different attitudes,
depending on the side to which it is induced to turn its
head by the offer of a bottle (fig. 23.45). Similiarly, when
its head is bent back, its arms may extend and its legs flex,
and conversely when its head is bent forwards. The body
takes up a posture appropriate for the head's position on

FIG. 24.45. Posture of supine baby when offered a bottle
from left or right side. From Gesell. A. (1938) *J. Paediat.*
13, 455.

he neck. These effects are not a matter of utricular re-
ponses alone. By suitable experiments in animals, con-
ributions can be distinguished from the utricle, from
receptors in the neck muscles, and also from the skin
surface of the body.

In the **semicircular canals** lie **semicircular ducts**, and at
the ampullae these too contain hair cells. The hair cells
here support jelly-like masses (cupulae) which are de-
ormed by the fluid in the semicircular ducts and enable
he hair cells to sense the fluid movements. When the head
tarts to rotate, fluid in one or more of these canals lags
behind. Which canals are affected depends on the axis
round which the head rotates. The lagging fluid distorts
he cupula, in which receptor endings are embedded.

When the fluid is at rest, the activity of most of these
receptors is not zero. If it were, then distortion to one side
would produce activity, but distortion to the other side
would produce no change; loss of one set of semicircular
canals would deprive the victim of information about
three of the six kinds of spin signalled by the canals, since
pin either way round, in each of three planes, makes six.
What actually happens is that there is a **resting activity**.
Activity is diminished by distortion of the cupula to one
ide and increased by distortion to the other side (fig.
4.46). When a rotation starts, it is signalled in this way.
When acceleration ceases and the rotation continues at a
teady rate, the cupula resumes its starting position, being
lastic. At the end of the rotation, the deceleration deflects
he cupula in the opposite direction and so the impulse
raffic alters in the opposite direction to its first change. In

20

fish it is possible to insert a globule of oil into the canal
and watch the mechanical changes going on. The semicircular canal system permits us to detect rotational acceleration so slight that it takes a whole minute, starting from
a stationary position, to complete the first full turn.

The response to stimulation of the semicircular canals
can be evoked by rotating a person in a special chair. But

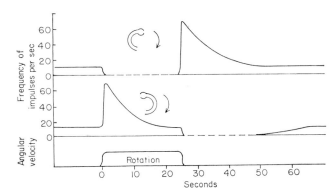

FIG. 24.46. Time course of discharge of vestibular neurones during rotation. From Adrian (1943). *J. Physiol.* **101**,
389.

it is easier to use warm or cold water syringed gently
into the external acoustic meatus; this method offers
the extra advantage of testing one ear at a time. The
lateral part of the lateral canal protrudes a little into
the middle ear cavity; when the adjacent tympanic membrane is heated or cooled and the head is tilted appropriately, the endolymph in this part of the lateral canal
undergoes a change of temperature and rises or falls in
relation to the rest of the endolymph. Thus the effect of
rotation on the canal is mimicked.

The response consists in **nystagmus**, i.e. repeated movements of both eyes together slowly to one side and then
rapidly back again. The direction of the nystagmus is
defined as the direction of the quick movement, right or
left, occasionally up or down if the head is not being held
vertical. Vertical nystagmus may occur during spinning
in a rotating chair. There is also **vertigo**, the sensation of
rotation, often associated with vomiting. The subject also
tends to misjudge the position of objects when he points
to them (**pastpointing**) as if he were spinning round and
round and making allowance for this.

As mentioned already, the semicircular canal system
produces a resting discharge when there is no rotation.
When rotatory acceleration occurs, this discharge grows or
diminishes, depending on the direction of the spin. If the
system on one side is damaged or removed, the effect is
the same as that of rotation one way. Vertigo, nystagmus,
nausea and vomiting occur and may take a month to
settle down; and even then, if the damage is permanent,
the control of eye movements may be deficient; the eyes

may not be accurately moved to compensate for head movements.

The vestibular portion of the eighth nerve receives the impulses from the semicircular canals. It enters the brain stem at the junction between pons and medulla, passing in front of the inferior cerebellar peduncle to terminate in the **vestibular nuclei** (fig. 24.47). These have been divided

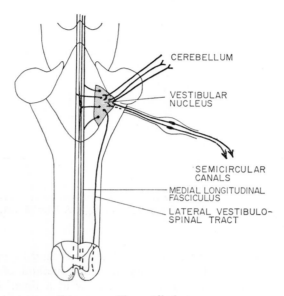

FIG. 24.47. The vestibular nerve.

into four. Some vestibular fibres, however, bypass them and enter the cerebellum via the inferior cerebellar peduncle. Fibres arising in the vestibular nuclei pass down the medulla and enter the cord as the vestibulospinal tract to end on the ventral horn cells; in this way they influence head, neck and trunk movements and to a lesser extent limb movements. Most of the vestibulospinal tract arises from the lateral vestibular nucleus. Other neurones arise from the vestibular nuclei and ascend the brain stem as an ill defined tract to end in the temporal cortex. An important connecting pathway is formed by fibres passing from the vestibular nuclei to the nuclei of the external eye muscles in the medial longitudinal fasciculus (fig. 24.39). Cerebellar nystagmus is due to impulses from the cerebellum and conveyed to the eye muscle nuclei via the deep cerebellar nuclei without relaying in the vestibular nuclei. Connection with other cranial nerves is also established through the medial longitudinal fasciculus. The importance of the connection between the vestibular and eye muscle nuclei cannot be overemphasized, as it assists co-ordination of head and eye movement so that fixation of the object on the fovea of the retina may be maintained despite head and neck movement. Many important vestibular connections are well illustrated by considering motion sickness.

HEARING

The **cochlea** resembles the helical cavity in a snail shell with the top of the shell pointing forwards and laterally. The cavity makes two and three-quarter turns round its bony axis, the **modiolus**, which is channelled to accommodate the fibres and cell bodies of the nerve cells of the cochlear division of the eighth nerve. The **cochlear duct** lies inside the bony cochlea. In cross-section (fig. 24.48) the top of one turn of the bony cochlea contains the **scala vestibuli**. This is the part of the cavity of the bony labyrinth which is continuous with the vestibule, where the footplate of the stapes introduces sound waves. The scala vestibuli is separated by a thin, easily deformed membrane from the cochlear duct which is part of the

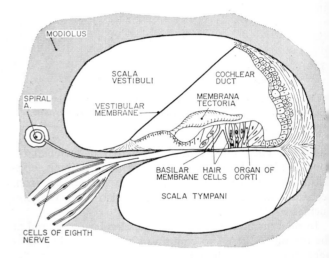

FIG. 24.48. Cross-section of cochlea showing organ of Corti and adjacent structures.

membranous labyrinth system. This thin membrane offers no obstacle to sound waves in the system.

The other side of the cochlear duct is bounded by a different type of membrane, the **basilar membrane**, which is strong and firmly mounted on bony ridges at each side. After deforming the basilar membrane, a sound wave can dissipate itself by entering the **scala tympani**, which is linked at the base of the cochlea to the inside of the round window in the inner wall of the tympanic cavity. The membrane filling the fenestra is flexible and so allows the fluid in the scala tympani to give.

Deformation of the basilar membrane is sensed by two rows of hair cells in the **spiral organ of Corti** which lies on the basilar membrane. On top of the hair cells is the soft padlike **membrana tectoria** which moves across the hairs when the basilar membrane is deformed, thus stimulating them. The hair cells are supplied by nerve fibres from cells lying within the modiolus of the cochlea. These neurones form the **spiral ganglia**, the counterpart of dorsal root ganglia at spinal level; they are bipolar and their central processes are the fibres of the cochlear division of the eighth nerve.

To enable hearing to take place, the middle and inner ears together have three operations to perform:

(1) transferring a sound wave arriving through air at the ear drum into a sound wave in liquid in the inner ear,

(2) providing a means of sensing the sound wave in the liquid of the inner ear,

(3) coding what is heard as nerve impulses passing along the cochlear division of the eighth nerve to the medulla.

Liquid is much less compliant than air. So to transfer a sound wave in air into one in liquid, a lever system is necessary. The lever reduces the movement but increases the force. Thus a wave of given amplitude in air is changed into a wave of much smaller amplitude in liquid. If there were no such lever system, sound in air would be able to produce hardly any wave disturbance in a liquid. Similarly sound waves in water cannot produce any perceptible sound waves in air unless some device is provided to match the properties of the two media; this is why we cannot normally listen to the conversation of porpoises.

The ossicles of the middle ear provide some leverage, about 1·3:1, but most of the leverage arises from the difference between the areas of the eardrum and the footplate of the stapes (p. 21.53). The ratio is about 15:1 and so the whole middle ear system gives a 20:1 reduction in movement and a 20:1 increase in force (fig. 24.49).

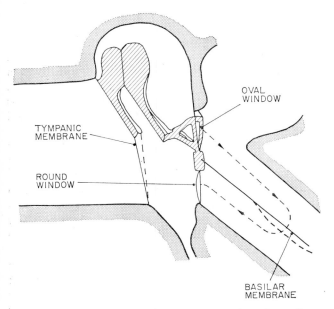

TYMPANIC MEMBRANE

ROUND WINDOW

OVAL WINDOW

BASILAR MEMBRANE

FIG. 24.49. Cross-section of the ear to show how displacement of the tympanic membrane is transmitted to the oval window, deforms the basilar membrane and then the fenestra cochleae (round window).

Extra stiffening of the middle ear mechanism is provided by the action of the two muscles **tensor tympani** and **stapedius**. Pulling on the ossicular chain, they restrict its mobility. They are brought into action in reflexes provoked by swallowing and yawning, but especially by loud sounds. Thus they can guard the hearing system against damage by overloading. But the reflex response to a loud noise has, like all reflexes, a latent period, in this case some 15 msec. This is a short time, but if a noise is very loud and abrupt in onset, it can slip through the reflex protection and damage the hearing mechanism before stapedius and tensor tympani can respond. Occasionally the stapedius may be paralysed by a facial nerve palsy. Then hearing on the affected side is too sensitive for comfort and the patient suffers from **hyperacusis,** or excessively acute hearing.

The sound waves in the liquid of the inner ear are sensed by the hair cells of the spiral organ of Corti, as already described; when the basilar membrane is deformed, the membrana tectoria 'strokes' the hairs. So far, one can understand how the ear senses whether a noise is occurring or not.

Even so, hearing is a very competent faculty. It can distinguish different pitches over a range of 10 octaves, from 20 to about 20,000 cycles/sec. It can distinguish loudness over a range of 120 decibels from the softest perceptible sound to the loudest that is not actually damaging; the loudest sound is a million million times more intense than the softest. And it can distinguish the direction of a sound with a precision which is partly due to the timing ability of the two ears working together. When sound reaches one ear 0.1 msec, or perhaps less, before it reaches the other, the difference is detectable and can be interpreted as indicating the direction of the sound.

The necessary information must be conveyed as trains of nerve impulses. The simplest way of indicating pitch would be to have one impulse per sound wave. But there is an upper limit to the frequency of impulses that a nerve fibre can carry. About 1100/sec is the highest possible frequency and pitch can be distinguished far above this limit.

The alternative method of indicating pitch is to have one nerve fibre for a particular pitch. There are plenty of fibres, since the cochlear nerve comprises some 25,000. The available sorting device is the basilar membrane. Although not taut, it is suspended in such a way that in different parts of the cochlea it is displaced furthest by different pitches of sound. At the basal part the preferred frequency is high and at the apical part it is low.

Thus different parts of the spiral organ of Corti respond maximally to sound of different pitches. A somewhat similar effect is shown by a piano; with the pedal depressed, it selects the frequencies in a sound and the appropriate strings of the piano resonate and are heard when the sound stops. The ear, however, is not so selective; the strings are coupled together in one basilar membrane and it is not true to say that one part of the membrane vibrates in response to a note of only a single pitch. One part vibrates maximally, the rest less.

So within the eighth nerve the information about pitch is probably derived by determining which fibre in the nerve is responding maximally; this fibre is linked to the hair cells in the part of the spiral organ tuned to the frequency. Loudness can be signalled by the overall amount of traffic in the nerve. Comparison between the times of arrival of sounds at the two ears can, of course be done only in the central nervous system.

Disorders of hearing

When the function of the middle ear is impaired, transfer of sound from air to the liquid of the inner ear is inefficient. This can happen because the external acoustic meatus is blocked by wax or because infection in the middle ear cavity has damaged the drum or locked the ossicles together. It can also happen because the footplate of the stapes has become rigidly fixed in the oval window by the process termed **otosclerosis**.

The affected ear hears sounds arriving in the air from a tuning fork poorly. But it is possible to transfer sound waves to the liquid of the inner ear directly by applying the base of a tuning fork to the scalp and thus causing the skull to vibrate. Tested in this way, the affected ear is just as efficient as the other, or even slightly better. The normal ear, during such a test, receives a variety of sound waves by the normal route plus the bone-conducted waves. To some extent the latter are masked by the former. The damaged ear will receive only the bone conducted waves, which are therefore clearly audible.

This is why the damaged ear seems actually to hear better when a tuning fork is applied by its base to the forehead, so that sound is being applied equally to both ears by bone conduction. The procedure is **Weber's test** and when one ear has faulty conduction from air to inner ear, the sound seems to be more in that ear than in the normal ear on the opposite side.

Simple, antiquated methods of testing hearing, using just tuning forks, produce reliable and prompt information when the subject is intelligent and the examiner experienced. More sophisticated testing can be done by **audiometry**. The instrument emits into one ear a pure tone of a selected frequency and the intensity can be altered so that the softest audible sound is measured for that frequency. When the procedure is repeated to cover the whole spectrum of audible frequencies, an **audiogram** is plotted. The plot shows the sensitivity of the ear against normal sensitivity for every frequency. The unit is the **decibel**; one bel represents a tenfold increase in intensity, and is divided into ten decibels, so that each decibel step makes a sound 7·9 per cent more intense than it was be-

fore. A curious choice of unit on first acquaintance, but convenient because to increase loudness by steps that seem equal to the listener the intensity of sound must be multiplied by approximately the same factor for each step (Weber–Fechner relation).

Besides, it might be supposed from the form of an audiogram that the ear is equally sensitive to sounds of any frequency. This is entirely untrue; it is far more sensitive to sounds of a frequency around 1000 cycles/sec

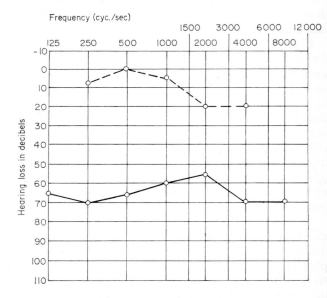

FIG. 24.50. Audiogram showing middle ear deafness. Continuous line, air conduction; broken line, bone conduction.

(about two octaves above middle C on the piano) than to sounds at the upper and lower limits of the audible range. But the audiogram compares the ear being tested with a 'standard ear' and exhibits any differences conspicuously. So it can be seen, for instance, whether a hearing loss is more marked at high frequencies than at low or confined to one small range of frequencies.

Impairment of conduction in the middle ear produces **middle ear deafness**. Damage of the cochlea, the eighth nerve or occasionally of the auditory paths in the central nervous system produces **nerve deafness**. The two can be distinguished by tuning fork tests, as already described. In addition, middle ear deafness tends to affect all frequencies of sound, but nerve deafness chiefly the higher frequencies.

Audiometry sometimes makes a further distinction possible. When the cochlea itself is at fault, then soft sounds are inaudible; there is a high threshold. But louder sounds may be heard just as well as by the normal ear or even apparently slightly better. This phenomenon is **recruitment**; it is as if the cochlea had lost its most sensitive receptors first, comparable to the rods of the retina (p.

24.57), but retained the less sensitive receptors in good order, at least until the disease progresses further. This is like 'night blindness' of the cochlea, with normal vision by day. Recruitment is not normally observed when the eighth nerve or central pathways are faulty. It is a characteristic of cochlear disease.

Central connections of the auditory system (fig. 24.51)
The fibres of the cochlear portion of the eighth nerve enter the brain stem at the lower part of the pons, dividing after

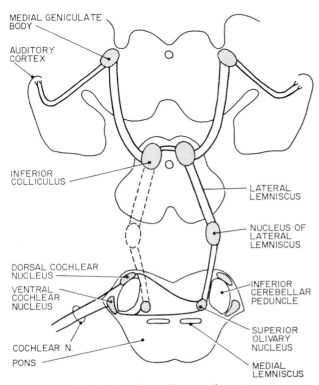

FIG. 24.51. The auditory pathways.

entry to synapse with cells in the dorsal and ventral cochlear nuclei; these lie posterior and anterior to the inferior cerebellar peduncle. Fibres from these nuclei cross the midline; those from the dorsal cochlear nucleus lie close to the ventricular floor and pass beneath the striae medullares, and those from the ventral cochlear nucleus cross at a deeper level and often relay with small cells which, together with the fibres form the **trapezoid body**. After crossing, both sets of fibres ascend together as the **lateral lemniscus** which is formed by crossed and uncrossed fibres arising from the cochlear nuclei. The lateral lemniscus is pushed laterally and anteriorly by the formation of the superior cerebellar peduncle and reaches the inferior colliculus from which it is relayed to the medial geniculate body. From here fibres pass in the auditory radiation of the internal capsule to enter the auditory cortex of the

temporal lobe (p. 24.49). Thus each temporal lobe receives fibres conveying impulses from both ears so that lesions of the central nervous system involving the auditory pathway do not produce deafness unless both sides of the brain are involved.

Vision and the midbrain

Most of the optic tract fibres from the eyes end in the lateral geniculate body (p. 24.33) but some pass directly through it to synapse on cells in the midbrain particularly in the superior colliculus. The colliculus also receives fibres from the occipital cortex and acts as a relay station of visual reflexes, co-ordinating head and eye movement so that, for instance, attention is paid by turning head and eyes to something seen out of the corner of one's eye. This is achieved by fibres which have arisen in the superior colliculus and pass down into the upper part of the spinal cord in the **tectospinal tract** ending in cranial and ventral horn motor nuclei. The **tectorubral tract** passes also to the red nucleus from which the **rubrospinal tract** arises and influences movement. The **pretectal nucleus** lies immediately anterior to the superior colliculus and just below the posterior commissure. It is an important component of the pupillary light reflex arc which constricts the pupil when light is shone into the eye (fig. 24.86). Just before entering the geniculate body, a few fibres leave the optic tract and enter the tegmentum of the midbrain to synapse with the pretectal nucleus. From this nucleus fibres pass to the Edinger–Westphal nuclei on both sides. From here fibres pass in the oculomotor nerve to synapse in the ciliary ganglion within the orbit from which impulses go by the ciliary nerves to the ciliary muscle and iris. Because fibres pass to both Edinger–Westphal nuclei from each pretectal nucleus a large stimulation in either eye results in bilateral pupillary constriction, the consensual light reflex (p. 24.58). In clinical neurology an understanding of this light reflex is of great importance in establishing the site of a lesion.

THE DIENCEPHALON

The forebrain has a central part, the diencephalon which is surrounded by the cerebral hemispheres or telencephalon.

The third ventricle (fig. 24.52) separates the two halves of the diencephalon, from the midbrain to the most anterior part of the third ventricle, the **lamina terminalis**. An evagination of the posterior wall of the third ventricle projects posteriorly and forms the **pineal body**. Beneath the pineal the posterior wall of the ventricle is thickened by many crossing fibres which form the posterior commissure. It is an important landmark in stereotactic surgery.

FIG. 24.52. Mid-sagittal section through third ventricle.

A large nuclear mass, the thalamus, occupies each half of the diencephalon with the epithalamus above, the subthalamus below and behind and the hypothalamus below and in front. The thalamus lies immediately lateral to the third ventricle, separated from the posterior part of the internal capsule by the thalamic reticular nucleus and the external medullary lamina. Its relation to the surface of the brain is shown in fig. 24.53.

FIG. 24.53. The position and connections of the thalamus.

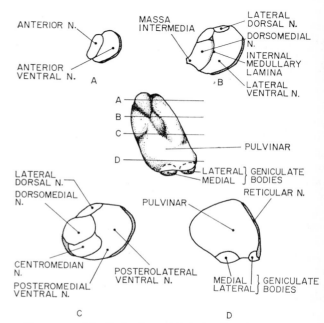

FIG. 24.54. The thalamic nuclei. A, B, C and D are cross sections at the levels shown in the central drawing, which is the right thalamus seen from above. Modified from Krieg W.J.S. (1966). *Functional Neuroanatomy*, 3rd Edition. New York: Blakiston–McGraw.

The thalamus

The thalamus is divided into anterior, medial, lateral ventral and central nuclear groups which are broken into subgroups. A Y-shaped internal medullary lamina encloses the anterior group and separates it from the medial and lateral groups. Fig. 24.54 shows the arrangement of these nuclei.

Nearly all the ascending sensory tracts from the spinal cord and brain stem end in the thalamus, from which they are relayed to the cerebral cortex. These tracts which include the spinothalamic tract, medial lemniscus and fibres from the reticular formation, naturally end in the lateral and medial portions of the ventral group. Fibres passing from the opposite cerebellar nuclei in the

superior cerebellar peduncle, of which some have relayed in the red nucleus, end in lateral and medial portions of the ventral group (fig. 24.55).

All groups participate in reciprocal connections with the cerebral cortex and the lateral group sends fibres to and from the basal nuclei. The anterior group, apart from its cortical connections through the anterior thalamic radiation, receives the mamillothalamic tract from the mamillary body (fig. 24.56).

The lateral group contains the **pulvinar**, the most posterior part of the thalamus which is thought to act as a co-ordinating link between visual somatic afferent and efferent systems giving and receiving fibres from the occipital, parietal and temporal lobes. The medial geniculate

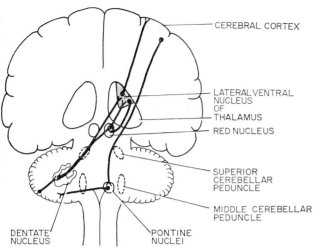

FIG. 24.55. Connections between the cerebellum and cerebrum.

body has been described in the section on the brain stem but is part of the thalamus lying at the junction between the diencephalon and midbrain. The lateral geniculate body lies immediately lateral to the medial geniculate and appears as a bulbous end to the optic tract. Its cells and fibres are arranged in definite layers, fibres from each retina interleaving with each other but probably remaining functionally separate. Binocular vision for example is not provided for in the lateral geniculate body but in the visual area of the cerebral cortex. The thalamic reticular nucleus together with the midline nuclei form part of the reticular formation and are thus concerned with arousal and attention. It lies between the external medullary lamina enveloping the thalamus and the internal capsule and inferiorly becomes continuous with the zona incerta. The spinothalamic tract and medial lemniscus have collateral connections with this reticular system which is multisynaptic and activates the cortex.

The subthalamus which lies below the thalamus is continuous with the mesencephalic tegmentum. Anteriorly and medially it becomes continuous with the hypothalamus. The subthalamus has connections with globus pallidus and midbrain structures and lies directly above the red nucleus. The **zona incerta** lies above the subthalamic nucleus. It is formed by fibres from the globus pallidus (the lenticular fasciculus) which penetrate the internal capsule before entering the subthalamus and passing downwards (fig. 24.56). The subthalamic nucleus receives the ansa lenticularis, which is a confluence of fibres from the globus pallidus gathering beneath the lentiform nucleus to pass in front of and beneath the anterior limb of the internal capsule.

FUNCTIONS OF THE THALAMUS

The thalamus receives sensory impulses from all parts of the body and, as already described, it has connections with most of the main masses of grey matter in the brain. Incoming sensory impulses are acted upon by impulses from other parts of the body, so that the organism can integrate a single stimulus with many other sources of information. This sorting out of the sensory impulses prevents incongruous reactions to particular stimuli. When the thalamus is damaged by disease, gross disorders of sensation or movement may follow and also disturbances of the emotions and changes in personality.

Using stereotactic methods neurosurgeons can make small lesions in discrete areas of the thalamus in man. Such lesions may be of great benefit to patients with various disorders. Thus lesions in the anterior nuclear

FIG. 24.56. A frontal section of the diencephalon.

group and in the anterior radiations from it are made for various mental disorders and may have profound effects on personality. Lesions in the central median nuclei of medial nuclear group influence both pain and movement, and lesions in the nucleus dorsomedialis have led to marked improvement in patients with mental disorders.

Experience with stereotactic methods, used both in human patients and in experimental animals, is likely to lead to much more accurate knowledge of the structural connections of the thalamus and their associated functions. This knowledge may allow a much greater use of neurosurgery in the treatment of disease.

The hypothalamus

This lies immediately in front of the thalamus and mesencephalic tegmentum. The hypothalamic sulcus on the lateral wall of the third ventricle separates the thalamus from the hypothalamus (fig. 24.52). Laterally the hypothalamus is contained within the optic tracts and the subthalamus and is divisible into medial and lateral regions.

The medial region is directly related to the third ventricle and can itself be subdivided into a number of nuclear groups. The lateral region, however, contains a less distinct nuclear arrangement and cells are separated by the fibres of the **medial forebrain bundle**. This bundle contains fibres passing from the lateral to the medial hypothalamic region and it has many connections to other parts of the brain. It passes through the lateral hypothalamus and enters the olfactory area to continue caudally into the mesencephalon. The medial forebrain bundle's numerous connections facilitate the co-ordination of visceral and olfactory pathways and it is probably via this system that pleasant odours evoke salivation and flow of gastric juices whilst disagreeable odours cause retching. The pyriform cortex and hippocampus and their underlying subcortical nuclei send fibres to the hypothalamus. The amygdaloid body forms the pyriform subcortical nucleus whilst for the hippocampus it is the septal system (p. 24.47). Complex pathways exist between all these systems, for example the amygdaloid body receives hypothalamic fibres and conveys them back to the pyriform cortex. Apart from this relatively intrinsic organization there is a well marked connection to and from the mesencephalic tegmentum.

The **supraoptic nucleus** lies in the anterior part of the hypothalamus behind the optic chiasma and sends fibres to the hypophysis which affect the pituitary (p. 25.9). Sympathetic and parasympathetic function is also anatomically differentiated. The supraoptic nucleus, for example, is probably related to parasympathetic function whilst the **paraventricular nuclei** are concerned with sympathetic function. Other hypothalamic nuclei appear to influence both parasympathetic and sympathetic activities.

FUNCTIONS OF THE HYPOTHALAMUS

The hypothalamus used to be described as concerned with vegetative activities. What vegetative means may be deduced by looking at the functions with which the hypothalamus is concerned.

Temperature regulation

Body temperature is precisely regulated by alterations in several physiological functions (chap. 40). When hot, we move into a cooler place if possible and reduce clothing; the blood circulation through the skin increases and sweating starts. When cold, we find a warmer place and increase clothing, the skin circulation is reduced and shivers may occur. These responses can be produced by electrical stimulation within the hypothalamus. But more important, they can also be produced by local cooling and heating in the hypothalamus. Evidently the hypothalamus contains cells which sense the temperature of the blood perfusing them and bring about appropriate responses. This is not the whole story, because the temperature regulating mechanism is certainly responsive to chilling of the skin, quite apart from any change in blood temperature. But the hypothalamus plays a cardinal role in controlling body temperature and damage here can put the regulating system out of action. The centre is also influenced by circulating pyrogens, e.g. bacteria, viruses and endogenous substances liberated from leucocytes; these are responsible for the fever of infections and other diseases.

Feeding behaviour

The human appetite is delicately controlled, so that body weight may vary little over periods of years, although in all a great deal of food is consumed. Hunger is often associated with uncomfortable contractions of the stomach, and hypoglycaemia causes a sensation of hunger. But it is impossible to believe that we eat only when we get hunger pangs or hypoglycaemia and stop eating when the pangs or the hypoglycaemia wear off, and so regulate body weight to the observed degree of precision.

In the rat's hypothalamus there is a large central region which is concerned with feeding and drinking behaviour. Evidence exists that the glucose level in the blood can be sensed here. After damage to this region rats overeat and gain weight until a plateau is reached at which the overeating levels off. It is natural to assume that overeating is proof of excessive hunger. But the two are subtly different; rats which have become obese from hypothalamic injury are less active in their cages than normal rats and are more fussy about the palatability of their food; their appetite depends upon opportunity, unlike natural hunger. Damage in a much smaller region in the lateral hypothalamus leads to a reverse effect; the rat refuses to eat enough and ultimately dies of starvation.

Osmolality of the blood

Drinking behaviour in rats is most effectively altered by electrical stimulation of the lateral hypothalamus; this provokes prompt and vigorous drinking which results in marked overhydration if stimulation continues. In goats the hypothalamus has been shown to be sensitive to the osmolality of the blood perfusing it, and when this rises drinking is stimulated.

The thirst provoking effect of stimulation of these hypothalamic cells differs from that of damage in the nearby supraoptic region. Here cells, also sensitive to the osmolality of the blood, are found lying in immediate relation to the capillaries surrounding them, unlike the usual arrangement in the nervous system where neuroglial cells intervene between capillary and neurone. They generate the hormone ADH and release it into the circulation, either in the hypothalamus or else at the termination of their axons in the posterior part of the pituitary gland, **the pars posterior**. Damage to these cells results in the polyuria and the dehydration of diabetes insipidus (p. 25.16).

Sexual behaviour

This is provoked by stimulation below the site where drinking is provoked, and oxytocin (p. 25.16) is produced in a closely similar fashion to ADH secretion. Thus the hypothalamus is involved in the regulation of renal and reproductive function.

Releasing factors

The hypothalamus regulates the activity of the anterior pituitary through the release of factors which are carried to the anterior pituitary by veins of the pituitary stalk (p. 25.10).

Cardiovascular regulation

The medullary vasomotor control system is able to maintain a normal arterial blood pressure even when cut off from the upper parts of the CNS. But this is not a sufficient degree of control for everyday life; for instance, during exercise an increased arterial blood pressure is maintained. This higher level is produced even in anticipation of exercise, when the need for it is foreseen. The medulla cannot organize an anticipatory response; it is quite possible that the hypothalamus can. Stimulation at some sites within it produces changes in the cardiovascular system which strongly suggest a function in regulating cardiovascular activity more effectively and flexibly than can be achieved by lower levels of the nervous system acting alone.

Fear and rage

Changes in the cardiovascular system are clearly seen in cats responding to stimulation of brain areas within the **limbic system**. This system includes not only the hypothalamus, but also the cingulate and hippocampal gyri,

the fornix, the mamillary bodies and the anterior part of the thalamus (fig. 24.57). The response begins with dilation of the pupils, pricking up of the ears and an increase in the rate and depth of respiration. Active vasodilation occurs in muscles and vasoconstriction in the skin and the gut. Pulse rate and cardiac output and arterial blood pressure rise, and the normal stabilizing effect of the baroreceptor reflexes is inhibited. Adrenaline is released into the blood stream and the animal behaves in a way suited for defence, exhibiting features of fear and rage. Similar stimulation has been carried out in the course of neurosurgical operations on patients who then reported that they felt these emotions.

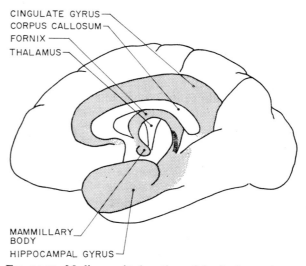

Fig. 24.57. Median sagittal section of forebrain to show structures of the limbic system (shaded).

Thus the hypothalamus takes part in important and complex reactions which are accompanied by powerful emotions of fear and rage, in the course of which the body is prepared for violent activity which has not yet begun; the usual prosaic control of cardiovascular and respiratory systems is temporarily overridden. These hypothalamic reactions alter the internal environment, for instance by reducing the P_{CO_2} in the blood through overbreathing.

Electrical stimulation in the lateral hypothalamus is in itself gratifying to rats, which rapidly learn to obtain the reward of stimulation by pressing a pedal connected to the stimulator, and then press it and stimulate their own hypothalamus until they are utterly exhausted, in complete disregard even of starvation. In a small central area of the inferior hypothalamus stimulation is evidently not attractive to the rat, which learns means of avoiding it.

Similar stimulation has been carried out in human beings at operation for the diagnosis or treatment of disease in this region. What they say and do is reminiscent of what might be expected from the results in rats; by stimulation here the surgeon can make the patient extremely angry with him. But the responses are not entirely in agreement with the rat results.

THE FUNCTION OF THE PINEAL GLAND

Rene Descartes (1596–1650), preoccupied with the idea of Animal Spirits and the analogy between them and liquids, surmised that the best place to control fluid flow in the brain would be at the pineal and posted the Rational Soul at this point. But long before, in the second century A.D., Galen thought that this part of the nervous system looked spongy, more like a gland. And recently, evidence from experiments in rats has led to the discovery that the pineal produces a hormone named melatonin, capable of antagonizing the effects of gonadotrophic hormones slowing the oestrous cycle and reducing the weight of the ovaries. Production of melatonin falls when a rat is in a constantly lit environment and an unexpected feature of the system is that the information about the amount of light seems to reach the pineal from the sympathetic chain in the neck, a strange path when one reflects how close the pineal is to the superior colliculus, itself closely linked to the retina. How far these findings in the rat relate to man is uncertain; but secreting tumours of the pineal in children lead to delayed sexual development, as if too much melatonin were being released, and on the other hand any damage to the pineal can give rise to precocious puberty as if melatonin release had been cut off.

THE WHITE MATTER AND BASAL NUCLEI OF THE CEREBRAL HEMISPHERES

The white matter (fig. 24.58)

Separating the head of the caudate nucleus and thalamus medially from the lentiform nucleus laterally is a thick layer of white matter, the **internal capsule**, containing both ascending and descending fibres. These radiate out as the **corona radiata** to all parts of the hemisphere and are intersected by transverse fibres of the corpus callosum whilst still maintaining a clear relationship to cortical areas. The internal capsule is indented and angulated by the lentiform nucleus to form the **genu** or knee which separates **anterior** from the **posterior limb** of the capsule (fig. 24.59).

The anterior limb is composed largely of fibres passing to and from the frontal lobe. The anterior thalamic radiation passes to the frontal cortex whilst fibres arising in the frontal cortex enter the anterior limb as the fronto-pontine tract.

The genu and anterior two-thirds of the posterior limb contain fibres from the precentral or motor cortex whilst the posterior one third contains temporo-parieto-occipito-pontine fibres. This arrangement ensures that when the internal capsule has lost its sensory component

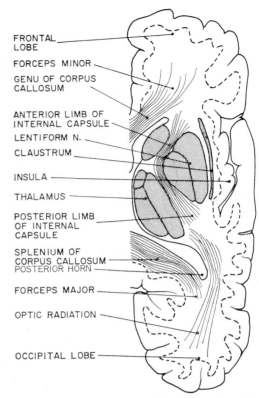

FIG. 24.58. The relations of the internal capsule.

FRONTAL LOBE
FORCEPS MINOR
GENU OF CORPUS CALLOSUM
ANTERIOR LIMB OF INTERNAL CAPSULE
LENTIFORM N.
CLAUSTRUM
INSULA
THALAMUS
POSTERIOR LIMB OF INTERNAL CAPSULE
SPLENIUM OF CORPUS CALLOSUM
POSTERIOR HORN
FORCEPS MAJOR
OPTIC RADIATION
OCCIPITAL LOBE

and formed the great motor pathway in the crus cerebri the fronto-pontine fibres lie anterior and the temporo parieto-occipito-pontine fibres posterior with the cortico bulbar and corticospinal fibres in between (fig. 24.38).

The auditory and visual radiations do not lie strictly within the internal capsule as they pass through white matter posterior to the lentiform nucleus; the auditor radiation runs from the medial geniculate body to the temporal lobe and the visual radiation from the lateral geniculate body to the occipital lobe.

The internal capsule is one of the projection pathways connecting cortex, basal nuclei, thalamus, cerebellum and spinal cord.

Different parts of each cerebral hemisphere are connected by **association fibres**, both short and long, uniting adjacent and distant gyri. **Commissural fibres** join the two hemispheres, the largest being the **corpus callosum** which radiates laterally and intersects the corona radiata. The callosum extends into the frontal lobes where it is called the **forceps minor** and into the occipital lobe as the **forceps major**.

The **anterior commissure**, connecting the temporal lobes is an important landmark in stereotactic surgery. The **hippocampal commissure** connects the hippocampus of each side by fibres passing through the fimbria to the opposite hemisphere (fig. 24.72).

INTERNAL CAPSULE

ANTERIOR LIMB

GENU

LENTIFORM PART OF POSTERIOR LIMB

RETROLENTIFORM PART OF POSTERIOR LIMB

THALAMUS

HEAD OF CAUDATE NUCLEUS

FIBRES

ANTERIOR THALAMIC

FRONTOPONTINE

CORTICOBULBAR

UPPER LIMB
TRUNK   } CORTICO-
LOWER LIMB } SPINAL

CORTICOTEGMENTAL

OCCIPITOTEMPORO PARIETOPONTINE

AUDITORY RADIATION

OPTIC RADIATION

FIG. 24.59. The fibre tracts in the internal capsule. Modified from Crosby E.C., Humphrey T. & Lawer E.W. (1962). *Correlative Anatomy of the Nervous System.* New York: Macmillan.

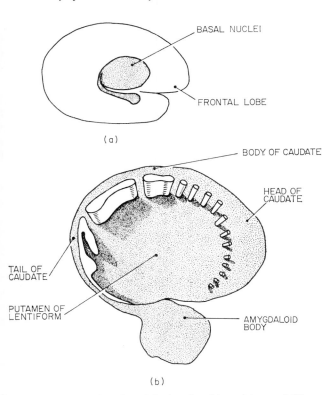

BASAL NUCLEI

FRONTAL LOBE

(a)

BODY OF CAUDATE

HEAD OF CAUDATE

TAIL OF CAUDATE

PUTAMEN OF LENTIFORM

AMYGDALOID BODY

(b)

FIG 24.60. The basal nuclei, showing (a) position and (b) component parts.

The basal nuclei (figs. 24.56 and 60)

These are large nuclei lying deep within the cerebral hemispheres lateral to the thalamus. They are the **putamen** and **globus pallidus** which together form the **lentiform nucleus**, the **caudate nucleus**, the **amygdaloid body** and the **claustrum**.

Of these the claustrum is a thin sheet of grey matter, which lies beneath the insula (p. 24.49). Little is known about its connections. The amygdaloid body lies at the tip of the tail of the caudate nucleus; it is functionally related to the rhinencephalon.

The caudate nucleus is composed of a head, body and tail. It is separated from the thalamus by a narrow groove in the walls of the lateral ventricle and by the internal capsule. The head lies close to the midline anterior to the thalamus and bulges into the lateral wall of the anterior horn of the lateral ventricle. It is fused with the putamen inferiorly and is then separated by the anterior limb of the internal capsule from the lentiform nucleus. The body of the caudate nucleus arches over the lentiform nucleus, separated from it by the internal capsule which is penetrated at many points by cellular bridges connecting the body of the caudate and putamen. These bridges of grey matter, amongst the white matter of the internal capsule, give a striated appearance and so the caudate and lentiform nuclei are sometimes called the **corpus** striatum. The tail of the caudate curves around the posterior part of the lentiform nucleus and lies in the lateral wall of the body of the lateral ventricle before entering the roof of the inferior horn of the lateral ventricle. The **stria terminalis**, a white fibre band, accompanies the tail of the caudate to end in the amygdaloid body. This band passes from the amygdaloid region of each side and crosses at the head of the anterior commissure to follow the course of the opposite striae and ends in the opposite amygdaloid region. Some of its fibres end in the anterior hypothalamus.

The lentiform nucleus lies between the insula and internal capsule divided by a sheet of white matter into a lateral portion, the putamen, and a medial portion of lighter colour, the globus pallidus. The external capsule separates the putamen from the claustrum.

The caudate and lentiform nuclei are parts of the extrapyramidal system. They have numerous connections between themselves and also with cortex and thalamus. The output from the lentiform nucleus is **ansa lenticularis,** and the **lenticular fasciculus** which divides into the thalamic fasciculus and the hypothalamotegmental fasciculus.

An aggregation of fibres arises in the globus pallidus and collects beneath it to form ansa lenticularis which passes under the ventral aspect of the anterior part of the internal capsule to the subthalamus (fig. 24.56). It descends the brain stem to enter the red nucleus and mesencephalic tegmentum and also has connections with the central tegmental tract.

The lenticular fasciculus arises in globus pallidus and passes horizontally through the internal capsule to enter zona incerta where some of the fibres synapse with zona incerta cells. A major part (the H2 bundle of Forel) connects with other nuclear masses of the extrapyramidal system including the red nucleus and the nucleus of the medial longitudinal bundle. This connection may explain how extrapyramidal disorders affect cranial nerve nuclei, especially those of eye movement.

The lenticular fasciculus descends into two main pathways, the **thalamic fasciculus** (H1 bundle of Forel) which turns first dorsally then laterally to enter nucleus ventralis lateralis of the thalamus, and the **hypothalamotegmental** tract which passes to the ventromedial nucleus of the hypothalamus and to the midbrain tegmentum. These connections may account for the unemotional facies of Parkinsonism since there has been shown to be a definite hypothalamic influence upon emotion (p. 24.35).

Thalamostriate fibres pass dorsally from the thalamus to enter the caudate and lenticular nuclei. The basal nuclei also receive many fibres from the cortex and transmit impulses to it. Most of these connections are to the globus pallidus, and are relayed to the caudate and putamen. A wide area of cortex is involved, especially from regions around the motor and sensory strip. Other fibres pass from these cortical regions to such thalamic nuclei as ventrolateralis which has connections with globus pallidus via the thalamic fasciculus. Other nuclei, the red nucleus, subthalamic nucleus and substantia nigra, also receive cortical fibres.

It is through this complex interconnecting system that motor function is affected profoundly through discharge pathways arising in many of the nuclei. Because these pathways are additional to the pyramidal or corticospinal pathway they are called **extrapyramidal** and are characterized by multisynaptic discharge pathways in contrast to the relatively long unisynaptic pathways of the pyramidal tract. Destructive lesions of the pyramidal system produce hypotonia whilst lesions of the extrapyramidal system produce hypertonia. In practice discrete lesions of these systems are uncommon, except those made deliberately by stereotactic surgery for the relief of spasticity.

Although much of this anatomy is complex and uncertain, an understanding of the basic arrangement and physiology of this extrapyramidal system is essential in understanding and treating extrapyramidal disorders such as Parkinsonism and other disorders (p. 24.65)

THE CEREBELLUM

The cerebellum lies behind and partly above the brain stem connected to it by the **inferior, middle** and **superior cerebellar peduncles**. It forms most of the roof of the fourth ventricle and partly surrounds the lateral aspect of the pons and medulla. It is separated from the occipital lobes by the tentorium cerebelli and thus lies entirely in the posterior cranial fossa.

External appearance (fig. 24.61)

The cerebellum may be divided grossly into a median portion or **vermis** and two larger lateral portions, the **cerebellar hemispheres**. On the superior surface, the vermis forms a midline ridge but on the inferior aspect the two hemispheres are separated by the vallecula, a hollow continuous with a posterior notch enclosing the falx cerebelli. The whole cerebellum is composed of folia, narrow curved gyri separated by numerous horizontal fissures, the deepest of which subdivide the cerebellum into various lobes.

The division into lobes by deep fissures is obvious in a midsagittal section for the median portions and in a parasagittal section for the more lateral portions.

The cerebellum has an outer layer of grey matter and a core of white matter containing nuclei. The central white core is formed by fibres entering and leaving in the cerebellar peduncles.

The middle cerebellar peduncles are the largest and contain pontocerebellar fibres conveying impulses from the opposite cerebral cortex.

The inferior cerebellar peduncle conveys afferent and efferent fibres to and from the spinal cord and medulla. In the medulla it ascends on either side of the fourth ventricle forming its lateral border and turning posteriorly at the lateral angles of the ventricle to enter the cerebellum. The dorsal spinocerebellar tract, originating in the thoracic nucleus, ascends the spinal cord and enters the

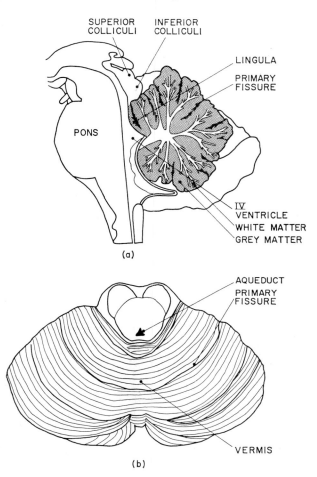

FIG. 24.61. External appearance of cerebellum. (a) sagittal section to show lobules and fissures, (b) as seen from above. Modified from *Cunningham's Textbook of Anatomy* (1964). London: Oxford University Press.

inferior cerebellar peduncle. Fibres also enter the cerebellum from the olive via this peduncle and go largely from one olive to the opposite cerebellar hemisphere. Fibres from the vestibular nucleus form the vestibulo-cerebellar tract and the reticular nuclei and other brain-stem nuclei, particularly the trigeminal spinal nucleus, also send fibres to the cerebellum. Apart from these afferent fibres, there are many efferent tracts descending in the inferior cerebellar peduncle to the reticular system, the olive, the vestibular nuclei and other brain stem nuclei.

The superior cerebellar peduncle consists almost entirely of efferent fibres which arise from the dentate, interpositus and fastigial nuclei. The small ventral spinocerebellar tract runs into the cerebellum through this peduncle.

Microscopic structure

Cerebellar cortex has a uniform structure and so differs from the cerebral cortex where parts can be identified by their cellular arrangement. Each folium has a core of white matter containing fibres going to and from the cerebellar cortex (fig. 24.62). The cortex is divisible into three layers.

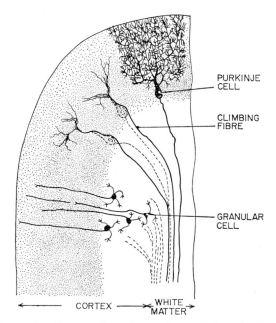

FIG. 24.62. Cross-section of a cerebellar folium, to show the relations of some of the types of cell.

The outer molecular layer contains the axons of the deeper granular cells and the dendrites of the Purkinje cells. Most of the few cells present are **basket cells**, named because of the way their processes surround the Purkinje cells. The axons of the basket cells run along and across folia. In this layer all these processes synapse together and so large areas of cortex are united functionally.

The inner granular layer contains small closely packed cells, each of which sends an axon into the molecular layer where they synapse with Purkinje cell dendrties.

The Purkinje cell layer lies between the other two layers. These cells are flask shaped with dendrites extending into the molecular layer where they divide in a transverse plane and axons projecting centrally to synapse with cerebellar nuclei in the white matter.

The white matter contains the axons of Purkinje cells and afferent fibres of two types, the **mossy fibres** and the **climbing fibres**. Mossy fibres arise outside the cerebellum from vestibular and pontine nuclei and are so named because their terminations have moss-like endings grasped by the claws of the granule cells. The origin of climbing fibres is uncertain. Probably most of them originate as collaterals of cerebellar cells, particularly Purkinje cells, although a few may arise outside the cerebellum. Within the granular layer large **stellate cells** connect with granule and basket cells and possibly act as reverberating circuits. These complex interconnections imply a widespread activation of cerebellar cortex, essential if it is to act as a co-ordinator of the muscles for the whole body.

The development of the cerebellum and its functional anatomy

The development of the cerebellum parallels its evolution through various species. Thus there is the **archicerebellum** of fishes which has rich connections with the vestibular apparatus. Higher in the evolutionary scale and with the development of extremities in the amphibia, reptiles and birds the **palaeocerebellum** appears with an afferent supply from limb movement receptors. With the development of the cerebrum, the **neocerebellum** establishes pathways for selective control of limb movement. The cerebellum is thus established as a co-ordinating centre for sensory impulses which then influence motor function.

The archicerebellum is composed of the **nodule** in the midline and the **flocculus** on either side. It has largely vestibular connections but with the formation of the palaeo and neocerebellum connections are established also with these parts.

The rest of the cerebellum is divided into **anterior** and **posterior lobes** by the **primary fissure** which is seen only on its superior surface. The anterior lobe is regarded as palaeocerebellum and the posterior lobe is largely neocerebellum.

The **anterior lobe** includes the anterior part of the vermis which is subdivided into lingula, central lobule and culmen, and the anterior parts of the superior surface of both cerebellar hemispheres.

The **posterior lobe** lies between the primary fissure and the archicerebellum and is subdivided by a number of horizontal fissures.

Most of the cerebellar nuclei can be seen in a cross-section through the middle cerebellar peduncle. The largest is the **dentate** which lies laterally, receiving fibres from the most lateral part of the hemisphere, and resembles the olivary nucleus. Immediately medial to the dentate nucleus lies the **interpositus nucleus** receiving fibres from the paravermal region.

On either side of the midline in the roof of the fourth ventricle lie the **fastigial nuclei** which receive fibres from

the vermis. Thus the nuclei manifest an orderly arrangement for the reception and transmission of impulses to parts of the cerebellar cortex (fig. 24.63). The archicerebellum (flocculonodular node) transmits fibres to the fastigial nucleus, and other parts of the vermis contribute and receive fibres from the vestibular apparatus. They enter through the inferior cerebellar peduncle and are distributed to the vermal cerebellar cortex. From thence efferent fibres go to the fastigial nucleus and on to the vestibular nucleus and the reticular formation. Both these give rise to descending tracts i.e. the vestibulospinal

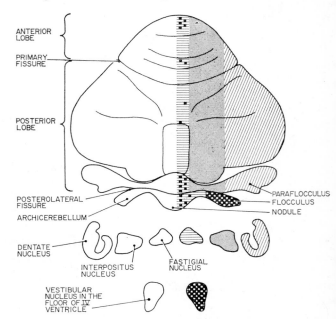

FIG. 24.63. Connections of cerebellar cortex with deep cerebellar and vestibular nuclei shown in corresponding tints. Modified from Krieg W.J.S. (1966). *Functional Anatomy*, 3rd Edition. New York: Blakiston–McGraw.

and reticulospinal, which pass down the cord to end on the ventral horn cells. The paravermal region, particularly the palaeocerebellum, transmits fibres to the dentate nucleus from which fibres pass in the superior peduncle to the opposite red nucleus and reticular formation; thence rubrospinal and reticulospinal pathways pass to the ventral horn cells. The dorsal and ventral spinocerebellar tracts are both distributed to the vermis and paravermal region.

The neocerebellum parallels the development of the cerebral cortex and has important connections with it. These are through the corticopontocerebellar pathway which relay in the pontine nuclei (fig. 24.55). Efferent fibres from the neocerebellum project largely to the dentate nucleus from which fibres pass to the reticular system and red nucleus. An important connection, however, is with the opposite ventrolateral nucleus of the thalamus from which fibres are projected to the cerebral cortex, the ventrolateral nucleus acting as a sensory relay station for proprioceptive impulses conveyed to the neocerebellum and transmitted to the dentate nucleus and thence to the thalamus. This pathway completes the afferent and efferent circuit between the cortex and cerebellum. It has been suggested that a functional arrangement exists in the cerebellum, the vermal zones being related to postural tone and equilibrium, a likely hypothesis in view of their rich vestibular connections. The paravermal zone similarly seems to be related to discrete movements and posture of the ipsilateral limbs, again highly probable since this is palaeocerebellum with connections through spinocerebellar tracts.

The lateral zone is largely neocerebellum and controls discrete voluntary movements of the limbs probably via its connections with the cerebral cortex. It is probable that extrapyramidal nuclei receiving impulses from vermal and paravermal regions influence movement pattern whilst impulses passing from the most lateral zones are concerned with more discrete movement projected to the ventrolateral nucleus of the thalamus and from thence to motor cortex. Although there is some evidence that afferent impulses other than those concerned with movement (touch, audition and vision) are represented in the cerebellar cortex there is little evidence for this in man.

The function of the cerebellum

The cortex of the cerebellum is a substantial mass of nervous tissue. If it were unfolded and spread flat, it would cover an area about 1.15×0.17 m. This is about three-quarters of the surface area of one cerebral hemisphere.

Mossy fibres

These afferents carry traffic from widespread origins i.e. from muscle, tendon and skin, from the labyrinth, from the cerebral cortex, including the visual and auditory areas and collaterals from the pyramidal tract, and from the reticular formation. The mossy fibres end in synapses with the granular cells, one fibre serving a number of granular cells, and one granular cell being served by a number of mossy fibres. However, in spite of this the arrangement of the information on the surface of the cerebellum can be made out to some extent. The information from muscle, tendon and skin is laid out in two maps of the body (fig. 24.64), one at the front, i.e. superior end, with the legs towards the cerebral hemispheres and the head down, and another at the back of the cerebellum, smaller and the other way round. Beside the face region of the front map, there is representation of information from eyes and ears, but it is not clear how this part is laid out. The link to retina and cochlea is indirect, and probably allows the cerebellum to play a part in the movements of eyes, head and body which shift attention about in space like a searchlight, but

does not permit the cerebellum to 'think about' what is seen or heard.

These maps no doubt describe the pattern of excitation in the axons of the granular cells; in other words, information from the legs arriving by the mossy fibre pathway excites granular cells with axons in the part of the cerebellum defined by the map. These axons end in the remarkable **parallel fibres**. A Purkinje cell (fig. 24.62) has a branching dendrite like a telegraph pole with a myriad crossbars and insulators, the crossbars all running transversely across the folium. Up and down the folium run the parallel fibres, hung upon the insulators of Purkinje cell after Purkinje cell, like telephone wires. There is, however, an important difference: the 'insulators' (**spiny branchlets** of the dendrites) are not insulators at all, but each is an excitatory synaptic knob.

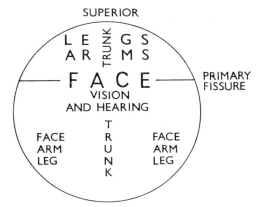

FIG. 24.64. The pattern of information on the cerebellar cortex.

Each of these telephone wires is around 5 mm long and is thin as nerve fibres go. Its conduction velocity is about 0.3 m/sec and so an impulse will take about 17 msec to go from one end to the other.

At the present time no account of the function of the cerebellum can claim to be complete. In a simplified account it is difficult to ensure that the selected features are the really significant ones. However, the working of the mossy fibre path might be summarized thus. It brings to the cerebellar cortex, via the granular cells, predominantly sensory information, about skin, muscles and tendons, about gravity and rotation and about what is seen and heard. The information arrives promptly, and although it is diffused by the granular cell synapses, it is displayed on the surface of the cerebellum as a pattern of impulses in the 'telephone wires' traversing the dendritic trees of the Purkinje cells, moving along the wires so that the impulse might take 17 msec to reach the end of any one wire. It is well worth pausing to calculate how far an impulse will travel in 17 msec over a fast-conducting sensory fibre in the central nervous system, moving at say 90 m/sec. The calculation emphasizes that mossy fibre information arrives fast and then initiates a slow moving ordered process in the cerebellum.

Climbing fibres

These are very thin and it is illuminating to realize how uncertain their origin still is, in spite of repeated attempts to discover it. Some people believe (p. 24.40) that they originate within the cerebellum, but others consider that their principal source is the olive. If this is so, then they carry traffic from the cerebral cortex, the corpus striatum, the red nucleus and some from the spinal cord.

Each climbing fibre is closely related to a single Purkinje cell. It branches like ivy to match the 'crossbars' of the 'telegraph pole' very precisely, and its terminal branches are intimately associated with the dendritic tree of one Purkinje cell, except for the 'insulators' bearing the parallel fibres.

The climbing fibre pathway is supposed to bring to the cerebellar cortex information about motor activity going on in the central nervous system, not only in the cerebral cortex, but also in the caudate and red nuclei. Each fibre is highly selective for its own Purkinje cell. The information arrives much more slowly than that in the mossy fibres, 10 or 15 msec behind, and is again probably displayed in an orderly fashion on the cerebellar cortex. So far as the surface of the body is concerned the map does not seem at present to agree closely with that of the mossy fibres.

Handling of information

This outline is concerned with the simplest excitatory paths, and there are also numerous other links involving other types of cell within the cerebellar cortex such as stellate and basket cells (p. 24.39). It will now be evident why it has been supposed that the cerebellar cortex can serve as a short term store of information, embodied in a slowly moving pattern of excitation, which can be assessed at any Purkinje cell by testing via its climbing fibre. The climbing fibre can readily excite the Purkinje cell if the Purkinje cell is already excited by the parallel fibres among its dendrites, but not otherwise.

It is not clear how this short term store of information is used. The anatomical arrangement seems to mean that activity in a group of climbing fibres is conveyed only to a proportion of the Purkinje cells up which they climb. The selection is directed by information which reached the cerebellum a short time before and depends on when it got there, since the longer the interval, the further transmission will proceed along the parallel fibres. Each Purkinje cell is like a safe which can be unlocked by its key, the climbing fibre, but only at a moment determined by its preset internal clock.

The outgoing paths from the cerebellum run to motor pathways in the central nervous system, especially to the motor areas of the cerebral cortex, and to the vestibular nuclei of the brainstem. They appear to be excitatory at their destinations. So one expects that the Purkinje cells will, for instance, excite the cells of the dentate nucleus and these in turn will (via the thalamus) contribute excitation to the motor area of the cerebral cortex. In fact this is not correct, for the Purkinje cells actually inhibit the cells of the deep cerebellar nuclei, a possibility which adds further complexity to the story. However, the fibres from the deep cerebellar nuclei certainly excite at their destinations in the motor area of the cerebral cortex. So it is clear that the cerebellum is closely concerned with motor activity and especially with voluntary motor activity, because of its particularly large output to the motor area of the cerebral cortex. And this output contributes excitation.

HUMAN CEREBELLAR DAMAGE

Firstly, conscious sensation remains unchanged. Although the cerebellum is liberally supplied with information from the sensory systems, it is not part of the arrangement for conscious sensation; information travels along other paths to the cerebellum, or is 'tapped off' by branching fibres from the paths that do contribute to consciousness. So after cerebellar damage the patient sees, hears and feels, just as before. So far as can be judged, he is as intelligent as before. A rat after cerebellar damage can still get through a familiar maze; if it is too unsteady to run, it rolls through the maze.

Secondly, a man walks clumsily, with a reeling drunken gait and feet wide apart. On reaching out to grasp anything, his arm trembles, and the nearer he gets to his target, the more his arm jerks and oscillates. He is not paralysed; all his joints can be moved at will, though not as strongly as before. The movements are **ataxic**, and are also slow to start and finish. When asked to make a movement, he starts later than normal by perhaps 200 msec and is similarly slow to stop. If the damage is one-sided, the effects are much more prominent on the same side of the body. However, in the minority of our movements both sides of the body must cooperate, and so movement of the other side may suffer from lack of properly timed cooperation. Affected movements are poorly balanced, tremulous and ill organized; they seem guided on inadequate and behind time information, their progress is not smoothly controlled, and their endpoint uncertain.

Speech may be similarly affected and be slow and deliberate. Of all voluntary movements, those of the eyes are the most delicately controlled. The eyes are affected very much like the limbs. The limbs, at rest and supported, do not tremble; neither do the eyes, while gazing straight ahead. But when turned to either side on request, they move too fast and too far and are corrected by a slower reverse movement; a rhythmic to-and-fro sequence is set up. This is cerebellar **nystagmus**. The eyes move together and one is not more affected than the other, even if the limbs are more affected on one side.

The limbs are more flacid than normal when the examiner moves them. This is **hypotonia,** since passive bending of joints is a method of assessing how much the normal 'tone' of muscles resists displacement of joints. The knee jerks (fig. 24.65) become pendular, and the legs

Normal   Cerebellar damage

FIG. 24.65. Movement of the leg during knee jerks produced thrice in a normal person and twice in a patient with cerebellar damage. From Holmes (1922). *Lancet,* **i,** 1181.

swing to and fro after the initial jerk more than normal. A knee jerk cannot be termed voluntary; here an involuntary reflex response becomes abnormal in cerebellar disease, and the active quadriceps and its antagonist hamstrings are not properly co-ordinated to damp the swing as effectively as usual. Suppression of swinging and oscillation of this kind is evidently much more necessary for movements in air than for movements in water, which are in more than one sense 'damped' by the surrounding water which prevents them from overshooting. In fact, animals with cerebellar damage swim remarkably well; a primitive fish like the lamprey possesses little in the way of a cerebellum.

Speculations
It is possible to interpret the cerebellum in general terms, as a device for metering excitation to the various levels of the motor pathways according to information about the body and its surroundings. When the level of excitation is too low, voluntary movements are slow to start; and once started, the excitation is turned off too slowly, if the cerebellum is absent. Involuntary movements are not so obviously affected, but are by no means immune. One keeps on one's feet by constant adjustments guided by information from the vestibular apparatus and eyes. The cerebellum, especially its flocculonodular lobe, is particularly intimately linked to the vestibular apparatus; anatomically, the intimacy is based on mossy fibres which run direct from the vestibular nerve and efferent fibres from the cerebellum which run direct to the vestibular nuclei, both contrasting with other connections which are multisynaptic. Thus in cerebellar damage the small movements of balancing start too late and then go too far.

Muscle spindle activity undergoes regulation by the cerebellum. The activity of the gamma motor neurones is normally increased by the cerebellum, especially by its posterior part; they make the muscle spindles more taut. Hence in cerebellar disease the spindles are less taut and sensitive than usual, and the limbs are consequently hypotonic. Further, a knee jerk is normally damped by the contraction of the hamstrings when they are stretched by the extending knee joint. If the muscle spindles in the hamstrings are less sensitive, the damping is not so effective and the knee jerk pendular. Also the muscle spindles are unable to signal a stretch to the nervous system as effectively as usual. As the cerebellum itself receives much information from this source, when damaged it tends to cut off its own source of information.

Correct setting of gamma motor neurone activity may depend on many factors. Suppose one sets out to keep pressing a button to summon a lift; the lift is coquettish and one maintains the pressure. Possibly this is achieved by an appropriate setting of the stretch receptors, not only in the upper limb pressing the button, but also in every muscle of the body which takes part in this complex action. The setting enables the stretch reflex to resist displacement during the action; any displacement tends to stretch the muscle spindles and the muscle responds by contracting further.

The setting must depend on the following.

(1) Gravity. The button may be at various heights, and the arm held accordingly against gravity requires adequate information about gravity. For this purpose the cerebellum has close connections with the labyrinth and is also linked to that other important source of information about gravity, the skin.

(2) The behaviour of the surroundings. People may give warning that they are going to jostle the button presser. Eyes and ears (presumably not nose) can record the warning and connections from the visual and auditory systems reach the cerebellum.

(3) The intentions and actions of the subject. The most extensive connections of the cerebellum are with the cerebral cortex and upper motor pathways, so that these structural features too can be included in the cerebellar calculation.

In conclusion, the cerebellum looks like a sophisticated regulator of the motor system and especially, but not exclusively, the voluntary motor system. It contributes to the correct setting of muscle spindles and to the adjustment of each level of motor function up to the cerebral cortex. Its remarkable and uniform structure suggests some one common process as its task, but the analysis of this process is hard, partly because its various parts although identical in structure, are linked to different parts of the nervous system. Not everyone will agree with the above interpretations.

THE CEREBRAL HEMISPHERES

The whole surface of the hemisphere consists of an external layer of grey matter, the **cortex**. This covers a mass of white matter surrounding the basal nuclei and thalamus which form the core of grey matter.

Gross anatomy

The cerebrum is divided into two hemispheres by the longitudinal fissure which is interrupted by the corpus callosum joining the two hemispheres together. Each hemisphere has a lateral, medial and inferior surface. The frontal poles project into the anterior cranial fossa, resting upon the roofs of the orbits. The occipital poles occupy the posterior part of the supratentorial compartment, resting upon the tentorium cerebelli which separates the occipital pole from the cerebellum. The temporal lobes occupy the middle fossa. The cortical area is vastly enlarged by folding, the summit of the fold being termed the **gyrus** and the space between each fold the **sulcus**. Particularly deep sulci are termed **fissures**.

The deepest and most obvious fissure apart from the longitudinal fissure is the posterior limb of the lateral sulcus separating the temporal lobe below from the parietal and frontal lobes above. This sulcus overlies a submerged portion of the cortex which is known as the insula.

THE LATERAL ASPECT OF THE HEMISPHERES
(fig. 24.66a)

The **central sulcus** separates the frontal and parietal lobes, with the precentral gyrus of the frontal lobe in front and the postcentral gyrus of the parietal lobe lying behind. It is an important landmark for the precentral gyrus forms the motor strip and the postcentral gyrus the sensory strip. The central sulcus is recognized by it tendency to continue on to the medial side of the hemisphere. No such sulci separate the temporal lobe from the posterior part of the parietal lobe or the occipital lobes.

The **frontal lobe** which comprises nearly 40 per cent of the cerebral hemispheres is roughly divided into three horizontal gyri by two sulci, the superior and the inferior frontal sulci.

The **parietal lobe** amounting to 20 per cent of the hemispheres is divided by a horizontal intraparietal sulcus which demarcates the superior and inferior parietal lobule. The inferior parietal lobule is itself subdivided into a supramarginal gyrus which embraces the extreme end of the lateral sulcus and behind it the angular gyrus.

The **temporal lobe**, also 20 per cent of the hemispheres is divided by two horizontal sulci, the superior and inferior temporal sulci.

The **occipital lobe** occupying about 20 per cent of the hemisphere has three sulci visible from the lateral aspect the transverse occipital sulcus which runs vertically from the intraparietal sulcus, the lateral occipital sulcus which lies horizontally below it and a curved lunate sulcus lying immediately in front of the occipital pole. The calcarine sulcus can often be seen notching the occipital pole.

THE MEDIAL SURFACE OF THE HEMISPHERES
(fig. 24.67a)

The medial surface is flat, each hemisphere being separated by the longitudinal fissure and falx cerebri. The corpus callosum forms a prominent feature and its divisions into the rostrum, genu, body and splenium can be readily recognized. The cingulate gyrus surrounds the corpus callosum separated only by the callosal sulcus. The cingulate sulcus in turn separates the gyrus from the superior frontal gyrus and superior

FIG. 24.66. Lateral aspect of cerebral hemisphere. (a) Sulci and gyri; (b) Cytoarchitectural map showing some of Brodmann's areas.

(a)   (b)

FIG. 24.67. Medial surface of cerebral hemisphere. (a) Sulci and gyri; (b) cytoarchitectural map showing some of Brodmann's areas.

parietal lobule, splitting as it passes posteriorly into the marginal sulcus which runs up, almost vertically, immediately behind the central sulcus. At the splenium the cingulate gyrus narrows and becomes the isthmus, uniting with the parahippocampal gyrus of the temporal lobe. Immediately behind the isthmus the calcarine sulcus passes posteriorly to notch the occipital pole, the parieto-occipital sulcus branching off it to demarcate the parietal and occipital lobes. The medial surface of the temporal lobe is largely made up of the uncus and parahippocampal gyrus.

THE INFERIOR ASPECT OF THE HEMISPHERES (fig. 24.68)

The olfactory tract lies in the olfactory sulcus forming the lateral boundary of gyrus rectus. Lateral to the olfactory tract lies the orbital sulcus in the shape of an H.

The inferior surface of the temporal lobe is angled towards the medial part of the hemisphere. It has a deep collateral sulcus which separates the parahippocampal gyrus medially from the rest of the surface.

Histological structure of the cortex

The cells and fibres are arranged in parallel layers and five types of cells can be distinguished (fig. 24.69).

(1) **Pyramidal cells** are classed according to their size as giant, large or small. The axon goes to the white matter giving off collaterals which ramify in various layers of cortex whilst the apical dendrite extends towards the surface of the cortex and ramifies there. Smaller dendrites arise from the sides of the pyramidal cells.

(2) **Granule cells** have short repeatedly branching axons which extend only short distances in the cortex.

(3) **Cells of Martinotti** which have axons travelling to the surface and ramifying in the superficial layer.

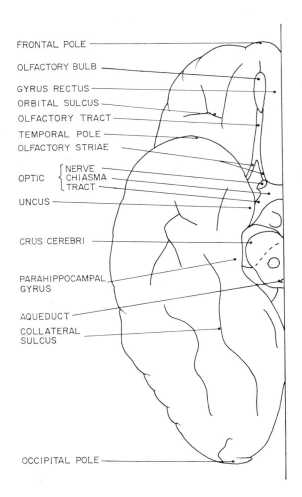

FIG. 24.68. Inferior aspect of cerebrum.

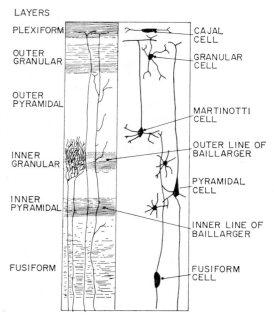

FIG. 24.69. Structure of the cerebral cortex.

(4) **Horizontal cells of Cajal** lie in the superficial layer and have axons which remain at the same level as their cell bodies.

(5) **Fusiform cells** lie in the deepest layer of the cortex with their axons entering the white matter.

Below a thin superficial band of white matter, the tangential layer, there are two well defined bands, the inner and outer lines of Baillarger. In the visual cortex (area 17, p. 24.45), the outer line of Baillarger is conspicuous. Apart from these gross appearances various parts of the cortex differ microscopically from one another.

In the older parts of the cortex, such as the rhinencephalon, only three layers of cells may be distinguished: the superficial molecular layer of fibres, the intermediate granular layer and a deep layer of pyramidal cells. In the neocortex six layers may be distinguished from without inwards (fig. 24.69):

(1) the plexiform or molecular layer containing horizontal cells of Cajal and granule cells within which the terminal branches of the apical dendrites of the pyramidal cells ramify,

(2) the outer granular layer containing short axons, granule cells and small pyramidal cells,

(3) the outer pyramidal layer containing medium-sized pyramidal cells and some granular cells,

(4) the inner granular layer of small granule cells,

(5) The inner pyramidal layer of large pyramidal cells which in the motor area are the giant cells of Betz,

(6) the fusiform layer containing fusiform cells.

Layers 2, 3 and 4 receive most of the afferent fibres to the cortex. Layers 5 and 6 are largely efferent and give rise to the main cortical tracts.

Histological studies have led to a subdivision of the brain into different areas, which have been given numbers or letters. The best known and most generally used map is that of Brodmann (figs. 24.66b and 67b). While these histological distinctions mirror functional differences revealed by experiment or disease, there is much functional overlap in many areas.

Functions of the cerebral hemispheres

To understand the function of the cerebral hemispheres is not far from understanding the behaviour of the whole person or animal. The methods used must match the diversity of the problem and the oldest (armchair speculation aside) is to determine the effects of injury. This was being used at least as long ago as the time of Galen (129–200 A.D.), who exposed the hemispheres in the living animal and noted in a general way the consequences of pressure and of incisions. Even earlier, war wounds of the head could be observed and the symptoms analysed. Modern methods of creating accurately placed injuries employ electric currents passed through fine electrodes inserted into the brain or freezing by miniature cooling devices.

Stimulation, instead of damage, can be achieved by applying drugs or even mechanically, but electrical stimulation is less damaging and better controlled. The results of electrical stimulation require cautious interpretation. Normally neurones do not fire synchronously as they do after electrical stimulation; this is hard to confine to a single neurone in the cerebral hemispheres; so the effects of electrical stimulation can rarely be identical with normal function.

The electroencephalogram (EEG)

Electrical recording of nervous activity in the cerebral hemispheres is another method of investigation. It falls into two categories. The first employs relatively large electrodes, lying on the surface of the brain or else externally upon the scalp. This type of record is called the electroencephalogram (EEG). Clearly it is convenient to use since no surgical operation is involved, but inevitably it cannot do more than record the summed activity of large amounts of neural tissue between the electrodes. Accordingly, in a normal alert subject, at first glance it seems to show small random and incomprehensible fluctuations, seen in the central parts of fig. 24.70. But several varieties of rhythmic activity appear in different circumstances. Berger noted in 1924 (though he waited five years to publish it) a rhythm with a period of 8–13 cycles/sec, noticeable when a healthy subject closed his eyes and chiefly present at the occipital pole of the hemispheres. This is the **alpha rhythm** and is shown at both ends of the traces taken from Lord Adrian and from a water beetle (fig. 24.70).

Sleep removes this rhythm and may substitute others in its place (p. 24.91). An epileptic convulsion is accompanied by gross rhythmic activity, suggesting the sort of synchronous discharge of neurones which is ordinarily absent, but which can be produced, for instance, by artificial electrical stimulation applied to the cerebral hemispheres; in fact, convulsions can be initiated in this way.

The precise origin of EEG rhythms can be traced to some one part of a hemisphere by recording from numerous electrode positions on the scalp and comparing the records so obtained. Their amplitude and time course bear little resemblance to those of an action potential. But they certainly depend on the integrity of the connections between the cerebral cortex and the underlying thalamus, for they are absent when these connections are

FIG. 24.70. Electrical rhythm (a) from the cerebrum of a water beetle in darkness and in light and (b) from the cerebrum of Lord Adrian with eyes closed and open. From Adrian and Matthews (1934). *Brain*, **57**, 373.

interrupted. Hence they are a feature more of the complete system of thalamus and cortex than of the cerebral cortex alone.

It is obviously desirable to remove the uncertainties of the EEG by recording the activity of single neurones in the cerebral cortex. However, there are formidable difficulties in the way, chief among which is the pulsation of the cerebral hemispheres when they have been exposed by removing the overlying bone. Techniques exist for overcoming this difficulty in animals, but they are as yet barely applicable to man.

THE OLFACTORY SYSTEM

High in the roof of each nasal cavity there is a patch of yellow-brown epithelium in which the olfactory receptors lie. They are very numerous (the rabbit has 50 million) and each consists of a neurone with fine processes on its superficial surface and a thin slow conducting axon running from its deep surface up through the cribriform plate of the ethmoid (p. 21.4).

Immediately above the cribriform plate the fibres penetrate the dura and enter the olfactory bulb of the brain. There they form synapses; their terminations are gathered together in groups to form conspicuous clusters or **glomeruli** (fig. 24.71) where they meet the dendrites of 'mitral' cells of the olfactory bulb. Some 25,000 single

olfactory receptor axons might meet the dendrites of some 24 mitral cells in each glomerulus. The axons of the mitral cells run back to terminate in the cerebral cortex and adjacent parts of the forebrain. Besides the mitral cells, other cells in the olfactory bulb link one glomerulus to another, and one olfactory bulb to the other across the midline. So the pathway from the olfactory receptors to axon terminations in the cerebral cortex has only one synapse, and the route is more direct than that of any other type of receptor. The **olfactory bulbs** are small flattened ovoid bodies narrowing to form a flat **olfactory tract** passing backwards along the orbital surface of the frontal lobe. Each tract divides into medial and lateral olfactory striae, which diverge to enclose the olfactory trigone lying immediately anterior to the anterior perforated substance. This is so named because when the many small vessels are pulled out they leave behind perforations. Immediately behind this substance lies the optic tract (fig. 24.68.)

The medial olfactory stria ascends anterior and lateral to lamina terminalis to become continuous with the grey matter of the para-olfactory area and subcallosal gyrus (fig. 24.71). Fibres from the medial stria end in the olfac-

FIG. 24.71. The olfactory pathway

tory trigone and medial part of the anterior perforated substance and also in the septum pellucidum, a thin sheet of fibres stretched between the corpus callosum and fornix. A few olfactory fibres pass into the anterior commissure and end in the opposite olfactory area, but most end in the uncus which also receives the lateral olfactory striae passing to the lateral part of the perforated substance.

The uncus forms the anterior boundary of the hippocampal fissure and becomes continuous with the parahippocampal gyrus bounded medially by the hippocampal fissure and laterally by the collateral sulcus. The anterior end of the parahippocampal gyrus, the uncus and the amygdaloid with the prepyriform area (a mass of cells lying along the lateral olfactory striae) together form the **pyriform area**. The para-olfactory area, subcallosal gyrus and septum pellucidum nuclei form the **medial olfactory area**. Fibres arising in this area arch over the thalamus as **striae medullares** and end in the habenular nucleus which lies lateral to the pineal in the region of the posterior commissure. From thence they pass to the interpeduncular nucleus (lying between the peduncles) as the habenulopeduncular tract. From this nucleus fibres pass to the midbrain where they synapse with the dorsal tegmental nucleus (fig. 24.73).

From this nucleus the dorsal longitudinal fasciculus passes caudally and connects with many cranial nerve nuclei especially those concerned with mastication (V) swallowing (V, X) and digestion (X). Other fibres pass from the habenular nucleus to the midbrain tectum coordinating olfactory and visual impulses. Thus the odour of food evokes olfactory memories and through connection with visceral neurones produces salivation and gut movement.

The **medial forebrain bundle** arises from the paraolfactory area and other parts of the medial olfactory area to end in the ventromedial nucleus of the hypothalamus. It correlates olfactory and gustatory impulses.

SMELL

This is the sense of a myriad theories, but of few established facts. Any complete account requires to explain a number of interesting features. First is the immeasurably large number of odours that can be distinguished by a competent dog. These may be present in extreme dilution in the air. How many a human being can distinguish is also hard to guess. The ability to distinguish scents is little valued, except among perfumiers, and there is evidence that labourers are better at doing this than members of learned professions.

> 'They haven't got no noses,
> The fallen sons of Eve.
> And even the smell of roses
> Is not what they supposes.'
> (G.K. Chesterton)

Four odours that have been recommended for testing the sense of smell are coffee, benzaldehyde (almond), tar and oil of lemon. There is nothing fundamental about these four. The merit they possess is simply that people can generally name them. Another test material is assafoetida, which possesses the advantage of smelling so unpleasant that the nose wrinkles uncontrollably.

Secondly, all smells cannot be made up by mixing a small number of components as in the case of vision or taste. Light of any colour can be matched by an appropriate mixture of three carefully selected wavelengths and many tastes can be made up from a similar mixture of four basic tastes, sweet, sour, salt, and bitter, although it is agreed that on due reflection we can separate out the components of a taste, but not those of a colour. The huge variety of smells, on the other hand, cannot be so simply created. There is no visible difference between one olfactory receptor neurone and another which would allow

them to be classified into a few simple types. Even if there were, the simple activity or silence of even, say, eight different types of receptor would in itself allow us to discriminate $2^8 - 1$ different smells, i.e. 255. This number hardly seems enough even for the disregarded human sense of smell. There must be facilities for recognizing different grades of activity in the receptors, not just its presence or absence.

Thirdly, there is some evidence that odour may influence behaviour even without being recognized, let alone being clearly named. For instance, half of a batch of boxes of nylon stockings, otherwise identical, were perfumed and the whole batch exhibited for sale in a selfservice store. For every unperfumed box chosen, three perfumed boxes were chosen by customers. Yet in retrospect no customer could recall being aware of the perfume at all.

The obvious approach to the olfactory system is to record the electrical activity of the receptor neurones while stimulating them with appropriate scents. This is singularly difficult; the neurones are small and inaccessible and their axons among the thinnest to be found in the nervous system. Besides, delivering only one kind of scent is not easy in practice. But evidence has been obtained that certain units in the frog's olfactory mucosa respond selectively to particular scents. Adrian was able to record the activity one stage further back, at mitral cell level, and show that it was more easily evoked by one of a group of five or six different odours.

Other investigators have looked for a physical or chemical basis underlying the resemblance in smell between different chemical compounds and have tried to define what it is about a molecule that determines its smell. The acid test of such an approach is its ability correctly to predict the odour of newly synthesized compounds and some success has been achieved, on the premise that there are about seven primary odours, each linked to a particular stereochemical configuration. A further line of approach is to look for individuals with impairments of smell corresponding to the varieties of colour blindness. Some ten varieties have been recognized, but recognition is not a simple procedure.

So the sense of smell can be assessed clinically only in the crudest way, but it may be a sense undervalued because it is difficult to talk about and difficult to investigate.

THE HIPPOCAMPUS AND FORNIX SYSTEM
(fig. 24.72)

During early development the hippocampus lies close to the olfactory and hypothalamic region but the later development of the temporal lobe draws it down and extends its olfactory and hypothalamic connections. The fornix system traces this development and remains as the connecting link between the hypothalamus and temporal lobe. During development the hippocampus rolls on it-self to enclose the dentate gyrus, which lies between the hippocampus and parahippocampal gyrus. Although the hippocampus probably receives some direct olfactory impulses from the nearby uncus, it is not primarily an olfactory centre but it may serve as a co-ordinating or association centre for olfactory and other impulses. It influences emotion and behaviour through its connections with other parts of the brain especially the hypothalamus. It appears also to be involved in recent memory (p. 24.93). The hippocampus lies in the floor of the inferior horn with its bulbous anterior end grooved to resemble a paw and therefore termed pes hippocampi.

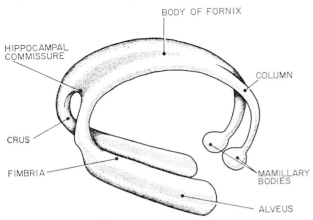

FIG. 24.72. The fornix.

Axons arising from the hippocampal cells form a thin layer of white matter, the **alveus** which covers the hippocampus and converges towards its medial side to form the **fimbria**. This is a narrow band passing backwards on the medial wall of the temporal horn to form the crus of the fornix. The two crura finally join to form the body of the fornix where fibres cross and make the hippocampal commissure. The fornix continues in the roof of the third ventricle before dividing again as the columns, which end in the **mamillary bodies** and hypothalamus.

The mamillothalamic tract arises from the mamillary bodies and ends in the anterior thalamic nucleus which in turn has connections with the cingulate gyrus. Other mamillary fibres pass to the midbrain tegmentum.

The cingulate region comprises areas 33, 24, 31, 23, the isthmus, 26, 29, 30; the para-olfactory area 25 is an anterior continuation of the cingulate gyrus, and although it extends to the frontal and parietal cortex, it is functionally part of the limbic system and therefore considered under that heading. The major connections are with the anterior thalamic nucleus through the anterior thalamic radiation, and with the mamillary bodies through the mamillothalamic tract. Gustatory impulses arising in the hypothalamus and impulses from the hippocampus are con-

veyed along the fornix and pass along the mamillothalamic tract to the anterior thalamic nuclei which probably co-ordinate and project them to the cingulate gyrus. The cingulate gyrus has important and rich connections with the frontal lobe and fibres also pass in the internal capsule from the gyrus to the basal nuclei. As well as receiving impulses from the anterior thalamic nucleus it also donates fibres to it. The connection between frontal cortex, thalamus, hypothalamus and hippocampus implies that the cingulate gyrus influences autonomic function and behaviour. Surgical extirpations of the cingulate gyrus (cingulectomies) have been made for mental disorders, especially obsessional states.

Closely associated with the hippocampus is the amygdaloid body which receives fibres from the medial olfactory striae. Fibres pass from the amygdala in the stria terminalis to end in the anterior hypothalamus (fig. 24.73).

FIG. 24.73. The connections of the hippocampus and fornix (limbic system).

The **insula** (fig. 24.58) is buried beneath the opercula formed by the frontal, parietal and temporal lobes. The buried island is roughly triangular, surrounded by an indefinite circular sulcus. Experimental and clinical evidence show that it is related to visceral motor and sensory function. Little is known of its anatomical connections. Impulses carrying taste sensations may reach the anterior part of the insula.

THE TEMPORAL LOBES

Apart from its contribution to the limbic system and rhinencephalon, the temporal lobe has a major function in **auditory appreciation**. Areas 41 and 42 occupy the part of the superior temporal gyrus that is largely hidden within the lateral sulcus. The auditory radiations arise from the medial geniculate bodies and pass laterally through the sublenticular part of the internal capsule, beneath the lower border of the insula, and enter the auditory cortex. This has many connections by association bundles with more distant parts of the brain. The auditory areas of the two sides are connected through commissural fibres in the corpus callosum. The superior temporal gyrus receives vestibular impulses and patients with lesions in this situation may have symptoms of vertigo or dizziness.

Like somatic sensation, hearing is represented on the cerebral cortex in a main auditory area, and just as in the somatic sensory area each part corresponds to a part of the body, so in the auditory area each part corresponds to part of the cochlea. Thus the front end of the area is concerned with high pitched tones, the back with low pitched tones. However, hearing differs from somatic sensation in being a much more bilateral sense. Thus damage to the auditory area in one of the two hemispheres is hard to detect at all; only when both hemispheres are affected does deafness become apparent.

Area 22 borders the auditory cortex and may be regarded as its association area. Lesions of area 22 produce word deafness or auditory receptive aphasia. Area 38 lies at the temporal pole and seems to be associated with recent memory. It has connections with surrounding cortex especially with the amygdaloid body, hippocampus and fornix.

THE FRONTAL LOBES

The precentral gyrus is largely occupied by primary motor cortex or area 4. Originally it was thought that only fibres originating in this area of brain contributed to the pyramidal tract, but in the human motor cortex the giant pyramidal cells in layer 5 of the precentral gyrus form only about 3 per cent of the corticobulbar and corticospinal tracts. Hence the cells of origin of the fibres in these tracts must lie either in other cells of the motor cortex or elsewhere in the cerebrum.

Perhaps assigning separate roles to the pyramidal and extrapyramidal systems may be confusing and unnecessary. The basal nuclei and other extrapyramidal nuclear masses not only receive fibres from extrapyramidal areas of cortex (areas 1, 2, 3 and 6) but also from the primary motor cortex area 4 itself. The only difference, therefore, between the two pathways is that the extrapyramidal pathway seems to be multisynaptic as compared to the relative absence of synaptic connections of the corticospinal pathway.

Stimulation of a discrete area in the motor cortex in man and other primates leads usually to a specific movement of only one part of the opposite side of the body. There is certainly some localization of function, which is indicated in fig. 24.74.

The amount of cortex given to each part of the body is

dependent more upon its function than its mass. Thus the hand occupies a greater cortical area than leg and trunk together whilst face, tongue and lips occupy an equally large area. All the voluntary muscles are represented with one striking exception, the external ocular muscles. These can be activated from central areas remote from area 4 and area 46 is often termed the frontal eye field since movements of the eyes are elicited by stimulation in this area.

Anterior to area 4 is a large cortical area, area 6, which possibly acts as a co-ordinator of muscle movement initiated by area 4, so that movements of many muscles produce a smooth action.

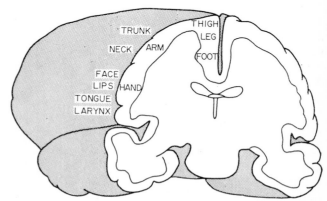

FIG. 24.74. Approximate representation of the body on the precentral gyrus. Note the position of the tongue and larynx below the face.

Damage of the main motor area of one cerebral hemisphere paralyses voluntary movements of the opposite side of the body, but there are reserve mechanisms. The face and mouth tend to have bilateral representation. Further motor areas certainly exist in animals and help to explain how relatively gross voluntary movements may be preserved, when fine movements are lost because of damage to the main motor area.

Areas 44 and 45 in the dominant hemisphere are related to speech (p. 24.52). This should not be surprising in view of its close relationship to the motor areas of tongue and lips. This region is often called Broca's area.

Prefrontal cortex

Areas 9, 10, 11 and 12 have many connections with other parts of the brain through association bundles. Fibres from areas 9 and 10 pass to the dorsomedial nucleus of the thalamus and influence the hypothalamus. Area 10 with 47 and 53, which lies deep, also have connection with each other by commissural fibres passing in the genu of the corpus callosum and with other parts of the brain by long and short association bundles.

If one compares a human brain with a monkey's, the

most obvious difference is the larger frontal lobes inside the high human forehead. But it is strangely difficult to allot a clear cut function to these lobes in front of the main motor area. They have no relation to reflexes, body posture, nor sensation. The celebrated case of Phineas Gage (1848) is to the point. An iron rod was accidentally driven across the front of his skull, severely damaging both frontal lobes. Yet intelligence-wise, he seemed little the worse. He was still able to carry out the tasks of road construction. But he was unfit to go on supervising his gang, which he had previously done. His character was the principal sufferer. He had become capricious, lazy and foul mouthed. Normal social restraints were lost and natural anxieties removed.

The damage was bilateral and in the frontal lobes function is so conspicuously bilateral that damage to one side alone often produces quite elusive symptoms and signs, such as subtle character changes, until or unless it extends to involve the motor area. Probably, as in animals, the frontal lobes are specialized to play some part in learning, though not as actual stores of knowledge, and are also involved in curiosity, affection and pleasure. A monkey without frontal lobes can barely remember for 10 sec in which cup it has seen food placed. Yet in other ways it is perfectly intelligent and can lay complicated plans. Such a monkey does not care much about its faulty memory or even about excessively difficult problems, which usually upset a normal animal considerably. This indifference to disturbing situations prompted the use of surgical removal or disconnection of the prefrontal areas (prefrontal leucotomy) for the relief of extreme human anxiety or emotional tension or to produce indifference to pain. When adult life is reached and learning processes become less rapid, these emotional changes become the most prominent if the frontal lobes are damaged.

THE PARIETAL LOBES

The sensory or postcentral gyrus contains areas 1, 2 and 3 which are often considered together as the **somaesthetic cortex**, receiving sensations from the opposite side of the body. It is overlapped, however, by areas which have been shown to be motor in function while a similar extension of the somaesthetic cortex into primary motor areas has also been demonstrated.

There is some localization of sensory function in the cortex. Thus when parts of skin are pressed or hairs are moved, the arrival of sensory traffic can be recorded in restricted areas of the cortex. The pattern in the postcentral gyrus is broadly similar to that in the motor cortex. Thus the genitalia are represented on the bottom of the medial part of the hemisphere close to the toes.

Besides this basic arrangement, there is also evidence that the skin surface of the body is related to the front part of the somatic sensory area and the deeper tissues to the part slightly further back along the cortex. Again, the

area on one hemisphere is concerned with the opposite side of the body, but the face is bilaterally represented.

So, when part of the sensory cortex is damaged, feeling may be impaired, but only in the part of the body corresponding to the cortical damage. The loss of feeling does not lead to loss of all responses. Lower levels of the nervous system are quite capable of jerking a limb away from harmful stimuli. The patient is often aware that something damaging is happening to him even though he does not know exactly where. When part of his sensory cortex is not working, the defect is far more subtle than the simple unresponding numbness that follows damage to a peripheral nerve. A test which helps is **two-point discrimination**. When the skin is touched by two points, they may seem one to him when they are a greater distance apart on the affected side than on the normal side.

The mechanism of two point discrimination is not so simple as a sensory cortex 'looking' at a map of the body surface to see whether two adjoining receptors are firing or only one. Some neurones in the sensory cortex increase their firing rate when their area of skin is stimulated, but actually decrease it when a nearby area is stimulated. A neurone of this kind responds to stimulation within its area and then decreases its response when stimulation is added outside; it fires particularly vigorously if the stimulus moves out of its area into the immediately adjoining 'inhibitory' area (fig. 24.75). A further practical test of the integrity of the sensory cortex is to look for **astereognosis**; a patient holding some simple object is aware that he holds it, but cannot identify it by touch, without looking at it.

FIG. 24.75. Response of a neurone in the somatic sensory cortex of a monkey to stimulation in different areas of the forearm. From Mountcastle & Powell (1957). *Bull. of Johns Hopkins Hospital*, **105**, 218.

Besides the main somatic sensory area, monkeys and cats certainly have at least one subsidiary sensory area on which the body is similarly laid out but on a smaller scale. It lies behind the main somatic sensory area of the cortex and rather lower down the cortical surface. It is connected to the spinothalamic system, which transmits chiefly information about temperature and pain; the localization of this secondary area is rather uncertain as each neurone can be influenced by a relatively large part of the body surface, compared with a neurone in the main sensory cortex.

If the arrangement in man is similar, then a ready explanation is to hand for patients with damage to the main sensory cortex, who may be still aware of painful stimuli, but not clear about exactly where they originate. Like other organs of the body, the brain possesses a large reserve of function and can provide alternative mechanisms when the principal system fails, but these are less precise. The somaesthetic areas of the hemisphere are connected through the corpus callosum and through long and short association bundles with many other parts of the brain. The most important connection is the sensory radiation from the nucleus ventralis posterior of the thalamus which passes in the posterior part of the internal capsule, projecting impulses of touch, proprioception, temperature and pain. The sensory cortex also has connections both direct and indirect to brain stem and spinal cord motor centres.

Speech

Speech is a feature of human beings, who have a highly-developed cerebral cortex, though even a dog can learn to obey several dozen verbal commands. It is linked with the cortex in one hemisphere only, commonly in right-handed persons the left hemisphere. Penfield of Montreal,

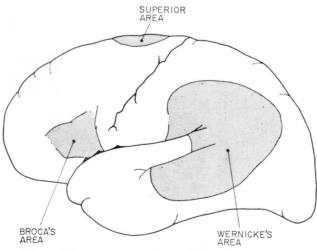

FIG. 24.76. The three speech areas shown on the left cerebral cortex. From Penfield & Roberts (1959). *Speech and Brain Mechanisms*. Princeton University Press.

described sites where electrical stimulation especially interfered with speech (fig. 24.76). Broca in France had long before defined one of these areas by finding that damage there led to a disorder of speech.

Although speech is dependent upon the co-ordination of large areas of cerebral cortex, certain parts, as has already been indicated, bear a special relationship. Although an undoubted simplification, clinical evidence tends to suggest that the region of the angular gyrus and supramarginal gyrus, namely areas 39 and 40, can be regarded as the co-ordinating centres, receiving and co-ordinating impulses received from the associative auditory areas (area 22) and visual associative areas (area 18) and projecting impulses probably through long association bundles to the expressive motor centre for speech or Broca's area (areas 44 and 45) in the dominant hemisphere.

Impairment in the use of speech can be as complex as speech itself. The simplest forms include **dysarthria** where the patient can marshal words perfectly but cannot operate his larynx with sufficient precision. Such a defect can result from damage to the vagus nerve when the cerebral cortex is normal, or else from certain types of cortical damage. Again, it is obvious that deafness or blindness due to cortical damage will interfere with understanding of heard or written speech. In the many less simple cases, which are varieties of **aphasia** or inability to speak, refined diagnostic methods can lead to localization of a cortical defect. The ability to read or to write is closely linked to speech.

We can use either hand for most tasks and so either hemisphere can organize the movements. But for the most skilled hand movements and for the highly skilled activity of speech, little reserve capacity exists in the opposite hemisphere once these abilities have been acquired. However, a baby can transfer his future speech area to the other side if injury to one side compels him. Adults cannot achieve this and cannot usually gain much skill in fine movements with the non dominant hand. So the Ambidextral Culture Society which once existed is now in abeyance.

THE OCCIPITAL LOBES

These occupy the posterior part of the brain and have two major areas, the primary visual cortex or area 17 and a visual association cortex, area 18.

Area 17 occupies the occipital pole and in man has been pushed largely on to the medial side of the hemisphere by the greater development of the rest of the brain. It occupies the superior and inferior lips of the calcarine fissure and may extend on to the occipital poles laterally and as far forward as the parieto-occipital sulcus. It is often called the **striate area** because it contains extra fibres which widen the outer lines of Baillarger into a broad white band.

Area 17 receives the visual radiations from the lateral geniculate body. Impulses from the superior retinal quadrant, that is to say from the inferior visual fields, pass to the medial half of the lateral geniculate body and from thence to the superior lips of the calcarine fissure. Fibres from the superior visual field or inferior retinal quadrant pass to the lateral half of the lateral geniculate body and end in the inferior lip of the calcarine fissure. Central vision passes in the macular fibres which end in the posterior part of area 17 whilst the more peripheral vision passes into the more anterior part of area 17. Central vision occupies a large part of area 17, i.e. the macula is greatly magnified; peripheral vision occupies very much less.

The visual radiations sweep behind the lentiform nucleus in the internal capsule. The fibres from the superior retinal quadrant pass almost directly posteriorly into the superior lip of the calcarine sulcus although the inferior retinal fibres pass forwards first looping into the anterior temporal region, before continuing posteriorly to join the superior retinal quadrant fibres and end in the inferior lip of the calcarine fissure.

After entering the visual cortex the fibres pass in the lines of Baillarger ending by synapse with cells in area 17 which connects with 18 and possibly 19 by association bundles.

The visual associative area or area 18 forms the parastriate area which lies immediately in front of area 17 and is distinguished by the absence of striation. Area 18 is richly connected with area 17 and also has a narrow strip adjoining area 17 which has many callosal fibres. The two halves of the field of view unite at the centre of gaze and along a line running vertically through it. So the two halves of the visual system, separate even in the cerebral hemispheres, must be suitably linked to create a functional whole. The link is the splenium of the corpus callosum, interconnecting the occipital poles of the hemispheres. From area 18, long association bundles connect the visual areas with the motor and sensory cortex, midbrain and tectum. Lesions of area 18 produce **visual agnosia** or the inability to recognize objects, a special form of which is **alexia** or inability to recognize written symbols, i.e. read. Stimulation of area 18 produces unformed visual images, flashes of light, colour and outline. In contrast, lesions of the temporal lobe and area 19 may result in formed images (hallucinations).

VISION

Movements of the eyes

The eyeball is nearly spherical and about 2·4 cm in diameter. It can be moved within the orbit by the external ocular muscles (p. 21.13). The range of movement is about 50° in any direction away from straight forwards. The muscles do not have their origin straight behind the eye and are not attached precisely round the vertical 'waist-belt' of the eyeball. So, as fig. 24.77 shows, the superior and inferior recti, and the obliques, have actions which are complex. It is evident from the diagram that the superior rectus elevates the gaze, and also directs it a little inwards and even twists it so that the eye rotates round the direction of gaze (torsion). Similarly, the superior oblique depresses the gaze, directs it outwards and twists it.

FIG. 24.77. The right eyeball seen from above to show muscle arrangements. The arrows show direction of pull.

If a similar diagram is constructed showing the muscles attached inferiorly to the eyeball, it is clear that the whole complex of six muscles can act together to turn the gaze in every possible direction, and also prevent any rotation round the axis of gaze, intorsion or extorsion. In fact these rotations are not always prevented, but occur as active movements of the eye to compensate for rolling movements of the head, which would otherwise rotate the gaze round its own axis.

PARALYSIS OF EYE MUSCLES

Careful consideration of the innervation and anatomy of the external ocular muscles makes it possible to deduce the consequences of their paralysis. These appear as double vision (**diplopia**) because if the most sensitive part of the retina, the fovea, of one eye is correctly aligned on some object, the fovea of the other will not be correctly aligned and so two images are produced, one in each eye, which are not on corresponding parts of the two retinae. This effect occurs during whatever movement of the eye is paralysed. It is also important to remember that the image on the retina moves in the opposite direction to any movement of the object seen.

Abducent paralysis

Applying these principles to paralysis of the right abducent nerve which supplies only the lateral rectus muscle, we find the pattern shown in fig. 24.78. Both eyes are

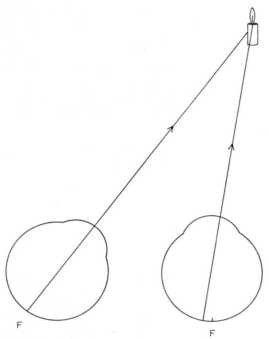

FIG. 24.78. Right lateral rectus palsy. Alignment of the eyes from above. F, fovea.

looking at a candle to the right of the subject; a candle is not only traditional, but has the advantages of a clearly defined vertical axis with top and bottom. The left eye is correctly lined up, but on account of the paralysis the right eye is unable to move into abduction. The lateral rectus muscle has no component of upward or downward movement, nor of intorsion and extorsion in its action. The image of the candle lies on the left fovea, but in the right eye it lies in the position normally occupied by the image of an object far to the subject's right side. The subject's double vision shows him two candles, a true candle, and a false candle to the right of the true one, level with it, and not rotated. This is the interpretation arrived at by the central nervous system when the image of the candle in the right eye lies medial to the fovea. The right eye's gaze is too far to the left; the false candle is seen as too far to the right.

TRUE CANDLE   FALSE CANDLE

FIG. 24.79. True and false images as seen during the double vision of a right superior oblique palsy.

Trochlear Paralysis

Only the superior oblique muscle is involved, but the outcome is much more complex because of its complex action. There is loss of depression, abduction and intorsion. So the false candle is seen displaced in these ways, as in fig. 24.79. The diplopia is most marked when looking down, as described on p. 21.14 since this is when the action of the paralysed muscle is most missed.

Oculomotor Paralysis

This nerve supplies the remaining four external ocular muscles, and so the deficiency is especially complex and variable. The two remaining muscles can move the eyeball only downwards and laterally, and if the gaze is directed any other way there is diplopia. Besides, the oculomotor nerve supplies levator palpebrae superioris, and so the eyelid droops; it also supplies the mechanism of pupillary control and accommodation inside the eyeball, which is paralysed. These effects of paralysis occur in the course of disease in varying combinations and with varying completeness.

Tears

The cornea is continually bathed by the secretion of the lacrimal glands (p. 21.16). This is a clear watery fluid with an electrolyte content similar to that of plasma. It serves the function of lubricating the eyeball and washing out dust, bacteria and other foreign particles. Tears contain less than 1 per cent protein, but, as Sir Alexander Fleming first reported, they contain an enzyme, **lysozyme**, capable of lysing many types of bacteria. Lacrimation may be caused by a variety of chemical and mechanical irritants. The increased secretion is mediated by the parasympathetic system and can be brought about by the drug pilocarpine. The lacrimal secretions drain from the eye into the nose through the nasolacrimal duct.

Pain and unpleasant emotion may promote a 'flood of tears' in man, but probably not in other animals, though Indian elephants have been reported by reliable observers to weep. Crocodile tears are a myth. Charles Darwin suggested that the flow of tears followed contraction of the muscles round the eye caused by pain or strong emotion, and his book *Expression of the Emotions* includes an interesting chapter on weeping.

The anatomy of the eyeball

The eyeball (fig. 24.80) has a tough opaque fibrous coat, the **sclera**, which is replaced in front by the transparent **cornea**. The cornea protrudes a little in cross-section, because its curvature is more marked than the curvature of the sclera. Inside the outer coat is a pigmented vascular layer, comprising the **choroid** at the back, more anteriorly the **ciliary body**, and in front the **iris**.

The interior of the eyeball is divided into three chambers, anterior, posterior and vitreous. The anterior chamber lies between the cornea in front and the iris behind; where the iris is absent at the **pupil**, the anterior chamber is bounded by the front surface of the lens. The iris is coloured usually blue or brown by pigment and prevents passage of light, which can enter the lens only through the circular pupil. The iris is provided with radially arranged smooth muscle fibres which enlarge the pupil and are innervated by fibres from the sympathetic trunk in the neck, entering the eyeball posteriorly in the long ciliary nerves. There are also circularly arranged muscle fibres which constrict the pupil and are supplied by the oculomotor nerve via the ciliary ganglion (p. 21.15). This nerve supply is part of the parasympathetic system.

FIG. 24.80. Horizontal section through the eyeball.

The **lens** is transparent and biconvex in shape, the front less curved than the back. It is elastic and becomes more globular and highly curved when released from its support in the eyeball, the **suspensory ligament**, which links it to the posterior surface of the ciliary body. The ciliary body incorporates a smooth muscle, the **ciliary muscle**; when it contracts, it reduces the pull on the suspensory ligament, thus enabling the lens to contract and become more globular. This increases the refractive power and the eye can then bring the image of nearer objects to a focus at the retina.

The ciliary body, together with the posterior surface of the iris, is the principal source of the intraocular liquid, known as the **aqueous humour**. This liquid is secreted into the **posterior chamber**, which is bounded by the anterior surface of the ciliary body, the posterior surface of the iris, and the anterior surface of the lens. At the margin of the pupil, the aqueous humour emerges into the anterior chamber and thus comes to fill both the anterior and posterior chambers of the eye.

The aqueous humour is like an ultrafiltrate of plasma, similar to the glomerular filtrate of the kidney, and is virtually free of protein, containing only 10–20 mg/100 ml. But although the capillaries of the ciliary body, like those of the glomerulus, contain blood at a relatively high pressure for capillaries (50 mm Hg), ultrafiltration is not the whole story. It fails to explain why the glucose content of aqueous humour is lower than in plasma, why the ascorbic acid content is some ten to fifty times higher and why carbonic anhydrase inhibitors, e.g. acetazoleamide, interfere with the production of aqueous humour. Active secretion is evidently involved.

The humour leaves the eyeball by fine channels lying in the angle between the margin of the cornea and the anterior surface of the iris. These channels lead into a path continuous with the venous system and named the **canal of Schlemm**. The mechanism is not unlike that for cerebrospinal fluid (p. 24.76).

The humour clearly plays a part in the maintenance of the avascular tissues bathed by it, the lens and the cornea. It is normally at a pressure of 10–20 mm Hg, which is the **intraocular pressure**. If the drainage channels are clogged or inadequate to carry the whole amount secreted, the intraocular pressure rises. The same outcome may appear when the path followed by the humour round the margin of the pupil is clogged by inflammatory adhesions. Raised intraocular pressure can seriously damage the retina and optic nerve disc in the condition known as **glaucoma**.

The **vitreous humour** lies behind the lens and occupies the vitreous chamber of the eye. It consists of transparent thin jelly. The **retina** lies against the back wall of the vitreous chamber, separated from the sclera by the pigmented **choroid**, which absorbs any light passing through the retina and prevents it from being reflected back from the lightly coloured sclera into the retina once more.

Accommodation

The optical system of the eye is capable of bringing entering rays of light to a sharp focus at the receptors in the retina. Most of the refraction occurs as the light passes from the outside air into the cornea, but part occurs at the lens, which is adjustable. When the ciliary muscle contracts, both curvatures of the lens increase, especially the anterior curvature, and so does its refractive power. This change is **accommodation**. In early youth, the lens is so elastic that objects can be sharply focused by accommodation when they are as near as 7 cm to the eye. A baby can in fact see clearly the toys which he holds so close to his nose, though he may look cross-eyed while he does it. The change in lens shape and in light paths during accommodation is shown diagrammatically in fig. 24.81.

By middle age the elasticity of the lens has become much less, and the unaided eye can no longer see near

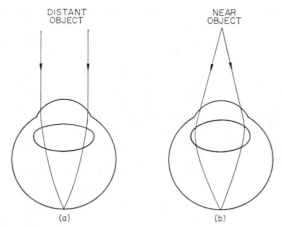

FIG. 24.81. Light paths in the (a) unaccommodated and (b) accommodated eye; note change in lens curvatures.

objects sharply, however well the ciliary muscle contracts (**presbyopia**). Accordingly, a convex spectacle lens is used and this provides the extra refractive power for close up vision which the eye can no longer supply. But this extra power is not required for distant vision and indeed blurs the distant scene. So when accommodation is lost bifocal lenses may be prescribed, the upper part for distant vision, the lower for reading.

ERRORS OF REFRACTION

A normal eye produces a sharp image at the retina of an object at infinity, without using any accommodation at all. However, all eyes are not normal; some are too long from front to back for their refractive power, or possess too much refractive power for their dimensions. These are termed **myopic** or short sighted and can be corrected by providing a negative, concave spectacle lens. Without the lens these eyes cannot bring the image of a distant object to a focus at the retina, but they have a 'far point'; inside the far point, an object can be sharply focused. A normal eye's 'far point' is at infinity.

Other eyes are too short, or have too little refractive power for their dimensions, and cannot provide a sharp image of near objects (**hypermetropia**, long sight). They are corrected by a positive, convex spectacle lens.

ASTIGMATISM

The curvature of the refracting surfaces, i.e. lens and cornea, is normally spherical, but if this is not so, then these surfaces may be more sharply curved, say, from above down than they are from side to side, just like the surface of a rubber ball on a table when it is pressed from above. The accommodation might then be correct for a vertical line, but incorrect for a horizontal line at the same distance; then the horizontal line would be poorly focused. This abnormality is astigmatism and can be corrected by providing a spectacle lens which is not spherical but

cylindrical. The axis of the cylindrical may be oriented vertically, horizontally or at any intermediate position according to the properties of the cornea-plus-lens refracting system.

PURKINJE IMAGES

The changes in accommodation can be observed in the human eye by the **phakoscope**. This is a device for shining twin spots of light obliquely into the eye, one above the other. The rays from each spot follow the paths shown in fig 24.82. A bright image of the spots can be seen due

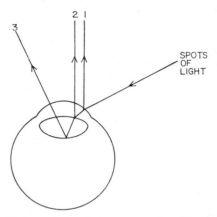

FIG. 24.82. Light paths in phakoscopy to show formation of Purkinje images 1, 2 and 3.

to corneal reflection; this is Purkinje image I. But by observing at a slightly different angle, another image of the two spots can be seen due to reflection at the anterior surface of the lens. It is much fainter, because the light has largely been reflected at the cornea since it has approached very obliquely. The separation of these two spots can be shown to be proportional to the radius of curvature of the anterior surface of the lens; in other words a more sharply curved lens means that the spots are closer together, and vice versa. Thus, by causing the subject to accommodate, one can actually observe the change in curvature of the front of the lens; the spots become closer together. With luck and a suitable subject it is possible to find Purkinje image III, reflected from the back of the lens, and verify that it changes little during accommodation. A further refinement is to black out one of the spots and confirm that images I and II are right way up, but III is inverted; this is a consequence of the fact that the cornea and the front of lens are convex, while the back of the lens is concave as seen from the front. We owe these observations to J.E. Purkinje (1787–1869), the Czech physiologist, who was also a distinguished histologist and gave his name to the Purkinje cells of the cerebellum and heart.

Retina

The retina can be seen in the living eye by using an ophthalmoscope. Very little light is reflected from the back of the eye and what is reflected follows the same path as it took on entering; in other words, it comes back exactly the way it went in. So the observer cannot normally see anything in the pupil of an eye except reflection of light from the cornea, the 'little doll', the image of himself which originally gave the pupil its name. To see the retina through the pupil, and to see it properly, three conditions must be met. The first is a dim light, which enlarges the subject's pupil, but not pitch darkness, because then the second condition cannot be met. This is that the subject must fix his gaze on some definite point behind the observer, so that his retina keeps still; naturally the observer must keep his head out of the way of the eye not being examined. The third condition is that the observer must project light into the eye along the same axis as he himself is looking (fig. 24.83).

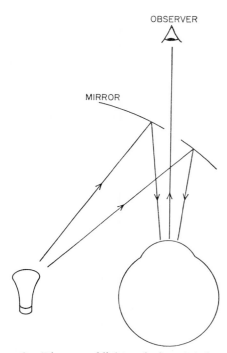

FIG. 24.83. Diagram of light paths in ophthalmoscopy.

This is done most simply by using a small mirror with a central hole in it, through which the observer looks. The light from a lamp is reflected by the mirror into the eye, and the observer's view is along virtually the same axis as the light entering the eye. Practical ophthalmoscopes usually provide their own illumination. They are used close to the subject's eye.

Thus seen the retina is red, the colour being chiefly contributed by the underlying choroid. At its posterior pole is the **macula lutea**, a yellow oval patch which contains at its centre the **fovea**. The fovea is a depression where the retina is thinnest and where vision is most acute; it is the point on the retina where the object at which we are looking is focused, and away from this point vision becomes rapidly less effective. The **optic disc** is some 3 mm to the nasal side of the fovea, and is about 1·5 mm in diameter; here the optic nerve leaves the eye. The disc is virtually flat, and of a light cream colour. The central retinal artery and vein reach the retina through the centre of the disc, where there is a depression which is not easy to see. The branches of these vessels are seen throughout the retina and supply all of it except the rods and cones, which are nourished by the separate ciliary system of vessels running in the choroid. The central retinal vessels and their branches have poor collateral connections, and a block here usually damages part or all of the retina irretrievably; though the rods and cones survive, this is not much comfort to the victim when their nervous connections are gone.

The optic disc is the **blind spot** within the retina, and is not sensitive to light; normally one is unaware of this gap in the seen world, as it is in a different position as seen by the two eyes, and each can fill in the other's gap. However, the blind spot is easy to demonstrate by closing one eye, fixing the other by looking steadily at a given point and noting that a pencil tip becomes invisible when moved into the part of the field of view corresponding to it.

STRUCTURE OF THE RETINA

The layer of the retina, lying against the choroid, consists of the receptors for light, about 120 million rods and 6 million cones (fig. 24.84). They are not scattered at random; the cones are present alone at the fovea, where they are about eighteen times as 'thick on the ground' as at the periphery. There are no rods at the fovea, but they are plentiful around it and less closely packed ($\times 1/5$) at the periphery.

Rods and cones each consist of an outer segment, a nuclear portion and a pedicle. The outer segment of a rod is cylindrical, about 24 μm long and 1 μm in diameter. The outer segment of a cone is shorter and more conical except near the fovea, where it may be so long and thin that it is hard to distinguish from a rod.

Inside the receptor layer (fig. 24.85) is a layer of bipolar cells, which as their name suggests are linked synaptically to a number of rods and cones on their outer side, and on their inner side to the cells of the next layer of the retina. This is the ganglion cell layer. Ganglion cells are larger than bipolar cells, and their axons are the fibres of the optic nerve. They run from their parent ganglion cell, forming the innermost layer of the retina, to the optic disc, where they assemble as the optic nerve and leave the eyeball. In the layer of these nerve fibres lie the branches of the central retinal artery and vein. Other

FIG. 24.84. Human rods and cones. A, rod; B, cone; C, cones in fovea centralis; D, nucleus; E, outer segment; F central connection. After Cajal.

FIG. 24.85. Diagram of principal neural elements and layers of the retina, as seen in cross-section.

types of cell are also found in the retina, e.g. amacrine cells and horizontal cells.

Thus light on its way to the rods and cones passes through all the other layers of the retina. These are transparent, but not completely so. Evidence of their being in the way can be found. For instance, when the sky is bright blue and one looks up, then the shapes of blood cells may be seen moving along. They absorb the blue light traversing them, and so shade some of the receptors enough to become visible. But this appearance is not seen exactly where one is looking, because at the fovea there are no blood vessels, and the bipolar and ganglion cells are displaced a little to one side as well.

It seems particularly odd that one cannot see one's own major retinal vessels. They are certainly not transparent and are conspicuous during ophthalmoscopy. They become visible through another manoeuvre discovered by Purkinje. With the eyes lightly closed, a lit torch bulb is gently applied to the lids near the outer canthus and vibrated to and fro. The retinal vascular pattern becomes visible as black lines upon a grey ground. The explanation lies in the peculiar properties of the retina. An entirely stationary image or shadow on the retina produces no response at all. If the retina were a photographic negative, the vessels lying on it would give rise to a contact print of their pattern. But as their shadow is normally stationary, there is no 'print' at all on the retina, which only responds when the shadow is artificially made to move, by illuminating the eye obliquely and intensely through the (normally) opaque coat of the eye and moving the illuminating light.

Function of the iris

The iris brings about **mydriasis** and **miosis** (enlargement and constriction of the pupil). It does so in response to the amount of light entering the two eyes together and reduces the size of the pupil in bright light. Since light is assessed by both eyes together, covering one eye makes the pupil of the other eye enlarge; no wonder that many centuries ago, when vision was attributed to a visual faculty proceeding out from the eye to meet the object seen, this phenomenon was regarded as an enlargement of the outward path, to let one eye emit more visual faculty when it had to work alone.

The light response

Shining a light into either eye alone makes both pupils constrict (**consensual reaction**). Often the constriction overshoots a little before becoming fairly steady. It can be neatly observed in one's own eye with Broca's pupillometer. With a pin make pairs of pinholes in a piece of aluminium foil 2 mm, 3mm and 4mm apart, set close together. Place the foil immediately in front of one eye. The pinholes are far too close to be focused, and give rise to blur circles on the retina. It can be shown that the pair of circles which just touch correspond to the diameter of the pupil. If the 3 mm pair just touch, the pupil diameter is 3 mm. Now shine a light into the other eye. The consensual reaction shrinks the pupil of the eye looking through the foil, and the change will be obvious, including its time course and the overshoot.

The light response is organized by the pretectal nucleus, just in front of the superior colliculus (fig. 24.86). The afferent path is by the optic nerve and

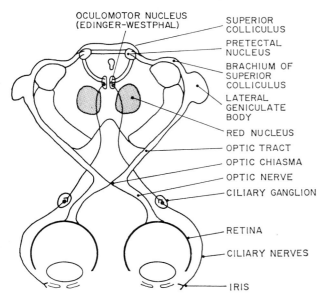

OCULOMOTOR NUCLEUS
(EDINGER-WESTPHAL)
SUPERIOR COLLICULUS
PRETECTAL NUCLEUS
BRACHIUM OF SUPERIOR COLLICULUS
LATERAL GENICULATE BODY
RED NUCLEUS
OPTIC TRACT
OPTIC CHIASMA
OPTIC NERVE
CILIARY GANGLION
RETINA
CILIARY NERVES
IRIS

FIG. 24.86. Pupil light reflex.

tract and is supposed to share exactly the same nerve fibres as are used in vision. Possibly the afferent fibres for the light response are different from those for vision. A stationary shadow or light patch on the retina is not seen, as already mentioned, but may be taken into account in regulating pupil size. The efferent path for constriction is by the oculomotor nerve and ciliary ganglion.

In a dim light, the maximum amount is allowed to enter the eye. But in bright light, vision is more acute when the pupil is smaller, as any optical imperfections in the cornea or lens have minimal effects when only a small part of the light carrying path is in use. Also the depth of focus is increased when the pupil is small. The depth of focus decides the distance an object can move towards the eye or away from it and still remain sharply focused without a change in accommodation. Just as in a camera, if the pupil is small and the eye 'stopped right down', there is a greater depth of focus. An eye with a large 7 mm pupil can see everything sharp from infinity to 3·1 m without any accommodation; but with a tiny 1 mm pupil it sees sharp from infinity right down to 0·6 m.

The near response

The eyes make **conjugate movements** together, from side to side and up and down. In addition they make **convergent movements** (fig. 24.87) for close work, superimposed

on the conjugate movements. Convergence is linked to the pupillary control system in such a way that miosis occurs with convergence. The eye gains greater depth of focus for close up work. The afferent path includes the cerebral cortex and is not identical with the afferent path for the light response. In the Argyll-Robertson pupil

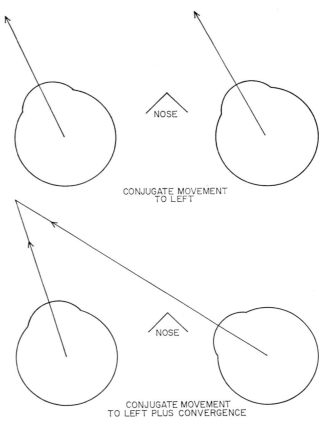

NOSE

CONJUGATE MOVEMENT TO LEFT

NOSE

CONJUGATE MOVEMENT TO LEFT PLUS CONVERGENCE

FIG. 24.87. Conjugate and convergent eye movements.

described in 1869 by an Edinburgh ophthalmologist and traditionally, though not always, associated with cerebrospinal syphilis, the near response survives and the light response is lost. It is clear that this can occur because the paths are in part distinct.

Visual pigments

The distal segments of the rods contain **rhodopsin**, a light-sensitive pigment, which is purple in the dark but becomes bleached in the light. It consists of one of the isomers of retinene (vitamin A-aldehyde) coupled to opsin, a protein. Its formation from vitamin A and the protein opsin, and the changes that occur on bleaching are given on p. 10.9.

Since the vitamin is necessary for the formation of rhodopsin, it might be supposed that lack of vitamin A would lead to blindness, and especially to night blindness, since the rods are predominantly concerned with vision in poor light. As it takes many months or even years to exhaust the store of the vitamin present in the liver of a well-fed European, night blindness from this cause is seldom found in prosperous countries. It is extremely common, however, in children in many parts of Asia and elsewhere where the diet is defective in vegetables and dairy products.

As rods are plentiful in human and animal retinas, rhodopsin has long been available in quantity for examination and its adsorption at various wavelengths has been measured. It is greatest for blue-green light at a wavelength of 510 nm. This can be compared with human vision in dim light. Here the sensitivity is greatest for blue-green light, although the colour of it cannot be recognized at all in such dim light. Fig. 24.88

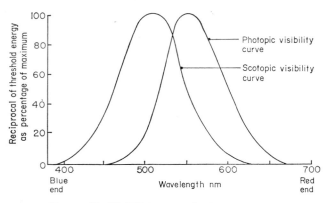

FIG. 24.88. Visibility curves for human vision.

shows the **scotopic visibility curve** of sensitivity against wavelength which, when appropriate corrections are made, is the same as rhodopsin's curve. So it is difficult to doubt that vision in dim light is concerned with the rhodopsin filled rods. Since there is only one pigment present, the eye cannot produce any information about colour. Everything is grey by moonlight, but the lightest grey is that of objects really blue-green by daylight.

Rhodopsin is certainly not the only visual pigment. Others, similar but with different adsorption curves, have been isolated in animals. So it is natural to expect that other pigments account for the **photopic visibility curve** (fig. 24.88). It is similar in shape, but displaced towards the red end of the spectrum; in daylight, yellow objects are the brightest.

COLOUR VISION

Early experiments in colour matching showed that any colour in the spectrum can be matched by some mixture of three pure spectral colours, each of a single wavelength,

for instance a blue of 460 nm, a green of 530 nm and a red of 650 nm. The intensity of each of the three varies according to the colour to be matched. Admittedly often the intensity of one of the three is negative, i.e. the match is made by adding it to the colour to be matched, not to the mixture. This seems like cheating, but in the end it has turned out that a negative contribution from one colour may have a real physiological meaning (p. 24.64).

Probably the first event in the process of vision is a change in visual pigments. From three pigments, each responding differently to any colour, the information can be drawn to account for all the colour matching that normal people do. Of course, given four pigments, still more elaborate matching could be achieved, and colours could be distinguished apart which to us seem identical though of different spectral composition.

So it is reasonable to expect three visual pigments besides rhodopsin, and to expect them in the cones. Cones are few and small compared to rods, and so the pigments have not been isolated from them. Two fruitful approaches have been made to the study of cone pigments. Rushton at Cambridge examined the tiny amount of light reflected from the human fovea, and by studying its spectral composition detected two pigments differing from rhodopsin, and probably a third. Marks, Dobelle and MacNichol at Johns Hopkins examined single monkey cones by refined spectroscopic methods; they too found evidence of three pigments.

Colour blindness of various kinds is common (8 per cent of all men and 0·4 per cent of all women). The possible varieties can be predicted from the three pigment hypothesis. Some people might have no cones at all and all colours would be grey to them, since they would have only rods to see with; they would be easily dazzled, and probably have a mere gap at the fovea, which is normally purely a cone domain. A few such people have been described.

A second group might have only one pigment in addition to rhodopsin; three varieties in this group are to be expected, since any one of the three pigments might be present, but only one has been found, and is very rare. A third group, dichromats, might have two pigments. Since any one of the three pigments might be absent, three varieties are to be expected, and three exist.

The largest group however, are the **anomalous trichromats**. Like normal people, they need mixtures of three spectral colours to achieve matches, but the intensities in the mixtures are different. This is one of the reasons why abnormal colour vision is not always obvious. Other reasons are that colour blind people can deduce a great deal from other clues. By distinguishing brightness differences they can guess colour differences, and they are aware that the top light at the traffic lights is red, but such deductions do not render them safe in fog as engine drivers or sailors. The best practical test is the **Ishihara plates** which show dots of one colour arranged as a letter or figure on a background of random dots of some other colour likely to be confused by the colour blind. Only those with normal colour vision can decipher the hidden letter or figure on all the plates.

Colour vision presents an intellectual problem which has fascinated clever minds for at least five centuries. Leonardo da Vinci, Newton, Goethe, Young (1802) and Helmholtz (1860) are among them. It is by no means entirely a theoretical problem; lighting engineering and dye technology are practical applications.

The sensitivity of vision

The dimmest light it is possible to see consists (if elaborate and approximate calculations are correct) of a single quantum in each of several (2–14) rods. More than this has to reach the eyeball, because of losses within the eyeball, but the receptors themselves appear to respond to amounts of the order of one quantum. The brightest light that can be dealt with is at least 10^9 times brighter. These extremes cannot be dealt with simultaneously. In the dark, the sensitivity becomes steadily greater as time passes, until within an hour it is maximal; most of the increase occurs within half an hour (fig. 24.89). The change is **dark adaptation**; it

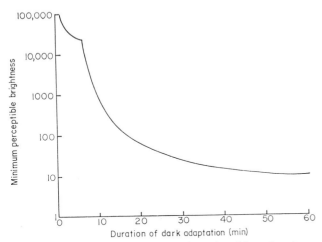

FIG. 24.89. Time course of dark adaptation. Note that the scale of brightness is logarithmic, not linear. After Kohlrausch.

raises the sensitivity ten thousandfold and is accompanied by the change in spectral sensitivity already mentioned (fig. 24.88).

The time course of the change is clearly biphasic. The first phase, levelling off after about 7 min. in fig. 24.89, is probably due to change in the organization of the cones, because when deep red (which rhodopsin can't 'see' at all) is used for testing, this is all the dark adaptation that is found; the second phase is not there at all for deep red

light. Again, the adaptation of the fovea itself does not seem to go any further than this first phase. In part, the changes in dark adaptation can be regarded as due to regeneration of visual pigments previously bleached by light. The change in the organization of ganglion cell fields is mentioned on p. 24.64.

Visual acuity

Whether a person can distinguish black and white patterns, such as letters, decides his visual acuity. It is impossible to measure the smallest point of light a person can see. Even if it is infinitesimal, it can be seen if it emits enough light. So instead the attempt is made to measure resolution, i.e. the ability to distinguish two points or lines close together (compare two point discrimination, p. 24.51). Foveal vision can normally do this when the space between the two lines subtends an angle of about one minute at the eye, for instance, when the space is one cm and the lines are just over 34 m away, or proportionally less if the distance is less. Really good lighting is compulsory; acuity falls off markedly in light which may seem adequate.

In practice, such a test method would be tedious. Instead, letters on a test card (Snellen chart) can be used

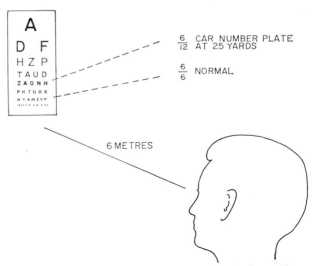

FIG. 24.90. Testing visual acuity by Snellen's charts. From Trevor-Roper P.D. (1965). *Lecture Notes on Ophthalmology* 2nd Edition. Oxford: Blackwell Scientific Publications.

(fig. 24.90). Each line of letters is marked with the distance at which the details will subtend one minute at the eye, and this distance is stated in metres. The top line is generally marked 60, and so should be legible at a distance of 60 m. Six metres is a practical distance for testing, and at this distance the normal eye does not need to accommodate. The acuity can then be expressed as a 'fraction'; the 'numerator' is the distance in metres at which the test is made (usually 6), and the 'denominator' is the number against the line of letters which are the smallest that can be read. Obviously this pseudo-fraction cannot be reduced by dividing top and bottom. Normal acuity is expressed as $\frac{6}{6}$. If the subject can read only the top line, acuity is poor and expressed as $\frac{6}{60}$; a more rough and ready test uses various sizes of reading type at the distance usual for reading. This is normally done using one eye at a time.

The ability to distinguish a space between two lines subtending one minute at the eye is not the supreme feat of the human visual system. Vernier acuity enables us to observe that two lines are slightly out of alignment with each other. This can be done when the discrepancy is a mere 5 seconds of arc, one twelfth of the 'minimum separable', and a distance at the retina of only 0·4 μm. The dimensions of the receptors are given on p. 24.57. To account for vernier acuity is much more difficult than to take advantage of it by using a vernier scale.

Illumination

As already mentioned, enough light is essential for all testing of visual acuity. The recommended amount is 100 lumens/ft² (foot-candles), which is comparable to what a 60 watt tungsten filament lamp sheds on a surface facing towards it and 24 cm away. Even more can be used with some improvement in acuity, so long as there is no local glare. But less light than this brings real impairment of acuity. Daylight in the open air gives over ten times as much throughout most of a summer day. In industry, the same standard of illumination is needed for the finest work as is needed for testing visual acuity (table 24.1).

TABLE 24.1. Some standards of illumination recommended by the Illuminating Engineering Society, or prescribed by law.

	Lumens/ft²	Approximately equivalent to a 60-watt tungsten lamp at
Fine work	100	24 cm
School rooms	30	44 cm
General office work	20	54 cm
Factory work (legal minimum at working level)	6	98 cm

Proper lighting involves other factors, such as glare and colour, too complex to discuss in detail. Colour can be used to real advantage; it ministers to morale and is an aid to safety when danger points are duly coloured. In laboratories and workshops, poor illumination leads to mistakes, inaccuracies and accidents. A well lit kitchen is also a safe and cheerful kitchen. Artificial light is never as satisfactory as daylight where patients are being examined and fails to disclose slight degrees of jaundice, because its spectral composition is different. The finest consulting rooms known to the writer, built by his former partners, provide a transparent dome admitting daylight above each examination couch.

Retinoscopy

Retinoscopy is the method of measuring the refraction of a human eye objectively. The word ought to mean looking at the retina but in fact it does not entail looking at the details of the retina at all. It contrasts with the subjective method of measuring errors of refraction which depends on placing lenses in front of the subject's eyes and requiring him to read Snellen's charts until he obtains the best possible acuity. Retinoscopy is an objective method and is useful, both for babies and for people who do not tell what they see as lucidly as the tester might wish.

The eye to be tested must not be accommodating. With

FIG. 24.91. Diagrams to illustrate retinoscopy (see text).

an ophthalmoscope mirror 1 m from the eye, a patch of light is moved across the eye from side to side. As the eye is unaccommodated, rays emerge from it parallel (upper part of fig. 24.91). So when the light has just left the pupil, moving in the direction of the arrow, it will be followed by a 'ray of darkness'; in other words, the shadow in the pupil follows the patch of light in the same direction as the patch moves over the eye. But if a convex lens of, say, 3 dioptres is placed before the eye, the parallel rays converge one third of a metre from the eye. The dioptre is the reciprocal of the focal length of a lens in metres and offers great convenience in calculation. When the patch of light is now moved in the same fashion across the eye, the 'dark ray' (lower part of fig. 24.91) appears when viewed from the mirror to have got ahead; in fact, the shadow is seen to chase the light patch across the pupil in the direction opposite to the actual movement of the patch.

Lenses are tried in succession until no movement of the shadow at all is seen. The mirror is then at the intersection of the light and dark rays shown in the lower part of fig. 24.91. If this occurs with a lens of 1 dioptre, the eye is emmetropic (neither myopic nor hypermetropic) and requires no correction. If the lens has some other value, a spectacle lens is required of that value minus one dioptre. The technique is not easy to master and the principles are too complex to present fully here.

Perimetry

From fig. 24.92 it is seen that the two eyes between them when gazing straight ahead command a field of view of

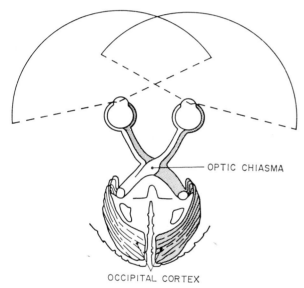

OPTIC CHIASMA

OCCIPITAL CORTEX

FIG. 24.92. The field of vision of the two eyes and the central connections of the retinae. Modified from Scott G.I. (1957). *Traquair's Practical Perimetry*. London: Kimpton.

about 200° from side to side. Each eye separately commands rather less, because the nose blocks about 35° medially. The field of each eye can be measured separately with a perimeter, a sophisticated protractor which enables the subject to fix his gaze at its centre and the operator to test him with stimuli of varying shape and colour at measured angles from the line of gaze in any direction. The field is markedly smaller for small or poorly lit stimuli than it is for large bright ones. It should contain only one gap, the **blind spot**, where the optic nerve joins the eyeball. The perimeter is invaluable for detecting defects in the field of vision, which can be due to disease of the nervous system or of the eye.

Central nervous pathways

The intracranial part of the **optic nerve** runs backward and medially to the **optic chiasma**, where it joins its fellow from the other eye. The chiasma forms part of the floor of the third ventricle of the brain, and it lies above the diaphragma sellae, the dura mater overlying the pituitary gland.

At the chiasma the two nerves cross over, but only in part. Behind the chiasma (fig. 24.92), the re-arranged optic nerve fibres continue back as the **optic tracts**. Each tract now contains the fibres from the temporal half of the retina of the eye on its own side and the fibres from the nasal half of the retina of the eye on the opposite side. So in a sense each tract 'sees' the world on the opposite side. The world is cut in two by a vertical line though the direction of gaze; the right optic tract 'sees' the left half, and vice versa.

The pituitary gland lies below the origins of the two optic tracts from the chiasma. It can be the site of tumours and it is well worth trying to deduce what effects on vision are to be expected if such a tumour enlarges forward, splitting the chiasma, or sideways, damaging the medial sides of one or both optic tracts.

Each optic tract continues back to the cerebral peduncle, winds round it, and terminates for the most part in the **lateral geniculate body**, but also in the **superior colliculus**. The latter is the major termination in birds, but when the cerebral hemispheres are predominant, as in man, the lateral geniculate body is the end station for most of the fibres of the optic tract. A few fibres end in the **pretectal nucleus** (fig. 24.86).

The lateral geniculate body is an outlying part of the thalamus and protrudes below its lateral part. Its neurones give rise to axons which form the **optic radiation** and run to the **striate area** of the cerebral cortex in the occipital lobe. The fibres of the optic radiation follow a path just lateral to the inferior horn of the lateral ventricle and very close to the posterior horn.

How pattern vision works

It is possible to record the electrical activity in a single ganglion cell in an animal's retina or in an optic nerve fibre, which is approximately the same thing, since the fibre is the axon of the retinal ganglion cell. It is also possible to record the activity of single neurones in the visual areas of the cerebral cortex. From such recordings a picture can be assembled of how the patterns in the seen world are analysed.

Each retinal ganglion cell deals with the traffic from a patch of the retina, a small patch at the fovea but a much larger patch at the periphery. The patch is round, and so when the sky is being looked at the cell can be thought of as 'seeing' a round portion of the sky. One might suppose that the ganglion cell would fire with vigour when the light falling on the many receptors in its patch of retina was bright, and slowly when it was dim. But the actual behaviour is more complex.

The round patch is not uniformly treated by the ganglion cell. It is divided into a circular core and an outer ring. Some ganglion cells (fig. 24.93, left) fire

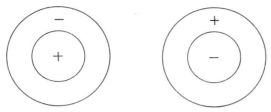

FIG. 24.93. Fields seen by retinal ganglion cells: two types of organization.

vigorously when light falls suddenly upon the inner core, but if light falls only upon the outer ring, they actually fire less than they would do in darkness. Even in darkness, the ganglion cell fires slowly. So here light can provoke a negative response.

Other ganglion cells (fig. 24.94, right) reverse this re-

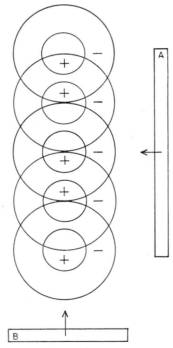

FIG. 24.94. Retinal ganglion cell field summed in the visual area of the cerebral cortex (see text).

lation; light in the centre slows their firing, but in the outer ring it speeds them up. It can be deduced that illuminating the whole area, core plus outer ring together, produces little result, because the two effects cancel each other. This is perhaps hardly surprising, since a uniformly lit surface which is entirely featureless excites

hardly any reaction in ourselves and gets no attention. It can also be deduced that anything moving across the patch of retina will produce a particularly brisk response in the corresponding ganglion cell, because before and after its central effect it produces the reverse; the central effect is made more prominent by what precedes and follows it.

Dark adaptation (p. 24.60) often abolishes the core-outer ring organization. The whole patch responds like its centre. The delicate balancing of core against outer ring is abandoned, and instead greater sensitivity to light over the whole patch is achieved.

In the cat, a ganglion cell's patch of retina in the most sensitive area might correspond to half a degree, which is about one quarter of the space between two knuckles when the fist is held at arm's length. In man, the patch may be a great deal smaller. The retina is not a simple mosaic of such patches, but each encroaches on its neighbours to a varying extent.

It will now be clear that the retina is much more than a camera film signalling the presence of light or darkness in any part of itself. It is part of the central nervous system, and carries out some of the necessary analysis of the information before transmitting it along the optic nerve. For instance, uniform light affects a camera film, but uniform illumination of the whole retina produces relatively little response, as already mentioned. Further, a special sensitivity to movement of light is already inherent in the traffic passing from retina to lateral geniculate nucleus.

The first stages of the processes in the cerebral hemispheres can also now be outlined. One neurone there certainly does not simply receive the incoming traffic from one patch of retina. It is coupled to a number of patches which are arranged (fig. 24.94) along a straight line in the retina. So it responds to a bar of light (A in fig. 24.94) falling along the centres of the patches along this line. A bar at right angles to this (B in fig. 24.94) excites no response; it does illuminate part at least of the centres of the patches, but it also illuminates the surround, thus cancelling the response. So there can be analysis of light patterns according to the slope of lines in the outside world and this part of the analysis occurs in the visual area of the cerebral cortex. It is continued with increasing elaboration outside the primary visual area. The whole story, as yet, is by no means clear. In particular, the eyes are in incessant movement and the machinery for dealing with a picture that does not keep still and is actually deliberately moved is hardly understood. Further, the central arrangements for colour vision are not at all plain.

Binocular vision

Each eye sees approximately the same world, but as already described, the world is bisected along a vertical ine through the centre of gaze because of the partial crossing of the optic nerves at the optic chiasma, and subsequently one cerebral hemisphere deals with the opposite half of the seen world. So each hemisphere receives and, in effect, analyses incoming traffic from one half of each retina; the other half is linked to the opposite hemisphere.

Stereoscopic vision thus becomes possible. Both eyes are normally directed so as to see the same thing and point in the same direction; in fact, the eye muscles are controlled so that this is the case, because the central nervous system monitors the view of the two eyes and provides for eye movements that will make the view the same. The monitoring arrangement can be upset by the simple and ingenious **Maddox rod**. This is a parallel array of small red glass rods. When placed in front of one eye, it distorts the image of a spot of white light in front of the observer into a long red line. The monitoring system is evidently unable to identify the white spot and the long red line as the same picture, and so can no longer align the eyes precisely with each other. While still pointing the same way approximately, they may show a 'latent squint' (**exophoria** if divergent, **esophoria** if convergent) which is not a squint, in the sense that during ordinary use the eyes point in the same direction. A latent squint of this kind is probably of no importance except perhaps where very fast responses have to be made to visual information, as by aircraft pilots.

Normally the views seen by the two eyes are made the same by appropriate eye movements, but never exactly the same. They cannot be, because the two eyes are in different places. Two photographs taken from closely adjoining positions are almost the same when correctly lined up, but never quite the same. When one looks at two such photographs in a stereoscope (simply a device enabling one eye to see one photograph and the other eye another one), one obtains an impression of depth in the picture which is otherwise absent. The impression of depth originates from the tiny differences between the two pictures. The nervous system is capable of recognizing these differences and this can be done only in the cerebral cortex, for only there does the traffic from the two eyes meet; it is still probably separate in the lateral geniculate body.

If only one eye is available, stereoscopic depth cannot be sensed. Stereoscopic vision is only one of the ways in which we can judge distance. A single eye can assess the angle subtended at the eye by any familiar object and allow for the known size of the object; it can take into account the amount of accommodation for very close objects, and compare with an extraordinary precision the angular velocities at which two objects are going past but it is still surprisingly difficult to thread a fine needle after closing one eye.

A squinting child, with eyes not pointing correctly in the same direction, loses stereoscopic depth and has double vision. But what is much worse, he often loses entirely the ability to see with one of his eyes, thus gaining single vision at the cost of a functionless eye. The reason is that if the two worlds presented to each cerebral hemisphere do not coincide as they should, then the nerve connections of one of the two eyes within the cerebral cortex, though already established at birth, become permanently ineffective.

MOTOR SYSTEMS

The pyramidal or corticospinal tract

If one looks at the medulla externally or in sections, the conspicuous pathway is the pyramidal tract, so named because of the prominences on the anterior surface created by the fibres of the corticospinal tract. Its origin lies partly in the main motor area of the cerebral cortex, where the largest fibres arise as the axons of the giant Betz cells. This is not its whole origin (p. 24.50). Contributions to the tract are made from the cerebral cortex in front of the main motor area and also from behind it, in the main somatic sensory area. The fibres run without synaptic junctions to terminations near the motor neurones. These motor neurones lie in the motor nuclei of the brain and spinal cord, and their axons run out in the ventral spinal nerve roots, or corresponding cranial nerve roots, to reach motor end plates in muscle. When discussing the motor system, one may call them **lower motor neurones**, and refer to neurones such as Betz cells (complete with axons) as **upper motor neurones**.

While the fibres of the pyramidal tract may terminate at lower motor neurones in the spinal cord, many do not; they end at interneurones nearby. At first sight it seems absurd that any interneurones should be interposed between the signals for action descending from the cerebral cortex to lower motor neurones. Time is lost at the synapses, though only in trifling amounts. What is gained is the better organization of movement. On flexing the elbow, for instance, one contracts brachialis and biceps, but simultaneously relaxes triceps; movements are controlled much better by the regulated slackening of antagonist muscles. This phenomenon, relaxation of antagonists when a muscle contracts to bring about a movement, is **reciprocal innervation** of the opposed muscle groups; as the impulse traffic to one muscle increases, the traffic to its antagonists is reduced. The interneurone systems of the spinal cord organize reciprocal innervation and are interposed in the pathway for voluntary movement.

Extrapyramidal system

The pyramidal tract is not the sole link between cerebral cortex and lower motor neurone. The remaining channels for voluntary movement run from much the same parts of the cerebral cortex as the pyramidal tract. The twin hallmarks of these channels are that they involve synaptic junctions in the basal nuclei or brain stem and that they do not run through the pyramids as they traverse the medulla.

Synaptic junctions involve relaying of the impulse traffic and again a slight delay. These functions do, however, allow two more complex forms of neuronal activity. First, traffic from many parts of the brain can gain access to the extrapyramidal pathway. Secondly, the cerebral cortex can act through extrapyramidal paths, not to excite neurones at intermediate junctions, but to inhibit their activity. The extrapyramidal system, like the pyramidal system, links the cerebral cortex to the motor systems of the spinal cord, but differs because it can function only by modifying, i.e. increasing or reducing, the activity of parts of the basal nuclei, thalamus, and brain stem. These structures can themselves produce movement, and the cerebral cortex need not be regarded as always stimulating them to action; the cortex can operate to prevent lower centres from producing or affecting movements.

What follows from all this in practice? If the pyramidal tract alone is interrupted, which can only occur at medullary level, where it is not intermixed with other tracts, some voluntary movements are still possible. The most delicate finger movements are lost and others may be slower and less nimble. In a monkey, after section of the pyramidal tracts, limb movements can still be evoked by stimulation of the motor areas of the cerebral cortex; the extrapyramidal system must be responsible.

Damage limited to the pyramids of the medulla rarely occurs, except deliberately in animal experiments. As a rule, damage due to disease or injury to voluntary paths occurs in the cerebral cortex or internal capsule, where extrapyramidal paths are interrupted as well as the pyramidal tract. Then, in addition to much greater loss of movements, **spasticity** develops. The normal stretch reflexes are exaggerated; the affected limbs are stiff and resistant to efforts to bend them by external force. The activity of lower motor centres is responsible, no longer restrained by cerebral cortical activity.

When there is spasticity, **clonus** is often present. It is produced by flexing a joint (for instance, dorsiflexing the ankle joint) by external force and keeping up the flexing force. The stretched muscles respond to the tension on their muscle spindles by contracting and do so excessively, so that for a moment they remove altogether the tension upon the spindles. This allows the muscles to relax again, but the examiner's continued pressure stretches the muscle once more, and the cycle restarts. So a maintained rhythm of contraction and relaxation persists as long as the examiner pushes.

In general, it is possible to distinguish damage to motor neurones proper (lower motor neurones) from damage to motor paths higher up (upper motor neurones) The principal distinctions are shown in table 24.2.

TABLE 24.2. Distinctions between lower and upper motor neurone lesions.

	Lower motor neurone lesion	Upper motor neurone lesion
Voluntary movements	None by affected motor units.	Gross movements are possible, especially at limb girdles.
Nutrition of the muscles	Wasted and atrophic	Normal
Tone	Limp.	Often spastic.
Spinal reflexes	None in affected muscles	Reflexes such as tendon jerks may be very brisk; clonus may be present
Plantar response (see p. 24.14)	None, if the relevant muscles are affected.	Upgoing.

When the human primary motor cortex is stimulated electrically, there is a movement, but the patient does not regard it as arising from his own will. Where does a voluntary movement really originate? Certainly the most highly precise movements depend particularly on the pyramidal tract. But coarser movements are not exclusively pyramidal, and extrapyramidal fibres arising from parts of the cerebral cortex well outside the main motor area can function not so much by exciting neurones in the corpus striatum and lower motor nuclei, as by releasing them. It is not possible to select a starting place in this network with any assurance. Neurophysiology cannot assign a definite site in the central nervous system for the initiation of voluntary actions.

SENSORY SYSTEMS

The sensory system deals with sensing what is happening to the body itself; what is touching or warming its surface, what is giving rise to pain in a viscus, the position of joints and so forth. Sight, hearing, smell and taste are 'special senses'. If one were designing such a sensory system, one would perhaps stud the skin with small pressure transducers and intersperse small thermometers and devices to detect tissue damage. Upon reflection, some means of signalling hair movement might be added in recognition of how sensitive we are to this stimulus, and how convenient the sensitivity must be in parts of the world where insects abound. So much for the body surface; such a system provides facilities for us to feel touch, heat and cold, pain or other damage. Pressure upon the skin and its temperature are signalled continuously from the skin to the nervous system, and anything damaging tissue starts an alarm discharge.

Organs deep to the surface must also be supplied with sensation. It is essential to know the angles of joints and the state of contraction of muscles and damage to tissue anywhere in the body must also be indicated. Processes such as the control of the circulation are conducted by the nervous system using sensory information from blood vessels which, like much of the other sensory traffic coming into the central nervous system, does not enter consciousness.

The reading of a thermometer can be signalled at a distance by, for instance, converting it to a D.C. electrical potential and reading this simple code at the end of a cable with a voltmeter. Sensory information must be coded in some way which can be conveyed along nerve fibres. There are two general possibilities: it might be coded in terms of the frequency of sequences of nerve impulses, each impulse being identical, and then perhaps 100 impulses/sec. would correspond to a skin temperature of 25°C, and 50/sec. to one of 15°C. Alternatively, special sequences might be used, like the Morse code, so that pairs of impulses from a temperature receptor indicated a temperature of 15°C, and triplets 25°C.

In fact the first method is used in the general sensory system, with important modifications which emerge later, and not the method of special sequences of impulses; indeed, if repetitive sequences of impulses occur, then the system is being stimulated by something itself repetitive, such as a vibration from a tuning fork applied to the skin.

The receptors

The skin is not a uniform sensitive surface. Touch it with a fine probe or with a small metal tip which is warm or cold, and it becomes clear that some points on the skin are much more sensitive than the intervening parts. Beside, the skin on all parts of the body is not equally sensitive. Fingers are highly sensitive, and two metal points very close together can be felt as two not one. In the middle of the back, two points feel like only one until they are widely separated. If follows that receptors in the fingers are likely to be much closer together than those in the back.

Two probable receptors for light touch, conspicuous in the hairless skin are: Merkel's discs and Meissner's corpuscles (fig. 24.95a). Merkel's discs lie in the deepest layer of the epidermis and consist of a disc shaped nerve plate, the whole being some 10 μm across, slightly larger than a red blood cell. Meissner's corpuscles are columns of interleaved nerve endings and flat cells and are about 20 μm across; they lie at the tips of the dermal papillae. These two receptors are not found in hairy skin and here the receptors for touch have not been identified.

Hair roots possess elaborate branched nerve endings of varying types, which respond to displacements of the hair, as when something brushes against it. Another type of elaborately organized receptor is the Pacinian corpuscle (fig. 24.95b), found not only below the skin but also in numerous other sites in the body and large enough to be visible to the naked eye, being some 3–4 mm long. It is very sensitive to pressure.

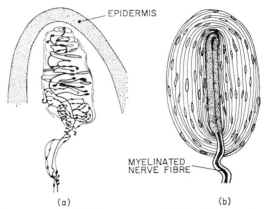

FIG. 24.95. (a) Meissner corpuscle in a human dermal papilla and (b) a human Pacinian corpuscle.

Although electrical recordings have often been done from nerve fibres which respond to temperature changes, temperature receptors have not yet been certainly identified. The hairy parts of the skin contain no specialized receptors for temperature, but they are not insensitive to heat and cold. It is not essential for a receptor to have an elaborate structure visible by light microscopy. The deepest layer of the epidermis itself, and indeed most parts of the body, contain large numbers of free nerve endings, lacking elaborate surrounding receptor structures.

Linking of receptors to nerve fibres

Does each receptor for touch, temperature, or other modality operate its own fibre? It seems at first sight strange that this is not so in general. While a receptor as large as a Pacinian corpuscle does have its own fibre, smaller receptors are often coupled several to one fibre. A motor unit consists of a motor neurone and the muscle fibres supplied by the motor neurone; similarly, sensory units are made up of several receptors and their common dorsal root ganglion cell and its bifurcating axon. In addition, one receptor can be coupled to more than one fibre, especially in the case of a complex system like that at a hair root. Overlap of this kind seems likely to scramble the information and give rise to vague and confused sensation, so the information must be disentangled by central processes.

The traffic entering the nervous system along each sensory fibre

It has already been explained that the code used is the frequency of impulses. Does this mean that when the skin is pressed by a given weight, impulses begin to travel along the relevant fibre at a frequency corresponding to the weight and continue until the weight is taken off?

When the skin becomes warmer or cooler, does the frequency along the appropriate fibre simply change accordingly and stay at the new rate as long as the temperature is steady? Neither of these simple statements is generally true; indeed, such an arrangement would be both wasteful of energy and, metaphorically speaking, boring for the central nervous system. From its origin at the receptors, the sensory system is especially sensitive to change, much more than it is to constant conditions. Many sensory fibres show a vigorous burst of impulses at the onset of a stimulus, and the firing frequency quickly falls away even though the stimulus persists, feature called **adaptation**. However, the final frequency is still often different from the starting frequency, so that there is an indication that the change persists, but it is the onset of the change that provokes the maximal activity.

FIG. 24.96. The behaviour of a fast adapting touch receptor in the sole of the foot. The upper trace shows the firing of the receptor and the lower trace the mechanical movement of the probe which stimulates the receptor. Lindblom (1963). *Acta Physiol. Scand.* **59**, 410.

The sensory fibres mostly fall into two classes; one carries traffic showing a marked response to a change when it occurs and very little or nothing later on, even though the change persists (fig. 24.96); the other is a much slower adapter and shows relatively little response to change at the time it happens, but does continue this smaller response for the duration of the change, or for a long time (fig. 24.97). The latter often shows a resting discharge, i.e. continuous firing, but rather faster during the application of pressure, a higher temperature or other appropriate stimulus.

Another question is whether there is a tidy separation of sensory fibres into those signalling touch, temperature and damage to tissue. The picture is not clear cut. Most of the touch fibres are highly specific and respond to nothing else, but some, usually of the slowly adapting type, respond to temperature change too, although they are perhaps a hundred times less sensitive than the specific temperature fibres. This is less surprising when one

FIG. 24.97. The behaviour of a slowly adapting touch receptor on the sole of the foot (see fig. 24.96).

remembers that the skin functions over a wide range of temperatures, and most biological processes are markedly affected by change of temperature.

The temperature receptors generally fire faster at the time that a change of temperature occurs; cold receptors respond in this way to a fall in temperature and warm receptors to a rise. In cats, the fall or rise can be as small as $0.2°C$, which is comparable to the smallest change sensed by one's own skin. These transient dynamic changes in frequency are superimposed on a continuous, static background discharge which depends also on temperature; the steady static background might for instance, be 15 spikes/sec at a temperature around 38–43°C for a 'warm' fibre, or around 15–34°C for a 'cold' fibre. Hibernating animals, interestingly enough are equipped with cold fibres reaching a maximum static discharge rate at only 4°C, which could function to awaken them if in peril of freezing. The dynamic response that signals the onset of a change may raise the rate temporarily to 150 spikes/sec. Just as touch receptors may respond with low sensitivity to temperature changes so temperature receptors may respond to pressure, but less sensitively.

Pain

What are the pain receptors and how does the system signalling pain behave? This question is easy to ask, but its solution is attended by two special difficulties. Firstly if the skin is stimulated in such a way as to bring pain receptors into action, this is likely to damage the system and so on repetition the same effect may not occur. Secondly, the smallest fibres have long been suspected of conveying information about pain, and recording from these fibres is especially hard as they are so small, although Iggo and a few other workers can do it. Worse still, it is virtually essential to carry out such recording on an animal. It is possible to decide fairly reliably whether anything painful has been done to an anaesthetized animal, even though it is unaware of the pain, but not when the fibres transmitting the pain have been interrupted for recording. Then the animal has not in fact been hurt since the relevant traffic has never reached the central nervous system.

So far, there are some points about the transmission of pain information which are reasonably well established. Firstly, pain is not just the increased responses of touch units when they are touched very hard. Such units generally reach their highest rate of firing before any evidence of damage occurs, and nothing makes them fire any faster. Secondly, small fibres certainly are not all pain fibres, so far as can be judged from their behaviour; small myelinated or unmyelinated fibres generally do not need harmful stimuli to excite them, but respond sensitively to touch or temperature change. Thirdly, the free nerve endings, without elaborate receptor structure, might be expected to be responsible for pain, but this is not necessarily the case at all; in the cornea, for instance, where they are found in isolation from any other sort of receptor, some of them respond only to cooling. There is certainly a close link between temperature sensation and pain; witness, for instance, the transient pain that water at very modest temperature (36–40°C) evokes. There is no tissue damage; one's bath feels comfortable in a few seconds. This sort of pain behaves like the dynamic component of a temperature receptor's response. So it is hardly surprising that pain and temperature are handled along the same pathways in the central nervous system.

In fact there are peculiar difficulties in the way of the belief that there are special receptors for pain alone; it is a matter of ordinary experience that sensitivity to pain varies from time to time in a fashion not at all explicable by supposing that one is at one time neurotic and at another hysterical, while all the time possessing a normal pain sensing mechanism. Normal skin can be quite roughly treated without pain; near a boil it is exquisitely sensitive. Those who have lost a limb may suffer from agonizing phantom pains which appear to originate in the absent limb, yet there can be no input of nerve impulses from the part to trigger the pain. In contrast, people under hypnosis undergo operations without anaesthesia and without seeming to sense pain. Lucretius (98–55 B.C.) wrote how in a battle with scythed chariots: such is the quickness of the injury and the eagerness of the man's mind that he cannot feel the pain'; or to come nearer home:

> 'For Witherington needs must I wail,
> As one in doleful dumps,
> For when his legs were smitten off
> He fought upon the stumps.'
> (Ballad of Chevy Chase)

So it is hard to believe that pain is the simple outcome of afferent traffic arising in free nerve endings and entering the central nervous system by slow conducting fibres. Admittedly, pain may follow only slowly after the responsible stimulus and not all tissue damage is necessarily an urgent matter. Anyone lying quite still, perfectly still, in a few hours develops bed sores, because pressure cuts off the blood supply of the skin on which the weight rests. Normally the skin receptors presumably prevent this by prompting a change of position, but seconds are unlikely to count.

What then is one to believe, if pain is not prompted by traffic along specific fibres entering the central nervous system? It may be supposed that pain is more like a deduction made by the central nervous system upon analysing the interplay of entering traffic, both fast and slow travelling. The deduction may take a very short or a long time to form, depending on the details of the entering traffic.

The handling of pain information in the central nervous system

If, then, pain is recognized after analysis, one might expect the analysis to start in the spinal cord, where the first organization of neurones exists which coordinates traffic entering at different times and along different fibres. If it does start there, it ought to be easier to single out the paths followed by pain traffic upwards in the spinal cord, than it is to define the paths by which it enters the spinal cord in the first place.

On the whole this is the case. The spinothalamic tracts convey traffic related to both pain and temperature from the spinal cord up to the thalamus. If they are interrupted, sensibility to pain and temperature is generally blocked below the level of the interruption.

Efforts to trace nervous traffic related to pain alone beyond the thalamus have never been successful. The sensory areas of the cerebral cortex appear relatively unresponsive to painful stimulation of the appropriate part of the body. Nor, if these cortical areas are stimulated electrically during operations on conscious patients, is pain often produced. And damage to the cerebral cortex does not abolish pain, at any rate after the first few days.

On the other hand, it cannot be shown that any part of the thalamus is the 'pain centre' and that its removal abolishes pain. There are widespread interconnections between the region where the spinothalamic tracts end and other parts of the forebrain, the frontal cortex and limbic system for instance. Damage to the thalamus occasionally brings about a state in which pain is not so easily provoked as before, but peculiarly disturbing when it occurs. In contrast, if the frontal cerebral cortex is severed from the thalamus on both sides (**leucotomy**), painful stimuli are just as easily appreciated, but the patient is much less disturbed by them than before. Pain is, it seems, the outcome of an analysis in which the final answer is not deciphered in any one part of the brain.

Referred pain

The correct interpretation of pain originating deep to the skin is a key problem in most branches of medicine. One automatically localizes precisely pain from the skin, or else learns to do so in earliest life. This precision is absent from deep pain. Several special features make its interpretation possible.

Firstly, what hurts a great deal on the skin may not hurt at all in muscles and viscera. The alimentary canal, kidneys, ureters, heart and lungs are normally insensitive to cutting or burning. On the other hand, these organs are sensitive to sudden distension or to ischaemia. In contrast, the parietal lining of body cavities (peritoneum, pleura, pericardium) is sensitive to mechanical damage.

The location of pain originating in deep tissues is often ill defined. It is sensed as in the midline when it arises from alimentary canal or heart, both of which originally developed in the midline. It also is often referred to the surface of the body corresponding to the spinal nerve roots concerned, yet the subject rarely doubts that the pain arises from some deep origin and not from the skin. This phenomenon of reference means that cardiac pain can be felt in the midline and in addition in the arms, because the afferent fibres from the heart reach the spinal cord in the roots T2 or higher, up to C5. It also means that pain arising in the pleura over the diaphragm is felt in the neck and shoulder, since the afferent fibres are in the phrenic nerve (C3–5), and on the appropriate side, since the diaphragm is not simply a midline structure. Similarly pain arising in a joint or muscle in the neck may be referred to the appropriate arm where the cutaneous branches of the same spinal root lie.

This reference is of course not simply a delusion in the patient's mind. The afferent traffic from body surface and from deeper structures converges in the nervous system. The skin surface may be hypersensitive to painful stimulation when a deep structure is also contributing a source of pain; for instance, lightly stroking the skin with a pin over an inflamed appendix may seem very painful. Conversely, pain from a deep structure may diminish if traffic from the skin surface at the corresponding root level is abolished by local anaesthesia of the skin surface. For instance, in the cervix and in the vagina above the hymen touch, heat and cold cannot be sensed, but pain can be produced by electrical stimulation of the cervix and is referred to the skin midway between the umbilicus and symphysis pubis. In Theobald's experiments, a stimulus strength above five units evoked pain, but he could abolish this by local anaesthetic infiltrated, not into the cervix, but into the abdominal skin at the site of reference. In this way stimulus strength could be increased up to ninety units without pain, but stronger stimuli produced pain in the abdominal wall which could not be abolished by local anaesthetics.

Vibration sense

The skin can detect that something pressing upon it is vibrating, and it is most sensitive to vibration at 200–400 cycles/sec, readily applied by a tuning fork. Bone underneath the skin makes the stimulation more effective, and so vibration sense is usually tested on skin overlying bone. Fast-adapting receptors for touch and pressure are clearly able to signal such vibrations, especially perhaps the Pacinian corpuscle, which is known to produce one nerve impulse per cycle over the appropriate range of frequencies. Vibration sense is thus closely linked to the sensation of touch and pressure and along with the sense of the position of joints is conveyed centrally by the dorsal columns and the medial lemniscus.

Stereognosis

This word means the ability to recognize by hand, blindfold, the shapes of solid objects, e.g. of a key or a threepenny piece. It involves not only analysing complex incoming traffic from the receptors, but also actively handling the objects. Clearly it depends on the traffic being adequate for analysis; numb fingers cannot be used for recognition. But it also depends on the analysing ability of the cerebral cortex, especially its posterior parietal part, and even when the receptor system cannot be faulted, stereognosis may be defective if there is damage to this part of the cerebral cortex (p. 24.51).

ARTERIAL BLOOD SUPPLY TO BRAIN

The arterial supply to the brain comes from the carotid and vertebral arteries which communicate through the circle of Willis and occasionally meningeal anastomoses.

Although each system has a relatively distinct territorial supply, the sequence of branching follows the same general plan. Thus each major vessel such as the internal carotid or vertebral artery gives off four large branches which in turn divide into medial and lateral perforating branches and terminal branches.

The **forebrain** (telencephalon and diencephalon) is supplied by the two internal carotid arteries which each divide into their four main branches; the **anterior cerebral**, **middle cerebral** and **posterior communicating arteries** which supply the superficial portion of the brain whilst the **anterior choroidal artery** supplies the brain core.

The **hindbrain** (mesencephalon, pons and medulla) is also supplied by two large arteries, the vertebrals which form the **basilar artery** so that the whole system is referred to as the **vertebrobasilar**. However, if the basilar is regarded as two fused vertebral arteries then the same general plan emerges. Thus each vertebral artery gives off four major branches, **posterior cerebral, superior cere-**

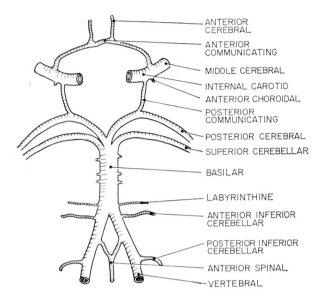

ANTERIOR CEREBRAL
ANTERIOR COMMUNICATING
MIDDLE CEREBRAL
INTERNAL CAROTID
ANTERIOR CHOROIDAL
POSTERIOR COMMUNICATING
POSTERIOR CEREBRAL
SUPERIOR CEREBELLAR
BASILAR
LABYRINTHINE
ANTERIOR INFERIOR CEREBELLAR
POSTERIOR INFERIOR CEREBELLAR
ANTERIOR SPINAL
VERTEBRAL

FIG. 24.98. The circle of Willis and principal arteries of the brain.

MIDDLE CEREBRAL

ANTERIOR CEREBRAL A.

POSTERIOR CEREBRAL A.

FIG. 24.99. Areas of the cerebral cortex supplied by the cerebral arteries. Above, lateral surface; below, medial surface.

bellar, **anterior inferior cerebellar** and **posterior inferior cerebellar arteries** (figs. 24.98 and 99).

The forebrain (carotid) and hindbrain (vertebral) circulations are connected through the circle of Willis by the **posterior communicating arteries**; the **anterior communicating artery** joins the two carotid systems.

The posterior communicating artery is one of the major branches of the internal carotid artery and communicates with the posterior cerebral artery of the vertebrobasilar system, whilst the anterior communicating artery connects the right and left carotid systems via the two anterior cerebral arteries. This is the major plan of the circulation and it readily explains the arterial supply to the fore- and hindbrain. Such apparent anomalies as the posterior cerebral artery supplying the forebrain (carotid territory) and yet arising from the hindbrain system (vertebrobasilar system) are due to enlargemen of the posterior communicating artery.

The carotid system

The left common carotid artery arises directly from the aorta, the right common carotid artery from the brachiocephalic artery. Each common carotid artery divides into external and internal carotids usually at the upper border of the thyroid cartilage at the level of the fourth cervical vertebra.

The **internal carotid artery** passes upwards into the intracranial cavity through the carotid canal in a forward and medial direction to enter the cavernous sinus (p. 21.9). It penetrates the dura lying lateral to the optic nerve and gives off the ophthalmic artery. The carotid artery then bends backwards to give off the posterior communicating artery, the anterior choroidal artery and finally bending forwards again divides into middle and anterior cerebral arteries (fig. 24.100).

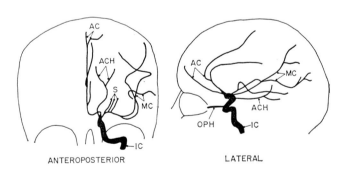

AC
ACH
S
MC
IC

ANTEROPOSTERIOR

AC
MC
ACH
OPH
IC

LATERAL

FIG. 24.100. Tracings of carotid arteriograms. AC, anterior cerebral; ACH, anterior choroidal; IC, internal carotid; MC, middle cerebral; OPH, ophthalmic; S, thalamostriate.

The **posterior communicating artery** passes backwards to join the posterior cerebral artery which usually obtains its major blood supply from the hindbrain circulation.

The **anterior choroidal artery** comes off either the internal carotid artery directly as its first branch or from one of its major branches. It passes posteriorly around the cerebral peduncles and supplies the medial aspect of the thalamus and basal nuclei before emerging at the trigone of the lateral ventricle to supply the choroid plexus.

The **middle cerebral artery** comes off the internal carotid artery and almost immediately enters the proximal part of the lateral sulcus. It soon gives off small **thalamostriate arteries** which penetrate the anterior perforated substance to supply the basal nuclei. The remainder of the artery ramifies on the surface of the insula and supplies the cortex of the lateral aspect of the frontal, parietal and temporal lobes.

The **anterior cerebral artery** comes off the internal carotid and passes between the two hemispheres above the optic nerves. Before joining the opposite anterior cerebral via the anterior communicating artery, it gives off perforating branches which pass to the septum and preoptic region of the hypothalamus. The **striate artery** is one of the larger perforating branches and supplies the medial part of the head of the caudate nucleus and putamen and the anterior part of the internal capsule. After the anastomosis, the anterior cerebral artery runs forwards and upwards around the genu of the corpus callosum, giving off arteries supplying the frontal poles before running backwards over the corpus callosum. The anterior two-thirds of the medial aspect of the hemisphere is supplied by the anterior cerebral and its branches.

The vertebrobasilar system

The vertebral arteries pass medially and forwards to enter the posterior cranial fossa through the foramen magnum via separate dural foramina closely related to the first tooth of the ligamentum denticulatum which is an important relationship in high cervical cordotomy. The artery then passes forwards to join its fellow artery in front of the pons to form the basilar artery.

The **posterior inferior cerebellar artery** is the first branch of the vertebrobasilar system and often projects in a loop down to the atlas. It may thus be easily damaged during operations unless the surgeon is aware of it. The artery supplies the inferior surface of the cerebellum and the dorsolateral aspect of the medulla.

The **basilar artery** lies in a shallow groove on the pons and gives off the **anterior inferior cerebellar artery** supplying the inferior cerebellar surface and a small part of the pons (fig. 24.101).

The **superior cerebellar artery** passes back around the cerebral peduncle beneath the tentorium to supply the dorsolateral aspect of the cerebellum and give a few small perforating branches to the pons.

The basilar artery finally divides into the right and left posterior cerebral arteries each of which supplies mesencephalic structures by perforating branches and receives

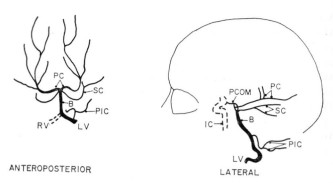

FIG. 24.101. Tracings of vertebrobasilar arteriograms. B, basilar; IC, internal carotid; LV, RV, vertebral, left and right; PC, posterior cerebral; PCOM, posterior communicating; PIC, posterior inferior cerebellar; SC, superior cerebellar.

the posterior communicating artery before continuing as the distal portion of the posterior cerebral artery. The main basilar trunk formed by the fusion of the two vertebral arteries supplies numerous medial and lateral perforating branches to the pons.

The **posterior cerebral artery** courses laterally and posteriorly around the cerebral peduncle to above the tentorium giving off a large branch to the thalamus and choroid plexus before dividing into occipital and temporal branches. It provides the main arterial supply to the visual cortex so that vascular lesions involving this artery are manifest by visual field defects.

THE MENINGES, VENOUS DRAINAGE OF THE BRAIN AND VENTRICULAR SYSTEM

The brain and spinal cord are protected and covered by membranes, the **meninges**, composed of three different layers. The intracranial meninges are continuous with those of the spinal cord already described. A thin delicate membrane, the pia mater, intimately envelopes the brain and spinal cord separated from the arachnoid by the subarachnoid space in which the cerebrospinal fluid circulates.

The **dura mater** is a tough fibrous envelope of connective tissue covering the brain and arachnoid and becomes continuous with the spinal cord dura mater at the foramen magnum. Intracranially, however, the dura mater is closely attached to the periosteum of the skull, forming an internal pericranium. This is in contrast to the spinal cord, where the dura mater is not attached to the walls of the spinal canal and where a large extradural space exists filled with veins and fat. In the region of sutures and at the base of the skull, the dura is closely attached to the bone and forms a sleeve to the nerves as they emerge from the foramina of the skull becoming continuous with the epineurium of the nerves outside the skull. The intracranial dura mater is united with the periosteum except where they are separated by the venous sinuses. Within the cranial cavity the dura mater has several projections often containing venous sinuses. These are the falx cerebri, the tentorium cerebelli and the diaphragma sellae described on p. 21.6.

The meninges have a rich nerve supply obtained largely from the trigeminal nerve. The floor of the anterior cranial fossa and the anterior part of the falx cerebri are supplied by the ophthalmic division of the trigeminal nerve which also supplies the tentorium cerebelli. This may account for the frequent association of frontal headache with lesions in the posterior fossa. The middle cranial fossa is supplied by the maxillary division of the trigeminal nerve which also supplies the vault of the anterior cranial fossa and by the mandibular division of the trigeminal nerve. The posterior fossa is innervated largely by meningeal branches of the vagus nerve and the second and third cervical nerves.

The **venous drainage** of the brain can be divided into deep and superficial systems which both drain into the venous sinuses of the cranial cavity (p. 21.7).

The superficial cerebral veins have variable origins, courses and terminations but mostly drain into the venous sinus system. The dorsal part of the cerebral hemispheres, for example, sends blood into the superior sagittal sinus and the medial part of the hemispheres sends blood into the inferior sagittal sinus. The orbital surface of the frontal lobe and the anterior parts of the temporal lobe are drained by a large vein passing along the lateral sulcus and known as the **superficial middle cerebral vein**. It drains into the cavernous sinus and also joins with the **superior anastomotic vein**, draining into the parietal part of the superior sagittal sinus, and the **inferior anastomotic vein** which passes inferiorly to the transverse sinus.

The **deep cerebral veins** drain the interior of the brain (fig. 24.102). The **septal vein** is formed by small branches draining the head of the caudate nucleus and the anterior horn of the lateral ventricle. The **thalamostriate vein** passes forwards between the caudate nucleus and thalamus draining both and then, arching backwards through the interventricular foramen, is joined by the choroidal vein and septal vein to form the **internal cerebral vein**.

The internal cerebral vein lies close to the midline in the pia mater forming the roof of the third ventricle. It joins the other internal cerebral vein posteriorly near the pineal gland to form the **great cerebral vein** which lies beneath the splenium and curves up around it to join the inferior sagittal sinus and form the straight sinus. The **basal vein** drains the anterior and posterior perforated substance and passes backwards around the cerebral peduncle to join the great cerebral vein.

The veins draining the brain stem pass largely to the cerebellar veins, most of which enter by short connections

into the adjacent sinuses or, as in the case of the **superior cerebellar vein**, connect with the deep cerebral veins.

The great cerebral vein therefore receives both internal cerebral veins and both basal veins. This venous system is readily demonstrated by cerebral angiography and a knowledge of its normal configuration enables the neuroradiologist to determine whether there has been any displacement of the deep structures of the cerebral hemispheres.

The **arachnoid** covers the brain and spinal cord separated from the dura by the potential subdural space. This space is filled only with a little tissue fluid but pus may accumulate there and form a subdural abscess either in the cranial cavity or the spinal canal. Although the pia covers the brain intimately, dipping into its sulci, the arachnoid does not do so, so that subarachnoid spaces are left between arachnoid and pia which enclose the cerebral vessels. In certain parts of the brain these spaces are large and termed cisterns containing collections of cerebrospinal fluid.

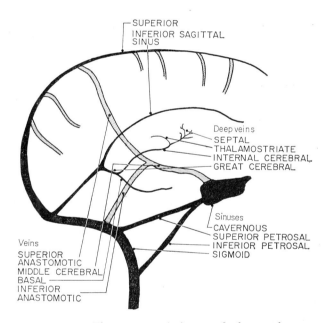

FIG. 24.102. The venous drainage of the cerebrum. Superficial veins are stippled and deep veins and sinuses are black.

The largest of these cisterns, the **cisterna magna**, is formed by the arachnoid leaving the under surface of the cerebellum to pass directly to the medulla. It is continuous with the pontine cistern which lies in front of the cord and both are continuous with the subarachnoid space surrounding the spinal cord. The arachnoid also bridges over the cerebral peduncles forming the interpeduncular cistern in which lies the circle of Willis. In the posterior part of the midbrain around the colliculi and the great cerebral vein lies another cistern which continues forward around the midbrain to become continuous with the cistern surrounding the optic nerves, the **chiasmatic cistern.** In the spinal column the subarachnoid space becomes enlarged as the lumbar sac which is traversed by the cauda equina.

The arachnoid granulations or villi are proliferations of arachnoid which project into the dural venous sinuses and are concerned with cerebrospinal fluid absorption.

The **pia mater** is the most delicate and vascular of the meninges and is separated from the arachnoid by the subarachnoid space containing cerebrospinal fluid. Many fibre strands pass between the two meninges.

The ventricular system

The brain and brain stem have hollow cores comprising the ventricular system. The lateral ventricles lie within the cerebral hemispheres communicating with one another through the interventricular foramen. The foramen also communicates with the third ventricle which occupies the diencephalon whilst a narrow aqueduct passes through the mesencephalon to widen out as the fourth ventricle behind the pons and medulla (fig. 24.103).

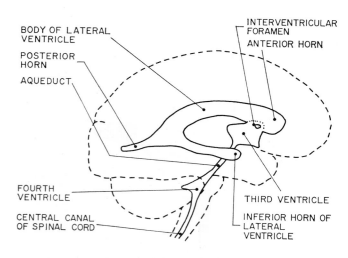

FIG. 24.103. Diagram of the ventricular system. Only the right lateral ventricle is shown.

The **third ventricle** lies between the thalami, often interrupted by a bridge of cells, the massa intermedia, connecting the right and left thalamus (fig. 24.104). The anterior part of its roof is interrupted by the interventricular foramen, and the anterior commissure, which may be regarded as a continuation of the corpus callosum, and more inferiorly the thin lamina terminalis both form the anterior walls of the third ventricle. The optic chiasma indents the anterior wall of the third ventricle, producing a superior recess known as the supraoptic recess. Immedi-

ately below the chiasma lies the pituitary stalk or infundibulum. The hypothalamus forms the lower anterior portion of the lateral walls of the third ventricle. The posterior portion of the floor and walls of the third ventricle are related to the subthalamic nucleus and its fibres, and finally the floor of the ventricle reaches the mesencephalon where it joins the aqueduct (fig. 24.52).

The roof of the third ventricle is complex and contains choroid plexuses. An invagination of pia mater, **tela**

FIG. 24.104. The tela choroidea and the roof of the third ventricle. After Last.

choroidea, passes anteriorly beneath the fornix and above the pineal body and the superior colliculi, extending laterally into the medial walls of the lateral ventricle to carry the choroid plexuses through the interventricular foramen down into the lateral ventricle. The superior part of the fold is attached to the body of the fornix and the lower part of the fold is fused with the thin roof of the third ventricle and the superior posterior surface of the thalamus (fig. 24.56). At the posterior part of the thalamus the two layers separate, the upper layer of the fold becoming continuous with the pia mater over the splenium and the lower part of the fold becoming continuous with the pia mater over the pineal gland and midbrain.

The **lateral ventricle** is composed of anterior, posterior and inferior horns interconnected through the body of the lateral ventricle. Separating the two lateral ventricles is the septum pellucidum lying between the corpus callosum and the fornix. The body of the fornix fuses

Not in accordance with plastic injection studies of Last & Tomsett (1952) Brit J Surg - 40 525-43 (Casts of the cerebral ventricles) ADC for a platocary

with the choroid roof of the third ventricle except anteriorly where it arches over the interventricular foramen and the third ventricle. The body of the lateral ventricle is roofed by the corpus callosum and the lateral boundary is formed by the caudate nucleus, separated inferiorly from the thalamus by a groove along which runs the stria terminalis. The thalamus forms the floor of the body of the lateral ventricle and also the posterior boundary of the interventricular foramen which is roofed by the fornix and bounded anteriorly by its anterior columns. Posteriorly the fornix divides into right and left parts (the crura) following the ventricular line into the inferior horns.

The **anterior horn** of the lateral ventricle is roofed over by corpus callosum which curves around the tip of the horn as the genu and extends beneath it as the rostrum. The head of the caudate nucleus forms the floor and lateral boundary of the anterior horn whilst medially the two horns are separated by the septum pellucidum and the medial frontal cortex on either side. The body of the lateral ventricle is somewhat triangular on transverse section and is roofed by the corpus callosum, its medial walls being formed by the septum pellucidum. Laterally lies the body of the caudate nucleus which also forms part of the floor of the body and, more medially, the thalamus and choroid plexus. The posterior horns extend from the body into the occipital lobe and the deep calcarine fissure of the medial surface of the occipital lobe forms a ridge in the medial part of the posterior horn known as calcar avis. A little above this protrusion another ridge marks the forceps major which contains callosal fibres uniting the occipital lobes.

The trigone is a triangular area in the posterior part of the body and the posterior and inferior horns (fig. 24.105).

The **inferior horn** curves downwards and forwards into the temporal lobe, the tail of the caudate nucleus forming its roof, and ends in the amygdaloid body which forms a small protrusion in the tip of the inferior horn. The hippocampal fissure forms a longitudinal projection in the medial part of the floor of the inferior horn whilst the fimbria lying in the floor and medial part of the horn close to the hippocampus passes backwards to form the fornix which joins with its fellow of the opposite side to form the body of the fornix.

The **aqueduct** connects third and fourth ventricles and is a short narrow channel lying within the mesencephalon.

The **fourth ventricle** is bordered anteriorly by the superior cerebellar peduncles and posteriorly by the inferior cerebellar peduncles. The superior medullary velum, stretching between the superior cerebellar peduncles and connecting the tectal region with the cerebellum, forms the roof of the fourth ventricle together with the cerebellum itself which forms the middle portion of the roof. The inferior medullary velum arches over the inferior lower part of the fourth ventricle perforated laterally by the lateral foramina and extends as lateral recesses which overlie the inferior cerebellar peduncles. Lateral foramina in these recesses open into the subarachnoid space. A median foramen is occasionally present.

A **choroid plexus** consists of a convoluted layer of simple cubical epithelium which forms from the ependymal lining. The associated pia mater provides a rich blood supply needed for the secretion of CSF.

Cerebrospinal fluid

The principal source of cerebrospinal fluid (CSF) is the choroid plexuses of the lateral and third ventricles of the brain. If the plexus is removed from one lateral ventricle and the interventricular foramen is blocked, that ventricle may collapse and the other lateral ventricle becomes distended by the fluid formed within it, dammed back at the interventricular foramen. It is, however, not possible to say confidently that the choroid plexus is the sole source of the fluid. It may well be that some is also formed at the ependymal lining of the ventricles. On the analogy of animal experiments, about 0·5 ml/min is produced in man by all the choroid plexuses together.

After secretion in the ventricles, CSF passes through the ventricular system and out from the fourth ventricle into the cisterna magna. Thence it reaches the outer surfaces of the brain and spinal cord. It is reabsorbed chiefly by a valvular mechanism in the arachnoid villi adjoining the superior sagittal venous sinus. The pressure in the sinus when one is upright is less than atmospheric pressure, but the arrangement of dura in the falx holds

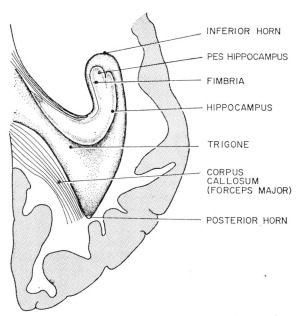

INFERIOR HORN

PES HIPPOCAMPUS

FIMBRIA

HIPPOCAMPUS

TRIGONE

CORPUS CALLOSUM (FORCEPS MAJOR)

POSTERIOR HORN

FIG. 24.105. The relations of the inferior and posterior horns.

the sinus open, and since in the upright posture the CSF pressure is above sagittal sinus pressure, CSF can traverse the valve, along with particulate matter, and enter the venous system. But return flow of blood out from the sagittal sinus into the subarachnoid space is prevented by the valve (fig. 24.106). Similarly, much smaller valves

FIG. 24.106. Frontal sections of the superior sagittal sinus and adjacent lacuna lateralis showing (a) the valve open and the lacuna filled with CSF and (b) the valve closed and the lacuna filled with blood. From Welsh & Friedman (1960). *Brain*, **83**, 459.

may exist allowing CSF round the spinal cord to find its way into the adjoining veins.

Blockage of the CSF circulation can occur. If the block is within the brain, the ventricular system becomes distended with CSF (**internal hydrocephalus**). If the block is at the drainage channels (for instance, when sagittal sinus thrombosis occurs), a general rise in intracranial pressure appears. In children, in whom the skull sutures are still not firmly united, distension of the skull and separation of the sutures may ensue (**hydrocephalus**).

SAMPLING

CSF can be removed for examination conveniently by **lumbar puncture**, which is a safe procedure except when the intracranial pressure is abnormally high. A needle is inserted into the subarachnoid space which contains the fluid by passing it between the spinous processes of lumbar vertebrae 3 and 4 or close to this level. Here the needle lies below the end of the spinal cord and cannot injure it, although it may occasionally meet a root of the cauda equina. It is also possible to remove fluid, though obviously more perilously, by inserting a needle into the cisterna magna between the atlas and the occiput, and fluid can be removed from the ventricles at operation.

PRESSURE

At lumbar puncture with the patient lying on his side the CSF pressure measured in a simple manometer is normally 6–15 cm. Compressing the jugular veins in the neck produces a marked rise in the pressure (**Queckenstedt's test**) because the venous pressure increases in the cerebral venous sinuses, and the increase is communicated directly to the CSF. No rise or a trivial one is seen if the subarachnoid space is blocked by, for instance, a

tumour round the spinal cord. In performing Queckenstedt's test, it is as well not to squeeze or even seem to squeeze the trachea, and it is not required to occlude the carotid arteries; firm widespread pressure on both sides of the neck but excluding the trachea is both kind and effective. The test is dangerous when intracranial pressure is high, because the medulla may become displaced down into the foramen magnum where it is subjected to pressure which impairs its blood supply.

COMPOSITION

Table 24.3 shows the normal composition of CSF. Protein is practically absent and so is any constituent of

TABLE 24.3. Composition of cerebrospinal fluid compared with plasma in a normal subject.

Constituent	Concentration of various constituents	
	in CSF	in plasma
Na$^+$ mEq/l	140	142
Cl$^-$ mEq/l	115	98
K$^+$ mEq/l	2·9	4·5
Mg^{++} mEq/l	2·1	1·6
Urea mg/100 ml	25	25
Glucose mg/100 ml	70	80
pH units	7·33	7·4
P_{CO_2} mm Hg	50·2	39·5
HCO$_3$$^-$ mEq/l	22	25

plasma adsorbed on protein, which includes for instance about half of the calcium present in blood. The absence of protein induces certain alterations in the concentrations of ions, in accordance with the Gibbs–Donnan equilibrium (p. 14.7). Is CSF then simply a filtrate of plasma, like the contents of Bowman's capsule in the kidney? This is not the case. Values for ions differ far more than the calculated Gibbs–Donnan alterations would indicate; there is less K$^+$, slightly less HCO$_3$$^-$, and more Cl$^-$ and Mg^{++}. Glucose (un-ionized) is clearly less. The P_{CO_2} is higher and pH lower. When the composition of plasma changes, [K$^+$] and [HCO$_3$$^-$] in CSF are slow to follow, but CO$_2$ enters the CSF rapidly. This distinction between HCO$_3$$^-$ and CO$_2$ may be significant in the control of respiration (p. 29.24), since receptors exist on the outer surface of the medulla which are linked to the respiratory control system and respond to changes in the composition of the CSF rather than to those in the blood.

These discrepancies between CSF and plasma make it clear that CSF is not a simple filtrate and active secretion must be involved. Further confirmation is available in the fact that CSF composition and rate of formation are influenced by drugs such as acetazoleamide and ouabain which influence Na$^+$ transport.

A few substances reach the CSF rapidly by diffusion from the adjacent brain tissue, besides entering more radually with the fluid secreted by the choroid plexuses. Ethyl alcohol is an instance. Others such as penicillin, even when present at a high level in blood, enter the CSF only slowly. So one pictures a blood–CSF barrier, surmounted by different substances with varying ease. Fortunately, infection (meningitis) lowers the barrier and penicillin then penetrates more readily into the fluid. (p. 24.86)

DEVELOPMENT OF THE NERVOUS SYSTEM

The development of the neural tube in embryos up to the 4th week is outlined on pp. 18.5 and 18.10.

THE SPINAL CORD

In the wall of the primitive neural tube three basic layers are identified:

(1) the **ependyma**, which retains its epithelial character and will do so throughout life;

(2) the **mantle zone**, a thicker layer of densely packed cells, the precursors of neurones and neuroglia; and

(3) a peripheral layer, the **marginal zone**, which contains few cells and consists mainly of the processes, axons and dendrites, of differentiating neuroblasts.

The ependyma serves as a germinal layer, mitoses being confined to it. The daughter cells produced there migrate to the mantle zone, where they differentiate into neuroblasts or glial elements.

The thicker sidewalls of the neural tube show a shallow longitudinal furrow facing into the neural canal; this is the **sulcus limitans**, a landmark of fundamental importance, since it demarcates a dorsal part of the tube, **alar lamina**, from a ventral part, **basal lamina**. The alar lamina will be concerned with sensory function, the basal with motor function. The dorsal wall (roof plate) and ventral wall (floor plate) are relatively thin.

Fig. 24.107 shows schematically the basic features in the further development of the neural tube and neural crest in the spinal region. Attention is directed in particular to the following changes.

(1) **Bipolar neurones** develop from the neuroblasts of the neural crest; these are **first order sensory neurones**, one of whose processes grows outwards to establish peripheral sensory terminations in skin, muscle, tendon, joint capsule, etc.; the other grows into the neural tube and synapses with the **second order sensory neurone** which develops from a neuroblast in the mantle zone of the alar lamina. Clusters of second order sensory neurones constitute a **sensory (somatic afferent) nucleus**. Groups of these nuclei form the main mass of the **dorsal grey column** of the adult cord. The nervous elements of the dorsal or sensory root of a spinal nerve are thus seen to be derived from the neuroblasts of the neural crest. **Lemno-**

blasts of neural crest origin migrate and apply themselves to the surface of developing peripheral nerve fibres, forming the Schwann cells, the source of the **myelin sheath**.

(2) **Multipolar (motor)** neurones develop from neuroblasts in the mantle zone of the basal lamina. Their dendrites ramify in the neighbourhood of the cell body; their axons grow outwards from the tube to innervate a group of skeletal muscle fibres at the periphery. This **somatic efferent neurone**, with the muscle fibres which it innervates, forms the **motor unit** (p. 15.7). Groups of these neurones form motor nuclei of the ventral grey column.

(3) **Sympathetic ganglia**, both of the paravertebral sympathetic chain and the prevertebral ganglia, e.g. coeliac and superior mesenteric, arise from sympathoblasts which migrate from the neural crest. The cells of these ganglia are **postganglionic effector neurones** (3a). **Preganglionic connector neurones** (3b) develop from multipolar neuroblasts in the mantle zone of the basal lamina, immediately ventral to the sulcus limitans. Their axons leave the neural tube via the ventral root to enter the spinal nerve which they leave to join the sympathetic trunk by way of a **white ramus communicans**. Groups of cell bodies of these neurones form the **intermedio-lateral column** of grey matter in the adult cord. These neurones are classified as **general visceral efferent**.

(4) The **white matter of the spinal cord** thickens as developing fibres grow up or down in the marginal zone.

(5) The **dorsal median septum** is formed by the fusion of the apposed surfaces of the ependymal lining of the dorsal part of the neural canal, brought about by increased bulk of the alar laminae.

(6) The **ventral median fissure** develops as the result of the expansion ventrally of the two sides of the neural tube on either side of the midline.

(7) The **central canal** of the adult cord represents the most ventral part of the original neural canal. It retains its lining of ciliated ependymal cells.

THE BRAIN

That part of the neural tube from which the brain develops shows the same features as those of the spinal cord. There are, however, even in the early stages, some differences between the two regions.

(1) The brain is ahead of the spinal cord in its development and grows more rapidly. It soon shows several bends or flexures, which presumably arise because it grows faster than its surroundings. These flexures demarcate three descriptive subdivisions of the brain, **fore-, mid- and hindbrain**.

(2) The sulcus limitans extends forwards only to the junction between midbrain and forebrain, and the alar and basal laminae are, therefore, recognizable only in mid- and hindbrains. Only the alar lamina is thought to be represented in the forebrain.

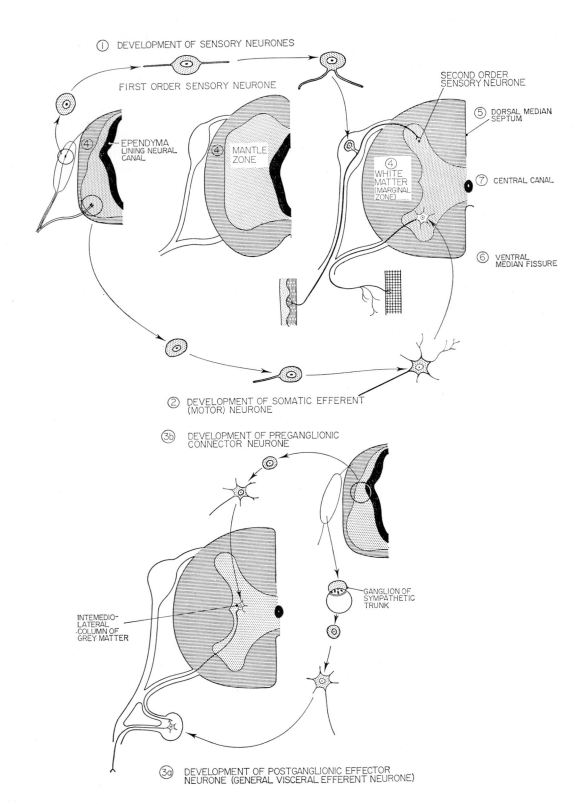

FIG. 24.107. Schematic drawing showing the main features in the development of the spinal cord and spinal neural crest.

(3) The roof plate remains thin, consisting only of ependymal epithelium, in the hindbrain and the forebrain. These are areas in which, at a later date, the choroid plexuses develop through the invagination of the ependyma by the layer of vascular pia mater which invests the neural tube.

(4) The neural crest forms irregularly disposed clumps rather than regular segmental masses.

(5) The sharp segregation of grey and white matter, so characteristic of the spinal part of the neural tube, is absent in the mid- and hindbrain where the grey matter forms nuclear groups lying in a complex network of nerve fibres with neurones and neuroglial elements, the whole constituting the **reticular formation.**

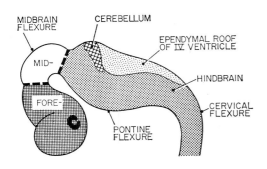

FIG. 24.108. The flexures of the brain and the fundamental subdivision into fore-, mid-, and hindbrain.

The hindbrain

The acuteness of the pontine flexure causes the lateral walls of the tube to splay apart, opening out like a hinge. The ependymal roof becomes diamond shaped, like that part of the neural canal (fourth ventricle) which it covers (fig. 24.108). The sulcus limitans now lies in the floor of the fourth ventricle; the alar lamina lies laterally, rather than ventrally, to the basal lamina. When nuclear groups develop in the hindbrain, they do so in the same general positions as in the spinal cord, i.e. motor nuclei in basal lamina, sensory nuclei in alar lamina. Their positions relative to one another have been changed, however, by the opening out of the tube. Moreover, two further categories of nuclei are found, in addition to the somatic efferent, general visceral efferent and somatic afferent groups which are equivalent to those already described in the spinal cord. The new groups are the **branchial (special visceral) efferent** motor nuclei which innervate the muscles of the branchial arches (p. 18.32) and the **special somatic afferent**, nuclei of termination receiving special sense afferents (auditory and vestibular). The pons, medulla and cerebellum are of hindbrain origin.

The cerebellum develops from paired thickenings of the alar laminae at the anterior end of the hindbrain; as it enlarges it overgrows the fourth ventricle, whose original ependymal roof is displaced, so that it covers only the posterior end of the ventricle and forms the **inferior medullary velum** of the adult (fig. 24.110). Here the choroid plexus of the fourth ventricle develops (fig. 24.109). Cells which migrate from the mantle zone establish the surface layer of grey matter, the cortex, while others remain deeply placed forming the **deep cerebellar nuclei.** The later development is described on p. 24.40.

The midbrain

This initially shows the typical basic pattern of neural tube. Its transformation to the adult condition is summarized in fig. 24.110. The neural canal narrows to form the cerebral aqueduct, the alar laminae thicken to

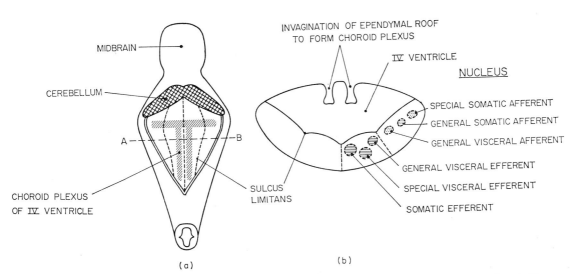

FIG. 24.109. Floor of the fourth ventricle viewed (a) from behind, and (b), in transverse section A–B.

FIG. 24.110. Parasagittal section of the hindbrain to show the developing cerebellum overgrowing the ependymal roof of the fourth ventricle.

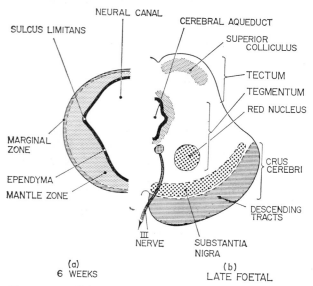

FIG. 24.111. Scheme to show the main features of the development of the midbrain.

produce the **tectum** from which arise the **superior** and **inferior colliculi**. The basal laminae form the **tegmentum** of the midbrain and the **substantia nigra**, while the **crura cerebri** become more prominent as more descending fibre groups, corticopontine, corticobulbar and cortico-spinal, grow down the neural tube. The **corticobulbar** fibres end synaptically on motor nuclei of mid- and hind-brain. **Corticopontine fibres** grow down into the hind-brain, where they continue to lie ventrally. They end on the **pontine nuclei**, which have migrated far ventrally from their origin in the alar lamina. Axons of cells of the pontine nuclei enter the opposite cerebellar hemisphere via the middle cerebellar peduncle. **Corticospinal fibres** continue growing inferiorly on the ventral surface of the medulla, where they form the **pyramids**, and on into the spinal cord, most of them crossing in the **pyramidal decussation** (figs. 24.9 & 38). Just as the crura are ventral additions to the tegmentum of the midbrain, so the basilar part of the pons, comprising corticopontine, cortico-bulbar and corticospinal fibres and the pontine nuclei, is a ventral addition to the tegmentum of the pontine part of the hindbrain.

The forebrain

The roof plate of the forebrain is thin, consisting only of ependymal epithelium, covered externally by vascular pia, the **tela choroidea** (p. 24.74). The cranial wall is thin; it is called **lamina terminalis**, and although in due course it loses its position as the most cranial part of the brain tube, it retains the name and is a valuable landmark in the adult brain. Several important outgrowths develop from the forebrain wall.

(1) The **optic vesicles** arise early, before the cranial neuropore closes completely (fig. 24.112). The walls of the vesicle show the same basic layers as the brain and its cavity is continuous with that of the third ventricle (fig. 24.112). From the start, its outer wall is in intimate contact with the surface ectoderm, which thickens, under its inductive influence, to form the **lens placode**. The outer wall of the vesicle invaginates, converting the vesicle into a **bilaminar optic cup**. The greater part of the inner layer of the cup forms light sensitive retina. Because of its invagination, the order of its constituent layers is now inverted; its ependymal layer faces into the narrow intraretinal space, which separates it from the outer layer of the cup; its marginal zone faces into the cavity of the bilaminar optic cup. The essential three-neurone chain, rods and cones, bipolar cells and ganglion cells, develops within the inner layer of the cup. Axons grow from ganglion cells towards the brain, running in the **optic stalk**, the narrowed derivative of the originally wide connection between brain and optic vesicle. Because the optic stalk developed as an outgrowth from the brain, optic nerve fibres which grow through it necessarily reach the wall of the third ventricle. Here the **optic chiasma** is

formed within the wall of the brain, near the ventral end of the lamina terminalis.

(2) The **posterior lobe of the pituitary gland** is formed from a downgrowth from the ventral wall of the third ventricle (figs. 24.113 and 25.9).

(3) The **cerebral hemispheres** develop as hollow outgrowths from the side wall of the most anterior part of the forebrain. The wall of the hemisphere initially shows the usual layers, and its cavity, the lateral ventricle is continuous with the third ventricle, through a large interventricular foramen. Part of the wall of the hemisphere consists only of ependymal epithelium. This is called the **choroidal fissure**; it lies, at first, in the **roof** of the hemisphere and is directly continuous with the thin, ependymal roof plate of the third ventricle (fig. 24.114. It marks the site of development, at a later stage, of the choroid plexus of the lateral ventricle.

The floor of the hemisphere thickens, to form a deeply placed mass of grey matter, the **corpus striatum**. Cells of the mantle zone also migrate to the surface of the hemisphere, where they form the **pallium**, a superficial layer of cells from which will develop the definitive **cortex**. The hemisphere grows rapidly forwards, dorsally and, more particularly, backwards, so that, although it develops

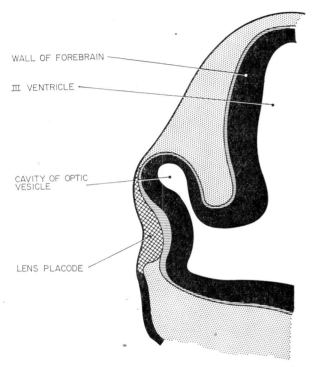

FIG. 24.112. Transverse section of the forebrain to show the optic vesicles and lens placode in an embryo of about 4 weeks.

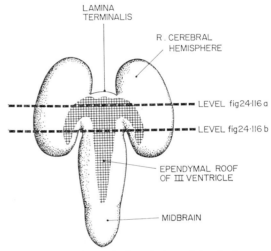

FIG. 24.114. Schematic dorsal view of developing cerebral hemispheres, to show the continuity between the thin ependymal roof of the third ventricle and the ependymal portion of the wall of the hemisphere, which will form the choroidal fissure. Based on Frazer, *Manual of Human Embryology.*

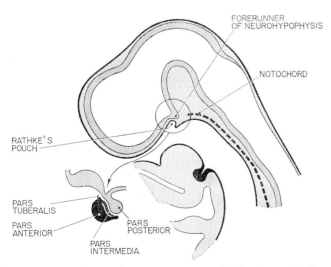

FIG. 24.113. Sagittal section to show the development of the pituitary gland.

originally as an outgrowth of the forebrain, it comes to overlie the midbrain and, later still, the hindbrain, including cerebellum. As the hemisphere expands in its growth, somewhat like an inflating balloon, the thick floor, corpus striatum, expands more slowly than the remaining thinner wall with the result that the hemisphere gradually assumes a C-shape (fig. 24.115). The C-curvature affects not only the hemisphere as a whole, but also the lateral ventricle within it and the choroidal fissure which, because of the expansion of the hemisphere, now lies on its medial wall. Two coronal sections through the midline part of forebrain and the two hemispheres, one passing through the interventricular foramen, the other somewhat behind it, make clear some important relationships (fig. 24.116).

(1) The thin roof plate of the third ventricle is continuous on either side with the choroidal fissure of the hemisphere, by way of the roof of the interventricular foramen, which is also ependymal.

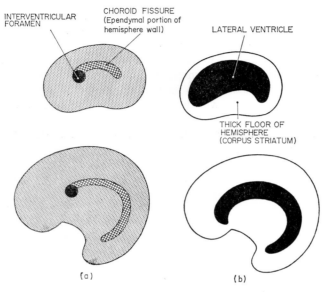

FIG. 24.115. The developing right cerebral hemisphere. (a) medial surface; (b) parasagittal sections.

(2) Behind the level of the interventricular foramen, the hemisphere is separated by a gap from the midline part of forebrain. This gap is obliterated, as if by adhesion between the two, although adhesion is apparent rather than real, and developing nerve fibres grow from the hemisphere to lower levels in the neural tube and in the opposite direction. These ascending and descending fibres form the **internal capsule** which cuts through the grey matter (corpus striatum) in the floor of the hemisphere, dividing it into **caudate** and **lentiform nuclei**. The internal capsule, like the lateral ventricle and the choroidal fissure, is bent into a C-shape by the curvature of the whole hemisphere. This means, of course, that the caudate nucleus also is C-shaped, with its head and body lying in the floor of the anterior horn and central part of the lateral ventricle and its tail lying in the roof of the inferior horn (fig. 24.117 and 120).

The lower part of the ependymal wall of the hemisphere becomes adherent to the **thalamus**. This has the result that part of the thalamus, a derivative of the midline part of forebrain, appears in the floor of the **lateral ventricle**.

The cerebral cortex

Mechanical factors probably play an important part in determining the complex pattern of fissures, sulci and

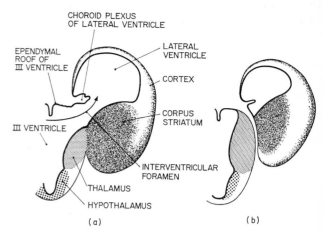

FIG. 24.116. Coronal sections of forebrain and hemisphere; (a) at the level of the interventricular foramen; (b) caudal to the interventricular foramen.

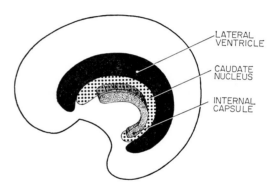

FIG. 24.117. Schematic medial view of the right cerebral hemisphere, to show the relationships of the lateral ventricle, caudate nucleus and internal capsule.

gyri of the adult cerebral cortex. As the hemisphere grows and becomes C-shaped, the cortex which overlies the outer surface of the corpus striatum is progressively hidden from view, in the depths of the lateral fissure, by the **frontal** and **temporal opercula**, and forms the **insula** (fig. 24.118).

The cortex grows more rapidly than the deeper tissue and becomes elaborately convoluted. Folding occurs at first between areas which differ in their structure, thickness and rates of growth e.g. between the uncus and hippocampus (archipallium) and the rest of the cortex (neopallium) and between primary motor and somatic sensory areas, at the central sulcus. These are called primary fissures. Secondary fissures are those which do not demarcate cortical areas of different structure and function.

The anterior and posterior horns of the lateral ventricle develop as secondary extensions of the original cavity of the hemisphere. They, therefore, lack the choroidal fissure, and the choroid plexus when it develops later does not extend into them.

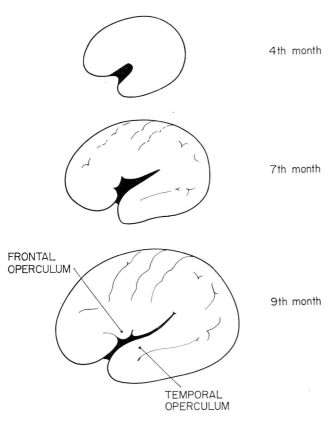

4th month

7th month

FRONTAL
OPERCULUM

9th month

TEMPORAL
OPERCULUM

FIG. 24.118. Lateral views of the left hemisphere to show successive stages in the formation of the frontal and temporal opercula.

The cerebral commissures

Several groups of nerve fibres serve to connect corresponding parts of the hemispheres with one another, forming the commissures. In early stages of development the natural and, indeed, the only convenient route for such commissural fibres to follow is the lamina terminalis, and it is here that the major commissures develop (fig. 24.119a). Two of these, the **hippocampal** and **anterior commissures** are called **archipallial**, because they connect phylogenetically ancient parts of the brain. The third, the **corpus callosum**, is the largest in man, and connects phylogenetically recent cortical areas, the **neopallium**. The corpus callosum at first lies within the lamina terminalis but, as more fibres are added, it extends beyond the lamina terminalis, the more dorsal part of which becomes stretched and thinned to form the **septum pellucidum** (fig. 24.119 b & c). The corpus callosum grows backwards, so that its **splenium** eventually lies close to the pineal gland, the most posterior derivative of the forebrain

roof. In its growth backwards, the corpus callosum carries with it the hippocampal commissure (fig. 24.119d).

Fig. 24.120 shows a coronal section through the forebrain at the conclusion of all these changes. Attention is drawn particularly to the space between the corpus callosum, dorsally, and the roof of the third ventricle ventrally. This is the transverse cerebral fissure; it contains pia mater (here called tela choroidea), which invaginates the ependymal roof of the third ventricle, to form the **choroid plexus of the third ventricle**, and the choroidal fissure of each **lateral ventricle**, forming the **choroid plexuses** there. The three plexuses are continuous with one another at the interventricular foramen, as a natural consequence of their development.

The midline part of the forebrain

This is divided into **telencephalon** and **diencephalon**, the line of demarcation being arbitrary; the telencephalon is that part of the forebrain from which arise the cerebral hemispheres, the diencephalon is the remainder.

On the inner surface of the side wall of the diencephalon is a conspicuous furrow, the **hypothalamic sulcus**, which separates two large nuclear masses, dorsally, the **thalamus**, ventrally the **hypothalamus**.

The thalami of the two sides thicken, and project medially into the cavity of the third ventricle; they often meet in the midline, forming the **interthalamic adhesion** (massa intermedia). It is worth stressing that this is no more than a chance contact, of no functional import; it is not a commissure.

The **hypothalamus** includes the hypothalamic nuclei, the optic chiasma, tuber cinereum, posterior pituitary and the mamillary bodies.

The **epithalamus** develops from the most dorsal and posterior part of the diencephalon, and consists principally of the **pineal body** and the **habenula**.

The **subthalamus** develops from the lateral wall of diencephalon, below the thalamus and lateral to the hypothalamus. It is continuous with the tegmentum of the midbrain, a continuity which emphasizes the essential unity of the neural tube.

The meninges

These develop from paraxial mesoderm which surrounds the neural tube. Experimental evidence from lower vertebrates suggests that some at least of these mesodermal cells arise originally from the neural crest. The **pia-arachnoid** arises from looser paraxial mesodermal tissue, **endomeninx**, closely investing the brain; the subarachnoid space is formed later by the coalescence of fluid filled spaces within the endomeninx, partially separating it into an inner pia and an outer arachnoid. The subarachnoid space contains CSF produced mainly by the choroid plexuses. The amount of fluid in the ventricular system is disproportionately large in the early

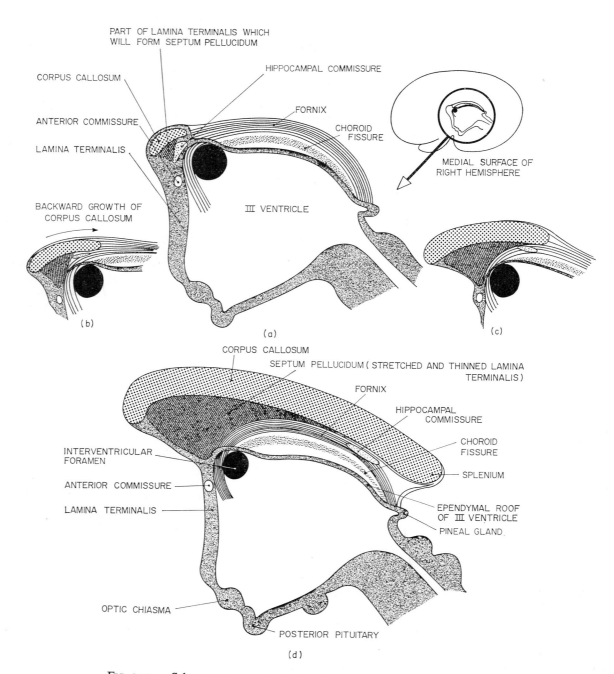

FIG. 24.119. Scheme to summarize the development of the cerebral commissures.

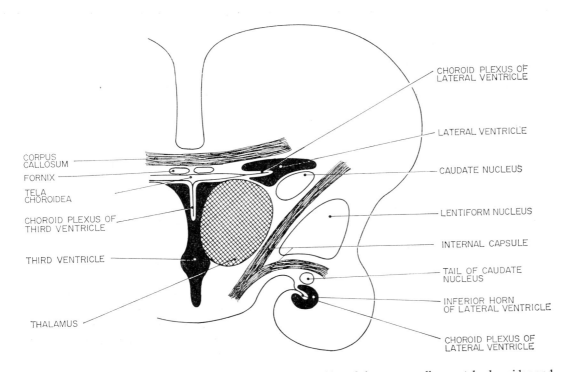

FIG. 24.120. Coronal section of the brain to show the relationships of the corpus callosum, tela choroidea and choroid plexuses of third and lateral ventricles, cf. fig. 24.56.

embryo, and studies of its electrolyte content relative to that of the blood show that it is formed first as a dialysate; it is only later that the ependymal epithelium of the choroid plexus actively transports electrolytes. The cerebrospinal fluid may play an important role in the early development of the brain, preventing collapse of the thin walled hemispheres.

The **dura mater** develops as a tough fibrous membrane from the **ectomeninx**, a denser mesenchymal layer lying beneath the membrane in which the bones of the skull vault ossify.

BIOCHEMISTRY OF THE BRAIN

The regional distribution of cell types accounts for some of the differences in the biochemistry of various areas of the brain. The neuronal cell bodies predominate in the grey matter and their dendritic processes occupy most of its volume, whereas myelinated axons and associated oligodendroglial cells are found mainly in the white matter. Much of the high respiratory activity of grey matter can be attributed to its mass of dendrites, and the relatively low oxygen uptake of white matter is now explained by its high content of myelin; although glial cells and axoplasm actively respire, myelin is metabolically virtually inert.

STUDIES ON ISOLATED COMPONENTS

Because of the morphological heterogeneity of nervous tissue further elucidation of the metabolism of each cell

FIG. 24.121. Differential centrifugation of the components of nervous tissue.

type and their components comes from studies of isolated single cells. Ultramicro methods of sufficient sensitivity have been devised to investigate the biochemistry of individual cells from histologically identified areas of the brain. An isolated cell can be weighed (0·1 ng) on a quartz fibre balance and optical methods, which can estimate 10^{-19} moles of a substrate, allow its chemical and enzymatic composition to be determined (fig. 24.121). The base composition of RNA from single nerve cells, from glial cells or even from isolated nuclei can then be determined. Samples are treated with ribonuclease and the depolymerized RNA extracted and hydrolysed; then the purine and pyrimidine base composition are determined by electrophoresis on a microscopic cellulose thread (diameter 20 μm). Additional information is obtained by differential centrifugation of cell free brain homogenates. The method leads to isolation of myelin and subcellular components such as nuclei, mitochondria and microsomes from mixed cell populations, and enables the part played by each component in the economy of the whole cell to be elucidated (table 24.4).

TABLE 24.4. Components of the neurones and their functions.

Structure	Constituents	Function
Nucleus	DNA, basic protein, mRNA	Genetic control
Myelin	Lipids and protein	Insulation (?)
Mitochondria	Citric acid cycle enzymes	Energy production
Synaptic endings	Acetylcholine	Neurohormonal transmission
Microsomes	Ribosomes, ATPase	Protein synthesis, lipid synthesis, active transport
Supernatant	Soluble enzymes	Glycolysis

The role of mitochondria in energy metabolism and of ribosomes in protein synthesis in cells of the brain is now established. Acetylcholine has been demonstrated in the vesicles of some isolated particles from synaptic endings, which supports current ideas of its role as a synaptic transmitter (p. 24.87). There is now a wealth of knowledge about chemical constituents and enzymic activities in discrete areas of the central nervous system, in individual neural cells, in groups of these cells and in subcellular particles from nervous tissue.

The metabolism of glial cells is probably closely linked with that of neurones. Thus, biochemical changes in neurones after physiological stimulation produce concomitant changes in the glial cell. It has been found by subjecting rats and rabbits to continual rocking movements that there is a significant increase of neuronal RNA, protein and respiratory enzyme activity in the vestibular nuclei. In contrast to these neuronal changes, RNA content and enzyme activity of the glia were found to fall.

Learning and conditioning experiments result in increased synthesis of nuclear RNA in cerebral neurones with specific changes in its purine–pyrimidine base composition; glia respond with similar but not identical base ratio changes. These experiments have focused interest on the DNA–RNA–protein system as a storage arrangement for information after molecular encoding. It appears that RNA synthesis and hence production of protein play a cardinal role in the expression of higher nervous control. This hypothesis is supported by the fact that neurones synthesize RNA and protein more rapidly than other cells and that the rate of biosynthesis increases on stimulation (p. 24.94).

THE BLOOD–BRAIN BARRIER

Apart from its cellular heterogeneity, the brain differs from other organs in the apparent inability of many substances to pass readily from blood to brain tissue; it admits or bars from the perfusing blood the same substances as the CSF admits or bars. For example, following injection of trypan blue all the tissues except brain are stained, and while glucose is readily utilized, entry of many other substrates into the brain is apparently impeded. The failure of many drugs to penetrate into the brain has lent support to the idea that a barrier protects the brain from the action of foreign substances. Account must be taken, however, of the fact that the cells of the central nervous system may be so closely packed that a gap of not more than 10–20 nm separates them, with an extracellular fluid space of about 4 per cent of the total brain volume. Thus protein-bound dyestuffs cannot readily cross into the astrocytes which invest brain capillaries, whereas in other tissues they pass directly into the extracellular space. The concept of a single blood–brain barrier may therefore be incorrect in the sense that the impediment may be due to the lack in the brain of extracellular space and to the special metabolic requirements of the central nervous system. If the cells of the nervous system cannot utilize fructose for example, we need no other explanation for the fact than that this sugar enters the brain very slowly.

VULNERABILITY OF THE BRAIN IN FOETAL LIFE

The general morphology of the brain is arranged quite early in embryological development and it is not long before the full adult population of neurones is established. The first phase of embryological development and neurone formation is of particular importance, for once the cell population is established, there is little possibility of forming fresh neurones. Growth and arborization of dendrites follows with the simultaneous onset of electrical activity and the appearance of respiratory enzyme activity.

The brain is therefore especially vulnerable to deprivation of nutrients and oxygen during development since in the adult brain myelin synthesis and the multiplication f neurones scarcely occurs at all. The premature human nfant may be particularly at risk because unlike the nature infant it is separated from intrauterine protection t a time of maximum development when it can be xpected to be most vulnerable.

ARBOHYDRATE METABOLISM

Glucose is the main energy source for the brain. Some of he glucose is converted by glycolysis to lactate but most, bout 4·5 mg glucose/100 g human brain/min, or 90 g/day or the whole brain, is oxidized via pyruvate and the citric cid cycle. Measurements of O_2 and CO_2 consumption f brain tissue *in vitro* and also of intact human brain p. 28.37) give a respiratory exchange ratio which approxinates closely to 1·0 and are consistent with the view that he metabolism is predominantly due to oxidation of lucose at the rate given above. The level of consciousness night be thought to be correlated with reduced oxygen nd energy utilization but no such changes have been ound during sleep, mental activity or in various mental tates including schizophrenia and drug induced psychosis. ince nervous tissue contains only a small carbohydrate tore of glycogen of doubtful lability and availability, it , particularly dependent on maintenance of normal lood glucose concentration. Hypoglycaemia or hypoxia, ven for a short period of time, result in coma and sometimes irreversible damage. The importance of carbohydrate metabolism in the brain is also apparent in the ccumulation there of pyruvate and lactate associated vith lack of cocarboxylase, which results from a dietary eficiency of vitamin B_1.

MINO ACID AND PROTEIN METABOLISM

Although net uptake of many amino acids from blood to rain is restricted, some free amino acids are found in ervous tissue in relatively high concentrations and the otal free amino acid concentration in brain is much higher han in most other tissues or blood plasma. Aspartic acid nd glutamic acid with its amide glutamine are the most bundant. As much as 75 per cent of the intermediary lycolytic metabolites are utilized within the brain for the ormation of dicarboxylic acids such as glutamic acid. ince these acids have a high rate of turnover, it is suggesed that the brain is especially adapted to utilize these mino acids and possibly also proteins in order to proide the energy required for functional activity. Moreover, he repeated synthesis of dicarboxylic amino acids esults in a conservation of amino N in the brain, thereby educing requirements for exogenous amino acids. Proeins account for about 10 per cent of the wet weight of he brain. They are found mainly as:

(1) soluble proteins constituting the numerous enzymes nd some of the hormones of the central nervous system,

(2) with lipids as lipoproteins in the insoluble membrane ystems of the organ.

The many different types of protein in the nervous system have a wide spectrum of metabolic activity. In general the soluble proteins undergo rapid synthesis and turnover, whereas the structural proteins are more stable. Cerebral phosphoproteins, for example, undergo very rapid exchange and may well be concerned in ion transport mechanisms within the organ, but the protein of the myelin sheath is exceedingly stable.

LIPIDS AND THEIR METABOLISM

The brain is rich in lipid, human grey and white matter containing about 10 and 30 per cent respectively. Table 24.5 shows the distribution of lipids in nervous tissue.

TABLE 24.5. Approximate values for the lipid content of parts of the vertebrate nervous system (μ moles/100mg wet tissue).

	Brain		Spinal cord	Sciatic nerve
	Cortex	white matter		
Cholesterol	2·4	9·4	18·6	4·9
Cerebrosides	0·3	4·7	9·2	1·5
Phospholipids	4·3	9·7	14·6	6·4
Sphingomyelin	0·4	1·7	3·6	1·2
Plasmalogen	0·8	4·0	—	1·3
Gangliosides	0·3	0·06	—	—

Some of this may be concerned in dynamic processes such as sodium ion transport, or provide essential cofactors in enzyme reactions, but the majority is structural. The most characteristic lipids of nervous tissue are cerebrosides (p. 10.5), galactose containing sphingolipids; they are found in high concentration in the myelin sheath. Cholesterol and phospholipids are also present in myelin. The relative metabolic inertness of the myelin lipids has been shown in experiments with isotopic labels. Extensive uptake of radioactivity into the brain lipids occurs only during development and this labelling is retained in the myelin lipids for years thereafter. Lipid and protein components of membranes of subcellular particles such as mitochondria undergo turnover but at a much slower rate than in other organs.

CHEMICAL TRANSMISSION WITHIN THE NERVOUS SYSTEM

There seems little doubt that chemical mediators are responsible for synaptic transmission in many parts of the central nervous system but the evidence for this is much less adequate than it is for transmission in the sympathetic ganglion or the myoneural junction, and with few exceptions the chemical nature of the transmitter is unknown.

Central presynaptic nerve endings contain granules and vesicles similar to those described in presynaptic terminals elsewhere (p. 14.26). Acetylcholine, choline acetyltransferase and acetylcholinesterase have been found in the central nervous system, particularly the motor cortex and ventral spinal horns, the thalamus and hypothalamus and the geniculate bodies. Acetylcholine and its associated enzymes are found in highest concentration in fractions of brain tissue containing separated nerve endings, and it has been collected from the surface of the brain in small cups in contact with the cerebral cortex of animals and from the CSF of patients who have died after generalized convulsions and epileptic fits. Microelectrodes inserted into the Renshaw cells (p. 14.28) of the spinal cord of the cat show that the cells undergo postsynaptic depolarization when the presynaptic fibres are stimulated, and acetylcholine introduced by iontophoresis through micropipettes into the neighbourhood of the cells can excite them to fire; their activity is also potentiated if the recurrent axon is stimulated electrically and acetylcholinesterase inhibitors are applied.

Besides acetylcholine it is possible that other substances which are detectable in the brain act as chemical mediators. These include noradrenaline and dopamine, 5-hydroxytryptamine (5-HT), histamine, γ-aminobutyric acid (GABA), ergothioneine and prostaglandins. Noradrenaline is found in highest concentration in the hypothalamus and the brainstem. Dopamine is found mainly in the caudate nucleus, substantia nigra and other nuclei of the midbrain. 5-HT is distributed in regions similar to those of noradrenaline but also in parts of the grey matter of the spinal cord, hippocampus, and pineal gland. 5-HT can be shown to be synthesized in the brain from its immediate precursors or 5-hydroxytryptophan and stored in subcellular particles. Histamine is also distributed in general like the monoamines and is present in highest concentration in the hypothalamus.

Substance *P* is a polypeptide containing about thirteen amino acids and present in large amounts in substantia nigra, the hypothalamus and the dorsal roots and columns of the spinal cord. It is also present in the intestines where it may be a transmitter for local reflexes. GABA arising from the decarboxylation of glutamic acid decreases the excitatory state in many parts of the nervous system and has been considered as a possible inhibitory transmitter.

The cerebellum contains little or none of the pharmacologically active substances found elsewhere in the brain, a surprising fact in view of its enormous number of synapses. Cerebellar extracts however, have been shown to contain ergothioneine, a derivative of histidine, injection of which increases the electrical activity of the cerebellum.

Brain extracts also contain pharmacologically active lipids, the prostaglandins, and evidence suggests that they too may act as chemical transmitters. Applied iontophoretically they may excite or inhibit certain neurones and can be detected in parts of the brain, notably the cerebellum, during electrical stimulation.

The concentration of most of these substances present in different areas of the brain can be altered by numerous drugs. The drugs which cause these chemical changes also affect emotional behaviour and the personality of the patient; they include tranquillizers and mescaline. Detailed study of the mode of action of these drugs is likely to enlarge knowledge of function of these amines and other substances. This is an important growing point in medicine.

AUTONOMIC NERVOUS SYSTEM

The nervous system controls not only the striated voluntary muscle, but in addition other tissues, such as smooth muscle, notably in the vascular and digestive systems, and also the secretion of many glands, especially salivary and gastric glands, the sweat glands and the adrenal medulla. The part of the nervous system supplying motor nerves to these tissues is called the **autonomic system**, a name based on the fact that the control of the vascular and digestive systems do not usually come to conscious attention, nor can it usually be consciously influenced. The autonomic nervous system therefore comprises the visceral efferent system.

Somatic and visceral systems differ in their anatomical arrangements. The cell body of a visceral efferent neurone lies in a ganglion outside the CNS, but the cell body of the somatic efferent neurone lies within the CNS. The visceral efferent cell bodies are collected in the course of the nerves forming small ganglia such as the ciliary ganglion and the otic ganglion, or are aggregated to form interconnecting masses lateral to the vertebrae (the paravertebral ganglionic trunks) or on the bodies of the vertebrae (the prevertebral ganglia) (p. 20.39). The intercalated neurones which connect the CNS with the peripheral cells have their cell bodies within the lateral column of grey matter, but their axons leave to synapse at the ganglion and are termed preganglionic. The fibres are myelinated and in respect of size are B fibres (p. 14.22). The trunk is therefore white and called the white ramus communicans. Postganglionic fibres are unmyelinated and therefore the trunk is grey and termed a grey ramus communicans (fig. 19.5). The length of the preganglionic fibre is variable. The parasympathetic or craniosacral outflow has preganglionic fibres with a long course within the somatic nerve before synapsing with ganglionic cells which are generally close to the organ innervated. Thus the postganglionic fibres are short. The sympathetic thoracolumbar outflow has relatively short preganglionic fibres and conversely often very long postganglionic fibres. Another difference between somatic and visceral neurones is that whilst somatic neurones only innervate one type of cell, namely striated muscle, visceral efferent neurones innervate a number of different cells such as smooth and cardiac muscle and secretory or glandular cells.

THE SYMPATHETIC SYSTEM (table 24.6)

This originates in preganglionic neurones emerging with the ventral roots from the first thoracic to the second lumbar segments. Their cell bodies lie in the visceral efferent column, the lateral grey matter of the spinal cord (p. 24.24) and the fibres reach adjacent ganglia where they synapse or pass through them to synapse with ganglionic cells higher or lower in the paravertebral chain. The thoracic fibres, for example, ascend to the cervical ganglia which lie in the neck, and in this way a very wide area of the body is covered, although the fibres retain a rough relationship to somatic areas. For example, the upper thoracic sympathetic fibres go to the eye, innervating the pupillary muscle, and the heart and lung receive fibres originating from the second to the ninth thoracic segments. Interruption of the cervical part of the sympathetic chain of ganglia produces a condition known as Horner's syndrome; the pupil is smaller on the affected side, because the radial fibres of the iris are denervated, and the eyelid droops because levator palpebrae superioris includes a small smooth muscle element which is now denervated. In addition, the side of the head concerned is incapable of sweating and its cutaneous blood vessels are dilated because normally the sympathetic system keeps them constricted (p. 21.15).

Table 24.6 shows the origin, destination and action of the sympathetic outflow. These fibres reach the organs innervated by the following routes.

(1) Some of the postganglionic fibres return to the spinal nerve, accompanying its various branches until it ends in its effector organ. Thus injury to a peripheral nerve may be accompanied by visceral changes, such as loss of sweating, within the distribution of that nerve.

(2) Other postganglionic fibres form discrete nerves or plexuses, often around blood vessels, following their course until they reach their terminations in other parts of the body. The postganglionic fibres arising from

TABLE 24.6. Origin, destination and action of sympathetic outflow. The levels of outflow may vary in different individuals. Striated muscle in the limbs receives from the sympathetic outflow vasodilator fibres (cholinergic) as well as vasoconstrictor fibres.

Spinal nerve roots carrying outflow	Destination	Action
T1	Iris	Produces dilation
T1–5	Head and Neck	Produces vasoconstriction and sweating (cholinergic)
T2–9	Upper limbs	Produces vasoconstriction and sweating (cholinergic)
T2–6	Heart	Increases rate and force of contraction
T5–9	Lungs	Produces bronchial dilation
	Adrenal medulla	Produces secretion
T6–L2	Abdominal viscera	Inhibits motility and secretion and constricts sphincters
T4–L2	Lower limbs	Produces vasoconstriction and sweating (cholinergic)
L1–2	Genitourinary tract	Contracts seminal vesicles and uterus and relaxes bladder

TABLE 24.7. Origin, route, destination and action of the parasympathetic outflow.

Origin	Leaves CNS with	Route	Ganglion	Destination	Action
Edinger-Westphal nucleus	Nerve III	With nerve III	Ciliary	Ciliary muscle	Accommodation for near vision
				Iris	Constricts pupil
Superior salivatory nucleus	Nerve VII	Greater petrosal nerve	Pterygopalatine	Lacrimal gland	Produces tears
				Nasal mucosa	Produces secretion
		Chorda tympani	Submandibular	Submandibular and sublingual salivary glands	Produces secretion
Inferior salivatory nucleus	Nerve IX	Lesser petrosal nerve	Otic	Parotid salivary gland	Produces secretion
Dorsal motor nucleus of vagus	Nerve X		Adjoining or in destination	Heart	Slows rate and conduction
				Bronchi	Produces constriction
				Alimentary canal down to proximal colon	Stimulates peristalsis and secretion
Spinal cord sacral segments	S2–4	Pelvic splanchnic nerves	Adjoining or in destination	Distal colon and rectum	Produces contraction
				Bladder	Produces contraction
				Genitalia	Produces erection

the superior cervical ganglion are an example, for they form a plexus around the carotid artery until they finally enter the orbit to supply the pupil.

(3) Not all preganglionic fibres end in the paravertebral ganglia, however, for in certain areas other ganglionic masses exist; the coeliac ganglion, for example, accepts preganglionic fibres from the splanchnic nerves and is a prevertebral ganglion. From these prevertebral ganglia arise postganglionic fibres which apply themselves to adjacent arteries and pass with them to various organs.

THE PARASYMPATHETIC SYSTEM

This arises from the brain stem and the sacral segments of the cord. The brain stem visceral efferents emerge with the oculomotor, the facial, the glossopharyngeal and the vagus nerves. Table 24.7 summarizes the origin, route, destination and action of the parasympathetic outlets.

The central connections of the autonomic nervous system have already been mentioned in the section on brain stem and spinal cord. Important connections exist with the hypothalamus via the hypothalamotegmental tract and the medial longitudinal fasciculus and also with the reticular system. Relatively little is known about the course of the tracts although there seems little doubt that the efferent spinal pathway is largely through the reticulospinal tracts.

DISTINCTIONS BETWEEN THE SOMATIC AND THE AUTONOMIC MOTOR SYSTEM

The transmitter substance at the motor end plate in striated muscle is acetylcholine. The transmitter in the autonomic system, however, is not everywhere acetylcholine. It is acetylcholine in the autonomic ganglia where the intermediate synapses of the autonomic system occur; but at the termination of the second, post-ganglionic fibre it is frequently noradrenaline (table 24.8).

So there are three distinctions between the somatic motor system and the autonomic system. (1) A synaptic junction is interposed between the CNS and the organ controlled by the autonomic system; the somatic system has no such interposed junction. (2) The transmitter in the autonomic system is not always acetylcholine. (3) The effect exerted by the autonomic system may be to reduce or slow activity or else to start it.

Visceral afferent fibres frequently accompany the efferent fibres of the autonomic system. For example, the vagus nerve contains many afferent fibres, e.g. those for the Hering-Breuer reflex (p. 29.22). Again, a peripheral nerve trunk usually contains some vasomotor efferent fibres, and so when it is cut vasodilation occurs in the skin area concerned. Painful stimulation of the skin provokes reflex vasoconstriction; the afferent path is in somatic sensory nerves, the efferent in the sympathetic outflow.

GENERAL ACTION OF THE SYMPATHETIC SYSTEM

Elements of the sympathetic part of the system can of course function in isolation from each other, but they can be thought of as a whole in some definite senses. The chief transmitter at the end organ is noradrenaline, a hormone which along with adrenaline circulates in the blood stream, especially in states of alarm or defence, because it is released by the medulla of the adrenal gland (p. 25.29). The cells of the adrenal medulla behave as neurones in sympathetic ganglia without axons, i.e. they respond to stimulation via the preganglionic fibres by secreting catecholamines into the blood stream instead of by originating nerve impulses in postganglionic fibres. When the whole system is active together the picture is one of increasing the defences of the body to protect itself: the heart rate and arterial blood pressure rise, the pupils enlarge, the bronchioles dilate, sweating occurs ready to dissipate extra heat production, hair is erected and peristalsis is inhibited.

GENERAL ACTION OF THE PARASYMPATHETIC SYSTEM

In contrast, overall parasympathetic activity corresponds roughly to the picture of an old man asleep after dinner, i.e. slow heart, small pupils, constricted bronchioles and noisy breathing, salivary secretion, vigorous peristalsis. In this case there is no circulating hormone in the blood, for acetylcholine is rapidly hydrolyzed by cholinesterase in the blood stream.

SLEEP

Sleep can be rather clumsily defined as: 'a reversible periodically recurring state of reduced muscular activity and sensory reactivity of an organism to the surrounding world'; the reversibility is obviously important, since sleep can be distinguished from coma by the relative ease

TABLE 24.8. Chemical transmission in the autonomic nervous system.

	Preganglionic fibres	Postganglionic fibres	Effector organs
Parasympathetic	Acetylcholine	Acetylcholine	Heart Smooth muscle Glands
Sympathetic	Acetylcholine	Acetylcholine	Sweat glands Blood vessels to skeletal muscle
		Noradrenaline	Heart Smooth muscle Blood vessels Some glands

with which the sleeper can be awakened. Beyond what common sense tells, little is known about why we need sleep in normal life. So it is impossible to calculate how many hours of it one needs. Explorers spontaneously take about eight hours when they are away from all social pressures and are pleasing themselves. Young children clearly need more and individuals vary greatly.

The requirement need not be taken in a single dose daily. In hot countries a siesta in the heat of the day is customary, except for mad dogs and Englishmen, as Noel Coward put it. Again, Oswald trained volunteers to sleep and wake on a 48 hour cycle instead of the normal 24 hours, and they grew accustomed to this. The sleep debt incurred in the first 24 hours was repaid during the second, and, unlike an oxygen debt, was not repaid in full; the extra sleep taken was not equivalent in length to the sleep lost.

No one is known to have died from lack of sleep. When people have been awake for long periods, it grows harder and harder to keep them awake and in the end practically impossible. Irritability, inattention and slowness of thought are well known consequences; delusions and liability to infective illness may be others.

Is sleep no more than a switching off of parts of the central nervous system? Since the plantar response (p. 24.14) becomes upgoing during deep sleep, it may be argued that the pyramidal tract is switched off. On the other hand, some individual neurones recorded in the pyramidal tract and the visual cortex of sleeping animals have actually been discharging more frequently than during resting wakefulness. Further, there is no apparent decrease in cerebral oxygen consumption and blood flow during sleep, although the measurements are not beyond criticism. The nervous system does not seem to be just switched off.

In fact this has long been clear. A mother, though asleep, is far more easily roused by her baby's cry than by other louder but less important noises. Pavlov painted the picture of a watchman still awake in the brain while the rest of him sleeps, and the watchman seems to be able to perform remarkable discriminations of this kind, wakening the sleeper if it is 'necessary'.

What does happen to the brain during sleep can be partly revealed by studying the electrical pattern shown in the electroencephalogram (EEG) (p. 24.46). During wakefulness, there is a pattern of waves of a frequency around 10/sec and of relatively low voltage, interspersed with much random activity. When sleep begins, these waves are displaced by slower waves, of greater amplitude. Later on, perhaps after an hour of sleep, intermittent episodes of **paradoxical sleep** occur, in which the EEG waves are much reduced in amplitude. Muscle tone is also generally reduced in these episodes but rapid eye movements may occur behind the closed eyelids. However, in spite of these eye movements, the sleeper is harder to wake during paradoxical sleep than during the rest of his sleep and it is then that he dreams. Electrical changes of this type make possible experimental work to determine what brings on sleep and arousal.

In the reticular formation of the brain stem the more medial part is concerned with facilitating stretch reflexes in the flexor rather than in the extensor muscles, and with reducing vascular tone. Flexion (curling up) and a lowered vascular tone and arterial blood pressure are features of sleep. So it is not surprising that damage to this region leads to insomnia. Further, 5-HT is demonstrable in some neurones here and in the brain of animals the level is related to the amount of time they spend sleeping. Hence it is suggested that 5-HT in the brain is important in ordinary sleep mechanisms.

On the other hand, paradoxical sleep depends in animals on the integrity of the locus coeruleus, which lies in the upper pons, 'north-east' of the median longitudinal bundle; it is named blue place because some of its cells contain melanin, but the region is also rich in both noradrenaline and monoamine oxidase (MAO) which can degrade noradrenaline and also 5-HT. It is thus a reasonable surmise that noradrenaline and the locus coeruleus are concerned in paradoxical sleep. Giving MAO inhibitors might be expected to raise the level of noradrenaline and increase the amount of paradoxical sleep taken by an animal. In fact, in man the use of MAO inhibitors suppresses paradoxical sleep, though not normal sleep, possibly by allowing levels of noradrenaline to rise too high. Such unexpected findings show, not that sleep is now well understood, but that it is less of a mystery than before.

ON LEARNING AND MEMORY

Memory and learning are topics that link physiology and psychology. Many difficulties arise in translating words and figures, the natural raw material for psychological experiments on memory, into the neurophysiological events in the nervous system. Memory can be studied by comparing it to the familiar processes of note-taking, note-storing, and note-reading, i.e. what we do when we expect memory to be inadequate without aid. The comparison raises at once a string of questions: how is the note made, how long does it take to make, what form of note is it, where is it kept, how are successive notes arranged in store, is it hard work making a note, and how is it read again? Psychological aspects are discussed on p. 36.18.

A series of useful experimental plans has been devised to study memory and learning in animals. These were inaugurated by the almost legendary figure, Pavlov (1849–1936). This Russian physiologist, who was born left-handed, taught himself to be ambidextrous and became an exceedingly skilful experimental surgeon. He studied

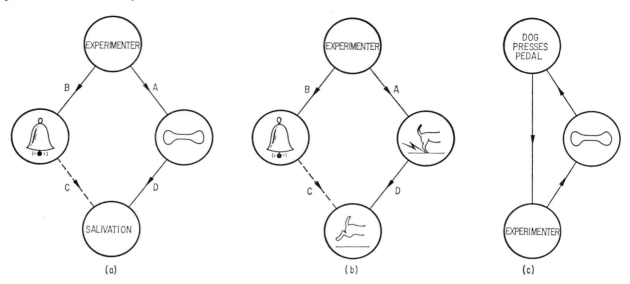

FIG. 24.122. Patterns of learning. See text.

the physiology of the gastrointestinal tract until he was fifty-six and devoted the remaining thirty-one years of his life to trail blazing experiments on the central nervous system.

In Pavlov's classical plan, the effectiveness of learning is assessed by measuring the volume of saliva produced by a dog. The pattern is shown in fig. 24.122a. The experimenter repeatedly first sounds a bell and then provides food for the dog. Salivation occurs in response to the food. The dog creates link C by learning, and will then salivate in response to the bell alone, a **conditioned reflex**. If the experimenter breaks link A and stops providing the food but goes on ringing the bell, link C gradually becomes broken again; the animal's conditioned reflex is said to be **extinguished**. This is not the same as simple forgetting. Forgetting is the much slower loss of link C occurring when the experimenter just provides food, when needed, over a long time with no bell at all, and link B is broken.

A further experimental pattern is shown in fig. 24.122b. Here, after the bell, the animal receives a shock, causing it to withdraw its leg, and so learns to avoid the shock by lifting its leg when it hears the bell. Thus by establishing link C it breaks link D. Here again extinction can occur, if the experimenter breaks link A, and shocks can no longer be received.

Yet another pattern is shown in fig. 24.122c. The animal learns that by pressing the pedal it can obtain food, and thus the sequence is established. The dog takes the initiative in pressing the pedal; coaxing it to do this at the outset may not be easy until the reward is recognized. The process is called **operant conditioning**. Here, as in the other patterns, the experimenter generally delegates his duties to a suitable machine which provides the food whenever the dog presses the pedal, and very large numbers of variations in the pattern have been invented.

In general, the animal requires quite a number of repetitions to learn the response. This slowness may seem unintelligent, especially since it is more marked in the less highly developed animals. For instance, the worm is a much slower learner than the rat, and the rat slower than the monkey. We fancy we can frequently learn from a first encounter. But this is not always so apparent. A person in the position of fig. 24.122b will learn to pull his limb out of the way within half a dozen trials, and this is fast learning. But suppose he receives a light shone into his eye instead of an electric shock, not a very bright light but enough to produce constriction of the pupil, and at the same time the bell rings. His nervous system will learn in time to constrict his pupil when the bell rings, even if the light fails to shine. But it takes a great many trials to learn this, perhaps four hundred or more. Even then, the conditioned reflex is very rapidly extinguished again. This is slow learning, but by a perfectly intelligent human nervous system. Keeping out of the way of an electric shock is, of course, a defensive reaction. Pupillary constriction is not the way we protect ourselves against bright lights; it is not a defence, because the protection against bright light consists in closing the eyelids. Pupillary constriction is the 'stop', if one considers the eye as a camera, but not the shutter.

A fourth pattern of learning is peculiar and is called **imprinting**. The duckling, 16 hours after hatching, has the characteristics of the mother duck imprinted into its responses, so that it persistently follows the mother duck. The duckling is only open to imprinting during a particular brief phase of development and then has 'learnt' the appropriate responses in a lasting way. Instead of the mother duck's characteristics, some other set can be imprinted during this critical phase, and the duckling may then follow a hen or a man. This pattern seems remarkable as a variety of rapid but lasting learning, possible only during a brief phase of life; both ducklings and chicks are capable of it.

However, it can be argued that the duckling only receives the imprint because it has not previously been able, in its first 15 hours of independent life, to distinguish one moving thing from another, and that it would follow anything that moved. As soon as it is able, it identifies its mother. On this interpretation, imprinting is a feature of very early life, when the bird has little previous experience; its choice of a mother to follow is one of the first it learns to make, and rapid and durable for that reason and not because of any special, qualitatively different mechanism of learning.

A memory can take a long time to become permanently stored. The storing can be prevented entirely within the first hour or so by an electric shock to the brain of an animal or by lowering the animal's body temperature. In man, a head injury damaging the brain may extinguish the memory of all events immediately preceding the accident (**retrograde amnesia**). What is going on during storing is uncertain, but seems to be related to the fornix, hippocampus and mammillary body, since damage there is especially likely to prevent storing; in addition rhythmic waves may be found in electrical recordings from these sites in animals learning a conditioned reflex, and vanish again when the reflex is extinguished.

During the process of storing, a memory is available; and even when it fails to be stored, it can be recovered for a short time. A phone number read for the first time is available long enough for dialling, but usually gone beyond recall 10 sec later. This kind of short term memory is easy to test by finding out how many numbers in a sequence a patient is able to recite back again at once (p. 36.19). A person with bilateral (it has to be bilateral) hippocampal damage can perform this test tolerably well, but he fails when his permanent storage of memory is tested by finding out whether he can recall memorable events which happened after the damage to his brain, such as political changes. Yet he can recover memories stored before the damage occurred.

How is the note kept and in what form? It was at one time supposed that the note might consist in electrical activity in the nervous system. Electrical activity is continuous both when awake and asleep and in certain cases it is known to 'reverberate', i.e. pass round and round a neuronal circuit or to and fro, so that its time course may repeat itself over and over again. But if this repeated activity corresponded to long term memory, then whatever arrested or seriously interfered with the electrical activity would also disrupt memory. This is not so, because chilling animal brains, or brief convulsions, do not necessarily remove memories, even though they interrupt the sequence of electrical activity. Memory can hardly depend on continuing electrical activity.

So it may depend on permanent changes in the structure of the system. The most plausible site is at the synaptic junctions between neurones. Enormous numbers are available, and new ones could form and old ones break down. The largest mass of neurones available to a mammal is the cerebral cortex. If the connections there are modified to create a memory, then damaging them should abolish the memories deposited in the damaged part. The synaptic links we see in a good microscopic section of the brain would thus be the sum of its inherited patterns of behaviour and its remembered experience.

This expectation does not work out in any simple sense. An animal's cerebral cortex can be sliced through repeatedly normal to its surface, severing the connections between each piece and its neighbour, without apparently abolishing memory. So a new piece of learning is unlikely to be just the 'soldering' of a new connection in the cerebral cortex. Certainly, actual loss of cerebral cortex that is widespread enough prevents the memory being available, so that memories are closely linked to the presence of enough functioning cerebral cortex.

How far can we believe that a memory is the establishing of a new connection, not in one place in the cerebral cortex, but in many places, so that it is available in any portion of cortex? This certainly cannot be entirely true. Some simple varieties of learning do not require the presence of the cerebral cortex at all. When deprived of it, an animal is still capable of learning the simplest conditioned reflexes. It can distinguish light from darkness and learn to act upon the difference, although no one knows whether a man can do this too. Learning is a feature of the nervous system which cannot be confined to one part of it; but naturally complicated kinds of learning require the most complicated part of the nervous system.

Learning can also be confined to one side of the forebrain by Sperry's fascinating 'split brain' experiments. In these, a cat or a monkey undergoes splitting of the optic chiasma from front to back. The neural connections are now such that what the animal sees with the left eye is fed to the left cerebral hemisphere, and what it sees with the

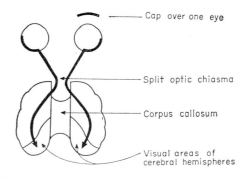

FIG. 24.123. Visual paths with split optic chiasma. After Sperry.

FIG. 24.124. Visual paths with split optic chiasma and corpus callosum. After Sperry.

right eye is fed to the right hemisphere. Normally (p. 24.62) what an eye sees is divided between the two hemispheres, but after chiasmal splitting this is no longer so.

After the splitting operation, one eye of the animal can be covered, and learning can be done through the other eye; for instance, the animal can learn to find food behind a door marked with one pattern and not with another. What is seen is being fed to one hemisphere and not to the other. The next stage is to find out whether the other hemisphere has 'learnt' as well as the trained one.

This is done by splitting the corpus callosum, the bridge between the two hemispheres, and changing the eye cover from one eye to the other. The position is now as in fig. 24.124. The hemisphere not originally trained is now being tested by allowing the animal to see only with the eye feeding that hemisphere.

It turns out that the untrained hemisphere has learnt from the trained one, and in the monkey very efficiently but not so efficiently in the cat. The memory has been transferred across from one hemisphere to the other, and it is possible to show that the corpus callosum effects the transfer, because if the corpus callosum is cut at the outset, then only the trained hemisphere has 'learnt the lesson'. The other hemisphere remains unaware of it, unless, as already mentioned, the lesson is so simple as not to require the presence of the cerebral cortex.

There are a very few people without a corpus callosum, either born without it or deprived of it by operation. They naturally have an intact optic chiasma, and it is not so easy to demonstrate that they have two independent hemispheres, but it can be done. Speech is a function confined to the 'dominant' hemisphere, and so the non-dominant hemisphere cannot speak or write. Is it then totally illiterate? It seemed at one time that there must be large amounts of vacant space in the non-dominant hemisphere, and then evidence from operations on the human brain suggested that the non-dominant hemisphere might contain maps and plans, instead of the words which were the prerogative of the dominant hemisphere. Clearly our memories come to contain vast amounts of information in plan and map form, and one of Penfield's cases, after

operation on the non-dominant hemisphere, could never find his way home unless he could actually see the house.

In addition, evidence is now appearing that the non-dominant hemisphere does perhaps recognize words when seen. The words cannot be spoken nor written; but the hand governed by the non-dominant hemisphere can reach out to something when the same hemisphere has seen and evidently read its name.

This is just one of a number of remarkable findings which have emerged from studies on 'split-brain man'. At times, the non-dominant hand may 'go off on its own' and have to be restricted by the dominant hand. One begins to doubt whether a split brain man is singular or plural. But in no sense does he resemble a schizophrenic, in spite of the layman's interpretation of that word.

Are we then to say that a normal piece of learning depends on synaptic connections in the hemisphere which did the learning, and that similar connections are established in the other hemisphere if the corpus callosum is intact. Before pinning our faith exclusively to synaptic connections, it is worth taking a look at another type of change.

When a new memory is stored, we presume that living tissue acquires new properties. Besides the formation of new synaptic connections, there is a quite different way in which living tissue can acquire new properties; this is by widening its spectrum of different protein structures. Living tissue can 'learn' to recognize and respond to an enormous variety of molecular structures and, having once 'learnt', remembers permanently. This model of memory does not in the least explain how nerve impulses can modify the structure of protein in neurones. It does, however, account in a way for the difficulty of locating a memory precisely, since a new molecular structure may become widespread throughout the body; but it does so most easily through cell multiplication, and neurones themselves do not multiply after birth.

So memory might depend on changes in neuronal protein structure. Changes in the structure of RNA could lead to synthesis of new proteins. Such changes have recently been sought in animals after training in new tasks like climbing along a wire, or getting food with an unaccustomed paw, and do appear to occur. But this type of explanation is not necessarily an alternative to synaptic changes. Both views may in the end turn out to be complementary; synaptic change and RNA change may both play a part.

Perhaps the number of new proteins we can 'learn' to form is quite limited. The number of antibodies of differing specificity that we can form may only run into thousands, and our repertoire depends on the genetic instructions we have received from our parents. Learning, and teaching what we have learnt, is the prized tool with which men hope in their wilder dreams to break through the limitations of human genetic make up and leave their mark upon the traditions of the future. Each of us grants readily that particular feats of learning are beyond us. But we are slow to agree that all human learning must be filed on any fixed number of shelves.

About the filing system for memory traces there is little clear knowledge. Experience confirms that they are somehow filed in the same order as they are made, so that they carry a time label with them. And artificial stimulation of the temporal lobe of a human cerebral hemisphere can summon into consciousness a series of memories correct in their sequence, one following another in the same order as the related events originally occurred. It must be admitted that this resummoning of memories by electrical stimulation has not yet been demonstrated in a normal cerebral hemisphere. It is also obvious that memories are labelled in the file in many ways in addition to order of time: witness how past events are recalled when the memory is jogged by every sort of diverse association between the present and the past.

It is hard to form any estimate of how large the filing system is. Ordinarily one is aware of recollections that do not come to mind when wanted, but report for duty later on. Again, hypnosis seems to provide access to far more recollections than one is ever normally able to draw upon. Even in old age, the store is never full up, whatever one may feel like just before an examination.

The reader may be awed by the demands of his course, and the pains he has to take to remember it. Must it take great effort or special trouble to record a memory? Can learning be effortless, involuntary? Certainly, as establishing a conditioned reflex is a form of learning. But it is the learning of even the lower animals; learning without understanding, learning without curiosity. It is not very different from the endless memorizing by children of scriptures they are too young to understand, a practice which still persists in the East, but dies out when paper and print become readily available. It leads later on to the endless memorizing of still meaningless textbooks by adults.

A reader ought not to sit passively in learned books, imbibing knowledge like a plant. He should prowl in them, scenting from far away the answers to questions in his mind, challenging the writer with his interest. Memories are often recorded with the utmost ease when interest gives her consent. Interest is a fickle goddess, but not too fickle to be successfully seduced. It is not enough to call loudly on the subject matter (or the teacher) to produce her. She can be lured by signs of affection, but she cannot be forced by threats or sacrifices. There comes a time to give up dogged persistence, put down the books and find another temporary mistress, till with time her feminine waywardness grows more amenable.

Finally, how is memory read back? This is just as difficult as any of the other features to explain in neurophysiological terms. The process seems rapid even when the memory is of a hoary antiquity. What is recalled carries a time label with it. All in all, memory presents problems difficult to reconcile with any one model proposed so far; it provides the facilities of an elaborate computer, but all on a mere 20 watts of power; this is the consumption of the whole brain, which has to cover numerous other facilities too.

MODELS OF THE BRAIN

Ever since the gross anatomy of the brain first became known, men have interpreted its function in terms of mechanical devices which they understood. Galen, working in the age of Roman aqueducts, was familiar with pipes and water channels and used cannulae in his experimental work. So he concentrated his attention on the ventricles of the brain as a fluid conducting system and on the nerves as pipes down which the active material could run. Squeeze the exposed brain, as Galen did, and convulsive movements may follow; vital spirits were being extruded from the ventricles down the nerves, and so movements were generated in the muscles to which the nerves run. The muscles were inflated by the vital spirits and bulged as they contracted, as Descartes held in the seventeenth century. Subsequent knowledge has outdated this crude model, which served its day; muscle volume does not increase upon contraction.

Electronic circuits nowadays provide the most complicated and versatile devices available to us, and so it is natural for interpretations of brain function to make full use of such analogies. Like Young, for instance, we may think of the brain as the controller of a homoeostat, keeping certain aspects of its surrounding organism continually the same. Certain aspects only? Presumably it is no part of the game to keep the thoughts of the organism always the same, and a constant effort to keep everything the same is more the picture of senility than of vigorous life.

However, it is important to recognize that no one method of study or kind of analogy is likely to provide the whole story. For instance, a detailed description of the constituent parts of a neon sign (its anatomy) can be combined with recordings of current and potential at every part of the sign (its electrophysiology); but even with all this information, the all-important message conveyed by the sign may fail to become apparent. We may still have no idea why it is as it is. As the distinguished American neurophysiologist, G.H. Bishop, put the matter recently: 'We are accustomed to think of cortical functioning in terms of two different sets of phenomena. One is physiological, involving analytic and integrative activity by means of which afferent information is organized to initiate and direct useful efferent responses. The other is psychological, involving such subjective phenomena as memory, sensory awareness and thinking. Often we mix these two languages and pretend that physiological and psychological categories can be correlated. But the one path leads inexorably to search for wiring diagrams and usually winds up with a presumed biological computer. The other eventually runs up against the little man inside'.

For a complete understanding, more than anatomy and physiology are likely to be required, and the brain will remain more than just a device which 'some fool made out of meat instead of wires'. Only in the simplest instances is enough known about structure and function in the central nervous system for its behaviour to be confidently predicted in time and space. Such prediction is an acid test of the adequacy of understanding. Another test consists in whether we can make nervous systems that synthesize themselves. Remarkable experiments by Weiss and Szentagothai show how small nervous systems can be induced to develop in a tadpole's tail and become capable of reflex action. But it is still easier to contrive mechanical or electronic models to the same purpose. However, a satisfactory model of the brain must be capable of having 'grown that way'.

When we look at man-made devices, we can often take it for granted that each component has one specific function, once we properly understand it. This assumption falls to the ground so often in neurophysiology that it can lead to serious error of a twofold kind. Any single component, nucleus, tract or other structure, is likely to be concerned in several functions which are hard to unify. And in addition these functions may be carried on elsewhere, apparently in duplicate. For an example, look at the section on the hypothalamus (p. 24.34).

A glance at possible models is useful. It binds together existing knowledge into a framework that can be thought about, and it stimulates experiments that add to knowledge. The **digital computer** has attractions. It is very fast, using pulses perhaps 10^{-7} sec long (how long is a nerve impulse?), and deals with information arriving in precise sequences and identical packets, like the mileage recorder of a car. It seems doubtful whether neurones are quite reliable enough to function exclusively in this way. Their temperature, for instance, may vary from time to time, though normally precisely controlled. Also the pulses are not always identical one with another, but can run so fast in normal function that the second of a series lies within the refractory period following the first and loses amplitude. Yet transmission along nerve axons is fundamentally digital. Each spike is like each other spike. What is transmitted is already coded, as digital computation requires.

Besides looking for adequate models of the brain, we can appreciate that in some senses the brain itself contains a model of features of the environment. This model of the environment is significantly biassed right at the beginning by the behaviour of the receptors. To take a simple instance: if one suddenly applies a pressure of a few grammes to a frog's skin and maintains it, the relevant receptor does not suddenly start firing with a frequency corresponding to the number of grammes applied, and go on doing so. The early high rate of firing soon falls to a low one. As Adrian showed long ago with tiny air blasts directed at a frog's skin, the frog soon ceases to pay any attention to a continuous constant stimulus that does no damage to it; the receptors no longer respond.

The **analogue computer** is a model also offering resemblances to the nervous system. It requires numerous small units, each varying in state over a continuous range as the speedometer of a car does, with variable interconnections. Numerous small units are just what the brain offers, 10^{10} of them, and their membrane potentials vary over a continuous range. Within limits, they generate spikes at higher frequency as the membrane potential falls; they can add and subtract in effect, and they can take account of differences in time between incoming pulses, because their postsynaptic potential changes long outlast the duration of the incoming pulse. What is to be said about the variable interconnections? For the purposes of anatomy, the connections are supposed to be fixed and immutable.

FURTHER READING

ADRIAN E.D. (1947). *The Physical Background of Perception*. London: Oxford University Press.

BATESON P.P.G. (1966). Imprinting *Biol. Rev.* **41**, 177.

BROWN-GRANT K. & CROSS B.A. ed. (1966). The Hypothalamus. *Brit. med. Bull.* **22**.

CHUSID J.G. & McDONALD J.J. (1967). *Correlative Neuroanatomy and Functional Neurology*, 13th Edition. Oxford: Blackwell Scientific Publications.

DAVSON H. (1966). Formation and drainage of the cerebrospinal fluid, in *Scientific Basis of Medicine Annual Review*. London: Athlone Press.

ELLIOT B. (1963). Lost bouquets (a vivid account of how it feels to lose the sense of smell). In *The Practical Management of Head Injuries*, by J.M. Potter. London: Lloyd-Luke.

GREGORY R.L. (1966). *Eye and Brain*. London: World University Library.

HARMON L.D. & LEWIS E.R. (1966). Neural modelling. *Physiol. Rev.* **46**, 513.

HILTON S.M. (1965). Emotion, in *The Physiology of Human Survival*, ed. Edholm & Bacharach. London: Academic Press.

HUBEL D.H. (1960). *The Visual Cortex of the Brain*. Scientific American offprint No. 168.

MacNichol E.F. (1964). *Three Pigment Colour Vision.* Scientific American Offprint No. 197.

McIlwain E. (1966). *Biochemistry of the Central Nervous System*, 3rd Edition. London: Churchill.

Olds J.E. (1967). Emotional centres in the brain. *Science Journal*, **3**, 87.

Oswald I. (1966). *Sleep.* Harmondsworth: Pelican.

Peterson L.R. (1966). Short-term memory. *Scientific American*, **215**, 90.

van Bergeijk W.A., Pierce J.R. & David jr. E.E. (1961). *Waves and the Ear.* London: Heinemann.

Walsh E.G. (1964). *Physiology of the Nervous System*, 2nd Edition. London: Longmans.

Wooldridge D.E. (1963). *The Machinery of the Brain.* New York & London: McGraw-Hill.

Wright R.H. (1964). *The Sense of Smell.* London: Allen & Unwin.

Wurtman R.J. and Axelrod J. (1965). *The Pineal Gland.* Scientific American offprint No. 1015.

Young J.Z. (1964). *A Model of the Brain.* London: Oxford University Press.

Chapter 25
The endocrine system

In the embryo, the primitive cells lining the body surfaces are called epithelial cells. Apart from being protective, their most important function is to absorb substances from the surrounding medium which are then modified and secreted in another form. As the embryo grows, certain epithelial cells develop this function to a specialized degree and are formed into structures called glands. This is achieved by invagination of a sheet of epithelial cells as shown in fig. 25.1. They may remain connected to the epithelial surface by means of a duct through which their secretion reaches the surface, thereby localizing its site of action, or they may lose their connection with the surface and secrete their products into the blood stream, thus making them accessible to all the body cells. Glands which have a duct and secrete externally are called **exocrine glands** (fig. 25.1b), e.g. the intestinal glands, the pancreas, sweat glands, lacrimal and mammary glands. Those without a duct have an internal secretion and are called **endocrine** or **ductless glands** (fig. 25.1c). These are listed in table 25.1, together with the names of their principal secretions and common abbreviations. Endocrinology is the study of the structure and function of these ductless glands.

Some organs have both exocrine and endocrine functions, e.g. the acinar cells of the pancreas secrete digestive enzymes through the pancreatic duct into the

TABLE 25.1. The principal endocrine glands of the body and their most important secretions.

Glands	Secretions	Chemical nature
Anterior pituitary or adenohypophysis	Somatotrophic hormone (SH) or growth hormone (GH)	Protein, mol. wt. 20,500–26,000
	Adrenocorticotrophic hormone (ACTH)	Polypeptide, of 39 amino acids mol. wt. 4500
	Thyroid stimulating hormone (TSH)	Glycoprotein, mol. wt. 25,000–30,000
	Luteinizing hormone (LH) ⎫ gonadotrophic	Glycoprotein, mol. wt. 26,000
	Follicle stimulating hormone (FSH) ⎭	Glycoprotein
	Prolactin	Protein, mol. wt. 20,000 (sheep)
Posterior pituitary or neurohypophysis	Vasopressin or antidiuretic hormone (ADH)	Polypeptide of 8 amino acids
	Oxytocin	Polypeptide of 8 amino acids
Thyroid	Thyroxine (T_4)	Iodinated amino acid
	Triiodothyroxine (T_3)	Iodinated amino acid
Parathyroids	Calcitonin	Polypeptide, mol. wt. about 3600
Adrenals	Parathyroid hormone	Polypeptide, mol. wt. 8500
Cortex	Cortisol	Steroid
	Aldosterone	Steroid
	Corticosterone and many other steroids, including androgens and oestrogens in small amounts	Steroid
Medulla	Adrenaline (USA epinephrine)	Catecholamine
	Noradrenaline (USA norepinephrine)	Catecholamine
Kidneys	Renin	Protein mol. wt. 40,000
	Erythropoietin	Glycoprotein
Testes	Testosterone and other androgens	Steroid
Ovaries	Oestradiol and other oestrogens	Steroid
	Progesterone	Steroid
Placenta	Chorionic gonadotrophin (Human CG)	Glycoprotein 30,000
	Oestrogens	Steroid
	Progesterone	Steroid
Pancreas	Insulin	Polypeptide, aggregates of 2–8 units each of mol. wt. about 5800
	Glucagon	Polypeptide, a single chain, mol. wt. 3500
Gastrointestinal tract		
Stomach	Gastrin	Polypeptide, mol. wt. 2100
Duodenum	Secretin	Polypeptide, mol. wt. about 2700
	Pancreozymin	Polypeptide, mol. wt. about 2700
Small intestine	Cholecystokinin	Polypeptide, mol. wt. about 2700

duodenum, and the pancreatic islet cells secrete insulin into the blood. Although exocrine and endocrine secretions can come from the same organ, they originate from different cell types.

Endocrine glands have a characteristic morphology consisting of secretory cells surrounded by connective tissue that bears capillaries, lymphatics and nerves. The secretory cells are rich in mitochondria and secretory granules. During a phase of activity, the nuclei enlarge and the secretory granules decrease in number with the appearance of vacuoles in the cytoplasm. The posterior pituitary gland is an exception to this general arrangement as its secretions are produced in neurosecretory centres in the hypothalamus and transported along nerve fibres into the posterior pituitary gland where they are stored and released as required.

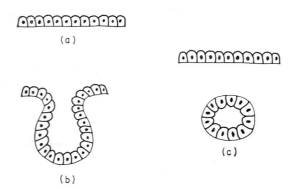

FIG. 25.1. (a) Primitive epithelial cells; (b) invaginations of epithelial cells to form an exocrine gland; (c) endocrine gland with loss of duct.

All endocrine glands have a rich blood supply into which they pour their secretions. The nerve supply to the glands appears to play little part in their function except for the adrenal medulla and posterior pituitary. The importance of the lymphatic drainage as a mechanism of hormone transport is not known but is probably small.

The internal secretions of the ductless glands were first called **hormones** (Greek *hormao*, I excite) in 1905 by Starling, after he and Bayliss had isolated the hormone, secretin, from the mucosal cells of the upper gastrointestinal tract. They regarded a hormone as a substance normally produced in the cells of some part of the body and carried by the blood stream to distant parts, so acting on the organism as a whole. This definition does not describe adequately present knowledge of the diverse actions of hormones, but it is difficult to be more precise.

The hormones maintain the constancy of the internal environment by affecting such variables as water and electrolyte balance, blood glucose level and metabolic rate. They also regulate cell metabolism, respiration, reproduction and neural activity. Hormones influence growth, development and ageing, and the responses to stress such as emotional disturbances, injury or infection. In certain instances their action is strictly localized, e.g. the pituitary hormone, thyroid stimulating hormone (TSH) stimulates only the cells of the thyroid gland, while others, e.g. the adrenal hormone, cortisol, affect the metabolism of most cells.

Of the hormones listed in table 25.1, those produced by the pituitary, thyroid and parathyroids, the adrenal glands and pancreas are discussed in this chapter. The placenta is also an endocrine gland, for it elaborates hormones that are necessary for the growth and function of both the pregnant uterus and the foetus. It is dealt with in chap. 37 together with the ovaries and testes. The hormones secreted by the upper gastrointestinal tract are all local hormones and regulate the supply of the exocrine digestive secretions. The actions of these hormones are described in chap. 30. The kidney secretes two hormones; erythropoietin regulates the production of red blood cells in response to hypoxia and renin plays an important part in salt metabolism and the maintenance of blood pressure (p. 33.21).

The thymus may produce hormones which are important in the development and function of the immunological mechanisms (p. 27.20). Whether the pineal gland has an endocrine function remains obscure after many years of conjecture (p. 24.36).

STUDY OF ENDOCRINE GLAND FUNCTION

The existence of the endocrine glands has been recognized since ancient times when views on their function were purely speculative and derived mainly from the site and morphology of the glands. For example, the adrenal glands, first illustrated by Eustachius in 1563, were thought to be active only in foetal life because of their large size at birth. Subsequently they were thought to act as a support for the stomach and even to help maintain potency. The thyroid gland was first thought to be part of the vocal apparatus and then to serve as a lubricating organ for the tissues of the neck. Some physicians considered it to be only an adornment of the neck. From the seventeenth century onwards, the study of endocrinology has been more scientific.

CLINICAL OBSERVATIONS IN MAN

This has been responsible for some of the most important landmarks in endocrinology and is still important today. In 1849 Thomas Addison read a paper to the South London Medical Society on 'a diseased condition of the adrenal glands which may interfere with the proper elaboration of the body generally'. This did much to dispel some of the false notions then prevailing as to the function of these glands and gave a strong impetus to further work.

Swelling of the thyroid gland (goitre) was recognized from early times to be associated in some cases with a condition now known as cretinism. It was also recognized that goitres were often endemic in populations living in certain mountainous regions. Despite this association, cretinism was still an obscure disease, even when Sir William Gull described in 1873 a similar disease, myxoedema, in adults. When thyroidectomy began to be practised at the end of the nineteenth century, it was found that symptoms resembling those seen in cases of myxoedema occurred, and this clinical observation led to the view that myxoedema and cretinism were both due to the same cause, namely loss of function of the thyroid gland.

By the beginning of this century, many of the diseases due to dysfunction of the pituitary gland had been described. For example, the condition of gigantism had been recognized, and acromegaly, characterized by overgrowth of certain parts of the skeleton, was described in 1886 by Pierre Marie. Apart from the observation that the pituitary fossa was enlarged, there was little to indicate that the pituitary gland was primarily responsible for these disorders. With the development of histological techniques, it was soon realized that acromegaly and gigantism were associated with an acidophil tumour of the pituitary gland.

THE PHYSIOLOGICAL AND EXPERIMENTAL APPROACH

Physiological investigations of the endocrine glands are based on studies of the effects of removing a gland and sometimes of transplanting it in the same animal. By these techniques, the effects of lack of the secretion of a gland can be observed and the status of the gland as an endocrine organ established by the demonstration that it produces its effects by humoral mechanisms independent of nervous connections.

Berthold, in 1849, demonstrated the existence of an internal secretion when he showed that transplantation of the testes of a cock to its peritoneal cavity prevented the atrophy of the comb that follows castration. Soon after, Brown–Sequard extended Addison's description of the effects of adrenal insufficiency in man, by showing that removal of these glands in animals was fatal, and that they were essential to life. Removal of the pituitary gland, hypophysectomy, in animals resulted in striking changes in which the animal failed to grow and the genital organs remained undeveloped. Changes also occurred in other endocrine organs such as the thyroid and adrenal glands which atrophied. These experiments indicated that the pituitary gland exerts a controlling influence over other endocrine organs.

Transplantation of the pituitary gland to other parts of the body was an exception to the rule about endocrine organs, since function was not restored unless the graft was replaced under the pituitary stalk. This was shown to be dependent on the tissue being revascularized by vessels of the pituitary stalk called the hypophysial portal vessels (p. 25.10). In this way, it became evident that the pituitary was itself controlled by a higher centre, now known to be the hypothalamus.

The work of Houssay, in Buenos Aires in 1924, on the relationship between the anterior pituitary and the pancreas is an example of how views on the aetiology of endocrine disease were influenced by experimental studies. Before this, diabetes mellitus was thought to be a disease caused by a simple failure of the β cells of the pancreas to secrete insulin, just as primary myxoedema resulted from inability of the thyroid to secrete its hormone. Houssay showed that after hypophysectomy an animal became very sensitive to insulin, and even small doses reduced the blood glucose dangerously. This hypoglycaemic action of insulin could, however, be prevented by injecting extracts of the anterior pituitary. He also demonstrated that in a dog from which the pancreas had been removed, the resulting diabetes could be alleviated by removing the pituitary gland. Later, Young in Cambridge gave repeated injections of anterior pituitary extract into dogs and induced permanent diabetes. It was apparent that the anterior pituitary gland produced hormones which were important in the regulation of carbohydrate metabolism and that other mechanisms, apart from simple failure of the β cells of the pancreas, might be responsible for diabetes mellitus.

THE ISOLATION OF HORMONES

After observing the effects of lack of the hormones of the endocrine glands in animals, the next step was to try to make good this lack by giving extracts of gland either orally or by injection. Murray, in 1890, successfully treated a Newcastle lady suffering from myxoedema with an extract of sheep's thyroid gland given subcutaneously. In 1929, Swingle and Pfiffner obtained a water-soluble extract of the adrenal glands from an ox and demonstrated that daily intraperitoneal injections of this extract, together with an adequate salt intake, could maintain in health dogs whose adrenal glands had been removed, whereas without the extract the animals died. This led to the isolation, in the 1930's, of the adrenal cortical hormones, which are steroids and are used in replacement therapy in patients whose adrenal glands have been destroyed and also in the treatment of many non-endocrine diseases.

In 1894, Schafer and Oliver showed that the adrenal medulla contained a substance which produced a rise in blood pressure. In 1901, this substance was isolated in crystalline form and called **adrenaline**; it was synthesized in 1904 and was thus the first hormone to be characterized.

A most important landmark in the history of endocrinology was the discovery of the pancreatic hormone, **insulin,** by Banting, Best and Macleod in Toronto in 1921. The practical importance of this hormone in the treatment of diabetes mellitus, which at that time was a fatal disease, led to the search for other hormones of therapeutic value.

One of the most recent hormones to be discovered is **calcitonin.** In 1962, Copp, in perfusion studies on dogs, produced evidence of a hormone apparently from the parathyroid glands which lowered the blood calcium. Further experiments showed that the hypocalcaemic factor was in fact released from the thyroid gland (p. 25.23).

HORMONE ASSAYS

A natural consequence of the isolation of hormones from the endocrine glands was the development of methods for measuring the concentration of these hormones in glands and body fluids. There are three types of assay procedure: (1) biological, (2) immunological and (3) chemical.

Biological assays

These involve the measurement of a graded or quantal effect following administration of the hormone to an experimental animal, in which the potency of the unknown preparation is compared with that of a standard preparation (p. 3.11). For example, the concentration of human pituitary gonadotrophins in the urine is assayed by injecting subcutaneously immature mice once or twice a day for 3 days with the test preparation. They are killed 72 hours after the first injection and the weight of the uterus is measured; the results are compared with those obtained from mice injected with postmenopausal urine. From this comparison, the gonadotrophic activity of the test preparation can be measured (plate 25.2f, facing p. 27.18).

A biological assay involving radioactive isotopes is used for studying another pituitary hormone, thyroid stimulating hormone (TSH). One method depends on the discharge of radioactive iodine, ^{131}I, from the thyroid glands of mice (fig. 25.2). Mice are fed on a diet low in iodine, which ensures a high uptake by the thyroid gland of any iodine given to the animal. ^{131}I is injected intraperitoneally, and each animal is then given large doses of thyroxine which suppresses the endogenous release of TSH from the pituitary gland. Under these conditions, the thyroid hormones become labelled with ^{131}I, but as the mice are being fed large doses of thyroxine the labelled hormones remain in the gland and little radioactivity is detected in the circulating blood, as thyroid hormone is not discharged from the gland under these

circumstances. When a standard preparation of TSH, or a test preparation containing TSH, is injected intravenously, some of the hormone labelled with ^{131}I stored in the thyroid gland is discharged into the circulation. The radioactivity is measured in blood samples taken two or three hours after the injection. The increases in the blood radioactivity following the injection of the test preparation and of a standard TSH preparation are then compared.

In biological assays, in view of the variation in response which may be obtained with different strains or even the same strain of animals in one laboratory at different times of the year, it is essential that results are related to those obtained with a single standardized preparation of the material in question. To this end, an international stan-

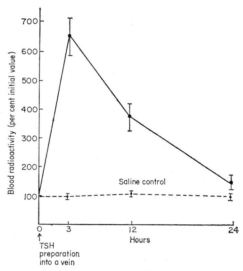

Fig. 25.2. The effect of a standard preparation of TSH on the blood radioactivity of mice (see text).

dard for TSH was established in 1955; one international unit (IU) is defined as the activity present in 13·5 mg of the standard material. International standards have been established for the bioassay of gonadotrophins and other hormones.

Certain tests of endocrine function used in clinical medicine are in fact a form of biological assay performed on the patient himself. For example, an indication of the circulating level of the thyroid hormones can be obtained by estimating the patient's basal metabolic rate. Studies on the uptake of ^{131}I by the thyroid are used to determine whether the secretion of TSH by the patient's pituitary is adequate. In pituitary hypofunction, with impairment of secretion of TSH, the uptake of ^{131}I is low.

Biological assays in animals are, in general, time consuming and expensive. The animals often require removal of major endocrine glands, e.g. hypophysectomy and pancreatectomy, to increase their sensitivity to the hormone being measured and, as can be appreciated, the care of animals in such circumstances may be difficult.

Bioassays may suffer also from the disadvantage that the chosen response may be influenced by hormones of different chemical structure. For example, one of the bioassays for growth hormone depends on the increase in width of the proximal epiphyseal cartilage of the tibia of hypophysectomized rats; this can be changed also by insulin, adrenocorticotrophic hormone (ACTH), cortisol or thyroxine as well as by growth hormone. Provided the response being measured is sufficiently specific, the success of bioassays depends upon the careful design of the experiment and the statistical analysis of the results.

Immunological assays

On repeated injection of a pure preparation of a protein hormone into an animal the substance acts as an antigen and produces antibodies in the animal's serum (p. 27.2); these can react with one or more binding sites on the hormone antigen. Antisera prepared in this manner can detect growth hormone, insulin, glucagon, parathyroid hormone, TSH and ACTH. Reliable quantitative assays for human growth hormone (HGH), ACTH and insulin in blood are now available. It is reasonable to expect that good assay methods for the other hormones listed above will be developed soon.

Immune assays depend on a reaction between a hormone labelled with ^{131}I or ^{125}I (radio-iodinated antigen) and an antibody specific to the hormone. This results in the formation of a labelled antigen–antibody complex. When unlabelled hormone in a test preparation is added to a known amount of labelled hormone and the two mixed with antiserum, there is competition between unlabelled and labelled hormone for binding sites on the antibody.

$$\begin{bmatrix} ^{131}I\text{-HGH} + \text{HGH} \\ \text{(test or} \\ \text{standard} \\ \text{preparation)} \end{bmatrix} + \text{Antibody to} \longrightarrow \\ \text{HGH}$$

$$^{131}I\text{-HGH-Antibody} \\ + \\ \text{HGH-Antibody}$$

The bound and free antigen can be separated by differential precipitation, electrophoresis or paper chromatography and the ratio:

$$\frac{^{131}I\text{-growth hormone}}{^{131}I\text{-growth hormone-antibody}}$$

can be determined. The ratios obtained with the test and standard preparations are compared. The more growth hormone the test preparation contains the less standard is absorbed and the higher the ratio becomes.

Immunological assays are potentially more specific than biological assays and can be extremely sensitive. They can be applied to large numbers of samples at one time and are much cheaper than biological techniques. Their one major disadvantage is that sufficiently highly purified preparations of all the polypeptide or protein hormones are not available for labelling with ^{131}I, so that the method is applicable at the present time to the measurement of only some of these hormones. Until more is known of the structure of some of the protein hormones, it is also difficult to be certain of the purity of the preparations used and, therefore, to be sure exactly what the immunoassay is measuring. Furthermore, the antibody may be reactive with a biologically inactive portion of the hormone amino acid chain. The results of immunoassay therefore require to be checked against bioassay.

Chemical assays

These are now in use for a number of hormones, e.g. colorimetric, fluorometric and gas chromatographic techniques have been developed for measurement of the three main oestrogens (oestrone, oestradiol and oestriol), and these methods have replaced bioassay of oestrogens. Other hormones which can be measured biochemically include progesterone and testosterone. The chemical estimation of groups of compounds that include the hormones under study provide a less specific but albeit valuable method of assay. Thus the fluorometric determination of 11-hydroxycorticosteroids in human plasma gives a good measure of the amount of cortisol and corticosterone in plasma, these substances being the major components of the 11-hydroxycorticosteroids. Other steroid metabolites may be less specific, for example, the 17-oxosteroids are derived from both the adrenal cortex and the testes, and their determination is, therefore, of little value in differentiating the activity of these two glands. The measurement of the catecholamines, (adrenaline, noradrenaline and related products) excreted in the urine provides a valuable index of the secretion in the body of adrenaline or noradrenaline. Likewise, while the level of free thyroxine can be measured in serum, it is much simpler to measure the level of the protein-bound iodine and use this as an index of circulating levels of thyroid hormone, bearing in mind the fallacies that may occur in this indirect measurement.

HORMONE SECRETION RATE

The concentration of a particular hormone in the plasma depends upon an equilibrium between its rate of synthesis in the endocrine gland, the amount bound in the tissues, the rate of destruction by cell metabolism and the rate of loss in the urine and other excretory routes. The measurement of hormone secretion rates provides a more accurate index of the metabolic activity of an endocrine gland.

The secretion rate of cortisol by the adrenal cortex can be determined by the technique of isotope dilution. Isotopically labelled cortisol is metabolized in the same way as the patient's own cortisol, and it is excreted in the urine in the form of metabolic derivatives. A known dose of ^{14}C-cortisol is given by intravenous injection to the patient. The patient's urine is then collected for a finite period of time, e.g. 48 hours. One of the metabolites of cortisol excreted in the urine, e.g. tetrahydrocortisone, is then extracted from the 48-hour collection of urine, its total amount measured chemically and its radio-activity also determined. The following formula then holds:

$$\frac{\text{Endogenous cortisol secretion}}{\text{Amount }^{14}\text{C-cortisol given to patient*}} =$$

$$\frac{\text{Urinary excretion of tetrahydrocortisone*}}{\text{Urinary }^{14}\text{C-tetrahydrocortisone*}}$$

Those variables indicated by an asterisk can be measured directly and hence the endogenous cortisol secretion rate over the period of study calculated. A similar technique may be used to determine secretion rate of aldosterone.

FIG. 25.3. Secretion, transport and metabolism of hormones.

Secretion, transport and disposal of hormones
(fig. 25.3)

Hormones are synthesized from precursors in the endocrine glands. Some hormones are then secreted into the blood almost as quickly as they are formed, e.g. the adrenocortical hormones. Other endocrine glands, such as the thyroid, store the hormone and secrete it over long periods of time. Hormonal secretion may follow a cyclical pattern, e.g. ovarian hormones and adrenocortical

hormones. In the blood many hormones are transported wholly or partly bound to plasma proteins. Their concentration there is determined by their rate of secretion, the rate at which they are taken up by and disposed of in the tissues and their rate of excretion.

Hormones exert their effects on the cells and tissues by a number of mechanisms only a few of which are understood. They may act by influencing enzymic mechanisms in the cells of the target organs, e.g. adrenaline increases the activity of the enzyme adenyl cyclase, which in turn raises the concentration of 3'5' AMP and hence affects the phosphorylase which catalyses the breakdown of glycogen to glucose in the liver (p. 9.9). Some hormones may act by changing the permeability of membranes. In this way insulin enhances the transport of glucose and amino acids from the extracellular fluid into the cell cytoplasm. Several hormones, e.g. thyroxine and cortisol, appear to act on DNA in the cell nucleus and thereby stimulate the production of messenger RNA; this may lead to the synthesis of specific enzymes which influence the direction of metabolism (p. 25.22).

Hormones are broken down either in their target organs or in other tissues, notably the liver, to biologically inert substances. These then undergo further chemical change, referred to as conjugation, to form more soluble compounds which can be excreted by the kidney (fig. 31.11).

Control of endocrine function

A primary function of hormones is maintenance of metabolic homeostasis. This is achieved at tissue level by a complex interaction of hormones in metabolic reactions which can be either antagonistic or synergistic, e.g. growth hormone promotes protein synthesis whereas the adrenocortical steroids promote protein breakdown. On the other hand, growth hormone and the adrenocortical steroids have a synergistic effect on fat metabolism, the synthesis of which is inhibited.

At a higher level, the maintenance of homeostasis depends on a close integration between the endocrine glands and the central nervous system. The influence of the nervous system on the endocrine glands is mediated through the hypothalamus and this is well seen in the reproductive system where different conditions are necessary for ovulation in various species. In the dog and humans, ovulation is spontaneous and independent of mating. In the cat and the rabbit however, ovulation requires the stimulus of coitus or an artificial stimulus of the vagina or cervix. In these animals, hypophysectomy prevents ovulation, thus indicating that the stimuli act through a higher centre which is probably the hypothalamus. This acts on the anterior lobe of the pituitary which in turn stimulates the ovary to liberate the ovum. Again in women it is well recognized that emotional disturbances may cause amenorrhoea. Any form of stress acts through the nervous system and has definite effects on the endocrine system, in particular on the adrenal glands, which counter the threat to homeostasis by preparing the person for 'fight or flight' through the secretion of increased amounts of adrenaline, noradrenaline and cortisol (p. 25.29).

Claude Bernard was probably the first to show that physical lesions of the central nervous system could result in endocrine effects; he demonstrated that puncturing the floor of the third ventricle resulted in hyperglycaemia and glycosuria, indicating that this area of the brain was involved in regulating the blood glucose level. It has since been shown that stimulation of the hypothalamus results in an increased secretion of certain pituitary hormones

capillaries of the portal vessels in the median eminence of the hypothalamus and are then carried by these vessels to the anterior pituitary where they regulate the secretion of its hormones. In man the releasing factors are:

(1) somatotrophin (growth hormone) releasing factor (SRF),
(2) corticotrophin releasing factor (CRF),
(3) thyrotrophic hormone releasing factor (TRF),
(4) luteinizing hormone releasing factor (LRF),
(5) follicle stimulating hormone releasing factor (FRF)

The hypothalamic releasing factors stimulate the pituitary gland to secrete its various trophic hormones (table

FIG. 25.4. Feedback mechanisms in the control of endocrine secretion.

mones while hypothalamic damage produces a decreased secretion (fig. 24.35). When the concept of the hypophysial portal system of veins connecting the hypothalamus and the pituitary gland became known (p. 25.10), evidence of a specific action of the hypophysial portal blood on the anterior pituitary gland was soon obtained. Only recently have nervous mechanisms for control of the endocrine glands been investigated in detail. It is now known that the hypothalamus exerts its specific action by means of humoral agents called **releasing factors.** Many such factors have been isolated and identified as small polypeptides, and investigations suggest that distinct hypothalamic nuclei are responsible for the synthesis of the various releasing factors. They are liberated into the

25.1). These then stimulate their target endocrine organs, e.g. the thyroid and adrenal glands and the gonads, to secrete their own individual hormones. In animals the hypothalamus may produce a factor influencing the secretion of prolactin.

Hormones themselves exert an important influence on the nervous system. For example, the sex hormones have a role in establishing psychological behaviour patterns. Diseases of the endocrine glands are also often accompanied by effects on the nervous system, e.g. the psychosis which sometimes accompanies hyperfunction of the adrenal cortex (Cushing's syndrome, p. 25.37). Hormones, however, by their influence on the hypothalamus and the pituitary gland, can regulate the rate of their own secretion by negative feedback control. Increased concentration of a particular hormone in the blood inhibits secretion of the appropriate trophic hormone from the pituitary gland within minutes, whereas a fall in the blood concentration removes this inhibition so that the secretion of the trophic hormone is facilitated; thus the level of circulating cortisol is in part controlled by a feedback mechanism by which a rise in cortisol level reduces ACTH secretion and hence cortisol output, and vice versa. The site of action of this feedback control of trophic hormone secretion includes both the pituitary and the hypothalamus and possibly even higher centres. The site of the feedback action of thyroxine, for example, is probably mainly the pituitary gland, whereas in the case of the adrenal and gonadal steroids it is thought to be the hypothalamus. This reciprocal relationship between plasma hormone level and trophic hormone secretion may become overridden under conditions of stress, for example hypoglycaemia, injury or infection in which ACTH is secreted independently of the circulating level of cortisol.

The problem of pituitary regulation has been further complicated by the discovery that certain pituitary trophic hormones, e.g. luteinizing hormone (LH), may act on the hypothalamus to inhibit their own secretion. These observations have given rise to the idea of the 'short feedback loop' theory of pituitary control. The relationship between the hypothalamic nuclei, anterior pituitary function and circulating hormones is shown in fig. 25.4.

Structure of hormones

Hormones can be classified according to their chemical structure and are either polypeptides or proteins, steroids or phenol derivatives.

The protein hormones are complex polypeptides and include the hormones of the anterior lobe of the pituitary gland, parathyroid and pancreas. The structure of the protein hormones may vary from one animal to another so that they may exhibit species specificity with regard to their hormone activity. Thus growth hormone is partly species specific and primate pituitary glands are the only

source of growth hormone effective in man. An example of a typical protein hormone is ACTH, the structure of which is shown in fig. 25.5.

Ser-Tyr-Ser-Met-Glu-His-Phe-Arg-Trp-Gly-Lys-Pro-Val-
1   2   3   4   5   6   7   8   9   10 11 12 13
Gly-Lys-Lys-Arg-Arg-Pro-Val-Lys-Val-Tyr-Pro-Asp-Gly-
14 15 16 17 18 19 20 21 22 23 24 25 26
Glu-Ala-Glu-Asp-Ser-Ala-Glu(NH$_2$)-Ala-Phe-Pro-Leu-
27 28 29 30 31 32 33   34 35 36 37
Glu-Phe
38 39

FIG. 25.5. The amino acid sequence of bovine ACTH. The abbreviations are given in full on p. 11.2.

Bovine ACTH is a polypeptide containing thirty-nine amino acids and by convention the constituent amino acids are numbered starting from the end of the molecule which has the free NH$_2$ group (the N-terminal end). The corticotrophin activity is probably not a function of the whole protein but resides in the N-terminal twenty-four amino acids. The structure of ACTH varies in different species of animals and the amino acids in positions 25–33, which are present in the C-terminal part of the molecule, are involved. When ACTH of animal origin is injected into man, the animal ACTH is likely to be antigenic, and may lead to allergic reactions. The immunological and hormonal properties of ACTH reside in different parts of the molecule. In some instances, e.g., parathyroid hormone, the antibodies so produced may interfere with the action of the injected hormone so that continued administration of the hormone becomes ineffective. The synthesis of the biologically active part of the corticotrophin molecule (1–24 corticotrophin) obviates the development of any untoward immunological reactions. The hormones of the posterior lobe of the pituitary are smaller polypeptides and are apparently not themselves antigenic in man.

The steroid hormones are secreted by the adrenal cortex,

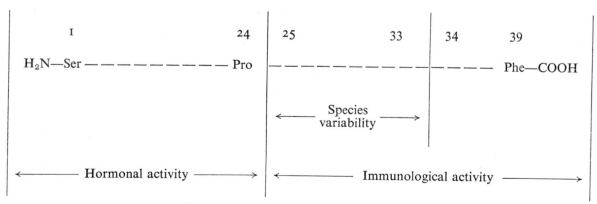

FIG. 25.6. Schematic representation of ACTH.

the testes and the ovaries. Steroids have a characteristic structure described on p. 10.5.

The hormones which are derivatives of phenol are thyroxine and adrenaline. The phenols are derived from the aromatic hydrocarbons benzene and nitrobenzene by the substitution of one or more hydroxyl groups for hydrogen atoms of the nucleus. They have distinct acidic properties.

THE PITUITARY GLAND

Anatomy

The pituitary gland is an appendage of the ventral surface of the brain and derives its name from the Latin word, *pituita*, meaning mucus, as originally it was thought to transfer mucus from the brain through the cribriform plate of the ethmoid into the nose. It is also called the **hypophysis**, from the Greek word meaning to grow under. The gland is oval in shape, weighing about 500 mg, although it gets smaller with advancing age. It lies in the base of the skull in a depression of the sphenoid bone called the hypophysial fossa or sella turcica (fig. 25.7).

The sella turcica is immediately behind the superior part of the sphenoidal air sinuses so that its floor forms part of the roof of each sinus. It is bounded laterally by the cavernous sinuses and the structures which they contain

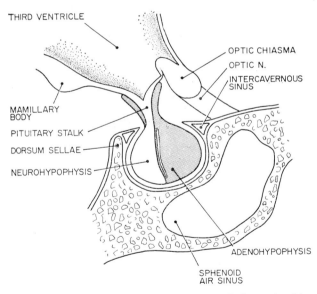

FIG. 25.7. A mid sagittal section of the pituitary gland in its fossa.

(fig. 21.6). The posterior boundary of the hypophysial fossa is a plate of bone forming the dorsum sellae (p. 21.4).

The arachnoid and pia mater blend with the capsule of the pituitary gland and so cannot be identified as separate layers in the fossa. Above, the gland is covered by a fold

of dura mater, the diaphragma sellae, which thus forms the roof of the hypophysial fossa. It is pierced by the **infundibulum** which is the stalk connecting the pituitary gland to the brain. Above the diaphragma sellae is the

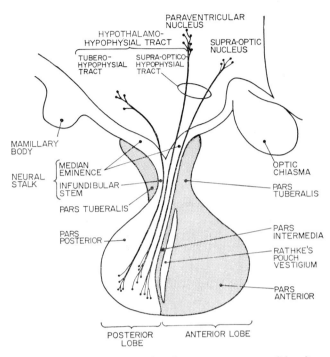

FIG. 25.8. Diagram showing the component parts of the pituitary gland and its connections with the nervous system.

hypothalamus and the third ventricle and slightly anteriorly is the optic chiasma. This proximity of the hypophysis to the optic pathways is of importance should the gland enlarge.

The pituitary gland consists of four different parts (fig. 25.8).

(1) **Pars posterior** or **neurohypophysis** is an outgrowth of the brain to which it is attached by the infundibulum.

(2) **Pars anterior** is the main part of the organ and is glandular in structure.

(3) **Pars intermedia** is rudimentary in man but is large in some vertebrates. It lies behind the pars anterior, separated from it by a small cleft, the remnant of Rathke's pouch.

(4) **Pars tuberalis** is an extension of pars anterior and encloses the infundibulum. It is also rudimentary in man and has no functional significance.

The **adenohypophysis** consists of the pars anterior, tuberalis and intermedia.

EMBRYOLOGY

The anterior lobe of the pituitary gland is derived from the ectoderm of the primitive mouth or stomatodeum, and the posterior lobe is derived from the neuroectoderm of the floor of the forebrain.

In the roof of the stomatodeum, a diverticulum forms which remains in contact with the under surface of the

(a)

(b)

(c)

FIG. 25.9. The development of the pituitary gland.

brain (fig. 25.9a). The surrounding mesoderm then constricts this diverticulum, which is also known as **Rathke's pouch**, cutting it off from the stomatodeum (fig. 25.9b). The ectodermal cells of the isolated diverticulum eventually develop into those of the anterior lobe (fig. 25.9c).

Behind Rathke's pouch, a hollow neural outgrowth extends from the base of the brain towards the mouth. The distal end of this outgrowth becomes solid and forms the pars posterior. The proximal part of the outgrowth, which is also solid, becomes the infundibulum and is covered by two dorsal extensions of the anterior lobe, the pars tuberalis.

The cleft separating the pars intermedia from pars

anterior is the remains of the original cavity of the stomatodeal diverticulum.

BLOOD SUPPLY

The internal carotid artery through its branches, the superior and inferior hypophysial arteries, supplies blood to the pituitary gland. The hypophysial arteries anastomose with each other on the surface of the adenohypophysis which is, therefore, richly vascularized (fig. 25.10).

The pituitary stalk or infundibulum is also supplied by a primary capillary plexus of the **hypophysial portal system**, as it is drained by a number of portal veins that lie on the anterior surface of the pituitary stalk. These veins are called the long and short portal veins. The long veins originate in the upper pituitary stalk and median eminence of the hypothalamus, and the short portal veins originate in the lower pituitary stalk a few millimetres below the diaphragma sellae. They penetrate the adenohypophysis and form a secondary sinusoidal plexus. The importance of this system in the

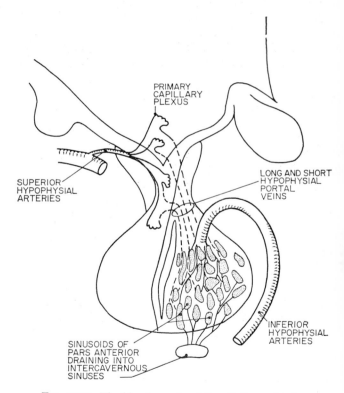

FIG. 25.10. The blood supply of the pituitary gland.

hypothalamic control of the anterior pituitary has already been referred to (p. 25.7).

The venous drainage of the pituitary consists of small efferent veins which drain into intercavernous sinuses in the dura mater surrounding the gland.

PLATE 25.1. Histology of the endocrine system.

(a) Pars anterior showing three types of secretory cell (1) basophil, purple; (2) oxyphil, orange; (3) chromophobe, grey-blue. Human, Slidder's Orange-G acid fuchsin (× 320).

(c) Thyroid. Human, haem & eosin (× 120).

(e) Parathyroid showing many chief cells, some enlarged and vacuolated, and a few oxyphil cells (arrow). Human, haem & eosin (× 240).

(b) Adrenal cortex and medulla showing collagenous capsule (1), zona glomerulosa (2), pale cells of the zona fasciculata (3), eosinophil cells of zona reticularis (4) and medulla (5). Human, haem & eosin (× 56).

(d) Thyroid showing groups of parafollicular cells (P), Human, haem & eosin (× 480).

(f) Islet of Langerhans from the pancreas. Blue β cells are numerous, reddish α cells are less conspicuous (arrows). The rich vascularity is demonstrated. Human, Gomori (× 280).

NERVE SUPPLY

Although nervous influences affect the function of the anterior pituitary gland, it has no direct nervous innervation. The neurohypophysis, however, has a well-defined nerve supply called the hypothalamo–hypophysial tract (fig. 25.8). This consists of two parts, the supra-optico–hypophysial tract and the tubero–hypophysial tract. The former arises from the supra-optic and para-ventricular nuclei of the hypothalamus and runs in the anterior wall of the infundibulum to end in the neuro-hypophysis. The tubero–hypophysial tract arises from the nuclei in the posterior hypothalamus and descends to the neurohypophysis in the posterior wall of the stalk. The hypothalamo–hypophysial tract is situated centrally in the neural stalk, being separated from the pars tuberalis by a zone relatively free of nerve elements. A few nerve fibres from this tract may enter the pars intermedia or the pars tuberalis but it is questionable whether any enter the pars anterior.

Sympathetic nerve fibres enter the pituitary gland from the perivascular plexuses which surround the gland. They are very few in number and probably have a vaso-motor function.

MICROSCOPIC STRUCTURE

Pars anterior

The glandular cells are arranged in columns, separated from each other by sinusoids. By means of haematoxylin and eosin stains, the cells can be divided according to whether they take up or reject the stain into two main types, (1) chromophil cells and (2) chromophobe cells.

The chromophil cells are large and contain granules which stain well. They can be subdivided further according to their staining reactions into two different types of cell, (1) acidophil cells or α cells and (2) basophil cells or β cells. The acidophil cells or eosinophils are so called because they stain red with eosin and have an affinity for other acid dyes. The basophil cells stain blue with haematoxylin and have an affinity for other basic dyes (plate 25.1a, facing p. 25.10).

The chromophobe cells are smaller, do not contain granules and stain very faintly. They are thought to be degranulated forms of the chromophil cells and are arbitrarily subdivided according to size. They are regarded as resting forms of the secreting chromophil cells.

With the use of more specialized staining techniques, the chromophil cells of the anterior pituitary have been divided into a greater variety of cell types These are designated α, β1, β2, δ1 and δ2. The α cells are the conventional eosinophil cells. The β1 cell is a large poly-hedral cell, usually heavily granulated, the granules being intensely PAS positive. The granules of the β2 cells have a strong affinity for the dye aldehyde thionin, staining a blue-black colour; they are fine and tend to aggregate irregularly in parts of the cell, giving a variable

staining effect. The δ1 cell is a small oval cell often found amongst the α cells. Its granules are stained by aldehyde thionin. The δ2 cell is also a small oval cell and, although PAS positive it is easily differentiated from the larger PAS positive β1 cell.

A functional classification of the chromophil cells based on clinical evidence is shown in table 25.2.

TABLE 25.2. Classification of the chromophil cells of the anterior pituitary gland.

Staining reaction	Function	Hormone
Acidophil or α cell	Somatotrophic	Growth Hormone
	?Lactotrophic	?Prolactin
Basophil β1	Corticotrophic	ACTH
β2	Thyrotrophic	TSH
δ1	Gonadotrophic	?LH
δ2	Gonadotrophic	?FSH

The acidophil cells almost certainly secrete growth hormone since an acidophil cell tumour of the gland results in the disease called acromegaly, known to be associated with hypersecretion of growth hormone.

The β1 cell is probably the source of ACTH, since patients with prolonged high blood levels of cortisol due either to overactivity of the adrenal gland (Cushing's syndrome) or to cortisone therapy develop a hyaline change in the β1 cells (Crooke's hyaline change). TSH is thought to be secreted by the β2 cells because marked hyperplasia of these cells has been observed in patients with myxoedema.

The δ cells are probably responsible for the secretion of the gonadotrophic hormones as they are not present in the pituitary glands of young children or during the last two trimesters of pregnancy. It is thought that the δ1 cell secretes LH and the δ2 cell FSH.

Pars posterior

The neurohypophysis consists of large branching spindle cells which resemble neuroglial cells. They are called pituicytes. Also in the posterior lobe of the gland are occasional mast cells and pigment cells as well as a rich network of nerve fibres and islets of basophil cells. These basophil cells have probably infiltrated from the adenohypophysis and are frequently found in the substance of the posterior lobe.

Pars tuberalis

This consists of a coarse network of nongranular chromophobe cells which have small pyknotic nuclei.

Pars intermedia

This is not sharply defined in man. It is the source of melanophore stimulating hormone (MSH) in amphibia and possibly in man.

Hormones of the anterior pituitary gland

Extracts of the anterior lobe contain polypeptides which are the trophic hormones secreted by the gland and are listed in table 25.1. They are all proteins or polypeptides but TSH, FSH and LH contain carbohydrate and so are glycoproteins.

SOMATOTROPHIC OR GROWTH HORMONE

In 1921, Evans and Long showed that extracts of bovine anterior pituitary gland when injected into rats caused an increase in growth. The active principle of these extracts was finally isolated in 1945 and most of the knowledge concerning GH was originally obtained using bovine GH in animals. This preparation, however, was ineffective in man due to a structural difference between bovine and human growth hormone (HGH). HGH was isolated from human pituitaries by Li and Papkoff in 1956 and produces metabolic changes similar to those of bovine growth hormone in animals.

GH is known to be secreted by the anterior lobe of the pituitary gland since removal of the lobe in animals or a failure of secretion in children retards growth; administration of extracts of the anterior lobe or preparations of GH or HGH to such animals or children improves their growth rate. GH is elaborated by the acidophil cells of the anterior lobe. Those from primates and ruminants all have molecular weights within the range 20,000–26,000 although they differ in their composition.

GH is necessary for the maintenance of the normal rate of protein synthesis in the body with a resulting increase in size of the body tissues. At the same time, the catabolism of amino acids is decreased. As a result of the positive nitrogen balance there is a decreased urinary excretion of nitrogen. This protein sparing effect is dependent on the presence of insulin and does not occur following destruction of the islet cells of the pancreas.

Growth hormone mobilizes the fat stores of the body and augments lipolysis with an increase in the plasma levels of free fatty acids. At the same time, fat synthesis is inhibited. The hormone when administered to the fasting subject is, therefore, ketogenic. This increase in the metabolism of fat depresses the respiratory quotient.

Growth hormone also has definite effects on carbohydrate metabolism. It inhibits the oxidation of carbohydrate in the tissues so that animals fed with carbohydrate develop hyperglycaemia and glycosuria, but in starving animals it induces depletion of liver glycogen. Prolonged administration of growth hormone together with carbohydrate ultimately results in the development of diabetes mellitus.

Growth hormone does not show a steady level in the plasma and is often not detectable (<1 ng/ml) but irregular bursts of secretion take place in people of all ages, when the level may rise to 60 ng/ml. On secretion its half-life in the plasma is only 25–30 min.

High concentrations are found in the umbilical vein blood of the newborn. The pattern of HGH secretion i children and in adults is influenced on an hour-to-hou basis by feeding and by energy expenditure. From obser vations in fasting subjects, the secretion of HGH tends t occur in a series of bursts at irregular intervals through out the day. Children may have three or four bursts c secretion at night but the reason for this is unknown.

A number of factors are, however, known to modif HGH secretion. These act by a feedback mechanis through the hypothalamus which controls the pituitar release of the hormone by means of the somatotrophi hormone releasing factor. Food and the consequent ris in blood sugar clear the plasma of any hormone that ma

FIG. 25.11. Plasma HGH, insulin, FFA and blood glucose for 2 hours before and 7 hours following a glucose load in a 30-year-old healthy male. From Hunter, Willoughby & Strong (1968). *J. Endocrin*, **40** 297.

be present. On the other hand, hypoglycaemia readil leads to secretion. If a normal subject is given or glucose the rise and fall of blood glucose is shortly followe by a marked elevation of the plasma concentration c HGH. These effects are shown in fig. 25.11 where th plasma HGH concentrations in a 30-year-old health male have been measured for 2 hours before and 7 hour following a glucose load. The levels of free fatty acids i the plasma can be seen to follow closely the rise and fa in the plasma HGH concentration. The changes in plasm insulin are also shown and are discussed on p. 25.40.

Exercise in the fasting state also stimulates HGI secretion and fig. 25.12 shows the plasma HGH respons in six normal adults during a 12·8 km walk. In additio plasma levels of FFA and glucose and values for RQ ar shown. These observations indicate that HGH secretion is associated with the mobilization of depot fat to meet the energy requirements of exercise. Although exercise is a powerful stimulus, if the subject takes glucose immediately before and during the walk, the HGH rises are not seen.

FIG. 25.12. The effect of exercise in the postabsorptive state on the levels of HGH, FFA and glucose in the plasma and on the RQ. From Hunter, Fonseka & Passmore (1965) *Science* (*N.Y.*) **150**, 1051.

Tissue growth is not completely dependent on growth hormone, being an inherent property of the tissues which is determined genetically. However, HGH appears to be necessary to support growth at normal rates and this is achieved at least in part by making available an adequate supply of fuel in the form of fat to the body, thus ensuring that proteins are not wasted as fuel.

Clinical abnormalities of HGH secretion
The first indication that the pituitary gland was concerned

in the growth of the body came from clinical studies of **acromegaly** and **gigantism** which are associated with acidophil cell tumours (plate 25.2d, facing p. 27.18). Acromegaly is characterized by continuous hypersecretion of HGH with no physiological control of the plasma level. Excessive production of HGH leads to overgrowth of the membrane bones and soft tissues, especially of the hands, feet and face giving the patient a characteristic appearance, but all organs of the body are affected. Because of the effect of HGH on carbohydrate metabolism some of the patients develop diabetes. Gigantism is due to a similar lesion occurring in younger age groups before growth is complete. The various parts of the body grow in proportion and the afflicted patient may attain a height of between 7 and 8 ft. Frequently the tumour responsible for these disorders causes pressure on the nearby optic chiasma which leads to bitemporal hemianopia (p. 24.63).

Deficiency in the secretion alone by the pituitary of HGH is rare but when it occurs gives rise to one type of **dwarfism**. Pituitary dwarfs show no deformity or mental inferiority. They grow at a reduced rate, are always small for their age and are often sexually undeveloped (plate 25.2a, facing p. 27.18).

THE ADRENOCORTICOTROPHIC HORMONE
Ascoli and Legnani, in 1912, found that hypophysectomy in the dog resulted in atrophy of the inner layers of the adrenal cortex. This dependence of the adrenal cortex on the pituitary gland was substantiated by Smith in 1927, who demonstrated in rats that the adrenal atrophy produced by hypophysectomy could be prevented by daily pituitary implants into the animal's tissues. It then became possible to separate this adrenal stimulating agent from pituitary gland extracts and eventually to purify ACTH.

As discussed on p. 25.8, ACTH consists of a single polypeptide chain containing thirty-nine amino acid residues. It is secreted into the circulation under basal conditions in very small quantities and is also rapidly removed. Pig ACTH injected into man has a biological half life of about 5–15 min. Because of the low secretory rate and the short half-life, the plasma content of ACTH is very low, ranging between 12–55 pg/ml. There is a diurnal variation in ACTH plasma concentration which is responsible for a similar variation in the level of plasma cortisol (p. 25.31).

ACTH is necessary for the maintenance and growth of the cells of the adrenal cortex and for the regulation of their secretory activity. It stimulates the synthesis of steroids in the adrenal glands which in man results mainly in an increased secretion of cortisol as well as of corticosterone. In man, ACTH can also increase the secretion of the salt retaining hormone aldosterone but other factors are more important in the secretory control of this hormone (p. 25.36).

If animals are injected with ACTH in increasing doses,

the cells of the adrenal cortex increase progressively in size and their lipid content falls. The nuclei also enlarge and the mitochondria increase in number. In addition, the ascorbic acid concentration of the adrenal cortex, which contains the highest concentration of this vitamin of any tissue in the body, is reduced and this effect is the basis of a biological method of assay for ACTH.

ACTH may stimulate steroid excretion from the adrenal cortex by making increased amounts of 3'5'-cyclic AMP available. This makes greater quantities of glucose-6 phosphate available for the hexose-monophosphate pathway and so provides $NADPH_2$ for corticosteroid synthesis. Alternatively it may act simply by speeding up the conversion of cholesterol to pregnenolone from which the corticosteroids are formed (fig. 25.6).

ACTH also has effects remote from the adrenal glands. For example, in amphibians and reptiles it causes dispersal of melanin as does melanocyte stimulating hormone, MSH of the pars intermedia of the hypophysis. It is now known that this common property is due to the possession of a peptide sequence containing seven amino acids in both the ACTH and MSH molecules. When given in large doses to adrenalectomized animals it mobilizes fat in certain species, but the physiological significance of this is in doubt. Through its action in increasing the secretion of the adrenal steroids, ACTH can also produce a fall in the blood eosinophil count.

The effect of ACTH on the rate of secretion of adreno-corticosteroids is now the basis of the best method of biological assay. The response to a dose of ACTH is measured in hypophysectomized rats by analysis of the corticosteroid content of adrenal venous blood. Immunological methods of assay have now been established.

The factors which influence the rate of secretion of ACTH are described fully on p. 25.36. High plasma levels are found after adrenalectomy in animals and in Addison's disease in man, in which the adrenal cortex is atrophied or destroyed (p. 25.31) and are due to the reduction in the concentration of circulating cortisol stimulating the β cells of the anterior pituitary. Because of the similarity of part of the amino acid chain to MSH pigmentation of the skin commonly develops in this condition.

THYROTROPHIC HORMONE

A relationship between the pituitary gland and thyroid gland was first recognized in the nineteenth century when cretins were found to have enlarged pituitary glands at post mortem. The pituitary control of the thyroid gland was then established by the demonstration that removal of the pituitary gland in rats resulted in atrophy of the thyroid gland, which was restored to normal on administration of simple extracts of the pituitary gland. When extracts of the anterior lobe of the pituitary gland were injected into guinea-pigs, the thyroid tissue became hyper-

plastic. The active principle of these extracts was called thyrotrophic hormone (TSH) or thyrotrophin and it is responsible for the maintenance of normal thyroid function. Although TSH has not been isolated, progress towards this has been achieved.

TSH may be assayed by a biological method (p. 25.4). This, however, lacks sufficient sensitivity to detect TSH in the majority of people with normal thyroid function. TSH can be convincingly detected by bioassay only in the serum of patients with primary hypothyroidism and not in hyperthyroidism. Recently immunoassay procedures for TSH have been reported sufficiently sensitive to measure normal circulating levels in man. These techniques have confirmed that the plasma TSH level is elevated in primary hypothyroidism and have shown it to be absent or reduced in hyperthyroidism.

Thyrotrophic hormone activity in the plasma appears to be located with the γ-globulin fraction of the serum proteins. At one time it was thought that the thyroid gland itself might inactivate TSH but more recently it has been shown that the kidneys may play a role in its excretion. Although the biological half-life of TSH in the plasma is about 10 min, the maximum effect on iodine uptake by the thyroid gland is apparent in 12–18 hours.

The injection of TSH or extracts of the pituitary gland into the guinea-pig increases the weight of the thyroid gland. The follicles (p. 25.17) are reduced in size due to the absorption of colloid and hypertrophy of the acinar cells which assume a columnar appearance. This increase in activity of the gland is accompanied by increased secretion of thyroid hormones. Constant stimulation of the guinea-pig's thyroid gland by injection of TSH results eventually in hyperthyroidism. There is evidence that the first step in the action of TSH is to become bound to a site on the plasma membrane of the thyroid acinar cell. Once this is achieved it stimulates the oxidation of glucose and increases the RNA content of the gland and the rate of purine and nucleotide synthesis. These biochemical and morphological changes may be due to a common primary event mediated by 3'5'-cyclic AMP.

As discussed on p. 25.7, TSH secretion by the pituitary gland is thought to be controlled by the hypothalamus through TRF. In conscious rabbits stimulation through electrodes implanted in the hypothalamus in the region of the supraoptico-hypophysial tract increases thyroid secretion and this is due to an increase in TSH secretion. TRF was postulated to explain these findings and in 1965 this factor was isolated from sheep. Administration of purified TRF to rats increases the weight of the thyroid gland and its rate of iodine uptake, while section of the pituitary stalk and electrolytic lesions in the hypothalamus are followed by depressed thyroid function.

The thyroid gland influences the pituitary secretion of

SH by a negative feedback mechanism. For example, SH secretion can be depressed by the administration of thyroid hormone and is stimulated in conditions where thyroid hormone synthesis is impaired, e.g. in iodine deficiency or when congenital biochemical defects of the gland result in a compensatory hypertrophy of the gland commonly called a goitre. The site of action of the feedback mechanism can be either the pituitary gland or the hypothalamus as it has been shown in the rabbit that the pituitary gland, freed of hypothalamic control by pituitary stalk section, maintains a physiologically significant level of TSH secretion which is below the normal basal level but which can be either decreased or increased by thyroxine (fig. 25.4).

THE GONADOTROPHIC HORMONES

In 1911, Harvey Cushing demonstrated from his observations on the effects of hypophysectomy in the dog that the gonads were dependent on the pituitary gland. It was later shown in hypophysectomized rats that the gonadal atrophy which occurred could be prevented by repeated implantation of pituitary tissue. Extracts of the pituitary gland were then found to have a similar effect on gonadal function and the hormone responsible for this effect, the gonadotrophic hormone, was detected in such extracts by Smith and by Zondek and Aschheim. In 1931, two active fractions in the crude anterior pituitary extracts were found, one having an action mainly on the growth of the ovarian follicle, and called the follicle stimulating hormone (FSH), and the other acting on the corpus luteum, and known as luteinizing hormone (LH). As LH was observed also to stimulate the interstitial cells of the testis, it is alternatively called the interstitial cell stimulating hormone (ICSH).

The physiological actions of the gonadotrophic hormones have been studied mainly in rodents. Biologically pure preparations of these hormones are not yet available, so that preparations of FSH, for example are usually contaminated by LH. For these reasons, and as both hormones have a synergistic action on the gonads, it is difficult to elucidate their precise effects. Despite these difficulties, however, much is known concerning the individual hormones. The main effects of these hormones and the control of their secretion are described in chap. 37.

PROLACTIN

This hormone, which is also called the lactogenic hormone, is essential for the development of the mammary gland during pregnancy and the production of milk by the gland following parturition (p. 37.52). It does this in conjunction with oestrogens, progestagens, the adrenocortical steroids, thyroid hormone and growth hormone which are known to influence the development of the mammary alveoli and ducts during pregnancy. Prolactin is also called the luteotrophic hormone because of its ability to maintain the corpus luteum. Although this luteotrophic action is present in animals, there is no evidence to indicate that prolactin has a similar activity in man. Indeed there is some doubt in man as to whether prolactin exists as a definite hormone and it is possible that the prolactin activity of the human pituitary gland may be due to growth hormone. For example, it is known that HGH preparations are active in biological tests for mammotrophic, lactogenic and luteotrophic activity in experimental animals. In animals, however, prolactin and growth hormone exist as separate entities.

Prolactin can be assayed biologically by making use of its property of stimulating the growth and secretion of the 'crop sacs' of the pigeon or by its mammotrophic effect on the rabbit. More detailed information of the role of prolactin will follow the use of recently developed immunoassay techniques.

PANHYPOPITUITARISM

Panhypopituitarism arises when the anterior pituitary is wholly or largely destroyed by disease. Such patients have a lowered metabolism due to failure of TSH secretion, and suffer from the consequences of adrenocortical insufficiency from lack of ACTH and so are unable to withstand any form of stress. They are sensitive to the action of insulin and develop hypoglycaemia on fasting. If the disease occurs before puberty they fail to develop sexually from lack of FSH and LH. If it develops after puberty menstruation ceases, the sex glands atrophy and pregnancy and milk production become impossible. When the disease is severe there is muscle wasting, hypothermia and somnolence. Most of these features may be dramatically reversed by appropriate hormone treatment.

Hormones of the neurohypophysis and posterior lobe of the pituitary gland

The neurohypophysis is a point of contact between neurological and hormonal control mechanisms. Two hormones, **vasopressin**, the antidiuretic hormone (ADH), and **oxytocin**, are synthesized in the perikaryon of nerve cells composing the supraoptic and paraventricular nuclei of the hypothalamus. The hormones, probably in combination with a polypeptide carrier, pass down the axons of the supraopticohypophysial tract in the pituitary stalk, within which they can be seen histologically as granular particles. In this way, they reach the posterior lobe where they are stored and from which they are released into the blood stream. The rate of their release is controlled by nervous impulses which originate, like the hormones, in the hypothalamus and which pass down the same axons in response to a variety of stimuli. Thus the nerve fibres of the pituitary stalk possess the dual function of hormone transport and secretomotor activity, though the final pathway of transport of the hormones to their target organs is by way of the blood stream. The neurological and humoral components of biological control are here indissolubly interwoven and the neuro-hypophysis may be regarded as an entity which includes the supraoptic and paraventricular nuclei of the hypothalamus, the nerve fibres of the pituitary stalk and the posterior lobe of the pituitary gland itself.

Vasopressin and oxytocin have been isolated, characterized and synthesized. Both are octapeptides and differ in only two amino acid residues:

```
Gly(NH₂)              Gly(NH₂)
   |                     |
Arg                   Leu
   |                     |
Pro                   Pro
   |                     |
Cys—Asp(NH₂)          Cys—Asp(NH₂)
 |    |                 |    |
 S   Glu(NH₂)          S    Glu(NH₂)
 |    |                 |    |
 S   Phe               S    Ile
 |    |                 |    |
Cys—Tyr               Cys—Tyr
  Vasopressin            Oxytocin
```

The structural similarity between the two hormones is matched, to some extent, by overlap of biological activity, and in the discussion of their effects this point must be borne in mind. The situation is further complicated by the fact that the two hormones appear to be liberated from the posterior lobe of the pituitary simultaneously, in response to stimuli which would be expected teleologically to give rise to secretion of only one of them. It is of interest that some non-mammalian vertebrates produce one posterior pituitary principle only, to which the name vasotocin has been given. This hormone has the ring structure of oxytocin, the side chain of vasopressin and possesses physiological activity in mammals intermediate between the two mammalian hormones.

VASOPRESSIN

The name vasopressin was given to this hormone when it was discovered that crude posterior lobe extracts raised the blood pressure. It is now known that vasopressin raises blood pressure by direct action on smooth muscle and contractile elements in the arterioles but only when given in doses far exceeding those required to cause enhanced renal conservation of water (antidiuresis); it is most unlikely that the hormone has any important physiological role in the regulation of blood pressure, whereas it is certainly of paramount importance in the control of water excretion. The name vasopressin is, therefore, an unsatisfactory synonym for **antidiuretic hormone**, but it remains the official name for the hormone, and both names are in common use.

The mode of action of vasopressin upon the kidney is indicated by the observation that addition of the hormone to the fluid bathing the inner surface of a variety of amphibian membranes increases their permeability to water molecules and accelerates the flow of water across the membrane in response to an osmotic gradient. Similar experiments show also that the hormone increases the net transfer of sodium across the membrane, an effect associated with an increase in the oxygen consumption of the membrane but independent of the influence of the hormone upon permeability. The increased permeability to water demonstrated in these experiments is widely believed to be the basis of the antidiuretic action of the hormone on the mammalian kidney (p. 33.16).

Two main theories attempt to explain this action in molecular terms. One view is that there is an interaction between the disulphide bond of the cystine residue of vasopressin and the sulphydryl groups of the proteins of the membrane such that permeability is increased. However, analogues of vasopressin that lack a disulphide bond retain reduced antidiuretic potency which renders the theory untenable. Nevertheless, it is possible that the disulphide bond influences the affinity of the hormone for its receptor site. The other view arises from the observation that vasopressin augments the production of 3'5' cyclic AMP in the renal tubular cells, presumably by activation of adenyl cyclase. Further, 3'5'-cyclic AMP itself alters membrane permeability to water though the mechanism by which this effect is mediated remains obscure. This theory has the advantage of being in accord with currently held concepts of the mode of action of several other hormones, notably ACTH, glucagon and the catecholamines.

In the mammalian kidney, vasopressin is believed to increase the permeability of the cells of the collecting ducts so that an increased amount of water is reabsorbed under the influence of the osmotic gradient which exists between the peritubular tissue and the collecting ducts. Thus, when the neurohypophysis is destroyed, either experimentally in animals or by disease in man, the absence of vasopressin causes large volumes of dilute urine to be produced. This condition is known as **diabetes insipidus**. If vasopressin is given, water conservation is enhanced by increased water reabsorption, the urinary volume falls and there is a corresponding increase in the concentration of urinary solutes (p. 33.16).

The secretion of vasopressin is dependent upon the osmolality of the ECF. This can be demonstrated by perfusion of the internal carotid artery with hyperosmolar solutions of sodium chloride. Raising the osmolality of the plasma by 1 or 2 per cent elicits an antidiuresis which can be abolished by destruction of the neurohypophysial system. Such experiments imply the existence of osmoreceptors within the tissues supplied by the internal carotid artery, and it is probable that they are situated within the supraoptic nuclei since micro-injection of hyperosmolar olutions in this region is also an effective stimulus for the antidiuretic response.

This servomechanism results in liberation of vasopressin from the posterior lobe of the pituitary in proportion to the osmolality of the ECF; a high osmolality leads to increased release of the hormone with production of small volumes of concentrated urine, and a low osmolality inhibits vasopressin release so that a large volume of dilute urine is secreted. The capacity of this system to ensure the constancy of ECF osmolality is evident.

The plasma volume is also a critical factor and when this is reduced by acute haemorrhage, antidiuresis regularly occurs, even if the plasma osmolality is low. Thus, the maintenance of plasma volume appears to take precedence over the regulation of osmolality. The nature of the receptors responsible for this effect remains obscure but it has been shown experimentally that distension of the left atrium of the heart inhibits the release of vasopressin, suggesting that atrial stretch receptors may be concerned (p. 28.40).

Other stimuli also can influence the release of vasopressin. Alcohol, for example, produces its characteristic diuresis apparently by inhibiting the secretion of the hormone. Conversely, vasopressin release is stimulated by a number of drugs, including nicotine, morphine and ether. The activity of the two latter agents may give rise to inappropriate water retention postoperatively.

Finally, direct stimulation of the breasts or genitalia, which might be expected to lead to secretion of oxytocin, also depletes the neurohypophysial stores of vasopressin and results in an antidiuresis.

The role of oxytocin on the contractility of the uterus and on milk secretion is discussed on p. 37.49.

THE THYROID GLAND

The thyroid gland is located in front of the trachea in the neck. It effects primarily the rate of metabolism by secreting into the blood the hormones **thyroxine** (T_4) and **tri-iodothyronine** (T_3) produced from tyrosine and inorganic iodine within the epithelial cells of its follicles. A second endocrine secretion, **calcitonin**, formed in parafollicular or C cells, influences the rate of bone breakdown. The thyroid gland stores its hormones, T_4 and T_3, bound to a glycoprotein, **thyroglobulin**, outwith the follicle cell in a viscid secretion, the colloid, contained within the lumen of the follicles. Iodine required for hormone synthesis is obtained from the small amounts present in food and drink. The colloid storage may be an evolutionary adaptation which guards against periods of low iodine intake.

Anatomy

The human thyroid has two lateral lobes connected over the third to fifth tracheal rings by a broad isthmus from which may arise a small pyramidal lobe. The adult thyroid usually weighs less than 30 g but its size and shape vary with factors such as sex, age and geographic position. The gland is surrounded by a fibrous capsule from which connective tissue trabeculae invaginate the gland substance so dividing it into numerous lobules. The position and relations of the thyroid gland are given on p. 21.51 and its development is described on p. 18.29.

The gland has a rich blood supply which, in an active thyroid, may be 7 ml/g/min and so is greater than the flow through any organ except active muscle. In cretins with big goitres observed in Switzerland in the early part of this century, the inferior thyroid artery was as large as the common carotid artery. The blood supply and follicle size vary with the activity of the gland.

MICROSCOPIC STRUCTURE

The thyroid follicle is a spherical structure composed of a single layer of cuboidal epithelial cells which surround and enclose the colloid (plate 25.1c, facing p. 25.10). A basement membrane encircles the follicle and is closely related to or even indented by the rich network of capillaries surrounding it. In the resting state the nucleus of the follicular cells is central, and only an occasional small microvillus can be seen in the EM projecting from the cell cytoplasm into the colloid. Occasional lymphoid cells, nerve fibres and lymphatic vessels are found in the interfollicular spaces. A few clear cells may be seen in the epithelial wall of the follicles but not in contact with colloid. These parafollicular cells, sometimes called C cells to distinguish them from the A cells of the thyroid follicle, produce calcitonin (plate 25.1d, facing p. 25.10). They are derived from the ultimobranchial bodies. In some species, e.g. the skink (South African lizard), pigeon and chicken, these are present in the adult as distinct bodies lying alongside the trachea below the thyroid gland. Large quantities of calcitonin have been extracted from these bodies, which appear to be true endocrine glands. In man and probably in most other mammals the ultimobranchial bodies fuse with the thyroid gland, though their cells do not form true thyroid tissue. Thyroid follicles are bound together in groups of twenty to forty to form a lobule, and groups of lobules are incorporated into lobes. A single artery supplies each lobule. In an overactive gland, the follicles are small and contain little colloid surrounded by tall columnar epithelium. A resting follicle has a flattened epithelium and a large store of colloid. The ultrastructure of thyroid is considered in relation to its function on p. 25.21.

Function of the thyroid gland

The secretions of the gland, thyroxine (T_4) and tri-iodothyronine (T_3) have a stimulatory effect on metabolism and increase oxygen consumption and thereby heat production. They are essential for normal skeletal growth and development, including metamorphosis in amphibia, and for cerebral maturation and normal mental activity. These and other physiological actions of the thyroid hormones are shown in table 25.3.

TABLE 25.3. Some actions of thyroid hormones (after Tata).

Growth promotion and development	Metabolic effects

Essential for:
  growth of many mammalian tissues,
  maturation of the central nervous system,
  maturation of bone,
  amphibian metamorphosis,
  synthesis of some cell enzymes and ultra-structures.
	Increase of the resting metabolic rate
	Increase of cholesterol and fat utilization
	Increase of protein metabolism
	Increase of calcium metabolism
	
	Effect on water and ion transport

The actions of thyroid hormones are best illustrated by the study of hypothyroid and hyperthyroid states as they occur spontaneously in disease or as induced in the experimental animal.

HYPOTHYROIDISM (CRETINISM AND MYXOEDEMA)

Removal, destruction or failure of development of the thyroid gland reduce heat production due to a decrease in the metabolic rate. Oxygen consumption and carbon dioxide production may fall by up to 40 per cent and this is reflected in a subnormal body temperature, decreased respiration, slow heart rate and listless behaviour. In the newborn animal or child, growth practically ceases and such a child is known as a **cretin** (plate 25.2b, facing p. 27.18). In the tadpole metamorphosis does not occur unless the thyroid hormone is replaced. The reduced rate of bone growth produces dwarfs with immature bones and a delay in ossification, epiphyseal union and growth of cartilage. There is a delay in normal development of the reproductive system at puberty.

Thyroid deficiency in the newborn baby results in mental retardation which is permanent unless hormone therapy is begun soon after birth. In the adult hypothyroidism (plate 25.2c, facing p. 27.18) produces mental apathy, an impairment of memory, lack of concentration and increasing sluggishness and somnolence.

Primary thyroid deficiency at all ages leads to the deposition of a viscid mucinous material in the skin which becomes characteristically thick and coarse. Unlike thickening due to the accumulation of extracellular fluid (oedema) it does not pit on finger pressure and it is called myxoedema. The hair becomes coarse and dry and tends to fall out. In part due to the diminished metabolic demands the body weight begins to rise and there is a general loss of muscle tone. In cretins this leads

to a pot belly, often with an umbilical hernia. The hypothyroid person is characteristically cold, sluggish and constipated and often has a mild anaemia due to depressed marrow activity. The pulse rate is slow and the cardiac output and electrical activity of the myocardium are diminished. The levels of lipids and cholesterol rise in the blood, with an increased tendency for fatty material to be deposited in the walls of the large arteries. This may further jeopardize cardiovascular efficiency.

HYPERTHYROIDISM

Hyperfunction usually arises spontaneously, but the onset of symptoms may follow an unusual stress such as an emotional crisis or exposure to excessive heat. The gland is often enlarged and vascular. The condition is known as thyrotoxicosis, and it can be induced by feeding thyroid extract or thyroxine. Oxygen consumption and heat production may be increased up to 80 per cent of the normal level. In response to the increased heat load there is vasodilation with a decreased peripheral resistance and a compensatory increased pulse rate. There is increased cardiac output due to tachycardia but no increase in stroke volume. Disordered cardiac conduction with fibrillation of the atrial muscle is a common complication. There is systolic hypertension with a raised pulse pressure. Mood changes occur, with irritability and restless behaviour, excitability and emotional instability. Altered electrical activity is seen in electroencephalograms. There is acceleration of the passage of nerve impulses with hyperactive limb reflexes. Both absorption from and movement through the gut are accelerated and diarrhoea is often present. Characteristically the appetite is voracious. Some loss of skeletal calcium occurs with increased faecal and urinary excretion.

An increased sensitivity to the effects of circulating adrenaline and noradrenaline can be demonstrated by intravenous infusion of these substances to normal and hyperthyroid animals. The thyroid hormones potentiate the effect of sympathetic nerves on heart rate, pulse pressure, oxygen consumption, etc. The retraction of the muscles of the eyelid with pupillary dilatation commonly seen in hyperthyroidism is probably due to this sympathetic effect. The eye changes of thyrotoxicosis also include swelling and damage of the extraocular muscles with an increase in orbital content of fat and fluid which leads to protrusion of the eye (exophthalmos).

An acceleration of intermediary metabolism takes place with increased rates of utilization of carbohydrate, breakdown of liver glycogen stores and an increased rate of gluconeogenesis from fat and protein sources. While protein synthesis may actually be increased, the total body protein stores diminish with damage to muscle fibre, wasting, weakness and increased creatine excretion in urine. Fat stores are mobilized and blood cholesterol falls lue to increased biliary excretion. There is progressive weight loss and finally cardiac failure develops.

Severe hypothyroidism and hyperthyroidism lead to characteristic clinical pictures, which can often be recognized at a glance. Minor degrees of both conditions are common and are more difficult to detect. It may also be hard to decide where normal variation in thyroid function ends and disease begins.

The thyroid hormones

The hormones L-tri-iodothyronine (T$_3$) and L-thyroxine (T$_4$) are iodinated derivatives of L-tyrosine. Their chemical structure and synthesis are given on p. 25.20. Optical isomers exist, but only the L-forms are found in nature.

The hormones are stored in the colloid vesicles of the follicles of the gland bound to thyroglobulin. This is a complex glycoprotein, mol. wt. 650,000, which is synthesized in the follicular cells and secreted into the colloid vesicles. It consists of four polypeptide chains and contains about 4 per cent carbohydrate (mannose, galactose, glucosamine and sialic acid) and 100 tyrosine residues/molecule.

IODINE METABOLISM

Iodine occupies a unique position in human physiology as its only function is to take part in the synthesis of

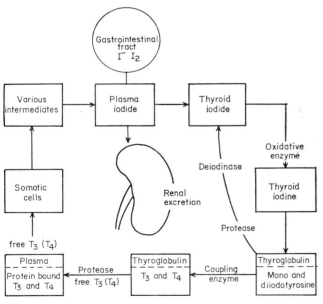

FIG. 25.13. The iodine pool. After Murray & McGirr (1964) in *The Thyroid Gland*, ed. Pitt Rivers & Trotter. London: Butterworth.

thyroid hormone. Dietary iodine is derived ultimately from the soil in the area from which the foodstuffs and drinking water come. A daily intake of 150 μg is normally sufficient to safeguard against the development of goitre.

The element enters the body in food or drink as ionic iodide, iodine, or as iodine in organic combination. Most forms are reduced during digestion and are absorbed as inorganic iodide, but some organic iodides, including thyroxine, can be absorbed from the gastrointestinal tract unchanged. Inorganic iodide is present in the blood in amounts below 1 μg/100 ml. The blood also contains T$_3$ and T$_4$, which are bound to protein. The level of protein bound iodine (PBI) in the blood is 3–8 μg/100 ml. Iodine is lost from the body chiefly through the kidney and to lesser extent in the faeces. The amount of iodine excreted daily in the urine depends on the dietary intake and is greater in an area where table salt is iodized or much fish consumed, and lower in areas where iodine deficiency is prevalent. T$_3$ and T$_4$ are secreted in the bile and because reabsorption from the small bowel is incomplete some iodine is present in the faeces. Most circulating hormone is de-iodinated and the iodine so released returns to the plasma iodide pool (fig. 25.13).

Inadequate dietary intake is the most important cause of iodine deficiency. Loss of iodine occurs with pregnancy, and rarely due to a familial absence of the de-iodinating thyroid enzyme. The human body contains 20–50 mg of iodine and about a quarter of this is in the thyroid. In the adult 60–120 μg of hormonal iodine is turned over per day, and the thyroid hormone store constitutes a 2–10 week supply.

SYNTHESIS OF THE THYROID HORMONES

T$_3$ and T$_4$ are formed by the following steps:

(1) the trapping and subsequent oxidation of inorganic iodide,

(2) the iodination of tyrosine to form monoiodotyrosine (MIT) and di-iodotyrosine (DIT).

(3) the coupling of MIT and DIT on the thyroglobulin molecule to form T$_3$ and T$_4$.

The thyroid hormones are then stored within the thyroglobulin of the colloid or released by hydrolysis and pass into the circulation. MIT and DIT do not normally escape from the follicle cell into the circulation.

The trapping of inorganic iodine

The first step is the accumulation of iodide in the thyroid by a concentrating mechanism or **iodide pump**. This active trapping produces a concentration gradient of 25:1 between the inorganic iodide within the cell and that in the plasma. The process requires energy and is presumably under enzyme control. The magnitude of the gradient depends on the quantity of stored iodine within the gland. Certain anions specifically inhibit the pump mechanism, e.g. thiocyanate and perchlorate. Although gastric mucosa, salivary and mammary gland share the ability to trap iodide, only the mammary gland can bind iodine in organic combination. The trapping of iodide by the thyroid is stimulated by TSH, and hence decreased by hypophysectomy or when TSH output is depressed by exogenous thyroid hormone.

The major site of concentration of iodine is in the colloid. Autoradiographs show that injected ^{131}I is taken up by the follicle cells within 30 sec and incorporated into colloid, where binding of the ^{131}I to protein appears to take place at the periphery of the cell. Later, within minutes, the ^{131}I is distributed uniformly throughout the colloid. Iodination of thyroglobulin probably occurs at the apical cell membrane between cytoplasm and colloid. Any iodide which has not been oxidized to iodine and bound to protein can be discharged by perchlorate which does not affect bound iodine.

globulin to form MIT. Under the influence of an enzyme iodinase, a second atom of iodine is added to form DIT. In the chick-embryo thyroid the formation of MIT can be shown to precede DIT by several hours. Subsequently coupling of MIT and DIT occurs on the surface of the thyroglobulin molecule to produce the metabolically active iodinated hormones, T_3 and T_4. One molecule of MIT and one of DIT, in the presence of a coupling enzyme give rise to one molecule of T_3, and two molecules of DIT to one of T_4. It is possible that T_3 is produced by removal of one iodine atom from T_4.

Autoradiographic techniques have shown the presence of protein-bound ^{131}I in the mouse thyroid within seconds of intravenous injection. The proportion of MIT and DIT

FIG. 25.14. The iodination of tyrosine to form T_3 and T_4.

The formation of thyroglobulin

Nadler, working in McGill University, traced the synthesis of thyroglobulin in rats by means of autoradiographs using labelled leucine, a constituent of thyroglobulin. After 30 min the label was seen to be incorporated into protein in the follicle cell, and by 36 hours it had all passed into the colloid. This suggests that follicle cells incorporate leucine from plasma in the manufacture of thyroglobulin which is subsequently secreted into the colloid. It is possible that the continuous formation and secretion of thyroglobulin by the follicle cell is the rate-limiting step in thyroid hormone formation. The formation of T_4 and T_3 occurs within the thyroglobulin molecule following the iodination of the tyrosine residues.

The iodination of tyrosine and the formation of T_3 and T_4

The inorganic iodide (I^-) trapped by the thyroid is first oxidized by hydrogen peroxide, formed by autoxidation of flavoproteins. This is catalysed by an enzyme, iodine peroxidase. Iodine (I_2) formed within the follicle cell is then added to the tyrosine component of thyro-

decreases and that of T_3 and T_4 increases with time after the administration of the tracer dose.

The steps involved in the synthesis can be demonstrated by using various antithyroid substances to interfere with the successive reactions. Perchlorate prevents iodide concentration and not only blocks the active trapping process but also discharges any inorganic iodide which is not bound to protein. Although iodine combines with free tyrosine *in vitro* the iodination of tyrosine to MIT and DIT on the thyroglobulin molecule requires the presence of an enzyme system. Thiourea compounds interfere with this step in hormone synthesis.

Further understanding of the enzyme steps involved has come with the study of the genetics of thyroid disease. Goitrous cretinism is associated classically with the iodine deficiency found in the endemic goitre areas in the world. Osler, in 1897, first drew attention to a familial tendency in rare cases in nonendemic areas. Thyroid disorders arising from genetically determined absence or deficiency of one or other of the thyroid enzymes are now well established. In a tinker family group studied by McGir nd Hutchison in Glasgow, the enzyme, dehalogenase, hich deiodinates MIT and DIT, was lacking. These dotyrosines were therefore excreted in the urine with ss of body iodine and the production of an iodine-eficiency goitre.

LTRASTRUCTURE OF THE THYROID FOLLICLE

is now possible to consider the role of the organelles in e cells of the follicle in relation to the synthesis of thyroid ormones. When the gland is overactive due to TSH

FIG. 25.15. The ultrastructure of the thyroid gland in relation to its function.

timulation in experimental animals or in human thyro-oxicosis, the characteristic feature of the stimulated cell is n increase in its height and a change in its shape from uboidal to columnar. The overactivity also leads to ypertrophy of the Golgi apparatus and increased numbers f mitochondria and of microvilli, which extend into he colloid and so increases the surface area of the cell; his facilitates transport mechanisms through the cell nembrane in either direction. Trapped iodine com-ines with the protein in thyroglobulin at the cell-olloid boundary, prior to storage or secretion of thyroid ormone. The microvilli appear to be concerned with ngulfing thyroglobulin into the cell as colloid vacuoles.

The vacuoles then fuse with lysosomes containing an acid protease enzyme system which splits the thyro-globulin by acid hydrolysis to release thyroid hormone into the basal cytoplasm of the follicular cell and thence into the blood capillary. A small amount of thyroglo-bulin escapes unaltered into the extracellular space and is removed by the lymphatics.

Protein synthesis in the cell is located in the rough-surfaced endoplasmic reticulum, where thyroglobulin formation is known to occur. In the overactive gland this area is much more prominent with increased numbers of ribosomes and many dilated cisternae. The number of mitochondria also increases in keeping with the higher rate of oxidative metabolism of the cell. Golgi bodies are thought to be the transport mechanism used by the cell to carry the manufactured thyroglobulin to the cell surface, and a carbohydrate moiety may be added to the protein molecule at this stage. At the cell surface iodine is seen to combine with the thyroglobulin which is either stored in the colloid, or hydrolysed within the cell to release thyroid hormone. The ultrastructure of thyroid cells is summarized in fig. 25.15.

THYROID HORMONE TRANSPORT

When the thyroid hormones are secreted from a follicle cell into the capillary lumen they attach themselves to chemical groups present on the surface of plasma protein molecules known as binding sites. This reaction between hormone and carrier protein is reversible and continuous so that there is always a certain amount of free thyroxine present. When a minute amount of radioiodine labelled thyroxine is added to serum and submitted to paper electrophoresis, separation of the serum proteins occurs. Thyroxine is carried by a protein migrating between the α_1 and α_2 globulins, called the **thyroxine-binding globulin (TBG)**. If the thyroxine content of serum rises above the physiological range, some spills over from TBG to other serum proteins, notably albumin. The amount of radio-activity associated with each protein fraction is a measure of its ability to bind and carry thyroxine. The biological potencies of T_4 and T_3 are therefore governed by their affinity for these protein binding sites. The lesser affinity of T_3 for globulin probably accounts for its more rapid action. This begins and ends sooner than T_4, with a smaller increase in the level of protein bound iodine but a greater inhibition of TSH secretion.

The concentration of circulating thyroid hormone is largely the result of an equilibrium achieved between thyroid hormone production and tissue utilization. However, the serum level is also dependent on changes in both free thyroxine and TBG. Thus in pregnancy a rise in protein bound iodine above the normal range occurs although thyroid function is normal. This might at first sight suggest a failure of TSH suppression, but is due to a rise in TBG which occurs in pregnancy and also after administration of oestrogen. The free thyroxine level remains normal. A fall in protein-bound iodine with normal free thyroxine may be seen when the serum globulins fall in disease. Displacement of thyroxine from its protein binding site can be caused by drugs, such as salicylates. It can be seen that it is the amount of free T_3 and T_4 (unbound fraction) circulating in the blood which determines the level of thyroid activity. This fraction also seems best able to reach the target peripheral cell and to exert its effect on cell metabolism.

THE METABOLIC FATE OF THYROID HORMONE

The daily requirement of thyroid hormone is approximately equivalent to that amount required to maintain a normal metabolic rate in the thyroidectomized animal. In the adult human this is 100–300 μg of T_4, or 40–80 μg of T_3. A small amount is not absorbed when given by mouth, and the maintenance dose by intravenous administration would be slightly less than the above. Half the thyroxine content of blood is metabolized every 6 days, and the half-life of T_3 is 2–3 days. A certain amount of conjugated thyroxine is secreted into the bile with partial reabsorption from the small intestine (enterohepatic circulation).

The ultimate fate of thyroid hormone is not clear but it is conjugated and excreted with glucuronide and sulphate, deiodinated and broken down in liver and peripheral tissues to a variety of iodinated compounds of varying activity. The iodothyronines, T_4 and T_3, are deaminated to their pyruvic acid derivatives which in turn may be decarboxylated and oxidized to acetic acid derivatives. Such derivatives may have various activities of the intact hormone in relatively different degree, and some of the effects of thyroid hormone may be produced by degradation products with specific metabolic effects.

MODE OF ACTION OF THE THYROID HORMONES

T_3 and T_4 have an effect on growth, metabolic rate, water and ion transport, nitrogen balance, sterol and fat metabolism. This makes it unlikely that they act at a single metabolic control point. While it is possible that the hormones influence these different metabolic processes by affecting different cell types in different ways, there is no evidence for this. Equally, there is little evidence that the hormones exert their effects by direct interaction with any enzyme system.

If T_3 or T_4 is given to a hypothyroid animal or patient, there is a slow return to the euthyroid state, provided the dosage is adequate and maintained. There is thus a lag phase between the start of the therapy and the first observable signs of a return to normal. The first observable change found in a treated animal is an increased synthesis of nuclear RNA. Thus the activity of the nuclear RNA polymerase, which is dependent on DNA, is increased by the hormone resulting in an increased rate of

synthesis of nuclear RNA. This newly synthesized messenger RNA (m-RNA) then leaves the nucleus and under the influence of the hormone, the rate of synthesis of ribosomal RNA (r-RNA) is increased. These events are followed in time by an increased rate of synthesis of protein by the ribosomes so that there is an increased protein content of some subcellular particles and in some cases these can be shown to have increased in size or weight (fig. 25.16). It is possible to explain the lag in the rise in the basal metabolic rate of a hypothyroid patient when given thyroid hormone on the basis that enough time must elapse to permit an effect of the hormone on the nuclear DNA for increased synthesis of m-RNA, to be followed later by increased r-RNA synthesis and yet later by increased

FIG. 25.16. Summary of data on the temporal relationships of RNA and protein synthesis in the liver of thyroidectomized rats following a single injection of 15–22 μg of triiodothyronine. Modified from Tata (1965) in *Mechanisms of Hormone Action*, ed. Karlson P. New York: Academic Press.

ribosomal protein synthesis. In this way the hormone may raise the level of the respiratory enzymes in the mitochondria and hence increase the rate of oxygen consumption by the tissues.

Thus it is likely that T_3 and T_4 exert their effect at the nuclear DNA level and, by some as yet unknown mechanism, control the transcription of information from the DNA to the m-RNA. This leads to the concept that their effect on metabolism may be exerted through the control of the amount of specific enzymes in cells by affecting the rate of enzymic synthesis. It is interesting that in the endoplasmic reticulum, RNA accumulates at a rate parallel to the rate of increase in membranous phospholipid.

CONTROL OF HORMONE SECRETION

The formation and secretion of thyroid hormones are influenced and controlled in a number of ways, but TSH of the anterior pituitary is the key factor in thyroid homeostasis. Iodine is not only a constituent of the hormone but affects gland activity by change in the concentration of plasma inorganic iodide.

After a reduction in iodine intake there is a fall in plasma iodide with a progressive diminution in the iodine content of the thyroid gland. Eventually this decrease results in diminished synthesis of T_3 and T_4 with a subsequent increase in TSH production. Thyroid iodine uptake is thus increased, which prevents a further fall in the thyroid iodine content. This stimulus returns hormone synthesis to normal. This functional overactivity of the thyroid is accompanied by an increase in size of the gland and is the mechanism responsible for the goitre in iodine deficiency; increased activity of the gland is required to maintain normal synthesis of hormone in the face of a continued shortage of iodine. A large excess of iodine on the other hand may partially suppress all aspects of thyroid activity with a reduction in gland size and vascularity by interfering with the actions of TSH and the formation of the iodothyronines.

Under physiological conditions the major factor determining the rate of thyroid secretion is TSH. The only other agent known to have a similar effect on thyroid cell activity is a long acting thyroid stimulator (LATS) found in the blood of most patients with thyrotoxicosis but not under physiological conditions. This substance, which is found in the γ-globulin fraction of the serum proteins, is distinct from TSH and not of pituitary origin. In thyrotoxicosis, blood levels of TSH are reduced or undetectable, and an increase in pituitary output of TSH is not the cause of spontaneous hyperthyroidism.

In the physiological control of thyroid hormone secretion, the actions of iodine, T_3 and T_4 and TSH are closely interrelated. The rate of peripheral disposal of T_4 is another factor to be considered. Sudden exposure to cold results in increased thyroid activity dependent on the hypothalamus and abolished by T_4. In prolonged cold exposure the rate of peripheral disposal of T_4 is increased. The thyroid gland is influenced by that fraction of thyroxine which is free in serum and is not bound to carrier protein.

Calcitonin

This is a polypeptide which can be extracted from the thyroid gland or more readily from the ultimobranchial bodies of certain species (p. 25.17). Various preparations have been reported to contain from forty-three to forty-eight amino acids and have a mol. wt. around 5000.

For a long time it was held that the hormonal control of the blood calcium was effected solely by variation in the rate of secretion of parathyroid hormone, which raises the calcium level. However, in 1962, Copp in Canada showed that in a dog given parathyroid hormone, total thyroparathyroidectomy did not lead to the expected fall in blood calcium, but to a rise. This observation led them to try the effects of extracts of parathyroid and thyroid on the blood calcium and these experiments demonstrated the presence of a hormone in the thyroid gland, which lowered blood calcium.

The calcitonin present in extracts can be assayed by measuring the fall in blood calcium which occurs after injection into a rat. An immunoassay has not yet been developed and there is little knowledge about the levels of hormone in the blood; as a consequence we do not know in detail how output is controlled.

Calcitonin probably has important roles in the maintenance of the skeleton and in calcium metabolism. These and other actions are discussed together with the roles of parathyroid hormone in the next section.

THE PARATHYROID GLANDS

Patients with goitres which are secreting excess thyroid hormone or which are so large as to be unsightly are often treated by surgical removal of a large part of the thyroid gland. At one time it was not unusual for the patient, after a few days, to complain of tingling and numbness in the face, hands and feet, associated with muscle cramps; occasionally convulsions followed, and in some cases were responsible for the death of the patient. Probably the first person to observe these complications of thyroidectomy was Raynard, a veterinary surgeon in Lyon, who reported in 1835 that dogs often died following the removal of a goitre. He wrote: 'the most meticulous examination of the cadavers has not revealed to this day any lesion to which one might be able to attribute the death.' The parathyroid glands were discovered in 1862 by Sir Richard Owens, who first dissected them in a rhinoceros. Their anatomy in man was described in 1880 by Sandstrom, to whom their discovery is usually attributed. By the beginning of this century, it was realized that the above complications of thyroidectomy were due to the removal of the parathyroid glands. Since then surgeons have been careful to preserve the glands at operation and nowadays these features are seldom seen.

Anatomy

As a rule, there are four parathyroid glands but there may be more and, very occasionally, fewer than four. They are small, yellow, oval bodies, about 5 mm long and 4 mm wide, situated on the posterior surface of the lobes of the thyroid gland. On each thyroid lobe, there are two parathyroid glands, one being placed superiorly about the middle of the lobe at the level of the lower border of the cricoid cartilage, behind the junction of the pharynx and oesophagus (fig. 25.17). The inferior gland may be situated at the lower edge of the thyroid lobe or may lie in relation to one of the inferior thyroid veins.

The development of the parathyroid glands is described on p. 18.29. The two lower glands arise in pouch 3 together with the thymus and migrate with it, crossing over the upper two glands. As they follow the same course as the thymus in development, aberrant inferior glands are sometimes found anywhere between the angle of the jaw and the anterior mediastinum.

Most parathyroid glands lie in the capsule of the thyroid gland but they may be actually embedded in the thyroid tissue. The gland cells, however, are still separated from the thyroid tissue by a connective tissue capsule. This capsule extends into the parathyroid gland, forming trabeculae which carry the vascular and nervous supply to the gland.

MICROSCOPIC STRUCTURE

There are two main cell types in the parathyroid glands, (plate 25.1e, facing p. 25.10). The **chief cells** (principal cells) are arranged in densely packed masses or columns supported by connective tissue and separated by numerous sinusoids. They are the more numerous and have a large centrally placed vesicular nucleus which stains poorly with haem & eosin and is embedded in a faintly staining cytoplasm.

FIG. 25.17. The relations of the parathyroid glands.

The chief cells are of two types, dark and pale. The dark cells secrete the hormone of the parathyroid glands. They contain much RNA, have a prominent Golgi apparatus and can be seen on EM to possess secretory granules. Their cytoplasm contains little glycogen or lipid. The pale chief cells have little RNA and a small Golgi apparatus; their cytoplasm contains much glycogen and some lipid. Pale chief cells sometimes show cytoplasmic vacuolation and are referred to as 'water-clear' (wasserhelle) cells. This term, however, is used for much larger vacuolated cells seen in tumours of the parathyroids, and it is probably better to reserve it for such pathological cells.

The **oxyphil cells** are larger than the chief cells. They have well-marked nuclei and their cytoplasm contains many eosinophilic granules. The oxyphil cells do not appear in the parathyroid glands until a few years before puberty and become prominent only after puberty. They do not secrete the hormone, and their function is unknown. They may, in fact, stem from the chief cells and be degenerate forms. However, the eosinophilic granules seen on light microscopy are mitochondria, and their large number suggests that the cells are metabolically active.

About one-half of the substance of the normal gland is made up of fat cells; when hyperplasia of the gland occurs the fat disappears, being replaced by active tissue.

BLOOD SUPPLY

The blood supply is from the inferior thyroid arteries derived from the thyrocervical trunks, which supply the lower and often the upper pair of parathyroid glands. Alternatively they may receive their blood supply from the anastomosis between the superior and inferior thyroid arteries. The blood supply to each gland is through a minute and delicate end artery which is, therefore easily damaged in operations on the thyroid gland.

NERVE SUPPLY

In contrast to their rich vascular supply, the nerve supply of the glands is very poor. Branches from the superior and recurrent laryngeal nerves innervate the glands. They accompany the blood vessels and are vaso-motor in function.

Functions of the parathyroid glands

By the start of this century, it was recognized that parathyroid insufficiency following thyroidectomy caused a fall in the serum calcium, which could be relieved by subcutaneous implantation of a normal gland in the experimental animal. The parathyroid glands, therefore became established as endocrine organs which secreted a hormone involved in the regulation of calcium metabolism. This hormone was eventually isolated by Hanson in 1923 and Collip in 1925 and called **parathyroid hormone**.

Most of our knowledge of the function of the parathyroid glands comes from studies of the effects of parathyroidectomy and the injection of parathyroid hormone. Removal of the parathyroid glands in the dog results within a few days in lethargy, anorexia, vomiting and a subnormal temperature. The muscles twitch and become stiff and spastic. The hind limbs may be fixed in extension with the head sometimes held in dorsiflexion. As muscular spasms develop, the animal becomes unsteady on its feet and falls to the ground, often with convulsions. Eventually cardiac failure or paralysis of the respiratory muscles leads to death.

Thyroidectomy is still the commonest cause of parathyroid insufficiency in man and the most usual manifestation is **tetany**. The patient develops tingling, numbness and spasms which affect particularly the forearm and hand muscles; this results in pronation with flexion of the elbow and wrist together with flexion of the metacarpophalangeal joints, the interphalangeal joints being extended and the thumb and little finger being drawn toward the palm. This appearance has been called '*main d'accoucheur*'. Carpal spasm may be induced in these patients by blowing up a sphygmomanometer cuff on the upper arm o above systolic pressure (Trousseau's sign fig. 25.18). The muscles of the larynx may also be affected by spasm giving rise to laryngeal stridor, and the abdominal muscles may be affected causing abdominal cramps. Spasm of the facial muscles can often be induced by tapping the skin over the facial nerve (Chvostek's sign).

FIG. 25.18. Trousseau's sign in a patient with tetany.

THE PARATHYROID HORMONE

The parathyroid glands appear only to secrete one hormone. This is a polypeptide, containing about eighty amino acids. There are slight differences in the sequence and number of amino acids in the hormone of different species. Tryptic digestion of the molecule shows that the physiological activity is dependent on a chain of about twenty acids.

Assay

The hormone may be assayed biologically using either the dog or rat in which the parathyroid glands have been removed. The parathyroid activity of the test preparation is measured by its ability to raise the plasma calcium concentration when injected into the animal. This form of assay, however, has the usual disadvantages associated with biological assays.

An immunoassay for bovine and human parathyroid hormone is now being developed. As yet only a few laboratories have a satisfactory technique and there is only limited information about the levels in the blood under various physiological circumstances and in disease. So rapid is progress in the immunoassay field that this statement may well be out of date before the printers can produce this book. The hormone appears to have a short half-life in the blood, where its concentration may change rapidly.

THE REGULATION OF THE PLASMA CALCIUM

The concentration of circulating calcium is controlled within narrow limits. When determined by chemical

methods, the variations in health lie between 9 and 11 mg/100 ml (4·5–5·6 mEq/l). More accurate analysis using the atomic absorption spectrometer may show that the range is even narrower. Rather more than half, 5–6 mg/100 ml, is ionized and freely diffusible. The remainder is bound to protein, mostly to albumin. It is the ionic fraction which is physiologically important and homeostatically controlled. The amount of protein-bound calcium depends on the concentration of plasma protein and is increased by a rise in pH. Under most circumstances, the amount of protein bound calcium in plasma remains fixed at from 4–5 mg/100 ml. As the determination

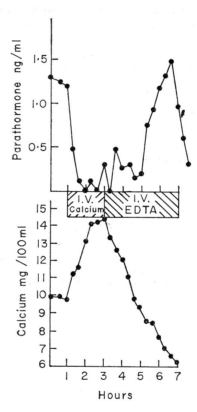

FIG. 25.19. Parathyroid hormone (parathormone) levels in the blood of a cow, determined by immunoassay, showing a fall when calcium is infused intravenously, and a sharp rise when the animal is given EDTA, a chelating agent that reduces the level of calcium in the blood. From Auerbach G.D. & Potts J.T. (1967) *Amer. J. med.,* **47,** 1.

of the ionic calcium in plasma is time-consuming, it is usual in both physiological and clinical studies to measure only the total plasma calcium. The calcium in the CSF, which is virtually free of protein, is almost all in the ionic form.

The ionic calcium in the plasma is regulated by the actions of parathyroid hormone, which raises it, and by calcitonin which lowers it. Figs. 25.19 and 20 summarize experiments which illustrate the switching off of parathyroid hormone and switching on of calcitonin in response to rises in the blood calcium level and the switching on of parathormone secretion in response to a fall.

Parathyroid hormone raises the blood calcium in three ways. Firstly and most important, is a direct action on bone, mobilizing calcium. Secondly, it has a direct effect on the kidneys, increasing tubular reabsorption of calcium. Thirdly, the hormone promotes the absorption of calcium from the intestine; in this respect the action of the hormone is much less important than vitamin D and plays only a small part in calcium homeostasis. These three actions of parathyroid hormone are complementary, but appear independent of each other. Calcitonin lowers the blood calcium by a direct effect on bone, inhibiting its breakdown. Effects on the kidney and on intestinal absorption of calcium have not been established.

FIG. 25.20. The effect on the plasma calcium concentration of a pig with perfusion of the thyroid gland *in situ* with a solution containing a slightly higher concentration of calcium than was present in the plasma. In the pig, the thyroid gland contains no parathyroid tissue and the fall in the level of plasma calcium in the general circulation must be due to a hormone secreted by the thyroid gland, presumably calcitonin. From Care A.D. (1965) *Nature (Lond.)*, **205**, 1289.

The secretions of parathyroid hormone and calcitonin are not controlled by trophic hormones of the pituitary but regulated by the calcium ion concentration of the extracellular fluid. When the calcium ion concentration is low, the parathyroid gland is stimulated to release its hormone. When the calcium ion concentration is raised, calcitonin is secreted. A clinical example is the enlargement of the parathyroid glands in response to a low plasma calcium found in severe rickets.

THE EFFECT OF PARATHYROID HORMONE AND CALCITONIN ON TISSUES

Effects on bone

The direct action of parathyroid hormone on bone has been demonstrated by transplanting a piece of bone together with parathyroid tissue into the brain of a mouse, the two tissues being placed adjacent to each other. After 2 weeks, the bone showed the histological changes of resorption. Similar evidence has been obtained from tissue culture experiments using bone and parathyroid tissue.

The means by which the parathyroid hormone mobilizes bone calcium is not completely understood. It may increase the amount of citrate and other organic acids at the surface of bone crystal. These produce a local increase in the solubility of the bone, removing calcium and liberating it into the circulation. It has been shown in the dog that bone is an important site of citrate formation which can be increased by administering parathyroid hormone. If a hole is drilled into the dog's femur so that blood can be obtained directly from the cancellous bone, the administration of parathyroid hormone increases the level of citrate in cancellous blood much more than in arterial blood.

The parathyroid hormone may also promote the breakdown of the bone matrix, thus liberating calcium and phosphate. It may do this by inducing depolymerization of polysaccharides in the matrix, these changes heralding the actual resorption of mineral from the bone.

The hormone also causes proliferation of osteoclasts which accompanies the resorptive process and removes the collagen framework which no longer has any bone tissue to support.

Calcitonin inhibits the breakdown of bone, perhaps by stabilizing the protein matrix. After injection of calcitonin into rats, there is a marked reduction in the urinary output of hydroxyproline, an amino acid largely derived from bone collagen.

Effects on the kidney

When the hormone is given to a parathyroidectomized animal, the first effects are on the kidney. Within a few minutes the urinary output of calcium and hydrogen ion is diminished and that of phosphorus and potassium increased. This is due to changes in renal tubular absorption. Later as calcium is mobilized from the bone and the plasma calcium rises, calcium excretion increases.

In man overactivity of the parathyroid glands often increases the urinary output of calcium up to 350–500 mg/day. The urine cannot easily hold such large amounts of calcium in solution and urinary stones tend to form. Overactivity of the parathyroid glands is the cause of a small proportion of the urinary stones arising in man. It is also sometimes associated with decalcification of the skeleton, which, if the disease is not treated, leads to gross keletal deformity. Calcitonin has an effect similar to that of parathyroid hormone in inducing increased urinary execretion of phosphate.

Miscellaneous effects

The effect of parathyroid hormone on alimentary absorption of calcium is slight and can be demonstrated only in the presence of large amounts of vitamin D. The hormone also effects magnesium metabolism and in patients who have parathyroid insufficiency the plasma magnesium level may be low and renal conservation diminished. Calcitonin when injected into man does not alter the plasma magnesium level.

The ionic changes in the extracellular fluid following secretion of the hormones may cause a variety of effects. A low plasma calcium increases the excitability of nerves and muscles, giving rise to tetany. A raised plasma calcium can result in cardiac arrhythmias.

Effects at the molecular level

Little is known of the action of parathyroid hormone at molecular level. It is possible, however, by using metabolic inhibitors, e.g. actinomycin, to block the effect of the hormone on bone without altering the renal response. This suggests that the action of the hormone on the kidney, which is immediate, differs from its action on bone which includes cellular proliferation of osteoclasts. The addition of the hormone to isolated mitochondria results in ionic effects similar to the action in the renal tubules, i.e. there is an increased uptake of phosphate, magnesium and potassium with release of hydrogen and calcium ions. As in the case of the effect on calcium absorption by the gut, the presence of vitamin D is necessary for the action of parathyroid hormone on calcium in the mitochondria, and is associated with an increase in oxygen consumption. It is postulated that the hormone, by influencing the uptake and release of ions in the mitochondria, induces changes in cellular metabolism which alter the rate of nucleic acid and protein synthesis and thus, in turn, the activity and number of bone osteoclasts.

THE ADRENAL GLANDS

In man, the two adrenal glands lie in the retroperitoneal space closely applied to the upper aspects of the kidneys. Each weighs about 5 g and is a composite structure comprising a central medulla and a surrounding cortex. In the lower vertebrates, however, these two components are anatomically separate and despite their intimate relationship in mammals they are totally distinct in developmental origin and structure. In common with the gonads, the adrenal cortex is developed from cells of the coelomic mesothelium. Two masses of these cells form on the medial side of each developing mesonephros (p. 34.1). The first

mass gives rise to the foetal cortex and the second, which envelopes the first, forms the true or adult cortex.

Meanwhile, ectodermal cells derived from the neural crest migrate to form the coeliac sympathetic ganglion and some, migrating still further, invade the developing cortical tissue to form the adrenal medulla.

Anatomy

The two glands differ in shape and relations (fig. 25.21). The right adrenal is pyramidal in shape with a concave base applied to the surface of the right kidney, whereas the gland on the left is flatter and semilunar in shape. Anteriorly the left adrenal is related to the stomach, from which it is separated by the lesser sac of the peritoneum. The right adrenal is related on its anteromedial surface to

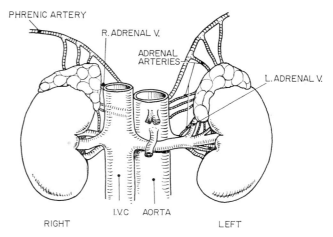

FIG. 25.21. The position and blood supply of the adrenal (suprarenal) glands.

the inferior vena cava and on its anterior surface to the liver. The upper portions of the posterior aspects of both glands are related to the diaphragm. The detailed relations of the adrenal glands vary somewhat according to the exact position of the kidneys but the glands are firmly attached to the posterior abdominal wall within their own fascial compartment so that, in the event of congenital malposition of the kidneys, the adrenals still occupy their normal situation within the abdomen, a fact of some importance in relation to the surgery of the glands.

Accessory glands are often found in the neighbourhood of the main gland. Usually they contain both cortical and medullary tissue.

MICROSCOPIC STRUCTURE (fig. 25.22 and plate 25.1 facing p. 25.10)

The whole gland is enclosed within a fibrous capsule from which trabeculae pass inwards to support the parenchyma. In section, the distinction between the dark red central medulla and the surrounding pale yellow cortex is clear.

The cortex is composed of large polyhedral cells rich in lipids, particularly cholesterol and a yellow pigment from which the cortex gets its characteristic colour. These cells are arranged in three zones. The outer **zona glomerulosa** (fig. 25.22a), lies immediately under the capsule and consists of cells arranged in irregular clusters. The intermediate **zona fasciculata,** which forms the main mass of

NAKED EYE

LOW POWER

(a)

(b)

(c)

(d)

(e)

HIGH POWER

FIG. 25.22. Various magnifications of human adrenal glands in section. In the section of highest magnification the cells of the zona glomerulosa (a) have small dark-staining nuclei and cytoplasm containing scanty lipid; the cells of the zona fasciculata (b) are filled with large globules of lipid, extracted during preparation for histological examination resulting in the formation of vacuoles (clear cells); at the border between zona fasiculata and zona reticularis (c) the cells are laden with lipid; the cells of the zona reticularis (d) are poor in lipid (compact cells); (e) medulla. After Ham.

the cortex, consists of cells arranged in long radial columns while the **zona reticularis** consists of branching and anastomosing columns of cells (plate 25.1b, facing p. 25.10).

The medulla is composed of a spongework of cell columns. The cells are known as **chromaffin cells** or **phaeochromocytes** since they possess intracellular granules which stain specifically with chrome salts. In addition, small groups of nerve cells are scattered throughout the medulla. Separate aggregations of chromaffin cells (paraganglia) are found retroperitoneally and also around various organs of the body. They are probably of little physiological importance.

BLOOD SUPPLY

The glands are highly vascular, each receiving three groups of arteries, the superior, middle and inferior adrenal arteries which are branches of the inferior phrenic artery, the aorta and the renal artery respectively. These vessels form a plexus under the capsule from which branches pass into sinusoids, running between the cortical and medullary cell columns. Each gland is drained by a single adrenal vein; the left one joins the left renal vein and the right one the inferior vena cava. Numerous lymphatics drain the lymph to the aortic lymph nodes.

NERVE SUPPLY

The adrenal medulla can properly be regarded as a specialized ganglion of the sympathetic nervous system and the secretory cells are richly innervated by cholinergic preganglionic sympathetic nerve fibres derived from the lower thoracic segments of the spinal cord. No nerve supply to the cortex has been demonstrated.

THE ADRENAL MEDULLA

In 1894, Oliver and Schafer prepared aqueous extracts of the adrenal medulla and these administered intravenously caused a striking rise in the blood pressure of animals. Later Abel isolated **adrenaline** as a crystalline compound from the medulla and for many years this was regarded as the only medullary hormone. Not until 1949 was the second hormone, **noradrenaline,** demonstrated and it was recognized that this hormone acts also as the transmitter substance at sympathetic postganglionic nerve endings (p. 14.28). The two hormones are both amino derivatives of the diphenol, catechol, and are frequently referred to collectively as the **catecholamines,** the normal ratio of adrenaline to noradrenaline being four to one. They are synthesized from phenylalanine and tyrosine by pathways described on p. 11.25. Two types of medullary cell exist, one producing adrenaline, the other noradrenaline.

Both hormones are stored in an inactive form in the chromaffin granules of the medullary cells, from which hey may be liberated *in vitro* by lysis with hypotonic solutions. *In vivo*, release of catecholamines from the medulla is controlled exclusively by nervous impulses arising in the hypothalamus and conducted via preganglionic sympathetic nerve fibres. Thus, section of the nerve supply to one medulla, followed by a stimulus normally producing catecholamine release, results in selective depletion of the hormones of the gland with the intact nerve supply.

Release of catecholamines from the medulla follows such stimuli as pain, emotional disturbance, hypotension, asphyxia, hypoglycaemia, exposure to severe cold and muscular exertion. These stimuli are sometimes described as 'stress situations' (p. 25.34). The normal rate of hormone release is probably of the order of 0·02μg/kg of body weight/min and this rate may be increased one hundred-fold. However, the adrenal medullae are in no way essential to life and patients may survive in good health after total bilateral adrenalectomy, if adequate substitution therapy is provided for adrenocortical function.

The adrenal medulla shares its origin with the cells of the sympathetic ganglia and of the central nervous system. Predictably therefore, the same biosynthetic pathway exists also in brain and in the cells of the peripheral sympathetic nervous system, with one important difference; the final step, i.e. the N-methylation which results in the conversion of noradrenaline to adrenaline, does not occur in nervous tissue so that synthesis ceases at the stage of noradrenaline. This limitation exists also in the foetal adrenal medulla and in a proportion of adult medullary cells. Adrenaline production may, therefore, be regarded as a sophisticated enzymic function of a restricted number of the medullary cells. The basic unity of the sympathetic nervous system and the adrenal medullae is illustrated in fig. 25.23.

Activation of preganglionic sympathetic nerve fibres results in the liberation of acetylcholine from the fibre terminals (p. 14.28). In sympathetic ganglia, this results in the transmission of an impulse along the postganglionic neurone and the release of noradrenaline at the target organ; in the case of the adrenal medulla, a mixture of adrenaline and noradrenaline is released from the chromaffin cells directly into the blood stream. The liberation of catecholamines from the medulla is accompanied by generalized sympathetic effects in all tissues of the body provided with catecholamine receptor sites. These effects are superimposed upon those exerted by the simultaneous local release of noradrenaline from postganglionic nerve fibre terminals. The medulla may thus be regarded as an endocrine luxury, available to reinforce, and to some extent modify, the effects of sympathetic nervous activity.

Actions of the catecholamines

The physiological functions of the catecholamines were summarized by Cannon in 1916 when he described the sympathetic nervous system as serving to prepare the organism for 'fright, flight or fight'. This preparation to meet the needs of stress is made by the combined effects of the catecholamines on receptors in the target organs. These receptors are divided into two groups: the **α receptors,** serving mainly excitatory functions such as vasoconstriction, and the **β receptors,** serving predominantly inhibitory functions such as vasodilation and bronchodilation, together with one excitatory function, stimulation of the heart with resultant cardioacceleration. The nature of these receptors is not understood, but they are not dependent upon the integrity of the sympathetic nervous system; denervated tissues, indeed, demonstrate enhanced responses to the action of the hormones (Cannon's law). The usefulness and significance of the

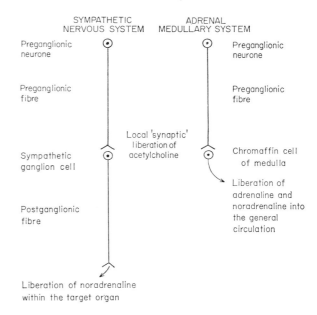

FIG. 25.23. Comparison of the sympathetic nervous system and adrenal medullary system.

receptor concept is best considered in relation to the action of drugs and is not discussed further here.

The effects of adrenaline and noradrenaline differ both qualitatively and quantitatively. In addition, different stimuli may result in preferential secretion of one or other hormone from the medulla so that the resulting response can be expected to vary.

HEART AND CIRCULATION

Adrenaline, given intravenously at physiological rates, produces a marked tachycardia with an increase in cardiac output and an overall fall in peripheral vascular resistance. As a result the systolic blood pressure rises while the diastolic pressure falls, the mean blood pressure remaining largely unchanged. The effect of adrenaline upon vascular resistance varies in different parts of the vascular bed. Thus, in the skin and splanchnic area, adrenaline constricts the vessels but dilates those in the skeletal muscle and, possibly, in the myocardium. All of these effects when taken together produce a lowered peripheral resistance, though individually the various effects lead to a redistribution of blood to those tissues whose requirements are likely to be high in situations of stress.

Noradrenaline stimulates the heart less than does adrenaline but greatly increases total peripheral vascular resistance. This in turn leads to a marked rise in systolic, diastolic and mean blood pressures which, by means of the carotid sinus reflex, results in a fall in cardiac output.

RESPIRATORY SYSTEM

Both adrenaline and noradrenaline increase the rate and depth of respiration. The minute volume increases and the alveolar carbon dioxide concentration falls. These effects are probably central in origin. Both hormones also produce peripheral effects on the respiratory system, the most important being bronchodilation. In this respect adrenaline is much more active than noradrenaline.

VISCERAL SMOOTH MUSCLE

Species differ in the effects of catecholamines on the gastrointestinal tract. In general both hormones lead to relaxation of the musculature of the gut, with the exception of the sphincter fibres, which are constricted. As a result the passage of intestinal contents is slowed.

A similar effect occurs in the case of the urinary bladder, with relaxation of the bladder wall and contraction of the sphincter.

METABOLISM

The medulla has important metabolic functions, adrenaline being about eight times more powerful than noradrenaline in this respect. The effect of adrenaline upon carbohydrate metabolism is of particular interest since its biochemical basis is known. The hormone activates the enzyme adenyl cyclase and so stimulates formation of $3'5'$-cyclic AMP. In the presence of magnesium ions this activates the enzyme phosphorylase kinase which, in turn, catalyses the conversion of inactive to active phosphorylase. The active phosphorylase so formed leads to the breakdown of liver glycogen with the formation of glucose 1-phosphate (p. 9.10). This compound is then acted upon by the enzyme, phosphoglucomutase, and the resulting glucose 6-phosphate then undergoes enzymic hydrolysis with the formation of free glucose which is released into the blood stream, raising the blood sugar. Muscle glycogen is also degraded by adrenaline stimulation to glucose 1-phosphate, but in the absence of phosphatase, hydrolysis does not occur and the hexose phosphate enters the glycolytic pathway with the produc-

tion of lactic acid and free energy available for muscular work.

Adrenaline and noradrenaline also accelerate the liberation of free fatty acids from the triglyceride stores of adipose tissue. In view of the limitation of available carbohydrate stores, this supply of oxidizable substrate is of great importance, especially to the fasting animal.

SKELETAL MUSCLE

Adrenaline increases the blood supply to skeletal muscle and the quantity of hexose phosphate available to the glycolytic pathway. The hormone also increases the force of muscular contraction and delays the onset of muscular fatigue, though the mechanism for these effects is not known.

OTHER EFFECTS

Adrenaline produces pupillary dilation and activates the arrector pili muscles of the skin leading to erection of body hair. These actions have been interpreted teleologically as mechanisms to enable the animal to appear more formidable to any would-be assailant. Their importance in man, however, is small. Adrenaline also exerts marked effects upon the function of the higher centres of the central nervous system, resulting in a state of increased wakefulness associated with sensations of anxiety and apprehension.

Metabolism of the catecholamines

Both adrenaline and noradrenaline are inactivated very rapidly in the body (p. 31.34), so that their effects are transitory, except in circumstances which lead to their

FIG. 25.24. Metabolites of adrenaline and noradrenaline in urine.

ontinuing liberation from the medulla. After intravenous
nfusion of the hormones, approximately four per cent of
he dose can be recovered unchanged from the urine, the
emainder being excreted in the form of a mixture of meta-
renaline, normetadrenaline and 3 methoxy-4-hydroxy-
nandelic acid (HMMA), end products of the ortho-
nethylation and oxidative deamination of the hormones.
IMMA can be estimated in the urine and provides a
onvenient means of estimating catecholamine produc-
ion.

THE ADRENAL CORTEX

arly experiments demonstrated that bilateral removal of
ne adrenal glands leads to a disorder of function so
evere as to be incompatible with survival under normal
ircumstances, though it was discovered that the fatal
utcome could be delayed by the administration of large
mounts of sodium chloride. In the mid-nineteenth cen-
ury, a similar clinical condition was described. **Addison's
isease** is characterized by weakness and muscle wasting
·ith a low plasma sodium. There is increased urinary
odium loss which leads to a reduction in the extracellular
uid volume and a low blood pressure. The fasting blood
ugar is low. The patient is nearly always pigmented.
Jntil modern therapy was available, the patients went
ownhill slowly and died. At post mortem the adrenal
lands were found to have been destroyed. These obser-
ations stimulated efforts to obtain extracts from
drenal glands which would sustain life in adrenalec-
omized animals. In 1931, the first active extract was
repared and subsequent research has led to the identi-
cation in such preparations of almost fifty closely
elated chemical compounds belonging to the chemical
roup of steroids and known, after their tissue of origin,
s **corticosteroids.** Only a few of this large number of
ompounds have been isolated from adrenal venous blood
nd it is likely that the remainder represent precursors or
egradation products of the physiologically active
ormones. The corticosteroids have diverse physiological
unctions, including the regulation of carbohydrate,
rotein, fat, water and electrolyte metabolism, together
·ith the normal homeostatic responses to all forms of
oxious stimulus and environmental change.

The adrenal cortex also synthesizes steroid hormones
aving the properties of androgens and oestrogens but the
hysiological importance of the glands in this respect is
mall, being overshadowed by the contribution of the
onads. For this reason, adrenal androgens and oestro-
ens are not discussed further here, but in chap. 37.

The corticosteroid hormones

he structure of the complex steroid nucleus has been
escribed on p. 10.5. The conventional lettering of the
ngs and the numbering of the carbon atoms is shown

again in fig. 25.25, together with the structures of the
corticosteroid nucleus and of the two physiologically
most important corticosteroids.

The basic steroid nucleus   The corticosteroid nucleus

Cortisol

Hydroxaldehyde   Hemiacetal
Aldosterone

FIG. 25.25. The structures of the corticosteroid nucleus,
cortisol and aldosterone.

The characteristic features of the corticosteroids are
the possession of a two carbon ketol side chain at position
17, representing carbon atoms 20 and 21, a ketone group
at position 3 and a double bond between carbon atoms
4 and 5. The hormones also possess angular methyl
groups at positions 10 and 13, representing carbon atoms
18 and 19. The corticosteroids, therefore, possess twenty-
one carbon atoms in all.

Spatial isomerism occurring in the steroid nucleus is
described on p. 10.6, together with the convention that
groups added to the steroid nucleus are designated β if
they project above and α if they project below the plane of
the ring structure; β substituents are shown joined to the
ring by a full line bond and α substituents by a dotted
line.

In the adrenal cortex, the synthesis of the hormones
occurs by means of enzyme-catalysed reactions and the

stereospecificity of the enzyme systems involved ensures that the synthesis of only one of the possible isomers occurs.

In man, the physiologically important corticosteroids may, at the risk of some oversimplification, be regarded as **cortisol**, sometimes known as hydrocortisone, and **aldosterone**. **Corticosterone,** a steroid identical with cortisol with the exception that it does not possess the 17 hydroxyl group, is secreted in small amount in man but, although its physiological importance in certain

hydroxyaldehyde and hemiacetal, between which an equlibrium state exists.

Biosynthesis of the corticosteroids

The corticosteroids are synthesized by the cells of the cortex from cholesterol. A summary of the pathways involved is given in fig. 25.26. The figures alongside the reaction arrows designate the number of the carbon atom at which each hydroxylation step occurs.

FIG. 25.26. Summary of the steroid synthetic pathway.

animal species is undoubted, its significance in human physiology remains uncertain and it is not considered further here.

Cortisol possesses a β hydroxyl group at C-11 together with an α hydroxyl group at C-17. Aldosterone also possesses the 11β hydroxyl group but is unique among steroids in having, in place of the 13β methyl group, a 13β aldehyde substituent. By virtue of this unusual molecular configuration aldosterone exists in two forms,

Where appropriate, an indication of the stereospecificity is included. The final step in the synthesis of aldosterone is a dehydrogenation reaction with conversion of the C-18 alcohol to the C-18 aldehyde function.

First cholesterol is converted to pregnenolone and thence to progesterone which then undergoes sequential enzymic hydroxylation to form the various corticosteroid hormones. The central position in this scheme occupied by pregnenolone and progesterone deserves special mention. Up to this point the synthetic pathway for all steroids is identical and the relative proportions of the final products, essentially cortisol, aldosterone and the sex hormones, are determined by the relative activities of the subsequent pathways. Since the activity of the enzymes involved is genetically determined, disorders of steroid biosynthesis can occur as congenital defects.

It is also of interest that the enzymic pathways involved appear to be distributed non-uniformly within the cortex so that different hormones are synthesized within the cells of the different cortical zones. Although conflicting evidence exists, aldosterone is probably synthesized by the cells of the zona glomerulosa, whereas cortisol is produced by the compact cells of the zona reticularis. The zona fasciculata is regarded as a non-secretory zone representing a store of steroid precursors; during periods of increased cortical activity, however, the clear cells of this zone undergo conversion to compact cells, this change beginning in the cells of the zona fasciculata adjacent to the zona reticularis. Thus the cells of the zona fasciculata may be regarded as a reserve of cortisol secretory activity which can be called upon as required.

ASCORBIC ACID AND THE ADRENAL CORTEX

The ascorbic acid content of the adrenal cortex is normally high. However, natural infections in man and experimental infections in animals reduce markedly the amount present in the gland, as does severe fatigue and the injection of ACTH. All these circumstances are associated with increased cortical secretion. Hence it is natural to postulate that ascorbic acid is associated in some way with the synthesis of cortical hormones. Possibly its role may be to exercise a tonic inhibition on steroid biosynthesis, which is reversed by the action of ACTH. Thus ACTH has been shown to deplete the cortical cells of the vitamin, which can be recovered quantitatively in adrenal venous blood, before any increase in steroid production can be demonstrated. Further, *in vitro*, high concentrations of the vitamin inhibit the enzymes responsible for the 21- and 11β-hydroxylation reactions essential for cortisol synthesis.

Actions of the corticosteroid hormones

It has been the custom to recognize two broad groups of corticosteroids, the **glucocorticoids,** regarded as exercising their principal effect upon carbohydrate metabolism and the **mineralocorticoids,** chiefly influencing electrolyte metabolism; the prototypes of these two groups were regarded as cortisol and aldosterone respectively. With increasing understanding of the corticosteroids, this arbitrary distinction becomes difficult to sustain since there is overlap in biological activity. The term glucocorticoid in particular is a misnomer because cortisol

exerts perhaps its most important influences outwith the sphere of carbohydrate metabolism.

CORTISOL

Cortisol given to adrenalectomized animals or to patients with Addison's disease increases the blood glucose and the urinary excretion of nitrogen; it influences carbohydrate metabolism by increasing the formation of glucose from non-carbohydrate precursors (gluconeogenesis), by promoting hepatic glycogen deposition and, possibly, by inhibiting peripheral glucose utilization. By virtue of its gluconeogenic effect, the hormone exerts a catabolic influence upon protein metabolism and amino acids are utilized for glucose synthesis and diverted from the pathway leading to protein synthesis. Although cortisol has a catabolic effect on the overall protein metabolism of the body, it has an anabolic effect on the liver, in which the incorporation of amino acids into protein is actually increased. Cortisol also modifies fat metabolism leading to liberation of FFA from the adipose tissue depots. The effect of the hormone is, however, complex since it causes mobilization of fat from some parts of the adipose tissue and deposition of fat in others. Thus, the action of the hormone results in the net availability of fatty acids for use as an energy source while at the same time exercising control upon the distribution of fat in various parts of the body.

From this point, the inappropriate nature of the term glucocorticoid becomes evident. Cortisol exerts important effects upon water metabolism by mechanisms which remain obscure. In adrenocortical insufficiency the distribution of body water is abnormal, so that extracellular dehydration and cellular overhydration may coexist. In addition, cortisol lack results in abnormal renal excretion of water shown by an inability to excrete a water load. Both of these defects are specifically corrected by cortisol administration.

The hormone also exercises effects upon electrolyte metabolism; both independently and by its synergism with aldosterone, cortisol promotes retention of sodium and loss of potassium and hydrogen ions by the kidney. It also influences the distribution of sodium and potassium ions between cellular and extracellular fluid although it is much weaker than aldosterone in this respect.

Cortisol also plays an important role in the regulation of blood pressure. This effect is independent of alterations in electrolyte metabolism and appears to be a permissive action of the hormone. Thus, in adrenocortical insufficiency a state of relative refractoriness to the pressor effects of noradrenaline leads to hypotension, which is particularly marked on the assumption of the erect position. This abnormality is specifically corrected by the administration of cortisol. The corticosteroids may also contribute to the maintenance of blood pressure by a direct action upon the myocardium since it has been demonstrated experimentally that very small amounts of the hormones can increase left ventricular work.

The hormone also exerts an influence upon erythropoiesis and the anaemia of adrenocortical insufficiency is corrected by cortisol. Conversely, excessive amounts of cortisol may lead to an abnormal increase in erythrocyte production. Injections of cortisol or stimulation of the cortex by ACTH lower the number of eosinophil granulocytes circulating in the blood but how this is brought about is unknown.

Cortisol also modifies the function of muscle cells and its administration corrects the muscle weakness characteristic of adrenocortical insufficiency. The hormone exerts an important influence upon the higher centres of the central nervous system, deficiency leading commonly to depression, excess to a state of euphoria. A more specific effect of cortisol upon the central nervous system is its capacity to modify the output of ACTH from the neurohypophysis, resulting in the feedback mechanism decribed on p. 25.7.

The hormone exerts diverse effects upon many other organs and systems, the mechanisms and significance of which are poorly understood; high concentrations of the hormone in the blood are required before these effects are seen. Thus, cortisol reduces capillary permeability, causes dissolution of lymphoid tissue with a coincident fall in antibody synthesis, reduces the intensity of inflammatory and allergic reactions and may retard normal wound healing. Cortisol may also stabilize the membranes of lysosomes (p. 13.8). In shock and many toxic conditions lysosomes are disrupted, with release of their enzymes and these may increase the severity of the illness.

In summary, observations of the effect upon the organism of cortisol lack or excess have demonstrated an almost bewildering variety of effects attributable to the hormone.

THE ADRENAL CORTEX AND STRESS

One of the most puzzling aspects of adrenocortical function is the increased secretion rate of cortisol in relation to **stress situations** of all kinds. This appears to be mediated by hypothalamohypophysial activity and is associated with the conversion of clear to compact cells and with as much as a five-fold increase in the rate of secretion of the hormone. Why the cortisol requirement should increase during periods of stress is unknown but failure of this mechanism impairs the resistance of the organism to the effects of the stressor. It is a not uncommon clinical experience that a patient, suffering from partial adrenocortical insufficiency but who, none the less, is capable of producing sufficient cortisol to meet the requirements of normal day to day life, is unable to increase significantly the output in

response to stress. In such a patient, relatively minor stress, e.g. a brief general anaesthetic for a dental extraction, may lead to profound collapse and rapidly to death unless treatment with cortisol is given. In a healthy person injury such as a fracture or a surgical operation leads to an increased urinary excretion of nitrogen and potassium with retention of sodium and impaired glucose tolerance. These effects are brought about by the pituitary-adrenal system and are associated with increases in the plasma levels of ACTH and adrenal steroids. The physiological nature of these normal adaptation mechanisms and the reasons for the serious consequences of their failure in adrenocortical insufficiency remain obscure. Psychological stress is also associated with increased adrenocortical activity and raised plasma levels of ACTH and cortisol

FIG. 25.27. Venous eosinophil counts made during a period of over 9 months on the leader of a British Antarctic base. During the first 'severe danger' period there were several crevasse incidents when dogs had to be rescued; also there were two occasions when his dogs charged downhill out of control in heavily-crevassed areas, since they could obtain no grip on the bare ice. In the second 'severe danger' period both tents were blown down simultaneously in the middle of the night and supplies in 50 lb (22·7 kg) boxes were blown away. Note the prolonged eosinopenia during the sledging period and return to control levels afterwards; also, since these are morning counts, they reflect the previous day's events or anticipation of the current day. From Simpson (1967) *Brit. med. J.* i, 531.

and it has been shown that the eosinophil counts of medical students fall as the time of their examination draws near.

In circumstances in which it is not possible to measure the level of plasma ACTH or cortisol, eosinophil counts have been used as an indirect field test of adrenocortical activity and its relationship to stress. Thus Dr Simpson of Edinburgh is an enthusiastic traveller and has become an expert at carrying out eosinophil counts under difficult circumstances. Fig. 25.27 shows his observations on a single subject during a long and arduous sledging journey in the Antarctic. The eosinophil count fell at the start of the journey but was reduced still lower in the course of the expedition when the subject encountered great dangers.

The value to the organism of the increased cortical activity accompanying prolonged stress is not immediately obvious, though it is certain that without it we would be restricted to a very limited life. To what extent the activity is adjusted to meet the stresses and strains of everyday life is not known. Almost every degenerative disease occurring in middle age has been attributed to stress at one time or another. It is certain that some people suffer much more than others from the after effects of either a severe psychological or physical stress. Whether this is due to excessive or prolonged cortisol responses to the stress is unknown. There is little or no evidence that such responses are either the direct or indirect cause of any disease that may subsequently arise. It is best to keep an open mind

minase appear to be activated or induced in this way. These reactions result in increased amounts of α keto derivatives and glutamate and so enhance the rates of synthesis of liver carbohydrate, urea and nucleotides. Fig. 25.28 shows the metabolic pathways which relate these actions of cortisol to urea, carbohydrate and purine nucleotide metabolism.

ALDOSTERONE

The function of aldosterone is much less obscure. It influences electrolyte metabolism by modifying the rate of active transport of sodium and potassium across membranes throughout the body. This effect has been most intensively studied in preparations of the toad bladder and in the distal tubules of the kidney. Here the hormone enhances the reabsorption of Na^+ from the tubular fluid in exchange for K^+ and H^+ whose excretion is enhanced. Thus in aldosterone deficiency sodium depletion and potassium intoxication result and in the presence of excess of the hormone the reverse situation

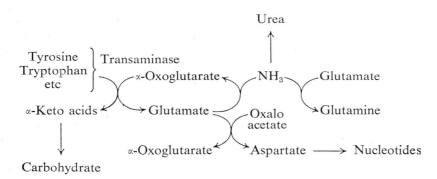

FIG. 25.28. Metabolic pathways influenced by glucocorticoids.

on this subject until we know much more in quantitative terms about individual responses to stresses of different natures.

The action of cortisol at the molecular level

In general, experiments in which glucocorticoids have been added to enzyme preparations *in vitro* have yielded negative or equivocal results. However, in the intact animal the release of cortisol causes a negative nitrogen balance. This must be due to a change in the rate of either synthesis or degradation of protein. The problem is to elucidate the site of action of the hormone in these reactions.

Cortisol may act by influencing a DNA-dependent RNA polymerase resulting in an increase in specific messenger RNAs, which in turn increase the synthesis of certain hepatic enzymes involved in protein metabolism, e.g. tryptophan pyrrolase and tyrosine transa-

occurs. Aldosterone is also known to decrease the ratio of sodium to potassium in sweat and salivary secretions and to promote the reabsorption of sodium chloride and water and the secretion of potassium by the cells of the ileum and colon.

In physiological amounts, unlike cortisol, aldosterone has little effect upon carbohydrate, protein or fat metabolism, is relatively inactive in protecting the organism against stress and does not influence the hypothalamo-pituitary axis.

The action of aldosterone at the molecular level

It is tempting to suggest that the hormone increases the uptake of sodium ions by activating or increasing the efficiency of the sodium pump. The toad bladder is an organ in which the mucosa fulfils a function comparable to the renal tubular cells in mammals and is amenable to investigations on the mode of action of aldosterone.

Since a preparation continues to pump sodium ions *in vitro* for many hours an approach similar to that developed for the study of the mode of action of thyroxine at the molecular level (p. 25.22) is possible. When aldosterone is added, increased sodium transport can be detected only after a time lag of about 1–2 hours. The aldosterone, however, is bound immediately to the cell nuclei, where it may effect changes in enzymic activities by stimulating RNA synthesis from precursor nucleotides. This newly formed m-RNA may be the control factor in the synthesis of some specific enzyme involved in active sodium transport. The localization of the hormone and the time course of the reactions are all compatible with this hypothesis.

Regulation of corticosteroid hormone synthesis

As the adrenal cortex contains negligible stores of the corticosteroid hormones, the regulation of the rate of steroid biosynthesis is synonymous with that of the rate of secretion of the hormones into the blood stream. In considering this regulation it is convenient to distinguish between cortisol and aldosterone, since separate mechanisms of control exist for each.

CORTISOL

The rate of utilization of the hormone may be calculated from the rate at which an intravenous dose of ^{14}C cortisol disappears from the blood. In this way it has been deduced that in a normal unstressed human subject cortisol secretion ranges from 10 to 25 mg/day, the value depending upon body weight, among other factors. Secretion is controlled by the action of ACTH, injection of which may raise the output of cortisol five or more times above the basal level. The nature of the stimulant effect of ACTH is discussed on p. 25.14. The feedback mechanism by which plasma cortisol modifies ACTH secretion is described on p. 25.7.

In normal circumstances the rate of cortisol secretion is not constant throughout the day but is highest in the early hours of the morning and lowest in the late evening (p. 44.2). This diurnal variation is a manifestation of the rhythmicity of the hypothalamus, the same rhythmicity which determines the diurnal variation in body temperature and the cyclical changes of the female reproductive system. The diurnal cortisol variation, which is reflected in plasma and urinary steroid levels, is merely a function of a diurnal variation in the production of the hypothalamic corticotrophin releasing factor.

The influence of the hypothalamus in determining adrenocortical function also explains the increase in cortisol secretion observed under conditions of stress. The hypothalamus receives afferent impulses from many parts of the central nervous system and its activity is modified by stress situations in such a way that liberation of CRF is increased.

ALDOSTERONE

Aldosterone is the most potent of all of the known naturally occurring corticosteroids and by using ^3H-aldosterone the average secretory rate of the hormone in man has been estimated as of the order of 200μg/day.

Aldosterone secretion is largely, though not absolutely, independent of ACTH and is increased by factors such as sodium depletion, potassium feeding, a fall in the plasma sodium to potassium ratio and by reduction in the extracellular fluid or blood volume, all situations in which the activity of the hormone tends to restore normality.

The mechanism by which these circumstances lead to increased secretion of the hormone remains controversial. However, the increased secretion of aldosterone in response to various stimuli can be abolished by bilateral nephrectomy. It is now thought that such stimuli lead to liberation of a protein named **renin** from the cells of the juxtaglomerular apparatus of the kidneys. Renin passes into the blood stream where it causes the hydrolytic cleavage of a circulating α-globulin with the formation of **angiotensin I**, an inactive polypeptide containing ten amino acids; this is then acted upon by a converting enzyme normally present in plasma to form **angiotensin II**, a polypeptide containing eight amino acid residues. In addition to possessing a powerful vasoconstrictor action, angiotensin II appears to act as a specific stimulus to aldosterone production by the adrenal cortex. The significance of this renin-angiotensin system remains controversial, though it is probably an important component of the volume control system (p. 33.20).

Effects of administered corticosteroids

Corticosteroids may be administered to patients for two reasons. The first of these is the replacement of defective endogenous secretion of the hormones due either to disease of the adrenal glands themselves or of the hypothalamo-pituitary axis. The second involves the use of cortisol or of one of its natural or synthetic analogues in pharmacological rather than physiological doses. Such therapy is employed with the intention of exploiting one or other of the actions of the corticosteroids usually in relation either to their effects in suppressing inflammatory or allergic reactions or in modifying the production of cells of the haemopoietic system. The use of corticosteroid hormones in this way, while often beneficial to the primary disorder, leads to a multitude of undesirable effects. The high doses involved interfere with the normal feedback control of adrenocortical function, causing inhibition of the hypothalamopituitary axis and leading to consequent depression of endogenous cortisol secretion. In these circumstances sudden withdrawal of the administered steroid, or indeed the advent of a severe stress may lead o adrenocortical insufficiency which may be so severe as o be fatal. The suppression of ACTH secretion may be rolonged. In addition other undesirable effects may ppear in patients kept on high levels of exogenous steroid or long periods; these include impaired glucose tolerance, wasting of muscle and loss of total bone substance esulting from negative nitrogen balance, accumulaion of sodium with secondary retention of water and rogressive loss of potassium. Exactly the same effects re observed in patients with adrenocortical hyperctivity who produce excessive quantities of steroid ormones, i.e. **Cushing's syndrome**. As may be antiipated on theoretical grounds, such adrenal hyperfuncion may be a reflection either of autonomous overactivity f the cortical cells themselves due to a secreting tumour vhich may be benign or malignant, or of overstimulation f otherwise normal glands by excessive production of \CTH by the anterior pituitary.

Numerous attempts have been made to elaborate ynthetic corticosteroids which would retain the desired herapeutic effects of the natural hormones without roducing unwanted and even dangerous side effects. Many synthetic steroids have been produced and are xtensively used in the treatment of disease but none is ree from adverse effects.

The metabolism of corticosteroids

ORTISOL

he peripheral blood contains from 5 to 25 μg/100 ml of ortisol, the level varying with such factors as the time f day at which the specimen is taken and the weight of he subject, levels being generally higher in the obese than n lean persons. Approximately 90 per cent of this cortisol xists in bound form, a small amount attached to the red ells and a much larger quantity bound to a circulating -globulin to which the name **transcortin** has been given. n the presence of high circulating levels of oestrogen, as n pregnancy and to a lesser extent after the consumption f the now fashionable oral contraceptives, the levels of ranscortin and cortisol in the blood both rise, the latter ften to abnormal values. Yet none of the expected ffects of excess cortisol are observed. Conversely in epatic disease the synthesis of transcortin by the ver cells is impaired, leading to a reduction in the irculating level of the protein with a parallel fall in he level of plasma cortisol; again, in such situations, no ffect attributable to cortisol lack occurs. Such observtions have led to the belief that only the unbound lasma cortisol is physiologically active, both in the xercise of corticoid activity and in participation in the eedback system.

From experiments carried out with ^{14}C labelled cortisol, t has been estimated that the half-life of the hormone in he body approximates to 80 min; in other words, half

of the cortisol circulating at any moment in time is inactivated within this period.

ALDOSTERONE

In plasma, the concentration of the hormone lies normally between 0·04 and 0·08 μg/100 ml. Aldosterone is significantly less firmly bound to protein than is cortisol, a greater proportion being carried in the free state in the plasma, and hence has a shorter half-life, of the order of 45 min.

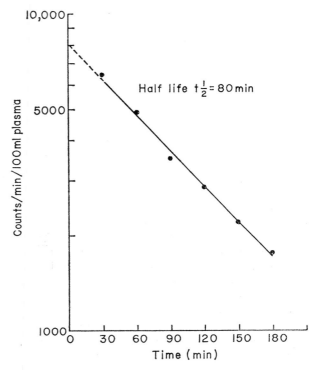

FIG. 25.29. Plasma levels of labelled cortisol after an intravenous dose of ^{14}C-cortisol. From Peterson R.E. (1959) *Hormone Research*, **15**, 236.

INACTIVATION AND EXCRETION OF CORTICOSTEROIDS

The inactivation of the corticosteroids occurs in the liver, the pathways involved being complex. The essential changes wrought in the steroid molecule, however, are the saturation of the double bond between carbon atoms 4 and 5, together with the reduction of the ketone group at carbon 3. This process is described on p. 31.11. The resulting metabolites then undergo conjugation with glucuronic acid or sulphate. These conjugated metabolites are devoid of hormonal activity and are, unlike the parent hormones, water soluble and negligibly bound to plasma proteins. The properties of the conjugates are such that they are rapidly eliminated from the body by the kidneys. In the urine they can be detected by chemical means as the '17–hydroxysteroids', providing a convenient and reliable method for the assessment of adrenocortical function.

THE ISLETS OF LANGERHANS
Development and microstructure

The development of the pancreas is described on p. 30.51. In the 3rd month two distinct types of cell can be seen around the developing ducts. The majority remain attached to the ducts and give rise to acini of serous cells whose secretion passes into the duodenum. A minority separate from the ducts to form isolated groups of cells clustered round capillaries, the **islets of Langerhans.** These cells contain secretory granules and as early as 3 months, two types of cells, α and β, can be distinguished on the basis of the staining reactions of the granules. With Gomori's special stain (plate 25.1f, facing p. 25.10), the granules in the α cells appear red, while those in the β cells are light blue. Both cells secrete hormones concerned with carbohydrate metabolism, the β cells **insulin** and the α cells **glucagon.** A few cells, δ cells, whose granules stain pale blue, are scattered in the islets; it is not known whether these are a separate type of cell or are a stage in the development of α and β cells.

At the earliest stage of development the close relationship of the β cells to the capillaries suggests that insulin is secreted directly into the blood stream. By the fourth month islet tissue constitutes approximately one-third of the total pancreatic mass and from the 30th week onwards in an increasing number of islets, the α and β cells intermingle as they do in the adult. Estimates of the ratio of the two types of cell vary but at birth the proportion of α cells is higher than in the adult. There is evidence that GH and ACTH influence the growth of both α and β cells and it is likely that the relative increase in the β cells in the adult, as compared with the foetus and newborn baby, is under hormonal control. In the adult β cells constitute about 75 per cent, α cells about 20 per cent and δ cells about 5 per cent of islet cells. Thus, most of the interior of the islet is made up of β cells which are in close proximity to the numerous capillaries, and this great vascularity led many years ago to the suggestion that they might be endocrine organs.

Islet tissue increases in size throughout childhood and adolescence and reaches a constant of about 1 g in adult life. The growth is due to an increase in both the number and size of the islets. In the first 3 years of life there is an increase in the number of islets from about 300,000 at birth to about 1,000,000. Thereafter, the increase in weight of islet tissue is due to an increase in the size of the individual islets which enlarge to three or four times their size at birth. The islet tissue grows more rapidly than the body as a whole during the first 2 years of life, lags behind the body in growth between the ages of 3 and 12 years, and

increases equally with the body from 13 to 21 years. It ha been suggested that the incidence of diabetes at these age may be correlated with these different growth ratios.

Ultrastructure

In serial EM studies on the β cells of the secreting pan creas of the rat, the earliest change observed is the migra tion of granules encased in their smooth membranou sacs to the membrane of the cell. This is followed by fusin of the two membranes with subsequent rupture, so tha the granules are liberated into either the intercellular o pericapillary space where they undergo rapid dissolution Prolonged hyperglycaemia, administration of insulin o starvation all lead to loss of granules from the β cells Resynthesis of β granules apparently occurs within th endoplasmic reticulum and ribosomes of the β cell.

Hormones of the islets of Langerhans
INSULIN

The discovery of insulin and its therapeutic application i one of the most dramatic stories in the history of medica science. It started in Germany in 1889 when Von Merin; and Minkowski removed the pancreas from a dog, whicl then began to pass large quantities of urine containin; sugar. This condition had already been recognized i man and first named by the Greeks **diabetes mellitu** (diabetes, a syphon, or running through; mellitus honeyed).

In 1902, Szobolew and Schultze found that if the mai pancreatic ducts are ligated in animals, the pancreatic acin rapidly disintegrate but the islets persist and even increas in number and the animals do not develop diabetes. Henc they concluded that the islet cells were the source of a antidiabetic principle produced by the pancreas and tha this must be an internal secretion or hormone. In 1909 de Meyer suggested the name 'insuline' for this hypo thetical hormone, but it was not until 1922, after severa attempts had failed, that Banting and Best, the latter medical student, working in Macleod's laboratory i Toronto, finally succeeded in extracting insulin from th pancreas. Banting, Best and Macleod shared a Nobe Prize, Banting was an imaginative genius who late turned from medical research to painting.

The Canadians succeeded where others had failed b following directly in the footsteps of Szobolew an Schultze. They used the same technique of ligating th pancreatic duct to induce atrophy of the acinar tissue anc so remove the source of proteolytic enzymes, which des troy insulin in extracts of whole pancreas. They were the able to extract insulin in relatively high concentratio from the islet tissue and to demonstrate that this extrac lowered the blood sugar in pancreatectomized dog (fig. 25.30). Applying the same reasoning they were alsc able to extract insulin from whole foetal pancreas, whicl contains functioning islets but has no digestive activity

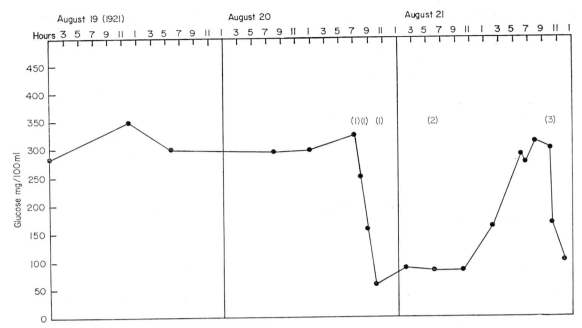

FIG. 25.30. Effect of insulin on the blood glucose level of a pancreatectomized dog. (1) Injection of extract of degenerated pancreas; (2) extract after incubation with pancreatic juice; (3) extract incubated without pancreatic juice. Redrawn from original data of Banting & Best (1921).

Later it was found that acid and alcohol not only extract insulin but also prevent proteolytic destruction and using these it is possible to obtain insulin from whole adult pancreas.

In 1926, Abel in the USA obtained insulin in crystalline form and it was found to be a protein. In 1955, the complete chemical structure of insulin was elucidated by Sanger working in Cambridge. Finally, in 1964, Katsoyannis in Pittsburgh synthesized the hormone.

Chemical structure

The molecular weight of insulin is about 6000. It is composed of two chains of amino acid residues, an A chain of twenty-one amino acids, and a B chain of thirty amino acids, joined by two disulphide bridges. A third disulphide bridge connects one part of the A chain with another part of the same chain.

In aqueous solution insulin exists as a polymer of several of these units. Theoretically polymerization could take place in a variety of combinations yielding a large number of products of different chain lengths and designs. However, experiments involving the cleavage of insulin by oxidative sulphitolysis and its subsequent resynthesis indicate that, under experimental conditions, there tends to be appropriate closure of the intramolecular disulphide ring in the A chain and that the A and B chains become reconjugated properly. The insulins from different animal species are identical in their biological and therapeutic effect but differ slightly in amino acid structure and immunologically.

Now that the structure of insulin is known it has been possible to devise experiments in which known parts of the molecule are broken off by controlled enzymic hydrolysis and the residue tested for activity. Nevertheless, little is known about the relationship of the physiological action of insulin to its chemical structure and it is not yet possible to state which amino acids make up the active centre. The following are among the more important facts known:

(1) the disulphide bridges are important and must be intact for biological activity,

(2) the exact sequence of the amino acids within the disulphide ring of the A chain is not important for biological activity since this varies among the insulins derived from different species,

(3) the residue that remains after splitting off the eight terminal amino acids from the end of the B chain of bovine insulin has only 15 per cent of the biological activity of the intact molecule,

(4) the presence of a carboxyl group from either asparagine or aspartic acid at the end of the A chain is necessary for full biological activity, but removal of this group does not bring about total inactivation.

Immunological behaviour

For many years insulin was regarded as only weakly or non-antigenic. However, it has now been discovered that insulin labelled by ^{131}I is retained for a long time in the blood stream of all subjects who have received insulin therapeutically and this behaviour is due to the presence in the blood of insulin-binding antibodies. When injected into man, beef insulin seems to be a much more potent antigenic stimulus than insulin derived from pigs which structurally resembles human insulin most closely. Furthermore, the antibody produced, although it partially neutralizes the biological effect of injected bovine insulin, shows little affinity for pork insulin. Homologous pancreatic insulin can, in some circumstances, act as a weak antigen and endogenous circulating insulin may differ antigenically from highly purified crystalline pancreatic insulin. These observations raise the possibility of auto-immune processes in disease of the pancreas. The antigenic behaviour of insulin is the basis of methods for the immunoassay of insulin.

ACTIONS OF INSULIN

Insulin is a powerful hormone whose actions affect the structure and function of every organ in the body. Not all tissues are, however, directly responsive. Among the responsive tissues muscle, liver and adipose tissue have been studied most extensively. Major physiological reactions stimulated by insulin are shown in table 25.4. In intact, fed animals, insulin is an anabolic hormone and promotes the storage of carbohydrate, protein and fat.

Under physiological circumstances insulin is secreted in response to the rising blood glucose concentration which

TABLE 25.4. Some major physiological reactions stimulated by insulin.

On carbohydrate metabolism

Insulin lowers the blood sugar:
(1) by promoting glycogen synthesis in liver and muscle,
(2) by increasing cellular utilization of glucose,
(3) by inhibiting gluconeogenesis from protein.

On fat metabolism

Insulin increases fat storage in adipose tissue:
(1) by stimulating lipogenesis,
(2) by inhibiting lipolysis.

On protein metabolism

Insulin increases protein synthesis:
(1) by promoting the utilization of amino acids,
(2) by promoting DNA and RNA synthesis,
(3) by inhibiting protein breakdown.

follows a carbohydrate meal (fig. 25.31) and the best known and most readily demonstrable action of exogenous insulin *in vivo* is its ability to lower the concentration of

FIG. 25.31. Blood glucose and plasma insulin values in a healthy, thin, young man measured for 2 hours before and 7 hours following 50 g glucose given orally. From data of Hunter, Willoughby & Strong (1968). *J. Endocrin* **40**. 297.

blood glucose (fig. 25.32). This is brought about by numerous actions which fall into two groups:

(1) those increasing the rate of withdrawal of glucose from the extracellular fluid into the peripheral tissues,

(2) those decreasing the rate of addition of glucose to the extracellular fluid by the liver.

Which effect predominates depends upon a number of factors which include the route of administration. In experimental animals, the action on peripheral tissues is encouraged by rapid intravenous injection of insulin and the hepatic action by a slow injection into the portal vein. Since infusion into the portal vein more closely resembles the way in which insulin enters the circulation naturally, it is likely that the hepatic action of insulin is as important as the peripheral one in maintaining the blood glucose level in the intact animal. Insulin increases the withdrawal of glucose from the ECF by direct or indirect actions on carbohydrate, fat and protein metabolism.

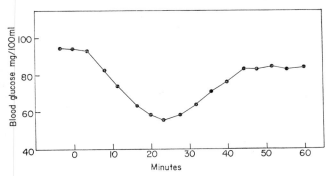

FIG. 25.32. Effect of an intravenous injection of insulin (1 unit) on the blood glucose concentration of a healthy, thin, young man. From data of Courtice, Douglas & Priestley (1939).

Effect on carbohydrate metabolism

Next to its ability to lower the blood sugar, the property of insulin that is best established is its action in **promoting glycogen deposition** in skeletal muscle. This glycogenetic effect is easily demonstrated *in vitro* using thin sheets of muscle from the diaphragm of young rats (table 25.5) and this preparation has been used for the bioassay of insulin. Glycogen can be formed from glucose by isolated tissue without insulin, provided the appropriate enzyme systems

TABLE 25.5. The effect of insulin on glucose utilization and glycogen formation by the isolated rat diaphragm. The figures are averages from nine experiments. Glucose concentration in the medium was 200 mg/100 ml. Data of Chalmers, Gemmill and Hamman (1941).

	No insulin	Insulin
Glucose utilization mg/g tissue/3 hr	5·4	10·3
Glycogen deposition mg/g tissue/3 hr	0·1	4·5

are present and in these circumstances the rate of glycogen formation depends on the concentration of extracellular glucose. However, for a given concentration of extracellular glucose, the rate of glycogen formation is increased by the presence of insulin. Insulin also has a glycogenetic effect on adipose tissue which can be demonstrated *in vivo* (fig. 25.33). It is important to remember that the glycogenetic effect of insulin *in vivo* is related to the concentration of blood glucose which in turn determines the amount of glucose available for deposition of glycogen. If hypoglycaemia occurs, glycogen is mobilized and enters the blood as glucose.

Insulin also **increases the rate of glucose utilization** in the tissues (table 25.5). However, glucose can be utilized in the absence of insulin. Experiments with eviscerated dogs have shown that within a certain range the rate of utilization is directly related to the level of blood glucose and that raising the concentration has an effect similar to that of insulin.

The effects of insulin on the liver are complex. In the diabetic state, glucose is produced in this organ both from protein and from glycogen in large amounts and insulin **inhibits this gluconeogenesis.** This action is additional to its effect on glycogenesis and the utilization of glucose, already described, which occurs in the liver as in other tissues. Administration of insulin can markedly decrease the glucose output of the liver, as has been shown in experiments in the dog when hepatic blood flow and glucose concentrations in the arterial and hepatic venous blood have been measured simultaneously. In this way

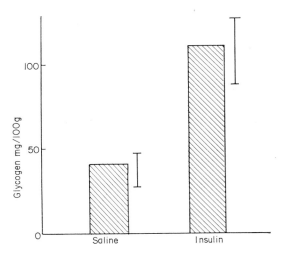

FIG. 25.33. Effect on glycogen deposition of injecting long-acting insulin (5 units) into the left groin fat of six diabetic rats compared with the effect of an equal volume of saline injected into the right groin. Glycogen measured 20 hours after injection. From data of Renold, Marble & Fawcett (1950).

the hepatic glucose balance can be determined (fig. 25.34).

Effect on fat metabolism

Adipose tissue is the major site for the regulation of energy storage and mobilization. Insulin plays a more essential role in the metabolism of adipose tissue than in liver and muscle, both of which can perform some of their major functions without insulin. The major metabolic reactions concerned with energy storage of fat are described in chap. 10, and the metabolic roles of adipose tissue are further discussed in chap. 32. Here it is sufficient to state that in isolated fat cells and in the isolated epididymal fat pad of the rat, insulin increases not only glucose uptake but also **stimulates lipogenesis** by the conversion of glucose into triglyceride. In addition insulin **inhibits lipolysis.**

FIG. 25.34. Mean changes in hepatic venous (▲) and arterial (●) glucose concentrations and hepatic glucose output (○) during the slow infusion of insulin into a dog, when hypoglycaemia is prevented by giving small amounts of glucose. An Eck's fistula, the anastomosis of the portal vein to the inferior vena cava, had been established some weeks before. In this preparation the liver is separated from the extrahepatic insulin-sensitive splanchnic tissues, so allowing direct measurement of hepatic glucose balance. From data of Madison, Combes, Adams & Strickland (1960).

It does this not only by increasing the availability of intracellular glucose and so supplying α glycerophosphate, but also by a direct effect on the release of FFA which is seen in the total absence of glucose (table 25.6).

Thus insulin is antiketogenic in two ways, firstly by reducing the quantity of free fatty acids delivered to the liver and secondly by increasing the rate of carbohydrate

TABLE 25.6. The effect of insulin in inhibiting the lipolytic action of noradrenaline on isolated adipose tissue. Mean values and standard deviations of observation on twenty-two rats. Data of Mahler, Stafford, Tarrant & Ashmore (1964).

	Glycerol released μmoles/g fresh tissue/hr
Control (no hormonal addition)	1·34 ± 0·06
Noradrenaline (0·08 μg/ml)	4·2 ± 0·12
Noradrenaline (0·08 μg/ml) + insulin (100 μU/ml)	1·72 ± 0·14

dissimilation in the liver so that the fatty acids which are delivered can be completely oxidized.

Effect on protein metabolism

Diabetes, whether produced by removal of the pancreas in animals or from destruction of the islets by disease in man, is a wasting condition. The tissues, especially muscle, atrophy and the cell components break down and increase the amount of nitrogen and potassium in the urine. These changes can be reversed by insulin (table 25.7).

TABLE 25.7. The effect of insulin on the urinary excretion of glucose, nitrogen and potassium in a diabetic patient. During the whole period the patient was on a formula diet which provided daily protein 90 g, fat 87 g, carbohydrate 190 g and potassium 80 mEq. The figures are the mean values for 4 days in each case. Data of Baird, Duncan and Passmore (1959).

	Glucose g/24 hr	Nitrogen g/24 hr	Potassium mEq/24 hr
Untreated	156	16	84
Treated (insulin 18 units twice daily)	15	11	37

The direct effect of insulin on **stimulating protein synthesis** by muscle can be demonstrated in the isolated rat diaphragm preparation (fig. 25.35). This effect is independent of the transport of glucose or amino acids into the cell and of glycogen synthesis. Insulin appears to stimulate intracellular protein synthesis at three sites, in the mitochondria by oxidative phosphorylation, in the microsomes by peptide bonding, and in the cytoplasm by the synthesis of RNA, especially messenger RNA.

Mechanism of action

The discovery of the chemical structure of insulin has not yet led to an identification of the combining site on the molecule which is biologically effective, nor has any specific receptor site or sites in insulin sensitive cells been identified. Levine has pointed out that: 'The reaction between these sites (hormone and effector) represents the primary chemical action of the hormone and all the innumerable effects of insulin observed under various conditions *in vitro* and *in vivo* should then be traceable back to this primary chemical event.' In broad terms insulin acts catalytically; minute amounts of the hormone are carried in the blood to the tissues where they permit the increased utilization of vast amounts of glucose. It has been calculated that one molecule of insulin promotes the extra utilization of 10^8–10^{10} molecules/min of glucose.

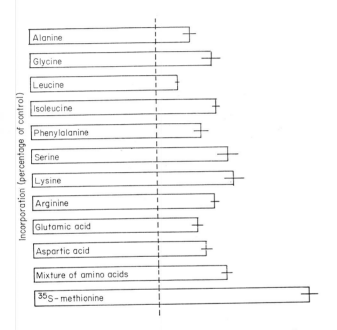

FIG. 25.35. Effect of the addition of insulin to a medium containing no oxidizable substrate on the incorporation of radio-activity from labelled amino acids into protein of the isolated rat diaphragm. The blocks represent incorporation in the presence of insulin; incorporation in the absence of insulin is shown by the dotted line. From data of Manchester & Young (1960).

Insulin promotes all the known pathways of glucose disposal and transformation including glycogen storage, fat formation, total oxidation and the use of the hexose-monophosphate pathway. Since the cell membranes must be intact for these effects to be obtained it is a reasonable hypothesis that insulin has a catalytic action on the transport of sugar into the cell. Further support for this view is provided by studies employing non-utilizable monosaccharides in eviscerated experimental animals, and by measurements of the amounts of free glucose inside cells. These methods allow separation of the initial transport step from the first intracellular enzymic reaction. Moreover, it has been shown that insulin stimulates pinocytosis at the cell surface of fat cells, indicating an interaction between insulin and membrane.

However, not all mammalian tissues require insulin for maximal glucose utilization, even though the same enzyme systems for carbohydrate metabolism are universal for almost all animal cells. For example, a sugar transport system with a high degree of species specificity which does not react to insulin exists in the red cells. Neither glucose reabsorption by the kidney nor glucose absorption by the intestinal mucosa is affected by insulin, although in both types of cell a sugar transport system capable of raising the glucose level above that of the blood exists.

In what way does an insulin sensitive sugar transport system differ from one on which insulin has no influence? Other factors such as muscular work, anoxia and certain drugs known to inhibit oxidative processes, influence the cell surface to facilitate sugar transfer in a manner similar to insulin. This lends support to the hypothesis that the sugar transport system in insulin sensitive tissues is normally inhibited and that this inhibition is either temporarily removed or altered in the presence of insulin so that more glucose can enter the cell. An insulin-sensitive sugar transport system thus enables a more active and finer control to be exerted on the metabolic activity of the tissues it serves.

The glucose transport theory of insulin action can account for most of the consequences of giving insulin to man or animals, such as increased glycogenesis and lipogenesis, enhanced oxidation of glucose, decreased lipid mobilization and formation of ketone bodies and protein sparing. However, it is difficult if not impossible to account for many other observations of the effects of insulin on this basis alone. The most important of these are as follows.

(1) It would be expected that if sugar entry could be enhanced in the absence of insulin, for example by raising the external glucose concentration in an *in vitro* system, the resulting metabolic events should be the same as those following the addition of insulin at lower concentrations of glucose. While this is broadly the case, it has been shown that insulin favours the formation of glycogen out of proportion to the other pathways and it has been suggested that insulin has a direct effect on glycogen synthetase.

(2) The fact that insulin has some metabolic effects which are specific to it and independent of its effect on blood glucose means either that insulin has a variety of totally unrelated actions in the cell or that a single type of chemical reaction underlies these widely varied metabolic events.

(3) Unlike muscle and adipose tissue cells, the liver cell does not appear to possess a sugar transport system and glucose permeates freely into it. After years of controversy it would now seem certain that *in vivo* insulin

directly affects both the intake and the output of the liver. Table 25.8 lists some of the enzymic reactions in liver cells that have been shown to be promoted by insulin *in vitro*. There actions are difficult to account for if enhancement of glucose transport were the only point of action of insulin.

Thus, there is at present no hypothesis which integrates satisfactorily all the diverse effects of insulin.

TABLE 25.8. Actions of insulin on enzymic reactions in liver cells.

Insulin stimulates:
  Deposition of glycogen – glycogen synthetase
  Glycolysis – glucokinase
          phosphofructokinase
          pyruvate kinase

Insulin inhibits:
  Gluconeogenesis – pyruvate carboxylase
          phosphoenolpyruvate carboxykinase
          fructose 1,6-diphosphatase
          glucose-6-phosphatase

CONTROL OF INSULIN SECRETION

The main natural stimulus to increased synthesis and release of insulin appears to be a rise in the glucose concentration of blood perfusing the pancreas. It has been shown in the dog that the rate of insulin secretion into the pancreatic vein is a continuous function of the blood glucose concentration. An increase in the concentration of insulin in the plasma occurs in less than one minute after giving glucose intravenously. Since the cells of the islets of Langerhans are freely permeable to glucose, the concentration of glucose in the intracellular water of these cells is the same as that in the blood.

It is far from clear how glucose controls the rate of secretion of insulin but it does not occur in the presence of substances such as 2-deoxyglucose which block the utilization of glucose. Utilization of glucose in the islet cell seems to be the necessary stimulus for synthesis and release of insulin and it is possible that a metabolite of glucose may be the triggering mechanism. The presence of calcium, magnesium and potassium significantly increase the rate of secretion of insulin in response to glucose.

Other factors are almost certainly involved in the secretion of insulin in response to glucose. When glucose is ingested the concentration of insulin in the plasma does not rise as rapidly as when it is given intravenously but the insulin levels eventually become much higher in spite of lower levels of blood glucose (fig. 25.36). This suggests the possibility of an insulin-releasing factor produced by the small intestine on contact with glucose, which enters the circulation and stimulates the release of insulin from

the pancreas. Glucagon (p. 25.46) has been shown to promote insulin secretion particularly in the presence of glucose and a biologically active glucagon-like substance has been demonstrated in different portions of the intestines of many species including man. The present view is that the presence of glucose in the stomach or duodenum releases a factor, possibly pancreozymin, which causes the secretion of insulin from the islets. This alimentary factor may also stimulate the secretion of glucagon which

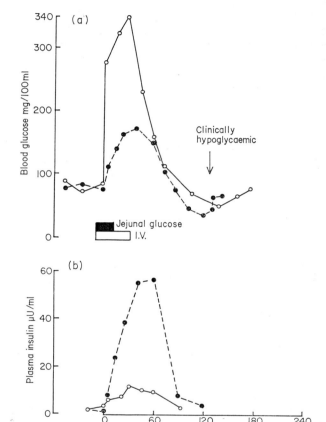

FIG. 25.36. Comparison of the effect on the blood glucose (a) and plasma insulin (b) of giving 60 g glucose intravenously (○) and into the jejunum (●) in a thin healthy young man. The intrajejunal route compared with the intravenous route causes a much smaller rise in plasma glucose, but a far greater increase in plasma insulin. From data of McIntyre, Holdsworth & Turner (1964).

in turn stimulates insulin release. Ketone bodies in physiological concentrations can also stimulate the secretion of insulin and this may be an important mechanism for protecting the organism from the development of severe keto-acidosis during prolonged fasting.

The insulin response to glucose is delayed in starvation and increased in obesity and in pregnancy. It is increased by growth hormone, ACTH, glucocorticoids, thyroxine, oestrogens, many types of proteins, polypeptides and certain amino acids, particularly arginine, and by vagal stimulation. Whether the latter is of any physiological significance is not known.

Exogenous insulin decreases endogenous insulin synthesis and secretion, which is increased by giving insulin antibodies.

ATP and cyclic 3'5' AMP increase the secretion of insulin *in vitro* and many of the influencing factors may act through these compounds.

Zinc plays an important role in the storage and secretion of insulin. It complexes with insulin, thus rendering it less soluble. Certain glucose metabolites such as oxaloacetate, as well as other compounds, e.g. organic phosphate, cysteine, L-histidine, glycine, L-leucine and glutathione, compete with insulin for zinc and thereby promote secretion of insulin.

DEGRADATION

The half-life of insulin in blood is short, probably a few minutes. Insulin is rapidly distributed throughout the body and most tissues contain some. Degradation occurs in some tissues under the influence of an enzyme, glutathione insulin dehydrogenase (insulinase), which catalyses reduction and cleavage of the disulphide bonds of insulin, resulting in the formation of the A and B chains of the insulin molecule. While most tissues have the capacity to destroy insulin, liver, pancreas, kidney and placenta are the most active. In man the liver removes 20–50 per cent of insulin from the blood during a single passage. Protein bound insulin is less subject to degradation than free insulin.

HORMONAL ANTAGONISTS OF INSULIN

An insulin antagonist may be defined as any substance capable of interfering with the action of insulin. Interference by an antagonist could occur during the synthesis of insulin in the β cell or at some point in its release into the portal circulation; an antagonist might

(1) modify or combine with circulating insulin so as to inhibit its biological activity,

(2) depress the response of the target organ,

(3) increase the rate of degradation of insulin in the tissues with or without the increased production of inhibitory degradation products.

The known anti-insulin hormones are growth hormone and glucocorticoids, adrenaline and thyroxine. How these hormones act is not precisely known but, broadly speaking, the anti-insulin hormones favour catabolic pathways, while insulin assists many aspects of anabolism.

Growth hormone is the most important physiological opponent of insulin action. It is known to be diabetogenic in the adult human subject, causing the rapid appearance of impaired glucose tolerance and depressed responsiveness to exogenous insulin. More prolonged administration of growth hormone, however, appears to stimulate the islet cells; this may represent a compensatory change resulting from the development of insulin antagonism. The overall effect of growth hormone is to preserve body protein and to favour the catabolism of fat to enable the body to withstand fasting.

Prolactin, like growth hormone, causes impaired glucose tolerance and even diabetes in experimental animals. During normal pregnancy, a substance sharing many immunological properties with growth hormone is produced in large amounts, probably by the placenta. Hence it has been designated placental lactogen. Little is known about its origin and biological properties but it is tempting to speculate that it may be responsible for the increased amounts of fatty acid and insulin in the plasma and the decreased responsiveness to insulin which are characteristic of normal pregnancy.

Following the administration of glucocorticoids for a few days some individuals have decreased glucose tolerance, despite a raised plasma insulin level. This suggests peripheral insulin insensitivity and an early and important action of cortisol may be to decrease the peripheral utilization of glucose by inhibiting glucose phosphorylation in muscle and adipose tissue. Following this initial effect hepatic glucose release is decreased. Changes in protein, amino acid and fat metabolism are probably secondary to these alterations in carbohydrate metabolism and can be prevented by giving glucose at the same time. Cortisol also facilitates and enhances the hyperglycaemic effects of both glucagon and adrenaline.

Adrenaline also blocks insulin release. This effect seems to be mediated through stimulation of sympathetic receptors since it is abolished by administration of phentolamine, a blocking agent for α receptors. Adrenaline also opposes the action of insulin by promoting liver glycogenolysis.

Although thyroid hormones lead to increased gluconeogenesis, proteolysis and glycogenolysis and so to increased glucose production, they also increase the secretion of insulin and glucose uptake in the periphery and promote lipid synthesis. The net result is that they do not usually exert a significant anti-insulin effect, although hyperthyroidism in man may aggravate the diabetic state.

NON-HORMONAL ANTAGONISTS

Ketone bodies and fatty acids inhibit glucose utilization by skeletal muscle *in vitro* and impair its sensitivity to insulin. In contrast these metabolites accelerate glucose utilization in adipose tissue and do not affect its responsiveness to insulin. A similar dissociation in the behaviour of these two tissues is seen in their response to growth hormone and can be demonstrated in diabetes, in hypopituitary subjects given growth hormone and in normal pregnancy, conditions where raised levels of plasma FFA are seen. It has been suggested that the anti-insulin effect of growth hormone is secondary to its lipolytic activity, and that a raised concentration of FFA in plasma is responsible for the impaired carbohydrate tolerance seen in many endocrine and nutritional disorders and represents a distinct biochemical entity, the glucose fatty acid syndrome. Moreover in normal man a sustained elevation of plasma FFA causes impairment of carbohydrate tolerance despite adequate secretion of insulin, suggesting a decrease in peripheral sensitivity to insulin.

The B chain of insulin has been shown to inhibit the action of insulin on skeletal muscle *in vitro* and it becomes attached to the albumin fraction in plasma when it is called synalbumin antagonist. The physiological significance of this antagonism is unknown, and it is probable that it is an artefact.

Glucagon

Glucagon is a pancreatic hormone, so named because on injection into an animal or man it causes a rise in the blood sugar. It has an important role in glucose homeostasis.

The evidence that glucagon is secreted by α cells of islet tissue is:

(1) It is found in pancreatic extracts obtained from animals previously treated with alloxan which produces diabetes by selectively destroying the β cells of the islets.

(2) Much less glucagon can be extracted from the pancreas after selective destruction of the α cells with cobalt.

Biologically active glucagon-like substances have also been identified in the gut of many species including man.

CHEMISTRY

Crystalline glucagon of high purity was obtained in 1953 and 3 years later its chemical structure was elucidated. It is a polypeptide containing twenty-nine amino acids (mol. wt. 3485). Unlike insulin, glucagon contains tryptophane and methionine but not proline, isoleucine and cystine. The absence of cystine probably explains the relative resistance of glucagon to treatment with alkali, a property used in obtaining glucagon solutions free of insulin activity. Like insulin, glucagon is antigenic and its concentration in plasma can be estimated by means of a radioimmunochemical assay method. The method is less reliable than that for insulin.

ACTIONS

The initial and outstanding effect of injecting glucagon into an intact animal is to raise rapidly the plasma insulin concentration (fig. 25.37). The insulinogenic effect of glucagon is greater than that of glucose and is not dependent on a rise in the blood glucose level, although it can be strikingly increased by giving glucose simultaneously. It is not known if the effect is due to direct or indirect action on the β cells of the islets.

Glucagon also raises the blood glucose level, provided adequate stores of glycogen are present in the liver. This is brought about by stimulating the adenyl cyclase system (p. 9.9) and so increasing the rate of glycogenolysis. This action requires the presence of adrenal cortex. It is likely

FIG. 25.37. Arterial glucose (a) and insulin (b) levels in a healthy subject during a constant intravenous infusion of glucose followed after 10 min by one of glucagon. From data of Samols, Marri & Marks (1966).

that a similar process occurring within the β-cell may be responsible for the insulinogenic properties of glucagon.

Glucagon also accelerates lipolysis and increases protein catabolism and gluconeogenesis.

CONTROL OF GLUCAGON SECRETION

Following oral glucose, the level of glucagon in the blood rises to reach a maximum after 30–45 min (fig. 25.38).

This almost certainly comes from the pancreas and alimentary absorption of glucose probably releases pancreozymin which in turn stimulates the pancreatic α cells. A second rise in plasma glucagon, probably originating in the gut, is observed 3–4 hours after oral glucose in some subjects and a marked increase in plasma glucagon invariably occurs during prolonged fasting. As growth hormone also rises in the blood 3–4 hours after a glucose load and during prolonged fasting, it may be responsible for promoting the secretion of glucagon from the gut. The anatomical arrangements contrive to make pancreatic

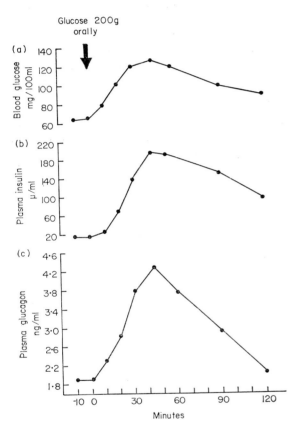

Glucose 200g orally

FIG. 25.38. Mean venous blood glucose (a), plasma insulin (b) and glucagon (c) levels before and for 2 hours following the administration of 200 g glucose orally in five normal subjects. From data of Samols, Tyler, Marri & Marks (1965).

glucagon primarily insulinogenic and gut glucagon predominantly glycogenolytic.

Glucose homeostasis and the 'glucoregulatory' hormones

The term glucoregulatory hormones has been applied by Unger to insulin, growth hormone and glucagon whose main function is to regulate the metabolic mixture and control the concentration of glucose in the blood.

Adrenaline and cortisol also play a part in glucose homeostasis under normal conditions and especially when the glucose supply to the brain is actually threatened under abnormal conditions, for example, those associated with disease or experiment. It appears that insulin is the hormone of glucose abundance, concerned with the storage of ingested glucose in fat and muscle, with glucagon playing a supporting role. The cells of insulin sensitive tissues are encased in a lipoid membrane which under basal conditions is highly impermeable to glucose. In times of glucose abundance insulin and glucagon are released and the net effect is to enhance glucose entry into the cell and to limit the formation of hepatic glycogen in favour of the deposition of glycogen in muscle.

There are several 'anti-storage' hormones secreted in situations of glucose lack. These include the glucogenolytic hormones, glucagon and adrenaline which act as a first line of defence in hypoglycaemia by releasing intact preformed glucose molecules from storage. Adrenaline also suppresses insulin secretion. Hormones concerned with gluconeogenesis, particularly glucagon and the glucocorticoids, provide reinforcements for the limited supply of preformed glucose by synthesizing new glucose from non-glucose precursors, and growth hormone spares glucose, in situations associated with glucose lack. Since during exercise muscle cells are capable of utilizing glucose even in the absence of insulin growth hormone is of particular importance in this situation. Growth hormone prevents glucose wastage for muscle energy in two ways; by a direct action on cellular glucose metabolism and by mobilizing FFA as an alternative and competitive substitute.

PROSTAGLANDINS

It has been known for a number of years that seminal fluid contains lipid-soluble substances which stimulate smooth muscle and Von Euler suggested that the active principle should be called prostaglandin. Employing a combination of bioassay on smooth muscle preparations and liquid-liquid chromatographic techniques, Bergstrom and his colleagues isolated the active principles from seminal fluid and tissues such as sheep seminal vesical and showed them to be unsaturated hydroxy acids. At first only two prostaglandins were characterized and called PGE_1 and PGF_1. They contain twenty carbon atoms and possess a structure shown in fig. 25.39. Subsequently a number of prostaglandins related to PGE_1 and PGF_1 were discovered.

While prostaglandins are present in highest concentration in seminal fluid they have been found in numerous other tissues such as kidney, iris, pancreas, lung, brain and human menstrual fluid, where they occur in concentration of from about 0·1–1 μg/g of wet tissue. In addition to the primary prostaglandins, tissues contain prostaglandin derivatives which appear to be normal metabolites of these substances and inactivation probably occurs

FIG. 25.39. Structure of two of the prostaglandins.

in the liver and the lungs. It has now been shown that these hydroxylated unsaturated fatty acids can be formed from the essential C_{20} unsaturated fatty acids present in the diet

acid is formed from linolenic acid ingested in the diet, and that linolenic acid and arachidonic acid are the precursors of PGE_1 and PGE_2 respectively.

Prostaglandins exert a profound effect on smooth muscle and this is shown in many species including man by marked changes in heart rate, blood pressure, intestinal motility, and contractions of the uterus; they also mobilize free fatty acids and affect the stickiness of platelets.

It has been established that PGE_1 given alone increases the level of cyclic $3'5'$ AMP in certain tissues. It is also known, however, that prostaglandins antagonize *in vivo* and *in vitro* the effects of a number of hormones such as adrenaline, noradrenaline, glucagon, ACTH and vasopressin which also increase the concentration of intracellular cyclic $3'5'$ AMP in selected tissues. These paradoxical effects suggest that prostaglandins may exert a control over the activity of the cyclase system and modulate the reactions which are initiated by this system. It has also been suggested that the prostaglandins may act as feedback inhibitors in metabolic processes since their precursors, the unsaturated fatty acids, are bound as triglycerides or phospholipids in a great many tissues. Thus an endocrine signal resulting in the release, e.g. of

FIG. 25.40. Conversion of unsaturated fatty acids to prostaglandins.

and normal tissues. A microsomal preparation of the prostate gland of sheep can convert labelled arachidonic acid, which is the best known C_{20} unsaturated fatty acid into an active prostaglandin, in the presence of oxygen and a reducing agent, glutathione. This unsaturated fatty acid is known as PGE_2. The oxygen introduced into the fatty acid at specific points in the molecule is derived from the gas phase and hence the reaction is typical of oxygenases. It was later shown that the reaction is in fact a di-oxygenase because the molecule of oxygen introduced into the molecule at one site provides two of the hydroxyls in the molecule. Fig. 25.40 shows how bishomo γ-linolenic-

free fatty acids by lipolysis, could then be followed by a local increase in the precursors of the prostaglandins. Assuming that the appropriate oxygenase enzymes were available for the conversion of the polyunsaturated fatty acids to prostaglandins the local concentrations of prostaglandins could then rise.

Prostaglandins are ubiquitous highly active substances and knowledge of their physiological role is still at an early and fragmentary stage. It is appropriate that they should be discussed here for it is likely that they will be shown to be metabolic modulators or regulators of the actions of hormones.

FURTHER READING

AUERBACH G.D. & POTTS J.T. (1964) The parathyroids, in *Advances in Metabolic Disorders*, Vol. 1. New York: Academic Press.

BERGSTRÖM S. (1967) Prostaglandins. *Science* (*N.Y.*) **157**, 382.

British Medical Bulletin (1960) Insulin **16** No. 3.

British Medical Bulletin (1966) Recent Studies on the Hypothalamus, **22**, No. 3.

COPE C.L. (1966) The adrenal cortex in internal medicine. *Brit. med. J.* **ii**, 847–53, 914–21.

COUPLAND R.E. (1965) *The Natural History of the Chromaffin Cell.* London: Longmans Green.

GREENWOOD F.C. (1967) Immunological procedures in the assay of protein hormones; in *Modern Trends in Endocrinology*, vol. 3, p. 288. London: Butterworth.

HARRIS G.W. & DONOVAN B.T. (ed.) (1966) *The Pituitary Gland.* Vols. 1–3. London: Butterworth.

JAMES V.H.T. & LANDON J. (1968) The investigation of hypothalamic pituitary adrenal function; in *Memoirs of the Society of Endocrinology*, No. 17. London: Cambridge University Press.

MACINTYRE, I. (1967) Thyrocalcitonin—Symposium on the thyroid gland. *J. clin. Path.* p, 399.

Parathyroid hormone (1967) *Amer. J. Med.* **4β**, 1.

McGOWAN G.K. & SANDLER, M. (1967) Symposium on the thyroid gland. *J. clin. Path.* Articles by I. Doniach, p. 309; R. Pitt-Rivers, p. 318; J.R. Tata, p. 323; K. Brown Grant, p. 327; Th. Temarchand-Béraud, p. 333; C. Osorio, p. 335.

UNGER R.H. (1966) Glucoregulatory hormones in health and disease: a teleologic model. *Diabetes*, **15**, 500.

VON EULER U.S. & ELIASSON R. (1967) *Prostaglandins.* New York: Academic Press.

WILLIAMS R.H. & ENSINCK J.W. (1966) Secretion, fates and actions of insulin and related products: the Banting memorial lecture. *Diabetes*, **15**, 623.

WOLSTENHOLME G.E.W. & PORTER R. (1967) *The Human Adrenal Cortex.* Ciba Foundation Study Group No. 27. London: Churchill.

Chapter 26
Blood

The first accounts of the functions of the blood were concerned with its role in disease; an excess of phlegm as set out in the Hippocratic code or plethora as held by Eristratus were both indications for bleeding and purging in early therapeutics. Galen added astrological reasons for blood letting and largely due to his great influence medical progress was halted for 1500 years. Then, in the sixteenth and seventeenth centuries the authority of the teachings of the Church and Medicine were challenged. Vesalius and Servetus discovered the pulmonary circulation, Harvey described the circulation of the blood and a little Dutch grocer, Leuwenhoek, gave an accurate account of the red blood corpuscles as seen by the microscope. The discoveries of Boyle, Lower, Priestley and Lavoisier all led to an understanding of the respiratory process and Liebeg many years later showed that a compound of iron within the red cell was capable of binding, reversibly, oxygen and carbon dioxide. The white corpuscles had been seen in the blood in the mid-eighteenth century. One hundred years later William Addison, a general practitioner in Malvern, observing diapedesis in inflammation, identified pus cells with granulocytes and emphasized their protective and reparative function. Addison is believed also to have been the first to see blood platelets and suggest that they had a role in coagulation. Hewson in 1770–73 described coagulation of the blood as being due to coagulation of the plasma. In 1845, Buchanan postulated the enzymic nature of coagulation and at about the same time Virchow, in introducing the concept of thrombosis and embolism, suggested that fibrin is present in the blood as fibrinogen which requires activation. The marrow was not recognized as the site of production of red cells and other blood cells until 1868. In 1878, Ehrlich revolutionized haematology by the application of dye staining techniques for studying the blood and marrow cells.

Although Thomas Sydenham was using iron, as iron filings steeped in cold Rhenish wine, with bleeding and purging, for the treatment of severe anaemia in the seventeenth century, iron was not known to be present in blood until 1747. This discovery led to the rational use of iron for the treatment of iron deficiency. Pernicious anaemia was described by Thomas Addison, who was no relation to William, in 1849, but its successful treatment had to wait until 1926 when the therapeutic effect of eating liver was discovered by Minot and Murphy in America. Later experiments of Castle demonstrated malabsorption of a food factor in consequence of a gastric defect and revealed the mechanism of production of this previously pernicious and fatal disease. As recently as 1948, Castle's extrinsic factor was identified as vitamin B_{12}; not long previously, folic acid had been isolated and synthesized and had also been shown to be an essential haematinic principle.

Harvey's discovery of the circulation of the blood was followed by attempts at blood transfusion but the perils of heterologous blood soon became apparent and the experiments were abandoned, particularly after a notorious legal action in France for murder. The reason for fatal transfusion reactions and the haemagglutinating power of normal sera became apparent when Landsteiner discovered the ABO system of blood group antigens in 1900; the description of the Rh system did not follow until 1940.

CELLS IN THE CIRCULATING BLOOD

The blood is a complex fluid which on standing or centrifugation separates into a pale, slightly opalescent yellowish liquid, the plasma, and a deposit of cells or formed elements. The blood cells are of three types, red cells or **erythrocytes**, white cells or **leucocytes** and platelets or **thrombocytes**. The deposit of the centrifuged blood is almost entirely red cells; above the red cells lies a thin layer of white cells and platelets, the buffy coat. It was this white layer, seen to be greatly increased in some diseases that attracted so much attention among early physicians.

The number of the different blood cells per unit volume of blood remains constant within narrow limits in health. The cells can be counted under the microscope when dilutions of blood are placed in a special glass counting chamber, comprising a ruled area of known dimensions in a trough of known depth. The number of cells is expressed per mm^3 of blood. Nowadays, much of the blood cell counting in large hospital laboratories is done mechanically. An electronic counter feeds diluted blood through a narrow jet orifice; as each cell passes through the orifice it changes the resistence in an electrical circuit and is thus recorded.

The size, shape and characteristics of blood cells are studied by making thin smears of undiluted blood on glass slides which are subsequently stained with one of the Romanowsky stains. There are several of these, e.g. Leishman, Giemsa, May–Grünwald, Wright, but all combine a basic dye, methylene blue, and an acidic dye, eosin, together with methyl alcohol for preliminary fixation of the blood film. They produce a wide range of shades between blue and red and are necessary for studying the maturity of the cells, details of their nuclei and, in some of the white cells, the granules in the cytoplasm.

Red cells

The red cells are by far the most numerous of the blood cells; for every white cell there are about 500 red cells and about 30 platelets. The mature red cell measures approximately 7 μm in diameter and appears as a biconcave disc with no nucleus. It is strongly acidophilic on staining because of its content of the red iron containing compound haemoglobin. The penultimate stage of erythrocytic maturation in the bone marrow (p. 26.5), the **reticulocyte**, appears transiently and in only small numbers in the peripheral blood accounting for <2 per cent of the mature red cells. Romanowsky stains containing methyl alcohol or other fixative agents cause reticulocytes to exhibit a faintly blue colour due to the diffuse precipitation of the last traces of RNA; the reticulocyte is however more easily recognized if it is stained with cresyl blue. Cresyl blue is a lipophilic dye and such dyes are believed to act by coagulating endoplasmic reticulum to produce the filaments by which the reticulocytes are recognized.

White cells

There are three varieties of white cell, the polymorphonuclear leucocyte or polymorph, the lymphocyte and the monocyte. The **polymorphs** are about 10–12 μm in diameter. In the adult, they account for approximately two thirds of the circulating white cells. When stained, the nucleus is a deep purplish blue and composed of coarse chromatin. It is divided into a number of lobes, usually 3 or 4, joined by thin strands; this segmentation has led to the term polymorph. The other feature of these cells is the numerous granules in the cytoplasm; the staining reactions of the granules allow a further division of the polymorphs into three types, the neutrophils, the eosinophils and the basophils (plate 26.1, pp. 27.2–3). Neutrophils usually account for more than 90 per cent of the polymorphs; they are recognized because they contain numerous small faintly purplish granules. The eosino-

phils and basophils have relatively fewer but coarser granules which stain distinctly reddish-orange and blue-black respectively. Approximately 1 per cent of the polymorphonuclear leucocytes in the blood of female subjects show a nuclear appendage like a drumstick or tennis racquet. This is believed to be another form of the nuclear sex chromatin body, the inactive X chromosome, which lies against the nuclear membrane in somatic cells in females.

The mature **lymphocyte** as seen in the circulation has a deeply basophilic nucleus with densely clumped chromatin, which is usually round or at most slightly indented. The most numerous cells, small lymphocytes, with a diameter of 7–10 μm, have very little pale blue cytoplasm, and a slightly eccentric nucleus. Large lymphocytes differ only in that they have more cytoplasm and may be up to 20 μm in diameter. It has been said that large lymphocytes are younger forms of small lymphocytes but this is uncertain. A few azure granules are not uncommon in the cytoplasm of the lymphocyte; they differ from polymorph granules in that they do not stain with peroxidase stains.

The **monocyte** is the largest of the circulating white cells, measuring 16–22 μm in diameter, and the least numerous. It possesses an abundant grey-blue cytoplasm with ground glass appearance. The nucleus has a stringy chromatin structure and tends to be indented, lobulated or otherwise mis-shapen. A few fine azure granules and an occasional vacuole are commonly present in the cytoplasm.

Platelets

Platelets are the smallest elements in human blood, their average diameter being 2–4 μm. When viewed by conventional light microscopy in a wet preparation they are colourless, rounded or oval, refractile bodies, though *in vivo* they are probably disc-shaped. Under dark field illumination they look translucent and granular. If they are stained by one of the Romanowsky dye techniques they show a pale blue cytoplasm and a central cluster of purplish granules. Like the red cells, they have no nucleus.

STANDARD MEASUREMENTS AND NORMAL VALUES IN STUDIES OF THE BLOOD CELLS

Red cells

The red cell count (RBC) ranges from 4·5–6·5 million/mm^3 in men and 3·9–5·6 million/mm^3 in women. Erythrocytosis denotes a raised red cell count. In the stained blood film the normal erythrocytes are spoken of as **normochromic**, due to a normal complement of haemoglobin, and **normocytic,** i.e. of normal size and shape. In disorders of the blood there may be variations in size of the red cells, anisocytosis, or shape, poikilocytosis. Small cells are said to be **microcytic** and large ones **macrocytic**. When a red cell has less than the normal complement of haemoglobin, it is described as **hypochromic**. The cells never have an excess concentration of haemoglobin.

Measurement of the haemoglobin (Hb) content of the blood is of enormous importance in clinical practice. It is achieved by converting the haemoglobin into a derivative, usually cyanmethaemoglobin, oxyhaemoglobin, acid haematin or alkaline haematin, which is then compared colorimetrically with a standard. The normal haemoglobin content of the blood in the adult ranges from 13·5–18·0 g/100 ml in men and 11·5–16·4 g/100 ml in women. When the haemoglobin level is low, as will happen if the number of red cells per unit volume of blood is reduced or the haemoglobin content of the red cell is reduced, the individual is said to have anaemia.

When blood is centrifuged in a tube under standard conditions, the height of the column of red cells is the **haematocrit** or **packed cell volume** (PCV). Normally the PCV is measured in a thick walled tube of 2.5 mm bore (Wintrobe tube) which is spun in a special centrifuge of 15 cm radius for 30 min at 3000 rev/min (1000–1500 *g*). Alternatively, a microhaematocrit centrifuge may be employed; for this, the blood is placed in a capillary tube which, when sealed at one end, fits into the head of the instrument. Since these instruments develop about 12,000 *g*, centrifugation for only 5 min is necessary. The PCV in health is 40–54 per cent in men and 36–47 per cent in women.

Having obtained the haemoglobin value, the red cell count, and the PCV, it is possible to derive, for the erythrocytes, the **mean cell volume** (MCV) and the **mean cell haemoglobin concentration** (MCHC). These indices, which are extremely useful in diagnosis, are obtained as follows:

$$MCV = \frac{PCV \text{ per cent}}{Red \text{ cell count} \times 10^6 \text{ per mm}^3} \times 10$$

$$MCHC = \frac{Hb \text{ in g per 100 ml}}{PCV \text{ per cent}} \times 100$$

The normal range for MCV is 75–95 μm^3 and for MCHC 30–36 g/100 ml of red cells.

A raised MCV occurs in macrocytosis and is a typical finding in anaemias due to deficiency of vitamin B_{12} and folic acid (p. 26.9). A low MCV and a low MCHC are typical of anaemia due to iron deficiency since in this condition the red cells tend to be smaller than normal and have a deficient content of haemoglobin.

The circulating **blood volume** remains very stable in health and is more related to body size than any other factor. The volume of the circulating red cells (the red cell mass) is found to be 30·3 ml/kg, *s* 4·5; the plasma volume is 42·1 ml/kg, *s* 5·8. The red cell mass is naturally low in anaemia; when it is raised the patient is said to have erythraemia. The plasma volume is increased in cardiac failure and for reasons not understood in pregnancy and in patients with marked enlargement of the spleen.

Because there tends to be more plasma in the capillaries than in the larger blood vessels, possibly due to axial flow of the cells in small tubes with layering of the plasma along the walls, the **body haematocrit,**

$$\frac{red \text{ cell mass}}{red \text{ cell mass} + plasma \text{ volume}}$$

tends to be lower than the haematocrit for venous blood. The body/venous haematocrit ratio in health is 0·91, *s* 0·026.

White cells

The total white cell count (WBC) in the adult is in the range 4000–10,000/mm³. Reduction of the white cell count, **leucopenia,** occurs for example in marrow failure and sometimes when the spleen is markedly enlarged, an effect known as hypersplenism. Increase of the leucocyte count is seen in most bacterial infections and after injury and is termed **leucocytosis.** White cell counts as high as 50,000/mm³ may be encounted in acute infections; much higher counts are typical of the malignant diseases of the white cell-producing tissues, the leukaemias.

Using a Romanowsky stained film, the proportions of the various types of white cell can be established. The range of values for the differential white cell count in adults is as follows:

Neutrophils,	2500–7500 mm³	(40–75%)
Lymphocytes,	1000–4500 mm³	(20–45%)
Monocytes,	200–900 mm³	(2–10%)
Eosinophils,	50–400 mm³	(1–6%)
Basophils,	0–200 mm³	(<1%)

Reference is made to the differential white cell count in children on p. 39.2.

Platelets

The total platelet count is in the range 150,000–400,000/mm³. Low values, **thrombocytopenia,** are encountered for example in marrow failure and when the marrow is involved in diseases such as leukaemia, in hypersplenism and when the platelets are destroyed abnormally rapidly in the circulation. Thrombocytopenia usually has no ill effect until the platelet count falls below 40,000–50,000/mm³. At this level there tends to be spontaneous bleeding into the skin and mucous membranes, a condition known as purpura. An increase of platelets, **thrombocytosis,** occurs transiently after injury, surgical operations and after splenectomy.

Erythrocyte sedimentation rate (ESR)

When blood is treated with an anticoagulant and allowed to stand in a tube, the cells sediment slowly. The rate of sedimentation is increased by changes in the proportion of the various plasma proteins, particularly if there is elevation of the concentration of fibrinogen and γ-globulin, and by some anaemias. The red cells aggregate in rouleaux like piles of draughts, probably because of changes in the surface charge of the cells; rouleaux formation is exaggerated in some diseases and this too accelerates the sedimentation rate.

An increased sedimentation rate is not diagnostic of any one disorder but is a good non-specific indicator of disease and is often used for this purpose in clinical practice. Serial estimation of the ESR is also valuable in following the progress of an illness. In the widely used Westergren method, blood anticoagulated with sodium citrate is allowed to stand in a 200×2.5 mm graduated glass tube and the fall of the blood cell column is measured after 1 hr. The normal ESR is less than 10 mm. in healthy young males and often slightly higher in females.

ORIGIN OF THE CELLS OF THE BLOOD

There is no unanimity of view regarding the genesis of the blood cells, and it is not known whether each cell has a separate progenitor or if all blood cells arise from a common parent cell. There is much to support the latter theory, and it helps to explain the pleomorphism (multicellularity) encountered in some malignant diseases of the reticuloendothelial system, e.g. the leukaemias and lymphomas. In recent years it has been suggested that the small lymphocyte is a pluripotential cell rather than an end stage mature cell, as previously believed. Ingenious experiments have shown that with appropriate stimuli the lymphocyte enlarges, assumes a variety of primitive appearances and proliferates. It has been postulated by Yoffey that in bone marrow the lymphocyte is transformed into other types of blood cell, in lymphoid tissue it is concerned with immune responses and in connective tissue, in addition to taking part in immune responses, it may become transformed into a monocyte and perhaps also into a connective tissue cell.

Blood cell production (haemopoiesis) in the foetus begins in the blood islands of the yolk sac and at this stage no distinctive cell type can be identified. The first recognizable cell is a primitive red cell precursor, a large cell with abundant cytoplasm. By the end of this first or mesoblastic period, definitive erythropoiesis is established and the various stages in maturation of the developing red cells can be recognized (p. 26.5); granular cells and megakaryocytes, which are the precursors of platelets,

also begin to appear. By the end of the second month of intrauterine development blood cell production has become established in the liver. Between the 2nd and 5th months lymphopoiesis and a small amount of erythropoiesis develop in the spleen. From about the 5th month, as the placental circulation is established, the myeloid tissues of the bones increasingly take over erythropoiesis, granulopoiesis and thrombopoiesis, and the lymph nodes become active with the spleen in lymphopoiesis. These various stages in the foetus are illustrated in fig. 26.1.

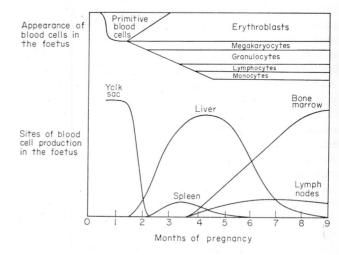

FIG. 26.1. The stages of development and the relative importance of the different sites of blood cell production in the foetus. From Wintrobe M.M. (1961) *Clinical Hematology*, 5th Edition. London: Kimpton.

Recent work in animals gives the thymus a special place in lymphopoiesis. There is evidence that this organ is active in lymphocyte production in the embryo and from it the other lymphoid tissues of the body may be seeded. Although the peripheral lymphoid tissues are fully organized around the time of birth or shortly afterwards the thymus may continue to exert a humoral effect on them, particularly in regard to immunological competence (p. 27.17).

At birth and during the first few years of life the marrow of practically all the bones is red and actively cellular. In the first year of life, fat cells begin to appear between the blood cells in the marrow of the long bones and as age advances the active marrow gradually recedes from the distal parts of the skeleton till at the end of the growing period active red marrow is found mainly in the flat bones, the skull, ribs, sternum and bones of pelvis; the other sites of red marrow are the vertebrae and the upper epiphyses of the humerus and femur.

Multipotential mesenchymal cells capable of returning to foetal and childhood patterns of erythropoiesis remain throughout life in the fatty yellow marrow of the long bones, in the liver, spleen and lymph nodes, and to a mall extent in the adrenal glands and intestinal wall; his potentiality for producing blood cells may be re-wakened when there are increased demands for them g. after haemorrhage and in certain disease states, e.g. aemolysis and leukaemia.

EVELOPMENT, FUNCTION AND FATE OF THE BLOOD CELLS

he description of the development of blood cells, par-cularly the erythroid series, has been confused by the se of different terminologies. The original nomenclature troduced by Ehrlich is used below and appropriate ommon alternatives are given in parenthesis.

Studies of normal and abnormal development of the lood cells depend on examination of the bone marrow. 1arrow can be obtained easily by needle puncture and spiration from the medullary cavity of certain bones, g. the shaft of tibia in infants, the spines of lumbar ertebrae in older children and the body of the sternum nd ilium in adults.

It is best examined as smears using Romanowsky tains.

The first and most primitive cell which can be distin-uished morphologically in the bone marrow, the spleen nd lymph nodes is the **reticulum cell**. This cell, which at he present time is believed to be the common parent lood cell, is large, about 20–30 μm in diameter with bundant pale, slightly basophilic cytoplasm. The ucleus is also large, usually filling about one half of he cell diameter; it is pale and basophilic showing a nely reticular chromatin pattern and containing one or 1ore nucleoli. Nucleoli, present only in very primitive lood cells are seen in the nucleus as areas of well demar-ated paler staining. The term blast cell is often applied o nucleolated cells and implies that the cell is of very arly type; normoblasts and megaloblasts, cells concerned 1 normal and abnormal erythropoiesis, do not contain ucleoli in the later stages of their maturation and are xceptions to this rule.

Red cells

rythropoiesis after normal full term birth occurs ex-lusively in the bone marrow in health and red cell pre-ursors normally account for one third to one tenth of he bone marrow cells. In children increased demands or red cells are met by using extramedullary sites; extra-1edullary haemopoiesis, however, is very rare in the dult. The first distinct erythroid cell is the **proerythro-last** (pronormoblast); it is a cell of about 15 μm in dia-1eter in which the nucleus leaves only a small rim of eeply basophilic cytoplasm. The nucleus still shows ucleoli or nucleolar remnants and contains thick strands f chromatin which may be clumped.

The time taken for the maturation process in the normal marrow from proerythroblast through the en-suing stages of normoblast to fully developed erythro-cyte is 7–10 days. This is achieved at first by mitotic division and then by progressive diminution in cell size. The nucleus is seen to become progressively more com-pact and dense (pyknotic), the cytoplasm becomes less blue and more pink due to reduction and disappearance of RNA on the one hand, and the synthesis of haemo-globin on the other. The present view is that the nucleus disintegrates and is largely absorbed within the cell and only the indigestible remains are extruded. In the next stage, strands of endoplasmic reticulum still remain which stain with cresyl blue. These are the reticulocytes (p. 26.2). When these strands have finally disappeared the red cell is fully mature. The endoplasmic reticulum is so altered by fixation when Romanowsky dyes are used that reticulocytes appear diffusely blue.

The **normoblasts** are spoken of as early (basophilic), intermediate (polychromatic) and late (acidophilic or orthochromatic). These terms are used arbitrarily and are based on cell diameter which decreases gradually from 15 to 10 μm, on the changes in colour which take place in the cytoplasm and on pyknosis of the nucleus which becomes increasingly marked till at the late normo-blast stage, it is like an ink spot. The early normoblast has cytoplasm which is still basophilic; in the intermediate stage it has a faintly purple colour as haemoglobin begins to appear; by the late normoblast stage the full com-plement of haemoglobin is present (plate 26.1, between pp. 27.2–3).

HAEMOGLOBIN

Comparison between red cells of lower vertebrates and those of mammalia shows gradual evolutionary improve-ment in their efficiency as oxygen carrying vehicles. According to Wintrobe the small mammalian corpuscles are more efficient oxygen carriers than the large corpuscles of the lower vertebrates and their biconcave form is be-lieved to be the optimum shape for the rapid and even diffusion of gases to all parts of the corpuscle. Although not easily measured, the total surface area of the circulat-ing erythrocytes appears to be much greater than the total surface area of the body. About one-third of the erythrocyte is haemoglobin; this is believed to be the highest concentration which will not interfere with reac-tion rates. Moreover the absence of a nucleus in the mature red cell leads to great reduction in its energy requirement as compared with other cells.

The precise structure of the red cell and the forces which preserve its biconcavity are poorly understood. It is a flexible elastic envelope which has a complex protein and lipid ultrastructure. Only about 2 per cent of the haemoglobin content of the red cell is near the plasma membrane and the remainder is uniformly distributed throughout the cell.

Haemoglobin is formed by the developing erythrocyte; in health, synthesis is virtually confined to the normoblasts, about 80 per cent being at the intermediate normoblast stage. Under normal conditions approximately 6 g of haemoglobin are formed per day in the adult and this productive capacity can be increased six or sevenfold after haemorrhage or haemolysis. Haemoglobin has a molecular weight of 66,700 and the molecule is believed to be ellipsoid in shape. The globin part consists of some 600 amino acids and the arrangement and sequence of these amino acids is now known to be genetically determined.

Globin is made up of two identical half molecules, each of which in the normal adult contains two different polypeptide chains, the α and β chains. Hence **haemoglobin-A**, the normal adult form, is sometimes designated $\alpha_2\beta_2$. In the early stages of foetal development **haemoglobin-F** is predominant and is designated $\alpha_2\gamma_2$. The γ chains differ from the β chains in their structure and by virtue of containing isoleucine, which is absent from haemoglobin-A. Haemoglobin-F has a higher affinity for oxygen than haemoglobin-A and in the 20-week foetus more than 90 per cent of the haemoglobin is Hb-F. At birth this has fallen to 55–85 per cent and thereafter it is usually rapidly replaced by haemoglobin-A. A third form **haemoglobin-A$_2$** also occurs normally; this is designated $\alpha_2\delta_2$; again there is a difference from the normal amino acid sequence of the β chain. The maximum proportion of haemoglobin-A$_2$ in the blood in health is less than 2–3 per cent.

The haemoglobin molecule comprises globin and four haem groups, each of which is a porphyrin ring structure made up of four pyrrole rings joined by methine bridges and containing a chelated iron atom. Haem is also part of the structure of myoglobin, the cytochromes, peroxidase and catalase. The four haem groups of haemoglobin lie in pairs on the surface of the molecule in pockets formed by the polypeptide chains. (Plate 11.1 facing p. 10.11).

The various stages of haemoglobin synthesis are illustrated in fig. 26.2. This shows that the basic building-blocks are succinyl-CoA from the citric acid cycle and glycine. The decarboxylation of α-amino β-oxoadipic acid forms δ-aminolaevulinic acid, a pyridoxal-phosphate enzyme complex being required at this laevulinic stage. The precise nature of the reactions from porphobilinogen onwards has not been established. However, it is known that porphyrin I and the porphyrin III series of isomers are synthesized in parallel.

Only the porphyrin III series is required for the production of haem; the porphyrin I series has no function and is excreted in the urine and faeces. An enzyme that catalyses the insertion of iron into protoporphyrin has been localized in the mitochondria. Haem is first formed from iron and protoporphyrin and then globin is added

The main function of haemoglobin is the transport of the respiratory gases and this is fully described on p. 29.17

In the red cell the ferrous porphyrin complex is continously being oxidized to the ferric form, methaemoglobin. This substance does not combine with oxygen and has no value in respiration. Hence methaemoglobin, which never constitutes much more than 1 per cent of the total haemoglobin in health, is continuously being reduced to the functional ferrous state. This reduction depends on the enzyme methaemoglobin-reductase, which utilises both NADH$_2$ and NADPH$_2$.

ENERGY METABOLISM OF THE RED CELL

The red blood cell is the site of numerous metabolic activities, most of which are concerned with maintaining the integrity of the cell membrane and preserving optimum osmotic conditions in the cell against steep ionic gradients. Many enzymes and intermediary products without known function are, however, present in the mature red cell, suggesting that it may have functions other than the transport of respiratory gases.

The normoblast is able to synthesize DNA, RNA, lipid, haem and proteins; it has an electron transfer system, a functional citric acid cycle, a hexose monophosphate pathway and the Embden–Meyerhof pathway. In the circulating non-nucleated erythrocyte most of these activities have been lost; the source of energy is glucose which has to be transported across the red cell membrane and only two energy producing reactions are retained; about 90 per cent of the glucose utilized is degraded to lactate by the Embden–Meyerhof pathway and the remaining 10 per cent is accounted for by the pentose pathway . The energy liberated in anaerobic glycolysis in the red cell seems to be stored in the high energy phosphate bonds of 1,3-diphosphoglycerate; such energy is subsequently used for preserving the cell membrane and for the transport of ions and nutriments into and out of the cell. The operation of the pentose pathway yields NADPH$_2$ and this is *inter alia* used in glutathione reduction and in preserving the cell against the effect of oxidant compounds.

Several studies indicate the wearing out of some enzyme systems as the cause of cell ageing. Measurement of the red cell survival time by different techniques show that its life span is 110–120 days; loss of cells is a linear process, the oldest cells being removed and replaced at the rate of about 1 per cent of the total red cell mass/day. Precisely what happens to the effete red cell is still not known. Sudden haemolysis in the circulation and erythrophagocytosis by reticuloendothelial cells are not proved and one theory is that the cell is gradually fragmented at the end of its days, before being cleared from the circulation by the reticuloendothelial system. Deficiency of one of several

Succinyl coenzyme-A ←—— Succinate ←—$\frac{\text{Citric}}{\text{acid cycle}}$— Acetate
+
Glycine-pyridoxal
phosphate
↓
α-Amino-β-oxoadipic
acid
↓
δ-Aminolaevulinic acid
↓
Porphobilinogen
↓
Dipyrrylmethenes
↓
Tetrapyrrylmethenes
(porphyrins)
↓
Uroporphyrinogen I   Uroporphyrinogen III
↓   ↓
Coproporphyrinogen I   Coproporphyrinogen III ———————→ Protoporphyrin
↓
excreted

Haemoglobin
↑
Globin
+
Haem
↑
Fe
+
Protoporphyrin

FIG. 26.2. The steps in the synthesis of haemoglobin. The synthesis of haem begins with the condensation of glycine and succinyl coenzyme A, the decarboxylation of the resulting product α-amino-β-oxoadipic acid and the condensation of two molecules of δ-aminolaevulic acid so formed to produce the pyrrole derivative, porphobilinogen. It is believed that polymerization of four molecules of porphobilinogen then leads to formation of porphyrin. Although four isomeric porphyrinogens could theoretically be formed in the next step only two, series I and III, occur in the body. Uroporphyrinogen I and coproporphyrinogen I have no known function and are excreted.

Porphyrins are ring structures composed of four pyrrole rings joined by methine (−CH=) bridges; porphyrinogens are similar but in these compounds the pyrrole rings are linked by methylene (−CH$_2$−) bridges; protoporphyrins are porphyrins in which the side chains contain carboxyl groups. Haem, the prosthetic group of haemoglobin, is a co-ordination complex in which a ferrous iron atom is firmly bound to protoporphyrin, type IX. Haem cannot combine reversibly with oxygen alone; this property is conferred upon it by its linkage with the basic protein globin to form haemoglobin.

Coproporphyrinogen III is converted to a protoporphyrin by dehydrogenation of the methylene bridges to methine bridges. In addition four methyl, two vinyl and two propionic acid side chains are formed and although this particular protoporphyrin has fifteen possible isomers, only one, type IX, is produced.

critical enzymes may lead to marked shortening of the red cell life span (haemolytic disease) either by premature ageing or by making the cell more susceptible to damage from environmental influences. Deficiency or defect of the enzyme glucose-6-phosphate dehydrogenase is common in Negro and Mediterranean peoples, being transmitted by a sex-linked recessive type of inheritance. This enzyme is concerned with $NADPH_2$ production and affected patients are liable to suffer bouts of haemolysis on exposure to certain drugs, e.g. the antimalarial drug primaquine, and sulphonamides and after eating the fava bean (favism). Other enzyme deficiencies now known to be implicated in congenital haemolytic anaemias are diphosphoglyceromutase, glutathione reductase and pyruvate kinase.

SUBSTANCES ESSENTIAL TO ERYTHROPOIESIS

Protein

Amino acids are required for the synthesis of the globin component of haemoglobin and for the construction of the red cell stroma. When the supply of amino acids is limited, priority appears to be given to the synthesis of haemoglobin. In consequence, in starvation and in children with protein deficiency (kwashiorkor) severe anaemia (Hb < 8 g/100 ml) is seldom found. Minor degrees of anaemia are common, in part due to haemodilution from an increased plasma volume, which frequently occurs in these conditions, and in part due to deficiency of other haematinic substances.

Iron

Iron is required for red cell formation because of its essential place in the haemoglobin molecule. The dietary sources of iron are described on p. 5.8. It will be remembered that a good mixed diet provides about 12–15 mg/day, most of which is unabsorbed and lost in the faeces. Of this dietary iron an adult male has to absorb about 1 mg/day, or slightly less than 10 per cent, to balance the iron that is lost from the body, mainly in desquamation, and women have to absorb about twice this amount during their reproductive life to meet the additional loss in menstruation, pregnancy and lactation (p. 5.8). The need for iron is increased in the growing child because of his expanding red cell volume and muscle bulk.

Factors which have been shown to determine the amount of iron absorbed are the rate of erythropoiesis and the state of the body stores of iron. More iron is absorbed when erythropoiesis is active and the body stores are depleted than when erythropoiesis is suppressed and the body stores are full.

Iron is transported in the plasma bound to a β_1 globulin, **transferrin**, and the level of iron in the plasma in health is of the order 80–180 µg/100 ml. This is mostly iron derived from the breakdown of haemoglobin (about 25 mg/day). The iron-carrying globulin is normally not fully saturated; the amount of globulin available for transporting iron can be measured and is spoken of as the total iron-binding capacity (TIBC). Information regarding the serum iron and degree of saturation of the TIBC is of value in the elucidation of some anaemias and diseases of iron overload.

The body stores contain enough iron to replace about one-third of the circulating haemoglobin in the event of haemorrhage. This iron, mostly in the form of ferritin, larger agglomerates being in the insoluble form haemosiderin, is concentrated in the reticuloendothelial cells of liver, spleen and bone marrow. The normal distribution of iron in the body is given in table 26.1.

TABLE 26.1. The disposition of iron in the adult. From Drabkin D. L. (1951) *Physiol. Rev.* 31, 245.

	Approximate percentage of total iron
Circulating haemoglobin	75·0
Iron in body stores	20·0
Myoglobin	5·0
Haem enzymes	< 0·5
Transferrin	< 0·1

The absorption of iron from the alimentary tract is discussed on p. 30.39. An active transport mechanism is involved and the upper small intestine is the main site. The capacity to absorb iron is often inadequate to meet physiological needs, particularly if the diet is poor in respect of iron-containing foods. Hence anaemia due to iron deficiency is common in women and children in all countries. On the other hand adult males seldom suffer from iron deficiency unless there is chronic loss of blood, e.g. from an ulcer or other lesion of the gastrointestinal tract or the presence in the bowel of blood sucking parasites, e.g. hookworms or schistosomes, such as are common in many tropical countries.

The person with iron-deficiency anaemia complains of weakness, tiredness and breathlessness, symptoms that are common to all anaemias. Diagnostic changes are found in the peripheral blood, where there will be a subnormal Hb level, reduced MCHC and low serum iron level; in the blood film the red cells vary in size and shape and are mostly hypochromic and microcytic. If body tissues, for example, liver or bone marrow, were to be examined for iron content they would be found to be grossly depleted.

Iron deficiency anaemia gives rise to much ill-health. Fortunately it can be treated easily by removing the cause if this is possible and by giving iron compounds, e.g. ferrous sulphate, medicinally.

Vitamin B₁₂ and folic acid

The nutritional properties of these two vitamins are discussed on p. 5.15. Despite their importance, particularly in relation to nucleic acid synthesis, the only proven functions of these two vitamins are that vitamin B₁₂ is concerned with the *de novo* synthesis of labile methyl groups from one carbon precursors such as glycine and formate (p. 11.27) while folic acid is concerned with the movement of methyl groups from one acceptor to another (p. 11.28).

Vitamin B₁₂ is the extrinsic factor which Castle described in 1929. The chemical structure (p. 7.14) shows it to be a porphyrin ring like haem but containing cobalt. An alternative name for the pure substance is **cyanocobalamin**. Related substances both naturally occurring and semisynthetic without the cyano group have been described; these are spoken of as cobalamins or corrins. The term vitamin B₁₂ is now used to describe all naturally occurring cobalamins with physiological activity.

Vitamin B₁₂ is synthesized exclusively by microorganisms. For all practical purposes, animal protein forms our only dietary source; pure vegetarians (vegans) get vitamin B₁₂ in their food only in tiny amounts from contaminating moulds. The daily requirement is less than 1 μg. In physiological amounts vitamin B₁₂ requires the action of **intrinsic factor** for its absorption. Intrinsic factor is a mucoprotein secreted by the glands in the body and fundus of stomach which is still to be identified chemically; it modifies the vitamin B₁₂ complexes in the food to a form suitable for assimilation but the precise mechanism of action is unknown. Vitamin B₁₂ is absorbed mainly in the ileum and is stored mainly in the liver. Studies with ⁵⁸Co vitamin B₁₂ indicate that in the liver it has a biological half life of about 1 year; this explains why patients after total gastrectomy, in which all intrinsic factor-bearing tissue has been removed surgically, may take several years to develop clinical vitamin B₁₂ deficiency. In the serum vitamin B₁₂ is mostly bound to globulin. The normal level is 170–1000 pg/ml (1 pg = 10⁻¹² g).

Folic acid is widely disseminated in nature both in the plant and animal kingdom. The main dietary source is probably green leafy vegetables; it was first isolated from spinach leaves in 1941 (*folium*, a leaf), hence its name. Its chemical formula (p. 7.13) shows it to be pteroylglutamic acid and therefore chemically related to the pterins, pigments in butterfly wings. The term folic acid is used to describe pteroylglutamic acid (PGA) and all naturally occurring substances with PGA-like activity.

The dietary requirement of folic acid is uncertain. However, in a patient with folic acid deficiency, e.g. from disease causing intestinal malabsorption, about 50 μg of folic acid per day are required therapeutically in order to keep the patient in health. Folic acid has no mediating absorptive mechanism like intrinsic factor and is assimilated throughout most of the small intestine but mainly from the upper part, the folic acid conjugates in the food, first having been broken down to monoglutamates. Absorbed folic acid is next converted to tetrahydrofolic acid, then to 5-methyltetrahydrofolic acid which is the main form in the serum. The normal serum level of folate is 3–20 ng/ml. The active principle, formiminotetrahydrofolic acid, acquires a formimino group (—CH=NH) from formiminoglutamic acid (FIGLU), an intermediary product in the conversion of histidine to glutamic acid. Both vitamin B₁₂ and ascorbic acid are believed to be concerned in the latter stages of tetrahydrofolic acid metabolism. In patients with folic acid deficiency FIGLU may accumulate in the body and be excreted in abnormal amounts in the urine. The rate of utilization of folic acid in the body is not known but is believed to be very much more rapid than that of vitamin B₁₂ and stores may last perhaps only a few weeks. The various steps in folic acid metabolism are shown in fig. 26.3.

FIG. 26.3. The main stages in the production of the active form of folic acid and its relationship to the conversion of histidine to glutamic acid. THF=tetrahydrofolic acid.

Deficiency of either vitamin B₁₂ or folic acid, due to dietary inadequacy, failure of alimentary absorption or increased metabolic requirement, produces a characteristic change in the blood known as **megaloblastic anaemia**. In the bone marrow the nucleus of the erythroid precursors matures more slowly than the cytoplasm, giving rise to abnormal cells, megaloblasts, which appear to be larger than normoblasts at a corresponding stage of development and show a nucleus with a characteristic spotted thrush breast appearance. In vitamin B₁₂ and folic acid deficiency the red cells in the peripheral blood are reduced in number and tend to be macrocytic and, provided there is no concomitant iron deficiency, they have their normal complement of Hb. This means that when the absolute indices are calculated, the MCV usually exceeds 95 μm^3 but the MCHC is in the normal range. In addition, vitamin B_{12}, but not folic acid, is essential for the integrity of myelin. Hence profound vitamin B_{12} deficiency can lead also to a specific neuropathy which consists mainly in peripheral neuritis and later a patchy degeneration in the spinal cord, particularly in the dorsal and lateral columns.

In many parts of Asia and Africa megaloblastic anaemia due to a dietary deficiency of folic acid is common. It is much less common in prosperous countries from any cause, but in Europe, the commonest is pernicious anaemia due to vitamin B_{12} deficiency. This is seen mainly after the age of 40 years and has an inherited basis. The cause is malabsorption of vitamin B_{12} due to failure of secretion of intrinsic factor consequent on atrophy of the gastric mucosa. Megaloblastic anaemia due to folic acid deficiency is seen in the later stages of pregnancy when the requirement for folic acid to meet foetal demands may outstrip the nutritional supply.

Vitamin B_6

A very rare anaemia showing signs of impaired utilization of iron for haem synthesis responds to administration of pyridoxine. It is believed to be due to interference with the porphyrin synthesis to haem at about the porphobilinogen stage where pyridoxal phosphate is implicated as a coenzyme (fig. 26.2).

Trace metals

There is no evidence in man that deficiency of any mineral other than iron can cause disturbance of erythropoiesis. However, veterinary studies indicate that certain elements in trace amounts are essential for normal blood production. Copper in particular seems to be important since copper deficiency in swine leads to an anaemia which is believed to result from interference with iron absorption and with red cell synthesis; there is also reduction in the red cell life span. Cobalt deficiency gives rise to a macrocytic anaemia in ruminants but this is because vitamin B_{12}, synthesized in the rumen, depends on an adequate supply of cobalt.

OTHER FACTORS INFLUENCING ERYTHROPOIESIS

Erythropoietin

At the beginning of this century two French workers, Carnot and Deflandre, postulated the existence of a humoral control of erythropoiesis on the basis of experiments in rabbits. This was discarded for the next 40 years mainly because the work could not be confirmed and it was believed that anoxia was the chief stimulus to an increased rate of erythropoiesis. However, a number of unconnected observations resuscitated the humoral hypothesis; for example, it was shown that anoxia actually inhibited erythropoiesis in tissue culture and that if one of a pair of parabiotic rats, i.e. rats with a shared circulation, was exposed to an atmosphere of low oxygen tension, both animals showed the same increase in marrow activity. Subsequently it was shown that the plasma from hypoxic, anaemic and cobalt treated animals was capable of enhancing erythropoiesis in other animals. The erythropoietic factor, named erythropoietin, appeared to be a polypeptide associated with α_2 globulin. Some workers thought that there might be at least two factors, one controlling haemoglobin synthesis and another red cell production. Experimental studies favour a renal source of erythropoietin; animals in which all the major viscera are removed can still elaborate this factor but production of erythropoietin ceases when the kidneys are removed. This is in accord with clinical experience; anaemia always occurs when there is renal failure of long standing, while some kidney tumours and cysts are associated with an increased red cell mass. (p. 33.21)

Observations on the levels of erythropoietin in the serum in man in various blood diseases are conflicting. This may be due to variation in the sensitivity of the animal assay techniques used, to the consumption of erythropoietin by an active marrow and to renal excretion. In one reliable study the titre of erythropoietin was found to be raised in all severe anaemias except that associated with chronic renal damage.

Age and sex

The newly-born infant has considerably higher values for PCV than at any later time in life (p. 39.2). After birth there is gradual reduction in Hb, RBC and PCV due to replacement of the larger foetal macrocytes of short life span by adult type red cells, final atrophy of erythropoietic tissue in the liver and the demands of rapid growth. The peripheral blood values continue to fall slowly until the infant is 2–3 months old. Thereafter marrow activity gradually increases and there is a progressive rise in Hb level until puberty when normal adult figures are reached. After the sixth decade there is commonly a slight decline in Hb and PCV. This is an inconstant finding and is probably due to malnutrition and iron deficiency rather than to any diminution in marrow activity from ageing.

During the reproductive period the Hb, RBC and PCV in the female tend to be about 90 per cent those of males. This difference between the sexes may be a hormonal effect but is more likely to be due to the difficulty which the female has in maintaining iron balance consequent on menstruation; it is not present before the menarché, or after the menopause.

A 15 kg child has about the same amount of bone marrow as a 70 kg adult but since the blood volume increases greatly during growth the rate of production of blood cells is much higher in childhood and adolescence than in later life.

Exercise and emotion

A transient increase in the concentration of circulating erythrocytes following strenuous muscular exercise and in emotional states such as fear and rage has long been recognized. In the dog this can be attributed to the discharge of blood of high haematocrit value from the spleen under the influence of adrenaline. In man, however, the blood changes are not easily explained since the spleen does not form a reservoir of red cells as in some animals. Cold baths in man are said to have a similar effect and it seems likely that the finding results from redistribution of cells in the circulation due to vasoconstriction in some regions, e.g. the skin, and vasodilation in others.

Physical changes in environment

No consistent effect on erythropoiesis has been observed from changes in environmental temperature, climate or season. Anoxaemia associated with a low barometric pressure does, however, within certain limits consistently increase the rate of erythrocyte production as measured by the rate of iron turnover in the plasma and red cells using radioactive iron techniques and the erythrocyte concentration in the blood. Healthy individuals show this effect within hours when ascending to altitudes above 6000 ft and the effect is maximal within 7–14 days. On the basis of the animal studies already mentioned these blood changes are believed to be due to erythropoietin. Natives residing at high altitudes have a rate of erythropoiesis about 30 per cent above normal. Since the red cell survival time is unchanged the Hb and PCV in the blood and the red cell mass are increased.

When a person who has been at a high altitude descends to sea level the rate of red cell production gradually returns to normal in about a month.

Very severe anoxaemia ultimately has a suppressive effect on erythropoiesis. Hurtado found that this occurred when the arterial oxygen saturation fell below 60–70 per cent, a degree of anoxaemia comparable with that obtaining at altitudes above 20,000 ft.

Endocrine factors

Deficiency of thyroid, adrenocortical and anterior pituitary function either from disease or surgical removal of secreting tissue produces mild anaemia which responds to the appropriate hormone. In Cushing's syndrome, a mild erythraemia may be a feature. Thyroxine, cortisol, androgens and prolactin promote erythropoiesis experimentally and oestrogens cause a fall in Hb, RBC and PCV probably by haemodilution from expansion of the plasma volume. The effect of hormones on blood cell production is complex. Not only do their actions appear to be inter-related but also they have indirect effects by altering nutrition and metabolic rates.

Degradation of haemoglobin and metabolism of bile pigments

The precise stages of haemoglobin catabolism are still uncertain; the initial reactions are, however, extravascular in the reticuloendothelial cells. It is believed that globin splits off and that the iron protoporphyrin ring of haem is opened by oxidative breakage of one of the joining methene bridges. Iron is next removed. Each day about 25 mg of iron is released to be mostly reutilized at once for new haemoglobin synthesis. The residual pigment is biliverdin, the main bile pigment in birds and amphibia. In man, reduction converts most of this to bilirubin.

Haemoglobin is released in small amounts into the plasma where it binds with haptoglobin. The haemoglobin-haptoglobin complex is then cleared from the plasma by the reticuloendothelial cells and the haemoglobin is thought to be metabolized as described. This is the only function so far ascribed to the haptoglobins.

After bilirubin is formed by the reticuloendothelial cells (about 200 mg/day in the adult) it is transported in the plasma bound mostly to albumin. This albumin bound bilirubin does not pass the glomerular filter. It appears in excessive amounts in the blood when there is increased catabolism of haemoglobin as occurs in the haemolytic states. In the liver cells, bilirubin is converted to water soluble forms and excreted in the bile. Most is conjugated with glucuronic acid into bilirubin diglucuronide, a small amount into monoglucuronide; a fraction of the bilirubin may also be converted into a sulphate.

In the intestine bilirubin is converted to stercobilinogen. Studies with ^{15}N glycine have shown that not all stercobilinogen is derived from haemoglobin. This is of great academic interest and of some clinical importance. The amount is of the order of 10–15 per cent in health and as high as 30–40 per cent in some diseases, for example pernicious anaemia. The observation may indicate that haem, not utilized for haemoglobin, and porphyrins other than haem, are also metabolized to bilirubin. The metabolism of bilirubin is described on p. 31.8.

White cells

GRANULOCYTE SERIES

After birth, the production of the granulocytic white cells takes place only in the red marrow where the proportion of granular to erythroid precursors is between 3:1 and 10:1.

The first stage of development is the **myeloblast** (plate 26.1, between pp. 27.2–3), a cell of 11–18 μm in diameter with a large nucleus, of fairly homogeneous chromatin containing 2–4 nucleoli, in a small amount of foamy cytoplasm. The next cell is the **promyelocyte**, a somewhat larger cell than the myeloblast, still with nucleoli in the nucleus and a few azurophilic granules in abundant cytoplasm. The **myelocyte** is a smaller cell with a round nucleus. It does not possess nucleoli and shows numerous cytoplasmic granules, like the mature polymorphs (p. 26.2) which are clearly identifiable using Romanowsky stains as eosinophilic (bright orange), basophilic (blue-black) and neutrophilic (faint purple). Mitosis does not occur after the myelocyte stage. The **metamyelocyte** shows commencing indentation of the nucleus producing a kidney shaped or horseshoe appearance leading to the lobulation seen in the next stage of maturation, the **polymorphonuclear granulocyte**. The time taken for maturation of a granulocyte in the bone marrow prior to its release into the circulation is believed to be of the order of 3–4 days. A mature polymorph is actively motile when studied in wet preparations. Pseudopodia form in the cytoplasm and the nucleus is capable of great distortion particularly in the neutrophils.

The survival time and fate of granulocytes is not well established. Probably only a small proportion, less than 5 per cent of the total number of granulocytes, are present in the blood at any one time and they may enter and leave the circulation many times in their life span. There is evidence that a large pool of granulocytes exists, mainly in the bone marrow, from which they can be rapidly discharged, giving an abrupt rise in the white cell count. This may occur with physiological stimuli such as exercise and after adrenaline injections.

Radioactive labelling indicates that most granulocytes spend only a few hours in the circulation, but their total life span is probably 6–11 days, most of which is spent in storage pools.

There is always a proportion of non-viable granulocytes in the circulation and it is believed that these are removed like red cells by reticuloendothelial cells (p. 27.1) in marrow, liver, spleen and lymph nodes. Granulocytes are lost in performing body defence functions and some pass regularly into the lungs, saliva and alimentary tract.

LYMPHOCYTES

Lymphocytes are produced in lymph nodes, the tonsils, the periarterial pulp of the spleen, the Peyer's patches of the intestine and lymph follicles in the bone marrow.

The first recognizable lymphocyte precursor, known as the **lymphoblast**, is similar to the myeloblast in appearance. Then follows the **prolymphocyte**, a cell approximately 15 μm in diameter with nuclear chromatin somewhat coarser than that of the lymphoblast and still showing nucleoli or nucleolar remnants.

Estimates of the life span of lymphocytes have ranged from 3 to 200 days. This may be because cells that appear morphologically similar in the lymphoid tissues and blood and bone marrow are in fact not the same in origin or function. There is good evidence for at least two populations of lymphocytes, a short lived group that are the main cells in bone marrow and thymus, and a long lived group in the lymphoid organs and lymph; the lymphocytes in the circulatory blood probably represent a mixture of the two. The lymphocyte is not now regarded as the end of a line of development but rather as a multipotential cell capable of transformation to a more primitive type which may then be a stem cell for other haemopoietic cells, a source of phagocytic cells and a source of antibody producing cells.

As with the granular cell there is evidence of a large pool of lymphocytes in lymphoid tissue, which has been estimated to be 25 times that in the blood. The output of thoracic duct lymphocytes per day is about 4 times the number in the blood. These thoracic duct cells are not short lived but recirculate from the blood and lymph via the lymph follicles of alimentary tract and lymph nodes; the time these cells spend in the blood is only a small part of their life span.

Lymphocytes are discussed more fully in chap. 27.

MONOCYTES

These cells are produced mainly in the spleen and lymph nodes. The parent cell, the **monoblast**, is like the myeloblast and lymphoblast, a cell of about 15 μm in diameter with a large nucleus, containing 2–3 nucleoli, filling much of the cell cytoplasm. Intermediate cells showing nucleolar remnants are recognized in the maturation process; they are sometimes termed **promonocytes**. The next identifiable cell is the monocyte. Production rates, life span and fate of monocytes are not known.

CHEMISTRY AND METABOLISM OF WHITE CELLS

When blood is centrifuged, the white cells separate as a layer on top of the red cells. By using a centrifuge tube shaped like a dumb-bell, it is possible to harvest a concentrate of leucocytes. The metabolic activities of such a suspension can be studied in the same manner as any other tissue. Much less is known about the metabolism of leucocytes than of tissues like muscle and liver, because only small amounts can be obtained from a sample of blood. However, now that micromethods are available for biochemical analysis, it is probable that in clinical practice studies of the metabolism of leucocytes will be made much more frequently, since the necessary material can be obtained by a simple venepuncture, whereas liver, muscle and other tissue can be obtained only by a biopsy.

Leucocytes have been shown to contain glycogen present in the cytoplasm of granulocytes, and they possess all the enzymic mechanisms for the degradation of carbohydrates both aerobically and anaerobically. Leucocytes obtained from malnourished children contain amounts of oxaloacetate, pyruvate, lactate and ATP which are significantly less than normal and this may be interpreted as evidence of impaired glycolysis.

So far two practical applications of analysis of leucocytes have been developed. Firstly their content of ascorbic acid is high, over 20 mg/100 g in a well nourished person, but falls to 1 or 2 mg/100 g when the dietary vitamin C is inadequate. This measurement is useful in the diagnosis of scurvy. Secondly, alkaline phosphatase, present in normal granulocytes, tends to be low or absent in abnormal cells and this measurement is useful in the diagnosis of leukaemia.

It has not yet been possible to make adequate preparations of the different leucocytes for quantitative measurements of their constituents.

FACTORS INFLUENCING THE NUMBER OF CIRCULATING LEUCOCYTES IN HEALTH

No specific nutrient is essential to the production of white cells as is iron for haemoglobin and red cells. However, vitamin B$_{12}$ and folic acid play some part in normal leucopoiesis since severe deficiency of either leads to leucopenia which responds to their administration.

The role of the spleen in white cell production is obscure. There is evidence for its having a remote effect on the release of white cells and platelets from the bone marrow and the existence of a splenic hormone has been postulated. When a normal spleen is removed in man, e.g. after injury, there is a rise in the leucocyte count in the blood, due mainly to neutrophils, which normally lasts for 2–3 weeks.

In the newborn infant the white cell count is usually in the region of 15,000/mm^3 in the first 24 hours of life. After 48 hours and for the first months the count is 10,000–12,000/mm^3; thereafter the normal white cell count is less than 10,000/mm^3. Lymphocytes are more numerous than polymorphs till about the age of 4 years; then the number gradually diminishes till adult proportions are reached.

The white cell count may fluctuate during the day and also vary from day to day but there is no consistent pattern. Environmental changes cause variable effects; anoxia at high altitudes produces a neutrophil leucocytosis but unlike the effect on the red cells this is transitory. Strenuous exercise, pain and severe emotional disturbance such as fear or rage produce a rise in the white cell count lasting at most a few hours, mainly due to a rise in the number of neutrophil polymorphs. In these circumstances the total count can exceed 30,000/mm^3. The effect is seen in the absence of the spleen and occurs within minutes; it is almost certainly due to the mobilization of white cells from the reservoirs. Since adrenaline and cortisol affects the white cell, many of the physiological variations in the blood picture

may be hormonally induced. Adrenaline produces first a polymorph leucocytosis and lymphocytosis and a later rise due to neutrophil increase accompanied by lymphopenia and eosinopenia. Noradrenaline appears to have no effect on circulating white cells. Cortisol causes neutrophil leucocytosis, lymphopenia and eosinopenia.

Since the main functions of the leucocytes are concerned with body defence, the most striking changes in the total white cell count and the relative proportions of the different white cells are seen in infections and inflammations.

FUNCTIONS OF THE LEUCOCYTES

Leucocytes are agents in the body's defence against infection. They are able to destroy or remove particles and micro-organisms and the lymphocytes are concerned with the formation and distribution of antibodies. They may well have other transport functions and the presence of many cytoplasmic enzymes suggests that numerous activities are still to be recognized.

Towards the end of last century Metchnikoff had suspected the role of phagocytosis, i.e. the ingestion of a particle by a living cell, as one of the main defence mechanisms. He showed the accumulation of mobile cells about a thorn placed under the skin of a starfish larva. Microscopic observation has shown that phagocytosis by leucocytes occurs in two ways. First, the cytoplasm in contact with the foreign particle flows round the particle at the site of contact and engulfs it; this is probably what happens with large and elongated bacteria. Second, the particle sinks into the cytoplasm without there being any observable flow around it.

The neutrophil polymorphs and monocytes are the most active phagocytic cells. Monocytes appear to be more important than neutrophils in engulfing protozoa and large particles, and they occasionally engulf red cells. Eosinophils and basophils are less adept at this operation and lymphocytes are not phagocytic. Most phagocytosis occurs extravascularly in the tissues. Aggregation of leucocytes at the site of bacterial infection or invasion by foreign particles is one of the earliest changes that can be seen microscopically. Apart from its motility, there is clearly some attracting force directing the leucocyte. This phenomenon, known as chemotaxis, has received much attention but its mechanism is obscure. In addition neutrophil polymorphs may release substances which help to generate the local response to inflammation and injury and the more general responses affecting the circulating leucocytes and the body temperature.

Because eosinophils are normally more abundant in tissue fluid than in blood and are found particularly in the bowel wall, the respiratory tract and skin, they are thought to be concerned with the degradation and removal of protein. They are most numerous in allergic reactions and histamine has been demonstrated to have a chemotactic effect on eosinophils.

Reference has already been made to studies which suggest that the lymphocyte is not an end stage cell but one capable of transformation into more primitive cells. The role of the lymphocyte in defence is related to this function. There is evidence of its ability to produce macrophages both *in vivo* and *in vitro* and there is some indication that it can give rise to giant cells and fibroblasts.

The complex functions of the lymphocyte and the relation of the thymus to immune responses are referred to on p. 27.16.

Platelets

Platelets are produced from megakaryocytes which lie outside the blood sinusoids of the bone marrow. The megakaryocytes are large, up to 180 μm in diameter, and when mature have a multi-lobed nucleus and a markedly granular, light blue cytoplasm (plate 26.1, between pp. 27.2–3). From their periphery processes develop which penetrate between the vascular endothelial cells lining the blood sinusoids and enter the blood stream. Platelets are believed to be formed when the ends of these processes are broken off into the blood.

Platelets are metabolically active, being rich in enzymes, particularly those concerned with glycolysis, oxidation, transamination and dehydrogenation and they contain a particularly high concentration of ATP. They are rich in phospholipid and in potassium and they contain virtually all the blood 5-hydroxytryptamine. Phospholipid and 5HT play an important part in blood coagulation.

Studies in man, using radioactive isotopic labels, e.g. ^{51}Cr, suggest that platelets have a life span of 8–11 days. There is good evidence that in normal man minute clots are continually being formed and dissolved, resulting in the random destruction of platelets, but death by senescence may also occur. The platelet life span can be artificially increased in a variety of ways as, for example, by the intake of a low fat diet, or by giving certain drugs, such as anticoagulants, and it can be shortened by smoking. Reduction of the platelet life span is also often associated with disease states. One of the most important functions of the platelet is the part it plays in haemostasis.

THE HAEMOSTATIC MECHANISM

Haemostasis is one of the most important protective mechanisms in the body and controls bleeding in the face of injury. Most of the early information concerning haemostasis arose from studies on the formation of a visible blood clot *in vitro* and in damaged vessels. More recently much has been learned from the study of diseases in which haemostasis is defective.

When a blood vessel is severed, the damaged end contracts and retracts; the diameter of the end of the cut vessel is thereby reduced. The damaged vascular endothelium undergoes a functional change and becomes water wettable; this is probably due to alteration in its electrical surface charge. Platelets become attracted to the damaged endothelium and they adhere to it and to one another. ADP appears to make them adhesive. In this process they change their shape from that of a disc to a sphere. The platelet aggregate thus formed seals the cut end of the vessel. At this stage, aggregation is a potentially reversible process. Normally it is rapidly followed by a further change in the platelets known as viscous metamorphosis. This consists of an irreversible fusion of the platelet aggregate into an amorphous mass, probably due to the action of thrombin on fibrinogen contained within the platelets. The platelets then discharge their content of 5HT which further enhances vascular contraction, and of phospholipid which is concerned in the early stages of the clotting mechanism.

The process of vascular contraction and retraction and the formation of a platelet plug together constitute the **initiation phase** of haemostasis and may stop blood flow from the damaged vessel. In capillaries, where the hydrostatic pressure is low, this mechanism alone may be adequate. It is reinforced by extrinsic pressure of the clot and by the normal turgor of the tissue. In larger vessels, however, where hydrostatic pressure is higher, the platelet plug is inadequate to stop the flow of blood. The contraction and retraction of the vessel wall soon passes off and a more secure and permanent plug is needed. A **blood clot** is produced by the conversion of circulating fibrinogen into an insoluble matrix of fibrin, in which blood cells are entrapped. This is known as the **maintenance phase**. Whole blood obtained by venepuncture and placed in a clean glass tube takes 5–10 min to clot at 37°C. A similar delay *in vivo* would explain the need for the initiation phase. Insoluble fibrin is formed from its soluble protein precursor fibrinogen through the action of the proteolytic enzyme thrombin. It follows that

FIG. 26.4. The final two stages of the clotting mechanism.

thrombin cannot be present in intact blood except perhaps in trace amounts. It is formed from an inactive soluble blood protein precursor, prothrombin. The final two stages of the clotting mechanism can therefore be written as in fig. 26.4. These reactions, first propounded by Morawitz as long ago as 1905, still hold good today.

In 1947, Owren in Norway clearly identified an additional factor in the normal clotting process and since then many others have been discovered. These are now known by Roman numerals assigned by an International Committee on Blood Clotting Factors. A full list of the factors together with synonyms is given in table 26.2; some use is still made of the older or original names.

The reactions illustrated in fig. 26.4 are explosive in their intensity once the necessary concentration of **prothrombin activator** (thromboplastin) has been achieved. The greater part of the time taken for the blood to clot is taken up in the first stage during which the activator is being formed. There is some dispute about the precise nature of these early events in intravascular clotting but Macfarlane has put forward the attractive hypothesis that all the clotting factors are involved in a chain reaction or 'cascade of enzymes'. The exact order of their action is still uncertain but it is believed that the process is initiated when Factor XII comes into contact with a foreign surface or an area of damaged tissue. Active Factor XII then activates Factor XI, i.e. the proenzyme is converted into an enzyme, which in turn activates Factors IX, VIII, X and V. Platelet phospholipid (platelet cofactor 3), which is released by damaged platelets, also takes part in the reaction. Calcium ions are required in this stage when prothrombin activator is being formed, as in the later two stages. Hence substances which remove calcium ions as insoluble salts, e.g. oxalates, or convert them to non-ionized organic salts, e.g. citrate, are anticoagulants. Sodium, potassium and ammonium oxalate, sodium citrate and disodium or dipotassium ethylenediamine tetraacetate (EDTA or sequestrene) are frequently added to whole blood for this pur-

TABLE 26.2. International nomenclature of clotting factors.

Factor	Common synonyms
I	Fibrinogen
II	Prothrombin
III	Thromboplastin, tissue juice
IV	Calcium
V	Accelerator globulin, proaccelerin, labile factor
VI	No longer used
VII	Proconvertin, stable factor, autoprothrombin I
VIII	Antihaemophilic factor (AHF), antihaemophilic globulin (AHG), antihaemophilic factor A.
IX	Christmas factor, plasma thromboplastin component (PTC), antihaemophilic factor B.
X	Stuart–Prower factor
XI	Plasma thromboplastin antecedent (PTA), antihaemophilic factor C
XII	Hageman factor, contact factor
XIII	Fibrin stabilizing factor (FSF)

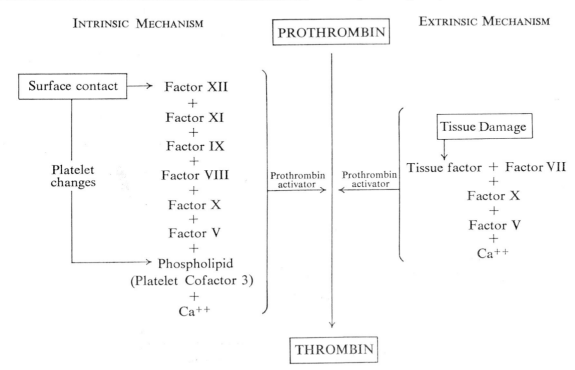

FIG. 26.5. The first stage in the clotting process; the production of prothrombin activator.

pose. Heparin, which acts as an antithrombin and anti-prothrombin agent may also be used.

The intravascular (intrinsic) clotting mechanism is the principal system involved in haemostasis. A separate extravascular (extrinsic) clotting mechanism also exists in the tissues. This is brought into play by tissue damage due to either trauma or inflammation. The main function of this extrinsic mechanism is probably to produce a fibrin barrier which helps to localize infections. The final two stages are the same in both the intrinsic and extrinsic clotting mechanisms, but the initial stage of the latter is a more rapid process due to the fact that tissue juice is almost a complete prothrombin activator in its own right. This extrinsic clotting mechanism is also illustrated in fig. 26.5.

Recent work in Great Britain and America has shown that the conversion of fibrinogen to fibrin is not as simple as previously represented. Thrombin is now believed to split fibrinogen into one major component, fibrin monomer, and several minor polypeptide components. The major components then polymerize, under the influence of Factor XIII and calcium ions, into fibrin threads that give stability to the blood clot (fig. 26.6).

$$\text{Fibrinogen} \xrightarrow{\text{Thrombin}} \text{Fibrin monomer}$$

$$\text{Fibrin monomer} \longrightarrow \text{Fibrin polymer}$$

$$\text{Fibrin polymer} \xrightarrow[\text{Ca}^{++}]{\text{Factor XIII}} \text{Fibrin}$$

FIG. 26.6. The conversion of fibrinogen to fibrin.

The catalytic production of thrombin in the clotting process at the site of injury could theoretically result in retrograde spread of the fibrin clot throughout the vascular tree were it not controlled. This is achieved partly by the inactivation of thrombin by the newly formed fibrin and partly by the lytic influence of the **fibrinolytic system** (fig. 26.7).

The active enzyme in this system, **plasmin**, is proteolytic but possesses a preference for fibrin as substrate. It is formed from an inactive soluble blood protein precursor, plasminogen, by the action of plasminogen acti-

vator; this is found in many tissues including vascular endothelium and in body fluids and is released locally into the blood at the site of vascular injury.

Intact blood contains at least two antiplasmins, one fast and the other slow acting. Their neutralizing capacity is great enough to cope with the conversion of the total blood plasminogen if this should be activated slowly. Fibrin, however, has a strong affinity for plasminogen and hence in a blood clot the concentration of plasminogen far exceeds that in intact whole blood. When activator from the damaged vascular endothelium diffuses into the clot matrix, plasmin is therefore produced in a concentration that exceeds the neutralizing capacity of the fast acting antiplasmin component and controlled lysis of the clot begins. No free plasmin is formed in the general circulation.

Occasionally in pathological states there is a rapid release of plasminogen activator into the general circulation. The plasminogen content of blood is so quickly converted to plasmin, that the fast acting antiplasmin component is overwhelmed and free plasmin is present in the blood. This fibrinolytic state leads to severe bleeding. Bleeding usually becomes aggravated not only from progressive destruction of the Clotting Factors V and VIII by the free plasmin but also because fibrinogen degradation products tend to inhibit the polymerization of fibrin monomer. This situation arises rarely after open heart surgery, in malignant disease and as a complication of pregnancy.

It is now believed that the sequence of reactions, platelet aggregation, coagulation and fibrinolysis is enacted constantly at myriad sites of vascular damage throughout the body resulting from the occult trauma of everyday life.

In haemostasis, the fibrin clot is in a state of dynamic equilibrium, there being a fine balance between coagulation and fibrinolysis until the reparative process is well advanced. The fibrinolytic system then becomes temporarily dominant at the site of injury and the fibrin matrix is lysed, thus aiding in recanalization of the vessel.

It is clear that any disturbances in the delicate balance of the dynamic haemostatic mechanism pose a threat

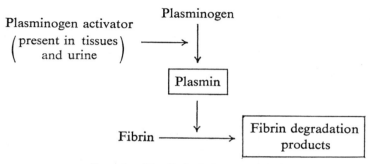

FIG. 26.7. The fibrinolytic mechanism.

to the survival of the organism. Indeed in some patients an overactive clotting mechanism with a normal fibrinolytic system can cause thrombosis. The term **thrombosis** is used for coagulation which occurs inside an intact vessel in flowing blood.

The haemostatic mechanism is so complex that no single or simple test can be used to assess adequately its function. A major defect anywhere in this mechanism usually results in clinical symptoms, for example easy bruising or prolonged bleeding after minor injury. The bleeding may also occur in unusual sites, e.g. into joints, and may result in permanent deformity or abnormality of function. Sometimes, as in haemophilia, the defect is genetically determined so that there may be a history of a similar abnormal bleeding tendency in some of the patient's relatives. When the defect is mild, the patient's history and clinical examination may not be significantly abnormal and laboratory tests become of prime importance. These can be divided into two groups, those which measure vascular and platelet functions and those which measure the clotting and fibrinolytic mechanisms. The first group includes determination of the bleeding time, Hess test for capillary fragility and the platelet count. The second group includes measurements of the whole blood clotting and lysis times, the 'one stage' prothrombin time and more complicated procedures which measure specific parts of the clotting and fibrinolytic processes or measure the actual concentrations of the various Factors present.

BLOOD GROUPS

In 1666, Richard Lower, a Cornishman, described to the Royal Society experiments in which he transfused blood from one dog to another. In the next year he demonstrated the transfusion of blood into a man before the Society. During the next 200 years these experiments were occasionally repeated, but they often resulted in a disastrous and fatal reaction in the recipient. No satisfactory explanation for these accidents was found until 1901, when Landsteiner discovered the first blood group system in man.

Mode of inheritance of blood groups

Human blood groups are inherited characters involving antigen-antibody systems. The antigens are carried on the surface of the red blood cells and are genetically controlled and first appear in the foetus. The antigen molecule has a chemical structure containing an amino acid complex which is capable of stimulating antibody formation, combined with a polysaccharide residue which usually confers specificity on the molecule.

There are at least nine principal human blood group systems, designated ABO, Rhesus (Rh), MNSs, P, Kell, Lutheran, Duffy, Lewis and Kidd, but only the ABO and the Rh systems are of major clinical importance. Each parent contributes a gene or a linked combination of genes for each of these blood group systems to the child. Each individual, therefore, possesses a pair of genes or a pair of linked genes, one from each parent, for each blood group system.

All the blood group genes, with the exception of those of the more recently discovered Xg system, where the genes are carried on the sex chromosome X, are carried somewhere on the twenty-two pairs of autosomes and are independent of one another; indeed it has been shown that most of them must be carried on different chromosome pairs.

ABO blood group system

This was the first blood group system to be discovered. Landsteiner, in 1901, published his classical experiments in which he showed that the population could be divided into three groups which he named A, B and O and to which he later added a fourth, AB. People in groups A, B or AB carry the respective antigen or antigens on the surface of their red blood cells, whereas those in group O possess neither of the antigens. Each individual has, in his serum, the naturally occurring antibodies named anti-A (α) and anti-B (β) to the red cell antigens that he lacks. The antigen frequency of the British population has been determined. These antigen frequencies vary even in different parts of Great Britain; for instance, the frequency of group A decreases and that of group O increases from South to North. Different distributions occur in other parts of the world and the frequencies of the antigens in populations are of value in anthropological studies (table 26.3).

TABLE 26.3. Antigen frequency of ABO blood groups in the British population.

Blood group	Antigen present on red cell surface	Antibody (agglutinin) normally present in serum	Antigen frequency (%)
A	A	Anti-B	42
B	B	Anti-A	9
AB	AB	Neither	3
O	Neither	Anti-A and Anti-B	46

Every person has a pair of chromosomes each of which carries the A, B or O gene and therefore the population can be divided into four phenotypes and eight genotypes (table 26.4).

BLOOD GROUP ANTIBODIES

Blood group antibodies are usually found in the γ fraction of the serum globulins. They may either occur naturally or

TABLE 26.4. ABO phenotypes and genotypes

Phenotype	Genotype
AB	AB
A	AA
	AO
B	BB
	BO
O	O

be acquired (immune antibodies) as a result of stimulation of the patient's antibody system from exposure to foreign red cells carrying blood group antigens which he normally lacks, e.g. in incompatible blood transfusion. Immune antibodies arising from exposure to foreign red cells are described as **isoantibodies**. Occasionally immune antibodies may arise spontaneously in a patient against his own blood group antigens in certain infections, diseases of lymphoid tissue and for reasons unknown; such antibodies are spoken of as **autoantibodies**. The immune antibodies are usually IgG (7S) globulins (mol. wt. about 160,000) and are of much smaller molecular weight than the natural occurring antibodies which are normally IgM (19S) globulins (mol. wt. about 1,000,000).

The naturally occurring blood group antibodies cause clumping together or agglutination in saline suspension of the red blood cells carrying the corresponding antigen; they are known as **complete antibodies**. Most immune antibodies, however, whilst combining with the specific antigen in saline do not produce visible agglutination of the red cells *in vitro* until protein, e.g. albumin is added; such antibodies are spoken of as albumin, blocking or **incomplete antibodies**. A diagrammatic representation of the possible modes of action of complete and incomplete antibodies is given in fig. 26.8. In clinical practice

incomplete antibodies can be detected by prior treatment of the red cells with a proteolytic enzyme such as papain which exposes the antigen to the action of the antibody in saline or by the antiglobulin (Coombs') technique.

Most naturally occurring antibodies react optimally with the appropriate red cell antigens *in vitro* at room temperature, whereas immune antibodies react optimally at 37°C. Sometimes sera from apparently healthy people contain agglutinins in low titre which react strongly in the cold (4°C) but which are usually inactive at body temperature; they are called **cold agglutinins**. Pathological cold agglutinins are found rarely in association with certain diseases and such agglutinins may be of clinical significance because they have a wide thermal range of activity and are still active at body temperature.

A AND B SUBGROUPS

There are several subgroups of group A of which the most important are A_1 and A_2. Subgroups of B are very rare. About 20 per cent of group A people belong to group A_2 and the same percentage of group AB people belong to group A_2B: the other 80 per cent belong to groups A_1 or A_1B respectively. The A_2 antigen is much weaker than A_1 and reacts less well with anti-A sera; this is very important in blood group testing and in the cross matching of blood. It is an axiom that no anti-A serum is considered suitable for typing purposes unless it gives a strong agglutination reaction with group A_2 as well as with A_1 cells. The naturally occurring anti-A and anti-B agglutinins vary in potency in individuals of the same blood group. They are absent at birth and do not become detectable until between the 3rd and the 6th months of life.

In addition to these naturally occurring complete anti-A and anti-B antibodies, immune or incomplete

FIG. 26.8. Diagrammatic mode of action of complete and incomplete red cell antibodies: (a) complete antibody, (b) red blood cell, (c) agglutination, (d) incomplete antibody, (e) red blood cell, (f) antigen sites blocked, no agglutination, (g) addition of protein molecules, agglutination.

anti-A or anti-B antibodies may be acquired. This can arise after transfusion with blood incompatible in respect of the ABO system or, in a pregnant woman whose own blood is group O but whose foetus is of groups A or B, through escape of foetal red cells across the placenta into the maternal circulation. These immune antibodies, being IgG globulins of relatively low molecular weight readily cross the placenta, whereas the natural antibodies do not because of their high molecular weight.

Rhesus (Rh) system

This was the second major blood group system to be discovered and resulted from the work of Landsteiner and Wiener who, in 1940, found that a rabbit antiserum prepared against Rhesus monkey red cells also agglutinated about 85 per cent of Caucasian human red cells; they called these cells Rh positive red cells. The other 15 per cent were said to be Rh negative cells. There are three principal Rh antigens which are said to be linked because they are found on one chromosome. The alleles (p. 38.3) are known as Dd, Cc and Ee. D is clinically the most important antigen because it is the most potent and accounts for more than 90 per cent of all reactions due to Rh blood group incompatibility. The existence of d antigen is assumed but so far remains unproved.

Whilst variants of most of these antigens are known, the main one of clinical importance is D^u. Red cells carrying this antigen are not agglutinated by all anti-D sera and can therefore be falsely grouped as d. When injected into a D negative person, D^u red cells behave like the D antigen and stimulate the production of normal anti-D antibody.

Naturally occurring antibodies in this system are rare and virtually all antibodies are acquired either from a pregnant Rh negative (d) mother carrying an Rh positive (D) child (see below) or by an incompatible Rh positive (D) blood transfusion. Antibodies to the antigens C, c, E and e are formed less frequently.

For laboratory purposes most Rh antisera are obtained from the blood of female patients immunized during pregnancy or from volunteers deliberately immunized. Whilst potent anti-D sera are plentiful, others such as anti-C and anti-e are less common and antiserum to the d antigen has not yet been discovered. This latter fact complicates the problem of Rh genotyping, and differentiation of the homozygote DD from the heterozygote Dd can be made only on a probability basis from family studies, though the effect *in vivo* of DD is greater than that of Dd. This, however, is an oversimplification of the problem in that it is also not possible to identify single linked gene complexes using an antiserum and each individual has two of the linked gene combinations making up his genotype, one from each parent. Thus genotypes CDe/cDE and CDE/cDe cannot be differentiated by antisera typing even though all the antisera needed are available. The probable genotype is best deduced from the frequency with which each occurs within a particular phenotype and in conjunction with family studies.

COLD ANTIBODIES AND THE Ii SYSTEM

As mentioned above, some sera contain non-specific cold isoagglutinins of no clinical importance. Occasionally, however, cold autoagglutinins may develop, sometimes complicating infection but often without known cause, and be of clinical significance. These autoantibodies can usually be detected in the plasma as well as attached to the patient's red cells. Often they are non-specific and react with the patient's own red cells and with practically all otherwise compatible donor cells. Sometimes the cold antibody is clearly specific for the I antigen. This minor antigen system is of particular interest in that foetal red cells, and those of the newborn, contain mostly the allele i and negligible I activity; the latter becomes fully potent only at the age of 18 months. The I antigen is so common in adults that it is almost universal and is sometimes referred to as a public antigen. The ii genotype is extremely rare in adults (less than 0·02 per cent). Hence cold antibodies with anti-I activity are detected *in vitro* if they agglutinate practically all red cells from adult subjects but not foetal red cells.

Medical application of blood groups

In clinical medicine their importance is due to the fact that profound damage to donor red cells can occur when a blood group antigen carried on the cell reacts with an appropriate antibody. Such an antigen antibody reaction can usually produce red cell destruction from agglutination or haemolysis or both. The effect of isoantibodies is seen in haemolytic transfusion reactions and haemolytic disease of the newborn; autoantibodies are the cause of autoimmune haemolytic anaemia.

Only the ABO and Rh blood group systems contribute significantly to isoantibody incompatibility in the giving of blood transfusions. With improved laboratory techniques and increased care in grouping and cross matching the blood of both patient and donor, reactions are now uncommon. However, repeated transfusions can lead to isoantibody incompatibility affecting the rarer blood groups and particular care is needed in the selection of blood for such patients.

Whenever possible before a transfusion, both donor and recipient blood should be tested in a well equipped blood transfusion or haematological laboratory. If this is impracticable, this is no contraindication to a transfusion which may be life saving. However, in all circumstances, compatibility of donor and recipient blood with respect to ABO groups must be assured. An approximate 5–10 per cent suspension of the donor red cells is made by diluting the donor blood, taken direct from the transfusion bottle, with the supernatant plasma or with physiological saline. One drop of this suspension is mixed on an opalescent tile or glass slide with two drops of the patient's heparinized plasma. The tile or slide is gently rocked and if no visible agglutination is seen after 5 min, the donor blood is compatible, but only for the ABO system.

Blood groups are useful genetic markers in identifying blood stains and in paternity disputes and also in anthropology.

Haemolytic disease of the newborn

This is nearly always due to Rh incompatibility between the mother and her foetus and 90 per cent of cases are caused by the D antigen. If an Rh positive (D) foetus is conceived by an Rh negative (d) mother she may become immunized by the periodic escape of foetal red cells across the placental barrier into her circulation. The immune anti-D antibody which she produces, being an IgG antibody globulin, crosses the placenta into the foetal circulation where it can cause haemolysis of the foetal red cells. Haemolytic disease of the newborn is rarely encountered in a first pregnancy, possibly because immunization of the mother, if it occurs, does so most frequently towards the end of gestation and during delivery. However, once the mother is immunized, the risk to a further Rh positive foetus may increase with each succeeding pregnancy. Fortunately foetal-maternal ABO incompatibility helps to minimize the risk of maternal Rh immunization because it enables the mother to destroy and remove foetal cells escaping into her circulation before the Rh antigen can become effective.

Very rarely haemolytic disease of the newborn can be due to one of the other blood group systems.

FURTHER READING

BIGGS R. & MACFARLANE R.G. (1962) *Human Blood Coagulation and its Disorders.* 3rd Edition. Oxford: Blackwell Scientific Publications.

BOORMAN K.E. & DODD B.E. (1966) *An Introduction to Blood Group Serology.* 3rd Edition. London: Churchill.

BRITTON C.J.C. (1963) *Whitby and Britton Disorders of the Blood.* 9th Edition. London: Churchill.

DE GRUCHY G.C. (1964) *Clinical Haematology in Medical Practice.* 2nd Edition. Oxford: Blackwell Scientific Publications.

MARCUS A.J. & ZUCKER M.B. (1965) *The Physiology of Blood Platelets.* New York: Grune & Stratton.

MOLLISON P.L. (1967) *Blood Transfusion in Clinical Medicine,* 4th Edition. Oxford: Blackwell Scientific Publication.

WINTROBE M.M. (1968) *Clinical Hematology.* 6th Edition. London: Kimpton.

Chapter 27
Reticuloendothelial system and thymus

The reticuloendothelial system (RES) is not an organic entity like the kidneys or the central nervous system. Instead its components are dispersed throughout the body in many tissues and organs. Reticuloendothelial tissue is of mesenchymal origin and consists of a scaffolding of fine reticulin fibres supporting large, irregular often stellate cells (fig. 27.1). The cells produce reticulin fibres,

Fig. 27.1. Reticuloendothelium. Note the three-dimensional network of reticulin, the reticulum cells and the endothelial-like lining which they form on the reticulin framework of the fluid channels or sinusoids.

and some form a loose lining for vascular or lymphoid channels and thus earn the description endothelial. However, the system is distinguished not so much by the histological features which give it its name but rather by the characteristic phagocytic activity of the cells; this property allows both its static and mobile cellular components to be recognized,

PHAGOCYTOSIS
This is the ability to ingest, concentrate and retain particulate matter, including certain vital dyes which

can be injected safely during life. Cells of the RES take up such material with differing degrees of avidity and marked differences are found between the uptake of particulate and of soluble material.

The cells of the RES may be listed as follows in increasing order of phagocytic activity:

(1) endothelium of blood and lymphatic vessels which take up only a little injected material;

(2) fibrocytes or connective tissue cells, the mesothelial cells of serous sacs and the endothelial cells of the splenic sinusoids which stain with vital dyes fairly readily;

(3) reticulum cells of the splenic pulp and corpuscles and those of the lymphoid tissue which are readily stained by vital dyes;

(4) the endothelial cells of the lymphoid sinuses and of the blood sinusoids which are found in the liver (Kupffer cells), bone marrow, adrenal and pars anterior of the pituitary;

(5) freely moving cells such as:

(a) macrophages, also known as histiocytes or amoeboid wandering cells of the connective tissues,

(b) mononuclear cells or phagocytes of the splenic pulp normally active in the phagocytosis e.g. of effete erythrocytes,

(c) blood monocytes.

An example of phagocytic activity which is easily demonstrated is the uptake of particulate carbon by the Kupffer cells of the liver sinusoids after an intravenous injection of dialysed India ink. Red blood cells, which may enter the alveoli of the lung during pneumonia, are phagocytosed by macrophages and their remains persist as golden-brown haemosiderin granules (fig. 27.2).

Because they take up dyes only feebly, groups (1) and (2) are sometimes not regarded as parts of the RES and the free-moving macrophages, group (5), are sometimes excluded, so that the system is confined to groups (3) and (4). However, because of the ability of mesenchymal elements, e.g. fibroblasts, mesothelial and endothelial cells to transform themselves into phagocytic cells in many pathological processes, the more inclusive definition of the RES is better.

Phagocytosis is not confined to experimental conditions. Effete red blood cells are normally destroyed and phagocytosed by the system, and phagocytosis is also an important defensive mechanism after invasion by bacteria and other parasites. As well as the immediate protective effect of phagocytosis there is also an important long term protection called the immune response.

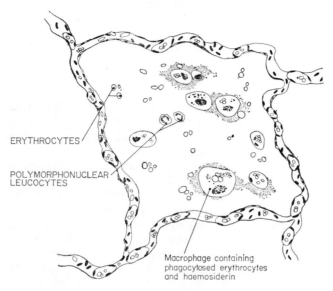

ERYTHROCYTES

POLYMORPHONUCLEAR
LEUCOCYTES

Macrophage containing
phagocytosed erythrocytes
and haemosiderin

FIG. 27.2. Phagocytes containing red cells and haemosiderin granules in a lung alveolus.

THE IMMUNE RESPONSE

This is a reaction by the body to the presence within it of foreign substances, mainly proteins, known as **antigens**. Commonly, the immune response consists of the synthesis of serum γ–globulins, **antibodies**, which react specifically with the foreign antigens of the invading organism and protect the host from its effects either by neutralizing it, destroying its cell wall or encouraging its more rapid phagocytosis. The antibodies take a little time to be produced after first exposure to the antigen but they remain or can be recalled very quickly to deal with subsequent attacks by the same organism, the **secondary** or **accelerated immune response**. The elaboration of antibodies which circulate in the blood stream is known as the **humoral type** of immune response. An equally important and specific immune reaction is the **cellular response**. This is often mediated by small lymphocytes which respond to certain antigens specifically. The lymphocytes acquire the ability to recognize the antigen, migrate from the blood stream to sites of high antigen concentration, and by gathering there in large numbers protect the host against its effects. Thus the immune response can be purely humoral, mediated by circulating antibodies, or cellular, mediated by small lymphocytes, but often mixtures of both mechanisms are found.

It is in the RES that the short term protective mechanism of phagocytosis is linked to the long term one of specific immunity. The specificity of the humoral and cellular immune response is ensured by the presence within the RE system of the mechanism of antigen trapping on the one hand, and the production of antibody and lymphocytes on the other. Aggregations of lymphoid tissue such as lymph nodes, tonsils, Peyer's patches and spleen are known as the **lymphoreticular organs** or **system**. In them a reticulin scaffolding acts as a framework to support densely-packed small lymphocytes and their precursors, and the endothelial cells form an incomplete or fenestrated lining to the lymphatic sinusoids of the lymphoid tissues and the blood sinusoids of the spleen. However, in the lymphoreticular organs the reticulum cells not only produce reticulin and differentiate into endothelial cells and phagocytes, but also differentiate into stem cells which divide and mature to form lymphocytes in the process known as **lymphopoiesis**.

The bone marrow, which is also largely made up of a reticulin and endothelial scaffolding, contains the maturing forms of the erythroid and myeloid circulating blood cells; lymphoid elements are scanty. The blood sinusoids of the marrow are lined by endothelial cells and once more reticulum cells differentiate into stem cells, this time for **haemopoiesis.**

The multipotential capacity of the RE cell is well shown in extramedullary haemopoiesis, (p. 27.11) where the reticulum cells of the lymph nodes, spleen and liver differentiate into haemopoietic cells.

The functional unity of the RES is also seen in the reticuloendothelial or lymphoreticular tumours. These are malignant transformations and multiplications of the reticulum cells (reticulum cell sarcoma) or lymphoid cells (lymphosarcoma). The process often starts simultaneously in widely separated representatives of the reticuloendothelial tissue and this also suggests that the scattered members of the system act as one.

LYMPHORETICULAR ORGANS

The organs of the lymphoreticular system consist of the lymph nodes, spleen and bone marrow. The bone marrow, as the site of haemopoiesis, is described on p. 26·5.

The lymph nodes are distributed widely throughout the body, and the spleen is the largest single lymphoid mass; they are encapsulated organs which contain large numbers of lymphocytes and germinal follicles in their reticulin framework. Numerous afferent lymphatic vessels drain into the lymph nodes and the lymph percolates through the lymphoid tissue in channels. It is thus exposed to phagocytic action and acquires additional lymphocytes before it leaves the node by the efferent lymphatic vessels (fig. 27.3).

In the spleen the lymphocytes and their germinal

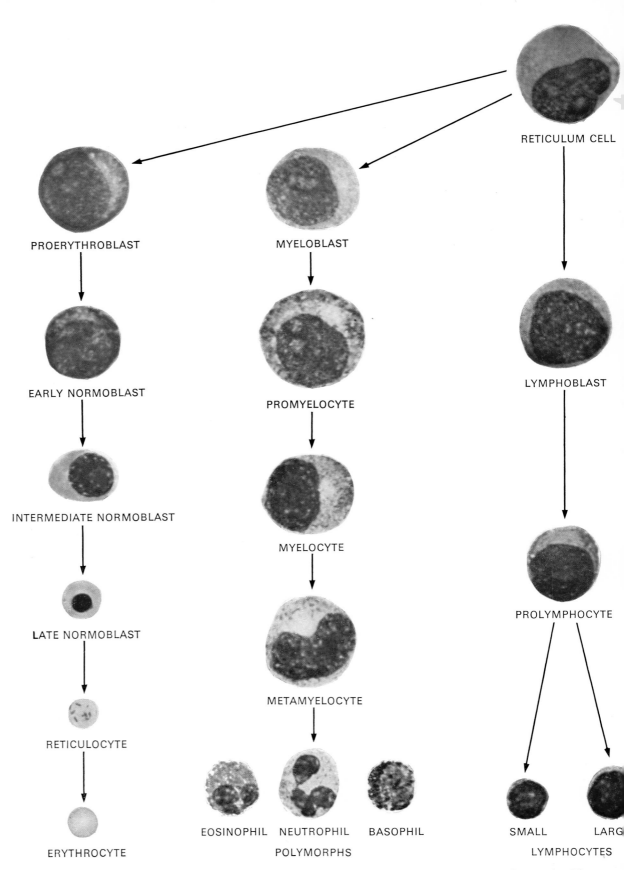

RETICULUM CELL

PROERYTHROBLAST

EARLY NORMOBLAST

INTERMEDIATE NORMOBLAST

LATE NORMOBLAST

RETICULOCYTE

ERYTHROCYTE

MYELOBLAST

PROMYELOCYTE

MYELOCYTE

METAMYELOCYTE

EOSINOPHIL   NEUTROPHIL   BASOPHIL

POLYMORPHS

LYMPHOBLAST

PROLYMPHOCYTE

SMALL   LARG

LYMPHOCYTES

PLATE 26.1. The stages

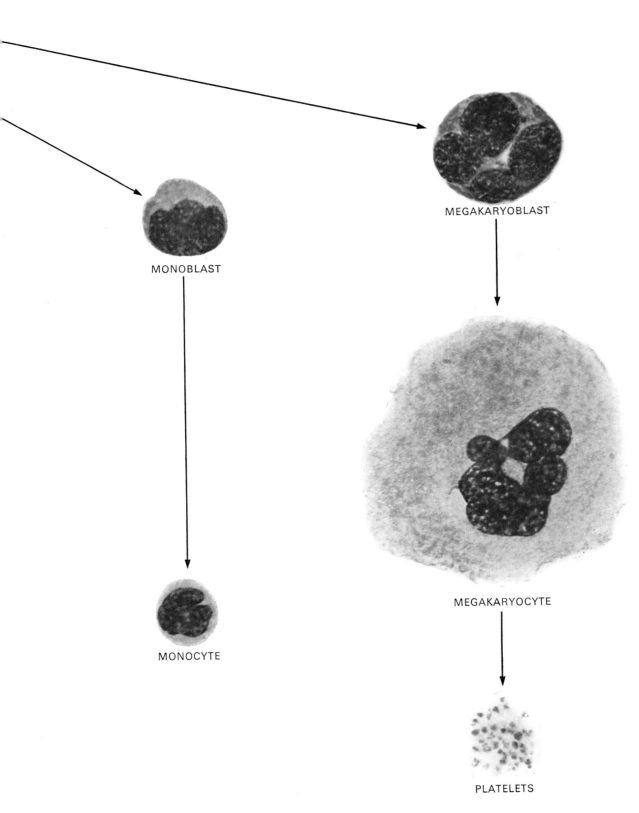

MEGAKARYOBLAST

MONOBLAST

MONOCYTE

MEGAKARYOCYTE

PLATELETS

blood cells.

follicles make up structures called **Malpighian corpuscles**; each corpuscle forms a cuff round a branch of the splenic artery before it ramifies into the innumerable blood sinusoids lined by RE cells of the splenic pulp.

The lymph nodes and spleen exert a filtering effect upon the lymph and the blood respectively, and during their passage through these tissues lymphocytes, macrophages or antibodies are added to them.

The lymphatic system

The lymphatic system is described on p. 28.25 and consists of myriads of tiny lymphatic capillaries which form plexuses in most tissues except the central nervous system. These vessels join together to drain the lymph into the subcapsular sinuses of the lymph nodes. From the lymph nodes larger lymphatic vessels commonly lead to other lymph nodes or groups of lymph nodes and ultimately to the thoracic duct (p. 20.37).

Although widely distributed in the body, the lymph nodes tend to form anatomically recognizable and clinically important groups. Thus in the limbs they occupy loose areolar fascial planes especially around the flexor aspects of the joints, e.g. in the popliteal fossa, inguinal region and axilla.

LYMPH VESSELS

An account of the regional systems of lymphatic channels and their groups of nodes is given in the appropriate chapter. In general the major lymphatic channels follow the routes of the main blood vessels and the lymph from the lower limb and the abdominal organs converges on a network of channels and nodes which run along the aorta (p. 20.32).

The lymphatic drainage of the small intestine differs from that of other organs in that it is an important route of absorption of fat from the intestinal mucosa in the form of chylomicrons which give its lymph a milky or chylous appearance (p. 30.37). The chyle passes through numerous nodes in the mesentery, reaches the superior mesenteric nodes which surround the origin of that artery and eventually enters the network of lymphatics around the aorta. Just below the diaphragm a confluence of all the channels forms a single dilated large lymphatic sac, the cisterna chyli (p. 20.37), which is the origin in the abdomen of the thoracic duct. The mesenteric lymph nodes often undergo inflammatory reactions as a result of infection carried from the intestine. Formerly, when bovine tuberculosis was rife, infected milk supplies often led to intestinal tuberculous infection, with involvement of the mesenteric lymph nodes. When the condition healed, the lymph nodes were left in a fibrosed and often calcified state, which rendered them opaque in radiographic examination of the abdomen.

Another important group of protective lymph nodes is situated in the hilum of each lung and around the bifurca-tion of the trachea. In city dwellers who inhale carbonaceous dust, finely-dispersed carbon particles drain to those nodes via the pulmonary lymphatics, and they acquire prominent black speckles which can be seen microscopically to consist of aggregates of macrophages containing ingested carbon.

Knowledge of the lymphatic drainage of the body is of practical clinical importance since regional involvement of the lymph nodes is often a clue to the site of infection, and since malignant tumours often spread along the lymphatic channels to involve the lymph nodes.

STRUCTURE OF LYMPH NODES (fig. 27.3)
Lymph nodes are pale grey and vary in size from a pinhead to a large bean, which they resemble by having flattened sides and a concave hilus or hilum. Each node

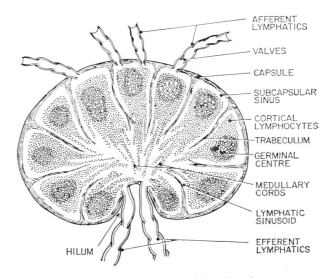

FIG. 27.3. Diagram of lymph node.

is surrounded by a fibrous capsule which sends trabeculae radially into the interior between masses of densely-packed lymphocytes with their prominent, pale, germinal centres. The germinal centres are rich in large pale staining lymphoblasts, the precursors of the small lymphocytes which are packed around their periphery Towards the hilus of the node the lymphoid tissue is not arranged in follicles around germinal centres but instead the region consists of interconnecting strands of densely packed lymphocytes. These medullary cords are surrounded by spaces which are much less rich in lymphocytes and are crossed by the processes of numerous RE cells. These are the sinusoids of loose RE tissue through which the lymph percolates on its journey to the hilus. This central area is often called the medulla to distinguish it from the peripheral cortex.

Lymphatic channels converge upon the convex surface of the node, penetrate the capsule and pour their lymph, usually through valved openings (fig. 27.3), into the subcapsular sinus. This is a loose RE space which separates the deepest layers of the capsule from the underlying densely packed lymphocytes. From the subcapsular sinus, sinusoids accompany the capsular trabeculae and pass radially towards the hilus where they eventually join the loose sinusoidal system of the medulla. From the medulla one or two large efferent vessels open from the concave aspect of the capsule to carry the lymph away from the node.

The lymph always flows from the large area of the capsule with its numerous afferent lymphatics to the narrow area of the hilus with its few efferent lymphatics, in keeping with the principle that lymphatic channels decrease in number but increase in calibre as they travel towards the thoracic duct.

The hilus serves also as the point of entrance and exit of the blood vessels and the nerves which supply the node. The main vessels run in the connective tissue trabeculae for a short distance before they ramify in the dense lymphoid tissue of the cortex. Thence drainage is to a system of post-capillary venules which are important as the sites of migration of lymphocytes from the blood stream into the node. This migration offsets the large number of lymphocytes which are lost to the node in the efferent lymph. The recirculation of the lymphocyte is considered on p. 27.5.

Sinusoids

The subcapsular, cortical and medullary sinusoids are made up of loosely arranged stellate RE cells which are continuous with the endothelial lining of the lymphatic vessels which penetrate the capsule. The stellate processes of the cells are joined to one another and some support is given by reticulin fibres. Because of the stellate nature of the endothelial cells the sinusoids are fenestrated; although they provide pathways of least resistance for the lymph, it is free to percolate back and forth into the adjacent lymphoid masses and lymphocytes gain access to the lymphatic sinusoids (plate 27.1a, facing p. 27.6). RE cells also frequently bridge across the lumen of the sinusoids and these cells are particularly active phagocytes. Even in health many of the traversing and lining cells of the sinusoid become free macrophages. In plate 27.1a, one of these can be seen to have ingested a red blood cell; small numbers of extravasated red cells are normally present in the tissues and gain access to the lymphatics. Especially after bruising, many extravasated red cells pass to the local lymph nodes where they are phagocytosed by macrophages which later show haemosiderin in their cytoplasm.

The production of free macrophages in the sinusoids is increased by irritation, inflammation or antigenic stimulation. In such circumstances the subcapsular and other sinusoids become packed with large round macrophages together with numbers of polymorphonuclear leucocytes which have migrated in with the lymph from the inflamed region. However, in health the polymorphonuclear leucocyte is not prominent in the sinusoids of the lymph node.

Another cell type not present in large numbers in the resting lymph node but easily found in the inflamed or reactive lymph node is the plasma cell.

The size of the sinusoids is variable and if lymphopoiesis is brisk the subcapsular sinus may be practically obliterated by the expanding cortex. It is therefore necessary to study sections in which the sinusoids are well expanded, for this is the only means of demonstrating the RE cells with their delicate processes; a suitable stain is Masson's trichrome, as shown in plate 27.1a. Elsewhere in the node the reticulum cells of the scaffolding are obscured by the density of the lymphocytes, although by silver impregnation methods its reticulin fibres can be shown.

The germinal centre and lymphopoiesis

Lymphocytes, or more properly small lymphocytes, to distinguish them from their immediate precursors, the medium and large lymphocytes, are formed in the cortex of lymph nodes by the maturation and division of lymphoblasts and lymphoid stem cells. The appearance of the individual cells is shown in plate 26.1a, facing p. 27.6.

The most primitive cells, the lymphoblasts and the scattered reticulum cells, are found chiefly in the germinal centres where a proportion of them can be seen undergoing mitosis (plate 27.1b, facing p. 27.6). Around the germinal centre, sometimes forming a dense band, are the more recently formed medium and small lymphocytes, the younger ones pushing the older ones out towards the periphery of the lymphoid follicle, as the whole lymphopoietic unit is sometimes called. In the germinal centres and among the surrounding lymphocytes the phagocytic action of the RE cells is not as prominent as in the sinusoids. Lymphoblasts are formed by differentiation and division of stem cells, thought to be derived principally from the reticulum cells which form the unobtrusive scaffolding of lymphoid tissue. When, however, the lymphoid tissue has been destroyed by x-radiation, it can be reconstituted by injections of cell preparations not only from lymph nodes, but also from non-lymphoid tissue such as bone marrow. Bone marrow is therefore considered to form stem cells, which enter the circulation and gain access to the germinal centres where they differentiate into lymphoid cells. It is improbable that the contribution from the bone marrow is important in health, but the production of stem cells in one RE organ and their maturation in another is a further example of the unity of the system.

As the lymphoid series matures, the power of cell division gradually declines, until in the small lymphocyte it is undetectable. The loss of mitotic activity with maturation would soon result in a dearth of mitotically active large and medium lymphocytes. However, a proportion of the divisions, e.g. of the large lymphocytes, are asymmetric; they result, not in two medium lymphocytes, but in one medium lymphocyte and one large lymphocyte whose proliferative capacity is thus preserved. The medium lymphocytes may divide similarly; in this way the demand for differentiation of reticulum cells along the lymphoid path is reduced.

In addition to the germinal centres, all lymphoid tissue contains scattered lymphoblasts which can differentiate and produce lymphocytes locally. Indeed, in the thymus, which has no germinal centres, lymphocytes are produced in very large numbers in this way.

In the young the continued development of lymphoid tissue is entirely dependent upon the presence of a functioning thymus which stimulates lymphopoiesis in the periphery by means of its humoral factor (p. 27.20). The lymphoid tissue of the late embryo and the newborn animal has no germinal centres and consists of loose sheets of lymphoid cells and their precursors. The germinal centres appear later in infancy, apparently as a response to antigenic exposure. Particulate and soluble antigens may be carried by the lymphatics of the alimentary and respiratory tract both to the local lymph nodes and perhaps eventually to the spleen where they stimulate germinal centre formation. In keeping with this idea is the finding that plasma cells, known to produce antibodies, appear in small numbers in the lymphatic sinuses about the same time. Also, if newborn animals are reared in an environment free of micro-organisms, neither germinal centres nor plasma cells appear until after exposure to normal conditions. The germinal centres are not static structures; their number and size wax and wane according to the prevailing lymphopoietic stimulus. They arise by the division of solitary lymphoblast cells and their number and size can be greatly increased when the node drains local areas of irritation or inflammation or if artificial immunizing agents are injected into the tissues; this is called the **reactive node.**

The lymphocytes produced by the germinal centres are immunologically competent, i.e. they are capable of mounting an immune cellular attack upon antigen localized elsewhere in the body, an activity in which they are joined by the antibodies produced by the plasma cells.

The epitheliolymphatic tissue

In certain sites lymphoid tissue is to be found directly under mucosal surfaces but not organized into lymph nodes. Areas where such large aggregations occur include the tonsillar ring in the mouth, oropharynx and naso-pharynx, the Peyer's patches of the small intestine and the appendix. In several other sites the lymphoid tissue is scanty, amounting perhaps to a solitary follicle with or without an active germinal centre; this is common in the mucosa of the rest of the alimentary tract, the urinary tract, and in the respiratory tract under the tracheal and bronchial mucosa.

None of the epitheliolymphoid collections has a fibrous capsule, a subcapsular sinus or a system of lymphatic sinusoids traversing its parenchyma. In many, quite a rich plexus of lymphatic capillaries is to be found in the surrounding connective tissue. Since all are situated in places where infection is a constant threat it is difficult to escape the notion that their function is protective.

THE LIFE SPAN AND CIRCULATION OF THE LYMPHOCYTES

Tritiated thymidine is rapidly incorporated in the DNA of reproducing large lymphocytes but very poorly by the small. Apparently the small lymphocytes are formed rather infrequently and since their numbers are fairly constant, they must have a long life. Continuous transfusion of the rat with tritiated thymidine labels only 50 per cent of the small lymphocytes after 1 month and even after 3 months not all are labelled. Calculations in man show that the average life of the small lymphocyte is about 100 days, but some probably live very much longer, possibly for years. Thus at any one time only a small percentage of circulating small lymphocytes is newly formed.

It has been shown that the number of cells which enter the blood from the lymph nodes via the thoracic duct each day is ten to fifteen times the total number in the blood at any given time; thus there must be a compensatory loss from the blood stream. The losses of lymphocytes from the surface of the alimentary and respiratory tracts are not sufficient to account for this loss and so lymphocytes must circulate back into the lymphatic system. Since the afferent lymphatics carry relatively few lymphocytes. and the number of lymphocytes in the nodes remains substantially constant, the outpouring of lymphocytes from the efferent lymphatics must be made good within the node. It is through the unusually tall endothelium of the post-capillary venules of its cortex that lymphocytes re-enter the node from the blood to maintain their constancy of number and distribution.

In animal experiments external drainage of the thoracic duct eventually abstracts fewer and fewer lymphocytes from the system, but the numbers draining away increase if viable compatible lymphocytes are given by intravenous injection. Simultaneous administration of tritiated thymidine confirms that virtually no lymphocyte synthesis goes on during this experiment. If radioactive labelled lymphocytes are injected about 80 per cent of the label turns up in the thoracic duct. The migration of lymphocytes from blood to lymph node is thus capable of balancing the loss from the node without the need for appreciable lymphopoiesis.

The principal route of lymphocyte transport from blood to lymph is shown by autoradiography with labelled lymphocytes. A striking accumulation of label is demonstrable in all the lymphoid tissue, nodes, Peyer's patches and spleen, but not in the thymus which is excluded from the circulation of the lymphocyte.

As well as maintaining the constancy of number and distribution of the lymphocytes their circulation has several important immunological implications considered on p. 27.14.

FUNCTIONS OF THE LYMPH NODE

The lymph node serves the following defensive and immunological functions:

(1) as a filtration mechanism where afferent lymph containing normal or inflammatory cell débris and bacteria is exposed to the reticuloendothelial macrophages;

(2) as a production centre for lymphocytes and as the site of re-entry of blood lymphocytes to the lymphatic system;

(3) as a centre for trapping and processing antigen and directing the immune response, both cellular, through the lymphocyte, and humoral, by antibodies which are produced by the plasma cell (p. 27.12).

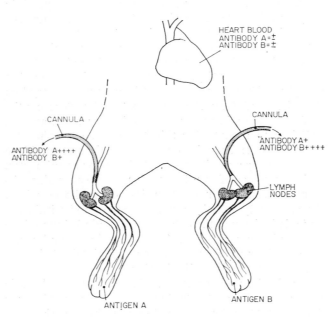

FIG. 27.4 The double antigen technique to show that antibody is produced in the lymph nodes which drain sites of local antigen injection.

The immunological activities of the lymph node and the spleen are so basically similar that a detailed account of the various cellular phenomena on which they depend is deferred until after the spleen is considered.

Meanwhile it suffices to prove, at the organ level, tha the lymph node produces antibody in response t local antigen and releases it into the circulation.

If an antigen is injected into the limb of an anima cannulation of the local lymphatics shows that antibod is absent from the afferent channels but present in hig concentration in the efferent channels of the regiona lymph nodes. Although suggesting strongly that antibod is formed in the lymph nodes these findings fall short c absolute proof since the antibody may have bee formed elsewhere and gained the efferent lymphatics vi the blood supply to the node, whose capillaries in th reactive state are unusually permeable. Conclusive proc of the synthesis of antibody within the lymph nod comes from an experiment based on the 'double antige technique' (fig. 27.4).

Using the hind limbs of a rabbit, antigen A is injecte into one foot and antigen B into the other. After a suitab interval the efferent lymphatics of the popliteal lymp nodes are cannulated and the concentration of antibod against A and B measured on each side. The effere lymphatics contain very high levels of antibody again the antigen which their nodes receive and scarcely an against the one injected into the opposite limb. In th blood, the antibodies against antigens A and B are preser in concentrations too low to account for those in th efferent lymphatics by mere diffusion; the distribution c antibody can be explained readily only by its productio in the local lymph nodes.

The spleen

ANATOMY

The spleen is a solid, encapsulated, deep red organ. It suspended by a medial pedicle in the upper left part c the abdomen where it lies in contact with and below th diaphragm, concealed anteriorly by the greater curvatu of the stomach and the left colic (splenic) flexure.

Its weight varies from 50 to 250 g. It is about 12 cm lon and 6 cm wide, and its long axis lies under the posterio part of the tenth rib from which it is separated, in turi by the pleural cavity, left lung, diaphragm and perito neal cavity (fig. 27.5). Its inferior and superior borders l along the eighth and eleventh intercostal spaces respe tively, and it is thus protected posteriorly by the thorac cage.

The spleen has a smooth convex posterior diaphragmat surface and a visceral surface which has a central hilu for the passage of the splenic artery and vein (fig. 27.6 The visceral surface is directed medially and is indente by the kidney posteriorly and the stomach and colc anteriorly. The posterior end of the spleen may reach th left adrenal gland.

The borders of the spleen are formed at the junctic of the diaphragmatic and visceral surfaces. The inferic border is related to the renal area and the superior to th

PLATE 27.1 Histology of the reticuloendothelial system.

(a) Loose reticuloendothelial tissue in a medullary lymphatic sinusoid. Note the stellate reticulum cells with their slender processes. Occasional macrophages show erythrophagocytosis, Masson trichrome (×650). Courtesy of the late H.S.D. Garven.

(c) The prominent ellipsoid of the cat. Perfused spleen, haem & eosin (×500). Courtesy of the late H.S.D. Garven.

(e) Thymic medulla to show Hassall's corpuscles. Note the large pale medullary epithelial cells which surround them, haem & eosin (×300). Courtesy of Dr A.M. MacDonald.

(b) Germinal centre, showing the mixture of large irregular reticulum cells and their derivatives, the lymphoblasts, which are rounded. A mitotic figure is seen in the centre of the field and another to the right above it, haem & eosin (×475).

(d) The endothelial cells (stave cells) of a splenic sinusoid which is beginning to branch into two. Perfused spleen, haem & eosin (×700). Courtesy of the late H.S.D. Garven.

(f) The 'blast' or pyroninophil transformation of the lymphocyte; the cell on the right is in mitosis (×1200). Courtesy of Dr Elizabeth Boyd.

gastric. The superior border is readily defined by the presence of a few notches which assist in the proper orientation of the excised spleen. Due to its position in the body the anterior end corresponds to the junction of the gastric and colic areas and extends forwards as far as the midaxillary line where it is in contact

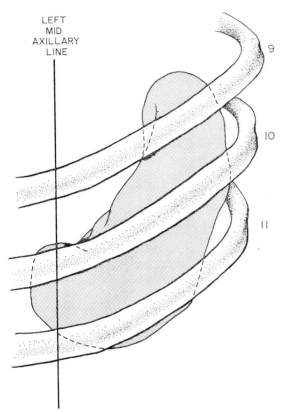

FIG. 27.5. Relations of spleen to the thoracic cage.

with the phrenicocolic ligament, which supports the adjacent colic flexure. Medially the spleen is attached, at the hilus, by two peritoneal folds derived from the dorsal mesogastrium (p. 30.52). The posterior fold, the lienorenal ligament, runs from the left kidney and carries the splenic vessels and tail of the pancreas, which makes a shallow concavity within the hilus. The anterior fold, the gastrolienal ligament, runs from the greater curvature of the stomach and carries the short gastric and left gastro-epiploic vessels.

In health the spleen is not palpable through the abdominal wall and it must be enlarged by at least 50 per cent before it is detectable in this way. It is protected from trauma by the thoracic cage, but in crushing injuries or in severe anterior blows to the left hypochondrium its capsule may rupture and fatal haemorrhage into the peritoneal cavity may ensue. The spleen enlarged by infection and protruding below the costal margin is prone to rupture from minor trauma. In parts of the world where

enlargement of the spleen due to malaria is common, assailants may contrive to rupture their victim's spleen by a swift blow with a small blunt instrument concealed in the hand.

Sometimes accessory spleens or spleniculi are found, usually attached to the hilus, but occasionally more remotely, e.g. in the root of the gastrolienal ligament. Although a harmless congenital aberration, it is important to search for spleniculi at operations for splenectomy aimed at relieving such conditions as haemolytic anaemia. If they are present and not removed they undergo compensatory hyperplasia and achieve a size and functional activity comparable to that of the spleen itself and thus vitiate the purpose of the operation.

The blood supply of the spleen comes from a midline visceral branch of the aorta and in this way it betrays its embryological association with the gut. The splenic artery is a branch of the coeliac artery and, more significantly, its venous return is into the hepatic portal system and not into the vena cava. In fact, the splenic vein first receives

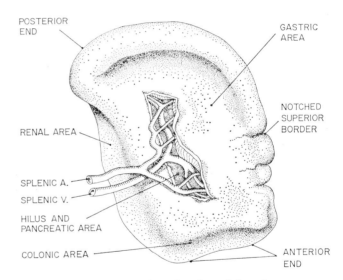

Fig. 27.6. The visceral surface of the spleen.

the inferior mesenteric vein and then joins the superior mesenteric vein to form the main trunk of the portal vein (p. 30.46). Like the rest of the portal venous system the splenic vein is devoid of valves.

MICROSCOPIC STRUCTURE OF THE SPLEEN
Under the low power of the microscope and even with the naked eye the two basic components of the splenic parenchyma can be made out (fig. 27.7). The **red pulp** forms the continuum of the organ and owes its deep red colour to large numbers of thin walled, blood filled sinusoids. The **white pulp** is dispersed as innumerable round white nodules of lymphoid tissue about a millimetre in diameter. In man, the spleen is bounded by a

fibro-elastic capsule from which trabeculae run radially into its interior, especially near the hilus where they serve to distribute the major intrasplenic vessels, nerves and lymphatics. In certain species, e.g. the cat and the dog, the capsule and trabeculae contain smooth muscle which contracts the spleen and makes the blood in its sinusoids available to the circulation in times of need, e.g. in shock, haemorrhage or anoxia.

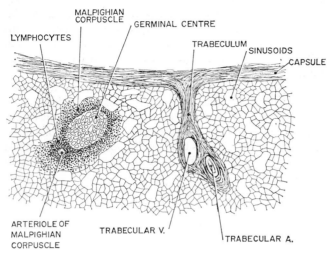

Fig. 27.7. Diagram of a section of spleen.

The lymphatics of the spleen are confined strictly to the capsule and trabeculae. As in the thymus, the lymphoid tissue of the spleen is of the dense type devoid of sinusoids.

The red pulp consists mainly of red blood cells and white cells of both lymphoid and myeloid series contained in irregular spaces lined by endothelium. In the interstices between these sinusoids silver impregnation methods reveal a complex reticulum scaffolding which contains large numbers of red cells together with reticulum cells, macrophages, which may show ingested red blood cells or iron pigment, lymphocytes, small and large, and occasional plasma cells, which are very numerous in times of active antibody formation. These richly cellular areas are called the **cords of Billroth**, and they are ramifications of a continuous celluloreticular scaffolding which extends throughout the organ. The cords of Billroth are in communication with the lumina of the sinusoids through deficiencies in their walls (fig. 27.9) which allow blood cells and injected particulate matter to pass into one of the most actively phagocytic areas of the spleen; phagocytosis by the endothelium of the sinusoids is poor, although free macrophages are to be found in their lumina. In the foetus and newborn child and in certain pathological states of the adult extramedullary haemopoiesis occurs in the cords.

The white pulp consists of ovoid collections of dense lymphoid tissue (Malpighian corpuscles) which form eccentric cuffs around the branches of the splenic arteries shortly after they leave the trabeculae. The lymphoid cuff does not end abruptly but tails off along the course of the vessel as a narrow sheath for an appreciable distance. Often, the Malpighian corpuscles contain a germinal centre, placed eccentrically to avoid the artery. The white pulp has a supporting scaffolding continuous with that of the red pulp but, just as in the follicle of the lymph node, the reticulum cells are concealed by the density of the lymphocytes and their precursors and, in this site, fail to take up much particulate matter.

The splenic blood vessels (figs. 27.8 and 30.51)
The **splenic artery** is a prominent muscular artery and has a rich baroreceptive innervation in its adventitia. In this way it resembles the carotid artery. Close to the hilus the artery divides into several branches which

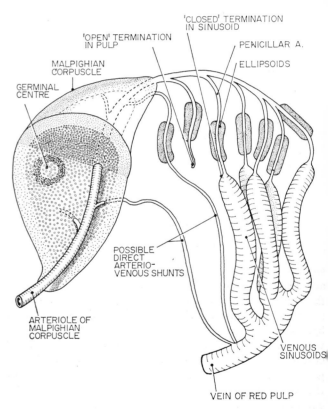

Fig. 27.8. The splenic circulation.

enter the capsule and pass into the organ along the trabeculae, accompanied by their veins and nerves. The **intratrabecular artery** soon parts company with the trabecula and its contained vein and, still with its nerve, traverses the red pulp where it is surrounded by the celluloreticular mesh and the venous sinusoids. The artery next acquires its lymphoid sheath which widens into the ovoid Malpighian corpuscle; it is now known as the **artery of the Malpighian corpuscle** and here it gives off a number of short capillaries which radiate through the lymphoid tissue and drain into the red pulp in the marginal zone of loosely arranged lymphocytes. Still with its nerve the artery emerges at the distal pole and when its lymphoid sheath is lost divides into several fine arterioles or **penicilli** which fan out with their nerves along straight courses into the red pulp. The penicillar arterioles soon reduce to capillary dimensions and become surrounded by a laminated concentric sheath of reticulum cells in a structure known as the **ellipsoid** (plate 27.1c, facing p. 27.6).

The **ellipsoid** is poorly innervated and has no detectable smooth muscle and so is not a sphincter. On the other

FIG. 27.9. The splenic venous sinusoid. Observe how the fenestrations can be closed or opened depending on whether the surrounding reticulum is expanded or contracted.

EXPANDED RETICULUM   CONTRACTED RETICULUM

hand, the sheath of reticulum cells around it is highly phagocytic. Like the marginal zone of the Malpighian corpuscle, the ellipsoid is one of the first areas in the spleen in which injected particulate matter appears. The wall of its central capillary is thought to be fenestrated and thus a good flow of blood past the phagocytes of its sheath may be expected. From the ellipsoid the **post-ellipsoidal capillaries** course into the red pulp. Considerable uncertainty surrounds their precise termination, whether into the venous sinusoids (closed circulation) or into the cords of Billroth (open circulation).

The **venous sinusoids** drain the blood to the trabecular veins; their walls are made up of longitudinally arranged strap-like cells (fig. 27.9) with prominent nuclei which protrude into the lumen. These are much less phagocytic than the endothelial cells of the sinusoids of the lymph node. The endothelial cells have sizeable spaces between them and are retained by circumferential bands

of reticulin which are in continuity with the reticular meshwork of the cords of Billroth. The arrangement is sometimes likened to the staves and hoops of a barrel, the cells being known as **stave cells**. It is not easy to demonstrate the reticulin fibres and the stave cells simultaneously, but plate 27.1d, facing p. 27.6 shows a longitudinal section of a venous sinusoid with the transverse semi-circles of reticulin appearing like the rungs of a ladder.

The spaces between the cells may widen if the spleen expands, and close up as it collapses or contracts. Thus cellular migration across the endothelium may be encouraged or hindered respectively. The venous sinusoids branch and anastomose in a complex manner and eventually drain into thin walled veins which enter the trabeculae after short courses in the pulp.

One of the functions of the spleen is to remove effete red cells from the circulation by phagocytosis. Although active free macrophages are found in the lumina of the sinusoids, many more are seen in the cords of Billroth, especially in times of excessive red cell destruction. It seems likely, therefore, that red cells are removed from the circulation by percolation through the cords of Billroth. If this is so, then the circulation through the spleen must have certain unusual features which permit the entry of red blood cells into the cords of Billroth.

The circulation through the spleen

If the splenic artery is injected with latex particles or nucleated red cells of the fowl which are easily recognizable in the red pulp, the material fills the capillaries, freely enters the cords of Billroth and, rather later, enters the venous sinusoids. If, however, the splenic vein is injected, the venous sinusoids and the cords of Billroth fill, but the arteries do not. The findings suggest that the post-ellipsoidal capillaries discharge their contents, not into the venous sinusoids, but into the cords of Billroth, so that the blood can percolate unidirectionally into the sinusoids through the interstices between its stave cells. This concept is known as the **open circulation** and is shown diagrammatically in fig. 27.10a.

An opposing theory, the **closed circulation,** considers that the postellipsoidal capillaries are continuous with the venous sinusoids in the normal way and that the blood cells in the cords of Billroth migrate through the interstices of the sinusoidal stave cells (fig. 27.10b). Movement of blood cells would therefore take the form of an ebb and flow between cords and sinusoids whose directions would depend upon local pressure gradients and would vary from time to time.

In scientific investigation it is a wise principle to postulate single rather than dual causes for any given effect. In fact, the venous sinusoid with its permeable wall makes it unnecessary to postulate any other reason to account for the number of red cells in the cords, and we can therefore regard the closed circulation as the like-lier of the two mechanisms.

A modification of the closed circulation is one in which control is provided by the degree of expansion or collapse of the spleen. In many animals the spleen has a definite function in storing blood in its sinusoids and releasing it when required, e.g. in shock or haemorrhage. When the blood pressure falls, the intra-splenic pressure declines, and in man the organ shrinks passively, perhaps aided by the elasticity of the capsule. Blood is therefore expelled from the cords into the sinusoids, and thence into

(2) The unusual system of venous sinusoids, coupled with the power of the spleen to contract, provides a method for expelling the contained blood to meet increased circulatory demands in certain animals e.g. cat and goat.

(3) The white pulp provides lymphocytes and a source of plasma cells and hence antibodies for the cellular and humoral specific immune defences.

Finally, certain more obscure functions of the spleen are partly revealed by splenectomy in the normal animal. These are dealt with in turn.

(a)

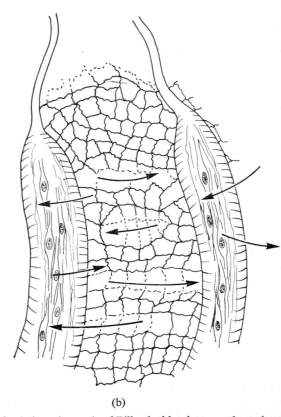

(b)

FIG. 27.10. (a) The open circulation; the postellipsoidal capillary opens freely into the cords of Billroth; blood returns through the fenestrations to the venous sinusoid. (b) The closed circulation; the postellipsoidal capillary joins the venous sinusoid in the usual way. Blood reaches the cords of Billroth by ebb and flow through the fenestrations of the sinusoids.

the veins. As the organ shrinks, the staves of the sinusoids become approximated and thus convert the vasculature into a closed state.

FUNCTIONS OF THE SPLEEN

The functions of the spleen reflect the three tissues which make it up.

(1) The reticuloendothelial scaffolding is concerned with phagocytosis of erythrocytes and cell débris from the bloodstream. In addition, in certain disease processes, the reticulum cells may exercise their multiple potentialities and produce foci of haemopoiesis.

Phagocytosis in the spleen

After intravenous injection of diffusible dyes or particulate matter, usually carbon in the form of India ink, there is a marked uptake of particles by the spleen, but diffusible dyes are taken up poorly. The latter are localized chiefly in the scattered mononuclear cells and reticulum cells of the cords of Billroth, and in the free macrophages of the sinusoids; the endothelial cells of the sinusoids are poorly phagocytic. Those macrophages which have already taken up red cells show a very poor uptake of dyes and of carbon particles and demonstrate the phenomenon of reticuloendothelial blockade, in which heavy uptake of one material prevents subsequent uptake of another.

On the other hand, intravenous injection of carbon particles is followed by rapid uptake and within ten minutes carbon appears in the RE cells of the marginal zone of the Malpighian bodies. The RE cells of the ellipsoids also take up injected carbon promptly and heavily. Further injections cause a more widespread uptake by the reticular macrophages of the cords of Billroth and the free macrophages of the sinusoids; the endothelial cells of the sinusoids take up the carbon poorly.

Physiologically the spleen removes from the circulation stray bacteria, cellular débris and the effete red cells, white cells and platelets of the blood. The uptake of effete red cells and the handling of the iron-containing haemosiderin which results from the degradation of their haemoglobin is readily seen in the normal spleen. It is possible to observe macrophages showing erythrophagocytosis, or bearing golden brown granules of haemosiderin which give the Prussian blue reaction for iron.

Phagocytosis by the spleen assumes great importance in diseases which are associated with excessive destruction of red cells or platelets or rarely in which the concentration of lipids in the blood, e.g. cholesterol, is increased. In these circumstances the macrophages multiply and the spleen gradually enlarges. Splenic enlargement is commonly found, for example, in countries where malaria is endemic, for in this disease the malarial parasite lives in and destroys red blood cells.

Extramedullary haemopoiesis

In the embryo, and in lesser degree in the newborn, many tissues other than the bone marrow are actively haemopoietic. The spleen and liver are particularly important. As the child matures, the marrow gradually emerges as the sole haemopoietic organ.

The spleen as a circulatory reserve

In man the spleen weighs up to 250 g and its content of blood does not amount to more than 1 or 2 per cent of the blood volume. The spleen is not therefore an important reservoir of blood. However, in many animals the spleen is relatively much larger and its intrasplenic volume is reduced by active muscular contraction of the capsule brought about by the sympathetic nerves and by release of adrenaline. Hence, its blood becomes available during vigorous exercise or after haemorrhage.

Lymphopoiesis and antibody formation in the spleen

In the spleen the Malpighian corpuscles make a modest contribution to the pool of circulating lymphocytes. The reticulum cells of the spleen, in the white and red pulp, also differentiate into plasma cells in response to circulating antigen. Their importance in antibody production

and resistance to infection is revealed by splenectomy.

SPLENECTOMY

Surgical removal of the spleen may be carried out in the experimental animal and it is necessary from time to time in the healthy patient whose spleen has been ruptured by trauma. In the long run splenectomy has no dire effects but certain changes are detectable.

(1) Partial removal is followed by a rapid regeneration of the retained part or accessory spleens until approximately its former weight is restored.

(2) Within hours of splenectomy in the normal animal there is a marked increase in the number of circulating leucocytes and platelets which lasts for many weeks. The effect is attributed to withdrawal of a humoral agent which is believed to inhibit the release of neutrophils and platelets from the marrow. In animals artificially joined together with a common circulation (parabiosis) splenectomy in one partner has no effect but splenectomy in both induces leucocytosis.

(3) In animals whose spleen has a significant contractile power, the loss of the storage function may diminish the tolerance to haemorrhage, shock, anoxia or exercise.

(4) After the spleen has been removed its haemodestructive powers are carried out by other RE organs, e.g. the liver and bone marrow.

(5) There is an increased risk of infection after splenectomy especially in very young children. In animals, the production of antibodies to certain intravenously injected antigens is reduced.

THE IMMUNE ACTIVITIES OF THE LYMPHORETICULAR TISSUE

The lymphoreticular system traps antigens and reacts to their presence by an immune response whose precise form depends on the nature of the antigen. In the **humoral response** antibodies are formed in the lymph nodes and spleen for release into the circulation in high concentration. On the other hand the response may be purely **cellular** where cells of the lymphoreticular system, chiefly the lymphocyte, acquire immune behaviour and come to recognize antigen, and migrate towards and mount a cellular attack upon it. Sometimes mixtures of humoral and cellular responses are found and in some local, essentially cellular responses in the tissues certain cells in the infiltrate can be shown to produce antibody but only in amounts too small to appear in the circulation.

Antigens which stimulate an immune cellular or humoral response in the lymph nodes or splenic lymphoid tissues bring about 'reactive changes'. The sinusoids of the lymph node become packed with macrophages, plasma cells appear and the germinal centres show increased mitotic figures and production of small lymphocytes.

The importance of each of those cell types in antigen trapping, production of antibody and as specific cellular effectors is now considered.

THE MACROPHAGE

The macrophage is a common cellular effector in local inflammatory responses but its phagocytic action is relatively indiscriminate. It ingests particulate material best and soluble substances are often poorly phagocytosed. Both antigens like bacteria and non-antigens like lipids, carbon and inorganic irritants are ingested. The non-specific phagocytosis of particulate antigens by the macrophage is enormously enhanced in those immune states where specific antibody is present. The ability of antibody to render antigen more readily phagocytosed is called **opsonization** and it depends largely on the amount and specificity of the antibody; macrophages from immune animals, if washed free of antibody, show only a modest increase in phagocytosis of the antigen. In states of purely cellular immunity a similar slight specific enhancement of phagocytosis may be detected and contributes significantly to the animals' immune defence.

The immune response requires the uptake of antigen and its processing in a way which stimulates the production of antibodies and cellular effectors. Since the macrophage takes up antigen avidly, investigators have postulated that this cell produces antibody. However, there is evidence that it does not but instead acts by instructing other cells to do so. Thus fluorescent tracers (p. 13.4) fail to show antibody in the cytoplasm of the macrophages which abound in the sinusoids of lymph nodes reacting to local antigenic stimulation. Circumstantial evidence for the absence of antibody formation in the phagocytic cells comes also from the finding that the liver produces very little antibody despite the uptake of antigen by its numerous Kupffer cells. Of course, it is possible that our inability to detect antibody in the macrophage is due to those cells which do produce it transforming into cells no longer recognizable as macrophages. However, if inert particles such as aluminium hydroxide are given along with the antigen they can never be demonstrated accompanying antibody in any cell which produces it, so it seems certain that the macrophage neither produces antibody nor transforms into cells which do. However, the macrophage can be shown to be capable of inducing other cells to produce antibody highly specific to the antigen which it carries. Macrophages from an immune animal, months after the antigen has disappeared from their cytoplasm, can confer specific antibody formation on a normal non-immune compatible animal.

Also, if antigens are given to peritoneal macrophages in tissue culture a population of cells results from which a cell-free extract rich in RNA can be made. Administration of the extract to cultures of certain lymphoid tissue leads to the appearance of antibody-forming cells in the culture. These suggestive experiments do not tell us precisely how the macrophage influences the antibody forming cells, but do point to some form of chemical mediation. However, direct cytoplasmic communications have been seen in EM between the cytoplasm of macrophages and other cells of the lymphoreticular system capable of antibody production. It is therefore suggested that the macrophage first processes the ingested antigen and then injects its ribosomes or messenger RNA into other cells. In this way the macrophage may direct their immune behaviour. Thus the plasma cells produce specific antibody and the lymphocytes acquire the properties of specific cellular effectors. If the macrophage should direct cell precursors rather than the mature forms its effect might persist for many generations by the operation of asymmetric mitosis.

THE PLASMA CELL

The plasma cell is without doubt the greatest producer of antibody (plate 27.2, facing p. 27.19). It has little or no phagocytic ability but, along with the lymphocyte, it may appear in local cellular responses both specific and otherwise. In those circumstances it sometimes produces antibody in amounts insufficient to be detected in the circulation. However in response to certain antigens numerous plasma cells appear in the sinusoids of the lymph nodes and spleen and large amounts of antibody may be released to circulate in the bloodstream often for lengthy periods. It usually differentiates from reticulum cells but may arise also from other immunologically important cells (p. 27.15).

The cytological structure of the plasma cell indicates its high protein synthetic powers, since it has basophilic cytoplasm, which in the EM is seen to contain a rich endoplasmic reticulum with its associated ribosomes (p. 13.8). A prominent Golgi body capping the nucleus is sometimes seen as a pale perinuclear halo in H and E preparations. Fluorescent tracer techniques confirm that the globulins which it produces on antigenic stimulation are indeed specific antibodies. The cytoplasm, containing large amounts of RNA, stains with pyronin and it is convenient to refer to such cells as **pyroninophil** even if they do not have all the characteristics of plasma cells. As the plasma cell ages, that area of its cytoplasm most synthetically active undergoes a hyaline change and turns into an eosinophilic, brightly refractile sphere which is often to be found free in the tissues in inflammatory states. It is known as the Russell body after William Russell (1852–1940), pathologist and physician who occupied the Chair of Clinical Medicine in the University of Edinburgh from 1913–19 and first described the structure in the inflammatory infiltrate around malignant deposits.

THE LYMPHOCYTE

Outside the lymph node small lymphocytes are easily recognized by their distribution and size. When stimulated by antigens the lymphocyte can transform into other cell types which scarcely resemble it. In a lymph node reacting to antigenic stimulation, the germinal follicles increase in diameter, show numerous mitotic figures, a high uptake of ^{32}P indicative of DNA synthesis, and often a rim of new lymphocytes. The centres themselves show few of the phagocytes and plasma cells which are such a prominent feature of the sinusoids of the reactive node.

Fluorescent tracers show much antibody in the plasma cells but none in any of the lymphocytes or their precursors. Only after a second injection of antigen can small amounts of antibody be found in the large and medium lymphocytes, but none in the small. However, although they make little or no antibody, the lymphocytes of the lymph node and circulation have now become immunologically primed. They are able to recognize the antigen, and react to it specifically by congregating round its local aggregations in injection sites and elsewhere. Here, the lymphocyte acts as a specific purely cellular effector. What precisely it does around antigen deposits is unknown but it is assumed to be protective to the host. How the lymphocyte recognizes antigen and how it retains this ability for lengthy periods (immunological memory) are equally not understood. It is possible that the lymphocyte or its precursors acquires the RNA messenger from the macrophages and retains it in generations of lymphocytes; the messenger may then serve simply as a complementary pattern allowing antigens to be matched for recognition.

Although it produces no antibody itself the lymphocyte plays an important part as a mediator of antibody formation, for it can transform itself, within 48 hours of exposure to certain antigens, into a large pyroninophilic cell which is virtually a lymphoblast with antibody-producing cytoplasm. Since the phenomenon can be demonstrated in vitro with pure suspensions of blood lymphocytes it is not dependent on the processing of the antigen by the macrophage. Indeed it probably provides an alternative method of antibody formation for soluble antigens which are poorly phagocytosed. It is important to realize that the transformation of lymphocytes into cells which form antibody does not preclude their cellular immune behaviour of migration and aggregation to antigen-rich sites. Indeed the large pyroninophilic cell and the plasma cell are often found at sites of predominantly cellular immune reactions when few antibodies can be detected in the circulating blood. (plate 27.1f, facing p. 27.6).

In addition, it is possible that the pyroninophilic cell may exert its lymphoblastic properties by dividing to yield medium and small lymphocytes. In this way the immunological specificity of the antibody-forming pyroninophil may determine the subsequent immune cellular behaviour of its daughter cells.

The lymphocyte as a cellular effector

Certain antigens have the capacity to evoke an immune cellular response in which antibody plays little part, e.g. infection with the organism of tuberculosis. The behaviour of the lymphocyte as a cellular effector in such cases is directed against the antigen with a high degree of specificity. Another example where cellular immunity is paramount and circulating antibody plays relatively little part is the mechanism of rejection of skin and other grafts.

The biology of grafts is important because work done on them has been responsible for most of our knowledge about the cellular immune response of the lymphocyte and kindred cells.

Grafting is a process alien to nature and skin taken from one animal and grafted on to another member of the same species, a homograft, is bound to be rejected except in certain special circumstances. After an interval of 8–10 days the graft sloughs off, leaving a raw area which is infiltrated with lymphocytes, medium-sized mononuclear cells and large pyroninophilic cells. The phenomenon has an immune basis and depends upon certain tissue antigens or histocompatibility antigens as they are sometimes called. Although members of the same species share many antigens in common, successful grafting of skin between any two unrelated individuals is impossible, since invariably either individual possesses tissue antigens not found in the other, and liable to evoke an immune response. Only by choosing identical twins or by using highly inbred animal strains do homografts 'take' successfully. So far our experimental system consists of a graft of skin, which has no appreciable content of immunologically active cells. Since this piece of graft tissue is rejected by the host it is called a **host versus graft reaction**. However, it is possible to graft preparations of lymphocytes or other immunologically active cells by injection intravenously. In the majority of cases they are destroyed in the spleen by a host versus graft reaction. However, by resort to genetic subterfuges it is possible to ensure that the host animal possesses antigens not to be found in the injected graft lymphocytes. To do so, a pure, inbred strain of animal is crossed with a wild one. By the Mendelian laws the resulting first filial (F_1) generation is bound to possess histocompatibility antigens not present in either parent. If lymphocytes are now taken from either parent and injected into the F_1 animal they find themselves exposed to antigens which they do not possess, during their circulation in the host. To those essentially foreign antigens, the donor lymphocytes react by mounting a cellular immune attack upon the tissues of the host, the **graft versus host reaction.**

The graft versus host reaction has easily recognizable signs and is useful because it allows known, defined parental cell populations to be tested for their immune competence in an F_1 animal. The graft versus host reaction leads to an infiltration of the tissues of the host with lymphocytic and pyroninophilic cells. Damage to the liver, lungs, kidneys and lymphoid system is severe, the latter leading to intercurrent infections and wasting similar to that found in the lymphoid atrophy which follows thymectomy of the newborn (p. 27.19); it is sometimes known as 'runt disease'. It is possible to be quite certain that the cells infiltrating the tissues of the F_1 animal are parental in origin by the use of a female parent whose X chromosomes may be identified in the cells invading the tissues of a male offspring.

The more familiar host versus graft reaction also provides useful information about the range of cellular types involved in a cellular immune reaction. It allows the histological study of the complete range of cellular types involved in rejection, and their host origin may be confirmed by the chromosomal marker or by isotopic labelling followed by autoradiography. Some examples of variations on the basic host versus graft system which confirm the importance of the lymphocyte and its pyroninophilic derivatives include the following.

(1) Lymphocytes from an animal which has already rejected a graft (usual time 8–10 days) cause accelerated rejection of a similar graft, perhaps in 2 to 3 days, in another animal with which they are compatible.

(2) Homografts applied immediately after birth in small rodents induce a curious state called tolerance which allows similar homografts to be accepted in adult life. If, however, injections of thoracic duct lymphocytes from a normal animal are given to a tolerant animal with an accepted homograft, rejection sets in.

(3) In tissue culture systems, lymphocytes from animals which have rejected grafts exert a marked cytopathic effect on cultured graft fibroblasts.

The transformation of the lymphocyte to antibody-forming cells

The transformation of the lymphocyte into cells capable of forming antibody does not prevent them joining in a cellular immune response to local antigen. In fact, in most cellular immune infiltrations of tissues injected with antigen, both antibody-forming plasma cells and other pyroninophilic cells are found even although little or no antibody is released into the circulation. In a graft undergoing rejection cellular particulate débris passes to the local lymph nodes and is phagocytosed by the macrophages which are responsible for directing lymphocyte immune behaviour. In addition, soluble antigens from the tissues bring about transformation of the lymphocytes directly in the lymph node. The immunologically primed lymphocytes and pyroninophils then gain the efferent lymphatics, reach the blood stream and migrate to the graft site. The pyroninophil almost certainly corresponds to the well known and long recognized Türk cell or 'irritation lymphocyte' which can be found in the peripheral bloodstream of patients in certain febrile infective states.

There is evidence that antigens, especially soluble antigens, have an immediate and early effect on the lymphocyte which may determine its future specific immune behaviour whether as a cellular effector or as a transformant to antibody-producing pyroninophilic cells. Some of the evidence is summarized as follows.

(1) Lymphocytes, incubated with antigen then washed free of it and injected into a compatible animal survive and confer antibody production on the recipient.

(2) Depletion of the lymphocyte population, by drainage of the thoracic duct, before intravenous injection of an antigen leads to a very poor antibody response. If, on the other hand, the antigen is given first and thoracic duct drainage is started immediately afterwards, antibody production is unimpaired. These experiments show that the lymphocyte is influenced directly by antigen and plays an important part in the earliest stages of the immune response.

(3) In vitro, blood lymphocytes from a subject immune to certain antigens transform into large lymphocytes and pyroninophilic lymphoblasts which show marked mitotic activity when exposed to the antigens. The reaction is easily observed and may be used as a test of previous exposure to an antigen. Lymphocytes from a subject who has not met the antigen do not transform in this way. There is one exception to this rule and it is of practical importance. Lymphocytes from one individual transform on exposure to the histocompatibility antigens of another which they do not share even although they have not met them before. Thus lymphocytes transform when exposed to tissue preparations from another member of the same species unless genetically identical. In practice, to test for compatibility of potential donors and recipients for grafting it is not necessary to use tissue preparations but merely to mix the lymphocytes of the two individuals together and observe their behaviour in culture. Transformation in culture shows the tissues of the two individuals are not compatible.

The re-circulation of the lymphocyte (p. 27.5) serves to prevent an excessive concentration of antigen round a static population of cells and it exposes all the circulating lymphocytes to the antigen and the processing macrophages of the reactive regional node. Interestingly the turnover rate of lymphocytes through the node decreases in the reactive state suggesting that the lymphocytes linger there longer, perhaps acquiring immune instructions.

The ease of transformation of the lymphocyte into large cells of more primitive type leads to the question of its ansformation into other recognizable mesenchymal ells. From time to time the transformation of the ʳmphocyte into macrophages, fibroblasts, and even ːem cells with multiple potentialities, including aemopoietic differentiation, has been suggested but has ot been substantiated.

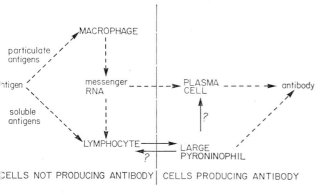

FIG. 27.11. Immunological relationships of the macrophages, plasma cells, lymphocytes and their derivatives.

The plasma cell commonly develops directly from ⸱ticulum cells like the macrophage, but the possibility ⸳ its formation from the lymphocyte via the large pyron- ʌophilic cells is considered probable by many workers nd is tentatively suggested in fig. 27.11 where the inter- ⸱lations of the immunologically active cells are sum- ʌarized.

THE THYMUS

n the past decade the thymus, formerly an enigma, has ⸱ome to be recognized as the foremost member of the ʌammalian lymphoid system; such is its importance that ʌe lymph nodes and spleen are now called the peripheral ʄmphoid organs. The thymus is necessary for the develop- ʌent and maintenance of the lymphoid system, especially ʌ the newborn and young animal. It is the first lymphoid ʳgan to develop and it secretes a humoral factor which ː essential for lymphopoiesis both in its own cortex and ʌ the developing lymph nodes and spleen. It makes a ʌall, but important, contribution to the pool of im- ʌunologically competent cells. Without its thymus, the ʾoung animal succumbs to chance infection because of ʰe failure of peripheral lymphoid development. The ʌajor activities of the thymus are in the neonatal and ʳowth periods: after puberty it undergoes involution, ʄith loss of its lymphocytes, gradual fibrosis and shrink- ʒe.

Anatomy

ʰe thymus is situated in the neck and anterior medias- ʴnum and reaches its greatest size in the child at about

9 years of age. At this time it is a bilobed triangular mass which represents the embryological fusion of bilateral downgrowths of the IIIrd branchial pouches (p. 18.29). It extends downwards from its apex, close to the lower border of the thyroid, to its base which is level with the fourth costal cartilage (fig. 27.12). In the neck it lies between the trachea and the origins of the sternohyoid and sternothyroid muscles. In the thorax it lies between the great vessels and pericardium posteriorly and the sternum anteriorly. According to an ancient view of Galen it serves as a cushion set between the violent pulsations of the one and the bony hardness of the other.

At birth, when it is largest in relation to the body weight, it weighs 10 to 15 g and at the age of 8–10 years it reaches its maximum absolute weight of 35–40 g. Thereafter it undergoes involution, and the fibrotic adult thymus is often difficult to recognize among the fibrofatty tissue of the anterior mediastinum.

The blood supply of the thymus is derived from branches of the internal thoracic artery and of the superior and inferior thyroid arteries. The venous drainage is chiefly by tributaries of the left brachiocephalic vein and of the thyroid veins.

Although a lymphoid organ, it is not concerned with the handling of lymph, and unlike a lymph node it has

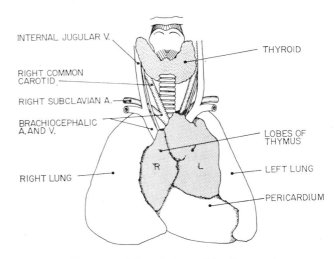

FIG. 27.12. The relations of the thymus.

no lymphatic channels of sinusoidal type in its paren- chyma. The lymphatic drainage of the thymus is confined to its capsule, from which channels drain ultimately to the deep cervical, tracheobronchial and internal thoracic groups of lymph nodes.

The thymic nerve supply consists of extremely fine branches of the vagi and sympathetic trunk. Branches from the phrenic nerve and the ansa cervicalis supply its capsule but not its parenchyma.

Microscopic structure (fig. 27.13)

The lobes of the thymus are made up of many lobules up to 2 mm in diameter which have a peripheral loose connective tissue capsule, an outer cortex densely packed with lymphocytes and a lightly staining medulla where lymphocytes are much less numerous. The lobules have a pyramidal shape with truncated apices directed centrally and are separated from one another by deep capsular septa which carry the vessels and nerves of the organ.

FIG. 27.13. Diagrammatic section of thymus to show cortex, medulla blood supply and the epithelial framework or sheath.

The medulla is a central continuous structure which ramifies into each lobule and is made up of large eosinophilic cells. The EM shows that the medullary cells form a continuum bounded by a prominent basement membrane wherever it is in contact with connective tissue. Accordingly, the medullary cells are known as epithelial cells. They are the probable source of the thymic lymphopoietic humoral factor which stimulates lymphopoiesis.

Hassall's corpuscles (plate 27.1e facing p. 27.6 and fig. 27.13), a feature of the medulla, are large spherical aggregates of eosinophilic cells and débris 30–100 μm in diameter. They are probably collecting points for degenerate epithelial cells. Lymphoid germinal follicles are not present in the normal thymus and plasma cells are scarce or absent.

Branches of the major arteries travel deeply in the interlobular clefts and eventually penetrate the lobules, usually on their deep or central aspects, to become the intralobular arterioles (fig. 27.13). The intralobular arteriole runs in the cortico-medullary zone and gives off

capillary branches which radiate outwards in the cortex. These radial capillaries anastomose freely and drain into the cortical radial veins which run back to the cortico-medullary zone to join the medullary vein. The medullary vein drains from the medulla and runs beside the intralobular arteries. In man, and in most species with a highly lobulated thymus, there is also a significant drainage from the peripheral cortical capillaries to superficial plexus of capsular veins.

THE THYMIC CORTEX

The framework of the cortex is an epithelial structure not readily seen in routine sections because of its cellular density. The epithelium radiates out from the medulla into the cortex in ramifying sheets which divide the lobule into numerous compartments in which the lymphocytes are produced (fig. 27.13). Like the cells of the medulla the cortical epithelial cells are probably of endodermal origin. Around the radial vessels the epithelium forms loose sheaths which electron micrographs show to be separated from the vessel wall by a narrow perivascular space. The sheath probably acts as a partial barrier to the passage of blood-borne antigens into the thymus. At the periphery of the lobule the epithelium lines the inner aspect of the capsule and completes the epithelial spongework in which the thymic lymphocytes are produced.

The epithelial cells of the thymus are different from the RE cells which form the scaffolding of the peripheral lymphoid tissue. They are most probably endodermal derivatives, not mesenchymal, and they are not phagocytic. They form a continuous sheet which EM shows to have the characteristics of an epithelium. Thus intracellular tonofibrils are present, and desmosomes link the adjacent cells into a sheet which is bounded by a prominent basement membrane. The epithelial cells produce no reticulin and when they gain support from adjacent reticulin fibres they are separated from them by a basement membrane.

THE CORTICAL LYMPHOCYTES

Lymphopoiesis in the thymus

The thymic small lymphocytes account for 90 per cent of the weight of the organ and are produced in the cortex from stem cells which appear to migrate there from the bone marrow. By a series of divisions the stem cell mature progressively to large, medium and finally small lymphocytes. Just as in the lymph node (p. 27.5) asymmetric division of the large and medium lymphocyte maintains the population of precursors in the thymus and reduces the demand for stem cells to less than 1 per cent of the total lymphoid population. Lymphopoiesis is stimulated in the thymic cortex and elsewhere by the humoral lymphopoietic factor secreted by the medullary epithelial cells. The paucity of lymphocytes in the medulla, where the lymphopoietic factor is present in highest concentration, merely emphasizes that lymphopoiesis depends also on other factors, e.g. the correct environment and the presence of stem cells. Indeed, even in the thymic cortex in which lymphopoiesis is about five times more active than in the average lymph node, mitotic figures and lymphoid precursors are not uniformly distributed, but are found in the subcapsular region and along the courses of the radial vessels, in particular around their peripheral segments. There the perivascular epithelial sheaths are fenestrated by lacunae through which stem cells and nutrients pass easily into the parenchyma. In addition the subcapsular region contains large vacuolated macrophages which are surrounded by dividing lymphoid precursor cells. Although these macrophages are present in most species they are especially prominent in the mouse where they are known as chromolipid or PAS cells. The name reflects their content of yellow insoluble lipid which stains with the PAS method and is a degradation product of phagocytosed effete lymphocytes. The chromolipid cells are thought to encourage lymphopoiesis in their surroundings by secreting soluble metabolites which stimulate the dividing lymphoid precursors. When lympholysis and subsequent phagocytosis of dead lymphocytes is brisk, e.g. after cortisol administration, the accumulation of chromolipid may give a yellow colour to the cortex. As the chromolipid accumulates in the macrophages at least some of them migrate to the medulla and become incorporated in Hassall's corpuscles.

Stability of thymic lymphopoiesis

Lymphopoiesis in the thymus proceeds at a rapid rate. It is stable and is not influenced by injections of antigen which stimulate lymphopoiesis in the lymph nodes and spleen. The failure of germinal centres to develop in the normal thymus despite potent antigenic stimulation suggests that thymic lymphopoiesis actually proceeds in an environment from which effective antigenic stimulation is excluded.

The immunological environment of the thymic lymphocytes

The lack of an effective antigenic stimulus to the formation of germinal centres may be due to defects in the uptake of antigen by the thymus or in its retention or ultimate processing by the macrophages. It is possible too, that cells capable of forming germinal centres are absent.

Although the basement membrane of the epithelial sheath may restrict blood-borne antigens to the perivascular space, the demonstration of lacunae in the sheaths of the peripheral regions of the radial vessels makes the idea of a complete anatomical barrier untenable. The haemothymic barrier is partial, and only the larger particulate antigens are successfully excluded.

Defects of phagocytosis also ensure that antigen is poorly retained in the thymus. Thus, in the neonatal rat, the macrophages of the entire RES take up labelled bovine serum albumin very poorly, a phenomenon probably related to immunological tolerance (p. 27.21). While the antigen readily crosses the haemothymic barrier and is exposed to phagocytosis, the uptake and retention of the antigen by the thymic macrophages is even smaller, perhaps due to increasing efficacy of the barrier. In the adult rat thymic uptake is similarly extremely poor and is in striking contrast to the avid and prolonged retention of the antigen in the macrophages of the spleen. Thus the lack of an effective stimulus to germinal centre formation may be due to inadequate retention of antigen by the phagocytes. However, in certain species some antigens are retained by the thymic macrophages in amounts which would stimulate germinal centre production in any other lymphoid organ. Presumably in this case either the macrophages fail to process antigen adequately or the thymus possesses no cells normally capable of forming germinal follicles. Since germinal centres appear in the medulla in certain auto-immune diseases it is possible that cells capable of forming germinal follicles are normally present there but remain latent due to the lack of effective antigenic stimulation. Support for this idea comes from the direct injection of antigen into the thymus, which evokes germinal centres confined to the medulla. Possibly the high concentration of antigen overcomes the inertia of the processing mechanism. No circumstances have been described in which germinal centres appear in the cortex.

In the thymus the epithelial barrier and defects of phagocytosis serve to protect its lymphocyte precursors from antigenic stimulation. Whereas the lymphocytes of the lymph nodes and spleen are committed immunologically to the antigens which stimulate their germinal centres, the thymus produces a corps of immunologically uncommitted cells.

The fate of the thymic lymphocytes

The vigorous lymphopoiesis in the thymus is offset by the death of 95 per cent after a life of 3–4 days which may represent the elimination of cells unsuited to the immunological needs of the body. The remaining 5 per cent of lymphocytes are long lived and identical with the lymphocytes of the circulating pool. They migrate to the medulla where they constitute a distinct population in which mitotic figures are absent. They are exported in small numbers, via the thymic capillaries, to make an important contribution of immunologically uncommitted cells to the pool of circulating lymphocytes.

THE THYMIC MEDULLA

The medullary epithelial cells

The thymic medulla is composed mainly of large epithelial cells of endodermal origin. They tend to aggregate together and in man it is probable that the Hassall's corpuscles are, at least initially, the result of their fusion. The epithelial cells of the medulla show certain similarities with those of the cortex. However, in the medullary epithelial cells, PAS-staining inclusions are prominent whereas in the epithelial cells of the cortical framework they are insignificant. The medullary epithelial cells have therefore been suspected of secretory activity.

Since there is good experimental evidence that the thymic lymphopoietic factor is secreted by the thymic medulla, attempts have been made to find out if the PAS-staining secretion has lymphopoietic activity. The evidence, so far, is indirect but when lymphopoiesis is rapid the inclusions are small and few and, when it is poor, they are large and numerous. These changes are compatible with the storage and release of a substance with lymphopoietic activity.

Hassall's corpuscles

Hassall's corpuscles are formed continuously in the embryonic and post-natal thymus and are especially prominent during involution. They are formed only in the medulla, probably by the aggregation of medullary epithelial cells.

The corpuscles begin in the medulla as a single epithelial cell which undergoes degenerative changes. Its nucleus becomes intensely basophilic, swollen and indistinct and a large crescentic perinuclear vacuole appears. The cytoplasm meanwhile becomes deeply eosinophilic and small basophilic granules of keratohyaline appear. Other epithelial cells approach, assume a crescentic shape and apply themselves to the central cell as shown in fig. 27.14a. The nucleus of the central cell then disintegrates and the vacuole enlarges to engulf some of the nuclear fragments, continues to expand slowly and compresses the cytoplasm and the keratohyaline granules against the cell membrane. At about the same time the surrounding cells fuse to form a syncytium, closely applied to the distended cytoplasmic membrane of the central cell (fig. 27.14b & c), and new cells become applied to the periphery of the corpuscle, while others enter the vacuole by parting its limiting cell membrane (fig. 27.14d & e). The central vacuole has the ability to digest the contained cells and their keratohyaline inclusions. The process of 'intrusion' of cells, in this way, may be repeated many times until the central vacuole becomes distended by fluid and ruptures. In keeping with their known attraction to sites of protein digestion, the eosinophil leucocytes of the medulla migrate into the ruptured cyst. Hassall's corpuscles become progressively larger with age, and their centres fill with amorphous débris and

eosinophilic hyaline lamellae. Nuclear fragments and keratohyaline granules are prominent and only the peripheral cells retain a normal nucleus.

The Hassall's corpuscles probably destroy effete thymic macrophages which migrate to the medulla with their loads of lymphocytic nuclear débris. Thus in times of involution or lympholysis the number and size of Hassall's corpuscles increase due to the rise in the number of macrophages which are destroyed.

FIG. 27.14. Stages in the formation of Hassall's corpuscles.

The functions of the thymus

The functions of the thymus may be summarized.

(1) In the newborn the thymus is necessary for the **development** of the peripheral lymphoid tissues. In its absence, lymphoid aplasia, lymphopenia and a failure of cellular immunity lead to wasting and death from infection. By adolescence the lymphoid system is fully developed and then the thymus involutes.

(2) In the adult the function of the involuted thymus is one of **maintenance**. It ensures the supply of fresh, immunologically uncommitted lymphocytes able to react to

PLATE 25.2. Clinical endocrinology.

(a) 18-year-old pituitary dwarf; (b) 44-year-old cretin; (c) patient with myxoedema; (d) patient with acromegaly; (e) patient with enlarged, easily visible, thyroid gland due to thryotoxicosis; (f) biological assay of human chorionic gonadotrophin using mouse uterus; from the top control, 0·2 i.u. and 2·0 i.u.

a

b

PLATE 27.2. Plasma cells.

(a) A light microscopic field containing a number of plasma cells, the two most typical indicated by arrows. The clumped pattern of nuclear chromatin is seen (× 1000). (b) An electron micrograph from a rat lymph node. The nucleus (N) is eccentrically placed; the cytoplasm is packed with rough-surfaced endoplasmic reticulum (RER). There is a large Golgi region (G) and a few mitochondria (M). Glutaraldehyde fixation, araldite embedding (× 6750).

PLATE 28.1. A radiograph of the normal chest. Several of the structures shown in fig. 28.6a (p. 28.) are easily seen. They include the ascending aorta, the pulmonary artery, the left ventricle, the right atrium and the shadow in the superior mediastinum showing the superior vena cava.

new antigens. Removal leads, not to severe illness, but only to a diminished response to new antigens.

(3) The thymus stimulates both its own and peripheral lymphopoiesis by a humoral factor produced by its medullary epithelial cells. The production of thymic lymphocytes is autonomous; the thymus governs its own lymphopoietic rate, its ultimate population of lymphocytes and the onset of its involution.

(4) The bone marrow supplies the stem cells from which lymphocytes develop in the thymus, under the influence of the humoral factor.

(5) The thymus is responsible for the gradual restoration of cellular immune competence in animals rendered experimentally tolerant to antigens.

(6) In auto-immune diseases the thymus often shows germinal follicle formation and in some of these diseases may play an initiating part. The thymus gives some protection against experimentally induced carcinoma.

The plasma cells and hence the antibody-forming system develop largely independently of the thymus.

THYMIC FUNCTION IN THE NEWBORN

In the embryo lymphocytes appear first in the thymus and many experiments have illustrated its leading part in the development of the lymphoid system. If the thymus is removed from newborn mice, they continue to grow for three to four weeks but thereafter develop a fatal wasting disease with loss of weight, severe respiratory and other infections and, most important, a marked lymphopenia and hypoplasia of the peripheral lymphoid organs, lymph nodes, spleen, tonsils and Peyer's patches in the intestine. The appearances are similar to those of the 'runt disease' which occurs in animals undergoing a graft versus host reaction (p. 27.13). There is no doubt that the failure to thrive is due to frequent infections since their lives can be prolonged greatly if they are treated with antibiotics or reared in a germ-free environment. The severity of the infection reflects a defect of cellular immunity due to the inadequate export of lymphocytes to the circulation from a lymphoid system which has failed to develop. The failure of cellular immunity in the thymectomized newborn mouse may be confirmed by observing the behaviour of skin homografts (p. 27.13). In a normal animal a skin homograft excites a local inflammatory response in which the host's lymphocytes mount an immune attack on the graft tissue and bring about its rapid rejection. The thymectomized newborn fails to reject homografts and indeed may even accept a heterograft from a related species, e.g. the rat.

The immune defects which follow thymectomy in the neonatal mouse are largely confined to the lymphocyte-mediated immune cellular reactions. In the atrophic lymphoid tissues the number of plasma cells is not significantly diminished and therefore antibody production is not seriously disturbed. Although they probably

25

differentiate from the same stem cells as the lymphocytes, plasma cells and the antibodies they produce are largely independent of the thymus.

A more positive approach to thymic function may be made by attempting to reconstitute the thymectomized neonatal animal. Two main methods have been used to reverse the lymphopenia and the defect in cellular immunity. In the first, lymphocyte suspensions from both thymic and peripheral lymphoid sources are injected intravenously to find out which are effective. In the second and more fundamental method, restoration is attempted by grafts of thymic tissue.

Restoration by cellular suspensions
With genetically compatible preparations the depleted lymphoid tissues, circulating lymphocytes and cellular immunity of thymectomized neonatal animals can be restored. Complete restoration limited only by the life-span of the injected lymphocytes is possible by the use of suspensions from lymph nodes, spleen and thoracic duct of normal animals. On the other hand, thymic lymphocytes restore lymphoid tissue and immune functions to only a small degree. It is therefore unlikely that the development of the peripheral lymphoid system is entirely dependent upon the receipt of thymic lymphocytes. Rather does the thymus stimulate peripheral lymphopoiesis by a humoral factor.

Restoration of function by thymic grafting
Compatible thymus grafts implanted in thymectomized neonatal animals restore their lymphoid and immune state after 3 or 4 weeks. After implantation the graft takes some time to acquire an adequate blood supply and during this period most of its lymphocytes die. Thereafter the epithelial frame of the graft gradually becomes restocked with healthy lymphocytes. Concomitantly the peripheral lymphoid tissues, which the graft saves from atrophy, acquire increasing numbers of lymphocytes and by the fourth week are restored to normal. To find out from where the new lymphocytes in the thymic graft and in the peripheral lymphoid tissue have come, grafts can be used which bear a marker chromosome so that the cells of the host can be distinguished from those of the graft. In this way the lymphocytes which re-stock both the thymic graft and the peripheral lymphoid system can be shown to be almost entirely of host as opposed to donor origin. Since the lymphocytes of the graft die off rapidly it is thought that the epithelial framework of the graft is in some way responsible for their re-appearance. The lymphopoietic effect of the thymic epithelium, in theory, could be exerted in two ways. Host stem cells may enter the graft and be induced to mature by close contact with the epithelium. Thereafter their progeny might be exported to repopulate the periphery. On the other hand if the thymic epithelium were to produce a

humoral lymphopoietic factor its effect could be exerted on stem cells throughout the lymphoid tissue. Most of the evidence favours this latter view which is also in keeping with the rather small numbers of lymphocytes which the thymus is known to export (p. 27.17). The dependence of peripheral lymphopoiesis on a humoral factor can be shown experimentally. To do so, thymic grafts are enclosed in a cell-tight capsule of 'millipore' filter membrane before implanting in a thymectomized newborn mouse. Despite the prevention of cellular traffic, the lymphoid population and its immune responses are adequately restored. The graft must therefore secrete a filter-passing, i.e. humoral, lymphopoietic substance. Examination of the encapsulated graft confirms the early death of its lymphocytes: the only component sufficiently viable to produce the lymphopoietic substance is the epithelial framework.

In summary, normal lymphopoiesis in the young is dependent upon the thymus. Maturation of stem cells, both in its own parenchyma and in the periphery, is stimulated by a humoral factor secreted by its epithelial framework. The source of the stem cells and the properties of the humoral factor are discussed later.

THYMIC FUNCTION IN THE ADULT

The adult animal has a fully developed lymphoid system and thymectomy does not give rise to the severe wasting and the infections found in the neonate. In fact, it has little evident effect upon growth, breeding, infection or longevity. Nor can changes be detected in humoral antibody formation or homograft rejection in the period soon after thymectomy. However, 6–9 months thereafter the adult animal loses weight and there is a fall of about 30 per cent in circulating lymphocytes. Although outwardly healthy the animal has an impaired cellular immune response to antigens not met previously.

Thymic function in the irradiated adult animal

Total body irradiation of sufficient dose kills an animal by destroying the haemopoietic bone marrow, but it can be kept in moderate health by injections of compatible bone marrow. This acts by providing stem cells which mature in the irradiated animal and repopulate it with blood cells and lymphocytes. If, however, the animal is thymectomized before it is irradiated restoration of haemopoiesis is unaffected but the lymphoid tissues fail to regenerate and the cellular immune response is lost. The restoration of lymphopoiesis and of cellular immunity in the irradiated adult is therefore dependent upon the thymus which must therefore retain lymphopoietic powers. Furthermore, since the thymus shares the total body irradiation the lymphopoietic effect must be relatively radio-resistant, in keeping with the origin of the thymic humoral factor in the relatively hardy epithelial framework.

The persistence of thymic lymphoiesis in adult life and the poor cellular response to new antigens after thymectomy suggest that the function of the adult thymus is to maintain a steady supply of immunologically uncommitted lymphocytes.

THE THYMIC HUMORAL FACTOR

Two experiments point to the medullary rather than the cortical origin of this factor. Cell-free extracts of thymus stimulate lymphopoiesis in thymectomized newborn mice and those from the medulla are more potent than those from the cortex. Also, experiments with small minced thymic grafts have shown that repopulation with lymphocytes is successful only if medullary epithelial cells are included. The humoral factor from the medulla is presumably secreted into the blood stream and stimulates lymphopoiesis wherever stem cells are present in the correct nutritional environment. Those conditions are not met in the thymic medulla but brisk lymphopoiesis goes on in the peripheral lymphoid organs and in the thymic cortex especially round the PAS-positive cells in the mouse.

The separation of the effects of the humoral factor into lymphopoiesis and induction of immune competence can be shown by grafting X-irradiated thymus into thymectomized newborn mice. Normal blood lymphocyte counts are restored by control grafts of normal thymus and by grafts previously exposed to both low and high doses of X-rays. However, only in mice grafted with the normal and the low-irradiated thymus is the immune competence restored. It therefore seems that the thymic humoral factor has two distinct effects, one radio-sensitive which induces competence and the other radio-resistant which is lymphopoietic.

The regulation of thymic lymphopoiesis

The thymic lymphocytes are regulated intrinsically by the thymus itself, the simplest and most telling evidence being the autonomy of the process of involution which no extrinsic agent can induce prematurely or arrest once it is under way. The lymphocytic population of the thymus appears to be limited only by the available epithelial framework since thymic grafts behave independently of the state of the host's thymus. Thus if neonatal thymus is grafted into adults at the time of thymic involution, the host thymus continues to involute and the grafts repopulate normally.

INVOLUTION OF THE THYMUS

During the growth of the young animal the supply of immunologically uncommitted lymphocytes is assured by the peripheral effects of the thymic humoral factor and also by a small direct export of lymphocytes by the thymus itself. By adolescence the lymphoid tissues are fully developed; most of the important antigens have been encountered and immunity to them established. The demand for immunologically uncommitted lymphocytes declines and the thymic lymphopoietic effect serves only as a mild stimulus to peripheral production of uncommitted lymphocytes. Concomitantly with the reduced demands upon it the thymus undergoes involution and becomes a barely recognizable fibro-fatty tag which contains many Hassall's corpuscles surrounded by greatly diminished numbers of pyknotic lymphocytes. The stimulus to involution probably comes from within the thymus itself, possibly by a decline in the secretion of humoral factor. As the gland involutes there is loss of lymphocytes, and also shrinkage of the epithelial framework both of the cortex and medulla. The epithelial cells form cords and islands which may become cystic or contribute to the enlarging size and number of the Hassall's corpuscles. The changes are irreversible and there is an infiltration of fatty and fibrous tissue.

The changes of natural involution must be distinguished carefully from the atrophy induced by giving corticosteroids. Unlike true involution, the effects of cortisone are largely confined to lympholysis with accompanying collapse but no permanent loss of the epithelial framework. The changes are reversible when the hormone is withdrawn. Similar atrophy is found in such stress situations such as burning, severe infection and prolonged illness. The weight of the thymus of young adults dying in such circumstances is less than in individuals who have died suddenly.

THE ORIGIN OF THE LYMPHOID STEM CELLS

The majority of the thymic lymphocytes are derived from precursors which arrive from elsewhere. That the thymus takes up cells from the bloodstream is shown by the repopulation of the framework of thymic grafts; likewise, in pairs of parabiotic animals, one having a marker chromosome, the cells of one can be found dividing in the thymus of the other. If the lymphoid organs are destroyed by total irradiation, injections of lymphocytes of peripheral or thymic origin lead to a repopulation of the peripheral lymphoid tissue only; the thymus is not repopulated. Only by injecting bone marrow cells can both the thymic and peripheral lymphoid tissue be adequately restored. Confirmatory evidence that the thymus receives its stem cells from the bone marrow comes from the finding that thymic grafts fail to repopulate in irradiated animals unless marrow is also injected. However in health peripheral lymphopoiesis is not entirely dependent upon marrow stem cells. The stem cells of the peripheral lymphoid organs probably differentiate in situ from local reticulum cells and only when these have been destroyed, e.g. by irradiation, is the contribution from the marrow important. The thymus, on the other hand, con-

tains no true RE cells in its lymphopoietic tissue and is therefore entirely dependent upon circulating marrow stem cells for its continued lymphopoiesis. The precise nature of the marrow stem cells has not yet been determined.

THE FATE OF THE THYMIC LYMPHOCYTES

The majority, perhaps 95 per cent of its lymphocytes die off rapidly without ever leaving the organ. If tritiated thymidine is administered to young mice and its distribution followed by autoradiography 50 per cent of the thymic lymphocytes can be shown to be heavily labelled in 1 to 2 days, which suggests a total replacement time (or life) of 3 to 4 days. The autoradiographs also show that after 5 days a significant 5 per cent of the lymphocytes, mostly situated near the medulla, remain unlabelled. They are probably a distinct population of long lived immunologically competent thymic lymphocytes which are exported in small numbers to join the lymphoid pool. The reason for the high death rate of the thymic lymphocyte population is unknown.

RESTORATION OF IMMUNOLOGICAL COMPETENCE IN THE TOLERANT ANIMAL BY THYMIC GRAFTS

Tolerance is the failure of the animal to respond immunologically to antigenic stimulation by a cellular or antibody response. The most familiar example is the inability of the immune system to react to the host's own antigens. Experimentally tolerance can be induced by exposure to antigens either in utero or, more practically, in the neonatal period. At this time, when the immune mechanism regards all antigens encountered as 'self', tolerance can be established. The mechanism of tolerance is ill-understood but must involve either the elimination of reactive or antibody-forming cells or the suppression of their immune action. Tolerance is specific to the antigen and operates only as long as it is present; on its withdrawal tolerance is gradually lost and competence restored. If, however, a tolerant animal is thymectomized before the withdrawal of the relevant antigen, competence takes very much longer to be restored and may be poor. Thymic grafts from normal animals to thymectomized animals break down tolerance in spite of continued exposure to the antigen. The thymus seems to restore competence in the tolerant animal not by making available its own cells but by the effects of its humoral factor on the periphery. Thus lymphocytes with new competence are produced, some of which respond to the antigen.

THE THYMUS IN AUTOIMMUNE DISEASE

In auto-immune disease the immune defences, both antibody and cellular, are stimulated by the individual's own antigens and mount a self destructive attack. Either abnormal cells competent to react with 'self' antigens appear in the body, or perhaps antigens which are normally concealed are released to stimulate a normal immune system. Both mechanisms might be encouraged by the thymus which could fail to destroy lymphocytes of 'self-reactive' type, or else render the lymphoid system hyper-reactive to 'self' antigens through its humoral factor. Certainly the thymus is involved in some way in auto-immune disease, for it shows proliferative changes in many of them. Thus germinal follicles commonly appear, and occasionally a benign thymic tumour or thymoma may arise, either alone or along with germinal follicles in the parent thymus.

THE THYMUS AND MALIGNANT NEOPLASMS

Many cancer cells, especially those induced by chemical carcinogens and tumour viruses, contain antigens which are foreign to the host. It is thought therefore that the immune response may play some small part in preventing the emergence of a malignant tumour e.g. carcinoma. Animals which have been thymectomized show an increased susceptibility to experimentally induced carcin-oma. Thus, after applying the carcinogen the interval before the development of carcinoma is shortened and the number of tumours is increased. It seems likely that the loss of the thymus diminishes the host's ability to deal with new 'tumour' antigens. It is possible also that the increased susceptibility to carcinoma in old age in human beings may depend ultimately on the waning of thymic function.

FURTHER READING

BURNET SIR M. (1962) *The Integrity of the Body*. Cambridge (Mass.): Harvard University Press.

ELVES M.W. (1966) *The Lymphocytes*. London: Lloyd–Luke.

METCALF D. (1966) *The Thymus*. Berlin: Springer Verlag.

MILLER J.F.A.P. (1964) Functions of the Thymus. p. 218. Scientific Basis of Medicine. *Ann. Rev.*

YOFFEY J.M. & COURTICE F.C. (1956) *Lymphatics, Lymph and Lymphoid Tissue*, 2nd Edition. London: Arnold.

Chapter 28
The cardiovascular system

Since the time of the Roman physician Galen, coherent accounts of how the animal body works have started with notions of the relation of the blood to the heart and the pulse beat and recognized their importance for life. The central role of the circulation, which was dimly realized in the Graeco-Roman and even in the Chinese, Hindu and Egyptian cultures, was made explicit in Harvey's small volume *De Motu Cordis*, published in 1628, itself a landmark in the development of procedure in natural science.

Harvey made measurements of the blood volume, and by showing that the output of the heart could exceed the total blood volume, proved the existence of a circulation. The function of the veins and their valves was demonstrated and confirmed the conclusion that the blood must circulate continuously in the body. The demonstration by Malpighi (1661) and by Loewenhoek (1703) of the capillaries connecting the arteries and veins, which were unknown to Harvey, completed the cycle of the circulation.

Current concepts of the function of the body continue to give the circulation of the blood a central role. The function of the cardiovascular system can be regarded basically as that of transport. Claude Bernard's *'milieu intérieur'* is protected and depends on a sequence of inter-relationships between events in cells, in fluid bathing the cells, in blood and in nerves, and in the external environment. Animals of more than a few million cells in size require a circulatory system to carry oxygen, carbon dioxide, nutrients and metabolites.

Functions of the circulation

OXYGEN TRANSPORT

The cells of the adult human require, in the resting state, some 200–250 ml/min of oxygen, all of which must be transported from the lungs to the cells throughout the body. At rest most oxygen is required by the brain and by the liver, and relatively little by the muscles (p. 4.9). During severe exercise the oxygen requirement rises to 4 or more l/min, most of the increase being used by the exercising muscles. More of the oxygen carried by the arterial blood is removed in the tissues under these circumstances, but this factor alone allows only a two or threefold increase of the oxygen supply, and there must also be a large increase in blood flow to the exercising muscles. The cardiac output in fact may rise six or sevenfold to 30 or more l/min. Thus, in one minute, the heart may pump round the circulation a volume five times the total blood volume and supply a volume of oxygen equal to the total blood volume to the tissues.

Extremely hard exercise of this type cannot, however, be continued for more than a minute or two. The oxygen consumption of the body during normal activities is discussed in chap. 4. Table 28.1 repeats some of the findings.

TABLE 28.1.

Activity	O_2 used ml/min
At rest	250
Standing	375
Walking	400–1000
Light work and exercise	750–1250

An adult usually complains of undue shortness of breath on effort if he is unable to increase his oxygen transport above 1000–1250 ml/min or treble the output of his heart on exercise. Such increases are sufficient to allow a man to earn his living in a light job and to enjoy light recreations and sport.

The cardiovascular system adjusts its rate of blood flow rapidly within these wide limits in response to metabolic need. Not only is the total heart output varied widely but the distribution of blood flow to the tissues, i.e. to muscle, skin, brain, liver and kidneys, can change greatly depending on local metabolic demand.

CARBON DIOXIDE TRANSPORT

The same considerations apply to carriage in the blood of carbon dioxide produced by the cells of the body. Its source and amount also vary according to metabolic activity, and a large excess carrying capacity is available in the form of changing blood flow.

NUTRIENTS AND METABOLITES

All the nutrients utilized by cells, including inorganic ions, glucose, amino acids, fatty acids, triglycerides and phospholipids, are transported via the blood stream. In contrast to oxygen, however, the utilization of these substances in the tissues is never so rapid as to be limited by the blood flow; in other words, the arteriovenous difference in the concentration of these substances is relatively small. Cell metabolites other than carbon dioxide, e.g. water, lactate, urea and creatinine, are transported by the blood stream and removed from it by the kidneys.

HEAT EXCHANGE

Many tissues of the body, particularly the brain, heart and viscera, function satisfactorily only within a narrow temperature range, and the central body temperature is stabilized closely around 37°C. An oxygen usage of 250 ml/min in the resting subject on an average diet means production of heat within the body of about 70 kcal/hr. About half of this heat is produced in the liver and brain and is distributed to other parts of the body via the blood stream. In exercise, heat is removed from the exercising muscles by the venous blood. Stabilizing the body temperature means that loss of heat at the surface of the body must be regulated in relation to ambient temperature. Excess heat is transported to the skin surface in the blood stream to be lost to the exterior by processes of conduction, convection, radiation and evaporation (chap. 40).

PHYSIOLOGICAL CONTROL SYSTEMS

Control of the concentration of many constituents of extracellular and intracellular fluid depends on a variety of negative feedback systems operating through the circulation. A good example is the control of blood glucose. A rise in the glucose level in the blood flowing to the pancreatic β cells is detected and stimulates an increased release of insulin into pancreatic venous blood. This insulin is then diluted and distributed to the tissues in the circulating blood. The increased insulin concentration acts to increase glucose uptake and thus to decrease glucose concentration in venous blood leaving these organs. This blood is again diluted and mixed with blood from other organs while travelling back through the heart and lungs to the pancreas. The whole system, typical of many in the body, is built up of a series of operations or **transfer functions**, each of which requires time. Each link in the system, including the circulatory link, affects the speed and accuracy of the total response. The importance of the general and local circulation to endocrine and neurohumoral organs and to metabolic processes is obvious.

Parts of the circulation

As though in response to the requirements mentioned above, the circulation is adapted to supply a widely varying volume flow of blood. A further adaptation is that this supply is fed into the distributing system of vessels under a stable head of pressure. There are obvious advantages in such an arrangement; it limits the tension which the walls of the blood vessels must withstand and thus permits stability of the vessels without unnecessary thickness of the wall. The brain is particularly sensitive to oxygen lack, and survives deprivation for hardly more than 3–4 min. Without a stabilized blood pressure the supply to the brain would constantly be endangered, particularly in erect animals, such as man.

As a closed hydraulic system, the circulation consists of a pump, which is called the heart, and a system of tubes, the blood vessels. After the neonatal period, there are in fact two pumps and two distributing systems of tubes, the systemic and pulmonary circulations, connected to each other in series. The two pumps, the left and right ventricles respectively, lie adjacent to one another in the heart, but the streams of blood passing through the right and left sides of the heart do not mix either within the heart or in the blood vessels (fig. 28.1).

The energy required to propel the blood through the circulation is supplied by the heart muscle. The mass of muscle in the heart of man is 250–400 g and the capacity of each of the pumping chambers or ventricles is about 100–150 ml. In addition to supplying energy the heart gives direction to the blood flow. The heart develops in the form of a folded tube, which contracts rhythmically, expelling its contents at each beat (p. 18.14). Valves are the non-muscular structures which allow flow to occur in only one direction. Finally, regulation of the heart beat is necessary to maintain constant input and output pressures and to vary the output according to requirement; various neural and humoral feedback mechanisms are involved in this regulation.

The systemic circuit may, from a functional point of view, be divided into:

(1) a distributing system (aorta, its branches and their final subdivision into arterioles),

(2) a system for the interchange of substances with the extracellular fluid of the tissues (capillaries) and

(3) a collecting and reservoir system (small and large veins, venae cavae and right atrium).

The pulmonary circuit similarly begins with the main pulmonary artery and ends in veins draining into the left atrium. Since the two circuits are in series, the volume flow through them must be equal if measured over any period longer than a few seconds. Pressures in the distributing systems of the two circuits are very different, however, being some five times greater in the systemic

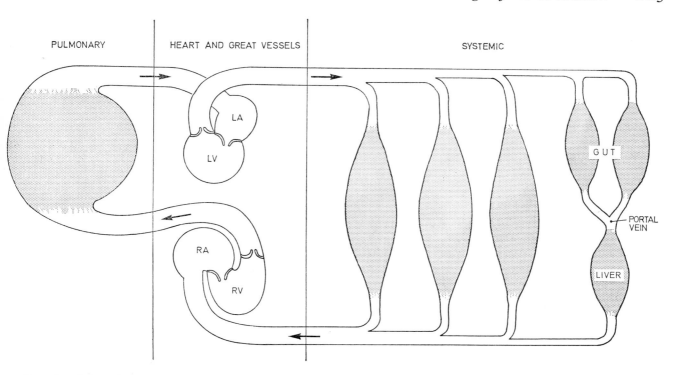

Fig. 28.1. Schematic design of the circulation. The systemic circuit consists of parallel vessel systems, e.g. cerebral, muscular, renal, splanchnic. LV, RV, left and right ventricles; LA, RA, left and right atria.

circuit than in the pulmonary. The latter is much the shorter circuit and offers much less resistance to the blood flow; also the effects of gravity are smaller than in the widespread systemic circuit.

Studying the circulation

As with any hydraulic system, there are basic quantities which are required to describe the system and measure its performance; these are as follows.

Volume is the blood contained in the whole system and its various segments.

Flow means volume flow, expressed in ml or l/sec, not velocity.

Pressure is measured in cm of water or mm of mercury. Pressure in the vascular system may be thought of as the height to which a column of saline or mercury in an open U-tube or manometer would rise if the system were connected to a cannula inserted into the vessel. This height is not affected by the bore of the manometer tube, and conventionally pressures are stated in terms of the height of the balancing column of mercury or water. Such heights, of course, can be measured only with reference to some zero level which, conventionally, is taken as heart level. Since the specific gravity of mercury is 13·6, a pressure of 1 mm mercury = 1·36 cm water. These basic measures of pressure, flow and volume yield various derived quantities.

Volume/pressure defines compliance or distensibility and the reciprocal, *pressure/volume* defines elastic resistance (dynes-cm^{-5}).

Pressure/flow is a measure of resistance to flow (dynes-sec-cm^{-5}).

Pressure × volume is work (dyne-cm or kg-m).

Since the main function of the circulation is to pump blood round the body, the most important measurements connected with it are the output of the heart into the distributing system and the pressure at which this supply is distributed. Second in importance is the input or filling pressure, which must be controlled within narrow limits, and third are measurements of blood flow through various organs and tissues, some of which are endangered by even a brief interruption of their blood supply.

CARDIAC CATHETERIZATION

The circulation in the heart and great vessels is studied in man by the technique of catheterization of vessels. A small flexible tube is inserted into a vein or an artery in the arm or leg, and the tip of the tube is advanced under radiological vision into the chambers of the right or left heart. Through these tubes pressures may be recorded and blood samples withdrawn for measurement of oxygen content; indicator dyes for measuring cardiac output and radio-opaque solutions for visualizing parts of the circulation may be injected through such catheters. This technique was first employed in 1929 by Forssman, who passed a catheter from his own antecubital vein into his right atrium. We owe the initial development of the technique to André Cournand of New York (1942). Cardiac catheterization is a safe procedure which has an established place in medical diagnosis. However, there is a very slight risk of severe disturbances of the cardiac rhythm. For this reason catheters should not be passed on healthy subjects, except under special circumstances and by experienced operators.

THE HEART

The heart lies in the centre of the thoracic cavity, above the diaphragm, behind the sternum, and flanked on each side by the lungs and pleurae. The posterior mediastinum, containing the oesophagus and descending aorta, separates the heart from the fifth to eighth thoracic vertebrae. Above are the aorta and pulmonary arteries and the two main bronchi into which the trachea divides.

The four **chambers** of which the heart consists, **right**

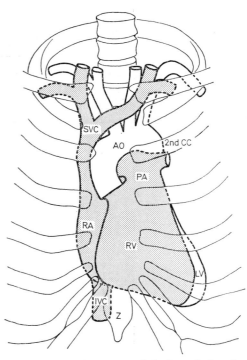

FIG. 28.3. Heart and great vessels in frontal view, in relation to thoracic cage; Z Xiphoid process. The apex beat is usually felt in the 5th intercostal space in the mid-clavicular line.

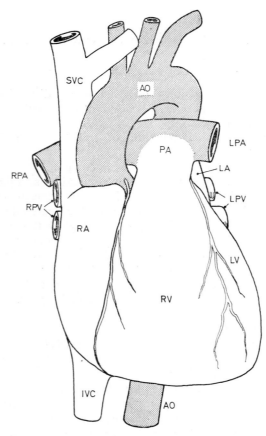

FIG. 28.2. Heart and great vessels in frontal view. LV, RV, left and right ventricles; LA, RA, left and right atria; PA, PV, pulmonary artery and veins; SVC, IVC, superior and inferior vena cava; AO, aorta.

and **left atria**, and **right** and **left ventricles**, lie as shown in figs. 28.2, 28.3, 28.4 and 28.5. The right ventricle lies in front of the left and therefore its profile cannot be seen in an anteroposterior view of the heart. The left ventricle, the most muscular of the four chambers, lies posteriorly and to the left of the right ventricle. The left atrium lies at the back of the heart almost in the midline of the body. The right atrium lies in front of the left atrium and to the right of the right ventricle and forms the right border of the heart in the anteroposterior view. All four chambers are in approximately the same horizontal plane.

The connections of the heart to the main blood vessels are as follows. The two **venae cavae**, superior and inferior, which return venous blood from the systemic circulation, enter the right atrium from above and below and form most of its upper and lower walls. The **coronary sinus** is the vein draining the heart muscle and also enters the right atrium. Having passed through the tricuspid valve and been pumped forward by the right ventricle the blood leaves the heart through the **pulmonary artery**. This vessel crosses in front of the root of the aorta and passes backwards and to the left of the aorta before dividing into a right and left branch. The **right pulmonary artery** passes to the right beneath the aortic arch and enters the hilum of the right lung. The **left pulmonary artery** continues to the left to supply the left lung.

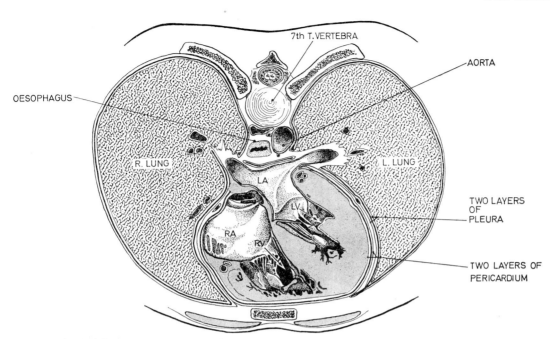

FIG. 28.4. Transverse section of thorax at heart level. LA, RA, LV, RV, left and right atria and ventricles. From *Cunningham's Textbook of Anatomy*, 10th Edition (1964) London: Oxford University Press.

The pulmonary venous blood returning from the lungs comes to the left atrium in four **pulmonary veins**, two on each side. These veins lie below the respective pulmonary arteries, and enter the left atrium on its lateral walls. This blood, oxygenated from its passage through the pulmonary circuit, is passed through the mitral valve into the left ventricle and then ejected into the **aorta** from which branches distribute it to the whole systemic circuit. The root of the aorta lies behind the pulmonary artery, and the aorta follows an arching course, upwards, backwards and downwards, first to the right of the main pulmonary artery, then above the right pulmonary artery and left main bronchus and finally downwards in the posterior mediastinum in front of and to the left of the vertebral bodies.

The relative positions of the chambers of the heart and the great vessels communicating with them are important, as are the projections they make on the cardiac outline, seen in the frontal and lateral radiographs of the chest (fig. 28.6). In the frontal view the right heart border is made up of the superior vena cava, right atrium and inferior vena cava. The left border is formed by, from above downwards, the aortic arch, the main pulmonary artery, a small portion of the left atrium, known as the left auricular appendage, and the left ventricle. In the lateral view the right ventricle and pulmonary artery are in front, and the left atrium forms the posterior border of the heart (Plate 28.1, facing p. 27.19).

Of the two separate streams of blood being pumped through the heart, the right stream, from the right atrium to the pulmonary artery, spirals round the left stream flowing from the left atrium to the aorta. This is partly due to the geometrical shapes imposed on the ventricles by their differing functions. The main core of muscle in the heart is the left ventricle, which is roughly cylindrical in shape. The right ventricle on the other hand is thin walled, triangular in the frontal projection, and rather flattened antero-posteriorly.

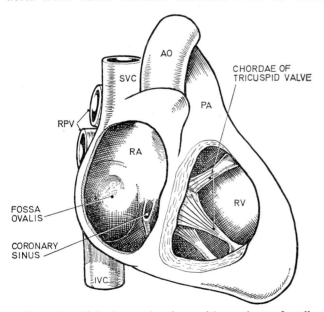

FIG. 28.5. Right heart chambers with portions of wall removed. From *Cunningham's Textbook of Anatomy*, 10th Edition (1964) London: Oxford University Press.

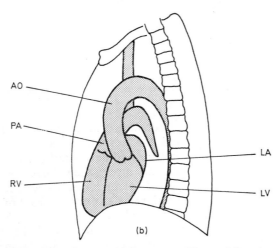

Fig. 28.6. Radiographic appearances of heart. (a) postero-anterior view, (b) lateral view.

Because of the oblique position of the heart in the chest, when in disease the atria enlarge they do so into the right side of the thorax. When the left ventricle enlarges it does so into the left hemithorax. When the right ventricle enlarges it does so in an anteroposterior plane.

The heart is a muscular organ. All muscles require some attachments if their contractions are to be translated into work. Some of the heart muscle is arranged in a circular form, in the wall of the left ventricle, and it therefore forms its own origin and insertion. The rest of the heart muscle spirals around the ventricles and works through its attachment to the fibrous stroma surrounding the four valve rings (fig. 28.7). The valves of the heart are set close together and in roughly the same oblique plane, with the ventricles on one side and the atria and great vessels on the other. When a ventricle contracts it does so concentrically, shortening its diameter, and also longitudinally, shortening its length by pulling on its attachment to the valve rings.

The circular layer of muscle lies innermost in the two ventricles, a thick layer in the left ventricle and a thin one in the right. Outside this are two oblique or spiral layers, arranged at right angles to one another and tending on contraction to pull the ventricular chamber towards the valve rings, or vice versa. That the latter movement is important may be seen by examining the heart radiographically, as it is beating; if a contrast medium is injected, the valves can be seen to move with contraction as do the cavities of the ventricles. Indeed, the silhouette of the heart appears remarkably immobile while it is contracting despite the volume of blood being ejected from it with each beat. The explanation lies partly in the reciprocal volume changes in the atria and ventricles; as the ventricles contract the atria fill with blood and as the ventricles fill the atria contract.

The differences between the left and right ventricles are related to the different conditions under which they

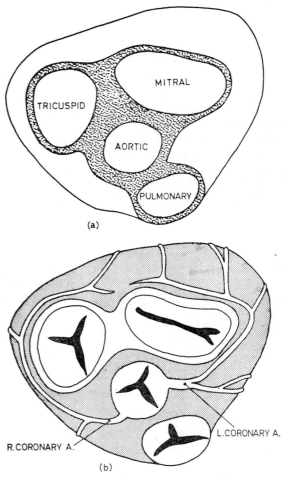

Fig. 28.7. (a) Diagrammatic section at level of atrioventricular groove to show from above the valve rings constituting the fibrous framework of the heart. (b) As in (a), with addition of valves and coronary arteries. The pulmonary and aortic valves are anterior to the mitral and tricuspid valves.

work. The left ventricle works against a pressure five times greater than the right. Its shape, roughly cylindrical, is mechanically the most efficient for pumping against pressure.

The right ventricle, on the other hand, bears the brunt of the transient fluctuations in volume of venous blood returning to the heart. Its shape and relatively poor muscularity give it a high compliance so that beat-to-beat variations in venous return are smoothed out as the blood is passed on to the low pressure pulmonary circuit. Before birth both ventricles work in parallel, against the same pressure, and their wall thickness is about the same. The difference in thickness develops in infancy and childhood.

Pericardium

The surface of the heart muscle is continually moving relative to the other contents of the thorax. Like the lungs, the heart is contained within a serous cavity, the pericardium, which allows free movement. The development of the pericardium from the early coelomic cavity is described on p. 18.14. In the adult, the pericardium has an outer fibrous layer which encloses the whole heart, and parietal and visceral layers of the serous sac; the fibrous layer blends with the tunica adventitia of the great vessels close to the heart. The central tendon of the diaphragm is fused to the inferior surface of the fibrous pericardium. In front it is attached to the sternum by weak fibrous bands, but the lungs and pleural cavities separate most of its anterior surface from the thoracic wall. The thymus gland occupies a variable portion of the space anterior to the pericardium. The phrenic nerves run downwards sandwiched between the pleura and the lateral aspect of the pericardial sac.

The serous pericardium which lines the fibrous sac is reflected on to the heart at the points where the great vessels pierce the fibrous layer. The visceral serous layer covers the heart completely and is separated from the parietal layer by a thin film of fluid. The potential cavity of the pericardium has two recesses, the **transverse sinus** which passes behind the aorta and pulmonary trunk, and the **oblique sinus** which passes up behind the left atrium between the openings of the four pulmonary veins. In inflammation of the pericardium excess of fluid may accumulate within the serous cavity.

The visceral layer of serous pericardium forms the outermost part of the **epicardium**. Between it and the myocardium, the coronary vessels and cardiac autonomic nerves course over the muscle. These are normally embedded in a layer of subepicardial fat. The inner layer of epicardium is fixed to the external surface of the heart muscle.

The inner surface of the heart muscle also has a smooth low friction lining which allows the blood to flow smoothly within the chambers. This is the **endocardium**.

This lining also covers the valves of the heart and is continuous with the endothelial lining of the great vessels.

Microscopic structure of heart muscle

The histology of cardiac muscle is described on p. 15.1 and here it is necessary only to mention one feature of physiological importance. From light microscopic studies, heart muscle was thought to be a syncytium consisting of cells fused together without separating membranes. The EM has shown, however, that heart muscle cells are separated by structures known as intercalated discs, so that the cytoplasm is not continuous. These discs differ from the cell membrane in that they offer a low resistance to the flow of electrical current. The result is that electrical excitation spreads throughout the muscle mass without the delay imposed by cell membrane resistance.

Valves

Two pairs of valves, one at the inlet and the other at the outlet of the ventricles, are necessary to give direction to the flow of blood through the heart. The inlet valves, or **atrioventricular valves**, are the larger in size and allow forward flow to occur with almost no resistance. The tricuspid valve is at the inlet of the right ventricle, and the mitral at the inlet of the left. The outlet or semilunar valves are the **pulmonary valve** for the right ventricle and the **aortic valve** for the left.

Valve mechanism is complex. The valve cusps are entirely passive structures which float into apposition and separate again in response to minute pressure gradients and eddies in the flow of blood. Particularly on the left side of the heart, they have to withstand high pressures when closed, and in combining delicacy of structure with efficiency they are better than any model made by man.

All the valves, except the mitral, have three flaps or cusps; the mitral has two. The nomenclature for the cusps of the heart valves is confusing and variable. The names serve little purpose except in the case of the aortic valve where they are used to define the origin of the coronary arteries (p. 28.36), and in the mitral valve where the two cusps are called anterior and posterior (figs. 28.9 & 10). When forward flow is occurring these cusps drift apart widely to allow unimpeded flow of blood. When forward flow slows and finally stops, the pressure gradient which propels the blood first becomes zero and then reverses its direction (fig. 28.8). The blood stream would then flow backwards if it were not for the valve cusps which float into apposition at the instant the flow tends to reverse. The aorta and pulmonary artery are dilated opposite the valves so that each valve cusp has a sinus which always contains some blood and so prevents the cusp sticking to the wall of the vessel (fig. 28.10). Thus, during ventricular relaxation the aortic and pulmonary valves support the column of blood which has been pumped into the corresponding arteries, and the

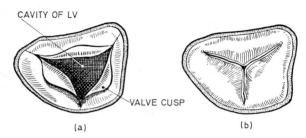

FIG. 28.8. Aortic valve from above, (a) open; (b) closed.

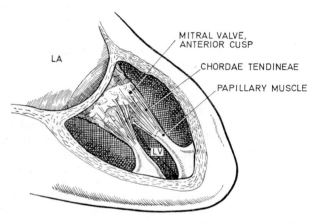

FIG. 28.9. Interior of LV to show the structure of the mitral valve.

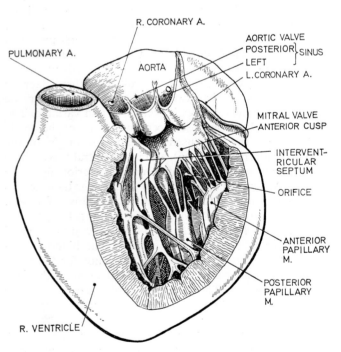

FIG. 28.10. The relation of the aortic valve to anterior cusp of mitral valve. From *Cunningham's Textbook of Anatomy*, 10th Edition (1964) London: Oxford University Press.

mitral and tricuspid valves prevent blood from being pumped backwards into the atria when ventricular contraction occurs. Clearly the semilunar and atrioventricular valves act reciprocally, one set being open when the other is closed and vice versa.

The atrioventricular valves are more complex than the semilunar. They have additional structures in the form of **chordae tendineae** attached to the margins of the cusps (fig. 28.9), which act as guy ropes and prevent them from being blown back into the atria on ventricular contraction. From the cusp margins the chordae come together and are anchored to the papillary muscles which arise from the inner walls of the ventricles and share in ventricular contraction. Thus tensing of the chordae at the moment of ventricular contraction causes the cusp margins to approximate closely to each other. The chordae from the adjoining halves of adjacent cusps are linked to the same papillary muscle; there are three such muscles on the inner wall of the right ventricle and two in the left.

The cusps of each valve are attached to the inner margin of a fibrous ring (fig. 28.7).

In the case of the left ventricle the inlet and outlet valves (mitral and aortic) are situated side by side, and in fact, only the anterior cusp of the mitral valve separates the inflow and outflow tracts (fig. 28.10).

Cardiac muscle contraction

AT THE CELLULAR LEVEL

Contraction of the myocardial cell differs from that of other muscle cells in some ways.

Chemically. The conversion of chemical energy in ATP to mechanical energy is mediated by actin and myosin in the same way as in skeletal muscle (p. 15.3). However, the fuel used by cardiac muscle differs somewhat. Thus, heart muscle can utilize to an unusual degree circulating lactate, free fatty acids and ketoacids and relatively little glucose is consumed. This is a clear adaptation to the circumstances of severe exercise, when the large amounts of lactate produced by skeletal muscle supply the fuel for cardiac muscle. The myocardium is also able to extract oxygen from its blood supply to an unusual extent; blood in the coronary sinus, the venous blood from the heart muscle itself, has an oxygen saturation of 30–40 per cent compared with 70–80 per cent in blood from the body as a whole.

Mechanically. The heart muscle cell contracts by shortening rapidly to approximately 70 per cent of its uncontracted length. It obeys the all-or-none law and shows the phenomenon of potentiation. In an isometric situation a plot of initial fibre length against tension developed on contraction shows that, up to a limit, stretching increases the force of contraction.

Electrically. The cardiac muscle cell shows the same phenomena of membrane potential and monophasic action potential as do other muscle and nerve cells. It differs, however, in some important respects. The action potential (fig. 28.11) shows a distinct plateau phase,

FIG. 28.11. Myocardial action potential curves showing 4 phases; (a) ventricular muscle cell; (b) atrial muscle cell; (c) SA node. R, repolarization phase of SA node which is not divisible into phases 1, 2 and 3.

repolarization being delayed in the case of the ventricle to 0·3 sec after depolarization, and in the atrium to 0·15 sec. In other words, the contraction is more sustained in the ventricle. Another consequence is that the refractory period, during which a second stimulus is ineffective, is relatively long. Ventricular muscle has a functional refractory period of some 0·25 sec and a relative refractory period of 0·3 sec. Because of their shorter refractory period, 0·15 sec, the atria can beat much faster than the ventricles.

The type of action potential varies in different specialized parts of the heart muscle. Variation in duration of the action potential affects the refractory periods of different parts of the heart, while the rate at which the membrane potential leaks away following repolarization influences the spontaneous rate of discharge. Certain areas, e.g. the SA node, have a slightly increased permeability to sodium ions, and therefore the membrane potential recreated at repolarization tends to leak away until a threshold value is reached at which spontaneous depolarization occurs. This phenomenon explains the spontaneous discharge rates of various parts of the heart, those with the highest rate of leakage of membrane potential (so-called prepotential) having the highest inherent rate of discharge.

The SA node (see below) has the highest inherent rate and so acts as **pacemaker**. Since other areas are discharged by the spreading contraction, their spontaneous discharge does not usually occur. Under certain circumstances, however, ectopic or unusual foci of excitation do arise and cause extra contractions (extrasystoles).

CO-ORDINATED CONTRACTION

The heart propels blood by alternately relaxing and contracting; it relaxes to allow the blood to flow in from the input reservoirs and contracts to expel the contents of the pumping chambers into the distributing systems. It is essential that contraction should occur in an ordered sequence and in a brief space of time. If contraction becomes uncoordinated, parts of the heart muscle contract

and relax in an apparently haphazard manner, known as **fibrillation**. Ventricular fibrillation causes the flow to stop in the circulation. Not only must there be nearly simultaneous contraction of all parts of the ventricles, but the atria too must contract at the appropriate time in the cardiac cycle, i.e. to complete ventricular filling just before ventricular contraction occurs.

The spread of the electrical impulse is assisted by the branching arrangement of heart muscle fibres, and in small hearts such as that of the mouse this alone is sufficient to ensure co-ordinated contraction. In larger mammals including man, however, contraction would be so slow as to be ineffective without an additional fast conducting system, conducting the electrical impulse rapidly throughout the muscle mass. This system was described by the Czech physiologist Purkinje, in 1839. The **Purkinje fibres** consist of specialized muscle cells, distinguishable histologically by their high glycogen content and electrically by a characteristic action potential (fig. 28.12).

Excitation must spread through the heart from a source which provides stimulation repetitively. As mentioned above, all cardiac muscle fibres have their own spontaneous rate of discharge or rhythmicity. The part of the heart with the highest spontaneous rate, therefore, provides the source of excitation of the whole heart, and this pacemaker is normally the **sinuatrial (SA) node**. It is situated high in the wall of the right atrium near the entrance of the superior vena cava. The SA node consists of a small group of specialized muscle cells embedded in connective tissue and surrounded by a rich plexus of autonomic nerve endings.

From the SA node (fig. 28.12) the excitation wave

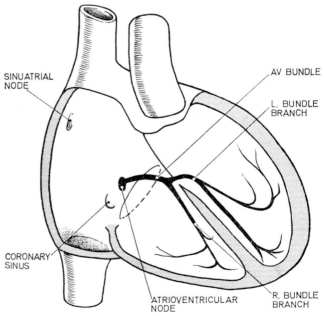

FIG. 28.12. Heart chambers opened to show specialized (Purkinje) conducting tissue.

spreads through the right and left atria. No specialized conducting tissue is involved here and the velocity of the depolarization wave is relatively slow, some 50 cm/sec.

Situated low in the right atrium, near the opening of coronary sinus and tricuspid valve, is another group of cells with a specialized conducting function, the **atrioventricular (AV) node**. This structure is the starting point of the specialized fast-conducting Purkinje fibres. These fibres are at first collected together in the AV bundle of His (1893) which passes from the AV node into the upper portion of the interventricular septum, and constitutes the only muscular connection between the atria and ventricles. Conduction in this specialized muscle tissue is 400–500 cm/sec.

High in the interventricular septum the bundle divides into left and right branches, which in turn arborize on the inner part of the walls of the corresponding ventricles, before the fibres finally dip into the muscle mass.

THE ELECTROCARDIOGRAM

Spread of depolarization and repolarization through a muscle mass is accompanied by measurable electrical potentials which, since the body is a conductor, may be recorded by electrodes placed on the skin. The electrocardiogram (ECG) is a recording of the potentials which accompany cardiac activity and the various stages of spread of excitation through the heart may be followed in the ECG (fig. 28.13).

FIG. 28.13. The spread of the electrical impulse through the heart from the SA node (pacemaker). The electrocardiogram, and the contraction (systole) of atria and ventricles. P, atrial depolarization; Q, initial negative deflection; R, first positive deflection; S, negative deflection; T, repolarization.

The discharge of the SA node causes no deflection on the ECG. Atrial depolarization, however, is recorded as a deflection which is conventionally labelled the P wave. It occupies 0.05–0.1 sec. The next deflection, or complex of deflections, corresponds to ventricular depolarization and is labelled the QRS complex. Q, initial negative

deflection; R, first positive deflection; S, negative deflection following R wave. Ventricular depolarization is normally complete in 0.08 sec. It starts approximately 0.1 sec later than the start of the P wave of atrial depolarization, and this interval, the **PR interval**, measures the time required for the following events to take place:

(1) the passage of the atrial depolarization wave to the vicinity of the AV node,

(2) the delay imposed by slow-conducting junctional tissue surrounding the AV node,

(3) the rapid spread of excitation via the AV bundle and its branches to the start of ventricular depolarization.

Most of the PR interval is occupied by delay in the junctional tissue.

Ventricular depolarization is rapid and is followed by an interval during which the muscle remains contracted, the ST interval. The T wave represents the spread through the ventricle of the repolarization wave, associated with relaxation of the muscle contraction. Atrial repolarization is usually not visible in the ECG as it is overlapped and obscured by the QRS complex.

It is thus possible to identify from the ECG the various stages of conduction, depolarization and repolarization in the heart and to note abnormalities. The relationship between the ECG and the individual cell action potential should be appreciated. The ECG represents the aggregate or resultant electrical activity of millions of individual cell action potentials directionally opposed to one another. It is easy to see, therefore, why the ST segment, corresponding to the plateau of the action potential, should be isoelectric.

Normally the SA node is the portion of the heart with the highest spontaneous rate of discharge, and therefore forms the pacemaker of the cardiac cycle. If the rate of discharge of the SA node is depressed, the portion of the heart with the next highest spontaneous discharge rate becomes the pacemaker, usually the AV node. **Sinus rhythm** is then replaced by AV **nodal rhythm**.

Again, if disease or drugs depress conduction through the AV bundle, the PR interval lengthens and a state of atrioventricular block exists. Impulses may fail altogether to be transmitted from atrium to ventricle, and the final or complete stage of block results in the ventricles beating independently of the atria at their own, much slower, spontaneous rate of discharge (20–30 beats/min).

Depolarization normally spreads rapidly through the ventricles in an ordered sequence, occupying less than 0.12 sec. (fig. 28.14). This is the effect of the rapidly conducting Purkinje fibres. Damage to one or other of the branches of the bundle, left or right, results in delayed activation of the left or right ventricles respectively. In this condition, which is called bundle branch block, the QRS complex is increased in duration (> 0.12 sec).

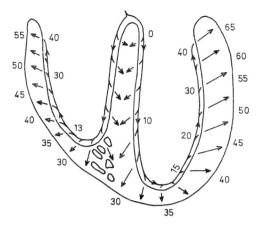

FIG. 28.14. Direction of wave of excitation through L and R ventricles and time of arrival (msec) of the impulse at various parts of the myocardium.

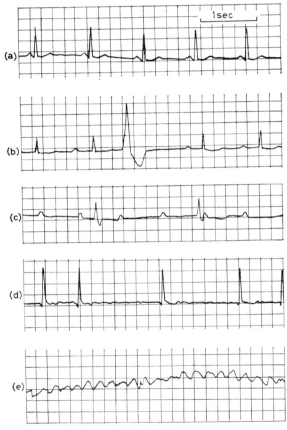

FIG. 28.15. Electrocardiograms illustrating some common disorders of rhythm. (a) Normal sinus rhythm; (b) prolonged PR interval (0·32 sec) and one extrasystole, i.e. irregular beat arising not from the normal pacemaker but from an abnormal irritable focus elsewhere in the myocardium; (c) AV block, atria and ventricles beating independently at 80 and 33/min respectively; (d) fibrillation or uncoordinated activity affecting atria only and (e) fibrillation affecting the whole heart.

The importance of co-ordinated contraction has been emphasized. Uncoordinated, haphazard contraction, **fibrillation**, destroys the effective pumping action of the affected chambers. Fibrillation may affect the atria, a common and not usually serious condition, or the ventricles, a terminal and rapidly fatal condition unless properly treated, or both. The electrocardiographic record of fibrillation is a rapid totally irregular series of spikes usually with no recognizable pattern (fig. 28.15).

THE CARDIAC CYCLE

By measuring simultaneously pressures and volumes of the heart chambers and recording the sounds of valve closure and the electrical phenomena of the electrocardiogram, it is possible to build up an accurate picture of how the electrical and mechanical events of the heart beat are related to one another in time. Pressure, sound and electrical potential present no difficulty, but recording of volume is not so easy. At first it was possible only in animals and involved opening the chest and enclosing the ventricles in a displacement recorder or plethysmograph. Now more sophisticated experimental techniques are available, such as dimension gauges implanted within the heart, or, in man, the technique of visualizing the ventricular cavity by injecting radio-opaque medium and taking radiographs in rapid succession in two planes at right angles to one another.

It is convenient to use the ECG as the reference for timing the other events.

PRESSURE CHANGES

It is not difficult to remember the intracardiac pressures if certain facts are recalled:

(1) venous or input pressure in both circuits is low in relation to the horizontal level of the atria (only a few mm Hg);

(2) a valve offers almost no resistance to the forward flow of blood, and when it is open pressures in the chambers on both sides of it are equal;

(3) the peak pressure in the systemic arterial system is approximately 100–150 mm Hg and in the pulmonary arterial system about one-fifth of this value.

Apart from the difference in pressure mentioned in (3) above, the pattern of pressure change is the same in the two sides of the heart, so it is convenient to consider only one, the left atrium, left ventricle and aorta, separated by the mitral and aortic valves (fig. 28.16).

The Q wave of the ECG signals the onset of ventricular contraction. Up to this point the atrium and ventricle have been in communication, the mitral valve being open, and pressures equal in these two chambers. When the ventricle contracts, pressure immediately rises within

FIG. 28.16. Relationship of electrical and mechanical events and heart sounds in the cardiac cycle.

latter part of the period of ventricular filling and adds a final boost to the filling of the ventricle, just before it contracts.

The period of ventricular contraction, occupying about four-tenths of the whole cycle, is known as **systole** and the period of relaxation or filling, occupying the remainder, is known as **diastole.** Ventricular contraction can be subdivided into phases:

(1) isometric contraction, the brief period at the start when both valves are shut, and pressure is rising in the ventricle without change in its volume,

(2) rapid ejection phase, when blood is being pumped into the aorta more quickly than it is running off into the peripheral circulation, and aortic pressure is therefore rising,

(3) slow ejection phase, when ejection is continuing

it and blood is prevented from being forced backwards into the atrium by closure of the mitral valve.

The rise in pressure in the left ventricle is very rapid, and as soon as it exceeds that in the aorta the aortic valve, which has hitherto been held closed by the pressure of blood in the aorta, is swept open and the blood in the left ventricle is expelled into the aorta. This ejection phase lasts as long as ventricular contraction persists.

The T wave of the ECG signals the repolarization of ventricular muscle which accompanies its relaxation. Pressure therefore falls in the ventricle, ejection stops, and since the aortic pressure now exceeds ventricular pressure blood would flow backwards into the ventricle were it not prevented from doing so by the aortic valve which is closed by the reversal of the pressure gradient. Pressure in the ventricle falls rapidly. As soon as it falls below that in the atrium, the mitral valve, which has remained closed during the whole of ventricular contraction, floats open, blood flows in from the atrium to refill the ventricle and the pressures in the two chambers, now in communication, are again equal.

The P wave, which signals the contraction of the atria, is really the first event of the cardiac cycle following discharge of the SA node. Atrial contraction occurs in the

FIG. 28.17. Pressure in LV recorded through fine tubes. Note standard pressures on the left. (a) The tube is withdrawn through the aortic valve into the ascending aorta. Note that in systole, pressure in LV and aorta is the same. (b) The tube is withdrawn through the mitral valve into LA. Note that in diastole, pressure in LV and LA is the same. (c) A patient in whom the aortic valve is narrowed by disease. Note high pressure in the LV and the pressure gradient between LV and aorta in systole.

but it is exceeded in rate by the run-off from the aorta into the periphery and aortic pressure is therefore falling.

The key to the pressure cycle is the behaviour of the valves. They are entirely passive structures and open and close in response to pressure gradients. If the pressure upstream to the valve is greater than that downstream even by a minute amount, the valve opens. If the downstream pressure exceeds that upstream the valve immediately closes. If the pressures in the upstream and downstream chambers are recorded, therefore, the crossover points of pressure determine the points at which the valve opens and closes (fig. 28.17).

Left atrial pressure changes are small and amount to only a few mm Hg (fig. 28.16). The **a wave** is caused by atrial contraction and therefore follows the P wave of the electrocardiogram. The **c wave** is a small deflection immediately following the QRS complex. It is caused by the mitral valve shutting and ballooning slightly into the atrium. The **x descent** occurs as the ventricle contracts and draws the mitral valve away from the atrium, thus lowering the pressure within it. Simultaneously the atrium is relaxing. The slow rise of pressure in the atrium as it fills from the pulmonary veins is called the **v wave**. Flow forward into the ventricle is prevented because the mitral valve is shut. The **y descent** is the fall in atrial pressure as blood rushes into the ventricle when the mitral valve opens.

VENTRICULAR VOLUME

The ventricle fills and empties alternately and both parts of this cycle have an early rapid phase and a later slow phase. The only brief intervals during which the volume of the ventricle is constant are the isometric contraction period and the period of falling pressure after the aortic valve closes and before the mitral valve opens. The volume of blood ejected during systole from the left ventricle into the aorta is the **stroke volume** (60–100 ml). The **output of the heart** per minute is clearly the product of the stroke volume and the heart rate per minute. Not all the blood contained in the ventricle is ejected; a variable part of the ventricular volume remains behind (20–50 ml). This is the **residual volume**. When lying at rest the residual volume is relatively large. On standing or on exercise it is smaller.

Activity and increased demands on the circulation also affect the diastolic volume of the ventricle. In exercise or stress atrial contraction is more forceful and the increment in ventricular filling produced by it at the end of the filling period becomes more important.

SOUNDS

Valves open inaudibly. When they shut, however, vibrations are set up which are transmitted through the chest and can be heard by the ear applied to the chest or indirectly through a stethoscope, or can be recorded by a microphone on the surface of the skin.

There are two audible sounds made by valve closure. The first is caused by closure of the mitral and tricuspid valves and occurs, therefore, just after the QRS of the ECG when ventricular pressure starts to rise and exceeds atrial pressure. It is normally difficult to distinguish by ear the mitral and tricuspid components of the first sound since they are so close together in time, but in fact mitral closure occurs slightly earlier. The first sound is usually best heard at the cardiac apex (fig. 28.18).

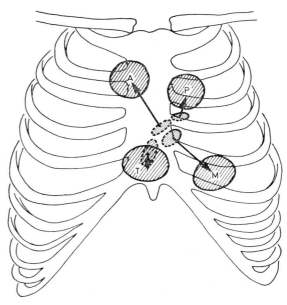

FIG. 28.18. Position of valves (dotted) in relation to thoracic cage and areas on the surface where valve sounds are best heard (lined). A, aortic; P pulmonary; M, mitral; T, tricuspid.

The second sound is caused by aortic and pulmonary valve closure. It occurs after the T wave of the ECG, at the cross-over points of left ventricular and aortic or right ventricular and pulmonary arterial pressures. Here, distinction of the aortic and pulmonary components is usually possible, the aortic being earlier. Deep inspiration increases right ventricular filling momentarily and prolongs right ventricular ejection, thus widening the degree of splitting of the aortic and pulmonary components and making their identification easier. The second sound is best heard, as might be expected, to the left or right of the upper sternum (fig. 28.18).

A third sound may sometimes be heard in health. It is soft and low pitched and occurs during the most rapid phase of ventricular filling. It is probably caused by rapid tensing of the ventricular walls. It is common in exercise, in pregnancy and in young persons.

Sounds caused by valves opening almost always denote an abnormality of the valve. The flow of blood through the heart in systole and diastole is usually silent. **Murmurs** are vibrations caused by turbulence or vortex formation in the blood stream and may be created in any part of the circulatory system, but most commonly in the heart. They indicate disease of valves, abnormal constrictions or communications in the central circulation, or occasionally, reduced blood viscosity as in anaemia.

Innervation of the heart

The frequency and strength of the heart beat is regulated through the autonomic nervous system. Both sympathetic and parasympathetic autonomic fibres are present in the cardiac plexus of nerves which surrounds the origin of the great vessels at the base of the heart. The **sympathetic supply** is derived from T2–T4 and travels via the middle cervical and cervico-thoracic ganglia and the first four ganglia of the thoracic sympathetic chain. In order to remove completely the sympathetic control of the heart it is necessary to remove the cervico-thoracic ganglia and the upper four thoracic sympathetic ganglia. The postganglionic fibres ramifying in the cardiac plexus supply the SA node in profusion, and also the whole cardiac muscle. The neural transmitter is predominantly noradrenaline and the cardiac effects of sympathetic stimulation can be blocked by the β-adrenergic blocking drugs.

The vagus nerve provides the **parasympathetic supply**. The fibres branch in the cardiac plexus and then supply the SA node and both atria. There is no sure evidence of parasympathetic fibres supplying ventricular muscle. The neural transmitter is acetylcholine, and the cardiac effects of vagal stimulation can be readily reversed by atropine. Normally both sympathetic and parasympathetic impulses reach the heart continuously.

The effects of autonomic nerve stimulation on the heart are threefold.

(1) On the rate of discharge of the SA node, consequently controlling the heart rate. Sympathetic stimulation increases and parasympathetic decreases the heart rate.

(2) On the speed of conduction of excitation within the heart. The junctional tissue surrounding the AV node is particularly affected. Here parasympathetic stimulation decreases the excitability of the junctional tissue and results in slower transmission. Strong stimulation may produce AV block (p. 28.11).

(3) On the speed of contraction of the cardiac muscle and the tension developed by the fibres for a given degree of initial stretching. Under sympathetic influence the rate of rise of pressure within the ventricle is increased and the residual volume decreased without any increase in the filling of the heart in the presystolic phase. This may be looked on in another way. If we construct a length-tension diagram for a particular muscle fibre this will be reproducible provided that the neurohumoral *milieu* is unchanged. When catecholamine concentration is increased by sympathetic stimulation, however, the length-tension curve is shifted to the left, i.e. for a given degree of initial stretch a greater tension is developed in contraction. This important mechanism operates not only on ventricular contraction via the sympathetic system, but also in the atria through both sympathetic and parasympathetic influences, the former enhancing and the latter diminishing the strength of atrial contraction. The effect of increased atrial contraction is to increase the pressure within the ventricle and therefore the degree of stretching of the myocardium before contraction. Sympathetic stimulation may therefore increase contractility in two ways, (1) by acting directly on the ventricle and moving its length-tension curve to the left, and (2) by increasing atrial contractility and hence increasing the initial stretch of the ventricular muscle fibres.

Ionic effects

The ionic composition of the extracellular fluid affects contractility as would be expected from the theory of action potentials. The main ions concerned in maintaining membrane potential are sodium and potassium, the former predominantly extracellular and the latter predominantly intracellular. The Nernst equation (p. 14.7) relates the membrane potential to concentrations of these ions and the permeability of the cell membrane to them. A decrease in the electromotive force (EMF) or membrane potential increases the readiness with which contraction occurs but weakens the contraction. An increase in EMF impairs depolarization and decreases the duration of contraction.

Potassium has a greater effect on contractility than sodium. Excess K^+ or Na^+ in the cell causes a slow, flaccid, dilated heart with a tendency to AV block, while a decrease in intracellular K^+ or Na^+ results in increased systolic tone of the heart. The characteristic changes in the ECG in K^+ deficiency are low voltages in the QRS complex and in the T wave and prolongation of the QT interval. Ca^{++} have an effect opposite to that of Na^+ and K^+. These effects are complex and not fully understood and cannot be explained simply in terms of membrane potential changes.

Tension

In any elastic spherical or cylindrical chamber the wall tension measures the force which would tend to separate the edges of a slit made in the wall. This important concept is related to the work done by the muscular walls of the heart or blood vessel to contain the blood within the vessel, and to the energy required. Also the thicker the wall, the greater the wall tension.

The relationship between pressure (P) within a chamber of radius (R) and the tension in the wall (T) is given by the law of Laplace.

$$T \propto R \times P$$

The same pressure can thus be contained in a small vessel with thin walls, e.g. a capillary, as within a large chamber, for example the aorta, with thick walls. The larger the size of the ventricular cavity the more tension must be present in its walls to generate the same pressure within. Thus when there is a high residual volume in the heart, the latter functions less efficiently.

ARTERIES

The systemic arteries provide a branching system of tubes taking the blood from the left ventricle and distributing it throughout the body. The pulmonary arteries similarly distribute the output of the right ventricle to the lungs; they are shorter, thinner walled, and contain blood under lower pressure than the systemic arteries.

In addition to the conduit function, arteries have a storage function. The output of the ventricles is discontinuous, occurring in ventricular systole only. The discontinuous blood flow from the heart is converted into a relatively smooth flow through the small blood vessels of the peripheral circulation. The effect of this is to conserve energy in accelerating the blood column and to reduce the pressures which the small vessels have to withstand. The arterial system, particularly the aorta, stores blood during systole and gives it up again during diastole so that the run-off of blood into the peripheral circulation is continuous. This function resembles that of a smoothing capacitor in an electrical circuit.

Structure

Arteries branch repeatedly and when their diameter is less than 0·1 mm they are called **arterioles**. Junctions between the branches are called **anastomoses** and they may occur between arteries and arterioles. In most organs these anastomoses ensure an adequate blood supply when one vessel is temporarily or permanently occluded. Occasionally anastomoses are absent or few in number, so the supply depends on a single vessel which is called an **end artery**. The central artery of the retina is a good example of an absolute end artery, but it should be apparent that as the number of anastomoses is reduced, functional end arteries increase.

Arteries are elastic tubes which are circular in cross-section because of the tension being equally distributed round their walls. These are composed of three coats or tunics.

(1) **Tunica intima** is the endothelial inner lining which provides a smooth, low friction, inner surface in contact with the blood stream.

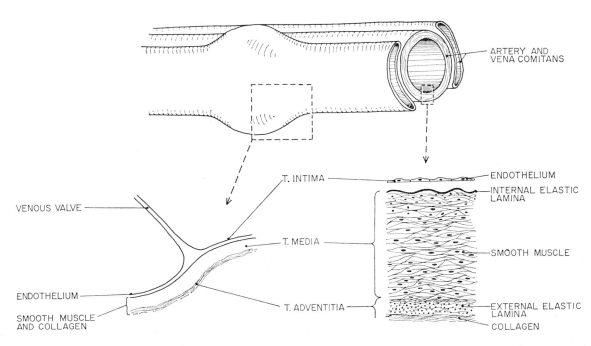

FIG. 28.19. The structure of a small, muscular artery and its accompanying veins. The tunica adventitia of the veins and artery are continuous with each other so that pulsation within the artery compresses the veins and so forces the venous blood towards the heart.

(2) **Tunica media** is a thick middle layer composed of smooth muscle and elastic fibres intermingled and arranged both lengthwise and circumferentially.

(3) **Tunica adventitia** is an outer layer of fibrous collagenous tissue.

The elastic tissue provides for the storage function by stretching and relaxing according to the pressure within the artery. The smooth muscle under autonomic nervous control regulates the diameter of the artery. The fibrous elements serve to limit the amount of stretch and prevent the wall rupturing under a surge of pressure (fig. 28.19).

The amount of elastic tissue in the walls of arteries varies with the vessel. Near the heart, the aorta and its large branches contain a large amount which is scattered through the whole thickness of the tunica media. These vessels are often called **elastic arteries**, and they dilate to accommodate the stroke volume. The remaining muscular arteries also have some elastic tissue but it is usually confined to the inner and outer aspects of the tunica media. At the junction of the tunica intima and media there is a perforated sheet of elastic tissue, the **internal elastic lamina**. Amongst the inner layers of fibrous tissue forming the tunica adventitia, there are discrete longitudinal elastin fibres called **external elastic lamina**. The adventitia and media are thinner in small arteries and the external elastic lamina is only present in large arteries. The internal elastic lamina, however, is present even in small arterioles. The pulmonary arteries have such thin walls that they are readily confused with veins.

Small arteries and arterioles are nourished by the blood they contain but such diffusion supplies only the inner layers of large arteries. The outer part of the walls of these vessels contain capillaries supplied by arterioles known as **vasa vasorum**.

Distribution

The **aorta** is the principal systemic artery (fig. 28.20). It starts at the aortic valve ring, passes in an arch upwards, backwards and finally downwards, crossing the pulmonary artery and left bronchus. The descending aorta lies in front of and to the left of the vertebral bodies and extends to the level of the fourth lumbar vertebra where it divides into the common iliac arteries. At its origin it is about 2·5 cm in diameter. Its main branches are as follows:

(1) two coronary arteries which supply the heart,

(2) the brachiocephalic, left subclavian and left common carotid arteries which supply the head and upper limbs,

(3) the intercostals, which supply the trunk,

(4) the coeliac, superior and inferior mesenteric arteries which supply the stomach, intestine, liver, spleen and pancreas,

(5) the renal arteries which supply the kidneys.

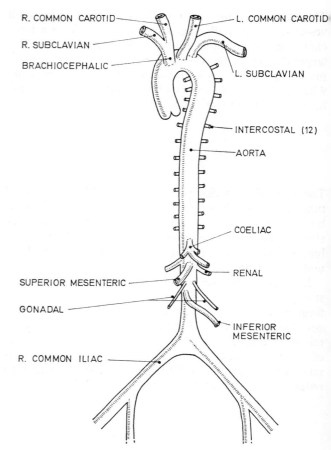

FIG. 28.20. Main branches of the aorta.

The common iliac arteries, into which the aorta divides, supply the pelvis and lower limbs.

The **pulmonary artery** starts at the pulmonary valve, passes backwards and slightly upwards for 5 cm and divides into right and left main branches. The right passes under the aortic arch and into the hilum of the right lung, there dividing into upper, middle and lower branches going to the corresponding lobes. The left main branch passes backwards and to the left into the hilum of the left lung where it divides into upper and lower branches.

Blood flow in arteries

The hydrodynamics of flow in the arterial system are complex, but some understanding of the theory is necessary if instruments are to be used correctly.

LAMINAR AND TURBULENT FLOW

Fluid flowing along a uniform tube at a fixed rate does so in laminar form, i.e. the stream can be looked upon as an infinite number of concentric laminae or layers sliding upon one another, the innermost or axial layer having the highest velocity of flow, and the outermost layer, touching the lining of the tube, having the lowest velocity. A velocity profile can be drawn for the whole diameter of the tube (fig. 28.21). The energy utilized in propelling

FIG. 28.21. The velocity profile in steady laminar flow.

$$V = \frac{P_1 - P_2}{4L\eta} (R^2 - r^2)$$

V, velocity of lamina at radius from axis, L, length; η, viscosity; R, radius of tube. The average velocity ($\overline{V}$) can be shown to be half the axial velocity. $y = r/R$. From McDonald, D. A. (1960) *Blood Flow in Arteries*. London: Arnold.

the fluid along the tube is required to overcome the internal friction of one layer on another. At a given viscosity, flow continues to be laminar as long as the product of velocity and diameter does not exceed a critical value. This is determined by the Reynold's number Re

$$Re = \frac{VD}{\eta}$$

where V = mean velocity, D is diameter and η is kinematic viscosity. In arteries, if Re exceeds 2000, laminar flow breaks up and becomes turbulent, i.e. forms eddies jets and whorls. The energy required to maintain turbulent flow rises greatly and the lateral pressure exerted on the tube also rises. Vibrations are set up which may be detectable as sound. Turbulent flow rarely occurs in the normal human circulation, except perhaps in the aorta under conditions of severe exercise.

POISEUILLE EQUATION

In a given rigid tube the physical factors upon which the volume flow of fluid depends are the pressure gradient from one end to another ($P_1 - P_2$), the radius of the tube (r), the length of the tube (l) and viscosity (η) of the fluid in question. The French mathematician Poiseuille wrote a thesis on the fountains in the town of Dijon in which he related these factors thus:

$$Flow = \frac{\pi r^4 (P_1 - P_2)}{8\eta l}$$

Since resistance (R) is $\dfrac{\text{Pressure gradient}}{\text{Flow}}$, the equation may be stated

$$R = \frac{8\eta l}{\pi r^4}$$

This equation illustrates the important fact that while flow is related linearly to pressure gradient and inversely to length and viscosity, it is related to the fourth power of the radius; i.e. doubling of the radius, other things being equal, increases the flow sixteenfold. It follows that quite a large variation in flow may occur with a scarcely perceptible change in the diameter of the tube. The application of the Poiseuille equation, valid for nondistensible tubes and continuous flow, to the human circulation is no more than approximate, yet the principles involved are worth careful consideration.

The pattern of flow in systemic arteries changes with distance from the aortic valve. The output of the heart is discontinuous; at the root of the aorta with each systole there is a rapid forward flow during ejection of blood, followed by standstill, or even some backward flow, during diastole. Progressively along the aorta this square wave pattern of flow becomes damped by the storage function of the aorta, and in the smaller arteries flow is much more continuous, though still roughly like sine waves (fig. 28.22). Here the instantaneous flow rate has been

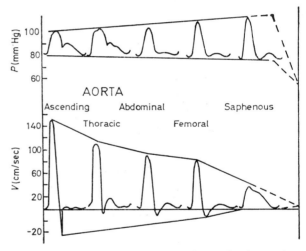

FIG. 28.22. Pressure and flow pulses in the dog in arteries at increasing distances from the heart. Pulse pressure increases while flow oscillation decreases markedly. From McDonald, D.A. (1960). *Blood Flow in Arteries*. London: Arnold.

recorded by a sensitive flow meter at different distances along the arterial system. If one were to time an actual corpuscle, or a dye particle, it would take some seconds to travel from the heart to the periphery. In the aorta it would move forward in jerks with each heart beat, as has been recorded by cinematography.

ARTERIAL PRESSURE PULSE

As seen in Poiseuille's equation the motive force propelling blood along the arteries is a pressure gradient. Pressure measured in the aorta or in a peripheral artery has a roughly triangular or saw toothed oscillation. With ejection of blood into the aorta from the heart, there is a rapid rise of pressure, as input into the arterial system exceeds the run off into the periphery. With slowing of ejection, pressure tends to fall again, and this continues after the aortic valve has closed, as flow continues from the aorta into the periphery. The point of closure of the aortic valve is marked by the **dicrotic notch**, a small transient rise of pressure as blood tending to fall back into the heart is rapidly decelerated by the closing aortic valve.

The peak pressure is termed the **systolic pressure** and the lowest point the **diastolic pressure**. The difference between the two is the **pulse pressure**. The mean pressure throughout the cardiac cycle may be found by planimetry, but may be approximated by the formula:

$$Pm = Pd + \tfrac{1}{3}(Ps - Pd)$$

since the wave form is nearly triangular. P, pressure; m, mean; s, systolic; d, diastolic.

This pressure pulse, starting in the root of the aorta, travels down all the branches of the arterial tree (fig. 28.23). The velocity of the pulse wave, which is to be

FIG. 28.23. Arterial pulses in the dog at various points (1–7) at increasing distances from the heart to the periphery. Note the change in wave form and the delay in arrival of the pulse wave. From McDonald, D. A. (1960) *Blood Flow in Arteries*. London: Arnold.

distinguished both from the velocity of blood flow, and also from volume flow of blood, is some 4–5 m/sec. The wave form changes somewhat as the wave travels distally.

There is a progressive delay corresponding to the velocity of the pulse wave. Energy is used in propelling the blood along the vessel, and therefore there is a small fall in the mean pressure along the arterial tree. Because of the geometry of the branching system, secondary waves are formed at points of branching which are reflected backwards along the arteries and which summate with the forward travelling wave. This explains why the pressure in a peripheral artery may show a higher systolic peak than does the central aortic pressure.

RELATION BETWEEN PRESSURE AND FLOW IN ARTERIES

Blood flows along an artery as a result of a pressure gradient. If pressure pulses are measured simultaneously at two points a fixed distance apart along a vessel the instantaneous pressure gradient between the two points can be estimated by subtracting the distal from the proximal pressure at each instant (fig. 28.22). The instantaneous flow along the segment of artery is a function of this pressure gradient. Paradoxically, it can be shown that if flow and pressure are measured simultaneously at a point in the vessel, the peak of flow slightly precedes the peak of pressure.

METHODS OF MEASURING PRESSURE

A simple liquid manometer in the form of a U tube filled with water or mercury is sometimes used as a pressure measuring device, connected on one side by tube and cannula to the lumen of the vessel. Because of its inertia such a system is useful only for measuring relatively static pressures, or where a mean pressure value only is required. The wave form of pressure pulses in the cardiovascular system contains frequencies as high as 30–40 cycles/sec, and to obtain a faithful record it is necessary to use a system which responds without distortion to frequencies higher than this, i.e. the system must have a high natural frequency. Such systems generally employ electromanometers; these are pressure transducers which operate by transforming minute displacements of a metal membrane into changes of electrical resistance or current flow in a bridge circuit which are then amplified and recorded. The frequency response of the whole system, catheter, transducer, amplifier and recorder must be carefully studied by exposing it to pressure oscillations at increasing frequencies when the point at which the response falls off can be determined. A system which has an inadequate dynamic frequency response yields a record which is overdamped, i.e. the true peaks are ironed out. On the other hand, the system may respond excessively to pressure oscillations so that overshoots and spurious oscillation of pressure appear in the record. Such a system is underdamped. Damping is introduced by narrowing a small

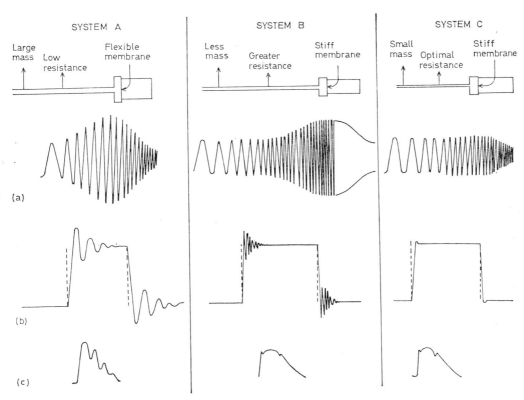

SYSTEM A   SYSTEM B   SYSTEM C

FIG. 28.24. The dynamic response characteristics of pressure recording systems, showing the effect of damping, i.e. increasing the frictional resistance of the system to match the frequency response of the measuring gauge; (a) frequency response, (b) square wave response, (c) pulse wave record.
System A is sensitive to changes in pressure but poorly damped and is unsuitable for recording intravascular pressures. System B is partially, and system C critically damped, i.e. the output is uniform over a wide frequency range. C reproduces intravascular pressures accurately. From Rushmer R. F. (1961) *Cardiovascular Dynamics*. Philadelphia: Saunders.

segment of the catheter system. Critical damping results in a faithful record of the pressure wave form without artefact or distortion (fig. 28.24).

The method of measuring systolic and diastolic arterial pressure in clinical use is the **sphygmomanometer**, introduced by Riva-Rocci in 1896. It consists of an inflatable cuff 13 cm wide, which is wound round the upper arm, the airfilled bag of the cuff being connected to a mercury manometer. The air pressure in the cuff is raised by means of a hand pump until it is well above the expected systolic pressure in the artery. The cuff pressure then exceeds the intra-arterial pressure at all times, and the brachial artery collapses and blood flow stops within it. The cuff is then allowed to deflate gradually. Below the true systolic pressure the artery reopens, allowing blood flow, but until the diastolic pressure is reached it opens for only a portion of the cardiac cycle and blood goes through intermittently. Below diastolic pressure the artery remains open continuously, and blood flow continues without interruption.

In order to detect when blood flow in the artery is intermittent, the brachial artery distal to the cuff is auscultated with a stethoscope. Intermittent jets of blood coming down the vessel at high velocity result in vibrations in the vessel wall audible as a slapping or cracking sound. The pressure in the cuff below which this sound begins to be heard is therefore the systolic pressure, and the pressure at which it becomes muffled and disappears is the diastolic pressure. This method is usually accurate to within 5 mm Hg.

The sphygmomanometer method measures the pressure, relative to atmosphere, in the brachial artery, which is approximately at heart level. In using methods involving direct recording through needles or catheters it is important to specify the zero reference level which is being used; this is generally the level of the middle of the thorax in the lying subject and the manubrium sterni in the erect. Pressures measured at any point in the arterial system, for example in the foot in a standing subject, are approximately the same if measured with reference to the same zero level. In absolute terms, however, i.e. using a zero level at the point of measurement, the pressure in a foot artery is greater than that at heart level by an amount corresponding to the hydrostatic pressure of the intervening column of blood.

VOLUME FLOW IN ARTERIES

This may be measured in a variety of ways;

(1) it may be computed from a knowledge of differential pressures measured at fixed distances apart, and the diameter of the vessel (fig. 28.22);

(2) an electromagnetic flow meter may be applied to the vessel. If the vessel is placed in a magnetic field, between the poles of a magnet, flow along the vessel sets up a potential difference between the electrodes placed on the vessel wall in the diameter at right angles to the direction of the field. This potential difference is a function of volume flow.

(3) an ultrasonic flow meter consists of an ultrasound generator placed on one side of the vessel and a detector on the other. Sound waves are transmitted across the vessel to the detector and also carried downstream by the blood flow; they are lost to the detector in a degree proportional to blood flow.

These last two methods involve exposing the artery surgically.

VEINS

The veins form a collecting system for blood returning from the periphery to the heart. In general, they follow the same pattern of distribution as the arteries and frequently run alongside them. The final destination of the venous blood from the systemic circulation is the right atrium of the heart, and from the pulmonary circuit the left atrium. The main exception to this is the venous drainage of the stomach, spleen and small and large intestine, which is carried by the portal vein not directly to the heart, but first to the liver. After passage through the liver the blood returns to the heart via the hepatic vein.

Structure

Like arteries, veins have three coats in their walls. There is, however, very much less muscle and elastic tissue and the wall is much thinner in proportion to the diameter of the vessel. They have the same smooth endothelial lining as arteries. Owing to the structure of their walls veins are much more distensible, more easily collapsed or compressed and less well adapted to holding high pressures within them than arteries (fig. 28.19).

One structure which is present in veins alone is the venous valve. At intervals on the long veins, particularly in the limbs, the endothelial lining is pulled out to form cup-shaped valve cusps, similar in design to the semilunar valves of the heart. These valves permit unidirectional flow only, i.e. towards the heart. This is a

functionally useful arrangement in that veins, being thin walled, are readily compressible by surrounding muscle. During muscular activity there is alternating compression and relaxation of the tissues surrounding the veins; one-way valves allow the muscles to act on the veins as a pump and thus expedite the flow of blood back towards the heart (the **muscle pump**, p. 23.41).

Distribution

The central venous system is shown in fig. 28.25. Veins from the head and neck, the jugular veins, join on each side the subclavian veins from the upper limbs to form brachiocephalic veins which unite in the superior vena cava. This main vein from the upper half of the body is joined by the vena azygos and vena hemiazygos from the chest wall, and ends in the right atrium.

The inferior vena cava, which drains the lower half of the body and ends in the right atrium is formed by the junction of the two common iliac veins and is joined by the renal and hepatic veins before passing through the

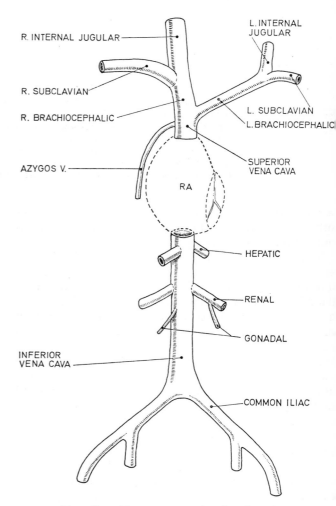

FIG. 28.25. Venae cavae and main tributaries.

diaphragm and into the right atrium. The portal vein is formed by the junction of the splenic and superior mesenteric veins and enters the liver at the porta hepatis.

The pulmonary veins are four in number, two on each side, draining the upper and lower parts of the lung and passing directly via the hilum of the lung into the left atrium.

Functions of veins

The veins provide low resistance conduits for transport of blood to the heart from the periphery. In addition, they perform a reservoir function for the circulating blood volume. The bulk of the blood volume is contained in the veins and venules which thus represent the **capacity vessels** of the circulation. As we shall see later, the neural regulation of the compliance of this system plays a part in circulatory homeostasis.

Innervation

Veins are supplied with autonomic sympathetic nerves to the smooth muscle in their walls. Venoconstriction can be demonstrated in response to sympathetic stimulation.

Venous blood flow

Flow in veins is much less phasic than in arteries and more continuous. However, the flow rate fluctuates with the pulse beat, as can be seen in the pulsations in retinal veins or demonstrated by cinematography of particles travelling in the inferior vena cava.

Velocity of flow is also less than in the corresponding arteries because of their greater cross-sectional area, though overall volume flow must be the same. Flow in the central veins, the cavae, varies to some extent with respiration. When the intrathoracic pressure falls on inspiration, and intra-abdominal pressure rises, blood tends to be drawn into the thorax by virtue of the increased pressure gradient; conversely, on expiration the intrathoracic pressure rises and blood flow slows. Forced expiration such as to raise the intrathoracic pressure considerably may arrest the return of blood to the thorax temporarily.

Venous pressure

The pressure in the venous system generally must be lower than that in the capillaries, and yet be high enough to fill the right atrium and ventricle and thus maintain cardiac output. When measured against a zero reference point at the horizontal level of midatrium the venous pressure is in health found to be remarkably constant at a few mm Hg (<5). The actual pressure at any point in the venous system is the pressure at the zero level plus any difference in hydrostatic pressure between the zero level and the point of measurement. Thus in the erect posture, if there is no muscle movement venous pressure

in the foot is over 100 mm Hg, while pressure in the head veins is negative.

The **transmural** or distending pressure is the pressure difference between the inside of the vessel and the tissues surrounding it. Veins are distended when the pressure within exceeds both the tissue pressure surrounding them and the elastic tension of their walls. They are circular in cross-section, visible or palpable if near the surface of the body, and constitute a reservoir of blood. When the pressure within them is less than the tissue pressure and wall elasticity veins are undistended, though blood flow continues in them. They are flattened or elliptical in cross-section, and poorly visible even when lying just below the skin. This difference provides a simple method of gauging roughly the central venous pressure. The subject lies with the head and chest inclined at an angle of 30° to the horizontal. In this position the external jugular veins, if distended, are easily visible, as may be pulsation in the internal jugular vein. The height to which they are filled above mid-chest level may be estimated and indicates the general level of venous pressure in the body (fig. 28.26). This manoeuvre is valuable clinically in patients with heart failure with a raised central venous pressure.

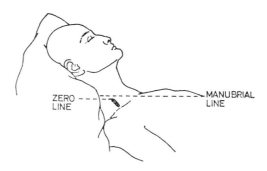

FIG. 28.26. Method of estimating central venous pressure from level of filling of neck veins.

Veins are low resistance channels and only a small pressure gradient exists along the major ones. Pressure in the venules, however, may be as high as 10 mm Hg. Because their walls are thin, veins are easily occluded by pressure. If in a limb a single vein is compressed, the blood by-passes the occluded vein by parallel or collateral venous pathways. If, however, a cuff is placed round the limb and inflated to a pressure of 40 mm Hg, flow in the vein stops. However, arterial flow continues and blood accumulates in the veins beyond the cuff. The rate at which it accumulates is the same as the rate of arterial inflow. This is the principle of the method of measuring flow by venous occlusion plethysmography. If the cuff pressure is maintained for more than a few seconds, the venous reservoir becomes filled, and pressure in the veins rises and finally exceeds the cuff pressure when blood again flows through the compressed veins and further trapping of blood ceases.

The general level of venous pressure is remarkably constant. It may be raised by manoeuvres which increase the pressure within the thorax, e.g. coughing, retching or blowing up a balloon. Failure of the heart to transfer all the blood presented to it on the input side to the output side also raises input (venous) pressure. A sudden excess of circulating blood volume may also raise venous pressure, but compensatory mechanisms which keep the venous pressure normal are remarkably effective (p. 28.40).

In general, the relationship of venous pressure and capacity is regulated by the tone of the veins, i.e. the degree of tension in the smooth muscle in their walls.

The pressure-volume diagram for a segment of vein may be contrasted with that of an artery (fig. 28.27).

FIG. 28.27. Comparison of pressure/volume relationships of short equal lengths of aorta and vena cava.

Increased tone in the vein shifts this curve downwards; the vein is less compliant and less distensible. For the venous system as a whole, wide variations in the volume of blood in the system may be accommodated by alterations of venous tone operating on the basal venous compliance, without alteration of the level of central venous pressure. This is important since the filling pressure of the heart, as such, is one determinant of cardiac performance.

CAPILLARIES

The part of the circulation of the greatest complexity, and about which the least is known, is the capillary network where the primary functions of the circulation, exchange of gases, nutrients, metabolites and heat, take place within the tissue. In general, the capillaries consist of fine tubes, approximately 7 μm in diameter, the same order of size as the red blood corpuscles. Their walls are one cell thick and arranged in a network throughout every tissue of the body except the cornea and cartilage. Blood from an artery passes first through the finer

arterial branches, the arterioles, which have relatively muscular walls, and then flows comparatively slowly through the capillary network, to be drained finally by venules or small veins which coalesce to form the main venous drainage (fig. 28.28).

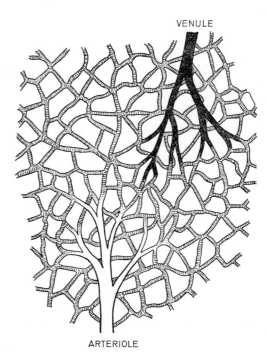

FIG. 28.28. Diagram of a capillary network and its supplying and draining vessels.

Structure

Capillaries *in vivo* are difficult to visualize satisfactorily They contain no muscle and their walls consist of a single layer of endothelial cells on a basement membrane. The capillaries themselves, which are long in relation to their diameter, appear to have no innervation though the arterioles and precapillary sphincters are innervated with autonomic nerves, as are the venules Controversy has surrounded the question of whether adjacent cells of the capillary wall are separated by a ground substance or cement; probably they are not and are in close approximation one to another (fig. 28.29).

The spatial arrangement of the capillaries varies with the tissue concerned. In muscle they are arranged longitudinally among the muscle bundles. In skin they appear as loops or arches coming up towards the surface, bending over and returning to the deeper tissues. In mesothelial structures like the pleura or peritoneum they form a horizontal network. One of the earliest and most important observations about the network was that it appears to be unstable or inconstant in that one capillary can be seen to transmit blood at one time and to close

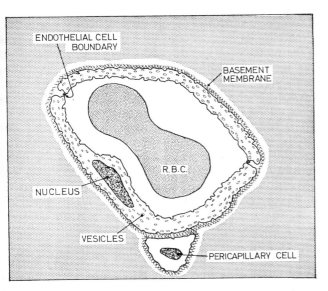

FIG. 28.29. Transverse section of single capillary shown by electron microscopy. Red blood cell shown for comparison.

shortly afterwards; different capillaries open and close in turn. This varies with the metabolic activity of the tissue. The Danish physiologist Krogh observed in microinjection studies of muscle capillaries with India ink that in active muscle the capillary count or number of capillaries open per unit cross section area increased many fold over that in muscle at rest. Another observation was that in the capillary circulation there occurs a separation of plasma and blood cells. Some capillaries appear to transmit only plasma while others of larger diameter allow blood cells to pass.

Gas exchange

All the respiratory gas exchange of the body occurs through capillary walls. In the lung capillaries oxygen passes into the blood and carbon dioxide out; the reverse process, quantitatively identical, takes place at the systemic capillary walls. Blood entering the capillary network from the arterioles is virtually identical in gas pressure and content with the blood leaving the lungs; its composition is shown in table 28.2. At the other end of the capillary network, in the venules and veins, the

TABLE 28.2. The oxygen and carbon dioxide content of blood.

	Arterial blood	Venous blood
Oxygen		
Content (ml/100 ml)	20	15
Saturation (per cent)	97	75
Partial pressure (mm Hg)	100	45
Carbon dioxide		
Content (ml/100 ml)	50	54
Partial pressure (mm. Hg)	40	45

composition has altered to a variable extent, depending on metabolic activity of the tissue and flow rate of the blood, in that oxygen pressure and content have fallen and carbon dioxide pressure and content have risen. The aggregate of values from venous blood from all over the body is the mixed venous blood which may be sampled only from the right ventricle or pulmonary artery. Its composition is also shown in table 28.2.

The process of exchange through the capillary wall between the blood plasma and the tissue fluid occurs by diffusion through the cell cytoplasm in the case of oxygen and carbon dioxide.

Movement across capillary wall

The chemical composition of interstitial fluid is closely similar to that of blood plasma as regards small molecules and the small differences in ionic composition are in accord with the Gibbs-Donnan equilibrium. Furthermore, changes in the ionic concentration of these molecules in the blood perfusing the tissue results in an almost instantaneous similar change in interstitial fluid concentration. It is apparent that the tissue fluid and blood plasma are virtually one space as regards ions and small molecules such as sodium, potassium, chloride, bicarbonate, urea, glucose and water and that the capillary wall offers no barrier to their passage.

Large molecules such as proteins pass with difficulty through the capillary wall under normal conditions and the tissue fluid contains very little of them. However, because of the vast area of exchange and flow of blood perfusing it, the amount of protein exchanged per day is a significant quantity, and has been estimated at 60–200 g, i.e. about a quarter of the plasma protein. Under conditions of damage resulting in increased permeability of both capillaries and venules, large amounts of protein may escape into the tissue fluid. These substances return to the circulation via the lymphatics rather than by reverse passage through the capillary wall (p. 28.26).

Red cells do not normally pass the capillary wall. White cells, which are capable of active movement, may be seen escaping into the tissue spaces through the capillary walls (**diapedesis**).

The mode of transfer of plasma constituents is uncertain. It was previously believed that pores existed in the intercellular ground substance of the capillary wall through which substances could diffuse freely. Electron microscope studies failed to reveal any such structures, but did show the presence of vesicles of fluid in the cytoplasm of the capillary endothelial cell, and these structures may be the main route for transfer of molecules across the capillary wall (fig. 28.29).

Capillary pressure

Direct measurement of pressure within a single capillary by micropuncture is difficult technically. The values which have been obtained in the capillaries of the nailfold are about 30 mm Hg. The validity of these measurements is, however, uncertain, in that they are in the larger capillaries and may be unrepresentative of the whole network. Most data about capillary pressure are based on indirect evidence. The important hypothesis of Starling (1895) depends on the fact that protein is present in the fluid on one side of the capillary wall and not on the other. This protein exerts a colloid osmotic pressure (COP) which is of the order of 25 mm Hg. This force tends to attract fluid into the capillary and must be balanced at equilibrium by an equal hydrostatic pressure forcing fluid out. This transmural hydrostatic pressure must be the difference between pressures within and without the capillary wall, i.e. capillary pressure minus interstitial fluid pressure.

The full Starling hypothesis is therefore:

$$P_{\text{capillary}} - P_{\text{tissue}} = \text{COP}_{\text{plasma}} - \text{COP}_{\text{interstitial fluid}}$$

where P is hydrostatic pressure and *COP* colloid osmotic pressure.

In interstitial fluid COP is negligible. A value could therefore be assigned to $P_{\text{capillary}} - P_{\text{tissue}}$. In those days as a result of micropuncture experiments it was thought that interstitial pressure was about 5 mm Hg above atmospheric pressure so that average capillary pressure would be 30 mm Hg. It is now known that interstitial pressure is normally slightly less than atmospheric pressure, so that average capillary pressure is approximately 20 mm Hg. This important observation regarding pressure in the interstitial spaces was the work of Guyton (1963), who implanted small perforated spheres in animal tissues so as to permit pressure measurement without mechanical distortion.

A further important corollary of the Starling hypothesis is that since hydrostatic pressure falls from the arteriolar end to the venular end of the capillary the average value applies only at a midway point. Proximal to this point there is a net balance favouring outward movement of fluid and distally an inward movement. The concept was thus of a circulation of fluid leaving the capillary for the tissues at one end and returning to it at the other.

This relationship between hydrostatic and osmotic pressure has since been validated by Landis in America in the case of a single capillary, and by Pappenheimer and others in studies on perfused tissues.

Control of the capillary circulation

Regulation of the flow through the capillaries must be adapted to two partially distinct functions. The primary function is that of exchange of substances to meet metabolic demands, and here it is clear that the critical factor is not the total volume of flow through the tissue capillaries, but the surface area of the capillary walls through which exchange takes place.

Secondly, since the capillaries are in series with the whole circulation their regulation cannot be independent of the requirements of the circulation as a whole. As we shall see, the regulation of the arterial blood pressure depends partly on control of the arteriolar resistance, i.e. the state of constriction of the arterioles, which in turn affects blood flow through the capillary network.

The obvious possibility of conflict between the demands of these two functions has led to a search for mechanisms allowing independent control of the functions in the capillary circulation. The scheme of control envisaged at present, for which there is much experimental evidence, involves two mechanisms.

(1) The arteriolar resistance is controlled by contraction of smooth muscle in the walls of the small arterioles. This governs the overall flow through the capillary bed.

(2) The precapillary sphincters, smooth muscle fibres controlling the mouths of capillary channels, determine by opening or closing the number of capillaries through which the blood circulates, i.e. the capillary exchange area. If many sphincters are closed the blood flows through the main capillary channels, few in number and relatively large. If the sphincters relax blood is diverted through a much denser network of channels and comes intimately in contact with the metabolizing tissues.

The small arterioles and precapillary sphincters appear to be resistances in series rather than in parallel as was earlier postulated.

In general, the arteriolar resistance is much more under neural control than is the precapillary. The latter is influenced mainly by locally produced vasodilator metabolites which readily diffuse through the tissues and cause the sphincters to relax. This occurs in conditions of metabolic demand such as exercise, local heating, and reactive hyperaemia following a period of arterial inflow occlusion. Although the metabolites primarily affect the precapillary sphincters, they diffuse around the arteriolar resistances, causing them to relax also.

Neural control of the arteriolar resistance is via the sympathetic supply. Sympathetic vasoconstriction takes place reflexly in response to a variety of stimuli, e.g. pain, cold, or a drop in blood pressure, exciting baroreceptors in the carotid sinus. Sympathetic tone may be reduced by general body heating or by section of sympathetic nerves. The vasodilation in these circumstances is less than the vasodilation produced by metabolites, and is not associated with opening up of large numbers of capillaries. Finally, in some tissues, especially muscle, there are special sympathetic vasodilator cholinergic fibres which on exercise or even anticipation of exercise cause arteriolar dilation.

The two resistances, arteriolar and precapillary, interact to some extent; a metabolic stimulus locally first causes precapillary dilation and then opens the rteriolar resistances. Severe arteriolar vasoconstriction may result in ischaemia and accumulation of metabolites ᴏ such an extent that the vasoconstriction is modified ᴀnd relieved. This mechanism provides the basis for the ᴘhenomenonon of **autoregulation of flow** which applies ᴡidely in the terminal circulation and which is made ᴘossible by the presence and interaction of two balancing ᴄontrol systems.

In a few areas of the body there are special communiᴄating channels between arteries and veins of larger size ᴛhan capillaries (**arteriovenous anastomoses**) which allow ᴘlood to bypass the capillary circulation to a large ᴇxtent. The best authenticated sites for these shunts are ᴏn the skin of the hands and feet and in the wall of the ᴛomach. Their function is obscure.

The effects of various stimuli on the peripheral circulaᴛion are now summarized.

(1) Local heat produces a marked local vasodilation ᴘoth of skin vessels and muscle vessels, while cold conᴛracts vessels locally.

(2) Generalized body heating such as to raise central ᴘody temperature results in a release of sympathetic ᴄonstrictor tone and generalized vasodilation, affecting ᴘarticularly the skin vessels. Chilling of the body results ᴎ reflex vasoconstriction.

(3) Muscular exercise results in a marked local vasodilation in the exercising muscles. Flow may increase ꜰrom resting values of 1–2 ml/100 ml/min to thirty or forty ᴛimes this value (fig. 28.30).

FIG. 28.30. Blood flow in the calf during rhythmic exercise. ×, rate of flow during a few seconds' relaxation; large blood flow; ○, rate of flow during a few seconds of sustained contraction; slightly increased blood flow; ●, mean rate of flow, average results in seven subjects. From Barcroft & Swan (1953), *Sympathetic Control of Human Blood Vessels*, London: Arnold.

(4) If blood supply is cut off for a period of time from an area of the circulation by arterial occlusion, release of the occlusion is followed by a large increase in blood flow over the control value which persists for almost as long as the period of occlusion lasted. This is **reactive hyperaemia**. It is probably caused by accumulation of vasodilator metabolites (fig. 28.31).

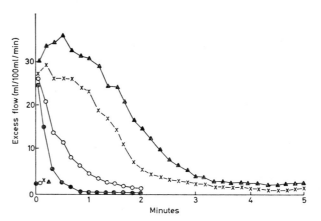

FIG. 28.31. Reactive hyperaemia following different periods of circulatory arrest. The averaged results of six experiments in which ●, 2-minute; ○, 5-minute; ×, 10-minute; and ▲, 15-minute periods of arrest were applied. The respective resting levels, indicated by the symbols at the left of the curves, have been subtracted. From Patterson & Whelan (1955), *Clin. Sci.* **14**, 197.

(5) Circulating catecholamines, adrenaline and particularly noradrenaline, cause vasoconstriction and elevate the blood pressure. Adrenaline, however, has a powerful action on muscle blood vessels, causing them to dilate.

THE LYMPHATIC SYSTEM

In a 65 kg man the exchange of fluid across the capillaries throughout the body into the interstitial fluid amounts to about 20 l/day. This moves in both directions and the great bulk is returned to the circulation through the walls of the capillaries and venules. About 2–4 l/day, however, is returned to the circulation by a circuitous route through the lymphatic system and is known as **lymph**.

The lymphatic vessels

The lymphatic system consists of lymphatic capillaries, larger lymphatic vessels and lymphatic trunks. Lymph passes from the interstitial fluid into the lymphatic capillaries which are found in specially large numbers near blood capillaries. They possess round blind ends and open into irregularly dilated thin walled channels which anastomose freely. The wall of the lymphatic capillary is composed of a single layer of endothelial cells with very little basement endothelium. Lymph passes from the capillaries into larger vessels most of which form a network surrounding blood vessels. The walls of these vessels are composed of three layers similar to those of veins but are thinner and the different components less distinct. The lymphatic vessels run from the limbs and all the organs of the body, including the lungs, and unite to form larger trunks; these join finally to form the right bronchomediastinal trunk and thoracic duct which open into the venous system at the junction of the internal jugular and subclavian veins (p. 20.37). The lymphatic vessels contain valves and these together with the muscle pump in the limbs and the low venous pressure within the thoracic veins, especially on inspiration, assist its drainage.

During their course lymphatic vessels pass through accumulations of lymphoid tissue called lymph nodes which are scattered in large numbers throughout the body and especially in the prevertebral region, the mesentery, the axillae and groins. The structure and function of lymph nodes are given on p. 27.3. They contribute lymphocytes to the lymphatic fluid which leaves the nodes by efferent lymphatic vessels.

Composition and function of lymph

The composition of lymphatic fluid draining the limbs is similar to that of interstitial fluid and contains less than 1 g/100 ml protein. Lymphatic fluid draining the intestine and liver, however, has a protein concentration of 3–6 g/100 ml.

The volume of lymph from different regions of the body varies with the protein content of the interstitial fluid. When this is small, e.g. in the resting limb, lymphatic flow is small. When it is larger, as in the case of lymph draining the liver and intestine, the flow is larger. The lymphatic capillaries are much more permeable to macromolecules than are the blood capillaries so that protein molecules which escape from the latter are taken up into the lymph channels. This is due to the thinness of the basement membrane in the lymphatic capillaries and to the fact that the endothelial cells are less firmly attached to each other. Pinocytosis may also play a part. In this way the lymphatic system operates as an overflow drainage system of interstitial fluid and plasma proteins which have escaped from the blood capillaries. Lymph draining the intestine also contains lipid and other substances absorbed from the gut while lymph from the kidney contains some of the sodium and water absorbed by the renal tubules.

THE PERIPHERAL CIRCULATION AS A WHOLE

The functional aspects of the vascular system as a whole are best considered in a simple system of an artery, the

capillaries supplied by that artery and the venous drainage from the system. Such a self-contained unit might represent the circulation through an organ such as a kidney or a lung, or a part of the body such as a limb. If smaller units than this are considered the situation may become complicated by collateral circulation, i.e. sharing to a greater or lesser extent of the blood supply among adjacent arterial territories by communications between them at arteriolar or capillary level. In such circumstances one unit of venous drainage is derived from several arterial supply units. If, however, a part of the body is chosen where the blood entering by the artery is identical with that leaving by the vein, a study may be made of the whole circulatory territory as shown in fig. 28.32.

FIG. 28.32. Schematic diagram of a single circulating system and the relation of its physical parameters.

Volume flow (in cm³/sec) is the same for each of the five verticals shown in the diagram

Area of cross-section (cm²) varies however, being relatively small at the arterial and venous ends and very large in the capillaries. In the case of the whole systemic circulation in a dog for example, the aortic cross-section vas estimated to be 0·8 cm² while the total capillary cross-section was 625 cm². This is a functional adaptation in that the surface available for exchange is small in the case of the supply and drainage vessels and larger in the case of the small exchange vessels.

Flow velocity (cm/sec) is inversely proportional to the cross-section (cm³/sec ÷ cm² = cm/sec). Flow velocity in the aorta in man may reach 500 cm/sec, while in the capillaries it is only about 0·07 cm/sec. This affords a relatively long time for metabolic exchange to take place. In using the term blood flow, it is volume flow that is generally understood rather than flow velocity.

Pressure (dynes/cm², or mm Hg). Flow always occurs down a pressure gradient, i.e. pressure is higher at the arterial than at the venous end. Fig. 28.22 shows the pattern of pressure through the system, the main drop in pressure occurring at arteriolar level. In other words, the arterioles constitute the main resistance to flow.

Resistance of any segment of the circulation is the ratio of pressure drop $(P_1 - P_2)$ along the segment to volume flow (F).

$$R = \frac{P_1 - P_2}{F}$$

Since in our model F is the same at all verticals, resistance is proportional to change in pressure, dP, i.e. to the slope of the line P in fig. 28.32. It is highest, therefore, where the pressure shows the greatest fall, at the arteriolar level.

Resistance represents energy lost as heat because of friction as blood is propelled along a vessel. Movement of all kinds implies loss of energy in this way and this is true for both liquids and solids. In a vessel with blood flowing through it, friction does not occur only at the inner surface of the vessel wall, as one might suppose, but throughout the thickness of blood. Flow takes place most rapidly in the centre of the stream, velocity falling progressively as the wall is approached until finally the layer of fluid in contact with the vessel wall is virtually motionless. In this way coaxial layers of blood may be thought of as sliding forward upon each other, the central core having the highest velocity. A velocity profile is shown in fig. 28.21. The shearing stress of one layer or lamina upon another uses energy and accounts for frictional loss.

The definition of resistance given above is a general one applying to any vessel or system of vessels. One may calculate, for example, the resistance of the femoral artery, or of an organ such as the kidney or lung, or indeed the resistance of the systemic or pulmonary circuits; in the latter cases the flow is, of course, equal to the cardiac output.

In a rigid physical system, such as a hollow tube, the relationship between flow and pressure is a straight line (fig. 28.33), and the line passes through the origin.

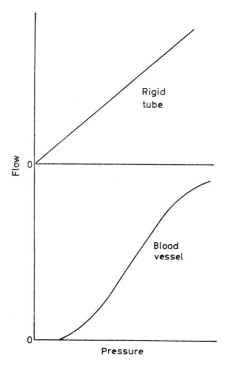

FIG. 28.33. Pressure-flow diagrams for a rigid tube and for a blood vessel *in vivo*.

Resistance is proportional to the slope of the line and is the same under all conditions. In the case of living elastic vessels, however, this relationship is only approximately true. A typical pressure flow diagram (fig. 28.33) shows a sigmoid curve with a positive intercept on the pressure axis. A certain threshold pressure is required to start flow, which then increases rapidly as the vessel expands, but finally the vessel resists further stretching and increase in flow tends to level off with further increase in pressure. This type of pressure-flow diagram is characteristic of living vessels. It implies that resistance alters to some extent with different perfusion conditions, and that a resistance value calculated for an observed flow and pressure is valid only within a certain range of pressures and flows. The threshold value of pressure, below which flow stops, is the **critical closing pressure**. It represents the point at which the forces within the walls of the smallest vessels become unstable and the lumen of the vessel is closed.

In practice, resistance is derived from the ratio of pressure to flow. What are the physical factors in any given system whose resistance is being measured which affect the observed values? The answer is given in the Poiseuille equation (p. 28.17) for conditions of uniform flow in nondistensible systems. These conditions are not fulfilled in the circulation, and so too much accuracy cannot be expected from such predictions. Calculation of resistance, which cannot be measured directly, as a ratio of pressure to flow is, however, useful in a variety of circumstances. Changes in blood flow in a limb, for example, may occur from three causes:

(1) alteration in the nervous control of the blood vessels,

(2) direct effects on the blood vessels due to circulating hormones or to local heat or metabolites,

(3) alteration in the pressure of blood $(P_1 - P_2)$ perfusing the limb.

In the first two cases a change occurs in the resistance of the vessels, while the third case represents a passive change in flow without any alteration in resistance. In analysing the effects of drugs or other forms of treatment it is necessary to distinguish between these possibilities, and a first step is to see by calculating resistance values whether any actual vascular change has been produced.

Another situation where reliance on measurements of pressure alone or flow alone is misleading is in certain forms of congenital heart defect in which, owing to abnormal communications in the heart, pulmonary blood flow and systemic blood flow may be widely different. In these circumstances high pressure in the pulmonary artery might be due either to a very large flow through lung vessels of normal resistance, or to a high resistance to flow through damaged lung vessels, the actual flow level being normal or low. In the former case surgical treatment is of great benefit; in the latter case it is often lethal. With all the reservations due to the approximate nature of the estimate, a resistance value, taking into account the two variables of average pressure and flow, is of immense value in clinical work.

If it is possible to measure **instantaneous** flow and pressure, a value for impedance rather than resistance may be calculated. One can then treat the problem not on the analogy of a D.C. circuit assuming a steady pressure and flow, but as a problem in A.C. theory to which the situation more closely approximates. since both pressure and flow are oscillatory. At present this approach has only research applications.

Resistances in parallel

The branching of the aorta and arteries divides the systemic circuit to supply different organs and tissues in parallel. Besides organs like the brain and kidneys which have an obvious individual blood supply, more widespread tissues such as skin and muscle may be regarded as individual organs since their vessels, and control of these vessels, are similar. Diagrammatically, therefore, the systemic circuit may be represented as in fig. 28.1, the parallel flows being cerebral, coronary, renal, splanchnic, muscular and cutaneous.

Clearly the output of the heart is the sum of the flows through the individual circuits.

$$F = f_1 + f_2 + f_3 + \cdots$$

What is the relation of the individual resistances to the total systemic resistance? The arterial and venous pressures are approximately the same for all, so each term in the equation may be divided by $(P_1 - P_2)$ or P.

Hence

$$\frac{F}{P} = \frac{f_1}{P} + \frac{f_2}{P} + \frac{f_3}{P} + \cdots$$

But

$$R = \frac{P}{F} \quad \text{and} \quad \frac{F}{P} = \frac{1}{R}$$

Hence

$$\frac{1}{R} = \frac{1}{r_1} + \frac{1}{r_2} + \frac{1}{r_3} + \cdots$$

In other words the resistances of the parallel circuits are individually greater than the resistance of the whole system.

Methods of measuring flow

On the one hand there are methods for measuring the entire cardiac output and on the other methods for measuring flow in one of the parallel circuits (fig. 28.1).

CARDIAC OUTPUT OR PULMONARY BLOOD FLOW Three methods are in use, all illustrating important general principles of the circulation.

Fick principle

The principle is that if a substance is added at a constant rate to the blood stream flowing past a point the volume rate of flow is inversely proportional to the increase in concentration of the substance in the down stream blood. In practice the pulmonary blood flow is measured and oxygen is the substance added to the blood as it passes through the lungs. The rate of oxygen uptake is measured (ml/min) and, simultaneously, the concentrations of oxygen (ml/l) in the blood arriving at and leaving the lungs:

$$F(\text{l/min}) = \frac{O_2 \text{ consumption (ml/min)}}{\text{Arterial} - \text{venous } O_2 \text{ concentration (ml/l)}}$$

Oxygen consumption is measured by collecting expired air and analysing it for oxygen content. Arterial blood is sampled, at a constant rate and during the same time interval, from the left side of the heart or from a peripheral artery. Mixed venous blood is similarly sampled from the pulmonary artery. The oxygen concentrations in blood samples are measured by Van Slyke analysis or by photoelectric oximetry.

The disadvantages of the Fick method are as follows:

(1) it requires catheterization of the pulmonary artery since venous samples obtained upstream from this point are not fully mixed and so are not representative of the body as a whole;

PLATE 30.1. Radiographs of the gastrointestinal tract. Courtesy of Dr C.K. Warwick.

(a) Oesophagus (right anterior oblique view); barium swallows. The impressions of the aorta (A), left main bronchus (B), and left atrium (LA) show clearly on the left photograph. The oesophagus on the right is well filled and shows the aortic and cardiac impressions. Vertebra (V), diaphragm (D).

(c) Stomach and small intestine (anteroposterior view), half an hour after a barium meal which has now entered the jejunum and proximal ileum. Their mucosal folds give the feathery appearance. The stomach lies almost transverse because patient is supine. Duodenojejunal flexure (DJ), diaphragm (D) and stomach (S).

(b) Stomach and duodenum (anteroposterior view). The patient is upright a few minutes after a barium meal. The duodenum is beginning to fill. Oesophagus (O), pyloric sphincter (P), breast shadow (B) and 2nd lumbar vertebra (L2).

(d) Large intestine (left anterior oblique view). A barium enema fills large bowel. The appendix is not visible. The splenic flexure (SF) is opened out because of oblique view and it is higher than the hepatic flexure (HF), caecum (C), pelvic colon (PC).

PLATE 33.1. Glomeruli from normal kidneys.

(a) A glomerulus showing how it communicates by a short neck with the proximal convoluted tubule (×270), by courtesy of Dr E.M. Darmady.

(b) and (c) Neoprene casts of cortical (b) and juxtamedullary (c) glomeruli showing the difference in calibre of the afferent (A) and efferent (E) vessels. From Trueta J. *et al.* (1947) *Studies of the Renal Circulation*. Oxford : Blackwell Scientific Publications.

(2) since it takes time to measure oxygen uptake (usually 2 min or more) the method is applicable only to steady-state conditions and is unsuitable for following rapid changes in output;

(3) the chemical analyses are tedious and do not lend themselves to automation;

(4) since blood sampling is at a constant rate, while blood flow in the vessels is phasic with the cardiac cycle, a small sampling error may be introduced.

The advantage of the Fick principle is its simplicity. It is essentially a dilution method, but has none of the problems of recirculation involved in most dilution methods using exogenous indicators.

Indicator dilution methods

Many exogenous substances and markers have been used as indicators. These include dyes such as indocyanine green, saline which alters electrical conductivity of blood and radioisotopes such as ^{131}I albumin or ^{85}Kr. A small volume of ice cold water may also be used and its dilution detected by thermistors. On the Fick principle these indicators may be continuously infused and blood sampled downstream. The rate of blood flow is then inversely proportional to the increase in concentration of the indicator in the blood flowing past the sampling point. Since these indicators recirculate, it is necessary also to ascertain the concentration in the blood arriving back at the point of injection and make a correction for this.

The indicator, usually a dye, is more conveniently given as a single injection into a large vein on the right side of the heart. Sampling is from a large peripheral artery. As dyed blood passes the sampling point the concentration of dye rises and falls (fig. 28.34). If the rate of flow is rapid, the appearance time of dye is relatively short; the dye has not had time to diffuse up and downstream and passes through as a single mass. Conversely, if flow is slow the appearance time is prolonged and dye has diffused up and downstream so that the recorded curve is broad though the peak is lower. The rate of flow is in fact inversely proportional to the area under the curve of indicator concentration:

$$F(\text{ml/sec}) = \frac{I(\text{mg})}{Ct\left(\dfrac{\text{mg}}{\text{ml}} \times \text{sec}\right)}$$

I is the amount of dye injected. Ct is the average concentration during the primary curve multiplied by the passage time of the primary curve. This is geometrically equal to the area under the curve.

A complicating feature is that the disappearance slope of the primary curve is often distorted by the secondary wave caused by dyed blood reappearing at the sampling site after circulating through the body. To correct for this distortion the upper, undistorted portion of the disappearance slope, which forms an exponential curve, is

26

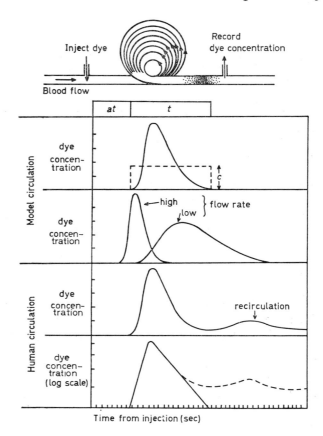

FIG. 28.34. Cardiac output by the indicator dilution method. *at*, appearance time; *t*, transit time; *c*, mean concentration. $c \times t$, area under primary curve. Output = dye injected (mg)/$c \times t$. Note the method of allowing for recirculation by extrapolating a logarithmic plot of dye concentration.

used to predict the subsequent course of the primary curve had there been no recirculation. This can simply be done by replotting the curve on logarithmic paper, when it forms a straight line, and projecting it towards the base line.

Advantages of the indicator dilution method are as follows:

(1) it is unnecessary to catheterize the pulmonary artery;

(2) the dye curve can be recorded in 30 sec; more frequent output measurements can therefore be made;

(3) by use of photoelectric densitometers concentration curves can be obtained continuously. Many estimates can be made by feeding the densitometer output into an analogue-digital converter.

Respiratory methods

The Fick method may be applied to figures for CO_2 output and A–V difference instead of O_2 uptake. The CO_2 content of arterial and venous blood may be calculated from partial pressures of the gas in arterial and venous blood. In arterial blood the P_{CO_2} equals, for practical purposes, that of alveolar air, which can be readily measured. An estimate of the mixed venous P_{CO_2} can be made by using the lungs as an aerotonometer. The subject rebreathes different mixtures of CO_2 and O_2 each for about 15 sec; when P_{CO_2} of the mixture is unchanged by the rebreathing, it represents that of the mixed venous blood. The advantages of the method is that no needles or catheters are required and it can be readily applied during muscular exercise. However, the subject needs to be trained in the experimental procedure. For these reasons the method is more useful to physiologists than to clinicians. The method also has theoretical difficulties because recirculation of the blood may raise the alveolar P_{CO_2} within 15 sec before the measurement is made.

The rate of uptake of N_2O by the lung capillary blood may be used to measure pulmonary blood flow or cardiac output. An ingenious method of doing so is to enclose the subject in a whole body plethysmograph, together with a bag of a N_2O and O_2 mixture from which he breathes. The atmospheric pressure within the plethysmograph decreases due to the reduction in gas volume as the N_2O is dissolved in the pulmonary capillary blood flow and from a knowledge of the partition coefficient of N_2O in blood and gas, the cardiac output can be calculated.

ORGAN OR LIMB BLOOD FLOW

Plethysmography

Volume flow of blood in the limb may be measured by a venous occlusion plethysmograph or volume recorder. This consists of a rigid container filled with air or water into which the limb is sealed; volume changes in the limb are recorded as displacements of the air or water from the container by a float recorder system. The limb is first raised above heart level so that the veins are undistended. If the venous outflow is occluded for a few seconds by a proximal cuff suddenly inflated to 60 mm Hg, which does not interfere with arterial inflow, the limb swells at a rate equal to the rate of arterial inflow. Since arterial inflow and venous outflow are normally equal, the rate of swelling measures the volume flow. Blood flow is expressed in ml/min/100 ml of tissue. Most of the blood flow to the hand or foot goes to skin, and in the forearm or calf to muscle. Plethysmograph records with a cuff over the wrist are used to measure changes in cutaneous blood flow. When flow to the hand is excluded by raising the pressure in a cuff at the wrist above the arterial pressure, a plethysmograph on the forearm measures muscle blood flow.

Clearance methods

If a rapidly diffusible exogenous substance is injected into a tissue, it is carried away by the blood stream. The amount

or concentration of the substance decreases exponentially, i.e. at a rate changing at each moment according to the concentration remaining. Thus the rate of decrease is a first rapid but then gradually slows. Exponential curves fall in a straight line when plotted logarithmically, and the slope of this line is therefore an index of the rate of removal and hence of the blood flow in the tissues. Fig. 28.35 shows the rate of removal of ^{24}Na injected into muscle, and how it alters with reactive hyperaemia.

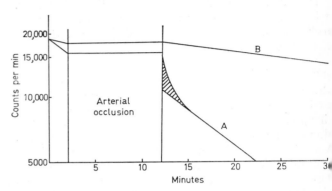

FIG. 28.35. Clearance of ^{24}Na from gastrocnemius muscle. A, normal subject; B, patient with impaired arterial circulation. Note reactive hyperaemia after arterial occlusion.

Similarly the rate of flow can be calculated if a tissue is saturated via the blood stream with some diffusible exogenous substance until equilibrium has been reached. The flow is then derived from the relationship between the changes with time in the arterial (Ca) and venous (Cv) concentrations and the partition coefficient between blood and tissues. Nitrous oxide, breathed in 15 per cent concentration for 15 min, or radioactive krypton are commonly used. In the case of the brain, internal jugular venous blood is sampled. In the case of the heart, coronary sinus blood is analysed.

$$F = \frac{100 \times Cv \times S}{\int_0^{15} (Ca - Cv)\, dt}$$

FIG. 28.36. Arterial and venous concentrations of nitrous oxide. (a) Saturation curves; (b) Ca−Cv plotted on a log scale; (c) desaturation curves. The slope of (b) is proportional to blood flow.

Fig. 28.36 shows the rise in Ca and Cv while the subject breathes nitrous oxide. Cv rises slowly to equal Ca when the tissue studied is fully saturated with nitrous oxide. When the subject stops breathing the gas, the curves again diverge. The area between the curves for Ca and Cv, in either case, represents the denominator of the equation above, which gives a measure of flow in ml/100 ml of tissue/min.

CONTROL OF THE CIRCULATION

The basic principles of the design of the circulation are twofold:
(1) a relatively stable perfusion pressure,
(2) wide variations in flow both as regards the cardiac output and its distribution to different organs and tissues under circumstances of varying demand.

Three main systems are involved. These are (1) control of the local circulation, (2) control of the blood pressure and (3) regulation of cardiac output. The local control of circulation, for example, on exercising muscles, has already been discussed (p. 28.24). Clearly these mechanisms are not independent but interact with each other, since blood pressure, for example, cannot be altered without altering either output or peripheral resistance. For purposes of illustration, however, individual mechanisms may be isolated and examined.

Control of blood pressure

The familiar closed loop negative feedback principle operates to control blood pressure. The misalignment detector consists of stretch receptors situated in the tunica media and adventitia of the main arteries of the body, the aortic arch, brachiocephalic artery and carotid arteries. In man the main site of the receptors is the carotid sinus, situated at the junction of the external and internal carotid arteries, p. 28.28. The importance of stability of pressure at this site is obvious for animals adopting the upright position.

These pressoreceptors or **baroreceptors** are stimulated by tension in the wall of the vessel which in turn is increased by pressure within the vessel. Thus a rise of intra-arterial pressure increases the rate of discharge in afferent fibres from the receptors, and a fall in pressure decreases the rate. The afferent fibres travel via the glossopharyngeal and vagus nerves to the centres in the upper medulla which are concerned with the nervous control of the heart and blood vessels. This control is mediated by both sympathetic and parasympathetic nerves in the case of the heart and by sympathetic constrictor or dilator nerves supplying arterioles and venules in the case of peripheral resistance. Control of the heart is exercised both as regards rate, through the sinuatrial node, and contractility. It is to be noted that an increased discharge rate of the baroreceptors results in depressor activity, i.e. inhibition of sympathetic cardiac stimulation and sympathetic vasoconstrictor activity (fig. 28.37).

FIG. 28.37. The effect of stimulation of the carotid sinus nerve on the blood pressure of a dog. Reflex bradycardia and hypotension arise. From Hering, H.E. (1927), *Die Karotissinus reflexe*. Dresden, Th. Steinkopf.

Blockade of the baroreceptor nerves by local anaesthetic results in a large though temporary increase in blood pressure and heart rate. Stimulation of the baroreceptors by local pressure on the carotid sinus slows the heart and lowers blood pressure. A few individuals have a hypersensitive carotid sinus mechanism. In them, even light pressure on the carotid sinus, e.g. with a tight collar, may induce reflex cardiac arrest and unconsciousness.

What is the norm of blood pressure towards which the baroreceptor mechanism adjusts? Fig. 28.38 shows the range of values in a group of male subjects aged 40–44 years. With age there is a gradual rise in pressures, mainly however, affecting the systolic component. To some extent this increase in pulse pressure with age reflects decreasing compliance in the arterial system, i.e. impaired storage function. Like any other biological variable, blood pressure has a fairly wide frequency distribution in the population. In western societies arterial pressure tends on average to rise with age. This tendency is not present in primitive peoples. There is no arbitrary dividing line between normal and abnormal pressures, although statistically the higher pressures carry a less favourable life expectation and life assurance companies allow for this. Table 28.3 gives an indication of the limits of pressure beyond which treatment should be considered.

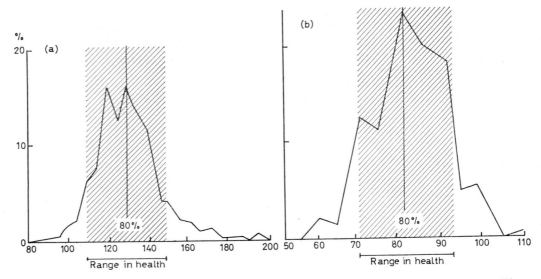

FIG. 28.38. Range of (a) systolic and (b) diastolic arterial pressures in males aged 40–44 years. The vertical line is the median and the shaded area represents 80 per cent of the population. Modified from Rushmer, R. F. (1961), *Cardiovascular Dynamics*, 2nd Edition. Philadelphia: Saunders.

Table 28.3. Upper limits of blood pressure which are considered normal, related to age. in western society (mm Hg). These pressures, if found consistently, are abnormally high. At any age, pressures below 100/60 are abnormally low.

Age	Systolic	Diastolic
20	150	90
30	150	100
40	160	100
50	165	105
60	170	105
70	170	110

The baroreceptors, although the most important, are not the only controlling mechanism of the blood pressure. There are chemoreceptors situated in the aortic arch and in the carotid sinus. Increased discharge of these receptors caused by a fall in Pa, O_2 or pH causes a pressure response via the medullary centres, i.e. sympathetic stimulation of the heart and peripheral vasoconstriction, which tends to elevate blood pressure.

The medullary centres are also under cortical control. Emotions, particularly fear or excitement, can cause large rises of blood pressure, and it is frequently difficult in normal individuals to measure the true resting blood pressure simply because the circumstance of having the pressure measured raises it. Pain and cold are other stimuli which regularly cause a pressor response and operate through cortical pathways on the medullary vasomotor centres.

The extent to which man is dependent on the baroreceptor mechanism for maintenance of consciousness in the upright posture and indeed for life itself is illus-trated by the cases in which this control breaks down. When a person changes from a lying position to a standing one, the effect of gravity is to pool a large proportion of the blood volume in the veins in the lower part of the body. This would continue if there were not a re-adjustment via the baroreceptors of the tone or compliance of the venous capacity vessels and of the arteriolar resistance.

In many elderly people this control mechanism is imperfect and postural hypotension, i.e. a drop in blood pressure on standing, is surprisingly common and accounts for many falls and fainting attacks. In young people also, sudden emotional stimuli of an unpleasant nature may produce fainting by inhibiting vasoconstrictor tone, but only in the upright posture. The situation is rapidly restored if the subject is allowed to lie flat, and only becomes dangerous through injudicious attempts by bystanders to hold him upright.

AUTONOMIC VASOMOTOR NERVES

What is the efferent pathway from the vasomotor centre in the medulla to the smooth muscle of the arterioles? The cardiovascular control or vasomotor centre is situated in the floor of the fourth ventricle (p. 24.21). From there fibres pass down the cervical cord in the lateral column to all the thoracic and upper two lumbar segments. Then they synapse with the connector cells of the sympathetic which lie in the lateral horn of the grey matter of the cord. From the connector cells the preganglionic fibres leave the cord in the ventral roots of segments T1–L2 and then enter all the mixed spinal nerves, p. 24.88. There is no parasympathetic supply to the peripheral vascular system.

The sympathetic supply of the heart (T2–T4) synapses in all three cervical ganglia and postganglionic fibres reach the heart via the cardiac branches of the sympathetic chain and the parasympathetic supply via the vagus.

Sympathetic constrictor tone is constantly present. Section of the cord below the medulla cuts off such tonic impulses and results in a fall of blood pressure. When the blood pressure is chronically elevated in disease, the activity of the baroreceptors seems to be normal, but set at a higher level of response. Drugs used to lower high blood pressure reduce vasoconstrictor tone, though they have different sites of action. Some act centrally, depressing the vasomotor centre. Others act by paralysing transmission in the sympathetic ganglia. Others again block the sympathetic postganglionic fibres, or deplete stores of catecholamine neural transmitter in the tissues. Finally, some act on arteriolar smooth muscle, blocking the catecholamine receptor, or cause relaxation of smooth muscle directly.

Control of cardiac output

The cardiac output is the product of the heart rate and the stroke volume. Change in output is therefore mediated by change in one or other of these, usually in both.

Changes in **heart rate** are effected through the SA node. Sympathetic activity increases and parasympathetic decreases the rate of discharge of this pacemaker. Circulating hormones such as adrenaline affect the node directly without neural linkage. The presence of a tonic parasympathetic effect, restraining the heart rate, is demonstrated by administering atropine which blocks the parasympathetic transmitter acetyl choline. The heart then speeds up to over 100 beats/min.

The stimuli altering rate are evoked by carotid sinus reflexes, by exercise or by the anticipation of exercise, and by emotion such as excitement or fear. Vagal stimulation by visceral pain slows the heart reflexly.

Stroke volume is determined by the extent of filling of the ventricles and the force and completeness of ventricular contraction. How these factors are controlled to produce required changes in output is complex and controversial. The difficulty in analysing the problem lies in the fact that several different control mechanisms may be seen to be operating depending on the extent to which the mechanisms are dissected.

The basic relationship between venous return and contractility is exemplified in Starling's law. Starling showed that in the individual muscle fibre the tension developed on contraction was a function of the initial length before contraction. Applying this relation to the myocardial fibres *in situ*, a more effective contraction should result from a greater degree of stretching of the fibres by increased filling pressure. It is difficult to measure fibre length in the intact heart, but easy to measure

end diastolic pressure, i.e. the pressure distending the ventricle just before contraction. In the uncontracted ventricle the pressure-volume relationship is non-linear and the pressure and fibre length cannot be directly related. The relationship is approximately as shown in fig. 28.39. Experimentally in the isolated heart, the ob-

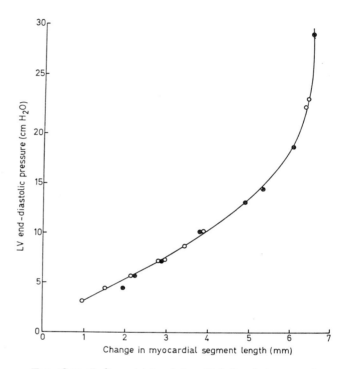

FIG. 28.39. Left ventricle of dog. Relation between end diastolic pressure and change in length of a segment of myocardium, before (●) and after (○) sympathetic stimulation. From Sarnoff & Mitchell (1960).

served change in left ventricular (LV) stroke work (measuring contractility) with change in LV end diastolic pressure is shown in fig. 28.40. Putting these two graphs together, and relating LV stroke work to LV fibre length, an approximate straight line relationship is obtained as in Starling's observation.

A simple feedback system such as this is capable of varying output in response to varying input (filling) and also to varying load (aortic pressure). It does so, however, with several disadvantages. Input pressure fluctuates widely and may have secondary effects, for example on the lungs. Varying degrees of stretch of the myocardium dilate the heart, and, because of Laplace's law, more tension is required for a given output pressure and hence the ventricle is operating at less than optimal efficiency.

The addition of a neurohumoral control increases the efficiency of the system. Sarnoff and others have shown that for an individual heart there is not one Starling

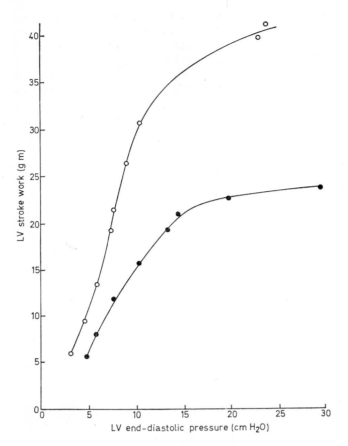

FIG. 28.40. Left ventricle of dog with constant heart rate. Relation between stroke work and end-diastolic pressure, ●, before and ○ after sympathetic stimulation. From Sarnoff & Mitchell (1960).

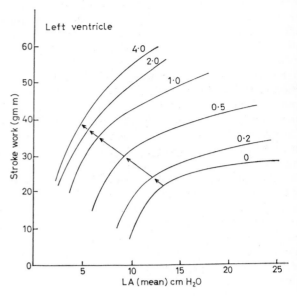

FIG. 28.41. Dog heart. Relation between LV stroke work and LA pressure, showing effect of stimulating the stellate ganglion at increasing rates. Sympathetic activity increases the work output for a given LA pressure. From Sarnoff and Mitchell (1960).

curve but a family of curves, and the heart's performance characteristics are transferred from one to another in response to neural stimulation, reflecting the amount of activity demanded or anticipated. Sympathetic stimulation or circulating catecholamines shift the length tension diagram to the left; impairment of myocardial efficiency as by coronary vasoconstriction shifts it to the right. This then is one mechanism whereby the LV stroke work may be increased without increasing diastolic pressure and hence atrial pressure (fig. 28.41).

There is another linked mechanism whose operation is one of the functions of the atrium. The atrium contracts towards the end of ventricular diastole and the strength of its contraction therefore affects the final stretch of the ventricular fibres. A vigorous atrial systole can increase end diastolic fibre length by increasing atrial pressure momentarily at the most effective time, while during the rest of the cardiac cycle it remains low. The vigour of atrial systole, controlled by sympathetic

and parasympathetic stimuli, is therefore an added mechanism controlling contractility of the ventricle.

Thus a simple regulator such as the Starling length tension curve (p. 28.33), which can be demonstrated in an isolated heart preparation, may be totally obscured when other regulating mechanisms are superimposed in the intact animal. This mechanism may still be operative, however, and demonstrable again when the more sophisticated regulators have broken down.

To summarize the neural control, therefore, sympathetic stimulation has three effects:

(1) to increase the frequency of the heart beat,

(2) to increase atrial contractility and thus ventricular filling,

(3) to shift the length-tension curve to the left, i.e. greater contractility for the same initial stretch.

Vagal (parasympathetic) stimulation has two effects (fig. 28.42):

(1) to slow the heart beat,

(2) to decrease atrial contractility and hence ventricular filling; it does not affect ventricular contractility (fig. 28.43).

These mechanisms explain the observed response to posture and exercise. In the resting recumbent state the heart rate is slow and the residual volume relatively high. Output is minimal. When the subject stands up the heart rate increases slightly and the residual volume decreases. Cardiac output is unchanged. On exercise, or anticipation of exercise, output rises greatly. At first the increase is mainly due to increased rate. With vigorous exercise stroke volume also increases however, and the contractions are faster and stronger although the input pressure does not rise. Residual volume is minimal. In the human it is possible to study LV stroke work and mean left atrial pressure which approximates to ventricular filling pressure. Fig. 28.44 shows such a plot and the effect of

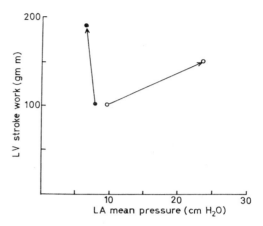

FIG. 28.44. Human heart. Response to exercise of LV stroke work in a normal subject (●) and a patient with myocardial failure (○).

exercise. The process may be looked upon as a shift to another Starling curve under neurohumoral stimulation.

CIRCULATION THROUGH SPECIAL AREAS

The arrangement of the systemic circulation into a number of parallel resistances has already been noted (p. 28.3). Each of these differs in some special respects from the others, and is described separately. In addition, the pulmonary circulation, which is in series with the systemic, has several distinctive features.

Pulmonary circulation

The flow of blood through the lungs is in normal circumstances equal to the systemic flow or cardiac output. The methods for measuring it are therefore the same as for the cardiac output. The pulmonary intravascular pressures can be measured by catheterization of the main pulmonary artery; here the pressure is approximately 20–10 mm Hg above left atrial zero reference level. The mean pulmonary venous pressure may be obtained by wedging the catheter in a pulmonary artery branch. It is 5–10 mm Hg approximately and is closely similar to the mean left atrial pressure. The left atrial pressure may be measured directly by puncturing the interatrial septum from right side to left with a hollow needle introduced inside a cardiac catheter.

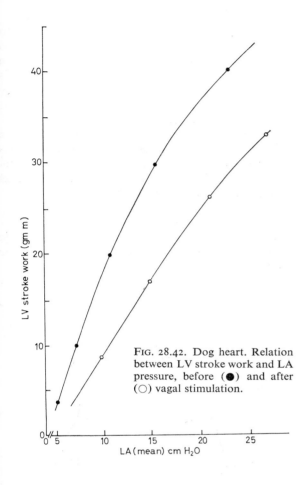

FIG. 28.42. Dog heart. Relation between LV stroke work and LA pressure, before (●) and after (○) vagal stimulation.

FIG. 28.43. Dog heart. Relation between LV stroke work and LV end diastolic pressure at constant heart rate. The open circles show that a vagal stimulation has no effect on the ventricle directly. From Sarnoff and Mitchell (1960).

Anatomically, the pulmonary artery branches follow the distribution of the bronchi throughout the lungs. The structure of the main pulmonary arteries is similar to that of the aorta but the wall is much thinner. There are no muscular arterioles normally in the pulmonary circuit, but a particularly dense capillary network.

The features of the pulmonary circulation are as follows:

(1) a very large blood flow in relation to the weight of the lungs;

(2) a low pressure gradient (5–10 mm Hg) driving the blood through the lungs. Thus there is a very low vascular resistance in the pulmonary circulation, which is only about one-eighth of the systemic resistance;

(3) a short pathway though the lungs in relation to the blood flow, and, compared with the systemic circulation, a low blood volume;

(4) great passive distensibility of the vessels, so that in conditions of increased flow the vascular resistance falls further. Thus a fourfold increase in flow on exercise may be accommodated without significant rise in pulmonary artery pressure.

Pulmonary blood flow is distributed to a vast network of capillaries which perfuse the respiratory exchange area of the alveolar walls. Exchange takes place through two cell layers, the alveolar epithelium and the capillary wall (p. 29.5). Blood passes from one end of the pulmonary capillary to the other in about 1 sec, and in that time gas equilibration is complete.

How is the blood distributed within the lung? The head of pressure under which the lung is perfused is relatively small. In the upright subject the hydrostatic pressure difference from the zero reference at atrial level to the top of the lung accounts for nearly all the available perfusion pressure, and hence blood flow is minimal at the apices of the lungs. Studies in which uptake of radioactive gas has been measured in three zones of the lung show that perfusion is poor in the upper zones and best in the lower zones in the upright subject. On recumbency this gradient disappears.

Arterial blood leaving the lungs is almost fully oxygenated (oxygen saturation 97 per cent). If some of the pulmonary blood flows through poorly ventilated areas of the lung, gas exchange cannot take place and arterial blood then contains an admixture of unchanged venous blood. That this does not occur despite the variations in the number of functioning alveoli known to take place implies that perfusion and ventilation are locally matched by some regulating mechanism. Probably the low PO_2 in poorly ventilated alveoli causes local vasoconstriction, thus shutting off perfusion. This mechanism has been observed in part of one lung, in both lungs, and after removal of the autonomic nerves to the lung vessels. Indeed, this local regulation seems to be the main vasomotor control in the lungs. Unlike the systemic circulation marked reflex effects do not seem to occur and autonomic denervation has little or no effect. The local hypoxic control, however, explains how in collapse or pneumonia of segments of lung, blood flow is shut down, and therefore unoxygenated blood is largely prevented from getting through to the pulmonary veins and so to the arterial side.

In addition to the pulmonary artery blood flow, the bronchi and bronchioles are supplied also via the bronchial arteries from the aorta. This supply is normally about 1 per cent of pulmonary blood flow. The venous drainage is via the pulmonary veins.

Coronary circulation

The two coronary arteries arise just above the aortic valve from the left and anterior sinuses (fig. 28.45). The posterior sinus has no coronary artery.

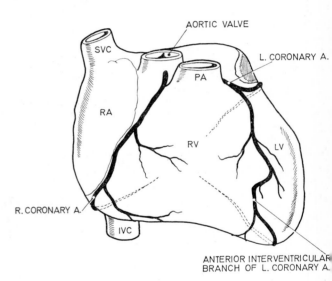

FIG. 28.45. Right and left coronary arteries in frontal view.

The left one divides soon into an anterior interventricular branch, which passes downwards toward the cardiac apex overlying the interventricular septum and a left circumflex branch which passes round the atrioventricular groove to become the posterior descending artery. The right coronary passes round in the same groove, giving a branch to the SA node, and supplying mainly the right ventricle. Normally, and unfortunately, there is little anastomosis between the right and left coronary arterial supplies in contrast to the rich anastomoses in skeletal muscle. Branches of the coronary arteries ramify on the surface of the heart in the epicardium and send penetrating branches through the myocardium.

Venous drainage of the territory of the left coronary artery, mainly the interventricular septum and left ventricle, occurs through the coronary sinus which opens into the right atrium near the tricuspid valve. The **coronary sinus** is a wide channel which represents the left horn of the embryonic sinus venosus (p. 18.18). It lies in the atrioventricular groove on the inferior aspect of the heart. The **great cardiac vein** begins at the apex of the heart and ascends in the anterior interventricular groove until it reaches the atrioventricular groove which it follows around the left margin of the heart to open into the beginning of the coronary sinus. The sinus also receives the middle cardiac vein from the inferior interventricular groove and a small cardiac vein from the right atrioventricular groove. Some of the right coronary artery blood returns via the anterior cardiac veins which open directly into the right atrium. A small amount of the venous drainage occurs directly into the ventricles via small venae cordis minimi.

Any increase in output of the heart calls for increased energy expenditure by the myocardium. All this energy has to be supplied as free fatty acids, lactate and glucose by the coronary artery blood, since the heart can run into metabolic debt for only a brief period. Hence increased cardiac output is dependent on increased coronary flow and the coronary circulation is frequently the limiting factor in exercise tolerance.

Coronary blood flow is measured by the nitrous oxide clearance method. A catheter is placed in the coronary sinus, and a peripheral artery is cannulated for sampling. The subject is given 15 per cent nitrous oxide to breathe for 15 min and the time concentration curves of nitrous oxide in arterial and venous blood are followed until equilibration is reached. Arterial concentration rises to a plateau at once. Coronary sinus blood rises slowly to the same concentration, this point being reached when the myocardium is fully saturated with nitrous oxide. The speed of this saturation is a function of coronary blood flow, which can be estimated in ml/100 ml/min by the formula given on p. 28.30.

Continuous measurement by electromagnetic flowmeter of flow in the left coronary artery shows that, as might be expected, inflow into the myocardium almost ceases during ventricular systole owing to compression of the vessels by the surrounding muscle. Flow in the coronary circuit, particularly the left, therefore takes place predominantly during diastole. A relatively slow heart rate is advantageous to an athlete on two grounds; long diastolic pauses lead to good coronary perfusion, and fewer contractions mean less cardiac work.

Control of coronary blood flow is not well understood. The venous blood in the coronary sinus is fairly fully deoxygenated, even in the resting state, and the arteriovenous difference for O_2 may be as much as 15 ml/100 ml. Hence increased oxygen can only be supplied by increased flow rather than by increased extraction of oxygen.

Coronary blood flow rises on exercise, and with hypoxic respiration. Autonomic stimulation affects profoundly the performance of the heart and thereby coronary flow. It is difficult, therefore, to detect separate coronary vasoconstrictor or dilator effects. Sympathectomy does not increase coronary blood flow. Local control via metabolites and hypoxia seems to be the main determinant of coronary flow.

Cerebral circulation

The brain is an area of relatively high and constant metabolism which is particularly vulnerable to interruption of oxygen supply. The cerebral circulation is adapted to meet these needs.

The whole blood supply of the brain is derived from the internal carotid and vertebral arteries and is described on p. 24.70.

The oxygen consumption of the brain is about 20 per cent of the whole body resting oxygen consumption, some 50 ml/min. Blood flow is normally of the order of 55 ml/100 ml/min or 750 ml/min for the whole brain. The most usual method in man of measuring cerebral blood flow is the nitrous oxide method, which is performed exactly as described under coronary blood except that in this instance the venous samples are taken from the jugular bulb.

The cerebral blood flow is remarkably constant. This constancy is achieved by three mechanisms.

(1) The cerebral vascular system is enclosed in a rigid container, the skull, together with the spinal dura enclosed in the vertebral canal. The volume of blood in this container must be relatively constant, inflow equalling outflow. The intracranial pressure is that of the CSF which is a few cm H_2O higher than the general venous pressure which it follows closely. Because the whole system is rigid, subatmospheric or negative pressure can exist in the venous channels without these channels collapsing.

(2) Though the arterial pressure at head level varies with changes in posture, the arteriovenous pressure difference in the brain remains constant because the pressure in the veins can be negative while the veins themselves remain patent. If the arm is held above the head, the pressure in the digital arteries is lower than the aortic pressure by an amount equal to the hydrostatic pressure difference. The veins of the arm and hand collapse, and pressure within them approximates to the local tissue pressure. The perfusion pressure at the fingers is therefore very low, and the blood flow through them correspondingly reduced. In contrast, however, in the cerebral circulation, while the CSF pressure is negative in the head on standing, the veins within the skull and the vertebral canal are held open and hydrostatic effects balance accurately on the arterial and venous sides. Perfusion pressure thus remains unaltered.

(3) Autoregulation seems to take place to some extent in the cerebral arteries, sudden increase in arterial pressure causing constriction and decrease relaxation of the smooth muscle in the walls.

The cerebral blood vessels appear to be relatively uninfluenced by the autonomic nervous system, and though strong sympathetic stimulation has been observed to cause constriction of pial vessels, sympathectomy does not alter cerebral blood flow. Local chemical control does seem to play a large role. Increase in $P\text{CO}_2$ or decrease in $P\text{O}_2$ of the arterial blood causes an increase in cerebral blood flow, as occurs clinically in chronic lung disease. Breathing high concentrations of oxygen or voluntary hypernoea reduce cerebral blood flow.

Renal circulation see p. 31.11 and **Splanchnic circulation** see p. 30.48.

Skin circulation

The skin represents the largest specialized organ in the body. Its vascular supply, which is described on p. 35.8, is governed not so much by the needs of its own metabolism but by its functions in regulating body temperature by losing or conserving heat. Under normal resting conditions a lightly clothed person in a room at 20°C has a skin blood flow in the region of 5–10 ml/100 ml/min. This value is greater per unit volume than muscle, and less than brain, heart or kidney. The skin blood flow is, however, sensitive to minor changes in sympathetic tone and varies widely from < 1 ml/100 ml/min with vasoconstriction to > 100 ml/100 ml/min with vasodilation in a hot bath.

Skin flow is most easily studied by venous occlusion plethysmography of the fingers of the hand. Less sensitive methods are those of measuring heat loss by calorimetry or change in skin temperature.

Skin blood flow is controlled in a variety of ways.
Local metabolism. When this is increased, for example by heating, locally produced metabolites cause arteriolar dilation and increased blood flow. The most important example of this is **reactive hyperaemia**. Following occlusion of arterial inflow, e.g. by a tourniquet, anoxia develops in the skin and metabolites accumulate. When the circulation is restored there is an immediate large increase in flow which subsides gradually as the metabolites are swept away.

Sensory nerves in the skin give off branches which arborize around the local skin vessels. Sensory stimulation results in local vasodilation via these antidromic impulses, the **axon reflex**. This mechanism persists after proximal section of the sensory nerve, proving its independence of central reflex pathways. The **triple response** to scratching the skin demonstrated by Lewis consists of:

(1) a white reaction, i.e. white streak caused by direct stimulation of vessels to constrict,

(2) a red reaction or flare dilation due to an axon reflex,

(3) a wheal, an elevated central area due to histamine release and capillary damage with extravasation of fluid.
Sympathetic nervous control of skin vessels is highly active and sensitive. Sympathetic constrictor tone is marked in the limbs and vasodilation is brought about by inhibition of this constrictor tone. The parasympathetic system is not involved. Another mechanism exists in addition in areas rich in sweat glands. Sweat gland activity, stimulated by the sympathetic, is accompanied by local production of bradykinin, which is a potent smooth muscle relaxant and this causes further local arteriolar vasodilation.

Mild pain, a sudden noise or a cold stimulus immediately causes reflex skin vasoconstriction. Radiant heat applied to the trunk causes reflex skin dilation. Body heating such as in a warm bath results in warm blood reaching the temperature control centre in the medulla which in turn inhibits sympathetic constrictor tone and increases skin blood flow (fig. 28.46). Blocking

FIG. 28.46. Forearm (●) and hand blood (○) (ml/100 ml/min) before and during indirect body heating. ▲, current (μA) flowing through the forearm skin as an index of sweat gland activity. From Roddie, Shepherd & Whelan (1957), *J. Physiol.* **136**, 489.

or section of the sympathetic nerve supply to a limb results in a large increase of skin blood flow, the hand being hot and, through inhibition of sweating, dry.
Hormones also affect the skin circulation. Adrenaline and noradrenaline both cause vasoconstriction. Oestrogen dilates mildly. Of the posterior pituitary hormones oxytocin dilates the vessels while vasopressin causes a marked skin vasoconstriction, if given in pharmacological doses, but its role in the circulation is doubtful.

Skeletal muscle circulation

A 65 kg man has about 30 kg of skeletal muscle. In the resting state blood flow through muscle is some 2–4 ml/100 ml/min, so that skeletal flow represents about one-fifth of the cardiac output. Under conditions of exercise, however, blood flow to muscle can be expanded to 30–40 ml/100 ml/min.

The artery supplying a muscle usually enters the muscle belly and breaks up into branches which run lengthwise within the muscle, these in turn giving rise to arterioles and capillaries which lie longitudinally between the muscle fibres.

When muscle contracts, the tension rises within and this cuts off the blood flow. During sustained strong contraction, therefore, an oxygen debt is built up and metabolites accumulate. Pain then develops in the muscle from sensory receptor stimulation. On release of the tension reactive hyperaemia occurs. During rhythmic contraction of muscle, flow stops during the contractions and is maximal during the short relaxation periods.

Muscle blood flow is controlled through the following mechanisms.

(1) Local control is effected by accumulation of metabolites and is believed to be dominant and represents a form of autoregulation.

(2) Sympathetic vasoconstrictor tone is present in muscle blood vessels; sympathectomy doubles muscle blood flow (fig. 28.47).

FIG. 28.47. A comparison of the effect of body heating on the blood flow through the nerve-blocked (○) and intact (●) forearm of one subject. From Roddie, Shepherd & Whelan (1957), *Clin. Sci.* **16**, 67.

(3) Sympathetic cholinergic vasodilator fibres are also present, originating not in the pressor centre but in the hypothalamic area. They are stimulated mainly during exercise. Fainting due to strong emotional stimuli is precipitated by muscle vasodilation resulting from discharge of these fibres.

(4) Adrenaline, but not noradrenaline, causes a large vasodilation in muscle vessels.

The distribution of the cardiac output

Measurements of regional blood flows have been made by many observers by the methods described above. Results naturally vary depending on the subject and to a lesser extent on the technique used. The data are, however, sufficiently consistent for the figures given in table 28.4 to be representative of normal men.

TABLE 28.4. An estimate of the distribution of the resting cardiac output in a normal man.

Organ	Weight g	Blood flow ml/min 100 g	Blood flow Total ml/min	Cardiac output %
Liver (including Splanchnic area)	1500	100	1500	30
Brain	1400	50	700	14
Kidneys	300	400	1200	24
Heart	350	63	220	4·4
Skeletal muscles	30,000	2	600	12
Remainder (by difference)			780	15·6
			5000	100

INTEGRATED RESPONSES OF THE CARDIOVASCULAR SYSTEM

Posture

When the subject changes from horizontal lying position to erect standing, the intravascular pressures, referred to atmospheric pressure, change. Pressure in the feet is higher by a hydrostatic factor affecting arteries, capillaries and veins. However, perfusion pressure, i.e. arteriovenous pressure difference, is unaltered. Following movement of water across the capillary wall pressure rises in the tissue spaces to balance the capillary pressure, and if the subject stands immobile for any length of time swelling of the feet occurs. Rhythmic muscular contraction of the legs pumps venous blood headwards by virtue of the venous valves and thus tends to keep venular and capillary pressure low. Veins in the upper part of the body are collapsed and pressure in them approximately equals tissue pressure. A negative pressure relative to atmosphere exists in the CSF and venous sinuses of the brain.

In order to counteract pooling of blood in the capacity vessels of the lower body and to maintain blood pressure at the carotid sinuses, reflex vasoconstriction occurs affecting arterioles, venules and veins. Similar reflex changes affect the heart. The rate of the heart increases slightly and the heart size, both in systole and diastole, decreases. In other words, although the stroke volume is not increased, the residual volume is smaller. The central venous pressure is unchanged and cardiac output is slightly reduced.

As regards regional flow, blood flow through the upper zones of the lungs is decreased through diminished perfusion pressure. Brain circulation is little affected because of the syphon effect, but renal blood flow shows a small reflex diminution.

Exercise

The response to exercise is mainly dependent on neural control mechanisms. It is extremely rapid, and in many instances is evoked before exercise starts by the mere anticipation of exercise. The response of cardiac output to increasing exercise is shown in fig. 42.12. The immediate increase in output is accounted for mainly by a rise in heart rate, though in more severe exercise stroke volume also rises greatly. Central venous pressure generally falls at the start of exercise. The total cardiac response is due to sympathetic stimulation increasing rate and contractility and altering the Starling length tension diagram to the left.

As stroke volume increases, systemic blood pressure usually shows a widened pulse pressure as might be expected, the systolic rising in severe exercise to as much as 200 mm Hg. The diastolic pressure usually rises a little. Since cardiac output increases up to fivefold in severe exercise in a trained athlete with little increase in systemic or pulmonary arterial blood pressure, it follows that both systemic and pulmonary vascular resistances fall. Considerable redistribution of regional blood flow takes place. Sympathetic stimulation reduces renal, splanchnic and skin blood flow, though with sweating, skin flow in certain areas may increase, overriding the constrictor tone. The exercising muscles show an enormous vasodilation, partly due to local metabolic causes and also via sympathetic cholinergic fibres. In prolonged exercise there is a demonstrable rise in the haemoglobin concentration and packed cell volume of the blood, mainly through extravasation of water by capillary filtration in exercising muscles. This circulation of fluid outside the vascular system is shown by the greatly increased lymph flow.

Altitude

Exposure to high altitudes ($> 10,000$ ft) results in circulatory changes. The P_{O_2} of the inspired air and consequently of the arterial blood is low and respiration and cardiac output are reflexly stimulated. Heart rate increases and a relative muscle vasodilation occurs. Other effects of acclimatization to altitude are described in chap. 43.

Blood volume changes

The normal blood volume is about 70 ml/kg or 4–5 litres. Sudden increase in the circulating blood volume as by rapid infusion of 1–2 litres of fluid evokes remarkable compensatory changes. If the fluid contains little or no colloid most of it rapidly passes out of the intravascular space and dilutes the body water. If it has a colloid osmotic pressure comparable with that of blood most stays in the intravascular compartment. Venous pressure tends to rise only after large volumes have been added; the capacity vessels can dilate to accommodate large volumes without rise in pressure. Stimulation of atrial stretch receptors results in inhibition of production of aldosterone and antidiuretic hormone, thus promoting diuresis (p. 33.17).

When a healthy individual donates a pint of blood, the compensatory readjustments within the circulation are so rapid and complete that there are no detectable effects although occasional reactions are psychologically produced.

Sudden loss of 1–2 litres, however, as in accident, burns, or gastrointestinal haemorrhage, results in changes due to the loss of circulating volume, and others to the body's efforts to compensate for it. When fluid is lost from the intravascular compartment, which is under elastic tension throughout, the immediate physical result is a drop in the intravascular pressure. The compensatory changes which occur have the effect of maintaining pressures, both arterial and venous, and of restoring the circulating blood volume.

(1) Baroreceptor reflexes are stimulated and produce a sympathetic discharge. This has four effects:

(a) peripheral systemic vasoconstriction occurs in all areas except the brain and heart, and affects arterioles, venules and veins alike,

(b) the heart rate is increased,

(c) sweating occurs and the skin is cold, pale and moist,

(d) renal blood flow is drastically reduced and urine output may cease.

(2) Beyond the arteriolar constriction, capillary pressure falls, and the remaining blood is diluted by interstitial fluid which to some extent restores the lost circulating volume. This is shown in lowering of the packed cell volume, haemoglobin content and specific gravity of the blood.

(3) Antidiuretic hormone, aldosterone and cortisol are secreted.

Though blood pressure may be well maintained, under filling of the arterial side of the circulation results in a lack of distension in the arterial walls and an easily compressible soft pulse. Sweating occurs through sympathetic discharge, and may cause unwanted skin vasodilation. If muscle vasoconstriction is intense it may be overridden by local dilator mechanisms. Compensatory changes, which are adequate in the horizontal position, may fail on sitting or standing, when venous pressure, cardiac output, blood pressure and brain perfusion pressure may fall in rapid sequence and fainting occur.

SHOCK

When blood loss is severe and blood volume is not restored by transfusion then compensatory changes are inadequate to maintain systemic blood pressure above a level needed to support tissue perfusion. Continuing anaerobic activity in the poorly perfused areas of the body results in metabolic acidosis, shown by a falling pH of the arterial blood and increased pulmonary ventilation. A state of shock is said to exist. Loss of blood volume is an important but not the only cause of shock; a similar state of shock occurs in acute heart failure and in severe infections in which the responsible haemodynamic mechanisms are different.

Temperature Changes

Local heat. If local heat is applied to a part of the body the result is a local vasodilation unaffected by reflex neural effects. The skin becomes red and hyperaemic and the large flow removes heat from the part so that local temperature does not rise so rapidly as it would if the circulation were stopped. This is thus a protective mechanism.

Exposure to a hot environment. The exposure of the body to a hot environment results in a great increase in skin blood flow which assists heat loss at the body surface. This vasodilation occurs in three ways:

(1) reflexly, through radiation falling on the skin surface,

(2) through warm blood reaching the thermoregulatory centre in the medulla; this causes inhibition of sympathetic constrictor tone in the skin vessels,

(3) by sympathetic cholinergic stimulation of sweat glands which, in addition to wetting the body surface and causing heat loss by evaporation, produce bradykinin which causes further arteriolar dilation in the skin.

The great fall in vascular resistance evokes an increase in cardiac output, to maintain blood pressure.

Local cold. If a moderate degree of local cold is applied to a finger, local vasoconstriction occurs. With exposure to severe cold, however ($<4°C$) the phenomenon of **cold vasodilation** occurs and the finger becomes red and feels warm. This is a fluctuating vasodilation which is independent of nerve supply.

Exposure to a cold environment. General exposure to cold results in skin vasoconstriction and piloerection (goosepimples), as a consequence of central increase in vasoconstrictor activities. Blood pressure may rise, and cardiac output fall, i.e. there is a rise in peripheral resistance. Muscle tone is increased and shivering takes place (p. 40).

When temperature homeostasis can no longer be maintained and central temperature falls, a condition of **hypothermia** is said to exist. Direct effects on the heart include (1) depression of the SA node, giving slowing of the heart (2) depression of conduction giving varying degrees of heart block and (3) finally ventricular fibrillation may occur below 30°C.

Increased intrathoracic pressure

When intrapulmonary and intrathoracic pressures are raised as in the **Valsalva manoeuvre**, where the subject takes a deep breath and blows against the closed glottis, or transiently in coughing, the pressure increment is applied to every intrathoracic structure including the vessels. Venous return to the thorax is therefore impeded, and if pressure is maintained, cardiac filling falls and stroke volume and pulse pressure also fall. The carotid sinuses produce fewer afferent impulses, and therefore reflexly sympathetic vasoconstriction and cardioacceleration occur. On release of the Valsalva manoeuvre and return of blood to the heart, the increased peripheral resistance results in a transient overshoot of blood pressure which in turn causes cardiac slowing. This normal pattern of response is obliterated when the venous pressure is abnormally high, since there is then an adequate reservoir under pressure to maintain cardiac filling. A prolonged Valsalva manoeuvre or bout of violent coughing may cause fainting through reduction of cardiac output.

Headward acceleration

One of the effects of exposure to acceleration exceeding the universal 1 g is that the blood becomes abnormally heavy, twice as heavy as normal in the case of acceleration at 2 g. Thus to support a column of blood 13·6 cm high a pressure of 10 mm Hg is required at 1 g (normal), 20 mm Hg at 2 g, 40 mm Hg at 4 g and so on.

Acceleration as in a centrifuge thus causes very high pressure in the lower limb vessels and stresses the body's power to resist pooling of blood in the limbs. Above 4 g an antigravity suit must be worn to prevent pooling. Blood pressure rises to maintain pressure at the carotid sinuses. Loss of vision and unconsciousness occur when the cerebral blood flow falls through lack of adequate perfusion pressure, and the retinae and visual cortex become anoxic.

Mental activity

Mental activity such as performing arithmetical tests is not associated with increased brain metabolism or increased cerebral blood flow (p. 28.37). It does, however, cause certain changes in circulation, all presumably mediated by centrally produced changes in sympathetic activity. Heart rate and cardiac output increase, and there may be a surprising increase in blood pressure. Muscle blood flow also increases, probably through activity of sympathetic vasodilator fibres.

Control and design

Many of the circulatory readjustments in response to changes in posture, activity or environment occur so smoothly and precisely that it is difficult to detect that a change has occurred. In the language of servomechanisms, misalignments are corrected almost before they can be measured. This adds to the difficulty of separating the sites of receptor and effector activity in circulatory control. Broadly speaking, however, certain features of circulatory regulation are apparent.

(1) There is a strongly autonomous local regulation of blood flow in the peripheral tissues. This control can in general override the central circulatory control.

(2) The two pumps which provide the energy of the system are input-sensitive, so that their outputs are precisely matched and venous pressure in both the systemic and pulmonary circuits is stabilized.

(3) A central nervous control, composed of a complex of reflex arcs and servomechanisms, modify the overall resistance to flow of the vessels and the volume and pressure of the venous return, and also the rate and contractility of the heart.

These three aspects of the circulation are all indispensable and damage to any one of them by disease results in a separate and serious disability.

FURTHER READING

BARCROFT H. (1963) Circulation in skeletal muscle, in *Handbook of Physiology*, Section 2, Circulation, ed. Hamilton, Vol. 2, p. 1353. Washington: American Physiological Society.

BING R.J. (1965) Cardiac metabolism. *Physiol. Rev.*, **45**, 171.

BURTON A.C. (1960) Haemodynamics and the physics of the circulation. *Medical Physiology and Biophysics*, 18th Edition, ed. Ruch & Fulton, p. 643. Philadelphia: Saunders.

EVANS J.R. (1964) Structure and function of heart muscle. American Heart Association, Monograph No. 9. *Circulat. Res.* Vol. XV, Suppl. II.

GREENFIELD A.D.M. (1963) The circulation through the skin, in *Handbook of Physiology*, Section 2, Circulation, ed. Hamilton, Vol. 2, p. 1325. Washington: American Physiological Society.

GUYTON A.C. (1963) Venous return, in *Handbook of Physiology*, Section 2, Circulation, ed. Hamilton, Vol. 2, p. 1099. Washington: American Physiological Society.

LANDIS E.M. & PAPPENHEIMER J.R. (1963) Exchange of substances through the capillary walls, in *Handbook of Physiology*, Section 2, Circulation, ed. Hamilton, Vol. 2, p. 961. Washington: American Physiological Society.

LINDEN R.J. (1963) The control of output of the heart. *Recent Advances in Physiology*, 8th Edition, p. 330. London: Churchill.

SCHER A.M. (1960) Electrical correlate of the cardiac cycle. *Medical Physiology and Biophysics*, 18th Edition, ed. Ruch & Fulton, p. 587. Philadelphia: Saunders.

Chapter 29

The respiratory system

Respiration consists of the utilization of oxygen and production of carbon dioxide by living cells, and the means by which the cells exchange these gases with the atmosphere. The basic process is the same throughout the animal kingdom. The atmosphere contains O_2 at a higher partial pressure than the interior of the cells. The direction of transfer of each gas is determined entirely by the pressure gradient between atmosphere and cell.

Fig. 29.1 shows the functional arrangement of the respiratory system in man. An open airway ABCD is

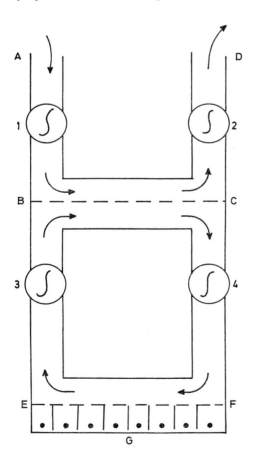

FIG. 29.1. Functional arrangement of the respiratory system. For symbols see text.

separated from a closed blood circuit BEFC by a membrane BC across which O_2 and CO_2 can diffuse. Another membrane EF separates the blood from the tissue cells G. The air at A has an O_2 pressure of about 150 mm Hg and a CO_2 pressure of almost zero. The cells at F have pressures of about 40 and 46 mm Hg for O_2 and CO_2 respectively. These differences in partial pressure between A and F impel O_2 and CO_2 in opposite directions. By itself, this would be an impossibly slow process owing to the distances entailed. Pumps (1, 2, 3, 4), which circulate both gas and blood, increase the speed of gas-transport enormously, and only at the membranes does the transfer of O_2 and CO_2 depend solely on diffusion.

An account of respiratory mechanisms and their operation must therefore cover the following topics:

(1) the **structure of the trachea, bronchi and lungs**;

(2) the **mechanics of breathing**, i.e. the pumps 1 and 2 which are the muscles of inspiration and expiration;

(3) the **pulmonary ventilation**, i.e. the circulation of air;

(4) the **carriage of gases in the blood**;

(5) **diffusion**, i.e. the transfer of gas across the pulmonary membrane;

(6) the **regulation of respiration**, i.e. the way in which the respiratory apparatus is made to serve the needs of the tissues.

Pumps 3 and 4 are of course the right and left ventricles described in the previous chapter.

STRUCTURE OF TRACHEA, BRONCHI AND LUNGS

The respiratory system consists of the lungs, the passages which convey air to and from the lungs, the muscles of the trunk which do the work of breathing and the pleural cavities which permit these movements.

The upper respiratory passages are considered as part of the head and neck (chap. 21). The construction of the thoracic and abdominal walls, including the respiratory muscles, forms a part of the anatomy of the trunk (chap. 20). Hence this account begins with the pleural cavities and then deals with the lungs, trachea and bronchial tree.

The pleural cavities

On each side of the mediastinum, there are two serous cavities with a smooth lining of simple squamous epithelium. These are the two pleural cavities and the lungs invaginate their medial walls, like fists pressed into the sides of almost empty balloons (fig. 29.2). The invagination is so complete that the space between the two layers of pleura is reduced to a narrow gap. The inner visceral layer covers the lung as the pulmonary pleura, while the outer or parietal layer is attached to the walls of the

connects the xiphisternal joint, eighth rib in the mid clavicular line, tenth rib in the mid-axillary line and twelfth thoracic vertebra. Along this curved line (fig 29.3), the pleura is reflected on to the diaphragm, so forming a narrow gutter known as the costodiaphragmatic recess. This is filled by lung only at the end of a deep inspiration. The posterior parts of the pleural cavities descend below the medial part of the twelfth ribs, where they are clinically important as posterior relations of the kidneys. The costal and mediastinal parts of the pleura join along the line of reflexion posterior to the sternum.

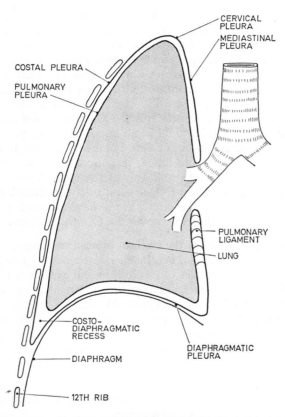

FIG. 29.2. A schematic coronal section through the right lung and pleural cavity.

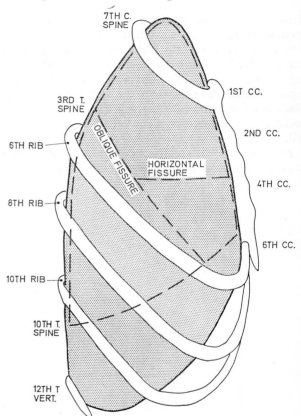

FIG. 29.3. The relation of the right lung and pleura to the thoracic wall.

thorax. When the thorax expands during inspiration, the volume contained by the parietal pleura increases and the air drawn into the lungs causes them to expand within the pulmonary pleura. Thus, with each breath, the pulmonary pleura slides on the parietal layer and a thin film of fluid between the two layers provides the necessary lubrication.

The extent of the parietal pleura determines the maximum possible distension of the lungs. The parietal pleura is named according to the structures which it covers, i.e. there are mediastinal, diaphragmatic, costal and cervical parts (fig. 29.2). The **costal pleura** lines all the ribs, costal cartilages and intercostal spaces down to a line which

These reflections are in the midline except at the upper end where they diverge to the sternoclavicular joints. Also, below the fourth costal cartilage on the left side, the heart and pericardium prevent the sternal reflexion reaching further medially than the left edge of the body of the sternum.

The **mediastinal pleura** passes on to the lung as the pulmonary pleura at the root of the lung. A thin pleural fold, which extends from the root of the lung almost to the diaphragm, is known as the pulmonary ligament (fig. 29.2). The structures covered by the mediastinal pleura are obviously different on the two sides. On the left side, it is applied to the arch and descending thoracic aorta, the pericardium in front of the lung root and the oesophagus close to its opening through the diaphragm. The right mediastinal pleura has only the azygos vein and the vagus nerve intervening between it and the trachea; in front of the trachea the superior vena cava descends to enter the pericardium at the level of the upper part of the root of the lung. As on the left side, the area below and in front of the lung root is related to the pericardium which, on the right side, contains the atrium. On both sides the pleura extends backwards around a broad groove on the sides of the vertebral bodies to join the costal pleura. The two phrenic nerves are closely applied to the mediastinal pleurae and pass in front of the lung roots on their way to the diaphragm.

The **cervical pleura** forms a dome-like projection into the neck through the thoracic inlet. It can be outlined on the surface by a curved line which ascends 2·5 cm above the medial third of the clavicle. The cervical pleura is strengthened by a sheet of connective tissue which runs from the transverse process of the seventh cervical vertebra to the inner margin of the first rib and costal cartilage. The subclavian artery arches in front of the cervical pleura as it passes from the superior mediastinum to the upper surface of the first rib.

The costal and diaphragmatic pleurae are supplied with sensory branches from the intercostal nerves. Pain from inflammation of the pleura is therefore referred to the distribution of these nerves in the thoracic and abdominal walls. The lowest part of the whole pleural cavity is the costodiaphragmatic recess in the mid-axillary line.

The lungs

The first breath, after birth, begins to expand the lungs and within two weeks the whole lung has the light spongy texture which it keeps during life. Its outer surface is covered by pulmonary pleura and the large amount of elastic tissue in the organ can be appreciated by handling a fresh lung.

The lung has an apex which occupies the dome of the cervical pleura and so can be examined clinically by auscultation and percussion above the medial third of the clavicle. The concave base rests on the diaphragm, and the sharp lower border, around the periphery, projects into the costodiaphragmatic recess. The sides of the lung conform to the shape of the pleural cavity; a thick posterior part fits into the broad groove at the side of the thoracic vertebrae and a convex lateral surface is separated by the pleura from the ribs, costal cartilages and intercostal spaces. The anterior border is a thin process pointing towards the midline. In the centre of the medial surface the **root of the lung** is surrounded by a sleeve of pleura which is formed by the continuity of the pulmonary and mediastinal pleurae. Within the root, the pulmonary veins are near the front, the main bronchus is at the back and the pulmonary artery is in the centre. Small bronchial

arteries, numerous lymph nodes and vessels and the pulmonary nerve plexuses are scattered in the connective tissue around these larger structures.

Since the volume of the lungs changes with each breath, it is impossible to define accurately the surface marking of the organ. The upper part of each lung is always in contact with the cervical, mediastinal and upper costal pleura. During inspiration the lower part expands downwards so that it occupies more and more of the costodiaphragmatic recess. At the mid-point of quiet respiration, the lower border of the lung can be marked on the surface by a line joining the tenth thoracic vertebra, the eighth rib in the mid-axillary line, the sixth rib in the mid-clavicular line and the sixth costal cartilage where it joins the sternum. The root of the lung also moves downwards with respiration and on standing erect; at rest, the root is behind a line joining the sternal ends of the second and fourth costal cartilages.

The two lungs are not identical because the heart and pericardium bulge more into the left side of the thorax and the right dome of the diaphragm, covering the liver, is higher than the left dome. Hence the right lung is shorter, broader and slightly larger than the left. Both lungs are divided into lobes by fissures which are lined with pulmonary pleura and which plunge into the substance almost as far as the hilum. An oblique fissure runs from the third thoracic vertebra at the back, crosses the axilla and ends at the lower border of the lung opposite the sixth costochrondral junction (fig. 29.3). The **lower lobes**, below this fissure, therefore include all the base and most of the thick posterior parts of the lung. On the left side the **upper lobe** is not usually divided again, but on the right a horizontal fissure runs from the oblique fissure at the axilla to the fourth costal cartilage at the sternum. This fissure produces a **middle lobe** which has a triangular surface directed to the anterior wall of the chest. The upper lobes are also mainly related to the anterior surface and they constitute the apices of both lungs.

To the left of the lower half of the sternum, the heart and pericardium press towards the chest wall. Hence, the anterior border of the left lung is attenuated and forms a tongue-like process, the lingula. In this region the reflexion of the pleura does not reach the mid-line and the lingula only partially fills the pleural pocket. So below the left fourth costal cartilage, the pericardium is separated from the chest wall only by two thin layers of pleura.

The air passages

The trachea (fig. 29.4), about 25 cm long, runs from the cricoid cartilage of the larynx, at the level of the sixth cervical vertebra, to its bifurcation at the level of the fifth thoracic vertebra. Its course is not vertical, since the upper end is practically under the skin of the neck

THYROID GLAND

6TH C. VERTEBRA

OESOPHAGUS

MANUBRIUM

5TH T. VERTEBRA

AORTA

OESOPHAGUS

FIG. 29.4. The course and main relations of the trachea.

muscles, sternothyroid and sternohyoid, separate the trachea from the deep fascia of the neck and jugular venous arch. The neurovascular bundles of the neck lie on the lateral sides of the trachea.

In the thorax, the arch of the aorta, its branches, the left brachiocephalic vein and the thymus gland intervene between the trachea and the manubrium of the sternum. The left lung and pleura are held away from the trachea by the arch of the aorta and its left subclavian branch, but the apex of the right lung is separated from the trachea only by the pleura, the arch of the vena azygos and the right vagus nerve. Hence, with the use of a stethoscope, breath sounds from the trachea can be heard clearly over the right apex. The bifurcation of the trachea is surrounded by lymph nodes and the pulmonary nerve plexuses.

In the **main bronchi** the rings of cartilage are replaced by irregular cartilaginous plaques. The right bronchus deviates only a little from the line of the trachea, but the left makes a more acute angle. The left bronchus passes under the arch of the aorta and in front of the thoracic descending aorta to reach the root of the left lung. It passes immediately in front of the oesophagus where it can arrest the swallowing of a large object. The branching of the pulmonary trunk and the left pulmonary artery are in front of the left bronchus. The right bronchus passes almost directly into the root of the lung, with the right pulmonary artery in front of it. Before reaching the lung, the right bronchus divides into two branches which pass above and below the pulmonary artery.

LOBAR AND SEGMENTAL BRONCHI (fig. 29.5).
Within the lung the bronchi branch repeatedly to form a tree of tubes carrying air to all parts of the organ. The pulmonary arteries and veins branch with the bronchi, so these three structures form an elastic scaffolding within

and the lower end is only just anterior to the vertebral column. The anterior and lateral walls of the trachea contain sixteen to twenty C-shaped rings of cartilage, while the posterior wall consists of smooth muscle, the trachealis muscle. The cartilaginous rings are joined together by fibroelastic tissue so that the length of this tube can alter with respiratory and neck movements. The oesophagus lies behind the whole length of the trachea; near the cricoid cartilage and at the bifurcation it lies slightly to the left of the trachea. The inferior (recurrent) laryngeal nerves ascend in the grooves between the trachea and oesophagus; on the left side this nerve hooks around the arch of the aorta to reach the groove, while on the right the loop is around the subclavian artery. In the neck the isthmus of the thyroid gland crosses in front of the third, fourth and fifth tracheal rings with the lateral lobes of the gland clasping the sides of the trachea. As the thyroid is attached to the trachea and larynx by the pretracheal fascia, it moves during swallowing. The inferior thyroid veins descend in front of the trachea below the isthmus. Anterior to these veins and the thyroid, the strap

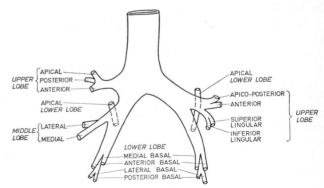

UPPER LOBE — APICAL, POSTERIOR, ANTERIOR

APICAL LOWER LOBE

MIDDLE LOBE — LATERAL, MEDIAL

APICAL LOWER LOBE

APICO-POSTERIOR, ANTERIOR

SUPERIOR LINGULAR, INFERIOR LINGULAR

UPPER LOBE

LOWER LOBE — MEDIAL BASAL, ANTERIOR BASAL, LATERAL BASAL, POSTERIOR BASAL

FIG. 29.5. The main lobar and segmental bronchi.

each lung. The larger branches of the bronchi are important clinically since they supply discrete segments of lung tissue. Fig. 29.5 shows the usual pattern of branching and each named branch leads to a bronchopulmonary egment. With dichotomous branching the diameter of he tube diminishes and when the lumen falls to about ›·2 mm in diameter the tube is known as a **bronchiole**. Further division of the bronchioles continues until the

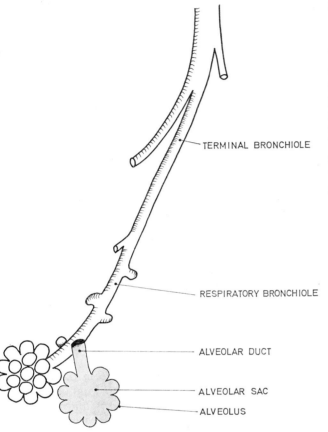

FIG. 29.6. The conducting and respiratory portions of the lung.

last division produces the **terminal bronchioles** (fig. 29.6). All the tubes mentioned so far have relatively thick walls and they form the **conducting portion of the lung**; the air contained in this portion does not exchange gases with the blood and this volume of air corresponds to the

'anatomical dead space' (p. 29.16). Beyond the terminal bronchiole, a more thinly walled tube, the **respiratory bronchiole**, has **alveoli** protruding from its wall; this is the beginning of the **respiratory portion of the lung**, which consists of the alveolar ducts, alveolar sacs and alveoli.

Microscopic structure

The lung is designed to expose the largest possible film of blood to moist air. The blood must be brought as close as possible to the air so that gaseous exchanges can take place. The contained air must be changed and the rate of change must vary according to the demand for oxygenation. The entry of foreign particles, such as dusts and bacteria, must also be prevented. It is interesting to consider how the histological structure of the organ fulfils these functions. A summary of the histology of the respiratory tract is given in table 29.1.

Gaseous interchange occurs in the respiratory portion of the bronchial tree, i.e. the **alveolar ducts** and **sacs** and the **alveoli** which lead from the respiratory bronchioles. The total area of the surface is over 50 m². All these cavities are lined by simple squamous alveolar epithelium, and they are surrounded by a meshwork of pulmonary capillaries. Thus, the blood–air barrier (fig. 29.7) consists of the alveolar wall and a capillary endothelium;

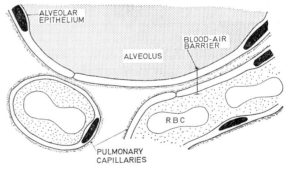

FIG. 29.7. The structure of the alveolar wall as shown by EM.

TABLE 29.1. The histology of the respiratory tract.

	Diameter mm	Epithelium	Goblet cells	Compound glands	Cartilage	Smooth muscle	Elastic tissue
Conducting portion							
Trachea	15	Ciliated stratified columnar	+	+	+ +	+	+ +
Large bronchi	8–2	Pseudo-stratified ciliated columnar	+	+	+ + +	+	+ +
Small bronchi	2–0·5	,, ,, ,,	+	—	+	+ + +	+ +
Bronchioles	0·5–0·2	Simple ciliated columnar	±	—	—	+ + +	+ +
Respiratory portion							
Respiratory bronchioles	0·2	Simple cubical	—	—	—	+	+
Alveolar ducts	0·2	Simple squamous	—	—	—	+	+
Alveolar sacs	0·3	,, ,,	—	—	—	+	+
Alveoli	0·1	,, ,,	—	—	—	?	+

both these layers are thin and the whole barrier is less than 1 μm thick. Each alveolus is a small cavity with its mouth opening into an alveolar sac; the whole substance of the lung, apart from the bronchial tree and its associated vessels, is composed of alveoli. The alveolar sac is the expanded end of an alveolar duct, three or four of which arise from each respiratory bronchiole. The bronchiole is lined by simple non-ciliated cubical epithelium, which probably does not permit gaseous exchange.

During its passage from the nostrils to the respiratory bronchioles, the air is filtered, moistened and warmed. The process starts in the conchi of the nasal cavities, with their richly vascularized epithelium, and continues throughout the whole length of the conducting portion of the lung. Particulate matter is removed by the lining of this portion through cilial activity and mucous secretion. In the trachea, the mucosa has a ciliated stratified columnar epithelium with goblet cells and numerous mucous and serous secreting glands with ducts opening through the epithelium. The mucous secretions provide a sticky slimy layer which traps the particles, and then the mucus and its contents are moved upwards by the beating action of the cilia. Coughing is a violent expiration which propels this material towards the larynx. After passing through the larynx it is usually swallowed, but if increased in quantity due to inflammation it forms sputum. Since the epithelium in the trachea is stratified, there is a supply of cells capable of regeneration to replace damaged tissue in this exposed lining.

The lining is similar with the same functions in the lobar and segmental bronchi. But as the liability to cell damage and replacement diminishes the epithelium becomes thinner with fewer undifferentiated regenerating cells. In the smaller bronchi the epithelium is reduced to a single layer of columnar ciliated cells; there are no compound glands so the only secretion is the mucus from the goblet cells in the epithelium itself. Goblet cells are not present in the smaller bronchioles, but the cilia continue as far as the terminal bronchioles and fine particles carried down to the terminal bronchioles are usually coughed up; if they pass further, they are ingested in the lumen of the alveoli by macrophages, known as 'dust cells'. These may pass up the bronchial tree and be ejected by coughing but some pass into the lymphatics and enter the lymph nodes at the hilum of the lung. The black, carbon-loaded lymph nodes in the lung of an adult city dweller contain inhaled particles which have escaped the protective process. Even heavily laden glands contain only a minute proportion of the particles inhaled during a lifetime.

Patency of the airway is ensured by the presence of rigid supports in the walls of the larger passages. If these were collapsible, any attempt to draw air into the lungs would seal them together; it would resemble trying to fill a rubber balloon by pulling outwards on the bag. Thus the nostrils are kept open by the nasal cartilages, the cavity of the nose is surrounded by bone and the larynx by cartilage. The trachea is braced by the incomplete rings of cartilage and the main, lobar and segmental bronchi have almost contiguous plates of cartilage in their walls. Occasional cartilaginous plaques are found in the walls of smaller bronchi and the bronchioles depend on the elastic tension of the surrounding lung substance to keep them patent.

The **diameter of the bronchial tree** is controlled by smooth muscle under autonomic nervous control. It is easier to control irrigation by damming the smaller streams than by regulating the main river. In the same fashion, the main control of the airway is exerted by circular smooth muscle around the terminal and other small bronchioles. It is this smooth muscle which contracts to produce the symptoms of asthma. In the larger bronchi, smooth muscle connects the cartilaginous plaques and in the trachea it is mainly longitudinally disposed in the posterior wall. In these larger tubes the smooth muscle assists the elastic tissue in keeping the tubes straight and taut in all stages of breathing. There is some muscle in the walls of the respiratory bronchioles and alveolar ducts but the main control is in the small bronchioles.

The ganglion cells and nerve fibres of the **pulmonary nerve plexuses** extend along the walls of the bronchi. Parasympathetic fibres are derived from the vagus nerves and sympathetic fibres are added from the upper four thoracic segments. Apart from the motor supply to the smooth muscle, secretomotor fibres are distributed to the glands of the bronchial tree and sensory fibres from stretch receptors in the lung pass through the plexus to serve reflex control mechanisms (p. 29.22).

The **elasticity** of the lung substance and bronchial tree provides the expiratory force in quiet breathing. The film of fluid between the two layers of pleura holds the lung out against the chest wall against the pull of the elastic tissue towards the hilum. If air is allowed to enter the pleural cavities, the lung collapses on to its hilum by the traction of its own elastic tissue (pneumothorax). The elastic fibres of the larger bronchi and trachea are arranged in two sheets, one inside and one outside the layer of muscle and cartilage. The inner layer keeps the mucosa corrugated in longitudinal folds. The alveoli and alveolar ducts also have an investment of elastic tissue.

The **lymphatic tissues** are widely distributed throughout the respiratory tract. The pharyngeal, palatine and lingual tonsils form a ring of lymphoid tissue around the entrance to the system. Numerous lymph vessels follow the bronchial tree to drain into the bronchopulmonary lymph nodes at the divisions of the larger bronchi. In turn, these drain into the tracheobronchial nodes at the bifurcation, from which the efferent vessels form the mediastinal lymph trunks. A superficial lymph plexus under the pulmonary pleura communicates with the lymph vessels in the lung substance.

DEVELOPMENT OF THE TRACHEA AND LUNGS

The mucosa of the lungs, trachea and larynx is developed from the endoderm of the ventral wall of the foregut. A longitudinal laryngotracheal groove appears in the ventral wall and later its lips begin to fuse at the caudal end. The fusion is not complete as the open upper end remains as the entrance to the larynx. Thus, a caudally projecting diverticulum is formed which lies on the ventral side of the developing oesophagus. The end of this diverticulum branches to form the two lung buds, which produce the definitive lung simply by growth and progressive branching.

The pleural cavities are derived from the primitive coelom and so they were originally continuous with the pericardium and peritoneum. The growth of the lungs causes the pleural cavities to enlarge into the chest wall until they almost completely surround the pericardium (fig. 18.23).

RESPIRATORY FUNCTIONS

SYMBOLS IN RESPIRATORY PHYSIOLOGY

In 1950, respiratory physiologists introduced a set of symbols (table 29.2) with which they developed ideas about the relation of the factors which determine respiratory exchanges. As a result, they have made their subject much more precise and scientific. The symbols are now widely used by physiologists and also by physicians and anaesthetists.

THE MECHANICS OF BREATHING

During respiration the lungs and thorax expand and contract rather like bellows. This requires the performance of mechanical work against forces which resist these movements. The truth of this statement will be obvious to anyone who has undertaken vigorous physical exercise, and we speak appropriately of 'laboured breathing'. Discussion of respiratory mechanics requires the use of physical terms. Force, pressure, work and energy are defined in chap. 4.

A **frictional force** is set up when one body moves over another, and its magnitude is determined by the nature and extent of the apposed surfaces. It does not exist until the moving force is applied, and opposes it. During the flow of liquids and gases, friction is set up between

TABLE 29.2. Symbols used in respiratory physiology.

Gases

Primary symbols		*Examples*	
V	gas volume		
$\dot{V}$	gas volume/unit time	$\dot{V}_{O_2}$	O_2 consumption/min
P	gas pressure		
F	fractional concentration in dry gas		
D	diffusing capacity		
R	exchange ratio (respiratory quotient)	R	$\dot{V}_{CO_2}/\dot{V}_{O_2}$

Secondary symbols			
I	inspired gas	F_{I,O_2}	O_2 concentration in inspired gas
E	expired gas	$\dot{V}_E$	ventilation rate/min
A	alveolar gas	P_{A,CO_2}	partial pressure of CO_2 in alveolar gas
T	tidal gas	V_T	tidal volume
D	deadspace gas	$\dot{V}_D$	deadspace ventilation rate/min
B	barometric	P_B	barometric pressure

Blood

Primary symbols			
Q	volume of blood		
$\dot{Q}$	blood-flow/unit time		
C	concentration of gas in blood phase	C_{a,O_2}	ml O_2 in 100 ml arterial blood
S	saturation of Hb, per cent		

Secondary symbols			
a	arterial blood	P_{a,CO_2}	partial pressure of CO_2 in arterial blood
v	venous blood	$S_{\bar{v}O_2}$	O_2 saturation in mixed venous blood
c	pulmonary capillary blood	$\dot{Q}_c$	pulmonary capillary blood-flow/min

In addition, we have:

f = respiratory frequency in breaths/min.
STPD = Standard temperature (0°C) pressure (760 mm Hg) and dry.
BTPS = Body temperature and pressure and saturated with water vapour.

Lung volumes and ventilation rates are expressed at BTPS, because they 'exist' in the body at this temperature and pressure. On the other hand O_2 uptake and CO_2 output are related directly to chemical reactions and must be expressed in absolute terms; they are therefore corrected to STPD.

— Dash above a symbol denotes a mean value.
· Dot above a symbol denotes a time-derivative, usually 'per minute'.

In respiratory physiology the chemical symbol N_2 includes the inert gases as well as nitrogen.

their molecules and between these and the wall of the conducting vessel.

Elasticity, a property of solid materials, may be defined as resistance to deformation. When a particular body, made of a given material, is being considered, the term **elastance** is used. Thus the elasticity of steel is constant, but the elastance of a steel spring depends upon its length, number of coils, diameter and gauge. Elastance, for practical purposes the more useful unit, is the stretching or compressing force which must be applied to a particular body in order to produce unit change in its length. In the case of a perfectly elastic body, equal increments in force cause equal increments in length (Hooke's Law). No material is perfectly elastic and there is always a limit to the range over which the law applies. The reciprocal of elastance is **compliance**, which expresses the 'stretchability' of a body as change in length per unit change in stretching force.

When an elastic body is stretched or compressed, work has been done since a force has acted over a distance. This work is stored in the body as potential energy which can be expended as work as the body returns to its original state. The work done in winding the spring of a clock is stored as energy, which is then expended as work against the frictional forces between the clock's moving parts. The energy of a deformed spring suddenly released is dissipated as heat and sound.

Although rubber is elastic, the relation between the pressure and volume within a rubber balloon does not conform to an elastic pattern. Anyone who has blown up a balloon knows that there is first a stage in which resistance to inflation increases steeply; when the balloon reaches a certain size the resistance 'gives' and inflation then becomes easier. A 'pressure-volume diagram' (fig. 29.8) shows first the steep increase in pressure with volume, due to elasticity, but at the inflection (*A*) the pressure within the balloon (the deforming force) actually falls as more air is introduced. Similarly, the pressure inside small soap bubbles is greater than that in big ones, and is in inverse ratio to their radii. Structurally, the

FIG. 29.9. (a) Laminar flow. Axial flow is faster than peripheral flow. (b) Turbulent flow.

lungs could be compared to clusters of tiny balloons and so might be expected to behave like a balloon or soap bubble on inflation. In fact they do not, but resemble a stretched spring.

Flow of gas through tubes is laminar at slow speeds, but at faster rates of flow molecular collisions set up eddies and the flow is then turbulent (fig. 29.9). Laminar flow obeys the Poiseuille equation (p. 28.17). The difference in pressure of the gas between the entry and exit of the tube is directly proportional to flow rate. The pressure/flow ratio is analogous to voltage/current in electricity, and expresses resistance to flow. For laminar flow, resistance is inversely related to the fourth power of the radius of the tube. For turbulent flow, the pressure-difference is proportional to the square of the flow rate and resistance inversely related to the fifth power of the tube's radius. Flow is usually partly laminar and partly turbulent, and pressure-difference is related to flow raised to the power *n*, where *n* lies between 1 and 2.

Physiological experiments cannot be controlled as precisely as physical ones, and while the laws of physics must be obeyed in biological systems no less than on the physicist's bench, the inability to allow for every variable makes physiology a relatively inexact science. The terms and concepts of physics are, however, useful in the description and understanding of many physiological processes.

FORCES AND PRESSURES ACTING ON THE THORAX AND LUNGS

Movements of the chest during the respiratory cycle are opposed by two kinds of forces which must be overcome by contraction of the respiratory muscles. These forces are (a) elastic and (b) non-elastic or 'viscous'.

Elastic forces

When a hole is made in the chest wall of a fresh cadaver, the lungs collapse and the thorax expands, air entering

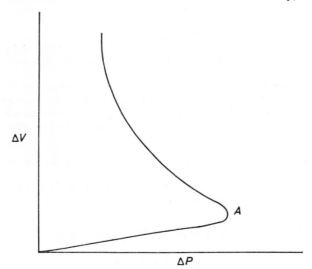

FIG. 29.8. Pressure-volume diagram during inflation of a rubber balloon.

the space formed by separation of the pleural membranes. These movements are due to elastic recoil of the lungs and chest. At the end of a quiet expiration, with the glottis open and the respiratory muscles relaxed, the elastic forces of the lungs and thorax are just balanced; the lungs then contain about 2 litres of air. The elastic forces of the lungs, if unopposed, would empty them; those of the thorax would expand it to correspond with a lung volume of about 4 litres. At lung volumes greater than this, the elastic forces of the thorax act inwards, towards their neutral position at about 4 litres. In apposition, the lungs and thorax form an elastic system on which work must be done by the respiratory muscles.

THE INTRATHORACIC (INTRAPLEURAL) PRESSURE
Imagine that a small amount of air has been introduced between the pleural layers, and that the pressure in this space is P_T (fig. 29.10). The pressure outside the thorax

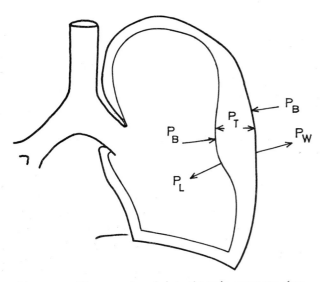

FIG. 29.10. The genesis of intrathoracic pressure (see text). P_B, Barometric and alveolar pressure; P_T, Intrathoracic pressure; P_L, 'Lung pressure' due to elasticity of lung; P_W, 'Chest wall pressure' due to thoracic elasticity with or without muscular forces.

is atmospheric, P_B, and when the airway is open and there is no flow of air into or out of the lungs the pressure within the lungs is also P_B. The retractile, elastic force of the lungs, when expressed per unit pleural surface area, becomes the 'lung pressure', P_L. The 'chest wall pressure', P_W, is derived from thoracic elasticity, with or without additional forces applied by the respiratory muscles. When no movement of air is taking place, and the airway is open, the pressures shown in fig. 29.10 must balance. Thus:

$$P_L + P_T + P_B = P_W + P_T + P_B \qquad (1)$$

Therefore

$$P_L = P_W$$

If we consider only the pressures acting on the visceral pleura, then under the same conditions these also balance. At two degrees of inflation, therefore:

$$P_1L + P_1T = P_B \qquad (2)$$

and

$$P_2L + P_2T = P_B \qquad (3)$$

Now if P_2L is greater than P_1L, as it would be at a greater lung inflation, P_2T must be less than P_1T. In other words intrathoracic pressure falls with inspiration. Further, since P_L is never zero, P_T is always less than P_B in the static condition with an open airway. P_T is usually measured with reference to P_B; it varies, during quiet breathing, from -2 cm H_2O in expiration to -7 cm H_2O in inspiration. This is what is meant by the term 'negative pressure', which is confusing and inexact, because pressure is never negative. 'Subatmospheric pressure' is a better term.

Under some conditions P_T exceeds P_B. During forced expiration P_T may have to be raised above P_B to propel air towards the mouth at high speed; this is achieved by contraction of the expiratory muscles so that P_W acts forcibly inwards. Again, even in the static condition, P_T can be raised above P_B by an expiratory effort against a closed glottis. A violent coughing attack, for instance, may raise P_T 200 mm Hg above P_B. Some wind instruments, notably the trumpet and oboe, require a high mouth pressure but a low volume flow of air; here the experts learn suitable tricks with soft palate and buccinator to avoid having to perform a continuous Valsalva manoeuvre (p. 28.41).

PRESSURE-VOLUME CHARACTERISTICS
OF THE LUNG
The pressure tending to inflate the lung (the **transpulmonary pressure**) is $P_B - P_T$ (fig. 29.10). The pressure opposing inflation (P_L) is due to the elastic recoil of the lung. The relation between lung volume and transpulmonary pressure gives information about the elastic recoil and is shown in fig. 29.11. Lung volume is measured with a spirometer and P_T through a saline-filled polyethylene tube, with its tip at mid-oesophagus, to avoid having to puncture the pleura; changes in oesophageal pressure adequately reflect changes in P_T. Each plotted point in fig. 29.11 represents a pair of measurements made with the chest stationary and the airway open.

The points fall on a straight line, like those for a stretched spring and not as for an inflated balloon (fig. 29.8). Elastance of the lungs (usually termed **elastic**

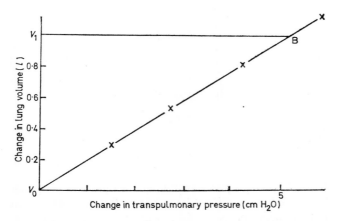

FIG. 29.11. Static pressure-volume diagram of lungs. V_0 and V_1 represent two degrees of inflation. B is the transpulmonary pressure at V_1.

resistance) is given by the change in transpulmonary pressure divided by the change in lung volume (BV_1/V_0V_1) in fig. 29.11. In absolute units, this means dyne cm^{-2} divided by cm^3, or dyne cm^{-5}. A spring's elastance is expressed as force divided by length, or dyne cm^{-1}. The physical parallel is therefore inexact. Also, since the absolute units of resistance are dyne sec cm^{-5}, it is, strictly speaking, no more accurate to use the term 'elastic resistance'. Compliance of the lungs, the reciprocal of elastance, is given by V_0V_1/BV_1 in fig. 29.11 and is normally about 0·2 l/cm H_2O. Elastance is therefore 5·0 cm H_2O/litre.

Elastic work is given by the area V_0BV_1 in fig. 29.11 for an inflation corresponding to V_0V_1. This area has the units pressure × volume, or in absolute units dyne cm^{-2} cm^3. These units reduce to dyne cm, or force × length. Physically, therefore, they are valid.

PRESSURE-VOLUME CHARACTERISTICS OF THE THORAX

If, instead of transpulmonary pressure in fig. 29.11, we were able to measure the effective distending pressure (**transthoracic pressure**) of the lungs and thorax combined, we could gain information about thoracic elasticity. To do this it is necessary to substitute an external source of energy for the respiratory muscles. The body is enclosed up to the neck in an airtight box (body respirator) inside which the pressure is varied by means of a pump. The muscles of respiration must be completely relaxed, either voluntarily or, since this is very difficult, by curarization. The difference between the pressure in the box and the atmospheric pressure is the transthoracic pressure. Thoracic elastic resistance is the difference between the resistance of the lungs and thorax combined (obtained from a pressure-volume diagram like fig. 29.11) and the resistance of the lungs alone. The measure-

ment of thoracic elastance is obviously rather difficult and it is fortunate that the elastic properties of the lungs are of greater clinical importance.

COMPONENTS OF LUNG ELASTICITY

Why the lungs behave more like a spring than a balloon or soap bubble is obscure, but is presumably related to pulmonary structure. The elastic properties of balloons are confined to their walls, corresponding in the lung to the pleura. On the other hand, the lung's elastic fibres form a system of branching springs, connecting the pleura with the hilum and also operating at right angles to this radial direction, parallel to the pleural surface. This may explain the difference in behaviour.

The honeycomb structure of the pulmonary elastic tissue ensures, in health, that not only the lung as a whole but each alveolus is endowed with the appropriate retractile capacity. This helps to equalize respiratory excursions in different parts of the lungs. Local destruction of elastic tissue in disease leads to grossly uneven ventilation.

Elastic fibres are not the only source of the lung's elasticity. Lining each alveolus is a liquid film, and surface tension exists in the interface between this film and the alveolar gas. This surface force tends to collapse the alveolus; the smaller the alveolus the greater should this tendency be, to judge from the ability of a small soap-bubble to blow up a big one connected to it. This behaviour of soap bubbles, however, depends on the fact that surface tension is independent of surface area. The surface tension of the liquid lining the alveoli, on the contrary, diminishes as the area gets smaller, thus reducing the tendency to collapse. This remarkable property probably helps to stabilize the size of alveoli. The surface tension in the alveoli may be lowered by the presence in the fluid lining the alveoli of a lipoprotein, which is a surface wetting agent and known as **surfactant**. Deficiency of surfactant may be a cause of the failure of the lungs to expand in the newborn (p. 39.4).

Non-elastic forces

Movement of air through the conducting passages and sliding of parietal and visceral pleural surfaces over each other set up frictional forces which must be overcome during the respiratory cycle. So far we have been careful to consider only the static condition. Movement of air immediately introduces frictional forces.

In fig. 29.12, change in lung volume is plotted against change in intrathoracic pressure (transpulmonary pressure with a minus sign) from measurements made continuously throughout a single respiratory cycle. V_0 and B again represent the static points at expiration and inspiration respectively, and correspond with V_0 and B in fig. 29.11. The line joining them is, however, no longer straight but forms a loop with upstroke and downstroke (V_0AB and

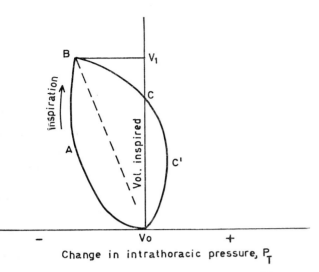

inspiration

Vol. inspired

B

A

V_1

C

C'

V_0

−   +

Change in intrathoracic pressure, P_T

FIG. 29.12. 'Dynamic' pressure-volume diagram of lungs. Redrawn from Cooper E.A., *Behaviour of Respiratory Apparatus*, Medical Research Memorandum 2. London: National Coal Board.

$BCC'V_0$). During inspiration, P_T falls considerably before pulmonary volume increases much, and during expiration the initial rise in P_T occurs without much change in lung volume. Changes in volume lag behind those in pressure. A pressure difference between mouth and alveoli must be established before air will move; friction must be overcome. Work against friction is given by the area V_0ABV_0 for inspiration and $V_0BC'V_0$ for expiration. The total inspiratory work, elastic plus frictional, is equal to the area $V_0ABV_1V_0$. This must be supplied by the inspiratory muscles. At volume V_1 the elastic work, $V_0BV_1V_0$, is stored in the elastic tissue and is available to do frictional work during expiration. Of the stored energy, V_0BCV_0 is used to provide expiratory frictional work, while the remainder (BV_1CB) is 'wasted' elastic energy which appears as heat. The remaining frictional work of expiration, $V_0CC'V_0$, has to be performed by the expiratory muscles.

In quiet breathing, the low airflow requires little frictional work and the loop $V_0ABCC'V_0$ is correspondingly slender; C' may, indeed, lie to the left of the line V_0V_1. In this case all the expiratory frictional work can be provided by the stored elastic energy and the expiratory muscles do no work. Expiration is passive. But area BV_1CB is bigger, representing a bigger waste of elastic energy.

Not all the frictional work $V_0ABCC'V_0$ is expended in moving air; some of it is used in moving viscera. Techniques have been devised by which the non-elastic resistance to breathing (termed, unhelpfully, **pulmonary resistance**) may be broken down into two components; (a) resistance to airflow or **airway resistance** and (b) resistance due to visceral displacement.

RESPIRATORY FREQUENCY AND RESPIRATORY WORK

Pulmonary ventilation rate, or simply **ventilation** ($\dot{V}E$) is defined as the volume of gas expired from the lungs per minute, and is expressed at BTPS. $\dot{V}E$ is slightly less than the inspired rate ($\dot{V}I$) because usually more O_2 is taken from the inspired gas than CO_2 added to it ($R < 1\cdot0$). **Tidal volume** (VT) is obtained by dividing $\dot{V}E$ by the respiratory frequency (f). At rest, $\dot{V}E$ is about 6 l/min, VT about 500 ml and f about 12 per min, but there is much variation in these figures (p. 29.13).

In fig. 29.12, tidal volume (VT) is ($V_1 - V_0$). If this is doubled, area $V_0BV_1V_0$ will increase four times; if trebled, inspiratory elastic work per breath (WEL) increases nine times. That is,

$$\text{WEL} \propto (VT)^2 \tag{4}$$

Let $\dot{V}E$ remain constant while VT is doubled; f must be halved. If VT is trebled, f must fall to one-third, and so on. That is,

$$\dot{V}T \propto \frac{1}{f} \tag{5}$$

The elastic work per min is equal to elastic work per breath multiplied by the respiratory frequency. Thus, from equation 4,

$$\dot{W}\text{EL} \propto (VT)^2 \times f \tag{6}$$

Substituting VT from equation 5, we have:

$$\dot{W}\text{EL} \propto \frac{1}{f} \tag{7}$$

In fig. 29.13 $\dot{W}$EL is plotted against f at constant $\dot{V}E$.

Consider now what happens to frictional work when VT and f are reciprocally altered, $\dot{V}E$ remaining constant. If f doubles, half as big a VT traverses the airway in half the time; the mean flow rate, $\dot{V}$, is the same. For laminar flow,

$$(P_2 - P_1) \propto \dot{V} \tag{8}$$

Now work equals pressure-change × volume-change, and work/min against flow-resistance equals pressure gradient × flow rate. For frictional work/min,

$$\dot{W}\text{FR} \propto (P_2 - P_1) \times \dot{V}$$

From equation (8)

$$\dot{W}\text{FR} \propto \dot{V}^2 \propto \dot{V}E^2 \tag{9}$$

and since $\dot{V}E$ by definition is constant, $\dot{W}$FR is independent of f.

We should therefore expect that for a given $\dot{V}E$, since only $\dot{W}$EL changes with f (equation 7), respiratory work would be minimal when f is high. Physiologically, however, the 'choice' of frequency involves a rather different

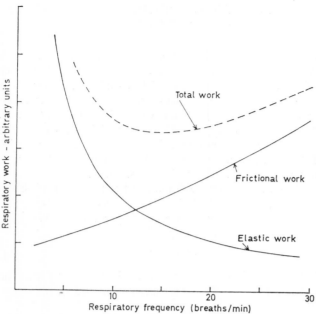

FIG. 29.13. The relation between respiratory frequency and respiratory work.

problem; it is to choose a $\dot{V}_E$, a V_T and a frequency which provides an **alveolar ventilation** ($\dot{V}_A$) appropriate to the needs of the moment. In the next section it will be seen that

$$\dot{V}_E = \dot{V}_A + V_D \times f$$

Then, from equation (9)

$$\dot{W}_{FR} \propto (\dot{V}_A + V_D \times f)^2$$
$$\propto \dot{V}_A^2 + 2\dot{V}_A . V_D . f + V_D^2 . f^2 \qquad (10)$$

Equation (10) shows that for a given $\dot{V}_A$, frictional work increases as a square function of f. Moreover, at constant $\dot{V}_A$, $\dot{W}_{EL}$ does not decrease quite so fast with increasing f as equation (7) would suggest, since $\dot{V}_E$ has to rise gradually. The situation is in fact quite complex. But we might expect that for a given alveolar ventilation $\dot{W}_{EL}$ should decrease and $\dot{W}_{FR}$ increase, with increasing frequency, in curvilinear fashion as shown in fig. 29.13. Adding elastic and frictional work, there should be an optimal frequency at which total respiratory work is minimal. Experiment bears this out, although there is a short range of frequencies over which total work changes little. The natural respiratory frequency falls within this range. How the adjustment is made is not understood, but respiratory work seems to be a factor in regulating the balance between V_T and f. A disease which alters elastic or frictional work is accompanied by the appropriate shift in respiratory frequency.

RESPIRATORY WORK DURING EXERCISE

Reasonable assumptions lead to the prediction that during exercise the following relationships should apply:

$$\dot{W}_{EL} \propto (\dot{V}_E)^2 \qquad (11)$$
$$\dot{W}_{FR} \propto (\dot{V}_E)^2 \quad \text{for laminar flow} \qquad (12)$$
$$\propto (\dot{V}_E)^3 \quad \text{for turbulent flow} \qquad (13)$$

From fig. 29.13 it has been shown that as $\dot{W}_{FR}$ increases less elastic energy is wasted during expiration; area $V_0ABCC'V_0$ approaches more and more closely to the total work per breath, $V_0ABV_1CC'V_0$. Thus at high $\dot{V}_E$ respiratory work is accounted for almost entirely by the frictional work, and equation 11 can be ignored. Combining equations 12 and 13, for all values of $\dot{V}_E$ found in exercise, we have approximately:

$$\dot{W}_{FR} \propto (\dot{V}_E)^n \qquad (14)$$

where n lies between 2 and 3.

Experiments in which $\dot{V}_E$ increased up to 120 l/min have shown a value for n of 2·12. This figure suggests that in the normal airway the flow of gas remains to a large extent laminar even during exercise, a tribute to good aerodynamic design.

THE OXYGEN COST OF BREATHING

A muscle's O_2 consumption is a good index of the work it is performing. Respiratory work can be expressed in this way. O_2 uptake has been measured in resting subjects, at each of several ventilation rates, during voluntary overbreathing. Fig. 29.14 shows the result. In health, $\dot{V}_{O_2}$ increases by 0·5–1·0 ml/min for every l/min increase in $\dot{V}_E$. The increase tends to grow as $\dot{V}_E$ rises,

FIG. 29.14. O_2 uptake of respiratory muscles at different ventilation rates in normal and diseased persons with emphysema. Redrawn from Campbell, Westlake & Cherniack (1957). *J. appl. Physiol.* **11**, 303.

consistent with equation 14. However, it remains relatively trivial; in heavy exercise $\dot{V}_{O_2}$ rises from a resting value of 250 ml/min to over 2500 ml/min, while $\dot{V}_E$ increases from 6 to 50 l/min and the O_2 cost of breathing rises by only 20 ml/min (fig. 29.14). This calculation assumes that the O_2 cost of breathing is the same, at a given $\dot{V}_E$ during exercise as at rest; this cannot be verified, but is probably valid.

The O_2 cost measures total respiratory work, including that done on the thoracic cage and viscera. The upper graph in fig. 29.14 shows how greatly respiratory work can increase when the lungs are abnormal, and in these conditions it may account for a significant part of total O_2 used and limit the ability to exercise.

PULMONARY VENTILATION

Ventilation of the lungs is the first step in the supply of O_2 to the tissues and the last step in the excretion of CO_2. The O_2 stores of the body are very small, and pulmonary ventilation must supply the body's needs from minute to minute if life is to continue. As an excretory organ the lung is of great importance and eliminates as CO_2 more than fifty times as much acid as the kidneys. These functions entail, in a resting subject, a daily ventilation of 8000–10,000 litres, from which about 360 litres of O_2 are taken and to which about 300 litres of CO_2 are added. All these figures may be doubled for a heavy worker.

THE SUBDIVISIONS OF LUNG VOLUME

The volume of air in the lungs and airways varies widely during respiratory movements. At the deepest possible inspiration they contain, in a healthy young man, some 6 litres. This is the **total lung capacity** (TLC). TLC is conveniently subdivided into four primary 'volumes' (fig. 29.15). At the end of a quiet expiration about 2 litres of air remain. Only 1 litre of this can be expelled by a

Fig. 29.15. The lung volumes.

deep expiration; this is the **expiratory reserve volume** (ERV) and the volume which remains, 1 litre or so, is the **residual volume** (RV). Starting again at the end of a quiet expiration, an average quiet inspiration draws in rather less than 500 ml; this is the ventilatory ebb and flow, or **tidal volume** (TV or V_T). In addition to this it is possible to take in a further 3.5 litres, the **inspiratory reserve volume** (IRV), before TLC is reached. ERV, TV and IRV together make up the **vital capacity** (VC) while ERV and RV form the **functional residual capacity** (FRC). The least important is the **inspiratory capacity** which comprises TV and IRV.

These volumes and capacities may be grossly altered in pulmonary disease and their measurement may help in diagnosis. Apart from RV, they are easily measured by means of a recording spirometer; this is a cylindrical bell floating in water, suspended by its dome from a pulley leading to a counterweight and kymograph pen; the interior air space is connected to a wide tube through which the subject respires. Vertical movements of the pen are proportional to respired volumes. RV cannot be measured directly and a dilution technique is used (p. 1.2). A known volume of helium can be used as a marker, or the N_2 contained in the lungs can be washed out, by breathing pure O_2, and estimated by analysis.

Forced expiratory volume (FEV)

When recording ERV, TV and IRV, no stipulation is made as to speed of performance. VC is taken as the biggest volume which can be expired, in three attempts, from full inspiration. In clinical work the 'timed vital capacity' or FEV is useful. This is the biggest expiration which can be made in a given time; usually 1 sec but sometimes 0.75 sec is chosen. In 1 sec a normal subject can expire 80 per cent or more of his vital capacity. Obstruction of the airway reduces this figure.

Maximal voluntary ventilation (MVV)

This is measured from a short spell of forced, voluntary hyperventilation, usually 15 sec. Stipulating frequency, e.g. forty breaths per min, MVV_{40}, improves reproducibility. Normal values lie in the range 100–150 l/min. MVV and FEV are related and tend to vary together in disease.

VENTILATION OF THE LUNGS

Partition of ventilation

Not all the inspired air takes part in respiratory exchange, for some of it travels no further than the conducting airway at each inspiration. This wasted volume is the **respiratory deadspace** (V_D). About 20–30 per cent of $\dot{V}_E$ is expended in ventilating the nose, mouth, pharynx, larynx, trachea and large and medium bronchi.

The rest ventilates the alveolar units and exchanges O_2 for CO_2 with the pulmonary capillary blood. This part of $\dot{V}_E$ is the **alveolar ventilation** ($\dot{V}_A$).

This concept is an oversimplification. Firstly, since many of the small conducting passages contribute significantly to respiratory exchange, it is impossible to set precise anatomical limits to the deadspace. Secondly, the alveolar ventilation is not distributed evenly to all alveoli, even in health, and we must distinguish overall alveolar ventilation from regional alveolar ventilation. The subject of deadspace is complex and simplifying assumptions are necessary. At the outset the deadspace can be regarded as a clearly demarcated zone in which gas is conducted but not exchanged, and we can assume that inspired gas is evenly distributed to the alveoli where gas is mixed and exchanged but not conducted. Qualifications of this simple model will be introduced later.

The respiratory deadspace

Fig. 29.16 depicts different stages of a respiratory cycle. Just before the start of inspiration (a), the alveoli and

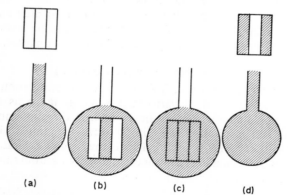

FIG. 29.16. Stages of a single respiratory cycle (see text).

deadspace are full of alveolar gas, i.e. gas which has undergone respiratory exchange. Three 'units' of atmospheric air are waiting to enter the lungs. At (b) these have been inhaled; two of them have reached the alveoli, washing in before them the alveolar gas which previously occupied the dead space, and one inspired unit now occupies the dead space. The two units which have reached the alveoli now undergo respiratory exchange and become two units of alveolar gas (c). The unit in the deadspace remains unaltered in composition. At (d) the three units have been expired; two are now alveolar gas (the 'expired portion of the alveolar gas') and one is unaltered inspired air ('deadspace gas'). Mixed, the three units are the 'expired gas'. Alveoli and deadspace are again full of alveolar gas.

Let the concentration by volume of any gas x in the inspired gas be F_{Ix}, in the alveolar gas F_{Ax} and in expired gas F_{Ex}. Let the volume of the expired portion of

the alveolar gas be V_A, of the tidal volume V_T and of the deadspace V_D. Then the volume of x in expired gas = volume of x in deadspace gas plus volume of x in expired portion of alveolar gas

$$V_T \times F_{Ex} = V_D \times F_{Ix} + V_A \times F_{Ax}$$

But

$$V_A = V_T - V_D$$

Therefore

$$V_T \times F_{Ex} = V_D(F_{Ix} - F_{Ax}) + V_T \times F_{Ax}$$

Solving for V_D,

$$V_D = V_T \times \frac{F_{Ex} - F_{Ax}}{F_{Ix} - F_{Ax}} \qquad (15)$$

Equation 15, the **Bohr Equation**, is a classical one in respiratory physiology. It tells us that if we can measure tidal volume and the concentration of any gas in the inspired, expired and alveolar gas, then the volume of the deadspace can be calculated. The only real problem is how to obtain a sample of alveolar gas for analysis. This will now be considered.

The composition of expired gas

When expiration starts, the first gas to emerge is inspired air from the deadspace. As expiration proceeds, the emergent gas changes to alveolar gas. The transition is not abrupt, because of the way one gas follows another along a tube. Smoke blown along a narrow glass tube has a spike-shaped 'front', because, during laminar flow, the velocity of the stream is greatest at the centre and least at the circumference (fig. 29.9). The CO_2 content of expired gas thus shows not a sudden change from inspired to alveolar levels (fig. 29.17, OFDBC) but an S-shaped curve (OABC). This may be shown by fractional sampling and analysis of successive portions of expired gas, or from the record of a rapid, continuous analyser such as the infra-red CO_2 analyser or the mass spectrometer. The curve has three phases: (1) the inspired gas phase (2) the mixing phase and (3) the alveolar plateau in which CO_2 content is almost constant.

FIG. 29.17. CO_2 concentration curve in relation to volume of air expired. Modified from Aitken & Clark-Kennedy. (1928) *J. Physiol.* **65**, 389.

The presence of phase (2) means that a volume some three times greater than V_D must be expired before one can be sure of obtaining alveolar gas, unmixed with deadspace gas. The composition of alveolar gas itself gradually changes as expiration proceeds, as shown by the gentle upward slope of the alveolar plateau. One cause of this change is the continued addition of CO_2 to alveolar gas from mixed venous blood during expiration; alveolar gas composition is never absolutely steady, but cycles with the respiratory tide. Another cause of the upward slope of the CO_2 plateau is uneven distribution of gas and blood to the alveoli, which is of importance in certain diseases of the lung.

In fig. 29.17, all the recorded CO_2 comes from alveolar gas. Assuming the extrapolation BD of the line CB is justified, and drawing FD so that area OFAO equals ABDA, the expired gas can be thought of as composed of volume OF of inspired gas and volume FG of alveolar gas, i.e. OF is the deadspace. The mean CO_2 content of the expired portion of alveolar gas is $(DF+CG)/2$. This is the CO_2 concentration used to derive equation 15 and when substituted in it must yield a value for V_D equal to OF.

The above discussion is limited to CO_2 but, with modifications, applies to O_2 or to foreign gases introduced into the inspired gas. It shows one way of determining alveolar gas composition, but the method needs special apparatus.

Direct sampling of alveolar gas

THE HALDANE–PRIESTLEY METHOD

A piece of smooth-walled rubber hose (fig. 29.18), about 2·5 cm in diameter and about 150 cm long, is fitted with a mouthpiece. Near the mouthpiece a small hole is made in the hose, into which the end of an evacuated gas-sampling tube fits snugly. The subject sits wearing a nose-clip, breathing naturally and holding the hose. At the end of a normal expiration the command 'Blow' is given. The subject quickly raises the mouthpiece to his lips and, without inspiring, blows as rapidly and deeply as he can

FIG. 29.18. Haldane–Priestley alveolar gas sampling tube.

into the hose. At the limit of expiration he seals the mouthpiece with his tongue, holds his breath, and signals to the observer who quickly opens the tap of the sampling tube for a second or two. Gas from the proximal end of the hose enters the sampling tube and can be analysed.

END-TIDAL SAMPLING

This is usually done by means of an automatic device which takes a few ml of gas from the end of each expiration. A cumulative sample may be collected over a set period or the end-tidal gas may be fed into a continuous rapid analyser. Tidal volume must exceed 450 ml before end-tidal gas is truly alveolar (fig. 29.17).

These methods are empirical but in healthy subjects, and in appropriate circumstances, they give values for alveolar P_{CO_2} in close agreement with arterial blood. They have the advantages of ease and great analytical accuracy, and avoid the very occasional risk attending arterial puncture.

The P_{CO_2} of arterial blood

For present purposes it can be assumed that, since alveolar gas is in CO_2 pressure equilibrium with end-pulmonary-capillary blood, the P_{CO_2} of arterial blood is equal to mean alveolar P_{CO_2} (see p. 29.16 for account of partial pressures). In health, arterial P_{CO_2} is the same (within experimental error) as the alveolar P_{CO_2} derived from Haldane–Priestley or end–tidal sampling. In certain lung diseases when the distribution of gas and blood to the lungs is markedly uneven, arterial P_{CO_2} is higher than mean alveolar P_{CO_2} and direct alveolar samples are unrepresentative of either. In these circumstances arterial P_{CO_2} becomes the basic measurement for calculation of deadspace and alveolar ventilation.

Volume of the respiratory deadspace

The derivation of the Bohr Equation assumes a deadspace equal to the volume of the conducting airway at the instant when expiration begins (fig. 29.16). X-rays show that the bronchi dilate and elongate during inspiration and shorten and narrow during expiration. Deadspace varies, according to the inspiratory level, from 120 to 180 ml. There is a tendency for V_D to increase with age.

Under some conditions, the value obtained for V_D depends upon the indicator gas used to measure it. The main differences are seen between the respiratory gases (O_2 and CO_2) and the non-respiratory gases (such as N, H and He). In exercise and hyperventilation, the non-respiratory gases yield a V_D corresponding to the inspiratory position of the chest, much the same as at rest. On the other hand, O_2 and CO_2 deadspaces may increase to 600 ml or more. This increase could not all be accommodated in the conducting airway, and represents an extension of deadspace into the alveolar units. The extension is termed **alveolar deadspace** and its functional nature is recognized by the term **physiological deadspace** used when V_D is measured with O_2 or CO_2. The non-respiratory gases, on the contrary, yield under all conditions a value for V_D much closer to that obtained by anatomical methods (plaster casts, direct measurement) and the non-respiratory gas V_D is referred to as **anatomical deadspace**.

The genesis of alveolar deadspace is too complex to be discussed fully, but at least two factors are involved. Firstly, non-uniformity of gas concentration within a single alveolar unit is more likely to occur with gases which are rapidly transferred across the alveolar membrane, that is, O_2 and CO_2 than with the non-respiratory gases, and in exercise rather than at rest. Secondly, non-uniformity of gas concentration between different alveolar units, arising from non-uniform distribution of gas and blood to the alveoli, also affects O_2 and CO_2 much more than the non-respiratory gases.

Functions of the respiratory deadspace

The walls of the deadspace moisten and warm inspired air, which is saturated with water vapour before it reaches the alveoli. All the heat lost from the respiratory tract at rest comes from the blood perfusing the walls of the deadspace, and none from the pulmonary capillary blood. This process is impaired by mouth breathing and especially by the operation of tracheostomy.

The deadspace also minimizes the results of uneven ventilation. The alveoli which fill first, during inspiration, are usually those with the highest ventilation in relation to blood flow. Since the deadspace is full of alveolar gas at the start of inspiration, these alveoli receive a preferential share of alveolar gas before inspired air reaches them. Their share of inspired air is thus more nearly equal to that of less well-ventilated alveoli.

RELATION OF ALVEOLAR VENTILATION $\dot{V}_A$ TO ALVEOLAR GAS PRESSURES

Partial pressure of a gas in a mixture of gases

If a mixture of gases $1, 2, \cdots n$ be contained in a volume V at a pressure P, then their partial pressures $P_1, P_2 \cdots P_n$ will in each case be the pressure exerted by the gas in question were it alone to occupy volume V. The pressure of a gas is proportional to its molecular concentration, and equal volumes of gases at the same temperature and pressure contain equal numbers of molecules. Partial pressure is therefore proportional to the concentration by volume of a gas in a mixture of gases, as determined by analysis of the mixture, and the sum of partial pressures of the constituent gases is equal to the pressure of the mixture. Thus, for alveolar gas:

$$P_{A,O_2} + P_{A,CO_2} + P_{A,N_2} + P_{A,H_2O} = P_B \qquad (16)$$

and

$$P_{A,CO_2} = (P_B - 47) \times F_{A,CO_2} \qquad (17$$

Gas analysis yields concentrations of dry gas, and the vapour pressure of water at body temperature i 47 mm Hg. Equations 16 and 17 ignore the small differences between P_B and alveolar pressure due to the movements of the chest.

Partial pressure of a gas in a liquid

If a liquid be exposed to a gas which is soluble in it molecules of the gas diffuse into the liquid. An equilibrium is reached when the pressure of the gas in the liquid equals that in the gas phase. If the gas phase contains a mixture of soluble gases, equilibrium will be reached according to the gaseous partial pressures. We may thus speak of the partial pressure of a gas in a liquid.

$\dot{V}_A$ and alveolar gas composition

CARBON DIOXIDE

When atmospheric air (which contains hardly any CO_2 is breathed, all the CO_2 in expired gas must come from alveolar gas. The CO_2 output per min ($\dot{V}_{CO_2}$) equals the volume of alveolar gas expired per min ($\dot{V}_A$) multiplied by its concentration of CO_2.

$$\dot{V}_{CO_2} = \dot{V}_A \times F_{A,CO_2} \qquad (18$$

When $\dot{V}_{CO_2}$ is constant, therefore,

$$F_{A,CO_2} \propto 1/\dot{V}_A \qquad (19$$

But F_{A,CO_2} is proportional to P_{A,CO_2} (equation 17) Therefore

$$P_{A,CO_2} \propto 1/\dot{V}_A \qquad (20$$

Equation 20 shows that when $\dot{V}_A$ is doubled, P_{A,CO_2} is halved, and vice versa, provided that CO_2 output is unchanged. This situation is very like the renal elimination of urea; when urea output is constant, halving the urea clearance doubles the blood urea concentration. By analogy, $\dot{V}_A$ is sometimes termed **alveolar clearance**.

OXYGEN

The corresponding 'clearance equation' for O_2 is a little more complicated because F_{I,O_2} is greater than F_{A,O_2} Another difficulty is that R is usually less than 1, which makes inspired $\dot{V}_A$ a little greater than expired $\dot{V}_A$. Assuming $R = 1$, the equation for O_2 corresponding to equation 20 is

$$(P_{I,O_2} - P_{A,O_2}) \propto 1/\dot{V}_A \qquad (21$$

The discerning student will see that what we are really doing by doubling $\dot{V}_A$ is halving the difference between inspired and alveolar gas pressures, and that this applies to both O_2 and CO_2.

Steady and changing states of $\dot{V}_A$

In the above calculations it has been assumed that $\dot{V}_A$, P_A,CO_2, P_A,O_2, $\dot{V}CO_2$ and $\dot{V}O_2$ are steady. When $\dot{V}_A$ is suddenly altered, equilibrium is temporarily upset and some time elapses before a new steady state is reached. Changing states in respiratory physiology are of interest and importance, but are too complex for discussion here.

THE CARRIAGE OF GASES IN THE BLOOD

SOLUBILITY OF GASES IN LIQUIDS

The concentration of a dissolved gas is related to its partial pressure in the solvent by a solubility constant (α) which is specific for the gas, the solvent and the temperature of the solution. Thus for oxygen

$$C_{O_2} = \alpha . P_{O_2}$$

C may be expressed as mM/l or as ml of gas (expressed at STPD)/ml of solvent. P is given in mm Hg or atmospheres.

OXYGEN

O_2 is held in blood in two forms, physical solution and chemical combination.

DISSOLVED O_2

At 38°C, 1 ml of blood dissolves 0·023 ml of O_2 when P_{O_2} is 760 mm Hg. Breathing air, P_a,O_2 is about 100 mm Hg and $P_{\bar{v}}O_2$ about 40 mm Hg. The volume of O_2 dissolved in 100 ml of arterial blood is thus 0·023 × 100 × 100/760 = 0·30 ml, and in 100 ml of mixed venous blood 0·023 × 100 × 40/760 = 0·12 ml. Breathing pure O_2 washes N_2 out of the alveoli and raises P_A,O_2 (and P_{O_2} in end-pulmonary capillary blood) to atmospheric minus the partial pressures of CO_2 and H_2O. 100 ml of end-pulmonary capillary blood then contain 0·023 × 100 × (760 − 40 − 47)/760 = 2 ml of O_2 in solution. P_A,O_2 is thus raised from 100 to 673 mm Hg and end-pulmonary capillary blood contains 1·70 ml more O_2 per 100 ml in solution. These facts are important in considering venous-to-arterial shunts.

COMBINED O_2

Erythrocytes contain a pigment, haemoglobin (Hb), which can combine reversibly with O_2, forming oxyhaemoglobin (HbO_2). Hb is a compound of a protein (globin) and haem (which contains Fe). Hb contains 0·34 per cent Fe, and since the atomic weight of Fe is 55·85, the molecular weight of Hb must be at least 55·85 × 100/0·34, or 16,232. 1 g of Hb combines with 1·38 ml of O_2; 16,232 g thus combine with 16,232 × 1·38 = 22,400 ml of O_2, or 1 mole of O_2. One molecule of Hb

therefore combines with one molecule of O_2 for every atom of Fe it contains. Suppose it contains one atom of Fe. Then the reaction between Hb and O_2 can be written:

$$Hb + O_2 \rightleftharpoons HbO_2 \qquad (22)$$

Applying the Law of Mass Action to equation 22, we have:

$$K'.[Hb].[O_2] = [HbO_2]$$

But $[O_2]$ is proportional to P_{O_2}. Therefore:

$$K.[Hb].P_{O_2} = [HbO_2]$$

or

$$[HbO_2]/[Hb] = K.P_{O_2} \qquad (23)$$

Now imagine a solution of haemoglobin in which some is present as Hb and some as HbO_2. The proportion of HbO_2 can be expressed as a percentage of the total haemoglobin present; this is the **per cent O_2 saturation.**

$$S_{O_2} = \frac{100\,[HbO_2]}{[Hb]+[HbO_2]}$$

$$= \frac{100}{1+[Hb]/[HbO_2]} \qquad (24)$$

Substituting for $[Hb]/[HbO_2]$ from equation 23, we have:

$$S_{O_2} = \frac{100}{1+1/K.P_{O_2}} = \frac{100K.P_{O_2}}{K.P_{O_2}+1} \qquad (25)$$

A graph based on equation 25, relating S_{O_2} to P_{O_2}, is a rectangular hyberbola (like the curve shown for myoglobin in fig. 29.20a). S_{O_2} can be estimated experimentally at each of a number of P_{O_2}s, and a graph relating S_{O_2} to P_{O_2}, so derived, is called an **oxyhaemoglobin-dissociation curve.** Figs. 29.19 and 29.20 show that this curve is not hyperbolic but S-shaped (sigmoid). The premise underlying the above calculation must therefore be wrong.

However, it is possible to arrive theoretically at a sigmoid curve, and even to fit the observed curve closely, by assuming that one molecule of Hb combines with more than one molecule of O_2, that each combination with an O_2 molecule is a discrete event, and that successive combinations have different dissociation constants. This line of reasoning, and more recent evidence from ultracentrifugation, have indicated that one molecule of Hb contains four atoms of Fe and can combine with four molecules of O_2. Equation 22 is therefore more accurately written:

$$Hb_4 + 4O_2 \rightleftharpoons Hb_4(O_2)_4 \qquad (26)$$

In passing, we have seen that the dissociation curve of oxymyoglobin ($MgbO_2$) is hyperbolic; this accords with the view that one molecule of Mgb combines with only one molecule of O_2. Mgb is the O_2-binding pigment of muscle.

Normal blood contains about 14·5 g of haemoglobin

FIG. 29.19. HbO_2 dissociation curves. (a) Influence of Pco_2. Redrawn from Bock, Field & Adair (1924), *J. biol. Chem.* **59**, 366. (b) Influence of temperature. Redrawn from Roughton (1964), *Handbook of Physiology*, Section 3, Vol. I. Washington: American Physiological Society.

FIG. 29.20. (a) Dissociation curves of carboxyhaemoglobin, oxymyoglobin and oxyhaemoglobin. (b) Dissociation curves of oxyhaemoglobin in presence of various amounts of HbCO. Redrawn from Roughton (1964) *Handbook of Physiology*, Section 3, Vol. I. Washington: American Physiological Society.

per 100 ml and this can combine with $14·5 × 1·38 = 20$ ml of O_2. The maximal volume of O_2 which can combine with 100 ml of a given sample of blood is called the **O_2 capacity** of the blood; this does not include dissolved O_2. The actual volume of combined O_2 in 100 ml of a sample of blood is the **O_2 content** (Co_2). When Co_2 is expressed as a percentage of O_2 capacity, the result is So_2.

The HbO_2 dissociation curve (figs. 29.19 and 29.20). So_2 is affected by several factors which shift the HbO_2 dissociation curve.

(1) A rise in H^+-ion concentration shifts the curve to the right. This is due to a link between the buffering action of Hb and its combination with O_2 (see below). The link may be symbolized as follows:

$$HHbO_2 \overset{(1)}{\rightleftharpoons} H^+ + HbO_2^- \overset{(2)}{\rightleftharpoons} HHb + O_2$$

$$HHb \overset{(3)}{\rightleftharpoons} H^+ + Hb^- \qquad (27)$$

Reaction (2) yields:

$$[H^+] = K . \frac{[HHb]}{[HbO_2^-]} . Po_2 \qquad (28)$$

Increasing $[H^+]$ at constant Po_2 must (and does) reduce the proportion of HbO_2 to total Hb.

(2) A rise in Pco_2 shifts the curve to the right (fig. 29.19a). This effect is due mainly to the direct acidifying effect of CO_2 but is partly specific and due to the formation of carbamino-CO_2, which is also linked to oxygenation and is a further source of H^+ (see below).

(3) Rise of temperature shifts the curve to the right

fig. 29.19b). Both [H$^+$] and temperature alter the curve in a way which can almost be duplicated by changing the scale of the P_{O_2} axis; the curve is compressed or stretched from side to side but does not change its fundamental shape, at any rate between 20 and 90 per cent saturation.

(4) The concentration of electrolytes affects the shape of the curve, which becomes more sigmoid, especially at the lower end, as salt concentration increases. The effect may be due to an action on the dissociation constants of $Hb_4(O_2)_4$.

(5) The curve varies markedly from one species of mammal to another. Even in man the P_{O_2} corresponding to half saturation (the 'P_{50}', a useful reference value) may vary by up to 25 per cent between individuals.

(6) Women, appropriately enough, have more rounded (sigmoid) curves than men.

Physiological implications of the HbO_2 and $MgbO_2$ dissociation curves

The steep part of the HbO_2 curve (fig. 29.20a) is directed, not towards the origin, but towards a P_{O_2} intercept of about 10 mm Hg. This means that S_{O_2} can fall to very low values before P_{O_2} becomes negligible; thus a useful diffusion gradient of P_{O_2} between tissue-capillary and tissue-cell is preserved to the point of almost maximal desaturation. It also means that Hb rapidly picks up O_2 as P_{O_2} rises; at 50 mm Hg, S_{O_2} is already about 80 per cent. The $MgbO_2$ dissociation curve, on the other hand, has no lower tail and rises steeply from the origin; this favours a transfer of O_2 to Mgb, at low P_{O_2}, which is presumably useful when the blood supply to the muscle is reduced intermittently by its contractions. The addition of CO_2 to blood in the tissue capillaries increases the yield of O_2 at a given P_{O_2} (shift of the curve to the right) and the converse effect occurs in the lungs; this is the **Bohr effect** which is probably not of great importance. The liberation of heat and lactic acid in exercising muscle also helps reduction of HbO_2.

CARBON MONOXIDE

This gas is very poisonous because the affinity of Hb for CO is very much greater than for O_2. Carboxyhaemoglobin ($Hb_4(CO)_4$) saturation is related to P_{CO} by a dissociation curve (fig. 29.20a) which is almost identical with the HbO_2 curve but for a lateral 'compression' of 200–250 times. Blood equilibrated with a mixture of CO and O_2 combines with both, but preferentially with CO, as follows:

$$[HbCO]/[HbO_2] = M.P_{CO}/P_{O_2} \qquad (29)$$

The constant M lies between 200 and 250 in different people. Let $P_{O_2} = 100$ mm Hg and $[HbCO] = [HbO_2]$. Then $P_{CO} = 0.5$ mm approximately. An alveolar and arterial P_{CO} of this order is reached if 0.1 per cent CO in air is breathed, yet this minute concentration is enough eventually to half saturate circulating Hb with CO. Heavy smokers commonly have a S_{CO} of 5 per cent or more.

The effects of given P_{O_2} and P_{CO} levels are not simply additive, for CO actually alters the HbO_2 dissociation curve (fig. 29.20b). Combination of Hb with CO increases the affinity of the remaining Hb for O_2, and release of O_2 in the tissues is greatly hampered. Reduction of the O_2 capacity by anaemia does not affect the HbO_2 dissociation curve. 'A person whose blood is half-saturated with CO is practically helpless, but a person whose haemoglobin percentage is simply diminished to half by anaemia may be going about his work as usual' (Haldane). This effect of CO is important if exercise is undertaken, and many a patient poisoned with CO has been discharged, apparently recovered, from hospital casualty departments, only to collapse in the street outside.

CARBON DIOXIDE

DISSOLVED CO$_2$

One litre of plasma at 38°C dissolves 0.0334 mM of CO_2 for every mm Hg of P_{CO_2}; the plasma of normal arterial blood thus contains $0.0334 \times 40 = 1.36$ mM of dissolved CO_2 per litre, compared with about 25 mM in combination.

COMBINED CO$_2$

This exists in blood in two forms, bicarbonate and 'carbamino-CO_2'. When CO_2 dissolves in water or plasma, the following reactions occur:

$$CO_2 + H_2O \rightleftharpoons H_2CO_3 \qquad (30)$$
$$H_2CO_3 \rightleftharpoons H^+ + HCO_3^- \qquad (31)$$

The equilibrium constant of equation 30, the ratio $[CO_2]/[H_2CO_3]$, is about 700. This means that a solution of CO_2 forms very little H_2CO_3. The enzyme carbonic anhydrase greatly speeds the reaction in either direction but does not affect the equilibrium constant. However, equation 31, by removing H_2CO_3, favours the combination of more CO_2 in equation 30. H_2CO_3 is a weak acid and dissociates very little (though about twenty times as much as acetic acid); thus equation 31 cannot get very far unless one of its products is removed by yet other means. This is achieved by the blood buffers, which remove H^+. The possession by blood of carbonic anhydrase, and of buffers which bind H^+, is the chief reason why blood is a better carrier of CO_2 than water.

'Carbamino-CO_2' is a compound of CO_2 with Hb through an amino group:

$$Hb-NH_2 + CO_2 \rightleftharpoons Hb-NHCOO^- + H^+ \qquad (32)$$

Reduction of HbO_2 favours the forward reaction and oxygenation of Hb the reverse. H^+ formed in the forward reaction is buffered. The buffer-systems of blood are described on p. 6.4.

Bicarbonate reacts with added H^+ as follows (B represents cation):

$$BHCO_3 + H^+ \rightleftharpoons B^+ + H_2CO_3 \qquad (33)$$
$$H_2CO_3 \rightleftharpoons H_2O + CO_2 \qquad (34)$$

The forward progress of these reactions in blood depends upon the excretion of CO_2 through the lungs. This system does not buffer H^+ produced by the addition of CO_2 to blood, which reverses reactions 34 and 33. The bicarbonate system is of course important in buffering acids other than CO_2.

Of the **blood proteins**, Hb is quantitatively a more important buffer than plasma protein. Haemoglobin contains many more histidine residues than plasma proteins (table 11.3, p. 11.9). The imidazole groups in these residues provide by far the greater part of the buffering action of haemoglobin in blood at pH 7.4 (equation 35).

$$(35)$$

The imidazole group of histidine is peculiar in that reduction of HbO_2 favours H^+ acceptance and oxygenation of Hb favours H^+ donation. Oxygenated haemoglobin (pK 6.7) is a stronger acid than reduced haemoglobin (pK 7.9) and so the pH in the erythrocytes tends to be raised when oxygen is given off in the tissues. This facilitates the buffering of carbonic acid and so the uptake of CO_2 by the red cells (fig. 29.21). The imidazole group is responsible for the link between oxygenation and buffer activity shown in equation 27. This link allows the exchange of O_2 and CO_2 in the tissues and lungs to take place with a smaller change in $[H^+]$ than would otherwise occur.

Uptake and release of CO_2 by blood

Fig. 29.21 summarizes the reactions which take place during the uptake and release of CO_2 by blood. Added CO_2 diffuses freely through the capillary and red cell membranes. Disposal of CO_2 is more extensive in the red cell than in plasma. This is because (1) the red cell is rich in carbonic anhydrase, which speeds reaction 30, whereas plasma contains none of this enzyme; (2) Hb can form carbamino CO_2; (3) Hb has a larger buffer capacity than plasma protein, and the removal of H^+ favours both reactions in the red cell. Consequently much more HCO_3^- is formed in the red cell and since the red cell membrane is freely permeable to HCO_3^-, this ion diffuses from the red cell into the plasma. This resolves the chemical gradient but creates an electrical

FIG. 29.21. Uptake of CO_2 from tissue cells into blood.

one. Since the red cell membrane is, in effect, impermeable to cation, K^+ cannot accompany HCO_3^- into the plasma. Instead, the electrical gradient is resolved by the diffusion of Cl^- from plasma to red cell; this is the **chloride shift**.

The sequence of reactions during the uptake of CO_2 is determined by the pressure gradient of CO_2 between tissue cells and red cells. In the lungs the gradient is reversed; red cells in mixed venous blood have a higher P_{CO_2} than alveolar gas. The reactions follow the direction of the pressure gradient, rather as a ball might run in alternate directions down a see-saw. Their speed is remarkable. During exercise, each red cell spends much less than 1 sec in a pulmonary capillary, yet 100 ml or more of CO_2 is transferred from each litre of blood. Drugs which inhibit carbonic anhydrase may interfere with CO_2 transport.

Distribution of CO_2 in blood

Table 29.3 shows arterial and venous contents of CO_2; the difference between these is the CO_2 carried from

TABLE 29.3. Distribution of CO_2 (mM) in 1 litre of arterial (A) and venous (V) blood, and venous-arterial differences (transported CO_2). The plasma is taken as 600 ml and erythrocytes as 400 ml. Values rounded to one decimal place. Modified from Davenport, H.W. (1958). *The ABC of Acid-Base Chemistry*, Chicago University Press.

	A		V		V−A	
Dissolved						
Plasma	0·7	⎫	0·8	⎫	0·1	⎫
		⎬ 1·0		⎬ 1·2		⎬ 0·2
Erythrocytes	0·3	⎭	0·4	⎭	0·1	⎭
Bicarbonate						
Plasma	15·2	⎫	16·2	⎫	1·0	⎫
		⎬ 19·5		⎬ 20·6		⎬ 1·1
Erythrocytes	4·3	⎭	4·4	⎭	0·1	⎭
Carbamino						
Erythrocytes	1·0		1·4		0·4	
Total CO_2	21·5		23·2		1·7	

tissues to lungs. Three points deserve notice: (1) three-quarters of the blood CO_2 is held in the plasma; (2) two-thirds of the carried CO_2 is held in the plasma (but most of it owes its appearance there to a reaction in the red cells); (3) most CO_2 in plasma, is carried as HCO_3^-, but in red cells as carbamino CO_2.

CO_2 dissociation curves of blood

A graph relating C_{CO_2} to P_{CO_2} of blood or plasma is a CO_2 dissociation curve (fig. 29.22). Four features need comment.

(1) Reduced blood takes up more CO_2 than oxygenated blood at the same P_{CO_2}. This is due to the greater capacity of reduced Hb for buffering and carbamino-CO_2 formation.

(2) All the CO_2 contained in blood is released when P_{CO_2} is reduced to zero. This contrasts with the behaviour of a simple bicarbonate solution which evolves only half

FIG. 29.22. CO_2 dissociation curves of blood and plasma. 'True plasma' is plasma separated from the red cells at the same P_{CO_2} at which CO_2 content is measured. Redrawn from Bock, Field & Adair (1924) *J. biol. Chem.* **59**, 366.

its CO_2, leaving half as carbonate. In blood, H^+ is freed from protein as the blood becomes more alkaline, driving equations 30 and 31 (p. 29.19) to the left.

(3) Although the curves are hyperbolic, they are fairly straight over the physiological range of P_{CO_2}. This is quite different from the HbO_2 dissociation curve.

(4) The dissociation curves for 'true plasma' in fig. 29.22 have much the same slope as those for whole blood. This is because whole blood was equilibrated with CO_2, and the plasma then separated; the difference from the blood curves reflects simply the greater CO_2 content of plasma compared to cells. When plasma is separated from red cells and then equilibrated with other P_{CO_2}, a less steep dissociation curve is obtained, and crosses the 'true plasma' curve at the P_{CO_2} of the blood at the time of separation. The flatter curve for separated plasma reflects

its inferior buffering capacity and inability to make carbamino CO_2.

The difference between the CO_2 capacities of reduced and oxygenated blood, at a given P_{CO_2}, helps in the exchange of O_2 and CO_2. More CO_2 can be transferred for a given fall or rise of P_{CO_2} when Hb is simultaneously oxygenated or reduced. This is the **Haldane effect.**

Application of the Henderson–Hasselbalch equation

As described on p. 6.3, this equation is expressed for CO_2 as follows

$$pH = \log \frac{1}{[H^+]} = \log \frac{1}{K'} + \log \frac{[\text{Bicarbonate}]}{0.03 \times P_{CO_2}}$$
$$= pK' + \log \frac{[CO_2] - 0.03 \times P_{CO_2}}{0.03 \times P_{CO_2}} \qquad (36)$$

$[CO_2]$ is the total CO_2 content of plasma as determined by analysis; [Bicarbonate] is $[CO_2]$ minus the concentration of dissolved CO_2. pK' is a constant which has had to be empirically determined by direct measurement of pH and $[CO_2]$ in plasma at a known P_{CO_2}. At 37.5°C, pK' averages 6.10. Knowing this, we can calculate any one of pH, $[CO_2]$ or P_{CO_2} if the other two are measured. However, pK' varies slightly but significantly with change in pH and in temperature, and quite possibly when the plasma is chemically abnormal.

DISTRIBUTION AND DIFFUSION

DISTRIBUTION OF GAS AND BLOOD TO THE LUNGS

In the preceding sections it has been assumed that alveolar ventilation and blood flow are evenly distributed throughout the lungs. This is far from being the case, even in health; in pulmonary disease, unevenness of distribution may be considerable.

If one lung is removed, the other receives the whole $\dot{V}_A$ and $\dot{Q}_C$ ($\dot{Q}_C$ is pulmonary capillary blood flow), twice as much of each as it received before. Yet, since the proportion of one to the other is well maintained in each part of the remaining lung, the disturbance of blood gases is minimal. This shows that it is not the absolute $\dot{V}_A$ or $\dot{Q}_C$ to any part of the lung which matters so much as the proportion of $\dot{V}_A$ to $\dot{Q}_C$ (**ventilation/perfusion ratio**). Although $\dot{V}_A$ and $\dot{Q}_C$ may each be normal, if they are not correctly matched the exchange of gases will be inefficient. In effect, some $\dot{V}_A$ will be wasted, and the wasted part appears as **extra deadspace ventilation.** Also, some $\dot{Q}_C$ will be wasted; it is as though some of the mixed venous blood had escaped gas exchange altogether and the arterial blood thus polluted by **venous admixture.** These effects are just detectable in healthy subjects by modern methods of investigation; they were clearly foreseen by Haldane 40 years ago.

ALVEOLAR-CAPILLARY DIFFUSION

Exchange of O_2 and CO_2 between alveolar gas and pulmonary capillary blood is accomplished by physical diffusion across the alveolar membrane. The rate at which a gas diffuses through a permeable medium is (1) proportional to the partial pressure gradient down which diffusion occurs, (2) inversely proportional to the thickness of the medium, (3) proportional to the solubility of the gas in the medium and (4) inversely proportional to the square root of the molecular weight of the gas. At the beginning of a pulmonary capillary, the Po_2 gradient between alveolar gas and mixed venous blood is $100-40=60$ mm Hg. The Pco_2 gradient in the opposite direction is only $46-40=6$ mm Hg. Yet CO_2 is so much more soluble than O_2 in the alveolar membrane that it diffuses twenty times faster, attaining complete partial pressure equilibrium well before the end of the capillary is reached. Po_2 equilibrium is not quite reached, though in health the Po_2 difference between alveolar gas and end-pulmonary capillary blood is very small; about 1 mm Hg.

The alveolar membrane is not the only barrier to diffusion. The whole process is so rapid that the transfer of gas through plasma, and even the speed of reaction of O_2 with Hb, become significant factors. Membrane resistance is about half the total resistance to the diffusion of O_2.

REGULATION OF RESPIRATION

NEURAL CONTROL

The respiratory muscles are supplied through a motor pathway consisting of upper and lower motor neurones. The upper motor neurones controlling respiratory movements originate in the reticular substance of the brain stem, predominantly from its lower end, in the floor of the fourth ventricle; they descend the cord in the lateral and ventral columns. The brain stem may be divided above, but not below, this level without abolishing (but not without distorting) respiration, and the 'respiratory centre' has been assigned to this position (p. 24.21). However, the whole reticular formation shows rhythmic electrical activity of a frequency corresponding to the respiratory cycle, even when all afferent impulses to it are blocked. It is now generally believed that a 'respiratory centre' cannot be localized precisely; normal respiration requires that the whole reticular substance is functionally intact. The unstable, oscillatory circuits which the reticular substance contains may be left for the enjoyment of neurophysiologists.

We may, therefore, think of the respiratory centre as a 'black box' occupying a large part of the brain stem generating spontaneous, rhythmic, inspiratory and expiratory impulses which may be modified by numerous afferent stimuli which reach the black box from outside. The rest of this section is concerned with these afferent stimuli and the effects they produce.

Impulses from other parts of the central nervous system
Breathing may be modified voluntarily, and pathways from the pyramidal and extrapyramidal systems to the respiratory centre are implicit in this fact. The over-breathing which accompanies excitement or anxiety is presumably mediated by these pathways. The neural component of the increased ventilation in physical exercise (p. 29.27) may consist partly of an irradiation effect in which impulses 'spill over' from the cortico-spinal tracts to involve the respiratory centre, but other factors are concerned. The coordination of respiratory movements, particularly during speech, demands a contribution from the cerebellum.

Impulses from the lungs
At least seven different types of receptor organ exist in the tracheobronchial tree, alveolar walls, pleura and pulmonary vessels, and numerous reflexes can be elicited by various pulmonary manipulations; the answer to the question which receptors serve which reflexes remains confused.

INFLATION REFLEX
An imposed, maintained inflation of the lungs delays the onset of the next spontaneous inspiratory effort. The delay is greater, relative to the length of the natural respiratory cycle, in rabbits than in monkeys, cats or men, in that order. Babies have a relatively powerful inflation reflex, which declines rapidly after the age of one week. This reflex is abolished when the vagus nerves are cut or cooled to $8°C$; the vagus carries the afferent fibres. Two types of response to inflation have been found in single fibres of the vagus, one slowly and the other rapidly adapting. The inflation reflex could be mediated by the first; the second may serve the paradoxical reflex (see below).

DEFLATION REFLEX
An imposed, maintained deflation of the lungs increases the frequency, or force, or both, of spontaneous inspiratory efforts. Afferent fibres are in the vagus nerves; single fibres, 'firing' on deflation, have been identified. The inflation and deflation reflexes together make up the **Hering–Breuer reflex**. Their role appears to be to supplement the cyclical inhibition and excitation of inspiratory neurones in such a way as to prevent undue distension or deflation of the lungs. The importance of these re-

flexes in man is uncertain; they may well become more powerful and significant when, in disease, the lungs are abnormally 'stiff'. The inflation reflex may, in addition, exert a tonic influence on inspiratory muscles, helping to set the 'level' of breathing.

PARADOXICAL REFLEX

An imposed inflation of the lungs induces a prompt and brief spontaneous inspiratory effort. Adaptation is rapid, unmasking the slowly-adapting inflation reflex. The paradoxical reflex has been demonstrated in various animals and in babies, and its afferents are vagal. The functional role of this reflex is not known, but it may be concerned in the production of the occasional deep breaths which characterize normal breathing. When tidal volume remains constant over long periods, progressive collapse of small groups of alveoli occurs; this process is reversed by a deep breath. It may be that alveolar collapse, which 'stiffens' the lung, gradually increases the discharge of the receptors responsible for the paradoxical reflex, and that when the discharge reaches threshold an inspiratory effort results in a bigger breath than usual. This big inspiration opens up the alveoli which have collapsed and the process begins again.

COUGH REFLEX

Two types of stimuli elicit the cough reflex, and appear to act through different receptor organs. (1) Mechanical irritation causes coughing most readily when applied to the larynx, posterior wall of the trachea, and bronchial branchings of the first degree, in order of decreasing sensitivity. (2) Chemical irritants induce coughing via receptors in the smallest air passages, the trachea and large bronchi being relatively insensitive.

The afferent nerves for both types of reflex are contained, probably entirely, in the vagus nerves. The reflex is potentiated by deep inspiration, probably by stimulating the same receptors. The cough reflex is highly organized; it consists of a deep inspiration, closure of the glottis, contraction of expiratory muscles (causing intrapulmonary pressure to rise), and finally opening of the glottis to allow an explosive discharge of air and the dislodging of secretions or foreign matter from the trachea. Intrathoracic pressure during violent coughing may exceed 200 mm Hg. Peak air-flow during expulsion may reach 6 l/sec and air velocity 250 m/sec. Bronchi are narrowed during expulsion by direct compression. A slower bronchial constriction also follows the inhalation of irritants and is presumably due to reflex contraction of bronchial muscle. The central connections serving the cough reflex are ill defined; there is little evidence of a 'cough centre'.

Impulses from the respiratory muscles

The diaphragm and the intercostal muscles contain muscle spindles, and Golgi tendon organs are present in the diaphragm. These structures must have functions but at present these are largely speculative. Proprioceptive stimuli from the respiratory muscles may be concerned in the appreciation of respiratory work, the adjustment of tidal volume and respiratory frequency to minimize work (p. 29.12) and the respiratory adjustments to imposed resistance to air flow.

Impulses from the systemic circulation

Baroreceptor reflexes from carotid sinuses and aortic arch probably include a specific respiratory component; baroreceptor stimulation is said to depress breathing and vice versa. It is, however, difficult to separate these responses from those due to concomitant carotid body effects and to secondary effects of induced circulatory changes. In man, there is no evidence that specific baroreceptor respiratory reflexes are important.

Temperature changes

A rise in body temperature causes hyperventilation, especially in animals which do not lose heat by sweating. The effect seems to be mediated partly by a reflex from warmed skin and partly by a rise in temperature of the blood. There are connections linking the heat regulating centre in the hypothalamus with the respiratory 'centre'.

Sudden cooling of the skin, as by a cold shower, causes a prompt inspiratory response, followed by hyperventilation and a rise in end expiratory level (FRC). Prolonged cooling of the body, as in hibernation, is accompanied by a fall in ventilation; since metabolic CO_2 production falls still further, a mild respiratory alkalosis results.

Impulses from exercising muscle

Crossed circulation experiments have shown that repeated contraction of limb muscles increases ventilation even when they have no vascular connection with the central or peripheral respiratory chemoreceptors. The effect is therefore presumably mediated by nervous pathways. Afferent impulses from muscle spindles may be concerned. The increase in ventilation which occurs in muscular exercise almost certainly includes such a 'neural' component.

Other impulses

Any sensory impression may modify breathing in the conscious animal; the response may be partly reflex, but arousal of the waking drive (p. 24.20) and gross voluntary interference are also involved. In the anaesthetized animal, stimulation of a somatic sensory nerve often alters breathing, but here it is not possible to say that a sensory modality is concerned.

Impulses from specific respiratory chemoreceptors

These impulses serve the chemical control of breathing, dealt with in the next section. There are two main receptor groups.

The **carotid bodies** and **aortic bodies**, supplied with afferent fibres by the glossopharyngeal and vagus nerves respectively, are the **peripheral chemoreceptors**. They consist of small nodules of pink or reddish-brown tissue, composed of bands and islands of specialized receptor cells supported by connective tissue cells and separated by numerous sinusoids through which some 20 ml of blood per g of tissue flows each minute, a very rich blood supply. The aortic bodies regress during childhood and their functional importance in man or animals is debatable. The carotid bodies are of great importance. They lie in close relation to the bifurcation of the common carotid artery on each side, and receive blood via branches of the occipital and/or ascending pharyngeal branches of the external carotid artery.

The adequate stimulus for the carotid bodies is thought to be an increase in H^+ concentration in or around the receptor cells. This may result from acidosis of the perfusing blood, due either to a primary rise in $[H^+]$ or a rise in blood P_{CO_2}. Owing to the rich blood supply of the carotid bodies, their large O_2 uptake normally causes only a small arteriovenous O_2 difference, and P_{O_2} in the carotid body cells and in the veins draining them is only slightly less than that in arterial blood. However, this balance is readily upset by a fall in blood flow, which results when arterial pressure is reduced. The arteriovenous O_2 difference increases markedly, and the P_{O_2} in the chemoreceptor cells therefore falls. A fall also occurs, without hypotension, when arterial blood P_{O_2} falls. In each case anaerobic metabolism in the carotid body cells probably releases lactic acid, and the local increase in H^+ concentration stimulates the receptors. At any rate, the carotid bodies are readily stimulated by hypoxia, as shown by the electrical activity in single fibre preparations of their nerves. Indeed, the response to a rise in P_{CO_2} and $[H^+]$ is not nearly so marked when P_{O_2} is high as it is during hypoxia; this accords with other evidence that the carotid bodies are primarily concerned with the ventilatory response to hypoxia. Stimulation of the carotid bodies by hypoxia, or electrical stimulation of the carotid body nerve, leads to an increase in ventilation.

The **central chemoreceptors** were originally thought to be the nerve cells of the respiratory centre itself. It is now known that intracranial receptors exist outside the centre. Of these, the best defined lie in the region of the lateral recesses of the fourth ventricle, close to the roots of the eighth, ninth and tenth cranial nerves. Perfusion studies have shown that these receptors are sensitive to change in $[H^+]$. A fall in pH of the perfusate, without change in its P_{CO_2}, causes an increase in ventilation. Surprisingly, an increase in P_{CO_2} without change in pH slightly reduces ventilation. Independence of P_{CO_2} and $[H^+]$ can be achieved in the perfusate by appropriately adjusting its HCO_3^- concentration; normally, of course,

a rise in P_{CO_2} of cerebrospinal fluid (CSF) reduces its pH, and a fall increases it.

The CSF bathes the intracranial chemoreceptors and changes in its composition presumably play an important part in ventilatory control. Normally, CSF (like intracellular fluid) is slightly acid with respect to arterial blood; its P_{CO_2} is about the same as jugular venous blood, its $[HCO_3^-]$ slightly lower than arterial blood, and its pK higher than blood. The blood–CSF barrier is freely permeable to CO_2 but much less so to H^+ and HCO_3^-; it appears that HCO_3^- moves out of CSF more readily than into it. Thus the acidosis of hypercapnia (raised P_{CO_2}) is shared by blood and CSF, and CSF cannot easily 'compensate' by gaining HCO_3^-. Acidosis due to NH_4Cl, on the other hand, by increasing ventilation, lowers P_{CO_2} in blood and CSF equally; since CSF cannot quickly lose HCO_3^- it becomes more alkaline. Subsequently loss of HCO_3^- does occur, and CSF pH falls, but the pH remains more nearly normal than that of blood. In all these situations ventilation seems to be determined partly by blood composition and partly by CSF composition. How the balance is set and achieved is at present under investigation.

CHEMICAL CONTROL

We now turn to the chemical regulation of breathing in the human subject. This is achieved by the integrated action of peripheral and central chemoreceptors, and is one of the most vivid examples of a negative feedback system in biology. Through it, a change in P_{CO_2}, P_{O_2} or pH of the body fluids produces a ventilatory response which tends to counteract the change.

The ventilatory response to CO_2

When a subject inhales a mixture of CO_2 in air or oxygen his ventilation increases. Fig. 29.23 illustrates this. When inspired P_{CO_2} is increased from 15 to 50 mm Hg, ventilation rises from just under 10 to over 60 l/min. If alveolar P_{CO_2} is measured as well, this is found to increase by less than 15 mm Hg for a 35 mm increase in P_{I,CO_2}. Both $\dot{V}$ and P_{A,CO_2} increase more and more rapidly as P_{I,CO_2} rises.

Fig. 29.24 is more informative. The curved lines in this figure are derived from equation 20 (p. 29.17), modified as follows:

$$(P_{A,CO_2} - P_{I,CO_2}) \propto 1/\dot{V}_A \qquad (37$$

When air is breathed, $P_{I,CO_2} = 0$ and we have equation 20. If we further assume that $\dot{V}_E$ is proportional to $\dot{V}_A$ we have

$$(P_{A,CO_2} - P_{I,CO_2}) \propto 1/\dot{V}_E \qquad (38$$

In words, if ventilation is halved we double the

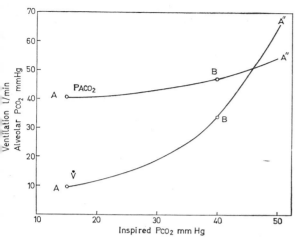

FIG. 29.23. Effects on alveolar P_{CO_2} and ventilation of increasing inspired P_{CO_2} from 15 to 50 mm Hg.

difference between alveolar and inspired CO_2 pressure; we double the first we shall halve the second, and so on, provided that CO_2 output remains constant (see p. 29.16). he left-hand curve in fig. 29.24 shows this relationship etween $\dot{V}E$ and P_{A,CO_2} when $P_{I,CO_2}=0$ and the CO_2 output is normal. We can now draw curves for P_{I,CO_2} values of 10, 20, $\cdots$, 50 mm Hg simply by moving the left-hand urve appropriate distances to the right. In fig. 29.24, oint A represents $\dot{V}=9\cdot5$ l/min, $P_{A,CO_2}=40\cdot5$ mm Hg, $_{I,CO_2}=15$ mm Hg; these are the values at the left-and ends of the curves in fig. 29.23. If now we raise

P_{I,CO_2} to 50 mm Hg, the new $\dot{V}$, P_{A,CO_2} point must lie somewhere on the curve representing this P_{I,CO_2}. If $\dot{V}$ does not increase, A will move to A' and P_{A,CO_2} will increase by 35 mm Hg; the entire increase of P_{I,CO_2} will be passed on to the alveolar gas. On the other hand, a rise of $\dot{V}E$ to 64 l/min brings A to A'', and the rise of P_{A,CO_2} is halved. The increase of $\dot{V}E$ has protected the alveolar gas, and thus the arterial blood, from the effects of a change in the environment.

Further comparison of figs. 29.23 and 29.24 shows that the values of $\dot{V}E$ and P_{A,CO_2} for an inspired P_{CO_2} of 40 mm Hg (B in fig. 29.23), when plotted at B in fig. 29.24, fall on a straight line joining A and A''. The same would be true for a pair of values taken from fig. 29.23 at any given inspired P_{CO_2}. In other words, the rise in ventilation due to an increase in the CO_2 stimulus is proportional to the rise in alveolar P_{CO_2}. The slope of the line ABA'' is a measure of the ventilatory sensitivity to changes in CO_2. A healthy adult's ventilation increases by 2–4 l/min for every mm Hg increase in P_{A,CO_2}; the rise is fairly constant from one day to the next in the same subject but varies a good deal from one subject to another. At inspired P_{CO_2} values below 15 mm Hg (2 per cent CO_2) the correspondence is not very close. But above 15 mm Hg the linear relationship suggests that ventilation is governed in a sensitive way by the level of alveolar or arterial P_{CO_2}.

So far we have considered only steady states of ventilation; each CO_2 mixture has been breathed long enough for $\dot{V}E$ and P_{A,CO_2} to become steady (this takes about 20 min). Ventilatory responses during changing states, e.g. the transition from one mixture to another, are complex. In general, the ventilatory rise lags about 2 min behind the change in arterial P_{CO_2} and is more closely related in time to change in jugular venous P_{CO_2}. This suggests an intracellular site for the true CO_2 stimulus, because venous blood is in P_{CO_2} equilibrium with the cells it drains.

Very high inspired CO_2 concentrations produce general anaesthesia, and the ventilation, having risen to high levels, begins to fall. This effect is seen when arterial P_{CO_2} reaches 80–100 mm Hg.

The ventilatory response to lack of oxygen (hypoxia)

Fig. 29.25 shows a magnified part of fig. 29.24. The line AB is the CO_2 response line, relating the change in ventilation to the change in alveolar P_{CO_2} as the inspired P_{CO_2} changes from 20 to 35 mm Hg. We shall assume that points A and B were plotted from an experiment in which alveolar P_{O_2} was kept constant at 100 mm Hg. If the experiment is now repeated with the same inspired CO_2 pressures, but with reduced inspired O_2 concentrations so that alveolar P_{O_2} is kept at 50 mm Hg, we find, at each inspired P_{CO_2}, a higher ventilation and a lower alveolar P_{CO_2} than before. Point A moves along the inspired

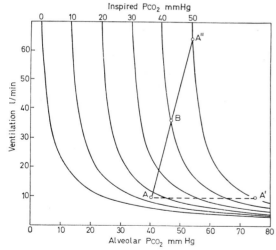

FIG. 29.24. Graph of ventilation in relation to alveolar P_{CO_2}. Each curved line shows the values for $\dot{V}$ and P_{A,CO_2} at a particular inspired P_{CO_2}, assuming CO_2 output to be constant. A, B and A'' are plotted from corresponding points in fig. 29.23 and a line joining these points is the CO_2 response line, showing the effect on ventilation of increasing inspired P_{CO_2}. If $\dot{V}$ did not increase, P_{A,CO_2} would rise to point A'.

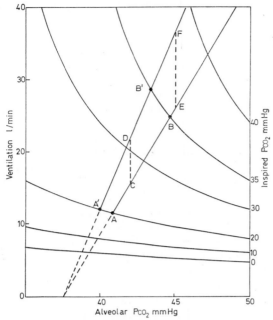

FIG. 29.25. Enlarged part of fig. 29.24, showing one CO_2 response line AB at a P_{A,O_2} of 100 mm Hg, and another, A'B' at a P_{A,O_2} of 50 mm Hg. Hypoxia increases the 'sensitivity' to CO_2 but leaves 'threshold' unchanged.

P_{CO_2} line to A' and point B to B'. The new CO_2 response line is A'B'. The distances AA' and BB' are such that, when BA and B'A' are produced to the left, they intersect at $\dot{V}=0$. We may say that the reduction of alveolar P_{O_2} from 100 to 50 mm Hg has increased the ventilatory sensitivity to CO_2, since a given rise in alveolar P_{CO_2} now causes a greater increase in ventilation. On the other hand, the threshold to CO_2, the alveolar P_{CO_2} below which ventilation is theoretically zero, has not been changed by hypoxia. Conversely, it is equally true to say that CO_2 increases the sensitivity to hypoxia; the rise in ventilation due to the hypoxia at an alveolar P_{CO_2} of 42 mm Hg (CD in fig. 29.25) is 6·5 l/min, but at 45 mm Hg (EF) it is nearly 11 l/min.

As the hypoxic stimulus increases, the line A'B' in fig. 29.25 becomes steeper. A limit (calculated from experimental data) is reached at an alveolar P_{O_2} of 20 to 30 mm Hg, when A'B' would become vertical, that is, infinite CO_2 sensitivity. It might be thought that increasing alveolar P_{O_2} above the normal air-breathing value of 100 mm Hg would have no effect, but in fact the line AB becomes slightly less steep. This means that, when air is breathed, there is a slight but significant hypoxic stimulus and that it is necessary to breathe high O_2 mixtures in order to abolish it. At an alveolar P_{O_2} of 250–300 mm Hg practically no hypoxic stimulus remains.

Very severe hypoxia (asphyxia) results in cerebral damage and respiration is depressed. Short periods of hypoxia down to alveolar P_{O_2} levels of around 40 mm Hg

can be tolerated, however, and it is between 40 and 7? mm Hg that the respiratory effects of hypoxia have chiefly been demonstrated. We may suppose that arteria? P_{O_2} is some 5–10 mm Hg lower than alveolar.

Chronic, tolerated hypoxia, as in the acclimatization t? altitude, produces more complex changes than does acut? hypoxia. There is a sustained rise in $\dot{V}$, leading to a sus? tained fall in arterial P_{CO_2}. A loss of HCO_3^- in th? urine occurs, and plasma and CSF [HCO_3^-] falls. Thi? change in acid-base state may be responsible for the fal? in CO_2 threshold and the rise in CO_2 sensitivity, i.e. i? the absence of hypoxia, which have been demonstrate? in experiments at altitude. The magnitude of the respons? to hypoxia itself seems to be unaltered. The effects o? high altitudes and other causes of hypoxia are discusse? in chap. 43.

The ventilatory response to H+

An increase in arterial P_{CO_2} due to inhalation of CO? mixtures is accompanied by a rise in [H^+] in both cell? and plasma, and it is probably by this effect that it cause? a rise in ventilation. But [H^+] can be increased in othe? ways. The ingestion of 8 g of NH_4Cl daily by a health? subject produces, in a few days, a marked extracellula? acidosis. Experiments have shown that this is accom? panied by a shift of the CO_2 response line to the left, tha? is, the CO_2 threshold is reduced while CO_2 sensitivit? remains the same (fig. 29.26). It is as though the ventila?

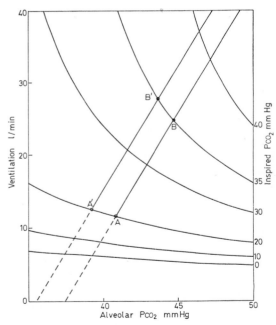

FIG. 29.26. Graph similar to fig. 29.25, but showing the effect on the CO_2 response line AB of metabolic acidosis induced by NH_4Cl. The new line A'B' is parallel to AB. Thus 'sensitivity' to CO_2 is not altered, while 'threshold' is reduced.

ion, during acidosis, has two components: (1) the $\dot{V}$ appropriate to the alveolar P_{CO_2} and (2) an extra $\dot{V}$ contributed by the increase in $[H^+]$. Unlike the response to hypoxia, which interacts with the CO_2 stimulus, the combination of an H^+-ion stimulus and a CO_2 stimulus seems to be simply additive.

Integration of chemical stimuli

Although the carotid bodies are stimulated by CO_2 and H^+, there is much evidence that in the intact animal they do not participate significantly in the ventilatory response to these stimuli. Far the greater part of the ventilatory drive due to CO_2 and H^+ is contributed by the intracranial receptors. On the other hand, the whole ventilatory drive due to hypoxia appears to be mediated via the carotid bodies.

The ventilatory response to rise in body temperature

The rise in ventilation when the body is heated has been mentioned. This effect seems to be mediated by an increase in sensitivity to CO_2, without change in threshold. The response to hypoxia *per se* is unaffected when the increase in CO_2 responsiveness is allowed for.

The control of ventilation during muscular exercise

The causes of the rise in ventilation during exercise are not yet fully understood. It seems probable that the rise can be largely accounted for in terms of the stimuli already discussed, but that individually these vary in importance according to the intensity and duration of the exercise.

(1) The **neural stimulus** is presumably involved in the abrupt rise in ventilation which occurs as soon as exercise begins. Irradiation from corticospinal pathways, or reflexes originating in muscle spindle afferents, have been invoked as mechanisms. The neural drive to respiration appears to increase according to the intensity of exercise.

(2) The **CO_2 stimulus.** Measurements of arterial P_{CO_2} during exercise have given conflicting results. There is a tendency for P_{CO_2} to rise in mild to moderate exercise; in severe exercise, with marked lactic acidosis, P_{CO_2} falls. However, there is little doubt that the combined stimulus from CO_2 and H^+ is increased at all but the mildest exercise intensities.

(3) The **lactic acidosis** of exercise is an obvious cause of an increase in ventilation, and becomes progressively more marked above an O_2 uptake of 1·5–2·0 l/min during walking up increasing gradients.

(4) **Hypoxia** occurs when severe exercise is performed and the subject breathes air. When 50 per cent O_2 is substituted for air, ventilation falls somewhat.

(5) **Body temperature** rises during exercise, and we have seen that heating increases ventilatory responsiveness to CO_2.

The five factors discussed above are partly additive, but hypoxia and rise in temperature both interact with the CO_2 stimulus, causing a disproportionately great ventilatory response. This fact has often been overlooked by those who find a significant portion of the ventilatory rise unaccounted for.

The control of ventilation during sleep

The response to CO_2 is depressed during normal sleep; the CO_2 threshold is slightly increased and the CO_2 sensitivity decreased. The degree of respiratory depression parallels the depth of sleep as judged by the electroencephalographic pattern. Breathing air, arterial P_{CO_2} may increase during deep sleep to 50 or 55 mm Hg and slight hypoxia may be present. How sleep affects the ventilatory response to hypoxia has not been fully investigated.

Conversely, any influence which increases wakefulness also increases ventilation. Ventilation, indeed, seems to be part of a 'package deal' delivered by the reticular formation, and it is probably idle to suppose that ventilation can be depressed or increased specifically. CO_2 itself, as we have seen, acts in high concentration as a general anaesthetic; in lower concentration it is an 'arousal' agent and at still higher concentration it causes convulsions. At rest, breathing air, ventilation is often not well correlated with alveolar or arterial P_{CO_2}; this may be because the so-called 'waking drive' to respiration supports ventilation at this level, making it relatively independent of CO_2.

FURTHER READING

CARO C.C. ed. (1966) *Advances in Respiratory Physiology.* London: Arnold.

COMROE J.H., FORSTER R.E., DUBOIS A.B., BRISCOE W.A. & CARLSEN E. (1962) *The Lung: Clinical Physiology and Pulmonary Function Tests.* 2nd Edition. Chicago: Year Book Publishers Inc.

CUNNINGHAM D.J.C. & LLOYD B.B. ed. (1963) *The Regulation of Human Respiration.* Oxford: Blackwell Scientific Publications.

HALDANE J.S. & PRIESTLEY J.G. (1935) *Respiration.* 2nd Edition. Oxford: Clarendon Press.

Handbook of Physiology, Section 3: *Respiration* Vol. I (1964) and Vol. II (1965). Washington: American Physiological Society.

'On the 1st August 1825, at 12 o'clock, midday, I introduced through the perforation between the ribs, into the stomach of Alexis St. Martin, the following articles of diet, suspended by a silk string . . . a piece of high seasoned à la mode beef, a piece of raw salted lean beef, a piece of raw salted fat pork, a piece of stale bread, and a bunch of raw cabbage. The lad continued his domestic employments about the house. 2 o'clock p.m.: withdrew and examined them: found the cabbage, bread, pork, and boiled beef all cleanly digested and gone from the string: the other pieces of meat but very little affected.'

This classical experiment was performed 150 years ago by William Beaumont on Alexis St. Martin, who was wounded in the stomach by a load of duck shot and was left with a fistula which failed to heal. It demonstrated the ability of the stomach to secrete a powerful digestive fluid for the breakdown of food. Equally remarkable is the resistance of the wall of the gut to its own digestive secretions, although the patient who suffers from peptic ulcer may testify that this resistance is not absolute.

The breakdown of food in the stomach is only one of many processes by which its constituents are assimilated into the body from the gut. The types of food in the diet vary greatly between individuals, depending on factors such as availability, economics, religious and social taboos and personal taste. In general about 500 g of solid matter and 2·5 litres of water are ingested each day. This passes down the hollow muscular tube of the gastrointestinal tract and appears at its lower end, after an interval of 24 to 48 hours, as faeces containing about 30 g of solids and 100 ml of water.

In this chapter we shall consider (1) the anatomy of this tube as it may be seen in the dissecting room or operating theatre, (2) the histology of the gut and the glands which manufacture the digestive juices, together with an account of the control mechanisms which ensure that each of the glands produces its secretion when the food reaches the appropriate place in its passage down the canal, (3) the processes of absorption by which the small molecules produced by the action of the digestive enzymes are transported from the lumen of the canal across the wall and into the veins and lymphatics, (4) the mechanisms by which the food is moved along the tract, (5) the blood supply of the digestive system and finally, (6) the embryology of the tract.

General organization and function of the alimentary canal

The gastrointestinal tract is a long fibromuscular tube stretching from the mouth to the anus, lined with an epithelium which in places is specialized for secretion and for absorption. The wall is composed of four concentric layers (fig. 30.1) from within outwards as follows:

(1) mucosa, consisting of epithelium, lamina propria and muscularis mucosae,
(2) submucosa,
(3) muscularis externa, consisting of outer longitudinal and inner circular fibres,
(4) serosa or adventitia.

The lining or **mucosa** consists of a surface epithelium, a lamina propria of supporting connective tissue and an inner thin layer of smooth muscle, the muscularis mucosae. The epithelium varies in different parts of the gut and is often richly glandular. Its surface is lubricated by a viscous adhesive layer of mucus. The lamina propria is a loose connective tissue layer which contains many capillaries where the epithelium is glandular. The muscularis mucosae is a thin sheet of smooth muscle with some elastic fibres; it causes local movements and folding of the mucosa and is innervated by sympathetic fibres.

The **submucosa** is a denser connective tissue layer with large blood vessels and contains a nerve plexus with parasympathetic ganglion cells which innervate the overlying mucosal glands. The plexus is especially prominent where the mucosa is very glandular, e.g. the stomach.

The main muscle coat, or **muscularis externa** is generally composed of an outer longitudinal and an inner circular layer of smooth muscle. In parts of the gut however, such as the oesophagus, stomach and colon there are local modifications of this arrangement. The muscle coat receives a parasympathetic innervation from the myenteric nerve plexus lying between its layers.

Much of the alimentary canal is covered with a **serosal layer**, mostly peritoneum. This layer consists of a smooth

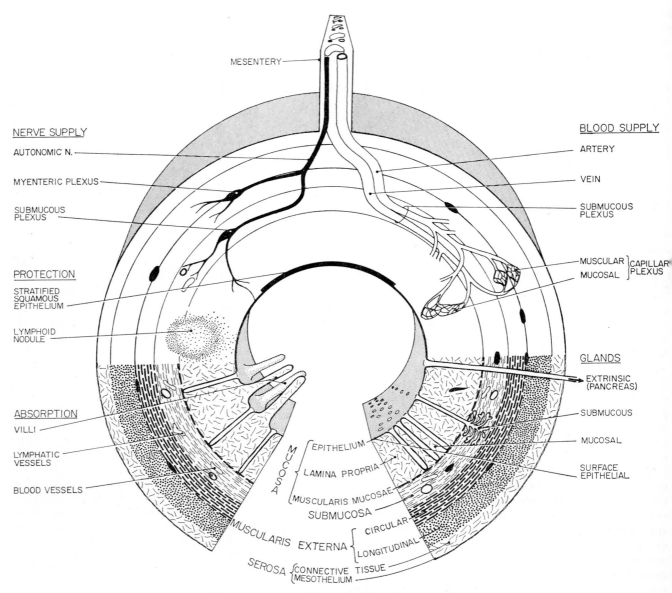

NERVE SUPPLY
AUTONOMIC N.
MYENTERIC PLEXUS
SUBMUCOUS PLEXUS

PROTECTION
STRATIFIED SQUAMOUS EPITHELIUM
LYMPHOID NODULE

ABSORPTION
VILLI
LYMPHATIC VESSELS
BLOOD VESSELS

MESENTERY

BLOOD SUPPLY
ARTERY
VEIN
SUBMUCOUS PLEXUS
MUSCULAR CAPILLAR
MUCOSAL PLEXUS

GLANDS
EXTRINSIC (PANCREAS)
SUBMUCOUS
MUCOSAL
SURFACE EPITHELIAL

MUCOSA { EPITHELIUM / LAMINA PROPRIA / MUSCULARIS MUCOSAE
SUBMUCOSA
MUSCULARIS EXTERNA { CIRCULAR / LONGITUDINAL
SEROSA { CONNECTIVE TISSUE / MESOTHELIUM

FIG. 30.1. Layers of the wall of the alimentary tract.

simple mesothelium of squamous cells with underlying loose connective tissue. Blood vessels and nerves supplying the gut often travel in this layer before entering the muscle coat. In parts where there is no serosa, loose connective tissue forms an **adventitious coat** which merges with the surrounding connective tissue.

The **intrinsic blood supply** varies in different regions of the gut, but is very rich in segments with high secretory or absorptive activities, such as the stomach or small intestine. Generally the arteries approach the gut at right angles to its long axis, enter the serosa or adventitia and after supplying the muscularis externa pierce it to gain the submucosa. Here the arteries form a plexus which supplies ascending branches to the capillary beds of the overlying muscularis mucosae, glands, and lining epithelium. Veins drain these capillaries into a large venous submucous plexus, which is the site of the splanchnic pool in which blood stagnates in some forms of shock and serious infection. The veins from the submucous plexus follow the path described for the incoming arteries.

The **nerve supply** consists of parasympathetic preganglionic, sympathetic postganglionic and general visceral afferent fibres. These run in the serosa for a variable distance before entering the muscularis externa where they form the **myenteric plexus of Auerbach**. This contains many parasympathetic ganglionic cells which are motor o the muscularis externa. Other nerve fibres leave the serosa and form a **submucosal plexus of Meissner** containing parasympathetic ganglion cells which are secretomotor to the mucosal glands. The sympathetic fibres are vasoconstrictor to the vessels of the gut and the parasympathetic fibres are vasodilator. Sympathetic fibres innervate the muscularis mucosae. The general visceral afferent fibres begin as free endings in the mucosa and also in the muscle where they act as stretch receptors (fig. 30.19).

GENERAL FUNCTIONS OF THE ALIMENTARY CANAL

The gut has a large secretory capacity because in addition to the many intrinsic glands within its walls there is the extrinsic group consisting of the major salivary glands, liver and pancreas. Many litres of fluid are secreted into the lumen of the gut daily, most of which is reabsorbed. This physiological recirculation of fluid explains how alimentary diseases causing vomiting or diarrhoea can lead rapidly to disturbances in water and electrolyte balance. Secretion in the main occurs in the upper part of the alimentary tract and absorption occurs mostly in the middle zone, chiefly but not exclusively in the small intestine.

Secretion and absorption are unconscious processes. The motor functions of the gastrointestinal tract disturb our daily existence; hunger and the desire to defaecate may arise from awareness of motility. Hunger contractions are a stimulus for food intake and arise when the stomach is empty. A few minutes after a meal food begins to leave the stomach, which is usually empty three hours later. On leaving the stomach the food passes fairly rapidly through the small intestine. Within about three to four hours the unabsorbed remnants begin to reach the colon and the residues of the various meals taken each day lie in the descending colon till expulsion. Defaecation usually takes place once per day, but the variation is great and it is not abnormal for it to occur three times per day or to be withheld for up to three days.

The muscle of the alimentary tract regulates the passage of the contents to allow adequate time for digestion and absorption. Mastication is a voluntary movement and swallowing can be initiated voluntarily so the oral and pharyngeal muscles are all striated, and the oesophagus contains both striated and smooth muscle. From the stomach to the anus there is only smooth muscle, except for the external anal sphincter which is again striated.

THE MOUTH, SALIVARY GLANDS, PHARYNX AND OESOPHAGUS

The gross anatomy of the mouth and pharynx are described on p. 21.13.

Salivary glands

The oral cavity is lubricated by saliva, which is secreted by numerous glands. Many of these are small glands in the lining mucosa of the oral cavity and pharynx including the soft palate, but the bulk of the saliva comes from the three pairs of major salivary glands, the parotid, submandibular and sublingual, which lie outwith the oral mucosa. Their gross anatomy is described on pp. 21.18 and 38. The salivary glands are composed of varying proportions of serous and mucous acini, the former producing the enzyme ptyalin, salts and water, and the latter mucus.

The **parotid gland** is the largest and is a pure serous compound tubulo-acinar gland. A fibrous capsule sends septa into the gland dividing it into lobules. The acini are composed of typical serous cells (p. 17.4) and drain into intercalated ducts lined with a low cubical epithelium; these unite and form intralobular ducts lined with cubical epithelium and are striated because of basal infoldings (p. 13.12), which indicate active transport. Thus the primary secretion of the acinar cells is modified as it traverses the striated ducts. On leaving the lobules these ducts become lined with columnar epithelium and lie in the interlobular septa with the vessels and nerves. The main parotid duct emerging from the gland has many goblet cells in its mucosa.

The nerves in the interlobular septa contain both parasympathetic postganglionic fibres from the otic ganglion (p. 21.34), which are secretomotor and end in close relation to the acinar and duct cells, and sympathetic fibres that accompany the arteries into the gland and are mainly vasoconstrictor.

The **submandibular gland** (fig. 30.2) is a mixed compound tubulo-acinar gland composed mostly of serous acini. The mucous acini are often surmounted by groups of serous demilunes (p. 17.4). The duct system is similar to that of the parotid, but the striated ducts are longer and therefore especially prominent.

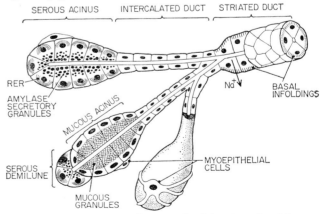

FIG. 30.2. High power diagram of acini and a striated duct in the submandibular salivary gland. RER, rough surfaced endoplasmic reticulum.

The **sublingual gland** is also a mixed compound tubulo-acinar gland but is mainly mucous. Although there are few pure serous acini, many of the mucous acini display serous demilunes. The parasympathetic secretomotor fibres of both the submandibular and sublingual glands come from the submandibular ganglion (p. 21.35).

SALIVARY SECRETION

Food in the mouth is broken up by chewing, moistened and mixed with the saliva. Since the food is present for only a short time before swallowing, there is little opportunity for digestion, but the salivary ptyalin continues to act after the food has passed to the stomach. The flow varies greatly from about 0·2 ml/min from the resting glands up to 4·0 ml/min with maximum secretion. In man an estimate may be made of the volume of saliva secreted in a given time by collecting the juice in dry dental swabs and weighing.

Composition of saliva

The constituents of saliva can be studied by cannulating the ducts of the glands and collecting their secretion. In this way it has been shown that different types of saliva are formed by the different pairs of glands. These types of secretion are related to the histological structure of the glands and whether they contain mainly mucous or serous cells. The secretion from the parotid glands is watery and contains a high concentration of the enzyme ptyalin. The submandibular glands secrete a viscous fluid, containing a variable amount of ptyalin and mucus, while the sublingual secretions contain little ptyalin, but a great deal of mucus and are therefore very viscous. The concentration of ions varies according to the rate of secretion (fig. 30.3). An estimate of daily secretion is given on p. 30.38.

Saliva is always hypotonic and at maximum rates of secretion has about two-thirds of the osmolality of the plasma; under these conditions [Na$^+$] is about 80 mEq/l and [K$^+$] 20m Eq/l. When the secretory rate is slow, there is a transport of Na$^+$ from the striated ducts into the surrounding capillaries and [Na$^+$] may fall to 20 mEq/l or less. This mechanism is under aldosterone control. The chief anion is HCO$_3$, which may be present at a concentration of over 50 mEq/l.

Functions of saliva

Ptyalin is an amylase which initiates the breakdown of starch and glycogen to maltose and a small amount of glucose. It is active over a wide pH range, with an optimum at 6·9. The high mucus content of saliva lubricates the mouth and pharynx and without it swallowing is impossible. By dissolving solids such as sugars it intensifies the taste of food; this may have important consequences on the secretion of other digestive juices. Since little digestion takes place in the mouth, it is not surprising that no absorption of nutrients occurs there. The thin mucosa barrier, however, allows some drugs to be absorbed directly from the mouth into the blood stream.

Control of salivary secretion

This is nervous and there is no chemical or hormonal mechanism since ingested food is present in the mouth for so short a time. In fact, secretion usually increases above the resting rate before food actually enters the mouth, particularly if the food is appetizing, when its sight and smell 'make the mouth water'. This response to a stimulus which is appreciated by the subject is a conditioned reflex (p. 24.92). The continuation of secretion after food has been taken into the mouth is due to an unconditioned reflex. A mechanical stimulus, the contact of food on the mucosa of the mouth, leads to afferent impulses passing via the glossopharyngeal and lingual nerves to a secretory centre in the medulla; efferent impulses pass via autonomic nerves to stimulate the effector organs, the salivary glands.

FIG. 30.3. Average composition of the parotid saliva of three young women as a function of the rate of secretion. From Thayson, J.H., Thorn, N.A. & Schwartz, I.L. (1954) *Amer. J. Physiol.*, **178**, 155.

Studies of what happens when the nerves to the glands are stimulated in experimental animals help understanding of the nervous control of secretion. Electrical stimulation of the parasympathetic nerves, e.g. chorda tympani, of the cat causes marked vasodilation, with a rise in blood flow of about 4–8 times; the oxygen consumption of the glands also increases showing that secretion is an active process, and a copious flow of saliva follows. Injections of small quantities of acetylcholine into the arteries supplying the glands have similar effects as would be expected since the nerves are cholinergic. However, acetylcholine is probably not a direct stimulus to the secretory cell. When released at the parasympathetic nerve endings, it sets free from the glandular tissue an enzyme called **kallikrein**; this enzyme acts on plasma globulins to form the polypeptide **bradykinin** which is an active vasodilator. This vasodilation may account for the increase in secretion. If the sympathetic nerves are stimulated, there is vasoconstriction and the glands secrete a viscous saliva containing a great deal of mucus; injection of noradrenaline into the arterial supply has the same effect. The sympathetic nerves affect mainly the mucous cells of the submandibular and sublingual glands.

When a meal is eaten, both the sympathetic and parasympathetic efferent pathways of the reflexes operate and the saliva is a mixture of the secretions of the three pairs of glands.

CHEWING

As the food is chewed, small quantities are separated by the teeth and tongue and passed into the oropharynx to be swallowed and passed down the oesophagus to the stomach. Chewing food is partly a voluntary and partly an involuntary process. Contrary to the teaching most people receive as children, the extent to which food is chewed has a negligible effect on digestion. Chewing breaks up the food and mixes it with saliva, thereby facilitating swallowing. Each portion of food entering the mouth is broken up voluntarily to start with, but the contact of the food on teeth, gums and palate produces a reflex opening of the jaw which is followed by contraction of the muscles closing the jaw. Thus an involuntary rhythm is produced. The extent of chewing depends on the type of food, e.g. soft foods are chewed for a shorter time than hard foods, and it is easily modified by external influences such as conversation.

Oesophagus

The oesophagus begins in the neck, just behind the cricoid cartilage, and is continuous with the lower end of the pharynx. It is a long fibromuscular tube which descends through the thorax, where it lies in the posterior mediastinum, and pierces the diaphragm to gain the abdomen. After a short abdominal course of about 2 cm it ends at

FIG. 30.4. Anterior view of oesophagus. Note relations to trachea, left main bronchus, aorta, diaphragm and the vagus nerves.

the gastro-oesophageal junction or **cardia**, the entrance to the stomach (fig. 30.4).

ANATOMICAL RELATIONS

The oesophagus is related anteriorly first to the trachea and then to the left main bronchus and the left pulmonary artery, and the pericardium separating it from the left atrium. Enlargement of any one of these structures may compress the oesophagus causing difficulty in swallowing (dysphagia). The normal oesophageal lumen, in radiographs taken after swallowing a radio-opaque substance, shows slight indentations opposite these structures (plate 30.1a, facing p. 28.28), and another on its left side caused by the arch of the aorta. Posteriorly the oesophagus is related closely to the lower cervical vertebral bodies, and so disease of the latter may also cause dysphagia. In the thorax the oesophagus is separated from the vertebral column by the meso-oesophagus, a double sheet of pleura containing oesophageal vessels from the aorta. On lateral radiographs, the space between the oesophagus and vertebrae appears as the retro-oesophageal window. On approaching the diaphragm the oesophagus swings forwards and to the left before piercing the left dome 2 cm to the left of the midline, at the level of the 10th thoracic vertebra.

Because the oesophagus in the mediastinum is surrounded by loose connective tissue which permits it to distend during swallowing, perforation of the oesophageal wall may lead to a spreading infection of the mediastinum, which is commonly fatal.

The vagus nerves descend behind the lung roots and then surround the oesophagus as a plexus (fig. 30.4). Near the diaphragm this oesophageal plexus forms anterior and posterior gastric trunks which lie on the corresponding surfaces of the oesophagus, and accompany it into the abdomen.

There is an important porto-caval anastomosis at the lower end of the oesophagus, which is described on p. 30.47.

STRUCTURE OF THE OESOPHAGUS (figs. 30.5 and 6)
The oesophagus, where no digestion occurs, is lined with a tough non-keratinizing stratified squamous epithelium similar to that of the pharynx. A few simple mucous glands lie in the mucosa at both ends of the oesophagus and the submucous nerve plexus is inconspicuous. The oesophageal glands proper are tubulo-

FIG. 30.5. Oesophagus T.S. The basic structure is typical of the alimentary tract.

FIG. 30.6. Oesophagus T.S. This higher power view shows the tough stratified squamous epithelium and the main oesophageal mucous glands in the submucosa.

acinar mucous glands found in the submucosa. During swallowing the oesophagus is also lubricated by the mucus from salivary, nasal, and bronchial secretions.

The muscle coat has the typical two layers, which consist of striated muscle in the upper third, both striated and smooth muscle in the middle third and only smooth muscle in the lower third. The inner circular coat is no thicker in the lower third of the oesophagus although there is a physiological sphincter above the cardia.

The cervical and thoracic oesophagus have an adventitia, except where related to pleura, but the intra-abdominal portion is covered by peritoneum.

There is the usual myenteric nerve plexus with parasympathetic ganglion cells which innervate the smooth muscle. The striated muscle is supplied by the vagus, fibres coming directly from the nucleus ambiguus (p. 24.24) similar to those which innervate the branchial striated muscle of the pharynx.

FUNCTION OF THE OESOPHAGUS—SWALLOWING
Swallowing involves both voluntary and reflex movements; it occurs in three stages.

(1) Small amounts of food are separated from the bolus being chewed and passed to the pharynx by the movement of the tongue (the voluntary phase).

(2) A reflex phase is initiated by the contact of food with the pharynx, soft palate and epiglottis. Impulses from these receptor sites pass via the glossopharyngeal nerves and the superior laryngeal branch of the vagus to the **deglutition (swallowing) centre** in the medulla. Here the motor response is co-ordinated and efferent impulses pass via the vagi and other nerves to the muscles responsible for the passage of food to the oesophagus. At the same time, contraction of other muscles prevents the bolus from entering the larynx or nasopharynx or passing back into the mouth (21.47).

(3) The third phase is also reflex, and the stimuli and reflex pathways are the same as for the second. After reaching the oesophagus the bolus is conducted along its length by peristalsis. A wave of contraction of the wall, preceded by a wave of relaxation, produces a pressure gradient which forces the bolus along the tube. The co-ordination of this movement depends on the parasympathetic myenteric plexuses present in the oesophageal wall. The bolus is thus passed towards the stomach, and impulses from the vagi relax the cardia and food enters the stomach. This is also assisted by the pressure built up in the terminal part of the oesophagus by repeated waves of peristalsis. The conduction of the food from the pharynx to the stomach is the only action of the oesophagus; no digestion and no absorption take place.

The motility of the oesophagus is easily studied in man. The subject swallows open-ended tubes from which by manometric techniques the intraluminal pressures are recorded. Three fine tubes are usually swallowed together, their distal apertures about 5 cm apart. As the subject swallows, a pressure wave may be recorded passing along the oesophageal lumen; that it is a propagated 'wave' may be deduced from its arrival opposite each tube in sequence. If the lowermost tube is placed in the most distal part of the oesophagus this zone is found to relax momentarily before the wave of contraction (fig. 30.7) reaches it. Respiratory variations, not shown in the figure, are superimposed on the general pressure patterns. If the multiple

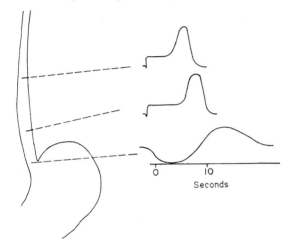

FIG. 30.7. Pressures in the lower part of the oesophagus during swallowing.

tube system is swallowed the length of the oesophagus and withdrawn upwards again, high pressure zones are detectable in the lowermost and uppermost areas. The lower sphincter prevents reflux of acid from the stomach into the oesophagus. The relaxation required at the upper zone before peristalsis is initiated in the oesophagus, and at the lower to enable the food to pass through the cardia, is reflexly induced.

Swallowing has been extensively studied by observing the passage of radio-opaque barium along the oesophagus using cine-radiography in man and animals. The time taken for food to reach the stomach from the mouth is about 5 sec, of which the transit time along the oesophagus is about 2 sec.

ABDOMINAL VISCERA OF ALIMENTARY SYSTEM

The major portion of the alimentary tract and its two main accessory glands, the liver and pancreas, are within the abdominopelvic cavity. Because of its great length the tract follows a devious course between the lower end of the oesophagus and its termination at the anus. The digestive organs are anterior to those of the genitourinary system which lie against the posterior abdominal wall.

The general disposition of the gastrointestinal tract is shown in fig. 30.8. The stomach, which starts just beneath the diaphragm on the left of the midline, sweeps down and to the right across the midline to join the duodenum at the pylorus. The C-shaped duodenum returns to the left side and becomes continuous, behind the stomach, with the jejunum and ileum. The latter are very convoluted, filling much of the lower part of the abdominal cavity and are attached to the posterior wall by the mesentery. The ileum ends in the right iliac fossa at the ileocaecal valve. The large intestine begins as the caecum which is the blunt cul-de-sac below the level of the valve,

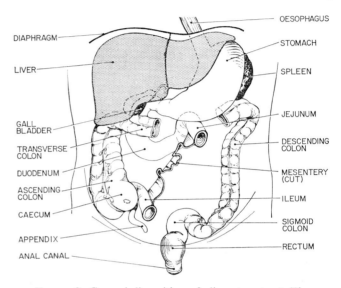

FIG. 30.8. General disposition of alimentary tract. The greater omentum, most of the small intestine and part of the transverse colon have been removed.

and gives off the vermiform appendix. Above, the caecum is freely continuous with the colon which ascends to the liver, where it turns medially at the hepatic flexure and runs transversely across the abdomen to the spleen, passing in front of the duodenum and pancreas but behind the stomach. From the splenic flexure the colon descends to the left iliac fossa, and then curves medially to enter the true pelvis. There it descends in front of the sacrum and joins the rectum, which ends at the anal canal. The liver is a large solid organ occupying the right hypochondrium beneath the diaphragm. The pancreas, omitted from fig. 30.8, stretches from the concavity of the duodenum across the posterior abdominal wall to the spleen.

PERITONEUM

Early in development the peritoneal cavity appears as a split in the lateral mesoderm which then forms two layers of peritoneum, the parietal layer lining the wall of the abdominal cavity, and the visceral layer covering the gut and its mesenteries (p. 18.13). This simple arrangement of the mesenteries is much modified before the adult state is reached, so that the relationships of the adult organs to the peritoneum differ from each other (fig. 30.11). The kidneys, for example, lie behind the parietal layer on the posterior abdominal wall and are therefore termed **retroperitoneal**. Much of the duodenum is also retroperitoneal because its mesentery has fused with parietal peritoneum

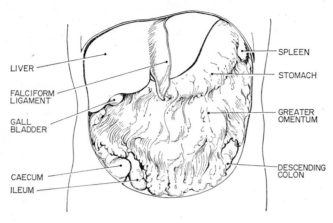

FIG. 30.9. Anterior view of abdominal contents. The greater omentum obscures much of the alimentary tract, but the stomach, ileum, caecum and descending colon are visible.

(p. 30.53). The jejuno-ileum however, is completely covered with visceral peritoneum, except for the thin linear attachment of the mesentery. It is important to appreciate that the peritoneal cavity is a potential space, containing only a thin film of fluid which lubricates the apposed surfaces, and that it does not contain abdominal viscera such as the small intestine. The basic relationships of peritoneum and gut can be simulated with a balloon for the peritoneum, and a pencil for the gut (fig. 30.10). If the pencil is laid along the balloon and gradually pressed down, it in-

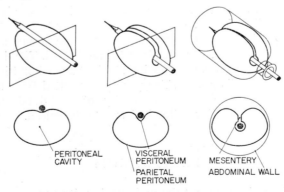

FIG. 30.10. Model of peritoneum. The balloon represents the peritoneum and peritoneal cavity and the pencil a portion of gut.

vaginates the balloon and various typical relations are established. Without pressure the pencil is 'retroperitoneal', but as pressure is applied, it becomes covered on three sides (cf. the ascending or descending colon), and with further pressure a mesentery is formed (cf. jejunum). Observe that the pencil (gut) is not inside the balloon (peritoneal cavity), unless the balloon bursts. Similarly the peritoneal cavity is empty, and does not contain viscera. Finally, if the manoeuvre is repeated with the balloon and pencil, within a bottle representing the abdominal walls, one can appreciate that both the pencil (gut) and the balloon (peritoneum) are within the cavity of the bottle (abdominal cavity), but the cavity of the balloon (peritoneal cavity) is empty.

The peritoneal cavity is a closed one in the male, but in the female it communicates with the exterior via the openings of the uterine tubes (p. 37.2). Thus in the female an ascending infection of the genital tract may involve the peritoneum.

A **mesentery** is a double layer of peritoneum containing blood vessels, attaching a viscus to the parietal peritoneum. The largest is that of the jejuno-ileum, which is known as the mesentery. Others sometimes have the prefix 'meso' followed by the organ to which they are attached, as in mesocolon, or mesoappendix. Some peritoneal sheets are somewhat arbitrarily termed ligaments or folds. The latter usually have a free edge, but many ligaments also have free edges. Such peritoneal structures possess elasticity which gives attached and related organs a high degree of mobility and allows the changes in shape, size and position of the hollow gut as ingested food and drink is stored, digested, absorbed and moved down the tract.

The peritoneal cavity extends from beneath the diaphragm down to the pelvic floor. Although a continuous cavity, it is partly subdivided into several compartments in which abnormal fluids such as pus or blood may accumulate and be localized to a greater or lesser degree. Thus a knowledge of these compartments or spaces is of value in predicting the spread of disease from a particular organ or alternatively of deducing the probable source of a collection of fluid in a given site. There are two important compartments called the **greater** and **lesser sacs**.

The simplest way to understand the peritoneal cavity is by a manual exploration of the abdomen. We shall now do this in imagination, looking first at the relations and attachments of neighbouring viscera and then try to appreciate the general features of the peritoneum.

EXPLORATION OF THE PERITONEAL CAVITY

On reflecting the anterior abdominal wall with its parietal peritoneum, the peritoneal cavity is entered. Without disturbing the viscera one can see (fig. 30.9) the liver, stomach, and the **greater omentum** which is a flattened pouch of peritoneum hanging down from the stomach anterior to the jejuno-ileum. Inferior to the omentum, coils of ileum are apparent and the caecum occupies the right iliac fossa. If the greater omentum is lifted upwards over the stomach, its attachment to the antimesentric border of the transverse colon is exposed (figs. 30.11 and 30.12). Examination of the transverse colon reveals that it is mobile because it is slung by a mesentery, the **transverse mesocolon**, from the posterior abdominal wall. Near the middle of the transverse colon, the jejunum starts. The jejunum and ileum follow a very convoluted course, but they are attached to the posterior abdominal wall by their sheet-like mesentery, which begins to the left of the midline inferior to the transpyloric plane, and runs obliquely down to the right iliac fossa where the ileum joins the caecum (figs. 30.8 and 30.11).

The caecum has a variable peritoneal relationship, but the lower end is usually completely invested and hangs free. The ascending colon is covered completely except where it rests directly on the posterior abdominal wall. The transverse colon has already been examined but note again that it is mobile as it has a mesocolon except at the two flexures.

The descending colon is bound to the posterior abdominal wall in the same fashion as the ascending colon.

The sigmoid colon is more mobile, and is attached by a mesocolon to the posterior and left side wall of the true pelvis. The upper part of the rectum is related in front and laterally to peritoneum but gradually it loses this coat as it descends towards the pelvic floor and becomes outwith the peritoneum like the anal canal (fig. 30.33).

In the upper abdomen, the **lesser omentum** is a double layer of peritoneum which runs from the right border of the stomach upwards to join the liver on its

FIG. 30.12. Median sagittal section through the peritoneal cavity, with viscera intact. Section is in plane A of fig. 30.11.

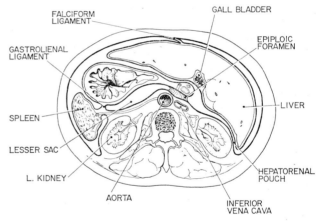

FIG. 30.13. Horizontal section of the peritoneal cavity. Plane B of figs. 30.11 and 12.

FIG 30.14. Horizontal section of the peritoneal cavity. Plane C of figs. 30.11. and 12.

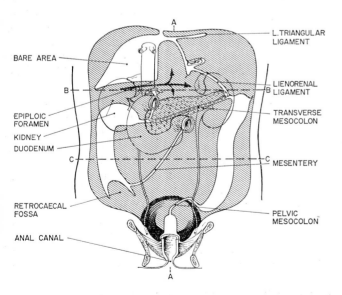

FIG. 30.11. Peritoneal relations of the posterior abdominal wall. The liver, spleen and most of the gut have been removed. Compare with fig. 30.8.

inferior or visceral surface. Traced superiorly towards the diaphragm behind the left lobe of the liver, it is found to have no free upper margin because it is reflected on to the diaphragm from the oesophagus (fig. 30.11). Following it towards the duodenum, note that it arises not only from the stomach but also from the proximal part of the duodenum and has a free right margin which leads up to the porta hepatis. The latter is so-called because it is the door of the liver where the two hepatic bile ducts, and major vessels leave and enter the liver.

From the left side and inferior border of the stomach another sheet, the greater omentum, runs posteriorly and eventually reaches the posterior abdominal wall. Begin at the oesophagus and confirm that the greater omentum is attached to the diaphragm and has no free upper border. Proceeding inferiorly, now run the right hand posteriorly and leftward again and you encounter the spleen (fig. 30.13) which is invested in the peritoneum of the left leaf of the greater omentum. Palm the spleen in the right hand so that the fingers are behind it and the thumb anterior, and feel between finger and thumb the narrow attachment of the spleen to the omentum (fig. 30.13). At this level the greater omentum is divided by the splenic attachment into an anterior portion, the **gastrolienal ligament**, and the **lienorenal ligament** which passes dorsally to fuse with the parietal peritoneum over the kidney on the posterior abdominal wall.

To check that the greater omentum is a thin sheet, cut a hole through the mesocolon from below avoiding damage to vessels) after lifting the omentum upwards. Now gently insert the left hand through the hole up behind the stomach, grasp the spleen in the right hand, and feel that only the thin membrane of the lienorenal ligament separates the right fingertips from the left hand, and similarly the gastrolienal ligament lies between the right thumb and left hand. Inferior to the spleen, the omentum hangs down from the lower border (greater curvature) of the stomach like a flattened pouch (figs. 30.9 and 30.14).

The greater omentum has free lateral and inferior borders where the anterior wall of the pouch curves backwards to form its posterior wall. The latter ascends and is attached to the transverse colon in the adult (fig. 30.12). In the embryo it rested on the superior surface of the colon and mesocolon before being reflected on to the parietal peritoneum over the pancreas, but fusion of its posterior surface to the adjacent surface of the mesocolon and colon moved its attachment to the adult position (fig. 30.64).

Push the right hand through the hole in the mesocolon and feel downwards into the pouch of the greater omentum; frequently it will be found that the cavity is obliterated by fusion of the adjacent walls.

The peritoneal relations of the liver are complex and are shown in figs. 30.15 and 30.16. The two layers of the

FIG. 30.15. Posterior oblique view of liver. This demonstrates the subdiaphragmatic spaces, and the peritoneal relations of the liver and lesser omentum.

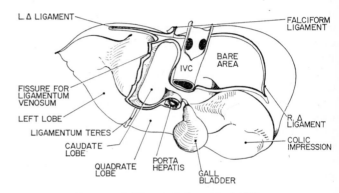

FIG. 30.16. The posterior aspect of liver.

lesser omentum separate and enclose the liver, before leaving its superior and posterior surfaces as the **coronary ligament** which ascends to the diaphragm (fig. 30.62). The liver develops in the ventral mesentery of the foregut between the stomach and the diaphragm (p. 30.51).

There are several important **subdiaphragmatic spaces** which lie between the diaphragm and the liver. To understand them, the peritoneal reflections on the liver must be traced out although not committed to memory. First pass the left hand into the **hepatorenal pouch** which is posteroinferior to the right lobe of liver (arrow 1). Next slide the other hand backwards above the right lobe (arrow 2). The **bare area,** which is devoid of peritoneum, and where the liver and diaphragm are in direct contact, separates the hands. Slide both hands to the right and they meet around the free border of the right triangular ligament. Withdraw the hand from the hepatorenal pouch, and pass it above the left lobe of liver (arrow 3) into the left triangular ligament. The hands are now on either side of the **falciform ligament,** which runs from the liver to the diaphragm and anterior abdominal wall as far down as the umbilicus. The lower free border is thickened because it contains the fibrous remnant of the umbilical vein, the **ligamentum teres** of the liver. This goes from the umbilicus *anterior ... be deleted ... in Davis (1968) Ann. Surg 168, 6.*

to the fissure for the ligamentum teres which is the boundary between the left and the quadrate lobes (fig. 30.16). Remove both hands and now place the left hand in the left anterior subdiaphragmatic space (arrow 3), and slide the other up behind the left lobe of liver in front of the lesser omentum (arrow 4); the fingertips are separated by the thin left triangular ligament. Now trace the attachment of the lesser omentum downwards from the back of the left triangular ligament, along the fissure for the ligamentum venosum to the porta hepatis (figs. 30.15 and 30.16). Notice that the omentum lies almost in the coronal plane and passes deeply into the fissure for the ligamentum venosum on the anterior aspect of the caudate lobe (fig. 30.16). Place the left hand in the hepatorenal pouch (arrow 1) and slide the forefinger medially along its upper limit (arrow 5) until it enters a narrow aperture, the **epiploic foramen** or entrance to the lesser sac.

The epiploic foramen is bounded anteriorly by the lesser omentum with the bile duct, hepatic artery, and portal vein within its free border. Posteriorly, the inferior vena cava ascends retroperitoneally on the posterior abdominal wall. The caudate process of the liver is above the foramen and inferiorly the hepatic artery runs forwards from the coeliac artery before ascending to enter the lesser omentum (fig. 30.37).

The **lesser sac of peritoneum** lies behind the stomach, and separates it from the structures on the posterior abdominal wall (fig. 30.13). It extends as the upper recess behind the lesser omentum and caudate lobe (fig. 30.12), and inferiorly for a variable distance as the inferior recess into the greater omentum. The narrow epiploic foramen is the only communication with the greater sac. In health it is only a potential space, but in disease may be filled with fluid, e.g. a gastric ulcer may perforate through the posterior stomach wall and pour irritant gastric contents into the sac.

The **greater sac of peritoneum** is the remainder of the peritoneal cavity, including the pelvic portion. It is partly subdivided into various compartments by the abdominal organs and their peritoneal attachments. We have already seen that there are subdiaphragmatic spaces between the liver and diaphragm and these may become the site of an abscess (fig. 30.15). The ascending and descending colons project from the posterior abdominal wall so that there are paracolic gutters alongside them which may determine the spread of infection from various organs (fig. 30.14).

The greater omentum and mesocolon form a large flap which divides the greater sac into supracolic and infracolic compartments which are in free communication via the lateral paracolic gutters.

The greater omentum varies in size between individuals, and may contain an enormous amount of fat. In local inflammation of the peritoneum there is often a sticky exudate to which the omentum adheres, and this helps to localize the infection. The omentum is brought sooner or

later to such sites as it is in a constant state of passive movement, produced by the muscular activity of viscera as they fill and empty, and by the respiratory and postural movements of the diaphragm and abdominal walls.

STOMACH

Once food has been swallowed it leaves the oesophagus and enters the stomach via the cardia. The stomach is a large fibromuscular bag with a capacity of $\frac{1}{2}$–1 litre, which stores the food and passes it on to the duodenum when required. The stomach also secretes gastric juice (Latin gaster = stomach) which partly digests the stored contents.

Gross anatomy

The stomach lies in the upper part of the abdominal cavity, inferior to the diaphragm and liver, and is separated from the posterior abdominal wall only by the lesser sac. The stomach begins at the gastro-oesophageal junction or **cardia** and extends down and right to end at the

FIG. 30.17. Stomach.

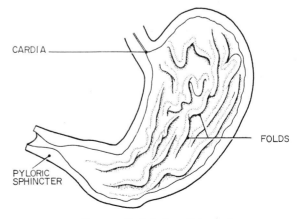

FIG. 30.18. Interior of stomach.

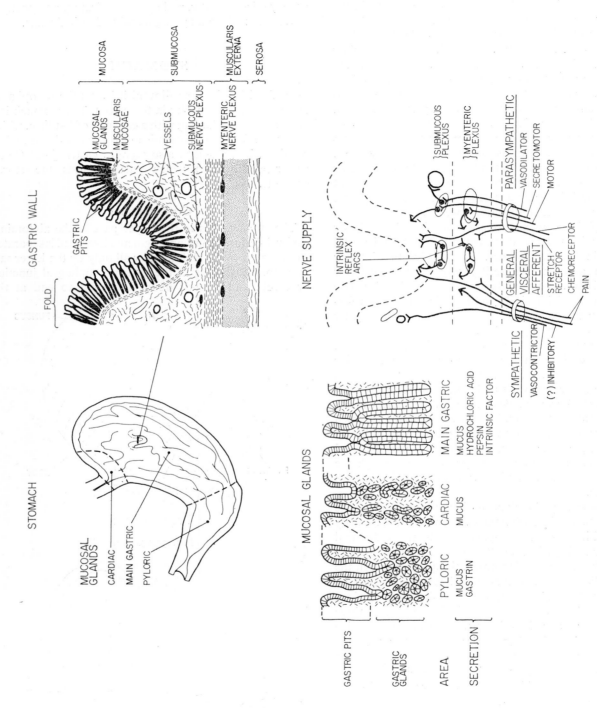

STOMACH

MUCOSAL
GLANDS
CARDIAC
MAIN GASTRIC
PYLORIC

GASTRIC WALL

MUCOSA
SUBMUCOSA
MUSCULARIS EXTERNA
SEROSA

MUCOSAL GLANDS
MUSCULARIS MUCOSAE
VESSELS
SUBMUCOUS NERVE PLEXUS
MYENTERIC NERVE PLEXUS

FOLD
GASTRIC PITS

MUCOSAL GLANDS

	PYLORIC	CARDIAC	MAIN GASTRIC
GASTRIC PITS			
GASTRIC GLANDS			
AREA	PYLORIC	CARDIAC	MAIN GASTRIC
SECRETION	MUCUS GASTRIN	MUCUS	MUCUS HYDROCHLORIC ACID PEPSIN INTRINSIC FACTOR

NERVE SUPPLY

SUBMUCOUS PLEXUS
MYENTERIC PLEXUS

INTRINSIC REFLEX ARCS

PARASYMPATHETIC
VASODILATOR
SECRETOMOTOR
MOTOR

GENERAL VISCERAL AFFERENT
STRETCH RECEPTOR
CHEMORECEPTOR
PAIN

SYMPATHETIC
VASOCONTRICTOR
(?) INHIBITORY

Fig. 30.19. Histology of the stomach. This composite diagram shows its regional variations and nerve supply.

PLATE 30.2. Histology of the gastrointestinal tract.

Body of stomach (dog). PAS, haem & aurantia. The lumen of the stomach is to the left in these photographs, and is visible in (a). (Cf. fig. 30.20.)

(a) Main gastric glands. Mucus in surface and mucous neck cells is red, parietal cells are yellow, and the serous pepsin cells have a blue cytoplasm.

(b) Isthmus and neck of gastric gland. Surface cells (S), and abundant parietal (P) and mucous neck cells (M).

(c) Base of gland. Serous cells (SE) predominate, but parietal cells (P) are also visible.

Liver (dog). Haem & eosin.

(d) A hepatic lobule containing a central vein lies in the midfield, bordered by one large and two small portal tracts (arrows).

(e) Portal tract. The bile duct tributary is on the right of the branch of the hepatic artery and above the branch of the portal vein (PV).

(f) Central vein, with irregular fenestrated liver sheets converging towards it. Sinusoids separate the sheets of hepatocytes.

gastroduodenal junction or **pylorus**, opposite the intervertebral disc between the bodies of L.1 and L.2, 2 cm to the right of the median plane (fig. 30.8). The stomach has an anterior and a posterior surface, and two blunt lateral borders, known as curvatures (fig. 30.17 and 30.18). The whole stomach bulges downwards and to the left, so the short right border is known as the **lesser curvature**, and the left as the **greater curvature**. The **fundus** is the portion of the stomach that is superior to the cardia, and usually contains a bubble of swallowed air. An oblique line running from an angular notch on the lesser curvature to the greater curvature divides the remainder into a main middle segment known as the **body**, and the **pyloric region**. Although the pyloric region is important functionally, the division between body and fundus is arbitrary and the gastric regions defined histologically are more useful. The pyloric region is also known as the **antrum.**

The stomach is attached to adjacent structures by the lesser and greater omenta which contain the gastric blood vessels and nerves. The lesser omentum runs upwards to be attached to the visceral surface of the liver and diaphragm. The greater omentum stretches from the greater curvature posteriorly to the posterior abdominal wall and transverse colon. The stomach is attached to neighbouring structures mainly by the oesophagus which is tethered as it passes through the diaphragm. The lesser and greater omenta are loose and so permit mobility. For instance the pylorus may descend by as much as 5 cm below the transpyloric plane on inspiration, sliding on the loose extraperitoneal connective tissue which holds it to the posterior abdominal wall. The shape of the stomach is also variable, tending to reflect the shape of its owner in a long thin person, but in the stocky person it is more oblique. The shape and position also depend on the degree of filling, posture, the tone of the abdominal muscles and on respiration. The greater curvature may descend to the level of the true pelvis in a thin erect individual. The tone of the muscle is also affected by emotion, and 'the heart sinking into one's boots' is more likely to be the stomach!

The anterior relations therefore vary according to its particular position, but include the greater sac and the left lobe of liver, left dome of diaphragm, and below these the anterior abdominal wall. The lesser sac is posterior and separates it from the structures shown in figs. 30.12 and 30.13.

The inner surface of the empty stomach is covered with irregular rugae, but these folds largely disappear on filling. Over the curvatures there are several longitudinal folds which are more permanent. When fluid is sipped it flows rapidly down the lesser curvature and into the duodenum within these folds. On palpating the intact stomach the walls are felt to thicken at the pyloric sphincter and, in the living, the prepyloric vein is a useful surgical guide to the pylorus.

Microscopic structure

The mucosa in the stomach is covered by many small pits which lead to gastric glands. Microscopically, a simple tall columnar epithelium covers the surface and dips down to line these gastric pits (figs. 30.19 and 30.20).

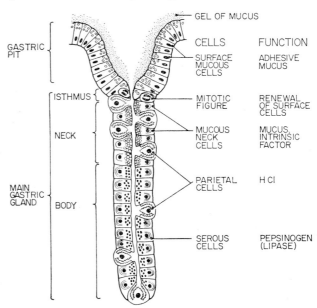

FIG. 30.20. Main gastric glands. These tubular glands are composed of serous, parietal and mucous neck cells, and more primitive cells near the gastric pits which undergo mitosis.

The epithelial cells contain many mucous granules above the nuclei, but in contrast to goblet cells they never become distended with mucus. The entire surface of the stomach secretes an alkaline sheet of mucus which adheres to and protects the epithelium. The lamina propria is very vascular, but is reduced to thin strands between the close packed glands, especially over the acid bearing area of the stomach. The muscularis mucosae is very thick in the human stomach. The submucosa contains many large blood and lymphatic vessels and a prominent submucosal nerve plexus with ganglion cells, which are secretomotor to the glands.

The smooth muscle coat is in three layers, a complete middle circular one which thickens to form the pyloric sphincter, an incomplete outer longitudinal coat confined mostly to the curvatures, and an inner oblique layer which extends from the cardia to the greater curvature.

The gastric mucosa contains three types of gland, which occur in different areas.

The **glands of the cardia** cover an area about 4 cm in diameter centred on the oesophageal orifice. Here the mucosa has gastric pits lined by short branched tubular glands with mucus secreting cells, but very few parietal cells.

The **main gastric glands** form the acid bearing area which amounts to 70–80 per cent of the mucosa. They are also called fundic glands, but as they are present in most of the body of the stomach as well as in the fundus, main gastric glands is a preferable term. The pits are relatively short and receive simple straight tubular glands, each with an isthmus, neck and body (fig. 30.20). **Mucous cells**, in the neck of the gland are low columnar with some cytoplasmic basophilia below the nucleus and many PAS positive mucous granules above. They secrete an acid mucopolysaccharide and may be the source of intrinsic factor, which facilitates the absorption of vitamin B_{12} (p. 26.9). **Serous** or **pepsin producing cells** form most of the gland body. On the luminal side they contain secretory granules and at the base the cytoplasm is intensely basophilic. Their structure is similar to that of other serous cells (p. 17.5). The secretory granules contain **pepsinogen**, the inactive form of the proteolytic enzyme **pepsin**, and precursors of other gastric enzymes. The **parietal** or **oxyntic cells**, which secrete hydrochloric acid, are large with eosinophilic cytoplasm and a central nucleus. They are abundant in the neck and isthmus of the gland. In the body of the gland their position on the wall of the gland gives them the name parietal; the secretion passes between adjacent cells to reach the lumen (fig. 30.20). The parietal cell has a unique system of intracellular canaliculi. These are deep invaginations of the apical cell membrane, which branch as they extend down into the cell. The cell membrane lining the canaliculi has many microvilli, which augment the secretory surface area (figs. 30.21 and 30.22).

Abundant mitochondria with close-packed cristae occupy as much as 40 per cent of the cytoplasm. This accounts for the exceptionally high metabolic rate of the parietal cell, which concentrates H^+ one millionfold, i.e. from pH 7·4 down to pH 1·4. The smooth endoplasmic

FIG. 30.22. Parietal cell, showing rectangular area in fig. 30.21.

reticulum is extensive, and the cells release their contents into the lumen of the gland by a reverse of pinocytosis. The parietal cell is rich in zinc, which is a component of the enzyme carbonic anhydrase. This enzyme catalyses the production of H_2CO_3 (p. 30.15). Argentaffin cells (p. 30.21) are found in the mucous membrane of both the pylorus and body of the stomach.

The **pyloric glands** occupy about 15 per cent of the gastric mucosa, approximately over the pyloric region already defined. The surface cells and pits are similar to those of the other two areas, except that the gastric pits are as long as the glands (fig. 30.19). The latter are branching coiled tubular mucous glands. The hormone gastrin (p. 30.17) is produced by the pyloric mucosa, but its cellular origin has not been identified. It is unlikely that the mucous gland cells are responsible as they appear to be typical exocrine cells.

Cell renewal of gastric epithelium

Mitotic figures are visible in the isthmus of the gastric glands, and in the mucous neck cells. The surface cells are shed at a high rate, but are replaced by fresh cells which arise in the isthmus and move upwards onto the surface. Both in animals and man complete renewal occurs every few days. The renewal rate of zymogenic and parietal cells is undetermined, but is very much slower. Experimentally, destruction in animals of a circumscribed area of gastric mucosa is followed by rapid spread inwards from the wound margins of a thin sheet of epithelium. This covering sheet is formed by division of cells in the isthmuses of the glands around the wound. Downgrowths from this sheet form new glands, which initially are composed solely of mucous neck cells, but later differentiate to form typical main gastric glands with the normal complement of

FIG. 30.21. Parietal cell.

parietal and zymogenic cells. The healthy gastric mucosa has therefore good powers of repair and regeneration.

The functions of the stomach

The stomach is not indispensable for life, though digestive disturbances may follow its removal (gastrectomy). Its main function is to act as a reservoir, in which a semi-solid mass known as the **chyme** is formed from the ingested food. Strongly acid juice kills many bacteria or restricts their growth. Digestion proceeds in the stomach until the chyme passes on to the intestine, but little absorption takes place, except for water and, if taken, alcohol.

Methods of study

Unlike the salivary glands, the gastric secretory glands cannot be cannulated directly and the study of gastric secretion is therefore more difficult because indirect methods must be used. In man, the most common methods involve passing a tube down the oesophagus into the stomach, so that the secretion may be aspirated. Either a 'test meal' or an injection of histamine is first given to stimulate secretion, and samples drawn off for analysis. Both methods are somewhat limited as a means of studying the normal composition of gastric juice, as after a test meal (usually a somewhat unappetizing gruel) the aspirated samples are contaminated with the food, and histamine is an artificial method of stimulating the glands which may not produce a normal secretion. Both tests have now been largely supplanted by the use of synthetic pentagastrin, which simulates the action of the natural gastric hormone (p. 30.17).

In experimental animals, more accurate studies can be made and it is on these that most of the knowledge of the control of gastric secretion is based. In a dog, a small pouch, separate from the main stomach, can be made and brought out through the abdominal wall at a surgical operation. Such a dog can remain in excellent health for many years. Gastric secretion can be stimulated in the normal manner and uncontaminated samples collected from the pouch without disturbing the animal. The pouch may be made in such a way as to leave its nerve supply intact (Pavlov pouch) or deliberately denervated (Heidenhain pouch).

COMPOSITION OF GASTRIC JUICE

The principal constituents are acid, mucus and digestive enzymes.

Acid secretion

The parietal cells secrete a fluid approximately isosmotic with plasma, in which the concentrations in mEq/l of the main electrolytes are about $[H^+]$ 153, $[K^+]$ 7 and $[Cl^-]$ 160. The concentration of electrolytes in the secretions of the other cells are approximately $[Na^+]$ 160, $[Cl^-]$ 120 and $[HCO_3^-]$ 40 mEq/l. The $[H^+]$ of the mixed juice

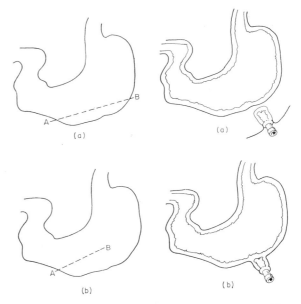

FIG. 30.23. Stomach pouches (a) denervated (Heidenhain) pouch and (b) innervated (Pavlov) pouch. A–B line of gastric incision.

FIG. 30.24. The relation between gastric acid secretion and parietal cell mass. From Card W.I. & Marks I. (1959) *Clin. Sci.* **19**, 147.

usually lies between 70 and 130 mEq/l, about pH 0·9–1·5, and depends on the number of parietal cells present. These cells have been counted in stomachs removed surgically and their number correlated with maximum acid secretion, as previously measured (fig. 30.24). It has been calculated that this amounts to 20 mEq/hr/10^9 cells. The number of cells, known as the **parietal cell mass,** varies widely. Low values for acid secretion are found in some healthy people, presumably due to congenitally few cells and in certain diseases, e.g. pernicious anaemia, when the cells are destroyed by an abnormal immune mechanism.

How the parietal cells manage to secrete a fluid with $[H^+]$ more than one million times that of the blood is an old, largely unsolved problem of ion transport. The cells contain large amounts of carbonic anhydrase which promotes the reactions

$$CO_2 + H_2O \rightarrow H_2CO_3 \rightarrow H^+ + HCO_3^-$$

The HCO_3^- passes into the plasma, from which Cl^- enters the cell to be excreted together with H^+ into the lumen of the stomach. In frog and dog gastric mucosa, a PD develops with the mucosal side about -40 mV relative to the serosal side during secretion; there is also evidence of active transport of Cl^-, which with the active transport of Na^+ out of the stomach may be partly responsible for the PD.

Details of the transport mechanisms for H^+, Cl^- and Na^+ are not known. To concentrate H^+ work, of course, must be done and oxygen is consumed. Secretion of HCl ceases in anaerobic conditions and under the influence of dinitrophenol which uncouples oxidative phosphorylation.

Consistent with the above outline are the old observations that at the height of gastric digestion there is a rise of plasma $[HCO_3^-]$, the **alkaline tide,** and a fall in RQ, due to retention in the body of a part of the metabolic CO_2.

Loss of the gastric secretion by repeated vomiting leads to water and electrolyte disturbances; the patients become dehydrated, deficient in sodium and potassium and develop metabolic alkalosis.

Mucus secretion

The gastric mucus contains a variety of mucopolysaccharides and mucoproteins. The mucopolysaccharides consist of fucomucins, and sialomucins. The mucoproteins contain mannose, galactose and hexosamine. As yet little is known about the relationship between their chemical structure and physiological action.

The mucus secretions of the stomach contain the AB blood group antigens, which are probably formed in the mucous neck cells of the glands. These may have a role in protecting the mucous membrane, since persons of blood group O, in whom they are absent, are more susceptible to duodenal ulceration than persons of other blood groups.

The mucus itself may also protect the stomach wall against the enzymes and acid. One component forms a gel which is partially adherent to the stomach wall and provides a barrier which might delay the diffusion of acid chyme. The extent to which mucus actually neutralizes gastric acidity is probably small.

Glandular mucoproteins also contain the intrinsic factor (p. 26.9). Doses of vitamin B_{12} as small as 5–15 μg when given orally with a mucoprotein fraction are rapidly absorbed and produce a striking response in the blood picture of patients with pernicious anaemia.

Enzymes

The chief enzyme present is **pepsin**. In many animals and in the human infant there is also **rennin**, which in the presence of calcium ions curdles the proteins of milk. Gastric juice may also contain traces of lipase.

Pepsin attacks many proteins, but only at a few points on the molecule. Protein digestion, therefore, does not proceed further than the polypeptide stage in the stomach. The stomach is not an important organ for enzymic digestion in man or for absorption. Indeed digestion often proceeds surprisingly well in patients after a total gastrectomy. The main role of the stomach is as a storage organ which receives large amounts of food at irregular intervals of time and passes on at regular intervals small amounts, graded in quantity to meet the capacity of the main digestive organ, which is the small intestine.

CONTROL OF GASTRIC SECRETION

Just as salivary secretion increases before food actually enters the mouth, so gastric secretion rises above the resting rate of about 0·5 ml/min before food reaches the stomach. The rate increases further when food is in contact with the gastric mucosa and this continues until all the food has passed into the duodenum. Several control mechanisms are involved, and secretion is usually considered in three phases which correspond to the site of the stimulus.

The **cephalic phase** is evoked before food reaches the stomach and is due to conditioned and unconditioned reflexes. These have their efferent path in the gastric branches of the vagus nerves. As with salivary secretion, the sight and smell of food and associated stimuli evoke secretion by conditioned reflexes. When food enters the mouth, a mechanical stimulus from its contact with the buccal cavity sets up an unconditioned reflex secretion again via vagal efferents. This phase has been convincingly demonstrated in dogs by the technique of **sham feeding**. Here, in addition to a gastric fistula for the collection of gastric juice, the oesophagus is divided and both cut ends brought out to the surface through the neck (fig. 30.25). When the dog eats, food does not pass to the stomach, but emerges from the neck. A large volume of gastric juice however, is secreted and can be collected from the gastric fistula. This does not occur if the branches of the vagus to the stomach have been divided and must therefore be due to a reflex mechanism mediated through the vagi. The dog must, of course, be given its normal food requirements through the fistula directly into the stomach. The volume of cephalic secretion is variable and it may last for an hour. In man it is susceptible to emotional factors and anxiety may reduce and anger increase the volume of secretion (see below).

The **gastric phase** begins when food enters the stomach from the oesophagus and lasts for up to 4 hours after a

FIG. 30.25. A dog used for 'sham feeding'.

large meal, when about 600 ml of strongly acid juice containing a high concentration of pepsin may be secreted.

A totally denervated stomach pouch of a dog secretes when food is present in the body of the stomach. Since nerve impulses cannot reach such a pouch, the stimulus to secretion is not a reflex and must be hormonal. Protein, alcohol and caffeine, when present in the stomach, are stimuli for this phase of secretion, but carbohydrate and fat have a much less marked action.

Soon after food reaches the stomach, a hormone, **gastrin**, is released from the pyloric region and passes via gastric veins into the general circulation. Acid in contact with the pyloric mucosa also releases gastrin into the circulation, but this release is reduced if the acid level becomes too high. When the circulating gastrin reaches the body of the stomach, the gastric glands secrete, as does also a denervated pouch. Gastrin has now been isolated and shown to be a polypeptide containing 17 amino acids (mol. wt. 2,150). There are minor differences in the peptide chain in gastrin from different species, but all the effects can be shown by the terminal chain of the last five amino acids, –Ala–Trp–Met–Asp–Phe. Two forms of gastrin have been isolated; I is unsulphated and II is sulphated. The active terminal pentapeptide has been synthesized and a chemical analogue, **pentagastrin,** is now available and is used experimentally. Gastrin II is 30 times more potent than pentagastrin on a molar basis and 250 times more potent than histamine, previously the most powerful gastric secretagogue known. Until the discovery of gastrin, it was thought probable that the gastric hormone was histamine. It has also been suggested that the vagal activity in the cephalic phase of secretion causes the release of histamine, which in turn stimulates secretion, but this now seems unlikely. Vagal activity augments the release of gastrin from the pyloric antrum; the action of the hormone on the parietal cells is furthermore greatly potentiated by concurrent vagal excitation. A further suggestion, which

has not been proved is that gastrin releases histamine, and that the latter is the ultimate stimulus to secretion.

The **intestinal phase** is much less important than the other two. If food is placed directly into the duodenum of a dog through a fistula, gastric secretion occurs after a latency of 1–3 hours, and may continue for several hours. Since a denervated pouch secretes in this way the stimulus must be hormonal, though the hormone concerned has not been isolated. In man, as well as in other animals, this phase is complicated by the inhibitory effect on gastric secretion and motility of the hormone **enterogastrone** which is released from the duodenum. The amount of secretion produced during the intestinal phase depends on the nature of the food eaten. The inhibitory effect of a meal rich in fat, which stimulates enterogastrone, may overcome the active intestinal phase of secretion.

Most of the experimental work on which early knowledge of the control of gastric secretion is based was, of necessity, carried out on animals. However, nowadays, more and more direct evidence is available in man. Reference has already been made to Alexis St. Martin, who had a fistula as the result of a gunshot wound. Beaumont noted that his gastric secretion increased when he was angry and hostile, and decreased when he was afraid or depressed. Similar results were seen by Wolf and Wolff in their study of Tom, an American who had a surgical gastric fistula provided after his oesophagus closed as a result of drinking excessively hot clam chowder! Another similar patient closed off his oesophagus by drinking a caustic solution. Carlson's observations on this subject confirmed that the fasting stomach secretes acid and that chewing food, even though it does not enter the stomach, induces gastric secretion.

In man, soup and meat extracts produce copious secretion and prolonged. It is less with carbohydrates and fat. The rate of secretion varies too with the type of food intake. Maximal rates, comparable to maximum stimulation of the stomach by gastrin or histamine, are achieved by meat meals.

GASTRIC MOTILITY

When the stomach is empty, it is small and relaxed but not totally quiescent. Movements may be studied in man or animals by passing a small balloon into the stomach and connecting it to a float recorder which registers changes of volume. When the stomach contracts, the balloon is compressed and the contraction recorded on either a kymograph or ink recorder. In the empty stomach small waves of contraction can be recorded passing from a pacemaker near the cardia and travelling towards the pylorus. These waves depend on the integrity of the intrinsic nerve plexuses. Some large waves of contraction may also be seen occasionally, together with changes in basic tone, which are thought to be due to activity of the vagi causing increased motor activity. Other spasmodic contractions occur and are called **hunger contractions**, although they are not always associated with feelings of hunger (fig. 30.26).

FIG. 30.26. Cessation of hunger and gastric contractions after giving glucose intravenously. The tracings are samples from a kymograph revolving at 2·54 cm/min (from Stunkard, A.J. & Wolff, H.G., (1956), *J. Clin. Invent.* **35**, 954).

An ingested meal distends the stomach though there is little change in pressure. There is, however, a rise in tension of the stomach wall. This causes a rise in the number of afferent impulses in the vagi, and also an increase in the efferent discharge in these nerves, which causes the onset of peristalsis. Waves of contraction sweep through the stomach from the fundus to the pyloric antrum and the chyme is propelled towards the duodenum. These contractions do not occur if the vagi have been cut. The waves of contraction raise the intragastric pressure above that of the duodenum and the chyme passes through the pylorus. The pylorus and duodenum act as a single functional unit rather than a true sphincter and do not constitute a barrier mechanism. The pylorus is normally open, but contracts with antral-contractions till the food bolus has been reduced in size and then it is allowed to escape. Gastric emptying may be measured in man using an isotopically labelled meal and scanning its emptying as it leaves the stomach. Emptying is controlled so that the pattern follows an exponential curve. The rate of gastric emptying is influenced by the volume of a meal, its osmotic concentration and fat content. As soon as the food and acid escape into the duodenum, receptors there lead to reflex pyloric closure until the pH rises again.

THE SMALL INTESTINE

The small intestine starts at the pylorus and ends at the ileocaecal junction, where it joins the large intestine. The major part of digestion and absorption occurs in this long and much convoluted region of the gut. The small intestine consists of the duodenum which is short and fairly fixed, and the much longer, more mobile and more convoluted jejunum and ileum, which are suspended by the mesentery from the posterior abdominal wall (fig. 30.8).

Gross anatomy

DUODENUM

The duodenum is the short, wide C-shaped segment which

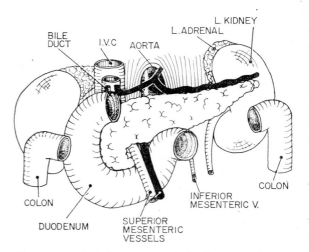

FIG. 30.27. Anterior aspect of duodenum and pancreas. The spleen has been removed.

begins at the pylorus to the right of the median plane, and curves around the head of pancreas on the posterior abdominal wall, to end at the duodenojejunal flexure to the left of the median plane (fig. 30.27). It is divided into four parts. The **first part** runs from the pylorus to the right upwards, and backwards to end by turning downwards abruptly to become the second, descending part. The first part has a 'free' portion continuous with the stomach which gives attachment to the right extremity of the lesser omentum above and the right margin of the greater omentum below. This means that its posterior surface faces the lesser sac, but its anterior surface faces the greater sac. Across the potential space of the lesser sac, the duodenum is related to the head of pancreas, and an ulcer penetrating the pancreas is an all-too-common complication of a chronic duodenal ulcer. The 'fixed' portion is covered with peritoneum on its anterior and superior surfaces. Above it is related to the epiploic foramen and posteriorly to the bile duct, portal vein and gastroduodenal artery (p. 30.51).

The **second part** descends on the pelvis of the right ureter and psoas major posteriorly, and is covered anteriorly with peritoneum except where crossed by the transverse colon. The bile duct and main pancreatic duct enter the second part by a single opening on the posteromedial wall. The **third part** sweeps leftward across the median plane lying in front of the inferior vena cava, aorta and psoas major muscles. Anteriorly it has a peritoneal coat except where crossed by the descending superior mesenteric vessels which occasionally cause duodenal obstruction. The short **fourth part** ascends on the left psoas major and turns forwards to end at the duodenojejunal flexure. The root of the mesentery is attached to its anterior surface.

The first part of the duodenum feels thin, but the remainder has thick walls because of tall circular mucosal folds. The duodenal papilla on the posteromedial wall of the mucosal surface of the second part discharges bile and pancreatic juice. An accessory pancreatic duct usually enters the duodenum about 2 cm proximal to the main duct.

Radiologically the duodenum is C shaped, but the first part is almost vertical, and conical like a dunce's cap (plate 30.1b, facing p. 28.28). This duodenal cap lies above the narrow pylorus and is often deformed or abnormally immobile in patients with duodenal ulcer.

JEJUNUM AND ILEUM

A long and deep mesentery attaches the jejunum and ileum to the posterior abdominal wall (fig. 30.8) and gives them their mobility. The root of the mesentery begins at the duodenojejunal flexure at the lower border of the body of the 2nd lumbar vertebra, to the left of the midline, and runs to the right and downwards for 15 cm before ending in the right iliac fossa. But the free border of the mesentery, where the two constituent peritoneal layers separate to enclose the gut, is much longer, as the jejunum and ileum are about three metres in length. The transition between the two is gradual and the division quite arbitrary, although there are distinct differences between the proximal jejunum and the distal ileum.

When compared with the ileum, the jejunum is broader, more vascular and therefore redder, and has thicker walls because of the high circular folds on its luminal surface. The ileum has sparse and low circular folds but has distinctive patches of lymphoid tissue, **Peyer's patches,** in its wall opposite the mesentery.

Another valuable distinguishing feature between the jejunum and ileum is the pattern of the arteries in the mesentery adjacent to the gut; at the jejunum the supplying arteries form a single arcade, but the arcades increase in number as the gut is followed distally, so that beside the ileum there are three or four vascular arches. The jejunal arteries are easily seen because the fat in the mesentery does not quite reach the gut, but the ileal arteries are often obscured by the fat which may even infiltrate the gut wall.

Many of the differences just discussed are minor, and the surgeon presented with a small loop of intestine protruding through a limited incision in the abdominal wall puts a hand on either side of the root of the mesentery and then slides them towards the gut, which untwists the mesentery and reveals its polarity.

Although the jejunoileum appears to lie at random, it is generally confined within the inverted U of the colon, with the jejunum above and to the left, and the ileum in the hypogastric region and true pelvis. The terminal ileum ascends out of the pelvis into the right iliac fossa where it joins the caecum.

The complex high circular folds of the jejunum produce a typical feathery appearance on a barium meal radiograph, whereas the lower and sparse folds of the ileum give a smooth outline (plate 30.1c, facing p. 28.28).

Meckel's diverticulum is a remnant of the proximal portion of the vitello-intestinal duct (p. 30.50) and is found in about 2 per cent of the population. Meckel's diverticulum is located on the anti-mesenteric border of the ileum, and is usually within 40 cm of the ileocaecal sphincter, although rarely this distance may be as much as 100 cm. The mucosa of the diverticulum is usually ileal, but almost half contain some ectopic gastric mucosa. Its clinical importance lies in the fact that the gastric mucosa secretes hydrochloric acid which leads to ulceration of the mucosa and this is occasionally the cause of obscure digestive symtoms.

Microscopic structure

Digestion takes place mostly in the small intestine, but does not depend on the secretions of its intrinsic glands, which secrete mostly mucus. Two large extrinsic glands, the liver and pancreas, discharge their secretions into the duodenum. The main function of the wall of the small intestine is absorptive and it has a number of specializations which provide the necessary large surface area.

ABSORPTIVE AREA OF THE SMALL INTESTINE

Determining the normal length of jejunum and ileum has been aptly compared to measuring a worm, because the difficulties are similar, namely that the length varies widely according to the tone of the intrinsic muscle and the tension on the two ends. At autopsy the measurement is usually about 7–8 metres, but this is an overestimate of the length in life. Results obtained by means of indwelling radioopaque intestinal tubes in man suggest that the small intestine is only about 3 metres long. The convolutions allow the gut to be about 20 times as long as its mesenteric attachment. A second factor increasing the surface area is the presence of circular folds on the mucosal surface of the gut wall (fig. 30.28). These folds begin in the second part of the duodenum, reach a maximum in the jejunum, and diminish in the ileum to become sparse near its termination. Thirdly, the surface of these folds is covered with villi, which are finger-like processes of mucosa 1 mm. long which project into the lumen of the gut. Finally, the epithelial lining of the villi is composed largely of columnar absorptive cells which have a brush border. This border consists of tiny microvilli (p. 13.12) which further increase the surface area twentyfold. Together the convolutions, circular folds, villi and microvilli result in a total surface area of approximately 20–40 m^2.

JEJUNUM

This is described first because it typifies the structure of the small intestine. The jejunal wall feels thick because of the permanent circular folds, and the mucosa forms villi and the intestinal crypts of Lieberkuhn.

FIG. 30.28. Small intestine showing regional variations. The circular folds and the height and numbers of villi all diminish towards the ileum. Aggregated lymphoid nodules characterize the lower ileum.

Intestinal villus

The villi of the jejunum are tall, slender and close packed (figs. 30.28 and 30.29). They are the absorptive units of the small bowel and defective villi are common when there is malabsorption. The delicate lining epithelium is only one cell thick, which facilitates absorption.

The submucosa is typical, with extensive vascular and nervous plexuses and the muscular coat has a prominent myenteric nerve plexus. The jejunum is completely enveloped by a serosa except where attached to the mesentery.

Columnar **absorptive cells** cover most of the villus and engage in absorption by a variety of active and passive transport mechanisms (p. 17.6). This tall columnar cell (fig. 30.30) has a basal nucleus, a supranuclear Golgi complex, and scattered short profiles of rough and smooth surfaced endoplasmic reticulum as well as many free ribosomes. There is a brush border over the apical surface of the cell. This border, across which all absorption probably occurs, is bounded by a thick and asymmetric cell membrane which is rich in several enzymes including alkaline phosphatase. At the bases of the microvilli many invaginations may represent pinocytotic vesicles, which could be involved in the absorption of certain substances. Laterally the cell membranes of adjacent cells are firmly attached to each other near

the lumen by junctional complexes (p. 13.11). The terminal web is a meshwork of fine filaments, lying parallel to the free surface, which are attached to the intermediate zone of the junctional complex. This web probably has a mechanical function, stiffening the apical part of the cell. Lateral to the nucleus the cell membranes are irregularly folded and provide a variable intercellular space which is utilized during fat absorption.

The **goblet cells** are the other main component of the lining epithelium and are typical mucus-secreting cells. Many dark staining nuclei of small lymphocytes are seen within the lining epithelium, but their significance is uncertain.

Intestinal crypts

The intestinal crypts are straight tubular glands which open on to the mucosal surface between villi (fig. 30.28). The epithelium of these crypts consists mostly of low columnar cells and developing goblet cells. Clusters of **Paneth cells** lie at the base of the crypt, and isolated argentaffin cells are wedged between the bases of crypt cells (fig. 30.29). The Paneth cell is a typical serous exocrine cell, with large eosinophilic secretory granules in its upper third, while basally there is cytoplasmic basophilia due to an extensive rough surfaced endoplasmic reticulum. The secretory granules are discharged in

CELLS

ABSORPTIVE COLUMNAR

GOBLET

LYMPHOID

MITOTIC

ARGENTAFFIN

PANETH

SUBEPITHELIAL CAPILLARY PLEXUS

EXTRUSION ZONE

ARTERIAL VENOUS LYMPHATIC

VESSELS

I HOUR   24 HOURS   48 HOURS

LABELLED NUCLEI

CELL RENEWAL

FIG. 30.29. Intestinal villus. The renewal of epithelium and the blood and lymphatic vessels are shown.

response to food entering the small intestine, but their nature is quite unknown. The cells are unusually rich in zinc which may indicate that the secretory granules are a metalloprotein enzyme. There are only about a dozen Paneth cells in each crypt, but because of the enormous number of crypts the total mass of Paneth cells is large. They are usually confined to the small intestine in health, but may occur in large numbers in the large intestine in various disease processes, for reasons which are obscure. **Argentaffin cells** are so named because they contain secretory granules which stain strongly with silver salts. These granules fill the cell, but the Golgi complex is on the basal side of the nucleus facing the capillaries, which gives a clue that the argentaffin cell is not exocrine but endocrine, and the granules are now known to be rich in 5-hydroxytryptophan. These cells are widely distributed throughout the gut, but are particularly numerous in the ileum and appendix.

Epithelial turnover in the small intestine

The presence of large numbers of mitotic figures in the crypts, and the fact that at the tips of villi the epithelial cells often appear degenerate and heaped upon one another suggests that there is a constant formation of cells within the crypts and loss of epithelium from the tips of the villi. If mice are killed after receiving a single dose of radio-active thymidine the movement of cells which divided shortly after the injection of thymidine can be traced. In mice killed within an hour of injection, labelling is confined to the crypts; after 24 hours labelled cells are observed over the upper parts of the crypts and the basal portion of the villi. After 48 hours the few labelled cells remain at the apices of the villi. Therefore complete renewal of villous epithelium occurs every two days in mice. In all mammals including man the villus is a dynamic organ existing in a delicate state of equilibrium, in which a high rate of epithelial cell renewal is balanced by correspondingly rapid loss. Disturbance of such a system would produce rapid change, and in animals blocking of mitosis by X-rays or antimetabolic drugs, causes collapse of the villi within a few days. In diseases such as idiopathic steatorrhoea where the villi are severely reduced or absent, there is a disturbance of this equilibrium. The population of absorptive cells is reduced due to flattening of the villi, and even the remaining cells may be abnormal, in that they lack their full complement of enzymes.

RESTING CELL   FAT ABSORPTION

LUMEN

MICROVILLI

JUNCTIONAL ZONE

SER
RER

GOLGI COMPLEX

INTERCELLULAR
SPACE

RIBOSOMES

LYMPHATIC LUMEN

① MICELLES OF FATTY ACIDS,
MONO-AND DIGLYCERIDES AND
BILE SALTS

② INDIVIDUAL MOLECULES
DIFFUSE ACROSS
MICROVILLI

③ TRIGLYCERIDE DROPLETS
SYNTHESISED

④ DROPLETS LEAVE CELL
(REVERSE PINOCYTOSIS)

⑤ ENTER LYMPHATIC

FIG. 30.30. Fat absorption across the columnar epithelial cells of a villus (p. 30.37).

Other components of the wall

The lining is supported by the lamina propria, a loose cellular connective tissue with many lymphoid cells and occasional lymphoid nodules, and this forms the core of each villus filling the interstices between the crypts. In addition, the lamina propria carries the villous blood supply, which comes from a branch of the submucosal arterial plexus which ascends in the long axis of each villus and supplies a widespread subepithelial capillary plexus (fig. 30.29). Venules from the latter end in the submucosal venous plexus and thereafter the venous drainage is typical of the gut. The lymphatics draining a villus are numerous and join a central lymphatic or lacteal (fig. 30.29) which descends in the villous core to a submucosal plexus and this in turn drains to the extrinsic lacteals of the intestines. Smooth muscle fibres from the muscularis mucosae, lying parallel to the central lacteal, shorten the villus rhythmically during digestion and may have a pumping action on the lacteals which speeds the passage of the lymph. The lymphatics often contain droplets of fat as they are the main pathway for lipid absorption (fig. 30.30).

DUODENUM

The wall of the first part of the duodenum feels thin because it lacks circular folds. The villi, however, begin immediately at the pyloroduodenal junction and are leaf shaped. The crypts also begin at the junction and resemble those of the jejunum. Additional glands, which developed as downgrowths from the crypts and invaded the underlying muscularis mucosae to lie within the submucosa, are a distinguishing feature of the duodenum. These **Brunner's glands** are numerous in the first part and diminish towards its end. They are branched, coiled glands which secrete alkaline mucus into the duodenum and thus reduce the acidity of the gastric chyme. Duodenal contents are made alkaline by the large amounts of pancreatic juice secreted into the second part. However, in the presence of a large acid secretion this local defence mechanism may prove inadequate and, as might be expected, it is in the first part of the duodenum that peptic ulceration may develop.

ILEUM

The general structure of the ileum is similar to that of the jejunum and the transition between them is gradual. The bulk of absorption occurs in the jejunum, although there is some regional specialization e.g. Vitamin B_{12} appears to be absorbed mostly in the distal part of the ileum. The villi of the ileum are less numerous and contain more goblet cells but fewer columnar absorptive cells than are in the jejunum. Lymphoid tissue however, is more plentiful, and forms lymphoid nodules in the mucosa. In the terminal ileum there are clusters of such nodules, several centimetres in length. These Peyer's patches extend into the submucosa, and the overlying epithelium which lacks villi, often contains numerous lymphocytes. In certain infections these aggregations of lymphoid tissue are particularly vulnerable, and in typhoid fever for example an intense inflammatory reaction may occur within Peyer's patches leading to necrosis of the wall.

An account of the functions of the small intestine is given on p. 30.36.

LARGE INTESTINE

The large intestine begins at the ileocaecal sphincter and ends at the anus (fig. 30.8). It consists of the following parts:

(1) caecum and vermiform appendix,
(2) ascending colon and hepatic flexure,
(3) transverse colon and splenic flexure,
(4) descending colon,
(5) sigmoid or pelvic colon,
(6) rectum,
(7) anal canal.

The proximal half, as far as the splenic flexure, absorbs water and electrolytes from the fluid chyme which enters through the ileocaecal sphincter. The distal colon, beyond the splenic flexure, stores the formed faeces until they are excreted.

As the name implies, the large intestine is usually wider than the small intestine. But this is not always true, and commonly the descending colon when empty after defaecation is narrower. Several other features characterize the large intestine. The taeniae coli are three whitish longitudinal muscle bands which start at the base of the appendix and run along the caecum and entire colon to the upper end of the rectum, where they spread out to form a complete muscle coat. The tension of these muscle bands puckers the large intestine, and with the activity of the circular layer of muscle, forms haustra or sacculations (plate 30.1c, facing p. 28.28). The appendices

28

epiploicae are little fat filled pouches of serosa that are scattered over the surface of the large intestine.

Gross anatomy

CAECUM

The caecum is a wide cul-de-sac of gut below the ileocaecal sphincter (fig. 30.31), lying in the right iliac fossa. Commonly it is completely invested in peritoneum and hangs free, but sometimes two vertical folds connect it to the posterior abdominal wall creating a retrocaecal recess (fig. 30.11). Occasionally this recess extends upwards behind the ascending colon to become the retrocolic recess.

VERMIFORM APPENDIX

This worm shaped appendage is developmentally the apex of the caecum (p. 30.51), but in the adult it opens on the posteromedial wall of the caecum inferior to the ileocaecal sphincter (fig. 30.32).

FIG. 30.31. Caecum and appendix.

FIG. 30.32. Blood vessels of caecum and appendix.

The appendix is less than 1 cm thick and from 2–20 cm in length. The mesoappendix is a peritoneal fold derived from the left layer of the mesentery which crosses posterior to the ileum to reach the base of the appendix. A second, bloodless fold joins the antimesenteric border of the ileum to the caecum, anterior to the mesoappendix. These two folds enclose the inferior ileocaecal recess.

The superior ileocaecal recess lies anterior to the terminal ileum and the bloodless fold, but behind a third fold which carries the anterior caecal artery from the mesentery to the anterior aspect of the caecum.

The appendix is freely mobile as the narrow mesoappendix exerts little restraint, and may adopt any position centred on its attachment to the caecum. According to Wakeley's famous studies of 10,000 cases the commonest position is retrocaecal or retrocolic (61 per cent), while of the remainder about one third were pelvic. Less than 5 per cent of the total were either subcaecal or related to the ileum. Gravity probably explains the high incidence of pelvic appendices, but the preponderance of retrocaecal cases is due to the appendix being less free than commonly described. It may lie within one of the three peritoneal recesses, which tends to localize infection in appendicitis.

Often the best method of finding the appendix surgically is to trace the anterior taenia down the ascending colon over the caecum to its beginning at the base of the appendix. The variable position of the appendix results in equally variable relations. A pelvic appendix may come into relation with the ureter in either sex, and with the ovary and uterine tube in the female. An inflamed retrocolic appendix may cause few symptoms other than diarrhoea due to irritation of the colon.

ASCENDING COLON

The ascending colon is continuous with the upper end of the caecum and extends up as far as the right lobe of the liver. Peritoneum covers its front and sides, but behind it lies on the posterior abdominal wall (fig. 30.11). A peritoneal fold, the right phrenicocolic ligament, connects the hepatic flexure to the diaphragm, but the flexure is not completely fixed in position and descends with the liver during inspiration. The colon has only limited mobility as it usually lacks a mesentery.

The right lateral paracolic gutter separates the colon from the abdominal wall, and the right medial paracolic gutter is occupied by coils of jejunum above and ileum below (fig. 30.14). Anteriorly it is in contact with the anterior abdominal wall or is covered by the omentum or small intestine (fig. 30.9).

The ascending, transverse and descending parts of the colon all possess the characteristics of the large intestine, namely haustra, taeniae and appendices epiploicae, but the haustra are most pronounced on the transverse colon (plate 30.1d, facing p. 28.28).

TRANSVERSE COLON

The transverse colon begins at the hepatic flexure low in the right hypochondrium and arches across the abdomen to the splenic flexure high in the left hypochondrium (fig. 30.8 and plate 30.1d, facing p. 28.28). Since the vertical parts of the colon lie in the paravertebral gutters well posterior to the vertebral bodies the transverse colon curves forwards as well as downwards (fig. 30.14). The splenic flexure is more acute than the hepatic, and is almost in a sagittal plane so that its two limbs are superimposed on an anteroposterior view of the abdomen. *Peritoneal relations*. These are complex and are more readily understood after its development has been described (p. 30.54). The first few centimetres or hepatic flexure has peritoneal relationships similar to the ascending colon, being invested completely except posteriorly where it lies directly on the right kidney and second part of duodenum (fig. 30.27). Antero-superiorly the flexure is in contact with the liver and gall bladder. Medial to the duodenum the transverse colon acquires a mesentery, the mesocolon, which is fixed along the entire anterior surface of the pancreas. The posterior wall of the greater omentum is attached to the antimesenteric border of the transverse colon. During development the pouch-like dorsal mesogastrium expands downwards over the upper surface of the transverse colon and mesocolon. The adjacent layers of peritoneum fuse so that in the adult the omentum, which is derived from the mesogastrium, is attached to the colon and not the posterior abdominal wall (figs. 30.12 and 64).

Visceral Relations. The posterior surface of the transverse colon faces into the infracolic compartment of the greater sac of peritoneum (fig. 30.12) and lies on the third part of duodenum, the mesentery, containing the superior mesenteric vessels, and the first few coils of jejunum (fig. 30.8). The anterior surface faces into the cavity of the greater omentum which is part of the lesser peritoneal sac, and is related to the posterior surface of the stomach. Observe that at both ends of the mesocolon the lateral borders of the greater omentum are attached vertically to the anterior surface of the mesocolon and transverse colon, so that the flexures are outwith the lesser sac. The splenic flexure is related to the diaphragm anteriorly and the spleen posteriorly (fig. 30.8).

DESCENDING COLON

The descending colon runs down from the splenic flexure on the posterior abdominal wall, crosses the iliac crest to enter the left iliac fossa and curves medially to end at the brim of the true pelvis, where it becomes the sigmoid colon. Peritoneum covers its sides and front, but its posterior wall rests on the structures in the posterior abdominal wall. The left phrenicocolic ligament is a peritoneal fold running from the diaphragm to the splenic flexure which fixes the position of the flexure and partly supports the spleen. The descending colon is fairly fixed.

The paracolic gutters are similar to those of the ascending colon. The omentum and jejuno-ileum cover it anteriorly, except in the iliac fossa where it may be related directly to the abdominal wall (fig. 30.9).

The descending and sigmoid colon constitute a storage unit which gradually fills with formed faeces from the proximal colon, and after an interval of some hours is emptied rapidly during defaecation. Obviously the size of the normal descending colon varies considerably; in a constipated patient it may be distended with hard faeces, because although normally there is negligible absorption of water from the faeces beyond the splenic flexure, further absorption does occur when faeces remains in the storage unit for long periods. In a thin constipated person, the descending colon can be palpated.

SIGMOID COLON

The sigmoid colon is mobile and convoluted, and has a mesentery. The root of the mesocolon forms an inverted V attached first along the pelvic brim and then on the front of the sacrum (fig. 30.33). As part of the faecal storage unit, the sigmoid colon varies in size; when empty it may lie entirely within the true pelvis. In the pelvis the sigmoid colon occupies the pararectal fossae between the rectum and lateral pelvic walls, and the rectovesical or rectovaginal fossa anteriorly. As it fills it rises out of the pelvis usually posterior to the coils of terminal ileum.

RECTUM

The rectum, following the sigmoid colon, starts opposite the third piece of the sacrum and follows its curve through the posterior part of the pelvis to the pelvic floor. The rectum turns sharply backwards as it pierces the pelvic diaphragm at the junction with the anal canal (figs. 30.12 and 30.33).

The rectum has a complete longitudinal muscle coat and lacks sacculations and appendices epiploicae; its dilated midpiece is the ampulla. The internal surface of the rectum is smooth except for three narrow crescentic transverse folds which project into the lumen, and serve as useful landmarks. The sites of these 'valves' are visible on the external surface as indentations.

The rectum is usually empty, but fills with faeces prior to defaecation. This stretches the rectal wall and reflexly stimulates the visceral muscle which contracts and expels the faeces. Thus the rectum has a function different from that of the storage unit described previously. The upper part of the rectum is enclosed in peritoneum except where it rests posteriorly on the areolar tissue covering the sacrum and emerging roots of the sacral plexus. Laterally, coils of the ileum or sigmoid colon may occupy the pararectal fossa. Lower down the rectum is extraperitoneal, and is related laterally to the sloping upper surfaces of the levator

FIG. 30.33. Coronal section of rectum and anal canal.

ani muscles. The pelvic nerve plexus passes forward on either side of the rectum between it and the levator ani (fig. 30.50), carrying the nerve supply to bladder, and may be damaged in operations on the rectum. Anteriorly the rectum is related to coils of ileum and in the female to the uterus, rectovaginal pouch, posterior fornix of vagina and cervix uteri, and in the male to the rectovesical pouch, bladder, seminal vesicles, and the prostate.

ANAL CANAL

The terminal 3 cm of the gut is the anal canal which runs downwards and backwards from the lower end of the rectum to the anus. The angle between the rectum and anal canal is controlled by the puborectalis muscle. This is the most medial portion of levator ani, and arises from the pubis passes around the side of the rectum and unites with its fellow to form the puborectalis 'sling'. Contraction of this voluntary muscle pulls the angle forwards exerting a sphincteric action on the gut.

The lining of the canal shows regional variations (fig. 30.34). The **anal** (rectal) **columns** are longitudinal ridges over the mucosal zone on the upper half of the canal. They contain the venous plexuses of the superior rectal vessels and are therefore a dark plum colour in life. The anal valves join the bases of adjacent anal columns enclosing little pockets, the anal sinuses. The valves are probably the remnants of the anal membrane (p. 30.51) and their upper sinuous border is the pectinate line. The transitional zone below the pectinate line is a shiny and bluish white. Near the lower end of the canal it gives way to the cutaneous zone which is lined with dull white or brownish skin.

Anal sphincters

The anal canal is guarded by a complex sphincteric mass composed of the puborectalis sling and the internal and external anal sphincters (fig. 30.34).

The **external sphincter**, composed of skeletal muscle, surrounds the anal canal throughout its entire length. It is

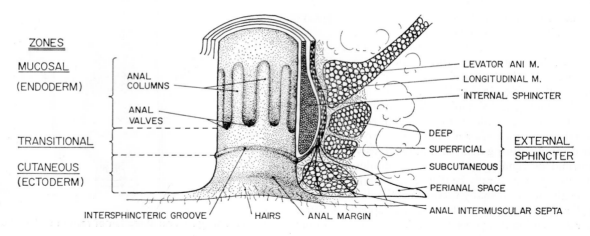

ZONES

MUCOSAL (ENDODERM)

ANAL COLUMNS

ANAL VALVES

TRANSITIONAL

CUTANEOUS (ECTODERM)

LEVATOR ANI M.

LONGITUDINAL M.

INTERNAL SPHINCTER

DEEP

SUPERFICIAL

SUBCUTANEOUS

EXTERNAL SPHINCTER

PERIANAL SPACE

ANAL INTERMUSCULAR SEPTA

INTERSPHINCTERIC GROOVE　　HAIRS　　ANAL MARGIN

FIG. 30.34. Coronal section of anal canal.

in three parts. The subcutaneous part encircles the lower half of the canal. The superficial part lies deeper and consists of fibres which arise from the central tendon of the perineum and arch around the canal to insert into the anococcygeal ligament which connects the anus to the tip of the coccyx. The deep part surrounds the upper third of the canal and merges with levator ani. The circular layer of muscle in the rectum thickens at its lower end to form the **internal anal sphincter**, which is accordingly smooth involuntary muscle, and encircles the upper two-thirds of the anal canal.

The longitudinal muscle coat of the rectum becomes increasingly fibro-elastic as it passes down the anal canal between the external and internal sphincters. Finally it splits into intermuscular anal septa which attach to the intersphincteric groove medially, and fan out laterally, piercing the subcutaneous sphincter and insert into the perianal skin. The longitudinal coat is not sphincteric.

Relations of the anal canal

The **ischiorectal fossa** is the large fat-filled space lying lateral to the anal canal, below the levator ani muscle and medial to the ischium and obturator internus muscle (p. 20.31). The semi-fluid fat allows the rectum and anal canal to distend easily during defaecation. Infection may spread into the fossa from the adjacent anal canal, forming an ischiorectal abscess. They may attain a large size before causing pain, because the fossa is readily distended. A **perianal space** surrounds the lower end of the anal canal. It is limited laterally by the most lateral of the intermuscular septa, and medially by the wall of the anal canal below the site of attachment of the most medial intermuscular septum. This space contains the subcutaneous sphincter and some loculated fat, and inflammation in it causes considerable tension in these septa and is therefore very painful.

Microscopic structure of the large intestine

COLON AND CAECUM

The colon lacks circular folds and villi so that the mucosa is fairly smooth. It is pitted with intestinal crypts which resemble those of the small intestine but have a much higher proportion of goblet cells, and normally lack Paneth cells. Numerous mitotic figures in the crypts form new cells which pass upwards and renew the surface epithelium every few days. The absorptive cells have a microvillous brush border that is less developed than that of the small intestine. The lamina propria contains some lymphoid nodules and lies on the muscularis mucosae. The submucosa is less vascular than that of the small intestine, and the submucosal nerve plexus is smaller.

The muscle coat varies in different parts of the large intestine. The circular coat is complete, but the outer longitudinal coat is thickened locally to form the three taeniae coli (fig. 30.31). Between these longitudinal bands it is thin or even incomplete. The myenteric plexus lies within the muscle coat. As far as the splenic flexure the parasympathetic component of this plexus is derived from the vagus and beyond that from the pelvic splanchnic nerves.

The serosal coat of peritoneum varies along the colon, being practically complete where there is a mesentery as in the transverse or pelvic colon. The appendices epiploicae are little fat filled projections of the serosal coat scattered over its surface.

VERMIFORM APPENDIX

The appendix is a narrow blind sac with a small lumen which is often irregular in outline due to folds in youth, but with age it becomes more rounded as the underlying lymphoid tissue undergoes involution. The mucosa is

FIG. 30.35. Colon. The mucosa has a flat surface and simple tubular mucous glands.

FIG. 30.36. Vermiform appendix showing the small lumen and abundant lymphoid nodules.

similar to that of the colon, but the intestinal crypts contain many argentaffin cells. These cells are present in the mucosa of the stomach and intestines (p. 30.21), but are abundant in the terminal ileum, appendix and caecum, where argentaffin tumours are more frequent. Many lymphoid nodules lie in the lamina propria and give rise to a stream of lymphocytes which infiltrate the surface epithelium (fig. 30.36). The submucosa is invaded by lym-

phoid tissue of the lamina propria which splits up the muscularis mucosae. A submucosal nerve plexus is present. The inner circular coat is thick, and the outer longitudinal coat, unlike that of most of the large bowel, is complete because the taeniae coli as they are traced down the ascending colon and on to the caecum converge on the base of the appendix.

The serosa presents no special features, and is complete except over the mesoappendix.

RECTUM AND ANAL CANAL

The structure of the rectum is similar to that of the colon except that the taeniae spread out and form a complete longitudinal coat over the rectum. Over the rectum and upper third of the anal canal, the mucosal epithelium is a typical colonic epithelium with many goblet cells and straight tubular mucous glands, but it becomes a stratified columnar epithelium for a short distance before becoming keratinized stratified squamous epithelium typical of true skin over the lower third of the canal.

Anal glands open into the canal between the anal columns. Their secretory acini usually lie in the submucosa but may extend through the internal sphincter into the substance of the external anal sphincter. It is believed that infection of these glands is an important cause of ischiorectal abscess.

Intestinal secretion

The secretions from the mucosa of the small and large intestines are increased by the direct mechanical stimulation from the presence of food. In the duodenum the secretion is mainly of mucus, whereas in the jejunum, ileum and colon, an isotonic fluid is secreted which is slightly alkaline. Some enzymes present in these secretions have come from the cells shed from the villi.

The most important secretions into the small intestine are from the pancreas and the liver and these organs and their contribution to the function of the alimentary tract are now described.

LIVER AND BILIARY SYSTEM

The liver is the largest gland in the body, and occupies the right hypochondrium (fig. 30.9). It is an important organ of intermediate metabolism and this role is described in chap. 31. It also has an exocrine secretion, the bile, which is conveyed to the duodenum by the biliary system (fig. 30.38).

The liver accounts for 5 per cent of total body weight at birth, and is largely responsible for the protuberant abdomen of infancy. As the growth rate slows during childhood there is a corresponding decline in metabolism and the liver becomes proportionately smaller until in the adult it is $2\frac{1}{2}$ per cent of body weight (1,500 g).

The liver is soft because of its vascularity (one-fifth of liver volume is blood) and friable because of a very low connective tissue content. Lacerations of the liver are therefore dangerous because they bleed profusely and are difficult to repair; try stitching two halves of a table jelly together with needle and thread.

The friable nature of the liver is altered radically by embalming, but the hard liver of the cadaver is useful as it records permanently, in the form of surface impressions, the relations of neighbouring adjacent structures. These relations approximate to those of a living recumbent supine patient who has expired deeply.

Gross anatomy

The liver is wedge shaped and is divided somewhat arbitrarily into four lobes by certain external features. The main division into a large right lobe and a smaller left lobe is marked by the **falciform ligament** on the anterior surface, and on the visceral and posterior surfaces by the fissures for the **ligamentum teres** and **ligamentum venosum**. The falciform ligament carries the ligamentum teres in its free border and is therefore continuous round the lower border of the liver with the fissure for the ligamentum teres which in turn ascends on the visceral aspect of the liver to end at the left end of the porta hepatis. Superior to the porta hepatis the fissure for the ligamentum venosum is the boundary between the two lobes (fig. 30.16). The quadrate lobe is an integral part of the right lobe bounded by the inferior border of liver, gall bladder bed, porta hepatis, and fissure of the ligamentum teres. The caudate lobe also belongs to the right lobe, and appears on the posterior surface of liver between the groove for the inferior vena cava and the fissure for the ligamentum venosum. It is connected to the main mass of the right lobe superficially by the caudate process, which forms the roof of the epiploic foramen (figs. 30.16 and 30.37).

The **portal vein,** carrying blood from the gut, enters the liver at the **porta hepatis** (fig. 30.37). It divides repeatedly within the liver into small branches which finally enter an anastomosing system of sinusoids. In the hepatic circulation 80 per cent of the blood is portal, and the remaining 20 per cent arrives in the hepatic artery. The hepatic artery also divides repeatedly within the liver, sending branches with those of the portal vein to the sinusoids. The sinusoids therefore contain mixed venous and arterial blood, which percolates past the hepatic parenchymal cells or hepatocytes before entering the central veins. These central veins are tributaries of the hepatic vein, which drain blood from the liver into the inferior vena cava (figs. 30.39 and 30.40).

The lobes are useful topographically, but are neither vascular nor biliary units. For example, although the right lobe is much bigger than the left, the main left and right hepatic ducts that emerge from the porta hepatis

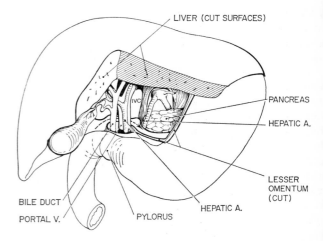

FIG. 30.37. A portion of liver has been resected to reveal the three structures in the free border of the lesser omentum. The arrow passes through the epiploic foramen.

have the same diameter, showing that the left hepatic duct drains half the liver tissue. The cleavage plane between the two drainage areas passes from the groove for the inferior vena cava and gall bladder bed posteriorly, to cut the anterior surface to the right of the falciform ligament, and therefore the left duct receives the bile from part of the right lobe and the entire left lobe. These two halves of the liver have been further subdivided into about a dozen segments. Each segment drains into a tributary of the hepatic ducts and is supplied by a corresponding branch of the hepatic artery and of the portal vein, and is both a biliary and vascular unit. These liver segments are not easily defined, because they are not surrounded by connective tissue septa, but as they are fairly constant in position their discovery has been of value to surgeons who can now perform local resection of certain segments with only minimal damage to adjacent hepatic tissue. Some of the liver segments cannot be removed separately, because they contain vessels or ducts going to other segments, which would therefore be damaged. In practice, therefore, several segments may have to be removed along with the diseased one, in order to leave only undamaged liver with an intact circulation and duct system.

POSITION AND RELATIONS

The bulk of the liver lies in the right hypochondrium, under cover of the lower ribs which protect it, but it also extends to the left across the epigastrium in the substernal angle (fig. 30.9). In the cadaver, the upper surface of the liver reaches to the 5th right rib, crosses close to the xiphisternal junction and is inferior to the 5th left rib. This cadaveric position is somewhat higher than that of the living bed patient who has exhaled fully. The inferior border passes obliquely from the left across the substernal angle to intersect the right costal margin at the right margin of the rectus abdominis and then continues under cover of the ribs a little above the costal margin. On inspiration the liver descends with the diaphragm, bringing the entire lower border inferior to the costal margin.

The upper, lateral, anterior and posterior surfaces of the liver together form a smooth convex area which is moulded by the overlying diaphragm. The intraperitoneal subdiaphragmatic spaces intervene between the liver and diaphragm (fig. 30.15), but over the bare area the liver is devoid of peritoneum and in contact with diaphragm, upper pole of right kidney, and adrenal gland (fig. 30.11). The right pleural cavity and lung are important relations above the diaphragm, as disease may spread from the liver to the thorax. The lower ribs are also significant because fractured ribs may lacerate the underlying liver. Anteriorly the liver is related near the midline to the anterior abdominal wall. The extensive visceral surface is in contact with many structures, the left lobe with the oesophagus, stomach and lesser omentum and the quadrate lobe with the first part of duodenum; finally the right lobe rests on the right kidney and hepatic flexure of the colon, separated only by the potential space of the hepatorenal pouch (fig. 30.16). It must be emphasized that these relations are only a rough guide to the changing ones in the living patient. In the upright posture, for example, a full stomach may descend by as much as 10 cm and then the pylorus and the first part of the duodenum are no longer related to the liver.

Anatomy of the biliary system

The ducts of the liver are known as the biliary system or apparatus and convey the bile from within the liver to the duodenum. In addition to this simple drainage function the biliary system stores, concentrates and periodically releases bile.

The intrahepatic ducts collect the bile as it is formed into many tiny channels, which converge and form larger but fewer ducts until finally two main hepatic ducts emerge at the porta hepatis. These intrahepatic ducts are described more fully with the histology of the liver (p. 30.30).

The extrahepatic biliary system consists of the following structures (fig. 30.38):

(1) right and left main hepatic ducts,
(2) common hepatic duct,   (4) gall bladder,
(3) bile duct,   (5) cystic duct.

The right and left main hepatic ducts, each draining half the liver, unite below the porta hepatis to form the common hepatic duct. This passes down in the free border of the lesser omentum for a few cm before receiving the cystic duct and becoming the bile duct. The bile duct leaves the lesser omentum and descends posterior to the first part of duodenum and then becomes embedded in the

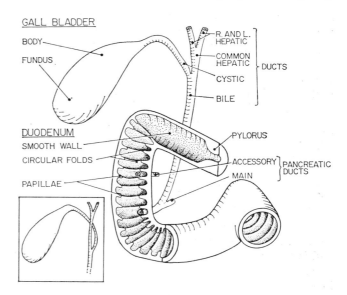

FIG. 30.38. Extrahepatic biliary apparatus. The smaller diagram shows a variation in which the cystic duct descends on the left side of the common hepatic duct before joining it.

back of the head of pancreas; there it curves laterally towards the posteromedial wall of the second part of the duodenum which it pierces obliquely to end on the duodenal papilla (figs. 30.27 and 30.38). Near its termination the bile duct joins the main pancreatic duct to form the hepatopancreatic ampulla before opening into the duodenum.

There are many important relations of the biliary system. The common hepatic and bile ducts lie in the lesser omentum lateral to the hepatic artery and anterior to the portal vein. Hepatic lymph nodes, which surround the biliary ducts near the porta hepatis, when enlarged by disease may compress the ducts and obstruct the flow of bile. The bile duct is an immediate posterior relation of the first part of the duodenum and is occasionally involved in duodenal peptic ulceration. In this situation it is accompanied by the gastroduodenal artery and remains anterior to the portal vein.

GALL BLADDER

The silvery blue and pear shaped gall bladder is found against the visceral surface of the liver along the right boundary of the quadrate lobe. The lower end, the fundus, is expanded, and the middle part, the body, tapers above to form the neck. The neck joins the stalk of the pear, the cystic duct, which ascends to the porta hepatis and then curves abruptly downwards into the lesser omentum, where it descends along the right side of the common hepatic duct for two or more centimetres before fusing with it.

The upper surface of the body of the gall bladder is in

contact with the liver but peritoneum covers its sides and inferior surface (figs. 30.16 and 30.37). The fundus is invested completely in peritoneum and projects freely beyond the lower border of the liver, where it is related to the anterior abdominal wall, at the junction of the right costal margin and the lateral border of the rectus abdominis. Inferiorly the gall bladder rests on the duodenum and transverse colon. The position varies in the living, but in a recumbent patient the fundus descends below the costal margin on inspiration and can then be palpated through the anterior abdominal wall, if the gall bladder is distended.

The normal gall bladder is radiotranslucent but can be outlined by injecting into the bloodstream organic iodine compounds which are radio-opaque and are excreted in the bile. Its position varies with posture and respiration, and is lower in thin individuals. A normal fundus may be as high as the transpyloric plane or below the right iliac crest.

Filling and emptying of the gall bladder

The bile duct is a wide, thin walled, distensible tube, containing little smooth muscle except at its lower end where it is surrounded by a well developed biliary sphincter. (fig. 30.46.) There is another more distally placed sphincter around the hepatopancreatic ampulla, the **sphincter of Oddi**. The third part of this complex is the pancreatic duct sphincter, which is often poorly developed or absent.

After the gall bladder has emptied and the bile has entered the duodenum, the biliary sphincter closes and freshly secreted bile flows down the common hepatic duct and fills the bile duct. The pressure in these ducts rises as the sphincter remains closed and bile refluxes up the cystic duct into the gall bladder. There is a curious spiral fold on the mucosa of the cystic duct and neck of the gall bladder which may facilitate the two way flow of bile; when the gall bladder relaxes, it accommodates the continuous inflow of bile so that the pressure within does not rise above that within the bile duct. A second factor which minimizes the pressure rise in the gall bladder is that the mucosa is continually withdrawing fluid from the bile and thus reducing its volume. For reasons that are described on p. 30.34 the smooth muscle coat of the gall bladder contracts and the biliary sphincter opens, so that bile flows down the cystic duct and through the bile duct into the duodenum.

There are two sites of constriction of the biliary passages where gallstones are liable to be arrested. The first is the cystic duct; the second, causing distension of the gall bladder, is at the biliary sphincter or in the hepatopancreatic ampulla.

Variations of the biliary ducts

The biliary ducts are so variable that it is arguable whether a normal pattern can be described. Although physiologi-

cally unimportant, some of these variations are dangerous surgically. For example, the cystic duct must be tied and cut to remove the gall bladder, so if the cystic duct passes behind the common hepatic duct and then descends on its left side for some distance before joining it, the common hepatic duct may be tied in error (fig. 30.38).

The structure of the liver

The liver consists mainly of hepatocytes (glandular epithelium) and blood filled sinusoidal capillaries with little connective tissue.

The three structures, which go through the porta hepatis, are the hepatic bile duct, the portal vein and the hepatic artery (fig. 30.39). These three all divide progressively within the liver substance, but remain associated with each other and form the **portal tracts**, which are easily visible on the cut surface of the liver with a hand lens. The tributaries of the hepatic veins run separately within the liver, between the portal tracts, and are seen as isolated structures. The liver of the pig is often used to illustrate the basic structure of the liver because adjacent portal tracts are joined by fibrous septa, which divide the tissue into lobules. At the centre of each hexagonal or polygonal lobule is a tributary of the hepatic vein, the **central vein**.

Several portal tracts lie at the periphery of a single hepatic lobule, and each consists of a large branch of the portal vein, a smaller branch of the hepatic artery, a tributary of the hepatic bile ducts, and some lymphatic vessels, all embedded in collagenous connective tissue (fig. 30.40 and plate 30.2, facing p. 30.12). The blood vessels of the tract give off branches which pass between adjacent lobules and ramify into little vessels which enter the sinusoids. The sinusoids therefore carry mixed blood, part venous and part arterial, which flows into the central vein. The sinusoids are surrounded by branching and anastomosing sheets of hepatocytes, to which they bring the products of digestion via the portal vein and oxygen via the hepatic artery. This classical picture of a hepatic lobule is based on the venous drain at the centre. In man and other mammals there are no fibrous septa and the outlines of the lobule are not so clear.

This classical concept has helped to explain the distribution of damaged areas within diseased livers in many instances, but sometimes only parts of a lobule are affected or adjacent parts of two lobules are damaged. The existence of a smaller unit, the **acinus**, is now established. This is the mass of tissue supplied by a **primary afferent branch** of the portal vein and hepatic artery. Each small portal tract gives off three branches which leave the connective tissue of the tract and running between the adjacent hepatic lobules, divide into terminal branches which enter the sinusoids of the lobules. Fig. 30.40 shows that the acinus is an irregular structure with a broad equator where the vessels enter, and two narrow extremities which end on two central veins. The fresh blood enters

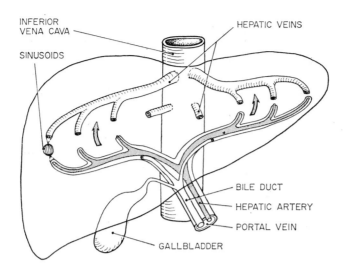

FIG. 30.39. Hepatic circulation. The liver receives a dual blood supply from the portal vein and hepatic artery. These two vessels end in the sinusoids that drain via the hepatic veins into the inferior vena cava.

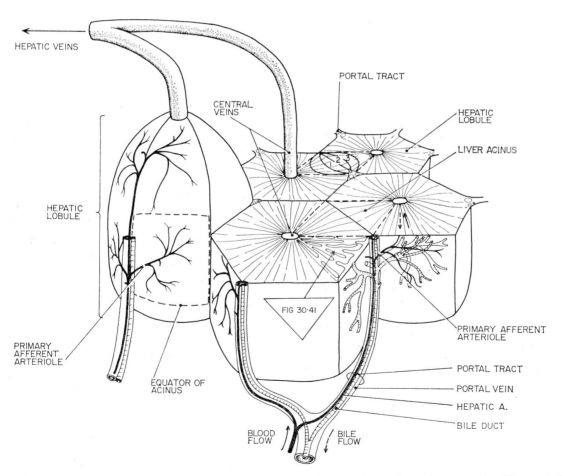

FIG. 30.40. Hepatic lobule. On section the liver parenchyma forms hexagonal or polygonal areas each with a central vein. Portal tracts lie between the areas. A classical lobule and a liver acinus are outlined.

the centre of the acinus and then diverges, passing along the sinusoids towards each central vein. These sinusoids are surrounded by sheets of hepatic epithelial cells. The entire acinus can be divided arbitrarily into three zones. Zone 1 receives the fresh blood supply, while zone 3 receives blood that has percolated along the sinusoids and lost oxygen and other substances to the adjacent epithelial cells of zones 1 and 2 (fig. 30.42). The concept of zones has been of value in interpreting liver disease; for example zone 3 is the most susceptible to certain anoxic states and this gives rise to a pattern of damage which was inexplicable on the classical view of liver structure (fig. 30.42). Conversely, certain toxic substances, carried in the hepatic artery or portal vein, might be expected to act on zone 1 as they reach it first.

FIG. 30.41. Liver acinus. Blood enters the sinusoids at the equator of the acinus and percolates past the plates of hepatocytes to enter the central vein. The hepatocytes secrete bile into the intercellular network of canaliculi which drain into biliary ductules.

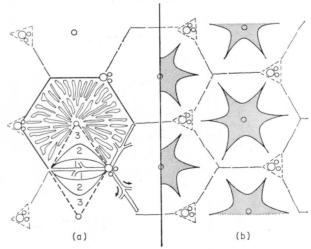

FIG. 30.42. (a) The acinar zones, (b) zonal necrosis of liver acini, showing the pattern produced by death of cells in zone 3 of acini.

Hepatic epithelium (*hepatocytes*)

This is arranged in the form of sheets one cell thick, which are fenestrated and branch and anastomose with each other. In general the sheets converge on the central vein, and the spaces between them are filled with sinusoids, which are capillaries lined with phagocytic reticuloendo-

thelial cells. Each hepatocyte has two surfaces that fac sinusoids and several surfaces in contact with other hepato cytes. The bile which is formed by the hepatocytes runs ii intercellular channels within the sheets towards the equato of the acinus to enter ductules which unite to form th tributary of the bile duct in the adjacent portal tract. Thu the flow of blood in the acinus is from the equator to th central vein, whereas the flow of bile is in the opposit direction.

The hepatocytes (figs. 30.43 and 13.17) where they fac the sinusoids are covered with microvilli, which projec

FIG. 30.43. Hepatocytes. High magnification view of rectangular area in fig. 30.41. Two surfaces of the hepatocyte face a sinusoid across the space of Disse. The remaining surfaces are contiguous with adjacent hepatocytes and are grooved to form a biliary canaliculus. The cytology and main functions are indicated.

into a narrow extravascular space between them and th sinusoidal endothelium (the space of Disse). The produc of digestion which are brought in the portal blood, as we as the oxygen in the arterial blood, cross this absorptiv surface. In addition many substances formed within th cell are secreted in the opposite direction into the sinusoic The lateral surfaces of the cell, which are contiguou with adjacent hepatocytes, have near their middle a groov which together with the similar groove in the neighbourir cell forms a cylindrical channel, the **biliary canaliculus.** Tł walls of these canaliculi also have microvilli and the membranes are rich in ATPase suggesting that some of tł bile constituents are actively transported. The bi canaliculi form an anastomosing and branching syste in which the flow of bile is away from the central vei towards the periphery of the lobule or equator of the acini where it enters biliary ductules.

Hepatocytes have an extensive and dispersed roug surfaced endoplasmic reticulum. The Golgi complex li between the nucleus and the biliary canaliculus, i. between the nucleus and the exocrine secretory surfa as with other exocrine cells. Glycogen is stored in the form of clusters of granules 50 nm in diameter and is therefore larger than the RNA ribosomes. There is an extensive smooth surfaced endoplasmic reticulum consisting of a network of interconnected tubules. This is diminished when the glycogen store is depleted by starvation, but expands on refeeding and glycogen granules first appear in close relation to it. Lipid droplets are present in normal hepatocytes and may increase in disease. Mitochondria are scattered throughout the cell. Lysosomes, first discovered in the hepatocyte, lie near the biliary canaliculi and vary in appearance according to whether they contain altered mitochondria, foreign material or granular debris (p. 13.8). Hepatocytes in zone 1, where blood supply is richest and aerobic metabolism predominates, contain many mitochondria and so have a high content of succinic dehydrogenase and cytochrome oxidase. In contrast, the cells in zone 3 have fewer mitochondria but a more extensive rough surfaced endoplasmic reticulum and are presumably more active in protein synthesis. Such differences between the cells of each zone, together with their differing blood supply, may account for their differences in susceptibility to noxious agents.

Connective tissue

The liver has a tough fibrous tissue capsule, which invests the vessels and the hepatic ducts as they enter the liver. In a reduced form it continues to support the portal tracts as they branch so that even the smallest tracts lie in a little collagenous tissue. A little connective tissue also surrounds the central vein (plate 30.2, facing p. 30.12). The lobule is supported by fine reticular fibres lying in the space of Disse. In cirrhosis of the liver fibroblasts lay down large amounts of collagen which forms scars; the lobular architecture of the liver is destroyed and there is interference with its blood flow.

Epithelial turnover

The number of mitotic figures in the adult liver is very low, but the response of the liver to reduction of its mass is prompt and effective. In rats 80 per cent of the liver can be removed experimentally and complete restitution occurs by proliferation of new cells. The most active and and earliest site of proliferation is in zone 1, where the blood supply is richest. The ability of the human liver to recover from damage to the cells by disease or injury is great and may be of the above order.

Sinusoids

Like other sinusoids, those of the liver are lined with reticuloendothelial cells which are phagocytic. Most of these cells appear as endothelial cells with flattened nuclei, but a small number have rounded nuclei and long radiating processes of cytoplasm which give them a stellate shape. These are the Kupffer cells which are rich in lysosomes. Intravenous injections of dye particles increases

the proportion of endothelial cells which appear as typical phagocytic Kupffer cells; this suggests there is only one cell type in the wall of the sinusoids. Normally these cells do not destroy effete red blood cells, as this process is confined to the sinusoids of the spleen. But if the spleen is removed, then the liver sinusoids assume this function.

The reticuloendothelial cells also synthesize the reticulin fibres in the space of Disse.

In foetal life the liver is an active site of erythropoiesis, but this normally ceases about birth. Stem cells persist in the liver, and in certain diseases these may cause erythropoiesis in the adult liver.

Microscopic structure of the biliary system

Biliary passages

In the portal tracts the bile ducts are lined with a clear cubical epithelium and some goblet mucous cells are found in the larger ducts.

The extrahepatic ducts have a simple columnar epithelium with some goblet cells and sparse mucous glands. There is a thin coat of smooth muscle consisting of an inner circular and outer longitudinal layer, similar to that of the rest of the gut. This muscle is innervated by the vagus and when in spasm causes the excruciating pain of biliary colic. The bile duct mucosa has several longitudinal folds when empty, as it is very distensible.

Gall bladder

This stores and concentrates hepatic bile. The mucosa has many irregular folds and is extremely vascular (fig. 30.44).

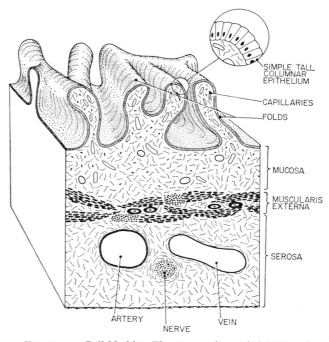

FIG. 30.44. Gall bladder. The mucosa is much folded and has a simple tall columnar epithelium.

SIMPLE TALL COLUMNAR EPITHELIUM

CAPILLARIES

FOLDS

MUCOSA

MUSCULARIS EXTERNA

SEROSA

ARTERY   NERVE   VEIN

The simple tall columnar epithelium, which concentrates the bile by absorption of salts and water, has inferolateral folds and a poorly-developed microvillous border (fig. 30.45). The former is of interest, because it is similar to that of the large intestine which also absorbs water and ions. There are a few mucous glands near its neck, which, together with the scattered glands and goblet cells already described, form the mucous component of the bile.

There is no muscularis mucosae, but there is a thick and vascular lamina propria. The muscular coat consists of loose bundles arranged in ill defined longitudinal and transverse layers. The serosa is thick with many large vessels and nerves. Although these include vagal branches that are motor to the gall bladder, the main stimulus to contraction is the humoral one of cholecystokinin.

FIG. 30.45. A diagram of the gall bladder epithelium, showing lateral infolding.

Bile secretion

Bile is continuously secreted by the hepatocytes, but is required for its digestive function only intermittently. Between meals it must be stored; it is diverted from the common hepatic duct into the gall bladder, where it is concentrated by the reabsorption of water and electrolytes, which keeps the volume of the stored bile low. The gall bladder bile is then released into the bile duct when required. Its composition is described in chap. 31 and its role in absorption on p. 30.37.

Control of bile secretion

Two aspects of the control systems concerned with bile secretion must be considered. First, its secretion from the hepatocytes and secondly the release of the stored bile from the gall bladder.

In the control of bile formation, nervous, hormonal and chemical influences are involved. The autonomic nervous system influences bile secretion, since in the dog vagal stimulation increases the flow of hepatic bile, and stimulation of the sympathetic supply to the liver reduces the flow. These are not, however, the main controlling factor, since division of the nerves does not stop the secretion from the liver. Both secretin and gastrin stimulate the flow of hepatic bile, but only double the resting rate of secretion and cannot be considered a major influence on bile secretion. The most potent stimulus is the presence in the blood of the bile salts themselves which are powerful **choleretics** (stimuli to bile secretion).

In the interdigestive periods, the biliary sphincter offers a resistance of about 20 mm Hg, so that bile secreted from the hepatocytes cannot pass into the duodenum, but is diverted to the gall bladder. Reabsorption of water reduces the volume of the bile in the gall bladder and the pressure does not rise sufficiently to overcome the resistance of the sphincter. About 30 min after the ingestion of food, the gall bladder contracts, the sphincter relaxes and the pressure exerted by the gall bladder bile is sufficient to overcome the lowered resistance of the sphincter, and bile pours into the duodenum. Both nervous and hormonal mechanisms are involved in this entry of the stored bile into the intestine. The nervous stimulus through the vagus nerves is part of the cephalic phase of digestion. In addition, the presence of foods, notably fats, meat and egg yoke cause the release of the hormone **cholecystokinin** from the duodenal mucosa into the circulation. The hormone then acts as a **cholecystagogue,** i.e. causes bile flow by contracting the gall bladder. The full chemical structure of this hormone is unknown, but the terminal sequence is the same tetrapeptide as in gastrin (p. 30.17). The gall bladder may be seen on fluoroscopy in man after administering radio-opaque, organic iodine compounds, which are excreted by the liver and concentrated by the gall bladder. It may be seen contracting after giving injections of cholecystokinin.

Another important aspect of bile secretion is the enterohepatic circulation (p. 31.9). The bile salts present in the secreted bile are nearly all reabsorbed in the small intestine, and re-secreted by the liver.

PANCREAS

The second main accessory digestive gland is the pancreas. This mixed exocrine and endocrine gland is elongated, and stretches across the posterior abdominal wall from the duodenum to the spleen. The exocrine tissue forms the great mass of the gland and secretes the pancreatic juice into the duodenum. The endocrine tissue consists of tiny spherical islets which account for less than 1 per cent of the whole. Their structure and function are described on p. 25.38.

Gross anatomy

The pancreas is a soft, lumpy organ with a large head, long body and tapering tail. The head lies within the concavity of the duodenum, and inferomedially gives off the uncinate process which passes behind the superior mesenteric vessels (fig. 30.27). The body extends leftwards from the upper part of the head across the vertebral column and on to the left kidney, where the tail turns forward into the lienorenal ligament to end at the hilus of the spleen.

The head and body of the pancreas are retroperitoneal and their posterior surface is directly related to several important structures. The head of the pancreas rests on the bile duct and inferior vena cava, and its neck on the origin of the portal vein. The body lies on the aorta and the left adrenal, renal vein, and left kidney. The splenic vein is also a posterior relation of the body of pancreas and the tortuous splenic artery runs along the upper border. The tail is surrounded by peritoneum as it lies in the lienorenal ligament. As the pancreas is retroperitoneal the anterior surface is covered by peritoneum, but the root of the transverse mesocolon is attached horizontally along the anterior border. Above this border, the pancreas is related to the lesser sac and stomach, and below it to the greater sac, small intestine and mesocolon, or if the latter is shallow, the transverse colon (fig. 30.12).

The **main pancreatic duct** begins at the tail and runs towards the head, receiving large oblique interlobular tributaries along its course (fig. 30.46). At the head, the main duct turns first caudally and then to the right to join the bile duct. The upper portion of the head is drained separately in most instances by the accessory pancreatic duct which runs horizontally and opens into the duodenum proximal to the main duct.

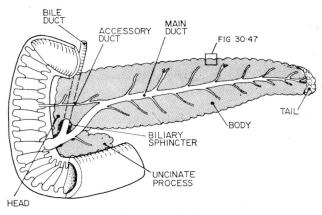

FIG. 30.46. Pancreatic duct system.

Microscopic structure (fig. 30.47)

The exocrine pancreas is a compound tubulo-acinar gland, enclosed in a very delicate fibrous capsule, through which the glandular lobules are readily observed. The capsule sends septa into the gland which divide it into lobules.

The lobule is made up of many acini, each draining into an intercalated duct. The acinar cells are excellent examples of serous cells which secrete enzymes. They are grouped around the lumen, into which they discharge their secretory granules. The lumen often appears to be filled by one or more cells with clear cytoplasm. These centro-acinar cells are the flattened epithelial cells at the start of the intercalated duct, which is partly invaginated into the acinus. The intercalated ducts unite forming the intralobular ducts, which are shorter than those of the salivary glands, and therefore appear to be less numerous.

FIG. 30.47. Pancreas. This low power diagram shows the typical features of an exocrine gland. The scattered islets or endocrine portion of pancreas constitute only 1 per cent of the total mass.

The intralobular ducts join interlobular ducts in septa alongside the incoming vessels and nerves. The larger interlobular ducts enter the main duct obliquely, in a herring bone pattern. The duct epithelium increases in height as the ducts become larger and in the main duct is a tall columnar epithelium with a few mucous glands.

Nerve and blood supply

There are many nerve fibres and parasympathetic ganglion cells in the interlobular septa which accompany the larger ducts. Postganglionic fibres end on the acini and islets. The sympathetic component is small and distributed mainly to the vessels. Visceral afferent fibres run with the sympathetic fibres.

The pancreas is a vascular organ with a rich capillary bed. The endocrine islets are particularly well supplied, so that a vascular injection makes the islets appear as berries on the stalks of their supplying vessels.

Pancreatic secretion

The exocrine secretion of the pancreas, the pancreatic juice, is secreted by the serous acinar cells and passes into the duodenum through the two pancreatic ducts. Experimentally, the secretion may be studied in the dog by providing the animal with a duodenal fistula which is carefully positioned opposite the main pancreatic duct. A cannula can then be passed through the fistula into the duct, and pancreatic juice collected for study. Between observations, the pancreatic juice flows normally into the duodenum, and the animal is not deprived of the digestive functions of the secretion.

COMPOSITION OF PANCREATIC JUICE

If the juice is collected from the duct of the gland, as described above, it is found to be isotonic with plasma, but much more alkaline. The constituents of the fluid are given in table 30.1. An estimate of the daily secretion of electrolytes is given on p. 30.38. The inactive enzyme precursor **trypsinogen** is converted to the active **trypsin** by the

TABLE 30.1. Composition of Pancreatic Juice.

Enzyme precursors	trypsinogen, chymotrypsinogen
Active enzymes	amylase, lipase
Cations	sodium, potassium, calcium
Anions	chloride, bicarbonate
pH	7·5–8·0

enzyme enterokinase, which is liberated from unidentified cells of the duodenal mucosa. Trypsin also acts on the precursor **chymotrypsinogen** to form the active **chymotrypsin**. The amylase and lipase are secreted by the pancreas in the active form without precursors.

FUNCTIONS OF PANCREATIC JUICE

The secretion has several functions.

(1) The alkalinity aids in the neutralization of the acid chyme passing into the duodenum from the stomach. This is an important function, since the enzymes of the pancreatic juice act optimally in an alkaline medium.

(2) Trypsin, when formed from its precursor trypsinogen, converts the proteins ingested to polypeptides and amino acids. The enzyme has its optimum pH at 8–9·7.

(3) Chymotrypsin, when formed from chymotrypsinogen, has the action of curdling milk.

(4) The secreted amylase breaks down polysaccharides mostly to disaccharides.

(5) The lipase converts neutral triglycerides to di- and monoglycerides and free fatty acids.

CONTROL OF PANCREATIC SECRETION

Like gastric secretion, the flow of digestive juice from the pancreas is controlled by both nervous and hormonal mechanisms. The nervous component is part of the cephalic phase of digestion, and is mediated by the vagus nerves. This can be demonstrated in sham feeding experiments, when the pancreatic ducts of a dog are cannulated through a duodenal fistula. When food is swallowed by the animal, the pancreas secretes, even though the food is emerging from the oesophageal fistula and never reaches the intestine. This secretion is not seen if the vagi are divided when the fistulae are made. In acute experiments, stimulation of the abdominal branches of the vagi causes pancreatic secretion to rise above the very small resting level.

If the pancreas is removed from its normal position and transplanted to another site, its blood supply becomes re-established, but it remains without extrinsic nerve supply. If food is then allowed to enter the duodenum, the transplanted pancreas will secrete. There must therefore be a hormonal control of secretion as well as a nervous component. This hormonal mechanism normally begins when the food eaten reaches the upper part of the small intestine. Extracts of the mucosa of the first portion of the small intestine will elicit pancreatic secretion if injected intravenously, but the cellular origin of the hormone is unknown. Two polypeptide hormones are in fact produced, having different stimuli for their release and different effects on the secretion of the pancreas. When acid enters the duodenum (as chyme from the stomach) the hormone **secretin** is liberated from the mucosa into the blood. When this reaches the cells of the pancreas a large volume of a watery secretion is produced, which contains a high concentration of bicarbonate ions, but little enzyme. Peptones and other digestive products reaching the duodenum cause the liberation of the other hormone **pancreozymin**, which stimulates the secretion of enzymes in the pancreatic juice. Both types of secretion, of course, occur after a normal meal. The neutralization of the acid chyme by the alkaline pancreatic juice reduces the stimulus to its secretion, and can be thought of as a self-regulating mechanism.

Secretin was the first hormone to be isolated, on January 16th 1902, by Bayliss and Starling, and its discovery paved the way for modern endocrinology.

ABSORPTION FROM THE GASTROINTESTINAL TRACT

Table 30.2 shows the quantities of different nutrients that may be eaten in a day and eliminated in the faeces. In

TABLE 30.2. An estimate of the different amounts of nutrients that may be eaten in a day and excreted in the faeces.

	In the diet	In the faeces
Protein (g)	100	6
Fat (g)	100	4
Carbohydrate (g) (excluding cellulose)	400	4
Sodium (mEq)	170	8
Potassium (mEq)	65	12
Calcium (mg)	1000	750
Iron (mg)	15	14
Total solids (g)	about 600	about 20

addition about 7 litres of digestive juices with their electrolyte and protein contents enter the gut and also the epithelial lining is shed into the gut, digested and largely absorbed. Clearly the intestines perform most of their absorptive functions efficiently.

Absorption is dependent on many physical factors, e.g. the area of the absorptive surfaces, concentration gradients, osmotic and intraluminal pressure. However for the most part, nutrients are actively transported from the lumen into the portal blood.

Ethanol is the only important nutrient apart from water which crosses the cells by simple diffusion. Consequently it may be absorbed by all parts of the intestines. The remainder of the nutrients are absorbed in the small intestines, in which digestion is virtually complete. Here absorption is favoured by the large surface area of plasma membrane.

The absorption of carbohydrates

Starch and other dietary polysaccharides are broken down by the amylases in the saliva and pancreatic juice mostly to disaccharides in the lumen of the gut. After a meal of starch very little monosaccharide is found in the lumen, yet only monosaccharides are found in the portal venous blood. The breakdown of disaccharides is effected within the brush border of the columnar cells. The enzymes responsible and their activity can be determined by biopsy samples, obtained by snipping off small pieces with an instrument which can be swallowed by man. Table 30.3 gives the enzymic activity found in such samples. The monosaccharides are then actively transported across the cell and enter the portal blood. The different sugars compete for the transport mechanism and so are absorbed

TABLE 30.3. The enzymic activity of human jejunal mucosa (units/g protein)

Enzyme	Activity mean	range
Maltase	593	(310–1120)
Sucrase	173	(70–325)
Isomaltase	159	(65–268)
Lactase	107	(39–258)

at different rates. The fastest rates are for galactose and glucose, followed by fructose, mannose, xylose and arabinose in diminishing order. The rates of absorption reach a maximum at high concentration. If the concentration of disaccharides in the lumen is high, hydrolysis proceeds faster than the transport mechanism can move hexoses into the blood; under these circumstances monosaccharides return temporarily to the lumen.

The nature of the transporting system, which is in the mucosal membrane, is not known accurately nor how it is coupled to a source of energy; it depends on the presence of Na^+, which may effect the supply of energy from ATP. Absorption is inhibited by phloridzin which also inhibits the uptake of glucose by the cells of the renal tubules.

A deficiency of disaccharidases may arise in congenital or acquired disease when carbohydrates are not digested, but pass into the large intestine where they are fermented by bacteria and cause diarrhoea. Owing to congenital lactase deficiency, some infants cannot tolerate milk and can be reared only on artificial milks containing other carbohydrates.

The absorption of lipids

Dietary fat leaves the stomach in the form of coarse undigested oily drops. In the duodenum these are emulsified by the action of the bile salts with the formation of particles not exceeding 0·5 μm diameter, which are susceptible to the action of pancreatic lipase. Hydrolysis does not go to completion; a mixture of di- and mono-glycerides with some free fatty acids is formed. The presence of conjugated bile salts makes the fatty acids more soluble in water. A clear microemulsion of molecular aggregations or **micelles** is formed in the lumen; each micelle consists of bile salts into which the lipids enter. They are absorbed by diffusion across the microvilli. Within the epithelium lipid droplets are enclosed in vesicles of the smooth and rough surfaced endoplasmic reticulum. Triglyceride is reformed, esterification taking place with free fatty acids, some of which reach the cells from the blood stream (p. 10.10). Large droplets, **chylomicrons**, are formed at the edges of the mucosal cells; these are 0·5 to 1·0 μm in diameter, consisting of over 80 per cent triglyceride with a little cholesterol and a small envelope of phospholipid (p. 10.11). These enter the lymph capillaries through pores and then pass along the larger lymph vessels and the thoracic duct to enter the general circulation (fig. 30.30).

In ruminants protozoa living in the rumen ferment the carbohydrate present in grass with the formation of short chain fatty acids. These are absorbed and pass in the portal blood to the liver. The only fats in human diets which contain significant amounts of short chain fatty acids are dairy fats (table 10.2). These may pass direct to the liver in the portal blood, but this route is of little significance in man.

Fat absorption is nearly complete in the small intestine. If on a normal intake, more than 5 g of fat appear in the faeces (a daily average over 5 days), then malabsorption is present and a diagnosis of steatorrhoea can be made.

The fat-soluble vitamins are absorbed with the lipids in the micelles and, if there is steatorrhoea the vitamins are not absorbed. The body contains only a small store of vitamin K and signs of deficiency, such as subcutaneous bleeding, arise in two or three weeks in patients who are jaundiced and have steatorrhoea owing to a failure of bile flow. Evidence of vitamin D deficiency and, rarely, of vitamin A deficiency occurs in patients with chronic steatorrhoea.

The absorption of protein

Pepsin and trypsin break down the dietary proteins in the lumen to a mixture of amino acids and peptides. After a meal rich in protein, the level of amino N in the blood rises from a fasting value of about 4 mg/100 ml to about 8 mg/100 ml in $1\frac{1}{2}$ to 2 hours and returns to normal in 3 to 4 hours. There are quantitative difficulties in accounting for protein digestion and absorption entirely in the form of amino acids. Studies of a few dipeptides and tripeptides provides evidence that peptide units are also taken up by the brush border and hydrolysed there, but more information is needed before it is possible to account for the absorption of all the protein in a meal.

Free amino acids are absorbed by active transport involving oxidative metabolism. As in the case of the renal tubules, different transport systems may exist for different groups of amino acids. Neutral forms are transported at 10 times the rate of basic amino acids, and the L forms are also absorbed more rapidly than are D forms, though apparently the two isomeric forms compete for the same transport system.

Absorption is normally very effective and less than 10 per cent of the dietary N is lost in the faeces.

The absorption of water and electrolytes

Table 30.4 gives an estimate of the large quantities that enter the alimentary tract daily. Of this no more than 2 per cent of the water, 2 per cent of the sodium and 10 per cent of the potassium appear normally in the faeces.

TABLE 30.4. Estimates of quantities of water and Na^+, K^+ and Cl^- entering the human intestine daily (Parsons (1967) *Proc. Nutr. Soc.* **26**, 47).

	Volume ml	Concentration mEq/litre			Electrolyte load mEq/24 hr		
		Na^+	K^+	Cl^-	Na^+	K^+	Cl^-
Saliva	1500	30	20	35	45	30	52
Gastric juice	3000	50	10	150	150	30	450
Bile	500	160	5	50	80	3	25
Pancreatic juice	2000	160	5	30	320	10	60
Internal load	7000				595	73	587
Dietary intake	1500				170	65	110
Grand total	8500				765	138	697

The net flux of water and electrolytes (the amounts secreted—amounts absorbed) between the gut lumen and the blood differs greatly in different parts of the tract. In the mouth there is a large salivary secretion, but no absorption; in the stomach there is a large secretion with little absorption; in the duodenum and upper jejunum the two processes are almost equal; the jejunum and ileum are the main sites of absorption, which is completed in the colon.

The bulk of the fluid in the alimentary tract comes from the digestive juices, which are approximately isosmotic with plasma; the dietary load may be either hypertonic or hypotonic. Hence there is no consistent osmotic gradient to facilitate absorption and fluid can be absorbed against an osmotic gradient. A basic mechanism exists for the transport of Na^+ and K^+ through the epithelial cells, which are functionally asymmetrical. Water probably accompanies the ions passively. The nature of the sodium pump is unknown, but active transport is probably achieved by a pump at the basal borders; ions which enter passively at the luminal border leak across the cell down an electrochemical gradient set up by the basal pumps. Whether Cl^- and HCO_3^- ions follow passively is not known, but probably active transport also takes place. The transport of Na^+ and K^+ is influenced by aldosterone in a manner similar to its action in the renal tubules.

It is probable that the transport mechanisms for sugars and amino acids are linked in some way to the transport of sodium.

Water absorption can be explained solely as a consequence of active transport of ions. Most of the water passes into the portal venous blood and only a small portion into the lymphatics.

Certain ions, e.g. SO_4^{--} and Mg^{++}, are not readily absorbed and these hold water in the intestines and prevent absorption and thus have a purgative action. Many natural waters contain these ions in small amounts and such mineral waters have acquired a great reputation. Perhaps the most famous came from a well near London and contained the original Epsom salt. Its owner made a fortune from the smart society of the seventeenth century.

The absorption of water-soluble vitamins

The amount of these vitamins available for absorption may be modified by the action of intestinal bacteria. In laboratory rats it is not difficult to alter the bacterial flora in the gut so that they either synthesize or utilize significant amounts of vitamin. Such synthesis of vitamins may be of practical use in animal husbandry. In a healthy man eating ordinary diets, the amount of available vitamins is probably not significantly altered by the intestinal flora, but when the bacterial flora is increased, as may happen in disease, this may not always be so. The bacteria are more likely to decrease than to increase the supply of any vitamin. Bacteria in the small intestine deconjugate bile salts and thus inhibit micelle formation and absorption of lipids. The absorption of water soluble vitamins may also be impaired for reasons unknown.

Since the water soluble vitamins are relatively simple molecules, easily soluble in water and freely diffusable, their absorption should present no problem and, in general, they are rapidly absorbed.

However, vitamin B_{12} is entirely dependent on a specific mucopolysaccharide secreted by the stomach (intrinsic factor, p. 26.9) for its absorption. The vitamin is probably absorbed largely, though not entirely, in the lower half of the ileum, but how the intrinsic factor operates at this site to permit the absorption of a few micrograms across the epithelium is not known.

By contrast with vitamin B_{12}, free folic acid is rapidly absorbed from the jejunum. The absorption of other water-soluble vitamins may not be as simple as it seems, for evidence of vitamin deficiency may occur secondary to a variety of alimentary disturbances and these cannot always be attributed to a deficient intake. The most common of these is an anaemia responding to injections of folic acid, which not infrequently occurs in disease of the small intestine.

Tests are available for assessing the absorptive capacity for a vitamin. In the case of folic acid, the subject is given the same dose of the vitamin on two occasions separated by an interval of a few days. On one occasion the dose is given by mouth and on the other by injection. The amount of vitamin or of one of its metabolites excreted in the urine is measured and, if absorption is defective, is much lower with the oral test. For testing vitamin B_{12} absorption, it is possible to give a small dose of the vitamin labelled with ^{60}Co and to measure the amount of radioactivity appearing in the faeces and compare this with normal standards. In health over 70 per cent of an oral dose is absorbed.

The absorption of minerals

Calcium and iron and probably also the other dietary minerals and trace elements (p. 5.9) differ from the nutrients already discussed in that the major portion of the dietary intake is excreted in the faeces and only a little absorbed. Further excretion of these substances by the kidney either does not take place (iron) or is limited (calcium). The minerals, if present in excess in the body, tend to form organic complexes which accumulate in the tissues and give rise to pathological states. These are fortunately rare. These facts suggest that the amount of a mineral present in the body is controlled by a mechanism which regulates intestinal absorption. No such control mechanism exists for other nutrients and any dietary excess is absorbed and either subsequently excreted in the urine (e.g. the N in protein, sodium and vitamin C) or stored (e.g. triglyceride and fat soluble vitamins). Here only the absorption of calcium and iron, which are the two most important dietary minerals, are discussed.

The absorption of calcium

Of the calcium present in most western diets, about 70 to 80 per cent is lost in the faeces (p. 5.6). However in eastern diets there is usually much less calcium (table 5.4), but the faecal losses are relatively smaller and the amounts absorbed are sufficient to allow the development and maintenance of healthy bone. Active and growing children absorb relatively more calcium than do adults. Calcium absorption thus appears to be related more closely to the physiological need than to the dietary intake. A proportion of the calcium in the faeces, estimated at 15 per cent, has been shown by using two isotopes of calcium, one given by mouth and one intravenously, the latter reaching the faeces via the intestinal secretions. Vitamin D is the most important factor influencing calcium absorption and in its absence this is negligible. How the vitamin effects the active transport of calcium is not known. Parathyroid hormone may also promote absorption.

The absorption of iron

Dietary aspects of this are discussed on p. 5.8, where it is stated that absorption is related to requirements and raised from the normal level of about 10 per cent of the dietary intake to up to 20–30 per cent when the need for iron for haemoglobin synthesis is increased, e.g. by severe haemorrhage. An early hypothesis sought to account for this control of iron absorption by reference to the fact that during absorption iron may be incorporated into the storage substance ferritin (p. 5.8). It was suggested that either the rate of formation of ferritin or the rate of removal of iron from it might be the controlling step in absorption: either lack of iron in the body fluids or local hypoxia caused by anaemia might stimulate iron release from ferritin and thus promote absorption.

Experimental evidence has failed to support this theory. More recent alternatives have not yet been adequately tested, although the basic fact that iron absorption is generally related to the need for haemoglobin synthesis, remains unassailed. Studies with ^{59}Fe have shown that iron may be absorbed against a concentration gradient and a transport mechanism involving oxidative metabolism must exist.

MOTILITY IN THE DIGESTIVE TRACT

Very varying rates have been reported for the passage of food down the gastrointestinal tract. In general when an opaque barium meal is followed, the passage is often slower than would be indicated by following the appearance and disappearance in the blood of the products of digestion after a normal meal. If a person taking 2,500–3,000 kcal. daily eats his food in 3–4 meals of about equal size and evenly spaced throughout the day, food begins to enter the small intestine a few minutes after the start of a meal; all may have left the stomach after 2–3 hours. The remnants that are not absorbed begin to reach the large intestine in about one hour and little remains in the small intestine after 4 hours. Digestion and absorption is probably complete for some time before the next meal is taken and we may spend a good part of each day literally starving.

Most of the remnants that reach the large intestine are evacuated in the faeces between 24 and 48 hours later, but studies using dyes or radioactive markers show that some usually continues to appear in the faeces for 5 days and occasionally later.

Food is moved along the tract by the contraction and relaxation of the muscular walls and sphincters, which also assist in breaking up the food, and mixing it with the digestive juices.

MOTILITY IN THE SMALL INTESTINE

Three distinct types of movement in the small intestine together serve to break up food particles, mix them with the secreted juices and move the food along the tract. The three types are called segmentation, peristalsis and pendular movement.

Segmentation is a series of rhythmic movements, of alternate constriction and relaxation of the gut (fig. 30.48), occurring at the rate of about 7/min in man. The alternating constriction and relaxation of each portion of intestine mixes and breaks up the food, but does not cause any movement of the food along the tract. Segmentation is apparently myogenic in origin, since it can be seen even after total nerve block which cuts off impulses from both the extrinsic and intrinsic innervation. Both the frequency and the amplitude of the waves are usually greater in the upper intestinal tract than in the lower.

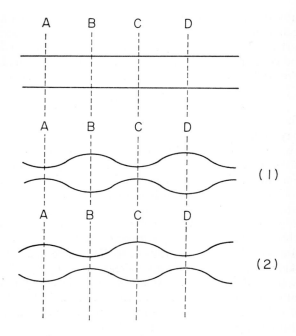

FIG. 30.48. Segmentation in the small intestine. The segments at A and C first contract (1) and then relax (2). At B and D relaxation occurs (1) followed by contraction (2).

Peristalsis is a type of motility already mentioned in connection with the oesophagus and stomach. Two types are distinguished in the small intestine, under experimental conditions, ordinary peristalsis and peristaltic rush. The former consists of slow waves of contraction preceded by relaxation, and in man the waves move at about 2 cm/sec. This type of movement was first described by Bayliss and Starling, and has been called the 'law of the intestines' or the 'myenteric reflex'. The peristaltic rush of more doubtful physiological significance and attributed by some to experimental artefact, is similar but the waves of relaxation and contraction are longer, and move at about 25 cm/min. Both types can move the food along the gut but have little or no effect on breaking up the food or mixing it. Peristalsis depends on local reflexes in the intrinsic plexuses, probably initiated by local distension, since it is abolished by the application of cocaine or stripping the mucosa, but not by section or blocking of the extrinsic nerves.

Pendular movements are waves of contraction sweeping backwards and forwards over the intestine and cause mixing up of the food rather than its propulsion. Like peristalsis, they depend upon the integrity of the intrinsic nerve plexuses.

The ileocaecal sphincter is normally closed, but opens as peristaltic waves reach the site. Like the pyloric sphincter, it appears to be opened by the pressure exerted by the peristaltic wave and not by nervous activity. Intestinal contents probably enter the colon passively.

MOTILITY IN THE LARGE INTESTINE

Two types of movement occur in the large intestine, propulsive and non-propulsive. The former consists of the contraction of one segment, with relaxation of the succeeding segment, and is therefore similar to peristalsis in the small intestine. A mass contraction affecting the left colon occurs before defaecation. The non-propulsive movement is not as clear cut as segmentation, but also results in a churning up of the gut contents. Approximately 24 hours after the ingestion of a meal mass peristalsis moves the faeces into the rectum and defaecation normally follows soon afterwards.

Defaecation

This is a reflex activity, but is under conscious control and normally occurs only when time and circumstances are suitable. The stimulus to the reflex is distension of the wall of the rectum, which gives rise to afferent impulses in the pudendal and pelvic splanchnic nerves. These travel to the 2–4 sacral spinal segments. From there efferent impulses pass back along the splanchnic nerves causing contraction of the colon and relaxation of the internal anal sphincter. The external anal sphincter is under voluntary control. During the process the levator ani contracts and lifts the anal canal over the descending faecal mass. Usually evacuation is assisted by an increase in intra-abdominal pressure caused by contractions of the diaphragm and abdominal muscles.

MISCELLANEOUS REFLEXES

Several reflexes have been demonstrated whereby food in one part of the digestive tract may influence the motility of other parts either by stimulating or by inhibiting muscle contraction.

The **gastroileal reflex** is evoked when food is present in the stomach, when the distension it causes leads to increased motor activity in the ileum. The **gastrocolic reflex** is a similar stimulus to the colon and is particularly active after the first meal of the day. The **ileogastric reflex** is evoked when food products distend the ileum and gastric motility and emptying inhibited.

In all these reflexes, the extrinsic and intrinsic nerve plexuses are concerned.

Vomiting

This is a reflex which may be caused by a wide variety of stimuli. These include irritation of the gastric mucosa by food or drugs, tactile stimulation of the throat, intestinal distension, compression or irritation of abdominal viscera, impulses from the vestibular apparatus (e.g. sea sickness), and by any severe pain or unpleasant emotion.

Impulses from many sites pass to a vomiting centre in the medulla, and give rise to a co-ordinated response. There is normally a deep inspiration with closure of the larynx and elevation of the soft palate, with relaxation of the oesophagus and stomach. This is followed by forceful contraction of the abdominal muscles, together with expiration which cause pressure on the walls of the stomach, and gastric contents are expelled. In prolonged vomiting, the duodenum may also contract, thus reversing the normal gastroduodenal pressure gradient, and its contents enter the stomach to be expelled with the gastric vomitus. Vomiting is usually, but not invariably, accompanied by feelings of nausea, and widespread autonomic activity, causing sweating, salivation and tachycardia.

Bacterial flora

The motility of the gut determines in part the bacterial flora. Large numbers of bacteria are taken in with the food, but the secretions of the upper alimentary tract are bacteriostatic and bacteriocidal. The upper part of the small intestine in consequence has a limited bacterial flora and may even be sterile. The colon has a large bacterial flora, which tends to pass into the small intestine through the ileocaecal sphincter. Thus the lower part of the small intestine may contain a number and variety of organisms. If motility in the small bowel is impaired, bacteria spread upwards and may become prolific in the whole tract.

Gas in the bowel

There is normally a gas bubble of up to 100 ml of swallowed air in the stomach. This passes quickly through the small intestine and becomes apparent only where there is delay in its transit as in obstruction of the intestinal tract. The gas reaching the colon contains less O_2, since some of it is absorbed via the intestinal mucosa, and more CO_2. In the colon gases are produced by fermentation and a healthy person may pass up to 1 litre of flatus daily. This contains little oxygen (about 10 per cent), some nitrogen (50 per cent) and an admixture of hydrogen sulphide and methane.

NERVE SUPPLY

The autonomic nervous system supplies the digestive tract from the mid-oesophagus to the anus, except for the striated muscle of the external anal sphincter. Although the parasympathetic and sympathetic divisions provide a dual innervation to the gut, normal digestion is almost completely controlled by the parasympathetic nerves, aided by the gastrointestinal hormones (p. 30.17). The nerves contain large numbers of general visceral afferent fibres which have their peripheral endings in the mucosa and muscle coat of the gut wall. They carry various forms of visceral sensibility, including pain, back to the central nervous system so forming the afferent limb for visceral reflexes, and are the basis of conscious visceral sensations.

PARASYMPATHETIC INNERVATION

The vagus nerves supply the gut from mid-oesophagus to the beginning of the splenic flexure and the pelvic splanchnic nerves supply the splenic flexure and remainder of the gut almost to the anus (fig. 30.49).

FOREGUT AND MIDGUT

ANTERIOR AND POSTERIOR GASTRIC VAGAL TRUNKS

COELIAC BRANCH

COELIAC PLEXUS

SUPERIOR MESENTERIC A.

TO MIDGUT

HINDGUT

SACRUM

PELVIC SPLANCHNIC N.

TO UROGENITAL SYSTEM

1ST SACRAL NERVE ROOT

PELVIC SPLANCHNIC N.

FIG. 30.49. Parasympathetic innervation. The lower figure shows the origin of the pelvic splanchnic nerves, X, Y and Z.

The parasympathetic fibres in both the vagi and the pelvic splanchnics are preganglionic and synapse on intrinsic ganglionic cells found in the myenteric and submucosal plexuses of the gut wall (p. 30.2). The postganglionic fibres of the myenteric plexus are motor to the main visceral muscle coats and those from the submucosal plexus are secretomotor to the glands.

Vagus

In the thorax, the left and right vagi form an oesophageal plexus around the lower half of the oesophagus. This plexus ends as the **anterior** and **posterior gastric vagal trunks,** which descend on the corresponding surfaces of the oesophagus as it pierces the diaphragm (fig. 30.4), where they are cut during abdominal vagotomy (p. 30.43).

The anterior vagal trunk is derived mainly from the left vagus, because the stomach rotates during development (p. 30.50). It divides at the cardia to be distributed to the foregut and its derivatives, anterior wall of stomach, liver, biliary system and pancreas.

The posterior vagal trunk divides into gastric branches which supply the posterior gastric wall. It has a large **coeliac branch** which passes inferomedially and retroperitoneally on the left crus of diaphragm to the coeliac plexus, which surrounds the coeliac artery at its origin, and descends through it to the superior mesenteric plexus, at the origin of the superior mesenteric artery. The parasympathetic fibres are then distributed from this plexus and run with the arteries to the small intestine and the large intestine proximal to the splenic flexure.

Pelvic splanchnic nerves

These are derived from S 2,3 spacing, and 4 segments of the cord and constitute the sacral parasympathetic outflow. They emerge from the pelvic sacral foramina and pass in two directions. First, many run ventrally into the pelvic plexus (fig. 30.50) which lies on the side of the rectum. The fibres continue through this plexus and are distributed to the rectum and upper half (mucosal zone) of the anal canal. The second group ascend out of the pelvis across the superior rectal artery and its sigmoid branches, and fan out to innervate the splenic flexure, and descending and sigmoid colon. The pelvic splanchnics are therefore distributed to the hindgut, from the splenic flexure to the anal canal, which is the segment of gut responsible for defaecation.

General visceral afferent fibres in parasympathetic nerves.

The parasympathetic nerves to the gut contain in addition to the parasympathetic (general visceral efferent) fibres, very large numbers of sensory fibres (fig. 30.19). As the major efferent control of the gut is parasympathetic, it is perhaps to be expected that the afferent nerves should use these pathways. For example, the fibres from the stretch receptors in the wall of the rectum that initiate reflex defaecation (p. 30.41) travel to the sacral cord in the pelvic splanchnic nerves.

SYMPATHETIC INNERVATION

The sympathetic nerve fibres for the abdomino-pelvic gut arise in the thoracic spinal cord, pass through the sympathetic trunk, and enter the three **thoracic splanchnic nerves** which descend into the abdomen and end in the **prevertebral ganglia** (p. 20.40). The latter ganglia send nerves which follow arterial pathways to the gut. The lumbar sympathetic ganglia send fibres to supply the more caudal part of the gut.

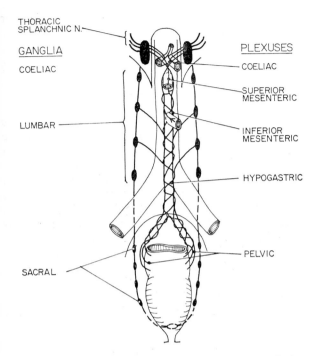

THORACIC
SPLANCHNIC N.

GANGLIA

COELIAC

LUMBAR

SACRAL

PLEXUSES

COELIAC

SUPERIOR
MESENTERIC

INFERIOR
MESENTERIC

HYPOGASTRIC

PELVIC

FIG. 30.50. Sympathetic innervation. The sympathetic supply from the prevertebral plexuses and lumbar sympathetic trunk accompany the arteries to the gut. Afferent fibres subserving pain also run in these nerves.

The preganglionic fibres traverse the sympathetic trunk without interruption and synapse in the prevertebral ganglia. The long postganglionic fibres leave the ganglia and run to the gut, where they are distributed via the myenteric and submucosal plexuses mainly to vessels, and possibly to visceral muscles (fig. 30.19).

Prevertebral plexuses and ganglia
These form a continuous network of sympathetic nerve fibres and ganglion cells over the ventral surface of the abdominal aorta, and continue down into the pelvis, in front of the sacrum, but are divided somewhat arbitrarily into the coeliac, mesenteric, hypogastric and pelvic plexuses.

The large **coeliac plexus** surrounds the coeliac artery and contains a well defined ganglion 1 cm in length on either side of the artery on the crus of the diaphragm. The preganglionic fibres for the abdominal part of the foregut and its derivatives travel to the coeliac plexus in the thoracic splanchnics and synapse in the coeliac ganglion. The postganglionic fibres emerge from the ganglion and accompany the branches of the coeliac artery to the stomach, part of the duodenum, liver and biliary system, and pancreas.

The **superior mesenteric plexus,** around the origin of the superior mesenteric artery, contains a smaller ganglion, and arises by numerous branches from the coeliac plexus

above. The preganglionic fibres for the midgut pass with those for the foregut as far as the coeliac plexus, where some synapse, and then all travel to the superior mesenteric plexus where the remainder synapse. Postganglionic fibres are distributed with the arteries to the gut from the caudal part of the duodenum to the splenic flexure.

The **inferior mesenteric plexus** contains many small groups of ganglionic cells. It lies at the origin of the inferior mesenteric artery, and is formed mainly from above by the downward continuation of the superior mesenteric plexus. Postganglionic fibres from the plexus go to the splenic flexure and descending colon.

The **hypogastric plexus** is the downward continuation of the inferior mesenteric, and as it passes in front of the sacrum it is sometimes called the presacral nerve. This plexus contributes to the bilateral pelvic plexuses.

The **pelvic plexuses** are large and lie within the true pelvis on both sides of the rectum, extending forwards on to the posterior aspect of the urogenital organs. These plexuses also get branches from the lumbar sympathetic ganglia (fig. 30.50). They innervate the pelvic viscera, including the sigmoid colon, rectum and mucosal zone of the anal canal.

General visceral afferent fibres in sympathetic nerves. Although the parasympathetic is accompanied by afferent fibres concerned with normal digestion, those subserving pain are carried along with the sympathetic nerves. The lower part of the anal canal, however, is innervated by the somatic inferior rectal nerves (p. 20.44).

Abdominal vagotomy
This surgical procedure eliminates completely the psychic secretion of acid gastric juice and pepsin, but the effect on mucus production is variable. The vagus nerve also affects hormonal responses, and it is usual in man to find that the secretory response to food and also to gastrin and histamine are reduced by vagotomy. Gastric emptying may also be delayed, but this is most obvious if there is narrowing of the pyloric region or of the duodenum, as a result of advanced peptic ulceration. There is little disturbance of small intestine motility but some subjects suffer from intermittent diarrhoea. Increased segmentation has been recorded, attributed to asynchronous discharge of local neural reflexes in the bowel wall, or to stagnation with subsequent production of the motor amines, as histamines and 5-hydroxytryptamine. Little is known about the effect on human physiology of the interruption of the afferent vagal pathways; in the dog the abdominal vagi have 35,000 fibres of which only 10 per cent are motor and 90 per cent serve a largely undetermined sensory role.

Sympathectomy
The splanchnic nerves are occasionally divided in the human to reduce blood pressure by relaxing arterioles of

the splanchnic vascular territory. The blood flow through the abdominal viscera is, however, not increased by this procedure which merely promotes pooling of blood. Little change in secretion or motility has been observed, but pain from certain viscera may be reduced or abolished.

ABDOMINAL PAIN

Abnormal contractions of the intestinal tract or its appendages can cause pain. The response is probably initiated by abnormal tension in the bowel wall or mesentery. Very severe pain arises when there is obstruction of ducts such as the biliary and pancreatic ones. On the other hand, the pain arising from the colon is less intense and often poorly localized in the lower abdomen. Stimuli from the viscera give rise to painful sensation by afferent impulses travelling to the cord with the sympathetic nervous system. Pain from various viscera is, therefore, appreciated on the basis of segmental distribution of this system, with inversion of the direction of their conduction. Fibres carrying pain impulses from the oesophagus reach the upper levels of the cord, where they overlap with the cardiac fibres (T1–4), thus explaining why oesophageal and cardiac pain are so confusing clinically. The stomach and intestines have their segmental representation in the splanchnic nerves, mainly T7–T9 for the stomach, bile and pancreatic ducts, T9–11 for the small intestine, and the proximal colon T9–L2. The distal colon and rectum have afferent fibres accompanying the sympathetic nerves.

Pain is not always necessarily felt in the appropriate segmental levels, but may be referred to segments above and below. Though commonly referred to the cutaneous segments, it may be felt also along the deep distribution of spinal nerves. This is characteristic of pancreatic and biliary pains (T7–T9), which are often felt in the back, near the scapula. Though pain from abdominal viscera is often felt bilaterally, this is not always the case, and some viscera rarely give rise to pain involving the whole segment; gall bladder pain is more often felt on the right of the midline.

In most disease states, visceral pain is soon supplemented or even supplanted by the more commanding pain of irritation of the exquisitely sensitive parietal peritoneum. This is innervated by the somatic nervous system, and pain is now experienced as sharp localized pain, in the immediately overlying surface area. Here too, there is variability, the pain of peritoneal irritation is almost unbearable when the peritoneum is diffusely irritated (e.g. when a perforated peptic ulcer leaks acid into the peritoneal cavity). It is severe when the peritoneum in the lower abdomen or under the diaphragm is irritated, but less so when the deeper pelvic or posterior parietal peritoneum is disturbed.

The viscera are however relatively insensitive; hence there is no pain when they are handled and cut at operations, in which the abdominal wall has been opened under local anaesthesia.

BLOOD SUPPLY AND LYMPHATIC DRAINAGE

The blood supply of the gut is a rich one, and accounts for about one quarter of the cardiac output at rest. The supply in secretory or absorptive areas, such as stomach and small intestine, is higher than in motor and excretory ones, such as oesophagus and rectum. The vessels reach the intestinal part of the alimentary tract in its mesentery, but in the case of the stomach the folds of peritoneum between the greater and lesser sacs serve as a similar means of access. Both the mesentery and these folds serve as pedicles, in which run the arteries, veins, nerves and lymphatics. The veins in the main accompany the arteries at first but diverge to form the portal system in the region of the pancreas. The intestinal lymph ultimately drains to the cisterna chyli and flows into the thoracic duct.

The arterial supply

The primitive foregut, midgut and hindgut each receive a branch from the dorsal aorta which runs ventrally in the dorsal mesentery to reach the gut (p. 30.54). In the adult the relationships of the primitive mesentery have altered, but the three unpaired visceral branches of the abdominal aorta remain as the coeliac, superior and inferior mesenteric arteries.

COELIAC ARTERY

This artery of the foregut supplies the gut from the lower part of the oesophagus down to the duodenum as far as the entrance of the bile duct, and also the biliary system, liver and pancreas. The spleen, although not functionally associated with the alimentary system, develops close to the stomach and is also supplied by this artery (p. 27.8).

The coeliac artery is a very short wide branch of the abdominal aorta; it arises just below the aortic opening in the diaphragm and divides into left gastric, hepatic and splenic arteries (fig. 30.51).

The **left gastric artery** is the smallest of the three coeliac branches; it runs up on the diaphragm and hooks forward near the gastro-oesophageal junction, in the superior gastropancreatic fold, to enter the lesser omentum and descend along the lesser curvature of the stomach, supplying it. It also gives off oesophageal branches.

The **hepatic artery** passes ventrally in the floor of the epiploic foramen and runs up in the lesser omentum where it gives off the cystic artery to the gall bladder and enters the liver at the porta. Although sometimes there is an accessory hepatic artery from the left gastric, usually the hepatic

FIG. 30.51. Coeliac artery.

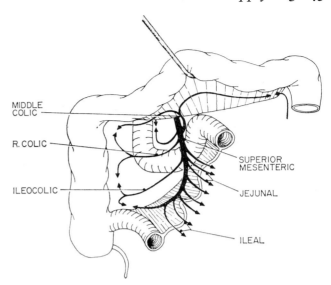

FIG. 30.52. Superior mesenteric artery.

is the sole arterial supply to the liver and it is an end artery. The **cystic artery** is also an end artery. The **gastroduodenal branch** of the hepatic descends behind the duodenum and gives branches to the lesser and greater curvatures, and to the duodenum and head of pancreas.

The **splenic artery** is the largest branch of the coeliac, and is the sole supply to the spleen and the major supply to the pancreas. Passing to the left, it follows a wavy course along the upper border of the pancreas, behind the lesser sac, and then accompanies the tail of the pancreas into the lienorenal ligament to enter the hilus of the spleen. The splenic gives off short gastric branches to the fundus of the stomach and a large **left gastro-epiploic artery** which follows the greater curvature and supplies both the stomach above and the omentum below.

The various gastric arteries form rich anastomoses on and in the wall of the stomach, so that one or more major branches may be tied without fear of ischaemia.

SUPERIOR MESENTERIC ARTERY

The midgut artery supplies the gut from the duodenum caudal to the duodenal papilla down as far as the splenic flexure of the colon (fig. 30.52). As this includes nearly all the small intestine actively engaged in absorption, it is the largest of the three gut arteries. In addition it furnishes some branches to the pancreas. The superior mesenteric artery arises about 1–2 cm below the coeliac, behind the pancreas and descends anterior to the left renal vein, uncinate process and third part of duodenum to enter the root of the mesentery which it follows to the right iliac fossa. Large **jejunal** and **ileal branches** run in the mesentery to the small intestine and a small branch ascends between the duodenum and head of pancreas supplying both, and anastomosing with a similar descending branch from the gastroduodenal artery. The large intestine is supplied by branches which arise from the right side of the vessel as it

lies in the mesentery and pass retroperitoneally to the caecum, ascending colon, and hepatic flexure. The lower of these, the **ileocolic**, gives off the anterior caecal artery (fig. 30.32) and the appendicular artery which is an end artery. The **middle colic artery** arises from the superior mesenteric just below the pancreas and passes forwards into the transverse mesocolon to supply the transverse colon as far as the splenic flexure.

INFERIOR MESENTERIC ARTERY

The hindgut artery is much the smaller of the three main arteries as it supplies a shorter and less active region of the gut, extending from the splenic flexure to the anal canal (fig. 30.53). The inferior mesenteric artery comes off the

FIG. 30.53. Inferior mesenteric artery.

aorta a few cm above its bifurcation and passes caudally and to the left where it enters the true pelvis medial to the left ureter and becomes the **superior rectal artery** which descends in the pelvic mesocolon and supplies the rectum. The **left colic artery** ascends from the left side of the inferior mesenteric artery and passes to the upper part of the descending colon. Several **sigmoid arteries** arise lower down and supply the remainder of the descending colon and sigmoid colon.

The various colic arteries from both the superior and inferior mesenteric vessels characteristically divide into two divergent branches as they approach the gut, and each branch then runs parallel to the gut and anastomoses with the corresponding branch of the adjacent artery. The linkage of these branches forms the **marginal artery** which establishes a good longitudinal anastomosis around the colon.

Venous drainage

The intestinal portal system of veins serves a wide area, including the entire alimentary tract from the lower end of the oesophagus to the upper part of the anal canal, and the spleen, pancreas and gall bladder (fig. 30.54).

The single portal vein carries all this blood to the liver within which it divides repeatedly into a plexus of capillary sized vessels termed sinusoids. The liver sinusoids empty into tributaries of the large hepatic veins which emerge from the back of the liver and immediately plunge into the inferior vena cava (fig. 30.39).

A portal venous system (Latin *porto* = I carry) is one which has a capillary plexus interposed on its pathway to the heart, and is a mechanism for carrying substances in the blood directly from one site to another without dispersing them into the general circulation. The hepatic portal system is the largest and is simply referred to as the portal system, but the hypophysial portal veins are another example (p. 25.10).

PORTAL VEIN

This starts at the union of the superior mesenteric and splenic veins behind the neck of the pancreas and passes upwards to the porta hepatis where it divides into right and left branches before entering the liver with the corresponding branches of the hepatic artery, and the hepatic ducts. In its course it lies behind the duodenum, gastro-duodenal artery and bile duct, and then runs up in the lesser omentum, anterior to the epiploic foramen, but posterior to the common hepatic duct and hepatic artery (fig. 30.37).

The **inferior mesenteric vein** corresponds to the artery of the same name, and drains the same area of gut extending from the splenic flexure to the anal canal. Its tributaries are also similar to the branches of the artery and are not described, except for the **superior rectal vein**. This

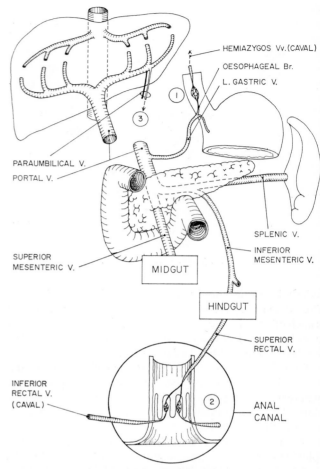

FIG. 30.54. Portal venous system. The three major porto-caval anastomoses are at the (1) oesophagus, (2) anal canal, and (3) umbilicus.

vein drains part of the anal canal, the rectum and the sigmoid colon. It is formed from venous plexuses within the anal columns and in the walls of the rectum. The superior rectal vein then accompanies its artery upwards, and becomes the inferior mesenteric vein as it leaves the true pelvis. The inferior mesenteric vein ascends retroperitoneally and lateral to the inferior mesenteric artery to join the splenic vein.

The **superior mesenteric vein** is a very large vein which corresponds to the artery of the same name and accompanies it from the right iliac fossa upwards in the root of the mesentery. It crosses anterior to the third part of duodenum and uncinate process of pancreas, before ending in the portal vein. It drains the midgut from the second part of the duodenum to the beginning of the splenic flexure, by tributaries which follow the branches of the artery.

The **splenic vein** drains the entire spleen, most of the pancreas, and some of the stomach. The arterial and venous patterns are similar for both the midgut and hindgut but the venous drainage of the foregut differs somewhat from the arterial supply. The details are not given, but it should be noted that the splenic vein accompanies the splenic artery over much of its course, and drains a similar area, except that it is joined by the inferior mesenteric vein behind the body of the pancreas. The remainder of the blood from the foregut, pancreas, and gall bladder, enters the portal vein by several tributaries including the **cystic vein** from the gall bladder and the left gastric vein. The **left gastric vein** follows a course similar to the left gastric artery and receives oesophageal tributaries from the lower end of the oesophagus (fig. 30.54).

PORTO-CAVAL ANASTOMOSES

The tributaries of the portal vein anastomose in certain sites with adjacent caval veins which return blood to the heart through either the superior or the inferior vena cava.

Little blood passes through these porto-caval anastomoses in health, but the portal system of veins has no valves, and therefore should the pressure within the portal system rise abnormally, e.g. due to liver disease then blood may flow in the reverse direction out of the portal area through these anastomoses. The porto-caval anastomoses dilate and may rupture causing haemorrhage.

The main sites are:

(1) An **oesophageal venous plexus** in the wall at the lower end of the oesophagus drains downwards into the (portal) left gastric vein via its oesophageal tributaries, but also anastomoses above with oesophageal veins that pass to the (caval) hemiazygos system and enter the heart by the superior vena cava (p. 20.36). When dilated these mucosal veins are liable to be damaged during swallowing and bleed into the lumen of the oesophagus.

(2) The **plexuses in the anal columns** of the anal canal drain upwards to the (portal) superior rectal vein but also anastomose with the inferior rectal veins which join the (caval) internal iliac veins (p. 20.36). Dilation of these venous plexuses causes local bulges of the mucosa known as 'haemorrhoids', which are likely to be damaged and bleed during defaecation.

(3) Small veins accompany the ligamentum teres from the umbilicus to where it joins the left branch of the portal vein (p. 30.55), and so connect the portal vein to the **veins of the anterior abdominal wall**. The latter, when dilated, radiate from the umbilicus and have a striking appearance known as the Caput Medusae.

(4) Many parts of the gut, such as the ascending colon, are devoid of peritoneum posteriorly where they rest directly on the **posterior abdominal wall**. Here, where areas of portal and caval venous drainage meet, there are many small porto-caval anastomoses.

Lymphatic drainage

Generally, lymph enters lymphatic vessels in the mucosa and other layers of the gut wall and passes into the peripheral group of lymph nodes adjacent to the gut. Their efferent vessels then accompany arterial branches back towards their origin from the aorta, sometimes entering a group of intermediate lymph nodes before reaching the proximal nodes which surround each of the three main arteries to the gut, at their origin from the aorta. The proximal nodes, which are the coeliac, superior mesenteric, and inferior mesenteric nodes, form two trunks which enter the **cisterna chyli** (p. 20.37). The **intestinal trunk** is formed by the efferent vessels from the coeliac and superior mesenteric nodes and therefore carries lymph derived from the stretch of gut between the lower end of oesophagus and the splenic flexure, and from the spleen, pancreas, liver and biliary system. The inferior mesenteric nodes are a component of the left para-aortic nodes which form the **left lumbar trunk,** and conveys lymph from the more distal part of the gut as far down as the anal canal. *Stomach.* The lymph from the stomach drains as shown in fig. 30.55 to the coeliac glands. The lymphatics in the oesophagus communicate with those draining upwards into the thorax.

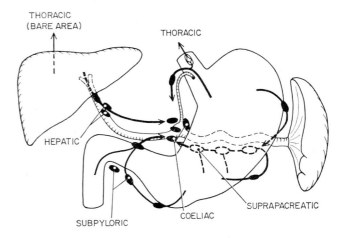

FIG. 30.55. Lymphatic drainage of stomach, pancreas and liver.

Liver. Most of the lymphatics emerge at the porta hepatis and enter hepatic nodes or pass direct to the coeliac group. Another group leave the bare area of the liver and drain into the thoracic nodes.
Pancreas. This drains to the pyloric and the suprapancreatic nodes and then to the coeliac nodes.
Small intestine (fig. 30.56). The three groups of nodes form almost continuous chains alongside the arterial branches of the superior mesenteric artery that supply the small intestine. The lymphatic vessels of the jejuno-ileum are

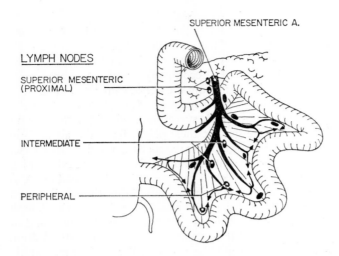

FIG. 30.56. Lymphatic drainage of small intestine.

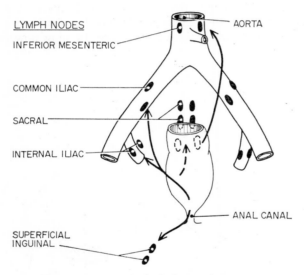

FIG. 30.57. Lymphatic drainage of rectum.

referred to as lacteals because they appear milky when they contain absorbed fat after a meal (p. 30.37).

Large intestine. Numerous paracolic nodes are distributed along the large intestine. As the lymphatics follow the arteries, those proximal to the splenic flexure end in the superior mesenteric nodes, and those distal to the splenic flexure go to the inferior mesenteric nodes.

Rectum and anal canal (fig. 30.57). Some lymphatics from the rectum drain upwards to inferior mesenteric nodes but others pass laterally to internal and common iliac nodes, and yet a third group pass dorsally to nodes on the sacrum. Below the pectinate line the anal canal drains across the perineum to the superficial inguinal nodes.

Blood flow

The Fick principle (p. 28.28) can be applied to measure the splanchnic flow in man in the following manner. The dye, bromsulphthalein, BSP, is excreted exclusively by the liver; if a solution of the dye is infused intravenously at a rate sufficient to keep the concentration in the blood constant, then the rate of clearance of the dye by the liver can be calculated. From a catheter passed from an arm vein through the right atrium, hepatic venous blood can be sampled and the concentration of the dye in it determined. Knowing now the concentration of dye in the blood entering and leaving the liver and the amount of dye removed, the flow rate can be calculated. In man at rest it is about 1500 ml/min or 30 per cent of the cardiac output.

The capacity of the splanchnic vascular bed is large and the big veins, the spleen and the liver sinusoids act as a store of blood, which can be shunted readily to other parts of the body, e.g. during muscular exercise. This is brought about by the constrictor action of the sympathetic nerves and by adrenaline. In a cat, the sympathetic nerves can be stimulated, causing visible contraction of the spleen, blanching of the gut and emptying of the large veins; at the same time a marked rise of systemic blood pressure may be recorded. The subsequent vasodilation is brought about by removing constrictor tone and there are no vasodilator nerves. Perhaps in man as much as 1 litre of blood may be removed from the splanchnic circulation by this mechanism.

At rest about one-fifth of the liver's blood supply comes from the hepatic artery and four-fifths from the portal vein. However, whereas the hepatic arterial blood is about 97 per cent saturated with oxygen, the portal venous blood is only about 60 per cent saturated in the post-absorptive state and probably less during digestion. Hence the hepatic artery supplies oxygen to the liver at a higher pressure than the portal vein; if the artery is injured or tied at an operation, fatal liver damage follows. On the other hand the portal vein can be anastomosed into the inferior vena cava, either in man to relieve an obstruction or in experimental animals (Eck's fistula), without serious impairment of liver function.

The mean pressure in the hepatic artery is about 100 mm Hg and in the portal vein about 5 mm Hg. Hence any increase in the capillary resistance to the portal flow, as may be caused by fine scarring of the liver due to past infection or chronic poisoning, may cause a marked rise in portal venous pressure. This leads to congestion of all the organs whose veins drain into the portal system and the subsequent enlargement of porto-caval anastomoses (p. 30.47).

The arteries supplying the wall of the whole gut anastomose freely. Hence only if there is obstruction to one of the large branches does the nutrition of the gut suffer. There are also many arterio-venous anastomoses, which acilitate the transfer of the blood from the gut to other organs when there is splanchnic vasoconstriction.

EMBRYOLOGY

The basic plan of the alimentary tract is established by the fourth week, when the lateral, head, and tail folds (p. 18.11) have incorporated the endodermal roof of the secondary yolk sac into the embryo, forming the gut. The definitive yolk sac opens only into the midgut (fig. 30.58). Cranially the midgut communicates

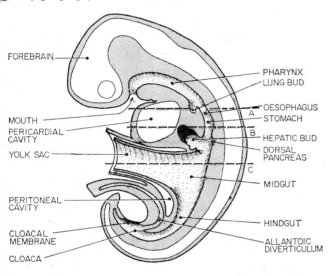

FIG. 30.58. Alimentary tract of 4-week embryo (4 mm). In this median sagittal section the secondary yolk sac communicates freely with the midgut, which in turn opens into the fore- and hindgut. The hepatic bud is present. The buccopharyngeal membrane has broken down, but the cloacal membrane is intact.

with the tubular foregut, the junction being marked by the hepatic diverticulum. The buccopharyngeal membrane (p. 18.11) has just broken down, so the foregut is continuous with the ectodermal stomatodaeum. Caudally the midgut opens into the tubular hindgut, which ends in a large chamber, the cloaca, which is shared with the urogenital system (pp. 34.1 and 37.53). The cloaca joins the mesonephric ducts posterolaterally, gives off the allantoic diverticulum ventrally, and is closed caudally by the cloacal membrane.

The endoderm differentiates eventually into epithelia, which form the lining of the gut and also the epithelium of the glands that arise as outgrowths of the endodermal gut, the liver and pancreas. The remaining layers of the gut wall are derived from the splanchnopleuric mesoderm, which enclosed the endodermal tube as a result of the folding and splitting of the lateral mesoderm (fig. 18.17).

DEVELOPMENT OF FOREGUT

At the end of the fourth week the foregut extends cranially from the hepatic diverticulum to the stomatodaeum. It consists of a branchial portion which gives rise to the buccal cavity, pharynx and the upper part of the oesophagus, and a postbranchial part which forms the rest of the oesophagus, stomach and duodenum as far down as the hepatic diverticulum (bile duct). The muscle of the branchial part is striated and supplied by the nerves of the branchial arches; in contrast the postbranchial portion has smooth muscle supplied by autonomic nerves.

The embryology of the branchial portion is given on p. 18.27. The postbranchial portion is slung from the dorsal wall of the embryo by a broad but shallow mesentery, which connects ventrally with the pericardium above and the septum transversum below. The lung bud descends in the mesentery ventral to the gut (figs. 30.58 and 30.59), and the pericardioperitoneal canals run on either side of the oesophagus to end in the peritoneal cavity inferiorly.

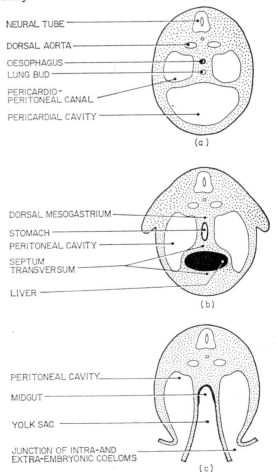

FIG. 30.59. Horizontal sections through alimentary tract at 4 weeks. These sections are through planes A, B and C of fig. 30.58.

Oesophagus. At four weeks the oesophagus is very short, but then it grows rapidly. Occasionally the laryngo-tracheal groove (p. 29.7) fails to separate completely from the ventral aspect of the gut, resulting in an abnormal opening between the oesophagus and trachea, through which ingested milk may enter the lungs. Frequently in such cases the oesophagus below the fistula is atretic.

Stomach. A slight fusiform swelling of the foregut caudal to the oesophagus denotes the beginning of the stomach (fig. 30.58). This broadens anteroposteriorly (fig. 30.59) and the posterior border grows rapidly forming the greater curvature. Simultaneously the anterior border rotates towards the right, converting the original left side to the anterior surface (fig. 30.60). This

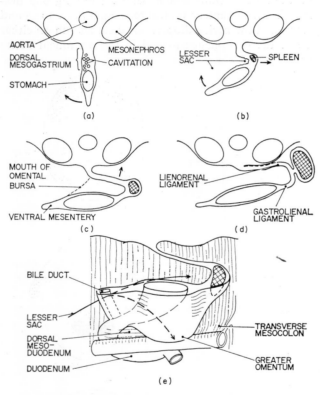

FIG. 30.60. Development of stomach and lesser sac. (a) The lesser sac forms initially by cavitation within the dorsal mesogastrium. (b) It increases as the stomach broadens ventrodorsally and rotates to the right. (c and d) With further growth the lesser sac becomes bounded by the mesogastrium which contains the spleen on the left, and ventrally by the stomach and ventral mesentery. (e) A stereogram of the developing lesser sac.

rotation explains how the left and right vagus nerves emerge from the oesophageal plexus as the anterior and posterior gastric trunks respectively.

Duodenum. The foregut caudal to the stomach grows and loops ventrally. The hepatic diverticulum arises from the

FIG. 30.61. Three stages in the development of the pancreas and biliary apparatus.

apex of the loop and marks the lower end of the foregut. The whole loop becomes the duodenum, which is therefore part foregut and part midgut (figs. 30.61 and 30.62).

DEVELOPMENT OF MIDGUT

The connection of the yolk sac to the midgut narrows in the fourth week forming the vitello-intestinal duct (fig. 30.62). Cranially the midgut becomes the caudal half of the duodenum, but the major portion elongates into a long loop towards the umbilicus that is attached at its apex to the vitello-intestinal duct. The cranial limb of the loop grows more rapidly and becomes coiled, while the caudal limb develops a bulge near the vitello-intestinal duct, the primordial caecum. Thus the coiled proximal limb becomes the jejunum and most of the ileum, and the caudal limb the terminal ileum, caecum and proximal colon. The vitello-intestinal duct atrophies in the sixth week, but occasionally persists as Meckel's diverticulum (p. 30.19). Rarely the entire duct may remain so that the intestinal contents leak from the umbilicus, or it may remain as a fibrous cord stretching from the ileum to the

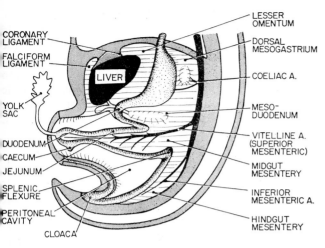

FIG. 30.62. Sagittal diagram of embryo showing mesenteries. In this 10 mm embryo the vitello-intestinal duct has narrowed, and the midgut loop has herniated into the intra-umbilical coelom. The growth of the liver into the septum transversum has formed a ventral mesentery consisting of the lesser omentum and the coronary ligament.

umbilicus. The caecal swelling becomes conical and later the apex of the cone lengthens to form the appendix, so that at birth the appendix arises from the apex of the caecum. Postnatally, further growth brings the base of the appendix to the posterolateral aspect of the caecum.

DEVELOPMENT OF HINDGUT

The hindgut extends from the midgut to the cloacal membrane. The cloaca becomes divided by the downgrowth of the urorectal septum into the rectum behind and the urogenital sinus in front. The part of the cloacal membrane which closes the rectum ruptures during the eighth week and the rectum then opens on to the ectodermal anal pit. Subsequently this pit deepens to form the lower ectodermal part of the anal canal, whereas the upper part is endodermal.

Imperforate anus results from a persisting anal membrane. Failure of the urorectal septum causes very serious fistulous communications between the gut and the urinary system, or vagina in the female. Atresia of the rectum may be associated with deficiency of the muscular anal sphincter.

DEVELOPMENT OF THE LIVER AND PANCREAS

The liver arises from a diverticulum at the junction of the foregut and midgut that grows ventrally into the septum transversum and divides into two primary branches (fig. 30.61). The stem of the diverticulum is soon joined by the ventral pancreatic bud, and becomes the bile duct. The caudal primary branch differentiates into the cystic duct and gall bladder, and does not divide further, but the cranial branch divides repeatedly and proliferates forming the remainder of the biliary system and hepatocytes. These consist of sheets of cells which invade the septum transversum and encounter the vitelline veins to transform them into a system of sinusoids (p. 18.17 and fig. 30.63). The fibrous and haemopoietic tissue of the liver is derived from the mesenchyme of the septum transversum.

The liver grows quickly so that at nine weeks it weighs 10 per cent of the whole embryo, and fills most of the abdominal cavity. The rapid growth is partly due to erythropoiesis within the liver (p. 26.4). The liver is 5 per cent of body weight at birth and declines to less than half that in the adult.

The pancreas develops from gut endoderm by two separate diverticula. The ventral one arises close to the hepatic diverticulum and soon fuses with it so that the main pancreatic and bile ducts share a common entrance into the duodenum in the adult. The dorsal pancreas

FIG. 30.63. Development of hepatic circulation. Three ventral views showing how the growing liver incorporates the vitelline veins and taps the umbilical veins, and how the portal vein forms in the region of the duodenum.

arises more cranially, and grows into the dorsal mesentery (fig. 30.61). Growth changes within the duodenum cause the ventral pancreas and hepatic diverticulum to swing to the right around the gut until they abut on the right surface of the dorsal pancreas. The pancreatic primordia fuse, so that the ventral outgrowth ultimately forms the inferior part of the head and uncinate process and the dorsal pancreas the remainder of the organ. The developing duct of the dorsal pancreas joins a tributary of the ventral duct so that the latter then becomes the terminal portion of the main duct (cf. figs. 30.61 and 30.46). The terminal dorsal duct usually separates off as the accessory duct from the newly developed main duct, and drains the upper part of the head into the duodenum more cranially.

The rotation of the bile duct around the duodenum explains its dorsal relationship to the first part of the duodenum and the head of pancreas in the adult (fig. 30.38).

Development of the mesenteries

By the end of the fourth week the gut is a midline structure which is suspended by a shallow median dorsal mesentery (fig. 30.58). Above the septum transversum, the oesophagus lies within a broad mesentery which contains the lung bud and attaches ventrally to the pericardium (fig. 30.59). The thick septum transversum has not yet become the ventral mesentery which connects the foregut and anterior abdominal wall. Subsequently, much of the gut deviates from the median plane, and certain parts of the mesentery increase in depth or fuse with the dorsal wall and are obliterated. The mesenteries are considered from above down.

MESO-OESOPHAGUS

This is a broad mass between the dorsal wall and the pericardium and contains the oesophagus and the lung bud. It forms the connective tissue of much of the mediastinum and associated pleura and the entire oesophagus except for its epithelium.

MESOGASTRIUM

The dorsal mesogastrium is in the median plane, but changes within it establish the lesser sac of peritoneum. Cavitation within its right side marks the beginning of the omental bursa (fig. 30.60). This cavity enlarges by active growth of the mesentery, which thins and bulges to the left. The rotation of the stomach to the right (p. 30.50) brings it to the anterior wall of the bursa, which is limited to the left and dorsally by the mesogastrium, but opens at the right into the general peritoneal cavity. The spleen develops in the mesogastrium and distends its left layer of peritoneum. The left surface of the mesogastrium fuses with the dorsal abdominal wall, to become attached over the left kidney and runs to the spleen as the lieno-renal ligament, and from the spleen to stomach as

the gastrolienal ligament (cf. figs. 30.60 and 30.13). Caudally the mesogastrium hangs down as a double fold from the greater curvature of the stomach over the developing transverse colon (fig. 30.64). The most posterior layer of the fold fuses with the adjacent mesocolon and colon, bringing its attachment to the antimesenteric border of the colon. This more caudal portion of the mesogastrium is the future greater omentum (cf. figs. 30.64 and 30.12).

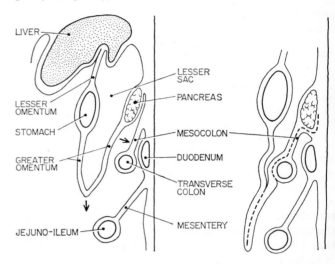

FIG. 30.64. Sagittal section through lesser sac. The dorsal mesogastrium projects caudally as a pouch which overhangs the transverse colon. This pouch is the greater omentum and fusion of its posterior wall with the adjacent transverse colon and mesocolon brings its attachment to the colon (compare fig. 30.12).

At four weeks the foregut is close to the lower part of the septum transversum (fig. 30.58), but as the embryo lengthens the septum becomes separated from the gut and thins forming the ventral mesentery which stretches from the foregut to the diaphragm and anterior abdominal wall (fig. 30.62). The liver has already distended the midportion of this mesentery (fig. 30.59), so that the thin part connecting the foregut to the liver is the lesser omentum, and the part joining the liver to the diaphragm is the coronary ligament. The free border of the latter part which carries the left umbilical vein from the umbilicus to the liver is the falciform ligament. Later cavitation of the septum transversum between the two organs establishes the sub-diaphragmatic spaces and reduces the area within the coronary ligament to the definitive bare area (fig. 30.16).

The cavitation in the dorsal mesogastrium extends cranially between the oesophagus and right lung bud as the pneumoenteric recess and this part becomes cut off by the closure of the diaphragm. The lower part persists as the upper recess of the lesser sac, which lies between the diaphragm posteriorly and the liver in front; it is

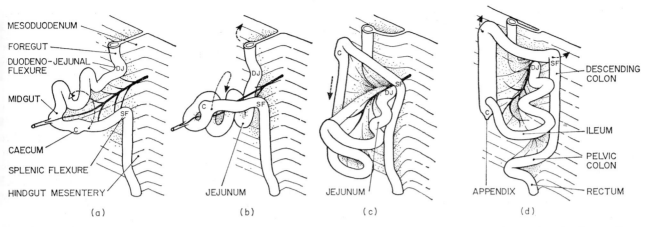

FIG. 30.65. Herniation and rotation of midgut. (a) The midgut loop herniates into the umbilical colon in the median plane. (b) The caudal and proximal limb rotated anticlockwise. (c) Further rotation and withdrawal of the hernia brings the proximal limb (jejuno-ileum) against the hindgut. The caudal limb (caecum and colon) presses the duodenum into the right posterior abdominal wall. (d) The caecum descends from the subhepatic position.

ounded on its right side by the caval fold which carries he inferior vena cava from the dorsal abdominal wall ⊃ the liver. Rotation of the stomach swings the lesser mentum into the coronal plane. It forms the anterior all of the upper recess of the lesser sac, and its free ight border bounds the entrance to the lesser sac, the piploic foramen (fig. 30.60).

The lesser sac of the peritoneum therefore communi-ates with the greater sac or general peritoneal cavity via he epiploic foramen, and arose by changes in the lorsal mesogastrium and ventral mesentery. The inferior ecess derived from the omental bursa is the large part hat lies behind the stomach and within the greater omen-um, while the upper recess is behind the lesser omentum nd liver.

MESODUODENUM

Growth of the duodenum caused it to loop ventrally, and he pancreas develops within the mesoduodenum (figs. 0.61 and 2). On reduction of the physiological hernia he returning colon displaces the duodenum to the ight, pressing it and the mesoduodenum against the ight half of the posterior abdominal wall where the ad-acent peritoneal layers fuse making the duodenum and nost of the pancreas retroperitoneal (figs. 30.11 and 66).

MIDGUT MESENTERY AND ROTATION OF MIDGUT

As the midgut grows, its mesentery deepens, so the gut forms a long loop towards the umbilicus (fig. 30.62 & 65). The fast growing liver comes to fill most of the ab-dominal cavity, so that in the sixth week the mobile midgut is pushed out into the umbilical coelom. This **physiological herniation** lasts about six weeks, until the liver becomes relatively smaller when the midgut re-turns to the abdominal cavity. As the gut continues to grow within the umbilical coelom, the cranial limb of je-

junoileum becomes very coiled, and the caecal swelling on the caudal limb enlarges. Simultaneously the midgut loop rotates through 90° around the axis of the superior mesenteric artery.

Little is known of the factors that initiate the reduction of the hernia, but the relative decline in the size of the liver and increase in size of the abdominal cavity probably both contribute. The jejuno-ileum returns first because the cae-cal swelling hampers the return of the caudal limb, and enters the lower left abdomen because of the liver in the upper right quadrant. The coils of jejuno-ileum displace the hindgut with its mesentery to the left against the posterior abdominal wall, where later the adjacent peri-toneal layers fuse, binding both the splenic flexure and descending colon to the posterior abdominal wall (figs. 30.65, 66 and 11).). The caecum and caudal limb return later and a further anticlockwise rotation through 180° brings them cranial to the jejunum and ileum. They enter above and to the right of the jejunum and ileum, with the caecum inferior to the liver. The colon pursues a straight course from the caecum to the splenic flexure. This rotation has brought the midgut colon ventral to the duodenum, and hence the superior mesenteric artery emerges ventral to its third part. Subsequently the liver rises away from the caecum and the ascending colon grows in length. The mesentery of the ascending colon is obliterated by fusion with the posterior abdominal wall in a similar fashion to that of the descending colon, but the transverse colon retains its mesentery.

The jejunum and ileum also retain their deep mesentery which permits mobility in the adult (cf. figs. 30.66 and 30.11).

MESENTERY OF HINDGUT

The development of the abdominal hindgut mesentery has

been described. The pelvic mesentery persists in part as the pelvic mesocolon, but the mesentery of the rectum diminishes so that the rectum rests directly on the sacrum. The most caudal part of the rectum and anal canal are outwith the coelom and so extraperitoneal.

The primitive dorsal mesentery of the gut is much modified since it grows in depth, fuses with the parietal peritoneum of the posterior abdominal wall, and deviates from the midline. There are two consequences of the fact that fusion occurs at a late stage of development. First, the gut remains ventral to the urogenital system on the posterior abdominal wall, and secondly the planes of fusion are natural cleavage planes that are not crossed by any major vessel or nerves, because the vessels reach the gut in the dorsal mesentery and their general pattern is established long before fusion occurs. These planes are therefore of practical value to the surgeon who can reopen them without fear of damaging vessels or

nerves. For example, the lower end of the bile duct whic[h] descends embedded in the back of the pancreas (p. 30.35) can be exposed by incising the peritoneum around th[e] convexity of the duodenum and reflecting it ventrally an[d] medially, which reverses the developmental fusion o[f] duodenum and posterior abdominal wall.

The extensive fusion and obliteration of the gut mese[n]tery is associated with an upright posture. In common wit[h] other recent evolutionary changes, it shows marke[d] variation. A quarter of the population have a persisten[t] mesentery on either the ascending or descending colon[.] More rarely, the duodenal mesentery may remain. Suc[h] faulty fixation of the gut, by allowing excessive mobility[,] predisposes to twisting of the gut or volvulus.

Varying degrees of incomplete rotation may occu[r] ranging from the extremely rare type of non-rotation wher[e] the jejuno-ileum is on the right side of the abdomen, an[d] the entire colon on the left, to the less severe varieties suc[h] as a subhepatic caecum. In the latter condition rotatio[n] stops at a late stage, but the caecum remains unde[r] the liver and there is no ascending colon. Complet[e] reversal of rotation is very rare and is usually associate[d] with similar reversal of the other abdominal and thoraci[c] organs.

Umbilical hernia is a common condition that result[s] from incomplete closure of the umbilicus by the developin[g] anterior abdominal wall.

Development of blood vessels

Three unpaired visceral arteries arise from the dorsa[l] aorta and enter the dorsal mesentery to reach the foregu[t,] midgut, and hindgut respectively (fig. 30.62). The **coelia[c] artery** of the foregut encounters the opening of the omen[tal] bursa as it runs ventrally within the mesogastrium, an[d] sends its branches around the margins of the entrance[.] The vitelline artery of the midgut originally supplied th[e] yolk sac, but its distal portion which accompanied th[e] vitello-intestinal duct atrophies with the yolk sac, leavin[g] the proximal portion to become the **superior mesenteri[c] artery**. The **inferior mesenteric artery** supplies the hindgu[t] as far as the proctodaeum, which forms the lower par[t] of the anal canal and receives a paired somatic segmenta[l] vessel, the inferior rectal artery.

The paired **vitelline veins** draining the yolk sac accom[]pany the vitello-intestinal duct to the midgut, and the[n] ascend in the mesentery on either side of the duodena[l] loop, and enter the liver. They emerge from the liver an[d] end in the sinus venosus of the heart (p. 18.16).

The vitelline veins form transverse anastomoses nea[r] the duodenum, and a plexus of sinusoids within th[e] liver (fig. 30.63). The decline in the yolk sac circulatio[n] results in the disappearance of the vitelline veins distally[,] but the differentiation of a new vessel, the superio[r] mesenteric vein, in the dorsal mesentery brings mor[e] blood to the proximal part of the system. This vein de[]

DUODENUM

TRANSVERSE MESOCOLON

(b and c)

MESENTERY

ASCENDING COLON

PELVIC MESOCOLON

(a)

ASCENDING COLON

JEJUNUM

(b)

R. PARACOLIC GUTTERS

MESENTERY

(c)

FIG. 30.66. Fixation of gut. (a) After withdrawal of the midgut from the umbilical coelom, parts of the mesenteries (shown in stipple) adhere to the parietal peritoneum on the posterior abdominal wall and fix the gut (b) before and (c) after fixation.

velops on the left surface of the caudal limb of the duodenal loop, which as the duodenum swings to the right (p. 30.53) becomes its ventral surface, and delivers blood into the left vitelline vein that follows a direct route into the liver. This direct channel becomes the **portal vein**, and consists of (1) part of the left vitelline vein (2) the transverse anastomosis within the duodenal loop (3) the proximal segment of the right vitelline vein and (4) another anastomotic vessel (fig. 30.63). The remainder of the vitelline system caudal to the liver atrophies.

INTRAHEPATIC CIRCULATION

The vitelline veins within the septum transversum are transformed by the ingrowing sheets of hepatocytes into a continuous system of liver sinusoids (p. 30.51). These sinusoids are therefore filled from the branches of the portal system, and drain cranially via efferent veins from the liver into the vitelline veins. After the disappearance of the left hepatocardiac segment of the vitelline vein (p. 18.17) these efferent veins, which are the future hepatic veins, converge on the right hepatocardiac vein. The latter forms the terminal segment of the inferior vena cava (fig. 18.30).

The vitelline veins therefore form the portal vein and its branches, the liver sinusoids, the hepatic veins and the uppermost part of the inferior vena cava.

The more laterally placed umbilical veins also become involved by the growing liver. First, the liver sinusoids tap the umbilical veins and provide a more direct route to the heart (fig. 30.63). Later as the placental flow increases a large shunt is established in the liver to by-pass the slow sinusoid circulation. This **ductus venosus** connects the definitive (left) umbilical vein with the right hepatocardiac vein. The umbilical vein ascends in the free border of the ventral mesentery between the umbilicus and the liver. After birth the fibrous remnant of the umbilical vein persists as ligamentum teres. The ductus venosus also fibroses after birth but remains as ligamentum venosum joining the upper end of ligamentum teres to the inferior vena cava.

FURTHER READING

CREAMER B. (1964) Variations in the intestinal villus: mucosal dynamics. *Brit. med. J.* **ii**, 1371.

DAVENPORT H. W. (1966) *Physiology of the digestive tract*, 2nd Edition. Chicago: Year Book Medical Publishers.

DE REUK A.V.S. and CUMSON N. (1962). *Exocrine Pancreas*. Ciba Foundation Symposium. London: Churchill.

PAVLOV I. (1910) *The Work of the Digestive Glands* (trans. W.H. Thompson) 2nd Edition. London: Griffin.

ITO S. (1967) Structure of Gastric Mucosa. *Handbook of Physiology*, Section 6, Volume 2. Washington: American Physiological Society.

ROUILLER C.R. (1963) *The Liver*, Vol. 1, chaps. 1–8. New York: Academic Press.

Chapter 31
Metabolic functions of the liver

The liver holds a key place in the metabolism of the body. It has important functions connected with the synthesis, storage, breakdown and interconversion of protein, fat and carbohydrate which it shares in varying degree with other tissues. The formation and secretion of bile, the synthesis of urea and the metabolism of various drugs and hormones, take place either solely or almost exclusively in the liver. Because of its important metabolic contribution, diseases causing dysfunction of the liver usually give rise to biochemical abnormalities, which may lead to serious illness. Death may occur from liver failure. The various activities of the liver may not all be affected equally by a disease process and, as there are large reserves of metabolic capacity in the normal liver, disturbance of essential functions may not be detectable until the organ has become severely damaged.

The hepatocytes in each acinus are subdivided into three zones dependent on the extent to which their blood supply is oxygenated (p. 30.32). Some degree of enzymic localization occurs within these zones. Thus zone 1, which has a relatively good supply of oxygen has relatively high concentrations of succinate dehydrogenase, cytochrome oxidase, ATPase and alkaline phosphatase, and zone 3, supplied with the least amount of oxygen is rich in diaphorase, $NADH_2$ and $NADPH_2$ reductases, 3-hydroxybutyrate dehydrogenase, lactate dehydrogenase, glutamate dehydrogenase and esterase. Zone 2 has intermediate properties. Owing to the predominantly venous nature of their blood supply liver cells must carry out their metabolic functions at relatively low Po_2. The cells in the zone 3 derive their O_2 mainly from venous blood further deoxygenated by passage through zones 1 and 2, which perhaps necessitates their predominance of dehydrogenase activities. Morphologically, differences are also present, mitochondria being more numerous in the cells of the zone 1 and microsomes in cells of zone 3. The remarkable regenerative capacity of the liver is described on p. 18.45 and p. 30.32.

The liver and protein metabolism

The liver is active in protein synthesis, in the interconversion of amino acids and in the formation of urea as the main nitrogenous end product of amino acid and protein metabolism in mammals. After total hepatectomy in experimental animals or severe liver failure in man the concentration of amino acids in blood rises, the amount in the urine increases and there is a fall in blood urea unless there is renal failure.

Amino acids for the hepatic synthesis of protein are derived partly from dietary protein and partly from the metabolic turnover of endogenous protein. The liver is important in the utilization of any amino acids present in excess of immediate need. Protein is only stored to a limited extent, and any imbalance between the availability of individual amino acids and those required for protein synthesis is partly offset, for the non-essential amino acids, by interconversions catalysed by the hepatic aminotransferases. The reactions have the following general form (p. 11.19):

$$\text{L-amino acid} + \text{2-oxoglutarate} \rightleftharpoons$$
$$\alpha\text{-ketoacid} + \text{L-glutamic acid}$$

There are several different aminotransferases, most of which are not confined to the liver. Of these, aspartate and alanine aminotransferase have been extensively studied in disease. These enzymes contain pyridoxal phosphate and catalyse reactions involving L-aspartic acid and L-alanine respectively. Alternative names for these enzymes used widely in the clinical literature are glutamic oxaloacetic transaminase (GOT) and glutamic pyruvic transaminase (GPT). Other aminotransferases localized to hepatic tissue include the ornithine, asparagine, and glutamine ketoacid aminotransferases; these are also proteins containing pyridoxal phosphate and catalyse the following reactions (p. 11.20):

$$\text{L-ornithine} + \alpha\text{-ketoacid} \rightleftharpoons$$
$$\text{L-glutamate-}\gamma\text{-semialdehyde} + \text{L-amino acid}$$
$$\text{L-asparagine} + \alpha\text{-ketoacid} \rightleftharpoons$$
$$\text{2-oxosuccinamate} + \text{L-amino acid}$$
$$\text{L-glutamine} + \alpha\text{-ketoacid} \rightleftharpoons$$
$$\text{2-oxoglutaramate} + \text{L-amino acid}$$

Collectively, the aminotransferases effect the deamination of most of the naturally occurring L-amino acids.

Several of these, on deamination, give rise to α-ketoacids (pyruvic, oxaloacetic or 2-oxoglutaric acids) which are intermediates that can be converted ultimately to glycogen by reversal of the glycolytic pathway. Examples of amino acids which can give rise to gluconeogenesis in this way are alanine, serine, cysteine, aspartic and glutamic acids.

In addition to the aminotransferases, liver cells contain an active glutamate dehydrogenase, which catalyses the following reaction:

$$\text{L-glutamate} + H_2O + \text{NAD (or NADP)} \rightleftharpoons$$
$$\text{2-oxoglutarate} + NH_3 + NADH_2 \text{ (or NADPH}_2)$$

Ammonia may also be formed from glutamine and asparagine by the action of the hydrolytic enzymes glutaminase and asparaginase. As one end result of these different transformations, ammonia is formed in the liver from the deamination of amino acids which are present in excess of immediate requirements for protein synthesis. Ammonia is also brought in the circulation to the liver, having been formed during similar reactions in other tissues, notably the kidney (p. 33.24).

THE SYNTHESIS OF UREA

Ammonia is a toxic product of nitrogen metabolism, which the liver converts into the relatively non-toxic end product, urea. The series of reactions which result in the synthesis of urea are often referred to as the ornithine cycle and associated with the names of Krebs and Henseleit. These reactions are shown diagrammatically in fig. 31.1. The cycle can go only one way because the hydrolytic reaction catalysed by arginase is irreversible.

In this sequence of reactions, the first synthetic step involves the transfer of the carbamyl group from carbamyl phosphate to the δ-amino group of ornithine. This is catalysed by ornithine carbamyl transferase, an enzyme which occurs in high concentrations in liver. The enzymic mechanism of formation of carbamyl phosphate is not completely understood, but synthetic carbamyl phosphate can replace it in the reaction with ornithine. The naturally occurring compound is formed, in the presence of N-acetylglutamate, from ammonium and bicarbonate ions by carbamate kinase, which requires ATP and Mg^{++}. The role of N-acetylglutamate in this reaction is unclear, and the intermediate formation of carbamic acid is assumed in the following description of events:

$$NH_4^+ + HCO_3^- \rightleftharpoons NH_4HCO_3 \rightleftharpoons NH_2COOH + H_2O$$

$$NH_2COOH + ATP \underset{}{\overset{Mg^{++}}{\rightleftharpoons}} NH_2COO\,\textcircled{P} + ADP$$

The synthesis of carbamyl phosphate, in fact, is largely irreversible and the above reactions oversimplify the process which results in its formation since, apart from the probable function of N-acetyl glutamate as an

FIG. 31.1. The ornithine cycle and the synthesis of urea. The cycle is unidirectional as the hydrolytic step catalysed by arginase is irreversible, but all the other reactions can be reversed under suitable conditions.

activator in the reaction, the overall stoichiometry of the synthesis requires two molecules of ATP.

In the next synthetic step citrulline condenses with aspartic acid, in the presence of ATP and Mg^{++}, to form argininosuccinic acid; the ATP is converted to AMP and inorganic pyrophosphate. Argininosuccinate synthetase catalyses this reaction, and the product is then split reversibly to arginine and fumaric acid by the enzyme argininosuccinate lyase. These enzymes are present both in liver and kidney extracts. The hydrolytic reaction catalysed by arginase gives rise to ornithine and urea.

There is an alternative though quantitatively less important route for the formation of ornithine from arginine, which is catalysed by glycine transamidinase.

Glycine + Arginine ⇌ Guanidoacetic + Ornithine
acid

Arginase occurs in highest concentration in the liver, but is also found in renal tissue. All the enzymes of the ornithine cycle occur in other tissues, but the high concentrations of each in the liver accounts for this organ's unique role in the synthesis of urea in mammals. The essentially cyclical nature of the process can be shown by the continuous production of urea for as long as ammonium and bicarbonate ions and an energy source to provide ATP are available, with only catalytic amounts of intermediates such as ornithine and citrulline being used. The net reaction of the ornithine cycle (omitting energy transformations) is as follows:

$$NH_4^+ + HCO_3^- + \text{L-aspartate} \rightleftharpoons$$
$$\text{urea} + \text{fumarate} + 2H_2O$$

THE LIVER AND PLASMA PROTEIN SYNTHESIS

Plasma proteins are mainly formed in the liver. Albumin is quantitatively the most important, and studies with ^{131}I-labelled human albumin show that the half-life of this protein is 20–26 days. Since the total plasma volume is approximately 3 litres, assuming an average normal serum albumin concentration of 4 g/100 ml, this means that the liver synthesizes about 3 g albumin *de novo* each day. Other proteins demonstrable in plasma and synthesized by the parenchymal cells of the liver include the α- and β-globulins (but not γ-globulins), several proteins concerned with the processes of blood coagulation (e.g. fibrinogen, prothrombin and Factors VII, IX, and X), and certain enzymes (pseudocholinesterase and caeruloplasmin). The formation of prothrombin by the liver depends on the supply and utilization of fat-soluble vitamin K.

The individual fractions of the serum proteins can best be demonstrated by zone electrophoresis. Plasma is not suitable for this examination, as fibrinogen produces a peak on electrophoresis which appears between the β- and the γ-globulin peaks, and which interferes with their interpretation. In this technique, as routinely employed, a sample of serum is applied to a solid supporting medium, e.g. filter paper or cellulose acetate strips

soaked in barbitone/sodium barbitone buffer (pH 8·6, ionic strength 0·1), and an electric field is applied across the strip. At this pH the plasma proteins carry a negative charge and move towards the anode, and differences in the net charge carried by individual proteins are largely responsible for their having different mobilities. At the end of the electrophoretic separation, the strips are dried, fixed and stained with a suitable dye, e.g., Amidoschwartz, Ponceau S; the different protein fractions can then be seen, and the amount of each determined by densitometry (see also p. 11.7).

Fig. 31.2 shows the electrophoretic pattern of normal serum. The areas under each peak are proportional to the

individual protein concentrations, and alterations in the electrophoretic pattern of serum proteins may be observed in many diseases. Table 31.1 shows some properties of plasma proteins.

In many parts of Asia, Africa, Central and South America levels of serum albumin are lower and those of γ-globulin higher than indicated in table 31.1. In a population with a low dietary intake of protein, serum albumin levels are likely to lie between 3·0 and 4·0 g/100 ml, but oedema or other evidence of protein deficiency is uncommon unless the level falls to below 2·5 g/100 ml. In populations exposed to many and repeated infections, particularly where malaria is endemic, even with severe protein deficiency, the γ-globulin level is often between 1·6 and 1·8 g/100 ml.

FIG. 31.2. Densitometer tracing of an electrophoretic separation of normal serum proteins.

TABLE 31.1. Properties of some individual human plasma proteins. After Putman 1960,

	Average Conc. mg/100 ml	Mol. wt.	Half-life days	Main functions or features
Albumin	4000	69,000	20	Large colloid osmotic pressure, plasma volume and tissue fluid balance. Transport function and buffer
α_1-Globulins				
Orosomucoid	50	44,100	6	A glycoprotein. Physiological significance unknown
α_1-Lipoprotein				
Density 1.093	100	435,000	—	Lipid transport
Density 1.149	350	195,000	—	Lipid transport
Haptoglobin Type 1-1	100	85,000	—	A glycoprotein; binds haemoglobin, and so helps to conserve iron.
α_2-Globulins				
α_2-Macroglobulin	200	820,000	—	A glycoprotein
Caeruloplasmin	25	151,000	4	Transports copper
β-Globulins				
β-Lipoprotein				
Density 0·98–1·002	160	5–20×10^6	—	Lipid transport; about 90% lipid
Density 1·03	220	3,200,000	—	Lipid transport; about 80% lipid
Transferrin	250	90,000	11	Transports iron
Fibrinogen	300	341,000	3	Precursor of fibrin
γ-Globulins				Antibodies or immunoglobulins
IgG (7Sγ)	1200	150,000	18	All glycoproteins
IgA	200	150,000 and 400,000	ca 5	
IgM (19Sγ)	100	900,000	ca 5	

The liver and carbohydrate metabolism

The liver also plays an important role in carbohydrate metabolism. Unless given glucose supplements, hepatectomized animals die quickly from hypoglycaemia. The liver maintains the level of blood glucose as summarized in fig. 31.3. The synthesis of glycogen from glucose-1-phosphate has already been described (p. 9.10).

Several hormones are concerned with the maintenance of normal levels of blood glucose. Following a meal rich in carbohydrates the blood glucose starts to rise and insulin release is stimulated. Insulin lowers blood glucose and facilitates the uptake of glucose into cells. In the liver, some of this glucose is converted to glycogen, the synthesis possibly also being stimulated by insulin. When increased amounts of glucose are needed as in muscular exercise, breakdown of glycogen occurs and glucose is released into the circulation. Phosphorylase, which catalyses the initial breakdown of liver glycogen to glucose-l-phosphate, is normally present in the liver in an inactive form. It is converted to the active form of the enzyme by the hormones adrenaline and glucagon, which exert their effect indirectly by stimulating the enzyme adenyl cyclase with the production of the cyclic adenosine–3′,5′-phosphate, cyclic AMP (p. 9.10).

In the liver, a specific kinase which requires cyclic AMP as cofactor phosphorylates inactive phosphorylase to form the active enzyme; this reverts to the inactive form on hydrolysis with the loss of inorganic phosphate from its molecule.

$$\text{Inactive phosphorylase} \underset{\text{hydrolysis}}{\overset{\text{Kinase}+\text{Cyclic AMP}}{\rightleftharpoons}} \text{Active phosphorylase}$$

GLUCONEOGENESIS

Normally, the adult human liver contains about 100 g glycogen, which provides a readily available, albeit limited, store on which the body can draw immediately for the maintenance of blood glucose levels. If the dietary carbohydrate intake is insufficient, gluconeogenesis helps to replenish the stores of liver glycogen, and several hormones include among their activities the promotion of gluconeogenesis, for instance the adrenal steroid cortisol, thyroxine and glucagon. The liver can also synthesize glucose from glycerol, formed during the breakdown of neutral fats and phospholipids. Glycerol enters the Embden–Meyerhof pathway through the action of glycerokinase and glycerolphosphate dehydrogenase. It is the only component of fat which has been shown to

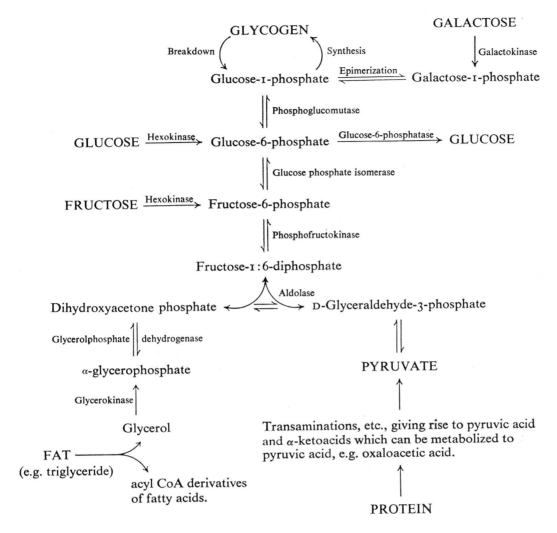

FIG. 31.3. Scheme of reactions involved in glycogen storage and gluconeogenesis by the liver.

give a net synthesis of glucose or glycogen in man; isotopic experiments with ^{14}C-labelled fatty acids demonstrate incorporation of isotope into glucose and glycogen, but on balance these experiments do not show any net synthesis of these compounds from fatty acids.

Glucose can also be formed by the liver from several monosaccharides and from various noncarbohydrate sources, since it contains enzyme systems which catalyse the conversion of galactose, fructose and several pentoses into glucose. In addition, those amino acids which after deamination form pyruvic, oxaloacetic or 2-oxoglutaric acids, either directly or indirectly as a result of further metabolism of their corresponding α-ketoacids, can give rise to glucose by reversal of the Embden–Meyerhof glycolytic pathway in the liver. Gluconeogenesis can lead to glycogen deposition in the liver or to the release of glucose into the blood for metabolism by other tissues.

Since the body's stores of carbohydrate are limited, any glucose absorbed from the diet in excess both of this capacity for storage as glycogen, and of the immediate requirements for oxidative metabolism, is mainly converted to fat and stored as such. Like adipose tissue, the liver is an important site for this conversion of carbohydrate to lipids, although other tissues, e.g. muscle, also contain the enzyme systems required for synthesis of fatty acids from acetyl coenzyme A.

The liver and fat metabolism

The principal dietary lipids of metabolic importance in man are triglycerides, phospholipids and esters of cholesterol. These are partly digested prior to absorption, and are partly absorbed in a finely emulsified state (p. 30.36). The liver is important in the normal processes of fat digestion and absorption since it is the source of bile;

bile salts act both as emulsifying agents and as activators of lipase. After absorption some of the dietary fat enters the portal circulation, and some goes via the lacteals and the thoracic duct to the systemic circulation and the fat depots.

The liver metabolizes lipids, whether brought directly to it in the portal circulation, or in the systemic circulation from the fat depots as a result of lipid mobilization. Synthesis of triglycerides and phospholipids takes place in the liver, free fatty acids being actively extracted from the plasma to take part in these synthetic reactions. Breakdown of long-chain fatty acids in the liver occurs in a series of stepwise reactions (p. 10.12), which result in the eventual overall production of several molecules of acetyl CoA and one molecule of acetoacetyl CoA, e.g.

$$CH_3(CH_2)_{16}COOH \longrightarrow$$
Stearic acid

$$CH_3COCH_2CO.SCoA + 7CH_3CO.SCoA$$
Acetoacetyl CoA   Acetyl CoA

The liver normally converts acetoacetyl CoA to two molecules of acetyl CoA, by the action of acetyl CoA acetyl transferase, and acetyl CoA itself then takes part

$$\text{Acetoacetyl CoA} + \text{CoA} \xrightarrow[\text{Acetyltransferase}]{\text{Acetyl CoA}} 2 \text{ Acetyl CoA}$$

in a number of different metabolic processes, mostly being oxidized to CO_2 and water via the citric acid cycle

KETONE BODIES AND KETOSIS

When the further oxidative metabolism of acetyl CoA in the liver is impaired, breakdown of fatty acids by the liver leads instead almost exclusively to the production of acetoacetic acid from which are derived, by further metabolism, 3-hydroxybutyric acid and acetone. These three compounds are collectively called ketone bodies although 3-hydroxybutyric acid is not in fact a ketone.

The reactions involved in the production of acetoacetic acid by the liver are shown in fig. 31.4. In the quantitatively more important process, two molecules of acetyl CoA first condense to give acetoacetyl CoA by a reversal of the action of acetyl CoA acetyltransferase, and acetoacetyl CoA then condenses with a further molecule of acetyl CoA to give a molecule of β-hydroxy-β-methylglutaryl CoA (HMG CoA). The presence of the enzyme HMG CoA synthetase is needed and the molecule of HMG CoA is subsequently split, by HMG CoA lyase with the formation of acetoacetic acid and acetyl CoA. Another enzyme, localized in the liver, can hydrolyse acetoacetyl CoA to acetoacetic acid, but this is the minor pathway for acetoacetate formation. The liver can only metabolize acetoacetic acid to a limited extent

Formation of acetoacetic acid (two routes)

Formation of 3-hydroxybutyric acid

Formation of acetone

FIG. 31.4. Formation of ketone bodies by the liver.

xcept by reduction to 3-hydroxybutyric acid. Non-enzymic decarboxylation of acetoacetic acid can also occur, giving ise to acetone. These reactions are also shown in g. 31.4. In bacteria the decarboxylation of acetoacetic cid is catalysed by acetoacetate decarboxylase, but the nzymic formation of acetone has not yet been demonstrated in mammals. Acetone is quantitatively the least nportant of the three ketone bodies and the decarboxytion of acetoacetate which results in its formation pparently occurs slowly and spontaneously under phyological conditions.

Acetoacetic acid and its derivatives are normally resent in blood and urine in small amounts, but when ese quantities increase sufficiently to give a wellarked nitroprusside reaction the condition of ketosis said to exist. Ketosis is associated with a low respiratory uotient (RQ), below 0·75, which reflects a predominance f fat metabolism. This state may develop in healthy dividuals after a period of 36–48 hours starvation at st, and its onset is promoted during starvation, vigorous ercise, severe cold, a difficult childbirth, fever or by veral other factors. Ketosis, however, is more severe patients with diabetes mellitus when the disease uncontrolled. Under these circumstances, high contrations of ketone bodies can be detected in the blood etonaemia), giving rise to a metabolic acidosis, and as uch as 25–50 g ketone bodies may be excreted daily in e urine (ketonuria) owing to the limited capacity of the trahepatic tissues to metabolize these compounds. cetone is volatile and is partly excreted in the expired r. Both acetoacetic acid and 3-hydroxybutyric acid are ong acids (p. 6.20) and contribute to the development the metabolic acidosis which is a common feature of controlled diabetes mellitus. Whether or not these acids e toxic in any other way than in causing disturbances of id-base balance is unknown.

IOLESTEROL SYNTHESIS

iolesterol is synthesized in the liver from acetyl CoA d HMG CoA has been shown, by isotopic experiments th ^{14}C-acetate, to be an intermediate in the synthesis of olesterol (p. 10.20); this is the normal route of HMG •A metabolism instead of being broken down to etoacetic acid (fig. 31.4). The reticulum cells and tiocytes of the liver are particularly active in the rmation of cholesterol, and the esterification of olesterol to form its acetate also takes place mainly in liver. Cholesterol in blood is mostly esterified (about per cent) and circulates as lipoprotein, the protein ving to maintain the lipid in colloidal solution. The er is an important site of formation of lipoproteins. Cholesterol is excreted into the bile in large amounts ble 31.3, p. 31.11); it is then reabsorbed from the estine, although some is converted to coprosterol bacterial action and excreted in the faeces. The

reabsorbed cholesterol enters the body's metabolic pool for cholesterol, and some is again excreted into the bile, giving rise to an enterohepatic circulation of cholesterol.

The liver and alcohol metabolism

Over 90 per cent of ingested alcohol is oxidized in the liver. Ethanol is rapidly absorbed from the gut and diffuses throughout the total body water and also into the urine and expired air. The kidneys and lungs do not actively excrete it. The amounts lost from the body by these routes are small and proportional to concentrations in the blood. Ethanol is not metabolized by resting or active muscle.

The liver possesses an alcohol dehydrogenase which acts on ethanol and NAD to produce acetaldehyde and $NADH_2$. An aldehyde dehydrogenase converts the aldehyde into acetyl CoA, which then enters the citric acid cycle. Ethanol is metabolized by these processes at a rate which is fixed and independent of concentrations in the blood. Hence after a loading dose blood levels fall linearly and not exponentially. Clearance from the body is at a rate usually between 50 and 100 mg/kg/hr, depending on the individual. A man weighing 65 kg can metabolize from 76 to 158 g daily. If larger amounts are consumed, the blood cannot be cleared in one day. As ethanol provides 7 kcal/g, an intake of 100 g meets about half the resting metabolism for a day. The alcohol content of various beverages is given on p. 5.23.

Bile salts, bilirubin and bile formation

BILE SALTS

One pathway for the metabolism of cholesterol in the liver is oxidation of the sidechain with formation of the primary bile acids cholic acid and chenodeoxycholic acid. These acids are formed approximately in a ratio of 4 : 1 and are conjugated by the liver with taurine and glycine. The salts of these conjugates are excreted into the bile; they are active emulsifying agents and play an important part in the digestion and absorption of fat from the intestine (pp. 10.10 and 30.36).

Cholic acid
(or R—COOH)

CH₃

$CHCH_2CH_2COOH$

HO   OH

Chenodeoxycholic acid
(or R¹—COOH)

O

R—C

NHCH₂COOH

Glycocholic acid

O

R—C

NHCH₂CH₂SO₃H

Taurocholic acid

(In the conjugates of chenodeoxycholic acid R¹ replaces R).

A portion of the cholic acid conjugates is lost in the faeces but about 80 per cent is reabsorbed from the intestine and subsequently re-excreted in the bile, thereby giving rise to an enterohepatic circulation of primary bile acid conjugates. A further portion of these conjugates is hydrolysed in the large intestine and the liberated cholic acid metabolized there to the secondary bile acids deoxycholic acid and lithocholic acid. These secondary bile acids are partly lost in the faeces but are also partly absorbed from the intestine and subsequently conjugated by the liver before being excreted into the bile. An enterohepatic circulation of secondary bile acids is

CH₃

OH $CHCH_2CH_2COOH$

HO

Deoxycholic acid

CH₃

$CHCH_2CH_2COOH$

HO

Lithocholic acid

thereby established. Quantitatively, the primary bile acid cholic acid, as its conjugates, forms the major fraction of bile acids in human bile.

BILIRUBIN

Bilirubin is formed mostly from haemoglobin breakdown (p. 26.11) and about 200 mg unconjugated bilirubin is brought to the liver daily in the adult. Its conjugation and excretion into the bile are two interrelated functions specific to the liver. Tests based on the effects of disturbances in these functions have a firmly established place in clinical investigation. Unconjugated bilirubin (prehepatic bilirubin) is transported in the plasma bound mainly to albumin. In the liver there are three stages in the transfer of bilirubin from the plasma to the biliary canaliculi (fig. 31.5) and involve:

(1) the transport of bilirubin from the plasma to the microsomes of the hepatocytes,

(2) the conjugation of bilirubin, which involves series of transfer reactions, resulting mainly in the formation of bilirubin diglucuronide and

(3) the transport of conjugated bilirubin from the site of conjugation to the biliary canaliculi.

Transport in blood	Protein-bound bilirubin
Conjugation by liver cell	Conjugation catalysed by microsomal enzymes
Excretion in bile	Bilirubin diglucuronide and sulphate

FIG. 31.5. Uptake, conjugation and excretion of bilirubin by the liver.

Bile only contains conjugated bilirubin (posthepatic bilirubin) and this is further metabolized by intestinal bacteria with the formation of a mixture of stercobilinogen stereoisomers and stercobilin. Haemoglobin breakdown ultimately accounts for most of the stercobilinogen and stercobilin in the faeces, but a proportion of these pigments also comes from by-products formed during the synthesis of haem, and some of the faecal pigmentation derives from other compounds such as mesobilirubinogen and urobilin IXα. In the present discussion, only the major pathways of bile pigment metabolism are described.

Some of the intestinal stercobilinogen is absorbed from the intestine into the portal circulation, and most of the

INTESTINES

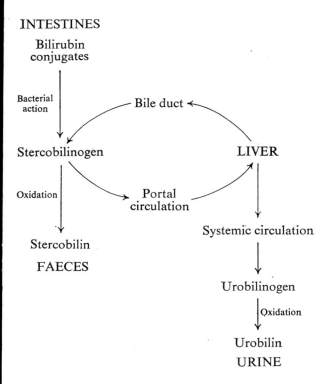

FIG. 31.6. Metabolism of bilirubin in the intestine and enterohepatic circulation of stercobilinogen.

pigmented material is excreted again into the bile, thereby giving rise to an enterohepatic circulation of bile pigment derivatives. Not all of the stercobilinogen in the portal blood is removed by this route and some is excreted into the urine (fig. 31.6). Normally, the faecal excretion of stercobilinogen is 40–280 mg/day, and the amount in

urine is 0–4 mg/day. Although its structure is the same as stercobilinogen, the urinary pigment is called urobilinogen.

Urobilinogen is oxidized to another urinary pigment, urobilin, which is structurally identical with the faecal pigment stercobilin, formed from stercobilinogen by oxidation in the intestine. Some authors use only the terms stercobilinogen and stercobilin, and others only use the terms urobilinogen and urobilin, prefixing them with the adjectives faecal or urinary to distinguish the site of the pigment under discussion, e.g. urinary stercobilin. In this book, stercobilinogen and stercobilin refer to faecal pigments and urobilinogen and urobilin to the corresponding urinary pigments.

The normal range of plasma bilirubin is 0·1–1·0 mg/100 ml, and this consists mostly of unconjugated bilirubin. Jaundice is a sign of liver disease and is liable to develop whenever the liver ceases to handle the daily load of bilirubin normally. Mild degrees of jaundice are often difficult to detect clinically but, by biochemical assessment, an individual is jaundiced whenever the plasma bilirubin is significantly raised above the upper limit of normal, i.e. if it exceeds 1·0 mg/100 ml. When jaundice occurs, it may be due to a raised level of either unconjugated or conjugated bilirubin in the plasma or to a mixture of both pigments.

Unconjugated bilirubin accumulates in the plasma as a result of over-production, for instance in haemolytic anaemia; it also occurs when hepatic uptake and conjugation of bilirubin are either incompletely developed, as in premature infants, or are abnormal due to an inborn defect of bilirubin conjugation or transport. Conjugated bilirubin accumulates in the plasma when the outflow of bile from the liver is obstructed, either in the bile duct

FIG. 31.7. Conjugation of bilirubin in the hepatocyte.

(extrahepatic) or bile canaliculi (intrahepatic) or when disease of the liver itself interferes with the conjugation of bilirubin and its excretion into the biliary canaliculi. Disease of the hepatocytes may adversely affect the uptake of unconjugated bilirubin, its conjugation with glucuronic acid and the excretion of conjugated bilirubin (fig. 31.7).

Obstruction to the outflow of bile often affects the hepatocytes and interferes with the normal processes of conjugation of bilirubin. Hence jaundice due to disease of the liver itself or due to obstruction to the outflow of bile may each result in a raised plasma bilirubin, part of which is conjugated and part unconjugated. Separate determinations of unconjugated and conjugated bilirubin have proved, therefore, of only limited assistance in localizing the site of the pathological process giving rise to jaundice. In practice, total plasma bilirubin is the single most widely performed bilirubin measurement in hospital laboratories; it provides a quantitative measure of the severity of jaundice and gives an objective index of the progress of the patient. Neonatal jaundice is the main group of conditions in which it has proved valuable to determine both total and conjugated bilirubin, and consequently unconjugated bilirubin by difference.

The causes of jaundice can be grouped on the basis of the diagram shown in fig. 31.8, which also contains a classification of the three chief sub-divisions of jaundice, based on the site of the lesion, namely prehepatic, hepatic and posthepatic. If a patient has prehepatic jaundice, unconjugated bilirubin accumulates in the plasma. Unconjugated bilirubin is bound to albumin and cannot be detected in urine unless the jaundice is very severe; even then bilirubin only occasionally appears in urine from uncomplicated cases of prehepatic jaundice, unless the patient has concomitant proteinuria. On the other hand, if jaundice is due to any process which interferes with the elimination of conjugated bilirubin from the body, this relatively small molecule circulates in the blood unbound to pro-

CLASSIFICATION OF JAUNDICE

Type of jaundice	Cause
(1) Prehepatic	Overproduction of bilirubin.
(2) Hepatic 2a.	Impaired uptake, transport defect affecting unconjugated bilirubin.
2b.	Disease of liver cell, which affects conjugation of bilirubin.
2c.	Transport defect affecting removal of conjugated bilirubin.
(3) Posthepatic 3a.	Intrahepatic obstruction to outflow of bile.
3b.	Extrahepatic obstruction to outflow of bile.

FIG. 31.8. Diagram of the metabolism of bilirubin as a basis for classifying causes of jaundice.

tein and is readily excreted in the urine, where it can be detected, e.g. by using Ictotest (Ames Co).

The diagnosis of the cause of jaundice can be assisted by the results of examinations of urinary and faecal pigment excretion, as shown in table 31.2, where the individual causes correspond to the classification in fig. 31.8. The detection of urobilinogen by Ehrlich's test is not easy if bilirubin is also present in the urine. Differentiation of jaundice into its three main types, depends both

TABLE 31.2. The bile pigments and jaundice. From Maclagan (1961).

Type of jaundice	Plasma bilirubin	Urobilinogen	Urine bilirubin	Faecal pigment	Other liver† function tests
(1) Prehepatic	Unconjugated	Increased	Absent	Increased	Normal
(2) Hepatic (a)	Unconjugated	Normal	Absent	Normal or reduced	Normal
(b)	Conjugated and unconjugated	Variable	Present	Reduced	Impaired
(c)	Conjugated*	Normal or reduced	Present	Reduced	Normal‡
(3) Posthepatic (a)	Conjugated*	Reduced or absent	Present	Reduced	Normal‡
(b)	Conjugated*	Reduced or absent	Present	Reduced	Normal‡

* Due to secondary effects on liver cell resulting from failure to excrete bile normally, some impairment of bilirubin conjugation may develop early in many patients, especially with posthepatic jaundice.

† Excluding tests of excretory function.

‡ Become impaired with onset of complications which adversely affect the hepatic parenchymal cells.

on the pigment tests summarized in table 31.2 and on the results of liver function tests. These chemical tests must be interpreted in relation to the history of the illness and to the signs of disease detected on examination, as well as results of other investigations.

BILE

The liver secretes bile continuously. It is a dilute aqueous solution of electrolytes, glucose, urea and other more complex molecules such as bilirubin conjugates, bile salts and cholesterol. It also contains some protein and the enzymes alkaline phosphatase and lactate dehydrogenase. Bile as secreted by the liver is approximately isotonic with plasma, but it does not all pass directly to the duodenum. When digestion is inactive, most of the hepatic bile is diverted to the gall bladder where it is concentrated by the reabsorption of water. Table 31.3 summarizes the main differences between hepatic and gall bladder bile. The mucosal cells of the gall bladder add mucus, sometimes in large amounts, and the high concentrations of cholesterol, bile pigment and calcium salts in gall bladder bile make these substances liable to be deposited as gallstones.

The rate of flow is related to the secretion of bile salts, and various substances, in the intestinal lumen stimulate the outflow of bile from the liver. These and the digestive functions of bile are described in chap. 30.

The biliary tract is also an excretory route. However, many compounds excreted in the bile are reabsorbed to a large extent from the intestine, and are later re-excreted in the bile. Substances which show this enterohepatic circulation include the bile salts themselves, cholesterol and stercobilinogen.

When the outflow of bile is obstructed to any marked degree, digestion and absorption of fat are seriously impaired and signs of deficiency of vitamin K may develop; if the course of the illness is very prolonged, symptoms of vitamin D and A deficiency may also appear. The excretory functions of the liver become deranged and jaundice develops with bilirubinuria and excretion of bile salts in the urine; stercobilinogen and stercobilin output are reduced. Plasma cholesterol and alkaline phosphatase levels are often considerably elevated. If obstruction is complete, the stools become very pale and urobilinogen is absent from the urine.

When parenchymal disease of the liver produces jaundice, swollen cells may obstruct the outflow of bile from the lobule and so produce many of the changes due to biliary obstruction. In addition, the diseased liver cells may be unable to excrete the stercobilinogen which has been absorbed from the bowel, and this disturbance of the normal enterohepatic circulation of stercobilinogen may result in an increased excretion of urobilinogen in the urine, even though the hepatic excretion of bilirubin conjugates is itself impaired. This is because the excretion by the liver of stercobilinogen absorbed from the intestine into the portal circulation is an activity which is rapidly impaired by disease of the liver cell. In hepatic jaundice, therefore, it may be possible to demonstrate an excess of urobilinogen in the urine at the same time as finding bilirubinuria.

Inactivation of hormones

STEROID HORMONES

Liver extracts contain several different enzyme systems which can modify the structure and inactivate the naturally occurring steroid hormones, and the liver is the main site of their metabolism. For instance, reduction of the Δ^4 double bond and of the 3-keto group to 3-hydroxyl convert cortisol to one of its major metabolites, tetrahydrocortisol; this physiologically inactive product is then mostly conjugated with glucuronic acid and excreted in the urine as tetrahydrocortisol glucuronide. These reactions are shown in fig. 31.9. Two dehydrogenases in liver can catalyse the first step:

(1) a soluble enzyme which gives rise to a dihydro derivative with a 5β configuration (fig. 31.9),

(2) a microsomal enzyme which gives rise to a 5α-dihydroderivative.

Both these steroid dehydrogenases require $NADPH_2$ and the soluble enzyme is quantitatively the important catalyst for the first step in the inactivation of cortisol. D-Aldosterone is similarly converted to inactive tetrahydro-aldosterone which is partly excreted as the corresponding glucuronide. Another major urinary excretion product of cortisol is cortol, formed by reduction of the 20-carbonyl group of tetrahydrocortisol. Other alterations to cortisol which are catalysed by hepatic enzymes include hydroxylations at C_2 and C_6, reduction

TABLE 31.3. Bile constituents. After Documenta Geigy, 4th edn.

	Hepatic bile	Gall bladder bile
Water content (per cent)	97–98	84
Colour	golden yellow to orange	dark brown to greenish brown
Specific gravity	1·008–1·016	1·008–1·060
pH	5·7–8·6	6·1–8·6
Total bile acids, g/100 ml (free and conjugated)	1·2–1·7	2·3–7·7
Bilirubin, mg/100 ml	20–70	50–1000
Cholesterol, mg/100 ml	90–180	100–900
Fatty acids, mg/100 ml	20–140	80–1600
Bicarbonate, mEq/l	20–25	8–12
Calcium, mg/100 ml	8–11	50–75
Phosphate, mg/100 ml	6–24	140
Mucin (per cent)	—	1–4

FIG. 31.9. Inactivation of cortisol.

FIG. 31.10. Excretory products of cortisol.

of the carbonyl group at C_{20} to a secondary alcoholic group and the reversible oxidation of the hydroxyl group at C_{11} to a keto group; this last reaction produces cortisone. A major fraction of the adrenal glands, output of cortisol is first metabolized to cortisone, which is then inactivated by reductive steps to tetrahydrocortisone. The reactions involving cortisol are summarized in fig. 31·10. Some of the steroid metabolites are excreted in the bile and are then partly excreted in the faeces and partly reabsorbed; the main route of excretion is in the urine.

Testosterone is metabolized to the isomeric 17-ketosteroids androsterone and aetiocholanolone and the main adrenal androgen dehydro-*epi*androsterone is also metabolized to these two compounds, which are mostly excreted as their 3-sulphate conjugates in urine (fig. 31·11).

Testosterone
(Testicular androgen)

Dehydro*epi*androsterone
(Adrenal androgen)

Androsterone

Aetiocholanolone

FIG. 31·11. Androgens and their principal metabolites. 17-oxosteroids are derived mainly from androgens and are excreted in urine principally as their 3-sulphate derivatives.

The various dehydrogenation and conjugation steps involved in these transformations are all catalysed by hepatic enzymes. Smaller amounts of testosterone derivatives hydroxylated in the two, six or sixteen positions have been described. The liver also inactivates the other androgens of gonadal and of adrenal origin. Oestrogens (oestradiol, oestrone and oestriol) are conjugated in the liver with glucuronic acid or with sulphate and then excreted in the urine. Progesterone is reduced to pregnanediol, which is excreted as sulphate or glucuronide conjugates.

In severe hepatic disease, the inactivation of steroid hormones may be impaired and side-effects may ensue because of this. The appearance of feminizing features in male patients and of masculinizing features in female patients with cirrhosis is due to impairment of the processes of metabolism and inactivation of the corresponding sex hormones.

THYROID HORMONES

Thyroxine and triiodothyronine are metabolized in several different ways and there is considerable variation between species as to the most important route. In man, both hormones are mainly metabolized by reactions involving deiodination, leading to excretion of iodine in the urine, and the liver is only one of several tissues that can effect this change. The mechanism of the deiodination is not yet understood. In addition, the liver takes up thyroxine from the circulation, conjugates it with glucuronic acid and secretes the conjugate into the bile. Quantitatively this is an unimportant route of inactivation and excretion and the majority of the thyroxine glucuronide in the bile is later hydrolysed in the intestine and the liberated thyroxine reabsorbed (another example of enterohepatic circulation); only about 10 per cent of an injected dose of radioactive thyroxine is excreted in the faeces in man. With triiodothyronine, sulphation appears to be more important as the hepatic conjugating mechanism, but this does not constitute a major pathway of inactivation for triiodothyronine.

OTHER HORMONES

The liver has not been shown to have any specific role in the metabolism of the peptide and protein hormones. For the metabolism of the catecholamines, noradrenaline and adrenaline, it is a rich source of both monoamine oxidase (MAO) and of catechol O-methyltransferase (COMT) but these enzymes are widely distributed and the liver has no special role in the inactivation of circulating catecholamines liberated from the adrenal medulla. On the other hand hepatic MAO and COMT both have an important function in the detoxication of dietary and bacterial amines absorbed from the intestine (see next section).

Inactivation of drugs and pharmacological agents

Many drugs and dietary or intestinal compounds with pharmacological activities are metabolized in the liver by processes which involve either oxidation, reduction, methylation or conjugation reactions. Most of these reduce the pharmacological activity of the compound and make the molecules more polar, thereby increasing their solubility in water and facilitating renal or biliary excretion. Tests of liver function based on the metabolism of drugs depend on these processes of excretion. It is necessary, therefore, for the excretory mechanism to be functioning normally before these tests can be satisfactorily applied. The conjugation and excretion of bromosulphthalein, for instance, is only useful as a test of hepatic function in the absence of jaundice, since bromosulphthalein is metabolized and excreted by the same pathway as bilirubin. Similarly, the hippuric acid synthesis test which depends on measuring the amount of hippurate excreted in the urine following the intravenous administration of sodium benzoate, and so assesses the liver's ability to conjugate sodium benzoate with glycine, is adversely affected if renal function is significantly impaired.

Certain chemical poisons give rise to liver damage and disturbances of lipid metabolism. These include chlorinated hydrocarbons, e.g. carbon tetrachloride, chloroform; various aromatic compounds, e.g. dinitrophenol, trinitrotoluene and inorganic poisons, e.g. phosphorus, arsenites. Histologically, droplets of fat can be demonstrated in the liver during the acute phase of poisoning and the liver may become enlarged and fatty; with large doses of poison, death (necrosis) of hepatocytes may occur on a large scale with serious failure of the liver's metabolic activities. The effects of poisons on the liver are more marked if the nutritional state of the individual is poor, associated with protein malnutrition or chronic alcoholism. Starvation by itself has little demonstrable effect on the liver other than to cause reduction in the glycogen and protein content and diminution in size. When fatty change occurs, the fat is mainly brought to the liver from the fat depots, and accumulates because of interference with its normal metabolism.

Sedatives such as barbiturates become less effective on patients if taken regularly over prolonged periods. This observation led to a study in which rats were repeatedly given phenobarbitone. This increased the activity of the hepatic microsomal system which hydroxylates the drug, as a result of increased production of the enzymes rather than the formation of an enzyme-activating substance. Accompanying these alterations in enzyme activity, ultrastructural changes occurred in the endoplasmic reticulum; new membranes were formed by outgrowth and budding off from tubules and cisternae of pre-existing rough surfaced endoplasmic reticulum. Inhibitors such as Actinomycin D and puromycin prevent the induction by phenobarbitone of this increase in the level of the drug hydroxylating enzyme system. The detailed sequence of reactions resulting in hydroxylation is not yet properly characterized, although one component would seem to be $NADPH_2$ cytochrome c reductase, the activity of which is itself increased by phenobarbitone.

Several common fruits and vegetables contain biologically active amines, for instance bananas are a rich source of catecholamines and 5-hydroxytryptamine, and intestinal bacteria produce amines by decarboxylating amino acids. After absorption these compounds are detoxicated in the liver by MAO or by COMT. Monoamine oxidase is a poorly characterized mitochondrial enzyme which catalyses the oxidation of primary, secondary and tertiary amines. For example, it inactivates noradrenaline and adrenaline as follows:

Catechol O-methyltransferase is one of several transmethylating enzymes detectable in hepatic tissue. For each reaction the liver provides S-adenosylmethionine as methyl donor, it being a rich source of the enzyme methionine adenosyl transferase. The formation of S-adenosylmethionine and other examples of hepatic transmethylation reactions involving naturally occurring compounds are set out on fig. 31.12.

Vitamin storage and metabolism

The liver contains the body's main store of the fat soluble vitamins A, D, E and K. It is also concerned with their absorption from the intestine, since this is promoted by the presence of bile salts. In the liver, vitamin K is required for the synthesis of prothrombin and several other clotting factors, e.g. Factor VII, Stuart–Prower factor; these factors are normally synthesized exclusively in the liver and any failure in supply of vitamin K, e.g. dietary insufficiency or failure to absorb, or interference in its utilization, e.g. due to drugs such as salicylates or indanedione derivatives, results in prolongation of the blood clotting process (p. 26.14). Storage of vitamins A and D in the liver is not associated with any specific

FIG. 31.12 Transmethylation reactions in the liver.

function of these vitamins in this organ, but the amounts of these vitamins stored under normal conditions of dietary intake are sufficient to require a prolonged period of dietary deprivation before signs of deficiency develop; as a result of its antioxidant properties, vitamin E protects the stores of A and D in the liver from destruction by oxidation.

Water-soluble vitamins are also stored by the liver, particularly vitamin B_{12} and folic acid, and the liver contains the various enzyme systems which can metabolize tryptophan to nicotinic acid. Both maize and rice are poor sources of nicotinic acid but rice proteins contain more tryptophan than maize proteins. The formation of nicotinic acid from this tryptophan accounts for the fact that pellagra is rare in rice eaters but common in maize eaters. In the sequence of reactions (fig. 31.13) which result in the formation of the nucleotide of nicotinic acid (NMN) the first enzyme, tryptophan pyrrolase,

is able to have its formation induced by administration of tryptophan, α-methyltryptophan or by glucocorticoids.

The liver is a rich source of enzymes which synthesize a range of coenzymes and prosthetic groups, NAD, NADP, FMN, FAD, thiamine pyrophosphate, pyridoxal phosphate, from members of the vitamin B group. Enzymes concerned with these various reactions are as follows:

$$NMN + ATP \xrightleftharpoons[\text{adenyltransferase}]{\text{NMN}} NAD + pyrophosphate$$

$$NAD + ATP \xrightarrow[\text{kinase}]{\text{NAD}} NADP + ADP$$

$$Riboflavine + ATP \xrightarrow[\text{kinase}]{\text{Riboflavine}} FMN + ADP$$

FIG. 31.13. Conversion of tryptophan to nicotinic acid.

$$FMN + ATP \underset{\text{adenylyltransferase}}{\overset{\text{FMN}}{\rightleftharpoons}} FAD + \text{pyrophosphate}$$

$$Thiamine + ATP \xrightarrow[\text{pyrophosphokinase}]{\text{Thiamine}} Thiamine \text{ pyrophosphate} + AMP$$

$$Pyridoxal + ATP \xrightarrow[\text{kinase}]{\text{Pyridoxal}} Pyridoxal \text{ phosphate} + ADP$$

Storage of vitamins becomes particularly important in the face of dietary deficiency and influences the ability to survive this period of deficient intake. The normal hepatic stores of vitamin A, D and B_{12} are sufficient to meet the body's needs for over a year, whereas signs of deficiency of the other water-soluble vitamins and of vitamin K can develop more quickly. In addition to vitamin storage, the liver is also an important storage organ for iron and copper.

Chemical tests of liver function

One or more of the wide range of liver functions may be impaired by disease. The liver function tests which are commonly performed to assess liver damage may be grouped under four headings.

TESTS OF EXCRETORY FUNCTION

There is no one test of excretory function that can be advocated as the most suitable for all circumstances since the various excretory activities of the liver may be mpaired to different degrees in individual patients. If the liver fails to excrete the bile pigments, they accumulate n the blood and measurement of the plasma bilirubin provides a quantitative assessment of the depth of jaundice; differential estimation of unconjugated and conjugated bilirubin is sometimes used for helping to delineate the type of jaundice. In the absence of jaundice, the liver's excretory function can be investigated by giving bromosulphthalein intravenously and measuring its rate of disappearance from the plasma.

Tests on urine for bilirubin (Ictotest, Ames Co.) and urobilinogen (Ehrlich's test) can provide valuable information and suffice to distinguish prehepatic jaundice from the other two groups in most cases and are simple to perform (table 31.2).

It is not clear how plasma alkaline phosphatase levels are related to hepatic excretory function but their determination is of value in the presence of jaundice. With posthepatic jaundice, the level rises markedly and usually exceeds 30 King–Armstrong (KA) units/100 ml. With hepatic jaundice, elevation of alkaline phosphatase is usually lower, results mostly falling in the range 13–30 KA units/100 ml, and with uncomplicated prehepatic jaundice results are normal (3–12 KA units/100 ml). These figures require modification in patients under the age of 20, because of the greater contribution by bone to the normal levels of plasma alkaline phosphatase in childhood and adolescence.

TESTS OF SYNTHETIC CAPACITY

The synthesis of serum albumin is often disturbed in liver disease, and a fall in serum albumin is one of the most characteristic chemical findings in chronic hepatic disease; it is an important factor in promoting the fluid retention and oedema that may develop in this condition. A reduction in serum albumin concentration due to disease affecting the hepatocytes is usually accompanied by an elevation of serum globulins. Specimens that show a rise in the γ-globulin peak often show abnormal turbidity on the addition of a buffered zinc sulphate or thymol solution; abnormal turbidity is associated with increases in both β- and γ-globulins. These turbidity tests are still used as empirical tests of liver function, but have now been largely replaced by serum electrophoresis.

Separate determinations of other proteins formed by the liver, for example, fibrinogen and other clotting factors, pseudocholinesterase, caeruloplasmin, do not usually provide useful information additional to that obtained from serum albumin determinations. However, it is important to investigate the coagulation mechanism, (p. 26.14) whenever liver biopsy or laparotomy has to be undertaken in a jaundiced patient. Hypoprothrombinaemia may be due either to failure to absorb vitamin K, as a result of obstruction to the outflow of bile, or to hepatocellular damage (and rarely to other causes), and

parenteral treatment with vitamin K preparations is frequently required before the liver biopsy or laparotomy is carried out.

TESTS OF METABOLIC FUNCTION

Despite its central place in metabolism, tests based on the liver's ability to metabolize protein, fat and carbohydrate have proved of only limited value, except in special circumstances. This is because the liver has such a large functional reserve. Thus liver failure does not lead to a detectable rise in the concentration of amino acids in blood or fall in blood urea until about 80 per cent of the organ has been destroyed by disease. With the development of improved methods for measuring blood ammonia, this examination may become a useful test of the metabolic functions of the liver. In patients suffering from severe disease of the liver, disturbances of function of the central nervous system which may lead to coma and death are common. The concentration of ammonia in the blood of such patients provides some measure of the degree of hepatic failure.

The only test of carbohydrate metabolism to have been widely assessed is the intravenous galactose tolerance test; this measures the liver's ability to convert galactose to glucose, but galactose is not metabolized exclusively by the liver and hepatic dysfunction has to be marked before the test becomes significantly impaired. The galactose tolerance test has a special place, however, in the investigation of relatives of a case of galactosaemia, a rare inborn error of metabolism due to deficiency of galactose-1-phosphate uridyl transferase.

TESTS OF LIVER CELL DAMAGE

These depend upon the presence in the blood of enzymes released from damaged parenchymal cells. Determinations of the activity in serum or plasma of several enzymes are used for this purpose, and the enzymes commonly measured are alanine and aspartate aminotransferases (GPT and GOT respectively), isocitrate dehydrogenase (ICD), ornithine carbamoyltransferase (OCMT) and lactate dehydrogenase (LD) combined with LD isoenzyme studies; the slowest isoenzyme on electrophoresis, LD_5, occurs in particularly high concentration in the liver. Few laboratories regularly undertake all these determinations. The activity of these enzymes is much greater in liver cells than in serum, and it is only necessary for a little of the intracellular enzyme to escape before a significant rise of serum enzyme activity can be detected. Measurements of enzyme activity in serum can therefore provide a sensitive index of liver cell damage. However, these enzymes are not found only in liver cells, and a rise in serum enzyme activity may follow damage to cells in other organs. Hence such findings need to be interpreted in relation to

TABLE 31.4. Liver function tests other than tests of bilirubin metabolism.

	Parenchymal disease		Obstruction to outflow of bile
	Acute	Chronic	
Bromosulphthalein excretion	Impaired	Impaired	Not indicated (jaundice present)
Alkaline phosphatase	Slight increases in most cases	Normal or slight increase in some cases	Marked increase in some cases
Serum albumin	Normal	Reduced	Normal
Serum globulins	Normal early, but later rise in β- and γ-globulins	Elevation of β- and γ-globulins	Normal; later may show rise in all fractions, especially β-globulins
Turbidity tests	Increased	Increased	Normal
Alanine aminotransferase (GPT)	Increased	Normal or slight increase	Normal or slight increase
Aspartate aminotransferase (GOT)	Increased if GPT markedly increased	Normal or slight increase	Normal or slight increase

No entries are shown for prehepatic jaundice; in this condition, normal results are observed for the various tests, except for excretion of bromosulphthalein.

clinical observations and the results of other laboratory investigations.

The damaged liver cell does not act like a leaky sieve. Alanine aminotransferase (GPT) for instance is more readily released than GOT, so serum GPT determinations provide a more sensitive index of liver cell damage than GOT, even though the activity of GOT measurable in liver extracts is much higher than GPT. Either GPT or ICD determinations on serum are commonly used for detecting liver cell damage; the information provided by these two measurements is essentially equivalent.

SELECTION OF LIVER FUNCTION TESTS

Students and doctors should become familiar with a limited number of liver function tests. Most hospital laboratories perform a selected group of tests as a routine, and these are generally sufficient for diagnostic purposes. Unfortunately, as yet the ideal set of tests has not been established.

Liver function tests are very frequently required for the assessment of patients with jaundice. They are also used in the investigation of suspected liver disease in many other clinical situations. Tests based on bile pigment metabolism are summarized in table 31.2 and examples of some other liver function tests are presented in table 31.4. In applying the information contained in table 31.4 it must be remembered that some of the tests,

e.g. serum albumin, serum alkaline phosphatase, serum aminotransferases, may be abnormal in the absence of liver disease. It is essential to interpret the results of chemical tests of 'liver function' in relation to the other information available concerning each patient (vol. III).

FURTHER READING

British Medical Bulletin (1957) The liver: some physiological and clinical aspects. **13**, No. 2.

LEEVY C.M. (1967) Observations on hepatic regeneration in man. *Advances in Internal Medicine*, ed. Dock & Snapper, **13**, 97. Chicago: Year Book Medical Publishers Inc.

MACLAGAN N.F. (1961) Changing views on jaundice. *Proc. Roy. Soc. Med.* **54**, 121.

Scottish Medical Journal (1964) The intelligent use of biochemical tests. **9**, 34.

POPPER P. & SCHAFFNER F. (eds) (1965) *Progress in Liver Diseases*, Vol. II. London: Heinemann.

READ A.E. (ed.) (1967) *The Liver*. Proceedings of Nineteenth Symposium of the Colston Research Society. London: Butterworths.

SHERLOCK S. (1968) Diseases of the Liver and Biliary System, 4th Edition, pp. 1–52, 253–74, Oxford: Blackwell Scientific Publications.

Chapter 32
Adipose tissue

The primary function of adipose tissue is the storage of triglycerides (TG), a potential source of energy. It also provides insulation against cold and mechanical damage and serves as the packing material for the internal organs. The amount and the distribution of adipose tissue largely determines our shape and general appearance and differs in adult men and women.

Amount and distribution

A healthy male contains about 7·5 kg of adipose tissue, a little more than half of which surrounds the organs in the abdominal cavity and elsewhere in the body; the remainder is subcutaneous. A healthy female has rather more than twice this amount. The total amount present is determined by the state of nutrition. Before death from starvation occurs, almost all visible fat disappears from the body. Many obese people carry around a load of 50 kg of adipose tissue and a few very much more. For instance, Mr John Cobb, who was featured in *Time* (30th July 1965) and who weighed 365 kg, probably had over 200 kg. He was in the habit of eating fifteen chickens at a sitting. Genetic factors also determine the amount of adipose tissue present. Several strains of fat and thin animals have been bred, but in the human, it is difficult to separate genetic and environmental factors responsible for an individual's degree of adiposity.

The distribution of fat differs markedly in the two sexes and also varies in individuals. This is partly controlled by the sex hormones. Administration of oestrogens to men leads to the deposition of fat round the hips and thighs, the characteristic female pattern. Conversely testosterone and corticoid hormones promote the male distribution, predominantly in the upper part of the body.

Microscopic structure

As a supporting and packing material, adipose tissue is often considered as a variety of connective tissue. It is of mesenchymal origin, but differs from other connective tissues in that its functions and properties are due to the cells themselves and not to the intercellular substances. Although the cells of adipose tissue may differentiate from and revert to cells which resemble fibroblasts, they are considered here as a separate tissue because of their characteristic structure and metabolic importance.

Ordinary adipose tissue is divided into lobules by collagenous and reticular septa, which carry the nerves and capillary blood supply to the closely-packed cells. The mature fat cell consists of a shell of cytoplasm, containing a flattened nucleus, which surrounds a single globule of lipid up to 50 μm in diameter. In routine histological preparations this lipid globule is dissolved during dehydration and embedding in paraffin wax (p. 13.3), so the empty shells which remain give the appearance of a honeycomb (fig. 32.1). Sections of frozen material,

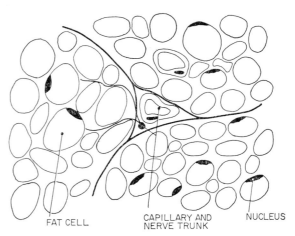

FIG. 32.1. Adipose tissue as seen in a paraffin section.

or techniques which render the lipid insoluble, reveal more details of the structure of the fat cell. During the accumulation of fat, numerous small globules appear which later coalesce into a single globule (fig. 32.2). Histochemical techniques and the EM show that the cytoplasm, surrounding the lipid, has all the usual enzymes and organelles of an active metabolizing cell; after starving and refeeding, glycogen can be demonstrated in the cytoplasmic rims (p. 32.2).

Some adipose tissue which is darker and more vascular is known as **brown fat**. Histologically this tissue also consists of closely-packed large cells, but each cell contains

32.1

many small lipid droplets which do not coalesce (fig. 32.3). The cytoplasm of brown fat cells contains numerous mitochondria and pigments which give it the dark colour. Small droplets of lipid have a larger surface area

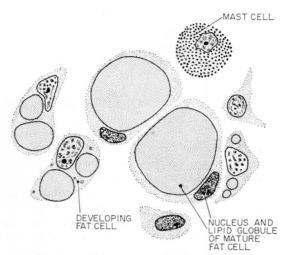

FIG. 32.2. The accumulation of fat in fat cells.

than the single globule of ordinary fat. This dispostion of the lipid allows its energy stores to become more freely available and the mitochondrial content suggests that the tissue can have a high metabolic rate. In hibernating animals there are large amounts of brown fat,

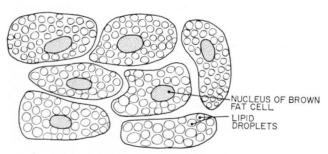

FIG. 32.3. Brown fat cells.

which promote the energy for the warming up process in the spring. Brown fat is found in the late human foetus where it serves as a small but easily mobilizable reserve for the energy demands of the neonatal period.

Chemical composition

Many samples of human adipose tissue removed at operation and by biopsy have been analysed. The fat content varies greatly, ranging from 65 to 90 per cent. Figures of 85 per cent for fat, 13 per cent for water and 2 per cent for protein are normal. Thus

7·5 kg of adipose tissue contains just over 1 kg of fat free tissue and about 150 g of protein. Therefore apart from its fat content adipose tissue is very substantial and is comparable in size and protein content to the liver. An obese person with 50 kg of adipose tissue probably has about 5 kg of fat free adipose tissue, metabolically equivalent to a very large organ. Excess food increases the size of the cells (hypertrophy) and also their number (hyperplasia). In man the hyperplasia appears the more important.

The greater part of the lipid, about 98 per cent, is TG, but there are traces of diglyceride, FFA, cholesterol and phospholipid. The cholesterol and phospholipid can be synthesized within the tissues and are probably present in the membranes. The phosphorus containing phosphatidic acids lie on the pathway of TG synthesis (p. 10.17) and might be expected to be present in small amounts. Of the total protein, up to 25 per cent is collagen and 12 per cent nucleoprotein and the remainder is probably mainly cytoplasmic and includes the enzymes needed for the metabolic processes. The glycogen content is normally less than 0·1 per cent, but many rise to as much as 1 per cent in the adipose tissue of animals who have been re-fed after a period of starvation.

For many years the body fat was considered to be a purely passive store of TG, not involved in the minute to minute energy metabolism of the body. When isotopically labelled fatty acids are administered to animals, the activity of adipose tissue becomes apparent. There is continuous formation and breakdown of TG. For these metabolic changes the immediate source of energy is ATP derived from oxidative processes. The oxygen consumption of adipose tissue, when expressed per unit of dry fat free tissue or tissue N is high and of the same order as that of kidney and liver.

Formation of fat stores
From non-lipid sources
It is common knowledge that a diet containing excess carbohydrate leads to obesity. Fat deposition is independent of ingested TG, since it occurs in young animals fed a fat free diet. It was once thought that lipid synthesis took place exclusively in the liver and that newly-formed TG was carried as lipoprotein in the blood to the depots in the adipose tissue. However, since lipid synthesis has been demonstrated in hepatectomized rats, this is not true. To study the relative importance of different tissues in the synthesis of TG from non-lipid sources, ^{14}C-acetate has been injected into rats, and the quantity of labelled TG in each tissue determined at different time intervals. The number of labelled molecules in the liver was found to be well below that in the intestinal cells and in the remainder of the carcass, suggesting that less TG synthesis occurs in the liver than elsewhere. However, this interpretation of the experiment is suspect since the

^{14}C-acetyl-CoA intermediate in the liver may be diluted with unlabelled molecules derived from the glycogen stores or incoming FFA and glucose. Consequently, the proportion of new TG molecules in the liver bearing the label would be expected to be lower than in other tissues. Nevertheless, the specific activity of TG in liver was higher than in adipose tissue, which seemed to support the original thesis that liver is the principal site of TG synthesis. Later this was refuted by repeating the experiment using rats whose fat stores had been depleted of TG by fasting. In these animals, the specific activity of the TG was higher in adipose tissue than in liver. It was therefore concluded that synthesis also occurs in the adipose tissue. The relative importance of the two tissues in the synthesis of fatty acids is still the subject of argument.

The bulk of the TG molecules formed in the liver are rapidly secreted into the blood stream as lipoprotein (p. 10.10), hence their turnover time is very short compared with that of the TG in adipose tissue.

The pathways of fatty acid and TG synthesis appear to be the same in adipose tissue as those in liver, but it has not yet been possible to isolate a fatty acyl carrier protein. Desaturation and elongation of injected ^{14}C-palmitic acid has been demonstrated in rat adipose tissue *in vivo*. These reactions occur in the microsomes.

The source of the TG formed from carbohydrate is the blood glucose and also glycogen in the adipose tissue. When pieces of adipose tissue are incubated with ^{14}C-glucose, the majority of the ^{14}C incorporated in the newly synthesized TG is in the glyceride moiety. Thus glucose provides α-glycerophosphate to esterify endogenous fatty acids. Addition of insulin increases the total quantity of glucose entering the tissue and also the amount converted into TG; the amount and the proportion of ^{14}C from labelled glucose incorporated into the fatty acid part of the labelled TG is also raised by insulin. However, the hormone does not affect the incorporation of ^{14}C-acetate or pyruvate molecules unless glucose is also added to the medium. This indicates that insulin acts prior to the oxidative decarboxylation of pyruvate and does not accelerate the conversion of acetate to fatty acid. Thus the incorporation of acetate rises only when glycolysis and hence the formation of α-glycerophosphate and ATP is promoted.

As in muscle, the incorporation of amino acids into the protein of adipose tissue is increased by insulin *in vitro*. This occurs if an energy source, e.g. pyruvate or glucose is present, although the insulin has no observed effect on pyruvate metabolism. Protein formation in both tissues is also promoted by growth hormone but inhibited by adrenocorticoid hormones. Carbon skeletons derived from amino acids by transamination can also be traced to the TG stores.

The pathways of glucose utilization have been studied in adipose tissue. The activities of the enzymes involved when expressed per mg of tissue N are usually one-third to one-fifth those of liver, but the enzymes for gluconeogenesis are absent and glucose-6-phosphate dehydrogenase is nearly six times as active as in liver. Comparison of ^{14}CO$_2$ formed when equal amounts of 1-^{14}C-glucose and 6-^{14}C-glucose were added to the incubation medium show that the hexose monophosphate pathway is active in adipose tissue. However, this does not appear to be the exclusive source of the large quantity of NADPH$_2$ required for fatty acid synthesis by the tissue (p. 10.13).

From incoming lipid

Both plasma lipoproteins and chylomicrons deposit some of their TG fatty acids in adipose tissue. The former are derived from the TG synthesized in the liver from fatty acids, while the chylomicrons originate in the intestine. Labelled FFA injected into human subjects have also been found 10 min later incorporated in the adipose tissue TG. However, this source of preformed fatty acid is quantitatively less important than the other two.

Most of the plasma TG taken up by adipose tissue is probably first hydrolysed to FFA and glycerol. The glycerol and the phospholipid, cholesterol and protein, which formed the shell of the lipoprotein, remain in the blood while the FFA enter the fat cell. There they are reconverted to TG by condensation with α-glycerophosphate formed within the cell from carbohydrate. As more TG fatty acid is taken up from the blood in the fed than in the fasted state, i.e. under conditions when lipoprotein lipase activity is known to be high (p. 10.12), this enzyme has been implicated in the hydrolytic process.

An adequate supply of blood glucose is of importance in the transfer of triglyceride FA from the plasma into the adipose cell. It promotes the re-esterification of the liberated FFA intermediates and also maintains the activity of lipoprotein lipase, perhaps by stimulating the secretion of insulin by the pancreas. When plasma lipoprotein labelled in the fatty acid moieties of the TG is perfused through rat adipose tissue, the FFA liberated by this process does not appear to mix with those of the blood. Consequently it has been suggested that hydrolysis of lipoprotein TG occurs within the fat cell rather than in the vascular bed, but this question has not yet been settled.

How TG enters the adipose cell from the capillaries is unknown. While lipid has been demonstrated by EM studies to pass through and between the epithelial cells of the intestine into the vascular and lymphatic systems, none is seen in the endothelial cells of the capillaries en route to or from the adipose cell. Investigators have concluded that the lipid observed adhering to the walls of the blood vessel passes through the perivascular space to the adipocyte in a manner not visualized by the EM. This could be as FFA bound to albumin or as micelles. It is possible that the small droplets seen at the periphery of the fat cell constitute the active TG compartment which

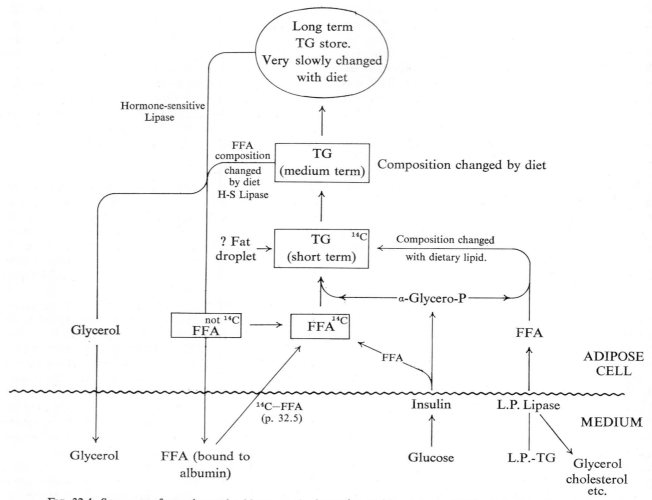

FIG. 32.4. Summary of experimental evidence on the formation and breakdown of TG within the adipose cell.

is functionally separate from the inert storage pool (fig. 32.4).

Under physiological conditions the major part of the fatty acid laid down as TG in adipose tissue is probably derived from plasma lipoprotein rather than by synthesis from glucose.

Composition of lipid stored in adipose tissue

The relative proportion of the major fatty acids derived by hydrolysis of adipose tissue from young healthy adults fed a random diet are as follows:

Fatty acid	Per cent of total
$C_{14:0}$	2·4
$C_{16:0}$	26·7
$C_{16:1}$	3·8
$C_{18:0}$	4·2
$C_{18:1}$	52·8
$C_{18:2}$	7·3
$C_{20:4}$	0·2

Six fatty acids account for 97 per cent of those present. The figure for arachidonic acid ($C_{20:4}$) is given so that a comparison may be made with liver where it amounts to almost 10 per cent of the fatty acid in the total lipid. The ratio of saturated to unsaturated fatty acids in adipose tissue TG is normally 1 : 2 in man. Saturated acids form a higher proportion in the ox and sheep which form a major dietary source of triglyceride for man.

Altering the dietary lipid slowly changes the pattern of fatty acids in the stores over a period of many months. A fat free diet produces no change within 10 weeks; a difference is observed only after 20 weeks of a diet containing 40 per cent of the calories as corn oil in which 50 per cent of the fatty acid is linoleic acid ($C_{18:2}$). As the stores do not closely resemble the dietary fat until about 160 weeks of the altered regime, it is apparent that most of the dietary fat does not mix readily with the main pool within the tissue. The half life of this store is calculated to be 1–2 years, while complete mixing of incoming TG FA in the total 10 kg of fat in a normal man would be expected to occur in 50 days if there was one uniform pool. This suggests the existence of an inert depot of TG and a small active compartment within the tissue (fig. 32.4). The serum TG alter rapidly and correspond with those ingested and hence can be in equilibrium with only a small tissue pool. Enzymes present in the intestine and liver and in the adipose tissue can elongate and desaturate dietary TG FA and help to maintain the pattern characteristic of the species. Nevertheless it is possible to alter the fatty acid composition of the fat depots if weight is being gained while on a diet of abnormal lipid composition. There is no change during weight loss, suggesting no preferential loss of particular fatty acids from the hydrolysed TG.

The composition of the fatty acid mixtures derived from samples of TG from various sites in an individual is similar; there is little difference between men and women and no change occurs with increasing age. Fatty acids are not distributed randomly in triglyceride molecules but in the following pattern:

$$CH_2OCO\text{-saturated chain}$$
$$|$$
$$CHOCO\text{-unsaturated chain}$$
$$|$$
$$CH_2OCO\text{-saturated or unsaturated chain}$$

This may result from specificity in the triglyceride synthesizing enzymes.

Release of FFA from fat stores

FFA are present in adipose tissue to the extent of $1-2\ \mu Eq/g$ in a fed rat and $2-3\ \mu Eq/g$ in a fasted animal. Reference has already been made to the rise in the plasma FFA level which occurs in the fasting human subject. FFA are liberated from the stores by the action of at least two enzymes, a triglyceride lipase and a monoglyceride lipase. The former is unable to hydrolyse lipoprotein substrates, in contrast to lipoprotein lipase from which it also differs in its response to activators and inhibitors. The triglyceride lipase may consist of two separate enzymes for attacking triglycerides and diglycerides successively. The monoglyceride lipase, being the more active enzyme, prevents the accumulation of monoglycerides. None of the adipose tissue lipases has been isolated in a highly purified form, probably due to their close association with structural lipoprotein. Glycerol the other product of hydrolysis is also carried away in the blood stream to the liver. It is unlikely that it is phosphorylated by adipose tissue to regenerate α-glycerophosphate to an important extent, as the necessary glycerokinase is present in only small amounts. In consequence esterification of fatty acids and therefore storage of triglyceride within adipose tissue only occurs when there is an adequate supply of α-glycerophosphate derived from glucose.

The FFA when released from TG are probably bound to cytoplasmic protein. They pass into an intracellular pool and then either leave the cell bound to plasma albumin, which makes them water soluble, or are re-esterified to TG (fig. 32.4).

FFA entering the cell from the plasma may not need to pass through this pool, but perhaps can be esterified directly close to the cell membrane. Some evidence for this was obtained from experiments in which adipose tissue was incubated with ^{14}C-FFA, which entered the cells and was found in the TG. The tissue was then immediately transferred to fresh buffer under conditions promoting lipolysis. Since the FFA released were not labelled, different molecules must be involved in short term formation and breakdown of TG (fig. 32.4). However, *in vivo* work shows that within a few days of altering dietary lipids, the FFA released into the plasma are similar in composition to those in the dietary TG. This is best explained by assuming the existence of a second longer term compartment of TG into which the newly-formed molecules pass and from which they are released after hydrolysis. This compartment may be simply those parts of the tissue lying near the blood vessels and need not be the compartment into which the TG is taken up intact in the *in vitro* experiment described earlier.

When isolated fat cells are homogenized and centrifuged the infranatant layer contains lipid droplets, resembling chylomicrons in size. If the cells have been previously incubated with ^{14}C-glucose, the specific activity of this lipid fraction is consistently higher than that of the fat which lies on top, but less than that of the microsomes and mitochondria. Hence these droplets may be newly-synthesized lipid in transit to the stores, which form the upper fatty layer in a centrifugate (fig. 32.4).

The activity of the enzyme involved in splitting TG stored in adipose tissue is enhanced manyfold by certain hormones. Hence it is named hormone-sensitive lipase, which differentiates it from lipoprotein lipase. This response is most clearly shown by a rapid increase in the glycerol present in the blood, or incubation medium. There is a concomitant rise in the output of FFA but as these, unlike glycerol, can be re-utilized in adipose tissue, the analytical data for FFA provide only a net picture, i.e. the difference between the quantity produced by hydrolysis of the TG and that disappearing due to re-esterification by α-glycerophosphate within the tissue. *In vitro*, provided glucose is not added, the ratio of change in FFA/change in glycerol for the total system (tissue plus medium) is approximately 3/1, corresponding to complete hydrolysis and no re-esterification. With glucose the ratio is lower. However, when isolated adipose tissue is perfused with diluted blood containing a lipolytic hormone, the ratio is found to be 5/1 to 7/1, provided the albumin content of the infusate is sufficiently high. The diglyceride content of the tissue is enhanced as well as the release of FFA and glycerol. This suggests that under conditions where the released FFA is efficiently carried away from the fat cells, 50 per cent is derived from partial hydrolysis to diglyceride. This is probably the situation *in vivo*. Similar high values have been found in human blood taken soon after exercise.

The lipase system, which probably resides in the microsomes, attacks all three positions in the TG molecule equally, in contrast to pancreatic lipase. Monoglyceride lipase does not appear to be under hormonal control.

The FFA released from isolated tissue consist of the seven major acids. The proportions of FFA found in the cell, relative to those in the total TG are highest for $C_{16:0}$ and $C_{16:1}$, and lowest for $C_{18:1}$ and $C_{18:2}$ acids. This may be due to an enzymic preference for the C_{16} acids. The fatty acid mixture which leaves the cells contains a higher proportion of the unsaturated acids and $C_{14:0}$ than is present in the cell, probably due to their higher solubility in the aqueous environment or to a lower affinity for cellular binding sites than the other saturated acids.

LIPOLYTIC HORMONES

The hormones known to activate the hormone sensitive lipase are adrenaline, noradrenaline, glucagon, ACTH vasopressin and 5HT. These also increase the activity of the glycogenolytic enzyme, phosphorylase. In addition the catecholamines appear to stimulate the uptake and utilization of glucose which promotes the removal of the FFA by re-esterification. The net effect, however, is an enhanced output of FFA from the tissue to the blood.

An increase in plasma glycerol and FFA also occurs in animals and man if sufficient growth hormone or cortisol is injected to achieve a high circulating hormone level. This response occurs very much more slowly than that due to catecholamines, which produce an effect on lipolysis within seconds after administration. The fast-acting hormones seem to activate an existing lipase or remove an inactivator. In contrast growth hormone and the adreno-corticoid hormones appear to promote the synthesis of more of the hormone sensitive lipase.

The activation of phosphorylase in liver and muscle by adrenaline has been shown to occur indirectly via stimulation of cyclic $3',5'$-AMP formation from ATP by adenyl cyclase associated with the cell membrane (p. 9.9). A cell-free extract of the cyclase from adipose tissue also promotes cyclic AMP formation in response to adrenaline. It is possible that the lipase is activated in a similar manner to phosphorylase, since the intracellular levels of lipase activity and of accumulated cyclic AMP both depend on the amount of adrenaline present, and are both increased by caffeine, which prevents the destruction of cyclic AMP. Addition of a more soluble derivative of cyclic AMP to isolated adipose tissue or free fat cells has

promoted FFA release, suggesting that cyclic AMP here too may be the intracellular mediator of hormonal action.

The hormones which activate the TG lipase under physiological conditions are probably noradrenaline, the adrenocorticoids and growth hormone. The other fast acting ones listed above have to be provided *in vitro* at too high concentration to be considered of physiological importance.

NERVOUS CONTROL

The nerve supply to adipose tissue plays a leading role in facilitating fat mobilization. Lipolysis and the increase in plasma FFA which occurs in the fasted subject is reduced after ganglionic and adrenergic blocking drugs are given. As these compounds also diminish the mobilization of fat in response to cold and psychological stress the nervous mechanism appears in part to involve noradrenaline release at the postganglionic sympathetic nerve endings. The fibres of the autonomic nerves terminate in close relation to the fat cells as well as the blood vessels. This innervation exerts a continuous control of the normal metabolism of the tissue, which is invoked in emergency states.

PROVISION OF FFA AS METABOLIC FUEL

The amount of FFA liberated from adipose tissue and transported to the peripheral tissues as a potential source of energy is the resultant of two processes operating in opposite directions: (1) FFA mobilization by lipolysis and (2) FFA re-esterification within the adipose tissue. The net release depends on which predominates at a particular time. The first process is influenced by the activity of the lipolytic hormones. There are antilipolytic hormones which oppose lipolysis in tissue in which TG lipase activity is raised. They include the prostaglandins formed from essential fatty acids (p. 25.47) and insulin, which even in the absence of glucose diminishes the enhanced output of glycerol and FFA from free fat cells incubated with noradrenaline. These hormones prevent the formation of cyclic AMP, the activator of the lipase. On the other hand the thyroid hormones promote the formation of cyclic AMP and reduce its rate of destruction (fig. 32.5). As a consequence the size of the lipolytic response to noradrenaline depends also on the quantity of thyroid hormones in the circulation. This provides an explanation for the low serum FFA levels after thyroidectomy and the high values in the hyperthyroid patient. In normal man, lower glycerol content of the blood after a glucose load is probably due to the consequent increased output of insulin by the pancreas, for the rate of removal of glycerol from the blood is not altered. However, provision of glucose within the cell, dependent on an adequate blood glucose level and the presence of circulating insulin, promotes a second process by providing α-glycerophosphate which also

FIG. 32.5. Mechanisms for increasing the activity of hormone-sensitive triglyceride lipase.

suppresses FFA release. Of consequence too, is the property of adrenocorticoid hormones of depressing the utilization of glucose by fat cells.

The mobilization or retention of FFA by the adipose tissue stores is therefore dependent on nutritional factors and the presence or absence of stress. Control is achieved by the ability of the body to alter the rate of blood flow through the tissue and to secrete the appropriate hormones.

Activity of the adipose cell under various physiological conditions

During absorption of carbohydrate and fat, TG are laid down in the fat stores. The plasma FFA level is low. Carbohydrate is used as the principal metabolic fuel and the major part of such TG as breaks down within the stores is regenerated. This continues until the blood glucose falls towards the fasting level.

During fasting FFA is increasingly mobilized from the adipose tissue. This is produced partly by stimulating the hormone sensitive lipase through release of catecholamines. Decreased availability of glucose to the cell due to the low blood concentration, a falling rate of insulin secretation and eventually the rise in circulating adrenocorticoid hormones also play important parts. Contributory factors may also be growth hormone, glucagon and a fat mobilizing substance isolated from the urine of fasting individuals and probably of pituitary origin.

The resulting rise in plasma FFA during fasting leads to their increased utilization, e.g. by the liver which resynthesizes TG, part of which appears as additional plasma lipoprotein. Fat becomes the main source of energy and the RQ falls to around 0·75. Gluconeogenesis besides providing carbohydrate for the nervous system acts as a brake on lipid mobilization by promoting insulin secretion. This leads to some reformation of TG and their return to the stores. Nevertheless, ketosis and triglyceridaemia eventually occur (p. 10.25). These changes are less frequently observed in the severely obese, perhaps because their output of growth hormone tends to rise to a smaller extent in response to fasting than in normal individuals.

Stress, such as fear, sudden cold, etc., results in rapid release of catecholamines with consequent activation of the hormone sensitive lipase. Stress also leads to secretion of increased amounts of ACTH and hence of adrenocorticoid hormones. The latter besides their gluconeogenic and glucose sparing effects slowly promote lipase formation. Thus an increased supply of FFA reaches the liver, muscles, etc., to provide the extra energy required in stressful situations.

The normal response to noradrenaline and to cold, in terms of increased lipase or phosphorylase action is not observed in adrenalectomized animals. It has been suggested that this is due to an adverse electrolyte pattern within the fat cell. Recovery is complete if cortisol is given and restored to 50 per cent of normal by giving saline or aldosterone. Phosphorylase activity was also restored in extracts of muscle from adrenalectomized animals by adding cyclic AMP. Hence the lesion may be an inability to form this compound leading to poor resistance to cold.

Exercise, even at a moderate level in fasting man produces a fall in plasma FFA within 10 min of onset. The level then rises, even in hypophysectomized or adrenalectomized individuals. The plasma glycerol concentration which is also enhanced can be reduced by administration of glucose or nicotinic acid, a compound which prevents

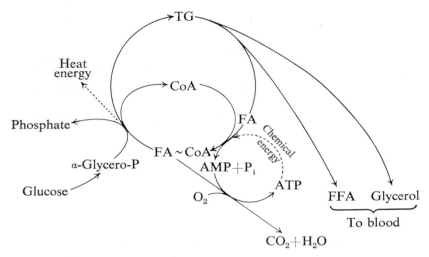

FIG. 32.6. Chemical processes involved in non-shivering thermogenesis in brown fat of infants. Modified from Dawkins N.J. & Hall D. (1965). *Scientific American*, **213**, 2.

the lipolytic effect of noradrenaline. This is consistent with the increased activity of the sympathetic nervous system during exercise. During the initial stage the primary adjustments are cardiovascular, causing an increased blood flow, and hence removal of FFA from the plasma. The reverse situation exists during the recovery stage. The RQ may fall to as low as 0·75, indicating the utilization of fat for provision of muscular energy. Some of this is not derived from the adipose tissue, but from TG lying between the muscle fibres. TG may also be taken up in greater amount from plasma lipoprotein by muscle.

INFANCY

The newborn infant overcomes his inability to shiver by using his supply of brown adipose tissue (p. 39.6). This, like white fat is a store of TG from which FFA are liberated in response to cold, noradrenaline, glucagon, etc. It differs by containing large numbers of mitochondria which are packed with cristae. As a result it has a higher rate of oxygen consumption due to its ability to burn FA locally.

The process involved in non-shivering thermogenesis can be visualized as follows (fig. 32.6). TG are hydrolysed to glycerol which escapes to the blood, and to FFA which is largely re-esterified within the tissue. The latter process involves formation of fatty acyl CoA and then replacement of the CoA by a glycerol moiety derived from blood glucose. Thus a cyclic series of reactions occurs in which a molecule of ATP is used to form the energy rich fatty acyl CoA. This is then broken with liberation of the energy as heat. Therefore, as each molecule of FA passes round the cycle, one ATP molecule is converted to heat. The ATP is generated by oxidizing some of the FA but since 1 palmityl CoA theoretically yields 131 ATP, only a small fraction of the liberated FA is oxidized rather than esterified. It is the presence of this small fraction of oxidized FA which is reflected in the raised oxygen consumption of brown fat in response to catecholamines. The TG–FA cycle is operative also to a small extent when FA of white fat is oxidized within the tissue, but their major outlet is export to the liver and other organs.

Brown fat becomes less important in the maintenance of temperature as the child develops neuromuscular control and the ability to call on heat energy associated with muscular activity.

Conclusion

Adipose tissue is an organ whose primary function is the storage of long chain fatty acids, potential sources of metabolic energy. These long hydrocarbon chains are deposited or withdrawn by precise nervous and hormonal control in order to overcome the fluctuations in nutritional and environmental conditions to which man may be subjected.

FURTHER READING

RENOLD, A.E. & CAHILL, G.F. eds. (1965) American Physiological Society's *Handbook of Physiology*, section 5, Adipose Tissue.

Chapter 33
The kidney

he structure and function of the mammalian kidney present the outcome of a long sequence of evolutionary changes. These have made it possible for complex organisms to live on dry land where water and salts must be conserved, waste products excreted in a concentrated form, nd tissue fluid regulated with respect to volume, chemical omposition and osmolality. The primitive ancestors of ne vertebrates, who lived in the brackish waters of the stuaries during the Cambrian period, were faced with the eed to conserve sodium and eliminate water. In response the need to excrete water, a filtering device developed onsisting of a coil of capillaries invaginated into the blind nd of a hollow tube. Under the influence of the arterial ressure, water and solutes were filtered through the capil-ry walls into the lumen of the tube where selective eabsorption of electrolytes and essential metabolites ccurred before the remainder of the filtrate drained to the xterior.

In the mammalian kidney the formation of urine still egins with the production of an ultrafiltrate of plasma and ach day a volume of fluid almost fifteen times the volume f the blood plasma is transferred by ultrafiltration from ne vascular system to the renal tubules. By far the greater art of this large volume of fluid, together with its salts, is eabsorbed by the cells lining the renal tubules and re-urned to the blood. This process involves a large number f complex chemical, physical and electrochemical mech-nisms which adjust the composition and the amount of ne fluid reabsorbed and so maintain the volume and the omposition of the body fluids within normal limits. The emainder of the filtered water, together with the waste roducts of metabolism and surplus salts, is excreted from ne body as urine (p. 5.27). The kidneys are therefore al-ost entirely responsible for the maintenance of the *milieu térieur*; while possessing some degree of autonomy, nese organs are under nervous and chemical control.

ANATOMY

he kidneys are paired organs and in the adult each eighs about 120–170 g. Their shape is so well known nat their name has passed into the common vocabulary.

They lie retroperitoneally and are loosely attached to the posterior abdominal wall by fat. In life their position is variable and they move with respiration. In the cadaver the hilum is usually opposite the second lumbar vertebra, the upper and lower poles reaching the twelfth thoracic and third lumbar vertebrae respectively. They are surrounded by a condensation of the retroperitoneal tissue, the renal fascia, which blends medially with the fascia over the psoas muscle and merges with the fascia around the renal vessels and ureters. Capping the upper pole of each kidney and enclosed within the fascia is an adrenal gland. The kidneys are covered by a tough almost inextensible capsule which in health is smooth and glistening. Blood vessels and nerves enter and leave the kidney and the ureter emerges at the hilum which is on the concave medial side. Fig. 33.1 shows a coronal section of the kidneys. The **renal cortex** is the paler, finely granular, outer region, while the **renal medulla** consists mainly of the **renal pyramids** which are striated columns of darker tissue continuous with the cortex. The apices of the pyramids project as renal papillae towards the renal pelvis. The ureter receives the urine from the

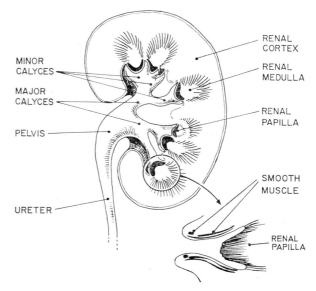

FIG. 33.1. Coronal section of the kidney.

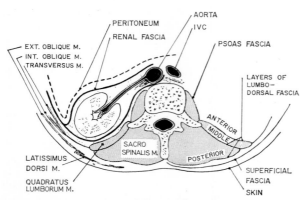

FIG. 33.2. A transverse section showing muscles on the left and fascial relations on the right.

renal pelvis, a funnel-shaped structure, the wall of which consists of muscle and connective tissue lined by transitional epithelium. The pelvis divides into several recesses or **calyces** which cover the tips of the renal papillae and are invaginated by them. At the papillary tips are the minute openings of the collecting tubules through which urine enters the recesses of the pelvis before passing to the ureter. The onward flow of urine is helped by rhythmical contractions of the smooth muscle in the walls of the calyces and pelvis.

The relations of the kidney are shown in figs. 33.2–5. Both kidneys are related posteriorly to the diaphragm, and to the muscles of the posterior wall of the abdomen, psoas, quadratus lumborum and transversus. The tips of the transverse processes of the first lumbar vertebra are also closely related to the kidneys. As fig. 33.3 shows, the kidneys extend up to the eleventh or twelfth rib so that, behind the diaphragm, the pleural cavities are posterior relations. The subcostal nerves and subcostal vessels and

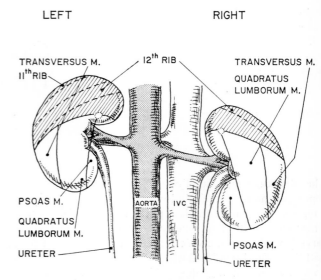

FIG. 33.4. The posterior relations of the kidneys. Shaded areas on both kidneys are in contact with the diaphragm.

the first lumbar nerves and vessels are close posterior re lations of both organs. More distant posterior relation are the sacrospinalis muscle, latissimus dorsi and parts of the external and internal oblique muscles.

The anterior relations of the kidneys are shown in fig 33.5. The left part of the body of the pancreas crosses th left kidney. Above this the kidney is covered by the per toneum of the lesser sac and lies behind the stomach. Th convex lateral part of the left kidney makes a large ren: impression on the spleen. Below the pancreas the kidne is covered by peritoneum of the greater omentum and is re lated to coils of jejunum. The peritoneum over the anterio surface of the pancreas is reflected across the kidney t form the **lienorenal ligament**. The upper part of the ante rior surface of the right kidney is closely related to th bare area of the liver while the duodenum covers the med

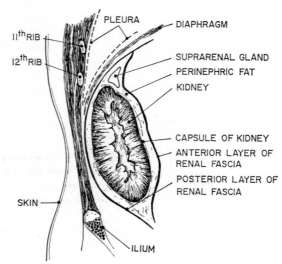

FIG. 33.3. A parasagittal section through the posterior abdominal wall.

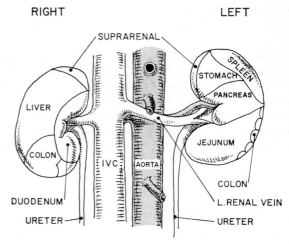

FIG. 33.5. The anterior relations of the kidneys.

l part. The right flexure of the colon and the beginning
' the transverse colon are in direct contact with the
iddle and lower lateral parts. Coils of small intestine
e related to the lower pole, but are separated from it
' peritoneum.

Microscopic structure

ach kidney is composed of a compact mass of about one
illion units called **nephrons** (fig. 33.6). After birth no

JUXTAMEDULLARY NEPHRON   CORTICAL NEPHRON   INTERMEDIATE NEPHRON

ORTEX

UTER VR ONE OF EDULLA H

NER ONE OF EDULLA

PAPILLA

FIG. 33.6. Diagram of nephrons and their blood supply. A
and V, arcuate artery and vein; C, collecting duct; H, thin
part of Henle's loop; VR, vasa recta; I, cell from proximal
convolution; II, cell from distal convolution; III, cell from
thin part of Henle's loop; IV, cell from collecting duct; N,
nucleus. Luminal surface is below, peritubular surface
above.

ew nephrons develop, though in certain circumstances
ae existing ones may enlarge. Each nephron consists of
small tuft of capillaries called a **glomerulus**, to which is
tached a thin tubule. Glomeruli are found only in the
ortex of the kidney while the tubules comprise the bulk
f the cortex and medulla. The glomerulus is surrounded
y a thin membrane of epithelial cells called after its dis-
overer, **Bowman's capsule**, and this is separated from the
omerulus by a narrow **capsular** or **Bowman's space**. The
apsule and glomerulus together are often named the
Ialpighian body** after the seventeenth century Italian who
rst described them. The **tubule** begins as a continuation
f the space around the capillary tuft and the capsular
oithelium is continuous with the cells lining the tubules.
ach tubule is 20–45 mm in length, coiled in parts and
aarply folded on itself in one place; it empties into a
ollecting duct shared by six to ten other nephrons. The
rst part of each tubule twists and coils to form the
roximal convoluted tubule (plate 33.1a, facing p. 28.29);

after straightening out to form the **pars recta** it then passes
into the medulla. There the tubules run straight for a
varying distance before making a sharp hairpin bend,
the **loop of Henle**, and return to the cortex in the neighbourhood of the glomeruli from which they arose; here
they again become coiled upon one another and form
the **distal convoluted tubules**.

Although all nephrons possess the same general configuration, they differ in their blood supply and in the
length of the loop of Henle. Most of the glomeruli are
located in the more superficial part of the cortex, and have
short loops which do not penetrate deeply into the medullary zone. About 15 per cent lie in the juxtamedullary
region of the cortex and to these are attached tubules
possessing long thin loops which pass deeply into the
medulla sometimes extending as far as the papillae before
they return to the cortex.

The distal convoluted tubules ultimately run more or
less parallel to the outer surface of the kidney to join a
collecting duct. These pass through the medulla and join
together with other collecting ducts to form larger ducts
which open into the pelvis of the kidney on the surface of
a papilla.

The tubule is by no means uniform in structure along
its length. The flat thin epithelium of Bowman's capsule
is replaced by low columnar cells in the proximal convolution. Under the light microscope the luminal surface
of these cells appears as a brush border. The EM shows
that this brush border consists of many thousands
of long, closely packed microvilli which project into the
lumen of the tubule. On the contraluminal side, the
basal surface of the cells is deeply indented and in the
cytoplasm between the indentations lie numerous
mitochondria (fig. 33.6). This type of cell continues
beyond the convolution into the pars recta. In the descending limb of the loop of Henle, the cells are thin and
flat. In all nephrons soon after the hairpin loop the cells
become cuboidal and possess basal invaginations and only
a few short villi on the luminal aspect. This type of cell
continues into the distal convolution which is shorter than
the proximal. The walls of the collecting ducts have low
cuboidal cells with central nuclei.

Embryology
The early development of the genitourinary system is
given on p. 18.17 and the formation of the mature kidney
on p. 34.1.

Blood supply
Renal arteries arise from the aorta opposite the second
lumbar vertebra and enter the hila of the kidneys. The
right renal artery passes behind the inferior vena cava. At
the hila the arteries divide into anterior and posterior
branches which further divide to form the **interlobar
arteries** lying between the medullary pyramids. When

these vessels reach the corticomedullary junction they lie parallel to the surface of the kidney and are called **arcuate arteries**. From these the **interlobular arteries** arise at right angles and penetrate the cortex radially giving off short side branches, the **glomerular afferent arterioles**. Each arteriole runs a short distance before it breaks up into the capillaries of the glomerulus. Here there are many anastomoses and the capillaries are arranged in loops. These reunite to form the **efferent arteriole** which is in close proximity to the point of entry of the afferent vessel. In the main cortical region the efferent vessel is always of narrower diameter than the afferent; in the juxtamedullary region the two vessels are of the same width (plate 33.1b & c facing p. 28.29). The efferent arteriole breaks up into a second set of capillaries which forms an anastomosing network closely applied to the proximal and distal convoluted tubules both of their own and of neighbouring nephrons. The capillaries coming from the efferent arterioles of juxtamedullary glomeruli form leashes of straight vessels called **vasa recta** (fig. 33.6). They run towards and through the medulla in close contact with the loops of Henle, and like the tubules make a hairpin bend to empty into the arcuate veins near the corticomedullary junction. There are anastomoses between the descending and ascending vessels. Transverse sections show the close intermingling of blood vessels and tubules which occasionally share a common basement membrane. Thus all tubules receive blood which has first passed through a glomerulus. Blood from the cortex and medulla passes

to the arcuate veins at the corticomedullary junction. These drain towards the hilum and into the renal vein.

Juxtaglomerular apparatus (JGA)

On the afferent arteriole close to its entry into the glomerulus, lying between it and a coil of the distal convolution of the same nephron, is the juxtaglomerular apparatus (fig. 33.7). The smooth muscle cells of the afferent arteriole enlarge to form an asymmetrical cushion or cuff at the vascular pole of the glomerulus which is separated from the blood stream by the endothelium. The cells contain granules and appear to be secretory. Beside this cushion of cells, those of the distal convolution change their character and become columnar with large prominent nuclei, and are referred to as the **macula densa**. In addition, a third type of cell is sometimes present in the form of small islets of epithelial cells adjacent to the afferent arteriole. Nothing is known about the function of the cells of tubular origin though it has been suggested that they may be involved in the control of sodium excretion. The function of the epithelial cell islets is also not known. The cells arising from the arteriolar smooth muscle are probably the source of renin, and their function is discussed on p. 33.18.

Lymphatics

The cortex has many lymphatics, some of which drain outwards to the capsule and others towards the corticomedullary junction. In the medulla, lymph channels run from the apex of the pyramids to the corticomedullary junction. From there larger lymphatic channels pass along the main blood vessels to the hilum and drain into the para-aortic lymph nodes.

Nerve Supply

The kidney is supplied with sympathetic nerves derived from the thoracic to the lumbar segments of the sympathetic trunk; most of them arise from the spinal cord between T12 and L2. The majority reach the kidney through the pre-aortic ganglia where they synapse. There are probably no parasympathetic nerves. The sympathetic fibres pass to the smooth muscle of renal blood vessels, particularly that of the afferent and efferent arterioles, and to the JGA. The cortex has many more nerves than the medulla. Afferent fibres arise in the kidney and ultimately enter the dorsal roots of T12 to L2. The nerves to the arterioles can exert a vasoconstrictor effect.

FUNCTIONS OF THE KIDNEYS

The kidneys are concerned in a number of activities, which include the removal of nitrogenous waste, mostly in the form of urea, maintenance of electrolyte and water

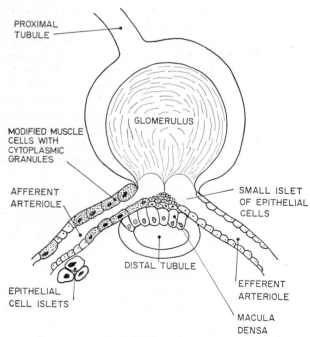

FIG. 33.7. Juxtaglomerular apparatus. Adapted from Cook W.F. (1963) in *Hormones and the Kidney*, ed. Williams. P. London: Academic Press.

d

PLATE 33.2. The structure of the capillary wall of the human glomerulus.

art of a glomerular capillary wall showing, (a) pedicel structure (P), basement membrane (BM), (c) pedicels with well-defined slit membranes ndicated by arrow; (b) endothelium lining internal aspect of the basement membrane showing several fenestrae (pores) indicated by arrow; d) tangential section of glomerular capillary showing endothelial fenestrae indicated by arrows.

PLATE 35.1. The histological appearances of the skin at various body surfaces
(a) back, (b) sole, (c) abdomen, (d) axilla, (e) scalp, (f) face.

Note the very thick layer of stratum corneum on the sole (b). The abdominal skin sample (c) contains a sweat gland but no hairs are included. The face (f) and scalp (e) contain large sebaceous glands and the axilla (d) shows apocrine sweat glands in the lower part of the field.

alance and regulation of the acid-base balance. In addi-on, two chemical substances are released into the blood. ne of these is the enzyme renin which is indirectly con-erned with electrolyte balance (p. 33.21). The second sub-tance may be a precursor of erythropoietin (p. 26.10) or a ubstance responsible for its formation. Without kidneys r treatment with an artificial kidney a man would die in bout 14–21 days. Thus, unravelling the function of the arious parts of this organ is as important as it is difficult.

There has been a variety of conflicting ideas about how ie kidney manufactures urine from blood plasma. owman (1842) and Ludwig (1844) both thought that fil-ation occurred in the Malpighian body but they differed their views over the function of the rest of the nephron. owman thought that the tubules secreted substances into ie urine, and Ludwig believed them to reabsorb some of ie filtrate. In 1874, Heidenhain proposed that the glom-ruli secreted water and salts and that other substances ere added by tubular secretion. This argument was not ettled until 1917 when Cushny published a famous mono-raph on the secretion of urine. He supported the idea, by ien fairly generally held, that urine formation began with process of simple ultrafiltration from the glomerular apillaries into the capsular space and suggested that iereafter tubular reabsorption could account for all the nown facts. In addition, he suggested that substances in ie glomerular filtrate could be divided into two groups. he first group consisted of substances such as glucose hich, after filtration, are completely reabsorbed pro-ded that the plasma concentration is below a certain ritical level. These were called **threshold substances.** In ie second group were unwanted, waste, no-threshold sub-ances which were not reabsorbed completely and which ere largely excreted in the urine. It was also assumed iat the renal tubules absorbed a fluid of constant com-osition resembling protein-free plasma. While it is now nown that this view is inaccurate, Cushny's book was nportant in that it summarized the evidence for and gainst many hypotheses, and put forward a theory of rine formation based on the concept of glomerular filtra-on and tubular reabsorption which could be tested. rom 1926 onwards Marshall published a series of papers which he showed that tubular secretion also occurs. A ajor advance took place in 1925 when Richards and his olleagues developed microtechniques by which fluid ould be collected from Bowman's capsule and individual ibules and analysed. This technique demonstrated rectly the reality of glomerular filtration and also showed at reabsorption was far more complex than had pre-ously been suspected.

Present concepts may be briefly summarized as follows. large volume of ultrafiltrate of plasma is produced by e glomerulus. As this passes from Bowman's capsule ong the proximal convolution most of the salt and water reabsorbed. Some substances are reabsorbed com-

30

pletely and others only partially. Thus, this part of the tubule roughly separates the substances which must be conserved from those which are to be rejected in the urine. Thereafter, the loop of Henle, the distal convolution and the collecting ducts are concerned mainly with the fine regulation of water, electrolyte and hydrogen ion balance. The processes involved in tubular reabsorption and secretion are chemical and physical and are under hormonal control.

GLOMERULAR FILTRATION

The importance of Richards' contribution lay in the fact that for the first time direct evidence was presented to show that urine formation begins by ultrafiltration. If the capsular fluid is an ultrafiltrate of plasma then it should contain all the substances present in plasma except the colloids and fats, and the substances passing the glomerular capillaries should be present in identical concentrations in both plasma and filtrate. Richards' studies were carried out on the frog and the South American mud puppy or *necturus*. Frog kidney is a thin elongated organ and transillumination under a dissecting microscope shows up many of the glomeruli and some parts of the tubules. Fine micropipettes were inserted into the capsular space and the fluid accumulating there was collected. To prevent contamination by retrograde flow of tubular fluid, the tubules were blocked below the capsule either by pressure from a glass rod or by injection of globules of mercury (fig. 33.8). The results showed clearly that the

FIG. 33.8. Illustrating the insertion of a micropipette for collection of tubule fluid from the beginning (A), the middle (B), and the distal (C) end of a proximal convoluted tubule of *Necturus*. Stippling at A represents a globule of mercury, stippling at B a column of coloured oil. From Richards A.N. & Walker A.M. (1937) *Amer. J. Physiol.* **118,** 111.

fluid taken from the capsules is almost protein free, in isosmotic with plasma and contains glucose, urea, creatinine, uric acid and the electrolytes of the blood. These observations left no doubt that in the frog and necturus capsular fluid was an ultrafiltrate of plasma (fig. 33.9). Some years later the difficulty of collecting capsular and tubular fluid from the more compact and less translucent mammalian kidney was overcome, and it has now been

FIG. 33.9 Showing that glomerular filtrate and proximal tubular fluid is essentially identical with plasma with regard to chloride concentration and osmotic pressure. Reabsorption of chloride occurs in distal tubule. From Walker A.M. *et al.* (1937) *Amer. J. Physiol.* **118**, 121.

FIG. 33.10. Ultrastructure of a glomerular capillary; (1) fenestrated capillary endothelium; (2) fenestrae (pores); (3) endothelial cell; (4) basement membrane; (5) epithelial cell (podocyte); (6) pedicel. Adapted from Pease D.C. (1955) *Histol. and Cytol.* **3**, 295.

shown that the capsular fluid is an ultrafiltrate of plasma in the rat, guinea-pig and dog. The observation that neither a reduction in temperature nor poisoning with cyanide affects the formation of this fluid indicates that it is produced by physical means.

Before considering this mechanism it is appropriate to discuss the structure of the glomerular capillary wall. It consists of two layers of cells and a basement membrane which lies between them. Endothelial cells line the capillary and constitute the endothelium. These cells lie on the basement membrane, which is covered externally by the **pedicels** (foot processes) of the highly specialized epithelial cells called **podocytes** (Greek, *podos*—a foot). Electron microscope examination shows that the cytoplasm of the endothelial cell contains irregularly placed rounded apertures or **fenestrae** which vary considerably in size, the majority being between 50 nm and 100 nm in diameter. Thus, they are sufficiently small to prevent blood cells passing out of the capillaries, but plainly do not hold back the protein molecules. The basement membrane is a homogeneous and continuous layer of mucopolysaccharide and glycoprotein gel, about 300 nm in thickness. The podocytes give off trabeculae which divide into fine pedicels and these lie against the outer aspect of the basement membrane. The processes from one cell interdigitate with those from a neighbouring one and between them are slit like spaces about 10 nm across (plate 33.2, facing p. 33.4 and fig. 33.10).

The glomerular filtrate is formed by the passage of water and solutes through these layers either by ultrafiltration or by diffusion. Ultrafiltration assumes that

some part of the glomerular wall acts as a porous membrane and that water and solutes penetrate pores and pass into the capsular space. The diameter of the pore determines the size of the filtered molecules. Haemoglobin in the plasma, mol. wt. 68,000, passes easily into the glomerular filtrate, but albumin, mol. wt. 69,000, only to a small extent, and larger proteins do not normally pass through at all. Taking into account the orientation of the molecules to the pore, frictional and electrostatic hindrances, functional pores of about 7·5 nm would account for the glomerular characteristics. The fenestrae and the slits between the pedicels are too large to hold back protein molecules, and it is likely that the basement membrane acts as the functional barrier. Since this is a continuous gel, in all probability the solutes pass through its aqueous phase.

An alternative theory is that substances pass through the basement membrane by diffusion, the rate being proportional to their diffusion coefficients in the membrane. According to this view, all solutes in plasma would be capable of crossing the basement membrane but in practice the rate of diffusion of the plasma proteins is negligible. Experimental observations of the rate of passage of the crystalloids, inulin and creatinine have shown a slight difference in the rates of transfer of these substances which would not be expected if the filtrate were formed by bulk filtration of micromolecules through pores. In spite of this, the pore theory is more widely accepted because of the similarity of the filtration characteristics between the glomeruli and artificial porous membranes.

The hydrodynamic force responsible for filtration is the

pressure within the glomerular capillaries. This is believed to be higher than in other capillaries and to be about 70 mm Hg. The colloid osmotic pressure of the plasma, some 30 mm Hg, opposes the hydrostatic pressure and tends to hold back water in the plasma. In addition, the pressure inside the capsular space is about 15 mm Hg and is a sum of the resistance in the tubules and the surrounding tissue pressure. Thus the effective filtration pressure is $70-30-15=25$ mm Hg. These values have been obtained in part from direct micropuncture in rats and in part from indirect observation on larger animals.

Abbreviations

V	volume of urine
U	concentration of solute in urine
e.g. U_{Na}	concentration of sodium in urine
$U_{Na}V$	rate of excretion of sodium
P	concentration of solute in plasma
e.g. P_{Na}	concentration of sodium in plasma
C	clearance
e.g. C_{in}	clearance of inulin $= \dfrac{U_{in}V}{P_{in}}$
GFR	glomerular filtration rate
RBF	renal blood flow
RPF	renal plasma flow
ECF	extracellular fluid
Tm	maximum rate of tubular transport
e.g. Tm_G	maximum tubular capacity for reabsorption of glucose
Tm_{PO_4}	maximum tubular capacity for reabsorption of phosphate
C_{PAH}	clearance of para-aminohippurate
C_D	clearance of diodone
E_{PAH}	extraction ratio for PAH = renal A-V difference for PAH
FF	filtration fraction $= \dfrac{C_{in}}{C_{PAH}}$
$\dfrac{TF}{P}$	$\dfrac{\text{concentration of solute in tubular fluid}}{\text{concentration of solute in plasma}}$
Tc_{H_2O}	rate of reabsorption of solute free water $= C_{osm} - V$

Glomerular filtration rate (GFR) and its measurement

How far does the rate of production of the ultrafiltrate affect the final volume and composition of the urine? This is an important question to which there is only a partial answer. The first essential step is to measure GFR in various circumstances. From the work of Richards and his successors it was clear that the volume of fluid filtered by the glomerulus was greatly in excess of the final volume of urine passed. Micropuncture techniques cannot be used in man or in intact animals and although indirect methods so far developed to measure glomerular filtration lack precision, they are valuable in properly controlled conditions. A non-toxic substance, soluble in plasma, not metabolized by the body, freely filterable at the glomerulus, and neither secreted nor reabsorbed by the tubules, could be used on the basis of the Fick principle to measure the volume of fluid removed from the plasma by glomerular filtration in unit time in intact animal or man. The quantity of such an ideal solute excreted in the urine in unit time would equal the amount filtered by the glomeruli in the same period. Furthermore, the volume of plasma filtrate which is formed in this period (GFR) is the amount of solute excreted divided by the concentration of the solute in the plasma.

The information needed to calculate the GFR is the concentration of the solute in 1 ml of urine (U), the volume of urine excreted in 1 min (V), and the concentration of the solute in 1 ml of plasma (P). Then $U \times V$ is the quantity of solute excreted in 1 min, and the ratio UV/P gives the number of ml of glomerular filtrate formed. Inulin, a polymer of fructose found in dahlia roots, is a substance which possesses nearly all the requirements of an ideal solute. Its colorimetric estimation is accurate and relatively simple provided proper care is taken. Using inulin, the value for GFR in young men is about 125 ml/min.

The ratio UV/P is called the **renal clearance** (C), of the substance. In the case of inulin, $C = GFR$. The clearance of a substance which is partly reabsorbed during its passage through the renal tubules is lower than the GFR; by contrast, clearance values which are higher than the GFR may be obtained for substances which are secreted into the urine by the tubular cells.

In measuring GFR the following points should be observed.

(1) The subject should be at rest and recumbent and 4 hours should have elapsed since the last meal.

(2) V should be 3 ml/min or more to minimize errors in the collection of urine samples.

(3) If the subject is unable to empty the bladder completely it should be washed out with air or known volumes of saline.

(4) The concentration of inulin in the plasma should be kept constant to ensure that P_{in} in the plasma sample taken for analysis represents the average concentration during the period of urine collection. To this end P_{in} is usually first raised with a priming intravenous injection and then maintained by a slower infusion in which inulin is given as near as possible to the rate at which it is being lost in the urine.

After a short period of time to permit the even distribution of the inulin through-out the ECF, accurately timed urine samples are collected at intervals of 10–15 min; the sample of venous blood is taken at the midpoint of each collection period.

UV_{in} is directly proportional to P_{in}. Since C_{in} is the ratio UV_{in}/P_{in} it is independent of P_{in}. This is part of the evidence favouring the belief that inulin is filtered by the glomerulus and is neither reabsorbed nor secreted by the renal tubules.

The measurement of the GFR using inulin requires considerable technical care and, for this reason, in clinical work GFR is often measured by the clearance of creatinine (C_{cr}). Creatinine was, in fact, the first substance to be used for this purpose and it was employed on the assumption that it was excreted by the kidney solely by glomerular filtration. While this is true in the dog, it is now known that in man in some circumstances it is secreted by the renal tubules as well and may therefore give values for GFR that are too high. C_{cr} is easier to measure than C_{in} because there is a continuous endogenous supply of creatinine and P_{cr} remains virtually constant throughout the 24 hours. No intravenous infusion is necessary and observations can be made over prolonged periods of time. The urine is usually collected for 24 hours and a single blood sample is taken at some time during this period. This method is sufficiently accurate for many clinical purposes.

A third substance which has been used to assess the state of renal function is urea. As the blood already contains urea the endogenous P_{urea} is readily determined and no infusion is necessary. Urea is freely filtered at the glomerulus but C_{urea} is always much less than C_{in}. When V is more than 2 ml/min C_{urea} is about 75 ml/min; when V is less than 2 ml/min C_{urea} falls in an unpredictable fashion. Since GFR is 125 ml/min some of the filtered urea must be reabsorbed by the tubules, and the slower the urine flow the greater is the time for reabsorption which, in this case, is due to passive diffusion.

Another substance used for the measurement of GFR is vitamin B_{12} (cyanocobalamine). Vitamin B_{12} is normally bound by plasma proteins, but if the proteins are first saturated, then the excess vitamin B_{12} is filtered through the glomeruli and is neither secreted nor reabsorbed. The values for GFR are similar to those obtained with inulin. If vitamin B_{12} containing ^{57}Co is used the estimations may be made simply and rapidly by measuring the radio-activity in samples of plasma and urine. This method cannot be used frequently in the same human subject as it is undesirable to give radioactive material repeatedly. ^{131}I sodium diatrozoate (hypaque) is also used to measure GFR.

The order of accuracy in the measurement of GFR is about ± 5 per cent. By relating the actual GFR to surface area or some other body standard, comparison of results in different subjects is made easier.

Factors affecting GFR

If the pressure in the glomeruli alters, other things being equal, the filtration rate changes in the same direction. Yet in man the GFR is remarkably constant over a wide range of levels of blood pressure because the diameters of the afferent and efferent arterioles alter independently and compensate for alterations in systemic blood pressure. On the other hand, in the perfused kidney isolated from nervous control, GFR is more susceptible to a change in blood pressure. After severe haemorrhage or shock and in violent exercise, sympathetic activity constricts both afferent and efferent arterioles and also reduces renal blood flow, with the result that all renal activity declines and blood is diverted to other sites. If, for any reason, the plasma protein concentration is reduced, then the osmotic pressure of the blood falls and filtration rises. For reasons unknown a diet rich in protein is accompanied by a rise in GFR and a diet low in protein by a fall in GFR.

TUBULAR ACTIVITY

Reabsorption

Since glucose is found in capsular fluid and is absent from urine, it must be reabsorbed somewhere in the nephron. The volume of urine is always far less than the volume of filtrate, so water also is reabsorbed; many dissolved substances present in capsular fluid are partly reabsorbed and, since the degree of concentration varies for different substances and is independent of the water removed, there must be a number of independent reabsorptive mechanisms. Again, the pH of capsular fluid fluctuates around neutrality, whereas urine is usually acid. Some information on where and how these processes occur has been provided by the micromethods introduced by Richards. Most of the glucose has disappeared halfway along the proximal convolution, and has virtually all gone by the end. In the proximal convolution large amounts of sodium, chloride, bicarbonate, about 80–85 per cent of the water and a variety of other substances are reabsorbed. Fluid that enters the descending limb of the loop is thus greatly reduced in volume and changed in composition, but it is still isosmotic with plasma (p. 33.13).

Many tubular activities involve the expenditure of energy, though some depend solely on chemical and electrochemical gradients. Where active transport is involved, its capacity may be limited by the supply of energy or by unfavourable ionic and pH gradients across the tubular wall.

The term **tubular transport maximum**, Tm, is applied to substances such as glucose which are actively reabsorbed by mechanisms capable of transporting a fixed amount in unit time. Sodium is also actively transported but its reabsorption is limited by the concentration gradient that can be achieved in the time available during which the glomerular filtrate is in contact with the tubular cells.

GLUCOSE

Glucose is an example of a substance which shows a Tm, and its transport mechanism was the first to be studied and defined. Normally no glucose appears in urine so that $C_G = 0$. However, it is excreted by healthy subjects given a large quantity by mouth or by infusion when P_G rises above a critical level of about 180 mg/100 ml. The higher the P_G the more glucose appears in the urine and, providing GFR is constant, the amount of glucose filtered bears a linear relationship to P_G. Clearly, the quantity of glucose filtered minus the quantity excreted in the urine equals the amount reabsorbed. If this value is determined when $P_G > 350$ mg/100 ml, the quantity of glucose reabsorbed by the tubules remains constant (Tm_G). $Tm_G = (C_{in} \times P_G) - U_G V$. At plasma concentrations between 180–350 mg/100 ml the gradual increase in the amount reabsorbed is shown by the dotted line in fig. 33.11. This is termed the splay of the curve. If all nephrons were identical, then there would be no splay but a sharp angle in the curve, as shown by the unbroken line. The

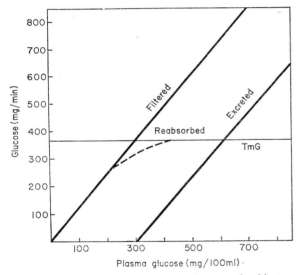

FIG. 33.11. Excretion of glucose in normal subjects.

splay is present because nephrons are not all exactly alike; their filtering surfaces vary in size so that the load delivered to a particular tubule is not precisely the same as that of its neighbour. In addition, transport capacities are probably not identical owing to differences in tubular length. Tm_G is unaffected by insulin. A normal value indicates a normal amount of reabsorbing tubular tissue.

A number of sugars use the same transport mechanism so that when more than one is present there is mutual interference. Glucose reabsorption can be prevented by phlorizin, a glucoside which also inhibits absorption of glucose by the gut.

PHOSPHATES (fig. 33.12)

Like glucose, phosphates are reabsorbed from the tubular fluid but Tm_{PO_4} is much lower and there is considerable splay in the curve. As a result, phosphate can always be found in the urine. Glucose and phosphate reabsorption bear a definite relationship to each other; phlorizin, which

FIG. 33.12 Excretion of phosphate in a normal subject in relation to rate of filtration of phosphate, normal (●), acidosis (○). From Schiess W.A. *et al.* (1948) *J. Clin. Invest.* **27**, 57.

prevents reabsorption of the former, increases reabsorption of the latter. It has been suggested that this is because both substances share a common energy source, so that when glucose reabsorption is blocked more energy becomes available for phosphate transport. Since Tm_{PO_4} is low, the amount in the urine depends more closely on the quantity filtered and on P_{PO4}, than is the case with glucose. The P_{PO_4} in turn varies with diet, exercise and the activity of the parathyroid glands. One of the actions of parathyroid hormone is to reduce Tm_{PO_4} and the excretion of phosphate is increased.

AMINO ACIDS

An adult excretes only traces of amino acids though they are filtered freely from the blood. In contrast, in the newborn infant there is a considerable excretion of the acids because the tubules are not completely functional at birth.

The blood plasma contains a variety of amino acids which the kidney must conserve. There seem to be at least three mechanisms for amino acid reabsorption, but knowledge of these is limited. If the plasma concentration of any of the amino acids is increased by an infusion then it overflows into the urine. All show a Tm, though at different levels. Probably arginine, lysine, ornithine and cystine are transported by the same mechanism, while another system deals with glutamic and aspartic acids and a third, or several more, transport the other acids. It is understandable that the infusion of arginine, for example, should depress the reabsorption of the similarly transported lysine, but it is more difficult to understand how acids with different transport mechanisms interfere with each other, as they have been shown to do. There is no competition between amino acid and glucose transport, suggesting that these are independent processes. The mechanism for the reabsorption of amino acids depends upon the presence of genetically determined enzymes. There is a variety of rare hereditary diseases associated with aminoaciduria. In one such disease the reabsorption of cystine, lysine, ornithine and arginine is reduced. Cystine is relatively insoluble and cystine stones are commonly formed in the renal pelves in patients with this inborn defect.

Creatine derives largely from muscle and is not usually found in urine. But for reasons unknown it occurs in the urine of children and of pregnant women. Its mode of reabsorption seems to be the same as that of alanine and glycine.

PROTEIN

Micropuncture shows that a small amount of protein, predominantly albumin, reaches the capsular fluid of mammals. The protein loss in the urine is normally of the order of 30–50 mg/day and is not detectable by routine clinical tests. Protein filtered by the glomerulus must be reabsorbed somewhere along the tubule and this is done in the proximal convolution. The Tm for albumin is about 30 mg/min, so that it readily appears in urine when an infusion of albumin is given. In certain circumstances, for example after severe exercise, it is found in the urine of healthy adults. This is probably because the circulatory requirements of the muscles lead to a fall in renal blood flow and temporary hypoxia in the kidneys with a consequent increase in permeability of the glomerulus. A long period of standing may lead to postural proteinuria. It has been suggested that the standing increases the curvature of the lumbar spine, causing increased pressure in the renal vein.

UREA

Urea is the form in which most of the waste nitrogen is excreted. It is an extremely diffusible substance which is relatively non-toxic, so that a healthy subject usually feels no ill effects if the concentration of urea in his blood is increased severalfold for a short period of time. Urea is reabsorbed from the tubular fluid by a process of back diffusion which is possibly facilitated by ADH (p. 33.16). In favour of the theory of passive diffusion are the observations that more urea is absorbed at low than at high rates of urine flow and that the rate of tubular reabsorption of urea is independent of P_{urea}. It is difficult to visualize an active transport process which would account for these findings. Although the diffusion of urea out of the tubular lumen is a passive process, work must be done to create and maintain a gradient for urea across the walls of the renal tubules. In fact this work is done by the active transport of sodium out of the tubule and is described on p. 33.13.

Tubular Secretion

This differs from tubular reabsorption only in the direction of movement. The transport may be active or passive and is subject to the same limitations as reabsorption. There appear to be only two active systems for secretion. The first substance proved to be secreted by the tubules, phenol red, is wholly foreign to the body as are a large number of other substances treated in this way. K^+ and H^+ are also secreted. Any substance whose clearance is higher than the GFR must be secreted, and provided it is freely filtered the extent of the secretion is the difference between its clearance and that of C_{in}. One transport system carries organic acids such as glucuronides and creatinine which are metabolic products, and also foreign chemicals such as PAH, diodone (D) and penicillin. The other system carries organic bases such as histamine and choline, and a number of foreign substances many of which are drugs used clinically. Some of the evidence for the existence of two active systems depends on the observation that a substance in one group interferes with the transport of another substance in the same group, but that substances in different groups do not interfere with each other.

Of the foreign substances secreted two are of practical physiological interest, PAH and diodone. At low values of P these substances are excreted rapidly and C approaches 600 ml/min. Up to a certain P value, C is constant, but above a critical concentration, UV no longer keeps pace with P and C falls. This is due to the active transport system for these compounds becoming saturated. Above this critical value for P the rise in excretion of PAH or diodone depends on their increased filtration alone; the value for tubular secretion remains constant at the Tm. These facts can be determined by making simultaneous measurements of C_{in} and C_{PAH} or C_D at various levels of P. When P_{PAH} or P_D is high, these two substances can be used to measure maximum tubular secretory capacity, Tm_{PAH} or Tm_D, and these values indicate the amount of the functioning tubular cell mass. For some years diodone was used, until PAH was found to give equally good results with the advantage that the chemical analysis is easier. In addition, a few people are hypersensitive to diodone.

URIC ACID

This comes from the breakdown of endogenous and dietary nucleoproteins and about 0·5–0·8 g/day is excreted in the urine. Since uric acid is filtered freely by the glomeruli and is normally present in the plasma in a concentration of 4–6 mg/100 ml, the quantity which appears in the urine is approximately 5–10 per cent of the amount filtered. Thus at least 90 per cent of the filtered uric acid is normally reabsorbed. Clearance studies have shown, however, that in certain circumstances the clearance of uric acid may exceed that of inulin. Uric acid is an example of a substance which is both reabsorbed and secreted by the renal tubules. The tubular transport of sodium, water, potassium and hydrogen ions is described on pp. 33.13 and 18.

RENAL CIRCULATION

At low plasma concentrations, the high clearance rates of PAH means that this substance is almost totally cleared from the plasma in a short period of time. This suggested the possibility that it might be used to obtain an indirect measurement of renal plasma flow (RPF). Theoretically what is needed for this purpose is a substance which is wholly cleared from the plasma and excreted in the urine as it passes once through the kidney. Direct measurements of plasma flow in animals and observations in man in which renal venous blood is sampled through catheters lying in the renal vein show that about 90 per cent of PAH is removed from the blood in a single passage through the kidney. Some of the remaining 10 per cent may be accounted for by blood which passes through non-secretory parts of the kidney, e.g. capsule, fat and connective tissue, and some more by blood supplying those parts of the tubules which are unable to secrete PAH. Secretion occurs mainly in the proximal tubule. In practice it is usual to ignore the 10 per cent error and refer to C_{PAH} as the effective RPF. The true value for RPF can be obtained by collecting renal venous blood and measuring the PAH A–V difference. This figure gives the extraction ratio (E_{PAH}) and thus the magnitude of the error. It is usual to measure C_{in} and C_{PAH} simultaneously and by the the same technique.

A second method of estimating RPF using nitrous oxide or radioactive krypton is identical with that described for the measurement of coronary and cerebral blood flow (pp. 28.36 and 37).

In man the effective RPF is about 600 ml/min, and the true RPF is about 700 ml/min; if the haematocrit value is 45, the whole blood flow is 1300 ml/min. This amounts to 25 per cent of the resting cardiac output and about 400 ml/100 g kidney tissue.

The ratio GFR/RPF is the filtration fraction (FF) and shows the proportion of plasma which supplies the filtrate. The usual figure is about 0·2 (125/600).

Factors affecting RPF

The RPF is greater when lying than when sitting or standing, because renal vasoconstriction occurs to maintain blood pressure against gravity. RPF is also reduced by vigorous exercise, pain and emotion, when a large volume of blood is diverted from the kidney to other parts of the body. RPF falls in water and salt depletion, when the blood volume is reduced. In pregnancy renal blood flow is increased, due to the increase in blood and plasma volume (p. 37.46). In conditions such as haemorrhage, shock and asphyxia, there is a marked reduction in RPF, in part due to increased vasoconstrictor activity in the sympathetic nerves. Mention has already been made of the fact that GFR is maintained to some extent in the face of a reduction in RPF.

Intrarenal circulation

The rate of blood flow through the cortex is five or more times faster than the rate through the medulla. Also, despite an overall constancy of GFR and RPF, the medullary blood flow is reduced during antidiuresis and is increased in diuresis, when the rate of urine flow is rapid. Measurements of this nature can be made by means of photocells, one in the cortex and one in the medulla, which monitor the arrival and disappearance of Evans blue injected into the renal artery. The dye is quickly washed through the cortex and only slowly through the medulla. The difference between the rates of flow is probably related to the rich anastomosis of capillaries round the tubules in the cortex and the long straight vessels offering more resistance in the medulla. Another factor is probably ADH to which the medullary vessels may be more sensitive.

The renal vessels are under the influence of vasoconstrictor sympathetic nerves and are also sensitive to adrenaline, noradrenaline and angiotensin. The last if injected produces a general vasoconstrictor response. The effects of adrenaline and noradrenaline depend on the dose given; in small doses the efferent arteriole constricts more than the afferent, so that there is a rise in GFR. With bigger doses all vessels, including the veins, are more or less constricted.

Autoregulation

A number of organs show some capacity for regulating their internal circulation regardless of the systemic blood pressure. In this respect the kidney is remarkable. The blood pressure can be changed over the range 80–200 mm Hg with only a small change in RPF and an even smaller one in GFR (fig. 33.13). How this is brought about is not clear, but its necessity is easier to understand. The regulation of water and electrolyte balance and many other renal activities would be almost impossible if renal haemodynamics were always changing. Autoregulation is preserved in the denervated kidney and even to some extent in the isolated organ. After denervation

GFR and RBF in man and dog are the same as in the innervated organ. The theory of plasma skimming is one of a variety of suggestions made to try to account for the facts. When blood flows along a vessel, the cells move in the axial stream and the plasma moves more slowly nearer the vessel wall. In the kidney a number of vessels arise almost at right angles from the parent branch, and these receive more of the plasma and fewer of the cells. To some extent this concentrates the cells in the parent

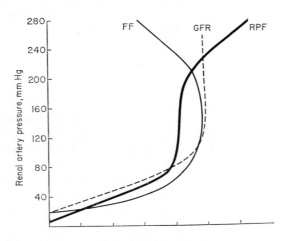

FIG. 33.13. Showing the range of systemic blood pressure over which the kidney demonstrates autoregulation. Adapted from Shipley R.E. & Study R.S. (1957) *Amer. J. Physiol.* **167**, 676.

vessels so that branches arising further along receive relatively less plasma and more cells. The more peripheral the blood, the more red blood cells does it contain and the more slowly it moves owing to its viscosity. With a rise in systemic blood pressure, plasma skimming is increased so that the blood in the peripheral part of the organ becomes even more viscous than before and offers a higher resistance to the raised blood pressure. This counteracts much of the effect of the rise in pressure and there is little alteration of the overall renal blood flow. Such at least is the ingenious hypothesis which accounts for some but not all the observations. In particular it does not explain the persistence of autoregulation in an isolated kidney perfused with a cell free solution or in severe anaemia when the cell content of the blood is reduced.

Another suggestion is that the smooth muscle of the renal blood vessels reacts to pressure changes even more vigorously than smooth muscle elsewhere. An increase in stretch, as when the systemic pressure rises, causes the muscle to contract, thus eliminating the effect of pressure changes. Yet another possibility is that the kidney has active internal reflexes which are still present after surgical denervation. Again the JGA, in particular the macula densa, may be involved.

WATER AND SODIUM

The osmolality of the body fluids is normally kept between 270 and 290 mOsm/l. This is achieved by adjusting the rate at which water is excreted in the urine. In a healthy individual, water deprivation leads to the release of ADH (p. 25.16), the rate of absorption of water by the renal tubules is increased and the osmolality of the urine rises to a maximum of 1200 mOsm/l. By contrast, in the hydrated individual in whom the release of ADH is suppressed, the osmolality of the urine may fall to a minimum of 30 or 40 mOsm/l; in these circumstances, proportionately less water is reabsorbed by the kidney.

The volume of the extracellular fluid is also regulated by the kidney. Since sodium is the principal cation of the ECF the retention of sodium raises its osmolality. A sensation of thirst follows which encourages the drinking of water. The release of ADH is also stimulated and water retention and expansion of the ECF follows. Loss of sodium induces the opposite chain of events leading to shrinkage of ECF volume. Despite wide variations in the intake of sodium, the total body sodium remains constant because the amount which is excreted in the urine can be varied from 1 or 2 up to 300 mEq/day, depending on the dietary intake. The maintenance of both the volume and the osmolality of the ECF depends upon the capacity of the kidney to regulate sodium and water balance.

As the GFR is about 125 ml/min, approximately 180 litres containing some 25,000 mEq of sodium are filtered daily. A person eating an ordinary diet excretes 1 or 2 litres of water daily containing about 100 mEq of sodium. Approximately 99 per cent of the filtered sodium therefore is reabsorbed and this process accounts for most of the energy used by kidney tissue. A large volume of water, approximately 178 l/day, is also reabsorbed by the tubules but water reabsorption is a passive process and follows the osmotic gradients created between the tubular lumen and the peritubular tissues during the active reabsorption of sodium.

Knowledge of the pattern of sodium and water reabsorption in the renal tubules has been obtained by micropuncture studies. The mammal commonly used for this purpose is the rat; this animal has a greater capacity than man for conserving both sodium and water so that the results obtained may not be entirely applicable to man. Under direct vision a micropipette is inserted into one of the surface tubules of the mobilized kidney. The minute amount of tubular fluid (TF) withdrawn is measured and subsequently analysed and the tubule is filled with a marker. Later, microdissection of the kidney enables the site of the puncture to be identified. Since inulin is neither reabsorbed nor secreted by the tubules, TF_{in}/P_{in} provides a measurement of water reabsorption. The TF/P ratio for sodium divided by the similar ratio for inulin provides information about the fraction of filtered sodium which remains in the tubular fluid at any point in the nephron.

Reabsorption of sodium and water in the proximal convoluted tubule

In the rat the deeply placed pars recta is inaccessible and only the first 60 per cent of the proximal convolution is available for micropuncture. Fluid withdrawn from here is always isotonic with plasma irrespective of whether the urine is more or less concentrated than plasma. This implies that the cells lining the proximal tubules cannot sustain an osmotic gradient. Furthermore, in fluid withdrawn from the last accessible point in the proximal tubule values of the inulin TF/P ratios are found to be around 3. This means that about two-thirds of the filtered water has been reabsorbed in the first 60 per cent of the proximal convolution, and if one assumes that reabsorption of water continues at the same rate in the remaining 40 per cent then about four-fifths of the filtered water must be reabsorbed in the proximal convolution. Because sodium is by far the most important osmotically active solute, four-fifths of the filtered sodium must also be absorbed together with an equivalent amount of anion. The reabsorption of sodium in the proximal tubule is an active process which occurs against an electrochemical gradient and the reabsorption of water is a secondary passive phenomenon.

EVIDENCE FOR REABSORPTION OF SODIUM AGAINST A CHEMICAL GRADIENT

Normally no chemical gradient for sodium exists across the wall of the proximal tubule and the concentration of sodium in the tubular fluid does not differ significantly from that of the plasma in the peritubular capillaries. Such a gradient, however, can be created artificially in animals receiving an infusion of mannitol which is excreted by the kidney in a way similar to inulin. The presence in the lumen of the proximal tubule of the osmotically active sugar reduces water absorption. Under these conditions fluid obtained by micropuncture shows that there is a progressive decrease in the TF/P ratio for sodium along the first two-thirds of the proximal convolution, so that a concentration gradient for sodium of 30–50 mEq/l is established between the tubular fluid and the peritubular plasma. This proves that sodium can be reabsorbed against a chemical gradient. The capacity of the cells of the proximal tubule to sustain such a gradient is limited and the concentration of sodium in the tubular fluid cannot be reduced below a value of 60 per cent of its concentration in plasma.

EVIDENCE FOR REABSORPTION OF SODIUM AGAINST AN ELECTRICAL GRADIENT

The electrical gradients which exist across the wall of the proximal tubule can be measured by means of micro-

electrodes inserted into proximal tubular cells. A potential difference of 72 mV between the interior of the cell and the peritubular fluid can be demonstrated, the intracellular fluid being relatively negative (fig. 33.14). A PD of

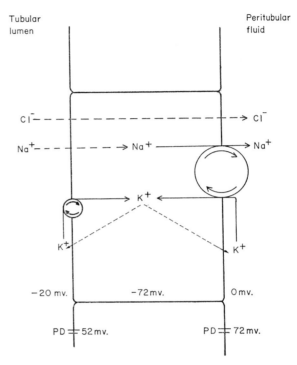

FIG. 33.14. Diagrammatic representation of ion transport in the proximal tubule. Broken lines indicate passive movement down electrochemical gradients. Solid lines indicate active transport. Adapted from Pitts R.F. (1961) *Prog. Cardiol. Dis*, **3**, 537.

52 mV is thought to exist between the interior of the cell and the lumen of the tubule. Both these potentials arise as a result of the tendency of K^+ to diffuse out of the cell and the PD across the luminal membrane is smaller because this membrane is more readily permeable to Na^+ which diffuses into the cell and shunts the potential. The PD between the lumen and the peritubular fluid is therefore believed to be 20 mV, the lumen being the more negative. Thus sodium reabsorption occurs against an electrical as well as a chemical gradient and must therefore be an active process.

Sodium ions from the tubular fluid are thought to enter the cell by moving passively down an electrochemical gradient and to be actively expelled into the blood against the electrochemical gradient which exists across the peritubular membrane. This is probably brought about by an ionic pump, situated in the peritubular membrane of the cell, which may also be concerned with the inward transport of K^+. Negatively charged chloride ions from tubular fluid follow sodium ions, moving passively down the transcellular electrochemical gradient and water follows the sodium.

EVIDENCE FOR THE PASSIVE REABSORPTION OF WATER

The proximal tubule of the amphibian *Necturus* can be perfused with solutions containing different concentrations of sodium chloride which are kept isotonic with the animal's plasma by adding varying amounts of mannitol. *Necturus* plasma contains 100 mEq/l of sodium and, since sodium can be reabsorbed against a moderate chemical gradient, it is reabsorbed from those solutions which contain more than 65 mEq/l of sodium. By contrast, when the

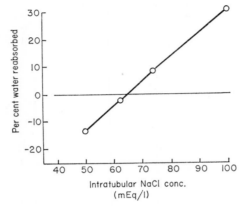

FIG. 33.15. The relationship which exists between the concentration of sodium chloride in the proximal tubular fluid of *Necturus* and the percentage of water reabsorbed. All solutions made isotonic with *Necturus* plasma by addition of mannitol. At concentrations of sodium chloride of less than 65 mEq/l sodium moves from the peritubular fluid into the lumen and water moves in the same direction, negative reabsorption. The percentage of water reabsorbed is corrected for movement of water due to the presence of mannitol in the tubular fluid. Adapted from Windhager E.E. *et al.* (1959) *Amer. J. Physiol.* **197**, 313.

sodium content of the perfusing fluid is less than 65 mEq/l it diffuses from the peritubular fluid into the lumen. As fig. 33.15 shows, the movement of water always takes place in the same direction as that of sodium, and one would not expect to find this if water were transported actively.

The osmotic pressure exerted by the peritubular plasma proteins cannot be of importance in determining the rate of reabsorption of water since water is reabsorbed at a normal rate from tubules in which the intraluminal colloid osmotic pressure has been raised above that of peritubular plasma by the infusion of albumin.

Reabsorption of sodium and water from the loop of Henle

The tip of Henle's loop is readily accessible for micropuncture in rodents such as the hamster which have elongated papillae. Fluid entering the descending limb is

isotonic with plasma and fluid at the tip of the loop i[s] markedly hypertonic. There is doubt as to whether sodium is reabsorbed from the descending limb of the loop bu[t] if so, water must pass, from the lumen of this limb int[o] the medullary interstitium at a rate considerably in exces[s] of that of sodium.

Fluid obtained from the early distal convolution is invariably hypotonic to plasma whatever the osmolality o[f] the final urine, the implication being that in the ascendin[g] limb of the loop the permeability of the cells to water i[s] reduced and the rate of reabsorption of sodium exceed[s] that of water. This in turn implies that in this part of th[e] nephron sodium is normally reabsorbed against a con[-] centration gradient.

Comparative studies have shown that the formation o[f] urine more concentrated than plasma depends on th[e] presence of the hairpin loops and that in mammals th[e] maximum urine concentration which can be achieved i[s] proportional to the length of the loop. The fluid emergin[g] from the loops, however, is more dilute than plasma an[d] no concentration occurs until it reaches the collectin[g] ducts, so that the old suggestion that the concentratin[g] process occurred in Henle's loop is untenable. It is no[w] generally accepted that the loops function as counter[-] current multipliers and establish a hypertonic environ[-] ment in the medullary interstitium. The collecting duct[s] pass through this medium and in the presence o[f] ADH water moves passively out of the ducts until th[e] urine comes into osmotic equilibrium with the hypertoni[c] medullary interstitial fluid.

Reabsorption of sodium and water from the distal con[-] voluted tubule and collecting duct

Active reabsorption of sodium continues in the distal con[-] volution and collecting duct. Samples of fluid obtained b[y] micropuncture from the distal tubules of normal rats sho[w] a steady diminution in the TF/P ratio for sodium which may fall to values of 0·1 indicating reabsorption o[f] sodium against a chemical gradient. When the urine is vir[-] tually free from sodium, even steeper chemical gradient[s] must exist in the collecting ducts. Experiments with micro[-] electrodes have shown that sodium may be reabsorbed i[n] the distal nephron against electrical gradients of as muc[h] as 120 mV (lumen negative to peritubular fluid). A propor[-] tion of the sodium reabsorbed in the distal system is take[n] up from the tubular fluid in exchange for hydrogen ion[s] or potassium ions (p. 33.19) while the remainder is re[-] absorbed along with chloride.

The pattern of water reabsorption in the distal part o[f] the nephron depends upon whether the final urine is t[o] be more or less concentrated than plasma.

HYPOTONIC URINE

During the formation of hypotonic urine micropunctur[e] studies show that the fluid entering the distal convolutio[n] remains hypotonic during its passage through this portion of the tubule and on entry into the collecting ducts. A similar picture is found in rats with diabetes insipidus under a variety of experimental circumstances. It seems that, in the absence of ADH, the permeability of the distal convolution to water is low, as is that of the collecting ducts. Hence in the hydrated animal the absorption of water in these areas lags behind that of solute and further dilution of the urine occurs.

HYPERTONIC URINE

During the formation of hypertonic urine the ratio TF_{osm}/P_{osm} shows a progressive increase along the length of the distal convolution. It is generally accepted that in the presence of ADH the cells lining the distal convolution become more permeable to water so that water is re-absorbed more rapidly than sodium. The osmolality of the fluid in the lumen steadily increases and on entering the collecting duct is isosmotic with the plasma. In the presence of ADH the collecting duct wall is permeable to water, and more water than solute is absorbed during the passage of the tubular fluid down the duct. The force leading to the absorption of water from the ducts is the osmotic gradient between the fluid in the ducts and the more highly concentrated medullary interstitial fluid.

The countercurrent mechanism for the concentration of the urine

Within the mammalian kidney the loops of Henle and the collecting ducts lie close together in the medulla while the proximal and distal convoluted tubules occupy the cortex. In 1942, Kuhn, a Swiss physical chemist, suggested that this spatial arrangement serves a specific purpose and put forward the hypothesis that the loops could act as countercurrent multipliers. A model of such a system is shown in fig. 33.16 and consists of two saline-filled tubes separated by a membrane (M) and joined at one end by a small pipe. A solution flows from left to right in the upper compartment, X, and from right to left in the lower compartment, Y (fig. 33.16a). If the membrane transports a finite amount of sodium from Y to X, a small concentration gradient will be established between the two tubes (fig. 33.16b). As the fluid flows onwards the position represented in fig. 33.16c is reached in which the right half of each tube is occupied by the more concentrated fluid and the concentration gradient across this portion of the membrane is abolished. Further transport of sodium from Y to X then occurs and re-establishes the gradient at a higher concentration of sodium in the fluid in the right half of compartment X, (fig. 33.16d); this in turn flows through the connecting pipe to establish the situation shown in fig. 33.16e. The whole process can be repeated indefinitely and the final result is the creation of a longitudinal concentration gradient for sodium many times greater than the small concentration gradient which

FIG. 33.16. Model of a countercurrent multiplier. Adapted from Wirz H. (1960) in *Water and Electrolyte Metabolism*, ed. Strengers & Gasthuis. London: Elsevier.

was originally established across the membrane. The final concentration attained at the tip depends upon the magnitude of the gradient which can be established between the two limbs, the length and cross section of the parallel tubes and the rate of flow through the system.

In the mammalian kidney the hairpin loops appear to function as countercurrent multipliers. Micropuncture studies indicate that the fluid in the descending limb becomes progressively more concentrated during its passage down to the tip of the loop. In slices of renal tissue taken from rats deprived of water the cortical tissue is isotonic with plasma but the osmolality of medullary slices cut perpendicular to the axis of the papilla rises progressively from the corticomedullary junction to the papillary tip (fig. 33.17). The descending limb of the loop and the medullary interstitial fluid are, therefore, together equivalent to compartment X of the model. Micropuncture experiments have shown that sodium is reabsorbed more rapidly than water from the ascending limb and the fluid

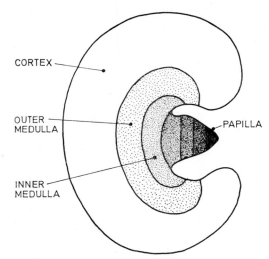

FIG. 33.17. Section of a rat kidney showing the progressive increase in tissue osmolality from cortex to papillary tip. The greater the depth of shading, the higher is the osmolality.

which leaves the loop is more dilute than that which enters it. The ascending limb thus corresponds to y in the model. The concentration gradient between the limbs is created by the transport of sodium unaccompanied by equivalent amounts of water out of the ascending limb into the interstitial fluid. Water then diffuses out of the descending limb, concentrating the contents until an equilibrium is reached in which the concentration of the fluid at any point in the descending limb is the same as that of the interstitial fluid at the same level and slightly higher than that at the corresponding point on the ascending limb (fig. 33.18). It is possible also that sodium may diffuse into the descending limb. The system establishes a longitudinal concentration gradient within the descending limb of the loops and the medullary interstitial fluid such that the concentration increases from values of about 290 mOsm/l at the corticomedullary junction to extremely high values at the tip of the papilla. In animals undergoing a water diuresis the gradient is greatly reduced. When tissue obtained from hydrated rats is examined with the EM swelling of the basement membrane is seen in the pars recta of the proximal convoluted tubule and the descending limb of Henle's loop. This may be due to hydration of mucopolysaccharides in the basement membrane, and is probably associated with reduced permeability to water. Any reduction in the rate at which water leaves the descending limb reduces the efficiency of the countercurrent multiplier.

The collecting ducts pass through this area and, in the presence of ADH, water diffuses from the collecting ducts into the hypertonic medullary interstitium so that the urine becomes progessively more concentrated and at the papillary tip its osmolality is the same as that of the fluid in the tip of Henle's loop. Under the influence of ADH, urea also diffuses from the collecting ducts into

→　ACTIVE TRANSPORT OF SODIUM
⇨　PASSIVE MOVEMENT OF WATER
⬛➤　UREA TRANSPORT

FIG. 33.18. Diagram illustrating possible mode of operation of a countercurrent mechanism for the production of a concentrated urine in the rat. The values represent mOsm solute/l.

the medullary interstitial fluid and the descending limb until the concentrations of urea in the urine and medulla are balanced. This allows the production of an even more highly concentrated urine since the concentration of solutes other than urea in the urine can be increased until it is equal to the concentration of sodium in the medullary interstitium.

The sodium entering the medulla from the ascending limb and the urea diffusing into the medulla from the ducts accumulate and are not removed rapidly because the medullary blood flow is relatively small and the blood supply consists of the vasa recta which are in the form of hairpin loops. This arrangement is thought to prevent loss of solute from the medulla because the loops act as passive countercurrent exchangers, solute in the ascending vascular limb diffusing into the descending limb and being re-circulated. Blood entering the descending limbs of the vasa recta contains solute at a concentration of approximately 290 mOsm/l. As the blood flows down towards the papilla solute diffuses into it and its tonicity increases. During its return to the cortex in the ascending limb, solute diffuses out again into the interstitial fluid so that the final concentration of solute in the blood entering the cortex is probably not much higher than that in the blood entering the loop.

Although it seems likely that a countercurrent mechanism for the production of concentrated urine exists in man there is little direct evidence that this is so. However, the few studies carried out upon human kidneys removed at operation or shortly after death show that a concentration gradient for sodium and for urea also exists in the medulla of the human kidney.

The capacity of the kidney to concentrate urine above the osmolality of the plasma is measured under hydropenic conditions or following the administration of ADH. It is expressed by the ratio U_{osm}/P_{osm} which has a normal value of 3–4. It is also possible to estimate the value of solute-free water reabsorbed by the renal tubules in unit time (Tc_{H_2O}). This is given by the formula:

$$Tc_{H_2O} = \frac{U_{osm} \times V}{P_{osm}} - V$$

REGULATION OF THE VOLUME OF THE EXTRACELLULAR FLUID

The maintenance of the circulation depends, among other things, upon the volume of the plasma together with the interstitial fluid. Reduction in the volume of the ECF is associated with a reduction in plasma volume and jeopardizes the circulation. It is, therefore, hardly surprising that homeostatic mechanisms exist to keep the volume of the ECF approximately constant by regulating the excretion of sodium and water. As long ago as 1935 the American physician, J.P. Peters, envisaged the existence of a mechanism whereby changes in the 'fullness of the blood stream' might start a train of events leading to changes in the rate of excretion of water and of sodium. There is much evidence in favour of the existence of such a mechanism; it has, for example, been shown that haemorrhage reduces the rate of salt and water excretion even when the loss of blood is too small to produce any measurable change in RPF or GFR. A similar reduction in sodium and water excretion occurs in man when he stands still or when venous tourniquets are applied to the thighs. It is seen in dogs after the distension of a balloon inserted into the inferior vena cava. These procedures result in pooling of blood in the lower limbs and hence underfilling of the great vessels of the thorax. Conversely an increase in the rate of excretion of sodium and water occurs when an individual lies down and when ECF is expanded by the infusion of saline, albumin, plasma or blood.

A homeostatic mechanism of this type requires the presence of receptor organs capable of detecting changes in the volume of the ECF and neural or humoral pathways capable of modifying the rate of excretion of salt and water by the effector organ, the kidney. It seems likely that there are a number of receptor areas each capable of reacting to a specific stimulus and that several integrated mechanisms exist to bring about the necessary changes in renal function. Knowledge of this important part of physiology is, however, fragmentary.

Volume receptors and their associated effector mechanisms

The circulation can be regarded as being made up of two components:

(1) the systemic arterial system which accommodates less than 15 per cent of the total blood at a high pressure in relatively indistensible vessels;

(2) a low pressure system consisting of the veins of the systemic and pulmonary circulations, the pulmonary arteries and the chambers of the heart, except for the left ventricle during systole.

About 85 per cent of the blood is in the low pressure system, the walls of which are 100–200 times more distensible than those of the arterial tree so that moderate changes in blood volume produce proportional changes in intravascular pressure. By contrast the arterial pressure is affected only by changes in blood volume large enough to alter cardiac output. For these reasons some of the early workers looked for receptors in the low pressure system. It was shown that normal men excreted water less rapidly when breathing against a positive pressure of 10–40 mm Hg, a procedure which displaces blood from the intrathoracic veins. This antidiuresis could be inhibited by alcohol which suggested it was due to the release of ADH. Further experiments showed that water excretion was increased during negative pressure respiration which leads to slight overdistension of the thoracic vessels and that this could be prevented by giving ADH. It was therefore postulated that receptors capable of responding to 'changes in the fullness of the blood stream' were situated in the thorax. An ingenious series of experiments designed to allow localized distension of different parts of the low pressure system have shown that distension of the left atrium induces a water diuresis and the impulses there are carried to the medulla by the vagus and ultimately relayed to the supra-optic nuclei. An increase in sodium excretion due to a reduction in circulating aldosterone has been reported to occur when the right atrium is stretched. The injection of veratridine, a drug sometimes used to lower blood pressure, into the left ventricle or into a peripheral vein produces an increase in urine flow which is abolished by vagal blockade. Injection of veratridine into the aorta has no such effect and it appears that veratridine stimulates sensory receptors in the heart.

The impulses from the atria cannot be the only ones concerned in the control of sodium excretion as section of the vagi does not prevent the sodium loss which occurs in response to expansion of the blood volume. Two sets of receptors in the arterial system can influence sodium excretion by altering aldosterone secretion. These are situated in the carotid arteries near the origin of the thyroid arteries and in the JGA of the kidney. These receptors are sensitive to changes in mean arterial pressure brought about by changes in cardiac output which in turn are influenced by the blood volume. Constricting the carotids low in the neck has been shown to increase aldosterone production by stimulating thyrocarotid receptors. Impulses from these receptors are probably carried by the vagus to a diencephalic centre concerned with control of aldosterone secretion. It is not known how such a centre might control the output of this hormone but impulses arising there could conceivably stimulate secretion of ACTH which can produce a small increase in aldosterone output. There must, however, be a mechanism capable of stimulating the release of aldosterone which does not involve higher centres because when decapitated dogs are bled their output of aldosterone increases. This increase occurs if the liver is also removed but is abolished by nephrectomy. Cells in the JGA are probably sensitive to changes in pressure in the afferent arteriole and angiotensin II, formed when renin is released, stimulates aldosterone production (fig. 33.19).

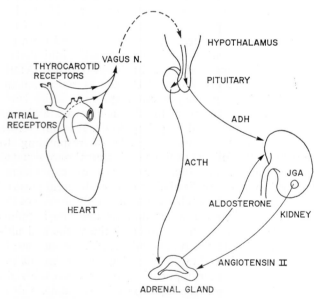

Fig. 33.19. System for volume control.

Changes in renal function

The changes in water excretion which occur in response to alterations in the circulating level of ADH are well established (p. 25.16). The rate at which sodium is excreted in the urine depends upon the balance struck between the amount of sodium filtered and the amount reabsorbed. Normally about 1 per cent of the filtered sodium is excreted and since variations in GFR of less than 5 per cent cannot be detected by present methods, conventional clearance studies are of little value in determining which of the two variables changes in a particular situation.

The adrenal steroids in general and aldosterone in particular are known to enhance reabsorption of sodium. Aldosterone and cortisol promote sodium reabsorption in exchange for potassium and hydrogen ions as well as increasing the rate of reabsorption of sodium chloride and they must therefore exert some effect upon the distal part of the nephron where these ion exchanges take place. It is not known whether they also promote the reabsorption of sodium in the proximal convoluted tubule. The presence of the adrenocorticoids is necessary to maintain sodium balance in the face of a variable intake of this ion. Their absence, as in Addison's disease (p. 25.31), leads to sodium depletion. Yet the actual fraction of sodium reabsorption affected by these hormones is quite small, being about 2 per cent. Experiments in which aldosterone was injected intravenously into adrenalectomized animals have shown that there is a delay of about 40 min before any effect is seen upon sodium reabsorption. It seems unlikely therefore that alterations in the amount of circulating adrenal hormones are responsible for rapid changes in sodium excretion. This is borne out by the fact that the usual rapid reduction in sodium excretion on standing up or after application of a tourniquet to the thigh occurs in patients who have undergone adrenalectomy and are being treated with a small fixed dose of adrenal hormone. Obviously there must be another mechanism which influences the rate of sodium excretion. The infusion of saline leads to an increase in the rate of sodium excretion, and micropuncture studies carried out on dogs show that the rate of sodium reabsorption in the proximal tubule is reduced during the infusion of saline even when the animal is receiving large doses of adrenal steroids and ADH. Moreover, in these experiments reduction of the GFR by the application of a clamp to the renal artery did not alter the findings. Other experiments have shown that the increased excretion of sodium which is seen after the infusion of saline can occur in the absence of changes in the plasma sodium concentration, or in the concentration of the plasma proteins or haematocrit; it also occurs in the denervated kidney. These results suggest that some unidentified humoral mechanism exists which can modify the rate of sodium reabsorption and that, in the dog at least, it acts upon the proximal tubule.

RENAL EXCRETION OF POTASSIUM

The urine of a healthy individual eating a mixed diet contains from 30 to 80 mEq of potassium each day. In persons with normal renal function this is equivalent to between 10 and 15 per cent of the amount filtered by the glomeruli.

The simplest explanation of this finding would be that 85–90 per cent of the potassium filtered by the glomeruli is reabsorbed by the tubules leaving the remaining potassium to be excreted in the urine. While this view was for long thought to be correct, it is now established that the filtered potassium is almost all reabsorbed in the proximal part of the nephron while the potassium which is found in the urine is secreted into the tubular lumen in exchange for sodium reabsorbed from the tubular fluid (fig. 33.20).

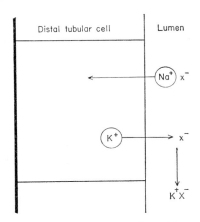

FIG. 33.20. Diagrammatic representation of the secretion of potassium in exchange for filtered sodium by the distal tubular epithelium.

Direct evidence about the excretion of potassium by the kidney has been obtained in micropuncture experiments. Fig. 33.21 shows the results obtained in rats receiving a diet containing normal amounts of potassium and ex-

Fig. 33.21. Micropuncture experiments on rats receiving a normal diet. (a) tubular fluid/plasma concentration ratios for potassium as a function of tubular length; (b), potassium/inulin tubular fluid/plasma concentration ratios as a function of tubular length. From Malnic G. *et al.* (1964) *Amer. J. Physiol.* **206**, 677.

creting about 17 per cent of the filtered potassium. The TF/P ratios for potassium in fluid obtained from different sites in the proximal tubule are all slightly less than one, indicating that the rate of potassium reabsorption is slightly greater than the rate of reabsorption of water. The ratio of TF_K/P_K to TF_{in}/P_{in} shows that at a point two-thirds of the way down the proximal tubule 70 per cent of the filtered potassium has been reabsorbed.

At the next site accessible to micropuncture, a point one-fifth of the way along the distal tubule, 95 per cent of the filtered potassium has disappeared from the lumen. It is clear therefore that most filtered potassium is reabsorbed in the upper portion of the nephron, and since the proximal tubular lumen is electrically negative with respect to the peritubular fluid and the concentration of potassium in the peritubular plasma higher than that in the tubular lumen, this reabsorption occurs against an electrochemical gradient and must be due to an active process.

In the distal tubule the potassium/inulin TF/P ratio increases steadily along the length of the tubule showing that potassium is added to the tubular fluid at this site and it can be calculated that at least 70 per cent of the potassium which appears in the urine is secreted by the cells of the distal convolution. The nature of this distal secretory mechanism is not known but the secretion of K^+ into the tubular fluid is linked with the reabsorption of Na^+ and influenced by the rate of secretion of H^+.

Fluid cannot be obtained from the collecting ducts by the micropuncture technique but the potassium/inulin U/P ratio suggests that in rats on a normal diet a small amount of potassium may be reabsorbed in the collecting ducts.

Factors which influence the rate of potassium excretion

Since the urinary potassium appears to be determined by the rate at which K^+ is secreted into the tubular fluid, information about the factors which influence the secretory process is needed in order to understand the changes in potassium excretion which occur in different physiological and pathological conditions.

POTASSIUM BALANCE

When potassium salts are given to a normal individual there is an increase in the rate of excretion of this ion in the urine. It is of interest that the capacity to excrete potassium appears to be enhanced when the substance is given in moderately large amounts over a long period of time. The mechanism of this is unknown. Conversely, when a normal person is placed on a diet containing very little potassium, e.g. 15 or 20 mEq/day, the rate of potassium excretion gradually declines until a balance is achieved, a process which may take up to 14 days.

The changes in P_K which occur in response to changes

in intake are usually small and in normal subjects $U_K V$ bears little relation to P_K but probably depends upon the concentration within the cells in general and the renal tubular cells in particular.

REABSORPTION OF SODIUM IN THE DISTAL TUBULE

The tubular secretion of K^+ appears to be linked with the reabsorption of Na^+ and numerous investigators have shown that in situations in which it is reasonable to infer increased distal tubular reabsorption of Na^+, the urinary potassium increases. Thus the administration to normal men of sodium-retaining hormones such as cortisol or aldosterone is accompanied by an increased urinary loss of potassium. This does not occur if retention of sodium is prevented by limiting the dietary intake of salt during administration of the hormones.

The administration of large quantities of sodium frequently increases the excretion of potassium. This is particularly likely to occur when the recipient has been depleted of sodium and consequently has a strong stimulus to absorb a large percentage of filtered sodium, or when the sodium is given along with an anion such as sulphate which is not readily reabsorbed, so that most of the sodium reabsorption must be effected by means of the ion exchange mechanisms.

The exact nature of the relationship between the reabsorption of Na^+ and the secretion of K^+ is not known.

SECRETION OF HYDROGEN IONS IN THE DISTAL TUBULE

In many situations the rate of $U_K V$ appears to be inversely related to $U_{H^+} V$. Thus giving a carbonic anhydrase inhibitor such as acetazolamide not only diminishes $U_{H^+} V$ but also increases $U_K V$. Patients with respiratory alkalosis in whom the P_{CO_2} is low have a low $U_{H^+} V$ and their alkaline urine contains increased potassium. In the same way giving $NaHCO_3$ not only makes the urine alkaline but also increases the $U_K V$. The exchange mechanism which has been proposed to account for K^+ secretion is very similar to that which is thought to be responsible for the excretion of H^+ and there is evidence which suggests that K^+ and H^+ compete in some way for Na^+, the outcome possibly being determined by the relative concentrations of K^+ and H^+ within the renal tubular cells (p. 33.26).

HORMONES AND THE KIDNEY

Certain hormones have a marked effect on renal activity.

(1) ADH which regulates water excretion is discussed on p. 25.16.

(2) Aldosterone and cortisol which modify sodium excretion are described on p. 25.33.

(3) Parathyroid hormone and calcitonin are concerned in renal regulation of phosphate excretion (p. 25.26).

(4) Growth hormone influences sodium excretion.

(5) The gonadal hormones indirectly affect sodium and water balance.

In addition, the kidney is itself responsible for the appearance of two hormones, angiotensin, which is functionally connected with aldosterone, and erythropoietin.

Renin-angiotensin aldosterone system

It has been appreciated for some time that there is a link between the kidneys, sodium balance and blood pressure. While some aspects of this complex relationship are now known, the extent to which the system serves a physiological purpose and the frequency with which its breakdown is responsible for disease remain uncertain. Bright of Guy's Hospital (1827) was among the first to realize that renal disease was often accompanied by an abnormally high blood pressure. Next came the observation of Tigerstedt and Bergman in 1898, that when saline extract of rabbit kidney were injected into normal rabbits, a slow and prolonged rise in blood pressure due to vasoconstriction occurred. Because the active material was extracted from the kidneys, it was called renin. In 1934 Goldblatt showed that when the renal artery of a dog was constricted by a clamp, hypertension developed. Later it was found that the renin content of the constricted kidney rose. Yet when renin was added to saline which was perfusing isolated organs the blood vessels did not constrict; the presence of blood plasma was also needed, showing that the kidney itself did not contain the active vasoconstrictor substance. This series of facts has now been explained as follows. Renin is an enzyme which on reaching the blood activates an α_2–globulin called angiotensinogen formed in the liver, making angiotensin I, a polypeptide containing ten amino acids. Another enzyme converts angiotensin I to angiotensin II by removing two amino acids. This last substance is the most potent pressor agent known. It constricts small arteries and arterioles and, in larger doses, veins. Renal blood vessels are highly sensitive to angiotensin, and for this reason it can act as an antidiuretic. It has little effect on the heart and does not constrict adrenal vessels. On injection into the circulation it is rapidly destroyed by the angiotensinase of the blood, so that the effect of a single injection is short lived. When low concentrations of angiotensin are infused the rise in blood pressure can be maintained for long periods. The action of renin is slow and prolonged because angiotensin has first to be formed and the process is not instantaneous. Another effect of angiotensin is that on injection into the venous system or into the adrenal artery it releases aldosterone from the adrenal cortex.

Important observations relating sodium and blood pressure level include the following. In man a low salt diet reduces the sodium content of the body and at the same time lowers the blood pressure. There is also a striking inverse correlation between the plasma renin and sodium concentrations. In rats a high salt diet can induce hypertension. In dogs a high salt diet combined with deoxycorticosterone, a salt-retaining substance formed in small quantities in the adrenal cortex, invariably causes hypertension. When, in addition, it is remembered that aldosterone causes sodium retention and potassium loss, the possible relationship between salt, the adrenals and the kidneys becomes clearer.

This series of facts has been interpreted as follows. A decrease in renal blood flow, as by renal artery constriction, liberates renin from the kidney. This enzyme is responsible for the appearance of angiotensin II, which acts upon the adrenal cortex and increases release of aldosterone. Aldosterone leads to sodium retention by the kidney. If sodium is retained so also is water, and this in turn leads to an increase in the ECF, including the plasma, so that the blood volume rises. The blood pressure rises because of an increased cardiac output and constriction of the resistance vessels.

To what extent a derangement of these sequences is responsible for the raised blood pressure so frequently found in middle-aged and elderly people, is not known.

SITE OF ORIGIN OF RENIN

Renin can be extracted from the cortex of the kidney, though little is found in the juxtamedullary part and none in the medulla. The JGA which lie in the cortex, became suspect as the source of renin for the following reasons. It was noticed that the granularity of the specialized arteriolar cells, the JG index, was less in hypertensive rats on a high salt diet, and was high on a low sodium diet. In a kidney whose artery was constricted the index rose at a time when it fell in the other normal kidney. There was a correlation between the granularity and the amount of renin that could be extracted. By an ingenious method glomeruli have been isolated and their renin content assayed. Iron filings were injected into the renal artery, and these jammed in the glomeruli; the kidney was broken up and slowly washed past a magnet which retained the glomeruli. It was found that renin was present in the glomeruli in large amounts, and only in small amounts in the other parts of the renal tissue. Later, individual glomeruli were collected and bisected; renin was found only in the half containing the JGA. This does not tell us whether the renin comes from the modified arteriolar cells or from the macula densa. These two are closely applied to each other and cannot be separated.

POSSIBLE PHYSIOLOGICAL ROLE OF RENIN

While renin may or may not be responsible for certain forms of hypertension, it would be interesting to know if it has a physiological role. Observations on normal man show that plasma renin rises in sodium deprivation,

and falls during sodium loading. This suggests that the renin-angiotensin system has some part in controlling sodium balance. Also, in normal animals following acute blood loss more aldosterone is released, and this does not occur if the kidneys have first been removed. Further, in rats the prolonged administration of renin leads to an increase in size of the zona glomerulosa of the adrenals which produces aldosterone.

The stimulus to renin production is still hypothetical. The possibilities are that the JG cells in the afferent arteriole act as stretch receptors, and that a fall in pressure releases renin, and a rise inhibits its release. Alternatively the macula densa cells may be osmoreceptors which react to the sodium concentration of the distal tubular fluid and pass the information to the JG cells.

Erythropoietin

Attention was first drawn to the importance of the kidney in blood formation because chronic renal failure is accompanied by an anaemia which cannot be attributed to a deficiency in the excretory processes. Conversely, in the presence of a renal carcinoma, a malignant tumour, there may be erythaemia, i.e. too many red cells. In normal people increased erythropoiesis follows haemorrhage or exposure to a low oxygen tension, and in these circumstances an erythropoietic substance can be found in the plasma. This substance is able to raise the red cell mass in normal people. Experiments on animals show that no erythropoietic substance appears unless kidney tissue is present. Its appearance is independent of excretory activity since the substance is found when the ureters are allowed to open into the peritoneum so that excretory products accumulate in the body. Most workers can find no active substance in extracts of the kidney or of kidney tumours. Erythropoietin has to be obtained either from plasma or urine. The situation somewhat resembles that in the early days of work on renin. An erythropoietic substance exists, the kidney is necessary for its appearance, but the kidney itself does not contain it (p. 26.10).

Growth hormone

The sodium-retaining properties of this hormone are effective in man as well as in preparations of isolated kidneys.

Gonadal hormones

Oestrogen administration leads to salt and water retention. This appears to be due to a general effect on the tissues and not on the kidney specifically. Oestrogens lead to some rise in both GFR and RPF, possibly owing to the rise in extracellular fluid volume. Progesterone can cause some sodium and water retention in animals, but in man it seems to have the reverse effect and increase the output. Androgen administration leads to a rise in RPF.

RENAL REGULATION OF ACID-BASE BALANCE

The concentration of hydrogen ions in the urine can be increased to 2,500 times that of plasma or decreased to one quarter i.e. from pH 4·0 to 8·0. This allows the kidney to regulate the reaction of the body fluids.

The healthy individual eating a mixed diet produces 60–80 mEq of hydrogen ions each day. These hydrogen ions are buffered by the bases throughout the body (p. 6.4). The conjugate acids formed are temporarily retained in the body except for carbonic acid, which is the conjugate acid of the bicarbonate buffer system. This breaks down to form CO_2 and water so that the protons remain in the body in water molecules while the CO_2 is eliminated by the lungs. The reconstitution of the body bases is achieved by the excretion in the urine of a number of protons equivalent to those formed in the course of metabolism and the simultaneous regeneration of the all-important base bicarbonate by the renal tubular cells.

Conversely, if an individual ingests a large amount of alkali the ingested base is buffered by the weak acids in the body. A proportion of the base reacts with carbonic acid according to the reaction.

$$OH^- + H_2CO_3 \rightleftharpoons H_2O + HCO_3^-$$

The bicarbonate ions formed in this reaction are then excreted in the urine because the tubular reabsorption of filtered bicarbonate ions is adjusted to maintain their concentration in the blood within defined limits. The kidney regulates the reaction of the body fluids in two ways:

(1) by controlling the rate of tubular reabsorption of filtered bicarbonate,

(2) by the excretion of hydrogen ions and the simultaneous regeneration of the base bicarbonate.

It will be readily appreciated that any change in the conjugate acid/conjugate base ratio of one buffer system leads to changes in the ratio in every other buffer system. Thus the alterations in the concentration of bicarbonate in the extracellular fluid which are brought about by the kidneys not only result in the restoration of the normal $\frac{1}{20}$ ratio of H_2CO_3/HCO_3^- (p. 6.4) but also restore the normal conjugate acid/conjugate base ratio in all the other systems.

Micropuncture studies have provided some evidence about the sites at which bicarbonate ions are reabsorbed and hydrogen ions added to the tubular fluid. Fig. 33.22 shows the changes in the pH of the tubular fluid found in different parts of the rat nephron. In the proximal tubule the changes are relatively small and the pH of the tubular fluid falls by about 0·5 to 1·0 units compared with that of the blood. This is due to the fact that HCO_3^- are reabsorbed more rapidly than water so that their concentration in the tubular fluid falls and P_{CO_2} remains

FIG. 33.22. The change in the pH of the tubular fluid obtained from rat nephrons by micropuncture technique. ΔpH = difference between pH of tubular fluid and that of arterial blood. pH measured by the quinhydrone microelectrode. From Gottschalk C.W. *et al.* (1960) *Amer. J. Physiol.* **198**, 581.

constant. Fluid obtained by micropuncture from the distal convoluted tubule is slightly more acid than that withdrawn from the proximal convolution. The urine, however, is much more acid than fluid obtained from the distal convolution so that the largest changes in pH must occur in the collecting ducts. This idea is confirmed by the results of experiments in which microcatheters were inserted into the collecting ducts of hamsters. In the studies shown in fig. 33.22 the pH of the urine fell to 5·4. Reduction of the urinary pH to 6·0 can be accounted for solely by the reabsorption of the base bicarbonate but in those animals in which the pH fell below this level, H^+ must have been added to the urine.

Some years ago Pitts and his colleagues carried out experiments upon normal human subjects in whom metabolic acidosis was induced by the administration of ammonium chloride. The presence of a large amount of buffer base in the urine was ensured by an infusion of a solution of neutral sodium phosphate. It was found that the rate of excretion of H^+ in the urine was greater than could be accounted for by the quantity of H^+ in the glomerular filtrate and it was concluded that H^+ were secreted into the urine by the renal tubules.

The tubular mechanism for reabsorption of bicarbonate and for formation of acid urine

It is now believed that the reabsorption of bicarbonate ions and the acidification of the urine are achieved by an ion exchange mechanism in which H^+ formed in the tubular cells are exchanged for Na^+ in the glomerular filtrate. This mechanism is shown in fig. 33.23. The source of the protons is not known but since the enzyme carbonic anhydrase is involved in their production (p. 6.4) it is possible that the hydration of carbon

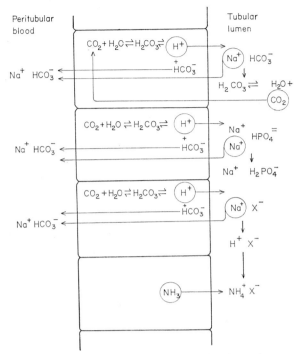

FIG. 33.23. Proposed ion exchange mechanism for reabsorption of sodium.

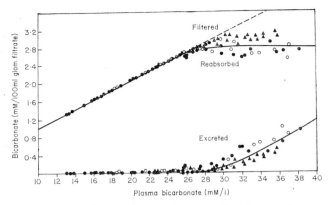

FIG. 33.24. The relationship between the plasma bicarbonate concentration and the rate of reabsorption of bicarbonate ions in normal man. ▲, ●, ○ represent 3 normal subjects. From Pitts R.F. *et al.* (1949) *J. Clin. Invest.* **28**, 35.

dioxide is catalysed in the tubular cells and that the carbonic acid formed dissociates to give H^+ and HCO_3^-. The protons are then secreted into the tubular fluid in exchange for Na^+ and the latter are reabsorbed into the peritubular blood along with the HCO_3^- formed from the dissociation of carbonic acid.

The fate of the H^+ which are secreted into the lumen depends upon the nature of the buffers present in the tubular fluid. These are as follows:

(1) filtered HCO_3^-,

(2) other filtered bases such as dibasic phosphate ion $HPO_4^=$, the hydroxybutyrate ion and creatinine,

(3) ammonia, which is also secreted into the tubular fluid by the renal tubular cells.

REABSORPTION OF FILTERED BICARBONATE

The base bicarbonate accepts a proton secreted by the tubular cells and forms its conjugate acid. Carbonic acid is unstable and breaks down to form water and carbon dioxide which is highly diffusable and passes readily out of the tubular lumen into the cells and the bloodstream. The net effect of this mechanism is therefore the reabsorption of sodium bicarbonate. In man the complete reabsorption of filtered bicarbonate requires the secretion of about 3500 mEq of H^+ each 24 hours.

The relation in normal subjects between the concentration of bicarbonate in plasma and its tubular reabsorption is shown in fig. 33.24. At low plasma bi-carbonate concentrations all filtered bicarbonate is reabsorbed and the urine contains none of this base. Bicarbonate appears in the urine in increasing amounts when the plasma concentration of the ion rises above 28 mEq/l. The amount reabsorbed may be calculated by subtracting the bicarbonate excreted in the urine from the bicarbonate filtered and is found to remain approximately constant at a value of 2·8 mEq/100 ml glomerular filtrate ($Tm_{HCO_3^-}$), i.e.

$$Tm_{HCO_3^-} = (C_{in} \times P_{HCO_3^-}) - U_{HCO_3^-} . V$$

FORMATION OF TITRATABLE ACID

When the concentration of HCO_3^- in the tubular fluid falls to very low levels, H^+ secreted into the lumen are taken up by the other bases which are present in the glomerular filtrate and their conjugate acids are formed. The most important of these is $HPO_4^=$ which accepts a proton to form its weak conjugate acid, monobasic phosphate ion $H_2PO_4^-$ (pK 6·8). Small numbers of H^+ are accepted by creatinine, but the acid form of creatinine is a relatively strong acid (pK 4·97) and only small amounts can exist in the urine. All the acids formed in this way are stable and accumulate in the tubular fluid so that the pH of the fluid falls. The lowest urinary pH which can be reached is 4·0, and the total number of H^+ which can be secreted into the urine before this limiting value is reached depends upon the total amount of filtered buffer base in the urine and upon the chemical nature of this base. When the conjugate acid formed as a result of the ion exchange process is relatively strong and dissociates readily to give free protons, the limiting value of urinary pH is reached much more rapidly than when the acid is weak. Thus at comparable rates of excretion $HPO_4^=$ is able to accept more protons than creatinine.

The contribution of this buffer mechanism is measured

by determining the amount of strong base which must be added to the urine in order to bring the urinary pH back to 7·4, the pH of the plasma from which the filtrate was derived. This gives a value for the so-called titratable acidity of the urine, and is usually 20–40 mEq of H^+/day. It is important to appreciate that for every molecule of titratable acid excreted one molecule of sodium bicarbonate is regenerated and reabsorbed into the peritubular blood.

Excretion of ammonium ion

Two-thirds of the H^+ excreted in the urine appear in the form of the extremely weak acid NH_4^+, the ammonium ion, which is formed when the base ammonia NH_3 accepts a proton. Ammonia is quantitatively the most important urinary buffer and unlike the other proton acceptors it is not present in significant amounts in the glomerular filtrate but is secreted into the lumen by the tubular cells. Micropuncture studies indicate that in the rat at least it is secreted throughout the length of the nephron although most of the ammonia is added to the urine in the collecting ducts where the pH is lowest. The importance of ammonia as a urinary buffer lies in the fact that the conjugate acid is very weak indeed (pK 9·47). Even in an alkaline urine most of the urinary ammonia is present in the form NH_4^+ and when the pH is low a large number of H^+ can be accepted by it. The rate at which ammonia is secreted into the urine depends on two factors.

(1) The rate at which ammonia is produced in the renal tubular cells. This is discussed in more detail below but, in general, the more H^+ that need to be excreted, the higher the rate of ammonia production.

(2) The pH of the urine influences the rate of ammonium excretion and the more acid the urine, the more ammonia is secreted into the tubular fluid.

In addition, the rate of urine flow has by itself a small influence on the rate of ammonia excretion, the amount of ammonia varying directly with the volume. It is possible that the concentration of NH_3 in the tubular cells may influence the rate of ammonia secretion.

THE MECHANISM OF SECRETION OF AMMONIA INTO THE URINE

Within the tubular cells the base ammonia is in equilibrium with the acidic ammonium ion.

$$NH_4^+ \rightleftharpoons NH_3 + H^+$$

Since the pH of the cells is about 7·0, most of the cellular ammonia must exist in the form of the weak acid NH_4^+ and only very small amounts of the free base NH_3 can be present. The cell membrane, however, is less permeable to the charged ammonium ion than to the uncharged ammonium molecule. The NH_3 therefore diffuses readily into and out of the cell, the direction of the diffusion being

determined by the pH of the intracellular water on the one hand and that of the plasma or the tubular fluid on the other. The accumulation of the NH_4^+ in an acid urine is most easily explained by assuming that the base enters the urine by passive diffusion down a concentration gradient. This diffusion continues until the concentration of NH_3 becomes the same in the urine as it is in the interior of the cell. The ammonia which enters the tubular fluid where the pH is lower than that in the cells is largely converted to the weak acid NH_4^+. This acid is then trapped in the tubular fluid because the cell membrane is relatively impermeable to it. Thus while the concentration of the base NH_3 in the tubular fluid is equal to that in the cells, the concentration of the acid ammonium ion in the cell fluid and in the urine are entirely different because they are determined by the relative concentrations of the H^+ in these fluids.

PRODUCTION OF AMMONIA BY THE RENAL TUBULAR CELLS

In 1921, Nash and Benedict showed that the concentration of ammonia in renal venous blood exceeded that in renal arterial blood and postulated that the kidney formed ammonia from some precursor in the arterial blood and that this ammonia was then added both to the urine and to the blood in the renal vein. Support for this idea was derived from the fact that the concentration of ammonia in renal arterial blood is not only far too low to account for the amount of this substance excreted but also does not increase in acidotic animals at a time when they are excreting large amounts of ammonia.

In 1943, Van Slyke and his colleagues noted that during the passage of blood through the kidney glutamine was removed from the blood to a greater extent than other amino acids. The kidney contains an enzyme glutaminase I which is capable of hydrolysing glutamine to form glutamic acid and ammonia,

$$\overset{\displaystyle NH_2}{\underset{\displaystyle |}{COOHCHCH_2CH_2CONH_2}} + H_2O \xrightarrow{\text{glutaminase I}}$$

$$\overset{\displaystyle NH_2}{\underset{\displaystyle |}{COOHCHCH_2CH_2COOH}} + NH_3$$

and these workers calculated that almost two-thirds of the urinary ammonia could be derived in this way from the amide nitrogen of glutamine.

Pitts and his colleagues have performed experiments upon dogs with acidosis in which tracer amounts of glutamine having the amide nitrogen labelled with ^{15}N were infused into one renal artery. Examination of the urine from the infused kidneys shows that 33–50 per cent of the urinary ammonia contained ^{15}N and must have been derived from the amide nitrogen of plasma glutamine. Similar studies using glutamine with a ^{15}N label in the amino group showed that 16–25 per cent of urinary ammonia was derived from the amino nitrogen of glutamine. A number of other amino acids have been shown to be capable of increasing the rate of ammonia excretion when they are infused and since the dog's kidney does not contain any significant amount of L-amino acid oxidase the ammonia cannot be derived from simple oxidative deamination of the amino acids. In all probability the role of such acids, whether they reach the tubules by the blood stream or are reabsorbed from the glomerular filtrate, is to supply amino groups to a nitrogen pool in the tubular cells.

It is possible to determine the overall rate at which amide and amino nitrogen are extracted by the kidney from the renal arterial blood and also the rate at which ammonia is added to the urine and to the blood in the renal vein. In dogs with acidosis the rate at which amine and amide nitrogen are removed from plasma is approximately equal to the rate of ammonia production.

FIG. 33.25. A simplified version of the major metabolic paths involved in the production of ammonia by the renal tubular cells. ● represents amino N_2, ○ amide N_2. Adapted from Pitts R.F. (1964) *Amer. J. Med.* **36**, 733.

Fig. 33.25 shows some of the metabolic pathways which are likely to be involved in the formation of ammonia in the renal tubular cells. It has been proposed that the immediate source of ammonia is glutamine and that this substance is split by glutaminase I to yield glutamic acid and ammonia. Since glutamic acid appears neither in the urine nor in the renal venous blood it must undergo further chemical change. At least two possibilities exist; glutamic acid may be broken down by glutamic dehydrogenase to form α-oxoglutarate and ammonia, the keto acid being subsequently oxidized in the citric acid cycle or else

reacting with an α-amino acid to resynthesize glutamic acid. Alternatively glutamic acid may undergo transamination reacting with an α-keto acid to produce the corresponding α-amino acid and α-oxo glutaric acid.

$$COOHCHNHCH_2CH_2COOH + RCOCOOH$$
$$\rightleftharpoons COOHCOCH_2CH_2COOH$$
$$+ RCHNH_2COOH$$

The kidney however contains a second glutaminase, glutaminase II, and under the influence of this enzyme which is, in reality, a transaminase, glutamine may react with an α-keto acid to form α-oxoglutaramate which cannot be detected in the cells because it is rapidly deaminated by an ω amidase to form α-oxoglutarate and ammonia.

FACTORS WHICH INFLUENCE THE RATE OF PRODUCTION OF AMMONIA

When an acidifying salt such as ammonium chloride is given to a normal subject the rate of excretion of H^+ in the form of ammonium ions and titratable acid is increased. If, however, the ammonium chloride is given for several successive days the rate of excretion of NH_4^+ rises progressively while the excretion of titratable acid and the urine pH remain the same. The kidney adapts to the stimulus of chronic acidosis by producing more ammonia. The means by which it does this are unknown. A similar pattern is seen in experimental animals and in some but not all species the concentration of glutaminase I in renal tissue increases during acidosis.

In summary, the total amount of H^+ secreted by the renal tubules may be calculated from the sum of the urinary ammonia, titratable acid (TA) and reabsorbed bicarbonate.

$$\text{Total } H^+ \text{ secretion} = U_{TA}V + U_{NH_4^+}.V$$
$$+ \{(C_{in} \times P_{HCO_3^-}) - U_{HCO_3^-}.V\}$$

The total urinary excretion of H^+ is given by the sum of the titratable acid and ammonium ion.

$$\text{Total } H^+ \text{ excretion} = U_{TA}V + U_{NH_4^+}.V$$

In order to calculate the net urinary loss of H^+ from the body it is customary to subtract the amount of bicarbonate excreted in the urine from the total H^+ excreted since the excretion of one HCO_3^- is equivalent to the addition of H^+ to the body fluid.

Net urinary loss of H^+ from body =
$$U_{TA}V + U_{NH_4^+}.V - U_{HCO_3^-}.V.$$

Factors which influence the rate of secretion of hydrogen ions

P_{CO_2}.

It has frequently been observed that when the P_{CO_2} of the arterial blood is elevated, as it is in certain forms of chronic respiratory disease, the concentration of bicarbonate in the plasma becomes stabilized at a higher level than normal. Experiments on dogs have shown that an increase in P_{CO_2} is associated with an increase in the rate of reabsorption of bicarbonate by the kidney and increased excretion of hydrogen ions in the form of titratable acid and ammonium ions. This increased secretion of protons is maintained even when steps are taken to prevent the fall in pH which normally accompanies the rise in P_{CO_2}. Conversely a reduction in P_{CO_2} is associated with a reduction in H^+ secretion. Carbon dioxide penetrates cells rapidly and the concentration of H^+ within the renal tubular cells must be influenced by the P_{CO_2}. It seems probable that the rate of secretion of H^+ is in turn dependent upon the intracellular concentrations of these ions.

POTASSIUM BALANCE

Potassium-depleted subjects usually have an extracellular alkalosis with an increased concentration of bicarbonate in the plasma. This high plasma bicarbonate must be maintained by an increased rate of bicarbonate reabsorption, i.e. an increased rate of H^+ secretion. Conversely the administration of potassium salts is associated with diminished reabsorption of bicarbonate. Like H^+, K^+ are secreted into the urine in exchange for Na^+ (p. 33.19) and it is possible that the relative concentrations of K^+ and H^+ in the cells are of importance in determining their relative rates of secretion.

CHLORIDE BALANCE

Filtered Na^+ are reabsorbed by the tubules along with an anion, Cl^-, or in exchange for K^+ or H^+. If the concentration of Cl^- in the filtrate is reduced a larger amount of Na^+ is reabsorbed by the ion exchange mechanism. The reabsorption of Na^+ unaccompanied by Cl^- results in an increase in the potential difference which normally exists across the luminal surface of the epithelial cells of the renal tubules. The rate of diffusion of positively charged H^+ out of the cells down this electrochemical gradient is increased, tubular reabsorption and generation of HCO_3^- increases and its concentration in the plasma rises. Thus the patient depleted of chloride develops a metabolic alkalosis and he is particularly likely to do so if his kidneys are under a strong stimulus to reabsorb filtered sodium.

Conversely, the administration of a large amount of chloride, almost invariably in the form of its sodium salt, leads to a diminution in sodium hydrogen exchange, an alkaline urine and a fall in plasma bicarbonate.

CARBONIC ANHYDRASE INHIBITORS

Substances such as acetazolamide which inhibit the action of the enzyme carbonic anhydrase have been shown to interfere with the secretion of H^+ in exchange for Na^+. Acidification of the urine and the reabsorption of bicarbonate are therefore reduced and the urine contains increased amounts of sodium bicarbonate.

ADRENAL STEROIDS

Hormones of the adrenal cortex which increase the reabsorption of Na^+ may also be necessary for normal rates of H^+ secretion.

DIURNAL RHYTHMS

Studies of renal function in man tend to fall into two categories, acute observations lasting for a few hours and prolonged studies of several days' duration during which all the urine excreted during each 24-hour period is pooled for analysis. If, however, the urine is collected at 3 or 4-hourly intervals for a period of several days, rhythmical changes in volume and composition can be detected and when the rates of excretion of substances such as sodium, potassium, chloride and phosphate are plotted against time a cyclical pattern with a mean period of 24 hours emerges. This phenomenon has been named the circadian (*circa die*) or diurnal rhythm, and its existence has been recognized for more than a hundred years, but the factors controlling the cyclical changes in renal function are by no means clear. A general account of biological rhythms is given in chap. 44.

FURTHER READING

DENTON D.A. (1965) Evolutionary aspects of the emergence of aldosterone secretion and salt appetite. *Physiol. Rev.* 45, 245.

METCALF J. (1963) *Angiotensin Systems and Experimental Renal Disease*. London : Churchill.

MILLS J.N. (1963). Mechanisms of renal homeostasis and Other aspects of renal function in *Recent Advances in Physiology*, ed. Creese. London : Churchill.

PITTS R.F. (1963). *Physiology of the Kidneys and Body Fluids*. Chicago : Year Book Medical Publications.

SELKURT E.E. (1963). The renal circulation, in *Handbook of Physiology*. Section 2, Circulation, volume II ed. Hamilton & Dow. Washington : American Physiological Society.

WILLIAMS P.C. (1963). *Hormones and the kidney* in Memoirs of the Society for Endocrinology No. 13. London : Academic Press.

Chapter 34
The urinary tract

The urinary tract extends from the minor calyces of the kidney to the external meatus of the urethra and can be divided into two parts. The upper part conveys urine from the collecting tubules of the kidney to the bladder and consists of the major and minor calyces and pelvis of the kidney, and the ureter. The lower part which stores and intermittently expels urine consists of the bladder and the urethra. In the male the urethra also has a reproductive function.

DEVELOPMENT OF THE KIDNEY, RENAL PELVIS, URETER, BLADDER AND URETHRA

Three structures, the **pronephros**, the **mesonephros** and the **metanephros** successively take part in the development of the urinary tract, and in mammals the last of these is retained as the permanent kidney (fig. 34.1). The development of the urinary and genital tracts are closely related and a full account of the development of the reproductive system is given on p. 37.53.

The mesoderm of the intermediate cell mass below the level of the eighth somite is called the **nephrogenic cord**. In the 23-day-old embryo a clump of cells appears in this cord at the level of the ninth somite. These proliferate and spread caudally forming a solid cord which reaches and fuses with the cloaca. At the cranial end a lumen develops and gradually extends throughout the cord to open into the cloaca about the twenty-eighth day of intrauterine life, thus forming the **nephric duct**. In some species, but not in man, vesicles appear in the cervicodorsal region of the embryo dorsal to the upper end of the primary excretory duct and connect this duct to the coelomic cavity; this is the pronephros.

The mesonephros develops caudal to the pronephros and consists of clusters of cells in the nephrogenic cord, each of which becomes a vesicle and communicates with the nephric duct, now called the **mesonephric duct**; the vesicle itself dilates and is invaginated to form a glomerulus. The glomerular capillaries arise from proliferation of these invaginated cells and are supplied with blood from lateral branches of the aorta. Some seventy to eighty mesonephric vesicles form but no more than thirty or forty are present at any one time and most eventually degenerate and disappear.

By the time the mesonephros has developed to its

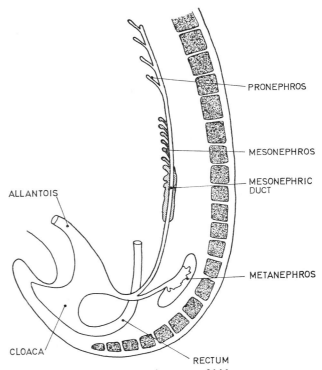

FIG. 34.1. Development of kidneys.

caudal limit, the cranial two-thirds of the tubules have degenerated and by the beginning of the 10th week few intact mesonephric tubules remain. Remnants of a number of these tubules do nevertheless persist to become part of the duct system of the testis. Some of these link up with the rete testis and form the efferent ductules of that organ. The corresponding set of tubules in the female form the epoöphoron. Others become separated from the mesonephric duct and form the paradidymis in the male and the paroöphoron in the female.

The metanephros, which becomes the permanent kidney, develops from two sources, the mesonephric duct and the metanephrogenic cap (fig. 34.2). When the embryo is 5 weeks old, an outgrowth called the **ureteric bud** arises from the mesonephric duct near its entry into the cloaca and grows into the mesoderm of the caudal end of the nephrogenic cord. The ureteric bud becomes the ureter and its cephalic end expands to form the pelvic calyces and the collecting tubules of the kidney.

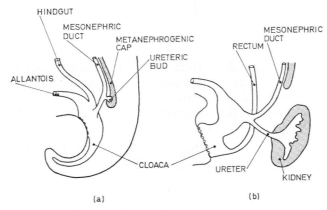

FIG. 34.2. Development of metanephros.

The mesoderm which surrounds this expanded end condenses to become the **metanephrogenic cap** from which the remainder of the kidney develops. Vesicles appear and elongate to form metanephric tubules which enlarge and convolute; one end of each tubule fuses with the collecting ducts and the other is associated with a tuft of capillaries and becomes a glomerulus. After the metanephros has developed, the cranial portion of the mesonephric duct is superfluous; it is available for incorporation into the genital apparatus (p. 37.58).

Each normal adult kidney contains approximately one million glomeruli at birth. Increase in the size of the kidney after birth is the result of hypertrophy and not of hyperplasia, i.e. it is due to an increase in the size and not the number of the nephrons.

At first the kidney lies in the pelvis but as the ureteric bud lengthens it gradually ascends and rotates to reach its adult position in the loin. It obtains blood from neighbouring vessels, which are the common iliac and median sacral arteries while it is in the pelvis, and from one of the adrenal arteries while it is in the loin until the renal artery appears in the third month. The kidney is a lobulated organ until the end of the first year of extra-uterine life.

The origin of the ureter moves from the dorsomedial to the lateral aspect of the mesonephric duct and the caudal end of this duct shifts downwards to be incorporated within the bladder. Thus the ureter comes to open directly into the bladder, lateral to the opening of the mesonephric duct. Because the mesonephric duct

continues to grow downwards the ureteric orifices gradually separate and eventually the mesonephric duct opens nto the p rostatic urethra (fig. 34.3).

A double ureter on one or both sides is one of many congenital malformations that may be found in the urinary tract. It occurs when two instead of one ureteric buds arise from the mesonephric duct. Because this duct shifts downwards the upper bud which forms the upper

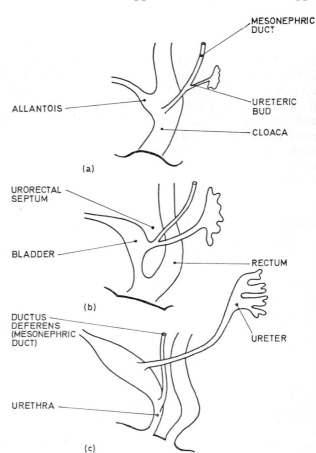

FIG. 34.3. Diagram to show development of ureter and ductus deferens.

renal pelvis eventually opens into the bladder below the bud which forms the lower pelvis (fig. 34.4).

The bladder is formed mainly from that part of the primitive urogenital sinus which lies above the mesonephric ducts, namely the vesico-urethral canal. In addition the absorbed caudal part of the mesonephric ducts form the bladder trigone and the dorsal wall of the prostatic urethra in the male and the trigone and part of the urethra in the female. The allantois passes from the ventral aspect of the urogenital sinus into the body stalk and later becomes the urachus which connects the bladder to the umbilicus. It persists into adult life as a fibrous cord called the median umbilical ligament.

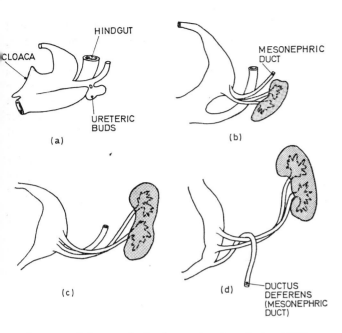

FIG. 34.4. Scheme of development when two ureters appear instead of one. (a) Two ureteric buds develop from the mesonephric duct. (b) Each bud elongates to form a pelvis and calyces inside the metanephrogenic cap. (c) The origin of the upper bud is carried below that of the lower bud as the mesonephric duct descends. (d) The ureter draining the upper pelvis enters the bladder below that draining the lower. Both are crossed by the ductus deferens.

Sometimes, however, its lumen does not disappear and then urine may leak from the umbilicus.

THE RENAL PELVIS, CALYCES AND URETER

The collecting tubules within the renal medulla drain into the minor calyces through the collecting ducts, sixteen to twenty of which open on to the surface of each renal papilla. There are usually six minor calyces but there may be as few as four or as many as thirteen in number. Several join together to form two or three major calyces and these, in turn, unite to form the renal pelvis which is the expanded upper part of the ureter (fig. 33.1).

The ureters are two narrow, thick-walled, muscular tubes which start from the renal pelvis, descend through the abdomen and pelvis and open into the base of the bladder. At first the ureter lies retroperitoneally on the psoas major muscle which separates it from the tips of the lumbar transverse processes, and is crossed by the testicular or ovarian vessels. It then enters the pelvis by crossing in front of either the common iliac vessels or the origin of the external iliac vessels from the common iliacs, and runs downwards in extraperitoneal tissue on the lateral wall of the pelvis as far as the ischial spine where, turning forward, it runs on the superior surface of the levator ani to the bladder. In the male it is crossed by the ductus deferens, and in the female it is very closely related to the uterine artery, the cervix of the uterus and the lateral fornix of the vagina (figs. 37.1 and 37.19).

The calyces, pelvis and ureter each have three coats. *The mucous coat* is smooth and contrary to what the term suggests is devoid of glands. Over the renal papillae it is a simple, cuboidal epithelium and is perforated by the openings of the collecting ducts; elsewhere it is transitional epithelium.

The muscular coat is smooth or involuntary muscle. In the calyces, the renal pelvis and the upper two-thirds of the ureters it is arranged in two layers, an inner longitudinal and an outer circular layer. The lower third of the ureter has an additional layer of longitudinal fibres outside the circular layer but where it pierces the wall of the bladder it retains only a longitudinal layer.

The fibrous coat or adventitia is continuous above with the renal capsule and below with the fascia on the surface of the bladder.

Blood supply and lymphatic drainage

The calyces and renal pelvis receive blood from the renal artery and return it to the renal vein. The ureter derives blood from the renal artery, lumbar arteries, testicular or ovarian arteries, common and internal iliac arteries, the vesical arteries and the uterine arteries, each supplying the adjacent part of the ureter. The lymphatics follow the veins draining the same part.

The ureterovesical junction

The ureterovesical junction allows urine to pass freely from the ureters into the bladder but prevents it from passing in the opposite direction. It does so by reason of its anatomical disposition rather than by neuromuscular activity. In fact since the muscle around the intramural part of the ureter is longitudinal it widens and shortens when it contracts and so cannot function as a sphincter. The ureters pass obliquely through the wall of the bladder, and whereas 10 cm separate them as they enter the bladder, they are only 5 cm apart when they open into the cavity. Their obliquity is increased as the bladder fills or contracts; in this way reflux of urine from the bladder into the ureter is prevented. Mucosal folds form where the mucosa of the ureter becomes continuous with that of the bladder and are important in preventing reflux in some animals but not, apparently, in man. The junction between the ureters and the bladder is of considerable clinical importance because of the relationship between recurrent urinary tract infection and the reflux of urine from the bladder into the ureters.

THE BLADDER

The bladder is a hollow muscular organ whose shape, size and relations vary with the amount of urine it contains. When empty it lies in the pelvis. It has a tetrahedral shape and possesses a superior and two inferolateral surfaces, a base, a neck and an apex. The superior surface is triangular in shape and is completely covered by peritoneum, which separates it from loops of ileum and the sigmoid colon. However, in the female a tiny area posteriorly is left uncovered as the peritoneum is reflected on to the anterior aspect of the junction of the body and cervix of the uterus. The inferolateral surfaces are separated by loose areolar tissue from the levator ani muscle of the pelvis posteriorly, and by the puboprostatic vesical ligament from the pubic symphysis anteriorly. The apex points forwards and continues into the median umbilical ligament which runs over the back of the anterior abdominal wall to the umbilicus. The base is triangular and faces backwards and downwards and is related in the female to the uterine cervix and anterior wall of the vagina and in the male to the rectovesical fold of peritoneum superiorly and the seminal vesicles and the two ductūs deferentes inferiorly which separate it from the rectum. The neck is the lowest part of the bladder and is pierced by the internal meatus of the urethra. It is continuous with the base of the prostate in the male (fig. 37.19) and with the loose pelvic fascia around the urethra in the female.

As the bladder fills it becomes egg shaped and expands upwards and forwards into the abdomen, pushing the peritoneum upwards and stripping it away from the anterior abdominal wall.

Interior of the bladder

When the bladder is empty its mucous membrane lies in longitudinal folds which gradually disappear as the bladder fills. The trigone is the triangular area bounded by the ureteric orifices and bladder neck. There the mucosa is firmly attached to the underlying muscle and is always smooth. The orifices of the ureters vary in appearance but are usually slit-like. They open into the bladder at the posterolateral angles of the trigone and are separated by the interureteric bar which is the base of the trigone. The internal urethral orifice, which is crescentic in shape, lies at the apex of the trigone.

Structure

The bladder consists of three coats.
The serosal or peritoneal coat is found only on the superior surface and has already been described.
The muscular coat is sometimes called the detrusor muscle. It is smooth muscle and consists of an internal and an external layer of longitudinal fibres and a middle layer of circular fibres. The layers intermingle with one another extensively. At the bladder neck the muscle

fibres run longitudinally and are not circularly disposed (fig. 34.5). Thus, there is really no internal sphincter, although this is frequently described. They pass through the bladder neck and surround the urethra as far as its membranous part in the male, and to within 0·5 cm of the external urethral meatus in the female. The muscle around the bladder neck contracts when the muscle of the bladder itself contracts, but being longitudinal it shortens and widens the lumen of the neck and urethra and thus allows urine to enter the urethra. When the bladder is relaxed the longitudinal muscle around the bladder neck is also relaxed. The urethra contains no urine except during micturition because its anterior and posterior walls are apposed. This is not due to contraction of

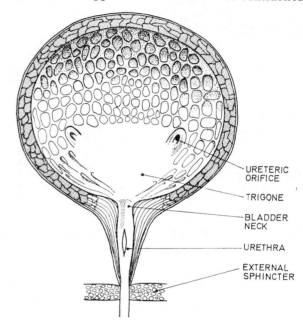

FIG. 34.5. Coronal section of bladder showing disposition of muscle at bladder neck.

a muscle sphincter around the bladder neck but results from the tension of elastic fibres which are liberally scattered between the fibres of the urethral muscle. It is also caused by the inherent tone of the urethral muscle, and to a lesser extent by the activity of the external sphincter of the urethra. Thus, the urethra proximal to the external sphincter is naturally closed and neuromuscular activity opens but does not close it. The external sphincter is striated muscle. *The mucosal coat* is transitional epithelium and is fixed over the trigone. In the subtrigonal and subcervical region some glands are found but they are probably prostatic in origin.

Blood supply

The bladder is supplied mainly by the superior and inferior vesical arteries, but it also receives small branches from the gluteal and obturator arteries and, in the female, from the uterine and vaginal arteries. Venous blood drains into the large venous plexus around the bladder neck and the prostate and then into the internal iliac veins. The lymph vessels run alongside the veins to lymph nodes around the internal iliac vessels.

THE URETHRA

The urethra extends from the neck of the bladder to the external meatus. The male and female urethra are so different that they are separately described.

THE MALE URETHRA

This consists of a prostatic, a membranous and a spongy part and is about 20 cm long (fig. 34.6). The prostatic urethra pierces the prostate gland from its base to its apex and is the widest and the most distensible part. Its transverse section is made crescentic by a longitudinal ridge on the posterior wall called the urethral crest. On

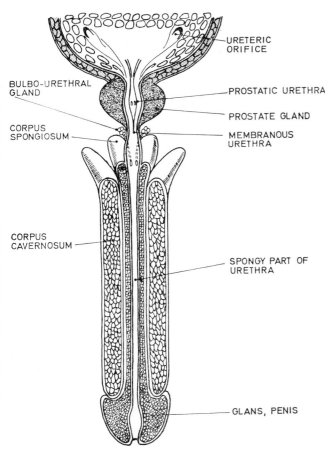

FIG. 34.6. Male urethra laid open.

either side of this crest is a gutter called the prostatic sulcus into which the prostatic glands open. At about the middle of the urethral crest is an eminence called the **colliculus seminalis**, on each side of which lies the opening of the ejaculatory duct and on its summit is a slit which is the opening of a cul-de-sac, the **prostatic utricle** (fig. 37.24).

The membranous urethra is the shortest, the least distensible and, after the external meatus itself, the narrowest portion of the male urethra. It perforates the urogenital diaphragm and is surrounded by the external urethral sphincter. This is a striated muscle and forms part of the urogenital diaphragm as it surrounds the membranous urethra (p. 20.32).

The spongy portion of the urethra is about 15 cm long and is contained in the **corpus spongiosum** of the **penis**. It extends from the inferior fascia of the urogenital diaphragm to the external urethral meatus. It varies in diameter, being widest at its start in the intrabulbar fossa and just before the external urethral meatus; the external meatus is the narrowest part of the whole urethra.

Structure

The transitional epithelium of the bladder continues through the bladder neck and lines the urethra as far as the opening of the ejaculatory ducts where it changes to a stratified columnar epithelium. Near the external urethral meatus the epithelium becomes stratified squamous and continuous with the skin of the glans penis.

The subepithelial layer is vascular erectile tissue and contains many mucous glands which open into the lumen of the urethra. The smooth muscular layer is longitudinally disposed and is continuous above with the detrusor of bladder and extends distally as far as the membranous urethra where it is replaced and partly surrounded by the striated muscle of the external sphincter urethrae.

THE FEMALE URETHRA

The female urethra is straight and only 4 cm long. It begins at the neck of the bladder and runs downwards and forwards. It is embedded in the anterior wall of the vagina and perforates the urogenital diaphragm where it is also enclosed by the external sphincter muscle. It ends anterior to the vaginal orifice as the external urethral meatus (fig. 37.5).

Structure

The mucosa is transitional epithelium near the bladder and stratified squamous epithelium elsewhere. The smooth muscle fibres which surround the urethra except for its last 1 cm are longitudinally disposed and continuous above with those of the bladder. Interspersed between the muscle fibres are many circular elastic fibres which help to keep the walls of the urethra apposed except when urine is passing. The striated muscle fibres of the external urethral sphincter surround the terminal part of the urethra and mix with the distal smooth muscle fibres. A layer of spongy, erectile tissue and veins lies between mucosa and muscle coat.

FUNCTION OF THE LOWER URINARY TRACTS

The flow of urine from the kidney down the ureter and into the bladder is caused by the co-ordinated contractions of the muscle coats of the urinary tract. Just as food is pushed down the oesophagus and along the bowel by peristalsis, so also is urine moved down the urinary tract. Gravity assists the flow and the kidneys do not empty as quickly in the supine position. The contraction wave starts in the circular muscle fibres of the minor calyces of the kidneys and spreads through the muscle fibres of the major calyces, pelvis and ureter, propelling urine downwards to the longitudinal muscle fibres of the lowest part of the ureter, which widens the lumen so that urine enters the bladder. That the contraction wave starts in the minor calyces and moves progressively downwards suggests the presence of a pacemaker which has not been identified. The efferent autonomic nerve fibres that can be demonstrated in the wall of the ureter supply only the muscle of the arterioles. The smooth muscle of the ureter has no motor nerve supply and contains no nerve plexuses. The contraction of this muscle and the propagation of the contraction wave result from inherent properties of the muscle fibres themselves.

MICTURITION

This is a complex act involving both autonomic and somatic nerves and is normally controlled by higher centres. It is one of the few visceral reflexes over which there is any conscious control. Three sets of nerves are involved.

The parasympathetic nerves travel to the bladder with the pelvic splanchnic nerves from the 2nd, 3rd and sometimes the 4th sacral segment. They emerge from the sacral foramina and pass through the pelvic plexus to the bladder and are the main motor nerves to the detrusor muscle. Afferent fibres also travel in the pelvic splanchnic nerves; these pass upwards in the ventral columns of the spinal cord and convey the sensation of the desire to micturate.

The sympathetic fibres come from the hypogastric plexus which lies anterior to the body of the fifth lumbar vertebra and join the pelvic plexus. Experimental stimulation of the sympathetic fibres in man may cause closure of the ureteric orifices and increase the tone in the trigone, but these effects play little, if any, part in normal micturition.

Afferent fibres travel with the sympathetic fibres and enter the dorsal horn of the spinal cord in the mid-thoracic region; they travel upwards in the lateral spino-thalamic tract and carry sensation, not of normal bladder filling, but of abnormal stimuli like overdistension or spasm.

The somatic nerves are the efferent and afferent components of the pudendal nerves (S2, 3 and 4) and consist of the efferent nerves to the external sphincter of the urethra and the afferent nerves from the posterior urethra which are stimulated by distension.

The sacral 2nd, 3rd and 4th segments of the spinal cord are the site of the spinal reflex for micturition and the parasympathetic and pudendal nerves derive from it. It connects with the higher centres by afferent and efferent pathways and is greatly influenced by them (fig. 34.7).

There is no sensation of bladder distention until it contains between 300 and 400 ml, when the need to micturate is felt. Although this can be temporarily suppressed, it soon returns and eventually becomes so strong and urgent that it must be obeyed. Once micturition starts it continues until the bladder is empty although the

FIG. 34.7. Nerve supply of bladder.

stream can be temporarily interrupted by voluntary contraction of the external urethral sphincter. Micturition can be started by voluntary effort, even though there is too little urine in the bladder to produce the sensation of the need to pass water.

The response of the bladder to filling can be studied by measuring the intravesical pressure produced in response to changes in bladder volume. This procedure (cystometry) is carried out by inserting a twoway catheter into the bladder through the urethra. The bladder is emptied and one limb of the catheter is connected to a reservoir of sterile water and the other to a recording manometer. Fluid is slowly run into the bladder from the reservoir and the intravesical pressure recorded continuously. Cystometry (fig. 34.8) shows that after a small

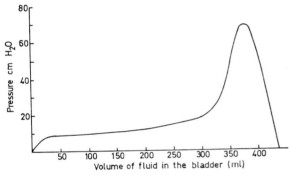

Fig. 34.8. Cystometrogram.

initial increase in pressure, the normal bladder accommodates increasing volumes of fluid with little, if any, change in pressure. When the volume of fluid inside the bladder exceeds 300 ml there is a small rise in pressure and the desire to micturate is experienced. If this is suppressed the pressure falls, but if micturition is allowed to proceed a marked rise in pressure follows. The ability to tolerate an increase in volume without a corresponding increase in pressure indicates progressive relaxation of the bladder wall. This is largely an effect of the properties of the muscle fibres but neuromuscular activity may contribute in the following manner. As the bladder fills, impulses pass from the stretch receptors in its wall, along the afferent fibres in the pelvic splanchnic nerves to the spinal cord. These would increase the excitatory state of the centre if they were not suppressed by inhibitory impulses from higher centres. When the bladder holds 300 or 400 ml of urine the intensity of these impulses overcomes the inhibition and they ascend to the sensory part of the cerebral cortex and the need to micturate is experienced. If it is socially inconvenient the desire can be suppressed because the higher centres can temporarily inhibit the spinal reflex. Otherwise the cortex lifts the inhibitory influences and micturition is initiated through a series of reflexes. These may originate in the

sacral centres but higher centres are essential for the accurate grading and control of the responses. Impulses from the sacral cord pass along the parasympathetic fibres of the pelvic splanchnic nerves and cause the bladder detrusor to contract. Urine can then enter and distend the posterior part of the urethra and so stimulate urethral sensory receptors. From these, impulses pass along the afferent fibres of the pudendal nerve into the sacral centre and there inhibit the ventral horn cells supplying the external urethral sphincter which relaxes, allowing urine to flow into the remainder of the urethra and on through the external urinary meatus. It is essential, however, that the bladder not only contracts but continues to contract until it is empty. This is achieved because the cerebral cortex, basal ganglia and reticular formation, which all inhibit the sacral centre while the bladder is filling, bombard it with facilitatory impulses once micturition begins so that it remains excited and, therefore, active until the bladder is quite empty.

DISORDERS OF MICTURITION IN NEUROLOGICAL DISORDERS

When the nerve supply of the bladder is damaged or involved by disease, micturition may be disordered in various ways and a description of these can help us to understand the physiology of micturition. Patients with disease of the nervous system may have one of four different abnormalities of micturition or, as is commonly but erroneously said of bladder function.

An uninhibited bladder results from a lack of inhibition by the higher centres over the sacral spinal centre. The desire to micturate is experienced when the bladder contains as little as 50 or 100 ml of urine; this volume excites the centre as much as 300 or 400 ml do when inhibitory influences are normal. The desire cannot be suppressed and becomes urgent. If it is not obeyed micturition starts precipitately. Once micturition starts it continues until the bladder is empty. The lesion that causes this disturbance is usually in the cortex and is frequently psychological in nature.

An atonic bladder develops when the sensory pathways from the bladder to the cerebral cortex are damaged as may occur for example in diabetes. All muscle contraction is absent. There is no sensation so the bladder fills until it is grossly distended when urine overflows down the urethra causing overflow incontinence; the bladder always contains a large volume of residual urine. This disorder occurs in spinal shock when the spinal cord is suddenly separated from the higher centre. This temporarily paralyses the sacral centre but local recovery occurs leading to an automatic or autonomous bladder.

An automatic bladder (upper motor neurone bladder) develops after complete section of the spinal cord above the sacral centre for micturition once the period of spinal shock is over. As sensory impulses cannot reach the sensory cortex no desire to micturate is felt. Inhibitory impulses from the higher centres cannot reach the sacral centre and the bladder automatically contracts when it contains as little as 100–200 ml of urine. The patient is incontinent, and because this is the result of bladder contraction, the incontinence is called active (1-1′ fig. 34.7).

An autonomous bladder (lower motor neurone bladder) results from lesions which separate the bladder from its sacral spinal centre by damage either to the spinal cord below the 2nd, 3rd and 4th sacral segments, or to the cauda equina, or the 2nd, 3rd and 4th sacral roots. If the bladder were striated muscle supplied by somatic nerves it would, in these circumstances, be paralysed and flaccid. Being smooth muscle, however, it responds directly to being stretched.

The absence of higher inhibitory influences makes the autonomous bladder tense and hypertonic, and it contracts when it contains only a small volume of urine. However, the contraction is weak so that little urine is passed and the amount of residual urine is high. There is active incontinence and the need to pass urine is not appreciated (2–2′ fig. 34.7).

The bladder is also concerned with a number of visceromotor and viscerosensory reflexes. These are most easily demonstrated in patients who have automatic or autonomous bladders in whom filling of the bladder sometimes causes marked disturbances in sympathetic nervous activity with changes in blood pressure, skin colour and sweating.

FURTHER READING

IRVINE W.T. ed. (1965). Chaps. 23 & 24 in *Scientific Basis of Surgery*. London: Churchill.

Chapter 35
Structure and function of skin

The primary functions of the skin are to encase and protect the other tissues and organs of the body and to supply sensory information concerning the external environment. As an organ with many different component parts the skin has other important functions which contribute to the health and comfort of the organism. In a normal adult male the skin and subcutaneous fat may weigh 9 kg, about 14 per cent of the body weight.

GENERAL ANATOMY

The skin covers the entire body surface, its epithelium being continuous with those of the digestive, respiratory and genitourinary systems at their external orifices. It is an elastic envelope which is under slight tension, and is freely mobile except where it is attached to the deep fascia as over the flexure lines of joints. The surface of the skin is traversed by branching lines which make up irregular geometric patterns. On the finger tips and toe pads, however, a regular pattern of ridges and sulci is found. The finger prints are so characteristic for each individual that they serve as an effective means of personal identification. In identical twins the patterns are similar but never identical.

The skin can be divided into two layers: (1) the surface epithelium or epidermis with its derived appendages, the cutaneous glands and hair, (2) the connective tissue or dermis which supports the epidermal appendages, vessels and nerves; under these is the adipose tissue or subcutaneous fat (fig. 35.1). There are regional variations of this basic pattern with regard to thickness of the layers, numbers of cutaneous appendages and vascularity. These are illustrated in plate 35.1, facing p. 33.5. Knowledge of these differences helps to explain the varying climatic conditions which exist on the skin surface in different areas of the body; it is also of value in assessing the reaction of the skin in disease and lays the foundation for a more rational approach to therapy. These structural variations may alter such factors as surface pH, composition of surface lipid film, and presence or absence of hair and sebum.

MICROSCOPIC STRUCTURE OF SKIN

The epidermis

The most superficial layer of the skin, the epidermis, is a keratinized stratified squamous epithelium of ectodermal origin. For descriptive purposes it is divided into five layers (fig. 35.2): (1) stratum corneum, (2) stratum lucidum, (3) stratum granulosum, (4) stratum spinosum, (5) stratum basale.

Only in the thickest skin, over the palms and soles, are there all five layers. Elsewhere only four are identifiable, the **stratum lucidum** being missing. The deepest layer, the

FIG. 35.1. The basic structure of the skin.

35.1

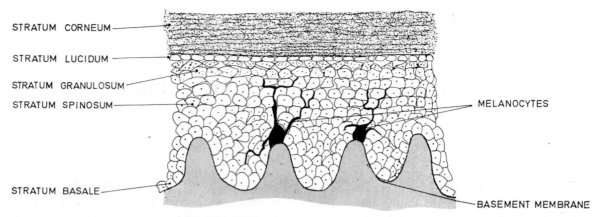

STRATUM CORNEUM

STRATUM LUCIDUM

STRATUM GRANULOSUM

STRATUM SPINOSUM

MELANOCYTES

STRATUM BASALE

BASEMENT MEMBRANE

FIG. 35.2. The detailed structure of epidermis.

stratum basale, consists of a single layer of cylindrical cells with deeply basophilic cytoplasm and centrally placed elongated nuclei. Their lower borders are attached to the underlying dermis by delicate cytoplasmic processes. Interspersed between the basal cells are the dendritic melanocytes, a specialized group whose function is the synthesis of melanin pigment (pp. 11.25 and 35.7).

Pigment in the form of a supranuclear cap of fine melanin granules is always found in some of the basal cells. In people with dark skins it is present in all basal cells and extends also into the upper cells of the epidermis.

Overlying the basal layer is the **stratum spinosum,** consisting of two to six rows of cuboidal cells, which become flattened as they approach the surface. This layer is so named because in fixed preparations viewed with the light microscope the cells appear to be joined together by intercellular bridges which give individual cells a spiny appearance. Electron microscopy (EM) has shown that these intercellular bridges are small areas of contact between the cells called desmosomes or maculae adhaerentes (p. 13.11) (fig. 35.3) and correspond to the points of attachment to the plasma membrane of bundles

of intracytoplasmic fibrous protein called tonofibrils. Similar fibrils are to be found in the cells of the stratum basale. Mitotic activity in the resting epidermis occurs mainly in the basal layer although in regeneration following injury it extends to the spinous cells. Above the stratum spinosum is the **stratum granulosum** which consists of one to three layers of diamond-shaped cells with darkly staining pyknotic nuclei and packed with irregularly shaped basophilic keratohyaline granules. This layer is best developed in the thick skin of the palms and soles where abundant keratin is produced. EM shows that the keratohyaline granules are an amorphous cytoplasmic precipitate adjacent to the tonofibrils.

In thick skin, immediately above and adjacent to the stratum granulosum there is a single layer of hyaline anucleated cells, the **stratum lucidum,** containing droplets of an oily substance, eleidin. This lipid is probably produced by disintegration of lysosomes (p. 13.8) since over pressure areas acid phosphatase activity increases progressively up to the stratum granulosum and then ceases abruptly.

The outer layer of the skin is called the **stratum corneum,** which consists of a variable number of flattened, anucleated, cornified, dead cells containing the fibrous protein keratin, bound together to form a tough, pliable membrane relatively impervious to substances passing in or out of the body (p. 17.3). Over pressure areas, such as the hands and feet, the keratin layer is dense and compact (fig. 35.4a), whereas over the general body surface it forms a loose, flexible covering resembling basket weave (fig. 35.4b).

Keratin can be considered as the metabolic end product of the epidermal cells and is of such importance as to warrant further scrutiny.

Keratinization

The fibrous protein keratin occurs in skin, hair, nails, claws and hoofs, and while these keratinized structures

NUCLEUS

PLASMA MEMBRANES OF ADJACENT EPIDERMAL CELLS

DESMOSOME

TONOFIBRILS

FIG. 35.3. Diagram of the electron microscope appearances of points of contact of adjacent epidermal cells.

PLATE 35.2.

(a) Photomicrograph of eccrine sweat glands. The pale tubules are the secreting acini, the dark ones the excretory ducts (× 350).

(c) Photomicrograph of apocrine gland acini. The glands are much larger than eccrine sweat glands and are lined by columnar epithelium (× 350).

(b) Photomicrograph of sebaceous gland lobule showing the foamy appearance of the secreting cells (× 200).

(d) Dendritic melanocytes at dermo-epidermal junction stained by silver impregnation. Note the numerous branching processes extending between the cells of the epidermis (× 350).

PLATE 37.1. Cervical mucus (× 170). Courtesy Dr R. R. MacDonald

(a) Normal mucus at time of ovulation. Typical salt crystallization showing the marked fern pattern.

(b) Normal premenstrual or pregnancy mucus showing endocervical cells and no crystals.

Vaginal smear (× 200). Courtesy Dr E. Little

(c) Pre-ovulatory, showing large flat discrete cells with pyknotic nuclei.

(d) Post-ovulatory, showing clumping of cells with folded edges.

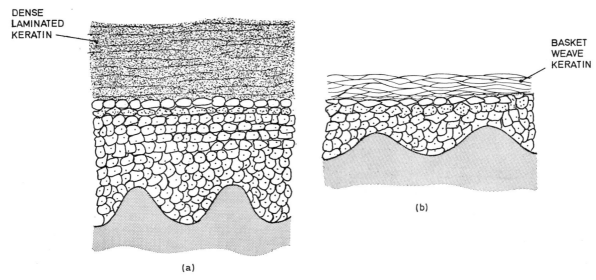

FIG. 35.4. The epidermis of (a) pressure areas and (b) general body surfaces.

differ greatly in their physical properties, the structure of the keratin molecule, as revealed by techniques such as X-ray diffraction, is constant.

Keratin is composed of eighteen different amino acids and the molecule exists in two forms, namely the α helical or spiral form (human keratins) and the β or straight form (bird feathers). The α helical molecule is kept in position by cross-linked hydrogen bonds. The durability of keratinized structures depends on a disulphide bond between the cystine molecules of adjacent polypeptide chains.

The first sign of the keratinization process is seen in electron micrographs of the stratum basale where **tonofibrils** of 5 nm diameter are present, coated with an osmiophilic sheath. As the cells of the stratum spinosum approach the surface the diameter of the tonofibrils increases to 10 nm and the sheath thickens. At the level of the stratum granulosum the bundles of tonofibrils are ensheathed by an electron dense matrix (keratohyaline granules); the fully keratinized cell of the stratum corneum consists of compact bundles of tonofibrils cemented together.

From the histochemical viewpoint the region of the stratum granulosum shows a concentration of —SH groups and it seems likely that the —S.S— bonds are formed from oxidation of the —SH group in two adjacent polypeptide chains.

In addition it appears that lipid is necessary for the orderly formation of the stratum corneum. The present concept is that the normal protein fibril from this stratum is surrounded by a thin layer of lipid. That keratinization and lipid synthesis are related is shown by the fact that some of the drugs used to lower blood cholesterol by interfering with its synthesis produce a serious upset in keratinization.

The dermis

The dermis is a fibro-elastic bed which supports and nourishes the epidermis and its appendages. Its deep aspect is ill defined as it becomes continuous with the subcutaneous fascia (fig. 35.1).

There are two distinct parts, the **superficial papillary bodies** and a deeper **reticular layer**. The papillary bodies project upwards, so that looked on from above there is a series of valleys and projections into which the undulating under surface of the epidermis fits (fig. 35.5). In fixed and stained tissue sections the dermis is seen to be composed of interlacing bundles of collagen fibres which give the skin its tensile strength. In the papillary body the fibres are very fine with abundant ground substance between them and tend to be orientated at right angles to the surface. Between the underside of the epidermis and the papillary body there is a basement membrane, rich in mucopolysaccharides derived from a condensation of the ground substance. Interspersed between the collagen bundles are spindle shaped cells of mesodermal origin, the fibroblasts. Normally these cells are inconspicuous but they proliferate rapidly after injury. In appropriately stained sections fine fibrils (elastic fibres) are seen forming a loose network around the collagen fibres. These elastic fibres anchor the collagen fibres and allow the skin to return to normal shape after it has been stretched. Overstretching, as may occur in pregnancy or obesity, may rupture the elastic fibres, allowing the collagen to become overstretched and resulting in the linear scars known as **striae**.

Cellular constituents of the dermis are the tissue macrophages and the mast cells. The latter are scant in human skin and situated in relation to blood vessels and hair follicles. Their granules, which stain meta-

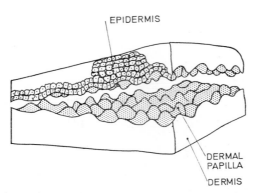

FIG. 35.5. Diagram of dermo-epidermal junction.

chromatically, contain histamine, heparin and hyaluronic acid. Mast cells are increased in number in some itching skin conditions.

Apart from the function of supporting the epidermal appendages, blood vessels, lymphatics and nerves, the dermis has a profound effect during development on the differentiation and structure of the epidermis. This influence appears to be continued into adult life as changes in the dermis often precede the development of epidermal cancers.

The epidermal appendages

The epidermal appendages are the sweat glands, apocrine glands, sebaceous glands, hair and nails.

These important structures arise during foetal life from the under surface of the developing epidermis. Here at about the third month of foetal life small buds of cells, primary epithelial germs, appear. From these structures develop the hair matrix, the sebaceous glands and the apocrine glands (p. 35.5). In the fourth month sweat buds appear on the palms and soles, to be followed at the beginning of the fifth month by those of the axillae and at the end of the fifth month by those over the remainder of the body surface. This pattern may have some functional significance as it is known that sweating varies between the palms and soles and the general body surface.

THE SWEAT GLANDS

These glands are found over the entire surface of the skin, being most numerous on the palms and soles and decreasing in number on the head, trunk and extremities in that order. There are between two and five million sweat glands in human skin, not all of which are active at one time. No sex difference in distribution or number has been observed but there is some evidence to suggest racial differences. The Japanese have more sweat glands on the extremities than on the trunk, in contradistinction to Europeans. Structurally the sweat glands are simple tubular glands extending down from the epidermis to the mid dermis, where they become coiled on themselves and in histological sections are seen as a nest of

transverse sections of tubes (plate 35.2a, facing p. 35.2). The secreting portion of the gland consists of a layer of cells the free borders of which are rather uneven. Two types of secreting cell can be identified, a smaller superficial dark cell, with a basophilic cytoplasm, and a larger deeper clear cell with an acidophilic cytoplasm. The dark cells contain RNA and mucopolysaccharide while the clear cells contain abundant glycogen. Glands from different areas of the body contain varying proportions of these two types of cell, but their functional significance is unknown. Along the base of the secreting cells and running parallel to the lumen are the 'myoepithelial' cells (p. 17.7) whose contraction is supposed to aid the expulsion of sweat (plate 17.1, facing p. 17.2).

The junction between the secreting coil and the duct is abrupt, the duct being lined by a double layer of darkly staining cuboidal cells which have a hyaline cuticle at their luminal border. The duct passes upwards through the dermis in a relatively straight line but then proceeds through the epidermis in a spiral fashion to open on to the surface.

The sweat glands are abundantly supplied by blood vessels which form an anastomotic network around the secreting coils and the intradermal part of the duct. These vessels are derived from a single arterial twig and are reminiscent of the supply to the glomerulus of the kidney. The secreting coils are profusely supplied by cholinergic nerve fibres from the sympathetic nervous system.

Sweating

Sweating is one of the ways in which man regulates his body temperature, and in tropical climates where atmospheric temperatures are high it is of prime importance (p. 40.4).

Sweating occurs in two distinctive patterns, each induced by a different stimulus. If a person is exposed to a warm atmosphere, within a few minutes sweat appears over the entire body surface, but most noticeably on the forehead, upper lip, neck and chest. While some does eventually occur on the palms and soles this is not conspicuous. This thermal sweating differs from emotional sweating, produced by anxiety and fear, which occurs mainly in the palms and soles and axillae.

At rest there is a steady slow loss of water through the skin called insensible perspiration. This is not a function of sweating but is related to diffusion and osmosis, the water passing through the epidermis.

Control of sweating

The nerve supply to sweat glands is, as already stated cholinergic fibres from the sympathetic nervous system and thus acetylcholine and cholinergic drugs such as pilocarpine induce sweating while it is inhibited by atropine. Adrenaline and noradrenaline have no significant effect on sweating. Bradykinin also promotes sweat production (p. 17.6). The general control of sweating is from the hypothalamus.

Composition of sweat

Sweat is a clear, watery fluid which is always hypotonic in relation to plasma. It contains approximately 0·5 per cent of solids, the chief one of which is sodium chloride (0·3 per cent), with small amounts of potassium, sugar, lactic acid and urea. The urea concentration is similar to that of blood. It is described more fully on p. 5.29.

THE APOCRINE GLANDS

These glands develop from the primary epithelial germ in close relation to the hair matrix. In the early stages of human foetal life all primary epithelial germs contain an apocrine bud; the majority of these fail to develop further except in the axilla, anogenital region, mammary areola and the canal of the external ear. Small irregular areas of development may be found on the scalp, face and trunk. This localization, as compared to hairy mammals in whom apocrine glands are universal, is probably an evolutionary change associated with regression of body hair.

Structure

Like the sweat gland the apocrine gland is a simple coiled tubule, but about ten times larger, so that it can be identified by the naked eye. These glands lie deeper than the sweat glands, being situated in the lower dermis and upper part of the subcutaneous fat.

On histological examination the secreting tubules (plate 35.2c, facing p. 35.2) are lined by a single layer of eosinophilic cells with a basal nucleus. The height of the cells varies from cuboidal to high columnar with a constriction at its tip. This variation in height is believed to indicate the cyclical nature of the secretion. The secreting cells are separated from a basement membrane by a layer of myoepithelium. The apocrine duct is similar in structure to the sweat duct. Instead of penetrating the epidermis, however, it opens into a hair follicle above the ducts of the sebaceous glands.

The blood supply is similar to that of the sweat glands but the innervation is different, being derived from adrenergic fibres of the sympathetic nervous system.

Apocrine secretion

Apocrine secretion is a turbid, milky, sometimes yellowish secretion. If allowed to dry it forms a thin plastic-like film around the hair follicle from which it has emerged. The glands begin to function only at puberty, as distinct from the sweat glands which are functional at birth. It has been stated that apocrine secretion is responsible for the characteristic body odour but it has been shown that this is due to secondary changes produced by bacteria.

Apocrine secretion is evoked by adrenergic stimuli such as fear or pain. Localized secretion may be induced by injection of adrenaline. Heat, acetylcholine and pilocarpine, which induce thermal sweating, do not affect the apocrine glands.

HAIR

Hair grows out of tubular invaginations of the surface epidermis called hair follicles. These follicles, with their associated sebaceous glands, are referred to as pilosebaceous units. The fact that the epidermis is continuous with that of the pilosebaceous follicles is of importance. Follicular and, to a lesser extent, sweat duct epithelium can proliferate and grow upwards to resurface the skin if the epidermis has been denuded by trauma or by the split skin graft of the plastic surgeon. The hair itself consists of a large, dead, keratinized **shaft**, at the bottom of which is a small growth area, the **hair bulb**. The junction between the dead and the living part of the hair is known as the keratogenous zone; this is of importance in limiting the spread of keratinophile fungi to the growing matrix and explains why children with hair ringworm do not lose their hair.

The hair bulb is expanded and claw-like and situated in the upper part of the subcutaneous fat (fig. 35.6). It is invaginated on the underside by a highly vascularized connective tissue, the **hair papilla**. The cells are darkly staining with large vesicular nuclei and, in people with dark hair, contain varying amounts of melanin. Interspersed between them are dendritic melanocytes similar to those in the stratum basale of the epidermis. Above

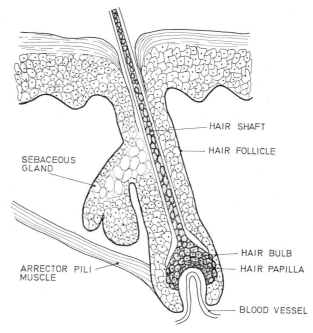

FIG. 35.6. Diagram of hair follicle and related sebaceous gland.

HAIR SHAFT

HAIR FOLLICLE

SEBACEOUS GLAND

ARRECTOR PILI MUSCLE

HAIR BULB

HAIR PAPILLA

BLOOD VESSEL

the hair bulb the cells become elongated with their long axis parallel to the direction of the shaft. They undergo keratinization without the intervention of a stratum granulosum. From this point upwards the hair shaft is a dead keratinized structure composed of an outer cortex where the keratinized cells are firmly cemented together and an inner medulla where larger keratinized cells are loosely connected and partially separated by air spaces.

Inserted into the walls of the follicles are strips of involuntary muscle, the **arrectores pilorum**. These are abundantly supplied by adrenergic nerve fibres, explaining the erection of hairs ('goose flesh') seen during cold and emotional stress.

Hair growth is cyclical in nature. The growth phase is followed by a phase of regression when the lower part of the follicle degenerates and the hair becomes loosened from the papilla. The hair bulb then passes into a resting phase when it is club shaped; this phase can be recognized by the much shorter length of follicle and the absence of a papilla. Subsequently this detached hair is pushed out by the growth of a new hair.

These stages vary in different species, in general being of shorter duration in hairy animals. In the young adult human scalp the growth phase is long (3 years) with a short rest phase (3 months), while in other parts of the body growth is measured in months with a long rest. In most hairy mammals the follicular cycles in each region are synchronous, waves of activity flowing outwards from one or more centres so that all the follicles in any one region are at the same stage of development. In man the activity is irregular and neighbouring follicles are at different stages in the cycle.

All the hair follicles on the human scalp are established at birth and in normal circumstances no new follicles are formed later. The pattern, distribution and, to some extent, the colour of hair are genetically determined and their growth sequence is closely linked to bodily growth and sexual maturity. The hair cycle may be modified by varying activity of the thyroid or adrenal glands.

THE SEBACEOUS GLANDS

Sebaceous glands are found over the entire skin surface with the exception of the palms of the hands and soles of the feet. They are most numerous and largest on the scalp, forehead, cheeks and chin where they are present in concentrations varying from 400–900/cm^2 of skin surface. Over the remainder of the body surface the content is about 100/cm^2. They are **holocrine** glands, forming their secretion by disintegration of the cell contents which are then discharged directly into the sebaceous duct which in turn enters the upper part of a hair follicle (fig. 35.6). Some ducts open directly on to the surface, such as those of the nipple and labia minora, and the Meibomian glands of the eyelid.

Structure

Each gland is a lobulated structure (plate 35.2b, facing p. 35.2), usually situated in the angle between a hair follicle and a strip of smooth muscle, arrector pili, which is thought to aid in the expulsion of the secretion. At the periphery of each lobule is a layer of basophilic cuboidal cells, similar in appearance to the cells of the stratum basale of the epidermis. Towards the centre of the lobule the cells become larger and more acidophilic and in fixed and stained preparations have a characteristic foamy appearance due to the contained lipid material being dissolved out by fat solvents during processing. Finally the cell breaks down and discharges its contents, **sebum**, into the sebaceous duct.

The function of sebum is to lubricate the skin and help to protect it against the effects of the elements. As it is difficult to collect sebum without contamination by surface lipids its chemical composition is not accurately known. It would appear to be a complex mixture of free fatty acids, glycerides, esters of higher aliphatic alcohols and of cholesterol and hydrocarbons including squalene.

Sebaceous gland activity is low until puberty when it increases rapidly. This change is due to androgenic hormones from the testis in the male, and presumably from the ovaries and adrenals in the female.

An androgen from the adrenal gland, 3β-hydroxyandrost-5-ene-17-one (DHA), stimulates sebaceous output in human subjects whose adrenals have been removed surgically. This hormone disappears from the circulation shortly after birth and reappears at puberty. The sebaceous glands on the face, chest and back contain steroid dehydrogenases, and human skin is capable of synthesizing testosterone from pure DHA. These findings from our laboratory appear to offer an explanation of the development of the common condition of acne vulgaris at puberty. It has been suggested that the sebaceous glands secrete vitamin D precursor but this has not been substantiated. More probably 7-dehydrocholesterol is produced in the stratum spinosum of the epidermis and its photoconversion to vitamin D occurs in the epidermis.

NAILS

Nails are composed largely of a semitransparent keratin plate surrounded proximally and laterally by folds of skin, the nail folds (fig. 35.7a and b), and arise from the **nail bed**, a modified epidermis. The nail plate is free at its distal border but is elsewhere firmly attached to the underlying epidermis. Under the proximal nail fold it is known as the nail root. The nail bed consists of a modified epidermis lacking a stratum granulosum, but with a highly vascular dermis which is continuous on its deep aspect with the periosteum of the distal phalanx.

In the region of the **half moon** or **lunula**, the root epi-

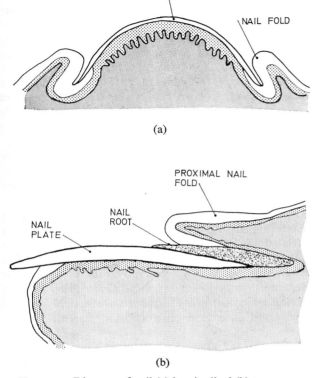

(a)

(b)

FIG. 35.7. Diagram of nail (a) longitudinal (b) transverse.

dermis is thicker and the underlying dermis looser and less vascular, features which cause its pale colour. Finger nails grow more quickly than toe nails, comparative times for replacement being about 6 months for finger nails and 12–18 months for toe nails, a fact to remember when treating fungus infection of the nail plate.

Pigmentation

While in many animals pigmentation serves as camouflage, its prime function in man is to protect the dermis from the harmful effects of sunlight. It seems probable that the dark-skinned races are an example of selective adaptation to extreme exposure to sunlight.

Mention has already been made of the melanin producing dendritic melanocytes which are to be found between the cells of the stratum basale at the junction of the epidermis and dermis (fig. 35.2 and plate 35.2d, facing p. 35.2). These cells, in conjunction with others found in the hair bulb, the iris and the leptomeninges, are known as the **melanocyte system**. They are derived from the neural crest and all have the faculty of synthesizing the black pigment melanin from the amino acid tyrosine by means of an enzyme tyrosinase. In fixed tissue preparations the melanocytes appear as pale cells with a small, darkly staining nucleus and a faintly basophilic cytoplasm (clear cells). In preparations stained specifically either to

show their contained melanin or to demonstrate their enzyme activity they appear as triangular cells with numerous fine branching processes which transfer the melanin granules to the surrounding basal cells. EM reveals in the cytoplasm of active melanocytes a rough-surfaced endoplasmic reticulum with numerous ribosomes adherent to it, indicating that the melanocyte is a secreting cell. These specialized organelles, called melanosomes, contain the enzyme tyrosinase. In normal secreting activity, melanin is deposited on the surface of the melanosomes until they become amorphous particles of melanin combined with protein and devoid of tyrosinase activity. Melanin is transferred to the surrounding basal cells by penetration of dendritic processes into them. Yet the basal cell may not be just a passive recipient of melanin and appears to take an active part in the process of transfer and in fact may be intimately connected with the control of melanin synthesis.

The basic steps in the synthesis of melanin from tyrosine may be summarized as follows.

The first stage of this reaction takes place slowly and for this reason the tyrosinase activity in melanocytes is more easily demonstrated by incubating skin with the substrate DOPA.

Melanin pigmentation is in general controlled by the melanocyte-stimulating hormone (MSH) which is produced by the anterior lobe of the pituitary gland. Excess MSH results in a generalized increase in melanin pigmentation.

Quantitative histological studies have revealed that irrespective of race the total number of melanocytes per unit area of skin is the same. This means that the increased pigmentation in coloured skins reflects an increase in melanin synthesis as the total number of melanocytes is the same as in white skin.

The protective aspects of melanin pigment in relation to the harmful effects of sunlight have already been mentioned. A practical aspect of this is seen in the sharp increase in the incidence of malignant neoplasms of the skin, in particular of basal cell carcinoma, which was seen in young white American soldiers who served in the Pacific theatre during World War II.

Blood supply

In addition to supplying nourishment to the skin the cutaneous blood flow plays a key role in the regulation of body temperature and blood pressure (pp. 40.4 and 28.31). The skin itself is not demanding as far as blood flow is concerned. It has been estimated that a minimum flow of 0·8 ml of blood/min/100 ml of tissue is adequate to supply its oxygen requirements. Despite this low consumption it has a very abundant blood supply and while there are considerable regional differences the basic pattern is similar. An arterial twig penetrates the subcutaneous fat and forms a plexus just above it. Another plexus is formed just below the papillary body and from here loops go up to supply individual papillae. Branches from these plexuses supply the glands and hair roots. Each arterial twig penetrating the subcutaneous fat supplies an inverted cone-shaped area, the base of which is towards the epidermis. This distribution is demonstrated on cold hands and feet, where a reticulate pattern may be seen. Blood is collected into venous plexuses which are situated below the arterial ones. Arteriovenous shunts, known as **glomus bodies**, are found in various regions of the skin, notably the pads of the fingers and toes, palms and soles, ears and central part of the face. These provide a means of short circuiting the capillary circulation and are concerned with temperature regulation.

Due to the fact that even the smallest cutaneous arterioles contain muscle fibres, in keeping with their thermoregulating function, the nourishment of the dermis is mainly via vessels which consist of a single layer of endothelial cells. The epidermis is avascular and receives its nourishment from the vessels in the tip of the papilla via the intercellular spaces. The dermis has a rich network of lymphatics which start at the tips of the papillae and pass between the connective tissue fibres, eventually joining up to run along with the larger blood vessels.

Innervation

Because it supplies much of our sensory information the skin is richly provided with sensory nerve fibres as well as autonomic fibres supplying secreting glands, smooth muscle and blood vessels.

The primary sensations are touch, pressure, pain and temperature and these are appreciated by a fine network of myelinated and non-myelinated fibres from which beaded terminals arise in the dermis. It is thought that each sensory area of skin is supplied by fibres subserving each of these sensations. The role of such specialized receptors as Meissner's tactile corpuscles and others is discussed on p. 24.67.

Itch is a common symptom of a diseased skin and while there is much evidence to show that it is closely related to pain, especially of a burning nature, travelling in the C fibres of sensory nerves and ascending the spino-thalamic tracts of the spinal cord in association with pain fibres, most doctors consider that it is a separate sensation from pain.

Itch may be invoked by a variety of physical stimuli, mechanical, electrical and thermal, provided these are below the threshold for inducing pain. It would seem that these stimuli cause enough damage to the skin to release histamine which in turn causes the itch. Itch may be elicited also by a number of exogenous chemicals such as weak acids or weak alkalis, presumably by releasing histamine or a proteolytic enzyme. Substances such as trypsin, papain, bradykinin and 'itch powder', which contains proteolytic enzymes, produce itch, probably by direct action on nerve endings, as no flare characteristic of histamine action is seen.

The spontaneous itch associated with some skin diseases appears to originate in different ways. That associated with urticaria (nettle rash or hives) is due to local release of histamine while that accompanying eczematous eruptions is probably due to release of endogenous proteolytic enzymes. Generalized itching may be a most distressing feature of obstructive jaundice but ceases at once if the obstruction is relieved.

Cutaneous permeability

The skin in its role as a protective organ relies mainly on an intact epidermis as an effective barrier. The concept of a distinct barrier layer in the epidermis is now generally accepted, and experiments involving the stripping off of the surface layer indicate that it is probably located in the inner part of the keratin layer. Much has yet to be learned concerning the mechanism of percutaneous absorption and recent work has suggested that specialized cell transport systems may be involved as well as simple diffusion through a membrane.

Substances may pass into the body directly through the epidermis or by means of the openings of the cutaneous appendages. This means, in fact, through the pilosebaceous follicles, as there appears to be no significant absorption through sweat ducts.

While molecular configuration and size may influence the ability of a substance to penetrate the epidermis, the main factor would appear to be determined by lipid and water solubilities. The skin is almost impermeable to water, but lipid-soluble substances such as alcohol penetrate by dissolving the lipid content of the cell wall. In practice it appears that substances which are equally soluble in water and ether penetrate the epidermis better than substances which are soluble in only one of these solvents. The intact skin is also virtually impermeable to electrolytes but permeable to gases to a small extent. Cutaneous respiration amounts to about 0.5 per cent of that through the lungs.

Absorption is enhanced by increase of skin temperature, hyperaemia and hydration of the keratin layer, and damage to the skin caused by physical means or by inflammatory changes.

FURTHER READING

GORDON M. (1959) *Pigment Cell Biology*. New York: Academic Press.

HURLEY G.H.J. & SHELLEY W.B. (1960) *The Human Apocrine Sweat Gland in Health and Disease*. Springfield, Ill.: Thomas.

MARPLES MARY J. (1965) *The Ecology of the Human Skin*. Springfield, Ill.: Thomas.

MONTAGNA W. (1962) *The Structure and Function of Skin*. 2nd Edition. New York: Academic Press.

MONTAGNA W. (1965) *Advances in Biology of Skin, Vol. 6. Ageing*. Oxford: Pergamon Press.

MONTAGNA W. & LOBITZ W.C. JR. (1964) *The Epidermis*. New York: Academic Press.

ROTHMAN S. (1954) *Physiology and Biochemistry of the Skin*. Chicago: University of Chicago Press.

Chapter 36
Human psychology

Contemporary psychology covers a wide canvas and deals with most aspects of human experience and behaviour, so it is not surprising that large portions can only be sketched with tentative strokes. There are still wide areas of ignorance in knowledge of the mental processes which motivate human behaviour. Fortunately other parts of the canvas may be painted more confidently. This is the case when dealing, not with theories, but with findings which have been verified by experiments. Indeed, it is the gradual emergence of a body of well-supported findings that encourages psychologists to consider the subject a science, albeit an embryonic one. This chapter is an introduction to aspects of psychological work which appear particularly relevant to the doctor. A condensed account of personality development with a brief description of the methods used in assessing personality is given first. Thereafter some of the mental processes used in dealing with the environment are considered.

PERSONALITY DEVELOPMENT

In psychology the term **personality** is normally used to denote the patterns of hopes, feelings, attitudes and beliefs which together make each individual a unique human being. This is different from the use of the term in everyday speech in phrases such as 'he is a striking personality' or 'she has lots of personality'. In this latter context personality is seen as the impact made by one individual upon another. This use of the term draws attention to the important fact that when we make judgements regarding another's personality we inevitably do so in the context of a human relationship. Our observations of another person are influenced by our feelings about him, by our own attitudes and beliefs, indeed by our own personality. In an attempt to make objective and reliable observations of personality, psychologists use techniques aimed at minimizing the errors introduced by subjective factors. It is, however, salutary to keep in mind that no matter how sophisticated psychological techniques become, observations and interpretations of another person's behaviour must always be influenced by our own personality.

At one time psychologists distinguished between **personality** and **temperament**, using the latter term to denote those personal characteristics of an individual which are determined by innate constitutional factors. During the last decade the word temperament has gradually slipped from the psychological vocabulary as psychologists became almost exclusively interested in the impact of learning on personality development. It is obvious that much of our personality is a product of the multitude of learning experiences occurring throughout life. Nevertheless, in the eagerness to assess the effect of the environment it is easy to underestimate the influence of constitutional differences. Most mothers who have reared a large family of children can testify that no two are alike and that individual differences are readily apparent from early infancy, before the environment has had much opportunity to modify the child's behaviour. Some studies of infantile behaviour tend to support this view. It has been demonstrated that in early infancy children can be differentiated in their level of physical activity, in their readiness to adapt to change and in their emotional responsiveness. Other studies have shown that some areas of future development can be predicted surprisingly well from observations made during the first two years of the child's life. Such observations serve as a useful corrective to those who regard the early environment and interpersonal relationships as the source of all later individual differences in personality. Even in early infancy the human infant cannot be likened to a piece of clay whose personality is moulded by the behaviour of others. Indeed parental behaviour is inevitably influenced by the infant's own responses. The finished product, which we call personality, is the result of a complex interplay between constitutional and environmental influences. This view is of particular relevance when faced with pathological deviations in normal human development. It has sometimes been said that 'there are no disturbed children—only disturbed parents'. While the emotionally disturbed child may be the product of conflict within the family group as a whole, a child reacts to disturbance in the family in his own characteristic way. In some cases such reactions are extreme, while in others a similar degree of stress may elicit little response.

The salient factors involved in personality development during the different stages of infancy, childhood, adolescence, adult life and old age are now briefly considered. More emphasis is placed on infancy and childhood as experiences during these formative years are likely to have a more lasting effect.

INFANCY

Although many fathers say that their child was not a personality until sometime during the second year of life, the majority of mothers date the emergence of the child's personality much earlier. They quote examples illustrating the infant's capacity to interact with mother within a reciprocal mother–child relationship. Psychologists have also disagreed as to when it is legitimate to speak of the infant as having a separate personality, capable of recognizing and relating itself to others in its environment. It is of course obvious that each infant is a separate person, reacting to the personal and non-personal environment in his own characteristic way. Some schools of thought take this much further and maintain that the infant is capable of sustaining a more complex relationship with specific people in his environment, e.g. mother, and that such early relationships serve as a prototype for future interpersonal reactions. Other studies of infantile development suggest that the infant is incapable of forming a personal relationship during the first six months of life. Genetic psychologists such as Piaget conclude that, during this period, the infant is still learning to discriminate between separate objects in 'the booming, buzzing confusion' into which he has been born. Even when objects are recognized and identified, his rudimentary memory does not allow him to recall the existence of an object when the object is not physically present. Although the infant may recognize mother when she is physically present, his inability to recall her when she is absent casts doubt on assumptions about infantile anxiety over separation from mother. The current view of the development of social relationships during infancy is well represented by the work of Schaffer in Glasgow, who discerns three temporal stages in the development of the infant's attachment to other people. During the first three months, the infant's main need is for a continuous flow of sensory stimulation from the environment. This includes all the auditory, visual and tactile sensations emanating from the environment, both personal and impersonal. At first the infant's limited motor development renders him dependent upon adults to supply stimulation and when this is not forthcoming he reacts to monotony by crying. Many mothers have learned the usefulness of the open window, the radio or even the sound of the washing machine and vacuum cleaner in obtaining a respite from baby's demands. Later, the more mobile infant explores his environment, searching out for himself the variety of sensations necessary for normal development. The fact that infants who are reared in a monotonous environment tend to lag behind in their development suggests that the human infant requires an optimum level of external stimulation. Somewhere between the third and seventh month of life the infant's social development reaches a second stage where he now differentiates between social (contact with people) and non-social stimulation. Now the infant encourages and responds to stimulation from other people but as yet he shows no attachment to any specific person. Around the seventh month of life the infant shows the first observable indications that he is able to discriminate among people and for the first time seeks mother's presence, rejecting the overtures of others. It is only now towards the end of the first year of life that we can safely speak of a fully reciprocal relationship between mother and child.

Such observations have more than academic interest. They are relevant to theories which relate a pathological breakdown in later life to early traumatic experiences within the mother–child relationship. John Bowlby and others have described the patterns of anxiety shown by children admitted to hospital and so separated from their mothers. If our earlier observations are correct one would not expect such reactions to separation to occur in an infant less than seven months old who has not yet formed any specific attachment to mother. Most observations of the reactions of infants to living in hospital confirm this suggestion. It is the child of over seven months who shows the overdependent and fearful behaviour on his return home. In the case of the older child around the age of two years living in hospital, separation has been said to exert a permanently damaging effect upon the child's social development. More careful studies suggest however, that many factors are involved and that the long-term effects of separation have been greatly over stressed.

While these observations serve as a corrective to over emphasis on the impact of the early mother–child relationship on later development, it must not be assumed that the mother's behaviour with her child during this time is of little or no importance. Studies of infant monkeys deprived of a mother show that they tend to be more inhibited and fearful in their later behaviour than monkeys who are reared normally. Harlow has shown that the presence of a mother substitute, a crude dummy figure to which the infant monkey can cling to in times of stress, is sufficient to allay anxiety but only if the substitute figure provides a soft, tactile contact. This suggests that the natural hugging and cuddling which most affectionate mothers give to their infants is a valuable and necessary source of stimulation.

Even in this area of infantile needs it is unwise to

generalize and neglect the wide measure of normal individual differences in infants. Some infants appear perfectly satisfied with much less stimulation than others who show an almost ravenous need for excitement. The former may be described by their mothers as contented babies who are easy to rear while the latter are regarded as demanding and exhausting in their insatiable desire for stimulation. Infants also vary in their need for particular types of stimulation. Schaffer found that a surprisingly large proportion of the infants did not react to tactile contact such as hugging, showing a preference for visual and auditory contact. He makes the important point that there are also wide individual differences in mothers' needs in the nursing situation. The optimum relationship is thus achieved when there is a mutual adaptation between the needs of both mother and child. Imbalance may occur when the mother is either unresponsive or overresponsive to the infant's needs. Such a disturbed relationship might, for example, occur when a mother with a strong need for physical contact attempts to relate herself to a 'non-cuddling baby'.

The existence of individual differences should also be recognized in specific areas of infant training such as feeding and toilet control. A number of psychological theories have stressed the importance of breast feeding, and of the timing of weaning. While some studies have indicated a relationship between bottle-feeding and later maladjustment, the findings of others have failed to support this view. Although breast feeding may possess physical advantages most studies suggest that these have been greatly exaggerated. In Aberdeen, Hytten found bottle-fed babies to be at least as healthy as those who had been breast-fed. He concluded that while 'we should help in every way possible the woman who wishes to breast feed ... we are not justified in putting pressure on those who are unwilling or unable to breast feed efficiently'. Other theories have suggested that either too early or too late weaning may cause later psychological difficulties although there is no evidence which convincingly links weaning with later personality development. The timing of the weaning may reflect the individual infant's readiness for this step rather than the mother's needs or beliefs.

Toilet training is another aspect of early rearing which has been related to later personality development. While grandmother may advise that this should be initiated as early as possible, many modern authorities stress the unfortunate repercussions of too early or too rigid training. The mother's dilemma is often solved by the child who trains mother in toilet training! Young children differ widely in the age at which they are capable of toilet control. If their rhythm of elimination is regular and predictable, toilet behaviour may be conditioned early, while irregularity renders any conditioning process ineffective. Some mothers feel compelled to establish training at a very early age because of their own disgust of normal excretory functions. This attitude, if extreme, may engender in the child an unhealthy aversion to his own bodily functions. Mothers who react in this manner are likely to introduce training which is not only ill-timed but also excessively rigid and harsh so that conflict develops between mother and child. Some studies indicate that where toilet training is initiated around fifteen months in a non-coercive, co-operative way the likelihood of later bed-wetting and soiling is greatly reduced. Perhaps the mother who trains early and harshly runs a greater risk of incurring a later breakdown in the child's toilet functions. The course of toilet training is, however, greatly affected by the child's personal rhythms and the ease with which he forms conditioned habits. It is deceivingly simple to relate all training difficulties to mother's own attitudes.

Implicit in much of what has been said is the problem of distinguishing between aspects of behaviour which are learned from those due to maturation. The term maturation here refers to development which occurs in an orderly, predictable pattern and independent of the child's experience. It is tempting to ascribe all behavioral changes in the infant as being a result of parental behaviour and other learning experiences and to overlook the possibility of a gradual unfolding of a predetermined sequence of development. Successful child rearing often depends upon the adequacy with which the parents match their teaching to the child's developmental readiness for change.

Observations indicate that the new-born infant has a very restricted emotional range, varying between generalized excitement and tranquillity (absence of emotion). At about the end of the third month the emotional state of diffuse excitement differentiates clearly into the two separate emotions of distress and delight. Thereafter, throughout the first year of development the emotions of anger, disgust, fear, elation and affection become observable. The suggestion that this sequence is due to maturation rather than learning and imitation is supported not only by its uniform regularity but also by the fact that the same sequence is observed to occur in infants who are deaf and blind from birth. While it must be admitted that we are restricted to observable emotions, these are reasonable indications that early emotional development is in the form of a predetermined pattern. Later learning does of course have unlimited influence upon the expression of emotions and on the linking of emotions with particular situations.

CHILDHOOD

The world to the young child is a fascinating if often somewhat bewildering kaleidoscope of rapidly changing experience. During the early stages of infancy his role is that of a relatively passive spectator engaged in assimilating each new experience. Gradually the individual learns to make appropriate responses to events and then begins a long apprenticeship in ordering, interpreting and finally attaining some degree of control over external reality. In this difficult task he is hampered, both by a very limited experience and the inability to apply the logical reasoning of the adult. Instead the environment is interpreted subjectively and he develops his own explanations and an **egocentric** system of thought. Whereas in adult thinking our ideas are altered to conform with reality the child tends to distort reality, moulding it to fit in with his own personal viewpoint. It is this prelogical way of interpreting events which, above all, creates the gulf between the world of the child and that of the adult. To bridge this gulf and understand the inner life and outer behaviour of the child some of the main features which categorize thinking during this egocentric phase of development must be considered.

Adults make a sharp distinction between animate and inanimate objects. The young child in contrast lives in an animistic world. In his egocentric way he imbues life to all objects in his environment, assuming that they are capable of the same feeling as he is. Gradually he narrows his definition of inanimate to include only objects which appear to move of their own volition. Thus, phrases such as 'a threatening sky' or 'a cheerful fire' have a very literal meaning for the younger child. It is not until between the ages of seven and nine years that the child is completely free of animistic traces in his thinking. The child's view of the world does protect him from one source of fear which haunts the adult world, i.e. the fear of death. Thus the irrational world of childhood is given up only at some cost. Of course, the younger child often experiences the death of pets or elderly relatives but he tends to interpret this as involving only temporary separation, the loved object being assumed to continue to exist elsewhere. It is not unusual to find eight to ten-year-old children reacting to their first appreciation of the implications of mortality by becoming morbidly preoccupied by death and showing fear and overconcern for the health of parents.

A central feature of the child's egocentric thinking is the constant confusion between internal mentality and external reality. During the latter stages of infancy, consciousness and selfawareness emerges as the infant learns to differentiate between itself and the rest of the environment. This distinction is not fully established for some time and the young child's thinking continues to be influenced by his tenuous hold on the difference between internal mental processes and external events. Parents are often faced with the difficult task of explaining to the young child why others cannot see his dreams while he sleeps. To the child the dream is an externally located

event and therefore must be observable by others. This confusion is by no means confined to the dream state, for the child constantly shows a similar failure to differentiate between his own thoughts and external events in his everyday activities. We may say that this only means that the child has a vivid imagination but there is a world of difference between the younger child's imaginings and that of the healthy adult who has no difficulty in separating his fantasies from his real life. To the young child his thoughts are omnipotent and at times as real as the deed itself. He may worry that he will be punished for unspoken thoughts or be convinced that what has been imagined has in fact happened. Not only the thoughts but the words by which they are expressed have, to the child, an independent and objective existence. I remember a father telling me how his young daughter was terrified of his tape recorder which she feared would 'take away my words and keep them shut up in the box'. Adults are often confused by the prelogical concepts used by the developing child to categorize objects in his environment. Like the adult, the child finds it more economical to arrange objects in groups but in this case the common denominator connecting the objects is personal and related to his own actions. Thus the young child may use the word 'door' to refer to doors, drawers, boxes and in fact to any object which he can open. His concept of 'car' may extend to any object which he can push along the ground.

So far we have been primarily concerned with cognitive aspects of the child's mental development, the manner in which he perceives and thinks about his environment. However, the young child is above all a creature of feeling and emotion. Indeed, a characteristic feature of his early behaviour is the degree to which his feelings guide his actions.

Freud referred to the child's life being dominated by the **pleasure principle** aimed at achieving the gratification of powerful emotional drives. Gradually through contact and repeated experience with the outside world, the child learns to conform to social demands and to control or delay the satisfaction of his primitive emotional drives. The child now ceases to live entirely for the moment and learns to appreciate the future consequences of his actions. In Freudian terminology the child now adapts to the **reality principle**. For some time, however, the child remains at the mercy of his uncontrolled feelings which are unaffected by considerations of reason or consequence. If his desires are realized he is happy, if they are baulked he is aggressive. He hates and loves with a passionate fervour although his passion may change from one moment to the next. Soon his emotional life becomes more complex in that he experiences the opposite emotions of love and aggression at the same time and towards the same objects. He loves his parents upon whom he is wholly dependent but at times they frustrate him in his desires and he responds in his characteristic way with aggression. All children must soon learn the difficult and painful lesson that life is a mixture of satisfaction and dissatisfaction, but the manner in which the individual child learns this lesson depends greatly upon his parents' reactions to his emotional demands.

One of the most difficult emotional crises which the child faces is in the resolution of the **Oedipus** situation. This psychoanalytic term denotes that stage of childhood development, occurring around the age of four to five years, at which the child forms an increasingly possessive and demanding emotional bond with the parent of the opposite sex, together with feelings of jealousy and aggression towards the parent of the same sex. Thus, for example, the little boy shows a need to monopolize fully the attentions of his mother, with corresponding jealousy and aggression towards his father who has become a hated rival. This external triangle can create an extremely difficult domestic situation and its resolution may depend on the emotional maturity of the parents themselves. A mother may welcome and indeed encourage this upsurge of demonstrative love on the part of a young son and even unconsciously play off son against father to gratify her emotional needs. On the other hand she may find her son's excessive demands tedious or embarrassing and react with aggression or complete rejection. The father may find himself entering the arena prepared to openly combat his son in the struggle for his wife's affections. It is believed by psychoanalysts that much of our later attitudes and feelings towards the opposite sex is decided by what happens during this crisis in development. It is normally around this time that the child shows the first signs of a rudimentary sexual curiosity. This preoccupation with his own body and that of others is usually transient and soon disappears until puberty when it reappears as a more fully developed sexual response. Again, however, it is only too easy for well-meaning parents to damage the child's normal sexual development by overstressing the impropriety of early sexual curiosity.

Whereas the younger child acts on impulse, translating his feelings and desires into immediate action, the elder child's behaviour is distinguished by his ability to inhibit behavioural responses which have been hitherto freely expressed. The emergence of this type of more controlled behaviour is gradual and its subsequent development naturally reflects individual differences in the life situation of each child. Some children appear to remain impulsive and uncontrolled in their behaviour. Although developing normally in other ways their social behaviour remains unpredictable and explosive, leading them into conflict with a society which tolerates such behaviour only in much younger children. Some experimental studies suggest that failure to develop the normal capacity to inhibit responses may sometimes be a consequence of minimal brain damage at birth. The Russian psychologist Luria has developed experimental techniques for measuring **response inhibition** and has used these to diagnose children who suffer from this developmental lag. In this country several investigations have used similar techniques to show that children who perform poorly on tasks demanding response inhibition tend to be unusually impulsive, anti-social and generally maladjusted.

To the young child the main factor which regulates his behaviour and prevents the immediate gratification of every need is that of external adult authority. He gradually learns that certain actions bring swift retribution and at this stage **wrong** actions are simply those which are punished. While this is equally true of the behaviour of the older child and adult, their behaviour is also under the more restrictive control of the inner-censor which we call our **conscience**. Here **bad** behaviour is no longer merely that which incurs punishment from others but also that which results in us feeling bad. By internalizing a set of moral standards we create our own punishment in the sense of shame or guilt which accompanies transgressions from our own moral code. While the behaviour of the very young child is not regulated in this way there is disagreement as to the age when conscience develops. According to the psychoanalytic theories of Freud and his followers the child takes his first step towards a more socially regulated mode of behaviour when he resolves the dilemma of the Oedipus situation by identifying with, and imitating his father. Others, such as Piaget, place the development of the moral sense later, about the seventh year. Certainly it seems that, before the age of seven years most children have no inherent sense of right and wrong, accepting without understanding the rules of conduct laid down by adult authority. The well-meaning parent who shows disappointment or annoyance at his youngster's lack of moral sense is simply expecting the child to function in a manner for which he is not yet ready. Because most children appear to develop a moral sense by the age of seven years, their moral standards need not be similar. Their moral codes reflect in a large measure their early environment, particularly the values of their parents. If the parents are themselves controlled by rigid and harsh moral principles then the child may be crippled by a conscience which is severe and overdemanding. Similarly, a lack of moral values in the parents may exert a different, although equally detrimental effect on the child's later development. Like every other aspect of our personality our conscience continues to develop and change after early childhood through the impact of new learning experiences.

Egocentric thinking and adult mental disorder

Many people have been struck by the resemblance between some aspects of egocentric thinking in children and the behaviour displayed by adults during mental illness. Psychoanalysts use the term **regression** to refer to this tendency to revert to an earlier, less mature type of behaviour when faced with a stressful situation. For example, older children when faced with a difficult situation fall back on thumb-sucking or some other primitive type of behaviour which relieved their tension when they were much younger. During a battle a weary and frightened soldier may break down and cry for his mother or even become temporarily enuretic. Illness, particularly if severe, is a stressful situation. Normally the healthy adult is a relatively independent being who adjusts to his environment in a mature manner. When he becomes unwell, particularly if he fears that his symptoms herald a serious illness, he becomes anxious, vulnerable, less mature and more dependent on the reassurance of authority figures around him. When such a patient goes to his doctor he is in a sense again in the position of the young child whose well being is totally dependent upon the understanding and experience of an all knowing authority figure. It is no exaggeration to say that the general practitioner's picture of his patients as individuals is seldom a fair reflection of the patient's normal personality. The more severe the illness and the more worried the patient the more childlike, demanding and dependent is his behaviour. If he has to enter hospital the adult patient's routine is disrupted and he is forced to surrender in a large measure many of the things which make him an independent adult. Such enforced dependency in an unfamiliar and sometimes frightening environment combined with the fears aroused by illness may result in the patient regressing to a childlike mode of behaviour. This regression can show itself in different ways, some patients becoming completely passive, over-dependent and demanding attention. Others may become peevish, irritable and irrational like spoiled children. Each patient, in fact, will tend to react in terms of his individual way of reacting to past emergencies in childhood. It is always worth remembering that the adult patient's behaviour in hospital is a poor reflection of his normal personality. An important task of doctors and nurses in hospital is to allay the patient's fears by reassurance and explanation in much the same manner as every parent has to do with young children.

The resemblance between adult and childhood behaviour is much more striking where the illness is mental rather than physical. Adult patients with a neurotic disorder often display childlike qualities, particularly in the emotionally uncontrolled nature of their behaviour. It is, however, in the behaviour of the more seriously disordered psychotic patient that we find the closest correspondence with the egocentric child. A progressive loss of distinction between fantasy and reality is one of the most characteristic features of schizophrenia. The adult schizophrenic constantly projects on to external reality his own inner wishes, fears and thoughts result-ing in the same type of reality distortion seen in early childhood. The omnipotence of thought already described may be found in the adult patient who feels others can see the thoughts in his head or that people are taking his words away from him while he speaks. Traces of animistic thinking, dormant since early childhood, may again reappear so that a patient imbues life and direction to inanimate objects and non-human creatures. Like the young child he may perceive and interpret events around him solely from his own perspective. In the more extreme and advanced stages of an illness the patient may show the same inability to differentiate between the self and the remainder of the environment as found in the adualistic phase of early infancy. In this condition he may show frequent confusions of identity, when his personality appears to merge with that of others around him. Some psychoanalysts think that the adult patient regresses back to a more primitive level of mental functioning because of his inability to adjust to the demands of adult life. Implicit in this point of view is the idea that patients who later develop such an illness had a particularly traumatic early childhood which renders later mature adjustment impossible. Regression in this sense means that the adult patient is pulled back to a more primitive mode of adjustment by the unresolved conflicts of childhood. However, the correspondence between childhood and adult mental illness may be interpreted in a rather different manner. An adult patient with a severe brain injury may show many regressive components in his behaviour in so far as he behaves in a childlike way. The main reason for such regression is that the injury has impaired his adult higher mental functions and caused him to function at a lower level. Many psychiatrists who regard severe mental disorders such as schizophrenia as being organic in origin, argue that the patient regresses in his behaviour not because of early unresolved infantile conflicts but because the illness has caused damage to the brain and nervous system. In this view the regressed patient is not so much pulled back to an earlier more primitive level of adjustment but is rather pushed back by his current condition.

Although the similarities between psychotic adult behaviour and normal childhood behaviour have been emphasized there are numerous differences. While the resemblances are useful in helping to understand the behaviour of the psychotic patient this should not lead us to treat a patient as a child. No matter how severe the illness or how destructive it is to the adult personality the patient still retains some residue of adult functioning. This point is also relevant to later discussion on ageing in that here again there is some resemblance between the mental changes which occur in old age and mental functioning in childhood. However, anyone who approaches elderly people as if he were dealing with children is apt to be quickly and forcibly reminded of his mistake!

ADOLESCENCE

By the time the child is twelve years of age his thinking is predominantly reality orientated and relatively free from egocentricity. He has developed a wide range of skills and aptitudes which allow him to deal competently with most situations in his limited environment. He is by now well adapted, integrated and enjoys the security of an established social status within his own age group. By this age parents are beginning to relax and feel with relief that out of the earlier turmoil has emerged a reasonably stable adult in miniature. Suddenly, their well earned tranquillity is shattered by a whole sequence of alterations in their child's behaviour. Integration and boyish confidence is replaced by disintegration, intense selfconsciousness and the domestic scene is rent asunder by a series of emotional explosions. Adolescence has arrived!

Adolescence is essentially a period of physical, mental and social change. The many physical changes which occur at this time cause him to be more aware of himself, more self-conscious in a literal sense. This new awareness of himself is intensified by the maturation of the secondary sexual characteristics, and a re-awakening of the long dormant sexual drive. How adequately youngsters learn to control and direct their sexual feelings partially depends upon the present and past attitudes of others, particularly his parents. Puberty also entails a new social adjustment in that popularity with the opposite sex is now an important symbol of social status.

The main mental change in adolescence is in the area of intellectual development. The young person of this age is equipped, not only with a new fund of physical energy, but also with a new fund of mental energy. In essence the adolescent becomes capable of a much more abstract mode of thinking and the capacity for new learning reaches its peak, slowly declining later in adulthood. These aspects of intellectual development help to explain some typical features of adolescent behaviour. The new found ability to reason in a wider context leads to endless speculations about abstract issues. The attitude to parents may be altered by the new capacity to question their reasoning and the realization that age does not necessarily bring wisdom. Finding that long established sources of authority have feet of clay, the young person is likely to seek new authority figures, often nearer to his own age level. This accounts to some extent for the rebellious, non-conforming attitude of the adolescent who constantly debunks all sources of the no longer infallible adult authority. Although this may be a trying period for the demoted parent, it is an essential and healthy part of development which aids the youngster in finding his own identity.

Adolescence is finally, and perhaps most importantly, a period of social change and adjustment. Although childhood and adulthood have their own problems they offer the individual a secure and clearly defined social role. The adolescent is asked to surrender the dependency of childhood without being offered the independency of adulthood. During this period of apprenticeship for manhood or womanhood the adolescent's social role is a vague, nebulous and often contradictory one. To some extent this long period of apprenticeship is imposed upon the young person by the society in which he lives. He may be criticized for being childish by the same adults who disparage and discourage his attempts to play a more mature role. It is not surprising that the adolescent in-betweens form their own social group or that their activities reflect their rootlessness and their insecure state of mind. In some less advanced societies adolescence does not exist as a distinct stage of human development. In such societies the child is accepted as such until he reaches a certain age. At this point he is fully accepted as a responsible adult member of his social group and assigned a clearly defined role to play. It is not surprising that many of the emotional and behavioural problems which appear to us as being a natural part of adolescence are much less evident in such societies.

What are the effects of such changes on the adolescent personality? Their main effect is probably summed up in one word—uncertainty. The adolescent suffers from a basic lack of direction. His own emotions are confused and ambivalent. He senses his own mental power but at the same time lacks the inner confidence to translate his beliefs into a definite course of action. His delight in shocking his parents' adult composure is matched by the feelings of guilt which his own behaviour invokes. Fantasies and day dreams are an easy substitute for action and in such imaginative reveries all problems are solved. In these he is sophisticated, sexually dominant, respected by others and decisive in action. Later, if he is to reach a more mature level of development, he must come to some sort of compromise between his inner desires and outward achievements. Out of this maelstrom of conflicting feelings and ideas the adolescent must find a new individual identity. He must find for himself what sort of person he is, where he is going in life and what are his personal limitations and potentialities. Some psychologists have called the adolescent period a crisis of identity, to stress the crucial process of social and personal readjustment involved. In these days when the adolescent has become a marketable (commercially viable) commodity we might easily conclude that adolescence is a purely contemporary social problem. Perhaps it is fitting to close our discussion of the adolescent period with the following quotation: 'The world is passing through troubled times. The younger people have no reverence for their parents; they are impatient of all restraint; they talk as if they alone knew everything, and what passes for wisdom with us is foolishness for them.'

This is taken, not from today's newspaper editorials but from the writings of Peter the Hermit in the eleventh century.

ADULT LIFE

Although a legal age for the onset of adulthood is easily decided it is less simple to denote its psychological onset. Adulthood carries with it a certain level of maturity that is not a necessary consequence of reaching any particular age. To some extent the criteria of mature adulthood have already been implied in our discussion of adolescence. Maturity involves a realistic adjustment, both to the environment and to one's self. By achieving insight into one's own limitations and potentialities we learn to accept the former and develop the latter. We turn aside from the unattainable day dream and employ our energies in a more realistic striving for the attainable. We learn to accept the responsibility for our actions, make our own decisions and learn by our mistakes. Gradually we learn to accept responsibility for others, this acceptance reaching its full development as the young adult himself becomes a parent.

Although any part of adulthood may contain stress, there are certain broad areas which may be distinguished as exerting particularly difficult demands upon the individual. The need to find some measure of success and satisfaction in work is not purely economic but is also an expression of man's need for a purposeful life. Unfortunately a modern industrial society does not provide every adult with an interesting and self-satisfying job. Many find, in their leisure time, activities which allow them to express their constructive needs. The adult who is unable to find personal satisfaction either in or out of work is unlikely to feel completely at ease with himself. Again, in a competitive society, the sense of achievement derived from steady vocational progress is not given to all. Marriage is another area of adult life which demands a great deal of individual readjustment. Immature adults may seek to re-establish in marriage the security and lack of responsibility of childhood. Unconsciously they seek not a partner but a father or mother substitute. Unfortunately a neurotic adult often marries a person who is also unstable. This may serve to contain the incidence of neurosis within certain families but it is poor recompense for the unhappy child of emotionally disturbed parents. Parenthood itself can be a stress for the immature adult who may dislike the competition for his wife's attention and the new responsibilities thrust upon him. The loss of one's parents is a naturally stressful experience which may be a catastrophic one for the immature adult

who has never been psychologically weaned. A final area of stress in adult life is the inevitable onset of middle-age. Rather than accept both the disadvantages and compensations of later life some individuals indulge in self-defeating attempts to prolong youth. Middle-age is often more stressful for women who have to cope with the biological and psychological changes of the menopause. Depressive illnesses are common at this period but it is uncertain whether physiological changes or social and psychological factors are mainly responsible. In discussing adult adjustment and earlier stages of development reference has been more to the effect of stress on the individual. It is worthwhile to pause and consider in more detail what is meant by psychological stress.

Stress

The question arises whether the apparent increase in mental breakdown is due to the stress of modern life. First, it is not certain that there has been a real increase in psychiatric illness. New psychiatric treatment, combined with public education, has lessened the stigma of mental illness and people are now more ready to seek psychiatric help. However, the query is raised as to whether all mental disorders do not arise in individuals subjected to too much stress. Knowledge of the more serious psychiatric conditions, the major psychoses, suggests that these illnesses are a result of biochemical changes affecting a genetically vulnerable nervous system. Although external stress may trigger off such illnesses as manic-depressive psychosis and schizophrenia, yet the basic cause is probably internal. However, what of the less serious, but often incapacitating neurotic illness, the **nervous breakdown**, which figures so prominently in contemporary life? May the onset of neurotic symptoms such as acute anxiety be due to continual exposure to an overdemanding and stressful environment? A difficulty in answering these questions is that circumstances, which provoke stress in one individual, another may take in his stride. What an individual finds traumatic reflects to a large extent his past experiences, from early childhood onwards. Thus marriage, promotion at work, parenthood, death of a parent, may or may not be stressful depending upon past experiences and the significance such events have for the individual.

Nevertheless, many people like Hamlet appear to break down under the 'sea of troubles' to which they have been exposed. The traumatic event which immediately preceded collapse may have no more significance than being the final link in a long and unremitting series of stresses. 'It is the last straw which breaks the camel's back,' expresses proverbially that when people are forced to make too many decisions at once or, to perform beyond their capabilities, performance deteriorates and adverse effects become evident. People differ widely in the amount of stress they can tolerate before they reach their breaking point. There is some evidence to suggest that the capacity to tolerate stress is partially constitutional, individual differences in which may be evident as early as the first few months of life. Neurotic symptoms develop out of two sets of antecedent conditions, the individual's capacity to tolerate stress and the amount of stress which is imposed upon him.

On the other hand some neurotic illnesses may be a reaction to apparent absence of stress. For example, a young housewife's symptoms of anxiety, irritability and depression may be related to the boredom of being confined in a house with young children as her main human contact. People often go out of their way to participate in stressful situations, from the thrill of the big wheel at the fairground to climbing dangerous mountains. The effects of monotony and the individual's need for some level of excitement and stimulation have been the subject of much psychological research. A practical problem in World War II was how to maintain the vigilance of men and women at anti-aircraft sites through long periods of idleness and boredom. Technological changes in industry have committed many workers to the important but monotonous task of monitoring dials and gauges of automated machines. Vigilance in such monotonous situations soon suffers as the operator developing involuntary lapses of attention, combined with subjective feelings of irritability, restlessness and boredom. Studies of the effect of different types of monotonous conditions have also confirmed the deleterious effects of boredom upon most adults. Some of these studies have gone to extreme lengths to create an artificial environment in which normal environmental stimulation is reduced to a bare minimum. In one such experiment the subjects were suspended in a tank containing water at body temperature. The experimental tank was constructed so that the subjects could neither hear, nor see, nor have any sense of pressure, movement or touch. In such extreme conditions the subjects quickly experienced failure in concentration, confused thinking, hallucinations and extreme feelings of panic. In interpreting the findings of such experiments the Canadian psychologist Hebb concluded:

'The well-adjusted adult therefore is not intrinsically less subject to emotional disturbance: he is well adjusted, relatively unemotional, as long as he is in his cocoon (his cultural environment). We think of some persons as being emotionally dependent and others not; but it looks as though we are completely dependent upon the environment in a way and to a degree that we have not suspected.'

All these observations suggest that man's adjustment to the environment is one of precarious balance. If we are asked to function continually at a level beyond our capacity our performance falls off and the effects of stress become evident. If, however, we are subjected to a non-stimulating, non-demanding environment similar reactions result. A severe reduction in contact with the outside world, as in the sensory deprivation experiments described above, produces, not a sense of tranquillity, but thought disorder and panic.

A healthy adjustment to an environment depends on achieving an optimum balance between these two opposing influences; the optimum level varies from one individual to another.

OLD AGE

This final stage of human development has been the focal point of a great deal of psychological study in recent years. As a result of medical progress and greatly improved social conditions more people are surviving into old age and their welfare is one of today's most pressing social problems. How much of this task still remains to be done is to be seen in the high proportion of elderly people who today live in mental hospitals. This fact raises the important question of whether the psychological changes associated with old age are an inevitable part of the biology of ageing or are avoidable consequences of social organization. As with growing up, it is difficult to link the onset of old age with any specific chronological age. The sequence of physical and mental changes in later life differs greatly from one individual to another. Indeed, perhaps the most striking feature of ageing is its individual variability.

Earlier categorization of adolescent changes into their physical, mental and social aspects provides a useful framework in which to examine the changes of later life. A reduction in physical energy is accompanied by increasing dimness in vision and hearing. Alterations in muscular control reduce mobility and the speed and dexterity with which movements may be made. These and other physical changes have a common psychological consequence for the elderly person in restricting his former pursuits and limiting his social relationships.

The mental changes in old age are many and complex, which is another way of saying that we have still much to learn about them. There is a reduction in the capacity to learn new principles, resulting in a progressive dependency on principles and ideas learned in the past. The older person tends to be more rigid in his thinking, less able to adapt himself readily to new ideas and experiences. There is a demonstrable reduction in the capacity to handle information. It takes longer to grasp information and less can be held at any one time. Retention of information in the short term is also easily disturbed by any other activity going on at the same time. These changes result in a tendency for the older person to be slower in grasp, poor in concentration and unreliable in his memory for recent events. Recall of events in the more remote past is seldom impaired, this being another factor in making the elderly person more comfortable and assured when dealing with the past rather than with the present. Earlier it was suggested that one of the hallmarks of successful development in late childhood was the capacity to control impulses and emotions. In old age there is often a noticeable decline in this control so that the old person may appear childish and overemotional in his responses.

The social changes in old age reflect in large measure the role which society offers to its older citizens. Normally retirement from work occurs at the age of sixty-five although today people may still have many years of life ahead. It is not until retirement that people realize how dependent they have been on their work, even though their job may have been uncongenial or dull. Retirement involves separation from familiar surroundings and friends and, most important, a negation of the lifelong pride of being an independent being contributing to society. It demands an abrupt change in established habits at a time when new adjustments are difficult to make. Such considerations do not similarly apply to the housewife whose job has no retirement age, although her own domestic routine is likely to be shattered by the continual presence of the former breadwinner. The social status of the elderly person has changed considerably outside the setting of work. Grandfather is no longer accepted as the head of the family. Indeed, slackening of family ties may result in there being no easily accessible family contact. In this age with its emphasis on youth's speed and flexibility the elderly are not respected or revered, merely tolerated. Where once the elders advised and guided others they are now themselves being looked after by others. By being denied a viable functioning role the older person is made to feel a social liability rather than an asset. It is impossible to estimate how many of the less fortunate changes associated with ageing are a direct and avoidable result of the social vacuum in which many elderly people are placed. In societies where the elderly are still given a clearly defined and useful social role, there tends to be a lower incidence in the mental and emotional disturbances of old age.

Many old people make an adequate adjustment to retirement by re-ordering their life around a rigid but secure pattern. Each hour of the day is fitted into a carefully planned programme of routine in which everything is expected. Such a repetitive pattern of living helps to compensate for their declining capacity to deal with change and the unexpected. Illness requiring admission to hospital or institution abruptly disrupts this well ordered existence and throws the old person into a completely alien and frightening environment full of uncertainties. It is then not surprising that some old people become emotionally disturbed or even deteriorate rapidly. Fortunately, hospital life is itself founded upon systematic routine and, given time to adjust, the elderly

patient may find security in its regularity. Most modern hospitals are also fully aware of the dangers of allowing the elderly patients to become too dependent and direct management towards as rapid a return to self-autonomy as possible.

STANDARDS OF NORMALITY

The terms **normal** and **abnormal** are commonly used by psychologists and psychiatrists but they are seldom defined precisely. Like many words in both everyday and technical usage, **normality** is given many shades of meaning. Perhaps the most common lay use is exemplified in the words of an American comedian who declared: 'My wife is abnormally immature, if I'm sitting peacefully in my bath she'll think nothing of walking right in and sinking all my little boats!' In this usage it is assumed that we are normal and that the behaviour of others may be judged abnormal to the extent to which it deviates from our own standards. Normality as a psychological concept has at least four different meanings, some of which have uncomfortably much in common with that expressed above.

THE DICHOTOMOUS CONCEPT

The history of psychiatry has involved much argument between those who measure mental health on a continuum and those who regard normality and abnormality as constituting a clear-cut dichotomy. In medieval times the latter view was well accepted. People were either healthy and normal or abnormal and possessed by a devil. Although this view has been greatly modified with increased understanding of mental illness it was not until the advent of psychoanalytic theory that the dichotomy between normality and abnormality was finally bridged. By viewing neurotic symptons as a product of unconscious conflict Freud demonstrated that the difference between normality and neurosis is one of degree and not of kind. Although few contemporary psychiatrists disagree with this argument as applied to the neuroses the dichotomous standard of normality is still often applied in the case of the more serious psychotic mental disorders. The conception of specific disease entities which has dominated European psychiatry since the time of Kraepelin denies that the psychotic process is merely an extension of normality. A person has or has not schizophrenia, just as he has or has not cancer. It is now appreciated that this all-or-none concept cannot always be correctly applied to physical illness and it may well be that the dichotomous approach may have to be abandoned in psychiatry. However, at the present time we do have two separate standards of normality operating in the field of mental health, depending upon the nature of the disorder. This double standard easily leads to double-talk in psychiatric diagnosis when we fail to distinguish which standard is being applied.

THE STATISTICAL CONCEPT

In discussing the distribution and measurement of intelligence a purely statistical approach to normality is utilized. Normal intelligence is here defined as being around an IQ of 100 and abnormal degrees of intelligence, low and high, lie on either side of the distribution curve. The **normal** may be the **average** in many aspects of human behaviour and this is an assumption used by the clinical psychologist in assessing mental health. This way of assessing normality is quite different from the dichotomous approach, for it implies a continuum between normality and abnormality, which differ only in degree. The whole idea of constructing standard psychological tests of behaviour is based upon a statistical approach to normality and in practice this often works well. A statement that a 1-year-old infant's physical development is abnormal because it deviates in certain ways from the average level of development of other 12-month-old infants is informative and useful. The parallel statement that a person's behaviour is abnormal because it deviates from the behaviour of others of a similar age and background is also useful but a great deal less simple to demonstrate. While it is relatively easy to assess the normal (average) level of physical development at different ages it is extremely difficult to assess what is the normal distribution of specific forms of behaviour. Another difficulty is that the norm of behaviour may vary in different social groups. If a statistical survey of the incidence of wife beating is made it will be found to occur sufficiently infrequently to call it abnormal behaviour. However, if the survey is confined to a particular social group it may be found to be statistically normal for this sample. Are we then to say that for members of this social group it is abnormal not to beat one's wife? This dilemma is perhaps more evident when we consider the third concept of normality.

THE ADJUSTIVE CONCEPT

A common denominator in all mental disorders is the inability of the individual to adjust harmoniously to others and to the society to which he belongs. Thus a common criterion of normality in psychiatry is the degree to which an individual is able to adjust to his environment. Inability to accept the prevailing social standards, either because of aggressive defiance, fear, withdrawal or personal deficiency, becomes the criterion of abnormality. This method of defining normality equates it with conventionality. The well-adjusted person is the conventional individual who conforms to the prevailing standards of conduct. This approach has much in common with the statistical method, both equating unusual and unconventional behaviour with abnormality. This

concept of normality has provoked the caustic comment that 'the capacity to share the delusions of the crowd is a sign of individual health'. If normality is measured in terms of adjustment to society, it is clear that mental health must be assessed with reference to a particular society. An individual, who is well adjusted and therefore normal in one society, may be maladjusted and abnormal in another society. As different cultural groups with differing standards exist within any one society, the decision as to whether an individual's behaviour is to be judged normal or abnormal requires detailed reference to his social background.

This problem is intensified by the fact that those who have to make such judgements (psychiatrists, social workers and magistrates) are frequently from a different social background from the individual whose normality is to be assessed. In some parts of the Scottish Highlands 'second sight' is not so much a sign of abnormal mental functioning as a matter of keeping up with the Mc-Donalds!

THE IDEAL CONCEPT

Some systems of measurement are based upon a flawless or ideal standard of normality. If the dentist used a statistical concept of normality he would remove healthy teeth in an effort to make his patient more 'normal' for his age. The dentist and the physician have in their mind an ideal set of teeth and a perfectly functioning human body which, although seldom seen, acts as a standard of normality. Unlike the other views, the ideal concept implies an absolute, rather than a relative criterion of normality. Although this approach avoids many of the pitfalls inherent in the other concepts it is seldom used in psychology. The reason for this is simply lack of adequate knowledge of the ideal qualities of human behaviour and mental health. Perhaps one day understanding of human nature will be sufficiently advanced to allow us to aim at an ideal level in human behaviour. Indeed it may be necessary to find a new yardstick for assessing human conduct independent of any one society if the survival of the race is to be extended.

ASSESSMENT OF PERSONALITY

All sciences strive to measure the material which they observe and psychology is no exception. The psychologist's task is especially difficult for the material which he seeks to measure is human behaviour. However, this has not prevented psychologists from constructing standard tests of selected aspects of mental functioning. Although such tests vary widely in the type of function which they seek to measure, they all have one thing in common. Each of them places the individual in a standard situation, defined by the nature of the individual test, and compares his responses with that of others in the same situation. As it is obviously impossible to obtain the test responses of the whole population, tests are standardized on a carefully selected sample of the population. This allows a reasonable comparison of an individual's test performance relative to that of others of his own age, sex and social background. The accuracy of the measurements always depends upon the reliability of the original standardization on the test population sample. The most generally accepted form of standard psychological test is the intelligence test and we shall begin by considering how it is constructed and what are its uses and limitations. Later psychological testing of other areas of personality are described.

Intelligence tests

It is doubtful whether any psychological instrument is more widely known and applied than the intelligence test. Such tests play a prominent part in education and in vocational selection for industry and commerce. Many psychologists have viewed the increasing use of such tests with disquiet, wondering if they have created a latter-day Frankenstein monster over which they have lost control. Certainly the IQ may be too easily regarded as a static and tangible part of the personality, a modern status symbol representing the individual's worth to society. It is important to realize that the IQ is simply a measure of an individual's performance at that time on a particular test. It is a relative measure in that it is based upon a comparison of the individual's performance with others of his age and background. Like many other measurements of behaviour, the IQ may fluctuate with mood changes, interest and co-operation or with any other factors which affect mental output. If the IQ varied too widely from test to test or from time to time it would have little value in predicting future behaviour. This indeed occurs with very young children where the IQ is too variable to use in predicting future progress. The younger the child the lower the predictive value of the IQ. However, the young child's performance on a standard intelligence test does offer an approximate comparison of his present level of ability to that of other children and this may often be a useful measure in itself. The child who is either developmentally retarded or precocious is spotted and the reasons for such findings may be discovered. In young children the capacity being assessed is still developing so that it is impossible to estimate accurately its final level. After the age of 9–11 years the probability of a marked change in ability is much less so that the IQ becomes a useful predictor of future intellectual level. Intelligence is of course only one factor in successful living and the estimation of a high or low IQ does not provide a ready means of predicting future progress. Selfconfidence, drive, emotional stability and specific non-intellectual talents have all to

be taken into account if such predictions are being made.

In older children and adults, the intelligence test is useful in assessing present ability and future possibilities. How is the IQ calculated and what does it actually measure? The first of these questions is much easier to answer than the second.

The IQ is a statistical conversion of the subject's test score to a number representing the relative position of his performance to others of his own age. The term **intelligence quotient** is a legacy from the older method of calculating the intellectual level by the ratio of mental age to chronological age. Mental age merely represents the age level corresponding to the score reached on the test. Thus, if a child of 10 years gives a test score appropriate to that of the average 11 year old child, his mental age would be 11 years and his IQ

$$\frac{\text{Mental Age}}{\text{Chronological Age}} \times 100 \quad \text{would be 110.}$$

This method works reasonably well for younger children but has grave disadvantages when applied to older children or adults. After the age of 13–14 years the gain in test scores per year is very small. It is for example impossible to find problems that an average 24-year-old person will pass and an average 23-year-old will fail. This limitation was formerly overcome by dividing the Mental Age by a constant figure, usually 15, when testing adults. Although this practice allows for the absence of improvement in test performance after the age of 15 years it is too crude to give consistent results. This method of calculating the IQ was found also to accentuate the difference between IQ's derived from different tests.

A more satisfactory way of designating a subject's test performance is to express his score in the form of a **percentile**. The percentile compares the subject's test score relative to that of others of the same age on a ranking scale from one to ninety-nine. Thus a child who scores at the 75th percentile is in the top 25 per cent of his own age group. Percentile gradings can then be statistically converted to standard scores with a mean of 100. Strictly speaking, the modern IQ is not a quotient at all but a standard score denoting the position of the subject's test score relative to others of his age.

The present method of calculating the IQ in terms of standard scores rather than quotients makes the assumption that intelligence is normally distributed in the community. In other words, the majority of the population are assumed to fall around the middle with only a few falling into the extreme of very high or very low IQ. While this assumption has never been verified there is sufficient evidence to suggest that it is a near enough approximation to the truth. The table below gives a rough idea of the distribution of IQ levels in the community.

It can be seen that the majority of people have an IQ

TABLE 36.1. Distribution of IQ levels in the community.

IQ Level	Per cent of Population	Designation
Above 145	1	Gifted, or genius
130–145	2	Superior
115–130	12	Above average
85–115	70	Average
70–85	12	Dull
55–70	2	Subnormal
Below 55	1	Severely subnormal

between 85–115. University entrants normally have a minimum IQ of 120 although there is much variation above this level among different faculties. Although many children, with an IQ below 80 require to be educated at a school for backward children, the normally accepted cut-off point for mental subnormality or deficiency is 70. The 1 per cent of the community with an IQ of under 55 require to be looked after in special institutions. It should be emphasized that the diagnosis of subnormality is never made solely on the basis of an intelligence test score. The ability of the individual to reach a resonable level of social adjustment is a much more important consideration.

The question as to what is actually being measured with intelligence tests becomes pertinent when the bewildering variety of tests in present-day use are considered. Many of the tests consist of the type of problems associated with academic success. Such items include defining words, reading, giving opposites, arithmetical problems and general knowledge. These tests tend to reflect the child's educational level and their emphasis on words and verbal reasoning favours the verbally fluent and well-read child. Although a good verbal knowledge and educational success is often synonomous with brightness this is not always the case. A child whose education has been interrupted by illness or who is reared in a home environment where learning is discouraged may falsely appear to be intellectually retarded on such a test. Other tests avoid this difficulty by being non-verbal in nature. Such **performance tests** provide a measure of the subject's ability to reason in a non-verbal setting. Thus the **Progressive Matrices** test presents a series of incomplete geometric patterns which can only be completed by an appreciation of the relationship within the pattern. Fig. 36.1 below illustrates a typical item from this test.

Many modern intelligence tests incorporate both verbal and performance sections within the one test. For instance the **Wechsler Intelligence Scale** is made up of six verbal and five non-verbal sub-tests yielding both a verbal and performance IQ, as well as a composite full scale IQ. Such tests may take longer to carry out but they provide a great deal more information.

There has been much debate as to whether intelligence is inherited or a product of the environment. Twin

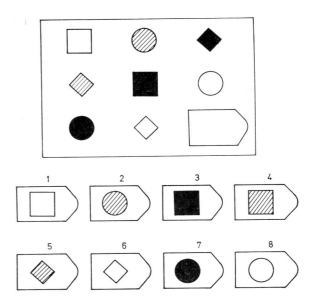

FIG. 36.1. An example of the Progressive Matrices test.

studies and other controlled investigations have suggested that there is a strong genetic loading in intelligence. Perhaps such discussions are fruitless and liable to lead to misleading conclusions. Our constitution may contain our developmental potentialities but the environment decides to what extent and in what ways these potentialities are realized. These two factors must always interact to such a degree that a clear distinction between their respective contributions is often impossible. The position regarding intelligence has been well stated by the Canadian psychologist Hebb who suggests that there are two aspects of intelligence, termed A and B. Intelligence A is constitutionally decided for each individual by the type of brain and nervous system with which he is born. This represents the individual's intellectual **capacity** or the range of his potential intellectual development. Intelligence B is a factor of experience and represents the stage of intellectual **development** within this range actually reached by the individual. The IQ regardless of the type of test used, will always be a measure of the developed ability of Intelligence B (we can never hope to measure a capacity or potential) although this will nevertheless be a function of the inherited capacity of Intelligence A.

Although we might go through life indefinitely expanding our knowledge, there is a good deal of evidence to suggest that the human brain's intellectual capacity falls off in later years. This is most evident in old age where the individual's test performance indicates a progressive inability to deal effectively with new learning and an increasing dependence upon knowledge acquired in the past. The differential decline in some forms of mental output with age occurs also in a more exaggerated form as a result of brain injury or organic cerebral disease. This finding allows psychologists to use modified forms of intelligence tests to assess the degree of intellectual deterioration due to pathological changes in the brain. However, the more complex matter of the psychological assessment of cerebral dysfunction is outside the scope of this discussion.

Personality testing

It would obviously be naïve to expect two people to behave in identical ways, just because they were of equal intelligence. The whole personality of the individual, his attitudes, his beliefs, his emotional stability, play a part in determining his behaviour. Psychologists have attempted to devise tests which assess such personality differences with the same accuracy achieved in testing intelligence. As might be expected this attempt has been much less successful. Intelligence is a complex enough concept to define and measure but personality is infinitely more so. Even if personality is reduced into its component parts the components to be measured are far from specific. Thus **emotional stability** or its converse **neuroticism** are themselves an amalgam of many personality traits. Here we shall consider some of the most frequently found forms of personality assessment.

THE INTERVIEW

The interview is perhaps the most common method of personality assessment, but unfortunately assessments are often unreliable. One of the main difficulties is that the personality of the interviewer tends to intrude and distort the picture of the interviewee. Interviewers adopt their own method of interviewing depending upon their interests, likes, dislikes and prejudices. Without being aware of it the interviewer may allow one aspect of the interviewee, for example, his dress or appearance, to colour and distort the general assessment of the person. Naturally, people vary greatly in their skill in interviewing but it is often the person who considers himself to be a good judge of character who is most subjectively biased. Some improvement can be brought about by **standardizing** the interview so that each interviewer adheres to a certain fixed framework. This is what the clinical psychiatrist does in his initial interview so that his impressions may be more easily compared with those of others. Such standardizing of the procedure brings it nearer to a personality test as it allows a comparative evaluation of the individual's responses on a standard situation.

The subjective factors in interviewing impressions may be reduced further by the application of **rating scales** which help to order the impression in a systematic manner. A rating scale simply lists on a graded scale the personality traits which we wish to assess. Thus, if we wished to include self-assertiveness in our evaluation, this trait could be rated on a five point scale from high to low degrees of assertiveness. Although this does not ensure the same standards for all interviewers, it does reduce the area of disagreement. Many standard rating scales are now usefully employed in hospitals to give nurses and other observers a simple and more reliable way of setting down their impressions of patients. If many individuals have been rated on such a scale, it is sometimes evident that certain clusters of traits are emerging. If, for example, we note that such items as self-consciousness, blushing, poor sleep, restlessness and anxiety tend to correspond in their rating value, we might feel that this cluster denoted the more general factor of **nervous disposition**. In some cases such clusters have been extracted by statistical analysis so that the rating scale provides assessments of more general areas of personality differences. Some such scales have been specially constructed as diagnostic aids in psychiatric assessment.

PERSONALITY QUESTIONNAIRES

To avoid the subjective errors inherent in the interview psychologists have constructed questionnaires on which the person is invited to rate his own personality. In most cases the subject's task is reduced to reading a series of statements and underlining a response indicating whether the statement could be applied to him, e.g. I sometimes get dizzy turns. YES : NO. Many of these questionnaires aim their sights ridiculously high in attempting to make a full personality assessment on the basis of the subject's responses to fifty or more such questions. The more successful types confine themselves to measuring one area of personality such as neuroticism, hostility, sociability, etc. Some of these, such as the **Eysenck personality inventory** developed at the Maudsley Hospital, are said to discriminate between neurotic patients and normal subjects with reasonable efficiency. The validity of such claims depends a great deal upon how neuroticism is defined and if it is thought reasonable to make a clear distinction between normal and neurotic. Nevertheless this type of questionnaire can be useful in psychological research as a speedy and reasonably reliable way of extracting from a group the two extremes of highly neurotic and highly stable individuals.

PROJECTIVE TESTS

In the eyes of some psychologists the preceding methods of personality assessment are too superficial and atomistic. They do not provide any information on the deeper, less conscious levels of personality. In projective testing the individual is presented with unstructured material and asked to organize and structure this in his own way. A group of people gazing at the dying embers of a fire may readily see pictures in the fire but it is unlikely that they will see the same pictures. Those which they do perceive will reflect their own inner preoccupations and fantasies because it is they who are projecting the meaning and significance into the situation. As in this age of central heating we cannot rely on a ready supply of dying embers, psychologists have devised their own standard projective situations. Thus, in one such test, **the thematic apperception test** the subject is asked to look through a series of twenty pictures and to construct his own story around each of the cards. In another, the well-known **Rorschach ink blot test** the material is in the even more amorphous form of ink blots and the subject is encouraged to describe what shapes and forms he perceives in them. There are many other types of projection tests but with the same general principle. The scoring and interpretation of projection tests is a much more complex and less objective procedure than with most other types of personality tests. The usefulness of the information elicited reflects the examiner's skill and experience to a much greater degree than in other simpler methods. Although projection tests are still popular in the U.S.A. they are going out of favour in this country. The contemporary emphasis on the scientific approach in British psychology has led to a critical appraisal of the claims made for such tests. Certainly, their interpretation is open to subjective abuse and sometimes it is difficult to see who is doing the most projecting—the subject or the examiner. However, in experienced hands they can yield useful information on the affective side of personality which is difficult to obtain by more direct and objective means.

This has been an unfairly short résumé of a very wide and diverse field of psychological testing. It is hoped that it has given the reader some idea of both the uses and limitations of intelligence tests. On the side of personality testing we might conclude that what these tests gain in scope they tend to lose in accuracy.

INTERACTION WITH THE ENVIRONMENT

Thus far we have been concerned mainly with the development of personality and with some of the effects of environmental changes upon the individual. The final section will consider some of the psychological processes which allow us to deal effectively with the environment. Although each of these processes will be considered separately, they are really different phases in the complex operation of processing information from the environment. In recent years these cognitive processes have been the subject of much experimental investigation and we are now much nearer to understanding their functioning.

Attending

Before we can deal with events in our environment we must first become aware of them. From the everyday environment a multitude of stimuli impinge upon our sense organs and are then relayed by the nervous system to the brain. All these stimuli are not taken in at once but rather certain stimuli are selected at the expense of others. The process of attention thus involves a selective filtering of the sensory input from the environment so that some stimuli are given priority over others. Psychologists have for long postulated a mechanism in the nervous system responsible for this selective filtering operation and have been encouraged by recent neurophysiological interest in the brainstem reticular system as a physiological correlate of attention.

Some stimuli are more attention-demanding than others, especially if they are unusual enough to stand out from the background. Thus a bright light, a loud noise or a totally unexpected event will claim our attention. Probably the most important determinants of attention are internal in that we will be more likely to attend to events which accord with individual interests and needs of the moment. To the hungry man the odour of food cooking will have priority over any other stimuli competing for his attention.

Selective attention, like most human processes, appears to develop gradually in early life. Indeed, one of the most characteristic features of the younger child is his inability to focus his attention on any one event for long. He is easily distracted by any change in his immediate environment. It is only as we grow older that we develop this capacity to ignore distracting stimuli. The efficiency of selective attention appears to fall off in old age so that the elderly person is easily distracted and unable to concentrate as well as before. Even in the healthy adult, attention fluctuates greatly. Fatigue, physical and mental, results in a less efficient filtering of the stimuli competing for attention so that it is more difficult to apply oneself to anything which requires rigorous concentration. On occasions when over anxious or preoccupied with personal worries, attempts to focus attention upon external tasks may be distracted by the competition offered by internal problems. A breakdown in the attentive process is a characteristic feature of some forms of severe mental illness. The deeply depressed patient cannot attend to everyday events in the outside world because his attention is fully occupied with his own thoughts and feelings. Indeed, the term **melancholia** literally means **full up** and is an apt description of the state of morbid preoccupation which isolates the patient from external events. A number of recent studies have demonstrated that one of the primary changes occurring in schizophrenia is a reduction in the capacity to attend selectively. The schizophrenic patient finds his mind being continuously bombarded by everything going on in the environment, so that his concentration is completely disrupted. It is possible that some of the success of the new tranquillizing drugs such as chlorpromazine is due to their action on the reticular activating system so as to bring the patient's attention nearer its normal effective level of performance.

Other studies have related individual differences in the process of attention to differences in personality structure. Thus, work carried out in the Menninger Clinic indicates that some people are particularly adept at directing their attention to relevant stimuli while ignoring irrelevant stimuli. Such people were found to be more self-controlled, assertive, confident and emotionally stable. Other individuals who were more passive in their attention and easily distracted were found to be lacking in confidence, less controlled in their emotions, more anxious and overconforming in their attitudes to authority. Although there is yet much to learn about the interaction between personality factors and cognitive processes such as attention, it would seem that the level of emotional maturity is an important factor in influencing the habitual mode of attending and concentrating.

Learning

If our environment is to have any lasting influence on us we must not only attend to events but learn from them and store the information for subsequent use. The capacity to store information and reproduce it after a period of time will be considered later when we turn to the process of remembering. Learning may be broadly understood as any process which modifies experience and behaviour. Life is thus itself a continual learning situation as we constantly modify our attitudes, opinions and behaviour in the light of each new experience. As we grow older we tend to become less receptive to new learning, more rigidly set in ways determined by prevously learned responses which have now become habitual. We have already seen that this resistance to change is one of the most prominent features of ageing. This is not due entirely to a natural reluctance to change established patterns of behaviour. Ageing also brings a falling off in the brain's capacity to utilize new information.

To the young child, however, there is no such brake on new learning and every day he faces a wide variety of new experiences which are consistently reshaping his view of himself and of his environment. As many of these influences are exerted long before the child is old enough to reason and to control his own behaviour, most early learning is without insight and does not require the active co-operation of the child. Although analogies between humans and animals are dangerous, studies of animal learning help us to understand the process of learning in early childhood. The training of animals by establishing conditioned reflexes and by operant conditioning is described on p. 24.92. Such procedures are used to teach circus animals new tricks but are also a reasonable description of how most parents train a young child. Parents constantly condition their child's conduct by reinforcing with either verbal or non-verbal signs of approval, those aspects of his behaviour which they wish to encourage. Alternatively conditioning may occur in a negative direction, parental disapproval being used to condition the child to inhibit certain types of behaviour because they have now become associated with displeasure. It is important to realize that this form of conditioned learning demands no insight on the part of the subject, who may be entirely unaware that his behaviour is being influenced. A number of psychological studies have shown how the behaviour of young children can be modified in a short space of time by planned conditioning techniques. When one realizes that the young child is exposed constantly to parental and other sources of conditioning throughout the lengthy period of his development it is easy to appreciate how much of early learning is of this type. Encouraged by such observations of the efficacy of conditioning techniques some psychologists suggest that all of our individual characteristics, likes, dislikes, our attitudes, opinions and indeed our whole personality is a product of the social conditioning process which begins in the home but continues throughout life.

The principles of conditioning may also be applied to the development of emotional responses. At the beginning of the present century, Watson suggested that the young infant displays only three basic emotional responses, fear, love and rage. At first these emotions are reactions to specific situations. Thus, fear is expressed as a response to sudden movements, loud noise or loss of support. Watson argued that, by a process of conditioning, these three primitive emotions are gradually extended to an ever increasing variety of new situations and experiences. He later gave a practical demonstration of this process in showing how a child could be experimentally conditioned to experience the emotion of fear to a new range of objects. This was done by the experimenters making a sudden loud anxiety provoking noise each time the child was playing with a pet white rat. After repeated conditioning sessions the child not only showed fear of the rat but later extended this to a fear of all white furry objects. An understanding of conditioned emotional responses is of value to a clinician, when treating neurotic patients who show inappropriate fears or **phobias** towards objects and situations which others experience as harmless. It may be argued that all abnormal fears can be understood as conditioned patterns of behaviour. To take a very simple example of this view we might visualize a young child who is bitten by a dog when walking under a tunnel. From this situation might develop a conditioned fear not only of dogs and other similar animals, but of enclosed spaces, darkness and any other aspects which were present in the original learning experience. This is of course in direct contrast to the psychodynamic view of the origin of neurosis which sees symptoms as a manifestation of unconscious conflict. The acceptance of the conditioned learning view of the development of neurotic symptoms has important practical repercussions on the treatment of such symptoms. If neurotic symptoms are learned responses, the most satisfactory treatment may be to help the patient to unlearn such responses by deconditioning them.

Deconditioning techniques are being used increasingly in the treatment of neurotic symptoms. Such **behaviour therapy** had an early success in the treatment of enuresis, bed wetting, in children. The child sleeps on a mat connected to electrodes so that the bed wetting produces a short circuit, causing the bell to ring. The child is trained to rise and go to the toilet when the bell rings. With repetition the child wakes and goes to the toilet in response to an increased bladder tension rather than to the sound of the bell. This technique is based on **reciprocal inhibition** one of the principles of modern learning theory, which aims at disrupting an unwanted behaviour pattern by introducing a new response incompatible with the old habit. Another form of conditioning, **aversion-therapy** has been extensively applied in the treatment of behaviour disorders such as alcoholism and drug addiction, sexual perversions and even compulsive gambling. Here the alcoholic patient might be presented with a noxious stimulus, such as an electric shock when drinking alcohol during treatment sessions. Repeated experience of this type lead to the taste of alcohol being associated with pain and displeasure. It is too early to assess the efficacy of these and other forms of Behaviour Therapy but such techniques may find a permanent place in the treatment of some neurotic symptoms and maladaptive habit patterns.

Much of human learning cannot be explained by the principles of conditioning and in later childhood and adult life it becomes progressively more self-directed and is accompanied by insight. Insightful learning involves a sudden understanding of the principle involved in solving a new problem and allows this principle to be applied to subsequent learning in similar situations. The point of insight in learning is usually derived from a **repatterning** of the various elements of the learning situation, leading to a new relationship between the different parts of the problem and so providing the solution. The information required to solve many problems in daily life is available, either externally in the nature of the problem itself or internally in the form of our stored memories of past learning. The point of insight is reached by first discarding items irrelevant to the solution and mentally reconstructing the relevant information to achieve the correct fit. Thus a doctor's information consists of his observations of the patient's signs and symptoms and his own previous learning of their diagnostic significance. He first discards features which appear irrelevant to this particular case and then mentally manipulates the relevant information until the correct

arrangement suggests the most likely diagnosis. Insightful learning therefore consists of a phase of **inhibition** which allows attention to be concentrated on what is relevant, followed by a phase of **organization** whereby the relevant information is put together. The efficiency of this organization is related to our intelligence and is largely a function of our individual intellectual capacity and acquired knowledge. The initial process of inhibition is related to attention and is more likely to be effected by our current state of mind. Tiredness, anxiety or any other temporary emotional state is likely to make us less effective in inhibiting irrelevancies and so reaching the heart of the problem.

It would be unrealistic to conceive of adult learning as always proceeding smoothly to a point of insight. Faced with an unfamiliar problem we may first proceed in an almost random manner, trying out possibilities and discarding them as they are found to be unsuccessful. Gradually, throughout these various trials we learn to reduce the number of errors made and improve performance. However, soon we reach a plateau where performance ceases to improve. Then a flash of insight into a better way of tackling the task may lead to a sudden improvement in performance. Most learning proceeds irregularly in this manner with periods of trial and error followed by sudden spurts. Someone learning to type, for example, will at first improve gradually through a process of trial and error and may soon reach a point where no further improvement in speed occurs. Later the elimination of inefficient work habits and the insight that all fingers may be used to type word units rather than individual letters may cause a sudden upwards spurt in performance, until once again a point of no improvement is realized. Human learning is thus a mixture of slow trial and error leading to points of insight where new principles are grasped and applied.

When any act is fully learned or overlearned by constant repetition it may become a skill which can now be reproduced without conscious deliberation. The child develops the skill of walking without pondering on each movement and of talking without deliberating upon the enunciation of each word. Conscious attention appears to be concerned mainly with the resolution of uncertainty, with acts which require decisions to be made. If something is learned so thoroughly as to become automatic, all uncertainty is eliminated and it can be carried out without thought or effort. Indeed, the focusing of conscious attention upon a skilled act which has become automatic may disrupt its normally smooth execution. The experienced driver often finds his expertise rapidly disappears when he attempts to teach someone else his skill. The well-practised radiologist or medical diagnostician may find similar difficulty in teaching his ability to others simply because it has become a highly developed automatic skill. We often use the word **intuition** as a poor expression of an act which is a result of many years of previous learning experience.

Remembering

The process of memory cannot be divorced from that of learning and it is often difficult to distinguish between a memory deficit and learning deficiences since we cannot expect to recall something inadequately learnt. As we have seen, learning is, in its turn, dependent upon the earlier phase of attention, so that all these factors operate in the learning process. Remembering is in fact the final stage in the learning process by which we are able to make use of the stored results of previous learning. Memory involves the capacity to retain in the brain a record of past experiences and to recall this record into consciousness when required.

Neurophysiologists and more recently, biochemists have speculated on the form in which this continuous recording of experiences is registered in the brain (p. 24.92). For many years psychologists have assumed the presence of a **structural memory trace** involving an actual modification in the brain cells. Biochemists have suggested that the memory trace may be recorded in the form of changes in the structure of RNA molecules contained in the individual neurones (p. 24.86). Whatever the form of the permanent record it soon becomes evident that the brain must possess a gigantic storage capacity to house all the experiences registered throughout life. Perceptual studies suggest that the human brain is capable of receiving around 1000 units of information in one-tenth of a second. If allowance is made for sleep this means that something in the nature of 15×10^9 units of information may be stored in a 70 year lifetime. This is rather more than a thousand times the available number of nerve cells in the brain. Any theory of memory storage must also account for the capacity to erase some of these records no longer of use to the individual. We do not need to clutter up the brain with telephone numbers and other items which need only to be remembered long enough for the appropriate action to take place. A somewhat different theory of memory suggests that memories are stored in the form of a **dynamic trace** which need not involve any structural alteration in the brain cells. This theory sees memories as consisting of active patterns of electrical impulses which have no specific static location. A nerve impulse travelling around a closed loop of connecting neurones might be the mechanism for such a dynamic memory trace.

Although it is difficult to assess directly the validity of these two theories, it is possible to make some indirect judgement of their comparative value. The electrical activity of the brain may be temporarily disrupted or stopped by freezing techniques or by electric shock. If the dynamic trace theory is correct such disruption should effect memory storage, while in the structural

trace theory no disturbance of memory need take place. We can then carry out a simple experiment in which an animal is trained in a new task, e.g. running a maze, and then given a strong electric shock. If it now performs the task as well or better than before, its memory has been unaffected and presumably did not depend upon reverberating patterns of neural activity. In fact, the findings from this sort of experiment do not completely contradict either theory. If the shock is administered some time after the initial learning of the maze, memory is completely undisturbed. However, if the shock occurs immediately or very soon after the initial learning, memory is disturbed. This is also in accordance with the known effects of electroshock in human beings where most recently stored events are more likely to be erased. Such results suggest that events may be recorded initially as electrical activity and subsequently transferred to a more permanent store in the form of structural changes in the nerve cells. An oversimplified model of this two-phase theory of memory is illustrated in fig. 36.2.

FIG. 36.2. The two-phase theory of memory.

As we can attend to only one source of stimulation at a time, attention may be regarded as a selective filtering of the sensory input from the environment. The information which is selectively attended to then passes into a short term memory store where it may be held for a short time before being passed into the more permanent and stable long term memory store. However, as it would be uneconomical for us to retain a permanent record of every event, information may be held in the short-term memory store only long enough to allow an appropriate response to be made. Thus we may wish to remember a telephone number only long enough to be able to dial it. In this case there would be no need to transfer the information to the more permanent long-term memory store.

This division of memory into two stages is of both theoretical and practical importance. It accounts for our capacity to store some events long enough to allow an appropriate response to be made without transferring such items into permanent storage. The two types of storage systems operate on quite different principles and most types of memory failure occur during the initial phase of short term storage. Although our long term memory appears to have an almost unlimited capacity for storing information this is certainly not the case with short-term memory, which is very restricted in the amount of information it can handle at any one time. Thus, most adults can adequately hold around seven digits but any digits arriving in short term memory in excess of this number interferes with the storage of the earlier digits and errors occur. Information held in short-term storage is thus very vulnerable to disturbance by the arrival of fresh information. If we are interrupted when dialling a telephone number by being asked a simple question this may be sufficient to wipe out our temporary storage of the required number sequence.

However, in everyday life we frequently require to hold in mind for a short time sequences of information which are much longer than the seven units said to be our maximum capacity. The writer would have no difficulty in memorizing the sequence of 10665844114226007372436, a total of twenty-three digits. The load on my short term memory is reduced greatly by the fact that this sequence is capable of being reorganized into fewer units of information. The first four digits are the date of the Battle of Hastings, 58441 is my telephone number, 14.2.26 my date of birth, 007 a familiar sequence to the James Bond fan and the last six numbers (37-24-36) represent some very significant statistics. In this way a sequence may be recorded and stored in six units without overloading available storage capacity. Normally, of course we should not require to memorize a long number sequence, but in listening to someone speaking we are constantly required to store very long sequences of words for a brief period. Studies of speech perception show that we perform a similar coding operation upon the language input so that the message is registered in groups of words or phrases, rather than as individual words. Another factor which further reduces the load on short term memory is that normal language contains many words which are re-dundant, in so far as they are unnecessary for adequate comprehension of the message. When listening to speech we need not burden our limited storage capacity with these redundant words which can easily be filled in later because they are determined by their context. The amount of redundant information in a verbal message will of course vary with the degree of conventionality of the statement. In the sentence; 'The canary escaped when his cage door was left . . .', it does not matter whether or not we hear or forget the last word as we can see from the context that it is probably 'open'. Indeed, the message 'Cage door open—canary escaped', conveys the same information adequately although 50 per cent of the ori-ginal words have been removed. If, however, the message to be conveyed is highly original, abstract and concise, as in a closely reasoned argument, we may require to register almost every word to be sure of grasping its significance. It is a useful, although a painful experience,

to examine the proportion of redundant words used in my own efforts to transmit thought to paper. The same process may be seen to operate in the act of speaking as in listening to speaking. A great deal of speech requires little or no thinking, being composed of con-ventional phrases and clichés which literally roll off the tongue. If, however, we attempt to express our thoughts on something new and original our speech requires more planning and is a great deal less predict-able. Studies of the normal speech process shows that spontaneous speech takes the form of phrases of four to six words followed by brief but measurable pauses. The words following such speech pauses are often more abstract and convey more information than the words preceding it. These pauses thus indicate the points in a person's speech when he is actively thinking. We often associate fluency in speech (the absence of pauses) with intelligence and original thinking. Such studies serve to remind us that lack of hesitation may often merely indicate that what is being said is either well practised or at a low level of thinking, or simply that the speaker is long winded.

Earlier in considering old age, comment was made upon the complaint of poor memory frequently made by elderly people. Studies of the way in which memory changes with age suggest that such difficulties are nearly always confined to the initial stage of short term storage. As we grow older the amount of information capable of being held in short term memory decreases and the likelihood of interference in initial registration is en-hanced. Older people also appear to have more difficulty, both in recoding information into more easily manage-able units and in screening out redundant information. Thus, in listening to speech the elderly person has to handle a greater volume of information and is more likely to be overloaded and confused.

Many of the effects of normal ageing on short term memory occur in a more exaggerated form in patients with organic cerebral disease. Indeed, a failure in short-term retention is often the first observable signs of an organic dementing process. A somewhat similar type of memory deficit has been demonstrated in some types of schizophrenia. Severely subnormal defectives have been shown to have surprisingly good powers of retention for material which has been adequately assimilated into long-term storage, whereas their short-term retention is extremely poor. Such findings help to explain some of the difficulties experienced by some patients in con-centrating and in communicating adequately with others. They also suggest some of the ways the patient may be helped to improve his performance. Patients with poor short term retention can function much more adequately in conversation if the speaker talks slowly, avoids long phrases and redundant words and gives the patient sufficient time to register their meaning and construct his own thoughts before replying. Other types of memory disordered patients show very little impairment of short term memory, their deficit being in the transfer of information from short to long-term storage. Thus in Korsakow's psychosis, an organic disorder of the nervous system, the patient may retain events well enough for short periods but be unable to form lasting durable memories. There is also some suggestion that the more durable long term memory store may sometimes be effected by the result of cerebral damage destroying specific structural memory traces and producing isolated islands of forgetting.

The majority of examples of normal forgetting in healthy adults can of course be explained without recourse to specific organic changes. Some cases of apparent forgetting are more the result of inadequate learning. Actions may be performed that are so habitual, e.g. winding one's watch, that they are never consciously registered and are therefore difficult to recall. From what has been said the impression may have been given that memories are static entities, which once fully registered are safe from any further influence. This would be a very false impression for we consistently modify our memories during the process of storage. Most types of inaccurate memory entail, not complete forgetting of an event, but its recall in a distorted form. This reshaping and falsification of memories is usually in the direction of changing the memory of the event to make it more pleasant and self-satisfying than the actual event itself. The longer the time interval between the event and its subsequent recall and the greater emotional involvement the more chance of such distortion. Thus, memories of central events in early childhood are likely to be highly distorted, both by the passage of time and the need to remember these days in the most pleasant manner. The summers of our childhood are always sunnier than those of today! Freud and the psychoanalytic school saw the influence of emotions on memory as the chief cause of forgetting and memory distortion. The term **repression** is used to denote the process by which impulses and memories unacceptable to us are barred from consciousness. Much of what we forget usefully helps us to avoid the unpleasant associations which remembering would bring. In some cases of a psychoneurotic nature, repression is a central feature of the patient's symptoms. During and after the last war many men suffered from symptoms motivated by their complete repression of a highly traumatic event. In such cases treatment is aimed at helping the patient to re-live the repressed event and to dissipate the feelings of anxiety associated with it. In cases of pathological repression it is possible for the actual memory of the event to be retained but the feelings associated with it to be repressed. A few cases of amnesia are caused by the complete repression of a period of life involving great stress, such as the unhappily

married man who may forget the whole period of his marriage. However, repression seldom works effectively. Although the memory or feeling associated with it may be shut out of consciousness its presence is displayed in the form of neurotic symptoms of anxiety and general feelings of dis-ease.

Thinking

Thinking is in a sense a continuous process in that it is doubtful if the mind is ever blank. On occasions when we might describe ourselves as thinking about nothing, we should more accurately speak of thinking about nothing in particular. We are not consciously directing our thoughts on to any specific issue but rather allowing them to follow their own, apparently random course. One might then begin by recognizing two different types of thinking. **Directed thinking** (rational thinking or reasoning) consists of the active focusing of thought on to a specific problem. **Undirected (autistic) thinking** is more passive, less conscious and less attuned to objective reality. This distinction is similar to that made in psychoanalytic theory between **primary** and **secondary process thinking**. Primary process thinking which may appear random is directed by unconscious fantasies, while secondary process thinking is consciously directed to dealing rationally with the external environment. One might also liken undirected autistic thinking to the primitive form of egocentric thinking already described as characteristic of early childhood.

In discussion of the learning process some of the factors governing directed thinking were mentioned. Effective reasoning involves both the inhibition of irrelevant information and the organization of the relevant information to allow a rational conclusion. Ineffective reasoning may be due to the distracting influence of irrelevant factors or to a failure in perceiving correct relations between the relevant items. Effective reasoning, directed towards the solution of a specific problem, is typical of that used by scientists, mathematicians and also by physicians in their efforts to reach a correct diagnosis. It is, however, quite unlike the type of thinking indulged in by the artist, the poet and the mystic. Such people deliberately relax their normal inhibitory process and detach their thoughts from objective reality in an effort to avoid the restrictions of logic and reach a deeper and wider level of subjective awareness. In some forms of modern art autistic thinking predominates so that the communication between the artist and his public is at a level beyond that of conscious logic. We may speak of finding a painting disturbing or uplifting without having a conscious knowledge of the causal factor at work. Much of our normal day-dreaming may be described as autistic in so far as it is concerned with inner fantasies rather than external reality. It is of interest that day-dreams carried out at a lower level of consciousness,

.g. when we are tired, become increasingly visual in nature. Our thoughts, free from their normal control, are translated into visual images, so vivid that they may even become confused with external events. At an even lower level of consciousness, during sleep, the pictorial representation of autistic thinking becomes more strikingly evident in the form of dreams.

As normal thinking fluctuates between these two objective and subjective poles it would be more accurate to speak of two **aspects** rather than two types of thinking. The thought process might be viewed as a continuum with wholly subjective thinking, as in dreaming, representing one pole and the deductive thinking of the mathematical scientist illustrating the opposite pole of directed thinking or reasoning. Thinking at different times occupies different positions in this continuum depending upon external circumstances and upon our inner mental state.

In times of stress or severe emotional strain thinking deviates markedly towards the autistic side of the continuum. Our thoughts are then less attuned to the world outside, more preoccupied with our inner fantasies and problems. Most of the time an adequate compromise is reached between personal desires and the restrictions of the environment. It is only when thinking becomes so autistic as to distort reality that our behaviour may be described as neurotic. If an individual's thinking becomes so dominated by autistic trends that he has literally lost control over the direction of his thoughts, contact with reality has been abandoned and a psychotic process is evident. The description of the psychotic patient as 'a dreamer in a world awake' aptly conveys the similarity between the undirected nature of psychotic thinking and the autistic world of the dream.

Since Freud first described the dream as 'the royal road into the unconscious' psychiatrists and psychologists have been particularly interested in the type of thinking occurring in dreams. Freud's experience with his patients led him to believe that a great deal of human behaviour was controlled by forces which normally lie outside of conscious awareness. The relaxation of conscious controls during sleep allows these unconscious impulses to slip through in the form of dreams. By examining the dreams of his patient the psychoanalysts hopes to widen his understanding of factors which influence his patient's behaviour. As the thoughts and wishes expressed in dreams are unacceptable to the conscious mind of the dreamer, the true meaning of the dream often remains hidden. Later recall of dreams is greatly distorted and frequently the dream may be completely forgotten or repressed. Thus the difference between the frequent and infrequent dreamer is regarded as one of accessibility of recall. In Freudian theory, dreams are seen as having a therapeutic function in so far as they allow the dreamer to discharge his inner conflicts

and tensions in a relatively harmless way. In recent years it has become possible to examine the process of dreaming more directly. The use of the electroencephalogram (EEG) provides a recording of the brain's activity which affords an objective measure of the depth of sleep. Close observation of normal adult subjects during sleep indicates the presence of sporadic scanning movements of the eyes at certain stages of sleep. The recording of such rapid eye movements (REM's) has led to the finding that these occur only during dream activity. By examining the occurrence of rapid eye movements it is now possible to chart the course of dreams, and by referring to the EEG record, relate these to the level of sleep at which they occur. Most studies agree that dreams tend to occur at the lighter levels of sleep and that the lighter the sleep level the easier the later recall of the dream. There would appear to be surprisingly little individual variation in the amount of dream activity, a total of approximately 90 min/night being spent in dreaming. The main difference between the person who recalls dreaming every night and the person who seldom recalls dreaming may then be that the former is a lighter sleeper. This may also help to explain the report of an increase in dreaming, commonly given by emotionally disturbed people. Emotional tension is likely to lead to a shallower level of sleep and thus to an increased recall of the normal quota of dreams. Freud's view of the dream as a safety valve which siphons off inner tensions is given some support by recent experimental studies of dreaming. Subjects who are deprived of dreaming, by being briefly wakened on the occurrence of REM, develop symptoms of irritability, apprehension and anxiety. Such changes do not occur in subjects who are also wakened briefly during the night at times when there are no rapid eye movements. If subjects are allowed to sleep undisturbed after a few nights of being dream-deprived they dream most of the night and awaken refreshed and symptom-free.

The context of the dream, the stage of sleep, is still by no means fully understood. The magic formula of eight hours each night is frequently put forward as a necessary component of healthy adult life. If their normal sleep rhythm is temporarily disturbed many people experience a rapid reduction in their general efficiency and sense of well being. The habitual insomniac will testify to the ill effects of a poor night's sleep. Studies of volunteers who have been kept awake for lengthy periods, demonstrate the almost psychotic-like symptoms which can occur through extreme sleep loss. On the other hand, some people appear to get by very well on only a few hours' sleep each night. A former colleague of mine never slept more than three hours a night but had the mental and physical energy of several men. Although a temporary disruption of the normal quota of sleep has adverse effects, these often disappear if the disturbance continues over a long period. People appear to adjust gradually to a new standard in their sleep rhythm. It seems likely that, like most other habits, the personal sleep rhythm is to some extent conditioned and, once well established, difficult to alter. Many parents have to make a temporary compromise between their own already established sleep habits and those of their young child who has yet to be conditioned into the acceptable pattern of slumber. The normal sleep pattern does not, however, remain static in adult life. Surveys of sleep habits show that most people sleep less as they grow older. The proportion of people, aged 25–34 years, who report sleeping less than five hours a night is around 10 per cent. By the fifties this proportion has risen to over 29 per cent, and after the age of 65 years to over 40 per cent. In contrast to this trend, older people complain less of the adverse effects of sleeplessness. This may mean that there is less need for sleep as we grow older. Some of these surveys show a strong sex difference in sleep habits. Where females are more likely to report insomnia in middle-age, the peak incidences for males is reported at 65–70 years. The steep rise in male insomnia at this time may reflect the disruption of normal daily habits consequent to retirement from work.

There is some indication that differences in sleep habits may be linked with the other personality measures. People who habitually waken quickly, feeling alert and bright tend to have many other personality traits which distinguish them from others who waken slowly feeling lethargic and irritable. It has been suggested, for example, that such differences are related to body build and that people with a long, thin physique are more likely to be at their best in the evening and at their lowest ebb first thing in the morning. In contrast to this, people with a heavier more rotund build are at their highest level of arousal in the early morning. Most students discover their own position in this dichotomy in planning the times when study is most productive.

In discussing the process of dreaming, reference has already been made to the effect of the emotional state on sleep. Anxiety and worry may prevent the relaxed state of mind which allows sleep. Sleep disturbance is such a common feature of many psychiatric conditions that sleep rhythm may be regarded as a reasonably sensitive barometer of our current state of mental health.

CONCLUSION

This introduction to a highly diverse subject is unavoidably sketchy and inadequate. Throughout the text no references have been given to the many workers in psychology whose findings have been quoted. Most busy preclinical medical students will have neither the time nor the mental energy to make use of such detailed references at this period of their studies. However, it is hoped that some may wish to extend their reading on aspects of psychology to which summary reference ha been made in this chapter. A short list of books for thos who wish to pursue the subject further is given.

GLOSSARY

All scientific subjects tend to develop their own vocabu lary which may be unfamiliar to anyone approachin a subject for the first time. Psychological vocabulary i perhaps particularly confusing in that many of its term are words in general usage which have been given a mor specific technical meaning. With this in mind a few of th terms used in the present text are here defined mor precisely.

Autistic thinking.   A form of associative thinking, con trolled more by the thinker's inner needs and desire than by reality, e.g. day-dreaming.

Behaviour.   Those activities of a person which ar capable of being observed by another person. Thi includes verbal reports of inner experiences.

Clinical psychologist. A psychologist who applies hi knowledge of human behaviour and experience to th clinical field. He has usually an undergraduate degre in normal psychology and post-graduate training i clinical psychology but has no medical training. Hi main work is in psychological assessments, teachin and research.

Constitution.   This term is used to indicate that part o the individual's personality which is basically inborn inherited, and present although sometimes in a laten form from birth. This is in marked distinction to th psychogenic or environmental attributes of personalit which are developed as a result of the impact an experience and learning on the individual. The dis tinction between those two terms is somewhat false i that all constitutional factors are acted upon and thei development influenced by the environment.

Deterioration.   An impairment of mental function or o personality. Intellectual deterioration is a term usuall used to describe an abnormal degree of deterioratio in an individual's intellectual capacity outside tha which one would expect through the normal proces of ageing.

Egocentric.   A person is described as egocentric when h responds to all situations from a personal viewpoint The term means literally self-centred. It is used b genetic psychologists, such as Piaget, to describe th nature of the child's thinking and to differentiate i from adult thinking which is more objective an orientated towards the outside world.

Emotion.   A state of mental excitement characterize by alterations in feeling.

Environment.   This is a general term embracing al

stimuli which, although external to the individual, affect his behaviour. It usually refers particularly to all objects and persons with whom the individual comes into some form of social contact.

Genetic psychology. That branch of general psychology which investigates human development, particularly in childhood.

Identification. An unconscious mental process which expresses itself in the form of an emotional tie with other people in which the individual behaves as if he were the person with whom he has this tie. This is one of the basic processes in childhood learning as the child imitates and strives to be like parents and other figures in his early environment.

Manic-depressive psychosis. A psychotic illness characterized by deviations of normal mood from depression (fatigue, despondency and sadness) to mania (overactivity, excitement and elation). Many patients during their illness remain in either the depressive or manic phase.

Neuroses. This term usually describes mental disturbance where the individual retains contact with reality. The term is contrasted with the more serious type of mental disturbance, the *Psychoses* (insanity), where the individual loses contact with reality.

Objective. Something which is localized outside the observer's body and is not dependent upon any special bias or judgement of the individual observer. This is in contrast to a subjective experience which is influenced by the individual's own internal feelings.

Psychiatrist. A medical doctor specializing in the diagnosis, treatment and prevention of mental disorder.

Psychoanalyst. A psychiatrist who has had special training in Freudian theory and practice and who applies his knowledge of psychotherapy mainly in the treatment of neurotic disorders.

Schizophrenia. Although meaning literally split-mind the term is often erroneously taken as indicating a split personality, e.g. Dr Jekyll and Mr Hyde. The split or disintegration is between different aspects of personality like emotion, thinking and behaviour. Perhaps the most malignant form of psychotic illness.

Standardization. The basic procedure in devising psychological tests which leads to the establishment of a fixed or standard procedure in the giving and scoring of tests as well as the establishment of adequate norms.

Stimulus. Any external or internal event which alters our experience and causes us to respond in a particular way.

Trauma. An emotional shock, usually of a severe nature.

Validity. The test as to whether a psychological test is truthfully measuring that which it sets out to measure.

FURTHER READING

For those who seek an authoritative and up-to-date account of the findings of present day psychology two paperback books are unreservedly recommended.

Foss B. (1966) *New Horizons in Psychology*. Harmondsworth : Pelican.

Miller G. (1966) *Psychology—The Study of Mental Life*. Harmondsworth : Pelican.

The following book is an introductory text for medical students.

Mowbray R.M. & Ferguson Rodger T. (1963) *Psychology—In Relation to Medicine*. Edinburgh : Livingstone.

Chapter 37
Reproduction

Four aspects of human reproduction are considered:

(1) reproductive mechanisms in the female, leading to the release of an ovum available for fertilization and the preparation of the reproductive tract for its accommodation,

(2) reproductive mechanisms in the male, leading to the deposition of spermatozoa in the female genital tract,

(3) pregnancy, i.e. the events which follow fertilization of the ovum by a spermatozoon,

(4) mechanisms of normal sex determination and development which provide the basis for sexual reproduction.

MECHANISMS OF REPRODUCTION IN THE FEMALE

ANATOMY OF THE FEMALE REPRODUCTIVE TRACT

The female reproductive tract consists of paired gonads, or **ovaries**, and a hollow duct system comprising paired **uterine tubes** and a single midline **uterus** and **vagina**. The ovaries are the source of germ cells and sex hormones and lie on each side of the pelvic wall. The uterus lies centrally in the pelvis between the bladder and rectum and is enclosed by a double fold of peritoneum lying in the coronal plane and known as the **broad ligament**. The uterus is predominantly a muscular structure and can both accommodate the products of conception during pregnancy and expel them at parturition. Its lower end communicates with the vagina and this in turn opens in the midline between the external orifices of the urethra and anal canal. The external genitalia disposed around the vaginal orifice are known collectively as the **vulva**. The vagina is a distensible tube which is the site of insemination and can transmit a mature foetus at parturition. Each upper angle of the uterine cavity communicates with a narrow tube which runs along the free border of the broad ligament towards the side wall of the pelvis where it opens into the peritoneal cavity. These uterine tubes act as conduits for the transfer of ova and spermatozoa.

The ovaries

The ovaries are flattened bean-like objects, measuring about 3–4 cm in length, 2 cm in breadth and 1 cm in thickness. Their surface is pearl white and their contours are scarred and wrinkled. During the reproductive years they are the site of cyclical changes with the regular formation and regression of cysts or follicles and these modify their naked-eye appearance.

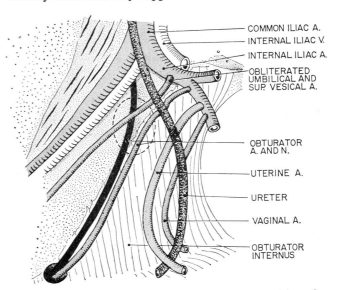

FIG. 37.1. Lateral wall of the pelvis, showing position of the ovaries. Dotted outline indicates position of ovary. From Smart C.F.V. & Jacoby F. (1948) *Gynaecological and Obstetrical Anatomy*, 2nd ed. London: Arnold.

The position of the ovaries in the pelvis is variable but in women who have borne no children (nullipara) they commonly lie on the lateral pelvic walls with their long axis vertical. Their lateral surface lies within the bifurcation of the common iliac arteries and in front of the ureters (fig. 37.1). The medial surface faces towards the pelvic cavity but is overhung by the uterine tube. The ovaries are attached to the posterior leaf of the

37.1

broad ligament by a short mesentery, the **mesovarium** (fig. 37.2).This mesovarian border constitutes the hilum of the ovary through which blood vessels, nerves and lymphatics pass. The lower end is attached to the angle of the uterus by the **ovarian ligament**, which lies in the free border of the medial part of the mesovarium and is attached to the uterus just behind the point of entry of the uterine tube. Laterally the mesovarium is continuous with the **infundibulopelvic ligament** which represents the continuation of the free border of the broad ligament extending towards the external iliac vessels.

The ovaries are covered by a single layer of simple cuboidal epithelium which is continuous with the mesothelium of the peritoneum. This is sometimes referred

The uterine tubes

Each uterine tube is approximately 10 cm in length. The tubal lumen communicates medially with the uterine cavity and the lateral end opens into the peritoneal cavity at the abdominal ostium. This provides direct communication between the exterior and the peritoneal cavity, a feature of considerable surgical importance.

Each tube is usually described as having four parts (fig. 37.2). The **interstitial part** runs obliquely through the uterine muscle and leads into a narrow muscular region known as the **isthmus**. This is followed by a tortuous segment, or **ampulla**. The lateral end of each tube is dilated to form the **infundibulum** which is fringed by a number of long mucosal processes, or **fimbriae**. The

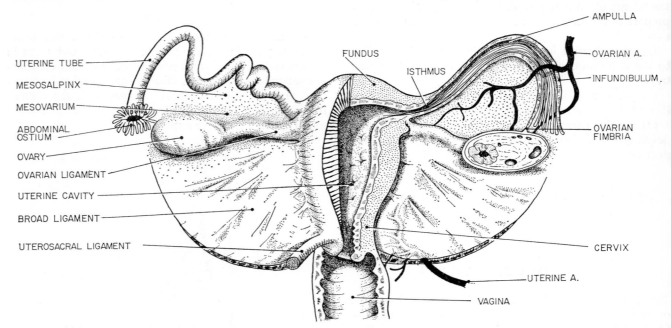

FIG. 37.2. Posterior view of the uterus and broad ligament. The broad ligament and ovaries are depicted as laid out on a flat plane, so that their vertical long axes appear horizontal, and the lower end lies medially. A more accurate position of the ovary in the pelvis is shown in fig. 37.5.

to as the germinal epithelium, on the incorrect assumption that it is a source of germ cells. Deep to this is a thin layer of connective tissue, the tunica albuginea, but this is much less prominent than the comparable layer in the testes.

On cross-section the ovary is seen to be composed of an outer cortex and an inner medulla although these two areas are not sharply demarcated. The cortex forms the bulk of the ovary and consists of a dense cellular stroma in which are situated numerous germ cells arranged in cellular formations known as follicles. These are described in detail on p. 37.8. The medullary stroma is loose and more vascular and within it may be found a number of 'hilus cells' which may be homologous to the testicular interstitial cells.

narrowest segment is the interstitial part where the diameter is only 1 mm, but the lumen widens to 5–6 mm in the ampulla. The tubes are too long to run in an extended form towards the side wall of the pelvis. As a result, the lateral half is looped over the ovary and largely covers its medial surface (fig. 37.5).

The tubes are composed of an outer serosal layer, a muscular coat and an inner mucous membrane (fig. 37.3). The mucosa is lined by a columnar epithelium. Most of the cells are ciliated and the cilia extend on to the tubal fimbriae. They produce ciliary currents which facilitate transport of ova from the ovaries towards the tubes. Other cells are secretory but little is known of the nature of these secretions. The mucous membrane is thrown into a complicated system of longitudinal folds which make the lumen a virtual maze. The muscular coat is continuous with the uterine musculature and increases in thickness in the isthmic segment.

Two groups of vestigial structures, the epoöphoron and paroöphoron, lie within the mesosalpinx (p. 37.6). They are not normally visible to the naked eye but they may be the site of origin of cysts.

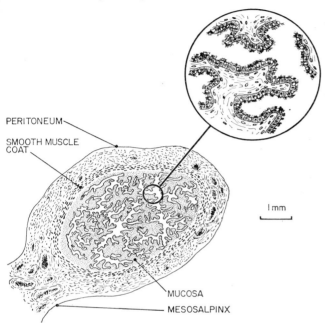

FIG. 37.3. Cross-section of ampullary part of the uterine tube. The low power view shows the mucosal folds. The high magnification shows the ciliated and secretory cells. From Netter F.H. (1954) *The Ciba Collection of Medical Illustrations.*

The uterus

The uterus is a pear-shaped organ whose narrow end projects into the vagina (fig. 37.4). The upper two-thirds constitute the **body** of the uterus and that portion of the body which lies above the insertions of the uterine tubes is known as the **fundus**. The upper lateral angles where the tubes enter are known as the **cornua**. The lower third of the uterus is the **cervix**. An intermediate zone between the cervix and body is known as the **isthmus**. However, this region is significant only in relation to the changes which take place during pregnancy and parturition. The non-pregnant uterus is flattened in an antero-posterior direction, weighs 50 g, and measures about 8 cm in length, 5 cm in breadth and 2–3 cm in thickness. The uterine muscle, or **myometrium**, is 1 cm thick so that the total length of the uterine cavity, or uterocervical canal, is 7 cm.

The cavity of the uterus is compressed between the anterior and posterior walls so that it is reduced to a mere slit when viewed from the side (fig. 37.5). The lumen of the cervix, or **cervical canal**, communicates with the cavity of the uterine body at the **internal os** and with the vagina at the **external os**. When viewed from the front,

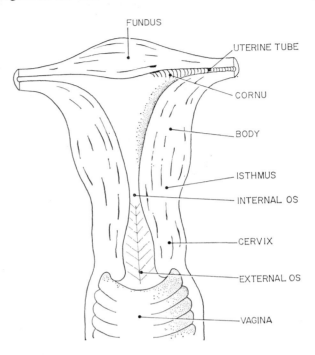

FIG. 37.4. Diagrammatic outline of the uterus. From Smout C.F.V. & Jacoby F. (1940) *Gynaecological and Obstetrical Anatomy*, 2nd ed. London: Arnold.

the cavity of the body is a triangle limited by the internal os and cornua.

The uterus is commonly slightly deviated towards the right side. When seen from the side, it is slightly bent forwards on itself in a position of **anteflexion** (fig. 37.6). Furthermore, the long axis of the cervix is inclined forwards to make an angle of about 90° with the long axis of the vagina in a position of **anteversion**. In about 10 per cent of women the uterus is angled backwards in a position of **retroversion**. The central position of the uterus within the pelvic cavity is largely dependent on the state of filling of the bladder and rectum. When a woman stands erect, the cervix is at the level of the ischial spines (fig. 37.5), but in gynaecological disorders the uterus may prolapse downwards well below this level.

The uterus is covered by peritoneum which is densely adherent to the underlying myometrium. At each side these peritoneal layers are continuous with the double folds of the broad ligament. Anteriorly, the peritoneum is reflected forwards, just above the junction of body and cervix, towards the bladder, forming a shallow utero-vesical pouch. Posteriorly, the peritoneum is continued downwards to cover the upper 2–3 cm of the posterior vaginal wall before it is reflected on to the rectum, so forming a deep rectovaginal pouch. The depth of this sac is variable but it usually extends to about 7–8

lined by a tall mucus-secreting columnar epithelium. There is a prominent longitudinal ridge on both the anterior and posterior walls of the canal and mucosal

FIG. 37.5. Median sagittal section of the female pelvis.

cm from the perineum, a distance which can be reached by an examining finger in the vagina or rectum.

The myometrium of the uterine body consists of bundles of smooth muscle fibres separated by connective tissue. These bundles are arranged in ill-defined layers, but the bulk of the muscle forms an interlacing meshwork of fibres. The mucosa of the body, the **endometrium**, lies directly on the myometrium so that the tips of endometrial glands burrow into the underlying muscle. During the reproductive years the endometrium undergoes cyclical changes which are described later in detail (p. 37.17).

The upper part of the cervix is cylindrical but that part which projects into the vagina is conical. The cervix contains much less muscle than the body; muscle forms no more than 15 per cent of its substance and is largely confined to the upper half. The remainder consists of connective tissue with a high collagen content. The cervical mucosa contains large, branched tubular glands

folds radiate out at angles from these ridges and interdigitate with each other. The surface of that part of the cervix which projects into the vagina is covered by stratified squamous epithelium and the line of junction between this squamous epithelium and the glandular

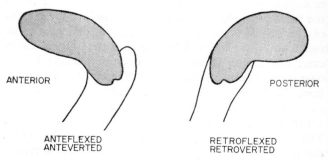

FIG. 37.6 Position of uterus in the pelvis. From Ellis, H. (1966) *Clinical Anatomy*, 3rd Edition. Oxford: Blackwell Scientific Publications.

epithelium of the cervical canal is usually just within the external os.

The uterus obtains most of its blood supply from the uterine arteries. Branches from both uterine arteries run medially and anastomose freely. It is a remarkable fact that both uterine arteries or even both internal iliac arteries may be ligated without prejudicing the viability of the uterus or other pelvic organs. This emphasizes the rich anastomoses between the branches of the internal iliac artery and the ovarian, inferior mesenteric and median sacral arteries. The branches of the uterine artery supply the myometrium, and their terminal branches also form the spiral arterioles which supply the endometrium and are involved in the mechanisms of menstruation.

The ureters have an important anatomical relationship to the cervix. As they pass forwards from the region of the ischial spines towards the bladder they incline medially below the root of the broad ligament, about 2 cm from the side of the cervix, and are crossed above by the uterine arteries.

The vagina

The vagina is a fibromuscular tube measuring about 8 cm in length. When a woman stands erect, the vagina does not descend vertically but is directed downwards and forwards from the uterus at an angle of 70° to the horizontal (fig. 37.5). The anterior and posterior walls are normally in contact except at the upper end, or **vaginal vault**, into which the cervix protrudes. The projection of the cervix allows the space of the vaginal vault to be divided into anterior, posterior and lateral **fornices**. The cervix enters the vault through the upper part of the anterior vaginal wall. As a result, the anterior vaginal wall is shorter than the posterior vaginal wall, and the posterior fornix is much deeper than the anterior fornix.

The epithelium of the vagina is thick and is thrown into prominent folds or rugae, some of which are disposed laterally and some longitudinally. It is lined by a stratified squamous epithelium which contains glycogen. It is not normally cornified and does not contain glands. Desquamation of this epithelium contributes to the normal vaginal discharge. The muscle coat consists of plain muscle bundles which run mainly longitudinally, and it is surrounded by an outer fascial coat. The vagina is richly supplied by branches from the internal iliac, uterine, middle and inferior rectal and internal pudendal arteries. The veins form a plexus around the vagina within the outer fascial sheath.

The anatomical relations of the vagina to other pelvic structures are important (fig. 37.5). Anteriorly, the upper half of the vagina is applied to the bladder base from which it is separated by a loose fascial plane. The urethra is intimately embedded within the substance of the lower half of the anterior wall of the vagina. The upper 2 cm of the vaginal wall in the posterior fornix are covered by the peritoneum of the rectovaginal pouch, so that this is a point of surgical access to the peritoneal cavity. The middle third of the posterior vaginal wall is closely related to the rectum, and the lower third to the central tendon of the perineum (perineal body). The ureters and uterine arteries cross just above the lateral fornices. The levatores ani blend with the middle part of the lateral vaginal walls and separate the vagina from the ischiorectal fossae.

The vulva

The **labia majora** are the most superficial structures of the vulva (fig. 37.7). They are normally apposed and so conceal the other external genitalia. They extend forwards

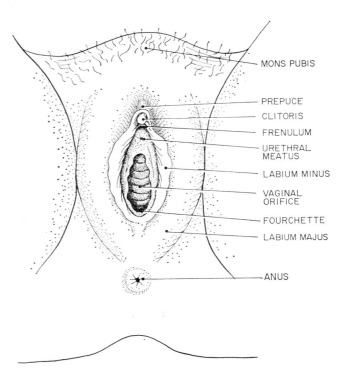

FIG. 37.7. The vulva. From Glenister, T.W.A. & Ross, J.R.W. (1965) *Anatomy and Physiology for Nurses.* London:Heinemann.

from the anus and fuse anteriorly in the **mons pubis**. The latter is a low eminence which covers the symphysis pubis and is covered by a triangular distribution of hair. The labia majora are composed of fibrous and fatty tissue and carry hair follicles and sebaceous and apocrine glands.

The **labia minora** are folds of skin which lie between the labia majora. Posteriorly they fuse with the medial surface of the labia majora and form a transverse skin fold, or **fourchette**. Anteriorly each splits into two components which surround the clitoris, forming the prepuce anteriorly and the frenulum posteriorly. The labia minora contain neither adipose tissue nor hair follicles.

The **clitoris** is the homologue of the male penis and has the same component parts in miniature. The body of the clitoris is 2–3 cm in length and it is acutely bent back on itself. It is enclosed within a fibrous coat and divided by an incomplete septum into a pair of **corpora cavernosa** which diverge at the root of the clitoris to form crura. The **crura** are attached to the pubic arch and are covered by **ischiocavernosus muscles**. A small **glans clitoris**, covered by a sensitive mucous membrane, fits over the body of the clitoris.

The **bulbs of the vestibule** are small masses of erectile tissue which lie alongside the lateral vaginal wall superficial to the inferior fascia of the urogenital membrane. They are expanded posteriorly but they narrow and fuse in front of the external urethral orifice. The **greater vestibular glands** (Bartholin's glands) lie posterolateral to the vagina, superficial to the inferior fascia of the urogenital membrane and concealed by the vestibular bulbs. They are racemose glands whose ducts open in the angle between the labium minus and hymeneal ring.

The **hymen** is a thin membrane which guards the vaginal orifice. It is normally perforated and so allows the escape of menstrual blood, but its thickness and rigidity are very variable.

The space bounded by the labia minora is the **vestibule** of the vagina. Its main contents from before backwards are the clitoris, external urethral meatus and vaginal orifice.

The vulva is richly supplied by branches of the internal pudendal artery and deep and superficial external pudendal arteries.

The broad ligament

The broad ligament forms a transverse mesentery across the pelvic cavity (fig. 37.2). It encloses the uterus in the midline, and laterally contains loose areolar tissue and smooth muscle elements known as the **parametrium**. It consists of a double fold of peritoneum. The anterior layers pass forwards towards the anterior abdominal wall and form shallow paravesical fossae, while the posterior layers form two prominent rectouterine folds which curve backwards from the cervix towards the posterior pelvic wall lateral to the rectum.

The medial attachment of the broad ligament to the uterus is almost linear. Laterally it is widened out to include the attachments of the round ligament, uterine tube and ovarian ligament.

The **round ligament** is a fibromuscular cord which extends from the lateral angle of the uterus to the deep inguinal ring, crossing the umbilical, obturator and external iliac vessels. It hooks round the lateral side of the inferior epigastric artery, traverses the inguinal canal, and terminates within the substance of the labia majora. The round ligament is the remains of the gubernaculum p. 37.56). Three structures are thus attached to each

uterine angle, the round ligament, uterine tube and ovarian ligament, in that order from before backwards.

The **mesosalpinx** is the part of the broad ligament which enfolds the uterine tube. Laterally it is continuous with the infundibulo-pelvic ligament. The lateral part of the mesosalpinx is loose and redundant and this allows the tube to cradle the ovary. The **mesovarium** is a fold of the posterior layer of the broad ligament which gives attachment to the ovary.

The parametrium is most abundant in the root of the broad ligament. It is attached medially to the supravaginal cervix and upper third of the vagina. Laterally it fans out, the posterior border sweeping back in the rectouterine fold towards the sacrum. This component of the parametrium is commonly known as the **uterosacral ligament**, but it is simply a fascial condensation around the nerve bundles passing between the sacral plexus and the uterus. The lateral part of the parametrium extends to the side wall of the pelvis blending with the fascia on the levatores ani. This is often called the **lateral cervical ligament** but again it is a fascial condensation around the uterine vessels. The most anterior part extends to the back of the pubic bones and is known as the **pubocervical ligament**.

The parametrium provides the main support to the uterus and upper vagina, preventing its downward prolapse. In this it may be aided by the tone of the levatores ani and the pelvic fascia. It is by virtue of these attachments that the uterus maintains its level in the pelvis. The position of anteversion is produced by the forward pull of the round ligaments on the fundus and the fixation of the cervix by the uterosacral ligaments.

Effects of age and parity

The preceding description applies to the reproductive tract of a nulliparous woman during the active reproductive years. However, these features may be considerably modified during the years which precede puberty and follow the menopause, and as a result of childbearing. Before puberty the vulva is not covered by hair; the labia majora are poorly developed and the labia minora are prominent. The vaginal epithelium is thin and almost translucent. At birth the uterus is small, and the cervix is as long as the uterine body. By puberty, the uterus has reached its mature size and proportions.

Following the menopause, the vulvar and vaginal epithelium again thins and all the external genitalia atrophy. As a result the introitus and vagina narrow. The uterus and cervix shrink in size and the cervix becomes almost flush with the vaginal vault. The ovaries are greatly reduced in size and their surface becomes increasingly wrinkled.

As a result of coitus, the hymen becomes torn and replaced by tags of epithelium surrounding the hymenal ring. During childbirth the perineum may become torn or stretched and the vaginal introitus gapes; the cervix is split, usually laterally, so that the circular external os is widened, and the cervix may be described as having anterior and posterior lips. After delivery, the uterus does not return fully to its non-pregnant dimensions. Following the distortion of the broad ligament and displacement of the ovaries during pregnancy, the ovaries rarely return to their original position on the lateral pelvic wall, and may take up a variable position behind the broad ligament.

Blood supply

The reproductive tract is supplied by the ovarian arteries and branches of the internal iliac arteries.

The **ovarian arteries** arise from the front of the aorta just below the origin of the renal arteries. They run downwards over the anterior surface of psoas major, anterior to the ureter and accompanied by the ovarian vein. They enter the pelvis by crossing the external iliac artery about 2 cm below its origin, pass between the layers of the infundibulopelvic ligament and enter the hilum of the ovary via the mesovarium. They supply the ovaries and tubes and anastomose with branches of the uterine arteries to supply the fundus and body of the uterus.

The **uterine arteries** are branches of the anterior divisions of the internal iliac arteries. They run medially and forwards over the levatores ani to the lower border of the broad ligament, then through the parametrium towards the cervix, crossing above the ureter. At the level of the cervix they give branches to supply the cervix and upper vagina. Each artery then follows a tortuous course along the side of the uterus towards the tube and anastomoses with branches of the ovarian artery (fig. 37.2).

The **vaginal arteries** may arise independently from the internal iliac artery, or from a common stem with the uterine artery. They run downwards and medially towards the vaginal vault to anastomose with vaginal branches of the uterine artery. From this anastomosis, they descend along the vagina to communicate with branches of the internal pudendal artery.

The **internal pudendal arteries** arise from the internal iliac arteries in common with the inferior gluteal arteries. Their branches supply the external genitalia and perineum (fig. 20.35).

VENOUS DRAINAGE

The ovarian and internal iliac veins provide the main venous drainage from the reproductive tract. Veins leaving the hilum of the ovary form a profuse **pampiniform plexus** in the mesovarium and unite to form the ovarian vein. These veins follow the course of the ovarian arteries, the right vein entering the inferior vena cava and the left vein draining into the left renal vein.

Uterine and vaginal venous plexuses drain by veins which follow the route taken by their respective arteries towards the internal iliac vein. However, there is a free communication between the vesical, uterine, vaginal and rectal venous plexuses, and these all communicate with presacral and lumbar channels of the vertebral venous plexus

Lymphatic system (fig. 37.8)

Although pelvic lymph nodes are usually situated along blood vessels, the lymph vessels from pelvic organs do not necessarily follow the path of the blood vessels that supply them.

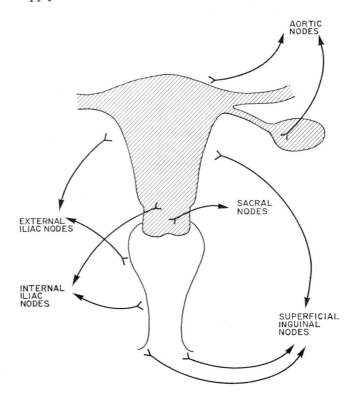

FIG. 37.8. Lymphatic drainage of the female genital tract. From Ellis H. (1966) *Clinical Anatomy*, 3rd Edition. Oxford: Blackwell Scientific Publications.

From the ovaries and tubes lymph vessels pass directly to aortic nodes along the course of the ovarian vessels. Lymph vessels draining the uterus are widely distributed. Some vessels from the fundus drain along the ovarian route, while a few follow the round ligament to reach the superficial inguinal nodes. Many lymph vessels from the body of the uterus pass directly to external iliac nodes. From the cervix, lymph vessels course through the parametrium to reach external and internal iliac or sacral nodes.

There is a free communication between lymph vessels draining the two sides of the vulva. Most vulvar lymph vessels run across the labia majora and mons pubis to reach the superficial inguinal nodes, from which they may communicate with the deep inguinal nodes or continue upwards towards the external iliac nodes. A few vessels from the clitoris may follow veins draining the clitoris and communicate with the vesical lymph plexus.

Innervation

With the exception of the vulva, the genital tract is innervated by the autonomic nervous system.

A parasympathetic component originates from the sacral segments of the spinal cord. Preganglionic fibres are distributed via the ventral primary rami of S2–4, and thence by the pelvic splanchnic nerves to the pelvic plexuses.

The sympathetic contribution is obtained in two ways. Postganglionic fibres from the thoracic sympathetic trunk and prevertebral ganglia reach the pelvis along the visceral branches of the abdominal aorta, particularly the ovarian and uterine arteries. Other fibres are derived from the hypogastric plexus. These descend to the pelvic plexuses where they mingle with the parasympathetic component.

These pelvic plexuses lie on each side of the rectum and fibres are distributed forwards along the uterosacral ligaments towards the cervix and thence to the uterus and vagina.

Both afferent and efferent fibres are included. Afferent fibres from the ovaries return along the ovarian arteries, whereas uterine sensory fibres run mainly towards the pelvic plexuses. These afferent fibres enter the spinal cord between segments T10 and L1. Sympathetic motor fibres arise from lower thoracic segments and parasympathetic fibres from S2–4. The ultimate site of termination of these efferent fibres in the uterus is unknown and their motor function is equally obscure.

The external genitalia are innervated primarily by the branches of the pudendal nerve (fig. 20.44). Additional innervation is obtained from the perineal branch of the posterior cutaneous nerve of the thigh, genital branch of the genitofemoral nerve, and the ilioinguinal nerve.

PHYSIOLOGY OF THE FEMALE REPRODUCTIVE TRACT

The ovaries play a central role in female reproduction and perform two intimately related functions, the production of gametes and the production of sex hormones. With respect to both functions, the ovaries are regulated by the hypothalamus and adenohypophysis. In turn, the principal site of action of ovarian hormones is the uterus, and ovulation may be followed by implantation in the uterine cavity. Reproduction in the female therefore may be studied at four closely integrated levels, hypothalamus, adenohypophysis, ovaries and uterus. This relationship is of crucial importance to an understanding of reproductive physiology and it is described in the following sequence

(1) the gametogenic and endocrine functions of the ovaries,

(2) the control of the ovaries by adenohypophysis and hypothalamus,

(3) the functional interrelation between the ovaries and the reproductive tract.

Functions of the ovaries

Both gametogenic and endocrine functions of the ovaries follow a strictly repetitive sequence and can be understood only in terms of the ovarian cycle. This cycle is based on the growth changes centred around the female germ cells. The origin of these germ cells is described on p. 37.54. It may be noted at present that some of these germ cells become surrounded by a single layer of somatic cells, the composite structure constituting a **primordial follicle**.

The ovarian cycle (fig. 37.9)

FOLLICULAR DEVELOPMENT

The ovaries change very little between birth and puberty, but each month thereafter successive waves of primordial follicles undergo a process of cyclical maturation and regression. The cell layer surrounding the germ cell is referred to as the **granulosa** layer, while the stromal cells immediately adjacent to this are differentiated to form the **theca interna**. As these two components proliferate, fluid accumulates between the granulosa cells and forms a small cavity containing follicular fluid. Only one or occasionally two of this group of follicles continue to develop, while the others regress. The mechanism by which a single follicle matures each month is unknown, but it becomes less efficient with advancing years, with the result that twin births due to multiple ovulation are more common in older mothers.

As the volume of follicular fluid increases, it displaces the germ cell to one side of the follicle where it lies in a small mass of granulosa cells, or **cumulus**. The cells immediately surrounding the germ cell are radially arranged and referred to as the **corona radiata**. The theca interna cells enlarge, assuming a polygonal shape, and are extensively vascularized, in contrast to the granulosa cells which have no direct blood supply before ovulation. As the follicle enlarges, it compresses the ovarian stroma and creates a false capsule of connective tissue, the **theca externa**.

The mature follicle is commonly known as the Graafian follicle in recognition of the Dutch scientist, Regner de Graaf, who first described it. The original primordial follicle has a diameter of only 30 μm, whereas the mature follicle measures from 10 to 30 mm in diameter, a 1000-fold increase.

OVULATION

When it reaches maturity, the follicle ruptures on the surface of the ovary discharging the germ cell, with its cumulus still attached, into the peritoneal cavity. The mechanism responsible for rupture of the follicle is unknown, but it probably occurs in the region of a thinned out, avascular area of the follicle wall. The phenomenon has been directly observed in women, and appears as a gentle oozing from a collapsed follicle.

At the time of rupture, the tubal fimbriae are approximated to the surface of the ovary and facilitate entry of the ovum into the abdominal ostium, while the ciliary activity of the tubal epithelium rapidly carries the ovum towards the ampulla, which is the site of fertilization.

steroid hormones for 8–10 days, following which, if fertilization has not occurred, it undergoes a process of degeneration or **luteolysis**, when its endocrine activities rapidly cease. Over the next few months it degenerates to a structureless mass, the **corpus albicans**.

PRODUCTION OF OVA

Ovulation occurs at the midpoint of each ovarian cycle and it is necessary to consider the processes which are involved in the production of ova.

Sexual reproduction involves much more than the addition of maternal to paternal chromosomes at fertilization. During gametogenesis, the actual genetic structure of the chromosomes of the germ cells is rearranged so

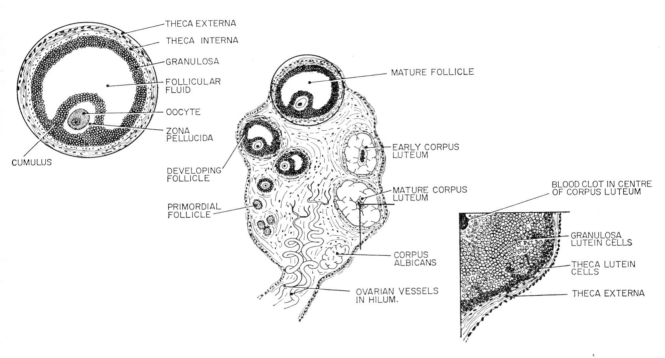

FIG. 37.9. The ovarian cycle. From Netter F.H. (1954) *The Ciba Collection of Medical Illustrations.*

The tubal entry is not always as direct as this because in some tubal pregnancies the corpus luteum is found in the contralateral ovary.

LUTEINIZATION

Following ovulation the follicle collapses, and the granulosa cells rapidly proliferate and at the same time become intensely vascularized so that each cell appears to be in direct contact with a capillary. This granulosa component forms the bulk of the growing **corpus luteum** and the intense yellow colour, from which this structure derives its name, is due to the presence of lipids in the luteinized granulosa cells. The thecal cells proliferate to a lesser extent and their physiological role is not clear.

The human corpus luteum actively synthesizes sex

that the chromosomes in the germ cells are genetically dissimilar from the corresponding chromosomes of somatic tissues. It is this structural alteration of chromosomes during gametogenesis, even more than the simple pooling of maternal and paternal chromosomes at fertilization, which determines the genetic uniqueness of the individual. A child is not simply the sum of a half share each of maternal and paternal chromosomes. The chromosomes which it inherits at fertilization are similar to, but not identical with the parental chromosomes. Furthermore, fertilization involves the fusion of an ovum and sperm. Therefore, in order to maintain the constancy of the chromosome number of human cells, it is necessary that the number of chromosomes in each gamete should be reduced by half prior to fertilization. This is achieved by two successive cell divisions known collectively as **meiosis**.

From these considerations it should be clear that two outstanding features of gametogenesis are the mechanism for the exchange of genetic material between chromosomes, and the reduction division from diploid to haploid number. Gametes are derived from diploid primitive germ cells known as **oogonia** in the female and **spermatogonia** in the male. The origin and differentiation of these primitive cells is described on p. 37.27. During the early months of intrauterine life oogonia proliferate by mitotic division. Some of these oogonia enlarge and become recognizable as **primary oocytes** which will proceed to undergo meiosis. The mechanisms and significance of meiosis are fully described on p. 12.16.

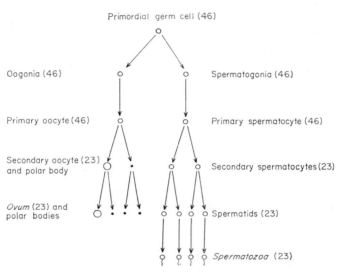

FIG. 37.10. Oogenesis and spermatogenesis. Numbers in brackets refer to chromosome number. Each diploid primary oocyte produces one haploid ovum. Each diploid primary spermatocyte produces four haploid spermatozoa.

During oogenesis, bivalent formation (p. 12.18) may be followed by a remarkably prolonged period during which pairing persists but the cell appears to enter a resting phase reminiscent of mitotic interphase. All oocytes reach this stage by the sixth or seventh month of intrauterine life. Many of these prophase primary oocytes are surrounded by a single layer of follicular cells, forming primordial follicles, and it may be that it is the presence of these follicular cells which arrests meiosis at this stage. Oocytes which fail to form follicles complete the first meiotic division and then degenerate and are lost.

There are no further developments in the oocytes until puberty. Thereafter, a few primordial follicles mature each month, and the primary oocytes contained within the developing follicles complete the first meiotic division. With completion of this cell division, each diploid primary

oocyte gives rise to two haploid cells, one **secondary oocyte** and one **polar body** (fig. 37.10). It should be recalled that as a result of crossing-over the genetic structure of homologous chromosomes of these two haploid cells differ from each other, and both may be different from the corresponding chromosome pair of the original primary oocyte.

Secondary oocytes immediately enter the second meiotic division, and this follows a sequence very similar to mitosis, although there are two important differences. Only twenty-three chromosomes are involved, and the two chromatids which form each chromosome are genetically dissimilar.

Three important features distinguish oogenesis from spermatogenesis (p. 37.26). First, the distribution of cytoplasm which accompanies each meiotic division during oogenesis is unequal, virtually all the cytoplasm being orientated around one nucleus. The smaller cells are known as polar bodies, which probably have no biological function. Thus, each primary oocyte can give rise to one large haploid cell, or **ovum**, and three polar bodies. The term ovum may be loosely applied to oocytes or even to the fertilized egg, but its correct use should be restricted to the major cell derived from the second meiotic division prior to fertilization. Secondly, the maturation of the female germ cell is complete following meiosis, and the oocyte undergoes no further changes prior to fertilization. By contrast, the spermatid emerging from meiosis must undergo a highly complex process of differentiation before becoming a mature sperm.

Finally, the time scales of oogenesis and spermatogenesis contrast dramatically (fig. 37.11). Oogonia undergo mitotic multiplication during the first six or seven months of intrauterine life. The final number of oocytes so formed in each ovary is about 200,000, although there is a wide individual variation. It is widely accepted that the production of oocytes ceases before birth, and it is unlikely that there is any postnatal oogenesis from the so-called germinal epithelium. On the contrary, there is a steady reduction in the number of follicles after birth until, at the menopause, the ovarian stock of oocytes is completely exhausted. Most of this loss of oocytes occurs by atresia rather than by ovulation. Thus, of the original total of 400,000 follicles only 400 may achieve ovulation, while the remaining 99·9 per cent degenerate.

All the primary oocytes so formed begin their first meiotic division before birth, but the completion of prophase is arrested until after puberty. During this time oocytes accumulate nutrients in the cytoplasm, and this storage process is probably essential for the subsequent viability of the zygote. Meiosis restarts in individual oocytes when their follicles undergo maturation in subsequent ovarian cycles. This means that the duration of the first meiotic prophase may range from 10 to over 50 years.

The remainder of the first meiotic division is completed by the time of ovulation, at which time a secondary oocyte is released into the tube. The second meiotic division follows immediately and proceeds to the metaphase stage, but this stage is not normally completed until the oocyte is penetrated by a spermatozoon. This indicates that the mature ovum normally has only a transient existence.

It will be appreciated that gametogenesis is an extremely complicated process, and meiotic errors are not infrequent (p. 38.10).

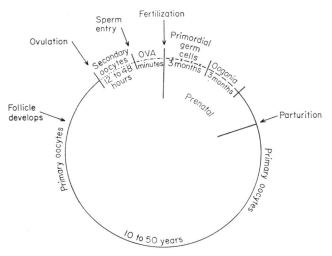

FIG. 37.11. The reproductive cycle. During the first 2 or 3 months after conception, primordial germ cells form and segregate. By the 6th intrauterine month, oogonia have divided and formed primary oocytes. The first meiotic division is not completed until ovulation occurs from the follicle within which the oocyte is contained, i.e. 10–50 years later. The second meiotic division and formation of the ovum is not completed until the egg is entered by a spermatozoon. Fertilization of the ovum by a spermatozoon starts another reproductive cycle.

PRODUCTION OF SEX HORMONES

The principal ovarian hormones are steroid in structure and fall into three broad functional categories, **oestrogens**, **progestagens** and **androgens**.

Ovarian production of oestrogens

The expression oestrus refers to cyclical phases of sexual excitement or heat demonstrated by many animals, and the word oestrogen originally implied the ability to induce this behaviour pattern. However, the human female does not exhibit any comparable oestrous behaviour, and there is no clear correlation between the secretion of oestrogens and sexual drive or libido. Oestrogen is now used to refer to any substance which is able to produce characteristic, changes in the reproductive tract, particularly in the vaginal epithelium. There are several naturally occurring oestrogens, the two most powerful being oestradiol-17β

and oestrone, and as these are the two oestrogens present in highest concentration in ovarian vein blood, it is probable that they are the principal active oestrogens secreted by the ovary.

Biosynthesis of oestrogens

Cholesterol is probably the precursor of all natural steroids (p. 10.5). However, it is not clear whether the ovaries utilize plasma cholesterol for this purpose or synthesize cholesterol from acetate. During steroid synthesis the cholesterol molecule is reduced in size, rearranged, and oxygen functions are added at a number of specific sites.

Cleavage of most of the side chain converts cholesterol to pregnenolone (fig. 37.12a). All steroid hormones are derived from pregnenolone and it has certain structural features which merit special attention. These are the double bond between C-5 and C-6 (the Δ^5 position), a two carbon atom side chain at C-17, a hydroxyl group at C-3, two angular methyl groups at C-10 and C-13, and full saturation of ring A. These are the features which are modified during steroid synthesis.

(1) Transfer of the Δ^5 double bond to the C-4–C-5 (or Δ^4) position, and dehydrogenation of the hydroxyl group at C-3 (by 3β-ol dehydrogenase) results in the formation of progesterone (fig. 37.12b).

(2) Hydroxylation at C-17 followed by cleavage of the side chain produces androstenedione (fig. 37.12c). By alteration in the sequence of these steps, androstenedione may also be produced without involving progesterone as an intermediate (fig. 37.12d).

(3) Aromatization of ring A and loss of the angular methyl group at C-10 leads to oestrone (fig. 37.12e). Alternatively preliminary reduction at C-17 may produce oestradiol-17β via testosterone (fig. 37.12f).

(4) Oestrone and oestradiol-17β are readily interconvertible by reversible dehydrogenation (fig. 37.12g).

This pattern of steroid synthesis provides basic pathways common to all steroid-producing tissues, adrenal cortex, testis and ovary. They all require the production of pregnenolone as the initial precursor. Thereafter, the essential step in the production of cortisol is hydroxylation at C-11 and C-21 (p. 25.32); androgens require cleavage of the side chain at C-17; oestrogens are characterized by aromatization of ring A. The steroid-producing potential of these organs can now be understood by a knowledge of their enzyme capabilities. The adrenal cortex possesses the enzymes for all of these steps and so is totipotent with regard to steroid hormones. The testis has very little ability to aromatize ring A. The ovary has aromatizing enzymes, but cannot hydroxylate at C-11 or C-21. The placenta, as shown later, is very highly specialized in so far as it has limited ability to cleave the side chain at C-17, but it is a plentiful source of 3β-ol dehydrogenase and aromatizing enzymes. It is not surprising that, even under

FIG. 37.12. Biosynthesis of oestrogens.

normal conditions, the ovary secretes small quantities of testosterone. Androgens must be considered both as primary virilizing agents in the male and also as intermediary metabolites in the female. Thus the normal sequence of steroid synthesis is cholesterol → progestagen → androgen → oestrogen.

Metabolism of oestrogens

Oestrogens enter the circulation by the ovarian vein, and their activity is regulated in the following ways.

(1) Conversion occurs to metabolites with less oestrogenic activity. The most important example is 16-hydroxylation producing the relatively inactive oestrogen, oestriol (fig. 37.12h). Other methods of inactivation include substitution by methylation at C-2, dehydrogenation at C-6, and hydroxylation at C-11. So far, over twenty naturally occurring oestrogens have been identified. These conversions occur mainly in the liver.

(2) Conjugation in the liver, almost exclusively with glucuronic acid, causes these steroids to become water-soluble and reduces their physiological activity. However, some steroid conjugates are retained in the body and serve as useful metabolic intermediates. This applies particularly to dehydroepiandrosterone sulphate of foetal origin which is an important substrate in placental steroid synthesis (p. 37.44).

(3) Oestrogens form complexes with plasma albumin, and the bound forms are probably inactive.

Excretion of oestrogens (fig. 37.13)

Oestrogens are conjugated and thereby rendered water-soluble before they are excreted. Approximately half is excreted from the liver via the bile into the duodenum, but the majority of this is reabsorbed via the portal circulation. This enterohepatic circulation of oestrogens is similar to that of the chemically allied bile salts. Despite reabsorption, there is an appreciable loss of oestrogens in faeces.

The main route of excretion of oestrogens is the urine. Quantitatively the most important urinary oestrogens are oestriol, oestrone and oestradiol-17β, but there are many others, some still unidentified. Because of technical limitations, oestrogen production is usually assessed by the estimation of these three oestrogens in the urine, but it will be clear that this is only a crude reflection of ovarian secretion rates.

Oestrogen levels during menstrual cycle

As levels of oestrogens in the blood during the menstrual cycle are difficult to measure accurately, most information has been derived from serial study of the urinary excretion of oestriol, oestrone and oestradiol-17β throughout normal cycles (fig. 37.14). These studies show a diphasic pattern. There is an initial rise which parallels the maturation of the follicle and reaches a peak at ovulation.

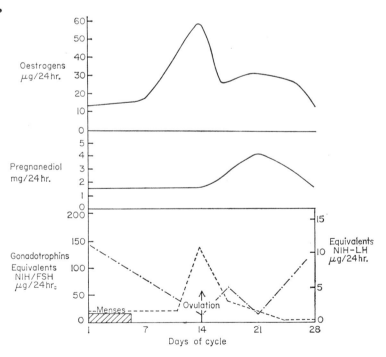

FIG. 37.14. Urinary excretion of oestrogens, pregnanediol and gonadotrophins in the normal menstrual cycle. Oestrogen data includes oestriol, oestrone and oestradiol-17β. — · — · —, FSH; - - - -, LH.

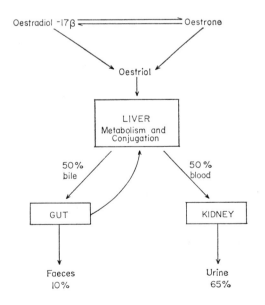

FIG. 37.13. Metabolism and excretion of oestrogens. Only 75 per cent of oestrogens can be accounted for as known urinary and faecal metabolites; the remaining 25 per cent of oestrogen metabolites have not been identified. From Brown J.B. (1959) *J. Obstet. Gynaec. Brit. Cwlth* **66**, 797.

There is then a transient fall followed by a second wave which corresponds with the growth and regression of the corpus luteum.

Site of production of oestrogens

This is uncertain. In the follicular phase of the cycle, the theca interna is probably the main source of oestrogens, while in the luteal phase the luteinized thecal cells may continue production. It is likely that the interstitial cells of the stroma can also produce small quantities of oestrogens.

Actions of oestrogens

This subject is complicated by the fact that there are so many naturally occurring oestrogens in the body. It may be an oversimplification to think of oestradiol-17β as the primary oestrogen which exerts a maximal oestrogenic effect, the other oestrogens having diminishing actions of an identical nature. On the contrary, oestrogens may vary in the nature of their action, and indeed there is good evidence that oestriol may inhibit some of the actions of oestradiol-17β. It is likely that oestrogen activity in the individual woman is the resultant of the concerted action of many different oestrogens.

Nevertheless, valuable information is accumulating about the nature of the biochemical actions of oestrogens at cellular level. It is known that steroid hormones alter the structure and activities of enzymically active proteins, although it has not proved possible to locate the primary site of action. For instance, pyridine nucleotide transhydrogenase is an important intracellular enzyme which catalyses the action,

$$NAD + NADPH_2 \longrightarrow NADH_2 + NADP$$

The activity of this enzyme is increased in the presence of oestrogens, and it is noteworthy that this oestrogen-dependent transhydrogenase is present in these tissues which are thought to be target organs of oestrogens, for example the genital tract epithelium and breast acini. Oestrogens also alter the polymerization of acid mucopolysaccharides and so modify the physicochemical properties of the ground substance of connective tissues. However, it is not yet possible to explain the widespread physiological effects of oestrogens in terms of their known biochemical actions.

The principal effects of oestrogens are as follows:
(1) the development of secondary sex characters at puberty,
(2) initiation of the cyclical activity of the reproductive tract and mammary gland; in general, they stimulate proliferation of the epithelia of the genital tract and produce hypertrophy and increased motility of its musculature,
(3) interaction with other endocrine organs; they regulate the pituitary release of gonadotrophins via the hypothalamus, and also increase the concentration of transcortin and thyroxine-binding globulin and so modify the physiological activity of cortisol and thyroxine,
(4) general metabolic effects on the retention of sodium and water (p. 33.21) and on the intermediary metabolism of carbohydrates and fats (p. 10.11).

Ovarian production of progestagens

The term progestagen or progestin or gestagen indicates the ability to maintain pregnancy, and this may be the primary role of these substances. However, a more useful pharmacological definition of a progestagen is a substance which induces secretory changes in an oestrogen-primed endometrium. Progesterone was the first naturally occurring progestagen to be isolated and identified. Other progestagens have been isolated from the ovary and ovarian venous blood, especially the C-20 reduced stereoisomers, Δ^4-3 keto-pregnen-20α ol and Δ^4-3 keto-pregnen-20β ol (fig. 37.15).

Biosynthesis of progestagens

Progesterone and its C-20 reduced forms are synthesized from cholesterol via pregnenolone (fig. 37.12). There is no problem in understanding these steps in the synthesis of progesterone, but it is more difficult to understand the mechanism by which steroid synthesis in the ovary is arrested at this stage.

Metabolism of progestagens

Progesterone is carried in the blood, some of it bound firmly to albumin, and as it is soluble in lipids it is present in adipose tissues.

In the liver, catabolism of progestagens principally involves reduction of the Δ^4-3-ketone group, giving rise to pregnanolone (fig. 37.15). Reduction of this double bond produces several asymmetric carbon atoms and as a result there is a large range of stereoisomeric metabolites. Further reduction at C-20 produces pregnanediol, the principal metabolite of progesterone. These metabolites are conjugated almost exclusively with glucuronic acid, but none of these compounds has any progestational activity.

Excretion of progestagens

Conjugated metabolites are excreted in both bile and urine, but as they are less readily absorbed in the intestines than are oestrogens, a larger fraction is lost in faeces. The remainder appears in the urine. The major urinary metabolite is pregnanediol, but this represents a very variable proportion of the ovarian production of progestagens.

Progestagen production during the menstrual cycle

The concentration of progestagens in the blood of nonpregnant women can now be measured accurately and progesterone and its C-20 reduced forms have been identified as the major steroids present in ovarian venous blood during the luteal phase of the cycle.

The only urinary metabolite which has been studied in detail is pregnanediol (fig. 37.15). During the follicular phase of the cycle, urinary pregnanediol excretion is roughly 1 mg/day. Following ovulation, there is a curve,

zation of the granulosa cells, and this permits the entry of progestagens directly into the blood. This two-cell theory implies that thecal cells have all the enzymic potential to synthesize oestrogens, whereas the granulosal component is unable to separate the side chain of progesterone.

FIG. 37.15. Metabolism of progesterone.

reaching 4–6 mg/day at its peak, which corresponds to the maturation and regression of the corpus luteum.

Site of production of progestagens

This is uncertain, but granulosa cells may be largely responsible for progestagen production. During the follicular phase, these cells are not vascularized, so that any progestagen produced by granulosa cells must filter through thecal cells on its way to the blood stream, and during this passage it is converted to oestrogens. Luteinization is characterized by intense vasculari-

Actions of progestagens

Knowledge of the action of progestagens is limited and the subject is highly controversial. In general, progestagens follow oestrogens in order of appearance during the menstrual cycle, and they must inevitably act synchronously with oestrogens.

(1) In the reproductive tract and breast, pr⌐ act on oestrogen-primed tissues. They ind⌐ pattern in the endometrium and m⌐ cervical secretions.

(2) They may reduce the excitabⁱ⌐

by hyperpolarization of the cell membrane. It is postulated that this represents a general effect of progestagens on all smooth muscle especially that of the ureter, gut and blood vessels.

(3) Progestagens, or their metabolites, raise resting body temperature.

Ovarian production of androgens

There is incontrovertible proof that the ovaries synthesize androgens. Both testosterone and androstenedione are present in ovarian vein blood in higher concentration than in peripheral blood. These androgens may be produced by thecal cells as a byproduct of the synthesis of oestrogens, but they are probably also specifically produced by stromal cells and hilus cells in the ovarian medulla. Further discussion of the metabolism and functions of androgens is found on p. 37.29.

Control of ovarian functions

The role of the adenohypophysis in the control of endocrine glands and the interrelations between hypothalamus and adenohypophysis have already been discussed (p. 25.6). This section is restricted to a description of the control of the ovaries by pituitary gonadotrophins, the hypothalamic control of pituitary gonadotrophins, and the relationships between the ovaries and the hypothalamus.

PITUITARY GONADOTROPHINS

Advance in this subject has been hampered by serious methodological limitations. In particular, there is no chemical method for estimating gonadotrophins, and it has been necessary to rely on bioassay techniques which are not specific for individual gonadotrophins. The recent introduction of an immunochemical assay may improve specificity. Similarly, no pure preparation of gonadotrophin is yet available for experimental studies.

There are at least two distinct gonadotrophins, **follicle stimulating hormone** (FSH) and **luteinizing hormone** (LH), also referred to as interstitial cell stimulating hormone (ICSH). These are both glycoproteins and are produced by the basophil cells of the adenohypophysis. Another pituitary hormone, **prolactin**, has been shown to have the ability to maintain the corpus luteum in rats and mice, and for this reason, it is sometimes called luteotrophin (LTH). However, there is no evidence to indicate that prolactin has any luteotrophic activity in man; its functions in relation to human lactation are discussed on p. 37.52.

Gonadotrophins control both the release of ova and the production of sex hormones, and the cyclical changes in the ovary are dependent on their intermittent release. FSH causes growth and distension of the ovarian follicle, but by itself it does not induce ovulation. LH, acting in conjunction with FSH, induces ovulation and following ovulation it initiates the formation of the corpus luteum and the subsequent production of both oestrogens and progestagens.

The factors which control the maintenance and regression of the corpus luteum are not understood, but during pregnancy a placental gonadotrophin exerts a powerful luteotrophic effect.

The cyclical activity of gonadotrophins is reflected in changes in plasma levels and urinary excretion of gonadotrophins during the menstrual cycle (fig. 37.14). The practical difficulties of assaying these hormones have been mentioned and there are no completely reliable data. FSH excretion probably reaches a peak during menstruation, declines before ovulation and rises again just before the onset of menstruation. LH excretion appears to be low during the follicular phase, but rises to a sharp peak at the mid-point of the ovarian cycle, falling to low levels again after ovulation. The data correlate reasonably with the concept of the major roles of FSH and LH in growth of the follicle and ovulation respectively.

The mechanisms by which gonadotrophins regulate the ovarian production of sex steroids are still not understood but it seems likely that LH acts at an early stage in steroid synthesis, possibly on the conversion of cholesterol to pregnenolone.

HYPOTHALAMO–HYPOPHYSIAL RELATIONSHIPS

The anatomical relations of hypophysis and hypothalamus and the hypothalamo–hypophysial portal system are described on p. 25.9. It is likely that neurones in the median eminence control the release of gonadotrophins from the adenohypophysis by the synthesis of specific neurohumoral transmitters which pass down the hypothalamo–hypophysial portal system. FSH- and LH-releasing factors have been extracted from the median eminence and identified as polypeptides.

The hypothalamus dominates and drives the adenohypophysis, certainly as far as the rhythmic release of gonadotrophins is concerned. In the adult female rat section of the infundibular stalk abolishes cyclical activity. Furthermore, if the hypophysis of an immature rat is transplanted to the hypothalamus of a hypophysectomized adult rat and allowed to revascularize, it exhibits normal adult cyclical activity. Thus, the rhythmic release of gonadotrophins which is the essential feature of adult female sexual activity is the function of the hypothalamus rather than the hypophysis, although the nature of this hypothalamic clock mechanism is unknown. The hypothalamus acts as a final common pathway for the convergence of stimuli which may influence sexual activity, and this information is translated into gonadotrophin activity by the mechanisms described above. These stimuli include a variety of visual and olfactory sensations together with the whole gamut of emotional experience, all of which modify the functioning of the reproductive system.

OVARIAN–HYPOTHALAMIC INTERRELATIONS (fig. 37.16)

There is good evidence that the ovaries exert a regulating influence on the release of gonadotrophins. For example, the urinary excretion of gonadotrophins is decreased by administering oestrogens and increased following bilateral oophorectomy. This indicates a negative feedback relationship between the ovaries and hypophysis.

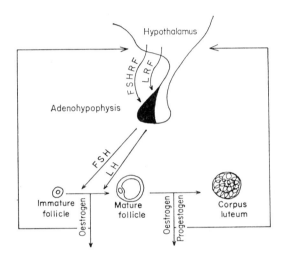

FIG. 37.16. Interrelations between hypothalamus, adenohypophysis and ovaries.

The afferent stimuli for this neurohumoral reflex are probably ovarian steroids and the central relay area is probably located in the hypothalamus. Thus, labelled oestrogens are taken up selectively by cells of the hypothalamus. Furthermore, in the rat, destructive lesions in the anterior hypothalamus abolish this feedback mechanism, whereas both ovarian grafts and oestrogen implants in this area reduce ovarian activity. The efferent side of this reflex comprises the median eminence, hypothalamo–hypophysial portal system and adenohypophysis. It is currently believed that oestrogens suppress the release of FSH but facilitate the release of LH, while progestagens suppress the production of LH.

This hypothesis provides a feasible explanation of the events of the menstrual cycle. During menstruation, the hypothalamus drives the hypophysis to release predominantly FSH and so induces growth of the ovarian follicle. Oestrogen secretion increases and this both suppresses FSH and facilitates the release of LH, as a result of which ovulation ensues and luteinization is initiated. The subsequent increase in progestagen secretion then suppresses LH secretion. As the corpus luteum regresses the production of sex steroids falls and a new

release of FSH initiates the beginning of another ovarian cycle. It must be emphasized that this hypothesis is partly conjectural.

There are other mechanisms which may interact with this hypothalamo–hypophysial–ovarian system. Ovarian steroids may have a direct action on the ovaries, and they may also act directly on the hypophysis. There is also evidence for a subsidiary component of the hypothalamo-hypophysial portal system which conveys blood from hypophysis to hypothalamus, and this may provide the anatomical basis for a direct short-loop feedback system between hypophysis and hypothalamus. Finally, the other endocrine organs, especially thyroid and adrenal cortex, may interact with all of these components.

Ovaries and the reproductive tract

If labelled oestrogens are administered systemically, they are taken up selectively by the hypothalamus, breast and genital tract. The actions of oestrogens on the hypothalamus have been described and their actions on the breast are given on p. 37.51. This section deals mainly with the interrelations between the ovaries and their principal target area, the reproductive tract. The component of the genital tract which undergoes the most marked cyclical changes is the endometrium.

FIG. 37.17. The endometrial cycle showing changes in glands and stroma during menstrual cycle. Vascular changes are not included in this diagram.

ENDOMETRIAL CYCLE (fig. 37.17)

The endometrium undergoes cyclical changes which reflect the activity of the follicle and corpus luteum, the duration and timing of each endometrial cycle usually being synchronized with the development and decline of a single follicle. Each cycle is characterized by a growth phase which parallels the maturation of the follicle and corpus luteum, and by a rapid regression which follows the decline of the corpus luteum. The growth phase provides a receptive endometrium suitable for the implantation of a blastocyst, and its exact nature and duration are influenced both by ovulation and implantation. In the absence of implantation, the corpus luteum undergoes involution, and the endometrium returns to its basal state. Regression of the endometrium is associated with uterine bleeding, and as this bleeding occurs at approximately monthly intervals in women it is known as menstruation.

The endometrium is a mucous membrane with some unusual features. It is composed of simple straight tubular glands lined by columnar epithelium. There is no submucosa intervening between endometrium and myometrium and the tips of endometrial glands burrow into underlying muscle. These glands lie in a stroma which is more cellular than typical connective tissue, and the stromal cells are responsive to ovarian hormones. This stroma is more than an inert structural framework and has an important part to play in implantation. The endometrium is vascularized by endometrial spiral arterioles. As these enter the endometrium, they supply subterminal branches to the deepest layers, while their terminal branches continue into the stroma of the superficial layers and terminate in subepithelial capillary networks. The spiral arterioles are specialized structures characterized by thick muscular and elastic layers, and they are destined to become the vessels which supply the placenta. Each of these constituent parts of the endometrium undergoes cyclical changes, and while the sequence of events in the glands and stroma is well documented, the vascular changes are equally important.

A useful preliminary concept is to recognize two functionally distinct layers within the endometrium. There is a **basal layer** which is in intimate contact with the myometrium. This layer has a separate blood supply, is relatively unresponsive to ovarian hormones, is not subject to menstrual disintegration, and is the layer from which regeneration of the endometrium takes place. By contrast, the **superficial layer** of the endometrium may be thought of as the **functional layer**. All the components of this layer respond dramatically to ovarian hormones and it undergoes cyclical growth and regression, being replaced after each menstrual loss by repair from the basal layer.

Menstrual bleeding normally lasts for 2–7 days and occurs at regular intervals of 21–35 days, the average duration of the menstrual cycle being 28 days. This interval is calculated from the first day of one menstrual flow to the day of onset of the next bleeding. To simplify description it is convenient to consider a typical 28-day cycle, day 1 referring to the day of onset of bleeding. In such a cycle, ovulation occurs around the 14th day, and it is possible to distinguish a follicular and a luteal phase of ovarian activity which precedes and follows ovulation respectively. This is reflected in corresponding phases of endometrial activity.

Follicular phase

Menstruation results in disintegration of the functional layer of the endometrium, leaving the residual basal layer no more than 1 mm thick. Regeneration begins even before menstrual loss is complete, by proliferation of the epithelium of the stumps of endometrial glands and possibly by conversion of stromal cells into epithelial elements.

Under the influence of oestrogens from the developing follicle, the endometrium enters a phase of rapid proliferation. The glands lengthen and become tortuous and the epithelium shows intense mitotic activity, while the stroma increases in cellularity, each cell being composed of a dense nucleus with little cytoplasm, so that the nuclei appear naked. This intense proliferative activity is indicated by an increase in the content of ribonucleic acid and alkaline phosphatase activity of the endometrium. During the follicular phase, spiral arterioles increase in length and tortuosity, each parent vessel giving rise to ten to fifteen arteriolar branches. The follicular phase is usually completed within 14 days from the onset of menstruation.

Luteal phase

Following ovulation and subsequent luteinization of the follicle, oestrogen synthesis is supplemented by the production of progestagens.

The luteal phase is characterized by secretory activity and the decline of cellular proliferation. The first signs of secretory activity are subnuclear vacuoles in the glandular epithelium which displace the basal nuclei towards the centre of the cells. These vacuoles contain glycogen and mucopolysaccharides and move towards the periphery of the cells where they discharge their contents into the glandular lumen. Histologically two zones in the functional layer of the endometrium can now be distinguished. In the deeper zone, the stroma becomes loose and oedematous while the glands become distended with secretory products. This zone is commonly referred to as the **spongy layer**. In the superficial zone, the stromal cells become polygonal with a prominent cytoplasm and are packed around the necks of endometrial glands. This gives the superficial zone a dense cellular appearance and it is referred to as the **compact layer**. This alteration in the appearance of the stromal cells in the compact layer becomes even more pronounced in the event of implantation. Spiral arterioles increase in length so that their distal ends approach very close to the surface of the endometrium. This increase in length of the arterioles is greater than the increase in depth of the endometrium, and this exaggerates their coiling.

MENSTRUATION

If implantation does not occur, luteolysis ensues and there is a rapid fall in the production of oestrogens and progestagens beginning about the 24th day.

With the withdrawal of steroid hormones, the spongy layer shrinks by loss of extracellular fluid, and the compact layer becomes infiltrated with polymorph and mononuclear leucocytes. This collapse of the endometrium causes further coiling of the spiral arterioles and results in vascular stasis and reduction of blood flow through the endometrium. Passive stasis is followed by active vasoconstriction, and the consequent reduction in blood supply causes the death of the endometrium (ischaemic necrosis). These arterioles subsequently relax and allow blood, under arterial pressure, to flow into vessels damaged by ischaemia. Rupture of these vessels produces uterine bleeding and the necrotic endometrium disintegrates. This process occurs patchily throughout the endometrium over a period of days, so that one area may have been shed and be in process of repair, while an adjacent area may still be viable. This process of ischaemic necrosis and shedding does not affect the basal layer.

Menstruation is seen to be due immediately to ischaemia, and the volume of bleeding is controlled by this constriction-relaxation sequence in the spiral arterioles. The factors which control vasoconstriction of the spiral arterioles are clearly of importance but are not understood, although a number of vasoconstrictor substances, such as prostaglandins, have been identified in the endometrium.

From the point of view of conception, the result of the growth phase is the preparation of the endometrium for implantation of the blastocyst. The secretion of glycogen into the uterine cavity produces nutrients before a placental circulation is established; the development of the spiral arterioles provides the basis for the maternal placental circulation, while the changes in the stromal cells are the beginnings of decidualization, which is probably of importance in determining the depth of implantation. Menstruation is a specific growth-limiting mechanism which supervenes whcn implantation fails to occur.

MYOMETRIUM

During the follicular phase, uterine contractions are of low intensity and occur at intervals of 30–60 sec, reaching maximum frequency at the time of ovulation. During the luteal phase, contractions occur less frequently but with greater intensity, the greatest amplitude occurring at the time of menstruation.

Little is known of the mechanisms which control uterine contractility. The molecular basis of a uterine contraction is actomyosin, and ATP is the immediate energy source. Oestrogens control myometrial work potential by determining the concentration of actomyosin in the uterus. Progestagens probably do not influence the contractile mechanisms but may reduce excitability and impair the propagation of impulses by hyperpolarizing the myometrial cell membranes. Catecholamines have an action similar to that of progestagens.

Oxytocin (p. 25.15) is a powerful myometrial stimulant but its physiological functions are still uncertain. This uncertainty is due largely to the fact that there is still no accurate method for the assay of oxytocin. It may be of importance in parturition, but its role in the non-pregnant woman is unknown.

There are several other naturally occurring substances which stimulate the uterus *in vitro*. Some of these, such as prostaglandins, may be important in sperm transport in the uterus, but their role in the overall control of uterine contractility is unknown.

CERVIX

There is no clear cut cyclical pattern in the cervical epithelium, and it does not undergo menstrual shedding. The mucus secreted by cervical glands, however, does show cyclical changes. Around the time of ovulation, and in response to rising oestrogen levels, there is an increase in the water and electrolyte content of cervical mucus. As a result, its volume increases and its viscosity is reduced. This produces a profuse, clear mucoid discharge which is typically thready in consistency. If a drop of mucus at this time is allowed to dry out on a clean slide, the crystallization of electrolytes produces a characteristic ferning or arborization pattern (plate 37.1, p. 35.3). In the later stages of the luteal phase, presumably under the influence of progestagens, these changes are reversed; the volume decreases, its viscosity increases and ferning cannot be demonstrated.

The changes in the nature of cervical mucus at the time of ovulation facilitate its penetration by spermatozoa following insemination.

VAGINA

The sequence of histological changes in the vagina is poorly documented, but there is much information on the nature of its exfoliated cells (plate 37.1, p. 35.3). During the follicular phase, under the influence of oestrogens, the vaginal epithelium proliferates and there is a continuous shedding of the superficial cells from the cornified layer. These desquamated cells have densely pyknotic nuclei and their cytoplasm has an affinity for eosin. Consequently, a vaginal smear in the proliferative phase is characterized by a preponderance of pink-staining cells with pyknotic nuclei, and the intensity of oestrogenic influence may be assessed by an eosinophilic index or by the karyopyknotic index (KI). Following ovulation the number of desquamated cornified cells is progressively reduced and those which are shed tend to form clusters, each cell having a typically curled edge, and there is an increased number of leucocytes in the smear. The vaginal smear gives a useful estimate of oestrogen activity but a much poorer assessment of progestational activity.

GENERAL SYSTEMIC CHANGES

Body temperature, especially if recorded under basal conditions, can be shown to be elevated during the luteal phase of the cycle. This is almost certainly a function of progestagens or their metabolites, possibly acting via the central nervous system. The precise time relation of this temperature shift to ovulation is not clear.

Evidence on changes in body weight and composition is conflicting. There is no evidence of a consistent increase in weight in the premenstrual phase, but there are subtle changes in blood composition throughout the cycle involving both cellular and plasma constituents. These are neither sufficiently pronounced nor consistent enough to influence the interpretation of most biochemical data for routine clinical purposes, but they deserve recognition for any more detailed research work.

Finally, the psychological repercussions of the ovarian cycle are of immense importance. At this stage, it is sufficient to note that 40–50 per cent of women experience varying degrees of pain with their periods, 20–30 per cent complain of irritability, depression and tension prior to the onset of bleeding (the premenstrual syndrome) and 70 per cent complain of general bodily discomfort, particularly a sensation of bloating or swelling, although this latter complaint is not associated with an increase in total body weight. In more general terms, it has been shown that both academic and athletic performance is slightly impaired in the immediate premenstrual period, while the incidence of serious crime, accidents and suicides is slightly increased.

Clearly, the menstrual cycle is not a phenomenon localized to the reproductive tract, but represents phasic activity involving the whole woman. It is important to recognize the teleological significance of the menstrual cycle. The follicular phase of the ovarian cycle initiates the preparation of the uterus for conception. At mid-cycle, an oocyte is deposited in the uterine tube and simultaneous changes in the cervical mucus facilitate the ascent of spermatozoa, thereby providing the opportunity for fertilization. The corpus luteum completes the preparation of the endometrium and myometrium for implantation of the blastocyst. If, however, fertilization or implantation fail to occur, the ovarian cycle is terminated and menstruation occurs.

Onset and cessation of menstrual activity

The menstrual cycle is the characteristic of sexual maturity and may be regarded as the unit of function in the female, each sequence representing a single concerted preparation for conception. The general problem of sex differentiation and development is described on p. 37.54

PUBERTY

The term **adolescence** refers to the attainment of physical and social maturity, the transformation of a child to an adult. This phase is not capable of exact definition but sexual maturation is only one aspect of adolescence. **Puberty** refers to the 'state of being functionally capable of procreation', and in the normal female this implies the presence of ovulation. The **menarche** refers to the onset of cyclical vaginal bleeding. This is a notable landmark during adolescence, but it will be shown that the menarche is not usually synchronous with the onset of ovulation.

At birth there is a transient phase of sexual pseudo-precocity. The breasts may secrete colostrum (p. 37.52), the internal and external genitalia are relatively enlarged, and a few infants bleed vaginally. These phenomena are due to the presence of a relatively high concentration of oestrogens in the foetus in the uterus, and their abrupt withdrawal at delivery. No further external signs of activity in the reproductive tract can be detected until the 10th or 11th year. During this time the ovary has been steadily increasing in size, and around the 10th year the uterus develops rapidly.

The breasts show the first external signs of sex development (fig. 37.18). The infantile breast consists of a nipple

FIG. 37.18. Development of the breast at puberty. From Hamblen, E.C. (1945) *Endocrinology of Women*. Springfield, Ill.: C.C. Thomas.

projecting from a pigmented areola. Around the 10th or 11th year, the areola becomes everted as a pigmented bud from which the nipple still projects. Thereafter, an increase in gland tissue and fat deep to the areola causes the areolar bud to become elevated on a non-pigmented hillock and, with further development, the areola becomes flattened over the underlying breast tissue. The onset of breast changes is rapidly followed by the appearance of pubic hair. This appears on the labia majora and spreads over the mons pubis to form a triangle of pubic hair. A year or two later, axillary hair appears.

The menarche is a relatively late feature of adolescence. The average age of the menarche in Great Britain is 13 years, but there is a wide scatter between the ages of 10 and 17 years. For the first year or two, menstruation is commonly anovular, i.e. it is associated with cyclical follicular development and regression, but ovulation does not occur.

The mechanisms involved in the onset of puberty are still unknown. It is clear that the prepubertal hypophysis contains and secretes small quantities of gonadotrophins, and the prepubertal ovary responds by secreting small quantities of oestrogens. However, the immature hypophysis is potentially capable of adult functions and similarly the ovary of an immature animal, when transplanted into a spayed adult, can release both ova and sex hormones. These observations suggest that prior to the menarche the hypophysial–ovarian system is held under restraint. It is possible that this inhibition is achieved via the ovarian–hypothalamic feedback system.

The reproductive axis in the immature female is similar to the adult in terms of structure and organization, but is set at a much lower level. The factors which alter this level and so initiate sexual development are unknown, but they may include changes in the production or metabolism of ovarian hormones, or alterations in the sensitivity of the hypothalamus to these hormones.

Finally, the adrenal cortex plays a part in sexual development, and is responsible for the growth of pubic and axillary hair.

CLIMACTERIC

The cessation of menstruation is known as the **menopause**, while the **climacteric** refers to the general physiological changes which occur at this time. The age of the menopause in Britain is about 48 years, with a normal range from 40 to 55 years.

The essential cause of the climacteric is ovarian failure. The hypophysis continues to secrete gonadotrophins in increasing quantities but the ovaries fail to release either ova or hormones. This is followed by permanent loss of powers of reproduction but there is usually no sudden reduction in active sexual behaviour. As a consequence of ovarian failure and the withdrawal of sex steroids, the genital tract and breasts atrophy and there are widespread physiological repercussions. The climacteric is sometimes associated with psychological disturbances.

MECHANISMS OF REPRODUCTION IN THE MALE

ANATOMY OF THE MALE REPRODUCTIVE TRACT

The scrotum

This is a pouch of skin situated below the root of the penis. It is divided internally by a median sagittal fibrous septum, and this division is marked on the surface by a median ridge, the **scrotal raphe**. The scrotal skin is dark and thin and contains numerous sebaceous glands and sparse hairs. Its subcutaneous tissue contains smooth muscle fibres, the **dartos muscle**. This muscle contracts in response to cold or exercise, and its contraction makes the scrotum smaller and causes its skin to be wrinkled.

The testis and epididymis

The two testes are smooth, ovoid structures which are laterally compressed. They measure about 2·5 cm from side to side, 3 cm from back to front and about 4 cm in length. The left testis is situated at a slightly lower level than the right testis.

Each testis projects forwards into a closed serous sac, the **tunica vaginalis**, so that only the posterior part of the testis is not covered by a double layer of tunica (fig. 37.20). The parietal and visceral layers of the tunica are usually separated from each other by only a thin film of fluid. The testis and the tunica vaginalis are attached to the lower part of the scrotum by a fibrous condensation, the **scrotal ligament**, which may be derived from the gubernaculum (p. 37.56).

The coverings of the testis are several because in the course of its descent to the scrotum it carries with it extensions from the different layers of the abdominal wall through which it has passed (p. 20.26). With the exception of the tunica vaginalis, which is related only to the testis and epididymis, the coverings of the testis are the same as those which invest the spermatic cord. The coverings from within outwards are as follows:

(1) the tunica vaginalis derived from the peritoneum,

(2) the **internal spermatic fascia** derived from the transversalis fascia,

(3) the **cremasteric muscle and fascia** derived from the internal oblique muscle,

(4) the **external spermatic fascia** derived from the aponeurosis of the external oblique muscle,

(5) the membranous layer of the superficial fascia (p. 20.29).

The epididymis is a comma-shaped structure which is closely applied to the posterior surface of the testis, overlapping its posterolateral aspect. The upper part is expanded and known as the head. The **head** overhangs the upper pole of the testis and tapers down to form the **body** which in turn becomes continuous with a thin **tail** which is related to the lower pole of the testis. The tail is continuous with the **ductus deferens** which then ascends on the medial side of the epididymis. The head of the epididymis is connected to the back of the testis by fifteen to twenty **efferent ductules**. The epididymis is in effect an extensively coiled duct which if straightened out would be 5–7 m long.

The **sinus of the epididymis** is an infolding of tunica vaginalis which partially separates the testis from the epididymis on the lateral side.

Embryological remnants of the mesonephric and paramesonephric ducts may be found in relation to the upper pole of the testis and the epididymis.

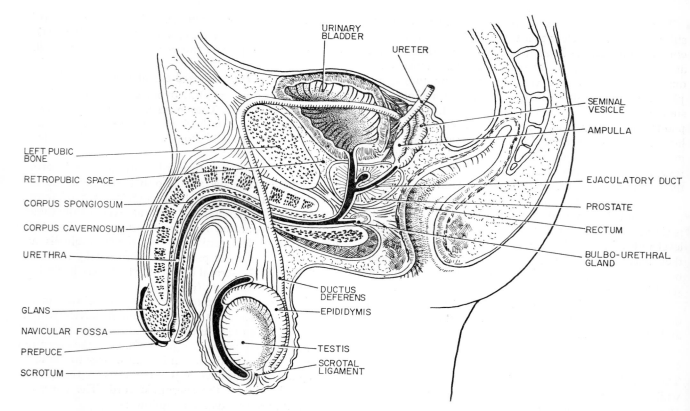

FIG. 37.19. Median sagittal section of the male pelvis. From Turner C.D. (1966) *General Endocrinology*, 4th Edition. Philadelphia: Saunders.

STRUCTURE

Each testis is completely invested by a dense, white, inelastic capsule, the **tunica albuginea**, which projects into the testicular substance at the posterior surface of that organ to form the **mediastinum testis**. From the mediastinum, where the testis is penetrated by its vessels and nerves, radiates a series of thin septa which reach out to the inner surface of the tunica and divide the testis into about 250 conical compartments, or **lobes of the testis**, and these contain the seminiferous tubules (fig. 37.20).

Each **seminiferous tubule** is highly coiled and when teased out is about 70 cm long. They are looped in such a way that both ends join a series of about thirty short, so-called **straight tubules** which converge on a network of vessels lying in the mediastinum, the **rete testis**. Within each lobe, the seminiferous tubules are embedded in delicate connective tissue which contains polyhedral **interstitial cells (Leydig cells)** some of which are swollen with lipids. These are the source of testicular androgens.

Each seminiferous tubule has a basement membrane on which are set numerous germinal cells in various stages of maturation (p. 37.32) interspersed with a smaller number of **sustentacular cells (Sertoli cells)**. Primary spermatogonia are attached to the basement membrane, and

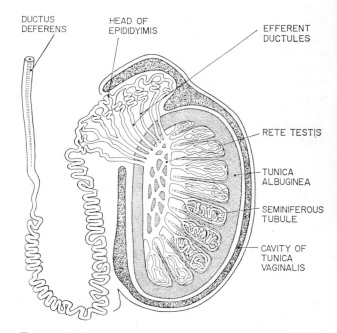

FIG. 37.20. Arrangement of tubules and ducts in the testis and epididymis. From Hamilton W.J., Boyd J.D. & Mossman H.W. (1962) *Human Embryology*, 3rd Edition. Cambridge: Heffer.

cells at successive stages of the spermatogenic cycle are pushed towards the lumen of the tubule so that mature spermatozoa reach the lumen. However, the arrangement of the cells is too irregular for intermediate types to be recognized simply by their position within the tubule (fig. 37.21).

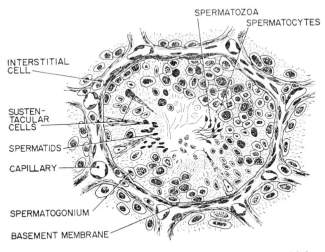

FIG. 37.21. Structure of seminiferous tubule and interstitial tissue. From Hamilton W.J., Boyd, J.D. & Mossman H.W. (1962) *Human Embryology*, 3rd Edition. Cambridge: Heffer.

The variable appearance of cross-sections of seminiferous tubules is partly explained by the fact that spermatogenesis occurs in waves which proceed along the length of the tubule. Before one generation of cells has matured completely at any point of the tubule another wave of growth is initiated.

The epithelium of straight tubules consists of tall columnar cells and that of the rete testis is cuboidal or low columnar. The rete testis is continuous with the efferent ductules and these in turn open into the ducts of the head of the epididymis. The epithelium of the efferent ductules consists of alternating patches of tall and low columnar cells. A thin layer of smooth muscle surrounds each ductule (fig. 37.22).

The duct of the epididymis is lined by pseudostratified tall columnar epithelium which is secretory and whose cells possess a long non-motile stereocilium (p. 13.13). This is concerned with the discharge from the cell of a secretion which plays a role in the maturation of spermatozoa. The duct is surrounded by circular smooth muscle, and its coils are held together by loose connective tissue.

NERVE SUPPLY

The testicular nerves originate from the tenth thoracic segment and contain both afferent and efferent fibres. The sympathetic nerves are derived from the plexus around the aorta at the level of origin of the testicular arteries. These testicular nerves communicate with those of the ductus deferens which are derived from the hypogastric plexus. The scrotal nerves are branches of the pudendal nerve and the perineal branch of the posterior cutaneous nerve of the thigh. The ilioinguinal nerve supplies the upper anterior part of the scrotum.

BLOOD SUPPLY AND LYMPH DRAINAGE

Each **testicular artery** arises from the aorta immediately below the origin of the renal artery. It runs down the posterior abdominal wall to reach the spermatic cord at the internal inguinal ring. Before reaching the testis it supplies branches to the epididymis.

Veins emerge from the posterior aspect of the testis as an anastomotic plexus, known as the **pampiniform plexus**, which passes up the spermatic cord. At the internal inguinal ring the plexus forms testicular veins which drain on the right side into the inferior vena cava, and on the left side into the left renal vein.

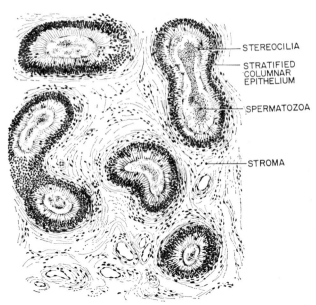

FIG. 37.22. Structure of the epididymis showing several sections through the duct. From Bloom W. & Fawcett D. W. (1962) *A Textbook of Histology*, 8th Edition. Philadelphia: Saunders.

The lymphatic vessels draining the testis and the epididymis accompany the veins and reach the lateral aortic lymph nodes near the origin of the testicular arteries.

The scrotum and coverings of the testis are supplied by the internal pudendal artery, by the cremasteric branch of the inferior epigastric artery and by the external pudendal artery. The veins follow the arteries, and the lymphatics pass to the superficial inguinal nodes.

The spermatic cord

This cord extends from the internal inguinal ring to the posterior border of the testis. Where it emerges from the inguinal canal at the external inguinal ring, it lies immediately under the skin and superficial fascia and is easy to palpate. It then passes in front of the pubis to reach the scrotum. The spermatic cord contains the ductus deferens (which has the consistency to touch of whip-cord), the testicular arteries, the pampiniform plexus and testicular lymphatics and nerves, all bound together by loose connective tissue.

The coverings of the cord have been described with the coverings of the testis. The cremasteric coat, including as it does striped muscle, has its own nerve supply from the genitofemoral nerve. By its contraction, the cremaster muscle raises the testis within the scrotum and the cremasteric reflex contraction is brought into action by stimulating the skin of the upper part of the thigh supplied by the femoral branch of the genitofemoral nerve.

The ductus deferens (vas deferens)

This fibromuscular tube is characterized by a very thick wall compared to the size of its lumen, and is 45 cm long. It begins at the tail of the epididymis as the continuation

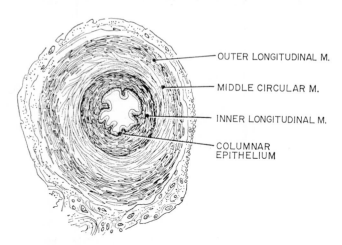

OUTER LONGITUDINAL M.

MIDDLE CIRCULAR M.

INNER LONGITUDINAL M.

COLUMNAR EPITHELIUM

FIG. 37.23. Structure of the ductus deferens. From Bloom W. & Fawcett D. W. (1968) *A Textbook of Histology*, 9th Edition. Philadelphia: Saunders.

of the duct of the epididymis and passes into the spermatic cord. It reaches the pelvic cavity after leaving the internal inguinal ring by hooking round the lateral side of the inferior epigastric artery. As it passes over the pelvic brim it becomes separated from the other constituents of the spermatic cord and runs backwards and medially under the peritoneum to reach the ureter close to where it enters the back of the bladder. It crosses above and in front of the ureter to converge on its fellow from the

opposite side and then runs down towards the prostate between the bladder in front and the rectum behind. Here the ductus deferens comes to lie medial to its corresponding seminal vesicle. Each ductus continues on its downward course and becomes dilated and tortuous to form an **ampulla**. Just above the prostate, each ductus narrows and is joined by the duct of the seminal vesicle, and so forms the **ejaculatory duct** which runs on through the substance of the prostate.

The ductus deferens has a thick muscular coat made up of outer and inner longitudinal, and a middle circular layer of smooth muscle. The total diameter of the duct is no more than 2·5 mm and the muscle coat is 1 mm thick so that it accounts for most of the thickness of the tube. It is peristalsis of this thick muscular coat which moves spermatozoa towards the ampulla. At the ampulla the muscular wall is much thinner. The lamina propria of the mucous membrane supports a pseudostratified tall columnar epithelium bearing non-motile stereocilia.

The arteries of the duct are derived from the testicular artery and from the vesical arteries; its nerves arise from the pelvic plexus.

The seminal vesicles

These apparently lobulated organs are placed symmetrically on each side of the midline behind the bladder and above the prostate. Each vesicle is about 5 cm long and is fusiform, the long axis being set obliquely with the upper extremities diverging. The upper end of each vesicle lies behind and lateral to the ureter as it enters the bladder. Between the vesicles lie the ampullae of the two ductus deferentes. The duct of the seminal vesicle joins the lower end of the ampulla of the ductus at an acute angle to form the ejaculatory duct.

Each vesicle is a coiled, elongated, blind sac measuring about 12 cm when dissected out, and is in effect a diverticulum from the lower part of the ductus deferens.

Up to ten blind diverticula extend from the main sac and the whole tortuous complex is held together tightly by connective tissue. Each component duct is surrounded by an elastic layer of connective tissue outside a muscular coat of smooth muscle. The mucous membrane is folded in an extremely complex fashion so that the folds break up the lumen into numerous intercommunicating spaces. These spaces are lined by stratified or pseudostratified columnar or cuboidal epithelium which is secretory. The secretory activity of the vesicles is under the control of androgens and the average capacity of a seminal vesicle is 2–3 ml of sticky fluid.

Before puberty its mucous membrane shows very few folds but at puberty under the influence of the testicular secretion the mucosa grows very rapidly and is thrown up into folds. Any subsequent decrease in the amount of androgenic stimulation leads to decrease in the size and secretory activity of the organ.

The nerve supply is derived from the pelvic plexuses. The vesicles are supplied with blood by the inferior vesical and middle rectal arteries. The veins drain into the vesico-prostatic plexus of veins.

The ejaculatory ducts

These are formed by the junction of the duct of the seminal vesicle with the ductus deferens of the corresponding side at the posterosuperior surface of the prostate. The ducts then pass obliquely forwards, medially and downwards through the substance of the prostate to open into the back of the **prostatic urethra** on either side of the opening of the **prostatic utricle** on the **urethral crest.** The elevation formed at the opening of the utricle and ejaculatory duct is known as the **colliculus seminalis.** The ejaculatory duct, which is about 2 cm long, is more in line with the duct of the seminal vesicle than with the ductus deferens.

The prostate

This organ is formed of muscular and glandular tissue. It is described variously as having the shape of a chestnut, or as being an inverted pyramid whose base is applied to the neck of the bladder. Its apex rests on the fascia covering the urogenital diaphragm and its posterior surface faces the rectum. Its convex inferolateral surfaces are related to the levator ani muscle of each side. The rounded anterior border of the gland is separated from the back of the pubis by a space of about 2 cm which is filled with the retropubic pad of fat (fig. 37.19).

The normal gland usually measures about 2·5 cm from front to back, 3 cm from above downwards, and nearly 4 cm from side to side. The connective tissue around the gland is condensed to form a fibrous capsule. There is a groove between the neck of the bladder and the base of the prostate which contains the vesicoprostatic plexus of veins, and the front part of the junctional area between the base of the prostate and the bladder neck is joined to the back of the pubis by a condensation of fibrous tissue, the **puboprostatic ligament.**

Because of these ligaments and the fact that its lateral surfaces are firmly gripped by the levator ani muscle, some of whose fibres gain attachment to the gland's fascial covering, the prostate is firmly fixed in the pelvis. In turn, the prostate fixes the neck of the bladder.

The prostate gland is traversed from top to bottom by the prostatic urethra which normally runs an anteroposteriorly curved course through the gland and lies closer to its anterior than to its posterior surface.

STRUCTURE (fig. 37.24)

The whole gland is enclosed in a dense fibrous capsule which adheres closely to the underlying tissue, and the stroma of the gland consists of fibromuscular tissue. The muscular component is smooth muscle.

The urethra appears as a semilunar split in horizontal sections through the gland. This is due to a projection into the posterior wall called the **urethral crest.** The prostatic glandular ducts, thirty on each side, open into the urethra on each side of the crest.

The glandular tissue consists of secretory acini of irregular shape and size surrounded by the fibromuscular stroma. The epithelium consists of pseudostratified or stratified columnar cells. After middle age, acini may contain concretions of secretion and desquamated cells.

That part of the prostate which is in front of the urethra is practically devoid of glandular tissue. The part of the prostate between the urethra and the ejaculatory ducts consists of glands that open near the opening of the prostatic utricle and constitute the **median lobe** of the prostate. The **prostatic utricle** is a blind glandular diverticulum which extends up the posterior margin of the median lobe between the ejaculatory ducts.

Although small mucosal glands open into the urethra at all points of its circumference, the main prostatic glands occupy chiefly the lateral and posterior portions and open on either side of the urethral crest by way of the prostatic glandular ducts described above.

The glands of the median lobe and mucosal glands constitute the glands of the **inner zone** in which senile enlargement usually starts. Carcinoma of the prostate usually starts in the **outer zone** which consists of the main prostatic glands.

At birth the prostatic utricle and particularly the median lobe show signs of stimulation by maternal oestrogens but these effects disappear within 2 months. The gland grows rapidly at puberty, and continues to grow till the age of 30 years. Involutionary changes, particularly at the periphery of the gland, start after about 40 years of age and the gland normally becomes smaller with increasing age.

The blood supply of the prostate is derived from the inferior vesical, middle rectal and internal pudendal arteries. The veins form a rich plexus in the fascial covering of the gland which contributes to the vesicoprostatic plexus. The gland is richly supplied by both pelvic sympathetic and parasympathetic fibres. The afferent nerves are linked to the lower three lumbar and upper sacral spinal segments.

The bulbourethral glands (Cowper's glands)

These lie deep in the deep perineal pouch, one on each side, between the lower margin of the prostate and the bulb of the penis. They are embedded in the muscle tissue which encircles the membranous urethra. Each is about the size of a pea and drains by a duct 2·5 cm long which pierces the inferior fascia of the urogenital diaphragm to enter the penis and opens into the bulb of the urethra. They consist of compound tubulo-alveolar secretory units.

FIG. 37.24. Sagittal and horizontal sections through the prostate. A and B are horizontal sections through lines A–A and B–B respectively. From Hamilton W.J., Boyd J.D. & Mossman H.W. (1962) *Human Embryology*, 3rd Edition Cambridge: Heffer.

The penis (fig. 37.25)

The male copulatory organ is composed mainly of erectile tissue arranged in three cylindrical columns, two dorsal **corpora cavernosa** and an inferiorly situated single **corpus spongiosum** which expands distally to form the substance of the **glans penis**.

The penis has a fixed root situated in the urogenital triangle of the perineum and a free shaft (fig. 37.26). At the root the corpora cavernosa diverge to be attached to the ischiopubic ramus as the **crura of the penis**. The corpus spongiosum expands proximally to form the **bulb of the penis**. The bulb is attached to the urogenital diaphragm and is enveloped by the **bulbospongiosus muscle**, while each crus is covered by the **ischiocavernosus muscle**.

The expanded glans is demarcated from the main shaft of the penis by the **coronary sulcus**. The corpus spongiosum and its glans are traversed by the penile urethra which in the glans is expanded to form a **fossa navicularis** from whose roof a diverticulum, the **lacuna magna**, extends. The skin of the shaft of the penis forms a fold, the **prepuce**, which projects from the coronary sulcus to cover the

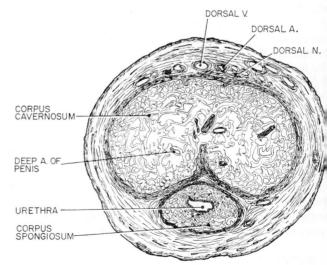

FIG. 37.25. Cross-section of the penis. The septum in the corpus cavernosum is incomplete as this section is in the distal part of the penis. From Bloom W. & Fawcett D. W. (1968) *A Textbook of Histology*, 9th Edition. Philadelphia: Saunders.

glans. On its inferior aspect the fold is tethered to the under surface of the glans as the **frenulum**. The skin of the penis is thin, distensible, devoid of fat and loosely attached to the underlying fascia. Proximally it is continuous with the skin of the anterior abdominal wall, and the scrotum and perineum.

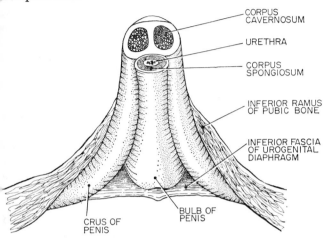

FIG. 37.26. Root of penis. From *Cunningham's Textbook of Anatomy*, 10th Edition. London: Oxford University Press.

The blood supply is derived mainly from the internal pudendal artery but the superficial part of the dorsum is supplied by the external pudendal branch of the femoral artery.

The veins run with the arteries, but in addition the superficial dorsal vein drains to the saphenous vein and the deep dorsal vein into the prostatic plexus. The lymphatics drain into the superficial inguinal nodes.

The sensory nerves are branches of the pudendal and ilioinguinal nerves, and a parasympathetic supply is derived from the pelvic plexus.

PHYSIOLOGY OF THE MALE REPRODUCTIVE TRACT

The testes fulfil a dual role analogous to that of the ovaries, being concerned with the production of sex hormones and male gametes. However, human testes function at a relatively constant rate so that their control by higher centres is less complicated. Furthermore, the male reproductive tract has relatively simple functions, being concerned almost exclusively with the production and transport of spermatozoa, and it has none of the complex cyclical changes characteristic of the female.

Functions of the testes

There is a greater degree of separation of gametogenic and endocrine functions in the testes than in the ovaries. They proceed in parallel in anatomically discrete sites.

PRODUCTION OF SPERMATOZOA (Spermatogenesis)
There are three successive stages in the production of spermatozoa. These are the continuous production of germ cells and their subsequent modification for fertilization by meiotic divisions and by structural modifications which render them actively motile.

Formation of germ cells
The origin of primitive germ cells and their migration to the testes are described on p. 37.54. As a result of these processes, the male germ cells or **spermatogonia** come to lie within the seminiferous tubules in close relation to the sustentacular cells. These cells are situated on the basement membrane and have a large irregular cytoplasm which comes into close contact with many spermatogenic cells. Their function is not clear, but they are probably concerned with the maintenance and co-ordination of developing germ cells. Spermatogonia show little sign of activity until puberty when they begin to multiply rapidly by mitotic division, and it is their active proliferation which ensures the continual renewal of germ cells. In the male, gametogenesis is a continuous process which begins at puberty and is maintained throughout adult life.

Meiotic divisions
Some spermatogonia enlarge in size and become recognizable as **primary spermatocytes**. Primary spermatocytes undergo reduction division to become haploid **secondary spermatocytes** and these in turn again divide, so that each diploid primary spermatocyte ultimately gives rise to four haploid **spermatids** (fig. 37.10). Meiosis has already been described in detail in relation to oogenesis and only two points of difference require attention. First, both the primary and secondary spermatocytes divide symmetrically with an equal distribution of nuclear material and cytoplasm in the spermatids, whereas the unequal division of the cytoplasm during oogenesis produces one ovum with a large volume of cytoplasm and three polar bodies with minimal cytoplasm. Secondly, the time scale of meiosis in the male and female is different. The first meiotic division in the female is prolonged over many years, whereas both meiotic divisions in the male are completed probably within two weeks.

Development of spermatids
A newly formed spermatid has a relatively simple cellular structure whereas a mature **spermatozoon** is highly differentiated to enable it to travel through the male and female reproductive tracts to fuse with the ovum. This development is highly elaborate and takes several weeks to complete. The two special functions of the spermatozoon, motility and fertilizing ability, are concentrated in two distinct regions; the sperm **head** contains the male pronucleus while the **tail**, comprising the neck, middle piece, main piece and end piece, is the organ of motility.

In fact, all else is sacrificed to subserve these two functions, and a mature spermatozoon is little more than a 'nuclear war-head' of paternal genes powered by an active tail.

The total length of the human spermatozoon is 50 μm (fig. 37.27). The sperm head is a flattened pear-shaped body compressed at its anterior pole into a flat edge, and

SIDE VIEW FRONT VIEW

ACROSOME

PLASMA MEMBRANE

NUCLEUS

HEAD

NECK

MITOCHONDRIAL SHEATH

AXIAL FILAMENT

MIDDLE PIECE

MAIN PIECE (greatly reduced)

CROSS SECTION OF TAIL

END PIECE

FIG. 37.27. Structure of the mature spermatozoon. The small diagram of a spermatozoon is included to show the relative sizes of the head and tail. Modified from Schultz-Larsen, J. (1958) The morphology of the human sperm. *Acta path. et microbiol. Scandinav.* suppl. 128.

occupied by the nucleus which contains the paternal contribution of genetic material. Anteriorly it is covered by the **acrosome** which is derived from the Golgi apparatus. Although the exact origin and nature of this structure are uncertain, the acrosome is poorly developed in man, and a human sperm head is composed almost entirely of a nucleus, densely packed with DNA, and only thinly covered by an acrosomal cap.

The tail is joined to the sperm head by a short fragile **neck**, probably derived from the centriole. It is traversed by the **axial filament**, which is itself composed of several long fibrils which run a straight course throughout its length and are arranged as a central pair of fibrils surrounded by two circumferential rings of nine fibrils each. In the **middle piece**, the axial filament is surrounded by the **mitochondrial sheath**, while the **main piece** is en-

closed by a thin but tough protein sheath which terminates a short distance from the end exposing the **end piece** The whole spermatozoon is covered by a plasma membrane. The tail is the organ of motility and the mitochondria in the middle piece contain oxidative enzymes which provide energy for this activity. Spermatozoa contain very little endogenous supply of energy, and certainly no glycolyzable substrates, and they obtain their energy from nutrients in their environment.

The time scale of spermatogenesis has been studied in two principal ways; by observing the time required for spermatogenic cells to disappear and reappear in the seminiferous tubules after acute radiation damage, or the time required for the formation of spermatozoa with radioactive nuclei after the systemic administration of radioactive labelled precursors of nucleoproteins. From these studies it is estimated that the whole process of spermatogenesis in man takes approximately 64 days to complete.

Spermatogenesis is a complicated process which frequently goes wrong, and this is reflected in a high incidence of grossly abnormal spermatozoa in fertile human semen. These include decapitated spermatozoa, spermatozoa with double heads or double tails, and multinucleate giant spermatozoa, and these may account for 4–20 per cent of spermatozoa in a normal ejaculate. Apart from these structural errors, anomalies may also occur during meiotic divisions and these may be important causes of male infertility.

Spermatogenesis is sensitive to environmental changes, particularly in temperature. The temperature of the scrotal testes in man is 1·5–2·5°C lower than the temperature of the abdominal cavity, and the testes appear to function optimally at this lower temperature. Even a slight elevation in temperature produces a transient impairment in sperm production. This phenomenon may be relevant to two clinical problems, cryptorchidism, where the testes fail to descend into the scrotum, and varicocoele, where there is dilatation of the testicular venous plexus, usually in the left testis. Both of these conditions are associated with defective spermatogenesis, and a factor common to them may be raised intratesticular temperature. Radiation can cause either a permanent or transient effect depending on the type, duration and intensity of exposure. Several drugs also interfere with the various stages of spermatogenesis and some of these may prove to be useful in the control of male fertility.

PRODUCTION OF SEX HORMONES

The principal testicular hormones are androgenic steroids, the most important of these being testosterone and, to a lesser extent, androstenedione. However, the testes also secrete small quantities of oestrogens, and both oestradiol-17β and oestrone have been identified in testicular vein blood. It has already been emphasized hat the patterns of steroid synthesis in testis and ovary ollow an essentially similar pattern and that each type of gonad produces both oestrogens and androgens. The endocrine distinction between the two organs is a simple quantitative one of degree rather than a fundamental qualitative difference. An appreciation of this fact is essential for an understanding of some intersex states, and is explicable in terms of the mechanisms of sex differentiation.

group, and most of these reduced metabolites of testosterone have very little androgenic activity. This conversion produces asymmetric carbon atoms at C-3 and C-5, and a number of stereoisomers are formed (fig. 37.28), the most important metabolites of testosterone being androsterone (a 5α compound) and aetiocholanolone (a 5β compound). Like the oestrogens, these metabolites are conjugated in the liver with glucuronic acid or sulphuric acid prior to their excretion.

FIG. 37.28. Metabolism of testosterone.

Biosynthesis, metabolism and excretion of androgens

The method of production of testosterone from cholesterol has already been described (fig. 37.12), although alternative biosynthetic pathways may also be involved. Testosterone is produced in the interstitial cells, but there is some doubt as to whether testicular oestrogens are also produced in interstitial cells or in the sustentacular cells.

The conversion of physiologically active steroids to less potent compounds takes place in the liver. The initial step in the deactivation of both testicular androgens and adrenal corticosteroids is saturation of the Δ^4-3 ketone

These two compounds are examples of 17-oxosteroids (or 17-ketosteroids), which may be easily measured collectively by a colour reaction, the Zimmermann reaction. As a result, the urinary excretion of 17-oxosteroids has been widely used as a measure of the excretion of androgenic met bolites. However, adrenal corticosteroids follow a similar pathway of conversion and the principal precursor of 17-oxosteroids is undoubtedly dehydroepiandrosterone derived from the adrenal cortex. Testosterone probably accounts for no more than one-third of urinary 17-oxosteroids and even castration produces little permanent effect on their level of excretion. For these reasons, the urinary excretion of 17-oxosteroids is a poor index of testicular endocrine function.

A more useful clinical test is proving to be the chemical assay of testosterone in plasma and urine. The level of plasma testosterone in normal adult males is 0·5–0·8 μg/100 ml as compared with 0·1 μg/100 ml in normal adult females. The urinary excretion of testosterone in adult males aged between 20 and 40 years is within the range 30–100 μg/24 hr.

Actions of androgens

The principal actions of androgens are as follows:

(1) the initiation and maintenance of male secondary sex features at puberty,

(2) the stimulation of growth of the male reproductive tract, and maintenance of its contractile and secretory activity,

(3) the maintenance of the germinal epithelium of the seminiferous tubules, in conjunction with pituitary FSH,

(4) a negative feedback relation with the adeno-hypophysis, inhibiting the release of LH,

(5) a powerful anabolic action, stimulating protein synthesis. The relation of this function to growth and skeletal development is discussed elsewhere (p. 18.42).

CONTROL OF TESTICULAR FUNCTIONS

Mechanisms for the control of the male gonads are essentially similar to those in the female. The same pituitary gonadotrophins, FSH and LH (or ICSH), are involved, and it seems likely that these have separate effects.

FSH promotes spermatogenesis by a direct action on the seminiferous tubules. In this it is aided by testosterone.

LH promotes the secretion of androgens by its action on the Leydig cells.

The relationship between the adenohypophysis and hypothalamus is similar in both sexes, specific releasing factors (FSHRF and LRF) mediating via the hypo-thalamo-hypophysial portal system. One major difference is the absence of cyclical fluctuations in the male. This steady state is determined by hypothalamic centres and ensures a maintained output of pituitary gonadotrophins and a constant level of both gametogenic and endocrine activity in human testes.

The reciprocal relations between testes, hypothalamus and adenohypophysis are still not understood. Two factors which have delayed progress are the lack of reliable assay methods for distinguishing FSH from LH, and the lack of application of accurate chemical methods for the estimation of testicular androgens. Despite this, a general picture has emerged (fig. 37.29).

Although the adenohypophysis maintains a constant secretion of gonadotrophins it is held under restraint.

The fact that castration increases the urinary excretion of gonadotrophins indicates that the testes are the source of this inhibition. In rodents, hypothalamic lesions abolish this effect of castration, and implants of minute quantities of testosterone in the hypothalamus, but not in the adenohypophysis, may cause testicular atrophy. Thus testicular inhibition is probably applied via the hypothalamus rather than directly on the adenohypophysis.

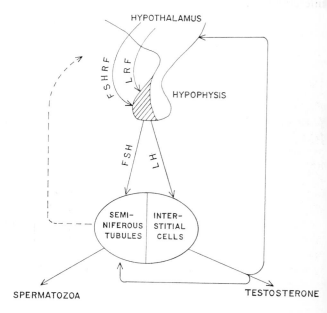

Fig. 37.29. Interrelations between the hypothalamus, adenohypophysis and testes. From Ganong W.F. (1967) *Review of Medical Physiology*, 3rd Edition. Los Altos: Lange.

It is still uncertain if there is a separate feedback system for each of the two testicular functions, gametogenesis and sex steroid production, mediated by FSH and LH respectively. It is thought that testosterone causes predominantly a fall in LH secretion, although large quantities of testosterone can impair spermatogenesis presumably by inhibiting FSH secretion. Castration in childhood, prior to the secretion of significant quantities of testosterone, causes a rise in gonadotrophin, predominantly FSH, excretion. Thus, testosterone may not be the only pituitary inhibitor of testicular origin, and it is probably not normally involved in the control of FSH secretion and spermatogenesis. The nature of this other factor is still uncertain. It is often referred to as a hypothetical substance, inhibin, and there are grounds for the belief that this may represent testicular oestrogen.

Fate of spermatozoa in male and female reproductive tracts

The fate of spermatozoa in the male reproductive tract constitutes a formidable problem, involving the management of a daily production of many millions of spermatozoa. At periods of sexual rest when ejaculation is not taking place, a method for the control of production and disposal of excess spermatozoa is required. For purposes of insemination and fertilization, spermatozoa must gain access to an oocyte by mechanisms which involve a number of complicated transport problems in both male and female reproductive tracts, from seminiferous tubules in the testes to the ampulla of the uterine tube.

As they leave the testes, spermatozoa are probably non-motile and incapable of fertilization, and require modification before they can enter an oocyte. This maturation occurs in both the male and female reproductive tracts.

Semen ejaculated by the male consists of two components, spermatozoa produced by the testes and **seminal plasma** formed by the secretions of the male reproductive tract. In man, the average volume of an ejaculate is 3·5 ml, of which only 10 per cent is formed of spermatozoa and 90 per cent of seminal plasma. From the time spermatozoa leave the seminiferous tubules they are entirely dependent on their fluid environment for their maintenance.

These three aspects, the transport, maturation and maintenance of spermatozoa are important functions of the reproductive tracts. In this context, it is logical to consider the fate of spermatozoa in both the male and female reproductive tracts as one overall problem.

TRANSPORT OF SPERMATOZOA IN MALE REPRODUCTIVE TRACT

Newly formed spermatozoa lie in the seminiferous tubules with their heads in contact with sustentacular cells. Under the influence of gonadotrophins, the cytoplasm of these supporting cells accumulates water in the form of vacuoles which subsequently discharge, shedding spermatozoa into the lumen of the tubules. The production rate of spermatozoa may be enormous, particularly under conditions of sexual activity. Seminal analysis on a 2-year-old bull ejaculating at a frequency of sixty times per week over a period of 5 weeks indicated a constant production rate of 7700 million spermatozoa daily.

Whether spermatozoa enter the rete testis intermittently or continuously is unknown, as is the mechanism by which this movement is achieved. Spermatozoa are propelled through the rete testis and efferent ducts to the epididymis by ciliary and smooth muscle activity. Although spermatozoa are potentially motile when they enter the ductus deferens, propulsion both here and in the epididymis is achieved by smooth muscle contraction. The distance from the efferent ductules to the urethra in man is approximately 6 m, and spermatozoa take approximately 7–14 days to traverse this distance, the time varying with the frequency of ejaculation.

The fate of non-ejaculated spermatozoa is still a mystery. In some animals, particularly the bull, the epididymis may be an important site of sperm resorption so that, at times of sexual rest, the rate of sperm resorption equals the rate of sperm production. In other animals, such as the rat, surplus spermatozoa simply leak away in the urine. The method of sperm disposal in man is uncertain.

INSEMINATION

The method by which semen is naturally deposited in the vagina is based on a complex of spinal reflexes. Three interrelated mechanisms are involved.

Erection

Erection of the penis is a necessary prerequisite for penetration of the vagina. Afferent stimuli for this reflex may involve either peripheral receptors on the external genitalia or stimuli from higher centres. Central connections are in the sacral part of the cord, and the efferent pathway is the parasympathetic component of the pelvic splanchnic nerves. The essential factor in penile erection is active arteriolar dilation which in turn compresses the venous outflow so adding to the distension of the erectile tissue. Loss of erection is due to sympathetic arteriolar vasoconstriction.

Emission

This refers to the movement of spermatozoa and secretions from the ductus deferens and seminal vesicles into the urethra. The afferent side of this arc is usually initiated by touch receptors in the glans penis via the pudendal nerves; central relays are in the upper lumbar segments of the cord, and the sympathetic outflow, via the hypogastric plexus, forms the efferent side of the arc. As a result of these stimuli, the muscle of the ductus deferens and seminal vesicles contracts and propels their contents into the urethra.

Ejaculation

Ejaculation indicates the propulsion of semen out of the urethra. The same afferent paths are involved; central connections are located in the lower lumbar and upper sacral parts of the cord, and efferent stimuli are conveyed by parasympathetic and somatic motor fibres in the pelvic splanchnic and the internal pudendal nerves. Ejaculation is caused by the rhythmic contractions of the bulbocavernosus muscles, while the internal bladder sphincter closes to prevent retrograde ejaculation into the bladder.

TRANSPORT OF SPERMATOZOA IN THE FEMALE REPRODUCTIVE TRACT

As a result of ejaculation a pool of semen is deposited in the vaginal vault around the cervix. This semen coagulates rapidly and the coagulum impedes sperm movement until clot lysis occurs 15–20 mins later. However, many human spermatozoa enter the cervix within 90 secs of ejaculation, presumably before coagulation traps them, and it is likely that these are the spermatozoa which achieve fertilization.

Cervical mucus is the first obstacle encountered by spermatozoa. Various mucoids give this mucus the properties of a visco-elastic gel, but at the time of ovulation it becomes less viscid and presents less resistance to sperm ascent. Active sperm motility is probably essential for ascent through the cervical canal.

From the time of ejaculation spermatozoa reach the ampulla of the tube in approximately 30 min, covering a distance of 15 cm. It is likely that the rate of forward propulsion of human spermatozoa is of the order of 1–3 mm/min, and so it is clear that spermatozoa do not ascend the uterus by virtue of their own motility. Uterine transport is aided by powerful contractions of the myometrium which carry spermatozoa towards the uterotubal junctions. The resistance presented by this junction varies between species, but it is unlikely that it offers a major hindrance to human sperm penetration. The rapid transport of spermatozoa in the uterine tubes is dependent on tubal contractility.

During sperm ascent there is an enormous reduction in sperm number. Over 100 million spermatozoa are ejaculated into the vagina, yet normally only one spermatozoon fertilizes one ovum. The initial reduction occurs at the cervix and perhaps only one million spermatozoa enter the uterus. Further elimination occurs at the uterotubal junction, so that a few thousand spermatozoa enter the tubes, and of these perhaps only about 100 spermatozoa reach the ovum in the tubal ampulla.

The fate of surplus spermatozoa in the female genital tract is still a mystery. Undoubtedly, many simply leak from the vagina and those which do enter the uterus disappear rapidly. Spermatozoa may be removed by phagocytosis within the lumen of the uterus and also by endometrial leucocytes. Despite this rapid removal, some spermatozoa may remain fertile and motile in the female reproductive tract for 1 or 2 days.

The origin of postcoital uterine activity is still uncertain. It may be a reflex stimulus mediated through the hypothalamus and effected via either the autonomic nervous system or neurohypophysial oxytocin. It may also be due to oxytocic properties of seminal plasma.

MATURATION OF SPERMATOZOA

During their passage through the epididymis spermatozoa undergo a process of ripening or maturation with respect to both motility and fertility. This is associated with demonstrable histological changes in the middle piece of the sperm, but the cause and nature of this process are unknown. Spermatozoa entering the ductus deferens are potentially motile and fertile, but they gain further

activation by contact with the secretions of the seminal vesicles and prostate.

In some animals, particularly the rabbit and rat, there is normally a delay of a few hours between insemination and fertilization which is not simply due to sperm transport. It has been shown that during this time spermatozoa undergo further changes, **capacitation,** in the female reproductive tract which enable them to penetrate the zona pellucida. The nature of capacitation and whether or not it occurs in human spermatozoa are unknown.

MAINTENANCE OF SPERMATOZOA

Following their release from the testes, spermatozoa are entirely dependent on their local fluid environment for maintenance, and this is the function of the secretions of the various regions of the male and female reproductive tracts.

Epididymal secretions are characterized by a high concentration of glycerylphosphorylcholine and a high K^+/Na^+ ratio which may approach unity. As spermatozoa enter the ejaculatory ducts the secretions of seminal vesicles and prostate are added. The outstanding feature of vesicular secretion is the high concentration of fructose, but it also contains sorbitol, which may contribute to fructose formation, inositol, ergothioneine and prostaglandins. By contrast, prostatic secretions contain virtually no fructose, but have a high concentration of citric acid and acid phosphatase. In man, the bulbo urethral and urethral gland secretions probably have a purely lubricant action.

The function of seminal plasma is still a mystery. A great deal is known of its chemical composition (table 37.1) and a variety of unusual substances have

TABLE 37.1. Approximate concentration of non-enzymic components of human semen (after Mann).

Fructose	225	Ergothioneine	trace
Citric Acid	376	Ascorbic acid	12·
Lactic Acid	35	Cholesterol	8
Pyruvic Acid	29	Potassium	c. 10
Glycerylphosphoryl-choline	c. 70	Sodium	28
		Chloride	15
Inositol	50	Zinc	1
Sorbitol	10		

All results expressed as mg/100 ml.

been identified, but virtually nothing is known of the function of these constituents. It is important to appreciate the short period of time during which spermatozoa are in contact with seminal plasma. Mixing begins at the time of ejaculation. If it is accepted that many spermatozoa leave the seminal pool and enter the cervix within 90 sec, then these will have been in contact with seminal plasma for no more than a few minutes. Consequently it is unlikely that seminal plasma contributes to the long-term welfare of spermatozoa in terms of energy production or maturation.

It is necessary to distinguish between essential and useful functions. Undoubtedly, spermatozoa removed from the ductus deferens are potentially motile and fertile without any contact with seminal plasma. However, seminal plasma has useful, if non-essential, functions. First, it normally acts as the carrier for spermatozoa. Secondly, fructose can act as a substrate for sperm energy metabolism. Thirdly, it may also have a role in relation to the female reproductive tract. Semen has been shown to exert a powerful oxytocic effect, and this may be relevant to the increased uterine and tubal contractility which follows coitus. However, this oxytocic principle has not yet been identified.

Ejaculated spermatozoa are likely to be dependent on the secretions of the female tract following insemination, but little is known of this aspect of uterine physiology.

Onset of reproductive functions in the male

The development of the male reproductive tract is described on p. 37.58. Here we are concerned with the changes in activity which follow birth.

The testes grow very slowly until the age of 10 or 11 years, following which there is a marked acceleration in growth rate. At birth the seminiferous tubules are compact cellular structures devoid of a lumen and they are not canalized until the age of 3 or 4 years. Interstitial cells are difficult to distinguish from fibroblasts. At the age of 10 or 11 years, mitotic activity can be identified in spermatogonia and this is followed by increasing evidence of spermatogenesis and proliferation of interstitial cells. These changes in the gonads are accompanied by increase in size and activity of the accessory glands and growth of the external genitalia. The characteristic male hair pattern is initiated by the appearance of pubic hair followed one or two years later by axillary and facial hair and then by the frontoparietal recessions in scalp hair. These latter changes in scalp hair do not occur in many Asiatic males. The voice characteristically 'breaks'; both sweat and sebaceous gland activity increases, and acne is a common feature of puberty.

The rate of skeletal growth begins to accelerate shortly before puberty, and it is the varying duration and intensity of this growth phase which is responsible for most of the sex differences in stature. In males the growth spurt is more rapid and lasts for a longer time due to the relatively late closure of epiphyses, so that the height of the adult male usually exceeds that of the female.

Seminal emissions usually follow the appearance of secondary sex characters, and early spermatogenesis is frequently irregular and prone to abnormal sperm formation. Thus, there may be a period of adolescent male infertility comparable to the early anovular menstrual cycles in the female.

It is difficult to time the onset of puberty accurately in the male because of the absence of any such clear-cut phenomenon as the menarche, but it is usually between the age of 10 and 15 years. Puberty is commonly said to occur at a later age in boys than in girls, but it is virtually impossible to make any valid comparison between the sexes on the basis of recognizable external features. This could be based only on a study of the time of release of hypophysial gonadotrophins or gonadal steroids, but there are no reliable data.

The mechanisms underlying puberty are essentially similar in both sexes. It seems likely that the testes exert some control over the hypophysial release of gonadotrophins via hypothalamic centres, and that unknown changes in this system may initiate puberty. It is possible that the steroids produced by the prepubertal testes may be different from those of the mature testes. Studies on bull calves have shown a preponderance of androstenedione production as compared with the dominant secretion of testosterone in adult bulls, but it is not known if these findings apply to man.

After testicular activity is established at puberty, it normally continues for the rest of life with only slight impairment in later years. There is a slight reduction in sperm and androgen production in old age and this is associated with some degenerative changes in the testes, but there is no abrupt testicular failure comparable to the female climacteric.

PREGNANCY

This section is concerned with the development of the foetus and placenta and their integrated functions, the physiological responses of the mother to gestation, the growth and behaviour of the uterus, and lactation.

Early embryogenesis and placentation

FERTILIZATION (fig. 18.1)

For obvious reasons there have been very few observations on *in vivo* fertilization of human ova, and most information has been derived from experimentation in other species. However, there is a wide variation between species, and consequently ideas about human fertilization are partly speculative.

Within one to two hours after ovulation, an oocyte is deposited in the ampulla of a uterine tube. It measures 120–150 μm in diameter and is enclosed by a plasma membrane, or **vitelline membrane**. This in turn is surrounded by a structureless shell, the **zona pellucida**, with a potential space between the two membranes. When it is shed from the ovary, the oocyte is surrounded by a loose fringe of granulosa cells, the **corona radiata**. Following ovulation, the primary oocyte completes its reduction division with extrusion of the **first polar body**, and immediately begins the second meiotic division.

Within one hour of insemination, about a hundred motile spermatozoa find their way to the tubal ampulla. There is probably a delay before these spermatozoa can penetrate the ovum while the process of capacitation is completed, unless insemination has preceded ovulation by a few hours.

After a period of time, ova lose their capacity for fertilization. This time varies from a few hours in rabbits to a few days in dogs, and although there is some uncertainty about the behaviour of human ova it is unlikely that they are readily fertilizable after 24–48 hours from shedding. Ageing of ova is a gradual rather than an all-or-none process; ageing ova may still be fertilized but are susceptible to anomalous mechanisms of fertilization. Spermatozoa probably also lose their ability to fertilize 24–48 hours after ejaculation. These factors are relevant to methods of family planning based on the safe period, and it is important to realize that, while they apply to concepts of optimal or adequate fertility, exceptional cases are well documented where both ova and spermatozoa appear to have remained functionally viable for longer periods of time.

The method of penetration of the ovum is still uncertain, but three stages have been recognized. Spermatozoa may first have to penetrate the granulosa cells of the corona radiata, and this has been claimed to be the function of hyaluronidase present in the acrosome. However, the acrosome is poorly developed in human spermatozoa and contains relatively little hyaluronidase. The second barrier is the zona pellucida and the sperm head contains enzymes which lyse this layer. Finally the spermatozoon penetrates the vitelline membrane, and it is likely that this occurs by fusion of the plasma membranes when the spermatozoon comes into contact with the vitelline membrane.

The ovum is normally surrounded by many spermatozoa and there must be an effective mechanism to limit penetration by more than one spermatozoon. This is probably achieved by the relative impenetrability of the zona pellucida. Ageing of the ovum is associated with a breakdown in this mechanism, so that more than one spermatozoon may fuse with the ovum, and more than one male pronucleus may combine with the female pronucleus. Thus, in the case of dispermic fertilization a triploid zygote is produced. Ageing of the ovum is almost certainly an important factor in human infertility and pregnancy wastage. In most animals, ovulation follows a short period of sexual excitement when the female accepts the male, or alternatively ovulation is reflexly triggered by copulation, and these mechanisms ensure that insemination and ovulation coincide. There are no comparable features in human reproduction to ensure the fusion of fresh spermatozoa and ova and

fertilization of ageing ova is likely to be a common occurrence. This is confirmed by the recent finding of many triploid embryos in spontaneously aborted conceptuses.

The immediate result of sperm entry is to activate the oocyte to complete the second meiotic division and extrude the **second polar body**. Both the spermatozoon and nucleus of the ovum undergo changes leading to the formation of male and female **pronuclei**, containing the haploid sets of paternal and maternal chromosomes. The pronuclear membranes are lost, a spindle forms, and the chromosomes come to lie along the equatorial plate. Each chromosome divides into a pair of chromatids, one of each pair segregates to opposite poles, and the first cleavage division results in the formation of two diploid cells, or **blastomeres**.

Successive mitotic divisions produce a cluster of blastomeres, or **morula**, within the confines of the zona pellucida. During these early cleavage divisions the blastomeres depend on the nutrients which were stored in the cytoplasm of the ovum prior to fertilization. As these nutrients are gradually metabolized, there is a progressive shrinkage in the volume of the total cytoplasmic material of the cell mass. Thus, although the number of blastomeres increases, there is no increase in the overall volume. This is essential to allow passage of the morula, with a diameter of 120–150 μm, to pass through the tubal isthmus.

Transport of the conceptus from the tubal ampulla to the uterus is due to a flow of tubal fluid induced by tubal peristalsis and ciliary action, and the morula arrives in the uterus three or four days after fertilization. Within the next two or three days, fluid from the endometrial secretions passes through the zona pellucida and accumulates to form a central cavity which becomes surrounded by blastomeres. As soon as the morula acquires this central cavity it is known as a **blastocyst**. The cells which constitute the blastocyst can now be differentiated into the surface cells, known as **trophoblast**, and cells which are attached to their inner aspect at one pole of the blastocyst where they form the **inner cell mass**.

IMPLANTATION

At this stage the blastocyst reaches a crisis of nutrition as the supplies of cytoplasmic nutrients rapidly become exhausted and it becomes essential for it to implant in the endometrium so that the trophoblast can obtain nutriment for the developing embryo from the maternal tissues. This process is a critical phase in embryogenesis and a large number of blastocysts fail to achieve it.

Implantation may be said to have started when the blastocyst becomes denuded of its zona pellucida, as the result mainly of trophoblastic activity, possibly aided by maternal secretions from the endometrium. In this way the trophoblast comes into direct contact with the endo metrium to which it can then attach itself. Thus, the persistence of the zona pellucida during the free-life or progestational phase of pregnancy not only binds the blastomeres of the morula together but also prevents the blastomeres from attaching themselves prematurely to the tubal mucous membrane.

The extent of trophoblastic penetration and the consequent degree of intimacy established between the embryonic trophoblast (later the **chorion**) and the maternal endometrium is of special importance in determining the thickness of the membrane (placental membrane) interposed between the embryonic (later foetal) blood stream and that of the mother, and across which the exchanges between mother and embryo (or foetus) must take place. In species in which trophoblastic penetration is minimal or non-existent the endometrial epithelium remains more or less intact so that the chorion merely lies in contact with it. Such a placenta is described as **epitheliochorial**. In other species the trophoblast erodes the maternal epithelium so that the chorion comes into contact with the endothelium of the maternal blood vessels. Such a placenta is described as **endotheliochorial**. In man, and in many other species, the trophoblast destroys not only the maternal epithelium and connective tissue stroma, but also the endothelium of the maternal blood vessels. In this way the maternal blood comes to bathe the chorion directly, and such a placenta is described as being **haemochorial**.

Maternal factors in implantation

Before implantation takes place not only does the blastocyst lose its zona pellucida, but the endometrium is modified. At the time of implantation, which begins about 7 days after ovulation, the endometrium is in the progestational stage corresponding to the 21st day of the cycle (p. 37.18). The stroma is oedematous, especially at the implantation site, the capillaries are especially prominent at this site, and the glands are extremely tortuous and actively secreting glycogen and mucus.

The maternal control of the implantation process appears to be exercised by ovarian progesterone although oestrogens may also play a role. In some species there is an oestrogen surge just prior to implantation. As soon as implantation begins, the endometrium becomes modified and gives rise to a phenomenon known as the **decidual reaction**. This transformation involves the surface epithelium, the glands, the stroma and the blood vessels. The stromal cells become polyhedral and dilated with glycogen and lipids. Mucopolysaccharides accumulate not only in these decidual cells but also in the ground substance of the endometrium. The decidual reaction is an exaggeration of the changes that take place in the postovulatory phase of the menstrual cycle and is probably an adaptation for the nutrition of the embryo. It may also be a defensive reaction on the part of the mother retarding and limiting the invasive activity of the embryonic trophoblast.

Embryonic factors in implantation (fig. 37.30 & 18.2)

About 6½–7 days after fertilization, the zona pellucida having disappeared, the trophoblast covering the inner

FIG. 37.30. Early attachment of blastocyst to uterine epithelium in macaque. From Hamilton W.J., Boyd J.D. & Mossman H.W. (1962) *Human Embryology*, 3rd Edition. Cambridge: Heffer.

cell mass (**polar trophoblast**) attaches the blastocyst to the endometrium, most frequently on the upper part of the posterior wall of the body of the uterus near the midsagittal plane.

The initial attachment has not been observed in man, but EM studies in other species indicate that the polar trophoblast fuses with the endometrial epithelium, penetrating its basement membrane to invade the underlying stroma. At this stage no plasma membrane is interposed between the embryonic and maternal cytoplasm so that a very intimate relationship is established, with possibilities for the exchange of molecular information which may have a bearing on the immunological relationship which exists between mother and embryo.

The polar trophoblast which effects the initial attachment acquires characteristics which distinguish it from the trophoblast covering those aspects of the blastocyst which are still unattached and exposed to the uterine lumen. The latter kind of trophoblast consists of flattened cells, whereas the polar trophoblast becomes invasive and consists of a mixture of variously sized basophilic cells, some of which are huge and some of which coalesce to form small masses of syncytium.

The youngest known attached human blastocyst has an estimated age of not more than 7½ days from ovulation and it is already partially implanted. The trophoblast has eroded the uterine epithelium and penetrated the underlying stroma which is congested and oedematous possibly

due to the liberation of some substance from the trophoblast. The trophoblast which invades the endometrium
has a thick plaque of primitive, invasive, pleomorphic
cells, while the free part of the blastocyst wall consists of
a layer of flattened cells.

By the 11th or 12th day after fertilization the human
blastocyst becomes buried beneath the endometrial
epithelium and is completely embedded in the stroma,
During this phase of implantation the endometrium is
digested by the trophoblast so that nutritive material is
supplied to the embryo which develops from the inner
cell mass of the blastocyst. Another result of this
digestive process is that the blastocyst sinks into the
endometrium 'like a hot marble placed on ice'.

As implantation reaches completion, the blastocyst
lies in the superficial part of the compact layer of the
endometrium (p. 37.18) and it produces a slight swelling
on the endometrial surface. In the vicinity of the trophoblast the stromal cells become transformed into decidual
cells and a zone of vascular congestion and oedema
spreads towards the deeper layers and also laterally. The
defect in the endometrial epithelium caused by the invasion of the blastocyst is gradually closed, first by a plug
of fibrin and subsequently by proliferation of the adjacent
epithelium.

During and after implantation changes occur in the
primitive invasive trophoblast. The innermost part in
contact with the embryonic tissues becomes organized
into a regular layer of uniform cells, or **cytotrophoblast**. At the same time isolated vacuoles appear in
the more peripheral pleomorphic trophoblast. These
vacuoles become confluent to form intercommunicating
lacunae (the future **intervillous spaces**). As a result,
this outer invasive trophoblast consists of irregular
trabecular strands of a mixture of pleomorphic cells and
small plaques of syncytium, **syncytiotrophoblast**. The
peripheral part of the primitive trophoblast continues to
invade and digest adjacent decidua, glands and blood
vessels and to absorb the extravasated blood.

By the 12th day the primitive trophoblastic trabeculae
and the lacunar spaces are well established but are not
uniformly developed around the conceptus. Whereas the
trophoblastic components are thick around the sides and
deeper parts of the embryo, there is only a thin layer
of trophoblast towards the endometrial surface, probably due to the poorer supply of nutriment in this
region. All round the embryo the junction between the
trophoblast and the maternal tissue has an irregular
contour, owing to the invasion of the endometrium by
irregular outgrowths from the trophoblast.

Implantation allows the embryo to establish a supply
of nutrients from the endometrium and its blood vessels.
The capillaries in the vicinity of the invading trophoblast
are congested and the blood in them tends to stagnate.
The trophoblast invades these capillaries so that blood
passes into the trophoblastic lacunae and soon circulates
through them. Although these capillaries are fed by
the coiled endometrial arterioles, the initial circulation
through the lacunae is sluggish.

*Functional interrelationship between embryo and mother
during implantation*

Implantation is the product of the interplay between
trophoblastic invasion and maternal tissue reactions.
The pre-implantation changes in the endometrium are
controlled by maternal hormones. However, once implantation has started the blastocyst probably produces
substances which not only affect the endometrium locally
(the decidual reaction) but also exert a systemic influence
on the mother.

The receptive property of the endometrium and the
invasive behaviour of the trophoblast are two complementary phenomena. The embryo-maternal relationship is biologically akin to a parasite-host relationship, and normally there is a balance between the
invasiveness of the trophoblast and the protective reaction of the endometrium.

Another relevant aspect of this interrelationship is that
whereas the primitive trophoblast is highly invasive
and irregular it subsequently becomes organized into
distinct layers of cytotrophoblast and syncytiotrophoblast. Cytotrophoblast consists of cellular layers with
intercellular boundaries separating the nuclei, whereas
syncytiotrophoblast consists of multinucleated masses of
cytoplasm in which the nuclei are not separated by intercellular boundaries. Other trophoblastic giant cells
invade deeper than this organized trophoblast but they
do not destroy maternal tissue but rather intermingle
with it. It would seem that as trophoblast differentiates,
it becomes less invasive. In some cases the balance between trophoblast and endometrium may be disturbed.
Overactivity of the trophoblast may result in the formation of hydatidiform mole or chorionepithelioma,
whereas if the endometrium is too resistant to trophoblastic invasion the embryo cannot become properly
established in the uterus and dies, being either absorbed
or aborted.

The blastocyst may implant in a number of abnormal
positions, most commonly in the uterine tubes, but
occasionally in the ovaries, abdominal cavity or cervix.
The occurrence of these ectopic pregnancies demonstrates
clearly that the embryo can implant in conditions which
differ from the optimal environment provided by the
progestational endometrium.

The decidua (fig. 37.31)

The endometrial lining of the uterus is greatly modified
during pregnancy and is called decidua because it is
shed at subsequent parturition. After implantation and
until about the 4th month of gestation, three parts of the

decidua can be distinguished. **Decidua basalis** is the part which is deep to the implantation site and forms the base of the developing placenta. **Decidua capsularis** covers or encapsulates the surface of the implanted embryo. **Decidua parietalis** lines the rest of the uterus.

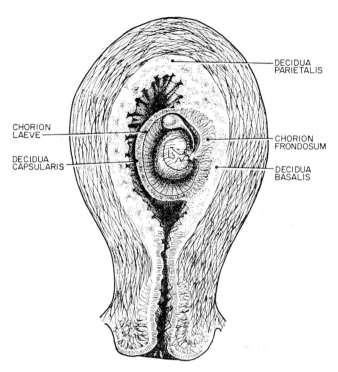

FIG. 37.31. Relation of chorion to different parts of the decidua. From Williams (1927) *Amer. J. Obstet. Gynae.* **31**, 1.

As the foetus grows and expands, the chorion becomes stretched, with a very thin covering of decidua capsularis and projects into the uterine lumen. Eventually the capsular decidua comes into contact with the decidua parietalis, so obliterating the uterine cavity. The decidua capsularis degenerates, and the chorion fuses with the decidua parietalis by the 5th month of pregnancy. At birth the decidua parietalis and basalis are torn away when the placenta is expelled.

Suppression of menstruation

The timing of implantation in relation to ovarian and endometrial cycles is critical. In an ovulatory 28-day cycle ovulation occurs around the 14th day, and the corpus luteum begins to regress about the 24th day resulting in endometrial shedding on the 28th day. Implantation begins about 7 days after fertilization, i.e. around day 21.

There is thus only a short period of three or four days between implantation and luteolysis during which subsequent menstruation must be suppressed. This is achieved by the production by the trophoblast of a powerful luteotrophin, **chorionic gonadotrophin** (p. 37.44), whose immediate function is to maintain the corpus luteum and ovarian production of steroids and so preserve and complete decidualization of the endometrium. Chorionic gonadotrophin has, in fact, been identified on day 25 of the menstrual cycle.

Development of the embryonic or foetal membranes and of the placenta (fig. 37.32)

In order to understand the development of these structures it is necessary to refer to the salient features of early embryonic development (chap. 18). By $7\frac{1}{2}$ days after fertilization the inner cell mass has developed into a disc of polyhedral ectodermal cells separated from the polar trophoblast by a space which will become the **amniotic cavity**. In relation to the inner surface of the disc some flattened endodermal cells have differentiated.

In the course of the next 4 or 5 days, the ectodermal cells form a disc of columnar cells in continuity with the flattened cells lining the amniotic cavity. The endodermal cells form a well defined layer of cubical cells related to the under surface of the embryonic ectoderm and together they form a bilaminar **embryonic disc**. While these changes are taking place, mesoblastic cells differentiate in relation to the inner aspect of the trophoblast and these mesoblastic cells proliferate to give rise to **extraembryonic mesoderm**.

By the 12th day after fertilization the inner aspect of the extraembryonic mesoderm facing the blastocyst cavity forms a well defined membrane of flattened mesothelial cells continuous with the margin of the endoderm of the embryonic disc. The space enclosed by endoderm and the mesothelial membrane is the **primitive yolk sac**. The trophoblastic cells with their lining of extraembryonic mesoderm constitute the **chorion**. As the chorion completely surrounds the developing embryo and its membranes the whole spherical structure is often referred to as a **chorionic vesicle**.

Expansion of the chorion is accompanied by an increase in extraembryonic mesoderm in which small cavities soon appear. These coalesce and an **extraembryonic coelom** is established as a space which eventually separates the yolk sac and the amnion from the chorion except at the future caudal end of the embryonic disc where the mesoderm persists as a solid cord, the **connecting body stalk**. As a result of the development of the extraembryonic coelom, the mesoderm is split into two layers. One covers the yolk sac and amnion, and the other lines the chorion. The layers are continuous with one another at the connecting stalk.

While the extraembryonic coelom is developing, endoderm originating from the embryonic disc grows round the inner aspect of the mesothelial membrane of the primary yolk sac to form a **secondary yolk sac**.

By the fifteenth day, the primitive streak (p. 18.4) has appeared in the caudal half of the embryonic disc and it gives rise to the intraembryonic mesoderm, but its caudal end also contributes mesoderm to the developing connecting stalk.

DEVELOPMENT OF THE YOLK SAC

As the result of the formation of the head and tail folds in the embryonic disc, parts of the secondary yolk sac become enclosed within the embryo as the foregut and hindgut respectively. The intervening part now forming the roof of the yolk sac is the midgut.

With the development of the lateral body folds in relation to the sides of the midgut the communication between the midgut and the yolk sac becomes constricted, and the latter is excluded from the inside of the embryo proper. The yolk sac, which now communicates with the

DEVELOPMENT OF THE AMNION AND UMBILICAL CORD

As already described, the amnion appears as a split in the inner cell mass. The size of the cavity rapidly increases and becomes lined by cells delaminated from the inner aspect of the related trophoblast and by ectodermal cells growing up from the margins of the embryonic disc.

The amnion is initially attached to the chorion by a very broad connecting stalk of extraembryonic mesoderm. With extension of the extraembryonic coelom into the mesoderm of the connecting stalk, the amnion becomes separated from the inner aspect of the chorion by the extraembryonic coelom except in relation to the caudal end of the embryo. Here the attachment of the embryonic disc and the amnion to the chorion persists as the definitive connecting stalk.

The separation of the amnion from the chorion allows

FIG. 37.32. Formation of the amnion and yolk sac. (a) and (b) represent successive stages of development.

midgut by means of a **vitello-intestinal duct**, is known as the **definitive yolk sac.** This structure reaches a size of about 5 mm diameter and persists until term as a small vesicle applied to the inner surface of the chorion. The vitello-intestinal duct normally disappears after the loop of midgut has returned to the developing abdominal cavity.

DEVELOPMENT OF THE ALLANTOIS

The allantois develops as a diverticulum from the caudal wall of the yolk sac and its site of origin comes to lie at the junction between the hindgut and the definitive yolk sac. The allantois grows into the mesoderm of the connecting stalk in which blood vessels develop which later become the paired umbilical arteries and the single umbilical vein. In man the allantois remains small, but as the vascularization of the placenta is effected through the blood vessels which differentiate in the mesoderm around the allantois, it is of great functional significance and the human placenta is described as being **chorioallantoic.**

the amnion to expand in the enlarging extraembryonic coelom. Growth of the amnion brings its superficial aspect into contact with the inner aspect of the chorion so that the extraembryonic coelom is progressively obliterated until only a cleft remains, separating the amnion and chorion.

With the development of head, tail and lateral body folds, and with the growth and differentiation of embryonic form, the junction between the amnion and the ectoderm of the embryo comes to be situated progressively on its ventral aspect. Thus a large **umbilicus** is established. In the early stages of its development the umbilicus transmits the vitelline duct, coils of intestine and possibly the allantois, all flanked by the communication between the intraembryonic and the extraembryonic coelom. As the amnion expands it comes to ensheath the connecting stalk, the vitello-intestinal duct and extraembryonic coelom, and the region contained within the resulting tubular sheath of amnion is the **umbilical cord.**

The mesodermal cells forming the core of the umbilical cord become converted into loose mesenchyme embedded in a jelly-like intercellular matrix. This is Wharton's jelly, through which the umbilical vessels and the allantois pass. At first the umbilical cord is short but it lengthens rapidly.

As pregnancy advances, the outer surface of the amnion fuses with varying degrees of intimacy with the inner aspect of the chorion so that at term the two membranes may be partially fused. From the foregoing description it will be realized that the amnion forms a closed bag which, because it is filled with a watery fluid, **amniotic fluid**, provides a supporting aquatic environment in which the embryo is free to move as it develops.

DEVELOPMENT OF CHORIONIC VILLI AND THE EARLY PLACENTA (fig. 37.33)

When maternal blood enters the lacunar spaces of the primitive trophoblast it constitutes a new source of nutrition for the embryo. For the first few days after

inner single layer of cytotrophoblast and an outer layer of syncytiotrophoblast, thus constituting **secondary villi**.

When an embryonic vascular system has become established in the mesodermal core of these villi, they are known as **tertiary villi**. These villous vessels link up with the embryonic cardiovascular system by way of vessels which differentiate in the mesoderm of the inner chorionic surface and in the connecting stalk. The first villous columns to be established constitute the **anchoring villi** or **stem villi** from which shorter branch villi subsequently develop. Cytotrophoblastic extrusions from the anchoring villi mushroom out from their distal points of contact with the endometrium and, by linking up with adjoining outgrowths, form a complete **cytotrophoblastic shell** which now attaches the chorionic vesicle to the maternal tissues. The endometrium adjoining this shell is known as the **boundary zone** and it is

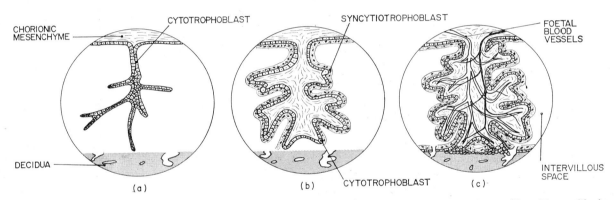

FIG. 37.33. Development of the placental villi. (a) primary villus; (b) secondary villus; (c) tertiary villus. From Glenister T.W.A. & Ross J.R.W. (1965) *Anatomy and Physiology for Nurses*. London: Heinemann.

implantation nutrient reaches the embryo by diffusion, but as the embryo grows, the development of a simple circulatory system becomes a necessity. The chorionic vesicle has become too large for diffusion to be able to provide for its metabolic processes adequately. The functioning of an embryonic heart and blood vessels starts 3 weeks after fertilization. During the period when the chorion is differentiating and growing vigorously, 9 to 20 days after fertilization, the villous character of the definitive placenta is established.

Whereas the trophoblastic trabeculae are initially arranged irregularly, they soon tend to be disposed radially round the chorion. They become recognizable as villous structures and the lacunae form the intervillous space. Soon these trabeculae acquire a core of cytotrophoblast and are called **primary villi**. The cytotrophoblastic cores extend gradually to the region where the primitive trophoblast reaches the endometrium. These villous stems subsequently acquire mesodermal cores and the trophoblast becomes organized around them as an

separated from actual contact with the trophoblast by a layer of fibrinoid deposit known as Nitabuch's membrane. This boundary zone is traversed by the maternal blood vessels on their way to and from the intervillous space.

It is the cytotrophoblastic shell which, by its interstitial growth, provides the mechanism for circumferential extension of the chorionic vesicle. Expansion of the cytotrophoblastic shell increases the volume of the intervillous space by encroachment upon the surrounding decidua. The area of trophoblast exposed to maternal blood in the intervillous space is also increased by the sprouting of branch villi from the primary stems. These pass through the successive stages of being primary, secondary and eventually vascularized tertiary villi.

These villi which are directed towards the decidua basalis enlarge and branch elaborately while those which are directed towards the decidua capsularis degenerate between the 3rd and 4th months of pregnancy. In this way the chorion which protrudes along with the decidua capsularis into the uterine lumen becomes the smooth, almost avascular **chorion laeve**, whereas the chorion in contact with the decidua basalis where the villi persist becomes the **chorion frondosum**. (Fig. 37.31.) The chorion frondosum progressively assumes the discoidal shape of the definitive placenta.

At implantation the decidua basalis is only 5–6 mm thick and the increase in the thickness of the placenta as it grows takes place by an increase in the number, length and size of the villi. Growth in thickness as well as circumference continues in the placenta until the end of the 4th month after which only circumferential growth continues until almost the end of pregnancy.

Once the cytotrophoblastic shell has been laid down in the 4th week of pregnancy, small multinucleated masses of syncytium known as trophoblast giant cells migrate from the periphery of the shell and extend into the decidua basalis and beyond it to the adjoining myometrium. Cytotrophoblastic elements also invade and extend up the spiral arteries of the endometrium, and sprouts of syncytiotrophoblast from the villi are shed into the intervillous space from which they are carried into the maternal veins and eventually reach the lungs. The cytotrophoblast which plugs the spiral arteries may play a mechanical role in preventing maternal arterial blood from reaching the intervillous space at too high a pressure.

THE MATURE PLACENTA (fig. 37.34)

The mature placenta has the form of a flattened circular disc, with a diameter of 15–20 cm and a thickness of 3 cm. At full maturity, the ratio of infant weight to placental weight is about 6:1, so that a placenta usually weighs about 500 g at term.

The attachment of the umbilical cord to the placenta is usually eccentric but it may vary from being near central to a marginal situation. The length of the umbilical cord varies from 30 to 100 cm with an average length of about 55 cm.

The placenta is essentially a structure which provides a large area of apposition between the maternal and foetal circulations for the exchange of materials. These transfers are controlled by the placental membrane which separates the two circulations.

FOETAL PLACENTAL CIRCULATION (fig. 37.35)

Foetal blood is conveyed to the placenta via paired umbilical arteries. The details of the circulation within the foetus are described on p. 39.2. The two umbilical arteries anastomose as they approach the placenta and their branches then ramify over the surface of the chorion. In the **disperse** type of vascular distribution the two umbilical arteries undergo dichotomous division and rapidly

diminish in calibre, whereas in the **magistral** type they give off only small branches and reach close to the placental margin before their calibre is reduced to any significant extent.

Branches of the umbilical arteries pierce the chorion and form the main stem vessels for the placental villi. Each stem branch is an end artery which does not anastomose with adjacent vessels, and each vascularizes a discrete group of villi which takes the form of an inverted cone or cylinder. These villous units are known as **foetal cotyledons**. They are approximately 200 in number and they vary widely in size. Each main stem artery divides repeatedly within its cotyledon to supply a complicated, root-like structure of villi. In the terminal villi the foetal vessels form an extensive arterio–capillary–venous system

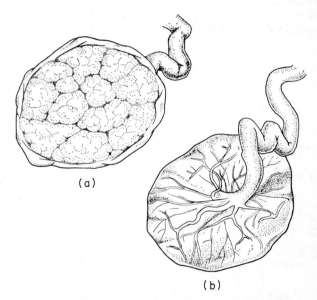

(a)

(b)

FIG. 37.34. Gross appearances of the mature placenta. (a) Maternal surface, (b) foetal surface. From Netter F.H. (1954) *The Ciba Collection of Medical Illustrations*.

such that the foetal capillaries come into very close proximity with the villous membrane. The veins which drain the villi track back along the course of the corresponding arteries and eventually reach the site of insertion of the umbilical cord where they fuse to form a single umbilical vein. Oxygenated blood is thus returned to the foetus via the umbilical vein. There are no valves in this extended umbilical venous circulation. The umbilical veins and arteries are muscular structures, but they are not innervated and little is known of the control of the foetal placental circulation.

The umbilical vessels follow a tortuous spiral course as they traverse the cord, and are embedded in the gelatinous matrix of Wharton's jelly. The amnion is fused with the external surface of the cord (fig. 37.36).

FIG. 37.35. A composite diagram of foetal and maternal placental circulations. (a) Villous architecture, (b) villous circulation in section, (c) maternal circulation, showing arterial jets entering intervillous space, (d) diagram of direction of maternal blood flow in intervillous space, (e) placental margin. From Eastman M.J. & Hellman L.M. (1966) *Williams Obstetrics*, 13th Edition. New York:Appleton-Century-Crofts.

MATERNAL PLACENTAL CIRCULATION (fig. 37.35)
It is convenient to regard the mature placenta as a blood-filled space, the intervillous or **choriodecidual space**, which is lined by trophoblast. This space is limited by a maternal surface, or **decidual plate**, and a foetal surface or **chorionic plate**, and these surfaces fuse around the circumference of the placenta. The villi of the foetal cotyledons project into the space from the chorionic plate. Some of these are anchoring villi which attach themselves to the decidual plate, while the branching villi extend freely in the intervillous space. The exact architecture of the villi is controversial but it is unlikely that there is any foetal vascular communication between adjacent villi. The villi are closely crowded together and must not be visualized as floating freely within a roomy space.

Septa extend from the decidual plate towards the chorionic plate, but they fail to reach the foetal surface. When the maternal surface of an expelled placenta is examined the placenta appears to be composed of 15–20 lobes, the clefts between these lobes representing the base of these placental septa. However, these lobes do not constitute subdivisions of the intervillous space and they are of no functional significance. They are sometimes referred to as cotyledons, but these must not be confused with the foetal cotyledonary villous unit.

Approximately 80–100 maternal arteries open haphazardly over the decidual plate into the choriodecidual space. Blood enters the placenta from these arteries

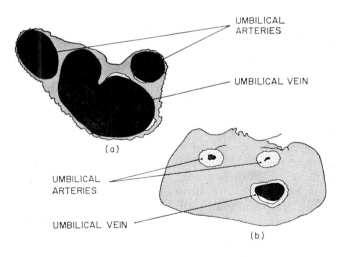

FIG. 37.36. Section through the umbilical cord. (a) Vessels distended with blood, (b) vessels constricted down after cord has been clamped. From Reynolds (1954) *Amer. J. Obstet. & Gynec.* **68**, 69.

under high pressure, and this jet of maternal blood reaches towards the chorionic plate before dispersing laterally through the interstices of the villi. The exact spatial relation of the decidual arteries to the foetal cotyledons is unknown. Blood leaves the intervillous space by veins which are scattered over the decidual plate. The previous belief that maternal blood drained only from the periphery of the placenta via a marginal sinus is incorrect. The so-called marginal sinus is no more than the peripheral limit of the intervillous space. This dynamic concept of the circulation of maternal blood through the placenta has been confirmed by cinematographic studies of uteroplacental blood flow.

The uterus contracts intermittently throughout pregnancy. The circulatory effect of these contractions is probably first to occlude the myometrial veins and only later may they obliterate the myometrial arteries supplying the placenta. Consequently, a uterine contraction does not squeeze blood out of the choriodecidual space and halt the transfer of oxygen to the foetus. However, the stronger contractions of labour temporarily impair maternal arterial blood supply and this may induce transient foetal hypoxia.

THE PLACENTAL MEMBRANE (fig. 37.37)

The placental or villous membrane is the structure which is interposed between maternal and foetal blood. The transfer of substances between mother and foetus is controlled by this membrane and it has, in addition, several important biosynthetic functions.

The villous membrane is composed of four components. Each villus has two layers of trophoblast, an outer layer of syncytiotrophoblast which is in contact with maternal blood, and an inner layer of cytotrophoblast. This trophoblast layer is supported by a basement membrane. Within the villus core there is a connective tissue stroma within which lie the foetal capillaries lined by their vascular endothelium. At this stage, four cellular layers separate maternal from foetal blood: (1) syncytiotrophoblast, (2) cytotrophoblast, (3) connective tissue fibroblasts, (4) foetal capillary endothelium.

As pregnancy advances there is a gradual thinning of this villous membrane. The number and size of foetal capillaries increases and the relative amount of villous stroma is reduced so that capillaries appear to abut directly on to the basement membrane. The cytotrophoblast becomes much scantier and by the end of pregnancy only a few scattered cytotrophoblast cells can be recognized by standard light microscopy. The syncytiotrophoblast thins and its nuclei clump into groups, or syncytial knots. Consequently, the villous membrane is greatly reduced in thickness, but at no time do the two circulations come into direct contact and there is always some representation of all four cellular layers.

Electron microscopy has contributed enormously to our knowledge of the placental membrane. The syncytiotrophoblast has an elaborate structure. Its free surface is covered by microvilli and it has a complicated system of intracellular canals, vacuoles and endoplasmic reticulum. In later pregnancy the syncytiotrophoblast makes direct contact with the basement membrane. This ultrastructure is suggestive of a major transfer and secretory role for the syncytiotrophoblast.

By contrast, the cytotrophoblast has a relatively simple structure with fewer intracellular organelles. It is the current belief that the syncytiotrophoblast is derived from the cytotrophoblast. The cytotrophoblast may be regarded as a relatively undifferentiated reserve cell which, under optimal conditions, produces a specialized syncytium.

This thinning of the placental membrane, the appearance of syncytial knots and the apparent loss of cytotrophoblast have been interpreted as placental ageing and assumed to indicate failing placental function. Undoubtedly these structural changes are paralleled by equally profound biochemical changes. Furthermore, there are other alterations which may be more conclusively degenerative, e.g. thickening of the basement membrane, degeneration and partial obliteration of the decidual arteries, the deposition of fibrin in the intervillous space, and calcification. However, some of the above histological changes in the placental membrane may constitute a useful adaptation to facilitate transfer. The correlation between placental ultrastructure and function is still poorly understood.

The immunological problems underlying pregnancy have already been indicated. A striking feature of pregnancy is the tolerance of a genetically dissimilar foetus within the maternal tissues. This confrontation takes place at the choriodecidual junction where the foetal trophoblast makes intimate contact with the endometrium.

Functions of the placenta

In physiological terms the placenta is a foetal organ and must be considered as an integral part of the foetus. This concept of the functional interdependence between the foetus and its placenta is conveyed by the expression foetoplacental unit. Anatomically the placenta is simply an extension of the foetal capillary bed covered by a layer of trophoblast, and provides a large surface area (10 m²) in intimate contact with maternal blood. A newborn infant acquires nutrients from, and excretes waste products into its environment at a number of specialized sites, lungs, kidneys and gut. By contrast, the only effective environment of the foetus is the mother's blood, and the placenta is the principal site for the exchange of all materials. It will be shown that the placental villi fulfil many of the functions of the lung alveoli, renal glomeruli and tubules and intestinal epithelium, in addition to which they also produce protein and steroid hormones. This versatile organ has a uniquely short life and rapidly becomes senescent if pregnancy proceeds beyond its normal span of forty weeks.

TRANSFER OF NUTRIENTS

For many years it was believed that the thin placental barrier separating maternal blood from foetal blood was little more than a semipermeable membrane, but this simple hypothesis has proved inadequate and more elaborate transfer mechanisms such as active transport or pinocytosis are involved. In view of the elaborate ultrastructure of the villous membrane and the synthetic and degradative biochemical reactions which it performs, it is misleading to think of simple concentration gradients across the placenta between maternal and foetal blood

transferrin, fibrinogen and IgS (19S) globulins do not reach the foetus.

Oxygen is unusual among nutrients in that it cannot be stored, and deprivation for even a few minutes is fatal. The oxygen requirement of the foetus can only be guessed, but it probably consumes oxygen at the same rate as comparable maternal tissues. In this respect it differs from the newborn infant whose relatively large surface area in relation to its body weight demands a higher metabolic rate. At term, the foetus utilizes oxygen at about 12 ml/min (4 ml/min/kg), and the placenta at about 4 ml/min (8 ml/min/kg). These figures indicate the high metabolic activity of the placenta.

The observed oxygen difference between uterine arterial and venous blood is 4–5 ml O_2/100 ml blood. Thus, to supply the foetus and placenta with 16 ml O_2/min, the mother must circulate 300–400 ml blood/min to the

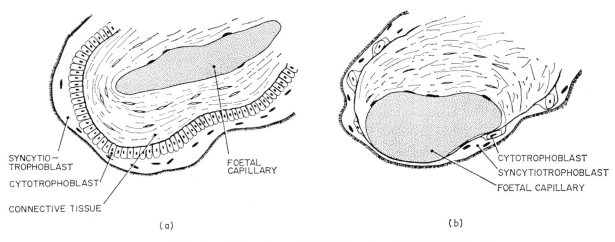

FIG. 37.37. Histology of the placental villi in (a) early and (b) late pregnancy.

according to which substances pass by passive diffusion. Simple diffusion can explain the transfer of gases and water between mother and foetus, but the transport mechanisms for other molecules are not understood in detail.

Sugars may pass directly from mother to foetus but in early pregnancy the placenta synthesizes glycogen from maternal glucose, and releases glucose into the foetus by glycolysis.

Amino acids also cross the placenta freely, and there is evidence that the placenta takes up some amino acids from the mother's blood selectively and more avidly than even the liver. Most proteins do not cross the placenta intact. For example, the albumin in foetal blood is structurally different from maternal plasma albumin. One exception to this rule is the IgG (7S) group of immunoglobulins which do cross the placenta in late pregnancy. Larger maternal proteins such as albumin,

placental site. This is less than the value of 500–600 ml/min obtained by most estimates of uterine blood flow at term. The rate of blood flow through the foetal side of the placental circulation is of a similar magnitude.

At term, foetal blood is relatively poorly oxygenated, the P_{O_2} of umbilical venous blood ranging from 20 to 50 mm. Yet there is no evidence of anaerobic metabolism and, under normal conditions, foetal plasma lactate levels are about 1 mEq/l, values similar to those found in resting adults. However, the foetus can compensate for this hypoxia in several ways. First, the foetus is, by adult standards, polycythaemic, with normal values of 4.35×10^6 red cells/mm^3 and 16·5 g haemoglobin/100 ml, thereby increasing the oxygen carrying capacity of foetal blood. Secondly, the oxygen dissociation curve of foetal blood is shifted to the left of that for adult blood (p. 29.18). This is not due to any chemical property of foetal haemoglobin, but possibly to the lower intracellular pH of the foetal erythrocyte. As a consequence, foetal blood can achieve higher degrees of oxygen saturation at low levels of oxygen tension. For example, if maternal blood with a Po_2 of 30 mm and 60 per cent saturation equilibrates with foetal blood, the foetal blood will be 70 per cent saturated. Finally, the human foetus probably shares the ability of most foetal animals to survive hypoxia more readily than the adult.

TRANSFER OF WASTE PRODUCTS

The major waste product of foetal metabolism, carbon dioxide, diffuses across the placenta even more readily than oxygen, and this process is aided by the low Pco_2 of the maternal plasma.

Urea and other waste products pass across the placenta for disposal by the mother. The foetus also uses its own kidneys and urine is passed into the amniotic fluid from early pregnancy onwards. However, it is unlikely that this is an important avenue of waste disposal, and solutes excreted in the foetal urine probably do not cross the amnion directly. The foetus swallows amniotic fluid and it is likely that waste substances are ingested by the foetus and ultimately eliminated by the placenta.

The heat of foetal metabolism must also be dissipated by the mother; hence the necessity for an increased maternal skin blood flow.

TRANSFER OF HARMFUL SUBSTANCES

Ideally, the placenta should permit the transfer of only nutrients and waste products and exclude harmful substances from the foetus, but its powers of discrimination are limited.

Most mineral ions cross the placenta freely, and their radioactive isotopes behave in a similar way. However, in the case of strontium, the mother rather than the placenta plays a protective role, binding the strontium in her own bones so that relatively little passes to the foetus. Gases pass through the placenta without hindrance. Carbon monoxide is a common example, and the carboxyhaemoglobin content of foetal blood is raised if the mother smokes cigarettes during pregnancy. The placenta allows most drugs to cross, and some drugs exert not only their normal pharmacological effect on the foetus, but may also cause malformations.

The placenta is more effective in excluding microorganisms. Bacteria, such as the tubercle bacillus or the syphilis spirochaete, reach the foetus only by first damaging the placenta. Some viruses, especially the virus of rubella or German measles, cross the placenta and damage the foetus.

The placenta prevents free mixing of maternal and foetal blood, but foetal red cells not infrequently cross over to the mother in small numbers, and are responsible for the occasional sensitization of a rhesus negative mother to her rhesus positive foetus (p. 26.19).

ENDOCRINE FUNCTIONS

The placenta is a major endocrine gland, but its inaccessibility has made it difficult to study directly. Most information has come from the study of hormones and their metabolites in blood and urine, from the study of isotopically labelled steroid precursors injected into mother or foetus in pregnancies which are to be terminated, and from incubation studies of placental homogenates and tissue slices. Although the placenta has been shown to produce both gonadotrophins and steroid hormones, nothing is known of the way in which these endocrine functions are regulated.

Gonadotrophin (human chorionic gonadotrophin or HCG)

EM and immunofluorescent studies suggests that the syncytiotrophoblast is the major source of HCG. Concentrations of HCG in the blood and in the urine follow the same course. It has been detected in the blood as early as the 25th day of the menstrual cycle. It reaches a peak around the 70th day, after which it falls to a relatively constant value which is maintained throughout pregnancy (fig. 37.38). Its supposed role in early pregnancy is to maintain the ovarian production of steroids until the placenta takes over this function. The function of HCG in later pregnancy is unknown. HCG can be detected in the urine about 14 days after a missed period and this provides the earliest test for pregnancy.

It is likely that the trophoblast secretes another protein hormone which is similar to, but not identical with pituitary growth hormone. This hormone may have some action in inducing breast development, and it is sometimes referred to as a placental lactogen. However, details of its production and functions are uncertain.

Steroid hormones

The syncytiotrophoblast is the likely site of production of steroid hormones. Steroid production in pregnancy provides an excellent illustration of the intimate interrelations between foetus and placenta.

The placenta has only a limited part to play in steroid production. It cannot split the side chain of C-21 steroids. Consequently, it requires a source of precursors such as dehydroepiandrosterone or androstenedione, and these are provided by the foetal and maternal adrenal glands. It is, however, a rich source of 3β-ol dehydrogenase and aromatizing enzymes, and so it can convert these precursors efficiently to oestrone and oestradiol-17β. Furthermore, the placenta probably cannot convert these oestrogens to oestriol. It is believed that the oestrone and oestradiol-17β produced by the placenta enter the foetal circulation, and that 16-hydroxylation occurs in the foetal adrenal and liver. The oestriol which has thus been formed by the combined activity of foetal and placental tissue (or foetoplacental unit) finally crosses the placenta into the maternal circulation.

The subsequent metabolism and excretion of placental oestrogens is similar to that already described for ovarian oestrogens. Quantitatively the most important urinary oestrogen in pregnancy is oestriol, and its excretion rises dramatically during pregnancy (fig. 37.38).

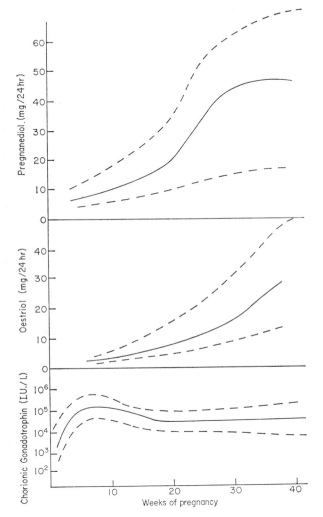

FIG. 37.38. Urinary excretion of pregnanediol, oestriol and chorionic gonadotrophin in pregnancy. Continuous lines indicate mean values. Broken lines indicate limits of 95 per cent probability. Ordinate on gonadotrophin diagram is on a logarithmic scale.

In late pregnancy the placenta secretes about 250 mg progesterone daily. The placenta cannot synthesize the steroid nucleus *de novo*, and it is dependent on steroid precursors. These are probably pregnenolone sulphate of foetal origin and maternal cholesterol and pregnenolone. However, the presence of a foetus is not essential for normal pregnanediol excretion, and maternal precursors

are adequate for the placental production of progesterone. This is in contrast to the intimate foetoplacental relations necessary for optimal oestrogen production in pregnancy. Pregnanediol is one of the principal metabolites of progesterone, and the urinary excretion of pregnanediol increases tenfold during pregnancy (fig. 37.38).

The role of these steroid hormones in pregnancy is not fully understood, although they have an important relation to myometrial growth and contractility, to the preparation of the breasts for lactation and to the systemic maternal responses to pregnancy.

The polypeptide hormone, relaxin, is probably also produced by the placenta. In small rodents, it has an important role in softening the uterine cervix and relaxing pelvic joints, but its function in human pregnancy is not known.

AMNIOTIC FLUID

Although amniotic fluid is one of the most readily accessible of all biological fluids, its production and functions are poorly understood. It provides the foetus with a favourable environment, absorbing mechanical pressures and yet allowing freedom of movement.

The volume of amniotic fluid increases from about 30 ml at the 10th week of pregnancy to a maximum of about 1000 ml at the 36th–37th week. Thereafter, it falls by approximately 150 ml/week, so that if pregnancy is prolonged until the 42nd week very little fluid remains. It should be emphasized that there is a wide variation in these values.

In early pregnancy, amniotic fluid is similar in composition to a dialysate of maternal plasma. At term the fluid is hypotonic. It also contains 0·25 g protein/100 ml, and these proteins have been shown to be of maternal origin. Tracer studies in late pregnancy indicate that a movement of water and sodium takes place between the mother and the amniotic fluid across the amnion and chorion. All of these facts imply that there is a major maternal contribution to the formation of amniotic fluid.

However, the foetus also participates by excreting urine into the amniotic fluid, and there is indirect evidence that the foetus may regulate the volume. Thus, in conditions such as congenital absence of the kidneys, where the foetus can excrete no urine, the volume of amniotic fluid may be abnormally small, whereas in other conditions such as congenital occlusion of the oesophagus, where the foetus cannot swallow, the volume of fluid may be excessive.

Physiological responses of the mother to pregnancy

The mother responds to the stimulus of gestation by widespread physiological changes involving most systems of the body in such a way as to provide a suitable environment for the growing foetus. However, the relationship between mother and foetus is not simply that of host and parasite, in that each maternal adjustment is not precipitated by the immediate demand of the foetus. Instead the mother anticipates the needs of the foetus, so that the response precedes the demand. The stimuli which initiate the maternal responses to pregnancy are unknown.

VOLUME AND COMPOSITION OF THE BLOOD

During pregnancy both plasma volume and red cell mass increase (table 37.2). Plasma volume begins to rise towards

TABLE 37.2. Plasma volume, red cell volume, total blood volume and haematocrit in pregnancy.

	Non-pregnant	Weeks of pregnancy			
		20	30	34	40
Plasma volume ml	2600	3150	3750	3830	3600
Red cell volume ml	1400	1450	1550	1600	1650
Total blood volume ml	4000	4600	5200	5430	5250
Body haematocrit per cent	35·0	31·5	29·8	29·5	31·5
Venous haematocrit * per cent	39·8	35·8	34·0	33·5	35·8

* Assuming a haematocrit ratio of 0·88.

the end of the 3rd month, reaching a maximum of 1250–1500 ml above non-pregnant values by the 34th week, and followed by a slight fall during the last few weeks. By contrast, red cell volume increases steadily from the 3rd month to term by about 250 ml, or more if medicinal iron is taken during pregnancy. Since the increase in plasma volume is disproportionately greater than the increase in red cell mass, packed cell volume and haemoglobin concentration fall. This fall in Hb concentration despite a rise in red cell mass has been described as a physiological anaemia of pregnancy, but this term is misleading as mean cell haemoglobin concentration remains unchanged, and there is normally no evidence of iron-deficiency anaemia.

There are also important changes in plasma composition. Their origin is complex and they are not due to simple haemodilution. For example, the concentration of total plasma proteins falls, due mainly to a drop in the albumin level. However, β-globulin and fibrinogen concentrations rise steadily throughout pregnancy, while α- and γ-globulin fractions show little change. The meaning of these changes is unknown. The altered pattern of plasma proteins raises the erythrocyte sedimentation rate to levels which would in other circumstances be considered to be pathological.

There are changes in blood concentrations of lipids, enzymes, inorganic ions, amino acids and vitamins, all of which illustrate the profound upheaval of the mother's metabolism. These are of considerable clinical importance,

because much confusion has arisen from interpreting blood composition in pregnancy in terms of non-pregnant standards.

CARDIOVASCULAR DYNAMICS

Cardiac output rises early in pregnancy to a level which is then maintained until parturition. The time of onset and magnitude of this rise are disputed, but an increase of the order of 1·5 l/min is probably reached before mid-pregnancy. It has been accepted for many years that cardiac output falls in late pregnancy, but it now seems certain that this observation is due to the fact that most measurements of cardiac output have been made with the patient lying on her back. In this position in late pregnancy, the pregnant uterus rests on the inferior vena cava and restricts venous return from the lower half of the body (supine caval occlusion). When cardiac output is measured serially during pregnancy with the patient lying on her side, there is no evidence of a terminal fall in cardiac output. This increase in output is achieved by an increase in both heart rate and stroke volume.

It is not possible to account entirely for the distribution of the extra 1·5 litres of cardiac output. Blood flow to the uterus rises throughout pregnancy to a mean maximum of about 500 ml/min, although this measurement is technically so difficult that the figure is only an approximation. Renal blood flow increases in early pregnancy by about 400 ml/min. It has been said to decline in late pregnancy, but this fall, like that in cardiac output, may be due to the fallacies of making clearance studies in the supine position. Blood flow through the skin is greatly increased and this is most obvious in the warm, moist extremities. It is not possible to estimate the increase in skin blood flow accurately, but it may amount to 500 ml/min. It may be noted that two major areas of increased blood flow, the kidneys and the skin, serve purposes of elimination, the kidneys of soluble waste and the skin of heat. Both processes require plasma rather than whole blood, which gives point to the disproportionate increase of plasma volume in the expansion of blood volume.

RESPIRATION

The resting minute volume increases throughout pregnancy by about 40 per cent. This is achieved by an increase in tidal volume rather than respiratory rate. Since oxygen intake increases by only 10 per cent, overbreathing results and alveolar P_{CO_2} falls from about 38 mm in non-pregnant women to little more than 30 mm in late pregnancy.

RENAL FUNCTION

An increase in renal blood flow has been described above. Glomerular filtration rate rises even more dramatically from a non-pregnant level of about 90 ml/min to 150 ml/min. This high level is reached in the first trimester and is maintained throughout pregnancy. Increased filtration may be related to the fall in plasma albumin concentration which lowers plasma colloid osmotic pressure. The rise in filtration rate contributes to changes in blood composition. For example, urea, uric acid and creatinine are cleared more effectively, and blood concentrations of these substances are reduced. Many nutrients are treated in the same way. Glucose is lost in the urine when blood levels rise, probably because the filtered load exceeds the tubular maximum reabsorptive capacity for glucose. Similarly as much as 1 g of amino acids may be excreted daily, with a consequent reduction in their blood concentration. Inorganic iodine and water-soluble vitamins are probably lost in the same way.

ENDOCRINE FUNCTIONS

The placental production of sex steroid hormones and chorionic gonadotrophin have already been described.

The hypophysis enlarges during pregnancy and there is indirect evidence of increased secretion of some trophic hormones. Melanocyte stimulating hormone (MSH) is produced in increasing amounts and may be responsible for the characteristic skin pigmentation of pregnancy.

The production of aldosterone by the adrenal cortex rises, but the significance of this increase in relation to renal function is not understood. There are also large increases in circulating blood levels of corticosteroids, especially cortisol, but this is partly due to increased binding of the hormone by transcortin and this bound component is not physiologically active.

The thyroid gland is palpably enlarged in the majority of pregnant women. Together with an increased oxygen consumption, raised pulse rate, heat intolerance and a rise in serum protein bound iodine (PBI), this has often been interpreted as evidence of hyperthyroidism. However, these signs are now recognized as physiological adaptations to pregnancy. The raised PBI is a reflection of increased hormone binding by plasma proteins. The thyroid enlargement is of the iodine deficiency type, and may be attributed to a low blood inorganic iodine level consequent on the loss of iodine by the kidney in pregnancy.

Carbohydrate metabolism is altered in pregnancy and almost invariably the insulin requirements of a diabetic are increased in pregnancy.

WEIGHT GAIN IN PREGNANCY

A normal British woman gains about 12·5 kg body weight during pregnancy, although there are enormous individual variations. On the average, her weight increases at a rate of about 0·5 kg weekly during the last two-thirds of pregnancy, the most rapid rate of gain occurring between the 16th and 24th weeks.

Fig. 37.39 shows the components of this added weight gain. At mid-pregnancy when the rate of increase is most rapid, and even at term, the uterus and its contents account for only one-half of the total weight gain. An increase in maternal blood volume and extracellular fluid accounts for another 2·5 kg. The remaining 4 kg represents body fat. The suggestion that large stores of protein are laid down by the pregnant woman can be discounted, because the body has little facility for storing protein. Fig. 37.39 shows that maternal fat is laid down early when other components are increasing very little, and that little more is accumulated in the last 10 weeks. This stored 4 kg of body fat remains after delivery, and represents the net weight gain of a normal pregnant woman.

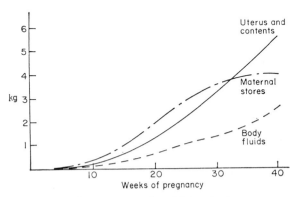

FIG. 37.39. Components of weight gain in pregnancy. From Hytten, F.E. & Leitch, I. (1964) *The Physiology of Human Pregnancy*. Oxford: Blackwell Scientific Publications.

NUTRITIONAL REQUIREMENTS OF PREGNANCY

The energy cost of pregnancy includes the building up of a reserve of fat, and the maintenance of the metabolism of the foetus and the additional maternal tissues. The storage of nutrients can be calculated with reasonable precision. By the end of pregnancy, the mother has gained approximately 1 kg protein, mostly in the uterus and products of conception, and 4 kg fat, most of it in her own fat depots. The running costs specific to pregnancy are required for the metabolism of the foetus and placenta, the metabolism of the additional uterine and breast tissue, and the cost of the extra cardiac and respiratory work (fig. 37.40). The cumulative energy requirement for a pregnancy is about 80,000 kcal, spread evenly at an almost constant rate over the last two-thirds of pregnancy. These specific costs, averaging between 300 and 400 kcal/day, refer to the woman at rest. If the mother continues her normal activities, these are almost certain to cost her more as her weight rises. In Western society, pregnant women tend to curtail their activities and may indeed subsidize the specific costs of pregnancy by a reduction of their normal non-pregnant energy expenditure.

Specific nutrient requirements are less easy to specify. The need for protein is greatest in the last 10 weeks, when it accumulates at a rate of about 5–6 g/day. With a high grade European diet, this would require no more than about seven extra grams of dietary protein, much less than would be found in any ordinary diet supplying the extra 300–400 kcal. The foetus accumulates about 30 g calcium throughout pregnancy, at a maximum rate of 250 mg/day. This requirement can be met by the

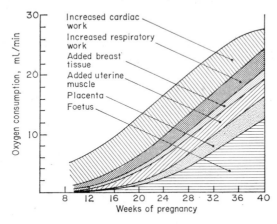

FIG. 37.40. Components of increased oxygen consumption in pregnancy. From Hytten, F.E. & Leitch, I. (1964) *The Physiology of Human Pregnancy*. Oxford: Blackwell Scientific Publications.

addition of 200 ml milk to the daily diet, but if this is not available, the maternal skeleton can easily provide this quantity of calcium. The gross extra requirement of iron is about 750 mg, of which one-third will be returned to store from the expanded maternal blood volume after delivery. The maximum demand is for 4 mg daily, and this should be provided by a good Western diet.

Uterus in pregnancy

The uterus has three principal functions in pregnancy, to allow implantation of the blastocyst, to accommodate the growing products of conception, and to expel these contents at parturition. Implantation has been described (p. 37.34), and parturition will be discussed in vol. III. Three mechanisms are involved in the accommodation of the foetus within the uterus; compensatory growth and distension of the uterus, restraint of myometrial contractility and the resistance of the cervix to stretch.

GROWTH AND DISTENSION OF THE UTERUS

The uterus has to make room for the rapidly increasing volume of foetus, placenta and amniotic fluid. Thus, the volume of the uterine cavity expands from a potential space in the non-pregnant state to approximately 5 litres at the end of the pregnancy. This expansion is the result of both active growth and passive distension. In the first half of pregnancy the uterus gains weight rapidly, partly by an increase in the number of muscle

fibres (hyperplasia) but mainly by an increase in the size of individual fibres (hypertrophy). The smooth muscle cells of the non-pregnant uterus are spindle shaped and measure 50–90 μm in length and 2–5 μm in breadth. By the end of pregnancy, the fibres are elongated to a length of 500–800 μm and increased to a breadth of 5–10 μm. Myometrial growth is initiated by oestrogens but is also stimulated directly by mechanical distension.

After mid-pregnancy the rate of uterine growth slows down but uterine volume increases rapidly (fig. 37.41). As a result, the uterus is passively distended and the thickness of the myometrium is reduced from 9 mm at mid-pregnancy to 6 mm at the end of pregnancy. This passive stretching is facilitated by alterations in the connective tissue framework of the uterus. During pregnancy, existing collagen fibres are replaced by new fine fibrils. These appear to be dispersed in random directions throughout the uterus within a loose, oedematous stroma. Thus, although the total content of collagen in the uterus is increased, its concentration is reduced.

FIG. 37.41. Growth of the uterus and products of conception during pregnancy. This diagram illustrates the disproportionate growth of the conceptus in the second half of pregnancy. Broken line, uterus; continuous line, conceptus (foetus, placenta and amniotic fluid).

MYOMETRIAL CONTRACTILITY

The measurement of uterine contractions (tocography) presents several technical problems. Internal tocography refers to the continuous recording of intra-amniotic pressure by catheters introduced through the abdominal wall into the amniotic fluid. This permits the measurement of the frequency, duration and maximum intensity of pressure waves, and an arbitrary index of uterine activity can be derived from the product, frequency (no. of contractions/10 min) × intensity (maximum pressure rise during contractions in mm Hg). The lowest intra-amniotic pressure between contractions is referred to as uterine tone.

This terminology is in general clinical usage but it is important to be aware of its limitations. In particular, uterine activity calculated in this way is a very arbitrary index. For example, contractions which occur every $2\frac{1}{2}$ min with a given intensity are not necessarily equivalent to contractions of twice that intensity occurring every 5 min. Furthermore, intra-amniotic pressure is the resultant of overall uterine activity and gives no impression of local patterns of motility throughout the uterus.

External tocography may be performed using strain gauges placed over the abdominal wall to record uterine contractions, and intramural tocography relies on the use of pressure transducers inserted percutaneously into the substance of the myometrium. Multiple external or internal leads may be used to study the propagation of contractions.

The pregnant uterus does not normally respond to distension by increased contractility. On the contrary, throughout pregnancy uterine contractions occur irregularly and are of low amplitude. Furthermore, in contrast to contractions during labour, they do not cause the cervix to dilate.

UTERINE CERVIX (fig. 37.42)

Whereas the upper half of the cervix is predominantly muscular, the lower half is largely fibrous in nature and has a high collagen content. Until the 12th–14th week of pregnancy, the expanding conceptus can be lodged in the space within the growing uterus. Thereafter, the upper half of the cervix unfolds and adds to the available volume of the uterine cavity. It is essential that this unfolding should not proceed to complete dilatation of the cervix as this would terminate the pregnancy prematurely. Unfolding is resisted by the fibrous lower half of the cervix so that complete effacement does not normally occur until parturition. This cervical mechanism is not due to a muscular sphincter but simply to the resistance to stretch of collagen fibres, and it is effective only if myometrial contractility is restrained.

ONSET OF PARTURITION

These three mechanisms allow the foetus to grow within the uterus for about 266 days before parturition. With a normal 28-day menstrual cycle and fertilization occurring at mid-cycle, this corresponds to a gestation period of 280 days or 40 weeks calculated from the 1st day of the last normal menstrual period. The duration of pregnancy is relatively constant, but the factors which determine the time of onset of labour are unknown.

Oxytocin stimulates the myometrium specifically, and it has been suggested that the release of this hormone by the neurohypophysis is responsible for the onset of labour. There is no doubt that the sensitivity of the myometrium to oxytocin increases in the last few weeks

of pregnancy as labour approaches, but assays of oxytocin in blood have not shown any rise in early labour. There is probably an increase in the later stages of labour when the cervix is widely dilated but it is likely that this represents a neurohumoral reflex release of oxytocin in response to cervical dilatation.

12 WEEKS   16 WEEKS

FIG. 37.42. Behaviour of the cervix and isthmus in pregnancy. The stippled area represents the fibrous position of the cervix. By the 12th week, the uterus has undergone hypertrophy and the amniotic sac does not yet occupy all the available space in the uterus. By the 16th week, the volume of the conceptus exceeds the available space in the uterus, and this is compensated by unfolding of the isthmus. This unfolding process is halted at the level of the fibrous part of the cervix. From Danforth, D.N. (1947) *Amer. J. Obstet. Gynec.* **53**, 541.

An alternative view is that the uterus is held under restraint during pregnancy, and that labour is due to escape from this inhibition rather than to oxytocic stimulation. This restraint is assumed to be exerted by progesterone. It has been demonstrated that progesterone causes hyperpolarization of the cell membrane of single myometrial fibres and so decreases excitability. However, there is no substantial evidence of a terminal fall in placental progesterone prior to the onset of labour.

The role of mechanical distension is not clear. There is a close relation between stretch of a muscle fibre and its contractility, and it has been shown that the muscle fibres of the body of the uterus reach their optimal length at the end of pregnancy. There is also evidence that experimental distension of the uterine cavity increases uterine contractility. However, it is relevant to recall that the volume of the amniotic fluid commonly falls in the last few weeks of pregnancy.

Lactation

The **mammary glands** are accessory reproductive organs and are modified sweat glands.

DEVELOPMENT

They develop from a linear thickening of ectoderm called the **mammary ridge** or milk line. By the 6th month of intrauterine life, this extends from the axilla to the groin in both sexes, but it soon becomes confined to the middle of the cranial third, where epithelial cells invade the underlying mesenchyme. In man, this invasion usually occurs at only this one site, but occasionally additional mammary gland rudiments develop along the milk line forming supernumerary breasts or nipples.

When the foetus is about 5 months old, 15–20 solid cellular cords grow out from the mammary epithelial bud into the surrounding mesenchyme of the developing dermis, pushing the component layers of the dermis before them. Each of these original cords becomes a separate exocrine gland, so that each breast is really composed of several glands which empty by separate ducts at the nipple and are separated from each other by partitions of connective tissue. These cords become canalized by the 8th–9th months so that by birth a nipple and rudimentary duct system have formed.

This infantile condition persists until puberty. At puberty in the female, the breast enlarges due to the accumulation of fat in the connective tissue. The epithelial duct system also develops further, but although cellular knobs form at the end of the ducts, probably no true secretory units develop until pregnancy.

FORM AND RELATIONS

The size and shape of the breasts of mature women vary between individuals and according to the functional state of the glands. Each **nipple** is surrounded by a disc-shaped **areola**, of darker colour than the surrounding skin, and usually protrudes below and lateral to the centre of each breast.

The nipples are usually situated at about the level of the fourth intercostal space. The gland extends vertically from the second to the sixth rib and horizontally from the sternal border to the mid-axillary line. From the upper outer quadrant there is a prolongation of mammary tissue along the anterior axillary fold, known as the **axillary tail** of the breast. The deep surface of the gland is related to the deep fascia covering the pectoralis major, and to a lesser extent the serratus anterior and external oblique.

BLOOD SUPPLY

The arterial supply is derived from perforating branches of the internal thoracic artery through the second, third and fourth intercostal spaces, from the external mammary branch of the lateral thoracic artery, and from the anterior intercostal arteries of the second, third and fourth intercostal spaces. The acromiothoracic artery may supply the upper outer quadrant.

Veins from the breast drain into the axillary, internal thoracic and intercostal veins. The rich subcutaneous venous plexus which connects with the veins of the stroma drains into the external jugular vein.

NERVE SUPPLY

Sensory fibres are conveyed by the second to the sixth thoracic nerves. Free and encapsulated nerve endings ramify in the gland stroma and in the subepidermal connective tissue. The nipple has a particularly rich sensory innervation. Sympathetic fibres are distributed with the sensory nerve fibres, and they innervate the smooth muscle fibres of blood vessels, ducts and nipple.

LYMPH DRAINAGE (fig. 37.43)

The lymphatics begin in the interlobular connective tissue as perilobular plexuses. Thence lymphatic vessels run:

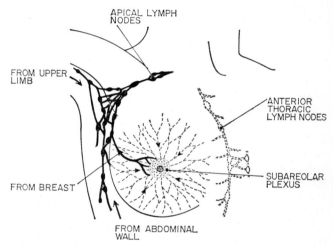

FIG. 37.43. Lymphatic drainage of the breast. From Glenister, T.W.A. & Ross, J.R.W. (1965) *Anatomy and Physiology for Nurses.* London: Heinemann.

(1) along the lactiferous ducts to join the subcutaneous plexus of the nipple and areola, or subareolar plexus,

(2) through the suspensory ligaments to reach the subcutaneous plexus of the skin overlying the breast,

(3) through the breast stroma to reach the deep plexus on the pectoral fascia.

From these subareolar and subcutaneous plexuses, lymph channels run towards the axilla over the surface of the gland and join the deep plexus at the lateral margin. Thus, the deep plexus receives most of the lymph from the breast either directly or indirectly. However, there is frequently a channel which drains the upper part of the subcutaneous plexus directly into the lower lateral deep cervical nodes by running across the clavicle.

The deep plexus drains as follows:

(1) along the external mammary blood vessels to the anterior (pectoral) group of axillary lymph nodes,

(2) along the perforating branches of the internal thoracic artery to the nodes along that vessel in the upper three intercostal spaces,

(3) along the mammary branches of the acromio-thoracic artery, through the pectoralis major and the clavipectoral fascia to reach the apical (subclavian) group of axillary nodes.

In addition there are anastomotic channels between the lymphatic plexuses of the two breasts, and others which pierce the rectus sheath between the xiphoid process and the costal margin to communicate with the lymphatics of the abdomen.

The main flow of lymph from the breast is to the anterior (pectoral) axillary nodes, but the subsidiary channels provide important routes for the possible dissemination of cancer cells.

STRUCTURE (fig. 37.44)

Each breast consists of fifteen to twenty **lactiferous ducts** which branch repeatedly and drain secretory **alveoli**. Each lactiferous duct is dilated to form an **ampulla** or sinus before it opens independently on the summit of the nipple. All the ducts and alveoli developing from a single lactiferous duct constitute one **lobe**, and this in turn is subdivided into **lobules**.

Ducts and secretory units are surrounded by connective tissue which acts as a supporting framework. The larger partitions between the lobes form strands which extend from the skin to the underlying deep fascia. These are known as **suspensory ligaments**. Fat accumulates in the connective tissue of the breast and between the parenchyma and the overlying skin.

The skin of the areola contains modified sweat glands and sebaceous glands.

Histologically, the non-lactating breast is seen to be made up of clusters of ducts set in cellular intralobular connective tissue derived from the papillary layer of the dermis, and widely separated by dense acellular inter-lobular connective tissue derived from the reticular layer of the dermis. The ducts are lined by two layers of epithelium. Spindle-shaped cells resembling smooth muscle cells, known as **myoepithelial cells**, surround the secretory alveoli.

BREAST DEVELOPMENT IN PREGNANCY

The duct and alveolar systems of the breasts develop during pregnancy, and as a result the breasts increase in size. There is a wide variation in the degree of glandular development. Examination of breasts of women dying at or shortly after delivery showed that in 30–40 per cent duct and alveolar development was grossly deficient, and the breasts consisted largely of fat and fibrous tissue.

Before pregnancy, the nipples are firmly bound to the underlying gland by fibrous tissue, and during pregnancy these bonds are loosened and the nipple becomes more mobile, making it easier for the suckling infant to grasp.

Alveolar and duct development in pregnancy is an extension of the growth which follows puberty. It is believed that oestrogens are primarily responsible for the

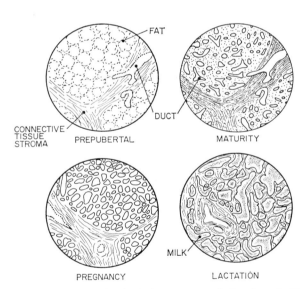

FIG. 37.44. Histological structure of the breast. From Netter, F.H. (1952) *The Ciba Collection of Medical Illustrations.*

growth of ducts, and progestagens for the growth of alveolar buds. Ovarian steroids can act directly on the breast in the absence of the hypophysis, but they require the presence of an intact hypophysis in order to exert their optimal effect. The principal hypophysial trophic hormone for the breast is prolactin. Prolactin both potentiates the action of ovarian steroids, and can itself induce mammary growth and even secretion in oopho-rectomized, hypophysectomized animals. Growth hormone and intact adrenocortical and thyroid systems are also required for optimal mammary gland development. A placental protein hormone, or lactogen, may play an important part in the development of the human mammary gland (p. 37.44).

CONTROL OF MILK PRODUCTION

The breasts secrete a small quantity of fluid, or colostrum, from early pregnancy onwards, and for the first two or three days after parturition. Colostrum differs from milk, especially in having a high fat and protein content. Milk secretion starts commonly on the 3rd day after parturition, but the factors which initiate lactation at this time are still not understood.

Prolactin is essential for milk production as well as breast development. Its production and release are controlled by the hypothalamus, although in a way different from that for other trophic hormones. The release of prolactin from the hypophysis is inhibited rather than stimulated by the hypothalamus, so that a transplanted hypophysis secretes an excess amount. It is likely that the hypothalamic control of prolactin secretion is modified by the rapidly falling levels of oestrogens and progestagens after delivery, although the exact nature of this stimulus is uncertain. Adrenal corticosteroids and thyroxine are probably also needed for continued lactation.

Regular milk ejection is also essential. The ejection of milk is stimulated by suckling via a neurohumoral reflex. The afferent side of this reflex is nervous, so that suckling a denervated gland is ineffective. The central area includes the neurohypophysis, and stimulation of the supra-opticohypophyseal tract will induce discharge of milk from the breast. The efferent mechanism is humoral. Thus, suckling an innervated gland causes release of milk from a denervated gland. The humoral factor is oxytocin, and administration of oxytocin causes the ejection of milk by stimulating contractions of the myoepithelial cells which surround the alveoli. These contractions force milk out of the alveoli into the ducts. The release of oxytocin during suckling commonly causes uterine contractions which may be noticeable or even painful to the mother. In women the cerebral cortex has an important overriding influence on all these mechanisms, and lactation is profoundly affected by emotions and psychological attitudes.

Under normal conditions, lactation continues as long as suckling is allowed. Breast feeding in Western countries is practised by only a minority of women, and then for only a few months, but in some countries in Africa and Asia lactation may be prolonged for two or three years. In many mammals, ovulation rapidly follows parturition, and lactation continues during the subsequent pregnancy.

However, the period of human lactation is a time of relative infertility. Ovulation is probably delayed, presumably due to a suppression of pituitary gonadotrophins. Yet, conception can occur during lactation, and in these circumstances milk secretion continues during pregnancy, although the quantity and quality falls off in late pregnancy.

MILK SECRETION

Milk secretion begins about 3 days after parturition, and gradually increases to a rate of about 850 ml/day although yields as high as 3 litres per day have been observed.

The principal constituents of milk are water, lactose, fat and protein. A table giving the composition of human and cow's milk is set out on p. 5.21. The production of lactose begins in early pregnancy, and it is demonstrable in maternal blood and urine. Milk fats are essentially triglycerides manufactured from circulating fatty acids by the mammary gland. Milk proteins are probably synthesized from circulating amino acids, although some plasma proteins appear in milk. Thus, the lactalbumin and lactoglobulin of milk differ structurally from analogous plasma proteins. The distinctive protein of milk is casein. Milk is an important source of calcium but has a low content of iron. All of the vitamins appear in milk. Most soluble constituents, including drugs, in the maternal blood appear in milk although generally in small amounts, e.g. barbiturates, alcohol and antibiotics. It must be emphasized that the contents of various nutrients shown are average figures and subject to considerable individual variation. The fat content of human milk, for example, may vary from under 1 to over 6 per cent and the fat content of cow's milk, though less variable, differs considerably between breeds of cattle. The levels of some other constituents notably the water-soluble vitamins, e.g. ascorbic acid, change conspicuously with variations in the maternal diet.

Apart from abnormal constituents, diet has relatively little influence on milk yield or composition, and established lactation is surprisingly little affected by short periods of severe deprivation. Similarly, fluid intake has little discernible effect on milk yield.

The energy cost of lactation must be met from the maternal diet. The efficiency of milk production is probably about 80 per cent, so that, for the production of milk with an energy value of 80 kcal, the mother must take in an extra 100 kcal in her diet if she is to remain in energy balance. A healthy baby may require 850 ml daily. At an energy value of 68 kcal/100 ml, this will provide 578 kcal daily. To meet this demand the mother requires extra dietary calories but she can also draw on the reserves of fat laid down during pregnancy. The recommended allowance for lactation (p. 5.25) provides a liberal safety margin to cover individual variations.

PRENATAL DEVELOPMENT OF THE REPRODUCTIVE TRACT

In chap. 34 the development of the urinary system is described and it is shown that the mesonephric duct and some of its tubules become available for incorporation in the genital apparatus, once the excretory function of the mesonephros has been taken over by the metanephros.

The cloacal region (fig. 37.45)

The caudal part of the hindgut which receives the allantois and the mesonephric ducts, is slightly dilated and is called the **cloaca** (chap. 18). It is separated from the exterior by a double-layered membrane, the **cloacal membrane** which consists of a layer of ectoderm on the outside and endoderm on the inside. Lateral plate mesoderm, spreading round from the caudal extremity of the primitive streak, passes round the edges of this cloacal membrane, insinuating itself between the ectoderm and endoderm. These bilateral sheets of spreading mesoderm meet in the midline anteriorly and spread on into the portion of the abdominal wall between the cloacal membrane and the attachment of the umbilical cord to form the infra-umbilical part of the abdominal wall.

This mesoderm extends round the cloacal membrane and raises slight elevations known as **genital folds** on either side of the membrane, and a **genital tubercle** at the anterior margin of the membrane. This genital tubercle enlarges to become the **phallus**. As a result of the development of these prominences flanking the cloacal membrane, the latter now lies in a depression called the **external cloaca**. More mesoderm extends into the region between the genital tubercle and the attachment of the umbilical cord and, as a result, the infraumbilical abdominal wall elongates. This lengthening together with the regression of the tail of the embryo causes the cloacal membrane to rotate so that its ectodermal surface, which originally faces forwards and upwards towards the umbilicus, comes to face forwards and downwards. When describing the further development of the urogenital system, particularly its lower portion, it is convenient to consider the foetus to be in the upright position with the phallus pointing forwards and the perineum facing downwards (fig. 37.53).

The deep part of this mesoderm contributes to the musculature of that part of the cloaca and allantois from which the bladder arises whereas the superficial somatic part contributes mesenchymatous components to the infra-umbilical abdominal wall.

In late somite embryos the cloaca, lined by endoderm, is joined on each side by the mesonephric duct which is of mesodermal origin. A transverse ridge, the **urorectal septum**, appears between the hindgut and the allantois. Its lower free edge, disposed in the coronal plane,

descends towards the cloacal membrane progressively dividing the cloaca into a smaller dorsal part, the **rectum**, and a larger ventral part, the **primitive urogenital sinus**,

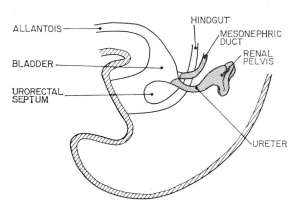

Fig. 37.45. Development of the cloaca and urorectal septum. From *Cunningham's Textbook of Anatomy*, 10th Edition (1964). London: Oxford University Press.

which is continuous with the allantois, and into which the mesonephric ducts open. When the urorectal septum reaches the cloacal membrane, the membrane itself disintegrates. The lower margin of the septum forms the

primitive perineal body. The remnant of the cloacal membrane in front of the perineal body is now called the **urogenital membrane** and the part behind it is called the **anal membrane.**

At this stage the primitive urogenital sinus may be divided into a portion above the level of the mesonephric ducts called the **vesico-urethral canal**, and a portion below the opening of the mesonephric ducts called the **definitive urogenital sinus**, which becomes markedly flattened from side to side. The vesico-urethral canal gives rise to most of the bladder in both sexes, apart from the trigone which is derived from mesonephric duct tissue. It is also the origin of the upper part of the prostatic urethra in males and of virtually the whole length of the female urethra.

Before proceeding further with a description of the development of the human genital system, it is necessary to stress that the same primordia and ducts originate in embryos of either sex, but the use made of these structures to produce the functional genital tract is very different in the two sexes. It is, therefore, usual to consider that the embryo passes through a neuter phase during which it possesses the rudiments necessary to develop the genital organs of either sex, but that, as development proceeds, progressive specialization occurs. Thus, although embryos of either sex develop both mesonephric and paramesonephric ducts, the functional adult male ducts arise from the mesonephric ducts, whereas those of the adult female are derived from paramesonephric ducts. Similarly, the external genitalia and the urogenital sinus are derived from the same embryonic structures in the two sexes, but their development is strikingly different.

It will be recalled that the sex of the embryo is determined at fertilization (p. 37.61). In presomite and somite embryos, the sex of the embryo can be established morphologically only by the presence or absence of sex chromatin (p. 12.16) in the resting nuclei of most embryonic cells. Apart from this, there is no morphological indication of the future sex of an embryo till late in the 6th week of intrauterine life when the gonads of male embryos begin to differentiate into testes. It is only when a foetus is about three months old that it becomes possible to determine its sex by examination of the external genitalia.

Development of the gonads (fig. 37.46)

The primordia of the gonads appear about 5 weeks after fertilization as thickenings of the coelomic epithelium, known as **genital ridges**, on the medial aspect of the mesonephros. Cords of cells proliferate from the thickened coelomic epithelium forming **sex cords**, and these extend into the underlying mesenchyme. Soon, cells of a very special kind appear in the genital ridges. These cells are larger than the surrounding mesenchymal cells; they are spherical and pale staining and possess large vesicular

nuclei. They are the **primordial germ cells** and are generally believed to have migrated by way of the mesentery from a restricted area of the yolk sac wall close to the allantoic diverticulum.

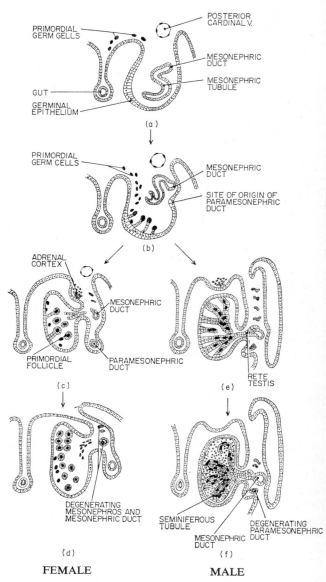

FEMALE   MALE

FIG. 37.46. Migration of germ cells and development of the gonads. (a) and (b) indifferent stage, (c) and (d) female, (e) and (f) male. From Hamilton W.J., Boyd J.D. & Mossman H.W. (1962) *Human Embryology*, 3rd Edition. Cambridge: Heffer.

Thus the gonads of both sexes are derived from three basic components: (1) the primordial germ cells, (2) the coelomic epithelium, (3) the mesenchyme of the adjacent part of the genital ridge.

The gonad overlaps approximately the middle two-quarters of the medial aspect of the mesonephros, which

ow projects well into the coelomic cavity and is connected to the posterior abdominal wall by means of a
thick mesentery. This mesentery suspends the gonadal
primordium as well as the mesonephros and so is known
as the **urogenital mesentery**. The mesentery, the mesonephros and the gonadal primordium together constitute
the **urogenital ridge**. As the gonad enlarges, it projects
more and more from the medial aspect of the urogenital
ridge. Deepening grooves on each side of the gonad
results in the formation of a **gonadal mesentery** (mesovarium in the female, mesorchium in the male) connecting
the gonad to the remainder of the urogenital ridge.

As a result of the growth of the metanephros,
gonad and adrenal gland the urogenital mesenteries, which originally lie parallel to one another,
become displaced laterally in their cranial portions. The
caudal parts, on the other hand, incline towards the
midline because of the medial inclination of the contained mesonephric ducts and particularly of the
paramesonephric ducts, which are approaching each
other to fuse in the midline. In this way the caudal
portions of the two urogenital mesenteries eventually
fuse with each other. This fusion results in the formation
of the **urogenital septum** (not to be confused with the
urorectal septum described above, which lies in the coronal plane between the bladder in front and the rectum
behind, and forms the basis for the development of the
broad ligament in the female.

As the tubal portion of the urogenital ridge passes the
brim of the developing pelvis, it becomes joined to the
anterior abdominal wall by a fold known as the **plica
inguinalis**, in which the gubernaculum of the gonad later
develops.

Histogenesis of the testis

A series of histological changes indicates the onset of the
differentiation of the male gonad. The sex cords become
distinct and are separated from one another by bundles
of fibrous tissue. At first the cords are continuous with
the coelomic epithelium on the surface of the gonad.
However, cells on the deep aspect of the germinal
epithelium proliferate and become converted into fibrous
tissue, forming the **tunica albuginea**, and this separates the
sex cords from the surface epithelium.

The male primordial germ cells become incorporated
within the sex cords so that these cords come to extend
inwards from the periphery of the gonad as distinct
columns containing germ cells. The innermost portions
of these columns extend into the region of the mesorchium
where they anastomose and branch to form a network
which will canalize and become the rete testis. It is in
this region that the gonadal tubular system communicates
with the mesonephric tubules bringing the rete testis
into communication with the efferent ductules and the
ductus deferens.

The sex cords canalize and form seminiferous tubules,
whose walls consist of cells derived from coelomic
epithelium which become the sustentacular cells, and
intercalated primordial germ cells which become
spermatogonia. The interstitial cells are probably
derived from the mesenchyme lying between the sex
cords. These interstitial cells show histological signs of
specialization when the foetus is 8–9 weeks old, and thus
this process precedes the onset of divergence in the two
sexes in the differentiation of the genital duct system by
about one week, and of the external genitalia by about
two or three weeks.

Histogenesis of the ovary

As in the male, the primordial germ cells reach the
gonadal primordium of the female in the somite stage of
development. However, in the female they come to be
situated only in the superficial cortex of the developing
ovary. Many of them are in contact with the superficial
germinal epithelium and the deeper medulla is almost
devoid of germ cells. When the foetus is 4–5 months old,
the sex cords become fragmented and the resulting small
groups of cells form **primordial ovarian follicles** in which
the primordial germ cells become encapsulated as primary
oocytes (p. 37.8). The encapsulating or follicular cells are
probably derived from coelomic epithelium. The
mesenchyme between the primordial follicles forms the
ovarian stroma and gives rise to the thecal cells. There is
no definite tunica albuginea in the developing ovary and
so the sex cords maintain some contact with the surface
epithelium, which is thus able to continue contributing
cells to the sex cords throughout foetal life. Although a
rete ovarii is formed it is only vestigial, but may occasionally form an imperfect union with mesonephric tubules.
The absence, in normal development, of any continuity
between sex cords, rete and mesonephric tubules is the
reason why, in the female, the mesonephric duct fails to
become the definitive sex duct and why ova can escape
only by rupture of ovarian follicles at the surface of the
ovary. This demands also the development of a new
duct, the paramesonephric duct, to convey the ova to the
site of fertilization and subsequent development.

Descent of the gonads (fig. 37.47)

Both the testis and the ovary come to occupy a final
position which is very different from their original site in
the embryo. The transposition of the testis is particularly
striking because it passes out of the abdominal cavity
into the scrotum. This descent of the gonads explains the
blood supply and lymph drainage of the gonads, which
are established prior to descent, while the passage of
the testis through the inguinal portion of the abdominal
wall explains the inherent weakness of this region in
males.

It is convenient to consider the descent of the gonad in

two stages, the first being common to testis and ovary, and the second affecting only the testis.

The first stage consists of the descent from the posterior abdominal wall to the pelvis, and is closely related to

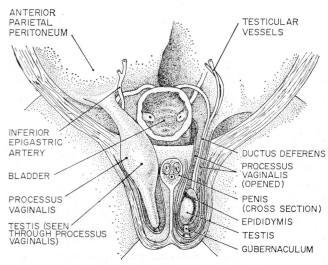

ANTERIOR PARIETAL PERITONEUM

TESTICULAR VESSELS

INFERIOR EPIGASTRIC ARTERY

BLADDER

PROCESSUS VAGINALIS

TESTIS (SEEN THROUGH PROCESSUS VAGINALIS)

DUCTUS DEFERENS

PROCESSUS VAGINALIS (OPENED)

PENIS (CROSS SECTION)

EPIDIDYMIS

TESTIS

GUBERNACULUM

FIG. 37.47. Descent of testis and formation of tunica vaginalis. Testis on left side is at a later stage of descent than on the right. Anterior parietal peritoneum has been removed on left side. From Hamilton W.J., Boyd J.D. & Mossman H.W. (1962) *Human Embryology*, 3rd Edition. Cambridge: Heffer.

changes in the mesonephros. The second stage consists of passage of the testis from an intra-abdominal to an extra-abdominal position.

Descent of the testis

In the 7th week of intrauterine life the testes are still attached to the posterior abdominal wall by the urogenital mesentery. The caudal pole of the testis is continuous with a mesenchymatous band which runs down toward the pelvic brim and skirts round it, so that it extends from the urogenital ridge to reach the inguinal region. As it descends, it raises the overlying coelomic epithelium to form the plica inguinalis. This band is continuous through the future inguinal canal with the mesenchyme of the genital fold. This whole column of mesenchyme extending from the lower pole of the testis to the genital fold constitutes the **gubernaculum testis**.

While the pelvis grows and the trunk of the foetus elongates, the gubernaculum does not grow in proportion, so that the testis, being attached to the gubernaculum, comes to lie in close proximity to the inguinal region. In other words this descent of the testis is only relative to the growing body wall. This stage is reached by the 3rd month of pregnancy. Meanwhile, the cremaster muscle differentiates in the gubernacular mesenchyme of the inguinal region and a diverticulum from the coelomic cavity, the **processus vaginalis**, extends into this mesenchyme. From the 6th month of intra-uterine life, the processus vaginalis grows into the mesenchyme of the inguinal canal and scrotum, and at the same time the cremaster extends downwards to the scrotum. The testis is still at the abdominal end of the inguinal canal at the beginning of the 7th month but it usually passes through the inguinal canal and reaches the scrotum by the end of the 8th month. The precise role of the gubernaculum is still unknown but it certainly provides a route along

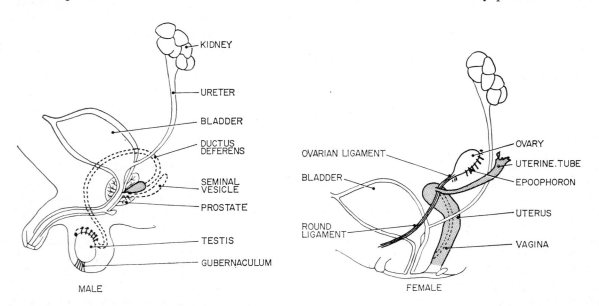

KIDNEY

URETER

BLADDER

DUCTUS DEFERENS

SEMINAL VESICLE

PROSTATE

TESTIS

GUBERNACULUM

MALE

OVARIAN LIGAMENT

BLADDER

ROUND LIGAMENT

OVARY

UTERINE TUBE

EPOOPHORON

UTERUS

VAGINA

FEMALE

FIG. 37.48. Definitive urogenital system in male and female. Dotted lines indicate derivatives of mesonephric ducts; stippled areas are derived from paramesonephric ducts. From Hamilton W.J., Boyd J.D. & Mossman H.W. (1962) *Human Embryology*, 3rd Edition. Cambridge: Heffer.

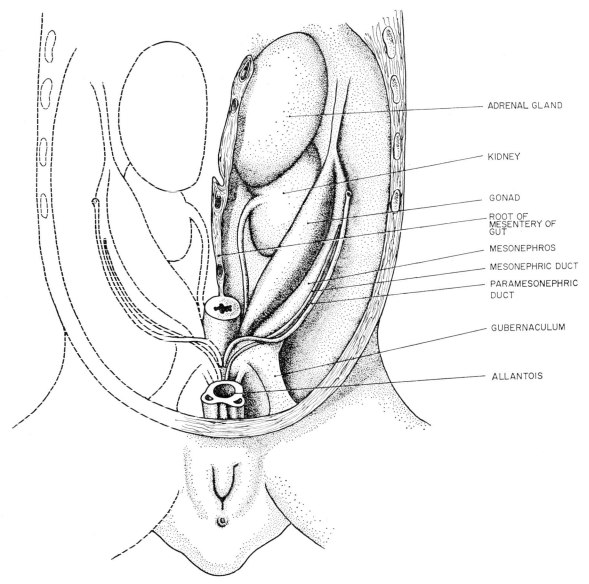

ADRENAL GLAND

KIDNEY

GONAD

ROOT OF
MESENTERY OF
GUT

MESONEPHROS

MESONEPHRIC DUCT

PARAMESONEPHRIC
DUCT

GUBERNACULUM

ALLANTOIS

FIG. 37.49. Posterior abdominal wall of embryo at 7 weeks. From Hamilton W.J., Boyd J.D. & Mossman H.W. (1962) *Human Embryology*, 3rd Edition. Cambridge:Heffer.

which the processus vaginalis and the cremaster muscle can develop without obstruction by the body wall. It also dilates and keeps open the pathway for descent and, by tethering the testis, it causes it to descend by differential growth. The gubernaculum does not actively pull down the testis. The lower portion of the processus vaginalis persists as the tunica vaginalis of the testis, but the upper part usually becomes obliterated at about the time of birth.

Descent of the ovary

The gubernaculum of the ovary becomes attached to the fused uterovaginal segments of the paramesonephric ducts at their junction with the free tubal portions, and so the ovary can effect only the first stage of descent and is unable to descend any further. This attachment of the gubernaculum to the uterus causes the ovary to enter the true pelvis, where it comes to lie on the dorsal (originally medial) surface of the urogenital mesentery which has descended with the ovary and now forms the broad ligament. The part of the gubernaculum persisting between the ovary and the uterus becomes the ligament of the ovary, and the part between the uterus and the labium majus becomes the round ligament of the uterus. A small processus vaginalis forms in the female and passes towards the labium majus, but it is usually obliterated by full term.

DEVELOPMENT OF THE GENITAL DUCT SYSTEM

The mesonephric duct

At first the mesonephric duct opens into that part of the cloaca which later becomes the primitive urogenital sinus. The length of this duct which is caudal to the origin of

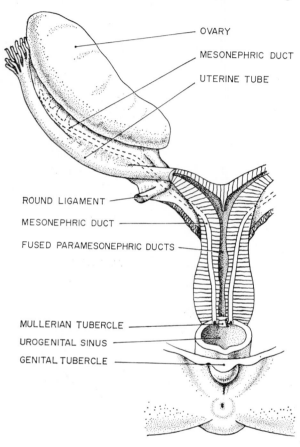

FIG. 37.50. Paramesonephric duct. From Hamilton W.J., Boyd J.D. & Mossman H.W. (1962) *Human Embryology*, 3rd Edition. Cambridge:Heffer.

the ureteric bud is known as the **common excretory duct** and it becomes absorbed into the posterior wall of the primitive urogenital sinus to form the trigonal area of the bladder.

In the male. The cranial portion of the duct becomes connected to the seminiferous tubules by way of some mesonephric tubules (these become the efferent ductules) and the rete testis. The part of the duct which is immediately adjacent to this point of junction with the efferent ductules becomes elongated and convoluted to form the epididymis and the remainder of the duct forms the ductus deferens. As it approaches the urogenital sinus, the duct becomes dilated and forms the ampulla from which a diverticulum arises to become the seminal vesicle.

That part of the original mesonephric duct which extends from this diverticulum to the urogenital sinus becomes the ejaculatory duct.

In the female. The caudal part of the duct gives rise to the ureteric bud and contributes to the formation of the bladder as in the male. However, the rest of the mesonephric duct degenerates, although part of it may persist in vestigial form as Gartner's duct which lies lateral to the uterus and in the anterolateral part of the vaginal wall.

The paramesonephric duct (fig. 37.50)

This duct appears in embryos of either sex at about 5 weeks after fertilization. It arises as an invagination of coelomic epithelium into the mesenchyme lateral to the cranial end of the mesonephric duct.

In the female. The original invagination persists as the abdominal ostium of the uterine tube. The caudal tip of the paramesonephric duct forms a solid cord which descends lateral to the mesonephric duct. As it descends, it canalizes in continuity with the abdominal ostium and the lumen extends progressively towards the solid growing tip. When it reaches the caudal extremity of the mesonephros, the paramesonephric duct crosses in front of the mesonephric duct and continues on its medial side. The two paramesonephric ducts meet and eventually fuse in the urogenital septum in the midline. This fusion is at first partial, so that a septum exists between the two

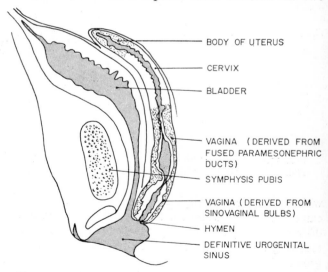

FIG. 37.51. Development of the vagina at 3 weeks. From Hamilton W. J., Boyd J. D. & Mossman H. W. (1962) *Human Embryology*, 3rd Edition, Cambridge: Heffer.

lumina. When the septum disappears, a single midline cavity is established and these fused segments of the paramesonephric ducts constitute the **uterovaginal canal.** The free parts of the ducts above the uterovaginal canal give rise to the uterine tubes.

The caudal tip of the uterovaginal canal remains solid and reaches the posterior wall of the urogenital sinus between the orifices of the mesonephric ducts. This solid cord is sometimes called the **vaginal cord** and where it reaches the urogenital sinus it produces an elevation in the posterior wall of the sinus called the **Müllerian tubercle** (fig. 37.51).

At about 3–3½ months, bilateral outgrowths from the Müllerian tubercle push back the vaginal cord, so increasing the distance between the lumen of the uterovaginal canal and that of the urogenital sinus. These outgrowths are called **sinovaginal bulbs** and together with the vaginal cord they constitute the **vaginal plate**. The vaginal plate is canalized by extension of the uterovaginal canal from above and by the breaking down of the epithelium of the sinovaginal bulbs from below. This process is not complete till late in foetal life.

The hymen is a partition which persists between the canalized fused sinovaginal bulbs and the urogenital sinus.

The future junction between the body of the uterus and the cervix becomes recognizable at about 10 weeks, but the uterine portion of the uterovaginal canal does not appear to be completely separated from the vaginal portion until 5–5½ months.

In the male. The paramesonephric ducts develop to the same extent as in the female until the 9–10th week. Thereafter they degenerate and lose their communication with the coelomic cavity.

DEVELOPMENT OF THE LOWER UROGENITAL TRACT AND EXTERNAL GENITALIA

The fate of the definitive urogenital sinus differs markedly in the two sexes. It may be divided into an upper **pelvic portion** which is widest in its transverse diameter and is continuous above with the primitive urethra, and a lower **phallic portion** which is related to the base of the phallic tubercle and is elongated in the sagittal plane. The urogenital membrane forms the floor of this phallic part.

Pelvic portion of the urogenital sinus

In the male. This forms the lower part of the prostatic urethra and the whole of the membranous urethra.

In the female. The pelvic portion of the urogenital sinus may contribute slightly to the lower end of the urethra.

The prostate gland

In the male. This gland develops when the embryo is about three months old as a series of buds growing from the primitive urethra and adjacent pelvic portion of the urogenital sinus. They grow into the surrounding mesenchyme which differentiates to form the fibro-muscular stroma of the gland. These buds arise from all sides of the urethra, both above and below the region of the orifices of the mesonephric ducts. An inner zone comprises the mucous and submucous glands and also the prostatic utricle, whilst an outer zone consists of the main prostatic glands.

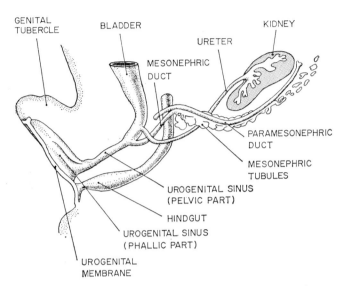

FIG. 37.52. Development of urogenital sinus at 7 weeks. From Hamilton W.J., Boyd J.D. & Mossmann H.W. (1962) *Human Embryology*, 3rd Edition. Cambridge: Heffer.

The prostatic utricle arises from the region of the Müllerian tubercle on the dorsal wall of the urogenital sinus, at the junction of the vesicourethral canal and the definitive urogenital sinus. In adult males the prostatic utricle ranges in size from a small blind diverticulum to a complicated glandular structure occupying most of the inner zone (median lobe) of the prostate. The Müllerian tubercle also gives rise to the prostatic glands of the inner zone, which comes to lie in the angle formed by the prostatic urethra and the mesonephric ducts on either side of the utricle, in other words, the glands of that part of the prostate called the middle lobe.

In the female. Comparable epithelial buds arise from the primitive urethra and the adjacent pelvic portion of the urogenital sinus to form the paraurethral glands, the latter being homologues of the median lobe of the male prostate.

EXTERNAL GENITALIA AND THE PHALLIC PORTION OF THE DEFINITIVE UROGENITAL SINUS (fig. 37.53)

In the neuter phase of sexual differentiation three small protuberances flank the external cloaca. These are the

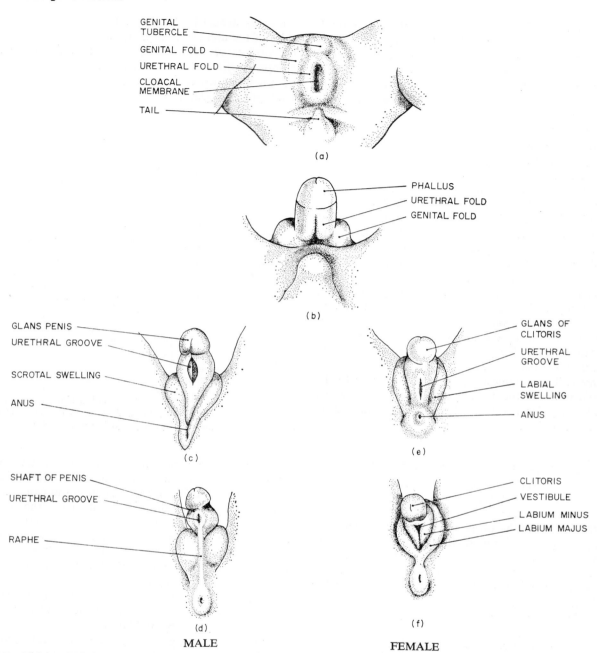

FIG. 37.53. Development of the external genitalia in both sexes. a and b—neuter stages; c and d—male; e and f—female. From Arey L.B. (1965) *Developmental Anatomy*, 7th Edition. Philadelphia: Saunders.

genital tubercle or phallus anteriorly, and the genital folds on either side. At about the 5th week, the endoderm which lines the inner surface of the urogenital membrane proliferates forwards into the mesenchyme of the phallus, forming the **urethral plate**. It grows forward in such a way that its lower margin remains in contact with the ectodermal epithelium covering the under surface of the phallus, and it eventually reaches the tip of the phallus in both sexes. The mesenchyme along each side of the

urethral plate proliferates and raises the overlying ectoderm to form primitive **urethral folds** between which the primitive **urethral groove** comes to lie (fig. 37.54).

The endodermal upper surface of the urogenital membrane forms the floor of the urogenital sinus, while its ectodermal aspect is continuous anteriorly with the ectodermal epithelium lining the primitive urethral groove. Thus, the urethral plate may be seen as a forward extension from the phallic part of the urogenital sinus.

After 6 weeks the urogenital membrane disintegrates with the result that the urogenital sinus comes to open to the exterior at the base of the phallus and an external opening is thus provided for the urogenital duct system. This converts the phallic part of the urogenital sinus into an open endoderm-lined trough flanked by the posterior portions of the primitive urethral folds and continuous along the phallus with the ectoderm-lined primitive urethral groove.

Later, the lower margin of the urethral plate (which lies in the floor of the primitive urethral groove) thickens and then disintegrates along with the ectoderm overlying it. This deepens the urethral groove which is now called the definitive urethral groove. This mode of formation accounts for the fact that the urethral grove is lined by endoderm in its deeper part and by ectoderm in its superficial part.

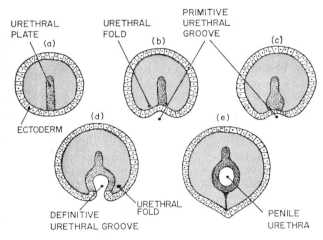

FIG. 37.54. Formation of the urethra. From Glenister, T. W. A. (1958) *Brit. J. Urol.*, **30**, 117.

In the male. The urethral folds begin to fuse in the midline when the foetus is about 2½–3 months old. Fusion starts at the base of the phallus immediately in front of the primitive central tendon of the perineum and extends towards the tip of the phallus. This converts the open phallic part of the urogenital sinus into the bulb of the urethra and the deeper part of the urethral groove into a tubular penile urethra. The urogenital orifice which was originally situated at the base of the phallus is thus carried progressively forwards towards the tip of the phallus or penis. A concurrent fusion of the genital folds forms the scrotum at the base of the penis.

After 3–3½ months, the urogenital orifice reaches the glans, which has become defined from the rest of the penis by the development of a circular coronary sulcus around the distal part of the shaft. The prepuce develops from folds which form just proximal to the coronary

sulcus. The urethral folds on the under surface of the glans are closely related to the prepuce and as they fuse to form the terminal part of the urethra a frenulum is formed on the under surface of the glans.

The terminal portion of the urethra is lined by an ingrowth of surface epithelium which extends into the substance of the glans to meet the distal extremity of the urethral plate. The urethral glands develop from the lining of the penile urethral walls, and the bulbo-urethral glands from the lining of the urethral bulb close to its junction with the membranous urethra.

In the female. The phallus and its glans develop to the same extent until about 2½–3 months, but the urethral folds do not subsequently fuse. In addition, the genital folds form labial swellings which flank the base of the phallus and the open trough of the phallic part of the urogenital sinus.

The phallus forms the clitoris, the labial swellings become the labia majora and the unfused urethral folds become the labia minora. The pelvic and phallic portions of the urogenital sinus are opened out to allow the vaginal orifice to reach the perineum and they both contribute to the formation of the vestibule. The greater vestibular glands (homologues of the bulbo-urethral glands) arise from the part of the vestibule derived from the phallic part of the urogenital sinus. Although a glans and prepuce are developed on the clitoris, failure of closure of the urethral groove causes the prepuce to be a hood-like structure which does not extend round the under surface of the glans.

The definitive form of the external genitalia is achieved in foetuses of both sexes when they are 4½–5 months old.

SEX DETERMINATION AND DEVELOPMENT

It should now be clear that there are fundamental structural and functional similarities between the reproductive tracts of the two sexes. At an early stage in development, sometimes called the neuter phase, each embryo possesses the potential to become either male or female. Development usually proceeds from this stage along separate lines so that the individual becomes unquestionably either male or female. However, in abnormal circumstances, this process of differentiation may deviate and produce a degree of intermediate or indeterminate sex, a condition known as intersexuality.

Sex is initially determined genetically at fertilization. In man, two special sex chromosomes can be identified, the female being homogametic, XX, and the male heterogametic, XY (p. 12.15). It is believed that there are female-determining genes on the X chromosome but that the male-determining Y chromosome predominates over the X chromosome. As a generalization, the female reproductive tract may be regarded as the basic unit upon which maleness may be superimposed. The absence of a Y chromosome permits the female system to develop. The presence of a Y chromosome induces male development. Nevertheless, a normal complement of two sex chromosomes is essential for normal sexual development. Thus, where there are three sex chromosomes, XXY, the individual is an apparent male but the testes fail to perform normal spermatogenesis. Conversely, in the presence of only one sex chromosome, XO, the individual appears to be female but the ovaries fail to develop normally.

Thus, initial sex determination is a function of the genotype, but genetic control of subsequent sexual development is not absolute. Somatic growth may be inappropriate to the genetic sex so that there may be a disparity between the genotype and its phenotypic expression.

The primary function of genetic sex determination is to control gonadal differentiation. At the neuter stage the gonads consist of both a cortex and a medulla. Testicular development is characterized by the appearance of a prominent tunica albuginea which cuts the cortex off from the surface epithelium, and by dominance of the medullary component. Seminiferous tubules are formed and diploid germ cells differentiate within these to produce spermatogonia. In the female, the tunica albuginea is inconspicuous in embryonic life, the cortical component dominates and the germ cells which accumulate in follicles within this zone form oogonia. The Y chromosome determines testicular differentiation, but a normal complement of two sex chromosomes is necessary for full gonadal development. Furthermore, local conditions in the genital ridge may also modify growth of the gonad.

The gonads in turn control the development of the genital duct system. The paramesonephric system is the basic unit which develops in the absence of testes. In this context, the foetal ovaries are probably simply permissive and are not necessary for paramesonephric duct growth. In the presence of testes, the paramesonephric ducts are suppressed and the mesonephric ducts take over the formation of the male genital tract. The testes exert this control by hormonal influence, but the effect of each

testis is confined to its own side and the effector substances are not necessarily androgens.

The testes also control the development of male external genitalia from the phallic part of the urogenital sinus by the release of sex steroids. Androgens cause the formation of the scrotum by fusion of the genital folds, enlargement of the phallus and development of a penile urethra. Again the foetal ovaries are probably passive and, in the absence of testicular androgens, the genital folds fail to fuse and persist as labia majora, the clitoris remains small, and the urethra opens directly into the vestibule.

Physical sexual maturation is completed at puberty by the development of secondary sex features and the onset of reproductive functions. These are determined by the release of testicular and ovarian sex steroids.

FURTHER READING

AUSTIN C.R. (1961) *The Mammalian Egg.* Oxford: Blackwell Scientific Publications.

CIBA Foundation Study Group No. 23 (1966) *Egg Implantation.* London: Churchill.

DONOVAN B.T. & VAN DER WERFF TEN BOSCH J.J. (1965) *Physiology of Puberty.* Monograph of the Physiological Society. London: Arnold.

FOLLEY S.J. (1956) *Physiology and Biochemistry of Lactation.* Edinburgh: Oliver & Boyd.

HAMILTON W.J., BOYD J.D. & MOSSMAN H.W. (1962) *Human Embryology.* Cambridge: Heffer.

HARTMAN C.G. (1963) *Mechanisms Concerned with Conception.* Oxford, London & New York: Pergamon Press.

HYTTEN F.E. & LEITCH I. (1964) *The Physiology of Human Pregnancy.* Oxford: Blackwell Scientific Publications.

MANN T. (1964) *Biochemistry of Semen and of the Male Reproductive Tract.* London: Methuen.

PARKES A.S. (1966) *Marshall's Physiology of Reproduction.* 3rd Edition. London: Longmans.

REYNOLDS S.R.M. (1945) *Physiology of the Uterus.* New York: Haffner.

YOUNG W.C. (1961) *Sex and Internal Secretions,* vols. I & 2, 3rd Edition. London: Baillière.

ZUCKERMAN S. (1962) *The Ovaries,* vols I & 2. London: Academic Press.

Chapter 38
Human genetics

To the nineteenth-century geneticists there appeared to be two general laws governing inheritance; firstly, like breeds like and secondly, inheritance blends. That black cats have black kittens and red antirrhinums crossed with white ones give pink antirrhinums are indisputable facts. These simple rules were used by live stock breeders over many centuries to produce the numerous breeds which are economically successful today. However, when inheritance is examined in detail, it is clear that such rules do not cover all situations nor do they even begin to suggest its mechanism. Many who attempted to explain the observed facts of inheritance failed to grasp one fundamental point, and not even Charles Darwin, whose theory of evolution required a rational theory of inheritance, realized that the essence of heredity is **genetic continuity**. Darwin's pangene hypothesis supposed that the germ cells contained material representative of all parts of the body and formed the basis from which a new individual emerged. This implied that one generation was formed *de novo* from the previous one. The idea of continuity, of a **germ plasm** set aside to preserve the characteristics of the species, arose from Mendel's demonstration that even when a particular character was not apparent in an organism, the factors controlling its inheritance might still be present and it might appear in later generations. The search for the mechanism which provides this continuity has formed the basis of modern molecular genetics. The concept of a molecule which has the capacity for self-replication provides a physical and chemical basis for the unbroken chain of life of which any individual is an ephemeral part. Such a sequence, however, would be a sterile perpetuation of the past if it were inflexible. This is not the case. There is an inherent variability in the system and mechanisms have evolved to ensure that variation occurs.

Human variation

In man there are striking differences in physical appearance, in stature and pigmentation, and possibly even more dramatic differences in intelligence and patterns of behaviour. This variation is determined by two main factors: the genetic constitution and the environment. The genetic constitution of an individual is the **genotype** and the sum of the physical and mental characteristics is the **phenotype**. While the phenotype is an expression of the genotype, it is in reality the interaction between the genetic constitution and the environment and it is not always clear how much each of these two components contributes to it. Certain characteristics, e.g. blood groups and eye colour, appear to be genetically controlled while other features such as behaviour and intelligence derive a major component from the environment.

ENVIRONMENTAL FACTORS

These operate on at least three different levels. Some exert their influence *in utero*. The genetic potentiality of a child to have normally developed limbs may not be realized if the embryo is exposed to a noxious agent such as thalidomide at a critical stage of morphogenesis. Such an influence has permanent effects on the physical form of the mature organism but does not affect the next generation. Secondly, environment may act directly in the adult. Severe haemolytic anaemia, arising after eating broad beans (*Vicia fava*) as already described on p. 26.8, occurs only in individuals who have a genetically determined deficiency of the enzyme glucose-6-phosphate dehydrogenase. It does not occur unless these individuals encounter the appropriate environmental stimulus. Thirdly, there may be a more subtle interaction over a long period of time between the genetic constitution of individuals in a population and their environment. A specific genetic constitution may be advantageous in a particular environment and by a process of natural selection individuals with this constitution become more numerous in the population. This concept of selection of the organism best adapted for life in a particular environment is the basis on which current notions of evolution are based and these have changed little since Darwin's time.

GENETIC FACTORS

Every individual within a species does not have an identical genetic constitution. There is variation from individual to individual and as discussed on p. 12.16 new combinations of these variations arise continually following crossing over during meiosis. Variation by recombination is, however, only a reshuffling of the existing genes. Totally new variants arise by mutation. Usually these are disadvantageous and are eliminated from the population; however, if the mutation rate is sufficiently high a population may always contain a small number of mutant individuals, there being a balance between mutation and elimination by selection. Sometimes a genetically determined variant becomes established in a population at a frequency that cannot be maintained by mutation alone. This must be the result of natural selection and where two or more variants of a single characteristic exist side by side in a single population then the population is said to show **genetic polymorphism** for this characteristic. Variation in blood groups is well known but more and more such polymorphic systems in blood proteins, red cell enzymes and tissue cell enzymes are being discovered.

Genetics in medicine

The study of human genetics is the study of human variation and of the interrelationship between genetic and environmental factors in causing this variation. Although the range of normality is wide, in some instances the variation falls outside the area which is considered normal. It is here that human genetics impinges on clinical medicine and this branch of human genetics is usually termed clinical or medical genetics. Human disease as with other features of man is determined partly by environmental and partly by genetic factors and again it is not always clear how much each contributes to the development of the disease. A disease, caused primarily by an environmental factor such as a micro-organism, a dietary deficiency or a mental stress may have manifestations which are in some individuals due to their genetic constitution. As environmental factors are controlled, the genetic component in human disease becomes relatively more important. It is important to stress the effect of environment on genetically determined disease; genetic disease is not untreatable disease.

THE GENE IN THE CELL

The Gene

This word was used by early geneticists to describe a factor controlling the inheritance of a particular characteristic. Although for many years this abstraction could not be related to any physical structure or chemical substance, the concept of a gene as a factor controlling a specific inherited feature was valuable in the study of heredity. Even now, when the chemical basis of inheritance is being elucidated in great detail, this concept is still of value.

The role of DNA as the genetic material of the cell is described on p. 12.1. What is the relationship between this molecular complex and the gene of classical genetics? This is most easily understood by considering briefly the mechanism of gene action. In 1908 A.E. Garrod published his monograph on *Inborn Errors of Metabolism* in which he formulated the concept that these errors were due to a block in the normal metabolism of the body and that this was due to the congenital absence of a particular enzyme. From this idea evolved, many years later, the idea that each gene controlled the production of a single enzyme, the one gene, one enzyme hypothesis. While this is a useful concept and undoubtedly contributed to the understanding of the mechanism of gene action, it now requires modification in certain circumstances, e.g. it is known that two or more independent regions of the DNA may be involved in the production of a single enzyme. This is reasonable in chemical terms since an enzyme, being a protein, may be composed of more than one polypeptide chain. Regions which code for different polypeptides of a single protein are often located close together, but this is not always so e.g. the two regions coding for the alpha and beta chains of the haemoglobin molecule are located on different chromosomes. Similarly the sequences of DNA which code for groups of associated enzymes in a series of biochemical reactions are frequently closely associated in the genetic material. Thus one can regard a gene as a region of the DNA which codes for a single polypeptide molecule. In this sense the word still retains its original meaning of a factor which controls a specific inherited characteristic, since, even if only one polypeptide of an enzyme composed of two polypeptides is involved in a genetic change the nature of the whole product is affected.

Control of gene action

The total number of genes of an organism such as man is very large, and it is clear, even in micro-organisms, that all of the genetic material is not active all the time. There must, therefore, be control mechanisms for switching on and switching off the gene action. The most widely held view is that the product of a sequence of DNA can have one of two functions. It may become a structural component of the organism or an enzyme concerned in the synthesis of such a component. Alternatively the product may exert an influence on other regions of the DNA and so modify or regulate the activity of that region. The former is a **structural gene** and the latter a **regulator gene**. One regulator gene controls the activity of a group of structural genes and is sensitive to the synthetic activity of the cell, which in turn is influenced by the external environment of the cell and of the organism, and hence exerts a feed back control on the structural genes. It is probable that the regulator gene makes a product termed a **repressor** which can exist in either an active or inactive state. When in the inactive state (combined with an **inducer**) it cannot interfere with the associated structural genes and the gene product is synthesized (fig. 38.1a). When in the active state (combined with a **co-repressor**) it appears to bind with a specific site termed the **operator** in or near the DNA of the structural gene. If the operator is blocked synthesis cannot proceed (fig. 38.1b). The grouping comprised of operator and the associated structural genes under the control of a single regulator gene has been termed an **operon** which is the basic unit of genetic function. This mechanism is probably

FIG. 38.1. Control of gene action (see text).

only one of the devices for controlling the activity of the genetic material and we do not yet know how the action of the regulator gene is controlled. It must also be borne in mind that this scheme for the control of gene action has been worked out almost entirely with bacteriophages and its applicability to higher organisms is at present a matter for speculation.

Genes at a locus

The DNA in higher organisms is organized into chromosomes and a particular region of DNA (or gene) is, with a few rare exceptions, always situated at the same site on the same chromosome. This site is termed a **locus**. Since the chromosomes are in pairs, one member of each pair being maternal in origin and one paternal, there are two **homologous loci** for each gene in every cell, with the exception of the sex chromosomes in the **heterogametic sex**, i.e. the sex in which the two sex chromosomes are unlike. In man and other mammals this is the male, but in birds

34

the female. The genes at a given locus are not always identical. Variants at a single locus are called **alleles**. The common situation is for one allele (the **wild type**) to be found in the large majority of the individuals in a naturally occurring population while other alleles have probably arisen as variants of the wild type. Such **mutations** may lead to an abnormal gene product with only partial function or to the total absence of a product and, very rarely, to a product which is as good as or better than the product of the wild type gene. In molecular terms a mutation is an alteration in the sequence of bases in the region of DNA coding for a polypeptide, while the smallest unit which can mutate is a single base pair

FIG. 38.2. Mutation. Linear sequence of bases in DNA, A: adenine; C: cystosine; G: guanine; T: thymidine. (a) Normal reading. Each triplet 'in frame'. (b) Substitution of a single base. One amino acid is altered. The remainder of the sequence still reads 'in frame'. The product may have some biological activity. (c) Deletion of a single base. All triplets to the right of the deletion now read out of frame. The amino acids are changed and the product will almost certainly have no biological activity.

(**muton**). The substitution of a single base pair leads to the alteration of a single amino acid and probably to an altered but related product (fig. 38.2b). For example, as described on p. 26.6, each of the several different normal and abnormal haemoglobins which have been adequately studied in man are the consequence of the substitution of a single base in the haemoglobin gene. Similarly a mutation can result from the omission of a single base (fig. 38.2c). Since this, however, results in all the succeeding triplets of the sequence reading out of frame, the whole sequence is now altered and no functional product can be detected. A similar consequence results from the insertion of a single base. One of the key pieces of evidence in determining the triplet nature of the genetic code was the finding that while one, two or four base deletions or insertions gave no meaningful products, three such deletions or insertions put the code back in frame and gave a modified but recognizable product. The causes of mutations are described on p. 38.9.

Interaction between genes

We have already seen that there are regulatory interactions between genes. The transfer of a gene to a new locus may modify its function (**position effect**). It is important, however, to consider the relationship between the two alleles at homologous loci in a single cell. These two alleles may be identical or they may differ. If they are the same the individual is said to be **homozygous** for this gene, and if they differ the individual is **heterozygous**. In a heterozygote the phenotype will depend on the interaction between the two differing alleles. At one extreme, a **dominant** allele may be expressed fully and the **recessive** allele not at all, so that the phenotype is the same as in the homozygous dominant individual. Dominance may not be complete so that phenotype is intermediate between that of the two homozygotes. A great many genes fall into this category of **intermediate inheritance** and provide a range of differing degrees of interaction. In some cases both alleles are expressed fully and more or less equally. Such a situation, termed **co-dominance** is found in the AB blood group in man.

GENES IN FAMILIES

The basic rules

The second main consideration concerns the transfer of genetic information from generation to generation. Despite many efforts to determine the rules which govern inheritance, it was not until 1900, when a number of workers independently came to reconsider and confirm the results which Gregor Mendel had obtained in 1865, that the basic laws became clear. Although these laws are still fundamental, many modifications and qualifications must now be made. One of the reasons for Mendel's success was his use of clearly distinct characters and his careful choice of stocks which bred true.

MENDEL'S FIRST LAW—INDEPENDENT SEGREGATION (fig. 38.3.)

When a male from a line which is pure bred for a particular character (a homozygous male) is crossed with a female from a line which is pure bred for a different but allelic character (a homozygous female) the offspring are all of one kind, i.e. all heterozygotes. The parents in such a cross are the **first parental (P1) generation**, and the progeny are the **first filial (F1) generation**. The phenotype of the progeny depends on the interaction between the two alleles. They may be identical with one or other of the parents if one allele is dominant, or intermediate in

FIG. 38.3. Mendel's first law: independent segregation. A and a are two allelic genes, where A is dominant to a. Note the 3 : 1 ratio of phenotypes in the F2 generation, but a 1 : 2 : 1 ratio of genotypes.

their phenotype if one allele is not completely dominant over the other, or show a mixed phenotype if there is co-dominance. When members of the heterozygous F1 generation are crossed with each other, the new progeny, **the second filial (F2) generation** are not all alike, but of three kinds always in the same proportion. There will be on average one individual like one of the original P1 parents, two like the heterozygous F1 generation and one like the other P1 parent. This is known as the 1 : 2 : 1 ratio. If, of course, one gene is completely dominant this will appear as a 3 : 1 ratio. When the gametes are formed in meiosis the members of each of the homologous pairs of chromosomes are distributed to separate gametes. Thus for a pair of allelic genes, the one derived from the maternal parent and the one derived from the paternal parent, go into different gametes. Thus the gametes from a homozygous parent are all alike, but those of a heterozygous parent are of two kinds. When the F1 cross is made there is one chance of a new homozygote being formed for each type and two chances of a new heterozygote being formed. One can say that the two alleles segregate independently in the offspring.

MENDEL'S SECOND LAW—INDEPENDENT ASSORTMENT

When a cross is made between two individuals, one homozygous for two different genes and the other homo-

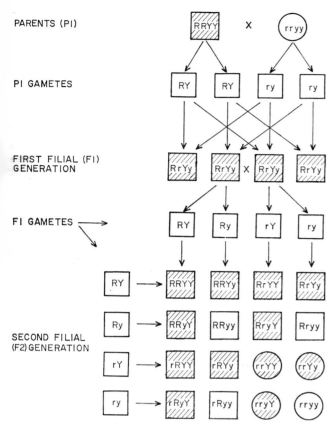

PARENTS (PI)

PI GAMETES

FIRST FILIAL (FI) GENERATION

FI GAMETES

SECOND FILIAL (F2) GENERATION

FIG. 38.4. Mendel's second law: independent assortment. R and r are a pair of allelic genes, where R is dominant to r. Y and y are a pair of allelic genes, where Y is dominant to y. In the F2 generation, the progeny are in the ratio—9 double dominant phenotype : 3 one dominant character : 3 the other dominant character : 1 double recessive phenotype.

zygous for two different alleles at the same loci, it can be shown that each obeys Mendel's first law without regard to the presence of the other gene (fig. 38.4). The FI generation must all be heterozygous for both genes. In the F2 generation there will be progeny of several different types again in definite proportions. Thus in Mendel's original experiment round (RR) yellow (YY) peas were crossed with wrinkled (rr) green (yy) peas. Nine of the offspring are like the dominant parent in respect of both characters. In spite of this phenotypic resemblance it can be seen that they are genetically of several different kinds and, if the relationship between alleles is not complete dominance, this will be expressed phenotypically. Three of the progeny are like the dominant parent in respect of one character only and three are like the dominant parent in respect of the other character. One of the F2 generation resembles the recessive parent in respect of both characters. This is the 9 : 3 : 3 : 1 ratio which refers to the phenotype only, in a straight double-dominant cross. In this experiment the characteristics

were free to assort themselves in a gamete independently of the other genes present. There is no general tendency for genes from one parent to remain together.

Factors which modify these ratios

LINKAGE

Although Mendel's second law holds good for most genes, it does not necessarily hold good for genes which are on the same chromosome. Loci which are situated on the same chromosome are said to be **linked loci**. In the fruit fly *Drosophila* the linkage groups and indeed the relationships between the linkage groups and the morphological chromosomes have been mapped out in detail. In the mouse there are a number of clearly defined linkage groups but these are not yet related to specific chromosomes. In man only one linkage group, the genes located on the X chromosome, has so far been demonstrated but a number of pairs of autosomal linkages are also known, for example, the linkage between loci for the ABO blood group and for an inherited malformation known as the nail–patella syndrome.

RECOMBINATION

Equally, there are exceptions to the rule that genes on a chromosome tend to stick together. Crossing over during meiosis causes genes on the same chromosome to be separated from each other. The further apart the genes the more likely they are to be separated by crossing over. This has enabled geneticists not only to construct linkage groups but to map, in relative terms, distances between genes; genes close together are a small number of cross over units apart, while distant ones are a large number of such units apart. It should be remembered that two cross overs between a pair of loci on the same strand does not result in their separation, for though one cross over separates them a second reunites them on the same chromosome. Similarly an odd number of cross overs separates genes but an even number keeps them together. Such multiple exchanges, of course, result in major rearrangements in the intermediate region. These are referred to as **recombinations** of the genetic material and the resulting progeny are the **recombinants**.

EXPRESSIVITY AND PENETRANCE

As already mentioned, genes are not always completely dominant and completely recessive and there are intermediate situations of two basic types. The factors controlling these are not always clear. First in a single individual the degree of expression of a dominant gene may vary. For example in certain malformations of bone in man some individuals carrying the dominant gene are severely affected and others only mildly. Such a gene is said to vary in **expressivity**. The second possibility is that under particular conditions the gene which is normally inherited as a dominant fails to be expressed at all in some individuals. This could be due, for example, to interaction with another non-allelic gene, but it does not alter the basic nature of the gene, which remains a dominant gene. If a dominant gene is expressed either in full or in part, in all individuals who carry it it is said to show **100 per cent penetrance**. When not all carriers of the gene are affected it is said to show **incomplete penetrance**. These two facts are of great importance in constructing human pedigrees for the purpose of determining the mode of inheritance of a particular characteristic or clinical syndrome.

AGE EFFECTS

Particular genes exert their effect at different stages of development. Some are concerned with morphogenesis and early life and are probably not used in the adult. In man, for example, the foetal blood contains a type of haemoglobin different from that in the adult. The manifestation of some genes may not appear until well into adult life, for instance Huntington's chorea a disorder causing uncoordinated involuntary movements. This makes the interpretation of human pedigrees and genetic counselling difficult in such cases.

PLEIOTROPY AND POLYGENIC INHERITANCE

In Mendel's experiments the characters were simple and clear cut. While many such characters exist, it is not uncommon for a single gene to affect many different characteristics (**pleiotropy**) or for many genes to control a single character (**polygenic inheritance**). Pleiotropy is easily explained in terms of enzymic reactions. If a mutation affects one enzyme, all the systems in the body utilizing it are affected. Phenylketonuria is an example

in which the primary deficiency is the inability to synthesize phenylalanine hydroxylase (p. 11.25). This single defect has different manifestations and the patient may be mentally deficient, and have the blue eyes and fair hair due to deficiency of pigment formation as well as excreting phenylpyruvic acid in the urine.

Similarly one can think of polygenic inheritance in terms of enzymic reactions. One end product may arise from a series of such reactions. Mutations of any one of the enzymes may cause the end product to be lost or be formed differently. In most cases the biochemical basis is not known, but it is clear that polygenic inheritance is of frequent occurrence and in some cases it can be quantitated. Where mating is random the number of genes in common for a character, determined by genetic factors is proportional to the degree of relatedness of the individuals in the family. Thus close relatives are more alike in respect of this character than distant relatives. On the other hand when a dominant gene is involved, the resemblance between affected cousins is just as great as that between affected brothers. Finger prints are one example of polygenic inheritance, for there is a correlation between the total ridge counts in the dermal pattern and the degree of relatedness in the individuals.

Patterns of inheritance

With these reservations in mind, let us look at the consequences of the laws of inheritance in terms of the patterns of inheritance which are observed in families. There are two fundamental types of inheritance. These are autosomal inheritance where the gene in question is on an autosome and sex-linked inheritance when the gene in question is on one of the sex chromosomes. The symbols used in recording pedigrees are given in fig. 38.5.

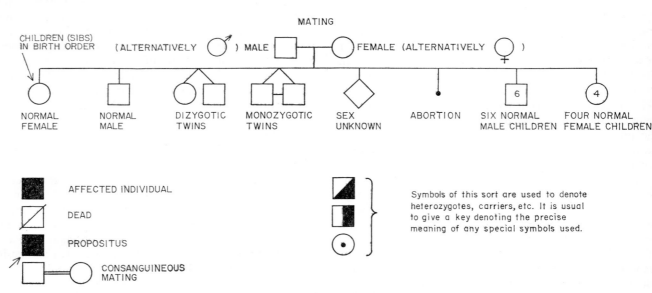

FIG. 38.5. Symbols commonly used in the recording of pedigrees.

AUTOSOMAL INHERITANCE

The main feature of this type of inheritance is that males and females are equally affected and it may be either

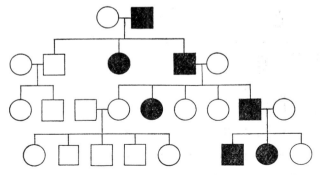

FIG. 38.6. Autosomal dominant inheritance. Composite pedigree demonstrating the main features: (1) the character appears in every generation; (2) half the offspring of an affected individual are also affected regardless of sex; (3) unaffected persons do not transmit the character.

| ■ | HETEROZYGOUS FOR AUTOSOMAL RECESSIVE GENE | ■ | HOMOZYGOUS AFFECTED INDIVIDUAL |

FIG. 38.7. Autosomal recessive inheritance. Composite pedigree demonstrating the main features: (1) the character does not appear in every generation; (2) unaffected heterozygotes (carriers) transmit the gene to half of their offspring regardless of sex; (3) both parents of an affected individual are carriers; (4) two carrier parents will have one child in four affected; (5) parents may be consanguineous.

dominant or recessive. An **autosomal dominant** gene will be manifested in the heterozygous condition. Fig. 38.6 illustrates three general rules, but these may be modified by all the factors already discussed, e.g. if a dominant gene has less than 100 per cent penetrance it may appear to skip a generation. However, the general pattern is still recognizable. **Autosomal recessive** inheritance has also a number of characteristic features which are a consequence of the fact that the effect of the gene is only manifested in the homozygous condition. A pedigree illustrating these is shown in fig. 38.7.

SEX-LINKED INHERITANCE

Characteristically one sex is affected more than the other, the predominant sex depending on whether the gene is X linked or Y linked. As Y-linked genes are so rare, X linked and sex linked are commonly used as synonyms. The most common type in man is **sex-linked recessive inheritance**. Examples are colour blindness, haemophilia, and Duchenne muscular dystrophy. The characteristic features are given in fig. 38.8. This type of inheritance arises because the female has two X chromosomes and the male only one and he is therefore **hemizygous** for genes on the X chromosome. Although the gene is recessive it will therefore be expressed in all males who have an X chromosome carrying the gene. In females a single X carrying the trait is masked by the normal X chromosome. Only when a female is homozygous will she be affected and consequently affected females are rare. Obviously such a female will transmit to all her sons, and all of her daughters will be carriers.

    Sex-linked dominant genes are rare in man. The best example is the Xg blood group. Characteristically a male who is phenotypically Xg(a+) transmits to all of his daughters but to none of his sons, while an Xg(a+) female transmits to all of her children if her genotype is homozygous (Xg^aXg^a) and to half of her children regardless of their sex if she is a heterozygote (Xg^aXg) (fig. 38.9). For **Y-linked** inheritance only males are affected (fig.

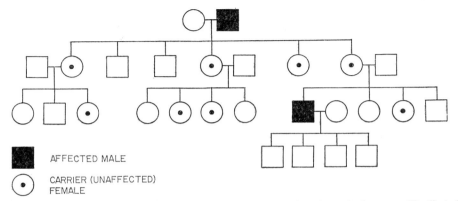

| ■ | AFFECTED MALE |
| ⊙ | CARRIER (UNAFFECTED) FEMALE |

FIG. 38.8. Sex-linked recessive inheritance. Composite pedigree demonstrating the main features: (1) affected males are more common than affected females; (2) an affected male cannot transmit to his sons but all his daughters will be carriers; (3) a carrier female transmits to half of her sons, and half of her daughters will be carriers.

FIG. 38.9. Sex-linked dominant inheritance. Composite pedigree demonstrating the main features: (1) an affected male transmits to all of his daughters and none of his sons; (2) a heterozygous affected female to half her children regardless of sex; (3) a homozygous affected female to all her children.

38.10). The only gene commonly accepted to be Y linked in man is the gene for hairy pinna of the ear. This character, described first in India, is transmitted by a father to all of his sons and none of his daughters, nor can the females be carriers.

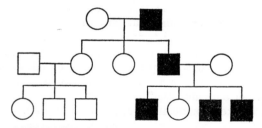

FIG. 38.10. Y-linked inheritance. A composite pedigree demonstrating the main features: (1) transmission by a male to all of his sons and none of his daughters; (2) females are not affected and cannot be carriers.

SEX LIMITATION

It sometimes happens that an autosomal gene affects one sex preferentially. This is probably because some factor in the other sex prevents expression of the gene. In the case of an autosomal dominant gene which is sex limited and expresses only in males, the pattern of inheritance has a superficial resemblance to that of a sex linked recessive gene but there are several important differences, e.g. a male can transmit to his son. However, if the condition renders the male patient infertile as in the testicular feminization syndrome the distinction between sex linked recessive inheritance and sex limited autosomal dominant inheritance cannot be made.

The typical modes of inheritance defined above are subject to all the modifications by the various factors previously described. Frequently in human genetics, sophisticated mathematical procedures are required to show that inheritance is of a particular kind.

TWINS

Dizygotic twins arise from the independent fertilization of two separate ova, and may thus be of like sex or opposite sex. **Monozygotic twins** arise from the separation of a single developing embryo into two independent parts and must be of like sex. They also have identical genetic constitutions. The diagnosis of zygosity is not always easy.

A study of monozygotic twins, especially comparison between those reared apart and those reared together, and the comparison between these two groups and dizygotic twins can yield useful information. For example, where environment plays a large part in the development of a particular character, a twin study may be the only way of determining whether or not the genetic constitution plays any part at all. The major factor in causing pulmonary tuberculosis is clearly the tubercle bacillus. Cases tend to occur in families but it is difficult to say whether this is due to the genetic susceptibility of the family or to their increased exposure to other cases of the disease. It has been shown that if a pair of twins are reared apart and one of them develops tuberculosis, the probability of the other developing the disease is higher for monozygotic than for dizygotic twins. This is evidence for a genetic component in the development of tuberculosis.

GENES IN POPULATIONS

Gene frequency

If it were possible to examine the genetic constitution of an entire population one could determine how many individuals had two copies of the same allele at the two available loci in the chromosome set, how many had one copy and how many had none. The ratio of the total number of copies of one particular allele to the total available loci in a population is the **gene frequency**. Obviously this figure cannot be determined directly but on theoretical grounds it can be predicted that if, in a population mating randomly, there are two alleles which have frequencies of p and q respectively, the proportion of individuals who are homozygous for p will be p^2 and those homozygous for q will be q^2 while the proportion of heterozygotes will be $2pq$. If the frequency of the homozygous recessive phenotype is known one can determine the gene frequency and also the frequency of heterozygotes in the population. For example, if the homozygous recessive phenotype occurs once in 10,000, i.e. $q^2 = 10,000$ then q (the gene frequency) is 1 in 100 or 0·01. The frequency of the wild type allele must therefore be 0·99 and the frequency of the heterozygotes will be 0·0198 or roughly 2 per cent. Similarly it can be shown that under conditions of random mating the gene frequency in the population will not alter from one generation to the next, table 38.1. The population where such an equilibrium holds good is said to be in **Hardy–Weinberg equilibrium**.

TABLE 38.1. Hardy–Weinberg equilibrium. Let *p* and *q* represent the gene frequencies of two alleles A and a. Assuming random mating the frequencies of the two homozygotes and the heterozygote will be:

AA	Aa	aa
p^2	$2pq$	q^2

The frequencies of the progeny in the next generation, assuming random mating, will be:

	AA	Aa	aa
AA × AA	p^4		
AA × Aa	$2p^3q$	$2p^3q$	
AA × aa		$2p^2q^2$	
Aa × Aa	p^2q^2	$2p^2q^2$	p^2q^2
Aa × aa		$2pq^3$	$2pq^3$
aa × aa			q^4

Total AA progeny $= p^2(p^2 + 2pq + q^2)$
Total Aa progeny $= 2pq(p^2 + 2pq + q^2)$
Total aa progeny $= q^2(p^2 + 2pq + q^2)$

Thus the ratio is still

AA	Aa	aa
p^2	$2pq$	q^2

Factors influencing gene frequency

The Hardy–Weinberg law is in fact the basis on which the study of population genetics is built. It gives a theoretical expectation of gene frequencies in a population and one can therefore determine factors which influence these frequencies.

NON-RANDOM MATING

We have already stated that random mating is necessary for the gene frequency to remain stable, and therefore non-random mating is one of the factors which influences this stability. In human populations non-random mating is a normal circumstance for a variety of socioeconomic and geographic reasons.

MUTATIONS

These arise through an alteration in the structure of the DNA and can be brought about by a number of environmental agents. Ionizing radiation is a potent mutagen and so are certain chemicals, such as nitrogen mustards. Work with experimental animals has also shown that temperature is a factor which can influence mutation rate. Mutation rates can be measured for genes in man but the calculation can be difficult, especially for autosomal recessive genes. For autosomal dominant genes, however, it is relatively simple. If the number of individuals born affected by an autosomal dominant gene to normal parents is measured and compared with the total number of births, the mutation rate can be calculated since an abnormal child affected by an autosomal dominant can only be born to normal parents following a mutation. Since mutations occur in a random way most of those produced are disadvantageous. Some are lethal, that is to say not compatible with life of the organism, while others are disadvantageous but not lethal. A small number, however, are advantageous and become established in the population by selection.

NATURAL SELECTION

The interplay between a large genetic variation and the environment leads to the selection of the best adapted phenotypes. As a result the best adapted individuals will tend to have more progeny than the others. It has been argued that, because man is to a certain extent in control of his environment, natural selection is no longer so rigorous for man as for other species. It would be more correct, however, to argue that selection is as rigorous as ever but that, because man is in control of his environment, the selection factors have been altered radically from those which operated before he reached his present level of sophistication. Medical science has undoubtedly played its part in this. For example, retinoblastoma, which is one of a very small number of malignant diseases that may be inherited and which until recently was usually lethal in early childhood, can now be treated successfully by surgery. Thus, this gene which is inherited as an autosomal dominant (sometimes irregularly) can now be passed on with a greater frequency from generation to generation because a higher proportion of those carrying the gene survive to child bearing age. Thus biologically this mutant is less deleterious than it was a short time ago. In a similar way many more haemophilic males now survive to reproductive age to pass on their mutant gene to the next generation. In these cases one can predict that the frequency of the gene will increase in the population. Instances of selection without the intervention of man are not hard to find. Sickle cell anaemia, a severe and often fatal haemolytic anaemia, is due to homozygosity for an autosomal recessive gene. However, in the heterozygous condition the sickle cell trait, which can be detected by an abnormality of the morphology of the red blood cells, is not associated with the anaemia found in the homozygous condition. Such individuals are very frequent in certain populations, e.g. in equatorial Africa, and unknown in others. It is now clear that the high frequency of the sickle cell trait in some populations is due to the fact that carriers of this trait have an unusual resistance to the malarial parasite; thus in areas where malaria is endemic carriers are at a selective advantage. The selection for the heterozygote results in a high frequency of an apparently deleterious gene. In areas where there is little or no malaria, selection factors operate against this gene.

GENETIC DRIFT

When a small population becomes separated from the main part of a population and remains separate for several generations, it is possible that its genetic constitution may show considerable divergence from that of the main population. This is because a small population is not necessarily a representative sample of the population from which it originated. These differences in the initial genetic structure of the population become accentuated over a long period of time. A group may be isolated for geographic reasons, e.g. the islanders of Tristan da Cunha, or for social reasons, e.g. religious minority groups in the U.S.A. These latter provide several interesting examples of genetic drift, e.g. the Dunkers of Pennsylvania have a distribution of ABO blood groups quite different from the population in Germany from which they originated. Similarly, in a classic study of the Old Order Amish of Lancaster County, Pennsylvania, McKusick has found that the frequency of a type of dwarfism associated with polydactyly is so high in this population of 8,000, that there may be as many cases as have been described in the entire world literature.

GENE FLOW

By this is meant the transfer of genes from one geographic region to another. In the past, local populations have developed their own pool of genes in response to the selection factors operating in their own area, but migration and intermarriage between adjacent communities has contributed to a flow of genes through the population. A good example is the distribution of blood groups in Europe where group B is common in eastern regions but becomes less frequent as one goes westwards.

Now that communication between different parts of the world is easier the flow of genes from one population to another has been dramatically speeded up.

CHROMOSOMES

"Point" mutations are only one kind of change in the genetic material of a cell. Alterations may come about by changes in the grouping of genes, by rearrangements of the existing chromosome material or by alteration in the number of chromosomes in the cell. Normal human chromosomes and normal cell division are described on p. 12.15.

Mechanisms of production of chromosome aberrations

Errors can occur at either mitotic or meiotic divisions and the consequences of these errors are quite different. Errors occurring during meiosis, i.e. during the formation

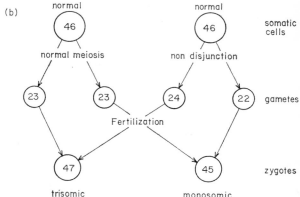

FIG. 38.11. (a) Mosaicism results from a mitotic error following fertilization. (b) Aneuploidy results from an error of meiosis prior to fertilization.

of the gametes result in the zygote being abnormal and hence all the cells of the individual developing from that zygote are abnormal. On the other hand an error of mitosis which occurs during development can lead to the production of an individual in whose body there are two or more kinds of cell with different genetic constitutions but which are derived from a single zygote. Such an individual is a **chromosome mosaic** (fig. 38.11a) which should be distinguished from a **chromosome chimaera** where two genetically different lines of cells in a single individual are derived from different zygotes, as in the mixing of blood cells which occurs regularly in cattle twins and rarely in human dizygotic twins following an anastomosis of the foetal circulation. Chromosome mosaicism results from an error of mitosis known as **anaphase lagging** where one chromosome fails to move from the equatorial plane of the cell at anaphase. This can result in the inclusion of the lagging chromosome in the wrong cell so that the daughter cells have forty-five and forty-seven chromosomes or its exclusion from either cell when the daughter cells will have forty-five and forty-six chromosomes. The exact composition of the individual depends on various factors such as the stage at which the error occurred, e.g. an error at the first cleavage division leads to a mosaic with two cell lines whereas a similar error at a later stage inevitably leads to a triple cell line mosaic provided that the cell lines are all viable and are included in the embryo.

Errors occurring during gametogenesis are of two kinds: those affecting chromosome number and those affecting chromosome morphology.

Those involving abnormalities of chromosome number probably all arise because of an error termed **nondisjunction**. If one pair of chromosomes fails to separate normally during meiosis both chromosomes of one homologous pair may be found in a single gamete or there may be no representative of that pair at all. In its simplest form these gametes have twenty-two or twenty-four chromosomes and, following fertilization, lead to the production of a zygote with forty-five or forty-seven chromosomes (fig. 38.11b). Such a zygote and the individual developing from it are said to be **aneuploid** (**euploid** cells are those containing exact multiples of the haploid number). The zygote with forty-seven chromosomes has three homologous chromosomes (**trisomy**) whereas the zygote with forty-five chromosomes has only one member of a homologous pair (**monosomy**). The effect on the developing individual will depend on which chromosome is involved. Some are lethal, e.g. no autosomal monosomies in man are known, but others lead to developmental abnormalities, e.g. children with Down's syndrome (mongolism) are trisomic for a G group chromosome. Nondisjunction can occur at the first or second meiotic division and it can occur in the male and in the female. Since most aneuploid individuals are sterile or of greatly reduced reproductive fitness these conditions are genetically determined but not inherited, with a few rare exceptions.

Abnormalities of chromosome morphology on the other hand can be inherited. These abnormalities all involve the breakage and incorrect rejoining of chromosomes and are of several different types. Probably the commonest is the **translocation** where a segment of chromosome is transferred to a different site. Most frequently such a transfer involves the reciprocal exchange of material between two chromosomes and may lead to the formation of chromosomes of abnormal morphology (fig. 38.12a). The available evidence in man suggests that such translocations are not associated with phenotypic abnormality in the balanced form, i.e. where all the genetic material is present but the offspring of such individuals may inherit the unbalanced form which is usually harmful. **Inversions** (fig. 38.12b) where the sequence of a segment of the chromosome is reversed have been described in man and no association with abnormality has been reported. On the other hand when a segment of the chromosome is entirely missing (**deletion**) there is usually some phenotypic abnormality (fig. 38.12c).

Aneuploidy involving the sex chromosomes occurs approximately once in every 600 births, and aneuploidy involving the autosomes is equally frequent. Translocations may be as common as 1 in 200 births and the other abnormalities relatively rare. Thus roughly 1 per cent of all children born have an abnormal chromosome constitution.

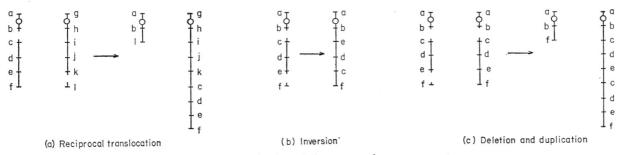

(a) Reciprocal translocation   (b) Inversion   (c) Deletion and duplication

Fig. 38.12. The production of chromosomal rearrangements.

Inheritance of chromosome aberrations

As with gene mutation the vast majority of chromosome aberrations are disadvantageous. In man, many cause infertility or defects so severe that reproduction, though possible, is highly improbable, but this is not an automatic consequence of chromosomal abnormality. For example, a female mouse with only one X chromosome instead of two (an XO sex chromosome constitution) is fertile and her offspring include further XO females. In man, a female with three X chromosomes instead of two (an XXX sex chromosome constitution) appears to be fully fertile but for some reason not yet understood all the children are normal, although on theoretical grounds half the offspring should have forty-seven chromosomes with an XXX, or an XXY sex chromosome constitution.

Rearrangements of the chromosome, as opposed to numerical aberrations, do not lead so regularly to diminished reproductive capacity. Some of these can therefore be passed on from generation to generation. The mode of transmission depends upon the precise nature of the rearrangement. A balanced translocation would in theory be passed on in the balanced form to 1 in 4 of the children, in one or other of the unbalanced forms to half the children, while the remaining quarter will have entirely normal chromosomes. In practice, however, this theoretical expectation is seldom, if ever, encountered, probably due to death of the unbalanced forms. This may be recognized as an increase in stillbirths or abortions in the families of carriers but if death occurs at a very early stage of embryogenesis they may not be recognized as abortions and there appears to be a 1 : 1 ratio of balanced translocation carriers to normal individuals.

In the case of inversions the abnormality should in theory be passed on to half of the children, but because of pairing difficulties at meiosis unbalanced forms would be expected. However, in the few cases known in man there appears to be little evidence for the production of such unbalanced forms.

Chromosome polymorphism

In some species, such as the common shrew, different subgroups are found within the species, each having a different karyotype. Frequently such polymorphisms are due to the end to end association of two telocentric chromosomes to give a single large metacentric chromosome, which results in a reduction in the chromosome number. It now appears that chromosome polymorphism also occurs in man. The frequency of aneuploid individuals discussed above is almost completely maintained by the occurrence of new aberrations. However, the situation for chromosomal rearrangements is quite different. For example, the D/D translocation occurs with a frequency of 1/1000 in the normal population and is transmitted from generation to generation with only a slight reduction in the fertility of the carriers. This frequency is probably higher than can be accounted for by the production of new aberrations and it seems that the population must be considered polymorphic for this rearrangement. This is an important practical point. Since there are relatively large numbers of individuals in the population with chromosome aberrations which have no apparent effect, these are encountered in patients from time to time purely by chance. Hence the frequency of such aberrations in the normal population must be considered before such an association is considered to be a causal factor of any disease.

FURTHER READING

COURT BROWN W.M. (1967) *Human Population Cytogenetics*. North-Holland Research Monographs, Frontiers of Biology, Vol. 5, Amsterdam : North-Holland.

HARRIS H. (1963) *Garrod's Inborn Errors of Metabolism*. Oxford Monographs on Medical Genetics. London : Oxford University Press.

MCKUSICK V.A. (1964) *Human Genetics*. New Jersey : Prentice Hall.

THOMPSON J.S. & THOMPSON M.W. (1966) *Genetics in Medicine*. Philadelphia : Saunders.

WATSON J.D. (1965) *Molecular Biology of the Gene*. New York : Benjamin.

Man in his environment

Chapter 39
On being born

During the last fifty years, improved social conditions and better maternal care have greatly reduced the hazards at the start of life, yet the transition from intrauterine to extrauterine life still has its dangers. In 1963 in England and Wales, thirty-one of every 1000 infants born did not survive the perinatal period, fourteen being stillborn and seventeen dying within a month. Physiologists are contributing to a reduction in foetal wastage by studying the adaptive processes during intrauterine life and in the perinatal period. Obviously, adaptive mechanisms vary depending partly on the stage of development reached at birth by different species. The groping, blind and naked newborn mouse needs and receives more protection from the elements than the active, upright, woolly lamb. The following account is mainly concerned with the human infant who is practically inaccessible in the uterus but is, when warm and well fed, a delightfully co-operative subject in the neonatal period. Fig. 39.1 shows how important it is for the human infant to be born

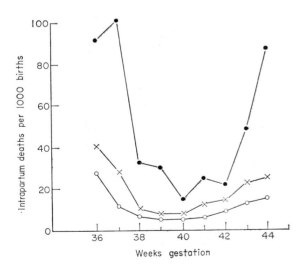

FIG. 39.1. Intrapartam mortality from asphyxia and/or trauma, at 36–44 weeks gestational age: ○, in infants of average weight (within 1 SD of mean); ×, underweight (−2 to −1 SD); ●, underweight (> −2 SD). From. Dawkins M. (1965). The 'small for dates' baby. In: *Gestational Age, Size and Maturity*.

after 40 weeks gestation and to have grown to the expected weight. Failure of a mother to adapt to pregnancy reduces the capacity of the infant to withstand the stress of labour and to adapt to its new environment.

The oxygen environment during labour

The supply of oxygen to the foetus during pregnancy is discussed on p. 37.43. Uterine contractions interfere with the placental circulation and so with the transport of the respiratory gases between mother and foetus. The frequency, duration and intensity of these contractions determine the extent of foetal asphyxia, and this changes the foetal heart rate. At term the rate is about 140 beats/min and the first indication of hypoxia is often an acceleration to 160–180 beats/min. However, this increase may not occur and the heart may slow down to 100–120 beats/min when the oxygen supply is reduced. A normal uterine contraction slows the heart for no more than 15 sec, and bradycardia lasting longer than this is evidence of more severe reduction in placental blood flow. Several mechanisms are responsible for these changes in foetal heart rate. The initial response of the cardiovascular centre in the medulla to hypoxia is tachycardia, but prolonged or severe hypoxia slows the foetal heart. Bradycardia is caused also by compression of the foetal skull. Compression of the umbilical cord can slow the foetal heart and this may be due to a transient rise in arterial pressure as a result of a reduced blood flow through the low resistance area of the placental vascular bed. This reflex bradycardia and that resulting from chemoreceptor stimulation are both abolished by atropine, a drug which paralyses the parasympathetic nerves. Animal experiments show no persistent bradycardia until the oxygen supply to the foetus is reduced to one-third of its normal value. This fact, together with the clinical evidence that infants may survive when the chorio-decidual blood flow has been reduced to one third of normal, suggests that there may be a large placental reserve. It is important to note that the foetal heart rate, which is the chief clinical guide to foetal welfare, may change only when this reserve is completely exhausted.

The oxygen debt incurred by the foetus during a normal

labour is small. At birth the plasma lactate level is slightly raised. It may double during the first minutes of life as lactate diffuses out of the tissues, but falls to normal levels within an hour. However, during difficult labours a large oxygen debt may cause metabolic acidosis with raised foetal plasma lactate at birth and this may not return to normal for many hours or even days. Acid base studies have been made on the human foetus during labour by sampling capillary blood from the presenting scalp of the infant. The blood collected from this source has an average pH of 7·36 during normal deliveries, and cardiac acceleration occurs when the pH falls below 7·26. The value of this method as a means of early detection of placental insufficiency and of consequent impairment of exchange between mother and baby depends upon repeated sampling. Measurements of Po_2 are of little value because they may change swiftly from minute to minute without any alteration in the circulation.

ALTERATIONS IN THE IMMEDIATE POSTPARTUM PERIOD

Normally the baby takes off to a flying start with the first good cry. The arterial Po_2 rises within minutes to 70–80 mm Hg and the haemoglobin is 80–90 per cent saturated with oxygen shortly after birth, reaching adult levels within hours or days.

The blood cells

Table 39.1 shows some normal haematological values in the new born. The red cells are usually a little larger than in adult life and they contain more haemoglobin, with MCHC values ranging from 30 to 35 per cent. Both the

TABLE 39.1. Some normal haematological values in the newborn.

Haemoglobin (g/100 ml)	
Capillary blood	14–22
Cord blood	13–18
Haematocrit value (%)	
Capillary blood	over 48
Cord blood	over 46
White cell count (cells/mm³)	
Capillary blood 1st day	15–45,000
8th day	8–16,000
Reticulocytes (%)	
Full term babies	4–6
Premature babies	up to 10

Hb concentration and the haematocrit rise during the first hours of life. The high values at birth are probably due to high levels of erythropoietin found in foetal blood, presumably in response to the low arterial Po_2. As the bone marrow becomes less active the Hb concen-

tration falls and by about 2–3 months of age the level has usually fallen to between 11 and 13 g/100 ml. This may be due to the low iron content of milk. The white cell count is high at birth, with a high proportion of polymorphs. During the 1st week of life the proportion of lymphocytes increases and the number of polymorphs falls. Platelets are small at birth and agglutinate more readily than in the adult, but their total number is similar to adult values.

The foetal circulation

Fig. 39.2 shows the course of the mammalian foetal circulation once the major channels have developed. The most oxygenated blood from the placenta reaches the foetus via the umbilical vein. The greater part of this umbilical venous blood perfuses the liver and then joins the inferior vena cava through the hepatic vein, but a small portion by-passes the liver and enters the inferior vena cava directly through the ductus venosus. On entering the

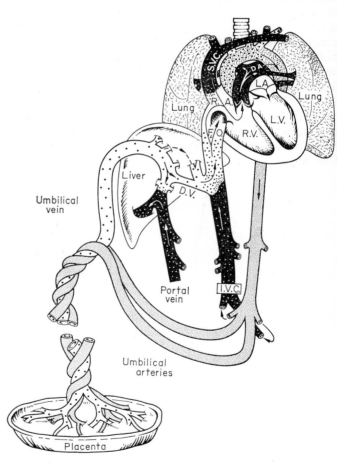

FIG. 39.2. Foetal circulation and probable course of the blood through the foetal heart. DV, ductus venosus; DA, ductus arteriosus; FO, foramen ovale. From Dawes G.S. (1964) *Textbook of Physiology and Biochemistry*, ed. Bell, Davidson & Scarbourgh. Edinburgh : Livingstone.

heart this inferior caval blood is divided by the septum secundum, forming the rim of the foramen ovale (fig. 39.3). The greater part of the flow is directed through the foramen ovale into the left atrium where it mixes with the small volume of pulmonary venous blood. This oxygenated blood leaves the heart by the left ventricle and is distributed mainly to the head and upper extremities.

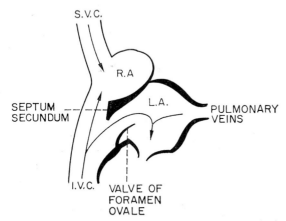

FIG. 39.3. Diagram of the great veins to show that the inferior vena cava blood divides into two streams in the foetus; one enters the right atrium and the other passes through the foramen ovale into the left atrium. From Dawes G.S. (1958) *Recent Advances in Paediatrics*, 2nd Edition. London: Churchill.

The smaller stream of inferior caval blood is diverted to the right atrium where it mixes with venous blood returning via the superior vena cava. After leaving the right ventricle, the greater part passes via the ductus arteriosus and so short-circuits the lungs to enter the descending aorta. This blood supplies the trunk and lower limbs or passes to the placenta for oxygenation.

FIG. 39.4. Schematic view of the foetal circulation, showing that both sides of the heart work in parallel; the flow through the main vessels is indicated in ml/kg/min. From Dawes G.S. (1958) *Recent advances in Paediatrics*, 2nd Edition. London: Churchill.

The distribution of the blood between the foetal tissues and placenta changes during growth. When the embryo is young the greater volume circulates in the placenta, but after mid-pregnancy when the placenta is approaching its maximum size, this distribution is reversed. Thus, the volume of blood which perfuses the foetal tissues steadily increases, while the capacity of the placental vessels remains relatively constant. Increased foetal requirements must then be met by an increase in flow of blood through the placenta. This is brought about by a reduction in placental resistance and by a rise in umbilical arterial pressure, which follows an increase in foetal vasomotor tone and foetal cardiac output. Fig. 39.4 shows the approximate distribution of the foetal blood flow at term as determined experimentally in the lamb. There is reason to think that the distribution of the cardiac output of the human foetus at term is similar.

The first breath

The immediate effect of delivery on the infant is the need for an abrupt transition from placental to pulmonary respiration and it is essential that adequate ventilation should be established without delay.

The infant's first breath establishes the respiratory mechanisms which subsequently maintain the ventilation-perfusion relationship in the lungs, so as to allow an arterial Po_2 of about 90 mm Hg. The capacity of the newborn to sustain this Pa,o_2 is of the utmost importance for survival, and it is important that the mechanisms required for respiration are developed long before they are normally brought into use. The rhythmic activity of the respiratory centre in adults is dependent upon a varied sensory input. At birth this centre receives a flow of new sensory impulses, notably from the skin and muscles as soon as the infant ceases to be 'weightless'. The mild acidosis which occurs during labour may also enhance the excitability of the respiratory centre, which becomes particularly sensitive to carbon dioxide once respiration is established. Since the carotid chemoreceptors show little activity until respiration is established, they probably play no part in initiating the first breath. The sensitivity of the pulmonary afferent endings is anomalous in early life and the Hering–Breuer reflex does not operate until 24–48 hours after birth. Gentle inflation of the newborn lungs causes a further increase in the depth of inspiration before expiration occurs and this may increase the effectiveness of positive pressure ventilation in aerating the alveoli.

MECHANICAL CHANGES IN THE LUNGS

Serial radiographs show that during the first few breaths the diaphragm plays a more important part than the other muscles in increasing the volume of the thoracic cage and developing a subatmospheric or negative pressure in the pleural space. Subsequent rhythmic breathing depends upon the expansion of the alveoli and the development of a functional residual capacity. Intra-thoracic pressures, as measured by an intraoesophageal manometer, fall to 40–60 cm H_2O below atmospheric pressure for about a second during the first few inspiratory efforts, and positive pleural pressures of 20–30 cm H_2O may also be developed during the first few expirations. These large inspiratory pressures are necessary to overcome resistance to the entry of air into the lungs.

One cause of this resistance is the viscous fluid which fills the foetal lung. Foetal alveoli have a glandular appearance and secrete a fluid with a pH about 6.4, low in protein and bicarbonate and with a high chloride content. Alveolar secretory capacity is sufficient to cause a rise in intratracheal pressure if the trachea is tied in experimental animals and it contributes to the volume of amniotic fluid. Amniotic fluid inhaled during labour may also be present, although some of this may be expressed through the mouth by the high intrauterine pressure transmitted to the foetal thorax during labour. This fluid disappears quickly once respiration is established, largely as a result of an increased pulmonary lymph flow.

A greater resistance to initial inflation of the lungs probably lies at the air–liquid interface in the terminal

FIG. 39.5. The pressure volume curves of an excised cat lung. ●, the low inflation pressure required with saline demonstrates the low resistance of the lung tissue; ○, the larger inflation pressure required with air demonstrates the high resistance at the air–lung interface.

small bronchioles. Fig. 39.5 shows the pressure–volume relations of an excised lung. When the lungs are filled with saline, complete expansion occurs in response to 2–3 cm H_2O pressure change because the compliance of lung tissue is high and offers little resistance to distension. However, when the lung contains air the pressure that is required to open the alveoli is higher by about 8 cm H_2O, and complete expansion requires an even

greater increase in pressure. When the pressure is reduced the volume changes do not follow the same curve. This suggests inherent instability of the system which is probably due to the different surface tensions at the air–liquid interface in alveoli of different sizes. The surface tension at the interface between liquid and air decreases lung compliance and increases the resistance to expansion. A surface-wetting agent, a lipoprotein known as surfactant, is present in the lung fluid at birth, and this has the ability to reduce surface tension at an air–liquid interface. Thus it stabilizes the alveoli so that those of different radius may remain connected without change in size.

THE INFLUENCE OF BIRTH ON THE PULMONARY CIRCULATION AND LARGE FOETAL CHANNELS

The umbilical arteries and vein all have thick muscular walls which are probably not innervated. This musculature is sensitive to cooling and mechanical stimuli, but the effectiveness of the contractile mechanisms is impaired by asphyxia. It is not known whether the hepatic blood flow changes at birth when the circulation through the umbilical cord ceases. The ductus venosus is still patent in the human infant at term but it must close soon after birth as otherwise the portal blood would short-circuit the liver and pass straight into the vena cava, as in an Eck fistula.

The first breath initiates changes in the course of the blood stream in the heart. Expansion of the lungs decreases the resistance in the pulmonary arterioles and so increases pulmonary blood flow. As a result, pressure in the left atrium rises above that in the inferior vena cava and this pressure gradient stops flow through the foramen ovale. Occlusion of the umbilical vessels helps by causing a temporary fall in inferior vena caval pressure. The whole inferior caval blood flow now joins the superior caval blood in the right atrium to maintain a high pulmonary blood flow. Because of the reduced pulmonary vascular resistance, pulmonary arterial pressure falls below aortic pressure and blood flow through the ductus arteriosus is diminished.

The reduction in pulmonary vascular resistance which follows the first breath depends upon inflation of the lungs with a gas of the correct composition since in the newborn the pulmonary arterioles are readily constricted by both hypoxia and hypercapnia. In the foetal lamb, pulmonary blood flow increases about tenfold following lung inflation. In the human infant, pulmonary arterial pressure is reduced by about half, to approximately 35 mm Hg, during the immediate postnatal period. How the ductus arteriosus closes is not yet clear. Its muscular layer resembles a sphincter but it is poorly innervated. Closure occurs when the Pa,O_2 is raised, but flow may start again if Pa,O_2 subsequently falls.

These changes in the small vessels and in the large cardiac channels all start abruptly, but take some weeks to complete. The unstriped muscle in the pulmonary arterioles gradually atrophies and their walls become thinner. After blood flow through the foramen ovale, ductus arteriosus and ductus venosus stops, all three channels gradually close. A mid-systolic murmur may be heard when listening to the heart sounds of normal infants during the first 2 weeks of life, indicating intermittent patency of the ductus arteriosus. The direction of flow depends upon the pressure difference between the aorta and pulmonary artery. In the neonate, flow should be from aorta to pulmonary artery, the reverse of the situation in the intrauterine circulation.

ALTERATIONS IN THE NEONATAL PERIOD
Respiration and circulation

LUNG MECHANICS

The important ventilatory values and subdivisions of lung volume in the newborn are summarized in table 39.2 and

TABLE 39.2. Ventilatory values in the newborn human infant compared with those of the adult.

	Newborn	Adult
Respiratory rate (min)	25–50	12
Minute volume (litres)	0·5	6·0
Alveolar ventilation (l/min)	0·38	4·0
Total compliance (ml/cm H_2O)	5	100
Airway resistance (cm H_2O/l/sec)	25	2
Oxygen diffusing capacity (ml/mm Hg/min)	2·5	30

fig. 39.6. It is difficult to collect expired air from the infant and many of the figures have been obtained by using the body plethysmograph (fig. 39.7). Advantage is taken of the infant's crying to measure the vital capacity. The respiratory rate is usually periodic and the work of respiration is minimal at a rate of about 37/min. The lung compliance is apparently low, but comparable with the adult when expressed in relation to the functional residual

FIG. 39.7. Diagrammatic longitudinal section through body plethysmograph for respiratory studies in infants. The head seal is shown and the outlet for pressure volume recording. The baby is clothed and covered with blankets. From Cross K.W. (1949) The respiratory rate and ventilation in the newborn baby. *J. Physiol.* **109**, 460.

capacity. Airway resistance is high due to the small diameter of the bronchioles.

CHEMICAL CONTROL OF RESPIRATION

This is similar in the newborn and the adult. The CO_2 sensitivity (p. 29.25) is the same as in the adult, provided the increase in ventilation for a given increment in alveolar PCO_2 is related to body weight. Arterial PCO_2 is low, about 32 mm Hg, for reasons unknown. Giving the neonate 15 per cent oxygen stimulates and 100 per cent oxygen inhibits ventilation, in each case only temporarily. These responses demonstrate the sensitivity of the peripheral chemoreceptor mechanisms and indicate that there is some resting tonic activity.

RESPONSES OF THE SYSTEMIC CIRCULATION

Table 39.3 sets out some normal haemodynamic values. In general, cardiac output and heart rate are high. As

TABLE 39.3. Circulatory values in the human foetus and newborn.

	Foetus	Newborn	Adult
Systemic arterial pressure (mm Hg)	70/45 (umb. art.)	70/45	120/80
Pulmonary arterial pressure (mm Hg)	—	35/15	30/10
Pulse rate/min	140	140	70
Cardiac output			
l/min	—	0·60	5
ml/kg/min	—	140	70
l/m²/min	—	2·5–3·0	2·5–3·0
Blood flow			
In pulmonary artery	small	large	
Through ductus arteriosus	large, to aorta	small, from aorta	nil
Limb blood flow (ml/100g/min)	—	4	2

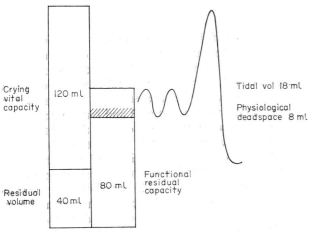

FIG. 39.6. Subdivisions of lung volume in the newborn human infant.

(figure labels: Crying vital capacity, 120 mL, Tidal vol 18 mL, Physiological deadspace 8 mL, Functional residual capacity, Residual volume, 40 mL, 80 mL) mean arterial pressure is low and peripheral blood flows are high, peripheral resistance is low. The blood volume forms a larger percentage of the total body weight than in the adult. The blood viscosity is also high due to the high haematocrit value.

The nervous pathways for cardiovascular reflexes are laid down early in intrauterine life, but their activity at birth is uncertain, and one cannot assume that the circulation behaves in the same way in the newborn as in the adult. In experimental animals, it can be shown that the carotid sinus reflex is present at birth. The change in peak frequency discharge of the baroreceptors in response to a given change in arterial pressure is the same in the newborn, with its low mean arterial pressure, as it is in the mature animal. However, in the intact newborn animal baroreceptor responses following a reduction in arterial pressure, induced by either haemorrhage or postural change, suggest that cardiovascular reflex activity is not yet fully developed. The response of chemoreceptors to stimulation by asphyxia also shows an increasing reflex activity with age. In the newborn arterial blood pressure is not well maintained when the blood volume falls or in asphyxia, suggesting that reflex vasoconstrictor activity is poorly developed, but there is a reflex increase in heart rate. Skin blood vessels constrict readily in a cold environment but vasodilation in response to a rise in body temperature is not regularly observed until the third or fourth day of life. The capacitance of the venous system must be large, for the infant's circulating blood volume can be increased abruptly by about 30 per cent at birth by transfer of blood from the placental circulation, and yet there is only a small increase in right atrial pressure.

Even if cardiovascular reflexes were as active in the young as in the adult, the final pattern of response might still be different for two reasons. Firstly, as an infant has a relatively larger head and smaller limbs than an adult, the relative size of the vascular beds subject to reflex control differ. Secondly, intermittent patency of the ductus arteriosus may modify the effects of changes in vasomotor tone and in cardiac output.

Temperature regulation

When the newborn leaves the tropical climate of the uterus, the change in environmental temperature provides another stress to which it must respond. The neonate has two special problems with regard to temperature control and this is reflected in the instability of its body temperature; these are the inadequacy of the heat-producing mechanisms and the fact that its large surface area relative to body weight increases the opportunities for heat loss.

HEAT PRODUCTION

In the newborn, oxygen consumption is only a little above intrauterine levels, but it rises to 8 ml/kg/min at 14 days, about double the value at birth. Fig. 39.8 shows the metabolic responses of kittens to cold at different ages. The critical environmental temperature which stimulates heat production falls during development. The neutral temperature range, in which heat loss is regulated by vasomotor and sudomotor responses with no change in heat production, increases with age. The human newborn cannot shiver because the nervous system is not sufficiently developed. However, heat production in response to cold takes place in brown fat

FIG. 39.8. The influence of environmental temperature on heat production and body temperature in newborn kittens aged (a) 3 hours, (b) 2 days, (c) 4 days, and (d) 7 days, showing the neutral temperature and critical temperature and the increase in maximum heat production with age. From Hill J. (1961) Reactions of the newborn animal to environmental temperature. *Brit. med. Bull.* **17**, 166.

(p. 32.2). The distribution and amount of brown fat in the newborn varies among different species. In the human infant it is found chiefly on the floor of the posterior triangle of the neck surrounding the subclavian and carotid vessels and in the perirenal areas. The mobilization of triglycerides is probably initiated and maintained within this tissue by the local release of noradrenaline at the sympathetic nerve endings. The free fatty acids are oxidized *in situ* and the glycerol liberated into the blood stream. A rise in blood glycerol concentration can be observed after exposure to cold. Stimulation of the sympathetic nerves which innervate brown fat increases local blood flow and local heat production, and removal of the brown fat abolishes the thermal response to cold without altering the metabolic rate. Heat production in response to cold is reduced by hypoxia and by starvation, which reduces the supply of substrates for the resynthesis of triglycerides.

HEAT LOSS

Environmental heat loss depends upon air temperature, air movement and radiant temperature, and can be modified by postural changes and alterations in tissue insulation under vasomotor control. In spite of the increase in heat production of which the newborn is capable, the battle to meet the losses from its large surface area is frequently lost. Thermal loss is enhanced by the high conductance of the skin since both skin and subcutaneous tissue layers are thin. In most climates some clothing is required to reduce these losses. In the immediate postnatal period evaporation from the wet surface of the skin may cause heat loss but this can be limited to some extent by skin vasoconstriction, especially in the human infant. A baby seal is unable to reduce its heat loss and it may drown in a pool of water formed from the snow which it has melted.

Premature infants are at a particular disadvantage if they are not kept in a warm environment, because heat losses are disproportionately greater owing to their relatively large surface. Although they can increase their heat production, their brown adipose tissue is not rich in lipid. Body temperatures may fall as low as 25°C in newborn infants who are insufficiently clothed and exposed to cold and the 'cold injury' syndrome may develop.

The liver

What fuel is available to meet the energy requirements of the foetus and newly born? There are ample carbohydrate stores in all foetal tissues. The glycogen concentration in early foetal life is high in the heart and lungs. During the second half of pregnancy, glycogen stores are built up in the liver (fig. 39.9). This provides sufficient energy to cover the needs of the infant during labour and the first few hours of extrauterine life. Immediately after birth the respiratory quotient (RQ) is about 1·0, but it soon falls as the reserve of carbohydrate is used up and it may be as low as 0·70 after 2–3 days before lactation is fully established. The liver glycogen store is replenished in a few days when carbohydrate become available in the diet, although the concentrations of the necessary enzymes, hexokinase, phosphorylase and glucose-6-phosphatase, are usually low in the neonatal liver, but increase to normal values within 2–3 weeks.

BLOOD GLUCOSE REGULATION

The blood glucose varies quite widely immediately after birth and often falls below 40 mg/100 ml. When glycogen stores are depleted the blood glucose can fall to levels which would cause neurological disturbances and coma later in infancy and certainly in adults. These

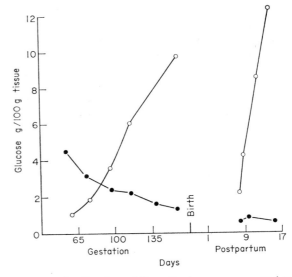

FIG. 39.9. Cardiac ●, and liver ○, glycogen, expressed as mg glucose/g wet weight, in the foetal and newborn monkey. From Shelley H.J. (1961) Glucogen reserves and their changes at birth. *Brit. med. Bull.* **17**, 138.

clinical features do not occur in the infant. The concentration of blood glucose rarely reaches adult values until the milk supply is established. Apnoea and cyanosis may occur when the blood sugar falls below 20 mg/100 ml for long periods and these may be relieved by giving glucose. The manner of control of the blood sugar in the neonatal period is unknown but it differs from that in adult life. Thus, if glucose is given by mouth to the normal infant it may not cause the expected rise in blood glucose. Glucose given by intravenous infusion is removed more slowly than in the normal adult. There is a delayed release of insulin, despite the fact that the pancreas has a large store of it. Gluconeogenesis must be important in the regulation of blood glucose in the newborn period because milk contains little carbohydrate.

PROTEIN AND LIPID METABOLISM

Foetal extracellular fluids, in common with other rapidly growing tissues, contain high levels of free amino acids. The liver accumulates amino acids early in intrauterine life and nucleic acid metabolism and protein synthesis are very active in both the foetus and newborn. Part of this hepatic activity may be concerned with its haemopoietic function which is not usually relinquished until the end of pregnancy. With the exception of the immunoglobulins, plasma proteins do not cross the placental membrane, nor are they synthesized by the placenta. Albumin synthesis has been demonstrated in early embryonic liver slices. In the newborn, plasma protein levels are usually below adult values, especially if the infant is premature. The plasma prothrombin level is often low but fibrinogen levels are normal. The activity of the enzymes required for amino acid breakdown and the urea cycle is low at term but increases rapidly after birth.

Significant amounts of lipid do not cross the placenta from the mother, but lipid synthesis occurs actively in foetal liver. The liver contains large stores of triglyceride at term but the plasma levels are low. Soon after birth the liver stores decline and plasma triglyceride and FFA rise. The RQ falls with the increasing utilization of fat.

BILIRUBIN EXCRETION AND DETOXICATION MECHANISMS

All foetal plasma bilirubin is in the free unconjugated form and is excreted slowly by diffusion through the placenta. Conjugated bilirubin in the maternal plasma does not cross into the foetal plasma. The activity of the foetal liver enzymes which conjugate bilirubin with glucuronic acid is low at term but increases rapidly after birth, and the water-soluble glucuronide begins to be excreted with the bile. Physiological jaundice is therefore common in the first 7 days of life. It usually appears on the second or third day and then fades. Many of the mechanisms for the detoxication of drugs are not fully developed in the liver at birth and the administration of drugs to the newborn presents many clinical problems.

Gastrointestinal tract

The gut becomes motile and capable of secretory activity by mid-pregnancy. Motility has been demonstrated by the intra-amniotic injection of a radio-opaque material, some of which is swallowed and can be followed in its passage down to the rectum. The transition from a placental to an intestinal route for nutrient intake constitutes another new task for the newborn. The whole gut is very distensible and is variable in size and activity. The muscle layers are thin in comparison with the adult, and the longitudinal muscle fibres of the stomach are particularly deficient over the greater curvature. The stomach is usually empty 3–4 hours after a feed. Emptying is not influenced by the large quantity of air which the infant may swallow.

SECRETIONS

Ptyalin is present in the salivary glands during the latter half of gestation. In the stomach, mucosal glands start to appear at the fourth to fifth month of intrauterine life and at term these glands are nearly as deep as in the adult. Despite this, the gastric contents at birth are practically neutral. After birth, gastric enzymes and hydrochloric acid are soon produced and the secretory mechanisms respond to gastrin. The acidity of the gastric contents of the newborn rises to a pH of 3 or less and this acidity, together with the gastric enzymes, readily digests milk. Intestinal, pancreatic and bile secretions are also adequate for the functions they have to perform.

Intrinsic factor and secretin are present in only small amounts in the gastric and intestinal mucosae.

The first stool is usually passed on the 1st day and consists of meconium. It may contain shed epithelial cells from the upper respiratory tract, together with epidermal cells and products of the intestinal secretions, while the bile pigments provide the characteristic dark colour. However, the major component is a mucopolysaccharide, which is the residue of the mucous secretions of the entire alimentary canal which has resisted the action of the proteolytic enzymes. Meconium gradually disappears from the stools about the 4th postnatal day.

ABSORPTION

Infants absorb their feeds well. A balance study on babies aged 5–7 days showed that of the dietary intake 17 per cent of the nitrogen, 8 per cent of the fat, 49 per cent of the calcium and less than 10 per cent of the phosphorus, sodium and potassium appeared in the faeces. Nitrogen and fat absorption increased after a few weeks. The percentage of calcium absorbed is, of course, much higher than in adults.

Endocrine regulation

GROWTH

Early intrauterine growth is slow and is determined predominantly by genetic factors which control cell differentiation. However, it is also influenced by the endometrial environment which is controlled in turn by ovarian steroids. Later in pregnancy, as the rate of foetal growth

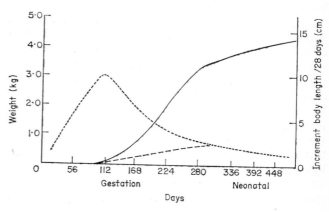

FIG. 39.10. Growth curves of the human placenta,------ and foetus and newborn ———; the mean weight is shown. The growth rate curve ------ of the foetus and newborn is the length increment.

increases, maternal nourishment becomes more important. Large amounts of both oestrogen and progesterone are also necessary to allow the uterus to accommodate the foetus (p. 37.48). The growth curve for the human foetus and newborn is shown in fig. 39.10.

ADENOHYPOPHYSIS

The regulation of foetal growth is dependent upon neither foetal growth hormone nor thyroxine. An anencephalic human infant with no adenohypophysis, and foetal rabbits which have been decapitated by tying the neck below the thyroid gland, may both attain a normal birth weight. Nevertheless, the foetal hypophysis stores growth hormone at an early stage in intrauterine development. The placenta contains a similar hormone (p. 37.44), and the foetal plasma levels of growth hormone are high at birth. Furthermore, although all the maternal protein hormones may cross the placenta they do so in only small amounts. Thus, excess growth hormone secreted by a mother with acromegaly and the insulin given to a diabetic mother have little direct influence on the foetus. The foetal hypophysis has no control over the early development of any of the endocrine organs or of the gonads although, together with the thyroid, it determines the ultimate size of the adrenal cortex and influences the deposition of glycogen in the foetal liver.

THYROID

Studies with ^{131}I show that the secretory activity of the foetal thyroid is dependent upon the hypophysis in late pregnancy. In the rabbit, if thyroxine is given to the mother or to the foetus it suppresses the development of the thyroid, but this may be prevented by giving TSH to the foetus. Conversely, goitre may develop in rabbit foetuses when the doe is given the thyroid antagonist thiouracil. This is due to an increased secretion of foetal TSH and is quite independent of the maternal pituitary. In goitrous areas, e.g. some Himalayan valleys, hypothyroid mothers often produce hypothyroid infants with goitres. The levels of protein-bound iodine are usually similar in the foetal and maternal bloods. The thyroid is very active just after birth; this is perhaps a response to cold, but the protein bound iodine level falls in a few days.

ADRENAL CORTEX

The foetal adrenal gland is a large structure relative to body weight, because of the large zone of foetal cortex. Birth, irrespective of conceptional age, is accompanied by rapid involution of this zone and the adrenal gland loses one-third of its birth weight in the first 2 or 3 weeks and half of it in the first 3 months of life. It may not return to birth weight until after the 2nd year. Development is unrelated to sex.

The possible role of the adrenal gland in stress is discussed on p. 25.34. Neonatal involution of the cortex was thought to imply temporary hypoadrenocorticism and poor or limited responsiveness to stress, but recent studies have shown that the urinary output of corticosteroids by new-born babies is considerable and that this is increased by stress even when the infant is prematurely born.

ADRENAL MEDULLA

The catecholamine content of the adrenal medulla at the end of gestation varies considerably amongst different species. The release of noradrenaline and adrenaline has been studied mostly in the lamb and calf, and it has been observed that the amine concentrations of the gland are inversely proportional to its capacity to release them. Early in intrauterine development the medulla can release noradrenaline in direct response to asphyxia. A reduction in arterial P_{O_2} to 5 mm Hg is required to stimulate this release, irrespective of P_{CO_2} and pH. When the gland becomes innervated by the splanchnic nerve, adrenaline is also released and, as development proceeds, the relative proportion of adrenaline to noradrenaline secretion increases. The splanchnic response to asphyxia is triggered at an arterial P_{O_2} of 10–15 mm Hg. Under normal intrauterine conditions the arterial P_{O_2} is well above that which would stimulate the medulla either directly or indirectly through the splanchnic nerves. During labour, if P_{O_2} falls very low, both catechol-amines might be released and cause peripheral vasoconstriction, so maintaining a circulation to the head without exhausting the metabolic reserves. In the newborn the secretion of noradrenaline probably initiates the metabolic response to cold by brown fat (p. 32.8).

Nervous system

CENTRAL NERVOUS SYSTEM

The growth rate of the human infant's brain increases during the 2nd and 3rd trimester, reaching a maximum just before birth (fig. 39.11), when it weighs one-quarter of the weight of the adult brain.

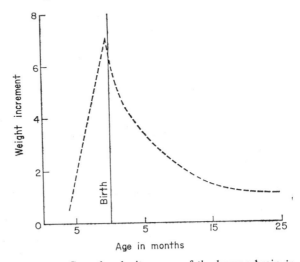

FIG. 39.11. Growth velocity curve of the human brain *in utero* and during the first two years of life; the weight increment is expressed as a percentage of the weight of the adult brain. From Davison A.N. & Dobbing T. (1966) Myelination as a vulnerable period in brain development. *Brit. med. Bul.*

REFLEX BEHAVIOUR

The area supplied by the trigeminal nerve is the first to respond to sensory stimulation *in utero*. Contralateral neck muscle responses occur as early as the 5th–6th week of gestation and by the 2nd month the motor response is widespread with flexion of the trunk and neck. The palmar and solar responses of the hand and foot also appear at this time. Pupillary responses occur at the 28th week, blinking at the 30th week and the stretch reflex at the 32nd week. Their development is related to postconceptional age, so they are a useful guide to foetal maturity.

The reflex responses which can be elicited from the newborn are legion. They operate largely at the level of the spinal and lower brain centres. Withdrawal of a limb in response to a painful stimulus, turning of the head to free the nostrils, crying when hungry, rooting for the breast, milking the breast and swallowing can all be observed. The grasp reflexes and the Moro embrace reflex may be phylogenetic hangovers, but the latter is useful clinically for it is readily abolished by cerebral disturbance in the newborn. Because the infant lies in a curled up position it is said to exhibit flexural tone. In the supine position, limb movements are gross and appear purposeless, but in the cuddling or prone positions these random movements are more organized and may resemble climbing or crawling. Some cerebral functions must also be present. The eyes are open and the infant appears awake, responding to light and sound in a variety of ways, changing the respiratory pattern, startling, blinking and sometimes turning the eyes and head. Smiling may also be observed.

The newborn sleeps for about 3 hours at a time with shorter periods of wakefulness. The first phase of sleep, as in the adult, is irregular, and continuous movements of eyelids and eyeballs are readily observed together with small movements of other parts of the body. In the second stage, eye movements cease, body movements occur only occasionally, and respiratory rhythm and heart rate become slower and more regular. Oxygen consumption is reduced. Sleep rhythms may first be observed in the electroencephalogram (EEG) at 34 weeks of gestational age. EEG patterns develop in the newborn irrespective of conceptual age. The adult pattern is not established until about puberty.

Body composition (table 39.4)

The water content of the early embryo is almost 90 per cent but the proportion of water in the body falls gradually during intrauterine life and the first postnatal year. These changes involve chiefly the extracellular fluid volume. The size of the various compartments has been measured by the conventional dilution methods used in adult physiology. The physiological weight loss in the first 2–3 days of life, which may be as much as 0·5 kg, is due to insensible loss of water from the skin and lungs and

TABLE 39.4. The composition of the human body at different ages.

	Foetus, 20–25 weeks gestation	Premature baby	Full-term baby	Adult man
Body weight (kg)	0·3	1·5	3·5	70
Fat (g/kg whole body)	5	35	160	160
Water (g/kg whole body)	880	830	690	600
Composition of fat free body tissue				
Water (g/kg)	880	850	820	720
Total N (g/kg)	15	19	23	34
Na (mEq/kg)	100	100	82	80
K (mEq/kg)	43	50	53	69
Cl (mEq/kg)	76	70	55	44
Ca (g/kg)	4·2	7·0	9·6	22·4
Mg (g/kg)	0·18	0·24	0·26	0·50
P (g/kg)	3·0	3·8	5·6	12·0
Fe (mg/kg)	58	74	94	74
Cu (mg/kg)	3	4	5	2

to renal excretion. Plasma levels of sodium and calcium ions are normal at term, but those of potassium, chloride, phosphate and some amino acids may be raised.

REGULATION BY THE KIDNEY

Urine may be found in the bladder by the third month of pregnancy and this contributes to the amniotic fluid volume (p. 37.45). However, renal excretion probably has no essential part in the regulation of the foetal *milieu intérieur*, and the placenta is responsible for maintaining intrauterine homeostasis. Thus, infants born with no kidneys may be otherwise normal.

At birth, the renal glomerular capsule is still covered by a tall columnar epithelium but the renal tubule appears well developed. The function of both these structures is immature, but there is a swift improvement after delivery and adult functional capacity is attained within a few weeks of birth. The newborn kidney is unable to eliminate water, salt and acid loads quickly or to conserve electrolytes. Because of these slow responses to their internal environment, infants readily become dehydrated when water intake is inadequate, or oedematous if the water or salt load is excessive.

The glomerular filtration rate, measured by inulin clearance, is low in the newborn, being about two-thirds the adult value when both are related to the volume of total body water.

The neurohypophysis contains vasopressin at an early stage in foetal life and releases it probably in the neonatal period, since ADH can be recovered in the urine during water deprivation. However, as urinary osmolality is not increased in these circumstances the neonatal kidney is insensitive to ADH. By the 6th day of age the human infant can respond to exogenous vasopressin. It can also respond to a water load with a diuresis by increasing GFR, although with little reduction in osmolality. This is in contrast to the adult mechanisms whereby a water load induces a diuresis with no change in GFR but by decreasing tubular absorption.

FOETAL RESPONSE TO ASPHYXIA

The mechanisms underlying the remarkable ability of the foetus and newborn to survive asphyxia are not fully understood. In an atmosphere of pure nitrogen, the survival time of young animals to the last gasp is directly related to the carbohydrate stores of the heart and liver. The energy requirements of the heart are provided by the anaerobic conversion of glycogen to lactic acid and survival time is shortened if this is inhibited by iodoacetate. So long as a circulation can be maintained, the liver glycogen stores can be mobilized to supply glucose to the brain. It is not known whether irreversible damage to the tissues is due mainly to the absence of oxygen and, therefore, the supply of energy, or to the fall in pH as the lactic acid accumulates. Survival time is prolonged if the acidosis is corrected with alkali; glucose enhances this action but is ineffective alone. The potassium content of anoxic foetal kidney slices is maintained longer than in adult tissue and if this is true for the foetal heart and brain it may explain the maintenance of excitability for long periods during asphyxia.

It is known that the circulation in the foetal lamb is capable of responding to asphyxia near term. The cerebral and placental flows can increase, probably at the expense of the rest of the body, for it is uncertain whether the cardiac output can rise in these circumstances. The lungs may play a large part in this redistribution, for their vessels are particularly sensitive to low P_{O_2} and to high P_{CO_2}.

In newborn animals, asphyxia causes general excitability, hyperpnoea, and marked bradycardia of vagal origin. These changes are followed initially by apnoea and succeeded, within a few minutes, by strong slow regular gasping, due to stimulation of arterial chemoreceptors, while the arterial pressure and heart rate decline further. Terminal apnoea then follows, but the heart continues to beat slowly and feebly, in contrast with the adult animal, in which the heart usually stops before the terminal apnoea. The newborn rat continues to gasp for 50 min in nitrogen, while the newborn guinea-pig will last 9 min and adult animals only a few minutes. Resuscitation after the last gasp is possible but it has been shown at autopsy that there is already damage to the subcortical centres, the midbrain and brainstem in the monkey. Infants delivered by Caesarean section 25 min after the death of the mother have lived, suggesting that the human foetus can withstand asphyxia relatively well.

FURTHER READING

AVERY M.E. (1964) *The Lung and its Disorders in the Newborn Infant*. Philadelphia: Saunders.

BARCROFT J. (1946) *Researches on Pre-natal Life*, Oxford: Blackwell Scientific Publications.

CROSS K.W. ed. (1961) Foetal and neonatal physiology. *British Medical Bulletin*, **17**, 2.

CROSS K.W. & DAWES G.S. ed. (1966) The foetus and the new-born: recent research. *British Medical Bulletin* **22**, 1.

DAWKINS M. & MACGREGOR W.G. ed. (1965) *Gestational age, size and maturity. Clinics in Developmental Medicine, No.* 19. London: Heinemann.

SMITH C.A. (1959) *The Physiology of the Newborn Infant*, 3rd edition. Springfield, Ill.: Thomas.

Chapter 40
Man in hot and cold environments

The human species has a great capacity to endure climatic stress. Men live and work in arctic regions where freezing temperatures prevail for most of the year and in desert areas where shade temperatures are often above 37·8°C (100°F). At the village of Verkhoyansk in Siberia, some of the coldest temperatures have been recorded. The mean for one January was −52°C (−62°F). On the other hand, temperatures over 49°C (120°F) are commonly experienced by nomads living in deserts and semi-desert areas in north and central Africa.

Even when man is exposed to extremes of temperatures in an arctic or desert environment, his internal deep body temperature is adjusted within a narrow range.

PHYSIOLOGICAL ADJUSTMENTS
Physiological adjustments involve changes in heat production, especially by muscles, and in heat loss by alteration in peripheral blood flow by which the heat flow to the skin surface is regulated, and by increased sweating. These make it possible for a naked man to work and survive over a range of temperatures. Even so extremes can only be tolerated for a very limited period of time without clothes or shelter.

A number of physiological responses based on specialized anatomical adaptations and involving particular genotypes are common in many mammals but are found in only a few races of man (p. 40.5).

CULTURAL AND SOCIAL ADJUSTMENTS
These involve the use of clothing and shelter which protect against extremes of climate and so permit physiological adjustments to operate successfully. In particular, the use of clothing provides a less demanding micro-environment for each individual.

NORMAL BODY TEMPERATURE

The internal or deep body temperature is normally maintained within a narrow range around 37·0°C (98·6°F). This is the temperature of the deep central organs of the body such as the heart, lungs, abdominal viscera and the brain. Under resting conditions these are also the areas

of high heat production (chap. 4). These organs are contained in a shell of peripheral tissues and skin, the temperature of which fluctuates in a nude subject within a wide range according to the environment. The temperature that is most narrowly controlled is neither the temperature of the body as a whole, nor even its average temperature, but that of the deep core.

ORAL TEMPERATURE
This measure of core temperature is easily obtained and sufficiently accurate for routine clinical purposes. It normally ranges between 35·8–37·7°C (96·4–99·8°F). Errors arise if the thermometer is not kept under the tongue for at least 2 min, if there is mouth breathing or talking during the measurement or if hot or cold drinks have been taken just previously.

RECTAL TEMPERATURE
Rectal temperature is frequently measured in infants or delirious patients and it normally ranges from 35·9 to 37·8°C (96·6–100°F). The thermometer must be inserted at least 2 inches deep in the rectum and kept in place for 2 min. Rectal temperatures measured at different depths may differ by up to 1·0°C. This suggests that the tem-

FIG. 40.1. The ranges in body temperature found in normal man. From Du Bois E. F. (1948) *Fever and the Regulation of Body Temperatures*. Springfield, Ill. : Thomas.

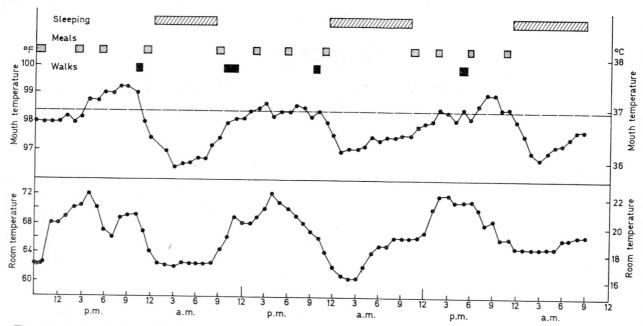

FIG. 40.2. Daily variations of body temperature in a healthy person related to external temperature, sleep, meals and physical activity. From Samson Wright (1949) *Brit. med. J.* **i**, 610.

perature may be influenced by that of the surrounding structures. The temperature of the venous blood returning from the legs has a marked effect on rectal temperature. Cold blood from chilled legs lowers the reading and warm blood from active leg muscles raises it by about 0·25°C over that of the blood in the right heart or femoral artery. For this reason rectal temperature records are unreliable for physiologists studying the temperature responses to exercise. Fig. 40.1 shows the normal ranges of oral and rectal temperatures under different conditions of heat production. The little arrow at a point on the scale of clinical thermometers gives a false impression of the normal range.

The internal body temperature of warm-blooded animals does not stay strictly constant during the course of a day. In man it may be 1°C higher in the evening than in the early morning (fig. 40.2). This is due in part to the drop in the temperature of the surrounding environment during the night and in part to an inherent circadian rhythm (chap. 44).

OESOPHAGEAL TEMPERATURE

This can be measured if a thermocouple is swallowed and allowed to descend to a depth of about 47 cm from the lips. The temperature recorded is usually about 0·1°C higher than in the mouth and about 0·2°C lower than the rectum. As the thermocouple lies in close proximity to the right side of the heart, this is perhaps the best site available to physiologists for recording deep body temperature.

SKIN TEMPERATURE

The skin eliminates at least 85 per cent of the total heat loss in man under ordinary conditions and a much higher percentage under conditions of stress. Most of the remainder is lost by evaporation from the respiratory passages which saturates the expired air with water vapour. Only a very small amount of heat is expended

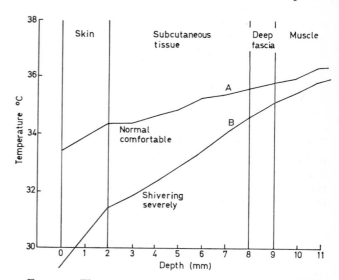

FIG. 40.3. The temperature gradient in the forearm between the skin and deeper tissues under (A) warm conditions with the subject comfortable and (B) under cold conditions which lead to shivering. From Bazett & McGlone (1927) *Amer. J. Physiol.* **82**, 415.

in warming food, and the heat lost in warming the inspired air is small even in cold weather. The extremities, peripheral skin and tissues may therefore be many degrees below core temperature and this temperate gradient facilitates heat dissipation. Thus when an individual is thermally comfortable the skin of the toes may be at 27°C, that of the upper arms and legs at 31–32°C with forehead temperatures near 34°C but a deep body temperature of 37·1°C. Between these cool surfaces and the deep central region of constant temperature there lies a mass of tissues whose temperature is variable (fig. 40.3).

Skin temperature is measured by applying thermocouples or thermistors to selected areas on the skin. The measuring instrument is applied as lightly as possible to avoid deforming the skin and creating a groove in which the temperature measured would be that of some tissue deep to the surface.

THE THERMAL BALANCE

This is expressed in the form of the equation

$$M - E \pm (R+C) \pm \Delta S = O$$

Where M is the metabolic heat production, E evaporative heat loss, (R+C) loss or gain of heat by radiation and convection and ΔS change in the store of body heat. Little heat is lost from the body by conduction as the surrounding air is a poor conductor. The accurate measurement of the four components of the balance is only possible in a laboratory specially equipped to study heat exchanges. For many years classical papers have come from either the Pierce Laboratory of Hygiene at Yale University or the Russell Sage Institute of Pathology at Cornell University. However, it is possible to draw up an approximation to the balance from measurements made with apparatus which is readily available.

METABOLIC HEAT PRODUCTION (M)

This can be derived from measurements of oxygen consumption, indirect calorimetry, as described in (p. 4.5). The minimum value of M in the resting or basal state is about 1·0 kcal/min depending on the size of the individual. Maximum values are obtained during severe exercise and may be as high as 20 kcal/min for a brief period of exercise; such a high rate can seldom be maintained for prolonged periods and the production of 600 kcal in an hour is very heavy exercise. M is largely determined by muscle activity and is increased by shivering, movements and carrying out physical work. A small increase in M follows the taking of a meal, the specific dynamic action of food SDA, and under certain circumstances heat production by the body can be increased without increasing the amount of physical activity. This chemical regulation of the heat balance is discussed on

p. 32.8. It plays a negligible part in maintaining body temperature under normal conditions.

EVAPORATIVE HEAT LOSS (E)

Evaporative heat loss is easily estimated from the change in body weight. At rest in a comfortable temperature a man will lose weight by evaporation of water from the skin and respiratory passages at approximately 30 g/hr. The latent heat of vaporization of water is about 580 cal/g of water and so the value for E is about 17 kcal/hr, approximately 25 per cent of M. Evaporative heat loss (E) is subject to physiological control and can be increased by sweating. A sweat rate of 1 kg/hr will give a value of E of about 580 kcal/hr. This, of course, is only obtained if all the sweat is evaporated. Sweat which drips off the body is not cooling. The sweat glands are under nervous control and sweating is the main physiological adjustment to an increased heat load. It becomes less effective in a humid atmosphere.

RADIATION AND CONVECTION (R+C)

These heat exchanges are determined by physical factors, mainly the temperature gradient from the surface of the body to the outer environment and the amount of air movement. Heat is normally lost by these means, but if the environment is at a higher temperature than the surface of the body, the body gains heat. Physiological adjustments modify these heat exchanges but only to a small extent. Stretching out the arms and legs and curling up the body increases or decreases the surface area over which heat exchange can take place and are familiar responses to warmth and cold. Vasomotor changes alter the skin temperature and so the temperature gradient from body surface to the environment. Movements of the body increase air movement and effect heat exchanges by convection. These adjustments are small and cannot protect the body from the inevitable losses that occur in a cold environment. (R+C) cannot be readily measured, but is calculated by difference, using measured values for the other components of the equation for the thermal balance.

THE CHANGE IN HEAT STORAGE (ΔS)

The specific heat of the human body is 0·83. If a 65 kg man has a change in mean body temperature of 1°C, the change in ΔS is $65 \times 0.83 \times 1 = 54$ kcal. In the equation for thermal balance ΔS can be either positive or negative and inspection will show the paradox that a fall in body temperature gives a positive value for ΔS and a rise a negative value. In determining ΔS the difficulty is to assess the change in mean body temperature. As already described, the superficial tissues have a lower temperature than the core temperature. The change in the reading of an oral or rectal thermometer cannot be taken as a measure of the change in mean body temperature.

Various formula have been suggested which combine measurements of skin and rectal temperatures, one such is the sum of 0·8 × the rectal temperature plus 0·2 × the value of skin temperatures, measured at several sites.

CHANGES IN HEAT EXCHANGE WITH VARYING ENVIRONMENTAL TEMPERATURES

OPERATIVE TEMPERATURE

Air temperature alone is not a satisfactory measure of the environmental thermal load. Outdoors the temperature of the soil surface as well as solar radiation affect the heat exchange between the human body and its environment. Indoors the body can lose or gain heat from the surrounding walls. Winslow and Herrington derived

FIG. 40.4. Factors in the thermal balance of the unclothed human body and its environment at various operative temperatures. From Gagge, Winslow & Herrington (1938).

a factor which they called operative temperature. It represents the combined influence of air temperature and the mean radiant temperature. Fig. 40.4 shows the changes in heat exchange of a resting naked man at various operative temperatures. M shows a slight tendency to increase with rising operative temperature.

R + C losses become negligible at 35°C and the body gains by these avenues at operative temperatures above this critical level. E shows a gradual decrease in the cold zone but above 33°C it increases very rapidly because of the onset of sweating. ΔS is positive at operative temperatures above 30°C when the mean temperature of the body tissue rises.

The naked subject studied in fig. 40.4 enjoyed a comfort zone of thermal equilibrium at operative temperatures between 30–34°C. At 30°C the value for M was 95 kcal/hr, for R + C 62 kcal/hr, and for E 35 kcal/hr, and there is no change in body heat. This comfort zone at rest shifts slightly up or down the operative temperature scale depending on body build, position of the body and clothing. Active work lowers it considerably to 19–10°C.

Immediate responses to heat

How the changes in body temperatures are sensed and the role of the hypothalamus as a co-ordinating centre are described in the chapter on the central nervous system (p. 24.34). Here the peripheral responses are considered.

VASODILATATION

On exposure to mild heat the peripheral regions of the body, which are cool initially, become perfused by warm blood flowing through a widely dilated peripheral network.

SWEATING

If the heat stress is great, the skin temperatures rise and approach 35°C over the whole body. At or near this point, despite increasing external heat load, the temperature tends to be stabilized. This results from the stimulation of the sweat glands, which pour large quantities of fluid on to the body surfaces. In a dry atmosphere the evaporation of sweat may maintain a relatively cool skin at 35°C and a stable deep temperature 37°C despite air temperatures greatly in excess of these.

Man's ability to tolerate temperatures higher than that of his body was dramatically demonstrated 200 years ago by Dr Blagden, then Secretary of the Royal Society. With some friends he went into a room at 126°C and remained there without ill effects for 7 min, but soon after he left because of a 'feeling of oppression in the lungs'. The greater part of steak placed in the room was found pretty well done in thirteen minutes. Such high temperatures can be withstood only if the air is absolutely dry and so allows evaporative cooling. In moist damp climates, such as a tropical jungle, the humidity of the air is high. With air saturated with water vapour, a temperature of 32°C (90°F) soon becomes intolerable.

Long term adaptations to heat

PHYSIOLOGICAL

The ability to sweat increases with repeated exposure to high temperature, and the highest sweating rates are reached only in man acclimatized by prolonged and severe heat stress. During a really hot day in the desert as much as 12 litres of sweat may be produced, giving an average rate of over 1 l/hr. But during shorter exposures sweating rates as high as 4·2 l/hr may be attained. Such high rates, however, cannot be maintained for longer than a few hours. An acclimatized man secretes sweat with a lower concentration of salt and thereby is able to conserve sodium to some extent.

There seems to be no inherent differences between different races in their physiological adaptations to heat. The ability of the tropical man to produce more sweat at lower skin temperatures can be maintained only by frequent exposures to heat, otherwise it is soon lost and disappears at the same rate as does the artificial acclimatization of non-tropical people.

A more important difference between native Africans and Europeans new to the continent is the possession of 'climatic know-how'. The African instinctively avoids exposure to the heat of the day and takes frequent rests after bouts of hard work. He thus saves some of his body water in dry hot environments and allows the body to cool when evaporation is not helpful, as in humid hot climates.

GENETIC

In tropical varieties of warm-blooded species there tends to be an increase in the relative size of protruding organs such as the ears and tail and in the length of the limbs. These rules are applicable to a large majority of warm-blooded species and are well illustrated by comparing the sheep normally seen in Scotland and in the Sudan.

The rate of heat exchange is influenced to some extent by body size and shape. The loss or gain of heat by convection and the loss by evaporation is greater the larger the surface area of the skin or, in the case of radiant heat exchanges, of the radiating surface.

Body shape affects heat loss in another way. Both convective and evaporative coefficients, i.e. the heat loss per unit area and per unit temperature or vapour pressure gradient respectively, approach constant values for large surfaces but increase rapidly as the diameter of the limbs is reduced below about 10 cm. At a diameter of 7 cm the coefficient of evaporative heat loss is nearly twice as great as at 15 cm.

The marked attenuations of the limbs of Nilotes, who live in a very hot part of the Sudan, and the linearity of their physique, seem therefore to serve a useful purpose in heat exchange. A linear build, i.e. a relatively greater height per unit of body weight, is attained by a delayed skeletal maturation and this appears to be related to the hot climate.

This action of climate on the growth and birth weight has been observed in successive generations of resident non-tropical people. Europeans in the tropics possess body weights lower on the average than those in colder environments. It may be that the morphological features of the Nilotes are advantageous and have appeared as a result of natural selection.

CULTURAL

The Arabian bedouins living in the deserts of North Africa and the Arabian Peninsula have developed a kind of clothing that does not impede the evaporation of sweat from the skin but still yields a maximum insulating protection against convection and radiation from the environment. These are loose fitting garments which are usually made of white cloth. They permit circulation of air between the skin and the garment so that sweat can evaporate from the skin surface and cool the body, rather than soak through the clothing and evaporate from there. The choice of colour is also useful because white clothing reflects more radiation in the visible spectrum. But this colour effect is not very great, for in the infra-red range which contains about one-half of the total energy of solar radiation even the whitest cloth acts as a perfect black body.

The housing problem has not yet been satisfactorily solved in the tropics. The nomads seek the shade of trees during the day for putting up their tents. The tent is usually open all along one side and ventilation is adequate. At night it may be cold and draughty. Other tropical people have also to choose between relative daytime comfort and comparative night time warmth. Malayans choose the former and their houses have loosely boarded walls and lightly thatched roofs which have a low thermal capacity and heat up quickly during the day but are cold at night. The West African builds a much more solid house with thick mud walls and small windows. Such a house becomes excessively hot by day, as the heavy walls slowly take up and store heat. At night the house remains warm and provides a relatively comfortable indoor climate for the family. The modern solution to the dilemma of tropical architecture is air conditioning.

Immediate responses to cold

VASOCONSTRICTION

A nude subject in a cold environment conserves heat by reducing the rate of blood flowing to the skin and superficial tissues. The skin temperature falls and if the exposure is prolonged heat production must increase by either voluntary movement or shivering to maintain body temperature. This increase is brought about by an increase in metabolic activity and is known as chemical control.

SHIVERING

Shivering may be considered from the thermodynamic point of view to be more efficient than voluntary muscular contraction, because only 80 per cent of the energy used in the latter appears as heat except when the mechanical work performed is also transformed to heat by friction. Hardy and Du Bois found that nude men begin to shiver after some time at operative temperatures of about 28°C. This critical temperature at which the chemical is added to the physical control of body temperature varies with age.

Long term adaptations to cold

Physical and chemical adaptations can be called upon to tide a subject over a period of artificial acclimatization or a newcomer to a thermally demanding environment. They are uncommon among indigenous populations because man largely meets his climatic problems by evading them. Thus the Eskimos might appear to be most subject to cold stress; but since they prepare both warm clothing and warm houses, in which the temperature may be 24°C or more, they are actually subject to limited demands for central thermoregulation and may be only adapted to maintain warmth in their exposed extremities.

PHYSIOLOGICAL

There are, however, more primitive races in South America and Australia who, lacking clothing and shelter, are directly exposed to the thermal stresses of their environments. Although temperatures in these regions do not approach those of the Arctic, they often fall below freezing in winter, thus constituting a severe stress to an unclothed man. Such people form isolated groups scattered over these continents and their initiation in modern technology has been slow. The aborigines of central Australia and Yahgan of South America are examples of such people.

These people are accustomed to severe chronic cold exposure and their primitive technology provides no adequate shelter or protection. They sleep unclothed on the bare ground between two fires, beneath a clear sky and protected only by low windbreaks. The night temperatures often fall below freezing and the temperature of the sky is always below that of the air. Even in summer time when the mean minimum night air temperature is about 21°C, the sky temperature may be only just above the freezing point or even below it.

The way in which the aborigine adapts to this environment can be summarized as follows. He allows a great amount of cooling both of his peripheral and deep-lying tissues, and his rate of heat loss may amount to 25–50 per cent of the basal metabolic rate and the heat content of his body consequently drops. The thermal conductivity of the body tissues between the centre and the skin surface drops and may average about 5 kcal/m²/hr/°C compared with a value of about 8 kcal/m²/hr/°C for a newcomer under the same conditions. Because of the lower metabolic rate and lower tissue conductivity, the average skin temperature drops, the temperature gradient between the skin surface and the ambient air falls and heat loss diminishes. The aborigines therefore can undergo considerable peripheral skin cooling with the temperature of their feet reaching regularly to 15°C or even 12°C before hypothermia awakens them. They then sit up, attend to the fire and go back to sleep.

This tolerance of exposure to cold can be elicited if the aborigine is exposed artificially to a low environmental temperature during the summer. It cannot therefore be considered as mere acclimatization to cold. Indeed, it appears to be a basic modification of the temperature-regulating mechanism consisting of a moderate reduction in the surface temperature and possibly of the deep organs, below which shivering occurs and a greater ability of the peripheral vessels to constrict.

CULTURAL

The Eskimos have succeeded in creating a micro-environment in which to live and work which provides them with a semi-tropical climate in the middle of the Arctic zone. Their houses are low and nearly round, about 10–12 ft in diameter. During winter the house is built of snow blocks. The entrance goes through a long tunnel sunk in the ground or snow. This passes under a wall and opens into a pit in the floor. On each side of the pit are low platforms for lamps of blubber (seal fat) and camp gear.

Ventilation in such a house is perfect. Hot air escapes through small apertures in the domed roof which can be stopped up at will. Cold air enters from below through the tunnel which often has no door. It can enter only as fast as the hot air is allowed to escape. As it rises, the cold air spreads slowly without noticeable draught. It is heated at the level of the blubber lamps and is at a comfortable temperature by the time it reaches the occupants of the house who are seated on the sleeping platform.

Stefanssen described the Eskimo indoor conditions as follows: 'when an Eskimo comes into such a house, he strips off all clothing immediately upon entering except his knee breeches and sits naked from the waist up and from the knees down. Cooking is usually going on continuously during the day and the house is so hot that great streams of perspiration run down the face and the body of every inhabitant and are continuously mopped up while the inhabitants drink cup after cup of ice water'.

Eskimo clothing is made of skins and fur, primarily because they are the only materials available and are also the best when comfort and warmth for weight are the main criteria. The winter costume for both men and women consists of two layers. Outside is a long loose hooded shirt, trousers, boots and mittens worn with the hair outside, and inside there is an underwear shirt, drawers and socks worn with the hair inwards. Caribou skin is the most widely used material for both layers. The clothes are tailored to fit the body loosely. The shirt and undershirt are worn hanging outside the trousers and are gathered around the waist with a belt when greater warmth is required. These two layers of fur clothing imprison the heat so effectively that the air in actual contact with the body is always at the temperature of a tropical summer. The Eskimo therefore moves about outdoors clad in well-chosen clothes and carries around with him a comfortable microclimate. When outdoors he can use his bare hands better than a newcomer to the Eskimo land. This may be accounted for partly by a higher sustained blood flow and partly by a more gradual initial decline in the skin temperature of the hands. This greater tolerance to cold hands seems to be the only physiological adaptation to the environment which the Eskimo has developed.

The spread of civilization to the cool temperature regions of the world can be directly linked with the discovery by man of the use of fire to keep a house warm. Burton and Edholm aptly state that: 'In human history, the new tool of evolution, the inheritance of how to control the climatic environment, has taken the place of the process of natural selection which presumably led to the development of homeothermy'.

FURTHER READING

ADOLPH E.F. *et al.* (1947) *Physiology of Man in the Desert.* New York: Interscience.

BURTON A.C. & EDHOLM O.G. (1955) *Man in a Cold Environment.* London: Arnold.

DARWIN C. (1890) *The Voyage of H.M.S. Beagle.* London: Murray

DILL D.B., ADOLPH E.F. & WILBER C.G. (1964) *Handbook of Physiology.* Section 4: Adaptations to the environment. Washington, D.C.: American Physiological Society.

DU BOIS E.F. (1948) *Fever and the Regulation of Body Temperature.* Springfield, Ill.: Thomas.

HARRISON G.A., WEINER J.S., TANNER J.M. & BARNICOT N.A. (1964) *Human Biology.* Oxford: Clarendon Press.

LEITHEAD C.S. & LIND A.R. (1964) *Heat Stress and Heat Disorders.* London: Cassell.

STEFANSSEN V. (1921) *The Friendly Arctic.* New York: Collier-Macmillan.

WINSLOW C.E.A. & HERRINGTON L.P. (1949) *Temperatures and Human Life.* New Jersey: Princetown University Press.

Chapter 41
On being lost on mountains, in deserts and at sea

Previous chapters have described the way in which man regulates his internal environment under the varying circumstances of everyday life. But when the conditions in the external environment are severe and his regulating mechanisms are overtaxed, how long can a man survive? The man who is lost faces this question, and his life can depend on his ability to adapt to a harsh situation. The physiologist can provide some answers which may improve his chances.

The essential physiological problems are the maintenance of the body temperature, the body water and reserves of energy. They are listed in this way because this is the killing order. Excessive falls or rises of body temperature can kill quickly before there is serious dehydration, and lack of water kills long before lack of food. However, these factors interact and often operate together.

The problems of survival are traditionally associated with the shipwrecked mariner, the explorer or the soldier. But airmen who land or crash in lonely country are now just as commonly involved and survival techniques are taught in most of the air forces of the world.

The problems arising from being lost do not affect only servicemen or travellers, nor do they arise only in remote and inaccessible areas of the world. Nowadays there are increasing numbers each year of people dying from exposure in the hills of Scotland, Wales and the Lake District, as well as on the moors of the Peak district and the Pennines. The number of deaths is fortunately still small, but there are many who suffer from some degree of exposure.

Exposure

Death from exposure can sometimes be very rapid and so protection is the first requirement. The Four Inns Walking Competition for British Rover Scouts is held every year on the moors of the Peak District. The course is 45 miles over rough country and there may be 240 competitors organized into three-man teams. In 1964, three of the Scouts died and another recovered after a period of unconsciousness. The weather was wet and cold, temperature about 1–4°C, with strong winds. These are not exceptional conditions for Britain, but because the temperatures are seldom below freezing, most people think the weather is merely unpleasant; on the contrary, it can be dangerous and even lethal.

The first competitors started at about 6.00 hrs. By 12.00 hrs one group of three had covered about 12 miles and were wet, cold and tired. One of the three began to flag and had to be helped. After a short time he had to rest and one of his companions set off for help, which arrived about 14.00 hrs. He was then able to walk with assistance, but after about an hour had to be carried and by 16.15 hrs was semi-conscious and incoherent. A little later he had a convulsion; the rescuers were then met by a stretcher party who carried him to a farm, which they reached at 19.15 hrs. At this stage the Scout was pale and rigid, but a pulse was detected at the temple. He was taken by ambulance to hospital, but on arrival at 20.15 hrs he was dead. Another group of three also got into difficulties after some 5–6 hours walking, when one of them developed cramp and had to be helped along by his two tired companions. Eventually, one of them went on alone to get help and met a rescue party, but he too was so exhausted that he could not give clear directions where he had left his companions. Their bodies were found 2 days later.

What happened to these three, and how did they die? The simplest answer is that they became cold, their body temperatures fell and they died of hypothermia. Direct evidence for this is lacking because the body temperature was not measured in these cases nor in similar ones which occurred elsewhere. Nevertheless, the success of rapid rewarming with hot water in restoring those who are unconscious and clearly near to death is very convincing. A boy of 14 was rescued in the Lake District and brought to shelter unconscious and moaning. He was immediately put into a very hot bath and within an hour had recovered consciousness and was talking rationally. These details and the account of the Four Inns Walk are taken from papers by Pugh.

The sequence of events is probably that as clothing becomes soaked its insulation falls almost to zero. Thus a man in saturated clothing, walking in a wind, is virtually naked. His heat loss increases, and body temperature is maintained only if he keeps up a high rate of heat production; in other words, a high level of physical work such as fast walking or rapid climbing must be continued. Sooner or later, depending on his physical fitness, training or drive, he begins to slow down and heat production falls. Although his central body temperature may still remain normal, his limb muscles will begin to cool, his movements become clumsy and he may stumble or fall. At this stage, unless heat loss can be substantially diminished, deep body temperature starts to fall. Consciousness may be retained until body temperature falls to within the range 30–32°C, but may be impaired at a higher level. Once consciousness is lost, death follows usually within 1–2 hr. As indicated above, it is remarkable how rapid and complete recovery can be if effective treatment is available.

There are several physiological aspects of the problem of exposure. Pugh has shown that a subject wearing saturated clothing has a markedly increased oxygen consumption when working on a bicycle ergometer in a climatic chamber at 10°C and an air speed of 14 km/hr, compared with work under the same conditions with dry clothing. The increase is so large that it is unlikely to have come from muscle, and possibly can be attributed to heat production in other tissues. This finding may be relevant to the observation that exposure cases are frequently associated with exhaustion. This latter term is unsatisfactory as it is difficult to define. It implies severe muscular fatigue, but its physiology is not clearly understood. Accounts vary of the mental state of victims of exposure, but it is not uncommon for errors of judgment and irrational behaviour to occur before there could have been a substantial fall of body temperature.

Although hypothermia is almost certainly the cause of death in exposure, it is worth emphasizing that recovery has been reported from very low body temperatures. The classic example is that of the Negress who was found unconscious in a Chicago street in winter; on admission to hospital her rectal temperature was under 20°C, yet she survived. However, in unattended cases it is likely that death occurs frequently from ventricular fibrillation at body temperatures in the region of 24–26°C.

Prevention of exposure

In wet cold, with temperature close to freezing point, the first essential is to protect clothing from rain or sleet by using an impermeable outer layer, such as a plastic mackintosh. Like all advice, this recommendation must be interpreted intelligently. Impermeable material may keep the rain out but it also prevents the evaporation of sweat, which is produced during hard work even in the cold. Sweat will then accumulate and can eventually saturate clothing within the impermeable layer. If you are caught out in wet and windy weather, put on the plastic mac before clothing becomes wet. If shelter is known to be near at hand, make for it; but if there is dangerous country ahead or a chance of getting lost, then get into the most sheltered position possible and stay there. Rescuers who are trying to carry a victim of exposure from a hillside to safety should remember that the rescue may take many hours, during which time the patient continues to cool and may die. It is often better for rescuers to carry a tent than a stretcher, and their first aim must be directed to preventing further heat loss and to raising body temperature. Hence the need for a tent and if possible a sleeping-bag and a plastic impermeable cover. Once the patient's temperature has returned to normal he will probably soon be fit to make his way back without the need for a stretcher.

Cold water immersion

Some of the features of exposure are similar to those seen in people immersed in cold water. The record of survivors of ships sunk during World War II shows that the length of survival is related to sea temperature; the colder the water the shorter the survival time. At a sea temperature close to freezing, most succumbed within an hour; at 15·5°C there were many who lived for up to 6 hours, and this appears to be the limit of tolerance. However, those who swim across the English Channel remain in the water for 12–20 hours and the sea temperature is usually close to 15·5°C. An investigation of Channel swimmers showed that they were fat and the thick layer of subcutaneous adipose tissue acted as an important thermal insulator. To swim successfully across the Channel demands a high level of energy expenditure maintained for many hours. These men and women were not only fat, but also highly trained athletes, for they needed a large heat production to balance their heat loss. As soon as they became fatigued and swimming speed diminished they got into difficulties. Heat production went down but heat loss continued, and so body temperature fell. In addition, limb muscle temperature fell and muscular movement became less efficient. Some, when close to exhaustion, became irrational, swam in circles, had various hallucinations and refused to leave the water. Such swimmers had body temperatures well below normal. Nevertheless, they had survived in cold water for double or more the expected survival time, and they succeeded in doing this by a combination of thermal insulation and the maintenance of a high level of energy expenditure.

This study was undertaken to try to determine the factors concerned in survival at sea. One of the problems was to decide on the best advice for survivors; should they be told to hold on to wreckage and stay passive in the water, or should they try to swim for as long as possible? Experiments have shown that for the ordinary individual, it is far safer to remain as motionless as possible and not to dissipate energy. Although swimming and struggling raises heat production, the movements in the water greatly increase heat loss. Only a very high level of heat production can prevent a net loss of heat from the body, and once physical exhaustion comes on, body temperature falls rapidly. Wearing thick clothing considerably delays body cooling in water, and if a plastic coverall is worn over the clothing, survival time is further prolonged. Survival time in water is dependent on water temperature; it has already been mentioned that in water close to freezing men can survive for up to 1 hr. There have been circumstantial accounts, on the other hand, of very rapid death on sudden immersion in cold water, and there is a widespread belief that this commonly occurred during World War II on the convoys through Arctic waters to Russia. Some pilots who had to bale out and were rescued within 15–20 min were dead when taken from the water. It is difficult to refute such evidence, but it can be stated with confidence that if rapid death does occur it is relatively rare. There have been many cases of accidental immersion in icy water on polar voyages, but no record of ill effects within 5–10 min of immersion. In experimental studies occasional extrasystoles have been observed, so it is possible that, exceptionally, there may be death from ventricular fibrillation.

As water temperature increases, so does survival time, and at a temperature of about 20°C death from hypothermia is unusual. In such relatively warm water it does not make much difference if the survivor swims or stays passive. However, when prolonged immersion is the rule, as in the case of diving instructors who may spend hours each day in the water, then the temperature has to be kept at 32°C for comfort.

Survival at sea

The castaway or survivor of disaster or accident at sea may be fortunate enough to be in a lifeboat or raft and so preserved from the immediate dangers of drowning or hypothermia. His problems are concerned with water and food, but water is the essential difficulty, especially as he is surrounded by water, which, naturally, he will be tempted to drink. 'Water, water, everywhere, nor any drop to drink'. There have been several claims that small quantities of sea water can be drunk with impunity or used to eke out an inadequate water supply. As this can literally be a matter of vital importance, a number of carefully planned experiments have been carried out under the auspices of the Royal Naval Personnel Research Committee. Groups of subjects, under otherwise identical conditions, lived for about 10 days on a small ration of fresh water, or a similar quantity of sea water, or sea water diluted with fresh water. Experiments carried out on rafts have shown conclusively that the dangers of drinking sea water are serious and have not been exaggerated. These experiments can be compared with the real life experiences of shipwrecked sailors and survivors in

World War II. Those who drank sea water had a death rate of 40 per cent compared with 4 per cent in those who refrained. The physiological basis for this finding is quite simple and depends on the fact that sea water, on the average, contains about 3·5 per cent salts. The kidney, on the other hand, cannot secrete a urine with a concentration greater than the equivalent of about 2·0 per cent sodium chloride. The difference between 3·5 per cent and 2·0 per cent means that the concentration of salts in body fluids must rise if sea water is drunk and this increased concentration will eventually cause death. Since urine is concentrated to the maximum when water intake is restricted, it is futile to drink urine as there will be no gain of water to the body.

Apart from the important negative advice not to drink sea water or urine, what is the wisest plan of action for the survivor in a lifeboat or raft? In many cases some supply of water is available; it is probably best to refrain from drinking for the first 24 hours and then to take as adequate a ration of water daily as possible. The preliminary day's abstinence will decrease urine flow, and a highly concentrated urine will be secreted.

The water intake required to maintain body water clearly depends on water loss; this varies greatly and depends mainly on changes in sweat rate. Because of differences in the environmental conditions and the amount of physical work, only approximate guides to water requirements can be given. The minimum water loss in temperate conditions, with little or no physical activity, is of the order of 1000 ml/day, made up of 400 ml urine, 300 ml insensible perspiration and 500 ml water lost in the expired air, which is partly offset by the production of 200 ml of metabolic water. This implies a minimum urine volume, and no allowance is made for faecal water loss. In conditions of water deprivation and lack of food, defaecation becomes infrequent and water loss in the stools can be ignored. However, if there is diarrhoea or vomiting, large quantities of water may be lost, so it is important to avoid anything which may cause these when water is in short supply.

If possible, a daily intake of approximately 1 litre of water should be taken after the first day without water. On this intake and provided there is little or no sweating, survival can be almost indefinite, and certainly is to be measured in weeks or months. Frequently, however, the initial water supply is small and the daily ration has to be reduced. It is important to avoid taking too small a ration, as there have been a number of tragic cases in which men have died from thirst with some of their water supply still available. The daily ration should be planned on a minimum intake of 500 ml/day. It is better to drink all the available water on this basis, even if the supply would last for only 10–15 days. When the water supply is nearly exhausted the survivor will still be physically and mentally capable of effective action; if he had been on a ration of, say, 250 ml/day, which would apparently have doubled his water-drinking days, then his condition would have seriously deteriorated and he might have been unable to take advantage of some improvement in his situation. Rescue is usual; this is worth emphasizing, because of the importance of maintaining morale within the first few days of disaster. Limiting water intake to only a few sips a day can prolong the water supply, but only at the expense of a faster rate of physical deterioration and decline in morale; also perhaps the chance of rescue may be missed. Fortunately, rain is not uncommon at sea and, if survivors are alert, water supplies can be greatly supplemented. In calm seas with heavy rain the top levels of water in the sea can be nearly fresh. This is the one exception to the rule of not drinking sea water; surface water can be drunk after heavy rain.

Apart from the bonus of rain, various methods have been devised to obtain fresh water from sea water. The **solar still** consists of a plastic balloon with a black cloth inside on which sea water drips from a reservoir. Water evaporates from the black cloth when it is heated by the sun, condenses in the inner surface of the plastic balloon and runs down to a trap at the bottom of the balloon. The yield from one still is of the order of 1 ml/min, depending on the amount of sunlight. Chemical desalting kits are also available and yield more water than their own bulk, but they are not simple to use and are relatively expensive.

All possible ways have to be adopted not only to conserve water supplies and to supplement them, but also to reduce water requirements. This means, in practice, reduction of sweating by diminishing physical activity and preventing body heating. In tropical seas, protection from sunlight is important, so any method of getting shade should be used. In addition, clothing can be soaked in sea water and this will reduce sweat rate because of the evaporative cooling of the wet clothing. The salt left in the clothing may, however, cause skin irritation.

Cold seas present the opposite problem of keeping clothing as dry as possible to prevent body cooling. Although the shipwrecked sailor greatly increases his chances of survival by getting into a boat or raft, he is still vulnerable to cold, and the survival time continues to be related to sea temperature. Apart from general body cooling and the risk of hypothermia, there is the hazard of immersion foot. This is a form of cold injury similar to trench foot which was commonly observed in World War I when men had to stand for many hours in the cold mud of the Flanders trenches. The condition is brought on by prolonged chilling of the feet and legs combined with inactivity and a degree of body cooling. It is not a form of frostbite as the temperature of the water need not be any lower than 5°C. The salient features are swelling and occasionally blisters, and loss of sensa-

tion. Frequently there is muscle damage, but degeneration of nerve fibres, leading to permanent disability, may be even more serious. As a result of general and local cooling, blood flow is virtually abolished. Although the metabolic needs of the tissues are greatly reduced by the lowering of temperature, if the reduction in blood flow is sufficiently great there will be local hypoxia which affects nerve fibres first, then muscle fibres, and also blood vessels. Prevention of the condition depends on keeping boots and socks as dry as possible and avoiding any constriction of the toes or foot. Deliberate exercising of the foot and leg at regular intervals is also important.

The most obvious hazard of all has not yet been mentioned, and that is drowning. Anyone who may face the risks of drowning should know the methods of resuscitation (p. 43.7).

Apart from drowning hazards at sea are those of cold and dehydration and, less important, lack of food. Cold is the greatest danger.

Lost in the desert

In the very different environment of the desert, the problems of survival are due to heat, lack of water and, less important, starvation. Since the last may be a feature of being lost in any environment, it will be dealt with separately.

High environmental temperatures not only introduce hazards because of the danger of heat illness and heat stroke, but also greatly increase the water requirement. The two factors of heat and water cannot really be separated.

Heat is gained in the desert not only from the high temperature of the air, but also from thermal radiation, both directly from the sun and reflected from the surrounding terrain. If air temperature exceeds skin temperature, heat loss by convection ceases and there is a heat gain. Heat loss by radiation also ceases and is replaced by heat gain when skin temperature is below the radiant heat temperature. In such conditions, heat loss can be achieved only by the evaporation of sweat.

Depending upon the severity of the environment and the amount of work, body temperature rises more or less rapidly. A slight increase in body temperature can be tolerated and men marching in the desert, even with adequate water supplies, commonly increase body temperature to 38°C or even as high as 39°C without serious consequences. But when temperatures go above this level ill-effects occur which increase in severity as the rise continues. Consciousness may be blurred at a body temperature of 40°C; commonly the subject is seriously ill and a further rise can provoke the onset of irreversible damage (heat stroke). Survival can occur from a body temperature of 42·5°C, but this is unusual and any higher temperature, unless treated almost within minutes, results in death or permanent injury to the brain.

There are virtually no natural climates in the world where the environment is such that the resting man with adequate water cannot survive. The most severe natural heat stress, in Death Valley, U.S.A., is compatible with life provided heat production is kept low and sweating continues. So the most important advice to the man lost in the desert is to conserve energy; don't walk in the heat of the day but rest in whatever shade is available; walk during the night if need be, or in the early morning before the temperature rises. There are two further points to remember about a desert climate. There is a large diurnal temperature swing, so night temperatures are low and it can be bitterly cold; the second concerns the widespread fear of the sun, a fear which led physicians to conceive that there was a mysterious component in sunlight, the actinic rays, which had the remarkable power of penetrating the scalp and directly injuring the brain. Such rays do not exist, at any rate in sunlight, and the effects of solar radiation are due essentially to temperature, with the important addition of the effect of ultra-violet rays on the skin. Sun beating on the unshaded head or neck can raise skin temperature to an uncomfortable or painful level, but damage to brain or spinal cord can result only from a rise of body temperature to 41°C or higher. It is sensible, of course, to protect head and neck and so reduce heat gain.

Water requirements are much greater in hot climates but only because of the need to sweat. So the advice to conserve energy by resting during the day and walking by night also conserves water as sweating is reduced. At moderately high work rates in the heat, such as marching with a load of 30 kg, sweat loss can exceed 1 l/hr and amount to a total of over 10 l/day. Anyone attempting such work without a water supply would probably die within 12–14 hr. Just as in the history of survival at sea, there have been exceptional people who have survived much longer, even while working.

The classic example of survival in the desert without water is of a Mexican named Pablo who was lost in the Arizona desert for 8 days and who covered 100 miles in that time. When he was found he had lost 25 per cent of his body weight, his skin was so dried and shrivelled there was no bleeding from cuts, and his blackened tongue was only a fraction of the usual size. Pablo made a complete recovery.

Survival is remarkable with such a degree of water loss. In general, death occurs with loss of 15–20 per cent of body water, which corresponds to a loss of 10–15 per cent of body weight. In a 65 kg man there are, on average, about 40 litres of water, and up to 2 litres can be lost without any significant change. During ordinary activities in a warm or hot climate such a deficiency at some period of the day would be common. Urine flow is reduced to a minimum, and sweat rate is probably also reduced. With further water loss deterioration begins but physical and mental activity are not seriously affected until the loss exceeds 5 litres. Then there begins dulling of perception and impairment of judgement, with some loss of physical endurance, but individual variation is marked and some show few signs of disturbance even at this level of water loss. However, a water loss of 8 litres for a 65 kg man would usually be fatal, and death may occur with a loss of 6 litres. Survival time without water will therefore depend on the rate of water loss, and could extend up to 10 days provided that there was no activity and sweating was at a minimum.

In the desert the water available is usually salty and unpleasant to drink, but provided the salt level is substantially below 2 per cent such water can be life saving. Obviously, the traveller lost in the desert is in no position to estimate the salt content of well water but the position is quite different from the problem at sea. As a rough generalization, it may be said that nearly all well water can be drunk, although there is often the risk of contamination with micro-organisms.

In the humid tropics, water is usually available and usually contaminated, so the wise traveller has means of sterilizing water, using tablets which release chlorine and others to neutralize excess chlorine. Severe as the heat may be in the humid regions, this is due to the high humidity which interferes with the evaporation of sweat rather than the air temperature which may not exceed 36–38°C. The same rules apply as in the desert, except that the diurnal temperature swing is much less and the advantage of travelling at night is small.

High altitude and the problem of frostbite

The special physiological problems of high altitudes are due to the lowered partial pressure of oxygen in the atmosphere and are discussed in chap. 43. The other problems of survival at these altitudes are also due to the diminished atmospheric pressure.

There is an extra need for water because the increased ventilation causes a larger water loss in the expired air. This water requirement is not always recognized and there is little doubt that one reason for the failure of the technically superb Swiss climbers to ascend Everest in 1952 was dehydration. Their fluid intake when they were on the South Col was less than 1 litre a day.

Oxygen lack impairs judgement, and this can lead to accidents. Any accident over 6000 m will be complicated by frostbite, which is due to the intense cold at this altitude combined with oxygen lack. An important additional cause is the immobility of any injured person.

Frostbite is not confined to high altitudes but it is all too common there and is difficult to treat. The relationship with the effects of oxygen is dramatically told by Herzog in his book *Annapurna*. He describes how he lost his gloves on his descent from the summit and forgot he had spare socks in his rucksack which he could have used instead of gloves. He came down, with bare hands, not unduly worried. In consequence he had severe frostbite and subsequently lost most of his fingers. It was hypoxia which made him lose his gloves, forget his socks and exacerbated the effects of cold. The prevention of frostbite both at altitude and in cold countries is essentially based on effective clothing, including gloves and footgear. Polar and Himalayan clothing are similar in many respects and aim at providing a maximum of insulation with low weight and a flexibility of insulation, so the need for varying heat loss with varying activity can be met. This is important, because even in polar regions men will sweat when working hard. The sweat can condense in the outer layers of clothing and freeze, greatly reducing the insulation.

The second precaution is to have a companion. Surprisingly, frostbite of the face and ears can occur without being noticed by the victim but should be spotted by the companion. Immediate rewarming by covering with a fur glove will prevent serious injury. Frostbite is difficult to treat but relatively simple to prevent. There are important don'ts in treatment. Don't rub the frostbitten part, and particularly do not rub with snow as this will damage rather than revive. Don't rewarm rapidly except in the first few minutes. Keep the frostbitten part carefully bandaged and protect it from further injury.

Other problems of cold

A description has already been given of the problem of cold at sea and in wet-cold climates. In the dry-cold of high altitudes, survival, as already mentioned, is largely a problem of equipment, i.e. good clothing. But shelter is vital, because the amount of insulation required to protect an inactive man is larger than can be provided even by the best clothing. Such shelter can include a proper sleeping bag, but further protection increases the chances of survival. Snow is a very effective insulator and digging into snow to a depth of a metre can provide a tolerable microclimate. It is for this reason that sheep may survive for days when buried in a snowdrift. At low temperatures, heat loss is greatly increased by wind and any form of shelter is a boon.

Although hypothermia and frostbite are the most important dangers, lack of water is once more a problem in spite of the fact that there may be plenty in the form of ice or snow. Although ice can be sucked and provide some water, it is difficult to satisfy thirst in this way. A water supply in frozen country depends on fuel. Unfortunately, the weight of fuel needed to melt snow and ice is almost as great as the weight of water gained from it. The early polar travellers suffered severely on this score from thirst.

Lack of food

Starvation is a less serious problem than dehydration, but can be a feature of being lost anywhere. Survival time, when water is plentiful but when there is no food at all depends on the degree of physical activity. At rest survival times of many weeks have been recorded. One of the best known cases is that of the Mayor of Cork Terence MacSwiney, who went on hunger strike when imprisoned during the troubles in Ireland in 1921–2. He died after 74 days of complete starvation. A number of cases have been recorded of survival up to 60 days without food. More frequently, men who are lost have some food but insufficient for their needs. The provision of survival rations for use in emergency is now routine in the armed forces, and most expeditions sensibly take similar precautions.

Although there are considerable variations in the composition of survival rations, they are based on two principles. In the first place laboratory experiment supported by experience in the field, has shown that compared with no food at all, a daily ration of 500 kcal even for a man doing moderate work, makes a disproportionately greater difference to survival than the difference between a ration of 500 and 1500 kcal. In other words, some food is very much better than no food at all; work capacity is better as is morale. Secondly, from the point of view of water conservation it is important to reduce as much as possible the solute load in the urine. Since the end products of protein metabolism are excreted by the kidney, protein is usually not included at all in survival rations. The simplest form of ration is carbohydrate alone, usually in some form of sugar. There are many ways in which the most palatable ration can be produced; fudge flavoured with rum has been predictably favoured by the Royal Navy. Since survival rations are reserved for emergencies they have to have a long store life in different conditions of temperature and humidity.

Even if the ration contains no protein, endogenous protein metabolism continues. To provide the needed calories the body tissues are metabolized, the fat stores being the main source, but muscle protein is also broken down, so the kidney continues to excrete nitrogenous end products. The solute load on the kidney is reduced but not abolished by cutting out protein intake.

The effect of a small ration on morale, amongst other advantages, has been mentioned. Nevertheless, even for a man who is resting all the time, 500 kcal/day represents semi-starvation. One of the most striking effects of food deprivation is the change in personality that develops. As calorie deficit increases, the subject becomes apathetic and listless, and physical activity is markedly reduced. He complains of weakness and giddiness, although measurements of muscle strength show that the weakness is partly subjective. There is also withdrawal from contact with others. Indeed, in one of the most famous studies of starvation carried out by Ancel Keys and his colleagues in the Minnesota experiment, after some 24 weeks of semi-starvation the subjects looked like and behaved similarly to concentration camp victims, although in this case there was no question of fear or brutal treatment.

Part of this behaviour may be regarded as a form of adaptation, reducing energy expenditure, and is associated with a fall in body temperature and a reduction of the basal metabolic rate.

The problems of survival are the need to maintain first, body temperature, secondly water balance and, finally, calorie balance. But man can survive very severe conditions for long periods provided he uses his resources wisely. The hardest factor to evaluate is the psychological, summed up in the term 'morale'. All travellers are convinced of its importance, and the will to live, determination and courage prolong life.

FURTHER READING

CHERRY-GARRARD A. (1948) *The Worst Journey in the World*. Harmondsworth : Penguin.

EDHOLM O.G. & BACHARACH A.L. (1965) *The Physiology of Human Survival*. London : Academic Press.

EDHOLM O.G. & LEWIS H.E. (1964) Terrestrial Animals in Cold: Man in Polar Regions, *Handbook of Physiology*. Section 4, Adaptation to the Environment, p. 435. Washington, D.C.: American Physiological Society.

KEYS A., BROZEK J., HENSCHEL A., MICKELSEN O. & TAYLOR H.L. (1950) *The Biology of Human Starvation*. Minnesota : University of Minnesota Press.

McGEE W.J. (1906) For an account of Pablo. *Interst. med. J.* **13**, 279.

PUGH L.G.C.E. (1964) Deaths from exposure on Four Inns Walking Competition, March 14–15, 1964. *Lancet*, **i**, 1210.

PUGH L.G.C.E. (1966) Accidental hypothermia in walkers, climbers, and campers: Report to the Medical Commission on Accident Prevention. *Brit. med. J.* **i**, 123.

PUGH L.G.C.E. (1967) Cold stress and muscular exercise, with special reference to accidental hypothermia. *Brit. med. J.* **ii**, 333.

WHITTINGHAM P. (1965) Problems of survival in *Exploration Medicine*, ed. Bacharach & Edholm. Bristol : Wright.

Chapter 42
On muscular exercise

The human organism is a complicated machine, the proper functioning of which can be fully tested only during exercise. No one would trust an automobile which had been constructed from parts that had been meticulously checked individually, but never tested after assembly; nor would anybody be satisfied by trying the car with the motor idling only. The wise driver would insist on observing the vehicle at different speeds, on different roads and, if possible, under different weather conditions.

Physicians must be at least as wise as the mechanic or the prospective buyer of a car. They should not be content to examine the functioning of only single parts of the patient's organism or be satisfied with observing the patient in the resting state only, e.g. lying in bed. Man was not made for rest! His muscles and bones, lungs and heart are proportioned for exercise and an active life. The good physician has this in mind, and his concern for his patient continues until he has seen him functioning as a whole machine and doing work. Knowledge of the physiology of exercise allows him to judge the degree of handicap that disease represents, and it also makes it possible to give advice concerning activities in which his recuperating patient may indulge and what job he will be able to carry out after recovery.

There is hardly an organ or a physiological function that is not involved when physical exercise is performed. Exercise causes considerable disturbances of the *milieu intérieur*. To counterbalance these and restore homeostasis, numerous regulatory functions are involved. These comprise circulatory and respiratory adaptations as well as hormonal and physicochemical changes. If these are adequate, a new steady state may be established, and the body functions satisfactorily though at a level different from that than during rest. There are many such levels of exercise, each characterized by the intensity of the work performed and by the adaptative changes following it. But, within limits, they may be considered steady states in the same way as the resting state.

There is, of course, an upper limit beyond which the body is no longer capable of adjusting to the exercise. Generally, it is not possible to select any single function as the factor which limits adjustment to work. It may vary from person to person and, in the same subject, from situation to situation. In patients, as well as with healthy persons at work and sport, it may be the physician's task to find out what this limiting factor is, whether it is the heart, the peripheral circulation, the lungs, the muscles, etc. Systematic training may be indicated, and the doctor's acquaintance with the effect of various work forms on the body should guarantee a proper selection of exercise.

The objective is to restore, or to maintain, a level of what is commonly called physical fitness, so that daily activities can be performed with a broad margin of safety. This presupposes that functional exercise tests can be performed and the results compared to the demands of the various occupational and leisure-time activities of the patients. The physiology of exercise is the theoretical background for the branch of medicine called physical medicine and rehabilitation.

The human machine

Strictly speaking, a machine is an apparatus that transforms one form of energy into another. In the animal body such transformations are performed by the muscles. Chemical energy, which is stored in the muscles or brought to them by the blood flow, is transformed in the muscle fibres into mechanical energy. Depending on the circumstances, the mechanical energy may be used to exert tension or perform external work.

STATIC WORK

In static efforts where no movement occurs, as in maintaining a position or holding a weight, no work in a physical sense is performed, because work is defined as the product of force and the distance through which it acts. But physiologically, the production and maintenance of muscle tension represents work. The quantity of static work performed may be expressed as tension × time. At maximum tension, fatigue soon sets in and may thus limit the time to a few seconds. Time can be prolonged at lower tensions, and experiments have shown that if human muscles develop less than about 15 per cent of their maximum tension, time becomes infinite (fig. 42.1). The energy cost of static effort is astonishingly

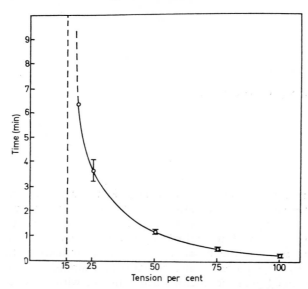

FIG. 42.1. The time a static contraction can be maintained related to the per cent of maximum tension. From Rohmert W. (1960) *Int. Z. angew. Physiol* **18**, 123.

low. One subject maintained a tension of about 100 kp with his leg muscles for 20 min with a metabolism of only about twice the resting level.

POSITIVE WORK

Positive work is performed when the muscles shorten and overcome resistance over a certain distance. The resistance to movement may be gravity, acting on the whole body or its single parts, or burdens, etc. The work performed can be expressed as the product of the weight (force) and the vertical distance it is lifted. The force of gravity acting on the mass 1 kilogram is called a kilopond. If the distance is measured in metres, the work will be expressed as kilopond-metres (kpm).

The human machine can produce work in practically unlimited amounts, provided adequate food is available and time for its performance is unlimited. If work has to be produced at a certain rate, however, there are limits. These are determined by:

(1) the mass of muscles taking part in the work,
(2) the fitness of the individual.

The latter is a convenient expression that covers the state of the muscles, their capillarization, the capacity of the circulatory and respiratory systems, etc. Big and fit, i.e. well-trained, young men, working with the big muscles of their legs and arms on a bicycle-ergometer, can work at a rate of 2250 kpm/min for 30 min or more. This corresponds to 0·5 horse power. It is estimated that the rate of work in a 100 m dash corresponds to about 3 hp. For most men these values are smaller, 600–1200 kpm/min during bicycling for up to about 10 min, and decrease with age, and they are smaller still in women. Work performed with the arms alone, as in cranking,

reaches rates corresponding to only about 70 per cent of those achieved with the legs alone.

NEGATIVE WORK

The expression negative work is used to describe the conditions when the muscles are resisting some outer force which overcomes their resistance and lengthens them. Actually, it is the outer force that does the work on the muscles, but physiologically they do work to resist the movement. Lowering the body weight or some burden at a constant speed is an example of negative work. Negative work can be performed with much less difficulty than the corresponding rate of positive work. This is due to:

(1) the fact that a muscle fibre being lengthened during contraction develops a much higher tension than when it shortens during contraction,
(2) the possibility that the muscle machine may reverse the transformation of chemical energy into mechanical energy, when this latter is supplied from the outside.

It is a fact that numerically identical rates of positive and negative work cost the organism different amounts of energy. The ratio cost of positive work/cost of negative work has been found to vary from 3 to 7 and upwards, depending on the velocity of the movements (fig. 42.2).

FIG. 42.2. Cost of positive and negative work, expressed in $\dot{V}_{O_2}$, related to the numerical work rates while riding a bicycle on an inclined treadmill. From Asmussen E. (1952) *Acta physiol. scand.* **28**, 364.

The maximum tensions in a muscle group during forced lengthening have been found to be about twice as great as during shortening over the same distance, at a speed of about 60 per cent muscle length/sec (fig. 42.3).

In daily life, the muscles carry out all three kinds of work, alternately or simultaneously. Static work is performed to fix parts of the body, while positive and negative work is performed by other muscles. While the capacity for performing actual work is best expressed by the ability to take up and use oxygen, which is discussed later, capacity for static work is closely correlated to maximum isometric muscle strength. This

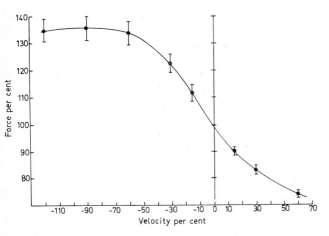

FIG. 42.3. Force-velocity curve from arm shoulder muscles of six young men. Ordinate, force in per cent of isometric maximum; abscissa, velocity in per cent of arm length/sec. Bars denote ± 1 standard error.

can be measured by the use of mechanical or electronic dynamometers applied to definite muscle groups in well-defined positions of the parts of the skeleton to which the muscles are attached. Such measurements show that strength depends on age, sex, size and other individual characteristics. Generally, strength increases with size, as large muscles have more or thicker muscle fibres. Males are stronger than females, the difference becoming obvious from the age of puberty, when boys undergo a strength spurt. In adults of the same age, women have only about 65 per cent of the strength of men; when size differences are eliminated the ratio is about 80 per cent. Maximum strength is attained at the ages of 25–30 years, when a slow and continuous decline begins (fig. 42.4). Some people apparently are inherently stronger than others, the standard deviation of normal averages are ± 15–20 per cent, and systematic training by often repeated, near maximum muscle contractions may increase strength slowly by 2–3 per cent per week.

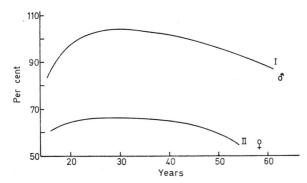

FIG. 42.4. Relative isometric strength of men and women in relation to age. Strength of men at age 22 set at 100. Averages of 360 men and 250 women, measured in 25 different muscle groups.

The passive elements in exercise

Bones, tendons, ligaments and other connective tissues were formerly regarded as passive elements. However, they are metabolically active and their component chemicals are being continually broken down and replaced. It is known that activity plays an important role in regulating this turnover. Bed rest, for example, is rapidly followed by decalcification of the bones. Inactivity also weakens the connective tissues in muscles, whereas mechanical stress induces production of mucoids and collagenous substance. Well-trained muscles are characterized by an abundance of collagenous intramuscular tissues and the tendons of wild rats are much stronger than those of laboratory animals. Bones and joints must endure tremendous mechanical strains, mostly due to the pull of the muscles. Let us consider the ankle joint. When standing on tiptoe on one foot, the ball of the foot carries the body weight, e.g. 70 kg. Assuming the distance from the point of support to the axis of the ankle joint to be twice as long as the distance between the Achilles tendon and the ankle joint, the pull of the calf muscles must be about 140 kp. The ankle joint, which may be considered the fulcrum of a two-armed balance, must carry both loads, i.e. a weight corresponding to 210 kp. Correspondingly, it can be calculated that the lower vertebrae and discs in the spine must withstand what may amount to 700–800 kp when weights are carried in the hands in a forward inclined position. These latter calculations have been verified by direct measurements of intradiscal pressures in humans. It is noteworthy that these pressures come close to the tensile strength of the vertebrae of young people and may surpass that of older people.

Sources of energy for the muscle contractions

The energy used directly by the muscle machine is set free by the splitting of energy-rich ATP which plays an important role in the actin–myosin reaction (p. 15.3). Energy must be supplied from other sources to resynthesize ATP. This may be provided either anaerobically or aerobically depending on the conditions.

ANAEROBIC WORK

If free oxygen is not immediately available in adequate amounts energy-rich substances, present in the muscle fibres themselves, split and thus provide energy for rebuilding ATP. Such substances are phosphocreatine and glycogen. Quantitatively, the latter is the more important. If lactic acid, its split product, is allowed to accumulate in the muscles, further muscle contractions are inhibited and it may thus be a cause of muscle fatigue. This occurs in sustained static contractions, when increased intramuscular pressure prevents blood entering the muscle and removing lactic acid. In near maximal static contractions, intramuscular pressures of 500–1000 mm Hg have been measured. If on the other hand the lactic acid can diffuse out into the blood and be removed, the muscles may continue to work even though the greater part of their energy supply comes from glycogen breakdown. The lactate concentration of the circulating blood then gives a qualitative measure of the conditions in the muscles. From a resting level of about 10 mg/100 ml it may increase to levels of up to 250 mg/100 ml shortly after the end of maximal effort with the larger muscle groups. At lower rates of work, a steady state of lactate concentration in the blood may be reached, indicating that removal, by oxidation in the aerobic metabolism and by rebuilding into liver glycogen, and formation are balanced. During the first 10–15 min of moderately heavy exercise, the lactate concentration is usually higher than subsequently, probably because muscle blood flow does not immediately adjust to the demands. An increased

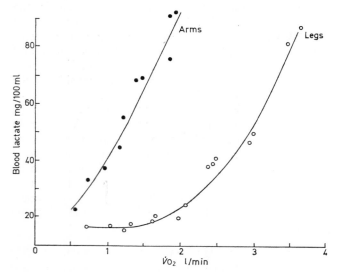

FIG. 42.5. Blood lactate concentration in relation to oxygen uptake during work performed with arms or legs. From Asmussen E. & Nielsen M. (1946) *Acta physiol. scand.* **12**, 171.

blood lactate concentration during exercise is thus a sign of an inadequate oxygen supply, not necessarily because the limits of the circulatory and respiratory capacities of the whole organism have been reached, but because the local peripheral oxygen transporting systems are inadequate. Work performed with the arms, for instance, gives rise to higher blood lactate concentrations than when performed at the same rate with the larger muscles of the legs (fig. 42.5).

The glycogen that is broken down in the anaerobic metabolism of heavy exercise cannot be rebuilt immediately. Experiments with biopsies of working muscles in human subjects have shown that the glycogen content diminishes with the duration of the work. In near maximal work on a bicycle ergometer it reached zero concentration after 60–90 min of exercise. The subjects

were then completely exhausted. On a carbohydrate-rich diet, it took a couple of days to restore the muscle glycogen, which eventually reached concentrations considerably above the pre-work values, only, however, in the exercised muscles. On a diet rich in fat and protein the muscle glycogen stores only showed a small and very retarded recuperation. The size of the muscle glycogen stores, usually 10–20 g/kg wet-muscle weight, thus is a limiting factor for the endurance of exercise that is performed partly anaerobically.

AEROBIC WORK

If oxygen is freely supplied to the muscles, the energy needed for resynthesis of ATP is derived from the combustion of nutrients brought to the muscles by the blood stream. Of the three possible energy sources, carbohydrate, fat and protein, the last named can be ruled out. Its oxidative breakdown presupposes a de-amination, which produces urea. But the excretion of urea, or nitrogen, in the urine is independent of whether work is performed or not. The two others are brought to the muscles mainly in the form of glucose and free fatty acids. Fully oxidized they give water and carbon dioxide as end products. Due to their different contents of oxygen their respiratory quotient (RQ) is different, being about 0·7 for fat and 1·0 for carbohydrates. In a steady state of exercise, when the body stores of carbon dioxide and oxygen have adjusted to the work conditions, the exchange of CO_2 and O_2 through the lungs is directly related to the oxidations in the body. In such a state the RQ may be used to estimate the ratio of fat and carbohydrate being oxidized (p. 4.6). Careful studies of the changes in RQ during exercise have shown that both fat and carbohydrate may serve as energy sources, but that their relative importance varies with the conditions. At light and moderate rates of work of not too long duration, the RQ is the same as during rest prior to exercise, i.e. the same mixture of fats and carbohydrates as in rest is burned, but in greater amounts. As the blood sugar concentration remains relatively constant, glucose must be released from the stores at the same rate as it is oxidized. As a store, the liver glycogen seems to be the most important. If the duration of exercise is extended, and the glycogen stores become exhausted, and relatively more fat is added to the fuel (table 42.1). Ultimately, the blood sugar concentration may decrease, and the subject may be unable to continue the exercise because of hypoglycaemia. Ingestion of glucose within minutes restores the blood glucose concentration and the working ability, without changes in the RQ, demonstrating that the muscles are capable of working on a high fat–low carbohydrate mixture. In the absence of a carbohydrate feed, failure to continue work is probably due to failure of the function of the central nervous system, which depends on a normal supply of blood sugar.

TABLE 42.1. From Christensen E.H. & Hansen O. (1939) *Skand. Arch.*

	$\dot{V}_{O_2} = 2\cdot7-2\cdot9$ l/min					
Minutes after start of work	0–30	30–60	60–90	90–120	120–150	150–162
RQ	0·91	0·89	0·875	0·855	0·84	0·825
Per cent energy from:						
Carbohydrate	69	63	57	50	45	40
Fat	31	37	43	50	55	60

At more strenuous rates of exercise, above 60–70 per cent of the maximum for the muscles at work, the RQ is found to be higher than in the previous rest period, approaching unity at the highest rates of work that can be sustained in a steady state. The muscles are then burning almost exclusively carbohydrate. The origin of this is probably still the liver glycogen, but another source, the muscle glycogen, adds increasing amounts in the form of lactic acid, as the local muscle metabolism increasingly becomes more anaerobic. Concomitantly with increasing values of RQ, the blood lactate concentration also rises. The estimated total amount of carbohydrate used during a prolonged bout of hard exercise greatly exceeds what is stored in the liver, but, as already mentioned, the content of glycogen in the working muscles decreases towards zero and this meets the discrepancy. For endurance, well-filled carbohydrate stores are of great importance. Subjects living for some days on an almost pure fat diet show decreased endurance for moderately strenuous work, with early onset of hypoglycaemia. On a carbohydrate-rich diet they are able to work two to three times longer without signs of hypoglycaemia. At higher rates of exercise, above 60–70 per cent of capacity, the content of muscle glycogen is the limiting factor. A previous complete emptying of a muscle's glycogen stores seems to be a necessity for an enhanced filling of that muscle's glycogen stores. The fat that is burned during exercise is probably delivered to the muscles in the form of free fatty acids (FFA). There are stores of fat both in the liver and in the muscles, and, of course, in the special adipose tissues. Direct measurements on exercising humans show no increase in the hepatic venous-arterial blood FFA difference during exercise. The splanchnic area thus cannot be the origin of the fat burned. Doubt has also been thrown on the intramuscular fat as the source of FFA. The numerous sites of adipose tissues, however, should be able to provide the necessary fuel for even prolonged periods of exercise with fat as the main supply of energy.

Oxygen uptake

In rest and in the steady state of exercise the liberation of energy from the nutrients takes place by means of oxidations. The oxygen uptake/min ($\dot{V}_{O_2}$) increases with the rate of exercise. If the work is measured when exercising on a bicycle ergometer or walking on an incline, $\dot{V}_{O_2}$ and rate of work are found to be linearly related up to a certain level. If the rate of work is raised further, $\dot{V}_{O_2}$ does not increase. This is the **maximal oxygen uptake** which varies from person to person according to his size, age, sex and state of training or fitness. In exercises such as running or walking horizontally the speed may be taken as a direct function of the rate of work. Values of $\dot{V}_{O_2}$ related to speed of movement tend to produce upward curving lines, suggesting that part of the mechanical work done takes the form of kinetic energy, which increases with velocity squared ($E_{kin} = \frac{1}{2} mv^2$). Tall and extremely well-trained male athletes, e.g. skiers and middle distance runners, have reached values of $\dot{V}_{O_2}$ exceeding 6 l/min. Average fit young men have $\dot{V}_{O_2}$ max of about 3·5 l/min, young women about 2–3 l/min. For qualitative comparisons the maximum oxygen uptake/kg body weight is a better expression. Average values are, for young men: 40–50 ml O_2/min/kg, and for young women: 30–40 ml O_2/min/kg. Systematic hard training combined with inherent talents may increase this value considerably, for example, up to above 80 ml/min/kg in male champion skiers. It decreases with age and there is also a tendency for it generally to diminish with the increasing degree of industrialization and motorization.

The limiting factors for the oxygen uptake may be of central origin, i.e. due to the oxygen transporting systems, or they may be of peripheral origin, due to a limit in the capacity of the muscles to take up and utilize oxygen. The maximal attainable oxygen uptake during work with the arms is only about 70 per cent of that attainable during work with the legs, so it seems justifiable to assume that in arm work the upper limit is due to peripheral factors, most probably the capacity of the local circulation. With combined leg and arm work the maximum $\dot{V}_{O_2}$ only slightly exceeds the $\dot{V}_{O_2}$ of maximal leg work and hence the limiting factor seems to be the capacity of the whole oxygen transporting system. A slight decrease in the inspired O_2 percentage immediately decreases $\dot{V}_{O_2}$ max, but a slight increase, e.g. to 22–23 per cent, has no noteworthy effect. Thus the actual diffusing capacity of the lungs is probably not the limiting factor. The addition of more oxygen to the inspired air, e.g. to 45 per cent, augments $\dot{V}_{O_2}$ max considerably, and more than would be expected from the extra physically dissolved oxygen in the arterial blood. A possible explanation is that the heart benefits from this extra oxygen in such a way that it can increase the cardiac output and thus further increase the amount of transported oxygen. Under these circumstances the work of the heart seems to be the limiting factor. In atmospheres with low oxygen pressures the total lung ventilation, which then may be greatly increased, is an additional limiting factor. The increased cost of breathing in hard work, estimated to be up to

10 or 20 per cent of the total oxygen uptake, can of course be a limiting factor for the external work output, but not for the maximum oxygen uptake. Finally, the total amount of circulating haemoglobin must be a limiting factor. This is indicated by the high correlation between $\dot{V}_{O_2}$ max and total haemoglobin (Hb) (fig. 42.6). As the

FIG. 42.6.   Relation between total haemoglobin and $\dot{V}_{O_2}$ max. ●, males; ○, females.

Hb concentration is not influenced by physical fitness, a high total Hb content is equivalent to a large blood volume, which gives good diastolic filling of the heart and thus a large stroke volume. This again points to the circulation as the main limiting factor for the oxygen uptake during work.

OXYGEN DEBT

The time relationship of oxygen uptake during and after light and moderate exercise at constant rate shows three distinct periods (fig. 42.7):

(1) an initial phase lasting a few minutes, during which the oxygen uptake per min is increasing and asymptotically approaches a certain level,

(2) a steady state, during which the $\dot{V}_{O_2}$ is constant,

(3) a recovery period after work, when $\dot{V}_{O_2}$ first rapidly, later slowly returns to the resting level.

FIG. 42.7. $\dot{V}_{O_2}$ during and after 20 min of heavy work.

The slow increase in the first phase is at least partly due to the unavoidable delay caused by the transport of the blood from the muscles to the lungs, where the oxygen uptake takes place, but partly also to delay in increasing the cardiac output. During this period the muscles do not receive enough oxygen to cover their demands and make up for this by utilizing the oxygen stores in the oxymyoglobin and by anaerobic breakdown of stored chemical energy. The whole organism may be said to have come into an oxygen debt to its muscles.

In the second phase the oxygen uptake is closely correlated to the work output and it must be assumed that aerobic processes in the working muscles themselves and in the resting organs cover the demands for free energy. Anaerobic processes may take place in the working muscles, but the formed lactic acid is oxidized at the same rate in the working muscles themselves and elsewhere in the organism. The blood lactate concentration, although elevated, therefore remains constant. In the third phase, the recovery phase, the total oxygen uptake in excess of the resting oxygen uptake is said to represent the repayment of the oxygen debt. The size of the oxygen debt depends on the intensity of the previous work but is independent of its duration. In light work, where no increased lactate formation occurs, it is probably used in reloading myoglobin with oxygen and in rebuilding the stores of ATP in the muscles. This oxygen debt is paid off rapidly, within some 5–10 min; it corresponds closely to the initial deficit, reaching values of 1·5–2 litres of O_2, and it is often called the **alactacid oxygen debt**. After more severe exercise, with increased blood lactate concentration, a **lactacid oxygen debt** is found. It is generally believed to represent the cost of retransferring some of the lactic acid produced into glucose and glycogen. Direct determinations of muscle glycogen contents after hard exercise have shown that this store is rebuilt very slowly over a period of 2–3 days; it must be concluded that glycogen reconstituted from lactic acid during the repayment of the lactacid oxygen debt is not muscle glycogen but liver glycogen. Direct measurements on exercising men by means of catheters in the hepatic vein have shown that lactic acid is taken up by the liver during heavy exercise. It seems justifiable to assume that this process continues also some time after exercise.

The actual size of the lactacid oxygen debt is difficult to determine, because $\dot{V}_{O_2}$ returns to the resting value slowly and gradually. It is disputed whether the pre-exercising resting value for $\dot{V}_{O_2}$ should be used, or whether a new, elevated level after exercise is more correct for the determination of the excess oxygen uptake. However, excess O_2 uptake after exhausting, short-lasting exercise has repeatedly been found to exceed 15 litres or more, even when only the first 20–25 min of the recovery period is used. With a blood lactate concentration of 200 mg/100 ml and assuming the lactate evenly distributed in the total body water, about 40 litres in an adult, a total of about 80 g of lactic acid must be present in the body. Its oxidation to CO_2 and H_2O would demand about 60 litres of oxygen. It is possible that an oxygen debt of 12–15 litres is used for burning about one-fifth of the total lactic acid thus providing energy for a chemical retransformation of the rest of the lactic acid into stored chemical energy.

INTERMITTENT WORK

It has been correctly claimed that work at a constant rate for prolonged periods is a phenomenon that is rarely met outside physiology laboratories or sports fields. The majority of practical jobs are performed intermittently, i.e. short bursts of work are interspersed with pauses or periods of rest or decreased work-rates. Laboratory studies of these kinds of activities have shown some important differences between constant work and intermittent work. If a certain task, measurable in kpm, is performed in short bursts of high intensity rather than at a constant rate, the same amount of work can be performed with much less strain. The active periods should

FIG. 42.8. Blood lactate concentrations during 30 min of intermittent work with different lengths of work periods. Total work output in all cases 15·120 kpm.

be short. It is then found that the blood lactate increases only slightly, even at very high work intensities, indicating that the energy for the work is liberated without glycogen breakdown (fig. 42.8). Possible explanations for this seem to be:

(1) energy is delivered aerobically by utilization of the oxygen stores present in the myoglobin,

(2) anaerobic breakdowns, not resulting in lactate formation, deliver the energy.

The effect of intermittent work on total output of work is demonstrated by the following example. A well-trained runner ran on the treadmill at 20 km/hr for about 4 min. He was then completely exhausted and his blood lactate

concentration reached maximal values. He then repeated the performance in short spells of 5–10 sec duration, interspersed with pauses of the same duration. In this way he ran actively for 20 min with only a slight increase in blood lactate concentration.

Pulmonary ventilation

If the oxygen uptake is used as a measure of the intensity of work, it is found that the pulmonary ventilation ($\dot{V}E$) increases proportional to $\dot{V}O_2$ up to a certain point, beyond which $\dot{V}E$ increases more than the corresponding $\dot{V}O_2$. This point varies for different subjects and is higher for well-trained than for unfit persons. It is also lower in the same subject if he works with the arms (fig. 42.9). The

FIG 42.9. $\dot{V}E$ in relation to $\dot{V}O_2$. ●, work with legs (pedalling); ○, work with the arms (cranking).

intensity of exercise at which this increase in the $\dot{V}E/\dot{V}O_2$ appears coincides with the point at which blood lactic acid rises above resting concentrations.

The values of $\dot{V}E$ during maximum exercise depends on the size and fitness of the subject. In average young men 100–120 l/min at body temperature and pressure saturated with water vapour (BTPS) is commonly found, but in athletes considerably greater values have been reached. The increase above the resting value is brought about by a rise in both depth and frequency of respiration. It has been found that the depth at maximum work comes very close to 50 per cent of the vital capacity. This value is usually reached at lower rates of exercise so that the further increase in ventilation is brought about mainly by increasing respiratory frequency.

The close adaptation of ventilation to metabolism results in an almost constant composition of the alveolar air at increasing rates of work. The P_{A,CO_2} may increase a few mm Hg until the point where $\dot{V}_E/\dot{V}_{O_2}$ begins to increase. Thereafter it decreases to considerably below resting values at the highest $\dot{V}_E$ (fig. 42.10). The P_{A,O_2}

FIG. 42.10. P_{A,CO_2} in relation to $\dot{V}_{O_2}$ in rest and exercise.

behaves correspondingly; it is nearly constant up to the highest work rate, when it may increase some 10 to 20 mm Hg above the resting value. The close adaptation of ventilation to oxygen uptake during exercise suggests the presence of a precise regulatory mechanism. However, it has not been possible to discover a humoral or nervous work factor that is responsible for the increase in ventilation during muscular exercise. The near constancy of the arterial gas pressures, and other observations, suggest that nervous pathways are involved but it is not known if these are of central or reflex origin. Receptors of some kind must play a role in the adjustment of ventilation to exercise, but none of the known receptors, chemoreceptors, thermoreceptors or mechanoreceptors, have been found responsible. The relation between the work

factor and the two best-known humoral factors, Pa,CO_2 and Pa,O_2, is best described by the statement that P_{CO_2} and the 'work factor' are additive stimuli for the ventilation, whereas the 'work factor' and the hypoxic drive potentiate one another (fig. 42.11).

FIG. 42.11. $\dot{V}_E$ in relation to $\dot{V}_{O_2}$. Top, P_{A,O_2} kept constant, P_{A,CO_2} varied; bottom, P_{A,CO_2} kept constant, P_{A,O_2} varied.

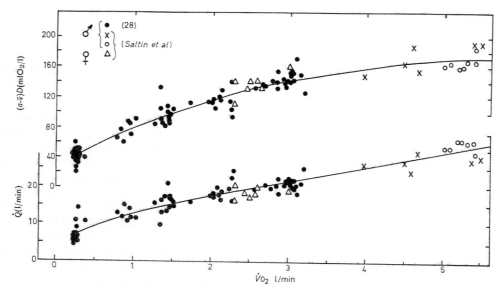

FIG. 42.12. $\dot{Q}$ and $(a-\bar{v})$ O_2-difference in relation to $\dot{V}_{O_2}$.

Cardiac output

In exercise, the cardiac output ($\dot{Q}$) is increased to correspond with the oxygen uptake. From a resting value of 5–7 l/min, $\dot{Q}$ has been found to reach values of about 30 l/min at oxygen uptakes of 5–6 l/min (fig. 42.12). It will be noticed that whereas the oxygen uptake may reach values of fifteen to twenty times the resting metabolic rate, the cardiac output reaches only values five to six times the resting value. This relatively smaller increase suffices because the utilization of the arterial oxygen also increases in exercise. The arteriovenous (a-v̄) O_2 difference increases with increasing rates of work from values of 4–5 ml O_2/100 ml blood at rest to values of up to about 18 ml/100 ml, i.e. close to the oxygen capacity of arterial blood (about 20 ml/100 ml). This is partly the result of better utilization of blood passing through the working muscle, but is mostly due to a diversion of a larger percentage of the cardiac output to the oxygen craving muscles away from the kidneys and splanchnic organs. The skin, which is not particularly oxygen demanding, still needs a comparatively large part of the blood flow because of its role in temperature regulation. The mixed venous blood, returning to the right heart, consequently never becomes completely de-oxygenized. Even at the severest rates of work the arterial blood is practically fully saturated with oxygen at a normal $Pa_{,O_2}$, indicating that the diffusion capacity of the lungs for oxygen is not a limiting factor for hard work at normal atmospheric pressures. The increased cardiac output is the result primarily of an increase in the heart rate, but under certain conditions an increase in the stroke volume of the heart also takes place. The heart rate increases linearly with increasing oxygen uptake up to a maximum value. The maximum heart rate has been found to be independent of sex and fitness but in adults it decreases steadily with age from an average value of about 200 beats/min at 20 years to a value of about 160 beats/min at age 65 years (fig. 42.13). Individual values are scattered around the mean with a standard deviation of about ± 10, and after short exhausting exercises heart rates above 250/min have been found in adolescents and youngsters. Hard training seems to reduce the maximum value, but as the resting pulse rate is even more reduced, to values around 30/min, the well trained still possesses a larger reserve of 'extra heart beats'.

Although training affects the maximum heart rate slightly, it has a considerable effect on the relation of the pulse rate to oxygen uptake. In the fit person a certain oxygen uptake is accompanied by a lower heart rate than in unfit persons. Therefore, the heart rate/oxygen uptake ratio is a practical measure for the fitness of a person, and several fitness tests are based on this phenomenon. Due to the rectilinear relationship, the line representing pulse rates over oxygen uptake may be extrapolated to the average maximum pulse rate of the subject, and thus provide a means of estimating the maximum oxygen uptake (working capacity or aerobic capacity) from measurements at submaximal rates of work (fig. 42.14).

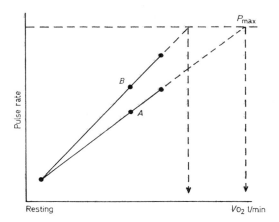

FIG. 42.14. Illustrating the method of estimating maximum oxygen uptake from measurements of pulse rate and oxygen uptake during submaximal work. *A*, fit subject; *B*, less fit subject.

There has been much dispute concerning the importance of an increased stroke volume as a means of increasing the cardiac output in exercise. Much of the disagreement is due to the fact that comparisons have been made between resting stroke volumes in an upright position, with the blood pooled in the more or less passive legs, and exercise stroke volumes. The pumping action of exercise, the venous pump, forces the pooled blood out of the legs and increases the diastolic filling of the heart and hence the stroke volume. If comparisons are made with the subject in a lying position, where the stroke volume is already large at rest, only a small increase is noticed during exercise. The evidence for a regulatory

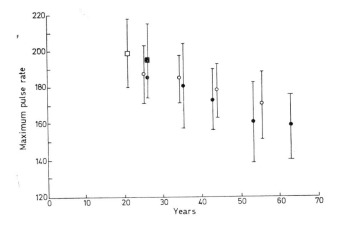

FIG. 42.13. Maximum pulse rates in relation to age. Vertical lines denote ± 2 standard deviations. ■, ●, male; □, ○, female.

increase in stroke volume is thus rather weak. Radiological studies of human hearts during vigorous exercise indicate an unchanged or slightly decreased diastolic heart volume. An increased stroke volume thus seems to be brought about by a more complete emptying of the ventricles during systole.

The arterial blood pressure, both systolic and mean, is increased in exercise, but less in fit than in unfit persons; it hardly ever rises to twice the resting value. As blood pressure is proportional to the product of cardiac output and peripheral resistance ($BP \approx \dot{Q} \times PR$), and the cardiac output may be five or six times larger in exercise than in rest, it follows that peripheral resistance must be lowered. This is probably due to the large increase in the number of open arterioles in the working muscles. The work performed by the heart in heavy exercise is considerable. The left ventricle alone pumps up to 30 l/min into the systemic arteries, against a mean pressure of say, 150 mm Hg, one-fifth of an atmosphere. That corresponds to lifting 30 kg 2 m/min or working at a rate of 60 kpm/min. Assuming a net efficiency of the heart muscle of between 10 and 20 per cent, the energy output for this part of the heart's work would correspond to between 300 and 600 kpm/min, say 427 kpm/min, which is equivalent to 1 kcal/min, i.e. of the same magnitude as the resting metabolism of the whole body. In order to do this under aerobic conditions the ventricle must receive about 200 ml O_2/min, i.e. the total volume of oxygen contained in one litre of arterial blood. The coronary blood flow alone to the left ventricle must thus be at least 1 l/min, and for the whole heart is probably about 1·5 l/min or 5 per cent of the total cardiac output.

Body temperature

Even under the best working conditions, only 20–25 per cent of the total energy output takes the form of mechanical energy that can be transferred to the environment as work. The rest produces heat. At an oxygen uptake of, say, 4 l/min, corresponding to about 20 kcal/min, 15–16 kcal/min of heat is produced. As the specific heat of the human body is about 0·8 kcal/kg, it follows that a man weighing 75 kg would increase his body temperature by 0·8°C every 5 min if the heat were not dissipated. In heavy exercise at normal conditions, most of the heat is given off by evaporation of sweat. Radiation and convection play only a minor part, since the temperature gradient between the skin and environment can be increased only slightly by elevation of the skin temperature (fig. 42.15).

During the first 30–60 min of exercise, not all the extra heat is given off, for a certain amount is stored in the body and the temperature consequently rises. Thereafter, the elevated body temperature is maintained within narrow limits. The temperature at which this plateau is reached is dependent on the metabolic rate and not on the

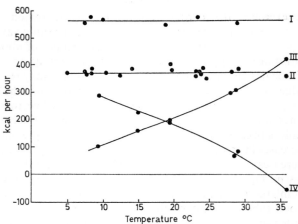

FIG. 42.15. Heat balance during one hour of exercise (900 kpm/min) at various environmental temperatures (abscissa). I, total energy production, from oxygen uptake; II, total heat loss; III, heat loss through evaporation; IV, heat loss through radiation and convection. I–II represents energy converted to mechanical energy (work) plus heat stored in the body during initial phase of work.

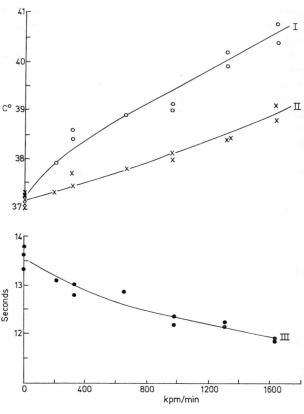

FIG. 42.16. I, deep muscle temperatures (vastus muscle); II, rectal temperatures after 30 min 'warming up' at work rates as shown on abscissa; III, time for a subsequent 'sprint' of 985 kpm on the bicycle ergometer.

temperature of the environment. Body temperature during exercise must consequently be a regulated function, but what actually sets the 'body thermostat' at a level corresponding to the rate of work is not known. It has been found that it is the relative load of work rather than the absolute value that determines the body temperature in exercise. At a certain percentage of their maximal working capacity, different people have approximately the same deep body temperature.

Sweat production in exercise is also a regulated function. It appears to vary with heat production, even when heat is produced in the body from other sources than from the metabolism. This happens for instance during 'negative work', where external work is absorbed by the muscles and turned into heat. One finds then that body temperature follows the metabolism, whereas sweat production follows total heat production.

A teleological explanation of the increased body temperature during exercise may be that the body machine works better at a higher temperature. The chemical processes are accelerated, the HbO_2 dissociation curve is flattened and viscous resistances in joints and muscles are decreased. Laboratory experiments have shown that subjects perform better, i.e. can work at a higher rate, run faster, etc., when their muscles are warmed up by previous exercise (fig. 42.16) or diathermy. This may partly explain the benefit that athletes derive from warming up before an event.

Fitness and training

The importance of being fit and physically well-trained can be seriously questioned in a society where hard labour, walking and running, and bicycling are becoming more unnecessary due to increasing mechanization, motorization and automation. Surveys of physiological working capacities show that this function is decreasing in industrialized societies, and that it is related to the physical demands of the occupation which are declining. However, the occurrence of certain diseases is actually curtailed by a systematic training of the body. Evidence is accumulating to show that degenerative diseases, including heart failure in middle age, are more common among persons who take little or no daily physical exercise, than among persons who indulge in some kind of sport or exercise. Also, cardiac patients who are given a suitable programme of physical exercise seem to get along better and live longer than patients who are recommended to take it easy. Many doctors of the old school are still reluctant to consider these trends. It is characteristic of our time that the disease and recuperation of a President of the United States brought the ideas of physical fitness as a means of rehabilitation and prophylaxis a long stride forward. A thorough study of the numerous functional adaptations of the human body to physical exercise thus seems a useful occupation for any medical student.

FURTHER READING

ASMUSSEN E. (1965) *Muscular exercise*, in *Handbook of Physiology*, Section 3, Volume II, ed. Fenn & Rahn. Washington D.C.: American Physiological Society.
ÅSTRAND P-O. (1952) *Experimental Studies of Physical Working Capacity in Relation to Sex and Age.* Copenhagen: Munkgaard.
JOHNSON W.R. (1960) *Science and Medicine of Exercise and Sports.* New York: Harper.

Chapter 43
Life at varying oxygen pressures

On the 1st August, 1774, Joseph Priestley used his new 12 in burning glass to focus the sun's rays on to mercuric oxide, and collected the gas evolved. This gas was oxygen, although Priestley called it 'dephlogisticated air' following the erroneous theory of chemistry in which he was an ardent believer. He noted that a candle burned with 'greater vivacity' in his new gas and proposed that it might be 'peculiarly salutory to the lungs in morbid cases'. The gas was named oxygen by Lavoisier, who was the first to show that it was used by the body in respiration. The role of oxygen in human metabolism was firmly established by the German physiologists of the nineteenth century, but the Frenchman, Paul Bert, showed that the effects of oxygen were dependent upon the partial pressure of oxygen (Po_2). The Po_2 of a gas mixture is directly proportional to the number of molecules of free oxygen present and is calculated by multiplying the percentage concentration of oxygen by the total pressure of the gas (p. 29.16). The Po_2 of a liquid is also directly proportional to the molecular concentration of free oxygen, but it is more difficult to measure. Air contains approximately 21 per cent oxygen, even at great altitudes, and many workers had attributed the symptoms of mountain sickness, which afflicts people at high altitudes, to the low barometric pressure. Paul Bert found that a bird in a bottle survived when given 90 per cent oxygen at 100 mm Hg total pressure (Po_2 90 mm Hg) but quickly died when given air (which contains 21 per cent oxygen) at this total pressure (Po_2 20 mm Hg). He concluded: 'Oxygen tension is everything'.

Oxygen secretion controversy

The manner in which oxygen in the air supplies the oxygen used up in biochemical mechanisms in the cell has continued to puzzle physiologists since Lavoisier and we still do not know all the answers to this problem. The passage of oxygen into the blood from the alveoli of the lungs is now accepted as being due to diffusion from a higher to a lower Po_2, this idea being proposed by August and Marie Krogh of Copenhagen in the early part of this century. J.S. Haldane of Oxford disagreed and held that active secretion of oxygen occurred in the lung. The crux of Haldane's argument was that on an expedition to the 14,000 ft Pike's Peak in 1912, he found evidence that the Po_2 in the alveoli was less than that in the arterial blood. This famous controversy later involved Sir Joseph Barcroft of Cambridge, who first defined accurately the form of the oxygen dissociation curve of haemoglobin (p. 29.18).

This secretion argument really hinged on the measurement of the Po_2 of arterial blood. In 1920, Barcroft lived in a glass chamber for 7 days under conditions of hypoxia and exercise similar to those endured by Haldane and others on Pike's Peak. Blood samples were taken directly from his radial artery, and the amount of oxygen in the blood was measured by the chemical methods then available. At the same time, his blood was mixed outside his body with samples of his alveolar air, and the amount of oxygen in the blood was measured when mixing was complete. This last oxygen content was greater than the first, and therefore his alveolar Po_2 must have been greater than his arterial Po_2. Cambridge and Copenhagen had triumphed over Oxford, at least in that controversy.

The modern development of a direct electrode method of measuring Po_2 has vindicated Paul Bert's thesis that the Po_2 is 'everything'. The direct measurement of Po_2 of the arterial blood is now an essential investigation in many patients with disease of heart or lungs who are thought to have deficient oxygenation of the blood.

Cellular oxygen usage

Chap. 8 describes the way in which cells use oxygen to provide the energy involved in living. It will be recalled that molecular oxygen is used to oxidize cytochrome a_3 which acts as the end receptor of the electron transfer series of interlinked enzymes in the mitochondria of the cell. This property of oxygen usage appears to be common to most cells in the body, although under conditions of oxygen deficiency cells can still obtain energy from metabolism of nutrients, but by this process (anaerobic glycolysis) they can produce much less energy than when using oxygen.

It is now known that oxygen must be supplied to the mitochondrial cytochromes at a Po_2 between 1 and 10 mm Hg. The famous aphorism of Claude Bernard: 'The constancy of the internal environment is the only condition of the free life', could be paraphrased to read: 'One essential condition of the free life is the provision of oxygen to the mitochondria at a P_{O_2} of 1–10 mm Hg'.

Capillary P_{O_2}

The supply of oxygen to the cell can be envisaged as the diffusion of oxygen molecules from areas of higher P_{O_2}, with more oxygen molecules, to areas of lower P_{O_2}, with fewer oxygen molecules; the lowest P_{O_2} results from the chemical conversion of oxygen to water at the cellular cytochromes. This idea is illustrated in fig. 43.1. The

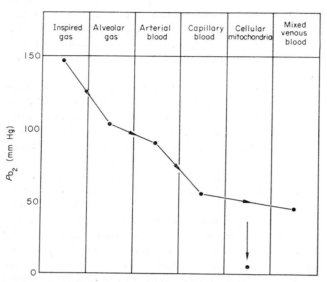

FIG. 43.1. The oxygen cascade illustrating the oxygen pressure at various sites in the body in a normal man breathing air at sea level.

immediate source of oxygen for the cell is of course the nearest capillary to that cell. How far is it from the capillary to the cytochromes in the mitochondria? This question cannot be answered definitely for the distance varies widely from tissue to tissue and depends also upon the number of capillaries open at any state of activity. Thus in the kidney there are large numbers of capillaries, and no cells are far removed from them, for the organ has a high blood flow. In resting skeletal muscle, on the other hand, there are few capillaries open and there is a low blood flow. The kidney has a high oxygen consumption, expressed as the volume of oxygen used each minute by each gram of tissue, whereas resting skeletal muscle has a lower oxygen consumption. However, when muscular activity starts, the capillary bed in the muscle expands enormously and as the blood flow rises the oxygen consumption increases. This careful matching of blood flow through an organ to its oxygen needs is one of the most beautiful examples of control mechanisms in physio-

logy. The mechanism is easily disturbed in disease. If the arterial blood supply to a muscle is limited, due to a partial blockage of the supplying artery, the patient may suffer pain when he exercises that muscle (intermittent claudication). This pain is due to the accumulation of some unknown products of anaerobic metabolism, for the blood supply cannot increase sufficiently to meet the demands of that tissue, and thereby provide enough oxygen to the muscle on exercise.

It is important to realize that the blood in the capillaries does not normally give up all its oxygen in passing from the arterial to the venous end of the vessel. If this did happen then the venous P_{O_2} would be zero. However, since the point of oxygen usage, the mitochondrial cytochromes, is the point of lowest P_{O_2}, unless the blood flow is completely obstructed the venous blood of a tissue will always contain some oxygen. In some varieties of heart failure, such as that due to severe mitral stenosis with a very low cardiac output which cannot be increased on exercise, the venous blood from exercising muscles contains very little oxygen. Such patients complain only of tiredness in the exercising muscles and breathlessness, and not of 'intermittent claudication', as the products of anaerobic metabolism are removed by the circulation.

Variation in inspired oxygen pressures

Man has evolved as an air-breathing mammal accustomed to an atmospheric P_{O_2} of between 160 and 150 mm Hg at sea level, and has never experienced higher levels of P_{O_2} from natural causes. In the conquest of new environments, however, he first ascended mountains, went up in balloons and later flew in aeroplanes and orbited in space capsules, as well as descending in mines, diving suits, submarines and bathyspheres. All these departures from sea level change the inspired P_{O_2}, ascents reducing it and descents increasing it.

LIFE AT REDUCED OXYGEN PRESSURE

Permanent residents at high altitude

About 10 million people live permanently more than 12,000 ft above sea level. At this height, the inspired P_{O_2} is about 90 mm Hg (fig. 43.2). These people live in the Himalayas and High Andes, where climatic limitations on the crops that can be grown seem to be of more importance than hypoxia. In Chile and Peru, mining is carried on at great altitudes. The highest place permanently inhabited by man is the mining camp on Mount Aucanquilcha at 17,500 ft. The actual sulphur mine is at 19,000 ft, but the miners refuse to sleep at this height and prefer to climb 1,500 ft to their work each day.

Acclimatization to these high altitudes depends upon the duration of the exposure and is most fully developed

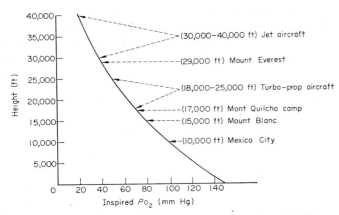

FIG. 43.2. The inspired oxygen pressures at various heights above sea level.

in permanent residents. Pulmonary ventilation is increased at altitude, particularly on exercise, and the arterial P_{CO_2} is reduced to about 30 mm Hg in the miners at 'Quilcha, compared with the standard of 40 mm Hg at sea level. Despite this low P_{CO_2}, the blood has a normal pH of 7·40 in these miners because blood $[HCO_3^-]$ is proportionately reduced. Newcomers to altitude, on the other hand, have a respiratory alkalosis with low P_{CO_2} and a high pH with $[HCO_3^-]$ only slightly below normal. The increased ventilation improves the distribution of gas to all parts of the lungs. An increase in haemoglobin concentration of the blood and in the red cell count has been known to occur in altitude acclimatized subjects since 1891. At 'Quilcha, the miners may have up to 23 g/100 ml Hb compared to a normal sea level value of about 15 g/100 ml. The oxygen capacity of this polycythaemic blood is about 30 ml oxygen/100 ml. Although the arterial P_{O_2} is only about 40 mm Hg at this altitude, the arterial blood contains about 22 ml oxygen/100 ml which is in fact more than that in the arterial blood of a normal man at sea level! This greater content of oxygen, however, is carried at a lower P_{O_2}, and it is the P_{O_2} which determines the ease of transfer of oxygen to the cellular mitochondria.

Permanent residents at high altitude have a normal cardiac output at rest, but the pulmonary artery pressure is raised, and the right ventricle hypertrophied, in comparison with subjects living at sea level. The media of the pulmonary arteries is thickened, the vessels appearing similar to those in the unexpanded foetal lung. On exercise, the cardiac output is greater than that at the same level of oxygen uptake at sea level, and this results in high pulmonary artery pressures and a consequent strain on the right ventricle.

Chronic mountain sickness, Mongé's disease, affects some people permanently residing over 14,000 ft. It is characterized by a higher arterial P_{CO_2} and a lower arterial P_{O_2} than is normally found in acclimatized residents at these altitudes. Right heart failure and severe poly-

cythaemia occur and seem to arise from the combination of the demands for an increased cardiac output, the narrowing of pulmonary vessels and the increased blood viscosity. The disease may be due to a reduction in the normal sensitivity of the carotid sinus chemoreceptors to hypoxia.

Acute exposures to high altitudes

The fighter pilot whose oxygen supply suddenly fails at 33,000 ft may lose consciousness without warning in 2 min. The tourist who motors from sea level to 12,000 ft in 1 day often suffers from headache and insomnia, whereas the mountaineer who climbs gradually to 19,000 ft notices only breathlessness, particularly on exertion, and Cheynes–Stokes breathing at night. The adaptive processes of acclimatization take time to develop.

Below 8,000 ft very few people are affected by altitude and most young adults notice nothing until 11,000 ft is reached, where the inspired P_{O_2} is about 95 mm Hg. The symptoms of **acute mountain sickness** consist of headache and breathlessness, with weakness and tachycardia and sometimes anorexia and vomiting; cyanosis is occasionally seen. However there is no correlation between the severity of the symptoms and the arterial P_{O_2}. These symptoms can develop within a few hours at altitude but usually improve in a few days.

Ventilatory regulation at altitude

The mechanisms underlying the increase in ventilation after acclimatization to high altitude are still incompletely understood. The increase is not entirely due to hypoxic stimulation, for reduction of the arterial P_{O_2} in a subject at sea level does not provoke such an increase in breathing. Conversely, administration of oxygen to the resident at high altitude does not reduce his ventilation to sea level values. When the ventilatory responses to CO_2 inhalation

FIG. 43.3. The response to CO_2 inhalation after acclimatization at 19,500 ft. ●, experiment at sea level; △, experiments on the same subject at 19,500 ft. $\dot{V}$ is ventilation in l/min. The figures above the lines are the P_{A,O_2} at which those lines are determined. From J.S. Milledge (1963) *The Regulation of Human Ventilation*, ed. Cunningham and Lloyd. Oxford: Blackwell Scientific Publications.

are studied, keeping the alveolar, or arterial, P_{O_2} constant (p. 29.24), the subject who is acclimatized to altitude is found to have an increased sensitivity to CO_2, which is expressed as a shift of his response line to the left and also as an increase in the slope (fig. 43.3).

The acidity of the cerebrospinal fluid (CSF) bathing the lateral surface of the medulla is also known to play an important role in the regulation of ventilation. The pH of CSF is, of course, dependent upon its P_{CO_2} and $[HCO_3{}^-]$. CO_2 molecules freely cross the blood-brain barrier, so that the arterial P_{CO_2} and the CSF P_{CO_2} are closely related. However, $[HCO_3{}^-]$ in the CSF is not always the same as that in the blood plasma. During acclimatization

FIG. 43.4. The pH in arterial blood and CSF in four subjects during acclimatization to 12,500 feet. The dotted line represents the CSF pH which would have resulted if the CSF bicarbonate concentration did not alter. From J.W. Severinghaus (1965) *The Cerebrospinal Fluid and the Regulation of Ventilation*, ed. McBrooks, Kao and Lloyd. Oxford: Blackwell Scientific Publications.

to altitude, the CSF bicarbonate decreases more quickly than that in the blood, and so the pH of the CSF is unchanged from that found at sea level. Thus, despite the fall in arterial P_{CO_2} during altitude acclimatization, which would be sufficient to stop breathing altogether in a normal subject at sea level, the CSF pH in the acclimatized subject is maintained at normal levels.

The ascent of Everest

The early attempts on Mount Everest (29,028 ft) were made mainly without oxygen breathing equipment, but these expeditions (1924–33) approached the mountain across the Tibetan plateau and became acclimatized during this march at over 13,000 ft. When the Southern route through Nepal was opened in 1951, Shipton found

that an ascent via the West Cwm and the South Col seemed possible. In 1953, Sir John Hunt led the successful expedition which culminated in the ascent by Hillary and Tensing. They climbed at a rate of 600 ft/hr from the South Col, at 25,800 ft, to the summit, using oxygen at 3 l/min (STP). In 1959, Mount Dawalaghiri (27,000 ft) was climbed without oxygen. Intense cold is as much a problem as oxygen lack in high altitude mountaineering, and dehydration from an insufficient fluid intake is a grave potential hazard.

Air transport

Modern commercial aircraft cruise most economically around 20,000 ft (prop jets) and 40,000 ft (pure jets) and yet their passengers and crew could survive for only minutes at these altitudes. The problem is overcome by maintaining the air pressure in the cabin at that of an altitude of between 5,000 and 8,000 ft. To pressurize the cabin to sea level when at 40,000 ft would greatly increase the demands on cabin strength and therefore in the weight.

Failure of cabin pressurization when at high altitude exposes everyone to severe hypoxia, and emergency oxygen must be instantly available to the crew, who must immediately bring the aircraft down to at least 10,000 ft, if this be possible. In addition to hypoxia, a sudden lowering of external pressure results in expansion of gas contained in closed cavities in the body, such as gas in the alimentary tract, or more seriously gas in a pneumothorax or an air-containing cyst in the lung. Air embolism is a serious but remote risk of such rapid decompression. Decompression sickness, the bends, (p. 43.6), can develop with rapid decompression of the cabin at 30,000 ft.

The problems involved in transport of invalids by air are more important to doctors. Infectious diseases are usually regarded as a complete contra-indication for scheduled passenger flights, as isolation is impossible. The inspired P_{O_2} at a simulated cabin altitude of 8,000 ft will be about 100 mm Hg. In patients with a decreased arterial oxygen pressure when breathing air at sea level even this degree of hypoxia may be dangerous. Such patients of course, include those suffering from chronic bronchitis and emphysema, or in an exacerbation of chronic asthma, and patients with pulmonary fibrosis or congenital heart disease with cyanosis. Patients with congestive heart failure and severe anaemia, particularly sickle cell anaemia, can also be at risk from hypoxia. In all these cases, supplementary oxygen can be provided on request. Patients who have had a myocardial infarction should not normally fly for 6–8 weeks. Divers who have been below 20 ft of water in the previous 24 hours are not advised to fly in pressurized aircraft as they may well develop decompression sickness even at simulated cabin altitudes.

Military pilots face other problems. They must be able to fly higher and to survive if their cabin is perforated. They wear oxygen masks, but at 40,000 ft, with a barometric pressure of 140 mm Hg, even when breathing 100 per cent oxygen, the inspired P_{O_2} will be only 93 mm Hg, after subtracting 47 mm Hg for the saturated vapour pressure of water at 37°C. To preserve efficiency at higher altitudes oxygen must be given under increased pressure.

Chronic respiratory disease

Hypoxia due to disease of the lungs is of far more importance to most doctors than the altitude hypoxia discussed above. Chronic bronchitis and emphysema affects over half a million people in Britain. In the advanced stages of this disease, the structure of the lungs becomes so disorganized, with narrowing of the airways leading to some alveoli and obstruction to the blood supply of others, that effective exchange of O_2 and CO_2 between gas and blood in the lungs is severely impaired. An increase in ventilation of alveoli that are perfused with blood removes more CO_2 from their blood, and thereby compensates for the inefficiency of other alveoli. However, such an increase in ventilation can add very little more oxygen to the blood leaving alveoli that are already adequately ventilated, due to the S-shape of the oxyhaemoglobin dissociation curve. Thus an increase in ventilation cannot compensate for hypoxia due to unventilated alveoli.

Ventilatory failure

In patients with chronic bronchitis and emphysema the respiratory centre becomes gradually less sensitive to CO_2 as a respiratory stimulant. As a result the patient tends to develop a raised arterial P_{CO_2}. The cause of this insensitivity to CO_2 is unknown. As the arterial P_{CO_2} rises, the arterial pH falls and a respiratory acidosis

develops. This high P_{CO_2} means that ventilation is insufficient to meet the metabolic production of CO_2 by the body, and a high P_{CO_2} is therefore always to be associated with a low arterial P_{O_2}, when breathing air. This combination of a low P_{O_2} and a high P_{CO_2} is known as ventilatory failure.

The high P_{CO_2} in ventilatory failure is very important, for not only does it demonstrate that the respiratory centre has lost some of its sensitivity to its most powerful stimulus, CO_2, but also the high P_{CO_2} acts as a very potent cerebral vasodilator. This protects the brain against oxygen deficiency at the mitochondrial level, for the vasodilation ensures a very short path for diffusion of oxygen from the capillaries to the mitochondria. Patients with chronic bronchitis often have chronic ventilatory failure, with an arterial P_{O_2} of about 50–60 mm Hg (fig. 43.5). Like residents at high altitude, some patients develop secondary polycythaemia in response to this hypoxic stimulus.

LIFE AT INCREASED OXYGEN PRESSURE

Diving

DIRECT EFFECTS OF PRESSURE

Water is more dense than air, so that at a depth of 33 ft the pressure is double that at the surface, and this pressure changes in simple proportion to the depth (fig. 43.6).

FIG. 43.6. The total pressure at various underwater depths below sea level.

Unless a man is protected by an unyielding vessel, such as a submarine hull, all the tissues of his body are exposed to this pressure. If the gas in any body cavity is maintained at the same pressure as the surrounding water, this pressure has no direct effect. The naval diver, who is supplied by air pumped into his helmet from the surface, can operate at depths down to 200 ft where the pressure

FIG. 43.5. Arterial ●, P_{O_2} and ○, P_{CO_2} in a man with chronic respiratory failure due to chronic bronchitis and emphysema. The vertical arrows represent episodes of severe chest infection.

is about six times atmospheric, although he is slightly hampered in hard work by the increased resistance to breathing resulting from the great density of air at this pressure. Excess air is continually bubbling from a non-return valve in his helmet. If gas is trapped, however, as in the bowel, it is compressed to a very small volume. Air in the middle ear can cause trouble, if the diver cannot keep his auditory tubes open, for then this gas is compressed and the inward displacement of the eardrum can cause it to rupture.

A swimmer without any apparatus may dive after taking a full inspiration. If his total lung volume is 6 litres, at a depth of 33 ft his lung would contain only 3 litres, and at 99 ft only 1·5 litres. At any greater depth his chest cannot collapse further, and pulmonary oedema and bursting of lung blood vessels will occur.

The popular 'Schnorkel' tube, which allows a swimmer to breathe underwater, is safe to breathe through only when floating horizontally at the surface. At any greater depth than 10 cm the effort to expand the chest against the water pressure is too great for continuous breathing. The Western cowboys who escaped from the Redskins by breathing through reeds whilst standing upright, but submerged in water, must have had superhuman respiratory muscles.

The self-contained open circuit breathing apparatus of the SCUBA diver, or sub-aqua club member, consists of one or two cylinders of compressed air (not oxygen), with a demand valve and face piece to allow the swimmer to breathe in from the cylinder, and out into the water. The cylinders usually hold 1200 litres, so that a diver using 30 l/min would be able to spend 20 min at 33 ft and only 10 min at a depth of 99 ft for each cylinder. If such apparatus becomes faulty in use and is discarded at depth for an emergency return to the surface, the swimmer must exhale as he ascends. Otherwise the gas in his lungs will expand as he ascends and result in 'burst lung' or rupture of the pulmonary blood vessels and grave danger of death from air embolism. In underwater escape from a damaged submarine, a sailor using 'free ascent' must also be taught to breathe out continuously as he ascends to avoid developing a burst lung.

INDIRECT EFFECTS OF PRESSURE
Nitrogen narcosis

The amount of gas dissolved in the body fluids is directly proportional to the partial pressure and, as this increases underwater, the gas in solution also increases. If the diver is breathing air then the partial pressure of both oxygen and nitrogen in his blood and tissues increase, but his $P\text{CO}_2$ does not rise, as this gas is produced by the body. This increased partial pressure of nitrogen may produce nitrogen narcosis, 'rapture of the deeps', or in Royal Navy slang, 'Narks'. The mental changes of this condition are very similar to drunkenness, and appear at depths around 150 ft and progress to unconsciousness at 350 ft.

Decompression sickness

In addition, the increased nitrogen dissolved in tissues causes problems on return to the surface. If the pressure falls too quickly the gas comes out of solution forming bubbles. These block small blood vessels and are the cause of decompression sickness, the major occupational hazard of diving and work at increased pressure (Caisson disease). Symptoms develop on return to the surface, and depend in severity on the depth of dive, the time spent at depth, and the time taken to return to the surface. Joint pains, the bends, occur in about 90 per cent of cases. More serious symptoms of spastic paresis of the legs, resulting in an unsteady gait, are called the 'staggers'. Dyspnoea, coughing and chest pain, with pallor or cyanosis, the 'chokes', are very serious and may occur some hours after ascent. Particularly in caisson workers aseptic necrosis of bone may develop years after the last exposure to pressure.

Rapid recompression is urgently required for all patients with symptoms, except those with trivial skin rashes. A very slow return to atmospheric pressure is then needed. The prevention of decompression sickness depends upon rigid adherence to stage decompression tables, which aim to give sufficient time at each pressure to allow nitrogen elimination without formation of bubbles in blood or tissues. These tables, originally developed by J.S. Haldane, prescribe the period that the ascending diver must spend at each depth. The theory underlying these tables is probably inadequate, but subsequent attempts to improve the tables by mathematical physiologists have not been entirely successful. There is no substitute for hard experience in this problem. The necessary decompression times for divers below 200 feet can be very tedious, and a submersible chamber is sometimes used. This is entered at depth, and then kept at the high pressure when hoisted on board ship. Decompression can then be continued, following the tables. For deep diving below 200 ft, gas mixtures of oxygen and helium have been used to avoid the dangers of both oxygen poisoning and nitrogen narcosis. Less helium is absorbed by the fatty tissues of the nervous system, and the gas also leaves the tissues more quickly than nitrogen. The world record dive is to 600 ft, where 4 min of useful work were achieved, followed by 6·5 hrs decompression (fig. 43.6).

Oxygen poisoning

From the armchair, it would seem simple to prevent decompression sickness altogether by giving divers pure oxygen to breath, and thus eliminating the risk of nitrogen bubbles. This idea is limited in practice by the development of oxygen poisoning, which affects both the central nervous system and the lungs.

When pure oxygen is breathed at pressures greater than atmospheric, epileptic fits can occur. This is known as the 'Paul Bert' effect after its discoverer. An individual's susceptibility to these fits varies both from day to day and with the duration of exposure to high levels of Po_2. The risk of developing a fit increases as the Po_2 rises, but they have never been recorded unless the inspired Po_2 is over 1300 mm Hg. The effect is probably dependent upon the actual Po_2 at the brain cells and this depends on the cerebral circulation as well as the inspired Po_2. High oxygen pressures cause some cerebral vasoconstriction. Although recovery from fits is complete they can be very dangerous to divers. In SCUBA diving, where a mouthpiece is used, drowning often results if oxygen fits occur. The only real protection from fits is to ensure that the inspired Po_2 never rises above 1300 mm Hg. It is for this reason particularly that pure oxygen must never be used to fill the cylinders of SCUBA divers.

The effect of oxygen on the lung is known as the Lorrain Smith effect. If an inspired Po_2 of more than 300 mm Hg is given continuously for longer than 36 hrs, retrosternal discomfort and cough may occur. Continuation of oxygen administration may result in severe bronchopneumonia and death. It is probable that the raised Po_2 interferes with the formation of the 'surfactant' protein lining the alveoli which is responsible for preventing collapse of alveoli (p. 29.10). Pulmonary oxygen toxicity in the early stages is rapidly corrected by allowing the subject to breathe air again. Recently it has been realized that patients being treated by continuous artificial ventilation with oxygen enriched mixtures run a grave risk of developing the Lorrain Smith effect.

Drowning and artificial respiration

Although gas exchange in the lungs ceases rapidly in drowning the situation is far more complicated than mere asphyxia. Swallowing and spasm of the glottis stops water entering the lungs at first, and this 'dry drowning' is said to happen in 40 per cent of cases. As unconsciousness develops, this reflex activity fails and water enters the lungs, where it provokes an intense reflex spasm of the terminal bronchioles. Sea water is hypertonic to blood, and haemoconcentration and pulmonary oedema rapidly develop as water is driven from the blood into the alveoli by osmotic forces. In fresh-water drowning, the water goes the other way and profound haemolysis can develop as water dilutes the blood. A rapid rise in the concentration of plasma potassium may then cause cardiac arrest and sudden death. In practice, however, severe haemodilution is rare in human drowning, and pulmonary oedema is commonly found in both salt- and fresh-water drowning.

In the treatment of the apparently drowned, it is imperative that mouth to mouth artificial ventilation, **the kiss of life**, should be started immediately after the airway has been cleared. Weed, vomit, false teeth and other obstructions should be scooped out of the mouth and throat with the fingers and the tongue pulled forward. The victim's head is then hyperextended with the mandible pushed upwards. The rescuer then blows into his mouth, keeping the victim's nose pinched, when the chest should be seen to expand. This is repeated at about twenty blows per minute, allowing the subject to exhale between each inspiration.

In most drowning accidents, the victim is dead before he is brought from the water. To have any chance of success, mouth to mouth breathing must start at once, for example whilst the victim is still in the water or being carried through the shallows. If a pulse cannot be felt closed-chest cardiac massage should also be started. Compression of the chest and therefore of the heart is best achieved by firmly pressing the sternum and anterior chest wall with the subject in the supine position. This is timed so that three chest compressions are given for one lung inflation. It is possible to detect a femoral or carotid pulse as a result of this manoeuvre, and both the kiss of life and cardiac massage can be carried out by one person. It is completely wrong to spend time bringing resuscitation equipment, such as oxygen cylinders, unless mouth to mouth ventilation and closed chest cardiac massage are already in progress. When these become available, usually following hospital admission, tracheal intubation and bronchoscopy may be needed, followed by intermittent mechanical positive pressure respiration if spontaneous breathing is still inadequate. Ventricular fibrillation can be treated by DC countershock. This is most effective in the well-oxygenated patient, in whom acidosis arising from the accumulation of lactic acid has been corrected by giving sodium bicarbonate intravenously. The haemoconcentration following sea-water drowning can be treated by hypotonic intravenous fluids, and in the unusual circumstance of severe haemolysis following fresh-water drowning fresh blood or exchange transfusion may be needed. Bacterial pneumonia from aspiration of infected water may require antibiotics.

Is all this worthwhile? It can be. A five-year-old boy fell into a freezing Norwegian river and was under water for 22 min. Despite prolonged unconsciousness and convulsions followed by a period of decerebration and blindness, he was physically normal 6 months later. Apart from some loss of visual fields, his nervous system appeared to have suffered no permanent damage.

Submarines

The world's first submarine was launched in 1897, and subsequent development has depended on solutions to three problems, withstanding water pressure, providing engines which run when submerged, and providing a habitable atmosphere for the crew. The first two problems belong to engineers, and the use of nuclear power has dramatically removed the limitation imposed by the engines. The third problem is one of biological engineering. The time of maximal submersion has increased from 6 hrs in 1900, to 6 weeks in 1940, and to many months in 1968. The submariner lives in an atmosphere at normal total pressure, and in a nuclear submarine this atmosphere is automatically replenished with oxygen, CO_2 is removed, and the temperature and humidity are controlled, so that it is the most rigidly stabilized atmosphere known to man. In 1944, a series of tests on prolonged exposure in submarines had to be discontinued because grease spilt on a galley stove formed acrolein vapour which caused incapacitating headache when rebreathed over a long period. A submariner's smells stay with him.

Space capsules

An astronaut is utterly dependent for all his physical needs on the contents of his capsule. The greatest of these needs is for oxygen, and its provision presents problems. If he lives in an atmosphere of pure oxygen at atmospheric pressure, the fire risk is very great and as the inspired Po_2 is about 700 mm Hg, the Lorrain Smith effect or pulmonary oxygen toxicity develops.

The total pressure in a capsule is therefore held below atmospheric and the oxygen concentration increased to give an inspired Po_2 of about 200 mm Hg. As the first American space tragedies have shown, pure oxygen, even at this pressure, poses a severe fire risk and future capsules may have an oxygen–helium atmosphere. For walking in space, however, the astronaut has his pressure suit filled with pure oxygen at a reduced total pressure. The exact details seem to be a military secret. The need for oxygen in prolonged space flight has led to the ingenious suggestion that a mixture of algae and bacteria, fed on CO_2 from the breath and urea from the urine, can produce enough oxygen by photosynthesis in sunlight.

Hyperbaric oxygen treatment

Oxygen is carried in the blood in two forms:

(1) in chemical combination with haemoglobin, the amount of oxygen at any blood Po_2 being determined from the oxyhaemoglobin dissociation curve,

(2) in physical solution in plasma, where the amount is directly proportional to the Po_2 so that 0·03 ml of oxygen are dissolved in each 100 ml of blood for each 1 mm Hg Po_2.

At a Po_2 of about 300 mm Hg, the haemoglobin is fully saturated with oxygen, but the oxygen content of the blood continues to rise as the Po_2 rises, due to the oxygen in solution. If the Po_2 can be taken to 1500–2000 mm Hg, the amount in solution is 5–6 ml for each 100 ml of blood. This is sufficient to provide for an oxygen consumption of 300 ml/min, if the cardiac output is 5 l/min, without using the oxygen combined with haemoglobin at all. Further-

more, at this arterial Po_2, the mean capillary Po_2 is of the order of 500 mm Hg. Thus the pressure differential driving oxygen to the mitochondria (where the Po_2 is 1–10 mm Hg) is about ten times normal. These facts are the basis of hyperbaric oxygen therapy.

This treatment requires a pressure chamber, which can contain the whole patient and also the doctors, surgeons and nurses looking after him, if his treatment is to be prolonged. Such chambers are available in Glasgow and Amsterdam in Europe and in various centres in the U.S.A. In the chamber, the patient breathes oxygen but the attendants breathe the chamber air. The pressure can be two or three atmospheres absolute or 1500–2200 mm Hg. These large chambers are very expensive and they need elaborate pumps and safety equipment. The attendants run the risk of developing the bends on decompression and later bone damage, but the patient is safe from this as he breathes oxygen although he is at risk from oxygen poisoning, and decompression must be very slow and carefully supervised. As in all work at high pressure involving oxygen, the fire risk is considerable. For example, all lighting must be from outside the chamber.

This treatment was first used as an aid to the treatment of cancer by X-rays. Some cancer cells are very resistant to X-rays, but this can be overcome if they are exposed to high Po_2. For this purpose, small one-man pressure chambers are in fairly wide use.

Hyperbaric oxygen treatment can be of value in treating carbon monoxide poisoning due, for example, to domestic coal gas. Here the haemoglobin combines with carbon monoxide much more firmly than it does with oxygen, but hyperbaric therapy can provide oxygen to the tissues without relying on haemoglobin at all. Excellent results are achieved in treating widespread infection with the gas gangrene organism, *Clostridium Welchii*, which cannot live at a high Po_2. Dramatic successes have been claimed in keeping limbs alive when the main artery has been severely damaged in an accident, but the treatment of arterial insufficiency due to chronic disease processes has not been so impressive. Despite the enthusiasm of the users of this new form of treatment there has been no objective assessment of its value, even in treating coal-gas poisoning, and it still remains an experimental form of therapy.

FURTHER READING

BATES D.V. & CHRISTIE R.V. (1964) *Respiratory Function in Disease*. Philadelphia : Saunders.

BERT P. (1878) *La Pression barometrique, recherches de physiologie*. Paris : Masson. English translation by HITCHCOCK M.A. & HITCHCOCK F.A. (1943) Columbus, Ohio : College Book Co.

FENN W.O. & RAHN H. ed. (1965) *Handbook of Physiology* Section 3. Respiration. Vols. I & II. Washington D. C.: American Physiological Society.

HALDANE J.S. & PRIESTLEY J.G. (1935) *Respiration*, 2nd Edition. London : Oxford University Press.

KVITTINGEN T.D. & NAESS A. (1963) Recovery from drowning in fresh water. *Brit. med. J.* i, 1315.

LASSEN H.C.A., NAHAS G.G., BATCO D.V. (1965) Respiratory failure. *Ann. N.Y. Acad. Sci.* 121, 651.

MILES S. (1962) *Underwater Medicine*. London : Staples Press.

Chapter 44
Circadian rhythms

All of us live in a world in which day and night follow one another in a fairly precise 24-hour cycle, even though the proportion of light and darkness varies with the seasons. Social life, work and leisure, sleep and meals are geared to this cycle, so it is not surprising that many physiological processes oscillate with a 24-hour period. All biological measurements vary, and the statistician analyses this variation into its component parts, random variation in any individual, variations between one individual and another, and variations linked with, and apparently caused by, some other measurable change. One such cause of variation which is commonly ignored is the **circadian** (Latin: *circa dies*) rhythm, or oscillation with a period of around 24 hours.

Every doctor knows that in health body temperature is usually lower on waking than at bedtime, and that this rhythm persists even when the temperature is raised in fever. Similar rhythmicity in many other functions may make a substantial contribution to biological variation, so that a measurement of, for instance, plasma phosphate or cortisol which is quite normal at one time of day may be of pathological significance at another time.

The first practical consequence of these rhythms is that, by elimination of one variable influence, diagnosis can become more precise. Thus a measurement of temperature or of plasma phosphate concentration is more meaningful if the time of day is known. For this purpose the cause of the rhythm does not matter. In the past it was once supposed, that urine flow is low at night because we neither eat nor drink at this time, body temperature is low because we are at rest, and that plasma and urine become alkaline after breakfast because the stomach secretes acid during the course of the meal. However, all these variations persist even if we abstain from the rhythmic circadian habits which have been held responsible for them, even if we remain recumbent for 24 hours, or indulge continuously in light work, or if we fast or take small identical meals regularly every hour. It appears that rhythmic variations in physiological function result from an underlying process which continues to oscillate with approximately a 24-hour rhythm, independently of the alternation of light and darkness and the many other circadian rhythms which surround us.

Rigid proof that a rhythm is endogenous requires elaborate investigations, for it is not easy in a civilized community in temperate latitudes to exclude all possible circadian influences. While light can be excluded by living in a cellar, it is more difficult to exclude noise. Social influences may have a considerable effect, and it is hard to avoid all clues indicating the alternation between a world quiet and at rest, and a busy world with noises of footsteps, voices and traffic; complete sound insulation is not an easy engineering feat. Since people become hungry and need sleep, absolute constancy of habit as well as of environment cannot be attained over long periods, but it is possible to alter deliberately either the phase or the cycle length of the habitual rhythmic activities. This may be done in an isolated community during the continuous daylight of an Arctic summer, or in a deep cave. The phase of habits may be shifted by a half cycle simply by pretending that noon is midnight and 6.0 a.m. is 6.0 p.m. With such a phase shift the rhythms adapt themselves to the new phase but only after some days, so that at first the persisting influence of inherent rhythm and habit is still shown. A similar abrupt shift of phase can be more perfectly attained by flying round the world into a different time zone. This is more satisfactory because the alternation of light and darkness and social activity, and all the external influences, shift to the same extent, so that every possible external influence conduces to good adaptation. Nevertheless, some physiological rhythms may take weeks to adapt after such a flight; observations, however, are still fragmentary considering how many people nowadays travel in this way. An alternative procedure in a uniform environment is to live a day of abnormal length. A day of 21, 22, 27 or 28 hours has been employed for this purpose, with a watch specially adjusted to gain or lose time, so that the subject is unaware of the passage of 24-hour time. In these circumstances, many rhythms continue to follow a 24-hour cycle for many weeks, even though the environment contains little or nothing in the way of 24-hour clues and any direct influence of habit, waking and sleeping, meal times, rest and exercise, the activities and rest of other people around all co-operate to cause adaptation to the artificial day (fig. 44.6).

Some have maintained that trifling residual circadian changes in the environment, such as fluctuations in the Earth's magnetism or in barometric pressure, provide a clue, but these oscillations are very small and below the limit of detection by any known human sense organ; furthermore they cannot account for the persistence of rhythms when one flies half-way round the world.

FIG. 44.1. Excretion of corticosteroids; □, during the first 6 hours of waking; ■, during sleep. Before, during and after a fortnight of sleeping by day in an Arctic summer. The slow adaptation to the artificial time and the equally slow return to normal are shown. From data of G.W.G. Sharp, S.A. Slorach & H.J. Vipord (1961) *J. Endocrin.* **22,** 377.

Another observation at variance with this suggestion is that when physiological rhythms have become adapted to a new time pattern, return to normal time does not cause them to revert immediately. They take about as long to change back as they took to depart from normal phase in the first place (fig. 44.1).

Species other than man can more readily be kept under constant conditions continuously, e.g. in a quiet room where light intensity is maintained at a uniform level, where food and drink are continuously available and where external activities such as supplying food or cleaning cages are randomized throughout the 24 hours. The easiest rhythm to study is that of rest and activity; small rodents such as rats and mice are normally active by night and inactive by day, and simple recording devices can register the amount of movement going on at any period throughout the 24 hours. Under uniform conditions, they maintain approximately a 24-hour periodicity, but after a time this begins to drift a little from precise adherence to a 24-hour clock, coming to adopt a cycle of slightly longer or shorter duration. The term 'circadian' was deliberately coined to cover such periods whose length was not precisely 24 hours. It thus appears that

there is a built-in clock which is not a perfect time-keeper, but tends to gain or lose slightly, and under ordinary conditions is constantly adjusted and set to keep good 24-hour time by the rhythmic alternation of light, darkness and so forth. Mice have been maintained in a constant environment for as long as three generations, and circadian behaviour still persisted. This indicates an inborn form of behaviour rather than one which is acquired by each animal early in life through exposure to a circadian environment. The most nearly comparable observations in man have been made on people spending long periods down deep caves in solitude, and the results have been essentially similar. The sleeping habits of people completely deprived of any indication of time follow a rhythm with a period rather longer than 24 hours, and usually somewhere around 25 hours (fig. 44.9). In contradistinction to the mouse, however, man appears to acquire these rhythms during the first year or so of life, and in Eskimos, who are exposed to a circadian rhythm of light and darkness only for a period around each equinox, circadian rhythms are notably absent (fig. 44.2; cf. figs. 44.6 & 44.7).

Of the factors which normally set the phase of a rhythm and adjust its timing, light appears to be of special importance. In most species the rhythms can be easily manipulated and their phase altered by artificial changes in the illumination of the cages. In human

FIG. 44.2. Excretion of water and potassium by Arctic subjects; (a) Eskimo subject; (b) white Arctic subject. From data of M.C. Lobban.

experiments in which subjects remained in complete darkness for 3 hours after getting up, various physiological changes normally occurring around that time of day have been postponed for roughly 3 hours (fig. 44.3). Blind subjects have rhythms which are disorganized as compared with those of sighted people, though the ability to distinguish light and darkness in those with no measurable visual acuity is sufficient to maintain normal rhythmicity. It is surprising, therefore, that there is so little alteration in the timing of physiological rhythms at different seasons of the year, when the time of sunrise can change so markedly.

In animals living in a natural state many physiological rhythms are critical for survival. For instance, animals which live in an intertidal zone depend upon rhythmic behaviour for their protection when the tide is in or out, for the possibilities of feeding at the appropriate state of the tide and for hatching and laying eggs. Lunar rhythms

FIG. 44.3. Eosinophil count. ○, control observations; ●, days when subject remained in complete darkness for 3 hours after getting up. From data of G.W.G. Sharp (1960) *J. Endrocrin.* **21**, 213.

are found in animals which depend upon the lunar variation in the height of tides. Similarly, most animals depend upon the alternation of light and darkness in their search for food or in their efforts to avoid being killed. Most small mammals are nocturnal and hide from their predators during the day in burrows, holes or other refuges. One might imagine that this behaviour is regulated by simple responsiveness to the changing illumination, leading them to retreat rapidly to security as the dawn appears and to emerge with the return of night. There are obvious advantages, however, in having some rhythmic process superimposed upon any direct response to the circadian stimuli. The mammal sleeping in a burrow by day would awake at around the appropriate time for safe emergence, rather than repeatedly coming out to see whether all is clear. Many of man's circadian rhythms are also beneficial. By and large, we are wakeful during the day when we are attempting to work or use our mind to maximum efficiency; we are tired and sleepy at night when we most commonly sleep. The early morning production of cortisol by the adrenals (fig. 44.8) has been held to be an arousal mechanism, and the low urine flow at night is conducive to continuous uninterrupted sleep. The higher temperature during the day is probably conducive to muscular and perhaps mental efficiency. By virtue of his ability to manipulate the environment and control, for example, temperature and illumination, man

has less need of these rhythms. He can store his food, and is virtually independent of restricted times of day for food gathering; he is also in most civilized communities relatively immune from predation and can venture forth at any hour of day or night. He is thus able to adopt habits which are strictly unnatural and to remain active long after dark and to lie abed after dawn. However, in so far as many of his physiological rhythms are endogenous and persist despite modification of habits or surrounding illumination, they do not accord with his wish to depart from the circadian behaviour which nature or evolution intended. The persistence of these rhythms and their functional significance thus becomes an important subject of study for all those interested in night or shift work. Having orginally devised machines for his benefit, man now finds himself increasingly the slave of these machines. Heavy capital investment in industrial plant demands that it shall operate continuously instead of merely in daylight hours. The provision of transport for those who wish to travel at different hours of day or night imposes a burden of work at unusual and irregular hours for the transport industries, and road congestion may make night travel desirable for heavy commercial transport. Aeroplanes and submarines work round-the-clock schedules. Those who rapidly fly long distances around the world subject their rhythms to a large enforced phase shift which creates its own problems. Such travellers, business men, statesmen, sportsmen, are often anxious to perform at maximal efficiency soon after arrival at their destination, and if they must spend days or weeks adjusting their internal rhythms to the sudden phase shift, the purpose of rapid travel is nullified. As soon as man travels in space he will be entirely isolated from the usual circadian fluctuations in light, darkness and other aspects of environment. Those who have already orbited the Earth have subjected themselves to the remarkable rhythm of a day–night alternation occupying 90 min. So far it has not been necessary for human beings to dwell underground for prolonged periods though a few have done so with the desire to break a record, but if an atomic war should ever occur it may become necessary.

Temperature

Temperature has been studied more extensively than any other component of human rhythms; very extensive observations have been made on small numbers of people, and more scanty observations on enormous numbers have accumulated in hospital records. The conventional hospital chart of an afebrile patient shows a regular pattern usually with an alternation between high evening and low morning temperature. In some subjects, however, this pattern is reversed and the temperature on waking is higher than on going to bed at night. The reason for this is seen at once if one studies fig. 44.4 which shows typical records of readings taken continuously throughout the 24 hours.

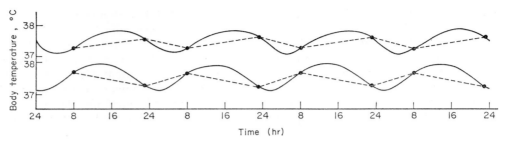

FIG. 44.4. Two examples of temperature rhythm, showing how a small shift in timing can result in a morning temperature above, instead of below, the evening value. Solid line, continuous record; broken line, readings only at bedtime and on waking.

The maximum temperature is usually observed in the afternoon and the minimum in the small hours, so that by bedtime the temperature is already declining from its peak and on waking it is already rising from its minimum value. A minor shift of the time of peak and trough may therefore result in the temperature being higher in the morning than in the evening, an apparent reversal of the usual rhythm which in reality is no more than a small time shift. The pattern is characteristic for the individual

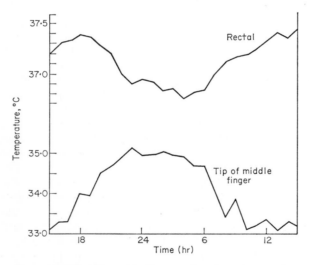

FIG. 44.5. Hourly record of temperature in rectum and on tip of middle finger. From data of G. Hildebrandt and P. Engelbertz.

and is much the same in summer and winter. Different people vary somewhat in the form of their curve and some individuals show a flat plateau during most of the day. This rhythm develops during the early months of life and the magnitude of the oscillation from minimum to maximum increases with age up to about two years, and, at the same time, the timing of the oscillation becomes more regular. This rhythm does not depend closely upon any variation in activity since it is as well developed in subjects recumbent throughout the 24 hours as in those active during the day. It appears to be due more to a variation in the heat loss than in heat production as is indicated by

the circadian variation in skin temperature shown in fig. 44.5; the minimum body temperature is attained shortly after the maximum skin temperature, at a time when heat loss is greatest.

Night workers often show circadian variations similar in phase to those of day workers, their temperature rhythm having failed to adapt to night work. Such workers in a civilized community are subjected to many influences indicating that the alternation of night and day is out of phase with their habits, and presumably one or other of these is responsible for the persistence of the usual pattern; moreover, they usually resume diurnal habits at the week-end; indeed in one study temperature was shown to adapt itself gradually to night work in the course of each week, only to lose the adaptation at the week-end. A more obstinate persistence of 24-hour rhythmicity in temperature has been shown in a subject who in an Arctic summer was living an artificial day of 18 or 28 hours. Many people, however, can adapt their temperature rhythm quite readily to night work within a few days and even to days of abnormal length, and it is generally supposed that temperature is one of the more adaptable of man's circadian rhythms.

The clinician using temperature measurement in diagnosis is aware of the circadian variation, and also of the fact that in febrile illness a high evening temperature is more characteristic than any elevation on waking. A more interesting possibility, as yet little explored and less understood, is a disturbance in the circadian temperature pattern in disease. This has been observed both in epilepsy and in cancer but has not as yet proved of any specific diagnostic value, and it is not known whether there is any association with particular diseases.

Kidney

The low urine flow at night is of obvious practical convenience and is a very ancient observation. The response to a standard water load is also greater in the morning than in the afternoon or evening. The factors determining urine flow are, however, complex, and include changes in excretory rate of the major solids of the urine and in the rate of production of ADH. Observations concerning rhythmic spontaneous variations in secretion of ADH are scanty and unreliable; most of our knowledge of circadian variations in renal function consists of information about excretion rate of the major solids, especially electrolytes. The rate of excretion of sodium, potassium and chloride, which is low at night, usually rises to a peak somewhere between 10.00 hours and 16.00 hours; the time is fairly characteristic for the individual and the peak time for these three electrolytes normally coincides. In subjects living a normal existence, the inherent rhythm may be modified by their habits, coffee and tea in particular having an influence upon the excretion of water, sodium and chloride. When the natural cycle of sleep and activity is altered, whether by deliberately sleeping by day in the Arctic, by flying a substantial distance around the world, or by living a day of abnormal length, the potassium excretory rhythm may maintain a 24-hour timing for many weeks, but sodium and chloride rhythms often adapt sooner, Fig. 44.6 shows an example in a subject living a 27 hour day over a period covering eight artificial, or nine real, days. Water excretion shows eight peaks, and has thus adapted to the

rhythmic variations in their excretion must be due to some other cause. That urine is acid by night and much less acid or even alkaline in the morning is another old observation, although the morning alkalinity used to be ascribed to the influence of breakfast. If hydrogen ion excretion is calculated as the sum of titratable acid and ammonium excretion minus bicarbonate excretion, it is found to be a close mirror image of potassium excretion (fig. 44.7);

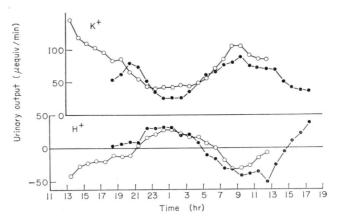

FIG. 44.7. Mean excretion of potassium and hydrion by subjects working in a laboratory for 24 hours; two series of observations.

this is due probably to competition of these two ions for exchange with sodium in the distal convoluted tubules of the kidney.

Phosphate excretion follows a different circadian pattern. When subjects sleep by night, it is commonly high during sleep and falls abruptly during the first hours of waking; when subjects remain awake and collect frequent samples during the night it is found that the fall in excretion has been proceeding steadily during the later hours of the night. Plasma phosphate analyses have been much less frequently performed, but they have been found to parallel very closely the rhythm of phosphate excretion, and a rhythm in plasma phosphate may therefore be the cause of the excretory rhythm. This rhythm is one of the most easily adaptable; thus in a subject changing over from night to day work, phosphate excretion fell abruptly when he awoke even during the transitional phase.

The immediate cause of the rhythmic changes in excretion of other electrolytes is unknown. Glomerular filtration rate (GFR) has been claimed to follow a circadian pattern though observations are not numerous, and most workers do not consider that GFR is a primary determinant of excretion of electrolytes. Of the endocrine factors said to play a part in their regulation, there is good evidence for rhythmic variations in cortisol secretion, but little for aldosterone secretion, diurnal variations in production of which are thought to be determined

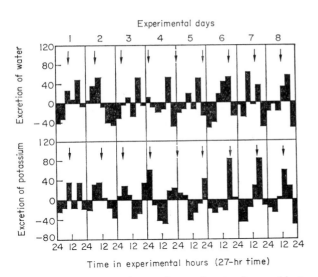

FIG. 44.6. Excretion of potassium and water by a subject living a 27-hour day, as percentage deviation from mean. Arrows indicate mid-day by real time. From data of P.R. Lewis & M.C. Lobban.

artificial time on which the subject was living, whereas potassium shows nine excretory peaks, occurring around mid-day by real time; it was affected by the subject's habits only in that the peak was low when real mid-day coincided with artificial midnight. This suggests the continued operation of a 24-hour clock from which water excretion has escaped under the influence of a 27-hour cycle.

There appears to be no circadian rhythm in plasma concentration of potassium, sodium or chloride, so the mainly by changes in posture. Cortisol increases the excretion of potassium and is produced mainly in the morning when potassium excretion rises. Since its own circadian rhythm is one of the most persistent when the subject's habits change, it could be responsible for the potassium excretory rhythm; but doubt arises whether quantitatively the circadian variations in cortisol production are sufficient to account for the large variations in urinary excretion of potassium. Uncertainty is greater over sodium since cortisol may either increase or decrease its excretion; the fact that sodium excretion may lose a circadian rhythm while that of potassium is maintained is evidence against their having a common mechanism. We are unlikely to understand the sodium excretory rhythm until ideas about those factors which normally regulate sodium excretion are clarified.

Of other urinary constituents, creatinine excretion often follows a circadian rhythm which probably reflects changes in glomerular filtration, and rhythm has also been claimed in the excretion of urea, uric acid, calcium, magnesium and a variety of other constituents. One practical implication of these findings is that if one is not specifically interested in circadian rhythms, but wants to use urinary excretion rates as an aid to diagnosis, nothing short of a complete 24-hour urine collection should suffice. Measurement of creatinine excretion affords a useful check on whether any substantial fraction of the 24-hour collection has been inadvertently discarded.

Adrenals

Circadian variations in the function of the adrenal cortex have been studied by measuring both plasma concentration of cortical hormones and their renal excretion, which lags about three hours behind. The various methods used, which measure mainly cortisol and its derivatives, all show peak plasma concentration in the early morning from 06.00 to 10.00 hours, though with sampling at 4-hourly intervals the precise time is difficult to define (fig. 44.8). Measurements have been made under carefully controlled conditions with indwelling cannulae to facilitate sampling without waking the subject, and consequently this is one of the best defined of human circadian rhythms, though it has been much less studied under abnormal circumstances. The normal rhythm may persist for a long time in subjects who deliberately alter their habits, as well as in people who have been working by night for years, though the week-end may disturb the pattern of night work. A reverse pattern with peak plasma concentrations around the time of starting work has, however, been observed in industries where night work is virtually universal and long established (fig. 44.8). Observations on man and other species suggest that these variations in adrenal activity are associated both with variations in adrenal sensitivity to ACTH and with variations in the rate of its production under the in-

fluence of the hypothalamic corticotrophin releasing factor. The rhythm disappears in some forms of brain damage.

Observations on rhythmic production of aldosterone are much fewer, though an isotope-labelling method has been used to measure rates of aldosterone production in

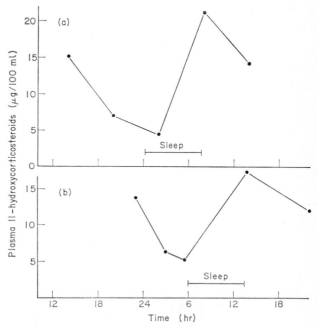

FIG. 44.8. Plasma concentration of corticosteroids; (a) subjects working by day; (b) night workers. From data of R.T.W.L. Conroy.

3-hour periods throughout the 24 hours, and has shown minimal secretion rates around midnight and maximal values during the morning. These observations were, however, upon subjects sleeping at night and ambulant during the day, and so may have resulted from the effect of posture. A rhythmic variation in adrenaline excretion which presumably reflects secretion rates has also been demonstrated in subjects remaining continuously alert throughout the 24 hours; high values were found in the early afternoon and minimal values in the small hours of the morning. This may be due to an action of glucocorticoids upon the adrenal medulla.

It is generally supposed that the adrenal rhythm is responsible for many other circadian rhythmic variations including the rhythm of the eosinophil count, which normally falls to a low level after waking, corresponding with the time of high cortisol production (fig. 44.3) and the sleep–wakefulness rhythm. One might suppose that we feel sleepy at night because we have been awake for a long time, and alert in the morning because we have slept; but people staying awake all night commonly observe similar fluctuations, from a very sleepy period in the small hours to a more wakeful one later on, even though they have not slept, coinciding with the time of high cortisol production. Furthermore some people are fully alert early in the morning, while others do not become alert till nearer mid-day, and it is interesting to speculate whether these variations reflect variation in the time of peak cortisol production. Variations in alertness may well be responsible for the variations which are claimed in a variety of aspects of psychomotor performance ranging from reaction time to incidence of errors in reading instruments. They may also be responsible for the altered excitability of the respiratory centre, whose activity is known to depend upon excitation from descending pathways; this activity diminishes in sleep, resulting in a small rise in alveolar CO_2 pressure. These respiratory changes are not the result simply of sleep itself since small circadian variations in alveolar CO_2 pressure are seen in subjects remaining awake all night, and it is claimed that other variations in alertness extend their influence to the respiratory centre.

Since one's sleepiness or wakefulness can be influenced by social contact, it is best studied on subjects staying in isolation in caves, whose times of going to bed and waking up can be recorded by a telephone line to the surface without their being aware of clock time. All who have done this have adopted a 'day' of somewhat over 24 hours, awaking a little later every day, until in the course of some months underground they may have lost several days. Fig. 44.9 shows records of three such subjects. The

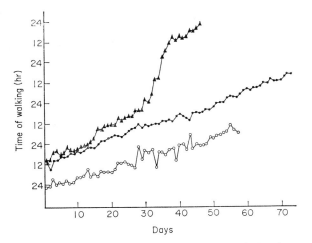

FIG. 44.9. Time of waking when living in isolation in a cave. ○, M. Siffre; ●, G. Workman; ▲, D. Lafferty. The time becomes progressively later day by day.

inference is that under these circumstances the supposed internal 'clock' fails to keep perfect time, losing slightly; more extensive observations on other mammals and birds confirm this general conclusion, except that the 'clock' sometimes gains. It would appear that under normal circumstances the 'clock' is repeatedly adjusted by

some factor in our habits or environment, just as it had to be re-set when we changed to or from Summer Time.

Circulation and blood

Pulse rate is simple to measure and record and many observations show its circadian periodicity, which adapts itself more readily than any other to a change of habits, such as sleeping by day or living a day of abnormal length. It is not entirely dependent upon habit, however, since it has been shown to remain rhythmic in subjects continuously recumbent and taking small regular meals. Periodicity has likewise been claimed for many other circulatory variables, such as blood pressure, pulse pressure, cardiac output, etc., as well as for most haematological values, including all those which would be affected by loss of fluid from the circulating blood into the interstitial tissues. It is probable that many of these changes result from a redistribution of body fluids due to posture. This is not an entirely adequate explanation, since some changes in haemoglobin concentration have been observed to occur independently of whether the subjects spent the day in bed or not. Among haematological measurements, plasma iron concentration has been most extensively investigated. It attains a maximal value around the time of waking and is low in the late evening and early night. The cause of this rhythm is unknown, but it is easily changed if the subject alters his habits and is one of the few rhythms which are known to be completely independent of the adrenal cortex.

Parasite rhythms

Among the more interesting of circadian rhythms are those of the parasitic nematode worms which give rise to elephantiasis and related diseases. The larvae of these worms, known as microfilariae, appear in the peripheral blood stream, whence they are conveyed to other subjects by biting-insects. If an attempt is made to assess the severity of infestation by counting the number of microfilariae in every ml of blood, it is found that this quantity varies very widely from none up to several thousand, and that these variations follow a regular circadian pattern. One of the commonest of such worms, *Wuchereria bancrofti*, appears in the cutaneous bloodstream during the night and retreats to the pulmonary capillaries during the day, whilst microfilariae of *Loa loa* behave in exactly the reverse way, appearing in the peripheral blood only by day. This complete difference in habits of these related worms reflects the fact that *Wuchereria* is conveyed by night-flying mosquitoes whereas *Loa* is conveyed by the day-flying mangrove flies, and hence it is an adaptation essential to the survival of the species. It would seem a safe assumption that the microfilariae react to one of the circadian changes going on within their host's body; indeed if subjects who have acquired the parasites in India come to England, their parasite rhythms are found to follow

English rather than Indian day and night. If the hosts then deliberately work by night and sleep by day, the parasites reverse their habits within a week or two. Observations on monkeys, which can also be infested with *Wuchereria*, have shown that deep body temperature determines the behaviour of the microfilariae. They can be made to retreat to the pulmonary capillaries by raising the temperature of the monkey during the night, or can be brought out of the pulmonary capillaries into the peripheral blood stream by lowering the animal's temperature during the day. Though it has not yet been investigated, it would seem a likely assumption that *Loa* reacts to temperature changes in the reverse direction, just as daylight causes some mammalian species to become more active, whilst it causes others to retire and go to sleep.

Circadian rhythms are also widespread throughout living organisms, being of equal importance in plants, which may depend upon daylight for their metabolic processes and upon the flying habits of insects for fertilization. As with animal rhythms, these can persist even if plants are kept in a constant environment, and they have even been shown in tissue cultures of plant cells.

Conclusions

It will be seen that circadian rhythms affect many human functions.

Even where they are least understood, the influence of circadian rhythms is pervasive. The popular description of the small hours of the morning as a time of lowest ebb is borne out statistically by the fact that death is more common then than at any other time; some variation also occurs in the sensitivity to drugs. Understanding of the mechanisms underlying these rhythms is rudimentary,

but it seems likely that they may reside in separate tissues and organs and under normal conditions are co-ordinated by some centre in the brain, perhaps in the hypothalamus.

The possibility that this co-ordination may break down so that different rhythms are no longer normally synchronized and cause disease is a speculation which is not yet founded on observation. Equally, the disturbances of rhythm found in some diseases are at present only empirical facts and of little diagnostic value. Further understanding is needed before we can manipulate the rhythms so that a man can fly half-way round the world, and, instead of imagining it is time for bed and feeling duly fatigued, accommodate at once to the new time and assume the alertness characteristic of the morning.

FURTHER READING

ASCHOFF J. (1963) Comparative physiology: diurnal rhythms. *Ann. Rev. Physiol.* **25**, 581.

BÜNNING E. (1964) *The Physiological Clock.* Berlin: Springer-Verlag.

HARKER J.E. (1958) Diurnal rhythms in the animal kingdom. *Biol. Rev.* **33**, 1.

HARKER J.E. (1964) *The Physiology of Diurnal Rhythms.* Cambridge: Cambridge University Press.

KLEITMAN N. (1963) *Sleep and Wakefulness.* 2nd Edition. Chicago: Univ. Chicago Press.

MILLS J.N. (1966) Human Circadian Rhythms. *Physiol. Rev.* **46**, 128.

SIFFRE M. (1965) *Beyond Time.* London: Chatto & Windus.

SOLLBERGER A. (1965) *Biological Rhythm Research.* New York: Elsevier.

Chapter 45
On living in society

It is only necessary to watch someone walking into a crowded room to realize that man is a social animal. His movements, his dress, his first words of greeting and the way he looks around his immediate environment, all have been shaped to varying degrees by myriads of past interactions with other human beings.

In studying this relationship social psychologists have used as a central concept the notion of **social group**, a simple definition of which is: '...two or more people who interact more with each other than with other people.' Such interaction must occur in order to achieve any objective beyond the reach of an individual. Early examples in evolution were probably moving rocks or lifting logs and later, hunting for food. Modern examples are the building with critical path technique of the first Polaris submarine and the construction of the Forth Road Bridge.

It is tempting to say that man's evolution has been influenced by living in herds for so long that he is now naturally gregarious and has a social instinct. This proposition cannot be tested and carries no useful practical implication; the facts may be accounted for more simply by saying that he joins social groups because he needs what he can get out of them in order to survive. His first social group after birth is based on food. Unlike many other organisms, the human neonate does not have pre-programmed behaviour that enables him to locate the nutritious parts of the environment. Instead, he enters a social group, usually a dyad, with his mother, which supplies this need and in so doing shapes his behaviour in more or less enduring ways.

It is a paradox that when one personality is compared with another many of the differences and the similarities are due to their involvement in a multiplicity of social groups. It is true, of course, that the blueprint of physical structure is laid down in the chromosomes and certain features of this physical structure have important repercussions on the personality. The endocrine system, for example, influences a basal level of temperament and the potential of intelligence and physical appearance are likely to influence social success. But these innate physical factors are inextricably interwoven with social experience. There are undoubtedly other elements about which little is known because they are never observed in pure form.

At the risk of oversimplification, we may describe this interplay by drawing an analogy between the adult personality and a furnished room. The dimensions of a room are fixed, but they interact to create a sense of proportion. This, in turn, depends very much on the way in which the room is decorated with planes of colour and on the arrangement of lighting. When the furnishings are added, they alter the general impression which is itself changed by what is there already. So the room assumes a unique and complex personality. It has been formed by interaction between the innate and acquired. It can be drastically changed, but refurnishing is laborious and limited by the basic structure of the room.

Every social group arises because a number of people want the same thing and none of them can achieve it alone. This is the **group goal** which members share in common. In addition different members stand to gain a wide range of subsidiary rewards. Most students in university groups want to achieve a degree or the learning which it symbolizes; in addition some want to get away from home, some to gain social status and others to meet girls.

If the value to an individual of the rewards drops below a certain level, membership lapses and he withdraws from the social system. If he wishes to attain the goals, however, he must continue membership of the group and conform to certain expectations. He may be informed of these by a threatening whisper or a printed constitution. The principle is the same.

The first kind of expectation is that in order to achieve the group goal, different members must restrict their behaviour to roles which complement each other. The second is that for the same reason the members are expected to conform to certain standards of behaviour, beliefs, opinion and attitude, called **norms**. Much human behaviour may be accounted for by saying that man learns the roles of father, businessman, husband, club secretary, one of the boys and many others, as prescribed by overlapping social groups. He also learns standards of honesty, punctuality, liberalism and aggressiveness, each of them the accepted norm of one or more social groups.

The process of conformity

An early systematic study of social conformity was made during the 1930's, using the **autokinetic phenomenon**. The subjects were asked to report the extent of movement of a pinpoint of light at the far end of a darkened room. When they did this by themselves there was a narrowing in their judgements over successive trials. If two people worked together publicly the estimates converged towards each other.

This approach was criticized because the stimulus was too ambiguous for the results to be relevant to judgements and opinions in real life. But in a classic and somewhat disturbing set of experiments, Asch subsequently revealed more of the power of group influence. His stimulus was a 20 cm line, drawn vertically on a piece of card. About 45 cm away were three more lines, one of 20 cm and the others differing by from 1·0 to 4·5 cm. The task was to identify the lines of equal length and subjects were asked to call their answers aloud, beginning from the left. Only one of the group of subjects was genuine and he had been manoeuvred into a seat on the right. The rest had been primed to give a pre-arranged wrong answer. Here, the stimuli were unequivocal, but just over one-third of judgements were given in a way that can only be described as contrary to the plain evidence of the senses. In more elaborate experiments subjects have been placed in booths with communication channels that purport to show decisions made by their colleagues in adjacent booths, but which are actually controlled by central switching. Under this pressure, 37 per cent of a sample of U.S. Army Officers agreed with the statement: 'I doubt whether I would make a good leader', although when questioned individually not a single one agreed.

Another study showed that the number of articles rejected by industrial inspectors could be changed greatly by manipulating the number of faulty articles ostentatiously put to one side by some members of the group.

There are many variables which have been shown to effect the degree of change in judgments, attitudes opinions and behaviour as a result of social interaction. For example, the greater the ambiguity of the stimulus or issue, the more readily can change be induced. Much of the information that the layman receives about politics and also medicine is of this kind.

The degree of privacy is obviously crucial. Many people go along with the group in public but privately know better. In an experiment in which judgements of modern paintings were recorded after a discussion with a dominant partner, half the final decisions were given in sealed envelopes and half declared publicly. The latter, needless to say, showed more conformity. A useful concept to describe double standards is **compliance**, but compliance is often the first step towards genuine conformity.

If a man submits readily and with conviction to group pressure, it is too facile to describe him as weak. Up to a point, conformity is a highly adaptive mechanism, because uncertainty is disruptive to the personality. Also, other people frequently do know better than oneself and unity of thought and action does bring strength to social groups and helps to achieve individual goals. However, unthinking compliance is sometimes maladaptive and society can only surmount this difficulty by purveying independence as a social norm for the behaviour of its members. This does not mean nonconformity, which is simply the irritating converse to conformity, but the ability to consider all available past and present sources of evidence before judging or acting.

Social pressure is insidiously strong when it issues from a group or person of high status. A programme of research at Yale explored the limits to which ordinary adults would go in obedient submission to the orders of an authority. The authority was a scientist who claimed to be carrying out an experiment on the effect of punishment upon learning. The results were alarming. Not only would many subjects obey commands to increase electric shocks to their partners up to points on a scale marked: '300 volts: Danger: Severe Shock', but they persisted, although obviously emotionally disturbed themselves, in spite of screams of pain and desperate pleas for release from the 'victims'. The latter were tape recorded!

The family

In the majority of societies, the family is the most powerful social group. When born into a family, we are involuntarily exposed to a particular set of cultural norms and role expectations. The leaders of the group control potent rewards such as love and affection. It is hardly surprising that in spite of the rebelliousness of the young, attitude surveys show a fairly high correlation between children and their parents on public issues. Because it is so obvious, it is easy to overlook the fact that we learn the language spoken in our family and this is probably the richest heritage of a transmitted culture. Although the language is a vehicle of exploration, it also selects and limits our attitudes and experience. Working class children in our society are hampered in the development of abstract thought processes which comprise intelligence because their early language has been limited to the expression of the concrete.

An important question is the effect of different regimes of child rearing on subsequent personality. This is a huge problem, bedevilled by the lack of valid methods for measuring personality on the one hand and the notorious difficulty of obtaining accurate information from mothers on the other. Most investigators have tried to do this retrospectively, but they encounter selective forgetting, repression and distortion which brings the past more into line with the idealized norms purveyed by neighbours and women's magazines. Many mothers are more sensitive about their choice of child rearing methods than about their choice of hats.

Attempts to relate specific practices like breast or bottle feeding, time of weaning and methods of toilet training, where a relationship is predicted by Freud's theory of psychoanalysis, have given conflicting results. It is too early to say that the theory is discredited on this account, because most studies have been looking for linear relationships whereas it is probably optima that are critical. Delayed weaning may be as harmful as premature weaning. These optima could differ for each child, depending on other factors, and this renders the conventional methods of statistics inappropriate.

However, abstraction of order from the complexity of social interactions between parent and child has only just begun, and those which attempt to relate broader and more persisting dimensions of maternal behaviour to the personalities of nursery and primary school children show an encouraging degree of consistency. For example, maternal behaviour has independent dimensions such as warmth to coldness (hostility), and permissiveness to restrictiveness. 'Independent' implies that the location of the mother on the scale of one dimension does not infer anything about her location with regard to the other. Two such dimensions can, however, be used to generate systematically a number of types of child rea ng. For example, a mother who is high in warmth can be classed as 'indulgent' if she is also high in permissiveness. If, on the other hand, she is warm and restrictive, then she is 'overprotective'.

One of the best known studies of the effect of such patterns of child rearing was carried out by Sears and his colleagues in a New England suburb. The family life of nearly 400 five-year-old children was studied in the home by ten trained interviewers. They used a schedule covering seventy-two items of behaviour and the full responses were tape recorded, transcribed and subsequently converted into scale forms for statistical analysis. Their findings included the correlation of maternal coldness with eating difficulties and persistent bed wetting. Maternal coldness also characterized homes where the children were retarded in conscience development and too aggressive. It is particularly interesting that these authors found overwhelming evidence that punishments, in contrast to rewards, were quite ineffectual in the training of children.

There are clearly national, racial and social class differences in child rearing and these are the real causes of many of the differences between people previously attributed to inheritance. Indeed the work of social anthropologists first stimulated the present interest in the social aspects of child development.

In a village in Ceylon, Straus found an apparent contradiction of the hypothesis that easy going demand feed-ing combined with an extreme casualness in elimination training (there was no prescribed place for defaecation except that the house was excluded) and much early affection would result in confident and emotionally secure adults. These Singalese, on the contrary, were tense, anxious and insecure. Straus ascribes this to a combination of two much broader features of their culture. The love and affection was withdrawn at about five years of age and replaced by an aloof relationship. There is also in Ceylon a loose social structure in which rights and duties are not rigidly defined but tend to be equivocal. This is in sharp contrast to Japan and Vietnam.

One of the difficulties of research on our own culture is that the mass media disseminate new thinking about child rearing with such rapidity that it is difficult to establish the existence of stable relationships. It appears, for example, from a careful reappraisal of studies going back to 1930, that there has been a radical change associated with social class. At present, it is the middle class mothers who are more permissive, who provide more warmth and are more likely to use reasoning, or merely expressions of disappointment in disciplining their children. Twenty years ago such parents were more inclined to impose restrictions and frustrations and to set high standards in the belief that such a regime 'builds character'.

Another problem is the perennial one of causality versus concomitancy. Does the permissive mother make the nonaggressive child or does the nonaggressive child allow the mother to be permissive? For psychology as for medicine, a method of experiment which circumvents this difficulty is seldom possible. It is obviously unethical to impose noxious psychological conditions on human beings or to restrict their freedom for experimental purposes. One study attempted to avoid this dilemma by the strategy of locating some deprived children in an institution and providing a remedy for the situation in respect of half of them. There were sixteen babies about 6 months; of these, eight were given a great deal of cuddling and attention over a period of 8 weeks by the same person. The other eight were treated by the prevailing socially sterile routine with essential feeding and cleaning by a rota of nurses. Subsequently, independent observers with no knowledge of the allocation of the children rated the experimental ones as more socially responsive, and they scored slightly higher on postural and ability tests.

This investigation was concerned with the well-known hypothesis, that separation of a child from its mother during the critical ages of infancy may affect emotional development. Research in this area, with which John Bowlby of the Tavistock Clinic has been associated, has led to profound changes in our attitude towards child care and hospitalization.

Intermittent separation from the mother, a less familiar situation, was investigated by the present writer and found to have harmful effects. There has been a widespread policy throughout the world to consolidate the administration of education in rural areas by closing small country schools with only one or two teachers and transporting the children by bus to schools in larger centres. There has always been ill-defined anxiety about the wisdom of this policy on the grounds that it makes too heavy demands upon the children and that it may sap the life from already weak rural communities. Until recently, however, there has been no evidence on either of these points and the economic and educational arguments have been strongly in favour of closure. It now appears from a study of population trends in several hundred Devon parishes that the anxieties on the second count were fully justified.

More pertinent to our present topic, however, was a study made of the emotional behaviour of children who at the ages of 7 and 8 years undertook long journeys to reach their schools. Teachers from fifty-seven rural primary schools made detailed assessments of 883 children on such dimensions of behaviour as concentration, eating difficulties, response to affection and depression. A clear relationship emerged between the majority of these behavioural characteristics and the length of journey to school. Less expected was the finding that if these journeys were made on foot, although walking is regarded as a physically fatiguing activity, they had less effect upon the child than journeys in a school bus. It appeared from supporting evidence that this could best be explained by assuming that a walk articulates the space between home and school, making it familiar and accessible and joining the two life spaces into a coherent, single whole. By contrast, the school bus transports the child over anonymous territory and after depositing him disappears until the time for departure. During the intervening period, whatever crises may arise to loom large in the children's minds, many of them will have no perceived access to their mother.

We generally persist in ignoring such psychological factors if they conflict with other more tangible values. A Swedish study of modern housing has shown that if multi-storey blocks are used to accommodate families with children, the younger ones either refuse to play outside or, if they do so, they reject the carefully provided spaces with expensive equipment and, exasperatingly, play in the area of the otherwise imposing entrance. This is the means of access to the mother. There are implications in these studies of an intimate link between the spatial, the social and the emotional which have hardly been explored.

Leadership

The most important role within social groups is that of leader. The leadership function, which is often spread over more than one person, is to help the group to clarify its goals, to devise plans for reaching them and to impose pressures on members to implement these plans. This is made possible because the group vests power in the leader and consents to carry out his orders, subject usually to certain safeguards. Again, members exchange a modification in their own behaviour for better group rewards in which they will share. Needless to say, most societies have speculated on the properties that distinguish leaders from followers. Ours is probably the first to carry out controlled experiments.

Early scientific research into the problem tried to identify traits of personality shown by established leaders but lacking in their followers. There are two major difficulties in this approach. The first is in specifying and measuring the traits in such a way that different observations are comparable. The second is that some of the followers may well have the relevant qualities to a high degree but have not been able to exercise them because circumstances have kept them from positions of leadership. Everyone knows that the converse sometimes obtains.

The results of this approach have been disappointing; each new study brings out a fresh collection of traits although some charateristics like dependability, intelligence, social participation and socio-economic status tend to recur. However, this diversity is not all due to error. Different qualities of leadership have been found critical to particular groups and investigation has tended to switch towards a situational approach to the problem. The man who is dumb and lost at a public protest meeting may be the born leader of a commando raid. Even the situational approach presents the difficulty that many social groups operate over a wide range of different situations, in all of which leaders must excel. A good example is the wartime search for OLQ, Officer Like Quality. This is a deceptively simple label for a motley of skills.

A series of studies carried out by the Survey Research Center at Michigan University were concerned with industrial foremanship. Eighty gangs of railway maintenance workers were divided into pairs each with a similar track section to maintain and similar conditions of work. Independent assessments of the quality and quantity of work performed by each gang were provided by the Divisional Engineer and by the Track Superintendent. Both the men and their leaders were questioned systematically on the ways in which the gang was run. The results for this study were similar to those in a tractor factory and in an insurance office and other organizations. Some of them were also confirmed by a study of British electrical firms carried out by a group from Oxford.

The effective leaders deployed a larger proportion of their time on planning or supervising the work of others and on tasks which only they could do, and correspondingly less on 'pitching in' with the men. Their supervision was not close or detailed and they allowed their men to get on with the job without frequent correction. They also were 'supportive', taking an interest in the men's domestic and work problems. They acted promptly to requests, communicated more freely about what was going on and made less use of punishment.

Although leadership of this kind is effective in contemporary work groups, it must be re-emphasized that there is no ideal type of leader. There are optimal leadership patterns to achieve the goals of given groups in given situations.

Other important facets of these patterns involved in differing proportions in many groups in our society have been named **initiation** and **consideration**. The first is a preoccupation with getting the job done; making plans, persuading people to execute them and generally getting the group ahead. The other is concerned with the human relationships, keeping members' morale high and meeting the subsidiary needs of human fellowship. A study of U.S. Army pilots in training showed that those who were high in consideration for their crews were independently rated the best leaders by instructors. But subsequently in combat conditions during the Korean war, those high in initiation were judged most effective. The complexity of the problem can be seen from the fact that when assessments were made by the crew members themselves instead of by instructors, the most effective combat leaders were those judged to be high in consideration. In a Japanese experiment industrial supervisors were trained by three alternative methods. One stressed productivity (P), one maintenance of morale (M) and the third a combination of both styles (PM). Productivity was highest in the order PM : P : M. Consideration (maintenance) appears as a catalyst that raises initiation (productivity) to the highest level.

Again, the question must be asked whether certain kinds of leader create good groups or whether good groups allow leaders to behave in certain ways. Churchill modestly claimed that he merely put the roar in the mouth of the British Lion. A leader can rarely impose his will on a group, except when he has access to external power. This was nicely demonstrated by a study of nursery school children, in which after careful observation the most dominant members of play groups were separated. The followers were then allowed to establish group goals and norms over a period and the leaders then re-introduced. Although some of them tried, they could not immediately change the patterns of play. Invariably they had to learn the ways of the group to gain acceptance and, through this, power. But this was power only to modify, not to recast. The group is stronger than its leaders but the leaders can influence the group within the limits of its goals.

Two industrial experiments have given further evidence of the influence of leadership. In one the leaders of clerical groups with high productivity were changed over with leaders of groups with low productivity. The result was that the output of the groups changed upwards or downwards in accordance with the new leader. In the other study detailed assessments of the leaders of telephone repair gangs in Montreal by men themselves were recorded. The approved leaders were then changed to the disapproving groups and vice versa. Four months later the groups' attitudes had changed and it seemed that the leaders could induce attitudes.

Group conflict and aggression

However efficiently a social group may be organized to achieve its aims, it has always to overcome many difficulties. One of the worst of these is that another group may have set itself the same goal. This is the basic condition for social competition. If one group reaches its goal, the other must fail, *ipso facto*. Both therefore devise strategies to increase their chances over the other. Up to a point this is fine. Competition is obviously a spur to effort and encourages innovation and the search for new paths, but it also leads to race riots and industrial strife. The strategies adopted for reaching the goal include actions that block the other group from getting there first. It is axiomatic that obstruction will be employed more by those who see themselves as losing by the more direct methods. One of the most common responses to frustration is aggression.

Conflict between groups, as between individuals, is aggravated further by the perceptual changes which it generates in its members. If the relationship between groups is one of enmity, then all the properties of an enemy are ascribed to all the members of the 'out-group' and not merely those properties which events have justified. These patterns of traits which are automatically switched on are called **stereotypes** and are acquired like other norms by social groups. Out-group members are firmly and consistently categorized even by members of the in-group who have never actually encountered them and the stereotype forms the first basis for interaction when they meet. Examples are 'nigger', 'bookie' and 'colonel'.

This narrowing of perceptions leads, of course, to less communication and perhaps even to segregation. Whichever group is the more successful is confirmed in its strategies and its members conform to them more readily. Increased cohesiveness gives greater power and success is accelerated. The losers, however, feel inferior. Their status appears to them to decline and their hostility increases. An ingenious study of group conflict was made by Sherif and his colleagues in the United States by setting up isolated summer camps for boys of about 12 years old. In one camp two groups who styled themselves the Eagles and the Rattlers were introduced separately, and deliberately ranged against each other in competitive tournaments of baseball, tug of war, treasure hunts, etc. Solidarity increased within each group and soon high rewards were being dispensed for vilifying the rivals. An Eagle against whom a Rattler had accidentally bumped was told by his friends to brush 'the dirt' off his clothes. Verbal abuse developed into scuffling and night raids on the enemy! Attempts at reconciliation were initiated. The usual methods of promoting contact and trying to correct false images were found to be insufficient. It was only when goals were instigated which could be attained only by the combined effort of both groups that progress was begun. Crises, such as a breakdown in the water supply and the need to push start a heavy lorry were manufactured surreptitiously by the experimenters. The unavoidable cooperation led to the formation of a new and larger social group and hostility quickly dissolved.

These processes, which are only part of a complex whole, can also be observed at the individual level. There is good evidence that generalized personality traits of hostility and aggression towards out-groups (such as anti-semitism) are derived from family emotional relationships and disciplinary methods during early childhood. The man with an 'authoritarian personality' is rigid and inflexible in his attitudes, considers power, status and dominance to be important matters and is scrupulous about the conventions. These are probably repressive mechanisms for disguising his own hostility and controlling his aggressive impulses. Research has shown that he is more likely to have been brought up under a harsh threatening discipline and in a family where love and affection are strictly conditional on submission to standards of good behaviour. Such families are much concerned with their status hierarchy and aggression towards parents is the unspeakable sin.

The authoritarian personality does not usually engage in overt aggression and is perhaps the more dangerous for that, because he deceives others as well as himself. By contrast, there are those who have simply learned techniques of physical aggression as a means of achieving their goals. Such techniques are class linked in our society.

The most obvious way for learning such responses is within a social group that dispenses rewards for excellence in aggression. The Iatmul head-hunters, for example, allocate prestige to members who are successful scalpers and give immediate reward in the form of celebrations and dances on what might be called a per-decapitation basis.

Experiments have shown that words of praise for hitting an inflated doll, establish a ferocious persistence in such behaviour among young children. In one study children were rewarded with coloured marbles for punching a Bobo clown and substantial differences in persistence were found for alternative 'schedules of reinforcement', i.e. the regularity with which the marbles were dispensed. After the withdrawal of rewards, children who had received one marble per punch were less persistent than those who had been rewarded only occasionally. This is a general finding in learning theory and explains the extraordinary tenacity of much human behaviour that appears to pay off only very remotely.

Another way in which aggressive behaviour is learnt is by imitation of a 'model'. This probably depends on a generalized habit of reproducing the behaviour of models of high status (particularly parents) which has been acquired by reward in early childhood. Bandura and his colleagues contrived a situation in which children observed adult models using novel forms of assault upon a large inflated doll, such as hitting it with a hammer or sitting astride it to punch the face. Subsequently, the children were put in different settings with the doll present and subjected to mild frustration. They tended to reproduce many of the responses they had seen earlier. Controls who had not been exposed to models showed only a conventional repertoire of aggression. A group who had seen non-aggressive models similarly reproduced their more inhibited responses. A disturbing feature of this study was that the children imitated behaviour seen on films as readily as that of living persons.

The urban neighbourhood

In the organization of collective behaviour the social group is the paradigm unit. However, although there are no sharp dividing lines, it should not be overlooked that there are many other social manifestations such as mobs, reference groups, crowds and crazes. The one chosen for description is less exotic to the point of being mundane, but it serves as a good example because it is more familiar and has been systematically studied. It is the urban neighbourhood.

Interest in the neighbourhood was stimulated by the postwar house building programme in Britain and particularly by the new towns. There was widespread acceptance by planners of the notion of **neighbourhood units**, which would be relatively self-contained residential areas with their own shopping and community centres and with distinct boundaries to promote a sense of belonging. It was hoped to create social communities that would be more satisfying than the faceless suburbs of pre-war years. There emerged a vocal opposition, however, which berated the concept as 'outworn parochialism' and 'village-green planning'. It was claimed that urban dwellers preferred anonymity and mobility. As is usually the case in social issues, neither side had any scientific evidence. It was generally conceded that neighbourhood behaviour was less than it had been, but two views prevailed about how to define neighbourhood. One was that it was a social group with 'nigh-dwellers' (a dictionary derivation) as members. The other view was that it was a piece of urban territory with commonly agreed boundaries.

When a random sample of residents were asked to describe their neighbourhood, however, it transpired that neither view was wholly correct. First and contrary to prediction, it was found that neighbourhood was still an important social concept. The majority of the housewives in the sample acknowledged that they had one, and for 75 per cent of them it was so highly salient that they could draw a map of it. To this extent it was a piece of territory, but when the maps were superimposed there was little coincidence of boundaries, even for a sample of people living in the same street. Furthermore, they were clearly influenced by a resultant of physical and social forces. The territory was partly determined by the need to include friends and other familiar people, who had acquired this status because they lived within the territory.

Thus the neighbourhood is a socio-spatial configuration. It differs from a social group mainly in that the social relationships are not necessarily reciprocal. A may be influenced by B but B is not aware of A's existence; she is influenced by C who also impinges on A.

It was found that the average concept of the size and composition of neighbourhoods is not affected by the density of population but there were large individual variations which depended on such factors as social class, age, length of residence, location of husband's work, etc. Physical factors, such as the siting of recreational facilities and shops, make a good deal of difference to the probability that people will use them. The **principle of least effort** is the main consideration, but what constitutes effort is determined subjectively. What is more, in the past we have greatly underestimated the influence of this principle upon social behaviour.

In a similar study of a housing project for married ex-service students at the Massachusetts Institute of Technology it was found that the positions of houses and the location of their front doors and such apparent trivia as the siting of post boxes and stairways affected the formation of friendships. Friendships in turn governed the channels of communication and these determined the way in which the residents aligned themselves on an issue of local politics.

In conclusion

We have glimpsed at man as a social animal in a number of settings but they all illustrate a few simple principles.

Men interact in social systems of varying degrees of elaboration in order to meet their needs. Group membership itself is not optional but universal. It is not 'instinctive' because this term is best retained for automatic sequences of behaviour triggered by specific stimuli and man possesses very few of these. The price of membership is the necessity to modify behaviour. This modification or learning seems to be mainly controlled by reinforcement, i.e. reward or punishment, however abstract and remote; groups purvey reinforcement and thus control much of the development of personality.

There are two final points that are worth emphasizing. The first is that learning, although to some extent reversible, is not ethereal. It is a biological process and implies real change in neural tissue. For example, the learned aspects of the sex role are no less physiological than the more obvious glandular aspects.

The second point is that some people find it distasteful and a reflection on the essential dignity of man to accept that he is a product of the processes of social conformity. But the palatability of a theory is not relevant to its validity. However, there are no grounds for a common cause of anxiety, which is the idea that conformity reduces us all to dull uniformity. On the contrary, convergence to one group sharpens the divergence from another. The number of groupings is infinite and idiosyncrasy is not in peril. What is certain is that none of man's achievements would have been possible unless he had been the most social of all known organisms.

FURTHER READING

BROWN R. (1965). *Social Psychology*. London: Collier-Macmillan.

KRECH D., CRUTCHFIELD R.S. & BALLACHEY E.L. (1962). *Individual in Society*. London: McGraw-Hill.

SECORD P.F. & BACKMAN C.W. (1964). *Social Psychology*. London: McGraw-Hill.

WATSON R.I. (1965). *Psychology of the Child*, 2nd Edition. London: Wiley.

Chapter 46
On being upright

It is a common fallacy to consider man as the only upright mammal and to suppose that he is ill adapted to this posture. However, all existing major groups of primates include species that sit or sleep with the trunk held upright. Indeed a tendency towards an erect trunk is a basic primate characteristic. Man's outstanding postural habit is not an upright trunk but his capacity to stand for long periods with extended knees. The popular idea that certain ailments, particularly of the trunk, arise from adoption of an erect posture, with failure of other parts of the body to adapt fully to such a change, may thus be incorrect and requires further examination.

Palaeontological evidence suggests that bipedal uprightness of the trunk has been a hominoid characteristic for a long period of time. 25–30 million years ago *Proconsul* had a well-developed calcaneal basal tubercle projecting backwards so that it could balance in an upright posture more effectively than do modern apes. *Proconsul africanus* had upper limb features indicative of a degree of brachiation and both these observations indicate that these early Hominoidea maintained trunk erectness for considerable periods of time. While not necessarily being in the direct line of hominoid descent, it is reasonable to suppose that they resembled fairly closely any co-existent human ancestor.

Some 15 million years later another apparently aberrant hominoid, *Oreopithecus*, possessed an enlarged heel, a broad trunk with a shortened robust lumbar region, a multisegmental sacrum and shortened hip-bone, and a large anterior inferior iliac spine, features characteristic of facultative, if not habitual, uprightness of the trunk. That *Oreopithecus* was not an habitual biped can be deduced from the relatively narrow sacral surface of the ilium and the possession of upper limbs longer than the lower.

It appears certain that a million or more years ago bipedal hominoidae existed, and it is likely that *Homo habilis* was in the direct line of human descent. The habiline foot has most of the specializations of the plantigrade foot of modern man and is clearly indicative of habitual bipedalism. A tibia and fibula, found in association with *H. habilis* and other contemporary hominoid remains, are straight and well adapted to a bipedal gait at the lower ends, although less well adapted at the knee.

The bipedal hominoid posture and locomotor habit were established in the early Pliocene, some 12 million years ago, and it seems certain that these were fully developed in human ancestral forms well over 1 million years ago. Such limb bones as exist of ancestors who lived half a million years ago indicate clearly that erect standing and walking were well established continuing features of man's descent at that distant time. If then, bipedalism has been evolving and becoming more efficient over such a long period, it is difficult to imagine circumstances in which many of the pathological defects attributed to the evolution of an upright posture could have persisted in the gene pool from which the modern human population has emerged. Such features as abdominal herniae, uterine prolapse, intervertebral disc lesions, varicosity of testicular and lower limb veins would appear to be susceptible to extinction by natural selection. If they were defects caused by the adoption of uprightness alone, sufficient time appears to have elapsed for them to have been selected out of the gene pool almost completely, and one would not expect them to occur so commonly today.

When assessing any factor in natural selection, one has to consider whether its possession will interfere with breeding. Adverse factors which appear in individuals only after they have produced and reared their family have little or no influence on future evolution. In human antecedents the shortening, broadening and fixation of the pelvis necessary for bipedalism restricted the size of the antenatal brain case and was strongly selective for birth to occur before fully independent existence could be established. This, exaggerated by the increase in brain and head size which followed the adoption of an upright posture, has led to the human nursing and rearing period being far longer than that of any other mammalian species. Even so, the existence of disproportion between foetal head and maternal pelvis is common, and labour in women verges on the extreme of natural mechanical processes. Since prolapses of the uterus and bladder occur in young adults following birth trauma, one can perceive a balance between the opposing selective forces of the need for as late a birth of the foetus as possible and reduction of the pelvic cavity for efficient bipedal loco-motion.

However, varicose veins, herniae and prolapsed discs may occur during the breeding period of life, and they would clearly have been lethal in pre-historic environments; furthermore one can see no advantage accruing to the human ancestor possessing them. It can only be inferred that their common appearance now is due either to the introduction of fresh genes into the pool or to some recent environmental change to which *Homo sapiens* has yet to adapt properly. Recent advances in functional anatomy and palaeontological thought suggest that this second alternative is probably correct. The divorce of the upper limb from locomotor function resulting from bipedalism not only promoted manual dexterity but also permitted adoption of a habit of moving things from place to place. The spread of grasslands and herbivores in the early Tertiary period reduced areas of the forest available to contemporary hominoids; this resulted in a strongly selective pressure towards bipedalism for those that changed to a partially or wholly carnivorous diet. The killing of wild ungulates at a distance from home necessitated and promoted the selection of transporting abilities, either the male having to carry the food to the mother or the mother having to carry the helpless infant to the food, or both. This hypothesis is attractive and suggests that the carrying of burdens in the hands is a long standing feature of human ancestry. When, however, one examines the magnitudes and frequency of transport of burdens, one realizes that it is only in very recent times that man has handled heavy objects with great frequency. A carnivorous diet is a concentrated and compact form of food, so that quite small and infrequent burdens would serve the dietary needs of an early human family. Modern 5-year-old children weigh only about 20 kg and can walk considerable distances long before this. Thus it is not improbable that, up to the beginnings of modern materialistic civilization, burdens in excess of an infant's weight were not transported with any frequency. It is only in the past 5 or 10 thousand years that frequent heavy load bearing has become part of the human pattern of behaviour. Although nowadays few industrial workers and housewives are required persistently to undertake heavy manual labour, occasions are common when they have to lift and carry burdens far in excess of 20 kg.

Stooping to lift and carry heavy weights is accompanied by a marked increase in intra-abdominal pressure. The ventral manual carriage of heavy burdens can induce forces in the spinal mechanism of very large magnitudes and if the vertebral column and erector spinae muscles were the only support for the load, then the necessary force could exceed what is known to be possible. Sir Arthur Keith proposed in 1923 that increase in intra-truncal pressure can supplement substantially the lifting power of the trunk and that such a raised pressure is required if loads of quite modest magnitudes are to be lifted with safety; this has since been verified experimentally.

The effects of raised intra-abdominal pressure are well known. Among them are the descent of abdominal contents into pre-existing hernial sacs, the breakdown of atrophying abdominal wall musculature to form new herniae, the appearance of perineal prolapses, and a raised venous pressure in the lower limbs; this leads to a breakdown of valve mechanisms, and once the valves have failed varicosity ensues. The prolapse of intervertebral discs and the early onset of other back derangements is clearly associated with excessive effort in manual operations. Almost all the disorders commonly associated with postural habitus are adversely affected by load bearing. It can properly be argued that in the male indirect inguinal hernia occurs only when there is a patent processus vaginalis and that this condition is seen in the newborn and very young. This is indeed true but it seems to be far less common than appearance at a later age, when herniation is commonly precipitated by excessive manual effort. In any case, the existence of a patent processus vaginalis is not associated with the adoption by man of the upright condition.

Collating these various observations, the conclusion emerges that the evolution of upright standing and walking, which are part of man's unique heritage, have not in themselves resulted in a bodily state ill adapted to such a posture. Rather has the increase in man's intellect led to new habits of weight transport, resulting from the use of elaborate and heavy machinery and furniture. It appears that it is the physical requirements of these new activities which have led to the increased incidence of a variety of postural disabilities.

FURTHER READING

BARTELINK D.L. (1957) The role of abdominal pressure in relieving the pressure on the lumbar invertebral discs. *J. Bone Jt. Surg.* **39B**, 718.

DAVIS P.R. & TROUP J.D.G. (1964) Pressures in the trunk cavities when pulling, pushing and lifting. *Ergonomics* 7, 465.

EISELEY L.C. (1953) Fossil man. *Scientific American*, **189**, 65.

KEITH A. (1923) Man's posture, its evolution and disorders. *Brit. Med J.* i, 451–454, 499–502, 545–548, 587–590, 624–626, 669–672.

KROGMAN W.M. (1951) The scars of human evolution. *Scientific American*, **185**, 54.

NAPIER J.R. (1967) The antiquity of human walking. *Scientific American*, **216**, 56.

STRAUS W.L. (1962) Fossil evidence of the evolution of the erect, bipedal posture. *Clin. Orthop.* 25, 9.

WASHBURN S.L. (1960) Tools and human evolution. *Scientific American*, **203**, 63.

Chapter 47
Adam and Eve

I know it will be said, continued my father, that in itself, and, taken simply—like hunger, or thirst, or sleep—'tis an affair neither good or bad—or shameful or otherwise—Why then, when we go about to make or plant a man, do we put out the candle? and for what reason is it, that all parts thereof—the congredients—the preparations—the instruments, and whatever serves thereto, are so held as to be conveyed to a cleanly mind by no language, translation, or periphrasis whatever?

The act of killing and destroying a man, continued my father, raising his voice and turning to my uncle Toby—you see is glorious and the weapons are honourable!

Tristram Shandy.

It will be clear from the title of this chapter that it concerns human sexuality. The euphemism itself provides evidence of the way we readily accept an idealized concept of the sexual relationship, shutting our eyes to the wide gap between the ideals of romantic love and mundane realities.

External influences on sexual behaviour

The spontaneous expression of the sexual instinct is greatly modified before and during marriage by social, economic, religious and cultural forces, acting in different ways in different societies. Whereas our title might suggest the existence of a uniform pattern of sexual behaviour common to all mankind, the range and diversity of human sexuality are, in fact, its most remarkable features. Even modern medical writers have tended to promulgate a stylized version of the marital relationship which gives little account of the varied forms which sexual behaviour may assume. Hence, if sexual behaviour is to be discussed in a realistic way, account must be taken of the modifying forces by which the sexual impulse is restrained, diverted, or even distorted. This dominant instinct, which is essential to the survival of the species, is one of the mainsprings of human motivation, and its fulfilment or frustration is closely bound up with human happiness or misery.

In many societies, however, the young child may acquire, through the attitudes of the parents, a sense of furtive shame towards the genital organs long before puberty. For economic, social and educational reasons marriage is often deferred for many years after complete physical sexual development. This is more likely to occur among those of higher social background, resulting in frustration

of the sexual impulse at a time when biologically it is most compelling. Even within marriage sexual behaviour is far from uninhibited. George Bernard Shaw declared that marriage was popular: 'because it combines the maximum of temptation with the maximum of opportunity', but only the most unnatural restraint or meticulous contraceptive discipline can result in an average family size of less than 2·5 children, which is now the pattern in Britain.

Development of the sex impulse

The age at which physical sexual maturation (**puberty**) occurs has become gradually lower in Britain during the last century, probably as a result of improved general health and nutrition. The girl of today, for instance, is likely to reach the **menarche** at an age ten months younger than did her mother. But psychosexual development is proceeding from the earliest years, shaped by the child's close relationships within the family and by the attitudes and precepts of the parents. During adolescence there is usually a passing phase of homosexual interest, and early sexual experiences are often of this nature, most commonly among those in single-sex boarding schools. The sexual segregation of adults in penal institutions also promotes homosexual behaviour. Some individuals of both sexes continue through part or all of adult life a sexual orientation of this type. The distinction between a hetero- or a homosexual interest is not, however, absolute and ambivalent dispositions are possible, so that an individual may be capable of enjoying sexual outlets of both types. For this reason, it is difficult to classify people as either homosexuals or heterosexuals, and hence estimates of the frequency of homosexuality in Western societies vary greatly from about one in seven to one in fifty.

After puberty, in the male, thoughts and fantasies of a sexual nature result in involuntary erection of the penis, and during sleep erection occurs from time to time as does seminal ejaculation. Erections during sleep occur too in infants, impotent males, and satiated males. Seminal ejaculation is usually accompanied by dreams of an erotic nature. The level of sexual tension, and hence the frequency of diurnal erections and nocturnal emissions, varies greatly among normal individuals. Voluntary relief from feelings of sexual tension may be sought through masturbation, i.e. by conjuring up fantasies of a sexual nature and simultaneously stimulating the sexual organs manually until orgasm results. This occurs almost universally among young males and a great variety of visual stimuli are published tacitly for this purpose. Masturbation is not physically harmful, but if an individual has come to feel guilty or anxious about its supposed effects, the conflict between these feelings and the compulsion to seek some outlet of sexual feeling may become emotionally disruptive. Among women, and particularly younger women, masturbation is less common and is less often associated with fantasies of an erotic nature. Masturbation allows some dissipation of sexual tension before, and to some extent during marriage.

Premarital relationships

The years between puberty and marriage are for many a time of intermittent sexual frustration. This sociobiological problem is exacerbated through the assiduous cultivation of erotic interest as an instrument of commerce in the fields of advertising, the cinema, fashion and publishing. At the same time, in Western societies, many of the conventional restraints such as chaperonage and educational segregation have been largely abandoned. Nowadays the young of both sexes mix freely in almost all social activities. Moral restraints also have tended to become less cogent. The authority of parental or ecclesiastical injunctions is often questioned or regarded with scepticism and ignored.

In this situation, it is not surprising that sexual relationships of some sort are common before marriage. Among those of higher educational level, who have a stronger motivation to defer marriage, this often takes the form of petting, which consists of intimate physical contacts designed to increase the intensity of erotic arousal, stopping short of coitus, but sometimes culminating in orgasm. However, it is not easy to drive with simultaneous pressure on the accelerator and the brake pedals, and some individuals are unable or unwilling to accept the restraint involved in petting and have intercourse before marriage. Premarital intercourse is more common among those of lower social class, who usually marry at an earlier age with conception preceding marriage in the majority of instances. About two-thirds of those women who marry

before the age of twenty are pregnant before marriage, and illegitimate birth is also most common in this age group (table 47.3).

A general survey, in 1965 throughout England and Wales by Schofield, indicated that in his representative sample about 30 per cent of young men and 16 per cent of young women aged 17–19 had experience of intercourse before marriage. Since opinion is often sharply divided, we should look objectively at the arguments for and against this behaviour.

In favour, it may be asserted that premarital intercourse is biologically natural when marriage has to be deferred, and that emotionally it is a helpful prelude to the marital relationship. Kinsey obtained information by questionnaires to American women on the degree of association between experience of premarital intercourse and success in achieving orgasm in marriage; table 47.1 is taken from the data in his report.

These figures show that among women who had never experienced orgasm from any source before marriage, those who had premarital coitus fared worse in marriage than those who had not. Among those who had experienced orgasm before marriage, those who had premarital coitus fared either somewhat better or much worse than those who had not, depending on whether they had or had not experienced orgasm during premarital coitus. These results suggest that premarital coitus does not promote the success of the sex relationship in marriage, but that there is a predictive correlation between the individual's response in the two situations, before and after marriage.

Table 47.2 taken from Schofield's report, provides more detailed evidence of the reactions of young people who have had premarital intercourse. The differences between the sexes are notable.

Schofield comments: 'Adults who criticise teenage morality always seem to assume that sexual intercourse is inevitable unless some form of restraint is put in the way. These figures show that other factors may be at work. Group pressures or a desire to be thought of as experienced and worldly may persuade some teenagers to take part in sexual intercourse although they do not really enjoy it; there may be strong pressures upon a boy to prove his masculinity, and upon a girl from the fear that she will lose the boy if she does not agree to intercourse.

TABLE 47.1. Premarital sexual experience in women correlated with degrees of marital satisfaction during first year of marriage (per cent). From Kinsey *et al.* (1953). *Sexual Behaviour in the Human Female.* Philadelphia: Saunders.

	Women who never had orgasm from any source before marriage		Women who had orgasm from some source before marriage		
	No premarital coitus	Premarital coitus	No premarital coitus	Premarital coitus no orgasm	Premarital coitus with orgasm
No orgasm	40	56	15	38	5
Consistent orgasm	29	17	44	29	54

TABLE 47.2. Reactions of teenagers to premarital intercourse. From Schofield (1965) *The Sexual Behaviour of Young People*. London: Longmans.

Question	Response	Males (per cent)	Females (per cent)
On the first occasion why did you have intercourse?	Sexual appetite	46	16
	In love	10	42
	Curiosity	25	13
	Drunk	3	9
Did you like it?	Yes	48	30
Did orgasm occur?	Yes	81	28
Do you usually experience a climax?	Always	54	14
	Usually	34	54
	Hardly ever	4	3
	Never	8	25
	Don't understand	—	4
Do you enjoy sexual intercourse?	Very much	72	52
	Sometimes	23	23
	To please other person	—	9
	Not really	5	16

One can imagine a situation where neither the boy nor the girl really wants it, but both of them feel impelled to participate.'

The less attractive consequences associated with premarital intercourse are the occurrence of pregnancy and a more remote risk of venereal disease. The information obtained in Schofield's survey makes it possible to estimate with some accuracy the risk of conception following premarital intercourse. Among young women aged 17–19 with experience of premarital intercourse, one in three is likely to become pregnant as a result. Impregnation may occur without penetration, and despite withdrawal (coitus interruptus). Wholly reliable methods of contraception are not often compatible with the circumstances of premarital intercourse. In Sweden, where contraceptives are more freely available, illegitimate births are more than twice as frequent as in Britain. Both illegitimate births and premarital conception have become more common in Britain during the last decade. About one-fifth of the children born to women under 20 years are illegitimate. Table 47.3 shows the figures relating to Scotland. This certainly suggests that premarital intercourse has become more common during recent years, but the incidence of premarital conception was almost identical a generation ago in 1939.

It is worth noting that transmission of venereal diseases can occur with either homosexual or heterosexual contacts. The incidence among young persons in Britain has increased over recent years. In Sweden, syphilis among young people was three times more common in 1964 than 1939.

Coital behaviour

In many species, mating takes place only at those restricted times when the female partner is in oestrus, and this may occur only during a limited season each year, or even at intervals of several years. However, human sexual union may take place at any time, even during menstruation. Desire may be greater in some women at the time of ovulation in midcycle, and just before and after menstruation, but there is no clear cut and universal cycle of human sexual responsiveness comparable with oestrus. However, the physiological phases of the menstrual cycle are accompanied by a pattern of more general emotional fluctuations, reflected in mood, behaviour and the content of dreams. Penal offences, suicide and impaired scholastic performance have all been shown to occur more commonly in the premenstrual and menstrual parts of the cycle.

In the later weeks of pregnancy, most women experience diminished sexual feelings following a period of enhanced sexual responsiveness in the midtrimester. In early pregnancy some women are less responsive, particularly if they are afflicted with nausea or vomiting.

TABLE 47.3. The percentage of births which were illegitimate and the percentage of births to women under 20 years in which conception occurred before marriage. Figures for Scotland.

	1939	1958	1959	1960	1961	1962	1963	1964	1965	1966
Illegitimate births	6·2	4·1	4·2	4·4	4·6	4·8	5·2	5·4	5·8	6·4
Premarital conceptions under age 20	70·0	54·0	55·5	57·8	59·3	61·1	61·7	64·5	66·2	

In both sexes the sexual impulse declines with ageing, but the general pattern differs in men and women. Male sex drive reaches a peak in the late teens, and thereafter progressively diminishes. In women, sexual feeling reaches its maximum less early in adult life, and is sustained in a plateau of responsiveness which tends to decline only in the fifties or sixties. There is not usually an abrupt loss of sexual feeling coincident with the menopause, as many women fear.

The frequency of coitus in the young married averages 3–4 times per week, decreasing to about once a week in the late forties and about once a month in the seventies. There is, however, great variation from couple to couple, and whatever is mutually acceptable cannot be regarded as abnormal.

Sexual display and arousal

Female moths release minute quantities of volatile sex attractants which may be effective over very great distances. It has been calculated that 0·1 μg. of glypure, the average amount of attractant in a female gypsy moth, would be adequate to excite and attract more than a billion male moths. In the customary social pattern of human sexual encounter in contemporary Western societies it is the female again who attracts, adopting modes of visual display (clothing, cosmetics, coiffure) and the male, in response to these, who first shows evidence of arousal. We may contrast this pattern with that of many species of birds and animals, where the female is dull and frowsy, and sexual display is exclusively the prerogative of the male, both in appearance and behaviour.

Although the psychic stimuli which arouse the man are predominantly visual, he readily becomes conditioned by his experiences and any objects or circumstances associated with sex may acquire the property of eliciting arousal. In this way, without any physical contact, male arousal occurs frequently and rapidly.

The female is usually aroused only when physical contact is established, and tactile stimuli are the most important in evoking her sexual response. Courtship may begin with touching fingers or holding hands, but it proceeds to more intimate embraces, culminating in the highest degree of epithelial contiguity during coitus.

Certain areas of the body surface are sexually particularly sensitive; these erogenous zones include the lips, and in women the breasts and nipples. Of the external genital organs the glans of the penis and the region of the clitoris are particularly sensitive. Tactile stimuli from these areas, accompanied by increasing intensity of emotion, lead to both local and general bodily changes.

It is a traditional belief that sexual arousal and response in women are inherently slower than in men. Both Kinsey and Masters and Johnson have challenged this opinion. Because she is less responsive to psychic stimuli, the woman may not become aroused until continuous physical contacts are established. For the same reason, the progress of her response can be arrested by any discontinuity of physical stimulation, and hence she may appear highly distractible at a time when the man's excitation is maintained by mental stimuli alone. The evidence presented by the investigators mentioned above demonstrates that, provided there is uninterrupted physical stimulation, the response of the female to the point of orgasm, whether during coitus or masturbation, can be no less rapid than that of the male.

Physiological changes during coitus

In men, erection of the penis may well have preceded any physical contact. With further stimulation, elevation and retraction of the testes takes place.

In women, the nipples become erect, and in women who have never lactated, hyperaemia of the breasts leads to engorgement and tumescence. These changes are minimal or absent in those who have lactated more than once. The clitoris enlarges and erection occurs. Intense vascular engorgement of the labia minora makes them pout and evert. The walls of the lower part of the vagina share in these marked congestive changes and their turgidity narrows the lumen of the vagina at this level. The upper vagina becomes elongated, presumably due to retraction of parametrial muscle fibres. A little mucus is secreted by the greater vestibular glands, but the important lubricant during coitus is a vaginal transudate which accompanies the hyperaemic changes. This allows penetration of the penis into the vagina to take place easily.

The intense sensations resulting from movement of the penis within the vagina culminate in mutual orgasm, i.e. a climax of sensation and emotional exaltation, followed by physical relaxation, mental tranquillity and often somnolence. With male orgasm, ejaculation of seminal fluid into the upper vagina takes place. In the female, orgasm is associated with irregular reflex contractions of the voluntary muscles investing the vagina. In some women, enhanced myometrial contractions occur, and it is possible that orgasm is accompanied by the release of oxytocin. There is no evidence that spermatozoa are aspirated into the uterus in this way.

We can infer that the thrusting movements of the penis within the vagina, in firm contact with the anterior vaginal wall, may milk secretions in retrograde fashion along the lumen of the female urethra, and hence introduce organisms into the bladder. 'Honeymoon cystitis' is a well recognized clinical entity, and bacteriuria is significantly more common in young married women than in virgins.

During coitus pulse rate and blood pressure are increased, as is pulmonary ventilation. At a later stage, patchy flushing of the skin is often evident, followed by increased sweating.

After male orgasm, erection rapidly disappears and there follows a refractory period during which further sexual stimulation will evoke no response. This refractory phase is not observed in women and some of them may experience a number of orgasms if stimulation is continued.

Intercourse takes place most commonly with the female lying supine. In some cultures, where the superiority of the male is emphasized, no other position for a married pair would ever be contemplated. However, coitus is possible in a great variety of postures, i.e. standing, sitting, kneeling and lying. In pregnancy, the lateral position, either face to face or a tergo, may be more comfortable for the woman.

The honeymoon

The traditional customs associated with marriage in British society do little to promote the immediate success of the physical relationship. Certainly marriage is a social institution in which both families and the community generally have an interest, but it often seems as though the emotional needs of the newly-married couple themselves receive scant consideration. Following the traditional eve-of-the-marriage bachelor party, through the protracted and exacting public rites of the ceremony, the tedious rituals of the reception, and the horseplay of the 'sending off', the wedding day often is completed by a tiring journey to a strange hotel. There the knowing looks of the staff and the evident thinness of the walls provide scant reassurance of true privacy to the anxious couple. The bridegroom is weary or, worse, inebriated; the bride is anything but relaxed.

Apart from these immediate factors, there are other reasons why the honeymoon is rarely the acme of marital experience. As we have already noted, the capacity of the woman to respond to the point of orgasm may only develop gradually over weeks, months, or even years, whereas the male partner tends at first to be precipitate in his reactions (premature ejaculation). If both are disappointed by their failure to achieve mutual satisfaction, this has a further adverse effect upon their responses. Patience and mutual understanding are often necessary.

Initial penetration is most readily effected when the woman is supine, with her thighs flexed and widely abducted. The hymeneal skin fold is torn at the time of first coitus, normally without any notable pain or bleeding.

Conclusion

In the past many assertions about human sexuality were based merely upon conjecture or supposition. Now it has become possible to describe the general outlines of sexual physiology from factual observations which have been collected by wide-scale questionnaires, and also by direct observations of coitus under laboratory conditions From all this data, a broad picture of the average man or woman's sexuality emerges.

At the same time, emphasis has been laid on the varied forms of normal sexual behaviour resulting from the adaptation of the sexual impulse to the social environment. It is important that the student, in this and other fields of scientific study should remain aware of this distinction between the average, and the range of normality. Such a recognition in the sphere of sexual behaviour is the foundation of a wise tolerance.

A description of the physiology of sex provides a very incomplete account of the pervasive importance of the sexual instinct in the development and fulfilment of human personality. It would be reasonable to claim that ability to create and sustain an unselfish relationship with a member of the opposite sex is a valid measure of emotional maturity.

FURTHER READING

KINSEY A.C., POMEROY W.B. & MARTIN C.E. (1948) *Sexual Behaviour in the Human Male*. Philadelphia : Saunders.

KINSEY A.C., POMEROY W.B., MARTIN C.E. & GEBHARD P.H. (1953) *Sexual Behaviour in the Human Female*. Philadelphia : Saunders.

MASTERS W.H. & JOHNSON V.E. (1966) *Human Sexual Response*. London : Churchill.

SCHOFIELD M. (1965) *The Sexual Behaviour of Young People*. London : Longmans.

VAN DE VELDE H. (1965) *Ideal Marriage—its Physiology and Technique*. London : Heinemann.

Index